Censorship

A World Encyclopedia

Volume 3

BOARD OF ADVISERS

CENSORSHIP

A WORLD ENCYCLOPEDIA

Volume 3
L–R

Editor

DEREK JONES

FITZROY DEARBORN PUBLISHERS
LONDON • CHICAGO

**British Library and Library of Congress Cataloguing in Publication
Data are available**

ISBN 1-57958-135-8

First published in the USA and UK 2001

Typeset by Florence Production Ltd, Stoodleigh, Devon
Printed and bound by Edwards Brothers

Cover design by Hybert Design

CONTENTS

ALPHABETICAL
LIST OF ENTRIES

THEMATIC LIST

Entries by Category

COUNTRIES

Africa
Asia (including the Middle East and Central Asia)
Australasia

Europe
North America
South and Central America and the Caribbean

TOPICS

Books
Book Burning
Booksellers, Printers, and Publishers
Bowdlerization
Libraries and Reference Books

Broadcasting and the Internet
General
Radio
Television

Film and Video

Law and Human Rights
Agreements, Laws, and Practices
Gender
Languages and Cultures
Race and Class

Literature
Country Surveys and Literary Genres
Biography, Letters, and Diaries
Fiction
Poetry

Performing Arts
Music, Song, and Dance
Theatre

Politics and Ideologies
Political Systems and Institutions
War, Diplomacy, and Secrecy

Press: Newspapers, Magazines, Advertising

Religion
Atheism, Blasphemy, Offence to Religion
Christianity
Islam
Judaism and Anti-Semitism
World Religions: General

Scholarship
Academic Freedom
History and Historians
History of Ideas
Science, Technology, Environment, Public Policy

Sexuality and Violence
Education and Practice
Children and Minors
Homosexuality and Lesbianism
Obscenity and Indecency
Violence and Media Effects
Moral Reformers and Pressure Groups

Theory and Practice of Censorship
Theories
Censors: Individuals and Institutions
Censorship: Forms, Methods, Processes
Exile
Imprisonment, Murder, Physical and Psychological Abuse
Resistance to/Subversion of/Writings against Censorship

Visual Arts
Caricature and Cartoons
Painting and Sculpture
Photography

COUNTRIES

Africa

Algeria
Algeria entries
Alleg
Harbi
Livre blanc sur la répression en Algérie
Pontecorvo

Angola
Angola

Benin
Benin

Botswana
Botswana

Burundi
Burundi

Cameroon
Beti
Cameroon
Mukong
Njawe

Central African Republic
Central African Republic

Chad
Chad

Comoros
Comoros

Democratic Republic of Congo
Bisikisi
Democratic Republic of Congo
Franco: *Hélène* and *Jacky*

Republic of Congo
Republic of Congo
Dongala

Côte d'Ivoire
Côte d'Ivoire

Djibouti
Djibouti

Egypt
al-Azhar
Chahine
Egypt entries
Fouda
Hamid
Husayn

Mahfuz
Moussad
al-Saʿdawi
Women Writers: Egypt

Equatorial Guinea
Equatorial Guinea

Eritrea
Eritrea

Ethiopia
Abyssinian War
Ethiopia
Hawariat

Gambia
Daily Observer
Gambia

Ghana
Ghana entries
Rouch

Guinea
Alata
Guinea

Kenya
Kenya entries
Maina wa Kinyatti
Nairobi Law Monthly
Ngugi wa Thiong'o
Wipper

Lesotho
Leselinyana la Lesotho
Lesotho

Liberia
Daily Observer
Liberia

Libya
Libya

Madagascar
Madagascar

Malawi
Malawi entries
Mapanje
Nqumayo
Odi

Mali
Mali

Mauritania
Hondo
Mauritania

Mauritius
Mauritius

Morocco
Chraïbi
Morocco

Mozambique
Mozambique

Namibia
Namibia
The Namibian

Niger
Niger

Nigeria
Achebe
Drumming
The Guardian (Nigeria)
Newswatch
Nigeria entries
Ogunde
Saro-Wiwa
Soyinka

Rwanda
Rwanda entries

Senegal
Senegal

Seychelles
Seychelles

Sierra Leone
Cheney-Coker
Kargbo
Sierra Leone

Somalia
Farah
Somalia

South Africa
Bandwagon
Biko
Breytenbach

Asia (including the Middle East)

Uzbekistan
Uzbekistan

Vietnam
Duong Thu Huong

Nguyen Chi Thien
Nha Ca
Tran Dan
Tu luc van doan
Vietnam

Yemen
Yemen

AUSTRALASIA

Australia
Australia entries
Clarke
Close
Glassop
Harcourt
Lindsay
Wowsers

Fiji
Fiji and the Pacific Islands

New Zealand
Cracker
Jarmusch
Mighty Morphin Power Rangers
New Zealand entries

Penthouse
Scrimgeour
Strick

Papua New Guinea
Papua New Guinea

EUROPE

Albania
Albania entries

Armenia
Armenia

Austria
Austria entries
Bernhard
Buber
Freud
Grillparzer
Holy Roman Empire
Kraus
Mahler

Azerbaijan
Azerbaijan

Belarus
Belarus entries
Svaboda/Naviny/Nasha Svaboda

Belgium
Belgium
Dutroux Case

Bosnia-Herzegovina
Bosnia-Herzegovina
Naši Dani/Dani
Oslobodjenje

Britain
Abortion: Britain
Aikenhead
Almanacs: Britain and the United States
Arms to Iraq

Austen
Banned
Barker
Baxter
The Beatles
Beckett
Berger
Biddle
Birth Control: Britain
Blount
Blyton
Bond
The Book of Common Prayer
Bowdlerization
Boxer
Brazil: Cinema, Sex and the Generals
Brenton
Britain entries
Brophy
Butler
Byron
Chesser
Children: Britain
The Chronicles of England, Scotland
    and Ireland
Clayton
Cleland
Clowes
Collier
The Committee
The Confessional Unmasked
Cracker
Crilly
Cronenberg
Cruikshank
Daily Worker
Darwin

Death on the Rock
Dryden
Ellis
Fielding
Foxe
Freethinker
Funding Restriction: Britain: Theatre
    and Visual Arts
Gay
Gibraltar
Godwin
Hall
Hardy
Hone and Cruikshank
Hook
Howard
Index on Censorship
Jack Sheppard
Janson
Jarman
Johnson
Jonson
Joyce
Kubrick
Lawrence
Libraries: Britain and the United States
Loach
Locke
Macklin
Maclean
McLibel
McNaughton
Martin Marprelate Pamphlets
Massinger
Master of the Revels
Med-TV
Middleton

Bardem
Basque Language and Culture
Buero Vallejo
Buñuel
Catalan Language and Culture
Death on the Rock
Ferreri
Franco, Francisco
García Berlanga
García Lorca
Gibraltar
Goya
Goytisolo
Els Joglars
León
Madrid
Maimonides
Picasso
Sastre
Saura

Servetus
Spain entries
Translation: Spain under Franco

Sweden
Folket i Bild/Kulturfront
Sjöman
Strindberg
Sweden

Switzerland
Küng
Rousseau
Servetus
Switzerland

Ukraine
Chernobyl
Dziuba
Kalynets

Shelest
Shevchenko
Stus
Svitlychnyi
Symonenko
Ukraine

Yugoslavia (including Serbia, Kosovo, and Montenegro)
Djilas
Djogo
Karadžić
Makavejev
Politika
Praxis
Radnička Borba/Borba/Naša Borba
War Reporting: Kosovo
Yugoslavia entries

North America

Canada
Canada
Cronenberg
Fraser
Klein
Little Sister's Book and Art Emporium
Québec
Smith
Zundel

Mexico
Aztec and Maya Culture
Excélsior
Mexico entries

United States
Almanacs: Britain and the United States
Amos 'n' Andy
Angelou
Anthropological Archives
Art, Design, and Barbie
Asch
Atomic Bombs
Barton
Batman and Robin
Biberman
Binford
Blume
Boston Chronicle
Bradbury
Bradford
Burroughs
Capra
Chaplin
Chicago

Children: United States
Comstock
Cummings
Curtiz
Damiano
Dreiser
Durang
Dworkin and MacKinnon
Eakins
Eliot
Federal Bureau of Investigation
Federal Theatre Project
Fitch
Fitzhugh
Franklin
Franklin-Trout
Funding Restriction
Ginsberg
Griffith
Hair
Heywood
Hughes
Hustler v. *Falwell*
Huston
The Hypocrisy of the United States and Her Allies
Ice-T
Jarmusch
Jefferson
Klein
Kubrick
Lang
Legion of Decency
Libraries: Britain and the United States
Lloyd

Luce, Time Inc., and Corporate Censorship
MacKinnon
McNaughton
Mapplethorpe
The Masses
Matthiessen
Maule
Mighty Morphin Power Rangers
Miller, Arthur
Miller, Henry
Morrissey
Morse
Ms.
Murrow
Mutual Film Corporation v. *Industrial Commission of Ohio*
National Campaign for Freedom of Expression
National Organization for Decent Literature
Native Son
Negro World
New-England Courant
New York Society for the Suppression of Vice
Odets
O'Neill
Parents Music Resource Center
Peckinpah
The Pentagon Papers
Penthouse
Playboy
Pound
Preminger

South and Central America and the Caribbean

TOPICS

Books

Broadcasting and the Internet

Film and Video

Kieślowski
Klein
Klimov
Kozintsev and Trauberg
Kubrick
Legion of Decency
Lloyd
Lukov
McNaughton
Maetzig
Makavejev
Makhmalbaf
Marker
Menzel
Milestone
Morrissey
Muratova
Mutual Film Corporation v. *Industrial Commission of Ohio*
Nachalo nevedomogo veka
Native Son
Němec
Nickelodeons
Olivera
Orko and Särkkä
Ōshima Nagisa

Panfilov
Peckinpah
Peng Ning
Petkova
Podnieks
Polaco
Pontecorvo
Powell and Pressburger
Preminger
Rambo Films
Rautenbach
Rocha
Room
Rossellini
Rouch
Russell
Russia: Historical and Factual Film
Russia: Film during and about World War II
Russia: The Shelf
Sanger
Sanjinés
Saura
Schorm
Scorsese
Shub

Shukshin
South Africa: Film
Spain: Film under Franco
Spielberg
Strick
Sun Yu
Tarkovskii
Tian Zhuangzhuang
Translation entrics
United States: Film entries
Vălčanov
Velasco Maidana
Vertov
Video entries
Wajda
Wang Xizhe
West
Wiseman
Wu Zuguang
Yihua Film Studio Incident
Z
Zhang Yimou
Zhelyazkova
Zhu Shilin

Law and Human Rights

Agreements, Laws, and Practices
Abortion entries
African Charter on Human and Peoples' Rights
Albizu Campos
Amnesty International
"Amnesty Lies International"
Anthropological Archives
Arab Charter on Human Rights
Article 19
Aung San Suu Kyi
Australia: Jehovah's Witnesses
Baha'ism
Bernhard
Birth Control entries
Blount
Brasil: nunca mais
Buddhism
Bulgaria: Religion
Burroughs
Cairo Declaration on Human Rights in Islam
Charter 77
China: Ethnicity, Religion, and Education
The Confessional Unmasked
Czechoslovakia: Religion
Déclaration des droits de l'homme et du citoyen

Defamation
Development versus Freedom of Expression
Dorje Shugden
Environment and Public Health
Europe: Human Rights and Freedom of Expression
Fang Lizhi
Faoro
Freedom of Expression Institute
Guatemala: Comisión de Esclarecimiento Histórico
Havel
Human Rights Watch
Hungary: Religious Censorship in Communist Hungary
Hustler v. *Falwell*
India: The Censorship of Religious Tracts in British India
International Centre for the Legal Protection of Human Rights
International Commission of Jurists
International Covenant on Civil and Political Rights
Journalism entries
Joyce
Khronika tekushchykh sobytii
Kravchenko
Lawrence

Literature and the Law
Luzac
McLibel
Martorell
Matthiessen
Mishima Yukio
Mutual Film Corporation v. *Industrial Commission of Ohio*
Obscenity and Indecency
Prior Restraint
Privacy
Private Property
Psychoanalysing Diana
Qin Shihuangdi
Romania: Religion
Russia: Religious Censorship after Gorbachev
Russia: Religion in the Soviet Union
Schlözer
Secrecy and State Security
Sedition and Public Order
Siwu Luntan
Skuodis
Truth Commissions
United Nations
United States: First Amendment to the Constitution
Universal Declaration of Human Rights

Literature

National Organization for Decent
  Literature
Novyi mir
Pornography
Pushkin
Qin Zhaoyang
Romania: Hungarian Literature
Russia: Treatment of Russian Literary
  Classics during the Soviet Period
Russia: Literature during World War II
Russia: Writers, Artists, and the Gulag
Science Fiction
Shouchaoben
Solzhenitsyn: Letter to the Fourth
  Writers Congress
South Africa: Literature
Spain: Literature and the Spanish
  Empire, 1920s
Translation entries
Wales: Welsh Language and Literature
Wang Ruowang
Wang Shiwei
Wu Nanxing

Biography, Essays, Letters, and Diaries
Alata
Angelou
Austen
Biography
Cummings
Dumitrescu
Franco, Francisco
Frank
Franklin
Hardy
Maclean
Mukong
Saidi-Sirjani
Salinger
Sarmiento
Strindberg
Wipper
Zuaytir

Fiction
Achebe
Andrzejewski
Arenas
Argueta
Babel'
Behan
Belinskii
Bernhard
Bibesco
Boccaccio
Borges
Bradbury
Breytenbach
Brink
Burroughs

Cabrera Infante, Guillermo
Chraïbi
Chukovskaia
Cleland
Colette
Conti
Dimitrova
Dimov
Ding Ling
Dongala
Dreiser
Duong Thu Huong
Echeverría
Flaubert
Fonseca
Gambaro
Gavelis
Glassop
Goethe
Gordimer
Gor'kii
Goytisolo
Grossman
Gruša
Haanpää
Hall
Hamid
Harcourt
Haşdeu
Hašek
Hedayat
Heym
Hrabal
Janson
Jin Ping Mei
Joyce
Kemal
Klíma
Konrád
Krohg
Kundera
La Guma
Lawrence
Lengyel
Leroux
Li Jiantong
Liu Shaotang
Lu Ling
McGahern
Mahfuz
Mais
Manas
Manea
Mann
Marker
Mercier
Miller, Henry
Mishima Yukio
Moussad
Moyano

Multatuli
Nasreen
Native Son
Nesin
Ngugi wa Thiong'o
O'Brien, Edna
O'Brien, Kate
O'Connor
O'Faoláin
Orwell
Panfilov
Pasternak
Pil'niak
Platonov
Prus
Rabelais
Radishchev
Rushdie
al-Sa'dawi
Sade
Salama
Salinger
Santareno
Santō Kyōden
Saro-Wiwa
Savoy Books
Selby
Shen Congwen
Shuihuzhuan
Shunsui
Sinclair
Siniavskii
Škvorecký
Tlali
Toer
Tolstoi
Tran Dan
Trocchi
Twain
Vaculík
Vargas Llosa
Vénus dans le cloître
Vizetelly
Wang Meng
Wilde
Wilson
Wolf
Xiao Jun
Z
Zhang Yang
Zola
Zoshchenko

Poetry
Ai Qing
Akhmatova
Apollinaire
Aresti
Barańczak
Barkov

al-Bayati
Bista
Brecht
Breytenbach
Brodsky
Brutus
Byron
Carter
Cheney-Coker
Correa
Dalton
Djogo
Faludy
García Lorca
Ginsberg
Goethe
Heine
Heredia
Hernandez
Hikmet
Huang Xiang

Husayn
Illyés
Jintian
Kalynets
Kliuev
Kunze
Lermontov
Madingoane
Mandel'shtam
Mapanje
Miłosz
Min Lu
Min-thuwan
Neruda
Nesimi
Nguyen Chi Thien
O'Connor
Ovid
Padilla
Petri
Plato

Pound
Praise Poets
Pushkin
Ritsos
Shalamov
Shelley
Shevchenko
Spenser
Stus
Swinburne
Symonenko
Thaker
Théophile de Viau
Tian Han
Tran Dan
Tsvetaeva
Tvardovskii
Whitman
Woroszylski

Performing Arts

Music, Song, and Dance

Anaphase
Babii Iar'
The Beatles
Beaumarchais
Biermann
Brecht
Buarque de Hollanda
Cruz
Czechoslovakia: Jazz Section of the
    Musicians' Union
Drumming
Estrella
Fandango
Ferrer
Flores
Franco: *Helène* and *Jacky*
Gubaidulina
Hair
Hindemith
Ice-T
Kubišová
Ligeti
Mahler
Maina wa Kinyatti
Mapfumo
Mendelssohn
Music entries
Nueva canción
Panufnik
Parents Music Resource Center
The Plastic People of the Universe
Prokofiev
Rostropovich

Schnittke
Sex Pistols
Shostakovich
Strauss
Tango
Tanzania: Music
Theodorakis
Top of the Pops
Verdi
Violence
Vysotskii
Wagner
Women Composers
Wu Han

Theatre

Aristophanes
Arrufat
Australia: Theatre
Barker
Barton
Beckett
Boal
Bond
Brecht
Brenton
Britain: The Lord Chamberlain
Britain: Theatre Clubs
Britain: Television Drama
Buarque de Hollanda
Büchner
Buero Vallejo
Bulgakov
Chénier

Clarke
Collé
Collier
Correa
Cuba: Popular Theatre, 18th–19th
    Centuries
Czechoslovakia: Theatre
Dorfman
Dryden
Dumas
Durang
Federal Theatre Project
Fielding
Fitch
France: Theatre
Fraser
Frei Volksbühne
Fugard
Funding Restriction
Gambaro
García Lorca
Gatti
Gay
Germany: Nazi Germany: The Nazi
    Canon
Ghana: Theatre
Grillparzer
Hauptmann
Havel
Hojas de Parra
Hook
Ibsen
Israel and the Occupied Territories:
    Theatre and Film

Jack Sheppard
Els Joglars
Jonson
Kabuki
Karagöz
Kargbo
Karvaš
Levin
Macklin
Malawi: Theatre
Massinger
Master of the Revels
Meyerhold
Mhlanga
Mickiewicz
Middleton
Mikhoels
Miller, Arthur
Mitra
Molière
Morse
Müller
Mystery Plays

Ngugi wa Thiong'o
Ogunde
O'Neill
Osborne
Ostrovskii
Panizza
Pavlovsky
Performance Art
Phrynichus
Piñera
Prynne
Ravenhill
Redford
Russia: Soviet Theatre
Santareno
Sastre
Schiller
Shadwell
Shakespeare
Shaw
Silva
Simpson
Soltanpour

Soyinka
Spain: Theatre under Franco
Strindberg
Synge
The Taganka
Ta'ziyya
Teatr Ósmego Dnia
Technical Evasions
Theatre
Tian Han
Tres Marías y una Rosa
Tret'iakov
Tsanev
Turgenev
Tynan
Uhde
United States: Theatre
Wedekind
Wu Zuguang
Ye Bare and Ye Cubb
Zinner
Zinsou

Politics and Ideologies

Political Systems and Institutions
Achebe
Almanacs entries
Amado
Argueta
Aung San Suu Kyi
Berger
Biberman
Biko
Boal
Brazil: *História nova do Brasil*
Brecht
Breytenbach
Brink
Britain: Anti-Nazi Films
Caricature
Cassius Severus
Chénier
The Cold War
Colonialism
The Committee
Conti
Daily Worker
Dante
Death on the Rock
Ding Ling
Eliot
Estrella
Exile
Federal Bureau of Investigation
Federal Theatre Project
Fielding

Flags
Fond zashchity glasnosti
Gandhi
Gay
Gill
Goma
Harcourt
Hauptmann
History: Rewriting History
Hondo
Howard
Illyés
India: Communist Party of India
India Ravaged
Johnson
Kenya: Mau Mau
Kozintsev and Trauberg
Kravchenko
Kundera
La Guma
Lang
Lèse-majesté
Liberal Democracy
Lietuvos Laisves Lyga
Liu Binyan
Lloyd
Luce
Makhmalbaf
Manea
Manet
Mann
Manufacturing Consent

Maps
Markov
Martí
The Masses
Maule
Miller, Arthur
Mitra
Mookerjee
Multatuli
Murals
Odets
Olivera
Panizza
Pe Thein
The Pentagon Papers
Perceval
Philipon
Prado
Red Channels
Ritsos
Rouch
Russia: Soviet Political Succession
Said
Sanjinés
Sex Pistols
Simplicissimus
Soltanpour
Solzhenitsyn
Soyinka
Spain: La Ley de Jurisdicciones
Stubbs
Su Shi

Press: Newspapers, Magazines, Advertising

Religion

Yugoslavia: Religion

Islam
Affendi
Albania: Religion
al-Azhar
Cairo Declaration on Human Rights in
    Islam
Fansuri
Fouda
Gardoon
Hamid
Heresy
Husayn
Iconoclasm
Islam
Kabiz
Livre blanc sur la répression en Algérie
Lutfi
Monitor
Nasreen

Nesimi
Observatories
Qur'an
Qurrat al-Ayn
Rushdie
Russia: Religion in the Soviet Union
Ta'ziyya

Judaism and Anti-Semitism
Askoldov
Babii Iar'
The Bible
Falk
Fassbinder
Frank
Germany: Nazi Germany: Degeneracy
Hasidism
Holocaust entries
Iconoclasm
Judaism entries
Levin

Mahler
Maimonides
Manea
Mendelssohn
Mikhoels
Spinoza
Tree of the Knowledge of Good and
    Evil
Wagner

World Religions: General
Australia: Jehovah's Witnesses
Ayodhya
Baha'ism
Buddhism
Confucianism
Freemasonry
Hinduism
Mormonism
Vodou

Scholarship

Academic Freedom
Donglin Academy
Fang Lizhi
Fei Xiaotong
Freire
Germany: Nazi Germany: School
    Textbooks
Krupskaia
Küng
Lunacharskii
Medvedev
Podzemní Univerzita
Political Correctness
Praxis
Race and IQ
Shakespeare in US Schools
Wang Dan
World University Service

History and Historians
Acosta
Anthropological Archives
Archaeology
Archives
Askoldov
Ayodhya
Aztec and Maya Culture
Babii Iar'
Bayer
Boxer
Brazil: *História nova do Brasil*
Chen Kaige
The Chronicles of England, Scotland
    and Ireland
Coloured Books
Comfort Women

Cremutius Cordus
Dai Qing
Galeano
Guatemala: Comisión de
    Esclarecimiento Histórico
Harbi
Heshang
History entries
Holocaust entries
The Inca
Japan: Official Japanese Attitudes to
    History since 1945
Li Jiantong
Maina wa Kinyatti
Medvedev, Roy
Nachalo nevedomogo veka
Ngugi was Thiong'o
Orwell
Qin Shihuangdi
Russia: *Bolshaia Sovetskaia
    Entsiklopediia*
Russia: Historical and Factual Film
Savarkar
Tacitus
Tarkovskii
Tian Zhuangzhuang
Truth Commissions
Vitale
Zhange Yimou
Zhu Shilin
Zundel

History of Ideas
Abelard
Anaxagoras
Aristotle

Bahrdt
Bruno
Buber
Chaadaev
Comte
Dante
Descartes
Diderot
Dolet
Encyclopédie
The Enlightenment
Erasmus
Feng Youlan
Franklin
Godwin
Gramsci
Humanism
Hu Ping
Illyés
Italos
Jefferson
Kant
Liberal Democracy
Li Zhi
Locke
Luxemburg
Machiavelli
Malesherbes
Mill, James
Mill, John Stuart
Montaigne
Montesquieu
Paine
Patočka
Pico della Mirandola
Plato

Protagoras
Raynal
Rheinische Zeitung
Rousseau
Sade
Said
Socrates
Spinoza
Su Shi
Totalitarianism
Valla
Voltaire
Yan Jiaqi
Yu Luoke
Zhu Xi

Science, Technology, Environment, Public Policy
Almanacs entries

Atomic Bombs
Belinskii
Brecht
Bruno
Butler
Chernobyl
Comte
Copernicus
Darwin
Descartes
Development versus Freedom of
  Expression
Drug-Trafficking
Encyclopédie
Environment and Public Health
Famine
Film: Medical Films
Galileo
Kapitsa

Lysenko
McLibel
Maps
Medvedev, Zhores
Observatories
Printing, Invention of: China
Printing, Invention of: Europe
Psychiatry Used in Censorship
Radishchev
Rocha
Russia: *Bolshaia Sovetskaia
  Entsiklopediia*
Science entries
Tree of the Knowledge of Good and
  Evil
Tuskegee Experiment
Vanunu
Wang Xiaoshuai
Xu Liangying

Sexuality and Violence

Education and Practice
Abortion entries
Australia: Attitudes to Sexuality
Barker
Birth Control entries
Butler
Chesser
Comfort
Cronenberg
Ellis
Hedayat
Institut für Sexualwissenschaft
Kubrick
Masturbation
Paedophilia
Rome, Ancient: Sexual Representation
Sadomasochism
Sanger
Schroeder
Sex Education
Sexual Morality East and West
Tabu
Your Pocket Guide to Sex

Children and Minors
Batman and Robin
Blume
Blyton
Bowdlerization
Britain: Television Drama
Children entries
Children's Literature
Dutroux Case
Ferrer
Fitzhugh
Fraser

Germany: Nazi Germany: School
  Textbooks
Ice-T
Internet: Online Service Providers
Kubrick
Moral Panic
Music: Rock
Nickelodeons
Oliver
Ovenden
Oz
Paedophilia
Parents Music Resource Center
Pirani
Plato
Polaco
Science Fiction
Shakespeare in US Schools
Smith
Top of the Pops
Twain
The V-chip
Violence
Your Pocket Guide to Sex

Homosexuality and Lesbianism
Arenas
Arrufat
Asch
Batman and Robin
Chen Kaige
Colette
Courbet
Ginsberg
Homosexual and Lesbian Expression
Lezama Lima

Moussad
O'Brien, Kate
Osborne
Pasolini
Puig
Ravenhill
West
Wilde
Zimbabwe: Gays and Lesbians of
  Zimbabwe

Obscenity and Indecency
Adam and Eve
Advertising
Anaphase
Apollinaire
Art
Bad Language
Barkov
Baudelaire
Bayle
Bertolucci
Boccaccio
Brazil: Cinema, Sex and the Generals
Brenton
Britain: British Board of Film Censors/
  Classification
Brophy
Burroughs
China: Pornography in Premodern
  China
Cleland
Close
Comic Books
Comstock
Cronenberg

Theory and Practice of Censorship

Resistance to/Subversion of/Writings against Censorship
Aesopian Writing
Aliansi Jurnalis Independen
Amnesty International
"Amnesty Lies International"
Andrzejewski
Angelopoulos
Apollinaire
Article 19
Association for the Promotion of the International Circulation of the Press
Beckett
Beti
Blount
Britain: Theatre Clubs
Britain: BBC World Service
Burma: Sar-pay haw-pyaw-bwe
Byron
Carnivalesque
Charter 77
The Committee
Committee to Protect Journalists
Cultural Boycotts
Dalton
Drugi obieg
The Enlightenment
O Estado de São Paulo
Fang Lizhi
Feminists for Free Expression
France: Vichy and Occupied France
Freedom of Expression Institute
Freedom of Information
Galeano
Global Internet Liberty Campaign
Gordimer
Goytisolo
Haraszti
Hardy
History: Historians
Holbach
Human Rights Watch
Illyés
Index on Censorship
International Centre for the Legal Protection of Human Rights
International Commission of Jurists
International Committee for Artists' Freedom
International Federation of Library Associations
International PEN
Khronika tekushchykh sobytii
Klíma
Lawrence
Licensed Fools and Jesters
Lietuvos Katalikų Bažnyčios Kronikas
Locke
Luzac
Mapanje
Medvedev, Roy and Zhores
Mercier
Mill, James
Mill, John Stuart
Milton
Min Lu
Montesquieu
Moore
National Campaign for Freedom of Expression
O'Faoláin
Paraguay: Radio Ñanduti
Pasternak
Patchwork Tapestries
Podzemní Univerzita
Printing: The Venetian Press
Project Censored
Radio Free Asia
Radio Free Europe/Radio Liberty
Radio Martí
Reporters sans Frontières
Samizdat entries
Saurin
Schlözer
Shouchaoben
Siniavskii
Solzhenitsyn
Sorel
South Africa: Street Arts
Soyinka
Staebroek News
Svitlychnyi
Tamizdat
Technical Evasions
Théophile de Viau
Tu luc van doan
Underground Press
United States: Voice of America
Uruguay : Radio Panamericana
Wajda
World Press Freedom Committee
World University Service

Visual Arts

Caricature and Cartoons
L'Assiette au Beurre
Caricature
Comic Books
Daumier
Feign
Gill
Hone and Cruikshank
Pe Thein
Philipon
Simplicissimus
Spain: La Ley de Jurisdicciones
Technical Evasions

Painting and Sculpture
Adam and Eve
Aretino
Art
Art, Design, and Barbie
Baumeister
Byzantine Empire: Iconoclasm
Chicago
China: Art
Colectivo de Acciones de Arte (CADA)
Courbet
Dada
Eakins
Falk
Filonov
Flags
Funding Restriction
Germany: Nazi Germany: Degeneracy
Gosudarstvennyi Institut Khudozhestvennoi Kul'tury
Iconoclasm
Islam
Kollwitz
Lawrence
Manet
Michelangelo
Murals
National Campaign for Freedom of
Expression
Nolde
Patchwork Tapestries
Performance Art
Pheidias
Picasso
Rome, Ancient: Sexual Representation
Sutherland
Tarkovskii
Thirty Years of Moscow Art
Utamaro
Veronese
Violence
Xingxing

Photography
Mapplethorpe
Oliver
Ovenden
Photography entries
Serrano

L

TITUS LABIENUS
Roman historian and orator, 1st century BCE

Labienus' style of oratory was praised for introducing vigour to old-fashioned gravity; at the same time, it was criticized for containing furious defamations of others. Coming from a very modest background himself, Labienus vilified people without regard for their class or status, and he thereby incurred for himself general odium. His invectives became so notorious that he was given the punning sobriquet "Rabienus". According to a famous dictum by the elder Seneca, Labienus' outspokenness exceeded even the proper boundaries of free speech.

No fragments of Labienus' historical writings survive, and little is known of their contents or scope. Doubtless they expressed his well-known republican sentiments – unwelcome to the regime in an era of increasing autocracy. Labienus declined to allow certain sections of his history to be published before his death; clearly he feared consequences for the free expression of his historical judgements.

Seneca states that Labienus was the first Roman author whose writings were proscribed under the law against treason (established 6 CE). Prosecution was initiated by his enemies; Labienus himself probably was not indicted, only his writings; by decree of the Roman Senate, all his works were condemned to burning (probably in 8 CE). The precise role of Augustus in Labienus' case is debated by scholars; this much can be said with confidence: the Senate, however eager it may have been to punish a vocal critic, would not have acted in a precedent-setting case without close consultation with the emperor.

After the senatorial decree, Labienus decided not to survive his writings, and promptly committed suicide. This too set a precedent for later Romans whose writings were officially proscribed. Not all copies of Labienus' works were destroyed, however, for they were republished during the reign of the emperor Caligula.

Two instructive ironies emerge from the case of Titus Labienus. He was responsible for the oft-cited opinion that in civil war the best self-defence is a state of obliviousness. Though he managed to survive the Roman civil wars, his outspokenness offered him no protection from the autocracy that was established thereafter. Also, the senator who sponsored the decree banning Labienus' writings lived to see his own works similarly proscribed.

PETER L. CORRIGAN

Sources (ancient)
Seneca the Elder, *Controversiae* 10 pref. 4–8, 10.3.5; Suetonius, *Life of Gaius* 16

Further Reading
Bauman, Richard A., *Impietas in Principem: A Study of Treason against the Roman Emperor with Special Reference to the First Century AD*, Munich: Beck, 1974

Hennig, D., "Titus Labienus und der erste Majestätsprozess de famosis libellis", *Chiron*, 3 (1973): 245–54

Peter, Hermann (editor), *Historicorum Romanorum Reliquiae*, vol. 2, Leipzig: Teubner, 1906

Syme, Ronald, *The Roman Revolution*, Oxford: Clarendon Press, 1939: 486–89; New York: Oxford University Press, 1960

Syme, Ronald, *The Augustan Aristocracy*, Oxford: Clarendon Press, and New York: Oxford University Press, 1986

ALEX LA GUMA
South African writer, activist, and diplomat, 1925–1985

Alex La Guma played a significant part in political and literary opposition to the white-dominated South African state during the apartheid years. He was a novelist and a leading member of the African National Congress (ANC), the Communist Party of South Africa (CPSA), and the Coloured Peoples' Congress (CPO); his political activities and writings drew state censure and persecution within South Africa, but earned him international recognition for his advocacy of human rights.

The son of trade union leader James La Guma, Alex was born in the 'Coloured' section of Cape Town known as District Six. He grew up with a family tradition of political activism and in a climate of increasing racial and class tensions as the white state intensified its oppression of African, Indian, and Coloured peoples from the 1940s and sought to crush opposition organizations. In addition to his experiences as a trade unionist and factory worker in Cape Town, his political consciousness was shaped through membership in the Young Communist League, the Franchise Action Council (which opposed the disenfranchisement of Coloured people), and by the example of his father, who led the South African Coloured Peoples' Organization (SACPO). In response to the election of the white Nationalist Party and its articulation of the apartheid policy in 1948, La Guma became a full member of the CPSA. In 1950, after the state had banned the CPSA, he joined the ANC and was active in that organization until his death. In 1955 he assumed the chairmanship of Cape Town SACPO and in 1957 was elected to the national executive of SACPO's successor, CPO.

The state police and security establishment targeted La Guma for suppression during the 1950s because of his work with CPSA and SACPO. Following his participation in the broad-based opposition movement of the Defiance Campaign in 1952 and in the 1955 Congress of the People's Declaration of the Freedom Charter (a multiparty policy document calling for non-racial equality and human rights in South Africa), the state intensified its harassment of La Guma, who was perceived to be spreading "subversive communist" ideology to the people. With the powers of the Suppression of Communism Act (1950), and the earlier Riotous Assemblies Act (1914, amended 1930) as well as various legislation under the "pass laws" (which governed the movement and residency of black people), the state had the arbitrary police powers it needed to strike.

In 1956 the police raided the homes of opposition leaders of all races, confiscated "subversive materials", and arrested 156 people from around the country on the charge of high treason. La Guma was among those "treason trial" defendants who faced state prosecutors in what was one of the largest and longest trials in history. Although the state granted bail to some of the defendants, and reduced the number of people charged to 91, La Guma remained accused and spent much of his time in court or prison from 1956 until charges were dropped in 1960. By that time, the still relatively independent judiciary ruled that South African state prosecutors had insufficient evidence to prove the case, and the remaining defendants were acquitted. However, the long trial had the significant effect of strictly limiting La Guma's political activities for some time. Moreover, as La Guma and other activists discovered, the trial illustrated the state's ability to enforce its will. This had a powerful impact on the lives and careers of opposition leaders who dared to express "radical" opinions. Indeed, while working at home during the trial in 1958, one of two bullets fired through La Guma's window by a suspected state-sponsored assassin grazed his neck.

Between 1960 and 1966, when he left South Africa, the police jailed La Guma several times for periods that ranged from ten days to seven months, and they placed him and his wife Blanche under a five-year house arrest. In 1962 he was banned as a "listed communist" under the Suppression of Communism Act. Under the provisions of the act and subsequent legislation, including the Publications and Entertainment Act (1963), as a banned person all his writings and publications were subject to complete censorship and he was prohibited from giving public speeches and from all political activities. In 1966 La Guma went into exile, spending the rest of his life in the UK, Russia, and Cuba, where he served as the chief representative of the ANC from 1978 until his death in Havana in

1985. He was awarded the Afro-Asian Writers' Association's Lotus Award in 1970, and served as the secretary-general of that association from 1979 until 1985.

Political persecution galvanized La Guma. He began his activist writing career as a journalist for the pro-ANC newspaper *New Age* (successor to *The Guardian*, which was banned by the government in 1952) from 1955 until 1962, when the state forced him to resign. In addition to penetrating articles in his own column, "Up My Alley", which condemned government policies and racial oppression, he also contributed caustic, satirical cartoons to various opposition publications, including *Fighting Talk* and *Africa South*.

Considered to be an authentic voice for the Coloured community, in *And a Threefold Cord* (1964) La Guma wrote passionately about the lives of the rightless and impoverished people of the ghettoes in the Cape region. Beginning with his work *A Walk in the Night* (1962), he hoped to expose the racism of the South African state, the oppression of black peoples, and to advocate political revolution. As a political prisoner, La Guma was able to bring personal insight into his stories of state repression, detention without trial, and torture in *The Stone Country* (1967) and *In the Fog of the Seasons' End* (1972). He believed he had shown that "we have now protested enough and . . . we should fight". The latter of these books drew enmity from South African state officials both for its portrayal of rising black militant activism and his dedication of the book to Zimbabwean revolutionaries. In *Time of the Butcherbird* (1979) he examined the plight of Africans forcibly removed from their homes and relocated under the "Bantustan" policy. He conceded however that his long years of exile had undermined his ability to "write meaningfully of the struggle against apartheid".

ARAN S. MACKINNON

Writings

A Walk in the Night and Other Stories, 1962
Quartet, with others, edited by Richard Rive, 1963
And a Threefold Cord, 1964
The Stone Country, 1967
Editor, *Apartheid: A Collection of Writings on South African Racism by South Africans*, 1971
In the Fog of the Seasons' End, 1972
A Soviet Journey, 1978
Time of the Butcherbird, 1979
Memories of Home: The Writings, edited by Cecil Abrahams, 1991

Further Reading

Abrahams, Cecil, *Alex La Guma*, Boston: Twayne, 1985
Abrahams, Cecil (editor), *Memories of Home: The Writings of Alex La Guma*, Trenton, New Jersey: Africa World Press, 1991
Asein, O., "The Revolutionary Vision in Alex La Guma's Novels", *Phylon*, 39 (1978): 74–86
Coetzee, J., "Alex La Guma and the Responsibilities of the South African Writer", *Journal of the New African Literature and the Arts*, 9/10 (1971): 5–11
Coetzee, J., "Man's Fate in the Novels of Alex La Guma", *Studies in Black Literature*, 5/1 (1984): 16–23
Couzens, Tim and Patel Essop (editors), *The Return of the Amasi Bird: Black South African Poetry, 1891–1981*, Johannesburg: Ravan Press, 1982
Horrell, Muriel *et al.* (editors), *A Survey of Race Relations in South Africa (1950–1972)*, Johannesburg: South African Institute of Race Relations, 1973

Karis, T., "Revolution in the Making: Black Politics in South Africa", *Foreign Affairs*, 62/2 (1983–84): 378–406

Lerumo, A., *Fifty Fighting Years: The Communist Party of South Africa, 1921–1971*, London: Inkululeko, 1971

"Obituary for Alex La Guma", *Sechaba* (January 1986)

Rabkin, D., "La Guma and Reality in South Africa", *Okike*, 8/1 (1973): 54–62

Scanlon, P., "Alex La Guma's Novels of Protest: The Growth of a Revolutionary", *Okike*, 16 (1979): 38–50

Shava, P.V., *A People's Voice: Black South African Writing in the 20th Century*, London: Zed, and Athens, Ohio: Ohio University Press, 1989

WALTER LANG
US film director, 1896–1972
THE KING AND I
Film, 1956: banned in Thailand

This musical film became a box office hit, secured for Yul Brynner an Academy Award for Best Actor, and brought him acclaim for his performance as the king of Siam. However, the film has never been shown in Thailand (as Siam is now known) itself.

The screenplay for the film was based on Margaret Landon's bestseller, *Anna and the King of Siam* (1944), a biography of Mrs Anna Leonowens (1834–1914), an English expatriate who, having lived in India, was hired by king Mongkut of Siam (1804–68) to teach English to his children and concubines in the palace school in Bangkok between 1862 and 1867. At that time, Siam was an absolute monarchy, ruled under ancient laws and customs that, among other things, legitimized both polygyny and slavery. Margaret Landon's novel portrays Anna Leonowens as a brave and virtuous woman who inspired a new generation's desire for progress. It also presents her relationship with king Mongkut in romantic terms.

The biography was based, in turn, on two books by Mrs Leonowens herself: *The English Governess at the Siamese Court* (1870) and *The Romance of the Harem* (1873). These books had received a mostly warm welcome from readers in the West, who saw in Mrs Leonowens an expert on "the Oriental". However, even at the time of their first appearance, some scholars criticized her work for plagiarism, exaggeration, distortion, and misunderstanding. In particular, it has been alleged, then and since, that she made king Mongkut and his court appear far more "backward" than was in fact the case. This became the major reason why the Siamese authorities attempted, without success, to prevent the circulation of both books in the United States. There was no ban on them in Siam itself, however, probably because only a small number of people in the country could read English and even fewer had enough money to order books from abroad.

The King and I was in fact the second Hollywood film to be based on Margaret Landon's book and thus, indirectly, on the writings of Mrs Leonowens. The first, *Anna and the King of Siam*, had been made in 1946 by John Cromwell, and starred Irene Dunne as Anna and Rex Harrison as king Mongkut. Only 14 years previously, Thailand had emancipated itself from the absolute monarchy that had ruled the country for centuries and had been regarded as a sacred institution. There had been times when people had resented, ridiculed, and revolted against the kings, but most people had accepted the monarchy as given, and not to be criticized. According to a review by the novelist M.L. Buppha Nimmanhemin (1947), the audiences who saw

Anna and the King of Siam in Thailand could be divided into three groups. One saw the monarchy as outdated and enjoyed the film as good entertainment. Another respected the monarchy, knew king Mongkut's biography very well, and therefore regarded the film as fiction, but believed it guilty of *lèse majesté*. A third group respected the monarchy, and, while not knowing much about Mongkut, were angry at his portrayal as a barbarian and a chauvinist. It was this third group that became the most vociferous. Nevertheless, this earlier film was a box office hit.

The King and I, with songs by Rodgers and Hammerstein, was originally a Broadway stage production (1951) before it was adapted for the screen. On the face of it, Lang and the studio might have expected a warm welcome for their film in Thailand, especially as field marshal Phibunsongkhram, known for his authoritarian and antimonarchist policies during his first term of office as prime minister (1938–44), had regained the premiership in 1948. In 1956, however, under pressure from the rising power of his political rivals, he was obliged to seek support from the monarchy, which still commanded a degree of popular respect. Phibun (as he was known) could see that, while Yul Brynner's portrayal of king Mongkut as exotic, erotic, droll, and stupid might impress millions of viewers around the world, it could cause great offence in Thailand. Billboards advertising the film had already aroused criticism. To avoid more controversy, the government banned the film outright. Those who could afford the trip went to neighbouring Malaya (now Malaysia) to see the film there and, in any case, the government did not resolutely enforce the ban. Since the 1970s, it has been easy to rent video cassette copies. Landon's book, meanwhile, was translated into Thai in 1962 and has been reprinted – an indication of continuing public interest.

On a trip to the United States in the 1980s, queen Sirikit of Thailand attended a Broadway performance of this controversial show. Thai journalists reported that she congratulated the actors on their performances, but then said that, although it was a good comedy, the story had nothing to do with her ancestors. The ban on the film remains in place in Thailand.

SUMALEE BUMROONGSOOK

Further Reading

Blofeld, John, *King Maha Mongkut of Siam*, Singapore: Asia Pacific Press, 1972

Bristowe, W.S., *Louis and the King of Siam*, London: Chatto and Windus, and New York: Thai-American Publishers, 1976

Griswold, A. B., *King Mongkut of Siam*, New York: Asia Society, 1961

Hamilton, Annette, "Cinema and Nation: Dilemmas of Representation in Thailand" in *Colonialism and Nationalism in Asian Cinema*, edited by Wimal Dissanayake, Bloomington: Indiana University Press, 1994

Kobkua Suwannathat-Pian, *Thailand's Durable Premier: Phibun through Three Decades, 1932–1957*, Kuala Lumpur, Oxford and New York: Oxford University Press, 1995

Landon, Margaret, *Anna and the King of Siam*, New York: Day, 1944; London: Harrap, 1945

Leonowens, Anna Harriette, *The English Governess at the Siamese Court, Being Recollections of Six Years in the Royal Palace at Bangkok*, London: Trübner, and Boston: Fields Osgood, 1870; reprinted Singapore, Oxford and New York: Oxford University Press, 1988

Leonowens, Anna Harriette, *The Romance of the Harem*, London: Trübner, and Boston: Osgood, 1873; edited by Susan Morgan, Charlottesville: University Press of Virginia, 1991

Moffat, Abbot Low, *Mongkut the King of Siam*, Ithaca, New York: Cornell University Press, 1961

Nimmanhemin, M.L. Buppha, "Anna and the King of Siam" in *Phuklin*, Bangkok: Phrae Phitthaya, 1962

Smithies, Michael, "Anna Leonowens: 'School Mastress' at the Court of Siam" in *Adventurous Women in South-East Asia*, edited by John Gullick, Kuala Lumpur, Oxford and New York: Oxford University Press, 1995

Thak Chaloemtiarana, *Thailand: The Politics of Despotic Paternalism*, Bangkok: Thai Khadi Institute, 1979

Wyatt, David K., *Thailand: A Short History*, New Haven, Connecticut: Yale University Press, 1984

LATVIA

(formerly Latvian Soviet Socialist Republic)

Population: 2,421,000

Main religions: Lutheran; Roman Catholic; Russian Orthodox

Official language: Lettish

Other languages spoken: Russian; Lithuanian

Illiteracy rate (%): 0.2 (m); 0.2 (f)

Number of daily newspapers: 24

Number of radio receivers per 1000 inhabitants: 715

Number of TV receivers per 1000 inhabitants: 496

The Teutonic Knights, crusaders who came mostly from Saxony and Westphalia, conquered the eastern Baltic littoral in the 13th century and imposed Christianity on the native Latvians. The first stirrings of the Reformation reached Riga (the capital of Latvia) in the early 1520s. A missal in Latvian, Estonian, and Livonian was printed at Lübeck in 1525, but was immediately destroyed by the Roman Catholic authorities. In the same year, some of the iconoclastic fury that was sweeping through other parts of Europe also arrived in Riga. In 1530, a new Lutheran church order was imposed from above and first administered by Johann Briesmann, a somewhat conservative colleague of Luther's. The first Latvian book, *Catechismus Catholicus*, was printed at Vilna in 1525; Luther's *Little Catechism*, printed in Königsberg, followed in 1585. The full Bible in Latvian was published during the 17th century.

Latvian national identity and language were, however, amorphous until the middle of the 19th century. Following periods of Polish and Swedish rule, the region passed into Russian hands during the reign of Catherine the Great (1762–96). Until then, Latvian censorship did not exist, because there was little or no written matter intended for Latvian serfs, who were regarded by the Baltic Germans as a simple peasant nation.

During the early 19th century a demographic explosion, urbanization, and industrialization were accompanied by a rise in literacy and the beginnings of a sense of national identity. The first newspapers were printed: the *Latviešu avize* (Latvian Newspaper) and the *Tas Latviešu ļaužu draugs* (Latvian Congregation's Friend). Both were generally conservative, both were subject to censorship. The authorities turned down a request from the editor of the *Latviešu avize*, Karlis Vatsons, for permission to print foreign news, on the grounds that the peasants did not need to know about such matters. The *Tas*

Latviešu ļaužu draugs, founded by Hermann Treija during the reign of Nicholas I was allowed to appear from 1831, but denied the right to publish political articles. Trouble came in the mid-1840s, when the paper ran an apocryphal story about a Lithuanian church congregation that abandoned Lutheranism for Catholicism after poor harvests, but quickly became disillusioned with their new faith. The censor passed the article as innocuous, but the Orthodox Church claimed that it was a thinly disguised warning to Latvians converting to Orthodoxy under similar conditions. The authorities confiscated the offending issues, dismissed the censor, and banished the editor.

In 1856 Ansis Leitans succeeded in founding a new paper, *Majas Viesis* (The House Guest), that for the first time included reports on politics, although they were couched in a "patriotic spirit appropriate for peasant understanding". This paper, subject like its predecessors to the censorship, usually reflected the ideas, not of Latvians, but of the Baltic Germans or the Russian imperial court. The first truly scandalous paper was the *Peterburgas avize* (Petersburg Newspaper), edited by Juris Alunans, which began its short but controversial existence in 1862. It contained the first overt expressions of Latvian nationalism and was published in St Petersburg because it would never have been allowed at home; its censor, Krišjanis Valdemars, was himself a Latvian. The Baltic Germans were incensed at the claim that the Latvians constituted a nation, rather than a peasant class, and managed to have the censorship of the paper transferred to Riga, where it was soon closed down. However, important lessons had been learned about how to circumvent the censorship laws.

On 6 April 1865 prior censorship was abolished throughout the Russian empire. Censorship after the fact took its place, with heavy fines for publishers who broke the rules. The Baltic

Germans were now able to control the spread of Latvian nationalism by denying newspaper concessions to those with "doubtful" pasts, but by the 1880s the spread of literacy prompted the arrival of another newspaper, the *Dienas Lapa* (Daily Page), which quickly garnered a widespread readership. Under Janis Rainis, its editor from 1891 to 1896, this paper surreptitiously introduced German social democratic thought to its readers, by debating the merits of books, plays, and other cultural events in terms intended to draw attention to the short-comings of society. Forbidden to use the term "Latvia", the paper referred to "homeland" or "Baltija" instead. A thorn in the side of the authorities, the paper was finally closed down in 1897, and Janis Rainis was arrested and deported to Siberia.

However, the state was losing the battle to control the press and thought. An underground press produced *Ciņa* (The Struggle) for the Latvian Social Democrats in 1904; books and articles were smuggled in from abroad, including even the works of Karl Marx. After the revolution of 1905–06, Latvians to the east of the Baltic provinces were at last granted the right to use their dialect, Latgallian. Censorship remained in place but could not cope with the flood of newspapers: 300 new titles were introduced between 1905 and 1922.

The independent republic of Latvia was established on 18 November 1918 in the wake of the Bolshevik revolution of 1917. Censorship ceased to exist during the first 15 years of the independent state. A liberal Press Law of 12 February 1924 resulted in an explosion of new newspapers and books. It became possible for many political parties and minority communities to publish their own journals. Between 1585 and 1918, about 12,500 books had been published in the Latvian language; between 1919 and 1929 14,038 books appeared in Latvia, of which 11,895 were in Latvian, with a total print run of 34 million. A further 12,716 were published between 1930 and 1939.

Latvia was a morally conservative society, and as early as 1926 concern was beginning to be expressed about the damage done by years of war, revolution, and drastic change. Two committees were formed to "safeguard youth from obscene . . . fiction", one of them under the chairmanship of the same Janis Rainis who had suffered censorship in the 1890s. Bans on works of a sexual nature were introduced, affecting everything from medical books that discussed birth control to racy novels about the sex life of Catherine the Great. Books about the Chicago gangsters of the 1920s were also ruled out, as were any that "raised the expectations" of young people too highly. Even Shakespeare was considered to contain subject matter that was too mature for anyone under 21.

Political censorship was never completely absent either. The new state had immediately banned the Communist Party and its publications, but the party continued to have materials printed in Moscow and smuggled into Latvia. They had little impact, however. It was the great multiplicity of other political parties that led to upheaval in Latvia as it began to be argued that they got in the way of stable government. On 15 May 1934 Karlis Ulmanis, leader of the Farmers' League and prime minister for the fourth time since 1918, claimed that civil war was imminent, suspended parliament, and took power as head of state. Pre-publication censorship was reinstated almost immediately. The Civil Code of 1938 decreed a huge fine and three months' imprisonment for the editor of any newspaper

that did not "strengthen the idea of 15 May". Latvia's fascist party, Perkoņkrusts (Thunder Cross), was banned, and Latvia was the only state in eastern Europe state to ban anti-Semitic works. Ulmanis saw himself as the father of the nation. The press dutifully reported his speeches and praised his visits to the countryside. Other publications carried his portrait and invoked the glory of united Latvia.

The Molotov–Ribbentrop pact of 23 August 1939 sealed the fate of the first independent republic of Latvia. Hitler assigned Latvia to the Soviet sphere of influence, and in June 1940 the Soviet Union occupied and incorporated the country, along with Estonia and Lithuania. Stalin sent Andrei Vyshinskii to oversee the process. Among other changes, schools and universities were purged of "harmful" influences, and libraries were ransacked for any books that suggested that Latvia might be independent. At least 34,000 Latvians (up to 2 per cent of the population) were deported to Central Asia or Siberia. Then the Germans turned the tables by invading the Soviet Union on 22 June 1941. Riga fell on 1 July, the Soviet forces left in a hurry, and Latvia was occupied by the Nazis for the next four years.

After the war, censorship in Latvia differed little from censorship throughout the rest of the Soviet Union. The Latvian branch of Glavlit imposed nearly absolute censorship. The state owned and controlled every printing press, radio station, and television station, and carefully scrutinized and scripted the presentation of all reports and creative ideas. By 1975 the Communist Party was employing around 63,000 people in the business of promoting Soviet ideology: 25,000 propagandists, 20,000 political information specialists, and 18,000 "agitators". This army of ideologists declared all existing histories of Latvian literature obsolete because they approached literature from an "aesthetic" point of view. Latvian writers were attacked for "pessimism, ethnographism, formalism, naturalism, mysticism, religiousness". The local literature was acceptable only in "isolated fragments". The work of a handful of Latvian writers, including Janis Rainis, were selectively edited to stress Latvian fraternalism with Russia and the legitimacy of the socialist struggle. Texts were rewritten to introduce new "consciously proletarian" characters.

By the early 1970s, however, some degree of cultural freedom was being allowed. Riga's hippy community made an underground film, *Pašportrets* (Self Portrait), complete with group nudity and sex, but realized, finally, that this was going too far for Soviet sensibilities. Meanwhile, the filmmakers Juris Podnieks, Gvido Zvaigzne, and Andris Slapiņš were pushing the acceptable limits of documentary-making. In 1991, before the Soviet Union collapsed, troops were despatched to Riga to seize press buildings and television stations, in an attempt to silence the more radical demands for complete independence for Latvia. In August that year, independence was achieved.

The last census of the Soviet era, taken in 1989, showed that Russians made up about 34 per cent of the population of Latvia, while Latvians accounted for only 52 per cent of the total; 60 per cent of the population of Riga could speak Russian. Latvian governments have sought to check this almost inexorable cultural mixing. They have cut state funding of the Russian-language press and television, arguing that Russia's own extensive resources are more than adequate. A few newspapers continue to appear in both Latvian and Russian versions, but they have failed to achieve reasonable market shares, for Latvia's Russian community reads newspapers and listens to broadcasts from Russia. There are two solitudes in Latvia.

The old Latvian moral conservatism is still alive, and its proponents stand ready to attack what they see as the "collapse of morality" in a society driven by market forces. Their targets have included the young visual artist Miķelis Fišers, who pays homage to homoeroticism and drug culture, as well as pornographic magazines, possession of which would have been a crime in Soviet times, but which are now commonplace. The one high-profile censorship case in Latvia since 1991 has concerned politics and anti-Semitism, not sex. In the spring of 1995, the police seized a Latvian translation of Hitler's *Mein Kampf*. Few came to the defence of the book in the name of intellectual freedom.

Latvia's state and society continue to struggle to find a balance between a free press and countenancing libel and slander. In recent years National Bolshevik and Latvian extremist nationalists have had newspapers censored for inflammatory articles.

ALDIS PURS

Further Reading

Dreifelds, Juris, *Latvia in Transition*, Cambridge and New York: Cambridge University Press, 1996

Ekmanis, Rolfs, "Soviet Attitudes towards Pre-Soviet Latvian Writers", *Journal of Baltic Studies*, 3/1 (Spring 1972): 44–70

Ezergailis, Andrew, *The Holocaust in Latvia, 1941–1944: The Missing Center*, Riga: Historical Institute of Latvia, and Washington, DC: United States Holocaust Memorial Museum, 1996

Kirby, David, *Northern Europe in the Early Modern Period: The Baltic World, 1492–1772*, London and New York: Longman, 1990

Kirby, David, *The Baltic World, 1772–1993: Europe's Northern Periphery in an Age of Change*, London and New York: Longman, 1995

Maryniak, Irene, "The Walls" and "Wanted: A Spirit of Unity", *Index on Censorship*, 21/10 (November 1992)

Misiunas, Romuald J. and Rein Taagepera, *The Baltic States: Years of Dependence 1940–1990*, updated edition, Berkeley: University of California Press, and London: Hurst, 1993

Plakans, Andrejs, *The Latvians: A Short History*, Stanford, California: Hoover Institution Press, 1995

Rauch, Georg von, *The Baltic States: The Years of Independence: Estonia, Latvia, Lithuania: 1917–1940*, London: Hurst, 1970; Berkeley: University of California Press, 1974

Thaden, Edward C. (editor), *Russification in the Baltic Provinces and Finland, 1855–1914*, Princeton, New Jersey: Princeton University Press, 1981

Treijs, Rihards (editor), *Latvijas Republikas Prese, 1918–1940* (The Press of the Republic of Latvia 1918–40), Riga: Zvaigzne ABC, 1996

D.H. LAWRENCE
British novelist and poet, 1885–1930

Censorship in Lawrence's lifetime

In a masterly essay to which he gives the title "D.H.Lawrence: A Suitable Case for Censorship", Damian Grant remarks that Lawrence's experiences of censorship do not begin and end with the forces of law. It is true that it was with the publication of *The Rainbow* in 1915 that Lawrence was first subjected to legal prosecution. However, Grant is undoubtedly right to argue that in a full consideration of Lawrence and censorship we would need to take into account all of the following factors:

... self-censorship (which Lawrence did learn to cope with – if only because others were keen to exercise that role on his behalf), his family (first his parents and siblings, and later Frieda), his friends (with a special category for his former friends), his typists (who had their own say in what should and should not be written), his agents (who often played a double game), his publishers (more active than most in 'toning down' Lawrence's work), booksellers and libraries (especially the private circulating libraries like Boots and Mudie's, who operated their own in-house system of censorship), reviewers (often eager to speak out on behalf of their readers' moral welfare), readers themselves (in so far as they made themselves heard), and, finally, the actual intervention of the law, in the shape of the police, the Post-master General, or customs officials.

This essay cannot address all the aspects of censorship to which Grant alludes. It is, however, necessary to note that Lawrence had been alert to the risks which his writing ran some years before *The Rainbow* fell foul of the law. His first novel, *The White Peacock*, had for the most part been generously praised, but it had offended at least one reviewer with its "physicality", "brutality", and "sick thoughts". He feared that his second novel, *The Trespasser*, was too erotic, and at one point he announced to the publisher Martin Secker that he had therefore decided to withdraw it. In the end, the novel was published by Duckworth on 23 May 1912 and received mostly favourable reviews. However, Heinemann, who had initially agreed to publish *Sons and Lovers* – or, as it was then called, *Paul Morel* – wrote to Lawrence on 1 July 1912 to say he had changed his mind; he felt that the novel's

... want of reticence makes it unfit, I fear, altogether for publication in England as things are. The tyranny of the Libraries is such that a book far less out-spoken would certainly be damned (and there is practically no market for fiction outside of them) (*Letters*, vol. 1, p.421, n.4).

Sons and Lovers was switched to Duckworth, and Edward Garnett, both as a reader for the publishing company and as a friend of Lawrence, made many suggestions for improving the manuscript. "What a Trojan of energy and conscientiousness you are!" Lawrence told him. "I'm going to slave like a Turk at the novel – see if I don't do you credit" (*Letters*, vol. 1, p.427). On the basis of this and further letters between the two men, it has sometimes been asserted that Lawrence bowdlerized his novel in order to make it safe for publication. This is not so, and although Duckworth ordered some cuts at proof stage, the novel finally appeared in a form of which Lawrence approved. Unfortunately, the libraries and booksellers did not at first share this approval. On 22 July 1913, Lawrence wrote to his friend Ernest Collins from Broadstairs, where he and Frieda were staying briefly, to say

> *Sons and Lovers* has been "well received", hasn't it? I don't know whether it has sold so well. The damned prigs in the libraries and bookshops daren't handle me because they pretend they are delicate skinned and I am hot. May they fry in hell. I don't like England very much, but the English do seem rather lovable people. They have such a lot of gentleness (*Letters*, vol. 2, p.47).

Lawrence was soon to think very differently of his fellow countrymen and women. Matters began to go wrong for him in 1914, when his collection of short stories, *The Prussian Officer*, was banned from Boots' Libraries. According to E.M. Forster's biographer, P.N. Furbank, this was at the explicit command of Sir Jesse Boot himself, who, "when pressed about it, sent subscribers a private copy in a special binding so they could see how disgusting the book was" (*Letters*, vol. 2, p.257, n.3). Whether this was true or not, Lawrence was sufficiently alarmed for the prospects of his new novel, *The Rainbow*, to write to his agent, J.B. Pinker, on 23 April 1915:

> I hope you are willing to fight for this novel. It is nearly three years of hard work, and I am proud of it, and it must be stood up for. I'm afraid there are parts of it Methuen won't want to publish. He must. I will take out sentences and phrases, but I won't take out paragraphs or pages ... Oh God, I hope I'm not going to have a miserable time over this book (*Letters*, vol. 2, p.327).

Methuen published *The Rainbow* on 30 September 1915. Just over a month later, on 3 November, a Bow Street magistrate's warrant to seize all copies of the novel was served on Methuen and Co., although Lawrence only learned of this three days later. At the same time he discovered that his publishers were unwilling to defend the novel.

The warrant may have been prompted by some pointedly hostile reviews. One of these was by James Douglas in *The Star*; in 1928, Douglas was to use his column in the *Sunday Express* to call for the banning of Radclyffe Hall's *The Well of Loneliness*. The other was by Clement Shorter in *Sphere*, who denounced the book as "an orgy of sexiness": Lawrence was, he said, worse than Zola, who "stood as a reeking symbol of pornography in the British mind". While there may be some doubt about who or what caused the law to act, it is certain that Lawrence was left more or less on his own. The Society of Authors considered intervening on the writer's behalf, but they were hamstrung by the readiness with which his publishers handed over all their copies of *The Rainbow* to the police, thereby accepting that they had erred in publishing Lawrence's novel. Indeed, they apologized in open court for having done

so. In this way, they made sure that there would be no trial and that the firm would therefore not be exposed to adverse publicity. So, although Philip Morrell, the husband of Lawrence's friend and patron Lady Ottoline Morrell, asked a question in parliament, it could do no good. Had the author of the book been given any opportunity of replying to the charge made against him? Morrell wanted to know. The home secretary, Sir John Simon, replied that "the publishers, and not the author, were the defendants, and they had the customary opportunity to produce such evidence as they considered necessary in their defence."

More than one commentator has pointed out that, as there was never a trial, *The Rainbow* cannot be considered to have been banned. In *D.H. Lawrence: A Biography*, Jeffrey Meyers has suggested that, had the case gone to trial, Lawrence and his publishers might well have emerged victorious. Perhaps this is so, but the evidence does not support Meyers's claim. Not only in Britain, but on the other side of the Atlantic too, Lawrence was becoming a danger to his would-be publishers. For example, on 30 November 1915, an expurgated American edition of *The Rainbow* was set to be published in New York by Huebsch, and an advance copy was sent to Lawrence, but the work does not seem to have been distributed. Lawrence was clearly considered too hot to handle. When Secker did republish *The Rainbow* in 1926, it was the Huebsch text which they used.

In 1917, Chatto agreed to publish a collection of poems, *Look We Have Come Through*, but only on condition that cuts were made in order to lessen the effect of "the continuously sexual tone". When Secker took *The Lost Girl* in 1920, he had to warn Lawrence that

> ... the lending libraries had refused to handle the book unless the accounts of the sexual encounter between Ciccio and Alvina were rewritten. Since the sale of 2000 copies was at stake, Secker urged Lawrence to comply. He did so and substituted a muted version (*Letters*, vol. 3, p.14).

The following year, Secker published *Women in Love*. The novel had been completed five years earlier; however, although in principle Secker was ready to publish the sequel to *The Rainbow*, he delayed for a number of reasons, most of which are spelled out by Paul Delany in his book, *D.H. Lawrence's Nightmare*. They include the fact that when the novel was circulated in manuscript form among a number of Lawrence's friends, they were understandably enraged to find themselves the objects of his satiric scorn. Ottoline Morrell apparently sent her husband to warn Pinker that, if the novel was published in the form in which it then existed, an action would be brought against the publishers for libel. Philip Heseltine also threatened action unless the name of his recognizable mistress was changed. When the novel was finally published, the journal *John Bull* excelled itself with a review under the headline "A Book the Police Should Ban: Loathsome Study of Sex Depravity – Misleading Youth to Unspeakable Disaster". The novel escaped prosecution, possibly because *John Bull*'s proprietor, Horatio Bottomly, was well known as a sensation monger. Nevertheless, reviews and sales were both depressingly poor.

By then, Lawrence was out of England, but the censors were not done with him. In March 1927, Lawrence wrote to Secker to tell him that he had finished a second version of *Lady Chatterley's Lover*. Although it was verbally "terribly improper", he said, "I don't think I shall alter it . . . [I] am not keen, somehow, on letting it go out. What's the good of publishing things!" (*Letters*, vol. 5, p.655). He must have known that the novel stood no chance of being published in England in unexpurgated form. A private, and error-strewn, edition was published in Florence in 1928, and in 1932, two years after Lawrence's death and contrary to his explicit instructions that there should be no such thing, Secker brought out a heavily expurgated edition in England. It was not until the famous trial in 1960 that the full text was finally cleared for publication. This was made possible by a change in the law to distinguish between erotic literature and commercial pornography, and of course by the priceless performance of the prosecutor Mervyn Griffith-Jones, of which more in section three below.

Before that time, the unexpurgated form of *Lady Chatterley's Lover* circulated in clandestine fashion. Soon after the publication of the privately printed Florence edition in 1928, copies began to be posted to England. Several were intercepted by the port authorities. One such interception netted the manuscript of *Pansies*, which Lawrence sent to Secker early in 1929. As soon as he heard the news, Lawrence wrote to Secker begging him not to give in to bourgeois morality: he said, "I want every poem included that is not open to legal attack." Nevertheless, 13 were omitted. This was also the unlucky number of Lawrence's paintings which were seized by the police when they raided the Warren Gallery on 5 July 1929. An exhibition of Lawrence's art had been mounted by Julia Warren in mid-June, and predictably enough it was greeted by a series of hostile reviews, most of which emphasized the "intimate nudes" on show. (By "intimate" was almost certainly meant the painting in of pubic hair.) The police raid resulted in the confiscation of 13 of Lawrence's paintings, and also of some by William Blake, although these were returned when it was explained to the police that Blake was dead and his paintings a national treasure.

On 8 August 1929, the gallery went on trial for exhibiting obscene material: Lawrence's paintings were described as "gross, coarse, hideous, unlovely and obscene". The cards were heavily stacked against Julia Warren and of course Lawrence. For one thing, the presiding magistrate was Justice Mead, aged 80, who at the beginning of the decade had behaved viciously to defendants in a drugs case. Mead declared that the pictures "should be put an end to, like any wild animal which may be dangerous". For another, the prosecutor, Harold Muskett, had had charge of the prosecution case against *The Rainbow*. There was a very real possibility that, in the event of the case being proved, Lawrence's paintings would be burnt. In the event, however, they were saved by the agreement of the gallery not to try to exhibit the paintings again in England, and by its promise to return them to the artist, thereby ensuring that England would be free of the taint of Lawrence's pornographic art. No wonder that, when Lawrence heard the court's decision, he wrote to a friend, "Let them burn their own balls, the fools. This has given me a great sickness of England."

Lawrence on censorship and pornography

The treatment of *Lady Chatterley's Lover*, of *Pansies*, and of his paintings roused Lawrence to write his powerful essays against censorship, *Pornography and Obscenity* and "My Skirmish with Jolly Roger", later retitled "A propos of *Lady Chatterley's Lover*". Lawrence wrote *Pornography and Obscenity* while taking what he hoped would be a rest cure in Bavaria in the late summer of 1929. The essay was first published in the July–September 1929 issue of the journal *This Quarter*, and was subsequently brought out in the autumn by Faber and Faber as part of a pamphlet series on issues of the day. In pamphlet form, it proved to be a considerable financial success. By 9 December, Lawrence was able to tell his friend Giuseppe Orioli that 12,000 copies a week were being sold. This encouraged him to expand "My Skirmish with Jolly Roger", which had appeared in the United States, and to offer the result, "A propos of *Lady Chatterley's Lover*", to the Mandrake Press, who published it in June 1930.

Lawrence's polemic in *Pornography and Obscenity* was in some ways an answer to a pamphlet in the same series by Lord Brentford, who – as Sir William Joynson-Hicks (Jix) – had been British home secretary and had instigated seizures for *Pansies* and searches for hidden copies of *Lady Chatterley's Lover*. A religious zealot, Brentford had proclaimed in *Do We Need a Censor?*,

> No silly prating about the necessity of elucidating problems, or that "to the pure all things are pure", or that the claims of art must be satisfied, which we frequently hear, can change the moral law, or alter the fundamental facts of human nature.

In his response, Lawrence sought to demonstrate his "high" view of human nature and sexuality. He was contemptuous of "Jix", declaring,

> The late British Home Secretary, who prides himself on being a very sincere Puritan, grey, grey in every fibre, said with indignant sorrow in one of his outbursts on improper books: "and these two young people, who had been perfectly pure up till that time, after reading this book, went and had sexual intercourse together!" One up to them is all we can answer. But the grey Guardian of British Morals seemed to think that if they had murdered one another, or worn each other to rags of nervous prostration, it would have been much better. The grey disease!

Only at the end of *Pornography and Obscenity* does Lawrence refer to the police raid on his paintings, and when he does so, his tone is one of weary contempt:

> They did not in the least know what to take. So they took every picture where the smallest bit of the sex organ of either man or woman showed. Quite regardless of subject or meaning or anything else; they would allow anything, these dainty policemen in a picture show, except the actual sight of a fragment of the human *pudenda*. This was the police test. The dabbing on of a postage stamp – especially a green one that could be called a leaf – would in most cases have been quite sufficient to satisfy this "public opinion".

Lawrence, like George Moore in *Literature at Nurse* before him, here takes his stand on the argument for the right of the artist to free expression. He also argues for sexual liberation, and this was a matter much debated during the 1920s. Sex, says Lawrence, is either "the dirty little secret", or it is "freedom from the vast lie of the social world, the lie of purity and the dirty little secret". He argues that freedom has to be fought for: he tells his readers that they must "fight the sentimental lie of purity and the dirty little secret wherever you meet it, inside yourself or in the world outside. Fight the great lie of the 19th century, which has soaked through our sex and our bones."

For Lawrence, sex was "the source of all real beauty, and all real gentleness. And those two things, tenderness and beauty will save us from horrors." He was less than confident that the young people of his day had yet achieved sexual health. If they had advanced from "fearing the body and denying its existence", they now treated it "as a sort of toy to be played with . . . these young people scoff at the importance of sex, take it like a cocktail." Lawrence, who accused the Victorians of puritanism, was himself at pains to condemn pornography, which he described as "the attempt to insult sex, to do dirt on it . . . you can recognise it by the insult it offers, invariably, to sex, and to the human spirit."

The *Lady Chatterley* trial

Lawrence's high view of sexuality was one of the main points seized on by the defence in the famous trial of the unexpurgated *Lady Chatterley's Lover* in 1960. The defence counsel, Gerald Gardiner, saw the novel as "a passionate and sincere work of the novelist in the puritan tradition, who believed he had a message for us in the society in which we lived". Richard Hoggart, then senior lecturer in English Literature at the University of Leicester, declared that the book was "highly virtuous, and, if anything, puritanical".

The previous year, publishers, writers, booksellers, and printers had come together to work out the Obscene Publications Act, whose express purpose was, as Damian Grant succinctly puts it, "to provide a distinction sustainable in law between erotic literature and commercial pornography". Their effort may in part have been fuelled by recent US experience. In 1959, the Grove Press of New York had decided to publish an unexpurgated *Lady Chatterley*, thereby testing the so-called Roth decision of 1957, which provided that a book charged with obscenity could be defended if it could be shown to have "redeeming social importance". The edition was distributed by Readers Subscription, a small-circulation book club whose members were mainly academics; however, this did not prevent its seizure by the Post Office, which declared the book obscene under the terms of the Federal Anti-Obscenity Act (the "Comstock Act", 1873). Grove Press claimed that this act was unconstitutional, and, in a counter-suit, denied the Post Office's right to judge any book obscene. The US District Court in the Southern District of New York found in Grove's favour. This decision was then challenged but was upheld by the US Court of Appeal, which affirmed on 26 March 1960, "This is a major and distinguished novel and Lawrence is one of the great writers of our age." Soon, a million copies of a Pocket Book edition had been sold, priced at 35 cents each.

Meanwhile, in Britain, Allen Lane decided to test the efficiency of the Obscene Publications Act, and to mark the 30th anniversary of Lawrence's death, by publishing the unexpurgated *Lady Chatterley's Lover* in Penguin. The Director of Public Prosecutions decided to take this edition to court, perhaps not least because the book was priced at three shillings and sixpence (17p) a copy. The five-day trial was, according to an article in the *New Statesman* at the time, "the most expensively mounted and high-powered course on D.H. Lawrence that money has been able to buy".

The prosecution was led by Mervyn Griffith-Jones, whose spectacular incompetence was epitomized by his now immortal question to the jury of nine men and three women. Was the book, he asked, one "that you would have lying around in your

LAWRENCE: Passenger on the London Underground reading *Lady Chatterley's Lover*, on the day that the full text of the novel went on sale legally in Britain: 3 November 1960. The book was first published in Florence in 1928 and in a heavily expurgated edition in England in 1932. The first unexpurgated edition of *Lady Chatterley's Lover* was published by Penguin in 1959 and taken to court under the Obscene Publications Act by the Director of Public Prosecutions. After a five-day trial the novel was cleared on the grounds that it was literature, not pornography, and that it did not tend to deprave or corrupt.

own home? Is it a book you would even wish your wife or your servants to read?" In his mind, the book was merely a "vicious indulgence in sex and sensuality", which might "tend to induce lustful thoughts in the minds of those who read it". Condemning its "bawdy conversation", he had counted 30 mentions of the word "fuck", together with "cunt 14 times; balls 13 times; shit and arse six times apiece, cock four times; piss three times".

The defence called 35 expert witnesses, including academics, writers, artists, teachers, clergy, and politicians: these all rejoiced in the work's high moral and literary purpose. Gerald Gardiner, the defence counsel, pointed out that some people "would describe *Antony and Cleopatra* as a play about adultery – the story of a sex starved soldier copulating with an Egyptian Queen". John Robinson, the bishop of Woolwich, made headlines with his assertion that Lawrence was trying "to portray the sex relationship as something essentially sacred . . . as in some sense an act of holy communion". *Lady Chatterley* was, of course, about the "life of a woman in an immoral relationship, in so far as adultery is an immoral relationship". It was, he concluded, "a book that Christians ought to read".

The jury retired for three hours and concluded that *Lady Chatterley's Lover* was literature, not pornography, and that it did not tend to deprave or corrupt. The 1960s had begun, in the words of Philip Larkin, with "the end of the *Chatterley* ban/And the Beatles' first LP". However, many were still cautious about the novel. For instance, Swansea Libraries decided to purchase a copy but to make it available by request only; also, there was one bookshop in Bromley, Kent, which would not sell the novel to schoolchildren without a note from their parents. Some refused to sell the book at all, but a mischievous pupil librarian at Lewes, Sussex, managed (temporarily) to get the book classified as "junior fiction". The book sold two million copies in 12 months.

JOHN LUCAS

Writings

The Prussian Officer and Other Stories, 1914
The Rainbow, 1915
Women in Love, 1920
Lady Chatterley's Lover, 1928; *The First Lady Chatterley* (first version), 1944; *La tre Lady Chatterley* (3 versions, in Italian), 1954; unexpurgated edition, 1959; *John Thomas and Lady Jane* (second version), 1972
Pansies, 1929
Pornography and Obscenity, 1929
"A propos of *Lady Chatterley's Lover*" in *Sex, Literature and Censorship: Essays*, edited by Harry T. Moore, 1953; revised edition, 1955
The Letters, edited by James T. Boulton, 7 vols, 1979–93
Works (Cambridge edition), edited by James T. Boulton and Warren Roberts, 1980–

Further Reading

Brentford, William Joynson-Hicks (viscount Brentford), *Do We Need a Censor?*, London: Faber, 1929
Coombes, H. (editor), *D.H. Lawrence: A Critical Anthology*, Harmondsworth: Penguin, 1973
Delany, Paul, *D.H. Lawrence's Nightmare: The Writer and His Circle in the Years of the Great War*, New York: Basic Books, 1978; Hassocks, Sussex: Harvester Press, 1979
Delavenay, Émile, *D.H. Lawrence: The Man and His Work: The Formative Years: 1885–1919*, London: Heinemann, and Carbondale: Southern Illinois University Press, 1972
Draper, R.P. (editor), *D.H. Lawrence: The Critical Heritage*, London: Routledge, and New York: Barnes and Noble, 1970
Gertzman, Jay A., *A Descriptive Bibliography of Lady Chatterley's Lover, with Essays Toward a Publishing History of the Novel*, New York: Greenwood Press, 1989
Grant, Damian, "D.H. Lawrence: A Suitable Case for Censorship" in *Writing and Censorship in Britain*, edited by Paul Hyland and Neil Sammells, London and New York: Routledge, 1992
Hoggart, Richard, *An Imagined Life, 1959–91*, London: Chatto and Windus, and New York: Oxford University Press, 1992 (Life and Times, vol. 3; chapter 3)
Hyland, Paul and Neil Sammels (editors), *Writing and Censorship in Britain*, London and New York: Routledge, 1992
Lucas, John, *The Radical Twenties: Writing, Politics, and Culture*, New Brunswick, New Jersey: Rutgers University Press, 1999
Moore, Harry T., *The Intelligent Heart: The Story of D. H. Lawrence*, New York: Farrar Straus, 1954, London: Heinemann, 1955; revised edition as *The Priest of Love*, Farrar Straus and Heinemann, 1974
Nehls, Edward (editor), *D.H. Lawrence: A Composite Biography*, 3 vols, Madison: University of Wisconsin Press, 1957–59
Rolph, C.H., *Books in the Dock*, London: Deutsch, 1969

LEBANON

Population: 3,496,000
Main religions: Shia Muslim; Sunni Muslim; Isma'ilite; Druze; Alawite; Roman Catholic (Maronite); Protestant
Official language: Arabic
Other languages spoken: French; Armenian; English

Illiteracy rate (%): 7.9 (m); 19.6 (f)
Number of daily newspapers: 15
Number of radio receivers per 1000 inhabitants: 907
Number of TV receivers per 1000 inhabitants: 375
Number of PCs per 1000 inhabitants: 39.2

The anthropologist Carlton Coon draws attention to the "mosaic" societies of the Middle East which are composed of distinct political, ethnic, and religious elements with only weak central authorities to hold them together. Lebanon is such a society: Maronite Christians, Eastern Orthodox Christians, Sunni and Shiite Muslims, and the Druze, among other groups, have coexisted there, often uneasily. For centuries Lebanon was under the tutelage of the Ottoman empire. Both its political history and socioreligious composition have bearing on its experience of censorship.

The Maronites trace their existence to St Maro; shortly after his death in the early 5th century, his disciples founded a monastery on the Orontes, from which the sect is said to have grown. More likely, they first arose in the 7th century as adherents of the Monothelite heresy (the notion that Christ, as both God and Man, had only one will), who were excommunicated at the Council of Constantinople in 680 CE. After the Arab incursion at the beginning of the 10th century, they looked increasingly westwards, uniting with the Roman Catholic Church during the 12th century, but retaining their own liturgy, customs, and religious law.

For much of Lebanese history, the Sunni Muslims have dominated the Shiites, both politically and numerically, but the Shiites have been numerically significant at least since the 16th century when Nur al-Din 'Ali al-Karaki (c.1466–1534) wrote about the dilemmas of adopting Shiism – which denies the right of political rulers to levy taxes – as a state religion.

The Druzes are an offshoot of Shiism, historically regarded as more extreme because they attribute near-divine powers to the imams, suggesting that 'Ali was of equal status to the Prophet himself, ideas that Sunni Muslims denounce in horror. For that reason, the Druzes developed elaborate systems of protection for what they regarded as "secret" truths: they could lie to unbelievers, but not to each other; they must renounce all other religions, including other forms of Islam, but, echoing an often-repeated practice in the history of censorship, they were allowed to conform outwardly to another religious tradition in order to avoid persecution.

Among these groups, there was, until the 19th century, some degree of common interest between the Maronites and the Druzes. Both groups were mostly landholders, and, although the Druze provided military support for the Ottoman government in Lebanon, they were said by a 19th-century traveller to Lebanon to be, if anything, more tolerant than the Maronites. In the early part of the century the Maronites grew in numbers, and the first intimation of sectarian discord came in the 1830s. Thirty years later the Druzes, increasingly of the opinion that the Maronites were planning to wipe them out, launched a first civil war (1860) during which many Christians were massacred.

At about the same time, considerable western, notably French, influence was brought to bear. The (Protestant) American Missionary College (later to become the American University of Beirut) was founded in 1867. The Jesuit University of St Joseph, which incorporated a French faculty of medicine, followed in 1875. An intelligentsia and a reading public emerged in a society that, until the early 1800s, had hardly known printing at all. Butrus al-Bustani (1819–83) published an encyclopedia of ancient and modern knowledge; according to Albert Hourani, "it speaks of Islamic subjects in tones not clouded by reserve or fear". Beirut was one of the main centres of publishing in the late Ottoman empire.

The first Lebanese newspapers appeared in the 1850s and 1860s, usually under official sponsorship, reflecting considerable Ottoman suspicion of "western" ideas. Moreover, the Ottomans adopted an on–off approach to censorship. Prior censorship was instituted to rule out any criticism of the government or any material that might harm their international relations. The Press Law of 1865 eased restrictions somewhat and, under Sultan 'Abdülhamid II (reigned 1876–1909), a constitution was introduced that guaranteed freedom for individuals in general and journalists in particular. However, as demands grew – such "western" ideas were, by now, not exactly foreign to the Maronites, even if their church still practised widespread censorship – so the Ottoman authorities drew back, reimposing government controls. Some Lebanese journalists now fled to Egypt to become prominent members of the press there, responsible for founding al-Ahram (Pyramids), which would become the best-known newspaper of the Arab world. Thus was inaugurated Lebanon's leadership of the Arab press, which continued through most of the 20th century.

A secret society pledged to oust the Ottoman Turks from Syria and Lebanon came into being in Beirut in the 1880s, publishing seditious pamphlets and posters. Members were the product of the Christian schools, but to succeed in their aims, they needed the collaboration of Muslims, with whom they hoped to make common ground with the demand that Arabic become the official language of Lebanon. The Muslims did not see that the breakup of the Ottoman empire was yet in their interest, a caution that seemed justified when, after the arrival of the Young Turks in 1908, the empire turned again towards centralization and made it clear that press freedom would be confined to the Turks themselves. Lebanese journalists then increased their opposition to the new Ottoman authorities; as participants in the growing movement for Arab nationalism, journalists were among those hanged by the Turks in Beirut and Damascus in 1915 and 1916.

With the end of the empire the League of Nations granted a mandate for the French to govern Lebanon from 1922. Not only did they introduce a law in 1924 that would permit the closure of opposition newspapers, they also fostered a system by which loyal journalists were rewarded. The French also created a "larger Lebanon", which significantly increased the number of Muslims in the country, causing alarm among the Christians (who thought that Lebanon was an essentially Christian state), and contributing to the conditions that threatened to tear the country apart later in the 20th century.

Lebanon was named a constitutional republic in 1926 and gained full independence in 1946. Elaborate arrangements were made to evolve governments that would reflect the ethnicities of the new country. The presidency and ministries of Education and Foreign Affairs were to be held by Maronites; the prime minister was to be a Sunni Muslim; and the speaker of the Chamber of Deputies to be a Shiite Muslim. A first, if minor, civil war took place in 1958, when both "sides" thought that the delicate political balance was being threatened by the other.

These arrangements did not at first suggest that Lebanon would become a major world centre for free publishing. In 1952 a Lebanese Press Union general strike was called when the government suspended several respected newspapers. In 1962 laws concerning press freedom were clarified and strengthened in a mostly liberal press decree, which was extended to nonprint media in the next decade. In the "golden era" – from the mid-1950s to the mid-1970s – 140 publishing houses printed 40 newspapers a day and more than 100 periodicals appeared regularly, extraordinary figures for a country of 3–4 million. The explanation lies in the fact that Lebanon provided printing and publishing facilities for the entire Middle East, at a time when regimes as different as Nasser's Egypt and Faisal's Saudi Arabia were making free comment impossible in their countries. Novelists took their work to Beirut to be published; their readers often had to travel there to obtain copies. Major newspapers switched production to the Lebanese capital. Ironically, some Lebanese newspapers offered expurgated versions for international distribution, to avoid offending the countries where they were widely read; and the 1962 law was amended to forbid criticism of heads of state, in response to protests from these countries.

The French radio station had been handed over to Lebanon in 1946, but failed to gain much popular support. Clandestine stations broadcast during the 1952 civil war, but did not survive it. Radio Cairo, on the other hand, where transmission capacity was increased in the 1960s, was both popular and widely available. Many Lebanese objected to the highly controlled nature of their national radio; a socialist deputy threatened to start his own radio station in 1972 because political advertising was forbidden on the government station; when another Lebanese purchased time on a Cyprus station the government jammed the broadcast. The situation with television was similar, although the service was commercial. Licences were granted on the condition that a station would transmit only news that had been provided by the Ministry of Information and Guidance free of charge; programmes that "threaten public security, or enhance the image of any political personality and party" were prohibited. These restrictions meant little, however, because only a small amount of local production was undertaken by either station. According to Douglas Boyd, profit-oriented stations were glad to be freed of responsibility for making choices about local news. International news was also cleared by a government censor.

Al-Adab (Literature), founded in 1953, was the most influential Arabic monthly, and featured socially committed literature. *Shï'r* (1957, Poem) promoted the "new poets". Much European existentialist literature was published. Literature by and about women began to appear, including that by Layla Ba'lbeki, whose first novel appeared in 1958. The Contemporary Theatre Troupe began in 1960. Lebanese cinema attendance was the highest in the Arab world in the 1950s and 1960s; state intervention in the Egyptian film industry drove producers into the Lebanese film community, with the result that 200 features were made in the decade before the civil war. Lebanon, in other words, appeared to many to be a beacon of urbanity and liberalism in the Middle East.

Such a flourishing culture could not mask for ever the forces of disintegration that were at work elsewhere in the society. The press, on the surface so open, was in reality permanently strapped for cash, leading publishers and journalists to accept support from special interest groups and to reflect their political agendas: an unofficial but powerful form of censorship. In turn, the practice contributed to the continuance of the political fragmentation that accompanied weak central government.

The civil war was waged intermittently between 1972 and 1989. In the first place, the Palestinian guerrilla organizations that operated in the country after the 1967 Arab–Israeli war posed a threat to Lebanon, but also polarized opinion along ethnic and religious lines. Maronite political leaders such as Camille Chamoun and Pierre Gemayel wanted to see the back of them. The Druze Socialist Party leader Kamal Jumblatt was prepared to offer them practical help as well as sanctuary. From June 1975 the right-wing Christian militia joined in what, it turned out, was only the first phase of the civil war. Writing in 1976, during a pause, Robert Fisk, then of the British *Times* newspaper, reported on:

the Lebanese government's newly-acquired, though perfectly legal control of the press. [Journalists] have found that almost anything they choose to report on the activities of the right wing Christian leaders . . . will be passed by the censor; but that almost any reference to Mr Kemal Jumblatt of the Leftist Alliance, and every reference to the Palestinians, is ruthlessly excised by government officials. This is scarcely surprising. Only two of the 20 censors working in Beirut are Muslims. Of the 18 Christians, several are known to have worked for the Phalangist party during the civil war; and the head of the censorship board, Colonel Antoine Dahdah, is a personal friend of the right-wing ex-President Franjineh.

Journalists left for Cyprus to "breathe some freedom outside the country", as formal pre-censorship was instituted in January 1977.

This was enacted in Legislative Decree no. 1. All material was to be submitted to a special police department on pain of a fine of 15,000 Lebanese pounds and/or up to three years imprisonment. Foreign newspapers, many of which had been banned during the war, were now similarly targeted by the censors, and even play scripts had to be submitted before performances. Even before the decree, some newspapers – *al-Nahar* and the official newspaper of the Communist Party *al-Difa'* – had been closed by order the Arab League peacekeeping force.

Despite all this, 42 national daily newspapers still appeared, many of them concentrated in West Beirut (as against 35 for the whole of Egypt, Saudi Arabia, Iraq, and Kuwait). Publishing also experienced a period of growth in the late 1970s. Thirty-one firms were registered, many of them entirely independent and thus still able to offer publication to Arab writers and scholars who could not be published elsewhere. The Egyptian writer Nawal al-Saddawi continued to be published there until Israel's occupation of Lebanon in 1982. On the other had, some of the Arab press started to be bought up by Saudi Arabians, who transferred production to London.

From 1978 Lebanon became increasingly embroiled in the wider conflicts of the Middle East. The presence of the Palestine Liberation Organisation (PLO) in the country provoked a first Israeli invasion, in alliance with a group commanded by a Lebanese Christian officer, and, more surprisingly, with Shiite Muslims in southern Lebanon. Violent sectarian clashes continued, compounded by the more sustained Israeli occupation of 1982. The civil war continued until 1989. It was little wonder in such circumstances that the most common form of "censorship" became the sectarian murder of journalists; nor that it was foreign journalists such as Terry Anderson and John McCarthy who ended up as hostages of militant Palestinian groups in 1988. Yet government radio at times experienced such extreme forms of more conventional censorship that listeners, had they not known better, could not have told that the country was at war. But in general, opposition to central control became increasingly vocal: cinemas ignored the laws and a range of radio stations grew up to become the mouthpieces of sectarian militias.

The 1989 Taif Accord ended the civil war, and modified the confessional political system to bring it closer to the actual proportions in the population of the religious/ethnic groups. The accord re-energized media pluralism. Generally speaking, in 1996 Beirut was again the seat of the most diverse media in the Arab world. On the one hand, Hollywood movies shown with voice-over critiques of their moral failings playing on a Shiite Hizbollah-sponsored television station; on the other, frank criticism of the Lebanese and Syrian governments shown on a low-budget independent television station, ICN.

Few governments would allow such a diversity of unofficial media, and, following a 1994 law designed "to organize the audio-visual media", the government licensed just four television stations and 11 private radio stations, ordering the rest (some 75 stations) to be closed. The television stations that were licensed were all linked financially to leading political figures. It was no wonder that during the outpouring of protest that followed the newspaper *al-Diyar* accused the government of "confiscating freedom", although it should be pointed out that economic and technical issues were also at stake. Finally, the government agreed to license an additional number of stations, including, temporarily, the Shiite *al-Manor*, with coverage restricted to anti-Israeli activities in southern Lebanon. Other new licences were issued to the Voice of Lebanon, backed by the Phalange Party, the communist station, Voice of the People, and Fadlallah, another Shiite station. An unknown number of unlicensed radio stations continue to operate.

Lebanon remains a complex society, and its recent censorship record defies simple description. On the one hand, it houses a most diverse range of media, reflecting its recent history and its religious and political reality. On the other hand, the government tries regularly to strengthen central control, including measures of censorship. Syria is said to retain considerable control and the Treaty of Fraternity between the two countries, signed in 1991, speaks of banning "harmful" media activity. Lebanese reporters exercise considerable self-censorship when reporting on Syrian affairs. In 1996 state prosecutors brought six libel suits against *al-Diyar* for its criticism of government policy. In 1998 opposition politicians condemned a government decision to ban television stations from showing any but government news bulletins. The rest of television, meanwhile, being mostly entertainment-oriented, is extending the boundaries of what would normally be permitted in the Arab world, especially in the area of sexuality, prompting calls for censorship of a different order than that overwhelmingly practised in the last 50 years.

Many recent sources agree that self-censorship on the part of Lebanese media continues to be significant, particularly regarding criticism of Syrian government figures and activities. Furthermore, some students were jailed in 2000 for leafleting against Syrian actions in Lebanon. In the same year, security officials banned seven foreign publications for allegedly insulting Syrian president Hafez al-Assad (now deceased). Access to information from government sources remains limited.

However, overall, privately-owned independent media are flourishing in Lebanon at the present time, and contemporary Lebanese media vividly express a wide range of opinion.

BARBARA M. ROOS

Further Reading

Badawi, M.M., *A Short History of Modern Arabic Literature*, Oxford: Clarendon Press, and New York: Oxford University Press, 1993

Boyd, Douglas A., *Broadcasting in the Arab World: A Survey of Electronic Media in the Middle East*, 2nd edition, Ames: Iowa State University Press, 1993

Dajani, Nabil H., *Disoriented Media in a Fragmented Society: The Lebanese Experience*, Beirut: American University of Beirut, 1992

Darwish, Adel and Haifaa Khalfallah, "Lebanon: Last Refuge of the Written Word Destroyed", *Index on Censorship*, 11/6 (December 1982)

Fisk, Robert, "Lebanon: Strict and Partial", *The Times* (10 January 1977)

Hourani, Albert, *A History of the Arab Peoples*, Cambridge, Massachusetts: Harvard University Press, and London: Faber, 1991

Hoye, Paul *et al.*, "Paradise Lost: Memories of a Golden Age", *ARAMCO World Magazine*, 33/5 (September–October 1982)

US Department of State, *Lebanon: Country Report on Human Rights Practices*, section 2: *Respect for Civil Liberties: Freedom of Speech and Press*, Washington, DC: Bureau of Democracy, Human Rights and Labor, 2001

Website

"Lebanon: 2000 World Press Freedom Review", at http://www.freemedia.at/

LEGION OF DECENCY
US moral crusaders and film censorship campaigners, 1935–68

In the spring of 1933 America was in the midst of the Great Depression. The film industry was reeling from a collapse at the box office and a chorus of demands from civil leaders, religious organizations, and politicans to clean it up. Will Hays, president of the Motion Picture Producers and Distributers of America (MPPDA), was desperately trying to maintain a coalition of support for self-regulation within the Hollywood film industry. While he continued to enjoy the support of numerous national organizations and women's clubs, the criticism of the industry remained unabated. The demands for federal censorship and increased state film censorship received a tremendous boost when in the spring of 1933 a sensational book published by Henry James Forman, *Our Movie-Made Children*, accused movies of corrupting youth. Forman boldly charged that 72 per cent of all movies were unfit for children and were "helping to shape a race of criminals". *Our Movie-Made Children* became a national bestseller.

The pressure on the film industry increased considerably when the newly appointed papal apostolic delegate to the United States, monsignor Amleto Giovanni Cicognani, declared that "a massacre of innocence of youth" was taking place in the movie theatres. "Catholics are", said Cicognani, "called by God, the Pope, the Bishops, and the priests to a united and vigorous campaign for the purification of the cinema, which has become a deadly menace to morals." The speech, written and inspired by Martin Quigley, an active lay Catholic who owned an important trade publication, *The Motion Picture Herald*, kicked off the Catholic campaign to create a Legion of Decency. In a matter of months, more than seven million people, mostly Catholics, had promised to boycott immoral movies:

I wish to join the Legion of Decency, which condemns vile and unwholesome moving pictures. I unite with all who protest against them as a grave menace to youth, to home life, to country, and to religion ... Considering these evils, I hereby promise to remain away from all motion pictures except those which do not offend decency and Christian morality ... I make this protest with the conviction that the American public does not demand filthy pictures, but clean entertainment and educational features".

When the church offered to soften its boycott if the industry would appoint a Catholic censor and give him the authority to enforce the production code written by Father Daniel Lord, Hays readily accepted. The Production Code Administration (PCA) was created in July 1934 and the Catholic church officially created a National Legion of Decency in November 1935. The legion and the PCA often worked hand-in-hand as film censors.

Administratively the National Legion office operated out of the Catholic Charities Office in New York. Father John Daly, from St Gregory's Church in New York and a professor of psychology at the College of St Vincent, was appointed executive secretary.

The task of determining the moral values of movies was given to the women's organization, the International Federation of Catholic Alumnae (IFCA). In 1922, under the direction of Rita C. McColdrick, the IFCA had created a Motion Picture Bureau, headed by Mary Looram. For 12 years Looram and her staff of volunteers had published reviews of good films which they urged Catholics to support. Films they considered vulgar, tasteless, or immoral were simply ignored.

The first task of the National Legion of Decency and the IFCA was to define a rating system that would be used to classify movies. After some debate the Catholic hierarchy agreed that only the National Legion, not local dioceses, would classify movies. The rating categories were to be: A. 1: Unobjectionable for general patronage; A. 2: Unobjectionable for adults; B: Objectionable in part for all; C: Condemned.

In February, 1936, the National Legion of Decency issued its first classification of films. Charlie Chaplin's *Modern Times* (United Artists, 1936) was placed in the A grouping despite "a few vulgarities". The Marlene Dietrich film *Desire* (Paramount, 1936) was approved for adults in spite of "a few long, drawn out kisses and suggestive remarks". No films were condemned but several were placed in the B classification including Boris Karloff's *The Walking Dead* (Warner Bros., 1936) because this Frankenstein spin-off implied that the mad doctor created life in his laboratory.

Within the year controversy had erupted within the newly created legion. Father Daly disagreed with Martin Quigley on the morality of a variety of films and was replaced as executive director by Father John McClafferty, who served until 1947. The Legion of Decency is often thought of as a huge bureaucratic arm of the Catholic church, but in fact it had a minuscule staff, consisting of a secretary, Mary Looram, and a handful of volunteers. The Hollywood studios submitted films to legion officials in New York before they had them duplicated for distribution and exhibition. After the reviewers saw a film they submitted written evaluations and recommendations for

classification to Looram. She and McClafferty tabulated them and made a final decision on a classification for each film they reviewed.

By mid-1937 there were only occasional differences of opinion between Breen's Production Code Administration (PCA) and the legion. In 1938, for example, only a small fraction – 32 out of 535 PCA-approved films – were given a B classification and no film from a major studio was condemned. In fact, no PCA-approved film was condemned by the legion for the remaining years of the decade.

It was in the post-World War II era, especially from the late 1940s to the early 1960s, that the Legion of Decency played a major role as film censor. In 1947, Father Patrick Masterson succeeded Father McClafferty as executive director of the legion. Masterson watched in horror when a film condemned by the legion, Howard Hughes's *The Outlaw*, enjoyed a bonanza at the box office. Masterson was determined to stop Hollywood from making similar films.

David O. Selznick was the first to experience the Legion's wrath. When the legion reviewed Selznick's lusty horse opera, *Duel in the Sun*, they slapped a condemned rating on the film because of the highly charged sexual relationship between Jennifer Jones and Gregory Peck. Selznick vowed to fight but recieved no support from the Hollywood community. In the end, he had to make all the cuts demanded by the legion in order to have the condemed rating changed. The legion's real power came from its ability to limit the distribution of films. Exhibitors were reluctant to book a film condemned by the legion because they feared local boycotts that would last far beyond the run of any particular film. When Selznick realized he could not book his film into first-run movie theatres he caved in.

It was an Italian film that brought legion activities to the attention of a national audience. In December 1950, Roberto Rossellini's *The Miracle*, starring Anna Magnani as a demented peasant woman who believes she has been impregnated by St Joseph, opened in New York City. The film was destined to fade quickly from the public view until it was condemned by the legion as a "sacrilegious and blasphemous mockery of Christian and religious truth". The controversy heated up when Cardinal Spellman, archbishop of New York, described the film as a "despicable affront" to Christianity inspired by communist propaganda. The New York state censorship board responded by banning the film as sacrilegious.

Catholics threw up pickets across the country to protest against the movie. But in the end, it was the Supreme Court that had the final say. In 1952 the Court ruled in *Burstyn v. Wilson* (343 U.S. 495) that films were "included within the free speech and free press guarantee of the First and Fourteenth Amendments". Nor could a state ban a film for religious reasons under the separation of church and state provisions of the Constitution. This action reversed the 1915 decision (*Mutual v. Ohio*) that had placed movies outside First Amendment protection.

The legion continued to condemn films considered to be immoral. Otto Preminger's *The Moon is Blue* (1953) and Elia Kazan's *Baby Doll* (1956) were condemned as immoral. Others, such as *A Street Car Named Desire* (1951), *Tea and Sympathy* (1956), and *Cat on a Hot Tin Roof* (1958), were threatened with condemnation. In return for a more favourable rating each was significantly altered by the legion before being released to the public.

By the late 1950s the legion was controversial even within the church. Monsignor Thomas Little was the executive director but the legion was under attack by such theologians as Father John Courtney Murray, who questioned whether or not the church had the authority under canon law to forbid individual Catholics from attending condemned films. Murray argued that a Catholic did not commit a sin by attending a condemned film. With such criticism from within, the legion's days were numbered. It was increasingly evident, even to legion officials, that by the early 1960s few Catholics paid much attention to its ratings. Moreover the legion itself changed under the pressure of liberalization: it condemned neither Federico Fellini's *La dolce vita* (1962) nor Mike Nichols's profane *Who's Afraid of Virginia Woolf?* (1966).

When Hollywood eliminated the Production Code Administration in 1968 and switched to a rating system, the legion all but disappeared. The church continued for a few years to review films under a newly created National Catholic Office for Motion Pictures (NCOMP), headed by Father Patrick Sullivan, but it lacked the authority of the old legion and was largely ignored by Hollywood and the general public.

GREGORY D. BLACK

Further Reading

Black, Gregory D., *The Catholic Crusade against the Movies, 1940–1975*, Cambridge and New York: Cambridge University Press, 1998

Morris, Charles R., *American Catholic: The Saints and Sinners Who Built America's Most Powerful Church*, New York: Times Books, 1997

Skinner, James M., *The Cross and the Cinema: The Legion of Decency and the National Catholic Office for Motion Pictures, 1933–1970*, Westport, Connecticut: Praeger, 1993

Walsh, Frank, *Sin and Censorship: The Catholic Church and the Motion Picture Industry*, New Haven, Connecticut: Yale University Press, 1996

LEMBAGA KEBUDAYAAN RAKYAT
(Lekra, Institute of People's Culture)
Indonesian arts and cultural organization, 1950–66

Lekra was established in Jakarta in 1950, less than a year after the transfer of sovereignty by the Netherlands to an independent Indonesia. In its original manifesto, the organization declared its aim to be the promotion of an Indonesian culture that would liberate the Indonesian people from the vestiges of colonial culture and resist efforts to impose imperialist and "feudalist" cultural practices within the framework of the post-colonial state. Among its founders were D.N. Aidit and Njoto, two leaders of the recently reformed Indonesian Communist Party (PKI). Njoto, elected to the politbureau of the PKI's Central Committee in 1951, also became one of six members of the initial Lekra secretariat, and retained leadership positions in both organizations until Lekra's demise at the end of 1965. The PKI claimed Lekra as one of its affiliated organizations, but the Lekra membership included non-communists who shared the organization's support for radical nationalist politics and identified with its democratic and populist cultural aspirations.

By 1951, Lekra had established branches throughout Indonesia, and was active in both national and regional cultural affairs. At the regional level it promoted the development of performance arts and other local cultural practices threatened with extinction. Nationally, it entered into debate with the "universalizing" tendencies in Indonesian language literature, and fostered a continuation of the "people-oriented" art of the 1945–49 revolution against the Dutch.

After 1959, a growing polarization of Indonesian artists and cultural workers along political lines involved Lekra in situations of increasing tension and conflict. As national politics under president Sukarno became more stridently anti-imperialist and Indonesia moved into closer alignment with China at the expense of United States' interests, the PKI came to occupy a more central position in national political life. The growing influence of the PKI and the indications that it was to be Sukarno's chosen successor increased the confidence and assertiveness of the party's affiliated organizations. By 1963 Lekra claimed a membership of 100,000 and was embarking on militant campaigns in support of its cultural and political objectives.

Especially in Java and Bali, regional cultural campaigns in support of land reform made extensive use of local performance traditions, while at the national level, Lekra entered into vociferous polemical debate with representatives of the opposing tendencies in literature, film, and art. Debate became particularly vitriolic after the declaration of the anti-Lekra Cultural Manifesto by various critics and literary figures in October 1963. This did not mention Lekra by name, but its carefully worded statement of adherence to religious and universalist values was intended – and perceived – as a direct challenge to the engaged art and literature, and the broader cultural politics, that Lekra represented.

By this time anti-Lekra writers and artists were seeking support from the Indonesian army, the main bastion of the anti-communist political forces. The military authorities had already on occasion banned performances of particular Lekra plays and dance dramas, and in 1962 the military commander of the Greater Jakarta Region issued a ban on a collection of poetry by the prominent Lekra poet Agam Wispi. After the banning of the Cultural Manifesto by president Sukarno in May 1964, however, Lekra influence was instrumental in acts of censorship directed at its opponents.

The anti-Lekra literary journal *Sastra* found itself denied access to printing supplies and was forced to cease publication by the middle of 1964. Literary critics and cultural figures associated with the Cultural Manifesto were dismissed from teaching positions in state universities, with the backing of left-wing student organizations. In mid-1965, the Department of Education and Culture issued bans on the books of many prominent writers and intellectuals associated with the anti-Lekra tendencies. These included older generation figures like S.T. Alisjahbana, Hamka, Idrus, H.B. Jassin, Mochtar Lubis, and Trisno Sumardjo, as well as young writers who were associated with the Cultural Manifesto, such as Wiratmo Sukito, Goenawan Mohamad, and Bur Rasuanto.

The military coup and counter-coup of October 1965 ushered in a dramatic reversal of Lekra's ascendancy. The events of October–November 1965 began the overthrow of Sukarno and his government and unleashed a military-backed campaign of mass murder and imprisonment directed at the PKI and its supporters. Officially, Lekra ceased to exist in March 1966, when general – later to be president – Suharto issued a decree in the name of president Sukarno, declaring the PKI and its affiliated organizations illegal. Shortly afterwards, a long list of bans on books by writers associated with or members of Lekra replaced the earlier bans on the work of anti-Lekra figures. These new bans included the work of prominent writers and critics like Pramoedya Ananta Toer, Utuy T. Sontani, Sitor Situmorang, Agam Wispi, H.R. Bandaharo, and Bakri Siregar, as well as publications of all kinds by numerous less well-known figures.

Lekra writers, artists, and intellectuals were taken into custody, to be imprisoned without trial under conditions of extreme suffering and deprivation for periods of up to 14 years. Meanwhile, in regional areas, it is likely that many thousands of Lekra members perished in the army-backed massacres that swept Indonesia between November 1965 and the early months of 1966.

The consolidation of the military-civilian "New Order" regime of president Suharto in the period before 1970 saw the continued denial of Lekra writers and artists from any role in the history of Indonesian national culture. For example, in a new edition of the standard anthology of literature by writers of the revolutionary period, *Gema Tanah Air* (Echo of the Homeland), the literary critic H.B. Jassin removed all writing by Lekra-associated figures, replacing it with the work of less well-known writers. No prints of films made with Lekra's support survived this period, and much painting and sculpture disappeared through destruction or neglect.

When Lekra figures began their "return to society" in the late 1970s, those still active as writers and artists continued to face informal censorship in the form of limited access to publication and performance channels, as well as the direct bannings imposed on the work of the most prominent writer formerly associated with Lekra, Pramoedya Ananta Toer. The continued demonization of Lekra, rooted in the resentments engendered by the bitter campaigns of the early 1960s, continued well into the 1990s as a means of censoring any public or printed evaluation of Lekra that portrayed it as other than an organization that subjected art to the interests of international communism and denied individual creative and intellectual freedom.

KEITH FOULCHER

Further Reading

Foulcher, Keith, *Social Commitment in Literature and the Arts: The Indonesian "Institute of People's Culture", 1950–1965*, Clayton, Victoria: Monash University, Centre of Southeast Asian Studies, 1986

Foulcher, Keith, *"The Manifesto Is Not Dead": Indonesian Literary Politics Thirty Years On*, Clayton, Victoria: Monash University, Centre of Southeast Asian Studies, 1994

Heinschke, Martina, "Between Gelanggang and Lekra: Pramoedya's Developing Literary Concepts", *Indonesia*, 61 (April 1996): 145–69

Hill, David T., *Who's Left? Indonesian Literature in the Early 1980s*, Clayton, Victoria: Monash University, Centre of Southeast Asian Studies, 1984

Holt, Claire, *Art in Indonesia: Continuities and Change*, Ithaca, New York: Cornell University Press, 1967

Maier, H.M.J., "Chairil Anwar's Heritage: The Fear of Stultification, Another Side of Modern Indonesian Literature", *Indonesia*, 43 (April 1987): 1–30

Sen, Krishna, *Indonesian Cinema, Framing the New Order*, London: Zed, 1994

Teeuw, A., *Modern Indonesian Literature*, The Hague: Nijhoff, 1979

JÓZSEF LENGYEL
Hungarian writer, 1896–1975

Lengyel was a novelist and journalist who devoted much of the latter part of his career to exposing the atrocities committed by Stalinists in the Soviet Union in the 1930s and 1940s. His personal life is representative of the career of radical left-wing intellectuals in central Europe in the early and mid-20th century, and his deeply autobiographical literary works were written with the intention of truthfully documenting human life against its historical backdrop.

Born into a wealthy middle-class family in the countryside, Lengyel gained recognition in Budapest in the 1910s as an avant-garde poet. He soon became sympathetic to radical leftist ideas, and chose to participate in the Hungarian Soviet Republic of 1919 by helping to edit two leading periodicals, *Vörös Újság* (Red Gazette) and *Ifjú Proletar* (Young Proletarian). His experiences during the brief period of communist rule were to be depicted in two of his novels, *Visegradi utca* (Visegradi Street, published in Moscow in 1932 and in Hungary in 1957), and *Prenn Ferenc hányatott élete* (1958, Penn Drifting).

Lengyel was forced to flee Hungary after the overthrow of the communist republic, and spent several years in Vienna and Berlin, supporting himself with journalism and writing film scripts. His political sympathies drew him to Moscow in 1930, where, like a number of his comrades and for no apparent reason, he fell victim to one of Stalin's purges in 1938. Lengyel subsequently spent 17 years in prison, in labour camps in Siberia, under police surveillance, and, eventually, in compulsory residence elsewhere in the Soviet Union. These experiences provided him with material for the second, belated stage of his career.

After his release from detention in the Soviet Union, in 1955, Lengyel returned to Hungary to find himself celebrated both by intellectuals and by the post-Stalinist, pro-Soviet government. He made a successful re-entry onto the Hungarian literary scene, and in 1963, at the age of 67, he was awarded the most prestigious of Hungarian literary prizes, the Kossuth Prize, for a volume of loosely connected short stories, *Igéző* (1961, Spell). These stories describe the horrors endured by exiled Hungarian communists under Stalin in the Siberian labour camps.

Lengyel's next major work, and the one that he himself regarded as his most important, was *Szembesítés* (1968, Confrontation). This strongly autobiographical novella describes the confrontation between two "true believers", Endre Lassu and István Banicza, in Moscow in 1948. They were close friends during the prewar years of illegality in Budapest, when Banicza was Lassu's political tutee and underground "contact", but their lives have diverged since then. Lassu fled to Vienna and subsequently to the Soviet Union, where, like his creator, he has been imprisoned and sent to labour camps. Meanwhile, Banicza has suffered similar incarceration at the hands of the Germans in Mauthausen, but, on his return to Hungary, he has been embraced by the diplomatic service of the victorious Communist Party and rewarded with the post of first counsellor at the Hungarian Embassy in Moscow. Their reunion, soon to turn into a confrontation, takes place at the embassy.

The disillusioned Lassu, who has returned to Moscow in secret from compulsory residence in a provincial Russian town, and Banicza, the confident representative of the victorious party, confront one another to evaluate the horrors of Stalinism and its effect upon the future of the ideals they once shared. Their critique, however, is markedly different from the views dominant in the West. Both hold that the crimes are integral to, and revelatory of the nature of communist dictatorships, but they also believe that they are incidental to the true nature of communism. Their debate revolves around the appropriateness of disclosing the Stalinist horrors. Banicza, the true and honest party bureaucrat, argues that premature disclosure of such atrocities would empower the "enemies" of the cause, and expresses his belief in the party's ability to purify itself bloodlessly. Lassu's stance is more complex: he too is certain that it is possible, at least in principle, to remove the elements of bloody dictatorship from communism, and thus realize a true workers' state, yet he makes his communist faith conditional upon immediate and complete moral purification. He insists that the party must honestly admit the atrocities of Stalinism and dismantle its stultifying bureaucracy. His faith in the possibility of a pure communism, however, is not based on previous experience or rationally conceived expectation. He knows that, in a sense, the Stalinist camps were worse than the German ones, for the Russians persecuted their own comrades, and he is fully aware that if he is caught in Moscow he will have to spend another 20 years in Siberia. Lassu's messianistic impulse, promising another incarceration, is contrasted with Banicza's less than radical subversion of the policies of the party, which is likely to reward him with a subsequent assignment in London.

Szembesítés is hardly subversive by contemporary western standards, or even by the standards prevailing in Hungary at a later period; yet only the first chapter of the novella was published in Hungary in 1968, in the government-financed literary periodical *Kortárs* (Contemporary). The subsequent chapters, due to be published from January 1969 onwards, were cancelled with no explanation. In 1971, following lengthy negotiations between Lengyel and the party bureaucrats in charge of cultural policy, the entire novella was published in the peculiar format of an "inner party *samizdat*", circulated for the benefit of politically reliable "inner party" members only, printed, without bibliographical information, under the heading "To be regarded as manuscript". As the unsigned preface to this edition explains, this arrangement was made necessary by the novella's dangerously subversive content. Although both characters share a commitment to the cause, Lassu's critique of the crimes of Stalinism lends itself to interpretations that would "generalize the exceptional", for its "debatable details" and its failure to "disclose the great historical connections" might allow readers to draw undesirable conclusions about the nature of the system. The misfortune of the novella lay in its timing: the attempt to publish it in *Kortárs* happened only a few months after the suppression of the Prague Spring by the forces of the Warsaw Pact (including Hungary's). Under these circumstances, even its mild critique of existing communist dictatorships was regarded as a threat to those in power.

The book reached the West in 1972, and Anna Novotny's English translation appeared in Britain in 1973. Its publication led to a cooling of the otherwise excellent relations between Lengyel and the party bureaucracy. In the long run, however, the writing of the novella did nothing to endanger Lengyel's position as a highly respected member of the Hungarian literary establishment, although he always regretted that his most important message concerning the necessity of separating communism from Stalinism did not reach the Hungarian public in time to influence their response to the events in Czechoslovakia.

So far, no complete edition of *Szembesítés* has been published for general circulation in Hungary. Ironically, its very content, which was initially felt to be threateningly subversive, soon came to seem dated and forgettable.

ZSUZSANNA VARGA

Writings

From Beginning to End, and The Spell, translated by Ilona Duczynska, 1966
Prenn Drifting, translated by Ilona Duczynska, 1966
The Judge's Chair, translated by Ilona Duczynska, 1968
Acta Sanctorum and Other Tales, translated by Ilona Duczynska, 1970
Confrontation, translated by Anna Novotny, 1973

Further Reading

Bédé, Jean-Albert and William B. Edgerton (editors), *Columbia Dictionary of Modern European Literature*, 2nd edition, New York: Columbia University Press, 1980
Books Abroad (Spring 1973, Summer 1975, Winter 1975)
Czigány, Lóránt, *The Oxford History of Hungarian Literature from the Earliest Times to the Present*, Oxford: Clarendon Press, and New York: Oxford University Press, 1984
Ignotus, P., "The Return of József Lengyel", *Encounter* (May 1965)
Lengyel József noteszeiből: 1955–1975, Budapest: Magvető, 1989
Révész, Sándor, *Aczél és korunk*, Budapest: Sík Kiadó, 1997
Tezla, Albert, *Hungarian Authors: A Bibliographical Handbook*, Cambridge, Massachusetts: Harvard University Press, 1970
Times Literary Supplement (6 March 1969, 21 December 1973, 28 April 1972)

LUIS DE LEÓN
Spanish theologian and poet, 1527–91

Any educated Spaniard is familiar with the tale of how this monk and professor of theology, on being released by the Inquisition after almost five years in jail, walked into his classroom at the University of Salamanca and began his lecture with the words, "As we were saying yesterday". The case of Fray Luis de León is notable not only as an example of the practice of censorship under the Spanish Inquisition but also of the petty jealousies that have always haunted universities in Spain and elsewhere.

Fray Luis was arrested in Salamanca on 26 March 1572, and sent to Valladolid, where he was incarcerated the next day. Among the reasons given for his arrest was that he was descended from a Jewish great-grandmother. The Inquisition also condemned him for having translated the Old Testament book *The Song of Solomon* into Spanish: the Council of Trent had expressly forbidden translations of the Scriptures into the vernacular. The Inquisition also denounced Fray Luis for having questioned the accuracy of the Vulgate, the Latin version of the Bible ascribed to St. Jerome (c.404). The Council of Trent (1545–63) had pronounced the Vulgate the only authentic text of the Scriptures, and the Inquisition did not take kindly to one who pointed out its flaws. (Yet in 1592, a revised text contained some 3000 corrections.)

Fray Luis had never intended his Spanish translation of *The Song of Solomon* to circulate publicly. He had prepared his translation and accompanying commentary around 1560 at the request of his cousin, Isabel Osorio, who was a nun in a convent in Salamanca. The text was discovered by a lay brother, Diego de León, who had been entrusted with cleaning Luis de León's monastic cell. Diego surreptitiously copied the text, which was then transcribed repeatedly. These copies of the translation circulated rapidly and widely, even to Peru by 1575. Nevertheless, Diego left the original manuscript of the translation in Fray Luis's cell, and the Inquisition confiscated it on 7 November 1573.

The Inquisition could not prove that Fray Luis was guilty of heresy; consequently, his prison term was prolonged while the Inquisition tried to garner evidence. In March 1574 the Inquisitorial Tribunal of Valladolid attempted to strengthen its case against him by enumerating 17 incriminating passages in his Latin writings and 30 such passages in his Spanish writings. However, the prosecution's new argument was based on minutiae that added nothing new to the original charges. On 7 December 1576, the Supreme Tribunal of the Inquisition intervened and ordered the provincial Tribunal of Valladolid to release Fray Luis.

The Inquisition had first become suspicious of Fray Luis because of public disputes that he had with some of his colleagues regarding the interpretation of the Scriptures. One of these adversaries was León de Castro, Professor of Latin, Rhetoric and Greek at Salamanca. Luis de León and León de Castro served together on a committee charged with revising François Vatable's version of the Bible; this committee provided the stage for their intellectual conflicts. (In 1545, Robert Stevens had published his Bible of Paris, based on Vatable's annotations. The Sorbonne had condemned it as bordering on Lutheranism.) Such was their rivalry that it divided the student body into two factions. Castro's chief ally in the debate was Bartolomé de Medina. Medina had been humiliated publicly by Fray Luis in a theological debate and thus academic jealousy, as much as controversial Scriptural interpretation, was at the root of Luis de León's treatment.

Luis de León resumed lecturing at Salamanca on 29 January 1577, less than two months after his release from prison. Undaunted by almost five years in jail, he was quick to attract the attention of the Inquisition again. In 1580 he published a Latin version of *The Song of Solomon*, accompanied by a Latin commentary on Psalm 26. On the title page, he included an etching of an oak tree and an axe, captioned, "Ab ipso ferro" (From the steel itself), a quotation from Horace's *Odes*, alluding to the holm oak's power to gain strength from the pruner's axe. The Inquisitorial Tribunal at Valladolid interpreted the etching and epigram as a challenge and wrote a letter of complaint to the Supreme Tribunal on 15 October 1580.

In 1582 Fray Luis took part in a theological debate about the reconciliation of the doctrines of predestination and free will. On 5 February Fray Juan de Santa Cruz denounced him before the Inquisitorial Tribunal in Valladolid, citing 16 passages in Latin taken from Fray Luis's pronouncements during the debate. Hoping to clear his name, Fray Luis appeared voluntarily before the Inquisitorial Tribunal in Salamanca on 8 March. The case was not resolved for two years; Fray Luis was finally summoned to Toledo on 3 February 1584, for the purpose of being reprimanded personally by the Grand Inquisitor, Cardinal Gaspar de Quiroga.

Luis de León again caught the attention of the censors when he was editing the writings of Teresa of Ávila, which had been denounced before the Inquisition in 1574. In 1589 Alfonso de la Fuente wrote to the Inquisition several times denouncing Teresa's writings. Fray Luis's name appears in some of these documents; so by editing Teresa's works, Fray Luis was said to have become an accomplice to her alleged heresy.

DOUGLAS EDWARD LAPRADE

Writings

De los nombres de Cristo, 1583; as *The Names of Christ*, translated by Manuel Durán and William Kluback, 1984

La perfecta casada (The Perfect Wife), 1583; in *La perfecta casada: The Role of Married Women in Sixteenth-Century Spain*, edited and translated by John A. James and Javier San José Lera, 1999

Obras completas, edited by Félix García, 4th edition, 2 vols, 1967

The Unknown Light: The Poems, translated by Willis Barnstone, 1979

Obra poética completa, edited by Miguel de Santiago, 1981

Further Reading

Alcalá, Ángel (editor), *El proceso inquisitorial de Fray Luis de León: edición paleográfica, anotada y crítica*, Junta de Castilla y León: Consejería de Cultura y Turismo, 1991

Durán, Manuel, *Luis de León*, New York: Twayne, 1971

Fitzmaurice-Kelly, James, *Fray Luis de León: A Biographical Fragment*, Oxford: Oxford University Press, 1921
Muñoz Iglesias, Salvador, *Fray Luis de León, Teólogo*, Madrid: Consejo Superior de Investigaciones Científicas, 1950

Pinta Llorente, Miguel de la, *Estudios y polémicas sobre Fray Luis de León*, Madrid: Consejo Superior de Investigaciones Científicas, 1965

MIKHAIL LERMONTOV
Russian poet, novelist, and dramatist, 1814–1841
SMERT' POETA (Death of a Poet)
Poem, 1837

Aleksandr Pushkin died in 1837 in his house in St Petersburg from a wound that he had sustained in a duel with Georges d'Anthès three days earlier. The poet's death occasioned an unprecedented outpouring of public grief, to which some of the best-known names in Russian literature endeavoured to give voice. Yet the most prominent contribution to these literary obsequies was made by a 23-year-old cornet in the Life Guard Hussars, with only one published poem to his credit. Lermontov's "Death of a Poet" became the most famous of the many eulogies on Pushkin, and launched its author's reputation.

Lermontov's threnody falls into three parts. He begins by describing Pushkin as a martyred rebel against "the opinions of society", a "prodigious genius" slain by a fortune-seeking, Russia-hating foreigner, a "killer" "with an "empty heart". After this magniloquent opening, the mood shifts to the elegiac. Pushkin's fate is compared to that of the "gentle-hearted" bard Lenskii in his own verse novel *Evgenii Onegin* (1833, Eugene Onegin), who falls prey to "blind-eyed jealousy". A further, hidden, allusion recalls Pushkin's elegy "André Chénier" (1825): "Why had he left kind friends and peaceful meditating / To move into a world of envy suffocating . . . ?" The last 16 lines are a sustained piece of rhetorical vituperation, and it was this part of the poem that got Lermontov into trouble. After denouncing the "arrogant" aristocrats clustered around the throne as the "executioners" of "Freedom, Genius, and Glory", he warns that God's judgement awaits these "minions of corruption", whose "black blood can't wash away nor shall it ever / Redeem the Poet's righteous blood!"

In fact, the first 56 lines had been composed while Pushkin was still alive. Lermontov had added the crucial 16-line postscript a few days after Pushkin's death, in a fit of rage at those who defended the conduct of d'Anthès. Two versions of the poem, with and without the postscript, were soon circulating in the capital. While it was extravagantly praised by Pushkin's friends and admirers, a sizable proportion of the city's *beau monde* found it personally or politically offensive. The notorious scandalmonger Anna Khitrovo, whose scheming and gossiping had won her the soubriquet "the leper of society", took particular exception to what she saw as an attack on the best Russian families. At a reception given by the Austrian ambassador, this malevolent soul pointedly asked count Alexander Benckendorff, the head of the Third Section (the secret police), whether he had read "Death of a Poet". She also sent a copy of the poem, with the superscription "A Call to Revolution", to emperor Nicholas I at the Winter Palace. Benckendorff himself had found nothing objectionable in the piece, at least in its original version, but Nicholas's younger brother, grand duke Mikhail Pavlovich, advised him to keep it from the emperor's eyes. Indeed, Nicholas was incensed by the poem. His anger at what he considered an act of political subversion may have been compounded by his concern over "his own involvement in the chain of murky events leading to the fatal duel" (according to Laurence Kelly).

Lermontov was placed under arrest at the General Staff headquarters. His lodgings at Tsarskoe Selo were searched and his papers were seized. In the "explanation" he wrote while he was in detention, he was to some extent apologetic, ascribing the violent language of his poem to a feeling of "spontaneous but strong indignation" against Pushkin's traducers, which he blamed on his "irritated nerves". He conceded that he had composed his verses "too soon" after the event and admitted that he had allowed his friend Sviatoslav Raevskii (who had also been arrested) to copy them out. It was the latter, Lermontov wrote, who was "probably" responsible for their dissemination. The "explanation" ended, however, on a note of restrained defiance: "I could not renounce them [the verses], even though I realized my lack of judgement: the truth has always been sacred to me."

Benckendorff wrote to Nicholas describing the first part of "Death of a Poet" as "impudent" and its conclusion as "shamelessly freethinking [and] more than seditious". On the margins of Benckendorff's report the emperor sarcastically referred to the poem as "pleasant verses" and, in a formulation that echoed his comments on Petr Chaadaev's first *Filosoficheskoe pis'mo* (1836, "Philosophical Letter") a few months earlier, added: "I have ordered the senior medical officer of the Corps of Guards to visit this young man and to ascertain whether he is insane; and then we shall deal with him according to the law". Count Chernyshev, the minister for war, informed Benckendorff that the emperor had decided to transfer Lermontov to the Nizhnii Novgorod Dragoons, at the same rank. This meant exile to the Caucasus, for the regiment in question was part of the expeditionary corps engaged in a bloody war against Shamil's mountain tribesmen. Raevskii was sentenced to a month's confinement, to be followed by an official assignment to Olonetsk Province in the north. In October 1837 Lermontov was transferred to the Grodno Hussar Life Guards, who were stationed in Novgorod province, and in April 1838 Nicholas I allowed him to rejoin the Hussar Life Guards. Raevskii's term of exile was lifted in late 1838.

RICHARD TEMPEST

Writings
Smert' poeta (Death of a Poet), 1837
A Lermontov Reader, translated by Guy Daniels, 1965
Major Poetical Works, translated by Anatoly Liberman, 1983

Further Reading

Kelly, Laurence, *Lermontov: Tragedy in the Caucasus*, London: Constable, and New York: Braziller, 1977

M. Iu. Lermontov v vospominaniiakh sovremennikov (Lermontov in the Recollections of His Contemporaries), Moscow: Khudozhestvennaia Literatura, 1989

Manuilov, V., *Letopis' zhizni i tvorchestva M. Iu. Lermontova* [Chronicle of M. Iu. Lermontov's Life and Creative Activity], Leningrad: Nauka, 1964

Manuilov, V.A. (editor), *Lermontovskaia entsiklopediia* [The Lermontov Encyclopaedia], Moscow: Sovetskaia entsiklopediia, 1981

Mirsky, D.S., *A History of Russian Literature, from Its Beginnings to 1900*, edited by Francis J. Whitfield, revised edition, New York: Knopf, 1958

ETIENNE LEROUX

South African writer (real name: Stephanus Petrus Daniel Le Roux), 1922–

MAGERSFONTEIN, O MAGERSFONTEIN!
Novel, 1976

Magersfontein, O Magersfontein! occupies a pivotal position in the relationship between Afrikaans literature and censorship. The censorship history of this work illustrates the growing discord within the Afrikaner community in the mid-1970s between the *verligtes* (liberals) and *verkramptes* (conservatives). The protracted battle around *Magersfontein* led to significant changes in the censorship law and its application.

The novel, written by an established Afrikaner author, is a satirical account of the expedition of a film crew to the battlefield of Magersfontein, to recreate the historic battle between the English and the Boers on 12 December 1899. The battle ends when a flood turns the Magersfontein plain into a vast lake. As is characteristic of Leroux's writing, the work abounds in hyperbole and irony. The victims of his biting sarcasm are among others: war, the apartheid system, the English, academics, and, not least the government officials who assure the population that everything is under control.

Magersfontein had already been approved by a publications committee when a group of moral vigilantes, the Aktie Morele Standaarde (Action for Moral Values), started a campaign to have the book banned. This small group of activists campaigned against what they viewed as the moral pollution of South Africa and had played a significant part in achieving changes to the Publications Act in 1974; in November 1975 its members had organized widely reported book burnings.

On 14 September 1977 Connie Mulder, minister of the interior, asked the Publications Appeal Board (PAB) to reconsider *Magersfontein*. The committee had earlier ruled that its literary value outweighed its uncivilized language and that it should be kept in circulation. The PAB now overruled that decision, declaring the work undesirable on moral and religious grounds. Leroux's reaction was one of shock. He was appalled that his work had been dissected in public by people without literary knowledge or interest. He feared a lasting impact on his writing career, although he vowed to continue.

As was to be expected, Mulder welcomed the ban. It would protect South Africa and ensure the survival of its people. Surprisingly, however, the Afrikaner newspapers, usually supportive of the Nationalist government, sided with the writers this time. When the ban was announced, *Beeld* ran a strongly-worded editorial: "When a brilliant novel by possibly our greatest writer – a satire whose literary value is undoubted – is summarily banned, our censorship system has become a monster, a threat to the creative artist, our intellectual life and the Afrikaans press" (22 November 1977).

A day later *Die Burger*, in milder words, also denounced the ban, but indicated how the law might be changed to avoid similar cases in the future: "What is apparently needed is legal protection for works of acknowledged literary value" (23 November 1977). The banning of *Magersfontein* actually did have far-reaching legal consequences. The Supreme Court, to which Leroux's publisher appealed, ruled that with regard to moral offence the PAB should have taken the "likely reader" into account instead of the "average man". *Magersfontein* did not immediately benefit from this decision because the court also confirmed that the book contravened the act's prohibition on blasphemy. But the introduction of the "likely reader" into the application of censorship was the first step in a process of relaxation of the rules for some literary works.

Two years after its publication *Magersfontein* received the most prestigious Afrikaans literary award, the Hertzog prize. The book was still banned, and this renewed the original controversy. On receiving the prize, Leroux recorded the effect censorship can have on an author:

> When the book was banned and I was asked whether I would continue to write, I boasted that I would write as though the law didn't exist. Don't kid yourself! This surely has an effect on a person. One cannot suppress the question, maybe these people were right? And then you start to check your style, your way of writing. You are very insecure and I believe all people whose books are banned feel the same (*Die Burger*, 8 May 1979).

The work remained banned. Even when resubmitted in 1979, *Magersfontein* was again considered blasphemous. By that time, however, significant changes in the censorship machinery were taking place. The new chairman of the PAB, Kobus van Rooyen, realized that the negative publicity surrounding some literary bans was more harmful to Afrikaner interests than the contents of the books concerned could ever be. To end the protracted stand-off between Afrikaans writers and the political establishment, Van Rooyen took steps to ensure that some forms of literature became less vulnerable to banning.

Three months after the PAB had declared *Magersfontein* undesirable for the second time, the ban was lifted. Van Rooyen explained:

> Two factors have made the new decision possible. The Supreme Court's ruling on *Magersfontein* now forces the Appeal Board to take into consideration the likely reader instead of the average man, and the institution of expert committees that advise the Appeal Board during the evaluation of a work (*Hoofstad*, 24 March 1980).

The amendments were a direct consequence of the *Magersfontein* case. Their function was to give "recognition to the minority rights of literature, art and language" (Van Rooyen 1987: 9). They began to take effect in 1980 when the ban was lifted on a number of other literary works.

MARGREET DE LANGE

Writings

Magersfontein, O Magersfontein!, 1976; as *Magersfontein, o Magersfontein!*, translated by Ninon Roets, 1983

Further Reading

Lange, Margreet de, *The Muzzled Muse: Literature and Censorship in South Africa*, Amsterdam: Benjamins, 1997
Magersfontein: Die Dokumente (Magersfontein: The Documents), Cape Town: Human & Rousseau, 1990
van Rooyen, J.C.W., *Censorship in South Africa: Being a Commentary on the Application of the Publications Act*, Cape Town: Juta, 1987

LÈSE-MAJESTÉ

Europe

Lèse-majesté is a concept derived from Roman law that, in its broadest terms, views as illegal all words or acts that might in any way harm either the reputation or the physical person of ruling officials, or the general authority of the state. Translated literally from the Latin *crimen laesae majestatis*, the terms refers to "hurt or violated" majesty or "outrage upon the rights and dignity" of the sovereign authority. *Lèse-majesté* is a French term, but the concept, if not necessarily this term, has been applied at one time or another in virtually every country to punish political dissent. In Britain it was known as "high treason", in the United States as "sedition", and in Wilhelmine Germany as *Majestätsbeleidigung*.

The concept is inevitably (and highly to the advantage of the state) an extremely vague one. As Montesquieu aptly warned in his *Spirit of the Laws* (1748), "It is enough for the crime of *lèse-majesté* to be vague for the government to decline into despotism", while a German historian of Rome noted that the offence was characterized by "juridic boundlessness". Under the English Treason Act of 1351, for example, treason even included "imagining" the death of the king, and Richard II (1377–99) made it treasonous to propose repeal of the treason laws themselves!

Although the concept of *lèse-majesté* could clearly theoretically be applied to virtually all dissident political activity at any time and in any regime in world history, for the purposes of this essay, this "crime" will be discussed in (and examples primarily drawn from) the narrower form that became increasingly common after the French Revolution, namely as verbal attacks upon the monarch or other personification of state authority; thus, in Wilhelmine Germany *Majestätsbeleidigung* was treated as a separate offence from high treason (*Hochverrat*) and treason (*Landesverrat*), with the former including physical attacks upon the emperor and the latter incorporating attempts to overthrow violently the constitution or structure of the state.

Such distinctions became possible and meaningful only with the gradual emergence of modern forms of constitutional government; during the Middle Ages the fusion of the monarch with the state and the idea that the monarch was divine rendered pointless any attempt to distinguish between verbal and physical assault upon him or between attacks upon the monarch and upon the state itself. Today, *lèse-majesté* (at least as applied to royalty) survives largely only in those states that have retained a functioning (rather than only symbolic) monarchy. Thus, such prosecutions are still common in Thailand (as noted in the accompanying article) where the monarchy still retains considerable political importance, while at least as late as 1987 Nepal retained a treason law that threatened up to three years imprisonment for those found guilty of promoting "hatred, malice, or contempt" for the royal family, and in December 1995 a Jordanian critic of his country's peace treaty with Israel was charged with *lèse-majesté*.

Elsewhere, *lèse-majesté*, like functional monarchy itself, is today largely a concept of the past even where (as in Britain) it may technically remain in statute or common law. As Albert Sorel notes in his history of the French Revolution:

> With majesty transferred from the king to the people, the crime of *lèse-majesté* is diverted from the person of the king, and there arises a conception of treason toward the State by which the king, who formerly could only be the victim, can now be imagined as the primary transgressor.

Indeed, in December 1792 the revolutionary French Convention prescribed the death penalty for anyone proposing to establish "royalty or any other power hostile to the sovereignty of the people", and Louis XVI was subsequently executed for "conspiracy against public liberty" and "assault against the general security of the state". (Under similar revolutionary circumstances, in 1649 the English king Charles I and in 1918 the Russian tsar Nicholas II paid the same price for having survived the winds of history.)

The original concept of *lèse-majesté* was deeply rooted in the conception that the monarch was the divine representative of God on earth and therefore that all assaults upon him, whether physical or verbal, represented a form of heresy and blasphemy that merits severe punishment. As the French jurist Cardin Le Bret explained in his volume *De Souveraineté de Roy* of 1632 (in words later echoed by the *Encyclopédie*, the 17th-century landmark of Enlightenment thought), to speak disparagingly of the king was an offence against God "because sovereign princes being vicars of God, his living images, or rather gods on earth . . . their persons should be respected by us as divine and sacred things . . . so that one may say that when one insults the king, one insults God himself".

Given this conception, those found guilty or even accused of *lèse-majesté* were normally subjected, throughout medieval and early modern Europe, to extraordinary legal procedures (including torture and trial by special courts) and extraordinary punishments, which, in the most egregious cases, often included the death penalty, the forfeiture of all personal property for the benefit of the king, and sometimes even the forced exile and forced renunciation of the family name of all close relatives of the accused. Invariably those found guilty of actual or planned physical assaults upon the monarch were subject to the death penalty, which, as in the case of the attempted assassination of the French king Louis XV by Damiens in 1757, was regularly carried out with incredible savagery. Brutal executions for *lèse-majesté* were also often effected in medieval and early modern Europe even in cases of mere verbal, written, and artistic criticism of the monarch. Thus, in 1664 the English printer John Twyn was hanged, drawn, and quartered for treason for publishing a "seditious, poisonous and scandalous" book whose most objectionable statement was that the king was accountable to the people. Citing provision of the Treason Act of 1351, Twyn's three judges agreed that "printing and publishing such wicked positions was an overt act declaring the treason of compassing [intending] and imagining the King's death". In 1694 two Frenchmen were executed for publishing a drawing that depicted Louis XVI in the guise of a statue enchained by four women who represented three of his mistresses and his wife, parodying the statue that the king had erected in the Place des Victoires in which he was surrounded by four enchained slaves who represented his foreign conquests.

The vagueness and malleability of the concept of *lèse-majesté* often led to its extraordinary manipulation for purely political purposes to allow the authorities to silence or rid themselves of subjects who proved troublesome for one reason or another. Such uses of the law perhaps reached their peak in England during the reign of Henry VIII, when the treason laws were modified as frequently as the king changed wives and religious denominations. As the historian Irving Brant noted:

> It was treason one year to call one of his marriages invalid; treason the next year to say the opposite. By one law his daughter Elizabeth was declared legitimate, by a later one illegitimate and woe to the unlucky subject who called her a bastard in the wrong year.

In the well known case of the king's former chancellor, Sir Thomas More, execution was the penalty for "high treason" in 1535 simply for silence, namely More's refusal to approve publicly of the Act of Supremacy which made the king head of the Church of England (this event is the central focus of Robert Bolt's play of 1960, *A Man for All Seasons*).

In 1519 Philibert Berthelier, a citizen of Geneva, who had led opposition to the encroachment of his fellow citizens' rights by a Savoyard-imposed puppet bishop, was summarily arrested and executed; and in 1772 the German-Danish physician and reforming statesman Johann Stuensee, the power behind the throne and the lover of the Danish queen Matilda during the reign of the mentally unstable Christian VII, was arrested by his enemies, convicted, and brutally executed.

Prosecutions for verbal and printed *lèse-majesté* seem to have been especially frequent in the wake of physical assaults upon monarchs. Thus, Damiens' assault on Louis XV in 1757 was followed by a wave of 100 such arrests, including that of one man who was among the few political prisoners who greeted the liberators of the Bastille in 1789. Similarly, in Germany, two failed attempts upon the life of the emperor Wilhelm I in 1878 were followed within a year by almost 2000 *lèse-majesté* prosecutions, with 521 such cases heard between July and August 1878 alone.

Although the concept of *lèse-majesté* became increasingly outmoded in western Europe during the 19th century, it continued to be enforced to some extent in most regimes, often disguised under new legal language. Thus, although the term itself seems to have been discarded in France after 1789, virulent criticism of the sovereign power continued to be targeted both in law and in practice. Thousands were executed for what might well be termed *lèse-nation* during the French Revolution's Reign of Terror, and suppression of opposition in France continued to be ruthless and persistent, if not nearly as bloody, under a long list of succeeding 19th-century rulers; following the final deposition of the "tyrant" Napoleon in 1815 literally all expression deemed hostile to the restored Bourbon dynasty, including singing the *Marseillaise* and displaying the tricolour flag, was outlawed, and such crimes were made subject to special military courts without juries or the right to appeal. About 6000 people were convicted for such political offences between July 1815 and June 1816 alone.

Even after the French political situation became more "regularized", similar laws and prosecutions remained the norm for another 65 years. For example, the press laws of 1819 outlawed criticizing the "person of the king, the succession to the throne or the constitutional authority of the King and the [legislative] Chambers", whether by "writings, printed matter, sketches, engravings, paintings, or emblems", as well as by the "removal or defacement of public symbols or royal authority, because of hatred of or contempt for said authority".

Following the "reform" Revolution of 1830 which brought Louis-Philippe of the Orléans dynasty to the throne, the press law of November 1830 similarly forbade all attacks against "royal authority" and the "inviolability" of the king, the royal succession, and the authority of the legislative chambers. Perhaps the most notorious of hundreds of victims of such laws was the great caricaturist Honoré Daumier, who was jailed for five months and fined 500 francs in 1832 for "provoking hatred and contempt against the government of the King and for offences against the person of the King", as the result of his *Gargantua* lithograph, which depicted a bloated Louis-Philippe sitting on a toilet-throne, consuming food and tribute from the poor and excreting boodle to his aristocratic supporters. Even the landmark French press law of 1881, which swept away the accretion of decades of repressive legislation, included an exception for defamation of the president of the republic, although in practice this provision has been rarely used.

As the entire concept that monarchs or other rulers should be legally immune from all criticism came under increasing attack after the French Revolution, attempts to impose or enforce *lèse-majesté* laws increasingly became subject to contention and sometimes embarrassment for the regimes involved. Thus, in Greece, when the hitherto obscure politician Charilaos Tricoupis was jailed in 1874 for publishing an article entitled "Who is to Blame?" in the Athens newspaper *Kairi*, which suggested that George I was responsible for his nation's chronic political crisis, he became a political martyr overnight. The king was forced by the weight of public opinion to appoint Tricoupis prime minister and to grant his leading demand: that the king accede to the principle of parliamentary responsibility.

An even more extraordinary case occurred in Sweden in 1834, where captain Anders Lindeberg, editor of the newspaper *Stockholms Posten*, was convicted under the medieval treason law and sentenced to death by decapitation. The obvious absurdity of this sentence was apparent even to king Karl Johan (who suppressed 60 newspapers during his reign between 1818 and 1844 and was no bleeding-heart liberal), who mitigated the penalty to three years in prison. However, Lindeberg decided to press his advantage by insisting upon his right to be beheaded and refusing to escape despite the government's encouragement that he do so. Finally, in desperation, Karl Johan issued a general amnesty to "all political prisoners awaiting execution", which applied only to Lindeberg. When the stubborn editor continued to insist upon the right to decapitation the regime finally locked him out of his cell while he was walking in the prison courtyard and then refused him re-entry.

In the newly created United States, the influence, and ultimately unpopularity, of the concept of *lèse-majesté* was reflected in the experience of the notorious Sedition Act of 1798, in which the Federalist Party of George Washington and the president, John Adams sought to suppress the emerging opposition of the Democratic–Republican party of Thomas Jefferson (forerunner to today's Democratic Party) by outlawing all verbal and written "false, scandalous, and malicious" comments about "the government of the United States, or either house of the Congress of the United States or the President of the United States" (no mention was made of vice-president Jefferson!) for the purpose of bringing them "into contempt or disrepute" or to "stir up sedition" or "excite" popular "hatred" against them. This law, which was enforced primarily against the Jeffersonian press, mostly succeeded in "stirring up" popular opposition to its enactment and was a significant factor in Jefferson's defeat of Adams in the presidential election of 1800 (the act automatically expired at the end of Adams's term – a ploy by Federalists to ensure that it could not be used against them if they lost the election – and Jefferson soon pardoned all of those convicted under it).

Despite this experience, the United States again enacted vague sedition laws during World War I and on the eve of its entry into World War II. The Sedition Act of 1918 was even more encompassing than its counterpart of 1798, outlawing printing or uttering any "disloyal, profane, scurrilous, or abusive language about the form of government", the constitution, the military, the flag, or even the military uniforms of the United States, as well as any language bringing these subjects into "contempt, scorn, contumely, or disrepute". This law, along with the less sweeping Espionage Act of 1917, was used to prosecute more than 2100 people (more than 1000 of whom were convicted) for purely written and verbal opposition to World War I, including for making such statements as: "We must make the world safe for democracy, even if we have to bean the goddess of liberty to do it", and "I am for the people and the government is for the profiteers".

In 1940 the more tightly drawn yet still vague Smith (Sedition) Act outlawed all advocacy of violent overthrow of the government; it was used during the Cold War to destroy the US Communist Party despite any showing that the party was actually planning violence of any kind. However, from 1957, rulings of the US Supreme Court effectively emasculated the Smith Act by requiring that the government demonstrate that alleged violators actually intended to overthrow the government rather than merely talk about it (or as in the case of the prosecuted communists, read books such as the *Communist Manifesto*, which talked about such acts as a theoretical possibility). In recent years, the US has repeatedly experienced attempts to enforce the concept of *lèse-flag*, with prosecutions of hundreds of dissidents for "flag desecration" during the Vietnam War and continual attempts to pass a constitutional amendment to outlaw such expression in the aftermath of twin Supreme Court rulings of 1989–90 striking down existing state and federal flag desecration laws.

Needless to say, although (despite exceptions such as those just discussed) the concept of *lèse-majesté* has gradually become discredited in Western democracies, modern totalitarian regimes have not hesitated to punish brutally those deemed guilty of such (written or unwritten) laws, with literally millions of victims collectively and barbarically slaughtered, usually without any legal procedures whatever, in Nazi Germany; in communist regimes in Stalinist Russia, Maoist China, and Pol Pot's Cambodia; and in Cold War right-wing military regimes in Guatemala, Chile, and Indonesia.

Among quasi-constitutional regimes, the implementation of *lèse-majesté* law has perhaps been studied most intensively in Wilhelmine Germany. Provision 95 of the German imperial penal code of 1871 (*Reichsstrafgesetzbuch*), entitled *Majestätsbeleidigung*, threatened an unlimited prison sentence of not less than two months for any subject whose written or spoken words were deemed to insult the emperor. As the German socialist leader August Bebel noted, exactly what this meant was a mystery to all; at any rate, under rulings of the German courts, the emperor was completely protected against all irreverent remarks, whether in public or private, whether or not the alleged criticism could be justified or proved truthful and even whether or not any injury to the monarch was intended.

This provision was implemented with extraordinary promiscuity. As noted earlier, during 1878, a year in which two assassination attempts were made upon Wilhelm I, almost 2000 prosecutions were effected, but even in relatively "normal" years hundreds of such prosecutions were regularly initiated: the average number of annual convictions was 439 during 1882–88 and 551 during 1889–95. Jail terms were mandatory and often extremely harsh: between 1889 and 1893 alone, 1239 years of imprisonment were inflicted upon violators, with sentences averaging 175 days. At the turn of the century in Germany, about 300 people were still being convicted each year for the offence; during the first six months of 1913 alone more than 100 socialist journalists were convicted of lèse-majesté and similar offences and sentenced to more than 40 years in jail and 11,000 marks in fines.

The law was, in practice, especially targeted against socialists and above all at the socialist press: between 1890 and 1900 the Hannoverscher Volksvwille was prosecuted 28 times, and the editor of the Hamburger Echo was convicted on 27 occasions between 1897 and 1906, spending two years in jail and paying almost 3000 marks in fines. In probably the most notorious such press case, the leading caricaturist Theodor Thomas Heine was sentenced to a six-month jail term in 1898 for a drawing that mocked the emperor's foreign policy; Heine responded with a brilliant caricature of himself in chains and under military supervision in jail, captioned, "Here's how I'll be doing my next drawing."

In a similar spirit of mockery, the socialist satirical journal Wahrer Jakob reported in 1904 that the police had seized a blank sheet of paper on the grounds that in the future an act of lèse-majesté might be committed upon it. When the Austrian socialist leader Victor Adler complained to him about Habsburg press restrictions, Bebel told him, "In this respect you enjoy almost ideal conditions. If your paper were to appear here [in Germany] in the same tone and with the same content, it would suffer daily at least six court cases and your editors would populate the prisons until the ends of their days."

Apart from the promiscuity of its enforcement, the most notable aspect of lèse-majesté laws in Wilhelmine Germany was the sheer absurdity of very many of the prosecutions (large numbers of which resulted from Germans taking advantage of the vagueness of the law to report alleged offences by personal enemies in order to settle private scores). In 1878 one woman was given an 18-month jail term for declaring, "The emperor is not poor, he can afford to care for himself"; subsequent sentences included a three-month jail term for a woman who made a gesture interpreted as an insult to the emperor while singing a song, and nine months for a Berlin worker who stuck out his tongue as the Emperor's motorcar passed by. In 1904 the editors of five different newspapers were convicted for re-printing an item from the Viennese press reporting that a stepbrother of the emperor had ended his days as a country pedlar.

Perhaps the single most notorious target of a lèse-majesté prosecution in Wilhelmine Germany was the young historian Ludwig Quidde (who received the Nobel Peace Prize in 1927), who became a sensation when it was realized that his article of 1894, Caligula: Eine Studie über römischen Cäsarenwahnsinn (Caligula: A Study of Roman-Caesarean Madness) was in truth a devastating portrayal of Wilhelm II. In instance after instance, the bizarre personality traits attributed to the clearly insane Caligula precisely matched characteristics widely ascribed to Wilhelm II. In pamphlet form, Quidde's article sold more than 150,000 copies. Although the government could not directly prosecute him for it without further identifying the emperor with Caligula, Quidde was subsequently jailed for three months for remarks critical of the emperor at a public

meeting in 1896, a prosecution that the regime made clear was really in retaliation for the Caligula affair.

Despite the severe penalties awaiting offenders, many others imitated Quidde's tactics. As Robert Brooks wrote in an article of 1904 on lèse majesté in Germany:

> To draw a cartoon so cleverly, or to hurl an epithet so deftly that everyone knows at whom it is aimed, while at the same time no possible ground is left upon which the State's Attorney can begin proceedings, is a decided feather in the cap of the journal which can accomplish the feat ... Certain comic papers especially are currently reputed to owe no small part of their circulation to the confident and seldom disappointed belief of their readers that each issue can be depended upon to come as near as possible to insulting the Kaiser without directly doing so ... The only apparent effect of the law is to increase the public demand for clever pictorial flings at royalty.

Among innumerable cartoons of this character may be mentioned one representing a scene at an alcove in an art gallery. Two gentlemen are standing before the portrait of a stocky personage in a rich Dutch costume of the 16th century. "This", remarks one of them, "is a picture of William the Silent." "I didn't know William [English for Wilhelm] was ever silent", responds his companion (a play on the Emperor's notorious affinity for sticking his feet in his mouth at every opportunity).

ROBERT JUSTIN GOLDSTEIN

Further Reading

Brooks, Albert C., "Lèse Majesté in Germany", The Bookman (June 1904)

Goldstein, Robert Justin, Political Repression in Nineteenth Century Europe, London: Croom Helm, and Totowa, New Jersey: Barnes and Noble, 1983

Goldstein, Robert Justin, Political Censorship of the Arts and the Press in Nineteenth-Century Europe, Basingstoke: Macmillan, and New York: St Martin's Press, 1989

Hall, Alex, "The Kaiser, the Wilhelmine State and Lèse Majesté", German Life and Letters (January 1974)

Kelly, G.A., "From Lèse Majesté to Lèse-Nation: Treason in Eighteenth-Century France", Journal of the History of Ideas, 42 (1981)

Streckfuss, David, "Kings in the Age of Nations: The Paradox of Lèse Majesté as Political Crime in Thailand", Comparative Studies in Society and History, 37 (1995)

Thailand

Thailand's absolute monarchy was overthrown in 1932 by a group of middle-ranking government officials. Half a century later, the threat of the lèse-majesté charges still looms over the country's political and academic spheres. Despite growing democratization and expanding economy since the 1970s, the state has promoted the institution of the monarchy as a part of its official nationalism. As in Europe, the charge of lèse-majesté has been used to suppress criticism not only of the monarchy, but of the government itself.

During the absolute monarchy, any act against the king was considered a threat against the state and the national security, since the king and the state were regarded as one and the same. According to the law of 1805, a crime of *lèse-majesté* – to defame, insult, or threaten the king – could be punished by death. A Print Act of the 1890s, influenced by Western laws, reduced the punishment to not more than three years imprisonment, but a criminal code of 1908 increased it again to seven years.

Before 1932 there were a few court cases involving censorship and *lèse-majesté* laws. A well-known case concerns a memoir published in 1878 by Nai Thim Sukkhayang, which described a disastrous military expedition to Nong Khai, a province in northeast Thailand, in 1875. The author described the miserable condition of the soldiers, which was largely due to corruption among the officials. He also harshly criticized a minister who had misled the expedition. The minister petitioned King Chulalongkorn to execute the writer, arguing that the claim that he failed in his duty amounted to criticism of the king who appointed the minister to supervise this expedition. King Chulalongkorn agreed that the author was guilty of a crime of *lèse-majesté* but he reduced the punishment to flogging and eight months imprisonment. Copies of the memoir were confiscated and destroyed.

Interestingly, in 1926 there was an attempt to re-publish the memoir. Even though all the parties involved were already dead, the government would not allow the re-publication because the royal decree of 1878 ordering the book to be destroyed still stood. It was not until the mid-1950s that the book was re-published, and then only after some offending passages were removed. Even now the uncensored version of the memoir is not available for the public to read.

After the revolution of 1932 *lèse-majesté* as a crime seemed to be in decline. There were struggles, conflicts, and distrust between the new government and king Prajadhipok and the royalists. The latter complained that the government did not respect and safeguard the honour of the monarchy; the government believed that the king and the royalists were plotting to overthrow it. The abdication of king Prajadhipok in 1935 did not end the conflicts, which continued until the late 1950s.

The open political struggles among the civilians and military elite in the various governments after World War II affected a change in the government's attitude and policy. The new monarch, Bhumibol Adulyadej, was popular, and both the civilian and military parties courted the royalists. The military set out to promote the monarchy as one of the three sacred pillars of Thai nationalism, along with Buddhism and the Thai nation. The state-controlled educational system and mass media promoted the monarchy as the sole source of the unity and strength of the nation.

In the revised criminal code of 1957 *lèse-majesté* became not only a crime against the reputation of the monarch but also an offence against national security. In 1976, under a military-backed dictatorial government, the law was revised to make the punishment not less than three years and not more than 15 years imprisonment, more severe than that of defamation. The law protects not only the king but also the queen, the heir-apparent, and the regent. The Thai people now dare not criticize the royal family and associated offices such as the Bureau of Crown Property and the Bureau of HM Private Property.

King Bhumibol Adulyadej has been highly respected and greatly loved by the Thai people owing to his commitment and dedication to the betterment of the public at large. None the less, since 1950 the number of the *lèse-majesté* cases increased from nine cases in the 1950s to an astonishing number of more than 100 cases in the 1970s. The accused were from all walks of life – ministers, politicians, government officials, journalists, writers, workers, and students, even a few foreigners. There is no official explanation for this increase. Critics maintain that the statistics confirm that the law of *lèse-majesté* has been misused by the authorities to suppress criticism of the government in general.

The ruling elite, and some palace officials, realized that these prosecutions tarnished the country's image in the eyes of foreign governments and human rights organizations. In October 1987 one of the king's deputy private secretaries gave an interview to Thai journalists in which he suggested that the prosecutions would gradually diminish and might be abolished if democracy in Thailand developed progressively. The interview resulted in an unprecedented round-table discussion in December 1987 involving a privy councillor, a noted human rights lawyer, and many distinguished legal scholars.

Supporters of the law argued that the monarchy represented the nation. If the reputation of the monarchy was defamed, the nation's honour was also insulted. Therefore the *lèse-majesté* law protected the interest of the general public, even against the human rights of individual citizens. However these supporters preferred a better and fairer administration of the law, free from political interference; public prosecutors and judges should be impartial and consider mainly the intention of the accused. One suggestion was that the Royal Household Department should have sole responsibility for filing *lèse-majesté* charges to the police. Critics argued that the popularity of the monarchy was proof that there was no need for such a law. They repeated the charge that the law was often abused by people in power to suppress opposition and to protect their own interests. The law was a deterrent to the development of democracy and yielded no benefits to the monarchy in the long run. The discussion made no reference to the fact that there are some in Thailand who either are not interested in the monarchy, or are part of a nascent republican sentiment that dare not speak its name.

The discussion had no effect on legal practice. The abuse of the *lèse-majesté* law by authorities continued. In 1991 Sulak Sivaraksa, a leading social critic and well-known monarchist, was charged with *lèse-majesté* after, in a speech to students, he had criticized the military leaders who staged the *coup d'etat* of 1991. Sulak turned the tables, accusing the coup leaders of themselves committing *lèse-majesté* by staging a coup against a legitimate government appointed by the king. A defender of equality and dignity of the common people, Sulak also criticized people's readiness to prostrate themselves on the road to pay respect to the king.

Sulak Sivaraksa and others like him believe that, to survive, the monarchy needs to be flexible, open to honest criticism, and adaptable. He urges the Thais to accept that the king and the royal family are ordinary people and not to give them false respect. Sulak's ideas are not popular among ultra royalists, who still consider the king and the members of the royal family as divine, virtuous, and superior to the common people.

In 1995 the criminal court decided in favour of Sulak Sivaraksa. The judges, having looked at the context of Sulak's words, found that Sulak was trying to teach the students the nature of constitutional monarchy and democracy. They considered that though some aspects of his speech were strong, impolite, and inappropriate, Sulak's overall intention was to give a talk that was respectful and loyal to the king.

The acquittal of Sulak was celebrated by the Thai and foreign advocates for democracy and human rights, not least because the court acknowledged the possibility that the *lèse-majesté* law could be used by people in power to silence opposition. However it should be noted that before the court made its decision in 1995 the general who ordered charges against Sulak was no longer in power. He and other former coup leaders had been removed by a popular uprising in May 1992. There are still no legal safeguards to ensure that the law is not used as a political tool in the future.

Thailand's *lèse-majesté* law of 1908, a model for other revisions, was based on the British sedition law, but the *lèse-majesté* laws in these two countries have developed in a strikingly opposite direction. A Thai lawyer who watched a BBC TV comedy programme in 1987 that ridiculed prince Charles's table manners confessed that he was confused. He told his British friend that if this kind of ridicule had been proposed in Thailand, it would have been banned and the television station attacked. It was his friend's turn to be puzzled. England has a long history of public scrutiny of the crown, and queen Elizabeth II herself acknowledged in 1992 that criticism was good.

SUMALEE BUMROONGSOOK

Further Reading

Hewison, Kevin (editor), *Political Change in Thailand: Democracy and Participation*, London and New York: Routledge, 1997

"Khwaamphit thaana minphraborom detchaanuphaap kap kaanpokkhraung rabaup prachaathipatai thii mii phramahaakasat pen pramuk" (The Crime of Lèse-majesté and a Democratic Governing System with King as Head of State), *Pajarayasara* 14/6 (1987): 12–45

Reynolds, Craig J., "Sedition in Thai History: A Nineteenth-century Poem and Its Critics" in *Thai Constructions of Knowledge*, edited by Manas Chitakasem and Andrew Turton, London: School of Oriental and African Studies, University of London, 1991

Streckfuss, David (editor), *Modern Thai Monarchy and Cultural Politics: The Acquittal of Sulak Sivaraksa on the Charge of Lese Majeste in Siam 1995 and Its Consequences*, Bangkok: Santi Pracha Dhamma Institute, 1996

LESELINYANA LA LESOTHO (The Little Light of Lesotho)
Lesotho newspaper, founded 1863

In 1860 the Swiss missionary Adolphe Mabille arrived in Lesotho with two important assets. His wife Adèle spoke Sesotho fluently, having been born in Lesotho as the daughter of one of the first French missionaries. The other asset was a printing press, which he was soon able to set up in the vestry of the Morija church. It was from this press that the first issue of *Leselinyana la Lesotho* was printed in November 1863; it was produced with the help of a Mosotho assistant, Filemone Rapetloane. The newspaper continues to be published today from premises located a mere 200 metres from the church vestry where it was first produced. Although it has remained, first and foremost, a church newspaper throughout this period, *Leselinyana* has at times also found itself acting as the conscience of the nation.

When the newspaper was founded, Lesotho was an independent kingdom. However, a four-year break in publication occurred from 1865 when the neighbouring Orange Free State Republic attacked Lesotho and expelled the missionaries. From 1868 Lesotho became British territory, and for a while was attached to the Cape Colony. By the late 1870s the Cape government wished to extend to Lesotho a "Peace Preservation Act" by which all fire-arms in the territory were to be surrendered. Mabille was not sympathetic to this act, and refused to translate or print the Disarmament Proclamation which extended the act to Lesotho. Nevertheless, in the January 1880 edition of *Leselinyana* he reluctantly printed advice that the Basotho should comply with the law. Mabille's misgivings about the law were borne out by subsequent events. In 1880, the so-called Gun War broke out and *Leselinyana* was again not published for 20 months, a time when Mabille was mainly absent in Europe.

Originally a monthly newspaper, *Leselinyana* gradually increased in frequency during the colonial period, becoming a weekly between 1909 and 1958, after which it was issued fortnightly. For the first 90 years its editors were expatriate missionaries. The first Mosotho to become editor was Z.D. Mangoaela in 1954.

In the early years after Lesotho's independence in 1966 *Leselinyana* was often subject to government harassment. An early test came after the January elections of 1970, when the defeated party seized power, banned the opposition newspaper, and ruled by decree. *Leselinyana*'s editor at the time was Seeiso Serutla, a Mosotho who had received his journalism training in Zambia. *Leselinyana* was the only newspaper which remained to provide an articulate voice of dissent. Serutla rose to the occasion, but *Leselinyana* was itself banned after its issue of 20 March and the editor was arrested and held without trial.

Publication resumed later in 1970 under a missionary editor, Albert Brutsch. He was followed in 1971 by Edgar Mahlomola Motuba. Motuba's period as editor was one of increasing political strife, culminating in political assassinations by a death squad believed to be sponsored by the government. The newspaper covered these events in detail. On 4 September 1981, apparently in response to this coverage, there was an armed attack on Ben Masilo, a former editor and current member of the *Leselinyana* Press Board. Although Masilo escaped, his grandson was killed in the attack. Three days later, Motuba was abducted together with two friends. Their bodies were found a day later. It was subsequently reported that his abductors were members of the paramilitary Police Mobile Unit, who were incensed that Motuba refused to name the contributors who had written articles about the activities of the death squads.

Leselinyana continued uninterrupted publication throughout this period of political turmoil. It managed to provide, but at terrible cost, an example of press freedom in a repressive state. Freedom of expression was again requested – and guaranteed – when elections were held and a new constitution adopted in 1993.

DAVID AMBROSE

Further Reading

Khaketla, B.M., *Lesotho, 1970: An African Coup under the Microscope*, London: Hurst, 1971; Berkeley: University of California Press, 1972
Smith, Edwin W., *The Mabilles of Basutoland*, London: Hodder and Stoughton, 1939

LESOTHO

(formerly Basutoland)

Population: 2,035,000	**Illiteracy rate (%):** 27.6 (m); 6.4 (f)
Main religions: Roman Catholic; Lesotho Evangelical; Anglican	**Number of daily newspapers:** 2
	Number of periodicals: 7
Official languages: Sesotho; English	**Number of radio receivers per 1000 inhabitants:** 52
Other languages spoken: Zulu; Xhosa	**Number of TV receivers per 1000 inhabitants:** 27

Lesotho emerged as a separate polity in the 1820s, as a result of the unification of peoples scattered by war into a coherent state under King Moshoeshoe. The people of the country adopted the name Basotho (singular Mosotho), and the royal dialect adopted as the national language became known as Sesotho. During the period of British colonial rule (1868–1966), the country was also known as Basutoland.

Missionaries of the Paris Evangelical Missionary Society began work in Lesotho in 1833, and from 1841 there was a mission printing press which produced books and periodicals in Sesotho. After earlier short-lived attempts, from November 1863 a regular mission newspaper, *Leselinyana la Lesotho* (The Little Light of Lesotho), was published in Morija. Originally a monthly, it was published weekly for many years, although since the 1960s the frequency has been fortnightly. During its history it has suffered periods of interruption due to wars (1865–69, 1880–81), a strike (1960), and a banning order (1970). Although *Leselinyana* was independent of the colonial government its content was filtered by its missionary editors. Throughout the late 19th century, there was no other forum where Basotho writers could present views critical of the parent mission, nor write of other matters which the mission editors thought inappropriate to ventilate publicly.

In 1904, the Morija Printing Works was equipped with a new power-operated press, and the old hand press was sold to two Basotho entrepreneurs, Solomon Monne and Abimael Tlale. They installed it in the town of Mafeteng, where in February 1904 they began publication of a fortnightly newspaper, *Naledi ea Lesotho* (The Star of Basutoland). The newspaper, which was written in Sesotho and English, circulated widely not only in Lesotho, but also in the adjoining Orange River Colony and in the Transvaal, where there were many Sesotho speakers and migrant workers. The paper was not afraid to print articles critical of white officials, although in some cases this resulted in legal action for defamation. In 1907, for example, articles had appeared about one Strydom, who was known to the Basotho as Raleting, a name which reflected his association with alcoholic liquor. He had been generally believed to have been guilty of illegal liquor dealing and had been dismissed from the colonial service, but in a court case had been acquitted on a technicality. Annoyed that he was still being pilloried in the press, Strydom sued the then newspaper editor, Simon Phamotse. Judgment was given against the paper which was fined £50, even though what it had reported was generally believed in Mafeteng to have been true.

By 1911 a third newspaper, *Mphatlalatsane* (The Comet), was founded, the first to be printed in the capital, Maseru. The enterprise was undertaken by members of the Tlale family, who established the firm S. Tlale & Sons. Abimael Tlale (formerly of *Naledi ea Lesotho*) was the founding editor. It was a time of intense interest for black South Africans, as they sought participation in the new Union of South Africa, created in 1910. Lesotho, following representations from its inhabitants, had been excluded from the Union. However, *Mphatlalatsane* and *Naledi* were able to include detailed coverage of the South African Native National Congress, convened for the first time in Bloemfontein in 1912. This was the founding meeting of the African National Congress (ANC), which, after a long struggle, became in 1994 the ruling party of the Republic of South Africa.

Basotho novelists had emerged by this time, of whom the most outstanding was Thomas Mofolo. A product of mission education, he also worked as a proofreader at the Morija Printing Works. However, in 1910 he had to depart from Morija because of disapproval by the mission authorities of an extramarital affair. His greatest novel, *Chaka*, languished unpublished for some 15 years, and might never have appeared at all if a change in management at Morija had not resulted in recognition of the novel's outstanding literary merit. It was published by the Morija Sesuto Book Depot in 1925, and has subsequently been translated into a number of European languages and also into Swahili.

The colonial administration kept a tight rein on the local press in Lesotho. This is exemplified by action taken in 1946 against the editor of *Mochochonono*, N.M. Tlale, on two counts of publishing seditious material. The paper had accused the resident commissioner of Basutoland of acting as an agent for the Union of South Africa; it also advocated non-compliance with a tax increase which had been implemented against the advice of the Basutoland National Council. Tlale received a £25 fine or a six-month term of imprisonment from the district commissioner; the sentence was later halved on appeal.

The missionary editor of *Leselinyana*, Georges Dieterlen, found himself in a similar predicament a few years earlier. He had been accused of printing a reader's letter which undermined the authority of the police. After receiving a similar punishment, he was at first ready to go to gaol. However, when his fine was paid by someone else, he threatened to return the Order of the British Empire (OBE) decoration which had been previously awarded to him by the British government.

The period following World War II was characterized by increasing expectations among Basotho of greater political participation. Formal political parties were established, and alongside these came new publications. Founded jointly by B.M. Khaketla, Ntsu Mokhehle, and Z.L. Mothopeng of the Basutoland African Congress (later the Basutoland Congress Party), *Mohlabani* was the first of Lesotho's politically oriented newspapers; it was edited by B.M. Khaketla throughout its publication history (1954–67). The newspaper established the tradition for such publications of using a passage of praise poetry on the cover, choosing a provocative couplet which referred to the loss of land by Lesotho in its 19th-century wars with the Orange Free State. *Mohlabani* was published in parallel columns in English and Sesotho. Its first three issues were mimeographed and prepared with assistance from a former colonial official, Patrick Duncan, whose sympathies led him eventually to join the Pan African Congress (PAC) of South Africa. These early issues contained articles sharply critical of the colonial administration, and they brought about a swift response. The three founders of the newspaper were summarily dismissed from their teaching positions at Basutoland High School in the capital, and were also banned from the Maseru urban area. Far from suppressing the newspaper, however, this action, by depriving its owners of a means of livelihood, provided a new stimulus for political activity in Lesotho. Ntsu Mokhehle became a full-time politician (eventually, in 1993, he became prime minister), and the newspaper itself, not risking a local printing which might be seized, came out in improved format, printed in Cape Town.

When a split occurred in the Basutoland Congress Party (BCP), *Mohlabani* no longer toed the party line, and a new BCP newspaper, *Makatolle*, was founded in October 1960. *Mohlabani* soon afterwards ceased publication, but re-emerged in 1963 as the paper of the Marematlou Freedom Party (MFP), of which B.M. Khaketla became the leader. It was a third party, however, the Basutoland National Party (BNP) which won the pre-independence elections and which led the country to independence on 4 October 1966.

During this period Lesotho was host to many refugees from South Africa, and in particular to publications representing their viewpoints, of which *The Africanist* is particularly noteworthy. This publication had been founded in Orlando, South Africa, in 1953 by Mangaliso Sobukwe and Potlako Leballo, who were its first editors. It represented the views of the Africanist wing of the ANC Youth League, and from 1959 those of the PAC. When the PAC was banned in South Africa in 1960, publication was suspended until the newspaper was revived in 1964 as a mimeographed monthly in Maseru, its cover showing a star over Ghana, radiating influence over the rest of Africa. From August 1966 *The Africanist* appeared as a 6-page printed paper in Maseru until 1969, after which it eventually moved to London, where Potlako Leballo was himself based.

The first post-independence elections in Lesotho were held in January 1970. They were won by the opposition BCP, which won 36 of the 60 seats, while 23 went to the BNP and one seat to the MFP. However, instead of relinquishing power, the outgoing BNP government of prime minister chief Leabua Jonathan declared a State of Emergency, "suspended" the constitution, and arrested the leaders of the victorious party. By Government Notice No. 32 of 1970 (5 February 1970), under what was called The Emergency (Amendment) Regulations Banning Order, the newspapers *Makatolle* (BCP), *The Range* (BCP), *Majammoho* (Communist Party of Lesotho), *Mohlabani* (MFP), *Seboholi* (BCP Youth League), and *The Commentator* (BCP) were subject to "prohibition of the importation, printing, publication, sale, offer for sale, distribution, reproduction, or possession". By Government Notice No. 33 of the same date, a similar prohibition was applied to all printed matter "propagating the principles or promoting the spread of Communism".

Criticism of government actions was thereafter left to the two church newspapers, of which the Catholic *Moeletsi oa Basotho*, under the influence of its French Canadian clergy, was at the time virulently anticommunist and sympathetic to the BNP (a party in whose foundation the church had participated). It could not therefore be expected to criticize the party's policies. *Leselinyana la Lesotho* of the Lesotho Evangelical Church represented the remaining source of articulate dissent, but this was suppressed when the newspaper was in turn banned on 31 March 1970, and its editor Seeiso Serutla detained. A further notice on 6 April 1970 prohibited the import and distribution of the ANC paper, *Sechaba*. As a result of these orders, the British-officered police force was given carte blanche to seize publications; books belonging to BCP leaders were burned in what were described by Radio Lesotho as a bonfire of "communist" books.

The newspaper *Leselinyana* was eventually un-banned by notice in the *Lesotho Government Gazette* of 12 June 1970, under conditions which were not explicitly stated, but which were known to include the replacement of the Mosotho editor, Seeiso Serutla, by a long-resident Swiss missionary, Albert Brutsch. In the following months, discussion of the current political situation was largely replaced in the newspaper by articles on mission history.

While political newspapers were proscribed in the early 1970s, the opposite applied to magazines and books with sexually explicit content. After the first modern hotel (part of the Holiday Inn chain) was opened in Maseru in 1970, its management soon realized that a profitable market existed in offering its clientele, who were mainly white South Africans, activities that were illegal across the border. These included gambling (casino and slot machines); the screening of films and shows (ranging from *Hair* and *Jesus Christ Superstar* to Miss Nude South Africa) which would not pass South Africa's censorship laws, and the selling of sexually explicit magazines such as *Penthouse* and *Playboy*. Although importation of some of the more extreme publications was later restricted by the Lesotho government, the Lesotho tourist industry was largely based on such activities (alongside which prostitution thrived), until the creation of "independent" homelands within South Africa in the late 1970s allowed similar activities closer to South Africa's main centres of population.

The attempt to crush dissent following the suppression of democracy in 1970 was not wholly successful, although it led to the departure of many Basotho into exile, including the former editor of *Leselinyana*, Seeiso Serutla. Edgar Mahlomola Motuba, recruited by Albert Brutsch in late 1970 as a columnist on the newspaper, assumed the editorship of *Leselinyana* in 1971, and the Lesotho Evangelical Church newspaper became again the main voice of the exiled and underground opposition. Even after the 1970 State of Emergency was repealed in 1973, when the publications banned could theoretically have resumed publication, the opposition had suffered so grievously through imprisonment, exile, and seizing of property that it did not have the resources to revive its newspapers.

Meanwhile, the initial peaceful opposition to the Jonathan regime developed into an increasingly violent confrontation, as Leabua Jonathan, desperate for international support and aid, reversed his earlier friendship with South Africa, and adopted a vigorous anti-apartheid stand. South Africa then followed suit to become a willing host to the Lesotho opposition, and the BCP, although by now suffering from its own internal strife, was able to attack government targets from bases situated close to the border. The ruling BNP reacted by strengthening the Police Mobile Unit, which in 1980 was renamed the Lesotho Paramilitary Force, and shortly afterwards developed into a full Lesotho Defence Force.

By 1981 *Leselinyana la Lesotho* was reporting on a spate of assassinations (and other repressive measures) being carried out by what was believed by many to be a government-sponsored death squad, generally known as "Koeeoko". It also printed statements by Ntsu Mokhehle and other exiled opposition leaders. On 4 September 1981 armed men attacked Ben Masilo, a prominent churchman who was then chairman of the Lesotho Council of Churches and was both a former editor of *Leselinyana* and also a member of the Press Board of the newspaper. Masilo went into hiding, eventually emerging in exile in Nairobi. Three days after the attack, the editor of *Leselinyana*, Edgar Motuba, was abducted with two friends from his home in Morija by persons thought to be policemen. The three bodies were found the following day 55 kilometres to the south of Morija at Siloe.

The army which had been created by the Jonathan regime to keep the BNP in power had by the mid-1980s to contend with a second armed force, the BNP Youth League, trained with North Korean assistance. In January 1986 a confrontation with South Africa led to the closure of the border; the Lesotho Defence Force, aware that South Africa would favour a change

of government, overthrew the Jonathan regime, disarmed the BNP Youth League, and instituted rule by a Military Council. The new regime was not accompanied by any resurgence of press freedom. A Zambian journalist, John Mukela, who was working in Lesotho and who was married to the daughter of a former minister of the BNP government, was arrested and detained without trial after his BBC report about events in January 1986. He was deported from Lesotho on 8 May 1986. A similar fate befell Johnny wa ka Maseko, a South African who was the editor of the Maseru English-language newspaper *The Mirror*. His newspaper's forthright reporting of alleged corruption and personal enrichment by senior members of the government resulted in his being arrested on 28 October 1988 and charged with criminal defamation. Before any trial could be held, however, he was detained under the Lesotho Internal Security Act of 1984, and after a month's detention was deported on 17 December 1988.

The military proclaimed itself as a caretaker government, pending restoration of civilian rule. There were, however, doubts about its sincerity in this regard. Meanwhile, the donor community, which was underwriting a substantial portion of capital development funds, provided repeated technical expertise directed at a restoration of constitutional parliamentary rule. A new constitution was eventually adopted in 1993, coming into force following parliamentary elections in March 1993, in which members of the BCP won all 65 seats; freedom of expression is specifically guaranteed (section 14).

The restoration of democratic rule and freedom of expression has resulted in the founding of a variety of new newspapers. Of these, *Moafrika*, edited by Candi Ramainoane has become the most controversial and also the paper with the widest circulation. A series of articles in *Moafrika* during 1996 covered the murky past of the ruling party, members of which were revealed as having links with the notorious Vlakplaas camp in South Africa (a centre for covert operations and base for apartheid murder squads), and with the internecine strife leading to the assassination of party members. Under a headline " 'Muso oa Mali" (Government of Blood) on 20 September 1996 the paper described a serious incident when police first tear-gassed and then shot down Lesotho Highlands Water Project strikers, killing seven of them (initial newspaper estimates were higher). The government took no action on the stories which were most damaging to its reputation, but concentrated on the factual content of a particular article, and this led in late 1996 to the editor being charged with libel, an action which eventually led to the editor being fired. The government also withdrew its advertising from the newspaper.

The right to publish a newspaper under a particular name was contested in the courts early in 1997, when the ruling Basutoland Congress Party split into two contesting factions, each of which claimed the right to publish the newspaper *Makatolle*. After a court order had been obtained by one faction against the other, there was a brief break in publication by the original editorial board, which had been supplanted by members of a newly elected National Executive Committee. Eventually, however, two different *Makatolle* newspapers appeared weekly, with almost identical mastheads, a situation which continued until June 1997, when the prime minister Ntsu Mokhehle broke with the BCP and formed his own new party, the Lesotho Congress for Democracy (LCD). The LCD achieved a parliamentary majority, which enabled Mokhehle to remain in power, even though the National Executive Committee of the party he had left (the BCP) had dismissed him as its party leader and could claim support from some 22 members of the 65-seat National Assembly. From June 1997 separate party newspapers appeared – *Makatolle* (BCP) and *Mololi* (LCD). Moreover, it was noticeable that Radio Lesotho was mainly reporting stories favourable to the LCD, and the BCP increasingly had to resort to a popular South African Sesotho radio station, Leseli FM, to acquire media coverage.

In the elections held in May 1998, although the main opposition parties, now the BNP and BCP, between them achieved some 40 per cent of the votes, the "first past the post" electoral system resulted in 79 per cent of the now 80 National Assembly seats going to the ruling LCD, now headed by Pakalitha Mosisili who had replaced the ailing Ntsu Mokhehle. Although independent monitors generally found the elections to be free and fair, the opposition parties claimed that there had been irregularities and held increasingly disruptive demonstrations in the capital, Maseru, the focus of attention being the palace gates. Ultimately opposition supporters managed to paralyse normal government activity, seizing government vehicles and driving them into the palace grounds. The police force vacillated in its allegiance, and the possibility of the Defence Force restoring order was nullified on 11 September by a mutiny by lower ranks that resulted in senior army officers having to take refuge in the South African border town of Ladybrand. The government radio station, Radio Lesotho, was also forced to close down, while enforced "stayaways" when no-one was supposed to come to work resulted in most newspapers missing one or two issues. The whereabouts of the prime minister and cabinet was far from clear, and by mid-September there was a complete power vacuum.

On 16 September, the prime minister, Pakalitha Mosisili, wrote a letter addressed to the heads of the four Southern African Development Council (SADC) countries, South Africa, Botswana, Mozambique, and Zimbabwe, requesting them to intervene to restore order in Lesotho and to avoid a military coup.

On 22 September an intervention force, led by South African troops, entered Maseru. It occupied the palace grounds, and the demonstrators, incensed by what they perceived as a South African invasion, started targeting South African shops and vehicles in Maseru, leading to a more general mayhem resulting in most of the central business district of Lesotho's capital, including several newspaper offices, being looted and burned. Meanwhile rebel soldiers systematically attacked and burned houses belonging to cabinet ministers. On the following days the orgy of destruction had spread to several of Lesotho's district towns.

After a few days order was eventually restored by units of the South African and Botswana defence forces, but there was massive damage to the economy, and even three years later the national wealth (as measured by Gross National Product) had still not recovered to the level in the year before the disturbances.

Following the disturbances, with South African prompting, an Interim Political Assembly (IPA) was set up to devise a new and more appropriate electoral system for Lesotho. Each of the 12 registered political parties was entitled to two seats on the IPA, and it was expected to make prompt recommendations, so that new elections could be held in 1999. Unlike the two Houses of Parliament, the Senate and the National Assembly, which each have a published *Hansard*, the deliberations of the IPA were not available for public scrutiny, nor were its meetings open to the public. Its members, who were due to hold office and to be paid until one day after new elections had been held, took very much longer in their deliberations than expected. The new electoral system was finally settled when the Fourth Amendment to the Constitution Bill became law on 16 March 2001. It provided for a 120-member National Assembly with 80 members being elected in constituencies by the familiar "first past the post" system, and the remaining 40 members being elected by proportional representation so that the Lower House of Parliament as a whole represents the proportions of those voting. By mid-2001, it was expected that elections would now be held in May 2002.

Despite the 1998 disturbances, which were the worst since independence, the freedom of expression guaranteed by the 1993 constitution was not seriously compromised during the late 1990s and at the turn of the millennium. There is indeed more freedom of expression since changes in legislation have since 1999 permitted private radio stations to operate in Lesotho, and some five stations, both religious and secular, have taken advantage of the opportunity. The Media Institute of Southern Africa in its 2001 report, *So This Is Democracy*, which records violations against the media, recorded only two incidents in Lesotho, the lowest of all among the southern African countries (report in *Mail and Guardian* [Johannesburg], 4 May 2001).

The only serious essay on censorship in Lesotho in recent years (Mda 1994) shows that the censors have been government departments or institutions aiming to protect their reputations. The Ministry of Education refused to allow the play *Bacha Malaeneng* (Youth in the Tenements) to be performed in schools and its accompanying comic book to be distributed to pupils. This was because in the play a teacher infected with AIDS seduces a schoolgirl. Such an incident was apparently judged to be prejudicial to the dignity of the teaching profession. Again, a video documentary in which an AIDS patient was filmed at a mission hospital was banned. This followed complaints by the mission authorities, who apparently thought that a government hospital should have been depicted rather then a "respectable Christian hospital".

DAVID AMBROSE

Further Reading

Khaketla, B.M., *Lesotho 1970: An African Coup under the Microscope*, London: Hurst, 1971; Berkeley: University of California Press, 1972

Kunene, Daniel P., *Thomas Mofolo and the Emergence of Written Sesotho Prose*, Johannesburg: Ravan Press, 1989

Mda, Zakes, "Another Theatre of the Absurd" in *Theatre and Performance in Africa: Intercultural Perspectives*, edited by Eckhard Breitinger, Bayreuth: Bayreuth University, 1994

Mukela, John, "My 28 Days in Captivity", *Index on Censorship*, 15/7 (August 1986): 26–27

HANOCH LEVIN
Israeli dramatist, 1943–

THE PATRIOT
Play, 1982

From its foundation, the state of Israel has been the scene of a conflict of values between the secularists, who want to see a modern Jewish country based on liberal values, and various strands of Orthodox religious tradition. At their most extreme, the ultra-Orthodox dispute whether the state should have been founded at all; now that this is an established fact, they take part in its politics to press for the strictest possible observance of the Torah.

Orthodox Jews have always insisted on the meticulous observance of the Sabbath, achieving legal status for this weekly commemoration; there are 39 categories of forbidden work, including both writing and playing a musical instrument. In the early days of the state, the Orthodox would stand at street corners on the Sabbath, throwing stones at passing cars thought to be violating the day.

The number of ultra-Orthodox Jews is increasing: in Jerusalem alone, by 1994, 52 per cent of Jewish children under 10 belonged to ultra-Orthodox families. It was not surprising that a decade earlier *The Patriot* caused a fierce outcry among them – the very title was hardly calculated to make them think well of it and many of them disapprove of theatre as such. Nor was it surprising that secular Jews mounted a passionate defence of freedom of expression, based on this particular case. The play, which was produced at the Neve Zadok Theatre Centre, satirised religious traditions, not least Sabbath rituals, which are bitingly questioned in a scene in which Shabbat candles are used to torture an Arab. The "patriot", Lahav Eshat, is, moreover, put under pressure to demonstrate his loyalty to Israel by murdering an Arab child.

The minister of the interior, Josef Burg, maintained that this kind of play was "a luxury we cannot afford". Hetzofeh, a branch of the National Religious Party, declared that the play should not be staged. On 23 October 1982 the play was pronounced "gravely offensive to the fundamental values of the State, both Jewish and Arab" by the Israeli Theatre and Film Censorship Board (established 1927), a fairly inactive body that had previously banned a mere two plays, one (*The Egg* in the 1950s) because, after 200 performances, it was found that the author was a Nazi. Nevertheless, the board agreed, by 11 votes to 7, to ban *The Patriot*; at this stage it would not even suggest cuts.

This was a signal to mount the defence. This was helped by the fact that, in the first instance, the theatre defied the ban: two performances took place in front of packed houses and were greeted with considerable acclaim. The police did not immediately enforce the ban, merely informing the theatre centre that criminal charges were being prepared. Two members of the Israeli parliament, the Knesset, then introduced a bill to abolish censorship of the arts; they argued that censorship was only required in cases of slander and the law already made sufficient provision for the protection of individual reputations. The Union of Performing Artists organized a rally, and the Hebrew Writers Association called for the abolition of the Censorship Board, which was "superfluous, and restricts the freedom of speech . . . [abolition was] a necessary condition for the social and intellectual development of the state."

The board made some limited concessions. A scene in which the "patriot" sings "Don't shoot me, I have a mother", while he is buying land on the West Bank had been widely considered blasphemous in its context, and was removed, as were the scenes which made use of Shabbat candles. With these and other amendments, the play was allowed to go ahead. In place of the deleted actions, the producer introduced a reader who stood at the front of the stage to intone the words.

This was not the first time that Levin, now one of Israel's most notable playwrights, had met with forms of censorship. A performance of his *Queen of the Bath* (1970), an attack on war and false heroism, was physically attacked by a crowd that had been assembled for the purpose; the songs that he wrote for this play are still banned by Israeli Radio. Much of his later work points up the contradictions between the idealism of Israel's early pioneering days and the well-heeled life of the modern Tel Aviv bourgeoisie.

DEREK JONES

Writings
Ya'akovi and Leidental: A Play with Songs, translated by Dennis Silk and Shimeon Levy, 1979
Mahazot (Plays), 1988–
The Sorrows of Job in *Modern Israeli Drama in Translation*, edited by Michael Taub, 1993

Further Reading
Armstrong, Karen, *A History of Jerusalem*, New York: Knopf, and London: HarperCollins, 1996; as *Jerusalem: One City, Three Faiths*, New York: Ballantine, 1997
Ben-Zeer, Noam, "Smashed Hits: Israel", *Index on Censorship*, 27/6 (November–December 1998)
Johnson, Paul, *A History of the Jews*, London: Weidenfeld and Nicolson, and New York: Harper and Row, 1987
Uscher, Nancy, "Unpatriotic *Patriot*", *Index on Censorship*, 12/3 (June 1983)

JOSÉ LEZAMA LIMA
Cuban poet, novelist, and essayist, 1910–1976

PARADISO
Novel, 1966

José Lezama Lima, poet, essayist, editor, and public speaker, is best known for a single work, *Paradiso*. According to the writer Reinaldo Arenas, "I do not think that Cuba has ever witnessed the publication of a novel so explicitly homosexual, so extraordinarily complex and rich in imagery, so idiosyncratically Cuban, so Latin American, and, at the same time, so unique."

Lezama Lima began to write the novel in the 1940s, when its first chapter appeared in the magazine *Orígenes*, which he edited. The writing and editing of the rest of the book were protracted and subject to considerable interruption. In *Paradiso*, the nature of Cuba – its language, customs, behaviour, sexuality, and historical or imaginary successes – is revealed through the story of a single family, and especially the central character of the book, José Cemi. *Paradiso* marks a considerable break with the conventional novel: it is as much poetry as narrative, almost an antinovel. It is full of obscure references, oblique metaphor, and surprisingly dramatic resolutions.

Despite the difficulties of the work, the 5000 copies of the Cuban edition were snatched up within a few days of its appearance. Successful translations appeared in Italy and France, and the book also won admirers in Mexico, Peru, and Argentina. However, in Cuba the novel had a peculiar fate. First, its original edition was held up at the printers until its distribution had been authorized. Then, after its initial success, the book was not reprinted for 25 years. Several reasons have been suggested for this apparently unofficial censorship. Lezama Lima's work hardly met the demands of the political system which demands of art a transparent and specific social function: *Paradiso* is elitist, inward-looking, and pessimistic. There was talk of Lezama Lima's political reserve, and of his failure to join the Communist Party, although, on more than one occasion, he had praised the social process that had begun in 1959. Lezama Lima was a Catholic, though hardly an orthodox one. Above all, in a period of homophobia in official

Cuban circles, it was the notorious chapter 8 of the novel, in which the author recounts homosexual relationships between his characters, that caused official displeasure, especially after the drastic antihomosexual resolutions of the Congress of Education and Culture in 1971.

The writer Ciro Bianchi has said, "*Paradiso* split Lezama Lima's life wide open . . . until then, he had used his skill to enable the creativity of his fluids to flow, and he had lived far away from the public gaze . . . With the appearance of this book, his private life became well known." Lezama Lima became practically a recluse in his home at Calle Trocadero, Havana, excluded from publication, reviews, conferences and literary competitions. He commented: "As I once endured indifference with complete dignity, so now I endure fame with complete indifference". He was, however, wounded by the silence.

LEONARDO PADURA
translated by Rupert Capper

Writings

Paradiso, 1966, revised edition, edited by Julio Cortázar and Carlos Monsiváis, 1968; as *Paradiso*, translated by Gregory Rabassa, 1978
Recopilación de textos sobre José Lezama Lima, edited by Pedro Simón, 1970
Obras completas, edited by Cintio Vitier, 2 vols, 1975–77

Further Reading

Alvarez Bravo, Armando (editor), *Orbita de Lezama Lima*, Havana: Unión Nacional de Escritores y Artistas de Cuba, 1966
Arenas, Reinaldo, *Before Night Falls*, New York and London: Viking, 1993
Espinosa, Carlos, *Cercanía de Lezama Lima*, Havana: Letras Cubanas, 1986
González, Reynaldo, *Lezama Lima: el ingenuo culpable*, Havana: Letras Cubanas, 1988

LI JIANTONG
Chinese novelist

LIU ZHIDAN
Novel, 1962

Although the draft for Li Jiantong's biographical novel of the revolutionary Liu Zhidan was completed in 1962, the novel was not granted publication in its entirety until 1979. For 17 years, the novel was effectively banned in the People's Republic of China. The author and her supporters were also subjected to censure and interrogation.

Liu (1903–36) had joined the Communist Party in 1925 and from the early 1930s was the recognized leader of communist guerrillas in northwest China. In 1932 Liu was instrumental in establishing the northwest Soviet District, and shortly thereafter

became its political and military director. Following the Long March of 1935, when Mao Zedong led the Central Committee of the Chinese Communist Party from the south to the northwest of the country, Liu was temporarily imprisoned on suspicion of "right-wing opportunism". He died in battle against the Nationalists in April 1936.

Li Jiantong was married to Liu Zhidan's younger brother, and depicted an accurate – if at times mawkish – picture of her brother-in-law's "devotion to the revolution". She was initially reluctant to write the novel, but was eventually persuaded by the Workers' Publishing House – the official publishing organ of the party-led Federation of Trade Unions – to embark upon a project that lasted from 1956 until 1962. Small sections of the novel were published in the newspapers *Gongren Ribao* (Workers' Daily) and *Guangming Ribao* (Guangming Daily) in July and August 1962.

Yan Hongyan, a leading party official connected with the military in Yunnan province, had been opposed to certain aspects of Liu Zhidan's leadership style in the 1930s, and strongly objected to the proposed publication of Li Jiantong's novel. Yan – whose name Li has never disclosed in public – voiced his objections directly to Kang Sheng, director of the Central Committee's Ideological Group and *de facto* head of Mao's secret police. This was the first time since the founding of the People's Republic that the secret police became involved in literary affairs (Wagner).

In September 1962, during the Tenth Plenum of the Chinese Communist Party in Beijing, Kang Sheng spoke in public about *Liu Zhidan*. He described the novel as "an anti-party poisonous weed" and warned of its negative ideological influence should it be published. Kang also claimed that the novel promoted the reversal of the party's verdict on Gao Gang. Gao, Liu Zhidan's successor as vice-director of the Military Committee, had been purged and denounced during the "rectification campaigns" of the early 1950s. Li Jiantong, writing three decades later, attempted to present a factual account, and had depicted Gao in a positive light in the novel.

The seriousness of Kang Sheng's accusations prompted Mao to speak out on the use of literature in the class struggle. At the Tenth Plenum, Mao warned of the continuing contradiction between the proletariat and the bourgeoisie in Chinese society: "Using fiction to engage in anti-party activity is a great invention. Those who intend to overthrow the government have to stir up public opinion before they can carry out ideological work. This remains the same for both the revolutionary and the counter-revolutionary classes." There is some doubt that Mao had even read the novel,

Following the Tenth Plenum, the Central Propaganda Bureau promptly issued a directive ordering publication of *Liu Zhidan* to cease. Mao also ordered that a "working group" be established under the leadership of Kang Sheng to investigate the "anti-party clique" that had coalesced around Li Jiantong. Initially, only Li and editors from the Workers' Publishing House were investigated, and made self-criticisms and recantations of their "erroneous" ideological views. However, Kang Sheng used the investigations as an excuse to interrogate all those interviewed by Li when preparing the novel. Between 1962 and 1966, thousands were brought to Beijing to be interrogated and to attend study sessions.

Li Jiantong and her supporters were arrested by the police and charged with "embellishing themselves" through the novel. As *Liu Zhidan* had extolled the revolutionary exploits of a guerrilla hero who had been based hundreds of miles away from Mao Zedong and the Party Central Committee, it was, so the critics maintained, in effect negating the victories achieved by Mao prior to the Long March. The novel was criticized as promoting the view that Liu Zhidan had saved the Central Committee, when in reality he had merely "stolen" Maoist thought for his own ends.

During the Cultural Revolution, Kang Sheng handed over his files on the *Liu Zhidan* affair to a Red Guard group in Beijing, encouraging them to continue persecution of those involved in what became known as "Special Case 62". Li Jiantong was arrested and detained in an underground cell. She was expelled from the Communist Party in 1970 and forced to undergo "reform through labour".

In late 1978, both Li Jiantong and Liu Zhidan were exonerated. The latter was promoted as a "revolutionary martyr" who sought to further – rather than subvert – the Maoist line. *Liu Zhidan* was granted official publication by the Workers' Publishing House in October 1979. The second and third volumes of Li's biography of Liu Zhidan were published in December 1984 and June 1985.

DESMOND A. SKEEL

Further Reading

Birch, Cyril, *Chinese Communist Literature*, New York: Praeger, 1963

Cheng, Jin (compiler), *A Chronology of the People's Republic of China, 1949–1984*, Beijing: Foreign Languages Press, and Metuchen, New Jersey: Scarecrow Press, 1986

Goldman, Merle, *Chinese Intellectuals: Advise and Dissent*, Cambridge, Massachusetts: Harvard University Press, 1981

Holm, David, "The Strange Case of *Liu Zhidan*", *Australian Journal of Chinese Affairs* (January 1992): 77–96

McDougall, Bonnie S. (editor), *Popular Chinese Literature and Performing Arts in the People's Republic of China, 1949–1979*, Berkeley: University of California Press, 1984

Wagner, Rudolf G., *The Contemporary Chinese Historical Drama: Four Studies*, Berkeley: University of California Press, 1990

Yen, Chia-chi and Kao Kao, *The Ten-Year History of the Chinese Cultural Revolution*, Taipei: Institute of Current China Studies, 1988

LI ZHI
Chinese philosopher, 1527–1602

The imprisonment (and suicide) of the unorthodox Confucian philosopher Li Zhi is the best-known instance of state censorship in the Ming dynasty (1368–1644). The impeachment of the man and the suppression of his writings were controversial at the time, but the judgement of most Confucians in the 17th century confirmed the state's intervention. They viewed the closing decades of the Ming as a time of decadence and immorality, and wove the denunciation of Li Zhi into a narrative of decline leading to the dynasty's collapse. Some historians of Chinese philosophy resurrected him as a representative of "anti-feudal" thought. Although this judgement has since been revised, Li Zhi did voice trenchant critiques against what he regarded as the intellectual shallowness and cowardice of his peers in the face of pressing moral choices, and suffered for it.

Li Zhi was born into a merchant family from coastal Fujian that had for centuries been involved in foreign trade. He was raised by his father, a reserved and proper man, who oversaw his conventional Confucian education. As his branch of the family was not able to support him past the provincial degree, Li Zhi applied for and gained the modest post of county director of studies in 1555, but his intellectual vigour eventually won him promotion to a place in the National Academy. He faced a series of career setbacks with the deaths of his father (1559) and grandfather (1563), for which he was required to take bereavement leave, compounded by personal tragedies with the death of his second son in 1563 and his second and third daughters in 1566. He was finally able to secure a posting in the Ministry of Rites that year and rose slowly through the ranks, retiring from a prefectship in 1581.

While working in Beijing in the late 1560s, Li Zhi began to explore the innovative teachings of Wang Yangming (1472–1529) and his disciplines, which called upon the individual to cultivate his mind to understand the nature of moral being rather than rely on book knowledge. In the 1570s during a long posting to Nanjing, Li enlarged his circle of philosophical acquaintants, absorbing the influence of more radical thinkers who looked to Buddhism for insights into the task of self-cultivation and advocated an accommodative blending of Buddhist elements into Confucian practice. In the 1580s, after retiring from public office, Li began to develop his own ethical position, which was to deny the possibility of absolute moral judgements and to question the necessity of relying on the teachings of Confucius to become a moral person. Truth could not be ascertained by following the standards set down in Confucianism, but was available only to the individual and only through careful introspection. The individual had to cultivate the mind in order to lay bare the innately good impulses with which people were born. The moral person did not cling to external standards of good and evil to become good, but did so by examining his own mind and establishing his own standards. In accordance with this belief, Li regarded all people, both men and women, as equal.

Li Zhi came increasingly to view the intellectual positions of most of his peers as pedantry rather than true philosophy, and he registered his impatience with their failure to strive for moral perfection by taking Buddhist tonsure in 1588. He did not formally become a monk but lived as a Buddhist Confucian for the rest of his life, much to the annoyance of Confucian conservatives, who distrusted the growing influence of Buddhism. Li did not withdraw from the world, however, but preferred to challenge what he regarded as the moral duplicity of many of the great thinkers of his age in full view. To ensure that his iconoclastic views did not remain within a small circle of philosophers, from 1590 onwards he actively published everything he wrote, including his forthright letters to intellectual sparring partners.

Evidence of his success appears in the impeachment memorial that landed him in prison in March 1602 at the age of 74. According to censor Zhang Wenda (died 1625), Li's ideas had become dangerous because they were circulating among the younger generation of the gentry, especially in the capital. At his trial, Li acknowledged that "the accused has written many books", but protested that his work "would benefit the propagation of the teaching of the sages rather than damage it". And yet the titles of his two most widely read collections of essays and letters – *Fen shu* (A Book to Be Burned) and *Cang shu* (A Book to Be Hidden Away) – suggest that Li anticipated that his writings would be regarded as transgressing "the teachings of the sages".

In the impeachment Zhang Wenda declared that Li Zhi had rejected the authority of Confucius; his embrace of Buddhism epitomized the unhealthy trend among the gentry of abandoning Confucian norms in favour of Buddhist practices. Zhang also charged Li with using his false monk's status to seduce the women who became his students. This charge cuts to the core of the impeachment. One of the female students was the daughter of Mei Guozhen, a high official who in 1602 was in conflict with the eunuch-backed faction surrounding the chief grand secretary, Shen Yiguan (1531–1615). Zhang Wenda was a member of Shen's faction. Since rumour had it that Li Zhi, who was living at the time just east of Beijing, was composing a diatribe against Shen, Zhang Wenda went on the offensive on behalf of his patron, pinning convenient charges on Li Zhi in order to embarrass Mei. "People never thought Li would delude the world or advocate licentiousness", a close friend of Li's observed shortly after his death. "Those who have heartlessly stirred up this business are clearly not after this old man."

The official judgement on Li Zhi was a suspended sentence and the burning of the printing blocks of his writings. The papers got held up at court, however, and the emperor did not confirm the judgement, leaving Li to languish in prison. Ill and unwilling to face the public humiliation of being sent home and placed under supervision, Li slit his throat with a razor, dying two days later on 6 May 1602. True to his vow that "they can kill me but they can't get rid of me", he provoked controversy in death as he had in life. His books continued to be printed and to be popular among younger readers, despite the ban. But orthodox opinion went against him once a more sober and conservative mood took hold of the country after the Manchu invasion in 1644, and many a 17th-century writer liked to quote the impeachment memorial and approve of the judgement.

Li Zhi has been rehabilitated in the 20th century. He was championed in the 1970s as a brilliant opponent of Confucianism and "feudalism" and a willing martyr for intellectual independence, and his death portrayed as the cruellest instance of state censorship in the Ming dynasty. Scholarly opinion in the 1980s has modified this assessment to suggest that Li was targeted for factional rather than intellectual reasons, and that he committed suicide out of a sense of having failed, despite his outspoken critique of the current orthodoxy, to formulate a moral and intellectual programme that could replace what it condemned. However he is assessed, Li Zhi was a spirited intellectual whose banned writings are among the liveliest and most incisive of his generation.

TIMOTHY BROOK

Further Reading

Billeter, Jean-François, *Li Zhi, philosophe maudit, 1527–1602: contribution à une sociologie du mandarinat chinois de la fin des Ming*, Geneva: Droz, 1979

Brook, Timothy, *Praying for Power: Buddhism and the Formation of Gentry Society in Late-Ming China*, Cambridge, Massachusetts: Council on East Asian Studies, Harvard University, 1993

Chan, Hok-lam, *Li Chih, 1527–1602 in Contemporary Chinese Historiography: New Light on His Life and Works*, White Plains, New York: Sharpe, 1980

de Bary, William Theodore and the Conference on Ming Thought (editors), *Self and Society in Ming Thought*, New York: Columbia University Press, 1970

Hsiao, K.C., "Li Chih" in *Dictionary of Ming Biography, 1368–1644*, edited by L. Carrington Goodrich and Chao-ying Fang, New York: Columbia University Press, 1976

Huang, Ray, *1587, a Year of No Significance: The Ming Dynasty in Decline*, New Haven, Connecticut: Yale University Press, 1981

LIBELLES
Slanderous pamphlets: France, 18th century

During the second half of the 20th century, in some societies, stories of the intimate lives of royalty and senior political figures have been said to "sell newspapers". Those who write for and edit these newspapers often argue that they are "acting in the public interest". These justifications for the invasion of prominent people's privacy – although the parallel should not be pressed too far – have a certain pre-echo in the *libelles* of 18th-century France, of which *Anecdotes sur Mme la Comtesse du Barry* is a prime example.

Libelles (from the Latin *libellus*, a small book) were pamphlets. During their long history, they became so associated with highly slanderous attacks on public figures that the Académie Française's dictionary of 1762 could define them more specifically as *écrits injurieux* (offensive works). They were, according to Robert Darnton, "the hack writers' staff of life, their meat, their favourite genre". Beginning as mere sexual titillation, they had so grown in scope and ambition during the 18th century that Mairobert, the presumed author of the *Anecdotes sur Mme la Comtesse du Barry*, was ready to pretend to a serious interest in history: "throughout our account, from her [the Comtesse's] birth up to her retirement, we have cited the sources of our information. We have followed, in this respect, the scrupulous principles of the historian". As for the writer's motives, he wished, he said, "to console the simple citizen, who, deprived by his obscure birth of access to the court and its glories, might sigh often after such things".

In fact, of course, *libelles* were usually "gossip . . . dressed up as history", as Darnton puts it, supposed eye-witness accounts of episodes in the victims' lives or extracts from memoirs. Because the victims were usually members of the court, the *libelles* sold well, though not necessarily to the "simple citizens". More likely buyers were other members of the court who could use the material against their rivals and enemies. The *Anecdotes* came second in the list of bestsellers published by the Société typographique de Neuchâtel (STN) based just across the French border with Switzerland. Buying and selling books which, like the *Anecdotes*, were offensive to the king, could be dangerous: a bookseller found guilty of trading in this area might be imprisoned. No wonder, by way of example, that Rigaud, Pons, and Company, of Montpellier, when placing orders with STN, felt it necessary to ask for "no risks, please", while making sure that they were well supplied with *nouveautés piquantes*, sexually revealing works on matters of topical interest and scurrilous accounts of the goings-on at court; the *Anecdotes* are specifically mentioned as desirable material for which there would be a quick sale.

Jeanne Bécu, Comtesse du Barry, the subject of one of the most popular *libelles*, had been successively a hairdressers' assistant, a companion to a wealthy widow, a salesgirl in a Paris dress shop, and a prostitute in Mme Gourdan's brothel. Her "virginity" had been sold many times over to clients holding prominent positions in the Church, the nobility, the magistracy, and the world of high finance. She assumed the title of countess after her association with Jean du Barry, a pimp for the nobility. When du Barry introduced Jeanne to Le Bel, first valet and procurer of bedfellows for Louis XV, she would crown her career, giving satisfaction, as the king is purported to have said, as "the only woman in France who has found a way to make me forget I am nearing 60". Unmarried, she might have been seen as harbouring an ambition to take away some of the king's powers. In 1768, therefore, an arranged (and sham) marriage to du Barry's own brother, the Chevalier Guillaume du Barry, was organized for her. From 1769, following her formal introduction at court, Mme du Barry embarked on her life of power, wealth, and influence as official mistress (*maîtresse en titre*) to the king.

It was the Comtesse du Barry's influence and her power as much as the wealth she acquired which singled her out as a suitable subject for a *libelle*. She made an excellent symbol for the corruption of the *ancien régime*. It is estimated that she had cost the French treasury some 18 million livres by the end of 1773, one pair of earrings alone costing 60,000 livres. For a comparison, the annual salary for a fashionable Paris physician was approximately 8000 to 10,000 livres. Her position also provided generous income for her pimp, who milked the treasury to pay off his gambling and brothel debts. A fellow-*libelliste* of Mairobert, Burzard de Mauvelin, wrote: "Louis XV always remained the same. Despite the desperation of his starving people and public calamity, his mistress grew so wild in her prodigality and pillaging that in a few years she would have brought the kingdom down, had not the death of the despot put an end to his extravagance".

Profligacy was not the only cause for jealousy or suspicion at court. Influence and coteries were too. Mme du Barry used her enormous influence first against the duc de Choiseul, Louis's secretary of state for foreign affairs, and then secretary for war, and later against Maupeou, one of the inheritors of Choiseul's power, to support the shift of power from the Parlements (which had power to veto royal decrees) to those who had demonstrated a closer loyalty to the king. All of this was grist to the mill of a *libelliste*, feeding off the desire of those who wanted to read privileged information about du Barry and the king.

Although the subject matter they chose was sensitive, the chances of Mairobert and his fellow-*libellistes* being caught were small. J.C.P. Lenoir, Louis XVI's chief of police, complained that "the Parisians had more of a propensity to believe the malicious rumours and *libelles* that circulated clandestinely than the facts printed by order or with the permission of the government". He attempted to have the offending works suppressed but was "undercut by courtiers who (also) had scandalous works printed and protected printers". All Lenoir could do was to put those who peddled the *libelles* in prison. A final push by the police was more successful; after 1784, booksellers decided that they must be more careful and their orders dried up. As for the Comtesse, she paid dearly for her allegiances and status. When King Louis XV had fallen victim to smallpox, she was invited to leave the court, and later, during the Revolution, she was executed.

LINDA WALSH

Further Reading

Barry, Joseph, *Passions and Politics: A Biography of Versailles*, London: Gollancz, and New York: Doubleday, 1972

Darnton, Robert, *The Literary Underground of the Old Regime*, Cambridge, Massachusetts: Harvard University Press, 1982

Darnton, Robert, *The Forbidden Best-Sellers of Pre-Revolutionary France*, New York: Norton, 1995; London: HarperCollins, 1996

LIBERAL DEMOCRACY

The basic tenets of the political philosophy of liberal democracy took shape and were refined in 18th and 19th-century Europe. These include adherence by government to a policy of toleration that stands opposed to the practice of censorship and to suppression in general. Toleration serves a more fundamental value in liberalism, that of individual liberty.

Historically, opposition to religious censorship and suppression provided the first opportunity to develop a systematic defence of toleration. John Locke's *Letter Concerning Toleration*, published in 1689, is a classic statement of the case for religious toleration. Locke argued for a separation of the religious and civil realms, insisting that the Church is "absolutely separate and distinct from the Commonwealth. The Boundaries on both sides are fixed and immovable." He described the Church as a "voluntary society" and religious belief as a private matter properly outside the scope of political authority. He was unwilling to extend toleration to Roman Catholics and atheists, but his argument represents an important step in clearing a space for liberty of conscience and freedom of thought. Toleration as a means of accommodation among people with deep religious disagreements was originally a mere *modus vivendi*. However, as the philosophical development of liberalism proceeded through the 18th and into the 19th century, moral justifications for toleration took shape.

Natural rights theory provides one way to ground toleration morally. According to this theory, individuals possess rights to such things as life and liberty simply by virtue of being human. Claims based on these rights are the strongest moral claims that can be made against government or other people. Natural rights, now normally named human rights, take priority over political authority and positive law, and thus have distinctive power as a moral foundation for toleration. The protection of individual natural rights provides the rationale for a limited government that respects a sphere of conduct outside the proper scope of political authority and within which personal freedom prevails. Control over public communication, conduct, or morals, unless necessary to protect the rights of others, is a violation of natural rights. The rights of conscience, speech, press, and assembly, referred to in such documents as the United States Constitution and the United Nations Declaration of Human Rights, have their roots in natural law and natural rights theory. For natural rights liberals, individual freedom is considered to be intrinsically valuable, regardless of how particular individuals choose to exercise their rights, and censorship in any form is considered inimical to such freedom.

Utilitarianism provides an alternative to natural rights theory as a moral foundation for toleration. In *On Liberty*, published in 1859, John Stuart Mill, like Locke, was concerned with the threat that political authority posed to individual liberty. But he was also concerned with the threat that stems from the pressure of convention and public opinion. He believed that people were more oppressed by unwritten laws and the prescriptive weight of tradition than they were by laws enforced by the state. Early in *On Liberty*, Mill makes it clear that his defence of toleration does not depend upon claims involving natural rights, but rests instead on utility. He regards utility "as the ultimate appeal on all ethical questions" and understands it "in the largest sense, grounded on the permanent interests of man as a progressive being."

Mill argued that once society had reached a certain level of intellectual development, freedom of thought, discussion, and action have positive utility both for society and for the individual. He believed that the only justifiable reason for restricting individual liberty is to prevent harm to others. Regarding freedom of discussion specifically, Mill argued that in censoring an opinion, no matter how unpopular, society assumes infallibility. He appeals to the historical record to demonstrate how ill-founded such an assumption of infallibility is. Tolerant societies have much to gain from the free and open discussion of all opinions. If the opinion is true – and this cannot be known in advance – society has the opportunity to exchange error for truth, but, if false, it loses "what is almost as great a benefit, the clearer perception and livelier impression of truth produced by its collision with error."

Regarding freedom of action, the liberty to chart one's own course in life, Mill argued that societies tolerant of a variety of "experiments" in living are more likely to develop and progress than repressive, tradition-bound ones. He emphasized the value of nonconformity, even eccentricity, and pointed to Socrates and Jesus as great social benefactors viewed as dangerous and subversive in their own times. For Mill, autonomy and originality are essential sources of social improvement and individual well-being. Toleration allows a variety of lifestyles to survive and flourish against the pervasive influence of convention and public morality.

Judith N. Shklar has written: ". . . liberalism is monogamously, faithfully, and permanently married to democracy – but it is a marriage of convenience". Only in a democracy is there sufficient equality of power for people to assert their autonomy and protect the conditions necessary for freedom. Democracy is the form of government most consistent with the values of liberalism, but there are strains in its marriage with liberalism. Majorities can be tyrannical and can seek to impose their religious, moral, or political views on the whole community. Constitutional limits on political authority may prevent majorities from achieving their goals through legal means, but cannot prevent public opinion and morality from operating informally in all areas of social life. Mill was probably correct that in a democracy it is this phenomenon, rather than official censorship, that poses the greatest threat to personal freedom.

Liberal democracy stands at the outset of the 21st century as the dominant political belief system around the world. Its global ascendancy has been particularly rapid since the end of the Cold War. But, problems and challenges for the liberal doctrine of toleration continue to demand attention. A particularly difficult problem arises with regard to the toleration of intolerance. How should liberals respond, for instance, to Christian fundamentalists who would ban certain school textbooks; or to the sentence of death pronounced on Salman Rushdie? John Rawls has addressed these issues in *A Theory of Justice* (1971). He argues that an intolerant group has no legitimate basis to complain when its activities are censored or it is denied equal liberty, because " . . . a person's right to complain is limited to violations of principles he acknowledges himself". Nevertheless, Rawls believes that tolerant groups do not have the right to suppress intolerant ones and that suppression can be justified only if intolerant groups present a considerable risk to others' freedom or to liberty itself. Is the German ban on the Nazi party, enacted after World War II, in violation of this liberal principle of extending equal liberty to intolerant groups? Perhaps, given Germany's history, it is possible to justify this selective suppression. It has not led to a general policy of suppression of dissident or unpopular viewpoints, and Germany is widely considered a healthy and stable constitutional democracy. The issue raises pressing concerns, particularly since religious and ethnic fundamentalism play an increasingly powerful role in world affairs and groups advocating and practising intolerance are increasingly visible. Contemporary defences of toleration must acknowledge and address the danger that this trend presents to liberal democratic values.

Communitarians have argued that liberalism neglects the critical importance of community and the extent to which individual freedom and well-being are dependent on society. Alasdair MacIntyre, for example, believes that an individual's good is inseparable from his or her social position or role, and Charles Taylor holds the view that autonomy can be developed only in a certain kind of social environment. Communitarians object specifically to the liberal doctrine of toleration which demands that government remains neutral regarding the intrinsic value or merits of particular lifestyles. They argue that certain individual conceptions of the good are preferable to others, because they conform to and support a particular society's way of life. According to this view, the state should favour these conceptions over others and should intervene to encourage people to adopt them.

In 1994, in the interest of cultural and linguistic preservation, a law was passed in France forbidding the sale of goods and services in any single language other than French. In the United States, public policy initiatives on issues as varied as abortion, pornography, and religious observances in schools have been taken by groups concerned to promote their conceptions of a common morality and to use the law to uphold them. How should liberals respond to such communitarian efforts? They can agree with communitarians that unbridled individualism weakens traditional forms of social cohesion, without agreeing that the state should actively favour particular conceptions of the good life. According to liberal theory, individuals should be free to make their own choices about the sorts of lives they lead, including choices about whether or not to support the dominant social practices. In addition, if the state were to intervene, the ways of life and corresponding definitions of the common good favoured would tend to reflect heavily the values of dominant groups. Politically and socially marginalized groups might be further excluded from participation in the life of society.

Toleration is essential not only for the development and expression of individual autonomy, but also for the proper operation of democracy. Meaningful political debate requires a plurality of interests and opinions which toleration helps to foster. Conflict and competition are the lifeblood of a healthy democracy. Competing interests and policy alternatives stimulate participation in the political process. This is important because democratic legitimacy depends upon participation by all groups in society.

Progressive and radical critics of liberal democracy charge that behind a formal commitment to toleration, political debate is informally constrained and excludes many dissident and minority points of view. Further, critics claim that the agendas of major political institutions reflect only the interests of the most powerful segments of society, particularly corporate and financial elites. Toleration is a necessary condition for democratic participation, but not a sufficient one. Political participation is not an isolated activity. It has its roots in the social, economic, and cultural conditions of the citizenry. Deep disparities between people diminishes democratic participation, especially for the socially most disadvantaged groups. Democracy requires a level of equality of political power among individuals which marked social inequality makes impossible.

Toleration is central to the liberal democratic creed, a necessary feature of a social environment in which individuals can develop autonomously. One crucial aspect of autonomy is democratic participation by each in the decisions binding on everyone. Tolerance is also a personal virtue, which, when widely possessed by the members of a liberal society, enables people with diverse and even incompatible conceptions of the good life to live together successfully.

DAVID T. RISSER

Further Reading

Bachrach, Peter, *The Theory of Democratic Elitism: A Critique*, London: University of London Press, and Boston: Little Brown, 1967

Goodin, Robert E. and Andrew Reeve (editors), *Liberal Neutrality*, London and New York: Routledge, 1989

King, Preston, *Toleration*, London: Allen and Unwin, and New York: St Martin's Press, 1976

Locke, John, *A Letter Concerning Toleration* (1689), edited by James Tully, Indianapolis: Hackett, 1983

Macedo, Stephen, *Liberal Virtues: Citizenship, Virtue, and Community in Liberal Constitutionalism*, Oxford: Clarendon Press, and New York: Oxford University Press, 1990

Macedo, Stephen, "Toleration and Fundamentalism" in *A Companion To Contemporary Political Philosophy*, edited by Robert E. Goodin and Philip Pettit, Oxford and Cambridge, Massachusetts: Blackwell, 1993

MacIntyre, Alasdair, *After Virtue: A Study In Moral Theory*, London: Duckworth, and Notre Dame, Indiana: University of Notre Dame Press, 1981

Mendus, Susan, *Toleration and the Limits of Liberalism*, Basingstoke: Macmillan, and Atlantic Highlands, New Jersey: Humanities Press, 1989

Mill, John Stuart, *On Liberty*, 1859; edited by Gertrude Himmelfarb, Harmondsworth and Baltimore: Penguin, 1974

Rawls, John, *A Theory of Justice*, Cambridge, Massachusetts: Harvard University Press, 1971, Oxford: Clarendon Press, 1972; revised edition, Harvard University Press, and Oxford: Oxford University Press, 1999

Rawls, John, *Political Liberalism*, New York: Columbia University Press, 1993

Raz, Joseph, *The Morality of Freedom*, Oxford: Clarendon Press, and New York: Oxford University Press, 1986

Rorty, Richard, "The Priority of Democracy to Philosophy" in *The Virginia Statute for Religious Freedom: Its Evolution and Consequences in American History*, edited by Merrill D. Peterson and Robert Vaughan, Cambridge and New York: Cambridge University Press, 1988

Rosenblum, Nancy L. (editor), *Liberalism and the Moral Life*, Cambridge, Massachusetts: Harvard University Press, 1989

Shklar, Judith N., *Ordinary Vices*, Cambridge, Massachusetts: Harvard University Press, 1984

Shklar, Judith N., "The Liberalism of Fear" in *Liberalism and the Moral Life*, edited by Nancy L. Rosenblum, Cambridge, Massachusetts: Harvard University Press, 1989

Taylor, Charles, *Philosophy and the Human Sciences*, Cambridge and New York: Cambridge University Press, 1985

Wolff, Robert Paul, "Tolerance" in his *The Poverty of Liberalism*, Boston: Beacon Press, 1968

LIBERIA

Population: 2,913,000
Main religions: Muslim; Christian; indigenous religions
Official language: English
Other languages spoken: Niger–Congo ethnic languages

Illiteracy rate (%): 29.9 (m); 62.3 (f)
Number of daily newspapers: 6
Number of radio receivers per 1000 inhabitants: 329
Number of TV receivers per 1000 inhabitants: 29

Liberia has never been a democracy. In 133 years of one-party rule, a decade of military rule, and seven years of horrific civil war, freedom of speech, expression or opinion has never flourished. Acts of censorship, such as the banning of a particular reporter or newspaper, accompanied by more gross violations, such as the massacre of people suspected of following a different warlord, have marked the country's history.

Africa's first republic was founded in 1847 by freed American slaves and other small non-indigenous groups. The views and attitudes of these "Americo-Liberian" colonialists towards the indigenous peoples were very much those of white Europeans. The indigenous people remained excluded from the development of the Liberian state economically, socially, and politically throughout the period of Americo-Liberian rule (1847–1980). Poorly governed by the quasi-hereditary leaders of the True Whig party, the country was "protected" by the United States and by a strategic concession to the American Firestone Company.

The Liberian state was unwilling to incorporate diverse social and political groups and forms of expression. Education infrastructure is undeveloped beyond the coastal regions; illiteracy stood at 75–80 per cent in the 1970s; an inaccessible "official" legal system was designed to benefit only Americo-Liberians; indigenous agricultural practices were destroyed; and the "tribal element" was marginalized. Limited reforms in the 1960s and 1970s certainly addressed some of the more glaring instances of discrimination but were widely regarded as either too little too late, or just plain cosmetic.

True Whig control of the political debate, principally through its powerful patronage machine, meant that Americo-Liberian rule was for a long time never called into question. Criticism of the authorities was always seen as a threat to cohesion and therefore to the security of the nation-state, over which William Tubman presided for 28 years (1943–1971).

The principal organs of control were the government-owned newspapers: the *Liberian Age*, the *Liberian Star*, and the *Daily Listener*. Any coverage of the weak, short-lived and half-hearted opposition was considered dangerous and therefore not permitted. Errant journalists and editors on these papers were quickly brought into line, as evidenced by the imprisonment of the editor of the *Liberian Star* in 1966.

Journalists on the independent papers were likely to fall foul of the strictly enforced libel laws and suffered almost systematic suppression from the 1930s onwards. The founder editor of the *African Nationalist*, for example, was found guilty of libelling president Tubman and sentenced to a lengthy prison term. He was released after 15 years in 1969. In 1955 the editor of the *Independent Weekly*, Bertha Corbin, was imprisoned, and the paper banned. Albert Porte, a long-term critic of the authorities, who wrote numerous pamphlets to publicize his dissent, suffered brief periods of imprisonment, job losses, public rebukes, and a massive civil damages lawsuit in the 1970s.

The use of radio as a means of control and indoctrination was barely taken up. There was one national broadcasting station, the state-run ELBC, but its coverage was not wide. However, Liberia did play its part in broader propaganda efforts when it agreed to allow the US to set up its Voice of America transmitter outside Monrovia in the 1960s.

Strains within the Americo-Liberian community emerged in the 1970s, stemming partly from economic difficulties but also from a growing sense that the political system was unjust and unsustainable. President Tolbert – who succeeded Tubman in 1971 – appeared not to understand what had taken place in the rest of Africa. In 1980 a coup d'état occurred which was led by sergeant Samuel Doe. The coup heralded 10 years of increasingly dictatorial rule, supposedly in the name of indigenous Liberians.

All political discussion was banned between 1980 and 1985 – this included the formation of political parties and discussion of political issues in the press. The silencing of the press was systematic and harsh. Decree 88A of July 1984 was said to be designed "to protect the Public against the spread of rumours, lies and discrimination". It was declared a felony to injure an official or his reputation, create disturbances, or to undermine security. This was applied to writing, engraving, drawing, the creation of effigies, and to broadcasts. Among those it was used against was Ezebiel B. Pajibo, who, in a leaflet called *React*, had aimed to rally student support for the presentation of "particular grievances" to the government. (The government had closed down the University of Liberia for three months during 1984.)

The new rulers continued the long Whig practice of subsidizing parts of the press, notably the *New Liberian*. On the other hand, they were extremely sensitive to criticism. The widely-read *Daily Observer* suffered particularly and was forced to suspend publication five times between 1980 and 1985. Its managing editor Kenneth Best was jailed after being accused of giving prominence to anti-government stories. After it resumed publication shortly after Doe's inauguration its premises were set alight. Similar harassment met the staff of *Footprints Today*. Before the 1985 election its publisher and president were detained for 55 days. In 1988, five journalists on the paper were detained for several days after articles critical of the government were published. These men were adopted as prisoners of conscience by Amnesty International.

Meanwhile the Doe government had rigged the 1985 election, closed down papers which threatened to expose him, and had Rufus Darpoh, the editor of the *Sun Times*, jailed and the paper banned after it had quoted his threat to use the army against Liberians of American origin, pejoratively called the "Congo". There were many political prisoners under Doe, including students opposed to the regime, political opponents, and former members of the government – people imprisoned solely because of the non-violent expression of their opinions.

Doe's rule was brought to a bloody end in 1990 by an invasion by the National Patriotic Front of Liberia, led by Charles Taylor. This developed into massive civil war that resulted in the collapse of the Liberian state, and, with it, the old institu-tions of state control of censorship. Warlords and faction leaders have exercised control over their fighters and civilians through acts of terror and massive human rights violations.

New elections took place in July 1997, as a result of which Charles Taylor came to power. The record on censorship remains patchy, however. In January 1998 the public prosecutor ordered *Heritage* newspaper to stop publication "until certain problems between [it] and the government have been solved". *Heritage* had criticized the government's relations with the West African peace-keeping force and reported on the kidnapping of a radio reporter, Alex Reid, who was researching human rights abuses. Meanwhile, in October 1998 posting information on the Internet "using unauthorized newspaper articles and gossip columns" was forbidden.

EMMA NORTON

Further Reading

Ajayi, J.F.A and Michael Crowder (editors), *History of West Africa*, 2 vols, London: Longman, 1971–74; New York: Columbia University Press, 1972–74

Amnesty International, *Urgent Action Appeals* (AFR/34/03/88, 34/04/88)

Amnesty International, *Liberia: Imprisonment of Opposition Leaders*, 1989 (AFR 34/01/89)

Amnesty International, *Liberia: Risk of Human Rights Violations as Conflict Increases*, 1992 (AFR 34/WU 02/92)

Amnesty International, *Liberia: No Chance for a Lasting Peace without Effective Human Rights Guarantees*, 1993

Chazan, Naomi et al., *Politics and Society in Contemporary Africa*, Boulder, Colorado: Rienner, and Basingstoke: Macmillan, 1988

Clower, Robert W. et al., *Growth without Development: An Economic Survey of Liberia*, Evanston, Illinois: Northwestern University Press, 1966

Cole, Henry B., "The Press in Liberia", *Liberian Studies Journal*, 4 (1971–72)

Cruise O'Brien, Donal B. et al., *Contemporary West African States*, Cambridge and New York: Cambridge University Press, 1989

d'Azevedo, W., "A Tribal Reaction to Nationalism", *Liberian Studies Journal*, 1–3 (1969–70)

Duodu, Cameron, "The Press Comes under General Doe's Boot", *Index on Censorship*, 14/6 (December 1985): 6

Economist Intelligence Unit, *Liberia Country Report*, 1995–

Ellis, Stephen (editor), *Africa Now: People, Policies and Institutions*, London: Currey, 1996

Fleischman, Janet, *Liberia: Human Rights Abuses by the Liberian Peace Council and the Need for International Oversight*, New York: Human Rights Watch, 1994

"Liberia, the Cycle of Abuse: Human Rights Violations since the November Cease-fire", *Africa Watch* (21 October 1991)

Liebenow, J. Gus, *Liberia: The Evolution of Privilege*, Ithaca, New York: Cornell University Press, 1969

Liebenhow, J. Gus, *Liberia: The Quest for Democracy*, Bloomington: Indiana University Press, 1987

Nelson, Harold D. (editor), *Liberia: A Country Study*, Washington, DC: Foreign Area Studies, American University, 1984

Reporters Sans Frontières, *Annual Report*, 1997

LIBRARIES: Britain and the United States

On the face of it, public libraries, known in some countries, felicitously, as "people's universities", are among the last places you would expect to find evidence of censorship. As with public service broadcasting "free at the point of use", their reputation is one of commitment to the open pursuit of knowledge and pleasure in books by all sections of a local community, administered by a profession that claims to base its selection of books on fair and objective criteria. However, public libraries do not exist in political or moral vacuums, and have been as subject as any other such public institutions to pressure, both formal and informal, and, as with the press and broadcasting, to direct political control in some countries.

This entry surveys examples of library censorship in two democratic countries – Britain and the United States; the next entry examines two countries where the state has taken a "hands-on" role in the administration of libraries – the former Soviet Union and South Africa under apartheid. Passing reference is also made to the practice of other countries. Specifically *public* libraries arrived only during the 18th century, growing exponentially from the mid-19th century as a result of mass literacy and the growing appetite for books. Their predecessors – for example, Suetonius has Julius Caesar seeking "to open to the public the greatest possible libraries of Greek and Latin books", and Pliny the Younger is recorded as founding a library for his native community – were either effectively censored by imperial patronage, or, literacy being rare, usable by the few.

Britain and the United States, 1750–1950

In Britain, the city of Newcastle on Tyne had a public library by the 1740s, with a librarian paid £25 a year and £5 available, by endowment, for the annual purchase of books. Such provision was exceptional, and, in any case, readers had to pay to borrow a book. Even so, following the intellectual and social turmoil of the French Revolution, the records show libraries in Wakefield (Yorkshire) and Bolton (Lancashire) being purged of any books that might inspire rebellious thoughts; and in a piece of direct action, familiar elsewhere in the history of censorship, a mob in Failsworth, now part of Greater Manchester, presented themselves at the entrance of a local library to demand the surrender of Tom Paine's *Rights of Man*.

More typical for the time, however, were the commercial circulating libraries, opened during the first half of the 19th century, of which the most famous were those of Thomas Mudie and W.H. Smith (whose chain of bookshops is still a familiar part of British High Streets). Subscribers paid around £2. 2s. a year, for which they were provided with as many books (usually novels) as they could read. Censorship was by no means absent. The circulating library at Broom Street, Manchester was forced to deny rumours that they were lending subversive literature. More notoriously, however, these libraries exercised their own censorship by refusing to circulate novels of which they disapproved. Even John Blackwood, publisher of George Eliot, had one eye on Mudie when he advised the excision of the description of Mrs Moss in *The Mill on the Floss* as "a

patient well hung, child producing woman"; instead, Mrs Moss became a "patient, prolific, loving hearted woman". George Moore's *A Modern Lover* (1883) and *A Mummer's Wife* (1885) were refused by both Mudie and Smith, who also turned down as indecent his most accomplished work *Esther Waters* (1894), based on the life of a single parent. Readers were deprived of the possibility of having the book in their hands, and authors of a decent income, because they depended on the circulating libraries buying their novels in bulk; publishers would not risk a book which had no guaranteed sales. Moore denounced these libraries for their censorship in *Literature at Nurse, or Circulating Morals* (1885). Matthew Arnold had already discerned a form of market censorship:

> As our nation grows more civilized, as a real love of reading comes to prevail more widely, this system, which keeps up the present exorbitant price of new books in England, the system of lending libraries from which books can be hired, will be seen to be, as it is, eccentric, artificial and unsatisfactory in the highest degree. It is a machinery for the multiplication and protection of bad literature.

Cheaper libraries – like those at Boots, the Chemist – gradually took their place. Public libraries multiplied from the middle of the 19th century, beginning with two in northwest England at Salford and Warrington, and one in the southeast, at Canterbury. The Public Library Act of 1850 allowed towns with a population of 10,000 or more to establish a library to be paid for by a small local rate. By 1911 libraries were available for around 62 per cent of the population, and by the 1920s they were universal.

Some interesting differences appear in the early history of public libraries in the United States. Administrators and benefactors appeared to agree with Thomas Jefferson that "an inordinate passion for novels" would poison people's minds. On average only around 10 per cent of funds available to subscription and sponsored libraries open from the 1730s onwards were devoted to the purchase of fiction, drama, and poetry. "Wholesome reading" was instead provided, that is, books on practical subjects, to encourage hard work at home and factory. Women, felt to be especially susceptible to the dangers of reading novels, were often excluded from libraries altogether. Community libraries, often based in schools, came into being during the 1830s, but took pains to ensure that only expurgated editions of such British writers as Dryden, Fielding, Pope, Shakespeare, and Smollett were available on the shelves. "Improper books" such as *Captain Kidd* were altogether excluded.

By the 1870s there were public libraries in eight large American cities, enough for the American Library Association (ALA) to be established in 1876. The new libraries inherited the paternalist spirit – as the Boston librarian reported to his board of examiners:

> There is a vast range of ephemeral literature, exciting and fascinating, apologetic of vice, confusing distinctions

between right and wrong; fostering discontent with peaceful, homely duties which constitute a large proportion of the average man and woman's lives; responsible for an immense amount of the mental disease and moral irregularities which are so troublesome as element in modern society.

It was "no business of a town library" to supply such books. Indeed, as William Pool, the first head of the Chicago Public Library, made clear, "The librarian who should allow an immoral book in his library for circulation would be as culpable as the manager of a picture gallery who should hang an indecent picture on his walls."

"Obscene" books remained a matter of concern to librarians on both sides of the Atlantic – though, of course, opinions changed radically on what should be so regarded between the late 19th and late 20th century. Gustave Flaubert's *Madame Bovary* appeared on the banned list of the ALA president in 1893. It was the policy of the Astor Library, funded from a bequest of Jim Crerar, that "dirty French novels, and all sceptical trash should never be found in this library. I want its atmosphere that of Christian refinement and its aim the building up of character." An even greater library benefactor (in both Britain and the US), Andrew Carnegie, remarked during the early 1900s that it was not usually librarians who closed the shutters: "I hesitate to differ with my good friends the librarians, but I would err on the safe side. Certain books I would consign to the flames and think I was doing God's service thereby, books in the category of pornography."

In Britain, books now regarded as classics – by Henry Fielding and Tobias Smollett, for example – were described by the Public Library Committee at Dewsbury, Yorkshire, as "disgusting, immoral, deceitful and shameful"; the committee laid down that such books could only be borrowed at the librarian's discretion. Each local authority established a public library committee, on which sat members of the council, who were, for the first two thirds of the 20th century, highly interventionist. At Beverly, south Yorkshire, H.G. Wells's new book *Ann Veronica* (1909) was said in 1910 to be "by no means food for babes", and withdrawn entirely. Wells had been on the ALA's banned list since 1904, along with Boccaccio, Ovid, Rabelais, and Voltaire, providing fuel for many local censorship campaigns, although no further such lists were compiled until 1924. By then Flaubert was thought admissible, but Emile Zola remained on the list and James Joyce, Marcel Proust, and André Gide were added to it. In Islington, London, on the other hand, the librarian wrote at this time, "Our job is to buy good books. Our job is to avoid bad books. But definitely it is not our job to deny our readers contact with the facts of life, and to help old ladies to preserve their chastity."

By the 1890s, meanwhile, questions of wider social importance were exercising librarians. A fundamental censorship by the denial of access to potential readers of certain social classes was implied in an ALA questionaire of 1894 about the provision of newspapers in public libraries. Evidently, some men came into libraries from the streets only to read the newspapers. "Are they not", wrote the ALA, "for the most part a vagrant and mal-odorous class whose presence in the reading room repels many who would receive more benefit from it?" Some suggested that vagrants should be encouraged to move

to "a more congenial games room where they would not feel embarrassed". James Whelpley of Cincinnati protested : the library was "in the broadest sense an institution for the betterment and education of that class which contains so many who came under the term mal-odorous".

Considerations of class later determined the choice of books. Theresa West, librarian at Milwaukee in 1895, took the view that "books proper for a large minority library might be essentially improper for the general mass of the people". Books of sociology – or rather, those dealing with the "morbid, diseased conditions of the individual man, or of society" – should be issued only to those making a special study of these matters. In 1905 the New York Public Library banned Bernard Shaw's *Man and Superman* from its shelves. It was

calculated to make light of dishonesty and criminality . . . How would a little eastsider react to a book that said "judges in general (not bad ones) were quite as bad as the criminals on whom they pronounced judgement"?

In the early 1920s, the ALA recommended that the Norwegian writer Knut Hamsun's *Hunger* be kept on closed shelves because of its description of "slow starvation with its attendant demoralization". Compton Mackenzie's *Youth's Encounter* and *Sinister Street* were likely to cause offence, and Somerset Maugham's *The Moon and Sixpence* was "unforgivably revolting". In Britain *Sunset Song*, Lewis Grassic Gibbon's account of rural and urban deprivation in northeast Scotland, was withdrawn from Aberdeen Public Library in 1934 (although nine copies were purchased by Glasgow; perhaps a case of a prophet having honour, but not in his own country).

John Shaw Billings, director of New York Public Library, warned in the 1890s of the danger that book selection could be influenced "by political party requirements which may vary at short intervals". His warnings became particularly relevant during World War I. From 1915 onwards US librarians were protesting that British censorship, for fear of spreading German propaganda, was preventing the import of books that they regarded as useful and educative. Readers were as entitled, they considered, to read about pacifism as they were to read accounts of the war. *Library Journal* took the view that books that currently appeared seditious would, after the war, be considered valuable historical documents; such books should certainly be available for purchase.

Interestingly, what was considered pro-British propaganda, but on a wholly different topic, was subject to pressure in the late 1920s. At issue were "politically incorrect" accounts of the American Revolution by Arthur M. Schlesinger, Jr and Alfred Bushwell Hart. The mayor of Chicago, William J. Thompson, threatened to remove such books from the library and have them burnt. A lawsuit was threatened and mayor Thompson agreed that the books should not be burned. Nevertheless, he sent officials to the library with orders to remove Hart's *The American Nation* (1907), which was "never to return". It never did.

At the beginning of World War II arguments in Britain about German propaganda reflected those in the US during World War I. The library committee at Eccles, near Manchester, withdrew Hitler's *Mein Kampf* in 1939. A neighbouring local authority, Swinton and Pendlebury, took the opposite view.

Libraries should, they considered, place at the disposal of their readers

> books reflecting all schools of thought on all subjects
> . . . the Nazi regime will not come to an end because of
> an attempt to prevent a small section of the British public
> from reading *Mein Kampf*. To ban a book is to give it
> wide publicity, and those who attempt to impose such
> restrictions are defeating their own ends.

Members of the committee nevertheless agreed to undertake the arduous task of reading this book before it was placed on the shelves. In the Lake District, Keswick Urban District Council wrestled with a proposal that "certain books bearing on the German nation" ought to be removed from the local library. They were overruled by Cumberland County Library Committee, who were adamant that this would constitute "a denial of the freedom of the reading public". More notoriously, many other library authorities reacted negatively to the comic novelist P.G. Wodehouse's 1941 broadcasts from Germany; he was considered a traitor, and his books were withdrawn from the shelves at Southport on the Lancashire coast, and from several other libraries in northwest England.

Meanwhile, in 1939 the ALA adopted a Library Bill of Rights, a political charter for librarians to be followed in normal (peacetime) conditions. The choice of books to be purchased by libraries should be based on objective criteria. The writer's politics, race, religion, and nationality were not relevant. Further, librarians should ensure that their shelves contained books on all aspects of a question, and that no barrier was placed in the way of any group that wanted to use the premises for public discussion.

DEREK JONES

Further Reading

Geller, Evelyn, *Forbidden Books in American Public Libraries, 1876–1939: A Study in Cultural Change*, Westport, Connecticut: Greenwood Press, 1984

Thompson, Anthony Hugh, *Censorship in the Public Libraries of the United Kingdom during the Twentieth Century*, Epping, Essex: Bowker, 1975

Britain since 1950

Neither in Britain nor the US would the high ideals of the Library Bill of Rights be always achieved. The *Library Association Record* reported in the early 1950s of the existence of the "Prison Shelf", containing books removed from general circulation because a complaint had been made about them: "I have seen *Candide* there, *The Decameron*, Rabelais, D.H. Lawrence, yes, even Chaucer. Support to the classics is given by Ernest Hemingway, Somerset Maugham, James Hanley . . . and many others of similar standing." Nor was the shelf confined to fiction. Mention was also made of anatomical textbooks that illustrated sexual relationships, if only diagrammatically, and books on forensic medicine where "the illustrations are rather gruesome to the layman".

Britain also had its McCarthyite period, during which any literature or newspaper that could be labelled communist was regarded with horror, even if nothing like the US House Un-American Activities Committee existed. Library policy continued to be entirely a matter for local authorities, as David Llewelyn, Conservative MP for Cardiff North, found in 1951 when he asked the minister of education whether he would introduce legislation making it illegal for local authorities to ban any political newspapers and periodicals under their control. The request was refused, making it possible, for instance, for Llandudno in north Wales to ban *Soviet News*, which had been available for perusal in the local library for the previous nine years (i.e. during the time when the USSR had been Britain's ally). The county of Caithness in northeast Scotland similarly withdrew the *Daily Worker*, organ of the British Communist Party, in 1952:

> We are a Protestant county and believe in the British way
> of living and dying. Why should the ratepayers of
> Caithness be asked to pay for this rag? It is seething with
> the atheism and communism.

The *Worker* was removed by many other library authorities.

Caithness's Protestant consciousness was not quite matched by Leamington's (Warwickshire) debates on whether to purchase for the library *The Rise of Christianity* by the modernist bishop Barnes of Birmingham in 1947. Barnes denied the Virgin Birth, miracles attributed to Christ, and his physical resurrection. Alderman Davies, noting that the archbishops of Canterbury and York disapproved of the book, did not see "how they could give the book their support". Councillor W.J. Duckworth claimed that if the book was circulated, it would give "grave offence to a large section of the public", offending "not only the Catholics, but also the Church of England and Non-Conformists". However, the mayor of Leamington won the day: "We do not need actually to ban the book. There is no need for people to have the book because it is in the library . . . it is our duty to have all sorts of books." Two years later, the town of Weston-super-Mare in Somerset decided to cease purchasing newspapers and periodicals that were associated with particular Christian denominations. This was in order "to keep clear of controversy".

As ever, however, it was "obscenity" that caused the most anguish, beginning with Alfred Kinsey's reports on sexual behaviour (1948 and 1953). Sensibilities were offended by his finding that women enjoyed sex as much as men. At Luton in Bedfordshire, librarians were instructed not to lend the book to unmarried people – though whether they had to produce a marriage certificate was not recorded. The chief librarian instructed:

> The book will be issued only on application. I shall decide
> if the person is suitable to read it. I think the only people
> who should read it are young married couples, doctors,
> marriage guidance counsellors and people with a scien-
> tific interest in it.

Banbury, Oxfordshire, on the other hand, made clear that if its citizens wanted the report "we should only be too willing to provide it for them".

The *Lady Chatterley's Lover* case of 1960 was, of course, of considerable importance for British librarians. Once the un-expurgated edition had been cleared, D.H. Lawrence's home county of Nottinghamshire responded in a manner typical of other library authorities. The chief librarian laid down: "Take particular care that junior assistants know how to deal with enquiries". In the city of Nottingham, the libraries committee decided not to implement their decisions to purchase the book; and in Liverpool, it was decided that *Lady Chatterley's Lover* was not to be issued to persons under 21 without a parent's written permission. Meanwhile, in North Wales librarians themselves were leading a censorship campaign. Denbighshire County Council withdrew 300 books from its shelves at the behest of the chief librarian, C.J. Luke, who even encouraged his wife to raise the matter at the local Women's Institute. She said:

> Librarians need all the help they can get to combat the danger of such [pornographic] books falling into the hands of innocent young people whose education has not been completed ... There are people who would condemn us for trying to set ourselves up as judges, but the public libraries are maintained through the rates and taxes we all pay and the books they contain should appeal to the majority and not to the sadistically-minded minority.

The Welsh Library Association conference held in Llandudno resolved

> That this Conference views with grave concern the alarming increase in publications relying on sex and violence as their *raison d'être*, and request the government as a matter of urgency to control the publication of books of a pornographic nature.

Although this resolution reflected the opinion of many in the early 1960s, it was rare indeed for librarians to demand that censorship take place.

British librarians had to exercise considerable flexibility during the 1960s while, following *Lady Chatterley*, a number of other books were "taken to court". In February 1964, Alexander Trocchi's exploration of heroin addiction in *Cain's Book* was held to be obscene by magistrates at Sheffield, south Yorkshire. Sheffield libraries had already purchased 20 copies of the book, some of which were out on loan. They had hastily to request the borrowers to return their copy immediately, even if they had not finished reading it. In 1967, after the *Last Exit to Brooklyn* decision, Birmingham had first to call in copies they had issued to readers, and then, after an appeal was launched in November 1967, restore copies to the shelves. The book was again convicted and again exonerated on a legal technicality, leaving librarians, until the row died down, in a considerable quandary.

Following an entirely different theme, librarians embarked in the 1960s on a campaign to purge libraries of what were considered dated and undemanding children's books by, among others, Enid Blyton, Richmal Crompton (author of the "William" books), and captain W.E. Johns (author of the "Biggles" books, excoriated for their attitudes to the "natives" in various parts of the British empire). Blyton was banned by St Pancras Library, north London in 1963, by all Hertfordshire libraries in 1968, and by all Wiltshire libraries in 1971.

Libraries in Australia and New Zealand followed suit. Of the three, Richmal Crompton appeared to have made a comeback by the late 1990s; Enid Blyton has remained in print, but Johns is barely remembered.

The British backlash against permissiveness clearly influenced the Middlesborough (Teeside) district librarian Frank Jenkins to call, at a weekend school organized by the Library Association in 1976, for librarians to "exercise positive discrimination against meretricious novels, including those with passages of sex and blood". The Republic of Ireland, meanwhile, had long known library censorship. According to the novelist Brian Moore, "in my day, it was said that if two old ladies went around to a library and said a book was dirty, it was withdrawn pending investigation of possible banning". John McGahern related that the parish priest of Ballinamore, County Leitrim, on his own authority simply removed from the library a book that contained descriptions of a married couple making love. Dermot Foley, once librarian at Ennis in County Clare, has confirmed their experience: librarians had little option but to remove books if objections were raised.

Similarly, "dumbing down" is now the main issue in studies of library censorship in Britain. Cultural democracy has often been interpreted in populist terms. Where money is short, libraries are tempted to purchase only books (and now compact disks and videos) for which there is a "market". Purchasing for a possible future market, in which tastes may have changed and educational standards improved, cannot be afforded. Thus we return to a question that has been implicit throughout this discussion. Democratically elected politicians, often in the past actively involved in book selection and rejection, cannot today possibly keep up with the details of book selection. If this is left to professional librarians, can we be sure that they always act even-handedly, or do other considerations – nowadays the budget but previously perhaps their own unspoken moral and political prejudices – play a part of a most unlibrary-like censorship?

DEREK JONES

Further Reading

Carlson, Julia (editor), *Banned in Ireland: Censorship and the Irish Writer*, London: Routledge, and Athens: University of Georgia Press, 1990

Holroyd, Michael, "Places of Opportunity", *Index on Censorship*, 28/2 (March–April 1999)

Malley, Ian, *Censorship and Libraries*, London: Library Association, 1990

Thompson, Anthony Hugh, *Censorship in the Public Libraries of the United Kingdom During the Twentieth Century*, Epping, Essex: Bowker, 1975

The United States since 1950

In spite of the "Library Bill of Rights" (1939), US librarians did not unanimously endorse the concept of free access to ideas on all sides of controversial issues, and little was done during the years of World War II to change that situation. Following the war, however, librarians responded to increasing external pressure with a strengthened "Library Bill of Rights" (1948) that not only continued the injunction to build collections containing many points of view but now also included a pledge to fight censorship. During the immediate postwar years, fear of communism increased. Spurred by governmental bodies like the US House Committee on Un-American Activities (HUAC) and its state counterparts, citizens' groups such as the American Legion, the Daughters of the American Revolution, and the Minute Women lodged many challenges against library materials they claimed were subversive or un-American. They targeted periodicals such as the *Nation* and the *New Republic* and demanded that books by "subversive" authors be labelled. Incidents involving libraries that resulted in prolonged political battles occurred from Boston, New York City, and Montclair (New Jersey), to Peoria (Illinois), Bartlesville (Oklahoma), San Antonio (Texas), and Los Angeles (California). The ALA responded with the formation of state intellectual freedom committees, a footnote that added all types of media to the "Library Bill of Rights", and a statement that declared that labelling was a "censor's tool". Nevertheless, some librarians agreed with Ralph Ulveling of the Detroit Public Library who declared in 1951 that the "Library Bill of Rights" was contrary to his responsibilities as a citizen, since it allowed access to propaganda and "subversive" materials. The ALA's Intellectual Freedom Committee had plenty on its hands.

In 1953 in the face of increasing domestic pressures on libraries and senator Joseph McCarthy's attacks on the US State Department's overseas libraries, the ALA joined the American Book Publishers' Council to create and adopt the declaration "The Freedom to Read". This statement publicized the ALA's stance against censorship and gave many librarians the support they needed to withstand censorship. The declaration stated that it was in the public interest for publishers and librarians to make available the widest diversity of views and expressions, including books that were unorthodox and unpopular; that publishers and librarians did not need to endorse every idea the books contained; that the views of authors were irrelevant in determining whether or not a book was acceptable on the shelves; that censorship, if regrettably it took place at all, was a matter for legislation – extra legal pressure on public taste was to be deplored; that librarians were "guardians of the people's freedom to read"; and finally, that the only way to deal with bad books was to counter them with good.

Despite the declaration, the famous research study reported in Marjorie Fiske's 1959 *Book Selection and Censorship: A Study of School and Public Libraries in California* revealed that many librarians tried to avoid conflict with governmental or special interest groups through self-censorship, or declining to select materials that might generate controversy. The Fiske study elicited much soul-searching.

The issue of racial segregation in southern libraries also caused librarians to search their souls. As the civil rights movement gained momentum in the late 1950s and early 1960s, even titles such as Garth Williams's children's book *The Rabbit's Wedding* came under attack by state segregation committees who said that a story describing the marriage of a black rabbit and a white rabbit encouraged miscegenation. In addition, a number of librarians brought to ALA, as an intellectual freedom issue, the denial of access to libraries for people of colour; surely denial of access to *all* books was as significant as denial of access to *one* book through censorship. The ALA membership agreed, and in 1961, the right of universal access to libraries was added to "The Library Bill of Rights".

Additional measures to bring about compliance were added in the next few years.

As the 1960s progressed, the "obscene" overtook the "subversive" as the leading cause for censorship of library materials. In spite of the Supreme Court's decision that a work had to be considered as a whole and that works with literary, social, political, or scientific merit could not be banned (*Roth* v. *United States*, 1957), the United States Postal Service and various congressional committees sought to prevent the distribution of materials they considered harmful to the morals of the nation. Although the postal service's ban on Henry Miller's sexually explicit *Tropic of Cancer*, published in 1961, lasted just a few days, librarians all across the country found themselves forced to defend their right to have the book in their collections. Citizens' groups focusing on "smut" – such as Charles Keating's Cincinnati-based Citizens for Decent Literature – made themselves felt. For the first time in its history, the ALA joined a court action opposing censorship when it filed a friend-of-the-court brief on behalf of a California bookseller arrested for selling Miller's book. The Supreme Court eventually overturned his conviction.

At the same time, perhaps because of heightened tension caused by the Cuban missile crisis, new conservative groups such as the John Birch Society, America's Future, and even the Conservative Library Association continued to press for removal of "subversive" titles and challenged selection policies. An article appearing in the right-wing magazine *Human Events* sparked challenges to library materials in such disparate states as Georgia, Louisiana, Illinois, and Idaho. In New York a library trustee removed from the shelves the Russian folk tale *My Mother Is the Most Beautiful Woman in the World*, alleging that it contained subtle communist propaganda. To varying degrees, such challenges continued throughout the decade.

Despite continued challenges, the ALA responded slowly to repeated requests from the membership and the Intellectual Freedom Committee to create an apparatus to support beleaguered librarians. Late in 1967, however, Judith Krug became the first (and so far only) director of the newly established Office for Intellectual Freedom. Its activities remained on the whole educational, until the intense social and political battles of 1968 and 1969 drew librarians into the crossfire. Gordon McShean lost his Roswell, New Mexico job after he had included hippie poetry in an otherwise well-received series of readings; in Richmond, California John Forsman battled to retain the counter-cultural *Berkeley Barb* in the library; and Joan Bodger, a Missouri state library consultant, lost her job for protesting at the seizure of a student underground newspaper and advocating the collection of similar materials in libraries. Finally, in 1969 the ALA formed the Freedom to Read Foundation (FTRF) and followed that in 1970 with the LeRoy C. Merritt Humanitarian Fund to support librarians – not just library users – involved in challenges to intellectual freedom. The precipitating event was a call for help from T. Ellis Hodgin, a Martinsville, Virginia public librarian, who had been dismissed because – as a private individual – he had joined a suit against religious instruction in the local schools. After much delay, the ALA not only moved to support intellectual freedom efforts in tangible ways, but embraced the defence of the civil rights of librarians as well.

In the nearly 30 years since the inception of the FTRF,

censorship challenges to public libraries have continued to come mostly from politically or religiously conservative groups, although in a few cases liberal groups lodged objections against such books as *Huckleberry Finn*, which were considered to be racist or sexist. Few, if any, challenges currently pertain to adult reading material; the protection of children is now the usual rallying cry for censorship efforts. With the end of the Cold War, materials perceived as communist are rarely proscribed. Socially sensitive or sexually explicit materials have become the primary targets. Congress and the states have passed laws designed to protect minors from sexually explicit materials disseminated electronically through the Internet. Groups claiming to speak for families, such as Family Friendly Libraries – a movement of the 1990s – demand the removal or restriction of materials pertaining to homosexuality and sex education, among other things. As the gay community has gained political strength and visibility, *Daddy's Roommate, Heather Has Two Mommies*, and other children's and young adult books that depict homosexuality in a positive light have increasingly come under fire in libraries, along with news-sheets published by and for the gay community.

Starting in 1996, a "family friendly" group in Oklahoma City targeted materials in the metropolitan library system. They wanted a number of titles removed or segregated on account of their sexual content. In spite of months of pressure, library director Lee Brawner and the board resisted the demands, saying that the restrictions limited adults' freedom of access to information. The pressure group charged that videos made available through the library were legally obscene, and asked a court to rule that the Academy Award-winning 1979 film version of Gunter Grass's *The Tin Drum* contained child pornography. When the court agreed, police armed with video store rental information raided several homes to seize copies of the tape. State librarians have outspokenly supported Brawner, giving him an award for upholding intellectual freedom. Nevertheless, the Oklahoma city council put pressure on the library to change its position. Brawner has since retired, but the pressure, although less, has continued.

This episode illustrates that public-library censorship in the United States is rarely accomplished without both private pressure group action and governmental cooperation. Librarians' self-censorship, when it occurs, results from the fear that these combined pressures – even with the considerable support of the professional association – will be too great to withstand.

Recently the American Library Association has joined with the American Civil Liberties Union and other groups to challenge successfully the Computer Decency Act, which required the use of filtering devices on library computers. A challenge to a subsequent version of the law is ongoing in 2001. Cyberspace appears to be the contested terrain for American libraries in the new century.

LOUISE S. ROBBINS

Further Reading
Busha, Charles, *Freedom versus Suppression and Censorship, with a Study of the Attitudes of the Midwestern Public Libraries and a Bibliography of Censorship*, Littleton, Colorado: Libraries Unlimited, 1972
Fiske, Marjorie, *Book Selection and Censorship: A Study of School and Public Libraries in California*, Berkeley: University of California Press, 1959
Geller, Evelyn, *Forbidden Books in American Public Libraries, 1876–1939: A Study in Cultural Change*, Westport, Connecticut: Greenwood Press, 1984
Index on Censorship, special issue: "Word Power" (on library censorship), 28/2 (March–April 1999)
Manguel, Albert, "Libraries and Their Ashes", *Index on Censorship*, 28/2 (March–April 1999)
Molz, R. Kathleen, "Censorship: Current Issues in American Libraries", *Library Trends*, 39 (Summer–Fall 1990): 18–35
Newsletter on Intellectual Freedom (various issues), Chicago: American Library Association, Office for Intellectual Freedom, 1952–
Robbins, Louise S., *Censorship and the American Library: The American Library Association's Response to Threats to Intellectual Freedom, 1939–1969*, Westport, Connecticut: Greenwood Press, 1996
Robbins, Louise S., *The Dismissal of Miss Ruth Brown: Civil Rights, Censorship, and the American Library*, Norman: University of Oklahoma Press, 2000

US School Libraries

Although censorship of materials in the school libraries (or media centres) of American public schools has occurred since their inception, it was not until after World War II that scrutiny of public school curricula and public school libraries' collections became a major public issue. McCarthyism, the civil rights movement, the feminist movement, the paperback revolution, the rise of the Moral Majority, and the AIDS epidemic, along with other social and cultural changes, led to greater censorship pressures on public school libraries than ever before. They now account for three-quarters of all book challenges in the United States.

Despite the fact that students are not generally required to read material available in school libraries, censors have not distinguished between libraries and the classroom. Librarians share responsibility with teachers, and both are overseen by the school principal, school district administrators, and the board of education. The library is part of a larger educational community whose goal is to mould young minds. These concerns determine the basis upon which challenges are mounted to material in the libraries of American public schools.

Books have been removed from elementary and junior high schools and placed in high school libraries because they were considered inappropriate for younger children, but censorship also includes requiring permission slips from parents or teachers, restricted shelves, closed collections, and labelling or expurgating works. Unwanted texts have been removed and never returned by students, parents, teachers, principals, and librarians. More often, principals and/or school boards have summarily banned controversial or challenged books.

Until the 1980s challenges to books and other media generally concerned profanity, pornography, anti-Americanism, and the theory of evolution. Those complaints lodged in the 1980s and 1990s have been markedly distinct from their predecessors and represent conflicting shifts in American moral, social, and political life. Objections have come from the entire ideological spectrum. The social agenda of the religious right has come into conflict with the "politically correct" movement of the left, with the result that the right has objected to perceived attacks upon parental authority, patriotism, capitalism, religion, and traditional family values while the left has fought against race and gender stereotypes and hate-speech. Environmentalism, "global education", gay and lesbian literature, sex education, violence, "secular humanism", "new ageism", witchcraft and the occult, creationism, racism, sexism, and ageism have also become grounds for exclusion from the public school library.

During the 1950s and 1960s objections came mostly from individual parents acting independently; books, periodicals, and films were quietly removed. By the early 1970s, however, parents began to be supported by local groups and, increasingly in the 1980s and 1990s, by national organizations such as Focus on the Family, the Traditional Values Coalition, and the Council on Interracial Books for Children. As parents, backed by such groups, became more willing to confront educational authorities, the battle for control of the public school media centre shifted from school board meetings to the courts. The 1970s and 1980s saw more legal and constitutional challenges to library and textbook decisions than in all previous American history.

Though there were some legal challenges to such censorship before the 1970s, no case directly addressed "the question of whether a school board could constitutionally remove from circulation school library books previously acquired and used by students for reasons pertaining to the controversial content of these books". The earliest case to handle the issue directly was *President's Council, District 25* v. *Community School Board No. 25* (New York City). In its 1972 decision, the United States Court of Appeals for the Second Circuit upheld the removal of a library book on the ground that court action against the board was precluded by the Supreme Court's evolution decision in *Epperson* v. *Arkansas*, because the elimination of the book did not involve an effort to aid or oppose religion, nor was the elimination of the book from the library analogous to a ban on nondisruptive silent speech (condemned by the Supreme Court in *Tinker* v. *Des Moines Independent School District*). Decided in 1976, *Minarcini* v. *Strongsville* (Ohio City School District) challenged the removal of Joseph Heller's *Catch 22* and two Kurt Vonnegut novels. Here, the Court of Appeals for the Sixth Circuit held that "[t]he removal of books from a school library is a much more serious burden upon freedom of classroom discussion than the action found unconstitutional in *Tinker*". In 1978, distinguishing "between the school board's power to control curriculum content and its power to control library collections as well as between the board's power to select books for the library and its power to remove books, once selected", a Massachusetts district court required the return of an anthology to the high school library (*Right to Read Defense Committee* v. *School Committee of the City of Chelsea*).

With the *Board of Education, Island Trees (New York) Union Free School District 26* v. *Pico*, the issue of school library book suppression reached the Supreme Court. One of the most important First Amendment decisions to be rendered by the Supreme Court in the previous 20 years, *Pico*, decided on 25

June 1982, denied the right of one junior-high-school and four high-school students to challenge the removal from school libraries by a Long Island school board of all copies of nine books because in the board's view that they were "anti-American, anti-Christian, anti-Semitic, and just plain filthy". The court held that the First Amendment prevents government officials, including public school officials, "from denying access to ideas with which they disagree". But when a regular system of review using standardized guidelines was followed, the court implied that censorship based on educational suitability would be upheld. In the 1988 *Hazelwood School District* v. *Kuhlmeier* case, the Supreme Court decided "that school-sponsored expressive activities can be subjected to content control as long as this is 'reasonably related to pedagogical concerns'". The *Hazelwood* decision seems to many to remove censorship motivated by educational purposes from the sphere of First Amendment protection. Critics fear that a rationale based on reasonable educational grounds could so camouflage unconstitutional censorship that legal challenge became impossible.

The ALA notes that the annual rate of complaints against books rose from 157 in 1990 to 762 in 1995, but warns that the actual number of such challenges may be five times as much – many of them are not reported. Across the 1990s as a whole, there were 1299 challenges against sexually explicit passages; 1134 against offensive language; 1062 against books considered "unsuited to age group"; 744 for mentions of Satan and the occult; 562 for violent content, and 474 for references to homosexuality.

PEACHES M. HENRY

Further Reading

Bender, David and Bruno Leone (editors), *Censorship: Opposing Viewpoints*, San Diego, California: Greenhaven Press, 1997

Burress, Lee, "Ten Reasons for the Recent Increase in School Censorship Pressures", *Elementary School Guidance and Counseling*, 17/1 (October 1982): 11–24

Burress, Lee, *Battle of the Books: Literary Censorship in the Public Schools, 1950–1985*, Metuchen, New Jersey: Scarecrow Press, 1989

Coetzee, J. M., *Giving Offense: Essays on Censorship*, Chicago: University of Chicago Press, 1996

DelFattore, Joan, *What Johnny Shouldn't Read: Textbook Censorship in America*, New Haven, Connecticut: Yale University Press, 1992

"Embattled Books", *Index on Censorship*, 28/2 (March–April 1999)

Noble, William, *Bookbanning in America: Who Bans Books and Why*, Middlebury, Vermont: Eriksson, 1990

Office for Intellectual Freedom of the American Library Association, *Intellectual Freedom Manual*, 5th edition, Chicago: American Library Association, 1995

Reichman, Henry, *Censorship and Selection: Issues and Answers for Schools*, 2nd edition, Chicago: American Library Association, 1993

Robbins, Louise S., *Censorship and the American Library: The American Library Association's Response to Threats to Intellectual Freedom, 1939–1969*, Westport. Connecticut: Greenwood Press, 1996

LIBRARIES: The Soviet Union and South Africa

The idea of libraries as "people's universities" would, on paper, have been entirely acceptable to the Soviet leadership, but 70 years after the revolution, even under glasnost, it was for the Communist Party to decide which books "the people" could read. South Africa under apartheid might have accepted the general idea, but made sure first (and in this its leaders of opinion were not entirely unlike their counterparts in Europe, merely some decades behind them) that only "decent" books were placed on library shelves, and then that library provision should be, like the education system, grossly unequal.

The Soviet Union

At the time of the revolution, only two in every five males in the Russian "empire" could read. Librarians were soon involved in the new government's literacy campaign: but, under the control of Nadezhda Krupskaia, deputy commissar for education and Lenin's wife, they also played their part in the politicization of the masses. On the one hand, at Lenin's insistence, a vastly increased number of books on practical subjects were written to order and introduced to library shelves. On the other, the great Russian literary heritage was subjected to considerable scrutiny; libraries were ordered to purge books by such pessimists as Dostoevskii, but allowed not only to keep but also to encourage the reading of authors whose work could be harnessed for the Soviet cause – not just Maksim Gor'kii, but also Pushkin, Tolstoi, and many others.

Libraries were soon part of the highly centralized hierarchical bureaucracy that characterized the organization of the country from start to finish. Library goals were codified in the Library Law of 1920, and with the foundation of Glavlit (Main Administration for Affairs of Literature and Publishing Houses – the central censorship board that decided which books could be published, banned, or altered to conform with the party's requirements) the state had control over each individual library's management, book selection, and circulation practices. The Congress of Political Education Committees noted in 1922: "The library must cease being an institution for storing books, and for lending them; it must rather become a weapon for the propaganda of Communism." To that end books that openly or indirectly contradicted Soviet doctrine were rigorously excluded. Librarians did not even have to interpret this doctrine: a writer who was *persona non grata* would not be published anyway, and when Andrei Zhdanov tightened ideological control of the arts in the late 1940s, instructions were quickly handed down; previously acceptable poetry and novels by (for example) Anna Akhmatova and Boris Pasternak were now to be removed from library shelves. Soviet literature was to "boldly lash and attack bourgeois culture".

Public libraries were controlled by the Ministry of Culture. Among the most famous of these 110,000 libraries was the V.I. Lenin Library in Moscow, and the Saltykov-Shchedrin library in Leningrad (now St Petersburg). There were also specialized humanities libraries and a vast network of republic, district, and village public libraries. The 130,000 school libraries came under the control of the State Committee on People's Education. Other, more specialist libraries (science, public health,

agriculture, etc) were maintained by the appropriate ministry; the 17,000 trade union libraries were controlled by the unions themselves, but had no more freedom than any other sector of Soviet life to create independent collections.

Some large Soviet libraries were allowed to house "special stacks" (*spetskhan*). The Lenin Library's special depository contained 298,239 books, 521,054 journal issues and 2,498,000 newspapers, some 25 per cent of its total stock; it contained writings by discredited political figures and dissidents, some foreign literature, both fiction and non-fiction, and books on such (for the Soviet Union) tricky subjects as religion, sexuality, and social deviance. Two card catalogues were maintained; one (which was for general readers) was limited, the other listed all the library's holdings. The number of those allowed to read from the special stacks was firmly controlled; those admitted to "room 13" to do so were obliged to sign a declaration that they would not use the information they gleaned for any anti-Soviet purpose.

Always, the first entries in library classification schemes were "Marxism-Leninism" and "Scientific Atheism". Soviet libraries received about five per cent of the world's printed material.

Just as the early Soviet government made sure that any dangerous tsarist literature was removed from libraries after 1917, so, when its successors acquired the Baltic republics (Estonia, Latvia, and Lithuania), they extended the Soviet system of library censorship to countries that had previously known an independent life. Maps that represented the states before 1945 were destroyed or placed in special stacks. In Lithuania 429,639 books were destroyed, many of them by Lithuanian authors; a further 600,000 library books were destroyed before 1989. In Estonia over 200,000 books were placed in areas of the library to which entrance was restricted. Lithuanian librarians had existing connections with the US Library of Congress, the Lund University Library in Sweden, and various German universities; but material sent to them under these agreements was, after 1945, mostly directed to larger libraries in Moscow. East Germany similarly suffered the depredation of its stock when, after World War II, the Soviet army removed up to five million volumes to restore library stocks in their own country damaged during the war (an estimated 100 million library books had been destroyed in the USSR).

By contrast, according to Brian McGee's 1999 report, in Cuba's *Biblioteca Nacional*, "a whole series of Russian encyclopedias, forlorn and dusty, end abruptly in 1990, the year before the Soviet withdrawal from Cuba; a monumental 42-volume 1958 edition of the complete works of Lenin in Spanish rests alongside, looking equally neglected". McGee also reports on the catalogue, where green lines have been ruled across books once available, which are so no longer. The absence of Shelley's *Prometheus Unbound* is of a piece with the classic censorship of Communism, which does not allow alternative forms of liberation. Books by the Peruvian novelist and politician Mario Vargas Llosa are completely excluded, even those written before 1971, when he became disillusioned with the Cuban revolution.

South Africa under Apartheid

Censorship by exclusion from the public library service had a long history in South Africa before apartheid was instituted. When libraries were introduced during the 19th century, they were open to non-whites in Cape Province only; elsewhere – in Natal, the Orange Free State, and Transvaal – the system was conceived on wholly racial grounds; blacks were not considered capable of participation, even by the few white administrators who devoted themselves to their educational advancement.

The history of South African libraries during the second half of the 20th century was in some senses one of facing up to the reality of a censorship based on an even more entrenched racial ideology and an ultra-conservative view of religion and morality. The South African Library Association (SALA) was founded in 1930. As early as 1938 they "viewed with apprehension the present method of censorship of books and periodicals in South Africa", and hoped that it would at least be regulated by the courts. By 1946 the results of a questionnaire sent to librarians revealed that many of them were not opposed to censorship; those who were more ambivalent thought that their best response was to ensure that the system operated with as few restrictions as possible.

No such relative openness was possible once the Nationalist Party, first elected in 1948 on a platform of wholesale racial segregation, began to establish its grip. Between 1956 and 1963, 5515 publications were banned, nearly 800 a year. Before the Publications and Entertainments Act (1962) established a formal censorship board, however, library censorship was mostly directed towards more perennial concerns with obscenity. Yet it was one of the founding fathers of apartheid, Geoffrey Cronjé (1907–92) who was appointed to chair a 1957 commission "to enquire into the evil of indecent, offensive and harmful literature". SALA refused to sit on this commission in the belief that their participation might well imply that they approved of censorship. They registered their concerns at "the dangers of a system in which ... no provision is made for appeal to the courts of law".

Libraries were directly affected by the Publications and Entertainments Act, which prohibited the publication but also the possession of material that was considered indecent or obscene, blasphemous, or disrespectful to the inhabitants of South Africa. Libraries might now possess banned books but could not casually display them. They were to be kept under lock and key and a register of usage was to be maintained. The books could not be copied. Certain books were classified as "possession prohibited"; they could not be perused without the written consent of the director of publications or the director of security legislation.

Censorship was further tightened during the 1970s and 1980s, as the government tried to stem the growth of opposition (generally called "communism") to its policies by the majority black population and by liberal whites. Some of the country's best authors – black and white –were on the banned list, and South African librarians struggled to keep up with the pace of censorship. There were reports of librarians feverishly checking the *Government Gazette* and *Jacobsen's Index of Objectionable Literature*, both issued weekly and listing the latest batch of banned books; they had then speedily to look at their catalogues, removing any offending titles from public gaze, and even burning them, according to newspaper reports from Cape Town and Durban. When it came to new books, librarians and their committees, anxious to avoid financial loss, took great care to vet the list before placing their orders.

Many librarians felt constrained – from fear, resignation, or personal conviction – to go along with censorship. In their submission to the 1974 Select Committee on Censorship, SALA merely requested that the provision for authors to appeal against a ban be retained, and that subject specialists be employed to help the courts in this areas; they even offered librarians as specialists in cases when the aims and objectives of libraries were at stake.

As individuals, librarians reacted to censorship with a similar range of views as the rest of the South African population. There were those who, like M.B. Gertz writing in the *Cape Librarian* in 1972, took the view that a library should consider itself a failure if all its readers approved of all its acquisitions. Many found themselves reluctant agents of the government. Others, in general agreement with apartheid, had no qualms. In one survey, 69 per cent of respondents considered that librarians exacerbated an already difficult situation; censorship would not have been possible without their help.

SETH MAGOT

Further Reading

Soviet Union
Greening, Joyce Martin, "Ten Years in the Life of Russian Libraries", *International Information and Library Review*, 27/2 (1995)
Gudauskas, Renaldas, "Lithuanian Library History", *International Information and Library Review*, 26/4 (1994)
Kuzmin, Evgenii, "From Totalitarianism to Democracy", *American Librarian*, 24/5 (1993)
Lisson, Paul, "Focus on Russia: History, Change and Libraries in the Soviet Union", *Canadian Library Journal* (February 1991)
McGee, Brian, "A Skewed Utopia: Letter from Havana, *Index on Censorship*, 18/2 (March–April 1999)
Raymond, Boris, "Former Eastern Bloc Librarianship in Transition: Hungary, the Czech Republic and Slovakia", *Canadian Journal of Information and Library Science*, 18/3 (1993)
West, Samantha and Michael Lowe, "Out of the Cold: Libraries in the Baltic States after Communism", *Journal of Librarianship and Information Science*, 30/1 (1998)

South Africa
Merrett, Christopher, "Librarians in a Police State: South African Academic Libraries and the Problem of Censorship", *Journal of Librarianship*, 20/3 (1988)
Merrett, Christopher, "Repression and Resistance: Lessons about Censorship and the Right to Know from the South African State of Emergency", *Focus on International and Comparative Librarianship*, 21/3 (1990)
Merrett, Christopher, "In a State of Emergency: Libraries and Government Control in South Africa", *Library Quarterly*, 60/1 (1990)
Sales, Digby, "The Interrelatedness of Book Selection and Censorship" (MA thesis), University of Cape Town, 1981
Sales, Digby, "Acquisitions and the South African Library Management", *Collection Management*, 19/2–4 (1995)

LIBYA

Libyan Arab Jamahiriya	
Population: 5,290,000	**Illiteracy rate (%):** 9.2 (m); 31.7 (f)
Main religions: Sunni Muslim	**Number of daily newspapers:** 4
Official language: Arabic	**Number of radio receivers per 1000 inhabitants:** 259
Other languages spoken: English; Italian	**Number of TV receivers per 1000 inhabitants:** 140

Like the rest of North Africa, Libya was settled, colonized, and subjugated by many peoples. These included the Berbers, Egyptians, Phoenicians, and the Greeks. Later Carthaginians, Persians, Romans, Vandals, and Byzantines attempted to take control. Each new invader sought to impose its own culture on Libya by force. During the early Christian era, the Jews of Libya were suppressed by emperor Hadrian (117 CE); and shortly thereafter, the Monophysites (who held that Christ was divine and not human) were violently put down as heretics. After a war of conquest, emperor Diocletian (284 CE) issued a statement declaring that the Nasomonian race no longer existed, thus putting his stamp of approval on one of the earliest recorded acts of genocide. The indigenous Berber tribes, the earliest known inhabitants of Libya, maintained their independent, intinerant life in the southern desert throughout these centuries.

The first key event of Libya's modern history was the invasion of eastern Libya by Arab Muslims, under 'Umar ibn al-'As, in 642 CE. All cults soon gave way to Islam. Although the Berbers became Muslims, they remained hostile to Arab culture, and strenuously resisted assimilation. In 1049, the Berbers revolted against their Arab rulers, and the Caliph responded by moving 200,000 Arab families into the coastal regions. Berbers today constitute only about 3–4 per cent of the country's population.

The Turks captured Tripoli in 1551. Indigenous Arab (and Berber) desires for autonomy were suppressed by the application of terror on the part of the Turkish authorities. The hegemony of the Turkish Ottoman sultan was periodically demonstrated by the slaughter of local inland tribes, and by the capture of local tribal leaders, who were summarily executed. Ottoman state schools imposed the use of Turkish language on the inhabitants of Libya.

When Italy invaded Libya in 1911, Turks, Arabs, and Berbers fought together to stave off the threat to Islamic culture. From 1911 to 1922, newspapers in Arabic, detailing the plight of Libya, had begun to circulate widely both within and outside the country. A nine-year resistance campaign against Italian fascist rule came to an end in September 1931, when Libya's most celebrated freedom fighter, 'Umar al-Mukhtar, was captured and publicly hanged.

During the period 1931–32, tens of thousands were executed, murdered, and starved to death in concentration camps. By 1945, some Libyan historians claim, more than half the Libyan population was killed as a result of the Italian occupation – either because of disease or deprivation in the internment camps, or because of the battles between the Axis and the Allies over Libyan soil during World War II. Some western scholars put the figure at 250,000 to 300,000, out of a population of "just over one million."

After the conclusion of World War II, Libya was jointly ruled by the occupying British and American military forces. The UN granted Libya statehood; and its new constitution, which came into effect in 1951, spelled out the rights granted to the people. Article 22 promised that: "Freedom of thought shall be guaranteed. Everyone shall have the right to express his opinion and to publish it by all means and methods. But this freedom may not be abused in any way which is contrary to public order and morality." The latter clause gave the US- and British-installed monarch, king Idris, a convenient escape clause to control the press as he saw fit.

By 1956 large numbers of Libyans began to feel that the presence of US and British bases on Libyan soil was an infringement of the nation's sovereignty. However, the people were not able to express their opposition to the bases, despite the written constitutional guarantees. According to historian John Wright:

> Political parties and clubs were officially banned and there was no political activity in the four-year intervals between general elections; there were no opportunities for public meetings or for the publication of messages and manifestos; and the press and information services were tightly controlled.

Elected officials had little power because "the Libyan Kingdom was from the outset little more than a benign despotism administered by an oligarchy of leading families and tribal and commercial interests".

Although the law banned political parties, citizens tested the limits of free expression and freedom of association through the organization of trade unions, which were legal. However, in 1961, when 4000 members of the Libyan General Federation of Trade Unions went on strike to protest deteriorating living conditions, the government took strong actions. The federation executive, Salim Shita, and other union leaders were arrested and held without trial. Police occupied union headquarters, and strike breakers were sent in. The labour laws were amended severely to restrict the right to union membership and the right to strike. Students began to organize clandestine opposition groups that focused criticism on Idris's servile attitude toward the west in general, and toward Britain and the US in particular. The government quelled internal opposition by killing street demonstrators and strengthening the internal security forces.

Gamal 'Abdul Nasser's 1952 revolution in neighbouring Egypt guaranteed that a variety of voices would be heard in the kingdom. Idris banned all literature he felt to be threatening. The most famous of the banned books was Nasser's *Philosophy of Revolution*, the prime tenets of which were Pan-Arab unity, anticolonialism, and socialism. Other significant banned works were those of the Ba'thists (whose socialist, Pan-

Arab ideology prevailed in Syria and Iraq), the tracts of the Muslim Brotherhood (who advocated Pan-Islamic, fundamentalist, antiwestern revolution), and the works of Marx, Engels, Lenin, and Mao. However, the Libyan government was not successful in cutting the country off from outside influences. The presence of large numbers of Egyptians and other foreign teachers in Libya severely undermined the government's attempts at censorship. The Arabic and foreign press circulated widely, while Cairo radio's "Voice of the Arabs" diffused the Nasserite revolutionary ideals throughout Libya.

The discovery of huge oil reserves in Libya dramatically altered the nation's self-image and socioeconomic structure: oil revenues grew from a mere $3 million per year in 1961 to $1.2 billion in 1969. Libyans came to believe that their right to self-expression was inextricably linked with other important demands, including the right to control their own oil resources and to be free of all foreign economic domination. The US and British bases were seen by many as the main threat to Libyan sovereignty. In 1968 prime minister Abdul Hamid Bakkush brought 106 people to trial on charges ranging from "plotting subversive and terrorist activities" to "inciting strikes and demonstrations."

On 1 September 1969 the "Free Unionist Officers" performed a coup within the space of four hours, which radically altered the structure of Libyan society. The first acts of the Free Unionist Officers included occupying all radio stations. They declared their intention to follow a Pan-Arabist, socialist, and anti-imperialist ideology. Leader Muʿammar al-Qaddafi's attitude toward press freedom is given its theoretical basis in part 1 of his most significant manifesto, *The Green Book*, which was widely disseminated after 1975.

In *The Green Book* Qaddafi puts forth the notion that society is composed of individual persons and corporate entities, both of which usurp and destroy the people's right to express themselves.

> Democratically speaking, it is inadmissible that a single person should own a means of diffusing information. [Likewise], a newspaper published by an association of entrepreneurs, or by a commercial entity, is only the means of expression of a particular social category. It expresses only one point of view and not the view of public opinion.

The solution proposed by *The Green Book* is a

> democratic press, one which is published by a popular committee composed of members of all social categories, including associations of workers, of women, of students, of farmers, laborers, civil servants, artisans, etc. In this case and in this case only, would the press or any other means of communication be the expression of the whole of society and reflect its general conception.

Qaddafi's theory of the press has gained adherents outside Libya, in both the developed and developing countries. The application of the theory is difficult to evaluate objectively because literature on the subject tends to be highly polarized. Ruth First, in *Libya: The Elusive Revolution*, points out several repressive measures taken by the officers' Revolutionary

Command Council during the early years of the new regime. In 1970 "restrictions were placed upon the operation of zawiyas and Sanusi religious education", because of their close ties to the monarchy. During the same year, journalists and editors were charged with corrupting public opinion. "The trials were televised at peak viewing times and the television station was besieged with requests for repeat showings . . ." The independence of the traditional press was radically curtailed. "Ten newspapers had their licenses suspended, and soon little remained of the Libyan press. In time even official press organs such as *al-Thawra* (*The Revolution*) were shut down for unstated errors . . ."

The censorship of the traditional press was justified by supporters of the revolution with a number of arguments: these papers had been tools of the monarchy; some represented an elite capitalist class; the owners were tied to foreign imperialist and non-Arab interests; or they were not faithful to the needs of the broad masses of Libyans. The Revolutionary Command Council, in order to fill the information gap, sponsored a series of public seminars, which were broadcast on Libyan television. Such open forums were hailed by some observers as unprecedented in Libyan society (and unprecedented throughout most of the Arab world). Workers, intellectuals, women, and religious figures were encouraged to debate several key issues that would define the course of the revolution. Critics pointed out that the scope of the conversations was limited, arguing that the debates were mere window dressing.

The launch of the so-called "Cultural Revolution" took place on 15 April 1973. Qaddafi called upon the masses to take over the government of society through the formation of "popular committees". Workers were called upon to take over many industries under the slogan "partners, not wage-earners". There were reports of book burnings; and at the instigation of some of the popular committees about 400 opponents of the government were arrested, including communists, Baʿthists, and members of the Muslim Brotherhood and the Islamic Liberation Party. The Libyan "Cultural Revolution" was not comparable in scale or duration to its Chinese namesake. In fact by August 1973 it ended, after a failed march to the eastern border to encourage union with Egypt.

During the 1980s opponents of the revolution could provide ample evidence to show that freedom of expression was severely curtailed for certain groups, especially entrepreneurs, landowners, and opposition political activists, including Islamists, Baʿthists, and communists. Nevertheless, supporters of the revolution could provide convincing evidence to show that other groups, namely women and working-class Libyans, had found their rights to free expression enhanced.

The Ghanaian journalist Kojo Yankah is perhaps the only reporter to write a book on the Libyan experiment. His *End of a Journey* (1984) contains a chapter on the media. Yankah writes:

> there is no private newspaper or publication in the Jamahiriya (State of the Masses). The Unions, People's Committees and Congresses and the various syndicates publish their own newspapers which reflect their particular views, opinions and decisions. Such publications are owned and controlled by the people themselves.

Writing eight years after the publication of *The Green Book*, Yankah argues that "freedom of expression is exercised by all the people through the basic congresses, people's committees, and unions ... The radio is 'the voice of the revolution' and is controlled by the General People's Committee for Revolutionary Information."

Workers do appear to have more say in the workplace than ever before. A survey of most of the literature could safely yield these conclusions. Press freedom is curtailed by the fact that, even though the people's committees are elected and granted real power, there exist numerous overseeing "revolutionary committees". The members of the revolutionary committees have the power to "cleanse" the people's committees. "Cleansing" appears to occur mostly at national level. Many scholars attest to the fact that on the local level, debate and free expression are relatively unhindered. There appears to be almost unanimous agreement that Libyan women have made great progress in obtaining the right to express their views. Under the monarchy they were denied rights to even walk in public, much less speak in public. Now they are given scholarships to universities, allowed to serve in the military, and given the right to speak and vote in basic people's congresses.

Libya continues to be criticized for its treatment of minorities, dissidents, and journalists. Berber groups throughout North Africa complain about being denied the right to speak, publish, and broadcast in their own languages. The internet is not currently available in Libya; but Berbers in exile are trying to counter censorship by designing websites to express their own cultural and linguistic uniqueness.

According to Amnesty International, the Libyan reporter ʿAbd Allah ʿAli al-Sanussi al-Darrat has been held without charge or trial since 1973, longer than any other journalist anywhere in the world. In 1978 Abu Mussa, a Shiite Muslim cleric from southern Lebanon allegedly made disparaging remarks about Qaddafi on Libyan television. He disappeared shortly thereafter, along with a compatriot journalist, al-Sayid ʿAbbas Nur al-Din. Another journalist, Mohamed Mostafa Rahan, was killed in 1980, while working for the BBC in London.

Libya's leading dissident, Mansour Rasheed al-Kikhia, former minister in Qaddafi's cabinet, and founder of the Arab Organization of Human Rights (AOHR) disappeared in Cairo on 10 December 1993. There are unconfirmed reports about his extradition to Libya where he may have been executed. Both the AOHR and the Libya League for Human Rights have accused the government of using terror and the threat of terror against opponents in exile, in order to silence criticism.

The noted media critic and scholar, and staunch defender of free speech, Noam Chomsky, declares that Libya is indeed a terrorist state. In spite of that fact, he argues, Libya's record must be put into perspective. Chomsky points out that between 1980 and 1985, while Libya was killing 14 of its citizens, and a handful of others, the US client regime of El Salvador killed some 50,000 of its people in what bishop Rivera called a war of extermination and genocide against an innocent civilian population. Libya is often singled out for extremely strong criticism of its censorship policy and of its human rights record by the western press. According to some commentators, this is not because Libya's record is even as bad as that of other nations in the Arab world. Saudi Arabia's record is arguably much worse. Instead, it may be because Libya's socialist policy of nationalizing its oil reserves threatens the interests of powerful constituencies within the western powers, especially in the United States, where loss of control over much of the Middle East's oil wealth is a key concern. Western hostility toward Libya has, in turn, been cited as a justification for further press restrictions.

In March 1998 the daily *al-Zahf al-Akhdar* (The Green March) was banned, because it published articles attacking fraternal Arab states and friendly countries and because of deviation from the revolutionary orientation that governs the media. In July 1998 human rights groups were demanding the release of more than 100 dissidents arrested for political oppositional activities that do not involve violence. Some of these individuals are members of professions where the right of free expression is paramount, such as Mohammad Faraj al-Qallal, an executive in a printing house in Benghazi, and ʿAbd Allah Ahmad ʿIzzeddin, a professor arrested in the middle of a lecture.

Religious freedom in Libya is continually in jeopardy, allegedly because the political stances of some Islamic sects threaten the regime. Qaddafi has stated that the Qur'an is the official law (shari'a) of Libya; but he has not done so in order to implement an Islamic revolution in the style of the Iranian fundamentalists. (He is greatly at odds with the fundamentalists, because he deduces from certain Qur'anic verses that men and women are political and social equals.) Qaddafi argues that every individual has the right to ijtihad (to reason), to think for himself on religious issues. By making the Qur'an the official law of society (and excluding traditional texts and commentaries), Qaddafi has effectively deprived the ʿulamaʾ (religious scholars) of its privileged position. Conservative and fundamentalist Muslim clerics have effectively been banned from national television and from circulating their ideas through written means.

When Qaddafi declared that Islam and socialism are one, he argued that the Qur'an calls for the elimination of poverty and the redistribution of wealth. Workers were encouraged to take over businesses; and the state proceeded to limit the acquisition of private property. The ʿulamaʾ denounced such a policy as contrary to Islam, because, according to Geoff Simons, the clerics had strong links to the commercial sector. Qaddafi responded to clerical opposition in 1978 by urging the masses to purify the mosques. The imam of Tripoli, shaykh al-Bikti, openly criticized the regime until he disappeared in 1980. The greatest active opposition to Qaddafi's Islamic socialism continues to come from underground fundamentalist movements, such as those in neighbouring Algeria. According to human rights activists, from 1995 until the present, clashes between armed Islamic groups and Libyan security forces occur sporadically. Such violent conflicts lend the authorities further pretexts to justify censorship and additional repression.

PAUL WELLEN

Further Reading

Ansell, Meredith O. and Ibrahim Massaud al-Arif, , *The Libyan Revolution: A Sourcebook of Legal and Historical Documents*, vol. 1 (September 1969–August 1970), Stoughton, Wisconsin: Oleander Press, 1992

Bessis, Juliette, *La Libye contemporaine*, Paris: L'Harmattan, 1986

El Fathaly, Omar I. and Monte Palmer, *Political Development and Social Change in Libya*, Lexington, Massachusetts: Lexington Books, 1980

El-Khawas, Mohammed A., *Qaddafi: His Ideology in Theory and Practice*, Brattleboro, Vermont: Amana, 1986

El-Kikhia, Mansour O., *Libya's Qaddafi: The Politics of Contradiction*, Gainesville: University of Florida Press, 1997

First, Ruth, *Libya: The Elusive Revolution*, Harmondsworth and Baltimore: Penguin, 1974

Giffard, Edward, "Libya's Libertarian Cloak", *Index on Censorship*, 19/5 (October 1981)

Henderson, George, "Free to Agree with Colonel Qadhaffi", *Index on Censorship*, 9/6 (December 1980)

al-Messaondi, Fadel, "The Media under Qadaffi", *Index on Censorship*, 16/5 (May 1987)

al-Qaddafi, Mu'ammar, *The Green Book*, London: Martin Brian and O'Keeffe, 1976

Rajab, Ahmed, "Criticise and Die", *Index on Censorship*, 9/4 (August 1980)

Simons, Geoff, *Libya: The Struggle for Survival*, London: Macmillan, and New York: St Martin's Press, 1993

Vandewalle, Dirk (editor), *Qadhafi's Libya, 1969–1994*, New York: St Martin's Press, 1995

Wright, John, *Libya: A Modern History*, London: Croom Helm, and Baltimore: Johns Hopkins University Press, 1982

Yankah, Kojo, *End of a Journey; or, A Journalist's Report from the Libyan Jamahiriya*, Accra: Dateline, 1984

LICENSED FOOLS AND JESTERS

It is a debatable point as to whether licensed fools ever provided effective subversion of censorship or whether, because they were licensed by some form of authority, they inevitably served the dominant hegemony. However, the reason that such household fools and later, jesters, were allowed was, surprisingly, the work of St Paul. In their time the Apostles were seen as a type of Eastern fool and mystic who had no concern for their material welfare, but spoke the truth as they saw it come what may. They were among the most determined breakers of censorship of their day and many of them died a death through torture. St Paul said, "We are fools for Christ's sake" (1. Corinthians 4:10), "for ye see your calling, brethren, how that not many wise men after the flesh . . . are called" (1 Corinthians 1:26).

The irony is that the Catholic Church became the monolithic authority in the Middle Ages that tortured heretics to death. But it maintained the concept of the Pauline fool. Examples, possibly safe examples, were the mentally handicapped who had no ability to consider their own welfare, and who were kept as moral reminders in houses of the great. They had no possessions and no human rights, eating and sleeping with the dogs, cuffed and caressed indiscriminately. But because they could not profit from what they said, they were allowed freedom of speech. On the Continent they were often known as *fooles sages* (wise fools) but an example from Britain reveals only wisdom *in extremis*. A year after a certain nobleman died his fool also fell sick, and on his deathbed bequeathed his soul to the devil because, he said, he wanted to rejoin his master. Other bequests were his bed to his master's wife, because she needed to lie so long in the morning, and his bauble to the man who gave charity to the poor, because when the poor pressed round him he beat them with his stick and the bauble was softer. Such breaking of taboos about criticizing masters was only really possible, and noticed, when the fool had arrived at a point when it no longer mattered whether he was licensed or not. There was one famous court fool, William Somer, who could influence his master Henry VIII at times when serious counsellors kept out of Henry's sight, but this was because of the careful psychology in Somers's approach. He never criticized the king, but, like the previous fool, offered him exempla in the form of moral riddles. More acerbic rebuttals were for the ambitious cardinal Wolsey, who once rebuked Somers in

rhyme, "a rod in the school/And a whip for the fool/Are always in season". To which Somers replied, "A halter and rope /For him that would be Pope/Against all right and reason". Whether Somers would have said this had Wolsey been his master is doubtful.

As this quip shows, Somers had all his faculties, and often acted purely as jester to cure his master of sadness. Towards the Reformation witty jesters became increasingly preferred to the naive kind, and in Britain they needed to be highly intelligent to judge how far freedom of speech could go. Erasmus wrote with greater confidence, "kings do dislike the truth, but the outcome of this is extraordinary for my fools. They can speak truth and even open insults and be heard with positive pleasure". This was in the *Praise of Folly* (paragraph 36) first published in Latin in Paris. However the fool's freedom of expression on the continent of Europe was more in evidence during licensed days in society than in courts of the great. Fool plays performed publicly at Shrovetide or midsummer could sometimes lampoon authority, though the writer always needed to know that he had a powerful patron to protect him. Pierre Gringore mocked the pope in 1512 in a Mardi Gras *sottie* (fool play), but with the protection of the king, Louis XII. Erasmus's *Praise of Folly* was printed the year before and in it he followed his own advice, seriously criticizing secular power, theologians, and the papal court under the guise of Mother Fool. It was always more dangerous to print criticism than to perform it, but through the convention of a fool's liberty and, more importantly perhaps, not writing in the vernacular, Erasmus achieved some breaking of censorship – it was reported that pope Leo X was amused by the work. Nine years later, however, the same pope was less amused by another theologian, Martin Luther, who styled himself "court jester" in the Preface to his first major reform treatise: "To the Christian Nobility of the German Nation". This contained a direct, comprehensive attack on the corruption, pride, and power of the papacy and was to lead to his excommunication. Luther linked his role of court jester to St Paul's letter to the Corinthians and was obviously aware that in terms of the outrage he was committing on papal doctrine, the fool title could not protect him. However, the date on the Preface is 23 June, midsummer eve, and it is possible, since he was writing to the German nobility rather than to the pope, that he sought the jester's traditional seasonal protection from men he preferred to consider his masters against the life-threatening wrath that was to come.

The only impunity guaranteed to fools was over trivial matters such as breaking pots on men's heads; in terms of criticism of authority there was never any certainty that "license" meant what it said. Risks were sometimes taken and using the title might provide an umbrella. The only "all-licens'd Fool" so-called by Shakespeare is in *King Lear* (I.iv.197), and he is thrown out of Goneril's house, whereas Feste in *Twelfth Night* cleverly jokes his way into favour. As Viola says: "He must observe their mood on whom he jests,/The quality of the persons, and the time . . ." (III.i.60–61).

SANDRA BILLINGTON

Further Reading

Billington, Sandra, *A Social History of the Fool*, Brighton, Sussex: Harvester Press, and New York: St Martin's Press, 1984

Billington, Sandra, *Mock Kings in Medieval Society and Renaissance Drama*, Oxford: Clarendon Press, and New York: Oxford University Press, 1991
Billington, Sandra, *Midsummer: A Cultural Subtext from Chrétien de Troyes to Jean Michel*, Turnhout: Brepols, 2000
Erasmus, Desiderius, *Praise of Folly; and, Letter to Martin Dorp, 1515*, translated by Betty Radice, edited by A.H.T. Levi, Harmondsworth: Penguin, 1971
Fo, Dario, *Mistero Buffo: Comic Mysteries*, translated by Ed Emery, London: Methuen, 1988
Green, Julien, *God's Fool: The Life and Times of Francis of Assisi*, San Francisco: Harper, 1985; London: Hodder and Stoughton, 1986
Gritsch, Eric W., *Martin – God's Court Jester: Luther in Retrospect*, Philadelphia: Fortress Press, 1983
Krueger, Derek, *Symeon the Holy Fool: Leontius's Life and the Late Antique City*, Berkeley: University of California Press, 1996
Otto, Beatrice K., *Fools Are Everywhere: The Court Jester around the World*, Chicago: University of Chicago Press, 2001
Welsford, Enid, *The Fool: His Social and Literary History*, London: Faber, and New York: Farrar and Rinehart, 1935

LIETUVOS KATALIKŲ BAŽNYČIOS KRONIKAS
(Chronicle of the Catholic Church in Lithuania)
Lithuanian underground journal, 1972–88

Over the whole history of Soviet *samizdat* there are a few initiatives that stand out above all others. The most systematic and long-lasting religious underground journal was the *Chronicle of the Catholic Church in Lithuania*, which ran for 78 issues from 1972 to 1988. Some issues came out bilingually, in Russian as well as Lithuanian, with the objective of more easily informing the Russian people, as well as the world outside. Despite allocating the unrestricted resources of the KGB to tracking down and rooting out the perpetrators, contingency plans were always in place and the title was never suppressed. In the event, the *Chronicle* was instrumental in providing a focus for Lithuanian nationalism, as well as the almost universal aspiration for religious liberty in the country. In doing this successfully, it unquestionably had a much wider significance as a trigger of the demands for Lithuanian independence, a key factor in the eventual collapse of the Soviet system.

The authors and editors of the *Chronicle* guarded their anonymity from the first. The *Chronicle* spoke authoritatively for the broad mass of Lithuanian bishops, clergy, and laity in the country, whose loyalty to the Vatican over 25 years of persecution and enforced atheism the regime had not managed to break.

The basic purpose of the *Chronicle* was very simple: to put the record straight and cut through the decades of libel to which Lithuanian Catholics had been subjected. Inspiration came also from the Russian human rights movement, communication with such figures as Andrei Sakharov or Sergei Kovalev being a priority. Lithuanians in the United States were often the first recipients of the *Chronicle*'s texts, sharing them immediately with Keston College (in Kent, England), the news service of which made their contents widely known. The precision and objectivity of the writing became a model for similar activities elsewhere. In the words of the seventh issue of the *Chronicle* itself:

Every news item, fact or event connected with the situation of the Catholic Church, the history of our nation past or present, the arbitrariness of government agencies, repression or other forms of discrimination, must be carefully verified, clear and specific. Numbers, dates, names of people and places, and other information must be especially clear, correctly recorded, and checked.

So outstanding was the response to this call, and so responsible was the editing, that the *Chronicle* appears never to have made a serious mistake. Among national minorities, only the Muslim Crimean Tartars used *samizdat* in a similar way to focus attention on nationality issues.

The primary instrument of production was the typewriter, secretly located and having escaped the mandatory KGB registration, which could lead to the identification of typescripts by analysis of the characteristics of individual typefaces. The originals in the Keston College archive are carbons stapled together between plain white covers of thicker paper (other issues are photocopies). At a trial in December 1974, one of the witnesses admitted using an "Era" photocopying machine to produce 20 copies of two consecutive issues. A defendant admitted distributing 100 copies of the sixth issue, but it is not definitively known how many copies were produced of any single issue. Secret printing presses were in use at the time in Lithuania, but these produced prayer books and catechisms, not issues of the *Chronicle*.

The impact of this publication on world opinion was nothing like as great as one might suppose, not even, it seems, in the corridors of the Vatican. Soviet propaganda was largely successful in persuading the world that the "nationality issue" in the Soviet Union had long since been settled. However, the reporting on some individual acts of barbarity did begin to reach world public opinion, and the Vatican began to take serious notice after the election of a Polish pope, John Paul II, in 1978.

Among the hundreds of noteworthy events that the *Chronicle* reported, perhaps the most momentous was published under the laconic title of "Case 345". From 1974 onwards, the KGB had some success in tracking down people associated with the production of the *Chronicle* and prepared a series of trials. The most dramatic opened on 2 December 1974 and lasted 12 days, not counting intermissions. Any casual observer permitted inside the Vilnius courtroom might have concluded that the charge was high treason or armed rebellion, as the five defendants were individually led in by three armed guards each. At no time were there fewer than six soldiers alongside the accused, with a further posse of guards at the door and in the street outside.

The five defendants, all male, ranged in age from 63 down to the youngest, Virgilijus Jaugelis, who was only 26 and was a product of an entirely Soviet education. The crime of which they were accused was the production and circulation of seven issues of the *Chronicle*, "the aim of which is to denigrate the Soviet system", according to the wording of the indictment. The leader was named as Petras Plumpa (35), but Jaugelis's conduct emerged as an equally serious challenge to the Soviet system. Having been refused entry to the one tiny Catholic theological seminary in Lithuania, he had become virtually a

full-time freedom fighter and openly admitted what he had been doing. He further incensed the prosecution by quoting the old Lithuanian national anthem: "Lithuania, land of our birth, our own dear country . . . How many times have the boots of foreigners trodden you down?" The KGB provoked a gang to attack Jaugelis in prison on the night of 10–11 February 1975. They broke his jaw, yet he was denied medical attention. His health was already fragile and he died five years later, having been released early in the vain hope of preventing his becoming a martyr. Case 345 was designed to crush the *Chronicle*, but the next issue appeared on time and contained a detailed account of the trial.

An extended run of complete issues of the *Chronicle* was published abroad in English, as well as in Lithuanian. Other Lithuanian *samizdat* publications included *Aušra* (Dawn), *Dievas ir Tevyre* (God and Country), *Rubintojelis* (The Suffering Christ), *Varkas* (The Bell), *Tiresas* (Way of Truth), *Alma Mater*, and *Perspektyros* (Perspectives).

MICHAEL BOURDEAUX

Further Reading

Bourdeaux, Michael, *Land of Crosses: The Struggle for Religious Freedom in Lithuania, 1939–78*, Chulmleigh, Devon: Augustine, 1979
Chronicle of the Catholic Church in Lithuania, Brooklyn, New York: Lithuanian Catholic Religious Aid, 1972–89

LIETUVOS LAISVES LYGA (Lithuanian Freedom League)
Underground organization, 1978–91

Certain key aspects of Lithuania's history were not allowed to be publicized during the period of Soviet occupation. These included the declaration of independence (16 February 1918); the Nazi–Soviet Pact (23 August 1939) and its secret protocols, which had assigned Lithuania to the Soviet sphere of influence; the partisan war against Soviet rule in the 1940s and 1950s; and the deportations, notably those between 1941 and 1951. The censoring of such historical issues maintained the myth of Lithuania's voluntary incorporation into the Soviet Union in 1940.

Thus, the Soviet account stressed "socialist revolution" and "the will of the people", glossing over the collusion between Nazi Germany and the Soviet Union, and denying that there were any secret protocols to the Nazi–Soviet Pact. Again, the 1918 declaration of independence was officially explained as the work of a small, self-interested group of non-patriots, who wanted to forge a union with Germany in order to shore up defences against "socialism". Similarly, information relating to the partisan war was censored because evidence of mass support for the resistance would contradict the account of Lithuania's voluntary accession to the USSR. Accordingly, the partisans were depicted as fascists, war criminals, and former landlords who, until they were defeated by Lithuanian supporters of the new, communist, regime, wreaked havoc among the populace. By portraying the war as an ideological struggle between classes, the Soviet ideologists denied any link between Stalinist terror, in particular by way of the forced collectiviza-

tion of agriculture, and partisan recruitment among the peasantry. The official account of the partisan war enabled the deportations to be mentioned only in the context of ridding Lithuania of class enemies. The Lithuanian press avoided discussing historical issues and only rarely mentioned Lithuanian dissidents or the growing Catholic protest movement.

The Lietuvos Laisves Lyga (Lithuanian Freedom League) was formed as an underground organization in Lithuania in June 1978. Its goal was to seek independence for the country by publicizing the way in which the Nazi–Soviet Pact had assigned Lithuania to the Soviet sphere of influence, and thus destroying the myth of voluntary incorporation into the Soviet Union. If it could be shown, in the Soviet Union's own words, that Lithuania had been occupied, then the claim for national self-determination became self-evidently just, a return to legality. Julius Sasnauskas, an active member of the group, noted later that "The Lithuanian Freedom League was a loose group of individuals united by one common goal – independence. Everyone who wanted Lithuania to be independent could consider themselves a member."

The League continued a tradition of resistance to Soviet rule in Lithuania. The first phase, of open resistance, had ended with the defeat in 1952 of the partisan movement, known also as the Forest Brothers, which had fought a guerrilla war since 1945, using the forests of Lithuania as a base for their resistance. Some cultural and economic autonomy was achieved in 1958–68, partly due to the policies pursued by Antanas

Sniečkus, first secretary of the Lithuanian Communist Party, but after 1968 Lithuania succumbed to a process of increased russification. Lithuanian dissidents learned from the failure of the Czechoslovak reform movement and the Warsaw Pact invasion of Czechoslovakia (1968) that legal opposition could easily be overcome with tanks. Those whose stance was to resist Soviet rule without any compromise had to face the problem of how they could practically do so. The solution was found in the publication of *samizdat*, and by the late 1970s Lithuania had the highest per-capita level of *samizdat* publications of any Soviet republic.

The League announced its existence in a statement dated 15 June 1978, published in the nationalist *samizdat* journal *Aušra* (The Dawn). It was to be "a non-partisan organization based on democratic principles and aiming at the restoration of Lithuanian independence". It was closely associated with the dissident historian Antanas Terleckas, and it is estimated that altogether about 200 supporters were actively involved. The risk of immediate arrest for the open conduct of their activities often led members to meet in small groups of five to ten in each other's homes and at various other sites, such as the forests near Vilnius. They discussed how to meet the organization's aims: "to raise the political and national consciousness of the nation, and to remind the world through political documents of Lithuania's occupation."

Realizing the impossibility of overcoming official censorship, the League never tried. Through the medium of its *samizdat* newspaper *Vytis* (the name refers to the "Mounted Knight", an emblem of the interwar Republic of Lithuania, which has been revived), first published on 1 June 1979, the League printed material relating to the Nazi–Soviet Pact, and the consequences of this breach of international law for the subsequent falsification of Lithuanian history. The Lithuanian identity of the nation was not construed by the League on ethnic lines, but by focusing on the myth of Lithuania's "voluntary" incorporation into the Soviet Union. The League described how hundreds of thousands of Lithuanians had been killed or deported to Siberia between 1941 and 1951. During the period of the Soviet occupation there was some immigration into Lithuania from Russia and other parts of the Soviet Union, but it was not on as great a scale as in Latvia and Estonia, and by 1979 ethnic Lithuanians comprised 80 per cent of the population, ethnic Russians 8.9 per cent, and ethnic Poles 7.3 per cent.

As a defiant gesture to mark the 40th anniversary of the signing of the Pact (23 August 1979), the League organized an open letter, the *Baltic Denunciation of the Stalin–Hitler Pact* – also referred to as *The Memorandum of 45* – which formulated demands for political independence, and was released in Moscow. Signatories to this document included a few Latvians and Estonians, but the majority were Lithuanians. The letter was published in the third issue of *Vytis* (August–September 1979) and also in the *Congressional Record: Senate* (28 September 1979) in the United States, where a substantial emigré community lived. Five Russian dissidents, including Andrei Sakharov, later added their signatures.

Contact was made with *The Chronicle of the Lithuanian Catholic Church*, to which the League gave occasional financial assistance, and it was possible, though difficult, to make contacts with the more developed underground movement in Poland. The League was particularly active in the publication of *samizdat* writings at least until 1980, when its activities were curtailed by arrest and imprisonment of many of the organizers and signatories to the *Baltic Denunciation*. Julius Sasnauskas was arrested on 11 December 1979, and spent one and a half years in the KGB prison on Gediminas Prospekt in Vilnius. Antanas Terleckas, arrested on 30 October 1979, was also imprisoned there. Sasnauskas was subsequently deported to Western Siberia and returned to Lithuania in 1986 after a seven-year absence. Terleckas was deported to the far north of Siberia.

Changes in the political climate were initiated by Mikhail Gorbachev after he came to power in 1985, including the freeing of political prisoners such as League activists. The League organized the first unofficial demonstration in Soviet Lithuania, on 23 August 1987, once again to commemorate the signing of the Nazi–Soviet Pact, and at that time "did not know if someone would shoot or arrest them". On 3 July 1988, the League announced its intention to work openly to re-establish Lithuania's independence. The resignation of Songaila, the First Secretary of the Lithuanian Communist Party, on 20 October 1988, and his replacement by Algirdas Brazauskas, was partly prompted by Songaila's decision to allow violence to be employed against a rally, on 28 September 1988, organized by the League. The group had been indicted by the authorities as "an anti-Soviet organization that could not be allowed to organize public meetings", but was now redeemed by those Lithuanian communists who condemned the use of violence against peaceful demonstrators: "One cannot throw troops against the people".

The League's refusal to contest the elections to the Soviet Congress of People's Deputies in March 1989, because it saw the new legislature as an imperialist body, meant that its political influence was reduced. However, its work was largely done. The League had kept alive the memory of independent Lithuania by opposing and undermining the vigorous censorship imposed by Soviet rule, and had helped to radicalize the Lithuanian national movement, leading to the restoration of Lithuanian independence in September 1991.

MARIA LENN

Further Reading

Lieven, Anatol, *The Baltic Revolution: Estonia, Latvia, Lithuania, and the Path to Independence*, New Haven, Connecticut and London: Yale University Press, 1993

Senn, Alfred Erich, *Lithuania Awakening*, Berkeley: University of California Press, 1990

Senn, Alfred Erich, *Gorbachev's Failure in Lithuania*, Basingstoke: Macmillan, and New York: St Martin's Press, 1995

Vardys, V. Stanley, "Lithuanians" in *The Nationalities Question in the Post-Soviet States*, edited by Graham Smith, revised edition London and New York: Longman, 1996

Vardys, V. Stanley and Judith B. Sedaitis, *Lithuania: The Rebel Nation*, Boulder, Colorado: Westview Press, 1997

GYÖRGY LIGETI
Hungarian composer, 1923–

How might Ligeti's music have developed if his formative years had not been lived in almost complete isolation from postwar modernism, the movement from which the leading composers of western Europe sprang? What could he have written if he had not been restricted by communist cultural repression? These questions are impossible to answer; but it seems likely that the originality of Ligeti's ideas, his emphatic detachment from "schools", and the freshness and clarity of his musical vision, which made a sensational impact on audiences, composers, and critics after his arrival in the west in 1956, were all conditioned by the lonely privacy of the creative experiments that he had necessarily had to hide from public and party as long as he was in Hungary.

Indeed, the four composers whose music most effectively dissipated the hegemony of the European avant-garde after 1960 all emerged from the confines of what may be called totalitarianism. The Greek composer Iannis Xenakis was the first, fleeing the death sentence pronounced on him in 1947 to settle in Paris, first as an engineer and architect, then as a composer. Ligeti escaped from Hungary in the turbulent late autumn of 1956, following the suppression of the Hungarian uprising, settling first in Vienna, later in Cologne and Hamburg. For Witold Lutosławski and Krzysztof Penderecki the transition was more gradual: they remained resident in Poland as leaders of a vigorous new school of textural composition that appeared in the wake of the cultural thaw of the late 1950s and soon influenced other composers around the world. In different ways, each of these four composers rejected the prevailing serial orthodoxy of the West (although their subsequent music was coloured by a brief dalliance with its methods), focusing instead, but from different standpoints, on the inner particles of sonic plasma, whether as statistical distribution (Xenakis), timbral contrast and modes of production (Lutosławski and Penderecki), or micropolyphonic counterpoint (Ligeti). Leaving aside the contradiction, identified by both Xenakis and Ligeti, between the apparent order of serialism, and the "fortuitous and irrational" impression of its audible result, one can say that it was extremely unlikely that such a pervasive dictatorship of compositional method would appeal to composers whose personal and creative freedom had been so dearly bought. As they emerged from totalitarianism into the light of freedom, they were as quick to reject, as they had been eager to learn, the common conventions of the west.

In any case, Ligeti had had no opportunity in Hungary to study the achievements of the Second Viennese School. After Stalin's clampdown on artistic freedom was imposed across the whole of the Soviet bloc in the second half of 1948, performances ceased even of Bartók's more "difficult" music, let alone of works by Schoenberg or Webern. Scores and recordings became unobtainable, books disappeared, information about developments in the West dwindled to nothing. Even the fine collection of French and Hungarian Impressionist painters was removed from Budapest's Museum of Art. The initial influences on Ligeti's music had been the works of Richard Strauss, Stravinsky, Bartók, and Kodály that he heard before the war and during the brief, heady cultural revival of his first postwar student days in Budapest. As this repertoire suddenly collapsed, and the communists imposed their agenda, Ligeti turned for inspiration to the uncensored free spirit of medieval and renaissance polyphony. It was a temporary means of escape but had the virtue of advancing his skill as a contrapuntalist.

Following his graduation from the Franz Liszt Academy of Music, Ligeti briefly followed the prescribed path of immersing himself in Romanian and Hungarian folk tradition. Many of his early compositions were for chorus, and they included numerous routine folk settings. He also wrote music of a more experimental kind, including a *Polyphonic Study* for piano duet as early as 1943, in which four independent rhythmic *talea*, each in its own tonality, circle each other as if in a mobile by Alexander Calder. However, by 1948, when he wrote his graduation compositions, the political climate had deteriorated. The uncertainty and ambivalence of Ligeti's feelings at this time are clearly evident. Early in the summer of 1948, still sharing the social idealism of his many left-wing friends, he began a *Youth Cantata* on an anti-imperialist text by Péter Kuczka, for soloists, chorus, and orchestra. Its manner was Handelian and boasted a large-scale fugue. By the time of the cantata's premiere, at a World Youth Festival in August 1949, he had come to understand the sinister motives of Soviet domination. Much disillusioned, he now hated the text, and felt acutely uncomfortable at contributing to an event stage-managed for maximum propaganda by the new government, but was powerless to prevent the performance. Not surprisingly, his final graduation piece, an *Andante and Allegretto* for string quartet, reveals a deeper uncertainty. Its cautious conformity lacks conviction.

By this time, the regime had set up a committee to vet new scores and reject any that showed the least trace of "bourgeois" or modernist tendencies. In 1950, Ligeti gained a teaching post at the Academy of Music. To retain this privileged position, he had to submit his works to the committee; its approval was, after all, the only means of obtaining a performance. Some of his choral pieces found favour, others did not. Ligeti has recalled how one was vetoed merely because it contained a musical joke, another because it ended with a minor second interval between mezzo-soprano and tenor. These were small irritations, but the rejection of his Cello Sonata was more serious and hurtful. Ligeti had composed its first movement, an expressive, melodically eloquent *Dialogo*, in 1948, for a fellow student with whom he was secretly in love, but she had not played it. The vigorous second movement followed five years later, when a well-known cellist, Vera Dénes, asked him for a composition; its addition gave the two-movement work an energy and expansiveness that is virtuosic but also lyrical, warm, and engaging. It is neither so ambitious nor technically as complex as Kodály's great solo sonata, yet it proved too advanced for the party conservatives:

Before the piece could be performed or I could be paid even a small commission, the Sonata had to be passed by the Composers' Union, in this case, one man who, it turns out, was a member of the KGB. I needed the money because I had only a small job at the Music Academy in Budapest and was a freelance composer. Had I been expelled from the Union, I would have had to do physical labour. Vera Dénes learned the Sonata and played it for the committee. We were denied permission to publish the work or perform it in public, but we were allowed to record it for radio broadcast. She made an excellent recording for Hungarian Radio, but it was never broadcast. The committee decided that it was too "modern" because of the second movement. ("A Tale of Two Movements", CD liner notes: DG 431 13–2, 1991)

After this experience, Ligeti realized that music of serious intent could only be written in secret, to be hidden in a drawer. In this private manner, he composed his *Musica ricercata* between 1951 and 1953. This set of 11 ingeniously rigorous piano studies was by far his most exploratory and distinctive music up to that time. Then, between 1953 and 1954, he wrote his first string quartet, entitled *Métamorphoses nocturnes*, his finest achievement before leaving Hungary. The quartet was given its first performance in Vienna in 1958 by the Ramor Quartet, whose members had also fled into exile. The *Musica ricercata* were not performed in their original form for over 15 years after completion, although five of the movements were played in Hungary in a version scored for wind quintet (*Bagatelles*) during the brief relaxation of constraints in the days of the uprising, shortly before Ligeti's departure. The sixth "bagatelle" was still omitted because of its many semitone clashes.

Those turbulent weeks showed Ligeti what he had been missing. Khrushchev's historic denunciation of Stalin at the 20th Party Conference in Moscow on 18 March 1956 undermined the prevailing policy of centralization and, especially in Hungary, fomented unrest among intellectuals and creative artists. Borne along on a tide of popular liberalization, contacts suddenly resumed with the west; scores, records, and information reappeared; the jamming of the air waves ceased, foreign radio music programmes could be heard; and, at last, at the age of 33, Ligeti discovered what his contemporaries outside the Soviet bloc had been doing. Particularly impressed by the music of Karlheinz Stockhausen, he wrote to the composer and immediately received a reply. With revived hopes and aspirations, Ligeti began to sketch ambitious instrumental and vocal works in an entirely new style. One that he completed was a

work for large orchestra symbolically entitled *Viziók* (Visions). Although its score was lost when the composer fled to Vienna a few weeks later, Ligeti was able to reconstruct it as the first movement of *Apparitions*, completed in 1959.

The thought of leaving Hungary had long been in Ligeti's mind, although escape without retribution for one's family had always looked impossible. Now, in the historic exodus that followed the arrival of Soviet tanks, and the ensuing chaos and street-fighting in Budapest, the opportunity occurred. Carrying what he could of his most important scores, hiding at one point under the bags in a mail train, Ligeti and his wife crossed the border to Austria, and to political and artistic freedom.

For Ligeti, escape from the dictatorship that had held him in check proved a watershed, the uncorking of a bottle bubbling over with a unique creative fantasy, all the more potent and idiosyncratic for being so long confined. Within weeks, Ligeti was in Cologne, staying at the Stockhausens' home, working in the new medium of electronic music, and engaging in the polemics of the avant-garde. His Hungarian compositions seemed suddenly far in the past, unworthy of this new company, "prehistoric Ligeti" as he would endearingly dismiss them. Everything he was to write in the next decade struck out adventurously into new and uncharted waters, expressing with the boldest conviction the personal freedom that he was at last able to enjoy.

Much later, in the more retrospective and pluralist climate of postmodernism, Ligeti's interest in the works of his Hungarian period revived. His reassessment of their quality coincided with a singularly bold project bestowed on no other living composer, the CD recording of his complete works, from the earliest juvenilia to the most recent masterpieces. As Ligeti's Hungarian compositions gradually reappear, we can judge their relationship both to the difficult circumstances in which they were composed, and to the developing maturity of a supremely original composer.

RICHARD STEINITZ

Writings
Ligeti in Conversation, with Péter Várnai *et al.*, 1983

Further Reading
Griffiths, Paul, *György Ligeti*, 2nd edition, London: Robson, 1997
Steinitz, Richard, *György Ligeti: Studies in Music and Mathematics*, London: Schott, 1996
Steinitz, Richard, *György Ligeti: Music and Imagination*, forthcoming
Toop, Richard, *György Ligeti*, London: Phaidon, 1999

NORMAN LINDSAY
Australian novelist, 1879–1969

REDHEAP (Every Mother's Son)
Novel, 1930

Redheap was written by the most celebrated member of the artistic Lindsay family, but the only copies of the novel to make it into Australia officially was a batch of 50 advanced to the distributor. The decision to ban *Redheap* was prompted by an unflattering review of the novel which appeared in the British *John o'London's Weekly* in April 1930:

> The assumption of the publishers that Mr Norman Lindsay's full-length novel, *Redheap* (Faber and Faber, 7s. 6d.), "will cause a stir in Australia for some years to come" is quite likely justified ... If *Redheap* is really a picture "of any Australian country town" then God help Australia! ... Mr Lindsay is an artist and presumably paints what he sees. But I wish he didn't see life in quite such grubby purples; and that his worship of truth did not impel him to make a song about some of life's most unpleasant details.

The publication of *Redheap* and its subsequent banning aroused intense debate in the Australian press. The *Sydney Guardian* took up the author's cause and later endeavoured to serialize the novel in an attempt to overcome any import restriction. At a time when the majority of Australian novels were published in London, local production meant that *Redheap* fell outside the ambit of the Trade and Customs Department. In an article "Commonwealth Hounding Norman Lindsay: Won't Trust State", the *Guardian* complained that "Once authority gets its teeth into this, it is relentless". The article argued that censorship regulations, once enforced, encouraged more regulation and surveillance. Norman Lindsay complained that the censorship of literature brought about its own "nemesis".

Complaints were forwarded by the state of Victoria police to the federal Trade and Customs Department. In the weeks before his book was banned Lindsay attacked censorship on the grounds that it choked local book production, contending that London publishers would waste no time dumping "conventional rubbish" on to a starving market. Lindsay made no mention of the fact that *Redheap* was published in London, though on a separate occasion he wrote that it was ironic that the government was considering the introduction of a tariff to protect the local product while hindering its development through censorship: "Amusing isn't it?" sneered Lindsay at what he saw as small-mindedness, "A proposal on the one hand to encourage the Australian novel, and, on the other an immediate outcry to stop it the moment it appears."

Until this time comparatively few books had been banned in Australia. In its consideration of *Redheap*, the Trade and Customs Department adopted as a model a judgement handed down in Britain in the 1920s by the Lord Chief Justice: "The test of obscenity is this: Whether the tendency of the matter is to deprave and corrupt those whose minds are open to such

immoral influences, and into whose hands a publication of this sort may fall". This raised explicitly the size of print runs as a determinant of authorial intention. In application censorship regulations in Australia followed Irish examples, which were far more severe than the British. In an attempt to decide whether or not *Redheap* contravened section 52c of the Trade and Customs Act a copy of the book was sent to the solicitor general Robert Garran, who maintained:

> This is not a general question of the censorship of morals. It is a particular question as to the application of the precise words 'indecent' or 'obscene'. And it may be added that, if a work comes within that category, even if its importation were not prohibited, its possession and exhibition for sale would be an offence against State law.
>
> The boundary line between what is indecent and what is not is difficult to draw, and depends upon the nature of a work but not on the nature of the publicity given to it. ... It is sometimes said that art is not concerned with morals; but when an artist (literary or other) exhibits his work to the public, he is not exempt from the law, which does concern itself with morals ... The matter, therefore, is one of policy as well as a strict interpretation of the law.

Garran posed a knotty problem for the Trade and Customs Department which was never satisfactorily settled until the legislation was repealed in 1957. Yet as a matter of policy the former solicitor general was in doubt as to what should constitute indecency; he described *Redheap* as indecent, obscene, and an infraction of morality. A second opinion from the attorney general's department did not share Garran's view: "The book contains here and there passages which are distinctly objectionable but it cannot be classed as an indecent or obscene work." However, mounting pressure from the Victoria authorities and from influential individuals within Victoria, resulted in the book becoming the first Australian novel to be banned in Australia. It became the standard against which all other publications would be judged.

RICHARD NILE

Writings

Redheap, 1930; as *Every Mother's Son*, 1930
My Mask, for What Little I Know of the Man behind It: An Autobiography, 1970
Letters, edited by R.G. Howarth and A.W. Barker, 1979
The World of Norman Lindsay, edited by Lin Bloomfield, 1983
Norman Lindsay on Art, Life, and Literature, edited by Keith Wingrove, 1990

Further Reading

Hetherington, John, *Norman Lindsay: The Embattled Olympian*, Melbourne and London: Oxford University Press, 1973

LITERATURE

Whether it is "performed" (as in ancient Greece or by the griots of West Africa) or read privately (its normal mode of transmission once literacy has been achieved), literature has rarely left moral or political authorities indifferent. Its authors have been expected, variously, to "praise" rulers, gods, and heroes – or to write in support of political "systems"; to extol virtue and to blame vice. Few authorities have valued poets and novelists as independent voices, and some may have feared reading's capacity to bring about an intimate relationship between writer and reader that cannot be externally controlled, and may lead people along new and disturbing paths. Italo Calvino warned: "When politicians and politically-minded people pay too much attention to literature, it is a bad sign . . . it is then that literature is most in danger . . . (politicians) are showing themselves afraid of any use of language that calls the certitude of their own language into question".

Virtue and vice

According to Plato, "the only poetry that should be allowed in a state is hymns to the gods and paeans in praise of good men; once you go beyond that and admit the sweet lyric or epic muse, pleasure and pain become your rulers instead of law and the principles commonly accepted as best". Out, then, from Plato's *Republic* went a considerable number of "false inventions" in Homer and Hesiod, both of them "guilty of the most serious misstatements about human life, making out that wrongdoers are often happy and just men miserable; that injustice pays, if not detected; and that my being just is to another man's advantage, but a loss to myself. We should have to prohibit such poems and tales and tell them to compose others in the contrary sense". It seems that, by the time Plato wrote, many Greeks had in any case begun to disbelieve many stories of the gods. Nevertheless, Plato's influence was long-lasting.

Thus, in his brief of 1896, pope Leo XIII justified the practice of the Catholic Church: "Nothing worse can be imagined for contaminating the minds of men, both by making them destitute of religion and by suggesting many incentives to sin. Wherefore the Church, the guardian and protector of the integrity of faith and morals, in fear of this great evil, long ago came to the conclusion that measures must be adopted to guard against the danger. To this end, it made continual efforts to prohibit men, as far as possible, from the reading of pernicious books, which are the worst form of poison".

Leo was attempting to justify the *Index Librorum Prohibitorum* (1596–1966), which, although dominated by works considered heretical or atheistic, had a fair sprinkling of poetry, stories, and novels, beginning with Giovanni Boccaccio's *Decameron* (1349–1351), copies of which had already been consigned to Savonarola's bonfire in 1498; it was now subjected to expurgation, including of those passages which imputed sexual excess to clergy and nuns, who became, retrospectively, conjurors and countesses. The *Decameron* was, however, highly popular and, at first, a blind eye was turned to the salacious aspects of many of its tales, actual cuts being applied only to passages considered heretical. It was finally completely banned under Sixtus V (pope 1598–1590), and remained so until 1900. (It continued to be the object of secular censorship, however,

copies being regularly refused by the US Customs, and ordered to be destroyed in Britain on eight occasions between 1951 and 1954 alone).

Leo XIII later laid down: "The books of classical authors, whether ancient or modern, if disfigured with the same stain of indecency are, on account of the elegant obscenity of their diction, permitted only to those who are justified on account of their duty or the function of teaching". Ovid's *Ars Amatoria* (c. 1 BCE) and Petronius' *Satyricon* (c. 60 CE) had been early casualties. Ovid's work, substantially more sexually explicit than the *Decameron*, had been lost to sight since the late Roman empire; when printers made it once more available, *Ars Amatoria* suffered a similar fate at the hands of Savonarola and the Index. An English translation by Christopher Marlowe was burnt at the Stationers Hall, London, in 1599.

What, later in the history of the censorship of literature would be called "literary merit" – skill, verbal exuberance, erudition – was, for some centuries, apparently of no consequence to the papal censors. François Rabelais's *Pantagruel* (1533), the first of many works in Western literature to take pleasure in human contradiction, having been first banned and then allowed in his own country, presumably because recognized as a true picture of peasant life, was placed on the Index from the beginning, and Rabelais named as an "author of the first class". Miguel de Cervantes's *Don Quixote* (1604) got away with an exceptionally minor excision – the sentence in part 2 which stated that "works of charity negligently performed are of no worth" – on a theological nicety.

Daniel Defoe's *Robinson Crusoe* (1719) was built around the principle that "God helps those who help themselves"; his *Roxana* (1724) might be considered a moral tale about the making of a criminal. Samuel Richardson's *Pamela; or, Virtue Rewarded* (1741) was explicitly on the side of ultimate moral justice: "The philosopher said true, when he looked upon the skull of a king, and that of a poor man, that he saw no difference between them. Besides, do they not know that the vilest of princes and the poorest of beggars are to have one great and tremendous judge at the last day". Pamela was indexed because it dealt with attempted rape; and Defoe's works for passages considered indecent; it is deeply ironic that *Robinson Crusoe* would eventually become one of the most popular of books considered suitable for children.

English novels, having originated in a Protestant country, were less noticed than French, which dominate the Index's fiction lists: Balzac, Dumas père et fils, Hugo, La Fontaine, Sand, Stendhal were all listed in the 19th century; Anatole France, Gide, and Sartre were added during the 20th. Not a single American or Russian novel was listed, but, in any case, the opinion of the church on matters of moral propriety in novels was now less important than the enforcement of national laws. The church had merely banned works considered indecent. In countries as different as Britain, France, Japan, and the United States, moralists and legislators had to wrestle with central questions: what was "obscenity"?, what literature?, and what pornography?

The French law of 1819 condemned, vaguely, *outrages a la morale publique et religieuse at aux bonnes moeurs*. The British

Obscene Publications Act (1857) was said by the Lord Chief Justice, Lord Campbell, to "apply exclusively to works written for the single purpose of corrupting the morals of youth, and of a nature calculated to shock the common feelings of decency in any well-regulated mind". The German empire legislated even more vaguely against "lewd" publications, and the US Federal Anti-obscenity Law (1873) similarly banned "every obscene, lewd, lascivious or filthy book", without attempting to define these words. It was no wonder that, at one time or another, Lord Byron, E.T.A. Hoffmann, Alfred de Musset, Mark Twain, and Guy de Maupassant fell foul of such imprecise definition. Peter Gay summarizes:

> Government censors, state attorneys, moral reformers intent on stamping out vice, sustained by their sense of mission or urgency in the face of danger, used such intemperate epithets quite indiscriminately. To their minds, a sensual lyric poem by Algernon Swinburne . . . and a pornographic story by Anonymous were all the same, all certain to corrupt and deprave the innocent. The most arresting and most controversial obscenity trials of the (19th) century were, therefore, not pornographic productions at all, but of candid, realistic, erotic poems, plays and novels

– of which perhaps the most notorious was Émile Zola's *La Terre*, the English publisher of which, Henry Vizetelly, was imprisoned in 1888.

Zola's *Paris* was banned in Japan in May 1908. A wholly different culture and literary tradition was exercised by the same questions. Nagai Kafu complained that for the censors, "fiction is nothing but a filthy abscess . . . they don't read our stories as literature or art; they treat them strictly as 'printed matter'". As early as 1721, the shogun Yoshimune Kyoto had ordered that erotic books (*koshokuba*) were to be allowed to go out of print "because they are not good for public morality". One of the first Meiji edicts (1869) was directed at books which "print lewdness and debauchery". The novelist Uchida Roen (1868–1929) complained that the words "injurious to public morals" were so vague that works of real value could easily be suppressed intentionally or by mistake. Of the ban on Saikaku Ihara's *The Life of an Amorous Man* (1682, published in 1894), he could not "help wondering whether the authorities themselves can understand Saikaku well enough to judge him obscene". The word "Zolaism" was now applied to this strand of Japanese writings, including *Tokai* (1908, The City) by Ikuta Kizan, for which the author was tried *in camera*, because the prosecutor judged the work too obscene for public hearing (its subject was adultery); and Mori Ogai's *Vita Sexualis*, banned in 1909. Ogai remarked: "If we cannot make a thing public because it is considered dangerous we will be unable to translate any works that express modern ideas, and that includes Tolstoy, Ibsen, Maeterlinck, and Hofmannsthal. You would have to reject the whole of modern literature and impose a kind of literary seclusion policy".

Such a policy could no more last in Japan than in the west, where, finally, it would be realized that Zola's intentions were serious rather than salacious, and where, increasingly, novelists would be drawn again to the tradition of Rabelais (James Joyce) or, for the first time, to write seriously about the act of sexual intercourse, without pornographic intent (D.H. Lawrence). The judgment of US judge John M. Woolsey, delivered on Joyce's *Ulysses* in 1933 seemed to settle the matter: "We think the same immunity should apply to literature as to science where the presentation, when viewed objectively, is sincere, and the erotic matter is not introduced to promote lust and does not furnish the dominant note of the publication. The question in each case is whether the publication, taken as a whole, has libidinous effect". In 1959, rejecting a judgment that Lawrence's *Lady Chatterley's Lover* was obscene, judge Frederick van Pelt Bryan declared that the novel had redeeming social merit and contained "descriptive passages of rare beauty". In Britain, Penguin Books were found not guilty under the 1959 Obscene Publications Act of publishing an obscene book; it was felt that "taken as a whole", the novel would not "deprave and corrupt persons likely, having regard to all relevant circumstances". For some years, arguments would rage on the literary quality or moral influence of such works as William Burroughs's *Naked Lunch* (1959), Alexander Trocchi's *Cain's Book* (1960), and Hubert Selby's *Last Exit to Brooklyn* (1966). Since then, over most of Europe, its former colonies, and in North America, there has been general agreement on the principle that to judge a work's literary quality takes precedence over any possibility that it may, variously, cause offence or contribute to moral decadence. The growth of other media – film, television and the internet – and that of publications that do not pretend to be other than pornographic has effectively laid the literary debate to rest in many countries.

Not all countries. Many communist regimes combined a rigorously enforced political control of literature with traditional views on the depiction of sexuality. Indeed, the two aspects of censorship could often scarcely be separated. Thus, when in 1980, Lin Xinwa, the Chinese novelist, was suspended as chief editor of *People's Literature* for her *Love Must Not be Forgotten*, the reason may partly have been its subject matter – adultery and incest – and partly its setting, Tibet. Similarly, in 1987, Zhang Xianlong was criticised, not only for suggesting, in *Half of Man Is Woman*, that capitalism should be considered with an open mind, but also for the novel's discussion of sexual impotence. And, even under perestroika, when the editor of *Atmoda* (issued in Riga, Latvia, then still part of the Soviet Union) published a poem which compared Russia to a whore with parted legs, he was taken to court for publishing pornography.

Conservative attitudes to literature and sexuality remained until comparatively recently in such countries as Ireland, Portugal, and Spain, influenced by Catholic practice, and South Africa and Malawi, whose leaders continued to believe that literature, however elevated its intentions, could deprave and corrupt. Among many writers of international repute whose work was banned in Ireland even after the abolition of the *Index Librorum Prohibitorum* were Saul Bellow, James Baldwin, Heinrich Böll, Angela Carter, Nadine Gordimer, and Jerzy Kosinski. An older generation of writers – William Faulkner, André Gide, Marcel Proust, and Émile Zola, among many others – were unbanned in 1967, under a ruling that previously banned "indecent" works could be released after 20 years, unless they were resubmitted to the Censorship Board; surprisingly, *Ulysses* was never banned in Ireland. Today, Ireland has joined the ranks of liberal countries, and even a writer with Catholic sympathies such as Peter Connolly notes first that it is foolish to suppose that the attitudes of the Victorian middle class towards literature were the ultimate expression of moral uprightness, and second that the presence of works previously considered indecent does not appear to have led other countries towards moral collapse, Connolly believes that human nature remains "always and everywhere the same", capable of both virtue and vice, influenced in either direction possibly by literature, but by no means more than by any other medium or social force.

At the other end of the Christian spectrum, South Africa's moral attitudes have changed in step with the abolition of apartheid. But, at the height of the Dutch Reformed Church's influence on the Publications Control Board, Aldous Huxley's *Island*, Mary McCarthy's *The Group*, Grace Metalious's *Peyton Place*, Henry Miller's *Tropic of Cancer*, and Charles Webb's *The Graduate*, among others, were banned for indecency in a country whose political and religious leaders considered themselves as among the last bastions of Christian morality. Of Etienne's Leroux's novel *Magersfontein, O Magersfontein!* the Publications Appeal Board concluded: "The writer built into (his) novel excessive filthy language, excessive idle use of the Lord's name, vulgar references to excretion, masturbation . . . the novel is highly regarded by literary experts. The broad public, however, as personified by the average man, regards the use (of such language) as an infringement of the dignity of the individual and an invasion of his respect for sexual privacy". The Malawi of Hastings Banda, who was also influenced by Calvinist morality, maintained similar lists; there, Saul Bellow's *Mr Sammler's Planet*, Graham Greene's *The Power and the Glory*, and Joseph Heller's *Catch-22* were among the casualties, not to mention Émile Zola's *Nana*. The Malawian system was known to be random and arbitrary; traces of it still remain.

Meanwhile, in western Europe and North America, it has been observed that some of the greatest works of literature have been created when writers have pitched their work against the taboos of their time – such as (and in wholly different ways) the works of Joyce and Proust. It has been argued in particular that a group of French works – Georges Bataille's *Histoire de L'Oeil* (first acknowledged publication, 1968), Pauline Réage's *Histoire d'O* (1954), Alain Robbe-Grillet's *Projet pour une révolution à New York* (1972) are modern masterpieces, using some of the conventions of pornography to extend the human imagination. Some feminists have argued that, as in pornography itself, any such extension of awareness is usually achieved through the exploitation of woman and the perpetuation of male dominance, and it cannot therefore be considered great literature. The works mentioned, some previously banned, are now widely available in numerous countries; on past form, arguments about their merits will continue for some time.

Indeed, the linguistic philosopher and critic George Steiner scorns the "new eroticists" whose products, he believes, mostly induce "nauseous boredom". The freedom they claim is illusory: "The sensibility of the writer is free only where it is most humane, where it seeks to apprehend and re-enact the marvellous variety, complication and resilience of life by means of words as scrupulous, as personal, as brimful of the mystery of human communication as the language can yield". The understatements of Tolstoi in *Anna Karenina*. and of George Eliot in *Middlemarch* "enrich and complicate our sexual awareness far beyond the douche-bag idylls of the contemporary 'free' novel".

This survey of the moral censorship of literature, which began with Plato's recommended prohibition of certain works because they were disrespectful to the gods, comes full circle with the ayatollah Khomeini's fatwa of 14 February 1989 against Salman Rushdie, whose novel *The Satanic Verses* (1988) was said to be "against Islam, the Prophet and the Qur'an". Clearly, the fatwa was a political as well as a moral act, but it raised in a new form a question implicit in all acts of literary censorship: can the author be identified with the thoughts and opinions of his characters? It can safely be asserted that all serious novelists would answer that they could not, that to suppose otherwise is entirely to misunderstand the nature of their art form. As, in a wholly different context, the Czech novelist Milan Kundera wrote in 1977:

> The novel is a game with invented characters. You see the world through their eyes, and then you see it from various angles. The more differentiated the characters, the more the author and the reader have to step outside themselves and try to understand. Ideology wants to convince you that truth is absolute. A novel shows you that everything is relative. Ideology is a school of intolerance. A novel teaches you tolerance and understanding. The more ideological our century becomes, the more anachronistic is the novel. But the more anachronistic it gets, the more we read it. Today, when politics have become a religion, I see the novel as one of the last forms of atheism.

Literature against ideology: central and eastern Europe

The control of literature for political reasons was one of the leading themes of what Eric Hobsbawn has termed "the short twentieth century" (1914–91), during which various forms of dictatorship dominated the world stage, demanding at least tacit, but often fervent support from poets and novelists. However, this was not the first appearance of such expectations. Once again, it is to Plato that we must turn for one of its first articulations. Literature should, he believed, inculcate respect and obedience towards political masters. In his ideal state, therefore, "impertinences" were to be removed from Homer's *Iliad*, especially passages in which Agamemnon was described as drunk, cowardly, or indecisive.

This was political censorship at its most primitive, but it was not absent from 20th century practice, as novelists and poets who delivered personal insults to dictators soon discovered. In Osip Mandel'shtam's description of the "Kremlin mountaineer", the Russian poet made reference to Stalin's "fingers as fat as grubs", and to his "cockroach whiskers", as well as naming him a "murderer and peasant slayer". Mandel'shtam's attack on the Soviet system went, of course, much deeper and was potentially much more subversive than name-calling; his fate far exceeded anything envisaged by Plato. He "stubbornly maintained", according to his wife Nadezhda Mandel'shtam, that "if they killed people for poetry, then they must fear and respect it – in other words, that it too was a power in the land".

Indeed, as Vitaly Shentalinsky has written: "Writers have always occupied a special position in Russia. For lack of democratic institutions, the Russian writer has never been just an artist, but a spokesman for the truth and a public conscience as well": Pushkin had written against autocracy, Gogol' against petty local officialdom, Dostoevskii, prophetically, against revolution and its consequences; all had suffered under tsarist censorship; all, after 1917, were subject to removal from the Soviet "canon". The critic V. Veresaev wrote in 1925:

> It is a terrible thing to say, but if Dostoyevsky were to appear now, so alien is he to the aspirations of our time and yet so indispensable because of his all-consuming fire, he would have to put up one after another of his novels' manuscripts, all bearing the protective stamp of glavlit [the state literary agency], into his desk drawer.

Franz Kafka was equally a hero of the young Czech democracy of the 1930s; after 1948, and again after 1968, his writings were proscribed, derided by the critic Vladimir Brett in 1974 for their "nonsensical search for an analogy for the alienation of man in capitalist society and in socialist society". Poland was proud enough of Joseph Conrad's origins to publish a 27-volume edition of his works in 1975, but they omitted the author's note to *Under Western Eyes* (1911), which referred to the "tyrannical lawlessness" of early 20th century Russia, which could, said Conrad, "be reduced to the formula of senseless desperation provoked by senseless tyranny".

Many of the earliest writers of the Soviet period became heroes, not because they set out deliberately to challenge the new order, but because they resisted the call to produce "party literature". Mandel'shtam's poetry and prose reflected instead his yearning for "world culture", for that which had animated Dante, or Goethe during his *Italian Journey*; this kind of "pilgrimage to the holy places of European culture seemed to him an essential and crucial event in the life of any artist", wrote his wife in *Hope Against Hope* (1971), but it was one which in no way connected to the utilitarian view of literature which Lenin had adumbrated in *Literature and Party Literature* (1905), let alone its more brutal expression under Stalin during the 1930s. The preoccupations of his friend and colleague Anna Akhmatova, later described as "half-whore, half-nun", were similarly antithetical to socialist realism for their supposed "other-worldliness". For most of the 1930s and 1940s, Akhmatova lived in obscurity. Mandel'shtam's rejection of Stalinism was complete, although, like Akhmatova, he did compose a few token eulogies of the dictator; when his real feelings about the "Kremlin mountaineer" came to light, his imprisonment and murder became inevitable.

By the 1930s, Isaak Babel' had decided his only possible stance against the brutalities of the regime was to practise "the culture of silence". He could not disclaim, however, his earlier work, including *Red Cavalry* (1923), a collection of 23 short stories based on his experience of the civil war and the war against Poland, which resulted, fifteen years later, in his condemnation for having a "wrong" view of history, one of the first in a long line of novelists so anathematized. When he was arrested in 1939, he confessed, under duress, to placing "emphasis on the cruelty and absurdity of the civil war", and to "the artificial introduction of an erotic element", and to "the depiction of only the most outrageous and sensational episodes". This did not help him. Accused of "sabotage and treason", he too was murdered in 1941. Among later writers whose work was banned for unorthodox or inconvenient, if fictional, accounts of historical events, one can also mention Vasilii Grossman's

accounts of events in Leningrad during World War II, *Life and Fate*, and Aleksandr Solzhenitsyn's *The Gulag Archipelago*. Even Mikhail Sholokhov's *The Quiet Don* (1926, published in two volumes in English as *And Quiet Flows the Don*, 1934, and *The Don Flows Home to the Sea*, 1940), considered one of the greatest of Soviet fictional achievements, had some 560 corrections imposed upon it before publication.

Writers were expected to praise Soviet heroes, and, not least, communist functionaries. Boris Pil'niak's *Mahogony* (1929) depicted the incompetence of provincial administrators and was refused by the literary magazine *Novi Mir* as "counter-revolutionary and anti-Soviet". Vladimir Maiakovskii wrote: "To me a finished literary work is like a weapon. Even if that weapon were above the class struggle – such a thing does not exist (though perhaps Pil'niak thinks of it like that) – handing it over to the White press strengthens the arsenal of our enemies". Pil'niak became the butt of many party attacks throughout the 1930s, and was executed on a trumped-up charge of espionage in 1938. Aleksandr Fadeev's *Young Guard* (1945), on the other hand, was said initially to contain a "superb representation of the Leninist-Stalinist type of statesman". Within two years, however, the party newspaper *Pravda* and the *Literaturnaia gazeta* were complaining that party leaders had been portrayed as "incapable, inexperienced, even foolish". Fadeev was always ready to submit to the party's will, became secretary-general of the Union of Soviet writers in 1946, and rewrote *Young Guard*, entirely removing suggestions of incompetence.

In the late 1940s Andrei Zhdanov was at the height of his powers; Fadeev's compliance was all too typical. A cycle of poems by Margerita Alliger, published at this time, was said by the critic Semen Tegub to be "full of diseased, despondent egoism – of oneself, for oneself, with oneself, 'how I feel' without perspective, without inspiration". Obediently, Alliger acknowledged her "mistakes", and revised the poems to stress courage and optimism, for her 1955 collection. Zhdanov had said: "Bolsheviks value literature highly. They see clearly its great historical mission and role in strengthening the moral and political unity of the nation".

Such sentiments might still have had some resonance in the Soviet Union 40 years after the Revolution, but not in some of the countries of central and eastern Europe, which had some experience of literary autonomy. The Czech novelist Bohumil Hrabal wrote his short story *An Ordinary Day* in 1953. It could not be published until after the fall of communism, because it reflected the attitudes of many whose "bourgeois" presuppositions could not be extinguished by ideology:

> I considered myself a citizen of this state and had not lifted a finger against it. I had done nothing except think freely, write, talk with friends. They'd have to operate on my skull to stop me thinking as I did, stop me loving or hating. No, no way could I live then, although I give to them what is Caesar's and what is mine I give myself and will continue to do so, myself, God, and man. But that's just the trouble, isn't it, they want it all, they think that everything, my thoughts, my innermost secrets, everything, even that which is human or divine should be Caesar's.

The Polish poet Zbigniew Herbert, speaking of the same period in an interview with Jacek Trznadel, recalled that he saw no end to Stalinism in his lifetime: "One has to choose internal emigration . . . When I was still a member of the Writers Union I told myself that I will never write anything according to party directions. I simply won't." A Romanian poet of the same generation, Maria Bauus, on the other hand, compared the early years of firm party direction favourably with that of the 1970s when censorship was said to have been abolished:

Previously, when censorship was official, openly there, you found on the manuscript the signs for what could not be printed. He would say, "Look, this can't be published for this or that reason" . . . At least it was pretty clear: this is OK, that is not. You made a compromise, he made another. You gave up a line, he allowed the poem to pass. The moment censorship was abolished, the first huge obstacle was the editor of the book. The publishing house was his living. If you persisted he could be left without a job.

Ana Blandiana, by contrast, exasperated by having to "write three, four, or five texts every week so that just one might be published in a literary review", resolved that she would never accept changes to her poetry: "I would rather forfeit the whole poem".

The "abolition" of censorship was never contemplated in the Soviet Union until the 1980s. Most writers and poets, never having known the possibility of free expression, continued to submit to party direction but, after the "thaw" of the 1950s and early 1960s, dissidence became a major theme of literary history. When Boris Pasternak published his *Doktor Zhivago* abroad in 1958 he was compared to "(a pig) who fouled the spot where he ate, and cast filth on those by whose labour he lives and breathes". Solzhenitsyn, having had official support for his *A Day in the Life of Ivan Denisovich* in 1962, lost it when he proposed the publication of *The First Circle*, and embarked on a long and direct confrontation which only ended when he was expelled from the Soviet Union in 1974. Lidiia Chukovskaia's *Sof'ia Petrovna* (written 1939–40), contracted for Soviet publication in 1964, fell foul of a renewed ban on works dealing with Stalinist repression, but was published abroad; the secretariat of the Writers Union resolved to expel her "with extensive press coverage". Under the pseudonym Abram Tertz, Andrei Siniavskii published abroad *A Voice from the Chorus*, his attack on socialist realism and plea for the autonomy of literature; along with Iulii Daniel', he was subjected to a show trial in 1966 and sentenced to hard labour. Looking back in 1980, after nine years in exile, Siniavskii noted the influence of dissident literature on official literature. He told Michael Scammell: "You have writers operating completely within the official limits who nevertheless write interesting works. And the state is obliged to tolerate them, because if they banned them completely they would all go straight into samizdat or emigrate to the West – the decision of so many writers to become dissidents is forcing the authorities to somewhat loosen the screws".

"Everything" by such writers as Ivan Klíma, Milan Kundera, Milan Uhde, and Ludvík Vaculík, all of whom had spoken for and rejoiced in the Prague Spring of 1968, were taken out of circulation during the years that followed. Czech literary dissidents had now to earn their living as window cleaners or taxi drivers, but some were published abroad by Josef Škvorecký (who established a Czech-language press in Toronto), and others at home in so-called Padlock editions, a form of Czech samizdat, perhaps the most developed in central Europe. The exiled writer Ota Filip, however, warned against "facile optimism": "The literary underground has the best critics in its ranks, but none of these can find it in his heart to slate an author who is now earning his living as an unskilled worker and has to do his writing in his spare time. The critical impulse is thus tempered by insight into human tragedy, losing its essential sharpness and irony". Meanwhile, as before 1968, "the more fervently an author follows the party line, the higher he stands in official estimation, the greater the praise lavished on him by the critics who do not even try to measure this 'progressive' literature with their own aesthetic yardstick, and of course the more money he earns" (*Neue Zuricher Zeitung*, 1–2 February 1975).

Many of the most eminent Polish writers could publish abroad without any of the penalties paid by their Soviet counterparts. At home, however, the poet Stanisław Barańczak reported that, from 1973 onwards, responsibility for the publication of unorthodox writings began to be seen not just as the author's, but a common responsibility of author, editor, publisher, printer, even proof reader. The very act of submitting an unorthodox manuscript to the censor could result in an editor's dismissal. Proof readers were adjured to be "ideologically vigilant". The result was, as intended, self-censorship, not dissimilar to that of Romania noted above. The fundamental taboos remained clear enough: nothing critical about Marxism-Leninism, the USSR, the police, or the army; but only by the experience of censorship could a writer know that he had offended certain other prohibitions: "You may not make too much use of words like 'democracy', 'freedom', 'tolerance', 'independence' or even 'face-saving' . . . you may not speak disrespectfully about Catherine the Great; you may not use the word 'totalitarianism'; you may not emphasize the role of the church in Polish history; you may not sink into pessimism and indulge in black humour". In response, Barańczak and other censored writers founded Zapis, a regular miscellany of work that could not be officially published; the Polish equivalent of samizdat.

At the eighth congress of Soviet writers in 1986, Evgenii Evtushenko demanded the opening of a Pasternak Museum, Andrei Voznesenskii called for the complete publication of works by Akhmatova, Pasternak, and Zamiatin. Glasnost had begun. Within four years, the works of Solzhenitsyn were freely available. Other communist countries followed suit and, by the end of the decade, literary censorship had virtually pre-deceased the system which had given rise to it. In all these countries, it is now possible, in theory, to publish anything – so long as its financial backers consider there is a market for it. Literary censorship has not wholly disappeared; it has merely changed its form.

Literature against ideology: East Asia

In the Chinese tradition, fiction and poetry had been less important than history and philosophy until around 1920 when, under the influence of the May Fourth Literature (an outgrowth of the modernizing May Fourth Movement) it was seen that literature could be used to promote national regeneration. Even less was there a tradition of literary dissidence. Li Chiang, a former Red Guard could write in *Le Monde* (26 February 1978):

> What do I have in common with Solzhenitsyn? I often wonder whether independent intellectuals in the Western sense have ever existed in China. In Chinese civilization, knowledge and power have always interlocked . . . it was the mastery of the classics which enabled one to become an official. Basically, little has changed; the only change is that there is a new canon of orthodoxy. The idea that the intellectual should perform the role of the critic towards those in power is inimical to Chinese civilization.

Dissidence – and consequent censorship – was not completely absent. The novelist and poet Ding Ling, though she was a convinced communist, criticized living conditions in areas controlled by the communists before the revolution; they were "like being shut in a dungeon, cut off from normal life". The beginnings of such independent observations provoked Mao Zedong to compose his "Talks at the Yan'an Forum on Literature and Art", in which, on the one hand, he asserted that there was no such thing as non-political literature, but on the other insisted that literature was to serve party ends. Unlike in Russia and central Europe, this was generally accepted in China. Such criticism as there was – it was allowed in 1956–57 for example – proceeded from a writer's membership of the party. Wang Meng's short story "Newcomer to the Organization Department" (1956) was about a young teacher, raised on films extolling the heroism of peasants and the revolution, who is sent to investigate conditions in a factory, and finds nothing but corruption and apathy; Lin Pin-yan's *Our Paper's Inside Story* (1956), similarly, describes the struggle of a newspaper reporter to file stories about conditions as they were rather than as the Party had laid down they should be. Even given that these conditions of relative freedom did not last long, it is hard to imagine that such stories would have been allowed in the Soviet Union at any time – those who were not with them were against them.

Until the Cultural Revolution of the 1960s, moreover, novelists and poets who stood out of line were mostly subjected to self-criticism sessions, or sent to the country to learn from the peasants rather than to the prisons and labour camps that might have been their fate in the Soviet Union. At the start of the Cultural Revolution in 1966, however, Tian Hian was named one of "four villains" (along with Zhou Yong, Yang Honshong, and Xia Yan), all of whom were imprisoned. Such old party stalwarts and veterans of the May Fourth Literature as Ding Ling, Ai Qing, Xiao Jun, and Hu Feng were actively persecuted, and sent off to labour camps in remote provinces. Of prerevolutionary novelists and poets, only Lu Hsun was allowed to be sold. Haroan, author of the optimistic *Bright Sunny Morning*, on the other hand, was praised as "the Gorki of China". After the publication of *The Second Handshake*, the story of the reactions of a group of scientists to the Cultural Revolution, the author Zhang Yong was arrested for spreading pornography. The following prospectus, couched as it is in wholly different terms, could have passed muster at various periods in the Soviet Union and east Europe:

Our publication (*Guan deng wei yei*) welcomes all manuscripts which . . . present revolutionary content in healthy ways. They must (1) Exalt the great chairman Mao with deep and warm proletarian feelings . . . (2) Follow the example of the modern revolutionary operas, zealously strive to create peasant and worker heroes, and (3) On the theme of the struggle between the two lines, reflect the people's revolutionary struggle.

Ding Ling had embodied, from the beginning, the tension which was allowed to come to the surface after the Cultural Revolution between party loyalty, revolutionary consciousness and creativity. She had written in 1950: "A writer is not like a child who cannot leave his nurse, he should grow independently. No matter how literary creation is guided, a work is created through an individual". Ding Ling was, however, disillusioned by the constant shifts of ideological orthodoxy. On the publication of works such as *The School Master* and *The Scar* in the late 1970s, she noted that "these young writers dare to speak out because they have not experienced as many twists and turns as we have. The older generation is used to keeping its mouth shut. We can no longer write as they do". Chen Johsi had been born in Taiwan, educated in the United States, but became an ardent supporter of Mao Zedong. Moving back to China during the Cultural Revolution, she was soon disillusioned. Her *Execution of Mayor Din and Other Stories*, published in 1979, was, by the standards of the time, certainly dissident, in that it was not written from a single point of view; that of officials who had to enforce the party line was given as much sympathetic treatment as that of individuals who wished to strike off on their own. Once again, there is a strong contrast with the dissident literature of the Soviet Union, which rarely gave a sympathetic voice to party hacks. Chen Jo-hsi, incidentally, refused to accept a Sun Yat-sen award from the Taiwanese government, in case it trapped her into too close an association with the authorities; Taiwanese censorship at this time was scarcely less severe than that on the Chinese mainland.

Ding Ling, Ai Qing, Hu Feng, and others were rehabilitated in the 1980s. The Cultural Revolution's wholesale dismissal of classic literature was reversed; it was accepted that works such as *Water Margin*, about rebellion against corrupt imperial officials, could be read as not wholly unsympathetic to communist ideas. Most surprising of all, and some years in advance of parallel actions in the Soviet Union. young writers were urged to study western writers, and massive reprints were ordered of works by Balzac, Chekhov, Dickens, Flaubert, Gogol, Heine, Ibsen, Pushkin, and Tolstoi.

At almost the same time, the opposite was taking place in the newly reunited Vietnam. Under Thanh doc, the "purification of culture", libraries and bookshops were being emptied of such "decadent foreign authors" as Albert Camus, Simone de Beauvoir, Erskine Caldwell, Herman Hesse, D.H. Lawrence, and Jean-Paul Sartre, and those Vietnamese novelists influenced by them, including Tran Sua Lam Le Xuyen and Nguyen thi Hoang, whose *Tay Hoc Tvo* (In the Arms of My Student), about a love affair between a student and teacher – a not uncommon occurrence in western universities – was considered to have promoted what amounted to incest. Carson McCullers and Somerset Maugham were said to encourage laziness and to ignore the miseries of their societies – as did, it was ruled, Dong Ho and Bong Ba Lin. Any novels which in any way opposed communism were removed; this list included works by Pearl Buck, André Gide, Boris Pasternak, and Arthur Koestler, as well as by Doan Quoc Sy, Hgiem Xuan Hong and Vu Dhas Khoan. Zola, Balzac, and Gor'kii, on the other hand, were considered healthy, constructive and progressive, as was Nguyen va Xuan's *Bao Rung* (Storm in the Forest) and the collection of poems by Mac Khai, *Mot The Ky Can Tho* (One Century, One Poem).

Following the earlier Chinese pattern, many of the novelists and poets from the former South Vietnam, condemned during the "purification" process, were sent for extensive re-education. Others were imprisoned: Hoang Hai Thu for publishing under a pseudonym, and for having translated into Vietnamese Solzhentisyn's *First Circle* and *Gulag Archipelago*, and Nguyen Chi Thien, who, in 1979, had thrown the manuscript of his poems through the gates of the British Embassy in Hanoi, in the (probably vain) hope that they might be published abroad.

Two years later, the "Barefoot Literary Group" of literary dissidents were complaining that "not a single work of art or literature has been produced which is worth talking about next to the great intellectual currents of modern times". They would not accept that "the creative work of writers and artists should be assimilated to that of 'bureaucrats and flunkies', nor that their productions should be required to conform with orders from above". They appealed to "our elders": "together we can defend and enrich our four thousand year old traditions".

Literature against injustice: Middle East, Latin America, and North Africa

The 11th century Islamic theologian Abu Hamid al-Ghazali warned poets: "Do not mix with princes and sultans. Do not see them. For in seeing them and associating with them is a great problem. If circumstances necessitate such contacts, then leave their praise and their flattering". Few Arab poets have taken his advice; in the second half of the 20th century as previously, poetry and politics have been inextricable. Roger Hardy wrote in 1980 that the Arab poet was "a public figure, the spokesman of a tribe, the mouthpiece of government against public, or of faction against faction. Throughout the Arab world, countless writers are in exile or in jail, or on a government payroll". The Egyptian novelist Nawal al-Saddawi told the London Conference on Censorship in 1984: "From my experience as a writer of fiction I believe that nothing is non-political. Even those who claim they're non-political are political, though in a very subtle and disguised way". In the communist countries, writing about the regime was, perforce, usually indirect; in Arab countries, it has been committed and direct, and has been treated as such.

The key political event in post-War Arab history was Israel's humiliation of Arab countries in the Six Day War of 1967. It gave rise to al-Adab al-Huzairani, the June Literature, well summed up by the Syrian poet Nizar Qabbani: "My grieved country/in a flash/You changed me from a poet who wrote love poems/To a poet who writes with a knife". His *Footnotes to the Book of the Setback* could only circulate in samizdat, and Qabbani himself could only exist as poet and publisher in the comparative safety of Lebanon. During the 1970s and early 1980s, the military censors of Israel took the view that any

Arab poetry was potentially subversive. That included selections from Qabbani and Mahmud Darwish, whose appearance in the collection *Adab al-Muqawama fi Filastin al-Muhtalla* (1966, Literature of Resistance in Occupied Palestine) alerted them to the power of his verse, which was soon translated into many other languages; harassed and imprisoned, he left the occupied territories in 1971. Such works as *Palestinian Poetry and the Tragedy of Palestine*, *Modern Arab Poetry*, and *Contemporary Arabic Literature in Palestine, 1860–1960*, as well as *Critical Studies in Modern Arabic Literature* all remained on the Israeli list of banned books. Elias Freij, the mayor of Bethlehem, noted how arbitrary was this censorship; the removal of "so many books in our native tongue left our bookshops and libraries very bare".

Elsewhere, Arab poets wrote about social conditions in their own countries. Ahmed Fouad Negm, a former labourer on Egyptian railways and a rural postman, attacked "the malaise of forbearance". He was imprisoned in 1959, 1969, and 1978. He could write in "Prohibitions": "Forbidden to discuss/forbidden to keep silent/And every hour in your life/the prohibitions grow". Soon afterwards he was imprisoned for a poem said to be "humiliating to the head of state", although president Sadat was not mentioned by name. Nor did the Syrian Muhi al-Din Lazibani refer directly to president Assad when, in 1971, he won first prize at a conference of young Arab poets for his poem attacking dictatorships and military regimes; within 24 hours he had been arrested and the poem condemned as "insulting to the public". On his release, he was made to go through the poem line by line, in a manner not unlike Chinese self-criticism, and to suffer further accusations of "hostility to religion", and "incitement of the masses". From then on unable to obtain work, he went into exile. In an interview he concluded: "They seem to be afraid of the written word, especially poetry. I think it is because our people respond to poetry, and it has always played an important part in political struggle. All opposition slogans are taken from poetry". In Iraq, on the other hand, every effort was made by Saddam Hussein to persuade poets to write verse for official occasions, praising the Ba'th Party and its leaders. Midhoffar al-Nawab, committed to writing about the sufferings of the peasants, declined to be so incorporated, and was forced into exile; had he stayed, he would undoubtedly have perished.

The Moroccan poets Abdellatif Laabi and Abdullah Zerrika fell foul of king Hassan in the 1970s. Both belonged to the Marxist-Leninist Frontiste movement. Both were firmly anti-monarchist. After he had been sentenced to ten years imprisonment for "conspiracy against the state" in 1972, Laabi wrote: "My friends/you have often wondered/how I got into this situation/how a poet/can descend from his clouds/walk on earth/and become a fighter ... my passion was devouring /it destroyed all urge for comfort/all the privileges brought me /by the condition of an intellectual". He spoke for many.

Latin America, different to the Middle East in so many respects, at least shares a 20th-century tradition of close relationships between politics and literature. Some major novelists and poets – Carlos Fuentes, Gabriel García Márquez, Pablo Neruda, Octavio Paz – have served their countries diplomatically; one, Mario Vargas Llosa, stood for the presidency of Peru; another, Ernesto Cardenal, became minister of culture after the Nicaraguan revolution of 1979. Vargas Llosa wrote in 1977: "In Peru, in Bolivia, in Nicaragua et cetera ... to be a writer means at the same time to assume a social responsibility; at the same time that you develop a personal literary work, you should serve, through your writing, but also through your actions, as an active participant in the solution of the economic, political and cultural problems of your society". Because of ubiquitous press censorship, "the realm of imagination became in Latin America the kingdom of objective reality; fiction became a substitute for social science, our best teachers about reality were dreamers, the literary artists".

Vargas Llosa, an early supporter of the Cuban revolution, moved to the centre of Peruvian politics, disillusioned by Cuba's perennially low level of freedom of expression. Elsewhere, socialism has been a convenient stick with which to beat dissident novelists and poets. The Paraguayan novelist Augusto Roa Bastos had to go into exile as early as 1947, because his work with the Guerani-speaking peasants was considered dangerous in this regard; he had never been a member of any political party, but when he briefly returned to the country in 1983, he was expelled as a "Marxist subversive". In exile from 1951, the Argentine novelist Julio Cortázar not only maintained "magical realism", the literary style for which Latin America became most notable during the second half of the 20th century, but also became a more committed socialist as he observed from afar the political distortions of the continent. Most of his work was banned in Argentina for that reason; yet he demanded "of no writer that he make himself a tribune of the struggle being waged against imperialism in its many forms; but I do demand that he be a witness of his own time ... that in his work or in his life (how can they be separated?) he be a witness in his own way".

The "way" of many was direct. The Uruguayan poet Mario Benedetti wrote in the early 1970s of the emergence of "protest poetry" – poetry which was specifically *revolucionaria*, *guerillana*, or *subversiva*, archetypally committed poetry. The El Salvadorean Roque Dalton, the author of *Poemas clandestinas*, acted on the belief that "literature as a calling holds the same risks as any other activity in society". The Nicaraguan poet-priest Ernesto Cardenal wrote the "documentary" poem *Zero Hour*, finally becoming committed to the violent overthrow of the Somoza government. Perhaps more subtly, Eduardo Galleano spoke of the Argentine authorities' "hatred" of the poet Juan Gelman, even as late as 1987, five years after the overthrow of that country's most recent dictatorship: "Juan's poems commit the unpardonable crime of marrying justice with beauty ... It isn't done. He isn't being realistic". Gelman, whose works remained banned, was charged with being a member of an illegal organization, the Monteneros.

In Argentina, Chile, and Uruguay, novelists and poets were among the many who "disappeared" during the 1970s. Many others were forced into exile; as the Chilean novelist José Donono, exiled in 1973, wrote in 1980: "the terror of those first years was not only the terror of being killed, it was also the problem of being intolerant of an intolerable situation". His compatriot, the novelist Isabel Allende, also in exile, resigned herself to the idea that "*The House of the Spirits* [1992] would not be read in my country ... that story which speaks of injustice, fear and suffering in a country like ours". In fact the novel entered the country minus its covers and split into parts in the suitcases of different travellers. Copies were made, and were passed from hand to hand until the book finally entered the country legally – and topped the bestseller lists.

Beneficent censorship?

The German poet Heinrich Heine notoriously exclaimed after the (temporary) abolition of censorship in 1848: "Ach! I can't write anymore. How can I write when there's no longer any censorship? How should a man who's always lived with censorship suddenly be able to write about it? All style will cease, the whole grammar, the good habits". He elaborated in *The Romantic School*: "Writers suffering under conditions of censorship and intellectual constraints of all kinds, who nevertheless cannot silence the promptings of their hearts are particularly dependent upon humorous and ironic modes of expression. These are the sole outlets still open to the honest man. In fact, it is through such dissimulation that honesty reveals itself in the most striking manner."

The argument has broadened during the 20th century. The Argentine writer Jorge Luis Borges took the view that censorship could help literature, teaching it how to cultivate subtlety and understatement. George Steiner, speaking on the Channel 4 television programme *Voices* in 1983, contrasted what he believed to be the pettiness and degeneracy of "western" writing, where there had been no literary censorship to match the scale of that encountered in central Europe, the Soviet Union, and Latin America, with the unquestionable quality of novels and poetry emanating from these countries since the 1950s.

Critics of Steiner have granted that, in the words of the journalist Neal Ascherson, "those writers (knew) more about extremes of good and evil than the mild, alienated westerner, and they also knew infinitely more about the nature of compromise and irony, of the importance and difficulty of simply behaving decently and attempting to preserve an ethic of truth". Ascherson noted however that, for example, little writing of any quality emerged from Czechoslovakia before Milan Kundera's *The Joke* in 1967. And the exiled Russian poet Joseph Brodsky pointed out that alongside the great writings of Pasternak and Solzhenitsyn, there was produced a considerable quantity of trash, which easily passed the censors.

In 1986, the El Salvadorean poet and novelist Claribel Alegría, who was forced into exile, dismissed as "absolute nonsense" the idea that poetry flourishes under repressive regimes; if this was occasionally so in the past it was "simply because the highly efficient, modern machinery of repression had not been brought to perfection". The Polish novelist Tadeusz Konwicki acknowledged in 1986 that "a censor can mobilize a writer to create ways of by-passing censorship ... but if, for years, everything one writes is at some stage taken to an anonymous office where some anonymous person, whom one never sees, submits it to some form of manipulation, there comes a moment when one starts to see red". The Hungarian novelist György Konrád has similarly written of the "slowly enveloping fatigue" of censorship, its "heavy atmospheric pressure".

Few would disagree with Steiner that major works of universal cultural importance were produced in these countries despite, and sometimes because of, "heavy atmospheric pressure". Twenty years later new censorial atmospheres have emerged, in which the very idea of universal culture appears to be denied. In 2001, a committee of teachers appointed by the education department in Gauteng province, which includes Johannesburg, South Africa, recommended that the works of Shakespeare be banned from classrooms because they "lack cultural diversity". *Julius Caesar* was said to "elevate men"; *Antony and Cleopatra* and *The Taming of the Shrew* to be "undemocratic and racist"; *Hamlet* to be "not optimistic or uplifting", and *King Lear* to lack "the power to excite readers", to be "full of violence and despair". The report was dismissed as not representative of government policy, but the fact that it could have been written at all caused considerable unease in some quarters. In Spring 2001, it was not yet clear whether the recommended bans would be enacted. This survey has shown that they would not be entirely unprecedented.

DEREK JONES

Further Reading

Alvarez, A., *Under Pressure: The Writer in Society: Eastern Europe and the USA*, London: Penguin, 1965

Ascherson, Neal, "Opinion", *Index on Censorship*, 12/1 (April 1983)

Baraheni, Reza, "The Perils of Publishing", *Index on Censorship*, 7/5 (September–October 1978)

Barańczak, Stanisław, "Introducing Zapis", *Index on Censorship*, 16/10 (November–December 1977)

Coetzee, J.M., *Giving Offense: Essays on Censorship*, Chicago: University of Chicago Press, 1996

Connolly, Peter, *No Bland Facility: Selected Writings on Literature, Religion and Censorship*, Gerards Cross, Buckinghamshire: Smythe, 1991

Eastman, Max, *Artists in Uniform: A Study of Literature and Bureaucratism*, New York: Knopf, and London: Allen and Unwin, 1934

Ermolaev, Herman, *Censorship in Soviet Literature, 1917–1991*, Lanham, Maryland: Rowman and Littlefield, 1997

Gay, Peter, *The Bourgeois Experience: Victoria to Freud*, vol. 1: *Education of the Senses*, New York and Oxford: Oxford University Press. 1984

Goldman, Merle, *Literary Dissent in Communist China*, Cambridge, Massachusetts: Harvard University Press, 1967

Ho Truong An, "Vietnam's Cultural Purge", *Index on Censorship*, 7/4 (July–August 1978)

Konwicki, Tadeusz, "The Delights of Writing under Censorship", *Index on Censorship*, 15/3 (March 1986)

Kundera, Milan, "Comedy Is Everywhere", *Index on Censorship*, 6/5 (November–December 1977)

Loseff, Lev, *On the Beneficence of Censorship: Aesopian Language in Modern Russian Literature*, Munich: Sagner, 1984

Meyer, Doris (editor), *Lives on the Line: The Testimony of Contemporary Latin American Authors*, Berkeley: University of California Press, 1988

Miłosz, Czesław, *The Captive Mind*, New York: Knopf, and London: Secker and Warburg, 1953

Phillips, John, *Forbidden Fictions: Pornography and Censorship in Twentieth-Century French Literature*, London: Pluto Press, 1999

Putnam, George Haven, *The Censorship of the Church of Rome and Its Influence upon the Production and Distribution of Literature*, 2 vols, New York and London: Putnam, 1906–07

Rubin, Jay, *Injurious to Public Morals: Writers and the Meiji State*, Seattle: University of Washington Press, 1984

Scammell, Michael, "Interview with Iosif Brodsky", *Index on Censorship*, 1/3–4 (Autumn–Winter 1972)

Siniavskii, Andrei, "Samizdat and the Rebirth of Literature", *Index on Censorship*, 9/4 (August 1980)

Steiner, George, *Language and Silence: Essays on Language, Literature, and the Inhuman*, New York: Atheneum, and London: Faber, 1967

Swayze, Harold, *Political Control of Literature in the USSR, 1946–1959*, Cambridge, Massachusetts: Harvard University Press, 1962

Vianu, Lidia, *Censorship in Romania*, Budapest: Central European University Press, 1998

Weissbort, Daniel (editor), *The Poetry of Survival: Post-war Poets of Central and Eastern Europe*, London: Anvil Press, and New York: St Martin's Press, 1990

LITERATURE AND THE LAW

Since therefore the knowledge and survey of vice is in this world so necessary to the constituting of human virtue, and the scanning of error to the confirmation of truth, how can we more safely, and with less danger, scout into the regions of sin and falsity, than by reading all manner of tractates, and hearing all manner of reason? And this is the benefit which may be had of books promiscuously read.

In this often-cited passage from *Areopagitica* (1644), John Milton summarizes his central argument for freedom of the press: since, he insists, we need some awareness of vice in order to be virtuous, reading takes on an extraordinarily important role. Reading, the private engagement of one individual mind with another, functions as a proxy for other kinds of experience; Milton's reader can "safely . . . scout into the regions of sin and falsity", and thus, presumably, be more effective in

avoiding those regions in other aspects of his life. Writing in 1644, Milton was protesting against a licensing order issued the previous year by parliament. In effect, the order had put into place a system of prior restraint, requiring that all English publications carry an indication that they had been licensed by parliament. Since he argues against the parliamentary order by which he had himself been targeted, the 17th-century writer imagines a modern reading process and a modern reader. This is a reader whose capacity for discernment can not only be relied upon, but can only be strengthened through exposure to "all manner of tractates and all manner of reason", one who will not mistake text for reality, and whose moral development can only be hindered by having the texts available to him mediated by government censors. Readers can be trusted to decide for themselves; they do not need the law to tell them what they can and cannot read.

Milton's argument has often been put forward in defence of

freedom of the press from legal constraints. The legal history of censorship, however, tells us that it has often been precisely those categories that make *Areopagitica* seem so modern and with which Milton defied a government in turbulent transition that came to be enormously problematic for later governments, judges, and students of jurisprudence. Once one supposes that the subjects of a given legal system are individuals, that reading is a private process and not a matter to be guided by religious authority, one also comes to see that in diverse ways this practice of reading can have real-world effects – and not always, in the eyes of governments at least, the salutory ones described by Milton. Examining the relations between law, literature, and censorship, we see the same questions arise: questions of the effects of reading, of morality, of the extent of law's dominion over the minds of those who are subject to it. However, they are posed quite differently depending on the geographical location, political context, and historical moment. The essay that follows will outline some of these broad issues, attempting to situate the complexity of relations between literature and the state that are raised by censorship. As it does so, it will draw on some specific examples, many of which come from the Anglo-American legal traditions; the examples, therefore, are by no means exhaustive and should be seen as illustrating general points in order to guide comparative investigations into the topic.

While state censorship is today often seen as the province of explicitly repressive regimes, it is historically inextricable from the rise of print culture and from the notion of the author as an individual solely responsible for his or her work, capable of attaining fame in the minds of numerous other individuals who read the work and the name affixed to it. Thus, as J.M. Coetzee writes, "since copyright law would not arrive until the eighteenth century, what forced the [early modern] writer to accept definition as a legal entity – to become an author with all the legal responsibilities thereby entailed – was the institution and the power of censorship." In *Areopagitica*, we see how complex this could become: Milton asserts himself as an author with the right to communicate with readers who likewise have the right to read precisely at the moment he is under parliamentary petition for having violated the law by publishing his tracts on divorce without having sought licensing. This in fact made him rather notorious. The larger point to be made here, however, is that as accustomed as we may be to thinking of the law and the writer as autonomous and often opposed entities, their relations have often been far more intricate. The law not only constitutes authorship, through censorship and copyright, but in the history of its agonistic relations with the author, law has taken upon itself the power to demarcate – or not – between the name of the author and his or her body, or between that body and the text.

As modern an example of the relations between the writer and the law as Milton can appear, it was not until the Enlightenment that law was instituted as the primary means of social organization in Western culture. During this period, a crucial distinction in censorship jurisprudence emerged: that between prior restraint and post-publication censorship. For instance, English common law understood freedom of the press as freedom from prior restraint. Thus in Blackstone's *Commentaries* we read that "every free man has an undoubted right to lay

what sentiment he pleases before the public", an apparent reversal of the 17th-century licensing disputes and an opinion seemingly consistent with Milton's. But what is crucial for Blackstone is the displacement of a civil sanction in favour of criminal prosecution; the way to suppress writers and publishers of offensive matter was to prosecute them criminally. In this instance, we see Enlightenment thinking on the subject move from restricting the circulation of texts themselves to the bodies and goods of those individuals legally responsible for them. On one reading, this seems to diffuse in some way the authority of the state over published materials. Yet since it claims centralized authority over publication, the state emerges as a more coercive authority, demanding that writers and publishers police themselves at the risk of criminal prosecution. "The law, including the law of censorship, has a dream", wrote Coetzee. "In this dream, the daily round of identifying and punishing malefactors will wither away; the law and its constraints will be so deeply engraved on the citizenry that individuals will police themselves. Censorship looks forward to the day when writers will censor themselves and the censor himself can retire". Of course, as the censors of oppressive regimes from pre-Revolutionary France to pre-1989 Czechoslovakia would attest, this is an entirely impractical dream. Centralized censorship, whether operating on a model of prior restraint or post-publication or some combination thereof, is hard work; it involves an ever more extensive bureaucratic structure, and it indirectly encourages black markets in pamphlets, books, and newspapers, making control all the more difficult.

The First Amendment to the constitution of the United States was passed by the First Congress in response to widespread concern about governmental involvement in publishing. "Congress shall make no law . . . abridging freedom of the press", it says in part. But the meaning of this is by no means transparent, as US jurisprudence from the 18th century to the present day demonstrates. Does no law mean no law at all? Or does it mean no federal law, leaving state legislatures to abridge freedom of the press as they see fit? The First Amendment was originally intended to condemn English laws that had been used to harass colonial dissidents, laws fresh in the minds of the framers of the constitution. Not only did it mean that there should be no prosecutions for "seditious libel", such as those that the Crown had engaged against colonial agitators for independence, but that there should be neither government licensing system, nor stamp taxes such as those used to suppress the circulation of newspapers and pamphlets. If the members of the newly established nation – or at least their founding fathers – sought to affirm positively the value of a free press, however, by the 19th century some of those values came into question. What was the extent of the First Amendment? Did it mean that all forms of speech were protected? Or were there some forms of expression that were not? The postal system then emerged as the principal site of struggle over censorship in the United States, to remain thus into the 20th century.

By 1836 the US Abolitionist movement was gaining strength, assisted by an array of the like-minded from Europe. Although still a comparatively small group, it was vocal and questioned a status quo that many Americans, including those in power, would prefer to have left uninterrogated. President Andrew Jackson was infuriated that these radicals, calling for the end of slavery, would be circulating their ideas via pamphlets and tracts courtesy of the US Government Postal Service. He asked the Congress to give the Postal Service the power to destroy abolitionist literature wherever it found it. The bill was rejected in both houses, accompanied by horrified comments on the part of some Congressmen. Passing Jackson's bill would open the way to using the still relatively new national Postal Service for precisely the political censorship the First Amendment had been framed to prevent. At the same time, however, the repudiation of Jackson's bill opened the field for questions that would persist: to what extent and under what conditions might the government censor what it carries in the mail?

During the 19th century there was an increase in literacy rates and in urbanization; industrial capitalism developed across Europe and in the United States. Imperialist endeavours were consolidated and thinking about the concept of nationhood and its parameters with them. The Enlightenment image of a relatively small reading public of middle- and upper-class men was giving way to an array of diverse groups of new readers: notably workers and women, but also children, principally those of the middle classes. The reader imagined by Milton, who could be trusted to sample all sorts of texts with virtuous discernment, was increasingly less imaginable by those concerned with the "social problems" presented by the modern industrial city. It was becoming clear that modern legal censorship could work indirectly, through state intervention into educational practices, for example. In 1803 a Prussian decree proclaimed that "the children of the working class are to read the catechism Bible and hymn book, to fear and love God and act accordingly, to honour authority. Whoever attempts to stuff them with more than this sets himself a useless and thankless task." Yet governmental understandings of education law varied as the century wore on; during the July monarchy in France in 1830, François Guizot encouraged primary education to the lower classes on the grounds that "the less enlightened the multitude, the more amenable it is to being misled and subverted".

In a revolutionary century, concern focused around the printed word: throughout the century of upheaval in France, for example, battles were waged time and again for freedom of the press. In 1789 the royal censors were deposed with the rest of the *ancien régime*, but after Thermidor restrictions returned. In 1810 the canny Napoleon, aware of how tenuous his power might be under a free press, put into place a strict new censorship code. This was a system of prior restraint: publishers were required to submit galley proofs to the imperial censorship prior to publication. Germaine Necker de Staël, the novelist and essayist, was about to see her work *De L'Allemagne* published when she found that the essay would be suppressed by the censor. On the face of it, *De l'Allemagne* is a discourse designed simply to introduce educated French readers to important German philosophical currents; in fact, initially the censor saw nothing wrong with it as a discussion of fairly obscure German Romantic thought. But the text had circulated via the salon culture prior to publication and the censor was given to understand that it was being read among the elite as a critique, a glorification of German culture with implicit negative comparisons to the French. Although the earlier parts of the text had been passed through the censor-

ship, it was abruptly suppressed. Despite de Staël's efforts to defend her work before the emperor, Napoleon demanded her exile. Her publisher, having already printed the first edition, went bankrupt. As she described events in a preface later appended to the book,

> at the moment when this work was about to appear, and when the ten thousand copies of the first edition had been actually printed, the Minister of Police . . . sent his officers to the house of the bookseller with orders to tear the whole edition to pieces, and to place sentinels at the different entrances of the warehouses for fear a single copy of this dangerous writing should escape.

A few copies indeed had already escaped and were safe in the hands of the German philosopher August Schlegel; the book eventually saw a new first edition in London several years later.

The example of *De l'Allemagne* and its author is suggestive of some central aspects of modern state censorship. Napoleon's persecution of a book read as politically threatening extended not simply to the suppression of a given text, but to the banishment of the author herself and the economic destruction of the publisher. *De l'Allemagne* was suppressed in France because it questioned the idea of nation and empire that Napoleon sought to install and it did so by praising the national culture of the neighbouring Germans.

The story of *De l'Allemagne* also conveys something of the particular situation of the literary in terms of censorship; where works of avowedly literary discourse are concerned, whether philosophical, belle-lettristic, or fictional, the censorship finds itself confronted with the choice of either over-reading – and thus putting forward an interpretation of a text that is arguable or even nonsensical – or under-reading, taking the text at face value, and perhaps missing the point. If censorship under-reads, it can look as if it does not know its job. Clearly Napoleon's censor realized, at the last minute, that he had committed such an error, thereby sending a message of incompetence to his employer on the one hand and to de Staël and other authors who might want to write critically of the government on the other.

State censorship in the 19th century came to be inextricably bound to the process that Benedict Anderson has described as "imagining" nationhood. As the idea, first advanced by the German philosopher Gottfried Herder, of national cultures grounded in a shared language and thus literature took hold, political boundaries came to be articulated with imaginary ones; a nation's identity could be buttressed and perhaps even instituted through its cultural products. Thus, for example, Guizot's working-class children could have French culture inculcated in them through their supervised reading, could become safely "French". But as this example also suggests, if the nation's fate was inextricable from that of the ever-expanding mass of readers, forms of control over these new reading publics would need to be devised.

The focus in the English and American legal systems during this period concentrated less on explicitly political censorship; in the American context, as we have seen, this seemed ruled out by the First Amendment and a crucial precedent was set by Congress's refusal of Jackson's bill. Instead attention turned to the matter of obscenity. As has often been the case in the history of censorship, claims were made for the protection of the public good. Here, though, we see a crucial shift by the middle of the 19th century; whereas there had been some common law tradition against blasphemy and obscenity in England and a few statutes on the books in New England against the diffusion of material deemed obscene, these cases had generally been prosecuted as disturbances of the peace or similar infractions. In other words, they were understood as behavioural infractions by particular individuals. But by the mid-19th century, the legal emphasis came to be not so much on the defendant's conduct but on the potential impact of the materials he or she was diffusing.

The much-vaunted Victorian concern over sexuality and obscenity played out in the courts as legal disputes over censorship. But it is important to see that very often what was at stake in these concerns was by no means simple prudery or naive Freudian-style sexual repression. For Victorian America and Britain, political concerns came to be articulated as concerns for "mental hygiene", anxieties about sexuality, gender difference, and the family. The nation could be understood, increasingly, as a nation of consumers of mass-produced images and texts; it could also be understood as a nation of urbanizing workers. If the image of the middle-class family, securely raising its children apart from the hustle-and-bustle of the marketplace, came to take on new ideological weight at this time, this must be seen against the image of the "dangerous classes", the anonymous urban masses that provoked fears, named and unnamed, of untrammeled desires, unclean habits, and contagion. No one had forgotten the lessons of Paris in 1789.

In 1857 the Lord Chief Justice John Campbell introduced the Obscene Publications Act in the British parliament, legislation spurred by his dismay at the circulation of materials "printed in Paris" and "more deadly than arsenic". Stored in London, the materials found a ready distribution network: back alleys, travelling salesmen, through the mail via advertisement. Opposition to the Act raised one of the critical questions: there was no legal definition of "obscenity" put forth in it or for that matter anywhere else in English law. The Tariff Act of 1842 was pointed to; the Americans were now confiscating art books that described putti in Italian sculpture and paintings. Surely Lord Campbell did not want this ridiculous practice emulated in his own country? Lord Lyndhurst reviewed excerpts from Restoration comedy, classical literature, and Shakespeare to illustrate his point that just about anything could fall under this bill's province, given the lack of clear definitions of obscenity. The bill was nonetheless passed.

Ten years later, the Obscene Publications Act was interpreted in a way that created a legal precedent for censorship law in both England and the United States. In *Regina* v. *Hicklin*, the defendant was brought to law for selling an anti-Catholic tract that he had also written and published. Hicklin was part of a campaign to keep Roman Catholics out of parliament and his tract depicted the depravity of Catholics by discussing in straightforward terms the vices of the confessional as he perceived them. The potential of the confessional for titillation had a long history and its representation as a site of depraved sexuality was not new. In *Hicklin*, the question revolved around the purpose of the representation: did Hicklin mean simply to induce sexual excitement in his readers or did he, as he claimed, have the goal of persuading his readers of the vices of the confessional and preserving the nation from the harms of depraved Catholics? His defence claimed that in order to achieve his rhetorical goal, Hicklin was obliged to instantiate with description the practices of priest and penitent, examples he could document amply. He had had to include objectionable material in order to prove a legitimate argument. Besides, argued the defence, these allegedly obscene passages constituted only a small percentage of the work as a whole.

The court's response began here: every passage in a book must be judged independently of every other passage; if any excerpt was judged in isolation to be obscene, it would be judged contraband, even if in its general argument and message the rest of the book were unobjectionable. The law in *Hicklin* emphasized what it termed the "tendency" of the printed word to corrupt or deprave; regardless of the larger discursive or narrative context in which it appeared, a single word or group of words in print could have what seemed to be an almost immediate imprinting effect on the minds of readers. The law furthermore would presume that any printed matter intended for public distribution could fall into the hands of children or others especially susceptible to the power of print. This was a group the court imagined to be a large one; implicitly it included newer groups of readers, young women, mothers of families, workers, and assorted other potentially dangerous minds. The law now saw itself as protector of these groups from the emergent perils of mass culture, especially those entailed in the power of print media.

Hicklin became standard not just in the English courts; in America, state legislatures enacted statutes using the Campbell Obscene Publications Act as a model and the courts adopted *Hicklin*, sometimes assuming it was an ancient common law precedent, in their reading of them. For a time, the power of print that so concerned the English court took a backseat in American jurisprudence to a concern about images; with the daguerrotype and photograph making images easily reproducible and diffusible, the Act of 1842 was amended in the 1850s specifically to name these as among the dangerous types of images that could not be imported. In the post-Civil War decades, the US Postal Service was given more and more leeway to censor the mails. In 1865 a bill was passed that authorized postmasters to confiscate obscene matter when it could be detected without breaking open sealed parcels and envelopes. This piece of legislation set the scene for the entry into public life of Anthony Comstock, who had for some time been perusing the back pages of newspapers and magazines, looking for suspicious advertisements, and upon ordering some of the "fancy books", turning them over to US marshals. Among the arrests he had instigated were those of the feminist agitator, journalist, and stockbroker Victoria Woodhull and her sister Tennessee Claffin, on the grounds that they had printed in their weekly newspaper allegations of adultery on the part of Henry Ward Beecher. Woodhull and Claffin were not only feminists, who would take part in the suffragist movement; they were also advocates of free love. It was Ward Beecher's hypocrisy that bothered them, not his extramarital activity. Ultimately the prosecution was dropped, but Comstock was made only more fierce in his desire to clamp down on the dirty.

Comstock now lobbied for an expanded law that would suppress circulation not only of books, but also gadgets and articles deemed obscene, advertisements, and all information on contraception, abortion, or instruments to be used for such purposes. Ultimately, what became known as the Comstock Act was passed in 1873. It expanded the powers of Congress and the Post Office enormously. According to it, no publications of any sort deemed obscene, lewd, or lascivious could be carried in the mails; anyone who knowingly sent or received these things would be subject to criminal prosecutions carrying penalties of up to 10 years in prison. Another part of this omnibus legislation dealt with importation; a redraft of the Tariff Act of 1842, it added to the list of images that could not be imported into the US books and pamphlets. Congress was asked to ban the importation of all foreign literature that might be deemed to be obscene.

Clearly Comstock and the prior legislation that enabled it were dangerously close to gutting the First Amendment. But for Congress, at least those members who passed the bill into law, the legal question was posed differently: was the US Postal Service and Customs obliged under the law to carry materials deemed obscene? In other words, citizens were protected under the First Amendment to say and write anything they wanted; the government was just not obliged to carry it for them. Comstock left open at least two significant legal questions: first, was this purely a criminal statute? Or did it also intend to authorize the postal service in an independent censorship operation? Second, were the criteria for obscenity clearly enough articulated? How was anyone to be clear on what constituted potentially harmful materials? Senator Casserly of California objected: "I do not know whether it can be left to employees of a custom house to determine with safety what kind of literature or what sort of matter is to be admitted."

Meanwhile the Comstock Act set the stage for the Hicklin standard to be imported into US law. In the 1870s, Comstock instigated the arrest of a fellow named Bennett, the author and publisher of a variety of free love and political books and pamphlets. Here, the two important aspects of Hicklin were brought to bear. The jury was instructed to read only the marked excerpts; if any one of them was found obscene the whole book was obscene. And obscenity was defined as in Hicklin: if the designated passages "tend to deprave the minds of those open to such influences" the jury should vote for Bennett's guilt. Bennett was convicted and served time in prison for circulating obscene materials.

It is far from established that Congress's intent for the Comstock Act was to authorize the Postal Service to become a censorship bureau. But in the years after the bill's passage, it became clear that this was what had happened. In the social and political context of the time, it was, furthermore, far from clear that prosecutions like that of Bennett could be understood purely as attempts to weed out "dirty" pictures and books. First, the obscenity standard was by no means lucidly defined. From one standpoint it was hopelessly subjective: how could any individual determine what was likely to harm anyone else when what was at stake were texts and images? And what constituted harm in this instance? How is a harm effected through reading and looking? More ominously perhaps, Hicklin invited not so much individual whim in determining the potentiality

for harm but rather a coercive consensus wherein the attitudes of a minority of good bourgeois men would designate for the rest of society what it was unable to read or see. And yet another point should be made here: in the second half of the century, "free love" positions were often held by those who also held unpopularly liberal political and religious views, including avowed atheists. The Hicklin standard, read into the Comstock Act, potentially authorized the censorship of minority political and religious stands and arguably worked to create the image of state morality, silencing all but those who would adhere to it.

By the end of the 19th century, expurgation, or as it had come to be known "bowdlerization", became the way around the Comstock law and the Hicklin standard. The instability of the obscenity criteria led such works as Tolstoy's Kreutzer Sonata, a novella with adultery and murder for themes, to be censored when it was serialized in a reputable newspaper. The attorney general upheld the privilege of the Post Office to refuse to carry whatever it saw as obscene; the newspaper publisher had no choice but to expurgate the problem passages or cease carrying the serial. The effect of publishing a literary work with pieces of text deleted is not dissimilar to that of hanging a painting with chunks of the image cut away.

The 19th-century history of legal censorship not only tells about the links between the assertion of boundaries of national culture and the imagining of that nation in terms of a small minority legislating the morality of those presumed susceptible to outside influences. It also begins to tell us another story about law and literature; that is, censorship in the law has had a significant role in the shaping of literary canons. Literary canons include the works usually taught in schools, given to students as examples of particular modes or genres. Up until relatively recently, at least, students were often instructed that these works were in some sense "classics", and that they achieved this status after having withstood the test of time, being read and appreciated for generations on account, presumably, of their excellence. This description proved to be problematic in many regards. One central way of rethinking canons is to see them as composed of works that have withstood not so much the test of time, as the vicissitudes of the censor.

Since national literatures have a legitimating function, they likewise have had a great deal to do with state censorship; through most of the 20th century, for instance, George Sand was known as the author of pastoral tales appropriate for children – as the narrator of Proust's À la Recherche du Temps Perdu reminds us as he recounts his childhood experience of them. But in her lifetime, Sand was known not only as the author of racy novels concerned with women's sexual and social freedom, but also as one of the most famous of European novelists, who influenced Dostoevskii and Flaubert among others. Under the Second Empire, her work was censored for both its political content – Sand was a socialist and her politics are quite legible in several of her novels – and its sexual content. Thus George Sand passed into history as a promiscuous and notorious woman writer, whose celebrity image seemed more intriguing than her "children's tales", the only works of hers available to late 19th- and early 20th-century readers. While there are a number of other factors influencing the aesthetic fate of George Sand's work, it is impossible not to see censorship as a factor in how it was inscribed in French literature.

Absolute suppression is not always what is at stake; partial suppression of a writer's work or of works dealing with specific themes can have profound effects on generations of readers' understanding of literary history. In communist Czechoslovakia, for example, three tiers of literature coexisted: the official literature, published within the geographic boundaries of the state by official publishing houses; *samizdat* writing published underground and often at great personal risk for the authors and publishers; and exile writing, such as that published in Canada through the enterprise of the *émigré* novelist Josef Škvorecký. While there was some coincidence between the last two groups, it was not entire. Since the events of the late 1980s and early 1990s, Czech 20th-century literary history has evidently had to be rewritten substantially, with the official canons displaced in favour of writers who were largely known through *samizdat*, most notably Václav Havel, taking on canonical importance.

Of course a primary distinction in the constitution of literary canon formation has involved the question of literariness itself. In the aftermath of the legal decisions of the Victorian era, British and American courts found themselves confronted with the legacy of the uses of the term "obscenity". One effect of the instability of this term as it was used in the law was to confront the courts with the need to distinguish the difference between the literary and the obscene. Indeed, 20th-century United States courts found themselves in the position of determining what constitutes literary value. If two major cases having to do with the suppression of novels led courts to unsettle the *Hicklin* standard, the resulting decisions are nearly as notable for the ways in which they do so, precipitating out of the fogginess of Victorian "obscenity" a valuable object: the literary work.

Bennet Cerf, an editor at Random House publishers in New York, wanted to publish James Joyce's *Ulysses* openly; in order to do so, he took a calculated risk of provoking legal action by importing a single copy. It was seized and Random House demanded the court hearing that the law provided for, petitioning for the exculpation of the work. In December 1933, Judge Woolsey of the US District Court handed down his opinion. Notably both parties to the action had waived their right to a jury trial, a fact Woolsey notes in his opinion with gratification, since "on account of the length of *Ulysses* and the difficulty of reading it, a jury trial would have been an extremely unsatisfactory, if not an almost impossible, method of dealing with it". Woolsey discusses the work as a whole, focusing on Joyce's intention. Was this book written with the purpose of "exploiting obscenity?" And he finds that it was not:

> But in *Ulysses*, in spite of its unusual frankness, I do not detect anywhere the leer of the sensualist ... Joyce sought to make a serious experiment in a new, if not wholly novel, literary genre. He takes persons of the lower middle class, living in Dublin in 1904 and seeks not only to describe what they did on a certain day ... but also tell what many of them thought about the while ... Joyce has attempted – it seems to me with astonishing success – to show how the screen of consciousness

with its ever-shifting kaleidoscopic impressions carries, as it were on a plastic palimpsest, not only what is in the focus of each man's observation of the actual things about him, but also in the penumbral zone residua of past impressions, some recent and some drawn up by association from the domain of the subconscious.

Reading this passage, the reader will not wonder that Cerf chose to include the opinion in lieu of an introduction in the 1934 edition of the work.

The opinion served then to unsettle the practice of isolating fragments of text and deeming an entire work obscene on the basis of them. By focusing on intention, Woolsey insisted on the necessity of examining an entire work, not just fragments. Within the frame of Joyce's intention, in Woolsey's reading, the words that were seen by the government as objectionable fail to meet any criteria for obscenity. Rather than focusing on the effect the book might have on its most impressionable readers, Woolsey claims that the criteria for obscenity must be tested out on a "person with average sex instincts – what the French would call *l'homme moyen sensuel* – who plays in this branch of legal inquiry the same role of the hypothetical reagent as does the "reasonable man" in the law of torts". Interpreting obscenity law into alignment with other branches of law, Woolsey puts into question the Victorian conception of law as the protector of the most vulnerable – or dangerous – minds. He posits an average reader, although why when it comes to discussion of the sexuality of the average reader, he resorts to French, we dare not conjecture.

US v. *One Book Called Ulysses* was a landmark in US obscenity law. It marked in clear terms that 20th century jurisprudence would erode the Victorian restrictions. It also suggested the extent to which the social world of Judge John Woolsey differed from that of his 19th-century forebears. Widespread literacy was assumed; universal elementary education was in place. If there were in the eyes of the middle class still "dangerous classes", they were not to be contained by censoring reading material for obscenity. And *Ulysses*, as Woolsey points out at least twice, is not likely to be picked up by someone looking for casual literary entertainment. As Morris Ernst, Random House's attorney in the *Ulysses* case, announced exuberantly in his own preface to the US edition of 1934: "A new deal in the law of letters is here." Insofar as the two central tenets of *Hicklin* were repudiated by Woolsey, this seemed to be true. But the Post Office still had the right to seize materials it found to be obscene; and while now there was an abstract average reader whose sensibilities the law had to imagine, the problem of defining obscenity remained.

By the 100th anniversary of the Obscene Publications Act, efforts were being mounted in Britain, by the Society of Authors among others, to replace it with more modern legislation. Lord Campbell's act and the *Hicklin* standard seemed hopelessly outdated. In the US, the *Ulysses* opinion had already undermined *Hicklin*; in 1957 the Warren Supreme Court gave it the death blow. Samuel Roth, a distributor of pornography, had been convicted under the Comstock Act; his conviction was affirmed on appeal and he then petitioned the Supreme Court. The court was faced, at last, with deciding whether criminal enforcement of Comstock violated the First Amendment. While the court affirmed the constitutionality of Comstock, it did so by adhering to a new definition of obscenity. Whereas previously obscenity had been legally defined as materials "having the tendency to arouse lustful thoughts or desires", Justice Brennan redefined it in his opinion as that which is "utterly without redeeming social value".

In 1959 the New York City postmaster seized unexpurgated copies of D.H. Lawrence's *Lady Chatterley's Lover* as well as a package of fliers announcing its availability. Grove Press, the US publisher, and The Reader's Subscription, through which some of the copies were to be distributed, petitioned the court to restrain the postmaster and to declare the novel not to be obscene. In this instance, the postmaster claimed that it was not for the court to decide obscenity; in effect, he insisted that he had already determined the work to be "non-mailable" according to the law. This attempt did not work; Judge Bryan cited the *Roth* decision of 1956 which had expanded and clarified somewhat Woolsey's standard of the "homme moyen sensuel": "whether to the average person, applying contemporary community standards, the dominant theme of the material taken as a whole appeals to prurient interest". This refinement of earlier law on obscenity moves the emphasis from the individual reader to a larger community of readers. While it seems positive that the court in *Roth* was recognizing that standards of what constitutes obscenity change over time, the term "community standards" is by no means unproblematic. Was the court supposing an abstract national community of readers who hold standards in common? Or could this be read to mean that determinations of obscenity could be local, implying that cities, towns, public school districts, or even smaller entities have the right to censor?

The force of Bryan's decision in this case is to challenge the authority of the postmaster in determining obscenity. "Plainly", writes Bryan, "*Lady Chatterley's Lover* is offensive to the Postmaster General, and I respect his personal views. As a matter of personal opinion, I disagree with him . . . But the personal views of neither of us are controlling here." He also points out that the postmaster general has used the *Hicklin* standard in deeming the book "non-mailable".

Bryan returns to the *Ulysses* opinion in order to elaborate on literary value, intention, and coherence. Acknowledging that intention is a problematic category in these matters, Bryan returns to the force of sincerity. Surely one might write a perfectly obscene book

in the mistaken belief that he is serving a higher moral purpose. The fact that this is the author's purpose does not redeem the book from obscenity. But the sincerity and honesty of purpose of an author as expressed in the manner in which a book is written and in which his theme and ideas are developed has a great deal to do with whether it is of literary and intellectual merit.

Thus, while in *Grove Press, Inc. And Reader's Subscription, Inc. v. Robert Christenberry, individually, and as Postmaster of the City of New York*, the power of the Postal Service to censor is undermined to some extent, it makes clear that defining obscenity in some objective manner was still a problem. Furthermore, despite the happy fate of Lawrence's novel,

exonerated in the action, Bryan's opinion makes it clear that obscenity standards were still bound to a notion of literary value that was fairly rigorous and highly institutionalized. In fact, reading Woolsey and Bryan together, one can trace Romantic images of authorship, intention, and sincerity combined with modernist theories of aesthetic form.

These are not the only instances of a dialectical relationship between literary style and legal authority. The mode of the pastoral – the innocent country tale, classically populated with stock figures of shepherds and shepherdesses – has often been updated by writers in order to offer veiled critiques of state authority, as has setting a novel, play, or discourse in the historically distant past in order to reflect on contemporary circumstance. In repressive regimes, authors have frequently deployed "Aesopian language", literary code modelled on the Greek fables that enabled them to say one thing and mean entirely another. To tell a fable, set outside of historical time and including characters that seemingly belong to no recognizable reality, ostensibly gives the censorship a harder job, insofar as interpretation becomes much less decidable. Under the Soviet government, Aesopian writing was extensively practised; Solzhenitsyn's *The Cancer Ward* is only one example. Literary tropes of all kinds can be recruited to the task of censorship evasion; irony is only the most obvious and under a system of centralized censorship, unless irony is extensively developed, it is perhaps the most easily detectable. Under some regimes, literary style has come to take on the aspect of a high stakes game with the censorship; can the allusions and tropes be understood by the government authorities reading the work? This is evidently more than gamesmanship bent on undermining the censor's authority as an official reader. Law marks out some forms of writing as material as it seeks to situate itself as a form of transcendent writing, free of individual authorship and determined by an abstract will. Of course, regardless of the nature of the regime, law is backed up by the machineries of a very material power. To test the censor-as-reader is to pit one form of writing against the other, to unveil the would-be transcendence of the law as an apparatus produced and sustained by material conditions.

Governments concerned about the free expression of their citizens can deploy the law, as we have seen, in diverse ways: pressure on publishers and booksellers, expanding the authority of diverse state agencies such as the Postal Service and the Customs Bureau are two familiar means. Stiff taxes for mailing bulk materials, which the American framers of the constitution were concerned about, is another example. Reducing or dismantling altogether state funding for the arts is another way, as is providing state monies only for those artists who will toe the line.

What seems crucial, however, in examining different ways in which law can be used to censor is the making of distinctions. In the British and US cases discussed above, for example, the publishers of the texts in question had the legal right to contest in the courts the decisions of the Postal Service and the Customs Bureau. While this is a highly problematic right, since it is prohibitively expensive and time-consuming and therefore available only to large corporate bodies or wealthy individuals, it is nonetheless a possibility that censorship can be challenged. The law can be changed. Distinction needs also to be made between the civil suppression of texts and the criminal prosecution of their authors. Clearly this is not the way in which authorship has been conceptualized by many other governments; writers may have only a narrow opportunity to defend their work, or none at all.

The Salman Rushdie affair recapitulates some of the issues we have been discussing since it also and more importantly makes clear the extent to which formerly dominant models of nation, empire, reading publics, and censorship law have been eroded. The legal questions presented by the affair were international in scope, bearing on the sovereignty of nations and the rights of individual citizens on the one hand, but on the other marking out the inadequacies of law's capacity either to restrain or protect expression in an era of globalized cultures and economies.

SARA MURPHY

Further Reading

Balmuth, Daniel, *Censorship in Russia, 1865–1905*, Washington, DC: University Press of America, 1979

Burt, Richard (editor), *The Administration of Aesthetics: Censorship, Political Criticism, and the Public Sphere*, Minneapolis: University of Minnesota Press, 1994

Coetzee, J.M., *Giving Offense: Essays on Censorship*, Chicago: University of Chicago Press, 1996

de Grazia, Edward, *Girls Lean Back Everywhere: The Law of Obscenity and the Assault on Genius*, New York: Random House, 1992

Dury, Maxime, *La Censure: la predication silencieuse*, Paris: Publisud, 1995

Goldstein, Robert Justin, *Political Censorship of the Arts and the Press in Nineteenth Century Europe*, London: Macmillan, and New York: St Martin's Press, 1989

Loseff, Lev, *On the Beneficence of Censorship: Aesopian Language in Modern Russian Literature*, Munich: Sagner, 1984

Peleg, Ilan (editor), *Patterns of Censorship around the World*, Boulder, Colorado: Westview Press, 1993

Sarat, Austin and Thomas R. Kearns (editors), *Law in the Domains of Culture*, Ann Arbor: University of Michigan Press, 1998

Siebert, Frederick Seaton, *Freedom of the Press in England, 1476–1776: The Rise and Decline of Government Controls*, Urbana: University of Illinois Press, 1952

Stewart, Susan, *Crimes of Writing: Problems in the Containment of Representation*, Oxford and New York: Oxford University Press, 1991

Travis, Alan, *Bound and Gagged: A Secret History of Obscenity in Britain*, London: Profile, 2000

Woodmansee, Martha and Peter Jaszi (editors), *The Construction of Authorship: Textual Appropriation in Law and Literature*, Durham, North Carolina: Duke University Press, 1994

LITHUANIA

(formerly Lithuanian Soviet Socialist Republic)

Population: 3,696,000	**Number of daily newspapers:** 19
Main religions: Roman Catholic; Lutheran; Russian Orthodox; Protestant	**Number of radio receivers per 1000 inhabitants:** 513
Official language: Lithuanian	**Number of TV receivers per 1000 inhabitants:** 459
Other languages spoken: Polish; Russian	**Number of PCs per 1000 inhabitants:** 54.0
Illiteracy rate (%): 0.3 (m); 0.5 (f)	

The Lithuanian Pranciškus Skorina established his first printing house in Prague in 1517, publishing a translation of the Bible and other books aimed at a Lithuanian readership. He later introduced printing onto Lithuanian soil, just as the Reformation was capturing the minds of some educated Lithuanians. Northern Lithuania was especially affected; the lesser gentry sent their sons to be educated in Königsburg and Wittenberg, where Lutheranism had taken particular hold. Put under pressure by the local Catholic clergy, grand duke Sigismund the Old forbade such studies. Prompted by complaints by the bishop of Vilnius against the prominent Lutheran man of letters Abraomas Kulvietis, Sigismund decreed in 1542 that there was to be no further dissemination of religious ideas condemned by the Catholic Church; these ideas were, he said, "littering people's minds", and "causing danger to Lithuania". Kulvietis was forced to flee to Königsberg, where he was free to teach. Despite the decree, prominent families such as the Radzivills offered protection for Calvinist ideas. Anabaptists and anti-trinitarians fared less well. Their ideas, which were attractive to the lower orders in the towns, threatened the

nobility, who had their exponents driven out of the country whenever they could. Meanwhile, Catholicism was reasserted in Lithuania through the presence of the Jesuits, who arrived in 1569 and opened a college in Vilnius, which became the University of Vilnius in 1578. The sons of those who had earlier supported the Reformation now turned back to the old church. Jurgis Radzivill even destroyed a translation of the Bible that had been published by his own father, and later became a cardinal.

Faced with the threats of Ivan IV (The Terrible) of Muscovy in the 1560s, Lithuania was formally united with Poland on 1 July 1569 in "the Most Serene Commonwealth of the Two Nations". Catholic censorship continued during the commonwealth years, and the church's *Index Librorum Prohibitorum* (Index of Prohibited Books) was applied in the predominantly Catholic north and west. After 1596, when the Uniate Church was formed by Orthodox Christians who acknowledged the primacy of the pope, those who remained within the Orthodox fold were subjected to severe censorship. In the same year, the Brotherhood of the Holy Spirit in Vilnius published the

Dialogue, a work by the patriarch of Alexandria, who was known to be an ardent enemy of any union between eastern and western churches. In 1610 the grand duke of Lithuania and the king of Poland, Sigismund Vasa, ordered the closing of the brotherhood's printing house, and the confiscation and burning of its books. As often in the history of censorship, however, it was merely a matter of moving the press elsewhere and starting again. The brotherhood established itself in Ukraine, the land of duke Oginskis, a supporter of Russian Orthodoxy who was so strongly opposed to the Uniates that he even considered a Protestant–Orthodox alliance to combat them.

The commonwealth lost part of Ukraine to Muscovy in 1667 and could not really be called a sovereign state after 1718, when a Russian protectorate was imposed on its vast territory. In 1733, the Seym (the legislature) expelled non-Catholics from its ranks and banned them from becoming judges. By 1794, the whole of what had once been Lithuania was ruled by Russia. After 1815 when the Napoleonic Wars ended, Lithuania was subjected to the full panoply of Russian censorship. Discussions of freedom could only be clandestine. At the University of Vilnius, the Society of Philomaths (1817), the Union of Friends (1819), and the Society of Philarets (1820) were formed to provide space for the exchange of ideas about the future of Lithuania. The Philomaths were eventually brought to book: some were imprisoned, while others, including the Polish poet Adam Mickiewicz, who had studied at Vilnius, were exiled. A failed uprising of 1830 was largely planned at the university, which was finally closed in 1832.

The so-called "Lithuanian movement" of the 1820s was championed by Józef Giedroic, bishop of Samogitia. He arranged for the New Testament to be translated into the Samogitian dialect, founded schools, and encouraged the written Lithuanian language. His efforts crumbled with the suppression of the uprising of 1830. His successor, Motiejus Valancius, at first felt constrained to go along with the official policies that laid down that Russian should be taught alongside Lithuanian in Catholic schools. He later changed his mind entirely when, in 1864, the Russians banned all writings in the Lithuanian language. Governor general Mikhail Muravev (known as "The Hangman") was instructed "not to allow the printing of a single Lithuanian textbook". Incensed, Valancius called for a boycott of Russian-language schools and for the use in teaching of all the old books still in people's possession. With his support, quantities of books printed in East Prussia were smuggled over the border.

The first Lithuanian-language newspaper had also been published in East Prussia, in the 1850s, and a Lithuanian Literary Society was founded in Tilsit in 1879. The nationalist newspaper *Ausra* (Dawn) was smuggled across the frontier, but formal bans on the Lithuanian press stayed in place until the Russian revolution of 1905–06.

Then followed what a leading intellectual called "an epidemic of newspapers", promoting ideas ranging from Lithuanian nationalism to extreme social radicalism. Lithuania again became independent in 1918. Censorship was not abolished, although the Peasant Populist and Social Democrat coalition of 1926, under M. Sleževicius lessened restrictions on the domestic press, and abolished the state agency that scrutinized and censored the foreign press.

Sleževicius was swept away in a military coup later in 1926. The new president, Antanas Smetona, styled himself "leader of the nation", and his new constitution of 1928 again tightened the press laws. Each region had a military commander whose duties included press censorship. The Communist Party was banned and its publications were suspended, although they continued to be circulated underground. Outside politics, on the other hand, a certain liberalization was allowed. The novel *In the Shadow of Altars* (1933) by Vincas Mykolaitis-Putinas contained explicit criticism of the Catholic Church, but was allowed to circulate widely uncensored.

The Soviet occupation of 1940 reinstated censorship at the centre of the Lithuanian experience, not least through the rewriting of Lithuanian history, notably in relation to the occupation itself, which was presented in the Soviet history books as the result of a free choice by the Lithuanian people. Within a few months publication of *The Lithuanian Encyclopaedia* was stopped, and libraries in seminaries and schools were confiscated. Initially, 250 specified books were taken out of circulation, and passages hostile to socialism were cut from textbooks. The museum of church art in Kaunas was closed. All publications were controlled by the Lithuanian branch of the censorship agency Glavlit, acting on instructions from Moscow. Particular care was taken with historical texts that might suggest previous hostility on the part of Lithuanians towards Russians, notwithstanding the fact that these works were often directed at pre-Soviet Russia. The first Lithuanian novel, *Algimantas* (1904) by Vincas Pietaris, was omitted from an edition of the author's selected works because it "depicted the endless battles that Lithuanians waged against the rulers of Russian lands".

In August 1972 Jonas Jurašas, the director of the Kaunas State Theatre, decided that he could no longer stay silent about the state's attitude to his art. A production of Slawomir Mrozek's play *Tango* had been made meaningless when its final scene was cut by the censor; Kazys Saja's *Mamutu Medziokle* (Mammoth Hill) had been banned just as rehearsals started; most important of all, Juozas Glinski's *Grasos namai* (Home of Terror), a play about the conflict between the 19th-century poet and songwriter Antanas Strazdas and the authorities of his day, with obvious contemporary resonance, had been subjected to severe cuts. Jurašas wrote an open letter to complain of:

> endless disputes with security-minded types, attempts to prove the future production's importance to society . . . the distortion of the creative work's texture by categorical demands for the removal of even essential emphases . . . the arbitrary limitation of a production's run, or its total prohibition, while ignoring the opinions of the broad theatrical community and of the audiences.

Once Jurašas had finally rejected compromise, the authorities made short work of him. He was dismissed from the theatre, his name was removed from the press and posters, and he had to get work as a stonecutter with a sculptor. Like some other troublesome artists in the Soviet Union, he was given permission to emigrate; he left for Munich in 1974.

Tomas Venclova, a poet and translator, was also permitted to leave (in 1977). He wrote in 1984 of his desire "to air out literature, to bring Lithuanian literature out of provincialism, to bring it to maturity, to modernize it". He too had waged constant battles with the censors, in his case about which novels could be translated. He had done his best to inject some humour into the situation. When he asked for permission to translate some stories by the Argentinian novelist Jorge Luis Borges, the censor enquired "Is Borges an enemy of the Soviet system?" Venclova replied that Borges "was against the solar system". The censor was probably baffled rather than amused.

The Catholic Church was also affected by Soviet censorship. *Kelione Petersburkan* (1895, Journey to St Petersburg) was omitted from a collection by the Lithuanian bishop and poet Antanas Baranauskas because it was said to be "dominated by an ideology foreign to our readers"; Baranauskas's poems had fiercely criticized Russia for keeping Lithuania poor and illiterate. The church itself once again adopted the cause of Lithuanian freedom when it founded one of the classics of Soviet samizdat, the *Chronicle of the Catholic Church in Lithuania*. In March 1972 17,000 people signed a petition to the United Nations drawing the world's attention to religious persecution in Lithuania. In the last decade of the Soviet Union's existence, the Catholic Committee for the Defence of Believers' Rights, the Helsinki Group, and, especially, the Lithuanian Freedom League joined the Lithuanian army of resistance to censorship.

After a visit to Lithuania in 1992, Irena Maryniak, former USSR editor at *Index on Censorship,* wrote that:

> the Lithuanians appear to have got compromise down to a fine art. When atheism was the obligatory doctrine, the Lithuanian government would repossess churches, turn them into museums, and restore them in the process. Now they are back in use. Many people joined the Communist Party to work towards genuine improvement in the social and economic state of things. Those who insisted on maintaining what they saw as their moral integrity often found they were paralysed, unable to contribute in any sphere at all.

The poet Vitalii Asovskii told Irena Maryniak that "there is no independent Russian press here". The newspaper *Ekho Litvy* (Lithuanian Echo) was an echo, indeed, of the government that supported it financially and whose views it represented. Czesław Okinczyc, a member of the Polish minority and president of the Centre for Mutual Understanding, told her "you are given the pro-government position and there is no opportunity to hear anyone express this own ideas. Lithuania is trying to become an open society yet it is closing up at the same time." The state-owned television company displays signs indicating which age group a particular programme is suitable for, while the private companies, which are more liberal in principle, try to avoid giving offence. Pornography is outlawed, but it rarely becomes a public issue. In 1992 Jurga Ivanauskaite's novel *The Witch and the Rain* was attacked as blasphemous

and the Vilnius city authorities sought to restrict its circulation, but the publicity that had been generated ensured that 20,000 copies were sold.

Political censorship ceased to exist as independence was re-established in 1990. Some indirect censorship remains, especially of state television. In 1992, the government denied that it had had any involvement in the pressure to drop such programmes as *Parliament Studio* and *News and Opinion*, but it reserved the right to be "dissatisfied with the network's output". The then-ruling Conservative Party forced *Krantas*, a series of investigative reports and studio discussions, off the air in 1997, but it was immediately snapped up by a privately owned television channel.

There was another challenge to press freedom in Lithuania in 2000 when a draft of a new law on media was introduced by a group of legislators. Among other things it aimed to establish the post of inspector/supervisor of media, whose functions would be somewhat reminiscent of those of a Soviet censor. After a heated media debate, Lithuanian president Valdas Adamkus spoke against the draft, and the idea of press supervision was eventually abandoned.

ALMANTAS SAMALAVIČIUS

Further Reading

Harrison, E.J. (editor), *Lithuania 1928*, London: Hazell Watson and Viney, 1928

Kirby, David, *Northern Europe in the Early Modern Period: The Baltic World, 1492–1772*, London and New York: Longman, 1990

Kirby, David, *The Baltic World, 1772–1993: Europe's Northern Periphery in an Age of Change*, London and New York: Longman, 1995

Maryniak, Irena, "The Uncomfortable Commonwealth", *Index on Censorship*, 21/10 (November 1992)

Miłosz, Czesław, *Native Realm: A Search for Self-Definition*, New York: Doubleday, 1968; London: Sidgwick and Jackson, 1981

Pirockinas, Arnoldas, "The Lithuanian Language: Hostage of Foreign Powers, 1940–1991", *Lituanus*, 42/2 (1996)

Samalavicius, Stasys, *An Outline of Lithuanian History*, Vilnius: Diemedis Leidykla, 1995

Šilbajoris, Rimvydas (editor), *Mind against the Wall: Essays on Lithuanian Culture under Soviet Occupation*, Chicago: Institute of Lithuanian Studies Press, 1983

Slavenas, M.G., "The Protestant Minority Churches in Lithuania", *Lituanus*, 43/1 (1997)

Stražas, A.S., "Lithuania 1863–1893: Tsarist Russification and the Beginnings of the Modern Lithuanian National Movement", *Lituanus*, 42/3 (1996)

Thaden, Edward C. and Marianna Forster Thaden, *Russia's Western Borderlands, 1710–1870*, Princeton, New Jersey, Princeton University Press, 1984

Vardys, V. Stanley and Romuald J. Misiunas (editors), *The Baltic States in Peace and War, 1917–1945*, University Park: Pennsylvania State University Press, 1978

Venclova, Tomas, "I am Grateful to Orwell", *Index on Censorship*, 13/4 (August 1984)

LITHUANIA: The Polish Minority in Soviet Lithuania

One of the consequences of the Molotov–Ribbentrop pact of 1939 was a boundary change that enlarged the territory of Lithuania in the southeast by the incorporation of the city of Vilnius and surrounding area, where many Poles lived. The Lithuanian share of the population under Soviet rule was 80 per cent, while the Polish share went up from 3 per cent to 7 per cent. As a result, Poles formed Lithuania's second-largest minority after the Russians.

Politically sensitive areas for these Poles included, in addition to the Molotov–Ribbentrop pact and its secret protocols, controversial events such as the massacre of Polish army officers at Katyn in 1940; the conflicts between Poland and Lithuania in the period 1918–45; and any form of opposition either to communism in general or to the communists who then dominated Lithuania's government. The Soviet line on Polish history in the interwar period was to depict the Poles as proxy agents for western imperialism.

Naturally, Poles in Soviet Lithuania were never allowed to challenge the territorial change of 1939 by referring to the Polish–Lithuanian conflict over Vilnius. The Lithuanian nationalist movement had always regarded Vilnius as the historic capital of Lithuania, but it had been occupied illegally and annexed by Poland in 1920. The aim of Józef Piłsudski, the nationalist leader of Poland between the world wars, had been to unite into a single nation the historic lands of both Poland and Lithuania, including Vilnius, much of Ukraine, and Belarus, which had comprised the Polish–Lithuanian Commonwealth during the 16th century. From 1944 onwards the communist regime in Poland cooperated with Moscow by severing its links with Poles in the Soviet Union, and this remained the case until the late 1980s. At the same time, the Polish government – and, indeed, its democratic successors – refrained from any attempt to revise the eastern frontiers established by the Molotov–Ribbentrop pact. Their intelligentsia having been decimated in Stalin's mass deportations, Poles felt marginalized by their exclusion from high positions in Lithuania.

No evidence has been found of publications in Polish distributed as samizdat in Lithuania before the 1970s. In 1966, however, the nucleus of an underground religious society, Promień (Sunbeam), was formed, consisting of about 100 members and using as its base a Polish-language secondary school in Nowa Wilejka, a district of Vilnius region. (The Soviet education system allowed Poles in Lithuania to be educated in the Polish language.) Between 1970 and 1974 this society published a samizdat periodical mainly addressed to Polish young people and their families, and entitled *My chcemy Boga* (We Want God), a quotation from a Polish religious song. The periodical contained information on Catholicism all over the world, reprints of articles from religious magazines published in Poland and elsewhere, religious verse, and articles written by Jan Mincewicz, the editor, who was a teacher at the school. In the words of the journalist Jan Sienkiewicz, the aim of the periodical was "to combat the atheistic, materialistic philosophy [of Marxism-Leninism] by presenting arguments for the truth of the Catholic faith". Altogether around 100 copies of each of the 12 eight-page issues was produced (all were in A4 format). Jan Mincewicz was also a founder of the Polish folk ensemble Wileńszczyzna, which helped to preserve and promote Polish culture in Lithuania, and is performing even now.

In January 1975 Mincewicz was dismissed from the school for participating in religious activities, but he managed to find work at another Polish-language secondary school in Niemenczyn, 20 kilometres from Vilnius. Here he organized another underground youth group, Świt (Dawn). In the late 1980s, when glasnost began to take effect, the two groups Promień and Świt were united into a legal religious youth club, which also still exists today.

Another underground organization, called Wileńszczyzna (but not connected with the group mentioned above), existed from 1972 until perestroika was introduced. It was a club of intellectuals who sometimes published religious declarations or translated articles from the underground Lithuanian Catholic press. This group had contacts with Lithuanian dissidents and also with Solidarność (Solidarity), the Polish independent trade union movement, and its members sometimes wrote articles for publication in Poland.

It was also possible to refer to Polish concerns in a coded way, as Jan Sienkiewicz found when he worked for the newspaper *Czerwony Sztandar* (Red Banner) – now the *Kurier Wileński* (Vilnius Courier) – the only Polish-language daily to be published in the Soviet Union. As he has recalled, "a very successful way to avoid censorship and to convey patriotic Polish ideas to readers was to strongly criticize Russian Tsarist policies towards the Polish people. The Communist censor apparently did not dare to interfere and readers could easily see parallels between Tsarist and Soviet politics."

In 1988, the Polish ethnic community emerged as a highly politicized group within Lithuania, determined to defend and promote its culture and rights. Mincewicz is a member of the Lithuanian Parliament, representing Polish interests; Sienkiewicz stood down from re-election in 2000. The Polish community is now free to explore and express its own history.

MARIA LENN

LITTLE SISTER'S BOOK AND ART EMPORIUM
Canadian bookstore, established 1983

To begin to understand the Little Sister's case in context, one needs to know that most of the printed materials sold in Canadian bookstores, whether books, magazines, or newspapers (other than the mainstream daily press), is imported, chiefly from the United States. Canada Customs, an agency of the federal government charged with the administration of the Customs Tariff, oversees the importation of goods of all kinds into the country and operates within guidelines set out in an internal interpretative document known as Memorandum D9-1-1. This Memorandum prohibits the importation of sexually explicit materials depicting or describing a variety of practices ranging from non-consensual sex to bondage and force in association with sexual gratification. Using the technique of "prior restraint" – i.e., seizing materials without first providing a rationale to justify the seizure and without allowing recourse to any public forum for debate – Canada Customs has consistently obstructed and prevented the circulation of gay and lesbian printed materials, apparently on the assumption that these materials can reasonably be assumed to be "obscene" within such terms of reference. The Little Sister's case records the attempt of Vancouver's leading gay and lesbian bookstore to challenge these practices as discriminatory. The history of this challenge is in itself complex.

After more than a decade of detention by Canada Customs of shipments of gay and lesbian books and magazines, the Little Sister's bookstore first attempted a legal challenge in 1987. The bookstore appealed against the seizure of issues of the *Advocate*, a gay news magazine, but two weeks before the trial Canada Customs reversed its earlier decision, determining that the magazines were not obscene. When Little Sister's requested that the seized materials be forwarded to them, they was told that the issues had been destroyed. Thus the opportunity for another challenge of this detention was lost.

In the face of Canada Customs' persistence in such practices, Little Sister's again mounted a challenge in 1990, this time assisted by the British Columbia Civil Liberties Association. Although the trial was set for 1991, it was delayed until a year later, when government lawyers first attempted to have the case dismissed and then, when it was scheduled to go forward, argued that insufficient time had been allocated for their presentation. After yet another postponement, the trial began in October 1994 when Justice Smith started to hear two months of evidence. His decision was handed down in the Supreme Court of British Columbia in January 1996. A partial victory at best, this decision was challenged in March 1998 by Little Sister's and the British Columbia Civil Rights Association and brought to the British Columbia Court of Appeal. In a 2–1 majority verdict, the Court of Appeal panel ruled that Canada Customs' practice was justified on the basis of legislation that nevertheless violates Canada's free expression rights. The owners of the bookstore, Jim Deva and Bruce Smyth, took the case to the final stage, the Supreme Court of Canada, in March 2000.

The issues in this case are complex, revolving around obscenity law after the *Butler* decision (on the criminalization of pornography), and constitutional law with respect to customs censorship or "prior restraint". J.J. Arvay, counsel for Little Sister's, argued in 1994 that violations of the constitutional right to freedom of expression and to equality had occurred and that it was unconstitutional for Customs to detain materials before a proper determination had been made as to whether such materials might be obscene. In *Butler*, the first case to mount a constitutional challenge to Canada's obscenity law which is contained in the Criminal Code, the Court stressed "community standards" as the arbiter of "harm" signifying that which "predisposes persons to act in an anti-social manner" (*R. v. Butler* [1992] 1SCR 452, at 454). In contrast, the Little Sister's case challenged the dominance of heterosexual relationships as a normative model of community, arguing for inclusiveness of representation and challenging the assumption that representations of gay and lesbian sexualities are any more or less "degrading", and thus obscene, than representations of heterosexuality. This argument adverts to the insistence in *Butler*, as in other recent Canadian obscenity cases, that what is represented is somehow "real" and thus that, as the Court asserted in *Butler*, "exposure to images bears a causal relationship to changes in attitudes and beliefs" (*Butler*, 455). The implication is clearly that the "community" is not yet ready for "exposure" to representations of the lives of its lesbian and gay members. One form this refusal takes is the construction as obscene of what is simply addressed to a gay and lesbian bookstore for it was argued that some shipments were detained before their contents had been perused and, further, that perusal sometimes took the form only of a quick scan to detect the use of certain words in the text.

In one of the most powerful demonstrations of the claim of discrimination, Duthie's, a mainstream Vancouver bookstore, successfully imported copies of books that had already been detained by customs officials when ordered by Little Sister's. Similarly, it was argued that the Vancouver Public Library unproblematically included in its collection books subject to prior restraint when shipped to Little Sister's. During the two months of court proceedings in 1994, Duthie's demonstration of censorship in action was repeatedly cited in connection with the argument that Canada Customs had operated within the framework of Memorandum D9-1-1 such that any presentation of gay and lesbian sexualities and identities may potentially be deemed obscene. It was argued that the very representation of gays and lesbians to themselves is thereby deemed obscene and, further, a potential danger to heterosexuals given the risk of contamination associated with "harm" as defined in *Butler*. To censor representation of those who are already subject to discriminatory treatment in mainstream society is, it was argued, for the Canadian government itself to become complicit in discriminatory practices, contributing to the silencing of those whose self-representations function in a distinctive way, and who might otherwise seldom encounter images of themselves in the world. Further, several expert witnesses set the detention of gay and lesbian materials by customs officials in the context of the ready availability of similar materials of interest to the dominant, i.e. heterosexual, market.

Justice Smith ruled that the Customs Tariff does not violate the rights of freedom of expression and equality enshrined in the Canadian Charter of Rights and Freedoms, that the unequal impact of the law is not discriminatory since "homosexual obscenity is proscribed because it is obscene, not because it is homosexual" (*Little Sister's* 1996), and that "obscene pornography produced for homosexual audiences causes harm to society" (*Little Sister's* 1996, para. 195). However, the Court also ruled that Canada Customs contravened the Charter in its exercise of seizure and harassment tactics focused on gay and lesbian bookstores. Nonetheless Canada Customs continued its usual practices and Little Sister's launched an action with the British Columbia Court of Appeal in March 1998. Acting for the plaintiffs, J.J. Arvay challenged Smith J.'s judgement in its complete "divorcing" of Customs' practices and the constitutional context from the discriminatory and homophobic effect of these practices. Further, Arvay asserted that there is a "heavy and compelling onus on the government to justify any limitations or infringements on our rights to free expression" (quoted by Stuart Blackley, *Xtra West* 121: 10, 2 April 1998). In December 2000 the Supreme Court of Canada held that the reverse onus on the importer of suspected obscene material to establish that the material is not obscene by the Customs Act violated the Charter of Rights and Freedoms. In the eyes of the majority, the targeting of gay and lesbian bookstores was clearly discriminatory and violated expression and sexuality rights. The Supreme Court result represents a partial victory:

although the burden of proof will shift, this may make little difference because of the costs incurred in challenges to Customs officials' decisions.

The Little Sister's case is one of the clearest manifestations of the ongoing struggle to achieve and enact freedom of expression in Canada. In the final analysis, the core issue may be seen to be not "obscenity" but the capacity of the courts to embrace the inclusiveness, diversity, and polymorphous vitality of "community" in contemporary Canada.

LORRAINE WEIR

Further Reading

Bakan, Joel, *Just Words: Constitutional Rights and Social Wrongs*, Toronto: University of Toronto Press, 1997

Cossman, Brenda, *Censorship and the Arts: Law, Controversy, Debate, Facts*, Toronto: Ontario Association of Art Galleries, 1995

Cossman, Brenda *et al.*, *Bad Attitude/s on Trial: Pornography, Feminism, and the Butler Decision*, Toronto: University of Toronto Press, 1997

Fuller, Janine and Stuart Blackley, *Restricted Entry: Censorship on Trial*, 2nd edition, Vancouver: Press Gang, 1996

Kinsman, Gary, *The Regulation of Desire: Homo and Hetero Sexualities*, revised edition, Montréal: Black Rose, 1996

Lacombe, Dany, *Blue Politics: Pornography and the Law in the Age of Feminism*, Toronto: University of Toronto Press, 1994

Rule, Jane, *Detained at Customs*, Vancouver: Lazara Press, 1995

Weir, Lorraine, "The Ethos of Censorship in English Canadian Literature: An Ontopornosophical Approach" in *Interpreting Censorship in Canada*, edited by Klaus Petersen and Allan O. Hutchinson, Toronto: University of Toronto Press, 1999

LIU BINYAN
Chinese journalist, 1925–

In the early 1950s Liu Binyan was working with the Communist Youth League newspaper *Zhongguo Qingnian Bao* (China Youth Gazette). In common with his contemporary the novelist Wang Meng, Liu was also greatly influenced by the developments in post-Stalin Soviet literature, especially the work by the essayist Valentin Ovechkin (1904–68). Ovechkin had made his name as a writer of the *ocherk*, sharply critical sketches that exposed party mismanagement on collective farms. Ovechkin visited Beijing in 1954; his lecture on the *ocherk* was immediately translated into Chinese by Liu Binyan and published in *Wenyibao* (Literary and Art Gazette).

Liu upheld Ovechkin's contention that literature should "write the truth" and "delve into life". In Liu's own words, the critical essays he wrote were aimed at "the tendency in literature to evade the contradictions and conflicts in reality and to cosmetize life".

Two pieces of reportage published in 1956 brought Liu Binyan to prominence. Both works were published largely as a result of the patronage of Qin Zhaoyang, the editor of *Renmin Wenxue* (People's Literature), the official literary organ of the Chinese Communist Party. "Zai qiaoliang gongdishang" (On the Bridge Construction Site), which appeared in April 1956,

told the story of the confrontation between a young engineer and his bureaucratic superior. Its publication was accompanied by an editorial comment from Qin Zhaoyang stating: "We have been waiting a very long time for just such an *ocherk*, with its incisive description of problems and its critical and satirical characters, and we hope that a great number of such works will follow." Qin was also alleged to have changed Liu's original text, as he did not consider it sufficiently bold. As it was, the reportage was certainly one of the first works of literature published since 1949 to portray "an unrevolutionary party member camouflaged as revolutionary". "Benbao neibu xiaoxi" (The Inside Story of This Newspaper) published in June 1956, centred on the attempts of a young reporter to persuade her editor to depict the seamier side of life, rather than merely regurgitating the party line. Qin Zhaoyang's praise of the work was again unequivocal: "You are opening your own road of realism and setting an example for others."

Liu Binyan's insistence on "delving into life" was audacious, even in the atmosphere of the "Hundred Flowers" period. When the Anti-Rightist Campaign was set in motion in the summer of 1957, Liu became one of the primary victims. The main characters in his reportage were denounced as "bourgeois individualists, undisciplined anarchists and totally negative". Liu was accused of having a total disregard for "party spirit", of embarking upon a crusade opposed to the rule of the Communist Party. Liu's close relationship to Qin Zhaoyang was described as unhealthy. He had spoken out against unwarranted attacks on other literary figures, in particular the novelist Wang Meng and the theoretician Hu Feng. And even after he had been hauled before the literary authorities to account for himself, Liu continued to accuse them of lacking feelings and being "chameleons who in spring allowed the youth to oppose the bureaucracy and then in the autumn called them anti-bureaucratic". That he fell victim to the Anti-Rightist Campaign came as no surprise to Liu. In early 1958 Liu Binyan was sent to a remote mountain district to engage in forced labour. He was allowed to return to work at *Zhongguo Qingnian Bao* in 1961, in the lowly position of a filing clerk, but between 1966 and 1975 the Cultural Revolution demanded that he again reform through labour.

Liu was officially rehabilitated on 24 January 1979. Unlike many of his colleagues who, in gratitude to the post-Mao regime, allowed themselves to become establishmentarians, Liu continued to champion the causes he had found so important two decades earlier. He used the Fourth Congress of Writers and Artists in November 1979 once more to advocate "delving into life" and "writing about the 'dark side'". In an emotive speech, "Call of the Times" (Shidai de zhaohuan), Liu maintained that "the writer must *actively* render a truthful reflection of the reality of life so that it exerts a powerful impact on the actual life of the readers". It followed hot on the heels of Liu's first post-Mao exposé of corruption: "People or Monsters" (Renyao zhijian), published in *People's Literature* in September 1979, described a female official who had woven a bureaucratic web around her encompassing bribery, corruption, backdoorism, and embezzlement. This work of reportage was not welcomed by many of Liu's contemporaries, who urged him to steer clear of politics.

During the 1980s Liu Binyan continued to act as "spokesman for the people", exposing those areas of life about which he felt the nation had a right to know. In 1985, Liu had great difficulty in having "Di'erzhong zhongcheng" (A Second Kind of Loyalty) published. This work of reportage depicted two patriotic intellectuals who dared to criticize aspects of the Communist Party's leadership. When the work eventually secured publication in *Kaituo* (Pioneer), all copies of the journal were immediately withdrawn from circulation and banned. Despite these setbacks, Liu continued to promote political reform.

Liu Binyan, the physicist Fang Lizhi, and the writer Wang Ruowang were held personally responsible for inciting students to demonstrate in late 1986. He became the first target of the Communist Party's Campaign against Bourgeois Liberalization.

He was denounced for the "negative portrayals of China" that filled his investigative reports. These portrayals, so the authorities maintained, were clear evidence of Liu's opposition to the party and to the nation as a whole. In January 1987 Liu Binyan was expelled from the Chinese Communist Party and dismissed from his position at *Renmin Ribao* (People's Daily).

Angered at the protests of foreign intellectuals, the authorities refused Liu permission to go abroad, despite many invitations from Western universities. The authorities finally relented in March 1988, and Liu went to the US to teach. In the autumn of 1988 Liu became a Nieman Fellow at Harvard University, and was therefore not in China at the time of the student demonstrations of June 1989. Liu, who speaks openly about the lack of press freedom in China, is editor of the influential émigré journal *China Forum*.

DESMOND A. SKEEL

Writings

People or Monsters? and Other Stories and Reportage from China after Mao, edited by Perry Link, 1983
Fragrant Weeds: Chinese Short Stories Once Labelled as "Poisonous Weeds", with others, translated by Geremie Barmé and Bennett Lee, 1983
Tell the World: What Happened in China and Why, with others, translated by Henry L. Epstein, 1989
A Higher Kind of Loyalty: A Memoir, translated by Zhu Hong, 1990
China's Crisis, China's Hope, translated by Howard Goldblatt, 1990

Further Reading

Barmé, Geremie and John Minford (editors), *Seeds of Fire: Chinese Voices of Conscience*, Hong Kong: Far Eastern Economic Review, 1986; New York: Hill and Wang, 1988
Chan, Sylvia, "The Image of a 'Capitalist Roader': Some Dissident Stories in the Hundred Flowers Period", *Australian Journal of Chinese Affairs*, 2 (July 1979): 77–102
Doleželova, Anna, "Liu Binyan's Come-back to the Contemporary Chinese Literary Scene", *Asian and African Studies*, 20 (1984): 81–100
Goldblatt, Howard (editor), *Chinese Literature for the 1980s: The Fourth Congress of Writers and Artists*, Armonk, New York: Sharpe, 1982
Goldman, Merle, *Literary Dissent in Communist China*, Cambridge, Massachusetts: Harvard University Press, 1967
Goldman, Merle, *Sowing the Seeds of Democracy in China: Political Reform in the Deng Xiaoping Era*, Cambridge, Massachusetts: Harvard University Press, 1994
Link, Perry, *Evening Chats in Beijing: Probing China's Predicament*, New York: Norton, 1992
Nieh Hualing (editor), *Literature of the Hundred Flowers*, New York: Columbia University Press, 1981
Wagner, Rudolf, "Liu Binyan and the *Texie*", *Modern Chinese Literature*, 2/1 (Spring 1986): 63–98
Yue Daiyun, *Intellectuals in Chinese Fiction*, Berkeley: Institute of East Asian Studies, University of California, 1988

LIU SHAOTANG
Chinese short story writer, 1936–

In 1953, after the publication of the short story collection *Qingzhi lüye* (Green Branches and Leaves), Liu Shaotang was hailed as one of China's most promising young writers. This accolade persuaded Liu to leave the Chinese Department of Beijing University and embark upon the road to professional writing. With the publication of *Shanzhacun de gesheng* (The Songs of Haw Village) in 1954, Liu once again attracted much positive reaction. These early works, clearly the immature efforts of a young writer, closely adhered to the literary line laid down by the Chinese Communist Party. Peasant heroes were depicted working selflessly for the good of the nation and of socialism.

By 1956, however, the tone of Liu Shaotang's writing had darkened considerably. The short story "Tianye luoxia" (Sunset Clouds in the Fields) painted a picture of dejection and hopelessness among farmers on rural collectives. Although such descriptions were apparently at odds with party propaganda, Liu was praised at the beginning of the "Hundred Flowers" period for adapting effortlessly to the more liberal political line. In early 1957 the short story "Xiyuan cao" (The Lawns of Xiyuan) showed that dejection and hopelessness were also afflicting urban students.

Liu came into his own during the latter months of the "Hundred Flowers" period. He was the leading spokesman in the campaign to reverse the criticism of the novelist Wang Meng and his short story "Zuzhibu xinlai de qingnianren" (The Newcomer in the Organization Department). He vociferously supported Wang during the course of numerous debates and meetings. In January 1957 Liu collaborated with his colleague Cong Weixi to write an essay entitled "Xie zhenshi – shehui zhuyi xianshi zhuyi de shengming hexin" (Write the Truth – The Living Core of Socialist Realism). The essay defended Wang Meng's brave decision to depict life as it really was and denounced the "vulgar sociology" of those literary officials who had criticized him. The essay concluded: "Literature which dares to participate in struggle, and be faithful to life and the truth, does not lie."

In the spring of 1957 Liu grew more audacious. His essay "Xianshi zhuyi zai shehui zhuyi shidai de fazhan" (The Development of Realism in a Socialist Period) was clearly influenced by the writings of Qin Zhaoyang, the controversial editor of *Renmin Wenxue* (People's Literature). The post-Stalin "thaw" in the Soviet Union was also an inspiration. Liu argued that the origin of cultural stagnation in China was Mao Zedong's "Talks at the Yan'an Forum on Literature and Art". The main problem lay in "emphasizing only the political nature of literature, not its artistic quality". Furthermore, the demands placed on writers at Yan'an were wholly inappropriate and "far behind the situation now developing".

In a second essay published in May 1957 and entitled "Wo dui muqian wenyi wenti de yixie yijian" (My Views on Current Literary Problems), Liu Shaotang continued his barrage against Mao's "Yan'an Talks". He criticized writers who focused on future ideals rather than present realities. His language was unforgivingly critical:

To carry on the tradition of realism, we must be truly faithful to the realities of life ... We should not white-wash life or alter its true face in the name of "realistic development of the revolution" ... The realities of life must have the characteristics of the age and the mark of the times.

Letters written to his publishers at the time – which were later to be used in evidence against him – revealed Liu's lack of interest in pursuing the "correct" ideology and his enthusiasm for developing a personal literary style.

Liu Shaotang was very influential among young would-be writers and gathered around him a sizeable band of followers. The group named itself the Beijing School, and made plans that were immediately quashed by the Anti-Rightist Campaign to set up its own independent literary journal. The Writers' Association could not understand how Liu, who had been nurtured almost exclusively by the communist regime, should have become a "rightist". They attempted to alert his followers to the error of his ways and on 3 August 1957 Liu presented his self-criticism, which concluded that the path to a better literature was "much more tortuous" than he had ever imagined.

Despite Liu's show of contrition, in October 1957 the propaganda section of the Communist Youth League continued to criticize him at some very well-attended discussions. He was said to be increasingly preoccupied with his own profession and with Soviet culture. Liu had never concealed the influence of "bourgeois" European films on his creative process. The year before he had revealed that Indian, Italian, and French films had "aroused in [him] the desire to search for the truth of life, its romantic flavour and its infinite beauty", sentiments that could hardly be reconciled with the cultural policy of the Communist Party.

Accusations against Liu Shaotang grew in intensity. It was alleged that following the positive reception of his early short-story collections he had become "conceited"; that he had left university early because political classes were interfering with his creativity; and that he had spent much of 1955 in the countryside not to "learn about life" but to escape Communist Party control. To cap it all, it was revealed that Liu's family had been wealthy landowners, which called in question his loyalty to the proletariat.

Liu spent several months working in the Beijing suburbs on railway and irrigation projects. In late 1958 he returned to the countryside to work on the land. Although he was allowed to publish again in the mid-1960s, Liu inevitably fell victim to the Cultural Revolution and spent a further lengthy period labouring in the countryside. Between 1962 and 1978, when he was rehabilitated, Liu's published works only amounted to three novels.

After the death of Mao, Liu Shaotang once again established himself as a writer of merit. Most of his writing from the 1980s reflects his experience of living among the peasants, and his refined use of folk tales and local colour has been praised by critics as "continuing and developing the legacy of classical literature". By the 1980s Liu had become very much an establishmentarian, yielding in order to "survive". As Merle Goldman writes: "because memories of his 1957 persecution were still fresh in his mind, Liu Shaotang expressed gratitude to the present leadership [and was therefore able to] publish his works relatively easily."

DESMOND A. SKEEL

Writings

Out of China, translated by Jack Chia and Henry Walter, 1953
Songs of Haw Village, 1956
Catkin Willow Flats (short stories), 1984

Further Reading

Fokkema, D.W., *Literary Doctrine in China and Soviet Influence 1956–1960*, The Hague: Mouton, 1965
Goldman, Merle, *Literary Dissent in Communist China*, Cambridge, Massachusetts: Harvard University Press, 1967
Goldman, Merle, *Sowing the Seeds of Democracy in China: Political Reform in the Deng Xiaoping Era*, Cambridge, Massachusetts: Harvard University Press, 1994
Hsu, Kai-yu (editor), *Literature of the People's Republic of China*, Bloomington: Indiana University Press, 1980
Nieh Hualing (editor), *Literature of the Hundred Flowers*, New York: Columbia University Press, 1981

LIU XIAOBO
Chinese writer and critic, 1955–

Liu Xiaobo comes from the city of Changchun, northeast China. His secondary education was truncated by the Cultural Revolution and he became a bricklayer. In September 1978 Liu enrolled at the Chinese department of Jilin University and embarked upon undergraduate studies. On graduation, he moved to Beijing Normal University to read towards a master's and a PhD degree.

Liu's first critical essay appeared in the literary journal *Zhongguo* (China) in April 1986. Entitled "Wufa huibi de fansi" (Unavoidable Retrospection), it denounced the portrayal of intellectuals in recent literature; they appeared too positive and untainted by the deep suffering they had endured during the Cultural Revolution.

On 3 October 1986 Liu's speech at a symposium on literary research was published in the *Shenzhen Qingnian Bao* (Shenzhen Youth Herald). The speech, "Weiji! Xinshiqi wenxue mianlin weiji" (Crisis! New Period Literature is Facing a Crisis) earned Liu the nickname "Dark Horse" (*heima*), and heralded a series of controversial articles in which Liu commented on philosophy, aesthetics, and literature. The aim of the symposium had been to praise advances in literature since the Cultural Revolution. Nobody had dared to offer a critical view until Liu stood up to say that literature was backward looking and had little to say about society's problems. Writers were prevented from using their imagination. In Liu's view, literature of the post-Cultural Revolution period (1976–86) compared most unfavourably with that of the Fourth of May period (1919–30). Students vied to purchase copies of the *Shenzhen Qingnian Bao*.

Later in 1986 Liu was invited to deliver a series of lectures in Beijing. At Qinghua University he said: "Chinese tradition has castrated the spirit of the Chinese intellectual . . . only by defeating [the classical poets] Qu Yuan [340–278 BCE] and Du Fu [712–70] has Chinese literature a way out." There was no way out through traditional culture or through blind or simplistic imitation of the West. Liu's comments so influenced his student audiences, that they invited him to participate in the demonstrations that took place in major Chinese universities at the end of the year. He declined but did not escape criticism during the 1987 Campaign against Bourgeois Liberalization.

By the summer of 1988 Liu Xiaobo had gained a PhD from Beijing Normal University. At the public viva for his doctoral thesis, which concerned aesthetics, Liu claimed that the Chinese education system had made students into slaves, and reiterated his view that contemporary Chinese literature was impotent.

In August 1988 Liu was invited to Oslo University, Norway to teach a course on contemporary Chinese literature. He soon fell out with the university authorities and, without fulfilling his contractual obligations, left for Hawaii in November.

Liu took up a position as lecturer at Columbia University in March 1989. While there he met with representatives from the émigré organization the Chinese Alliance for Democracy, including its leader Hu Ping. Under the pseudonym "Dark Horse" Liu contributed several articles to the alliance's US-based journal (*China Spring*). By means of the articles, Liu reappraised modern Chinese culture and wrote in particular about the failure to liberate the individual. One of the articles, "Zhongguo dangdai zhengzhi yu Zhongguo zhishifenzi" (Contemporary Chinese Intellectuals and Politics) was highly critical of China's older intellectuals.

In April 1989, in support of the burgeoning student demonstrations in Beijing's Tiananmen Square, Liu sent an open letter to the Chinese government urging that it heed the students' demands. He also published an article in *China Spring* claiming that political prisoners such as Wei Jingsheng and Xu Wenli were much more important for China than political leaders like Hu Yaobang, whose death had precipitated the demonstrations.

Liu returned to Beijing on 26 April. Although he initially intended merely to observe the student demonstrations, by the middle of May he openly supported active involvement: "Students are suffering for our ancient people – Chinese with any sense of justice or sympathy shouldn't just watch coldly on." On 2 June Liu began a high-profile hunger strike with Hou Dejian, a Taiwanese rock singer, Gao Xin, an editor, and Zhou Duo, department head at the Stone Corporation. Liu announced:

> Through our hunger strike, we also want to tell people that what the government media refer to as a small bunch of troublemakers is in fact the whole nation. We may not be students, but we are citizens whose sense of duty makes us support the democracy movement started by the college students.

Following the 4 June crackdown on the popular demonstrations, Liu was swiftly arrested. He was denounced as an "evil backstage manipulator" and accused of being sent to China by the Chinese Alliance for Democracy to lead students astray. Articles in *Renmin Ribao* (People's Daily), the official daily newspaper of the Chinese Communist Party, excoriated Liu as an "historical criminal" who was "resolutely opposed to socialism" and "stubbornly supportive of bourgeois liberalization".

In November 1990 Liu agreed to write a "letter of repentance", which secured his release from the high-security Qincheng Prison in Beijing two months later. Under constant surveillance by the police, he found it impossible to obtain meaningful employment. Eventually he was again given permission to travel abroad and accepted a temporary position as visiting scholar at Canberra University, Australia. He also gave speeches at Harvard and Berkeley universities, speaking mostly on such safe subjects as popular culture. An account of his experiences during the student demonstrations was published in Taiwan under the title *Mori xingcunzhe de dubai* (Monologue of a Survivor of Judgement Day). In general it followed the Chinese government line and was, for that reason, universally criticized in the West. Liu returned to China in 1994.

Liu was sentenced to three years' "re-education through labour" on 9 October 1996 for a statement he had jointly issued with the democracy activist Wang Xizhe. The statement, published in Hong Kong's *Ming Pao*, claimed that while the Communist Party was the sole legitimate ruler of China, it had reneged on many of the rights given to citizens in the constitution. Liu was released before the end of his sentence.

DESMOND A. SKEEL

Further Reading

Barmé, Geremie and John Minford (editors), *Seeds of Fire: Chinese Voices of Conscience*, Hong Kong: Far Eastern Economic Review, 1986; New York: Hill and Wang, 1988

Barmé, Geremie and Linda Jaivin (editors), *New Ghosts, Old Dreams: Chinese Rebel Voices*, New York: Times Books, 1992

Cheng, Chu-yuan, *Behind the Tiananmen Massacre: Social, Political, and Economic Ferment in China*, Boulder, Colorado: Westview Press, 1990

Goldman, Merle, *Sowing the Seeds of Democracy in China: Political Reform in the Deng Xiaoping Era*, Cambridge, Massachusetts: Harvard University Press, 1994

Ogden, Suzanne et al. (editors), *China's Search for Democracy: The Student and the Mass Movement of 1989*, Armonk, New York: Sharpe, 1992

LIVRE BLANC SUR LA RÉPRESSION EN ALGÉRIE
(White Book on Repression in Algeria)
Testimonies by Islamists: published in Switzerland, 1995

A civil war in Algeria started in January 1992 after the cancellation of a second round of elections that would probably have resulted in victory for the Front Islamique du Salut (Islamic Salvation Front, FIS). The FIS was dissolved and several Islamist groups began a guerrilla war against the Algerian government by attacking presumed enemies of Islam: politicians, journalists, intellectuals, women who did not wear a veil, and foreigners.

During the 1990s, it was extremely difficult to get accurate information on the civil war in Algeria, for the Algerian regime controlled the entire Algerian press, and very few foreign journalists were allowed into the country. *The White Book on Repression in Algeria*, published by the Comité algérien des militants libres de la dignité humaine et des droits de l'homme (Algerian Committee of Free Fighters for Human Dignity and Human Rights), was one of the first publications that challenged the official Algerian version of the conflict. The book, in two volumes plus a supplement, gives detailed inside information on the persecution of Islamist groups by the state. The first volume covers the themes of justice, killings, disappearances, and torture during the years 1991–94. The second volume covers the period 1991–95 and looks in detail at the carnage in the Serkadji Prison on 21 February 1995, when many Islamist prisoners were killed or wounded after an alleged mutiny. The supplement is an overview of judicial errors and of the reactions of the media and human rights organizations in Algeria and France.

The writers of *The White Book*, a committee of Algerian men and women, were close to the FIS, in favour of "une Algérie souveraine, démocratique et sociale, dans le cadre des principes Islamiques" (a sovereign, democratic, and social Algeria, based on Islamic principles). The book contains testimonies by former FIS members allegedly subjected to arrest, torture, and forced confessions.

The book was published in Switzerland by Hoggar in 1995, but a truck containing 300 copies was stopped at the French border so that its contents could be "re-examined". At that time, it was becoming clear that the French government, which officially took no side in the conflict, in fact supported the Algerian government in trying to eradicate all opposition in Algeria, especially of Islamist groups. Thus it was no surprise that, in August 1995, Jean-Louis Debré, the French minister of the interior, prohibited the distribution of the book in France. *The White Book* was said to contain *appel à la haine* (incitement to hatred) against the Algerian government, and also a distinct anti-French tone. Algeria was a former French colony, and the French immigrant community, mostly of North African origin, could, it was said, be susceptible to the "violent language" of the book and even act upon it. This French fear was increased by several bombings that took place in Paris during the summer of 1995, and it was suspected that these acts were the work of small Islamist groups such as the Groupe Islamique Armée (GIA, Armed Islamic Group).

Four French publishing houses, La Découverte, Arléa, Esprit, and Éditions de Minuit, protested at the ban on 11 September. They acknowledged that the testimonies were pro-FIS and pro-Islamist, and that the book stays silent, for instance, about the killings carried out by Islamist groups themselves. But they pointed out that *The White Book* broke no French law. The prohibition implicitly acknowledged that the French government was hardly neutral in the conflict, despite the official position. The publishers Hoggar deplored the ban by stating a few days later that the book in no way threatened public safety in France.

Despite these protests, the ban on the *White Book* was not lifted. Since its publication in 1995, however, more attention has been paid to the crimes committed by the Algerian government during the civil war. Hoggar has published several other books on contemporary Algeria, and the first volume of the *White Book* has even been published on the Hoggar website, in response to widespread demands for the book to be freely available.

MIRA VAN KUIJEREN

Further Reading

Aït-Embarek, Moussa, *L'Algérie en murmure: un cahier sur la torture*, Plan-les-Ouates: Hoggar, 1996

Bedjaoui, Youcef, Abbas Aroua and Méziane Aït-Larbi (editors), *An Inquiry into the Algerian Massacres*, Plan-les-Ouates: Hoggar, 1999

Comité algérien des militants libres de la dignité humaine et des droits de l'homme, *Livre blanc sur la répression en Algérie, 1991–1994* and *1991–1995: les vérités sur une guerre cachée*, 2 vols, Plan-Les-Ouates: Hoggar, 1995; vol. 1 at www.hoggarbooks.org

Comité algérien des militants libres de la dignité humaine et des droits de l'homme, *Livre blanc sur la répression en Algérie, 1991–1995, Supplément: Les Complicités*, Plan-Les-Ouates: Hoggar, 1996

"Jean-Louis Debré interdit un livre dénonçant le pouvoir algérien", *Le Monde* (14 September 1995)

"L'Algérie en contrechamp", *Peuples Méditerranéens*, 70–71 (January–June 1995)

Vergès, Jacques, *Lettre ouverte à des amis algériens devenus tortionnaires*, Paris: Michel, 1993

HAROLD LLOYD
US film actor, director, and producer, 1893–1971

WELCOME DANGER
Film, 1929: censored in China, 1930

Harold Lloyd had been popular with Chinese audiences, but the premiere of *Welcome Danger* in Shanghai immediately sparked protests. The film was said to portray the Chinese in an extremely negative light, not least because it had been shot in Chinatown and, it was thought, ridiculed Chinese characters. An article signed by 36 people appeared in *Minguo Ribao* (National Daily), which denounced the film as hostile toward the Chinese, and called for public action against further screenings. However, the two theatres where the film was playing were located in the foreign concessions and did not heed the public reaction. On 23 February 1930 Hong Shen, a professor at Fudan University, stood up before the audience in the Grand Theatre where the film was being shown and asked them to boycott the film. The theatre manager called the police and Hong was arrested.

The next day, Hong requested that the Shanghai branch of the Nationalist Party penalize the Grand Theatre for showing a film that insulted the Chinese people. Nine theatre groups in Shanghai published a joint manifesto in his support. The manifesto decried the "cultural invasion" from the West and blamed the Chinese government for allowing the film to play in China. It condemned Hong's arrest as an insult to Hong himself and to all Chinese. The government responded quickly. The Shanghai Board of Film Censors, the Nationalist Party's Shanghai branch and Nanjing's Central Department of Propaganda jointly issued an order banning *Welcome Danger* throughout China. Since the two theatres were located in the foreign concession area and thus beyond the jurisdiction of the Chinese authorities, Hong took the case to the Shanghai Mixed Court. After a year of legal struggle, he won the case. The court ruled

that (1) the film should never be shown in China again, (2) the American ambassador should make a formal apology to China's Ministry of Foreign Affairs, (3) Harold Lloyd, the director and star of the film, should write a formal letter apologizing to the Chinese people, (4) the Capitol Theatre, which also showed the film, should make a public apology in the newspapers, (5) the Grand Theatre be banned from advertising in newspapers, (6) the Grand Theatre donate 5000 yuan to schools, and (7) films shown in the foreign concession areas should also be subject to Chinese film censorship.

This incident marked the beginning of Chinese government censorship of foreign films. Soon after the ban on *Welcome Danger*, the Nationalist government's Department of Propaganda and Board of Film Censors in Shanghai banned all Harold Lloyd films. Lloyd then wrote to the US consulate in China, explaining that "the comedy was not intended as a reflection against Chinese dignity, but was simply made in the spirit of fun". But that did not allay the Chinese audience's indignation. Several years later when another of Lloyd's films was brought to China, someone threw tear gas into the theatre where the film was being shown. A note was found which read: "We have not yet forgotten the *Welcome Danger* incident!" In August 1936 two further American films were banned for their negative portrayals of Chinese people. One of them, *Cat's Paw*, was by Lloyd. The US consulate protested to the Ministry of Foreign Affairs, which in turn sent a letter of inquiry to the Central Film Censorship Committee (CFCC). The CFCC answered quite explicitly that Lloyd's previous offence was a factor in the ban on *Cat's Paw*.

ZHIWEI XIAO

Writings

An American Comedy (autobiography), with Wesley W. Stout, 1928; revised edition 1971

Further Reading

Jones, Dorothy, *The Portrayal of China and India on the American Screen, 1896–1955*, Cambridge, Massachusetts: Center for International Studies, Massachusetts Institute of Technology, 1955

Xiao, Zhiwei, "Anti-imperialism and Film Censorship during the Nanjing Decade" in *Trans/national Chinese Cinemas: Identity, Nationhood, Gender*, edited by Sheldon Hsiao-peng Lu, Honolulu: University of Hawaii Press, 1997

KEN LOACH
British film and television director, 1937–
QUESTIONS OF LEADERSHIP
Television series, 1983

There are certain topics which British television has found it extremely difficult to treat without falling foul of either self-censorship or state interference, whether direct or indirect. Traditionally, these topics have been the nuclear issue, anything which could be construed as having a bearing on "national security", Northern Ireland, and labour relations. This last was a particularly hot potato in the early years of the Thatcher government.

During the 1970s, both Conservative and Labour governments had come into conflict with the trade unions. By 1979, the Conservative opposition, aided by a partisan press (which had its own commercial reasons for wishing to limit the power of organized labour) had turned the whole issue into one of "who governs Britain?" After a so-called "Winter of Discontent", during which the Conservative party and press waged a campaign to persuade people that the unions had made Britain "ungovernable", the Conservatives were elected and proceeded drastically to reduce the power of trade unions. Their theme was that the "moderate" rank and file was constantly being "led astray" into industrial action by the "militant" leadership of the unions, and that power needed to be "handed back" to the members.

The trade union issue had been central to some of Ken Loach's most notable television films, namely *The Big Flame* (1969), *The Rank and File* (1971), and *Days of Hope* (1975). In all of these films, Loach's point of view, and that of his scriptwriter Jim Allen, had been diametrically opposed to that of the Conservatives: they had argued that, when it came to the crunch, craven and reformist trade union leaders and their allies in the Labour Party had consistently sold out and betrayed the activist, militant, rank and file membership. This was the theme which Loach wished to explore, in a straightforward documentary form, in *Questions of Leadership*. The experience was to be a painful and frustrating one.

A hint of what was to come was provided by *A Question of Leadership* (1980), Loach's first attempt to examine the impact of Thatcherism on the unions. This programme was made for the commercial television company Associated Television (ATV), the forerunner of Central Television, for whom *Questions of Leadership* was later made. It was basically a discussion among a group of steelworkers and other trade unionists, filmed just after the former were defeated in the 1980 steel

strike and became the first victims of the government's anti-union strategy. However, the expressly political and overtly left-wing nature of the analysis presented by the trade unionists in the programme seems to have set alarm bells ringing both at ATV and at the Independent Broadcasting Authority (IBA), which at that time regulated commercial television (Independent Television, ITV). As Loach himself put it at the time,

> I think there's nervousness in television about ordinary people showing articulate political views. They like working class people to be complaining about unemployment or bad housing, they like social distress, but they don't like numbers being added up and conclusions drawn. Conclusions have to be drawn by experts in studios, because "ordinary folk can't talk politics".

The IBA expressed concern that the programme contravened the Broadcasting Act's requirements for objectivity and balance, even though the programme could itself be regarded as a piece of "balance", offsetting the much-heard views of the trade-union leadership, as well as counterbalancing what was widely felt to be the media's routine demonization of industrial action. Thus this unassuming film languished unseen for over a year. It was never shown on network television, and was cut for its ATV transmission in order to tack on a "balancing" discussion at the end, a discussion which Loach argued "anaesthetizes the rest of the programme" and is "entirely redundant".

Undaunted and still eager to pursue his enquiries into trade union politics, Loach, via Central, approached the recently established Channel 4 with a proposal for *Questions of Leadership*, four 50-minute films with the subtitle "problems of democracy in trade unions: some views from the front line". The story of their banning is a labyrinthine one, but revealing of the way in which censorship in British television works.

The programmes dealt with a number of industrial disputes, including the above-mentioned steel strike. One programme concentrated on the assault by management and media on the shop stewards' movement at the car firm British Leyland. Another looked at democracy within the electricians' union, the EETPU: this included an interview with the EETPU leader Frank Chapple, which he cut short by walking out when he didn't like the questions. The series also included an edited version of a day's discussion at Warwick University, in which the issues raised by the films were debated from a number of different positions. Taken as a whole, the series suggested that large unions such as the AUEW (the engineering union) and the EETPU were undemocratic and did not adequately represent the interests of the rank and file; furthermore, it argued that the TUC (Trades Union Congress) and the Labour Party establishment had a vested interest in preventing the formation of inter-union solidarity and the emergence of direct challenges to government in the course of industrial disputes. Unusually for the British media, it is the voices of radical union leaders and activist shop stewards and convenors which set the agenda, and the trade-union leaders who have to respond. As the campaigning journalist John Pilger pointed out, "nothing like this perspective of the trade unions has been seen in a sustained form on television". And indeed, as things turned out, it was to remain unseen.

The finished series was passed from Central to Channel 4 in May 1983. However, because the series was felt to be so "unbalanced" as to contravene the Broadcasting Act, Loach was asked to reduce it to three programmes, each of which would be followed by a half-hour "balancing" discussion made by someone else. The whole series was to be concluded by another programme, which would not be of Loach's making. In the event, however, union leaders showed little inclination to become involved in the "balancing" act. Both Channel 4 and the IBA agreed that union leaders could not in effect censor the series by refusing to appear in the "balancing" programmes, but nonetheless their heel-dragging meant that the whole thing had to be pulled from the originally scheduled dates in September 1983.

By this point, the dispute over *Questions of Leadership* was becoming public. On 14 October, David Glencross, the IBA Director of Television, explained in *The Guardian* that the problem with the programmes was not simply a matter of "balance" but that they "make specific charges about specific individuals and trade unions in connection with specific industrial disputes". Consequently, "those directly involved should be offered an opportunity to comment immediately following the films. That is the reason for postponement . . . No right of veto has been given to those who may still decline to take part." However, Frank Chapple and Sir John Boyd of the AUEW had been given the opportunity to comment on the "charges" during the actual programmes; prevarication by union leaders was holding up the transmission of the series. Loach complained in *The Guardian* on 31 October, "effective censorship is best achieved not by an outright ban but by delay and inaction, by passing the item from one desk to another, from one Board to another, so that the programme gradually loses its topicality and relevance." He also outlined what he saw as the unspoken objection to the films, namely that

> . . . working people are allowed on television as long as they fit the stereotype that producers have of them. Workers can appear pathetic in their ignorance and poverty, apathetic to parliamentary politics, or aggressive on the picket line. But let them make a serious political analysis based on their experiences and in their own language, then keep them off the air.

While Glencross had suggested that the question was less one of "balance" than of giving certain individuals the chance to answer specific "charges", Edmund Dell, Channel 4's chairman, put the "balance" issue firmly back on the agenda in *The Guardian* on 14 November: "we will stick to the view that balance within one particular programme is not required", since "where a producer is heavily committed to a particular point of view, his opponents may not be prepared to have their answers mediated through his editorial judgement." However, he argued, "In a case like this it is necessary, in fairness, to provide additional balancing material produced by someone else." Loach replied, "I am no more committed to allowing the issues which seem to me to be of fundamental importance to be discussed than any news editor or current affairs producer. Each makes editorial judgements according to his perception of events" (*The Guardian*, 22 November).

In December 1983, Central asked Loach to cut down the series to two programmes of 50 minutes each. Central would add one "balancing" discussion, and the package was scheduled for transmission in March 1984. Loach did as requested, merely shortening each programme item, but Central did not record their part of the deal until April 1984, thereby causing yet another postponement. Union leaders Frank Chapple, Terry Duffy, and Bill Sirs all apparently declined to take part, but those present included the miners' leader Arthur Scargill, and the MPs Ian Wrigglesworth (Social Democrat), Peter Bottomley (Conservative), and Bob Clay (Labour).

On April 17, Loach and various Central representatives (including Central's solicitor) met with a leading QC. Loach agreed to make one small cut in one programme; otherwise, it was his impression that the programmes were pronounced a fair risk. However, the programmes still did not appear in the schedules. Channel 4 chief executive Jeremy Isaacs and Charles Denton (director of programmes at Central) spoke of "legal difficulties". The miners' strike had begun. Loach commented,

> Clearly the union leaders who are criticised in this film are the ones who at present are intent on leaving the miners isolated. They are the ones the Government and the Coal Board are relying on to leave the miners isolated. Anything which criticises them now is really too sensitive to broadcast (*Television Today*, 26 July).

Shortly afterwards, Central announced that they were seeking fresh legal advice, and then issued the following statement:

> The board of Central Independent Television has been advised that the programme *Questions of Leadership* is defamatory and would have no adequate defence at law . . . After extensive legal argument has been heard the board has reluctantly concluded that the clear risk of a successful action for defamation precludes the programmes being offered to Channel 4 for transmission.

Arguably, this decision represented political censorship masked by legalistic pretext. As Loach himself pointed out,

> The films were edited under the guidance of an expert lawyer, and we conceded to every request for changes. If

there were elements in the two remaining films which are still thought to be libellous, then there is additional material which could be put in its place, so the argument simply does not stand up. The only explanation therefore is that this is not a legal decision but a political one, and therefore of concern to anyone who is concerned with freedom of speech (*Screen International*, 4 August).

Like *The Animals Film*, *The Friday Alternative*, *Brazil: Cinema, Sex and the Generals*, and others, the fate of *Questions of Leadership* demonstrates that, in its early days, the new fourth television channel could be hindered from carrying out its unique statutory remit by the timidity of the IBA. The 1981 Broadcasting Act required the IBA to ensure that Channel 4 would show "a suitable proportion of matter calculated to appeal to tastes and interests not generally catered for by ITV", and it also imposed a statutory duty on the channel "to encourage innovation and experiment in the form and content of programmes". In practice, however, the IBA's treatment of Channel 4, in the matter of pre-broadcast censorship, differed less from its treatment of ITV than one might have expected, given the existence of the channel's remit.

More generally, however, the *Questions of Leadership* controversy illuminated the limits of what was politically possible on British television in the 1980s. As critics and broadcasters such as Stuart Hood, John Pilger, the Glasgow University Media Group, and many others have argued, the way in which the IBA (and, for that matter, the BBC) interpreted the requirements for "balance" and "objectivity" tended to favour the *status quo* and a consensual view of society. Indeed, this was the position of many who lobbied for Channel 4 in the first place, in the hope that it might broaden the range of views available on British television. To a certain extent, their hopes were fulfilled, unhelpful IBA interventions notwithstanding. However, it is hard to avoid the conclusion that, of all the channel's disputes with the IBA, the *Questions of Leadership* affair most clearly illustrates Ralph Miliband's point that, as far as broadcasting in Britain is concerned, "impartiality and objectivity stop at the point at which the political consensus itself ends – and the more radical the dissent, the less impartial and objective the media". It may be that, with the transformation of the IBA into the "lighter touch" ITC, the general weakening of political consensus, the changing nature of the main political parties, and a widespread loss of faith in Westminster-style party politics in general, these strictures apply less readily to contemporary broadcasting. However, they undoubtedly shed useful light on the broader context in which *Questions of Leadership* was banned.

JULIAN PETLEY

Writings
Loach on Loach, edited by Graham Fuller, 1998

Further Reading
Beharrell, Peter and Greg Philo, *Trade Unions and the Media*, London: Macmillan, 1977
Isaacs, Jeremy, *Storm over 4*, London: Weidenfeld and Nicolson, 1989
McKnight, George (editor), *Agent of Challenge and Defiance: The Films of Ken Loach*, Trowbridge, Wiltshire: Flicks, and Westport, Connecticut: Greenwood Press, 1997
Miliband, Ralph, *The State in Capitalist Society*, London: Weidenfeld and Nicolson, 1969
Pilger, John, *Heroes*, London: Jonathan Cape, 1986

JOHN LOCKE
English philosopher and political theorist, 1632–1704
FIRST LETTER CONCERNING TOLERATION
Treatise, 1689

As secretary to the Earl of Shaftesbury, John Locke had become involved in Protestant politics; as a result he spent the years 1683–89 in exile in the Netherlands. It was from that vantage point that he wrote the first and greatest of his *Letters Concerning Toleration*, which was published anonymously in Latin in late April or early May 1689, by the printer Justus van Hoeve of Gouda. By that time, however, Locke had been sufficiently emboldened by the Revolution of 1688 to return to England, from where he discussed the appearance of the *Letter* with his friend, Philip van Limborch, the Dutch theologian who had arranged for its publication and to whom it was enigmatically dedicated. The frontispiece read: *Epistola de Tolerantia ad Clarissimum Virum T.A.R.P.T.O.L.A. Scripta a P.A.P.O.I.L.A*; that is to say, "to the most famous Theologiae apud Remonstrantes Professorem, Tyrannidis Osorem, Libertatis Amentem" by "Pacis Amante, Persecutionis Osore, Joanni Lockio, Anglo". Locke was so cautious, however, that he continued to discuss the *Letter* with van Limborch as though it had been written by someone neither of them knew; and, as with his *Two Treatises of Government*, he acknowledged his authorship of the *Letter* only in a codicil to his will, bequeathing it to the Bodleian Library, Oxford.

When Thomas Jefferson sat down in 1776 to prepare his speeches in connection with the disestablishment of the church in Virginia, he made for himself a commonplace book out of Locke's *Letter*, supplemented with Milton's *Of Reformation* and *The Reason of Church Government*. At one point Jefferson noted, "It was a great thing to do so far (as he himself sais of the parl. who framed the act of tolern.) but where he stopped short, we may go on". "Where he stopped short" applies to the section in Locke's *Letter* that withholds toleration from certain groups whose opinions make them incapable of peaceful cooperation with civil society – atheists who cannot take a binding oath, and (though Locke does not identify them as such) Catholics, whose religion requires them to define as heretics, and hence disobey, all Protestant monarchs.

The *Letter Concerning Toleration* has been the subject of controversy among modern scholars, the central questions being about these restrictions within Locke's theory of toleration, and to what extent he promoted complete toleration as distinct from indulgence or comprehension. At issue also is whether the English translation by William Popple, the nephew of Andrew Marvell, was faithful to Locke's intentions, and indeed whether Locke had authorized its appearance. Locke's notorious statement in that codicil, that the translation had been carried out "without my privity" was as ambiguous as his other disclaimers, and the notion that Locke disapproved of the translation has been effectively demolished. Some Locke scholars are made uneasy by Popple's dramatic address "To the Reader", which not only broadened the *Letter*'s implications for the political sphere, but by using the second person plural strongly suggested an English context: "We have need of more generous remedies than what have yet been made use of in our distemper. It is neither declarations of indulgence, nor acts of comprehension, such as have yet been practised and projected among us, that can do the work . . . Absolute liberty, just and true liberty, equal and impartial liberty, is the thing that we stand in need of." But the historical circumstances in which the *Letter* was finally published suggest that this language, though less cautious than Locke might have preferred, was appropriate to his tolerationist agenda.

According to van Limborch, the *Letter* was written in Amsterdam during the last weeks of 1685, in the context of the final revocation of the Edict of Nantes on 18 October of that year, and subsequent intensification of the persecution of Huguenots in French dominions. Yet it was not published until nearly three and a half years later, by which time it had acquired a compelling new set of contexts. The first of these was the Declaration of Indulgence issued by the English king, James II, in 1687, suspending all penal laws and giving Catholics equality with Protestants. The *Epistola* appeared just as the first Williamite parliament was about to pass a compromise Act of Toleration, conciliating the Anglican clergy by merely exempting Nonconformists from the penal laws while leaving those laws intact. On 12 April 1689 Locke had received from van Limborch a long letter filled with advice as to what he should work for in the toleration debates. That same day Locke wrote back, informing van Limborch that the tolerationist agenda was inhibited by the "disposition of the prelates", but that he still had hopes. And on 6 May, van Limborch informed Locke that a most pertinent treatise had just appeared (*non expresso autoris nomine*) and that "in the present state of affairs it could be read with great profit in England". This scenario, along with the failure of a projected Comprehension Act later in 1689, helps to explain not only why and when Popple's translation was conceived, but also his preface's insistence on "more generous remedies".

The main arguments of the *Letter* have been by now so incorporated into Western culture that their dazzling inventiveness can scarcely be recuperated. Locke's fundamental point is that the European Reformation had so divided the churches against each other that religion should no longer be subject to state regulation. Geopolitical relativism makes a mockery of this premise – which was, of course, taken for granted by almost every European government, that of the Netherlands being an important exception. The formula that Locke arrived at – the separation of church and state, or, in his language, that the civil magistrate should not interfere with religious belief and practice – was brilliantly supported by a series of memorable aphorisms, many of which Jefferson jotted down: "every church is orthodox to itself; to others, erroneous or heretical"; "a church then I take to be a voluntary society of men . . . a free and voluntary society"; "the business of laws is not to provide for the truth of opinions, but for the safety and security of the commonwealth"; "he jumbles heaven and earth together . . . who mixes these societies".

Despite Locke's notorious restrictions on toleration, he actually went further than John Milton in imagining a tolerant society. Thinking perhaps of the more liberal attitudes to Jews in Amsterdam, Locke (through Popple) declared that "neither pagan, nor Mahometan, nor Jew, ought to be excluded from the civil rights of the commonwealth, because of his religion . . . Shall we suffer a pagan to deal and trade with us, and shall we not suffer him to pray unto and worship God". It was this position, among others, that horrified Jonas Proast, who attempted to refute Locke's arguments in a series of increasingly hefty pamphlets. Locke's need to refute Proast resulted in three more *Letters Concerning Toleration*, which were published under the pseudonym "Philanthropus". Unfortunately they do not begin to equal the first *Letter* in originality of argument or zest of style – the latter, of course, being partly attributable to William Popple.

ANNABEL PATTERSON

Writings

Epistola de tolerantia (first letter on toleration), 1689; as *A Letter Concerning Toleration*, translated by William Popple, 1689, 2nd edition 1690; edited by James H. Tully, 1983
A Second Letter Concerning Toleration, 1690
A Third Letter for Toleration, 1692
Posthumous Works, 1706 (includes part of a *Fourth Letter*)
Correspondence, edited by E.S. de Beer, 8 vols, 1976–89
The Locke Reader, edited by John W. Yolton, 1977

Further Reading

Ashcraft, Richard, *Revolutionary Politics and Locke's Two Treatises of Government*, Princeton, New Jersey: Princeton University Press, 1986
Cranston, Maurice William, *John Locke: A Biography*, London and New York: Longman, 1957
Gough, J.W. "Introduction: Locke's Theory of Toleration" in *Epistola de Tolerantia / A Letter on Toleration*, by Locke, edited by Raymond Klibansky, Oxford: Clarendon Press, 1968
Horton, John, and Susan Mendus (editors), *John Locke: A Letter Concerning Toleration, In Focus*, London and New York: Routledge, 1991
Marshall, John, *John Locke: Resistance, Religion, and Responsibility*, Cambridge and New York: Cambridge University Press, 1994
Montuori, Mario, *John Locke on Toleration and the Unity of God*, Amsterdam: Gieben, 1983
Patterson, Annabel, *Early Modern Liberalism*, Cambridge and New York: Cambridge University Press, 1997
Schochet, Gordon, "John Locke and Religious Toleration" in *The Revolution of 1688–1689: Changing Perspectives*, edited by Lois G. Schwoerer, Cambridge and New York: Cambridge University Press, 1992

LU LING
Chinese novelist (real name: Xu Sixing), 1923–

Xu Sixing began writing fiction in the early 1940s under the pen-name Lu Ling. He enjoyed the patronage of the literary theoretician Hu Feng (1902–85), and when Hu was first censured by the Chinese communist literary authorities in 1945 he was eager to shield Lu, then a lecturer at the Nationalist Central University, from denunciation by association. Hu advised his protégé: "Insults are people's nourishment; suffer them for a while . . . and complete your own work."

Lu Ling was indeed not spared scathing attacks. His novels *Caizhu de Ernümen* (Children of a Rich Man) and *Ji'e de Guo Su'e* (Hungry Guo Su'e) attracted much negative criticism in the early 1950s. The criticism was levelled primarily against Lu's portrayal of revolutionary cadres as "lacking in knowledge and ability" and as "having lost their revolutionary stance". He was accused of having failed to reform his bourgeois views. In 1952 Ding Ling, editor of *Wenyibao* (Literary and Art Gazette), the official organ of the Chinese Federation of Literary and Art Circles, condemned Lu's "non-idealistic" depiction of the working masses.

Lu Ling and a number of other protégés of Hu Feng were officially urged to reform their "subjective" ideologies and learn from their mistakes. But Feng Xuefeng, the veteran critic and editor, commended Lu Ling for daring to explore new literary themes, although he was not uncritical of Lu's immature attempts at depicting "primitive feelings".

Lu Ling found it difficult to secure publication for his new works. Editors were understandably reluctant to risk the writings of a recently censured artist. Moreover, Lu was forced to attend a series of "struggle meetings" aimed at encouraging him to recant his "bourgeois thinking". On 11 September 1952 an open letter addressed to Lu was published in *Wenyibao*. The letter, written by Zhou Yang, begged Lu to abandon his individual ideas, to learn from Mao Zedong's "Talks at the Yan'an Forum on Literature and Art", and to acknowledge his mistakes. Under relentless pressure, Lu yielded.

For a while, Lu Ling found it easier to get his works published. His short story "Wadishang de zhanyi" (Battle in the Lowlands) appeared in *Renmin Wenxue* (People's Literature) in March 1954. It is a love story from the time of the Korean War. A soldier agonizes over whether he should indulge his feelings of love for a Korean peasant girl or follow army discipline. The question is never solved, for the soldier dies in an enemy skirmish.

"Wadishang de zhanyi" was criticized almost as soon as it appeared in print. Lu Ling wrote a 40,000-word apology, but this failed to save him from an extended period of "thought reform through living with the peasants". By concentrating on the soldier's personal feelings, Lu was "advocating individualism" and "glorifying excessive individual tenderheartedness". Would a patriotic soldier really sacrifice duty for his personal feelings?

When Hu Feng became the victim of a protracted ideological campaign in 1955, Lu, having penned a four-part essay in defence of Hu Feng published in *The Literary and Art Gazette*, was again denounced. Along with the critics A Long and Jia Zhifang, and the poets Lu Yuan and Zhang Zhongxiao, Lu was found to be a member of the so-called "Hu Feng Counter-revolutionary Clique".

Lu Ling was officially exonerated from all his previous "crimes" by the Chinese Communist Party in 1979. "Wadishang de Zhanyi" and other works were reappraised for their literary and artistic merit. Since then Lu has written a number of drama and poetry collections.

DESMOND A. SKEEL

Further Reading
Birch, Cyril, *Chinese Communist Literature*, New York: Praeger, 1963

Fokkema, D.W., *Literary Doctrine in China and Soviet Influence, 1956–1960*, The Hague: Mouton, 1965

Goldman, Merle, *Literary Dissent in Communist China*, Cambridge, Massachusetts: Harvard University Press, 1967

McDougall, Bonnie S. (editor), *Popular Chinese Literature and Performing Arts in the People's Republic of China, 1949–1979*, Berkeley: University of California Press, 1984

McDougall, Bonnie S. and Kam Louie, *The Literature of China: The Twentieth Century*, London: Hurst, 1997

Nieh Hualing (editor), *Literature of the Hundred Flowers*, New York: Columbia University Press, 1981

MOCHTAR LUBIS
Indonesian journalist and novelist, 1922–

Born in Padang, West Sumatra, Mochtar Lubis is a journalist by profession and a teacher by inclination. He is also well known as a writer of novels and stories for adults and children and as a liberal and middle of the road cultural critic. Mochtar Lubis's fight for democratic institutions and the democratic rights of the nation as well as his environmental and social concerns are informed by fervent nationalism.

Lubis was one of the founders of the Indonesian News Agency, Antara, which would not mention his name for several years in the 1970s and 1980s, but as a journalist he is now best known for his editorship of the daily *Indonesia Raya* (Greater Indonesia) which appeared with interruptions from 1948 until 1974 when its licence to be published was permanently cancelled by the authorities. Previous interruptions had been caused by president Suharto's ban in 1956. These actions were provoked by the articles Mochtar Lubis had written in the name of democratic rights and principles, publishing politically unwelcome stories that were deemed to threaten national stability. In consequence he spent the years between 1957 and 1966 in prison and under house arrest.

When Lubis was allowed to attend an International PEN Congress in Tel Aviv, he smuggled out of Indonesia the manuscript of his novel, *Twilight in Jakarta*, which denounces the moral bankruptcy of the Sukarno regime. While the English translation of the novel appeared in 1963, and a Malaysian edition in 1964, the Indonesian edition was not published until 1970. His critical assessment of Indonesian character, culture, and society found its expression in *The Indonesian Dilemma*, first published in 1977, while *Indonesia: Land under the Rainbow* is his own account of Indonesian history.

Indonesia Raya was one of 12 daily newspapers ordered out of existence in the clampdown that followed the student demonstrations against the Suharto regime's relationship with Japan in late 1973. At a time when foreign capital investment was flooding into Indonesia, Lubis had aroused the particular ire of the regime by the publication of his environmental concerns. As well as having his newspaper shut down, he was again placed under house arrest in 1975.

Mochtar Lubis is the recipient of several prestigious national literary prizes and, as a journalist, the holder of the Magsaysay Prize (1958) and the Golden Pen of the World Federation of Editors and Publishers (1967). A life member of the Jakarta Academy since 1970, he is also a co-founder of the Indonesian Legal Aid Institute (1970) and past president of the Press Foundation of Asia. In 1995 he returned the Magsaysay Prize when it was awarded to Pramoedya Ananta Toer, who had been connected with the discrimination against liberal writers during the period prior to 1965, when the influence of the political left had been particularly strong.

E. ULRICH KRATZ

Writings

Twilight in Djakarta, translated by Claire Holt, 1963
A Road with No End, edited and translated by Anthony H. Johns, 1968
We Indonesians, translated by Florence Lamoureux, 1979; revised edition as *The Indonesian Dilemma*, 1983
Indonesia: Land under the Rainbow, 1987; edited by E. Ulrich Kratz, 1990
"Literature and Liberation: An Awareness of Self and Society" in *Literature and Liberation: Five Essays from Southeast Asia*, edited by Edwin Thumboo, 1988
Tiger!, translated by Florence Lamoureux, 1991
Budaya, masyarakat, dan manusia Indonesia: himpunan "catatan kebudayaan" Mochtar Lubis dalam majalah Horison, 1992

Further Reading

Atmakusumah (editor), *Mochtar Lubis, wartawan jihad*, Jakarta: Harian Kompas, 1992
Chambert-Loir, Henri, *Mochtar Lubis: une vision de l'Indonésie contemporaine*, Paris: École Française d'Extrême-Orient, 1974
Hill, David T., "Mochtar Lubis: The Artist as Cultural Broker in New Order Indonesia", *Review of Indonesian and Malayan Affairs*, 21/1 (1987): 54–88
Hill, David T., "Interpreting the Indonesian National Character: Mochtar Lubis and Manusia Indonesia" in *Text/Politics in Island Southeast Asia: Essays in Interpretation*, edited by D.M. Roskies, Athens: Ohio University, 1993
Hill, David T., "The Changing Revolution: Three Novels by Mochtar Lubis", *Tenggara*, 33 (1994): 51–67

HENRY R. LUCE, TIME INC., AND CORPORATE CENSORSHIP

Two American journalists, A.J. Liebling and Dorothy Sterling, were leftist victims of corporate censorship imposed by the publishing company led by the legendary Henry Luce.

By the late 1940s, Henry R. Luce (1898–1967), the editor-in-chief of Time Inc., had become the most influential American publisher of his day. *Time* (co-founded by Luce in 1923), was essential reading for millions of middle-class Americans. *Fortune*, which first appeared in 1930, reached America's managerial and corporate elites, and often moulded their views. Luce's picture magazine *Life* (1936) quickly became America's favourite advocate of consumerism in the ever-more prosperous decade that followed World War II. All told, Time Inc. claimed that 40 million Americans each week read or saw one or more of Henry Luce's publications. Robert Hutchins, the famous and controversial president of the University of Chicago, even argued that Luce's magazines did more to mould the American character than "the whole education system put together".

The architect of *The American Century* series (1941), Harry Luce looked forward to a "reorganization of the world" resulting in the global primacy of the US. But suddenly, Soviet Russia stood in the way, and by 1945 Time Inc. became the earliest mainstream advocate of what was soon called the cold war. By 1947 Henry Luce had become ever more anxious to rid himself of leftist writers, unless they changed their line from antifascism to anticommunism.

Luce, a vehement opponent of government censorship, would go to extraordinary lengths when Time Inc.'s reputation was at stake. He tried to make sure that the American public did not receive any uncensored information about the people who ran the company. In this effort, Luce's primary tool was Roy Edward Larsen (1899–1979), who was in charge of Time Inc.'s business operations. Larsen's role in censoring critics of Luce and Time was not devoid of irony. In 1938, *Life*, thanks in some measure to civil libertarian Roy Larsen, published photographs made from the film *The Birth of a Baby*. After the production was banned as obscene in the Bronx, New York, Larsen publicly sold a copy of the magazine. Arrested, he was acquitted of the charge of selling "indecent" material, and thereby struck a blow for freedom of the press. More than a decade later, Roy Larsen denounced violations of due process in the case of a blacklisted actress who resided in his own area of Fairfield County, Connecticut. But Roy Larsen was also in informal charge of rooting out communists at Time Inc. Though Larsen detested the vulgar Joseph R. McCarthy, at times he was willing to use questionable methods himself. As a colleague later confirmed, Larsen "did a lot of the dirty chores".

In 1949 Roy Larsen learned that *Collier's* magazine intended to publish media critic A.J. Liebling's essay on Time Inc. Liebling, aided by a young researcher named James Munves, had his own agenda: he set out to expose Time as anti-labour and pro-authoritarian, or even pro-fascist. Liebling also mocked Time's pretentious, biased, omniscient style. But his research was meticulous and without precedent, based as it was upon textual analysis, ideological inquiry, and 15 major interviews. On 7 November 1949, Liebling submitted his piece to *Collier's*. But as Munves noted, "*Collier's* felt that A.J. Liebling's first draft on their planned series about Time, Inc., was too rough." Liebling revised his article, but to no avail. The essay disappeared, and in 1988 Munves noted that "No one seems to know what became of the Time pieces". Moreover, Liebling was paid, so he could not publish the piece anywhere else. In fact, Larsen had taken advantage of *Collier's* financial troubles (the magazine folded a few years later), and pressured the president of Crowell-Collier into killing the article. A year later, Time Inc. again applied its heavy hand, but as far as the public could see, it was once again devoid of incriminating fingerprints.

Dorothy Sterling had joined Time Inc. in 1936 as a secretary assigned to *Architectural Forum*; she worked as a researcher at *Life* from 1941 to 1949. (As Sterling later wrote, at Time Inc. "men were writers, women researchers".) Upset by the company's political and gender bias, Sterling began to accumulate material for a book of her own. By 1950 she had left *Life*, and was intensely involved in writing her manuscript. An inside story of Time Inc.'s editorial bias, the proposed book was highly critical of Luce's ardent anti-communism. Far more detailed than Liebling's work, it too represented an attack on former senior editor Whittaker Chambers's influence upon Time. It was, however, well documented, and profited from countless hours of interviews with former and current Time Inc employers. Unaware of the *Collier's* fiasco, one friendly editor even suggested that A.J. Liebling turn Sterling's material into a manuscript, "but somehow it never happened". In at least one instance involving the Sterling manuscript, a publisher overruled the favourable recommendation submitted by an editor-in-chief. Why?

The evidence reveals corporate collusion among Time Inc., top New York publishers, and the Federal Bureau of Investigation (FBI). The chronology of this Cold-War alliance is uncertain, but at the FBI, Louis Nichols and Clyde Tolson, top aides to director J. Edgar Hoover, made sure that prospective publishers discovered that Sterling had been a communist when she joined Time Inc. back in 1936. Once Hoover acted, agents and publishers (among them such giants as Little Brown, Doubleday, and Random House) rejected Sterling's manuscript. Time Inc.'s editorial director John Shaw Billings soon gloated that Hoover had killed Sterling's "scurrilous book". Though Sterling went on to pursue a successful literary career, her manuscript sits in a dusty carton in Eugene, Oregon, where it bears silent witness to Time Inc.'s effective censorship. Indeed, it was not until the publication of W.A. Swanberg's *Luce and His Empire* in 1971, and of Robert E. Herzstein's *Henry R. Luce* more than 20 years later, that the American public gained access to the kind of information first unearthed by A.J. Liebling and Dorothy Sterling during the Cold War heyday of Time Inc.

ROBERT EDWIN HERZSTEIN

Further Reading

Elson, Robert T., *Time Inc.: The Intimate History of a Publishing Enterprise*, edited by Duncan Norton-Taylor, 3 vols, New York: Atheneum, 1968–1986

Heiskell, Andrew, "The Reminiscences of Andrew Heiskell" in the Oral History Research Office, Columbia University, 1990

Herzstein, Robert E., *Henry R. Luce: A Political Portrait of the Man Who Created the American Century*, New York: Scribner, 1994

Kobler, John, *Luce: His Time, Life, and Fortune*, New York: Doubleday and London: MacDonald, 1968

Luce, Henry R. *et al.*, *The American Century*, New York: Farrar and Rinehart, 1941

Luce, Henry R., *The Ideas of Henry Luce*, edited by John K. Jessup, New York: Atheneum, 1969

Sokolov, Raymond A., *Wayward Reporter: The Life of A. J. Liebling*, New York: Harper and Row, 1980

Swanberg, W.A., *Luce and His Empire*, New York: Scribner, 1972

LUDU KYI-BWA-YAY PRESS
Burmese publishing house, established 1938

Ludu U Hla, who co-founded the Ludu Kyi-bwa-yay Press with his wife Daw Amar, is remembered as a pioneering Burmese journalist, a supporter of social reform, a social historian, and, perhaps above all, a recorder of folk tales, which he collected from the minority peoples of Burma as well as from the majority Burmans. He died in December 1982, and the last in his series of folk-tale collections was published by Daw Amar in 1996.

Daw Amar was a member of the Burmese Communist Party for many years and Ludu U Hla may have been a member too, although it is claimed in some memoirs that he never joined. The couple set up the Kyi-bwa-yay Press as a radical left-wing publishing house, working, even under the Japanese during World War II, to promote their vision of Burmese nationhood

based on socialist principles. As independence approached, Daw Amar produced a Burmese version of Maurice Collis's book *Trials in Burma*, which found great favour with the public because it was critical of the British. The couple also launched the newspaper *Ludu Thadin-Za* (The People) in Mandalay in 1946.

At independence in 1948, Burmese political parties ranged from conservative Buddhist, through various forms of nationalism, to radical Marxist. U Hla and Daw Amar were among those who considered the politics of "self-reliance", pursued by U Nu's government in the 1950s, inadequate. During these years of instability, U Hla was arrested and imprisoned on five occasions, including for three years from October 1953, when he was found guilty of having published a seditious news item.

The "Burmese Way to Socialism" pursued by the Revolutionary Council, led by Ne Win, that seized power in 1962 was not U Hla's way. He succeeded in keeping *Ludu Thadin-Za* in being while many other newspapers were closed down, but in 1964 the Revolutionary Council announced that it had "resolved the problem of the country's main newspapers" – by nationalizing them. The Ministry of Information now controlled what could be published and in 1967 *Ludu Thadin-Za* was closed down.

U Hla and Daw Amar had established a family tradition of opposition to Burma's increasingly repressive governments. Two of their sons joined the underground communist movement: Their eldest son, Soe Win, was "purged" from the party in the 1970s, while the second son, Than Chaung, was forced into exile. The couple's youngest son, the writer Nyi Pu Lay (1952–) became popular after his father's death for his satirical short stories, published in 1989 and 1990. He was arrested, along with three other writers, in December 1990, as he returned to Mandaly after a visit to Pagan. Charged under section 7 of the Unlawful Association Act of 1908, he was sentenced to ten years' imprisonment, primarily because of his family's political pedigree, but also for his satirical writings. Nyi Pu Lay was released from prison in February 1999 and has been able to publish new short stories since, though not all that he has written has been passed by the censors.

Kyi-bwa-yay's printing press and paper store were destroyed in the great Mandalay fire of 1984. Publication did not begin again until 1987. In the 1990s, financial constraints forced the press to abandon its traditional commitment to dissidence and to concentrate on commercial contracts. Only a severely limited number of other work now sees the light of day.

ANNA ALLOTT

Further Reading

Allott, Anna J., "Half a Century of Publishing in Mandalay: The Ludu Kyi-bwa-yay Press", *Burma Studies Journal*, 1/1 (1997): 83–106

Hla, Ludu U, *The Caged Ones*, Bangkok: Tamarind Press, 1986

LEONID LUKOV
Russian film director, 1909–1963

BOL'SHAIA ZHIZN' (A Great Life)
Film, 2 parts, 1940–46

Bol'shaia zhizn' (*A Great Life*) was made and shown in two parts, a practice that was not uncommon in Soviet cinema in the 1940s. Part 1 was completed and released to a warm reception in 1940, before the Soviet Union entered World War II, and Leonid Lukov was awarded the Stalin Prize; part 2 followed six years later. Both parts of the film starred three popular actors: Boris Andreev, Petr Aleinikov, and Mark Bernes.

Part 1 depicts the "great life" of miners in the Donbass region, who had played a crucial role in the rapid industrialization of the 1930s. They were in every sense "key" workers, and their activities were held up as a role model for others. Part 2 represents a continuation and development of the themes of part 1 in the light of the experience of the war. Set in 1943, after the Donbass region had been recaptured by the Soviet army from the German invaders, the film depicts the reconstruction of the mining and other industries by the workers themselves.

The film might well have been forgotten if it had not become the subject of a notorious decree issued by the Communist Party's Central Committee on 4 September 1946, "O fil'me *Bol'shaia zhizn'*" (On the Film *A Great Life*). Although the decree mentions three other films – *Prostye liudi* (1945, Simple People), directed by Grigorii Kozintsev and Leonid Trauberg; Vsevolod Pudovkin's *Admiral Nakhimov* (1946); and part 2 of Sergei Eisenstein's *Ivan Grozni* (1946, *Ivan the Terrible*) – it concentrates its wrath, as its title suggests, on *A Great Life*. The decree was one of a series of postwar edicts on various aspects of cultural life issued at the instigation of Andrei Zhdanov, who had by then become Stalin's "cultural commissar". The consequences of these edicts were to some extent mitigated, at least for some cultural activists, by Zhdanov's death in 1948, although it was not until some time after Stalin's death in March 1953 that some semblance of normal creative activity began to return.

The decree of September 1946 argues that *A Great Life* is "ideologically and politically flawed, and artistically extremely weak". Furthermore, "the reconstruction of the Donbass is of minor importance in the film, where attention is focused on a primitive depiction of all manner of personal experiences and scenes from daily life". It was a fairly common complaint on the part of the Soviet authorities that films concentrated on the personal at the expense of the political, but audiences might well have complained if the the films had done otherwise. The decree further declares that "two different epochs in the development of our industry have evidently become confused in the film". As a result, reconstruction is depicted as involving the kind of "application of brute physical strength, superannuated technology, and old-fashioned work methods" characteristic of the early Soviet period after the end of the Civil War in 1921, instead of the "sophisticated technology and advanced production culture" that the propaganda myth required in any depiction of postwar reconstruction.

Reconstruction is also depicted, according to the decree, out of its proper historical context. On the one hand, *A Great Life* implies that the war came to an end in 1943, with the recapture of the Donbass; on the other, the workers appear to be labouring without the support of the Soviet state, so that "party workers have been falsely portrayed in the film". However, the most stringent criticism is reserved for the depiction of the workers themselves:

The film *A Great Life* champions backwardness, coarseness, and ignorance. The film-makers have shown workers who are technically barely literate, and hold outdated views and attitudes, being promoted *en masse* to management positions. This is entirely unjustified and incorrect . . . The film *A Great Life* shows Soviet people in a false, distorting light. The workers and engineers who have reconstructed the Donbass are shown as backward people with very low moral qualities. For most of the time, the heroes of the film are idle, engaging in empty chit-chat or drunkenness. The best people, in the film's scheme of things, are inveterate drunkards.

Such realism, especially in the portrayal of the workers, had no place in "socialist realism", which, according to the decree, is required through "revolutionary romanticism" to depict didactically "not reality as it is, but reality as it will be". Lukov's film had fallen foul of that requirement by depicting reality as it almost certainly was.

Lukov was not a director of the first rank and, despite being singled out for opprobrium in this decree, he continued his film-making career until two years before his death. Although the decree was not officially rescinded until the period of pere-stroika in the 1980s, *A Great Life* was finally released on 21 December 1958, nearly three years after Khrushchev's secret speech (February 1956) denouncing the excesses of Stalin's "cult of personality". It has more recently been shown on Russian television.

RICHARD TAYLOR

Further Reading

Eisenstein, S.M., *Selected Works*, vol. 3: *Writings 1934–1947*, edited by Richard Taylor, London: BFI Publishing, and Bloomington: Indiana University Press, 1996

Leyda, Jay, *Kino: A History of the Russian and Soviet Film*, 3rd edition, London: Allen and Unwin, and Princeton, New Jersey: Princeton University Press, 1983

Margolit, Evenii and Viacheslav Shmyrov, *Iz"iatoe kino* (Withdrawn Cinema), Moscow: Double-D, 1995

Mar'iamov, Grigorii, *Kremlevskii tsenzor: Stalin smotrit v kino* (The Kremlin Censor: Stalin Keeps Watch on Cinema), Moscow: Kinotsentr, 1992

Taylor, Richard and Derek Spring (editors), *Stalinism and Soviet Cinema*, London and New York: Routledge, 1993

Volkova, Nina et al. (editors), *Sovetskoe kino, 1917–1978: Resheniia partii i pravitel'stva o kino*, vol. 2: *1937–1961* (Soviet Cinema, 1917–78: Party and Government Decisions on Cinema, vol. 2: 1937–61), Moscow: NIITIK and TsGALI, 1979

ANATOLII LUNACHARSKII
Russian politician and educator, 1875–1933

Lunacharskii was born at Poltava in Ukraine, the illegitimate son of a senior civil servant, state counsellor A.I. Antonov. After schooling in Kiev, where he became a member of a Social Democratic student group, he studied philosophy at the University of Zurich. While he was in Switzerland, he came into contact with Georgii Plekhanov, then the leading Marxist theoretician in the Russian Social Democratic Workers' Party. On his return to Russia in 1898, Lunacharskii became active in a Social Democratic group in Moscow, and was arrested, imprisoned, and sent into exile in Siberia. After his release from exile, Lunacharskii again went abroad.

Lunacharskii met Lenin for the first time in Paris in 1904, and later joined Lenin's Bolshevik faction within the Russian Social Democratic Party. He was to be active intermittently in Bolshevik circles in western Europe for the next few years. However, his friendship and intellectual cooperation with Aleksandr Bogdanov, who was his brother in law, and whose Vpered (Forward) Group was in philosophical and political dispute with Lenin, led to Lunacharskii's break with the Bolsheviks in 1908. His association with Vpered was confirmed by the publication in the same year of the first volume of his work *Religiia i Sotsializm* (Religion and Socialism). This work, which eventually filled two volumes, is an idealistic appeal for the rediscovery of the moral and ethical strands in socialist thought. As such, it aroused the censure of Lenin, who was always a resolute defender of the materialist position in philosophy and politics.

In 1909 Lunacharskii made his first direct contribution to the political education of working people. Interested in the possibility of developing political awareness didactically, he was instrumental in organizing a Social Democratic Party school on the Italian island of Capri. The purpose of the school was declared to be the education and training of "permanent cadres of party leaders from the working class". The students were chosen by local Social Democratic committees within Russia and smuggled across Europe to Italy. Lunacharskii insisted on a nonpartisan programme, without censorship of the curriculum. Leading members of all the Russian Social Democratic groups in exile were invited to give lectures. Nevertheless, the school soon fell victim to the internecine struggle being waged within the Russian party. In practice, only members of the Forward Group actually taught at the Capri school. Lunacharskii himself lectured on social and labour history. A second party school was organized by Lunacharskii and his associates at Bologna in 1910. This managed to attract lecturers from outside the Forward group, notably Lev Trotskii. Lenin remained opposed, seeing the experiment as an instrument of factional struggle. No more such schools were held until after October 1917. The experience made Lunacharskii aware of the potential problems of censorship and indoctrination in the curriculum and conduct of workers' political education.

For the next few years, Lunacharskii continued to develop his theoretical understanding of educational and cultural questions in general, and of working-class adult education in particular, and edited the Forward Group's theoretical and discussion journal. He was particularly keen to secure the recognition and development of an independent proletarian culture. He believed that the shaping of such a culture through independent working-class educational initiatives would be an important method of developing proletarian class consciousness and political militancy. This placed him very close to the programme of the postrevolutionary "Proletkul't" movement, which was to be vigorously opposed by Lenin for what he regarded as its naivety and idealism.

Lunacharskii returned to Russia in May 1917 and was imprisoned during the disturbances known as the "July Days". Readmitted to membership of the Bolshevik Party (as Lenin's faction had since become) on his release, he became chairman of the newly formed Cultural and Educational Commission of the Petrograd Bolshevik Party Committee. After the October revolution, he was appointed People's Commissar for Popular Enlightenment. His political record prevented him from becoming a member of the party inner circle but he was recognized nonetheless, together with his deputy Nadezhda Krupskaia (Lenin's wife), as the leading party authority on educational and cultural matters. Henceforward, he received Lenin's consistent support, although the latter remained critical of Lunacharskii's continuing tendency to favour Bogdanov and the Proletkul't movement. Indeed, in 1920, when Lunacharskii was instructed by Lenin to reduce the Proletkul't to a subsidiary of his own People's Commissariat of Enlightenment (Narkompros), Lunacharskii failed to do so, maintaining that the Proletkul't "must preserve its quality of independent activity".

Lunacharskii's attitude to "proletarian" censorship of so-called "bourgeois art" was in fact ambiguous. A demand from the revolutionary poet Vladimir Maiakovskii that "the firing squad" should give its attention to the "classical generals" of culture, including Aleksandr Pushkin, caused Lunacharskii to protest against "the destructive tendencies in regard to the past and the attempt, while speaking in the name of a particular school, to speak at the same time in the name of authority". It has been observed that Lunacharskii felt uncomfortable in the role of censor. In an article written in 1921, he was to say that:

The person who tells us that censorship is necessary, even when it prevents the publication of great works of art when these hide obvious counter-revolution, is correct. So is the one who says that we must choose, and we must give only third or fourth priority to undoubtedly necessary works in comparison with books for which we have the greatest need. But the person who says, "down with all those prejudices about the freedom of expression. State leadership in literature corresponds to our new Communist order. Censorship is not a terrible component of our time of transition, but a regular part of socialist life", the person who draws the conclusion that criticism should be turned into some kind of denunciation, and that artistic work should be turned into primitive revolutionary slogans, he only shows that under the Communist exterior, if you scratch him a bit, you will find in reality *Derzhimorda* (Shut your gob).

Peter Kenez regards this statement by Lunacharskii as the closest to a defence of the freedom of expression any Bolshevik leader was to make in the early 1920s. Yet Lunacharskii accepted Lenin's principle that censorship was sometimes a revolutionary necessity. Also in 1921, in the context of the introduction of the New Economic Policy, Lunacharskii stated plainly, in a manner reminiscent of Krupskaia's justification for her purging of workers' libraries, that: "We in no way shrink from the necessity of applying censorship even to belles-lettres, since, under this banner and beneath this elegant exterior, poison may be implanted in the still naive and dark soul of the great mass of the people, which is constantly ready to waver."

As People's Commissar of Enlightenment, Lunacharskii was responsible for the administration of all forms of education. His first proclamation, on 29 October 1917, had declared the intention to mount a major struggle against the mass illiteracy and popular ignorance that had prevailed in prerevolutionary society. This meant, of necessity, a massive programme of popular adult education. In 1919, the educational policy detailed by Lunacharskii and Krupskaia, and supported by Lenin, was confirmed as part of the programme of what was now the Communist Party. It was a truly revolutionary educational manifesto. The basic principle of Lunacharskii's programme was to be the encouragement of mass initiative, "the inducement of all the working population to participate in the spread of enlightenment". The Soviet state was given the task of constructing a network of adult education facilities, including libraries, museums, art galleries, and cinemas, in an effort to raise the level of mass popular culture. The rapid building of a socialist education system was seen by Lunacharskii and the Communist Party at this period as essential to maintaining Soviet proletarian power, and overcoming the dangers of bureaucracy and reliance on bourgeois "expertise".

Although considerable progress was made, the political and economic circumstances of the difficult postrevolutionary years carried serious implications for educational policy. The first party conference on popular education (December 1920 to January 1921) indicated a trend away from Lunacharskii's radical early decrees towards a more narrowly pragmatic policy. Over the next decade, Lunacharskii and Krupskaia saw their objective of a high level of mass general education, linked with productive work, steadily eroded by a programme aimed at producing an elite of highly trained specialist cadres for the party, the state, and the economy. The consolidation of Stalinism after 1927 hastened and intensified this process.

The new policy did see a massive expansion of the education system, but mass initiative had been replaced by mass direction, including central control and censorship of both academic and vocational curricula in the interests of the Soviet state. Once again, Lunacharskii's uncomfortable ambiguity may be seen in his guarded defence in November 1927 of a non-party intelligentsia who were, he said, "awaiting a call from Soviet power to bring the most valuable elements of the aristocracy of mind into the highest organs of the government". This led to accusations of "cultural rightism". In 1929 Lunacharskii was replaced as People's Commissar for Popular Enlightenment by Andrei Bubov, a former Red Army political commissar. During the remaining years of his life, Lunacharskii held various titular offices, including director of the Institute of Literature, Art, and Language, where once again he became involved in questions of literary and artistic censorship. In poor health after 1930, he died in the south of France in 1933, while on his way to take up an appointment as Soviet Ambassador to Spain. A warm and cultured man, and a key educational theorist and administrator, he was himself a victim of censorship: his works were not published again in the Soviet Union until after Stalin's death in 1953.

W. JOHN MORGAN

Writings

*Self-Education of the Workers: The Cultural Tasks of the Proletariat;
also a Brief Account of the Educational Work of the Russian
Soviet Republic*, 1919
On Literature and Art, translated by Avril Pyman and Fainna
Glagoleva, 2nd edition, 1973
On Education: Selected Articles and Speeches, 1981

Further Reading

Carr, E.H., *Socialism in One Country, 1924–1926*, 3 vols, London
and New York: Macmillan, 1958–64

Fitzpatrick, Sheila, *The Commissariat of Enlightenment: Soviet
Organization of Education and the Arts under Lunacharsky,
October 1917–1921*, Cambridge: Cambridge University Press,
1970
Fitzpatrick, Sheila (editor), *Cultural Revolution in Russia,
1928–1931*, Bloomington: Indiana University Press, 1978
Kenez, Peter, *The Birth of the Propaganda State: Soviet Methods of
Mass Mobilization, 1917–1929*, Cambridge and New York:
Cambridge University Press, 1985

MOLLA LUTFI
Ottoman theologian and mathematician, died 1494

Molla (or mullah) Lutfi was a leading member of the Ottoman learned elite and at times an intimate of sultan Mehmet II (reigned 1451–81), before being sentenced to death and executed for heresy. His was a case of "censorship" resulting from professional jealousy and hurt pride.

As with many other personalities of the time, our knowledge about Molla Lutfi is full of gaps. We know that he came from the central Anatolian town of Tokat, but we do not know the year of his birth. We also know that he studied under some of the greatest scholars of the Ottoman empire. One of these was Sinan Pasha, who became Lutfi's most important patron, and also had excellent relations with sultan Mehmet II, who conquered Constantinople in 1453. At first, Sinan Pasha taught at the most prominent religious colleges of the Ottoman empire, and then became the Conqueror's personal instructor. Sinan Pasha is said to have been of splendid intelligence, tolerant and open-minded, the leading member of a group of scholars who shared his intellectual inclinations and were in part his pupils: Lutfi was one of them. They were opposed by another group of religious scholars, whose members are described in the sources as tradition-loving, narrow-minded, and intolerant. To this second group belonged Hatibzade, Molla Zari, and Molla Ahaveyn, who later on were the chief advocates of Molla Lutfi's execution. Both groups struggled for position and the sultan's appreciation (which in the end meant money and a good career).

On Sinan Pasha's recommendation, sultan Mehmet made Molla Lutfi the keeper of his personal library in 1470. Lutfi retained this position for six years. This was an honourable post and the sultan's collection offered Lutfi the chance to read rare books that were not accessible to other people, including most of the 'ulama' (senior scholars), a privilege calculated to draw out their invective against him. Lutfi was involved indirectly in teaching the sultan, for at Sinan Pasha's request, he had taken mathematics lessons from 'Ali Kuščū in order to teach the Pasha, who then in turn would instruct the sultan in Kuščū's teachings. Lutfi was soon on very familiar terms with Mehmet.

In 1476, however, a dramatic event interrupted the careers of both Sinan Pasha and Lutfi, when the former was dismissed from his position and imprisoned. We do not know the reason, but Sinan Pasha is believed to have drawn upon himself the personal anger of the sultan. Following petitions from his friends among the Ottoman learned class, Sinan Pasha was released from prison shortly afterwards, but he was then appointed qadi (judge) in a place remote from power and influence. According to some, he was also imprisoned and tortured there on the pretext that he had lost his mind. Molla Lutfi, himself known to his enemies as "the mad", followed him into exile, living there with him for five years.

It was only after the death of sultan Mehmet in 1481 and the accession of the new ruler, Bayezid II, that Lutfi and his teacher were rehabilitated. They returned to Istanbul. Lutfi became a teacher at some of the important religious colleges of the empire before being assigned to one of the top Ottoman religious colleges at the Court of the Eight (Sahn-i seman) in about 1493. The Court of the Eight was a conglomeration of eight religious colleges around the courtyard of Fatih mosque in Istanbul. Each of the eight had its own teacher. This was an important step towards the highest state offices, but his presence led to intense competition between him and the other teachers. Lutfi is reported to have been not only intellectually brilliant but also ready to expose the shortcomings of the other seven teachers, in a highly derogatory manner. His enemies, infuriated by his criticism, accused him of heresy and demanded his execution.

Their first attempt to persuade the sultan to have Lutfi executed failed. Bayezid refused to decide the matter himself. He referred the matter to the experts, who included, however, the very conspirators who sought Lutfi's punishment. His enemies reported that he had called the ritual prayer, which is obligatory in Islam, "worthless rising and bowing". For that alone, they argued, he deserved to be condemned for heresy. However, it appears that Lutfi had spoken out only against a degenerate form of the prayer, bodily movements without spiritual engagement and therefore without value. Lutfi was also accused of "insulting the Prophet Muhammad", but we do not know on what grounds these accusations were founded, nor whether a charge of having stolen books from sultan Mehmet's library had substance.

In the end, despite Lutfi's declaration that he adhered to the orthodox Muslim creed, his opponents were able to persuade the rest of the assembled scholars that he deserved death. The sultan bowed to the learned men's decision, and Lutfi was beheaded in the Hippodrome of Istanbul, probably on 24 December 1494.

Arguably, the execution of Molla Lutfi resulted from an ideological conflict between a more traditional school of scholars and the sceptical, rationalistic views of the Molla. However, it seems more likely that the "court" that was summoned against him was really a vehicle for his enemies' personal hatred. Among the reasons for adopting this view is the role played by Hatibzade, a member of the "jury" and long-standing enemy of Molla Lutfi. Under sultan Mehmet, Hatibzade had attained a post as teacher in one of the Eight Colleges, but had been dismissed due to some dispute with the sultan. Rehabilitated, he then even became Mehmet's personal teacher for some time, before being dismissed after another quarrel with the sultan. Under Bayezid, he had to endure Lutfi's occupation of a post that he himself had once held. Lutfi had recently written a tough review of one of Hatibzade's books, and had announced his intention to do so with another of his works. When Hatibzade came home from watching Lutfi's execution, he reportedly said that he had just saved the second book from being ruined by Molla Lutfi.

The works of Molla Lutfi that have come down to us deal with Islamic theology, logic, rhetoric, mathematics, astronomy, engineering, the theory of science, and ethics. Molla Lutfi had a number of pupils, the most important of whom was Ibn Kemal (or Kemalpashazade), one of the greatest Ottoman scholars of the 16th century.

MICHAEL REINHARD HESS

Further Reading

Adnan-Adivar, Abdülhak Adnan, Osmanlı Türklerinde ilim (Science Among the Ottoman Turks), Istanbul: Maarif Matbaası, 1943

Çoruh, Hakkı Şinasi, "Fatih'in kütüphane memuru, Büyük Türk Ansiklopedisti Molla Lutfi (?–1494) (The Librarian of Mehmed the Conqueror, The Great Turk Encyclopedist Molla Lütfi), Türk Kültürü, 115 (1972): 35–42

Gibb, E.J.W., A History of Ottoman Poetry, edited by Edward G. Browne, vol. 2, London: Luzac, 1902

Gündüz, Irfan, Osmanlılarda devlet-tekke münasebetleri (The Relations between the State and the Dervish Lodges under the Ottomans), Ankara: Seha Neşriyat, 1984

Mumcu, Ahmet, Osmanlı Devletinde Siyaseten Katl (Political Murder in the Ottoman Empire), Ankara: Birey ve Toplum Yayınları, 1985

Ocak, Ahmet Yasar, Osmanli Toplumunda Zindiklar ve Mülhidler, 15–17. Yüzyıllar (Heretics in the Ottoman Society, 15th to 17th Centuries), Istanbul: Tarih Vakfi Yayinlari, 1998

Zelyut, Rıza, Osmanlıda karšı düšünce: Düšünceleri Nedeniyle Idam Edilenler (Oppositional Thinking under the Ottomans: Those Who Were Executed Because of their Thoughts), Istanbul: Alan Yayıncılık, 1986

MARTIN LUTHER
German theologian and reformer, 1483–1546

On 31 October 1517, Martin Luther, an Augustinian monk and, since 1512, professor of bible studies at the University of Wittenberg, posted his *Ninety-five Theses; or, Disputation on the Power and Efficacy of Indulgences* at about noon on the door of the town's Castle Church. He thereby initiated, quite unintentionally, the Protestant Reformation.

Luther was concerned about abuses perpetrated by the church in general and outraged in particular about the sale of indulgences by Johann Tetzel, a Dominican friar, in nearby Magdeburg. Indulgences were certificates that those who had repented their sins and been forgiven for them could purchase from the church, giving them, according to the prevailing doctrine, remittance from certain numbers of days that after death they would otherwise have to spend in Purgatory. Luther seems to have intended merely to provoke some academic debate about the doctrinal justification for indulgences. Almost immediately, however, the church, along with the Holy Roman Emperor and, eventually, a host of other secular authorities, attempted to have him silenced. Luther was not the first to challenge the church, of course, but, as he himself explained it, "others have attacked the life" of the church, while "I attack the doctrine".

Luther's act of posting his theses was not unusual in itself. Such disputatious theses were often posted on church doors to communicate information about significant matters. Yet Luther did not intend that his theses should have a widespread circulation and wrote them in Latin for his fellow-scholars to read. He wrote in the preamble:

Out of love and zeal for the truth and the desire to bring it to light, the following theses will be publicly discussed at Wittenberg under the chairmanship of the Reverend Father Martin Luther, Master of Arts and Sacred Theology, and regularly appointed lecturer on these subjects at that place.

Luther requested that those who could not be present in person to debate should do so by letter. Not a single person arrived to debate the theses.

Luther then sent a copy of the theses to Albert of Brandenburg, archbishop of Mainz, along with a letter requesting his help in the fight against the sale of indulgences. Tetzel, according to Luther, was perpetrating a "great swindle", assuring his victims that "as your money into the coffer rings, a soul from Purgatory springs". Understandably, the archbishop, who not only supported, but benefited financially from, Tetzel's activities, did not respond directly to Luther's letter. Instead, on 1 December 1517 he asked theologians at the University of Mainz to study Luther's theses and tell him their opinion. The archbishop sent a copy of the theses, with the theologians' conclusions, to Rome in mid-December 1517: by this point he wanted the heretic Luther stopped. Tetzel and others, such as Dr Johannes Eck, a professor at Ingolstadt University, also denounced Luther.

Within a few months, Luther's individual concerns had become a matter of controversy all over Europe. Three editions of the theses were printed in Nuremberg, Basel, and Leipzig, and many more followed: no wonder Luther described printing as "God's highest and extremest act of grace". As professor De Lamar Jensen has argued, "In a very real sense it could be said that the Reformation was a result of the invention of printing".

Calls to silence Luther and efforts to censor his writings became ever more frequent and determined. As early as 3 February 1518, pope Leo X ordered Luther's monastic superior, the prefect of the Augustinians, Gabriel della Volta, to exert his control over Luther. Reportedly, Leo referred to the reformer as some "drunken German who will amend his ways when he sobers up". However, the elector of Saxony, Frederick III – known to later Protestants, but hardly to Catholics, as Frederick the Wise – had installed Luther as a teacher at Wittenberg and now promised to protect him. In a letter dated 31 March 1518 the "Wittenberg Reformer" refused to recant unless convinced on the basis of scripture and claimed his right to dispute as a university professor.

The controversy intensified. Luther was prolific, writing tracts, treatises, sermons, devotionals, commentaries, and other theological pieces, denouncing, among other practices and institutions, clerical celibacy, pilgrimages, religious orders, and the admission of the laity to communion in one kind only. Scholars have claimed that Luther kept three printing presses busy.

On 15 June 1520, pope Leo published his bull *Exsurge, Domine*, which cited 41 of Luther's "heresies", called for the burning of his books, and gave him 60 days to recant: "A wild boar has invaded thy vineyard", the pope wrote, addressing God, and his teachings were "poisonous, offensive, misleading for godly and simple minds, uncharitable, and counter to all reverence for the Holy Roman Church, the mother of the faithful and the mistress [*magistra*] of faith". Public burnings of Luther's books took place at the Sorbonne in Paris, St Paul's churchyard in London, and elsewhere in western Europe. Luther replied by burning the bull and other writings hostile to his positions. Pope Leo then issued a bull of excommunication, *Decet Romanum pontificem*, on 3 January 1521.

Luther was thus excluded from the church and should have been executed by secular authorities. Instead, probably because of political concerns and manoeuvrings, and perhaps also because of the increasingly powerful popular support for Luther, it was arranged that he be summoned to appear before the emperor, Charles V, and the Diet of the Holy Roman Empire at Worms. Safe passage was promised. Luther arrived at the Diet on 17 April 1521. His books were piled up on a table. Members of the Diet asked two questions: was he their author? and if so, would he recant? The next day, Luther confirmed his refusal, first in German, then in Latin:

Since then Your Majesty and your lordships seek a simple answer, I will give it in this manner, neither horned nor toothed: unless I am convinced by the testimony of the scriptures or by clear reason (for I do not trust either in the Pope or in councils alone, since it is well-known that they have often erred and contradicted themselves), I am bound by the scriptures I have quoted and my conscience is captive to the Word of God.

Luther would not be silenced. He continued, "I cannot and I will not retract anything, since it is neither safe nor right to go against conscience. I cannot do otherwise, here I stand, may God help me: Amen." Charles V offered Luther three more days to consider his position, but Luther stood firm. Finally, on 26 May 1521, Charles V signed the Edict of Worms, which declared Luther an "outlaw who could be killed with impunity".

Luther was not killed, for he continued to enjoy the protection of the rulers of Saxony and of the increasing numbers of other "Lutheran" princes. He passed the rest of his life writing and teaching at the University of Wittenberg. He was always amazed at how quickly his writings spread among the general population. He wrote in 1541, "So my theses against Tetzel's articles, which you can now see in print, were published. They went throughout the whole of Germany in a fortnight, for the whole world complained about indulgences."

The significance of the Lutheran Reformation for the history of censorship lies partly in its early demonstration of the subversive power of print. Those who would have censored Luther could hardly keep up as his works were reproduced on all the printing presses of central Europe and beyond. According to Lewis Spitz, "the Reformation was the first historical movement in the post-Gutenberg era and the printing press made it possible". Luther himself taught that "we must continue to be disciples of those speechless masters that we call books". For those who have sought to defend freedom of thought and expression, the blunt declaration that Luther is supposed to have made at the Diet of Worms – *Hier stehe ich, ich kann nicht anders* ("Here I stand, I can do no other") – has become a landmark, whether he actually said it in precisely those terms or not.

Nevertheless, Luther was unquestionably a man of his time when it came to the rights of others, and it would be anachronistic to see him as defending freedom of thought or expression in the abstract. His support for the German princes and his opposition to those who rose against them in the Peasants' War (1524–25) indicated his contempt for the uneducated and for advocates of social rather than religious reform; while in *On the Jews and Their Lies* (1543), for example, he urged that "synagogues should be set on fire and whatever is left should be buried in dirt so that no one may ever be able to see a stone or cinder of it". For all that, Luther was one of the first western thinkers to insist on the primacy of the individual conscience, a constant theme in the history of censorship from then on.

JESSE L. SCOTT

Writings

Werke (Weimar edition), edited by J.C.F. Knaake *et al.*, 1883–
Works (American edition), edited by Jaroslav Pelikan and Helmut T. Lehmann, 1955–
Selections, edited by John Dillenberger, 1961
Selected Political Writings, edited by J.M. Porter, 1974

Further Reading

Bornkamm, Heinrich, *Luther in Mid-Career, 1521–1530*, edited by Karin Bornkamm, Philadelphia: Fortress Press, 1983
Brecht, Martin, *Martin Luther: His Road to Reformation, 1483–1521*, Minneapolis: Fortress Press, 1993
Edwards, Mark U. Jr, *Luther's Last Battles: Politics and Polemics, 1531–46*, Ithaca, New York: Cornell University Press, 1983
Eisenstein, Elizabeth L., *The Printing Press as an Agent of Change: Communications and Cultural Transformations in Early Modern Europe*, Cambridge and New York: Cambridge University Press, 1979
Jensen, De Lamar, *Confrontation at Worms: Martin Luther and the Diet of Worms, with a Complete English Translation of the Edict of Worms*, Provo, Utah: Brigham Young University Press, 1973
Jensen, De Lamar, *Reformation Europe: Age of Reform and Revolution*, Lexington, Massachusetts: Heath, 1981

Kittelson, James M., *Luther the Reformer: The Story of the Man and His Career*, Minneapolis: Augsburg, 1986; Leicester: Inter-Varsity Press, 1989

McGrath, Alister E., *Luther's Theology of the Cross: Martin Luther's Theological Breakthrough*, Oxford and New York: Blackwell, 1985

Oberman, Heiko A., *Luther: Man between God and the Devil*, New Haven, Connecticut: Yale University Press, 1989

Ozment, Steven, *Protestants: The Birth of a Revolution*, New York: Doubleday, 1992, London: Fontana, 1993

Spitz, Lewis W., *The Protestant Reformation, 1517–1559*, New York: Harper and Row, 1985

ROSA LUXEMBURG

Polish intellectual and socialist revolutionary, 1871–1919

From her schooldays in Russian-ruled Warsaw to her violent death at the hands of German soldiers in revolutionary Berlin, Rosa Luxemburg regularly faced censors of various kinds. Although not exactly a matter of free choice, her confrontations with opponents trying to stifle her freedom of expression were not accidental either. In part, they stemmed from her rebellious character. She was not a person to shun conflict. But Luxemburg's struggles with censorship also derived from the culture in which she spent her entire adult life: the fiercely faction-ridden and discordant world of international socialism. Finally, just as her position on the radical fringe of the socialist movement compounded Luxemburg's problems with party censors, socialism's own outsider status in Poland and Germany around 1900 created another censorship source: that of the established order, or the imperial German and Russian state machineries.

The main cultural influences in the close Luxemburg household of assimilated Jews were Western and German. As a teenager the gifted Rosa attended the second girls' high school in Warsaw, where she first experienced official oppression. First, the students were not allowed to speak Polish at this highly Russified institution, not even among themselves. Second, and more significant, upon graduation in 1887 Rosa did not receive the gold medal for academic achievement that she had earned on academic merit, reportedly because of a rebellious attitude toward the authorities. Although in part a matter of character, this episode can also be explained by her membership by this time of the "Revolutionary Party Proletariat", a Marxist grouping of mainly intellectuals.

In 1889, fearing arrest, she left Poland for the Swiss city of Zürich, a haven for left-radical exiles from the Russian empire. Almost immediately she became active in Polish socialist circles, while in 1890 she also enrolled at the university. Emphasizing the socialist cause over Polish nationalism, Luxemburg came into conflict with the established Polish Socialist Party (PPS), which tried to silence Rosa and her group. The PPS succeeded in this at the Congress of the Socialist International in August 1893, when the meeting denied Luxemburg and her friends a mandate as members of the Polish delegation, even though Rosa managed to get in a passionate plea for her cause. In a movement already leading a beleaguered existence Rosa Luxemburg often managed to occupy an extreme position, exposing herself to more than one kind of censorship.

In 1897 she received her doctorate, *magna cum laude*, with a dissertation entitled *The Industrial Development of Poland*, and the next year she moved to Berlin. She was determined further to expand her influence in the socialist movement through membership of the leading party, the Socialist Party of Germany (SPD). Although free from the restrictions placed on its activities by Bismarck's anti-socialist laws, and in spite of its growing support among the working population, the German party at this time remained an outcast in German politics. In part this was by choice, as became clear in 1903 when the party rejected the so-called revisionist doctrine that argued for a gradual, pragmatic, and parliamentary strategy, as opposed to a radical, anti-bourgeois, revolutionary course based on classic Marxism. From the time she joined the German party, Rosa Luxemburg polemicized vehemently against revisionism and its most prominent proponent, Eduard Bernstein. In her *Social Reform or Revolution* she accused Bernstein and his supporters of bringing bourgeois values into the party and argued for a radical form of censorship: if the revisionists did not leave the party of their own regard, they should be evicted: "We cannot commit suicide in the name of freedom to criticize." Around this time, Luxemburg also had her first run-in with the German imperial authorities. In 1904 she was sentenced to three months in jail for arguing that the emperor, Wilhelm II, had "no idea of the real facts" when he claimed to understand the problems of Germany's workers better than any Social Democrat.

In December 1905, at what turned out to be the high point of her influence in the SPD and the International, Rosa Luxemburg went to Warsaw to participate in the revolution that had begun in Russia that same year. She was arrested and jailed the following March, but became an even greater proponent of revolution as spontaneous mass action, for Germany as well. In the SPD, however, the trend was toward moderation and bureaucratization. As a result, Luxemburg became rather isolated in her party, received fewer opportunities to publish her work, and by 1911 even faced efforts to cut her out of party leadership correspondence. Meanwhile, she had served another prison term, in 1907, for a speech in 1905 in which she had called for mass strikes.

By 1913 Rosa Luxemburg's prominence, aggressive style, and anti-militarism made her a formidable adversary for the German imperial government. When, in a speech in September, she implored German workers not to take up weapons against their French brothers, the authorities were quick to charge her with calling for public disobedience of the law. She was tried the following year and sentenced to a one-year prison sentence. She began serving her term in early 1915, right after the first and only issue of a left-radical anti-war journal she had co-founded, *Die Internationale*, had been confiscated by the censor. By this time, the SPD executive, itself under pressure from the imperial government, was also cracking down on left-radical dissent in the party. These combined censorship campaigns made it ever more difficult for Luxemburg and her associates to distribute their views. Through clandestine ways, however, they managed, most famously in the form of the so-called *Spartakus Briefe* (Spartacus Letters), to which Luxemburg contributed heavily during her second prison term during World War I (in July 1916 she had been re-arrested on security grounds). While in prison she also composed her critique of the methods of the Bolshevik revolution, denouncing Lenin's dictatorial methods. In Luxemburg's view there could be no socialist revolution without the spontaneous and autonomous participation of the great majority of the masses.

Rosa Luxemburg met with the ultimate act of censorship – physical elimination of an opponent – on 19 January 1919 during the ill-fated Spartacus uprising in Berlin. However, the controversies over her work did not end there. Well into the era of the Cold War, Luxemburg's legacy was deformed, defamed, and otherwise manipulated, all according to the political needs of the Soviet government, the German Communist Party, the rulers of the German Democratic Republic, and Western leftist activists during the 1960s and 1970s – among others. But no matter where one stands on the significance of Rosa Luxemburg's work or the wisdom of her policies,

there is no question that in 19th- and 20th-century revolutionary socialist theory and practice she was, in Lenin's phrase, "an eagle".

RUUD VAN DIJK

Writings

Die industrielle Entwicklung Polens, 1899
Sozialreform oder Revolution, 1899, revised edition 1908; as *Reform or Revolution*, 1937
Gesammelte Werke, 5 vols, 1970–75
Selected Political Writings, edited by Dick Howard, 1971
Selected Political Writings, edited by Robert Looker, 1972
The Letters, edited by Stephen Eric Bronner, 1978

Further Reading

Ettinger, Elzbieta, *Rosa Luxemburg: A Life*, Boston: Beacon Press, 1986; London: Harrap, 1987
Fröhlich, Paul, *Rosa Luxemburg: Her Life and Work*, New York: Monthly Review Press, 1972
Hirsch, Helmut, *Rosa Luxemburg in Selbstzeugnissen und Bilddokumenten*, Hamburg: Rowohlt, 1969
Nettl, J.P., *Rosa Luxemburg*, 2 vols, London and New York: Oxford University Press 1966

ELIE LUZAC
Dutch publisher, 1721–1796

ESSAI SUR LA LIBERTÉ DE PRODUIR SES SENTIMENS
(Essay on Freedom of Expression)
Treatise, 1749

Elie Luzac was a young publisher of Huguenot descent living in Leiden, where in 1747 he brought out Julien Offroy de la Mettrie's *L'Homme machine* (Man a Machine). The book espoused an extreme materialism; people did not have immortal souls and there was no immaterial God. Luzac was immediately called before the Walloon Consistory in Leiden and ordered to turn in all copies of the book for burning, to reveal the name of the author, and to apologize and promise to never print anything like that again. He delivered most of the copies, said he could not name the author, apologized, and promised as requested. The book was also banned and burned elsewhere, and became one of the most notorious tracts of the Enlightenment.

Luzac's submission, however, was not as abject as the Consistory believed. Soon he was sending copies that had been spared from the fire to booksellers for sale, and defending himself in print. In 1749 he brought out his own *Essay on Freedom of Expression* in 124 pages, octavo. In 1750 he published a shorter defence of freedom of the press in the *Nouvelle Bibliothèque germanique* and, many years later, returned to free-press issues in Dutch debates. Luzac's name did not appear on the *Essay on Freedom of Expression*, surely for fear of further trouble. The place of publication was given as "A Free Country", and instead of an official privilege, it read "With privilege from all true philosophers". It was dedicated to the English nation as a truly free people who enjoyed freedom of the press.

In the foreword Luzac positions himself in the natural-law

tradition, according to which self-love guides our judgement and a drive for domination makes us want to control other people's ideas. He examines the question whether by nature some can have a natural right to limit the expression of others, concluding that the public good demands that all views be examined in the search for truth. Although he defends the rights of atheists and immoralists to expound their position, Luzac insists that his own views are firmly grounded in religion and morality. Here, and elsewhere, he makes it clear that he is defending serious attempts to communicate ideas, not novels and lampoons or indecent and insulting material.

Luzac then argues that the expression of ideas can never be harmful to society; the only danger is the way in which they may be used. If everything which can be abused were prohibited, however, very little could be permitted. Anticipating J.S. Mill by over a century, Luzac argues that false ideas destroy themselves, and that people cannot be fully convinced of a truth unless they have seen both sides of the matter and weighed the objections against it. He defends the publication of la Mettrie's book despite its erroneous contents. When they see prohibitions of ideas instead of counter-arguments, people will suspect that the truth is being suppressed. The third chapter concludes that since the only rights that rulers have are those which benefit their subjects, and since ideas cannot be harmful, no ruler can have a right to limit the expression of ideas. Since no ruler can be infallible, they must listen to the opinions of their subjects.

Luzac then refutes objections, noting that prohibition of books seldom prevents the clandestine circulation of them, that rulers cannot be fully informed unless they have heard everyone, and that suppression of atheists violates religious principles. The final chapter is the most ad-hominem, arguing that those who seek to censor others usually do so out of laziness, ignorance, and fear or for the sake of selfish ambitions: Frederick the Great of Prussia is held up as an example of a forthright ruler who has no need of censorship.

Throughout the book, Luzac's chief targets are the clergy, and the chief writers he mentions in need of defence are philosophers whose orthodoxy had been questioned, from Spinoza and Leibniz to Collins. No mention is made of John Milton's *Areopagitica*. There is no sense that unlimited freedom of the press will undermine monarchy or oligarchy and actually lead to rule by public opinion.

JOHN CHRISTIAN LAURSEN

Writings

Essai sur la liberté de produir ses sentimens, 1749
"Reponse a l'imprimeur" in *Nouvelle Bibliothèque germanique*, 6/2 (1750): 431–41
Man More than a Machine . . . in Answer to a Treatise by M. de La Mettrie, 1752
"Memorie" in *Nieuwe Nederlandsche Jaerboeken*, 5/2 (1770): 809–96

Further Reading

Kossman, E.H., *Verlicht Conservatisme: over Elie Luzac*, Groningen, 1966

Laursen, John Christian, "Impostors and Liars: Clandestine Manuscripts and the Limits of Freedom of the Press in the Huguenot Netherlands" in *New Essays on the Political Thought of the Huguenots of the Refuge*, edited by John Christian Laursen, Leiden: Brill, 1995

Velema, Wyger R.E., *Enlightenment and Conservatism in the Dutch Republic: The Political Thought of Elie Luzac, 1721–1796*, Assen: Van Gorcum, 1993

TROFIM LYSENKO
Russian geneticist and agronomist, 1898–1976

Lysenkoism is perhaps the best-known case of pseudoscience in the 20th century. It emerged in the Soviet Union in the late 1920s and early 1930s, and became a dominant trend in biology in the late 1940s. By then, it was also prominent in Poland, Czechoslovakia, Bulgaria, Romania, Hungary, and the German Democratic Republic (East Germany). During the early 1950s Lysenko's theories were also officially supported in North Korea and the People's Republic of China.

In the Soviet Union, Lysenkoism was part of a more general pseudoscientific trend, which emerged in 1929–31 under the influence of the campaign of terror against several groups of prominent representatives of the pre-revolutionary scientific and technical elite. During this period, Iosif Stalin started his programmes of rapid industrialization and collectivization of agriculture. A considerable number of prominent scientists, designers, and engineers were arrested, and falsely accused of attempts to sabotage and wreck industrial and rural projects, in order to discredit the "socialist" system. Several prominent agricultural economists were accused of organizing an opposition "Peasant Party", while prominent engineers and designers were accused of creating an "Industrial Party" with the purpose of restoring the capitalist system. After several show trials, most of those arrested were sentenced either to death or to long terms in prison. (They were rehabilitated posthumously after 1956.) The forced collectivization of agriculture in 1929–32 was also linked to a mass terror campaign against more prosperous peasants (*kulaks*). More than a million *kulak* families were uprooted and deported to the Urals, Siberia, and the Soviet Far East; thousands were shot or sentenced to prison or labour camps.

These campaigns of terror made a serious impact on science in general, dividing scientists into different camps. The Communist Party postulated the inevitable existence of two conflicting scientific systems, the one "reactionary" and "bourgeois", the other "progressive", "socialist", and materialistic. According to this theory, the sciences were fields for "class struggle", just as much as other areas of human activity. Attempts were made to identify progressive, materialist, and socialist ideas in physics, chemistry, biology, and medicine. In 1936–37, during the main waves of Stalin's political terror, it became common to declare the theories of western scientists reactionary and idealistic, in contrast to the progressive ideas of "people's scientists", even though many of the latter were neither well-educated nor versed in research techniques. Trofim Lysenko was one such "people's scientist".

Lysenko became famous for his "discovery" that winter wheat could be harvested, even if sown during the spring, by keeping wet seeds under snow for several weeks. In fact, the technique had long been practised in other countries. However, Lysenko gave it a special name, *iarovisatsia* (vernalization) and promised that if it was used widely it would increase crop yields (which turned out not to be the case). He also developed a new theory of the "phasic development of plants", which paid great attention to the role of temperature and light patterns. This theory also was not a new one: once again, Lysenko merely used new terminology.

In 1935 Lysenko was appointed scientific director of the All-Union Institute of Selection and Genetics in Odessa. He boldly promised the government that his institute would create special winter wheat that would be super-resistant to cold, even that of the severe winters in Siberia. Lysenko's promise to solve the endemic problem of Russia's winters in exactly four years was all he needed to gain the attention and support of Stalin. In reality, of course, no such special winter wheat was ever created.

Lysenko also undertook to carry out his promise, not by classic methods of hybridization and selection, which needed more time, but by exploiting the direct effect of environmental factors on plants, on the false assumption that acquired characteristics could be inherited. In 1936, he declared that Mendelian genetics, based on the chromosomal theory of heredity and the existence of genes as chromosomal particles responsible for the specific characteristics of each organism, was not merely mistaken, but "bourgeois, Mendelist–Morganist pseudoscience". Lysenko redefined heredity as development under the control, not of genes, but of external and internal complexes of influences that are "assimilated" by cells. His ideas represented a revival of the long-discredited notions of the French biologist Lamarck.

Lysenko started to organize well-publicized debates on the problems of heredity, and finally split the Soviet biology fraternity into two conflicting camps. Opposition to Lysenko was led by the geneticist and plant breeder Nikolai Vavilov, director of the Institute of Cultivated Plants in Leningrad and the Institute of Genetics in Moscow. The debates spread into human genetics as well. In 1937 all fields of human and medical genetics were declared reactionary, and linked to Hitler's racial theories. Politicians who participated in the debates considered it impossible that humanity's many capabilities could be determined wholly or mainly by genes. All branches of human and medical genetics were duly banned, and the most prominent scientists in these fields (I. Agol, S.G. Levit, and others) were arrested and sentenced to long prison terms. Vavilov, despite the great international reputation that he then enjoyed, was arrested in 1940 and died in prison in 1943.

However, despite the physical elimination of Lysenko's most serious critics, the debates in genetics resumed in 1946, stimulated by the explosion of the atomic bombs over Hiroshima and Nagasaki, which represented an apparent "success" for "reactionary" western science. Stalin promised that Soviet scientists would "catch up" with their US counterparts. This statement encouraged the younger generation of Soviet geneticists to challenge Lysenko's theories. Perhaps surprisingly, Stalin continued his personal support for Lysenko's ideas, approving Lysenko's formal report *On the Situation in Biological Science*.

All aspects of Mendelian genetics, and particularly the theory of genes as chromosomal structures responsible for inheritance of individual characteristics, were now simply banned from both research and education. The state censorship body Glavlit was instructed to stop all publications in this field, but the existing censorship infrastructure, comprehensive as it was in the Soviet Union, was not enough. Ordinary censors could not understand the specific problems of genetics in particular or biology in general – or, indeed, of any other scientific discipline. Lysenko became a kind of "little Stalin" for biology and associated agricultural sciences. He was now in charge not only of the Lenin Academy of Agricultural Sciences and several other institutes, but also of a special commission that made authoritative recommendations to different ministries and committees about the measures that were needed to purify Soviet science of the negative and corruptive influence of "Mendelism–Morganism".

The teaching of genetics based on previous textbooks was banned in all schools and institutions of higher education. Textbooks on genetics and biology, and other related sciences, were taken out of the libraries and destroyed. Hundreds of university professors and dozens of other teachers who were not supporters of Lysenko's theories were dismissed. All others were under obligation to declare support for Lysenko. Directors of many research institutes were also dismissed, as well as many ordinary scientists. Some institutes and laboratories were closed down. Practically all editors of biological journals were replaced by supporters of Lysenko, and the editorial boards of these journals were also reorganized. These measures made certain that any paper containing any criticism of Lysenko's ideas, however indirect, would be rejected. Publishing houses that dealt with biological literature were also reorganized: well-known geneticists lost any chance to get their work accepted for publication at the preliminary stages. Between 1948 and 1964 not one graduate student was able to select a "classic" genetic problem for research or as the basis of a doctoral thesis, because the special "expert commission" on biology at the Ministry of Education, which made the final decisions about the award of science degrees, had also been reorganized and staffed with Lysenko's supporters.

Eventually, foreign books on genetics were also removed from science libraries and destroyed. Foreign scientific journals that had previously arrived through library or private subscriptions were also censored, and papers or articles that were critical of Lysenko's theories or considered "Mendelist–Morganist" were simply cut out. It was forbidden to subscribe to specialized journals in genetics, such as *Heredity*, *Genetics*, or *Mutations*.

Nikita Khrushchev, who became Soviet party and state leader after the death of Stalin in 1953, continued support for Lysenko's ideas and for repressive measures against "Mendelists–Morganists". The ban on western genetics and criticism of Lysenko's theories was lifted only after the fall of Khrushchev in October 1964. The Academy of Sciences appointed a special commission to investigate Lysenko's claims and experimental results. Most of them were found to have been falsified. Nevertheless, Lysenko remained a full member of the Academy and director of its agricultural experimental station until his death in 1976. Soviet biology was never able to recover fully from the negative effects of Lysenkoism.

ZHORES A. MEDVEDEV

Writings

Heredity and Its Variability, translated by Theodosius Dobzhansky, 1946
Soviet Biology: Report to the Lenin Academy of Agricultural Sciences, 1948

Further Reading

Graham, Loren R., *Science and Philosophy in the Soviet Union*, New York: Knopf, 1972; London: Allen Lane, 1973
Joravsky, David, *The Lysenko Affair*, Cambridge, Massachusetts: Harvard University Press, 1970

M

MACAU
See Hong Kong and Macau

MACEDONIA

(formerly Yugoslav Republic of Macedonia)

Population: 1,230,000
Main religions: Macedonian Orthodox; Muslim
Official language: Macedonian
Other languages spoken: Albanian; Turkish; Serbo-Croatian

Number of daily newspapers: 3
Number of periodicals: 37
Number of radio receivers per 1000 inhabitants: 206
Number of TV receivers per 1000 inhabitants: 257

The Slavs of Macedonia – an area coinciding, more or less, with ancient Macedonia – until the end of the 19th century called themselves Bulgarians, and many of them continued doing so until World War II. A large segment of them, however, developed a Macedonian national awareness. After the Congress of Berlin in 1878, Bulgaria and Greece, as well as Serbia, laid territorial claims on Macedonia and tried to prove that the population consisted predominantly of their respective co-nationals. All deviating opinions were suppressed. In Serbia, the pro-Macedonian weekly *Balkanski Glasnik* (Balkan Herald), which started appearing in 1902, was prohibited after a few issues. In Bulgaria, most copies of Krste Misirkov's *Za makedontskite raboti* (Sofia 1903, On Macedonian Matters) were confiscated and destroyed.

In 1913, after the Second Balkan War, Macedonia was divided between Bulgaria, Greece, and Serbia. In none of these countries were the Macedonians recognized as a separate national community, and all expressions of Macedonian national consciousness were prohibited. In Bulgaria, periodicals such as *Makedonski Vesti* (Macedonian News) and *Makedonska Zemja* (Macedonian Land), promoting an independent and united Macedonian state, ceased publication on censor's orders. In Yugoslavia (the Kingdom of the Serbs, Croats, and Slovenes), publications in Macedonian were forbidden (they were distributed illegally, mostly by the Communist Party); only stage performances by amateur companies were, informally, allowed. In Greece, even speaking Slavic was punishable under the dictatorship of Metaxas (1936–41).

After World War II, the communist government of Yugoslavia recognized the Macedonian nation and created a Republic of Macedonia as part of the Yugoslav Federation. Political opinions and works of art were censored in the same way as in the rest of Yugoslavia. In addition, with a view to the consolidation of Macedonian national consciousness, all manifestations of Bulgarianhood were forbidden – partly under the guise of measures against those who had collaborated with the Bulgarian fascist occupiers during World War II. Historians, linguists, folklorists, and literary historians seem to have been forced by (self-)censorship to distort or conceal any facts which appeared to support the Bulgarianhood of the Macedonians. In a notorious example, the title of the 19th-century anthology of folk songs compiled by the brothers Miladinov, *Bulgarian Folk Songs*, was systematically avoided; the book was usually referred to as "the collection of the Miladinovs". Macedonian citizens were sentenced to prison terms if they declared themselves Bulgarians or denied the existence of the Macedonian nation.

In 1991 the Republic of Macedonia became an independent state. Article 16 of the constitution guaranteed the freedom of press and speech. About 150 newspapers and magazines and nearly 200 radio and television stations quickly emerged. There is now potentially unlimited artistic and ideological freedom. Publications and broadcast programmes produced in minority languages by private companies are also allowed. There is no official censorship; journalists are entitled to protect their sources of information and the public has the right to be properly informed. There is, however, still no press law providing a legal framework, and the state still has many ways to manipulate the media, to exert pressure, and to muzzle journalists. Printed and electronic media have to be officially registered and to obtain a "work permit". Through the employee-owned, but state-subsidized (and actually state-controlled) company *Nova Makedonija* (New Macedonia), which has a near-monopoly on the printing, distribution, and sale of newspapers and periodicals, the Macedonian government has an efficient tool to influence the news coverage of an uncompliant editorship. Moreover, *Nova Makedonija* publishes the four main Macedonian newspapers. Reporters critical of the government are not dismissed but may be transferred to positions where they can do no harm. Dailies published by opposition parties – such as *Dnernik* (Journal), the privately owned paper of the main nationalist opposition party – fell victim to customs duties on newsprint and other costs. The Euro 92 printing plant, co-financed by the Soros Foundation, printed at lower cost, enabled opposition publications to appear, and thus substantially contributed to the pluralization of the Macedonian printed media; however, the plant was also struck by customs duties, from which the pro-government papers are exempted. Finally, major enterprises, which depend on the government for licenses, mostly advertise in pro-government papers, thus depriving the opposition papers of a part of their revenue. In this way, the latter are put under economic pressure to soften their tone. Papers from neighbouring countries such as Greece, with which Macedonia has strained relations, can be imported only with the approval of the Ministry of Internal Affairs.

The only broadcast corporation with nationwide capacity, the Macedonian Radio and Television, has remained state property; the general manager is appointed by the parliament. There are many alleged instances of government interference and pro-governmental bias in the news coverage. The government, which authorizes the use of broadcasting frequencies, decided in May 1995 to close down nearly half of the private radio and television stations, apparently for technical reasons. Accusations that the government attempted to muzzle the opposition by exerting "censorship through cleaning the airwaves" are not convincing. However, according to Human Rights Watch, about 70 per cent of the affected stations were owned by representatives of ethnic minorities, particularly Albanians (TV ART in Tetovo).

Finally, it should be mentioned that all the media (including the opposition papers and broadcast stations) have displayed a considerable amount of self-censorship when attacking the government and dealing with minorities issues. This attitude is inspired by the precarious international situation of Macedonia, whose name is not even recognized by the Greek government, and the ethnic tensions within the country. The government has to a large extent profited from the journalists' (declining) fear of endangering the country's stability. On 31 March 1992 100,000 ethnic Albanians demonstrated in favour of opening schools and media using the Albanian language. The police cracked down on one Albanian movement (which was demanding the establishment of an Albanian university in Tetovo) and arrested its leader, Farid Sulejmani, in February 1995. In 2000 the Macedonian authorities prohibited the distribution of the Albanian newspaper *Bota Sot* (The World Today) because of its "partial" covering of ethnic issues.

RAYMOND DETREZ

Further Reading

Abrahams, Fred, *A Threat to "Stability": Human Rights Violations in Macedonia*, New York: Human Rights Watch, 1996

Geroski, Branko, "Waiting for a Second Chance in Macedonia", *Transition*, 1/18 (6 October 1995): 42–45

Perry, Duncan M.. "The Republic of Macedonia: Finding Its Way" in *Politics, Power, and the Struggle for Democracy in South-East Europe*, edited by Karen Dawisha and Bruce Parrot, Cambridge: Cambridge University Press, 1997

JOHN McGAHERN
Irish novelist, 1935–
THE DARK
Novel, 1965

The banning in Ireland of John McGahern's second novel was announced on 1 June 1965. The novel, which had been published in Britain, was detained and forwarded to the Irish Censorship of Publications Board by customs officials. It had been reviewed in Ireland when it was published in May and compared by Terence de Vere White to the work of James Joyce. Nevertheless, the Censorship Board, although it was required to consider the literary merits of a work, recommended banning *The Dark* as "indecent or obscene".

The Censorship Board was not obliged by law to give any further explanation for its decision. It was generally assumed, however, that *The Dark* was banned on the basis of several passages that dealt with the central character's discovery of his sexuality. Set in rural Ireland, the novel portrays an adolescent's struggle to understand and escape the claustrophobic, puritan-ical Catholic society in which he has grown up. It is a society characterized by sexual repression, and the novel outlines the nature of this repression in detail. It opens with a scene in which the boy's father challenges his son for using the word "fuck". In other scenes the boy is subjected to sexual abuse, first by his father and then by a priest whose appearance in the boy's bedroom on his first night at boarding school reminds him of his father's nocturnal visits. Later, a chapter is devoted to a scene in which the boy masturbates while reading advertisements for stockings and depilatories.

Defenders of the novel praised it both on artistic grounds and on the basis of its realism. Anticipating the moral outrage that the novel would provoke, de Vere White argued that it had "the wholeness of artistic integrity" and that it was not "written to titillate or to shock." It was, he claimed, "the best novel to come out of Ireland for many years". Those who defended the novel's realism insisted that it was "serious, sensitive, and true." It was praised for the way in which it "deals starkly, honestly, with several varieties of Irish darkness: sexual frustration, religious zeal and power, ignorance, brutality and the stultifying narrowness of rural life in Ireland".

In a broader context, there was concern that the novel was banned because it did not conform to an official view of "Holy Ireland". One letter writer to *The Irish Times* appealed, "When, one asks, are we going to be allowed to see ourselves as we are, and not as others think we are?" John Jordan, a lecturer in English at University College, Dublin, wrote that the banning of the novel clearly suggested that there was a need within Irish society to suppress the subversive imagination: "there are still forces in the Shamrock Establishment (Church, State, lay pontificate) that hate, despise and fear the sincere artist".

The McGahern Affair, as it came to be known, did not end with the banning of *The Dark*. At the time of the ban, McGahern was on leave of absence from his position as a national school teacher at St John the Baptist's National School, Clontarf, Dublin, where he had taught for seven years. He had gone abroad for a year after winning the Macauley fellowship for his first novel, *The Barracks*, and during that year had married a Finnish theatre practitioner, Annikki Laaksi.

When McGahern returned to resume his teaching responsibilities in October 1965, he was told that the parish priest, the Reverend Patrick J. Carton, had forbidden him to enter the classroom. McGahern had not violated the terms of his contract, but there was no place where he could state his case. He immediately made representations to the Irish National Teachers' Organization (INTO), but no protest followed and the union did not act until December, when a letter was written to Father Carton seeking a reason for McGahern's dismissal. The response contained no specific explanation; instead the INTO was informed that McGahern was "quite well aware of the valid reason which would render his resumption of duties" inadvisable.

The Department of Education gave McGahern no support, and did not offer to compensate him, arguing that by law Father Carton had "exercised his right of dismissal." The case was raised by senator Owen Sheehy Skeffington in the Irish Senate on 9 February 1966, but he was blocked from discussing it on a point of order. Nevertheless, he managed to challenge the way in which the case had been handled, arguing that the Minister for Education had relinquished responsibility in the case and had allowed the church to dictate McGahern's

future: "... are we really to understand that in respect of a teacher ... the Minister has no power, no responsibility, no capacity to see that this man is not deprived of his right to earn his living in this country?"

Although it was never stated officially, it was generally assumed at the time that the Catholic archbishop of Dublin, John Charles McQuaid, was behind McGahern's dismissal, and that it had occurred not only as a result of the banning of *The Dark* but also because he had married in a civil ceremony. What was perhaps most interesting about the case, as Peter Lennon, a journalist with *The Guardian* (a British newspaper), pointed out in *The Irish Times*, was the extent to which an attempt was made "to avoid leaving any official trace of the dismissal".

In this regard, both the banning of *The Dark* and McGahern's loss of his job were similar: in neither case was a detailed official statement required to be made available for the historical record. Secrecy surrounded both actions, causing protestors to raise the issues of the Censorship of Publications Board's accountability to the public and the way in which power was abused and public debate of social issues blocked in Irish society.

JULIA CARLSON

Writings
The Dark, 1965

Further Reading

Carlson, Julia (editor), *Banned in Ireland: Censorship and the Irish Writer*, London: Routledge, and Athens: University of Georgia Press, 1990
Duffy, M.J., "Letters to the Editor: In The Dark", *The Irish Times* (19 June 1965): 13
Hill, Tracy, "Letters to the Editor: In The Dark", *The Irish Times* (18 June 1965): 7
Jordan, John, "Letters to the Editor: In The Dark", *The Irish Times* (16 June 1965): 7
Lennon, Peter, "Letters to the Editor: The McGahern Affair", *The Irish Times* (14 February 1966): 9
"McGahern Loses His Post as Teacher", *The Irish Times* (5 February 1966): 1
Seanad Éireann, *Parliamentary Debates*, 60
Sharpe, R., "Letters to the Editor: In The Dark", *The Irish Times* (9 June 1965): 7
Skeffington, Owen Sheehy, "McGahern Affair", *Censorship*, 2 (Spring 1966): 27–30
"Tone Values", *The Irish Times* (10 February 1966): 9
White, Terence de Vere, "Five to One", *The Irish Times* (8 May 1965): 8

NICCOLÒ MACHIAVELLI
Italian statesman, political theorist, and historian, 1469–1527

Machiavelli was born into an old, but not wealthy Florentine noble family. Little is known of his early life and education. He entered the Florentine government following the execution of Girolamo Savonarola in 1498, when he became head of the second chancery under the republican regime of Piero Soderini. For the next 15 years in this office, Machiavelli undertook diplomatic missions on behalf of the Florentine republic to king

Louis XII of France, pope Julius II, the Holy Roman emperor Maximilian, and Cesare Borgia, who, as the son of pope Alexander VI, was charged with the pacification of papal Romagna. Distrustful of mercenary troops, Machiavelli oversaw the training of a Florentine militia according to the canons of ancient military science, which were later set forth in his *Arte della guerra*. When Medicean rule returned to

Florence with the election of Giovanni de' Medici as pope Leo X in 1512, the Soderini regime was toppled and Machiavelli was discharged from his post.

After brief imprisonment and torture on the charge of treason, Machiavelli was exiled to his family's farm at San Casciano outside Florence. There he resolved to apply the lessons of politics he had learned as a statesman and his study of ancient history to Italy's political problems. The results were his famous *Il principe* (The Prince) and *Discorsi sopra la prima deca di Tito Livio* (Discourses on the First Decade of Titus Livius), which established his reputation as the foremost political thinker of the Renaissance.

Only a few of Machiavelli's works were published during his lifetime, including his *Arte della guerra* (1521) and his comedy, *Mandragola*. Soon after his death on 22 June 1527 his more famous works were issued in Rome by A. Baldus and in Florence by Giunti: the *Discorsi* in 1531 and the *Historie fiorentine*, dedicated to pope Clement VII, and *Il principe* in 1532. The immorality of his political views (perhaps most of all his claim that the end justifies the means, the meaning of which has been much disputed), pervasive secular outlook, and rampant anticlericalism soon attracted critics both within and outside Italy. Among his first critics was his sometime friend and younger contemporary Francesco Guicciardini, whose *Considerations on Machiavelli's Discourses* remained unedited until the 19th century. Machiavelli's works, however, remained popular, and in 1550 a complete edition of his *Opere* was issued at Genoa in several printings.

But by this time critics, both lay and clerical, became vocal in their condemnation of Machiavelli's ideas. Opposition to the publication of his works soon crystallized in the oppressive censorship of the Counter Reformation. In 1557 pope Paul IV entrusted to the Congregation of the Inquisition the task of drawing up a complete catalogue of forbidden books. This first comprehensive list, known as both the Roman and the Pauline Index, was issued in 1559 and condemned all Machiavelli's works. Thus the reading of his *Opera omnia*, along with the works of 550 other authors, including such major heresiarchs as Luther, Calvin, and Melanchthon, was forbidden to the faithful. This blanket condemnation of Machiavelli's works continued under the Index issued by the Council of Trent in 1564. After a plan to issue expurgated versions of some of Machiavelli's works came to naught in the late 16th century, all subsequent Indexes of Prohibited Books down to the 20th century placed Machiavelli among those writers, heretics, and freethinkers whose works were available to the faithful only under the special authority of the pope. So far, Machiavelli's posthumous fate was similar to that of many thinkers of his time. To the historian of censorship, it is the continued appearance of his works despite the bans that makes interesting reading.

The publication and reading of his works continued in both Catholic and Protestant Europe. In that home of surreptitious printing, Venice, many of Machiavelli's writings were secretly published despite the efforts of the Roman Inquisition to hunt out and suppress these clandestine printers. In the early 17th century the Venetian publishers Marco Ginammi and Marc Antonio Ottobon issued the *Discorsi* by the blatant expediency of simply placing a transparent anagram of the author's name, given as Amadio Niecollucci Toscano, on the title page. North of the Alps, Protestant publishers moved to meet the demand

for editions of Machiavelli's works in their Italian originals. Working in London in the 1580s, the English printer John Wolfe published surreptitious editions of the *Historie fiorentine*, the *Discorsi*, and *Il principe*, placing a false city, Palermo or Piacenza, and publisher on the title page. These Italian-language editions were then smuggled into Italy, where they were studied by both admirers and critics of Machiavelli.

Translations provided another important means of disseminating Machiavelli's condemned writings and ideas in northern Europe. His popular work of military science was printed as *The Arte of Warre* four times in London in the late 16th century, often dedicated to queen Elizabeth I, while the *Florentine Histories* were published in 1595 and the *Discourses* and *The Prince* with *The Life of Castruccio Castracani* appeared in Edward Dacres's English version in London in 1636 and 1640, respectively. French, Dutch, and German translations of almost all of Machiavelli's works appeared throughout the late 16th and 17th centuries, with Paris, Leiden, and Frankfurt the main cities of publication. But ironically Machiavelli's revolutionary message of political realism circulated most widely in that ancient language of church, learning, and diplomacy, Latin. *The Prince* was first issued in Latin at Basel in 1560 as *De principe*, to be followed by more than ten editions over the next century. Thus Machiavelli's ideas attracted a wide audience from both scholars and lay readers in the principal Protestant lands.

Here opposition took the form of reasoned rebuttal instead of prohibition and condemnation. An early critic was the Swiss Protestant thinker Innocent Gentillet, whose *Discours contre Machiavel* marshalled detailed arguments against the supposed immortality and efficacy of Machiavelli's idea of rulership. This work was followed by many condemnations of Machiavelli's "godless state" and underhanded politics, which perhaps culminated with the *Anti-Machiavel* of Frederick the Great of Prussia. Written in collaboration with Voltaire, the chapter-by-chapter refutation of *The Prince* stressed that rulership was essentially honourable, glorious, and moral.

Even in the late 20th century the term "Machiavellian" remains a synonym for callous, cynical, and immoral politics, though several generations of historians, led by Hans Baron and John Pocock, have emphasized Machiavelli's *Discorsi* as a major contribution to Western republicanism and Anglo-American liberal thought.

BENJAMIN G. KOHL

Writings

The Chief Works and Others, translated by Allan Gilbert, 3 vols, 1958

The Portable Machiavelli, edited by Peter Bondanella and Mark Musa, 1979

Further Reading

Bertelli, Sergio and Piero Innocenti, *Bibliografia Machiavelliana*, Verona: Valdonega, 1979

De Mattei, Rodolfo, *Dal premachiavellismo all'antimachiavellismo*, Florence: Sansoni, 1969

Frederick of Prussia, *The Refutation of Machiavelli's Prince; or, Anti-Machiavel*, Athens: Ohio University Press, 1981

Gerber, Adolph, *Niccolò Machiavelli: die handschriften, ausgaben und über setzungen seiner Werke im 16. und 17. Jahrhundert*, 3 vols, Gotha: Druck, 1912–13

Grendler, Paul F., *The Roman Inquisition and the Venetian Press, 1540–1605*, Princeton, New Jersey: Princeton University Press, 1977

Meinecke, Friedrich, *Machiavellism: The Doctrine of Raison d'État and Its Place in Modern History*, London: Routledge, and Paul, and New Haven, Connecticut: Yale University Press, 1957

Raab, Felix, *The English Face of Machiavelli: A Changing Interpretation, 1500–1700*, London: Routledge, and Paul, 1964

Woodfield, Danis B., *Surreptitious Printing in England, 1550–1640*, New York: Bibliographical Society of America, 1973

CATHARINE A. MacKINNON
See **Andrea Dworkin and Catharine A. MacKinnon**

CHARLES MACKLIN
Irish dramatist, 1699–1797

For some 11 years the British Lord Chamberlain refused to license Charles Macklin's *The Man of the World*, a comedy castigating greed, hypocrisy, and political corruption. Originally entitled *The True-born Scotsman* and performed in Dublin in 1764, Macklin's play was first denied a licence in 1770; even the title was prohibited. In 1779, Macklin submitted a revised version, *The Man of the World*, but the Lord Chamberlain again refused to grant a licence. In 1781, Macklin put forward a further revision, which the Lord Chamberlain finally passed. Performed at Covent Garden Theatre, *The Man of the World* won immediate acclaim, and for nearly 50 years it remained in the repertory. Some critics regard it as one of the most stageworthy 18th-century comedies. In 1936, the critic Dougald MacMillan wrote that *The Man of the World* "is commonly considered one of the more aggravated instances of governmental interference with the stage".

In at least ten plays – full-length comedies and farces or afterpieces – Macklin dramatized a range of middle-class attitudes, values, and behaviour patterns, believing that the theatre should offer moral lessons. He used domestic and social relationships to reveal the conflicts growing out of the accelerating economic and social change, which had brought an increase in education and culture. Macklin's dramatic interests, combined with his understanding of the close connection between the stage and the social life of his time, made him a vehicle of public opinion; he readily perceived changes in public taste and in politics. Along with newspapers, the London theatre had been gaining importance as a political medium. The government failed to recognize the growing complexities of public opinion.

In *The Man of the World*, Macklin attacks political patronage, bribery, bartering parliamentary boroughs, and the methods used to form new boroughs. Scottish politician Sir Pertinax Macsycophant (formerly Sir Hector Mackcraft in *The True-born Scotsman*) has determined that adjusting to society requires hypocrisy, immorality, duplicity, and expediency. His steadiness of purpose, despite personal hardship, results in wealth, status, and fame. However, his native accent and crude manners keep him from gaining social acceptance. Warned by experience, he provides his eldest son Egerton with the education necessary for social acceptance and high political office. Egerton, however, had been made the heir of his mother's uncle on condition that he drop the family name. His father, intend-

ing to put "the House of Macsycophant" on a par with families of rank, arranges for Egerton to marry Lord Lumbercourt's daughter Lady Rodolpha. Egerton's proposed marriage will bring him membership of parliament and social advantage. Nevertheless, Egerton, having learned from the good example of his clergyman-teacher Sidney, rejects his father's plan; instead, he marries the virtuous and beautiful Constantia, a working-class woman. Macsycophant fails to learn from his humiliation and continues with the same viewpoints, prejudices, and intolerances. Although some critics have dismissed it as "sentimental", Macklin's play unrelentingly explores the struggle to make one's way in the world. In addition to exposing political decay, it raises perplexing issues of personal and social conduct.

The examiners in the Lord Chamberlain's office, Edward Capell in 1770 and John Larpnet in 1779, evidently thought that recent political events had not sufficiently receded in the public memory and that Macklin's *The Man of the World* would therefore offend political and governmental leaders. For example, through Macsycophant, Macklin had satirized the Earl of Bute, who assumed power as prime minister in 1761 and advocated George III's policy of the supremacy of monarchy. Bute consolidated his power through political patronage, filling offices with Scots who had followed him to London. He resigned in 1763, owing to his unpopular policies. Like many of his contemporaries, Macklin thought that Bute's actions on behalf of the government abridged accepted freedoms. He advocated a stronger sense of individual morality and civic responsibility than his society either accepted or expected, and he stressed patriotic nationalism. Macklin's play also implied support for John Wilkes, the foremost critic of the Crown's policies. In 1763, in an issue of the anti-Tory weekly *North Briton*, Wilkes criticized a speech by George III; the government imprisoned Wilkes for seditious libel and confiscated his papers. Macklin, like many others, regarded Wilkes as an opponent of tyranny and an advocate of freedom of the press and of individual rights.

The government's response to *The Man of the World* confirmed Lord Chesterfield's view that the 1737 Theatres Act virtually ended the freedom to make political references on stage. In opposing the act, Lord Chesterfield reminded parliament that the stage did not cause the vice it reflected, and that the act threatened the "Liberty of the Press, which will be a long Stride toward the Destruction of Liberty itself". His potent argument did not deter the sponsor of the act, Sir Horace Walpole, from securing its approval. Walpole had been embarrassed by plays satirizing political underhandedness; he personally prevented the licensing of John Gay's comedies, which brought acts of political deception to light. Also, the Lord Chamberlain refused to license plays such as Joseph Reed's *The Register Office* (1761), Samuel Foote's *A Trip to Calais* (1776), and Lady Eglantine Wallace's *The Whim* (1795). Of course, such censorship only sharpened public interest in the manoeuvrings of politicians.

In 1779, prior to resubmitting *The Man of the World* to the Lord Chamberlain, Macklin wrote to a friend that "the business of the stage is to correct vice and laugh at folly". In a letter to the Lord Chamberlain which accompanied his revised version, he indicated that his play "inculcates the love of liberty, and hatred of oppression; it satirizes the abuse of law; it reprobates a corrupt, tyrannical, over-reaching, fawning, booing Scotsman, and extols the liberal, virtuous, independent, honest, conscientious conduct of his son". The approved 1781 version differs little from the 1779 version.

Some 20th-century critics think that political necessity forced the Lord Chamberlain to suppress *The Man of the World*, and that it was this suppression, more than his developing skill, which led Macklin to improve it.

TIMOTHY C. MILLER

Writings

The True-born Scotsman, produced 1764; revised version as *The Man of the World*, produced 1781, published 1785 (reprinted 1951)
Four Comedies, edited by J.O. Bartley, 1968

Further Reading

Appleton William Worthen, *Charles Macklin: An Actor's Life*, Cambridge, Massachusetts: Harvard University Press, 1960

Baker, David Erskine (continued by Isaac Reed and Stephen Jones), *Biographia Dramatica; or, a Companion to the Playhouse . . .*, 3 vols, London: Longman, 1812; reprinted New York: AMS Press, 1966

Cooke, William, *Memoirs of Charles Macklin, Comedian*, London: Asperne, 1806; reprinted New York: Blom, 1972

Findlay, Robert R., "The Comic Plays of Charles Macklin: Dark Satire at Mid-Eighteenth Century", *Educational Theater Journal*, 20 (1968): 398–407

Fowell, Frank and Frank Palmer, *Censorship in England*, London: Palmer, 1913; reprinted New York: Blom, 1969

MacMillan, Dougald, "The Censorship in the Case of Macklin's *The Man of the World*", *Huntington Library Bulletin*, 10 (1936): 79–101

Nicoll, Allardyce, *A History of Late Eighteenth Century Drama, 1750–1800*, Cambridge: Cambridge University Press, 1927

Parry, Edward Abbott, *Charles Macklin*, London: Paul Trench Trubner, and New York: Longman, 1891

JOHN MACLEAN
British revolutionary socialist and popular educator, 1879–1923

John Maclean has achieved legendary status in the annals of the Scottish working class. He was born at Pollokshaws, an industrial settlement near Glasgow, on 24 August 1879, into a family which knew economic and social oppression. His parents, Daniel and Anne, had been uprooted from their homes in the north of Scotland by the continuing aftermath of the Highland clearances. Daniel was a casual, itinerant worker before finding relatively steady employment at Lockhart's Pottery in Pollokshaws. Anne was a weaver. John Maclean was the sixth of seven children brought up in a strict but caring Scottish working-class Calvinist family. This gave Maclean his sense of personal responsibility and social duty. His public life was to be characterized by honesty and unwavering adherence to principle.

Maclean was educated at Pollok Academy, Queens Park, while working at casual jobs and at the Thornliebank Print Works. At 17 he became a pupil teacher at Polmadie School in the south of Glasgow; then, after two years at the Free Church Training School, he became a certified teacher. He continued to study at Glasgow University part time, graduating as an MA in 1904, and he attended science and mathematics classes at Glasgow Technical College regularly until 1907.

This appears to be the upwardly mobile progress of an intelligent young man of the working class. However, this was not the case. Maclean's combination of personal experience, humanity, and historical circumstances drew him to Marxism and to revolutionary socialism. In 1903, he joined the Social Democratic Federation (SDF), which became part of the British Socialist Party in 1911. An inspiring teacher, pamphleteer, and orator, he launched himself into a tireless campaign of revolutionary propaganda and militancy.

His first pamphlet, *The Greenock Jungle* (1906), was an outspoken attack on local butchers who threatened public health by selling meat cut from putrid carcasses; this set the tone for his polemical writing. Maclean understood the political necessity for agitation and propaganda. Realizing that capitalism would not simply collapse under its own contradictions, he emphasized the need for a massive creative effort by the working class. Like his Sardinian counterpart, Antonio Gramsci, Maclean was a dedicated popular educator. The pattern that he followed was to alternate winter evening classes for workers with open-air summer meetings. Between 1906 and 1916, he taught a regular class in political economy to workers in Greenock, encouraged women-only meetings and organizations, and was a central figure in the plans for a Scottish Labour College. In 1909 he married Agnes Wood, a nurse, by whom he had two children.

He opposed H.M. Hyndman, the founder of the SDF, because of the latter's support for World War I, and it was during the conflict that Maclean's outstanding reputation as a socialist militant and "organic intellectual" of the Scottish working class was consolidated. He appeared to be everywhere: he was a leading figure in the Clyde Workers' Committee, in the cooperative movement, in the 40-hour week campaign, and above all in the struggle for workers' education. As editor of *The Vanguard*, he presented an uncompromising Marxist perspective on World War I.

Maclean's relentless militancy brought him, as he intended, into collision with the authorities, and inevitably also with his employers, the Govan School Board. It was Maclean's hope and belief that he would take the rest of the working class with him into the struggle. He was dismissed from his post as a teacher and blacklisted following his conviction and imprisonment for sedition in October 1915 under the Defence of the Realm Act (1914). Maclean's outspokenness allowed him to turn his trial into an indictment of capitalism, and he aroused great popular support both for himself personally and for the socialist, anti-imperialist principles for which he stood. This led to the formation of the socialist-led Free Speech Defence Committee in Scotland. In 1916, he was sentenced again, this time to three years' penal servitude for publishing a seditious pamphlet. Released in June 1917, he was arrested, convicted, and imprisoned on three more occasions. His final sentence was a year in prison between October 1921 and October 1922 on a charge relating to his public agitation in support of the unemployed.

Maclean was recognized as a revolutionary leader by Lenin and was appointed Bolshevik Consul in Glasgow in 1918 for his work on behalf of Russian political refugees. He was also elected honorary president of the First All-Russian Congress of Soviets. Nevertheless, he opposed the formation of a Communist Party of Great Britain that would be under Moscow's control. Instead, he campaigned for an independent socialist republic of Scotland and formed the Scottish Workers' Republican Party in 1923, for which he was bitterly criticized by the communists.

Maclean died of double pneumonia on 30 November 1923, after a lifetime of socialist commitment for which he paid a heavy personal cost. His wife, who had left him in 1919 declaring that she would not return until he gave up revolutionary work, nursed him during his final illness. Maclean's lasting significance is hard to assess. A tireless agitator and propagandist, he published a number of biting polemics, of which the best known is *The War after the War* (1918?), and he contributed a great deal to the movement for a class-based workers' education programme. But such work was ephemeral, designed to energize the revolutionary potential of the working class, and it brought down on Maclean the weight of reaction and repression which he expected. On 1 December 1923, his obituary appeared in *The Times*, while in Glasgow thousands of workers filed past his coffin. The memory of John Maclean persists as an inspirational legacy to the Scottish working class. His personal papers are in the National Library of Scotland.

W. JOHN MORGAN

Writings

The War after the War in the Light of the Elements of Working-Class Economics, 1918?
Condemned from the Dock: A Burning Indictment of Capitalism, Being an Authorized Account of the Trial and Sentence of John Maclean, Including a Verbatim Report of His 75 Minutes' Speech from the Dock, 1918
In the Rapids of Revolution: Essays, Articles and Letters, 1902–23, edited by Nan Milton, 1978

Further Reading

Aldred, Guy Alfred, *John Maclean: Martyr of the Class Struggle: The Man, His Work, and His Worth*, Glasgow: Bakunin Press, 1932
Bell, Tom, *John Maclean: A Fighter for Freedom*, Glasgow: Communist Party, Scottish Committee, 1944
Howell, David, *A Lost Left: Three Studies in Socialism and Nationalism*, Manchester: Manchester University Press, and Chicago: University of Chicago Press, 1986
Milton, Nan, *John Maclean*, London: Pluto Press, 1973
Obituary, *The Times* (1 December 1923)
Scottish Marxist, special issue: "John Maclean", 5 (November 1973)

McLIBEL
The McDonald Corporation v. Steel and Morris, 1990–2000

In 1992, George Pring and Penelope Canan of the University of Colorado noted that "a new and very disturbing trend is happening in America, with grave consequences for politically active citizens and for our political system" (quoted in Rowell, 1996). This they termed the SLAPP, or Strategic Lawsuit Against Public Participation, a form of legal intimidation or gamesmanship, usually in the form of a threatened libel action, undertaken by large corporate interests with the aim of frightening and harassing their critics into silence, and discouraging potential ones from voicing their views in the first place. In most cases, the threat of a SLAPP is sufficient, but should the critics persist and the case proceed to court, they are equally liable to find themselves silenced by being forced to become full-time participants in a lengthy, complex, exhausting, and potentially bankrupting legal process.

A company that has frequently had recourse to this tactic is the fast-food chain McDonald's, which, as Fiona Donson (2000) has pointed out, has sought to deal with its critics by way of an aggressive policy of self-protection. Instead of adopting an approach which seeks to make a reasonable response to criticism, accepting fair comment and ignoring and/or rebutting the more extreme challenges, the corporation has responded in a manner that appears to seek to silence its critics.

The recipients of such treatment have been many and various, as both Donson and David Hooper (2000) illustrate; a lengthy list is also contained in Franny Armstrong's documentary *McLibel: Two Worlds Collide* (1997), discussed below. A criticism about which the company has appeared particularly sensitive is the charge that their beef-buying policies have encouraged farming practices that have helped to destroy tropical rainforests; this has led to action against, among others, a 1984 BBC *Nature* programme, the Vegetarian Society's magazine *Greenscene* over an interview with the singer Morrissey, a 1983 documentary, *Jungleburger*, broadcast in Britain by

Channel 4 in 1989, and the 1994 Polish school book *Biology 4 Man and Environment*. The most common response to a letter from McDonald's lawyers threatening libel has been to capitulate to their demands, which have included providing public apologies for and corrections to published statements. The company has then relied upon the ever-growing pile of such responses to reinforce and legitimize its demands for future ones. As Donson argues:

> By invoking the law in support of its reputation, McDonald's has been able to create an impression that any criticism that is withdrawn as a result of a threat of a libel action must in some way have been 'unlawful', and in particular must have amounted to a defamation of the character of McDonald's.

In 1990, however, this policy came badly unstuck, from McDonald's point of view, when it decided to sue five members of the tiny activist group London Greenpeace (no relation to Greenpeace International) for publishing and distributing a leaflet entitled *What's Wrong with McDonald's: Everything they Don't Want you to Know*. This attacked every aspect of the corporation's business, accusing them of exploiting children via their advertising, promoting an unhealthy diet, exploiting their staff, and being responsible for environmental damage and the ill treatment of animals. McDonald's offered the five the chance to retract and apologize for the leaflet's allegations, or else to go to court. Three reluctantly apologized, but Helen Steel, a 25 year old former gardener, and Dave Morris, a 36 year old former postman and a single father, each living on around £40 per week income support, decided to fight on.

From the very start, Steel and Morris were faced with what looked like insuperable odds. Firstly, there is no legal aid available to either side in libel cases in Britain, thus making the contest of two individuals with few resources against a giant corporation a grotesquely unequal one. Secondly, and equally seriously, the British libel laws reverse the normal burden of proof so that it is the defendant who has to prove that the words complained of are true and not the litigant who has to prove that they are false. Nor do litigants have to prove actual financial damage, nor are corporate interests debarred from suing for libel, unlike local authorities in Britain which, following a 1993 judgment by the House of Lords, are denied this course of action on the grounds that freedom of speech requires that people should be able to criticise government bodies. It is these factors that have made Britain an extremely popular place for the libel litigant and turned London into what one legal expert has called "a town called Sue". And it was for these reasons that, at the start of the legal action, McDonald's looked to be in an insuperable position. As Hooper puts it:

> they could set the agenda of what London Greenpeace had to prove and sit back in the knowledge that this tiny pressure group was most unlikely to be able to fly in witnesses and testify, for example, about the state of rainforest areas in Central America or labour disputes around the world.

In 1991 the defendants took the British government to the European Court of Human Rights to demand the right to legal aid or the simplification of libel procedures. They lost; paradoxically, the court ruled that as they had put up a "tenacious defence" of their case they could not justly claim that they were being denied access to justice. Meanwhile, when McDonald's came to realize that Morris and Steel were deadly serious about fighting the case, they hired top libel lawyer Richard Rampton QC, for a reputed fee of £2000 per day plus a six-figure briefing fee. He led a team consisting of a junior barrister and at least six other solicitors and assistants. Steel and Morris represented themselves, with occasional *pro bono* back-up from barrister Keir Starmer.

However, worse was to come for the defendants. In late 1993, Rampton applied for the trial to be heard by a judge only, arguing that the scientific evidence necessary to examine the links between diet and disease would be too complicated for a jury to understand. That, by the same token, it might also have been too complicated for a former gardener and a former postman to defend entirely unaided, and in the face of the massive resources of a giant corporation, did not trouble Rampton – nor, apparently, the trial judge, Mr Justice Bell, who granted his request. Rampton also applied for certain parts of the defence – concerning environmental damage and the way in which McDonald's treated its workforce – to be struck out on the grounds that they were not sufficiently supported by the Steel and Morris's witness statements. Bell agreed. Steel and Morris appealed to the Court of Appeal (the first of seven appeals), in which they were helped by the civil rights organization Liberty, again on a *pro bono* basis. They lost on the matter of the jury but, in a move which significantly extended the rights of future libel defendants, the Appeal Court restored all parts of the defence struck out by the judge, arguing that his ruling placed an unrealistic burden on the defendants and that they were entitled to rely for justification of their claims not only on their own witness statements but also on those of McDonald's witnesses, the future discovery of McDonald's documents, and on what they might reasonably expect to discover under cross-examination of the company's witnesses.

Nonetheless, the prospects for Steel and Morris looked bleak. As legal commentator for the BBC and the *Guardian* newspaper Marcel Berlins put it at the time: "I cannot think of a case in which the legal cards have been so spectacularly stacked against one party". The scene seemed set for a classic SLAPP; as Helen Steel put it in court on 29 June 1994, the second day of the trial:

> We feel there is one word which can sum up what this case is about, and that word is 'censorship'. McDonald's are using the libel laws of this country to censor and silence their critics. During this trial we intend to show that the public face of McDonald's is a fraud; that the truth that lies behind their image is far from savoury.

> As Mr Rampton has admitted, their aim in taking this case to its conclusion is to gain a legal seal of approval for their business practices. This is a show trial against unwaged, unrepresented defendants. McDonald's hope that because of our lack of resources and legal experience they will gain an easy victory and a detailed judgement in their favour which they can then use to say to all their critics that they have proven, to the satisfaction of the court, they are squeaky clean (quoted in Vidal, 1997).

McDonald's hopes were, however, effectively dashed, as Steel and Morris fought the company on every point, calling on as many expert witnesses as they could afford, and, equally importantly, cross-examining McDonald's own array of witnesses with the thoroughness and confidence of professional barristers. In the process, a vast amount of information which the corporation would have rather remained hidden came out in open court and became publicly available through the court transcripts and, later, on the McSpotlight website. Undoubtedly this was one of the main reasons why, twice during the trial, Steel and Morris were offered a secret deal by McDonald's whereby they would agree never again to criticise the company publicly in return for the company dropping the case and paying a substantial sum to a third party. However, Steel and Morris came up with a counter-deal whereby McDonald's would undertake never to sue anyone again for making criticisms similar to theirs, and would also apologise to those they'd already sued. No deal was struck.

On 13 March 1995 the case became the longest libel trial, and on 11 December the longest civil case, in British legal history. On 16 February 1996 the McSpotlight website was launched, receiving more than a million visits in its first month. On 17 July 1996 the hearing was finally completed; 40,000 pages of documentary evidence had been amassed, along with 20,000 pages of court transcripts. In October the two sides returned to court to start their closing speeches. Steel and Morris began theirs on 21 October and carried on for six weeks, taking the opportunity to argue once again that the British libel laws are oppressive and unfair, citing in particular their denial of legal aid and the abuse of process involved in allowing multinational corporations to use the libel laws to sue their critics as a means of silencing them in matters of public interest.

On 1 November 1996 the case became the longest trial of any kind in English legal history; in British terms it was exceeded only by the 391-day Piper Alpha disaster case in Scotland. Judgment was finally delivered on 19 June 1997, day 314 of the trial. It had taken the judge six months to write his 762-page judgment, and even the 45-page summary took two hours to read out. In brief, Mr Justice Bell ruled that Morris and Steel had not proved the allegations against McDonald's on rainforest destruction, heart disease and cancer, food poisoning, starvation in the developing world and bad working conditions. But they had proved that McDonald's exploit children with their advertising, falsely advertised their food as nutritious, risk the health of their most regular, long-term customers, are "culpably responsible" for cruelty to animals, are "strongly antipathetic" to trade unions, and pay their workers low wages.

Steel and Morris were fined £60,000 – only half of the damages claimed by McDonald's as they had proved a number of their allegations. However, as Helen Steel summarized their response: "McDonald's don't deserve a penny and in any event we haven't got any money". The company had now discovered the full price of suing over each and every allegation in the original leaflet, as David Hooper puts it:

McDonald's no doubt feared that if they did not sue for every allegation, they would be perceived to be admitting that parts of the pamphlet were true, but they were wrong to follow this path. They had well-paid lawyers and PR men to explain why they had chosen the worst allegations without conceding that any of the others were true. It seemed they simply wanted to crush their opponents.

And as *UK Marketing* concluded: "McDonald's took a serious wrong turn in bringing the McLibel trial . . . this not only brought many issues about its corporate behaviour into the public eye for the first time, it also had the effect of making it look paranoid and power-crazy". Meanwhile Channel 4 News called the trial "the biggest corporate PR disaster in history", for which it is estimated that McDonald's paid out at least £10m in costs.

That day the McSpotlight site was accessed 2.2 million times, and work began on a CD-Rom version. By the end of the trial the site had grown to 21,000 files and had been visited 7 million times. It remains the prime source of information for anyone interested in this case and its ramifications, and by early 2001 had been visited over 65 million times. In the days following the end of the trial, the offending leaflet was reprinted and 400,000 copies were distributed outside 500 of McDonald's 750 UK stores. However, McDonald's never pursued any claim for costs and damages, nor their originally stated intention of gaining an injunction preventing further leafleting. By then over 2 million leaflets had been circulated worldwide, and the final total would top 3 million.

Two months later the defendants launched their appeal. This challenged the specific handling of the case by Mr Justice Bell, but also raised once again the oppressive nature of the British libel laws, in particular the way in which they provide corporate interests with significant protection from the criticisms which they, like public authorities, ought to be able to withstand without recourse to law in a democratic society. They also argued that it was wrong that in British libel law there exists no defence which would allow for defendants having a "reasonable belief in the truth of the words complained of", nor a defence of "qualified privilege" which should be available to any publication, such as the original leaflet, which amounts to a "reasonable and legitimate response to an actual or perceived attack on the rights of others, in particular vulnerable sections of society who generally lack the means to adequately defend themselves". They also argued that the judge should have stopped the case, as an abuse of process, before it ever came to trial.

The Appeal Court hearing started on 12 January 1999 and ended on 31 March. The defendants had prepared over 700 pages of legal submissions, and challenged the judge's rulings and findings on 63 closely argued points. The result was a 309-page judgment and another £200,000 in legal costs. The Appeal Court found against Steel and Morris on the general points relating to the libel laws. However, they also concluded that it was fair comment to say that McDonald's employees worldwide "do badly in terms of pay and conditions" and that McDonald's food was linked to a greater risk of heart disease. Steel and Morris's liability for damages were thus reduced from £60,000 to £40,000.

In April 2000 Steel and Morris were refused leave to appeal to the House of Lords over the conduct of their trial, having submitted a 43-point petition, and on 20 September 2000, ten years to the day after the original writs were served, they lodged an application to take the British Government to the European Court of Human Rights on the grounds that their trial breached Article 6 of the European Convention on Human Rights (the right to a fair trial) and Article 10 (the right to freedom of expression), among others, and that the British libel laws are incompatible with the Convention. As of May 2001 this case remains to be heard, but could have very far-reaching implications.

David Pannick QC stated in *The Times*: "the McLibel case has achieved what many lawyers thought impossible; to lower further the reputation of our law of defamation in the minds of all right-thinking people". But it also demonstrated that those who attempt to use the laws of libel for censorship purposes risk the whole enterprise blowing up in their faces – especially when faced with determined and formidably well-informed defendants with almost nothing to lose in material terms. If McDonald's wanted to suppress criticisms of its business practices, its libel action had precisely the opposite effect of revealing those practices in considerable detail, first of all in court and then to an audience of millions on the world wide web.

Nonetheless, the chilling effect of McDonald's formidable reputation as an assiduous litigant appears to have survived the embarrassment of the McLibel trial. Thus, for example, although Channel 4 commissioned and broadcast a three-hour reconstruction of the trial, they refused to sell it to overseas buyers unless these indemnified it against possible libel action

by McDonald's, thus losing at least one foreign sale. Nor would they, along with the BBC, screen Franny Armstrong's hour-long documentary *McLibel: Two Worlds Collide*. This refusal then caused the distributor Jane Balfour to decide that she could not sell the programme abroad in case foreign television broadcasts led to her being prosecuted under English libel law. It would thus appear, the epic McLibel trial notwithstanding, that the spectre of the SLAPP remains as baleful as ever for the mainstream media, and a sharp spur to self-censorship.

JULIAN PETLEY

Further Reading

Armstrong, Franny, *McLibel: Two Worlds Collide* (video), One-Off, 1997

Donson, Fiona J.L., *Legal Intimidation: A SLAPP in the Face of Democracy*, London and New York: Free Association, 2000

Hooper, David, *Reputations under Fire*, London: Little Brown, 2000

Petley, Julian, "An Unsavoury Business", *Index on Censorship*, 27/5 (1998)

Rowell, Andrew, *Green Backlash: Global Subversion of the Environmental Movement*, London and New York: Routledge 1996

Vidal, John, *McLibel: Burger Culture on Trial*, London: Macmillan, and New York: New York Press, 1997

Website

www.mcspotlight.org/case/index.html

JOHN McNAUGHTON
US film director, 1950–

HENRY: PORTRAIT OF A SERIAL KILLER
Film, 1986

Henry: Portrait of a Serial Killer was made during 1985 and 1986 on the extremely low budget of $200,000, the money coming from the Chicago-based company MPI Video. The story is loosely based on the life of the Texan serial killer Henry Lee Lucas, who also served as the model for Mark Blair's *Confessions of a Serial Killer* (1987). Its public debut, in its original 16mm form, was at the 1986 Chicago Film Festival. Atlantic Releasing showed an interest in distributing *Henry*, but this rapidly evaporated when the Motion Picture Association of America (MPAA) insisted on giving it an "X" rating. This rating is usually reserved for hard-core pornography and spells commercial death for any non-porn movie, as the mainstream exhibitors refuse to show "X"-rated products. Indeed the film's producer Steve Jones suggested that *Henry*'s problems might well be connected with its independent status, "since the ratings board is run by the studios it enables them to control the independents and the small pictures. What they're trying to do is to prevent any situation wherein people might possibly start to go out to theatres and really like something that's beyond their control."

However, *Henry* began to garner an underground reputation on the cult and independent repertory circuit; it was also brought to the Telluride Festival in Colorado in 1986 by Errol Morris (of *The Thin Blue Line* fame) where it deeply divided the audience but won the support of critic Roger Ebert and

director Arthur Penn, among others. The film was then resubmitted to the MPAA, who confirmed their original "X". McNaughton signalled his willingness to make cuts, but the MPAA made it very clear that it was the whole film, not individual scenes, that constituted the problem; in particular, they took exception to what they described as its "disturbing moral tone". MPI decided to distribute *Henry* unrated, and the film continued its limited circulation of the independent exhibition sector. In 1991 they also released it on video, but the notoriously censorious, Mormon-owned Blockbuster chain refused to stock it.

If *Henry* encountered a form of economic censorship in the United States, elsewhere it met censorship of the more direct kind. In Switzerland it was refused a certificate, and in New Zealand the censors refused to allow it to be screened at the Wellington and Auckland Film Festivals.

However, it was in Britain that *Henry* faced its biggest difficulties. For the British cinema, *Henry* was cut by 62 seconds; to begin with, James Ferman, the director of the British Board of Film Classification (BBFC), had wanted to ban the film outright. In the end, it was passed for cinema showing in April 1991, after a year of agonized deliberations within the BBFC, which also took advice from a forensic psychiatrist and two forensic psychologists who had studied serial killers. Three scenes suffered cuts: the opening montage of Henry's victims,

McNAUGHTON: Still from McNaughton's violent horror film *Henry: Portrait of a Serial Killer* (1986). The film, based around the life of Texas serial killer Henry Lee Lucas, was given an "X" rating by the Motion Picture Association of America and as a result was screened only at independent venues in the US. The British Board of Film Classification, after a lengthy delay, insisted on making cuts to the film before passing it for general release in 1991, because of its perceived exploitative depiction of sexual abuse and violence. The film was cut more severely and one scene re-edited for its release on video.

which lost a shot of a dead woman sitting on a lavatory with blood between her exposed breasts and a broken bottle pushed into her face; the murder of a TV warehouseman; and the infamous "home invasion", in which Henry and his sidekick, Otis, video themselves murdering a couple and their son, during the course of which Otis sexually abuses the woman. It was this last scene which most disturbed the BBFC; as stated in its 1991 *Annual Report*, it and the opening montage were cut because "the Board is always careful to remove the links between sexual availability and violence towards sexually exposed and terrified women". Tom Dewe Mathews also quotes from a BBFC examiner's report to the effect that in the "home invasion" scene,

... the woman is totally depersonalised. The camera gives us no lead-in to the assault from her viewpoint and therefore no feel for her as a person. Otis and Henry we already know, however, and accordingly we see her through their eyes. Conventions from the standard repertoire of filmic sex and violence also operate here, such as the positioning of the woman towards the camera. By these devices viewers are invited to participate, to see the titillatory nature of such cruelty and the film is therefore truly exploitative.

Ferman himself also noted that

All the material we cut was violence connected with sexual abuse of a victim. Therefore it could have got past the guard of the audience. Once you're into sexual images you can turn people on because whatever one part of their mind is thinking, another part is telling them something else.

However, there was rather more to the censorship of *Henry* than this, since the Board, like the MPAA, also confessed itself perturbed by the film's neutral moral tone. As Ferman put it,

"*Henry* was always a difficult film because it didn't contain its own moral context; it's totally up to the viewers to bring their own moral viewpoint from the outside. It's been described as a morally blank film." Not content with leaving it as such, however, Ferman fretted, "how does one get the audience to take a properly moral view about the violence that's shown on the film?" On the one hand, Ferman admitted that one of the forensic psychologists whom the BBFC consulted had said that the film was "remarkably accurate"; the psychologist had added that it was "a film he would like to send his students to see because it shows the cold, detached personality of the serial killer who can't engage with the world, who has no strong feelings himself and can't see that anyone else's feelings are real". On the other hand, Ferman was concerned because the film was "so quiet. My biggest worry was that, because it is so realistic, with no aesthetic distance, you enter into the psychology of the psychopath." However, arguably, it is precisely the film's ability to make us see the world through Henry's eyes (though most certainly not to sympathize with him), allied with its refusal to pass overt moral judgement, offer easy explanations, or reassure by having Henry finally caught and punished, that makes *Henry* so remarkable and so intensely disturbing. As McNaughton himself put it, "I hate it when a film-maker tells me what moral judgements to make, when everything is pre-packaged for me. What we tried to do was say, 'What do *you* think the morality of this piece is? What do *you* think the morality of Henry's soul is?'"

When *Henry* was submitted for video classification, further cuts were imposed. In Britain video classification is also carried out by the BBFC; however, its video classifications, unlike its cinema classifications, carry statutory force. Thus Britain is one of the very few countries in the world which enjoys state video censorship; this is also extremely strict, stricter even than film censorship, as the video fate of *Henry* demonstrates.

After *Henry*'s cinema release, James Ferman made it clear, publicly, that the Board would be highly unlikely ever to pass it on video. According to the BBFC 1992 *Annual Report*, this was "because of the obsessional manner in which disturbed individuals might use the replay facility within the home". Or, as Ferman himself put it,

> We were worried about the small proportion of viewers who would use the family murder scene in the way that the forensic experts feared, which was to feed their own fantasies, to play them again and again; because on video you can control the fantasies, just as Henry and Otis are controlling their own fantasies when they relive their killings on video.

However, after more lengthy deliberations within the BBFC, Ferman decided that it could, after all, be released on video, but only with a further 51 seconds of cuts, and the crucial "home invasion" scene not only cut but "rearranged" (without the director's permission). In a very real sense, then, the British video version of *Henry* is the "BBFC cut".

To gauge the full significance of this remarkable intervention, it is crucial to understand how this deeply shocking scene actually works. McNaughton himself has described it as "the key scene of the picture"; he continues,

> We used video, because the emotional content of a video image is different from a film: with a film you believe in the surface illusion, but with video you don't. We knew that by using that video image, it would make that act seem absolutely, terrifyingly real. And then the idea was to put parentheses around parentheses. We set it so that you see Henry and Otis about to enter the house, and then you see the image on the TV. And because you know they have a video camera, you think you're seeing them murder the family as they're taping it. But then you realise that you're sitting there watching it on the cinema screen, just as they're sitting there watching it on the video. And that's where the whole picture turns things inside out, where it says to you: "you think this is graphic, but you're sitting here watching it, waiting to be entertained. Now what do you think about yourself, and what do you think about watching this kind of violence on the screen?"

Indeed, even the BBFC examiner quoted above seems to have understood the significance of having these intensely disturbing images shot on video. As their report puts it, "the effect of a film within a film here is not to distance it but rather, through the home movie feel, give the impression that this could be located anywhere, including one's own home". However, obsessed with grim visions of what video viewers might be up to within the privacy of their own homes, the BBFC cut this scene in the video version even more severely than in the cinema version. As Ferman put it,

> Additional cuts were made to remove precisely that material which lent itself to obsessional viewing and re-viewing in the home. We believe that, in its final form, the video no longer offers the stuff of masturbatory fantasies about violence or sexual violence of the kind indulged in by those whose private fantasy worlds represent a significant danger to society.

Not content with this, however, Ferman then set about destroying the very effect which McNaughton had striven so determinedly to create, inserting what should be the later shot of Henry and Otis watching the video of the "home invasion" into the actual scene as shot by Henry's video camera. This curious piece of re-editing was unearthed by the *Time Out* writer Nigel Floyd, who aptly concluded that "this radically alters the structure of the scene: by pre-empting the crucial moment at which our guilty complicity is exposed, Ferman's version subverts this moment of subversion".

JULIAN PETLEY

Further Reading
Floyd, Nigel, "Charnel Knowledge", *Time Out* (3 July 1991): 20–21
Floyd, Nigel, "Video", *Time Out*, 1172 (3 February 1993): 151
Gire, Dann, "Henry: Portrait of a Serial Killer", *Cinefantastique* (March 1990): 27–30
Guttridge, Peter, "In Defence of a Serial Shocker", *Daily Telegraph* (9 July 1991): 12
Kermode, Mark, "Slice of Life", *Fear*, 17 (May 1990)
Mathews, Tom Dewe, *Censored*, London: Chatto and Windus, 1994

MADAGASCAR

(formerly Malagasy Republic)

Population: 15,970,000
Main religions: Animist; Christian; Muslim
Official languages: Malagasy; French
Illiteracy rate (%): 26.4 (m); 40.3 (f)

Number of daily newspapers: 5
Number of radio receivers per 1000 inhabitants: 209
Number of TV receivers per 1000 inhabitants: 22
Number of PCs per 1000 inhabitants: 1.3

Oral histories and folklore have long dominated Madagascar's cultural expression. Eighteen distinct dialects today attest to the diverse creolization of culture which resulted from the immigration of Indonesians to the island beginning in the 6th century, and the movement of Africans from the eastern side of the continent.

Literacy was important in the 17th century, when the Antemoro, or People of the Banks, wrote Malagasy on bark paper and created the *Sorabe*, the Sacred Books, by using the Arabic alphabet. Transcribing this originally oral work onto paper, royal scribes of the Antemoro controlled the historical narrative. Writing became one means of legitimizing the reign of the Antemoro. Royal and popular oral histories still constitute the most reliable source of information about early Madagascar; verbal arts have become the most succinct expression of Malagasy identity. Stories circulated as early as the *Sorabe* have provided a means of communication and resistance in political struggles. Some examples can be found in the strategies of coastal groups in maintaining autonomy against the Imerina, or the Imerina's opposition to French colonialism during the Rising of the Red Shawls in 1896.

Malagasy religious systems vary widely according to ethnic group, or community of belonging. In addition to influences from traders, missions (established from the 16th century onward), and new immigrants (beginning with Muslims in the 12th century), the island is unified by the *fomban-drazana*, a respect for ancestors which derives from beliefs that people are created and transformed through interpersonal relations through life into death and the future. Leading up to and during the period of the French protectorate, Protestant and Catholic missionaries outlawed the practices stemming from these religious convictions at funerals or ceremonies of spirit possession. Religious pluralism none the less prevails throughout the island.

In the 18th century Imerina inhabitants of the central highland region established dominance over coastal groups, as can be seen in the Imerina royal histories, the *Tantaran'ny Andriana*. Recorded by the French Jesuit priest Callet from 1862 to 1866, these histories narrate the consolidation of Merina power on the island beneath the imperial system of Andrianampoinimerina (1783–1810). This ruler suppressed narratives that conflicted with official versions of history so that the history of the Imerina became the most authoritative version of national history, eclipsing those of other communities.

During the 19th century, the consolidation or national integration of the kingdom of Madagascar was often met with resistance. Religion became a tool of persecution in the hands of political leaders in numerous ways. King Radama I (1810–28) created an alliance with the British and encouraged the Protestant education of a literate Merina bureaucracy in schools of the London Missionary Society. Queen Ranavalona I (1828–61) massively repressed popular versions of Christianity, enforcing a nationalism based in Imerina tradition. Forced labour and institutionalized massacres dominated her reign; supporters of religious symbols other than traditional Imerina talismans were considered sorcerers and enemies of the state.

In 1861 Radama II opened the island again to European missionaries and traders. Persecuted Christian factions flourished, strengthened by their clandestine survival. After Radama, queen Ranavalona II and her husband, prime minister Rainilaiarivony, constructed a Christian state, profiting from the modern tools of the press and the railway. The Protestant press, an arm of the state, published works by both European and Malagasy authors. Propaganda was widely distributed through periodicals like the Protestant journal *Teny Soa* and the government gazette *Ny Gazety Malagasy*. The Malagasy press grew in the 1870s and 1880s under the influence of Protestant missionary organizations like the London Missionary Society and the Société des Missions Évangéliques de Paris.

Ranavalona II outlawed traditional symbols and forced the conversion of those professing a belief in the power of talismans. Compulsory education and forced labour became organized tools of church and state. Minorities like the Betsileo and Betsimisaraka were treated as colonized peoples. Opposition grew rapidly in countless cults and secret societies, whose members still valued the talismans.

The Franco–Malagasy War (1883–85) initially left Madagascar independent, but France and Britain continued to compete for a colonial foothold, eventually signing a treaty which recognized French rule. Malagasy opposition grew in the form of a mass revival of tradition and nationalism. For example, the possession cult or *ramanenjana* of 1894, enacted to keep away demons, showed signs of a collective spiritual crisis; even former Protestant preachers among the Malagasy brought out talismans in public for the first time.

French troops landed in October 1895 to establish protectorate rule. Malagasy resistance to French occupation reached its apogee in the Rising of the Red Shawls in March 1896. The *menalamba* (red shawl-wearers) expressed a fierce sentiment of nationalist unity, refusing to recognize the French. General Gallieni finally put down the insurrection in 1897, and exiled queen Ranavalona and her husband to Algeria.

The French protectorate established rigid control. The extremely politicized Malagasy press was abolished, and, in place of the English-language press, French became the compulsory language for communication, administration, and education. The Catholic church, schools, and the army were the principal institutions of French dominance and censorship, to which few Malagasy had access. From 1896 to 1905 governor-general Gallieni's system of compulsory education was one representative strategy of suppressing Malagasy culture. The Malagasy language was prohibited in school, with the result that few Malagasy went beyond primary level education.

By the beginning of the 20th century, privately owned French-language newspapers addressed an expatriate or elite Malagasy audience, but remained otherwise deaf to indigenous interests. Radio was introduced in 1931, principally serving a French settler audience. In opposition to such cultural infiltration, most Malagasy continued to rely upon traditional chains of communication in town meetings (*fokolohana*), ignoring French colonial institutions.

National organizations such as the Union Chrétienne des Jeunes Gens (YMCA), banned in 1906, grew in strength during the 1920s. The nationalist movement Vy, Vato, Sakelika (VVS, or Iron, Stone, Organization), with the support of the French Communist Party, also advocated Madagascar's sovereignty. The VVS leader Jean Ralaimongo, who spent time in France during World War I as a member of the *tirailleurs*, an elite African section of the French army, began to organize resistance against colonialism upon his return to France in the 1920s. At first he sought equality between French and Malagasy, but later formed the Mouvement Démocratique de la Rénovation Malgache (MDRM). The colonial regime condemned VVS collaborators and outlawed the group in 1915. The artist Émile Ralambo, for example, was one of many exiled from Madagascar for his participation in resistance movements.

During the 1930s Ralaimongo was imprisoned in France, yet in Madagascar itself the influence of the Front Populaire brought about the lifting of trade union bans, provisions for freedom of the press, and cessation of forced labour. Many Malagasy, like Ralaimongo, began to focus on the issue of suffrage in response to the fact that so many Africans had served in World War I despite not having French citizenship.

Malagasy men were again conscripted in World War II. However, soon after the war the Malagasy obtained the right to send representatives to the French National Assembly, due in part to the gains of the Brazzaville Conference of 1944. Delegates Ralaimongo (1945), Ravoahangy (1945), and Rabemanjara (1946), discovered that French parties completely opposed Malagasy independence and autonomy. In 1946 the Malagasy became French citizens and Madagascar an overseas territory of the French Republic.

On 29 March 1947 the struggle for Malagasy independence erupted in the so-called Malagasy Revolt. Communications links were severed, public and mission buildings destroyed. Malagasy rebels killed 400 French, but the French suppression of the rebellion over the next 20 months led to at least 90,000 deaths. The French banned the MDRM and arrested its three deputies, who returned to Madagascar only in 1960. Approximately 2000 nationalists were branded traitors and imprisoned until 1957.

Independence was negotiated from 1954, and the Franco–Malagasy accords we signed in 1960. Throughout the rule of Philibert Tsiranana (1960–72), the French maintained control of cultural and political life in Madagascar. Tsiranana's favour for the French was visible in the number of French advisers and expatriates who remained in Madagascar and in his anti-strike legislation. Yet cultural life seems to have flourished. Immediately following independence, the Malagasy press included at least 200 titles. By 1967 publications reached one person in 150, giving Madagascar the fourth largest readership in Africa.

In 1971 fighting between medical students and unemployed led to a strike, to which Tsiranana responded by closing down the medical school, banning the students' union, and on 12 May arresting and imprisoning more than 400 students and sympathizers. A further strike forced the release of students and brought about Tsiranana's resignation, in response to which general Gabriel Ramanantsoa established a military government, authorized the establishment of relations with communist and Arab countries, instituted the Malgachization of education, and secured the complete withdrawal of the French. These rapid changes profoundly affected sociocultural life. By 1972, only seven daily newspapers were being published, all in Malagasy (though one was bilingual). Between 1972 and 1975 rigid censorship was established.

Between 1972 and 1975 Ramanantsoa negotiated for the closure of all French bases in Madagascar and for all French public property to be relinquished. The government began studying local dialects in search of a common Malagasy language. In December 1974 political parties that opposed Ramanantsoa's bourgeois oligarchic government attempted a coup. The following February colonel Richard Ratsimandrava took over from Ramanantsoa. Ratsimandrava was assassinated six days later, after which Didier Ratsiraka was appointed head of state. Apart from one three-year break he has remained in power ever since.

The nationalization of the Malagasy economy, of politics, education, and culture which followed was communicated by radio, and the new ideology was later issued in printed form as "The Little Red Book of the Malagasy Socialist Revolution", or the *Boky Mena*. There was a slight relaxation in the intellectual climate. The works of Plato, Rousseau, Marx, and Mao, banned during Tsiranana's time, were introduced in 1973 into

philosophy classes at the University of Madagascar. Yet eventually Ratsiraka's regime eliminated certain civic liberties; for example, overseas mail was opened, and incoming air passengers were thoroughly searched for foreign papers. Several pro-government newspapers existed in what was a time of heavy editing and censorship. The French-language daily *Bulletin de l'Agence Nationale d'Information 'Tanatra'* remained the only source of foreign news. The French- and Malagasy-language daily *Nouveau Journal de Madagascar* has continued to follow the government propaganda line.

A notorious victim of censorship during this period was the periodical *Jeune Afrique*, banned by Ratsiraka for conducting "a campaign of systematic denigration and diffusing lies about the Malagasy Revolution". While few Malagasy journalists spoke out against Ratsiraka, one particular *Jeune Afrique* journalist, the Malagasy Sennen Andriamirado, remained undeterred.

The Ratisiraka regime muzzled journalists and authors. Writing and instruction in Malagasy was enforced and French discouraged. Government publications ceased in 1984. By 1985 only four daily newspapers existed; these were privately published.

Michèle Rakotoson's plays were broadcast on the radio in the early 1980s. After *Un jour ma mémoire* was banned, she began to show her dramatic works in Benin and France. Writing in French made Rakotoson a counter-revolutionary. Censors found certain topics of her writing subversive: child labour, reproductive rights, etc. She explained in an interview that voicing these issues offends the dominant culture – the Protestant puritanism of the plateau. Her works raise questions about power relationships in Madagascar, contradicting the objectives of the Malagasy revolution, which pretends to have abolished traditional castes.

In 1984 a famous 34-page pastoral letter entitled "The Anatomy of a Dictatorship" gave voice to much protest against Ratisiraka. The letter, chiefly written by cardinal Victor Razafimahatratra, alluded to the many mysterious deaths of Catholic priests in Madagascar and quickly became a rallying point for religious Malagasy who had until this time had supported the government.

Ratsiraka's re-election in 1989 led to protests in 1991. When 400,000 protesters marched on the presidential palace, Ratsiraka's guard opened fire, killing 31 people. Trade unions stopped organized trade, and the protests continued. In response, the president increased the freedom of the press and allowed the growth of opposition parties. In November 1992 and February 1993, Malagasy elected a new president, Albert Zafy, who during his three-year term reversed the policy of nationalization. However, Ratsiraka was re-elected to the presidency five years later.

The visual art of the comic strip may constitute one of the most persistent forms of resistance against abuses of power in Madagascar. Often going against the grain of official literature, the first comic strips or *tantara an-tasry* were produced in 1961 and written in Malagasy, since their writers and readers had little access to the French language. Most popular were the "Ny Ombalahibemaso", printed in the newspaper *Madagascar Matin* in the 1960s; these mythic stories based on the folk hero Andrianampoinimerina were forms of social satire. While the 1980s proved to be the golden age of the Malagasy comic strip or *bande dessinée*, their readers were particularly frustrated by the Marxist control of the media, which filtered out any pro-Western messages.

HEATHER BRADY

Further Reading

Bourgault, Louise M., *Mass Media in Sub-Saharan Africa*, Bloomington: Indiana University Press, 1995

Deleris, Ferdinand, *Ratsiraka: Socialisme et misère à Madagascar*, Paris: L'Harmattan, 1986

Ellis, Stephen, *The Rising of the Red Shawls: A Revolt in Madagascar, 1895–1899*, Cambridge and New York: Cambridge University Press, 1985

Gow, Bonar A., "Madagascar" in *The Cambridge History of Africa*, vol. 8: *From c.1940 to 1975*, edited by Michael Crowder, Cambridge and New York: Cambridge University Press, 1984

Haring, Lee, *Verbal Arts in Madagascar: Performance in Historical Perspective*, Philadelphia: University of Pennsylvania Press, 1992

Harovelo, Janine, *La SFIO et Madagascar, 1947*, Paris: L'Harmattan, 1995

"Madagascar 2: La Littérature d'expression française", *Notre Librairie*, 110 (July–September 1992)

Middleton, John (editor), *Encyclopedia of Africa South of the Sahara*, New York: Scribner, 1997 (Republic of Madagascar entry in vol. 3)

Rajoelina, Patrick, *Quarante années de la vie politique de Madagascar, 1947–1987*, Paris: L'Harmattan, 1988

INGOAPELE MADINGOANE
South African poet, 1950–1996

Active in the anti-apartheid struggle as actor, playwright, poet, and cultural organizer, the "people's poet", dubbed "poet laureate of Soweto", attracted the attention of the South African government's censorship apparatus with the publication of *Africa My Beginning*, which is in two parts: the long poem "Black Trial" and the short poem which gives the work its title.

Africa My Beginning contains 21 sections and recounts the narrator's psychological and physical progress from a state where, he says, "had I known the fruits of being/black as i am/i would have chosen to be/human/so as to avoid the chains of this/black trial" ("Black Trial/*One*"); he describes a journey towards consciousness and liberation that must be undertaken by himself and all black people. The result, also implied for the audience, is that "the speaker is a new man" ("Black Trial/*Five*").

This progress is described through the juxtaposition of a vast array of images, metaphors, and tropes, some familiar, some defamiliarized, often appearing ideologically contradictory in such proximity, like the numerous references to Christian and biblical events and themes that are placed alongside evocations of ancestors and African gods. Fatalistic and existential worldviews, as well as European and African languages, interpenetrate, as do militant nationalism and the pan-African flavour of "i talk about me/for/i am africa" ("Black Trial/*Twelve*"); while metaphysical and spirit ideals coexist with disturbingly concrete images of suffering and exploitation. All these elements may be apprehended as loose and separate, but the poem strives to integrate their diversity.

Much of the cohesion attained in the course of the poems in *Africa My Beginning* is derived from their structured vocal intonations and rhythms, supplemented by percussive beats in performance. Rhythmic influences range from "traditional" indigenous drumming and poetry to contemporary local urban and black American styles, and rhythms are often epitomized by the repetition of simple yet provocative phrases such as "*go man go/black man go*" ("Black Trial/*Six*").

The style of the poems ranges from lamentation to exhortation, from declamation to laudation, from invocation to incitement to collective mobilization, but the underlying theme is that there is really only one choice, one that begins with the recog-

nition and acceptance, of self- and collective identity, leading to liberationist activism based on this principle, as at the close of the poem: "azania here i come/from apartheid in tatters/in the land of sorrow/from that marathon bondage/the sharpeville massacre/the flames of soweto/i was born there/i will die there/in/*africa my beginning* / *africa my ending* / let's do something/*mbopha*".

Africa My Beginning attacked the sanctioned injustice of apartheid and was a commentary on a particularly volatile time in South African history. The Soweto riots of 1976 had left many dead and ignited resistance to government policies throughout the country. Increasingly, from the mid- to late 1970s, social and cultural organizations linked to the Black Consciousness (BC) movement had been making headway in persuading urban black South Africans to become conscious of their identity as oppressed black human beings, so that they might actively transform their environment.

The government perceived BC activity as a major threat to the stability of its repressive policies. Steve Biko, its leading figure, was arrested and killed in detention on 12 September 1977; just more than a month later, on 19 October, the Internal Security Act extinguished legal resistance with a blanket ban on 17 organizations, many of them with BC affiliations.

Africa My Beginning was first published in Ravan Press in March 1979, with a second impression following a month later (Rex Collings published a London edition in 1980). In May it was banned under the Publications Act of 1974, but the ban applied to distribution, not possession – 2000 copies had already been sold.

Once performed and published, mostly to a black urban audience, *Africa My Beginning* made a considerable contribution to the development of oral poetry performance in South Africa. Oral poetry played an integral conscientizing role in the broad-based liberation struggle of the 1980s, which was mobilized by elements of BC, pan-Africanist, and African nationalist and trade union organizations. Poetry performances, as part of a broader range of cultural performances such as theatre, song, music, and dance – which were at times linked to social and political events, such as speeches at rallies and funerals – both contributed to, and were a sign of, ferment in the townships. Poems were often recited – largely from memory – on stage or in a crowd, and, if the occasion sanctioned it, performed as choreographed sequences to the accompaniment of music, or as part of a play or in between speeches.

Madingoane was arrested in early 1984 after a search of his house by the Special Branch security police brought to light so-called "undesirable publications", which included his own volume and a publication by the Medu Arts Ensemble (based in Gaberone, Botswana). He was acquitted four months later for insufficient evidence. *Africa My Beginning* was eventually unbanned in 1985 and a third impression of the volume was published in April of that year – three months before the State of Emergency was proclaimed – while a fourth impression followed in 1988. By then, the poem was no longer threatening. BC, which had operated best when it could speak legally about its opinions, had been in decline since the early 1980s. Although Madingoane continued to involve himself in cultural activity, he never regained his popularity and influence, and during the last 10 years of his life his work was regularly turned down by publishers: a casualty of censorship indeed.

RICHARD BOWKER

Writings

Africa My Beginning, 1979
I Talk about Me: I am Africa (video), BBC2 *Arena* programme (March 1980)
"Run Africa" in *The Two Rivers: A South African Documentary* (16mm film), directed by Mark Newman, produced by Edwin Wes, 1986
"Khumbula My Child" in *Ten Years of Staffrider, 1978–1988*, edited by Andries Walter Oliphant and Ivan Vladislavić, 1988
"Mother Spirit" in *Matatu*, special issue: "Towards Liberation: Culture and Resistance in South Africa", 1988

Further Reading

Brown, D., "Black Consciousness, Tradition and Modernity: Ingoapele Madingoane's 'Black Trial'", *Current Writing*, 9/1 (April 1997)
Lange, Margreet de, *The Muzzled Muse: Literature and Censorship in South Africa*, Amsterdam: Benjamins, 1997
Marcus, G., "Censorship under the Emergency", *South African Human Rights and Labour Law Yearbook*, 1 (1990)
Msimang, C.T., "Ingoapele Madingoane's 'Black Trial': A Contemporary Black Epic" in *Soweto Poetry*, edited by Michael Chapman, Johannesburg and New York: McGraw Hill, 1982
Mzamane, M.V., "New Poets of the Soweto Era: Van Wyk, Johennesse, and Madingoane", *Research in African Literatures*, 19/1 (1988)
Mzamane, M.V., "Mtshali, Gwala, Serote and Other Poets of the Black Consciousness Era in South Africa, 1967–1984" in *Perspectives on South African English Literature*, edited by Michael Chapman, Colin Gardner and Es'kia Mphahlele, Johannesburg: Donker, 1992
Tucker, J., "The Minstrels of Africa: Review of Ingoapele Madingoane's *Africa My Beginning*" in *Perspectives on South African English Literature*, edited by Michael Chapman, Colin Gardner and Es'kia Mphahlele, Johannesburg: Donker, 1992
Visser, N. "Censorship and Literature" in *Perspectives on South African English Literature*, edited by Michael Chapman, Colin Gardner and Es'kia Mphahlele, Johannesburg: Donker, 1992
Vivan, I, "Black Poets of South Africa: Witnesses of Suppressed and/ or Forgotten History" in *The Writer as Historical Witness: Studies in Commonwealth Literature*, edited by Edwin Thumboo and T. Kandiah, Singapore: UniPress, 1995
Walmsley, A., "Speaking for Africa", *Index on Censorship*, 9/5 (1980)
Welz, Dieter, *Writing against Apartheid: South African Authors Interviewed*, Grahamstown: National English Literary Museum, 1987

MADRID
Spanish newspaper, 1960–71

Madrid flourished in the late 1960s and early 1970s, a turbulent period in Spain's intellectual history. A generation of students, born too late to have any direct experience of the Civil War that had torn Spain asunder between 1936 and 1939, was beginning to demand the democratic freedoms enjoyed by the country's European neighbours, yet it was still in the grip of an authoritarian regime in which the victorious factions of 1939 – Church, Army, Falange – continued to pose as the guardians of "eternal" Spanish values. The propaganda of the regime had served it well throughout the 1940s and 1950s, staving off social and political reform. Contentious literature had been banned, and liberal and leftist opponents had been demonized. However, these incantations began to ring hollow as the memories of the Civil War faded and Spaniards began to see their political future as inseparable from that of the emerging European Community (now the European Union).

The press law of 1966, introduced by Manuel Fraga Iribarne, Minister of Information and a former ambassador to London, was the outcome of a compromise strategy to persuade Spaniards and foreign observers that there was now genuine freedom of expression. The previous press law, passed as an emergency measure in wartime Spain, had unashamedly decreed that newspapers were to be "at the permanent service of the national interest". Perhaps the most welcome measure in the new law was the abolition of pre-publication censorship of the press, although all newspapers and weeklies still had to be deposited with the Ministry at least 30 minutes before they were distributed.

This was the climate in which two university professors, Rafael Calvo Serer, who presided over *Madrid*, and its editor, Antonio Fontán, attempted to make their paper a platform for democratic debate. Together with magazines such as *Cuadernos para el Diálogo*, *Triunfo*, *Destino*, and *Indice*, *Madrid* offered social and political commentary that was intended to challenge the official rhetoric. Its third page, in particular, became famous for the contributions of a host of liberal intellectuals. Calvo Serer was a member of the Catholic lay order Opus Dei, as well as being a supporter of Don Juan, the pretender to the Spanish throne, against Don Juan's son, Juan Carlos, who had been chosen by Franco as his successor. Calvo Serer gathered around him journalists of considerable talent, constituted as a *sociedad de redactores* ("editorial company") for greater solidarity, and gave access to a wide range of outside contributors.

Over the short life of the newspaper, some 180 writers contributed 2375 articles to its third page, on a range of political, social, and cultural themes. Comparisons with values and practices abroad were common, with the intention of highlighting the immobilism of Franco's regime. Headlines were devised to embarrass without courting official intervention: thus, "Franco, as always, was authoritarian", turned out to be a reference to a football referee, not the Caudillo. In private suppers with Calvo Serer, Fraga occasionally warned the paper away from such sensitive topics as public order, the legitimacy of the regime, the European Community, and political parties. However, the paper continued to attack unexpectedly and then move on to other topics, making it difficult for Fraga to counter. Contentious material often appeared on Saturdays, in the knowledge that Franco was usually away from Madrid on official business.

Despite its pretensions to enabling press freedom, article 2 of Fraga's press law included a list of conditions designed to gag the opposition, among which were

compliance with the Law on the Principles of the National Movement and other fundamental laws . . ., the maintenance of internal public order . . ., due respect for institutions and persons in criticism of political and administrative action . . ., and the protection of personal and family intimacy and honour.

Moreover, the Penal Code was amended in April 1967 to provide penalties for infringements of these conditions, including imprisonment and fines of up to 100,000 pesetas. The Official Secrets Act of 1968 prohibited the reporting of student conflict, meetings of the regime's National Council, and colonial skirmishes in Equatorial Guinea, to name but a few taboos of the time. Finally, the old version of censorship was reimposed whenever a state of emergency was declared, as in the period January to March 1969. (The defensiveness of the regime is illustrated by the fact that Spain led the world in 1968 and 1969 in banning issues of the British weekly *The Economist*, not normally seen as a seditious publication.)

The end came for *Madrid* on 25 November 1971, following the publication in *Le Monde* in Paris, on 11 November, of an article by Calvo Serer in which he wrote that "the confusion between politics and news in Spain, produced by censorship, [and] manipulation of the law on the press and official propaganda, is chiefly due to Admiral Carrero Blanco". Carrero Blanco was Prime Minister, and second only to Franco himself within the regime's hierarchy, until he was assassinated in 1973. (Intriguingly, like Calvo Serer he was a member of Opus Dei.)

While *Madrid* never attained the circulation figures of other evening newspapers such as *Pueblo* (maximum circulation about 200,000), with a maximum circulation of around 66,000 it clearly earned the respect of intellectuals in the capital, and it can be argued that, despite Calvo Serer's contacts with Fraga and others, it represented a threat to the credibility of the regime. It consistently refused to take part in orchestrated hysteria against enemies of Francoism, even when these were members of the Basque nationalist group ETA, charged with terrorism in the Burgos trials; and it relegated coverage of pro-Franco rallies to the inside pages. On one occasion it even dared to suggest that the time had come for Franco to retire, in the manner of Charles de Gaulle in France – bringing upon itself yet another suspension. Moreover, in rejecting the triumphalism of the regime, it brought to journalism a freshness of linguistic expression, in which a "technical stoppage" (*paro técnico* in the officialese of the National Movement) became known for what it was: a strike (*huelga*).

GARETH THOMAS

Further Reading

Barrera, Carlos, *El diario Madrid: realidad y símbolo de una época*, Pamplona: Eunsa, 1995
Beneyto, Antonio, *Censura y política en los escritores españoles*, Barcelona: Euros, 1975
Blaye, Edouard de, *Franco and the Politics of Spain*, Harmondsworth: Penguin, 1976
"Death of a Newspaper", *The Economist* (28 April 1973)

KURT MAETZIG
German film director, 1911–

DAS KANINCHEN BIN ICH (The Rabbit Is Me)
Film, 1965

Das Kaninchen bin ich is one of the "forbidden films" that were produced in the German Democratic Republic (GDR) in 1965–66, but were not screened until after the collapse of the GDR in 1989.

Kurt Maetzig was one of the best-known and most experienced directors working for the GDR's state film production company DEFA. Born in Berlin, he had studied sciences and law in Munich, but had been prevented from entering the film industry during the Nazi period because of his Jewish background. In 1944 he joined the Communist Party and, after the war, was one of the founders of DEFA. In 1947, he directed his first film, *Ehe im Schatten* (Marriage in the Shadows), which deals with the true story of a German actor who committed suicide, together with his family, in order to save his Jewish wife from being deported to a concentration camp. Maetzig's uncompromising pro-socialist stance was made particularly apparent in two later films, *Thälmann – Sohn seiner Klasse* (1954, Thälmann – Son of His Class), which concerns the Communist leader Ernst Thälmann, and *Septemberliebe* (1961, September Love), widely interpreted as presenting a justification for the building of the Berlin Wall through its story of a young woman who approaches the authorities when her boyfriend attempts to flee the country. By 1965 Maetzig not only had earned a high reputation for his feature and documentary films, but was esteemed as a professor at the Film Academy in Babelsberg and for his work with younger filmmakers.

Maetzig has always believed in tackling controversial topics head on. He sees cinema as having an educative function, and considers that the mission of the artist is to point out weaknesses and make suggestions for improvement. According to Maetzig, the artist has to activate and challenge his audiences, and carries an enormous social responsibility. It was in this spirit that in 1965 he started to address the problems of everyday life in the GDR, and to expose some of its many complexities and contradictions. He aimed to contribute to a more open and tolerant atmosphere. Past mistakes by the judicial system were being admitted and some of the extremely harsh sentences that had been passed in the 1950s were under review.

The fact that Maetzig chose to make a film from Manfred Bieler's novel *Maria Morzeck* illustrates his self-confidence and his hope for a more democratic development. The novel had hitherto been withheld from publication because of its controversial treatment of corruption and careerism in the courts. The Minister for Film and others voiced their doubts about the project, but Maetzig got permission to start work on the film.

Maria Morzeck, a self-confident and intelligent young woman living in Berlin with her aunt, is not allowed to go to university because her brother is serving a three-year sentence for "anti-state activities". She gets to know Paul Deister, the judge who sentenced her brother to jail, and falls in love with him. She finds out not only that he is married but that he increased her brother's sentence because he wanted to further his own career by appearing to be uncompromising towards enemies of the state. Maria leaves Deister when he tries once again to use her brother's case for his own advantage: she still loves him but she realizes that he is an opportunist who uses people. When her brother is released and finds out about her relationship, he beats her up. The film ends with Maria moving to a room of her own and enrolling at university to become an interpreter.

Maetzig made important changes to the plot and characters of Bieler's novel. The author's criticism of old judicial practices is transformed to become an affirmation of some positive changes through which society is rid of officials who abuse their power. As in the book, the story is told consistently from Maria's perspective, through an ironic interior monologue directed straight at the viewer. The film derives its strength from

Maria's character as a witty, lively young woman, and from its realistic depiction of everyday life in the bars, theatres, and streets of East Berlin.

Already completed by the time the 11th plenary session of the Central Committee of the ruling Socialist Unity Party of Germany (Sozialistische Einheitspartei Deutschlands, or SED) had taken place, *Das Kaninchen bin ich* was the first film to be attacked there and at subsequent party meetings. Maetzig was accused of "nihilistic propaganda, a whorehouse standpoint", as well as of "generalizing conflicts and neglecting the dialectics of social development". According to a report published after the Plenum, Maetzig had failed to capture the true nature of socialist life, and had presented state and party as unfeeling powers alienated from the people. The film was also criticized because it lacked a "positive hero", a character with whom the audience could identify, the presence of which was one of the criteria by which "socialist realist" art was judged.

Maetzig considered the film to be a good one and was deeply shocked by the accusations. In a futile attempt to take the edge off the attacks on "forbidden films", he admitted to various errors of judgement. He also wanted to make it absolutely clear that he did not regard himself as a dissident. In an open letter to Maetzig, Walter Ulbricht, the General Secretary of the party, clearly defined the rigorous rules of behaviour for artists that were to shape film production at DEFA in the future.

Kurt Maetzig's next film, *Das Mädchen auf dem Brett* (1967, The Girl on the Diving Board) tells the story of a young sportswoman at a critical point in her career. Compared to *Das Kaninchen bin ich*, it lacks commitment and urgency, and is stylistically more conventional.

Das Kaninchen bin ich was "rehabilitated" in the autumn of 1989 and was first screened in 1990.

GABRIELE MÜLLER

Writings

Filmarbeit: Gespräche, Reden, Schriften, edited by Günter Agde, 1987
"Auferstehung des Kaninchens: Kurt Maetzig im Gespräch mit Rolf Richter" (Resurrection of the Rabbit: Kurt Maetzig in Conversation with Rolf Richter), *Film und Fernsehen*, 5 (1990)
Discussion with Martin Brady and Helen Hughes in *DEFA: East German Cinema, 1946–1992*, edited by Séan Allen and John Sandford, 1999

Further Reading

Mückenberger, Christiane (editor), *Prädikat, besonders schädlich*, Berlin: Henschel, 1990

THE MAFIA
Secret criminal society, southern Italy

In the late 20th century there was a considerable increase, around the world, of the most basic form of censorship: the murder of those journalists, writers, and broadcasters whose activities threaten an oppressive status quo. Murders of this kind are rarely perpetrated directly by governments, who prefer to use semi-criminal gangs to do their dirty work. The Mafia – which has wide interests in the worlds of gambling and

narcotics, but which has often had connections with governments and political parties – has regularly employed "censorship" in this sense against journalists who threaten to reveal the true face of this organization, who simply "know too much".

The Mafia was born out of a situation recurrent in the history of southern Italy: centuries of foreign domination had progressively weakened any sense of wider loyalty to the peninsula, and engendered an endemic localism. In 1870 the newly constituted Italian state needed to develop systems to sort out local disputes; in the absence of any alternative solution, the government gave the Mafia *de facto* recognition to run Sicily, and turned a blind eye to the extension of its activities elsewhere in south Italy. The name Mafia is given to several organized groups: Cosa Nostra works in Sicily, Camorra in the Campania area (Naples), 'Ndrangheta in Calabria, and Sacra Corona Unita in Puglia. Mafiosi, the "godfathers", were often charming; people turned to them to solve their problems and in return accorded them considerable popular legitimacy.

The Mafia is best known, however, as an army for organized crime. It is estimated that some 18,000 men are directly involved. Trade officials estimate that Mafia business accounts for some 12 per cent of Italy's gross national product; its system of "taxation" (in reality, extortion) nets around £1 billion per annum, and is equivalent to a 20 per cent surtax on the whole population of southern Italy. With such physical and material resources behind them, it is hardly surprising that it aspires to rival or neutralize the state, or, at least, to influence it. It is also in a position to silence – permanently – those who threaten to expose its illegal activities.

In the mid-1970s Giuseppe Impastato, a militant of the far left, was in charge of a local radio station in Cinisi, Sicily. He used the radio to attack the violence and corruption of the Mafia, especially the local boss, Gaetano Badalamenti, supporting his campaign with posters throughout the town. He was killed by the Mafia on 9 May 1978, ironically the same day on which Aldo Moro, the leading Italian politician, who had been kidnapped by the Red Brigades, was found dead in Rome. In many other parts of Europe the death of a popular and well-liked journalist would have generated considerable media coverage, but very little space was given to Impastato's fate, and the influential *Il Corriere della Sera* went so far as to describe him as a terrorist, albeit one who had challenged the Mafia.

A new film about the life and death of Impasto, *I centro passi* (One Hundred Steps), was released in 2000. Directed by Marco Tullio Giordana, this independent film has won, unexpectedly, numerous prizes including the Golden Lion for the best screenplay at the Venice International Film Festival 2000 (one of the screenwriters is Claudio Fava, son of the murdered journalist Giuseppe Fava), and the Golden Globe nomination for the Best Foreign Language Film of the year, 2000.

Giuseppe Fava, from Catania in Sicily, was the editor of *I Siciliani*, a local newspaper that disclosed what it believed to be an interlocking system of power, money, and interest: the politicians in power, steered by governments in Rome; the murderers and drug traffickers of Cosa Nostra; and a consortium of local businessmen, Cavaliere del Lavoro (*cavalieri* = knight or horseman), described by Fava as "the four horsemen of the Mafia apocalypse". Fava was gunned down in January 1984.

Once again, the media failed to name this as murder: it was "an act of vengeance in a matter of honour".

Mauro Rostagno presented nightly programmes at the local television station at Trapani. In 1988 he began to reveal Mafia corruption, quoting names and dates, interviewing magistrates and those who had suffered at the Mafia's hands. The only free voice, he was violently silenced.

Il camorrista (1986), a film directed by Giuseppe Tornatore (who later directed *Cinema paradiso*) is a fictional account of the criminal career of Raffaele Cutolo, head of the Camorra, and particularly of his part in the Cirillo affair (1981), when a prominent Christian Democrat politician was kidnapped by the Red Brigades and released, unharmed, after three months. The film revealed the obstruction and vilification of the seven-year judicial investigation that followed. The film was withdrawn when Cirillo threatened a lawsuit – a more "traditional" form of censorship; it disappeared from the cinema and from home video screens; television transmission was delayed until March 1994.

The elimination of courageous journalists – as well as clergy, magistrates, and other defenders of the people – on the one hand, and the self-censorship of the rest indicate the intractability of the problem. Progress is only likely as, gradually, the cultural code that underpins the Mafia, and which is, consciously or unconsciously, widely shared, is altered.

SALVATORE COLUCCELLO

Further Reading

Arlacchi, Pino and Nando Dalla Chiesa, *La palude e la città*, Milan: Mondadori, 1987

Behan, Tom, *The Camorra*, London and New York: Routledge, 1996

Blok, Anton, *The Mafia of a Sicilian Village, 1860–1960: A Study of Violent Peasant Entrepreneurs*, Oxford: Blackwell, 1974; New York: Harper and Row, 1975

Deaglio, Enrico, *Raccolto Rosso: la mafia, l'Italia e poi venne giù tutto*, Milano: Feltrinelli, 1995

Gambetta, Diego, *The Sicilian Mafia: The Business of Private Protection*, Cambridge, Massachusetts: Harvard University Press, 1993

Hess, Henner, *Mafia and Mafiosi: The Structure of Power*, Farnborough, Hampshire: Saxon House, and Lexington, Massachusetts: Lexington Books, 1973

Lewis, Norman, *The Honoured Society*, London: Collins, and New York: Putnam, 1964

Stille, Alexander, *Excellent Cadavers: The Mafia and the Death of the First Italian Republic*, New York: Pantheon, 1995

Tranfaglia, Nicola, *Mafia, politica e affari nell'Italia repubblicana, 1943–1991*, Rome: Laterza, 1992

Vulliamy, Ed, "Mafia Face the Music", *The Guardian*, (15 June 1993)

Websites

http://www.centroimpastato.it
http://www.mafianews.net/
http://www.svileg.censis.it

MAHATHIR MOHAMAD
See **Mohamad**

NAJIB MAHFUZ (Naguib Mahfouz)
Egyptian novelist, 1911–

Najib Mahfuz is a seminal figure in contemporary Arabic literature; the winner of the 1970 State Prize for Literature, and in 1988 a Nobel Laureate. He has written over 40 novels and short story collections, in addition to newspaper articles on politics and society, which are collected in three volumes. Mahfuz's fiction often reflects his powerful engagement with social and political issues, and his deep concern for the freedom of expression. Unafraid to unmask corrupt practices, Mahfuz has suffered from several potentially catastrophic clashes with political and religious authorities. His public life has often been marked by a problematic relationship between his twin careers as an artist and a government employee.

In 1946, Mahfuz published al-Qahira al-jadida (New Cairo), the story of a government employee who prostitutes his wife to win favour with his superiors. Individual and institutional corruption are presented in the novel in a 1930s context of general poverty, unemployment, and widespread moral degeneration. Coincidentally, a scandal involving some high-ranking officials at the time of publication exposed Mahfuz to suspicion and he was called in for questioning. Mahfuz reports that he was interrogated by sheikh Ahmad Husayn, mufti of the Ministry of Awqaf (Religious Endowments), who understood that Mahfuz was the student of his brother, the celebrated Taha Husayn, and consequently cleared Mahfuz of suspicion in a favourable report.

A more threatening brush with the authorities came as a result of the publication of Tharthara fawq al-nil (Chatter on the Nile) in 1966, which exposed Mahfuz to the anger of president Nasser and vice-president 'Abd al-Hakim Amir. The novel depicts a group of men and women from a cross-section of society who regularly meet in a boathouse on the Nile to indulge in sex, drugs, and drunkenness – an escapist response to their existential sense of futility in a bleak, amoral social environment. Under the influence of narcotics, they engage in rambling conversations about politics; in particular, the opportunism and rampant corruption of high government officials is subjected to scathing criticism. At one point, a hallucinating character invokes the figure of an ancient Egyptian sage, who sings a warning song to the pharaoh and accuses him of turning a blind eye to the misdeeds of his subordinates. The significance of this was not lost on Nasser, and Amir, who was also minister of defence, is reported to have threatened to punish Mahfuz. However, as Mahfuz recounts, Nasser asked Tharwat 'Ukasha, minister of culture, his opinion about the book. The latter said to Nasser, "Mr President, I tell you frankly that if art is not allowed this kind of freedom, it will not be art." Nasser replied, "Very well, consider the matter closed."

After Egypt's defeat in the 1967 war with Israel, the regime's tolerance for criticism became minimal and more stringent censorship was imposed. In 1969 Nasser visited the offices of the semi-official daily al-Ahram (Pyramids), of which Muhammad Hasanayn Haykal, Mahfuz's patron and Nasser's close friend, was in charge, and where Mahfuz himself was then employed. Nasser joked about putting both Haykal and Mahfuz in prison.

It was not until after Nasser's death in 1970 that Mahfuz could treat, in al-Hubb tahta al-matar (1973, Love in the Rain)

and al-Karnak (1974, The Karnak), thorny issues such as state-sponsored police violence, the torture of political detainees, the collapse of morale as a result of the defeat in the Six-Day War, and general apathy and distrust in the regime. Nevertheless, an entire scene dealing with the battlefront in al-Hubb tahta al-matar was deleted when the novel, which had first been serialized in al-Shabab newspaper, was about to be published in book form. Mahfuz says that he was tempted to withdraw the novel from publication, but that the publisher threatened to charge him the printing costs. Mahfuz laments that "the published novel was like a single-winged bird since we do not see the draftee [on the battlefront] to understand the reason for his anger."

Mahfuz's most controversial work, though, has proved to be Awlad haritna (Children of Our Alley), originally published in 1959. It is a philosophical and political allegory modelled on the Qur'anic stories of the Fall, Moses, Jesus, and Muhammad, and concluding with the advent of the age of modern science and the "death of God". The setting, however, is an alley near the Muqattam hills on the eastern outskirts of Cairo, and the time of narration spans several generations in an unspecified, semi-mythic past. The story is concerned with the conflict between descendants of the mysterious God-figure Gabalawi over control of his waqf, or family endowment, which all too often falls into the hands of rapacious futuwwat, or strong-arm men. Thus the spiritual history of humankind is brought to bear upon the history of Egypt and its rulers from the beginning of time to the present.

The novel was first serialized in al-Ahram newspaper, then edited by Haykal. According to Mahfuz, the novel was the result of intense reflection on the new situation after the coup d'état led by Nasser in 1952:

> I started to feel that there were many faults and mistakes that worried me, actions of terrorism, torture and imprisonment . . . I asked the men of the Revolution, do you want to follow the road of the prophets or the road of the futuwwat? The story of the prophets is the artistic frame, but the purpose of it was to criticise the Revolution and the prevailing social order.

In order to have his work published, however, Mahfuz was forced to employ various literary techniques to conceal its implications. "I have always been sincere in my writing", Mahfuz observed later. "There have never been any circumstances which made me lie to myself or to my readers. There were, however, circumstances when, in order to express my ideas, I had to employ subterfuges of which literature . . . has always availed itself, such as symbol and allegory." The use of allegory to avoid censorship was so successful a strategy that the regime took no notice of the political significance of the book. In the event, it was the religious establishment, represented by the Islamic university al-Azhar, that began to attack it even before its serialization was completed, on the grounds that it blasphemed the sacred history of the prophets. According to Mahfuz:

several petitions were sent to al-Azhar as soon as the novel appeared. For the first time the sheikhs of al-Azhar had to read a novel. And one must remember that the work was considered highly innovative even among the intellectual circles of the time. So the sheikhs cannot be blamed for their interpretation. The petitions had made reference to the Prophet Muhammad, and accordingly the sheikhs condemned the work as blasphemous and demanded that it be banned.

Haykal suggested to Nasser that the book be examined by a committee of al-Azhar sheikhs. They recommended banning the book. Interestingly, Mahfuz was, at that time, the director of censorship on art media (cinema, theatre, sound recordings, etc.). His office, in fact, was in the same building as that of Hassan Sabri al-Khuli, who was the chief censor on publication, and hence Mahfuz's colleague. Al-Khuli told him: "We do not want a fight with al-Azhar. We will ban the book itself and anything written about it. But if you want to publish it outside Egypt you may do so." Mahfuz "considered this a reasonable solution given the attacks on the book". Thus the matter was concluded without legal or administrative action.

By this time the entire novel had been published in *al-Ahram*. However, Mahfuz refrained from publishing it in book form abroad out of respect for the decision by al-Azhar and the protection he had received from the government censors. In 1967 the novel was published, slightly expurgated, in book form in Beirut without Mahfuz's consent. It has been readily available on the black market in Egypt ever since with author's knowledge and with the government taking no action.

The matter was more or less forgotten until the Swedish Academy announced that the novel was among the works it reviewed before reaching the decision to award Mahfuz the 1988 Nobel Prize for literature. In the wake of this announcement, attacks on Mahfuz were renewed, this time by Egyptian fundamentalists, not al-Azhar. Meanwhile, several Egyptian intellectuals asked president Mubarak to lift the ban on the novel. He declared that it had never been officially banned in the first place. When this became known, the daily *al-Masa'* (Evening) began to serialize the novel, once more without Mahfuz's permission, although eventually publication was stopped at his request. Another newspaper, *al-Ahali*, published the entire novel (also without the author's consent) in a special issue which was sold out in a few hours.

Matters became more complicated a few months later after the declaration of Ayatollah Khomeini's *fatwa* (legal opinion) condemning Salman Rushdie's *The Satanic Verses*. Both Rushdie and the fundamentalists linked the two books together. Sheikh Omar 'Abdul Rahman, who was later convicted for his role in the 1993 World Trade Center bombing in New York, issued the following statement:

Salman Rushdie has wronged Islam. He has wronged the wives of the Prophet and has abused the Qur'an. In doing this he found appreciation in the West. From an Islamic point of view, Salman Rushdie, like Naguib Mahfuz, is an apostate. Anyone who wrongs Islam is an apostate and the religious jurisdiction in this case is that they repent. If they do not repent, they must be killed, since the Prophet himself said, "Kill him who changes his

religion." Accordingly, Khomeini's *fatwa* is correct. Salman Rushdie must be killed. Had this sentence been passed on Naguib Mahfuz when he wrote *Awlad haritna*, it would have served as a lesson to be heeded by Salman Rushdie.

Dr Muhammad Sayyid Tantawi, Egypt's chief mufti (Muslim legal expert), responded: "I am totally opposed to this *fatwa*, for it cannot have been decreed by a sane human being . . . Mr Naguib Mahfuz is an important literary figure. Should he do wrong, we must question him. But should he do right, we must thank him." Mahfuz commented, "The Mufti of al-Azhar has responded to the *fatwa* of my death. This is the Islamic point of view. But the fundamentalists do not want to listen".

As to the association made between himself and Rushdie, Mahfuz issued the following statement in *al-Ahram* (2 March 1989):

I have condemned Khomeini's *fatwa* to kill Rushdie as contrary to international law and to the treatment of the apostate in Islam . . . Islam's message is not one of terrorism and calls to murder. I believe that Khomeini has done as much, if not more, harm to Islam and to Muslims than the author [Rushdie] himself . . . During the debate [surrounding *The Satanic Verses*], I have supported the ban on the book in order to preserve social peace, on the condition that such a decision may not become a pretext to constrain thought. I have even upheld al-Azhar's decision to ban *Awlad haritna*, as long as the sheikhs have not changed their opinion of it. I have assured my interlocutors that my novel contains not the least insult to religion or to the prophets, that to compare it to Rushdie's would be a grave mistake, and that I have always hoped to be able to explain to my detractors its real significance.

The affair culminated on 14 October 1994 with a physical attack on the 83-year-old Mahfuz by a group of young fundamentalists armed with knives; he survived, and the assailants were quickly apprehended. They were tried and sentenced to death.

WAÏL S. HASSAN

Writings

al-Qahira al-jadida (New Cairo), 1946
Tharthara fawq al-Nil, 1966; as *Adrift on the Nile*, translated by Frances Liardet, 1993
Awlad haritna, 1967; as *Children of the Gebelawi*, translated by Philip Stewart, 1981; as *Children of the Alley*, translated by Peter Theroux, 1996
al-Hubb tahta al-matar (Love in the Rain), 1973
al-Karnak, 1974; as *Al-Karnak*, translated by Saad el-Gabalawy, in *Three Contemporary Egyptian Novels*, 1979
Najib Mahfuz yatazakkar (Mahfuz Remembers), edited by Jamal al-Ghitani, 1980

Further Reading

El-Enany, Rasheed, *Naguib Mahfouz: The Pursuit of Meaning*, London and New York: Routledge, 1993
Jacquemont, Richard, "L'Affaire Mahfouz, 1959–1994", *Nasser, 25 ans, Peuples Méditerranéens*, 74–75 (1996): 281–92

Mehrez, Samia, *Egyptian Writers between History and Fiction: Essays on Naguib Mahfouz, Sonallah Ibrahimi and Gamal al-Ghitani*, Cairo: American University in Cairo Press, 1994

Shukri, Ghali, *Najib Mahfuz: min al-Jamaliyah ila Nubul: muwajahah nagdiyah* (Najib Mahfuz: From Jammaliyya to Nobel), Beirut: Dar al-Farabi, 1991

Stagh, Marina, *The Limits of Freedom of Speech: Prose Literature and Prose Writers in Egypt under Nasser and Sadat*, Stockholm: Almqvist & Wiksell, 1993

GUSTAV MAHLER
Austrian conductor and composer, 1860–1911

Gustav Mahler entered the Vienna Conservatory in 1875, studying harmony with Robert Fuchs and composition with Franz Krenn. He also attended courses at the University of Vienna under Anton Bruckner. After graduating, Mahler occupied numerous conducting positions in opera houses throughout Germany and the Austro-Hungarian empire, the most important being at Leipzig, Budapest, and Hamburg. In 1897 he converted from Judaism to Catholicism in order to secure the post of music director at the Vienna Court Opera. After 10 years in Vienna, he went to New York to become principal conductor of the Metropolitan Opera. Mahler's compositions include 10 symphonies of epic proportions and the song cycles *Kindertotenlieder*, *Lieder eines fahrenden Gesellen* and *Das Lied von der Erde*.

During his lifetime Mahler undoubtedly received greater recognition as a conductor than as a composer. Although engendering support from many influential musicians including Richard Strauss and Arnold Schoenberg, his music aroused great controversy for its disturbing juxtapositions of profundity, irony, and banality, for its excessive length and emotionalism, and for its modernity, which in places prophesies the breakdown of conventional tonality. Anti-Semitic musicologists and critics declared that many of these elements betrayed his Jewish origins and tried wherever possible to undermine his influence. Nonetheless, after his death, and in particular during the early 1920s, Mahler's music enjoyed considerable popularity both in Germany and in the Netherlands, although British and American audiences were initially more reluctant to embrace his work.

When Hitler came to power in 1933, all performance of Mahler's music in Germany was banned on racial grounds. After the Anschluss (March 1938) it was also suppressed in Austria, and a similar veto existed during the war in occupied Netherlands, despite the fact that the influential principal conductor of the Concertgebouw Orchestra, Willem Mengleberg, had been one of the most enthusiastic proponents of Mahler's work.

In order to give intellectual credence to such a ban, the Nazis mounted a virulent propaganda campaign against his work. Music history books and articles of the period invariably reiterated the familiar anti-Semitic arguments posed by Mahler's early detractors. Perhaps the most widely disseminated and notorious work of this nature was Karl Blessinger's monograph *Mendelssohn, Meyerbeer, Mahler: Drei Kapitel Judentum in der Musik* (1939, Mendelssohn, Meyerbeer, Mahler: Three Cases of Judaism in Music) in which the composer was a depicted as a fanatical oriental Jew who deliberately wreaked havoc on western traditions through his development of atonality on the one hand, and his cynical cultivation of cheap popular music on the other.

Perhaps partly in reaction to the racist theories postulated by the Nazis, postwar reception of Mahler's music has been far more widespread and tolerant than ever before. Indeed, the composer is now widely regarded as one of the most significant figures in 20th-century music.

Erik Levi

Further Reading

Adorno, Theodor W., *Mahler: A Musical Physiognomy*, Chicago: University of Chicago Press, 1992

Blessinger, Karl, *Mendelssohn, Meyerbeer, Mahler: Drei Kapitel Judentum in der Musik als Schlüssel zur Musikgeschichte des 19. Jahrhunderts*, Berlin: Hahnefeld, 1939

Franklin, Peter, *The Life of Mahler*, Cambridge and New York: Cambridge University Press, 1997

Hefling, Stephen E. (editor), *Mahler Studies*, Cambridge and New York: Cambridge University Press, 1997

La Grange, Henry-Louis de, *Gustav Mahler*, vol. 2: *Vienna: The Years of Challenge, 1897–1909*, Oxford and New York: Oxford University Press, 1995

Levi, Erik, *Music in the Third Reich*, London: Macmillan, and New York: St Martin's Press, 1994

Namenwirth, Simon Michael, *Gustav Mahler: A Critical Bibliography*, 3 vols, Wiesbaden: Harrassowitz, 1987

Walter, Bruno, *Gustav Mahler*, London: Kegan Paul Trench Trubner, 1937

MAIMONIDES (Moses ben Maimon)
Spanish-born Jewish philosopher and rabbi, 1135–1204

Maimonides was born in the Jewish community of Córdoba where his father was a respected rabbi and judge. The Jewish community of Spain at that time was well established and on the whole thoroughly integrated into Andalusian culture. During Muslim rule there were long periods during which both Jews and Christians were tolerated and were allowed to rise to high positions in the state. It was quite possible for someone to remain faithful to his own religious traditions and study the work of Muslim intellectuals on medicine, mathematics, astronomy, philosophy, and political thought. Maimonides was a perfect example of this multiculturalism.

However, living on the frontier also had less positive results in the form of invading regimes from North Africa that were more fundamentalist and less tolerant to religious minorities. During such an invasion in 1148 by the Almohads, Maimonides and his family had to flee from Andalus and after seven years of wandering settled in Fez. After 1165 they left Morocco, travelled to Palestine, and in 1165 took up residence in Fustat (near Cairo). Here Maimonides rose to become one of the main physicians of the ruler's vizier Al Fadil.

Maimonides is considered as a great renewer of the Jewish tradition. He systematized the complicated and comprehensive Jewish laws and became an authority on the Halachah (Jewish law containing the rules and ordinances of Jewish religious and civil practice). Furthermore he tried to connect Jewish thinking with the ideas of Aristotle and to give a scientific basis for the Bible and its tradition.

Guide of the Perplexed is his most famous and most philosophical work, written in Arabic and published in 1190. The book seeks to reconcile the contradictions between biblical doctrines and the rationalist-scientific philosophy of Aristotle. In the words of Maimonides: "it is designed for thinkers whose studies have brought them into collision with religion", for men who "have studied philosophy and have acquired sound knowledge and who, while firm in religious matters are perplexed and bewildered on account of the ambiguous and figurative expressions employed in the holy writings". "Thus the book is not meant to convince the unbeliever, but rather, to correct the believer."

To calm these intellectual doubts, he set out to demonstrate that reason and faith were the twin sources of revelation. Far from his critics' fears that his rationalist approach might in the end lead to questioning the truth of the Bible, the book was meant to strengthen belief. According to Maimonides, "all truth is one". The Bible and the writings of philosophy were in harmony with each other, not in conflict with reason but in harmony. The *Guide of the Perplexed* was soon translated into Hebrew and Latin and was widely read. Catholic theologians such as Albertus Magnus and Thomas Aquinas were deeply influenced by it.

Maimonides criticized the way in which theologians addressed metaphysical problems. His criticism was mainly based on their lack of logical rigour. He strongly disapproved of the practice of astrology and occult rituals that he had observed in certain Provençal Jewish communities and which came – in his point of view – close to idolatry. Finally he wanted the hierarchical, aristocratic leadership within Jewry replaced by an intellectual, personal leadership.

Maimonides himself was criticized for his "excessive rationalism" by conservatives from inside and outside the Jewish community who feared heretics and disbelief. Non-Jews also disapproved. After studying the *Guide*, Aegidius Romanus (1244–1316), an Augustinian theologian and a pupil of Aquinas, drew up a list of 11 "errors" that Maimonides made in his work. They vary from a too negative understanding of God to his rationalist views on morals and his vision of providence. After issuing their own Jewish ban in 1232, Solomon ben Abraham of Montpellier and his associates denounced the *Guide* to the Dominican inquisitors. At the order of the papal legate all copies in the hands of Montpellier Jewry had to be delivered to the authorities who, in December 1233, destroyed them in a public bonfire.

The fear of an over-rationalistic approach to the holy writings can be illustrated by a *herem* (decree) that the Jewish community of Barcelona issued on 26 July 1305 against "any member of the community who, being under the age of 25 years, shall study the works of the Greeks on natural science or metaphysics, whether in the original language or in translation". The ban was intended to prevent young men from being influenced by Greek philosophy to turn away "from the Torah of Israel which is above these sciences".

STEFAN VAN DER POEL

Writings

Dalalat al-ra'rin, 1190; as *The Guide of the Perplexed*, translated by Michael Friedländer, 3 vols, 1881–85
The Code of Maimonides, translated by Jacob J. Rabinowitz *et al.*, 9 vols, 1949–72
A Maimonides Reader, edited by Isadore Twersky, 1972
Ethical Writings, translated by Raymond L. Weiss, 1975
Ramban: Readings in the Philosophy of Maimonides, edited and translated by L.E. Goodman, 1976
Letters, edited by Leon D. Stitskin, 1977

Further Reading

Cohn-Sherbok, Dan, *The Blackwell Dictionary of Judaica*, Oxford: Blackwell, 1992
Hayoun, Maurice-Ruben, *Maïmonide: ou, l'autre Moïse*, Paris: Lattès, 1994
Herlitz, Georg and Bruno Kirschner (editors), *Jüdisches Lexikon*, 4 vols, Berlin: Judischer Verlag, 1929–30; 2nd edition Frankfurt am Main: Judischer Verlag bei Athenaum, 1982
Jacobs, Louis, *The Jewish Religion: A Companion*, Oxford and New York: Oxford University Press, 1995
Kraemer, Joel L. *et al.* (editors), *Perspectives on Maimonides: Philosophical and Historical Studies*, Oxford and New York: Oxford University Press, 1991
Leaman, Oliver, *Moses Maimonides*, London and New York: Routledge, 1990
Leibowitz, Yeshayahu, *The Faith of Maimonides*, New York: Adama, 1987
Roth, Cecil (editor), *Encyclopaedia Judaica*, 16 vols, Jerusalem: Encyclopaedia Judaica, and New York: Macmillan, 1972: vol. 11

Maimonides in 19th-Century Russia

The works of Maimonides had a following in eastern Europe by the late Middle Ages, were in widespread use in Poland from the 16th to the 18th century, and, after 1772, became an integral part of the spiritual life of Russian Jewry. For much of the 19th century, however, his works – urbane, tolerant, and open-minded – gave a certain amount of work to the Russian censors.

Even in the 18th century it was considered necessary that imports of his work from elsewhere in Europe should be at least examined by the censorship. In the 1780s it was reported that it was being imported, along with other works, at the port of Riga, where the committee of Jewish censors – M. Iesekiel, D.E. Levi, and L. Elkan – appear not to have opposed its circulation among scholars and rabbis. Again, in 1828 formal permission was given by V. Tugenhold for the importation of Maimonides' *Moreh Nevukhim*, in a Venetian edition of 1561.

In the same year, however, *Untersuchungen über die Seele* was prohibited, since "the book's contents could shake the foundations of, and lure into error inexperienced people, who are not sufficiently educated and are morally doubtful". That this was a notable period for the censorship of Jewish religious books is indicated by the ban on *Maaseh HaRambam*, published by the famous Jewish typographer Schapiro, which was said to have been "full of superstitious fables and dangerous morals". The official line was that Jews were entitled to their classical literature, but in practice it appears that such books could undermine people's Christian convictions.

From the 1840s, Russian policy changed. It was now felt desirable that the Jewish population should be fully assimilated. To that end, "jargon" (Yiddish) should be replaced by the "clean" German language. It was hoped that the appointment of a Jewish representative at the Ministry of Education would help this process. This official certainly made it clear that the work of Maimonides was necessary for the education of Jewish youth. This was accepted, but only a censored and "cleaned up" version, with a parallel text in German, was ordered. This work, prepared by L.I. Mandel'shtam, was under the supervision of V.A. Levison, a converted Jew, who finally allowed only three books to be published out of a possible fourteen. Among the passages excluded was one on marital purity, considered "acceptable for adults, but cannot be studied by youth". Levison explained that some passages would have been ruled out by general censorship regulations in any case, and that others needed to be supplemented by "precautionary notes".

Some critics thought that the censorship had not, even then, been sufficiently rigorous. P.A. Shirinskii-Shikhmatov declared that the works of Maimonides were "anti-Christian" in places. The reviewer A.S. Norov, on the other hand, claimed to have found 1000 places in which the text had been cut; if this trend continued, he considered, Talmudic study would soon be wiped out altogether.

He underestimated the tenacity of the rabbis, who considered Mandel'shtam's edition entirely unacceptable. They not only denied permission for its use in everyday religious life, but continued to regard as authentic the foreign editions which, they knew, would never be passed by the censors. By the 1880s, the government had accepted reality: Jews could not be "corrected", and nor could censored Jewish literature be imposed. From then on, Maimonides' work was allowed to be imported and circulated freely.

DMITRY A. ELYASHEVICH

Further Reading

Carmilly-Weinberger, Moshe, *Censorship and Freedom of Expression in Jewish History*, New York: Sepher-Hermon Press, 1977

El'iashevich, D.A., "Pravitel'stvennaia politika i evreiskaia pechat' v Rossii, 1797–1917" (Government Policy and Jewish Printing in Russia, 1979–1917), St Petersburg: Gesharim, 1999

MAINA WA KINYATTI
Kenyan writer, editor, and translator 1944–

THUNDER FROM THE MOUNTAINS: MAU MAU PATRIOTIC SONGS
Collection of songs, 1980

The French philosopher Ernest Renan (1823–92) wrote that an important prerequisite for a nation is to get its history wrong. On several occasions this thesis has been related to the historiography of the Mau Mau war, fought in Kenya during the 1950s. The direction which this falsification should take, however, has been a matter of intense debate and bitter conflict in postcolonial Kenya. Mau Mau's history has been forged into a weapon with which an ideological war is waged about the nature and legitimacy of Kenya's postcolonial state.

After decolonization the Kenyan government headed by Jomo Kenyatta referred to Mau Mau in largely negative terms. Fearing a large-scale departure of white settlers, an increase in ethnic antagonism, and incriminating questions about the role of many current politicians during Mau Mau, the government launched the slogans "Forgive and forget" and "We all fought for freedom". As Kenyatta had been imprisoned during Mau Mau, an emphasis on his role as "Father of the nation" necessitated a denial of the importance of Mau Mau for the decolonization process. The demands of the former fighters were seen as a threat to stability and order: in the course of time many of their organizations were forbidden. A positive interpretation of Mau Mau increasingly came to be regarded as politically subversive. These politics of loyalism, initiated by Kenyatta, were continued under the leadership of Daniel arap Moi, who became president in 1978. A number of historians have remained close to the government interpretation. These liberals have emphasized the ethnic dimensions of Mau Mau and held that instead of being a nationalist movement, Mau Mau had been a violent expression of Kikuyu expansionism.

This interpretation was vehemently opposed by radical historians, who stressed the nationalist character of Mau Mau. The Mau Mau war, according to them, belonged to a long tradition of resistance of the oppressed against the forces of domination. As the revolution was being betrayed by a selfish *comprador* class, Kenya's independence became no more than a farce. Fearing for their position, the ruling classes have done everything within their power to suppress Mau Mau and its legacy, but – the radical historians predict – they will not be able to break the spirit of resistance: "Mau Mau is coming back" (Ngugi 1983).

Ngugi wa Thiong'o and Maina wa Kinyatti are the most outspoken and well-known exponents of the radical view. Both authors write about Mau Mau from a class perspective and stress the continuing importance of Mau Mau in Kenya's history. Both authors experienced government interference in connection with their work: Ngugi for his radical literary projects, Maina because of his work as a historian concerned with Mau Mau.

Although Maina wa Kinyatti was too young to play an active role in Mau Mau himself, his father and eldest brother were both detained during the Emergency. As his family was not able to raise his school fees, Maina applied for overseas funding and won a scholarship to attend high school in the United States. After completing his history studies there, he returned to Kenya in 1974 and started working at the History Department of Kenyatta University College. Shortly before his arrest in 1982 he had been promoted to senior lecturer.

In *Thunder from the Mountains* Maina wa Kinyatti has published just over one hundred Mau Mau songs. As he refrains from discussing his research methods, it is difficult to establish the sources the author has used. From the introduction it becomes clear that a number of the songs were recorded in the homes of former guerrillas, whereas others stem from hymn books which were published in the early 1950s and after decolonization. Although the early hymn books were banned by the colonial government in 1952 and 1953, the songs knew a wide dissemination and were sung at rallies, in guerrilla camps, and during detention. The translation of the songs is described as "a collective effort" and, although Maina takes full responsibility for the translations, he maintains that "the views expressed in the songs are entirely those of the thousands and thousands of Kenyans, who, because of their patriotism, joined the struggle against the British colonial occupiers". In *Thunder from the Mountains* Maina clearly takes class analysis as his leading principle and, what is more, has infused the songs with concepts stemming from Marxist terminology. John Lonsdale's and my own comparisons reveal that Maina has adapted the songs in a manner concordant with his interpretation of Mau Mau. Not only has Maina made the choice to translate Kikuyu concepts as "the Kenyan masses", and "imperialists" he also omitted references to Kikuyu ethnicity, God, and Kenyatta.

Thus far such accusations of partiality have hardly been expressed with regard to the liberal interpretation. Yet, Kenyan liberals have, like the radicals, taken Renan's words literally. Ogot's condemnation of Mau Mau songs as being too exclusive to "be regarded as the national freedom songs which every Kenyan youth can sing with pride and conviction" is also based on rewritten sources. Thus Ogot argues that the songs call upon leaders of other ethnic groups to humble themselves before Kikuyu politicians. Yet the word Ogot has decided to translate with "humility" is usually translated as "kindness, generosity".

All parties try to "get history wrong", but as the outcome of the Mau Mau debate has implications for the legitimacy of the Kenyan government, representatives of the radical school of interpretation have been hindered in the expression of their views. Shortly before the coup attempt in 1982, Maina wa Kinyatti was apprehended during a wave of arrests. As his lawyer S.M. Otieno had access to the confiscated documents only a few days before the trial, there was no time to build up a strong defence. Maina wa Kinyatti was sentenced to six years imprisonment on the charge of possession of seditious literature. The leaflet on the basis of which he was convicted might never have been in his possession. At the trial, however, *Thunder from the Mountains* was extensively quoted by the prosecution, suggesting that Maina's interpretation of Mau Mau formed the ground reason for his detention. During the six years of his imprisonment, wa Kinyatti suffered from severe malnutrition and illness. After his release in 1988 he fled to the United States.

It seems that *Thunder from the Mountains* was never officially banned. Yet, Maina wa Kinyatti had problems in finding a local publisher. Furthermore, the book was not included in the Kenyan school lists, which are the most important means to connect with a local audience. *Thunder from the Mountains* can be found in the tourist bookshops in Nairobi, the capital of Kenya. This reveals the importance of assessing the local distribution network in connection with censorship, especially when large parts of the population have only limited access to transport, literacy and a budget for the acquisition of books.

Censorship is often equated with the banning of books. Such a standard definition fails to include more subtle processes of censorship. By addressing the historical and cultural context of such processes, other factors come to the fore which hinder and inhibit the freedom of expression.

INGE BRINKMAN

Writings

"Mau Mau: The Peak of African Political Organization in Colonial Kenya" in *Kenya Historical Review*, 5/2 (1977): 287–311

Thunder from the Mountains: Mau Mau Patriotic Songs, 1980

Editor, *Kimathi's Letters: A Profile of Patriotic Courage*, 1986

Editor, *Kenya's Freedom Struggles: The Dedan Kimathis Papers*, 1987

Mau Mau: A Revolution Betrayed, 1991

A Season of Blood: Poems from Kenya Prisons, 1995

Mother Kenya: Letters from Prison, 1982–1988, 1996

Further Reading

Barnett, Donald L. and Karari Njama, *Mau Mau from Within: Autobiography and Analysis of Kenya's Peasant Revolt*, New York: Monthly Review Press, and London: MacGibbon and Kee, 1966

Benson, T.G., *Kikuyu–English Dictionary*, Oxford: Clarendon Press, 1964

Berman, Bruce and John Lonsdale, *Unhappy Valley: Conflict in Kenya and Africa*, Nairobi: Heinemann, London: Currey, and Athens: Ohio University Press, 1992

Buijtenhuijs, Robert, *Mau Mau, Twenty Years After: The Myth and the Survivors*, The Hague: Mouton, 1973

Gakaara wa Wanjau, *Nyimbo cia Mau Mau*, Karatina: Gakaara Press, 1988

Kabira, Wanjiku Mukabi and Karega Mutahi, *Gikuyu Oral Literature*, Nairobi: Heinemann, 1988

Kahengeri, G., *Nyimbo cia wiyathi wa Kiri-Nyaga*, n.d.

"Maina wa Kinyatti: Prisoner of Conscience", *Index on Censorship*, 6 (1987): 22–25

Mirugi, Mathenge, *Nyimbo cia Gikuyu na Mumbi*, Nairobi: Gakaara, 1952

Mugia, D. Kinuthia, *Urathi wa Cege wa Kibiru*, Nairobi: Kenya Literature Bureau, 1979

Ngugi wa Thiong'o, *Barrel of a Pen: Resistance to Repression in Neo-Colonial Kenya*, London: New Beacon, and Trenton, New Jersey: Africa World Press, 1983

Ogot, Bethwell A., "Politics, Culture and Music in Central Kenya: A Study of Mau Mau Hymns, 1951–1956", *Kenya Historical Review*, 5/2 (1977): 275–86

ROGER MAIS
Jamaican novelist, 1905–1955

Roger Mais is best known for his novels *The Hills Were Joyful Together* (1953) and *Brother Man* (1954), which are distinguished for their sympathetic portrayal of the urban poor in Jamaica's capital, Kingston, and for *Black Lightning* (1955), which moves away to some extent from social realism to explore the nature of artistic creation.

Mais was born in Jamaica, which was then a British colony largely stratified by class and colour, where the majority of the population served as a source of cheap labour for the production of export commodities for the metropolitan market. Mais himself came from a comfortable middle-class background. At the time of the working-class riots of 1938 he was, as he later claimed, on his way into Kingston to volunteer as a special constable to help preserve the status quo when he suddenly changed his mind and decided he must support the working-class cause. He had already had some experience as a reporter for Jamaica's leading paper, the *Daily Gleaner*. From 1940 he began to contribute short stories and articles on a regular basis to *Public Opinion*. This was the organ of the People's National Party, which was committed to changing the colonial system, not only by improving the material conditions of the working class, but also by securing more say for all Jamaicans in the running of their country.

In 1944 the British government promulgated a new constitution for Jamaica. This gave all adults the right to vote for the first time without the property qualifications, that were still in force in other British West Indian colonies, and it gave the island a significant measure of internal self-government. Many Jamaicans were prepared to hail this as real progress. For Mais, on the other hand, it was clear that the new constitution did not go far enough. After the constitution had first appeared in draft form, he wrote an article in *Public Opinion* (11 July 1944) which denounced it as a "piece of hypocrisy and deception", and claimed that it was intended to support "the real official policy" implicit in statements made from time to time by the British prime minister, Winston Churchill. At a time when many Jamaicans and other West Indians were supporting Britain in World War II by serving in the British armed forces, Mais claimed that Churchill had openly avowed that "what we are fighting for is that England might retain exclusive prerogative to the conquest and enslavement of other nations", and that the war effort aimed at "the non-dissolution of a colonial system which permits the shameless exploitation of those colonies across the seas of an Empire upon which the sun never sets."

For some, Mais's outspokenness made him a national hero. In a colony of an empire at war – even an empire supposed to be fighting fascism in defence of democracy – the authorities felt that he had gone too far. Mais's reward was arrest and conviction on a charge of seditious libel, and he served six months in prison. After his release he produced very little journalism. Instead, he threw himself into his creative work, which, it is clear, he saw as an extension of political struggle by other means. He had begun to achieve success as a writer of fiction when his career was cut short by an early death from cancer. His novels have long been recognized as classics of Caribbean literature.

JOHN GILMORE

Writings

And Most of All Man, 1939
Face and Other Stories, 1942
The Hills Were Joyful Together, 1953
Brother Man, 1954
Black Lightning, 1955
The Three Novels, introduction by Norman W. Manley, 1966
Listen, the Wind, edited by Kenneth Ramchand, 1986

Further Reading

Brathwaite, Kamau, "Brother Mais" in his *Roots*, Ann Arbor: University of Michigan Press, 1993
Hearne, John, "Roger Mais: A Personal Memoir", *Bim*, 6/23 (December 1955): 146–50

DUSAN MAKAVEJEV
Yugoslav filmmaker, 1932–

Dusan Makavejev has experienced two types of censorship – the repressive censorship of communism and the subtle one of capitalism. Under communism he made films which were later shelved; under capitalism nothing was shelved, but many of his projects never materialized.

By the time he made his most controversial *W.R.: Misterije organizma* (*W.R.: Mysteries of the Organism*) in 1971, Makavejev was internationally acclaimed. *W.R.*, which in addition to explicit sexual content makes daring nonconformist political statements, was found outrageous by the Yugoslav Ministry of Culture and shelved. Makavejev's further projects did not receive approval for production. As travel abroad for Yugoslav citizens was not restricted at the time, the director and his wife, Bojana Marian (musical editor of all his films), chose to leave the country. They set up home in Paris, but also worked in the USA, Canada, Sweden, the Netherlands, Germany, Australia, and Israel. Since leaving Yugoslavia, Makavejev, who has also written all his films, has had a hard time securing finance for his projects. While in Yugoslavia (1965–71) he was able to make four feature films; over 30 years in the West he has only realized six more. Since 1994 he has tried in vain to find finance for a feature project called *Yugoslavia*.

Born in Belgrade, Makavejev graduated in psychology from the University of Belgrade and made amateur documentaries. He was strongly influenced by the Yugoslav Marxist-humanist group Praxis, which itself was subject to censorship. In his early work, Makavejev set out to explore the extent to which individual behaviour is determined by social and political influences. His first feature, *Covek nije tica* (*Man Is Not a Bird*, 1965), is a love story with a sad ending. The lovers copulate to the accompaniment of Beethoven's Ninth Symphony. His second film, *Ljubavni slučaj ili tragedija sluzbenice PTT* (1967, *Love Affair; or, The Tragedy of the Missing Switchboard Operator*), again a love story with a tragic end, received international acclaim. In this film Makavejev daringly experimented with nonlinear narrative and Godard-inspired techniques of associative montage. In a scene which was supposed to be the prelude to the first screened sexual intercourse, Makavejev showed his Yugoslav protagonists watching television footage of Russians pushing down church crosses (from Esphir Shub's *The Fall of the Romanov Dynasty*). By using this seemingly unrelated documentary footage, Makavejev was not only setting up a sociopolitical context for the love story but creating a complex allegory. The challenge to the previously erect but now falling symbols of the religious establishment was a visual equivalent to the vulnerability of phallic power which the film examined. Scenes containing nudity were cut when the film was released in France and Britain.

In three of his next five films, *Nevinost bez zastite* (1968, *Innocence Unprotected*), *WR* (1971), and the Canadian–French co-production *Sweet Movie* (1974), Makavejev abandoned straightforward narrative altogether and switched to complex associative montage to make statements about the complex interaction of personal libidinal inclinations, national character, and world politics. *Nevinost bez zastite*, incidentally, was

based on an original work by Dragoljub Aleksič, a Serbian acrobat who had not been allowed to perform in public during the Nazi occupation. Aleksič, a childhood hero of Makavejev, made the film clandestinely, and, after it had been reworked, apparently took the film around Yugoslavia by bicycle before it was banned. Makavejev's version – which includes interviews with Aleksič – mocks Nazi and Communist politics.

W.R.: Misterije organizma opens with a 20-minute documentary on the American period in the life of one of the leading members of the Frankfurt School, Wilhelm Reich (1897–1957), and combines feature and documentary to make a nonconformist statement on social and sexual liberation, totalitarianism and imperialism, communism, and free love. The director meshes together subplots about Yugoslavs, Soviets, Chinese, Americans, and Germans. *W.R.*, standing for both Wilhelm Reich and World Revolution, was avant-garde, unconventionally structured around a wide array of cinematic techniques – mostly musical collages and associative montages of documentary and feature film (from documentary footage of crowds cheering Mao Zedong to feature excerpts from a 1948 Soviet glorification of Stalin, and "shock corridor"-style scenes from an American mental institution). The film is, in fact, an attack on communist prudery. One of its characters, Milena, believes that "communism without free love is a wake in a graveyard".

W.R. was shown at the Yugoslav film festival in Pula, but then withheld from distribution initially after Soviet pressure. Graphic sex was one of the concerns of the Ministry of Culture. Another was the ridicule of socialist kitsch, and the generally incomprehensible appeal to sexual and social liberation, considered to be a harmful Western influence. Reportedly, Tito himself found the film to be a perverted work of art and left before the end of a private screening, along with writer Miroslav Krleza. In 1973 a lawsuit was launched against Makavejev by a veterans' association in Vojvodina who had felt offended by the film's preoccupation with masturbation, homosexuality, and exhibitionism. In the West, *W.R.* played mostly within the festival circuit and had a limited theatrical release, even then censored for sexual content in Britain, France, and the USA.

Makavejev's subsequent *Sweet Movie*, made in the west, went even further in applying the approaches of *W.R.* and has a visceral disturbing effect on the viewer. It is one of his most controversial films and has caused public outcry in western Europe and North America for its bold treatment of sexuality and politics. The film has had limited release in the West and exhibitors, fearing audience outrage, refrain from scheduling it. Since *Sweet Movie*, Makavejev has had enormous difficulties in finding sponsors for his work. In his later films (such as *Montenegro*, 1981; *The Coca-Cola Kid*, 1985; and *Manifesto*, 1988), he gradually abandoned associative referencing and stopped making political statements. He maintained his interest in human sexuality, but now treated it with less intensity. Makavejev returned to using associative political referencing in *Gorilla Bathes at Noon* (1993), dealing with the end of the Cold War.

It is not just the sex but rather the cross-referencing of sex and politics that censors of Makavejev's films have found difficult to handle. There is nothing as brazen as Makavejev's daring montages, which overload his simple plots with numerous layers of significance. He does not hesitate to use stereotypical images, like the stiff Russian lover in *W.R.*, or the hygiene-obsessed Texas oil tycoon and the sensual, glamorous Latin singer in *Sweet Movie*. Makavejev's stance is to defy traditional stereotypes by placing them in a nontraditional sequence of other cultural icons and signifiers which allows him to subvert the commonplace pillars of historical imagination. He has not always been successful. Nevertheless, it is Makavejev's trademark to challenge popular understanding by confronting commonplace mentality with frivolous subversive collages. Makavejev's oeuvre is routinely part of the curriculum for film production students.

DINA IORDANOVA

Films

Covek nije tica (Man Is Not a Bird), 1965
Ljubavni slučaj ili tragedija sluzbenice PTT (Love Affair; or, The Tragedy of the Missing Switchboard Operator), 1967
Nevinnost bez zastite (Innocence Unprotected), 1968
WR: Misterije organizma (WR: Mysteries of the Organism), 1971
Sweet Movie, 1974
Montenegro, 1981
The Coca-Cola Kid, 1985
Manifesto, 1988
Gorilla Bathes at Noon, 1993
Hole in the Soul, 1994

Writings

"Film Censorship in Yugoslavia", *Film Comment* (July–August 1975)

Further Reading

Blazevski, Vladimir (editor) *Dusan Makavejev: 300 Cuda*, Belgrade: Studenski kulturni centar, 1988
Eagle, Herbert, "Yugoslav Marxist Humanism and the Films of Dusan Makavejev" in *Politics, Art, and Commitment in the East European Cinema*, edited by David W. Paul, New York: St Martin's Press, and London: Macmillan, 1983
Eagle, Herbert, "The Films of Dusan Makavejev" in *Before the Wall Came Down: Soviet and East European Filmmakers Working in the West*, edited by Graham Petrie and Ruth Dwyer, Lanham, Maryland: University Press of America, 1990
Goulding, Daniel, "Makavejev" in *Five Filmmakers: Tarkovsky, Forman, Polanski, Szabo, Makavejev*, edited by Goulding, Bloomington: Indiana University Press, 1994
Horton, Andrew, "The Mouse That Wanted to F—K a Cow" in *Comedy/Cinema/Theory*, edited by Horton, Berkeley: University of California Press, 1991
O'Grady, Gerald (editor), *Makavejev Fictionary: The Films of Dusan Makavejev*, Boston and New York: Harvard Film Archive/American Museum of the Moving Picture, 1995
Udovicki, Svetozar, "Dokumentacija za internu upotrebu", Neoplanta film, 1971 (1009-page long mimeo report containing all important documents pertaining to the controversy over *WR*)

MOHSEN MAKHMALBAF
Iranian film director and writer, 1957–

Mohsen Makhmalbaf began his eventful cinema career in 1982 as a "state filmmaker". A devout Muslim all his life, he had experienced a short spell in the shah's political prisons for attempting to disarm a police officer. He had a lot to learn and catch up with as a young director, since, on his own admission, he – like many other devout Muslims – totally boycotted cinema before the Islamic Revolution of 1979.

During the early years, Makhmalbaf was one of the handful of filmmakers who did not need the state's "guidance, supervision, and control" to observe the rules of the new cinema. His early films, all produced by the state-owned and controlled Arts Bureau of the Islamic Publicity Organization, encapsulated the new regime's key political and ideological themes: the war with Iraq, the Islamic nature of the struggle against the shah, and the remaining threat of "un-Islamic ideologies". *Baycot* (1984, Boycott), for instance, was about a leftist anti-shah campaigner becoming disillusioned with his brothers in arms and eventually finding salvation by embracing Islam.

Around 1985, with the publication of a number of film scripts and a novel, *Bagh-e Bolur* (Crystal Orchard), Makhmalbaf began to reveal signs that he no longer had an unquestioning faith in the ability – or, for that matter, the will – of the "Islamic state" to fulfil the revolution's pivotal promise to transform social, economic, and political relations in Iran. For instance, in a script called *Madreseh-ye Raja'i* (Raja'i School),

Makhmalbaf voices his grievance with the dominant position that rich people still enjoy in Iran and their ability to pull the strings to safeguard their interests. In 1996, after *Dastforush* (The Peddler), a bitter and hard-hitting commentary on poverty, inequality, violence, and fatalism, Makhmalbaf broke acrimoniously with the Arts Bureau and chose a new state patron, the Foundation for the Oppressed. His next two films were the product of the natural progression of his state of disenchantment with what was taking place in Iranian society. *Arusi-ye Khuban* (1988, The Wedding of the Righteous) tackles the sensitive subject of devout young revolutionaries (*Basijis*) returning from the war front and finding out that their ideals were being trampled upon by the rich and the "unfaithful", with the tacit support of the state. In *Bicycle Raan* (1988, The Cyclist), the rich are blamed again for the prevailing poverty and other dire economic bottlenecks, although this time in less direct language. For the first time a Makhmalbaf film was subjected to censorship. The film, about a penniless Afghan man's bicycle marathon, was partly shot in Pakistan, because, in Makhmalbaf's own words, "some people objected that there was no poverty, deprivation and other such miseries in Iran, and forced me to shoot the film abroad".

There were two central characters in *Shabha-ye Zayandeh Rud* (1990, Zayandeh Rud Nights): a disabled intellectual teaching history at the university and his westernized daughter studying psychology. The history lectures reflect Makhmalbaf's preoccupation with social and political change, or indeed the lack of it. The daughter, however, represents a new Makhmalbaf fascination, first with the theme of love and romantic relationships, but also with the idea that the "truth" is relative and cannot be monopolized by a single political and ideological camp. A relationship grows between the daughter and a disillusioned *Basiji*, and she then has to make a choice between him and her westernized fiancé. Romance and truth are also at the centre of the plot of *Nonbat-e Asheqi* (1990, Time to Fall in Love). A married woman forms a romantic relationship with another man. The jealous husband catches them together and kills the lover. Following his arrest, a court sentences him to death but lets him choose the manner of his execution. The story is repeated in three different versions, each with a different conclusion. The film employs a highly symbolic and allegorical language to underline the prevalence of prejudice and self-righteousness in society.

Both these films were banned after their premieres at the Ninth Tehran Fajr Film Festival. Clearly, as the critics argued at the time, had it not been for Makhmalbaf's reputation as a trusted Muslim filmmaker, these two scripts would have never been granted production permits in the first place. The films' premieres were greeted with strong complaints from various *Basiji* individuals, some sections of the hard-line press, and the conservative clerics, who strongly objected to the "trivial and frivolous portrayal of love and sexuality" in the films as well as to what was called "the promotion of sexual liberalism and promiscuity". The films were also attacked because of their alleged attempts to "tarnish" the image of the devoted *Basiji* youth and the families of martyrs. This time Makhmalbaf had gone too far to argue his case that the Islamic Revolution had brought about little change. In particular, critics mentioned a sequence in which a number of portraits of various Iranian leaders adorn the lecture hall wall. The camera pauses on each picture, depicting first the Qajar kings, then the two Pahlavi shahs, and finally a blank picture frame. The "revolutionaries" were incensed that by the unfilled frame Makhmalbaf had really meant Khomeini.

Significantly, critics, in particular on the influential hard-line newspaper *Kayhan*, used Makhmalbaf's "transformation" as proof that the country's arts and media policies as a whole had failed miserably. Political factions now made virulent attacks on each other; in particular, the Ministry of Islamic Culture and Guidance and its minister, Mohammad Khatami, were singled out for criticism. Khatami finally resigned in 1991 and entered a period of political isolation that lasted until his election as president in May 1997.

The ban on the two films is still in force. They have been shown in a limited number of foreign film festivals, but, according to officials, without the permission of their private producers. Limited copies of the films are available on Iran's extensive film and video black market.

Makhmalbaf moved away from direct and explicit political films after the controversy and began concentrating on films about different aspects of cinema. For example, his next film, *Nasereddin Shah, Actor-e Sinama* (1991, Once upon a Time, Cinema), is a satirical account of the early history of Iranian cinema, not failing to mention various restrictions imposed by the political elite on Iranian filmmakers at different junctures. The majority of Makhmalbaf's other film projects in the 1990s were "art films" which were largely ignored by Iran's mainstream cinema-going public, but were screened and acclaimed widely in prestigious foreign film festivals.

ALI SHAHABI

Films

Tobeh-ye Nasuh (Nasuh's Repentance), 1983
Do Cheshm-e Bisu (A Pair of Sightless Eyes), 1983
Este'azeh (Fleeing from Evil to God), 1984
Baycot (Boycott), 1984
Zangha (script; The Bells), 1984
Madreseh-ye Raja'i (script; Raja'i School), 1985
Dastforush (The Peddler), 1986
Bicycle Raan (The Cyclist), 1988
Arusi-ye Khuban (The Wedding of the Righteous), 1988
Nowbat-e Asheqi (Time to Fall in Love), 1990
Shabha ye Zayandeh Rud (Zayandeh Rud Nights), 1990
Nasereddin Shah, Actor-e Sinama (Once upon a Time, Cinema), 1991
Honarpisheh (The Actor), 1992
Salaam Sinama (Salaam Cinema), 1994
Nan va Goldun (Bread and Flowerpot/A Moment of Innocence), 1996
Gabbeh, 1996
Sokut (Silence), 1998
Dar (The Door), 1999
Safar-e Kandahar (The Kandahar Journey), 2001

Writings (novels)

Hoze-Soltun, 1984
Bagh-e Bolur (Crystal Orchard), 1985
Gung i khvabidah (The Sleeping Ganges; collection), 3 vols, 1993

Further Reading

Farasati, Mas'ud, *Dah Film, Dah Naqd* (Ten Films, Ten Criticisms), Tehran: Barg, 1991
Haydari, Gholam, *Filmshinakht-i Iran* (Filmography of Iran), vol. 1, Tehran: Intisharat-i Pazhohash-ha-ye Farhangi, 1992
Kayhan (February–March 1991)
Sureh (film issue; Spring 1991)

MALAWI

(formerly Nyasaland)

Population: 11,308,000

Main religions: Protestant; Roman Catholic; Muslim;
indigenous religions

Official languages: English; Chichewa

Illiteracy rate (%): 25.5 (m); 53.5 (f)

Number of daily newspapers: 5

Number of periodicals: 4

Number of radio receivers per 1000 inhabitants: 258

Malawi, under its eccentric "President-for-Life", Dr Hastings Kamuzu Banda, had the most elaborate and comprehensive legal apparatus of censorship in postcolonial Africa. Although since the 1960s Africa has seen many single-party or military dictatorships, in most instances the power of the state has been unable to assert itself effectively over a recalcitrant civil society. Banda, by contrast, moved rapidly after independence successfully to crush his political rivals and stem the development of the institutions of civil society.

The British colonial administration in Nyasaland (as Malawi was known prior to 1964) had extensive powers to restrict the circulation of material regarded as politically offensive, notably under the penal code. Nyasaland had a vigorous nationalist movement. There was early opposition to colonial rule in the form of the 1915 uprising led by John Chilembwe, which had been sparked by a combination of economic and political grievances and millenial expectations on the part of his followers. In the inter-war period, Nyasaland was a cradle of militant Watch Tower sects – a movement related in name only to the quietist Jehovah's Witnesses. The Central African Watch Tower movement opposed colonial rule and organized workers in the Rhodesian mines. The nationalist movement became more explicitly political in 1953, after the imposition of the Central African Federation, in which Nyasaland and Northern Rhodesia (now Zambia) came under the thrall of the white settlers of Southern Rhodesia (now Zimbabwe). Nationalist activity in Nyasaland was strictly circumscribed. In 1959 a state of emergency was imposed and hundreds of members of the now banned Nyasaland African Congress arrested, including Banda. Reorganized as the Malawi Congress Party (MCP), however, the nationalists eventually succeeded in breaking the federation and achieved independence in 1964, with Banda as prime minister.

One-party states were the norm in early postcolonial Africa, facilitated by the usually overwhelming popular support for the victorious nationalist party. Yet in neighbouring Tanzania and Zambia, for example, the single party was generally fairly benign and contained within it differing political strands. Malawi, by contrast, was an entirely personal dictatorship in which the party, although apparently omnipresent, played little political role except as an instrument of Banda's rule. The comprehensiveness of Banda's control is explained, at least in part, by the swiftness with which he moved against his potential rivals and critics. Within weeks of independence, in the so-called Cabinet Crisis, Banda drove into exile almost the entire younger generation of nationalist leaders – the very men who had called the ageing physician back from self-imposed exile in Britain to lead the struggle against the federation. He ruled for nearly a decade through a network of African chiefs – para-

doxically the only significant grouping in Malawian society that had supported colonial rule. At the same time, Banda depended upon the repressive legal framework inherited from the reviled federation. By the early 1970s the MCP had been remoulded in Banda's image, although it was still not trusted as an independent entity. Until the end of his rule, the chiefs, through the "traditional court" system, provided a check on the politicians, while the party and various intelligence services kept the chiefs under control.

Some commentators – usually those who had only known the country under Banda's rule – concluded that Malawians were a docile people who suffered repression and censorship because they had no inclination to do otherwise. Thus the American writer Paul Theroux wrote in 1989: "In my youth I had misread the mood of the Malawians. It had taken me all that time to see that they are essentially conservative and quiet-minded and somewhat puritanical. The last thing they want is radical change."

This turns the history of Malawi on its head. Rather, Banda's ferocious suppression of all alternative voices was a testament to the lively effectiveness of oppositional politics in Malawi under colonialist rule. Indeed resistance to Banda, including armed rebellion and unofficial labour unrest, continued well into the 1970s. Banda's opportunistic alliances with colonial Portugal and apartheid South Africa were partly to provide him with the means to crush such dissent. He was intolerant of any signs of independence whatsoever. This could take the form of religious persecution – his vicious treatment of the Jehovah's Witnesses was the most serious example. Hundreds died and many thousands more were imprisoned or exiled. Meanwhile, those who posed a political threat were quickly neutralized. Opponents, or potential rivals within the party apparatus, were detained without charge, or else imprisoned, or even executed after show trials in the "traditional courts".

Banda's control over the mass media differed in extent, but not in kind, from other African countries. The only daily newspaper, the *Daily Times*, was owned by the ruling party, as was the one weekly paper that addressed political matters. Banda himself acquired ownership of Malawi's principal publishing company in 1972. One of the great hazards for Malawian journalists was inadvertent "misreporting". Perhaps the most notorious example of this occurred in 1985, after Banda's mistress, the Official Hostess Cecilia Kadzamira, made a speech to a UN conference in which she used the words "Man cannot live without a woman". This bland quip was duly reported by the Malawi News Agency (MANA) and relayed by the other official media. By the following morning, however, Kadzamira had concluded that these words were offensive to the unmarried life-president and therefore that she could not have said them.

The three journalists who had reported them were detained without charge for a year. An earlier instance of detention without trial had occurred in 1973, when eight journalists were arrested for reporting clashes between Malawian and Portuguese troops on the Mozambique border.

Banda retained tight control over all forms of the media in Malawi. The Malawi Broadcasting Corporation was a state-owned monopoly. It relayed the comings and goings of the head of state with predictable deference. Until the 1980s, Banda was the only government minister allowed to broadcast in voice. Meanwhile, Malawi was more successful than many of its neighbours in restricting the activities of foreign journalists in the country. On a number of occasions journalists were expelled, often after a short period behind bars.

The MCP's control of press and broadcasting differed little in scope and intention from what was going on in neighbouring countries. However, Malawi's formal censorship structure was highly distinctive. In most of its repressive laws, especially those connected with freedom of expression, Banda appeared to take a "belt and braces" approach. Thus the government had powers to ban publications under at least three separate laws. Section 3 of the Preservation of Public Security Regulations allowed it to ban the publication or dissemination of matter deemed "prejudicial to public security". Section 46 of the penal code gave it the power to prohibit the import of publications "contrary to the public interest". Possession of a banned publication was a criminal offence carrying a sentence of imprisonment. The Censorship and Control of Entertainments Act overlapped both these provisions. Under section 23, publications were to be banned if they were: "likely to give offence to the religious convictions or feelings of any section of the public, bring anyone into contempt, harm relations between sections of the public or be contrary to the interests of public safety or public order". A Censorship Board determined which publications were acceptable. Any imported book, record, publication, or film had to be submitted for approval. All set textbooks for schools or the university had to have the prior approval of the Censorship Board. Books by Malawian authors did not, strictly speaking, have to be submitted; however, as the chief censoring officer observed, it was in an author's interest to do so: "A work that is banned after publication is of no use to anyone, least of all the writer. Most publishers in Malawi prefer to have manuscripts vetted first before they are sent to the printers". This presumably accounts for the fact that only a tiny proportion of the works formally banned were of Malawian origin.

Not surprisingly, given the breadth of the criteria, hundreds of publications were banned: 1350 books alone between 1968 and 1985. According to Catherine Chimwenje, Chief Censoring Officer in the mid-1980s, 90 per cent of banned books and 85 per cent of magazines were "pornographic or substantially obscene". It should be borne in mind that the criteria for pornography or obscenity were extremely broad. *Drum* magazine was banned following a series of articles on human reproduction; *Parade* because it contained pictures of girls in bikinis. Meanwhile, whether on grounds of obscenity or for other reasons, dozens of works by giants of 19th- and 20th-century literature were banned. These included: James Baldwin, Okot p'Bitek, J.P. Donleavy, Graham Greene, Ernest Heming-way, Bernard Malamud, George Orwell, Wole Soyinka, Tennessee Williams, and Émile Zola.

The grounds upon which a work was banned were often misinformed. For instance, *The Second Sex* by Simone de Blauvoir (*sic*!) was on the banned list sandwiched between *The Nymphet* and *The Dangerous Games* and in close proximity to *The Leather Scene* and *The Kinky Crowd*. One of the rules of thumb was apparently to ban anything with a remotely risqué title. Another was that if an author was banned once, all subsequent works should be banned as well. The poet Jack Mapanje recalled an occasion when Banda recommended to his cabinet a book that had been presented to him on his return to Meharry Medical College, Tennessee, where he had trained as a doctor, only to find that it was on the list of banned books. In a similar incident in 1987, the British Prince of Wales, on an official visit to the country, publicly commended the film of E.M. Forster's *A Room with a View*, which had also been banned from public showing – much to the embarrassment of his ultra-royalist hosts.

The rationale for censorship was largely to do with protecting national culture from pollution by immorality: "The Board is appealing to the writers not to look at it as a body that is there to ban things, but as a body that is there to safeguard the moral conduct of the Malawian society." The Censorship Board files from the latter years of MCP rule are littered with such claims. It is a major theme of Chimwenje's 1988 paper bearing the Orwellian title "The Role of Censorship in Promoting Books and Reading in Malawi", although she at least had the honesty to admit: "The Censorship Board may be said to be not in the business of promoting reading of books in Malawi."

The arguments for censorship were of a piece with the Decency in Dress legislation of the early 1970s, which banned women from wearing short skirts or trousers and men from wearing flared trousers or hair over their collars. This law was generally popular, yet it reflected a spurious and invented notion of tradition. For Muslim women, for example, wearing trousers is "traditional", yet they did not conform to Banda's notion of Malawian culture. Banda's notion of the "traditional" owed more to European missionaries than to historical practice.

By the 1980s the more sophisticated advocates of censorship perceived that the Censorship Board was open to ridicule. By this time the board's chairmen included men such as bishop Nathaniel Aipa of the Anglican Church and Reverend Silas Ncozana of the Blantyre Presbyterians, who were more intelligent and liberal men than the first chairman, the rather absurd figure Reverend Tobias Banda, who banned Samuel Beckett's *Waiting for Godot* because he was upset by "the man with the rope around his neck". The chief censoring officer in this period was also politically more acute. Catherine Chimwenje attempted to develop an ideology of censorship reflecting local conditions and which helped writers be in tune with their society: "Because censorship deals with social issues and sometimes political issues, censorship policies are of necessity dynamic, responding to the contemporary social and political climate and the level of enlightenment of the people."

In 1987 Chimwenje visited the British Board of Film Classification to help her develop standard criteria for the board's readers, as well as computerizing the records. Some books were quietly unbanned and very few new books were suppressed. In 1989 the university was allowed to submit a list of books that it wanted unbanned. However, despite the supposed centrality of protection against immorality, in fact the area where the Censorship Board never wavered was in keeping books on Malawian history out of circulation. Works by Landeg White, Philip Short, Robert Rotberg, John Pike and others remained on the banned list. However, poverty and illiteracy meant that very few Malawians read books anyway, so unbanning Okot p'Bitek's *Song of Lawino* (which was proscribed on account of its allusions to excrement), for example, made little difference to anyone.

Paradoxically, although Malawi was one of Africa's most highly censored countries it also produced a number of fine writers who wrote some distinguished literary works. One of those who flourished was Jack Mapanje. He was a founder, and the most eminent member, of the Writers' Group, which met weekly at Chancellor College from 1970 onwards. Although the group numbered journalists and others among its members, it met at the university and was regarded as part of the academic teaching programme – a loophole through which it evaded the attention of the censors. It was a group of writers – many of whom were poets – yet it also occupied a unique position, especially in its early years, as a general forum for critical views of government policy, albeit in a highly cryptic and metaphorical fashion. From early in its life, the group's writings were circulated to some 400 people.

The Writers' Group rapidly developed a series of metaphors commonly used to deal with sensitive political topics. The Malawi Congress Party with its slogan of *kwacha* or "dawn" would be represented by dawn or daybreak or by the cockerel (*tambala*). Chingwe's Hole is a cleft in the rock of Zomba Plateau where – in myth though not in fact – a Yao chief is supposed to have thrown his prisoners to their deaths. This served as a metaphor for imprisonment or detention, or more generally for Malawi under Banda: "Chingwe's Hole, how dare I praise you knowing whose Marrow still flows in murky Namitembo River below you?"(from Jack Mapanje's *Of Chameleons and Gods*). Mapanje, for one, was always amused by the idea that the Malawi Censorship Board might actually have improved his poetry.

There is a long history in Malawi of the use of ambiguity or metaphor as a means of communicating critical or potentially offensive messages. For example, women's pounding songs among the Ngoni communicate explicit messages about sex, in a way which can be generally understood, but without using *zotukwana* or obscenities. Among the Ngoni this is known as *kukulawika*. For the Tonga the same phenomenon is known as *chambula njiwi ching'ongo*. The meaning and purpose of such techniques is to communicate criticism in a veiled manner. This allowed the problem to be resolved without loss of face. Similar techniques were used in the anticolonial struggle – not to save face but to communicate politically subversive messages without the colonial authorities getting wind. Thus broadcasters at the Central African Broadcasting Corporation in Lusaka used "seemingly harmless folk-songs as instruments of nationalism" (Kerr 1993).

The approach of the Writers' Group belonged firmly in this tradition. It could also trace its roots back to the praise song.

Such an approach was theorized most coherently by Mapanje, who advocated a return to "traditional literature and modes of thought as the source of metaphor and inspiration." Mapanje argued that traditionally the praise poet had a licence to criticize the chief, whereas the new songs in praise of Banda had become "watered down propaganda to praise the new leaders with very little poetic insight" (Vail and White 1991).

The first post-independence generation of Malawian writers had already fallen foul of the new order. Legson Kayira, the country's leading novelist, went into exile after having several books banned in Malawi. His book *The Civil Servant*, published in the early 1970s, contained a thinly disguised satire on Malawian politics. The prominent poet, novelist, and playwright David Rubadiri served as ambassador to Washington and then the United Nations in the 1960s, but afterwards went into exile.

Although the Writers' Group did succeed in creating some critical space, the next generation of writers was equally under threat. In 1975 a Writers' Group member, Felix Mnthali, was arrested on the very day that he was to have been promoted to a professorship at the university. He was detained for a year at Zomba Central Prison. When he was arrested, police Special Branch officers searched his house and seized some of his collection of classical music on gramophone records. They appeared to single out those works by Russian composers or featuring Soviet musicians. After his release Mnthali was eventually re-employed at Chancellor College, but left the country in 1982. Like David Rubadiri before him, he left to teach in Botswana. Another prominent Writers' Group member, Frank Chipasula, also went into exile in 1973, followed in the early 1980s by Lupenga Mphande. Chipasula left only days before sitting his final exams and slipped across the Tanzanian border disguised as a peasant. However, he could not resist taking his typewriter with him, hidden in an old sack. On 25 September 1987, Jack Mapanje himself was finally detained. His imprisonment for more than three and a half years drew international attention to censorship and broader human rights violations in Malawi and probably thus helped bring about the end of single-party rule.

In May 1994, the Banda era finally drew to a close with multi-party elections and a new democratic constitution which provided a clear protection of freedom of expression for the first time. Yet many of the restrictive old laws remain in force, and there is still a Censorship Board. The new government decided not to lift the ban on all publications that had been listed by the board under Banda, so, in principle, Malawians are still highly restricted in their reading and viewing. Recent years have seen a gamut of attempted censorship, familiar elsewhere, based on alleged defamation of public officials, and especially of president Bakili Muluzi.

RICHARD CARVER

Further Reading

Carver, Richard, *Where Silence Rules: The Suppression of Dissent in Malawi*, New York: Human Rights Watch, 1990

Carver, Richard, *Malawi under Banda: A Lost History*, forthcoming

Gibbs, James, "Of Kamuzu and Chameleons", *Literary Half-Yearly*, 23/2 (1982)

Gibbs, James, "Singing in the Dark Rain", *Index on Censorship*, 8 (1988)

Kerr, David, "Ideology, Resistance and the Transformation of Performance Traditions in Post-Colonial Malawi" (dissertation), Gaborone: University of Botswana, 1993

Malawi: Communications Reform and Freedom of Expression, London: Article 19, 1998

Mapanje, Jack, "Censoring the African Poem", *Index on Censorship*, 18/8 (September 1989)

Vail, Leroy, and Landeg White, *Power and the Praise Poem: Southern African Voices in History*, London: Currey, 1991

MALAWI: Theatre

During the long and repressive regime of Hastings Kamuzu Banda, particularly in the 1970s, Malawian theatre suffered from repeated intervention by the state. Under the terms of the Censorship and Control of Entertainments Act (1968), the Censorship Board would vet each text being considered for performance, licence every venue at which a performance was planned, and issue permits for every individual performance. The permits had to be obtained by the person responsible for the venue from the regional representative of the Censorship Board. During the 1970s that post was filled by Tobias Banda, a Roman Catholic priest with a doctorate in canon law.

The elaborate procedure inevitably impeded the development of Malawian theatre. For example, it tended to confine drama to schools, community centres, and colleges; to institutions run by well-connected individuals who were in a good position to apply for licences and permits. The system was run with ruthless efficiency by civil servants, who in turn were closely monitored by the president's office. However, grey areas existed. As far as the University of Malawi was concerned, there was the feeling that there were advantages in allowing some doubt, some lack of definition. For instance, it was not clear at what point an improvisation became a performance. Was work prepared in a practical drama class liable to vetting by the board?

In practice the leeway allowed varied, and it became clear that the board's response was partly affected by reports received. Any complaint caused alarm at the board and led to very strict imposition of the rules. Thus, in the wake of the *Odi* affair, productions of plays mentioned in that publication that had been staged up to nine years earlier were checked against the records of permits issued. Such a response was indicative of the anxieties and uncertainties of board officials, fearful of incurring the displeasure of those on high. As soon as the prospect of exposure loomed the over-zealous enforcement of rules ensued.

The issuing of licences and permits was a fairly mechanical operation. That of reading scripts and deciding whether or not to allow performances was far more complex. The act under which the Board operated provided some guidance by listing grounds for complaint. Works "likely to give offence to the religious convictions or feelings of any section of the public, bring anyone into contempt, harm relations between sections of the public or be contrary to the interests of public safety or public order" were singled out in the act.

The kinds of changes required provide the clearest insight into the thinking of the board and its readers. Generally, it seems decisions were motivated by a sense of the power of the theatre to influence lives, and by acute sensitivity on matters of sex, religion, and politics. There was an attempt to eliminate any discussion of sex or of criminal behaviour, to exclude polit-ical comment, and to remove any reference to Banda other than those which portrayed the Life President in entirely positive terms. Mixed up with this political expediency and puritanism was an idealized view of Africa, one in which, for example, all old men were wise, all women modest, and all young people respectful. Objections often focused on language, on particular words, such as "anus" and "buttocks", that had to be removed. Meanwhile, Banda's firmly-held opinions as to what constituted "correct Chichewa" discouraged playwrights from writing in local languages, and many of the battles were fought over English words.

Evidence of the workings of the board indicates confused thinking and arbitrary decision-making. Tobias Banda confessed to passing everything by the Greeks and Elizabethans without reading them. It was against this background that *Antigone* was approved – though Wole Soyinka's *Kongi's Harvest* was rejected on political grounds. Meanwhile, *Julius Caesar* was acceptable even though Wisdom Kamkondo's *Vacant Seat* had been rejected because it included a scene of "cold-blooded murder". Texts by African writers were read carefully and with a certain irritation. According to Tobias Banda, Wole Soyinka – a substantial portion of whose work was banned – was "a bad man who had been chased out of his own country".

It should be noted that the reasons given for rejecting material were not always those that actually motivated the board to take action. Nikolai Gogol's *The Government Inspector* was supposedly rejected because it contained the line "All Frenchmen are thieves". This was deemed insulting to nationals of a friendly state. However, the reasoning was so far-fetched that Professor James Stewart of the University's English Department confronted Tobias Banda. After pointing out that the play had been performed "hundreds of times" in France without provoking protest, he added, tactlessly, that the board chairman's interpretation of the text would not have been accepted from a first year student at Chancellor College (University of Malawi). It is likely that the "thieving Frenchman" angle was only a pretext. *The Government Inspector* provided many insights into the political situation in Malawi at that time.

Examples of the arbitrary treatment of diverse texts are numerous. Brecht's *The Good Woman of Setzuan* was rejected, apparently because the eponymous heroine is a prostitute. Meanwhile the same playwright's *Caucasian Chalk Circle*, with its dangerous message that everything should "belong to the person who is good for it", was approved. Soyinka's *The Jero Plays* were rejected for ridiculing "some religious denominations"; while his *The Lion and the Jewel* was deemed to make "a mockery of our African customs, eg, open breasts, carrying things on the head, bride-price, etc. ... calling them savage, barbaric etc. [and] . . . is sexually objectionable". The Tanzanian play *Kinjikitile*, about an uprising in the colonial period, was passed subject to the removal or replacement of the rape scene near the beginning and of the "loose talk of the women on page 11". Athol Fugard's play *Sizwe Bansi Is Dead* was simply "Not approved". Steve Chimombo's drama about the Maravi rainmaking cult, *The Rain-Maker*, was "approved provided that two lines are altered: 'They flaunt their nakedness' and 'Two buttocks cannot avoid rubbing against one another'." *The Wonderful Doctor*, based on Molière's *The Doctor in Spite of Himself*, was "Approved provided 'slut' and 'stupid priest' are replaced."

Among the reasons given for rejecting a collection of sketches this writer had compiled under the title *Ethiopian Opera* were the following:

> Play 1 and 2, where a woman is depicted defrauding a nut-seller and deceiving her husband. There are already such practices and I do not see why new ones should be added to the detriment of the country.

Old Man, *Young Wife*:   I do not see why the European way of life should be encouraged on our African youth and young girls marry old men for their money. The practise on the contrary should be discouraged.

Thangata: Africans being oppressed by Europeans.

The Preacher: Abandonment of European and Christian influence and return to the old African tradition. Here it should be remembered that the days of colonialism are over and past, and the past oppression should be forgotten for the unity and stability of our country.

The examples given above come from between 1972 and 1978. After 1978 there was something of a "thaw". For example, Catherine Chimwenje was appointed as chair of the board, while Tobias Banda returned to parish work. Some plays were "unbanned", and influential productions of *Waiting for Godot* and *Sizwe Bansi is Dead* were staged. In addition to the "unbannings", drama for development teams led by Chris Kamlongera – who had links with the Malawi Congress Party – took theatre into the rural areas, where it was used, even though licences and permits had not been obtained, to challenge communities to address issues affecting them. Under this more relaxed dispensation there were two other shifts: the more widespread use of African languages for plays, and the emergence of an increasing number of urban-based drama groups.

JAMES GIBBS

Further Reading

Horn, Andrew, "African Theatre: Docility and Dissent", *Index on Censorship*, 9/3 (June 1980)

MALAYSIA

(comprising Malaya, Sabah, and Sarawak)

Population: 22,218,000
Main religions: Muslim; Buddhist; Confucianist; Hindu; Christian
Official language: Bahasa Malaysia
Other languages spoken: English; Chinese; Tamil; Iban
Illiteracy rate (%): 8.6 (m); 16.5 (f)

Number of daily newspapers: 42
Number of periodicals: 44
Number of radio receivers per 1000 inhabitants: 434
Number of TV receivers per 1000 inhabitants: 172
Number of PCs per 1000 inhabitants: 58.6

Modern cultural and media institutions in Malaysia originated during British colonial rule, along with censorial and other restrictive methods, a circumstance Malaysian politicians emphasize when criticized for contemporary constraints on freedom of expression. The first newspaper, *The Government Gazette* of Penang, started in 1806 under "certain conditions" laid down by the East India Company, which granted its publishing permit. There was to be "no gossip, no criticism of government, individuals or policies". Proof sheets were to be submitted before publication.

For the next century and a half, Malaya remained colonized (and briefly during World War II, occupied by the Japanese), one result being that there was no widespread consciousness of democratic values, a national film unit, a radio network, and newspapers in Malay, English, Chinese, Tamil, and Punjabi notwithstanding. When independence came in 1957, a state of

emergency was still in effect (until 1960) because of the threat from communist insurgents. The constitution referred to freedom of speech but did not mention the press. Restrictive laws enacted by the British at the onset of emergency in 1948 remained in force, including the Printing Presses Act, requiring annual licences to operate presses and publish periodicals, and the Sedition Ordinance, specifying, among other things, that publications must not bring into hatred or contempt or excite disaffection against any ruler, government, or state. Other laws limiting the freedom of Malaysians to read and view what they wished came in swift order: the Undesirable Publications (Prohibition of Importation) Act (1951), the Cinematograph Film Ordinance (1952), the Defamation Ordinance (1957), the Public Order (Preservation) Ordinance (1958), the Control of Imported Publications Ordinance (1958), and the Internal Security Act (ISA) (1960). The ISA, which makes special provisions relating to "subversive" publications, is considered especially alarming, since it allows for the preventive detention of suspects without formal charges and gives them no opportunity to challenge the grounds for their detention. Harry E. Grove has commented that the Malaysian parliament's power to restrict freedom by ordinary legislation is almost without limit.

Other legislation in the 1960s included the Essential Control of Publications and Safeguarding of Information Regulation (1966) and the Societies Act (1966), the latter providing for the legal existence of organizations. For the most part, however, during the first 12 years of independence there was a high level of freedom, with media and the intelligentsia openly criticizing the government and its policies.

This came to an abrupt halt on 13 May 1969 when race riots erupted, resulting in hundreds of deaths. The ruling party, the United Malays National Organisation (UMNO), which had suffered major losses in the general elections a few days earlier, suspended democracy (eventually for 21 months), a policy that successfully arrested the momentum built up by the opposition. In the aftermath of the riots, the government instituted new policies, altered laws, and restructured society – and mass media – to force all Malaysians to assist in implementing UMNO goals. The Printing Presses Act was amended in 1971, adding further conditions for the issue of licences, and stipulating that incidents involving public order must not be reported in a distorted, prejudicial, or inflammatory manner. In 1974, a further amendment granted the right to deny a licence to publications not owned by Malaysians. The Sedition Ordinance was toughened in 1971, prohibiting all discussion of four sensitive issues: national language policy, the special rights granted to the Malay ethnic group, the special roles of sultans and other royalty, and the discriminatory citizenship policy.

Other post-1969 government pronouncements had chilling effects upon culture and media. Malaysians were expected to follow without question the tenets of the Second Malaysia Plan, which was highly favourable to the Malays, and the vaguely stated *Rukunegara* (National Ideology). Throughout the 1970s, the many repressive laws facilitated the suspension of newspapers, all with no reason given, the revocation of publishing licences, the imposition of fines and imprisonment on journalists and intellectuals, and censorship of materials of all types. Foreign periodicals, including *Time, Far Eastern Economic Review*, and *Playboy*, films, and broadcasts were (and still are) banned, mutilated, or censored. Ministers regularly went to the podium or used the telephone to "guide" those in charge of cultural, educational, and media institutions on their proper role in a pluralistic, developing country such as Malaysia. The government took the view that in Malaysia, a young country, the media's main role was to support national economic policy and national ideology (*Rukunegara*: united nation, democratic society, just society, liberal society, progressive society; all bestowed by belief in God, loyalty to king and country, upholding the constitution, rule of law and good behaviour and morality).

To force its points home, or to tide itself over rough times, the government has occasionally staged purges where groups of individuals are rounded up under the ISA, held for periods ranging from 60 days to several years without legal recourse,

charged with subversion or other serious crimes, and then released after they recant in television "confessions" or otherwise show they are rehabilitated. Two examples will suffice. In 1976, the award-winning writer and managing editor of the *New Straits Times*, A. Samad Ismail, was detained for more than four-and-a-half years under the ISA, charged with being a long-time communist subversive. He was never brought to trial despite two televised "confessions" in 1976 and 1981. On 27 October 1987, the Mahathir Mohamad government arrested and held without trial 119 political opponents – social and church activists, and dissidents – and the following day, revoked the licences of three prominent newspapers. Gradually, the detainees were released, and in March 1988, the newspapers' licences were returned, but the impact was devastating, as journalists lacked the confidence in their freedom to publish, reporting was influenced by the demands of secret policemen or politicians, and the small group willing to venture an opinion different from the authorities became even smaller.

When Mahathir became prime minister in 1981, he envisaged that Malaysia would join the ranks of Asia's newly industrialized economies. Mahathir and his deputy, Musa Mitam, in both official and informal statements, suggested ways this could be achieved – "Look East" and emulate Japanese work habits, attract investment and trade from the United States and other large countries, and encourage privatization and the development of an information society. At times, accomplishing these goals meant trampling on the right to freedom of expression.

Mahathir spoke out regularly about his expectations of mass media. What the pronouncements boiled down to was that he required media and cultural forms to be even more supportive of government policy than the already sycophantic purveyors of information had been since 1969. In a 1985 speech, the prime minister said that so long as the press "conscientiously limits the exercises of its rights", it should be allowed to function without government interference, and that press freedom is really just the right of a few editors to express *their* "views and prejudices".

In other speeches, even into the mid-1990s, Mahathir and other ministers urged that more self-censorship was needed, and perhaps a clampdown, accusing some newly established dailies of raising sensitive issues to increase circulation; that the role of the press as a catalyst of development must take priority over ideals of democratic rights; and that the press should be seen as a supporter of governmental aims. Mahathir's view of the media was clearly stated from the beginning of his administration. In an unsolicited essay for the *New Straits Times* in 1981, Mahathir wrote that "journalists' righteousness is usually a gimmick they employ for the sake of their jobs – not for democracy", that press people have too much influence since they are not elected by anyone, that the practices of Western journalism were not suitable for Malaysia, that press freedom is a myth invented by "so-called liberal West," and that the foreign press monopolizes and distorts information about Malaysia.

To restructure mass media more to its liking, the Mahathir government moved to counteract what it perceived to be negative foreign reports, and increasingly controlled the domestic discourse by strengthening the government news agency, revamping media ownership, and further tightening press legislation.

To deal with the foreign press, which Mahathir saw as reporting only bad news about Malaysia and acting under the control of "Jews" to denigrate Islam, the government temporarily banned foreign periodicals from time to time, and discredited or sued foreign correspondents. In mid-1988, the Information Ministry sent a letter to all editors, suggesting in effect, that they smear particular foreign countries. Promoting a positive image of the country was obviously the goal when in 1990, the government offered news clips to American and European news organizations to give their viewers a "correct" picture of Malaysia. In 1984 and again in 1990, the state-controlled news agency, Bernama, became also the sole distributor of news from foreign news services.

After the passing of the 1974 Printing Press Amendment Act, which required majority local ownership in the mass media, newspapers scrambled to restructure their equity distribution, often seeking support from one of the components of the ruling coalition (Barisan) government – most frequently, UMNO or MCA (Malaysian Chinese Association). For many years, Star Publications has been tied to MCA, and New Straits Times Press and Utusan Group, the largest media combines, to UMNO. Other Chinese- and Tamil-language dailies have been strongly associated with UMNO, MCA, or another major Barisan partner, the Malaysian Indian Congress (MIC). Media connections to the government and ruling political elite involve entanglements with a number of national and transnational corporations, which own sectors of the hotel, real estate, plantation, gambling, trading, finance, shipping, and other businesses. *New Straits Times*, via its parent, was linked through ownership to about 150 corporations in telecommunications, public relations, magazines, computers, transport, resorts, hotels, insurance, development, and banking, among others.

With most mass media owned, controlled, or otherwise closely affiliated with the government, which issues constant exhortations about the proper role of the press, editors quickly complied. They practise strict in-house censorship that usually does not require government intervention; however, since they monitor themselves, they are fully aware of the abundance of press and other legislation at the government's disposal. Many press acts were added in the 1980s. The basic publishing law, the Printing Presses and Publications Act (PPPA), was amended in 1984 and 1987, and the Official Secrets Act and Broadcasting Act were strengthened in 1986 and 1987 respectively.

The 1984 amendment to the PPPA discouraged local and foreign publications from producing materials derogatory to Malaysian principles. Under the amendment, printers are liable for any news item they print that is distributed in Malaysia. The law further states that if a foreign publication is found prejudicial to public order, morality, security, the relationship with any foreign government or country, or public or national interest, the importation of that publication can be prohibited. Foreign publishers must pay a deposit before their periodicals can be distributed in Malaysia, and the deposit may be forfeited if publishers do not abide by government policy. By consolidating already existing legislation – PPPA, Control of Imported Publications Act, and Section 22 of the ISA – the act was seen as a violation of the constitution and a further step toward authoritarianism.

The Official Secrets Act was amended soon after, further intimidating journalists. New requirements stated that public officials must report immediately to the police if approached by anyone seeking classified information. Officials who fail to do this face possible five-year prison terms. "Secret" is defined as any information entrusted to an official in confidence by another official, or obtained by virtue of a position in the public service. Associating with a "foreign agent" makes an individual liable to prosecution, whether or not information is passed on. The maximum penalty is seven years' imprisonment and/or M$10,000 fine. The new act's catch-all phrasing made it particularly open to bureaucratic abuse.

The 1987 amendment to the PPPA gave the minister of home affairs absolute discretion to prohibit the publication or importation of any publication that is "likely to alarm public opinion" and provided stiff penalties for "maliciously publishing fake news". The minister's decisions in these matters are "final and shall not be called into question by any court on any ground whatsoever". The amendment also forces all newspapers to apply for a new licence annually (the licence was previously renewable). Another change in 1988 empowered the home minister to amend a paper's permit "at any time by notification in writing". This was invoked in 1991, when the government amended the licences of opposition party papers, changing their status from newspapers to "in-house" publications, thus restricting their circulation to members only.

The Broadcasting Act was strengthened to empower the information minister to monitor all radio and television programming to ensure their content was "consistent with government policy".

Throughout the 1990s, media and cultural institutions and individuals were harassed in various ways. *Aliran*, organ of the National Consciousness Movement, fought for seven years for permission to publish in the national language; three Chinese dailies received stern warnings in 1995 that their licences would be revoked if they did not stop publishing articles undermining the government's efforts to create a multiracial society; and in 1994, the editor of *Dewan Sastera* magazine was moved to another position at Mahathir's request after he had published a short story by Shahnon Ahmad that parodied the prime minister. In 1993, the poet Cecil Rajendra had his passport impounded as he prepared to give readings in London, the government response to his poems supporting anti-logging activities. In 1997, Ahmed Nazri Abdullah was asked to resign after criticizing the government economic policy in his newspaper *Berita Harian*.

Media laws have been further modified to limit freedom of expression. In 1997, the government reviewed the national broadcasting policy to give priorities to information and education rather than entertainment; two years earlier, the Film Censorship Board announced it would not countenance any appeal from television stations to be lenient when reviewing programmes depicting sex and violence. The censors outlaw depictions of most types of kissing (mouth-to-mouth, passionate, on suggestive parts of the body, and even as expression of sympathy, condolence, or affection) and embracing (between men and women that shows passion and lust, while someone is lying down or sleeping). It also looks askance at what it terms "Jewish propaganda"; *Schindler's List*, the American-made movie, was banned temporarily on those grounds, and in the early 1980s, a musical piece by the Jewish composer Ernest Bloch was found to be "unsuitable" when the visiting New York Philharmonic proposed to perform it. For a time, the government banned ownership of television receiver dishes to prevent Malaysians from tuning in to uncensored films emanating from regional satellite networks.

In the mid-1990s, the government adopted a more relaxed attitude (usually associated with times of political harmony and economic plenty in Malaysia), allowing the Instant Café Theatre to continue its satires of Mahathir, the government, and society; permitting broadcast talk shows to mention hitherto taboo topics, and allowing leading politicians to write newspaper columns calling for an investigative, critical press. Such instances are deceptive, however, since Malaysia serves as a model of a conditional democracy, where all aspects of society are hemmed in by a tradition of uncritical discourse and executive dominance. To oppose Mahathir continues to be dangerous, as the recent treatment of his former deputy, accused and convicted on the trumped-up charge of sodomy, shows.

JOHN A. LENT

Further Reading

Byrd, Cecil K., *Early Printing in the Straits Settlements, 1806–1858*, Singapore: Singapore National Library, 1970

Committee to Protect Journalists, *Press Abuse in Malaysia and Singapore*, New York: CPJ and Article 19, 1988

Glattbach, Jack, "Malaysia" in *Broadcasting in Asia and the Pacific: A Continental Survey of Radio and Television*, edited by John A. Lent, Philadelphia: Temple University Press, 1978

Groves, Harry E., *The Constitution of Malaysia*, Singapore: Malaysia Publications, 1964

Lent, John A., "Malaysia's Guided Media", *Index on Censorship* (Winter 1974): 65–75

Lent, John A., "True (?) Confessions: Television in Malaysia and Singapore", *Index on Censorship* (March–April 1978): 9–18

Lent, John A., "Malaysia" in *Newspapers in Asia: Contemporary Trends and Problems*, edited by John A. Lent, Hong Kong: Heinemann Asia, 1982

Lent, John A., "Restructuring of Mass Media in Malaysia and Singapore: Pounding in the Coffin Nails?", *Bulletin of Concerned Asian Scholars* (October–December 1984): 26–35

Lent, John A., "Human Rights and Freedom of Expression in Malaysia and the Philippines", *Asian Profile* (April 1989): 137–54

Lim Kit Siang, "Press Freedom in Malaysia" in *Malaysia: Crisis of Identity*, by Lim Kit Siang, Petaling Jaya: Democratic Action Party, 1986

Mahathir Mohamad, "Freedom of the Press: Fact and Fallacy", *New Straits Times* (9 July 1981)

Slimming, John, *Malaysia: Death of a Democracy*, London: John Murray, 1969

Sussman, Gerald and John A. Lent (editors), *Transnational Communications: Wiring the Third World*, Newbury Park, California: Sage, 1991

CHRÉTIEN-GUILLAUME LAMOIGNON DE MALESHERBES
French censor, 1721–1794

Few people were more intimately aware of the vagaries of censorship in 18th-century France than Chrétien-Guillaume Lamoignon de Malesherbes. From 1750 to 1763 he was Directeur de la Librairie, a post which gave him administrative charge of the nation's book trade. His practical experience in this role formed the basis of two detailed works on the need for censorship reform. His liberal views and reforming instincts make him a prominent Enlightenment figure, but his loyalty to the crown and his scrupulous sense of duty reveal a more conservative side.

The job of Directeur de la Librairie was an enormous and extremely delicate one. In this post, Malesherbes was obliged to adhere to a set of regulations which were outmoded, draconian, and frequently unenforceable. The 1723 *Code de la Librairie*, still in operation in the mid-18th century, had attempted to rationalize the laws governing book production, but it was flawed in several respects and abuses were legion. A move to amend the *Code* in 1757 resulted in the sweeping – not to say ridiculous – declaration that any book able to "émouvoir les esprits" (stir the emotions) should be punished with the death penalty. With some ingenuity, and doubtless benefiting from his training as a lawyer, Malesherbes succeeded in negotiating his way through the obstacles in his job as Directeur de la Librairie, fully aware of when the establishment could and would turn a blind eye. In general, his position was one

of cautious pragmatism: he strove to avoid confrontation and only intervened when it was wholly necessary.

The old system of preventive censorship which Malesherbes inherited, whereby all book-printing was illegal unless royal permission in the form of a *privilège* was granted, needed to be supplemented for practical reasons. Consequently Malesherbes made extensive and consistent use of the *permission tacite*, a form of unofficial permission whereby a book did not gain full royal approval but was not considered to require a total ban. Where necessary, Malesherbes also resorted to the *tolérance*, a mere verbal approval. It would be wrong to see Malesherbes as compromising his position through his recourse to these means; rather, he acted with a heightened sense of expediency in ensuring the smooth course of book production.

Malesherbes's sympathy with the more progressive thinkers of his day is revealed in his treatment of Diderot and d'Alembert's *Encyclopédie* (Encyclopedia). In a notorious incident following the banning of the first two volumes in 1752, Malesherbes prevented the authorities from seizing the manuscripts by hiding the drafts in his own home. Although he was responsible for the revocation of the work's *privilège* in 1758, he was aware that this step would assist the enterprise in the long run, preventing a total ban and allowing the work's publication in secret. Malesherbes also facilitated the publication of many of Rousseau's works and did his best to protect

Helvétius from the storm of controversy surrounding *De l'Esprit* (Essays on the Mind) in 1758.

In 1758 Malesherbes began writing his *Mémoires sur la librairie* (Memoranda on the Book Trade), a thorough analysis of the inadequacies of the system of censorship in his day together with proposals for reform. Although he did not deny outright the principle of censorship in these memoranda, Malesherbes argued forcefully for a relaxation of the rules, believing that greater tolerance of minor abuses would focus attention more effectively on large-scale wrong-doing. He also emphasized the role of the public in distinguishing right from wrong. He judged censorship to be necessary only for works on religion, morals, and sovereign authority. Among the practical improvements proposed by Malesherbes were a more precise definition of the censor's job, a fairer system of punishment, and more effective policing through the restriction of presses to big cities. He also advocated greater rights for authors over their works, but argued that they should at the same time show responsibility by practising self-censorship. Finally, Malesherbes argued for official endorsement of the *permission tacite*.

Most of these reforms were not put into place, for in 1763, when his father fell from grace, Malesherbes resigned as Directeur de la Librairie. In 1788 he retired fully from public life and wrote his *Mémoires sur la liberté de la presse* (Memoranda on the Freedom of the Press). This work discussed the advantages and disadvantages of freedom of the press in general terms but also in the context of the forthcoming meeting of the States General. Here, as before, Malesherbes was reluctant to do away with all forms of censorship; yet he was aware that at this important moment in history the French nation required a national assembly with press freedom. He argued that French censorship law had to be changed since it was patently unworkable, and in particular that France should do away with the requirement that every book be submitted to the censor before publication. However, he considered that a system where there was no preventive censorship, such as that

in operation in England, would be unsuitable for France because of the peculiarities of its judicial system; in France, the spirit rather than the letter of the law was applied and therefore legal power was much more arbitrary and volatile. Malesherbes's proposed solution was a compromise: authors should have the freedom to decide whether to submit their works voluntarily to the censor or whether to suffer possible legal consequences after publication.

Some evidence suggests that Malesherbes was not as liberal as it would seem in the fulfilment of his duties. More authors and publishers were imprisoned in the Bastille under his directorship than under previous holders of the post. But although Malesherbes was not himself responsible for far-reaching reform, his skilful pragmatism as Directeur de la Librairie and his perceptive, broad-minded reflections on the book trade undoubtedly paved the way for the abolition of censorship in 1791. During the Revolution, Malesherbes remained faithful to his monarchist principles, defending Louis XVI at his trial and subsequently being arrested and tried himself by the revolutionary tribunal. He was guillotined in 1794. His views on censorship were rapidly overtaken by those of more radical thinkers such as Mirabeau and Chénier.

MELISSA PERCIVAL

Writings
Malesherbes: Mémoires sur la librairie et sur la liberté de la presse, edited by Graham E. Rodmell, 1979

Further Reading
Birn, Raymond, "Malesherbes and the Call for a Free Press" in *Revolution in Print: The Press in France, 1775–1800*, edited by Robert Darnton and Daniel Roche, Berkeley: University of California Press, 1989
Grosclaude, Pierre, *Malesherbes: témoin et interprète de son temps*, Paris: Fischbacher, 1961
Pottinger, David T., *The French Book Trade in the ancien régime, 1500–1791*, Cambridge, Massachusetts: Harvard University Press, 1958

MALI

(formerly French Sudan)

Population: 11,351,000	**Illiteracy rate (%):** 51.1 (m); 65.6 (f)
Main religions: Muslim; Animist; Christian	**Number of daily newspapers:** 3
Official language: French	**Number of radio receivers per 1000 inhabitants:** 55
Other languages spoken: Bambara; other indigenous languages	**Number of TV receivers per 1000 inhabitants:** 4.3
	Number of PCs per 1000 inhabitants: 0.7

Mali is located in central West Africa, a region that has benefited from a rich and varied trade in both goods and ideas for centuries; however, geography has also been a factor in the many wars of conquest that have impeded such trade. Perhaps this helps to explain Mali's paradox – both cultural beacon and model of despotism, Mali has a highly uneven history when it comes to freedom of expression. Various states in the area have alternately promoted freedom, then suppressed all dissent. This

is also true across time. That celebrated centre of learning in medieval West Africa, Timbuktu, became a beacon, while the postcolonial city of Bamako became a centre for the brutal repression of dissent under Moussa Traoré's dictatorship (1968–91).

Of course, notions of censorship and freedom of expression change over time and space. Medieval Timbuktu did not share the Enlightenment values that inform many contemporary definitions and condemnations of censorship, but the fact that scholarly debate took place there shows a certain respect for what is prized today. At the same time, the social hierarchies typical of the region probably restricted freedom of expression according to social rank. Caste, slavery, and economic class probably limited the right to express one's views publicly.

The current borders of Mali enclose areas once part of the medieval empires of the western Sudan – Ghana, Mali, Songhay, Kingi, Bure, Kaarta, Maasina, Segou, and Jenne, among others. We know that states of this type controlled speech and behaviour to some extent. Religion was a matter of state, given the institution of divine kingship. In addition, the caste structure made public speaking primarily a matter for *griots*, or bards, who were the "masters of the word". The king did not speak directly to the people; rather, he spoke through his *griot*. Bards did exercise some freedom of speech, however, for they were free to satirize, as well as to praise, important figures in society.

Some scholars have portrayed the political system of the Mali empire as being flexible and tolerant, with imperial subjects enjoying certain forms of freedom of speech. Ideas and goods from North Africa, the southern savannah, and the forest regions of the areas now known as Ivory Coast and Ghana (not to be confused with ancient Ghana, which lay between today's Mali and Mauritania) were exchanged in the many trading posts located in Malian territory. Islam first came to the region through trade. Under Mansa Musa in the 14th century, Islam became a state religion, although religious tolerance appears to have continued to be practised in Mali. By the 15th century, the University of Timbuktu had a reputed 25,000 students and a renowned collection of Arabic manuscripts, and was home to many scholars and their libraries. It was reported that "books sell very well here".

In spite of this tradition, the right to religious freedom has been an issue in the history of civil rights in the region. In the 15th century, Mohamed Torodo gained control of the Songhaï empire (a successor to the empire of Mali). He used his authority to order forced conversions to Islam and to persecute the tiny Jewish minority. Much later, religious wars continued to threaten ordinary people's lives. The Pulaar jihads of the 19th century, while partly motivated by the desire for gain, arose from the desire to spread a "pure" Islam in regions their leaders considered partly pagan. These crusades threatened all prior social structures and clearly led to further restrictions on freedom of speech. When Sheku Amadou took Jenne in 1825, for instance, he established a puritanical social order that banned even dance and song. However, leaders did not have total control over their followers. For example, dissension among his troops influenced the policies of the 19th-century Muslim warlord Cheikh Umar.

The French conquest of West Africa in the 19th century transformed the region. French Sudan, with Mali at its centre, was created in the 1890s. Forced labour, harsh taxation, and other forms of repression led to several popular revolts even after the early "pacification" of the Sudan. In 1916, for instance, several rebellions took place in protest against forced labour and the conscription of young men for the battlefields of World War I. The Bambara of Beledougou, the Bobo of San, the Minianka of Koutiala, and nomads in the Timbuktu region all revolted at this time, but each of these protest movements was ended by French military action. One colonial administrator who served in the French Sudan from 1930 to 1940 asserted that blind repression of dissidence in the colony, in addition to forced conscription, had decimated local leaders.

Although open protest was unsuccessful, criticism of French rule continued in popular theatre and performance genres. Notably the Sogobò masquerade theatre provided a public space for commentary on power relations, as it had in the pre-colonial era. Its popularity among several ethnic groups, including the Bozo, the Bambara, the Somono, the Maraka, and the Malinke, attests to the vitality of this tradition of political commentary in Mali. It is a multimedia form of entertainment, many different art forms being used to criticize and ridicule the authorities. Sogobò and similar forms of art still permit people in Mali to express themselves in the public sphere with relative freedom. Other forms of popular theatre, poetry, and song are highly topical and allude to power relations as well.

During French rule, the contradictory nature of the story of freedom of expression in Mali was heightened. Alongside their rigid restrictions the French attempted to spread literacy through assimilationist education. Ironically, the very "civilizing mission" of the French thus made it possible for anti-colonialist associations, newspapers, political tracts, and literary production to have a national and regional influence that they would not otherwise have had. Of course, the colonial administration attempted to control these developments, and newspapers and associations had to register with the French authorities in order to publish. In spite of administrative obstacles, though, the Malian press flourished in the 1940s and 1950s. Magazines such as *Le Mali* and other ephemeral publications were created at this time. Modibo Kéïta and Jean-Marie Koné founded one such newspaper called *L'Oeil du Kénédougou*, which was highly critical of the colonial government. They soon learned, however, that they were not free to voice their criticisms of the administration as they chose, even when sending private messages. Kéïta, later to become the first president of Mali, was arrested in 1947 and sent to prison for six months for sending telegrams in which he denounced the "slave system" of the French administrator of Sikasso.

In addition to the African press, Malians had access to the official press. *L'Essor*, still the official newspaper today, began publishing in 1949. Other publications included official colonial newspapers such as *Soudan français* and the *Bullétin de l'A.O.F.* Radio programming was exclusively in French, and aimed primarily at French residents. Tight regulation of film production at the time under the Laval decrees effectively censored both French and African filmmakers.

After World War II colonial controls were loosened as African subjects gradually gained political representation and the right to a public voice. Thanks to the creation of the French Union (1946) and the ratification of the *loi cadre* (1956) anti-colonialist leaders such as Modibo Kéïta were able to create political parties. Eventually Kéïta went on to become the first leader of the new state of Mali after formal independence in 1960.

Modibo Kéïta's era introduced a new form of censorship to Mali: after independence censors took on the task of controlling thought. According to Sanankoua, early independent Mali was dominated by party slogans, suspicion, and lies. As in other one-party states of the time, citizens were expected to participate in mass rallies in praise of Modibo Kéïta and the socialist state. Cheikh Oumar Diarrah has compared Modibo Kéïta's Mali to Maoist China; ideological dissenters were purged without hesitation. In 1961, when respected leaders of the colonial period, such as Fily Dabo Sissoko and Hammadoun Dicko, joined protests against the government's decision to leave the French monetary union and create a new Malian currency, they were imprisoned along with 89 other demonstrators and accused of treason. Sissoko and Dicko were condemned to death, then pardoned and sentenced to forced labour for life. Both died in 1964 while serving this sentence.

According to Sanakoua, "No one dare say anything at all, for fear of being convicted of treason or suspected of slowing the forward march" of the regime. Although many party members reacted to the situation with a mixture of self-censorship and extravagant avowals of loyalty, Kéïta foreclosed any possibility of public debate by cancelling all party congresses after 1962. In 1967 he dissolved the party's political bureau and replaced it with the Comité National de Défense de la Révolution (National Committee for the Defence of the Revolution, CNDR). He also created a popular militia that intimidated and terrorized citizens. On the other hand, Yombo Ouologuem's controversial novel *Bound to Violence* (1971), though it contained much that was violent and sexually explicit, and stirred up some controversy in Muslim circles, was not censored. In a country with a low literacy rate, it was presumably considered that such a novel would make few waves.

The Kéïta regime grew progressively more dictatorial as its economic policies failed. The National Assembly was dissolved in 1968, after which Modibo Kéïta 'governed by ordinance'. Since the regime's central planning failed to alleviate the economic malaise and essentially taxed rural peasants to subsidise the urban population (a process that continues today), failed economic policies became the subject of rural dissent at this time. The peasants of Ouolossébougou revolted against the fixed prices of the government boards in June 1968: 15 peasants and merchants were arrested. A day later, when many of their fellow villagers attempted to liberate the prisoners, the police shot and killed two people and injured several others. Although people basically seem to have supported Kéïta's ideological goals, they did not accept his failed economic policies. In November 1968 Kéïta's government fell to a military junta; he was sentenced to forced labour in the desert camp of Kidal, where he died in 1977. Ironically, under the new regime, hundreds of people were arrested simply for attending his funeral.

Moussa Traoré, the new president, quickly intensified the state's repressive control of the population. First the constitution was suspended, then in 1969 the Union Nationale des Travailleurs Maliens (National Union of Malian Labourers) was dissolved. The police quelled student-organised strikes in 1969, 1971, and 1977, and in 1970 seven intellectuals were condemned to 18 months in prison for offending president Traoré. The following year a teachers' strike was targeted, and teachers were arrested and intimidated. In 1974 12 people were condemned to prison and sent to the desert concentration camp of Taoudénit for writing and distributing a tract criticizing the conduct of the elections held that year. Similarly, the leaders of

a group called the Malian Patriots were sentenced to two to four years in prison in 1975 after distributing a tract that criticized the 1974 constitutional referendum.

According to several sources, the state remained relatively disorganized. Individual members of the junta, and of the police and military, often acted arbitrarily and independently, brutalizing dissenters who had insulted them by criticizing the regime with which they were identified. Tiékoro Bagayoko, chief of police, is still remembered as one particularly notorious individual from this period. In the context of this arbitrary and uncontrolled repression, self-censorship quickly became common.

The media, at this time, served primarily as a vehicle for propaganda. In 1974, Radio Mali's various programmes all had "one thing in common: the furtherance of party policy", reports Wilcox. The same could be said of the official newspapers of the time (*L'Essor* and *L'Essor Hebdomadaire*, *L'Informateur*, *Le Journal Officiel de la République du Mali*, and *Kibaru*). The Imprimérie Nationale and Les Éditions Populaires were the only publishers available until Alpha Oumar Konaré, the current president, organized the cultural cooperative *Jamana* in 1983. Meanwhile, outside sources of information were censored in Traoré's Mali as well; foreign periodicals and films were censored or banned, and cinemas were arbitrarily closed.

The many trials for attempted coups d'état during this period even limited freedom of expression within the inner circles of the junta. By 1978, however, Traoré seems to have gained more power and more confidence. A new constitution was put into place. This formal change did not end repression, which indeed increased in severity. In 1979, Mamadou Gologo and Idrissa Diakité, political figures from the days of the Union Soudanaise–Rassemblement Démocratique Africain (US-RDA), were condemned to four years in prison for organizing a political association and offending the head of state. In 1980 12 teachers were arrested for organizing an unauthorized meeting, planning a strike, and opposing "legitimate authority". From July 1980 to January 1981 other teachers were arrested for various reasons. Later in the decade, in 1989, a peaceful political demonstration led to the arrest of at least 10 people, some of whom were sentenced to death.

Touré Kéïta, a Malian writer in exile, wrote in 1986: "the least allusion [by a journalist] to a corrupt affair which may be common knowledge to the man in the street; the reporting of the most timidly dissenting opinion; a photo inadvertently published in the wrong size or in the wrong column; a speech summarised or reproduced in faint type – any of these will bring down sanctions on the journalist's head". The "common knowledge" which Kéïta refers to became known as *Radio Trottoir* (the rumour machine – a phenomenon not confined to Mali). However, people were far more ready to believe rumours than the official channels of communication.

Students represented the most tenacious opposition to the regime. The consequences of the student strikes of 1979–80 deserve special attention, for they led to a backlash against a regime that habitually used terror and torture to control the population. Several students were arrested, but the death of their leader, Abdoul Karim Camara, touched off protests among normally reticent middle-class adults. Even though adults had not supported the students' strike, this death touched a nerve. In response, the government closed the secondary schools and the École Normale of Bamako, which did not re-open for another two years. In 1980 when teachers organized a gathering in memory of Camara, 32 of them were sentenced to internal exile in the desert regions of Gao and Timbuktu.

In spite of government repression, student protest continued in the 1980s. Six people, mostly students, were detained in January 1986 because they had received letters from political exiles. In 1989, students of the École Nationale d'Administration (National School of Administration) went on strike; the same year, eight students were arraigned for belonging to the banned Association des Scolaires et Universitaires Maliens (Association of Malian Students and Academics). In spite of the students' opposition to the regime, self-censorship remained a survival strategy for adults, especially after the party established ideological classes, civic education, and "cellules de surveillance" (surveillance groups) in the workplace in the 1980s. Nevertheless, the cultural organization Jamana published a cultural review of the same name, and created two more publications in 1987 (*Grin-grin* and *Jekabaara*). In addition, Jamana reached those unable to read by providing an audio newspaper on cassette (*Sorofe*). Moreover, the group dared to create an independent newspaper, *Les Echos*, in 1989. This newspaper was a clear sign of the growing movement that would eventually lead to democratization and the end of the Traoré regime in 1991. According to Clark, "groups such as Jamana provided Malians with subtle yet meaningful avenues of political criticism and debate".

Jamana's importance became clearer in the 1990s, when it merged into a coalition that actively lobbied for democratization. However, both international pressure and popular revolt were required in order to make the regime yield concessions in this area. The summit of African leaders at La Baule in 1990 certainly influenced Mali, just as it did other francophone states, for president François Mitterrand clarified France's new policy which tied financial aid to democracy. Traoré could conceivably have given way to this pressure without changing the regime very much, had it not been for the demonstrations and riots that broke out in Bamako in March 1991. The state's first response was to use armed forces, who killed an unspecified number of demonstrators. Many others were arrested. Violent insurrections in other cities were repressed just as violently. Traoré then declared a state of emergency, closed borders, and imposed a dusk to dawn curfew. In spite of the state of emergency, thousands of women protesting the killings tried to march on president Traoré's residence. Approximately 65 protestors who sought refuge in a shopping centre were burned to death when security forces set it on fire.

These events stiffened the resolve of the opposition to Traoré. Alpha Oumar Konaré and other opposition leaders met in Bamako and formed the Committee for the Coordination of Opposition (also known as Adema). The group called for Traoré's resignation and supported the nationwide strike led by the National Workers' Union. Although the regime freed about 30 prisoners of conscience, this did not appease Malians, and new riots broke out in Bamako. These protests, too, were crushed by the armed forces. The crisis was revolved on 26 March 1991, when the army, led by lieutenant colonel Amadou

Toumani Touré (often called A.T.T.), arrested Traoré and established a military National Reconciliation Council. ADEMA's resistance to military rule led Touré to compromise and create a coalition with civilian leaders. An effective national conference then opened the way for democracy. The 1992 elections were clearly free and fair. Since this time, Mali has shone as a beacon for other francophone states involved in the delicate process of democratization.

Nevertheless, freedom of expression remains a vexing question in post-Traoré Mali, for the line between freedom of expression and misuse of that right is often hard to draw. For example, student dissenters sacked and burned government buildings in Bamako in 1996, when the government refused to give in to their demands for increases in scholarship funds. More recently, the arrest of opposition leaders whose followers beat and killed a police officer assigned to maintain order at their meeting has led to renewed protest. In such cases, it is difficult to determine whether the government has overreached itself or whether it is simply fulfilling its role of maintaining public order.

According to the perhaps rather optimistic United States Bureau of Democracy, Human Rights and Labor report of January 30 1998, the Malian government in 1997 "generally respected constitutional provisions for freedom of speech, press, assembly, association, and religion". Approximately 40 private newspapers are available in French, Arabic, and national languages. Two of the five dailies are government-controlled. The government also controls one television station and many radio stations, but these stations do present views critical of the government. 15 independent radio stations now exist in the capital, and there are forty more private radio stations in the country.

Although the current constitution protects freedom of expression, however, laws instituted in 1993 regulate the press and allow for penalties, including imprisonment, for slander and public injury of the head of state and other officials. Since the laws are ill-defined, cases actually depend upon judicial discretion. In practice, they have restricted freedom of speech. For example, several journalists have been detained and interrogated, as was Mamadou Dabo of the daily *Nouvel Horizon* after the publication of an article critical of the president in 1995. In 1997, such intimidation occurred repeatedly: in August, 15 journalists attending an opposition press conference were arrested and detained; Yero Diallo, director of publication of *Le Tambour*, was seriously wounded, and other journalists were also assaulted.

Political expression has been restricted as well. For the first time since Traoré was deposed, all demonstrations were prohibited in May 1997. This measure was taken after the opposition, which numbers as many as 48 different parties, organized political meetings questioning the procedures and results of the April elections. The police arrested dozens of members of the political opposition. Meanwhile, protestors who demonstrated against the public investiture of president Konaré were dispersed in June; and the following month police shot and killed two opposition militants. Other events echo the previous regime. In September 1997, 30 members of the Association des Travailleurs Volontaires Partant à la Retraite (Association of Voluntarily Retiring Workers) were arrested for demonstrating peacefully in protest at the government's failure to keep its promises. Amnesty International reports that many ordinary citizens have been tortured or ill-treated by security forces recently because of their political involvement. Repression of the press has not abated of late, according to Reporters sans Frontières. Indeed, in August 2000 a parliamentary representative of the party in power attempted to strangle a journalist, and in 2001 the director of the Office for Radio and Television Mali was sentenced to a month in prison for defamation because guests on a programme had accused magistrates of corruption. One guest, Bamako's mayor Ibrahima N'Diaye, was fined 4573 euros, and Radio Television Mali was fined 1524 euros for airing the interview. Given Mali's recent history of repression and censorship, it may take some time for a sustainable tradition of free expression to develop.

LISA McNEE

Further Reading

Amnesty International, *Mali*, London: Amnesty International, 1981–

Amnesty International, "Mali", *Amnesty International Newsletter*, 11 (1981): 7

Amnesty International, "Mali: Internal Exile for 32 Teachers", *Amnesty International Newsletter*, 11/4 (April 1981): 5

Amnesty International, *Mali: Arrests of Student Leaders*, London: Amnesty International, 1986

Amnesty International, *Mali: Basic Liberties at Risk*, London: Amnesty International, 1997

Arnoldi, Mary Jo, "Political History and Social Commentary in Malian Sogobò Theater", *Africa Today*, 41/2 (1994): 39–49

Bertrand, M., "Un An de transition politique: de la révolte à la troisième République", *Politique Africaine*, 47 (1992): 9–22

Clark, Andrew F., "From Military Dictatorship to Democracy: The Democratization Process in Mali", *Journal of Third World Studies*, 12 (1995): 201–22

Decraene, Philippe, *Le Mali*, Paris: Presses Universitaires de France, 1980

Diarrah, Oumar, *Mali: bilan d'une gestion désastreuse*, Paris: L'Harmattan, 1990

Gaudio, Attilio, *Le Mali*, Paris: Karthala, 1988

Imperato, Pascal J., *Mali: A Search for Direction*, Boulder, Colorado: Westview Press, and London: Dartmouth, 1989

Kéïta, M.K., "Réflexion sur la presse écrite", *Politique Africaine*, 47 (1992): 79–90

Levtzion, Nehemia, *Ancient Ghana and Mali*, London: Methuen, 1973

Le Pluralisme radiophonique en Afrique de l'Ouest, Paris: L'Harmattan, 1993

Sanankoua, Bintou, *La Chute de Modibo Keïta*, Paris: Chaka, 1990

Sandbrook, Richard, "Transitions Without Consolidation: Democratization in Six African Cases", *Third World Quarterly*, 17/1 (1996): 69–87

US Department of State, *Mali: Country Report on Human Rights Practices for 1997*, Washington, DC: Bureau of Democracy, Human Rights and Labor, 1998

Vengroff, Richard and Moctar Koné, "Mali: Democracy and Political Change" in *Democracy and Political Change in Sub-Saharan Africa*, edited by John A. Wiseman, London and New York: Routledge, 1995

Wilcox, Dennis L., *Mass Media in Black Africa: Philosophy and Control*, New York: Praeger, 1975

MALTA

Population: 390,000	**Number of periodicals:** 4
Main religions: Roman Catholic	**Number of radio receivers per 1000 inhabitants:** 669
Official languages: Maltese; English	
Other languages spoken: Italian	**Number of TV receivers per 1000 inhabitants:** 735
Illiteracy rate (%): 8.6 (m); 7.2 (f)	**Number of PCs per 1000 inhabitants:** 260
Number of daily newspapers: 2	

The island of Malta has been conquered and ruled by numerous alien powers who have sought to impose their culture on the indigenous population: the Byzantine empire (from 395 CE), the Arabs (from 870), the Normans (from 1091), the Knights of the Order of St John (from 1530), the French (from 1798), and the British (1802–1964). Maltese culture and language are believed to have originally been of Punic (or Phoenician) origin. After centuries of development, the language has retained many Semitic elements from both Phoenician and Arabic, though it has many Romance elements and is written in a Latin script. Maltese did not become the official language until independence in 1964.

Little is known about Christian practices on the island before the 11th century. Re-christianization proceeded under the Norman Sicilian occupiers, who treated remaining Arabs with a degree of tolerance until the Holy Roman emperor, Frederick II (1211–50), at the pope's behest, forced all who would not embrace Christianity to leave. During the rule of the Knights of the Order of St John, the foreign nobles constituted a ruling class that held absolute sway. This governing class was divided into eight *langues*, which represented the dominant European tongues; the language of the majority Maltese had no place in the halls of power.

In 1574, Malta received its first "Inquisitor," whose task was to punish heresies against the Catholic religion. The Inquisitor possessed the sole power to determine what forms of thought and speech constituted heresy. His closest rivals for the authority to exercise cultural control were the bishop and the grand master. When the first printing press arrived in Malta, the grand master attempted to reserve the rights of censorship to himself and the Inquisitor. After the bishop protested, the Holy Office in Rome intervened and granted the sole power of press censorship to the Inquisitor alone.

During the next two centuries, the Maltese peasants and labourers would not assert themselves or assemble to express grievances unless clear signals came from within the ecclesiastical hierarchy. For example, during the period of the revolt of 1637, peasants wished to protest inordinate rates of taxation imposed by the grand master. The bishop encouraged local parish priests to allow the villagers to organize. The people were put down when the bishop, the grand master, and the Inquisitor all came to an agreement: the ringleaders were summarily arrested, and the old order was restored.

The 1775 "Rising of the Priests" also illustrates the extent to which the Maltese people were dependent upon the authorities to express themselves. Priests, dissatisfied with the fact that political power was being increasingly gathered in the hands of aristocrats, enlisted the peasants on their behalf; peasants were once again aggrieved at higher rates of taxation. The uprising was quashed by the aristocracy, and the pope was compelled to accept the limitation of ecclesiastical privileges. The separation of church and state had begun in Malta.

However much the power of the church was challenged by the knights, it was not seriously curtailed until the arrival of Napoleon Bonaparte in 1798. Still gripped by the spirit of the French Revolution, Bonaparte radically altered the Maltese social order: the aristocracy was abolished, foreign clerics and nuns were expelled, civil marriages were introduced, indigenous priests were no longer allowed to charge for services, and the power of the bishop was limited to the purely ecclesiastical domain. The first newspaper in Malta, printed in Italian and French, *Journal de Malte*, was introduced. Displeased by such innovations, the indigenous priests invited the British to intervene. The French were driven from the island, and the British assumed formal control in 1802.

The declaration of a Maltese Congress made His Majesty the King the protector of the Catholic faith, and provided that freemen have a right to choose their own religion. Toleration of other religions is therefore established as a right. Such proclamations were seen by many Maltese as self serving. Henry Frendo entertains the notion that "the British wanted to annihilate the power of the [Catholic] clergy and to create a national religion on a Protestant basis which could spread from Malta and ultimately percolate throughout the whole Empire." The colonial government's decision to permit the publication of a New Testament in the Maltese language was seen as part of this strategy. But proselytization was unwelcome, and education remained in the hands of the Catholic clergy. Language, too was a matter of dispute. In civil administration, the judicial system, and in education, Italian was mostly used. During the early 1800s the anti-British elite class relied on Italian as its mainstay in the struggle for cultural expression; while the rising pro-British middle class sought the promotion of the English language. In 1813, the British secretary of state for the colonies urged the governor of Malta to ensure by any means that "the English may be brought to supersede the Italian tongue."

In 1898, to divide the competing groups and maintain control, the governor approved a measure allowing elementary school children to be taught in the Maltese language in the first two grades; afterwards parents could choose to have their children study in English or Italian; though of course, English was more strenuously promoted. The rise of pro-Maltese nationalist sentiment was thus inadvertently encouraged. Gradually a working-class movement began to develop for the first time in the history of the island, a movement which expressed popular aspirations that had been stifled for centuries by a multitude of ecclesiastical, aristocratic, colonial, and competing national interests.

The most famous of the early 20th-century working-class dissidents was Manwel Dimech. Trained as an artisan, and largely self-educated, Dimech began in 1892 to teach foreign languages to the lower classes, and shortly thereafter founded *Il Bandiera tal-Maltin* (The Flag of the Maltese), a newspaper intended to "arouse the poor people to an awareness of their possibilities". Later he founded a mutual self-help society called the Circle of the Enlightened and a trade union. In 1911 Dimech was excommunicated for espousing socialist doctrines and for advocating the equality of women.

In 1914 colonial officials, equally displeased with Dimech's activities, arrested him during a demonstration protesting the government's refusal to grant a permit for a concert to benefit the unemployed. One official was quoted as saying, "England was not going to have any trouble-makers like Dimech running around her strategic colony in the centre of the Mediterranean." Dimech remained in custody in a prisoner of war camp in Alexandria for the duration of the World War I, and died a few years after his release.

Dominic Mintoff took on the mantle of his dissident predecessor Dimech, and sought to challenge the uneasy alliance that had developed between the British colonial administration and the church. Mintoff was a staunch opponent of clerical censorship, and of the church's frequent recourse to moral suasion and the threat of excommunication to attain political ends. During the 1950s the church had asserted its right to censor "morally reprehensible" magazines, books, and films through the presence of their representatives on the official censorship boards. The church was also permitted to own cinemas in many village areas. Many were outraged by the case of six "penitents", who in 1956 had been denied absolution for refusing to vote in accordance with church doctrine. Only after independence did the church give its assurance that Maltese who voted for the Maltese Labour Party (MLP) would not receive the sanction of having committed a mortal sin.

During the 1962 electoral campaign, the pro-Catholic conservative party and the MLP were permitted to record 20-minute speeches to be broadcast on cable radio. After censors excised all of his anti-ecclesiastical remarks, Mintoff withdrew his speech, and made sure that copies were played on tape recorders in localities that he could not visit. When independence was finally achieved in 1964, Mintoff became prime minister.

Article 32 of the post-independence constitution allows, subject to respect for the rights and freedoms of others, "freedom of conscience, of expression and of peaceful assembly and association". Article 41 states, "Except with his own consent or by way of parental discipline, no person shall be hindered in the enjoyment of his freedom of expression, including freedom to hold opinion without interference, freedom to receive ideas and information without interference, freedom to communicate ideas and information without interference. However, exceptions are made in the interests of defense, public safety, public order, public morality or decency, or public health" and for the purpose of protecting the reputations, rights, and freedoms of other persons.

Between 1966 and 1991 the two main political parties, one conservative and one socialist, alternated in power. Whichever party held the majority made use of its power to manipulate the official state-controlled electronic media. The island's print media remained relatively free whichever government was in power. Malta has, compared to other former Mediterranean colonies, been rated quite free of censorship for most of its post-independence history. In fact, Maltans have been able to exercise their press freedoms in a manner comparable to the citizens of most west European countries. The conservatives have accused the socialists of monopolizing the state media for their own ideological purposes when in power, while the socialists have accused the conservatives of dominating the private media through their alliance with the business leaders that own the majority of media outlets.

Between 1975 and 1985, freedom of expression came under pressure, when the Labour Party enacted legislation that penalized journalists who spread false news, when officials tolerated attacks on the offices of opposition newspapers (such as the English-language *Times of Malta*), and when, on occasion, they banned the entry into Malta of British print journalists. The Labour government was accused of acting heavy-handedly when it suspended the British Forces Broadcasting Station. Such measures were viewed as justified in socialist, and in some nationalist circles, as part of a strategy to thwart neocolonialist designs on the newly independent nation.

Since 1991 private media have proliferated and the state's control over the airwaves has weakened considerably. Some observers say that a larger number of radio and television stations, along with the advent of cable television will guarantee more freedom of expression. Others argue that the privatizations and multiplication of media outlets have created a "sterile diversity," which is virtually uniform in its procorporate and commercial bias. Meaningful political dialogue in the electronic media, some critics say, is rare.

Malta's constitution contains provisions to protect the free market and private ownership, and clauses to encourage the development of cooperative enterprises. Very little has been done, however, to encourage the development of cooperative, worker-run, or worker controlled media outlets. Nevertheless, the development of the internet has begun to offer new possibilities for free expression in Malta. The island nation has joined 12 other Mediterranean basin countries to work out the framework for InterMed, "a cooperative network", which finds inspiration in certain Spanish syndicalist approaches to organization.

Maltese computer scientists and ethnographers, along with representatives of the other Mediterranean countries, are working to develop a "deeper understanding of the so-called 'networked communities,' and their implications for the new international model of cooperation ..." Participants in InterMed make a distinction between two modes of disseminating information: the older method, which is traditional and encourages hierarchical structures, and the new method of organization, which stresses international cooperation and "the leadership of the civic society in this process, with respect for cultural diversity". The development of the internet along cooperativist lines promises to reduce the possibility of censorship in Malta, and throughout the Mediterranean region, by either the government or the owners of the corporate media.

PAUL WELLEN

Further Reading

Frendo, Henry, *Malta's Quest for Independence: Reflections on the Course of Maltese History*, Valletta: Valleta Publishing and Promotion, 1989

Koster, Adrianus, *Prelates and Politicians in Malta: Changing Power-Balances between Church and State in a Mediterranean Island Fortress, 1800–1976*, Assen, Netherlands: Van Gorcum, 1984

Navarro, Leondro, *The InterMed Network: Changing Cultural Patterns with a Large-Scale Cooperative Internet Network in the Mediterranean*, Barcelona: Universitat Politècnica de Catalunya, 1996

Rossi, Enzo, *Malta on the Brink: From Western Democracy to Libyan Satellite*, London: Alliance, 1986

MANAS
Kyrgyz folk epic

Manas is the greatest monument of the Kyrgyz oral tradition. It is 20 times longer than the *Iliad* and the *Odyssey* combined, five times longer than the Persian *Shahnameh*, and two and a half times longer than the Indian *Mahabharata*. The first known reference to its existence is in the writings of Khudud-Al-Alam, an Arab physician of the 10th century, but fragments of the epic were not written down until the 19th century. They were discovered by Choqan Valikhanov (1811–1865) on an expedition organized by the Russian Geographical Society in 1856, and published under the title *Koketoidun ashi* (The Funeral Feast for Koketai-Khan).

Manas, a tribal hero with titanic power, defends the Kyrgyz people and leads them from Altai to their historic motherland in Ala-Too (Tian Shan in Chinese), there to enjoy freedom, tolerance, and harmony, the major themes of the epic. Valikhanov concluded that *Manas* is an "encyclopedia of all Kyrgyz myths, folk tales, and legends, placed in one epoch and grounded around one man-hero, Manas". Indeed, in full it covers events from the 6th century to the 19th. Recited by a single performer, known as a *manaschi*, the epic has been used to rally people in times of hardship. In the 20th century, the Soviet leadership used the epic to buttress its own ideology. For that reason, Valikhanov's version is of considerable significance, since it contains no imported features.

Even before the Bolshevik revolution, the most complete version of *Manas*, a set of around 500,000 lines compiled by Manaschi Sagymbai Orozbakov (1867–1930), was influenced by Russian traditions and intended to please Russian officials. Their Soviet successors understood the power and uniqueness of the myth, but on their own terms. Study and interpretation of the epic were selectively censored to prevent its use in connection with "anti-Soviet" sentiments, not least calls for liberation and struggles for independence. Stress was placed on Manas's visit and subservience to the "White Tsar" of Russia, who alone made it possible for him to attack the Uigurs. Soviet symbolism was also introduced into the wording of the epic, as in the following excerpt:

Like a wild mountain stream we ran down, against the
     cities
We moved, we destroyed the idolatrous temples . . .
At night we attacked them, on all sides we lay in
     ambush,
Their locks we cut off . . .
The red flag rose, the black dust rose . . .

During World War II, the *manaschis* were encouraged to emphasize the parallels between Manas and modern Kyrgyz warriors fighting for the Soviet Union. However, after 1949, when China was admitted to the Communist bloc, the stress on warfare was abruptly abandoned: fraternal nations could hardly encourage the recitation of stories telling of the heroic military exploits of Kyrgyz warriors in western China. Now the *Manas* was presented as anything but a suitable vehicle for party ideology. It was said to contain "feudal-patriarchal remnants", to be aggressive and militaristic towards China, to be nationalistic and socially undesirable. Scholars who wanted to mark the millennium of Manas's great march, said to have occurred in 847, were attacked for paying excessive attention to the traditional epic while ignoring Soviet folklore.

In 1991 Kyrgyzstan became a sovereign nation. *Manas* ceased to be subject to state censorship and manipulation, and its national significance was restored. The millennium of the first epic by Khudud-al-Alam was proudly celebrated in 1995, which was declared by Unesco to be the "International Year of the *Manas* Epic". Archives were opened, numerous books were published, and fragments of the epic appeared in several languages.

JAMILYA UKUDEEVA

Text
The Manas, translated by V.V. Radlov (Wilhelm Radloff), edited by Arthur T. Hatto, Wiesbaden: Harrassoqitz, 1990

Further Reading

Abramzon, S.M., *Kirgizskii geroicheskii epos "Manas" kak etnograficheskii istochnik* (The "Manas" Heroic Epic as an Ethnographic Source), Frunze: Ilim, 1968

Aliev, S. *et al.*, *Encyclopedic Phenomenon of Epos Manas*, Bishkek: Muras, 1995

Chadwick, Nora K. and Victor Zhirmunsky, *Oral Epics of Central Asia*, London: Cambridge University Press, 1969

Jirmunskiyi, V.M., *Vvedenie v izuchenie "Manasa"* (Introduction to *Manas* Studies), Frunze: Ilim, 1948

Maldybaev, I., *"Manas": Istoriko-kulturnyi pamiatnik Kyrgyzov* (*Manas*: Historic Cultural Monument of the Kyrgyz), Bishkek: Kyrgyzstan, 1995

OSIP MANDEL'SHTAM
Russian poet, 1891–1938

Murder may be regarded as the ultimate form of censorship. That is effectively what Stalin and his henchmen did to Mandel'shtam in 1938 (or soon after), by sending him to the camps from the Samatikha sanatorium, where he and his wife Nadezhda had been sent by the Writers' Union to "recuperate", via the Butyrki prison. Stalin had already played cat and mouse with Mandel'shtam in 1934, exiling him to Cherdyn and then Voronezh after interrogation in the Lubianka, the headquarters of the security police, as a direct result of an unpublished epigram against Stalin.

Osip Mandel'shtam was born in 1891 in Warsaw. Soon afterwards, his family moved to Pavlovsk near St Petersburg. His first book of verse, *Kamen'* (*Stone*), was published in 1913. His second, *Tristia*, was first published in Berlin in 1922, and Mandel'shtam disowned this collection. These two books were republished (*Tristia* as *Second Book*) and expanded, then finally came out, expanded again by the addition of *Poems 1921–1925* in a single volume, simply called *Poems* (1928). This was the last book of verse that Mandel'shtam was to publish in his lifetime. We can assume that all three books were not subjected to censorship. Mandel'shtam's last publication was "Journey to Armenia", which appeared in 1933 in the magazine *Zvezda*. Its editor, Caesan Volbe, was sacked as a result of the ending of this piece, which, as Clarence Brown has put it, "must be one of the most unmistakably derogatory references to Stalin published in the Soviet Union in the 1930s". Mandel'shtam was warned to repudiate the piece, "or you will be sorry". As early as 1926 he was suffering from an enforced poetic "silence": both Anna Akhmatova and Boris Pasternak also suffered from similar "silences" this time. Mandel'shtam was forced to translate and undertake journalism until his "silence" ended in 1930. In his interrogation at the Lubianka in 1934, Mandel'shtam stated that the liquidation of the *kulaks* (affluent peasants) in the late 1920s had thoroughly depressed him. In 1930, there was a bitter and orchestrated scandal about the misattribution to Mandel'shtam of a translation of Charles de Coster's *Thyl Ulenspiegel*, which he had only edited, and which was to be the inspiration for his own dynamic piece, *Chetvertaia proza* (1930, "Fourth Prose"). Partly to escape from this scandal, Mandel'shtam visited Armenia with Nadezhda, on a journey sanctioned by his powerful ally Nikolai Bukharin. On his return, he started his *New Poems*, the first section of which became *The Moscow Notebooks*. None of these verses, written down in private notebooks, was published in the Soviet Union until 1973, when some of them appeared in the long-delayed Biblioteka Poeta edition of Mandel'shtam's verse, with an introduction by a party hack, Aleksandr Dymshits, who even got Mandel'shtam's place of birth wrong. The publication in the Soviet Union of the complete notebooks had to wait until 1989 (Tallin) and 1990 (Georgia), and then they appeared in an authoritative two-volume edition given a 200,000-copy print run, again in 1990 (Moscow). This effectively superceded the Struve and Filipoff Western Edition that had been the standard edition since the 1960s. The one untitled poem that stands out from the *Moscow Notebooks* is what has become known as "the Stalin epigram" (as translated by Richard and Elizabeth McKane):

> We are alive but no longer feel the land under our feet,
> you can't hear what we say from ten steps away,
> but when anyone half-starts a conversation
> they mention the mountain man of the Kremlin.
>
> His thick fingers are like worms,
> his words ring as heavy weights.
> His cockroach moustache laughs,
> and the tops of his tall boots shine.
>
> He is surrounded by his scrawny-necked henchmen,
> and plays with the services of nonentities.
>
> Someone whistles, someone miaows and another
>   whimpers,
> he alone points at us and thunders.
>
> He forges order after order like horseshoes,
> hurling them at the groin, the forehead, the brow, the
>   eye.
>
> The broad-breasted boss from the Caucasus
> savours each execution like an exquisite sweet.
>
> November 1933

Under interrogation, Mandel'shtam admitted that he had read this poem to a dozen friends, named most of them, and gave brief descriptions of their reactions (although he did not include Pasternak, who was to defend him soberly and, where he had to, evasively, when Stalin subsequently telephoned him about Mandel'shtam). One of the listeners had leaked the poem to the OGPU (as the security police were then known). Mandel'shtam's defiant, suicidal act, which amounted to permanent self-censorship, was to cost him dearly.

Despite the "counterrevolutionary" nature of his crime, it did not suit Stalin to destroy Mandel'shtam immediately, for the important first Congress of Soviet Writers was approaching. Instead, in an act that can only be called merciful, he was exiled, with his wife, first to Cherdyn, where he threw himself from a window in the hospital ("I jumped into my mind"). He may have been suffering from what is now called post-traumatic stress disorder after the tortures in the Lubianka, where he had also tried to commit suicide by slashing his wrists with a blade that he had concealed in his shoe. Then he was allowed to choose Voronezh, where he broke a poetic silence of 18 months after a concert by a young violinist, Galina Barinova. Her music released him into the most fertile phase of his writing, during his last two years in exile, when he wrote the 90 poems in the three *Voronezh Notebooks*. The "Ode to Stalin" was written during this period. There was a chance later for Nadezhda Mandel'shtam, who preserved his poetry, to impose her own censorship on this poem by destroying it, but she did not, despite the fact that Mandel'shtam had said: "It was an illness".

Recently Russian critics (notably M.L. Gasparov and Victor Krivulin) have made a case that Mandel'shtam was striving to accommodate himself to "the people" in his late poetry, especially in "Stanzas" and the "Ode to Stalin". Indeed, Stalin was perhaps hoping to tame Mandel'shtam by giving him that "one extra day" (a phrase to be found at the end of *Journey to Armenia*). He wrote the "Ode to Stalin" at a table with pencil in hand, in contrast to his usual method of moving his lips while in motion and dictating later to Nadezhda. However, whereas there is a case for excluding Akhmatova's "In Praise of Peace", her poems in (false) praise of Stalin, from editions of her work (see the article on Akhmatova), there is a strong argument that the "Ode to Stalin" should be included in Mandel'shtam's. Far from adulatory, it was written to save his life and that of his wife.

Nadezhda Mandel'shtam had this to say about the cult of the martyr that can surround Mandel'shtam in her book *Hope against Hope*, as translated by Max Hayward:

What would have become of Mandel'shtam if he had not been forced into a "different channel"? Being stronger than either me or Akhmatova, he would have accepted any channel, but suffering did not enrich him. It only destroyed him. He was hounded and stifled in every possible way, and the camp was merely the logical culmination of all he had been made to endure through the years. In effect, he was cut off before he had come to maturity – he was a slow developer – and he was still in the process of reaching it. His voice came through not because he was being hounded and smothered, but in spite of it ... Considering the dynamic force with which he was endowed, he had no need of prison, exile and the camp as the main elements of his biography.

Nadezhda's own courage should not go unremarked. At the end of the second volume of her memoir of those times, published in 1972, she wrote,

This book ... may never see the light of day. There is nothing easier than to destroy a book ... But even if it is destroyed, it may, perhaps, not have been entirely in vain. Before being consigned to the flames, it will be read by those whose expert task it is to destroy books, to eradicate words, to stamp out thought. They will understand none of it, but perhaps somewhere in the recesses of their strange minds the idea will stick that this crazy old woman fears nothing and despises force. It will be something if they understand that much ...

RICHARD MCKANE

Writings

Selected Poems, translated by David McDuff, 1973
Selected Poems, translated by Clarence Brown and W.S. Merwin, 1973
50 Poems, translated by Bernard Meares, 1977
Stone, translated by Robert Tracy, 1981
The Noise of Time, translated by Clarence Brown, 1986
Poems from Mandelstam, translated by R.H. Morrison, 1990
Selected Poems, translated by James Greene, 1991
The Collected Critical Prose and Letters, edited by Jane Gary Harris, 1991
The Moscow Notebooks, translated by Richard and Elizabeth McKane, 1991
A Necklace of Bees: Selected Poems, translated by Maria Enzensberger, 1992
The Voronezh Notebooks, translated by Richard and Elizabeth McKane, 1996

Further Reading

Baines, Jennifer, *Mandelstam: The Late Poetry*, Cambridge and New York: Cambridge University Press, 1976
Brown, Clarence, *Mandelstam*, Cambridge and New York: Cambridge University Press, 1973
Mandel'shtam, Nadezhda, *Hope against Hope: A Memoir*, New York: Atheneum, 1970; London: Harvill Press, 1971
Mandel'shtam, Nadezhda, *Hope Abandoned: A Memoir*, New York: Atheneum, and London: Harvill Press, 1974
Shentalinsky, Vitaly, *The KGB's Literary Archive*, edited and translated by John Crowfoot, London: Harvill Press, 1995; as *Arrested Voices: Resurrecting the Disappeared Writers of the Soviet Regime*, New York: Free Press, 1996

NORMAN MANEA

Romanian novelist, 1936–

PLICUL NEGRU (The Black Envelope)

Novel, 1985–92

Norman Manea was deported at the age of five to a Nazi internment camp in the Ukraine; he later spent much of his adult life in Romania under the communist regime. Accordingly, much of his writing is concerned with the Holocaust, with life in a totalitarian state, and with the anti-Semitism – to which he himself was subject after some of his critical writings – and the xenophobia that were manifested both in Nazi-occupied Europe and in communist Romania. Lucid in his critical prose, but sometimes more indirect in his creative writing, Manea has enjoyed a more objective reputation in the west than in his homeland.

Manea did not write during the Stalinist period. He publicly turned against the notion of Romanian protochronism – the idea (promoted by many communist critics) that developments in Romanian culture had anticipated events in the better publicized cultures of western Europe. Manea also voiced criticism of predominant political and aesthetic categories. The reaction from the communist mainstream was a series of articles that appeared in 1981 and 1982 declaring or insinuating that, because Manea was Jewish, he could not write properly, was unpatriotic, and had no proper god.

Manea's problems with Nicolae Ceauşescu's regime

(1965–89) culminated in the censorship of his novel *Plicul negru* (*The Black Envelope*). At the end of the 1970s, the Press Department, the organ of Romanian censorship, had been officially abolished and the regime had begun to rely on self-censorship by authors and editors. By the mid-1980s, however, when Manea was writing *Plicul negru*, censorship had been reinstated. A group within the Council for Socialist Culture and Education was charged with overseeing and advising individual editors. The recently established notion of the need for self-censorship was thus combined with a renewal of direct government control: a lethal combination.

Manea's novel centres on a deaf-mute association, "organized according to the principles of democratic centralism", which, as Manea has acknowledged, represents "an attempt to find a metaphor for our blocked and handicapped society". Tolea, an intellectual, comes into contact with the association in his quest to find out the truth about his father's death 40 years before, during World War II. The details of the allegory are sometimes obscure, and have become more so with the passage of time, but the novel is stylistically accomplished and effectively evokes life under Ceauşescu.

In December 1985 the editor assigned by Manea's publisher to read the novel in manuscript told him that it had not been accepted. The galley proofs that Manea eventually received had about 80 per cent of the text marked with the censors' objections: even entire chapters were said to be at fault. Among the offending words were "food lines", "informer", "anti-Semitism", and "homosexual", words that approached the reality of contemporary Romanian life. Although the censors' hostility toward single words and phrases such as these reveals a form of paranoia, Manea's own account of censorship always stresses, even if with a degree of irony, the intelligence and education of the censors.

Manea made some changes and cuts, but his revised text was returned untouched, apparently because the censors considered the corrections "trivial and hypocritical". The publisher then found a former censor who was asked to write a substitute censor's report (Manea had not been allowed access to the actual report, but simply the marks on the text). The idea was that, if Manea submitted another version, this time following the recommendations of the substitute report, his novel would be accepted.

The substitute report demonstrated that all Manea's implied parallels between Nazism and Romanian communism had been perfectly understood. This terrified the author. It also indicated that, if the book was to be published, a structural revision would be necessary, so that ideologies could be clarified. Some evocation of a "powerful antifascist" movement would have to be included, even though there was, in fact, no large antifascist movement in Romania before or during World War II.

The overwhelmingly negative view of daily life, of dirt and aggression in Bucharest, would have to be eliminated. A character would have to be changed so that his marginal position could be seen as resulting from a misunderstanding of "the new problems and needs of our socialist period". There could be no detailed mention of the contemporary resurgence of nationalism and fascism. It should not be implied that a real Holocaust took place in Romania. The distinction between Hitler and Stalin should be made clear.

In April 1986, Manea submitted a revised version to the censor's office. He received further requests for changes, such as eliminating the idea that two characters were on the point of suicide. Manea carried out his third set of changes and the book was passed. The 26,000 copies of its first edition sold out in a few days and received many favourable reviews. The regime seemed well disposed towards Manea. In October 1986, for example, he won a prize awarded by the Romanian Writers' Union for his book *Pe contur* (On the Fringes), published in 1984. However, Manea's statements elsewhere turned the tide against him, and the prize was withdrawn. In December 1986, the author emigrated to the United States via Berlin. In retrospect, Manea had adopted a cynical, pessimistic view (not unlike that of the Hungarian writer Miklós Haraszti) of the all-encompassing nature of communist censorship. He thought that, although *Plicul negru* had been published, the regime had won, because the book had become "corrupted by the very artifices . . . used . . . as a defence against the censor's office".

Since 1986, Manea's books have been translated into English and other major languages, and have been praised in the western press, but tensions remain within Romania. For example, an essay he wrote on the Romanian thinker Mircea Eliade (1907–86) discussed Eliade's support for fascism. When the text was published in Romania in 1992, some elements of the democratic press that had emerged after the fall of Ceauşescu in December 1989 called Manea "a traitor" and "the dwarf from Jerusalem".

JOHN LONDON

Writings

Plicul negru, 1986; as *The Black Envelope*, translated by Patrick Camiller, 1995
On Clowns: The Dictator and the Artist: Essays, 1992
October, Eight O'Clock, translated by Cornelia Golna et al., 1992
Compulsory Happiness, translated by Linda Coverdale, 1993

Further Reading

Verdery, Katherine, *National Ideology under Socialism: Identity and Cultural Politics in Ceauşescu's Romania*, Berkeley: University of California Press, 1991
Volovici, Leon, "Norman Manea and the Rumanian Jewish Renaissance", *Jewish Quarterly*, 34/4 (1987): 41–47

ÉDOUARD MANET
French painter, 1832–1883

THE EXECUTION OF THE EMPEROR MAXIMILIAN
Painting, 1867–69

Edouard Manet cultivated an image of himself as dandy, provocateur, and magus of the Realist avant-garde. His paintings, appreciated by an elite circle of Parisian writers, critics, and painters, often caused either confusion or outrage among the conservative bourgeois audiences who attended the official exhibitions of the Paris Salon in the 1860s and 1870s. Although his art frequently provoked critical debate, Manet was censored only twice by the French government – first for a painting, then for a lithograph, both of which depicted a political event, the execution of the Emperor Maximilian in Mexico.

Manet's style embraced *and* rejected the past, as it both demonstrated his thorough knowledge of artistic tradition and yet subverted convention through his depiction of modern subject matter in a bold visual syntax of flattened space, broad brushwork, and a limited palette of starkly contrasting light and dark tones. For Manet, artistic success was not just an intimate affair of labour in the studio. He craved the official recognition and the critical attention accorded to artists who exhibited at the Salon. For him, the making of modern art was a public affair, and the true "painter of modern life" (to borrow a phrase from Baudelaire) should make his name in the crucible of the Salon (or in its wake, at the Salon des Refusés).

In the early 1860s Manet provoked considerable debate over his deployment of the female nude in shocking takes on modern

Parisian life – in an outdoor picnic with young men (*Déjeuner sur l'herbe*; Salon des Refusés, 1863), and in the bedroom of a courtesan (*Olympia*, Salon 1865). Moreover, he tackled the long-standing conventions of religious art in his deflation of hallowed Christian themes, submitting to the Salon a moving yet unheroic image of the collapsed body of the crucified Christ mourned by angels (1864) and an image of a meek Christ mocked by soldiers (1865). Having thus updated major iconographic traditions of the nude and of Christian painting in western art, he turned to the challenge that had occupied Gustave Courbet in the previous decade: that of making history painting modern.

In 1867 Manet started painting several images of a key political event – the execution of emperor Maximilian in Mexico that same year. Although this event occurred on the other side of the Atlantic, it reflected upon the vainglorious and expansionist foreign policy of Napoleon III and the Second Empire, and thus held a controversial place in the political debates taking place in Paris in 1867. The execution was the climax of a European political folly in the New World. Napoleon III had hoped to establish a Catholic empire in Central America, and joined the English and Spanish in a joint military invasion of Mexico in 1861. By 1864 Napoleon III had helped orchestrate the selection of a European emperor for Mexico – the archduke

MANET: *The Execution of the Emperor Maximilian*. Manet worked on the painting, his third version of the subject, in late 1868 and early 1869, with the intention of exhibiting it in the Paris Salon. He was advised by the Salon authorities, however, that the finished painting would be rejected because of official discomfiture about Manet's implied critique of French imperialist policy in the work: the Mexican soldiers are dressed in uniforms provocatively similar to those of the French army, thus alluding to the French government's indirect political responsibility for Maximilian's execution. After completing the painting, Manet hid the work away, showing it only once in his lifetime, in the United States in 1879–80.

Maximilian of Austria. Maximilian arrived in Mexico in 1864 to embark on what would be a tumultuous three-year reign. Under pressure from the USA, Napoleon III withdrew his support for Maximilian, whose fragile regime was threatened by resistance from Mexico's president Juarez and his supporters. Juarez's troops captured Maximilian and executed him (along with two of his generals) at Querétaro, Mexico, on 19 June 1867. The European press, notably *L'Indépendance belge*, blamed this bloody debacle on Napoleon III, who was seen as having hand-picked the puppet emperor and then abandoned him in his hour of need. Although official reports in France attempted to deflect this attack (Napoleon III's Press Law of 1868 still left many restrictions on newspapers), any discussion of the subject was necessarily tinged with the unresolved question of the French government's responsibility and guilt in the matter.

Soon after receiving illustrated news reports, Manet began work on a canvas depicting the execution. He prepared two versions in 1867–68. The first, left unfinished, is in the Museum of Fine Arts, Boston. The second is in the National Gallery, London. His scene depicted Maximilian's death by firing squad. In the first version, the Mexican riflemen appear in sombreros and Mexican flared pants. In Manet's third (and final) version of the scene, painted during the winter of 1868–69 (Städtische Kunsthalle, Mannheim, Germany), the Mexican soldiers appear in uniforms that are suggestively close to French military costumes, a reference that implied that the ultimate responsibility for the execution lay with the French themselves. In this detail, Manet made overt a critique of French imperialist policy. His modernist style of rendering the scene in all three versions also raised challenging questions. In these canvases he refused to endow the scene with the comforting topographic or narrative detail, common to the academic painting of the day, that might allow the viewer to dismiss his representation as simply documentary or realistic. Moreover, he refused to follow the strategy of some contemporary Salon painters who heroicized Maximilian as a martyr. Rather, Manet's uncompromising scene of execution blurred the boundaries between the calculated actions of a military squad carrying out orders and the bald inhumanity of political murder. Manet set out to trouble the viewer.

Manet's depictions of the event disturbed the authorities of the Salon, and as he worked on his third version in the winter of early 1869 he was warned by Salon officials that if he submitted his canvas it would be rejected. The suppression of this painting from public exhibition might not be termed a case of literal censorship, in that government officials neither removed his picture from a display nor destroyed the canvas. One might even argue that they accorded this famous artist a certain respect by warning him ahead of time what consequences he could expect if he submitted the picture to the Salon. But for Manet, who cared deeply about exhibiting in this particular venue, this rejection by the Salon had almost the same effect as destroying his work: thereafter, he only showed the picture once during his lifetime, and that was outside France at an exhibition in New York and Boston in 1879–80. Otherwise, he kept it hidden in his studio, turned to the wall, and out of the realm of both the public and the private art-world debate. In early February 1869 he was also denied permission to print a lithograph that depicted the same scene (examples of this lithograph are in the collections of the Rijksmusum, Amsterdam, and the Bibliothèque Nationale, Paris). The print remained unpublished during Manet's lifetime.

ELIZABETH C. CHILDS

Writings

Manet by Himself: Correspondence and Conversation, edited by Juliet Wilson-Bareau, 1991

Further Reading

Boime, Albert, "New Light on Manet's *Execution of Maxmilian*", *Art Quarterly* (Autumn 1973): 172–208
Courtauld Institute Galleries (London), "The Hidden Face of Manet", special issue of *Burlington Magazine*, 128 (1986)
Edouard Manet and the Execution of Maximilian, Providence, Rhode Island: Bell Gallery, Brown University, 1981 (exhibition catalogue)
House, John, "Manet's *Maximilian*, Censorship and the Salon" in *Suspended License: Censorship and the Visual Arts*, edited by Elizabeth C. Childs, Seattle: University of Washington Press, 1997
Wilson-Bareau, Juliet *et al.*, *Manet: The Execution of Maximilian: Painting, Politics, and Censorship*, London: National Gallery Publications, and Princeton, New Jersey: Princeton University Press, 1992

THOMAS MANN
German novelist and essayist, 1875–1955

Thomas Mann, widely seen as the last representative of Germany's *Bildungsbürgertum* (cultivated middle class) and the ultimate exponent of its cultural traditions, may seem to have been an unlikely candidate for censorship. A scion of an established dynasty of Hanseatic merchants, he married into one of the most fully assimilated German-Jewish families in Munich, fathered six children, wrote several of the canonical works of German literature in the 20th century, and won the Nobel Prize for literature in 1929. A proud Prussian and archmonarchist in imperial Germany, Thomas Mann turned democrat under the Weimar Republic (1919–33) and became an increasingly outspoken critic of rising National Socialism. As an exile from

Nazi Germany after 1933 and, later, a citizen of the US, he campaigned unstintingly for liberal democracy, and emerged as the most prominent representative of Germany's humanist legacy. No matter how dramatic the sea changes of modern history, Thomas Mann always seemed to ride the crest of its tumultuous waves. Yet over the course of his long career he was to experience not only conventional censorship by state institutions, but also censorship within his own family, censorship by his most celebrated translator, and, perhaps most effective of all, his own self-censorship.

What increasingly strikes latter-day readers of Thomas Mann's works is his persistent deployment of racial and cultural stereotypes. A master of social satire, he imbricated the texts of his early works with popular caricatures that spared none of his culture's various "others", whether Bavarian or Prussian. Germany's most prominent "others" of that period were the Jews, who began their most successful phase of assimilation and integration into German culture and politics around the turn of the 19th and 20th centuries. Repeatedly typecast as *parvenus* and *nouveaux riches*, they make more or less comic cameo appearances in Mann's *Buddenbrooks* (1900) and *Tonio Kröger* (1902), before taking centre stage in his novella "Wälsungenblut" (1905, "The Blood of the Walsungs"). This story celebrates and caricatures Berlin's Jewish upper class, as modelled on his wife's family, presenting them as decadent arrivistes whose glamorous world and cultural sophistication are repeatedly refracted by vestiges of their humble origins in the *shtetls* of eastern Europe. The novella culminates in the incestuous embrace of the Jewish Aarenhold twins, which is staged with a mock-heroic tempestuousness parodying Wagner's opera *Die Walküre* (the "Walsungs" of Mann's title being a reference to that opera's doomed lovers, Siegmund and Sieglinde). However, their forbidden passion is ultimately driven by their shared desire to cheat on the sister's future husband, a bourgeois bore, attractive only as a conjugal conduit into the Prussian Protestant establishment. Thomas Mann's father-in-law prevented the publication of this story at the last minute. When it was finally published, in a limited edition, in 1921, the concluding sentence appeared with the two most offensive expressions, *beganeft* (Yiddish for "to cheat") and *goy* (Yiddish for "Gentile") expunged.

The frivolous highjinks of this German-Jewish family romance soon became eclipsed by the unspeakable horrors of the Holocaust. In 1965 a film version of the novella made in West Germany did not dare to mention, let alone depict in detail, this historically compromised story of the German-Jewish symbiosis gone terribly awry. In this film version, the Aarenholds, renamed the von Arnstatts, are neither Jewish nor *nouveau riche*, but members of the respectable old German aristocracy. Well-intentioned as it may have been, it can be argued that this recasting of a daring and doomed German-Jewish history amounted to another erasure of Jewish identity, as it inadvertently recapitulated what may be seen as the last chapters towards the "Final Solution" of German Jewry: assimilation, "Aryanization", annihilation. This grim and fatalistic version of events was clearly not shared by the coauthors of the film script, Georges Laforêt and Erika Mann. The latter was Mann's favourite daughter and the trusted executor of his literary legacy. As a talented author in her own right, she is a telling testimony to the German-Jewish symbiosis – fortunate enough, it might be said, to have escaped her own prescribed destiny.

The scandalous tale of "Wälsungenblut" may be taken as emblematic of the many censorial injunctions that permeated and punctuated Thomas Mann's life and work. More specifically, his censorship experience *en famille* illustrates both the problematic production of his works, and their reception at home and abroad.

With the loss of his audience and authority in Nazi Germany, Thomas Mann quickly had to refocus on an English-speaking culture, relying on the often hurried translations of Helen Lowe-Porter. Although serviceable at the time, more recently her work has become a veritable case study for the problematics of translations. Whereas Thomas Mann's original works reflect an increasingly countercultural agenda, undermining the patriarchal paradigm of western civilization by challenging its various social, sexual, and spiritual premises, Lowe-Porter's English translations represent a systematic suppression of Mann's complex cultural critique and a reaffirmation of cultural conventions (for a detailed analysis see Lubich, 1994, cited below). In this context, one example from Mann's social philosophy must suffice. In his public speech "German Address – an Appeal to Reason" (1930), Thomas Mann links his explicit denunciation of fascism with an emphatic allegiance to *Idealismus und Sozialismus* ("idealism and socialism"). Lowe-Porter reduces this utopian project, so symptomatic of the dreams and delusions of the Weimar Republic, to the "social and the ideal".

The most effective form of censorship has always been silencing. Mann's early political reflections, such as the fervent anti-French polemics that he wrote during World War I, remained untranslated throughout his years in the US. Only as an uncontroversial citizen, leaving all former national and utopian aspirations behind him, and thereby, some might say, exchanging personal authenticity for political expediency, could Mann rise to become the most prominent German exile in the US and the most persuasive advocate of western democracy. Enlisted by the British Broadcasting Corporation, he was able to address Nazi Germany in numerous radio speeches during the years 1941–45, thus penetrating the silence, and vociferously wooing and warning his deluded nation. Defying fascist censorship through modern technology, he could come home again while his enemies were still ruling and ruining his country.

With the beginning of the Cold War, Mann's political fortunes in the US changed again as his growing left-liberal leanings met with heightened suspicion. Increasingly associated with left-wing causes, the ageing author finally decided to return to the Old World for good, and settled in Switzerland, the mythical motherland of all modern democracies. Thus, the politics of calumny and censorship had expelled Thomas Mann twice from his home countries, Hitler's Germany and Joseph McCarthy's US, and a central figure of cultural representation had been transformed into a representative figure of political resistance.

As much as the conflicts of race relations and ideological convictions shaped and deformed Mann's reality and creativity, nothing affected and inflected his life and work more deeply and immediately than his own suppressed homosexuality. As early as the completion of his early novella *Der kleine Herr Friedemann* (1897, Little Herr Friedemann), Mann confided to his friend Otto Grautoff that he had discovered the literary masks that would allow him to hide his complex sexuality. With the extensive publication and exhaustive interpretation of his voluminous diaries since the 1980s, his literary work has emerged as an exemplary inventory of the multiple dialectics of Eros and Logos, sexuality and textuality. His many modern and mythical protagonists may all be seen as sexual personae through which he voices erotic desires and challenges moral conventions. What censors would cut, he pasted together again in his narrative montages, using ingenious techniques that delighted even his earliest and most conservative hagiographers. Again, Lowe-Porter's translations provide an array of examples that can illustrate the various levels of expression and repression possible and necessary in the respective German and English texts. She not only cleansed metaphors and *double entendres*, she purged whole passages. The most prominent example can be found in Mann's still contested lecture *On the German Republic* (1922), in which he elaborately delineates his political conversion from monarchist to democrat. Lowe-Porter's translation undercuts his arguments by removing almost two pages in which Mann enthusiastically invokes Walt Whitman's democratic vistas of homoerotic bonding.

Lowe-Porter does not stand alone with such practices of censorial cutting of seminal texts. In Charles Neider's anthology *The Stature of Thomas Mann* (1947), a collection of representative essays by influential critics designed to introduce Mann's literary work to a larger public, we find an essay by Bruno Frank about Mann's *Tod in Venedig* (1912, *Death in Venice*). In the English translation of this essay, the reference to Tadzio, Gustav Aschenbach's passionately pursued object of desire, is changed from "him" to "her".

Such editorial cuts and censorial cosmetics in the portrait of Thomas Mann and his art were – for better and for worse – the *sine qua non* for readers deemed not to be ready for socialist experiments, let alone different sexual experiences. It was not until the 1990s that Mann's masterworks, *Buddenbrooks*, *The Magic Mountain*, and *Doctor Faustus* appeared in new, uncensored English translations.

FREDERICK A. LUBICH

Writings

Buddenbrooks, 1900; as *Buddenbrooks*, translated by H.T. Lowe-Porter, 1924, and by John E. Woods, 1993
Tonio Kröger in *Tristan: Sechs Novellen*, 1903; as *Tonio Kröger*, translated by H.T. Lowe-Porter in *Death in Venice and Seven Other Stories*, 1936; translated by David Luke in *Tonio Kröger and Other Stories*, 1970
"Wälsungenblut" (The Blood of the Walsungs), 1905

Der Tod in Venedig, 1912; as *Death in Venice*, translated by H.T. Lowe-Porter, 1928, and by David Luke, 1990
Der Zauberberg, 1924; as *The Magic Mountain*, translated by H.T. Lowe-Porter, 1927, and by John E. Woods, 1995
Order of the Day: Political Essays and Speeches of Two Decades, translated by H.T. Lowe-Porter *et al.*, 1942
Doktor Faustus, 1947; as *Doctor Faustus*, translated by H.T. Lowe-Porter, 1948
Tagebücher, 1918–55, edited by Peter de Mendelssohn and Inge Jens, 10 vols, 1979–95; selection as *Diaries, 1918–1939*, translated by Richard, Clara, and Krishna Winston, 1982
Gesammelte Werke in dreizehn Bänden, edited by Hans Bürgin and Peter de Mendelssohn, 1990

Further Reading

Adolphs, Dieter Wolfgang, "Thomas Manns Einflussnahme auf die Rezeption seines Werkes in Amerika", *Deutsche Vierteljahrsschrift für Literaturwissenschaft und Geistesgeschichte*, 64 (1990): 560–82
Bloom, Harold (editor), *Thomas Mann*, New York: Chelsea House, 1986
Buck, Timothy, "Neither the Letter nor the Spirit", *Times Literary Supplement* (13 October 1995): 17
Heilbut, Anthony, *Eros and Literature*, New York: Knopf, 1996
Lubich, Frederick, A., *Die Dialektik von Logos und Eros im Werk von Thomas Mann*, Heidelberg: Winter, 1986
Lubich, Frederick, A., "Thomas Mann's Sexual Politics: Lost in Translation", *Comparative Literature Studies*, 31/2 (1994): 107–27
Lubich, Frederick, A., "Horrible Humanist – Hippest Humanist: Recent Thomas Mann Biographies (Donald Prater, Ronald Hayman, Anthony Heilbut)", *German Studies Review*, 21/1 (1998): 105–13
Neider, Charles (editor), *The Stature of Thomas Mann*, New York: New Directions, 1947
Reed, T.J., *Thomas Mann: The Uses of Tradition*, Oxford: Clarendon Press, 1974
Thirlwall, John, C., *In Another Language: A Record of the Thirty-Year Relationship between Thomas Mann and His English Translator Helen Tracy Lowe-Porter*, New York: Knopf, 1966

MANUFACTURING CONSENT
The propaganda model of the media

It was in their book *Manufacturing Consent: the Political Economy of the Mass Media* that Edward Herman and Noam Chomsky first elaborated their "propaganda model" of the media. They set out to show, with a wealth of empirical detail, how massive inequalities of wealth and power, within both the media and wider society, make it possible to "filter out the news fit to print, marginalize dissent, and allow the government and dominant private interests to get their message across to the public".

To this end, Herman and Chomsky identified five sets of "filters" that squeeze out certain kinds of news and actively encourage the production of others; this they do by fixing the "premises of discourse and interpretation, and the definition of what is newsworthy in the first place". According to Herman and Chomsky, the operation of these filters has become so much a "natural" part of the taken-for-granted daily reality of news production that:

media people, frequently operating with complete integrity and goodwill, are able to convince themselves that they choose and interpret the news "objectively" and on the basis of professional news values. Within the limits of the filter constraints they often are objective; the constraints are so powerful, and are built into the system in such a fundamental way, that alternative bases of news choices are hardly imaginable.

Thus are set what Chomsky has described in another book, *Necessary Illusions*, as "the bounds on thinkable thought".

The first of the five filters is the "size, concentrated ownership, owner wealth, and profit orientation of the dominant mass-media firms". These firms constitute an increasingly exclusive rich man's club, and rich men tend to hold a fairly narrow range of views and to appoint like-minded managers to run their businesses. However, even firms with a relatively liberal ethos are likely to find their media output shaped and constrained by the profit-orientation of the market system within which they operate. As businesses first and foremost, giant media firms have vested interests in low business taxes and interest rates, employer-friendly labour policies, deregulation, and weak antimonopoly legislation, and it would be surprising if such firms did *not* use their media interests, particularly in broadcasting and the press, to propagandize on behalf of such policies and those political parties that pursue them the most ardently. Meanwhile, those media organizations that depend to any extent on state support of one kind or another (such as public service broadcasters) have always to bear in mind that there may be a significant price to pay if their output regularly alienates the government of the day.

Advertising is the second filter: it is the main, and in some case sole, source of income for an ever-increasing number of the world's media. For those media dependent on advertising, the advertisers are the latter-day version of the patrons, their funding being endlessly solicited and media products carefully tailored to meet their needs. These, of course, consist in reaching audiences with buying power – not necessarily the largest numbers, but those known to be high spenders on consumer goods and services. This dependence on advertising quite clearly has significant consequences for media content; as Grant Tinker, a former head of NBC-TV put it, television in the United States is an "advertising-supported medium, and to the extent that support falls out, programming will change". Herman and Chomsky conclude that:

> with increasing market pressure for financial performance and the diminishing constraints from regulation, an advertising-based media system will gradually increase advertising time and marginalize or eliminate altogether programming that has significant public affairs content. Advertisers will want, more generally, to avoid programmes with serious complexities and disturbing controversies that interfere with the 'buying mood'. They seek programmes that will lightly entertain and thus fit in with the spirit of the primary purpose of programme purchase – the dissemination of a selling message.

The third filter comprises the reliance of the media on information directly provided by the government and big business, and not least on "experts" funded and approved by these primary sources and agents of power. Because the media are voracious, needing a constant flow of the raw material of news to meet their tight deadlines and the imperatives of "immediacy", news organizations tend to concentrate their resources at the points at which events deemed the most "newsworthy" tend to occur, where important briefings, leaks, and rumours abound, and where regular press conferences are held – in other words, the centres of national and local government, and the headquarters of business corporations and trade groups. All of these specialize in churning out vast amounts of rapidly digestible and apparently reliable material that perfectly meets the endless demands of news organizations for regular and easily processed flows of information, in effect providing the media with a considerable "information subsidy". Such sources rapidly become routine and less subject to critical scrutiny than they should be, either because journalists are under pressure of

time or because they are simply insufficiently sceptical of information carrying the "official" imprimatur. What this means is not only that these sources may be more trusted than they deserve to be, but also that non-routine or alternative sources may find themselves at a considerable disadvantage by comparison. This is not only because they are competing for access with far more powerful players, but also because they run the risk of being excluded from media debate altogether, either on the grounds that their inclusion might alienate a regular and valuable official source, or because the official view of a subject has become so coterminous with the views of the media gatekeepers that any dissent from it is automatically regarded as extreme, eccentric, demagogic, or some form of "special pleading" by sectional interest groups, and thus not worthy of inclusion.

"Flak" makes up the fourth filter, and consists primarily of organized negative responses to media items, personalities, or interests. When carefully organized, either by governments or by large corporate interests, or both, "flak" can be extremely uncomfortable and costly, and can act as a significant deterrent to certain kinds of media output – which is usually its central purpose. For advertising-funded media, the most serious forms of "flak" are consumer boycotts, and withdrawal of sponsorship and other forms of commercial support; for public service broadcasters, it is government threats of deregulation or even outright privatization. In the latter case, government "flak" is frequently augmented by "flak" from commercial media interests, keen to weaken their public service competitors and even keener to see them entirely dismembered so that they can scavenge the remains for the richest pickings.

"Anti-Communism as a control mechanism" accounts for the fifth and final filter. When Herman and Chomsky first elaborated their propaganda model the Cold War was still being fought, and opposition to communism was still, as they put it, a "first principle of western ideology and politics". However, they also noted that: "this ideology helps [to] mobilize the populace against an enemy, and because the concept is fuzzy it can be used against anybody advocating policies that threaten property interests or support accommodation with Communist states and radicalism". It is this very "fuzziness" that ensures that this filter still stays firmly in place, despite the collapse of the Soviet Union and most other communist regimes.

Herman and Chomsky conclude their discussion of the five filters by arguing that they:

> narrow the range of news that passes through the gates, and even more sharply limit what can become "big news", subject to sustained news campaigns. By definition, news from primary establishment sources meets one major filter requirement and is readily accommodated by the mass media. Messages from and about dissidents and weak, unorganized individuals and groups, domestic and foreign, are at an initial disadvantage in sourcing costs and credibility, and they often do not comport with the ideology or interests of the gatekeepers and other powerful parties that influence the filtering process. Thus it is that many stories never even make it to the starting gates in the first place, let alone suffer overt bans, cuts or other forms of interference after they have entered the race. The process whereby this takes place is not random,

it is institutionalized and systemic. That is why it can be considered as censorship.

The most consistent criticism of the propaganda model is that it is based on a conspiracy theory of the media. However, Herman and Chomsky devote the opening pages of *Manufacturing Consent* to distancing themselves quite explicitly from any such approach. As they put it:

> our treatment is much closer to a "free market" analysis, with the results largely an outcome of the workings of market forces. Most biased choices in the media arise from the preselection of right-thinking people, internalized preconceptions, and the adaptation of personnel to the constraints of ownership, organization, [and] market and political power.

In other words, what they are describing is a decentralized system in which control, such as it is, is exercised largely by the market, and in which the filters work mainly through the independent actions of many different but nonetheless like-minded individuals and organizations. In this respect, they describe the media as constituting a "guided market system",

> with the guidance provided by the government, the leaders of the corporate community, the top media owners and executives, and the assorted individuals and groups who are assigned or allowed to take constructive initiatives. These initiators are sufficiently small in numbers to be able to act jointly on occasion, as do sellers in markets with few rivals. In most cases, however, media leaders do similar things because they see the world through the same lenses, are subject to similar constraints and incentives, and thus feature stories or maintain silence together in tacit collective action and leader–follower behaviour.

Of course, the charge of conspiracy theorizing could still be laid at Herman and Chomsky's door if it was warranted by their analyses of the ways in which the media deal with specific stories, as opposed to the way in which they claim to carry out such analyses. However, their critics conspicuously fail to deal with the analyses in *Manufacturing Consent*, which focus on, among other things, the media's role in helping to ascribe the shooting of Pope John Paul II in 1981 to a plot by the Soviet and Bulgarian security services; a comparison of media coverage of the murder of the Polish priest Jerzy Popiełuszko by the Polish police in 1981 with coverage of the killings of more than 100 priests within the US sphere of influence in South America; and a comparison of media coverage of elections in El Salvador, Guatemala, and Nicaragua. These take up by far the greater part of the book and demonstrate, through detailed and meticulous empirical work, that the propaganda model is a highly productive way of analyzing the media that precisely does not rest on a crudely conspiratorial view of their role within society. (Nor are these analyses confined to *Manufacturing Consent*: equally detailed ones can be found in, among others, Chomsky's *Necessary Illusions*, *The Fateful Triangle*, and *Pirates and Emperors*, and Herman's *The Real Terror Network*, and *The "Terrorism" Industry*, written with Gerry O'Sullivan.)

A second, and related, criticism is that the propaganda model represents the media as more monolithic than they actually are. Again, this objection is actually anticipated by Herman and Chomsky in *Manufacturing Consent*, in which they expressly state that "the mass media are not a solid monolith on all issues. Where the powerful are in disagreement, there will be a certain diversity of tactical judgments on how to attain generally shared aims, reflected in media debate." Herman and Chomsky argue, as we have seen, that the media reflect the consensus of the powerful elites that make up the state–corporate nexus, but they are also quite clear that the consensus is broad enough to contain within it views that may well be in disagreement with specific aspects of government or corporate policy, albeit on tactical as opposed to substantive strategic or principled grounds. They also show that when non-elite groups are interested in, well-informed about, and effectively organized to fight on certain issues, then, as long as these issues do not challenge fundamental political, ideological, or economic premises, the media are not entirely closed to such groups. Indeed, many of the facts that Herman and Chomsky draw on to back up their analyses are themselves taken from the mainstream media, which has led some of their critics to claim that those media thus cannot be as propagandist as is apparently being claimed. However, the authors foresaw this charge too:

> That the media provide some facts about an issue, however, proves absolutely nothing about the adequacy or accuracy of that coverage ... More important in this context is the question of attention given to a fact – its placement, tone, and repetitions, the framework of analysis in which it is presented, and the related facts that accompany it and give it meaning (or preclude understanding). That a careful reader looking for a fact can sometimes find it with diligence and a sceptical eye tells us nothing about whether that fact received the attention and context it deserved, whether it was intelligible to the reader or effectively distorted or suppressed. What level of attention it deserved may be debatable, but there is no merit to the pretence that because certain facts may be found in the media by a diligent and sceptical researcher, the absence of radical bias and de facto suppression is thereby demonstrated.

A third criticism of the propaganda model is that it grants more power to the media than they actually possess; in other words, Herman and Chomsky stand accused of both endorsing a version of "media effects" theory and instilling a sense of what Philip Schlesinger calls "political fatalism" in the radically inclined. However, as Herman points out in his essay "The Propaganda Model Revisited", what he and Chomsky actually elaborated was:

> a model of media *behaviour and performance*, not of media *effects*. We explicitly pointed to alternative media, grassroots information sources, and public scepticism about media veracity as important limits on media effectiveness in propaganda service, and we urged the support and more effective use of these alternatives ... In fact, we would like to think that the propaganda model can help activists understand where they might best deploy

their efforts to influence mainstream media coverage of issues.

Herman and Chomsky would be the first to admit that the propagandist initiative conspicuously failed to persuade many of, for example, the morality of the Vietnam War or the desirability of the US campaign against Nicaragua in the 1980s. That does not mean, however, that the media did not perform a propagandist role in the first place. To follow their critics down this particular road would, *mutatis mutandis*, end up with the argument that, because many Soviet citizens did not believe everything they read in *Pravda* or *Izvestiya*, then these newspapers were not the organs of state propaganda that they clearly were.

Finally, the propaganda model has been portrayed as a blunt instrument that is difficult to apply to particular media instances or, alternatively, to media other than those of the United States. Leaving aside the fact that, as noted earlier, Herman and Chomsky's own detailed case studies of media reporting decisively invalidate the charge that the model is inoperable, it is important to note that in his "revisiting" article Herman stresses that the model "deals with extraordinarily complex sets of events, and only claims to offer a broad framework of analysis that requires modification depending on many local and special factors, and that may be entirely inapplicable in some cases".

In conclusion, the most important tests of the model must surely be, first, whether it can still perform a useful analytic and predictive function today, and, second, whether it can be applied to the media systems of other democratic countries as well as that of the United States. Clearly this is a vast issue, detailed empirical consideration of which is beyond our scope here. Perhaps the best way to approach it, however, would be to revisit, albeit briefly, the five filters in the light of these two crucial tests.

Examining the first – the size, concentrated ownership, and market-orientation of the dominant media companies – it appears that the model's applicability has been greatly enhanced almost everywhere. The decline of public service broadcasting in Europe, the "merger mania" that has led to the growth of global cross-media empires, the powers that moguls such as Silvio Berlusconi and Rupert Murdoch clearly exercise, either directly or indirectly, over the content of the media that they own: these are all inescapable developments that have clearly "filtered" what actually appears in the media themselves, not least in the domain of news and current affairs, which is Herman and Chomsky's main (although not sole) concern. If the interests of advertisers are placed before those of audiences, if the highest possible numbers are routinely chased by offering content representing the "lowest common denominator", and if audiences are generally treated as consumers to be wooed and sated, as opposed to citizens to be informed – in short, if an increasing number of the largest media players put purely commercial considerations before all else – this is powerful ammunition for the argument that market forces do indeed act as filters and, in so far as they militate against the presence of certain kinds of material, as spurs to an insidious form of self-censorship. A particularly worrying development in this respect has been the ousting of serious journalism by "infotainment" of one kind or another, both in broadcast and print journal-

ism, coupled with the narrowing of journalistic autonomy that has taken place in many media organizations as a result of deunionization, casualization, budget cuts, and so on.

The situation outlined above puts more power than ever in the hands of the advertisers, and thus strengthens the second filter too. Indeed, one of the main reasons why many European governments deregulated and commercialized their public service broadcasting systems in the 1980s and 1990s was because of sustained lobbying by the advertising industry. Advertisers have more power over more areas of the media than ever before, but they in turn are only one part of a greatly enhanced industry of public relations, which is a key component of the third filter. Today the best-known representatives of this news-creating and news-manipulating industry are "spin doctors", but their high-profile activities should not blind us to the fact that a worryingly large proportion of news today originates, less dramatically but equally directly, from press and public relations releases of one kind or another. The diminution in journalistic resources mentioned above plays directly into the hands of those who are only too ready to dole out the ever-increasing "information subsidies" noted earlier.

The production of "flak", the fourth filter, also makes things easier for the public relations industry. Today, large corporate interests are more adept than ever at handling the media, employing large and intimidating legal departments to help them do so and, in particular, to discourage the media from even tackling certain stories in the first place. Even at the best of times, but especially when journalistic resources are limited, the threat of a long and costly legal action can be a powerful incentive for leaving a story well alone, especially in Britain with its notoriously plaintiff-friendly libel laws. There are also times when sections of the media themselves act as powerful "flak"-producing machines – witness the routine attacks on the allegedly liberal bias of the US media by its decidedly illiberal members; the endless hostility shown by Rupert Murdoch's newspapers in Britain to public service broadcasting, as part of his News International group's concerted campaign to establish its satellite television service, BSkyB, as a serious commercial rival; or the similarly motivated attacks in Italy by Berlusconi's numerous media on the state broadcaster RAI.

As noted earlier, the fifth filter, anticommunist ideology, does present certain problems today, in the light of the demise of so many communist regimes. However, as was clearly demonstrated by the reporting of the "Battle of Seattle", around the meeting of the World Trade Organization in that city in 1999, and of other protests against the depredations of global capitalism, the media have been only too willing in most cases to swallow the official line and pin the label of "anarchist" on the protestors as a means of delegitimizing and demonizing their causes. Again, however, we should note that the success in Europe – but not, significantly, in the United States or Canada – of campaigns against genetically modified organisms shows that government and big business do not always have it all their own way. Similarly, rhetorical invocations of threats to "national security" are still regularly used by governments to silence awkward and embarrassing stories of one kind or another. Finally, one might note that, among the elites of Europe and North America at least, there now seems to be such an absolute, unquestioned, almost religious faith in the beneficence of the market that non-market options are made to seem hopelessly utopian by comparison, and thus find themselves increasingly filtered out of media debate altogether. This is what Herbert Marcuse aptly referred to in *One-Dimensional Man* as "the closing of the universe of discourse". It would indeed be hard to think of a better description of the workings, not only of this filter, but of the five filters in their totality.

JULIAN PETLEY

Further Reading

Chomsky, Noam, *The Fateful Triangle: The United States, Israel, and the Palestinians*, Boston: South End Press, 1983; updated edition, 1999

Chomsky, Noam, *Pirates and Emperors: International Terrorism in the Real World*, New York: Claremont, 1986

Chomsky, Noam, *Necessary Illusions: Thought Control in Democratic Societies*, Montréal : CBC Enterprises, Boston: South End Press, and London: Pluto Press, 1989

Herman, Edward S., *The Real Terror Network: Terrorism in Fact and Propaganda*, Boston: South End Press, 1982

Herman, Edward S. and Gerry O'Sullivan, *The "Terrorism" Industry: The Experts and Institutions That Shape Our View of Terror*, New York: Pantheon, 1989

Herman, Edward S. and Noam Chomsky, *Manufacturing Consent: The Political Economy of the Mass Media*, New York: Pantheon, 1988; London: Vintage, 1994

Herman, Edward S., *The Myth of the Liberal Media: An Edward Herman Reader*, New York: Peter Lang, 1999

Marcuse, Herbert, *One-Dimensional Man: Studies in the Ideology of Advanced Industrial Society*, Boston: Beacon Press, and London: Routledge and Kegan Paul, 1964

Schlesinger, Philip, "From Production to Propaganda?", *Media, Culture and Society*, 11/3 (1989)

MAO ZEDONG
Chinese leader, 1893–1976

TALKS AT THE YAN'AN FORUM ON LITERATURE AND ART
Political statements, 1942

Whether viewed as "the most important and brilliant Chinese Marxist statement on literature and art" (the view of the Chinese authorities) or a "dogmatic and mechanical . . . narrowly determinist ideology" (Michael S. Duke), Mao Zedong's seminal statement provided a justification for the Chinese Communist Party's extensive censorship of writers and artists for over 40 years.

The "Talks" were delivered at the communist base of Yan'an, northwestern China, on two occasions in May 1942, but were not published until October 1943. Intellectuals such as Wang Shiwei and Ding Ling, who had followed the communist armies of the Long March to Yan'an, had dared to suggest that writers should be free to explore ideas, unfettered by the restraints of politics and ideology. Mao responded with a "rectification campaign" designed to purge such "bourgeois thinking".

Mao insisted that the Communist Party should control literature and art. Writers should serve the interests of the people. They should write for and be guided by the people, developing a popular and intelligible style, and seeking out the "rich deposits of literature and art [that] exist in popular life itself". Writers were not to expose shortcomings among the people or to dwell on the dark side of society. Rather they should "awaken and arouse the popular masses, urging them on to unity and struggle and to take part in transforming their own environment". Political acceptability took precedence over artistic technique; writers were merely "mechanical reproducers" of party policy. Words were weapons to be used to deliver the "correct" message; complexity and ambiguity were to be eradicated. No wonder that so much officially approved Chinese writing read as if it were the verbatim regurgitation of official party documents rather than as the expressive language commonly associated with literary creation.

Mao's ideas combined the socialist realism of the Soviet literary czar Andrei Zhdanov (1896–1948), who from the 1930s had been demanding that literature should "boldly lash and attack bourgeois culture", with the notion of Qu Qiubai, Chinese Communist Party general secretary in the 1920s, that Marxist literature should properly only be produced for mass consumption. Mao failed to credit these ideologues; *he* was the architect of the "new literary line".

He made it clear that any departure from his policy would be "duly corrected". After 1949, any work of literature that "deviated" from the party line was immediately pounced on by literary bureaucrats and the author forced to make a self-criticism. The "Talks" were used to justify the exclusion of any dissenting opinion in a series of successive crackdowns in the 1950s – the campaign against Hu Feng (1955) and the Anti-Rightist Campaign (1957) – culminating in the Cultural Revolution of 1966–76. By this time Mao had published a new collection of his pre-1950 writings, heavily revised and with substantive changes. After 1953, this was the version referred to.

By prescribing the role of writers and artists in socialist society, defining the themes that could (or could not) be treated, and even giving directions on style, Mao was establishing norms that were to stifle literary creation beyond his lifetime. Even in the early 1980s when a number of his other policies were being called into question, the ideas of the "Yan'an Talks" remained sacrosanct. By the middle of the 1980s, however, with the appearance of "roots-seeking literature" (*xungen wenxue*) and then "avant-garde fiction" (*xianfeng xiaoshuo*), the Maoist line began at last to be challenged; its dominance, diluted for a while, it was again asserted as party policy by He Jingzhi, the conservative minister of culture, in the years after the suppressions of Tiananmen Square in June 1989.

DESMOND A. SKEEL

Writings

Talks at the Yenan Forum on Art and Literature, 1956; 4th edition 1965
Selected Works, 5 vols, 1961–65

Further Reading

Fokkema, D.W., *Literary Doctrine in China and Soviet Influence, 1956–1960*, The Hague: Mouton, 1965

Goldman, Merle, *Literary Dissent in Communist China*, Cambridge, Massachusetts: Harvard University Press, 1967

McDougall, Bonnie S., *Mao Zedong's "Talks at the Yan'an Conference on Literature and Art": A Translation of the 1943 Text with Commentary*, Ann Arbor: University of Michigan Press, 1980

McDougall, Bonnie S., *Popular Chinese Literature and Performing Arts in the People's Republic of China, 1949–1979*, Berkeley: University of California Press, 1984

Nieh Hualing (editor), *Literature of the Hundred Flowers*, New York: Columbia University Press, 1981

JACK MAPANJE
Malawian poet, 1943–

John Alfred Clement Mapanje is not only his country's foremost poet, but also a towering figure in contemporary African letters. Ironically, many knowledgeable observers credit the Malawi Censorship Board with honing his skills. Mapanje himself has approvingly quoted the Polish novelist Tadeusz Konwicki on this subject:

> [W]riting under censorship has positive aspects. It can be like gambling or doing battle. The fact of having to face a censor can mobilize a writer to create ways of bypassing censorship; it forces the writer to employ metaphors which raise the piece of writing to a higher level ("Censoring the African Poem").

Those of Mapanje's contemporaries who were driven into exile probably fared less well. The critic James Gibbs has written of the sad impact that exile had on the work of Legson Kayira and David Rubadiri, the leading figures of Malawi's early post-independence literary generation:

> It is easy to wax eloquent over the literary impetus given to authors by leaving their native lands – and it is certainly necessary to be aware of the literary tendencies stimulated by exile. However, there is a price which often has to be paid in terms of creativity. And it seems that Kayira is paying it . . . Like Kayira . . . [Rubadiri's] . . . talent has not flourished in foreign fields and he can be seen as another of Banda's victims (Gibbs 1988).

Mapanje gained international recognition during his four years of detention without trial in the late 1980s. Yet he had been playing an extended game of cat and mouse with the censors for many years prior to his incarceration. He was one of the founders of the Writers' Group, which met weekly at Chancellor College in the University of Malawi from 1970 onwards. Mapanje, a theoretical linguist, was first a student at the college and later a lecturer, rising to become head of the department of English language and literature. The Writers' Group developed a collective fund of metaphors and allusions to describe the travails of life under the quirky and deeply authoritarian regime of Dr Hastings Kamuzu Banda.

Mapanje was aware of the temptation, like the chameleon, "to bask in one's brilliant camouflage", but generally the necessity to employ the heightened use of metaphor strengthened his individual poetic voice, as Konwicki suggests it could. Mapanje, like many of his contemporaries, drew heavily on Malawian oral traditions and popular tales. To the outside reader, his poems are sometimes dense and difficult to decode. To a Malawian, especially one who lived through the Banda years, the poems speak very clearly.

There is a long history in Malawi of the use of ambiguity or metaphor as a means of communicating critical or potentially offensive messages. For example, women's pounding songs among the Ngoni communicate explicit messages about sex, in a way that can be generally understood, but without using *zotukwana* (obscenities). Among the Ngoni this is known as *kukulawika*. For the Tonga the same phenomenon is known as *chambula njiwi ching'ongo*. The meaning and purpose of such techniques is to communicate criticism in a veiled manner that allows the problem to be resolved without loss of face (Kerr 1993). The approach of Mapanje and the Writers' Group belonged firmly in this tradition. As a result of his poetic output – in which he employed these techniques – Mapanje achieved a quite unusual celebrity. In 1983, when he delivered a university lecture on the dry-sounding topic "Aspect and Tense in Chiyao, Chichewa and English", the audience was so large that they had to move to a different hall.

In 1981 a collection of Mapanje's poems entitled *Of Chameleons and Gods* was published. Under the Censorship and Control of Entertainments Act, works by Malawian writers did not formally have to be submitted to the Censorship Board. The book was not submitted for authorization, and copies circulated privately. In 1985, however, the Ministry of Education and Culture issued a circular banning it in schools and colleges. The Censorship Board – in response to Mapanje's complaints that the book had been banned – informed him that the book had merely been "withdrawn from circulation". He was told that anyone could possess a copy of the book. "How", Mapanje responded, "could anyone have the book in their house when it has been withdrawn from circulation; when it's not even available?"

A serious confrontation with the authorities was imminent. In the 1980s Mapanje's poetry was becoming more explicitly political. "The Cheerful Girls at Smiller's Bar, 1971" is a playful dig at the hypocrisy of "Presbyterian prudes" (Banda was a strict Presbyterian). Its 1983 sequel is dark and angry in tone, dealing with the official murder of four prominent political figures.

On 25 September 1987, police arrested Mapanje at the Gymkhana Club in Zomba and took him in handcuffs to Mikuyu Prison. He was held, without ever being charged, for three years, seven months and 16 days (as he reminds us in one of his post-release poems). Under Malawian law, a person could only be detained on the individual order of the Life-President, yet Mapanje's detention order had a signature "visibly photocopied from the Malawi Congress Party Card of 1960, perhaps for security reasons!" (*The Chattering Wagtails of Mikuyu Prison*).

His incarceration was marked by many of the casual cruelties of detention without trial. He was denied any visits by family or friends for the first 20 months. A practising Roman Catholic, he was denied access to a priest for his entire period in detention. His mother died while he was in Mikuyu and he was not allowed out for the funeral. And he was denied reading or writing materials on pain of severe physical punishment.

Mapanje survived his ordeal. He emerged into a world where the power of Life-President Banda was rapidly waning and Mapanje's own reputation had soared. He produced *The Chattering Wagtails of Mikuyu Prison*, a collection of poems which is an important addition to the canon of prison literature. But, although the esteem in which he is held in Malawi has never been higher, he has not returned from self-imposed exile in Britain.

RICHARD CARVER

Writings

Of Chameleons and Gods, 1981
Editor, with Landeg White, *Oral Poetry from Africa: An Anthology*, 1983
Editor, with Angus Calder and Cosmo Pieterse, *Summer Fires: New Poetry of Africa*, 1983
"Censoring the African Poem", *Index on Censorship*, 18/8 (September 1989)
The Chattering Wagtails of Mikuyu Prison, 1993
Skipping without Ropes, 1998
Editor, with James Gibbs, *The African Writers' Handbook*, 1999

Further Reading

Gibbs, James, "Censorship and Felix Mnthali, Jack Mapanje, Frank Chipasula and Others", *Index on Censorship*, 17/2 (February 1988): 18–22
Kerr, David, "Ideology, Resistance and the Transformation of Performance Traditions in Post-Colonial Malawi" (dissertation), Gaborone: University of Botswana, 1993

THOMAS MAPFUMO
Zimbabwean musician, 1945–

Thomas Mapfumo, one of Zimbabwe's best-known composers and singers, established his reputation for incisive political and social commentary during the country's war of liberation (1972–79). He emerged as the leading proponent of the *Chimurenga* (Liberation War) music genre, fusing traditional Shona music and poetry with more modern instruments and forms. Mapfumo's songs, vaguely worded in the vernacular to avoid suppression by the Rhodesian security apparatus, exhorted nationalist guerrillas and African patriots to advance the struggle against the white minority regime, and gained immense popularity. Inevitably this attracted the attention of the state, its security agencies, and its censoring mechanisms.

Mapfumo started out as a struggling musician in Rhodesia after UDI playing local versions of American rock and roll and Zairian rumba. He became a professional musician in 1973, and soon his music started to shift in the direction of indigenous rhythms and forms. The contemporary political and cultural context helped create the space for this move. Internationally, interest was growing in "Third World" music, and successful African groups like Osibisa led the way in demonstrating the viability and potential of new Afro-fusion forms. More importantly, however, the intensification of the nationalist political struggle inside Rhodesia in the mid 1970s gave rise to new opportunities for artistic and cultural expression. Mapfumo and his band began experimenting with more traditional Shona musical forms – reinterpreting old songs, often imitating the sound of the traditional "mbira" or "finger piano" with distinctive guitar picking – while injecting nationalist politics into their lyrics.

Mapfumo's first "traditional" releases were *Ngoma Yarira* and *Murembo* in 1973. The latter record, whose underlying theme was one of commitment and sacrifice, had an immediate impact on the local music scene and proved influential in the development of what would become known as *Chimurenga* music. It also received a direct and rapid response from the Rhodesian authorities, who, deeming the song subversive, banned its broadcast on the state-owned radio monopoly, the Rhodesia Broadcasting Corporation (RBC). *Murembo* set the tone for the Rhodesian regime's future relations with *Chimurenga* musicians. Over the years, many of Mapfumo's releases were banned by the Rhodesian Board of Censors and denied airplay on RBC.

However, musicians responded to increasing pressure from the state with ingenuity. As Mapfumo would later recount, his songs supporting the guerrilla fighters and nationalists were couched in metaphorical terms in order to avoid a complete clampdown by the government: "I couldn't do it direct; I had to sort of go at it vaguely and conceal what I was trying to say. But our own people understood the language that the whites didn't understand, and that was an advantage."

By 1976 Mapfumo's music – mainly within the emerging *Chimurenga* genre – was increasingly popular. His hit satire on the bravado of the Smith regime, *Pamuromo Chete* (Mere Big Mouth), was followed by the landmark 1977 album, *Hokoyo!* (Watch Out!). *Hokoyo!* was a major commercial, artistic, and political success, and along with *Tozvireva Kupiko?* (Where Shall We Tell It?) and *Pfumvu Paruzeva* (Trouble in the Rural Areas), established Mapfumo as both a leading struggle singer and a target of the Rhodesian authorities.

Most of Mapfumo's more strident lyrical assaults on the minority rule regime were not released to the RBC, on which they stood no chance of being broadcast. Instead they found their way onto the airwaves by means of ZANU-PF's Voice of Zimbabwe (VOZ) station, based in Maputo, Mozambique. Each evening the VOZ broadcast across the border, carrying programmes which included political speeches, commentary, news, and music. The *Chimurenga Requests* programme became a popular favourite, and Thomas Mapfumo's records were one of its major attractions. Inside Rhodesia, Mapfumo's records were often distributed directly to record stores and bars, thereby maximizing their chances of avoiding banning orders from the state. Most observers consider his best work to have come from this period (roughly 1976–80), during which he often recorded using poor quality equipment and distributed through direct-to-market methods.

Mapfumo was unable to escape the attentions of the security police. The police demanded that subversive songs should not be recorded or released by his record company, Teal Recording. "The one they really didn't like was *Tumira Vana Kuhondo* (Send Your Children to War)", recalled a Teal Recording company executive, adding that he despatched security officials by arguing that the tune was "an old (Rhodesian) military marching song". In *Tumira Vana Kuhondo* Mapfumo exhorted parents to support the struggle: "Children to war, children to war. Fathers, mothers, send your children to war, We are all sending out children to war. We may be eliminated, but our children are fighting; This year we send our children to war."

Unable to prevent the distribution or external broadcasting of Mapfumo's incantations for the intensification of the *Chimurenga*, the Rhodesian security police moved to directly silence the singer in 1977. He was detained by the Special Branch for one month without charge, accused only of being "the *Chimurenga* singer". When confronted with being a composer and singer of *Chimurenga* songs, Mapfumo pleaded ignorance and asserted that his music was merely "traditional African". Though record company officials, musicians, and human rights activists attempted to intervene to secure his release, their pleas fell on deaf ears. When Mapfumo was finally released, it was on condition that he perform at a rally for bishop Abel Muzorewa, one of Ian Smith's "Internal Settlement" political partners. But the singer used his enforced participation in the event to strike back once again. "At the rally we deliberately played all the songs on my banned album to see what the government would do next. But nothing happened."

Mapfumo's role in the liberation war was later recognized when he and his band, the Blacks Unlimited (formed 1978), were invited to play at the ZANU-PF rally welcoming future head of state Robert Mugabe back to the country, in January 1980. Mapfumo continued to compose songs about African liberation in the 1980s, commenting on struggles against colonialism and terror in Namibia, South Africa, and Mozambique. At the same

time he developed an international following, and occasionally recorded overseas.

He did not lose contact with his own country, though, and in the late 1980s came to address emerging problems in Zimbabwe. Once again this led him into conflict with the state. His 1989 hit single *Corruption* was recorded soon after revelations emerged of a high-level scandal that saw a number of ruling party politicians leave their government jobs in disgrace. Mapfumo observed at the time, "We've read a lot about corruption in our country. People have been afraid to point out the mistakes made by the chiefs, but that is changing and the new openness we see now is healthy. I wanted to contribute to that openness so I pushed the song forward at the peak of the controversial goings on" (*The Sunday News*, 12 March 1989). The ZBC – the successor to the RBC – was less open-minded. The song was swiftly removed from the station's playlist.

In the 1990s Mapfumo has continued to provide critical social commentary through his music, and he remains a core fixture of the Zimbabwean recording and live music scene. Recent work continues to explore fusions of traditional African, choral, jazz, and pop forms, while the deepening poverty which is now being experienced under structural adjustment economic reforms in Zimbabwe has become a recurring theme in his lyrics.

RICHARD SAUNDERS

Recordings

Ngoma Yarira, 1973
Murembo, 1973
Pamuromo Chete, 1976
Hokoyo!, 1977
Mr Music Africa, 1985
Chimurenga for Justice, 1986
Zimbabwe–Mozambique, 1987
Varombo Kuvarombo, 1988
Chamunorwa, 1989
Corruption, 1989
The Chimurenga Singles, 1976–1980, 1989
Hondo, 1993
Vanhu Vatema, 1994
The Best of Thomas Mapfumo, 1995

Further Reading

Frederikse, Julie, *None but Ourselves: Masses vs. Media in the Making of Zimbabwe*, Harare: Zimbabwe Publishing House, and London: Heinemann, and New York: Penguin, 1982
Pongweni, Alec J.C., *Songs That Won the Liberation War*, Harare: College Press, 1982
Zindi, Fred, *Roots Rocking in Zimbabwe*, Gweru, Zimbabwe: Mambo Press, 1985; as *Music YeZimbabwe. Zimbabwe versus the World*, Harare: Zindi and Chirumiko, 1997

ROBERT MAPPLETHORPE
US photographer, 1947–1989

Not knowing that seven of his photographs were about to become the main topic of a prosecution by a coalition of right-wing Christians and politicians, Robert Mapplethorpe died of AIDS approximately 100 days before the Corcoran Gallery of Art, in Washington, DC, cancelled an exhibition of his pictures, *The Perfect Moment*, in July 1989. This show of 175 photographs had originally been organized by Janet Kardon when she was director of the Institute of Contemporary Art in Philadelphia, and had then been mounted, successfully, at the University of Pennsylvania (December 1988) and the Chicago Museum of Contemporary Art (February 1989). The photographs that led to the arrest on 7 April 1990 of the director of the Cincinnati Arts Center, Dennis Barrie, had been publicly displayed in museums, galleries, and books before they were brought to court in Ohio in September 1990.

Mapplethorpe had first become known for his photographic representations of sadomasochism and homoeroticism in New York and San Francisco during the late 1970s. Working in New York, he had also photographed flowers and nude black men, which had been featured in the exhibition *Black Holes* in Amsterdam in 1980. Of the works produced in this period, Edward Lucie-Smith writes:

> The fact that the male nude now invoked a much more powerful taboo than the female one was realized and cannily exploited by Mapplethorpe . . . the black body, his photographs consistently tell us, is interesting for the shape it makes, for the way the light falls upon black skin, for the sexuality it exudes, rather than for the personality which inhabits it. He conquered the liberal establishment by flouting some of its most cherished conventions.

An exhibition of some of Mapplethorpe's pictures, described by a hostile critic, Hilton Kramer, as "tamer", had been held at the Whitney Museum of American Art in New York in 1988. At that stage, Kramer, writing in the *New York Times*, had confined himself to an attack on what he regarded as Mapplethorpe's imposition on the public of photography "designed to aggrandize and abet erotic rituals, involving coercion, degradation, bloodshed, and the infliction of pain". *The Perfect Moment*, a full-scale posthumous retrospective, was to cause much louder reverberations.

In March 1989 the Reverend Donald Wildmon of the American Family Association (AFA) had seen a museum catalogue featuring Andres Serrano's *Piss Christ*, a representation of the Crucifixion, the central icon of Christian belief, immersed in yellow liquid that was apparently Serrano's own urine. Senator Jesse Helms of South Carolina had denounced on the Senate floor a grant of $15,000 made by the National Endowment for the Arts (NEA) for a group installation that included *Piss Christ*, housed at the South Eastern Center for Contemporary Art (SECCA) at Winston Salem, North Carolina. *The Perfect Moment* was caught up in what had already become a national row on arts funding.

Also at play, arguably, was the traditional antipathy of American puritans towards the iconography and art of Catholicism: the loathing of anything that suggests idolatry has always been present in that tradition. Although Mapplethorpe was non-practising, he was a lifelong Catholic, greatly influenced, like his intimate peer Andy Warhol, by western religious sculpture and painting. Mapplethorpe's photographs – designed, he said, as "little altars" – can be seen to be related, in matter and form, to the doctrines of the incarnation (his faces), transubstantiation (his flowers), and martyrdom (his figures), and to such expressions of Christian belief as mysticism (his fetishes) and ritual (his formalism).

On 12 June 1989, Christina Ohr-Cahill, director of the Corcoran Gallery of Art, claimed that the Serrano case had made the $30,000 funding of the first posthumous Mapplethorpe exhibition a political issue. Wishing to protect the Corcoran's financial position, she decided to cancel *The Perfect Moment*, arguing that "I don't think there was censorship at all . . . the exhibition has been seen elsewhere and will be seen elsewhere. I think censorship would have been editing the show."

MAPPLETHORPE: *Man in Polyester Suit*, photograph, 1980. Mapplethorpe's photographs of black men, often nude studies or explicit depictions of homosexual activity, became the focus of protest by conservative antipornography organizations, culminating in 1990 in the trial of the director of the Cincinnati Contemporary Art Center, where Mapplethorpe's works were being exhibited. Copyright © The Estate of Robert Mapplethorpe. Used by permission.

A "culture war" ensued. On the night that *The Perfect Moment* was cancelled, members of the Washington arts community projected some of Mapplethorpe's most explicit photographs, including self-portraits, to billboard size on an outside wall of the Corcoran. The exhibition was then accepted by the Washington Project for the Arts, provocatively located near Capitol Hill and the office of Senator Helms. Meanwhile, the conservative television talk-show host Pat Buchanan was equating the new culture war with the Cold War (the Berlin Wall had come down that autumn): there was, he implied, a new "enemy within".

The Perfect Moment moved next – and without incident – to Hartford, Connecticut, to Berkeley, California, and eventually to the Contemporary Art Center (CAC) in Cincinnati, Ohio, the home of the National Coalition against Pornography and of Citizens for Community Values. These two organizations quickly went to work with mass mailings of the photographs and threatening telephone calls to the arts centre. They failed, however, to dislodge the CAC, whose only concession was to post warnings about the nature of the imagery and to decline entry to people under 18. The show opened on 7 April 1990, with members of the Hamilton County grand jury among its first visitors.

The grand jury selected the seven photographs that would form the basis of a prosecution against the CAC and its director, Dennis Barrie, who were charged with "pandering" obscene images and using a minor in nude materials. The photographs in question were a portrait of a boy nude (*Jesse McBride*, 1976); a portrait of a girl with her genitals exposed (*Honey*, 1976); and five photographs typical of Mapplethorpe's homoerotic or sadomasochistic images of the late 1970s: his signature self-portrait with a whip inserted in his anus (*Self Portrait*, 1978); a duo of a man urinating into another man's mouth (*Jim, Sausalito*, 1978); a fisting shot of a man's arm inserted in another man's rectum; a close-up of a man with a finger inserted into the head of his penis; and a shot of a man with a cylinder inserted in his rectum. While the case was being prepared, the show completed its Cincinnati run and moved on to Boston.

The defence case for *The Perfect Moment* was formidable. Janet Kardon and Jacqueline Baas, arts academics and curators, testified to the quality of the photographs as art, and some 50 other museum curators signalled their agreement. Moreover, the parents of the children whose photographs had been taken all confirmed that they had given permission for this to take place and regarded Mapplethorpe's intentions as innocent. Only one witness was called for the prosecution, Dr Judith Reisman, a former researcher for the AFA, who claimed that the photographs were an apology for child abuse. The defence arguments carried the day, and both the CAC and Barrie were acquitted.

In Boston, meanwhile, the First Amendment Common Sense Alliance, a newly formed coalition, had failed to persuade the authorities to take any legal action against *The Perfect Moment*. Donald Wildmon also failed in his attempt to have WGBH, the Boston-based television station that forms part of the Public Broadcasting Service, disciplined, after photographs from the exhibition had been shown in a news programme broadcast at 10 p.m. The pressure group Queer Nation demonstrated against homophobia and the exhibition went ahead without further incident.

Politically, however, the issue of funding of allegedly obscene material was far from dead. Senator Helms introduced a provision prohibiting the NEA from funding "depictions of sadomasochism, homeroticism, the sexual exploitation of children, or individuals engaged in sex acts". Even when this was found legally faulty, John Fromayer, who had been appointed chairman of the NEA by President George Bush, tried to get potential recipients of grants to sign a "pledge" that they would not feature this kind of material. This too was found unworkable, and the culture war dragged on.

Meanwhile, Robert Mapplethorpe's many books of photography, as well as books written about him, continue to be published and republished, despite censorship carried out privately in bookshops and libraries. In 1998, the vice-chancellor of the University of Birmingham in England had to face down local police who wished to prosecute the university over the presence of one of these books in its library. Photographs by Mapplethorpe are now to be found in the permanent collections of more than 30 major museums around the world.

JACK FRITSCHER

Books of Photographs and Exhibition Catalogues

Robert Mapplethorpe Photographs, text by Mario Amaya, 1978
Fotografie, edited by Germano Celant, 1983
Lady: Lisa Lyon, text by Bruce Chatwin, 1983
Robert Mapplethorpe, 1970–1983, text by Sandy Nairne *et al.*, 1983
Certain People: A Book of Portraits, text by Susan Sontag, 1985
Black Book, text by Ntozake Shange, 1986
The Power of Theatrical Madness, text by Jan Fabre, 1986
Robert Mapplethorpe: The Perfect Moment, text by Janet Kardon, 1988
Mapplethorpe Portraits, 1975–87, text by Peter Conrad, 1988
Some Women, text by Joan Didion, 1989
Flowers, text by Patti Smith, 1990
Early Works, 1970–1974, edited by John Cheim, 1991
Mapplethorpe (catalogue of exhibition held at Louisiana Museum of Modern Art, Humlebaek, Denmark and elsewhere), text by Germano Celant, 1992; translated by Joachim Neugroschel, 1996 (for exhibition at Hayward Gallery, London: three images removed)
Mapplethorpe, text by Arthur C. Danto, 1992
Altars, text by Edmund White, 1995
Pistils, text by John Ashbery, 1996
Mapplethorpe: The Catalogue Rainonné (disk), 1996 (abridged version as *Robert Mapplethorpe: An Overview*, 1995)
Pictures, edited by Dimitri Levas, 1999

Further Reading

Adams, Laurie, *Art on Trial: From Whistler to Rothko*, New York: Walker, 1976
Bolton, Richard, *Culture Wars: Documents from the Recent Controversies in the Arts*, New York: New Press, 1992
Chernoff, Maxine and Paul Hoover, *Censorship and the Arts: New American Writing*, Chicago: OINK! Press, 1989
Danto, Arthur C., *Playing with the Edge: The Photographic Achievement of Robert Mapplethorpe*, Berkeley: University of California Press, 1996
Dubin, Steven C., *Arresting Images: Impolitic Art and Uncivil Actions*, London and New York: Routledge, 1992
Dubin, Steven C., "The Trials of Robert Mapplethorpe" in *Suspended License: Censorship and the Visual Arts*, edited by Elizabeth C. Childs, Seattle: University of Washington Press, 1997
Fritscher, Jack, "Caro Roberto" in *Corporal in Charge and Other Stories*, San Francisco: Gay Sunshine Press, 1984

Fritscher, Jack, *Mapplethorpe: Assault with a Deadly Camera: A Pop Culture Memoir, An Outlaw Reminiscence*, Mamaroneck, New York: Hastings House, 1994

Heins, Marjorie, *Sex, Sin, and Blasphemy: A Guide to America's Censorship Wars*, New York: New Press, 1993

Lucie-Smith, Edward, *Sexuality in Western Art*, revised edition, London and New York: Thames and Hudson, 1991

Paglia, Camille, *Vamps and Tramps: New Essays*, New York: Vintage, 1994; London: Viking, 1995

Philanthropy and the Arts after Mapplethorpe: The Standards for Private Funders, New York: Institute for Educational Affairs, 1990

Smith, Patti, *Robert Mapplethorpe*, New York: Bellport Press, 1987

MAPS

Cartographic censorship involves the deliberate removal, omission, or inclusion of map features in order to divert the reader's attention and accretion of information. Mapping is a fundamental way of representing spatial knowledge and location. As such, the control of cartographic input has long been used as a highly effective visual means to direct knowledge and ultimately to project power relations. Today's increasing emphasis on visual mass media and graphic imagery has heightened the importance of cartography to project political, social, and consumer information across societies.

In essence, mapping is a form of spatial censorship. The cartographer and map-user share an assumed cultural understanding from which to interpret the graphics, but, in most cases, the latter perceives the map to be a realistic representation of space or territory. Herein lies the power of cartography to direct and focus knowledge. Map-users generally trust maps, establishing fertile ground for visual propaganda, whether it be for political, military, social, or business purposes. Information may be suppressed, exaggerated, contradicted, or reactions provoked according to the purpose of the map and the scale, symbols, or colours used. The London Underground Journey Planner, for example, designed by Harry Beck in 1931, deliberately manipulates physical distance in order to represent a connected, commutable urban sphere. Suburbs and city merge on a colourful, visually direct map that substitutes direction and distance for readability and reference.

A town map delineates spatial variance in terms of street or land-use patterns, but tells the map-user little about the inhabitants and their socioeconomic reality or living conditions. A singular road or bypass is represented by a line, but beyond that image may lie an untold local history of personal and political upheaval, contested plans, and active dispute. In this way, maps de-socialize space. Town plans present the living space of anonymized denizens, and vast tracts of territory marked by state boundaries suggest an uncontested and uniform social space. Populations have been "colonized" on paper by the will of the colonial politician and the quill of the cartographer. The pen may indeed be mightier than the sword. The concept of *terra nullius* was formerly used by colonial powers to lay claim to vast tracts of land in North America, Australia, and Africa. Maps were drawn to emphasize these claims over the "discovered" territories which were presumed legitimate conquests, ignoring the existence or the existing territorial claims of indigenous populations. Colonial place names have frequently brushed aside indigenous or existing nomenclature in order to impose a new sense of belonging. Not only names, but conceptions of space and map-forms themselves vary greatly across societies and lead to diverse cartographic

interpretations. The sand drawings of Aboriginal groups in Australia illustrate not only the terrain, but also the history of the land according to ancestral dreamings. The principal issues of cartographic representation are therefore scale, orientation, symbolism, and purpose.

By its nature, cartography must be selective in what it represents. Maps are thus always value-laden. Selective representation, the inherent censorship of certain mappable features, challenges the notions of mathematical and cartographic objectivity which the reader expects or assumes to be true in most cases. Landsat images derived by remote sensing from orbiting satellites may appear to be actual photographs of the earth, but they are selective maps that register different wavelengths of electromagnetic radiation, decipherable only by the accompanying text or indices.

Mapping distortions may be deliberate or unconscious "noise". Medieval maps designed in Europe portrayed the Mediterranean region as the "navel of the world", incorporating images that were formed, and in effect censored, through contemporary religious ideological filters and orthodox representational hierarchies. The belief by certain peoples that they themselves were situated at the centre of the universe, the so-called omphalos syndrome, similarly influenced the earlier maps of Mesopotamia which centred on Babylon, and Greek maps with Delphi as the central location. Cartography delineated a psycho-physiological approach to spatial representation, where the external, the territory that lay beyond mapped boundaries, was deemed mysterious and heathen.

The European Renaissance heralded a far-reaching reconceptualization and cartographic reconstruction of space. Mercator's projection of the earth, devised in the late 16th century to aid navigators in their task by following true compass directions, reshaped visions of the world, but within a framework in which two-thirds of the land mass appears in the high latitudes. During the early 1970s, as an attempt to modify this bias, Peters popularized an equal-area map projection that was adopted by Unesco and various international development agencies. While the latter removes the exaggerated land mass of the northern hemisphere, it achieves a real fidelity at the expense of demographic representation. The publication of the *State of the World Atlas* in 1981 has been seminal in socializing representations of the contemporary world space. The selective use of symbols and colour projects a humanistic orientation on cartographic illustration.

Cartography can produce emotive images that may carry political messages. Map propaganda involves the deliberate use of cartography to portray a biased, and usually incorrect, image of space or territorial possession. Map-making, as J.B. Harley outlines, can become a specialized intellectual weapon to gain, administer, or legitimize power. A succession of caliphs and sultans of the Ottoman empire and Mogul emperors in India were careful to patronize cartographic practice as a means of knowledge production and power brokerage. In more recent times, Nazi maps produced during the late 1930s and early 1940s aimed to show that Germany was more the victim of Allied aggression than the aggressor itself. A series of maps, issued by the German Library of Information in New York through the journal *Facts in Review*, depicted an isolated Germany surrounded by hostile countries with a history of empire-building. The purpose of the periodical was to encourage the then non-aligned US not to enter the war. Contemporary maps have used cartographic symbols to illustrate the threat of a global nuclear war. Suggested zones of destruction and the size of competing nuclear arsenals depict the threat of annihilation in an emotive and challenging visual manner.

Perhaps military matters have provoked the keenest use of map censorship. During periods of actual or potential conflict the publication of accurate land surveys is often restricted or false maps deliberately produced to confuse enemies. Soviet maps produced during the Cold War projected incorrect settlement patterns, and the US Geological Survey still makes limited reference to nuclear waste sites or certain military installations due to the sensitive nature of the subject matter.

The visual images of cartography clearly shape our mental maps or social imaginary in a direct manner through delineated areas of territorial control, with aggressive arrows of military advance, or through the more subtle use of symbolism. For example, the British maps of South Africa before the Boer War were printed in two colours on a white background – the red roads and blue rivers crisscrossed the British colony, guilefully imitating the patterns and colours of the Union Jack.

During the last two decades, Geographical Information Systems (GIS) have revolutionized the concept of mapping by creating a new electronic space for cartographic imagery and projection. The power of the map is increasingly apparent in the scramble for representation on the Internet. The pages of the World Wide Web provide infinite access to an increasingly global electronic map of visual graphics whereby the cartographer's pen is now a "mouse" with which millions of users can themselves direct others and follow predetermined routes of information. The constantly changing map of the Internet, its longevity and ease of modification compared with paper maps, make the electronic media an increasingly contested space for the production, control, and censorship of knowledge.

DAVID HOWARD

Further Reading

Black, Jeremy, *Maps and Politics*, London: Reaktion, and Chicago: University of Chicago Press, 1997

Bunge, William, *The Nuclear War Atlas*, Oxford and New York: Blackwell, 1988

Dorling, Daniel and David Fairbairn, *Mapping: Ways of Representing the World*, London: Longman, 1997

Gilbert, Martin, *Atlas of the Holocaust*, London: Joseph, 1982; revised edition, Oxford and New York: Pergamon Press, 1988

Harley, J.B., "Maps, Knowledge and Power" in *The Iconography of Landscape: Essays on the Symbolic Representation, Design, and Use of Past Environments*, edited by Denis Cosgrove and Stephen Daniels, Cambridge and New York: Cambridge University Press, 1988

Kidron, Michael and Ronald Segal, *The State of the World Atlas*, London: Heinemann, and New York: Simon and Schuster, 1981

Kidron, Michael and Dan Smith, *The War Atlas: Armed Conflict – Armed Peace*, London: Heinemann, and New York: Simon and Schuster, 1983

Monmonier, Mark, *How to Lie with Maps*, Chicago: University of Chicago Press, 1991

CHRIS MARKER
French film director, 1921–

Chris Marker's numerous documentary films are characterized by their socialist leanings, their innovative visual and narrative styles, and their expression of Marker's concern for the human condition. Born Christian François Bouche-Villeneuve ("Chris Marker" being only the best-known of several pseudonyms he has used), Marker came from a relatively privileged background. However, like his former schoolmate Simone Signoret and their former teacher Jean-Paul Sartre, he developed leftist opinions during World War II, when he was a resistance fighter, and in the early postwar years, when he tried his hand at being a novelist, poet, and essayist. He turned to films, initially writing scripts for short documentaries, in the late 1940s. His Marxist sympathies have greatly influenced his choices of subject matter and location, which have included China, Cuba, North Korea, and Siberia, although he has also made less explicitly political films about Paris, Tokyo, and other major cities. He has maintained his interest in places where life is (as he has put it) in the process of "becoming history", but his obvious support for the "socialist" societies that have emerged in some of the nations he has studied has sometimes laid him open to the charge of being a propagandist for the governments of such societies.

Until the 1960s and even beyond, many in Marker's own country, France, were acutely sensitive to criticism of its colonial policy, believing that the export of the French language and culture was humane and civilized, and therefore in the colonies' best interests. Marker's second film as a director, *Les Statues meurent aussi* (1953, Statues Also Die), which he co-wrote and co-directed with Alain Resnais, presented an entirely opposite perspective. It is a study of African art and its decline under colonialism. The film suggests that such art had once made possible what he calls (in the film's narration) "a harmony between the world and man", which was being destroyed by colonialist impositions. The film was banned for 10 years and then released only in a severely cut version.

The footage for what is probably Marker's single most controversial film, *Cuba si!* (1961, Cuba, Yes), was shot in 1960 and early 1961, during and after the celebration of the second anniversary of the Cuban Revolution. The film is structurally divided into two parts: Marker's Cuba and Fidel Castro's Cuba.

The first shows Marker as less a documentarist or historian than a tourist, sending his thoughts and impressions to people back home. He displays the everyday details of existence: a parade, going to work, observing the death of a child, going to the shops. In the second half he deliberately abandons this style; it is as if the camera suddenly retreats, leaving the stage open for the Cuban president. Castro is allowed to put his own case without editorial interference. The Catholic Church's claim that he is a dictator is answered by archive footage of the Spanish dictator Francisco Franco, surrounded by cardinals. In a postscript Marker celebrates the defeat of the US-backed invaders at the hands of Cuban forces at the Bay of Pigs on 15 April 1961.

On 31 July 1961 the French Commission de contrôle des films cinématographiques agreed to ban *Cuba si!*, by a vote of five to three, with six abstentions. Those who voted for the ban took the view that the film was a naked apologia for Castro's regime:

> Certainly everything that is recalled or reported concerning the previous regime conforms to historical truth, but the change from an extreme right-wing totalitarian system to an extreme left-wing totalitarian system has not prevented any new excesses or deprivations of liberty, which the film in question in no way reports.

The majority's opinion was stiffened by the observation that the Cuban government had given its full collaboration and support – rare indeed in any communist country – allowing Marker access to a remarkably wide range of subjects. The film's anti-American postcript was judged to be particularly inappropriate. Finally, the commission returned to the French establishment's traditional readiness to defend its colonial policy. Martinique and Guadeloupe are on Cuba's doorstep, and the press in both these territories was showing, it was thought, an inordinate interest in the activities of Castro's regime. The commission was determined not to give the Cuban leaders another public forum for their opposition to the maintenance of colonies anywhere in the western hemisphere. (The two islands remain parts of France to this day.)

The effect of the commission's judgement was to ban the film abroad as well as in France. Marker responded with a series of clandestine showings for foreign journalists and critics, in and around Paris. He also published the first of his volumes of *Commentaires* (1961, Commentaries), which includes the text of the commentary accompanying *Cuba si!*, a selection of stills, and the texts of the narrative tracks of his six earlier documentaries, together with copies of his correspondence with the Ministry of Information pertaining to bans on his films.

Later in the 1960s clandestine screenings and the circulation of illicit prints caused the film to be seen and reviewed in Germany, Scandinavia, and, ultimately, Britain (in 1969). It has never been publicly screened in the United States, where uneasiness about the presence of Cuba so near to its southern edge has hardly lessened since the general demise of Communism at the beginning of the 1990s.

In 1967 Marker organized the making of *Loin du Vietnam* (Far from Vietnam), a film composed of episodes directed by himself, Resnais, Jean-Luc Godard, Agnes Varda, Joris Ivens, and others, which attacked US policy on Vietnam and was in turn attacked by supporters of that policy. However, the fact that calls for it to be banned went unheeded in France was perhaps an indication that, even in relation to a country that had been a French colony until only 13 years before, opinion was becoming less hostile to radical critics such as Marker and his colleagues. Alternatively, it may have been an indication that denouncing the US government was more acceptable in France than denouncing the French government.

SANDRA GARCIA-MYERS

Films

Les Statues meurent aussi, 1953
Cuba si!, 1961
Loin du Vietnam, with others, 1967

Writings

Commentaires, 2 vols, 1961–67

Further Reading

Cameron, Ian, "Cuba Si! Censor No!", *Movie*, 3 (October 1962): 14–21
"Cuba si", *Monthly Film Bulletin*, 36 (May 1969)
Van Wert, William F., "Chris Marker: the SLON Films", *Film Quarterly*, 32/3 (Spring 1979): 38–46

MARKET CENSORSHIP

Market censorship refers to a broad class of economically driven constraints or interdictions on the cultural production of ideas and creative works that shape what can be said, written, published, distributed, broadcast, or communicated in visual form. It encompasses both overt actions by cultural producers and the systematic effects of production practices that subordinate content to commercial considerations. The term amends and extends Adam Smith's classic metaphor by suggesting that "the invisible hand of the market" is as pro-active as the visible hands of church or state censors. By virtue of its invisibility and its capacity to operate automatically, market censorship is, however, more efficient and insidious than other forms of censorship.

Market censorship includes the direct interventions by the private owners of the organs of cultural expression or their agents that suppress, expurgate, or "spin" aural or visual messages. The most common and pervasive forms of intervention occur as a result of the media's dependency on advertising. In the United States, about two-thirds of the revenues of newspapers and magazines come from advertising, while broadcasting is almost entirely dependent upon advertising for its profits. Media that serve local markets, newspapers, and local broadcast news are especially vulnerable to such interventions. For example, automobile dealers are major advertisers in local media markets. Some local newspapers and television news organizations that have undertaken investigative reports of the unethical practices of car dealers have had their stories suppressed by management. Where the stories have been allowed to run, the reporters and producers responsible have sometimes been reassigned or dismissed. Experienced journalists learn not to waste time or take career risks by pursuing such stories.

Self-censorship of this kind frequently becomes a routine procedure in the organizational practices of the commercial media, where it functions automatically and largely invisibly as "business-as-usual". Standard conventions for framing news stories filter out stories that cause "flak" for journalists and thereby interfere with the efficiency of news organizations.

The category of overt market censorship encompasses self-censorship by writers and artists who fear that their work will not be published, exhibited, or distributed. For example, long before the advent of modern economies of scale in publishing and marketing, the American writer Herman Melville complained: "Dollars damn me . . . What I feel most moved to write, that is banned, it will not pay."

Under the constraints of commercial pressures, self-censorship frequently becomes a natural and normal practice. Individual writers and artists internalize market imperatives and produce what they think will sell; and commercial media organizations coordinate their production practices in order to maximize their financial returns. What is not considered to be marketable is not produced.

Many routine business practices are constituents of market censorship when they operate in the area of cultural production. For example, economies of scale may preclude the production of specialized or esoteric forms of knowledge or other cultural products unless the production costs are subsidized by cultural workers, producers, or public or private grants.

Economies of scale in the mass media also affect the production of cultural products for young children. Pre-school children constitute a small percentage of the population and they do not directly control consumer purchasing decisions. Consequently they are not a profitable market for commercial television broadcasting. In the United States the main commercial television networks have produced very little television programming for children.

Economies of scale may reinforce psychologies of dominance and submission. For example, broadcasters know that girls will watch children's programmes in which male figures play all or most of the major roles, but boys will not watch programmes that feature female characters. To increase the size of this already proportionally small audience, programmers will develop shows in which male characters significantly outnumber female ones. The same logic applies in much adult prime-time broadcasting. The newer technologies that facilitate narrow-casting, for example, cable, pay-per-view, and the Internet-based communications, are alleviating some of these pressures for economies of scale and making way for programming that is more age and gender specific, or featuring minority and non-dominant languages. Nevertheless commercially driven alternative or target-marketed programming is as tightly bound to the systematic constraints of the economic bottom line as broadcast media.

The cross-ownership patterns of the big conglomerates can facilitate the control of supplies or the pricing of essential resources, such as paper for print media and access to spectrum or band-width in broadcasting. Suppliers of paper, ink, and other manufacturing materials that give discounts on large orders favour large producers, and in some culture industries such as publishing this may force small producers who serve specialized or minority markets out of business.

In the book trade, distributor discounts favour retailing chains over small independent bookshops. Distributor discounts exert pressure for the production of trade books over academic books, for blockbusters over modest runs, and for books by writers with recognized names (even if ghost-written) over works by talented but unknown authors. The huge advances given by the publishing industry for books by newsmakers are compensated for by cost-cutting measures in other areas of a publishing operation. These advances, for example $6.5 million to General Colin Powell, the former US military chief, $5 million to General Norman Schwartzkopf, director of the 1989 war against Iraq, $4.2 and $3 million for the leading attorneys in the footballer O.J. Simpson's murder trial, also exert pressure to keep the news stories that precipitated the advances on the public agenda. Chain distribution diminishes the "shelf-life" of books; rapid turnover of stock maximizes shop profits.

In the film and television industries, the profitability of residual rights through syndication and increasingly through global marketing encourages formulaic productions that will succeed in export markets. That is, they favour homogeneous, action-based plots that are easy to translate into other languages and culture-contexts. This encourages investment in formulaic scripts featuring stock characters and high levels of violence and sex. As a result, fewer scripts with complex plots and nuanced character development are produced by the major film and television studios.

Lawsuits or threats of protracted and costly litigation by big businesses have a chilling effect on media organizations, especially the producers of news and documentaries. Investigative reports, even when demonstrably true, are subject to this kind of litigation. In the United States, for example, two of the main commercial television networks, the American Broadcasting Company (ABC) and the Columbia Broadcasting Company (CBS), experienced substantial legal pressures to soften or cancel stories about the tobacco industry in 1995. Even scientific researchers increasingly face pressure, including attacks on their professional reputations, from patent advocacy groups and drug companies that have vested financial interests in suppressing their findings.

Corporations, like governments, sometimes wage active disinformation and propaganda campaigns. Censorship by corporations and industry-wide associations seeks to shape public opinion and influence news coverage by structuring information strategically and first testing the potential responses to it in focus groups. In recent years, for example, major corporations have employed the public relations firm Hill and Knowlton to develop pro-China campaigns in an effort to influence the American public and to pressurize Congress into renewing China's trade status as "most favoured nation". The tobacco industry has a long and widely documented history of both suppressing and actively misrepresenting information about the health risks of smoking.

Copyrights and patents are, technically, forms of market censorship. They protect the capital investments of the producers of cultural products, including authors, artists, and performers as well as the patrons, sponsors, manufacturers, and share-holders. Workers in cultural fields often complain about the specific terms of their arrangements with their publishers, exhibitors, or distributors; but few could afford to write or create without copyright constraints on the reproduction or circulation of their products.

In an absolute sense, piracy allows for a freer flow of ideas than the protected markets of advanced capitalism. Non-copyrighted forms of expression, materials in the public domain, and share-ware are therefore, in theory, freer from market censorship than the cultural products actively stocked by the cultural industries. Some constraints on the free exchange of cultural products were built into the founding assumptions of the legal reasoning that secures freedom of expression in liberal societies.

The term "market censorship" is of recent origin, coined around 1980, but the practice is as old as capitalism. The term has wider currency in critical media discourses in the United States than in other countries because there the practice is more ubiquitous and intractable. In addition to the enormous size and global reach of the American media industry, two other important factors contribute to the pervasiveness of the practice there.

First, in the United States, the ideology, if not always the reality, of the separation of the powers of government and of press is almost as sacrosanct as the American constitutional commitment to the separation of church and state. The First Amendment to the constitution formalized this separation, and prohibited Congress from making any laws that might curtail the freedom of the press. Although Congress does have an oversight capacity in broadcasting, the United States is the only major industrial nation that has relied completely on private, commercial interests to develop and manage its broadcasting industry. Consequently, press and broadcast organizations have traditionally exercised extraordinary power in the country. Some media critics have compared the cultural power of American television to the power of religion in medieval Europe. In the United States this cultural power has been exercised with considerable autonomy. The regulatory agency established by Congress in 1934, the Federal Communication Commission, has generally served the interests of the industry; and the industry has often served as a training ground for future regulators.

Second, in the United States, the deregulation and privatization initiatives of the Reagan–Bush era have proved to be particularly fortunate for the media and telecommunications industries. The omnibus Telecommunications Bill of 1996 was written at the behest of long-distance telephone companies, the local telephone carriers, and the cable television industry. These interests funded multi-million dollar lobbying and advertising campaigns to promote the passage of the legislation, while at the same time pouring several million dollars into political contributions to both the Democrats and Republicans to keep the bill moving through Congress. Conversely, some media outlets, for example Cable Network News (CNN), refused to carry advertisements by public advocacy groups against the bill. The legislation dismantled the long-standing regulatory principle that had separated control of the conduits from the contents of electronic media. It allowed telecommunications, cable, and broadcasting interests to diversify their holdings and it lifted many restrictions on cross-ownership of media in local markets.

The United States is the leading force in the current globalization of the marketplace, and cultural products are among its leading exports. The deregulation and privatization of the media are, however, now global processes. As a result, market censorship is becoming a worldwide experience. Governments of weaker states are unlikely to possess either the resources or the will to regulate large global corporations that operate without borders and recognize no government as sovereign.

Even in an era when media industries are dominated by huge global corporate conglomerates, however, market self-censorship does not control or suppress all the messages that challenge the authority, interests, or profits of media moguls. Ralph Miliband's distinction between democratic and elite pluralism is useful in describing the slippage within the system. He maintains that elite pluralism has replaced democratic pluralism but that competition among elites still permits some openings in the system of corporate control. Elite pluralism does, however, result in the formation of a dominant economic class, which has a high degree of cohesion and common interests and goals that greatly outweigh their competitive differences. The slippage created by competition among elites appears to be more volatile in the post-Fordian economy than it was under the Cold War economic conditions that Miliband analysed. This volatility creates greater risks for elites and greater pressure on opportunities for market censorship, including overt interventions in news operations.

Because market values are constituent values of liberal societies, free markets and free expression have sometimes been equated as, for example, in Justice Oliver Wendell Holmes's valorization of a "marketplace of ideas". The restrictive templates that market values impose on the production of knowledge are usually invisible to those who hold these values in common.

Karl Marx and Frederick Engels explored the distortions imposed on language and philosophy by market imperatives in *The German Ideology* (written 1845–46, published posthumously). The 19th-century humanist Aleksandr Herzen directly equated market forces and censorship and abandoned his native Russia in protest against tsarist censorship, but he later expressed deep disillusionment with the extremely narrow limits of permission imposed on freedom of expression by market censorship in the West. A century later, another Russian, the Soviet exile Aleksandr Solzhenitsyn, would express similar disappointment at what he viewed as the moral bankruptcy of Western materialism.

Every powerful force in social formation, whether church, state, or corporation, creates order, stability, and continuity by suppressing disorder. Gaining control over communications has always been a vital move in securing social order. From the tablets of Moses to computer encryption codes, human communications and communities have been governed by rules. This proclivity for order has imposed a fundamental or constituent censorship on all human communities, even those that provide legal protections for freedom of speech and freedom of the press.

Some global corporations are now larger, richer, and more powerful than many individual nations. Like nations, corporations seek to preserve and advance their own interests by controlling communications. They are, in effect, private governments. Unlike democratic governments, which are formally accountable to citizens, corporations are only accountable to their principal shareholders.

SUE CURRY JANSEN

Further Reading

Bagdikian, Ben H., *The Media Monopoly*, Boston: Beacon Press, 1983

Epstein, Jason, *Book Business: Publishing Past, Present and Future*, New York: Norton, 2001

Gerbner, George, "Television: The New State Religion?", *Et Cetera* (June 1977): 145–50

Herman, Edward S. and Noam Chomsky, *Manufacturing Consent: The Political Economy of the Mass Media*, New York: Pantheon, 1988; London: Vintage, 1994

Herman, Edward S., "The Propaganda Model Revisited", *Monthly Review*, 48/3, (1996)

Jansen, Sue Curry, *Censorship: The Knot That Binds Power and Knowledge*, New York and Oxford: Oxford University Press, 1988

Jansen, Sue Curry, *Market Censorship Revisited: Press Freedom, Journalistic Practices, and the Emerging World Order*, Thousand Oaks, California: Sage, 1994

Johnson, Nicholas, "Freedom, Fun, and Fundamentals: Defining Digital Progress in a Democratic Society" in *Invisible Crises: What Conglomerate Control of Media Means for America and the World*, edited by George Gerbner, Hamid Mowlana and Herbert I. Schiller, Boulder, Colorado: Westview Press, 1996

Keane, John, *The Media and Democracy*, Cambridge: Polity Press, 1991

McChesney, Robert W., *Corporate Media and the Threat to Democracy*, New York: Seven Stories Press, 1997

McChesney, Robert W., *Rich Media, Poor Democracy: Communication Politics in Dubious Times*, Urbana: University of Illinois Press, 1999

McManus, John H., *Market-Driven Journalism: Let the Citizen Beware?*, Thousand Oaks, California: Sage, 1994

Marx, Karl and Frederick Engels, *The German Ideology*, Moscow: Progress, 1964; London: Lawrence and Wishart, 1970 (written in German, 1845–46)

Miliband, Ralph, *The State in Capitalist Society*, New York: Basic Books, 1968; London: Weidenfeld and Nicolson, 1969

Miller, Jonathan, *Censorship and the Limits of Permission*, London: Oxford University Press, 1972

Phillips, Peter and Ivan Harslof, "Censorship within Modern Democratic Societies" in *Censored 1997: The News that Didn't Make the News*, edited by Peter Phillips and Project Censored, New York: Seven Stories Press, 1997

Sanders, Beth and Randy Baker, *Fear and Favor in the Newsroom* (video documentary), 1996, http://www.fearandfavor.org

Schiffrin, André, *The Business of Books: How the International Conglomerates Took over Publishing and Changed the Way We Read*, London and New York: Verso, 2000

Smythe, Dallas W., *Dependency Road: Communications, Capitalism, Consciousness, and Canada*, Norwood, New Jersey: Ablex, 1981

Stauber, John and Sheldon Rampton, *Toxic Sludge Is Good for You: Lies, Damn Lies, and the Public Relations Industry*, Monroe, Maine: Common Courage Press, 1995

Website

http://www.fearandfavor.org/

GEORGI MARKOV
Bulgarian novelist, dramatist, and broadcaster, 1929–1978

Georgi Markov was a prolific and successful literary figure in Bulgaria before he defected to the West in 1969. His first novel, *Muzhe* (Men), was published to highly favourable reviews in Sofia in 1962 and won the year's most prestigious literary prize. The novel, which concerns a Bulgarian teenager's psychological problems before entering military service, was translated throughout eastern Europe and was made into a film. Two other novels followed: *Portretut na moya droynik* (1966, Portrait of My Double) and *Zhinite na Warshawa* (1968, The Women of Warsaw). Markov also became a successful dramatist with the play *Gospozhata na gospodin Furgovetsa na Sirene* (1963, The Cheese Merchant's Good Lady). He entered the privileged world of the Bulgarian literary and intellectual elite, and joined the officially approved Bulgarian Writers' Union. Communist Party leaders who mingled with theatre and literary circles also accepted Markov into their fold. He attended their parties and knew the intimate details of their personal lives, which were carefully hidden from the public.

In the early 1960s a roof under construction at a huge showpiece steel works collapsed, killing and injuring several workers. The party failed to inspire or lead workers in the search for victims. Years later, Markov wrote a novel entitled *Golemiyat pokriv* (The Great Roof), which was not approved by the censorship. He called the novel "an allegory and docu-

ment of the moral degradation" of Bulgarian socialist society: "In the fall of the roof, I perceived a symbol of the inevitable collapse of the roof of lies, demagogy, fallacies, and deceit that the regime had constructed over our country". He also wrote a play entitled *Ubiytsite* (The Assassins), which depicts a plot to kill a leader in a police state. That play was censured in a party newspaper article signed by Todor Zhivkov, then president of Bulgaria. Markov's career took another turn for the worse on 15 June 1969, when his play *Chovekut koyto beshe az* (The Man Who Was Me) was previewed before an invited audience, including party officials. Reportedly, most of the audience responded enthusiastically to the play; the party members did not. Further performances of the play were cancelled and a close friend warned Markov to leave Bulgaria.

Georgi Markov defected to the West the next day with a "sense of the unbearable". He later explained that: "I tried to compromise as much as I could and it was eventually too much. And the whole atmosphere was in deep disagreement with myself." As a defector, he was branded a "traitor" by the Bulgarian media. Five years later, a Bulgarian court tried him *in absentia*, sentenced him to six and a half years in prison, and ordered the confiscation of all his personal property. His books, which had once been bestsellers, were banned and his plays were no longer performed.

After living in Italy with his émigré brother, Markov settled in Britain, where he renewed his literary career. In 1974, a version of a play that had been granted only 13 performances in Sofia was staged in Britain as *Let's Go under the Rainbow*, and *The Archangel Michael*, his first new play, won an award at the Edinburgh Festival. The play, set in central Europe, is a dialogue between a policeman and a physician as they look for refugees wounded during an insurrection.

Georgi Markov now became a broadcast journalist for the BBC World Service and a freelance scriptwriter for Radio Free Europe in Munich, Germany. His first programme, broadcast on 8 June 1975, was called *Dulgovete na suvremmenata bulgarska literatura* (The Debts of Contemporary Bulgarian Literature). Over the following three years, he wrote more than 130 prime-time Sunday-evening programmes for Radio Free Europe, largely consisting of his memoirs, in a series called *Zadochui reportazhi za Bulgariya* (In Absentia, Reports about Bulgaria). Not only were these memoirs informative about cultural life in Bulgaria, but they also revealed the otherwise hidden life of Communist Party leaders, especially Todor Zhivkov. Markov's listening audience was estimated to be about 60 per cent of the Bulgarian adult population, even though Radio Free Europe's Bulgarian-language broadcasts were heavily jammed. A collection of these programmes was translated into English and published posthumously as *The Truth That Killed*.

Georgi Markov used words in their original meanings and attacked the regime's use of a highly formal, disingenuous "anti-language" to distort the truth. For example, in "Where are You, Dear Censor?" Markov explained that "stopping" was a synonym for censorship or banning: "In Bulgaria, nothing is censored and nothing is proscribed. Some works are merely stopped." He added:

> The regime can, I think, be very proud of its dialectical conjuring trick – the shifting of the functions of censorship from an outdated, historically compromised, and ineffective institution to a multitude of private, voluntary censorships established inside individual people.

In another programme, "The Dialectic of Censorship", Markov exposed the absurdity of the Bulgarian censors:

> during the 1960s Bulgarians were subjected to censorship of Soviet works that Bulgarian dialecticians found insufficiently "Soviet". Soviet films dealing with this or that not particularly praiseworthy aspect of Soviet reality, or deviating from the clichés of "socialist realism", were released in the Soviet Union but not shown in Bulgaria.

Markov compared living in Bulgaria to living under a lid:

> Every word spoken under this lid constantly changes its meaning. Lies and truths swap their values with the frequency of an alternating current. We have statesmen who have no state ... politicians who have no policies ... shops in which nothing is sold, writers who do not write, elections in which there is no choice ...

In 1977, when Georgi Markov learned that his father was dying of cancer, he asked for permission either to return to Bulgaria, or to have his father visit him in the West. The regime denied both requests. His father died in June 1977. The tone of Markov's programmes on Radio Free Europe changed, notably in a bitingly satirical series, broadcast from November 1977 to January 1978, called *Shreshti c Todor Zhivkov* (Personal Meetings with Todor Zhivkov). Markov wrote:

> I have stressed over and over again that the principal evil in the life and work of Bulgarian writers, painters, composers, [and] actors ... was interference by the Party ... And behind the Party's interference stood its chief organiser and executive – Todor Zhivkov ... as a result of Zhivkov's general, arbitrary and often quite unwarranted interference, Bulgarian cultural life became permeated by an atmosphere of insecurity and chaos ...

In July 1977, Zhivkov had signed a Politburo decree stating that "all measures could be used to neutralise enemy emigrés". Markov received various warnings and anonymous threats to stop broadcasting his inside knowledge of Zhivkov and of the obsequious circles of Bulgarian intellectuals and government officials. Markov persisted, peeling away the layers of lies and corruption in Bulgaria until his death.

A grotesque black comedy followed during 1978, when three attempts were made to kill Markov. The first was in Munich in the spring, when Markov was visiting friends and colleagues at Radio Free Europe. An agent failed in an attempt to put a toxin in Markov's drink at a dinner party held in his honour. The second attempt occurred on the Italian island of Sardinia, where Markov was enjoying a summer holiday with his family. Farce turned to tragedy with the final and successful attempt in London, on president Zhivkov's 67th birthday, 7 September 1978. Markov had parked his car below Waterloo Bridge and climbed the stairs to a bus stop. As he neared the waiting queue, he experienced a sudden stinging pain in the back of his right thigh. He turned and saw a man bending to pick up a dropped umbrella. Later that evening, Markov developed a high fever and was taken to hospital, where he was treated for an undetermined form of blood poisoning. He went into shock and, after three days of agony, he died.

In January 1979, after months of investigation, research, and experimentation, a coroner's court in London ruled that Markov had been unlawfully killed by the use of 450 micrograms of a lethal biotoxin, ricin, implanted in a sophisticated and minute pellet found in Markov's leg. The case lay dormant until after the collapse of communism in Bulgaria in 1989, when Bulgarian and British investigators reopened it. Their efforts were hampered, however, by a lack of coordination, documentary evidence, and witnesses. Any evidence of the crime has apparently been removed from Bulgarian government archives. In 1998 president Stoyanov told the British foreign secretary, Robin Cook: "It is painful for every Bulgarian democrat, but, leaving the scene, communism has taken to its grave also some secrets, such as the files about the murder of Georgi Markov".

Georgi Markov was almost certainly a victim of the ultimate form of censorship: political murder. Today, one can read on his gravestone, in a small churchyard in Whitchurch Canonicorum, Dorset, that he died in the "cause of freedom".

RICHARD H. CUMMINGS

Writings

The Truth That Killed, translated by Liliana Brisby, 1983

Further Reading

Kostov, Vladimir, *The Bulgarian Umbrella: The Soviet Direction and Operations of the Bulgarian Secret Service in Europe*, Hemel Hempstead, Hertfordshire: Harvester Press, and New York: St Martin's Press, 1988

JOSÉ MARTÍ
Cuban writer and revolutionary leader, 1853–1895

José Julián Martí y Pérez is widely regarded as the apostle of Cuban independence. He was a particularly gifted writer who wrote poetry, novels, plays, literary and artistic criticism, essays, and journalism, and was also a gifted orator.

Martí was born in Havana and, despite his parents' Spanish origins, began to embrace separatist ideas from an early age. Among his first poetic compositions, published in a clandestine student publication, was a sonnet dedicated to "10 October", the date when the Ten Years' War (1868–78), aimed at Cuban independence, began. In this sonnet the young poet gives "thanks to God who, finally, with honesty/broke Cuba away from the noose that oppressed her/and proud and free she raised her head."

In 1869, with some friends, Martí founded the newspaper *La Patria Libre* (The Free Country), only one issue of which was published. It contained his one-act drama, *Abdala*, written in verse and dealing once again with the subject of freedom. Martí then encountered a form of censorship when he wrote a letter accusing a fellow student of apostasy after he had enlisted in the Spanish army. The Spanish authorities found the letter and brought him before a military court, where he was sentenced to six years of forced labour in the quarries. The sentence was later commuted to confinement on the island of Pinos and, some months later, he was deported to Spain, where he began his studies of law, literature, and philosophy in 1871.

In Madrid, Martí associated with other Cubans with separatist ideas and published the leaflet *El presidio político en Cuba* (Political Imprisonment in Cuba), based on his own experience. He wrote: "Dante was not in prison. If he had experienced the depths of that torment crushing down on his head, he would have refrained from writing his *Inferno*."

When the first Spanish republic was proclaimed, Martí drew up a memorandum that he sent to the new heads of government, as well as to journalists and public figures. *La república española ante la revolución cubana* (The Spanish Republic Faced with the Cuban Revolution) as it was called, had as its main purpose the exposure of the contradiction between the newly proclaimed republican government in Spain and the continued maintenance of colonies in the Americas. The memorandum went unanswered.

At the end of his studies Martí left for Mexico, where he began to write for various newspapers and wrote the play *Amor con amor se paga* (1876, Love Is Repaid with Love), which was performed successfully. After a short stay in Guatemala he returned to Cuba where the Ten Years' War had ended without Cuba gaining its independence. After one of Martí's patriotic

speeches, captain general Ramón Blanco commented: "I believe that Martí is a madman, but a dangerous madman." In 1879 Martí's involvement in the preparation for what became known as the "Chiquita War" was discovered, and he was deported to Spain. From there he left for New York and, eventually, Venezuela, where he received some recognition for the quality of his oratory and the success of his *Revista Venezolana* (Venezuelan Review), although only two issues were published. He also wrote for the newspaper *La Opinión Nacional* (The National Opinion). It soon became obvious that his presence was not welcomed by the government of Antonio Guzmán Blanco. Martí therefore left for the United States, where he was to devote himself to preparing for what he called Cuba's "necessary war". In 1882 he published *Ismaelillo*, a poem written in Caracas and dedicated to his absent son. Nine years later the *Versos sencillos* (Simple Verses) were published. This was also the period of *Versos libres y Flores del destierro* (Free Verses and Flowers of Exile), which remained unpublished in Martí's lifetime. However, Martí's literary importance was recognized in the US and he came to be regarded as one of the key figures in the modernist movement.

Martí's journalism supported his political, ethical, and aesthetic pursuits. His writing found audiences in Argentina, Mexico, Honduras, Panama, Colombia, Uruguay, and the United States. In 1892 he also founded the periodical *Patria*, a publicity organ for the Cuban Revolutionary Party, which he created in order to organize the revolution that eventually began in 1895.

From 1891 practically all of Martí's activities were devoted to preparing for war. He was untiring in his efforts to bring together disparate groups in the common cause of independence; his oratory and his journalism were basic weapons for this purpose. However, when the preparations for the uprising were complete, Martí was betrayed when the three ships prepared to take the first leaders of the revolution to the island were seized. Undeterred, Martí and Máximo Gómez, head of the liberating army, went ashore. Within days, on 19 May 1895, Martí was killed in battle.

Despite the wider importance of Martí's written works and his oratory, his obituary stated that "his influence in his country was secondary and weak ... The speeches by the exiled orator scarcely reached the ears of his compatriots; the writings that were brought to the island were seized by the police ..." Almost all his intellectual work was indeed done in exile without reaching his own country, where he was always regarded as an enemy of the colonial system. It was only after

1900, when Cuba's independence had been achieved, and after the efforts of Gonzalo de Quesada, that the patriot's works began to be published in Cuba.

LEONARDO PADURA
translated by Rupert Capper

Writings

Obras completas (Nacional de Cuba edition), 28 vols, 1963–73
Inside the Monster: Writings on the United States and American Imperialism, edited by Philip S. Foner, 1975
Major Poems, edited by Philip S. Foner, translated by Elinor Randall, 1982

Further Reading

Abel, Christopher and Nissa Torrents (editors), *José Martí: Revolutionary Democrat*, Durham, North Carolina: Duke University Press, and London: Athlone Press, 1986
Griñán Peralta, Leonardo, *Martí, líder, politico*, Havana: Montero, 1943
Lizaso, Félix, *Martí, místico del deber*, 3rd edition, Buenos Aires: Losada, 1952
Mañach, Jorge, *Martí, el apóstol*, Madrid: Espasa Calpe, 1933; 5th edition 1968
Marinello, Juan, *José Martí, escritor americano: Martí y el modernismo*, Mexico City: Grijalbo, 1958

MARTIN MARPRELATE PAMPHLETS
Anonymous tracts: England 1588–89

The Martin Marprelate controversy surrounded seven pamphlets by Puritans which attacked the bishops of the Church of England. These pamphlets were ostensibly written by "Martin Marprelate", "Martin" referring to Martin Luther and "Marprelate" referring to Martin's intent to "mar" the bishops, or prelates. English Puritans found the hierarchy of bishops too close to Catholicism and resented the bishops' unwillingness to move the English church further towards Protestantism. The first Marprelate pamphlet was probably conceived of as a temporary answer to a defence of bishops by John Bridges. However, the pamphlets quickly took on a life of their own.

The pamphlets were designed pre-eminently to appeal through satire. Their colloquial style has been described as "witty, rumbustious, savage, and extremely effective" and it entertains, while making fun of the bishops' ponderous books. Martin usually appears as a fool or country bumpkin, seemingly a naive observer of the bishops; this allows him to launch a savage attack on the bishops' characters and personal lives. He says that a fool is best qualified to discuss their arguments, quotes them out of context, and uses their words against them, and feigns intimacy with them, treating them with jocular familiarity. Martin often takes his cues from Richard Tarlton, a popular jester, and uses language which is rambling, punning, and inventive. He switches topics suddenly, twists bishops' titles into satanic appellations, and invents words and satiric catalogues. Martin himself is not a consistent *persona*; sometimes he drops the fool's mask to condemn the bishops and passionately defend English Puritans, as in "A Dialogue wherein is plainly laide open the tyrannical dealing of Lord Bishops against God's Church . . ." Also, the supposed authors of the later pamphlets are Martin's sons, Martin Junior and his older brother Martin Senior. The Marprelate pamphlets are a "consciously constructed parody of established written and oral rhetoric", written more to popularize reform than to debate the substance of the bishops' position.

Although the complete story of the Marprelate pamphlets is still not known, it has been established that John Penry, a Welshman, Job Throckmorton, and John Udall were closely involved in writing, financing, and managing the pamphlets; Robert Waldegrave and John Hodgkins printed them clandestinely. The pamphlets were extremely popular, especially after

the government condemned them. They were also well regarded among Protestants in court, despite queen Elizabeth's and the archbishop of Canterbury, John Whitgift's, hatred of them. At the same time, they shocked many people for their indecorum and their lack of respect. Interestingly, despite this disapproval, the bishops commissioned professional writers, including Thomas Nashe and John Lyly, to write Martinesque responses to Marprelate.

In November 1588 the archbishop began the search for the originators of the pamphlets, and in February 1589, Elizabeth issued a proclamation against "certain seditious and euill disposed persons" who had produced "schismatical and seditious bookes, diffamatorie Libels and other fantasticall writings . . . against the persons of the Bishoppes . . . in rayling sorte and beyond the boundes of all good humanitie". The government made an enormous effort to apprehend Martin Marprelate, conducting massive surveillance efforts, searching carts, carriers, and inns, granting officials the authority to arrest anybody on suspicion, and sending spies into Puritan areas with copies of the pamphlets in their hands. In order to continue printing, the Marprelate press was forced to move constantly and to restrict knowledge of it to a very few. The press barely escaped detection on several occasions; on one such occasion, Robert Waldegrave saved the letters of his press by smuggling them out under his cloak; on another, the press was transported in farmer's carts, covered with hay or turnips. Penry, Throckmorton, and others went by aliases or dressed in disguises.

The press began at a Mrs Crane's house in East Molesey, near Kingston on Thames, where the first pamphlet, *Oh read ouer D. John Bridges*, was printed in October 1588. The search then forced the press to move to Fawsley in Northamptonshire, estate of Sir Richard Knightley, at which the second pamphlet, *The Epitome*, was printed in November. It then moved to John Hales's house, White Friars, in Coventry, Warwickshire, which saw the production of *Certain Minerall and Metaphisicall Schoolpoints* (February 1589) and *Hay, any worke for Cooper* (March 1589). At this point, Waldegrave decided that he could no longer bear the life of constant alarms, and he fled to Scotland. John Hodgkins took over the press and moved it near Warwick to Wolston Priory, which belonged to Roger Wigston. Hodgkins printed *Theses Martinianae* (or Martin Junior) and

The Just Censure and Reproof (or Martin Senior) in July 1589. He then left for Lancashire, intending to print *More Work for the Cooper* there. Along the road, some type fell out of the cart as it was being unloaded. Onlookers recognized it and reported it to authorities. Hodgkins set up a mile from Manchester, and started printing *More Work* but was quickly arrested, along with his two assistants. As authorities were closing in, Penry and Throckmorton printed *The Protestatyon of Martin Marprelate* in September 1589.

Hodgkins and his assistants were tortured into revealing everything they knew; this and the testimony of Henry Sharpe, an assistant printer, were the basis of the government's case. Hodgkins and Humphrey Newman, who distributed the pamphlets, were imprisoned and sentenced to death, although the sentences were not carried out. John Udall was imprisoned and sentenced to death, and died in prison. Mrs Crane, Sir Richard Knightley, John Hales, and Roger Wigston and his wife were called before the ecclesiastical High Commission and endured months of imprisonment and enormous fines. Robert Waldegrave, safe in Scotland, eventually became James VI's official printer. Job Throckmorton inexplicably escaped punishment, perhaps through the connections of his family or friends. John Penry escaped to Scotland but was ultimately executed in 1593, although it is not clear if this was because of his Marprelate involvement, or his subsequent affiliation with Robert Browne's separatist cause, or both.

The identity of "Martin Marprelate" is still unknown, although the best candidates are John Penry and Job Throckmorton. Martin Marprelate left a lasting legacy: he swayed the English people towards Puritanism, he left the Elizabethan authorities permanently suspicious of popular pamphlets, and

he gave leaders of the Puritan revolution, 50 years later, a potent name and prose style to use in their resistance to ecclesiastical authorities.

ALZADA TIPTON

Texts

7 tracts: *The Epistle, The Epitome, Mineral and Metaphysical Schoolpoints, Hay Any Work for Cooper?, Martin Junior, Martin Senior, The Protestation*; as *The Marprelate Tracts, 1588–1589*, edited by William Pierce, 1911 (reprinted 1967)

Further Reading

Anselment, Raymond A., *"Betwixt Jest and Earnest": Marprelate, Milton, Marvell, Swift and the Decorum of Religious Ridicule*, Toronto: University of Toronto Press, 1979

Black, Joseph, "The Rhetoric of Reaction: The Martin Marprelate Trials (1599–89), Anti-Martinism, and the Uses of Print in Early Modern England", *Sixteenth Century Journal*, 28/3 (Fall, 1999): 707–25

Clegg, Cyndia Susan, *Press Censorship in Elizabethan England*, Cambridge and New York: Cambridge University Press, 1997

McGinn, Donald Joseph, *John Penry and the Marprelate Controversy*, New Brunswick, New Jersey: Rutgers University Press, 1966

Pierce, William, *An Historical Introduction to the Marprelate Tracts: A Chapter in the Evolution of Religious and Civil Liberty in England*, London: Constable, 1908; reprinted New York: Burt Franklin, 1963

Poole, Kristen, "Facing Puritanism: Falstaff, Martin Marprelate, and the Grotesque Puritans", in *Shakespeare and Carnival: After Bakhtin*, edited by Ronald Knowles, Basingstoke: Macmillan, and New York: St Martin's Press, 1998

Van Eerde, Katherine, "Robert Waldegrave: The Printer as Agent and Link between Sixteenth-Century England and Scotland", *Renaissance Quarterly*, 34/1 (Spring 1981): 40–75

FRANCISCO MARTORELL
Chilean writer, 1963–

IMPUNIDAD DIPLOMÁTICA (Diplomatic Impunity)
Investigation, 1993

Diplomatic Impunity presents the results of a newspaper investigation into the activities of Oscar Spinoza Melo, the Argentinian ambassador to Chile between 1989 and 1992. After 17 years of dictatorship in Chile it again seemed possible to investigate freely cases of official corruption.

Martorell's book alleges that Spinoza and various prominent Chileans had been involved in drug trafficking and illegal trading using exemptions granted by the Chilean foreign ministry, leading to the purchase of luxury vehicles, liqueurs, and pornographic material; and that 20 people at the foreign ministry were infected with AIDS, from which seven officials had already died. The book also refers to the links between Spinoza, the former dictator Augusto Pinochet, and businessmen with investments in Argentina.

Eight legal actions were brought against Martorell. Hopes that Chile had abandoned the practice of censorship were soon dashed. President Patricio Aylwin, on his own initiative, laid down the bases of the so-called "Aylwin Doctrine" regarding freedom of expression. According to this view, the public

honour of individuals and their entitlement to privacy come before freedom of opinion or information. Since the appointment of judges in Chile lies in the hands of the president, this might have been taken as a clear direction on their verdict in this case. It was viewed by many as a setback to the progress made towards complete freedom of expression since the departure of Pinochet.

The courts decided to ban the book and to bring an action against its author. The Third Criminal Court even ordered that Martorell should be detained. The chairman of the State Defence Council, Luis Bates, had already expressed the view that Martorell should be imprisoned for three to five years.

Francisco Martorell went into exile in Argentina. In Buenos Aires he was supported by the Press Workers' Union (UTPBA) and various human rights organizations. The International Organisation of Journalists (OIP) also took up his case. In sharp contrast, the Board of Journalists of Chile avoided speaking in his defence.

According to Martorell, the book served

to open up a discussion which, unfortunately, the leaders of opinion reduced to its lowest form. However, many people discussed the real state of freedom of expression in Chile seriously. It also served to show up certain matters; for example, many people had to put aside their masks, and to go out and defend their financial interests. We are a country with virtues and faults, and I believe

that it is right that we should learn, once and for all, to look at ourselves in the mirror and to see ourselves as we are.

MARCELO ALVARADO MELÉNDEZ

Writings
Impunidad diplomática, 1993
Interview in *Full Stop* (October 1993): 8
El caso de Gloria Stockle: otra historia de impunidad, 1998

THE MASSES
US magazine, 1911–17

Founded by Piet Vlag, and subsequently reaching its journalistic apex under publisher Max Eastman, *The Masses* was a medium for socialist thought in the United States, and became a critical test case for state censorship during World War I.

Vlag founded the magazine as a vehicle for encouraging the formation of consumer cooperatives, but the narrowness of his political goals contributed to the magazine's failure to find a popular audience, and he suspended publication in 1912. A handful of radical artists and journalists convinced him to sell the magazine to them, and *The Masses* resumed publication under the editorship of Max Eastman, a trained academic then with little experience in publishing or political mobilization. Under Eastman's guidance, however, the magazine assumed a coherent political mission based on "revolution, not reform" of the capitalist system. Eastman made the magazine free of advertising, so as to remove any potential influence on its editorial content. Writers such as Sherwood Anderson, Mabel Dodge, and John Reed, and artists such as John Sloan, Cornelia Barns, George Bellows, and Art Young all worked for the magazine under Eastman's helm. The magazine's distinctive aesthetic sensibility made it popular in leftist circles. It also made it a visible target for critics, who referred to its staff as "them asses".

In 1916 *The Masses* began to devote substantial editorial space to criticizing pro-war sentiment in the nation, just as intolerance to such criticism began to emerge. To curb the influence of pacifists and leftists, Congress passed the Espionage Act (1917), which expanded the list of treasonable offences to include not merely action against the government's war policy, but criticism of that policy.

The federal government began immediately to take action against *The Masses* and similar leftist publications. First, the US Post Office attempted to remove the magazine from the mails for being in violation of the Espionage Act. The Post Office cited four cartoons and four pieces of text as the basis for the charge, all of which were typical of the level of war criticism present in the magazine. Boardman Robinson's drawing, entitled "Making the World Safe for Capitalism", depicted a man labouring at the Workman and Soldier's Council while US secretary of war Elihu Root and pro-war socialist Charles E. Russell stand behind him holding a noose; a menacing man labelled "Japan" threatens him from the door. Art Young's cartoon "War Plans" portrays a group of businessmen discussing war strategy, while a congressman at the door queries,

"Where do we come in?" Two drawings by H.J. Glintenkamp were also listed in the charge: one depicted a decaying liberty bell; the other portrayed soldiers as slaves, with the heading "Conscription". A poem by Josephine Bell entitled "A Tribute" lauded Emma Goldman and Alexander Berkman, two anarchists jailed for their anti-war beliefs. Two editorials by Max Eastman were also cited: "Friends of American Freedom", which supported Goldman and Berkman, and "A Question", which encouraged support for conscientious objectors. Also listed as violating the Espionage Act was Floyd Dell's introduction to "Conscientious Objectors", an article consisting of letters by imprisoned British men resisting conscription.

In a landmark decision contributing to the formation of modern American civil liberties law, federal district judge Learned Hand decided in favour of *The Masses*, citing its cartoons and writing as falling "within the scope of that right to criticize, either by temperate reasoning or by immoderate and indecent invective, which is normally the privilege of the individual in countries dependent upon the free expression of opinion as the ultimate source of authority". Moreover, Hand found that only Congress had the right to exclude the magazine from the mails, not Post Office officials, and therefore ordered that distribution of *The Masses* be reinstated for the August issue. However, a US circuit court judge then ordered a stay on Judge Hand's decision, and the issue was never mailed. Shortly thereafter, the Post Office threatened to revoke the magazine's second-class mailing privileges because of irregular publication.

In November 1917, while waiting to appeal the stay of execution of Hand's decision, the federal government indicted Max Eastman and six staff members for violating the Espionage Act by interfering with the recruitment and enlistment of servicemen and conspiring to cause mutiny in the US Army and Navy. Eastman, Floyd, and Bell were charged for the same materials cited in the Post Office case. John Reed was indicted simply for adding the title "Knit a Straight-Jacket for Your Soldier Boy" to a reprint from a *New York Times* article on mental illness among servicemen. This time, H.J. Glintenkamp was indicted for a cartoon depicting a skeleton taking the measurements of a recruit for his coffin, and Art Young for a cartoon entitled "Having Their Fling", which depicted figures representing the press, business, government, and the church doing a war dance. The government also charged Merrill Rogers and *The Masses* Publishing Company for conspiracy to use the mail system illegally. The trial ended in a hung jury, as did a second trial.

Though federal prosecutors failed to obtain convictions for any of *The Masses* staff, the government's systematic harassment of the magazine did succeed in putting the magazine out of existence. With mail privileges suspended from July 1917, the magazine had only newsstand sales to sustain it; and because of long-standing conflicts with distribution chains that objected to its content, newsstand sales were erratic at best. With no advertising revenues to fall back on, the magazine's production resources quickly dried up while the court cases dragged on until the autumn of 1918. Though the November /December 1917 issue promised future issues, it was the last issue to be published. Of course, the US was not alone in the censorship and harassment of pacifists and leftists. Most of its European allies – not to mention Germany – did the same.

STEPHANIE DYER

Further Reading

Diggins, John Patrick, *The American Left in the Twentieth Century*, New York: Harcourt Brace, 1973

Diggins, John Patrick, *The Rise and Fall of the American Left*, New York: Norton, 1992

Fishbein, Leslie, *Rebels in Bohemia: The Radicals of The Masses, 1911–1917*, Chapel Hill: University of North Carolina Press, 1982

Jones, Margaret C., *Heretics and Hellraisers: Women Contributors to The Masses, 1911–1917*, Austin: University of Texas Press, 1993

Maik, Thomas A., *The Masses Magazine, 1911–1917: Odyssey of an Era*, New York: Garland, 1994

Zurier, Rebecca, *Art for The Masses: A Radical Magazine and Its Graphics, 1911–1917*, Philadelphia: Temple University Press, 1988

PHILIP MASSINGER
English dramatist, 1583–1640

English drama developed in two distinct ways in the quarter-century before the English Civil War: some playwrights tirelessly debated the aristocratic codes of love and honour in never-never-land settings remote from reality; others produced work showing new levels of political and constitutional sensitivity and sophistication. Philip Massinger, who for much of the period wrote for London's premier theatre company, the King's Men, falls in the latter group and his plays were several times subject to the attentions of the court censor, the Master of the Revels.

The first such encounter concerned *Sir John van Olden-barnevelt*, written in collaboration with John Fletcher, a tragedy about current political conflict in the Netherlands. Written in the summer of 1619, the play concludes with Oldenbarnevelt's execution the previous May, still a subject of intense interest in London. Though not published at the time, the text survives in the manuscript annotated by the Master, then Sir George Buc.

Buc's most striking intervention was provoked by a sequence in which the Prince of Orange is prevented from entering the council chamber during a conspiratorial meeting of Olden-barnevelt's faction. Buc not only marked the passage for omission, but added a marginal note: "I like not this; neither do I think the Prince was thus disgracefully used. Besides, he is too much presented." Although in the case of the prince of Orange, Buc could not invoke the usual ban on representing kings on stage during their lifetimes, his courtier's antennae twitched at the abusive treatment of a head of state, and whether or not the incident was authentic, it was unacceptable as stage material and could cause diplomatic problems; many of Buc's subsequent interventions were to tone down offensive references to the prince by his opponents.

The play's censorship problems did not end there. After the King's Men had gone to some expense preparing the production, it was banned outright by the bishop of London, John King (c.1559–1621), using his general executive power as a member of the Privy Council rather than any specific instru-

ment of censorship. The bishop's reasons are not documented, though it seems likely that he was concerned at the play's linking religious dissidence with political subversion. In any event, after about a fortnight the actors succeeded in circumventing the prohibition, and *Sir John van Oldenbarnevelt* was on the London stage by the end of August.

Massinger was next in censorship difficulties in January 1631, when his tragedy about Sebastian of Portugal was refused a licence by the Master, now Sir Henry Herbert. When the play was resubmitted in May, however, under the title *Believe as You List* and with a classical setting substituted for the modern, Herbert passed it with virtually no changes. He must have known that it was in essence the same play he had rejected four months before: even if the actors had tried to conceal it, the surviving manuscript, with his handwritten licence on the back, has several points where Massinger inadvertently copied down "Sebastian", omitting to substitute the character's new name, Antiochus.

The play's problems lay in its original subject matter and its timing. In 1629 Charles I had dismissed parliament, leaving himself no means of raising taxes; he was therefore compelled to pursue a less active foreign policy, and peace with Spain was proclaimed on 5 December that year, probably while Massinger was writing the play. It was this treaty which made Herbert disallow the first version; he was probably wary of the kind of diplomatic pressure which had followed the performance of Middleton's *A Game at Chess* in 1624. Although Massinger's play was less bluntly anti-Spanish (its villainous Spanish ambassador, who poisons people through "necessity of state", is eventually disowned and punished by his political superiors), it dealt with a sensitive topic. The historical King Sebastian of Portugal was killed in 1578 during a disastrous military adventure in Morocco, following which his kingdom was annexed by Spain. Subsequently, a number of pretenders claimed Sebastian's identity and the throne, and the belief in the *Principe encubierto* (hidden prince) remained a powerful focus for sedition decades later. The problem of Massinger's play, which was evidently not resolvable by the censor's usual selective cutting, was that it treated one such pretender as the real Sebastian; in doing so it implicitly questioned Spain's right to its Portuguese territories at a time when its grip on them was growing insecure (Portugal was eventually liberated in 1640).

A foreign setting did not disguise the application to domestic politics of Massinger's 1638 play, *The King and the Subject*. Now mostly lost but probably drawn from 13th-century Spanish history, the play was evidently so controversial that Herbert felt unable to license it on his own authority, and referred it upwards. It was eventually read and annotated by King Charles I, who took particular exception to a speech in which King Pedro arrogantly declares his royal prerogative to levy whatever taxes he pleases: "We'll mulct you as we shall think fit." Charles, himself unable to raise direct taxation without summoning a potentially hostile parliament, was then keeping the exchequer afloat with such dubious and unpopular fiscal devices as ship money and forced loans, and understandably took the passage personally: "this is too insolent, and to be changed". (Ironically, the seven lines in question are the only part of the play now extant, preserved in Herbert's

records.) Herbert later received special permission to allow the play, subject to specified revisions and a change of title, presumably to avoid directing attention to the touchy constitutional issues the play must have raised.

MARTIN WIGGINS

Writings

Sir John van Oldenbarnavelt, with John Fletcher, produced 1619; edited by T.H. Howard-Hill, 1979
Believe as You List, produced 1631; edited by Charles J. Sisson, 1927
The Dramatic Works in the Beaumont and Fletcher Canon, edited by Fredson Bowers *et al.*, 1966–96
The Plays and Poems, edited by Philip Edwards and Colin Gibson, 5 vols, 1976

Further Reading

Clare, Janet, *Art Made Tongue-Tied by Authority: Elizabethan and Jacobean Dramatic Censorship*, 2nd edition, Manchester: Manchester University Press, 1999
Dutton, Richard, *Mastering the Revels: The Regulation and Censorship of English Renaissance Drama*, Iowa City: University of Iowa Press, and London: Macmillan, 1991
Gross, Alan G., "Contemporary Politics in Massinger", *Studies in English Literature*, 6 (1966): 279–90

MASTER OF THE REVELS
England, 16th–17th centuries

Originally the title given to the member of the English royal household responsible for staging entertainments for the court (*Magister Jocorum Revelorum et Mascorum omnium et singulorum nostrum vulgariter nuncupatorum Revelles et Maskes*), the Master of the Revels came to be one of the officials involved in censorship of the theatre. The title probably dates from the reign of Henry VII, the earliest surviving mention of a Master occurring in 1494. The first permanent Master was Sir Thomas Cawarden, who held the office between 1545 and 1559, when the responsibilities of the post were expanded to include authorizing the performance of plays and other productions at the court. The Master of the Revels was responsible to the Lord Chamberlain.

Cawarden oversaw the revels for the coronation of Elizabeth I in 1558, and it seems that her hand lay behind the efforts to exert more effective control over the subject matter of drama. Such intervention seems initially to have been prompted by a desire to prevent religious and political upheaval, for only a year after coming to the throne the queen decreed that her representatives in the localities were to forbid plays "wherein either matters of religion or of the governaunce of the estate of the common weale shall be handled, or treated". As her reign proceeded, it became clear that it would be from court that censorship would be imposed, and the office of the Master developed accordingly. In 1581 a patent stated that the Master was required "to order and reform, authorize and put down, as shall be thought meet unto himself, or his deputy" any piece which was deemed derogatory to the Crown. In order to carry out his duties he was authorized to read and approve plays and to license theatres. A later act in 1606 required the Master to excise profanity from performances.

The effect of the supervisory role of the Master upon the theatre, particularly in London, could be both positive and negative. On the one hand, the Master's approval could protect a theatre troupe from further interference by other authorities; however, the Master's consent could only be gained after intense scrutiny of the work to be performed, and there is ample evidence of plays being revised as a result of his suggestions. For example, the text of *Sir Thomas More* (c.1594) contains an instruction which may have been an attempt by the Master, or some other official, to remove a controversial scene: "leave out ye insurrection and the cause". In more serious cases, some playwrights were incarcerated for plays deemed to be seditious. Ben Jonson, George Chapman, and John Marston were imprisoned as a result of their collaboration on *Eastward Ho* (1604), since their outspoken criticism of corruption at the royal court aroused the ire of James I.

However, it would be wrong to view the Master as simply imposing fiats from on high, for the office and its activities were shaped considerably by the interests of the individual holding it. Masters of the Revels worked for their own profit as well as for the good of the realm. Sir Edmund Tilney, who served as Master from 1579 until 1610, received seven shillings for each work he read in addition to £3 a month and £100 a year from the queen. Sir Henry Herbert was willing to pay £150 for the office when he took it up in August 1623. Herbert, perhaps in an effort to recoup that sum, interpreted his duties as broadly as possible. He declared that he had the right to license every form of public entertainment performed within the kingdom. Indeed, the earliest entries in his register, only part of which survives, reveal that he was authorizing exhibitions of exotic beasts such as elephants, beavers, and camels, as well as the public displays put on by quack doctors. He even attempted to exert his authority over the printed word, authorizing the publication of a number of books in 1632. His broad view of the powers with which he had been entrusted certainly paid off, for he received £2 for every new performance that was staged and £1 for the revival of older plays. However, the breadth of his activities sometimes interfered with the care and conscientiousness with which he carried them out. In November 1632 he was summoned before the royal court to explain why he had provided Donne's *Paradoxes* with his approval.

The closing of the theatres in 1642, although they would be reopened during the Restoration, heralded the decline of the Master of the Revels' authority. On the accession of Charles II, Sir Henry Herbert still held the office but found it difficult to maintain its power in the face of encroachments by other courtiers, not least the Lord Chamberlain himself. Thomas Killigrew, who had gone into exile with Charles II during the Interregnum and who in 1660 was granted a monopoly patent which he used to close down all other theatre companies, in effect exercised the Master's functions, although Herbert retained the title. Killigrew's newly established King's Company now dominated the theatre scene. Upon Herbert's death in 1673 the title of Master of the Revels passed to Killigrew, and, in 1677, was granted to Killigrew's son Charles. The Mastership of the Revels was eventually made defunct by Robert Walpole's 1737 Licensing Act, which gave the Lord Chamberlain responsibility for licensing theatres and for the censoring of dramatic performances.

ANDREW ROBERT WINES

Further Reading

Clare, Janet, *Art Made Tongue-Tied by Authority: Elizabethan and Jacobean Dramatic Censorship*, 2nd edition, Manchester: Manchester University Press, 1999
Dutton, Richard, *Mastering the Revels: The Regulation and Censorship of English Renaissance Drama*, Iowa City: University of Iowa Press, and London: Macmillan 1991

MASTURBATION

Few sexual practices have stirred so much controversy and debate as masturbation. Depending on the historical period and the cultural context, masturbation has been hailed as an excellent cure or treated as a vicious disease, approved as perfectly normal or condemned as utterly perverse, despised as the worst of sins or glorified as the royal road towards individuation. The judgement passed on masturbation by philosophers, medical doctors, and religious authorities has often varied according to the sex, the age, and the social status of the individual. Views on masturbation have always been influenced by the perceived goal of sexuality and the function accorded to men's semen.

In ancient Greece, masturbation was generally tolerated in women, who were regularly portrayed with artificial phalluses (*olisboi*); in men, however, it was only acceptable for those who were deprived of opportunities for sexual intercourse, such as slaves and idiots. The main reason for the negative evaluation of masturbation in adult male citizens was that the emission of semen that it inevitably brought about did not contribute to procreation and thus involved an irrecoverable loss. Similar reasons underpinned the repudiation of male masturbation in Roman, Jewish, Indian, Chinese, and Islamic cultures, the restrictiveness of the attitudes being directly proportional to the preciousness attributed to the semen. Ruth Benedict, on the other hand, reports that the Japanese regarded masturbation as "a pleasure about which they feel no guilt . . . sufficiently controlled by assigning it a minor place in a decorous life".

Until the 18th century, western views on masturbation were dominated by the teachings of St Augustine (354–430) and St Thomas Aquinas (1225–74), who denounced the practice as an unnatural vice. To Aquinas, masturbation was one of the four "sins against nature" (alongside bestiality, homosexuality, and oral/anal intercourse), because it contravenes "the natural order of the venereal act", which is derived from God and which puts sexuality within the plan of procreation. During the late Middle Ages and the Renaissance, this violent condemnation of masturbation by one of the founders of Christian theology was hardly criticized, yet masturbators were not a major concern for the church councils, and penances for those who were caught were fairly lenient. Despite the sinfulness of the act, some authoritative medical doctors, such as Ambroise Paré and Nicholas Culpeper, even recommended masturbation as a remedy against illnesses which they attributed to an overabundance of semen in both men and women. In the earliest sexual advice literature, which appeared during the late 17th century, masturbation was largely neglected.

These conflicting positions of religious and secular authorities with regard to masturbation disappeared during the first decades of the 18th century, when moral and medical objections converged and masturbation became the principal bugbear on both sides of the Atlantic. Instrumental in the definition of this sexual scourge was the publication of a concise brochure entitled *Onania, or the Heinous Sin of Self-Pollution* in 1708. This anonymous work was hugely successful and went through numerous expanded editions until 1760, when it was superseded by *Onanism: or, a Treatise upon the Disorders Produced by Masturbation*, an anti-masturbation treatise by the Swiss doctor Samuel-André Tissot (1728–97), which was even more influential than its predecessor. These two works are responsible for the erroneous equation of masturbation and onanism – the act of Onan described in the book of Genesis (38: 7–10) is actually coitus interruptus – and for the dissemination of myriad myths about masturbation, some of which remain vivid to this day. The key message of *Onania* and *Onanism* was that masturbation (self-abuse, self-pollution, the vicious habit, the solitary vice, etc.) represents the *fons et origo* of moral corruption, and exposes an individual to a cornucopia of physical and mental diseases, ultimately leading to complete decay and premature death. To strengthen his claim, Tissot referred to "medical evidence" produced by various early 18th-century doctors which showed that the expenditure of semen is detrimental to overall mental and bodily health. In this way, he paired the age-old theme of male semen-economy with the conservative mores of medieval Christian theology, thus also applying the Enlightenment principles of rationality and moral discipline to the realm of sexuality. Tissot and other 18th-century writers of anti-masturbation literature were well aware that their works might induce the very behaviours they wanted to fight, but they relied on the Church fathers to legitimize their explicitness in sexual matters and disclaimed responsibility for such unintended effects by punctuating their texts with regular warnings addressed to the reader. In general, self-censorship was restricted to the use of a different language (Tissot's book was originally written in Latin) or extensive circumlocutions.

With the rise of psychiatry and sexology during the 19th century, masturbation became associated with every possible disorder (as a cause, symptom, effect, or complicating factor), and especially with neurasthenia. Masturbation (including involuntary nocturnal emissions) in men and women was considered more dangerous than fornication or buggery, and medical doctors and quacks invented complicated mechanical devices to prevent or curtail the activity. Hermann Rohleder, one of the leading late 19th-century sexologists, went so far as to suggest circumcision and clitoridectomy without anaesthetic as the most effective treatment procedures. Books, pamphlets, and flyers alerting the public to the risks of masturbation circulated widely and were only censored if their descriptions did not convey disapproval. One striking example of such selective moral censorship concerns the practice of "Comstockery" in the United States during the last decades of the 19th century. Under pressure from Anthony Comstock, the American congress passed a law in 1873 that ordered the confiscation of obscene materials in the US mail. Comstock watched over the entire enterprise, yet his definition of "obscene" applied to how something was presented rather than to the actual topic. Therefore, he only confiscated materials on masturbation in which the behaviour was not sufficiently condemned.

This grim picture gradually lost its colour during the 1920s, under the influence of the sexually liberalist theories of Sigmund Freud, Havelock Ellis, and Magnus Hirschfeld; these writers questioned the link between masturbation and disease, emphasized the normality of autoerotic behaviours in children and adolescents, and drew attention to their frequency within the population. The public attitude towards masturbation changed from fear and condemnation to reassurance and tolerance. Nonetheless, D.H. Lawrence (1930) viewed masturbation as "certainly the most dangerous sexual vice that society can be affected with in the long run"; and the continued scientific belief in the potentially harmful effects of "excessive" masturbation, especially in adulthood, prevented practitioners and educationists from encouraging the practice as a sexual outlet or as part of the healthy exploration of the body. The latter development did not occur until the publication of the Kinsey reports after World War II and the dissemination of Masters and Johnson's ideology of sexual adequacy in the 1960s.

Nowadays, the sex-education literature generally supports masturbation in children and adolescents, and sex-advice manuals are reasonably tolerant concerning masturbation in adults, as long as the practice is not accompanied with "deviant" sexual fantasies, images, or behaviours. Nevertheless, prejudices about masturbation, for example that it causes deafness, are still widespread, albeit often in the guise of folk-

wisdom. In addition, the Catholic Church continues to denounce all forms of non-procreative sex, including masturbation. One of Shere Hite's informants in 1976 recalled: "Being Catholic, I was brought up to think that I should not obtain power and pleasure from my body and neither should anyone else." The extent to which masturbation remains a delicate topic for American scientists and government officials can be measured first from the fact that the US surgeon general Jocelyn Elders had to resign in 1994 following the outcry that greeted her statement that masturbation at least prevented the spreads of AIDS and teenage pregnancy; and second from the methodology used in a large-scale survey on sexual behaviour that was published in 1994. Without following the advice of the government review body, which suggested deletion of all items related to masturbation, Laumann and his colleagues decided to use paper-and-pencil techniques for these questions, because they expected both interviewers and interviewees to feel very uncomfortable about the issue.

DANY NOBUS

Further Reading

Benedict, Ruth, *The Chrysanthemum and the Sword*, Boston: Houghton Mifflin, 1946

Bennett, Paula and Vernon A. Rosario (editors), *Solitary Pleasures: The Historical, Literary, and Artistic Discourses of Autoeroticism*, New York: Routledge, 1995

Brenot, Philippe, *Eloge de la masturbation*, Cadeilhan: Zulma, 1997

Bullough, Vern L., *Sexual Variance in Society and History*, Chicago: University of Chicago Press, 1976

Duché, Didier-Jacques, *Histoire de l'onanisme*, Paris: Presses Universitaires de France, 1994

Emch-Dériaz, Antoinette, *Tissot: Physician of the Enlightenment*, New York: Peter Lang, 1992

Engelhardt, H. Tristram Jr, "The Disease of Masturbation: Values and Concept of Disease", *Bulletin of the History of Medicine*, 48 (1974): 234–48

Hall, Lesley A., *Hidden Anxieties: Male Sexuality, 1900–1950*, Cambridge: Polity, 1991

Hare, E.H., "Masturbatory Insanity: The History of an Idea", *Journal of Mental Science*, 108 (1962): 1–25

Hite, Shere, *The Hite Report: A Nationwide Study on Female Sexuality*, New York: Macmillan, 1976; London: Collier Macmillan, 1977

Hite, Shere, *The Hite Report on Male Sexuality*, New York: Knopf, and London: Macdonald, 1981

Jordanova, Ludmilla, "The Popularisation of Medicine: Tissot on Onanism", *Textual Practice*, 1 (1987): 68–80

Laqueur, Thomas W., "The Social Evil, the Solitary Vice and Pouring Tea" in *Fragments for a History of the Human Body*, edited by Michel Feher *et al.*, 3 vols, New York: Zone, 1989

Laumann, Edward O. *et al.*, *The Social Organization of Sexuality: Sexual Practices in the United States*, Chicago: University of Chicago Press, 1994

MacDonald, Robert H., "The Frightful Consequences of Onanism: Notes on the History of a Delusion", *Journal of the History of Ideas*, 28 (1967): 423–31

Marcus, Irwin M. and John J. Francis (editors), *Masturbation: From Infancy to Senescence*, New York: International Universities Press, 1975

Neumann, R.P., "Masturbation, Madness, and the Modern Concepts of Childhood and Adolescence", *Journal of Social History*, 8 (1975): 1–28

Porter, Roy and Lesley A. Hall, *The Facts of Life: The Creation of Sexual Knowledge in Britain, 1650–1950*, New Haven, Connecticut and London: Yale University Press, 1995

Sarnoff, Suzanne and Irving Sarnoff, *Sexual Excitement/Sexual Peace: The Place of Masturbation in Adult Relationships*, New York: Evans, 1979

Soble, Alan, *Sexual Investigations*, New York: New York University Press, 1996

Stengers, Jean and Anne van Neck, *Histoire d'une grande peur, la masturbation*, Brussels: L'Université de Bruxelles, 1984

Tarczylo, Théodore, *Sexe et liberté au siècle des Lumières*, Paris: Presses de la Renaissance, 1983

Thody, Philip, *Don't Do It! A Dictionary of the Forbidden*, London: Athlone Press, and New York: St Martin's Press, 1997

PETER MATTHIESSEN
US novelist and essayist, 1927–

IN THE SPIRIT OF CRAZY HORSE
Reportage, 1983, revised 1991

On 25 June 1975, two agents from the Federal Bureau of Investigation (FBI), special agents Jack Coler and Ron Williams, were shot and killed when they followed a red and white vehicle onto land on the Pine Ridge Indian Reservation in South Dakota. A shoot-out had occurred between the agents and members of the militant American Indian Movement (AIM), and a Native American man also died in the gunfire. After an exhaustive manhunt, four men were indicted for the killings. One was released, two were acquitted when a jury concluded that they had fired in self-defence, and the fourth, a Chippewa Sioux named Leonard Peltier, was tried separately after extradition from Canada, convicted of the murders of both agents, and sentenced to two life sentences in prison. Peter Matthiessen, strongly moved by what he called "the ruthless persecution of Leonard Peltier", by the long history of inequity for Native Americans, and by what he perceived as a signal failure of the United States judicial system, was led to tell the stories of Peltier, AIM, and the systematic oppression of Native Americans in his book *In the Spirit of Crazy Horse*. Two public figures, South Dakota governor William Janklow and FBI agent David Price, objecting to Matthiessen's partisan stance and to their characterizations in the work, brought libel suits against the author, against his publisher Viking Press, and against booksellers stocking the book. These suits, asking a total of $44 million in damages, effectively repressed *In the Spirit of Crazy Horse* for eight years in one of the longest and most expensive libel suits in publishing history.

Although Matthiessen takes as his particular subject the plight of the various indigenous peoples known generally as the Sioux, their story is reproduced across the Americas: in exchange for concessions of land or behaviour, time and again Native Americans were granted the right to certain lands by treaties with the US government – at least until those lands seemed valuable to white settlers or prospectors, at which point the Native Americans were confined to reservations and attempts were made to integrate them into white mainstream society at the expense of their culture and traditions. In the 1970s, however, young Native Americans began to rise up in opposition to the continued repression of their peoples. They encouraged a renaissance of Native American pride and began to take a militant stance against the US government. Members of AIM carried out several daring operations, among them the occupation of the deserted island of Alcatraz – formerly a maximum-security federal prison – and the occupation of the Bureau of Indian Affairs office in Washington, DC. Reactions to AIM varied widely, even among Native Americans. Some saw the members of the organization as heroes, while others saw them as interlopers. The government response to AIM, however, was unambiguous. The members of the organization were treated as domestic terrorists, and when in February 1973 a group of them took over the historic village of Wounded Knee on the Pine Ridge Reservation – the site of a 19th-century massacre of Native American men, women, and children by the Seventh Cavalry – for 71 days, the government ringed the community with helicopters, armored personnel carriers, and automatic weapons.

Matthiessen argues that the FBI, following the siege of Wounded Knee, took aim at the American Indian Movement, harassing its members with the intention of destroying it as a functioning entity. When on 25 June 1975, agents Coler and Williams drove onto an Indian farm, following several men who they reported seemed to be carrying guns, their action precipitated the firefight in which they were first wounded by rifle fire from a distance and then shot at close range.

Matthiessen's reading of these events prompted Janklow and Price to sue for libel. Janklow argued that he had been portrayed as a bigot and a sexual offender (Matthiessen reported, truthfully, that the governor had twice been charged with sexual offences), while Price objected to his characterization as an agent involved in many of the FBI's most sinister anti-AIM operations. Some analysts suggested that the suits were unconcerned with the truth or falsity of Matthiessen's account, but were simply intended to keep the book from being read. Janklow, still sitting in the governor's mansion when he filed his suit, named several local bookstores as co-defendants along with the author and publisher, suggesting an attempt to frighten outlets by the magnitude of his office and the threat of damages.

Both cases were dismissed, although not without years of acrimonious legal wrangling and the expenditure of more than $2 million by Viking for legal expenses. Price's suit was ultimately settled in January 1990 when the US Supreme Court refused to hear his appeal from the summary judgement granted by the US Court of Appeals for the Eighth Circuit. In the Price ruling, the Court of Appeals ruled that "Sometimes it is difficult to write about controversial events without getting into some controversy along the way. In this setting, we have decided that the Constitution requires more speech rather than less." Janklow's suit was resolved in November 1990, when after the dismissal of his case in South Dakota Circuit and Supreme Courts, he allowed the deadline for appeal to the US

Supreme Court to expire. Viking rushed an updated hardcover version of the book into print in May 1991. Martin Garbus, attorney for Matthiessen and Viking, contributed an afterword on the legal battle over the book's publication and freedom of the press.

Although in his epilogue to the revised edition Matthiessen suggests that another man – a mysterious "Mr. X" whom he has interviewed – may have been the person who actually pulled the trigger for the close-up shots that killed the FBI agents, Leonard Peltier's guilt or innocence is not the primary concern of the book. Like many others, Matthiessen considers Peltier a martyr to a cause. Partly on the strength of the passionate convictions expressed in *In the Spirit of Crazy Horse*, Peltier has been nominated for the Nobel Peace Prize and been designated a political prisoner by Amnesty International, the former Soviet Union, and Desmond Tutu. Film director Michael Apted has made a documentary film produced by Robert Redford, *Incident at Oglala*, about Peltier, as well as the feature film called *Thunderheart*, which is loosely based on his story. Although these things have brought a heightened visibility to Peltiers case, and outgoing president Bill Clinton briefly considered issuing a presidential pardon to Peltier in early 2001, he remains in Leavenworth Federal Penitentiary.

GREG GARRETT

Writings

In the Spirit of Crazy Horse, 1983; revised edition 1991
Indian Country, 1984
"Who Really Killed the FBI Men?", *The Nation*, 252 (13 May 1991): 613ff.

Further Reading

Anderson, Scott, "The Martyrdom of Leonard Peltier", *Outside*, 20/7 (July 1995): 44ff.
Churchill, Ward, "Goons, G-Men, and AIM", *The Progressive*, 54 (April 1990): 28–29
"'Crazy Horse' Suit Ends; Viking to Publish New Edition in 1991", *Publishers Weekly*, 237 (9 November, 1990): 12
Dowie, William, *Peter Matthiessen*, Boston: Twayne, 1991
Garbus, Martin, "The FBI Man Who Cried Libel", *The Nation*, 249 (13 November 1989): 564–67
Peltier, Leonard, *Prison Writings: My Life is My Sun Dance*, New York: St. Martin's Press, 1999
"Viking, Matthiessen Win in Price Libel Suit", *Publishers Weekly*, 236 (1 September 1989): 8

THOMAS MAULE
Colonial American writer, 1643–1724

TRUTH HELD FORTH...
Theological treatise, 1695

The primarily theological treatise *Truth Held Forth and Maintained According to the Testimony of the Holy Prophets Christ and His Apostles Recorded in the Holy Scriptures* was written by Thomas Maule, a Quaker of Salem, Massachusetts, during the years 1690–94. The 268-page book, printed by William Bradford of New York, contained, for the most part, explanations and justifications of selected religious beliefs and practices of the Society of Friends (Quakers). It also, however, included caustic denunciations of Puritanism as practised in Massachusetts, condemned their mistreatment of Quakers, and accused the Puritan authorities, particularly the clergy, of being no less guilty than the persons who had been charged and convicted of witchcraft during the Salem trials a few years earlier. Maule suggested that the witchcraft hysteria and conflicts with the Native American tribes were a direct consequence of Puritan persecution of Quakers and evidence of God's adverse judgement on the colony and its leaders. Maule asserted that the Salem trials stopped only because the accusations had begun to focus on ministers and eminent Puritans.

On 12 December 1695, after copies of *Truth Held Forth* appeared in Massachusetts, the lieutenant-governor and council determined that the book contained not only lies about specific persons and the government but also subversive religious doctrines. They ordered Maule's arrest, the search of his properties for copies, and the seizure of any copies found. Two days later the House of Representatives acted likewise. On 14

December the sheriff reported that he had arrested Maule and seized 31 copies of the book. On 19 December Maule was presented to the governor and the council, and admitted that the copies were his and that he wrote the book. The seized books were ordered to be burned, Maule was held for trial at the next session of the Court of Assize and General Gaol Delivery, and he was directed to give bond as assurance for his appearance. On the next day, Maule appeared to present the required bond, but also demanded a trial by jury of his peers in Essex County, a demand to which the court assented. No indictment was presented.

The authorities' reaction to Maule's book reflected the intolerance prevalent not only in late 17th-century Massachusetts but also throughout post-Reformation Europe. So long as each denomination considered itself the "one true church", it was inevitable that each sect would seek and then exercise political power to advance theological supremacy. Consequently, religious questions became political ones and devices designed to protect governments, such as the charge of seditious libel, were used to shield the power-holding church from words expressing dissent from the theology of those controlling the government. In the climate of the times, the Massachusetts authorities probably had no choice but to seek suppression of Maule's expression of his opinions.

Maule's trial began in Ipswich in May 1696 before Judges Thomas Danforth, Elisha Cook, and Samuel Sewall. Asked if he was responsible for the publication of *Truth Held Forth*, Maule asked to see a copy of the book, and after looking at it, replied that everything in the book was true except for printer's errors and some author mistakes. Judge Danforth then charged Maule to answer for printing the book without Licence of Authority. Maule's response was that if he were so responsible, he owed accountability to the bishops of the English church because the king allowed to him the same liberty to have his book printed as was allowed to any of the king's subjects regardless of their religious denomination. Further pressed, Maule contended that the books were his lawful goods to be distributed as he saw fit, to which the king's attorney answered that the books were illegal because they contained lies about the colony's church and government. After repeating some of the accusations he had made in the book, Maule demanded that he receive a copy of the particulars of the charge against him. The court agreed, and continued the trial to the next session at Salem. It appears that despite the posting of bond, Maule remained in prison from December 1695 until the resumption of the trial in Salem in the autumn of 1696.

The grand jury's presentment, when finally made, included charges based not only on what was in the book but also on what Maule had said during the May 1696 portion of his trial. When the trial resumed, a jury of 12 residents of Essex County was empanelled and all pleas to the indictment entered on Maule's behalf were overruled for lack of technical merit. Maule then argued on his own behalf, rejecting the court's jurisdiction over theological disputes and again castigating the government for mismanaging the care of the people entrusted to it. Following the court's charge to the jury, in which it demanded conviction, Maule made a closing argument, contending that he had not violated the king's law nor any law of the English nation, that he had not written anything contrary to sound doctrine nor inconsistent with Scripture, and that the printer's placement of his name on the book no more proved him to be the author than spectral evidence proved a person of being a witch. The jury quickly returned a verdict of "Not Guilty according to Indictment", explaining that the book was insufficient evidence, given that the printer had placed Maule's name on it, and also asserting that the matter was not within their jurisdiction, belonging instead to a "Jury of divines".

Maule's trial was the first seditious libel case in Massachusetts involving written (in contrast to oral) publication of opinions critical of the authorities. It was the first such case in colonial America in which the defendant was acquitted. Despite his lack of formal education, Maule relied on a five-part defence. First, he essentially denied the court's jurisdiction by accusing the court of usurping the power of the Bishop's Court. He then argued that the jury had the right to decide law as well as facts. Third, he asserted that he had put nothing in the book contrary to sound doctrine and the truth of Scripture. He tapped the jury's misgivings about the attitude of the same judges in the witchcraft trials, by alluding to the use of spectral evidence, knowing that popular sentiment at the time was that the use of such evidence had led to the conviction and execution of innocent persons, and also knowing that the jury was familiar with these judges' subsequent determination to exclude spectral evidence from those trials. Finally he suggested that the appearance of his name on the book was not proof of his authorship, deftly comparing its appearance to the appearance

of a spectre. Though the first two prongs of his defence were in conflict with the law then in effect, Maule was doing no more than what professionally trained attorneys must do when the case requires arguing against precedent. Knowing that the jury in Bradford's case four years earlier had divided on the jurisdiction issue, Maule gave his jury the obviously contrived name-placement excuse as a justification.

Maule's trial was the first case – in Massachusetts, at least – in which the jury effectively asserted its independence from the judges and disregarded the court's virtual direction to convict in a matter involving printing and authorship. The jury's denial of Maule's culpability under the seditious libel law when the elements of the crime had been proven demonstrates that the jury objected to using seditious libel as a tool to suppress a person's expression of religious and political opinions.

In practical terms, Maule's acquittal opened the door for a growth in the local printing industry. Printers limited the items for which they sought government licence, and no longer were compelled to send works controversial in one colony to a printer in another colony. The acquittal gave printers the courage to be more aggressive in their decisions.

Although erroneously praised as the "first victory for freedom of the press in America", Maule's acquittal nonetheless presaged the consequences of the expiration of the Licensing Act, namely, a rapidly fading success of the Massachusetts authorities in attempted press restrictions following Maule's trial. Thus, Maule's subsequent book, *New England Pe[r]secutors Mauled with Their Own Weapons*, provoked no official sanctions despite the fact it was more political in character and less theological than *Truth Held Forth*.

Maule's acquittal contributed to the idea that there were at least some matters on which a person could comment without being punished by the government. Maule highlighted the public distrust of the combination of ecclesiastical matters with the secular, and the jury's refusal to convict him coincided with the evolving formation of the 18th-century political philosophy that treated liberty of expression as essential to preservation of a person's civil, political, and religious rights.

In this regard, Maule's acquittal was a significant precursor to that of the colonial printer John Peter Zenger, though it is unclear whether Maule's dealings with William Bradford and Bradford's retention of Zenger as apprentice served as a link between Maule and Zenger (and possibly Hamilton). Both Maule and Zenger faced insurmountable obstacles, in part because authorship could hardly be denied. Both juries reached results contrary to the judges' preference. Maule's acquittal diminished the threat of seditious libel charges to printers in Massachusetts; Zenger's did the same for printers in New York. Neither trial caused a change in doctrinal law, because they were simply jury verdicts. Maule's trial meant for the freedom of religious expression what Zenger's did for the freedom of political expression.

The acquittal influenced the development of First Amendment rights in general and, in particular, contributed significantly to the establishment of the freedom of religious expression. Maule persuaded his jury to reject secular control of religious expression. Maule was tried not for verbalizing criticism of political issues but for expressing dissent with respect to theological matters. That a seditious libel charge, a politically empowered reaction, would be brought in response to expressions of religious belief reflected the degree to which the government was unwilling to tolerate suggestions of ecclesiastical manipulation of political power and the degree to which suppression of expression was a prerequisite to maintenance of the theocracy. Thus, by agreeing with Maule, the jury hastened the detachment of secular authority from the control of theological debate and the removal of ecclesiastics from the halls of government.

JAMES EDWARD MAULE

Writings

Truth Held Forth and Maintained According to the Testimony of the Holy Prophets, Christ and His Apostles Recorded in the Holy Scriptures, 1695
New-England Pe[r]secutors Mauled with Their Own Weapons (as Theo. Philathes), 1697
An Abstract of a Letter to Cotton Mather, 1701
For the Service of Truth against George Keith (as Philalethes), 1703

Further Reading

Adams, James Truslow, *A History of American Life*, vol. 3: *Provincial Society, 1690–1763*, New York: Macmillan, 1927
Chandler, Peleg W., *American Criminal Trials*, 2 vols, Boston: Little Brown, and London: Maxwell, 1841–44
Channing, Edward, *A History of the United States*, 6 vols, New York: Macmillan, 1905

Duniway, Clyde Augustus, *The Development of Freedom of the Press in Massachusetts*, New York and London: Longman, 1906
Goddell, A.C., "An Account of Thomas Maule", *Historical Collections of the Essex Institute*, 3 (1861): 238
Jones, Matt Bushnell, "Thomas Maule, the Salem Quaker, and Free Speech in Massachusetts Bay, with Bibliographical Notes", *Historical Collections of the Essex Institute*, 72 (1936): 1
Levy, Leonard W., *Emergence of a Free Press*, Oxford and New York: Oxford University Press, 1985
Maule, James Edward, *Better That 100 Witches Should Live: The 1696 Acquittal of Thomas Maule of Salem, Massachusetts, on Charges of Seditious Libel and Its Impact on the Development of First Amendment Freedoms*, 1996
Murphy, Lawrence W., "Thomas Maule: The Neglected Quaker", *Journalism Quarterly*, 29 (1952): 171
Nicholson, Richard L., *Genealogy of the Maule Family with A Brief Account of Thomas Maule of Salem, Massachusetts*, Philadelphia, 1868
Perley, Sidney, *The History of Salem, Massachusetts*, 3 vols, 1924–28
Thomas, M. Halsey (editor), *The Diary of Samuel Sewall, 1674–1729*, 2 vols, New York: Farrar Straus, 1973
Winsor, Justin (editor), *Narrative and Critical History of America*, 8 vols, Boston: Houghton Mifflin, 1884–89
Worrall, Arthur J., *Quakers in the Colonial Northeast*, Hanover, New Hampshire: University Press of New England, 1980

GUY DE MAUPASSANT
French novelist and short story writer, 1850–1893

Maupassant was a master of the short story, and also an acclaimed novelist and journalist. Mentored by Gustave Flaubert and aligned early in his career with Émile Zola, Maupassant is most often grouped with the Naturalist school. Although he was a deft and elegant stylist, much of his writing concentrated on the seamier side of life. As a writer he focused on the art and craft with which an object or event was depicted, regardless of how sordid or coarse the subject matter. This daring and amoral aesthetic assured Maupassant's notoriety, and he repeatedly tested and pushed the limits of official condemnation throughout his writing career.

Maupassant's first and only encounter with the censor occurred at the beginning of that career, and happened in a peculiar and round-about way. In the late 1870s Maupassant was employed by the Ministry of Education as an administrative assistant while he was honing his skills as a writer under the tutelage of Flaubert. The latter introduced him to a number of publishers and editors, including Catulle Mendès, editor of the literary journal *La République des Lettres* (The Republic of Letters), with whom he had a long and fruitful association. In 1876 Mendès agreed to publish Maupassant's poem, "Au Bord de l'eau" (The Water's Edge). The poem appeared, under the pseudonym of Valmont, without incident, although its subject matter clearly invited controversy. It is the tale of an obsessive love affair between an oarsman and a washerwoman in which the focus is on unbridled sensual and carnal pleasure. Eventually the couple destroy themselves in their pursuit of sex. Maupassant's own estimate was telling: "My poem, chaste in

language, is completely immoral and indecent in images and subject matter."

Maupassant's difficulties with the law arose when the poem was reprinted in his own name with the title "Une Fille" (A Girl) in the *Revue Moderne et Naturaliste* (Modern and Naturalist Review) of November 1879. He later claimed the poem was printed without his permission, but the damage was done. Maupassant and Auguste Allien, the printer, were charged with *outrage à la morale publique* (outrage to public morals) by the Office of the Public Prosecutor of Étampes, near Paris, on 22 December 1879. That charges were filed in Étampes illustrates one of the quirks of censorship under the Third Republic. It so happened that the *Revue Moderne et Naturaliste* was printed there, and that according to the law the printer was considered equally liable, along with the publisher and the author, for the offensive piece. The authorities had difficulties in locating Maupassant in Paris, and it was not until February 1880 that he caught wind of the subpoena and appeared voluntarily before the court on the 14th. Although it remains unclear what transpired at the initial deposition, Maupassant took immediate steps afterwards to organize his defence. In a revealing set of letters to Flaubert, Maupassant confessed that he was less concerned with incarceration or injury to his literary career than with jeopardizing his position and livelihood at the Ministry of Education.

Maupassant pleaded with Flaubert to write a letter in his defence and place it in the influential and widely read newspaper, *Le Gaulois*. Flaubert, normally loath to step into the public arena, complied with his request, and also penned a number of private letters to influential people. Flaubert's strategy was to avoid legalistic argument, instead employing sarcasm and ridicule in arguing that the state had no business in dictating artistic expression. *Le Gaulois* published Flaubert's letter on 21 February 1880. It opened with Flaubert's praise of his "disciple" and immediately engaged the question of why the charge was filed in Étampes three years after the initial publication of the poem in Paris. Flaubert explicitly asked: "Is there one kind of justice for Paris and another for the provinces?" For further irony, Flaubert recalled the censorship trial of *Madame Bovary* which "received enormous publicity and to which I attribute three quarters of my success". The brunt of Flaubert's charge, however, was that it was the nature of the state, which, he maintained, had remained the same in its essentials from monarchy to empire to republic, to command a "monopoly of taste", and that if the authorities were indeed able to exercise aesthetic control then there would have been no Shakespeare, Rabelais, Voltaire, Goethe, or Byron. Flaubert concluded that it was unthinkable that a poem could provoke criminal charges, but added: "Yet who knows? The earth has its limits, but human stupidity is infinite."

Flaubert's bravura performance had its intended effect and the charge was promptly dropped for lack of evidence on 28 January 1880. Maupassant was clearly relieved to be rid of the ordeal, yet for the remainder of his career he was fearless in courting controversy and in his adamant refusal to relinquish any editorial control over his work. He did however recognize that some publications were more appropriate than others, especially for racier items, of which he wrote many and which covered a remarkable range of topics. Particularly favoured was the literary journal, *Gil Blas*, that prided itself on its daring reputation and was prosecuted and fined for overstepping the bounds of decency numerous times.

On two separate occasions Maupassant brought suits against parties which, he felt, had restricted access or maligned his writing. In the first instance, he protested against the prominent publisher Hachette, which monopolized sales in train station bookstalls, and had refused to stock his novel *Une Vie* (A Life). Maupassant pursued the case all the way to the Chamber of Deputies, where a petition was presented on 28 May 1883 arguing that Hachette was exercising *de facto* censorship of the novel. The Minister of Public Works, whose responsibility extended to railway stations, would neither confirm nor deny that Hachette was practising censorship, but did say that his understanding was that certain passages in *Une Vie* were "indelicate, to put it mildly". The Chamber voted overwhelmingly not to act, but Maupassant received considerable coverage and sales of his work were brisk. Late in his career, in 1888, he was outraged that the newspaper *Le Figaro* extensively edited an essay, "Le Roman" (The Novel), without seeking his permission. Maupassant was not immune to editorial advice, but it was inconceivable to him that an artist would surrender editorial control without consent. Eventually the suit was dropped after *Le Figaro* printed an apology, yet Maupassant never published with the newspaper again. Maupassant repeatedly pushed the bounds of what was acceptable, and many of his finest stories are marked by a brutal sensuality. However, the legal authorities of the Third Republic distinguished sharply between works of art and popular writings aimed at a broad public. Maupassant's unquestioned stature as an artist shielded him from further prosecution.

JIM MILLHORN

Writings

The Collected Novels and Tales, translated by E.A. Boyd and Storm Jameson, 18 vols, 1922–26
Selected Short Stories, translated by Roger Colet, 1971
Contes et Nouvelles, edited by Louis Forestier, 2 vols, 1974–79
"Une Fille", reprinted in *Crimes Écrits: la littérature en procès au 19e siècle*, by Yvan Leclerc, 1991
Mademoiselle Fifi and Other Stories, translated by David Coward, 1993
"Au Bord de l'eau" reprinted in *Correspondance: Gustave Flaubert–Guy de Maupassant*, edited by Yvan Leclerc, 1993

Further Reading

Hamelin, Jacques, *Hommes de lettres inculpés: Mérimée, Barbey d'Aurévilly, Maupassant, Flaubert, Baudelaire, les Goncourt [et] Diderot*, Paris: Minuit, 1956
Steegmuller, Francis, *Maupassant: A Lion in the Path*, New York: Random House, 1949; London: Macmillan, 1972

MAURITANIA

(formerly part of French West Africa)

Population: 2,665,000	**Number of daily newspapers:** 2
Main religions: Muslim	**Number of radio receivers per 1000 inhabitants:** 146
Official language: Arabic	
Other languages spoken: Poular; Wolof; Solinke	**Number of TV receivers per 1000 inhabitants:** 25
Illiteracy rate (%): 47.2 (m); 67.9 (f)	**Number of PCs per 1000 inhabitants:** 5.5

The history of civil rights in the Islamic Republic of Mauritania is indissolubly linked to other themes – most notably, those of ethnic discrimination and slavery. Bidan of Arab and/or Berber descent dominate the country's other ethnic groups through control of the government and the military. Meanwhile, while repeated attempts have been made to rid the country of slavery, these have had little practical effect. Religious rights are another contentious issue in this Islamic republic, while the country's vulnerable borders are a further relevant theme. Given the extremely complex history of the region now known as

Mauritania, these themes will serve as guidelines for an exploration of the history of censorship and freedom of expression in the area.

Modern Mauritania is a product of French colonialism. The fragile nature of the polity which has emerged over the past century has often been used as a justification for censorship and repression. The region was "pacified" by the French military over a period of about 50 years. Colonial administrators, reports Francis de Chassey, had "the right to hand down penal sanctions at will – days in prison and fines – for reasons as vague as subversive speech or unwillingness to pay taxes". In addition, the administrator's chief role was to spy on the population and keep "interminable lists of 'dangerous persons to be put under surveillance' which were drawn up frequently".

In the postcolonial period as well, Mauritania's fragility has been invoked as a reason for limiting freedom of speech. The war for the independence of Western Sahara – the Sahraoui conflict, in which Mauritania was involved between 1975 and 1984) – almost destroyed the country. Earlier, Morocco had offered part of the disputed territory in return for diplomatic support. When Mokhtar Ould Daddah, the first post-independence leader of the country, signed accords in 1969 with king Hassan II of Morocco, there was great disagreement within Mauritania. The editors-in-chief of two publications, *al-ʿAlam* and *L'Opinion*, were sent to jail for eight days for daring to report on the incident.

Although some of Mauritania's borders, like that which runs along the Senegal River, constitute obvious natural boundaries, others are simply lines drawn in the sand of the Sahara. These borders were demarcated for a very specific reason. French administrators defined this large region lying between north Africa and the outer reaches of the Sahelian areas of west Africa as a buffer zone that would be used to contain Islam. It would be interesting to consider whether this policy constituted an attack on freedom of religious faith. In any case, Islam has played an important, if uneven, role in the history of censorship and free expression in Mauritania.

The country has been the home to active Muslim scholars whose written documents seem to indicate that relatively free intellectual exchanges took place in the past. The Malekite school of jurisprudence which is followed in Mauritania led scholars to argue that Islamic law must be interpreted within a historical framework, rather than in a literalist fashion. Mauritanian legal traditions thus offered some support for freedom of expression, as well as protection against libel. On the other hand, some intellectuals disputed the rights of various Islamic brotherhoods. The legal scholar Muhammad Yahya-al-Walati proposed banning them altogether.

Religious conflicts in Mauritania have been violent. In August 1940 the conflict between Hamallists (Laghal) and Qadria (Tenonajiou) followers led to 300 deaths in one day. The French colonial authorities reacted with violent repression. They established two concentration camps, executed 33 members of brotherhoods, and sentenced four men to forced labour.

Today, Islam is the official state religion of Mauritania. Indeed, Mauritania was the first state in the world to be officially styled an Islamic Republic. Official imams have state approval, and are thus distinguished from the marabouts (hermits, saintly men) whose positions are hereditary. Constant Hamès suggests that this "bureaucratization" of imams is intended to subordinate them to the state and thus contain their political influence. All parties formed on a religious platform are illegal. In 1991 a party named al-Umma (Muslim Nation) was banned in pursuance with this policy.

In the Islamic Republic, Arabs and the Arabic language enjoy great prestige among all ethnic groups for religious reasons. However, many of the conflicts in postcolonial Mauritania are related to the dominance of the Moors, who claim Arab ancestry and speak a dialect of Arabic (Hassaniya). More than any other, the ethnic factor affects freedom of speech in postcolonial Mauritania. The June 1966 decision to make Arabic the official language of secondary instruction was the first formal action that opened a period of ethnic conflict that continues up to the present.

During the colonial period, many more non-Arab – "black" – Mauritanians than Moors received a French education. (Use of the term "black" is problematical in Mauritania as the Moors themselves are broken down into the dominant Bidan group, known as the "white" Moors, and the Harattin minority, who are known as the "black" Moors. In this entry the term "black" refers to negro Africans.) In contrast to most Moors at the time, black communities tended to be sedentary, and thus more vulnerable to French demands that children be sent to French schools, even if they resisted on religious grounds. This meant that most of the educated Mauritanians employed by the French colonial service were black. The 1966 decision can be seen as an attempt to reverse this historical development by giving Hassaniya-speakers an advantage. Observers have compared Mauritania's Arabization policy to the decision by the South African apartheid government to restrict black students to instruction in Afrikaans.

On 4 January 1966, the students of the high schools in Nouakchott and Rosso, as well as those of the normal school of Nouakchott (École Normale) organized a strike in protest. The strike spread among black members of the government. Nineteen professionals wrote and circulated the "Manifesto of the Nineteen", which detailed the grievances of the students and of black Mauritanians generally. The reprisals were brutal. Moors attacked and wounded eight high school students on 6 February (two suffered severe knife wounds). On 9 February Harattins attacked black residents in Nouakchott. The army's eventual intervention in these attacks resulted in four deaths and 70 injuries (20 of which were serious), as well as to the closing of the secondary schools. Twenty-six bureaucrats and students were suspended from their work or studies and imprisoned for six months without charge or trial in the interior of the country at N'beika.

These events prompted the government to curtail freedom of speech by banning any reference to ethnic conflict. It was even forbidden to speak of "Moors" and "Blacks". Nevertheless, student strikes continued on a regular basis for several years. The government reacted by expelling student leaders, closing schools, and assigning army and police officers to permanent duty in schools in order to quell protests. After a 1972 strike, the government conscripted students by force and sent other students to military prison. The students protested against their incarceration by engaging in a prolonged hunger strike. In 1973 the government again attempted to make Arabic the primary language of instruction; this time making French an option only after two years of obligatory instruction in Arabic. In 1979 the number of subjects taught in Arabic was again increased; marks would thus be more heavily weighted toward Arabic. Strikes followed, only to be repressed. The government's efforts to Arabize the Mauritanian media have accompanied the school reforms. Television and radio broadcasts in languages other than Arabic are severely limited. Meanwhile, in the July 1991 constitution only Arabic is considered the official language, and French is not even mentioned.

Arabization has many consequences in Mauritania, which remains a multicultural and multiracial society. It has resulted in limits on freedom of speech by giving an official linguistic advantage to native speakers of Arabic. In addition, the policy has been used to actively repress efforts to promote other languages. Groups for the promotion of literacy in other national languages have been forced to go underground. It is easy to target such groups, simply because black Mauritanians have almost no right to assembly or association. "Authorization is officially required for all such gatherings of blacks and Arabs alike, although in practice only the blacks need such permission." Even unauthorized family celebrations of events like the birth of a child have led to the arrest of black Mauritanians.

In spite of government support for Arabization, pan-Arabist parties loosely based on Baʿathist (Iraq) or Nasserite (Egypt) Arab nationalist ideologies have also been banned. It is illegal to form a political party whose platform is based purely on ethnic or clan identity, just as it is illegal to create a purely religious party. These parties seem to have been banned in part because they were a threat to the one-party system that Ould Daddah put into place in the 1960s. In 1989 Amnesty International reported that at least 100 supporters of the Baʿath party were detained; many were tortured. When twelve of these detainees were brought to trial, the prosecutor claimed that "by enrolling police and soldiers into the Baʿath party, the defendants had undermined the security of the state". Several other opposition parties were also forced to remain clandestine. The Mouvement National Démocratique (MND), or National Democratic Movement, was formed in 1968; the Parti des Kahidines (PKM), or Proletarian Party of Mauritania, was formed in 1973.

November 1973 was "one of the high points of repression", when arrests, property seizures, night patrols, and curfews were used to prevent opposition groups from expressing themselves, either through tracts or through public demonstrations. More than 100 political prisoners were taken in the capital alone, and torture was used during interrogations. In spite of this severe repression, clandestine newspapers such as *Zouerate*, *L'Élève Mauritanien*, *L'Étudiant en Lutte*, *Jeunesse Ouvrière*, *Flambeau*, and *Tarik al-ʿUmal* managed to operate between 1971 and 1975.

By the early 1990s the changing political climate in the region made such overt political repression unacceptable. In response to these changing conditions a new constitution was passed in 1991 formally allowing multipartyism. However, the government continues to circumscribe political rights. For example, 100 arrests and three deaths were reported in 1992 in relation to the first multiparty elections. In 1997, one activist was sentenced to six months in prison for "activity opposed to Mauritania's relations with Israel". The right to freedom of association now has constitutional protection, yet the government has continued to limit this right. Non-governmental

agencies must be registered; the government tends to control NGOs by denying permits. It has denied permits to groups such as SOS-Esclaves (SOS-Slaves) and the Mauritanian Association for Human Rights, whose activities are primarily of benefit to black Mauritanians.

The workers' movement has also faced government repression. Although the Union of Mauritanian Workers (UTM) is connected to the state, it has acted independently in the past. In May 1968 workers at the Miferma iron mines in Zouerate went on strike and organized a demonstration. The army fired on the crowd, killing at least eight people and wounding about 40. Several other strikes took place in the following years, and the government continued its strategy of violent repression. In August and September 1971 90 per cent of all workers in Mauritania went on strike. According to Francis de Chassey, union leaders were arrested, put under house arrest, or simply transferred to other regions. The police, the army, and the prefects were all mobilized to intimidate striking workers. Government repression of legal trade unions has a certain continuity. The secretary general of the UTM, al-Kory Ould H'Meitty, was arrested and tried in 1986, receiving a suspended prison sentence of six months. Forty-five people were arrested in a related demonstration, 15 of whom received prison sentences. The situation has eased in the 1990s. Several trade unions now exist. However, labour rights are not yet respected in practice. In April 1997 the government arrested secondary school teachers and cut their salaries because they threatened to strike.

Although repressive measures affect many opposition groups, they are used most brutally against groups defending black rights. In the 20 years between the 1966 Manifesto of the Nineteen and the 1986 Manifesto of the Oppressed Black Mauritanian, distributed by the Forces de libération des Africains de la Mauritanie (Mauritanian Africans' Liberation Force – FLAM), this brutality appears to have increased. Many black intellectuals, including members of the Institute for National Languages and teachers of classes in national languages, were arrested on the suspicion that they might have been involved in producing the manifesto. Of the 40 arrested in September 1986, 21 were brought to trial. The defendants were charged with holding unauthorized meetings (law 73.008 of 1973); the display and distribution of publications harmful to national interest (law 63.109 of 1963); and making propaganda of a racial or ethnic character (law 66.138 of 1966). All pleaded not guilty, but the defendants were convicted and received sentences ranging from six-month prison sentences to five or ten years of internal exile with the loss of all civil rights. The trial took place in Arabic, although only three of the defendants spoke that language. Meanwhile, prior to the trial the defendants had been tortured. It is significant that one of them was a television journalist (Ibrahima Sarr) and another an important writer (Tène Youssouf Guèye, writer and former diplomat). Guèye died in prison as a result of the harsh conditions he experienced there.

This trial did not signal the end of reprisals for publication of the Manifesto. On 24 September captain Abdoulaye Kébé was tried because he allegedly provided statistics used in the Manifesto concerning the army's ethnic composition. He was held in detention, denied access to counsel, and sentenced to two years in prison and twelve in internal exile. In October, another group was arrested on the same charges as those levelled at the Manifesto defendants. Four of the prisoners died while in custody. The following year, several prominent members of the black community were arrested and tortured because they protested the execution of three black military leaders.

Other organizations that have attempted to defend poor Mauritanians' rights also met with severe repression. The Harattins, who are descended from slaves (though ethnically there is little distinction between themselves and the dominant Bidan Moors), founded a group called al-Hurr in 1974 in order to put pressure on the government to abolish slavery. Instead, the government chose to suppress al-Hurr. Many of its leaders and members were arrested and severely tortured. In 1979–80 some were exiled; an action which "signalled the government's unwillingness to allow the existence of an independent forum agitating for the rights of haratines". These events were a reaction to March 1980 demonstrations calling for greater rights for the Harattin and for the release of four Harattin arrested for protesting against the sale of a young woman in Atar. Seventeen members of al-Hurr were tried and convicted, and a further 18 Harattin were arrested for interfering with the sale of a slave. Other Mauritanians who protest against abuses of slaves on an individual basis have been silenced as well. In 1983, a black officer of the military police was transferred to another post after protesting against the sale of a slave at Boutilimit. Censorship of any organization that protests against slavery continues.

Government repression of black Mauritanians was most brutal during a period of ethnic cleansing that began in April 1989. Thousands of black Mauritanian citizens were forcibly dispossessed and expelled from the country after the government argued that they were simply illegal aliens from neighboring countries. Many were killed, raped, or tortured during this period. These citizens represented a threat to Moorish hegemony for several reasons. First, their existence made an ethnically-based Moorish state impossible. Second, they offered direct political opposition to the regime. Finally, they were gaining economic power in relation to the Moors, for they traditionally hold the most fertile lands in Mauritania. Most of their lands were taken by Moors and Harattins after the events of 1989. In 1990 many of the remaining black officers in the army were arrested and tortured. Others disappeared.

It was around this time, however, that some positive changes in Mauritania's human rights record occurred. Because it had sided openly with Iraq, international donors isolated the country as a "rogue state." In order to regain donors' confidence, Mauritania agreed to follow its neighbours in instituting a process of democratization. As a result, Mauritania now has several political parties and several independent newspapers. Christian Roques counted 39 independent newspapers, in addition to the official newspaper, *Chaab/Horizons*, in 1992. Although some of these have folded – or appear irregularly because of printing problems, or because their clientele is too small – many have survived. The United States Bureau of Democracy, Human Rights, and Labor reported 42 independent privately-owned newspapers in 1998. The radio and television stations remain under government control, but opposition candidates have had equal access to electronic media during electoral campaigns, even though their access is otherwise limited.

Nevertheless, many new cases of censorship and repression have also been reported. In June 1991 the Front Démocratique Uni pour le Changement (United Democratic Front for Change, FDUC) was formed in opposition to the government, which quickly arrested its leaders and put them under house arrest in the interior of the country. A week later, a solidarity committee of women held a demonstration in Nouakchott that "was broken up by police, who reportedly kicked and beat the women, at least 10 of whom were hospitalised". In April and May 1991 several open letters calling for the government to allow independent investigation of the 1989–91 massacres were published. In June, several Moors who had signed one of the letters were arrested. All were held in detention until 25 July 1991.

On that date new laws easing restrictions on press and parties were enacted. However, all parties must abstain from propaganda "in contradiction with the principles of true Islam", and are prohibited from being formed on racial, ethnic, or religious basis alone. If they do not comply, the government can dissolve them. The press law states that the press must adhere to principles "based on tolerance, respect for others, fairness, just treatment and upholding the principles of freedom, social justice and the defense of human rights and for justice among nations". Insulting the president is an offence punishable by imprisonment and fines.

These laws have been used to censor many journalists. All newspapers are published at the national printing press, so the government can seize them or delay production quite easily. In addition, newspapers must pass the scrutiny of a censor commission. The commission has been quite active since it was established. A September 1991 issue of *Mauritanie Demain* was banned for reporting that black detainees had been tortured to death. *Le Calame* has been seized repeatedly; in 1995 it was seized three times in one month. In 1996, *Mauritanie-Nouvelles* was repeatedly censored, and its editor, Bah Ould Saleck, was harassed. Distributors of that newspaper and *La Tortue* were harrassed as well.

The African Commission on Human and Peoples' Rights stated in 1997 that the Mauritanian government has "increasingly sought to silence opposition to its policies by detaining government critics for short periods". As many as 40 people were detained in 1997 for criticizing the government. Only six were given due process. Those arrested included students, members of the union for secondary school teachers, supporters of a campaign to expose slavery, and members of opposition parties.

The press also faced government repression in 1997. *Mauritanie-Nouvelles* was seized again, as was *La Tribune*. In June, the police raided the offices of two newspapers, *al-Bouchra* and *La Vérité*. Both have been permanently shut down. On 26 April *Mauritanie-Nouvelles* was censored and banned for a month; on 22 April *La Tribune* was banned; and on 3 March *L'Éveil Hebdo* was censored for printing an article on slavery (it had been censored the previous September as well). Journalists have also been expelled from press conferences, as they were in September 1997, during the visit of the French president Jacques Chirac. Seventeen journalists were arrested between 1991 and 1997. Meanwhile, attacks on freedom of expression continued in 1998. In January *Mauritanie-Nouvelles* was again banned for three months, just as the previous ban expired. The same week, *Le Calame* was seized. A month later, five human rights defenders were convicted and five others detained without charge. The government has also denied applications to establish private radio stations, perhaps because the radio is the most powerful tool for reaching Mauritania's largely illiterate population.

Indeed, the government has also attempted to prevent Mauritanians from listening to international short-wave broadcasts that criticize the government's policies. In November 2000 broadcasts of Radio France Internationale were interrupted, and in April 2001 the radio journalist Mohammed Lemine Ould Bah, a correspondent with Radio France Internationale, Radio Monte Carlo Moyen-Orient, and Abou Dhabi TV was denied permission to continue working for these organizations while in Mauritania. According to the minister of communication, his "subjects run counter to the interests of Mauritania".

Although Mauritania, like many of its neighbours, initiated a democratization plan in 1991, the new constitution appears to reflect diplomatic strategy, rather than true policy change. This is the conclusion of many Mauritanian journalists. In an issue of *Mauritanie-Nouvelles*, Hamoud ould Salihi stated that the democratization simply shows how dependent African nations are on international aid. Seen from this angle, democratization in Mauritania has led to little substantive change. Freedom of speech remains a privilege, rather than a right, in Mauritania.

LISA MCNEE

Further Reading

Amnesty International, *Mauritania*, London: Amnesty International, 1981–

Amnesty International, *Mauritania, 1986–1989: Background to a Crisis: Three Years of Political Imprisonment, Torture, and Unfair Trials*, New York: Amnesty International, 1989

Amnesty International, "Mauritania: Government Should Do More than Host Human Rights Conference", *Amnesty International* (16 April 1997)

Amnesty International, "Mauritania: Trial of Four Human Rights Defenders", *Amnesty International* (30 January 1998)

Amnesty International, "Mauritania: Serious Attack on Freedoms of Expression and Association", *Amnesty International* (6 March 1998)

Baduel, Pierre Robert, "Mauritanie 1945–1990; ou, l'état face à la nation", special issue: "Mauritanie entre arabité et africanité", *Revue du Monde Musulman et de la Méditérannée*, 54 (1990): 11–52

Belvaude, Catherine, *La Mauritanie*, Paris: Karthala, 1989

Belvaude, Catherine, *Ouverture sur la littérature en Mauritanie: tradition orale, écriture, témoignages*, Paris: L'Harmattan, 1989

Belvaude, Catherine, *Libre Expression en Mauritanie: la presse francophone indépendante, 1991–1992*, Paris: L'Harmattan, 1995

Bouboutt, Ahmed Salem ould, "L'Évolution des institutions de la République Islamique de Mauritanie", special issue: "Mauritanie entre arabité et africanité", *Revue du monde musulman et de la Méditérannée*, 54 (1990): 130–40

Chassey, Francis de, *Mauritanie, 1900–1975*, Paris: Anthropos, 1978

Cheikh, Abdel Wedoud ould, "Des voix dans les désert: sur les élections de l'ère pluraliste'", *Politique Africaine*, 55 (1994): 31–39

Daddah, Amel, "Le Fragile Pari d'une presse démocratique", *Politique africaine*, 55 (1994): 40–45

Hamès, Constant, "Le Rôle de l'islam dans la société mauritanienne contemporaine", *Politique Africaine*, 55 (1994): 46–51

McNee, Lisa, "The Black and the White: Race and Oral Poetry in Mauritania" in *The Desert Shore: Literatures of the Sahel*, edited by Christopher Wise, Boulder, Colorado: Rienner, 2001

Mauritania's Campaign of Terror: State-Sponsored Repression of Black Africans, New York: Africa Watch, 1994

Ould Bah, Mohamed El Mokhtar, *La Littérature juridique et l'évolution du Malikisme en Mauritanie*, Tunis: l'Université de Tunis, 1981

Reporters without Borders, "Letter of Protest" (11 April 2001)

Roques, Christian, "La Mauritanie au miroir de sa presse", special issue: "Mauritanie entre arabité et africanité", *Revue du Monde Musulman et de la Méditérannée*, 54 (1990): 171–76

Roques, Christian, "Essor et difficultés d'une presse indépendante en Mauritanie", *Revue du Monde Musulman et de la Méditérannée*, 63/64:1–2, (1992): 245–55

Soudan, François, *Le Marabout et le colonel: la Mauritanie de Ould Daddah à Ould Taya*, Paris: Jeune Afrique, 1992

US Department of State, *Mauritania: Country Report on Human Rights Practices for 1997*, Washington, DC: Bureau of Democracy, Human Rights and Labor, 1998

MAURITIUS

Population: 1,161,000	**Illiteracy rate (%):** 12.1 (m); 18.6 (f)
Main religions: Hindu; Roman Catholic; Muslim; Protestant	**Number of daily newspapers:** 6
Official language: English	**Number of periodicals:** 29
Other languages spoken: Creole; French; Hindi; Urdu; Hakka; Bhojpuri	**Number of radio receivers per 1000 inhabitants:** 371
	Number of TV receivers per 1000 inhabitants: 228
	Number of PCs per 1000 inhabitants: 87.1

Arab traders may have known about Mauritius as early as the 10th century. The first European contact came with the arrival of the Portuguese in the 16th century. From 1598 to 1710 the Dutch took possession of the island, but departed after several failed attempts at settlement. Then, in 1721, the French East India Company occupied the island, renaming it Île de France

and establishing sugar plantations there. The British captured the island in 1810. It remained under British stewardship until 1968, when Mauritius became independent.

Although the British were technically in control of Mauritius from 1810 onwards, the earlier French influence proved enduring. French remains the dominant language for both printed and audiovisual material. Another profound influence on the development of Mauritius was the massive influx of Indian indentured labour which was necessary for the plantation economy to function. By the mid-1800s there were over 330,000 indentured labourers on the island. Today, over half the population is of Indian descent. Diversity is one of the hallmarks of Mauritius, and may be partly responsible for the culture of tolerance that has arisen there. The presence of a large Indian population, alongside those of African, Chinese, or European ancestry, has sometimes in the past resulted in occasional flare-ups. In general, though, governments have been able to maintain tolerant coexistence between these groups.

The news media and the press in Mauritius have functioned in a relatively uncensored environment for decades, testimony to the liberal nature of the political system. This does not mean that no problems have arisen. There have been occasional attempts by the government to restrict the media through the use of such tactics as forcing the print media to post bonds against potential defamation suits. However, such efforts met with widespread public protest and were ultimately unsuccessful.

In the 1970s, the revolutionary Mouvement Militant Mauricien's (MMM) sudden rise to prominence in Mauritian politics prompted the government to delay elections, and pass a public order act which allowed it to declare a state of emergency and shut down unions, press, and other organizations it considered threatening. As a consequence, for much of the first half of the 1970s freedom of expression was curtailed in Mauritius. Eventually the MMM and the government were able to resolve the situation. Political stability returned, and with it the freedom of speech and the press to which Mauritians had become accustomed. Indeed, in 1982 the MMM and its partners, the Parti Socialiste Mauricien (PSM), won a landslide victory in a general election.

High literacy rates have encouraged the proliferation of printed media. Numerous privately-owned media exist, with daily news available in French, English, Creole, and other languages. Freedom of speech and of the press is guaranteed by the constitution. Although libel laws do exist, the government has not made use of them to silence its critics. Occasional attempts at book censorship have occurred when the government deems the material to be threatening to "national security".

Until 1997 there was a government monopoly on the broadcast media, but this was overturned by the Supreme Court with the result that private broadcasters now exist, although they are still nascent. Internet access is available and unrestricted, though costly. Academic freedom is generally respected, as is freedom of religion. Although permits are required for demonstrations, these are routinely issued. Again, there have been sporadic incidents where permits were denied, but these have been isolated events.

Ethnic and religious tensions have arisen between the diverse communities of Mauritius. A significant example of this occurred in 1995, when a fatwa (religious edict) was issued against the editor of the Mauritius weekly L'Indépendant in response to the printing of an article calling for the liberalization of the meat industry, which was interpreted by Muslim fundamentalists as an attack on the Prophet Muhammad. This resulted in the firebombing of the paper's offices, threats, and the flight of the editor from the country. Supporters of L'Indépendant burnt other papers – L'Express, Le Mage, and Le Mauricien – for being anti-Hindu, among other things. This rare form of Mauritian censorship was approved by the Movement against Communalism.

DANA OTT

Further Reading

Area Handbook for Indian Ocean: Mauritius, Washington, DC: Library of Congress, 1994

Bowman, Larry W., Mauritius: Democracy and Development in the Indian Ocean, Boulder, Colorado: Westview Press, and London: Dartmouth, 1991

IFEX (International Freedom of Expression Exchange Clearinghouse), Action Alert, various years

US Department of State, Mauritius: Country Report on Human Rights Practices, Washington, DC: Bureau of Democracy, Human Rights and Labor, various years

MED-TV
Kurdish satellite television channel, established 1995

Med-TV was named after the Medes, who lived in the upper Mesopotamian region between the rivers Tigris and Euphrates around 4000 years ago; the peoples known today as the Kurds are believed to be related to them. There are substantial Kurdish communities today in Iran, Iraq, Turkey, and the Russian Federation, and many other Kurds live in exile in western Europe and the United States.

Med-TV was the Kurds' only television outlet. Licensed in Britain by the Independent Television Commission (ITC) in late 1994, the station began test transmissions on 30 March 1995, broadcasting three hours daily and transmitting via Intelsat to a potential audience of 35 million Kurds throughout Europe, North Africa and the Middle East. Broadcasting mostly in the main Kurdish dialects, Kirmanci, Sorani and Zazaki, the station provided television for Kurdish people from all parts of divided Kurdistan, and also drew on an existing market of Turkish-speaking viewers. Its European headquarters and main production studio were in Brussels, and there was a second production studio in Cologne. Foreign-language films were dubbed into Kurdish in Med-TV's studios in Stockholm. Major financial support came from the Kurdish Foundation Trust.

The idea of a satellite television station for a nation without a recognized homeland was unique, and highly charged politically. Turkey regards all expressions of Kurdish identity as illegal, and regularly suppresses them. The Turkish government claims that Med-TV supported the Kurdish Workers' Party (PKK) which had carried out acts of terrorism against Turkey, discounting entirely the station's affirmation that it was "a privately-owned and funded organization with no political or financial links to any organization making use of violence for political purposes". Nevertheless, the emergence of Med-TV inspired considerable media interest as well as high-level diplomatic debate. It was hailed as a historic achievement and a defeat for political censorship.

Med-TV's output included music programmes, animations and films, and live political debate. As early as April 1995 the British Foreign Office received a complaint from the Turkish government about Med-TV's coverage of the "Kurdish Parliament in Exile", which was trying to gain international recognition. The Foreign Office asked that the station's licence to broadcast be withdrawn, but the ITC refused because it had "no reason to believe that it has broken any UK broadcasting regulations", such as being owned by a political party or promoting violence.

There followed a campaign to intimidate those who watched Med-TV in Turkey. The Turkish press gave full coverage to the destruction of satellite dishes and the detention of suspected viewers. The Turkish government also pursued a vigorous campaign in European capitals to have the licence withdrawn. The prime minister, Tansu Çiller, first asked the British government to support her request that the station be taken off the air during her visit to Britain in November 1995; she then asked the German authorities to prevent cable broadcasts. Turkish pressure led France Telecom to refuse to renew Med-TV's contract with the Eutelsat satellite in April 1996. Portugal Telecom followed suit in June 1996. Med-TV was unable to transmit for 45 days when a third Eutelsat provider, Polish Telecom, broke its contract. The US State Department described the station as "the voice of terrorists". In September 1996 the Brussels and London studios of Med-TV were raided by police in searches for evidence of money laundering and drug trafficking; nothing was found.

In December 1995 an unprecedented attempt was made to censor transnational satellite broadcasting when Med-TV's transmission was disrupted by a pirate signal during a live debate from Brussels. There is no firm evidence to show who the perpetrator might have been, but similar interference took place in October 1998. Med-TV claimed that the jamming contravened the European Union's Television without Frontiers directive, as well as many other international covenants and conventions that guarantee the right to seek, impart, and receive information and opinions freely, in all media, and without regard to borders. In the Vienna Declaration of 9 October 1993, the Council of Europe explicitly affirmed that national minorities must "be able to use their language both in private and in public and should be able to use it, under certain conditions, in their relations with the public authorities". At present, there are no Kurdish-language newspapers in Turkey, and Kurds have no rights to use their language on radio and television even during elections.

Turkey is also a signatory of the European Convention on Human Rights. Article 10(1) protects freedom of expression, but does not provide an absolute right to free speech. Thus Turkey might argue that its actions against Med-TV are justified under article 10(2), which states that "the exercise of these freedoms . . . may be subject to such formalities, conditions, restrictions or penalties as are prescribed by law and are necessary in a democratic society in the interests of national security". Turkey believes that Med-TV "stirs up racial hatred and is against the territorial integrity of Turkey". In January 1999 it did not object to attempts by the Iraqi Kurdistan Democratic Party to establish a television station in northern Iraq as long as the station did not support separatist terrorism.

Med-TV received two formal warnings from the ITC for breaches of its programme code: in November 1996 (for two occasions on which it was said to not to have observed "due impartiality"), and in March 1998 (for having incited crime). In January 1998 the ITC fined the station £90,000 for further offences against "due impartiality"; and in June 1998 it gave the station a formal warning about a further case of incitement to crime. Then, in November 1998, the ITC issued a notice to Med-TV that its licence would be revoked if, over the following six months, its service failed to comply with its terms: the station had, the ITC maintained, allowed a "recurrent lack of balance in political coverage". It must not "give preference to the views of representatives or supporters of any political party or parties, including the PKK", and "politicians must not be used as news reporters".

Hikmet Tabak, managing director of Med-TV, argued that Turkey had carried out a disinformation campaign, the influence of which was now being felt. Med-TV was trying its best to be a democratic channel and he did not think that the licence would be revoked. However, on 23 April 1999 the ITC served a notice of revocation following four broadcasts said to have encouraged acts of violence in Turkey and elsewhere. The ITC stated that:

> Whatever sympathy there may be in the United Kingdom for the Kurdish people, it is not in the public interest to have any broadcaster use the UK as a channel for broadcasts which incite people to violence. Med-TV has been given many opportunities to be a peaceful voice for their community; to allow them to continue broadcasting after such serious breaches would be to condone the misuse of the UK's system for licensing broadcasters.

Several weeks of demonstrations outside the ITC headquarters followed. A press release on the Med-TV website reassured Kurdish people that "we will be back on the air before long", and that an appeal to the High Court was being considered. No such appeal has been lodged. Med-TV remains, in the words of Hikmet Tabak, an example of "how satellite technology of the modern world, often seen as an implement to abolish cultural differences, can also be a tool to preserve them".

ABDULLAH TANAY

Further Reading
Drucker, Catherine, *Kurdish Voices from the Sky*, London: Article 19, 1997
Imset, Ismet, "Turkish Roulette", *Index on Censorship*, 25/2 (March–April 1996)
Ryan, Nick, "Television Nation", *Wired* (March 1997)

ROY MEDVEDEV and ZHORES A. MEDVEDEV
Russian intellectuals, 1925–

Roy and Zhores Medvedev, twin brothers, were born in 1925. Their father, Aleksandr Medvedev, a historian and philosopher, was one of millions who was arrested during Stalin's purges in 1936–38: he died in a labour camp in the Russian Far East in 1941. Roy, who graduated from Leningrad University, became a historian. Zhores, who graduated from the K.A. Timiriazev Agricultural Academy in Moscow, became a biologist. They were among the few Soviet intellectuals who decided to fight censorship in their home country by deliberate publication of their major works and their papers in western countries, both in Russian and in foreign languages. The best-known among their books secretly delivered to western publishers are probably Zhores's *The Rise and Fall of T.D. Lysenko* (1969) and Roy's *Let History Judge: The Origins and Consequences of Stalinism* (1972). Repressive measures taken against them by Soviet authorities included dismissal from their positions, confiscations of their papers and archives, detention in mental hospital (Zhores), a form of house arrest (Roy), and expulsion from the Soviet Union and deprivation of Soviet citizenship (Zhores, in 1973). Because they both remain active authors, they themselves now tell their stories of confrontation with Soviet censorship.

Zhores A. Medvedev

Everybody in the Soviet Union knew something about censorship, despite the fact that its existence and functions were considered to be state secrets. People knew perfectly well what could be said in public and what could not, because many forms of criticism, or mere deviation from the official line in the analysis of events or personalities, could be treated as a political crime and lead to arrest or a prison sentence.

I first became acquainted with the workings of Soviet censorship from 1946 onwards, when I contributed articles to *Timiriazevez*, the students' weekly newspaper at the K.A. Timiriazev Agricultural Academy. I discovered that even this paper, with a circulation as small as one or two thousand readers, had to be approved before it was printed by an official from Glavlit, the Main Administration for Affairs of Literature and Publishing Houses. This state organization operated through both local and specialist offices, including one attached to the main publishing house for agricultural literature in Moscow. General censors could understand and implement the constantly updated secret instructions when it came to literary magazines and newspapers, but they needed further help with academic texts on physics, mathematics, chemistry, or biology. Books on tuberculosis, power station turbines, or mineral fertilizers, for example, had to pass through two stages of censorship, the first general, the second carried out by specialists at the Ministry of Health, the Ministry of Electric Power, or the Ministry of Agriculture. It was also of relevance to a future scientist that his professional correspondence with colleagues abroad had first to be presented to the director of his institute, and then, if approved, to the "foreign" section of the appropriate ministry, which finally sent all such letters once it was satisfied that they contained nothing dangerous to the state or its ideology.

My first direct confrontation with the censors happened in 1961 when my book *Protein Biosynthesis and Problems of Development, Heredity, and Ageing*, which was already under contract with the publishing house Soviet Science in Moscow, was returned because the chapter on heredity considered DNA and the role of genes, and was critical of the then dominant theories of T.D. Lysenko. The publishing house was attached to the Ministry of Higher Education and Lysenko's pseudoscientific theories were still compulsory for biological education. I then offered the same book to Medgiz, which was attached to the Ministry of Health. It was accepted and published, but the whole print run of nearly 4,000 copies was "arrested" only a few days later, because a high official in the agricultural department of the Central Committee of the Communist Party had discovered that my chapter on heredity contained direct criticism of Lysenko. At first, Medgiz came under pressure to destroy the whole print run. However, about 400 copies had already been sold. Protracted negotiation between the director of Medgiz and the agricultural department of the Central Committee followed, and it was finally agreed that the pages that directly challenged Lysenko's ideas would be removed. The book now exists in two slightly different versions. This experience revealed that, in addition to all the different censors, every leading official of the state and party apparatus (ministers, members of the Central Committee, regional party secretaries) received relevant books for pre-publication review, and had the power to stop sales if they found reasons to do so.

At the end of 1961, partly as a result of my problems with this book, I decided to write a new book on the history of Lysenkoism in the Soviet Union and the fate of many scientists who lost their lives or their freedom in the 1930s and 1940s after fighting Lysenko's theories. Lysenko was still the "Tsar" in biology and agriculture: he was president of the Lenin Academy of Agricultural Sciences, director of the Institute of Genetics, and deputy chairman of the Supreme Soviet of the Soviet Union. He had the full support of Nikita Khrushchev. I knew quite well that my second book could not be published in the Soviet Union. The book, completed in the middle of 1962 under the title *Biological Science and the Cult of Personality*, was intended not for officially sanctioned publication but for clandestine circulation. About 20 typewritten copies were prepared, and distributed among prominent scientists, writers, and journalists whom I trusted. Twenty copies happened to be enough to start the process that was later called samizdat ("self-publishing"). Within two or three months, with the help of typewriting or photocopying, there were already several thousand copies in circulation. I was receiving comments and new materials from all parts of the Soviet Union, which enabled new versions of the book to be constantly updated.

By the end of 1963, the manuscript was apparently known in the relevant departments of the KGB and the Central Committee, and Lysenko himself got hold of a copy. My position as a senior scientist in the K.A. Timiriazev Agricultural Academy became untenable. A special commission of the local party committee was created to investigate my "anti-Soviet activity", but I preferred to resign rather than be investigated.

I moved to a research position at the Institute of Medical Radiology at Obninsk in the Kaluga region, but the pressure was felt there as well. However, in 1964, Khrushchev was dismissed and replaced by Leonid Brezhnev. Without political support, Lysenko also lost his influence and many of his positions.

In 1965 I received an offer from the publishing house of the Academy of Sciences to publish my book on condition that I added a chapter on the fall of Lysenko and the rehabilitation of his critics. The new version was put before a special commission of 12 members of the Academy of Sciences, under the chairmanship of professor N.N. Semenov, a winner of the Nobel Prize for Chemistry. In 1966, this commission unanimously recommended publication and I naturally expected that this decision would be implemented. However, the publishing house was still unable to get the manuscript through all the levels of censorship. The new political leadership clearly preferred to forget, rather than expose, the crimes of the Stalin era. Many other books about political repression in Stalin's time experienced the same fate.

There were only two possible choices for me, either to wait for a better time or to publish my book abroad. Publication abroad without official permission was considered a political crime, but since the book had already received considerable support among Soviet scientists, I decided to take the risk. In November 1967, a special conference to commemorate the 80th anniversary of the birth of the geneticist Nikolai Vavilov was organized in Leningrad. Vavilov had been Lysenko's main opponent and victim: he had been arrested in 1940 and had died in prison in 1943. An old friend of Vavilov's, Åke Gustafsson from the Institute of Genetics in Sweden, volunteered to send my manuscript to Columbia University Press in New York. In the United States, the book was translated into English by Michael Lerner, a geneticist who had known Vavilov. The book was published in New York in April 1969, under the title *The Rise and Fall of T.D. Lysenko*, and by 1971 it had been translated into ten other languages.

The consequences of such "illegal" publication were predictable: I was dismissed from my position as head of the institute's molecular radiobiology laboratory. However, no investigation was launched against me, apparently because a book of this kind could no longer be considered as "anti-Soviet". I had violated the rules, not the law.

My attempts to find a new research job were not successful. I therefore decided to continue writing. Before the end of 1969 I had completed another book about international cooperation among scientists, which criticized Soviet restrictions on foreign travel and the isolation of Soviet science. It too was offered for publication in the West. At the beginning of 1970 I wrote a study of postal censorship and exchange of literature, even among libraries. These two books were published in one volume by Macmillan in London in 1971, under the title *The Medvedev Papers*. Russian versions were also published in London.

In May 1970, when it became apparent that I would continue to write and publish, I was arrested without charge and put into a mental hospital in Kaluga. However, this action created so much negative publicity for the Soviet authorities that I was released three weeks later. This experience also gave me material for a book on the misuse of psychiatry in the Soviet Union, *A Question of Madness*, which was published in

London and New York in 1971, both in Russian and in English, and has been translated into many languages. My next project was a book about Aleksandr Solzhenitsyn and about more general problems of censorship in the Soviet Union.

In 1972, I was invited by the National Institute of Medical Research in London to conduct a year's collaborative research on molecular aspects of ageing. This invitation had no connection with my political writing. I was given official permission to travel to London with my wife and younger son. Soon after we arrived in Britain in January 1973, I was invited to the Soviet Embassy to be informed that I had been stripped of Soviet citizenship for "anti-Soviet activity", and that my passport was to be confiscated. Fortunately, my research work at the institute in London was successful and I was able to work as a full-time senior research scientist in its genetics division until retirement in 1991. I became a British citizen in 1984, but my Soviet citizenship was also restored in 1990 by a decree of president Mikhail Gorbachev.

ZHORES A. MEDVEDEV

Roy Medvedev

In 1956, after Nikita Khrushchev's "secret" speech about Stalin's crimes to the 20th congress of the Communist Party, I decided to join the party because I felt that it would be possible to work toward democratic socialism within it. At that time, I was head of a secondary school in the Leningrad region and I was also researching the possibility of combining general education with vocational education. This research was the subject of my first published book and of my Ph.D. thesis in pedagogical sciences.

At the beginning of 1957, I was offered the comparatively senior position of deputy to the editor-in-chief of the Uchpedgiz (Learning and Pedagogical Literature) publishing house, which was the largest in the country, being responsible for publication of all textbooks for primary and secondary schools, as well as for books in pedagogical sciences. There were dozens of subjects for pupils aged between 7 and 17, and millions of copies of each textbook were printed every year. I was put in charge of the history textbooks department. The history of Russia before 1917 and the history of the Soviet Union were most important, and were compulsory for every school. I now had the task of signing off on manuscripts that were considered ready for printing.

However, as Zhores reveals above, printing could start only if a second signature, from an official of Glavlit, was added. A section of Glavlit was actually located inside the main building of our publishing house. I was allowed to read numerous instructions from the censors and to argue with them when I felt it was necessary. I worked in this publishing house for nearly four years, at a time when the history of Russia and the Soviet Union was being rewritten virtually every year because of the changing attitudes of the party leadership and Khrushchev himself toward the Stalin era, reflecting the constant struggle for power within the leadership. I noted Glavlit's instructions to remove the names of Viacheslav Molotov, Georgii Malenkov, and other members of the "anti-party group" from all history textbooks. I got to know the censorship rules and the censorship system quite well.

I also knew that there were clear distinctions among three different kinds of censored information. First, there was information that was simply suppressed and not recommended for disclosure, such as descriptions of life in labour camps and prisons. If an editor or author somehow released suppressed information he could face disciplinary action or reprimand, or, in serious cases, expulsion from the party and dismissal from his position. Second, there was information that was strictly forbidden for publication, such as criticism of Lenin or (at that time) Khrushchev. The release of forbidden information was treated as a criminal offence and could lead to a sentence of between one year and seven years in prison for "anti-Soviet activity". Finally, there was highly classified secret information, which included not only military or state secrets, but also many party secrets hidden in special archives. The disclosure of classified information was regarded as treason and incurred much heavier sentences. In my subsequent research work as a historian I mostly revealed suppressed information, rather than forbidden or classified materials. I never tried to work in the many special archives or receive internal documents from party or state officials. My main sources of information were previously published materials that had appeared in relatively obscure provincial, regional, or republican newspapers. I also collected oral testimonies, private diaries, or memoirs from those who had survived Stalin's prison camps, show trials, and exiles.

In the Soviet Union, private memoirs were often a more valuable source of information than archives, which were, as a rule, selective and distorted. After Khrushchev's speech in February 1956, more than 1 million political prisoners, some of whom had survived more than 20 years in labour camps, were released and rehabilitated. Many of them started to write memoirs, papers, or articles, but this great volume of important information was suppressed. The censorship rules did not allow the publication of any information about prisons and labour camps, or the show trials of the 1930s. Even Khrushchev's speech remained "secret" and was never published in the Soviet Union. At the end of 1962, the publication of Aleksandr Solzhenitsyn's novella *Odin den' Ivana Denisovicha* (*One Day in the Life of Ivan Denisovich*) was allowed in a literary journal, *Novyi mir*, but only after a special decision of the Politburo and Khrushchev, and because it was a literary fiction, not a documentary account. In this situation – and because no single account of Stalin's life had yet been written by a Soviet historian – I decided to write a more comprehensive book that would combine a biography of Stalin with an analysis of his reign of terror. Initially I hoped that so long as the trend towards greater openness about Stalin continued, my book might be published in the Soviet Union.

The first version of this book, to which I gave the title *Let History Judge*, was ready at the end of 1964. However, in October that year, as Zhores has mentioned above, Khrushchev was replaced by Brezhnev. Some of Khrushchev's "mistakes" were corrected, particularly in agricultural policy, but as far as the history of the party was concerned, Brezhnev was a more conservative leader. He did not want to disclose the real picture of Stalin's era because he was afraid that this might undermine the party's monopoly of power. Glavlit received new instructions, and quite a few literary and historical works already approved for publication, or in print, were suppressed. The KGB even started to confiscate some manuscripts. It was clear now that my book never could be published in the Soviet Union. Nevertheless, I decided to continue to collect the necessary materials, and to discuss new versions of my book with friends, colleagues, and many former inmates of the labour camps. I showed a new version of this work to Solzhenitsyn, Aleksandr Tvardovskii (editor of *Novyi mir*), Vladimir Lakshin, Konstantin Simonov, and others whose comments were also very helpful. By the middle of 1968, about 200 people had read and commented on the manuscript, which constantly grew in size. By then it amounted to about 1,000 pages of typewritten text, making it difficult to distribute in samizdat form.

At the end of 1968, moreover, after the Warsaw Pact suppression of the "Prague Spring", political repression resumed inside the Soviet Union as well. Because my work was not confidential and was known even to some of the more liberal party officials, I did not exclude the possibility that my papers might be confiscated and repressive measures taken to stop my research. I therefore decided to send my book abroad for publication. I knew, of course, that my brother Zhores had already done this with his book on Lysenko. Zhores prepared three copies of my manuscript on microfilm – photography was his hobby – and two of them were taken by foreign colleagues and delivered to historians in Austria and the United States whom we knew and who could read Russian. David Joravsky, the head of the history department at Northwestern University in Evanston, Illinois, who was an expert on Soviet history, agreed to be my representative in the United States. He arranged for the reproduction of the microfilm and on my behalf signed an agreement with Alfred A. Knopf in New York to publish an English translation.

We had managed to do all this only just in time. In the middle of 1969, the KGB somehow managed to get hold of one of the 20 or so copies of the book that were then in limited circulation, mostly in Moscow. A special commission of the Moscow party committee was created to analyse the book and decide my fate. Because my work was strictly factual, it was impossible to accuse me of "slander" or to treat it as a "criminal" document. Nevertheless, I was expelled from the party and later dismissed from my position as a department head at the Institute of Vocational Education. A few months later, when information emerged about foreign publishers' interest in the book, a KGB team arrived at my flat in Moscow. They searched my books and papers for several hours, and confiscated the whole archive on Stalin and many other papers.

A few days after that, I was invited to the Procuracy (the prosecuting authority) for interrogation. This could mean that, after interrogation, the investigator had the right to arrest me. I therefore decided to go into hiding. For several months I lived in different places in the Black Sea area, where some of my close friends from university years helped me to stay undetected. I returned to Moscow during the spring of 1972, when I got the news that my book would be published in New York and would be on sale shortly. The book received very good reviews. This was the first comprehensive work on Stalinism written by a Soviet author.

After 1971, I wrote exclusively for foreign publishers, and several of my books were published in France, Britain, or the United States, not only in foreign languages but also in Russian. It was also during 1971 that I managed to send abroad a microfilm of the samizdat journal *Politicheskii dnevnik* (Political Diary), which I had been composing and editing since 1964.

Issues of this journal were prepared monthly, usually containing my review of the main political and cultural events of the month and also samizdat works and contributions from some of my friends. This journal's circulation was limited to between 50 and 100 trusted readers, making it possible to keep the project undetected for many years. However, during another KGB raid on my flat in October 1971, some issues of this journal and materials related to it were confiscated. Because three copies of the microfilm version were kept elsewhere, Zhores managed to send them abroad via friendly foreign journalists in Moscow. Selected issues were subsequently published in two large volumes in Russian in the Netherlands in 1972 and 1975, and an English version of some materials from the journal was published by W.W. Norton in New York, under the title *An End to Silence*.

In 1975, I decided to start a new samizdat journal and to do so more openly. The title of this journal was *The Twentieth Century*. It was composed mainly of some samizdat works whose authors were not able to publish them openly. By this time, Zhores was living in London. We hoped that it would be possible to make a printed Russian version of this journal in London and later distribute it in the Soviet Union. However, this journal had a much shorter history than its predecessor. In 1976 I was officially invited to the Procuracy once again and told by the deputy procurator general to cease publication. A person from the KGB was also present. They had obtained the first issue of selected works from this journal published in London. I knew that if I did not stop, I could be arrested. A few days later, my flat in Moscow was again raided, and all materials related to the journal, along with a lot of other materials and books, were confiscated. Therefore, I had to stop. I did manage to issue 11 Russian-language editions of the journal in which about 70 works of different authors were made available for samizdat. Two volumes of selected works were published in London in Russian and also in English. English versions had been titled as *Samizdat Register* and published by Merlin Press in London. There were also Italian and Japanese translations. Some other works from this journal (among them two novels and several works on history or

political polemic) were also published as separate books by different publishers in France, Britain, and the US.

In 1983, after I had published two more books in Britain and the United States – *Khrushchev: A Political Biography* and *All Stalin's Men* – I was put under a form of "house arrest". A permanent KGB post was kept at the door of my flat and all visitors were turned away apart from my close relatives. If I left the flat, I was always followed by KGB agents in a car. This, of course, restricted my activities, because I did not want to get my friends and assistants into any trouble, and therefore did not visit them. This permanent close surveillance was ended only in the middle of 1985. I was able to publish some of my works and articles in the Soviet press only after 1988, when Gorbachev's policies of perestroika and glasnost finally led to the abolition of political censorship in the Soviet Union.

ROY MEDVEDEV

Writings

Medvedev, Zhores A., *The Rise and Fall of T.D. Lysenko*, translated by I. Michael Lerner, 1969

Medvedev, Zhores A., *The Medvedev Papers: Fruitful Meetings between Scientists of the World; and Secrecy of Correspondence Is Guaranteed by Law*, translated by Vera Rich, 1971

Medvedev, Zhores A. and Roy, *A Question of Madness*, translated by Ellen de Kadt, 1971

Medvedev, Roy, *Let History Judge: The Origins and Consequences of Stalinism*, translated by Colleen Taylor, 1972

Medvedev, Roy (editor), *The Twentieth Century: A Socio-political Digest and Literary Magazine*, 2 vols, 1976–77

Medvedev, Roy (editor), *The Samizdat Register*, 2 vols, 1977–81

Medvedev, Roy (editor), *Politicheskii dnevnik, 1964–1970* (Political Diary, 1964–70) (nos. 3, 9, 25, 30, 33, 43, 46, 55, 63, 67, 72), 1972; and *Politicheskii dnevnik, 1965–1970* (Political Diary, 1965–70) (nos. 7, 28, 31, 48, 50, 54, 64, 75), 1975; selections as *An End to Silence: Uncensored Opinion in the Soviet Union from Roy Medvedev's Underground Magazine Political Diary*, edited by Stephen F. Cohen, translated by George Saunders, 1982

Further Reading

Tökés, Rudolf L. (editor), *Dissent in the USSR: Politics, Ideology, and People*, Baltimore: Johns Hopkins University Press, 1975

MEIROKU ZASSHI (The Meiji Six Magazine)
Japanese journal, 1874–75

The *Meiroku Zasshi* was produced by a group of reformist Japanese intellectuals early in the Meiji period (1868–1912). The group took the name Meirokusha (Meiji Six Society), "Meiji Six" signifying the sixth year of the Meiji period, 1873, in which it was founded. The journal first appeared in 1874 and ceased publication the following year after only 43 issues. Contributors tackled many of the most fundamental issues of the "Meiji enlightenment", such as the future role of women in Japan, political systems and forms of government, political freedoms for citizens, and so on. The contributors, who were all men, included many who had had first-hand experience of western countries and/or worked for the government, seeking to reform it from the inside, as well as individuals who preferred to retain their independence and criticize from the outside.

The sixth issue contained a plea for freedom of the press from Tsuda Mamichi, one of the most radical members of the Meirokusha, who also advocated the formation of a popularly elected assembly. However, the strict new press and censorship regulations introduced by the Meiji government in 1875 demonstrated that the government was moving in the opposite direction and caused something of a crisis among the membership of the Meirokusha. Those within the government, such as Mori Arinori, who was later to be minister of education, urged that political issues be avoided in future, to forestall the possibility of censorship and to keep the journal going. Others, especially the enlightenment pioneer Fukuzawa Yukichi, who vigorously preserved his independence of the government, argued that they had no choice but to halt publication, since they could not engage in free discussion in print any more. A vote was taken and it was decided to suspend publication. Three further issues did appear, with articles written mostly by those who had opposed suspension, but this was the end of the journal. To some extent, the demise of the *Meiroku Zasshi* was a consequence of the diverging interests of the members, but the immediate cause was the opposition of the majority to the government's restrictions on the expression of views in print.

P.F. KORNICKI

Further Reading

Braisted, William Reynolds (translator), *Meiroku Zasshi: Journal of the Japanese Enlightenment*, Cambridge, Massachusetts: Harvard University Press, 1976

FELIX MENDELSSOHN (Jakob Ludwig Felix Mendelssohn-Bartholdy)
German composer, 1809–1847

The grandson of the philosopher Moses Mendelssohn, Felix Mendelssohn was born into a prosperous Jewish family that had converted to Christianity on settling in Berlin. He was precociously gifted, writing masterpieces such as the Overture to *A Midsummer Night's Dream* and the Octet in E flat major for strings in his teens. During his lifetime, he enjoyed great success throughout Germany, and was particularly venerated in Britain. In 1835 he became conductor of the Gewandhaus Orchestra in Leipzig and eight years later founded the Music Conservatory in the same city. Among his best-known works are the oratorio *Elijah* (commissioned by the Birmingham Festival), the Overture *The Hebrides,* the Violin Concerto, and the Italian Symphony.

A staunchly conservative musician, Mendelssohn continued to exert enormous influence over musical developments in Germany and Britain well after his death. However, his reputation declined somewhat after the turn of the century, partly as a result of changing tastes which found some aspects of his music infused with Victorian sentimentality. Wagner's controversial pamphlet *Jews in Music* (1851, revised 1869) may also have been influential.

While recognizing Mendelssohn's undoubted talents as a musician, Wagner accused him of superficial imitation of the great classical composers and of being incapable of achieving real depth of feeling on account of his racial origins. It was an argument that was frequently reiterated by some German musicologists and critics even before the Third Reich.

When the Nazis came to power in 1933, they managed to suppress performance of music by the majority of Jewish composers within a matter of months. The removal of Mendelssohn's work proved more troublesome. For example, when in 1934 the National Socialist Cultural Community (NSKG) offered leading composers generous commissions to write incidental music to *A Midsummer Night's Dream* to replace the much-loved score by Mendelssohn, they met with firm refusal and had to settle for scores by the lesser-known Julius Weismann and Rudolf Wagner-Régeny. Needless to say, neither work gained widespread acceptance, and further attempts to replace Mendelssohn's work, including the 1939 score by Carl Orff, suffered a similar fate.

In the early years of the regime, there were isolated examples of defiance of official policy. In 1934, the conductor Wilhelm Furtwängler presented an all-Mendelssohn concert with the Berlin Philharmonic Orchestra in celebration of the 125th anniversary of the composer's birth. The German company Telefunken issued a commercial recording of the Violin Concerto with the violinist Georg Kulenkampff, although it was only available for export. But by and large, musicians maintained the party line. Although Mendelssohn could not be tarred with the brush of degeneracy, every attempt was made to undermine his significance, either through removing his name from reference books and historical surveys or by challenging his achievements. The most grotesque distortions of historical fact occur in Karl Blessinger's book *Mendelssohn, Meyerbeer, Mahler: Drei Kapitel Judentum in der Musik* (1939), where Mendelssohn's success is attributed entirely to Jewish vested interests. Thus, according to Blessinger, Mendelssohn revived Bach's *St Matthew Passion* in 1829 so that Judaism could claim the management of Germany's greatest creations, and his oratorios were composed primarily to impose Jewish ideals upon Christianity. In addition, citing Joachim's espousal of the Violin Concerto, Blessinger suggested that Jewish performers artificially maintained Mendelssohn's music in the repertoire, in order to prevent rival composers from achieving success.

The Czech Jewish writer Jiří Weil's story *Mendelssohn on the Roof* is said to have some basis in fact. In the story, Reichsprotektor Richard Heydrich is angry when he finds there is a statue of Mendelssohn along with other composers on the roof of the Rudolfinum in Prague. Workmen are quickly despatched to remove it, but, when they reach the roof, they are unable to identify which is Mendelssohn. They decide that it must be the one with the biggest nose. They topple the statue – but it depicts Richard Wagner!

ERIK LEVI

Further Reading

Blessinger, Karl, *Mendelssohn, Meyerbeer, Mahler: Drei Kapitel Judentum in der Musik als Schlüssel zur Musikgeschichte des 19. Jahrhunderts*, Berlin: Hahnefeld, 1939

Levi, Erik, *Music in the Third Reich*, London: Macmillan, and New York: St Martin's Press, 1994

Werner, Eric, *Mendelssohn: A New Image of the Composer and his Age*, New York: Free Press, 1963

JIŘÍ MENZEL
Czech film director, 1938–
SKŘIVÁNCI NA NITI (Skylarks on a String)
Film, 1969

Jiří Menzel began his career as a film director in 1965, with "Smrt pana Baltazara" ("The Death of Mr Balthazar"), his contribution to the episodic film *Perličky na dně* (Pearls of the Deep), which has become known as the "manifesto" of the Czech "New Wave". Like the other episodes, it was adapted from a short story by Bohumil Hrabal. In 1966, Czechoslovakia received its second US Academy Award when *Ostře sledované vlaky* (Closely Observed Trains), directed by Menzel from a screenplay by Hrabal based on his own novel, was awarded the Oscar for best foreign-language film. *Skylarks on a String* was their third collaboration – and Menzel's first film after the Warsaw Pact invasion of 1968. Like Karel Kachyna's *Ucho* (The Ear, 1969), it was not released until after the fall of communism; in 1990, it was awarded the Golden Bear at the Berlin Film Festival.

Unlike many of the other banned films from the 1960s, *Skylarks on a String* makes an overt attack on Stalinism. It opens with a title referring, with what must have been obvious irony, to the achievement of power by the working class and the need to incorporate the defeated classes into the new society. The setting is a steel reprocessing plant to which various remnants of the bourgeoisie have been sent for "re-education". They include a lawyer who believes in applying the law, a saxophonist whose instrument has been banned as "bourgeois", a Seventh-Day Adventist, Pavel, who refuses to work on Saturdays, a dairyman who "closed his dairy and volunteered to work for Socialism", and other assorted "enemies of the people".

As in Hrabal's other work, the characters remain resolutely human and defy the simplistic ideology imposed on them. They discuss the philosopher Immanuel Kant, keep fish, and find ways of meeting the female detainees who have been arrested for "desertion of the republic" (trying to escape to the West). Each character lives in the best way he or she can, with a perverse kind of internal freedom. The men's supervisor is mercilessly pilloried as he talks about his working-class past and encourages them to labour by example (revealing a remote acquaintance with reality). He only comes into his own when lurking proprietorially behind the factory railings to observe the latest secret police arrest, or assisting a campaign for bodily cleanliness by helping to sponge a naked Roma girl. References to the glorious future are interspersed with such events as a polka in honour of a record smeltdown, a tour by young Pioneers (members of the communist youth movement) who come to look at "faces soaked in imperialism", and a visit from the minister of culture (a caricature of the musicologist, Zdeněk Nejedlý), with his sentimental references to Smetana and Dvořák. The union representative arrives in a chauffeur-driven car and puts on a workman's hat on arrival. The romantic and optimistic vision of socialism is constantly juxtaposed with the seedy realities, self seeking, and absurdities of a police state.

The narrative, which is based on a number of Hrabal stories, is punctuated by the arrests of the dairyman for initiating a strike against an unnegotiated increase in work norms, the librarian, for asking what happened to him, and Pavel the Adventist, for asking the Minister what had happened to the good old days. As the prisoners descend a mineshaft at the end of the film, the light recedes behind them, and the film's final words echo: "They stole our truth". Menzel contrasts this unpleasant reality with the omnipresence of love between the sexes. In the main, the treatment is romantic, but the lyrical romance between Pavel and one of the women detainees, Jitka, does not have a happy outcome. Their eventual marriage is carried out through surrogates and bureaucrats, and unconsummated due to his arrest.

Despite the subject matter, Menzel opts for an apparently incongruous lyricism that resembles the tone of his *Rozmarné léto* (1967, Capricious Summer) rather than *Closely Observed Trains*. Most of the men are lovable and the women magical. The comedy is delicately timed, with the underplaying of comic points seeming to owe more to René Clair and Jacques Tati than to more contemporary trends. Perhaps the classic sequence here is the one in which Andel, the prison guard, pursues his Roma bride through the rooms of their new house, and the lights are switched on and off with a balletic precision and romantic humour.

The film has been criticized for using laughter and absurdity to characterize a period that saw political purges and the consigning of thousands to labour camps. However, like *Closely Observed Trains*, it does not deny reality, but uses comedy and lyricism to face the otherwise unfaceable. *Skylarks on a String* has no place for the tragic heroes of Polish and Hungarian films. Imbued with the spirit of the Good Soldier Švejk, its heroes are ordinary folk, survivors and anti-heroes. Also, like the characters in *All My Good Countrymen*, *The Firemen's Ball*, or *The Party and the Guests*, they share a group identity. It is surely telling that it is anti-Stalinist films such as these that provide some of the most persuasive characterizations in European cinema of the interaction between the individual, the social, and the political.

There is a legend that *Skylarks on a String* was kept under permanent guard at the Barrandov studios. In fact, it was one of the three films most widely disseminated on underground videos during the 1980s, the others being Jaromil Jireš's *Žert* (The Joke) and Jasný's *All My Good Countrymen*. However, it could have no public impact until 1990, when it was one of the year's top ten box office films.

Both Menzel and Hrabal were eventually able to continue their careers after the Warsaw Pact invasion but not without compromises and adjustments. Two of Hrabal's "permitted" novels, *Postřižiny* (Cutting It Short) and *Slavnosti sněženek* (The Snowdrop Festival) were filmed be Menzel in 1980 and 1983 respectively. Unloved by the authorities, they kept alive both a sensibility and a tradition. The exiled critic Jan Uhde described *Cutting It Short* as a flower in the desert of the Barrandov studios. After the "Velvet Revolution", Menzel filmed an adaptation of Václav Havel's play *Žebrácká opera*

(1990, *The Beggar's Opera*) and Vladimir Voinovich's Russian novel *Život a neobyčejná dobrodružství vojáka Ivana Čonkina* (1994, The Life and Extraordinary Adventures of Private Ivan Chonkin). After failing to set up a film version of Hrabal's novel *Obsluhoval jsem anglického krále* (I Served the King of England), he has devoted himself to theatre.

PETER HAMES

Writings

Closely Watched Trains: A Film, with Bohumil Hrabal, translated by Joseph Holzbecher, 1971; as *Closely Observed Trains*, 1971

Further Reading

Bluestone, George, "Jiri Menzel and the Second Prague Spring", *Film Quarterly*, 44/1 (Fall 1990): 23–31

Hames, Peter, *The Czechoslovak New Wave*, 2nd edition Trowbridge, Wiltshire: Flicks, 2001

Hames, Peter, "Reality Czech", *The Guardian* (23 February 2001): 12–13

LOUIS-SÉBASTIEN MERCIER
French dramatist and novelist, 1740–1814

L'AN DEUX MILLE QUATRE CENT QUARANTE: RÊVE S'IL EN FÛT JAMAIS
(The Year 2440: A Dream If Ever There Was One)
Novel, 1771

Long known to scholars of 18th-century France through his published journals, *Tableau de Paris* and *Nouveau Paris*, Louis-Sébastien Mercier's utopian novel *L'An deux mille quatre cent quarante: rêve s'il en fut jamais* holds great interest in the history of French *ancien régime* censorship, both for the publishing history of the book and for the views it expresses about the interaction between state power and cultural production. The son of a Parisian diamond merchant of Huguenot origins, Mercier was first exposed to literary life while a student at the Collège des Quatre-Nations, through family connections, and by attending the Comédie Française. He completed his studies in February 1763, briefly taught rhetoric in Bordeaux, then returned to Paris, where he translated poetry and wrote several short, classically inspired verse pieces. Between 1766 and 1772 Mercier penned a series of plays, none of which was performed by the royal theatre, perhaps in part because of their anti-absolutist political overtones, and more certainly because Mercier lacked a patron to introduce him to the troupe. He also worked regularly on a series of prose essays about the state of society, politics, and culture in contemporary France, which, by late 1770, he had stitched together into the manuscript of a novel set as a dream taking place almost 700 years in the future *L'An 2440: rêve s'il en fût jamais*.

The story is recounted by an unnamed narrator who awakes to discover himself in Paris in the year 2440. He proceeds to tour the city with a guide with whom he engages in lengthy conversations on topics ranging from religion to literature to government. He consistently finds that many of the faults in the France of 1770 (evoked in footnotes, which make some of the most interesting reading in the book) have been rectified by simplifying matters so that the goodness of human nature can express itself readily. For example, upon visiting a courtroom, the narrator is pleased to learn that legal pleading is no longer made by professional lawyers arguing cold technicalities but rather by each individual arguing the morality of his own cause. Moreover, he learns on several occasions how one of the most significant changes has been the greater recognition given to men of letters, who have used their influence to advance the cause of humanity by spreading virtue, so that the people have become largely self-policing and no longer need a powerful government to oversee their behaviour.

The utopian future has clearly done away with censorship such as it existed in Mercier's day, as evidenced by the narrator's ability to view (in chapter XXV) a performance of Charles Collé's *La Partie de chasse de Henri IV* and by the liberty of the press described in a supplementary chapter added to the 1786 edition. Yet the people of 2440 have preserved an important role for censors – not as a general cultural police, but to preserve the enlightened philosopher-king from "everything which would incline him to irreligion, to libertinage, to lying . . .", thereby ensuring his continued devotion to his people.

The other form of censorship which the narrator encounters – and is pleased to discover – is in the royal library (chapter XXVII), which houses only a "small cabinet of several books" rather than the thousands of volumes one might expect. Over several hundred years, countless books had been printed by writers who wrote before thinking. These books contained nothing original in them, serving not to instruct at all but only to pander to the vanity of authors perpetuating "miserable controversies". An enlightened monarch, realizing that so many questions had been answered definitively thanks to the effort of "good minds" aided by the technology of print, ordered that only what was truly useful and beautiful should be distilled into a few books and the rest burnt on a public bonfire.

A 20th-century reader might ask if this is really a representation of censorship, and one would have to answer yes, precisely because it illustrates the 18th-century meaning of *censure* not as a repressive state practice against civil society but as a matter of critical judgement exercised by those with proper "taste" on behalf of those lacking it. Mercier differed from most of his contemporaries in believing that taste was best cultivated not in salons and academies but by men of letters mixing among the people. In his utopian dream of the future, this mixing had worked to perfect both a sense of duty on the part of writers and the willingness of the people (and government) to learn from them.

In part to avoid running foul of the chancellor at a time when the monarchy was trying to stifle opposition and political tensions were therefore high, Mercier published *L'An 2440* anonymously and clandestinely. Having completed his manuscript in late 1770 or early 1771, he sent it out of the kingdom to be produced by the Huguenot printer E. van Harrevelt, who had previously published a series of his verse works and some of his plays, and who would the next year issue his *Du Théâtre*. Unable or unwilling (or more likely both) to obtain even a *permission tacite* to circulate *L'An 2440* legally in France, Mercier and his printer distributed the edition, beginning in mid-1771. It became an immediate *succès de scandale*. By the end of 1772, over 18,000 copies were circulating in three languages, leading to a revised 1774 edition, which similarly came out anonymously and without censorial approbation. In 1786 an enhanced, three-volume edition was published by the influential Swiss publisher, the Société Typographique de Neuchâtel (STN), which had also been putting out Mercier's *Tableau de Paris*. By 1789, according to Robert Darnton, the work had become the title most in demand on the STN's list and may well have been the biggest of what he calls the "forbidden best-sellers" of the *ancien régime*, with some 30,000 copies in circulation. This work, then, is a good example of how dissident ideas were circulating in pre-revolutionary France not just in the works of the *"philosophes"*, which have become the canon of the Enlightenment (and which generally managed to enjoy official endorsement from the royal censors) but also in the many clandestine works circulating, as Darnton puts it, "under the cloak" of *ancien régime* censorship.

GREGORY S. BROWN

Writings

L'An deux mille quatre cent quarante: rêve s'il en fût jamais, 1771; as *Memoirs of the Year Two Thousand Five Hundred*, translated by William Hooper, 1772
Panorama of Paris: Selections from Tableau de Paris, edited by Jeremy D. Popkin, 1999

Further Reading

Darnton, Robert, *Édition et sédition: l'univers de la littérature clandestine au XVIIIe siècle*, Paris: Gallimard, 1991
Darnton, Robert, *The Forbidden Best-Sellers of Pre-Revolutionary France*, New York: Norton, 1995; London: HarperCollins, 1996
Rufi, Enrico, *Le Rêve laïque de Louis-Sébastien Mercier: entre littérature et politique*, Oxford: Voltaire Foundation, 1995
Wilkie, Everett C. Jr, "Mercier's *L'An 2440*: Its Publishing History during Its Author's Lifetime", *Harvard Library Bulletin*, 32 (1984): 5–25 and 348–400

MEXICO

Population: 98,872,000	**Number of daily newspapers:** 295
Main religions: Roman Catholic; Protestant	**Number of periodicals:** 23
Official language: Spanish	**Number of radio receivers per 1000 inhabitants:** 329
Other languages spoken: Mayan dialects	**Number of TV receivers per 1000 inhabitants:** 272
Illiteracy rate (%): 6.7 (m); 10.6 (f)	**Number of PCs per 1000 inhabitants:** 47.0

The Conquest

Most current ideas of 16th-century Europe's violent intrusion into Mexico and the larger region known as Mesoamerica have a western perspective and are shaped by Spanish chronicles of the time, as well as later historical overviews. That is, the "official" history of the event has, until recently, failed to respect the indigenous view and is therefore evidence of effective and long-standing ideological suppression or even outright censorship. Only in recent decades has the process of repair begun.

Indigenous accounts exist in both native and alphabetic script. They are to be found first of all in native annals that follow the format of the ancient screenfold books of Mesoamerica, as well as in historical maps and large cotton *lienzos*. These native script texts were then transcribed into the alphabet imported from Europe in lengthy histories written in native languages and in Spanish by authors representing the local point of view, among them Tezozomoc and Cristóbal de Castillo, from the capital, Tenochtitlán; Chimalpahin of Chalco; Ixtlilxochitl of Texcoco; Diego Muñoz of Tlaxcala; and various authors from the Maya highlands and lowlands. This tradition was drawn upon in part in the work of such Spanish clerics as Diego Durán, Toribio Motolinía, and Bernardino de Sahagún.

The indigenous cultures of Mesoamerica were far from being backward or unenlightened, in the way that the invaders claimed when advancing their own cause. Knowledge in such areas as astronomy, mathematics, and writing was extremely sophisticated, a fact that is increasingly being recognized by scholars today. Writing using pictographic, ideographic, and phonetic signs had been practised for more than two thousand years. Painted books recorded large amounts of information on various topics such as history, genealogy, tribute rolls, astronomy, calendrics, and almanacs. These books were kept in libraries and were highly prized documents.

The Spanish, unable to comprehend these books and fearing that they contained a form of idolatrous worship, burned them in large quantities. In 1521 Cortés's allies burned the archives of Texcoco. The first archbishop of Mexico, the Franciscan Juan de Zumárraga, is also known to have destroyed books. In 1539 he was responsible for having the native ruler of Texcoco, Carlos Mendoza Ometochtzin, son of Nezahualpiltzintli, burned at the stake, along with his books, as part of the Inquisition's proceedings against native people suspected of religious violations. On 12 July 1562, in an *auto-da-fé* at Maní, Diego de Landa burned more than 5000 idols and 27 books. One hundred and seventy indigenous Mexicans were said to have died under torture while confessions were extracted. Ironically, having perpetrated so much destruction, Landa wrote the *Relación de las cosas de Yucatán*, a chronicle that safeguarded early information about the inhabitants of the Maya region.

The book burning was severely lamented by all native authors, whether otherwise sympathetic to the Spanish or not, and even certain Spanish authors felt unhappy about it. The *mestizo* Diego Muñoz denounced the total failure to distinguish between the ritual books, "pagan" in Christian eyes, and the histories that told of the New World's millennial past. Chimalpahin and others noted that, even on the evidence that remained, it was clear that biblical history must be in error on several accounts, not least the age of the world, and the spread over its surface of languages and humankind. The great American creation story told in the *Popol Vuh* of the highland Maya refers to the need "within Christendom" to conceal and judiciously transcribe the ancient books that escaped destruction; similar observations are made in the *Chilam Balam* books of the lowland Maya.

Upon arriving in Mexico in 1524, the Franciscan friars informed their Aztec counterparts that they were bringing them a religion whose authority was guaranteed by the "book" or Bible. The Aztec replied that they too had books, which told a very different story. Undaunted, the missionaries embarked upon a systematic destruction of temples and idols in and around the area of the Aztec capital from 1525 onwards. The Dominican and Augustinian orders arrived and the process of evangelization continued apace. During this period public forms of worship were forbidden and existing Aztec schools closed. These schools, the *calmecac*, had been responsible for safeguarding and transmitting knowledge through the sons of nobles. The Spanish were eager to replace the existing system with their own. Thus in 1536 the Colegio de Santa Cruz was founded in Mexico City to teach the indigenous nobility. The Spanish were quick to replace established forms of education and religious worship in order to consolidate their position within New Spain by controlling the dissemination of knowledge and belief.

Adaptation to new forms of government and religion was to be a long and painful process, involving much exploitation of indigenous labour through the *encomienda* (forced labour) system and church tithes. Yet it was accompanied by a concerted attempt on the part of the Spanish crown, defending its interests against those of the *encomenderos* (land agents) and the church, to institute the rule of law. To this end the Real Audiencia was set up, being instructed to receive evidence, written in native as well as European script, which would directly represent the other side of the case. Such documents were later used in legal disputes to settle claims and safeguard traditional lands against unscrupulous immigrants. The religious responsibilities of the Spanish monarchy were taken very seriously, and numerous edicts were issued to protect the rights of the indigenous Mexicans and to shelter them from exploitation. Yet these laws, while admirable in principle, were unenforceable since the colonial administration (the Council of the Indies) was based in Spain, powerless to act as corruption in the distant colonies increased.

The Spanish conquest of Mexico represented the displacement and censorship of established indigenous societies. The construction of churches and chapels on top of pyramid mounds, in a process known as "topping", has, for example at Cholula, left a visual legacy of conquest. The chaos of the Spanish world displaced the order of indigenous Mexico, leading to protests from both Spaniards, such as the celebrated Bartolomé de las Casas, and indigenous Mexicans.

The subsequent neglect and suppression of the native side of the story has, in part, been compounded by the inability of Europeans at that time to read native documents or to understand the complexity of the information they contained. Along with the censoring of native versions, history can be seen to have been tailored to European priorities so that the most popular and accessible accounts have formed our perspective to the exclusion of other important chronicles. This process began with the hugely popular and successful *The Conquest of New Spain* by Bernal Díaz del Castillo, one of the conquistadors under Hernán Cortés. Significantly this account was edited, in the popular shorter edition, to conclude with the Spanish capture of the capital city of Tenochtitlán, whereas the original version continues through the various campaigns that took the conquistadors west to Michoacan and east to Nicaragua. This has served to give the erroneous impression that the fall of the capital city was enough to bring about the capitulation of the whole country.

In addition historians have tended to present Mexico as a unified country, thus further exaggerating the success of the Spanish expeditionary force. By concentrating on the Aztecs we form an image of regional unity that did not exist. In central Mexico, for example, the Aztecs or Mexica, the founders and inhabitants of Tenochtitlán (now Mexico City), maintained power through the Triple Alliance between themselves and the inhabitants of the city-states of Tacuba and Texcoco. Yet they never subdued Tlaxcala, which fiercely defended its independence against attacks from the Triple Alliance. Tlaxcala was quick to see the chance of defeating its old enemies by allying with the Spaniards, a factor crucial to the success of the invading force that is brought out in their own account of events, the *Lienzo de Tlaxcala*.

In their histories the Spanish ascribe their victory to the dictates of the Christian religion, and to the superiority of European technology over that of the indigenous Mexicans. The power of gunpowder, the horse, and steel – for swords and armour – are indeed also noted in the native annals. So are far less glorious factors, such as the use of attack-trained mastiffs, which played a major role in the campaign of terror. Above all, native as opposed to European accounts bring out the devastating effect of imported diseases and plagues. For example, the Aztec ruler, Cuitlahuac (who succeeded Moctezuma II), was a victim of the smallpox epidemic that decimated the Valley of Mexico in 1520; native annals show that he ruled for only 80 days. The advantage the Spanish gained from a weakened population, the ability to ally themselves with local forces against the Triple Alliance, and the disparity in tactical warfare swung the military balance heavily in favour of the Spanish even before taking into account technological differences.

Our understanding of the conquest of Mexico, even our unthinking use of the term "conquest" rather than "invasion", has been subject to a form of censorship, in that we, as readers, have been conditioned by a select view of events – that of the victors. This point is brought out in the different versions of the story of Malintzin or La Malinche, baptised Doña Marina, who knew Maya and Aztec, and at first communicated with Cortés through Gerónimo de Aguilar. Without her aid, the progress of the Spanish would have been harder, even impossible, yet she is scarcely mentioned by them, and Cortés, who relied on her most, disparagingly refers to her as just his mouth-piece or "tongue". By contrast, native texts – historical maps from the Gulf Coast, the *Florentine Codex*, the irreverent poems in the *Cantares mexicanos* manuscript – have things the other way round and show Cortés as her creature, one who receives less tribute and respect than she; here, Cortés is even displaced by her in the designing of strategy and the actual issuing of military orders.

By reflecting traumatic events and, indeed, by their very existence, native accounts of the invasion bring out one last difference. Rather than affirm the fall and total end of an ancient civilization, they point the way forward to the resistance that in fact has carried on right through the colonial and independence periods, up to the present. The continuing oppression of indigenous groups, recently brought to worldwide attention by the Zapatista movement in Chiapas, and the reluctance of communities to reveal the painted books and maps they still possess are two examples that represent the ongoing process of conquest and resistance begun five centuries ago. The ability of these indigenous populations to resist such severe pressure stands as testament to the strength of, and their belief in, their own history and the pre-Hispanic order which, though heavily censored, retained its form over centuries of abuse. It also reveals the failure of the Spanish to transform Mexico totally, despite severely suppressing the indigenous culture.

ADRIAN LOCKE and GORDON BROTHERSTON

Further Reading

Brotherston, Gordon, *Painted Books of Mexico: Codices in UK Collections and the World They Represent*, London: British Museum Press, 1995

Díaz del Castillo, Bernal, *The Discovery and Conquest of Mexico, 1517–1521*, New York: Harper, and London: Routledge, 1928; as *The Conquest of New Spain*, Harmondsworth and Baltimore: Penguin, 1963 (written 1568)

Gruzinski, Serge, *The Conquest of Mexico: The Incorporation of Indian Societies into the Western World, 16th–18th Centuries*, Cambridge: Polity, 1993

León Portilla, Miguel, *The Broken Spears: The Aztec Account of the Conquest of Mexico*, Boston: Beacon Press, 1962; expanded edition 1992

Lockhart, James, *The Nahuas after the Conquest: A Social and Cultural History of the Indians of Central Mexico, Sixteenth through Eighteenth Centuries*, Stanford, California: Stanford University Press, 1992

Ricard, Robert, *The Spiritual Conquest of Mexico: An Essay on the Apostlate and the Evangelizing Methods of the Mendicant Orders in New Spain, 1523–1572*, Berkeley: University of California Press, 1966

Thomas, Hugh, *The Conquest of Mexico*, London: Hutchinson, 1993; as *Conquest: Montezuma, Cortés, and the Fall of Old Mexico*, New York: Simon and Schuster, 1993

Colony and Country from 1520

When Hernan Cortés conquered the region in 1520, 24 million indigenous people lived in Mexico and northern Central America. The Spanish population had risen to a mere 300,000 by the time of Mexican independence in 1821; a thin Hispanic veneer covered a foundation of indigenous culture.

The conquering Spanish had imposed a fiercely hierarchical system on empires that were themselves profoundly hierarchi-cal. The power of the Spanish monarchy was long unchallenged; whereas North America had imbibed the questioning spirit of Europe's intellectual revolutions, Spain retained strong centralized control in its colonies through its viceroy and through satellite *audiencias* (law courts with some administrative and executive powers). The church provided a further arm of government, especially after the establishment of the Tribunal of the Inquisition at Mexico City in 1571.

Mexico's first printing press was established in the capital in 1535. Strict censorship was applied, including a ban on the importation of fiction. However, Bartolomé de las Casas was allowed to publish his history of the Indies (published between 1522 and 1561), despite his defence of indigenous ("Indian") rights. A university, modelled on that of Salamanca (central Spain), was established in Mexico City in 1553. Some degree of cultural pluralism was possible, despite the tightness of political control. It is remarkable that the colonial writer Sor Juana Inés de la Cruz was encouraged to pursue her wide intellectual interests by the viceroy, until she was persuaded by her confessor that a woman's pursuit of learning could damage her eternal prospects – an extraordinary case of censorship by gender.

The original idea of the independence movement was that Mexico should become an independent monarchy. The Plan of Iguela (1821) carefully provided a balance of various interests. Catholicism would remain the official religion, and the whole population would enjoy equality before the law, but a Mexican king would indicate some degree of reverence to Spanish custom. The Plan also attracted the allegiance of other Central American provinces, but was wrecked when Spain refused to recognize Mexico's independence, ushering in a century of coups d'état and civil wars. The constitution of 1824 proclaimed press freedom, but the idea was constantly undermined by arbitrary governments; the privileged position of the church was maintained until its complete separation from the state in the 1860s. A new liberal constitution was passed in 1857, under president Benito Juarez, but was followed by the curious interlude when Napoleon III of France imposed on Mexico the archduke Maximilian of Austria as emperor of Mexico; he lasted three years until his death by firing squad in 1867, an event which led to censorship in France.

General Porfirio Díaz, who became president in 1877, imposed law and order, with total censorship. Newspapers were expected to base their coverage on the government's *Diario official*. The few who dared to criticize were closed down, and the occasional rebel editor would not only be removed from his publication, but tied round the neck with a rope and forced to trot behind a galloping horse until he was strangled. This indeed discouraged political criticism. Newspapers and magazines fawned over the "great leader". During the long dictatorship of the general, known as the *Porfiriato* (1877–1910), Mexico seemed to be prospering as railways and other technical improvements were introduced, but the suffering of the *peones*, the peasant farmers who remained in lifelong debt to the owners of the large *haciendas* (estates), was not reported in the Mexican press.

A civilian reformer, Francisco I. Madero, arose to challenge the dictator. The champion of the *peones*, he published *La Sucesion Presidencial en 1910* (The Presidential Succession in 1910), which called for the restoration of the democratic principles of 1857, including the provision that a president should not be re-elected. Evading the Porfirian police and soldiers, Madero's friends managed to circulate the book in 13 states before extra copies, brought in from the United States, began to be seized. In 1909 Madero toured Mexico on behalf of the Anti Re-election Movement, and became its presidential candidate for 1910. Díaz put the "apostle of democracy" in prison for sedition, and the first stirrings of what is now known as the Mexican Revolution were heard.

The revolution promised press freedom, and, in the new constitution of 1917, freedom of speech, assembly, and the press were specified. Article 7 proclaims: "Freedom to write and publish on any subject is inviolable. No law can establish pre-publication censorship, nor can press freedom be curtailed. The only limits are that individual private rights must be respected by spoken words and written materials." Press freedom was not, however, among the priorities of president Álvaro Obregón (1920–24), but his appointment of José Vasconcelos as minister of education was of great relevance to the creation of a society that would respect the constitution. A school system was built up and the national university rejuvenated. Literacy rates rose, as did magazine and newspaper circulations, if modestly. Vasconcelos's belief in the formation of a "cosmic race", which would at last make indigenous people and *mestizos* (those of mixed race) feel that they belonged in Mexico, began to remove the racial legacy of the Spanish conquest. The great Mexican muralists – Diego Rivera, David Alfaro Siquieros, and José Clemente Orozco – were commissioned to paint frescoes on revolutionary subjects, regardless of the fact that some of them were Marxists.

Rural Mexico remained overwhelmingly Catholic, and the attempts to replace church education with secular schooling created some disaffection. A law of 1926, promulgated by Obregon's successor, Plutarco Elías Callas, that further reduced the power of the church, met with complete opposition from the hierarchy, who promptly suspended church services throughout the country. This led to peasant uprisings in the so-called Christmas War. Finally, the 1926 law was allowed to lapse and services resumed. Anti-clericalism was not dead, however, and, within a few years, the governor of Tabasco State established extreme anti-Catholic laws, and employed fascist-style, church-burning "Goldshirts" to enforce them. Lázaro Cárdenas (1934–40) consolidated the control of the National Revolutionary Party over Mexican affairs and strengthened the corporatism of the system, but maintained the 1917 constitution. There was little overt press censorship, and some degree of international openness: Leon Trotskii, the former Soviet leader, was granted political asylum in Mexico in 1937, and a considerable number of defeated Spanish republicans were allowed to settle there after the Spanish Civil War in 1939. During World War II Mexico sided with the Allies, taking German agents off all borderland radio stations, where, from 1938, they had been propagandizing for the Third Reich. A Mexican Supreme Court decision in early 1942 held that the government could take pro-Nazi broadcasts off the air.

Over the next four decades Mexico enjoyed high public expenditure on health, welfare, and education, managing to keep violence at bay by a system of generally benevolent control. The general corporatism was extended to the media under the presidency of Miguel Alemán Váldes (1946–52),

whose family had business connections with the media empire of Emilio Azcarragan, owner of most of the film, radio, television, and press interests in Mexico.

Mexico has always sought the good opinion of other nations, and has exercised informal control of the media to that end. This was severely shattered by the events of 1968, during the presidency of Gustavo Díaz Ordaz (1964–70). For two years student strikes over a variety of issues had brought some turmoil to the campus of the National Autonomous University of Mexico (UNAM); its rector had to resign when he lost control of the situation, and the government, preparing to host the 1968 Olympic Games, was seriously concerned. Already it had effectively silenced *Politica*, the news magazine which, in May 1962, had run a series of articles calling on young people "to take matters into their own hands". *Politica*, which claimed street sales of 257,000, reprinted the articles in November 1967, distributing an additional 300,000 copies. It followed in December with an article calling for riots to prevent the Olympic Games taking place. Questioned by the Associated Press (AP), Edmundo Jardon, former chief of the Mexican bureau of *Prensa Latina* news service of the Cuban government, admitted to "some subsidies" for the magazine. The admission allowed the government agency, Paper Producers and Importers Inc (PIPSA), to end paper supplies to *Politica*. The law allowed a publishers to purchase newsprint abroad, but imposed an 80 per cent *ad valorem* tax on the transaction. *Politica* announced its own demise on 3 January 1968, the victim of a technique which, if it could not strictly be called censorship, was closely related to it.

A week before the Olympic Games, serious street violence resulted in the deaths of 400 students and police. A number of Cubans were shown to have been involved. *Excelsior* duly published photographs of their passports, together with printed instructions from the strike committee on how to provoke violence. The radical paper *La Prensa* made no mention of the Cuban involvement. The government, meanwhile, suggested that the Televisa network play down the violence in favour of the many Olympic stories that were available. Attempts at manipulation and control were to no avail internationally, as newspapers described a regime using excessive force to bolster its own power.

Other major attempts to control the media took place under the presidency of Luis Echeverría Alvárez (1970–76). *Porqué* was closed down because it was about to publish an account of the rescue of a kidnapped senator which contradicted the government's account. Towards the end of his presidency, during a severe economic crisis, Echeverría was subjected to vigorous criticism in the columns of *Excelsior*. Martin Luis Guzman, author of *El estilo personal*, had pointed out that Echeverría was tolerant of criticism, but only when it was friendly. The newspaper was (and still is) a cooperative with policy shaped by its own staff, but its board of directors could choose, retain, or change editors and columnists. At a meeting of shareholders on 8 July 1976, it emerged that the chairman and all those allowed to speak were members of Echeverría's political machine. Armando Vargas, then *Excelsior's* chief Washington correspondent, described the meeting as a "scenario of intimidation". The publisher, Julio Scherer García, and five senior editors were dismissed, and some 200 others promptly walked off the job. The government now took over Channel 13, clearly an attempt to see that the criticisms went no further. However, the internationally known critic Octavio Paz, editor of *Plural*, and his staff, who had given general support to the government, now resigned in protest. Three years later, when the government nominees to the *Excelsior* board had floundered, all those who had been dismissed were reinstated.

After the devaluation of the Mexican peso in 1982, president Lopez Portillo was depicted as a defeated boxer in the weekly newspaper *Processo*. By June of that year, the government had refused to place advertising in it, or in *Critica Politica*; both of these papers had been established by journalists dismissed from *Excelsior*. Herberto Castillas, columnist on *Proceso*, commented, "we used to think that the government brought advertising to publicize its products and services, not to buy consciences".

Two issues – alleged electoral fraud and the war against drugs – dominated the history of the Mexican press and media in the late 1980s and the 1990s. During the 1988 election campaign, opposition parties claimed that the ruling party's control of the media was limiting their rightful access to a platform for putting their case to the people. They decided to boycott the sponsors of 24 *Horas*, the main news programme. A historical series, *Path to Glory*, which praised the former president, Lázaro Cardenas, was taken off air, evidently because his son, the leader of the *Cuauhtemoc*, the Revolutionary Democratic Party, was an opposition candidate in the election. In 1990, the daily newspaper *La Jornada* began to investigate ballot-rigging in two Mexican states; as described previously in different contexts, the government threatened to withdraw its advertising.

In June 1990, in its report *Human Rights in Mexico: The Politics of Impunity*, Americas Watch charged that murder, torture and police mistreatment, election-related violence, and abuse of independent unions and journalists had "become an institutional part of Mexican society". Indeed, 39 Mexican journalists were assassinated between 1984 and 1990. Many of them were apparently targeted because they had threatened to expose abuses by the narcotics police. In 1990 the journalist and academic, Jorge Casteneda, wrote about the issue in *Proceso*, as well as in *Newsweek*, *El País*, and the *Los Angeles Times*. Apart from receiving death threats himself, he was subjected to an orchestrated campaign of abuse. The *Los Angeles Times* ran a letter from Wayne Cornelius, director of the Center of Mexican–US Studies at the University of California, San Diego, and a friend of president Salinas. Casteneda was, he wrote, "a spokesman for Cuauhtemoc, a plagiarist, a person who is neither honest nor honourable, and an enemy of the administration". Inside Mexico, he was labelled "an enemy of the president". Throughout, Salinas sought to distance himself from the violence and personal attacks. On 6 June 1990, announcing the creation of a National Commission on Human Rights, he proclaimed, "Protecting human rights is not a luxury for society. It is the first obligation of the Mexican government."

The PRI (Institutional Revolutionary Party) continued to be the party of government, but was now much more strongly challenged. In the 1997 nationwide election for the lower house of the federal Congress, the PRI received 36.6 per cent of the votes, its conservative opposition 27.1 per cent, and the leftist opposition 25.6 per cent. The PRI still got more airtime, but the other parties received more objective coverage. The PRI was finally defeated in the presidential election of June 2000.

MARVIN ALISKY

Further Reading

Alisky, Marvin, *Latin American Media: Guidance and Censorship*, Ames: Iowa State University Press, 1981

Camp, Roderic Aí, *Political Recruitment across Two Centuries: Mexico, 1884–1991*, Austin: University of Texas Press, 1995

Girwan, Tim, "Murder with Impunity", *Index on Censorship*, 19/1 (December 1990)

Grayson, George W. (editor), *Prospects for Democracy in Mexico*, New Brunswick, New Jersey: Transaction, 1990

Merrill, John C. (editor), *Global Journalism: Survey of International Communication*, 3rd edition, New York: Longman, 1995

"Mexico: Readjusting the Veil", *Index on Censorship*, 4/1 (Spring 1975)

Meyer, Michael C. and William L. Sherman, *The Course of Mexican History*, 6th edition, New York: Oxford University Press, 1999

Needler, Martin C., *Mexican Politics: The Containment of Conflict*, 2nd edition, New York: Praeger, 1990

Riding, Alan, *Distant Neighbors: A Portrait of the Mexicans*, New York: Knopf, 1984; as *Mexico: Inside the Volcano*, London: Tauris, 1987

Sierra, Justo, *The Political Evolution of the Mexican People*, Austin: University of Texas Press, 1969

Taylor, John, "Mexico: The Guessing Game", *Index on Censorship*, 5/4 (Winter 1971)

Thayer, Frank, *Legal Control of the Press*, Chicago: Foundation Press, 1944; 4th edition 1962

Thomas, Hugh, *The Conquest of Mexico*, London: Hutchinson, 1993; as *Conquest: Montezuma, Cortés, and the Fall of Old Mexico*, New York: Simon and Schuster, 1993

MEXICO: LA COMISIÓN CALIFICADORA DE PUBLICACIONES Y REVISTAS ILUSTRADAS (Classifying Commission for Illustrated Periodicals)
Mexican government censorship office

La Comisión calificadora de publicaciones y revistas ilustradas is responsible for approving the titles and contents of new comic books and other magazines in Mexico. It has monitored Mexican periodicals for slang, depictions of crime, and images of nudity and sex since 1944. In theory, it enforces stringent legal regulations on the content of periodicals. In practice, it does very little.

Comic books were among the most popular forms of mass media in Mexico between 1935 and 1955. The best-selling *Pepín* sold hundreds of thousands of copies while also supporting a huge market in second-hand comics; its 64-page issues appeared eight times a week. And *Pepín* had hundreds of competitors, some nearly as successful. Mexican comic books were aimed at a far broader audience than comics in the United

States or Europe at the time, and contained no super-heroes and relatively little crime-fighting. Instead, they told long, episodic romances. They were not very different from the soap operas that dominated Latin American radio (and eventually television) in this era.

Conservative groups in Mexico, especially those associated with the Catholic Church, often took up cultural issues as an indirect way to argue or negotiate with a "revolutionary" government that espoused at least a nominal anticlericalism. By the 1940s opposition to comic books had become a key conservative rallying point. Conservatives objected to the use of slang and to depictions of women working outside their homes, as well as to crime and violence, but above all they complained about the references to sexuality even in these relatively chaste stories.

The government of President Manuel Avila Camacho bowed to popular pressure in 1944 and announced that it would begin to censor comic books, setting up an elaborate bureaucracy to do the job. The commission was defined legally as an interdepartmental committee under the supervision of the Department of Public Education, whose members would be drawn from several different branches of government, including the powerful interior ministry (Gobernación). The commission was empowered to weed out those comic books and magazines that discouraged devotion to work or study or encouraged laziness and faith in luck; portrayed their protagonists succeeding in life by breaking laws or disrespecting established Mexican institutions; provoked disdain for the Mexican people or for their history or abilities; and used dialogue or texts with slang or offended "modesty and good manners" or were contrary to the "democratic concept". These strictures also covered any published photograph or drawing that in itself infringed the code. Thus, in the process of writing the regulations the commission expanded the scope of its interests to include more directly political aspects of these periodicals, and it extended beyond comic books to include any periodical sold in Mexico. Only after this expansion of the commission's legal mandate did conservative protestors begin to raise questions about other kinds of magazines and tabloids, like sports papers, movie magazines, true-crime tabloids, collections of song lyrics, newspaper supplements, and, eventually, photonovels.

The rules allowed publishers complete freedom on a provisional basis – that is, they were allowed to print what they liked until the inspection period was complete, as long as a copy of every issue was sent to the commission. The commission, in turn, was required promptly to grant or refuse licences to the publishers on the basis of its inspection. After the 1951 revision of the law, the regulations required two certificates: a title licence, signifying that the title itself was not immoral and could be sent to the copyright office and a content licence, certifying that the contents of the publication infringed no rule and that it could go on being published unchanged. Title licences were usually granted immediately. Almost all publications eventually received content licences too, but these sometimes required weeks or months of extended discussion within the commission and between the commission and the publisher.

The commissioners, in theory, have enormous power. They are entitled to levy moderate fines and request that federal judges send stubborn editors to jail; they can also ask that the government paper monopoly deny cheap, subsidized newsprint to outlawed publishers, so that one racy publication could, in theory, put a whole company out of business; they can withhold certification of a licit title so that no copyright be granted; they can request that the post office deny publishers permission to use the mails at cheap rates, or at all; and they can ask the Mexico City police to collect fines from or arrest newsstand operators who deal in banned publications.

However, the commission cannot enforce its rulings. It can announce draconian punishments, but it needs the courts and the federal and local police to impose the penalties, and it has no power to force other government agencies to honour its demands. The commission has not usually received their support. No publisher has ever gone to jail; no publisher has ever lost his or her access to government-subsidized newsprint at the request of the commission; no publisher has permanently lost bulk-mailing privileges; no publisher has ever paid more in fines than a week's gross income from an offending periodical. The commission has forced some periodicals to change their titles, but it has put none out of business. This lack of reliable power of enforcement is the clearest evidence that the politicians who wrote the laws bringing the commission into existence never intended that comic books, or any other form of periodical, be suppressed by this highly visible public body. Instead, the commission serves to absorb and redirect conservative anger over the content of mass media. Meanwhile, Mexican print media have grown increasingly open in their depictions of sex and violence since 1940.

There is, of course, substantial censorship of print and electronic media in Mexico for political reasons, including the murder of journalists (39 were murdered between 1984 and 1990). At least one comic-book artist, Eduardo del Rio (who works under the name Ríus), has also been threatened with death by agents of the state. All of this is unofficial – and unconstitutional. Ironically, the only official censorship of print in Mexico appears to have been entirely toothless.

ANNE RUBENSTEIN

Further Reading

Alcocer, Marta and Alicia Molina, "Mexican Comics as Culture Industry" in *Comics and Visual Culture: Research Studies from Ten Countries*, edited by Alphons Silbermann and H.-D. Dyroff, Munich and New York: Saur, 1986

Aurrecoechea, Juan Manuel and Armando Bartra, *Puros cuentos: la historia de la historieta en México*, 3 vols, Mexico City: Grijalbo, 1988–94

Bartra, Armando, "The Seduction of the Innocents: The First Tumultuous Moments of Mass Literacy in Postrevolutionary Mexico" in *Everyday Forms of State Formation: Revolution and the Negotiation of Rule in Modern Mexico*, edited by Gilbert M. Joseph and Daniel Nugent, Durham, North Carolina: Duke University Press, 1994

Curiel, Fernando, *Mal de ojo: iniciación a la literatura icónica*, Mexico City: Universidad Nacional Autónoma de México, 1989

Foster, David William, *From Mafalda to Los Supermachos: Latin American Graphic Humor as Popular Culture*, Boulder, Colorado: Rienner, 1989

Herner, Irene and María Eugenia Chellet, *Mitos y monitos*, Mexico City: Universidad Nacional Autónoma de México, 1979

Hinds, Harold E. Jr and Charles M. Tatum, *Not Just for Children: The Mexican Comic Book in the Late 1960s and 1970s* , Westport, Connecticut: Greenwood Press, 1992
Knight, Alan, "Revolutionary Project, Recalcitrant People: Mexico, 1910–1940" in *The Revolutionary Process in Mexico: Essays on Political and Social Change, 1880–1940*, edited by Jaime E. Rodríguez O., Los Angeles: Mexico/Chicano Program, University of California, 1990

Rubenstein, Anne, *Bad Language, Naked Ladies, and Other Threats to the Nation: A Political History of Comic Books in Mexico*, Durham, North Carolina: Duke University Press, 1998

VSEVOLOD MEYERHOLD
Russian theatre director, 1874–1940

Meyerhold was an internationally respected avant-garde director who also made landmark contributions to western performing arts as set designer, theoretician, teacher, inventor of cinematic techniques, actor, opera director, and musician. Meyerhold's students called him, simply, "The Master". After his execution his name was forcibly obliterated for 15 years, causing colossal damage to theatre history, which is still being slowly repaired. His influence remains the invisible underpinning of cutting-edge western theatre even today.

Almost from the beginning of his professional life, Meyerhold collided with official censorship. From 1904 until the Bolshevik revolution of October–November 1917, the following plays directed by Meyerhold were either heavily cut by the censor before performance, banned outright after performance, or both: Ibsen's *An Enemy of the People*, Aleksandr Kosorotov's *Spring Torrent*, Maksim Gor'kii's *Summer Folk*, E.N. Chirikov's *Jews*, and Frank Wedekind's *Spring's Awakening*. Any hopes that the revolution would inaugurate the free flow of ideas in Russia were astoundingly short-lived, and the imperial censorship would soon look benign compared to what lay ahead.

In 1917, when all Soviet theatres were put under the control of the newly formed Commissariat of Enlightenment (Narkompros), its head, Anatolii Lunacharskii, invited 120 of Russia's most prominent artists and intellectuals to a meeting. Only five accepted, one of whom was Meyerhold, the only theatre director to attend. To cast his lot so openly with the communists in such uncertain times was a brave gesture; the following year he joined the party and remained, as he wrote in his last letter from prison, "an honest communist to the end".

In the history of Soviet theatre censorship, Meyerhold was himself not without sin. When in 1920 Lunacharskii put him in charge of Narkompros's Theatre Section, Meyerhold used his newfound authority to campaign shrilly against practitioners of traditional theatre. Judging by his rhetoric, he was bent on obliterating all performances that did not conform to his style of "Cubo-Futurist Bolshevism", and he might have done so if the somewhat more tolerant Lunacharskii had not reorganized the Theatre Section, thus encouraging Meyerhold to resign after only one year. From 1921 until his arrest in 1939, Meyerhold devoted himself to his true calling as a director, in his own and other companies, and a teacher in his theatre workshops.

Meyerhold tried to fulfil the official demand for plays by Soviet writers on Soviet themes, but there was an abysmal dearth of first-rate material, and with the beginning of the 1930s, he began to lose his few good writers and other valued

colleagues to suicide (Vladimir Maiakovskii, 1930), arrest (Nikolai Erdman, 1933), and execution (Ivan Aksenov, 1935). Moreover, starting in the mid-1920s, the official censorship office for theatre, Glavrepertkom, became increasingly repressive, with the result that talented playwrights whose works Meyerhold had successfully produced were now having their newest and perhaps best scripts turned down by the censor.

For example, Maiakovskii's satire on Soviet bureaucrats, *Bania* (*The Bathhouse*), finally reached the Meyerhold Theatre's stage after four years (1926–30) of negotiations with the censor and heavy cuts, but the official criticism was severe and – perhaps coincidentally, perhaps not – Maiakovskii committed suicide less than a month after the premiere. Sergei Tretiakov's *Khochu rebenka* (*I Want a Baby*), with its radical suggestions about the proper role of sex and parenthood in socialist society, was also submitted in 1926, rejected by the censor, rewritten to pass muster, and finally passed by the censor in 1928, but it was not staged until 1980 (in Germany). In 1927 Meyerhold's plans to adapt and stage Andrei Belyi's novel *Moscow* also foundered against the rocks of censorship. As with *Khochu Rebenka*, Meyerhold enjoyed the author's wholehearted, even excited cooperation in, and enthusiasm for, the project, and the scenic designs promised astounding visual power and surprise. "If he succeeds in staging [*Moscow*]," Belyi wrote, "this will represent a new achievement not only for the stage but also for dramatic art; dramatists will be able to write differently." Perhaps it was this very "difference" that the censor feared. Although plans and negotiations continued at least until 1930, and textual revisions were made in response to Glavrepertkom's many objections, the play "fell victim to an increasingly hostile critical climate" before rehearsals ever started, and Meyerhold never staged it.

Even when Meyerhold was belatedly permitted to take his company on tour to Germany and France (1930) he could shake off neither censors, would-be censors, nor Stalin's long arm. Two of his most successful productions about revolution – Tretiakov's *Roar, China!* and Ilia Selvinskii's *The Second Army Commander* – were banned in Paris, where his most elegant work, a radical reworking of Gogol''s *The Government Inspector* provoked angry demonstrations from Russian émigrés. When Meyerhold applied to the Soviet authorities for permission to take his company on a tour of the United States, he was ordered to return home quickly, which he did, to an ever deeper, more treacherous vortex of smear campaigns, accusations, censorship, and "disappearances".

Erdman's tragicomedy *The Suicide*, a play about "why some of us decided to go on living even though everything was pushing us to suicide" (Nadezhda Mandel'shtam, translated by Max Hayward, *Hope against Hope*), was submitted to Glavrepertkom in 1930. This represented Meyerhold's last and best hope for a worthy Soviet play, but in 1932 that hope was quashed by Stalin, via his henchman Lazar Kaganovich.

An intense official campaign against "formalism" (modernism) in general and Meyerhold in particular opened in 1936 with press excoriations of his work, but throughout the attacks Meyerhold remained intransigent, publicly denouncing his denouncers. He also remained unbowed through the humiliating public accusations of 1937, but in 1938 his theatre was closed and in June 1939, after an apparent remission of official displeasure when Meyerhold's star seemed to be rising again, he was arrested. Three weeks later his wife and star actress, Zinaida Raikh, was stabbed to death through the eyes by unknown but probably officially approved assailants. After horrific bludgeonings with a rubber club, and a meaningless conviction for leading an anti-Soviet conspiracy within the arts and spying for Japan, Britain, France, and Lithuania, Meyerhold was shot. In a letter to Stalin written after his arrest (it is not known whether it was posted), Raikh wrote, "Since theatre people could not understand politics, politicians probably could not understand art."

KATHERINE BLISS EATON

Writings

Stat'i, pis'ma, rechi, besedi (Articles, Letters, Speeches, Interviews), 1968
Meyerhold on Theatre, edited and translated by Edward Braun, 1969
Perepiska (Correspondence), 1976

Tvorcheskoe nasledie V.E. Meierkhol'da (The Creative Legacy of V.E. Meyerhold), 1978

Further Reading

Braun, Edward, "Meyerhold: The Final Act", *New Theatre Quarterly*, 9/33 (February 1993): 3–15, 95–96
Braun, Edward, *Meyerhold: A Revolution in Theatre*, Iowa City: University of Iowa Press, 1995
Eaton, Katherine B., *The Theater of Meyerhold and Brecht*, Westport, Connecticut: Greenwood Press, 1985
Gladkov, Aleksandr K., *Meyerhold Speaks, Meyerhold Rehearses*, edited by Alma Law, Amsterdam: Harwood, 1997
Hoover, Marjorie L., *Meyerhold: The Art of Conscious Theater*, Amherst, Massachusetts: University of Massachusetts Press, 1974
Hoover, Marjorie L., *Meyerhold and His Set Designers*, New York: Peter Lang, 1988
Law, Alma and Mel Gordon, *Meyerhold, Eisenstein, and Biomechanics: Actor Training in Revolutionary Russia*, Jefferson, North Carolina: McFarland, 1996
Law, Alma and Mel Gordon, *Gosudarstvennyi teatr imeni V.E. Meierkhol'da, 1920–1938 gg.: iz fondov Rossiiskogo Gosudarstvennogo arkhiva litertury i iskusstva* (The Meyhold Theatre, 1920–1938: from the holdings of the Russian State Archive of Literature and Art), Woodbridge, Connecticut: Research Publications, 1999
Leach, Robert, *Vsevolod Meyerhold*, Cambridge and New York: Cambridge University Press, 1989
Picon-Vallin, Beatrice, *Meyerhold*, Paris: Éditions du CNRS, 1990
Rudnitsky, Konstantin, *Meyerhold, the Director*, edited by Sydney Schultze, Ann Arbor, Michigan: Ardis, 1981
Schmidt, Paul (editor), *Meyerhold at Work*, Austin: University of Texas Press, 1980
Symons, James M., *Meyerhold's Theatre of the Grotesque: The Post-Revolutionary Productions, 1920–1932*, Coral Gables, Florida: University of Miami Press, 1971; Cambridge: Rivers Press, 1973

CONT MHLANGA
Zimbabwean playwright, 1958–
WORKSHOP NEGATIVE
Play, 1987

When Zimbabwe won independence in 1980, Cont Mhlanga was a factory foreman in the country's second city of Bulawayo who ran a township karate club for local boys. That year Mhlanga was annoyed when his club's regular meeting was cancelled because their hall had been requisitioned for a National Theatre Organisation (NTO) workshop. He called in to see what was going on and was enthralled. In 1983 he wrote his first play, *Children, Children*. By 1986 the playwright had formed an impoverished but professional theatre company, Amakhosi Theatre Productions, working out of the black Bulawayo township of Makakoba, though in great demand throughout the country.

Up to 1980 any artistic endeavours which sought to raise political issues were strictly suppressed by the white politicians who then ruled the country. A divide-and-rule policy was in force whereby even the anodyne offerings which were permitted were often allowed only in local languages, and there was strict censorship of all publications. However, the liberation forces had called upon theatre and music as powerful tools of politicization, and, after independence, theatre was fostered both by indigenous artists and by a number of foreigners who had worked in politicized people's theatre movements in Kenya and South Africa, and who sought refuge in Robert Mugabe's new socialist state. Consequently Zimbabwe now has an impressive indigenous theatre movement which encompasses some 200 amateur and professional companies.

Amakhosi's plays are based on their director's observations of everyday life, out of which he produces themes and scripts from which his actors work to create dramas with which they too can identify. When he found that the action-oriented style of *Children, Children* attracted an almost exclusively youth audience, Cont Mhlanga set out to find how to attract older members of the community. This resulted in the company commissioning an old man to teach them the traditional dances their generation had never learnt for incorporation in future plays. When the playwright found that he had a turnover of seventy female performers in the space of four years, he went to all the women's parents and then held a party to which he invited their boyfriends, in order to explain the ethos of his company and to break down preconceptions which commonly regarded women actors as immoral.

In 1986 the policy of action-packed people's plays bore fruit when Amakhosi's *Nansi le ndoda* (Behold the Man) won the NTO's festival award and toured successfully both in Zimbabwe and Botswana. *Nansi le ndoda* deals with contemporary Zimbabwean problems of youth unemployment, nepotism, and the sexual abuse of women. The play combines tragedy, melodrama, comedy, and karate – an eclectic blend which possibly only a man of Mhlanga's training-through-practice would dare attempt and successfully bring off.

Workshop Negative was produced by Amakhosi in 1987. By then, the government of Robert Mugabe had become wary of theatre. As the populace became increasingly disillusioned with government failures to transform life for the mass of the black population, and as stories of government corruption spread, theatre became a significant tool for public criticism of the state. A number of plays such as T.K. Tsodzo's *Shanduko* (1983), Gonzo Musengezi's *The Honourable MP* (1984) and Andrew Whalley's *Platform Five* (1987), to name only a few, had strongly criticized the government. The row over *Workshop Negative* represented a turning point when the state first openly intervened by denouncing a theatre production.

Workshop Negative examines the issues of political corruption and race relationships. Roy Graham is a white ex-soldier and Zuluboy is an ex-guerrilla. Both find themselves employed in the workshop of a black MP who proclaims his socialism in public while practising the grossest exploitation of those whom he employs – besides being involved in numerous corrupt business practices. *Workshop Negative* examines the tensions and contradictions of post-independence Zimbabwe in an extremely critical light. In particular, the issue of continuing racial tensions in an officially non-racial nation had never been addressed on stage before.

Workshop Negative became the cause of considerable political debate conducted in a number of newspapers. It was also the subject of a debate at the University of Zimbabwe, where a government spokesman attracted boos and laughter when he argued that the play misrepresented Zimbabwean history. Amakhosi conducted a successful tour of Zimbabwe with the play, but when they tried to take *Workshop Negative* abroad the government announced not an outright ban, but a formal denial of the state's blessing, because there were "serious flaws" in the play's view of the state of the nation.

So far this remains an isolated example of overt government interference with the arts, and plays which are extremely critical of the government have continued to be written, published, and performed. However, the state has drastically reduced its support for local theatre, and discourages the form by a failure to provide funding or premises and by discouraging reporting of many black theatre performances. More worryingly, playwrights such as Cont Mhlanga have been approached by government officials and warned not to get involved in politics. In Mhlanga's case the warning has not been effective. He continues to write and produce works which are critical of prevailing social and political conditions, although only *Workshop Negative* has been published. Amakhosi Theatre Productions has received several major funding awards from foreign donors, and recently Mhlanga has diversified into making and renting videos of his own and other African works.

In recent years Zimbabwe has experienced a rapidly worsening economic situation and significant intimidation of those opposed to the government. However, theatre seems to have experienced less censorship than other cultural forms, and Amakhosi has continued to engage with political issues as evidenced in their 2001 play, *Witnesses and Victims*, which explores the controversial question of land ownership in Zimbabwe. Cont Mhlanga left Amakhosi in 2001 in order to form a separatist Ndebele political party. The Ndebele constitute 20 per cent of the population and have often been discriminated against by the Shona-dominated government.

JANE PLASTOW

Writings
Workshop Negative, 1992

Further Reading

Chifunyise, Stephen, "Trends in Zimbabwean Theatre since 1980" in *Politics and Performance: Theatre, Poetry, and Song in Southern Africa*, edited by Liz Gunner, Johannesburg: Witwatersrand University Press, 1994

Kaarsholm, Preben, "Mental Colonisation or Catharsis? Theatre, Democracy and Cultural Struggle from Rhodesia to Zimbabwe" in *Politics and Performance: Theatre, Poetry and Song in Southern Africa*, edited by Liz Gunner, Johannesburg: Witwatersrand University Press, 1994

Plastow, Jane, *African Theatre and Politics: The Evolution of Theatre in Ethiopia, Tanzania and Zimbabwe: A Comparative Study*, Amsterdam: Rodopi, 1996

Rohmer, Martin, *Theatre and Performance in Zimbabwe*, Bayreuth: Bayreuth University, 1999

MICHELANGELO BUONARROTI
Italian painter, sculptor, and architect, 1475–1564

Commissioned in 1501 for one of the buttresses of Florence Cathedral, Michelangelo's *David*, when completed in 1504, was placed instead in front of the principal entrance to the Palazzo Vecchio, the building that housed the government, as a symbol of the growing pride the Florentines had in their city. Michelangelo depicted the biblical hero at the moment before he challenged the giant Goliath; like the city itself, he is poised for greatness. The *David* differs from earlier versions in its synthesis of total nudity and strength. Donatello's bronze *David* (1430s) is a nude boy; Verrocchio's bronze *David* (1470s) is partially dressed, sensuous, and youthful. Considered "the ideal of aristocratic *kalokagathia*" (Hauser), Michelangelo's *David* exemplifies the ideals of the Neoplatonic circle of the High Renaissance: physical beauty reflects intellectual beauty. Defying the medieval disdain of physical beauty, the concept of *kalokagathia* revelled in the beauty and divinity of the naked

MICHELANGELO: Detail from *The Last Judgement* fresco for the Sistine Chapel, Rome, painted between 1535 and 1540. Officials were shocked by the nudity in the work, which was felt to be unsuitable for the pope's domestic chapel. In the lower right-hand corner is Michelangelo's retaliatory portrayal of Biagio da Cesena, Paul III's papal master of ceremonies, who was vehement in his disapproval of the "shameless" nakedness in the unfinished work. He is represented as Minos, the snake-entwined judge of souls in Hades. The frescos suffered repeated overpainting on the orders of successive popes over the course of the following four centuries, in order to hide the offending nudity with draperies. The paintings were mostly restored to their original state in the late 20th century.

human body. Citizens threw stones at the statue when it was moved in 1504, but the motive for the animosity remains unknown; either the pagan nudity or the political implications (anti-Medici) could have aroused their anger.

Modern depictions and protests against the *David* focus on its nudity (not least, the marble genitals and unmistakable pubic hair), reflecting the conservative values of the society making the protest and revealing ignorance about the statue's original intent. On 19 July 1969, a 22-foot high marble copy of the *David* was displayed at Forest Lawn Memorial Park in Cypress, California – without a figleaf for the first time since 1937. Park officials explained that changed times and social attitudes justified the removal, although a few residents in the Orange County community did protest. Similar statues in the company's Memorial Parks in neighbouring Glendale and West Covina kept their protective covering, however. Other California communities were equally conservative. In 1966 the Beverly Hills police had removed a replica of the statue from an art gallery; its crime was "appearing in public without a figleaf".

On the other side of the world, in Australia in November 1969, a poster of the statue that had been on display in a bookshop in Sydney was seized by vice squad officers, and the manager was charged with an obscene display; the charge was dropped after the curator of the New South Wales Art Museum explained the full historical context. The vice squad maintained their vigil: in January 1970 four men were arrested in another Sydney bookshop for selling obscene publications: prints of three drawings by Aubrey Beardsley and a print of a photograph of the *David*. The statue was also used in 1970 in Brazil, to advertise the Rio de Janeiro art fair; the government had held up distribution of the posters with the statue on them.

In 1995 an offer by the city of Florence to give the city of Jerusalem a replica of Michelangelo's *David* to commemorate the 3,000th anniversary of its conquest by David was turned down by the city council, who feared that its nakedness would offend ultra-orthodox Jews; Verrocchio's *David* was chosen instead.

Misunderstanding of the implications of nudity also created problems for Michelangelo's *Last Judgement*. The Medici pope Clement VII (1523–34) had commissioned Michelangelo to paint the wall behind the altar in the Sistine Chapel, first discussing the project on 22 September 1533 in Florence. Clement died in 1534, and Michelangelo hoped to be released from the obligation. His hopes were unfulfilled, however, and work on the fresco started on 16 April 1535, with the construction of the scaffolding. The previous decoration (two frescos flanking an altarpiece of the *Assumption of the Virgin*, all by Perugino, and two of Michelangelo's own lunettes from the ceiling) had to be destroyed. Although Clement VII had envisioned a depiction of the Resurrection, pope Paul III and Michelangelo decided on the Last Judgement.

The Last Judgement had been used as a subject for frescos before this; it was a common subject in northern Europe, and had appeared in Italy in the 11th century. Michelangelo's *Last Judgement*, however, differed from earlier depictions in its composition and style; it also differed from Michelangelo's earlier works in its mood. Earlier, medieval Last Judgements depicted all the figures clothed, according to their social position: Christ, the Virgin Mary, and the apostles sit in Heaven. No such structures exist in Michelangelo's version. There are no thrones and no clothing to signify rank. Some structure does, however, exist in Michelangelo's fresco; divided into three

MICHELANGELO: *David*, completed in 1504 as a commission for a buttress in Florence cathedral, but placed instead in a prominent position outside the city's Palazzo Vecchio to symbolize Florentine civic pride. The uncompromising nudity of the work and its many replicas and reproductions in various historical and geographical contexts have aroused protest and occasionally official censorship.

zones, the composition shows the kingdom of Heaven at the top, the realm of those who have been judged in the middle, and Charon and the demons at the bottom. But the main impression is of teeming masses of twisted bodies, contorted in pain and suffering. The fresco presents a pessimistic view of humanity, different from the idealistic and optimistic portrayals of Michelangelo's earlier works. Rome had been sacked, Europe was at war, and papal authority was questioned. The heroic nudity of Michelangelo's earlier works was replaced by a nudity reflecting the belief that all humans are naked on the Day of Last Judgement.

The work raised eyebrows even before it was officially unveiled, primarily because of the nakedness of the figures in an era no longer in touch with the Neoplatonic views of the High Renaissance. The fresco also depicted a man being pulled to Hell by his testicles and possibly some kind of sadistic activity between St Blaise and St Catherine. After viewing the three-quarters completed work in 1540, the papal master of ceremonies, Biagio da Cesena, told pope Paul III that it was "a very improper thing to paint so many nude forms, all showing their nakedness . . . in shameless fashion"; the picture was "better suited to a bathroom" or a roadside tavern, and not a pope's chapel. (It was, however, dangerous to criticize an

artist who was painting Judgement Day. Michelangelo retaliated by depicting Biagio as a figure in Hell: he is Minos, the snake-entwined judge in Hades at the lower right-hand corner of the painting.)

Michelangelo's contemporaries were shocked by the fresco when it was unveiled on 31 October 1541. Most critics felt that the nudes – unclothed human bodies – were unsuitable for the pope's domestic chapel. Pietro Aretino, the infamous satirist, author of the *Sonnetti lussuriosi*, who attacked powerful figures of the time, wrote Michelangelo a letter with a tirade on the "licentiousness and impurity" he found in the painting, which made him, "as a baptised Christian", blush. Vasari, who otherwise had nothing but praise for Michelangelo's work, wrote in the second edition of his *Vite* (1568) that he felt the nudity was unsuitable for the pope's chapel. Pope Paul III, however, is said to have broken into prayer when first seeing the wall: "Lord, charge me not with my sins when Thou shalt come on the Day of Judgement."

The frescos were repeatedly "censored" between the 16th and early 20th centuries. Under Paul IV's pontificate (1555–59) Michelangelo was denounced as a heretic. In 1558 the pope told Daniele da Volterra, one of Michelangelo's pupils, to paint draperies over the "especially provoking" naked figures such as St Catherine and St Blaise. By obeying these orders, Volterra earned the nickname "The Breeches-Maker". Successive popes also contributed additional layers of veils, draperies, skirts, and clouds. Accusations of immodesty led to the Council of Trent's decision decreeing the correction of indecent parts of the fresco in 1564. Interestingly enough, not only nudity was questioned. The theologian Andrea Gilio published *Dialogo degli errori dei pittori* (Dialogue on the Errors of Painters) in 1564. This work supported and clarified the directives established by the Council of Trent, which ended painters' freedom to interpret biblical stories as they wanted. Artists were to conform to official interpretations of questions of dogma. All nudity in ecclesiastical art, even when the Bible might describe someone nude, was to be avoided. Clearly Michelangelo's *Last Judgement* went far beyond what was now allowed, but the work was also criticized for other "faults". These included the representation of Christ (he was shown unbearded and standing instead of sitting, as he should be, on his throne); the Charon ferry is a theme from mythology; the angels have no wings; the apocalyptic angels stand next to each other, when they should be at the four corners; the saints' gestures are appropriate for a bullfight, not the Last Judgement; and the draperies of some of the figures indicate wind, and on the Day of Judgement the wind would have stopped blowing. The main criticism, however, was the nudity.

Pope Pius IV (1559–65) had further offensive portions of Michelangelo's fresco painted over with draperies in 1566, ignoring El Greco's recommendation that the fresco be destroyed and replaced with one of his own. Michelangelo's work was not without its supporters, however, for when Veronese defended his own artistic licence before the Inquisition in 1573 by citing *The Last Judgement* as an example of the free imagination, he was told: "Do you not know that in these figures by Michelangelo there is nothing which is not spiritual?" Nevertheless, the work continued to be denounced. Pope Clement VIII considered destroying the fresco in 1596 because of the supposed obscenity of its figures, but reconsidered after receiving a petition from the Accademia di San Luca. Further overpaintings were undertaken in 1625 and 1712; in 1758 pope Clement XIII ordered the artist Stefano Pozzi to add yet more draperies to the figures, which were completed in 1762. The cover-ups continued in the 20th century; in 1936 Pius XI ordered the artist Biago Diaetti to paint draperies on several of the nudes, considered daring and offensive to Catholic morals.

Not only religious leaders were offended by the nudity. In 1931 the United States Customs Bureau in New York City banned a postcard of the Sistine nudes. The law at the time considered all pictured nudity indecent. Two years later the New York Office of the United States Customs detained a series of copies of the fresco by the 16th-century artist Marcello Venusti, who made them before Volterra painted loincloths on the figures according to Paul IV's order; the pictures were reproduced in 10 pamphlets of 30 rotogravure reproductions and had been ordered by the Weyhe Gallery in New York. Customs at first requested the Gallery to waive rights to the reproduction and allow them to be destroyed, but withdrew their request after the intervention of a senior officer.

Recent restorations have removed many of the superfluous layers and unoriginal garments, returning the work to Michelangelo's own intentions. When the restoration was unveiled, John Paul II declared the Sistine Chapel "a sanctuary of the theology of the human body", a statement entirely in keeping with the Neoplatonic ideals of the High Renaissance.

ELISABETH L. VINES

Writings

Complete Poems and Selected Letters, translated by Creighton Gilbert, 1963
The Complete Poems, translated by John Frederick Nims, 1998

Further Reading

Barnes, Bernadine, "Aretino, the Public and the Censorship of Michelangelo's Last Judgement" in *Suspended License: Censorship and the Visual Arts*, edited by Elizabeth Childs, Seattle: University of Washington Press, 1997

Bazin, Germain, *The Avant-Garde in Painting*, New York: Simon and Schuster, 1969

Clapp, Jane, *Art Censorship: A Chronology of Proscribed and Prescribed Art*, Metuchen, New Jersey: Scarecrow Press, 1972

De Vecchi, Pierluigi, *Michelangelo: The Vatican Frescoes*, New York: Abbeville Press, 1996

Gimpel, Jean, *The Cult of Art: Against Art and Artists*, New York: Stein and Day, and London: Weidenfeld and Nicolson, 1969

Goldscheider, Ludwig, *Michelangelo: Paintings, Sculpture, Architecture*, London: Phaidon Press, 1964; 6th edition 1996

Hauser, Arnold, *The Social History of Art*, 3rd edition, 4 vols, London and New York: Routledge, 1999

Salinger, Margaretta, *Michelangelo, 1475–1569: The Last Judgment*, New York: Abrams, 1954

JULES MICHELET
French historian, 1798–1874

One of France's greatest historians, Jules Michelet is best known for his 17-volume *Histoire de France* (1833–67) and for his 7-volume *Histoire de la Révolution* (1847–53). His attitude to history was much influenced by Giambattista Vico's *Scienza nuova*, which he translated in 1817. His first brush with the Catholic censor followed his translation *Mémoires de Luther*, which was placed on the *Index Librorum Prohibitorum* by pope Gregory XVI in 1840.

Michelet's father was a follower of Voltaire, but, for whatever reason, the historian began his career with a romantic study of the crusades and a portrait of St Thomas Aquinas. Michelet lectured at the École Normale Supérieure (1827–38) and at the Collège de France (1838–51). He was in charge of the national archives between 1830 and 1852. The death of his wife in 1839 changed his attitude towards the past in general and towards the Church in particular. His long conflict with the ecclesiastical authorities began. "The past, that is the enemy – the barbaric Middle Ages – and its representative, Spain . . . the Spain that burnt the books of Voltaire and Montesquieu. The future, that is the friend; progress and the new spirit, 1789 distantly appearing on the horizon," he wrote significantly in volume 15 of the *Histoire de France*. In his journal he also explained tellingly: "I came out of the 18th century. I left the 18th century for a time. Then I returned there for ever, to find there always my own father, that is to say, the true France of Voltaire and Rousseau". The Roman Church, well used since

the 18th century to attacks on the plausibility of Christian doctrines, found Michelet's attacks on the ethics of Christian belief difficult to deal with. According to Owen Chadwick, Michelet "assailed not the truth of Genesis, nor the probability of miracles, but the doctrine of the atonement for its lack of justice; the inequality of the doctrine of predestination to death; the diminution of freedom through the doctrine of grace; the inquisition, the contrast between Christian ideals for humanity and the church's failure to promote these ideals in society".

Early in his career, Michelet had praised the institution of clerical celibacy. Then, in *Du Prêtre, de la femme, de la famille* (The Priesthood, Women and the Family, published in 1845), he attacked the power of the priesthood, especially as it was wielded in the confessional. Priests with no personal experience of marriage presumed to tell women in particular how to behave towards their husbands and family, thereby undermining family relationships. The Church was desperate to hold on to its role as moral guardian. If the loss of authority of the confessional were to follow the Church's earlier loss of political power, how then could the Church exercise its mission? The book was promptly removed from the faithful's hands by being placed on the *Index*. Interestingly, when Michelet returned to the topic in his later writings he was at pains to amend his earlier work, removing passages which had praised the celibate priesthood.

Michelet had particular animus against the Jesuits for their hold on social life and on education in France. His attacks on them began in a series at lectures at the Collège de France in 1843 and continued well into the 1850s. To Michelet, the Jesuits were the enemies of liberty and enlightenment. They had kept the people of France in a perpetual state of ignorance and poverty, alleviated only for a moment at the Revolution. They had failed to tackle the class divisions which their educational system perpetuated, in particular the gap between the literate and the illiterate. Doubtless Michelet, who believed in the power of education to bring about social change, was glad when, under the Orléans Monarchy (1830–48), the Jesuits were banned from French classrooms, but he was aware that the battle between Church and state for the control of education was far from over. The Jesuits would fight to keep their influence. Michelet's outspoken republicanism may not, however, have helped his campaign for secular education. He was suspended from the Collège de France in 1848, and, although later reinstated, he remained under suspicion. Government agents posing as students attended his lectures in 1849, and at one stage even packed his classes with bourgeois students to preempt riots. Michelet was finally dismissed for good by Louis Napoleon in 1851. In the same year, Louis Napoleon ordered that books by Michelet's heroes, Voltaire and Rousseau, should be removed from libraries. Once Michelet had refused to sign the oath of allegiance to the new regime, his fate as a teacher and curator of the archives was sealed.

Michelet continued to write. His *Histoire* was still in progress. In 1858 he wrote *L'Amour* (*Love*), in which he contrasted the love and morality which existed in ordinary families with their absence in the institutional Church. This work, too, was placed on the Index, but the action of the censors hardly prevented the book's immense popularity among the reading public. *La Sorcière* (*Satanism and Witchcraft*), published in 1862, a defence of medieval witches against the superstition and zealous oppression to which they were subjected, was given the same treatment by Church censors as his previous work, as was *La Bible de l'humanité*, an exploration of ancient religions, published in 1864, in which Michelet proposed that

ancient Indian myths and folklore provided a foundation for a humanistic and fraternal religion.

Michelet's real loyalty was to the people: "The deeper I have dug, the more surely I have satisfied myself that the best was underneath, buried in obscurity". This belief drove his historical studies, fuelled his anti-clericalism, and led to the censorship of his writings and teachings by Church and state alike. Most of his writings remained on the *Index* for the rest of the 19th century and through the early 20th century. *Mémoires de Luther* was still there when the Index was abolished in 1966.

DOUGLAS PALMER

Writings

Histoire de France, 17 vols, 1833–67; abridged translation as *History of France*, 2 vols, 1844–46
Translator, *Mémoires de Luther: écrits par lui-même*, 1835
Les Jésuites, 1843
Le Peuple, 1846; as *The People*, translated by John P. McKay, 1973
Histoire de la Révolution française, 7 vols, 1847–53; as *History of the French Revolution*, translated by Charles Cooks, 1967
La Sorcière, 1862; as *Satanism and Witchcraft: A Study in Medieval Superstition*, translated by A.R. Allinson, 1939
La Bible de l'humanité, 1864; translated as *The Bible of Humanity*, 1877

Further Reading

Chadwick, Owen, *The Secularization of the European Mind in the Nineteenth Century*, Cambridge and New York: Cambridge University Press, 1975
Kippur, Stephen A., *Jules Michelet: A Study of Mind and Sensibility*, Albany: State University of New York Press, 1981
Mitzman, Arthur, *Michelet, Historian: Rebirth and Romanticism in Nineteenth-Century France*, New Haven, Connecticut: Yale University Press, 1990
Orr, Linda, *Headless History: Nineteenth-century French Historiography of the Revolution*, Ithaca, New York: Cornell University Press, 1990
Walch, Jean, *Les Maîtres de l'histoire, 1815–1850: Augustin Thierry, Mignet, Guizot, Thiers, Michelet, Edgard Quinet*, Geneva: Slatkine, 1986
Wright, Gordon, *France in Modern Times*, 5th edition, New York: Norton, 1995

ADAM MICKIEWICZ
Polish poet, 1798–1855

DZIADY (Forefathers)
Dramatic cycle, 1823–32

In a letter to his fellow exile, the historian Joachim Lelewel, dated 23 March 1832, Adam Mickiewicz wrote:

I place great hopes in our nation and in a course of events unforeseen by any diplomacy ... I think only that our aspirations should be given a religious and moral character, distinct from the financial liberalism of the French and firmly grounded in Catholicism.

The third part of *Dziady*, which Mickiewicz wrote in Dresden later that spring, develops these ideas in dramatic form, moving in a quite different direction than that taken in the enigmatic

fragments of the earlier parts, which had been published as volume 2 of Mickiewicz's *Poezje* (1823, Poetry).

These earlier parts – 2 and 4 only, since the draft of part 1 was discovered only posthumously – are known as the Wilno (or Vilnius)–Kaunas *Dziady*, with reference to the cities in which Mickiewicz wrote them. They demonstrated Romanticism "in action" for a literary culture that was still largely dominated by classical aesthetics. The action of part 2 draws on a Belarusian folk rite in honour of the dead, when the spirits are summoned to commune with and receive sustenance from the living, in a ceremony conducted by the village wizard (the *guślarz*). In part 4, a hermit visits the home of a Uniate priest and delivers a long monologue on his wretched life. He turns out to be Gustav, an old pupil of the priest's, and perhaps even a ghost himself, and he intercedes with the priest not to interfere in the folk rite.

Part 3, which is artistically and structurally more complex, received fulsome praise from Georges Sand (1839): "since the fears and imprecations of the prophets of Zion, no voice has been raised with such power to sing so vast a theme as that of the fall of a nation". The starting point is Mickiewicz's own life. Its central character, Gustav, who assumes the name "Konrad" in a mysterious ritual, is, like Mickiewicz, a victim of Russian oppression in the Vilnius of the early 1820s. The drama reaches for universal significance when Good and Evil wage a titanic struggle over his and Poland's soul. As he awaits trial in his cell, Konrad questions the existence of divine justice, given the monumental crimes committed against Poland. His blasphemous conclusion is that God is in fact in league with the Devil (identified with the Russian emperor). However, Gustav is saved from damnation by Father Peter, who leads him to understand the need for expiation and suffering, introducing ideas that Mickiewicz was to expand upon in the *Księgi narodu i pielgrzymstwa polskiego* (1832, Books of the Polish Pilgrimage and Nation), specifically that Poland is the "Christ of Nations", whose collapse was a necessary sacrifice in the coming moral regeneration of Europe.

The mystical Vilnius scenes are complemented by a series of realistic, satirical scenes set in Warsaw, showing members of Polish society collaborating with the Russian oppressor. What was to exercise the Russian censors particularly, however, was the "Ustęp" (Digression), a series of long poems following the drama that depict the despotism in St Petersburg in all its horror. "The Monument of Peter the Great" focuses on the human costs of Peter's great enterprise – it stung Aleksandr Pushkin to respond with *Mednyi vsadnik* (1833, The Bronze Horseman) – while "Review of the Army" shows the dehumanization created by the autocracy, as exemplified in a military parade.

The Russian censorship's repression of Mickiewicz's works began in earnest after the publication of part 3, which was kept secret for several weeks to mislead Russian spies in Paris. The Russian authorities had been alerted to the subversive nature of his earlier historical poem, *Konrad Wallenrod* (1828 and 1829, St Petersburg), and now it was the open attack on the autocracy that made part 3 unpublishable in Russia proper or in the Kingdom of Poland (the section of the historical Poland occupied by Russian troops). Nevertheless, shortly after part 3 went on sale, in January 1833, it made its way into Russian Poland. On 6 March, the Government Commission for Internal and Religious Affairs and Public Education ordered searches to be conducted on the territory of the Kingdom itself. This initiated an unconditional ban on the work, extended to the Russian empire as a whole on 1 September. In December, the St Petersburg Committee of Foreign Censorship confirmed the ban, defining the work as "an outpouring of poisonous bile against the Russian government and the imperial family". Rewards were offered for handing in copies and fines were imposed for possession. The arbitrariness of Russian imperial justice allowed for sentences of 25 years military service for individuals caught with the work.

In the period of limited liberalization after the Crimean War,

the possibility arose of publishing Mickiewicz's works openly. In the eight-volume Warsaw edition of 1857–58, parts 2 and 4 found places, but the still unconditionally banned part 3 did not. Instead, it had to be published clandestinely around 1860, in lithograph form, in Kyiv, by students of the university, and in St Petersburg. The first official publication of part 3 occurred in the Austrian sector – Lwów (or Lemberg, or Lviv, 1885) and Cracow (1890) – where the Poles had enjoyed cultural and increasing political autonomy after the passing of the Fundamental Laws of 1867. In the Russian sector of Poland, even during the relatively liberal period after the revolution of 1905–06, the censor, V.M. Ivanovski, could still justify confiscating a whole print run thus: "The poem is imbued with a desire for vengeance against, and profound hatred of, Russia, particularly of the Russian emperor as the chief cause of the sufferings of the Polish nation".

Dziady became a politically contentious work again following the Soviet occupation of eastern Poland at the start of World War II. Obvious comparisons were made between earlier Russian imperialism and oppression and what the Soviet Union was doing. Accordingly, compilers and teachers of school readers stressed other elements: the minor social criticism in part 2 and the pro-Russian sentiments in "To My Russian Friends". The distinction that Mickiewicz makes there between opposition to Russian imperialism and opposition to the Russian people was employed in propagating Polish–Soviet friendship. In this way, given the Nazi destruction of monuments in the western portion that they had conquered simultaneously, the Soviet authorities could at least pose as defenders of Polish culture.

These Soviet-inspired readings continued after the war, particularly during the years when the doctrine of socialist realism was most stringently enforced (1948–55), when the party's desire to exploit the national tradition as a source of legitimacy also applied to literature. In accordance with president Bolesław Bierut's exhortations, in January 1950, to "extract, reveal and bring out the real popular democratic, social and ideological bedrock of [Mickiewicz's] creative work", party critics devised class-conscious interpretations:

There is no hint of the ideology of passivity, expiation, sacrifice, grace. The drama exudes passion for the struggle. This is not altered by comparisons scattered throughout between the sufferings of the conspirators and those of Christ.

The Censorship Office ensured that introductions to, and commentaries on, editions of Mickiewicz's works explained any unacceptable "reactionary" elements in class terms and, it was hoped, neutralized their effect.

The history of theatre productions of the work was almost as fraught as that of its publication. A fragment of part 3 was performed in Cracow in 1848, but it was only in 1901, again in Cracow, that the first complete production was staged, by the "Young Poland" poet and playwright Stanisław Wyspiański. In newly independent Poland from 1918, a flurry of performances celebrated national survival, but it was the left-wing director Leon Schiller (1887–1954) who is generally credited with reinventing the play as theatre in a series of productions throughout the 1930s (Lwów 1932, Vilnius 1933, Warsaw 1934, Sofia

1937). In postwar Poland, Schiller's dream of reviving the play foundered on the party's caution about the nationalism inspiring Romantic works in the new political conditions of the Cold War: productions planned for 1948 and 1950 were quietly dropped. It was not until 1955 that Aleksandr Bardini, one of Schiller's pupils, mounted the first major postwar production.

The most renowned production, directed in 1967 by Kazimierz Dejmek at the National Theatre in Warsaw, seemed to bear out the party's earlier anxieties about *Dziady* as theatre. Because of the undesirable audience reaction – the loudest cheers were for the "anti-imperialist" passages in the play – the authorities decided to curtail performances after several weeks. The closure of the play on 30 January 1968, officially due to the illness of its main actor, Gustaw Holoubek, resulted in a march by students of Warsaw University in protest at what was widely seen as Soviet interference. Members of the Warsaw branch of the Writers' Union supported them, drafting a motion criticizing the authorities. The subsequent repression of writers, students, and lecturers – in effect, a cultural clearance of the intelligentsia, with some choosing to emigrate – came to be known euphemistically as the "March events".

JOHN MICHAEL BATES

Writings

Gems of Polish Poetry: Selections from Mickiewicz, translated by Frank H. Fortey, 1923
Konrad Wallenrod and Other Writings, translated by George Rapall Noyes et al., 1925
Poems, edited by George Rapall Noyes, 1944
Selected Poetry and Prose, translated by Stanisław Helsztyński, 1955
Adam Mickiewicz, 1798–1855: Selected Poems, edited by Charles Mills, 1956
Pan Tadeusz; or, The Last Foray in Lithuania, translated by Kenneth Mackenzie,1966
Forefathers, translated by Count Potocki of Montalk, 1968
Forefathers' Eve, part 3, in *Polish Romantic Drama*, edited by Harold B. Segel, 1977

Further Reading

Fik, Marta, *Marcowa kultura* (The Culture of March 1968), Warsaw: Wodnika, 1995
Inglot, Mieczysław, *Polska kultura literacka Lwowa lat 1939–1941* (Polish Literary Culture in Lvov, 1939–1941), Wrocław: Pryjaciół Polonistyki Wrocławskiej, 1995
Kopczyński, Krzysztof, *Mickiewicz i jego czytelnicy: o recepcji wieszcza w zaborze rosyjskim w latach 1831–1855*, (Mickiewicz and His Readers: The Reception of the Bard in the Russian Partition, 1831–1855), Warsaw: Semper, 1994
Prussak, Maria (editor), *Świat pod kontrolą* (A World under Supervision), Warsaw: KRĄG, 1994
Timoszewicz, Jerzy, *"Dziady" w inscenizacji Leona Schillera: Partytura i jej wykonanie* (Forefathers in the Stagings of Leon Schiller: The Score and Its Performance), Warsaw: Panstw. Instytut, 1970
Weintraub, Wiktor, *The Poetry of Adam Mickiewicz*, The Hague: Mouton, 1954

THOMAS MIDDLETON

English dramatist, 1580–1627

A GAME AT CHESS

Play, 1624

Thomas Middleton shocked and delighted audiences with *A Game at Chess*, a thinly disguised allegory of the failed marriage alliance between the thrones of England/Scotland and Spain in 1623. The play was an expression of national pride and one which was so powerful that it threatened already tenuous relations between England and Spain.

By the 1620s England and Scotland had become accustomed to a Protestant monarch, church, and government. In 1624 this stability appeared to be threatened by an impending marriage between the heir to the thrones, prince Charles, and the Spanish princess Donna Maria. James I wanted a Spanish match for his son, as it would result in a magnificent dynastic alliance and trade advantages with the New World. These prizes were not to be had without a cost. The Spanish insisted upon the suspension of penal laws against Catholics in England, and that all children born to the couple were to be raised Catholic for the first 12 years of their life.

In February 1623 prince Charles and the duke of Buckingham left for Spain in hopes of returning with a Spanish bride. The talks collapsed after five months as a result of Spanish reluctance to promise extensive military aid to England. Although he had been insulted and embarrassed, Charles was greeted with unrestrained jubilation upon his return to England. Virulent anti-Catholic sentiment had been whipped up by the prospect of a Catholic princess of England, which was perceived as a Spanish attempt to plant a foothold in England.

In the euphoria that followed, Middleton was inspired to write *A Game at Chess* (1624). A chess game was used for the backdrop in which the "Black House" seeks to corrupt members of the "White House" through the use of romantic entanglements and clever subterfuge. Unflattering characters from the Black House were clearly caricatures of influential Spaniards, including the Black Knight (Count Gondomar), the Black King (Philip II), and the Black Bishop (the Father General of the Jesuits). The White House was presented far more sympathetically with trusting characters who wish to deal honourably with the Black House. The White Knight is clearly prince Charles, the White Duke is Buckingham, and the White King is king James. In the course of the play the Black House has occasional success in seducing pawns of the White House, but in the end their plotting is discovered. The White Knight exposes the corruption of the Black House and literally bags up the offending players in an exultant finale.

The play was audacious on a number of fronts. By tradition, it was forbidden to portray on stage living monarchs in a hostile manner. Living persons, if portrayed at all, were to be depicted at a distance and with respect. The 17th century was a period in which political intrigue flourished and authorities believed it was their duty to halt the circulation of any ideas that were likely to provoke unrest and upset the delicate political balance. *A Game at Chess* did all those things.

As was required by law, the play had been submitted to the Master of the Revels for approval prior to the performance. The Master of the Revels was a servant to the Lord Chamberlain, and together these two officials were responsible for the regulation and licensing of theatres, plays, and entertainment. They had the power to censor plays or disband acting companies that disturbed the peace or threatened public health. It is a matter of some surprise that *A Game at Chess* ever obtained a licence for performance. It has been suggested that Sir Henry Herbert, the Master of the Revels, was in sympathy with the content of the play, and may even have secretly obtained permission from prince Charles and the duke of Buckingham to allow it to proceed.

The first performance was on 6 August 1624 at the Globe Theatre, London and was an immediate success. It was customary for acting companies to perform a different play each day, but the overwhelming popularity of *A Game at Chess* allowed the play to run on nine consecutive occasions to a packed house until it was abruptly suppressed. The authorities could hardly ignore the sensation. The king himself ordered the acting troupe to cease performance while an investigation was conducted. The Spanish ambassador angrily informed the king that the play was intended to show "the cruelty of Spain and the treachery of Spaniards", and that anti-Spanish feeling was so high that he no longer felt safe in London; he demanded that the actors be punished, or else the king should be prepared for a severance of all relations between Spain and England.

King James ordered Middleton and the actors to report to the Lords of Council on 21 August 1624. The actors appeared and were rebuked and forbidden to continue performances. Middleton failed to appear and a warrant was issued for his arrest. When he could not be found, his 20-year-old son, Edward, was brought in for questioning but was unable or unwilling to provide information on the whereabouts of his father. It is believed that Middleton was in hiding and rapidly preparing transcriptions of the play for private sale since three separate editions were available within the year. When Middleton did resurface, tradition claims, he spent some time in Fleet Prison awaiting formal pardon by the king. The length and circumstances of Middleton's imprisonment are unknown, but contemporary sources claim that he was released after submitting a witty epigram to the king. But no further performances of the play were allowed.

It could hardly be said that the people associated with the production of *A Game at Chess* were severely punished. Middleton and the actors were protected because the play had been licensed by the Master of the Revels, who, in turn, was protected by his close association with the Lord Chamberlain and prince Charles. The king knew that the vast majority of his subjects were fervently sympathetic to the play and his primary loyalty had to be to his subjects rather than to a foreign king.

DOROTHY AUCHTER

Writings

A Game at Chess, produced 1624, published 1625; edited by M.A. Buettner, 1980
Works, edited by A.H. Bullen, 8 vols, 1885–86

Further Reading

Albright, Evelyn May, *Dramatic Publication in England, 1580–1640: A Study of Conditions Affecting Content and Form of Drama*, New York: Heath, and London: Oxford University Press, 1927
Clare, Janet, *Art Made Tongue-Tied by Authority: Elizabethan and Jacobean Dramatic Censorship*, 2nd edition, Manchester: Manchester University Press, 1999
Gildersleeve, Virginia Crocheron, *Government Regulation of the Elizabethan Drama*, New York: Columbia University Press, 1908; reprinted New York: Burt Franklin, 1961
Howard-Hill, T.H., *Middleton's "Vulgar Pasquin": Essays on A Game at Chess*, Newark: University of Delaware Press, 1995
Power, William Longford, "Thomas Middleton vs. King James I", *Notes and Queries*, 202/4 (1957): 526–34

MIGHTY MORPHIN POWER RANGERS
US television series, censored in New Zealand, 1994

Mighty Morphin Power Rangers (also known simply as *Power Rangers*) is a television show aimed at 9- to 12-year-olds. Developed from a Japanese programme, it features six teenagers, four boys and two girls, who *morph* (transform themselves) into superheroes. These superheroes are either uniformed ninja fighters or robotic dinosaurs, who protect Earth from Godzilla-like monsters sent by the wicked Rita Repulsa or the evil Lord Zed. *Power Rangers* has been shown in about 30 countries around the world, generally with little controversy. However, in 1994 the programme was declared too violent for Canadian television, and pulled from screening on several free-to-air channels, although Canadians with cable continued to receive the programme through the Fox network. Some Scandinavian countries also dropped the programme, and it became a focus for New Zealand debate over the influence of television on younger viewers.

In New Zealand, *Power Rangers* was screened in the late afternoon on weekdays, on Television New Zealand's TV2, a national free-to-air TV channel. The programme ran for 12 weeks, from 9 May until 29 July 1994, with a total of 60 episodes transmitted. During this period, four formal complaints about *Power Rangers* were referred to the television watchdog the Broadcasting Standards Authority (BSA), including two that represented the views of parents and teachers of kindergartens. One was from the Children's Media Watch, a lobby concerned with children's television programming, and another from the mother of young children. The Authority also received a large number of informal written and telephone complaints about the series. The complaints focused on the Power Rangers' use of violence as a means of resolving conflict, and the negative impact of the programme on the behaviour of children, particularly preschoolers, who were imitating the martial arts sequences. The Children's Media Watch noted that in the 25-minute duration of one episode, more than 50 violent or aggressive acts occurred.

Following established procedure, the complainants were initially referred by the BSA to the broadcaster, in this case Television New Zealand (TVNZ). Each of the four complainants alleged that *Power Rangers* was in breach of Standard V10 of the Television Code of Broadcasting Practice, which reads: "The cumulative or overall effect of violent incidents and themes in a single programme, a programme series or line-up of programmes back to back, must avoid giving an impression of excessive violence." TVNZ countered by arguing that the series empowered children, with the Power Rangers offering positive role models and demonstrating values such as self-esteem, courage, responsibility, teamwork, and respect for individual differences. Along with other defenders of the programme, they observed that vigorous play had always been part of growing up, and that fantasy adventure had always been a popular children's genre.

The complainants also alleged a breach of standard VI of the Television Code of Broadcasting Practice: "Broadcasters have a responsibility to ensure that any violence shown is justifiable, i.e. is essential in the context of the programme." For example, the Bayfield Kindergarten submission, on behalf of 55 parents and staff, cited research indicating that when children were exposed to violent modes for resolving conflict, it became part of their own means of responding to such behaviour. The kindergarten noted the increased incidence of playground violence, imitating the Power Rangers martial arts moves. TVNZ countered by noting that the series complied with the stringent regulations set in the United States for children's programmes, and also with series producer Fox Network's additional set of rules. These stated that the Power Rangers may only use science-fiction-style weapons and that the monsters must be clearly fictional creations. The Rangers could not start fights, nor escalate them, and they must never fight people. Further, each programme contained a social message (given at the end).

The complainants were not satisfied with TVNZ's defence of *Power Rangers*, and the BSA now became more closely involved. After considering the complaints, and the broadcaster's response to them, the BSA decided in favour of the complainants. Its decision noted that "the heavy concentration of episodes every week day for twelve weeks overwhelmingly contributed to an impression of excessive violence", with each episode "centred around incidents of karate-style sparring between the heroes and their adversaries." The BSA does not have the power to direct the broadcasters, but its decisions are clearly not to be ignored, especially when the government controls broadcasting licensing in New Zealand. Accordingly, TVNZ did not repeat the original *Mighty Morphin Power Rangers* programmes, even though repeats are a common local programming strategy to keep costs down. The channel had already acted to modify the series, by reducing the number of incidents of martial arts sparring, and were screening public service announcements by members of the cast which alerted children to the difference between fantasy and reality, and the dangers of violent behaviour in the playground. This strategy was continued with the screening of further episodes of *Mighty Morphin Power Rangers*, and there were no further formal complaints about the programme to the BSA.

ROY SHUKER

Further Reading

Davies, Máire Messenger, *Television Is Good for Your Kids*, London: Shipman, 1989

Gunter, Barrie and Jill L. McAleer, *Children and Television*, London and New York: Routledge, 1990; 2nd edition 1997

Hendershot, Heather, *Saturday Morning Censors: Television Regulation before the V-Chip*, Durham, North Carolina: Duke University Press, 1998

SOLOMON MIKHOELS
Russian actor and theatre director, 1890–1948

As an actor, theatre director, and public figure, Solomon Mikhoels was a leading figure in Soviet Jewish cultural life under Stalin. Born into an Orthodox Jewish family in Dvinsk in 1890, Mikhoels received a typical Jewish education before studying jurisprudence at St Petersburg University. Following the Bolshevik revolution in 1917, he joined the Yiddish Chamber Theatre of Petrograd, which was led by the Symbolist director Aleksandr Granovskii. After the theatre received the official support of the newly created commissariats of Nationalities and Enlightenment, it moved to Moscow. In 1924 the theatre was nationalized and renamed the Moscow State Yiddish Theatre (GosET or MGET).

Mikhoels's talent as an actor was first recognized in his portrayals of 19th-century Russian Jewish life when the theatre presented a series of productions based on stories by pre-revolutionary Yiddish writers. Plays such as Sholem Aleichem's *200,000* or Avrom Goldfadn's *The Sorceress* attracted the praise of the communist authorities for mocking the futility of capitalist life, the decadence of the *nouveaux riches*, and religious fanaticism. With the film *Yidishn glikn* (1924, Jewish Luck) and the play *"Banakht ofn altn mark* (1925, Night in the Old Market), the company cooperated with the Jewish Section of the Communist Party to entice Ukrainian and Belorussian Jews to abandon their "petty bourgeois" occupations, and to join instead the urban proletariat or the collective farm movement.

In the late 1920s party and state censors began to attack the Yiddish theatre for failing to incorporate contemporary Soviet productions into its repertoire, and for promoting pre-revolutionary Jewish "bourgeois" music. It was realised that, for the purposes of survival, more subtle approaches were needed. In 1926 the company presented *137 Children's Houses* by the

Soviet playwright Avram Veviurka. While this play ostensibly resembled typical Soviet propaganda, the title clearly alluded to Psalm 137 ("By the rivers of Babylon . . ."), in which the Jews lament their inability to sing songs of Zion while being held captive in a foreign land. The following year Mikhoels starred as Benjamin in the theatre's adaptation of Mendele Mokher Sforim's *Masaes Vinyomin hashlishi* (1927, The Travels of Benjamin III), a play about a naive simpleton who sets out in search of the land of Israel only to find himself back at his Ukrainian home. The play was praised by the communist press for showing the futility of the Zionist dream. However, it also served to ignite Zionist aspirations among some members of the audience.

After the defection of Granovskii during the theatre's European tour in 1928, Mikhoels became its director. The recent formation of a Central Arts Administration to monitor the activities of all Soviet artists further decreased his already limited independence. Mikhoels was instructed to perform plays on the theme of socialist construction in the Soviet Union. Once again, Mikhoels inserted allusions to Jewish national history into otherwise typical propaganda plots. For instance, in David Bergelson's *Der toyber* (1930; The Deaf), which concerns a proletarian rebellion in a factory, Mikhoels, as the deaf protagonist, stuttered only 30 words in the play and stood with his right hand resting limp over his head – an allusion to Psalm 137:5, "If I forget thee O Jerusalem let my right hand lose its cunning and let my tongue cleave to the roof of my mouth". Similarly, M. Daniel's *Fir teg* (1931, Four Days) told of a group of Bolsheviks who commit suicide while under siege rather than be captured by the enemy – an allusion to the siege of Masada. These allusions were comprehensible to a Yiddish-speaking audience familiar with Jewish history and the scriptures, but were hidden from the secular Soviet censors, who understood neither the Yiddish language nor Jewish culture.

In 1935, Mikhoels starred in his most famous role, as Shakespeare's King Lear. Mikhoels was determined, however, not to allow his theatre to abandon its Jewish heritage by performing exclusively world classics. His adaptation of Goldfadn's *Bar Kokhba* (1938), for instance, told of the Jewish revolt against Roman rule in second-century Judaea. While the play is often interpreted as a Jewish call to arms against oppressive rule, Mikhoels disguised it as a historical example of the class struggle. Only the Yiddish-speaking members of the audience saw it as a glorification of Jewish nationalist heroism. Mikhoels's roles as Tevye in Sholem Aleichem's *Tevye der milkhiger* (1938, Tevye the Dairyman) and as Zayvl Ovadis in Peretz Markish's *Mishbokhe Ovadia* (1937, Family Ovadis) helped to paint an optimistic picture of Jewish life in the Soviet Union, but implicitly reinforced Jewish national distinctiveness.

During World War II Mikhoels was appointed chairman of the Soviet Jewish Anti-Fascist Committee (JAFC), an organization established with the goal of soliciting international Jewish support for the Soviet war effort. In this capacity, Mikhoels helped end years of Soviet Jewish isolation by calling for world Jewish unity and travelling abroad to meet Jewish community leaders. During his travels, Mikhoels, increasingly sympathetic to Zionist causes, met Chaim Weizmann, president of the World Zionist Organization. Mikhoels also began collecting information for a book on Nazi atrocities against the Jews. After he arranged for the book to be published in the United States in

1946, the Soviet censors refused to allow its publication in the Soviet Union, on the grounds that it exaggerated Nazi crimes against the Jews.

Following the war, Mikhoels's theatre performed a number of plays, such as Peretz Markish's *Oyfshtand in geto* (1947, Uprising in the Ghetto), depicting Jewish heroism during the war. However, he was not permitted to single out Jews as Nazi victims, and was forced to downplay the anti-Semitism that the war had ignited within the Soviet Union. At the same time, Mikhoels continued to work with the JAFC to help rebuild Jewish life, and to retain contact with western Jewish communities. The Soviet state no longer needed to attract the support of western Jewry, however, and viewed Mikhoels's continued contacts with suspicion. Following the passage of a resolution favouring partition of Palestine between Jews and Arabs at the UN General Assembly in November 1947, Mikhoels spoke in favour of the establishment of a Jewish state at a public ceremony. The next day, when the ceremony was broadcast on the radio, Mikhoels's speech had been removed; he had failed to recognize that Soviet diplomatic support for the partition plan was not intended as an endorsement of Zionism, and his outspoken defence of Jewish national interests disturbed the Soviet authorities. In the early hours of 13 January 1948, Mikhoels was killed after being run over by a truck, in what was portrayed as a tragic accident but was actually arranged by the Ministry of State Security, acting on direct orders from Stalin. The murder of Mikhoels preceded an anti-Jewish campaign that left the most prominent members of the Soviet Jewish community dead.

Beginning in 1949, the state began attacking Mikhoels's heritage by burning his archives, removing his scenes from popular films, and disbanding his theatre. Publication of a collection of his writings became possible during the "Thaw" of the late 1950s, and in 1989 the Mikhoels Jewish Cultural Centre was established in Moscow. An official commemoration of the 50th anniversary of his murder was held in 1998.

JEFFREY VEIDLINGER

Writings

Stat'i, besedi, rechi (Articles, Conversations, Speeches), 1964

Further Reading

Altshuler, Mordechai (editor), *Ha-teatron ha-yehudi be-brit ha-moatsot* (The Jewish Theatre in the Soviet Union), Jerusalem: Hebrew University, 1996

Borshchagovskii, Aleksandr, *Obviniaetsia krov'* (Blood on Trial), Moscow: Kultura, 1994

Dobrushin, Yehezekiel, *Mikhoels der aktior* (Mikhoels the Actor), Moscow: Der Emes, 1940

Geizer, M., *Solomon Mikhoels*, Moscow: Prometer, 1990

Goldenberg, Mikhail, *Zhizn' i sud'ba Solomona Mikhoelsa* (The Life and Fate of Solomon Mikhoels), Baltimore: Vestnik, 1995

Grinvald, Iakov, *Mikhoels: kratkii kritiko-biograficheskii ocherk* (Mikhoels: A Short Critical-Biographical Sketch), Moscow: Der Emes, 1948

Markish, Peretz, *Mikhoels*, Moscow: Der Emes, 1939

Picon-Vallin, Béatrice, *Le Théâtre juif soviétique pendant les années vingt*, Lausanne: La Cité, 1973

Veidlinger, Jeffrey, *The Moscow State Yiddish Theater: Jewish Culture on the Soviet Stage*, Bloomington: Indiana University Press, 2000

Vovsi-Mikhoels, Natalia, *Mon père Salomon Mikhoels: souvenirs sur sa vie et sur sa mort*, Montricher, Switzerland: Noir sur Blanc, 1990

LEWIS MILESTONE
US film director, 1895–1980

ALL QUIET ON THE WESTERN FRONT (Im Westen nichts Neues)
Film, 1930

Erich Maria Remarque's novel was published in 1929, was translated into 12 languages, and became a bestseller in Germany and worldwide. It provoked bitter controversy between those who praised it as an indictment of the futility and horror of war and those who condemned it as pacifist propaganda and commercial exploitation. *All Quiet*, set during World War I, follows a group of German recruits who gradually become disillusioned with the war and are killed one by one.

The film rights were bought by Universal, founded by the German-American Carl Laemmle, who actually approached UFA, the largest German film producer and exhibitor, which was owned by the right-wing media magnate Alfred Hugenberg, to see if they would be interested in cooperating on *All Quiet*. The company's point-blank refusal was an early indication of the film's future troubles in Germany. *All Quiet* was released in the United States in May 1930, and elsewhere shortly thereafter. In general the film was very well received, and in the US there were even suggestions that Laemmle, Remarque and Lewis Milestone should receive the Nobel Peace Prize. However, *All Quiet*'s reception in Germany was another matter, and even in countries where the film was well received it occasionally encountered censorship problems. In Britain a two-minute bedroom scene between the central character, Paul Bäumer, and a young Frenchwoman, Suzanne, was cut out entirely. The Canadian print suffered five cuts, mainly to remove lewd soldierly talk, but the famous scene in which Bäumer stabs a French soldier in a shell-hole was also trimmed, and a one-minute scene showing German soldiers fraternizing with French women was removed. Unsurprisingly, the last two alterations were also made in France. The film lost seven minutes in Australia; again, raw dialogue and sexual scenes fell victim to censorship but so too, more seriously, did sequences illustrating the horrors of trench warfare and aerial bombardment. In New Zealand the film was initially banned outright and was released only after appeal and in a version shorn of some six minutes.

When *All Quiet* was viewed by the Berlin Censorship Board on 21 November 1930, a representative of the Defence Ministry argued for a total ban on the grounds that the film damaged Germany's image and cast aspersions on its army at a time when its position as defender of the Republic was being emphasized. However, a representative from the Foreign Office, perhaps fearing reaction abroad to a ban, defended its showing, and his view prevailed. None the less, a number of cuts were made in scenes which showed the German army and establishment in a negative light. The premiere was set for 4 December at the Theater am Nollendorfplatz.

All Quiet was assured the stormiest of receptions, for a number of reasons. Firstly, in the September elections the Nazis had increased their seats in the Reichstag from 12 to 107; they were thus in fighting mood, and the parties of the conventional, conservative Right were terrified of losing any more support to the "radicals" by appearing soft on "national" issues. Secondly, the film raised in an especially acute form the issue of American

cultural imperialism, an issue that the parties of the Right, both old and new, never tired of exploiting. Nowhere was this battle more fiercely fought than in the cinema, where it was exacerbated by the frequent departures of indigenous talent to Hollywood and by what was perceived as a steady flow of American anti-German films. Thus in July 1930 the Defence Minister General Groener wrote to Chancellor Brüning demanding the banning of 37 foreign films which, he claimed, represented Germany in a negative light. These included *The Big Parade*, *What Price Glory?* and the 1927 re-release of Chaplin's *Shoulder Arms*. Thirdly, as already noted, the UFA media empire, itself involved in rivalry with Hollywood, was particularly hostile to *All Quiet*. In June the board of directors had received a report from a UFA representative in London

MILESTONE: Scene from *All Quiet on the Western Front*, showing a young German soldier fraternizing with a local French girl. Scenes such as this were cut in a number of countries, including France and Canada, before the film was released in 1930. In Germany the film was banned after its initial release provoked a stormy reaction to its portrayal of the German army. *All Quiet* was re-released, with significant cuts, by its producer, Carl Laemmle, in 1931; this version was passed by the Berlin Censorship Board, but banned when the Nazis took power in 1933.

describing the film as "thoroughly hostile" towards Germany, and had thus decided that an "appropriate stand" would be taken against it being shown there. The Hugenberg-owned newspapers the *Berliner Lokalanzeiger* and the *Nachtausgabe* began to campaign vociferously against it, and other right-wing newspapers soon followed suit. In December 1930 Hugenberg wrote to President Hindenburg himself urging him to ban the film. The whole situation has been clearly summed up by Modris Eksteins, who points out that:

> in December, many of the frustrations and fears, and much hatred and resentment, prevalent in various sectors of German politics and the economy, would converge dramatically on *All Quiet*. The fate of the film in Germany would illustrate eloquently the acuteness of the crisis that country was facing and would suggest the direction the government would follow in the next years.

All Quiet's premiere, before an invited audience, passed off peacefully. However, the first public performance was severely disrupted by a large number of Nazis in the audience. These included various Reichstag deputies; among them was Goebbels, who made a speech from the balcony. Eventually the screening was abandoned, and the following one also cancelled. For the next few days the film was shown under police protection, but on 8 December rioting broke out in the streets around the cinema. This happened again on 9 December, and that day the German Federation of Cinema Owners voted to boycott any films that provoked public disturbances, expressing their regret that "Carl Laemmle, a German-American, should have seen fit, 12 years after the conclusion of peace, to produce a war film that cannot be shown in Berlin in the same version as that exhibited in London and Paris." At the same time, the main student association of Berlin University, the League of German Officers and the veterans' organization, *Stahlhelm*, all called for the film to be banned. On 10 December the police president of Berlin announced a ban on all open-air demonstrations, provoking an outcry from extreme Left and Right alike.

On the same day members of the cabinet took the unprecedented step of viewing the film. By now it was being alleged that the foreign office had changed its mind and favoured a ban. Brüning's state secretary commented, after the screening:

> deeply shocking and yet accurate. In the end, nevertheless, I too favour banning the film. For peace and order would be affected by its showing. Moreover, a longer film is said to be running in America, in which, apparently, parts are anti-German and inflammatory. Certain sections, because of their prominence, tend to standardize and falsify, and thus to create one-sided impressions.

Meanwhile five Länder (states), Saxony, Braunschweig, Thuringia, Württemberg, and Bavaria, had invoked their legal right to ask the Supreme Censorship Board to reconsider the passing of *All Quiet*. At a meeting of the Board on 11 December the Länder argued that the film posed a threat to public order, that it damaged Germany's image and that it could encourage political extremism at a time when democracy in Germany was already endangered. A representative of the Defence Ministry stated that *All Quiet* was but a more sophisticated version of the old anti-German propaganda films; the foreign ministry argued that it had changed its mind about the film because of reports of the effects of screenings in Britain and the US; while Dr Hoche of the Interior Ministry wished to see it banned in case it worsened still further Germany's "profound spiritual distress and inner strife" and "destructive and lamentable ideological struggle".

Almost inevitably *All Quiet* was banned, the Board deciding that the film presented German soldiers in negative, stereotypical fashion. It was dishonest, malicious and slanderous. "Ours the Victory!" rang the headline in the Nazi paper *Der Angriff*, while the *Neue Preussische Kreuz-Zeitung* congratulated the "success of the national resistance". The liberals and the Left were, of course, outraged, and the SPD newspaper *Vorwärts* warned that this "victory of terror" clearly demonstrated that Germany was now in the grip of a momentous "final struggle". The foreign press, equally predictably, were largely hostile; the British newspaper *The Manchester Guardian* summing up the general mood by condemning this "capitulation before the organized mob" as a "betrayal of the world's peace". Within Germany itself, however, outside the left-wing stronghold of Berlin, opinion tended to support the ban.

In the summer of 1931, Carl Laemmle announced that *All Quiet* was to be re-released throughout the world in a version even shorter than that shown for those few days in Berlin the previous year. In September the Berlin Censorship Board passed this version without further cuts and with very little public reaction. (Needless to say, when the Nazis seized power in 1933 this too was banned outright). It is now impossible to ascertain whether or not Laemmle's announcement of a worldwide release of this truncated version was simply a ploy to get the Germans on-side, given how sensitive they had been to the original's foreign screenings. Whatever the case, Universal did release a version running at approximately 100 minutes in 1934. This was re-released in 1939 with an anti-Nazi commentary, plus a documentary section on World War I and the rise of Nazism tacked onto the front; this increased the running time to about 110 minutes. The 1950 re-release ran to only 103 minutes, and this also was used as the basis for the 16mm print and, later, video release. The version shown on British television was a considerable improvement at nearly 126 minutes, but it was not until 1984 that the film could finally be seen once again in its full, uncut glory, thanks to painstaking restoration by the German broadcaster ZDF. Ironically, one of the prints used in this process came from the private collection of none other than Goebbels himself.

Remarque moved to Switzerland as the Nazis came to power and was deprived of his German citizenship in 1933. He became a US citizen in 1939, continued writing, and, after World War II, returned to Locarno, Switzerland, where he lived until his death in 1970.

JULIAN PETLEY

Further Reading

Eksteins, Modris, "War, Memory and Politics: The Fate of the Film *All Quiet on the Western Front*", *Central European History*, 13/1 (1980): 60–82

Kelly, Andrew, "All Quiet on the Western Front: 'Brutal Cutting, Stupid Censors and Bigoted Politicos' (1930–1984)", *Historical Journal of Film, Radio and Television*, 9/2 (1989)

JAMES MILL
British political philosopher, 1773–1836

Political theorist, political economist, and utilitarian, James Mill was the contemporary of Jeremy Bentham and David Ricardo and is best known for his *Essay on Government* (1821), largely because of the debate with T.B. Macaulay that followed its publication. Mill was one of the founders of utilitarianism, and his views on freedom of the press are contained in his *Essay on Liberty of the Press* (1821), one of several essays he wrote for the 5th edition of the *Encyclopaedia Britannica* (1823). This essay received less attention than his *Essay on Government*, which was reprinted in the *Encyclopaedia*, but it articulated a defence of the press that can be seen as a precursor to his son John Stuart Mill's famous *On Liberty* (1859). In the *Essay on Liberty*, the elder Mill addressed the question of which acts capable of being committed by the press should be prohibited by the government through the use of penalties. Since, he argued, offences by the press are of the same kind as all types of offences, what should be addressed is how to prevent injury. Mill characterized press offences as libel, because the press is primarily a danger to reputation, and may commit libel against private individuals or against the government.

Mill defined libel against private individuals as a violation of that individual's right to the character he deserves according to his actions. An offence occurs when the publication attributes actions to the individual that he did not commit, or accuses him of a disposition toward behaviour where evidence for this does not exist. Such claims are decided on fact. If the claim of offence is true, compensation for the injuries should be required with the goal of returning the reputation of the individual to its level prior to the libel. The writer should be required to print the judgement to repair the reputation. If this is not enough to convince the public, it must be because the public is privy to evidence the judge was not, or the public is of an improper mind. It is the duty of the legislature to correct the latter problem through education. Libel, no matter what the motive, can be prevented when the legislature ensures that compensation will negate any benefits the writer hopes to achieve, and that execution of such compensation will be certain.

If the publication is true, no restrictions should be placed on its printing. It is useful to have evil acts of individuals brought to public attention, since the certainty of discovery is the best way to prevent them. This usefulness outweighs the harm that may come from printing actions by individuals that do not harm society, but can bring them personal harm when exposed. Since it is not possible to separate these, all printing of the truth must be allowed.

With respect to libel against the government, the dilemma arises that if all activities of government are allowed to be obstructed then government cannot function, but if no criticism is allowed the people are oppressed. To solve this dilemma, Mill distinguishes printing that targets all the powers of government and printing that obstructs the operations of government. Printing that targets all the powers of government is not offensive: the press itself does not have the power to overthrow the government since it must have the cooperation of the general will to succeed. Legitimate government must have the support of the general will; if the general will does not support it, the overthrow of the government in favour of one more in keeping with this will is legitimate. If the general will does not support overthrow, such publications will not succeed and are not a danger. Thus publications targeting all the powers of government should not be considered offences. By contrast, publications which target detailed operations of government can be dangerous, and may thus be considered offences. It is possible for a publication to arouse action against specific government operations, such as judgement in a trial that may impede the workings of government at a critical juncture. To allow such action could seriously undermine the ability of government to rule. For this reason, publications against the detailed operations of government can be punished as offences.

However, if the publication targeting government operations is implied and constructive rather than detailed, it should not be punished. Such publications of opinion and recommendation rather than detailed demands for specific action are not as dangerous. They are an important check by the people on vicious governments, since such actions by the press are needed to reach the conformity of opinion required to overthrow these types of governments. The freedom of the press is essential for good government, because to make good choices for leaders the people need to have knowledge about whom they are choosing. Without a free press, the government could limit information about leaders so that it could control choices by the people. Unless there is a press free to expose all truths about the functionaries of government, any choice by the people may not be in their best interest. It is therefore dangerous to allow any party to have the power to choose what information is available to the people.

What should be punishable are claims, without supporting evidence, that public officials are guilty of criminal acts. This type of libel should be treated in the same way as libel against private individuals, in that judgements about whether it is an offence should be based on fact. Mill also argued that false opinions should not be restricted because freedom of discussion implies both true and false opinions. In every discussion there is a right side and a wrong side. To place a restriction on one side would restrict all discussion.

Indecency should not be used as a standard because indecency really means what is not liked by the judge. Indecency for the government means what requires punishment. To classify false opinion as indecent classifies all discussion as indecent, since all discussion contains false opinion. Passionate critiques of government should not be restricted, since it would be inconsistent to allow passion in defence of government and not allow it for criticism. To allow for the suppression of publications based on this criteria would allow any publication to be suppressed on the grounds of passion. Therefore, none of these restrictions should be instituted. Opinion can only legitimately be impeded by evidence on the other side.

The only two restrictions that can be allowed for publications criticizing government are to punish and prevent direct obstruction of the operations of government, and the allegation of criminal acts by functionaries of government where there is no evidence.

BRENT STEWART LERSETH

Writings

An Essay on Government, 1821
*Essays on Government, Jurisprudence, Liberty of the Press, Prisons
   and Prison Discipline, Colonies, Law of Nations and Education*,
   1825 (reprints from the supplement to the 5th edition of
   Encyclopaedia Britannica)
Political Writings, edited by Terence Ball, 1992

Further Reading

Fenn, Robert A., *James Mill's Political Thought*, New York: Garland,
   1987

JOHN STUART MILL
British philosopher, 1806–1873

John Stuart Mill, the son of the utilitarian philosopher James
Mill, is probably best-known today for his essay *On Liberty*
(1859), a classic statement of western liberalism against the censorship of thought and in favour of the utmost diversity of
human beings, epitomized in the ringing sentence:

> If all mankind minus one were of one opinion, and only
> one person were of the contrary opinion, mankind would
> be no more justified in silencing that person than he,
> if he had the power, would be justified in silencing
> mankind.

Mill took the argument for freedom of expression several
stages beyond that of John Milton's *Areopagitica* (1644).
Milton's experience was of the tyranny of kings and parlia-
ments. He believed that the opinions of Catholics and atheists
were so beyond the pale that freedom of expression could not
be extended to them. By contrast, Mill, living in an age when
the Licensing Act (which had been allowed to lapse in 1695)
was, at most, a distant memory, and the Catholic Emancipation
Act (1829) had, at last, accorded full political and religious
freedom to Catholics, excludes no set of opinions or beliefs. It
is of the utmost significance that *On Liberty* was published in
the same year as Charles Darwin's *On the Origin of Species*
and Karl Marx's *Critique of Political Economy*. Just as important as the intellectual context in which the work was written,
however, was its social and political context. Although universal adult suffrage had not yet been fully achieved (and Mill
wrote elsewhere about women's rights), Mill was concerned
about the possibilities of tyranny by democratic majorities in a
rapidly growing urban and industrial society.

Mill took it for granted that it was no longer necessary to
defend the proposition that freedom of the press was useful to
good government, and "one of the securities against corrupt
and tyrannical government". He noted that, just as he was
preparing *On Liberty* for publication (in 1858), the British government had launched prosecutions against newspapers that
had defended the legitimacy of tyrranicide, but he remained
convinced that, except in extreme circumstances ("panics"), by
which he presumably meant periods of war or insurrection, the
government "never thinks of exerting any power of coercion
unless in agreement with what it conceives to be (the people's)
voice". No group has the right to coerce others to comply with
its views, whether or not it uses the government to do so. Right
or wrong, minority opinion has value to all humanity: "The
peculiar evil of silencing the expression of an opinion is that it
is robbing the human race: posterity as well as the existing

generation; those who dissent from the opinion still more than
those who hold it".

Mill's argument is that the majority may be – and often is –
absolutely certain that its opinion is correct, but there is always
the chance that it is wrong. There is a great difference between
presuming an opinion to be true, because it has not been refuted
when there is every opportunity to do so, and not permitting
its refutation. The ideas and opinions of Socrates and of Jesus
were forcibly suppressed by authorities who considered themselves infallibly right, but were considered afterwards by vast
millions of people in every generation to have been true.
Nobody can be justified in the belief that his or her opinion is
correct unless they have submitted it to the disciplines of argument and refutation.

Before Mill's time, Samuel Johnson, who had "refuted" the
idealist philosophy of Bishop Berkeley by kicking a stone – "I
refute it thus" – had taken the view that the persecution of
people for their ideas had beneficial side-effects: "persecution
is an ordeal through which truth ought to pass, and always
passes successfully, legal penalties being, in the end, powerless
against truth". Related arguments for the supposed "benefits"
of censorship have also been deployed in the 20th century by
those impressed by the quality of some of the literature produced under tyrannical and censorious regimes. Mill will have
none of this: "The propounder of a new truth, according to
this doctrine, should stand, with a halter round his neck, to be
instantly tightened if the public assembly do not, on hearing
his reasons, then and there adopt his proposition". In case any
of his readers might think that the world had put aside the persecution of people for their beliefs, Mill pointed out that in
1857 a Cornishman had been imprisoned for 21 months for
writing insulting words about Christianity on a gate, and that
a person who freely confessed that he was an atheist had, in
the same year, been rejected as a juror. Suppression of heretics
and unbelievers, Mill asserts, hurts those who are not heretics
and unbelievers, because their mental development is cramped
for fear of heresy: "both teachers and learners go to sleep at
their post, as soon as there is no enemy in the field".

According to Mill, even if majority opinion is true, it must,
if it is to be held with conviction, be vigorously challenged: "if
it is not fully, frequently and fearlessly discussed, it will be held
as a dead dogma, not a living truth". Subjects that provoke
little debate, such as mathematics, inspire little conviction in
defence of principles, but in subjects "infinitely more complicated, such as morals, religion, politics, social relations, he who
knows only his own side of the case knows little of that".
Ninety-nine per cent of those who argue "have never thrown

themselves into the mental position of those who think differently to them".

Mill then moves on to an argument that has irritated fundamentalists of all descriptions: no argument is ever completely right or wrong. Mill writes:

Heretical opinions ... are generally some of those suppressed ... and neglected truths, bursting the bonds which kept them down, and either seeking reconciliation with the truth contained in the common opinion, or fronting it as enemies, and setting themselves up, with similar exclusiveness as the whole truth.

Far from seeking to suppress the ideas of those who oppose them, politicians need to recognize that a party of order and a party aiming for radical change each "derives its utility from the deficiencies of the other; but it is in great measure the opposition of the other that keeps each within the limits of society". A multiplicity of religions, likewise, allows one religion to provide answers for subjects that another may not even address.

According to Mill,

Liberty, as a principle, has no application to any state of things anterior to the time when mankind have been capable of free and equal discussion. Until then, there is nothing for them but implicit obedience to an Akbar or a Charlemagne, if they are so fortunate as to find one.

Is liberty, in Mill's sense, applicable to the real world? Is *On Liberty* any more than a clarion call? A decade after Mill wrote, Fitzjames Stephen thought not. In his view (as expressed in the work cited below), Mill, trained in the disciplines of academic discourse, must have been dreaming if he thought that any but a tiny minority really exercised their minds and came to individual conclusions. In the real world, according to Stephen, articulate groups become so convinced of the truth of their opinions that, consciously or unconsciously, they impose them upon the rest of us, and we accept them passively and uncritically. Moreover, Mill's notions would lead to profound indecision rather than clear progress.

Many subsequent political leaders have effectively agreed with Stephen, sweeping aside Mill's hymn of praise as yet another example of "woolly liberalism". Even those who are committed to the struggle against the censorship of opinions have felt constrained, considering the history of the 20th century, to ask whether or not there are some ideas that are quite simply intolerable, that cannot be admitted into the rather cosy world envisaged by Mill, in which all respect each other. However pressing these questions may be – and doubtless Mill would have welcomed the chance to debate them – his short book continues to challenge the equally cosy certainties of those who are so convinced of the rightness of their cause that they are prepared to censor those who do not agree with them.

BRENT STEWART LERSETH and DEREK JONES

Writings

On Liberty, 1859
Considerations on Representative Government, 1861; revised edition 1861
Utilitarianism, 1863, revised edition 1871; edited by Roger Crisp, 1996
Collected Works, edited by J.M. Robson *et al.*, 33 vols, 1963–91

Further Reading

Berlin, Isaiah, *Four Essays on Liberty*, London and New York: Oxford University Press, 1969
Donner, Wendy, *The Liberal Self: John Stuart Mill's Moral and Political Philosophy*, Ithaca, New York: Cornell University Press, 1991
Gray, John, *Liberalism*, 2nd edition, Milton Keynes: Open University Press, 1995
Gray, John, *Mill on Liberty: A Defence*, 2nd edition, London and New York: Routledge, 1996
Miller, David (editor), *Liberty*, Oxford and New York: Oxford University Press, 1991
Rawls, John, *Political Liberalism*, New York: Columbia University Press, 1993
Ryan, Alan, *J.S. Mill*, London and Boston: Routledge, 1974
Stephen, James Fitzjames, *Liberty, Equality, Fraternity*, 1873; edited by R.J. White, London: Cambridge University Press, 1967

ARTHUR MILLER
US dramatist, 1915–

Born in Harlem but raised in Brooklyn, New York, in a Jewish middle-class family, Arthur Miller catapulted to fame in 1949 with the publication and Broadway production of his play *Death of a Salesman*, which won numerous prizes, including the Drama Critics Circle Award and the Pulitzer Prize. Following graduation in 1938, Miller briefly worked for the (much censored) WPA Federal Theatre Project before turning to writing radio and film scripts. In 1945 he published his only novel, *Focus*, about anti-Semitism in an American community. *All My Sons* (1947), which also won the Drama Critics Award, brought him national recognition and expanded the themes Miller had introduced in his first Broadway production, *The Man Who Had All the Luck* (1944): the responsibility of the individual to the world and his fate within society.

Over the next decade, Miller wrote successful plays – *Death of a Salesman* and *The Crucible* (1953) – amidst the intensification of the Truman Doctrine and, fuelled by the activities of the Republican senator from Wisconsin, Joseph R. McCarthy, the domestic anticommunist purges. Supported by Executive Order 9035, which contained a list of subversive organizations, including the US Communist Party, loyalty oaths spread from government agencies throughout American society. Congressional investigating committees, notably the House Committee on Un-American Activities (HUAC), held hearings to investigate subversive activities; fear swept the country as accusations ruined careers and lives. Banned in Hollywood and television, Miller and many of his colleagues were mired in the insidious effects of McCarthyism, the national hysteria of "indiscriminate allegations" and "unsubstantiated charges".

According to the playwright, he probably first came under scrutiny when he participated as a moderator in the Cultural and Scientific Conference for World Peace in 1949 in New York City. A year later in Hollywood, Miller came up against the national anticommunist campaign when Harry Cohn had *The Hook*, Miller's film script about the Brooklyn waterfront to be directed by Elia Kazan, vetted by the FBI and demanded a pro-American rewrite turning the union racketeers and gangsters into communists. Miller withdrew the script.

At the same time, critics began to attack *Death of a Salesman* as Marxist for its implied critique of capitalism and material-ism (ironically, Soviets criticized the play as not Marxist enough). The play shockingly inverts the ethos of the American belief that hard work will bring success; its protagonist, Willy Loman, despite his belief in that system and 30 years of loyal service, loses his job as an on-the-road shoe salesman, and, bewildered by his inability to fulfill his dreams, eventually com-mits suicide. In an interview with Griffin Fariello, Miller tells of having to close down the Middle West touring company of *Salesman* because of American Legion picketing. In fact, Miller recalls most of his out-of-town productions being picketed.

Nor did *The Crucible* (1953), his most frequently produced play, escape scrutiny. Based on documents from the Salem (Massachusetts) Witch Trials of 1692, the play portrays the mass accusations of witchcraft and ennobling struggle of John Proctor, who is falsely accused and condemned. Offered amnesty if he will name other witches, Proctor maintains his integrity, but loses his life, by his refusal. The parallels between the Salem hysteria and McCarthyism were not lost on *The Crucible*'s audience and critics.

In 1954, the Belgo-American Association, a business group, invited Miller to the European premiere of *The Crucible* in Brussels. His application for a passport renewal was turned down by the chief of the passport division as "not in the national interest". Miller speculates that his signature on left-wing petitions and attendance at unacceptable meetings met with State Department disapproval, as would his dissolved friendship with Elia Kazan – who earlier had directed several of Miller's plays, but in 1952, accompanied by much publicity, appeared as a friendly HUAC witness. Miller recalls that the Belgian audience embraced the play as a protest against McCarthyism and against the State Department's prohibiting his travel.

Additional problems arose in 1955 with a screenplay Miller wrote about gang warfare based on research in Brooklyn. The producer of the projected film project had a contract with the city of New York for filming on location; however, attacks in several papers and protests by the American Legion and Catholic War Veterans, as well as intervention by HUAC, forced Mayor Wagner to subject Miller to a political means test. After a narrow vote by department heads, the city with-drew its backing of police cooperation; the film did not get made.

In June 1956, Miller was called to testify before the House Un-American Activities Committee concerning unauthorized use of passports. Knowing that he had attended "four or five" meetings of communist writers, HUAC expected Miller to name the meetings' attendees; he freely answered questions about himself but, like his character John Proctor, he refused to impli-cate others. In 1957 Miller was convicted of contempt of Congress, fined $500, and given a suspended 30-day jail sen-tence; ironically, his passport was renewed for six months; on appeal the next year, the citation was reversed. Miller believes his national reputation and the publicity surrounding his impending marriage to Marilyn Monroe prompted the rela-tively low-key HUAC hearing. (Indeed, Miller recalls that HUAC chairman Walter offered to cancel the hearing in exchange for a photo opportunity with Miller and Monroe.)

In 1965, Miller was elected president of PEN, the inter-national literary organization that provides a forum for express-ing views and fighting government repression. He helped negotiate entry of Soviet writers into the organization and shaped PEN as the conscience of the world's writing commu-nity. Miller personally intervened in incidents involving Fernando Arrabal and the young Wole Soyinka.

JUDITH C. KOHL

Writings

Death of a Salesman: Certain Private Conversations in Two Acts and a Requiem, 1949
The Crucible, 1953
"The Testimony of Arthur Miller, accompanied by Counsel, Joseph L. Rauh, Jr.," United States House of Representative, Committee on Un-American Activities, *Investigation of the Unauthorized Use of United States Passports*, 84th Congress, part 4, June 21, 1956, Washington, DC: United States Government Printing Office, November 1956: 4660–4690
Collected Plays, 2 vols, 1957–81
The Portable Arthur Miller, edited by Harold Clurman, 1971; revised edition with an introduction by Christopher Bigsby, 1995
"The Year It Came Apart", *New York* (30 December 1974–6 January 1975)
The Theater Essays, edited by Robert A. Martin, 1978
Timebends: A Life, 1987
Conversations with Arthur Miller, edited by Matthew C. Roudané, 1987

Further Reading

Bentley, Eric, *Thirty Years of Treason: Excerpts from Hearings before the House Committee on Un-American Activities, 1938–1968*, New York: Viking, 1971
Fariello, Griffin, *Red Scare: Memories of the American Inquisition: An Oral History*, New York: Norton, 1995
Welland, Dennis, *Miller, The Playwright*, 3rd edition, London and New York: Methuen, 1985

HENRY MILLER
US novelist, 1891–1980

Henry Miller described his first novel *Tropic of Cancer* (1934) as a "gob of spit in the face of art". But it was not his desire to affront social values and critique an American homeland he despised that disturbed moral majorities in the US. *Tropic of Cancer* was published in Paris, where Miller lived until 1939, by Obelisk Press, a low-brow company providing English-speaking tourists with smutty books. On its release Miller's book received widespread critical acclaim from such modernist notaries as Marcel Duchamp, Ezra Pound, and T.S. Eliot, but due to its sexually explicit content it could not legally be imported into the US. Any subsequent efforts to publish Miller's work in the US aroused the attentions of the police. In Boston police raided the offices of the *Harvard Advocate*, destroying an issue in which the young editor, James Laughlin, had

MILLER: Cover of Henry Miller's first novel, *Tropic of Cancer*, published in Paris in 1934 by the lowbrow Obelisk Press, financed by the writer Anaïs Nin with money borrowed from the psychoanalyst Otto Rank. Because of its sexually explicit content the book was illegal in the US and Britain: it was issued with a wraparound cover band which read: "For Subscription: Not to be imported into Great Britain or U.S.A." For the second printing, in 1935, the book was issued with a plain wrapper around the dust jacket as a result of copies of the earlier printing of the book having been confiscated. Without a visible dust jacket, the book would be rendered anonymous and inoffensive.

reprinted the first pages of Miller's journalistic piece, *Aller Retour New York*. The limits censorship had placed on circulation of his first novel had compounded its fame worldwide, while it remained banned in English-speaking countries until the early 1960s. Miller continually resisted offers to have expurgated versions published in America. For many years he continued his writing career surviving on handouts and the sale of his paintings, until returning to the US and settling in 1944 in a rent-free log cabin in Big Sur.

By 1945 five of his more palatable novels had been published in the US by James Laughlin, now at New Directions, though the income he gained from these was minimal. In France, however, postwar royalties from *Tropic of Cancer*, and the equally contentious and acclaimed follow-up, *Tropic of Capricorn* (1939), made Miller a fortune and consolidated both his critical reputation and his infamy. In March 1946, however, both these works received complaints in Paris from Daniel Parker, president of the Cartel d'Action Sociale et Morale, citing France's antipornography law of 1939. To his surprise a committee found against Miller, labelling him a pornographer and proposing sanctions against his works in France. An appeal by a host of French writers, including André Breton, Camus, Sartre and Gide, provoked a fierce public debate in the French press. A suit was subsequently brought against Parker himself which saw the case against Miller dismissed. However, he received no such support when following this furore he unwisely published the more sexually explicit and violent *Sexus* in 1949. A critical failure, the book was immediately suppressed for offence given to the morals of the French public. In 1950 the French interior minister declared that *Sexus* could not be published in France in any language.

Nevertheless, Miller's fame and critical reputation remained such that by 1957 he was inducted into America's National Institute of Arts and Letters and could rightly claim to have the greatest international reputation of any living American writer. There continued to be reminders of the fact that he was also the most famous living author of banned books. In May 1957 the attorney general of Norway ordered the seizure of *Sexus* on grounds of obscenity, and brought charges against two booksellers. Despite Miller's own growing reservations about the book, he wrote a long letter to the trial's defence attorney, subsequently published in the *Evergreen Review* (September 1959) as "Defense of the Freedom to Read". It was this article that brought Miller to the attention of Barney Rosset, the owner of *Evergreen*'s publishers, Grove Press. Rosset actively sought Miller's help in attacking US censorship laws.

For two years following Rosset's initial approaches Miller delayed engaging in direct provocation of the US authorities. He felt that the status quo regarding the banning of his major works in the US acted to highlight America's distance from true democracy, and furthermore underlined its peoples' complaisant acceptance of that situation. A victory in the courts would he felt only confirm his reputation as "King of Smut" rather than come as response to a nonexistent public demand for the release of his books. It was Rosset's determination that ultimately swayed Miller, willing as he was to guarantee to bear all legal expenses and damages, and protect the author from court appearances.

As an undergraduate at Swarthmore, Rosset had been intrigued by Miller's work, and following his success at Grove Press defending publication of *Lady Chatterley's Lover* he now felt the time was right for pushing Miller's *Tropic of Cancer* into the US. Though his judgement ultimately proved to be correct, the unprecedented furore following publication of a hardcover edition on 24 June 1961 was much worse than either author or publisher had anticipated. A rash of litigation spread from state to state, with Rosset encouraging booksellers by letting it be known that Grove would defend those prosecuted regardless of whether there was any legal obligation to do so. In the autumn of 1961, police officials in Chicago and its vicinity systematically intimidated stockists of *Tropic of Cancer*, making several arrests. Grove's chief counsel, Elmer Gertz, took action whenever a suit was filed, and acted under the auspices of the American Civil Liberties Union to restrain officials from interfering with the sale of the novel. During the first year of publication Grove Press spent more than $100,000 fighting 60 cases nationwide.

It was not until 1964 that the US Supreme Court finally declared *Tropic of Cancer* not to be obscene and its sale protected by the US constitution. Underestimating the extent of the victory he had won, Miller was subsequently fearful of the consequences of the publication of *Sexus*, a book he now regarded as pornographic. The publication of that book and other previously suppressed works by Grove in 1964 raised no concerted complaint. Miller had lived to see a landslide victory for the circulation of sexually explicit material in the US. Miller was a lifelong critic of America and a fierce advocate of liberation in all guises; his victory nevertheless secured the notoriety he had feared and the label of America's "King of Smut".

IAN D. COPESTAKE

Writings

Tropic of Cancer, Paris 1934; New York 1961
Black Spring, Paris 1936; New York 1963
Tropic of Capricorn, Paris 1939; New York 1962
The Rosy Crucifixion
 Sexus, 1949
 Plexus, 1953
 Nexus, 1960
Quiet Days in Clichy, 1956
Henry Miller: Years of Trial and Triumph, 1962–1964: The Correspondence of Henry Miller and Elmer Gertz, edited by Elmer Gertz and Felice Flanery Lewis, Carbondale: Southern Illinois University Press, 1978

Further Reading

Gertz, Elmer, *A Handful of Clients*, Chicago: Follett, 1965
Hutchison, E.R., *Tropic of Cancer on Trial: A Case History of Censorship*, New York: Grove Press, 1968
Karolides, Nicholas J., *100 Banned Books: Censorship Histories of World Literature*, New York: Checkmark, 1999
Martin, Jay, *Always Merry and Bright: The Life of Henry Miller*, Santa Barbara, California: Capra Press, 1978
Sova, Dawn B., *Literature Suppressed on Sexual Grounds*, New York: Facts on File, 1998

CZESŁAW MIŁOSZ
Polish poet, 1911–

Among the Polish literati of the 20th century a special place belongs to Czesław Miłosz, a poet of Lithuanian birth who eventually made his home in Berkeley, California. Miłosz studied law at the Stefan Bathory University in Wilno (as Vilnius, now the capital of Lithuania, was then generally known). His first poems appeared in print while he was still a student. At the time he was a member of a left-wing poetry group, Żagary, and his first book of verse, *Poemat o czasie zastygłym* (1933, A Poem on Time Frozen) shows his concern with the "course of history" and social issues. From 1935 to 1939 he worked for Polish Radio, first in Wilno and later in Warsaw. At the beginning of World War II he stayed for a few months in Wilno from where in 1940 he returned to Warsaw. It was during the German occupation that Miłosz had to confront censorship for the first time not as a mild nuisance (as before 1939 in Poland) but as an everyday fact of life. The occupiers closed down all Polish journals and publishing houses, one German-controlled news bulletin-type newspaper excepted, and Miłosz, as indeed most writers, had no choice but to publish his work illegally. In 1940 he published (under the pseudonym Jan Syruć) a collection of his own poems, and in 1942 he edited an anthology, *Pieśń niepodległa* (Independent Song), containing verse by a number of Polish poets.

The kind of poetry cultivated by Miłosz before the war was neosymbolist. As he had used it to try to warn readers of impending catastrophe, the epithet "catastrophist" has also been applied to most of his prewar work. Yet these poems were distant in their coded, classical rhetoric; human suffering of a previously unimaginable kind had to engulf the poet to make him write in a simpler, more dramatic and tormented way, as, for example, in "A Poor Christian Looks at the Ghetto" or "Campo di Fiori". Although he did not take part in the Warsaw Uprising of 1944, Miłosz was in the city, the burning of which he compared in a poem to the destruction of Troy.

In his first book published after the war, *Ocalenie* (1945, Rescue), Miłosz had to face one of the central ethical problems of survival, as in "Dedication":

What is poetry which does not save
Nations or people?
A connivance with official lies,
A song of drunkards whose throats
will be cut in a moment

The end of the war did not lift the weight of the moral commitment that the German occupation had placed on him. While making a pledge not to become "a wailing woman" over "the terrible wounds of his nation", Miłosz preserved for himself the right to empathize with Antigone, as in the poem "In Warsaw":

How can I live in this country
Where the foot knocks against
The unburied bones of kin?

However, these postwar poems also reflected a new problem:
the communists slandered the memory of the Warsaw Uprising
and were unwilling to honour those who had fallen in the
fight against the Nazis. Miłosz's postulates of "truth and justice"
were to be ignored from the very beginning of the new regime.
Although at the time the communist takeover of central and eastern Europe seemed a historical necessity to many intellectuals,
and Miłosz himself accepted a post in the new Polish diplomatic service, he did not stop questioning the right of the authorities to break moral laws. A poem such as "Child of Europe"
(1946) verges on the cynical with its wry admonitions –

Love no country: countries soon disappear.
Love no city: cities are soon rubble –

and would have become unpublishable within a few years.
Meanwhile, the dramatic fragment "Antygona" (written in
1949 but published in the Paris journal Kultura only in
December 1956) shows that Miłosz did not believe in the long-
term stability of communist rule in Poland:

Creon shall not be able to build
His kingdom on our graves.
He will not establish it just by the rule of the sword.
Great is the power of the dead.

What Miłosz did fear was communism's short-term force and
powers of persuasion.

It was in February 1951 that Miłosz, then cultural attaché
in Paris, broke with the communist authorities. Although his
reasons for this break had already been given in an article,
"Nie" (No), published in Kultura, it was only in his political-
psychological study Zniewolony umysł (1953, The Captive
Mind) that he explained the secret of dialectics and its impact
on Polish writers who had swallowed the pill of submission.
Part of the book deals with individual cases of adaptation to
the new regime through case histories of Jerzy Andrzejewski,
Tadeusz Borowski, Jerzy Putrament, and Konstanty Gałczyński,
disguised as "Alpha", "Beta", "Gamma", and "Delta". Each
writer had different reasons for submitting to the alleged laws
of history; the communist regime is shown to be based both on
naked fear and dialectical persuasion.

In The Captive Mind Miłosz also confesses his personal fear
of exile. For a poet his native tongue is his highest asset and
although 19th-century Polish poetry abounds in great figures
who created some of their best work in emigration, for a long
time Miłosz was reluctant to follow their example. It was only
the pressure of the absolute conformism forced on Polish literature in the name of "socialist realism" that forced him "to
defy history" and choose the loneliness of freedom in another
country.

During the first few years after his break with Warsaw, in
spite of the success of The Captive Mind Miłosz had to struggle to eke out a living as a writer. His writings continued to
appear in Kultura and further books came out under the
imprint of the publishing house Instytut Literacki, also based

in Paris. It was the latter that published the novel Zdobycie
władzy (1955, The Seizure of Power), which is devoted to contemporary Polish history, and the essayistic intellectual autobiography Rodzinna Europa (1959, Native Realm), both
attempts at self-definition. Native Realm is a story of the artist's
development from innocence to a complex understanding of the
world and one's place in it.

Both these books and all of Miłosz's postwar poetry were
banned in Poland until 1980. Yet only the first collection produced in exile, Światło dzienne (1953, Daylight) has strong
political undertones: in his short foreword Miłosz writes that
"there are quite a few things here that I could not print in
Poland". He is not a political poet by definition. In one poem,
"In Milan", he answers a friend's accusation that "I was too
politicized" as follows:

If you have a nail in your shoe, what then?
Do you love that nail? Same with me.
I am for the moon amid the vineyards
When I see high up the snow on the Alps.

Miłosz's move to Berkeley in 1960, to take up a professorship of Polish literature at the University of California's campus
there, allowed him to concentrate on matters more permanent
than politics, although a perception of the dialectics of history
remains even in his most private and surrealistic poems.
On only one other occasion, in 1968, when a group of hard-
line communists launched a vicious anti-Semitic and antiwestern propaganda campaign in Poland, did Miłosz take up
the challenge of protest. In a moving confession, "My Faithful
Mother Tongue", he dwells on his love for the Polish language
that had now become "a tongue of the debased/of the
unreasonable . . ./a tongue of informers", but that he hopes
to be able to save it through his continuing service. On the
other hand, lecturing on 19th-century Polish literature and on
Dostoevskii's novels led Miłosz to conclude that there was an
uncanny similarity between the beliefs of the nihilistic Russian
intelligentsia of the past century and those of some of his young
American students.

Until the 1970s, Miłosz was known mostly to Polish readers
and to a handful of students in Berkeley. The publication of his
Selected Poems in English (1973) led first to the award of the
Neustadt International Prize for Literature in 1978 and then to
the Nobel Prize for Literature in 1980. After the latter had been
awarded, all resistance to Miłosz's work in Poland crumbled,
and during the bloodless revolution led by Solidarność
(Solidarity) in 1980–81 he was hailed as one of Poland's greatest cultural assets. Ever since then his books have been published in large print runs.

It is possible that Miłosz derived his greatest satisfaction
from the decision by Solidarity to adopt one of his poems,
written in 1950, as the inscription under the Workers'
Memorial in Gdańsk, which is dedicated to the memory of
the 48 rebellious workers shot dead by police in December
1970. The poem, "You Who Have Wronged . . .", includes the
following lines:

You who wronged a simple man . . .
Do not feel safe. The poet remembers.
You can kill one, but another one is born.

Although after 1980 most of Miłosz's work was published in Poland, until 1989 he was still subject to censorship. In his collection *Ogród nauk* (1986, The Garden of Sciences, Lublin), the censor intervened twice, deleting entire essays from the collection. One of these "unpublishable" pieces was the essay "Brognart", the story of a young Frenchman caught up in the cogwheels of Stalinist Russia during World War II.

GEORGE GÖMÖRI

Writings

The Captive Mind, translated by Jane Zielonko, 1953
Native Realm: A Search for Self-Definition, translated by Catherine S. Leach, 1968
The Witness of Poetry, 1983
Collected Poems, 1931–1987, translated by Miłosz et al., 1988

Further Reading

Błoński, Jan, "Poetry and Knowledge", *World Literature Today*, 52/3 (Summer 1978): 387–91
Davie, Donald, *Czesław Miłosz and the Insufficiency of Lyric*, Cambridge: Cambridge University Press, and Knoxville: University of Tennessee Press, 1986
Fiut, Aleksander, *Moment wieczny: Poezja Czesława Miłosza* (Eternal Moment: Miłosz's Poetry), Paris: Libella, 1987; 2nd edition, Warsaw: Literackie, 1993
Gömöri, George, "Notes on Czesław Miłosz's Life Writing", *World Literature Today*, 73/4 (Autumn 1999): 672–74
Krzyżanowski, Jerzy R., "*The Captive Mind* Revisited", *World Literature Today*, 73/4 (Autumn 1999): 658–62
Nathan, Leonard and Arthur Quinn, *The Poet's Work: An Introduction to Czesław Miłosz*, Cambridge, Massachusetts: Harvard University Press, 1991

JOHN MILTON
English poet and prose writer, 1608–1674
AREOPAGITICA
Pamphlet, 1644

Areopagitica: A Speech ... for the Liberty of Unlicenc'd Printing, has acquired a special place in the history of censorship for reasons which have little to do with its arguments and nothing to do with its efficacy, at least not at the time. Even its magnificently metaphoric style might not have ensured its survival as a classic of liberal thought without Milton's two other claims to fame, which have often been seen as mutually exclusive: his nearly 20 years as a polemicist for what it is perhaps still best to call the Puritan revolution of the 1640s and 1650s in England; and his writing of *Paradise Lost*.

Milton was born in 1608 into a Calvinist family, the son of a scrivener. A Cambridge education and a rather prolonged period of study at his father's home, some early poetry-writing and a European tour – all of this might have prepared him for a comfortable clerical position. In fact, while he was still in Europe (having visited Galileo, as he tells us in *Areopagitica*, "grown old, a prisoner to the Inquisition, for thinking in Astronomy otherwise than the Franciscan and Dominican licencers thought,") war broke out at home between Charles I and the Scots over the imposition of the Laudian prayerbook and in 1640 the king, forced after 11 years to call a parliament, was soon facing more serious trouble.

When Milton wrote *Areopagitica* the political revolution to be accomplished by the new and ferociously determined parliament was already well advanced. In particular, they had on 5 July 1641 abolished the Star Chamber, the royal prerogative court which from 1637 had taken over censorship legislation and, with the Stationers' Company, regulated all printing by way of a licensing system, or pre-publication censorship. With Star Chamber abolished, there was a sudden flood of unregulated press activity. The Stationers petitioned parliament for a return to the restrictions that ensured their monopolies, and on 14 June 1643 parliament passed a new Licensing Act that was almost identical with the 1637 Star Chamber decree, the only difference being that the licensers were now to be parliamentary appointees.

At the level of principle and logic alone, Milton would have been outraged by this hypocrisy. But among the "many false forged, scandalous, seditious, libellous, and unlicensed Papers, Pamphlets, and Books to the great defamation of Religion and government" which were embarrassing the parliamentarians were earlier pamphlets of Milton's own, on the subject of divorce. Milton seems to have tried unsuccessfully to obtain a licence for his first pamphlet on this topic, *The Doctrine and Discipline of Divorce*, which sold well in two unlicensed editions, the first anonymous, the second carrying his initials. In August 1644 there were hostile references to his tract in a sermon delivered before parliament and the Westminster Assembly, arguing that his book should be burned, and attacks on him continued during November. In a postscript of his pamphlet *Judgement of Martin Bucer concerning divorce*, licensed in July 1644, Milton protested that, while the century-old views of Bucer and Erasmus on divorce circulate freely, his own, "containing but the same thing, shall in a time of reformation, a time of free speaking, free writing, not find a permission to the Presse". On 23 November 1644 *Areopagitica* appeared in the booksellers; a "scofflaw" text, it was unlicensed, unregistered, and issued without the imprint of either publisher or printer, yet carried the name of JOHN MILTON in large letters as an act of personal defiance. It seems clear that the provocation given to reason by the Licensing Act had been intensified and personalized by writerly adversity: the criticism of those he thought his friends – the Presbyterian ministers – rubbed salt in the wound of political disillusionment.

The graecized title is usually assumed to allude to the seventh oration of Isocrates, written around 355 BCE. Isocrates too was a private citizen addressing a legislative court, the Areopagus. Yet Milton's argument is almost the reverse of that of Isocrates, who wanted the Areopagus to reclaim its former control over education and culture. The other classical precedent flagged on the title page was, however, more conceptually *apropos*. A quotation from Euripides' *The Suppliants* advised the reader:

"This is true Liberty when free born men
Having to advise the public may speak free . . .".

This republican theme-word returns in the opening paragraphs, where Milton explains his pamphlet's objective. He brings "gratulation . . . to all who wish and promote their Country's liberty":

> whereof this whole Discourse proposed will be a certain testimony, if not a Trophy. For this is not the liberty which we can hope, that no grievance ever should arise in the Commonwealth, that let no man in this World expect; but when complaints are freely heard, deeply considered, and speedily reformed, then is the utmost bound of civil liberty attained that wise men look for.

Milton wanted to establish from the outset that the new Licensing Act was incompatible with the aspirations to right and liberty that had inspired the parliamentarian cause. Licensing was associated with the Catholic Church and the Inquisition, the tyrannies the Puritan cause had to oppose, whereas Greek and Roman culture, and even early Christianity under the emperors, was, he claimed, comparatively unrestrictive. Without religious toleration, the new reformers in both church and state would quickly become indistinguishable from their earlier oppressors.

Yet even as he pursued his argument further towards what we now recognize as liberalism than the argument against licensing may have required, Milton hesitated: not only did he restrict his appeal for a free press to the licensing issue – being willing, even eager, to have ideas suppressed *after* they had been tested in the intellectual marketplace – the Commonwealth should watch "how books demean themselves as well as men; and thereafter to confine, imprison and do sharpest justice on them as malefactors". There were limits to toleration:

> Yet if all cannot be of one mind, as who looks they should be? This doubtless if more wholesome, more prudent, and more Christian that many be tolerated, rather than all compelled. I mean not tolerated Popery, and open superstition, which as it extirpates all religions and civil supremacies, so it self should be extirpate, provided first that all charitable and compassionate means be used to win and regain the weak and the misled.

One can explain this passage as typical of the times. Even John Locke, in the first great *Letter Concerning Toleration*, agreed that *political* Catholicism was dangerous to the state because it required its adherents to substitute obedience to the papacy for national allegiances, and rendered men incredible as oath-takers. The vacillations of this passage in *Areopagitica* have been used to argue that Milton was no liberal; or, in a more perverse because more sophisticated version of the same point, that liberalism empties itself out conceptually whenever it introduces an exception to the rule of non-interference.

Milton's reputation as a reformer has also been impugned on the grounds that he acted for a few months as government licenser, and may even have had some responsibility for the Commonwealth Licensing Act passed in 1650, which called for strict censorship of all newsbooks. But again, his apologists point out, the record is confusing. In April 1652 he was investigated by Parliament for allowing the publication of the Polish *Racovian Catechism* translated by the notorious anti-Trinitarian John Biddle; his answer was that in doing so he had merely stuck to his principles, since "he had published a tract on that subject, that men should refrain from forbidding books". Later still, in the *Second Defence* of the regicides against their European critics, Milton had the courage to face up to an Oliver Cromwell whose commitment to toleration he was beginning to doubt, addressing to the Protector the wish:

> . . . may you permit those who wish to engage in free inquiry to publish their findings at their own peril without the private inspection of any petty magistrate . . . May you always take the side of those who think that not just their own party or faction, but *all citizens equally have an equal right to freedom in the state*.

The truth of the matter is, surely, that Milton – like William Walwyn, Roger Williams, John Saltmarsh, Henry Robinson, John Lilburne, and, in the next generation, John Owen, Andrew Marvell, and John Locke – was moving with very little guidance from the past towards a position that at least in the West is now taken for granted; and that while freedom of the press and religious toleration are today seldom challenged as principles, in the arena of practice they constantly require, at the highest juridical levels, the formulation and testing of exceptions.

Milton's immediate successors in the evolving liberal tradition were less concerned with these inconsistencies than we are today. At the end of the 17th century he was promoted as a champion of freedom by Edward Phillips and John Toland, a role expanded in the mid-18th century by Richard Baron, Thomas Hollis, and the poet James Thompson, who in 1738 wrote an ardent preface for a new edition of *Areopagitica*, in the context of the renewal of the laws for licensing the stage, which it was widely feared would bring back the press licensing that had lapsed in 1694.

Areopagitica stands as a remarkable document with many passages that sum up the nature of freedom of expression. This one will suffice as example and epitome:

> Behold now this vast City; a City of refuge, the mansion house of liberty; . . . the shop of war hath not there more anvils and hammers waking, to fashion out the plates and instruments of armed Justice in defence of beleaguered Truth, than there be pens and heads there, sitting by their studious lamps, musing, searching, revolving new notions and ideas wherewith to present . . . the approaching Reformation: others as fast reading, trying all things, assenting to the force of reason and convincement . . . We reckon more than five months yet to harvest; there need not be five weeks, had we but eyes to lift up, the fields are white already. Where there is much desire to learn, there of necessity will be much arguing, much writing, many opinions; for opinion in good men is but knowledge in the making.

ANNABEL PATTERSON

Writings

The Doctrine and Discipline of Divorce, 1643; revised edition
1644
Translator, *The Judgement of Martin Bucer Concerning Divorce*,
1644
Areopagitica: A Speech for the Liberty of Unlicensed Printing, 1644
Pro populo anglicano defensio, 1651
Pro populo anglicano defensio secunda, 1654
Works, edited by F.A. Patterson *et al.*, 18 vols, 1931–38
Complete Prose Works, edited by D.M. Wolfe *et al.*, 1953–

Further Reading

Achinstein, Sharon, *Milton and the Revolutionary Reader*, Princeton,
New Jersey: Princeton University Press, 1994
Haller, William, *Liberty and Reformation in the Puritan Revolution*,
New York: Columbia University Press, 1955
Hill, Christopher, *Milton and the English Revolution*, London: Faber,
1977; New York: Viking, 1978
Jordan, W.K., *The Development of Religious Toleration in England*,
4 vols, Cambridge, Massachusetts: Harvard University Press,
1932–40
Norbrook, David, "Liberty, the Public Sphere and the Sublime:
Areopagitica" in his *Writing the English Republic*, Cambridge and
New York: Cambridge University Press, 1999
Patterson, Annabel, *Early Modern Liberalism*, Cambridge and New
York: Cambridge University Press, 1997
Sirluck, Ernest, Introduction to vol. 2 of Milton's *Complete Prose
Works*, 8 vols, New Haven, Connecticut: Yale University Press,
1953–59

MIN LU
Burmese poet and novelist (real name: Nyan Paw), 1954–

Min Lu is the pen-name of Burmese writer and poet Nyan Paw, who was arrested in September 1990 and sentenced to seven years in jail. His crime was to have written a satirical poem entitled "What Has Become of Us?" and to have distributed it, with the help of editor U Myo Myint Nyein and U Sein Hlaing, in three instalments, each handwritten and cyclostyled on a single sheet of paper. The poem is one of the few examples of *samizdat* literature to have been produced in Burma since the May 1990 election. Min Lu was released on 22 September 1992, but his colleagues remain in prison, having been sentenced to a further term for attempting to convey messages to the outside world about prison conditions in Rangoon.

Min Lu is the third son of a famous Burmese film director, Tha Du, who died during Min Lu's imprisonment (Min Lu was let out of jail just long enough to attend his father's cremation). His older brother U Thu Maung is a popular film actor, and another, Maung Wunna, a film director. It is thought that Min Lu's early release was the result of the influence of his family who undertook that he would not engage in further political writing. Since his release, his novels have been reprinted and he has recently been able to publish new work.

Min Lu began writing poetry and short stories when he was at university. His first novel was published in June 1977, and between 1978 and 1979 he published four books of poems. By 1983 he had published his seventh novel. The novels are mostly about young people and are very popular with university students. *Little Bird* (1981) is a simply written, very moving story, told as seen through the eyes of a child, and as far as possible in the language that a child would have used to express its thoughts. A young boy, an only child just into his teens, tries to understand his parents' behaviour as their marriage is breaking up. The boy's love for his father leads him to run after his father when the latter leaves home, with tragic consequences. *Ties of Affection* (1983) draws a charmingly humorous and faithfully observed picture of student life on the campus of Rangoon University and follows a young student through the pitfalls and misunderstandings of his first innocent relationship with a fellow girl student. Neither of these works could be described as political.

By 1988, however, Min Lu had become a popular speaker at the open-air *sarpay haw-pyaw-bwe* (literary gatherings) that are a feature of Burmese cultural life during the months of December and January. His audience especially looked forward to hearing him recite his own poems at these gatherings.

While "What Has Become of Us?" may not be technically skilful, it is a very accurate reflection of the mixture of cynicism, humour, anger and despair with which the Burmese people view their government and their situation, and the endless insults to their intelligence which appear regularly in the government-controlled media. The poem mocks the members of the State Law and Order Restoration Council (SLORC), and in particular the then chairman, general Saw Maung, who was retired in April 1992 on grounds of "ill-health" and died in July 1997. By the time this poem was written in June/July 1990, Saw Maung had already acquired a reputation for giving two-hour, off-the-cuff rambling speeches, during which he would recommend books that he had read, while waving them in the air, whether they were on Burmese history or on the life of Jesus Christ. During the preceding two years, the public had also become used to watching SLORC first secretary, lieutenant general Khin Nyunt, inspecting drainage ditches and building sites, and giving, in the words of the *Working People's Daily* – renamed in 1993 the *New Light of Myanmar* – "necessary instructions to responsible personnel".

The poem catalogues the actions of the SLORC since taking power: changing the name of the country, moving hundreds of thousands of poor squatters in shanty towns and slum areas of Rangoon to new satellite towns outside the city far from their places of work. Tribute is paid to those who have been arrested, in particular the writer and satirist Maung Thawka (arrested in 1989) who was a close friend of those involved with the poem. Reference is made to the cynical denial of the army's massacre of students in 1988, to the elections in May 1990, and to the reasons the SLORC subsequently invented for not transferring power.

The following extract shows the flavour of the poem and its relevance to the study of contemporary Burmese censorship:

Although they have abolished the one-party system in
  Burma
We still live in a single paper dictatorship
Where the *Working People's Daily*
Leaves a bitter taste in our mouths.
Some people say that
There is not a single true news item
in the *Working People's Daily*.
But it's not really that bad.

There is some news which is fifty percent true.
(I mean the weather forecast, of course.)

(translated by VJB)

ANNA ALLOTT

Further Reading

Allott, Anna J., *Inked Over, Ripped Out: Burmese Storytellers and the Censors*, New York: PEN American Center, 1993

MINBAN KANWU (People-Run Journals)
Unofficial publications, China, 1978–80, 1990s

"People-run journals" grew out of the Democracy Wall movement in China in 1978–79. Campaigners for democracy formed small groups with specific political standpoints and demands and produced journals which they posted on walls or sold in the streets of Beijing and other cities, sometimes under the shadow of the Communist Party headquarters. Denied access to official publishers, paper, and printing equipment, the amateur publishers mimeographed their journals on poor-quality stencils. Editions came out irregularly and the cover price was often higher than that of their official counterparts. Although they were sold quite openly – and journals usually included contact addresses – to purchase them was considered a rather shady business.

In total, more than 100 people-run journals existed, at least one-third of which were based in Beijing. Journals from other cities included *Minzhu Zhi Sheng* (Voice of Democracy) from Shanghai and *Renmin Zhi Sheng* (Voice of the People) from Guangzhou. They always ran the risk that official permissiveness could, without wavering, be replaced by repression. To begin with, however, encouragement from the top leadership led the activists to believe that what they were doing was acceptable. Therefore they were opposed to being labelled "dissidents" and refused to allow their journals to be known as "dissident" or "underground" publications, preferring the more euphemistic "people-run journals".

It is important to distinguish people-run journals from such genuinely underground publications as "hand-copied literature" (*shouchaoben*) which circulated during the Cultural Revolution, were created under different circumstances, and circulated in different ways. Writers for people-run journals might well previously have contributed to privately circulated works, but when the opportunity arose, they made the step from underground to non-official. Similarly the phenomenon of people-run journals did not parallel *samizdat* in the Soviet Union or central and eastern Europe. For a short while Chinese activists enjoyed civil relations with the government and saw themselves as supporters rather than opponents. Whereas *samizdat* literature was generally created by established writers forced underground, people-run literature was written by young aspirants striving to be accepted above ground. Indeed, these journals were often seen by their youthful contributors as stepping stones to the regular official press.

People-run journals generally fall into two categories: those with a political bias and those with a literary bias. Of the political journals, *Beijing Zhi Chun* (Beijing Spring), which was published between January and October 1979, was the least dissident. The editorial statement in the journal's first issue was unequivocal: "This journal will use Marxism-Leninism as its guide and will support the Chinese Communist Party ... It aims at attaining democracy and promoting order and unity, and makes a modest contribution towards realizing the 'four modernizations'." *Beijing Zhi Chun* was printed, without official consent, by the government's Foreign Language Press, and was edited by leading members of the capital's Communist Youth League. It ran political commentaries, poetry, and short stories. In May 1979, when the authorities began their crackdown on many of the people-run journals, *Beijing Zhi Chun* sharpened its focus to concentrate on Deng Xiaoping's failure to democratize the political system and curb bureaucratic malpractice.

Other politically biased people-run journals were less supportive. *Siwu Luntan* (Fifth of April Forum) (December 1978–March 1980) adopted a middle position. After the suppression of the movement, the journal became a source of information on the fates of the arrested activists. *Tansuo* (Explorations) was very militant, and openly critical of Marxist ideology and the Chinese government. The most prominent contributor to and cofounder of *Tansuo* was Wei Jingsheng, whose well-crafted yet highly provocative essays demanded democracy as the "fifth modernization" and denounced Deng Xiaoping as a "new dictator". Wei's personal attacks angered Deng so much that he had Wei arrested and the editors of other people-run journals put under police surveillance. By the early summer of 1979, under the pretext that they had not registered with the Bureau of Publications, most of the political journals had been forced to close down and their editors were facing jail sentences. Deng had clearly used them and the Democracy Movement in general as catalysts in an intra-party power game. When they became a liability – even a threat – to his regime, he immediately moved to suppress their influence.

People-run journals with a literary bias, such as *Wotu* (Fertile Soil), *Qiushi* (Autumn Fruits) and, more importantly, *Jintian* (Today), fared a little better than their political counterparts. These journals carried literary reviews, original short stories and poems, and Western literature in translation. That they avoided direct political comment ensured their relative longevity, but by the summer of 1980 they too had been closed down.

At the end of the 1980s, people-run journals made a come-back in China. The acceleration of commercialization in the literary realm meant that many poets and writers found themselves alienated and marginalized; their experimental works failed to make money. With a more relaxed attitude to private publication and the relative tolerance shown by the political establishment, people-run publications sponsored by the private sector began to appear. Like their antecedents they were only available through private vendors. The number of copies available varied greatly. For example, *Xiandai Hanshi* (Modern Chinese Poetry, 1991–94) had a printrun of only 300, while *Feifei*, from Sichuan province, ran to 2000.

The people-run journals of the 1979 Democracy Wall movement were marginalized and closed down for political reasons. Those of the 1980s and 1990s were marginalized and closed down for commercial reasons – that is, the sponsors ran out of money.

DESMOND A. SKEEL

Further Reading

Barmé, Geremie and John Minford (editors), *Seeds of Fire: Chinese Voices of Conscience*, Hong Kong: Far Eastern Economic Review, 1986; New York: Hill and Wang, 1988

Brodsgaard, Kjeld Erik, "The Democracy Movement in China, 1978–1979: Opposition Movements, Wall Poster Campaigns and Underground Journals", *Asian Survey* (July 1981): 247–74

Chan, Peter, "Popular Publications in China: A Look at *The Spring of Peking*," *Contemporary China*, 3/4 (Winter 1979): 103–11

Goodman, David S.G., *Beijing Street Voices: The Poetry and Politics of China's Democracy Movement*, London: Boyars, 1981

Kinkley, Jeffrey C. (editor), *After Mao: Chinese Literature and Society, 1978–1981*, Cambridge, Massachusetts: Harvard University Press, 1985

Link, Perry (editor), *Stubborn Weeds: Popular and Controversial Chinese Literature after the Cultural Revolution*, Bloomington: Indiana University Press, 1983

Link, Perry (editor), *Roses and Thorns: The Second Blooming of the Hundred Flowers in Chinese Fiction, 1979–80*, Berkeley: University of California Press, 1984

Nathan, Andrew J., *Chinese Democracy*, New York: Knopf, 1985

Seymour, James D. (editor), *The Fifth Modernization: China's Human Rights Movement, 1978–1979*, Stanfordville, New York: Human Rights Publishing Group, 1980

Widor, Claude (editor), *Documents on the Chinese Democratic Movement, 1978–1980: Unofficial Magazines and Wall Posters*, Paris: Ecole des Hautes Etudes en Sciences Sociales, 1981; Hong Kong: Observer Publishing, 1984

Yeh, Michelle, "The 'Cult of Poetry' in Contemporary China", *Journal of Asian Studies*, 55/1 (February 1996): 51–80

MIN-THUWUN
Burmese poet and scholar (real name: U Wun), 1909–

The creative life of poet U Wun, better known in Burma by his pen-name Min-thuwun, spans the years of colonial Burma, the wartime years under Japanese rule, Burma's independence under parliamentary democracy, and the period of military rule from 1962 until the present. He is widely recognized to be one of the best, perhaps the greatest modern Burmese poet. However in 1968 a public disagreement between him and general Ne Win took place during a meeting concerned with the preparation of new Burmese dictionary. He fell out of favour and was soon after demoted from his headship of the Department of Translation and Publication at the University of Rangoon. By 1971, aged 62, he had been retired from government service, and, from then on, was given no official honours or appointed to the educational and cultural positions that were his due.

Born in a village in the delta south of Rangoon, he began his formal schooling at the national school in his village at the age of 11. From there he went to St John's College in Rangoon and then to the University of Rangoon, which he attended from 1929 to 1936. Awarded a scholarship to study in Britain, he obtained a B.Litt in linguistics from Oxford University and also spent some time at the School of Oriental and African Studies, University of London, returning to Burma in 1939. During the Japanese occupation he served as chief editor of the government-sponsored Burmese dictionary compilation project; when the project was transferred to the University of Rangoon he became head of the Department of Translation and Publication, and also for a short time took over the headship of the Department of Burmese Literature.

After his retirement, he became visiting professor in Burmese at the University of Osaka, Japan, where he worked from 1975 to 1979, and helped, *inter alia*, to prepare a Burmese–Japanese dictionary. On his return to Burma he continued his work as a poet, translator, literary critic, and historian, and in 1984 published a masterly translation of Shakespeare's *King Lear*, which he had toiled over for more than 10 years. (The translation appeared first in instalments in a monthly magazine, and rumour has it that when permission was sought for the whole to be published as a book, this was only granted because a junior official was on duty at the time.)

In 1989, aged 80, Min-thuwun joined the National League for Democracy (NLD), stood as a candidate in the May 1990 election, and was elected in his Rangoon constituency. During the time of Daw Aung San Suu Kyi's house arrest the military forced him to resign from the party. Military Intelligence are alleged to have asked him, "What is an old man like you doing getting involved in politics?"

In 1995, *Sarpay Gya-neh* (Literature Journal) a leading Burmese literary journal, prepared a special number for Min-thuwun, as part of a series honouring outstanding writers. At the last moment, an order was received from the Press Scrutiny Board, Burma's main censorship body, that the cover showing his portrait was not to be used, and the four pages inside containing his biographical data were to be removed. However by May 1997, another magazine, *Maha* (Great Big), devoted mostly to fashion and the loves and lives of pop stars, was able to publish a short article in praise of Min-thuwun, including the banned portrait. Some have seen this as a deliberate attempt on the part of this government-supported magazine to attract a larger circle of readers. At the same time a weekly news-sheet (*Shat-tabyet*) had prepared its front page with a large portrait of the poet, but was ordered to overprint it with text and cartoons.

It seems that the military government is unable to decide how to treat their great national poet, who, since 1926 has been writing poetry admired and loved by all Burmese, poetry that has consistently reflected his fellow countrymen's moods and aspirations.

ANNA ALLOTT

Further Reading
Saw Tun, "Political Themes in the Poetry of Min-thuwun", *Journal of Burma Studies*, 1/1 (1997)

MISHIMA YUKIO
Japanese novelist, playwright, and nationalist, 1925–1970

Certain incidents from the career of Mishima Yukio, one of the best known and most discussed of the Japanese writers who came to prominence after World War II, cast an interesting light on the varied forms that censorship can take in modern societies overtly committed to defending freedom of expression. In addition, a consideration of what Mishima was permitted to do with impunity, and what he was punished for doing, may help to highlight both the few remaining specific differences between Japan and the West, and the far-reaching similarities between them.

In Japan as in the West, it has long been customary to permit greater freedom of expression in "literary" works aimed at "educated" readers than in popular works for the supposedly excitable and unpredictable masses (possible explanations of this divergence are discussed below). Anyone who knows even a little about the history of the media in the West will find little to be astonished by in the fact that Mishima – a graduate of Tokyo University, the most prestigious in Japan, and an extremely erudite literary scholar in his own right – was allowed to describe masturbation, homosexual love, and sado-masochistic rituals in his novels, the first of which appeared in 1949, at a time when the Japanese film industry was still reeling from the shock of its first onscreen kiss (in 1946). Intriguingly, he was thus in a position to explore territory that remained off limits to his literary counterparts in many western countries for another decade or so.

Mishima was by no means unique in this respect. Indeed, for Mishima as for others of his generation, the model of a renowned "highbrow" novelist testing the limits of respectability had been set by Tanizaki Jun'ichirō (1886–1965) before most of them were born. Tanizaki's *Chijin no ai* (*Naomi*), a clinical study of adultery and – what was then truly shocking – female promiscuity, had appeared as early as 1924. In a celebrated incident during World War II, the monthly journal *Chūō Kōron* (Central Review) had effectively been compelled to abandon its serial publication of Tanizaki's greatest novel, *Sasameyuki* (1943–48, *The Makioka Sisters*) – but it did so in response to informal pressure from the military, rather than any official intervention by censors. It is also significant that no steps were taken to prevent Tanizaki from having the work printed and distributed privately soon afterwards. For the rest of his life, Tanizaki continued to explore foot fetishism, masochistic voyeurism, and other extremes of human sexuality in novels that display an exemplary zest for life. It is telling that one of these, *Kagi* (1956, *The Key*), was adapted for the

cinema soon after publication, not in Japan but in Italy – and even there the sexual content had to be considerably toned down.

Many critics, both in Japan and in the West, have speculated at length on the reasons why Mishima, Tanizaki, and other Japanese novelists have been able and willing to depict human sexuality in relatively explicit ways. Indeed, there has been something of a critical consensus that their openness, which presented such a contrast to the prevailing practices of their western counterparts until remarkably recently, is to be connected with the absence, or near-absence, of Judeo-Christian ethics from Japanese culture. This claim in turn raises some very large questions. For one thing, to adopt this approach is to risk overlooking the undoubted fact that Mishima and Tanizaki, for all their appreciation of national traditions and inherited values (those of the samurai in Mishima's case, those of the merchant class in Tanizaki's), were both greatly influenced by their extensive reading in European literature. More broadly, this claim makes it difficult to explain why, even today, the mainstream popular media of films and television in Japan have as little overt sexual content as (say) British and American films and television of the 1950s, with even soft-core pornography being relegated to dedicated cinemas showing the output of specialist companies. It may make more sense to avoid concepts as abstract as "Judeo-Christian ethics" altogether, and attend instead to the social context of forms of expression. From this point of view, it is sufficiently clear that, in Japan as in the West, self-censorship and official regulations alike are framed on the assumption that the depiction of sexuality should be curbed in the mass media, since they are accessible even to children and others who are thought to need protection, while novels and other specific forms aimed at educated adults can be permitted a greater degree of freedom. In this light, the differences between Japanese and (some) western approaches to the depiction of sexuality appear to have more to do with the relative weight of conservative and liberal opinions among decision-makers, which vary from time to time within each country, than with alleged divergences over metaphysics, all too often described in suspiciously ahistorical terms.

Nevertheless, even writers of the stature of Mishima can occasionally fall foul of the law in Japan. Unlike with some of his predecessors, the possibility of official censorship of his publications hardly arose. The Japanese government's system for vetting books had been formally abolished in 1945, and rendered unrestorable, at least in principle, by the guarantee of freedom of expression in Article 21 of the 1947 Constitution; while the censorship system operated by the Allied Occupation authorities (1945–52) was too busy monitoring the press, films, and school textbooks to pay much attention to literary publications. Nor was Mishima ever likely to have been confronted with even the relatively mild pressure that Tanizaki had faced during the war, given the greatly reduced social influence of the military and other traditionally prestigious institutions in postwar Japan (which, indeed, was one of the postwar changes that Mishima himself most vociferously objected to). What eventually trapped Mishima was the application of a doctrine of *puraibashii* (privacy) that was entirely new to Japanese jurisprudence and has remained controversial ever since.

Like many other Japanese novelists, Mishima had frequently included elements drawn directly from life in his works, partly because the *roman à clef* has a distinguished tradition in Japan, partly too, no doubt, because Japan's libel laws were (and are) extremely lax by comparison, for example, to Britain's (and even now, the vast majority of libel cases are settled out of court through arbitration). Thus, his first novel, *Kamen no kokuhaku* (1949, Confessions of a Mask), a detailed study of a young man's sexual awakening, includes depictions of people and institutions in the upper-class circles of prewar and wartime Tokyo that must have been easily recognized by its first readers. To take another example, *Kinkakuji* (1956, The Temple of the Golden Pavilion) is an imaginative but also highly plausible reconstruction of the thoughts of the novice monk who really did burn down the Kyoto landmark of the title in 1950, causing a sensation that was still reverberating when the novel appeared. Mishima had no trouble from government officials, lawyers, publishers, or critics over either of these novels. By contrast, *Utage no ato* (1960, After the Banquet) landed him in the Tokyo District Court, facing the charge that the candidate for governor of Tokyo who is its main character amounted to a portrayal of Arita Hachirō, a Socialist politician and former foreign minister who had lost his fight for that very post the year before the novel first appeared (as a serial in none other than *Chūō Kōron*).

Tellingly, Arita did not sue Mishima for libel alone. This would have been difficult to prove anyway, given that the politician in the novel is shown to be a man of principle and integrity who resists all advice to mount a negative campaign against his rival. Instead, Arita brought his case not only under the libel law but also under article 13 of the Japanese constitution, which states that "all of the people shall be respected as individuals". On this somewhat slender basis the court proceeded to build a wholly new right to privacy, insisting that readers must not be permitted to take fiction as fact, and that matters considered by "the average man" to be private should stay private.

Many commentators pointed out at the time that Arita's life was hardly private by anyone's definition. In particular, it had been well known to Tokyo voters that he had a longstanding and, in Japanese terms, perfectly respectable relationship with the hostess of a bar and nightclub located in an expensive and socially exclusive part of the capital. (Her counterpart in the novel is one of Mishima's few entirely convincing female characters.) Nor did it go unnoticed that the winner of the election for the governorship, who could easily be assumed to resemble the corrupt conservative who wins in the novel, made

no complaint about it. Nevertheless, Arita was almost certainly extremely embarrassed by what could be seen as an inconsistency – or even a yawning gulf – between his quasi-Marxist rhetoric and his ostentatious lifestyle. In 1964, the court awarded Arita damages of 800,000 yen (about US$2200), which, although it may seem low, in fact set a record for such damages for another 10 years.

Interestingly, however, the novel remains available in Japan (as does Donald Keene's translation of it in English-speaking countries). As for Mishima, he hastened to make a formal act of reconciliation with the Arita family and was invited to an imperial garden party soon afterwards, an indication that his social standing had not been affected by the case. Accordingly, he remained free to continue his increasingly bizarre career as a nationalist campaigner up to 1970, when he performed his startling but politically ineffective ritual act of *seppuku* (self-disembowelment or "harakiri") at a military barracks in Tokyo. In short, the case had amounted to a rap on the knuckles for Mishima and a warning to less well-connected writers, partly, perhaps, because anything more severe would have carried the risk of turning Mishima into a martyr for free speech.

Despite its essentially trivial nature – this was a dispute between social equals, not a challenge to the state – the case has had a long-term impact. This has been felt, not so much in the courts of Japan, which remains a relatively nonlitigious society, but, as it were, on their thresholds, through what the Japanese themselves call the *jishukusei*, the "self-censorship system". As in the West, this system is operated by editors and publishers rather than state officials, and enforced by advertisers and press officers rather than the police. Like its western counterparts, it is sometimes misunderstood as being applied exclusively in favour of government bodies or large corporations. For example, western journalists visiting Japan frequently express (or feign) surprise that reporters who do not belong to the press clubs attached to the various ministries are prevented from investigating them. More generally, the system has been blamed, for example, for the failure of the mainstream press to challenge Tanaka Kakuei and other politicians who took bribes from Lockheed in the early 1970s, until shortly after western newspapers started doing so; or to expose the industrial pollution, and the consequent horrific diseases, caused by Chissō Corporation and other companies, until long after the victims had started suing in the notoriously slow-moving courts. However, the system also operates at the level of individuals. Prominent actors, singers, and politicians will release details of their private lives only to publications regarded by their press officers as "sympathetic" and respectful of the right established by Arita against Mishima. No Japanese publication has yet dared to examine the finances or the private lives of the imperial family, even though the crime of *fukei – lèse-majesté* – is no longer on the statute books.

Mishima's experiences suggest, then, that Japan is not so very different from the West. Freedom of expression is largely unrestricted when that expression involves works that it is generally agreed have literary or artistic merit. Indeed, to a greater extent in Japan than in some western countries, but much the same as in some others, novels, documentary films, educational videos, and "highbrow" magazines can include material that mainstream mass media would hardly dare even to refer to, except, perhaps, to expose it as evidence of decadence. Yet a distinguished novelist, the winner of several prizes and a well-known figure in the "establishment", who was already famous for intruding with impunity on the privacy of a deranged and defenceless novice monk, could not be allowed to embarrass a high-ranking politician and get away with it.

Finally, the development of freedom of expression in Japan since the court decided in Arita's favour suggests another, broader conclusion. The case set a powerful precedent, yet it has barely been tested in the courts in the intervening years. Hence, the limits of freedom of expression and, accordingly, the impact of forms of censorship in practice, are not easy to trace. Even the most obvious and basic question – how far can a constitutional guarantee of freedom of expression be reconciled with a doctrine of respect for privacy? – remains without a definitive answer, in Japan as in the western countries from which the new doctrine was borrowed. However, even in more litigious societies, neither statute law nor case law can encompass the whole range of forms of censorship, and social realities are much less tidy than the philosophical or legal abstractions that are supposed to explain and direct them. Official censorship, based on written law and open to challenge for that very reason, is dead and buried in Japan, as in most western countries – with the notable exceptions, of course, of television, films, computer games, and other forms of popular entertainment. Self-censorship, meanwhile, continues to thrive, and may

even be more effective, perhaps precisely because it is less overt and less easy to challenge, but also because it is more flexible in its responses to the changing social consensus on sexuality, privacy, and other matters of controversy.

PATRICK HEENAN

Writings
Kamen no kokuhaku, 1949; as *Confessions of a Mask*, translated by Meredith Weatherby, 1958
Kinkakuji, 1956; as *The Temple of the Golden Pavilion*, translated by Ivan Morris, 1959
Utage no ato, 1960; as *After the Banquet*, translated by Donald Keene, 1963

Further Reading
Beer, Lawrence W., "Defamation, Privacy, and Freedom of Expression in Japan", *Law in Japan: An Annual*, 5 (1972)
Scott-Stokes, Henry, *The Life and Death of Yukio Mishima*, New York: Farrar Straus, 1974; London: Owen, 1975
Tanizaki Jun'ichirō, *Chijin no ai*, 1925; as *Naomi*, translated by Anthony H. Chambers, New York: Knopf, 1985; London: Secker and Warburg, 1986
Tanizaki Jun'ichirō, *Sasameyuki*, 1943–48; as *The Makioka Sisters*, translated by Edward G. Seidensticker, New York: Knopf, 1957; London: Secker and Warburg, 1958; revised edition, Knopf, 1993
Tanizaki Jun'ichirō, *Kagi*, 1956; as *The Key*, translated by Howard S. Hibbett, New York: Knopf, 1960; London: Secker and Warburg, 1961

DINABANDHU MITRA
Indian writer, 1830–1873
NIL DARPAN (The Mirror of Indigo)
Play, 1861

Nil Darpan is a powerful political play. It highlights the oppression perpetrated by European indigo planters in the rural areas of Bengal in the late 19th century, and portrays the plights of the cultivators. The play focuses on two planters, J.J. Wood and P.P. Roge, who force the cultivators to sow indigo without appropriate remuneration, unleash violence on defiant peasants, and even violate Indian maidens and encourage prostitution. The indigo planters are patronized by the local magistrate who appears to be more interested in the favours of the planter's wife than delivering justice. A highly educated young Bengali villager known as Nobinmadhab Bosu emerges as the organizer of peasant resistance; he dies from a wound caused by a planter during a fracas. Soon Nobinmadhab's peace-loving father and the head of the family, Golukchandra Bosu, is incarcerated under a court order. This incident so much distresses the old patriarch that he commits suicide. At the end of the play, Nobinmadhab's younger brother Bindumadhab returns to the village after completing his college education in Calcutta and finds his family ruined.

Nil Darpan captured the spirit of Indigo Rebellion in colonial "lower" Bengal – an area coterminous with the modern state of Bangladesh and the Indian province of West Bengal. The autumn of 1859 was an extremely disturbing time for colonial rulers. Cultivators refused to sow the commercially unprofitable indigo crop, and peasants resisted fiercely when

armed retainers of the planters tried to compel its cultivation. The Indigo Rebellion occurred at a time when the Bengali intelligentsia of Calcutta was awakening to the first stirrings of national sentiment. Becoming aware of peasant resistance, as did English philanthropists and missionaries, they began to articulate the grievances of the cultivators. *Nil Darpan*, written a year later, was a distinctive product of this national awakening.

The author of the play, Dinabandhu Mitra (1830–73), was an Indian official in the colonial postal service. He travelled widely in rural areas of Bengal in connection with his job, gaining a rare insight into the social life of the villages. His concerns for the rural population were repeatedly expressed in his literary works.

Ironically, the Bengali version of the play did not provoke hostile comments from the planters. The trouble started as soon as an English translation of the play was published. An enterprising English missionary and a champion of the interests of the Bengal peasantry, the Reverend Long, drew the play to the attention of W.S. Seton Carr, secretary to the Bengal government. Carr, who knew that several important government officials wished to read the play, authorized an English translation, which was organized by Long. The lieutenant governor, Halliday, sanctioned Carr's printing and circulating the play at private expense. Five hundred copies were printed and distributed to officials of the Bengal government, prominent philanthropists, retired Indian officials, newspaper editors, and even members of the parliament.

Soon the play reached the hands of the secretary to the European-dominated Landholders and Commercial Association of Bengal, who promptly wrote a protest letter to the Bengal government, which denied any responsibility. The Commercial Association decided to prosecute the printer of the book, C.H. Manuel, on a charge of libel against the planters as a body. Long then claimed all responsibility for the publication of the book. *The Englishman*, mouthpiece of European businessmen in Calcutta, quickly decided to prosecute Long, accusing him of knowingly encouraging a rebellious spirit among Indians. Sir Mordaunt Wells, known for his hostility to Indians, was assigned the responsibility of trying the case. In an earlier judgement he had observed that Indians were a nation of forgers and perjurers, and he now gave extremely biased advice to the jury of 12 Englishmen, a Portuguese, an Armenian and a Parsi. Long was found guilty and at a hearing before full bench sentenced to one month's imprisonment and a fine of 1000 rupees.

This judgement and the English translation of *Nil Darpan* became a landmark in colonial history. Indian newspapers expressed their enthusiastic support for Long's solidarity with the indigo cultivators. Moreover, they felt alarmed at the manipulative power of the European commercial lobby, which could influence justice in Calcutta by playing upon the fear of rebellion. The judgement was the first of a series of regular suppressions of the performance of *Nil Darpan* in India. In 1872, for example, *The Englishman* opposed an attempt to stage the play in Calcutta. In Lucknow in the same year, resident British audiences disrupted a performance. Dinabandhu Mitra, meanwhile, was said to have been denied promotion and to have been transferred from job to job until his early death in 1873.

The *Nil Darpan* affair contributed to the government's decision to pass the Dramatic Performances Act in 1879, instituting a theatre censorship that persisted well into the 20th century – and was used to ban *Nil Darpan* itself in 1908.

SUBHO BASU

Writings

Nil Darpan; or, The Indigo Planting Mirror, translated by "A Native", 1861; translated by M.M. Dutt, 1958; translated in *The Blue Devil: Indigo and Colonial Bengal* by Amiya Rao and B.G. Rao, 1992

Further Reading

Brown, Judith M., *Modern India: The Origins of an Asian Democracy*, Delhi and New York: Oxford University Press, 1985; 2nd edition, Oxford and New York: Oxford University Press, 1994

Chaudhuri, Sashu Bhusan, *Civil Disturbances during the British Rule in India, 1765–1857*, Calcutta: World Press, 1955

Day, Lal Behàri, *Bengal Peasant Life*, London: Macmillan, 1909

Guha, R., "Neel Darpan: The Image of a Peasant Revolt in a Liberal Mirror", *Journal of Peasant Studies*, 2/1 (October 1974): 1–46

Guha, Ranajit, *Elementary Aspects of Peasant Insurgency in Colonial India*, Delhi: Oxford University Press, 1983

Guha-Thakurta, P., *The Bengali Drama: Its Origin and Development*, London: Trench Trubner, 1930; reprinted Westport, Connecticut: Greenwood Press, 1974

Kar, S., *British Sashone Bajeapta Bangla Boi* (Bengali Books Proscribed during the British Rule), Calcutta: Ananda Publishers, n.d.

Kling, Blair B., *The Blue Mutiny: The Indigo Disturbances in Bengal, 1859–1862*, Philadelphia: University of Pennsylvania Press, 1966

Mitra, L.C., *History of the Indigo Disturbances in Bengal with a Full Report of the Nil Darpan Case*, Calcutta, 1903

Sanyal, Ram Gopal, *Reminiscences and Anecdotes of Great Men of India*, 2 vols, Calcutta: Herald, 1891; Calcutta: Riddhi, 1980

MLADINA (Youth)
Slovenian weekly newspaper, established 1943

Originally the paper of the Slovenian Socialist Youth Alliance, (ZSMS), *Mladina* served as a mouthpiece for the communist authorities of Yugoslavia's northernmost republic, voicing the political dogmas of the Yugoslav state until the early 1980s.

After Tito's death in 1980, however, a new generation of journalists and editors rose to the fore, to whom socialist symbols and slogans meant less, and who were more interested in liberalization of both society and their chosen profession. When, later in the 1980s, the communist authorities of Slovenia loosened their stranglehold, even allowing a limited measure of pluriformity, *Mladina* transformed itself into a newspaper highly critical of socialist imagery, and in particular, the privileged position of the Yugoslav People's Army (JNA). However, it refused to publish letters, reports or editorial comments with an explicit nationalist bias, a policy it maintained into the late 1990s.

In 1987 and 1988, *Mladina* led the Slovenian media in criticizing the activities of admiral Branko Mamula, the federal minister of defence. *Mladina* described the details of how Mamula used federal conscripts to construct a private villa on the Adriatric coast. Mamula was also named as "the salesman of death" because of his arms sales trips to Africa. The paper questioned how Yugoslavia could invest two billion dollars in the development of a new supersonic fighter while the country faced its biggest economic crisis of the century. In 1989, *Mladina*'s editors openly concluded that the socialist revolution had failed.

The JNA leadership could not possibly ignore statements that questioned its prestige and authority and that of the Yugoslav state. The army saw itself as the sole protector of Yugoslav unity and felt the Slovenian publications eroded the very foundations of this unity. It decided to have *Mladina* silenced. By early 1988, it had collected over 200 "incriminating" articles. At the same time, the Federal Minister of Defence, general Veljko Kadijević, who had replaced admiral Mamula, accused the Slovenian authorities of supporting the activities of *Mladina*, concluding that "if they'd wished to silence them, it would have been not too much of an effort".

The conflict between the federal army leadership and the Slovenian press intensified. A first climax was reached in April as *Mladina* published JNA plans for a coup d'état in Slovenia if the local liberal communist leadership proved to be incapable of controlling the press. Within a month, another explosive piece entitled *Noč dolgih nožev* (Night of the long knives) described how the JNA was preparing numerous arrests among reporters and politicians. Infuriated, the Federal Ministry of Defence brought charges against journalists Janez Janša, David Tasič, and Franci Zavrl, and soldier Ivan Borštner, the presumed source of the information.

Under federal law, the four were charged with possession of military secrets and brought to trial at a military court. The Slovenian Central Committee supported *Mladina* but was unable to prevent the trial. The trial was held in Ljubljana, capital of Slovenia, but since it fell within the jurisdiction of the army, whose language of command was Serbo-Croat, that language was used instead of Slovene. Although this procedure was formally correct, the Slovenian public was enraged. During the trial, thousands of citizens demonstrated their sympathy for the defendants by laying flowers at the doorstep of the court. A human rights committee managed to collect about 100,000 signatures demanding the immediate release of the defendants. Slovenian citizens felt the trial against *Mladina*'s editors was a battle about the very essence of "Sloveneness". Thus the trial, rather than the fact the four were convicted to prison terms ranging from one and a half to four years, greatly contributed to Slovenia's taking the road towards independence.

Mladina itself was not altogether happy with this outcome and, in its own words, "assumed cynical distance towards the rush into Slovenia's independence". Accordingly, when independence from Yugoslavia was proclaimed in 1991, *Mladina*'s journalists covered the ensuing war from both Yugoslav and Slovenian points of view. It was the only Yugoslav newspaper to do so.

The newspaper continued to play a controversial role in independent Slovenia. Ironically, it was Janez Janša, who in December 1992, in his new role as Defence Minister, accused *Mladina*'s editor-in-chief Robert Bottieri of having collaborated with the former Yugoslav Army's security service. This happened after *Mladina* had extensively reported on Slovenia's arms trade. The Ministry of Defence announced that it would press charges against the newspaper for "manufacturing stories". *Mladina* responded by announcing that it would sue Janša for libel. In May 1996, a Ljubljana judge suspended *Mladina* contributor Bernhard Nezmah for one month for having made "insulting comments" in an article published in February 1995.

JAN R. BLAAUW and FLORIBERT BAUDET

Further Reading

Gow, James, *Legitimacy and the Military: The Yugoslav Crisis*, London: Pinter, and New York: St Martin's Press, 1992

Meier, V., *Wie Jugoslawien verspielt wurde*, Munich: Beck, 1995

Ramet, Sabrina Petra, *Nationalism and Federalism in Yugoslavia, 1962–1991*, 2nd edition, Bloomington: Indiana University Press, 1992

Ramet, Sabrina Petra, "Democratization in Slovenia: The Second Stage" in *Politics, Power, and the Struggle for Democracy in South-East Europe*, edited by Karen Dawisha and Bruce Parrott, Cambridge and New York: Cambridge University Press, 1997

Silber, Laura and Allan Little, *The Death of Yugoslavia*, London: Penguin/BBC Books, 1995; revised edition, 1996

Website

http://www.mladina.si/

MODERNISM
Catholic heresy, 19th–20th centuries

The Christian church has always claimed the authority to define the authentic content of the revelation with which it claims to have been entrusted. After the credal formulations promulgated in the first centuries, the Catholic Church, from the 16th century to the mid-20th, relied heavily on defining its core tenets by a process involving the condemnation of what seemed incompatible with its revelation. The practice of censorship became therefore structurally essential to its continuing quest to define the implications of its beliefs. It erected a perimeter fence round an enclosure that left room for theological debate to define orthodoxy more closely within the newly set limits.

Modernism was referred to by Pius X in his consistory allocution of 17 April 1907 as "constituting not a heresy, but the epitome and poisonous venom of all heresies". In the sense in which it was condemned in a series of papal documents and made the subject of an antimodernist oath imposed on 1 September 1910 on all holders of ecclesiastical office and ordinands, it consisted first of all in the application of critical methods to the study of scripture in such a way as to derogate from normative authority for belief. Second, essential to modernism was the study of the history of dogma in such a way as to suggest that doctrine had developed as a by-product of the process by which spiritual experience within the Christian community achieved intellectual expression. The most important figures at the centre of the movement in the form in which it was condemned were the French dogmatic historian Alfred Firmin Loisy (1857–1940) and the English Jesuit spiritual writer George Tyrrell (1861–1909).

Modernism, to which religious fundamentalism was a reaction, can be extended to include liberal Protestantism, and it can be seen to develop from the scientific discoveries of Charles Darwin, who had published *The Origin of Species* in 1859, threatening the doctrines of monogenesis and original sin, and from the philosophy of the French idealists Maurice Blondel (1861–1949) and Henri-Louis Bergson (1859–1941), which threatened the power of rationality and promoted reliance on moral conviction in preference to defined teaching. The tightly imposed antimodernist oath stipulates acceptance of the rational demonstrability of God's existence, the institution of the Church by Christ, the immutability of dogma, and the rationality of faith.

As early as 1864 Pius IX had issued the *Syllabus of Errors*, attacking the growing hegemony of scientific rationalism and insisting that theology was itself a rational discipline. His successor, the liberally minded Leo XIII, thought it necessary to check the paths being traced in biblical criticism, on which he issued the encyclical *Providentissimus* in 1893. Loisy was dismissed from the teaching post at the Institut Catholique, which he had held since 1881. It was later to become clear that, in defending Catholicism from Alfred Harnack's Protestant view, later expounded in *Das Wesen des Christentums* (1900), Loisy had himself exceeded the bounds of orthodoxy in a series of articles from the *Revue du Clergé*, published as *L'Évangile et l'Église* in 1902. He had regarded dogmas, hierarchy, and liturgy as dependent less on divine, or divinely established ecclesiastical, authority, than on a largely natural growth in response to changing spiritual, social, and cultural environments.

An encroaching rationalism continued to permeate scriptural interpretation, and in order to adjudicate on the permissibility of interpretations of scripture Leo XIII instituted the Biblical Commission in 1902. Its decisions were to be made binding in 1907. Loisy sporadically continued a distinguished academic career as professor first at the Collège des Hautes Études (1900–04) and then at the Collège de France (1909–30), publishing *Le Quatrième Évangile* in 1903, and in 1908, the year of his excommunication, *Les Évangiles synoptiques*. He had openly contested the authority of the episcopacy to grant or to withhold the ecclesiastical *imprimatur* which permitted publication, and had at least seemed to compromise the divinity of Christ with his statement "le Christ est Dieu pour la foi" (Christ is God in the light of faith).

George Tyrrell taught philosophy as a Jesuit until he was assigned in 1896 to the Jesuit journal *The Month*, for which he wrote 39 articles over seven years. He was also in demand as a spiritual director, and his interests turned increasingly to spirituality. His *Hard Sayings* (1898) and *External Religion* (1898), written for Catholic undergraduates in the hostile environment of Oxford, attracted no comment, but in 1899 his article "A Perverted Devotion" in *The Weekly Register* was harshly criticized by the censors of the Jesuit curia in Rome, and in 1901 he was removed from the staff of *The Month* to a quiet parish in Yorkshire. A collection of articles, *The Faith of Millions* (1901) was deemed acceptable, but a further work attracted such strong disapprobation from Jesuit censors in London and Rome that Tyrrell's next two works were published pseudonymously: *Religion as a Factor of Life* (1902) and

The Church and The Future (1903). Religion was becoming grounded for him in a "sense of the absolute" translated by the intellect into moral values, rather than on a revelation and a teaching authority, and he was beginning to regard dogmas merely as mental ideas approximating to the truth. The function of the pope and the bishops was simply to interpret the consensus of the faithful.

None the less, Tyrrell's *Lex Orandi* (1903) was passed by the censors and appeared with an *imprimatur*. A counterweight, *Lex Credendi*, was to appear in 1906. Meanwhile, however, Tyrrell had in 1904 written a *Letter to a Professor of Anthropology*, of which a leaked copy had appeared in 1906 in Italian translation in the *Corriera della Sera*. It was Tyrrell's refusal to accept the doctrine of the Assumption of the Blessed Virgin Mary at the demand of the order's general which caused his dismissal from the order and suspension as a priest. He failed to find a diocese that would accept him, or allow him to exercise his priestly functions again.

There had been further censures in France. Loisy's five latest works were put on the *Index Librorum Prohibitorum* in 1903, to be followed by works by La Laberthonnière, Edouard Le Roy, and A. Houtin in the course of 1906. In July 1907 Pius X issued the encyclical *Lamentabili*, whose text had first been drafted in 1903 and which finally condemned 65 propositions concerned with teaching authority, inspiration, revelation, the development of dogma, the sacraments, the Church, and Christian doctrine. It was followed by *Pascendi* of 8 September 1907, primarily announcing a tightening of discipline, but also denouncing agnosticism and the view that faith is the perception of God's presence in the human consciousness, which historically gave rise to dogmas and sacraments. The Church was not simply instituted by the collective consciousness of the early Christians.

Tyrrell attacked *Pascendi* in the London *Times* on 30 September and 1 October 1907, and was thereupon excommunicated, although he received conditional absolution and the last sacraments before his death of Bright's disease in 1909.

ANTHONY LEVI

Further Reading

Ranchetti, Michele, *The Catholic Modernists: A Study of the Religious Reform Movement, 1864–1907*, Oxford and New York: Oxford University Press, 1969

Ratté, John, *Three Modernists: Alfred Loisy, George Tyrrell, William L. Sullivan*, New York: Sheed and Ward, 1967

Reardon, Bernard M.G. (editor), *Roman Catholic Modernism*, Stanford, California: Stanford University Press, and London: A. & C. Black, 1970

Vidler, Alex R., *A Variety of Catholic Modernists*, Cambridge: Cambridge University Press, 1970

MAHATHIR MOHAMAD
Malaysian politician and writer, 1925–

THE MALAY DILEMMA
Political book, 1970

Dr Mahathir Mohamad, now prime minister of Malaysia, was born in Alor Setar, the capital of the state of Kedah. He had his early and secondary education in his home town. In 1947 he was admitted to the King Edward VII College of Medicine in Singapore. After graduating, he joined the Malaysian Government Service as a medical officer. He left government service in 1957 to set up his own practice in Alor Setar and began his political career.

Although he has written two other books, his most important work remains *The Malay Dilemma*, published in 1970. The bulk of the book was written after Mahathir had been expelled from the ruling United Malays National Organization (UMNO) shortly after communal riots in 1969. The book examines relations between the Malays and the Chinese, the most sensitive issue in Malaysia. It was banned by the Malaysian government, which feared that the contents might lead to further communal discord. Mahathir was especially critical of the then prime minister, Tunku Abdul Rahman, indirectly blaming him for the riots. Mahathir argued that the Tunku had gone too far in giving in to the demands of the Chinese, to the detriment of the Malay community. The decision to ban the book was almost certainly taken by the prime minister himself. Several other books, mostly academic works dealing with ethnic relations between the Malays and the Chinese, were banned at the same time.

The ban on *The Malay Dilemma*, however, was not effective, as the book was easily available in Singapore. Copies were widely distributed among politically active Malaysians, such as university students. Mahathir was rehabilitated politically into UMNO after Tunku Abdul Rahman's removal in 1972, but the ban on *The Malay Dilemma* remained in deference to the Tunku, and was not officially lifted until 1981, when Mahathir took office as prime minister. Since then, the book has been reprinted several times, including a Malay-language edition, and it remains influential.

The Malay Dilemma seeks to justify official racial discrimination against the Chinese or the non-Malay communities in Malaysia. Under the current system, Malays and other indigenous peoples are given preferential access to such economic and social benefits as special government contracts, heavily subsidized business loans, business quota, cheap shares (often sold below market price to fulfil the legal requirement that 30 per cent of listed companies must be owned by Malays) and scholarships.

Mahathir claims that the 1969 race riots happened because "the government started off on a wrong premise. It believed that there had been racial harmony in the past and that Sino-Malay co-operation to achieve Independence was an example of racial harmony. These dubious assumptions led to policies that undermined whatever superficial understanding there was

between the Malays and the non Malays." Mahathir believes that the Malays are the original inhabitants of the Malay Peninsula and that the "Malay economic dilemma" is caused by "hereditary environmental" factors.

His suggestion that the Malays are the original inhabitants of Malaya is, of course, wrong. Many aborigine tribes had settled on the Malay Peninsula long before the Malay migrated there. The only claim the Malays could sustain was that they were earlier migrants than the Chinese – large-scale Chinese migration to Malaya only occurred in the 19th century, when the British colonial authorities imported Chinese labour to work in the mines and on plantations.

Mahathir argued that all immigrants were "guests" until they were "truly absorbed". Absorption would occur only when the immigrants adopted the Malay language, culture and religion. Because of "the lush tropical plains [of the Malay peninsula] with their plentiful sources of food", the Malays had never had to fight hard to survive, so the observation that only the fittest would survive did not apply. Heredity also played a part, since "the absence of inter marriage . . . the habit of family in-breeding" through "first cousins", produced a "cumulative effect . . . In this sort of society, enterprise and independence are unknown".

Contrast this, commented Mahathir, with "the history of the China . . . littered with disasters . . . For the Chinese people life was one continuous struggle for survival" which led to "survival to the fit only". "As if this was not enough . . . Chinese custom decreed that marriages should not be within the same clan. This resulted in more cross-breeding. The result of this . . . was to reproduce the best strains and characteristics that facilitated survival and accentuated the influence of environment." Thus, Mahathir argues, "the Malays whose own heredity and environment influence had been so debilitating, could do nothing but retreat before the onslaught of the Chinese immigrants. Whatever the Malays could do, the Chinese could do better and more cheaply. Before long the industrious and determined immigrants had displaced the Malays . . . [in] all branches of skilled work." For this reason alone, Mahathir advocated discriminatory policies in favour of the Malays in all social and economic fields.

In an interview in 1997, Mahathir was asked if he still harboured the views he espoused in *The Malay Dilemma*. Mahathir replied that "some parts" of it were wrong, but he refused to elaborate or state which part of the book he was referring to.

JAMES CHIN

Writings
The Malay Dilemma, 1970
The Early Years, 1947–1972, 1995

MOLDOVA

(formerly Soviet Socialist Republic of Moldova; Moldavia)

Population: 4,295,000
Main religions: Eastern Orthodox; Jewish
Official language: Moldovan
Other languages spoken: Russian
Illiteracy rate (%): 0.5 (m); 1.7 (f)

Number of daily newspapers: 4
Number of radio receivers per 1000 inhabitants: 736
Number of TV receivers per 1000 inhabitants: 288
Number of PCs per 1000 inhabitants: 6.4

The territory now called Moldova, formerly part of the Ottoman empire and, after 1812, under Russian suzerainty, was claimed by Romania at the end of World War I. However, by 1924 the Soviet Union had taken back land east of the river Dniester, which now became the Moldavian Autonomous Soviet Socialist Republic (ASSR), and in 1940, Transnistria (Bessarabia and the Bukovina) were ceded to the Soviet Union under the terms of the Molotov–Ribbentrop pact (with Nazi Germany). Recovered by Romania between July 1941 and August 1944, Moldavia was again annexed by the Soviet Union and remained part of it until the latter's fall in 1991. The new country, Moldova, has opted to remain independent, rejecting proposals for reunion with Romania, notably in a referendum in 1994.

Romanian and Moldovan are closely related languages, and the two territories have obvious cultural and historical links. The Soviet Union made every effort to break these links. Thus, for example, use of the Roman alphabet was forbidden and Cyrillic was imposed instead. The *Great Soviet Encyclopedia* attempted both to justify the Russian acquisition of Bessarabia in 1812 and to "russify" Moldovan history, claiming that the Moldovans had welcomed the arrival of the Soviets. Russian and Ukrainian immigration was encouraged, a recurring Soviet strategy to weaken national identity. When Leonid Brezhnev came to power in 1964, he declared Russian the official language for education and the media. Orthodox churches and Jewish synagogues were closed down. On the other hand, some selected works of Romanian literature were allowed to be published in the 1950s and in the 1960s a 1000-kilowatt radio transmitter in Iasi, the historic capital of Moldavia (now situated just over the Soviet border) allowed for the broadcasting of programmes on Romanian history and literature.

It was only with glasnost, introduced by Mikhail Gorbachev in 1986, that russification was reversed. Decrees issued in 1987 and 1989 established a more intensive study of Romanian in schools. Moldova achieved its independence in 1991, and there followed a period of "national awakening", including the re-introduction of the Roman alphabet. Article 13 of the constitution, promulgated in 1994, establishes that "the national language of the Republic of Moldova is Moldovan, and its writing is based on the Roman alphabet". However, the constitution allows parents to choose the language of education for their children and it remains the case that Russian is the language understood by most people.

The country's search for unity has been hampered by the presence of two regions seeking autonomy: Gagauz-Yeri, the homeland of the Orthodox Christian and Turkic-speaking Gagauz; and Transnistria, the area on the west bank of the Dniester river where Russian is strong. Some local autonomy was granted to Gagauz-Yeri in 1994, but no final compromise

has been reached with the Transnistrian authorities, whose ideology remains close to that of the Soviet Union, and who demand "statehood" and the recognition of Moldova as a two-state federation.

Although the Moldovan government formally controls only three national daily newspapers, *Moldova Suverana*, *Patria Tanana*, and *Momentul*, it has indirect financial interests in several others. More than 20 publications are owned and directed by political parties. *Moldova Suverana* made a bid for independence in October 1994, but this was overwhelmed when the government confiscated equipment, hindered printing, and expelled journalists from the newspaper's office building. The broadcasting service Teleradio Moldova is financed by advertising and the government; a plan for the introduction of a licence fee, modelled on the system used in Britain to finance the BBC, has not yet been implemented. Catalan TV, the first private station, was established in 1995 and at first, according to Gheorge Straistenu, its head of economic affairs, was under "consistent pressure from state bodies and top officials from the parliament, the presidential office, and the government".

Between 1992 and 1997, 277 of the 801 cases of litigation examined by the Moldovan Supreme Court were directed against the media. The numbers of cases decreased considerably after 1997, but even then *Cuvinyul*, an independent newspaper in Rezina, was sued for defamation after it had published a story, already on record at the public prosecutor's office, concerning three men who used public funds to pay their private telephone bills. Former president Mircea Snegur (who was replaced by Petru Lucinschi in December 1996) also used the law to stifle critical comments or unwelcome stories.

The Moldovan Press Law of 1994 made this possible. It guarantees "everybody the right to free expression of opinion and ideas, and the right to truthful information from periodicals and press agencies"; but it provides penalties for the publication of "materials that ... defame the state and the people", or "false materials, whether or not they disparage the honour and respect of a person". Clearly, all depends on who is defining what "defames" and what is "false". The Law on Television and Radio, passed in 1995, states, similarly, that "the freedom of audiovisual expression ... does not allow" the broadcasting of material to "the detriment of other people's honour, dignity, private life".

The writ of the government does not, apparently, run in the "Transnistrian Republic of Moldova", where the two main newspapers are owned by the authorities, "national" and local. Journalists on one of the independent papers, *Novaya Gazeta*, were made to register by Boris Abulov, the head of ideology, and in February 1999 two issues of the paper were confiscated without explanation. Journalists on a second independent newspaper, *Dobrii Den*, have, reportedly, been subjected to physical threats. As in the rest of Moldova, the law has been used to prevent comment, as when in April 1998 a local court sued *Dobrii Den* after it had suggested that the sentences passed in a corruption case had been too lenient.

Also in Transnistria, Asket, a private television station, has been subjected to jamming and other forms of harassment, not least when it reported in 1992–93 on remarks critical of the regime made by general Aleksandr Lebed, then commander of the Russian 14th Army, which was stationed in Transnistria. Forced to close down by the threat of lawsuits, Asket reinvented itself as TiViK Asket and gained a licence from the central Moldovan authorities, which, of course, was not acceptable in Transnistria. Harassment by telephone continued, although the Tiraspol city authorities now allow coverage of official events. When in 1998 the station aired a young people's discussion on the subject of "patriotism", and refused to supply a copy of the programme to the authorities before transmission, the programme presenter was called in for questioning.

The international watchdog group Article 19 reported in 1999 that "the situation of the media in Moldova (excepting Transnistria) has seen a marked improvement in recent years". The report drew attention to the Moldovan government's attempts to reduce its statutory control of newspapers and the broadcast media. However, the report also pointed out that:

there remains a large gap between the law and practice in many areas of Moldovan life. This is largely due to severe

financial impoverishment combined with a significant black market economy, and aspects of the Soviet legacy – for example, that Russian remains the language of most citizens. This allows the penetration of the Moldovan media by Russian language organizations based outside the country, primarily in Russia.

FEDERICA PRINA

Further Reading

Article 19, *Moldova: Media in Transition*, London: Article 19, 1999
Bosatikova, Nadezhda, "Summer in Trans-Dniester", *Index on Censorship*, 22/4 (April 1993)
Brezianu, Andrei, *Historical Dictionary of the Republic of Moldova*, Lanham, Maryland: Scarecrow Press, 2000
Bruchs, Michael, *Nations, Nationalities, People*, New York: Columbia University Press, 1984
Byelostechnik, Alla, "Freedom of Speech and Freedom of the Press in the Republic of Moldova", *Balkan Media*, 6/2 (Summer 1997)
Deletant, Denis, "History as Nemesis: An Overview", *Index on Censorship*, 22/4 (April 1993)
Dima, Nicholas, *From Moldavia to Moldova*, Boulder, Colorado: East European Monographs, 1991
Lange, Yasha, *Media in the CIS*, Brussels: European Commission, 1997
"Moldova", *East European Constitutional Review* (Fall 1997)
US Department of State, *Moldova: Country Report on Human Rights Practices*, Washington, DC: Bureau of Democracy, Human Rights and Labor, 1997

MOLIÈRE (Jean-Baptiste Poquelin)
French dramatist, 1622–1673

The fate of *Tartuffe*, persecuted (to use Molière's own term) at the behest of the Compagnie du Saint-Sacrement or Cabale des Dévots (the School for Bigots), which felt itself targeted by the play, exemplifies the subtle manoeuvering for power between the monarchy and the Church in 17th-century France. The play, first produced in 1664 as a three-act farce in prose before king Louis XIV at Versailles, relates how a credulous bourgeois is duped by a fraudulent spiritual director. It was immediately attacked by the Compagnie du Saint-Sacrement with which the Queen Mother, Anne of Austria, was in sympathy. This powerful group consisted of Catholic supporters of the counter-reformation, Jansenists, bourgeois parliamentarians, and anti-court aristocrats. The king, under pressure from his religious adversaries, adopted a compromise position towards the play that reflected the strategic lines around which the struggle concerning the censorship of theatre was fought throughout the century. Invoking his rights as a *personne privée*, the king allowed private performances for himself, the court, and certain *personnes de qualité*. At the same time, respecting the demands of Hardouin de Péréfixe, Archbishop of Paris, he prohibited public performances. This ruling implicitly supported the position of the Compagnie du Saint-Sacrement, which maintained that theatre was a public danger from which the populace must be protected. But it made an exception for the court and the aristocracy, for whom theatre and spectacle remained an important political and cultural instrument.

In spite of Molière's efforts to have the play produced on the public stage, this state of affairs remained in effect for the next five years. In 1667, Molière attempted to stage a five-act re-working of the play, in verse, entitled *L'Imposteur*, in which Tartuffe appeared under the pseudonym of Panulphe. But Molière's adversaries were not fooled. The day after the first performance, *L'Imposteur* was banned by order of Guillaume de Lamoignon, President of the Parlement and member of the Compagnie du Saint-Sacrement. Five days later Hardouin de Péréfixe issued an order banning the play and forbidding attendance at any performance whatsoever under pain of excommunication. This order was to be posted on all church doors as well as read from the pulpit. Lamoignon's argument, that even if the intentions of the play were not suspect the stage was not the proper place to debate questions of religion, appeared to hold the day until 1669, when La Paix de Clément IX or Paix Clémentine, a truce between Jansenists and the mainstream church, provided the king with the opportunity of authorizing public performances.

During the ban on *Tartuffe*, further difficulties were placed in Molière's way. In 1665 he attempted to stage *Dom Juan; ou, le Festin de Pierre*, in which, among many targets, he certainly took aim at the persecutors of *Tartuffe*. *Dom Juan* quickly provoked cries of outrage from the religious authorities, even inspiring the curate of Saint-Sulpice to demand Molière's punishment both by the fires of hell and the more immediate fires of the stake. Aware of the very real danger that threatened him, and unable in this case to rely on the protection of the king, Molière succumbed to the pressure and quickly withdrew *Dom Juan* from the boards. The play virtually disappeared for 200 years, existing only in a bowdlerized version in verse by Thomas Corneille (younger brother of Pierre) which excised all the material deemed offensive to piety. This watered-down adaptation of Molière's *Dom Juan* was the sole version produced until the middle of the 19th century.

Dom Juan occasioned one of the most virulent pamphlets written against Molière, entitled *Observations sur une comédie de M. intitulé le Festin de Pierre, par B.A. Sr de R[ochement], avocat en parlement*. Polemical tracts such as these, although masquerading as the work of a single individual, were often produced collectively, and the author may be considered to have been an unofficial spokesman for the Cabale des Dévots. This pamphlet is thus of particular importance since it rehearses for us the major arguments of Molière's adversaries.

De Rochement argued that he was defending the "interests of God", which Molière had "openly attacked". He claimed that Christians must be distressed at seeing the theatre "in revolt against the altar" and "farce at war with the gospel". He accused the play of "dragging into the gutter everything which is most saintly and sacred in religion". Molière had created a "School for Libertinage" and "visibly betrayed the cause of God by creating an occasion in which God's glory is visibly attacked". Using another theme popular with the anti-theatre party, the polemicist compared Molière to a serpent who poisons his spectators while making them laugh (the author appears to have mistakenly transferred to the serpent the legendary effects of the tarantula's bite).

Not content with attacking *Dom Juan*, de Rochement took advantage of the occasion to attack other plays by Molière, and in particular *L'École des femmes* (1662, The School for Wives). Even before *Tartuffe*, Molière had run into problems with this play, for which he was accused of immorality. About *L'École des femmes* de Rochemont wrote that "the malicious naiveté of his Agnès has corrupted more virgins than the most licentious written works". Molière was thus castigated as a corrupter of morals, and was held particularly responsible for undermining Richelieu's call, some 30 years earlier, for a purification of the theatre. In Molière's hands, theatre had once again become a "courtesan", a "coquette", and a "libertine", whose lascivious air and dissolute gestures were the opposite of the well-regulated modesty of honest women.

Although never formally banned, *L'École des femmes*, because of the character of Agnès, who was seen as a reprehensibly independent example for young French womanhood, caused Molière as many difficulties with the enemies of theatre as any of his plays. Well before *Tartuffe* and *Dom Juan*, this play defined him in the eyes of the moralists as a corrupter of morals and a dangerous influence on public behaviour. The Cabale des Dévots, which crusaded against theatre throughout the 17th century, often used Molière as its most persuasive

illustration of the impiety and infamy associated with both producing and going to the theatre. For example, the Prince de Conti, Molière's former patron and protector, in his *Traité de la Comédie et des Spectacles selon la tradition de l'Eglise* (1666), accused theatre of displaying "an open and unbridled immodesty", and used *L'École des femmes* as his specific example: "There is nothing more scandalous than the fifth scene of the second act of *The School for Wives*." Conti retained the image of a "school" when in the same text he accused Molière of atheism: "Is there a more flagrant school of atheism than *Dom Juan*?" Molière countered with his celebrated formulation that the purpose of theatre was both to please and to instruct. His detractors maintained that Molière's lessons were those of immorality and impiety.

Molière's reputation among the moralists for impiety, libertinage, immorality, and atheism was to remain throughout the century, even after his death. Thus Bossuet took Molière to task in his *Maximes et réflexions sur la comédie* of 1694, stating that Molière's plays were filled with impiety and infamy. Bossuet conceivably had Molière in mind too when he referred to a playwright "recently expired who still filled the stage with the most vulgar ambiguities ever to have infected Christian ears".

Bossuet's remarks show that Molière remained throughout the 17th century the primary example for the moralists of all that was pernicious and scandalous in theatre. He was indeed at the centre of a subtle struggle for power between throne and altar. Seen by his adversaries as one of the primary contributors to a monarchical program of festivals and spectacles which the moralist wing of the Church identified as a barely disguised counter-religion of a pagan character, intended to give the king an authority claimed by the church, Molière was threatened and harassed by their constant surveillance, a surveillance that could be evaded only by the subtle wit of the playwright and the frequent complicity of the monarch.

MICHAEL SPINGLER

Writings

Oeuvres complètes, edited by E. Despois and Paul Mesnard, 14 vols, 1873–1900
Tartuffe and Other Plays, translated by Donald M. Frame, 1967
Don Juan and Other Plays, translated by George Graveley and Ian Maclean, 1989

Further Reading

Gabaudon de Cortès, Paulette, "La Cassette de Monsieur Organ" in *La Fronde en questions*, edited by Roger Duchêne and Pierre Ronzeaud, Aix-en-Provence: Université de Provence, 1989
Howarth, W.D., *Molière: A Playwright and His Audience*, Cambridge and New York: Cambridge University Press, 1982
Mongrédien, Georges, *Recueil des textes et des documents du XVIIe siècle relatifs à Molière*, 2 vols, Paris: Centre National de la Recherche Scientifique, 1965
Mongrédien, Georges (editor), *Comédies et Pamphlets sur Molière*, Paris: Nizet, 1986

MONG TANG MUM (Looking from Different Perspectives)
Thai television programme, 1991–96

Although Thai television generally had a poor track record of encouraging political awareness and promoting free expression, one programme stood out from the rest before, during, and after the May 1992 events. This was *Mong Tang Mum*, a weekly panel discussion on Channel 11, hosted by Dr Chermsak Pinthong, an associate professor of economics at Bangkok's Thammasat University. The programme was first broadcast in July 1991, in the middle of the NPKC period: thus it was a child of dictatorship rather than of democracy, a deliberate attempt to stimulate public debate about pertinent issues of the day. Modelled on the BBC television programme *Question Time*, *Mong Tang Mum* was the brainchild of three Thais, Chermsak himself, leading journalist Peter Mytri Ungphakorn, and Abhisit Vejjajiva, a young Thammasat economics lecturer who subsequently became a Democrat MP and minister. The programme was produced by a team of academics under the auspices of the Creative Media Foundation. Each week, four prominent people took part in the discussion; unscripted questions were posed to the panel by a studio audience, who could then make their own comments on the replies. Though never confrontational in his manner, Chermsak ensured that participants were not allowed to dodge the issues. This was a radical departure from the traditional norms of Thai political television, according to which the politician was able to use the medium as a personal platform.

The programme received strong personal support from another Anglophile, Cambridge-educated premier Anand Panyarachun, but others in the establishment were less sympathetic. It was not long before right-wingers, soldiers and bureaucrats began to claim that the programme was biased against them. While those who making *Mong Tang Mum* disputed this charge, arguing that conservatives were welcome to advance their views on the programme, the values of *Mong Tang Mum* were clearly those of western-educated liberal intellectuals. For the Thai viewer, the sight of ordinary members of the public questioning senior figures – and challenging their replies – was a novel experience. *Mong Tang Mum* quickly developed a "cult" following, watched by many people who would never normally have switched over to Channel 11 at all.

The programme experienced its first serious crisis in November 1991, at the height of the uproar over the new constitution. On 26 November, Channel 11 director Wichit Wuthi-ampol announced that transmission of *Mong Tang Mum* would be stopped "for improvements to be made". Wichit went on to say that the programme had over-concentrated on "limited issues", and had failed to give specific information on the topics discussed. Clearly, Wichit was not acting on his own initiative, but under pressure from above. Deputy prime minister Pow Sarasin, in his capacity as head of the Broadcasting Directing Board, had earlier issued "advice" to all television stations, asking them to be careful not to invite party politicians to appear on programmes, since an election was not far off (though elections were not in fact held for another four months). In the event, *Mong Tang Mum* went back on air after a couple of weeks, by which time the new constitution had been successfully promulgated, and the political tension greatly eased. The reason for

the suspension was never clear: had Pow wanted the programme banned? or had Wichit over-reacted to a vague hint of displeasure from his superiors ? At the end of his first administration, Anand admitted that some people had wanted to ban the programme, but insisted that they were not members of his cabinet. All too often, censorship of Thailand's electronic media took the form of vague injunctions to station directors, along the lines of "Do as you think fit". At any rate, the ban on *Mong Tang Mum* produced an immediate clamour of popular opposition, testifying to the programme's success in promoting a climate of public debate.

When general Suchinda Kraprayoon succeeded Anand as prime minister in April 1992, *Mong Tang Mum* experienced a second crisis. It was clear that certain members of Suchinda's administration were extremely hostile to the programme: according to Chermsak, one prospective minister was threatening to have the show banned even before he had been officially appointed. On 20 April, the minister of the prime minister's office, Piyanat Watcharaporn, declared that "adjustments" would have to be made to *Mong Tang Mum*, in order to make it "more balanced". On 1 May, Chermsak was reported as having said that the programme had been under the scrutiny of a censor for the past two weeks. Nevertheless, *Mong Tang Mum* continued to appear in its usual format throughout the May crisis. On 24 May, however, after the violence of the previous week, the production team decided not to broadcast a new programme, screening a repeat instead.

Following the May 1992 events, threats to the future of the programme receded. All this was to change during a special edition of the programme broadcast on 25 June 1995, shortly before the 2 July general election. The participants on this edition were the leaders of various political parties, Thailand's prospective prime ministers. At one point, Chermsak asked Banharn Silpa-archa, leader of the Chart Thai Party and the front-runner in the election, to name some of the ministers he would like to appoint to his Cabinet. Superficially, this appeared to be a reasonable question, but Banharn's party contained virtually no credible figures since it was largely dominated by provincial gangsters. Banharn complained bitterly afterwards that Chermsak had been biased against him during the programme.

When Banharn became prime minister, he appointed Piyanat Watcharaporn as the minister responsible for overseeing Channel 11. Although admired by leftists for his strong anti-military stance in the 1970s, Piyanat had later become a pugnacious populist with a miscellaneous collection of private grievances. An old enemy of *Mong Tang Mum* from the Suchinda government, Piyanat brought in another former Suchinda apologist, well-known broadcaster Somkiat Onwimol (not coincidentally, a native of Banharn's own province of Suphanburi) to revamp Channel 11. This included axing the channel's most popular current affairs programme, *Mong Tang Mum*. According to Piyanat, Chermsak was becoming increasingly "violent" and "arrogant", though he did not elaborate on these allegations (interestingly, Piyanat himself had once lost his parliamentary seat after being expelled from the Social

Action Party and because of his aggressive personality, no other political party was willing to accept him as a member). According to Piyanat, *Mong Tang Mum* was like an "independent country", and too much freedom of this kind could damage society. The claims reflected a common Thai tendency to focus on questions of personality and style, which were irrelevant to the core issues of media freedom and open debate. Chermsak alleged that general Prem Tinsulanond, a former prime minister and close aide to the king, had been one of those instrumental in bringing about the programme's closure by lobbying donors to the Creative Media Foundation. *Mong Tang Mum* had succeeded in enraging a coalition of conservative forces, and made its final broadcast in February 1996.

DUNCAN MCCARGO

Further Reading

Fairclough, Gordon, "Shut Up or Shut Down: Government Pulls Plug on Current Affairs Show", *Far Eastern Economic Review* (29 February 1996)

McCargo, Duncan, "The Buds of May", *Index on Censorship* (April 1993): 3–8

Samudavanija, Chai-Anan, "Old Soldiers Never Die: They Are Just Bypassed" in *Political Change in Thailand: Democracy and Participation*, edited by Kevin Hewison, London and New York: Routledge, 1997

MONGOLIA

(formerly Outer Mongolia)

Population: 2,533,000	**Number of daily newspapers:** 4
Main religions: Tibetan Buddhist; Muslim	**Number of periodicals:** 30
Official language: Khalkha Mongolian	**Number of radio receivers per 1000 inhabitants:** 142
Other languages spoken: Kazakh; Turkic; Russian; Chinese	**Number of TV receivers per 1000 inhabitants:** 47
Illiteracy rate (%): 0.8 (m); 0.7 (f)	**Number of PCs per 1000 inhabitants:** 5.4

The Chinese constructed the Great Wall in the 2nd century BCE in an attempt to repel the Xiongnu, the direct antecedents of the Mongols. These same Xiongnu, known in the West as Huns, terrorized Europe some 600 years later under the leadership of Attila. At best, the Mongols were a loose confederation of warring clans who fought against each other while attempting to subjugate their neighbours. The lack of a centralized government precluded the necessity for any form of censorship.

Temüjin (1162–1227), leader of the Borjigin Mongol clan, was given the honorary epithet Genghis Khan (meaning "universal king") in 1206, after uniting most Mongol tribes under his leadership. Within 30 years, the Mongol empire stretched from the Caspian Sea in the west to the Yellow Sea in the east. Genghis Khan is perhaps usually considered a bloody warrior, yet from his capital of Karakorum he played the role of unifier. He promulgated a number of edicts, including the *Yasa*, a code that "enacted religious toleration, exempted the clergy of all faiths from taxation, forbade washing or urinating in running water, and prescribed the death penalty for spying, desertion, theft and adultery". The latter provisos of this code were deliberately ambiguous, and Genghis Khan had many of his citizens executed on suspicion or hearsay. Nonetheless, modern Mongolian historians, especially those operating within the Stalinist system, have continued to view Genghis in an overwhelmingly positive light.

Kublai Khan (1226–94), Genghis's grandson, established the Yuan dynasty and ruled over the whole of Mongolia and China from Dadu (present-day Beijing) from 1279. By the time of his death, the people resented the special privileges and exemption from taxes of the elite official class. Any attempt to speak out was, however, curtailed by immediate execution. The Mongols were driven out of China by the Ming dynasty in 1368.

In the mid-16th century, in an attempt to reunite the Mongol clans, the Altan Khan (1507–83) made Tibetan Lamaism the state religion of Mongolia. No deviance in religious belief was tolerated.

In the 18th century, Mongolia fell under Chinese rule. The emperors of the Chinese Qing dynasty grew despotic and corrupt. They exploited the people, levying exorbitant taxes and meting out brutal punishment for the slightest offence or resistance to authority. The 1911 revolution in China resulted in Mongolia declaring its independence with the establishment of a theocracy headed by the 8th Living Buddha (Bogd Haan) on 1 December 1911. China granted Mongolia limited autonomy through the Treaty of Kyakhta in May 1915.

A series of events resulting from the Russian Revolution of 1917 plunged Mongolia into 70 years of repressive socialist government. In 1919, a Chinese warlord dispatched troops to capture the Mongolian capital Ulaanbaatar. In February 1921, White Russian troops entered Mongolia at the request of the Bogd Haan to expel the Chinese. Although initially welcomed, these Russian troops soon became a ruthless army of occupation. The Mongolians requested the assistance of the Bolsheviks, who successfully re-captured the capital in July 1921.

A number of purges began among supposed "heroes of the revolution" following the declaration of the People's Government of Mongolia on 11 July 1921. Prime minister Dogsomyn Bodoo, leading official in the Mongolian People's Party, was executed in 1922, along with 14 other "dissenters", for engaging in counter-revolutionary activities and for advocating the restoration of theocracy. Bodoo had expressed his concern about the increasing presence of Russian troops. In August 1924, the party chairman Horloogiyn Dandzan denounced Russian influence at the 3rd Congress of the Mongolian

People's Party. He was promptly arrested and executed for advocating capitalism. At about the same time, Damdiny Sühbaatar, the minister of war, died of a mysterious illness at the age of 29. Horloogiyn Choybalsan, Sühbaatar's deputy, claimed that the minister had been poisoned by "enemies of the people" headed by Dandzan. These claims were refuted when it became clear that Choybalsan had designs on the leadership himself.

The Mongolian People's Republic was founded on 26 November 1924. Mirroring the events and policies of the Stalinist Soviet Union, in the late 1920s moves were undertaken to purge Mongolia of so-called "rightists". As a result, many party officials were exiled on trumped-up charges. The most important victim was the party chairman Tseren-Ochiryn Dambadorj, who was exiled to Moscow in 1928. Stalin himself is said to have selected Choybalsan as Mongolian leader in his place.

Stalinist politics continued to influence Mongolia into the 1930s. In 1932, the country embarked upon a disastrous scheme aimed at rural collectivization. Land was seized from landowners, primarily monks, and redistributed to the peasants. Over 700 people were imprisoned, murdered, or had their property seized. The resulting famine and concomitant popular rebellion in western Mongolia was brutally suppressed and scapegoats found *pour encourager les autres*.

By the end of the 1930s, "the final destruction of the Church was ruthlessly carried through, all opposition to subordination to the USSR was stifled, and the ranks of the party, government, army and intelligentsia were brutally and thoroughly purged". In 1937, Choybalsan's secret police descended upon the monasteries and arrested all but the youngest monks. Those arrested – some estimates put the figure as high as 17,000 – were either executed or died in Siberian labour camps. The monasteries were closed down, looted, and then burned. There were a number of reasons behind Choybalsan's purge of monks: their religious ideology was incompatible with Marxism; they could be sent to work in labour-intensive Siberia without damaging the Mongolian economy; they were celibate and therefore were not increasing the nation's population; and, quite simply, as monasteries had been the centre of traditional political and economic power, Choybalsan was merely eliminating the opposition.

By 1939, more than 27,000 people had been executed – almost 3 per cent of the entire population – in the purges to eliminate "rightist elements" and against religion. Among the prominent victims were the premiers Genden and Amar, who were executed in 1937 and 1939 respectively, and the minister of war, marshal Demid, who was poisoned while travelling by train to Moscow. As World War II broke out in Europe, Choybalsan had consolidated his power over Mongolia. Although he never viewed himself as a puppet manipulated from Moscow, he claimed that the party's enemies had been eliminated and the party had grown in strength "through the great aid of the Soviet Union . . . and thanks to the fatherly solicitude of the great Stalin".

Following Choybalsan's death in 1952, power passed to Yumjaagiyn Tsedenbal. In the Soviet Union, Khrushchev's criticism of Stalinist policy initiated a few years of comparative freedom. A similar thaw occurred in Mongolia with Tsedenbal condemning Choybalsan for his extremist policies. During the 1960s and 1970s, the Soviet Union consolidated its grip on

Mongolia, with at least the positive result of an increase in literacy rates and the use of technology.

Information on literary and other cultural censorship in Mongolia is scant. Much of the literature from the imperial period was oral and therefore difficult to censor. Many of the written documents of the oral legends were lost or destroyed during Mongolia's turbulent history.

During the period of Soviet domination from 1924 to 1990, the official literary line in Mongolia was but a regurgitation of the socialist realist dicta advocated in Moscow. This marked a complete break from Mongolian literary tradition. Any deviation from this line was discouraged. Tentative literary experimentation in the 1930s was halted in 1937 with the execution of S. Buyannemekh. In 1929, Buyannemekh had formed a Writers' Circle with the poet and novelist Byambin Rinchen, which advocated a literature that went beyond the black-and-white of socialist realism. Following his death, Buyannemekh's work was completely suppressed until his rehabilitation in 1962. Rinchen evaded the wrath of the Mongolian regime by appearing to toe the political line. Nevertheless, despite winning the nation's top literary prize in 1944, his script for the historical film *Tsogtu Taiji* was temporarily banned.

In 1973, at the 5th Congress of Mongolian Writers, the Central Committee of the Mongolian People's Party spelt out its preferred literary line: "The creation of works with a lofty ideological content which are artistically advanced, worthy of the heroics of socialist construction, and promote the education of the working people in a high political consciousness and communist morality, and boundless faith in Marxism-Leninism and the principles of proletarian internationalism." Such comments were not uncommon at literary congresses in Moscow or Beijing. At the congress, Byambin Rinchen was condemned by the leadership for publishing an article allegedly displaying "narrow nationalistic views" and praising "backward customs and habits". Rinchen had made the mistake of believing his Mongolian heritage to be more important than policies determined in Moscow.

At the 7th Congress of Writers in 1984, the official view was still that Mongolian literature was based on "socialist realism" and that its main task was "to raise the ideological and artistic standards and meet the people's ever-growing spiritual needs". A reiteration of the official line was thought necessary following the installation of Gorbachev and his more liberal policies in Moscow. Indeed, shortly before the Congress, the police ordered that all typewriters and duplicating machines be registered and certificated at local militia offices. This was clearly an attempt by the authorities to prevent the printing and circulation of *samizdat* literature.

Tsedenbal was forcibly retired as Mongolian president in 1984. He was replaced by Jambyn Batmönh, a reformist who criticized his predecessor for supporting an authoritarian government. Inspired by Gorbachev's policy of *glasnost*, Batmönh advocated *il tod*, a hastily conceived programme of reforms. In March 1990, a huge popular protest broke out in the square before the parliament building in Ulaanbaatar. Demonstrations and hunger strikes continued for days. The leaders of the protest were mostly young intellectuals who had spent time in eastern Europe. They urged the government to go beyond *il tod*, and to adopt real democracy.

By July 1990, Batmönh had been replaced by Gombojabyn

Ochirbat, who initiated Mongolia's first multiparty elections. In 1991, the country's name was changed from the Mongolian People's Republic to the Republic of Mongolia. A state committee was established to rehabilitate all the victims of repression, a process that had officially begun in 1956. However, between 1956 and 1990 only 5100 victims had been rehabilitated, whereas between 1990 and 1992 that figure rose to more than 22,000. Subsequently, Mongolia has passed a number of liberal laws protecting human rights – yet not all without incident. An "unofficial" hunger strike in April 1994 was used to force the government to enact a law guaranteeing the freedom of assembly.

As Buddhism once again became dominant, a 1997 law restricted the organized introduction of religions from abroad. Customs staff have impounded a number of Christian videotapes and 10,000 children's Bibles; the Bibles were released in January 1998.

The Mongolian language was traditionally written in a cursive vertical alphabet adopted from the Uighurs in the 13th century. In 1946, under Soviet influence, a resolution was passed by the Mongolian government to introduce the Cyrillic alphabet to transcribe the Mongolian language. This move effectively ruled out the use of the traditional script for all officially sanctioned and published literature. With the collapse of authoritarian rule in the 1990s, the new government began to advo-

cate the use of the traditional script. It is being taught in schools and it is hoped that full implementation can be achieved by 2005. Despite the move to rid Mongolia of many of the vestiges of Soviet dominance, many argue that re-adopting the traditional script may serve to isolate Mongolia even further.

DESMOND A. SKEEL

Further Reading

Akiner, Shirin (editor), *Mongolia Today*, London and New York: Kegan Paul, 1991

Bawden, C.R., *The Modern History of Mongolia*, London: Weidenfeld and Nicolson, and New York: Praeger, 1968

Bawden, Charles R., "Mongolian Literature" in *A Guide to Eastern Literatures*, edited by David M. Lang, London: Weidenfeld and Nicolson, and New York: Praeger, 1971

Becker, Jasper, *The Lost Country: Mongolia Revealed*, London: Hodder and Stoughton, 1992

Brent, Peter, *The Mongol Empire: Genghis Khan – His Triumph and His Legacy*, London: Weidenfeld and Nicolson, 1976

Bruun, Ole and Ole Odgaard (editors), *Mongolia in Transition*, Richmond, Surrey: Curzon Press, 1996

Dashpurev, D. and S.K. Soni, *Reign of Terror in Mongolia, 1920–1990*, New Delhi: South Asian Publishers, 1992

Sanders, Alan J.K., *Mongolia: Politics, Economics and Society*, London: Pinter, and Boulder, Colorado: Rienner, 1987

MONITOR
Indonesian weekly magazine, 1986–90

In April 1991 Arswendo Atmowiloto, editor of the weekly magazine *Monitor*, was sentenced to five years in jail for violating Article 156A of the Indonesian Criminal Code. This law, which relates specifically to religious sensibilities and offences, is one of a number collectively known as the *Haatzaai Artikelen* (The Spreading of Hatred Articles). These are a set of draconian libel and slander laws that are a relic of colonial times but have so far remained part of the repressive repertoire of all postcolonial Indonesian governments. *Monitor* had published the results of a poll of its readers' most admired figures, which placed the prophet Muhammad in 11th position, behind among others, the Indonesian president, Suharto (no. 1), Saddam Hussein of Iraq (no. 7), the pop singer Iwan Fas, and in 10th position, Arswendo Atmowiloto himself. The publication of the poll resulted in loud protests from sections of Indonesia's Islamic community, the ransacking of *Monitor*'s office, and finally the arrest and imprisonment of Arswendo himself. The way the *Monitor* affair was handled by the Indonesian government, the Kompas-Gramedia group (*Monitor*'s publishers), and Islamic groups provides a valuable window on to the problems of media and censorship in Indonesia.

Until its closure in October 1990, *Monitor* had been a remarkably successful commercial venture. It appeared under Arswendo's editorship in 1986, using the name and publishing permit of an earlier, unsuccessful magazine and achieving a large circulation by Indonesian standards (figures ranged between 470,000 and 720,000). *Monitor*'s format and style were tabloid and down-market, with salacious photographs,

film, and television gossip being its staples. Although this content may have offended some more conservative elements in Indonesian society, this played little or no part in the magazine's final demise.

Of greater significance was the perception among some Indonesian Muslim groups of government favouritism towards Indonesia's Christian and Chinese minorities. This factor affected both the Kompas-Gramedia Group, and Arswendo himself. Kompas-Gramedia is seen in the wider Indonesian community as representative of "Catholic" and "Chinese" interests. Arswendo, an indigenous Indonesian, is a Roman Catholic. This perception of Christian–Chinese advantage was further amplified by the relative weakness of the Islamic press in Indonesia at the time. In broader political terms, Muslim political organizations (like all other civilian political forces) had also been effectively tamed in Indonesia's carefully stage-managed political processes. These factors, along with the presence of an ageing president and an unclear succession, created in this restricted political system both a volatile opportunity and a potential political space for particular Islamic groups and individuals to gain some temporary political concessions.

The reaction of organized Islam to the *Monitor* poll was neither immediate nor unanimous. Direct action by Muslim groups grew in intensity over several days, culminating in the sacking of the magazine's office and Arswendo's being spirited away from the scene in a police vehicle to the safety of a police station. Arswendo was described as "the Salman Rushdie of Indonesia". While demands by some Muslim activists for harsh punishment to be meted out to Arswendo and his publishers grabbed the headlines, other Muslim leaders were more measured in their response, fearing a setback to the small signs of openness and democratization that were beginning to appear in Indonesian political discussion and mass media.

Indonesian government reactions to the affair grew in intensity and in the seniority of those involved. Government responses were largely reactive – suggesting it had not foreseen the depth of Muslim anger at the *Monitor* poll. The initial official response came from the Department of Information in the form of a strong warning to the magazine. This warning failed to assuage Muslim anger. Three days later, following a meeting with the president, the state secretary issued a statement condemning *Monitor*. Later that day, the Indonesian Press Council met and decided to withdraw *Monitor*'s publication permit – a decision assumed to have been at the behest of the president himself. On subsequent days, national figures from the president down issued statements condemning *Monitor* and calling for the full force of the law to be brought down on the offenders. This ultimately led to Arswendo being charged with various offences under Indonesia's Criminal Code and Press Laws.

The Kompas-Gramedia Group's response to the affair was revealing. Rather than rushing to defend either Arswendo or the principles of press freedom, the group acquiesced to the banning of the magazine and dismissed Arswendo from his many positions within the organization. *Kompas*, the group's flagship, even editorialized against *Monitor*. The company's reaction can be interpreted either as a recognition of the sensibilities at work in a complex society like Indonesia, or as a pragmatic attempt to limit potential economic and political damage to Indonesia's largest media conglomerate.

The *Monitor* affair points to the weak and fragmented state of Indonesian civil society, where principles of press freedom (regardless of religious or ethnic colouring) can be set aside for temporary sectional gains, and where the authoritarian forces in control of the Indonesian state can then claim to be working in the interests of the Indonesian people. Arswendo Atmowiloto was released from prison in August 1993. *Monitor* itself has not reappeared.

PAUL G. TICKELL

Further Reading
Asia Watch, "Monitoring the Opinion Polls", *Index on Censorship*, 20/1 (July 1991)

MONOPHYSITES
Christian dissidents, from 5th century

Monophysitism was the opposite heresy to Nestorianism. Whereas Nestorianism, exaggerating the theology of the Church of Antioch, emphasized the duality of divine and human natures in Jesus and led to a belief that there were two persons in Christ, the Monophysites exaggerated the Church of Alexandria's tendency to emphasize the divinity to the detriment of real human experience in Jesus, such as learning and suffering. Historically, the doctrinal disputes involving Monophysitism, such as those that culminated in the condemnation of Nestorius, were compounded by political hostilities, and, like the Nestorian debates, were exacerbated by the difficulty of expressing in Latin terminology a doctrine originally conceived in Greek.

After the council of Ephesus in 431, the patriarch Cyril of Alexandria, certainly himself holding Christ to be not only divine, but also fully human, with rational body and soul, was allowed to hold that Christ had a single *physis*, a word usually translated as *natura* in Latin. After his death, he was succeeded in 444 by Dioscorus, whose views were even more extreme. The episcopal succession at Constantinople, where the anti-Alexandrian Antiochene theology ruled, went in 446 to Flavian, who began by antagonizing the eunuch Chrysaphius, who dominated the emperor Theodosius and who was linked to the Alexandrian party through his godfather Eutyches.

Dioscorus, Eutyches, and Chrysaphius conspired at once to overthrow Antiochene theology, and to demonstrate that Alexandria, not Constantinople, was the second-ranking bishopric in the church. The Antiochenes saw the threat, but in 448 Eutyches attacked the doctrine of two natures, and successfully appealed against the ensuing condemnation by Flavian. When Dioscorus joined in the controversy, the emperor called a council (the so-called *Latrocinium*, or "Robber Council") to meet in August 449. The pope, Leo I (the Great), sent a letter (the "Tome of Leo") strongly attacking Eutyches's formula, "one nature after the union", taken from Cyril of Alexandria, but the council was controlled by Dioscorus, and it rehabilitated Eutyches, condemning Flavian and deposing other "Nestorian" defenders of the duality in Christ. Leo's Tome was not allowed to be presented at the synod.

Leo was enraged against the Alexandrians; and at the same time the emperor's sister, Pulcheria, favourable to the Antiochenes, regained ascendancy at court. Flavian's successor at Constantinople, although beholden to Dioscorus, also seized the chance to reassert Constantinople's second rank over Alexandria. When Theodosius died in 450, Pulcheria took control; she had Chrysaphius executed, Dioscorus deposed, and Eutyches declared a heretic and exiled. She then summoned the great council of Chalcedon in 451, which reversed the decision of the assembly of 449, received Leo's Tome, restored some Antiochenes to their former offices, and attempted to define the union of two natures in one person in Christ.

The formula was contested by the Roman legates who represented Leo, because it still allowed of a Monophysite interpretation. They also protested at the reassertion of the privileges of Constantinople, voted in their absence. Egypt and Palestine remained strongly Monophysite, and when the emperor Marcian died, the successor of Dioscorus at Alexandria was killed by the mob for his acceptance of the Chalcedon formula. He was replaced by an exaggerated Monophysite.

The process of reconciling Monophysites and Chalcedonians

took well over a century. Under the emperor Zeno, a formula of union was devised in 482. Known as the Henoticon, it condemned both Nestorius and Eutyches, explicitly approving Cyril of Alexandria's 12 anathemas against Nestorius, and was promulgated without specifically ecclesiastical involvement, on the authority of the emperor alone. Only the extreme Monophysites were left alienated, but the author of the document, the patriarch of Constantinople, had, to Rome's fury, entered into communion with the Monophysites without Rome's leave. The pope excommunicated him, together with the Byzantine emperor, opening a schism between East and West that lasted until 518.

The difficulty was as much political as theological. The emperor needed the loyalty of Egypt and Syria more than he needed the support of Rome and the West, while the pope needed to cultivate the Goth, Theodoric, who was an Arian, in order to retain his independence in the West. A desire for theological harmony ceded to more imperative political necessities. However, theological debate continued. Extreme Monophysites argued for the physical incorruptibility of Jesus's body even before the resurrection. Other Monophysites concentrated on demonstrating the incompatibility of Cyril's theology with that of Leo and Chalcedon, while the Chalcedonians attempted to show the opposite.

Justinian's ambition to reimpose Roman control in the West and in Africa depended partly on the acceptance there of Chalcedonian theology, which he therefore sought to promote in spite of the Monophysite sympathies of his wife Theodora. He attempted to reassure the Monophysites by persuading pope Vigilius to condemn proportions of some Antiochene theologians, however illogical it was to combine these condemnations with support for Chalcedon. Vigilius did condemn one Antiochene theologian and propositions from two others, but then changed his mind and withdrew the condemnations.

Another general council, Constantinople, had to be called in 553, but the Monophysites refused to be trapped by the anti-Antiochene condemnations, now formally passed, and surreptitiously created their own episcopacy. Like the Nestorians, they have survived in isolated pockets up to the present. The Syrian Jacobites, the Armenians, Copts, and Ethiopians all reject Chalcedon. Historically, a final attempt to reconcile the Monophysites was made when the emperor proposed a formula according to which Christ had two natures but only one will. The whole controversy was eventually swamped by the Islamic invasions of the 7th century, which concentrated Christianity in Western Europe, where the theology of Chalcedon was accepted.

ANTHONY LEVI

Further Reading

Chadwick, Henry, *The Early Church*, revised edition, Harmondsworth and New York: Penguin, 1993

Grillmeier, Aloys, *Christ in Christian Tradition*, 2nd edition, London: Mowbray, and Atlanta: John Knox Press, 1975–

Kelly, J.N.D, *Early Christian Doctrines*, London: A. & C. Black, and New York: Harper, 1958

Loofs, Friedrich, *Nestorius and His Place in the History of Christian Doctrine*, Cambridge: Cambridge University Press, 1914

Pelikan, Jaroslav, *The Christian Tradition*, vol.1, Chicago: University of Chicago Press, 1971

MICHEL DE MONTAIGNE
French essayist, 1533–1592

On 30 November 1580 Montaigne's books were seized in Rome to be "visited", as his secretary words it in the *Travel Journal*, by the censor. Among those books was the edition of 1580 (that is, the first edition), of his *Essays*. Four months later, on 20 March 1581, Montaigne remarked that his *Essays* had been "corrected according to the opinion of the learned monks". During the conversation that Montaigne had with the ecclesiastical authority and during a second interview on 15 April 1581, both of which are recorded in the same *Travel Journal*, the essayist was instructed to delete, before republishing his work, whatever he found either "licentious" or "in bad taste". More specifically, the Roman censor objected to Montaigne's use of the word "fortune" or chance; the naming of heretics in a list of good poets; excusing the Roman emperor Julian the Apostate; stating that persons who pray should be free of all vicious inclinations during the time of prayer; claiming that cruelty is anything that goes beyond simple death; and noting that children should be raised with the ability to do all things, both good and bad.

Montaigne never changed any of these statements. He continued to use the word "chance" (*la fortune*) rather than "providence"; he never retracted his view of Julian; he increased his condemnations of cruelty and the use of the rack; he even boasted that he stood his ground in Rome: "And I did not concede even to the magistrate that he was right to condemn a book for having placed a heretic among the best poets of this century."

He did, however, take greater measures to protect the heterodox passages in the *Essays*. In 1580 he had already given the innocuous title "A Custom of the Isle of Cea" to a very dangerously ambiguous essay on suicide that explicitly contradicts the *Catechism of the Council of Trent* of 1563, which formally proscribed suicide "without any exceptions". But now, having unquestionably noticed that the condemned passages were found in essays bearing direct titles that announced dangerous subject matter ("Of Presumption", "Of Freedom of Conscience", "Of Prayers", "Of Cruelty", and "Of the Education of Children"), he more frequently assigns these "façade titles" (titles that conceal more than they reveal about the subject matter of an essay), as in "Of Coaches", which contains a vivid condemnation of contemporary French politics both at home and in the New World, and "Of Cripples", which constitutes a forceful attack on cruelty, superstition, torture, witchhunting, and the death penalty.

In addition to the use of façade titles, before expressing unorthodox views, Montaigne now more often wrote precautionary prefaces ("I put forward formless and unresolved notions, as do those who publish doubtful questions to debate in the schools, not to establish the truth but seek it. And I submit them to the judgement of those whose concern it is to regulate not only my actions and my writings, but even my thoughts"); expresses rigid formulas of submission ("I hold it as execrable if anything is found which was said by me, ignorantly or inadvertently, against the holy prescriptions of the Catholic, Apostolic, and Roman Church, in which I die and in which I was born"); and sets up false dichotomies ("I do not teach, I tell"), all of which are designed to exculpate the narrator in advance for the heterodox views he is about to expound.

Montaigne's *Essays* were ultimately placed on the Roman *Index Liborum Prohibitorum* on 28 January 1676. Since the document, however, gives no explanation of why the *Essays* were placed on the Index, at least two interesting questions arise. First of all, why were the *Essays* not placed on the Index earlier? The soundest explanation seems to be that Montaigne's fideism – the grounding of faith in scepticism or the separation of faith and reason – was not originally deemed objectionable. The Roman censors of 1580–81 never even mentioned the "Apology for Raymond Sebond", where Montaigne extols the doctrine of Pyrrho. Indeed, fideism was to function for an extended period of time as an unofficial Catholic position against the faith in reason of the Protestants. One finds it still later in the works of Pierre Charron and Jean-Pierre Camus, both priests and disciples of Montaigne.

The second question, of course, is: why were the *Essays* put on the Index in 1676? Here a whole network of events, philosophical, theological, and historical, seems to converge to point a damning finger at Montaigne, whose *Essays* were now the breviary of libertines such as Saint-Evremond, and who was attacked in different camps for being a Stoic, an Epicurean, and a Pyrrhonian. More specifically, the rehabilitation of reason by Descartes seemed to undercut the fideistic viewpoint, while the Jansenists waged a veritable war against Montaigne. Pascal, for example, attacked his egoism, his Pyrrhonism, his pagan views on suicide and death. Arnauld and Nicole, too, in *The Logic of Port Royal* in 1666, proscribed Montaigne's Pyrrhonism, his *amour propre*, his Epicureanism, his libertinage, and his lack of repentance, finding in his work "a complete eradication of any religious sentiment". In addition, Bossuet in 1669 took issue with Montaigne for praising only our lower instincts, those that make us similar to the animals, without praising our higher instincts that lead us to God. Finally, in *Search For The Truth* of 1674, Malebranche underscores the danger of reading Montaigne because the pleasure one draws from him wakes up and fortifies the passions in an imperceptible manner. Once

more, he attacks Montaigne's "criminal vanity" and his sins against humility.

These attacks all took place between 1655 and 1674. It is also possible that the religious politics of Louis XIV played a role in the condemnation of the *Essays* in 1676. No edition of the *Essays* appeared in France between 1670 and 1723. Furthermore, if Montaigne's ideas on suicide played a role in the ultimate condemnation of the *Essays*, additional evidence points to the same decade as a moment of increased concern regarding "self-slaughter". Not only had Pascal underscored Montaigne's "pagan" views on "voluntary homicide", but the Jansenists, Descartes, Gassendi, and La Mothe Le Vayer had all condemned suicide which, in 1670, was outlawed by new and reactionary criminal ordinances.

Censored in 1580–81, the author of the *Essays* changed nothing of substance in the subsequent editions. His Pyrrhonism apparently kept him in good stead with the church well into the 17th century. The man who had had an audience with pope Gregory XIII on 29 December 1580 ultimately had his book condemned in 1676 under Innocent XI. When the Index was finally abolished on 14 June 1966, the *Essays* of Montaigne was still listed on it.

PATRICK HENRY

Writings

Essais, 1580, revised 1588
The Complete Works: Essays, Travel Journal, Lettters, translated by Donald M. Frame, 1957
The Complete Essays, translated by M.A. Screech, 1991

Further Reading

Bernoulli, René, "La Mise à l'Index des *Essais* de Montaigne", *Bulletin de la Société des Amis de Montaigne* (October–December 1966): 4–10
Bonnet, Pierre, "Les *Essais* à l'Index", *Bulletin de la Société des Amis de Montaigne* (October–December 1966): 11–12
Daniel-Rops, Henri, "Montaigne et l'Index", *Bulletin de la Société des Amis de Montaigne* (January-March 1959): 4–5
Frame, Donald M., *Montaigne: A Biography*, New York: Harcourt Brace, and London: Hamish Hamilton, 1965
Henry, Patrick, *Montaigne in Dialogue: Censorship and Defensive Writing, Architecture and Friendship, The Self and The Other*, Saratoga, California: Anma Libri, 1987
Popkin, Richard H., *The History of Scepticism from Erasmus to Spinoza*, revised edition, Berkeley: University of California Press, 1979
Sayce, R.A., *The Essays of Montaigne: A Critical Exploration*, Evanston, Illinois: Northwestern University Press, and London: Weidenfeld and Nicolson, 1972
Smith, Malcolm, *Montaigne and the Roman Censors*, Geneva: Droz, 1981

MONTENEGRO
See **Yugoslavia: Serbia, Kosovo, and Montenegro**

MONTESQUIEU (Charles-Louis de Secondat, baron de La Brède et de Montesquieu)

French philosopher and historian, 1689–1755

LETTRES PERSANES (Persian Letters)

Satire, 1721

Montesquieu was a political theorist whose works on constitutionalism and institutions have greatly influenced modern forms of democratic governance. He was an aristocrat and a magistrate, a landowner who studied law and was actively involved in the political and legal life of Bordeaux during his early adulthood. He is best known for his *De l'Esprit des lois* (The Spirit of Laws, 1748), where he advances his theory of the separation of powers, but the *Lettres persanes* is itself a powerful work and Montesquieu's first major text. Although both works were eventually put on the Catholic Church's *Index Librorum Prohibitorum*, *Lettres persanes* is the more significant in the history of censorship, because of Montesquieu's use of satire to put the censor off the scent of his penetrating criticisms of the Christian religion and French society.

The events in the *Lettres persanes* are set between 1711 and 1720, during the last years of the reign of Louis XIV and the subsequent regency of Philippe d'Orléans for the young Louis XV. At the centre of the work are Usbek and Rica, two Persians of high social standing who travel to Paris. In writing letters to each other and to their friends and family, the Persians criticize French society in acute and often humorous ways. Letters had been incorporated in numerous French prose romances of the 17th century. Other works, including La Bruyère's *Les Caractères*, had been written in the same vein of social satire as the *Lettres persanes*. And Montesquieu's book has been likened in some respects to *The Spectator*, the contemporary British periodical produced by Joseph Addison and Richard Steele.

Early in the *Lettres persanes* Montesquieu attacks regal figures and religious institutions. His character Usbek suggests that the king and the pope are magicians of persuasion. Usbek claims that France's king is full of contradictions, strange priorities, and suspect policies. Monarchy is "a violent state which invariably degenerates into despotism or a republic". Turning to theological matters, he asks: "Is it possible for those who understand nature and have a reasonable idea of God to believe that matter and created things are only 6000 years old?" The Catholic Church is severe in accusing and punishing heretics, Montesquieu intimates, while its theologians are a dense black mob forwarding unclear arguments and false conclusions. Montesquieu's Usbek admonishes those who hate and persecute people who do not conform to a particular religion, conceding that intolerance has lessened among Christians, but noting that the proselytizing spirit is still present. It is a spirit of dizzy madness, Usbek declares, the spread of which can only be regarded as leading to the total eclipse of human reason.

By putting these ideas into the mouths of Persian characters, Montesquieu distanced himself to a degree from his polemic. Montesquieu was also careful to have the first printing of the *Lettres persanes* released under the name of a non-existent publisher, with a false place of publication, and without an author's name anywhere in the edition. Censorship in France was carried out at that time under the crown's authority. Montesquieu's publisher had applied for tacit permission to distribute the book; this required that the book bear an imprint showing that it had been published outside of France. The censor neither granted nor opposed the request and this silence indicated to Montesquieu and his publisher that they could introduce the *Lettres persanes* to France without much risk.

The first pressing of the *Lettres persanes* was made in the Netherlands, whereupon it was snatched up quickly, living up to the expectation of Montesquieu's friend Pierre Desmolets that it would sell like bread. The book went through 10 printings in its first year of publication, with a new printing in each of the eight years that followed. The attendant fame drew Montesquieu to Paris. He stayed there on and off for six years, forming relationships with some of the great intellects of the day. Montesquieu was an aspirant to the Académie Française, but he had made fun of the Académie in the *Lettres persanes* and was considered by some to have written an irreligious book. The influential Cardinal Fleury had caught wind of the reputation of the *Lettres persanes* and could have opposed Montesquieu's election to the Académie. Montesquieu visited the cardinal to discuss the matter with him, convincing Fleury that the work was innocuous. He was elected to the Académie in late 1727, unopposed by the cardinal or Louis XV. He subsequently travelled for a few years before returning to France to write *De l'Esprit des lois*, which was put on the *Index Librorum Prohibitorum* in 1751. The *Lettres persanes* would suffer the same fate a decade later, but only after they had been widely read for years in France and abroad.

LUCAS A. SWAINE

Writings

Persian Letters, translated by C.J. Betts, 1973; reprinted 1993
Selected Political Writings, edited and translated by Melvin Richter, 1990

Further Reading

Harrison, Nicholas, *Circles of Censorship: Censorship and Its Metaphors in French History, Literature, and Theory*, Oxford: Clarendon Press, and New York: Oxford University Press, 1995
Shackleton, Robert, *Montesquieu: A Critical Biography*, Oxford: Oxford University Press, 1961
Shklar, Judith N., *Montesquieu*, Oxford and New York: Oxford University Press, 1987
Swaine, Lucas A., "The Secret Chain: Justice and Self-Interest in Montesquieu's *Persian Letters*", *History of Political Thought*, 22 (2001)

S.P. MOOKERJEE
Indian educationist and politician, 1901–1953

Shyama Prasad Mookerjee was elected to the Bengal Legislative Council in 1939 as a Congress candidate representing Calcutta University, under the provisions of the 1935 Government of India Act. In 1941 he joined the Progressive Coalition Ministry of Fazlul Haq as finance minister; he resigned from the ministry on 20 November 1942, emerging as a spokesman for Hindu opinion, organized separately from the mainstream of the Indian nationalist movement. He presided over the annual sessions of the All India Hindu Mahasabha in 1943 and 1944, and in November 1945 stood as a Hindu Mahasabha candidate for the Central Assembly. He died on 23 June 1953 while under detention in Kashmir.

Mookerjee was extensively censored during World War II under the Defence of India Rules, as a member of the Bengal Ministry, and as a member and later as president of the Hindu Mahasabha. His movements were restricted, his letters frequently opened as they passed through the Special Branch, a wing of the Intelligence Bureau of the Indian Police. Mookerjee's speeches and public statements against the government in the press did not escape censorship, and an interesting instance is provided by the censorship of his letter of resignation. In this letter of 20 November 1942 to Sir John Herbert, governor of Bengal, Mookerjee charged the British government with wishing to hold on to India at any cost, and objected to the government's repressive policy during the Quit India movement and the governor's interference in the working of the Bengal Ministry. He wrote, "India wants that she should be a free country and she should fight along with other free nations for the liberation of humanity against the onslaught of Axis Powers ... We want to be rid of alien rule altogether. We want this country to belong to and to be governed by ourselves."

Mookerjee drew attention to actions that had drastically affected the lives of the people of Bengal. One was the government's "denial policy", intended to slow down a potential Japanese invasion by removing sources of supply and transport in eastern India, which was leading to the suffering of thousands of people. The second issue was the suppression of the Quit India movement of 1942, which, said Mookerjee, had resulted in indiscriminate arrests, and assaults on innocent people, notably in Midnapore, "in a manner hardly creditable to any civilized Government". He compared repression in Midnapore to "the activities of Germans in occupied territories as advertised by British agencies. Hundreds of houses have been burnt down by the police and the armed forces. Reports of outrages on women have reached us. Moslems have been instigated to loot and plunder Hindu houses; or the protectors of law and order have themselves carried on similar operations." He also criticized the government's attempt to censor information about natural calamity in the region, following a devastating cyclone.

The resignation letter caused much consternation in government circles because it was directed at the British administration itself and had little to do with Fazlul Haq or his ministry. The viceroy stated that "in fairness to his colleagues as well as to the governor it would not be proper to publish Cabinet secrets" and that "the wise course would be for the governor to see Mukerjee and ... endeavour to dissuade him from publishing any portions, publication of which would be open to exception". The governor of Bengal wrote back to the viceroy that the ministers were against publication of the letter. Moreover, the press had been forewarned that publication of Mookerjee's resignation statement was to be undertaken at their own risk.

Mookerjee issued a statement to the press which was published in full in the *Amrita Bazar Patrika* and other papers on 24 November 1942. The governor of Bengal wrote to the viceroy after the publication of Mookerjee's statement: "The published statement omits some of the more noxious expressions which found place in the original draft, and this omission is due to the persuasion of Mookerjee's former colleagues." At the time of his resignation, Mookerjee wrote in his diary, the governor had been extremely anxious that correspondence between the two "should not see the light of day and he wanted an assurance from me to that effect".

Mookerjee's letters were published shortly afterwards but were proscribed by the government under the Defence of India Rules. During these years, the police confiscated letters at random and dispatched them after copying them verbatim, without the knowledge of the correspondents. Postal censorship under the Censorship Regulations of 1939, was concerned with "packets conveyed by the public posts", which included individual communications, private and commercial documents, printed matter, samples of goods, literature for the blind, insured boxes, and money orders. The authorities aimed "to stop all communications ... which are injurious to the national cause, more especially communications to and from the enemy", and "To collect information of value to the national cause from all communications subject to censorship or examination". Some of this correspondence was detained, deleted, or returned to the sender. Mookerjee was one of those whose letters were regularly processed for information.

SULAGANA ROY

Writings

Integrate Kashmir: Mookerjee, Nehru and Abdullah Correspondence, 1953
Leaves from a Diary, 1993

Further Reading

Bhattacharya, Sanjoy, "'A Necessary Weapon of War': State Policies towards Propaganda and Information in Eastern India, 1939–1945" (dissertation), University of London, 1996
Chatterji, Joya, *Bengal Divided: Hindu Communalism and Partition, 1932–1947*, Cambridge and New York: Cambridge University Press, 1994
Das, Suranjan, *Communal Riots in Bengal, 1905–1947*, Delhi and New York: Oxford University Press, 1991
Sarkar, Sumit, *Modern India, 1885–1947*, Delhi and Basingstoke: Macmillan, 1983; New York: St Martin's Press, 1989

GEORGE MOORE
British novelist and essayist, 1852–1933

In 1883 George Moore, newly arrived in London from Paris, published his first novel, *A Modern Lover*. In accordance with standard practice of the day, the novel, published by the small firm of Tinsley, was put out in three-volume form. At a guinea-and-a-half, the price was beyond most pockets, but the circulating libraries, chief among them W.H. Smith and Mudie's, operated a scheme whereby, for an annual fee of one guinea, subscribers could have access to any novels the libraries chose to buy. This meant, of course, that novels the libraries chose *not* to buy had virtually no chance of commercial success; and it inevitably followed that publishers were very unlikely to take on novels the circulating libraries would in all probability reject. Mudie's, who were the biggest and therefore most powerful of all the circulating libraries functioning in the latter half of the 19th century, were tender of their reputation for upholding respectable morality. They bought 50 copies of *A Modern Lover* but refused to circulate them after two ladies objected to a scene in which a young girl sits as Venus for the protagonist, Lewis Seymour, artist and hard-hearted seducer.

Moore's novel is modelled on French naturalist fiction, which he had come greatly to admire during his years in Paris. Such fiction had already established a bad name for itself in Britain, as had French art, of course: Ruskin had not long before emerged as moral victor from the libel case brought against him by Whistler. Whistler, Ruskin asserted, was a coxcomb whose especial impudence was to charge 200 guineas for throwing a pot of paint in the public's face. Whistler sued and for his pains was awarded a farthing damages: so much for French-derived impressionistic art. In 1898, that august journal, *The Nineteenth Century*, carried "A Familiar Colloquy on Recent Art" by W.H. Mallock, in which Gage Stanley, the spokesman for decent English values, attacked Swinburne for writing a sonnet in praise of Gautier's *Mademoiselle de Maupin*. According to Stanley, Gautier's novel is "the foulest and filthiest book that ever a man put pen to. It is the glorification of nameless and shameless vice". At which point a women friend interjects to say that "I never read *Mademoiselle de Maupin*; but my brother horsewhipped a man because he lent it to my sister."

It is hardly surprising that Moore's next novel, *A Mummer's Wife*, published two years later, would cause problems. Moore had anticipated as much and had cleverly offered it to a sympathetic publisher, Henry Vizetelly, who enjoyed taking risks. He was the English publisher of Zola, reckoned far more immoral than Gautier, and he outwitted the unofficial censorship of the circulating libraries by publishing in one-volume form and even in paperback. (His distinctive yellow-paper covers led to coining of the phrase "yellow-back publishing", applied to whatever was *risqué* or louche. He was at one point handed a term of imprisonment for publishing disreputable material.) *A Mummer's Wife* is about a woman who leaves her respectable marriage to go off with a troupe of actors. She becomes the mistress of one, sinks into alcoholism and prostitution, and dies. A moral tale, it might be thought. But Mudie's blacklisted the novel.

Following Mudie's handling of his first novel, Moore had written an article called "A New Censorship of Literature", which appeared in *The Pall Mall Gazette* for 10 December 1884. There, Mudie is attacked as "Mr. X", a philistine businessman solely concerned with the wishes of his clients. Earlier that year, Henry James had published his great essay on "The Art of Fiction", in which he had challenged the argument of the first president of the Society of Authors, Walter Besant, that writers should consider the needs of their readers. No, James said, a writer's sole responsibility is to his art. Moore agrees with James. He also announces that he intends to publish his next novel "in a cheap form and challenge a popular verdict". And he adds for good measure that *A Mummer's Wife* will be issued "at 6s.; 4. 6d. at a discount bookseller's – still too high a price, in my opinion, but undoubtedly a great literary improvement on the thirty-one-and-six system. I shall now, therefore, for the future, enjoy the liberty of speech granted to the journalist, the historian, and the biographer, rights unfortunately in the present day denied to the novelist."

With the blacklisting of *A Mummer's Wife* the novelist returned to the attack. In the summer of 1885 Vizetelly published, with a cover price of threepence, Moore's pamphlet, *Literature at Nurse; or, Circulating Morals*. Here, Mudie is explicitly identified as the powerful enemy of artistic freedom. He is, however, the friend of the British Matron and "The British Matron has the public by the ear, and her evidence on the subject of impure literature will be as greedily listened to as were her views on painting from the nude." "Greedily listened to" is a neat thrust: Mudie has no moral concern with impurity, Moore implies: he is solely motivated by avarice. Accordingly,

> although I am willing to laugh at you, Mr. Mudie, to speak candidly, I hate you; and I love and am proud of my hate of you. It is the best thing about me. I hate you because you dare question the sacred right of the artist to obey the impulses of his temperament; I hate you because you are the great purveyor of the worthless, the false and the commonplace; I hate you because you are a fetter about the ankles of those who would press forward towards the light of truth ... I hate you because you impede the free development of our literature.

Moore's best novel, *Esther Waters* (1894), describing the life of an unmarried mother, was, hardly unexpectedly, again excluded by Mudie's and Smiths.

It is difficult to be sure how to assess Moore's part in the declining influence of the circulating libraries. The three-decker novel was on its way out, and cheap publishing was bound to become more widespread. Nevertheless, Moore's attack is an important moment in the war between what Whistler called the British and the artists. And Arnold Bennett always regarded Moore as hugely important in freeing novelists from the yoke of "the British Matron". Writing in anger to Middleton Murry in 1924, in response to some disparaging remarks Murry had made about Moore, Bennett told him,

> All the younger generation owe a lot to G.M., who fought for a freer code & established a certain freedom

which you & others now enjoy – in deplorable ignorance of how you came to enjoy it. At any rate he is now over 70; he has always been absolutely unvenal; he has cared for nothing but literature; & I think he is entitled to some respect from serious persons – even if they are young.

Moore continued to be subject to censorship. *A Story-Teller's Holiday* was turned away by the US customs in 1929.

JOHN LUCAS

Writings

A Modern Lover, 1883, revised edition 1885; as *Lewis Seymour and Some Women*, 1917

A Mummer's Wife, 1884, revised edition 1886, 1917; as *An Actor's Wife*, 1889
Literature at Nurse; or, Circulating Morals, 1885; edited by Pierre Coustillas, 1976
Esther Waters, 1894, revised edition 1899, 1920; edited by David Skilton, 1983
A Story-Teller's Holiday, 1918; revised edition, 2 vols 1928

Further Reading
Owens, Graham (editor), *George Moore's Mind and Art*, Edinburgh: Oliver and Boyd, and New York: Barnes and Noble, 1968

MORAL PANIC

The term "moral panic" refers to the process in which public condemnation of a particular item or category of cultural products, or forms of behaviour, escalates to the point where authorities find themselves under considerable pressure to prohibit the article or activity in question. Since the 1970s the notion has come to be associated with the waves of concern about screen violence expressed by politicians, the press and others, which have led to often rather hurried and flawed attempts to control the distribution of the films or videos in question.

Stanley Cohen introduced the concept in his study *Folk Devils and Moral Panics* (1972), in which the moral panic is described as a situation in which

a condition, episode, person or group of persons emerges to become defined as a threat to societal values and interests; its nature is presented in a stylized and stereotypical fashion by the mass media; the moral barricades are manned by editors, bishops, politicians and other right-thinking people; socially accredited experts pronounce their diagnoses and solutions; ways of coping are evolved or (more often) resorted to; the condition then disappears, submerges or deteriorates and becomes more visible.

As a theoretical tool the idea of "moral panic" may lack real *explanatory* power, but it provides an uncanny description of the controversies over screen violence that have been seen in such countries as the United States, Britain, Canada, and Australia – although, contrary to Cohen's definition, the condition has shown little sign of disappearing. The consequences of such panics for the practice of censorship are widely recognized, but recent products of the concerns about screen violence include the British Video Recordings Act of 1984, and the "V-chip" legislation in the United States in 1996. Delays and cuts introduced by censors throughout the world can often be seen to result from moral panics, but this occurs most often in those countries where there is scope for vocal groups to feel that there is generally too *little* censorship in their society.

The case against there being any good evidence that the mass media can cause imitative behaviour – in any predictable sense, at least – has been forcefully argued by various commentators over the decades. However, many researchers, often from uni-

versity departments of psychology, have been equally resolute in their protestations that their studies *do* demonstrate the kind of causal link that is generally presumed by the agents of moral panic. The counter-argument is that only contrived or poorly-executed studies have actually suggested this: more careful, sociological and longitudinal studies have shown that fictional depictions of violence in the mass media cannot really be seen as causes of actual violence. Socio-economic, psychological, and developmental variables that are nothing to do with the media appear, in such studies, to be substantially better predictors of antisocial behaviour. Other research has suggested that the fears about young offenders being influenced by the media lack a basis in reality, as such criminals have less interest in, and less access to, such media than other young people.

Moral panics, unsurprisingly, are nothing new. Cheap novels, Victorian music hall shows, comics, jazz, and even bicycles have all been the subject of controversy in the past two centuries. In the more recent case of concern about the effects of screen violence, however, it has been demonstrated that both the moral panic, and the empirical research on that subject, have had unusually little to do with the supposed topic of concern. Instead, both the expressions of public disquiet and the reports of research findings feed into a "spiral of panic" that largely ignores any study of the actual depictions of violence. A particular panic may start to roll when a politician, critic, or "moral entrepreneur" publicly condemns some seemingly unprecedented example of depravity in the media. The condemnation is reported by the media, cultivating further expressions of concern, which leads to academic interest and research funded by broadcasters, governments or other bodies. The claims and findings of this research are then interpreted and reported by the media, and so may fuel more expressions of moral panic, leading to further (but usually similar) research, and so on. Studies that suggest that effects do occur are clearly more "newsworthy" than those that do not, and so more sophisticated academic approaches to the problem are unlikely to have the media impact necessary to halt the spiral.

Assumptions and fears about class also feed into these processes. The history of numerous censorship bodies has shown that cultural products that are seen as "artistic" works for a middle-class audience are much less likely to be considered for restriction than those more obviously aimed at a mass market – hence the hope of Penguin Books that they might be allowed to publish D.H. Lawrence's novel *Lady Chatterley's Lover* in the 1950s if they pledged not to release it in paperback, or the furore over a British video release for *Reservoir Dogs* in 1993, while the more violent but foreign and subtitled *Man Bites Dog* was uncontroversially released uncut at the same time.

DAVID GAUNTLETT

Further Reading

Barker, Martin (editor), *The Video Nasties: Freedom and Censorship in the Media*, London: Pluto, 1984

Barker, Martin and Julian Petley (editors), *Ill Effects: The Media/Violence Debate*, London and New York: Routledge, 1997

Cohen, Stanley, *Folk Devils and Moral Panics: The Creation of the Mods and Rockers*, London: MacGibbon and Kee, 1972; New York: St Martin's Press, 1980

Gauntlett, David, *Moving Experiences: Understanding Television's Influences and Effects*, London: Libbey, 1995

Gauntlett, David, "Ten Things Wrong with the 'Effects Model'" in *Approaches to Audiences: A Reader*, edited by Roger Dickinson et al., London: Arnold, and New York: Oxford University Press, 1998

Hagell, Ann and Tim Newburn, *Young Offenders and the Media: Viewing Habits and Preferences*, London: Policy Studies Institute, 1994

Klapper, Joseph T., *The Effects of Mass Communications*, Glencoe, Illinois: Free Press, 1960

Milavsky, J. Ronald, *Television and Aggression: A Panel Study*, New York: Academic Press, 1982

Pearson, Geoffrey, *Hooligan: A History of Respectable Fears*, London: Macmillan, 1983

MORAL REFORMERS AND PRESSURE GROUPS

This essay surveys a range of organizations in Australia, Britain, Germany, and the United States that, since the end of the 17th century, have been formed to defend a certain view of public morality, decency, and purity. Many of them have placed the censorship of obscene or violent material at the centre of their campaigns, leading their opponents to accuse them of prudery or "podsnappery", after Charles Dickens's *Our Mutual Friend* (1865). (This covers persons who, according to the *Oxford English Dictionary*, embody "insular complacency and self-satisfaction and refusal to face unpleasant facts".) Mostly influenced by evangelical Christianity in the 19th century but supported internationally by the Catholic Church in the 20th, "watchdog groups" claim to be acting in the interests of a better, more healthy society. They have had a considerable influence on governments, citizens, and media alike.

According to John Disney, a Nottingham vicar writing in 1710, "There is nothing we need to blush at in turning informers against Vice; 'tis an honourable undertaking, and cause of God, and whosoever is ashamed of it deserves neither the work nor the reward." He was a member of a Society for the Reformation of Manners, the first of which had been founded in London in 1690 under the patronage of Queen Mary. By 1700 there were 20 societies in London, 13 in Edinburgh, and 42 in the provinces, as well as outposts in Europe, North America, and the Caribbean. Centrally concerned with such matters as drunkenness and lewd talk, these groups also campaigned against theatres because of their capacity to encourage "prophane" behaviour. They influenced, for example, the prosecutions of the actors Thomas Betterton and Anne Bracegirdle, convicted of using the name of God as an expletive in William Congreve's *Love for Love* (1695), and Sir John Vanbrugh's *The Provok'd Wife* (1697). By 1738, they were claiming to have brought about some 101,683 prosecutions in London alone, the majority of which, it should be noted, were concerned with general behaviour rather than with the censorship of the theatre or literature. Few organizations devoted to moral reform last more than a generation – but, as will be seen below, new organizations with similar aims quickly arise to take their place.

William Wilberforce (1759–1833) lamented the disappearance of the Societies for the Reformation of Manners. Under his influence, and with the support of John Moore, Archbishop of Canterbury, George III issued on 1 June 1787 "A Proclamation for the Encouragement of Piety and Virtue and for Preventing and Punishing of Vice, Profaneness and Immorality". Specific reference was made to the need to suppress "all loose and licentious prints, books and publications, dispersing poison to the minds of the young and unwary, and to punish ... the vendors thereof". Wilberforce then followed up with the Proclamation Society, insisting that "it thus becomes to us, like the ancient censorship, the guardian of religion and morals of the public". Among his supporters was Beilby Porteus, bishop of Chester, already a bowdlerizer, and now particularly vigorous in the prosecution of "obscene libels". Many of these libels were said to be perpetrated in pornographic classics, such as John Cleland's *Memoirs of a Woman of Pleasure* (1748–49, generally known as *Fanny Hill*) and *A Dialogue between a Married Lady and a Maid*, for which the publisher, James Hodges, was convicted in 1780. Unlike its predecessor, the Proclamation Society's conviction rate was low, and, by the turn of the 19th century it had ceased active campaigning.

Its place was promptly taken by the Society for the Suppression of Vice and the Encouragement of Virtue, an altogether more effective body, which reflected the manners and morals of the emerging middle classes, and was active during the heyday of the circulating libraries. At this time, the central tenets of the Christian faith were being questioned, as in Thomas Paine's *Age of Reason* (1794–95), and as the population of British towns and cities grew, there were fears that their inhabitants would be corrupted by the increasingly ready availability of "licentious and obscene books and prints". Sydney Smith described the new moral watchdog as "a society for suppressing the vices of persons whose incomes do not exceed £500 per annum".

In its 1868 report, the "Vice Society" claimed that in 34 years it had been responsible for the destruction or seizure of 129,481 prints; 16,220 books and pamphlets; five tons of letterpress sheets; 16,005 sheets of obscene songs, catalogues, and handbills; 5503 cards, snuff boxes, and so forth; 844 steel or copper engraving plates; 428 lithographic stones; 95 woodblocks; 11 printing presses; and 28 hundredweight of type. This was an organization of considerable power and influence. If it was the courts that imposed the fines and prison sentences, it was the Society that selected the works to condemn, identified the people to be prosecuted, filed the charges, supplied the prosecuting counsel, and paid for the legal procedings. It even attempted to grapple with what would be the continuing ploy of pornographers – publishing the transcript of trials of "adultery, fornication and other criminal convictions", as in Alexander Hoff's *A New and Complete Collection of the Most Remarkable Trials for Adultery* in 1795. It almost certainly influenced the enactment of the Obscene Publications Act of 1857. Finally, however, it ran out of funds, and ceased its operation in 1870.

Its first US counterpart and namesake, the New York Society for the Suppression of Vice, was established on 16 May 1873, mostly through the energy of its secretary Anthony Comstock (1844–1915), said to have been personally responsible for the prosecution of 3500 individuals and the destruction of 160 tons of obscene literature in his 40 active years. The New York Society, like its British predecessor, influenced legislation, notably the 1873 act that banned from the mails "every obscene, lewd, lascivious or filthy book, pamphlet, picture, paper, letter writing, print or other publication of an indecent character". Again, the line between governmental and non-governmental action was blurred – Comstock could not arrest people, but police officers had a legal obligation to follow his directions. Comstock's notoriety soon led to the formation of similar "vice societies" in San Francisco, California and Portland, Oregon. The Western Society for the Suppression of Vice had its headquarters in Cincinnati, Ohio. The New York Society also put pressure for legislation against obscene material in Kansas, New Hampshire, and Vermont, among other states.

Meanwhile, in Britain, the National Vigilance Assocation (NVA) had stepped into the shoes of the Vice Society in 1885. With similar aims and a network of regional branches, it was in the forefront of campaigns against the "French novels" of the late 19th century, notably Émile Zola's *La Terre* (1887; published in English in 1895) and Guy de Maupassant's *Une Vie* (1883; as *A Woman's Life*, 1885), for which the British publisher, Henry Vizetelly, was imprisoned. In the regions, the Leeds Vigilance Association had the name of Dr Henry Allbutt removed from the medical register for publishing *The Wife's Handbook* (1886), which provided information about contraception. The NVA was chaired by the bishop of Southwell, Nottinghamshire, and included on its board an archbishop, three other bishops, and numerous clergy.

In Germany, at about the same period, the Morality Leaguers drew together a wide variety of groups ranging from the small Verein zur Hebung der öffentlichen Sittlichkeit (League for Raising Public Morality) in Munich to the Allgemeine Konferenz der deutschen Sittlichkeitsvereine (General Conference of German Morality Leagues). Here there was considerable emphasis on gaining political power and influence in pursuit of their aims; Hermann Rösen founded a Sittlichkeitverein in Cologne in 1898 and went on to support censorship statutes as a legislator. The founder of the Münchener Mannverein zur Bekämpfung der Öffentlichkeit (Munich Men's League for Combatting Public Immorality), Armin Kausen, followed the examples of Comstock and the NVA, taking out private prosecutions against particular books.

The Jugendbewegung was an institution peculiar to Germany. It had similar aims to all the other "watchdog groups" so far mentioned, but its members were all school and college students, 100,000 of whom met in Thuringia in 1920 to discuss the possibility of making the movement international. They condemned smoking and drinking, posted protests against films and plays they opposed, and organized burnings of juvenile fiction they disapproved of. In 1926, they worked for the Schund- und Schuttgesetz, the Literary Trash and Filth Law. From that, it was but a short step to the Hitler Youth, membership of which was compulsory from 1933.

In Britain, the NVA had been joined by the Public Morality Council (PMC) and the National Council of Public Morals (NCPM), formed in 1900 to combat prostitution and promote sexual purity. The council, under the bishop of London, A.F. Winnington-Ingram, was notable for its opposition to sex-education manuals and working-class entertainments (music halls and tableaux vivants). In 1915, by contrast, D.H. Lawrence held it responsible for the censorship of *The Rainbow*; it certainly sought – unsuccessfully – for the suppression of Aldous Huxley's *Point Counter-Point* in 1929.

In Australia, meanwhile, the Catholic Federation had established an Indecent Literature Committee following some of the same lines as their British predecessors, but also demanding the suppression of books "harmful to faith and morals", by which they meant anti-Catholic literature, such as Charles Chiniquy's *The Priest, the Woman and the Confessional* (1880). Now caught up in an unseemly argument with their Protestant brethren, the Committee left the field of literature for that of dirty postcards. The Australians would later call all such groups "wowsers".

In the US, Anthony Comstock had developed the most powerful non-governmental censorship group in the world. His successor, John Sumner, presided over its decline. First the Society for the Suppression of Vice began to lose cases – for example against Théophile Gautier's *Mademoiselle de Maupin* (first published in 1835) in 1917. In October 1922, a judge took pains to praise the "unusual literary merit" of James Branch Cabell's *Jurgen and the Censor* (1920). Sumner similarly failed to persuade the Authors' League and 20 leading publishers of the usefulness of his idea that a panel of 500 citizens should be formed from which "book juries" would be selected to approve, expurgate, or reject manuscripts submitted to the publishers. Sumner then formed the Clean Books League (1923), made up of religious leaders, including from the Salvation Army and the Manhattan Free Synagogue. Seeking to reverse recent legal decisions, they proposed a statue that would have allowed an indictment on only part of a book, banned the use of expert witnesses in any case brought against a book, and made possible the censorship of "filthy" and "disgusting" books even if they were not sexually stimulating. The proposal was voted down in the state legislature and the Clean Books League had disappeared by 1929.

A similar organization, The Watch and Ward Society, was founded in Boston in 1891. In 1915, it joined forces with booksellers to form the Boston Booksellers Committee, which examined new books and made recommendations. If they condemned a book, it was not reviewed, and newspapers would refuse to advertise it. If an individual bookseller rebelled, the Watch and Ward Society would seek prosecution. Within ten years, the

Committee had been responsible for the suppression of nearly 70 works, including Theodore Dreiser's *An American Tragedy* (1925), William Faulkner's *Mosquitoes* (1927), Ernest Hemingway's *The Sun Also Rises* (1926), and Sinclair Lewis's *Elmer Gantry* (1927). The phrase "Banned in Boston" entered the language. When, however, the hubris of the Watch and Ward Society became conspicuous (it tricked the proprietor of the Dunster House Bookshop, James Delacy, into selling a copy of *Lady Chatterley's Lover* (1928), causing his prosecution and mental breakdown), the group lost any moral authority it had, and it too had to leave the field.

An Australian Protestant group, the Council for Civil and Moral Advance, formed in 1919, was one of the first watchdog groups to take note of the cinema, and especially of cinema advertisements, which they wanted regulated. When this campaign failed, the group went into decline. The Legion of Decency, formed in 1933 by the Roman Catholic Church in the US to monitor films, was both long-lasting and influential. It was the first of 42 Catholic film offices around the world. The legion had a central role in the drafting of the Production Code of the Motion Picture Association of America. It still exists, but its influence beyond the Catholic world in a wholly changed moral world is now minimal.

In Britain the moral changes of the 1960s provoked a considerable backlash, and the arrival of a new generation of watchdog groups. In January 1964, Mary Whitehouse formed the Clean Up TV Campaign (CUTV), which, within six months, had produced a manifesto that was signed by 250,000 and aimed at the revival of the "militant Christian spirit", which would attack television programmes containing "sexy innuendoes, suggestive clothing and behaviour; cruelty, sadism and unnecessary violence . . . excessive drinking and foul language; undermining respect for law and order; unduly harassing and depressing themes". Despite its following, the CUTV was regarded as too negative and soon transformed itself into the National Viewers and Listeners Association (NVLA), aiming to "ascertain and collate public opinion on radio and television items and bring positive and constructive criticisms, complaints and suggestions" to a proposed Viewers and Listeners Council. Despite the positive noises, NVLA continued to attack individual TV programmes, with Mrs Whitehouse a national figure until at least the 1980s, not confining herself to television. In 1971, the Festival of Light, supported by well-known figures such as Lord Longford, Malcolm Muggeridge, broadcaster and recently converted Christian, the singer Cliff Richard, and Trevor Huddleston, bishop of Stepney, made a brief, spectacular appearance in a campaign of social purification. Some of its members prophesied the imminent end of the world if Britain did not purge itself of obscenities; when this did not take place, the festival itself went into decline (its Australian counterpart continues a "non-denominational Christian ministry which promotes family values"). Since the 1970s, moral watchdogs have struggled to make a similar impact, although Mrs Whitehouse's personal efforts produced the Protection of Children Bill (1977). Her campaign against the National Theatre's production of *The Romans in Britain* (1980), on the other hand, was a costly failure and damaging to her more general cause. Nearly 20 years after the formation of the Clean Up TV Campaign, an American equivalent with the same name was established in 1978 "to insist that television programs be reviewed so that they are no longer an insult to decency and a negative influence on young people".

It is indeed to the US that we must mostly look for continuing evidence of the ability of watchdog groups to promote their moral agendas. The National Office for Decent Literature, sister organization of the Legion of Decency (founded in 1938), examined and listed works that offered the by-now familiar gamut of "objectionable" features (indecency and blasphemy). In 1956, Charles Keating founded Citizens for Decent Literature, which, within four years, could mount a national conference attended by 400 delegates from 18 states. It continued under different names – Citizens for Decency through Law, the National Coalition against Pornography, the Children's Legal Foundation – for the rest of the 20th century. In 1990, it cooperated with Citizens for Community Values of Cincinnati in a campaign for the closure of a notorious exhibition of photographs by Robert Mapplethorpe, *The Perfect Moment*.

Among the many prominent opponents of Mapplethorpe's work was the American Family Association (AFA), run by the Reverend Donald Wildmon, a United Methodist minister. Its purpose is to promote "traditional family values, primarily on the influence of television and other media – including pornography". At its height, when Ronald Reagan was US president, the AFA engaged in a massive fundraising campaign using "immoral art" as a starting point; in 1990, it supported its work with revenues of $6 million, way beyond the resources of previous moral pressure groups. It promoted boycotts of companies that sponsored television programmes it had condemned, and claimed to have caused the American Broadcasting Corporation to lose about $1 million per episode of *NYPD Blue*, and to have caused Pepsi to drop sponsorship of a world tour by Madonna.

Other moral pressure groups have attacked violent videos (The Movement for Christian Democracy, under David Alton in Britain) and violent music (the Parents' Music Resource Center, under Tipper Gore and other wives of leading politicians in the US). It seems likely that new groups will arise to campaign against pornographic websites. These pressure groups have all the defects of other single-issue campaigners, and they do tend to die away when they run out of steam rather than because they have fully achieved their goals – which, in the nature of the case, is impossible. Politicians have often used them as allies in wider programmes, but they are also wary of adopting all the campaign goals of moral pressure groups in the knowledge that, in pluralistic societies, what they gain in the moral sphere they may lose in the political one.

DEREK JONES

THOMAS MORE
English writer and public servant, 1478–1535

Thomas More is one of the most celebrated among the many victims of the repression of individual conscience in Tudor England. He died proclaiming that he had been "the king's good servant, but God's first". However, his status as a martyr (at least among Catholics) should not obscure the fact that he was a severe opponent of contemporaries whose consciences had led them in different directions, and – at the very least – he did not intervene to stop their imprisonment and execution. In the words of one of the leading British historians of Tudor England, G.R. Elton, "tolerance he would have abominated as treason to God".

As a student at Oxford from 1492 to 1494, More came into contact with the "New Learning", meeting the humanists John Colet and Erasmus, and studying Greek, Latin, French, theology, and music. Then, between 1501 and 1505, in the words of William Roper, his contemporary and biographer, "he gave himself to devotion and prayer in the Charterhouse of London, religiously living there without vow about four years". His preference for the austere, traditional observance of the London Carthusians, many of whom later also died as martyrs, is telling. When it came to the abuses of the church – the existence of which he did not deny – More preferred a purification of the time-honoured ways of Catholicism, rather than attempts to remove them.

More was first elected to parliament in 1504 and became under-sheriff of London in 1510. He then turned his attention to literary and philosophical matters, publishing his most famous work, *Utopia*, in Latin in 1516. Returning to public service, he became a councillor to the young king Henry VIII, his unofficial secretary and, in 1525, chancellor of the Duchy of Lancaster. These were the years of Henry's enthusiastic support of Catholic orthodoxy: for his tract *Assertio septem sacramentorum* (1521, Assertion of the Seven Sacraments) attacking Martin Luther and praising Pope Leo X, he was awarded the title "Defender of the Faith" (which has been retained by English and British monarchs ever since). Some scholars have claimed that More actually wrote the *Assertio*, but he admitted only to having helped Henry to organize its contents. We may in any case assume that, as the king's collaborator, More supported the burning of Luther's books, which took place during this period.

However, More was perhaps more suited to being a polemicist than to service as an active scourge of heretics. When Luther responded with his *Contra Henricum regem Angliae* (1522, Against Henry, King of the English), it was More who wrote a *Responsio ad Lutherum* (Response to Luther), a violent and sometimes crude attack, not only on Luther, but on other persons and ideas that challenged the authority of the church. In language worthy of Luther himself at his worst, More described the reformer as speaking with a "beshitted tongue", best suited to lick "the very posterior of a pissing she-mule". Inadvertently, however, as Richard Marius has pointed out, More's printers, by setting Luther's words in block type, drew attention to them, and, ironically, provided a text of Reformation ideas that their supporters could possess without incurring

the wrath of the authorities. Nevertheless, according to William Roper, More was so effective "in setting forth of divers profitable words in defence of the true Christian religion against heresies secretly sown abroad in the realm" that the English bishops in Convocation voted him "a sum of four or five thousand pounds at least, to my remembrance, for his pains to recompense". More declined the offer.

According to Christopher Haigh, "after More became [Lord] Chancellor, in October 1529, the emphasis shifted from burning books to burning those who bought them and those who held to their ideas". We cannot say that he was in any way directly responsible for these executions, since the lord chancellor was responsible for the proper conduct of the secular rather than the ecclesiastical courts. However, we know that he was aware that they were taking place, and as an orthodox Catholic of his time he cannot be entirely absolved of helping to create the climate in which they could take place.

We also know that in some cases More was somewhat more than peripherally involved. Thomas Bilney, an earlier supporter of Luther, had recanted in 1527, but, troubled by his conscience, he set out again in 1531, walking through Norfolk distributing copies of William Tyndale's banned translation of the New Testament and preaching against images. The relapsed heretic was again brought to trial and was sentenced to execution; he is said to have quietly recanted once more at the stake. As a lawyer and a Christian, More may (or may not) have been disturbed at the thought that an innocent man might have gone to his death. He instituted a Star Chamber investigation, which concluded, first, that Bilney had been properly tried, but, secondly, that he had indeed recanted. More's self-exculpating version of the event is contained in his *The Confutation of Tyndale's Answer* (1532–33).

It was also in 1531 that an attempt was made in parliament to secure the release of Thomas Patmore, who had been imprisoned on the orders of the bishop of London, John Stokesley, earlier that year for preaching and publicizing the forbidden works of William Tyndale. According to Patmore's servant, More quashed the effort on the grounds that, because he was a heretic, it was entirely proper that Patmore should be in prison.

In both these cases, More certainly appears to have shown a greater concern for the letter of the law than for individual conscience. So far as other cases of the persecution of heretics are concerned, evidence for More's complicity is not conclusive, but some have argued that on more than 20 occasions More used his influence to ensure that Lutherans were imprisoned.

More's own steadfast adherence to the truth as he saw it appears not to be in any doubt (at least within the limits of the available evidence for what might have been going through his mind). Unable to support Henry VIII's divorce from Catherine of Aragon and the declaration of the English church's independence from Rome, More resigned the chancellorship on 16 May 1532. He could not sign the statement that Henry's first marriage was "against the laws of Almighty God", and refused to sign the succession oath: "Unto that oath that was offered me I could not swear, without [jeopardizing] of my soul to perpetual damnation". More, ready to suffer "in and for the faith of the holy Catholic Church", was beheaded on 22 June 1535.

ANDREW ROBERT WINES

Writings

A Dialogue Concerning Heresies and Matters of Religion, 1528; edited by Thomas Lawler *et al.*, 1981
A Dialogue of Images, Praying to Saints, Other Things Touching the Pestilent Sect of Luther and Tyndale, 1529
A Confutation of Tyndale's Answer, 1532; 2nd part 1533
The Answer to the Poisoned Book Which a Nameless Heretic Has Named the Supper of the Lord, 1534

Complete Works (Yale edition), edited by R.S. Sylvester *et al.*, 1963–
Responsio ad Lutheram, edited by J.M. Headley, 1969

Further Reading

Elton, G.R., "Sir Thomas More and the Opposition to Henry VIII", *Bulletin of the Institute of Historical Research*, 41 (1968): 19–34
Marius, Richard, *Thomas More: A Biography*, New York: Knopf, 1984; London: Dent, 1985
Roper, William, "The Life of Sir Thomas More" in *Two Early Tudor Lives*, edited by Richard S. Sylvester and Davis P. Harding, New Haven, Connecticut: Yale University Press, 1962

MORMONISM
Church of Jesus Christ of Latter-Day Saints

In 1827 Joseph Smith, Jr, a young farmhand and visionary, announced that he had discovered a set of golden tablets on which was written the Book of Mormon (published 1830). The tablets, translated from "Reformed Egyptian" by Smith, recalled the legend of the lost tribes of Israel who came to the US and established a Christian civilization, only to be exterminated by hostile natives.

In April 1830 Smith acted upon his belief that God had selected him for a special purpose by founding the Church of Jesus Christ of Latter-Day Saints. Unfortunately for Smith's followers, scornfully called Mormons by outsiders, their attempts to institute a government in which the godly ruled ran counter to the democratic pluralism of American society. As a result, non-believers persecuted Mormons wherever they ventured. Hostile mobs drove the Saints from western New York to Kirtland, Ohio, and from Ohio to Jackson County, Missouri. After riots erupted throughout northwestern Missouri in 1838, the governor, Lilburn Boggs, announced that "the Mormons must be treated as enemies and must be exterminated or driven from the state".

Persecuted Mormons fled the state and created the settlement of Nauvoo, Illinois. Once again, however, the "gentiles" gradually grew weary of the Saints' political and economic clout. To make matters worse, rumours of polygamy outraged Nauvoo's neighbours and some Mormons. Those opposed to plural marriages responded by establishing a newspaper, the *Nauvoo Expositor*. The first issue of the opposition paper, published on 7 June 1844, alleged that Joseph Smith was a fallen prophet. Smith, charging libel, directed the town marshal to destroy the "public nuisance".

Word of the subsequent riot and destruction of the *Nauvoo Expositor* enraged Smith's opposition. Hoping to avoid violence, Smith and three others surrendered to the authorities on the charge of inciting a riot after state officials promised them protection. On 27 June 1844 an angry mob stormed the Carthage jail and murdered Joseph Smith. The majority of Mormons, hoping to avoid continued persecution, believed that they could ensure their religious independence and safety only by leaving the United States. Brigham Young, head of the Quorum of the Twelve Apostles, led the exodus to the sunscorched plains of northern Utah where the Latter-Day Saints set to work erecting the kingdom of God.

In 1849 the Mormon pioneers created the State of Deseret with Brigham Young as governor and applied for admission to the Union. Congress, wary of establishing a Mormon theocracy, rejected the application, preferring instead to create the Utah Territory in 1850. Although Utah residents could select their own governor, political and judicial officers were appointed in Washington. As a rule, Mormons refused to cooperate with these "outsiders", who denounced many of their beliefs. In 1857 repeated cries of Mormon lawlessness forced president James Buchanan to declare that "a state of substantial rebellion" existed in the territory. Buchanan responded to the crisis by dispatching soldiers to seize control.

Federal lawmakers were also determined to stamp out polygamy in the western territories. In 1862 Congress passed a law making bigamy in a territory a crime punishable by a fine and a prison sentence. Realizing that proving cohabitation was easier than obtaining testimony about Mormon wedding ceremonies, lawmakers later enacted the Edmunds Act, a law of 1882 that made bigamous cohabitation a misdemeanour charge and barred people living in polygamy from jury service, public office, and voting. Some 1300 Mormons defied the law and went to jail. Legal attacks against the Mormon faithful culminated with the Edmunds–Tucker Act of 1887. This legislation authorized the seizure of church property not directly used for religious purposes, disincorporated the church, placed regulation of elections in the territory in the hands of a presidential commission, and disenfranchised Mormon women. In the Idaho Territory a test oath of 1885 banned Mormons (and former Mormons) from voting because of the church's position regarding polygamy. After a long legal battle involving First Amendment freedoms, the Supreme Court of the United States ruled in 1890 that both the confiscation of church property under the Edmunds–Tucker Act and the Idaho test oath were legal. President Wilford Woodruff, realizing the futility of further resistance, responded to the court's ruling by abolishing polygamy. As a result, political persecution of the Mormons subsided, confiscated church property was returned, Utah became a state, and the Latter-Day Saints prospered.

While the church continues to grow rapidly (it currently has more than 10 million members), Mormon leaders have taken an uncompromising stand against the influence of "so-called intellectuals", feminists, homosexuals, and other dissenters within the church. "Like the high priests of old", notes Malcolm Thorpe, a history professor at Brigham Young University, "the traditionalists would exclude from the temple all who do not understand Mormonism in quite the same way as they do." The church even employs a Members Committee to monitor the speeches, writings, and activities of those suspected of undermining the doctrinal purity of Mormonism. Although Mormon leaders have excommunicated controversial members in the past, including the famous historian Fawn McKay Brodie and the feminist Sonia Johnson, recent developments seem to indicate that an orchestrated purge is under way.

In 1993 church courts excommunicated five outspoken dissidents, including thinkers on the ultra-liberal and ultra-conservative fringes of the church. D. Michael Quinn, a former history professor at Brigham Young University, was excommunicated after a long battle with individuals who wanted to control and sanitize the church's history by restricting access to its records and censoring historians who explored controversial themes or advanced alternative interpretations from those of the accepted story. Quinn commented: "I find it one of the fundamental ironies of modern Mormonism that the general authorities who praise free agency, also do their best to limit free agency's prerequisites – access to information, uninhibited inquiry, and freedom of expression."

Another dissident, Maxine Hanks, was excommunicated for her outspoken feminist views. Hanks ran foul of church elders when she turned to the "public marketplace of ideas" with her book *Women and Authority: Re-Emerging Mormon Feminism* (1992). Hanks, who ignored orders from church leaders not to speak publicly about Mormon feminist issues, believes that her excommunication was a small price to pay for her voice. The recent excommunications, instead of silencing the dissenters, have helped to increase the visibility and discussion of controversial topics.

Jon L. Brudvig

Further Reading

Anderson, Robert D., *Inside the Mind of Joseph Smith: Psychobiography and the Book of Mormon*, Salt Lake City, Utah: Signature, 1999

Arrington, Leonard J. and Davis Bitton, *The Mormon Experience: A History of the Latter-Day Saints*, 2nd edition, Urbana: University of Illinois Press, 1992

Bitton, Davis, and Maureen Ursenbach Beecher (editors), *New Views of Mormon History: A Collection of Essays in Honor of Leonard J. Arrington*, Salt Lake City: University of Utah Press, 1987

Bringhurst, Newell G. (editor), *Reconsidering No Man Knows My History*, Logan: Utah State University Press, 1996

Brodie, Fawn M., *No Man Knows My History: The Life of Joseph Smith, the Mormon Prophet*, revised edition, New York: Knopf, 1971

Givens, Terryl L., *The Viper on the Hearth: Mormons, Myths, and the Construction of Heresy*, New York: Oxford University Press, 1997

Hanks, Maxine (editor), *Women and Authority: Re-Emerging Mormon Feminism*, Salt Lake City, Utah: Signature, 1992

Hansen, Klaus J., *Mormonism and the American Experience*, Chicago: University of Chicago Press, 1981

Launius, Roger D. and Linda Thatcher (editors), *Differing Visions: Dissenters in Mormon History*, Urbana: University of Illinois Press, 1994

Quinn, D. Michael (editor), *The New Mormon History: Revisionist Essays on the Past*, Salt Lake City, Utah: Signature, 1992

Quinn, D. Michael, *Early Mormonism and the Magic World View*, revised edition, Salt Lake City, Utah: Signature, 1998

Shipps, Jan, *Mormonism: The Story of a New Religious Tradition*, Urbana: University of Illinois Press, 1985

Smith, George D. (editor), *Faithful History: Essays on Writing Mormon History*, Salt Lake City, Utah: Signature, 1992

MOROCCO

Population: 29,878,000	**Number of daily newspapers:** 22
Main religions: Muslim; Christian; Jewish	**Number of radio receivers per 1000 inhabitants:** 247
Official language: Arabic	**Number of TV receivers per 1000 inhabitants:** 115
Other languages spoken: Berber; Spanish; French	**Number of PCs per 1000 inhabitants:** 2.5
Illiteracy rate (%): 38.1 (m); 63.9 (f)	

"The Maghrib is the country of the setting sun. In *The Arabian Nights*, the Maghribians were users of magic, of everything that Islam forbids and bans." The sociologist Fatima Mernissi thus suggests that Morocco's difference from other Islamic countries in the region may be due in part to its Berber heritage – "before the Arab conquest, we spoke a different language, and had different cults and rites". From a strong and self-confident Berber culture sprang a tradition of dissidence, which regularly did battle with more centralizing movements driven by orthodox Sunni kings and sultans. At the same time, Morocco is at the frontier of the Muslim world, "close to the border of Christianity – Tangier is only a few miles from Spain". The country was under French and Spanish "protection" between 1905 and 1958. Dissidence was at first inspired by traditional Islam, but developed more modern political forms. These have continued under the conservative monarchy, which again took charge when independence was achieved.

The Berbers entered Morocco in the second millenium BCE, developing over the centuries an intense localism that has endured despite the disturbances of the Arab conquest and the introduction of Islam in the 7th century CE. The Berbers did not find Islam unamenable, so long as they could maintain their own ways alongside what was becoming an international religion. There followed regular attempts to impose monarchy, which were intermittently successful.

The Berbers remained independent of such dynasties as the Umayyads and the 'Abbasids, preferring local confederations and shifting control, but in the 780s Idris ibn 'Abd Allah, claiming descent from Fatima, Muhammad's daughter, and 'Ali, his first cousin, began to build a kingdom based on the city of Fez.

From his efforts grew the Fatimid dynasty, its power stretching from Morocco to Egypt. The Almoravids, militant and puritanical tribal Berbers, succeeded them in the late 11th century, creating an empire that included the whole of Morocco as well as Muslim Spain.

Localism reasserted itself when the Hasmuda tribes of the High Atlas revolted in the 1120s. They were followers of Ibn Tumart (d. 1130), sternly forbidding alchohol, music, and dancing, preparing the way for the Almohads (a name derived from an Arabic word *al-muwahhiddun* conveying unitarianism), who, although they classified Muslims not of their persuasion as infidels, were sufficiently open-minded as to allow the emergence of some of Islam's greatest philosophers, such as Ibn Tufail (d. 1185) and Ibn Rushd (Averroes, d. 1198). In what was now a familiar pattern, however, centralization gave way to more anarchistic ways. Berber tradition took naturally to Sufism, with its yearning for a more direct relationship with God and a readiness to use methods to obtain it – singing, dancing, cults of saints, shrines, and brotherhoods – regarded by most other Muslims as abhorrent, and usually banned. Such movements, at their height in the mid-15th century, had little place for central authority.

Outside interference began with invasions from Portugal, from about 1415, but their influence was confined to the coastal regions. The Sa'idi dynasty, from 1525, restored some elements of central control, the *makhzan*, but was not economically strong enough to develop an elaborate bureaucracy, relying instead on political manipulation and the prestige of the descent they claimed from Muhammad. They did, however, remain independent of the Ottomans, as did their successors, the Filalis, who from the 1660s laid the foundations of the modern monarchy, not without continuing challenges from Berber areas in the south, later to be known as *blad siba*, the "land of dissidence". Ernest Gellner describes the situation as "a mildly unstable stalemate between dynastic central power, based on towns and the plain, and the hill and desert tribes who successfully defied it".

Morocco's vulnerable geographical position made it necessary to keep on reasonably good terms with European powers, taking care, however, not to emulate their ways. Wasil al-Ghassani was Moroccan ambassador to Charles II of Spain in the early 1690s. He would not address the king in the ways Muslim leaders might address each other, saying "Peace be with you", preferring the less than fulsome "Peace be with those who follow the right path". He was shocked to see couples dancing at the balls that were held in his honour:

> When the party dispersed, we returned to our lodgings and we prayed to God to save us from the wretched state of those infidels who are devoid of manly jealousy and are sunk in unbelief. We implored the Almighty not to hold us accountable for our offence in conversing with them as the circumstances required.

Al-Ghassani also reported on a "writing mill" (printing press) and on the newsletters that it produced: according to him, "they are full of sensational lies". As elsewhere in the Islamic world, printing was not introduced into Morocco until the 19th century.

Morocco had finally to succumb to forms of outside control in 1860, when the Spanish invaded, demanding an indemnity against further incursion which the sultan could not pay. France too developed considerable interest in the area, and in 1907 it was agreed that France and Spain should have control over its administration and finance. By an agreement of 1912, Morocco was divided between French and Spanish protectorates, although both remained formally committed to the legal sovereignty of the sultan, 'Abdülaziz. Owing to the extraordinary persistence of Berber localism, France did not achieve unified control of the territory until 1934. They did so by negotiating the *dahir berbère*, by which the tribal rulers were allowed to administer customary law – secular and subject to alteration – in areas under their control. This was dismaying to orthodox Muslims, who believed that the agreement was tantamount to legalizing heresy and schism. Violent protests followed, the first stirrings of nationalism being expressed, unusually, by religious sheikhs, but there was little they could do at this stage to change the agreement.

Acting through residents-general, the French also introduced the elements of a modern economy, with all its by-products – people uprooted, underemployed, poorly housed, subject to the influence of their well-educated fellow Moroccans who had passed through the "Franco-Muslim" secondary schools and universities instituted in the 1930s. Many of these educated Moroccans believed that various forms of socialism were the answer to the country's predicaments. They were opposed by the religious nationalists, who called for statehood based on a reformation of *shari'a* law. The sultan, Sidi Muhammed, was generally in favour of the latter position, and when Morocco's independence was restored in 1958 his own power was fully restored with it. He now styled himself *malik* (king) and abrogated the *dahir berbère*.

In the press code of 1958, Sidi Muhammed left no further room for doubt about the limits of dissidence. The king, a descendant of the Prophet, was the "commander of the faithful" (*Amir al-Mu'minin*). His speeches must be reproduced in full, and any newspaper or other medium that "threatened the institutional, political or religious basis of the kingdom" would be prohibited. Driss Chraïbi's attack on feudalism, social exploitation, and religious hypocrisy in *The Simple Past* (1954), for example, was considered treasonable, and led to his permanent exile in France.

Given this, it was surprising that recruitment to political parties was initially considerable. Indeed, the total number of people claimed to have joined one party or another exceeded that of the entire population. The main opposition groups were Istiqlal (Independence), founded in 1945 by 'Allah al-Fasi, the author of *Self-Criticism*, a critique of Muslim thought; and the Marxist-Leninist Frontiste movement. Failed military coups were used to justify the postponement of constitutional monarchy and parliamentary democracy, but at least the parties provided the organization for the exchange of information between localities and the capital.

Enormous contradictions characterized the succeeding decades. King Hassan II had succeeded to the throne in 1961, but 11 years passed before the constitution was proclaimed. While it guaranteed "freedom of opinion, expression, assembly, and association", the king instituted a determined sweep against dissident intellectuals, notably including the poet and painter 'Abdellatif Derkaoui. After an attempted coup on 16 August 1972, several newspapers were confiscated, including

L'Opinion, which had presumed to publish a declaration by Istiqlal in favour of the physical extension of Moroccan territory into the Western Sahara, then ruled by the Spanish. In what was to become a continuing practice, Moroccan poets were arrested and imprisoned, not directly for their writings, but for their political sympathies. Thus, 'Abdullatif Laabi (1942–), a leader of the Frontistes and founder of the literary review *Souffles* was tortured and then imprisoned in 1973 for 16 years on the grounds that he had "conspired against the state". Abraham Serfaty, similarly, was condemned to life imprisonment for "anti-state articles".

The position of the king was continually reasserted. The constitution contained prohibitions against any criticism of his person; the monarchy was "inviolable and sacred"; his speeches could not even be debated, let alone criticized. A further decree of 1973 widened the areas of prohibition. It now became impossible to publish any article "considered offensive" to the king or members of his family. Transgressors were liable to 20 years' imprisonment and substantial fines. Such imprecision allowed the newspaper *al-'Alam* to be seized regularly, without explanation, during the 1970s. This did not preclude its confiscation for its deliberate challenge to the king's authority in an article, published in 1976, commenting on the seizure of the Spanish Sahara under the headline "How we link the Saharan problem with the organization of democracy".

The government was not entirely impervious to criticism, internal and external. Formal censorship was abolished in March 1977, during the run-up to legislative elections. *Al-Bayone*, daily newspaper of the Progress and Socialist Party, felt able to applaud the end of "illegal censorship", but it also condemned continuing bans on the French papers *Libération*, *Le Monde,* and *Le Monde Diplomatique*. *L'Humanité*, the newspaper of the French Communist Party, had never been allowed on Moroccan streets. Censorship was, *al-Bayone* maintained, "a weapon of the weak", and in any case sufficient power remained in the government's hands to induce considerable self-censorship.

Within two years, petty censorship had returned. *Al-Bayone* was suspended on the order of the minister of the interior merely because it had failed to report on the ceremonies marking the 18th anniversary of Hassan's accession. In February 1981, similarly, an issue of this newspaper was again seized, because it had questioned the usefulness of a conference on agricultural policy then being chaired by the king.

In June 1981 riots and demonstrations took place against price increases on basic foodstuffs. Six hundred people were killed, and many more were arrested and given long prison sentences. Prior censorship was again in force, the government at last understanding the real consequences of its abolition. Major left-wing papers were suppressed, and the leaders of left-wing parties were imprisoned until they were released by royal clemency in February 1982. For the first issue of *Amazigh*, published that year, 'Ali Gadki wrote an article arguing that the Berber and Arabic languages should have equal status; the magazine was seized and Gadki was accused of publishing "false information liable to harm public order and institutions". As had been the case ever since independence, the government sought once again to emphasize the position of the king. Poems by 'Ali Idrissi Kaitouni, inspired by the Casablanca riots, were judged "harmful to the king" and resulted in a 15-year jail

sentence. Meanwhile, compliant newspapers continued to be dominated by stories of the king's doings and sayings.

When political parties were suppressed, other groups stepped in to take their place, not least Islamic fundamentalists, who then amounted to only a relatively small part of Moroccan life. Religious censorship came to the fore in 1984–85. The writer and publisher 'Abd al-Salam Yassin, a former Sufi, had become a preacher, denouncing injustice and corruption. He was sentenced to two years' imprisonment for his critical articles. Death sentences were handed out to 13 people convicted of distributing unauthorized religious literature. Fatima Mernissi's *The Political Harem*, published in France, which discussed the political role of Muhammad's wives, was banned in her native Morocco. Sixteen Baha'is were imprisoned for trying to convert Moroccan citizens to their faith. In 1986, 26 people were charged with membership of a subversive fundamentalist organization, having been discovered distributing the magazine *al-Sarayan*.

More direct political censorship continued. Food riots again took place in 1984, while Hassan was chairing the Fourth Islamic Conference. Foreign journalists were not allowed into Nadar, the centre of the disturbances, and local journalists were not even allowed to mention them. The more radical but technically ill-equipped press was weakened and commercially threatened by the government's welcome to foreign, ideologically conservative papers such as the Saudi Arabian *Sharq al-Awsat* (Middle East), printed in London, Jeddah, Riyadh, and Washington, and to the French conservative papers *Le Figaro* and *Le Soir*. Such was the success of this indirect censorship that the government felt confident enough once again to abolish formal predistribution censorship in 1985.

However, the system was temporarily reimposed in 1988, when *al-Bayan* and *al-Ittihad al-Ishtiraki* reported on clashes between troops and students at Fez University. *Al-Massur*, organ of the Union Socialiste des Forces Populaires, was ordered to cease publication by the court of appeal after a reader's letter complaining that a public official had stolen the land of local people in al-Jedida had been found to be libellous. *Lamalif*, a monthly magazine, was also forced to close down after the king had complained about a series of articles describing the poor condition of public services. An exception to the general rule occurred in 1990, when the director and editor of *al-Ittihad al-Ishtiraki* was found to have been acting in the public interest by publishing an article describing corruption in the Casablanca courts.

From 1989 criticism of Morocco's human rights record began to be the subject of censorship. The director of *L'Opinion*, Muhammad Idrissi Kaitoumi, was convicted and sentenced to two years' imprisonment for publishing "false news likely to disturb public order", having printed a statement by human rights groups holding the government responsible for the deaths of four people in detention. Morocco was gaining an international reputation for its use of torture. To offset this, Hassan agreed in May 1990 to the establishment of a National Council for Human Rights, consisting of jurists, ministers, academics, and human rights activists. However, in October, Giles Perrault's book *Notre Ami le Roi* (Our Friend the King), published in France, blamed the king personally for the human rights situation, as well as criticizing his unchallengeable power. France refused a Moroccan request to ban the book, leaving the only option available of a local ban, which was also applied to the circulation of French newspapers that serialized the book and to the transmission, by the French-Canadian satellite channel TV5, of an interview with Perrault. The National Council for Human Rights was accused of excessive secrecy and in 1994, according to the entertainer Ahmed Sanoushi, the government banned one of his plays that satirized its human rights record.

Sensitivity to the dignity of the king remained high until the end of Hassan's long reign. In 1999, Maaki Mounjob's *The Moroccan Monarch and the Struggle for Power* was withdrawn because it was claimed to contain "inaccuracies". The newspaper *Anwal* defied an attempt to censor its serialization of the book, refuting the charge, but its issue of 29 January 1996 was confiscated. On 28 July 1999, the French satirical weekly *Le Canard Enchaîné* was refused circulation for its disrespectful treatment of Hassan's death.

DEREK JONES

Further Reading

Article 19, *La Liberté de la presse et l'information en Maroc*, London: Article 19, 1995

"Eliminating the Outspoken Press in Morocco", *Index on Censorship*, 14/2 (April 1985)

Gellner, Ernest, *Muslim Society*, Cambridge and New York: Cambridge University Press, 1981

Henderson, George (pseudonym), "How Morocco Treats Its Dissidents", *Index on Censorship*, 11/6 (February 1981)

Henderson, George (pseudonym), "Morocco at the Crossroads", *Index on Censorship*, 11/4 (April 1982)

Joffe, George, "Morocco's Saharan Policy", *Index on Censorship*, 10/1 (February 1981)

Lewis, Bernard, *The Muslim Discovery of Europe*, New York: Norton, and London: Weidenfeld and Nicolson, 1982

Mernissi, Fatima, *Islam and Democracy: Fear of the Modern World*, Reading, Massachusetts: Addison Wesley, 1992; London: Virago, 1993

Rajab, Ahmed, "Profile of Abdullah Zeriba", *Index on Censorship*, 9/3 (June 1980)

PAUL MORRISSEY
US film director, 1939–

FLESH
Film, 1968 (released in Britain, 1970)

Flesh, a film about a day in the life of a New York hustler, was made by Factory member Paul Morrissey with some input from Andy Warhol, and must be one of the few films in any country whose attempted suppression was roundly criticized by a censor.

The censor in question was John Trevelyan, who was secretary of the British Board of Film Censors (BBFC) when he saw *Flesh* privately in 1969. Though regarding it as "in many ways amateurish" (it was shot over four days for $4000), he liked its quality of compassion and the fact that "these people, however alien their lives were to us, were real people behaving not in the stylized way that people in films usually behave, but as they really were, talking as they really talked". However, for the BBFC , such naturalism also posed a problem in that it embraced "unabashed nudity", "uninhibited talk about sex", and "implied fellatio". Regretfully, Trevelyan concluded that the film "was probably true of life in Greenwich Village; it was possibly true of life in Chelsea; but it was certainly not a true picture of life in Hornsey, Catford or Northampton. I believed that this film would shock and offend a great many people". Therefore, he advised its distributor, Jimmy Vaughan, not to submit it to the Board, who would almost certainly refuse to pass it. Instead, he suggested to Vaughan that he should try to show the film in a cinema club, thus avoiding the need for a BBFC certificate. To this end, he introduced him to Charles Marowitz and Thelma Holt, the directors of the Open Space Theatre Club, which had a reputation for staging radical new work; they readily agreed to screen *Flesh* under cinema club conditions.

The film opened to good reviews and full houses. Then, on 3 February 1970, the club was raided by 32 policemen, led by a chief inspector and armed with a warrant under section 3 of the Obscene Publications Act 1959. A member of the public had apparently complained that the film was obscene. The film, the screen, and parts of the projector were seized, as was the club's register of members, and the names and addresses of all audience members were taken down.

Vaughan rang Trevelyan while the raid was in progress, and the latter immediately phoned Scotland Yard, headquarters of the Metropolitan Police, because, as he himself put it, "as a result of private consultations I knew that this action conflicted with prevailing attitudes at Scotland Yard which seemed to me both intelligent and reasonable". Discovering that they knew nothing at all about the raid, he then went round to the Open Space, only to discover that the police had already left. The raid, however, had already become national news, and Trevelyan spent the evening telling the media that he

> . . . thought this police action unjustified and preposterous, that the Open Space was a reputable theatre club, supported by the Arts Council, with a membership of intellectuals, and that [he] thought that the film was entirely suitable for showing to audiences of this kind but would have little interest or profitability in commercial cinemas.

In his memoir, *What the Censor Saw*, on which this account draws heavily, Trevelyan described the police raid as being "without parallel in contemporary history".

The police raid was condemned by the press and in the House of Commons. In the House of Lords, Lord Norwich arranged a screening for his fellow peers. He declared, "I am well aware that the police have not in this matter infringed any regulations; they were perfectly within the law"; however, he asked

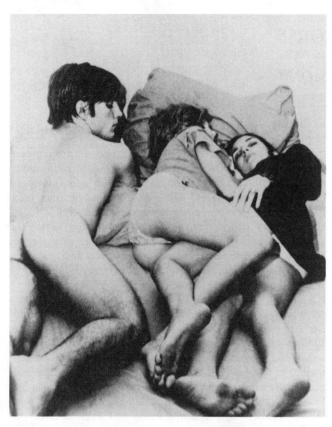

MORRISSEY: Still from the 1968 film *Flesh*, directed by Morrissey and produced by the Pop artist Andy Warhol. The Secretary of the British Board of Film Censors, John Trevelyan, after seeing the film, advised against submission to the board for a certificate for general release of the film in Britain because of its explicit sex scenes and potentially shocking and offensive nature. He suggested screening *Flesh* at a private cinema club venue, where it opened to critical acclaim. The club was subsequently raided and charged unsuccessfully under the Obscene Publications Act in February 1970. The club was then taken to court a month later by the Greater London Council and the owners found guilty of allowing non-members admission. The film was passed uncut for general release by the BBFC later that year.

for the print to be returned or for reasons to be given for its continued retention. He was told by Lord Beswick that "the Commissioner of Police had sought the advice of the Director of Public Prosecutions about possible offences relating to licensing and obscenity". Three days later, on 27 February 1970, Vaughan was advised that there would be no prosecution under the Obscene Publications Act but that papers were being referred to the Greater London Council (GLC) "for consideration as regards the question of proceedings for any offence under the Cinematograph Act of 1909". Parliamentary unease about the case continued. On 11 March there were calls for an independent enquiry, and it was asked whether "a repressive Mrs Grundy campaign in London" was in progress.

In reply, the home secretary, James Callaghan, stated that "there is a great deal of pornography about that is causing a great deal of concern to many people in this country. It is the general desire of the average person in this country that it should stop." He said that "the police must enforce the law as it now is" and added, "I want the House to know that I will support the police when they act in response to complaints from the public in investigating these matters." However, both Callaghan and Lord Norwich were in fact wrong to suggest that the law had not been abused, although neither was challenged on this point in parliament at the time. It was left to the legal expert Graham Zellick to demonstrate conclusively that "with one small exception, films fall right outside the scope of the Obscene Publications Act, so that the issue of the warrant was entirely without legal foundation".

On 20 March it was reported that the GLC had taken out summonses against the Open Space for non-observance of the rules governing clubs. In other words, like the numerous neighbouring strip joints, they had let in non-members. The case was heard at the end of May, and Holt and Marowitz pleaded guilty. John Trevelyan himself actually appeared as a character witness and to explain that it was at his suggestion that the film was shown at the Open Space in the first place. All to no avail. The defendants were lectured on their wickedness by the magistrates and fined £200 with £20 costs. As the theatre had no money, Trevelyan suggested that Holt and Marowitz appealed to Andy Warhol himself to pay, which he did.

In October 1970 the British Board of Film Censors passed *Flesh* uncut.

JULIAN PETLEY

Films

Lonesome Cowboys, 1968
Flesh, 1968
Trash, 1970
Women in Revolt, 1972
Heat, 1972

Further Reading

Trevelyan, John, *What the Censor Saw*, London: Joseph, 1973
Zellick, Graham, "Films and the Law of Obscenity", *Criminal Law Review* (March 1971)
Zellick, Graham, "Two Comments on Search and Seizure under the Obscene Publications Act", *Criminal Law Review* (September 1971)

SALMI MORSE
US writer, 1826–1884

THE PASSION
Play, 1879

One of the earliest attempts to claim First Amendment protection for theatrical expression in the US came in 1879 in San Francisco. A professional theatre company produced a pageant depicting the trial, crucifixion, and resurrection of Jesus Christ. With lavish settings and innovative lighting effects (now credited to David Belasco), with over 600 in the cast, and starring James O'Neill as Christ, the production was, by all contemporary accounts, impressive and moving. Nevertheless, it would become one of the most controversial stage productions of the time, provoking nationwide protests from pulpit and press, bringing public cries for censorship, and prompting legislators to attempt to suppress it by law.

Intended in part as a means of correcting what its Jewish author, Salmi Morse, perceived as "errors" in the Oberammergau *Passionsspiel* in Bavaria (especially its depiction of the Jews), *The Passion* was a reverent and respectful if dramatically weak play. First publicly read in January 1879, the work received the blessings of the Catholic prelate of California and was praised by critics as "a literary labor of importance".

Immediately upon the announcement two weeks later that *The Passion* was to be staged by a professional theatre company, Morse's "labor of importance" became "blasphemy", an "impiety", "sinful", "irreverent", "sacrilegious", and "a burlesque of everything we hold Sacred", in the words of editorials and Protestant Sunday sermons across the city. Protestant reaction to the depiction of Christ was of a piece with such activities of the early Reformation as the smashing of images and the banning of Mystery plays.

Embodying as it did the church's traditional anti-theatrical biases, the entire controversy revealed how easily offended was 19th-century America's concept of the Christian religion as the bedrock of society. But the controversy also saw Morse fall victim to local politics. His play was caught in the violent Protestant/Catholic power struggles gripping San Francisco at that time.

The Protestant leaders turned to the city's mostly Protestant Board of Supervisors to suppress the Catholic-tainted production and thus protect by law "the Christian religion". Their resolution made it a crime to "exhibit ... in any theatre, or other place, ... any play, or performance, or representation, displaying ... the life or death of Jesus Christ, or any [representation] ... calculated to profane or degrade religion". This action came just as the play completed its run, closing after 10 performances. Morse immediately announced that it would reopen during Lent, ordinance or no. In fact, now he began to argue   that the US Constitution gave him the right to produce his play, despite any moral objections. It was his intention, he said, to "test whether the municipal ordinance is constitutional or not", a radical challenge in an era in which most playwrights willingly censored themselves.

To force the issue, the play reopened on Easter Tuesday; as expected, O'Neill was jailed for impersonating Jesus Christ in violation of a city ordinance. Ultimately, ten other members of the company would be arrested, charged, and fined. Morse, however, was not allowed to pursue his proposed constitutional challenge in court. The prosecution, unwilling to countenance the larger church versus state or free-speech issues, dropped the charge of "immorality" and instead pursued the more technical charge of the production's illegality. Morse lost the case and the play closed. He returned to journalism, where he defended his First Amendment rights in print (wherein his "anarchist" notions were constitutionally protected).

The following year, New York producer Henry E. Abbey considered the play for performances at Booth's Theatre, again to star O'Neill. And, in a virtual reenactment of the San Francisco controversy, Abbey was immediately denounced by the moralists – this time including the Catholics. Harrison Grey Fiske, William Winter, and other theatre notables also vehemently fought the production, seeing their actions not as moral censorship of the stage but as a means of "protecting" their struggling profession from falling into further disrepute. As in San Francisco, the New York Board of Aldermen proposed a resolution "prohibiting the introduction and exhibition of this play". At that point, only eight days before the scheduled opening, with even his theatre colleagues against him, Abbey suspended production.

For three more years, beset by legal battles, court appeals, and setbacks, Morse struggled on. Denied a theatre licence by the mayor because he would certainly produce *The Passion*, Morse turned to the courts complaining of "prior censorship". He lost case after case. In March 1883, the Court of Special Sessions ruled that a dress rehearsal for a nonpaying audience was legal, as it did not constitute a "public" presentation, and under those conditions Morse finally staged a complete performance without police interference.

With *The Passion*'s resurrection imminent, the Society for the Prevention of Juvenile Delinquency – which by law received all licensing monies charged New York City theatres – petitioned the state supreme court to halt the production. While their motivation was clearly censorious, they argued that *The Passion* was indeed a dramatic performance and therefore needed a theatre licence, the fees for which should go to the Society (but which, conveniently, no mayor would grant). Morse was served the restraining order minutes before the curtain rose on his first public presentation.

At the same time, the controversy reached the state senate, which passed an act outlawing any stage representation of "Jesus Christ, the Saviour of Mankind". With the state now playing censor, Morse reluctantly accepted the inevitable.

Morse briefly continued to pursue his career as a dramatist. In February 1884 his body was found floating in the Hudson River.

Over the next two decades, several attempts by O'Neill and others to revive *The Passion* regenerated community outrage, which meant continued suppression of the play in cities across

America. Ironically, in 1898 it was filmed secretly, and deliberately exhibited as the "Oberammergau Passion Play", to great public and priestly praise.

It is not surprising that courts in 19th-century America were unreceptive to Morse's "anarchic" First Amendment claims, especially as they challenged the very nature of religion's empowerment by the state. Not until the 1940s and 1950s would the US Supreme Court move toward Morse's thinking, embracing First Amendment protection for speech that offends, and more specifically extending such protection to film and drama (in *Burstyn v. Wilson*, 1952).

ALAN NIELSEN

Writings
The Passion: A Miracle Play in Ten Acts, 1879

Further Reading
Flaherty, David H., "Law and the Enforcement of Morals", *Perspectives in American History*, 5 (1971): 203–53
Issel, William and Robert W. Cherny, *San Francisco, 1865–1932: Politics, Power, and Urban Development*, Berkeley: University of California Press, 1986
Kalven, Harry Jr, *A Worthy Tradition: Freedom of Speech in America*, New York: Harper and Row, 1988
McArthur, Benjamin, *Actors and American Culture, 1880–1920*, Philadelphia: Temple University Press, 1984
Nielsen, Alan, *The Great Victorian Sacrilege: Preachers, Politics and the Passion, 1879–1884*, Jefferson, North Carolina: McFarland, 1991
Winter, William, *The Life of David Belasco*, 2 vols, New York: Moffat Yard, 1918

RAOUF MOUSSAD
Egyptian writer, 1937–

BAYDAT AL-NAʿAMA (The Ostrich Egg)
Novel, 1994

The history of censorship must sometimes touch on work which might, given the history, politics, and culture of a country, have seemed almost certain to be banned, but which was, in the event, allowed to be published. *The Ostrich Egg* is such a work.

Baydat al-Naʿama is a very frank, semi-autobiographical novel; the life story of a communist who grew up as a Christian and was in fact intended for the priesthood. Moussad became a communist at the age of 16, just a year after Gamal ʿAbdul Nasser, who was profoundly anticommunist, came to power in Egypt. Moussad was imprisoned for his political activities between 1960 and 1964. It was here that he was first exposed to theatre, acting the part of a woman in a play performed by the prisoners. After his release from prison he attempted to put on a play, however, it was banned on the grounds that it threatened state security.

From 1970 to 1975 Moussad studied drama in Moscow. Avoiding a return to Egypt – where the new president, Sadat, was even more anticommunist than his predecessor – he worked in Iraq and the Lebanon. He returned to his home country in 1982, shortly after Sadat's assassination, and set up as a publisher. Many of the books he hoped to publish were banned, including one on the Palestinian issue and another on the Egyptian bread riots of 1977. In 1994, his own play *Urshalim, Urshalim* (Jerusalem, Jerusalem) was also banned, not only because it included ideas about the Palestinian peace process that were "contradictory to the higher national interests", but also because it contained quotations from the Bible, a practice thought to be lacking in respect to sacred literature.

Moussad turned his energies towards autobiographical writing, eventually producing *The Ostrich Egg*. The book contained the story of a life which had been dominated by what Egypt regarded as subversive activities. Moreover, in it Moussad discussed other sensitive subjects, which elsewhere would have caught the censor's eye: the place of religion, and, not least, sexuality (his account of homosexual relationships in work camps would been particularly shocking to his Arab

readers). For these reasons, coupled with the fact that Moussad had a known "record" of being censored, it would not have been surprising if the book had been banned with no further argument.

Publication was certainly not easy. The recent censorship of *Jerusalem, Jerusalem* convinced him that he could not publish the work himself. Meanwhile, state publication houses in Egypt have long experience of discerning what would not be acceptable to the regime, and simply turn away books that would run into political trouble. Moussad had to resort to getting *The Ostrich Egg* published in London, from where it was imported into Egypt. This was not a foolproof way of avoiding censorship. Egyptian censors usually inspect foreign-produced works and they are sometimes banned. However, in this case, the book was let through.

Non-government newspapers like *al-Ahrar* and the London-based daily *al-Hayat* considered it to be one of the best books of the year. The semi-official *al-Ahram* gave a much more reserved account. The book was completely neglected by Egypt's left-wing press, perhaps because it was felt to tarnish the image of communists jailed by Nasser. Communists are often depicted as morally depraved, and a description of homosexual relationships between detainees could have been considered embarrassing.

How then could a book which used biblical quotations as much as *Jerusalem, Jerusalem* had done, which was published at a time when Egyptian Islamism was resurgent, and which had been written by a known and previously censored opponent of the government, escape censorship this time? The author has remarked that the application of Egyptian censorship is like a lottery – little consistency is discernible. To his astonishment, after the book's publication Moussad was for the first time described as a Coptic, rather than a left wing writer. Extreme Islamists had, during the previous decades, physically attacked members of the Coptic minority. To more liberal critics, and perhaps even to the government, a book which provided an insight into the Copts' way of life, their fears and feelings of inferiority, might have seemed useful at that particular time.

On the other hand, after runaway sales, it proved difficult to achieve a second printing – a device often employed to suppress unwanted books, and *de facto* censorship. *The Ostrich Egg*, meanwhile, is entirely banned in Saudi Arabia, Kuwait, and Syria.

ROB LEEMHUIS

Writings
Baydat al-Náama, 1994

DANIEL MOYANO
Argentine journalist and novelist, 1930–1992

Daniel Moyano trained to be a plumber at a technical college and then learned to be a bricklayer. He was told by his grandparents, who brought him up in Córdoba province, that there are times in life when a trade is more in demand than all the knowledge in the world. When he went into exile on 24 May 1976, he took with him his plumber's toolbag because it might be more useful than a typewriter to start a new life in Madrid. He had been severely shaken by a short and brutal imprisonment ordered by the military dictatorship that seized power in Argentina in March 1976.

The typescript of his last novel at that time, *El vuelo del tigre* (The Flight of the Tiger), remained in Argentina, buried in the back yard of his home in La Rioja, the impoverished northwest province where he had made his home. Irma, his wife, had buried the book immediately following his arrest on the day after the March coup d'état, and, although they dug up the garden on his release they never found the roll of typewritten papers. The novel was rewritten in exile.

Moyano's first book was *Artista de variedades* (Variety Artiste), a collection of short stories published in 1960. His second book of stories, *La lombriz* (The Worm), published in 1964, had the advantage of a preface by the Paraguayan writer Augusto Roa Bastos, who associated Moyano's writing with that of Franz Kafka and Césare Pavese. Moyano's first novel, *Una luz muy lejana* (A Distant Light), followed in 1966. That was the year in which his novel *El Oscuro* (The Dark) won the prize for fiction awarded by *Primera Plana* magazine (banned in August 1969). The judges were the Colombian writer Gabriel García Márquez and the Argentines Jorge Luis Borges and Julio Cortázar. It was the best and most astounding career launch for any writer in Latin America.

Nevertheless, Moyano returned to his work in La Rioja province, where he was on the staff of the newspaper *El Independiente* (The Independent), perhaps the only and certainly the most successful genuine co-operative newspaper in Latin America, banned by the military in 1976). He was also a stringer for the Buenos Aires newspaper *Clarín* (Trumpet), as well as playing the viola in the provincial symphony orchestra.

The combination of all these activities made Moyano a suspect intellectual subversive to the provincial military commander – the most reactionary of the breed in the republic, because such men were out of touch with changes in the capital, and had considerable power in local politics, backed by the force of their barracks. Moyano's novel *El trino del diablo* (The Devil's Trill), was launched in Buenos Aires in 1974, as Argentina slid into its age of darkness. The fact that such a novel (which is the tale of a young musician who travels to Buenos Aires and there finds the squalor of life in the big city alongside the hope of glory and success) might be considered subversive had only struck Moyano after the local La Rioja radio station (LV-14) ran a series of readings from the book: an anonymous caller threatened to blow up the station if the readings continued. Moyano was then threatened at his home and called on governor Carlos Menem – who in 1989 became president of Argentina – for help. The governor gave him a police guard at his home.

In spite of the difficulties, Moyano remained a local personality, an immensely warm and humorous man, and very witty about the ways of bureaucrats and authority. In 1976, before and again immediately after his imprisonment, he was witness to the burning of his own books by the army in the provincial capital La Rioja. He looked upon the episode as an honour: "Fancy being burned alongside Julio Cortázar, Gabriel García Márquez, Juan Carlos Onetti, and all those greats."

In exile in Spain Moyano rewrote *El vuelo del tigre* from memory in a desperate drive to recover his power of recall and to write, as he said, so as not to lose his sanity or his sense of place. He stopped there. His next novel, *Libro de Navios y Borrascas* (Book of Ships and Storms), published in Madrid in 1984, was a fictionalized memoir of his journey into exile with his family, and had in it all the characters of expatriation. It was the first full-length book he was able to write after seven years in exile.

Although Moyano travelled back to Argentina after the restoration of constitutional rule in 1983, and in 1985 made a film about his life for Spanish television, he said that he could never be at ease again in a land that had murdered so many of his friends, including the novelist and journalist Antonio Di Benedetto (1922–86), who was arrested in Mendoza in 1976 on fabricated charges of subversion, and was so ill-treated that he never recovered. In Spain Moyano wrote some journalism, and lectured on Latin American literature and creative writing at several colleges, before dying of cancer in 1992.

ANDREW GRAHAM-YOOLL

Writings
The Devil's Trill, translated by Giovanni Pontiero, 1988
"Aunt Julia" in *The Faber Book of Contemporary Latin American Short Stories*, edited by Nick Caistor, 1989

"The White Wall and the Spiders" (interview with Andrew Graham-Yooll) in *The Forbidden Rainbow: Images and Voices from Latin America*, edited by Amanda Hopkinson, 1992
"Movements" in *Hand in Hand alongside the Tracks and Other Stories: Contemporary Argentine Stories*, edited by Norman Thomas di Giovanni, 1992
The Flight of the Tiger, translated by Norman Thomas di Giovanni, 1995

Further Reading

Graham-Yooll, Andrew, *After the Despots: Latin American Views and Interviews*, London: Bloomsbury, 1991 (includes interview with Daniel Moyano)
Graham-Yooll, Andrew, "Obituary: Daniel Moyano", *The Independent*, London (3 July 1992)

MOZAMBIQUE

Population: 18,292,000	**Illiteracy rate (%):** 39.9 (m); 71.3 (f)
Main religions: Roman Catholic; Muslim; indigenous religions	**Number of daily newspapers:** 2
	Number of periodicals: 4
Official language: Portuguese	**Number of radio receivers per 1000 inhabitants:** 40
Other languages spoken: Ronga; Shangaan; Muchope; other indigenous languages	**Number of TV receivers per 1000 inhabitants:** 4.9
	Number of PCs per 1000 inhabitants: 1.6

Home to a number of important medieval African kingdoms, and connected to Arabia and India by the trading activities of Islamic merchants, the area today known as Mozambique was visited by the Portuguese navigator Vasco da Gama after he rounded the Cape of Good Hope in 1498. Over the following centuries the Portuguese exercised a loose influence over the territory. Up to its abolition by Portugal in 1869, the trade in slaves formed the principal economic activity. Between 1729 and 1800 some 125,000 slaves were said to have been taken from Mozambique en route for Brazil and European-controlled islands off the East African coast. Meanwhile, settlers from Portugal and Goa (where the Portuguese had also settled), including the Jesuits and Dominicans, profited from the *prazo* landholding system by which they controlled Africans in semi-feudal fashion.

After the Berlin Conference of 1884–85, Portuguese power in Mozambique was consolidated and a period of "pacification" ensued. Chartered companies were employed to create a Portuguese colony, with the emphasis on exploitation rather than any "civilizing mission". The Mozambican nationalist Edouardo Mondlane asserted: "The chief consideration was utility to Portugal; the concept of mission could be left to theorists or apologists." At best, Africans were considered "children", as in the words of Antonio Eanes, governor-general of Mozambique in the 1890s : "I even feel an inner fondness for the Negro, this big child, instinctively bad like all children . . . though docile and sincere. I do not consider him something to be exterminated because of the necessity for the expansion of the white race, although I may believe in his natural inferiority."

The Native Assistance Code of 1921 began to define a specifically Portuguese colonial policy, designed to lead Africans towards "civilization". Marcelo Caetano, later to be president of Portugal, envisaged that Africans would in time be equal citizens, but a civilized African "must read, write and speak Portuguese fluently ... have the necessary education and social habits to make it possible to apply the public and private law of Portugal to him". It should be noted that when Caetano wrote this, some 40 per cent of the population of Portugal itself was illiterate. "Schools are necessary", wrote cardinal Cerejeira, patriarch of Lisbon, in a pastoral letter of 1960, "but schools where we teach the native the path of human dignity and the grandeur of the nation which protects him." The Catholic Church was empowered to run mission schools providing rudimentary education for Africans (the state ran parallel schools for Europeans and *assimilados* [educated or mixed race Africans]), but as late as 1959 it was estimated that between 90 and 95 per cent of the Mozambican population was illiterate. Of the 280 students enrolled at the new university college of Lourenco Marques in 1962, there were fewer than a dozen Africans.

One bishop stood apart from the rest. Mgr Sebastiao Soares de Resende, bishop of Beira in the 1950s, criticized colonial policies in pastoral letters which he published regularly in a church periodical, and later in a daily newspaper. He was in favour of liberal reform, hoping that Mozambique could evolve into nationhood as Brazil had done. At length, he so angered the Salazar dictatorship in Portugal that the Vatican ordered him to cease publishing the letters; he was also dismissed as the director of the only secondary school in Beira, the country's second city.

African resistance had been growing since the period of the new republic in Portugal (1910–1926). Informal resistance is epitomized by the following lines sung of the Chope people in protest at the dominance of the Portuguese language:

> Listen to the song of Chigambe village
> It's tedious saying *bom dia* all the time
> Macarite and Babuane are in prison
> Because they did not say *bom dia*

More formally, groups like Gremio Africana (African Guild) started newspapers in which to campaign against colonial abuses and for equal rights. The Salazar government sought to intimidate or to infiltrate both groups. Meanwhile, the newspaper *O Bianda Africana* (The African Cry) was shut down under Portuguese press laws in 1936.

A new generation of intellectuals came of age artistically and intellectually in the 1950s. They included the painters

Malangatana Valente and José Craveirinta, who created images of liberation; the short story writer Luis Bernado Henwarra; and the political poets Marcelinma dos Santos and Noedia de Sousa. All were to suffer censorship of some sort. Craveirinha and Hanwara were imprisoned, for example, while Malangatana was subject to official supervision and suffered harassment by the police.

Edouardo Mondlane, meanwhile, was developing a Marxist philosophy which would inspire the Nucleo dos Estuanates Africanos Secundarios de Mocambique (NESAM). NESAM spread ideas of resistance and independence under the cover of social and economic activities, and printed a magazine, *Alvar*, which continued to be published despite the censorship to which it was subjected. Mondlane subsequently formed Frelimo, the Mozambique Liberation Front, in Lourenço Marques in 1962. Justifying the organization's resort to armed struggle, Mondlane maintained that the Portuguese had proved impervious to persuasion – "the only reaction . . . was prison, censorship and the strengthening of the PIDE, the secret police". Frelimo was more than a liberation army. Among its stated aims were "to promote at once the literacy of the Mozambican people, creating schools wherever possible", "to promote by every method the social and cultural development of the Mozambican woman", and "to organize permanent propaganda by all methods in order to mobilize world public opinion in favour of the Mozambican people".

The Mozambique Institute in Dar es Salaam, Tanzania, was established in 1963, teaching Portuguese, basic literacy, political education, and tactics, as well as the background to the liberation struggle, to Mozambicans who had been forced into exile by the suppression of NESAM. When war eventually broke out in 1964, broadcasting was organized via Radio Tanzania. Radio sets were distributed so that listeners could hear the news in Portuguese and African languages, and be better informed on politics, hygiene, and public health. Entertainment came in the form of revolutionary songs, traditional, and popular music.

Throughout the war Frelimo was "preparing for government" by developing embryonic departments, such as the one for Information, Publicity and Propaganda, which kept people informed about the aims of Frelimo and current events. At the same time, it formulated counter-propaganda against the Portuguese, who, by contrast, allowed in only a few selected reporters who could be trusted to see events from their point of view. One result of these restrictions was that the conflict received negligible coverage in the international media – becoming known as "the forgotten war".

The war ended and independence was granted to Mozambique in 1975, after a change of government had occurred in Portugal. By this time, however, Mondlane had become a casualty of the liberation struggle; assassinated by a Portuguese bomb in Dar es Salaam in 1969. Frelimo, now led by Samora Machel, formed the first government of independent Mozambique. One of its main policies concerned the necessity, as it saw things, for a Marxist-influenced one-party state. There were mixed reports on their attitude to censorship and the control of information. Matias Manuel Kaphese, the national director of education, could write in the London-based *Times Higher Education Supplement* in April 1976: "We accept that we must clear the minds of those who do not accept our principles . . . if students and teachers persist in disagreeing with our aims it must be because they are linked with internal or external reactionary elements." Up to 1981, the directors of the press, radio, and television participated in the meetings of the Party Central Committee and the Council of Ministers. This could be interpreted as either positive or sinister: an indication that they were themselves trusted members of the party, not likely to step out of line in their newspaper columns and broadcasts, or that the government was relatively open. The Mozambican writer Mia Couto, once head of the Mozambique Press Agency, was positive about the government record, observing: "Ever since independence there have been popular meetings in which the government ministers discussed and debated with people in the street". Couto's own play *The Tale of the Two Who Returned from the Dead*, one of whose themes was government abuses, generated considerable debate among its audiences without provoking government intervention.

Then in 1981 it was decided that openness should be checked. In future, information for journalists would be made available only through the Ministry of Information. This was in part due to the outbreak of civil war, provoked by the activities of armed guerilla bands under the auspices of Resistancia Nacional de Mozambique (Renamo), funded and encouraged by the apartheid regime in South Africa, which was intent on destabilizing African regimes to its north. The civil war gave rise to some international debate about censorship in Mozambique. The "front line states" of which Mozambique was one, met at Kadoma, Zimbabwe in 1983 to consider how best they could counter South African propaganda. When South Africa carried out a bombing raid at Motala in Mozambique, they had claimed that they were merely "taking out" buildings which they knew housed forces of the African National Congress (ANC), the principal opposition force to the apartheid regime. In fact, they had demolished housing and a jam factory. The minister of information had gone to the scene, accompanied by international journalists who were free to report on what they could see. However, in a follow-up meeting at Maputo, Mozambique, delegates appeared to have failed to learn the lessons of Motala. They announced that any correspondents who were based in South Africa were not to be allowed into Mozambique to cover the war, thus "censoring" reporting that might have been to their advantage. In the 12 years of civil war 600,000 people are said to have died, and more than a third of the population fled abroad.

As the war drew to a close, Frelimo began to draft an amended constitution (1990). Among other things, it stated:

All citizens should enjoy freedom of expression, assembly and association. The exercise of this basic right should be regulated by law and may only be limited if public order or individual rights, freedoms or guarantees are endangered, or if the use of force is implied or proposed.

"All citizens", it continued, "shall have the right to freedom of scientific, technical or artistic creation." From 1989 Mozambique had ceased to be a Marxist state, a decision influenced by events in eastern Europe. Having agreed a peace settlement with the Frelimo government, Renamo now become a political party, competing for the allegiance of Mozambicans, although it was not clear that they had equal access to the media. In 1991 president Joaquim Chissano (who had taken over from Samora Machel after he had died in a mysterious plane crash in South Africa) made it clear at the National Organization of Journalists annual conference that citizens had the right to receive information which was "as objective as possible"; multi-party politics demanded "greater responsibility".

Censorship continued to occur, arising from the activities of both the government and Renamo, who in 1992 threatened to arrest any journalists accompanying Medecins sans Frontières, who were reporting on health conditions in areas "controlled" by them. More positive was the arrival in 1993 of *Mediafax*, a three-page daily newspaper distributed down telephone lines, which received an enthusiastic response from both readers and journalists for whom it acted as an outlet for opinions which could not be expressed in the existing media. A representative of Renamo told Jean Chichizola in 1995: "*Mediafax* is the most independent medium possible in this country."

DEREK JONES

Further Reading

Article 19, "Mozambique: Freedom of Expression and the Elections", *Censorship News*, 36 (1994)

Caetano, Marcelo, *Colonizing Traditions, Principles and Methods of the Portuguese*, Lisbon: Divisão de Publicações e Biblioteca, Agência Geral do Ultramar, 1961

Chichizola, Jean, "*Mediafax* – The Right Number", *Index on Censorship*, 24/1 (January–February 1995)

Couto, Mia, "Lack of Access Makes the Press More Bureaucratic", *Index on Censorship*, 19/5 (May 1990)

Duffy, James, *Portugal in Africa*, Cambridge, Massachusetts: Harvard University Press, and London: Penguin, 1962

Mondlane, Eduardo, *The Struggle for Mozambique*, London and Baltimore: Penguin, 1969

Thomas, Hugh, *The Slave Trade*, New York: Simon and Schuster, and London: Picador, 1997

ES'KIA MPHAHLELE (Ezekiel Mphahlele)
South African writer, 1919–

Es'kia Mphahlele is a scholar, educationist, fiction writer, critic and journalist. His views have been shaped by Africanist perspectives which seek to counteract the negations of colonialism by restoring African culture as an important part of world culture. He describes himself as "the personification of the African paradox, detribalized, Westernized, but still African."

In the first part of his autobiography, *Down Second Avenue* (1959), he recounts his childhood of squalor and hardship, and the prejudice of growing up in Cape Location in Pretoria, South Africa. At the age of five he was taken to live with his paternal grandmother in Mphahlele, a village some 50 kilometres northeast of Petersburg. Later he was to return to Pretoria with his mother, to live in Second Avenue, Marabastad.

After various jobs he became a teacher. His first serious experience of repression occurred as a result of his opposition to the Bantu Education Bill of 1950. In the words of the then prime minister, Hendrik Verwoerd, this bill aimed to make the African understand that "there is no place for him in the European community above the level of certain forms of labour". In 1952, following Mphahlele's active opposition to this type of education, he was prohibited from teaching in South Africa.

He worked as a messenger and later as a fiction editor on the popular magazine *Drum*. In 1957, at the age of 37, Mphahlele left South Africa for Nigeria. In the early 1960s he settled in Paris, where he co-edited the journal *Black Orpheus* with Wole Soyinka and Ulli Beier. In 1967 he went to lecture at the University of Denver in the USA. He returned to Africa in 1968 for a teaching spell at the University of Zambia. In 1971 he returned to Denver. He lived in the USA until 1977.

In the meantime, the Government Gazette Extraordinary of 1 April 1966 banished Mphahlele along with Mazizi Kunene,

Can Themba, Todd Matshikhiza, Bloke Modisane, and Lewis Nkosi. All their past and future writings were outlawed, and it was a crime to quote from their works.

The African Image (1962) is perhaps his most important critical study of race and prejudice in South Africa. The book is organized around four themes: the African personality; the philosophy of négritude; nationalism in Africa and Europe; and literary portrayals of blacks and whites in fiction. The book was examined by the Publications Control Board in 1977. It was found to be "undesirable" in terms of the Publications Act of 1973. In 1982 the decision was reviewed and the book again found undesirable. Four reasons are provided in the two Afrikaans transcripts.

The 1977 report cites the writer's refusal to refrain from participation in politics. He dreams of returning to South Africa. At the airport he surrenders himself to an official. Mphahlele writes:

> I want to teach in South Africa, I won't make any trouble. I'll keep out of politics. They make me sign an agreement. I don't see their faces clearly. They don't say a word either. They wave me goodbye with a neutral smile, like mannequins. I'll poison the minds of your youth. I think, I promise you that, you stinking Boer Bastards. You can take that agreement I have just signed and tear it into pieces enough for you to stick a few pieces up each of your pink and purple arses. I fought your stinking educational politics in the fifties and I'll fight them again.

Both reports mention that "whites and especially Afrikaners are represented as despicable". The 1977 report cites the following passage referring to whites: "Well fed, full of himself, his arse frothing with privileges . . . Calvinist trash". Mphahlele is accused of "inciting revolution and uprising". The 1977 and 1988 reports mention a quotation by the author from the Manifesto of Mkhonto we Sizwe, the military wing of the ANC. The writer's view that "The ANC have spent too much time, effort and money in representations across the globe and too little, if any, on strategy and intelligence based on the science of guerrilla warfare" is adduced as further evidence of his revolutionary attitude.

The writer is charged with "slandering" and "defaming the authorities and the police" by accusing them of injustice, oppression, brutality, terror, "torture, hangings, banishments, evictions, starvation, extermination, imprisonment aimed at the terrorising of Africans". Reference to "a bunch of fascists in the houses of Parliament" and the threat by police: "Kaffir your life is worth nothing . . . you will die," are cited as evidence of his antipathy to the state and its officers.

In April 1991 the publication was again submitted on review and was found to be "not undesirable". The committee that made the finding did not explain it except to reject the previous ruling and the motivation for it. This ruling must be seen against the background of the fact that Mphahlele was allowed to return permanently to South Africa in 1977. He first returned in early July 1976 to speak at a conference in Soweto. It was a mere 2 weeks after the Soweto uprisings of June 1976. In October that year 17 organizations, including cultural groups and two newspapers with predominantly black readerships, namely The World and the Weekend World, were banned under the terms of the Internal Security Act. It was the second wave of repression since the banishment of the liberation movements in March 1960.

Mphahlele returned to South Africa because exile had become unbearable. When the Publications Act of 1974 was amended in 1978 to make provision for a committee of experts to advise on the literary merits and likely readership of a publication, Mphahlele served as an expert on black literature. In 1983 he advised the censors against the banning of Why Are We So Blest? by Akyi Kewi Armah and other writers, on the grounds that their works are complex and because in his view, there is no proven relationship between political unrest and fiction.

ANDRIES WALTER OLIPHANT

Writings

Man Must Live and Other Stories, 1947
Down Second Avenue (autobiography), 1959
The Living and the Dead and Other Stories, 1961
The African Image (essays), 1962; revised edition, 1974
Editor, with Ellis Komey, Modern African Short Stories, 1964
Editor, African Writing Today, 1967
In Corner B and Other Stories, 1967
The Wanderers, 1971
Voices in the Whirlwind and Other Essays, 1972
Chirundu, 1979
Afrika My Music: An Autobiography, 1957–1983, 1984
Bury Me at the Marketplace: Selected Letters, 1943–1980, edited by
    N. Chabani Manganyi, 1984

Further Reading

Lodge, Tom, Black Politics in South Africa since 1945, Johannesburg: Ravan Press, and London and New York: Longman, 1983
Manganyi, N. Chabani, Exiles and Homecoming: A Biography of Es'kia Mphahlele, Johannesburg: Ravan Press, 1983
Thuynsma, Peter N., Footprints along the Way: A Tribute to Es'kia Mphahlele, Braamfontein: Skotaville, and Yeoville: Justified Press, 1989

MS.
US magazine, established 1972

Founded by Gloria Steinem, Elizabeth Forsling Harris, and Patricia Carbine, Ms. was created as a medium for the American feminist movement, then undergoing a rebirth. Its struggles between reliance on advertising revenues and its editorial mission illustrate the difficulties of maintaining a principled stance, free of the "censorship" of the advertising industry in the US mass circulation magazine market.

The magazine covered controversial and often-ignored topics from a feminist perspective, including abortion rights, equal pay, job discrimination, domestic violence, and lesbianism and gay rights. Its treatment of such issues antagonized many conservatives, who protested to school boards across the United States to have the magazine removed from school libraries. In 1979, a US district court ruling found that Ms.'s right to freedom of speech had been violated by its removal from a New Hampshire high school library, and that the magazine was a valuable educational tool. Similar victories were obtained in cases brought against Bennington, Vermont and the Mt Diablo, California school district.

In seeking to have a magazine whose advertising policies matched its editorial agenda, Steinem, Carbine and their col-

leagues struck a blow for change in the way that advertisers dealt with women's magazine publishers and the type of advertising they directed towards female audiences. Steinem insisted that advertisers pay the same premium prices for ad space in the magazine that they did for Time or men's magazines such as Esquire, which was several times the standard rates in women's magazines. Moreover, the publisher Patricia Carbine and her staff sought to convince major advertisers for products such as cars, alcohol, and electronics that women made consumer decisions about these items, not just about beauty and fashion products. Despite market research data showing that Ms. readers were affluent, highly educated, and had careers, the magazine was a tough sell to male-dominated advertising agencies suspicious of feminism. One media director of a large advertising agency vehemently rejected the magazine's first market research study. Nonetheless, Ms. magazine was successful in attracting companies such as Ford, McDonnell-Douglas, and Hublein Liquors to have major accounts with the magazine – the first women's magazine to do so.

Carbine also sought to make sure the messages contained in these ads did not contradict the magazine's feminist agenda, and frequently requested changes in what they deemed to be sexist language and imagery. Even so, ads perceived as offensive led to vociferous responses from angry readers. One ad for Hublein Liquors, in which a woman appeared with a black eye, generated an intense outpouring of letters from readers who accused the firm of joking about domestic violence and demanded its immediate withdrawal. *Ms.* staff presented the letters to Hublein, who changed the campaign and printed an apology to readers in the next issue.

Despite its success in increasing the range and quality of advertising to female audiences, *Ms.* fell victim to the market pressures of the American magazine publishing industry. Even with growing advertising rates during the 1970s, *Ms.* increasingly lost money because its ethical advertising practices, which dictated a level of selectivity that kept the total number of ads per issue low, simply could not keep pace with the costs of production to a growing readership base. In order to salvage the magazine, *Ms.* applied for and was given nonprofit status in 1980. In return, the magazine had to adhere to an educational mission that prevented it from endorsing specific political candidates or platforms – one of the strongest components of its feminist mission during the 1970s. For most of the 1980s, *Ms.* barely survived on grants from charitable donors. Finally, in 1987, Gloria Steinem was forced to sell the magazine or cease publication. She sold the publication to Fairfax Communications, an Australian conglomerate, which, under its new editor-in-chief, Australian feminist Anne Summers, sought to make *Ms.* a commercially profitable venture. Summers attempted to broaden the magazine's appeal by remaking it into a general-interest news magazine for women, combined with features more like those in traditional women's magazines. The new *Ms.* resorted to carrying fashion and beauty advertising previously omitted from the magazine's pages. Movie stars and talk show hosts appeared on the cover. This strategy alienated long-time feminist readers, and failed to win greater acceptance among advertisers. The venture proved unsuccessful; *Ms.* was losing $150,000 a month, and circulation dropped from a peak of 550,000 to under 100,000. The magazine was sold twice more, and in 1990, new owner Lang Communications temporarily suspended publication.

The magazine's future uncertain, Steinem appealed to publisher Dale Lang to keep it going. To avoid the long-standing advertising problem, she suggested that it be run as an advertising-free bi-monthly, paid for by high cover prices and yearly subscription rates. This strategy proved successful, as first and second printings of 25,000 copies each sold out within days. In the first issue of the new *Ms.*, Steinem wrote a scathing editorial on Estée Lauder, Philip Morris, Pillsbury, Carnation, and General Mills who previously had refused to advertise in the magazine because of objections to editorial content. She specifically cited an incident in 1980, when Revlon pulled its advertising from the magazine because it ran a cover photo of Soviet feminists who were not wearing make-up. Steinem asserted that advertisers controlled almost all the editorial copy in women's magazines. "That nothing-to-read feeling comes from editorial pages devoted to 'complimentary copy'; to text or photos that praise advertised categories, instruct in their use, or generally act as extensions of ads," she wrote. The issue also revived an old feature, "No Comment", which focused on objectionable advertising, this time featuring ads that *Ms.* itself had previously run. Within a year of foregoing advertising, *Ms.* turned a profit, albeit on a circulation base much lower than when supported by advertising. By 1999, *Ms.* was reaching a niche market of devoted subscribers, and was also sold in bookstores alongside specialized journals.

STEPHANIE DYER

Further Reading

Echols, Alice, *Daring to Be Bad: Radical Feminism in America, 1967–1975*, Minneapolis: University of Minnesota Press, 1989

Heilbrun, Carolyn G., *The Education of a Woman: The Life of Gloria Steinem*, New York: Dial Press, 1995; London: Virago, 1996

Steinem, Gloria, *Moving Beyond Words*, New York: Simon and Schuster, 1994

Thom, Mary (editor), *Letters to Ms., 1972–1987*, New York: Holt, 1987

Thom, Mary, *Inside Ms.: 25 Years of the Magazine and the Feminist Movement*, New York: Holt, 1997

ALBERT WOMAH MUKONG
Cameroonian writer, bookseller, and political activist, 1928–

Albert Womah Mukong has long been a thorn in the side of successive Cameroonian governments, and has suffered incarceration and censorship on account of his political convictions. It is Mukong's view that Cameroon has been under a dictatorship since independence. He is also critical of the position of the Anglophone minority – of which he is a member – in postcolonial Cameroon. According to Mukong, Francophone Cameroon has colonized the Anglophone areas. His political vision of Cameroon proposes a solution for the Anglophone community. He advocates a return to a federated state, where Anglophone Cameroonians would be able to determine their own destiny free of interference from Francophone politicians.

A founding member of the One Kamerun Congress, he was elected its general secretary in July 1961 in Kumba. The following year, rumours of his arrest as a member of the One Kamerun Movement made him take refuge in Ghana, where he worked for Nkrumah's Convention People's Party newspaper, and later in Togo, before returning to Cameroon in 1964.

Between 1964 and 1970 he was arbitrarily detained on two occasions. The arrests appear to have been motivated by a desire on the part of the government to curb his political activities and to curtail his freedom of expression. In October 1970 Mukong was detained once again without charges, despite the fact that by this time he was politically more or less inoperative. His arrest was part of president Ahmadou Ahidjo's attempt to eradicate any form of opposition whatsoever in Cameroon. He was thrown into a 3.75m × 2m cell, with 18 other inmates, suffering horrendous living conditions including artificial light on 24 hours a day and extreme overcrowding.

Mukong spent three months in the secret services detention centre (BMM) before he was called for questioning. Although physical and psychological abuse in order to extract confessions was routinely used at the BMM, Mukong was not tortured at that time. While under arrest, he never hid the fact that he was against the government; hence there was no need to torture him to discover his opinions. His honesty and bravery won him some respect from his captors. Mukong was not exempt from the occasional caning, however.

In February 1971 he was sent to Mantoum detention centre for an indefinite period. He hoped for an early release, but it would be two years before he left Mantoum to receive medical treatment in Yaoundé. In his book *Prisoner without a Crime* Mukong documents the brutality and constant humiliation he and other prisoners suffered at Mantoum. Officers at the prison had created a forced labour camp that operated for their own personal benefit. Meanwhile, conversations among prisoners were routinely monitored, and the use of certain words, if reported to the authorities, could get one in trouble. At one point Mukong was sent into solitary confinement for having petitioned the head of state about his detention, for which he still had not received any explanation. Life in the detention centre became more difficult. Mukong fell ill, but the director would not allow him hospital treatment. Eventually, however, in late April 1972, he was taken to Founban Hospital. However, reports of conversations in which Mukong criticized the government filtered back to the prison director who sent him back – while he was still ill – to Mantoum. After more time in solitary confinement, he was finally moved to Yaoundé for medical attention in late 1972.

While in Yaoundé, Mukong enjoyed relative freedom to move around the city. At this point he could have gone into exile. Instead, he decided to remain in Cameroon in order to fight for people's rights and greater political freedom. On his return to Mantoum he went on a hunger strike to protest against the reunification of Anglophone and Francophone Cameroons, an arrangement which he believed was heavily slanted against the anglophone community. He fasted for nine days, refusing to give in to attempts by authorities to make him stop. He also petitioned the government about his case, but once again was unsuccessful. His name was omitted from a list of prisoners to be released in January 1974. In March of that year, Ahidjio's government tried to bribe him with a political appointment, which he rejected. Shortly afterwards he was transferred to another detention centre at Tcholliré in north

Cameroon, where he remained until his release on 6 October 1976, by which time he had served a six-year sentence without ever being formally charged or convicted of any crime.

After his release Mukong continued to receive the unwelcome attention of the government. All those associated with him were investigated by state security agents, which resulted in his complete isolation. Meanwhile, his written work – like that of fellow Cameroonians Mongo Beti and Jacques Ndongo – was censored and/or suppressed. The autobiographical work *Prisoner without a Crime* (1985), for instance, was banned a few months after its publication. He wrote in 1992:

> I was running a bookshop and doing quite well until the police harassment started. They came for my works which were critical of government, including copies of *Prisoner without a Crime* (his autobiographical work) which they took to the Commissariat Spécial. Other works were returned, but all copies of *Prisoner without a Crime* were confiscated and no compensation paid . . . These events scared away many customers from our bookshop . . . Gradually we lost business and fell short on our loan repayments; soon we could not pay for the books we got on credit from other bookshops . . .

The political demise of Ahmadou Ahidjo in the early 1980s offered Mukong no respite. Under the new president, Paul Biya, Mukong's writings remained banned. In addition, he was forced to close his bookshop. After an interview given to the BBC in 1988, he spent another eleven months in prison. He was also detained for three months in 1990, because of his association with the Social Democratic Front (SDF). This time Mukong enjoyed the relative luxury of being tried, and was eventually acquitted by a military tribunal and released. In the face of this high degree of victimization Mukong finally resolved to leave the country and continue his political activities abroad. He now lives in England.

DIEUDONNÉ DANG

Writings

The Problem of the New Deal, 1984
An Open Letter to the First Ordinary Congress of the New Deal, 1985
Prisoner without a Crime, 1985
What Is to Be Done, 1985
Editor, *The Case for the Southern Cameroons*, 1990
"The Tale of a Lesson Learned Too Well", *Index on Censorship*, 2 (1991)
My Stewardship in the Cameroon Struggle, 1992

Further Reading

Breitinger, Eckhard, "'Lamentations Patriotiques': Writers, Censors and Politics in Cameroon" *African Affairs*, 92 (1993): 557–75

HEINER MÜLLER
German dramatist, 1929–1995

Heiner Müller was the leading playwright to emerge in the German Democratic Republic (GDR) between the death of Bertolt Brecht in 1956 and the collapse of the regime in 1989. Müller, like Brecht, had welcomed the establishment of the GDR in 1949, as an antidote to Nazism, but came to realize that "really existing socialism" in this "Stalinist colony of Moscow" had no connection with the utopian socialism he believed in. Having grown up under a fascist dictatorship, he found himself living most of his life under a communist one.

The first of Müller's plays to be performed was *Der Lohndrücker* (The Scab), which was premiered in Leipzig in 1958. At first, it seemed to be a standard piece of "socialist realism" and was treated as such, but a year later it became the subject of a campaign by the ruling Socialist Unity Party of Germany (Sozialistische Einheitspartei Deutschlands, or SED) against unsound drama, and it was not performed again in East Germany until 1988. Müller's next play, *Die Umsiedlerin; oder, Das Leben auf dem Lande* (1961, The Incomer; or, Life on the Land), which deals with the collectivization of agriculture, was written, tried out, and rewritten during two years of rehearsals with a student company. Müller recalled that "we thought we were doing something really socialist, the students too, they were having great fun". The authorities, however, viewed Müller's attempt at constructive criticism as an attack on the system and *Die Umsiedlerin* was banned after just one performance (1961). The Berlin Wall had been completed on 13 August, just a month beforehand, so the authorities were particularly sensitive. Under official pressure, the Academy of Arts denounced the play as counter-revolutionary, students who had taken part in it were forced to repudiate it, and B.K. Tragelehn, who had directed it, was sent to the mines. The Writers Union duly expelled Müller and he was not reinstated until 1988.

For the next two years Müller and his writings were taboo, and with contemporary topics closed to him he turned to classical subjects. In his *Philoktetes* (Philoctetes), Odysseus stands for political realism and Neoptolemos for idealism. Being banned in the East made Müller attractive in the West, and *Philoktetes* was premiered in Munich in 1968. Western commentators condemned Odysseus as a depiction of Stalin, whereas Müller had considerable sympathy with this pragmatic figure.

In 1968, Müller wrote *Der Horatier* (The Horatian) in response to the events in Prague, where an attempt at limited liberalization of a system much like the GDR's was stifled by a Warsaw Pact invasion in which units from the GDR participated. A conflict between Rome and Alba is decided in single combat. The Horatian kills the Alban champion, who is also his sister's fiancé. When she complains he kills her too. Should he go down in history as a hero or as a murderer? *Der Horatier* is the nearest Müller came to a parable play. In the GDR discussions of Stalin's crimes were still subject to the strictest censorship: Müller's play is a coded plea for the revelation of historical truth. When *Philoktetes* was finally performed in East Germany in 1977, a Stasi agent reported that Müller was clearly using the classical myth to attack political expediency and the betrayal of ideals in the GDR. However, there was no attempt to make the production explicitly topical, so no action was taken.

The authorities in the GDR issued either a "directive" or a "recommendation" in relation to a suspect play: a directive represented an outright ban on performance, but a recommendation effectively left the decision to the theatre that proposed to stage the play. A recommendation was enough to make most directors give up on a play, but in 1973 Ruth Berghaus disregarded a recommendation and began Müller's rehabilitation by staging his *Zement* (Cement) with the Berliner Ensemble at the Theater am Schiffbauerdamm. Similarly, Benno Besson ignored a recommendation, and staged both *Die Schlacht* (1975, Slaughter) and *Die Umsiedlerin* (disguised as *Die Baueren* [1975, The Peasants]), at the Volksbühne, another theatre in East Berlin, in the late 1970s.

In the early 1970s Müller had turned to German history. *Die Schlacht* deals with Hitler's Germany in five short, bloody scenes. In *Germania Tod in Berlin* (1977, Germania Death in Berlin), scenes set in the GDR between 1947 and 1953 are alternated with scenes from German myth and history; the play shows the workers' uprising of June 1953 – still a taboo subject 20 years later – and paints a dismal picture of the GDR, while West Germany is presented as the child of Adolf Hitler and Joseph Goebbels, in a mock nativity presided over by the three wise western powers. *Leben Gundlings Friedrich von Preussen Lessings Schlaf Traum Schrei* (1977, Gundling's Life Frederick of Prussia Lessing's Sleep Dream Scream) identifies the roots of German militarism in the 18th century and focuses on the role of Frederick the Great. All these plays were performed in West Germany but only *Die Schlacht* was performed in the GDR, where it caused a sensation because its picture of life under the Nazis was so different from the official version taught in schools. These are postmodern plays that move rapidly through different styles, ranging from circus pastiche in one scene to naturalism in the next.

In 1977, Müller went through an intellectual crisis. The risings in East Germany (1953), Hungary (1956), and Czechoslovakia (1968) had demonstrated the gulf that separated the people from their communist rulers, posing a dilemma for Marxist intellectuals that Müller confronted in his *Die Hamletmaschine* (Hamletmachine). This short, allusive, non-linear text based on *Hamlet* was premiered in Paris in 1979 and has since been an enduring success with experimental companies everywhere. The central figure imagines himself as both protester against, and defender of, the Budapest regime. *Hamletmaschine* established Müller's reputation among the western avant garde, but it remained unperformed in the GDR as long as that state existed.

By 1980, Müller was an international celebrity. The GDR allowed him to travel freely, but continued to censor his plays as "subversive" or "formalist" or both. In West Germany, of which he was highly critical, he was showcased as a dissident, while his early "socialist realist" plays were ignored. He happily bestrode the Berlin Wall, calling a plague on both their houses.

In 1988, Müller directed a revival of *Der Lohndrücker*,

which was now officially hailed as a socialist classic. Müller had realized that the Stalinist roots of the GDR were inscribed in the text, and he proceeded to expose them. A lifesized dummy of Stalin watches events from a box; Stalin's face appears illuminated in the doorway of a party office; when a strike is threatened the rumble of Soviet tanks is heard. Müller commented, "If they let this through, the GDR's days are numbered". The play had a sell-out run and in 1989 the Wall came down.

It had taken an average of 15 years for each of Müller's plays to reach the stage in the GDR, and as we have seen some never made it. Publication had not been any easier. The only official ban on publication was applied to *Mauser*, Müller's response to Bertolt Brecht's "agitprop" play *Die Massnahme* (1930, The Measures Taken), but publishers in the GDR knew better than to risk publishing *Germania Death in Berlin* or *Hamletmachine*. Müller himself supervised the edition of his works published by Rotbuch Verlag in West Berlin.

In 1993, Müller admitted that he had had some contact with the Stasi, the GDR's state security police, during the 1980s. Examination of the record shows that he did so in the hope of effecting some improvement in relations between the authorities and individual artists, but his attempts to explain his motives went largely unheeded amid the free-market triumphalism that prevailed in newly unified Germany.

HUGH RORRISON

Writings

Der Lohndrücker, 1958; as *The Scab*, translated by Carl Weber in *The Battle*, 1989
Die Umsiedlerin; oder, Das Leben auf dem Lande, 1961, revised version as *Die Bauern*, 1975
Philoktet, 1966; as *Philoctetes*, translated by Oscar Mandel and Maria Kelsen Feder, 1981
Zement, 1974; as *Cement*, translated by Helen Fehervary *et al.*, 1979
Der Horatier, 1975; as *The Horatian*, translated by Carl Weber in *The Battle*, 1989
Die Schlacht, 1975; as *The Battle*, translated by Carl Weber in *The Battle*, 1989; as *Slaughter*, translated by Marc von Henning in *Theatremachine*, 1995
Mauser, produced in English 1975, in German 1980; published in German 1976; as *Mauser*, translated by Carl Weber in *The Battle*, 1989
Germania Tod in Berlin, 1977; as *Germania Death in Berlin*, translated by Carl Weber in *Explosion of a Memory*, 1989
Leben Gundlings Friedrich von Preussen Lessings Schlaf Traum Schrei, 1977, as *Gundling's Life Frederick of Prussia Lessing's Sleep Dream Scream*, translated by Carl Weber in *Hamletmachine*, 1984
Die Hamletmaschine, 1977; as *Hamletmachine*, translated by Carl Weber in *Hamletmachine*, 1984
Hamletmachine and Other Texts for the Stage, translated by Carl Weber, 1984
The Battle: Plays, Prose, Poems, edited and translated by Carl Weber, 1989
Explosion of a Memory: Writings, edited and translated by Carl Weber, 1989
Theatremachine, edited and translated by Marc von Henning, 1995

Further Reading

Fischer, Gerhard (editor), *Heiner Müller: Contexts and History*, Tübingen: Stauffenberg, 1995
Kalb, Jonathan, *The Theater of Heiner Müller*, Cambridge and New York: Cambridge University Press, 1998
Wallace, Ian, *et al.* (editors), *Heiner Müller: Probleme und Perspektiven, Bath Symposium 1998*, Amsterdam: Amsterdamer Beiträge zur neueren Germanistik, 2000

MULTATULI
Dutch civil servant and novelist (real name: Edouard Douwes Dekker), 1820–1887

Eduard Dekker, who used the pen-name "Multatuli" (Latin for "I have borne many things"), belongs to a group of civil servants or former civil servants, in various countries, who have broken the "code" that people in such positions are expected to adopt by revealing matters that governments find politically embarrassing. Most examples, perhaps, have arisen in the 20th century, when issues of official secrecy and the public's right to information became unprecedentedly prominent. Multatuli's case is therefore unusual for its relatively early date (1860). It is also noteworthy because of Multatuli's subject matter, given that radical criticism of the colonial system was rarely put into print in the 19th century; and for its form, since, while most civil servants who feel constrained to tell what they know have resorted to journalism, Multatuli wrote a novel, *Max Havelaar*.

Dekker joined the civil service of the Dutch East Indies (now Indonesia) in Java in 1838, and became a district officer at Natal, on the west coast of Sumatra, in 1842. A year later, he was suspended for irregularities in his bookkeeping and suspected fraud, but was found to have been inept rather than dishonest.

In 1853, Dekker and his wife, Everdine, baroness van Wijnbergen, returned to the Netherlands on two years leave. He lived far beyond his means, borrowed a considerable amount of money, and came up with various schemes, all unsuccessful, that he hoped would allow him to achieve the standard of living and prestige that he felt he was entitled to. Returning late from his leave, he was appointed assistant resident of Lebak, the scene of recent corruption by the native Regent. Dekker, under the impression that he had been given the task of bringing the Regent to justice, had him charged, regardless of the politics of the situation. The principal authorities in the Dutch East Indies – the governor-general and the Council of the Indies – both regarded this as overhasty, and the Council recommended that Dekker be dismissed. Before this could occur, however, Dekker tendered his resignation, which was accepted.

After some unsuccessful attempts to obtain other work, Dekker returned to Europe and began to write *Max Havelaar* in Brussels. The characters and the narrative are clearly drawn from his personal experiences. The action is set in Lebak, and the individuals involved in the Havelaar (Dekker) affair are disguised by pseudonyms. More importantly, however, Multatuli draws attention to the essential injustice of the Dutch colonial *Kultuurstelsel* (known in English either as the "Culture System" or as the "Cultivation System"):

> If anyone should ask whether the man who grows the products receives a reward proportionate to the yields, the answer must be in the negative. The government compels him to grow on *his* land what pleases *it*; it punishes him when he sells the crop so produced to anyone else but *it*; and *it* fixes the price it pays him . . . and . . . since the entire business *must* yield a profit, this profit can be made in no other way than by paying the Javanese just *enough* to keep him from starving, which would decrease the producing power of the nation.

Dekker sent the novel to Jacob van Lennep, a prominent Dutch novelist and man of letters, who was impressed by its quality as literature and promised to find a publisher for it. Dekker wanted more, however, than publication: he wished to be reinstated in Java, to have his pension rights restored, and to receive a knighthood. He asked van Lennep to negotiate with the minister for the colonies, Jan Jacob Rochussen, to these ends, and even stated that, if all three conditions were met, he would not proceed with publication of the novel. Perhaps not surprisingly, none of them was, although Dekker was offered an "honourable, independent and lucrative" position in Suriname, which he rejected.

The government appears to have taken no steps to prevent the publication of *Max Havelaar*. Censorship, such as it was, was carried out by van Lennep, who maintained his admiration for the work but sought to soften its political impact. He succeeded, first, by persuading Multatuli to disguise the connections between people and places in the novel, and members of the colonial service. He then persuaded the author to sign over his copyright in the work, suggesting that he would otherwise be unable to represent Multatuli when dealing with publishers. Compounding this betrayal, he then made changes of his own.

The novel caused a considerable sensation on its first publication, in 1860. Whether or not the novel was directly responsible for the abolition of the *Kultuurstelsel* is not known for certain, but the abolition occurred gradually between 1862 and 1866.

Only in 1875, however, after various changes in the ownership of the copyright, did Multatuli have an opportunity to remedy van Lennep's corrections. As he commented:

> The pestilential dots with which Mr van Lennep thought fit to spoil my work have here of course been replaced by readable words. I have left unaltered the pseudonyms Slymering, Verbrugge, Duclari, and Slotering, because these names have become common property. The real names of Controleur Verbrugge and Commandant Duclari were van Hement and Collard. The Resident of Bantam was Brest van Kempen, and the petty Napoleon at Padang was General Michiels . . . I was certainly not out to observe secrecy – as, if it comes to that, is apparent from the whole purport of the book – but I found it distasteful to expose certain persons to criticism by the lay reading public. I considered that in the *official* world – and the matter was *their* concern – people would know who they had to approach for further information on the facts I revealed. And they *did* know; for, after *Havelaar* had reached the Indies, Governor-General Pahud went post haste to Lebak "to investigate complaints about abuses there."

DEREK JONES

Writings
Max Havelaar; of, de koffieveilingen der Nederlandse handelsmaatschappij, 1860; as *Max Havelaar; or, The Coffee Auctions of the Dutch Trading Company*, translated by Roy Edwards, 1967
Volledige werken (Complete Works), edited by G. Stuiveling, 25 vols, 1950–95
The Oyster and the Eagle: Selected Aphorisms and Parables, translated by E.M. Beekman, 1974

Further Reading
Keijsper, Chantal (editor), *K. Ter Laan's Multatuli Encyclopedie* (K. Ter Laan's Multatuli Encyclopedia), The Hague: Sdu, 1995
Straten, Hans van, *Multatuli: van blanke radja tot bedelman* (Multatuli: From White Rajah to Beggar), Amsterdam: Bas Lubberhuizen, 1995
Veer, Paul van 't, *Het Leven van Multatuli* (The Life of Multatuli), Amsterdam: Arbeiderspers, 1979

MUNNANSI/THE CITIZEN
Ugandan newspaper, founded 1980

The Citizen was the English-language newspaper of the Uganda Democratic Party (DP). This was the official parliamentary opposition after the fraudulent elections of 1980, which had brought president Milton Obote and his Uganda People's Congress (UPC) to power. Shortly afterwards the National Resistance Army (NRA), led by Yoweri Museveni, launched an armed rebellion against the UPC government, based largely in the "Luwero Triangle" to the northwest of Kampala. Luwero became a byword for gross and vicious human rights violations.

Obote's army massacred hundreds of thousands of civilians over a five-year period.

The Citizen was one of four newspapers that the government banned in early 1981, before the Luwero war was properly under way. *The Citizen* neatly sidestepped the ban. The Luganda version of the paper, *Munnansi* (which means "The Citizen"), continued to be published. The Democratic Party simply launched an "English-language edition" of *Munnansi*. Official harassment and threats to the printers soon reduced the English

Munnansi to a typewritten, cyclostyled A4 newsletter, but it continued to appear fortnightly throughout Obote's rule. The paper soberly documented human rights abuses in the Luwero Triangle and elsewhere, publishing lists of political detainees and victims of army killings. Given the extraordinary difficulties of access for outside human rights investigators, *Munnansi*'s reports were a vital source of information in building up the indictment against the Obote regime.

The paper's staff were regularly arrested and often held for long periods without charge. When Obote was finally overthrown in a military coup in 1985, four *Munnansi* journalists were among the hundreds of political detainees released. The editor Anthony Ssekweyama was a particular target, being detained without charge on a number of occasions. He was also charged several times with sedition, although none of the cases ever came to court. He only finally appeared before the high court in 1987, facing a charge of treason against the new NRA government, of which he was finally acquitted. By then the English-language *Munnansi* had reverted to its original masthead and was published as a tabloid newspaper. But it never regained the pre-eminence it had enjoyed during its most difficult years.

RICHARD CARVER

Further Reading

Amnesty International, *Uganda: The Human Rights Record, 1986–1989*, New York: Amnesty International, 1989

Carver, Richard, *Truth from Below: The Emergent Press in Africa*, London: Article 19, 1991

MURALS

The origins of modern muralism lie in the Mexican Revolution of 1919, when "Los Tres Grandes" – José Orozco (1883–1949), David Siquieros (1898–1974), and Diego Rivera (1886–1957) – painted pro-revolution murals. In their public art they had the support of the revolutionary government. As mural painting progressed during the 20th century, censorship became a consistent phenomenon. Its likelihood has been influenced by two interrelated variables: first, whether the mural was merely decorative, or had an explicit or implicit political message; second, the extent to which the artist's politics ran counter to those of powerful groups in the society, including state, semi-state, and corporate sponsors.

In 1932 Rivera was commissioned to paint a mural in the showpiece building of US capitalism, the Rockefeller Center on Fifth Avenue, New York. John D. Rockefeller Jr specified an exact title for the mural: "Man at the Crossroads Looking with Hope and High Vision to the Choosing of a New and Better Future". Rivera's response was to design, in Rochfort's words, "a eulogy to revolutionary socialism". He included a portrait of Lenin, which, crucial to subsequent developments, had not appeared in the preliminary sketch approved by Rockefeller. Rockefeller personally requested that Rivera remove the portrait of Lenin, but the artist refused. Despite the fact that the mural was near to completion, he was paid his full commission of \$21,000 and summarily dismissed, the work draped in canvas. It was later proposed that the entire wall on which the painting existed could be moved to the nearby Museum of Modern Art, but Rockefeller had the mural chipped from the wall in 1934.

At the same time a mural painted by Siquieros in Los Angeles was also destroyed. The Plaza Art Center had commissioned him to paint on the theme "Tropical America", but Siquieros felt that what was envisaged was an innocuous portrayal of happy peasants and palm trees. He therefore introduced references to US imperialism in Latin America, including, in the centre of the mural, an indigenous South American crucified underneath an imperialist eagle; elsewhere Mexican and Peruvian revolutionaries were portrayed. In 1934 the mural was

MURALS: Diego Rivera's mural *Man at a Crossroads Looking with Hope and High Vision to the Choosing of a New and Better Future*. The original mural was commissioned for the Rockefeller Center in New York in 1932 by John D. Rockefeller, Jr, and completed in 1934. Rockefeller ordered the destruction of the unfinished work after Rivera refused to remove the portrait of Lenin in the painting. This is the final version that Rivera painted at the Palace of Arts in Mexico City after his return there in 1934.

MURALS: Examples of loyalist and republican murals in Northern Ireland, both dating from the early 1980s. The Loyalist mural, top, shows the red hand of Ulster and the royal crown, flanked by the flag of Ulster and the Union flag. The dates on the mural commemorate the struggle for control of Ireland: 1688, the date of the Protestant William of Orange's taking of the English throne, and 1690, when, at the Battle of the Boyne, the deposed Catholic ruler James II was defeated by the English. The colours of the Union are echoed in the painted kerbstones below, a common feature in loyalist areas in the North. The Republican mural, bottom, shows a hunger striker in the infamous H Block of Long Kesh prison, shown in the background. The figure of Mary, Mother of God, the rosary beads and the legend "Blessed are those who hunger for justice" lend a religious dimension to the imagery of the independence struggle.

partially whitewashed and eventually it was entirely painted out at the behest of the owner of the building.

The New Deal era in the United States led to a proliferation of murals, some of which were censored. The Public Works of Art Project in 1933 commissioned unemployed artists to produce art for federal buildings, including approximately 400 murals. Its successor, the Federal Art Project, between 1938 and 1943 saw the production of more than 2500 murals. The programmes were designed to be politically safe, but there were major controversies. The most celebrated concerned murals painted for the Coit Tower, San Francisco, which included a miner reading a Communist Party newspaper, books by Marx on library shelves, and images of street crime. Despite a public outcry, the murals remained and can be viewed to this day. Other murals at the time were short-lived. For example, the

artist August Henkel was accused of including a portrait of Lenin in his mural at Floyd Bennett Airport, Brooklyn, New York. Despite his insistence that it was a portrait of Franz Reichelt, an early parachutist, the Federal Art Project administrators had three of the four panels of the mural burned. Although murals made up a minority of the works produced under federal sponsorship during the New Deal era, they accounted for a disproportionate amount of controversy and consequent censorship.

Censorship has been particularly widespread in situations where murals are part of a struggle against dictatorship or imperialism. At times this has meant injury or death for the artists concerned. Countless murals were painted in Chile during the period of the Popular Unity government under president Allende between 1970 and 1973. With the subsequent military coup the widespread censorship included murals that were systematically whitewashed, and posters that were destroyed. As Kunzle (1978) concludes: "Seldom in recent history have workers and their expression, artists and their art been subject to so cruel a repression."

A popular socialist government in Nicaragua in the 1980s inspired a similar explosion of mural painting. Almost every street corner of every town and village had paintings celebrating the Sandinista victory and its successes in land reform, education, literacy, etc., as well as condemnation of the previous Somoza regime and the support given by the United States to Contra attempts to overthrow the Sandinistas. But, with the electoral defeat of the Sandinista government in 1990, an official systematic campaign of painting out the pro-revolutionary murals began in Managua, spearheaded by the Somocista mayor. Within two years most of the murals throughout the country had gone (Kunzle 1995).

A similar explosion of mural painting occurred in Northern Ireland beginning in the spring and summer of 1981. A hunger strike by republican prisoners demanding prisoner-of-war status led to unprecedented support within nationalist areas. As 10 prisoners died in succession, hundreds of murals were painted as part of the successful political mobilization of large numbers of nationalists in support of the prisoners. Loyalist murals had existed in the North since 1908, often pro-British and opposed to a unified Ireland. The themes of the republican murals were oppositional, often rooted directly in the military campaign of the Irish Republican Army. No republican muralist has been shot, badly injured, or indeed arrested while painting; but it was not uncommon for people from loyalist areas, as well as members of the police and British army, to destroy the murals under cover of darkness. Loyalist murals tended to survive longer, being less oppositional in content and intent; occasionally, however, they were similarly damaged by people from republican areas.

What Chile, Nicaragua, and Northern Ireland have in common is the existence of murals making direct political statements against powerful political forces both inside and outside the country. But even in the absence of such stark political divisions, there is scope for political murals to be "censored" by opposing political groups. Even murals ostensibly articulating no other message than ethnic pride can be read as politically offensive by other groups. Two examples, a continent and a decade apart, will suffice to illustrate such censorship. In 1983 a mural in East London commemorating a street battle 50 years earlier when local leftists and Jews had blocked a fascist march through their area was destroyed by skinheads and had to be redesigned and repainted. In 1996 a mural of the black campaigner Malcolm X at San Francisco State College was sandblasted after the artist refused to remove a Star of David, which some students took to be an anti-Semitic symbol.

Murals should not be confused with graffiti, despite a blurring of the distinction at the edges, particularly in the case of some of the more ornate spraycan art in the United States and elsewhere. That said, censorship has been closely associated with spraycan art. With arrests of graffiti artists as well as major programmes of obliteration of "pieces", as the paintings are called, from trains, public buildings, bridges, etc., spraycan artists have probably faced more systematic opposition from official sources than most muralists of the 20th century.

BILL ROLSTON

Further Reading

Barnett, Alan W., *Community Murals: The People's Art*, Philadelphia: Art Alliance Press, 1984

Chalfant, Henry and James Prigoff, *Spraycan Art*, London and New York: Thames and Hudson, 1987

Cockroft, Eva Sperling and Holly Barnet Sánchez, *Signs from the Heart: California Chicano Murals*, Albuquerque: University of New Mexico Press, 1993

Hurlburt, Laurance P., *The Mexican Muralists in the United States*, Albuquerque: University of New Mexico Press, 1989

Kunzle, David, "Art and the New Chile: Mural, Poster and Comic Book in a Revolutionary Process" in *Art and Architecture in the Service of Politics*, edited by Henry A. Millon and Linda Nochlin, Cambridge, Massachusetts: MIT Press, 1978

Kunzle, David, *The Murals of Revolutionary Nicaragua, 1979–1992*, Berkeley: University of California Press, 1995

McKinzie, Richard D., *The New Deal for Artists*, Princeton, New Jersey: Princeton University Press, 1973

Prigoff, James and Robin J. Dunitz, *Walls of Heritage, Walls of Pride: African American Murals*, San Francisco: Pomegranate Communications, 2000

Rochfort, Desmond, *The Murals of Diego Rivera*, London: Journeyman, 1987

Rolston, Bill, *Drawing Support: Murals in the North of Ireland*, Belfast: Beyond the Pale, 1992

Rolston, Bill, *Drawing Support 2: Murals of War and Peace*, Belfast: Beyond the Pale, 1996

KIRA MURATOVA
Russian (Moldovan) film director, 1934–

Kira Muratova's career as a film director has been based at the Odessa film studios in Ukraine. Her first two films, *U krutogo iara* (1962, By the Steep Ravine) and *Nash chestnyi khleb* (1963, Our Honest Bread) were co-directed with her then husband, Aleksandr Muratov. Her first solo feature, *Korotkiye vstrechi* (1967, Short Meetings) concerns the triangular relationship between Valentina, a woman who organizes the water supply in a Soviet city, played by Muratova herself; a geologist, Maksim, played by Vladimir Vysotskii; and a young village girl, Nadia, played by Nina Ruslanova. The film is remarkable for the ordinariness of the characters, and the authentic mundanity of their dialogue and their interrelations. Muratova's is emphatically not a political vision, unlike that of so many of the directors whose films ended up on the infamous "shelf" during the Brezhnev years. However, as she recalled in a 1987 interview with Viktor Bozhovich (a key source on the fates of her films), it was precisely this surface banality, this absence of "drama", "clarity", a "central idea", that irritated the few critics who wrote about the film. "Very few copies were made of the film, in fact it scarcely got shown to audiences at all. It was shown in film clubs". Limited distribution was an effective method of censorship in the Brezhnev years.

Muratova then spent three years trying to get permission to film a script about a woman artist. Only after she had conceded the hopelessness of this endeavour did she team up with the scriptwriter Natal'ia Riazantseva, who had been having her own problems with a screenplay entitled *To be a Man*. The film that they made from this script which was eventually given the title *Dolgie provody* (The Long Farewell, or The Long Goodbye), traces the relationship of a divorcée in her early 40s with her teenage son, who thinks he wants to leave and live with his father, an archaeologist. Muratova's method of filming the ordinary lives of ordinary characters with a sympathetic acuteness and rigour that makes them unforgettable reaches its apogee in this brilliantly original work. However, it demands a sympathetic readiness in its viewers to work out for themselves an assessment of its characters. The film was therefore difficult to accept for viewers used to films with clearcut moral assessments.

After the usual process of discussion within the studios, the film was passed almost without cuts, but about ten days later the decision was mysteriously reversed. Muratova was accused of succumbing to bourgeois influences and her characters were found to be "too gloomy". Even their dancing was somehow "not right". In the words of the minister of culture of Ukraine:

> Kira Muratova . . . has filmed her subject in such a way as to produce a very gloomy film. In her choice of actors, in their look, in the way their surroundings are depicted . . . she has created an atmosphere of the unsuccessful life of a "little person", her "loneliness", her "drama" . . . This is unsocialist, bourgeois realism.

These words are eloquent evidence not only that in the Soviet Union all possible film subjects were ideologically sensitive, but also that questions about how a film was constructed and shot, even about how it looked, were just as likely to provoke the incomprehension, and therefore the ire, of those on whom their fate depended. The film was shelved, despite the eloquent support of Muratova's fellow filmmakers.

As Muratova sardonically recalls, the banning of *Dolgie provody* "interrupted my fate as a director for a long time. That was the first time that I was disqualified." After five years she was persuaded to turn to the theoretically safe Russian classics and attempted to make a film based on part of Mikhail Lermontov's novel *Geroi nashego vremeni* (1840, A Hero of Our Time), but the footage she shot to test her actors was found to contain "allusions" and "modernization", and this project, too, was closed down.

Eventually, in 1979, Muratova made *Poznavaia belyi svet* (Getting to Know the World), a triangle drama set on a building site. This was followed in 1983 by *Sredi serykh kamnei* (Among the Grey Stones), an adaptation of a story written in the late 19th century by V.G. Korolenko, set among beggars and other social outcasts. As Muratova recalls: "*Among the Grey Stones* was more unlucky than my other films, which were just closed down. But this one they started cutting . . . Some scenes were cut out and destroyed." She removed her name from the titles and the film was released as directed by "Ivan Sidorov".

In retrospect, Muratova, along with Aleksei German and Aleksandr Sokurov, can be seen as having been among the directors whose careers were comprehensively distorted by the censorship, delays, and bannings of the Brezhnev period. As she laconically told Bozhovich: "I started looking at life more pessimistically". She is also one whose artistic achievement, like German's and Sokurov's, was subsequently revealed to be enormous. *Korotkie vstrechi* and *Dolgie provody* were released after the intervention of the "conflict commission" set up by the Filmmakers' Union after its fifth congress in 1986, with the express purpose of removing banned films from the shelf, and both were greeted with lavish international praise.

Meanwhile, unlike many other banned filmmakers, Muratova found a way to respond to the changed circumstances of the Soviet Union in the late 1980s. In 1987 she made *Peremena uchasti* (Change of Fate), a version of W. Somerset Maugham's short story "The Letter" set in Central Asia, and in 1989 she directed *Astenicheskii sindrom* (The Asthenic Syndrome), an extraordinarily ambitious evocation of the ambiguities of the perestroika period that also represents a rejection of her earlier aesthetic. In its vigour and originality, *Astenicheskii sindrom* has come to be seen as the most profound and wide-ranging analysis of the confusions of late Soviet society, but its astringency brought it the by now rare distinction of being banned by the still-functioning State Cinema Committee (Goskino). Most specifically, Goskino objected to a scene at the end of the film in which a well-dressed woman on the metro utters a stream of foul abuse to no one in particular. Despite the intervention of the "conflict commission" and the appearance of a number of articles defending the film in the Soviet press, it could not be shown until after it had won the Special Jury Prize at the Berlin Film Festival in 1990. At this point, Goskino agreed that the film could be shown exclusively in clubs – just as Muratova's first film had been – with obligatory introductory lectures explaining Muratova's intentions. This system remained in force until October 1990, when Goskino finally removed all bans on its showing.

In the post-Soviet period Muratova has made three further films, continuing to develop both her moral analysis and her bold formal experimentation. Her recent work shows her to be as acute and unillusioned an observer of human hopes and fears, strengths and frailties, as ever.

JULIAN GRAFFY

Further Reading

Bozhovich, Viktor, "Rentgenoskopiia dushi" (X-Raying the Soul), *Iskusstvo kino*, 9 (1987): 51–70

Bozhovich, Viktor, *Kira Muratova: tvorcheskii portret* (Kira Muratova: A Creative Portrait), Moscow: Soiuzinformkino, 1988

Fomin, Valerii, "*Dolgie provody*" (The Long Farewell) in "*Polka*": *Dokumenty, Svidetel'stva, Kommentarii* (The Shelf: Documents, Evidence, Commentaries), Moscow: Nauchno-issledovatel'skii institut Kinoiskusstva, 1992

Graffy, Julian, "Conflict Resolution", *Index on Censorship*, 20/3 (1991): 24

Graffy, Julian, "Private Lives of Russian Cinema", *Sight and Sound*, 3/3 (March 1993): 26–29

Taubman, Jane A., *Asthenic Syndrome*, Trowbridge, Wiltshire: Flicks, 2000

EDWARD R. MURROW
US journalist and broadcaster, 1908–1965

Edward R. Murrow is the most distinguished and renowned figure in the history of American broadcast journalism. He was a seminal force in the creation and development of electronic newsgathering as both a craft and a profession. His career began at Columbia Broadcasting System (CBS) in 1935 and spanned the infancy of news and public affairs programming on radio through to the ascendancy of television in the 1950s, as it eventually became the nation's most popular news medium. In 1961, Murrow left CBS to become director of the United States Information Agency (USIA) for the new Kennedy administration.

David Halberstam observed in *The Powers That Be* (1979) that Murrow was "one of those rare legendary figures who was as good as his myth". Murrow was apparently driven by the democratic precepts of modern liberalism and the more embracing *Weltanschauung* of the American Protestant tradition. Murrow's imagination and the long-term effects of his early home life impelled him to integrate his parents' ethical guidelines into his own personality to such an extensive degree that Edward R. Murrow became the virtual fulfilment of his industry's public-service aspirations.

Ed Murrow's rich, full, and expressive voice first came to the attention of America's listening public in his many radio reports during the Battle of Britain in 1939. Churchill himself gave the approval for these broadcasts after Murrow produced two weeks of test recordings from the rooftop of Broadcasting House in London, demonstrating that he could deliver eye-witness accounts of the bombing without compromising general security. Murrow exercised self-censorship about military information as he used the airwaves to revivify and popularize many of the democratic ideals that resulted from a broader liberal discourse in Britain, France, and the United States, such as free speech, citizen participation, the pursuit of truth, and the sanctification of individual liberties and rights.

Edward R. Murrow, of course, was only one of many heroes to emerge from World War II, but he became the eminent symbol for American broadcasting. At the outset of the Korean War, Murrow's first policy censure occurred when CBS news officials suppressed his 14 August 1950 radio newscast for criticizing the American offensive: "so far as this reporter is concerned, he doesn't see where or when this conflict will end". Ann Sperber recounts that the army denied any formal action, although "General Douglas MacArthur had gone after CBS to get Murrow out of Korea" and to cease any "unwarranted criticism" of command decisions. Murrow's willingness to tackle controversial issues slowly exacerbated his relationship with CBS executives throughout the 1950s.

Murrow's initial foray into television was as the on-camera host of *See It Now* (1951–58). This series was an adaptation of radio's popular *Hear It Now* which was also co-produced by Murrow and Fred W. Friendly. *See It Now* began in a half-hour format on 18 November 1951. By 20 April 1952, it had been moved to prime-time where it stayed until July 1955, when sponsor Alcoa Aluminum finally withdrew its support after a series of high-profile telecasts challenging McCarthyism and its impact on American liberties. After that point, *See It Now* was expanded to an hour but scheduled more irregularly on a special-events basis.

Through the course of its run, many of *See It Now*'s broadcasts were duly considered breakthroughs for the medium. For example, "This is Korea . . . Christmas 1952" was produced on-location "to try to portray the face of the war and the faces of the men who are fighting it". Murrow's most celebrated piece was his 9 March 1954 telecast, when he engaged Senator Joseph R. McCarthy in a programme "told mainly in [McCarthy's] own words and pictures". In his review, the *New York Times* television critic Jack Gould wrote that "last week may be remembered as the week that broadcasting recaptured its soul".

Edward R. Murrow also produced lighter, less controversial fare for television. His most popular success was as host of *Person to Person* (1953–61) where he chatted informally with a wide array of celebrities every Friday during prime-time, such as Marilyn Monroe, John Steinbeck, and Harry Truman. Murrow remained with this programme through 1958–59, the same season he excoriated the broadcasting industry in a speech before the Radio and Television News Directors Association (RTNDA) for being "fat, comfortable, and complacent" and television for "being used to detract, delude, amuse and insulate us". Murrow had long revelled in his role as broadcasting's Jeremiah. By October 1958, though, the viewing public and the television industry were less inclined to accept yet another of his ethical reprimands, especially since his RTNDA speech was directed at them and their shortcomings. As the business of television grew astronomically during the 1950s, Murrow's priorities fell progressively out-of-step and his role at CBS was gradually diminished to such a point that he departed to the USIA in 1961.

Surprisingly, one of Murrow's first acts as USIA director was to attempt to suppress the BBC telecast of "Harvest of Shame" (*CBS Reports* series), a muckraking exposé about migrant workers in America hosted by the former newsman himself. Murrow even tried to use his previous familiarity with BBC director-general, Hugh Carleton Greene, to prevent the telecast, but Greene refused his old friend's request and the programme was aired as scheduled. In response, "there was . . . a slightly gleeful note [in the US media] in catching the Great Man in a contradiction" (Sperber). This episode was uncharacteristic of Murrow's overall tenure at the USIA, however, which ended with his resignation on 19 December 1963 following the onset of lung cancer.

GARY R. EDGERTON

Writings

This Is London (radio broadcasts August 1939–December 1940), edited by Elmer Davis, 1941
Editor, with Fred W. Friendly, *See It Now*, 1955
In Search of Light: The Broadcasts, 1938–1961, edited by Edward Bliss Jr, 1967

Further Reading

Baughman, James L., "*See It Now* and Television's Golden Age, 1951–1958", *Journal of Popular Culture*, 15 (1981): 106–15

Bliss, Edward Jr (editor), *In Search of Light: The Broadcasts of Edward R. Murrow, 1938–1961*, New York: Knopf, 1967

Bliss, Edward Jr, "The Meaning of Murrow", *Feedback*, 25 (Winter 1983): 3–6

Bliss, Edward Jr, *Now the News: The Story of Broadcast Journalism*, New York: Columbia University Press, 1991

Cloud, Stanley and Lynne Olson, *The Murrow Boys: Pioneers on the Front Lines of Broadcast Journalism*, Boston: Houghton Mifflin, 1996

Edgerton, Gary R., "The Murrow Legend as Metaphor: The Creation, Appropriation, and Usefulness of Edward R. Murrow's Life Story", *Journal of American Culture*, 15/1 (1992): 75–91

Friendly, Fred W., *Due to Circumstances Beyond Our Control . . .*, New York: Random House, 1967

Gould, Jack, "TV and McCarthy", *The New York Times* (14 March 1954): 2, 11

Halberstam, David, *The Powers That Be*, New York: Knopf, and London: Chatto and Windus, 1979

Kendrick, Alexander, *Prime Time: The Life of Edward R. Murrow*, Boston: Little Brown, 1969

Kuralt, Charles, "Edward R. Murrow", *North Carolina Historical Review*, 48 (1971): 161–70

Leab, Daniel J., "*See It Now*: A Legend Reassessed" in *American History, American Television: Interpreting the Video Past*, edited by John E. O'Connor, New York: Ungar, 1983

Lichello, Robert, *Edward R. Murrow: Broadcaster of Courage*, Charlotteville, New York: SamHar Press, 1971

Merron, Jeff, "Murrow on TV: *See It Now*, *Person to Person*, and the Making of a 'Masscult Personality'", *Journalism Monographs*, 106 (1988)

"Murrow's Indictment of Broadcasting", *Columbia Journalism Review* (Summer 1965): 27–32

Persico, Joseph E., *Edward R. Murrow: An American Original*, New York: McGraw Hill, 1988

Smith, R. Franklin, *Edward R. Murrow: The War Years*, Kalamazoo, Michigan: New Issues Press, 1978

Sperber, A.M., *Murrow: His Life and Times*, New York: Freundlich, 1986

Wershba, Joseph, "Murrow and McCarthy: *See It Now*", *The New York Times*, 128/6 (4 March 1979): 31–38

Winfield, Betty Houchin and Lois B. DeFleur (editors), *The Edward R. Murrow Heritage: Challenge for the Future*, Ames: Iowa State University Press, 1986

MUSIC

Music has served to instil religious or moral feeling; to create a sense of community; and to stimulate both cerebral and sensual experiences. It has a unique capacity to take people "out of themselves" in corporate or individual ecstasy. So far, so apparently benign. At intervals throughout history, however, music has also been seen as subversive of established values. Plato considered Dionysian ecstasy incompatible with the ordered state, and recommended banning the music that inspired it. His successors across the centuries have condemned certain kinds of music believed to undermine religion and encourage sexual licence. In the 19th and 20th centuries music that challenged prevailing political orthodoxies or theories of racial superiority, protested against social conditions or incited political action, was censored on much the same basis as other arts that disturb the *status quo*, authoritarian or otherwise.

The words have been more often censored than the music. Sometimes textual censorship has been prompted by forbidden words, sometimes by the use of words to sing of proscribed ideas. Censorship of music alone, however, has been far from absent. The so-called tritone, the interval of three tones, very awkward to sing, was subject to considerable prohibition in both East and West: "Mi contra fa diabolus est in musica", (e against f is the devil in music). Similarly, Western musical convention dictated the use of the diatonic scale for centuries; the introduction, by Arnold Schoenberg, of the 12-tone system early in the 20th century was considered in some societies to be an act of subversion whose implications extended well beyond music.

The Ancient World, and Medieval and Early Modern Europe

It seems that the earliest music was part of a clan's or tribe's self-image and self-definition: integral to ritual, heard on cere-monial occasions. Early music censorship involved tribal or religious interdictions against playing or singing specific pieces or deviating from officially recognized musical styles. As civilizations arose, each developed musical traditions, protected by convention and sometimes by law. When musical notation was invented in ancient Babylon, restrictions soon extended to the circulation of tablets or papyri on which the music was transcribed.

In ancient China, music regulated both cosmic harmony and public morals. Modes, pitches, and tempos corresponded to emotional and moral states in human beings. Music, according to Confucius, was one of the four main functions of government, along with rites (*li*), punishment (*xing*), and administration (*zhong*). Certain kinds of music were considered dissolute and were to be punished. The Chinese administrators were strikingly modern in their practice of collecting popular songs, in which they believed they could discover what people were really thinking: that way rebellion could be forestalled and good and harmonious behaviour promoted. Compare the British magazine *The Spectator* of 7 October 1712:

> A certain Elizabethan Minister of State was invariably at pains to discover the drift of public opinion before embarking on any new policy, to which end, we read, "he had all manner of books and ballads brought to him, of what kind soever, and took great notice how they took with the people; upon which he would, and certainly might very well judge of their present dispositions and proper way of applying them to his own purpose".

In ancient Greece, similarly, music was both an aspect of the workings of the universe ("the music of the spheres") and closely related to human behaviour. According to his biographer, Porphyry, Pythagoras believed that music "soothes the passions of the soul and body by rhythms, songs, and incantations". Porphyry, writing in the 3rd century CE, related the anecdote of the young man listening to the Phrygian mode at a drunken party; leaving the party in the early hours, he sees his girlfriend leaving the home of his rival for her affections; incensed, he prepares to burn her house down; Pythagoras, taking the night air, and believing that it was Phrygian pipe music that gave rise to such extreme violence, suggested that the disappointed lover should listen instead to spondees, which conveyed calm – an arresting rehearsal of modern arguments about the effects of music on young people.

Music was deeply embedded in the civic, artistic, and religious life of ancient Greece. Theatre and poetry were unthinkable without it, and it was central to the joyful worship of the gods at public festivals. To Plato, however, music was a decidedly mixed blessing. From his ideal state, described in the *Republic* and the *Laws*, all musical modes that appealed to the baser instincts – the Mixolydian, Hyperlydian, Lydian, and Ionian – were to be excluded in favour of those that promoted refinement, sobriety, courage, and discipline: views of the Phrygian mode had changed 200 years after Pythagoras, and it, along with the Dorian, was to be allowed. In the 12th century CE the great Arab scholar Ibn Rushd (Averroes) wrote, in his commentary on Plato's *Republic*:

There is nothing at all in common between a sound mind and pleasure. That is because pleasure throws a sharp-minded man into perplexity resembling a madman's, all the more when he goes to excess . . . pleasure should not be mixed with the desire of the musical one; rather he shall desire only the beautiful with self-control . . . this is the end at which the activity of music aims.

A generation after Plato, the future Alexander the Great enjoyed, during his childhood, the poetry and music of Timotheus of Miletus. Alexander is said to have questioned whether it mattered if he played with one string rather than another. Timotheus told him that musicians had to care about these matters, but to a future king it was an issue of no importance. When, however, the composer added four strings to the kithara, the seven-stringed lute, the innovation – and Timotheus' music with it – was condemned by Aristotle; in Sparta, the restructured kithara was seized and hung at the side of a thoroughfare leading to the central marketplace.

Music, often highly ceremonial, played a prominent part in ancient Hebrew religion: "Make a joyful noise to the Lord all the earth; break forth into joyous song and sing praises! Sing praises to the Lord with the lyre, with the lyre and the sound of melody. With trumpets and the sound of the horn make a joyful noise before the King, the Lord" (Psalm 98:4–6, Revised Standard Version). King David appears once to have been carried away in musical ecstasy before the Ark of the Covenant: "And David danced before the Lord with all his might and . . . was girded with a linen ephod. So David and all the house of Israel brought up the ark of the Lord with shouting and with the sound of the horn" (2 Samuel 6:14–15). For this, however, his predecessor Saul's daughter, Michal, "despised him in her heart" – outraged at the indignity of a king exposing himself before servants.

Later, in their Babylonian exile, the Jews had greater reason to fear the power of music: "O peoples, nations and languages . . . when you hear the sound of the horn, pipe, lyre, trigon, harp, bagpipe and every kind of music, you are to fall down and worship the golden image that King Nebuchadnezzar has set up" (Daniel 3:5). Shadrach, Meshach, and Abednego, who refused to comply, were sentenced to the "burning fiery furnace". Later Jewish practice has been wary of music, especially secular music. Anxious to defend their own beliefs and practices against the pagan cults of Syria and Mesopotamia, the rabbis (4th–16th centuries CE) forbade the use of musical instruments in worship: only the ram's horn was allowed and that only on special occasions.

Christian churches have been similarly ambivalent about music, their worship ranging from the austere to the flamboyantly elaborate, and their attitudes to secular music varying from a belief in its transcendent power as a "path to God" to wholesale condemnation of music thought to foster sinfulness. In the first place, as Christianity grew, it absorbed much of Plato's legacy, including the suppression of music considered low, secular, heretical, or pagan. Early Christian worship, mostly clandestine, could hardly be other than chaste and austere, though hymns appear to have been sung. It was felt necessary, none the less, to warn believers to keep their distance from secular music. Clement of Alexandria (died 215 CE) affirmed:

It must be banned, this artificial music which injures souls and draws them into feelings snivelling, impure and sensual, and even a Bacchic frenzy and madness. One must not expose oneself to the powerful influence of exciting and languorous modes, which, by the curve of their melodies, lead to effeminacy and infirmity of purpose. Let us leave coloured [chromatic] harmonies to banquets where no one blushes at music crowned with flowers and harlotry.

St Augustine of Hippo (354–430), writing after Christianity had become the official religion of the Roman empire, explained the ban on musical instruments in worship as the result of their association with the "sensual heathen cults . . . and shameless performances of the degenerate theatre and circus". The ban persisted until 670, when pope Vitalian at length allowed the organ to be played at the Eucharist. In Byzantium, where the Eastern Rite had nurtured its own musical traditions, the ban endured – and has endured in the Eastern Orthodox Church down to the present day.

In the West, St Gregory the Great (pope, 590–604) is credited by his biographer John the Deacon (c.872) with "sitting on the papal throne and dictating to a scribe the melodies that a heavenly dove, perched on his shoulder, is whispering into his ear". However fanciful the legend, it is certain that by the time that the Frankish king Charlemagne was crowned Holy Roman emperor in 800, Gregorian chant ("plainsong") had official status. It was not seriously challenged as the official liturgical music of the Roman Church until the 17th century; and the exclusive use of Latin as the language of the Mass endured until the second half of the 20th century.

In the world outside, however, more popular forms flourished. Minstrels entertained with harp and viol, the troubadours sang of love and despair, and altogether more bawdy forms were sung at fairs and in the marketplaces. And new musical thinking – *ars nova* – also invaded worship, bringing, in the 14th century, polyphonic motets into the Mass, causing some concern to the Avignon pope, John XXII (1316–34), who issued a bull against the innovation, fearing that it would disturb the plainsong.

The Reformation challenged papal hegemony in music as in every other aspect of Christian living. Luther introduced the vernacular to worship and encouraged the setting of hymns to secular tunes. The Calvinist synod of Edam (Netherlands, 1586), on the other hand, prohibited "thoughtless and worldly songs . . . [being] played on church bells or organs". The synod of Dokkum (1591) excoriated: "bell ringing to call young people together, erecting maypoles, hanging up gardens and singing carnal songs and choruses beneath". Privately, it seems, Calvinists liked tunes: if there could be no organ in church, one could at least be introduced into the town hall, and if bells were at first dismissed as papist excess, carillons could take their place. The council of Trent (1544–63), meanwhile, decreed that sung Mass should include nothing "profane . . . but only hymns and divine praises". Musical modes that "give empty pleasure to the ear" were condemned. When Pius IV became pope in 1559, echoing earlier practice, he threatened to exclude music from worship altogether, claiming that settings for the Mass were frivolously ornamental. In response, the Italian composer and choirmaster Giovanni Pierluigi da Palestrina (1525–94) produced settings specifically to demonstrate the efficacy of music in helping worshippers to memorize the liturgy. Convinced, Pius changed his mind; fortunately for posterity, Claudio Monteverdi, Joseph Haydn, and Wolfgang Amadeus Mozart could each contribute their genius to the Church as well as to the world. The English composer William Byrd (1543–1623), meanwhile, who was a Catholic, in a typical piece of resistance to censorship, composed both for his own church, at great risk to his life, and for the Anglicans.

DEREK JONES

Further Reading

Grout, Donald J. and Claude V. Palisca, *A History of Western Music*, 5th edition New York: Norton, 1996

Hucker, Charles O., *China's Imperial Past: An Introduction to Chinese History and Culture*, Stanford, California: Stanford University Press, and London: Duckworth, 1975

James, Jamie, *The Music of the Spheres: Music, Science, and the Natural Order of the Universe*, New York: Grove Press, 1993; London: Little Brown, 1994

Janson, H.W., Dora Jane Janson and Joseph Kerman, *A History of Art and Music*, Englewood Cliffs, New Jersey and New York: Prentice Hall/Abrams, 1968

Kennedy, Michael, *The Concise Oxford Dictionary of Music*, 4th edition Oxford and New York: Oxford University Press, 1996

Robertson, Alec and Denis Stevens (editors), *The Pelican History of Music*, 3 vols, London: Penguin, 1960–68

West, M.L., *Ancient Greek Music*, Oxford: Clarendon Press, and New York: Oxford University Press, 1992

18th- and 19th-Century Europe

By the beginning of the 18th century, churches were no longer the dominant force in music censorship. Censorship was now used to protect political virtue. In 1704 the Scottish patriot Andrew Fletcher wrote to a friend: "If I were permitted to write all the ballads, I need not care who makes the laws of the nation". Expressing a similar sentiment, the minutes of the revolutionary French constitutional assembly of 21 December 1793 state that "every occasion should be celebrated with the singing of hymns praising the fatherland, liberty, equality and fraternity, because hymns have the power to endow the citizens with all manner of virtues". These comments capture the widespread sense that the stirring power of music, especially when accompanied by words, makes a powerful means of influencing public feelings.

In Britain, opera was specifically mentioned as a form of theatre subject to censorship when the stage censorship laws were comprehensively revised in 1737, and modified in 1843. John Gay's *The Beggar's Opera* (1728) successfully combined words and music to lampoon the prime minister, Sir Robert Walpole. The sequel, *Polly* (1729), was promptly banned. In the Habsburg empire, where opera censorship dates at least from 1770, Joseph II had to give his personal approval before Mozart's masterpiece of 1786, *The Marriage of Figaro* (based on Beaumarchais's play of the same name, which had originally been banned in France and was still banned in Austria due to its mockery of the nobility), could be performed. In his foreword to the libretto, Lorenzo da Ponte explained that he had made an "adaptation" from the play, partly due to "prudent considerations and exigencies imposed by morality, place, and spectators".

Beethoven's *Fidelio* could be performed in Vienna in 1805 only after censorship amputations to its theme: a political prisoner unjustly imprisoned by a tyrant. In France during the Revolution, on the other hand, the Committee of Public Safety banned an opera, *Le Tombeau des Impositions et l'inauguration du Temple de la Vérité*, along with other musical and dramatic works that were considered "counter-revolutionary manoeuvres designed to disturb public tranquillity", and to promote views "inimical to the Revolution".

The monarchy restored (1815–30), even the present French national anthem, *La Marseillaise*, was banned due to its obvious appeal to republican sentiment – the ban was repeated during the Second Empire of Napoleon III (1852–70). All over Europe, meanwhile, opera emerged as by far the most important forum in which large numbers of people could gather together, hear the same lyrics, and be influenced by them. Like the dramatic theatre, moreover, it was accessible to the illiterate; the general consensus was that a live performance could have a specially powerful impact in moving crowds to immediate action. Rossini's opera *Le Siège de Corinthe* (1826), a clearly supportive allusion to the Greek revolt against the Ottoman empire, was approved only after several appeals to liberal sentiments were attenuated. Thus the phrase "Liberty! All our sons will rise up in your name" became "O fatherland! . . ." etc.

In 1830 revolutionary outbreaks in both France and Belgium were partly attributed to the impact of operas. In France, during a rehearsal of Rossini's *William Tell* on 29 July 1830, the hero's cry of "Independence or Death" was taken up by everyone in the theatre: musicians, stagehands, and even soldiers on guard rushed into the street to join in the ongoing revolt that succeeded in overthrowing Charles X. Daniel Auber's *La Muette de Portici* (1828), which portrayed a commoner's rebellion in Naples against Spanish rule in 1647, was widely interpreted as a general call for democracy and nationalism. According to the opera historian William Croston, performances of this work, which began in Paris in 1828, were "almost an accessory to the 1830 Revolution". After the French regime was overthrown, the authorities in Brussels and in German towns near the French border banned the opera. However, the ruling Dutch authorities soon lifted the Brussels ban, and, during a performance on 25 August, members of the audience began to stream into the streets destroying symbols of Dutch rule, and helping to touch off the revolt that brought Belgium its independence.

In 1852 the French government banned an opera about the rebellion known as the *Fronde Parlémentaire* (1648), because any such theme was viewed as dangerous, and because it was feared that the phrase "Aux armes" might be picked up in other theatre bands on the streets. Reflecting a similar concern, a 19th-century Italian journalist defended opera censorship because some experiences "when sung, produce an impression not to be tolerated, though they might be tolerated in reading". Even music without words could be banned: in Austrian-controlled Hungary during the 1850s, the Habsburg authorities banned all performances of Hector Berlioz's "Rakoczy March", which had strong links with Hungarian nationalism.

Especially in Italy, but also in some other European countries, such as Russia and Germany, the opera house was an important venue for social gatherings, a place not only to be feared by the authorities but also one to be used by them for secret police surveillance, or, hopefully, to divert public attention away from matters of politics. Thus, the chief minister of the Austrian-ruled Italian state of Lombardy–Venetia urged, during the early 19th century, that La Scala opera house in Milan be kept busy since "it attracts to a place open to observation during the hours of darkness a large part of the 'educated population'". Similarly, an advisory committee in Rome in 1837 recommended that the pope increase his support of opera since "in order for the people to be more calm and content with the government to which it finds itself subjected, it is absolutely clear and confirmed by the experience of the centuries that the means most fitting and conducive to this end is a suitably distracting theatre, decently entertaining and soberly diverting".

Opera censorship was notably strict in Italy, where the Austrian, papal, and Bourbon authorities who dominated the peninsula lived in perpetual fear of appeals to Italian unity, democracy, or anything else that might threaten their rule. In Bourbon-ruled Naples, libretti had to be submitted a year before the proposed opening night, while in Rome, where there were separate ecclesiastical, political, and municipal censors, 41 copies of libretti had to be submitted for clearance. In general, censors struck out virtually all overt political and religious comment and forbade even the mention of such words as "tyrant", "liberty", "regicide", "revolution", "fatherland", and "treason".

Censors in Italy and elsewhere banned some operas entirely, and in many other cases imposed major surgery on the libretti, frequently requiring that characters, times, and places be changed so that they would seem to have no bearing on contemporary political events. While *William Tell* was allowed in France, in Austria, where the censors were sensitive to the portrayal of a Swiss revolt against Habsburg rule in the Middle Ages, the opera could be performed only after the setting was shifted to Scotland, and William Tell became William Wallace. The German-dominated but multinational Austrian empire similarly banned any appeals to local nationalist sentiment in the Hungarian, Polish, and Czech lands.

Verdi's opera *Un ballo in maschera* (1859), based on the assassination of Gustav III of Sweden in 1792, could be performed in Rome only after its setting was shifted to 17th-century North America, and the assassin's target changed into the "colonial governor" of Boston, Massachusetts. In Germany, the Saxon censorship butchered Wagner's *Rienzi* (1842), about a 14th-century Roman revolutionary, by striking out all references that might be interpreted as a call for liberation or national unity in Italy, and, by implication, in Germany also, then divided into nearly 40 petty tyrannies. Thus Rienzi's cry, "Not only Rome shall be free! All Italy shall be free! Hail to United Italy", was changed in Dresden to "Not only Rome is great! All Italy shall be great! Hail to the ancient greatness of Italy!". (It should be noted that, later in German history, *Rienzi* was one of Adolf Hitler's favourite operas.)

Despite formal censorship, and the censorship that composers and librettists imposed upon themselves, Italian audiences frequently interpreted operas set far into the past as bearing on current events, and, by stormy applause or boos, made their views clear. Thus, when Verdi's *Nabucco* was performed in Milan in 1842 the audience quickly identified their plight under Austrian rule with that of the ancient Hebrews under Babylonian rule. The chorus of Hebrew slaves, "Va Pensiero", with its reference to "my country, so lovely and so lost", aroused storms of applause and demands for encores – despite a ban on encores – and soon became something of a national anthem. The Milan police commissioner upbraided the conductor, and even threatened him with arrest for giving Verdi's music "an expression too rebellious and hostile to the imperial government".

An extraordinary document, dated 1870, from the French censors to Napoleon III, recommended a continuation of the ban on *La Marseillaise*. While describing the anthem as the "French song *par excellence*" with an "indisputably heroic and grandiose character", the censors declared that it had, in practice, become "the symbol of revolution", and was "no longer the song of national independence and liberty but the war chant of demagogy". Repeated performances of it, they claimed, would cause "new and dangerous excitation" because "its exclusively revolutionary character is too universally known and accepted today to hope for the government's generosity (in allowing it to be played) to change this at all". As the 20th century would show, revolutionaries themselves would, in their turn, be among the censors.

ROBERT JUSTIN GOLDSTEIN

Further Reading

Arblaster, Anthony, *Viva La Libertà!: Politics in Opera*, London: Verso, 1992

Goldstein, Robert Justin, *Political Censorship of the Arts and the Press in Nineteenth- Century Europe*, Basingstoke: Macmillan, and New York: St Martin's Press, 1989

Kimbell, David R.B., *Verdi in the Age of Italian Romanticism*, Cambridge and New York: Cambridge University Press, 1981

Perris, Arnold, *Music as Propaganda: Art to Persuade, Art to Control*, Westport, Connecticut: Greenwood Press, 1985

The 20th Century

The themes of 20th-century music censorship cut across national and musical boundaries even more radically than before. Ideologies developed on an international scale, and everywhere music was used as a form of resistance to tyranny and oppression. The convergence of musics was in part due to a fresh realization, fuelled by international media, of their power to move and energize.

Ideologies of class

Like the Christian church before it, the Communist Party of the Soviet Union (CPSU) set out to control how people thought and felt. Music was among its first targets, at first in a conventional manner: as the 19th-century Italians and French had sought to eradicate any musical challenges to monarchy, so now the Soviets sought to remove any references at all to the institution it had overthrown; Mikhail Glinka's *A Life for the Tsar* was banned, and the melody "God Save the Tsar" was excised from Tchaikovsky's *1812 Overture*. A campaign against church music was mounted; it was said to be "class hostile".

On the other hand, the full panoply of musical ideology evolved slowly over the decade that followed the Revolution. First a dichotomy between "proletarian music" and "decadent" and "petit-bourgeois" music had to be established. Then the regime sought to distance itself from "modernism"; already the Russian émigré Igor Stravinsky had created a sensation in Paris with his *Rite of Spring* (1913), and by 1923 the Austrian-born Arnold Schoenberg had developed his technique of twelve note music (dodecaphony). This was, according to Maksim Gor'kii, "the music of the fat". By the late 1920s ORKIMD (Association of Revolutionary Composers and Musicians) and Glavrepertkom (Chief Directorate of the Repertoire Committee) were in place. From then on, concert programmes had to be submitted and given a certificate to perform in advance. The abortive Russian Association of Proletarian Musicians, which set out to foment "class struggle on a musical front", made way in 1930 for the Union of Soviet Composers.

In effect, the Union of Soviet Composers, to which all who aspired to official recognition had to belong, now became the sieve through which all new music had to pass. It was proclaimed that, in the new socialist society, composers were working together to create music that reflected "Soviet reality". In practice, under its secretary-general, T.N. Khrennikov, the reality that could be "reflected" was extremely circumscribed – and did not include any expression of misery or pessimism at a time when masses of Soviet citizens were being forcibly removed from their homes, sometimes to the camps.

Dmitrii Shostakovich's opera *Lady Macbeth of Mtsensk* hardly conformed. Premiered in 1934, it met with great success in both Leningrad and Moscow, until Stalin and other officials heard it in January 1936. According to *Pravda*, it was "chaos instead of music". It was banned, the *Fourth Symphony* was withdrawn, and Shostakovich constrained to "apologize" to the party for what had been described as "freakishness" and "unmelodiousness". The two works remained unperformed in the USSR for several decades, and the composer, along with Nikolai Miaskovskii, a former pupil of Rimsky-Korsakov, Vissarion Shebalin, Sergei Prokofiev, and the Armenian, Aram Khachaturian, were the targets of the cultural commissar Andrei Zhdanov's attack on "formalism" at the First Congress of the Union of Soviet Composers in 1948. The Central Committee of the CPSU again attacked "the cult of atonality, dissonance, and disharmony"; it consisted only of "confused, neuro-pathological combinations that transform music into cacophony, into a chaotic conglomeration of sounds".

Given such wholesale rejection, it was surprising that any musical exploration at all took place. Shostakovich himself, departing from the prescribed boundaries in ways that more conventional composers – and censors – failed to understand, created outstanding music that reflected the terror of his times, and, highly subversive, individual despair. Edison Denisov composed *Sun of the Incas* (1964), based on verses by the Chilean Nobel prizewinner Gabriela Mistral; baffled, the censors disparaged the work. Alfred Schnittke could hardly be described as anything else but "formalist", and the Latvian composer Arvo Pärt and the Tartar Sofiia Gubaidulina had the temerity to explore religious themes. It was wisest to work quietly; performers such as Mstislav Rostropovich, Vladimir Ashkenazy, and Gidon Kremer, inevitably in the public eye, had finally to go into exile to achieve artistic freedom; in their homeland they became non-persons.

Meanwhile, from the 1970s, the Soviet Union was forced to take into account the increasing invasion of popular culture from elsewhere in the world, and, courtesy of modern technology, the ability to circulate forbidden music clandestinely on tape: *magizdat*, the musical equivalent of *samizdat*. Songs by Vladimir Vysotskii and Aleksandr Gallich reached wide audiences of young people, now rebelling against the constraints of a system they had had no part in constructing. Andrei Romanov of the rock group Voskresenie (Resurrection) was imprisoned in the early 1980s. In 1984 the Ministry of Culture banned public performance by 41 indigenous rock bands and instituted proscriptions on 34 popular Western artists. In 1985 the Georgian rock group Phantom (so-called because they were, in their words, "phantoms, insubstantial spirits, without much hope of leaving and without rights so long as we remain") came to official attention. The group members Tenghiz Gudava and Emmanuel Tualadze were charged with "anti-Soviet agitation and propaganda", and then with "treason", a capital offence.

Elsewhere in the Soviet bloc, rather paler versions of socialist realism prevailed, but they were stifling enough to force Witold Lutosławski of Poland into semi-exile, or, when he returned, into the performance of more popular music in cafés. His compatriot Andrzej Panufnik and the Hungarian György Ligeti departed for permanent exile, the latter to become a disciple of Anton von Webern and to compose in strikingly "formalist" mode. Hanns Eisler of the German Democratic Republic moved back to his homeland, whence he had fled into exile during the Nazi period; a convinced Marxist himself, he found the libretto for his opera on Faust banned as "negative and formalist" even before the music was written.

The GDR was also the home of the musical dissident Wolf Biermann, again not entirely unsympathetic to Marxism, but whose cabaret songs were too political for the authorities. Banned in 1965, he pointed out:

> My live contact with many people in the GDR is the logical – if paradoxical – result of precisely that official policy of isolation that has been pronounced over me;

the gag that the state has stuffed into the mouth of the song writer acts like a microphone, the official campaign of defamation like an enormous amplifier.

Biermann was deprived of his citizenship in November 1976. Anne McElvoy records that it took another 10 years for the GDR to accept rock music:

> In 1986, I had the dubious honour of acting as interpreter to the first punk-rock group allowed to play in the East. The Neurotics from Harlow New Town caused fervent excitement in Leipzig and Dresden but received a cooler reception from an audience of horrified middle-aged functionaries at the Party Institute in Mittelweida, summoned to see for themselves the musical product of alienated capitalist youth.

In Czechoslovakia, meanwhile, jazz was a primary instrument of resistance, its origins in the resistance of black people to racist oppression more than just obliquely resonant after 1968. The Jazz Section of the Union of Musicians had 7000 members. Jazz clubs openly promoted "bourgeois culture" and the Section even published a three-volume *Rock Dictionary*. It was disbanded on spurious legal grounds in 1986. "Red Music", the foreword to Josef Škvorecký's *The Bass Saxophone* (1978), describes the history of jazz censorship in Czechoslovakia from the Nazi period onwards. He writes: "The police guns of all dictatorships are aimed at the men with the horns".

Members of the Plastic People of the Universe, a rock band, were regularly imprisoned and harassed, but determined to continue with their repertoire. Their leader, Ivan Jivons, affirmed: "It is better not to play at all than to play music that does not flow from one's own convictions. It is better not to play at all than to play what the establishment demands."

Of the communist countries of Asia, we can be reasonably sure that North Korea applied its restrictive ideology to music – it is known that the government systematically destroyed all indigenous musical instruments as feudal survivals; and that in Cambodia under the Khmer Rouge music did not escape the general vandalism and genocide. Details are at present scarce.

The Chinese People's Republic inherited not only a set of attitudes that their leaders had imbibed from Soviet writers, but also a mixed musical tradition: the coastal areas had been greatly influenced by Western occupation, adopting such forms as hymn singing and marching bands; inland, Chinese music was said to lack a developed idea of harmony, relying on memory. The Chinese Communist Party (CCP), in this at variance with its Soviet counterparts, decided at first on a policy of "walking on two legs". The composer Xian Xingai was charged with the task of reworking Chinese folk music along Western lines, and with the development of "Chinese harmony". Significantly, ornament and improvisation were not to be allowed. After Mao Zedong's "Talk to the Music Workers" in 1956, such compositions as the *Yellow River Cantata* and the *White Haired Girl* clearly owed something to Soviet models.

All was thrown into confusion again by the Cultural Revolution (1966–69). "Music workers" and students were despatched to the countryside to learn from the peasants. Jiang Qing, Mao Zedong's wife, arranged for the radicalization of the Beijing Opera, showing that even the "most stubborn of strongholds"

could be taken by storm and revolutionized. Western music was excoriated, Schubert and Beethoven coming in for special vituperation; the effect was still apparent in a statement by Jiang Qing in 1974:

> Some people talk about bourgeois classical music with great relish, are mesmerised by it and prostrate themselves before it, showing their slavish mentality for all things foreign. They are nihilists with regard to national art. Their reverence for foreign things is actually reverence for the bourgeoisie.

Officially sanctioned mass music (*qunzhong yinyue*) and revolutionary song (*geming gequ*) continued to be the norm.

Unlike in the Soviet Union, however, music policy see-sawed. In the early 1980s, as well as considerable recording of folk and traditional music, Western music was again welcomed. The expatriate pianist Fou T'song was allowed to visit – and to play Chopin. In a society hitherto known for ideologically driven musical austerity, "light music" (*qing yinyue*), originating in Taiwan and Hong Kong, was allowed to circulate; indeed, a state-run popular music industry emerged. *Xibei feng* (northwest wind) combined folk music and disco, while commenting on Chinese culture, ancient and modern. Yet, on 12 March 1982 the party resolved to forbid "the import, reproduction, sale, and transmission of reactionary, yellow, obscene recordings, and video recordings". Some 250 cassettes were confiscated and destroyed in Shaanzi province, including 41 from the period of the Cultural Revolution.

Nevertheless, rock music emerged in the late 1980s, and was closely associated with the student rebellion in Tiananmen Square of June 1989. The heavy metal guitarist Gao Qi said:

> In China, we have several thousand years of feudalism, which makes people's thinking all alike, conformist, without individuation. Now, after reform and liberalization, we have a generation of youth that are familiar with all sorts of Western thinking and Western literature ... and this has resulted in a complete cultural transformation ... And rock belongs to this younger generation.

After Tiananmen, rock shows were banned every year during the month of June, lest they be used to revive the memory of the massacre. Rock music was also excluded from radio and television – but the Hong Kong-based Star TV aired it, and it could be received by any Chinese household with a satellite dish. Rock musicians got financial support from Star and from Rock Records of Taiwan. Andrew F. Jones commented: "As a result mainland rock music is imported home ... *and* exported abroad to Hong Kong and Taiwan. Ironically, though, the music's principal market is abroad, largely because the domestic market is saturated by Hong Kong and Taiwanese imports." That was in 1994, before Hong Kong's return to Chinese sovereignty. Doubtless the movement has continued. On the other hand, when, in 1998, Chen Shizhang tried to revive the traditional Chinese opera *Mu Dan Ting* (Peony Pavillion), 55 acts lasting 22 hours, in its day (c.1598) seen as a call for individual freedom, he was told by the Shanghai Bureau of Culture: "You are not allowed to re-interpret Chinese culture." The Shanghai performance and an international tour had to be abandoned.

Racism and racist ideology

In the US, the strongest challenge to musical convention came from the vibrant culture of Africans transported to the New World as slaves. Traditional African drumming was banned by the slaveholders, much as it was by the colonists in its lands of origin, but African influences survived. By the end of the 19th century, "negro spirituals", the blending of the words of European Protestant hymns with African rhythms, largely tolerated because of their biblical base, had given rise to jazz – notably the blues – and ragtime.

Jazz attained respectability only after decades of repudiation by white Americans. In one typical diatribe, Anne Faulkner described jazz in the *Ladies Home Journal* August 1921 as "voodoo" licentiousness, "stimulating the half-crazed barbarian to the vilest deeds". "Vile" in this context perhaps referred to the blues' considerable sexually explicit content, used by black singers not only to entertain but also to subvert established values. Those considered most obscene were excluded from the collections, and songs such as Dinah Washington's "Long John Blues" are still rejected for broadcast in the US, and, for many years, were only marginally available. Black singers such as Paul Robeson, who chose a mainstream political approach to register their protest against discrimination, were bullied, harassed, and, in Robeson's case, branded "communist".

Jazz was hardly the main plank in the construction of Adolf Hitler's racist ideology, but it was among the musics singled out for elimination in 1933: jazz was "perverse". The saxophone was prohibited as an example of "negroid lewdness" and such "negroid excrescence" as the swing, the "Hot Dance", and the Lambeth Walk were excluded. Unfortunately for the National Socialists, jazz remained popular in Germany. They found it necessary, in 1937, to draw attention in an official paper to "impudent swamp flowers of negroid pandemonium in German dance halls, regrettably abetted by so-called German dance-bands". "German jazz", a feeble imitation of the real thing, was allowed to take its place.

However, it was the Jews who were the real target of Nazi music censorship. Posthumously, Mozart's *Marriage of Figaro*, *Don Giovanni*, and *Cose fan tutti* were consigned to the dustbin because Lorenzo da Ponte, their librettist, was a baptized Jew. Mendelssohn and Mahler followed. Handel's *Judas Maccabaeus* was reworked and renamed *Wilhelm von Nassau*, and *Israel in Egypt* became *Mongol Fury*. Among the living, Arnold Schoenberg was rejected as much for his Jewishness as for his atonal revolution – he slipped out of the country in 1933 – and Kurt Weill, who also fled to Paris in 1933 to avoid arrest, was similarly on the Nazi index. The conductors Bruno Walter, Otto Klemperer, and Erich Kleiber, unable to stomach racist censorship, emigrated as "non-Aryans". In 1937 Severus Ziegler, manager of the Weimar Theatre, mounted the Degenerate Music (*entartete Musik*) exhibition, which featured, along with Jewish music, Gypsy music, and jazz, much of European music since Wagner: Stravinsky, Milhaud, Hindemith, Bartók, and others. "We do not", wrote Ziegler in the programme, "reject dissonance *per se*, or the enrichment of rhythm, but dissonance as a principle, an irruption of alien rhythms". One long-term result of Nazism remained in Israel, where the music of Richard Wagner was still banned 50 years after the Holocaust, until the ban was broken recently. The composer Oded Zehavi has also reported: "There were red lists which were, we all knew, mostly the music of Nazi collaborators."

In the early 1990s the government of reunified Germany began to censor the work of extreme right-wing musicians: in October 1992 the music of *Storkraft* (Disturbing Force), and, two months later, the performance, manufacture, distribution, and sale of music by four more *oi* bands considered to be neo-Nazi propaganda. A song called "Kanaken" – a derogatory term for foreigners – was banned for encouraging the murder of Turkish immigrants. The Federal Inspection Office for Writings Endangering Youth placed various albums off-limits to minors. Other western European countries also fear the reactionary right. Bands expressing Nazi sentiment or using Nazi symbols – Swedish Death Metal, its Norwegian counterpart, and Finnish skinheads – have been curbed, although some argue that this is a cover for restrictions on other aspects of youth culture.

Nazism had its admirers among the progenitors of apartheid in South Africa from the early 1950s. There are also, hardly surprisingly, connections with the US and German censorship of jazz: Julian Bahula (malombo drums), Philip Tabane (guitar), and Abe Cindi (flute) toured South Africa, but at one show had to wear masks because black and white were not allowed to appear together. Bahula left South Africa in 1979, but did not lose his commitment to the anti-apartheid struggle. Most songs performed by Jabula, which he formed, including "Afrika Awake", were banned in South Africa. Abdullah Ibrahim, of Dollar Brand Trio, the jazz piano player, left South Africa in 1976. He told the *International Herald Tribune* in 1982: "I'm a citizen of that country but the law says that if I play for whites my own mother cannot come to hear me. It is impossible for me to make a living there because of my colour."

Under apartheid, music censorship was carried out under the auspices of the Publications Act which banned music considered "harmful to the relations between any sections of the inhabitants of the Republic", or "prejudicial to the safety of the state, the general welfare or the peace and good order". The rubric barred such records as "Fire in Soweto" (Sonny Okosun) and "Biko" (Peter Gabriel). Pink Floyd's "Another Brick in the Wall, part 2", used by black children in the campaign against segregated education, was, hardly unexpectedly, prohibited.

As elsewhere in the world, radio broadcasting was a prime agent of music censorship. The South African Broadcasting Company (SABC) insisted that every record purchased had an accompanying lyric sheet, and a committee decided which music should be played to which audience. One of its more notorious bans was that on Creedence Clearwater Revival's "Have You Seen the Rain?", the "rain" being a commonly used synonym for the "revolution". Double censorship was commonplace: companies would not record music which, they judged, would not get airtime.

Ideologies of religion

As noted above, there is a long, but far from consistent, history of music censorship within and by the Christian church. In no society today, however, does the Church have other than an indirect influence on the practice.

Historic attitudes to music in Islam are similarly mixed.

There have always been legalists who have condemned all music whatsoever, but the religion was born in the Arab world, where poetry and music were of central importance. The Qur'an itself is recited wherever Muslims gather, and the Sufis search for truth in ecstatic states, aided by music. Mystics are depicted in religious painting learning about the rhythms of the bazaar, where the tapping of the metalsmiths inspired them to new forms of gesture and dance. On the one hand, the 11th-century Sufi theorist Hujwiri, an inhabitant of what are now Afghanistan and Pakistan, complained that the great writings of his movement had been distorted by such bawdy lyricists as Aby Nuwas (died c.810). On the other hand, seeking to silence those who feared the capacity of music to induce loss of control, he took the view that the hearing of instrumental and vocal music was a primary way to discover God.

It is commonly assumed that the rise of Islamism in the second half of the 20th century has included a condemnation of music as such (and, perhaps, particularly Western music), but once again the evidence is mixed. The first ruler of Saudi Arabia, Ibn Saud (1932–53), whose family had adopted the Wahhabi version of Islam, a notably restrictive branch of the religion, employed the Committee for the Advancement of Virtue and the Elimination of Vice to enforce his ban on singing; this was considered the work of the devil and was punished by on-the-spot floggings. In Egypt, the lyricist Ahmed Fouad Negm worked with the blind singer Sheikh Iman on a synthesis between two traditions: recitation of the Qur'an and the group singing of the peasants. Their subjects, however, included poverty and unemployment, as well as the humiliation inflicted on Egypt by Israel during the war of 1967; when they made their presence felt at theatres and other public gatherings, they were frequently harassed. Refusing to bow to pressure, they made cassettes and put them in the hands of students.

When some of the more zealous pressed for a total ban on music at the time of the Islamic Revolution in Iran (1978), however, the ayatollah Khomeini is said to have remarked that there was nothing wrong with music unless it was "intoxicating"; this is presumably only a reiteration of fears dating back as far as Plato, but may have some special reference to Western adulation of pop stars, which the Ayatollah may have observed during his exile and did not want to see develop in Iran. At any rate, however, according to Kareh Basmenji, Reuters correspondent in Iran, "for nearly 15 years . . . the only legal music in Iran was hymns, traditional songs, or anodyne instrumentals". Andranik "Andy" Madadian, the "Persian Elvis", a popular pre-revolutionary singer of Armenian descent, is now resident in the United States, where he continues to produce records for the international community of Iranian exiles. Inside Iran, bootleg copies of albums by Madadian and other expatriate artists circulate clandestinely. Basmenji reports that in the late 1990s there was a growing tolerance of western-style music, and of a new Iranian popular music that combines Western melodies with the traditional music of the country.

An "Islamization of Art" programme has been carried out in the Sudan since the coup by the National Islamic Front (NIF) in 1989. The director-general of Radio Omdurman has forbidden the broadcast of any music that does not contribute to the strengthening of religious devotion. Music must now be approved by Islamic jurists. Abu Araki al-Bakheit's songs have been banned from broadcast and the singer himself arrested. In 1994, during one of the NIF campaigns against secular music, a schoolteacher entered the Musicians' Club in Khartoum, fatally stabbed the popular singer Khogali Osman, and wounded the musician Salah Ahmed Osman and the *oud* virtuoso Abdel Gadir Salim.

Algerian Islamists have been less successful politically. The government's cancellation of elections that Islamic fundamentalists were expected to win in 1992 pre-empted more direct "censorship" of *raï*, a popular musical form uniting Euro-pop with traditional Arabic music. The singer Cheb Khaled was accused of "infringing sacred taboos" and was forced into exile. In 1994 Cheb Hasni was shot to death in Oran. In 1995 the *raï* music producer Rachid Baba-Ahmed was killed in Tlemceu.

The Taliban, who seized substantial areas of Afghanistan, including the capital Kabul in 1996, are, like the rulers of Saudi Arabia, greatly influenced by Wahhabism, highly conservative and ready to impose their ideology by force: Afghanistan too has its department and local committees for the Promotion of Virtue and Prevention of Vice. Seeking to govern by exclusive reference to Shari'a, Islamic law, they have banned all music, recorded or otherwise, along with television, video cassette recorders, and satellite dishes. Singers and musicians, many of whom fled, are "enemies of God". Audio and videotapes, records and compact disks are considered to be contraband and are widely confiscated. Tapes, wrenched from their cassettes, are hung on trees to remind passers-by of the ban. Only recitation of the Qur'an is allowed; all other music is said to be corrupting, and to distract believers from their religious duties.

Australia is one of several countries trying to deal with racism and racial expression in music. In 1996, following a campaign by the B'nai B'rith Anti-Discrimination Committee, the Australian Recording Industry Association agreed to a voluntary rating system. Such offensive material as "Exterminate You" by No Remorse, whose lyrics include passages like "We've gotta get rid of the niggers and the Asians, we've gotta hang the reds/ we've gotta make sure the Jew is finally dead", were specially targeted. The Australian Federal Race Commissioner, Zita Antonios, stated in 1996 that people in possession of racist music could be prosecuted and the offending material destroyed.

Protest songs

The use of song to protest against social and political conditions again blossomed in the second half of the 20th century, but this was not new. In the 17th century, after the monarchy had been deposed in England, it was an offence even to whistle the royalist song "Hey Boys". In the early 20th century, the tune of "The Wearing of the Green" was banned by the British in Ireland for its call for Irish independence. The fate of more modern protest songs has often been similar.

In Brazil, the songs of Chico Buarque, Gilberto Gil, and Caetano Veloso, exponents of *musica popular brasiliensa*, made direct attacks on the military regimes in continuous power from 1964 until 1985. Their songs were memorized, and, when banned, as was "Vai Passar" (It Will Pass), hummed and whistled by their many fans. Between 1974 and 1979 alone, some 840 songs were banned or bowdlerized. Mikis Theodorakis, the Greek composer and singer, embodied in his songs the revulsion of most of his compatriots towards the Colonels who had seized power in 1967; fearing to touch such a popular figure for some time, the military dictatorship finally arrested him and despatched him into exile. And in a third example of the power of song against military regimes, in Chile, the *nueva cancion* (new song) had sought to promote the ideals of Salvador Allende before his murder in 1973. One of the leading lights of *nueva cancion*, Victor Jara, was murdered soon after general Pinochet's coup, and the instruments on which musical protest had been played, the *quena* (Andean flute) and *charango* (guitar), were banned. The music itself was banned from radio and television, and public performances were hedged about with bureaucratic restrictions.

In Israel, Si Heiman's protest songs against the treatment of Palestinians during the first Intifada were banned from the radio. In Kenya, the very Mau Mau songs that called for the country's independence in the 1950s were banned by the country's second president, Daniel arap Moi, in the 1970s. The authorities closed down performances of the musical *Maiti Njugira* (Mother, Sing for Me) at least partly because it echoed the concerns of the songs in a new setting. One of the play's progenitors, the novelist and essayist Ngugi wa Thiong'o, commented: "There are some people who seem really scared of any transformation of people's lives especially when it has come about as a result of people's common efforts". Since 1986, the Kenya Broadcasting Corporation has banned songs in any of the 40 vernacular languages of the country, in an attempt to curb what is known as "ethnic nationalism"; the Kikuyu, the largest group, from which Mau Mau was largely drawn, can hear their language sung only on juke boxes. When the Berber singer Matoub Lounes protested against the Algerian imposition of Arabic as the sole official language, all his songs were banned, and he was assassinated in June 1998. In Pakistan, during the late 1990s, the rock group Junoon (Obsession) was often censored for "belittling the concept of the ideology of Pakistan". Their song "We Have No Nationality" was banned.

In Mauritania, meanwhile, Malouma Mint El-Meidah has been banned from broadcast for precisely opposite reasons: for departing from the griot tradition, for parodying traditional Arabic songs, and for reducing their length. Earlier, in the 1970s, the Zairean president Mobutu demanded, in the name of *authenticité*, the indigenization of music and the adoption of African names by Zairean musicians; and in 1973 the otherwise liberal president Julius Nyerere of Tanzania prohibited broadcasts of popular foreign music by the national radio station; music advocating Zanzibarian separatism has also been banned there.

The Nigerian Fela Anikulapo Kuti blended jazz, African percussion and drums, and the chanting of traditional African songs ("Afro-beat"). He set out to "question, agitate, advocate, harangue, mock, taunt, satirize, lecture, compare and contrast" (Moore 1982) – a heady brew for the succession of military regimes that have ruled Nigeria since independence. From the 1970s onwards, the initials NTBB (Not to Be Broadcast) were placed against his name. Often arrested, he replied with the establishment of his own nightclub, the Afrika Shrine, and the creation of his own record label, Kalakuta Records, whose premises were destroyed by bombs in 1977 but re-established in 1986. Anikulapo Kuti affirmed: "Music is one of the neces-

sary means to carry out the struggle for a better world. I am an artist, with my music I create change."

Protest music of an even more strident kind emerged in rap, first in the US, and then internationally, from the 1980s. Abrasive, angry, ribald, and politically astute, rap addressed the black American underclass. In 1990 a Florida attorney, Jack Thompson, began a crusade against the genre, beginning with 2 Live Crew and moving on, via the sedition laws, to prosecute artists such as Ice-T of the band Body Count (whose heavy metal song "Cop Killer" provoked as much rage as it expressed). However, rap has been more subject to censorship for its moral than for its political content.

Moral censorship of music

When the Chinese authorities have commented on Western or Western-inspired popular music they have regularly named it "spiritual pollution". They are offended not only by its preoccupation with sex, which they consider vulgar, but also forbid broadcasters to show bands featuring long-haired men or women with very short hair. In Pakistan, similarly, the prime minister Nawaz Sharif banned jeans and long-haired men on television in 1997. When, after a 10-year exile in the US, Tabu Ley Rochereau returned to Congo (Zaire), now ruled by Laurent Kabila, he was attacked as an "obscene musician", despite his enthusiastic support for the new regime, for a song that read: "Since the beginning of time, everyone dances/let the one who can't dance raise his hand/some do it in the bar, some in the nightclubs/and there are some who dance and grind in the bedroom." The fear of sensuality is today a product of the generation gap.

In Britain the moral campaigner Mary Whitehouse was instrumental in the prosecution of the Anti-Nowhere League in 1982 for their song "Secrets of London/So What?", and in the prosecution of the anarchist band Crass in 1984 for their "Bata Motel". The BBC, which kept "hot music" off the air from 1935 onwards, banned Scott Walker's version of Jacques Brel's "Jacky" in 1968. The Corporation denied airtime to songs suspected of fomenting violence, such as Eric Clapton's cover of Bob Marley's "I Shot the Sheriff", and to sexually explicit songs like Serge Gainsbourg's and Jane Birkin's "Je t'aime".

In 1977 Argentina's military junta embarked on a crackdown against subversive musicians, following the rise in popularity of *Rock Nacional*. Admiral Massera, a member of the junta, condemned rock music as a "race towards the most extreme heightening of the senses", a hedonist ideology intended to undermine the state. Concerts where musicians played forbidden songs were broken up by the police and concertgoers detained for questioning.

But it is in the United States that some of the most widespread moral concern, leading sometimes to forms of censorship, has developed. When rock and roll emerged in the 1950s, it was first branded a communist plot, and then named by Asa Carter of the Alabama White Citizens Council and other southern segregationists as consciously intended to bring white youth "down to the level of the negro". Congressional hearings on the destructive effect of popular culture took place in 1956 and a close watch was kept on rock performers like Elvis Presley, whose gyrations were considered salacious. In 1959 Link Wray's instrumental single "Rumble" was banned by radio stations across the US for encouraging gang violence through aural suggestions. In 1964, the Kingsmen's cover of Richard Berry's song of 1957, "Louie, Louie", was excluded from broadcast because its indecipherable lyrics were said to evoke lust.

In 1970 after the vice-president Spiro Agnew had denounced popular music as "blatant drug culture propaganda", the Federal Communications Commission (FCC) sent a memorandum to US broadcasters warning that failure to exercise caution in the selection of drug-related songs would invite "serious questions as to whether the continued operation of the station is in the public interest". Most stations promptly removed the 22 songs listed by the FCC, including "With a Little Help from My Friends" (The Beatles), "Puff, the Magic Dragon" (Peter, Paul, and Mary), and the explicitly anti-drug "The Pusher" (Steppenwolf).

Parents looked for guidance from hostile critics such as David Noebbel, author of *The Marxist Minstrels*, and Joe Struesy, who wrote *Heavy Metal Users Manual*. In 1985 the wives of various senators, led by Tipper Gore, outraged by the content of Prince and Madonna albums, formed the Parents Music Resource Center (PMRC) which successfully campaigned to have certain albums labelled, warning parents of their content.

Among PMRC's targets was the satirical, anti-authoritarian music of the Dead Kennedys and Jello Biafra, its lead singer, who was arrested in California in 1985 on obscenity charges, stemming from the inclusion in the *Frankenchrist* album of an H.R. Giger poster "Penis Landscape". But it was rap, already mentioned above, which aroused most concern and litigation. 2 Live Crew and a Fort Lauderdale record dealer were indicted on obscenity charges for the album *As Nasty as They Wanna Be*, and, in particular, for the sexually explicit song "Me So Horny". In 1997 the PMRC brought together people at the opposite ends of the moral and political spectrum – Dolores Tucker, chairwoman of the National Political Congress of Black Women, and the right-wing morality crusader William Bennett – in a media campaign against it.

White musicians have been attacked for blasphemy, morbidity, and "anti-family" themes. Ozzy Osbourne's "Suicide Solution", Metallica's "Fade to Black", and Judas Priest's "Better by You, Better than Me" were alleged to have provoked suicides and suicide attempts. Marilyn Manson, said to have incorporated activities as diverse as animal slaughter, live sex, and devil worship into his act, was subjected to American Family Association-inspired demonstrations and cancellations.

Popular music has also fallen foul of particular pressure and interest groups. Protests from feminists drove the British band Prodigy's "Smack My Bitch Up" (1996) out of record shops and off the air. The Country and Western singer Tom McGraw's "Indian Outlaw" was dropped from playlists when Native American groups accused it of stereotyping. Reggae albums by Shabba Ranks and Buju Banton, whose "Boom Bye Bye" seems to advocate shooting gay men, were pulled off the shelves or not carried at all by some retailers.

Many states have sought legislative solutions, whose constitutionality has been widely questioned. Washington state's "erotic music law", which would have criminalized the sale to minors of record albums with parental advisory labels, was struck down by the state Supreme Court in 1992. A divestiture law of 1997 required all agencies of the Texan government to withdraw their investments from any corporate entity responsible for music that "describes, glamorises or advocates violence, drug abuse, or sexual activity". This scheme was soon under consideration in other states.

Perhaps the most effective censorship is that now practised by Wal-Mart, the largest music retailer. It demands – and obtains – expurgated versions of albums from musicians and record companies. Its editions of popular albums alter cover art, transcriptions of lyrics, and the content of albums themselves. Those not censored according to its specifications are not stocked. When Sheryl Crow declined to delete the line "Watch our children kill each other with a gun they bought at Wal-Mart discount stores", the album was excluded from these stores.

Thus, after the best part of three millennia, would-be censors still echo Plato's concern that certain music leads to licentiousness. Now, however, music is produced and disseminated on an international scale; even the most restrictive political and musical environments are not immune from penetration by independent radio transmissions and the Internet. Resistance is both local – as with the Massachusetts Music Industry Coalition and Rock Out Censorship – and global – the first world conference on Music and Censorship was held in Copenhagen in late 1998. The conference declared its intention to establish an international network for the support of musicians under pressure, and appealed to governments, human rights organizations and all individuals, organizations and media involved in music to end censorship and apply the principles of free expression to this ancient and universal medium.

DEREK JONES

Further Reading

Clarke, Donald, *The Rise and Fall of Popular Music*, London: Viking Press, and New York: St Martin's Press, 1995

Cloonan, Martin, *Banned! Censorship of Popular Music in Britain, 1967–92*, Aldershot, Hampshire: Arena, 1996

Garofalo, Reebee (editor), *Rockin' the Boat: Mass Music and Mass Movements*, Boston: South End Press, 1992

George, Nelson, *Hip Hop America*, New York: Viking, 1998

Grunberger, Richard, *A Social History of the Third Reich*, London: Weidenfeld and Nicolson, 1971

Holden, D., "Pop Go the Censors", *Index on Censorship*, 22/5–6 (May–June 1993)

McElvoy, Anne, *The Saddled Cow: East Germany's Life and Legacy*, London and Boston: Faber, 1992

Martin, Linda and Kerry Segrave, *Anti-Rock: The Opposition to Rock 'n' Roll*, Hamden, Connecticut: Archon, 1988

Moore, Carlos, *Fela, Fela: This Bitch of a Life*, London: Allison and Busby, 1982

Palmer, Roy (editor), *A Touch on the Times: Songs of Social Change, 1770–1914*, Harmondsworth: Penguin, 1974

Škvorecký, Josef, *The Bass Saxophone*, translated by Káča Poláčková-Henley, Toronto: Anson-Cartwright, 1977; London: Chatto and Windus, 1978; New York: Knopf, 1979

Škvorecký, Josef, *Headed for the Blues: A Memoir with Ten Stories*, translated by Peter Kussi et al., London and Boston: Faber, 1997

"Smashed Hits", special issue of *Index on Censorship*, 27/6 (November–December 1998)

Theiner, George, "Music Is Dangerous", *Index on Censorship*, 12/1 (February 1983)

Wasserstrom, Jeffrey N. and Elizabeth J. Perry (editors), *Popular Protest and Political Culture in Modern China*, 2nd edition, Boulder, Colorado: Westview Press, 1994

Wilson, Elizabeth, *Shostakovich: A Life Remembered*, London: Faber, and Princeton, New Jersey: Princeton University Press, 1994

MUSIC: Jazz and Blues

The collector of the blues, Alan Lomax, has written of the profound reluctance of black people in the United States in the 1930s to speak of their treatment at the hands of whites. Blacks were "poorly paid, badly housed, constantly insulted and bullied, and were without equal rights before the law". Their "self-censorship" proceeded from the fact that "working-class blacks who talked ran the risk of losing their jobs, if not their lives. Blacks who hobnobbed with strangers might also land in serious trouble." The net result was that "In the South I grew up in . . . almost everyone had convinced themselves that the blacks were happy".

Against this background, blacks invented forms of resistance that most whites only dimly recognized. In their work songs, slaves had insulted their overseers without the overseers realizing what was being said: the full impact of the songs was hidden in the anonymity of the group. The blues picked up on this tradition, disguising black fury with officialdom by addressing mules and other farmyard animals in ribald and satirical songs; there are strong relationships here with the use of Aesopian language to defy censorship. This was one answer to oppression.

Another was to develop, however unconsciously, subtleties of expression to respond much more directly to everyday life than was possible for those nourished in the predominantly Puritan culture of the United States in the early 20th century. The blues made no concessions to decorum or respectability. It was, according to Paul Oliver, "this open declaration of subjects that the conventions of polite society thought should be kept hidden from view which has caused so much offence, and, incidentally, added the term 'blue' to the English language as a word synonymous with 'pornographic'."

Today, most people would probably regard blues lyrics as erotic rather than pornographic:

When we reach th'Atlantic Ocean, the sea may be a
    little rough
But I will steady your boat, ooh well, 'cause I really
    knows my stuff.

Many would regard some of the lyrics as sexist:

I been a mighty good bull cow, oh Lord, but I got
    to go
I found me a pig meat heifer, I can tell by the way
    she lows.

Homosexuals are referred to as "freaks", "sissies" or "drags"; hermaphrodites are called "peaches". Nevertheless, most lyrics could be printed today without raising eyebrows.

In 1960 Paul Oliver wrote: "To those only accustomed to the conventions of the printed and recorded word, the blues sometimes seems violent and coarse, but its expression is a natural and uninhibited use". In contrast, in 1925 two early collectors, Howard Odum and Guy Johnson, had declared that much of what they had collected could not be printed because of "its vulgar and indecent content": "These songs tell of every phase of immorality . . . and filth; they repeat the superstructure of repulsion". Believing, mistakenly, that other forms of

folk song were less "indecent", their books censored those lyrics they considered "unfit for publication" by the simple expedient of shortening them.

Yet, as the black American novelist Richard Wright pointed out, "the most astonishing aspect of the blues is that their burden of woe and melancholy is dialectically redeemed through sheer force of sensuality, into an almost exultant affirmation of life, of sex, of movement, of hope". That explains the attraction of the blues, and of jazz, to people living under many different forms of oppression, including Nazism.

The Nazis banned blues and jazz for racist reasons, and their counterparts in Japan for nationalistic reasons. Modern dancing, according to the Nazis, arose from "Jewish confections of meretricious trash crossed with jungle emanations of Negro jazz". Their prohibitions extended to all the territories they conquered, including Czechoslovakia, discussed below, where jazz became then, as later under communism, a form of resistance. In Japan, jazz was officially considered to be "enemy music". The Nippon Music Culture Association promised in January 1943 to devote every third Friday to discussions of ways of "ousting the degenerate American jazz music". Bans appear to have been ineffective, however, mostly because the police could not tell the difference between jazz and other forms of music, but also because many Japanese liked the form, continuing to listen, despite the ban, with the volume turned down.

DEREK JONES

Further Reading

Grunberger, Richard, *A Social History of the Third Reich*, London: Weidenfeld and Nicolson, 1971

Lomax, Alan, *The Land Where the Blues Began*, New York: Pantheon, and London: Methuen, 1993

Odum, Howard and Guy B. Johnson, *The Negro and His Songs: A Study of Typical Negro Songs in the South*, Chapel Hill: University of North Carolina Press, 1925

Odum, Howard and Guy B. Johnson, *Negro Workaday Songs*, Chapel Hill: University of North Carolina Press, 1926

Oliver, Paul, *Blues Fell This Morning: Meaning in the Blues*, foreword by Richard Wright, 2nd edition, Cambridge and New York: Cambridge University Press, 1990

Shillony, Ben-Ami, *Politics and Culture in Wartime Japan*, Oxford: Clarendon Press, and New York: Oxford University Press, 1981

Jazz in Czechoslovakia

Jazz arrived in Czechoslovakia immediately after World War I, in the shape of modern dances, fairly syncopated rhythms, and then-unusual instruments, such as saxophones and drumkits. A group could be called a "jazz band" then even if all it played was a set of drums. Jazz differed strikingly from the Czech, Slovak, German, and Hungarian popular music familiar to audiences in the new republic, and was met with violent opposition from professional musicians who felt threatened by this new style. A contributor to one of the trade papers wrote in 1927 of a jazz band as "undisciplined" and "violent", attracting people with "bobbed hair kept in vicious disorder, thick rouge on the lips and faces of our ladies, trinkets on their necks". The writer deplored "the way of thinking of our youth, the declining value of human life, all those . . . barbarian qualities, mocking all humanism and cultivation of the human spirit". Yet Czechoslovakia was a democratic country and jazz suffered no censorship at that time.

Jazz found strong support among avant-garde artists, who saw in it a recipe for dismantling middle-class cultural clichés. Most of them were close to leftist political movements. Jaroslav Ježek, to some extent the embodiment of Czech jazz before World War II, was music director of the Liberated Theatre, which launched a passionate campaign against Hitler's Nazi ideology during the mid-1930s. In consequence, after the Munich agreement of 1938 the theatre was closed down by the authorities to avoid conflicts with Czechoslovakia's powerful neighbour. Ježek fled to the United States, becoming the first of many jazz musicians to go into exile in order to avoid censorship or worse. From the 1940s until the late 1980s, jazz was regarded as a form of music with strong political connotations.

Thus, for instance, during the Nazi occupation, jazz grew from a protest by urban youth against their teachers and parents into a hidden anti-Nazi revolt. The Nazis opposed jazz on musical grounds, regarding it as degenerate, a distortion of "Aryan" principles, and as a reflection of the values of the United States.

They issued formal written rules about its performance – a fixed percentage of syncopations, a ban on muted instruments – which Josef Škvorecký has paraphrased in his novels. Škvorecký also relates how the rules were circumvented and resisted by swing fans: the names of American composers were replaced by those of fictitious Czech composers; the original titles were changed into nonsensical Czech phrases. During inspections by the German authorities, the bands changed their way of playing, only to return to the jazz idiom as soon as the officials had left. When the Prague swing arranger Fritz Weiss was sent to the Terezín concentration camp because of his Jewish origins, bands continued to play his arrangements. A swing guitar player, Gustav Vicherek, was arrested by the Gestapo, on the concert stage itself, while he was scatting Louis Armstrong's vocal chorus in *Tiger Rag*; he was sent to a concentration camp, which he survived.

When the war ended, jazz enjoyed three years of complete liberty, with no censorship at all, although it was still disliked by most of the older generation, their attitude epitomized by the head of the police service, who had written to a newspaper during the occupation: "I'm not a musician to utter any opinion on the subject. But, Mr Editor, this is not our Czech music." This was a mild enough comment compared with the cultural policy of the communists after 1948. Pamphlets by Soviet music writers such as A. Gorodinskii and V. Shneierson described jazz as an "utterly reactionary, utterly antidemocratic and utterly perverse kind of music"; it was part of "that spiritual leprosy that has long since been nourishing itself on western science, philosophy, and all forms of creative arts".

The Czech Marxist critic Dušan Havlíček stressed the incompatibility of jazz with ideas of socialist realism:

> Jazz feeling . . . cannot be squeezed into the framework of our realistic music. The modern jazz principle of improvisation . . . works against the creative effort of our authors of dance songs and compositions . . . to submit to its influence . . . would place obstacles in the way of the independent development of *Czech* dance music.

Some of the leading jazz bands emigrated or disbanded. Kamil Běhounek's big band failed to return from Germany after playing to the court at the Nuremburg war crimes trials. Members of the bop group Rhythm '48 left the country. Gustav Brom, considered by the communist regime as "as exponent of bourgeois, decadent culture", was not only dismissed from Bratislava Radio, but "forever denied access to its building".

However, unlike the Nazis, the communists tried to avoid clear regulations or punishment for offences against ideology and cultural policy. They preferred to use more subtle methods. Only "socialist institutions", such as factories, trade unions or political organizations, could issue licences to bands or groups that wished to perform in public, and it was very easy to withdraw the licence of any that did not comply with the opinions or taste of the local party boss, forcing them virtually to disband. Thus, for example, the local authority in the town of Hranice sent the following letter to the trade union at a cement works under whose auspices a "dubious" band was performing:

> It is quite clear that the further existence of this ensemble is not desirable . . . It contributes nothing to our present efforts. On the contrary . . . its improvisations are fostering musical pornography . . . Eighty per cent of its music is cosmopolitan music of western provenance, which had the effect of driving even a soldier of our army on to the stage to perform a tap dance . . . It is not desirable for their ensemble to perform again in public, as neither the leader nor the members can offer any guarantee that they will free themselves from the remains of their former education.

Such a letter would have been placed in the personal files of each member of the band and would have effectively banned not only their performances but also access to any kind of higher education or decent job.

More conventional forms of censorship were also present. A collection of essays called *Jazz 1958*, the first Czech publication on the subject since 1928, was confiscated at the printers after a Marxist critic had read and commented unfavourably on his preview copy. In 1962, an international jazz festival held at Karlovy Vary was severely criticized in the party newspaper *Rudé Právo*, and had to be discontinued. Preparations for a similar event in Prague were also stopped.

The generally hostile attitude to this kind of music continued to shape trends in Czech jazz even when, after the death of Stalin in 1953, open repression diminished. Musicians were conditioned to "play it safe", avoiding any music that might be disapproved of by party functionaries. Thus "free" jazz was only very rarely performed, and the "apologists of jazz" movement found it easier to follow the general European trend of regarding jazz as part of "highbrow" culture, preferring styles such as West Coast or Third Stream.

The political climate was rarely stable: periods of relative liberalization were followed by periods of repression, making it difficult to maintain the sense of continuity necessary for the healthy development of music. Around the middle of the 1960s, for instance, a period of liberalization led to the acceptance of jazz as a normal part of national cultural life. This was halted following the Warsaw Pact invasion in 1968, leading to a new wave of emigration, especially of young musicians such as Miroslav Vitouš, later a founding member of the group Weather Report, and Jan Hammer, later of the Mahavishnu Orchestra. The Jazz Section of the Musicians' Union (discussed in a separate entry) kept flying the flag of cultural opposition, and the jazz clubs of Prague were known to be meeting places for musical and other kinds of dissidents. However, during the 1970s and 1980s, the authorities switched their attention to music regarded as yet more decadent: rock, new wave, and politically orientated folk music. Jazz ceased to be an object of open censorship and has so remained.

LUBOMÍR DORŮŽKA

Further Reading

Dorůžka, Lubomír and Ivan Poledňák, *Čskoslovenský jazz minulust a přítomnost* (Czechoslovak Jazz, Past and Present), Prague: Supraphon, 1967

Dorůžka, Lubomír, "Jazz in der Tschoslowakei 1945 bis 1993" in *Jazz in Europa*, edited by Wolfgana Knauer, Hofheim: Wolke, 1994

Dorůžka, Lubomír, "Jazz under Two Totalitarian Regimes: Problems of East European Jazz Historiography" in *Jazz und Sozialgeschichte*, edited by Theo Mäusli, Zürich: Chronos, 1994

Dorůžka, Lubomír, *Panoráma paměti* (Panorama of the Memory), Prague: Torst, 1997

Kouřil, Vladimír, *Jazzová sekce v čase a nečase, 1971–1987* (Jazz Section in Good and Bad Times), Prague: Torst, 1999

Škvorecký, Josef, *The Bass Saxophone*, translated by Káč Poláčková-Henley, Toronto: Anson-Cartwright, 1977; London: Chatto and Windus, 1978; New York: Knopf, 1979

Škvorecký, Josef, *Headed for the Blues: A Memoir with Ten Stories*, translated by Peter Kussi *et al.*, London and Boston: Faber, 1997

Srp, Karel, *Výjimečné stavy* (Exceptional Situations), Prague: Pragma, 1994

MUSIC: Rock

From its inception, rock music has aroused scorn and contempt around the world for its threatening articulations of race, class, ethnicity, sexuality, gender, and youth rebellion. The wide array of fears and anxieties elicited by the music and the activity of its fans quickly inspired fervent attempts at censorship by the self-appointed gatekeepers of white middle-class culture. In their bid to restrain this form of expression, religious and community-based organizations as well as government and industry forces have focused their wrath on almost every aspect of rock since the 1950s. These efforts consolidated around 1955 at a time when the music industry began to distribute rock and roll records widely and, additionally, television started bringing entertainers into the domestic arena.

Because of the many distribution channels in which the music is able to circulate, rock censorship assumes many forms. Banning artists or songs from radio broadcasts and censoring specific lyrics for broadcast are common modes. There are also point-of-sale techniques, such as censoring album art or refusing to stock certain records. Forbidding rock in certain venues (or rock concerts in general) became a popular way for many towns to prevent rock bands from performing their music. Campaigns directed against specific artists also have a censoring effect, creating negative publicity for their music. Most recently, courtroom battles and congressional hearings have been the site of attempted repression in cases of alleged obscene lyrics in rock songs. The censorship arena is continually expanding: as the forms of rock and roll expression proliferate (music video, Internet concerts, etc.), so do the efforts to control it.

Rock and roll first arrived on the scene in the US as a hybrid that evolved out of rhythm and blues, gospel, folk, and country music. The producers and consumers of these genres were primarily poor and working class. Although they had appeal that transcended racial lines, these forms of music were traditionally linked to Southern blacks. This inspired early rock to be termed "race music", "jungle music", and "off color". The music's rhythm and the dancing it inspired were described as "savage and primitive". These racially motivated designations underscored early objections to rock as "black" music that should be kept out of white society. Although explicit race-related attacks on rock are no longer prevalent, they were crucial strategic elements of the early censorship campaigns against the music.

Coinciding with the birth of rock music was the emergence of a socially significant youth culture. Rock and roll created an empowering space for this new market that was quite threatening to the established order. The music acknowledged teenage desires that were antagonistic to the strictly coded gender roles of the 1950s. Rock articulated sexuality as an active expression which defied repressive attitudes towards teenage sex, love, and pleasure. The definitive pulsating beat of rock and roll was also associated with sex, inspiring fear in middle-class culture that the music was encouraging teenage promiscuity.

In April 1955, Chicago teenagers sent 15,000 letters to local rock stations accusing them of playing "dirty" records. The letters, patterned on a model suggested by a Catholic high school newspaper, were part of their "Crusade for Decent Discs". In March 1957, rock and roll music was banned from Catholic schools in Chicago, because the local church authorities felt that "rock's tribal rhythms encourage young people to behave in a hedonistic manner". These events mark the beginning of censorship efforts generated by religious groups, a formidable battle that the rock music industry has faced ever since. While mainstream religion was instrumental in early attacks on rock music, it has progressively given way to fundamentalist and right-wing groups who have adopted the cause with increasing intensity.

Attempts to restrain rock became more vigilant as the music's popularity and influence grew. In 1955 the entertainment industry trade paper *Variety* denounced rock and roll's "leer-ics" in an influential series that was picked up and printed in papers across the country. In Boston, six disc jockeys formed a censorship board with journalists and religious leaders employed to screen new records. Rock and roll dances were banned in Bridgeport and New Haven, Connecticut. Civic groups in San

Antonio, Texas, assembled a list of objectionable records, and all the radio stations in the town reportedly banned those songs from airplay. Also at this time, the Alabama station WABB ran editorials about "The Music You Won't Hear on WABB". The station enacted a self-censorship policy, promising not to play any records considered off-colour, offensive, or those containing double entendres.

Elvis Presley emerged as an icon of the threat posed by rock and roll to cultural mores. He came from working-class roots with a background in blues, country, and gospel music. His dark sexuality and gyrating hip movements inspired gleeful hysteria among teenagers while causing authority figures to panic. Police vice squads were dispatched to his concerts, and religious organizations held prayer rallies to counteract the evil influence of "Elvis the Pelvis". When the singer appeared on the Ed Sullivan Show in 1957, network censors instructed the camera crew to show Elvis only from the waist up to avoid broadcasting his "lewd and vulgar" dancing.

Since rock and roll was largely an American export in the 1950s, international reaction to the music depended largely on a country's political and ideological affiliation. Rock and roll was forbidden in Cuba, Yugoslavia, and Egypt. A nationalistic spirit characterized the initial reactions of Argentina, when the government banned dancing and demanded that only native music be played in public places. Rock and roll was also banned from the Soviet Union, as were Western performers. South Vietnam banned the twist music that was introduced by American soldiers in 1963 because "it was not compatible with the country's morality law and its anti-Communist struggle". In Britain, the BBC's Radio One regularly censored music containing offensive language or references to sex, radical politics, specific brand names, or drugs. The American army would soon forbid pop music at European bases because of the anti-Vietnam War sentiments of many rock songs.

Banning music initially proved to be more difficult than most countries anticipated, however. Black markets and bootlegging flourished, and the rock and roll broadcasts on the Voice of America could be picked up by short-wave radio. One of the more inventive methods of overcoming the prohibition on rock music was known as "rock on bones". This emerged in the Soviet Union when an underground movement used exposed X-ray films of organs and bones and converted them into rock records that would last a few months.

In the 1960s rock culture became increasingly associated with drug culture, infusing its already threatening image with new hostility. Rock and roll artists of this era were viewed as aggressively antisocial, and considerably more pernicious than the teenage idols of the 1950s. The FBI had extensive files on numerous musicians, including John Lennon, Jim Morrison, and Janis Joplin.

As rock concerts grew in popularity, so did the efforts to censor them. The Rolling Stones, James Brown, Jimi Hendrix, the Beatles, the Doors, Chuck Berry, Bill Haley, and Janis Joplin all had concerts shut down by government mandate in America and Europe during the 1960s. Jim Morrison of the Doors exposed his genitals at a Miami concert in 1969 and six warrants for his arrest were filed. He was found guilty in court, fined for his behaviour, and policed vigilantly at subsequent shows. The city of Houston, Texas, banned the free-spirited rocker Janis Joplin from performing there simply for "her attitude in general". Government, police, and civic organizations confronted the perceived threat of rock music and its "seething mob" of teenage fans by closing certain venues to rock concerts (such as the Albert Hall in London) or banning them altogether. They cited uncontrollable fans, the destructive reputations of the artists, and antagonism towards police as justification.

In March 1966, the Beatles provoked hostility when John Lennon commented that the Beatles were more popular than Jesus Christ. His statement was taken out of context, however, and widely misquoted in the media. Record burnings, radio bans, and communal outrage ensued, especially in the Southern United States. The band's albums were also removed from many stores. A forced apology from Lennon relieved some of the anger, but animosity from the religious community remained high towards the Beatles. As a result of the incident, the South African government enforced a ban on all sales and radio programming of Beatles music that was not repealed until the group split up in 1971.

The Rolling Stones was another group that amassed a siege of angry tirades from community and religious groups for the way they wore their hair, their suggestive lyrics, and overtly sexual stage mannerisms. Many of their songs were banned from radio for being "sexually suggestive". In 1968 the mayor of Chicago, Richard Daley, ordered local radio stations not to play their single "Street Fighting Man" during the Democratic National Convention because he feared that the song would fuel anticipated rioting during the event. The plan failed, riots arose anyway because of the politically charged situation, and the single set records in airplay and sales that week in Chicago.

Record cover art also became a censorship target in the 1960s. The Rolling Stones's *Beggar's Banquet* was censored by their own record companies, deeming the bathroom stall with graffiti that was originally intended for the cover "in poor taste". In June 1966, the Beatles released the album *Yesterday and Today* with the famous "butcher cover". It showed the Beatles surrounded by bloody chunks of meat and decapitated baby dolls. This was withdrawn after Capitol Records was deluged with complaints by disk jockeys and replaced with a nondescript picture of the band. In 1969 J. Edgar Hoover attempted to suppress the cover of John Lennon's and Yoko Ono's *Two Virgins* album, which showed the couple in full-frontal nudity. However, the Justice Department and FBI decided that they could not censor an album cover legally on the grounds of obscenity. Nevertheless, Newark police seized 30,000 copies of the record upon its arrival at the Newark airport and a retailer in Chicago was shut down by the vice squad for carrying the album. That same year, the self-titled *Blind Faith* LP was released with a nude 11-year-old girl on the cover. It was quickly replaced with an alternative photo that featured the band.

In October 1970, the US president Richard Nixon told radio broadcasters that rock music lyrics should be screened for content and suggested that any music with drug references should be banned. This campaign against drug lyrics in the early 1970s was abetted by FCC and Congressional investigations into rock music. In March 1971 the FCC notified commercial broadcasters that it was their responsibility to refrain from glorifying or promoting illegal drug use in their programming. Stations were to censor music of that type or risk having their licence revoked because they were not acting "in the public interest". A suit was brought against the FCC by a group of broadcasters charging that this censorship violated the First Amendment. The plaintiffs appealed all the way to the Supreme Court but were struck down in 1973 when the court ruled in favour of the FCC, effectively allowing the government to require broadcasters to censor their music.

Elsewhere in the world, rock was not faring much better. During the late 1960s it was banned from Japanese television, denounced in Greece, and restricted to only 25 per cent of the airtime on radio stations in Spain. In 1975 South Korea issued a list of 261 songs (mostly American rock) that were to be blacklisted from airplay in the country. The reason given was that these songs were morally and politically harmful to the country's youth. The Soviet Union also maintained a hostile stance towards rock and roll, a position adopted by many communist countries fearful of western ideology creeping into their countries via record albums and "vulgar" dancing.

In the late 1970s and early 1980s, punk rock and heavy metal had to contend with a renewed vigour in the censorship campaign. Punk music emerging from Britain in the 1970s spoke directly to the unemployed and politically disenfranchised youth of the UK. The angry rock of the Sex Pistols was vilified by the British press and banned by the BBC. Even their advertisements were barred from commercial radio and television. Nevertheless, "God Save the Queen", the band's anti-government anthem recorded in time for Elizabeth II's Silver Jubilee in 1977, topped British sales charts despite censorship efforts. The Pistols were prohibited from performing at most rock venues in London, as were many other punk groups, such as the Jam and the Clash. At the same time, the religious right and political conservatives in the US were waging an incessant cultural war against the "Satanic influences" of heavy metal music.

With the introduction of music video in 1980 and the inauguration of MTV in 1981, a new arena for censorship emerged. Interestingly, music videos initially suffered from the same racially motivated censorship as rock music had done in the 1950s. Videos by white artists monopolized the medium for many years. Of the 750 videos shown in MTV's first 18 months, less than 24 featured black artists. Only after Michael Jackson began making extremely popular videos was this barrier broken in a significant way. Censoring gratuitous sex, violence, obscene lyrics, and nudity has since become the focus for MTV, albeit an inconsistent one. Their arbitrary and undefined guidelines create the same *ad hoc* discrimination as those embraced by the radio industry.

The BBC's *Top of the Pops* has also banned videos, for their politics ("Invisible Sun" by the Police) and their sexuality (Frankie Goes to Hollywood's "Relax" and George Michael's "I Want Your Sex"). Madonna's video of 1990 for "Justify My Love" was banned by both MTV and the BBC for its "overall tone" and graphic sexual content. In this case, the record company parlayed censorship into a financial windfall; after being banned, Madonna's video was released as a single and sold more than 250,000 copies.

Censorship battles moved into the courtroom in the 1980s. The music industry, however, has won almost every high-profile case. All those records that have been brought to trial for obscenity, including the Dead Kennedy's *In God We Trust, Inc.*, Ice Cube's *AmeriKKKa's Most Wanted* and N.W.A.'s *Efil4Zaggin* as well as 2 Live Crew's *As Nasty as They Wanna Be* have been acquitted. Judas Priest was unsuccessfully sued for causing the suicide attempts of two fans in 1985 through "backward masking" subliminal satanic messages in their songs. The Dead Kennedys were found not guilty of distributing pornography with their *Frankenchrist* album, which featured a poster enclosure of artwork by H.R. Giger.

Also during the 1980s, one of the most prominent forces in the history of rock and roll censorship emerged: the Parents Music Resource Group (later known as the Parents Music Resource Center or PMRC). It was formed in 1985 by Tipper Gore, wife of senator Al Gore, and Susan Baker, wife of treasury secretary James Baker. The "Washington wives" founded the group in 1985 to put pressure on record companies to censor "pornographic" rock music and institute a ratings system. Their campaigning and political connections led to the Senate Commerce Committee's hearings on "porn rock" in 1985. Representing a wide spectrum of musicians, John Denver, Frank Zappa, and Dee Snider of Twisted Sister were on hand to defend their music, oppose the ratings system, and fight against music censorship. Eventually, the PMRC's efforts resulted in the Record Industry Association of America's adopting a sticker reading "Explicit Lyrics – Parental Advisory". They agreed to sticker certain albums voluntarily rather than face enforced government legislation. Frank Zappa, a vehement opponent of the PMRC, holds the distinction of having the only instrumental album (*Jazz from Hell*) to receive a warning label.

"Tipper stickers", as they became known in the industry, have had a dual effect. Most significantly, two of the largest music retailers in the US, K-Mart and Wal-Mart, refuse to stock any stickered product. Since rap and heavy metal are largely singled out by the stickering campaign, they have suffered the most from this form of censorship. American record companies are sometimes wary of signing up acts that are likely to be stickered, fearing customer boycotts and being shut out of major record chains.

As is familiar in the history of censorship, fans have begun to value albums that are stickered, making them more desirable to many teenagers because of their status as "forbidden fruit". As a result, many record companies have been reported to use stickers or parodies of them in order to boost sales, since they are widely recognised as the "Bad Housekeeping Seal of Approval". Until a standard definition of "explicit lyrics" is adopted, record companies are free to sticker whatever they want. Conversely, the policy is voluntary so they are also free *not* to sticker. The victory for the PMRC was a dubious one.

Consequently, point-of-sale censorship assumed renewed strength in the 1990s. The retail clout of "family-oriented" chain stores has inspired record labels and bands to omit songs from their albums, redesign cover artwork, and rewrite lyrics in order to secure a spot on the shelf. Beck, John Mellencamp, Nirvana, the Fugees, and Jane's Addiction are among the groups that have altered their work specifically to be stocked at Wal-Mart. However, with the advent of internet retailers, this will likely become less important.

Rap music and "gangsta rap" in the 1980s and 1990s also established themselves as prime targets for censors because of the sex, violence, and aggressive antisocial behaviour glamorized in their lyrics. 2 Live Crew achieved a great deal of their fame for being the first rap artists to be banned. An Alabama record store owner was taken to court in 1987 for selling their allegedly obscene album *Move Somethin'* but later acquitted. In 1990 the group was also arrested for performing their album *As Nasty as They Wanna Be* in Florida. That same year, the FBI sent a letter to the rap group N.W.A. stating the agency's disapproval of their song "Fuck tha Police". Law enforcement agencies across the country hassled the band on their tour. Rapper Ice-T eventually removed the single "Cop Killer" from his *Body Count* album (1992) after record company employees received death threats and Time-Warner was besieged by outraged police departments and unhappy stockholders. The single was banned by state radio in Ireland and removed from his shows in Australia and New Zealand. In June 1997 the rap group Insane Clown Posse was dropped from their Hollywood Records label shortly after their album was released. Disney, the label's owner, decided that the album was too offensive for the company's image.

Threats of US government censorship loomed large at the start of the new millennium, when the music business came under fire, along with other sectors of the entertainment trade. A Senate committee and the Federal Trade Commission reviewed the marketing practices of the music, film, and video game industries, denouncing them for advertising violent and "inappropriate" entertainment to children. The lyrics of Marilyn Manson and Eminem were read aloud by senators as evidence of music targeting teenagers that is depraved and violent. Congress urged industry leaders to "clean up their act" and adopt a stricter system of self-policing with standardized guidelines or risk possible prosecution and restrictive legislation. The initial response by the music business was to set up a parental advisory task force in the the hopes of averting government intervention.

The hallmark of rock and roll censorship has always been inconsistency. There has never been any standard or rule that determines what is obscene, dangerous, or inappropriate. Some groups have been allowed to include "indecent" language or imagery in their songs while others were censored for doing the same thing. Largely tied to contemporary sociopolitical climates, rock censorship is best understood within its specific cultural context. In the US, the disparate realms of the Federal Trade Commission (FTC), Federal Communications Commission (FCC), Congress, recording industry, broadcasters, civic organizations, lobbyists, and public opinion have all been factors in the decisions on what should and should not be heard. However, the government's wishes figure most prominently with broadcasting, since the pressure of the FCC's warnings, red tape, and ability to deny licence renewals is usually enough to induce most stations to institute a practice of self-censorship. In Britain, the process is equally arbitrary, but the decisions are largely made by the BBC and the (independent) Radio Authority.

Specific programme producers usually decide on which records to ban and there is little recourse for those artists shut out of broadcasting.

Today, rock songs, artists, and fans remain the targets of efforts to silence this form of musical expression all over the world. Rock music is still blamed for glamorizing an impressive array of social evils including violence, drug use, misogyny, and the occult. Records have been banned and burned since the 1950s and musicians have been subjected to government harassment. Rock and roll has been accused of causing everything from teenage pregnancy, suicide, copycat murders, and drug addiction to juvenile delinquency, "sexual deviance", and mental illness. The demonization continues unabated. Recently, however, the newsletter *Rock and Rap Confidential*, and watchdog groups such as Rock Out Censorship, Massachusetts Music Industry Coalition, and Parents for Rock and Rap have arisen. While they do not yet have the political clout of their rivals, they are a growing force with chapters in the US, Britain, and Canada lobbying against restrictive laws and challenging censorship attempts.

JENNIFER HOLT

Further Reading

Cloonan, Martin, "Popular Music and Censorship in Britain: An Overview", *Popular Music and Society*, 19/3 (1995): 75–104

Cloonan, Martin, *Banned! Censorship of Popular Music in Britain, 1967–92*, Aldershot, Hampshire: Arena, 1996

Denselow, Robin, *When the Music's Over: The Story of Political Pop*, London: Faber, 1989

Frith, Simon, *Sound Effects: Youth, Leisure, and the Politics of Rock 'n' Roll*, New York: Pantheon, 1981; London: Constable, 1983

Gaar, Gillian G., *She's a Rebel: The History of Women in Rock & Roll*, Seattle: Seal Press, 1992

Garofalo, Reebee (editor), *Rockin' the Boat: Mass Media and Mass Movements*, Boston: South End Press, 1992

Holden, D., "Pop Go the Censors", *Index on Censorship*, 22/5–6 (May–June 1993)

Martin, Linda and Kerry Segrave, *Anti-Rock: The Opposition to Rock 'n' Roll*, Hamden, Connecticut: Archon, 1988

Nuzum, Eric D., *Parental Advisory: Music Censorship in America*, New York: Perennial, 2001

Savage, Jon, *England's Dreaming: Sex Pistols and Punk Rock*, London: Faber, 1991, New York: St Martin's Press, 1992; revised edition, Faber, 2001

"Smashed Hits", special issue of *Index on Censorship*, 27/6 (November–December 1998)

Ward, Ed, *et al.*, *Rock of Ages: The Rolling Stone History of Rock & Roll*, New York: Rolling Stone Press, 1986

Winfield, Betty Houching and Sandra Davidson (editors), *Bleep! Censoring Rock and Rap Music*, Westport, Connecticut: Greenwood Press, 1999

Website

A brief history of banned music: http://www.ericnuzum.com/banned/

MUTUAL FILM CORPORATION V. INDUSTRIAL COMMISSION OF OHIO
US Supreme Court decision, 1915

Is film censorship constitutional under United States law? When the US Supreme Court first addressed this question, in *Mutual Film Corporation* v. *Industrial Commission of Ohio*, its answer was a decisive "yes". At issue was a 1913 Ohio statute that established a board of film censors to approve for exhibition in the state only films of a "moral, educational or amusing and harmless character". Exhibitors of unapproved films faced criminal penalties. A unanimous Supreme Court upheld this statute, explaining that movies, not being part of the nation's "press", did not warrant constitutional free-press protection.

Many observers have viewed the *Mutual* decision as a betrayal of the "deeply rooted Anglo-Saxon antagonism to censorship". In the law of films and theatres, however, it was censorship itself, not antagonism to it, that was "deeply rooted". In fact, official control over US theatrical amusements was a tradition as old as the nation itself. Nineteenth-century Ohio, for instance, was typical in banning outright certain types of shows (e.g., puppetry), and requiring that exhibitors of all other types of shows obtain permits prior to exhibition. "An inquiry has to be made as to the character of those who propose to exhibit", a state judge explained in 1860, "and as to the nature of the thing exhibited."

Did such measures violate constitutional speech and press guarantees? Nobody at the time thought to ask. Prior to the 20th century, few if any appellate litigants argued that laws regulating theatrical amusements violated free-expression clauses. This being the case, judges did not rule on the matter one way or another. Theatrical regulation was not yet a free-speech issue.

The Mutual Film Corporation, therefore, was something of a pioneer when it launched its free-press campaign. At the outset, however, its motivation for attacking the Ohio censorship law had less to do with free expression than with free enterprise. As a film distributor that purchased films from producers and rented them to exhibitors nationwide, Mutual viewed state-by-state censorship schemes – never more than minor irritants to small-scale theatre troupes – as major nuisances. For one thing, given the massive scope of Mutual's operation, even nominal censorship fees could quickly add up (Ohio charged one dollar per original or duplicate reel). In addition, patchwork censorship delays threatened the effectiveness of the nationwide advertising blitzes that the company launched in support of coast-to-coast, same-day film releases. Finally, unlike producers of live shows, who could easily excise a line here or alter a costume there to appease local authorities, Mutual strove to deliver identical copies of its films to movie theatres across the country. If films confronted "many boards of censors, and possibly, eventually, one in every state, each board having its own ideas", Mutual president Harry Aitken worried, "it will be almost impossible to run a film distribution concern profitably". By no accident, then, did US history's most comprehensive attack on the constitutionality of state regulation of theatrical amusements come only after the entertainment business had outgrown its traditional, local scale.

During 1914 and 1915, the Mutual Film Corporation distributed its top attorney, Walter Seligsberg, almost as widely as it distributed its movies. Seligsberg went from Chicago to Pennsylvania, to Kansas, to Ohio, attacking state and local film censorship measures each step of the way. In the Ohio case, which made it to the US Supreme Court, Seligsberg argued that the state's censorship law was unconstitutional on three grounds: first, because it unconstitutionally interfered with interstate commerce; second, because it delegated an unacceptable degree of discretionary, "legislative" power to an unaccountable administrative body (the state censorship board); and, third, because it "directly contravene[d] the guaranties of freedom of publication and liberty of the press".

Writing for the Court, Justice Joseph McKenna rejected all Seligsberg's arguments and upheld the censorship statute. Once inside Ohio's borders, McKenna explained, rebuffing the company's interstate commerce claim, out-of-state films "mingled ... with the other property of the state" and immediately became subject to Ohio law. Regarding the delegation of legislative discretion to an administrative body, McKenna ruled that the statute's descriptive terms for acceptable films – "moral, educational or amusing and harmless" – constituted sufficient legislative guidance.

The bulk of the opinion, however, answered Mutual's contention that the censorship law violated constitutionally protected freedoms of expression. In words that would subsequently exasperate entire generations of civil libertarians, the Court ruled that films did not qualify for constitutional protection. "It cannot be put out of view", McKenna wrote, "that the exhibition of moving pictures is a business, pure and simple, originated and conducted for profit." As such, movies were "not to be regarded, nor intended to be regarded" as "part of the press of the country". State censorship of motion pictures, in other words, was constitutionally unobjectionable.

The *Mutual Film* case exemplifies the general indifference of Progressive Era courts to free-speech claims. It also illustrates, however, something quite different: the increasing tendency of the day's litigants to make such claims. Prior to *Mutual Film*, precious few had conceived of the censorship of theatrical amusements as a free-speech issue. The Mutual Film Corporation's failed legal crusade raised and changed the nation's constitutional consciousness regarding this issue. In 1919, for instance, the National Association of the Motion Picture Industry, inspired by Mutual's example, proposed a constitutional amendment to protect "freedom of the screen". When this failed, industry leaders and civil libertarians began contemplating a follow-up test case. The ultimate result was *Burstyn* v. *Wilson* (1952), in which the United States Supreme Court overruled its holding in *Mutual Film* by ruling that motion pictures indeed warranted First Amendment protection. With this decision, the so-called "*Mutual Film* Period" of American film history, marked by scores of state-and-local censorship measures, came to an end.

JOHN WERTHEIMER

Further Reading

Jowett, Garth S., "'A Capacity for Evil': The 1915 Supreme Court Mutual Decision", *Historical Journal of Film, Radio and Television*, 9/1 (1989): 59–78

Randall, Richard S., *Censorship of the Movies: The Social and Political Control of a Mass Medium*, Madison: University of Wisconsin Press, 1968

Rosenbloom, Nancy J., "Between Reform and Regulation: The Struggle over Film Censorship in Progressive America, 1909–1922", *Film History*, 1/4 (1987): 307–25

Schiller, Reuel E., "Free Speech and Expertise: Administrative Censorship and the Birth of the Modern First Amendment", *Virginia Law Review*, 86 (February 2000): 1–102

Wertheimer, John, "*Mutual Film* Reviewed: The Movies, Censorship, and Free Speech in Progressive America", *American Journal of Legal History*, 37/2 (1993): 158–89

MYANMAR
See Burma

MYSTERY PLAYS

The mystery plays were religious drama that was performed annually throughout Britain from the late 14th to the late 16th century on the annual feast of Corpus Christi. They were written in the vernacular by the clergy to bring the Christian story to the people, at a time when few could read and books were scarce. They fell foul of changes in religious doctrine at the Reformation, and increasing state control of performance under the Tudors. The prohibition of religious drama kept them from the stage for more than 300 years and dogged early 20th-century attempts at revival. Late 20th-century performances were subject to demands for "political correctness", and anti-Semitic references, sexism, and anti-Islamic sentiment were sometimes cut.

The mystery plays sprang from an impulse both to embellish an existing ceremony and to aid its comprehension. Adopted in 1311, the feast of Corpus Christi commemorated the institution of the Eucharist. Early celebrations were organized by the church and mounted by town guilds. These included street processions (first held in 1318) featuring wooden tableaux illustrating biblical figures. These developed into *tableaux vivants* of mimed action and eventually some dialogue. In 1376 the guilds of York produced the first recorded example of the Corpus Christi pageant or mystery play – a series of short biblical plays performed on wagon carts around the city.

The Corpus Christi performances traced the Christian epic, from the Creation and the Fall to the Last Judgement, and also featured tales from the Apocrypha (including the Fall of Lucifer, the Harrowing of Hell, and the Assumption of the Virgin). Growing out of the missionary fervour of the 12th and 13th centuries, the plays used drama as a means of encouraging moral behaviour. Similar religious dramas were also enacted in France (the *mystères sacrés*), Germany (the *Osterspiele* at Easter and the *Fronleichnamsspiele* at Corpus Christi), Italy (the *sacra rappresentazione*), and Spain (*representacións*), as well as the Low Countries and some parts of eastern Europe.

Four cycles of mystery plays are extant (from York, Wakefield, Chester, and the N-Town cycle from East Anglia), although fragments of plays from Coventry, Newcastle, and Norwich exist and there are records of many more – in Beverley, Hereford, Ipswich, and Louth. Variations on the cycles also survive from Scotland, Ireland, and Cornwall. There were regional variations in number (at Chester some 25 plays were performed over three days while at York there were 50 in one day) and method (the N-Town plays are believed to have had a fixed staging, while the rest are thought to have used rolling carts). But records suggest a similarity in means and methodology.

Written in rhyming, alliterative verse the plays had a popular appeal. Set in the present they reflect the environment in which they were performed – thus Pilate and Herod are feudal figures, addressed as "Sir"; the shepherds keep watch in the hills of the Cotswolds; while God wears the triple crown of the pope, and Christ in majesty appears in rich episcopal costume. Special effects add to the spectacle and include fire for the Holy Spirit, fireworks for devils, lightning for the Last Judgement, and flight for supernatural characters.

The comedic, acrobatic, and musical tradition of secular drama also had an impact on the mystery plays. Some of the best moments of the cycles, and certainly the most memorable characters, are comic, including Mak the sheep stealer from the famous Wakefield play *The Second Shepherd's Pageant* and Noah's argumentative wife. The lazy soldiers of the York *Crucifixion*, moaning about poor workmanship and the weight of the cross they have to fix, bring a blacker humour to proceedings and suggest the strength of creative intelligence behind some of the writing.

It was the doctrinal purpose of the mystery plays, however, that proved their undoing. Subject to continuous revision and additions during their 200-year lifespan, the scripts kept pace with developments in religious teaching. The Reformation of the 1530s had an inevitable impact on their performance: Chester dropped all references to the pope from the banns that opened the cycle in 1531, while plays on the life of the Virgin ceased in the 1540s. In 1543 the "Act for the advancement of the true religion and for the abolishment of the contrary" banned all plays likely to offend against Protestantism and in 1548 Corpus Christi and its attendant festivities were suppressed.

But the plays' decline was not just a matter of a change of religious belief and emphasis. From the time of Henry VIII's accession in 1509 the state had tightened its grip on publishing and performance. In 1529 proclamations appeared against seditious and heretical books, while the licensing of books was introduced in 1538. Restrictions on touring players were also instigated by Henry, under whom a company needed a patron's livery and letter of authorization to travel around the country and perform. Edward VI continued his father's work against "popish" books and in 1549 introduced the licensing of plays.

Although the mystery plays, and Corpus Christi, were briefly revived during the counter-reformation of Mary I, Elizabeth I decisively ended the tradition. According to an injunction of 1559, no interlude or play was to be performed unless previously licensed by the mayor of the locality, while local authorities were empowered to prohibit plays "wherein either matters of religion or of governance of the state of the common weale shall be handled or treated". In 1574 the Chester cycle was suppressed. Two years later the York and Wakefield plays were banned (a final, unsuccessful attempt was made to revive York in 1580). The last appearance came in 1581 at Coventry, and coincided with Elizabeth's prohibition of all Corpus Christi plays and a ban on scriptural or religious drama. A similar fate befell the religious drama of Protestant Europe, while in Catholic areas the plays survived, albeit in more sophisticated forms, into the 17th and 18th centuries.

Elizabeth's ban, enacted as much for her political security as for her religious beliefs, was in force for more than 300 years. The first revival, by the theatre antiquarian William Poel in 1901, was a private (unlicensed) production which paired the morality play *Everyman* (c.1508) with the mystery play *The Sacrifice of Isaac*. Five years later Poel's disciple Nugent Monck produced the Chester *Shepherds* and *Magi* plays but when he attempted to mount the Passion sequence of the N-Town cycle in 1909 he was arrested for selling tickets for a performance of an unlicensed play in an unlicensed theatre and read the blasphemy laws. The representation of Christ on stage (prohibited by the Censorship Act of 1737) was his real offence – so sensitive was the representation of the Cruxifixion that it was even bowdlerized from printed versions of the texts in the 1920s. Monck was not able to produce the Passion sequence until 1938 (in a private performance). The ban on performance was lifted in 1951, with the revival of the York plays for the Festival of Britain, and Monck's production was licensed in 1952.

No longer subject to the blasphemy laws or theatrical censorship (the latter abolished in 1968), today the mystery plays are prized for their theatricality. They are performed regularly in York (once every four years) and Coventry (once every two years) and have been reworked to critical acclaim in Tony Harrison's adaptation of the York cycle (*The Mysteries*, Royal National Theatre, 1985).

Modern sensibilities have brought a different type of censoriousness. Poel had cut "offensive material" (usually sexual) from the texts, while revivals in Toronto in 1985 removed anti-Semitism from the Wakefield plays. A production of 1997–98 by the Royal Shakespeare Company in Stratford-on-Avon and London went further, however, removing not only uncomfortable lines such as "But Jews, cursed may they be, damned him and nailed him to a tree" but all references to the race. Thus in Edward Kemp's version, Jesus is persecuted by an unnamed politico-religious establishment. Such tactics not only sacrifice the medieval sentiment of the plays but beg the question of their revival.

SARAH A. SMITH

Further Reading

Beadle, Richard (editor), *Cambridge Companion to Medieval English Theatre*, Cambridge and New York: Cambridge University Press, 1994

Cawley, A.C. (editor), *Everyman, and Medieval Miracle Plays*, 3rd edition, London: Dent, and Rutland, Vermont: Tuttle, 1993

Harris, John Wesley, *Medieval Theatre in Context: An Introduction*, London and New York: Routledge, 1992

Twycross, Meg (editor), *Festive Drama: Papers from the Sixth Triennial Colloquium of the International Society for the Study of Medieval Theatre*, Cambridge: Brewer, 1996

Tydeman, William, *English Medieval Theatre, 1400–1500*, London and Boston: Routledge, 1986

Wickham, Glynne, *The Medieval Theatre*, 3rd edition, Cambridge and New York: Cambridge University Press, 1987

N

NACHALO NEVEDOMOGO VEKA (The Beginning of an Unknown Era)

Russian film, 1967–88: now consists of *Angel* (Angel), directed by Andrei Smirnov (1941–),
Rodina elektrichestva (Homeland of Electricity), directed by Larisa Shepitko (1938–79),
and *Motria*, directed by Genrikh Gabai (1923–)

Films on historical subjects were always crucially important in the Soviet Union. Several such films were commissioned to mark the 50th anniversary of the Bolshevik revolution in 1967, including Gennadii Poloka's *Interventsiia* (*Intervention*), Aleksandr Askoldov's *Komissar* (*The Commissar*), and a portmanteau film to be directed by a number of young film makers, *Nachalo nevedomogo veka* (*The Beginning of an Unknown Era*). It is a measure of the sensitivity of historical subject matter that none of these three films could be released at the time, and that all ended up on the infamous "shelf".

The Beginning of an Unknown Era was planned in the new Experimental Creative Studio, and the initial proposal sent to the State Cinema Committee, Goskino, in April 1967 was for five "novellas" to be based on the revolutionary stories of Iurii Olesha, Isaak Babel', Aleksandr Malyshkin, Konstantin Paustovskii, and Andrei Platonov, and directed by the young filmmakers Andrei Smirnov, Elem Klimov, Dzhemma Firsova, Genrikh Gabai, and Larisa Shepitko, some of whom had already experienced censorship difficulties with earlier projects. This plan was initially accepted by Goskino, but its enthusiasm was shortlived. Its deputy chairman, Vladimir Baskakov, soon halted work on Klimov's section of the film, based on Babel''s story "The Betrayal" from the cycle *Konarmiia* (1926, *Red Cavalry*), with the revealing words "Why the Hell do we need this Babel'?" Babel''s Jewish subject matter was particularly sensitive at the time, and publication of his writings was itself subject to censorship. Firsova's version of a story by Malyshkin was also stopped soon afterwards.

Vladimir Ognev, who worked in the administration of the Experimental Studio, has recalled that, initially, there were plans to connect the novellas with documentary footage, and that Shepitko's film of Andrei Platonov's story "Homeland of Electricity", about a young idealist trying to bring electricity to a drought-stricken village, was to be preceded by footage of the famine along the Volga in 1921. The film was shot in Astrakhan with nonprofessional actors, using an innovative, almost "documentary" visual style that draws attention away from the central characters to give a picture of the revolutionary epoch in all its tragic bleakness. Ognev suggests that the reason for the eventual shelving of the film was that, at its end, the drought

is overcome, not by the young man's motor, improvised from a motorcycle engine, but by a sudden rainstorm, which the censors interpreted to imply that God and nature had watered the land, not the Bolsheviks. Valerii Fomin, the leading historian of film censorship in the Brezhnev period and the source of most of our knowledge of the subject, quotes a Goskino document confirming its realization that the very expressiveness of Shepitko's cinematic means had brought out the full tragedy of the people's fate. By thus going counter to the official myths of the revolutionary period, she had inadvertently consigned the film to 20 years of oblivion.

The fate of Andrei Smirnov's film *Angel*, based on a story by Olesha, was just as harsh. In a memoir, Smirnov has recalled how he wanted to give his film the look of "early Bergman" and to portray all the savagery of the Civil War. In Olesha's story, set in 1920, a group of passengers travelling on a train are attacked by a counter-revolutionary group led by the eponymous Angel and the commissar among them is brutally murdered. When the film was shown in the studio it provoked a scandal. Smirnov had captured the horror of the period only too vividly, and the film was rejected as "ideologically diversionary" and "unsuitable for an anniversary". Repeated attempts to salvage it by making minor changes were doomed; the film was written off and the studio bosses were reprimanded. To quote again from a document published by Fomin, Goskino found that the film showed "only the terrible and bloody destruction of the normal flow of life" caused by the revolution.

After these rejections, all attempts to release the planned portmanteau film were abandoned. Shepitko went on to make her most brilliant film, *Voskhozhdenie* (1976, *Ascent*), which brought her tragic vision of her country's modern history to a tale set in World War II. She died in a car crash in 1979, soon after beginning work on an adaptation of a short novel by Valentin Rasputin. This film was completed by her widower, Elem Klimov, as *Proshchanie s Materoi* (1983, Farewell to Matera). Smirnov's career continued to be beset by censorship problems, to the extent that at the end of the 1970s he decided to abandon his directorial career, and to concentrate on writing scripts and plays. It was only in 1986, with the changes to the

Soviet film industry inaugurated by the fifth congress of the Filmmakers' Union, that he was elected to the new board of the union, for which he acted as first secretary in 1988–90. With the unshelving of banned films that resulted from these changes, *Angel* and *Homeland of Electricity* were finally released together, under the title *The Beginning of an Unknown Era*, to great acclaim. Their startlingly original visions, combining a poetic sense of place and time with an almost documentary intensity, the very qualities that had so alarmed the artistically unsophisticated censors of the Brezhnev period, were to exert considerable influence on the film-makers of the late 1980s, who continued their preoccupation with establishing a true picture of the history of their country.

Genrikh Gabai's "novello" *Motria*, based on the work of Konstantin Paustovskii, was finally shown together with the novellos by Shepitko and Smirnov at the 22nd Moscow International Film Festival in July 2000.

JULIAN GRAFFY

Further Reading

Fomin, V.I., *Kino i vlast´: Sovetskoe kino, 1965–1985 gody* (Cinema and Power: Soviet Cinema 1965–85), Moscow: Materik, 1996
Ognev, V., "Dvadtsat´ let nazad" (Twenty Years Ago), *Iskusstvo kino* (Cinema Art), 1 (1988): 32–39
Rosenberg, K., "Shepitko", *Sight and Sound*, 56 (1987): 119–22

NAIROBI LAW MONTHLY
Kenyan magazine, founded 1987

Nairobi Law Monthly, launched by Gitobu Imanyara, a practising lawyer, covers current affairs and political news but specializes in documenting violations of human rights and freedom of expression together with the abuse of power and constitutional law in Kenya. Unsurprisingly, the response from the authorities has included intimidation, violence, banning, and imprisonment aimed at the publishers, journalists, printers, and street vendors. Gitobu Imanyara, the main target of attempts to censor the *Nairobi Law Monthly*, has received international acclaim for his journalism and bravery including the Lyon Award and the International Pen Award. He has been arrested and jailed repeatedly. Charges against him have included treason and violating publishing laws.

The magazine came into being in response to two developments in the 1980s. First, the growing authoritarianism of Kenya's political leaders. After the attempted coup d'état in 1982, the country reverted to a single-party constitution under the rule of president Daniel arap Moi. This heralded a period of consolidated rule by the Kenya African National Union (KANU) which saw constitutional freedoms further eroded. The government's disregard for law grew steadily, as did the ruling party's appropriation of the state. The introduction of queue-voting in 1986 culminating in the large-scale rigging of the 1988 election began to provoke widespread criticism. Second, the launch of Gitobu Imanyara's magazine reflected the increasing confidence of the country's legal community. By the mid-1980s, Kenyan lawyers were speaking out against what they saw as the undermining of their legal system and constitution. Part of the reason for this lies in the changed profile of the Kenya Law Society, a body established in 1962 by an act of parliament to assist the government and judiciary on issues relating to the practice of law and justice, and to assist the public on issues that touched upon the law. At first, many members were British expatriates seconded by the departing colonial power. By the 1980s a new generation of African lawyers had emerged, some of whom were much more willing and able to criticize the political establishment. However, very few were, and still are, willing to take "political cases" – for fear of the personal consequences. The widespread powers of detention under the Preservation of Public Security Act passed after the attempted coup in 1982 have not been abandoned, and the fear of detention, torture, and unfair trials continues to create a climate of intimidation.

One of Gitobu Imanyara's early articles, which resulted in his arrest, was the publication of an interview with the lawyer Gibson Kamau Kuria – pictured on the front cover – who had recently been released from detention, together with a letter sent to the commissioner of police calling for his resignation and the acceptance of blame for alleged incidents of police brutality and the death of people in custody. Kuria was a lawyer who had filed a case on behalf of four detainees in March 1984 arguing that their detention was illegal. It was the first time such an application had been made. Gitobu Imanyara was subsequently arrested.

Following his release, he continued to raise questions about the constitution, the decline of parliamentary supremacy, the lack of an independent judiciary, torture, inhumane prison conditions, freedom of worship, and threats of the independence of the bar. The *Nairobi Law Monthly* was also at the forefront in the campaign to restore a multi-party system in the country. Along with a number of other lawyers, he was detained without trial for three weeks July 1990. The government justified its action thus: "You are the editor or proprietor of a Nairobi magazine known as *The Nairobi Law Monthly*, in which you have repeatedly written and published articles which denounce, ridicule, and discredit the government of Kenya, its activities and its established constitutional leadership ... You have aligned yourself to and associated with known anti-government characters and personalities ... to lay ground work for the formation or creation of another political party contrary to the provision of the Constitution of the country." In September 1992, the *Nairobi Law Monthly* became the fourth publication in the country to be prohibited. Nevertheless, the magazine has remained at the forefront of efforts to reform the legal, constitutional, and administrative framework of the country in order to secure the respect for human rights, a fair electoral system, and freedom of speech. Imanyara also became secretary general of an opposition party.

Tactics used by the authorities to censor the *Nairobi Law Monthly* have been varied and typical of the measures employed to censor other independent magazines such as *Finance*, *Society*, and the *Economic Review*. In March 1991 the head of Fotoform Ltd, which at that time was printing the magazine, was detained and charged with violating the Books and Newspapers Act and with working in Kenya illegally. Some of the measures used clearly fall outside the legal framework of the state. Pressure is not just applied to the printers of the magazines and those companies who pay to advertise. Vendors are also harassed. For example, in October 1990 newsvendors were injured and arrested and copies of the magazines seized by the police. This followed the first successful repeal of a ban in the high court which had been issued against the *Nairobi Law Monthly*. Imanyara successfully argued that the ban was unconstitutional. Even so, vendors were still told the publication was illegal, despite the high court order. Poor and often vulnerable street sellers offer easy targets for harassment and intimidation.

Other tactics fall within the state's recourse to censor through the law as it currently stands. On a number of occasions, including after his first arrest in 1988, Imanyara has been charged with failure to file annual sales return to the Registrar of Books and Newspapers. When detained in February 1991 at Kamiti Maximum Security Prison, he was charged with printing a seditious publication. In April he was found unconscious in his cell, having been kept in solitary confinement since being remanded, with only 30 minutes exercise and light a day. A medical report, used later in court, recorded severe bouts of left-sided headaches, leading to loss of consciousness, possible epilepsy, blood-clotting and high blood pressure. In May 1991

he was released unconditionally and all charges against him (apart from two of theft) were dropped.

Section 56 of the Kenyan Penal Code includes in its definition of a "seditious intention" the deliberate intention "to raise discontent or disaffection among the inhabitants of Kenya" or "to promote feelings of ill-will or hostility between different sections or classes of the population of Kenya". The problem with this rule is that while a publication is not seditious merely if it points out mistakes by the government, the charge of sedition cannot be defended by the claim of being truthful, since according to the code, "every person shall be deemed to intend the consequences which would naturally follow from his conduct". Such a law sustains an overall climate of self-censorship which Gitobu Imanyara through the *Nairobi Law Monthly* has confounded.

JOANNA LEWIS

Further Reading

Article 19, "Kenya: Continued Attack on the Independent Press", London: Article 19, 1993

"Kenya: News from Africa Watch", *Africa Watch* (5 April 1990)

Kenya: Shadow Justice, London: African Rights, 1996

Kenya: Taking Liberties, New York: Africa Watch, 1991

"Report on a Visit to Kenya, 27–31 January 1997", International Committee of the Law Society of England and Wales (4 June 1997)

Throup, David, "Elections and Political Legitimacy in Kenya", *Africa*, 63/3 (1993): 371–96

NAMIBIA

(formerly South West Africa)

Population: 1,757,000	**Number of daily newspapers:** 4
Main religions: Lutheran; Christian; indigenous religions	**Number of periodicals:** 2
Official language: English	**Number of radio receivers per 1000 inhabitants:** 143
Other languages spoken: Ovambo; Nama; Kavango; Afrikaans; German	**Number of TV receivers per 1000 inhabitants:** 37
Illiteracy rate (%): 17.2 (m); 18.8 (f)	**Number of PCs per 1000 inhabitants:** 18.6

The early history of the region that constitutes contemporary Namibia reveals an area characterized by an abundance of societies, cultures, and political units. There were numerous highly centralized kingdoms similar to those found in West Africa, though smaller in scale; as well as smaller clan groupings, all of which were linked by intricate trading routes.

Contact with Europeans first occurred in the late 15th century, when Portuguese traders arrived in the area. However, it was not until four centuries later that European colonization took place. In 1884, the Germans acquired sovereignty over South West Africa, as the territory was known, in exchange for conceding British control over Walvis Bay and the surrounding area. The Germans actively encouraged settlement in the area, and a land allocation system which disenfranchised the African population was put into place. African resistance to colonial rule in Namibia culminated in the Herero–German war of 1904. After a particularly brutal defeat of the Herero, the

Germans continued to annihilate the Herero people resulting in a loss of nearly 80 per cent of the population.

During World War I, the British invaded South West Africa, and set up an interim military administration in 1915. In 1920 the League of Nations decided that South West Africa was not ready for independence, and the international community granted the guardianship of the territory to the Union of South Africa in a quasi-colonial arrangement (it was stipulated, however, that South Africa could not set up military bases). Following World War II and the establishment of the United Nations, there was pressure from nascent nationalist organizations to remove South West Africa from its "colonial" status and move it towards independence. This was strongly resisted by the South African government, which continued to administer the area as part of South Africa, and implemented the same pass laws and reserve system as applied there. With the ascent to power of the Malan government in the late 1940s, the

Namibian population was subject to the apartheid laws of Afrikaner nationalists.

Labour activism became one path of resistance, with strikes occurring frequently in the 1950s. Meanwhile, the international community was unable to get a clear mandate for action on South West Africa from the International Court of Justice, which argued in 1950 that South Africa and the United Nations had to decide jointly on any alteration of South West Africa's status as a trusteeship territory. This effectively hamstrung the United Nations from taking action on the territory.

In Namibia itself, following the shooting of 11 protesters in Windhoek in 1959, the indigenous resistance movement was energized. The major player in this fight was a former labour organization called the Ovamboland People's Organization (OPO), which reorganized into the South West African People's Organization (SWAPO) in 1959. In 1966 the UN General Assembly terminated the South African mandate, but South Africa was defiant and in 1968 SWAPO took up arms against its presence. For the next decade, these clashes became a part of the daily life of South West Africa. Colin Leys and John S. Saul record:

> A political activist who fell into the hands of the police, the army or the counter-insurgency unit Koevoet (Crowbar) was very likely to be beaten, if not systematically tortured and quite likely (especially when taken by Koevoet) to be killed. Atrocities were "censored", obviously in South Africa itself but also by default through lack of reportage in the world press. The resistance press in Namibia itself – the *Namibian* for instance – was subject to threats and intimidation.

In 1976 the UN General Assembly recognized SWAPO as the "sole and authentic representative of the Namibian people".

South Africa's intransigence proceeded partly from its anxiety over events in Angola, which it invaded in the mid-1970s in support of the opposition UNITA party. Namibia became the base from which military operations were planned, in clear defiance of the mandate. It was no wonder that a barrage of censorship measures were instituted. The Defence Act (1983) forbade reports that might cause "alarm and despondency"; any account of SWAPO military activity was to be referred to the Ministry of Defence press department. Information on the bases, and on casualties, was strictly controlled. The Protection of Information Act could be used against any person "who obtains or compiles information for disclosure . . . to any foreign state or hostile organisation". The Police Act declared illegal any "false" statement about the police "without having reasonable grounds for believing it to be true".

Most censorship was directed at the independent press. Broadcasting was a monopoly of the South West Africa Broadcasting Corporation and had always been under government control. Most resistance came from the *Windhoek Observer*, which insisted on covering SWAPO activities (SWAPO was not illegal) and exposing official corruption. The South Africans took particular exception to columns by Gwen Lister, who returned from a UN conference in Paris (March 1984) with a suitcase full of UN literature (drawing attention to the UN viewpoint on Namibia) and also some SWAPO literature. Two months later the *Observer* was banned until it signed up to an agreement that it would "steer a course clear of the undesirable aspects of the 26 May edition" (which reported the talks with SWAPO then being held in Lusaka). Lister had to resign, went freelance, and had her personal mail intercepted. She went on to found *The Namibian*, even more of a thorn in South Africa's side.

Namibia achieved independence on 21 March 1990, becoming now a multi-party democracy with an independent judiciary, freedom of speech, the right to organize, a free press, and a generally free and fair electoral process. Freedom of speech and the press is provided for in the constitution and generally respected by the state, as is academic freedom and freedom of religion. The government-owned Namibian Broadcasting Corporation (NBC) operates most radio and television services, but provides significant coverage to opposing points of view. Its radio phone-in programmes are regarded as particularly irreverent. There have, however, been sporadic accusations of censorship when NBC management has refused to release or air footage of certain interviews. Several private radio and television stations exist, and generally operate without interference. Reporters for independent newspapers criticize the government openly and do not engage in self-censorship.

Nevertheless, there remain some sensitive issues which can and have provoked a harsh response from the government, particularly the question of the fate of persons detained by SWAPO prior to independence. For example, the publication of a book on the detention and torture of SWAPO detainees, *Namibia: The Wall of Silence*, was attacked by the government, although no attempt was made to ban the publication. The government has also been accused of stalling investigations of corruption within its own ranks, and failing to punish those responsible. Meanwhile, the Bushmen, or San people, descendants of the country's earliest known inhabitants, have been arrested when staging demonstrations to protest against government policy regarding their ancestral lands and other issues. Generally the government has not pursued these cases.

Namibia's first post-independence presidential and legislative elections were held in December 1994. President Sam Nujoma and SWAPO were the overwhelming victors, securing over two-thirds of the seats in the legislature: enough to modify the constitution if they chose, though this has not happened. However, the government has taken an increasingly harsh approach in its dealings with the media, mostly through unprovoked verbal attacks on the press. In December 1996 Nujoma called the independent media an "enemy", claiming it was run by "foreigners", in an interview with a state-run newspaper. The following year SWAPO refused to allow press coverage of the party's second congress in May 1997, and president Nujoma reportedly made denigrating remarks about the press in his opening statement to the congress.

In 1996 the Powers, Privileges and Immunities of Parliament Act was introduced. The original act gave parliamentary committees the right to subpoena journalists in order to force them to reveal their sources, and to prohibit journalists from interviewing MPs about pending legislation that is controversial. The publication of "false information" about parliament or its proceedings was defined by the act as an offence, as was the intentional or negligent publication or disclosure of information placed before a parliamentary committee. These offences were punishable by a maximum fine of USD $5000 or five years' imprisonment. In April 1996 the National Assembly passed the act, but removed the provisions which restricted the media in response to criticism from the Media Institute of Southern Africa, other civil liberties groups, and foreign diplomats. The government subsequently proposed a Film Commission Bill which would require a film production licence for the production of any film in Namibia. Concerns were expressed by industry representatives that there needed to be a clear separation between the government and the licence-granting body of the commission itself.

In July 1997 the National Assembly passed a Central Intelligence Service bill, which permits the use of wiretaps, the interception of mail, and other covert activities in the interests of "national security". This appears to pose a definite threat to freedom of expression in Namibia, particularly for opposition groups. Also in July, in response to protests by ex-fighters urging the government to provide jobs, Nujoma banned all public demonstrations that lacked police permission. In October 1997 the Ministry of Information and Broadcasting issued new regulations requiring foreign journalists seeking to visit Namibia to provide one month's advance notice to the ministry, stating the purpose of their proposed visit. The government and media are struggling to come to terms with the role of the media in a democratic state and how they can develop a working relationship that serves the needs of both parties.

Three issues have dominated the censorship agenda recently. In 1997 parliament took powers to subpoena and to demand sources of information from journalists; Hannes Smith, editor of the *Windhoek Observer* was imprisoned for four months in 1999 for failing to produce confidential documents relating to the assassination of the SWAPO activist Anton Lubowski ten years previously: they were required for the coroner's inquest. In 1998 Namibian forces were sent to support the new government of Laurent Kabila in the Democratic Republic of Congo. The prime minister, Hage Geingob, admitted that the minister of defence was deliberately withholding information on the topic; he had "instructed his staff not to release any informa-

tion to the media generally because of a number of reasons". And in November 1998 various groups in the "Caprivi strip" demanded secession; a film crew from the South African Broadcasting Corporation covering the crisis had their video footage confiscated.

Finally, and on an entirely different note, legislation has recently been introduced to ban the practice of male and female homosexuality. The language used by the president and other ministers in this regard has been discussed by Namibian gay groups as hate speech: homosexuality has been described as a "hideous deviation" which needs to be "uprooted totally".

DANA OTT

Further Reading

Committee to Protect Journalists, *Attacks on the Press in 1997*, New York: Committee to Protect Journalists, 1998

Herbstein, Denis, "Namibia: How South Africa Controls the News", *Index on Censorship*, 14/4 (August 1985)

Herbstein, Denis and John Evenson, *The Devils Are among Us: The War for Namibia*, London: Zed, 1989

Leys, Colin and John S. Saul, *Namibia's Liberation Struggle: The Two-Edged Sword*, London: Currey, and Athens: Ohio University Press, 1995

Media Institute of Southern Africa, "Ruling *SWAPO* 'Bars' Media Coverage of Its Congress", *Action Alert* (7 June 1997)

Media Institute of Southern Africa, "President Sam Nujoma Bans Demonstrations", *Action Alert* (17 July 1997)

Media Institute of Southern Africa, "Recommendations and Proposals on the Development of the Namibian Film/Video Industry" (press release) (11 September 1997)

"Namibia" in *Africa South of the Sahara*, 26th edition, London: Europa, 1997

Press Freedom Worldwide: 1997, New York: Freedom House, 1997

Soggot, David, *Namibia: The Violent Heritage*, London: Collings, and New York: St Martin's Press, 1986

Sparks, Donald L. and December Green, *Namibia: The Nation after Independence*, Boulder, Colorado: Westview Press, 1992

US Department of State, *Namibia: Country Report on Human Rights Practices for 1997*, Washington, DC: Bureau of Democracy, Human Rights and Labor, 1998

THE NAMIBIAN
Namibian newspaper, established 1985

Censorship takes many forms under a repressive regime, and *The Namibian*, and its staff, were subject to a variety of attempts to silence the newspaper during the South African occupation of Namibia. In addition to enforced editorial changes, censorship at this time encompassed various attempts to intimidate journalists physically and psychologically, as well as to destroy the premises of the newspaper itself.

Censorship ruled the lives of reporting staff, and there was no privacy from the prying eyes of security police and army intelligence units which read all correspondence, monitored telephones, conducted surveillance on homes, infiltrated the staff, carried out telephonic death-threat campaigns, and conducted other surveillance duties.

This "censorship" started before the inception of the newspaper in 1985. The authorities were aware that we were intent on establishing an English-language newspaper that would

challenge South African control and influence over the media in Namibia, would advocate self-determination from South African rule and the implementation of the United Nations settlement plan (Resolution 435 of 1978), and would expose the atrocities committed against civilians by the forces of apartheid occupation. They were intent that the paper would never get off the ground.

Under the guise of fighting what were variously termed the "terrorists" or "communists" of the South West Africa Peoples' Organization (SWAPO), who were fighting a war for the liberation of Namibia, South African security forces waged a campaign of terror against the civilian population. This went largely unreported because foreign media showed scant interest in Namibia, and home-based media were either muzzled by, or in concert with, the authorities. The emergence of an independent newspaper threatened to focus attention on atrocities committed, as well as more generally on the coercive nature of the South African regime.

In the process of working towards setting up the newspaper, our mail was intercepted. I was arrested under the Official Secrets Act, jailed, and later confined to the Windhoek magisterial district, with my passport confiscated and under order to report to the police three times a week. This was in force for several months, effectively prohibiting me from travel abroad to raise funds for the newspaper. The charges were eventually dropped.

Working clandestinely we managed to draft a proposal to solicit funds, and were finally successful in our efforts. On 30 August 1985 the first edition of *The Namibian* appeared on the streets, and while it was greeted with jubilation by war-weary Namibians, its inception meant the start of another, more sustained campaign by the South African authorities in an attempt to silence what was from the outset a critical voice. The interim government cabinet decided to levy a deposit of 20,000 Rand (in those days a large sum of money), citing the terms of the Newspaper Imprint and Registration Act. The act normally required a much smaller 10 Rand deposit for new publications. *The Namibian* immediately urged the interim government to reconsider, without success, and was finally forced to pay the deposit.

In an attempt to have the decision of the interim government set aside on the grounds that it conflicted with the then bill of rights, *The Namibian* took the matter to court. The case was a historic one. In a landmark judgement, judge Harold Levy ruled that to hold a government in contempt did not necessarily constitute a danger to the security of the state or the maintenance of public order, as the government had claimed. The judge also ruled that constructive criticism was fundamental to a healthy democratic society, and that if public figures felt they had been unfairly attacked, they had access to redress in the courts. He then ordered the interim government cabinet to pay back to *The Namibian* the 20,000 Rand deposit and to pay the costs of the court application.

This did not deter the authorities. When they failed to thwart publication of *The Namibian* by means of financial impediment, a concerted campaign of more drastic measures was put into force. The five years preceding Namibian independence in 1990 were characterized by a host of dirty tricks which including two firebombings of the newspaper premises, as well as a campaign of intimidation and harassment of staff. I was detained without trial for a week for refusing to reveal the source of our report on a secret document which gave sweeping new powers to the police and was published by the newspaper. Our revelations seem to have contributed to the bill not becoming law in its original form.

One edition of the newspaper was banned after a revealing photograph, showing the bodies of several SWAPO fighters strapped to the sides of armoured military vehicles being paraded to civilians, was published on the front page. The police attempted to deny that such incidents ever occurred.

Despite firebombings (5 August 1986), tear-gas being thrown into the airconditioning units of the newspaper, and other such intimidation, publication did not cease. Staff worked in fire-blackened premises to ensure *The Namibian* appeared. Frequently, the glass façade of the building was shot at, resulting in the need for bullet-proof windows, which also became perpetually scarred by attacks from unknown sources. Charges laid with police on a number of occasions failed to bring forth the perpetrators, and it was an open secret that authorities would not pursue those responsible since they tacitly approved of the campaign.

Staff members were subject to continuous telephone death threats, arbitrary arrests, confiscation of passports, and intimidation of friends and family members. In some areas of the country, members of the armed forces would confiscate entire editions of *The Namibian*, particularly those which carried reports of atrocities against civilians, in an attempt to keep the newspaper from its audience. Advertisers were intimidated, with the result that donor funding became more necessary than ever to keep the newspaper afloat.

When Namibian independence finally arrived in 1990, the transition was not an easy one. Under apartheid *The Namibian* had been viewed as a pro-SWAPO campaigning newspaper, and supporters of the ruling party had difficulty coming to terms with the newspaper's critical watchdog role – in keeping with its independent editorial policy – when the liberation movement assumed power. Nevertheless, since independence the media environment has improved dramatically. Although politicians and the public are sometimes impatient with the principle of freedom of speech, and although democracy in Namibia remains vulnerable, there are now constitutional guarantees in place concerning press freedom and freedom of speech. The free flow of information, which is essential for development and democracy, remains an elusive goal. The ruling party, itself finding difficulties with the transition from being a liberation movement to becoming a democratic government, has yet to be convinced that transparency, accountability, and only minimum secrecy are essential components of a democracy. As a result, the general lack of tolerance towards free and independent media is less than ideal.

GWEN LISTER

Further Reading
Herbstein, Denis, "Namibia: How South Africa Controls the News", *Index on Censorship*, 14/4 (August 1985)

NAŠA BORBA
See Radnička Borba

NASHA SVABODA
See Svaboda

THOMAS NASHE
English pamphleteer and satirist, 1567–1601

On 1 June 1599, John Whitgift, archbishop of Canterbury and Richard Bancroft, bishop of London, issued the order that "all Nasshes bookes and Doctor Harvyes bookes be taken wheresoeuer they maye be found and that none of theire bookes been euer printed hereafter". This order came as part of a larger censorship decree, the "Bishops' Ban", which concentrated on several kinds of literature, as well as individual authors. First, it decreed that "no Satyrs or Epigrams be printed hereafter". Second, it provided that no English histories or plays be printed except as allowed by governmental authorities. Other authors and works also mentioned specifically in the decree are John Marston, Edward Guilpin, Joseph Hall, Thomas Middleton, and John Davies, for satirical works, and Christopher Marlowe, Thomas Cutwode, and two anonymous books for sexually explicit works.

Many critics have seen the Bishop's Ban as concerning itself mainly with suppressing satire for its political content. Lynda Boose, however, argues that the ban was also concerned with sexual explicitness and the way satire combined with pornography in these works to offer a violent expression of sexual and political aggression.

Why is Nashe included? Nashe's and Harvey's "bookes" seem to be referring to a war in print that the two had waged for several years. It began with Gabriel Harvey's brother Richard, who mentioned Nashe and Robert Greene disparagingly in his pamphlet, *The Lamb of God* (1590). Richard then came under attack in Greene's *Quip for an Upstart Courtier* (1592), to which Nashe may have contributed, and in Nashe's *Piers Penniless, His Supplication to the Divell* (1592). Gabriel Harvey entered the fray with his *Four Letters and Certain Sonnets* (1592). Nashe replied in kind with *Strange Newes on the Intercepting of Certain Letters* (1592), but then offered an apology and a chance to end the quarrel with *Christ's Teares over Jerusalem* (1593). Harvey either did not see or did not accept Nashe's apology and published *Pierce's Supererogation* (1593) as a continued attack on Nashe. Nashe counter-attacked in a second edition of *Christ's Teares* (1594) and added the finishing stroke with *Have With You to Saffron-Walden* (1596).

All these pamphlets, but especially Nashe's, are exuberant and endlessly inventive in the abuse that they heap on their enemy. The language has often been described as "scurrilous" and "railing"; a characteristic passage of Nashe's from *Strange Newes* describes Harvey as:

> this indigested Chaos of Doctourship, and greedy pothunter after applause, . . . an apparent Publican and sinner, a self-loue surfetted sot, a broken-winded galdbacke Iade, that hath borne vp his head in his time, but now is quite foundred and tired, a scholer in nothing but the scum of schollership, a stage soker at Tullies Offices, the droane of droanes, and maister drumble-bee of non proficients.

Nashe continually invents ridiculous names for his enemy, including Gabriell Howliglasse, Gilgilis Hobberdehoy, Gregory Haberdine, Gabriel Hangtelow, Gibraltar, and Galpogas. The style of these pamphlets is very different from the graceful balance of Euphuism and is probably designed to appeal to a wide audience in its virtuoso display of wit in name-calling and invective.

It still remains somewhat unclear as to why these books were named by the Bishops' Ban. The traditional answer that critics have given is that the ban was concerned about Nashe's and Harvey's connection to the "Martin Marprelate" controversy (1588–89). Nashe was commissioned to write a Martinesque response to the Marprelate pamphlets, while Harvey could be seen as supporting some of "Martin's" Protestant agenda. Nashe's anti-Harvey pamphlets certainly used the same kind of humour and linguistic excess as the documents surrounding the Marprelate pamphlets. It has been suggested that the quarrel could be seen as a continuation of the Marprelate controversy; necessarily in a personal vein because overtly political discussion had been disallowed by authorities.

Elizabethan authorities found the Marprelate pamphlets disturbing partly because of their popularity, and the Nashe–Harvey pamphlets also excited public interest. That their popularity might have brought about their censorship is supported by a critical interpretation of the pamphlets as less a forum for personal feeling than an attempt, especially by Nashe, to establish himself as a professional writer with a large reading audience. Perhaps we can connect this to the fear that the Bishops' Ban manifests that the materials banned are being too widely disseminated because they are printed. The ban can be read as specifically directed at (and was enforced by) printers rather than authors.

Another answer lies in the "scurrilous" nature of the works, especially Nashe's. The vigour of the attacks mounted against each other by Nashe and Harvey could be seen as exhibiting the same kind of aggression that Boose identifies in other works targeted by the ban. This aggression does sometimes take on political or sexual overtones.

Finally, Nashe's work as a whole sometimes fits the parameters which the Bishops' Ban used. Nashe wrote other satires; a passage about aldermen in *Christ's Teares* caused Nashe to be "piteously persecuted by the L. Maior & the aldermen" and forced to leave London. Nashe contributed to *The Isle of Dogs* (1597; lost); when the authorities found it a "sclanderous", "lewd", and "seditious" play, they raided his lodgings and seized his papers, and he was once again forced to flee. Nashe also wrote sexually explicit works, such as *The Choise of Valentines* (1590?). Perhaps the authorities seized all his work for fear of its potentially subversive nature. Certainly, Nashe's contemporaries, as well as many critics, see Nashe primarily as a satirist.

Nashe died in the year or two after the ban; he is mentioned as deceased in 1601. One work, *Summer's Last Will and Testament*, appeared in print in 1600, although it was written eight years earlier; perhaps it was published posthumously. It appears as though Nashe wrote nothing else after the Bishops' Ban, although whether this is because of the ban or because of poor health is impossible to tell.

ALZADA TIPTON

Writings

The Choise of Valentines; or, The Merie Ballad of Nashe His Dildo, written 1590?; edited by John S. Farmer, 1899
Pierce Penniless His Supplication to the Devil, 1592; edited by G.R. Hibbard, 1951
Strange News on the Intercepting of Certain Letters, 1592; as *The Apology of Pierce Penniless*, 1593
Christ's Tears over Jerusalem, 1593; revised edition 1594
Have with You to Saffron Walden; or, Gabriel Harvey's Hunt Is Up, 1596
The Isle of Dogs, with others, 1597 (lost play)
Works, revised edition, edited by F.P. Wilson, 5 vols, 1964

Further Reading

Boose, Lynda, "The 1599 Bishops' Ban, Elizabethan Pornography, and the Sexualization of the Jacobean Stage" in *Enclosure Acts: Sexuality, Property, and Culture in Early Modern England*, edited by Richard Burt and John Michael Archer, Ithaca, New York: Cornell University Press, 1994
Clegg, Cyndia Susan, *Press Censorship in Elizabethan England*, Cambridge and New York: Cambridge University Press, 1997
Crewe, Jonathan V., *Unredeemed Rhetoric: Thomas Nashe and the Scandal of Authorship*, Baltimore: Johns Hopkins University Press, 1982
Hibbard, G.R., *Thomas Nashe: A Critical Introduction*, Cambridge, Massachusetts: Harvard University Press, 1962
McCabe, Richard, "Elizabethan Satire and the Bishops' Ban of 1599", *Yearbook of English Studies*, 11 (1981): 188–93
Nicholl, Charles, *A Cup of News: The Life of Thomas Nashe*, London and Boston: Routledge, 1984
Rhodes, Neil, "Nashe, Rhetoric, and Satire" in *Jacobean Poetry and Prose: Rhetoric, Representation, and the Popular Imagination*, edited by Clive Bloom, Basingstoke: Macmillan, and New York: St Martin's Press, 1988

NAŠI DANI (Our Days)/*DANI* (Days)
News magazines in Bosnia-Herzegovina, 1950–91 and since 1992

Considered by many to be the most independent-minded of all Bosnian news magazines founded in the 1990s, *Dani*, like its predecessor *Naši Dani*, is aimed at a young and progressive readership, and contains political features, satire, gossip, interviews, and cultural reviews. According to Mark Thompson, "its tone is lucid and rather hard-bitten, avoiding the pleading and dogmatic victim-laden rhetoric which often marked the Sarajevo media".

Naši Dani was the official organ of the Youth League of Bosnia-Herzegovina during the communist period. For 30 years, it could be relied upon to reproduce the party line. It was, however, greatly influenced by revelations, in 1987, of corruption in high places in the course of the Agrokomerc affair, in which Hamdija Pozderac, a vice-president of Yugoslavia, and Fikret Abdić, a member of the Central Committeee of the Bosnian League of Communists, were found to be involved in the issue of promissory notes without the financial ability to deliver on them. *Naši Dani* not only became openly critical of Bosnian politicians in its last few years of publication, but also began to publish opinions that differed from the official line. The magazine skilfully trod a difficult path between exploiting the regime's uneasy tolerance of dissidence and provoking it into banning those media outlets that were considered to have gone too far.

After publishing an interview with Branko Horvat, a social democrat known for his dissenting opinions, the editor-in-chief of *Naši Dani* was summoned before a commission of the Central Committee, which, however, acquitted him of deliberate wrongdoing. Nevertheless, pressure was now placed upon the Youth League to ensure that its magazine behaved according to party precepts. On 3 March 1989, in an article entitled "Journalism is a Dangerous Profession", *Naši Dani* drew attention to the persecution being suffered by such journalists as Milovan Brkić, a Belgrade-based reporter who had been arrested on no less than 200 occasions. An issue featuring an article critical of a local party boss, written by a journalist from Sisak in Croatia, resulted in a ban on the distribution of that issue and three months' imprisonment for the journalist. In the spring of 1990, with Bosnia-Herzegovina's first free elections imminent, the Youth League broke away from official control so that it could campaign for political and economic change. However, with freedom came financial ruin, and *Naši Dani* was forced into liquidation early in 1991.

Dani quickly took its place. It was independent, owned by a private company headed by Senad Pečanin, its editor-in-chief, and financed by Alija Delimustafić, a former communist but now an entrepreneur, who had joined the Stranka Demokratske Akcije (Party of Democratic Action, or SDA), the party supported by most Muslims (and many non-Muslims) in Bosnia-Herzegovina and led by Alija Izetbegović. *Dani's* independence was further enhanced when Delimustafić fell out with the party leadership in the autumn of 1992, after which he retired to Austria, but continued to support the magazine. After the Dayton Accords of 1995, *Dani* became one of the most prominent magazines in the Muslim–Croat Federation.

Critics objected that Delimustafić had kept *Dani* going in a spirit of revenge against the government, and that the journal had built up its critical independence at the expense of demoralizing the public. It certainly continued its predecessor's campaign against corruption, and was ready to criticize army commanders for incompetence that resulted in the loss of soldiers' lives. It was soon subject to censorship, as when, in 1993, it published an interview with Fikret Abdić, whose allegedly corrupt commercial dealings had previously been revealed by *Naši Dani* and who was now working towards a further partition of Bosnia-Herzegovina. At the same time, however, *Dani* was the only magazine to respond positively to the government's call, in 1993, for criticism of what was considered to be a growing threat of Islamic radicalism. It has further enhanced its reputation for investigative journalism, revealing diplomacy that the authorities had hoped to keep secret, and, on 24 October 1997, it published the confessions of Ramiz Delalić

Celo, who, as commander of the North Mountain Brigade, had witnessed war crimes by the Bosnian army against Croatian civilians.

ROBERT STALLAERTS

Further Reading

Delalić Celo, Ramiz, "Idem U Haag!", *Dani* (24 October 1997)
Mras, Dadi, "Nova Sarajevska škola: *Naši Dani* nevješćuju moguće medijsko proleće u BiH" (The New Sarajevan School: *Naši Dani* Heralds the Possible Media Spring in Bosnia-Herzegovina), *Danas*, 333 (5 July 1988)
Pečanin, Senad, "On the Road: A Bosniak in Banja Luka", *WarReport: Bulletin of the Institute for War and Peace Reporting* 55 (October 1997)

Ramet, Sabina Petra, *Nationalism and Federalism in Yugoslavia, 1962–1991*, 2nd edition, Bloomington: Indiana University Press, 1992
Thompson, Mark, *Forging War: The Media in Serbia, Croatia and Bosnia-Hercegovina*, London: Article 19, 1994; revised edition, Luton: University of Luton Press, 1999

Website

http://www.bhdani.com

TASLIMA NASREEN
Bangladeshi novelist and poet, 1961–

Known in some quarters as "the female Salman Rushdie", Taslima Nasreen denies that she is any such thing: "Salman Rushdie wrote against the prophet Muhammad, whereas I have mainly highlighted the plight of women." She has, however, admitted that she regards all forms of religion as "anachronistic" – "I dream of a world without religion. Religion gives birth to fundamentalism as surely as the seed gives birth to the tree. While the seed remains we cannot root out fundamentalism."

Nasreen trained as a doctor, and has been married twice. She had written 15 novels before *Lajja* (1993, Shame) was subjected to a sustained campaign by Bangladeshi Islamists, which has still not abated. The novel depicts a Hindu family who are attacked by Muslims after Hindu extremists had burnt down the Babri Mosque in Ayodhya, India, in 1992. As it happened, Maulana Azizul Haque, a mullah and leader of the group The Council of the Soldiers of Islam, had led a protest of several hundred thousand Bangladeshis to the Indian frontier where they protested against the destruction of the mosque. He now turned his attention to Taslima Nasreen, having been given extra fuel by an interview she gave to the Indian newspaper *The Statesman*, in which she called for changes to Shariʿa (Islamic law) which, she believed, paid insufficient attention to the rights of women. This was interpreted as an attack on everything that Islam stood for, and on the Qurʾan itself. Haque responded:

> She is worse than a prostitute. She demands "freedom of the vagina". She says that if a man can have four wives, a woman should have the right to four husbands. Even within marriage she says a woman should have the right to other men. This is against the Qurʾan, and it is blasphemy.

He put a price on her head of 50,000 taka (£850) and convened regular demonstrations of about 5000 people to denounce the writer. Taslima Nasreen was forced to go into hiding in fear for her life.

Bangladesh is a secular society and therefore the Shariʿa is not legally binding. There were calls for Bangladesh to pass a blasphemy law like that of Pakistan which prescribes execution for those who disobey it. Politicians said that they had more important things on their minds. Abdul Hassan Chowdhury, shadow foreign minister for the opposition party, the Awami League, was reported as saying, "We have such tremendous problems – poverty, illiteracy, the environment, and so on – that we don't want to get bogged down with Taslima Nasreen. Only the intellectual elite of Dhaka knows about her and she's doing secularism a lot of harm." The latter was hardly the case; Chowdhury knew the power of the Islamists and was unwilling to lose his party's credibility by direct confrontation with them: "We're against all death threats, and we believe in freedom of speech, but it's very difficult for us to support her on the issues she raises. It would be politically improper and probably fatal. We won't comment until the government does."

The government was finally forced to act. Five months after it was published, *Lajja* was banned because it might "create misunderstanding and mistrust". Nasreen herself was charged with "insulting Islam", but allowed bail of 5000 takas by the Dhaka high court. She had been offered asylum by the European Parliament, but at first replied that that she had no plan to leave. Finally, however, she felt compelled to depart for the safety of exile in Sweden. While she was there, her parents' house was attacked, and her father, a medical doctor, lost patients. Having won the European Union's Sakharov Prize for freedom of expression, she returned to Bangladesh in 1998 to look after her mother who was seriously ill. Her trial (in absentia) had been postponed on numerous occasions, but she found that it was still not safe to show her face in public, and had, before long, to return to Sweden.

Condemning the renewed demonstrations against her and the book, Abdul Mamad Azad, the foreign minister, said: "The religious sentiment of the people should be respected, but we cannot allow any excesses in the name of religion." Nevertheless, in 1999 the government banned an issue of the Bengali-language magazine *Desh* because its publication of a poem by Nasreen, "Amar Mayer Glapo" (My Mother's Story) was considered "a potential affront to the religious feelings of Muslims which could cause unrest". In August 1999, they banned the importation, distribution, and sale of Nasreen's *My Childhood* because it might have "adverse effects", and cause "hurt". A further novel concerns a Muslim woman whose family forbids her to study.

Some Bangladeshi intellectuals believe that Taslima Nasreen has suffered because of her confrontational tactics. Serajut Islam Chowdbury, professor of English at Dhaka University, said in 1993: "After all, more than 70 years ago, Robeya Begum was writing about women's emancipation without being attacked, and it wasn't so different. But she wrote in a more serious vein." Nasreen retorts that "What I have done is protested against the system which is against women. I have seen that, in the name of tradition, society wants to keep women in ignorance and slavery."

Elsewhere, she has written:

I do not mind being persecuted and hunted by the mullahs and their frenzied followers. I am happy that I have penetrated a bastion of patriarchy guarded by fanatical religious orthodoxies. As a free human being, I have

entered this courtyard not with a sword in my hand, but with a simple instrument, called "the pen".

DEREK JONES

Writings
Light Up at Midnight: Poems, translated by Carolyne Wright *et al.*, 1992
Lajja, 1993; as *Shame*, translated by Tutul Gupta, 1994; translated by Kankabati Datta, 1997
The Game in Reverse: Poems, translated by Carolyne Wright *et al.*, 1995
"Tongues of Fire", *New Statesman and Society* (17 February 1995)
100 Poems, translated by Kabir Chowdhury, 1997

Further Reading
Granty, Linda, "Public Lives", *The Guardian* (14 December 1994)
"La Mystification", *Figaro* (13 December 1994)
Rettie, John, "Bangladesh's Threatened Writer Wins Police Guard but No Champions", *The Guardian* (10 December 1993)
Whyatt, Sara, "Taslima Nasreen", *Index on Censorship*, 23/4–5 (September–October 1994)

NATIONAL CAMPAIGN FOR FREEDOM OF EXPRESSION
US organization opposed to censorship, 1989–2000

The National Campaign for Freedom of Expression (NCFE) was an educational and advocacy network of artists, arts organizations, audience members, and concerned citizens that was formed to protect freedom of artistic expression throughout the US. The organization's work reflected an understanding that true democracy is dependent on the right to free artistic expression for all. NCFE was the only national organization exclusively dedicated to promoting First Amendment rights as applied to the support, presentation, and creation of the arts in American culture.

NCFE started in 1989 as a regular group telephone call by a collection of artists and arts activists who recognized the growing political antagonization to freedom of artistic expression, and the hesitation with which members of the mainstream and established arts communities defended the arts against these challenges. The founders, representing alternative arts spaces, small arts organizations, and media artists, understood the need for the arts community to organize and actively promote the principles of artistic freedom, especially in light of the attacks waged across the American cultural landscape by ultraconservative organizations and politicians. NCFE was incorporated as a nonprofit organization in 1990. It played a critical role in promoting freedom of expression, both artistic and other, in the face of challenges from all shades along the socio-political spectrum.

NCFE's first major effort was to initiate litigation against the National Endowment for the Arts (NEA), the US government agency that awards arts grants, on behalf of four performance artists: Karen Finley, John Fleck, Holly Hughes, and Tim Miller. Each artist was recommended for fellowships by an NEA peer panel. However, the recommendations were overturned by then-NEA chair John Frohnmayer for what were seen by many as political reasons. The American Civil Liberties

Union (ACLU) and the Center for Constitutional Rights joined with NCFE attorneys in filing the lawsuit in September 1990. The lawsuit was later amended to challenge the constitutionality of the clause added to the NEA's enabling legislation in 1990 that required the NEA to consider "general standards of decency and respect for the diverse beliefs and values of the American public" in awarding grants. The artists ultimately settled the part of the case dealing with their individual grants and were awarded the amount of their fellowships plus additional damages. In the summer of 1998 the US Supreme Court upheld the decency and respect provision, emphasizing that it was advisory only; the NEA could not use it "to leverage a penalty".

NCFE developed and implemented a variety of programmes to assist artists who faced challenges to their freedom of expression. Its scope expanded beyond the issue of governmental funding for the arts to all forms of censorship and challenges to the rights of artists and audience members to create and experience art. The heart of NCFE's mission was its one-on-one work with artists seeking to promote, or facing challenges to, their artistic freedom. It aided over 200 artists and arts organizations and became recognized as an invaluable resource for assistance and information. Among the services NCFE provided were strategic advice, grass-roots organizing, national coalition-building, media advocacy, legal referrals, and mediation. The organization also supplied artists with educational and other resource materials. It assisted artists in all disciplines – visual, performance, media, and literary arts.

NCFE played a prominent role in a variety of censorship incidents. In 1993, it organized protests against the decision of Cobb County, Georgia, to restrict arts funding to those organizations that endorsed "traditional family values". In 1994, the organization assisted two artists whose photographs were removed from a competition in Pennsylvania because the works contained, or implied, nudity. As one of the photographs had been judged "Best of Show", the judges were dismissed and the exhibit rejudged by the organizers. The artists ultimately prevailed in their legal action against the organizers. In 1995, NCFE came to the assistance of a Tennessee artist whose painting of a partially nude woman was removed from public display following a complaint that its display violated a local sexual harassment law. The artist successfully sued the censors. In 1996, NCFE organized a national coalition to protest against the removal from an Illinois school curriculum of a book detailing a former gang member's experiences because it was considered too violent for young adults. In the following year, NCFE helped organize grass-roots and national response efforts in opposition to a judge's ruling in Oklahoma that the award-winning film, *The Tin Drum*, was obscene, and the rejection in California of a public mural image because of its alleged negative views on law enforcement.

NCFE was a founding member of the Free Expression Network, a coalition of more than 40 national organizations representing artists, record companies, the film industry, booksellers, civil liberties groups, libraries, museums and theatres, publishers, and the Internet community, all concerned with defending the First Amendment.

In addition, NCFE produced a number of publications and educational tools. Its chief publication was the *National Campaign for Freedom of Expression Quarterly*, a 12-page periodical that reported on issues and incidents of art censorship nationwide, and provided detailed examination of pertinent legal and cultural issues. The *Quarterly* was regarded as an invaluable source of news and information for free speech and arts advocates. In 1998, NCFE released the *Artistic Freedom Handbook*, a guide to understanding, preparing for, and responding to challenges to freedom of artistic expression.

After the conclusion of the NEA lawsuit, however, many of the progressive foundations that had supported NCFE turned their attention to other projects. NCFE was unable to sustain an adequate level of philanthropic support to continue its operations and closed at the end of 2000. Its programmes were transferred to the National Coalition against Censorship's Arts Advocacy Project and the First Amendment Project and its archives to the National Association of Artists' Organizations.

DAVID GREENE

Publications by NCFE

National Campaign for Freedom of Expression Bulletin (journal; Spring 1991–Winter 1996)
Arts Voter Mobilization Guide, Washington, DC, 1994
How Democracy Works: A Guide to Civil Rights, Civil Liberties, and the Issues of the Day, Washington, DC: Blue Mountain Working Group, 1996 (with Lambda Legal Defense and Education Fund, Women's Project, Washington Education Association, North Carolina Mobilization)
National Campaign for Freedom of Expression Quarterly (journal; Spring 1996–)
Artistic Freedom Handbook: A Guide to Understanding, Preparing for, and Responding to Challenges to Freedom of Artistic Expression, Washington, DC, 1998

Videos

State of the Art: Art of the State, 1990 (produced by Branda Miller for NCFE and Deep Dish TV)
Vote Anyway (parts 1–3), 1996
What Are Your First Amendment Rights?, 1996
When Democracy Works, 1996 (with National Gay & Lesbian Task Force, Public Research Associates, Interfaith Alliance)

Further Reading

Dubin, Steven C., *Arresting Images: Impolitic Art and Uncivil Actions*, London and New York: Routledge, 1992
Heins, Marjorie, *Sex, Sin, and Blasphemy: A Guide to America's Censorship Wars*, New York: New Press, 1993
Hunter, James Davison, *Culture Wars: The Struggle to Define America*, New York: Basic Books, 1991
Marsh, Dave et al., *50 Ways to Fight Censorship, and Important Facts to Know about the Censors*, New York: Thunder's Mouth Press, 1991
Mendoza, David C., "The Future of the Cultural Landscape" in *The Cultural Battlefield: Art Censorship and Public Funding*, edited by Jennifer A. Peter and Louis M. Crosier, Gilsum, New Hampshire: Avocus, 1995
Pally, Marcia, *Sense and Censorship: The Vanity of the Bonfires*, New York: Americans for Constitutional Freedom, and Chicago: Freedom to Read Foundation, 1991

NATIONAL ORGANIZATION FOR DECENT LITERATURE
US moral crusaders, 1938–70

From the late 1930s through the 1960s, the National Organization for Decent Literature (NODL) was to printed materials what the better-known Legion of Decency was to films in the US. NODL was a Catholic pressure group, which attempted to restrict public access to objectionable magazines and, later, comic books and paperbound books. Like the Legion of Decency, NODL was officially sponsored and supervised by the US Catholic bishops. Bishop John F. Noll of Fort Wayne, Indiana, who was a founder of both of these organizations, was the driving force behind NODL until his death in the early 1950s.

According to the 1939 NODL code, which originally applied only to magazines, materials that glorified crime or had content, illustrations, or advertising that were sexually explicit or suggestive were objectionable. In order to keep these materials out of the hands of children, NODL believed that they also had to be made unavailable to adults. The 1956 NODL code, which applied to comic books and paperbound books (hardbacks were thought inaccessible to young people and therefore not considered) in addition to magazines, declared objectionable those publications that:

(1) Glorify crime or the criminal. (2) Describe in detail ways to commit criminal acts. (3) Hold lawful authority in disrespect. (4) Exploit horror, cruelty or violence. (5) Portray sex facts offensively. (6) Feature indecent, lewd

or suggestive photographs or illustrations. (7) Carry advertising which is offensive in content or advertise products which may lead to physical or moral harm. (8) Use blasphemous, profane or obscene speech indiscriminately and repeatedly. (9) Hold up to ridicule any national, religious or racial group. (*NODL Newsletter,* all issues, 1957–69)

To avoid legal complications, NODL did not label particular publications obscene, which only the courts could do, but simply declared them in violation of the NODL code. The goal was to persuade public opinion to do what the courts and law enforcement would not: to eliminate publications that were offensive to traditional moral values. On the basis of its code, NODL published monthly lists of materials currently disapproved of by the organization. They were also printed separately and distributed to interested groups and individuals. The response of magazine publishers was various. Some, in the 1930s and 1940s, would meet Bishop Noll, hoping to persuade him to have their titles taken off the NODL list. A few voluntarily sent dummies or page proofs for approval before publication. Others threatened lawsuits, but none of them sued.

By the early 1940s, most of the nearly 100 Catholic dioceses of the US had local NODL organizations, which were almost always directed by priests. Local NODL members, a few of whom were non-Catholics, performed two main functions: serving as reviewers and as members of vigilance committees. The reviewers, who were mostly women, read materials and recommended titles for blacklisting. Starting in the 1950s, NODL also recommended good books for young readers. The members of the vigilance committees canvassed local stores selling magazines, comic books, and paperbacks and monitored them for compliance with the NODL code and list. This second function of NODL volunteers, which varied in effectiveness from place to place and over time, but which was probably most zealously carried out in the early years, was sometimes the source of serious friction, particularly when NODL volunteers used coercive tactics such as the threat of boycott and, in at least a few known cases, when public officials enforced the policies of this private organization.

In the 1950s, when NODL started blacklisting paperbound editions of books by prominent authors (as well as less reput-

able ones), it incurred the opposition of the American Civil Liberties Union, *Harper's Magazine,* and other organizations. Among the authors appearing on the NODL list of books disapproved for youth in the 1950s and 1960s were James Baldwin, John Cheever, John Dos Passos, James T. Farrell, C. S. Forester, William Faulkner, Thomas Heggen, Joseph Heller, Ernest Hemingway, Evan Hunter, James Jones, Jack Kerouac, Jerzy Kosinski, Norman Mailer, Grace Metalious, James Michener, Vladimir Nabokov, John O'Hara, J.D. Salinger, John Steinbeck, John Updike, Leon Uris, Robert Penn Warren, Nathanael West, Tennessee Williams, Kathleen Winsor, and Richard Wright.

By the 1960s, changes both in US society and the Catholic church made NODL's work more difficult. Censorship decisions of the US Supreme Court and other federal courts had been proceeding steadily in a more liberal direction since the 1930s. The Catholic church, which was also changing after the decisions of the Second Vatican Council (1962–65), stopped publishing the *Index Librorum Prohibitorum* (the Index of Forbidden Books) in 1966. Although NODL was more moderate under the leadership of monsignors Thomas J. Fitzgerald and Joseph J. Howard, who successively directed the national office in Chicago from in 1955, its public image, even among some Catholics, was negative as a coercive censorship group. At the same time, even NODL's supporters had to admit that the organization, which was never well funded, was losing its effectiveness against the multi billion-dollar pornography industry.

In late 1969, bishop Joseph L. Bernardin, the general secretary of the US Catholic Conference (USCC), the secretariat of the Catholic bishops in Washington, DC, announced the closing of NODL. He left open the possibility of NODL's work being transferred to some other unit of the USCC, as the Legion of Decency's work later was, but that never happened in NODL's case, and it became defunct on 1 January 1970.

THOMAS F. O'CONNOR

Further Reading
Gardiner, Harold C., *Catholic Viewpoint on Censorship,* New York: Hanover House, 1958
O'Connor, Thomas F., "The National Organization for Decent Literature: A Phase in American Catholic Censorship", *Library Quarterly,* 65/4 (1995): 386–414

NATIVE SON
Novel, 1940, by Richard Wright (US, 1908–1960); film, 1951, directed by Pierre Chenal (Belgian, 1904–1990)

Described by James Baldwin as "everybody's protest novel", *Native Son* tells the story of three individuals: a young, poor black man, Bigger Thomas, who murders a rich white girl, Mary Dalton; Mary herself, who believes in economic and racial equality; and a poor black girl, Bessie Mears, who concludes that little can be done to reverse the injustice in the world.

Richard Wright had moved from his birthplace near Natchez, Mississippi, first to Memphis, Tennessee, and then in 1934 to Chicago. A sense of isolation – his own and other people's –

in the black ghettos of the city led him to join the Communist Party around 1933. *Native Son* is a classic statement of the individual's sense of alienation, caused, according to Max, Bigger's attorney, by the social environment.

Such explanations were less important for the Book-of-the-Month Club than the description of Bigger's sexual responses to Mary. The club required Wright to attenuate these scenes before they would adopt *Native Son* as one of their alternate selections. More than 50 years later, Arnold Rampersad, editor of the Library of America's two-volume collection of Wright's fiction, noted the following in an article that appeared in the *New York Times Book Review*:

> Bigger's vibrant sexuality had historic significance. Never before in literature, except in scurrilous attacks on black men as rapists or likely rapists, had black male sexuality been represented with such frankness.

Wright understood that, with few exceptions, there could be no serious discussion of race in the United States without reference to sexuality ... To nullify Bigger's sexual drive was to dilute or even to sabotage the central power of *Native Son* as a commentary on race in this country.

As might be expected, the Library of America edition restored the cuts.

Censorship of Pierre Chenal's cinematic version of *Native Son* was even more drastic 2500 feet of film were cut to meet the requirements of the Production Code Administration (PCA), which declared "Miscegenation is forbidden". This aspect of the code explains why certain sections of the trial scene were excised, since much of Buckley's cross-examination of witnesses insinuates that miscegenation between Mary and Bigger did indeed take place.

The code also specified that "The treatment of bedrooms must be governed by good taste and delicacy". The scene in which Bigger and an inebriated Mary are kissing each other, as she lies sprawled on the bed, was subjected to the censor's scissors, although the PCA did permit Bigger's subsequent act of smothering Mary to remain intact.

Finally, in a section on "Crimes against the Law", the code laid down that "the presentation must not show sympathy with the crime as against the law, nor with the criminal as against those who punish him". It is reasonable to infer that other major parts of the trial scene, which takes up nearly one-third of the book but is reduced to a few minutes in the film, were deleted because Wright's screenplay has Max argue, at length, that society is as culpable as Bigger for the horrific crimes committed.

Factors unconnected with the film itself were also clearly at work. Wright had been a member of the Communist Party until 1942, and the pursuit of the House Un-American Activities Committee (HUAC) of actual and supposed communists was at its height when the cinematic adaptation of *Native Son* appeared. The PCA, in all likelihood, was heavily influenced by HUAC's hearings.

Quite butchered, the film was released in 1951. The cuts were insufficient for the Ohio Censorship Board, which banned the film in 1953 because it considered that showing it would lead to "immorality and crime". The distributor, Classic Films, appealed to the US Supreme Court, which, despite the spirit of the times, confirmed the ruling it had made in 1952 on Roberto Rossellini's film *The Miracle* that films are protected by the First Amendment.

Other cinematic treatments of *Native Son* have been suggested and/or accomplished. Rossellini, in fact, wanted to make the film, and the Hollywood producer Joseph Fields was keen to adapt it, but only, Michel Fabre reports, if Bigger Thomas could be "recast as a member of a white ethnic minority".

Despite what may be seen as the universality of the film's message, Wright refused such "censorship". Richard Wesley's adaptation was completed in 1986; it too emasculated the trial scene and did not treat Mary's decapitation, the racist dialogue among the newspapermen after they discover that Bigger has killed Mary, or the rape of Bessie. Despite the considerably changed society of the 1980s, questions remained as to whether the omissions were due to the director's sense of the film's grammar, or to self-censorship.

RUTH ELIZABETH BURKS

Writings by Richard Wright

Uncle Tom's Children: Four Novellas, 1938; augmented edition 1940
Native Son, 1940
Twelve Million Black Voices: A Folk History of the Negro in the United States, 1941
Black Boy: A Record of Childhood and Youth, 1945
The Outsider, 1953
Savage Holiday, 1954
The Color Curtain: A Report on the Bandung Conference, 1956 (French translation 1955)
Pagan Spain, 1957
White Man, Listen!, 1957
The Long Dream, 1958
Lawd Today!, 1963
American Hunger (autobiography), 1977
The Wright Reader, edited by Ellen Wright and Michel Fabre, 1978
Works, edited by Arnold Rampersad, 2 vols, 1991 (Library of America)

Films

Native Son, directed by Pierre Chenal, screen adaptation by Wright and Chenal; with Wright as Bigger, 1951
Native Son, directed by Jerrold Freedman, screen adaptation by Richard Wesley, 1986

Further Reading

Bloom, Harold (editor), *Richard Wright*, New York: Chelsea House Publishers, 1987
Bloom, Harold (editor), *Richard Wright's Native Son*, New York: Chelsea House, 1988
Bloom, Harold (editor), *Bigger Thomas*, New York: Chelsea House, 1990
Brunette, Peter, "Two Wrights, One Wrong" in *The Modern American Novel and the Movies*, edited by Gerald Peary and Roger Shatzkin, New York: Ungar, 1978
Burks, Ruth Elizabeth, "The Effects of Censorship and Criticism on the Film Adaptations of Richard Wright's Native Son" (dissertation), Los Angeles: University of California, 1993
Fabre, Michel, *The Unfinished Quest of Richard Wright*, 2nd edition, Urbana: University of Illinois Press, 1993
Gates, Henry Louis Jr and K.A. Appiah (editors), *Richard Wright: Critical Perspectives Past and Present*, New York: Amistad, 1993
Kinnamon, Keneth (editor), *New Essays on Native Son*, Cambridge and New York: Cambridge University Press, 1990
Rampersad, Arnold, "Too Honest for His Own Time", *New York Times Book Review* (29 December 1991): 3, 17–18
Ray, David and Robert M. Farnsworth (editors), *Richard Wright: Impressions and Perspectives*, Ann Arbor: University of Michigan Press, 1973
Sklar, Robert, *Movie-Made America: A Social History of American Movies*, New York: Random House, 1975
Walker, Margaret. *Richard Wright, Daemonic Genius: A Portrait of the Man, a Critical Look at His Work*, New York: Warner, 1988

NAVINY
See Svaboda

NEGRO WORLD
US newspaper, 1918–33

Founded in New York in 1918 as the newspaper of Marcus Garvey's Universal Negro Improvement Association (UNIA), *Negro World* built a circulation of over 50,000 readers by 1920, gaining praise even from Garvey critic Claude McKay, who called it "the best edited colored weekly in New York". The paper sold for five cents in New York, seven cents in other parts of the United States, and ten cents abroad. Edited by William H. Ferris, its 10 to 16 pages carried a variety of stories in English, French, and Spanish, most of them devoted to developing Garvey's philosophy of black nationalism and unity. With the slogan "One Aim, One God, One Destiny – A Newspaper Devoted Solely to the Interests of the Negro Race", it regularly included historical stories on the exploits of African warriors and civilizations, front-page editorials by Garvey addressed to "Fellowmen of the Negro race", a column written by John Bruce, and a section titled "Poetry for the People". Alone among the major African-American publications of this period, *Negro World* did not publish advertisements for skin whiteners or hair straighteners, products it denounced as degrading to the dignity of the race.

The strongly anti-colonial tenor of the newspaper led a number of governments around the world to ban its publication or distribution, including those in Barbados, Trinidad, and British Guiana (now Guyana), and in African colonies under Italian, French, and Portuguese rule. In the United States, the Department of Justice identified *Negro World* in 1919 along with other radical African-American newspapers in attorney general A. Mitchell Palmer's report, "Radicalism and Sedition among the Negroes as Reflected in Their Publications". The next year, the state of New York's Lusk Committee, which had been created to study seditious activities, named *Negro World* in its 44-page section on the black press. The UNIA survived these attacks, however, and continued to publish *Negro World* until it finally suspended operations in 1933.

In addition to these formal denunciations, a number of other government agencies attacked both Garvey and *Negro World*. In 1919, New York district attorney Edwin P. Kilroe forced Garvey to publish a retraction of his charge that Kilroe had made a concerted effort "to hound and persecute" the UNIA. Then in August 1921, William J. Burns, director of the Federal Bureau of Investigation (FBI), helped delay the maiden voyage of a UNIA Black Star Line steamship by claiming that the UNIA had affiliations with the Communist Party, informing the New York Shipping Board that Garvey "advocates and teaches the overthrow of the United States Government by force and violence". In 1922, authorities from the United States Post Office charged Garvey with using "fraudulent representations" and "deceptive artifices" to advertise stock for the UNIA's steamship company, leading to Garvey's arrest, conviction, and eventual imprisonment for mail fraud. The next year, following the assassination of one of Garvey's critics, the New Orleans Department of Justice raided the UNIA's state headquarters and arrested ten workers. They claimed to have found "evidence of a nation-wide anarchistic plot", although they never produced this evidence and all of those arrested in the incident were eventually acquitted.

The popular success of *Negro World* coincided with a generational shift in African-American leadership following Booker T. Washington's death in 1915. Rejecting Washington's accommodationist policies and the slower, court-centred strategy of W.E.B. DuBois and the National Association for the Advancement of Colored People (NAACP), "New Negro" leaders like William Bridges, Cyril V. Briggs, William H. Ferris, Hubert H. Harrison, Chandler Owen, and A. Philip Randolph concentrated on building a radical African-American press. Many of these leaders also organized local groups devoted to political activism and spreading black nationalist views through street-corner oratory. Although internally divided and lacking a cohesive platform for change – many of these leaders openly criticized Garvey and his philosophy – this small group of radical leaders had a wide influence among African-Americans across the country, in part because they targeted urban African-American masses rather than the black middle-class constituency of older organizations.

Garvey's *Negro World* was not alone among the radical black publishers in facing censorship. In addition to *Negro World*, Palmer's "Radicalism and Sedition Among the Negroes" cited the *Veteran*, the *Crusader*, the *Challenge*, the *Messenger*, the *New Negro*, and the *Crisis* among New York publications, and the *Broad Ax*, the *Favorite Magazine*, and the *Half-Century Magazine* from Chicago publishers. Georgia, Mississippi, and South Carolina all made it a crime to read the Chicago *Defender*, which encouraged black migration to the North in its editorials, and the mayor of Pine Bluff, Arkansas blocked the newspaper's distribution by injunction. As with *Negro World*, these newspapers survived regional censorship and continued publication.

Censorship of this segment of the African-American press took place in the context of World War I, heavy black migration to the North, and numerous race riots. Reflecting the widespread racism of the period were D.W. Griffith's popular film *The Birth of a Nation* (1915), which glorified the Ku Klux Klan, and the revitalization of that organization by William J. Simmons that same year. Southern hostility to black troops led to small-scale riots in Houston and Spartanburg, South Carolina, in late 1917, resulting in the quick trial and execution of 13 African-American soldiers and the lifetime imprisonment of 41 others. African-American migrants to northern industrial cities, driven by racism and the boll weevil (a beetle that destroyed cotton crops), and drawn by wartime demand for labour and the hope of a better life, created anxiety among whites and heightened tension between the two races.

Palmer's condemnation of *Negro World* can be attributed in large part to the newspaper's vigorous editorial responses to over 20 bloody race riots that broke out around the country that year – dubbed "the Red Summer of 1919" by the African-American poet James Weldon Johnson. In Palmer's view, "the more radical Negro publications have been quick to avail themselves of the situation as cause for the utterance of inflammatory sentiment – utterances which in some cases have reached the limit of open defiance and a counsel of retaliation", leading him to conclude that leaders like Garvey "constitute themselves a determined and persistent source of radical opposition to the Government, and to the established rule of law and order". Ironically, in carefully documenting Garvey's call "to prepare to match fire with hell fire" and "administer to our oppressors their Waterloo", Palmer's published report, along with the Lusk Committee's documentary account, now constitute two of the most valuable sources preserving the very texts they sought to suppress.

CHRISTOPHER W. WELLS

Further Reading

Cronon, Edmund David, *Black Moses: The Story of Marcus Garvey and the Universal Negro Improvement Association*, Madison: University of Wisconsin Press, 1955; 2nd edition 1969

Fax, Elton C., *Garvey: The Story of a Pioneer Black Nationalist*, New York: Dodd Mead, 1972

Garvey, Marcus, *Philosophy and Opinions of Marcus Garvey*, edited by Amy Jacques Garvey, 2 vols, 1923–26

Locke, Alain (editor), *The New Negro: An Interpretation*, New York: Boni, 1925; 2nd edition New York: Atheneum, 1969

Palmer, A. Mitchell, "Radicalism and Sedition among the Negroes as Reflected in Their Publications", Exhibit 10 of *Investigation Activities of the Department of Justice*, vol. 12 of Senate Documents, no. 153, 66th Congress, 1st Session, 1919: 161–87

Revolutionary Radicalism: A Report of the Joint Legislative Committee of New York Investigating Seditious Activities, 4 vols, Albany: Lyon, 1920

Vincent, Theodore G., *Black Power and the Garvey Movement*, Berkeley, California: Ramparts Press, 1972

JAN NĚMEC
Czech film director, 1936–

O SLAVNOSTI A HOSTECH (The Party and the Guests)
Film, 1966

Jan Němec, who believes that the film director should create his own world, started his career as a feature film director with *Demanty noci* (1964, Diamonds of the Night), adapted from a novel by Arnost Lustig, which won the Grand Prix at the Mannheim Festival. Němec developed the original novel's flashback structure to create a film that mirrors the mental world of two youths being sent by train to a Nazi death camp during World War II. Dependent almost entirely on images and using only natural sound effects, the film has only one line of dialogue.

Němec followed *Diamonds of the Night* with two films in the same year, *The Party and the Guests* and *Mučedníci lásky* (Martyrs of Love), both of which were cowritten by Němec and Ester Krumbachová. While the second courted controversy by drawing on the traditions of Czech poetism and surrealism, the first was rightly perceived as one of the foremost political films of the 1960s. A group of middle-class people sets off through the woods to attend an open-air banquet in honour of the birthday of a political leader. Eventually, they are escorted to the celebration by members of the secret police, who also interrogate them. The film examines the process by which they learn to adjust and accommodate themselves to oppression. At the centre of the system is the leader himself, whose sadism is masked by an outward show of affability. Beneath him is his psychotic "adopted son", Rudolf, head of the secret police, whose purpose is to ensure order, to make sure that everyone sits in the right place, and to hunt down the guest who leaves without permission. At the end of the film, the screen turns black and we hear the barking of dogs and the fake gaiety of fairground music.

Unlike Němec's other two early films, *The Party and the Guests* relies heavily on dialogue, but it is dialogue that is superficially meaningless. As Ester Krumbachová has said:

> I tried to create a conversation in which the characters said nothing meaningful about themselves, as if they had walked suddenly into the midst of a sophisticated party ... I tried not to mimic real speech but to suggest its pattern.

While Krumbachová refers to Eugène Ionesco as an influence, it is worth noting that, in addition to Ionesco, the period 1963–65 had seen the production of plays by Samuel Beckett, Edward Albee, and Friedrich Dürrenmatt in theatres in Czechoslovakia, as well as work by Václav Havel and Josef Topol. Like Havel's *The Memorandum* and *The Garden Party*, *The Party and the Guests* can be seen as a contribution to what might be termed "the politicized absurd". Thus, the baffling dialogue is in fact about a great deal, and the scenes in which Rudolf interviews the "guests" are concerned with the interplay of power and weakness, the quest for different kinds of collaboration and accommodation. The film also gains a visual dimension from its use of images from the public domain of political ceremony and newsreel. In this as in other ways, it can also be linked to the surrealist vision and social satire of Luis Buñuel, an acknowledged influence on Němec.

The Party and the Guests is not just a coded reflection of Czechoslovakia under communism, for its observations have a much wider resonance, but it was inevitably interpreted as such. Filmed with the involvement of many friends, *The Party and*

NĚMEC: Still from the 1966 film *O slavnosti a hostech* (The Party and the Guests), showing party henchmen preparing the table for the banquet to celebrate a political leader's birthday, to which the middle-class guests are being escorted. The film, co-written by Němec and his wife, Ester Krumbachová, was widely interpreted as a sinister commentary on Czechoslovakia under communism: it was initially banned for two years by president Novotný and again after the Warsaw Pact invasion in August 1968. It was banned "for ever" in Czechoslovakia in 1973.

the Guests was seen almost as a collective statement by the intelligentsia and, according to Němec, a virtual rogue's gallery of "counter-revolution". Among many others, the cast includes the novelists Josef Škvorecký and Zdena Salivarová (Škvorecký's wife), the composer Jan Klusák, the psychologist Jiří Němec, and not least, the film director Evald Schorm, who plays the guest who says nothing, refuses to engage in meaningless dialogue, and simply decides to leave.

Together with Věra Chytilová's *Sedmikrásky* (1966, Daisies), *The Party and the Guests* was one of the films that formed the basis of an attack by a parliamentary deputy, Pružinec, in 1967: "How much longer do they intend to poison the lives of the honest toilers, how much longer do they mean to trample underfoot the achievements of socialism . . . ?" Initially banned on the instructions of president Novotný, *The Party and the Guests* was due to be shown at the 1968 Cannes Festival, but the event was abandoned when Jean-Luc Godard and others prompted its closure in support of the May events in Paris. The film was, of course, banned again following the Warsaw Pact invasion and, in 1973, it joined *The Firemen's Ball*, *All My Good Countrymen*, and *End of a Priest* as one of four films to be banned "for ever".

Němec subsequently worked for television, although *Oratorium pro Prahu* (Oratorio for Prague) and *Strahovská demonstrace* (The Strahov Demonstration), both made in 1968, were banned from screens inside Czechoslovakia until 1990.

Nevertheless, *Oratorio for Prague* provided the rest of the world with many of its principal images of the Warsaw Pact invasion. Němec left Czechoslovakia in 1974 but was unable to sustain his career on a regular basis. He returned in 1989 to work on a project he had first prepared in the 1960s, *V žáru královské lásky* (1990, In the Heat of the King's Love/The Flames of Royal Love), based on Ladislav Klíma's novel *Utrpení knížete Sternenhocha* (The Sufferings of Prince Sternenhoch), following this with the poetic parable *Jméno kódu: Rubin* (1996, Code Name: Ruby). His semi-autobiographical and dreamlike *Noční hovory s matkou* (2001, Night Talks with Mother) combines the personal and the political and includes footage from *Oratorio for Prague*.

PETER HAMES

Further Reading

Hames, Peter, *The Czechoslovak New Wave*, 2nd edition Trowbridge, Wiltshire: Flicks, 2001

Liehm, Antonín J., *Closely Watched Films: The Czechoslovak Experience*, New York: International Arts and Sciences Press, 1974

Škvorecký, Josef, *All the Bright Young Men and Women: A Personal History of the Czech Cinema*, Toronto: Martin Associates, 1971

Škvorecký, Josef, *Všichni ti bystří mladi muži a ženy: osobní historie českého filmu*, Prague: Horizont, 1993

Žalman, Jan, *Umlčený film: Kapitoly z bojů o lidskou tvář československého filmu*, Prague: Národni filmový archiv, 1993

NEPAL

Population: 23,043,000	**Illiteracy rate (%):** 40.8 (m); 76.1 (f)
Main religions: Hindhu; Buddhist; Muslim	**Number of daily newspapers:** 29
Official language: Nepali	**Number of radio receivers per 1000 inhabitants:** 38
Other languages spoken: Maithir; Bhojpuri	**Number of TV receivers per 1000 inhabitants:** 5.8

Nepal has existed as a unified nation state since 1769, but a modern intellectual class did not emerge within Nepali society until the 20th century, and so the question of "censorship" as it is understood today did not really arise until then. Nepal was never a British colony, but a group of inter-related families usurped the shah king's authority in the mid-19th century, secured British approval, and assumed the quasi-royal title Rana. The Rana regime lasted until 1951, arrogating all facilities and privileges to itself while taking measures to exclude foreigners and reformist ideas. When the regime fell in 1951 the national literacy rate was probably around two per cent.

Rana censorship was not guided by constitutional rules, because there was no constitution, only a Legal Code (*Muluki Ain*) that was silent on such matters. Some rulers were more enlightened than others, but all were dependent on the support of the Brahman priestly class, and concerned to uphold orthodox Hinduism in the world's last Hindu kingdom. Thus, the ideas of reformist Hindu sects such as the Arya Samaj were anathema: one Madhav Raj Joshi made many efforts to promote Arya Samajist ideas, but in 1905 he was paraded through the streets of Kathmandu in disgrace and sentenced to two years' imprisonment.

A small educated elite began to emerge between the world wars, with a political outlook influenced by the Indian nationalist movement. In 1920 Krishnalal Adhikari was jailed for nine years for his role in the production of a booklet entitled *The Cultivation of Maize*, and died before his prison term had been completed. No copies of the booklet are extant, and it is difficult to ascertain what it was that offended the government of the day: Nepali sources state that it contained allegorical statements that were interpreted as criticisms of the Ranas. Several other persons are said to have been arrested, fined, or dismissed from government service in connection with this controversy. Because of the Ranas' censorious tendencies, Nepali writers usually published their work in India, and many lived in exile. In 1930, the poet Lakshmi Prasad Devkota and several others raised a petition calling for the establishment of a public library, an "offence" for which they were fined and given suspended jail sentences.

In 1941 three members of Nepal's first political party, the Praja Parishad, were executed publicly for the crime of distributing leaflets critical of the Rana government; a fourth man was hanged for spreading a reformist message in his religious lectures. The four men are commemorated at "Martyrs' Gate", a monument in central Kathmandu.

The basis for a tradition of journalism was laid during the Rana regime when Nepal's national newspaper, *Gorkhapatra*, was established in 1901. Twelve years later the Ranas established the Gorkha Language Publications Council, which had the dual roles of encouraging the production of literature in the national language, Nepali, and also censoring the content of all books.

The regime could not outlast the end of British rule in India, and the 1950s saw the first attempts to establish democratic institutions and processes in Nepal, with a Nepali Congress government elected in 1959. The palace retained emergency powers under the 1959 constitution, however, and in December 1960 king Mahendra dissolved the government and reestablished direct monarchical rule. In 1962 a new constitution was promulgated, inaugurating an era of "partyless" Panchayat democracy that was to last until 1990.

Freedom of public expression was severely curtailed during the Panchayat period, though the authorities made a tacit distinction between public speech and activity and the private expression of opinion. A national news agency (the RSS) was established in 1962, controlled by the press secretariat of the royal palace; Nepal's newspapers were unable to use other agencies, and the state-owned organs *Gorkhapatra* and *The Rising Nepal* fed their readers the official line. Similarly, the state-controlled Radio Nepal monopolized the airwaves, and in all media the only languages used were Nepali and English, despite the existence of large communities speaking other languages, notably Maithili, Hindi, and Newari. All new privately owned papers were required to register with the government, and registration was withdrawn if they reported the activities of the banned political parties or criticized the monarchy or the Panchayat system. During the Panchayat period, journalists were usually charged under the Treason (Crime and Punishment) Act of 1962, the Public Security Act of 1961, or, latterly, the Freedom of Speech and Publication Ordinance of 1980.

During the Jan-Andolan ("People's Movement") of February–April 1990, which led to the dismantling of the Panchayat system, the privately owned media were severely harrassed, with print runs confiscated and around 50 journalists arrested. However, articles 12 and 13 of the new democratic constitution promulgated in November 1990 provide safeguards for freedom of thought and expression, and press and publication rights, provided that these do not prevent the making of laws that protect the sovereignty and integrity of Nepal and the harmonious relations between its peoples, or laws that prevent sedition, defamation, contempt of court, crime and acts against public decency or morality. Article 13 guarantees that no news item, article or other reading material shall be censored and that no press shall be closed or seized, and that the registration of a newspaper or periodical shall not be cancelled merely for publishing any news article. Since 1990 privately owned newspapers have proliferated: a typical Kathmandu street stall is able to provide a customer with more than 15 daily and 10 weekly papers, while Nepali viewers can now watch Nepal TV (established in 1986), CNN, and BBC World TV. The state-controlled media now also make some concessions to the kingdom's linguistic minorities; Radio Nepal, for example, now broadcasts in several minority languages as well as Nepali and English.

The temporary arrest in 1996 of two prominent leftist writers on charges of alleged "vandalism" suggests that, despite the existence of constitutional safeguards, the relationship between journalists and the government still contains potential problems. There is a constitutional ban on the religious conversion of others (Article 19.2), and the Christian and Muslim minorities cannot market their literature openly.

The serious nature of the Maoist "People's War" launched against the government by Nepal's extra-parliamentary Left in February 1996 has become more clearly apparent in recent years. The insurgency, and the government's response to it, had led to the deaths of more than 1500 people by mid-2001, and the government lost control of a substantial portion of the western part of the kingdom. Although no newspapers had been closed down, the sale and distribution of certain publications was prevented in some districts. The printruns of particular issues of certain pro-Maoist newspapers were seized, and allegedly pro-Maoist journalists were subjected to arbitrary arrest, detention, and assault on numerous occasions.

MICHAEL HUTT

Further Reading

Amnesty International, *Nepal: A Pattern of Human Rights Violations*, London: Amnesty International, 1987

Constitution of the Kingdom of Nepal 2047; and Electoral Laws, Kathmandu: Legal Research Associates, 1991

Fisher, James F., *Living Martyrs: Individuals and Revolution in Nepal*, Delhi and New York: Oxford University Press, 1997

Hutt, Michael (editor), *Nepal in the Nineties: Versions of the Past, Visions of the Future*, Delhi and New York: Oxford University Press, 1994

Raeper, William and Martin Hoftun, *Spring Awakening: An Account of the 1990 Revolution in Nepal*, Delhi and New York: Viking, 1992

Shaha, Rishikesh, *Modern Nepal: A Political History, 1769–1955*, New Delhi: Manohar, and Riverdale, Maryland: Riverdale Company, 1990

PABLO NERUDA
Chilean poet and diplomat, 1904–1973

Neruda (born Neftali Ricardo Reyes Basoalto) adopted his pseudonym in 1920 and was a well-published poet and critic before his appointment as honorary Chilean consul in Rangoon, Burma, in 1927; he then served successively in Sri Lanka, Java, and Singapore. In 1934 he was appointed as consul in Spain, first in Barcelona and then in Madrid. He was already a close friend of Federico García Lorca, Rafael Alberti, and Miguel Hernandez. During the Spanish Civil War he openly sided with the Republicans, having been deeply affected by Lorca's murder. He started writing poems for *España en el corazón* (Spain in the Heart; published in Chile, 1937, in Spain, 1938). At the end of 1936 he was dismissed from the Chilean foreign service. After returning to Chile, he established the Alliance of Chilean Intellectuals for the Defence of Culture in November 1937.

Neruda returned to consular service and became consul general in Mexico in 1940, publishing a single issue of the magazine *Araucania*; he was called to order by the Chilean government following what he later described as "absurd racial claims" about a photograph of an Araucan woman that was used on the cover.

While in Mexico, Neruda wrote a poem that savagely criticized Getúlio Vargas, the president of Brazil, who had prevented Luis Carlos Prestes, the jailed leader of the Communist Party, from attending his mother's funeral. The Brazilian government protested and it was rumoured that Neruda would be penalized. In reply, he wrote:

As the Consul General of Chile (and not a diplomatic representative), my duty is to work in strengthening the commercial relationships between Mexico and my country. However, as a writer, my duty is to defend freedom as an absolute rule of the civil and human condition and neither protests nor incidents of any type will change my actions or my poetry . . . We Chilean writers have a tradition: when we accept a public position or a duty in the government, however great or small it may be, we are not in the habit of surrendering our freedom or our dignity as free men and, even less, of varying the fidelity to the ideological or social principles which each one represents in his sphere. (*Excelsior*, Mexico City, 1 June 1943).

Neruda, who identified without reservation with the anti-fascist cause, that year published the *Nuevo canto de amor a Stalingrado* (New Love Song to Stalingrad), which was displayed as a poster in the streets of Mexico City and later published by the Society of Friends of the USSR. Some time later, as he was dining with some friends in Cuernavaca, Neruda was attacked by a group of Nazi sympathisers.

In 1945, Neruda was elected senator by the provinces of Tarapaca and Antofagasta in the extreme north of Chile. In the same year he joined the Communist Party, taking a prominent part in the presidential campaign that culminated in the triumph of Gabriel González Videla in September 1946. Despite having been elected with a decisive Communist vote, González Videla broke with the Communist Party in 1947, accusing it of subversive activities and agitation on behalf of the Soviet Union. Press censorship was instituted, but Neruda went ahead with the publication of his *Carta intima para millones de hombres* (Private Letter to be Read by Millions) published in the Caracas newspaper *El Nacional* (27 November 1947). He wrote:

The whole of the press in my country is censored. However, by the authority's impositions, the press is not able to tell the public that its publications have been brutally eliminated. The purpose of the government is to feign a state of normality that does not exist.

On 25 December the government began proceedings against the poet for treason. Still in the Senate, Neruda made a famous speech "I accuse" (6 January 1948), which circulated in hundreds of thousands of copies. He said:

> I accuse Señor González Videla of taking measures against freedom of opinion, as in the case of the action of deprivation of privileges against myself, and of attempting, by means of the most brutal censorship, and police and financial measures, to silence the newspaper *El Siglo*, the official organ of his candidacy and the fruit of many years of struggle by the Chilean people, *El Popular*, and six other newspapers.

On 3 February Neruda was deprived of his seat in the Senate and ordered to be detained. He went into hiding, but, constantly changing his address, he completed his great *Canto general*. In February 1949 he crossed the cordillera of the Andes on horseback and reached Argentina via the south; he then travelled to Buenos Aires and from there to Europe. Meanwhile, the Communist Party produced a clandestine edition of *Canto general*. Five thousand copies, with an introduction by Calo González, general secretary of the banned Communist Party, and with illustrations by the painter José Venturelli, were produced by Imprenta Juarez in Mexico City.

Neruda spent the next few years travelling widely, including to the Soviet Union, on which he still looked kindly even in his *Memoirs* published many years later: "The existence of a Soviet dogmatism in the arts for long periods of time cannot be denied but it should also be mentioned that this dogmatism was always considered a defeat, and contested openly . . . We know that life is stronger than precepts."

Neruda was allowed to return to Chile after 12 August 1952, but over the last 20 years of his life, despite his international eminence, he continued to be subjected to acts of censorship. In 1956 the Argentine authorities refused him permission to read his poems at the General San Martin Theatre, Córdoba, because of his political beliefs. It was many years before he was granted a visa to enter the United States – McCarthyism was at its height.

Neruda was active in the presidential campaign of Salvador Allende in 1970 and was awarded the Nobel Prize for Literature in 1971, having been appointed Chilean ambassador to France. In a final political speech, given at the PEN Club in New York in 1972, he condemned the US economic blockade of Cuba. Ill with cancer, he resigned his ambassadorship and returned to Chile. On the day of the military coup against the Allende government, 11 September 1973, he was at his seaside home, Isla Negra. He was seized by troops and taken by ambulance to a clinic in the capital. In hospital he managed to add a powerful attack against the military to his *Memoirs* before he died on 23 September.

Meanwhile, many of Neruda's works had been publicly burned on 21 September. His town house was ransacked, with books hurled to the ground and pictures daubed with crude slogans. His widow, Matilde Urrutia, and the writer Miguel Otero Silva arranged for publication of his memoirs in Venezuela with the title "I Admit to Having Lived".

HERNAN SOTO

Writings

España en el corazón: himno a las glorias del pueblo en la guerra, 1936–1937, 1937
Nuevo canto de amor a Stalingrado, 1943
Pablo Neruda acusa, 1948
Canto general, 1950; as *Canto general*, translated by Jack Schmitt, 1991
Confieso que he vivido, 1973; as *Memoirs*, translated by Hardie St Martin, 1974
Five Decades: Poems, 1925–1970, translated by Ben Belitt, 1974
Late and Posthumous Poems, translated by Ben Belitt, 1988

Further Reading

Aguirre, Margarita, *Las vidas de Pablo Neruda*, Santiago: Zig-Zag, 1967
Teitelboim, Volodia, *Neruda: An Intimate Biography*, Austin: University of Texas Press, 1991

SEYYID ʿIMAD AL-DIN NESIMI
Azeri/Ottoman poet, ?1340–?1418

Nesimi was one of the most influential representatives of the Hurufiya religious movement which flourished for a brief period around the year 1400 in a region that stretches roughly from the south flank of the Caucasus mountains to an imaginary line connecting modern Tehran and Aleppo. Nesimi's fame is based on his poetry: he wrote in a Turkic dialect related to modem Azerbaijani, and is regarded as one of the earliest master poets of that language, but he is also remembered for his martyrdom at Aleppo where he was flayed alive.

The Hurufiya was founded by Nesimi's teacher Fadl Allah, who received the epithet "al-Hurufi". Although the Hurufiya movement saw itself as a development within Islam and made explicit reference to the Qur'an, it met severe persecution from Muslim officialdom. Even today, most orthodox Muslim references place the Hurufiya outside Islam. Fadl Allah taught that letters (Arabic *huruf*) are more fundamental than the divine Word, because the Word is composed of letters. Further, he stated that the word "Allah" was written in human faces (because their lines resemble the letters of the word in Arabic). In its belief in the significance of letters and numbers (in the Oriental tradition each letter has a numerical value), the Hurufiya clearly shows resemblance to the Kabbalah school of Jewish mysticism. Besides, Fadl Allah is said to have read the Jewish and Christian scriptures. Among the statements that led to his being executed for heresy one probably has to list his suggestion that the word "Allah" in the Muslim prayer call be replaced by the letters that, in the quasi-Kabbalistic views of the Hurufiya, symbolize Fadl Allah.

After being given the rank of successor (khalifa), Nesimi wandered through the petty emirates of northern Iran and Anatolia in order to gain supporters for the new teaching, which included the Hurufi conviction that "God is man himself". His activity gained him a large following and also the support of some of the rulers. However, his success in small principalities such as Dhu'l-Kadr might also have paved the way to his death penalty, for these princedoms were the arch-enemies of the Mamelukes, whose sultan al-Mu'ayyad eventually had him executed. Thus, there was probably a political as well as a religious motive behind Nesimi's death. Others have linked the event with the downfall of the pro-Hurufi dynasty of the Ğalayirs in 1410. Although the extant sources do not explicitly state a political background for the events, one has also to keep in mind that to be doctrinally "pure" was an important legitimation of power for medieval Muslim rulers and that the suppression of the Hurufiya therefore necessarily had political implications.

As to the method of execution, most references state that Nesimi was flayed alive. One contemporary account even states that Nesimi, while already having his skin torn off, sang a verse mocking his judge. This verse is interesting also because it may give us some hint as to why the method of flaying was chosen. The judge, we learn from the verse, considered the sinfulness of Nesimi to be so great that every body part that came in contact with his blood had to be cut away. However, the sources report another reason for the skinning: Nesimi was blamed for having brought things to the surface (i.e. revealed his mystical knowledge) that should not have been made public according to the Islamic orthodoxy of his time. Since Islamic law was concerned only with the outer aspects of Nesimi's wrongdoing, not the interior, it was deemed appropriate by the executioners to punish Nesimi by the destruction of his skin. Modern Muslim historians emphasize that execution by torture is against the spirit and letter of Islam, yet the famous Muslim mystic and theologian al-Hallaj (857–922 CE), had similarly suffered a cruel death imposed by an orthodox Muslim court.

Although the Hurufiya remained quite marginal, many of its prominent representatives such as Fadl Allah 'Ali al-A'la (died 1420) being killed by Muslim authorities, it had and has still a great influence upon other Muslim heterodox sects such as the Alevis in Turkey, among whom Nesimi is still revered as a great mystic and martyr.

MICHAEL REINHARD HESS

Writings

The Quatrains, translated by Kathleen R.F. Burrill, 1972
Poems, translated by Peter Tempest, 1984
Seyyid Nesîmî Dîvâni'ndan seçmeler (A Selection from the Divan of Seyyid Nesimi), edited by Kemâl Edib Kürkçüoglu, 1985

Further Reading

Algar, Hamid, "The Hurufi Influence on Bektashism" in *Bektachiyya*, edited by Alexandre Popovic and Gilles Veinstein, Istanbul: Isis, 1995
Babinger, Franz, "Nesimi" entry in *The Encyclopaedia of Islam*, new edition, Leiden: Brill, 1993
Çamuroğlu, Reha, *Sabah rüzgârı: Enel-Hakk demişti Nesîmî* (Morning Breeze: Nesimi said, "I am the Truth"), Istanbul, 1992
Çiftçi, Cemil, *Maktul Şairler* (The Murdered Poets), Istanbul, 1997
Geoffroy, Eric, *Le Soufisme en Egypte et en Syrie sous les derniers Mamelouks et les premiers Ottomans: orientations spirituelles et enjeux culturels*, Damascus: Institut Français de Damas, 1995
Mitler, Louis, *Ottoman Turkish Writers: A Bibliographical Dictionary of Significant Figures in Pre-Republican Turkish Literature*, New York: Peter Lang, 1988

AZIZ NESIN
Turkish novelist and short story writer, 1915–1995

The author of more than 100 novels and collections of short stories satirizing political life in Turkey, chairman of the Writers' Union of Turkey, and the cofounder and columnist of a leftist daily newspaper which defended Kurdish rights and attacked Islamic fundamentalism, Aziz Nesin (born Nusret Nesin) was jailed for his opinions, and harassed by the authorities for many years.

Nesin's first experience of the hostility that was regularly to be directed at him came when he was a columnist for *Tan* (Dawn) in the mid-1940s. The Republican People's Party founded by Atatürk had enjoyed unchallenged rule for 20 years. The offices of *Tan*, which published articles by politicians who would soon lead the new Democrat party, were violently attacked by nationalist students on 4 December 1945. Following that event, nobody would employ Nesin if he wrote under his own name, so he used various pseudonyms, throwing the authorities into confusion. He later recalled:

At my first arrest, the question the police asked me continually was this – "Who is the real writer of articles that come out under your name?" They wouldn't believe that I wrote them. Not long after this event – two years – the opposite occurred. This time the police claimed I wrote the articles with other signatures. The first time I'd tried to prove I wrote, the second, that I didn't write. On one such occasion, an expert witness testified that I'd written an article under another name, so I was imprisoned 16 months for an article I didn't write.

Despite his experience on *Tan*, Nesin joined the Turkish Socialist Workers' and Peasants' Party, and wrote for *Gercek* (Truth), which lasted for a mere 25 issues in 1946, until it and the party were closed down under martial law regulations that were still in force after the end of World War II. Undaunted, he now started a satirical newspaper, *Markopasha*, soon to have a circulation of 25,000, but to be equally short-lived; Nesin was picked up by the security police and held under severe conditions for 17 days, without being charged.

Although Nesin was to spend some five years in jail, he was probably more successful than other dissident writers in avoiding imprisonment. As Mübeccel Kıray wrote in the foreword to Nesin's autobiography:

Aziz Nesin's real genius . . . is in his incredible capacity to observe the ridiculous and ludicrous in all situations, and to describe it without exaggeration . . . He represents an unprecedented victory of the written word in exposing intolerance, absurdity, cruelty, and stupidity.

It is probably less dangerous to disparage the authorities for their incompetence than to confront them head-on with accounts of their cruelty and injustice. Moreover, Nesin extended his assessments to his fellow citizens. He once said that "60 per cent of Turks are fools", but later increased the proportion when he saw the progress of Islamism. An avowed atheist, he was alarmed at the prospect of an intolerance even more powerful than political intolerance.

He was a founding member of the Writers Union of Turkey in 1974, succeeding Yasar Kemal as chairman in 1976. The union was pledged "to defend the rights of people who have chosen writing as a profession, to protect their legal, cultural and economic rights and freedoms, and to struggle, by all possible legal means, to achieve and safeguard full freedom of speech and expression". These were brave aims for 1974; in the previous three years some 5000 people, including writers, journalists, and trade unionists, had been arrested in the witchhunt of Nihat Erim's regime against leftists and liberals. After the military coup led by general Kenan Evren in 1980, the new authorities continued the repression of trade unions; in 1982 Nesin and all the members of the union's executive were charged with forming an "illegal organization" and "defaming the security forces". Their trial lasted from January 1983 until the end of 1984, and resulted in acquittal.

Nesin and his colleagues had to defend themselves against charges that they had "set up clandestine organizations to achieve the supremacy of one class over another", that they had organized commemorative events for Nazim Hikmet, "whose thoughts and ideology are banned by law", and for their support of certain strikes. While on trial Nesin drafted a petition, which was in due course signed by 1383 intellectuals, *Observations and Demands for a Democratic System in Turkey*. They asserted the right "to be free to produce and circulate artistic work of any kind"; censorship should be abolished and no subject should be taboo; the press, radio, and television should be free and autonomous. It was not surprising that at first no news of this petition was allowed in the Turkish press. It was finally made public in June 1984, not before president Evren had attacked its signatories as "traitors" who wanted to embarrass Turkey abroad.

The Turkish government banned publication of Salman Rushdie's *The Satanic Verses* on 24 August 1989. On 27 May 1993 Nesin defied the ban by publishing extracts in *Aydınlık* (Illumination), which he had helped to found earlier that year. Further extracts were published on the following day, leading to seizure of the paper by government security forces and to

the arrest of four members of the staff; meanwhile, Hezbollah, Islamic militants, prevented distribution in southeast Turkey. Despite telephone threats, further extracts were published on the following two days, prompting police confiscation and a call from the imam of an Istanbul mosque for a holy war against *Aydınlık*. A Turkish government appeared to come down on the side of a dissident newspaper. On 1 June the deputy prime minister Erdal İnönü commented that *Aydınlık* was "fighting for freedom of expression", and on the following day Ismet Sezgin, minister of the interior, ordered provincial governors to ensure distribution of the paper. On 7 June members of the Aczüzümendi sect were refused entrance to Ankara, where they wished to protest against *Aydınlık*.

However, on 2 July a group of Alevi Muslims (a liberal Islamic sect) invited Nesin and other writers, along with musicians, artists, and dancers to attend a cultural festival at the Madimak Hotel, Sivas. A statue was unveiled to a poet who had been stoned to death for blasphemy some centuries previously. These events proved to be too much for local extremists, who, after eight hours of violent demonstrations, set fire to the hotel. A police film showed that the authorities stood by while the fire caused the deaths of 37 delegates to the festival, including several writers, a cartoonist, and 22 actors and dancers of the Pir Sultan Abdal Association. Nesin escaped, unrecognized. He denied that the protests had occurred because of his involvement; he had, in fact, written to apologize that he could not attend but had changed his mind. Erdal İnönü announced that "the secular state order our republic has introduced in Turkey cannot be changed through such fundamentalist reactions". On 15 August Nesin met Rushdie in Germany, where they called for opposition to fundamentalism and chided western governments with "indifference to the terror of religious fanatics".

Nesin believed that Turkish governments had a double standard: "When they deal with the Europeans, they present themselves as secularists. When they deal with the electorate, they make all kinds of concessions that in turn help fundamentalists in Turkey." On the other hand, on 2 July 1994, the anniversary of the fire, the deputy prime minister laid a wreath in Sivas in front of a statue of Atatürk, the founder of secular Turkey.

CHRISTINE L. OGAN

Writings
Istanbul Boy: The Autobiography of Aziz Nesin, translated by Joseph S. Jacobson, 2 vols, 1977–79
Turkish Stories from Four Decades, translated by Louis Mitler, 1991
Gomu Arayan Adfam, 1998

Further Reading
Bedford, Carmel, *Fiction, Fact and the Fatwa: 2000 Days of Censorship*, London: Article 19, 1994
Can, Hasan, "Turkish Writers on Trial", *Index on Censorship*, 13/5 (October 1984)

NESTORIANS
Christian dissidents, 5th century

Once Jesus' followers had decided to proselytize among the Gentiles, the early development of Christian theology was conditioned by the need to graft Hebrew monotheism on to Greek philosophical categories that had been developed in a pagan context. There were major difficulties in finding ways to state that there were three persons in one God, and that Jesus was both fully divine and fully human. One of the main obstacles, at least from the 3rd century when western theological documents were produced in Latin, derived from the greater richness of nuance of which the Greek philosophical vocabulary had been capable. The Greek *hypostasis* meant more than the Latin *persona*, as the Greek *physis* meant more than the Latin *natura*. Latin orthodoxy demanded three persons in God, and two natures in Christ, although there are orthodox Greek documents that speak of a single *hypostasis* in God, and of a single *physis* in Christ.

With Constantine's victory on the Bosphorus in 324, the empire could be split, leaving Latin Rome supreme in the West, with the Greek-speaking patriarchates of Alexandria and Antioch, to which were added Constantinople and Jerusalem, in the East. Constantine hoped that it might be possible to rule both eastern and western empires from Constantinople, the town he built to replace Rome as the capital of the empire on the site of the former Byzantium. The Eastern Church was, however, riven with doctrinal dissent, and Constantine had had difficulty in getting agreement concerning the consubstantiality of the Father and Son.

After the final rejection of Arianism, which subordinated the Son to the Father, the disputes culminated again in a quarrel at once theological and political. The bishopric of Constantinople had been declared second in rank to Rome, which infuriated the Alexandrians, and, while the Church of Antioch so insisted on the duality of natures in Christ as to endanger the unity of his person, the Church of Alexandria so emphasized the divinity as to obscure the reality of Christ's humanity.

When the Syrian Nestorius, a distinguished preacher trained at Antioch, was appointed patriarch of Constantinople in 428, he began to query the doctrine, dear to the Alexandrians, that Mary was the *theotokos*, the mother of God. He held, true to the Antiochene position, that Mary was the mother of the earthly Jesus, but that the assumption of the human nature into the person of the *Logos*, or Son of God, did not make her the mother of God. He was accused of denying the divinity of Christ, and Cyril of Alexandria, hostile on account not only of the jumped-up status accorded to Constantinople, but also on account of the opposed theological traditions, did not wait long before intervening. He stirred up trouble where he could, among his clergy, among the dissidents at Constantinople, and within the emperor's family. Theodosius' sister Pulcheria, hostile to Nestorius, who had once snubbed her, was quarrelling with his wife, Eudokia, who was on Nestorius' side.

Cyril denounced Nestorius to Rome as a rationalist who denied the divinity of Christ and man's need for grace. Pope Celestine, already annoyed that Nestorius had received a group of Pelagians condemned at Rome, and as jealous as Alexandria of the upstart status accorded to Constantinople, sent Cyril a formal letter to be passed on to Nestorius. It demanded recantation within 10 days and imposed the *theotokos* title.

Nestorius was to be excommunicated if he did not accept this, and the retraction was to be enforced by Cyril, who also demanded that Nestorius accept 12 anathemas he had drawn up. Nestorius was to admit that the Word of God suffered in the flesh. Nestorius, who could rely on the support of John, bishop of Antioch, and the Syrians riposted with a counter-excommunication, creating a situation that only a council could resolve.

The council was held in 431 at Ephesus, where Nestorius arrived with 16 bishops and an army, and Cyril with 50 bishops. The disorderly proceedings ended in a strong vote against Nestorius in a session that was declared invalid by the emperor. Other bishops arrived, and extensive lobbying dominated numerous sessions and counter-sessions, until the emperor had both Cyril and Nestorius imprisoned while he listened himself to the arguments. Siding with the majority, he eventually deprived Nestorius of his bishopric, although Cyril, who had bribed his way out of prison, was forced to make concessions. He was not allowed to impose his anathemas, and was forced to sign a declaration stating that Christ was "perfect God and perfect man". Nestorius retired to his monastery at Antioch until 435, when the emperor banished him to the Egyptian desert. He appears to have been captured and later freed by nomads. He wrote memoirs, *The Book of Heraclides*, before his death in 450.

Nestorianism as a heresy went beyond anything that can be attributed to Nestorius personally, who merely felt obliged to take a stand against the exaggerated implications attendant on the sudden upsurge in Marian devotion in the early 4th-century Church. If Mary was the mother of God, it would have seemed farcical to refer to *her* mother, St Anne, as God's grandmother. Nestorius was no doubt right to wish to withstand the incursions of a piety that made Mary quasi-divine, but his remark that God is not a baby two or three months old caused immeasurable offence. However, "Nestorianism" did see two complete persons in Christ, compromising the integrity of the incarnation, and insisting to its detriment on the reality of Christ's humanity.

ANTHONY LEVI

Further Reading

Chadwick, Henry, *The Early Church*, revised edition, Harmondsworth and New York: Penguin, 1993

Grillmeier, Aloys, *Christ in Christian Tradition*, 2nd edition, London: Mowbray, and Atlanta: John Knox Press, 1975–

Kelly, J.N.D., *Early Christian Doctrines*, London: A. & C. Black, and New York: Harper, 1958

Loofs, Friedrich, *Nestorius and His Place in the History of Christian Doctrine*, Cambridge: Cambridge University Press, 1914

THE NETHERLANDS

Population: 15,864,000
Main religions: Roman Catholic; Protestant
Official language: Dutch
Other languages spoken: Frisian
Number of daily newspapers: 38

Number of periodicals: 63
Number of radio receivers per 1000 inhabitants: 980
Number of TV receivers per 1000 inhabitants: 519
Number of PCs per 1000 inhabitants: 317.6

To modern eyes, the late 15th-century Netherlands would seem like fertile ground for the growth of intellectual freedom. Its provinces enjoyed considerable local autonomy. It possessed the second largest university in Europe after Paris. Lutheranism, with its stress on individual responsibility, had a foothold. Erasmus of Rotterdam was advocating personal growth through literacy and the pursuit of scholarship. Printing arrived in the 1470s and the press at Deventer quickly became a leading centre for the production of humanist books in northern Europe.

Erasmus would have long-term influence, and not only in his own country, but humanism was too tender a plant to withstand what was, in the words of Jonathan Israel, "the most sustained attempt to suppress the Reformation by administrative means seen in sixteenth century Europe". Charles V, ruler of the Habsburg empire, regarded himself as the defender of Catholic orthodoxy, and determined to suppress Lutheran ideas by force. In March 1521 he prohibited the "books, sermons and writings of the said Luther, and of his followers and adherents", and appointed Franz van der Hulst as his inquisitor-general to enforce the ban.

Erasmus "never approved of the suppression of Luther in this way by public uproar, before his books have been read and discussed". He left, permanently, and the Dutch version of his *Enchiridion* (1523) was banned. Van der Hulst proceeded to censor by fear – heretics were burnt, and clergy, booksellers, and schoolmasters who had adopted or propagated Lutheran doctrines were intimidated. From 1526 no book could be produced without a licence, on pain of banishment and loss of property. For a religious book to be published, from 1529, a bishop's approval was necessary. Punishments became progressively more extreme; printers of heretical material were exposed on scaffolds, branded, or had an eye poked out or a hand chopped off. People thought it best to keep their opinions to themselves, and Lutheranism's roots withered.

Next to feel Charles's lash were the Anabaptists, who, believing that the Second Coming was imminent, had little regard for secular rulers. From 1523 to 1566 some 1300 of them were executed for their beliefs. Many fled with other Protestants to the England of Elizabeth I, only to face her inquisition of 1568. At the same time, the Anabaptists themselves were not exactly noted for open-mindedness; Jan Bochelson of Leiden ("King Jan"), on behalf of his followers, banned and burnt all books except the Bible. Finally, under the leadership of Menno Simmons (1496–1561), in the interests of survival they adopted a more private and pious discipline and, in the Netherlands, were generally left alone.

Calvinism was to prove much more durable. It arrived in the Netherlands in the 1550s, and by the middle 1560s many of its followers were ready to use violence against Catholic art

and literature. In August 1566, often with the support of local authorities, altars and images were stripped from churches all over the Netherlands, and the library of the Friars Minor at Utrecht was burnt. Charles V's successor Philip II sent in the duke of Alva to restore his authority, which he did by executing a thousand people. Calvinists went into exile or worshipped clandestinely, but their day was imminent. Their membership increased. After the Dutch Revolt, "the true Reformed Christian Religion" quickly became the dominant Church of the United Provinces of Holland and Zeeland. Immediately, the practice of the "Roman religion" was forbidden, triggering further iconoclasm in the 1590s (there was not, perhaps, a hostility to art itself, for some of the paintings removed from churches ended up on the walls of town halls, as in Delft).

Many of the heroes of Dutch history – William the Silent, Dirck Coornhert, Jacob van Oldenbarneveldt, Johann de Witt – campaigned and manoeuvred for religious toleration. It was slow to arrive, not only for Catholics but even for unorthodox Calvinists. Jacob Arminius (1560–1609) questioned predestination. His followers were pursued and in places silenced as recusants. Major church parties emerged, with attitudes familiar to modern ears: the "fundamentalist" Voetians, determined to maintain the pure faith, and to punish those who departed from it; and the more "liberal" Coccians, who stood for freedom of conscience. As elsewhere in Calvinism, the Reformed Church kept its members in theological and moral order by means of consistories and synods, and they expected – but did not always get – support from the secular authorities. The Synod of Dordrecht (1618) affirmed Voetian attitudes and forbade trade in Catholic religious books, prints, and engravings – a prohibition which lasted 150 years, although it was never universally applied.

The two centuries of the Dutch Republic are, nevertheless, in some respects a byword for urbanity and freedom. It was the most literate country in Europe. As early as 1593 the humanist scholar Joseph Scaliger reported that even servant girls could read. The Sephardic Jews, who had fled the Inquisition in Spain and Portugal and had settled in Amsterdam, were shown relative tolerance, being allowed to build synagogues in 1597 and 1639. There was a flourishing book trade in Dutch and other languages, with an emphasis on travel and navigation. In keeping with the status of the republic as an international power, an oriental press with the capacity to print in Syriac, Ethiopian, Arabic, and Hebrew was installed at Leiden in 1625.

There was no other country, wrote Descartes, "where you can enjoy such complete liberty". The republic was, according to the engraver Romeyn de Hooghe, "the freest, and safest state . . . of all those known in the world". Certainly, by comparison with many of its neighbours, the republic was relatively free. But, ironically, both of these commentators were to experience censorship in one form or another, and the position was far more complicated than they allowed. The wealth-creators, for example, were more liberal-minded than the leaders of the Reformed Church. The record of censorship was patchy; what was allowed in one province could be forbidden, or evaded, in another.

The targets of religious censorship changed. Dordrecht had deplored the drift to "liberty and pleasure" and Willem Teeldinck (1579–1629) wrote of the need for a "further Reformation", which would combat sexual immorality and drunkenness; he and those who came after him were hostile to music, theatre, and "amorous books" (see below). The most overt religious censorship of the 17th century, however, was directed at the Socinians, whose denial of the Trinity was felt to be beyond toleration. If found, their books would be destroyed. In 1653 the States of Holland instituted large fines for printers (3000 guilders) and booksellers (1000 guilders) who handled such literature. But a request by the synods that the States institute provincial boards of censorship (*vistadores librorum*) was rejected on the grounds that "such practices would have dangerous consequences".

Dordrecht having deplored the drift to "liberty and pleasure", theatre became a major target of the "further Reformation". It was even banned entirely for a time in Leeuwarden. William III was a patron of the stage, but *Lucifer* (1654) by the republic's most celebrated playwright, Joost van den Vondel, and the first appearance of a woman – Adriana Nozeman – on stage (1655), provoked a renewed campaign against profanity and paganism. The Dutch were allowed much less theatrical licence than the citizens of Restoration London. Unsuccessful attempts were made to get music and dance halls closed down in Amsterdam, but as late as the 18th century actors could still be discredited in a court of law because they were said to belong to a disreputable profession.

Dutch painting enjoyed its golden age, but individual painters could fall foul of the authorities. Erotic pictures could be obtained under the counter but not displayed. The above-mentioned Romeyn de Hooghe was brought before the Amsterdam magistrates for producing and selling such pictures (among other work, he had produced engravings for Aretino's *Ragionamenti*). In 1628 Jan Torrentius, best known as a painter of still life, was sentenced at Haarlem to 20 years in prison, ostensibly for blasphemy, but actually for a series of pornographic paintings. *L'École des filles*, a pornographic book imported from France, was banned for a century from 1669.

Attitudes to pornography in the 17th and 18th centuries appear to have been generally relaxed. Such books as *Het Amsterdomsch Hoerdom* (The Amsterdam Whore, 1681) and *D'openhertige Juffrouw* (The Outspoken Mistress, 1679) were regularly reprinted. On the other hand, the humanist Johann de Bruno failed to see why Aretino's *Postures* were needed when most people could enjoy "the real thing" without such aids. An edict of 1726 excluded pornography from a list of categories of books it was forbidden to print. *Papekost Obgedist in geuse Schotelen* (Popish Cooking in Beggar's Dishes) was condemned not, mostly, for obscenity but because it might cause offence to Catholics and thus be a threat to order. However, changes are discernible from the 1740s onwards; *Venus Miasebe Gasthuis* (Venus' Guesthouse for Love) was more often banned and expurgations more regularly carried

out. Moral decline, it was said, might be responsible for the economic and political decline of the republic.

The independence of Dutch printers was well known. They managed to obtain copies of Catholic Indexes and, on the forbidden fruit principle, used them as a marketing tool. Galileo's *Discorsi e dimostrazioni*, for example, was published by Louis Elsevier. However, new scientific and philosophical ideas had a mixed fate. To avoid the French censorship, works by Bayle, Locke, Hume, and Voltaire could be published in the republic and smuggled back over the border, but the Dutch were extremely wary of what they would allow to circulate at home. Descartes, having initially found a safer intellectual home than in France, was accused of atheism and corrupting young people following his *Discours de la méthode* (1636). University senates attempted – unsuccessfully – to prohibit his ideas. Like Erasmus before him he decided to leave. To avoid similar treatment Spinoza, already anathematized by the Synagogue, had his *Tractatus Theologico-Politicus* (1670) published in Latin; it was banned by the States General in 1674. Ingrid Weekhart has concluded: "That the practice (of censorship) was less drastic was not so much the result of a principled attitude of tolerance as of a decentralized structure of authority and the persistent antagonism of the several authorities".

So far, freedom meant mostly religious and intellectual freedom. The stadholderate of Holland was first abolished in 1667 in the interests of what was then understood to be political freedom, but, until well into the 18th century, the idea had generally a passive, rather comfortable quality: "every man minding his own business and little enquiring into other men's" (Sir William Temple, English ambassador, 1672). Books such as Rousseau's *Du Contrat social* and Voltaire's *Traité sur la tolérance*, which challenged the political status quo, were prohibited by the States.

Wider influences, notably the American Revolution, began to challenge Dutch stability. *Aan het Volk van Nederland* (To the Netherlands People, 1781), published anonymously under a false imprint, became the rallying call for the so-called "Patriots". It promised to lead the Dutch "out of bondage" to Orangist stadholders, and demanded a free press. The States of Holland immediately prohibited the reading of it. The *Politieke Kruijer* (Political Courier, Amsterdam), and *De Post van den Neder Rhijn* (Utrecht) emerged, while their editors and publishers were fined for denouncing decrees of the States of Utrecht or attacking the Regents. For their part the Orangists believed that the "true freedom" of the Dutch proceeded from their respect for religion; the only press freedom worth having, which was not the same as licence, was already achieved.

When the tables were turned, and the Patriots had their brief taste of power (1786–87), they themselves drew lines. Orange was declared the "colour of sedition"; there was to be no singing of Orange songs or display of banners and pennants. When they regained control, the Orangists instituted stringent, though not entirely effective press censorship; in a reversal of the Dutch printing industry's traditional hospitality to foreign work, editions of Thomas Paine's *Common Sense* and Condorcet's *Avis des bataves* were produced in France, smuggled in, and circulated to the growing number of reading clubs where French ideas were discussed. In 1794 the States of Holland closed all unlicensed presses and attempted suppression of reading societies as "disturbers of public peace and inciters of sedition".

Despite the instability of the times, the press was not greatly muzzled during the years of the Batavian Republic (1795–1805). Writers took care to avoid criticizing the Constitution, and even the opposition paper, *Constitutioneele Vlieg* (Constitutional Fly), was allowed to appear. Severe censorship was reintroduced with the French annexation of the Netherlands and the rule of Louis Bonaparte (1806–14). No newspaper could publish an article on matters of state or politics unless it had been submitted to the government, translated into French, and passed; all books were subject to prior censorship. Offenders were brought before a tribunal of nine judges and could be sentenced to the pillory, to deprivation of civil rights, and to fines. The system was only slightly modified when the Kingdom of the Netherlands (incorporating what is now Belgium) was imposed in 1814. The Kingdom, unpopular in both parts of the Low Countries, was notable, among other things, for its failed attempt to enforce Dutch as the official language.

Press freedom, along with freedom of worship for all denominations and the right of public meeting, was finally enshrined in the Constitution of 1848: "Without prejudice to liability under the law, no person requires advance permission to express thoughts or feelings by means of the printing press." This basic principle has continued to apply, suitably adapted, for other mass media, film, radio, and television: 150 years on, the established practice is to make the media responsible for their own products, so long as they do not break the law.

The Dutch model of press freedom has not always made for a fearless pursuit of truth. In 1940 Adriaan J. Barnouw could write:

> The daily press of Holland is a very dull, strait-laced and respectable old lady. Her conduct is hemmed in by inhibitions. She practises an aristocratic self restraint, shows a puritanical estimate of the kind of news that is fit to print . . . uses headlines in moderation and makes them conform to the substance of their story.

The same "safe" approach may perhaps be deduced from the record of Hollandia Filmfabrieck, which, during the years of World War I, when Holland was neutral, produced 21 feature films and never once made reference to the war. The press (and broadcasting) may not endanger state security or breach official secrets. On at least one occasion a journalist (C.L. Hansen of *Het Waterland*, 1938) was charged with the mere breach of *confidentiality*, and, when he refused to name his informant, was jailed for contempt.

The history of broadcasting in the Netherlands, as in Belgium, has been greatly influenced by the system of pillarization (*verzuiling*), whereby a group of organizations based on some religious or spiritual principle (ever more broadly interpreted) can be licensed to broadcast. Here, too, it has been charged that the system makes for safety rather than risk. Every organization which is given broadcasting time is answerable for its observance of broadcasting legislation; programmes may not endanger state security, public order, or morality. In 1967 the government commissioner for broadcasting (later replaced by the Commissariaat voor de Media, 1987) was empowered to ensure that organizations toe the line. The Broadcasting Council (Mediaraad), whose 17 members are appointed by the Crown to advise the government, found it necessary in the 1970s to warn the minister of culture, recreation, and social work against excessive interference in the form and content of programmes, but the minister can, in an extreme case, withdraw an organization's right to broadcast. So far as television and other advertising is concerned, the Foundation for Advertising may issue directives on content.

Citizens have no legal right of reply if they are wrongly or unfairly reported in the media, but broadcasters must issue a retraction if a successful application is made to the Amsterdam Court of Justice. The Council for Journalistic Conduct hears complaints against the press and issues reports, but it cannot impose penalties. These forms of self regulation do not exempt offenders from facing the consequences of breaking the law.

Censorship of films in the Netherlands is concerned only with audiences under the age of 16. Films must be submitted to a panel of educators and psychologists, which may restrict audiences to those over the age of 12, or over 14, or otherwise order cuts of violent scenes.

As elsewhere in Europe, the Churches have experienced declining influence as well as declining membership, although the Dutch Reformed Church may still be said to enjoy a "leadership of honour". Protestant Christians range from traditionally rigid Calvinists to lovers of moral and religious freedom. It was still possible in 1966 for two books by Gerard Reve to be described by a Protestant deputy in parliament as "blasphemous, bestial and even satanic". (Reve was prosecuted, but acquitted, and the victory party was held in a Catholic Church.) Dutch Catholics have been among the most rebellious of their co-religionists since the late 1960s; one of their leading theologians, Edward Schillebeeckx, a Belgian resident in Holland, was summoned to Rome to be tried for heresy following his writings against the papal encyclical *Humanae Vitae*, which forbids the use of all forms of birth control. Others do not appear to have been deterred by the fear of pontifical censorship.

Along with Denmark, the Netherlands now enjoys the reputation of having a radically liberal approach to sexual expression in books, films, video, and sex shows. It is still, formally, an offence to produce and distribute writings and pictures which "offend decency", but in practice the meaning of "decency" has been seen to change in a liberal direction. Cardinal Alfink, Catholic primate of Holland in the 1960s, said: "There is perhaps no country in the world where the transition from closedness to openness was experienced as dramatically as it has been in Holland".

Lines are, however, drawn. In the early 1970s, 15 photographic collages by Joop Schafthuizen were acquired by the art lending library of the Rotterdam Borough of Schiedam. The artist had used magazine pictures of naked young boys, some of them engaged in overt sexual behaviour. In August 1998, following international concern about child pornography, a library user declared the collages to be pornographic. The Rotterdam police had them removed from the browsing collection, and the library itself decided that they should no longer be loaned. G. Kruijt, director of culture for Schiedam, declared that the purchasing committee today normally rejected "art that is currently being experienced as controversial or shocking", including not only pictures of young children but "explicit violence against women". Schafthuizen himself avowed that he would no longer make such work.

Covert censorship may also remain, some of it perhaps due to the country's colonialist past. *The Observer* (London, 27 October 1996) reported that children's books published originally in Britain could be discriminated against by Dutch publishers (along with counterparts in France and Denmark) if their covers depicted images of non-white children. According to the report, British publishers then made alterations in the interest of sales.

DEREK JONES

Further Reading

Barnouw, Adriaan J., *The Dutch: A Portrait Study of the People of Holland*, New York: Columbia University Press, 1940

Boxer, C.R., *The Dutch Seaborne Empire, 1600–1800*, London: Hutchinson, and New York: Knopf, 1965

Geyl, Pieter, *History of the Low Countries: Episodes and Problems*, London: Macmillan, and New York: St Martin's Press, 1964

Haak, Kees van der and Joanna Spicer, *Broadcasting in the Netherlands*, London and Boston: Routledge, 1977

Israel, Jonathan, *The Dutch Republic: Its Rise, Greatness and Fall, 1477–1806*, Oxford: Clarendon Press, and New York: Oxford University Press, 1995

Schama, Simon, *Patriots and Liberators: Revolution in the Netherlands, 1780–1813*, New York: Knopf, and London: Collins, 1977; revised edition, London: Fontana, 1992

Schama, Simon, *The Embarrassment of Riches: An Interpretation of Dutch Culture in the Golden Age*, New York: Knopf, 1987; London: Collins, 1988

Smith, Anthony, *The Shadow in the Cave: A Study of the Relationship between the Broadcaster, His Audience and the State*, London: Allen and Unwin, 1973; Urbana: University of Illinois Press, 1974

Weekhout, Ingrid, *Boekencensuur in de noordelijke Nederlanden: de vrijheid van drukpers in de zeventiende eeuw*, The Hague: Uitgevers, 1998

Wigbold, Herman, "Television and Politics: The Netherlands", *Index on Censorship*, 8/2 (March–April 1979)

THE NETHERLANDS: The Netherlands under the Nazis

On the night of 9–10 May 1940, German troops invaded the Netherlands. Rotterdam was bombarded, approximately three-quarters of Dutch Jews were murdered, and numerous hostages were executed. Censorship, Nazi-style, was in force for the five years of the occupation, and the whole experience was one of enormous trauma for the Dutch people. Since 1945, however, the Dutch have built up a myth of collective resistance, to which many historians have contributed. Some have argued that this amounts to censorship, since certain unpalatable facts about the Dutch–German relationship have been either forgotten or suppressed. This essay summarizes what, it is argued, is "censorship by omission".

It is important to note, first of all, that even before the war the Dutch press practised censorship for the sake of the country's economic self-interest. According to the historian Pieter Geyl, who was also a journalist for the *Nieuwe Rotterdamse Courant*, this very influential newspaper dismissed its Jewish foreign editor and acting editor-in-chief, Marcus van Blankenstein as early as 1936, because as a journalist he had taken too critical and close a look at developments in Germany. Geyl believes that to have "a Jew as foreign correspondent was considered dangerous in Rotterdam"; the port was the major centre for Dutch trade and clearly central to the economy, then as now.

Just before the invasion, the journalist Menno ter Braak made some critical comments about Hitler in a preface to *Hitler's eigen woorden*, the Dutch translation of Hermann Rauschning's book *Hitler Speaks* (1940). He was charged on 1 May 1940 by the head of the Dutch legal service, Professor Gerbrandy, with "slander of a friendly head of state", and was summoned to appear in court on 14 May, the day on which he committed suicide.

Many postwar accounts of the occupation have, unwittingly or not, suppressed the full facts of Dutch–German collaboration. Louis de Jong points out in his standard work *Het Koninkrijk der Nederlanden in de Tweede Wereldoorlog (The Kingdom of the Netherlands in the Second World War;*

1969–91) that Dutch industrialists went further than they need have done in fulfilling 84.4 per cent of German orders (the comparable figure in France was 70 per cent). For whatever reason, little attention was given to the scant support given to Jews during the occupation, from actual betrayals in some cases (for example, Anne Frank), to the stubborn fact that, while it was claimed that the Dutch did all they could to protect Jews, it was considered easier to look after non-Jews, tens of thousands of whom avoided forced labour by going underground in the Netherlands.

"Censorship by omission" in the accepted history of the Netherlands under the Nazis has included the failure to mention or the playing down of the facts that many members of the Dutch civil service had signed the so-called "Declarations of Aryan Origin", that it was Dutch policemen who arrested Jews, and that it was Dutch field security who guarded them in the "Westerbork" transit camp, from where they were deported to their death by Dutch railway personnel. When the historian Nanda van der Zee described in her book *Om erger te voorkomen* (1997, To Prevent Worse), queen Wilhelmina's unheroic role and the consequences of her flight for the persecution of the Jewish Dutch, she was fiercely attacked by virtually every Dutch historian.

The historian Graa Boomsma was charged in 1994 with slander when he compared the employment of military personnel in the Dutch East Indies after the war with the conduct of the German SS. It was pointed out that there was circumstantial evidence that some Dutch who had served in the SS were despatched to Indonesia at the end of the 1940s to maintain "colonial order". Boomsma had the support of International PEN, who wrote to the Dutch justice minister, Hirsch Ballin. The case was dismissed for a second time at the beginning of 1995.

Fifty years after the war "censorship by omission" has taken on an altogether new turn, now drawing attention to Dutch complicity in Nazi crimes, while focusing at the same time on Germany's postwar democracy. The former Dutch ambassador to Germany, A.P. van Walsum, has said that the time has passed when Dutch–German relations need be strained by memories of World War II. The future king, crown prince Willem Alexander, a qualified historian, has suggested that the 5th of May, the day on which the liberation is celebrated, should no longer be a public holiday. Some argue that it is once again the health of the Dutch economy, dominated by its relationship to Germany within the European Union, that is considered more important than the pursuit of historical truth. The historians who think differently believe that it is part of their professional responsibility, with Milan Kundera, the Czech novelist, to promote "the struggle of memory against forgetting".

JAN HERMAN BRINKS

Further Reading

Amerongen, Martin van, "Contrapunt: Reclassering anno 1949", *De Groene Amsterdammer* (15 September 1993)

Brinks, Jan Herman, "About Mammon and Morals: The Ambivalent Relationship of the Dutch with the Germans", *Mediterranean Quarterly*, 8/4 (1997): 123–30

Brinks, Jan Herman, "Die Niederländer und das grössere Deutschland", *Blätter für deutsche und internationale Politik* (July 1997)

Brinks, Jan Herman, "The Dutch, the Germans and the Jews", *History Today*, 49/6 (June 1999): 17–23

Dunk, Hermann von der (interview with), "Eine Art Antisemitismus: Der Historiker von der Dunk über Hollands Deutschlandbild", *Der Spiegel* (5 April 1993): 161

Esterik, Chris van, "Het litteken van een scheermes, SS'ers in Nederlands-Indië tijdens de politiële actes", *NRC-Handelsblad*, 24 (November 1984)

Geyl, Pieter, *Pennestrijd over staat en historie* (Controversy about State and History), Groningen: Wolters-Noordhoff, 1971

Jong, Louis de, *Het Koninkrijk der Nederlanden in de Tweede Wereldoorlog*, The Hague: Nijhoff 1969–91: vols 2 and 7

Presser, Jacob, *Ashes in the Wind*, London: Souvenir Press, 1968; as *The Destruction of the Dutch Jews*, New York: Dutton, 1969

Vree, Frank van, *De Nederlandse Pers en Duitsland, 1930–1939: Een studie over de vorming van de publieke opinie*, Groningen: Historische Uitgeverij, 1989

Zee, Nanda van der, *Om erger te voorkomen: de voorbereiding en uitvoering van de vernietiging van het Nederlandse jodendom tijdens de Tweede Wereldoorlog*, Amsterdam: Meulenhoff, 1997

NEUTRALITY IN WAR

Wartime censorship in a democratic neutral country is heavily influenced by the nature of the neutrality involved. The contrasting cases of Ireland and Switzerland during World War II illustrate this well.

Switzerland was a traditional neutral which took seriously its defensive obligations. Ireland, on the other hand, was a new state whose neutrality was primarily rooted in pragmatism (Ireland had no imperialist interests under threat; it made sense to want to avoid the horrors of war; and neutrality was the policy that divided the people least in a state that had emerged from civil war only 16 years previously); it also had symbolic importance as an expression of sovereignty. Ireland failed to mount a defence effort remotely comparable to that of Switzerland (or that of the other successful European democratic neutral, Sweden) and relied on other strategies, as well as a large dose of good fortune, to ensure the survival of its status.

Ireland was lucky that it lay outside the path of the various advancing war machines, that the province of Northern Ireland gave the Allies a foothold on the island, and that British and American requirements at an operational level could be satisfied without provoking German retaliation. The benevolence of Irish policy towards the Allies went beyond the normal tendency of neutrals to be neutral for the power that threatened them most, as in the case of Switzerland and Germany. Indeed, the extent of the partiality has led to the conclusion that Ireland was not a neutral in the generally accepted sense of the term, but merely a non-belligerent.

This situation, however, could not be revealed to the Irish people and an image more fitting to prevailing popular expectations and the rhetoric of the ruling Fianna Fáil party was presented. The neutrality that came to dominate public perception was an illusion of strict impartiality, the crowning glory of independence, untainted by the hidden realities, particularly

the close links with the "old enemy", Britain. The Irish wartime censorship was a crucial player in this area. The Swiss had no need for such political conjury. Another difference between Irish and Swiss neutrality was the emotional dimension that became attached to the Irish policy and the sense of moral superiority that became a corollary of it. The Irish refused to allow the conflict to be placed in a moral framework and denied publicity to reports, such as those of the Holocaust, that revealed a variety of behaviour among the belligerents, for to have admitted a difference between them would have undermined the basis of Irish moral superiority and the "moral neutrality" that the Irish authorities believed was necessary.

For most of the war no Allied newspapers were sold in Switzerland and virtually all the external newspapers that circulated were German. In addition, Nazi propaganda papers were distributed freely, while Swiss newspapers were provided with material by the German Legation. British propaganda was carried in a legation bulletin and by the BBC. The Swiss situation thus resembled that in Ireland, with one side – in the Irish case, the Allies – being in a dominant position with regard to propaganda. The principal difference was that the Swiss had their own agencies and correspondents covering the war and were not reliant, as the Irish media were, on one particular side for an account and interpretation of events.

Both censorships were directed against internal disruption and subversion; the authorities were concerned to enhance the states' reliability and deter powers tempted to fish in troubled political waters. In Switzerland, communists and anarchists were the main target, while in Ireland the Irish Republican Army (IRA) was the main focus of censorial attention. Both states were also concerned with the maintenance of domestic morale and censorship was used to minimize publicity for matters that might undermine it.

While the Irish censorship set out to create "a truly neutral outlook among newspaper readers", by preventing or confining expressions of partiality, treating neutrality as sacrosanct, and prohibiting matter that was contrary to it, in Switzerland freedom of expression on the war, its participants, and the issues at stake was not regarded as being incompatible with neutrality; hence, what an Irish official described as "the shockingly pro and anti articles to be found in any Swiss paper". The Swiss authorities originally took a line – in direct contrast to the Irish – that the press should be discouraged from influencing the creation of a state of public opinion described as "neutralization"; one paper was actually punished for advocating a policy of press reticence on the war with the object of making the Swiss "neutral-minded". From early 1942 some measures were taken against partiality in the Swiss press and in August the existing provisions against internal disruption were extended to include persons who carried on propaganda for the abandonment of neutrality. Despite these new restrictions, however, the press was still free to express views about the war of a character and to an extent that was never tolerated in Ireland.

The decree of August 1942 was seen by the Irish authorities as demonstrating that the Swiss regarded pro-war propaganda as more harmful than anti-belligerent propaganda, and that mere unfriendliness towards a belligerent – in this case, Germany – on the part of a small group of Swiss newspapers entailed no risk of war, unless it actually created a body of opinion in favour of Switzerland going to war. The Irish censorship did not make such fine distinctions and saw the exclusion of belligerent propaganda as a precondition for the maintenance of "moral neutrality", the unity of the people behind the policy of neutrality, and the handicapping of efforts to create a condition of "warm-mindedness" among the population.

Film censorship was also applied with far less vigour in Switzerland. German features and newsreels dominated the market, but British and American war films were also shown. In Ireland, where British and American films enjoyed a virtual monopoly, war newsreels were excluded and most war films were mutilated or banned.

DONAL Ó DRISCEOIL

Further Reading

Ó Drisceoil, Donal, *Censorship in Ireland, 1939–1945: Neutrality, Politics, and Society*, Cork: Cork University Press, 1996

NEW-ENGLAND COURANT
Colonial American news-sheet, 1721–26

The publisher of this "vigorous little sheet", James Franklin (older brother to Benjamin) would take the first steps to "unshackl[e] . . . the American press from the licenser".

When the elder Franklin started the *New-England Courant*, there were already a number of newspapers in Boston, and the publishers of those papers had greater access to the news of the day from traditional news sources. To make his paper viable Franklin decided to make it lively and entertaining. He had an unofficial editorial board made up of liberal and educated Bostonians, and the content of the paper was highly literary and engaging. Franklin appealed to his readers with information they were interested in obtaining, told in a bold style. In fact, Benjamin Franklin, at the tender age of 16, wrote as "Silence Dogood" a series of excellent essays that imitated the styles in the London coffee-house papers the *Spectator* and the *Guardian*. The *Courant* was, as one writer put it, "a fresh breeze in the stale journalistic atmosphere in Boston".

Not everyone liked the *Courant's* spirited style. The *Boston News-Letter*, the second oldest newspaper in the colonies and the oldest Boston paper, described it as "full freighted with Nonsense, Unmannerliness, Railery, Prophaneness, Immorality, Arrogancy, Calumnies, Lyes, Contradictions, and what not, all tending to Quarrels and Divisions, and to Debauch and Corrupt the Minds and Manners of New England".

A rebel spirit was apparent in the *Courant* from the beginning as well. As one commentator put it, "The *Courant* was born out of anger and prospered in it". Franklin began to challenge the power and influence of the Puritan group, led by Increase Mather and his son, Cotton. Censorship was not only the province of governmental authorities; church doctrine and orthodoxy had a strong influence, too. The strong-willed Franklin chafed against the strict disciplinarian Mathers and the forceful Congregationalism that dominated the Massachusetts Bay colony.

Sadly, Franklin took issue with one of the few topics on which the Mathers were proved correct. This was smallpox inoculation. The Mathers had heard about blood from surviving smallpox victims being injected into uninfected individuals and encouraged a Boston doctor to try the technique. Zabdiel Boylston inoculated two of his sons and a slave, and the results were dramatic. But Franklin lambasted inoculation in the pages of the *Courant*, claiming that the practice was "doubtful and dangerous" and had derived from "the Greek old women". Inoculation thus became a political as well as medical subject. Other young Boston intellectuals signed on to write for the *Courant*.

Cotton Mather called the *Courant's* writers "the Hell-Fire Club" and insisted that "the practice of supporting and publishing every week a libel on purpose to lessen and blacken and burlesque the virtuous and principal ministers of religion in a country . . . is a wickedness that was never known before in any country, Christian, Turkish, or Pagan, on the face of the earth". Eventually, however, the Mathers won out: inoculation was successful, and the smallpox epidemic waned.

As the epidemic diminished, so did the *Courant's* interest. It continued to publish light news and witty letters from Bostonians. The Mathers, who with the magistrates of the Boston Council viewed Franklin as a troublemaker, continued to be watchful. One commentator notes that the fact that the *Courant* was not arbitrarily shut down showed how much freedom the press already had. Twenty years earlier there would have been no need to wait for an opportunity to suppress a printer, but the *Courant* was popular, and the magistrates were careful.

Then the elder Franklin ran afoul of the authorities. He printed a fictitious letter claiming that there were pirates off the coast of New England and accused the government of ineffectual defence against them. The Boston Council called James Franklin to appear in 1722. Franklin was defiant and rebellious, and the council found him in contempt and threw him into jail. He repented and was released, but within a few months he was back to his old tricks. After a few other attacks on the magistrates, the Boston Council issued a decree against Franklin: he was forbidden "to print or publish the *New-England Courant* or any other pamphlet or paper of the like nature, except it be first supervised by the secretary of the province". This was a return to licensing; the press was not yet completely free.

Courant followers and supporters were not about to let the paper cease publication. A scheme was concocted by which 17-year-old Benjamin Franklin would be the sole official publisher, but he would have to sign papers of apprenticeship to his elder brother in secret. James Franklin would appear to relinquish control. The paper took on a more light-hearted style, and indeed appeared to have toned down the political attacks.

But relations between the Franklins deteriorated. Open admiration from other *Courant* writers for Benjamin's writings as "Silence Dogood" irritated his elder brother. Benjamin saw

his opening in 1723: James could not pursue him for abandoning his apprenticeship without revealing that he was in fact publisher of the *Courant*. So Benjamin Franklin left for New York under cover of night and ended up eventually in Philadelphia, where in 1729 he began the *Pennsylvania Gazette*. James Franklin left the *Courant* three years later and moved his press to Rhode Island to start the first newspaper there, the *Rhode Island Gazette*.

The *Courant* was a lesson for the press and for dissidents who came later. They saw how a printer with courage and support could withstand governmental tyranny against its freedoms, as well as become a means of attacking authority. Should the printer even be jailed, the friends and supporters of the paper could continue its work anonymously, and "when a newspaper is aggressive and readable in serving the public cause, it will elicit support sufficient to protect it from powerful foes".

GENELLE I. BELMAS

Further Reading

Emery, Michael *et al.*, *The Press and America: An Interpretive History of the Mass Media*, 9th edition, Boston: Allyn and Bacon, 2000

Ford, Edwin H. and Edwin Emery (editors), *Highlights in the History of the American Press: A Book of Readings*, Minneapolis: University of Minnesota Press, 1954

Smith, Jeffery A., *Printers and Press Freedom: The Ideology of Early American Journalism*, New York: Oxford University Press, 1988

Tebbel, John, *The Compact History of the American Newspaper*, 2nd edition, New York: Hawthorn, 1969

NEW STRAITS TIMES
Malaysian newspaper, established 1845

Hailed as one of Asia's longest-lived daily newspapers, the *New Straits Times* has had its share of censorship and other restrictive measures. Founded in Singapore on 15 July 1845 as *The Straits Times and Singapore Journal of Commerce*, the newspaper has survived British colonialism, Japanese occupation, the splitting-up of Malaysia and Singapore, and internecine politics. It was not, however, the first newspaper in what is now Malaysia; that honour belongs to *The Government Gazette* of Penang, established in 1806.

Early newspapers of the three colonies that eventually made up Malaysia – Malacca, Penang, and Singapore – suffered restrictions from the colonial authorities, but by the time *The Straits Times* came along, censorship had been lifted, although it was reapplied for a year in 1857.

The Straits Times was originally financed by Martemus T. Apcar and edited by lawyer Robert Carr Woods, described as a "pompous, self-important and frivolous writer" who thought so highly of his sense of humour that he underlined his printed puns. Woods promised to uphold "the integrity of national institutions, laying bare to the eye whatever abuses spring up or exist . . . and by faithful advocacy of public rights secure to

the governed protection against the innovation or misrule of the governing". The paper was criticized frequently during its first decades, either because it took its role as critic of government too seriously, or because it practised irresponsible journalism. In 1849, *The Straits Times* was said to err so often that a volume of "*Straits Times* Obituaries" could be compiled of all living people embalmed in its pages during their lifetimes. Another complaint was that slanted and misleading articles were giving false impressions in Europe where they were copied by London papers.

The paper was sold to Wynter and Company in 1860, and the following year John Cameron, an unsuccessful mariner who had lost his last two ships, became editor. Cameron put *The Straits Times* in an unassailable position until a fire in 1869 forced him into bankruptcy. The remains of the paper fetched $40 at public auction, but it carried on nevertheless, not missing an edition. By 1900, at a second auction, ten partners subscribed $10,000 each to form a private company.

Editorial policy and content remained most important to *The Straits Times* and other newspapers of the colony until the 1930s, when big business practices seriously began to erode those of journalism. To attract more Malayan readers, *The Straits Times* purchased both the *Penang Gazette* and *The Times of Malaya*, the mouthpiece of British mining interests in Ipoh, transferred to Penang soon after. But these manoeuvres were not financially rewarding and the two papers were sold in 1939.

When the Japanese took control of all mass media in February 1942, *The Straits Times* was converted into a propaganda organ, *Syonan Shimbun*, that resounded with the themes of a new Malai, attacks on Anglo-Americanism, and calls for an Asia for Asiatics. Although it had been forbidden by the British Military Administration, which wanted its own paper to be the chief English-language periodical in the first six months of liberation, *The Straits Times* resumed under its old name, as a single sheet, on 7 September 1945.

The paper circulated freely in both Malaya and Singapore, but when the two states split in 1965, the Malaysian authorities decreed that Singapore newspapers circulating on the mainland had to obtain a special permit and be free of anti-Malaysian material. *The Straits Times* was in a favourable situation as it maintained separate editorial and production offices in both countries, a result of its 1952 purchase of the *Malay Mail*, located in Kuala Lumpur. From the *Mail* office, the company initiated Malayan editions of *The Straits Times* in June 1956 and of *Berita Harian* in 1957. In addition, the paper broadened its publishing interests, so that by 1958 *The Straits Times* in Singapore published its daily and Sunday editions and eight other periodicals, as well as *The Straits Times*, *Malay Mail*, and *Berita Harian* in Kuala Lumpur. It also owned Federal Publications, a textbook publisher.

After the stringent restrictions placed on Malaysian life in 1969–70, particularly the call for local ownership of newspapers, *The Straits Times* was renamed *New Straits Times*, and 80 per cent of its ownership was placed in the hands of a government body, Pernas. This meant that in effect, the New Straits Times Press newspapers were controlled by the ruling party, United Malays National Organisation (UMNO).

New Straits Times Press has been strongly linked to UMNO-based conglomerates ever since. In late 1983, the press group underwent a major management reshuffle that resulted in a number of politically motivated appointments. The changes occurred after Fleet Holdings (an UMNO firm) and its arm, Fleet Group, which owned 55.9 per cent of New Straits Times Press, were placed under the chairmanship of member of parliament Daim Zainuddin, then a close ally of prime minister Mahathir and chair of important state-owned banking and investment corporations. In the restructure the New Straits Times Press board was reconstituted, loaded with friends of the government. Although Mahathir claimed these moves were intended to improve efficiency, critics believed the changes

were aimed at securing appointments more sympathetic to the prime minister at the paper's helm and at strengthening the role of Daim. In early 1984, the Fleet Group increased its holdings in the New Straits Times Press, when the 20 per cent held by Singapore's *Straits Times* was sold. Since then, another conglomerate closely aligned to UMNO has taken over the press group.

Because the *New Straits Times* has been owned and controlled by elements of the ruling National Front government, its coverage has been lopsidedly pro-government. Surveys have shown the bias of the *New Straits Times* in a number of ways: it devotes a high percentage of its content to information favourable to the government and national development; carries four times as much content supporting the national coalition rather than the opposition during elections and obscures election issues; distorts reports of demonstrations to avoid mentioning peasant demands and to promote fear about demonstrations; legitimizes those in power, determines who can speak and which views are credible; promotes a male, adult world, ignoring the political views of women and youth; represents anti-working-class opinions, emphasizes urban life in a society that is 70 per cent rural; and portrays the world from a capitalist perspective.

Linked by ownership to more than 100 other companies, the New Straits Times Press practises strict self-censorship on business and financial matters, as well as those of a political and governmental nature. Furthermore, since the newspaper has much influence in the journalistic community, it has set the standard for other media on how stories are to be covered or buried, which individuals are in favour, and the "correct" editorial stance on all major issues.

JOHN A. LENT

Further Reading

Buckley, Charles Burton, *An Anecdotal History of Old Times in Singapore*, Singapore: Fraser and Neave, 1902; reprinted Singapore and New York: Oxford University Press, 1984

Byrd, Cecil K., *Early Printing in the Straits Settlements, 1806–1858*, Singapore: Singapore National Library, 1970

English, John W., "Malaysia: Chilling Press Freedom", *IPI Report* (August 1982): 5

Kennard, Allington, "1845 to 1970: We're 125 Today", *Straits Times* (Malaysia), 15 July 1970

Lent, John A., *Malaysian Mass Media: Historical and Contemporary Perspectives*, Amherst: Council on International Studies, State University of New York at Buffalo, 1978

Lent, John A., "Restructuring of Mass Media in Malaysia and Singapore: Pounding in the Coffin Nails?", *Bulletin of Concerned Asian Scholars* (October–December 1984): 26–35

Seow, Alex, "*New Straits Times*: The News Machine", *Fijar* (October 1980): 10–14

NEW YORK SOCIETY FOR THE SUPPRESSION OF VICE
US moral crusaders, 1873–1939

Industrialists, Protestant professionals, businessmen, and financiers of the upper and upper-middle classes funded the New York Society for the Suppression of Vice on 16 May 1873. Many of them, such as Morris Jessup, William E. Dodge, David Dows, and J.P. Morgan, were founders and trustees of the Young Men's Christian Association (YMCA). Concerned ever since the 1860s about working men's access to obscene literature and images, these men had successfully passed an anti-obscenity law in New York state in 1868. Inspired to work for similar federal laws, the YMCA's Society for the Suppression of Vice funded shop-clerk Anthony Comstock's successful lobbying campaign in the US Congress to pass a national bill outlawing the distribution of "obscenity" through the US mails. Comstock was made an agent of the US Post Office in order to help enforce the new regulations.

The primary activity of the New York Society for the Suppression of Vice was reporting "obscene" materials to legal authorities – including postal inspector Comstock himself – for search and seizure. Early on, the society was involved in a number of notorious arrests, lawsuits, and impoundments. The YMCA officially disassociated itself from Comstock's anti-obscenity organization in 1874 because of the sensational publicity he was receiving. By this point, however, the new vice society was able to thrive independently from an open affiliation with the YMCA. In 1878, men as wealthy and respected as those who had founded the New York Society, including church leaders and presidents of prestigious universities and colleges, founded in Boston the New England Society for the Suppression of Vice (after 1890, the Watch and Ward Society). This organization worked in tandem with Comstock's group to make vice societies an important force in cultural regulation and censorship.

At the turn of the century, when censorship regulations went largely unchallenged by judges and lawmakers, neither a single man nor a group of elites could simply impose censorship upon a majority of Americans. The New York Society for the Suppression of Vice relied upon a broad network of reformers to enforce extant laws by informing it of any legally repressible materials as well as by lobbying for stricter censorship regulations. Vice societies collaborated with middle-class organizations and women's groups that promoted censorship. From the 1880s through to the 1930s, the vice societies had similar censorship goals to the Woman's Christian Temperance Union (which had a Department for the Promotion of Purity in Literature and Art), the Young Men's Christian Association, the Christian Endeavor, the Protestant churches, the Catholic church, the League of American Mothers, the National Congress of Mothers, the American Literary Railway Union, the Society for the Prevention of Cruelty to Children, the General Federation of Women's Clubs, the National Association of Colored Women, and the International Reform Bureau. Each organization favoured the enforcement and often expansion of censorship laws.

Able to reduce distribution of pornography through the mails relatively quickly, the New York Society for the Suppression of Vice turned its attention to advertisements that catered (however ineffectively) to the needs of those men and women engaging in sexual intercourse, by discreetly offering everything from cures for venereal diseases to birth control devices and abortifacients. As pornographic materials were effectively confiscated and then abortion advertisers and providers were arrested and driven further underground, the society directed more of its attention to campaigns against other "impurities", including gambling at slot machines or through lotteries.

During the 1880s and early 1890s, furthermore, activity against cheap crime story papers and dime novels was at its height. The society typically sent word to other reform organizations, informing them that in addition to the national obscenity laws, there were often state or local laws covering the sale or exhibition of the papers. The vice societies, in league with women's reform groups and some mainstream newspapers, then attempted to have the crime story papers removed from the stands of newsdealers.

In its public campaigns, vice society leaders highlighted the ways that "sensational" literature negatively influenced youths. They focused rhetorically on the masturbating boy. Youths who read "sensational" stories, they argued, were sure to become addicted to the "solitary vice" of masturbation. Metaphors of disease appear in almost every vice society discussion of "impure" literature; indeed, moral reformers exploited medical knowledge about the germ theory and the spread of disease to impress upon their audiences the dangers of impurity in literature. Not only the mind and subsequent behaviour, but the physical body too, would be damaged by "impure" reading.

As the leader of the New York Society for the Suppression of Vice, Comstock held to a basic central argument: "Without morals no public order". A guest speaker at the conventions of a variety of other reform organizations, he warned of the evils of "sensational" literature – even crime reports in the daily papers. "Evil thoughts are an introduction to every debasing practice", he claimed. This assertion put "immoral" literature in the forefront as the "great crime breeder", thereby ensuring the necessity of pro-censorship campaigns (NYSSV, *Annual Reports*). Effectively mobilizing around these concerns, the New York Society for the Suppression of Vice for over 40 years facilitated the suppression of "impure" literature as well as the arrest and prosecution of free-love advocates, abortion providers, printers of cheap pornography, and those who advertised birth control devices or wrote sex education manuals. In 1924, Comstock's successor, John S. Sumner, reported that the society had "confiscated an average of 65,000 obscene pictures per annum".

ALISON M. PARKER

Further Reading

Beisel, Nicola, *Imperiled Innocents: Anthony Comstock and Family Reproduction in Victorian America*, Princeton, New Jersey: Princeton University Press, 1997

Bennett, D.M., *Anthony Comstock: His Career of Cruelty and Crime*, New York: Bennett, 1878; reprinted New York: Da Capo Press, 1971

Boyer, Paul, *Purity in Print: The Vice-Society Movement and Book Censorship in America*, New York: Scribner, 1968

Broun, Heywood and Margaret Leech, *Anthony Comstock: Roundsman of the Lord*, New York: Boni, 1927; London: Wishart, 1928

D'Emilio, John and Estelle B. Freedman, *Intimate Matters: A History of Sexuality in America*, New York: Harper and Row, 1988

Friedman, Andrea, *Prurient Interests: Gender, Democracy, and Obscenity in New York City, 1909–1945*, New York: Columbia University Press, 2000

Haney, Robert W., *Comstockery in America: Patterns of Censorship and Control*, Boston: Beacon Press, 1960

Kilpatrick, James Jackson, *The Smut Peddlers*, New York: Doubleday, 1960

MacMillan, P.R., *Censorship and Public Morality*, Aldershot, Hampshire: Gower, 1983

Parker, Alison M., *Purifying America: Women, Cultural Reform, and Pro-Censorship Activism, 1873–1933*, Urbana: University of Illinois Press, 1997

Paul, James C.N. and Murray L. Schwartz, *Federal Censorship: Obscenity in the Mail*, New York: Free Press, 1961

Pivar, David J., *Purity Crusade: Sexual Morality and Social Control, 1868–1900*, Westport, Connecticut: Greenwood Press, 1973

Trumbull, Charles Gallandet, *Anthony Comstock, Fighter: Some Impressions of a Lifetime Adventure in Conflict with the Powers of Evil*, New York: Revell, 1913

NEW ZEALAND

Population: 3,778,000
Main religions: Anglican; Presbyterian; Roman Catholic; Methodist; Baptist
Official language: English
Other languages spoken: Maori

Number of daily newspapers: 23
Number of radio receivers per 1000 inhabitants: 997
Number of TV receivers per 1000 inhabitants: 512
Number of PCs per 1000 inhabitants: 282.1

According to the settlement story of the Maori, the indigenous people (*tangata whenua*) of New Zealand (Aotearoa), they first began to arrive in canoes from the north about 1000 years ago. Europeans first came ashore with Abel Tasman in 1642, but a full exploration of the coast did not take place until the late 18th century, when the British explorer captain James Cook made three voyages during which he drafted coastal survey maps of the three main islands that make up the country. Sporadic settlement took place almost immediately, largely by whale and seal hunters, followed closely by Christian missionaries.

In 1840, the founding treaty between the British and the Maori was signed at Waitangi, and European migration began apace. The New Zealand Company attempted to attract a cross-section of British society, but in the main the migrants dispatched were artisans, small farmers, and labourers. Only the Canterbury settlement, centred on Christchurch, attracted numbers of the "gentry", who set up large farms ("runs") based on rearing sheep for wool. This particular settlement was closely tied to the Anglican Church and a large cathedral was built as a first priority. Further South, Dunedin was peopled by large numbers of settlers with Scottish ancestry; here the Presbyterian Church was prevalent. In the far North, the area where the Europeans first settled, the Anglican Church Missionary Society and the Catholic Church were each strongly represented. The missionaries attempted to introduce a veneer of Christian "respectability" over Maori customs. For example, they bowdlerized many of the post carvings that marked the frontages of the *marae* meeting houses, removing the penises that were prominent features, and, as throughout the rest of the Pacific, they made women wear enveloping clothes. The most radical censorship of Maori culture, however, was the "censorship" of land, discussed in a separate entry below.

At first administered from New South Wales in Australia, New Zealand became a self-governing crown colony in 1852. It was granted dominion status within the British Empire in 1907 and full autonomy in 1931, although this was not fully accepted until 1947. A few substantial landowners from Hawkes Bay and Canterbury Province dominated politics in the early years, when voting was based on property qualifications, but by the end of the 19th century government was becoming increasingly democratic, with universal male suffrage being introduced in 1879, and women being given the vote in national elections earlier than in any other country in the world, in 1893. The Maori were dispossessed of their land, but not disenfranchised politically, although their population declined through ill health and impoverishment.

Historically, censorship has been mostly underpinned by Protestant, lower-middle class mores, with women as influential players in legislation affecting values. The Presbyterian Church had most members until 1938, but the Catholic Church, comprising around 15 per cent of the population, has also had an impact, subjecting its members to directions on reading and viewing, and actively opposing the dissemination of information on contraception and abortion. Only in recent years have modern technology and contact with the rest of the world helped some New Zealanders to challenge a mostly puritanical ethos, and even then moral liberalism has been regularly challenged. The swing of the pendulum has a relatively short range and swift movement in New Zealand.

The press and literature

Newpapers arrived with the first settlers, starting with the publication from 1840 of the *New Zealand Gazette and Wellington Advertiser*, and the *New Zealand Advertiser and Bay of Islands Gazette*. Almost immediately, they were in trouble with the authorities. The lieutenant-governor, William Hobson, needed them to publicize his decrees, but the editors of both papers considered that they had an equal responsibility to discuss local controversies, such as what was generally regarded as the tortuous process demanded before the purchase of Maori land was recognized and a government grant was released. Hobson was notoriously sensitive to criticism, and, after a mere 27 issues, the editor of the *Advertiser*, the Reverend Barzillas Quaife, was summoned to the Colonial Secretary in New South Wales to explain himself. The draconian regulations of a previous New South Wales governor, Ralph Darling, issued in the mid-1820s but much criticized on legal grounds, were revived and applied to New Zealand. The newspapers had now to obtain a governor's licence to print; two sureties of £300 each had to be deposited with the Supreme Court, which would be forfeited if the newspapers were felt to have gone too far. The *Spectator* regarded the new regulations as "arbitrary, oppressive, and inapplicable to the state of society in this colony".

This did not stop the publication of further newspapers, one of which, the *New Zealand Herald and Auckland Gazette*, founded in 1841, tackled the problem of government interference head on (in an editorial, 10 July 1841):

> We feel extremely anxious that no erroneous impression should prevail in consequence of the *Government Gazette* being published weekly from our press. It may consequently be imagined that this journal has been established under its auspices. We beg, most unqualifiedly, to deny such an imputation ... this journal will be conducted entirely upon independent principle.

The *Gazette* sought immediately to put its principles into action, complaining on 31 July about "the extraordinarily high price" of an allotment, which could militate against "the rapid and ultimate prosperity of this colony". This was too much for the newspaper trustees, who gave the editor, William Cobbett, three months notice.

Cobbett's successor, Samuel Morton demanded some assurance that he would have full control of the newspaper, but in February 1842 the trustees prevented the printers from inserting the following editorial comment:

> Dr Morton cannot view the circumstances in any other light than as an attempt, on the part of some persons connected with the government, to suppress the expression of public opinion through the press.

With little further delay, Morton was dismissed and the *Gazette* was closed down. The government now took the extraordinary expedient of setting up their own newspaper, the *Auckland Standard*, under the editorship of William Swainson, the Attorney General. However, while it could now rely on subservience, it could not compel people to read what was generally regarded as a dull publication.

Samuel Morton, having sued for the balance of his contract, used the money to establish the *Southern Cross*, printed on his own premises. Henry Falwasser, editor of the *Auckland Times*, was allowed to use government presses for only nine issues, that is, only until the publication of an advertisement headed "New Zealand in 1842; or the Effects of a Bad Government on a Good Country". Undeterred, Falswasser printed his paper by means of a mangle, until he obtained access to a suitable press in Sydney, Australia, from which he published 159 issues of the *Times*.

The proliferation of New Zealand newspapers indicated that the government was fighting a losing battle. Over the next decade, independence from Australia and freedom of expression were achieved, at the same time as the territory began to be governed from a local base. The *New Zealander* editorialized in October 1853 on "the advantage of Her Majesty's subjects in these islands that there should be occasional excesses on the part [of] the Press, rather than continual restraint", not least in a situation in which, as yet, "freeborn men" had "no direct voice in the government of the country".

The free press partly arose from a general lack of regulation in early colonial New Zealand. Paul Christoffel has observed that there was only limited censorship legislation, that it was based on the example of Britain and the Australian colonies, but that "it was generally passed years, or even decades later". This was due, in part, to the fact that settlements were in separated clusters, and dominated, not by legislation, but by ideas of respectability held by the middle classes and colonial gentry.

In 1858, however, more direct censorship began to be imposed when new customs regulations banned the importation of indecent material, and were supported by local measures taken by several provincial councils. A provision of the Vagrant Act of 1866 made it a criminal offence "wilfully to expose to view" in public "any obscene book, print, picture, drawing or representation". However, it was not until 1890 that any prosecution took place. Five booksellers were arrested for selling the works of Émile Zola, which had already fallen foul of the authorities in several European countries, and in Australia. In New Zealand, despite the fact that one of the novels seized had not been translated from the French, all five men were convicted.

Suddenly, there was a plethora of legislation, the most important measures being the Offensive Publications Act of 1892, the Police Offences Act of 1908, the Indecent Publications Act of 1910, and the Customs Act of 1913. Paul Christoffel attributes this flurry to the "greater availability of pornography and erotica, accompanied by the growth of socially conservative movements, and a more interventionist style of government". Among the popular publications prosecuted were the "penny dreadfuls", short, illustrated novels, with garish covers, presented on cheap newsprint. In 1901, the *New Zealand Observer* speculated that some of these might be a major cause of juvenile crime:

> the thrilling deeds of *Revolver Dick* or *Jim, the Slayer of the Prairies*, as related in the picturesque and dramatic language of the penny dreadful, are calculated to fire the blood and stimulate the adventurous ambition of the youthful mind to an extraordinary degree. And this class of literature has a marvellous sale in the colonies.

Caught up in the push for censorship were publications that today might be lauded for promoting safe sex. Indeed, the Offensive Publications Act of 1892, which was the first law passed in New Zealand solely for censorship purposes, specifically prohibited "any picture or printed or written matter which is of an indecent, immoral or obscene nature", including

> any advertisement or other publication relating to any venereal or contagious disease affecting the generative organs or functions, or having reference to any nervous disability, or other complaint or disability arising from or relating to sexual intercourse.

Despite the fact that venereal diseases were creating a major health problem, Ettie Rout's *Safe Marriage*, published in 1922, was banned.

Comics, considered to have negative influences, particularly on children, became available in New Zealand from the 1930s onwards. Concern about their content reached a peak in the early 1950s, with numerous complaints from a wide range of community groups, public meetings, and investigations by government committees. Like the penny dreadfuls before them, comics were said to contribute to juvenile delinquency. Even the *Lone Ranger* series of comics was banned because of the prominence of pistols in the pictures and because the hero always wore a mask, a practice that was an offence under New Zealand law. The Indecent Publications Amendment Act of 1954 insisted that the distributors of printed matter be registered. From 1956 until 1963, a Comics Advisory Committee exercised informal censorship.

The Indecent Publications Act of 1963 established the Indecent Publications Tribunal, an institution unique in the English-speaking world that, until the end of the 1980s, was regarded by some liberals as a model of how these matters might be publicly discussed and decided upon. "Indecency" was defined as "describing, depicting, expressing, or otherwise dealing with matters of sex, horror, crime, cruelty, or violence in a manner that is injurious to the public good". Publishers, police, or customs officers could bring such a publication before the tribunal, which met in public, took evidence from experts, and considered representations by authors and readers alike. The tribunal was required to consider not only the dominant effect of the work as a whole, but also its literary or artistic merit, or otherwise, and whether it displayed an "honest purpose"; it had also to consider those whom the work was aimed at, their ages and backgrounds, and whether they were likely to be corrupted. The Act stated unequivocally: "Where the publication of any book . . . would be in the interest of art, literature, science or learning and would be for the public good, the tribunal shall not classify it as indecent". Such was considered the case with *The Little Red Schoolbook* (1972), much censored elsewhere but regarded by the New Zealand tribunal as containing useful advice on sexual matters for young people. Publications were sometimes restricted by age, and it became a criminal offence to sell them to people under 18.

A whole genre of comics went "underground" during the 1960s and were no longer available in traditional outlets, such as dairies or stationery shops. Comics aimed at students, and dealing with such themes as free speech, recreational drug-taking, uninhibited sex, and opposition to war, especially the Vietnam War, could sometimes be found in university bookshops. Their popularity waned towards the end of the 1970s, when they were replaced by the more sophisticated "alternative" comics, the most elegant of which came from Europe and were often known as "graphic novels". Violence and sexuality were treated as graphically as in novels, but with the added impact of pictorial depiction. A third period of concern with the effect of publications on young people now began. Although alternative comics were often encased in hard covers, were purchased by adults rather than children, and were offered for sale in specialized comic shops, they fell foul of the Indecent Publications Act, which stated that:

When the Tribunal decides that any picture-story book likely to be read by children is indecent in the hands of children under a specified age, that picture-story book shall be deemed to be indecent in the hands of all persons.

In November 1990, a series of "adult comics" came before the tribunal, having been seized by customs officials on their way to bookshops. Expert witnesses on one side argued that children chose not to buy such comics; they were loyal to particular genres rather than eclectic readers of all that was available. On the other hand, Patricia Bartlett of the Society for the Protection of Community Standards held that, if children came across such a comic by chance, they would be drawn to it because it "looked familiar" and would thus be exposed to sexually explicit material that was originally not intended for them. The tribunal agreed with the second point of view, but in his summing up, the chairman, Judge Cartwright, pointed to a fundamental dilemma:

It is not easy to consign works intended for adults, which are not injurious, and which, in many cases, have artistic, literary or social merit, to the banned pile simply because they are likely to be read by children and indecent in children's hands.

In the Films, Video and Publication Classification Act of 1993 (discussed below), no such distinction was made. Adult comics now face the same constraints as are applied to other media.

Films and videos

Films were introduced to New Zealand on 13 October 1896, at the Auckland Opera House. By 1917, Auckland alone had 17 film theatres. Film censorship arose from concerns similar to those being expressed in the United States, Britain, and Australia, chiefly fears about increased crime and declining moral standards, especially among young, working-class people. National legislative and institutional responses were also similar. It was usually the same films that generated controversy in each country. With New Zealand often being the last in this group of countries to receive particular titles, the country's censors were able to take into account the treatment already accorded to them abroad.

One of the first calls for censorship came in 1909, when the National Council of Churches asked the government to ban the showing of the world heavyweight boxing championship match between Tommy Burns and Jack Johnson. Prime Minister Ward, a boxing fan himself, declined to do so. In 1910, however, there were calls to ban a film of another Johnson fight, supported by the editor of the *New Zealand Observer*, who argued that it would be "an unnecessary agitation"; while "it would probably be injurious to the small boy inhabitant of the community, who is generally panting for gore and plenty of it . . . in the case of adults it is a different matter". This comment foreshadowed what was to become the central legislative justification for film censorship: that it was necessary in cases where the film content could be "injurious to the public good". The editorial also reflected the view, cited in discussions of the censorship of magazines and comics, that censorship was required in the best interests of children, who, as the Royal Commission of Education complained in 1912, were being allowed to "loiter about in the streets at night, or gather in the neighbourhoods of theatre picture shows at hours when they should be at home in their beds".

The official response to such concerns was, as elsewhere, regulation of the cinemas, regulation of their patrons, and regulation of the films. The Cinematograph Film Censorship Act (1916) provided for the appointment of a national film censor, with the power to reject films considered to be unfit for public viewing. The guidelines were extremely general: no film was to be approved that, in the censor's opinion, depicted "any matter that is against public order and decency, or the exhibition of which for any other reason is, in the opinion of the censor, undesirable in the public interest". Although this wording gave the censor sweeping discretionary powers, film distributors could appeal against his decision to a three-person board of review appointed by the Minister of Internal Affairs. The Minister said in Parliament that the censor was to be:

the clean average man – the man who knows what things are clean, and who . . . realizes that he is not put there for the purpose of destroying the capital of those who are importing the films, but for the purpose of protecting the public mind, especially children, against things that may do harm.

William Jolliffe was appointed to be the first censor.

Jolliffe faced his first major controversy soon after taking office, when church groups protested against his passing of D.W. Griffith's *Intolerance* (1916), which has scenes showing bare breasts and industrial unrest, as well as depictions of Jesus. Jolliffe resisted the pressure and refused to adopt a list of unacceptable subjects, as was suggested by his political masters. Robin Kay and Dallas Moore observed that: "It became a tradition of New Zealand film censorship to avoid any enunciation of strict principles (which could be applied in all cases), but to judge all sequences in the context of the whole film" (unpublished paper for Department of Internal Affairs, 1969). This approach, which foreshadowed the later treatment of literature, was in contrast to the procedure in Britain and the United States, where the censor's counterparts were guided by restrictive "shopping lists". Equally progressive for its time, after many had advocated the appointment of a woman censor, who would, it was argued, be more in tune with the values of the community, two women, one of them a prominent feminist, Mrs A. Atkinson, were appointed to the board of review.

Jolliffe died in 1917 and was succeeded by his assistant, W.H. Tanner. "Talkies" had arrived and, under the Cinematograph Films Act of 1918, the censor could take into account any sound track or accompanying sound recordings. At the same time, however, the censor was made a public servant, more directly under the authority of the Minister of Internal Affairs and less able than Jolliffe had been to take a strong independent line.

Anticommunism made its mark on censorship in New Zealand, as it did elsewhere. Sergei Eisenstein's depiction of a successful revolt against authority, *The Battleship Potemkin* (1925) was not allowed to be released; it was not granted a certificate until 1946, and even then could only be shown to film societies. However, there was strong criticism of Tanner's apparent political bias. His dismissals of *Turk Sib* (1929), one

of a group of films featuring the transformation of the Soviet Union, and of *Road to Life* (1932), a Soviet documentary about homeless children, were both taken to the Board of Appeal, which rejected his decision on the first but upheld his ban on the second.

Lewis Milestone's film *All Quiet on the Western Front* (1930) was the subject of a major controversy over film censorship in New Zealand. Tanner's office rejected it as antiwar propaganda, and his decision was upheld by the Board of Appeal. The issue was debated in Parliament and discussed in a number of press editorials, with most being in favour of the film being exhibited. The promoters, Universal Film Manufacturing Co. (Australia) Ltd., organized a private screening and invited several parliamentarians to attend. A "reconstructed" version of the film, effectively the same film with several scenes cut out, was then submitted, thus constituting a "new" film for the purposes of the Act. Tanner again rejected the film, but this time, the Board of Appeal passed it.

Love on the Dole had been rejected at script stage by the British film authorities in 1936, but was passed in 1941. In New Zealand, it was rejected in 1942 because it was said to set out

to show that immorality is justifiable under stress of economic pressure and that honesty in certain circumstances is not the best policy. Marriage is held up to ridicule and disparaged, and the heroine's lapse from virtue is apparently condoned by her mother.

Clearly, the influence of the churches was still strong in New Zealand.

Following World War II, most films with which the censor had to deal addressed "adult themes". Concern with the effects of films on young people continued, particularly during the 1950s, when "juvenile delinquency" again emerged as an international phenomenon. However, the orientation of films now began to shift away from "family entertainment" to subjects for more adult audiences. Film censorship became focused on the refinement of classification systems, tackling the question of the nature and desirability of content restrictions. Gordon Mirams, chief film censor from 1949 until 1958, had been a writer and film critic. He argued for tolerance of "art films" and had sympathy for products that could be described as part of "high culture". He passed many of the European classics that came before him. Adolescent audiences, meanwhile, preferred films that portrayed youngsters as rebels, engaged in behaviour that often offended adults. Certain of what David Considine described as "juvenile delinquency films" became *causes célèbres* of the genre. Laslo Benedek's *The Wild One* (1954) was banned in New Zealand; Nicholas Ray's *Rebel without a Cause* (1955) was restricted to those over 16; and Fred Sears's *Rock around the Clock* (1956) was passed, reluctantly.

Under Doug McIntosh, chief censor from 1960 until 1976, it was decided that Joseph Strick's adaptation of James Joyce's *Ulysses* (1967) could be shown only to segregated adult audiences, but the main criticisms levelled at McIntosh were that he frequently cut films instead of giving them the restrictive certificates that had been pioneered by Mirams, and that he had sought to ban Bernardo Bertolucci's *Last Tango in Paris*, which was eventually passed by Bernie Tunnicliffe, his successor, in

1977. These and other practices eventually caused a public outcry against strict film censorship, which led to the introduction of the Cinematograph Films Act of 1976, under which Tunnicliffe was able to operate. The discretionary clause that had allowed the censor to rule on films on the basis of "his opinion" was removed and films were to be cut or banned only if they were "injurious to the public good".

Alan Highet, Minister of Internal Affairs from 1976 to 1984, commissioned a public opinion poll in 1980, the results of which demonstrated that the general populace of New Zealand was actually very liberal in its approach, preferring classification to censorship. Thus, Section 13 (2) of the Films Act of 1983 specified that "in determining whether the exhibition of any film is likely to be injurious to the public good, the Chief Censor shall consider . . . the dominant effect of the film as a whole". Working under this act, Arthur Everard decided to rely on "expert" advice that some harm was likely to be suffered as a result of viewing a film before he would cut or ban it. It proved extremely difficult to determine whether injury had actually occurred, with the result that on the basis of psychological opinions, he passed for public viewing films with explicit sexual content that would have been described by Linda Williams as "hardcore"; authorities such as Edward Donnerstein and Varda Burstyn had asserted that no harm would come from watching adult couples engaged in nonviolent consensual sex. A coalition of feminists and fundamentalist Christians believed that Everard, by following these authorities, had "opened the floodgates to pornography". By promoting an amendment that limited the tenure of censors to three years, they were able to have him and his deputy, Anthony Hill, removed in 1990. Everard was replaced by New Zealand's first female chief film censor, Jane Wrightson. She continued to operate under the same act, although by this point almost all sex films on video were being sent to the video censor.

The call for video censorship emerged later in New Zealand than in some other countries, because video players were originally subject to heavy taxation and only the rich, who seldom subject themselves to censorship, could buy them. When tariffs were reduced and ownership spread through all social classes (27 per cent of New Zealanders had access to the technology by March 1987), concern began to grow. At first customs officers intercepted videos that they regarded as pornographic and pursued prosecutions through the local courts when they considered them warranted, but court judgements were not uniform: what was passed in one jurisdiction might be banned in another. Importers began to send tapes to the film censor in order to obtain expert opinions on whether they were likely to be "injurious to the public good". If he passed them, it was less likely that customs officers would seize them. With Arthur Everard of the opinion that the depiction of consensual sex had not been shown to be injurious, the way was open for "hardcore" pornographic tapes to be imported and sold openly.

After complaints from the Society for the Protection of Community Standards in 1984, police had seized 30 copies of *Electric Blue* from video shops, but by 1987 such tapes were to be seen on stands labelled "adult", bearing fluorescent vermilion stickers saying "R18: Explicit Sexual Content May Offend". The printed covers on the boxes often carried images that would probably have been banned if they had been presented to the Indecent Publications Tribunal. A strong lobby group, Women Against Pornography, took particular exception to such videos being publicly available and worked with other interest groups to get the controls tightened. This happened, but only to a limited extent, when the Video Recordings Authority was established at the end of 1987. The decision-makers were now largely women. Pornographic tapes could still be passed for viewing, but the decision was based on whether or not they were "indecent", rather than "injurious". So far as the depiction of rape was concerned, Lois Hogg, a temporary video censor in 1988, reported: "It is when a video is seen to use this factor to titillate viewers, to suggest that women ultimately enjoy or deserve this treatment, that the video is banned, or, more likely, a portion is subject to cutting".

The most interesting development was that the industry was now charged with evaluating its own products. Anything that was not controversial was to be given a sticker by the "labelling authority", intended to indicate the minimum age of the audience for which it had been judged suitable. The censors had to see only those tapes that had been rated overseas as only suitable for adults.

In 1987, Joanne Morris, a law lecturer, was invited by the Labour government to chair a committee of enquiry into pornography. Its main recommendation was that there should be a single body to censor films, videos, and publications, including audio recordings, computer software, and CD-Roms. This was established under the Films, Video and Literature Classification Act, 1993, which now governs what may be seen, read, and heard, apart from broadcast media, in New Zealand. The act continues to insist on the prohibition of material "injurious to the public good", but goes on to say that this can be a matter for the expert opinion of the censor himself or herself. For the first time, the act lists specific behaviours that are considered "objectionable" and therefore proscribed. These include:

> the exploitation of children; the use of violence or coercion to compel any person to participate in . . . sexual conduct; sexual conduct with, or upon the body of a dead person; the use of urine or excrement in association with degrading or dehumanizing conduct . . . bestiality or acts of torture or the infliction of extreme violence.

Attacked by liberals as a "shopping list" of offences, it was insisted upon by conservatives who wished to constrain the powers of the censor to operate in a subjective manner. In practice this has resulted in the banning of sex videos which commonly include urination and which had been passed by Arthur Everard as not "injurious", but otherwise it is pretty much "business as usual". The act prohibits nothing on political grounds and appears to be more in favour of classification than censorship. Pier Paolo Pasolini's *Salo, o le contovente di Sodoma* (1975, *Salo, or The 120 Days of Sodom*), having been banned in 1976 and 1993, and seized by Wellington Customs as recently as February 1997, was passed for exhibition in a travelling film festival later that year, despite containing examples of almost all the prohibited acts.

A giant cut-out sign of an almost naked "Vegas Girl" above a strip club became a landmark in Auckland's red light district. In 1997, after complaints from a local antipornography campaigner, the Classification Office consulted with several groups, including the sign's owners, nearby schools, and local businesses. The Chief Censor, Kathryn Paterson, decided that, because of the public nature of the display, the sign could be considered "objectionable" and "injurious to the public good". The owners sought a review, which classified the display "unrestricted", satisfied that, on the evidence, the sign did not "degrade, dehumanize or demean any person".

Radio, television, and the internet

Censorship was applied to what was once called the wireless well before the advent of broadcasting. The new invention was of obvious relevance to a country physically so isolated from the rest of the world, and within which citizens often had no near neighbours. Yet New Zealand and the Falkland Islands were the only territories in the world to deny their citizens the right to transmit radio messages. Like telephones and telegraph messages, the wireless was declared, in the Wireless Telegraphy Act of 1903, a government monopoly. All three of these media were strictly censored during World War I, and an act passed in 1920 set out "to license and suitably regulate the operation of wireless stations of all kinds".

"Broadcasting" was first mentioned in the New Zealand parliament in 1922. The government had no desire to prevent its introduction and was even willing to agree to the principle of public access, but it remained nervous of the greater freedom implied by private ownership, issuing the Radio Telegraph Regulations for Amateur, Experimental and Broadcasting Stations in 1923. The real source of its worries was now made explicit:

> Broadcasting stations shall not be used for the dissemination of propaganda of a controversial nature, but shall be restricted to matters of an educative or entertaining character, such as news, lectures, useful information, religious services, musical entertainment, and such other items of general interest as may be approved by the Minister from time to time.

While the government had no aspirations to run radio directly, it had a firm intention of remaining in control of the medium: broadcasting was seen as a function of the Posts and Telegraphs Department, and there was to be no seditious, profane, obscene, libellous, or offensive material on air. Broadcasters were to ensure that religious services were provided on Sundays between 11 a.m. and 12.30 p.m., and between 6.30 p.m. and 8 p.m. Advertising was absolutely prohibited. However, of all these regulations, it was the implied ban on controversy that was to last longest: it was still being invoked more than two decades later.

In 1925, four radio stations were licensed and accorded wavelengths, one for each main district of the country. They were required to broadcast for at least 12 hours a week and, in keeping with the now established tradition of government influence, they had to "broadcast any announcement of the New Zealand government or any department thereof". The ban on advertising remained, but religious programmes were no longer compulsory. The four stations operated under the umbrella of the Radio Broadcasting Company.

The ban on controversy became yet more explicit in 1927, when the United Victuallers Association complained that certain programmes had touched on the question of prohibition of alcohol. The secretary of the Posts and Telegraph Department was adamant:

> Violent or definite remarks for or against prohibition should not be allowed. Further, nothing should be said having for an object the inflaming of political feeling. While not wishing to hold the Broadcasting Company to any hard and fast rules in the matter, I certainly look to it to exercise a wise discretion.

"Discretion" evidently led to boredom, but when a Listeners League was formed in Auckland to express dissatisfaction at the service provided, its proposed remedy was to urge the government to take "immediate and complete control" – hardly a recipe for better programmes.

In its aversion to controversy, the New Zealand government was clearly following the example of the BBC under John Reith, but its ban on live horse-racing commentaries, issued in 1928, was perhaps more distinctively local. It was the ruling body of the sport, the Racing Conference, that insisted on it, fearing that broadcasting would prevent people attending the meetings, but actually claiming that it would encourage illegal betting, and would "create and maintain an attention to the happenings at race meetings during the progress thereof by many persons not present, which [would] result in disadvantage to the business community". A member of parliament, R.W. Smith, commented: "The claim that the broadcasting may lead to an increase in gambling is sheer hypocrisy, because, after all, the racing clubs look to the gambling ... through the totalizator as the chief source of their income". Live outside broadcasts at races was banned for the time being.

New Zealand radio was again remodelled, on BBC lines, under the Broadcasting Act of 1931. A "public service", under the New Zealand Broadcasting Board (NZBB), was to be at the heart of it, but this would coexist with "B" stations, small operations that had been transmitting local programmes since the 1920s. The ban on controversy was reaffirmed and, as in the early BBC, broadcasters were not allowed to originate their own news, since news was still regarded as the property of the newspapers.

The NZBB proposed that "the regulation prohibiting the broadcasting of controversial matter should be relaxed so as to give the Board similar liberty in this respect to that of BBC", where the ban had by then been removed. Such a freedom seemed as far away as ever in New Zealand when it was laid down that the Workers Educational Association (WEA), which began presenting educational material in 1932, was to deposit copies of programmes on "doubtful subjects" with the NZBB before they were delivered. The WEA, which prized its own independence from the adult education service, ceased to broadcast a year later. Meanwhile, a certain leeway was allowed to religious broadcasters, "Christian values" being interpreted fairly widely. At the 1ZR station, the Reverend Colin Scrimgeour, known as "Uncle Scrim", took full advantage of the station's relative freedom, starting a series called *Man in the Street*, addressed in particular to those unemployed as a result of the worldwide Depression.

The ban reached its apogee in the mid-1930s, when New Zealand was visited by, among others, major Douglas, the advocate of social credit, Jiddu Krishnamurti, then regarded as one of the world's foremost spiritual teachers, and Bernard Shaw. Douglas and Krishnamurti were refused broadcasting time outright, but the NZBB was allowed to invite Shaw to appear without a requirement to submit a script in advance. Speaking at a civic reception in his honour, Shaw remarked that "the question [of censorship] has not arisen, but I would have no objection if I knew what I should say". The 2YA station asked him to speak about "Drama", but he "flatly refused" and "warned that he would be as controversial as Hell, we could take it or leave it". His subject was "Observations Pertinent and Impertinent". Not even Shaw, however, could stop a broadcast of his play *Androcles and the Lion* from which the epilogue had been cut; *Androcles* is an account of a secular "conversion".

When the ban on controversy was temporarily revoked in 1936, broadcasters were so used to being cautious that they would not allow air time to the Friends of the Soviet Union or to the Theosophical Society. On the other hand, New Zealand was the first country in the world to introduce the broadcasting of legislative proceedings. James Shelley, director of the newly named National Broadcasting Service, said in 1936:

> The radio, if properly used, should provide a means whereby the sympathetic influence of the actual human voice of ancient Athens can be added to the intellectual facilities of the widespread communication of the printing press.

The appointment of Colin Scrimgeour as director of the Commercial Broadcasting Service also appeared to herald a new era.

This new era was not to arrive. The Labour government that had abolished the ban on controversy reintroduced it in 1937 and, in 1939, the ostensibly liberal Shelley wrote to Oliver Duff, the editor of the *New Zealand Listener* (modelled on the now defunct BBC magazine *The Listener*):

> In general, any contemplated material which involves politics, religion, or foreign countries should be submitted to me before publication. The whole content of the journal should be submitted to me before printing . . . to ensure that matters of broadcasting policy are checked . . . in matters of taste – if in doubt cut it out.

Duff replied: "If I have no freedom, I can show no initiative, and the *Listener* will become a dull official journal which the public will not buy".

Less exception seems to have been taken to the wartime censorship of radio, especially of the broadcasting of parliament, after 1939. The Speaker was given the power to cut any broadcast parliamentary speech:

> I do not think that any member can trust himself when speaking in the heat of debate, to be absolutely discreet, and we would never forgive ourselves if we uttered a single word that would endanger the lives of our boys.

Music was specially targeted for censorship, and bans were imposed on broadcasts of such songs as "The Fleet's in Port Again" and "There's a Boy Coming Home on Leave". The

jokes in a comedy programme, *Chuckles with Jerry*, were also carefully scrutinized and sometimes censored.

After the war, growing dissension within the Labour Party forced some concessions on the issue of controversy. In 1947, Shelley instituted a weekly discussion programme, the aim of which was "to stimulate public thought and discussion, and [not] to reach conclusions". Speakers were carefully chosen to give as nearly as possible a balanced presentation of the various aspects of the question under discussion; this was cautious certainly, but not more so than, say, the BBC's approach. In the same year, a schools programme, *How Things Began*, was attacked by the Evolution Protest Movement, who demanded the right to put the literal biblical view of creation. Shelley suspended the series, and, after consideration by numerous committees and by the Minister himself, who was sympathetic to the anti-evolutionist case, the programme was not reinstated.

The fact that the fear of controversy was not entirely banished from New Zealand broadcasting was demonstrated in 1980, when the National Broadcasting Service decided not to screen the British documentary *Death of a Princess*, on the grounds that it misrepresented and distorted "the values and way of life" (of Saudi Arabia) with which it dealt, and was therefore not reliable. Television censorship in New Zealand today is bound by the Television Code of Broadcasting Practice, which is monitored by a quasi-autonomous government body, the Broadcasting Standards Authority (BSA). The code is very broad and includes such vague notions as "currently accepted norms of decency and taste". Individuals can relay complaints to the BSA, which must investigate them. While only around one third of complaints are upheld, these set a precedent for the treatment of particular types of programme by the television channels' in-house "assessors". The two main free-to-air national broadcasters are Television New Zealand (TVNZ), a state-owned enterprise that operates TV1 and TV2, and Can West, largely foreign-owned, which operates TV3 and TV4. Programmers at all four channels attempt to "second guess" what will be acceptable to the BSA. Sky Television, available on subscription, is subject to a different code of practice, and uses a consumer card to enable films that are rated as suitable only for people over 18 ("R18") by the film and video censors to be blocked out. They also broadcast two encrypted channels, Playboy and Spice, for those subscribers willing to pay extra for coded access.

In 1998, after four years in the position, Kathryn Paterson, the first chief censor of all New Zealand media (except Broadcasting), left for a similar post in Australia. It had been pointed out, to the parliamentary select committee studying the bill that resulted in the Films, Video and Literature Classification Act of 1993, that the limitation of a chief censor's term to three years with the possibility of a single extension of a further three years would result in an incumbent looking for alternative employment as soon as the second term began. So it proved. The regulation (which had been designed to get rid of liberal Arthur Everard) was then amended so that her successor, Bill Hastings, a Canadian law lecturer from Victoria University in Wellington, was not subject to a limited tenure.

The authorities in New Zealand, like their counterparts elsewhere, have been exercised by the availability of sexually explicit material on the Internet. Having been advised that it was breaking the law, Telecom Xtra cut Internet access in 1996, despite the fact that it was already providing its customers with filtering software. A report by the Internet Society estimated that it would cost NZ$7.4 million to put a wholesale block on such material, but suggested that it could be funded by increasing classification charges for books, magazines, and CD-Roms. However, interception and excision have proved impossible to date, although there have been successful prosecutions of those linked to international groups trading child pornography.

New Zealand has a "Bill of Rights" that protects "freedom of expression". Although this bill does not have the paramountcy of the American First Amendment for "free speech" it has had a significant effect on New Zealand legislation. The officers working on film, video and literature classification must consider the effects of their decisions on the submitter's rights to freedom of expression. Kathryn Paterson said that it was just possible that the High Court might one day rule that the bill could negate any attempt at censorship. Although this has not happened, some rulings of the chief censor have been challenged by the courts.

In December 1999 the appeal court ruled that the censor had made an error in law in classifying an item as objectionable without giving adequate consideration to the Bill of Rights. The Film and Literature Board of Review had endorsed Bill Hastings's ruling that a book detailing sexual escapades between children and men, along with photographs of naked boys, should be banned as "objectionable". However, Justice Tipping sent the decision back to the board for reconsideration on the grounds that the provisions within the Bill of Rights had not been given sufficient weight.

The next year the chief censor, who is himself openly gay, banned two anti-homosexuality videos *Aids: What You Haven't Been Told* and *Gay Rights/Special Rights Inside the Homosexual Agenda*, which had been imported by fundamentalist Christian groups. He did so in terms of the Bill of Rights constraints on material that "discriminates against a section of the public". His decision was supported by both the Film and Literature Board of Review and by the High Court. But, in September 2000, the court of appeal referred the issue back to the Board of Review for reassessment on the basis that the UK House of Lords and the European Court of Human Rights had both cited "freedom of expression" as an essential "foundation of democracy". The appeal court ruled that whereas the Bill of Rights was against discrimination, it was necessary to give greater emphasis to the provision guaranteeing freedom of expression.

These set-backs for the censor's office resulted in calls by some politicians for a tightening of the legislation so that "child porn" was not given carte blanche, while Sir Geoffrey Palmer, the former prime minister and largely responsible for the Bill of Rights, asked for further clarification of the meaning of "objectionable" as used in the Films, Video and Literature Classification Act.

Bill Hastings himself would welcome further clarification. He has pointed out that while publications that "promote or support the sexual exploitation of the young, necrophilia, bestiality, rape and torture" should be declared "objectionable", and therefore banned, there were two other provisions citing "the use of urine and excrement during depictions of sex" that, although offensive to many people, were not, in themselves, illegal.

In some sex videos it was difficult for Bill Hastings to determine whether he was watching copious ejaculation or micturition. He added: "under the law, the censor must consider urination between consenting adults in a sexual situation as being directly equivalent to the sexual abuse of children. Which I think, personally, is bizarre. That's where I think the lawmakers have slipped away from a harm-based to a more morality-based legislation".

These contrasting tensions, between liberality and conservatism, are certain to be the continuing story of censorship in New Zealand in the 21st century.

CHRIS WATSON and ROY SHUKER

Further Reading

Burstyn, Varda, "Beyond Despair: Positive Strategies" in *Women against Censorship*, edited by Burstyn, Vancouver: Douglas and McIntyre, 1985

Campbell, Gordon, "The New Brutality: An Interview with Bill Hastings", *The Listener* (10 April 1999)

Christoffel, Paul, *A Short History of Censorship in New Zealand*, Wellington: Department of Internal Affairs, 1989

Day, Patrick, *A History of Broadcasting in New Zealand*, vol. 1: *The Radio Years*, Auckland: Auckland University Press, 1994

Dickinson, Garry, Michael Hill and Wiebe Zwaga, *Monitoring Community Attitudes in Changing Mediascapes*, Palmerston North: Dunmore Press, 2000

Donnerstein, Edward *et al.* (editors), *The Question of Pornography: Research Findings and Policy Implications*, New York: Free Press, and London, Collier Macmillan, 1987

du Fresne, Karl, *Free Press, Free Society*, Wellington: Newspaper Publishers Association of New Zealand, 1995

Eldred-Grigg, Stevan, *Pleasures of the Flesh: Sex and Drugs in Colonial New Zealand, 1840–1915*, Wellington: Reed, 1984

Holden, Lewis, *The General Public's Attitude to Film Censorship in New Zealand*, Wellington: Department of Internal Affairs, 1983

Morris, J., *Pornography: Report of the Ministerial Committee of Inquiry*, Wellington: Department of Justice, 1989

Paterson, K., *Report of the Office of Film and Literature Classification*, Wellington: Office of Film and Literature Classification, 1997

Watson, Chris and Roy Shuker, *In the Public Good? Censorship in New Zealand*, Palmerston North, New Zealand: Dunmore Press, 1998

NEW ZEALAND: Maori Language and Culture

The Maori culture in New Zealand dates from around the year 1000, when East Polynesian migrants became the first people to arrive in Aotearoa (The Land of the Long White Cloud), later renamed New Zealand by Europeans. Colonization by the *Pakeha* (non-Maori) from the late 18th century threatened Maori identity, or the *Maoritanga*, the culture, customs, and language of the indigenous population.

It may seem that the ownership of land occupies an area of study unrelated to censorship, but *whenua*, Maori land, is essential to Maori language and culture, and its acquisition, still a controversial issue in New Zealand, is regarded, by many Maori, as every bit as much an act of censorship as the more direct varieties of the practice explored in this encyclopedia. From the beginning of its occupation, Britain sold land gained from the Maori to the predominantly English and Scottish settlers, and the need to define land rights soon emerged. The *Tiriti o Waitangi*/Treaty of Waitangi was signed by representatives of the British crown and more than 500 *rangatira* (Maori chiefs) in 1840. The three articles in the treaty are written in English and Maori, and there has been continued debate about the linguistic discrepancies between the two texts, leaving the suspicion that the British used their position to manipulate the actual words to their own benefit.

The first article, for instance, says (in the English text) that the *rangatira* give "all the rights and powers of sovereignty" over their territories to the Queen of England. J.M.R. Owens has commented: "Today the term 'Maori soverignty' has become one of considerable controversy. Did they have an equivalent concept before the Treaty, did they understand the word?"

The second article pledges that Maori will have "the full exclusive and undisturbed possession of their Lands and Estates Fisheries and other properties", a promise that the Pakeha found themselves increasingly unable or unwilling to fulfil, as they strove to satisfy the demands of a growing number of settlers. This led to a Maori uprising and the start of the Land Wars in 1860, which were won decisively by the Pakeha. They then confiscated even more *whenua*. One hundred years later, the Maori have been seeking to reclaim possession of their property and to pursue compensation through the Waitangi Tribunal, established in 1975 (its aims were extended in 1985).

Much of the Maori population had by then been urbanized and even, to some extent, assimilated into European culture. This did not prevent the emergence during the 1970s of Maori activism. For instance, Raglan Golf Course was built on former tribal land that had been appropriated by the government in 1941 for war purposes but never returned. Overnight, a *marae* (ceremonial and ancestral assembly ground), which is *tapu* (sacred) and regarded as *turangawaewae* (a place to stand and to belong by ancestral right), had been bulldozed. Struggles over this land, led by Eva Rickard, were recorded in Barry Barclay's seminal six-part television series, *Tangata Whenua* (1974, The People of the Land). In 1975, the *Te Matakite o Aotearoa* (Maori Land March) was filmed by Geoff Steven for a documentary of the same name. Bastion Point, on Auckland Harbour, had been the tribal land of the Ngati Whatua, and when the government tried to sell the property, in 1977, protest-

ing Maori occupied the land. A 507-day siege ended in 1978 with homes being demolished by a government backed by the courts, and with 150 protesters, as well as media personnel, being removed by 600 policemen. The events were captured in Merata Mita's documentary *Bastion Point – Day 507* (1980).

There followed, in the 1980s and 1990s, a Maori renaissance: a growing acknowledgement of the concept of *taha Maori* (the Maori dimension), and some recognition and respect for Maori cultural heritage. The present is understood through a strong connection to an ancestor past, and arts, crafts, traditions, history, storytelling, and memory are seen as *taonga tuku iho* (highly prized possessions, or treasures, handed down from ancestors), which carry meaning through the *taha wairua* (spiritual element). The British Museum holds around 3000 Maori artefacts, making up the largest collection outside New Zealand, which remained for generations in storage. When, finally, a small part of the collection was displayed in 1998, the implied censorship of displaying it in a glass case and far from its place of cultural origin was remarked upon. Unique artefacts, such as the only surviving sail for a *waka* (canoe), regarded by Maori as a crucial part of their enculturation, have been kept distant from researchers. In New Zealand some have argued that the indigenous culture is now being plundered and its exoticism exploited for the populist, postcolonial tastes of local Pakeha and tourists. Traditional arts, crafts, and rituals have begun to attract significant commercial interest, and Maori iconography is appearing on various domestic products and souvenirs.

There is, finally, the censorship of language itself. It was not until 1987 that *te reo Maori* (the Maori language) was recognized, along with English, as an official language of New Zealand. Some mountains and regions are now known again by their original names, and many *kohanga reo* (kindergartens) and *kura kaupapa Maori* (primary schools), providing only Maori language and culture education, have been established. Maori radio stations have emerged, there are a number of Maori television programmes, and the first Maori feature film, *Ngati*, was made in 1987. Yet, as Paul Spoonley and Walter Hirsh have argued:

> There are more dogs shown on [New Zealand television] commercials than there are Maoris and Polynesians. It is deliberate . . . the view is that they have no image appeal – except in association with fast food. There is a whole class of clients who would be horrified if you showed a Maori or a Polynesian.

In the opinion of many, and despite biculturalism, the Maori remain marginalized.

IAN CONRICH

Further Reading

Awatere, Donna, *Maori Sovereignty*, Auckland: Broadsheet, 1984
Belich, James, *The Victorian Interpretation of Racial Conflict: The Maori, the British and the New Zealand Wars*, Montreal: McGill–Queen's University Press, 1989
Bell, Claudia, *Inventing New Zealand: Everyday Myths of Pakeha Identity*, Auckland: Penguin, 1996

Conrich, Ian and David Woods (editors), *New Zealand: A Pastoral Paradise?*, Nottingham: Kakapo, 2000

Duff, Alan, *Maori: The Crisis and the Challenge*, Auckland: HarperCollins, 1993

King, Michael, *Being Pakeha*, Auckland: Hodder and Stoughton, 1988

Owens, J.M.R., "The Treaty of Waitangi: Event and Symbol", *British Review of New Zealand Studies*, 3 (1990): 6–14

Reihana, Lisa, "Skinflicks: Practices in Contemporary Maori Media" in *Disrupted Borders: An Intervention in Definitions of Boundaries*, edited by Sunil Gupta, London: Rivers Oram Press, 1993

Sinclair, Keith, *The Origins of the Maori Wars*, Wellington: New Zealand University Press, 1957

Spoonley, Paul and Walter Hirsh (editors) *Between the Lines: Racism and New Zealand Media*, Auckland: Heinemann Reed, 1990

NEWS AGENCIES

News agencies date from the mid-19th century. Charles-Louis Havas opened a modest newspaper-translation bureau in Paris in the early 1830s; Paul Julius Reuter, after failures on the European continent, set up a telegraphic institute in London in 1851 (the year that London was linked by electro-magnetic cable to the Continent); and Bernhard Wolff opened a news agency in Berlin in 1849, at a time when governments – in Prussia as elsewhere – were repressing the revolutionary movements of 1848. Then, as now, news agencies operated as professional and commercial organizations for whom reporting the news accurately and fast depended in part on the geopolitical context, "state-of-the-art" technology, and perceptions of market demand for news and data. Now, as then, there are three leading international news agencies: Reuters, based in London; the Associated Press (AP), based in New York (1848); and Agence France-Presse (AFP), based in Paris (1944). Whereas in the 1850s the three leading agencies considered the international news to flow primarily from the European or imperial perspective of a capital city, nation state, today all three leading agencies collect, process, and distribute news, sometimes directly, sometimes via national news agencies and other news outlets, from the perspective of a supplier of news worldwide.

For three-quarters of a century – from the 1850s to the 1930s – the leading European agencies, with Havas and Reuters to the fore, pooled their resources for the gathering and distribution of news with the result that, together, they dominated the international news flow: the AP joined this news-agency alliance, cartel, or ring, in the 1870s. At the start of the 21st century competition exists between the leading international agencies based in the West, which have assumptions in common about news values and factual reporting, and which were often united in opposition to the concept of the news flow favoured by the official news agencies of the Soviet Union (TASS) and of Communist China (Xinhua). With the end of the Soviet empire, Western news agencies increased their presence in central and eastern Europe and in Russia itself: many Moscow dailies, for instance, take much of their reporting of international news from Reuters, AP, or AFP. Reuters, for example, develops services in Cyrillic for media and – especially – non-media markets. Agencies help to fashion the professional perceptions of news values, writing skills, and presentational styles across the world. And as international purveyors of news, agency journalists battle against self-serving or self-censorship constraints that the authorities may strive to impose on national media. International news agencies, literally, help to get the story "out".

Agencies are attentive to their role in alerting the media, diplomats, and public opinion throughout the world. In the late 1980s famine in Somalia and nascent conflict in Yugoslavia were covered by the agencies long before they became top international news stories. A Reuters man in Somalia noted the words of praise from a UN relief official: "you alerted an indifferent or apathetic international community" to the consequences of famine and civil strife for the Somalis. Words, data, photos, computer graphics, and newsfilm produced by the agencies are quickly seen by the world's news outlets. Some of their visual material becomes icons encapsulating a situation: the AFP photo of 1997 of grief-stricken women in Algeria, for instance. Most agency output has a shorter shelf life. Production, however, is geared to furnish subscribers with fast and accurate news and data; pains are taken to ensure that it can be accessed in a "user-friendly" mode – formatting and presentational skills are as important as accuracy and speed; news is, among other things, a commodity whose shelf life is brief indeed; some reports or news items that are less than an hour old become "historic data", and are recycled as such. This said, within its brief, prescribed "life-span", a news report may have considerable impact; news agencies compete worldwide to secure the cutting edge that comes with meeting "deadlines every minute".

News agencies produce words, digits, still photos, news-film, computer graphics – including visual reconstructions of how an event happened – sound recordings and reports, etc. A single agency may produce more than a million words per day. Agencies also do not just provide systems applications – the terminals and state-of-the-art technology that enable customers to access their data streams. They have websites and feed online services; some observers wonder whether, in a world of deregulated, cheap telecommunications, of the Internet and of electronic commerce, their traditional role as primary international purveyors of fast and accurate news is being endangered. Similar concerns were voiced with the growth of CNN and international television broadcasting organizations purporting to carry live "real-time" news. Such outlets, however great their impact – including on the agencies: CNN coverage of the Gulf War caused much rethinking of agencies' television stategies – are major users of agency video material.

Historically, agencies have played an important role in ensuring that "the outside world" learned of developments that national authorities tried to ensure were given "low to no" coverage in their domestic media. In Israel, censorship about the military affects domestic media coverage of sensitive defence issues; at the same time the Israelis are perceived by agencies as news junkies. Thus, in the course of "hard news reporting" about Israel and the Arab world – a top international ongoing news story of many years – agencies have been attacked by the Israeli authorities for being hostile and for misreporting; when Reuters television carried news film of an air collision in which several Israeli troops were killed (1997), such attacks redoubled. For decades, there have been difficulties in reconciling the secrecy and news-management strategies of authorities – in western, parliamentary democracies, as in totalitarian (and other) regimes – with the agency demand for accurate news fast for an international audience. There are international conflicts where western governments themselves become belligerents; in the Falklands (Malvinas) conflict of 1982, with British and Argentine forces at war, Reuters – like the BBC – took pains to ensure that it reported the positions of both the Argentinian and British governments; it explained to the Argentinian representative at the United Nations that it was a truly international organization and took "no position, national or otherwise, in any situation or conflict" (6 June 1982).

A story that moves to the top of the international news agenda sees agencies boost the resources allocated to its coverage: staff from world or regional headquarters reinforce the staff reporting to the "local" office. This happened in Moscow in August 1991, when the long-feared "coup" occurred, as in countless other instances – such as in Yugoslavia – Belgrade, Zagreb, and elsewhere – which moved from being a story that agencies alone reported – via their bureaux on the spot – to a top story. The local agency bureau relies on a host of local sources, but also on its agency's network of sources across the world. The Moscow bureau of Reuters, in April 1986, was alerted to the nuclear explosion at Chernobyl in the Ukraine (Saturday, 26 April), not by the Moscow authorities or by TASS – which delayed putting out a statement – or even by one of its correspondents who happened to spend the weekend in Kiev, where there was no mention of the explosion that had occurred 80 miles away, but by a phone call from the Swedish embassy in Moscow, on the Monday, reporting on findings by the body in Sweden that monitored nuclear tests. International news agencies and broadcasters – the BBC, for instance – monitor domestic and international media and agency reports and indeed those of other "carriers" and sources relaying data worldwide; this militates against censorship, restricted access, and other attempts to ensure that events and issues do not enter the public domain and figure on the international news agenda.

In many regions of the world, in the past, authoritarian governments subscribed to the services of the international news media, and primarily to the news agencies; an edited, filtered version of AP, Reuters, or AFP reports was then relayed by the national news agency, which – in some countries – had a monopoly of the distribution of news to the domestic media. This was the case in the USSR. It is still the case in some regimes in Africa and Asia. The development of international television news channels, whose signals are beamed by satellite (CNN, BBC World, Sky News, etc.), lessens the effect of such "censorship". Another type of imbalance in the flow of international news was much criticized in the 1970s and early 1980s during what became known as the "NWICO debate": international news agencies were particularly targeted by advocates of a "new world information and communication order"; agencies purportedly purveyed some 80 per cent of the news circulated worldwide; they were accused of over-reporting the northern hemisphere and under-reporting the south; such news that they carried about, say, sub-Saharan Africa, was alleged to stress "bad news" – news of catastrophes, disasters, and deaths, whether perpetrated by man or by nature. Such criticism, relayed in international bodies – governmental (such as Unesco) and other – sensitized agencies to the impact of their output in different regions of the world. Throughout the 1980s and 1990s, AFP and Reuters reinforced the "regionalization" of their copy: for instance, material produced in the English-language service of AFP and distributed in "Asia-Pacific" (covering more than 20 countries, from Islamabad to Sydney, and whose news priorities are overseen from the regional headquarters in Hong Kong), reflects a news agenda that is not the same as that of the English-language service distributed elsewhere. Even within a given world region, the coverage by an international news organization of events concerning two neighbouring countries with a complex ethnic mix and with fraught relations – Pakistan and India, for instance – presents news-editorial difficulties that are in part resolved by adherence to the tenets of factual "hard news" reporting.

In the middle and late 19th century, most national news agencies were created in Europe; in the 1950s to 1980s, many news agencies were set up in newly independent sovereign states, often located in the south, in the post-colonial world; in ex-Soviet bloc states, in the 1980s and 1990s, again new national agencies emerged. Some governments consider national agencies as news-propaganda outlets: indeed, a national official agency may be part of the ministry of information. Some national agencies report news from official sources first, at length and sometimes exclusively: such official agencies confine themselves to the role of government mouthpiece – this was the case of TASS and of the French official news agency during the Vichy regime, l'Office français d'information (1940–44). But news from government sources of country "A" interests governments in countries "B to H", if not those of countries "I to Z"; news from official sources (the White House, the State department) in the US interests governments and media worldwide. The media (among others) may discount or criticize the stress on government sources. In 1858 *Punch*, the satirical London magazine, poked fun at a Reuters telegram from Madrid that stated the obvious:"the Royal speech will express very clearly the intentions of Government on the political and economical questions of the day".

Today, many national agencies remain under government control: their chief executive is accountable, in some instances, to the minister of information. Their output, accordingly, is used by other agencies as a reflection of official attitudes; this needs to be complemented by news from other sources. Consider, for example, past situations in the USSR, from which international agency correspondents were frequently expelled, and where they were not allowed unauthorized contacts with private citizens: in 1968 Adam Kellett-Long, a Reuters Moscow correspondent, explained how the Andrei Siniavskii–Iulii Daniel' trial of February 1966 changed matters; previously, Moscow intellectuals opposing the authorities were too afraid to speak to Western correspondents, and any such news leaked out to the West through émigré and other foreign-based organizations; during the trial, Western correspondents made some contact with friends and relatives of the accused outside the court; although the information was limited, the contacts continued subsequently, despite Soviet foreign office warnings, prompted by the KGB. Kellett-Long knew he might be expelled or tried for anti-Soviet activities: he argued that his reports were true and accurate, and that Soviet charges of false reporting related to stories "which the authorities do not like". Ten years later, international news agencies, such as Reuters, the AP, and AFP, covered news about dissidents in Soviet Russia while TASS only reported Soviet statements about them.

In China, likewise, Western agency correspondents operated in the context of changing geopolitical relationships: the Reuters correspondent Anthony Grey lived under house arrest for 806 days (1967–69), in retaliation for the arrest and imprisonment of Chinese journalists after rioting in Hong Kong. There was no formal censorship as such. Thirty years later, Reuters was distributing services in English and in Chinese to clients in China: there were fears, in 1996, that the authorities might ensure that the official Xinhua agency restricted the ability of foreign news organizations to market services of economic and financial news-feeds.

Ongoing agency debates about the need for a variety of sources, for (at least) "two pairs of eyes" for any one story, and about which stories to carry in which service, and the classification of news items help to fashion the international flow of news, data, and information. Agencies declare that they normally comply with the law relating to the media in each country in which they operate, but may act otherwise so as to circumvent censorship affecting news of major significance. Censorship impinges insofar as authorities impose silence, restrict access, give "spin-doctor" presentation, and fashion

news agendas; agency journalists, in reply, seek to be not merely reactive, but proactive, and investigative, with varying degrees of success. In the developed world, the international news agenda is less heavily and overtly political than a century ago; the various markets that news agencies serve lead some to highlight "market-moving news" and techniques and norms of news presentation. There is, for some, a concern that – in response to clients' demand – the stress on "human interest" angles, user-friendly material, and news-as-a-commodity leads, despite the appearance of an information glut, to a situation reminiscent of Lamennais's "Silence aux pauvres!"; "pauvres", here, signifies poor in news access and news management skills. Sophisticated public relations and information strategies replace the heavy-handed (but often effective) news censorship of yesteryear. Agencies strive both to monitor and to cut through the cackle.

MICHAEL B. PALMER

Further Reading

Boyd-Barrett, Oliver, *The International News Agencies*, London: Constable, and Beverly Hills, California: Sage, 1980

Boyd-Barrett, Oliver and Michael Palmer, *Trafic de nouvelles*, Paris: Moreau, 1981

International Commission for the Study of Communications Problems, *Many Voices, One World*, London: Kogan Page, 1980

Read, Donald, *The Power of News: The History of Reuters*, 2nd edition, Oxford and New York: Oxford University Press, 1999

Schwarzlose, Richard A., *The Nation's Newsbrokers*, 2 vols, Evanston, Illinois: Northwestern University Press, 1989–90

Tunstall, Jeremy and Michael Palmer, *Media Moguls*, London and New York: Routledge, 1991

NEWSWATCH
Nigerian weekly magazine, established 1985

Nigeria's leading weekly magazine, *Newswatch*, was proscribed by the military government of general Ibrahim Babangida on 12 April 1987. The six-month ban came suddenly and without warning. The government accused the magazine of publishing materials which it considered "sensitive".

At issue was a secret report prepared by professor S.J. Cookey, pro-chancellor of the University of Benin, who had been the head of an 18-member political bureau appointed by the government to ascertain the wishes of Nigerians on a broad range of issues concerning the country's future. The bureau moved around the country hearing oral testimonies and receiving representations from Nigerian citizens. The concerns were wide ranging and included the future administrative structure, ideology, economy, types of political parties, and education system of the country. On completing its assignment the Bureau had submitted its report to the government in March 1987, who were expected to announce their views on it in a "white paper". *Newswatch* managed to obtain a copy of the Cookey report and decided to make it public, hoping that their action would help assist the government to draft a more profound white paper. Nigerians were anxious to know the contents of the report. The government had given the impression that the Third Republic, which was to emerge in 1990 after decades of

military rule, depended to a large extent on the commission's recommendations.

The *Newswatch* report reviewed the conclusions reached by the bureau, reporting that it had recommended the creation of six new states, upheld secularism as opposed to theocracy, and advocated a socialist ideology in preference to what it believed "were the pernicious attributes of capitalism". By socialist ideology it meant the "socialization of the commanding heights of the economy", such as full nationalization of Nigeria's oil industry.

The government said that the magazine's method of acquiring the sensitive document was "illegal" and the publication of it was "irresponsible", in part because it would prejudice an objective assessment of the report by the public. The government dusted off a rarely used law – the Official Secrets Act of 1962 which, it alleged, the magazine had contravened. The act makes it an offence to obtain, reproduce, or transmit any classified matter to unauthorized persons.

The ban was challenged in court. Olu Onagoruwa, for *Newswatch*, sought a declaration that the decree was unconstitutional. The court refused and held that it had no jurisdiction and competence to declare the decree unconstitutional or null and void. The Constitution Suspension and Modification

Decree no. 1 of 1984 and the Federal Military Government (FMG) Supremacy and Enforcement of Powers Decree no. 13 of 1984, laid down that no decree could be questioned on the ground that the military government had no competence to make it.

Significantly, the publishers of the *Newswatch* were not brought before a court of law to defend themselves. Rather the publication was banned by a military decree. The decree, known as the *Newswatch* (Proscription and Prohibition from Circulation) Decree 1987, stated that (1) "not withstanding anything contained in the Constitution of the Federal Republic of Nigeria of 1979 or any other enactment or law, the weekly news magazine known as *Newswatch* and published by the Newswatch Communications Limited is hereby proscribed from being published and prohibited from circulation in Nigeria or any part thereof" and (2) "the premises where the weekly newsmagazine referred to in Section I of this Decree is published shall be sealed up by the Inspector General of Police or any officer of the Nigeria Police Force authorised on that behalf during the duration of this decree."

General Babangida and other members of the Armed Forces Ruling Council (AFRC) eventually approved the release of a 168-page white paper in July 1987. The Government disagreed in some respects with the Bureau report; such differences were not totally unexpected in commission reports of that nature. The government rejected "socialization of the commanding heights of the economy" and said that the level of state participation in economy was already sufficient. It also rejected the "imposition of a political ideology" and said that government "believes an ideology will eventually evolve with time and a political maturity of the country".

In a country where more than 70 per cent of all newspapers and 100 per cent of the electronic media were under government ownership, an independent voice trying to assert its independence was anathema. A year earlier (1986), the editor of *Newswatch*, Dele Giwa, had been killed by a parcel bomb under circumstances that were as murky as they were unprecedented in the history of political violence in Nigeria. *Newswatch* had established itself in the country as a forthright, independent magazine imbued with a spirit of investigative journalism modelled on *Time* and *Newsweek*, the US and international news magazines. It built on the foundations laid by *Newbreed*, a magazine started in 1972 by chief Christ Okolie with Tony Lee Onyisi as its first general editor, which itself had been subject to censorship in 1978. In a country where the government controlled the bulk of the media, such truly independent voices were both unusual and unsettling.

TONY EZENWEZE ONYISI

NGUGI WA THIONG'O (James T. Ngugi)
Kenyan writer, 1938–

As a novelist, playwright, essayist, and scholar, Ngugi has since the publication of his first novel, *Weep Not, Child*, in 1964 been a forthright critic of both British colonial rule as well as of its postcolonial legacy of neocolonialism in independent Kenya. A motivating factor behind all his writings is the desire to reassert the autonomy of the Kenyan people, lost at the time of European conquest in the late 19th century.

His first novels emphasized historical themes. *Weep Not, Child* was set at the time of the Mau Mau rebellion in colonial Kenya. *The River Between* (1965) focused on the way in which Kikuyu traditions were undermined by colonial rule. His third novel, *A Grain of Wheat* (1967), is set during the four days leading up to Kenyan independence (1963), although it celebrates "more than 60 years of Kenyan people's struggle to claim their own space", making special reference, in a series of flashbacks, to the Mau Mau period. In *Petals of Blood* (1977) he turned to the problems of contemporary Kenya, attacking prevailing injustice in the country, and in particular the venality of the political and commercial elite. This theme was continued in the allegorical novel *Caitaani Mutharaba-ini* (1980; published in English as *Devil on the Cross*, 1982), which was written on toilet paper in cell 16, Kamiti Maximum Security Prison, where Ngugi was held in 1977–78.

His beliefs and attitudes first aroused the hostility of the political authorities in 1969, when he resigned as a lecturer in English at University College, Nairobi, in protest against Jomo Kenyatta's suppression of academic freedom. In 1976 he and Micere Mugo were members of a group which produced the play *The Trial of Dedan Kimathi*. Dedan Kimathi led the Kenyan Land Freedom Army (Mau Mau), and was seen by Ngugi as a neglected national hero. He was warned by the CID not to stage the play at the National Theatre because of its "Communist slant", and because it interfered with "European theatre" (which concentrated on such musicals as *Annie Get Your Gun* and *Jesus Christ Superstar*). The group transferred the production to Kameriithu community theatre, involving audiences in rehearsals and performances.

Both the publication of *Petals of Blood* and the performance of Ngugi's next collaborative play, *Ngaahika Ndeenda* (I Will Marry When I Want, 1977) were thought to have resulted in Ngugi's imprisonment in 1977. The play, which examined the social conditions of working people, and the history of their resistance to authority, was banned, and Ngugi detained without trial under the Public Security Act. He described his experiences in *Detained: A Writer's Prison Diary* (1981). He was released in 1978.

Ngugi continued to suffer the attentions of the Kenyan authorities. In 1982, during a production of his play *Maitu Njugira* (Mother Sing for Me), the National Theatre was put under police guard, and the company of performers barred from entry. Public rehearsals were held at the University of Nairobi, but the police moved in again after 10 performances, closing the university theatre and subsequently burning down the community theatre at Kameriithu.

In 1982 Ngugi went to London to promote his prison diaries, fully intending to return to Kenya. However, while he was in England, a failed coup against the Kenyan president Daniel arap Moi occurred, in which several of Ngugi's friends were implicated. He decided it was unsafe to return, and has since lived abroad, in London and Connecticut. Despite his exile, though, the Kenyan authorities continued to target his work, including the London production of *The Trial of Dedan Kimathi* at the Africa Centre in 1984. The High Commissioner declared that the Kenya government did not want to gag the author, but that the play had been altered, and was anti-Kenyan. Having failed to persuade the British foreign secretary, Sir Geoffrey Howe, to get the play banned, Kenyan security agents attended every performance.

Ngugi's novel *Matigari* (1986) was also written in London. It is concerned with the activities of a former freedom fighter who roams the land seeking "truth and justice", neither of which he encounters. Matigari, the eponymous hero, is led in the end to dig up his weapons and resort to force to try to achieve his ends. The publication of the novel in Kenya resulted in anxiety and confusion in government circles there. According to Ngugi: "People who had read the novel started talking about Matigari and the questions he was raising as if Matigari was a real person in life. When Moi heard that there was a Kenyan roaming round the country asking such questions, he issued orders for the man's arrest. But when the police found that he was only a character in fiction, Moi was even more angry, and he issued fresh orders for the arrest of the book itself" (Ngugi, "Matigari and the Dreams of One East Africa", *Geo* magazine, Hamburg, October 1989; reprinted in *Moving the Centre*). Every bookshop was raided and remaining copies seized, but 3346 copies had already been sold.

Perhaps Ngugi threatens the current regime most fundamentally by challenging the official version of the struggle for independence in which the role of the Mau Mau movement is downplayed. He believes that it was the Mau Mau above all, who achieved independence, through their fight for land and freedom. By retelling the story he hopes to inspire present-day Kenyans to rebel against continuing injustice. According to Ngugi: "Tyrants and their tyrannical systems are terrified at the sound of the wheels of history. History is subversive . . . so they try to *rewrite* history, make up *official* history" ("In Moi's Kenya, History is Subversive", first published as foreword to *Kenya's Freedom Struggle: The Dedan Kimathi Papers*, edited by Maina wa Kinyatti, London: Zed, 1987).

Ngugi believes that first Kenyatta and then Moi betrayed the ideals of both Mau Mau and the wider nationalist movement, delivering up "independent" Kenya to the IMF, the World Bank, and to western interests in general (both the UK and the USA, since 1980, have been allowed to keep military bases in Kenya). Openly a Marxist, he writes in *Matigari* of "the ogres now running the country". As far as the regime is concerned, Ngugi is, like other fellow academics, one of the "misty eyed revolutionaries whom the Soviet Union was openly backing" (*The Express*, Nairobi, November 1984).

Ngugi believes that the writer has a crucial role in revolutionary struggle as mythogizer, scholar and interpreter. He has described his understanding in such books as *Writers in Politics* and *Barrel of a Pen*. From exile, he has pursued a wider campaign against the censorship of language and culture. Since *Caitaani Mutharaba-ini* he has written his imaginative work in Gikuyu – a necessary step, in his view, in the struggle to reverse the imposition of colonial literatures and languages.

DEREK JONES

Writings

Homecoming: Essays on African and Caribbean Literature, Culture and Politics, 1972
Detained: A Writer's Prison Diary, 1981
Writers in Politics: Essays, 1981; revised edition, 1997
Barrel of a Pen: Resistance to Repression in Neo-Colonial Kenya, 1983
Decolonising the Mind: The Politics of Language in African Literature, 1986
Moving the Centre: The Struggle for Cultural Freedoms, 1993

Further Reading

Boehmer, Elleke, *Colonial and Postcolonial Literature: Migrant Metaphors*, Oxford and New York: Oxford University Press, 1995
Rutherford, Anna (editor), *From Commonwealth to Post-Colonial*, Sydney: Dangaroo, 1992
Said, Edward, *Culture and Imperialism*, New York: Knopf, and London: Chatto and Windus, 1993
Sicherman, Carol, *Ngugi wa Thiong'o, The Making of a Rebel: A Sourcebook in Kenyan Literature and Resistance*, London and New York: Zell, 1990

NGUYEN CHI THIEN
Vietnamese poet, 1939–

Born in Hanoi, Nguyen Chi Thien was educated at one of the major high schools that used both Vietnamese and French as the basic language of tuition. Despite the war, his schooling continued until 1956, when he obtained his baccalaureat. But by then he had contracted tuberculosis and moved to live with a sister in the port city of Haiphong. During his convalescence, he engaged in part-time teaching but his courses, particularly in modern history, conflicted with the Communist Party line and he was arrested in May 1961. Conditionally released three years later, Nguyen Chi Thien then found work as a translator of French and English. He was re-arrested in 1966 on the grounds of being a reactionary and subsequently detained

without trial in various prisons and labour camps, often in solitary confinement, until 1977.

During that period, deprived of any writing materials, he composed and committed to memory a series of poems, which he wrote down on his release when he went once more to live with his sister in Haiphong. Knowing that these poems would never be published in Vietnam because of their bitterly anti-communist content, he sought to get them out of the country. Although some foreign ships, mostly Chinese and Soviet, visited Haiphong, Nguyen Chi Thien decided it was too dangerous to approach their crews. Instead, he made several trips to Hanoi to see whether any of the foreign embassies there was accessible. His first choice was the French embassy but that proved to be too strongly guarded. The much smaller British mission seemed to have greater potential, so on 16 July 1979 he burst in through the front door, much to the consternation of the staff, who thought they were under attack from a madman. Trying to calm them, he then produced from inside his underwear a sheaf of poems, together with an introductory letter in French explaining his background. There was no possibility of being granted political asylum in the British embassy; Nguyen Chi Thien was immediately arrested and taken to the Central Prison in Hanoi for interrogation.

British diplomats forwarded the poems to London, where they were recognized as having literary merit as well as being the first of their type to emerge from Vietnam. *Hoa Dia Nguc* (The Flowers of Hell) contains not only denunciations of the Communist Party and its leaders but also descriptions of the degradation of the body and the mind induced by the prison camp system in North Vietnam. The poem "From Ape to Man, From Man to Beast" points out that the process of human evolution took millions of years but can be reversed in a matter of days "when naked inmates crouch in their jungle jails . . . Ready to fight for a root, to kill for a yam, Chained up, shot, broken, smashed at their captors merest whim". Another poem includes the repetitive refrain "Leaving aside, the hunger and the terror, the Ho Chi Minh era appears in two forms, graves of prisoners, tombs of soldiers."

A Vietnamese edition of Nguyen Chi Thien's anthology was quickly published in the United States and was also set to music by the well-known musician Pham Duy. Some of the 150 and more poems were also translated into French and English, although in the process they lose a lot of their classical symbolism but not the political message. Nguyen Chi Thien was to spend another 12 years in various camps, and was adopted as a prisoner of conscience by Amnesty International. It seems that it was only through international pressure and the desire of the Hanoi government to present a more humane face to the world at large that he was finally released in October 1991. Even then, when he returned again to live in Haiphong, access to him was restricted and, as he tried to regain his health, he was not allowed to accept donations of medicine sent from abroad. Eventually in November 1995, Nguyen Chi Thien was granted a passport and allowed to visit the United States for health reasons. Since then he has travelled widely in North America, Europe, and Australia, speaking about his experiences while composing more poems for a second anthology. This has evoked an angry response among official circles in Hanoi, although individually some Vietnamese have expressed surprise and shock that a man could spend so many years in prison with his name never being mentioned in public and his work remaining unknown in his native country.

JUDY STOWE

Writings

Chants de prison, 1982
Flowers from Hell, translated by Huynh Sanh Thong, 1984
The Will of a Vietnamese: The Poetry of Nguyen Chi Thien, translated by Hang T. Nguyen, 1984

NHA CA
Vietnamese journalist and short story writer (real name: Tran Thi Thu Van), 1939–

Nha Ca (literally, Sweet Water) is the pen-name of Tran Thi Thu Van. She was born in Huê, the former imperial capital, situated in central Vietnam. She was educated at a Buddhist school for girls, married at a fairly young age, and moved with her husband, Tran Da Tu, to Saigon, where there was far more opportunity for them to make a living as writers, something to which they both aspired.

As the fighting in southern Vietnam escalated during the early 1960s, Nha Ca made a name for herself as the first Vietnamese woman to become a war correspondent. Her breakthrough came in January 1968, when she returned to Huê for the traditional lunar New Year festival and witnessed at first hand the communist onslaught on the city in what is known as the Têt Offensive; the bitter battle lasted three weeks until Huê was recaptured by Saigon government troops aided by US marines. In a semi-fictional account of the battle entitled "A White Turban for Huê" (the white turban being the traditional symbol of mourning in Vietnam), Nha Ca recounted the horrors of war perpetrated on both sides, although she did not disguise the fact that she was particularly appalled by the mass graves of thousands of prominent Huê citizens whom the communists massacred before they were forced to retreat.

When the book was first published in serial form in Saigon, Nha Ca received death threats from the communist side but also warnings from the South Vietnamese administration that she should not write anything to suggest that there had also been brutality on their side since this might "damage the morale of the troops". Henceforth she found herself treading a very fine line in the many articles and short stories she continued to write, being praised and denigrated in Hanoi and Saigon in turn. At the same time, the American press came to regard her as one of the most important South Vietnamese writers.

When communist forces took control of Saigon on 30 April 1975, Nha Ca made no attempt to escape. Realizing that she could no longer write – all the press and publishing houses were immediately closed down – she retired quietly to live with her husband and family, which now numbered six children, keeping in touch with the literary friends who had remained in South Vietnam. This domestic peace prevailed until the night of 3 April 1976, when a series of police raids took place throughout Saigon. Nha Ca and her husband were among the many people arrested. Their children, aged between 13 and only one year old, were left to fend for themselves, and their home was confiscated. Fortunately the children were looked after by relatives, but Nha Ca did not know this when she was separated from her husband and interrogated about her supposed links with the CIA; she had previously given interviews to the American press.

After a year, during which she was often subjected to solitary confinement, Nha Ca was released "for the sake of the children". To support them and also make occasional visits with food parcels to her husband, Tran Da Tu – who along with many other writers had been sent to a so-called "re-education camp" remote in the central highlands of Vietnam – Nha Ca resorted to becoming a street vendor. Even then she was frequently threatened with re-incarceration and her two eldest children were ejected from the music school where they were studying because of their "bad family background".

Eventually the Swedish branch of International PEN came to hear of the plight of this family and entered into negotiations with the authorities in Hanoi to allow them to emigrate. It took about four years until Tran Da Tu was finally released in 1988, after 12 years under detention without trial, and the family was given permission to leave on a flight to Sweden. Since then Nha Ca has resumed writing. Apart from a volume of memoirs recounting various episodes in her life and that of many of her friends in the literary world of Saigon in the 1960s and 1970s, she has written several volumes of short stories. They have been published in California, where she now lives, but her testimonies to life as it was in South Vietnam before and after April 1975 have not been translated.

JUDY STOWE

Writings

At Night I Hear the Cannons, translated by James Banerian, 1993

NICARAGUA

Population: 5,071,000	**Number of daily newspapers:** 4
Main religions: Roman Catholic; Protestant	**Number of radio receivers per 1000 inhabitants:** 265
Official language: Spanish	
Other languages spoken: English	**Number of TV receivers per 1000 inhabitants:** 68
Illiteracy rate (%): 33.1 (m); 29.8 (f)	**Number of PCs per 1000 inhabitants:** 7.8

Under Spanish rule, Nicaragua belonged with Guatemala, Chiapas, El Salvador, Honduras, and Costa Rica, and was administered as part of the *audiencia* (administrative and legal court) of Guatemala. For discussion of censorship during that period, see the entry on Guatemala.

As in Guatemala, agitation for independence in Nicaragua at the beginning of the 19th century was largely fuelled by *pasquínes*, or informal news-sheets. In 1811 the soldier Encarnacion Balladeres was charged with distributing *pasquínes* which spread news of anti-Spanish insurrections in El Salvador and Guatemala, and for reporting that Nicaragua too was about to join the movement for independence. When, finally, the Spanish yoke was broken in 1821, Nicaragua was at first part of the shortlived Central American Federation. Arguments about the future raged between the conservatives – largely based in the city of Granada, and in favour of annexation by the Mexican empire – and the liberals of León, who supported full independence. José Antonio Chamorro's *pasquíne* in favour of the Mexican solution earned him prosecution in Granada, and Nicaragua formally achieved statehood in 1826, and seceded from the federation in 1838.

In the mid-19th century the exercise of intellectual and political freedom was adversely affected by direct US military intervention. In 1855 the US millionaire Cornelius Vanderbilt funded the expedition of the freebooter William Walker, who landed with a mercenary force, declared himself president of Nicaragua, made English the official language, reinstituted slavery, and closed down opposition newspapers. The newspaper editor Mateo Mayorga was executed by firing squad, but Walker was defeated and himself executed in 1860, after he had failed to capture Costa Rica.

The first daily newspaper, *El Diario de Nicaragua*, appeared in 1884; Rigoberto Cabezas, its founder, promised that the paper would "defend the people against unauthorized attacks by the government, and to confront power whenever it goes beyond its assigned bounds".

The 1893 "Liberal Revolution" of general José Santos Zelaya promised initially an era of new freedom for Nicaragua. Newspapers proliferated – *The Liberal*, *The Democrat*, *The Dawn*, and *Independent Ideas*. But Zelaya proved corrupt, compelled the newspapers to follow his directives, and closed them down when they resisted – as was the fate of the respected *Diario Nicaragüense*. Soon the conservative journalist Enrique Guzman was the only dissident voice in the choir of liberal dailies; the only possible resistance was the publication of *folletas*, clandestine pamphlets published abroad.

The United States overthrew Zelaya in 1909, under the pretext that he was negotiating canal treaty rights with the Japanese. Marines occupied the country intermittently until 1933, propping up a series of governments that restricted the flow of information running contrary to US corporate interests. In the late 1920s, Augusto César Sandino emerged as leader of the resistance to US imperialism, and was a considerable influence on later Nicaraguan thinking. Sandino was a revolutionary, but not a doctrinaire communist. According to Alejandro Bendaña, Sandino's views were "as far away from the dictatorship of the proletariat as from the dictatorship of capital, as opposed to plutocracy as to party-bureaucratic rule". His attempts to organize democratic workers' collectives inspired later revolutionary journalists to set up "information collectives", in order to free the press from domination by the financial elite. Sandino was murdered in 1934 by members of the Nicaraguan national guard, under their commander Anastasio Somoza, who took over the government in 1937, establishing both a family dynasty and a US fiefdom. Among his first acts was the destruction of Sandino's "moral treasure", his archive of El Ejército Defensor de la Soberania Nacional de Nicaragua (The Defending Army of Nicaragua's National Sovereignty).

The dictatorship of the Somoza family lasted from 1937 until 1979. Using anticommunism as a pretext, they enriched themselves, censored the press, and eliminated journalists who stood in their way through torture, imprisonment, and extra-judicial killings. Resistance was expressed in a "journalism of the caves" (*el periodismo de las catacumbas*), which, inspired by the example of the *pasquines*, reported the struggle of ordinary working people to overcome poverty and resist the regime. The more orthodox (and conservative) *La Prensa* supported and encouraged the middle-class opposition. The assassination of its editor Pedro Joachin Chamorro on 10 January 1978 was a watershed event. Chamorro's martyrdom brought about an alliance between the middle classes and the poverty-stricken majority, represented by the Sandinista Front for National Liberation (FSLN), which spearheaded the revolution of 1979.

Upon coming to power, the FSLN annulled the Somozan legal framework and in their "Fundamental Statute of the Republic" guaranteed liberty of expression and other basic rights. During the first two years of the revolution new voices became part of the journalistic mainstream. *El Nuevo Diario* was founded as an independent "workers' information cooperative", allowing reporters and printers to participate in the decision-making. *Barricada* (Barricade) was founded in 1981 as the revolutionary voice of FSLN; it was run as a "cooperative editorial enterprise", where workers also took part in making decisions. These cooperativist papers were founded and run by many journalists who had worked for *La Prensa*. That paper was finally left with only 15 per cent of its original staff. Many had left *La Prensa* because it retained the top-down management style, a style now viewed as reactionary and restrictive of the rights of the journalists to express themselves freely.

In 1980 workers at *La Prensa* had gone on strike to protest at the stockholders' control over the editorial line. Journalists contended that press freedom would be enhanced if the means of communication were less subject to control by an elite that determined content in line with their special interests. Outright expropriation of all the means of communication was rejected because this was inconsistent with Sandino's brand of pluralist libertarian socialism. The Sandinista Front was trying to steer between the extremes of capitalism and orthodox communism's system of one-party rule.

Their task became increasingly difficult as the US began to intervene directly, through the sponsorship of armed insurgents, and covertly, through Central Intelligence Agency (CIA) operations to manipulate the Nicaraguan press. In March 1982 the *New York Times* confirmed that millions of dollars were being given by the Reagan administration to "covert individuals and private organizations inside Nicaragua". The purpose was "to destabilize" the country. *Barricada* reported that several editors of *La Prensa* had met with W.E. Rooney, the CIA station chief in Managua.

The US funded an armed insurgency, the contras, to destabilize the Nicaraguan revolution. Some 30,000 people died as a result, mostly civilians. According to Fred Landis, the CIA set out to manipulate the flow of information by offering modernization of printing presses to papers that followed the "correct" ideological line, by compelling press organs to fire dissenters, and by employing propaganda and disinformation to create artificial divisions. The FSLN declared a State of National Emergency in March 1982. The Statute of Rights and Guarantees was suspended – except for article 2, which stated that the government was not authorized to suspend, even in times of emergency, "basic rights and guarantees", such as "the right to life; the physical, psychological and moral integrity of the person; the prohibition of torture; freedom of thought, conscience and religion".

Abuses occurred nevertheless. According to staff at *La Prensa,* 30 to 40 per cent of their copy was cut. Jaime Chamorro Cardenal, editor at that time, has claimed that staff were subjected to considerable intimidation. But the human rights group, Americas Watch, claimed that "what *La Prensa* was actually allowed to publish was the harshest criticism of its government that could be read in any newspaper in Central America in 1985".

Members of the Front justified the use of censorship on several grounds. How could free expression flourish in a small country like Nicaragua, the Sandinistas asked, if a wealthy superpower was left free to take control over important media organs? The US, it was argued, would certainly not have allowed the German government to fund or control US newspapers during World War II. *El Nuevo Diario* reported at the time what Fred Landis only later confirmed: that *La Prensa*, in cooperation with the CIA, was engaged in a "systematic, continual, and preplanned [attempt to deceive and disinform] . . . Nothing is impossible when that much money is available."

Restrictions were lifted during the election campaign of 1984. Private radio and TV stations were allowed free rein – many of them, according to Michael Parenti, "giving the government a daily pounding".

Voted back into power with 67 per cent of the vote, after what observers agreed was a fair election, the Sandinista Front began work on a new constitution. The document was approved by the National Assembly and promulgated in 1987. Article 30 stated that "Nicaraguans have the right to express their thought freely, in public and in private, individually and collectively, in written or in oral form or by any other means." Article 3 guarantees the existence of pluralism in the country, i.e. "the participation of political organizations in social, economic and political matters, without ideological restrictions". An exception is made, however, in the case of those organizations "which attempt a return to the past or abet the establishment of a system similar to that of the past". This clause served to justify censorship, exercised haphazardly from 1984 until 1990, as long as the US-backed insurgents and CIA operatives posed a threat to the revolution.

In 1990 the FSLN was voted out of power, and the US ended its support of armed insurgents. The new policy towards freedom of expression of president Violeta Chamorro, widow of the assassinated editor of *La Prensa*, pleased even her critics in the FSLN. In 1996 Sandinista Carlos Tunnerman said that "with Chomorro's government in power Nicaraguans enjoyed unrestricted freedom of the press". Tomas Borge, one of the most prominent Sandinistas, admitted that while in power the FSLN committed "many errors which cost them power" in 1990. Among these was "censorship of the press", which could only partly be excused because the government was under military pressure from "the most powerful country in the world".

After the expiration of Violeta Chamorro's mandate, the presidency was assumed by Arnoldo Alemn, who defeated the Sandinista opposition in 1996. The political chasm immediately widened with severe repercussions for Nicaragua's stability. As the state began to teeter on the brink of an open class war, freedom of speech, of association, and of the press came under threat. Whereas Violeta Chamorro had agreed to give legal status to many of the expropriations made by the Sandinistas for the poorer classes, Arnoldo Alemn decided to return many properties to their pre-1979 owners. Carlos Tunnerman, who had praised "Violeta", spoke of Alemn's government as one with "authoritarian features". The leader of the FSLN, Daniel Ortega, said: "If the government continues to advance its dictatorial program we will have no other alternative but to take up arms again. We will not allow a return to the dictatorship. Since he came in, Alemn has closed all the democratic spaces."

In March 1997, after the Sandinistas sponsored a paralyzing general strike, their main bureau of information was burned to the ground. An FSLN radio broadcast announced that the building was torched "presumably by liberals who were irritated by the Sandinista's campaign of protest". A few days later, the young son of a reporter working at La Prensa was kidnapped.

Alemn caused a stir in media circles when he fired 56 employees of the Office of Social Communication to pre-empt a possible strike by the television workers to protest the new government's political line. Even more provocative was the statement issued on 30 April 1997, by El Consejo Superior de Empresa Privada (The High Council for Private Enterprise, or COSEP). COSEP alleged that the Nicaraguan media was displaying increasingly strong "leftist tendencies," and warned businessmen to be "prudent", urging them to withhold advertising revenues from offending media outlets. Daniel Ortega accused COSEP of wanting "to suppress the publication of acts of corruption". The cooperativist paper, Barricada, alleged the existence of an "illicit cohabitation" between COSEP and the government, directed against the more democratically organized forms of media. In 1998 Barricada was forced to close, because many advertisers followed COSEP's direction and boycotted the paper.

The Committee to Protect Journalist (CPJ) Year 2000 report describes "a tense state of confrontation between the means of communication and the government, which continues to use its its power to punish the more critical news organs". According to the CPJ, the government practices favoritism in alloting state advertising revenues. "In 1999, a new paper called The News, with less than 2% of the national circulation, was granted 25% of the state 'anouncements'." Meanwhile, La Prensa suffered an audit, "because, unlike The News, it had roundly criticized senior government officials, accusing them of corruption".

PAUL WELLEN

Further Reading

Article 19, *Information, Freedom and Censorship: World Report 1991*, London: Article 19, Library Association Publishing, 1981

Bolaos G., Enrique, *Como Negar la Información al Pueblo: Recordando la Censura*, Managua: COSEP, 1987

Cardenal, Roberto, *Lo que se quiso ocultar: 8 años de censura sandinista*, San José: Libro Libre, 1989

Chamorro Cardenal, Jaime, *La Prensa: The Republic of Paper*, New York: Freedom House, 1988

Cross, Nigel, "Revolution and the Press in Nicaragua", *Index on Censorship*, 11/2 (April 1982)

Cuadra, Pablo Antonio, "Full Circle to Dictatorship", *Index on Censorship*, 15/10 (November–December 1986)

Jiménez Ruvulcaba, Maria del Carmen, *El estado de emergencia y el periodismo en Nicaragua*, Guadalajara, Mexico: Universidad de Guadalajara, 1987

Landis, Fred, "CIA Media Operations in Chile, Jamaica and Nicaragua", offprint from *Covert Action Information Bulletin*, 1981

Ramirez, Sergio (editor), *El pensamiento vivo de Sandino*, San José, Costa Rica: Universitaria Centroamericana, 1974

Rushdie, Salman, *The Jaguar Smile: A Nicaraguan Journey*, London: Pan, and New York: Viking, 1987

NICKELODEONS

On 19 June 1905 Harry Davis opened a storefront theatre on Smithfield Street, Pittsburgh, and called it a Nickelodeon. Unlike previous venues it offered a fixed exhibition site specifically for the screening of films and frequent programme changes; its name was taken from the entrance fee of 5 cents. Similar exhibition sites were quickly established, initially in the industrial cities of the Midwest, such as Chicago, or in those cities with a large population, such as New York and Philadelphia. The "nickel madness" offered great entrepreneurial opportunities, with many exhibitors and proprietors experiencing significant daily receipts with relatively small fixed expenses. It has been estimated that, by 1907, between 7000 and 10,000 nickelodeons had opened in the United States.

The boom lasted only three years, with the number of sites having reached a point of saturation by 1908. This, also, was when the first picture house appeared. A more sophisticated and commodious theatre for film, it led to the demise of the nickelodeon. By 1914, the number of storefront theatres had declined considerably and the era of the nickelodeon was over.

From the beginning, nickelodeons were the subject for concern and condemnation. It was easy to open a nickelodeon and many emerged in unused or empty buildings, shops, and tenement lofts. Expenditure on fixtures was, in many, minimal and they were frequently seen to be violating building and fire regulations; nitrate film is inflammable and theatres were overcrowded and lacked sufficient fire exits and fireproofing. Charles Musser writes that "by the summer of 1907 two to three film fires were occurring each week in the State of Ohio, where the press reported '75 disastrous fires within the past year'" and that "following the fires in Birmingham [Alabama, August 1907], electricity was cut off in all but one of the city's nickelodeons until they conformed to newly adopted fire laws".

The nickelodeons were noisy. Many businesses complained about the playing of outdoor music and the cry of outside barkers to attract customers. In some cases even "ballyhoo wagons" were pushed on to the streets to promote the films. In St Louis, an ordinance was passed "that required anyone desirous of setting up a nickelodeon to obtain signed permission from the owners of neighbouring stores and homes, not only next door but also across the street, stating that they would not object to noise" (May 1980).

Many nickelodeons were respectable, but as venues for a new cheap form of mass entertainment, which was often open all night, they became an easy target for campaigns from the press and the pulpit. The *Chicago Tribune*, for instance, in 1907 maintained a series of daily denunciations of the nickelodeons. They were regarded as dens of vice, and women and children were seen to be in the most danger. The yellow press, in particular, fuelled stories of the white slave trade and of young women being drugged and kidnapped in darkened theatres. This led to a call, from Dr Anna Shaw, for a woman police officer to be positioned outside and inside the theatres (May 1980). Such spaces were also seen to aid promiscuity and provide a cloak for courting couples. However, as Lauren Rabinovitz has noted, the nickelodeons created a venue that promoted sexual egalitarianism and the danger of the theatres was that they "may well have liberated women from familial constraints and Victorian sexual restraints".

Large numbers of children regularly attended nickelodeons and concern was expressed that many were not accompanied by adults and that they were viewing obscene and immoral films. In 1907 a suit was brought by the Children's Aid Society (founded in 1853) against George E. Watson, the owner of a nickelodeon on Third Avenue, New York. He was successfully prosecuted and fined $100 "on a charge of imperiling the morals of young boys" (Czitrom 1996). Four boys under the age of 14 had viewed the film *The Unwritten Law*, a dramatization of the crimes of Stanford White and Harry Thaw of 1946, which had depicted White drugging a woman and later his being shot. Another New York nickelodeon proprietor, William Short, was arrested for screening to children a scene that had depicted a Chinese opium den. The case was heard by a police magistrate who stated that "If any man should show that picture to my child I would kill him. The town is full of these sort of places and they are doing incalculable harm. The police should close every one of them" (Czitrom 1996).

The content of films concerned religious leaders greatly and with screenings on Sundays, nickelodeons were also seen to be breaking the Sabbath. Campaigns and public meetings were organized by religious groups. One such organization, the Interdenominational Committee for the Suppression of Sunday Vaudeville, was established in New York in late 1906 by canon William Sheafe Chase of the Christ Episcopal Church and the Reverend F.M. Foster, a Presbyterian. They campaigned for the enforcement of a New York state law of 1860 prohibiting Sunday theatre performances.

Under sustained pressure from social reformists Chicago became the first local council to censor films when it passed a city ordinance on 4 November 1907. This decreed that all films to be shown in Chicago had to be first screened to the police for approval. Meanwhile, in New York, a new police commissioner, Theodore Bingham, had been appointed. He promised a tough approach to the nickelodeons and that he would personally review all applications that were made for an entertainment licence. The mayor of New York, George H. McClellan Jr, needing to take swift action against the city's nickelodeons, did so in dramatic style. Famously, on Christmas Eve 1908, he revoked the licences of the 550 film theatres in New York. Soon after, on 25 March 1909, a Board of Censorship for New York City had its first meeting. The Board was funded from within the film industry, then predominantly based in New York, and it established a voluntary form of film censorship aimed at reducing the direct influence of politicians and the police. This was the basis for a national code for film censorship.

IAN CONRICH

Further Reading

Allen, Robert C., "Motion Picture Exhibition in Manhattan, 1906–1912: Beyond the Nickelodeon" in *Film before Griffith*, edited by John Fell, Berkeley: University of California Press, 1983

Allen, Robert C., "Manhattan Myopia; or, Oh! Iowa!", *Cinema Journal*, 35/3 (1996): 75–103

Bowser, Eileen, *History of the American Cinema*, vol. 2: *The Transformation of Cinema, 1907–1915*, New York: Scribner, 1990

Czitrom, Daniel, "The Politics of Performance: Theater Licensing and the Origins of Movie Censorship in New York" in *Movie Censorship and American Culture*, edited by Francis G. Couvares, Washington, DC: Smithsonian Institution Press, 1996

Fuller, Kathryn H., *At the Picture Show: Small-Town Audiences and the Creation of Movie Fan Culture*, Washington, DC: Smithsonian Institution Press, 1996

Higashi, Sumiko, "Dialogue: Manhattan's Nickelodeons", *Cinema Journal*, 35/3 (1996): 72–74

May, Lary, *Screening Out the Past: The Birth of Mass Culture and the Motion Picture Industry*, Oxford and New York: Oxford University Press, 1980

Merritt, Russell, "Nickelodeon Theatres, 1905–1914: Building an Audience for the Movies" in *The American Film Industry*, edited by Tino Balio, Madison: University of Wisconsin Press, 1976; revised edition 1985

Musser, Charles, *History of the American Cinema*, vol. 1: *The Emergence of Cinema: The American Screen to 1907*, New York: Scribner, and New York: Macmillan, 1990

Rabinovitz, Lauren, "Temptations of Pleasure: Nickelodeons, Amusement Parks, and the Sights of Female Sexuality", *Camera Obscura*, 23 (May 1990): 70–89

Singer, Ben, "Manhattan Nickelodeons: New Data on Audiences and Exhibitors", *Cinema Journal*, 34/3 (1996): 5–35

Singer, Ben, "New York, Just Like I Pictured It . . .", *Cinema Journal*, 35/3 (1996): 104–28

Staiger, Janet, *Bad Women: Regulating Sexuality in Early American Cinema*, Minneapolis: University of Minnesota Press, 1995

PETER NIESEWAND
Rhodesian journalist, born 1944

In 1973 freelance journalist Peter Niesewand paid a high price for exposing the secret involvement of Ian Smith's Rhodesian Front regime in military operations in neighbouring Mozambique. In a case which was to signal the rebel Rhodesian regime's growing censorship of the domestic and foreign media, Niesewand was detained under Emergency Powers regulations and brought before a secret court. In the event, the case proved a political disaster for the Smith regime – and a sign of things to come.

Niesewand, a 28 year-old naturalized Rhodesian of South African origin, was one of the best-known foreign correspondents reporting from Rhodesia. In late 1972, following his reports for Britain's *Guardian* and the BBC on Rhodesia's military assistance to Portugal in the fight against FRELIMO nationalist insurgents, Niesewand's house was raided by security police. Documents and notes were carted away for inspection. In February 1973 he was detained under the Law and Order (Maintenance) Act, which allowed "preventive detention" of those "believed likely to commit or incite acts endangering public safety". The following month he was tried *in camera* under the Official Secrets Act in the first secret trial in Rhodesian legal history (many more would follow).

Previously, journalists in Rhodesia had been allowed to attend *in camera* cases involving national security issues, as long as they agreed not to publish sensitive details of the cases. But for Niesewand's trial reporters were barred from the court proceedings, and prevented from publishing even the details of the charges laid against him. Niesewand was kept in solitary confinement in an 8ft by 10ft cell for a total of 72 days before and during his trial, and was adopted by Amnesty International as one of 110 Rhodesian prisoners of conscience.

The main charge against Niesewand involved Section 3(a) (ii) of the Rhodesian Official Secrets Act of 1970, which made it an offence to "obtain, collect, publish or communicate to any other person information calculated to be or which might be useful directly or indirectly to an enemy of the country". His reports on Mozambique had quoted unnamed Rhodesian military intelligence sources, and it is likely that the legal case against the journalist arose when he refused to reveal these to the authorities. However, as the journalist's lawyer argued, the news of Rhodesian activity in Mozambique did not constitute a threat to national security, as it had been common knowledge among both Rhodesian journalists and Mozambique's freedom fighters that Rhodesian troops were operating across the border.

The real reason for the attack on Niesewand, as the journalist later argued in exile, was the growing need of the Rhodesian state to clamp down on political criticism and perceived "dissent" in the media. His revelations of Rhodesia's increasing vulnerability to nationalist guerrillas, and its resort to covert military operations, had proved a major embarrassment to the Smith regime, threatening to deflate white morale in the sanctions-hit country. "The local press is listless and self censoring, fearful of the prospect of nationalism", Niesewand wrote in *The Guardian* (5 May 1973). "Journalists working for newspapers and broadcasting outside Rhodesia posed the threat. I was selected to be made an example of ... I was lucky.

I was white and a journalist. In other (jails) ... scores of African detainees were incarcerated. Some had been held without trial or charge for a decade."

Niesewand's case proved a benchmark in the Rhodesian government's attack on "unfriendly" foreign journalists – of whom more than 60 were deported or declared prohibited immigrants between UDI in 1965 and 1973. Intimidation was now extended beyond summary deportation to include legal harassment and assault. This was underlined by the unusually harsh sentence handed down upon his conviction in April 1973. Niesewand was sentenced to two years hard labour with one year suspended, and held incommunicado while an appeal was launched. Bail was set at 20,000 Rand (£13,000), which several observers claimed was a record. At the sentencing, journalists described the "extraordinary" measures taken by police to seal off the courts from observers. Special Branch police photographers took pictures of demonstrators gathered outside the court.

However, Niesewand's trial and subsequent sentence soon represented more of an embarrassment than his initial news reports, and it became apparent that the Smith regime had badly misjudged the local and international response. A widespread and strong international outcry ensued, led by a range of political interests, media, and human rights organizations. In Britain, Harold Wilson (then leader of the opposition) expressed his disgust with the "blatant attack on Press freedom and human rights", and noted "this trial has clearly been staged for the purpose of intimidating any other journalist who seeks to find and print the truth about Rhodesia". Mounting pressure in Britain led to an official government protest registered through back-door diplomatic channels in South Africa. In Salisbury, Niesewand's journalist associates approached Commonwealth secretary-general, Arnold Smith, demanding intervention. Even the normally docile *Rhodesia Herald* condemned the case, saying that secret trials were alien to the "Rhodesian way of life".

Most observers reported surprise on the part of the Smith regime over the strongly negative world reaction, which was a serious setback at a time when it was anxious to prove the openness and stability of the political situation in sanctions-beleaguered Rhodesia. Niesewand's High Court appeal, which proved successful on 1 May 1973, therefore offered government a means out of the immediate crisis. After winning his appeal, again held under extraordinary *in camera* circumstances, Niesewand remained in detention under the original Law and Order (Maintenance) Act regulations.

Eventually, two days later, following rising demands for his release and free passage out of the country, Niesewand was put on a plane to exile in Europe. In a last attempt to keep a lid on his reportage, Rhodesian authorities demanded that the journalist sign a document promising not to reveal military intelligence or information surrounding his detention and trial, in order to win his freedom. In exile in London, Niesewand argued that his "consent" in this regard had been extracted under duress, and was therefore invalid. In late 1973 he published the full details of his case in *In Camera: Secret Justice in*

Rhodesia. The book was immediately banned in Rhodesia and South Africa.

Inside Rhodesia, the Niesewand case pointed the way to a bleak future. The president of the Rhodesian Guild of Journalists, Bill McLean, noted that despite the vindication and release of Niesewand local journalists remained concerned about the political intentions of the government. "We want an assurance that the general working journalist in this country will be able to do his job without the threat of deportation hanging over his head," McLean wrote in the domestic media.

This did not come to pass. Rather, Rhodesian press censorship and other constraints placed on the media would increase throughout the 1970s, as several local media were muffled and then banned; freedom to report on a broad range of political and economic issues was further curtailed; and scores of journalists were banned, deported and otherwise harassed.

RICHARD SAUNDERS

Writings

In Camera: Secret Justice in Rhodesia, 1973

Further Reading

Catholic Commission for Justice and Peace in Rhodesia, *Rhodesia: The Propaganda War*, London: CIIR, 1977

Caute, David, *Under the Skin: The Death of White Rhodesia*, London: Allen Lane, and Evanston, Illinois: Northwestern University Press, 1983

Fothergill, Rowland, *Mirror over Rhodesia: The Rhodesian Press, 1962–1980*, Johannesburg: Argus, 1985

Frederikse, Julie, *None but Ourselves: Masses vs. Media in the Making of Zimbabwe*, Harare: Zimbabwe Publishing House, 1982; London: Heinemann, 1983; New York: Penguin, 1984

International Defence and Aid Fund for Southern Africa, *"Civilised Standards" in Rhodesia: The Law and Order (Maintenance) Act*, London: IDAFSA, 1976 (Fact Paper on Southern Africa 1)

Parker, John, *Rhodesia: Little White Island*, London: Pitman, 1972

Ranger, Terence, "Rhodesia: The Propaganda War", *New Statesman* (22 June 1979): 919–22

Windrich, Elaine, *The Mass Media in the Struggle for Zimbabwe. Censorship and Propaganda under Rhodesian Front Rule*, Gwelo, Zimbabwe: Mambo Press, 1981

NIGER

(formerly part of French West Africa)

Population: 10,832,000	**Number of daily newspapers:** 1
Main religions: Muslim; Christian; indigenous religions	**Number of periodicals:** 5
Official language: French	**Number of radio receivers per 1000 inhabitants:** 70
Other languages spoken: Hausa; Tuareg; Djerma; Fulani	**Number of TV receivers per 1000 inhabitants:** 13
Illiteracy rate (%): 76.2 (m); 91.6 (f)	**Number of PCs per 1000 inhabitants:** 7.8

Once part of the 16th-century Songhaï empire, whose centres of scholarship were unequalled in sub-Saharan Africa, the land-locked state of Niger is, at the beginning of the new millennium, one of the world's poorest countries. By 1934, after 50 years of colonial rule, only 2872 children attended school; by 1980 only 13 per cent of school-age children had the chance of attending classes; by 1997 86.4 per cent of the country's people could still neither read nor write.

Over twice the size of France, whose colony it once was, Niger is a desert country whose southern Sahelian rim borders the vastly more populous and richer Nigeria, with which it shares most of its cross-border trade and a sizeable Hausa population (56 per cent of Niger's total). Its northern neighbours Mali, Algeria, and Libya share with Niger desert borders and the nomadic Tuareg people, or Tamasheks. To the west the fertile bend of the Niger river from which the country derives its name links it to francophone west Africa through Benin, Burkina Faso, and Mali. This region contains the Djerma people who, with the Fulbe or Peuls, make up another third of Niger's ethnic mix. The country is predominantly Muslim, with French its official (but minority) language.

During the 1970s chronic instability in Chad to the east and the designs on its mineral-rich northern borderlands by Libya highlighted Niger's vulnerable strategic situation at the crossroads of west and central Africa. Economic development was boosted by the discovery of uranium reserves, but hampered by

the lack of qualified local technicians. The slump in uranium prices and ensuing financial crisis from the early 1980s, coupled with severe droughts in 1973–75 and 1985–86 saw Niger become overwhelmingly dependent on western aid. By the mid-1990s over 20 per cent of its annual budget went on servicing its debts. A pro-democracy movement asserted itself from 1989, with a National Convention in 1991 creating new civil society structures, only to be thwarted by a military coup in January 1996. The "accidental" assassination of the president in April 1999 ushered in a further period of uncertainty for the country.

Niger's independence in 1958 took place in the context of heated rivalry between Diori Hamani's Niger Progressive Party and the Sawaba (Liberty) Party of Djibo Bakary, which claimed it had been cheated of victory by electoral manipulation by the French. A call to insurrection made by Sawaba leadership in exile led to quick extinction of the revolt and a period of political repression. The ensuing years of Diori's personalized rule were marked by corruption and stagnation, with sporadic student unrest and strike action. The ill-acquired wealth of Diori's entourage was in stark contrast to the country's poverty and proved particularly intolerable when severe drought struck in 1973, driving hordes of destitute nomads out of the desert into the barely more fertile Sahel lands to the south.

The unscrupulous diversion of relief aid into the pockets of government officials led directly to lieutenant colonel Seyni Kountché's military coup on 15 April 1974, ushering in a régime of austerity and the almost complete stifling of political life. These repressive tendencies were reinforced after the suppression of coup plots in 1975, 1976, and 1983. While a return to civilian rule was promised, no deadline was given and the military continued to rule through a Conseil National de la Société de Développement. The adoption of a new National Charter, scheduled for 1983, was constantly delayed on the pretext of the acute economic crisis into which the country had plunged by the mid-1980s.

These circumstances created an environment in which information was subject to complete state control, the country's 60 working journalists operating in conditions of self-censorship with no leeway for personal initiative. There was no apparent need for direct censorship: the country's sole television and radio stations, its press agency, and two press titles being 100 per cent state-owned, the fear of instant dismissal for journalists was sufficient dissuasion. No foreign journalists were based in Niger, and those who visited the country found that even ministers were unwilling to speak, on or off the record, for fear of reprisals. The taciturn president Kountché remained the country's only official spokesman.

When general Kountché died in 1987 after 13 years in power, the more outgoing army chief Ali Saïbou replaced him, pronouncing a general amnesty but ruling out any progression towards a multiparty system. Government remained based on a de facto alliance between the military and powerful Hausa traders. A new constitution in 1989 consecrated one-party rule under a Mouvement National pour une Société de Développement (MNSD), which designated Ali Saïbou president for the next seven years. However, this "Second Republic" was to be severely discredited by two key events: the deaths of a dozen striking students on the Kennedy Bridge across the River Niger in February 1990, and in May of that same year the severe repression meted out to unarmed Tuareg citizens following an armed attack on a remote northern military outpost at Tchin Tabaraden. These events signalled, on the one hand, the reassertion of civil society through a new generation of intellectuals and activists impatient for change; and on the other, the start of a rebellion triggered by the enforced return of some 20,000 Tuaregs from neighbouring countries. Having worked as migrant labourers or fought in Libya's "Islamic Legion", these *ichomeren* (or *chomeurs* – unemployed) now found themselves denied assistance and excluded from society in their own country. Their revolt came against a backdrop of economic slump, cereal and livestock deficit, crushing debt burden, and continued desertification. 1990 also saw a five-day general strike called by the trade unions for an end to IMF-imposed austerity and the installation of multiparty democracy, in line with the wave of reform that was sweeping through French-speaking Africa after starting in neighbouring Benin.

Under this pressure, Ali Saïbou agreed to a constitutional revision which would allow the creation of political parties and non-governmental organizations (NGOs), with the military stepping down from the ruling MNSD party. Some 20 parties and numerous NGOs formed in anticipation of the July 1991 National Convention, while a free press was able to set up in business openly, drawing many of its contributors from the state-controlled press – some of them working for both systems simultaneously. The independent journal *Haské*, founded in 1990, attracted a circle of independent critics of government

who helped spearhead the changes in favour of democracy. By the time the "Sovereign National Convention" brought together over 1200 representatives of civil society, the country was almost bankrupt. The delegates drew a bitter picture of 30 years of misrule since independence. They suspended the constitution, elected a prime minister, but kept on Ali Saïbou as a figurehead president until the end of the transitional period in December 1993. Among other acts of the National Convention was the creation, in October 1991, of a Conseil Supérieur de la Communication (CSC), whose function was to guarantee press freedom from all forms of interference and censorship, and to ensure equal access to the media.

The first challenge to the transitional regime was to come from the army, which by now was engaged in a desert war against the Tuareg rebels and who seized control of the national radio and television on several occasions during February 1992 in order to put pressure on the government to pay arrears of salary and to release one of their number imprisoned for the Tchin Tabaraden killings. This virtual coup attempt was finally thwarted only after a general strike action by an alliance of "Niger Democratic Forces" representing civil society. In August that same year, following the murder of a policeman in the northern town of Agadès, local law-enforcement agents acting on their own initiative seized a large number of alleged suspects including the local prefect and ordered the town's radio station to broadcast a declaration condemning the "inactivity" of the transitional government faced with the Tuareg rebellion. They called for media coverage of their action, and it was given on national television news. The independent press made much of this showdown between uncontrolled elements of the security forces and the transitional government, whose authority suffered in consequence. A general conference of media practitioners, the États Généraux de la Communication, in session two months later called for a self-regulating code of professional ethics for journalists, autonomous status for all public broadcasting and print media, and the creation of a fund to assist the private press sector.

The accession to the presidency of Mahamane Ousmane, Niger's first democratically elected head of state, in April 1993 ended the transitional period and opened the way for resolution of the Tuareg rebellion by the release of the last of the Agadès hostages and the start of talks with the rebel front. The adoption of the new democratic constitution in December 1992 and the subsequent victory at the polls of the Alliance of Forces for Change (AFC), gave a strong impulsion to a government programme intent on overcoming the country's ethnic and regional divisions in order to tackle the long-standing economic crisis. This meant renewal of dialogue with the IMF and World Bank, which had been broken off in 1991, and signature in January 1994 of a structural adjustment programme, which led directly to debt-service relief, but also prompted further social unrest.

Under the new regime the independent press was able to operate without interference, and a dozen new publications made their appearance in Niamey, the capital, including a satirical weekly *Le Paon africain* (The African Peacock). However, these journals spoke only to the country's small French-language elite, and distribution beyond the capital proved uneconomic and logistically difficult. Similarly, the Télé-Sahel television service – which now gave equal airtime to parties during the elections – only functioned in urban centres. Only the radio station, La Voix du Sahel, could claim national coverage over this vast country. Even here, levels of extreme poverty meant that possession of a transistor radio was a luxury, and the purchase of batteries problematic. Listeners were as likely to tune in to the Hausa-language services of international broadcasters and of Nigeria. Media staff were also living close to poverty, and their concerns for securing a living wage risked eclipsing the movement to establish new press legislation. In March 1993, all 430 staff members of the Office de Radiodiffusion et Télévision du Niger went on strike to obtain salary arrears and the adoption of texts guaranteeing media freedom. In September 1993 the Syndicat des Agents de l'Information (SAINFO) joined 39,000 striking civil servants in a five-day strike against renewed economic austerity measures and a five-month delay in payment of their salaries.

The devaluation of the CFA franc in January 1994 struck a further blow to the information sector, where lack of advertising revenue hindered development, and technical incidents and strike action interrupted the public-service broadcast media. A new and disturbing element, however, was a marked increase in tension between the government and the independent media in 1994–95, as competition for access to dwindling resources was exploited in some quarters by the manipulation of ethnic differences. Thus some leading press titles, and a number of new and more extreme ones, yielded to the temptation to adopt ethnic stereotyping to explain the country's troubles, rather than engage in serious political analysis. The ongoing confrontation with the Tuareg rebels, which had not yet achieved a settlement, contributed to this vindictive atmosphere. Le Républicain, one of the few journals to cover this war with some degree of impartiality, was discounted by others on the sole grounds that its director was a Tamashek (Tuareg). In February 1994, the director of the left-wing (and anti-Hausa) Tribune du Peuple was arrested and fined for publishing a defamatory letter questioning the competence of a minister; while in April and May the weeklies Alfazar and Anfani received heavy fines for reporting an alleged coup attempt, after being charged with libelling two army officers said to have been involved. Radio journalists also complained when their weekly round-up of the press was dropped in November, and only won its reinstatement after threatening strike action.

From October 1994 this heated atmosphere was compounded by the enforced "cohabitation", after a vote of censure and the collapse of the ruling coalition, of the elected head of state Mahamane Ousmane with a prime minister, Hama Amadou, imposed by the former ruling party MNSD. The ensuing conflict exacerbated the divisive tendencies of the print media, and undermined the authority of state institutions, including the state-controlled media. In July 1995 leading members of the pro-presidential party burst into the CSC headquarters after publicly threatening its secretary-general Abdoulaye Souleye at a press conference, apparently for disrespectful remarks he was said to have made about the president during an earlier television broadcast. That same day the CSC banned the broadcast media from making any statement about the political "cohabitation" of the country's leaders until the crisis cooled down. It claimed the spate of broadcast reports were likely to threaten public order and national unity. This

prompted the main trade union grouping, USTN, to charge that the CSC had yielded to political pressures and was defaulting on its statutory functions of guaranteeing press freedoms by depriving citizens of their rightful access to the news. The upshot of this turmoil was a draft press law presented to parliament in December 1995, which both the CSC and the press union SAINFO condemned as an attack on press freedom, depriving journalists of their prerogative to treat information in an honest and independent spirit. Similarly, the government announced its intention to "restore order" to the state media. These intended measures were interrupted, as was the entire democratic process, by the military coup staged by the army chief of staff Ibrahim Maïnassara Baré on 27 January 1996.

In the name of "saving Niger from chaos" colonel Maïnassara called a state of emergency, suspending all democratic institutions, including political parties. The army occupied the three private radio stations in Niamey, and closed down the CSC (until April). Under pressure from donors, a new constitution was introduced in May 1996 as a prelude to presidential elections in July, which Maïnassara won by a small margin after dissolving the independent National Electoral Commission and placing his three opponents under house arrest for the duration of the vote. The media continued to operate, but in a climate of threats and intimidation, with the private radio station Anfani being forcibly closed down on orders from the interior minister for three weeks during and after the July elections. Journalists and editors of both written and broadcast media were repeatedly held for questioning without warrant and beyond the legal limits of police custody, interrogated, and sometimes charged, though never brought to court and usually released after a few rough days in detention. Accusations included "insulting and defaming the ruling council", "inciting rebellion and public hatred", and so on by articles touching on the presidential aspirations or private life of colonel Maïnassara. In May public broadcasting employees condemned the "increasingly overt attacks on press freedom in the public sector media", while SAINFO raged against what it termed "the confiscation of state media for the sake of individual self-promotion".

Threats and aggression reached their height during the July elections, when journalists were prevented from covering civil unrest in the provincial town of Zinder. In mid-July the local correspondents of both the BBC and Radio France-Internationale were given a "last warning" by the interior minister, who described them as "stateless persons" (apatrides). On 30 July the BBC's correspondent Abdoulaye Seyni was held for three days at the Intelligence Service headquarters for reporting the suspension of American aid to Niger, on the grounds that this information might "sow confusion within national and international public opinion".

The independent radio station Anfani was singled out for particular attention. Its director Gremah Boukar was questioned in late 1996 about interviews with opposition spokesmen and the former president, Mahamane Ousmane. Anfani then announced that it was ceasing its news bulletins "as a result of intimidation", because it was proving "impossible to inform the public in an objective fashion". In January 1997 police burst into its studios to prevent a statement by the Magistrates' Union being broadcast, and on 1 March uniformed men ransacked its offices. Three staff members were held following an item blaming the army for this wilful damage, while Boukar was arrested for attempted fraud after the authorities claimed he had organized the attack himself. All were later released.

The Press Freedom Law adopted on 23 June 1997 was Niger's first legislation designed to regulate the media. It sought to license journalists through a restrictive press-card system, required pre-publication delivery of journals and periodicals to the public prosecutor's office, and rendered defamation of any public official a criminal offence, prescribing fines and imprisonment for offenders, and their professional deregistration. This prompted an outcry from international rights groups and national civil society bodies alike. However, the law failed to stifle either the outspokenness of local journalists, or the zeal with which they were (sometimes literally) pursued by the authorities. Anfani was again closed down in April 1998 after broadcasting a joint statement by Nigerian and foreign journalists denouncing press censorship. Moussa Tchangari, who read out the statement, was beaten by state security agents both publicly and in detention before being released without charge. Other journalists, including international correspondents, were subjected to violence, and their equipment was confiscated. A printing works used by the independent press was set ablaze, and other opposition publications were closed for non-payment of taxes. By October 1998 the CSC, the body originally set up to ensure respect for press freedom, announced moves designed to deregister several newspaper editors and to prevent the retransmission of live news from international radio networks. The last bulwark against official abuse of the media had itself fallen prey to it.

The unexplained accidental death of president Maïnassara in April 1999 did little to dispel the concerns of those few outsiders who followed Niger's loss of its late-won freedoms. He was succeeded as head of state by the commander of the Presidential Guard.

A new constitution was adopted in July 1999, leading to parliamentary and presidential elections that brought Mamadou Tandja to power. On International Press Freedom Day in May 2000, the chairman of the Observatoire National de la Communication or media ombudsman reported that Niger's press was in "good health" within a positive legal environment, but that financial and tax constraints still inhibited its functions. However, a year later the ombudsman was himself taken to task by the independent press for criticizing the reborn *Canard Libéré*, which the government pursued relentlessly in the courts for allegedly "undermining army morale". Journalists from another independent paper, *L'Enquêteur*, were detained for "disturbing public order" after reporting a border dispute with neighbouring Benin, which effectively closed down the paper. These unwelcome developments prompted local and international protests.

MARGUERITE GARLING

Further Reading

Biarnès, Pierre, *L'Afrique aux africains: 20 ans d'indépendance en Afrique noire francophone*, Paris: Colin, 1980

L'État du monde, annual reports by Amnesty International and Reporters sans Frontières

Fugelstad, Finn, *A History of Niger, 1850–1960*, Cambridge and New York: Cambridge University Press, 1983

Ki-Zerbo, Joseph, *Histoire de l'Afrique noire: d'hier à demain*, Paris: Hatier, 1972

Maja-Pearce, Adewale (editor), *Directory of African Media*, Brussels: International Federation of Journalists, 1995

Observatoire de l'Information, *L'Information dans le monde: 206 pays au microscope*, Paris: Seuil, 1989

Websites

Centre d'Etudes d'Afrique Noire (CEAN), University of Bordeaux, http://www.cean.u-bordeaux.fr/etat/chronologie/niger.html

Niger Human Rights Watch (section on censorship) under Focus on Niger at http://www.txdirect.net/users/jmayer/fon.html

NIGERIA

Population: 113,862,000	**Number of daily newspapers:** 25
Main religions: Muslim; Christian; indigenous religions	**Number of radio receivers per 1000 inhabitants:** 226
Official language: English	
Other languages spoken: Hausa; Yoruba; Ibo; Fulani	**Number of TV receivers per 1000 inhabitants:** 66
Illiteracy rate (%): 27.6 (m); 44.2 (f)	**Number of PCs per 1000 inhabitants:** 5.7

With a land area of 923,768 kilometres, a population of over 100 million, around 250 peoples and languages, and 400 dialects, Nigeria is a truly diverse federation. It is divided into 30 states, although there are three principal ethnic conglomerations: Yorubaland (in the southwest), Igboland (in the southeast), and Hausaland (in the north). Relations between these regions have been tense, playing a significant part in Nigeria's faltering start to independent nationhood.

Modern Nigeria emerged after the imposition of British colonial rule beginning in the 1860s. Early newspapers tended to toe the government line. The British nevertheless employed

measures to silence the nascent Nigerian press. These included the Official Secrets Ordinance (1891), the Criminal Procedure Ordinance (1900), the Wireless Telegraph Ordinance and Newspaper Ordinance (1903), and the Seditious Offences Ordinance (1909). Despite this, the press grew in size, influence and daring. Between 1890 and 1937 no fewer than 51 newspapers were founded (all but three of them based in Lagos), laying the foundations for what was to become the most prolific press in Africa, and providing openings to oppose the British presence. Among them were the *West African Pilot* and the *Daily Comet*, which reported controversial events such as the anti-tax disturbances of the 1920s and 1930s, the Enugu colliery workers strike of 1949, and political unrest in the 1950s.

When Nigeria achieved independence in 1960 the north had a population which was larger than the south and east put together. It held half the seats in the Federal Assembly. Each region was ruled by a different political party. The new constitution guaranteed "freedom to form and hold opinions and to express them, subject to laws that are reasonable, justifiable in a democratic society in the interest of defence, public safety, public order, public morality and public health". However, within two years new legislation was introduced. The Official Secrets Act of 1962 prescribed two years' imprisonment or a fine for obtaining and reproducing classified information. Then in 1964 an amendment was introduced designed to "curb recklessness or irresponsibility of certain sections of the press". A £200 fine or one year in prison was now to be imposed for publishing rumours which later proved to be false.

These were the actions of a beleaguered government. The alliance between the conservative northerners and a radical southern party, which had held the federal assembly together, collapsed in 1964. There was serious disorder in the west. Two years later, in 1966, after pogroms against southerners living in the north, the first of Nigeria's military coups resulted in the murder of the federal prime minister, Abubakar Tafawa Balewa, and two other regional leaders. General Ironsi, an Ibo, took control, but lasted only a short time, to be replaced by general Yakubu Gowon, a northerner and a Christian. Gowon failed to quell unrest in the north. In 1967 colonel Chukwuemeka Ojukwu, a prominent Ibo officer, announced the secession of east Nigeria, and the short-lived republic of Biafra was born.

The Biafran secession led to the declaration of a state of emergency. The government warned that "no political statements in the press or other publicity media will be tolerated ... the military and the police are empowered to deal summarily with any offenders". Even to mention Biafra's declaration of secession was regarded as unpatriotic. Meanwhile, Decree no. 17 of 1967 prohibited the circulation of newspapers whose content was judged to be detrimental to the federal government or that of any individual state. The novelist Chinua Achebe, who sympathized with Biafra, was forced to leave the country, having been warned that soldiers would test "which was stronger, your pen or my gun". Wole Soyinka, the playwright, was arrested after it was alleged that he had seized the western region radio station. The press and broadcasting media became, to all intents and purposes, the mouthpieces of the federal government.

The secession eventually collapsed in 1970, although general Gowon's military rule continued until 1975, when he was replaced by general Murtala Mohammed. Mohammed promised to produce a timetable for the return of Nigeria to civilian rule, but was shot in 1976 before it could be implemented. Another military officer, general Olusegun Obasanjo, took his place, eventually handing over to an elected civilian government in 1979.

By 1978 only three of the twelve national daily newspapers were privately owned. What was more, journalists on these newspapers were appointed through the Public Service Commission, and thus liable to dismissal if they displayed too much independence. Other, less subtle forms of "censorship"

also existed. Minere Amakiri of the *Nigeria Observer* was arrested and tortured for having run a story about teachers' grievances on the birthday of the governor of Rivers State. *New Breed* had published an interview with the former Biafran leader colonel Ojukwu, then in the Côte d'Ivoire, and printed a further article, "The Uses and Abuses of the Nigerian Security Organisation". It was banned. Following this incident, the government attempted to establish a "press council", which would register journalists and impose fines on erring reporters and editors; however, the Nigerian Press Organisation refused to participate and the initiative collapsed. It was not for nothing that on the gate of his farmstead general Obasanjo placed a sign "No dogs or journalists allowed".

With the return to civilian administration in 1979 a new constitution laid down that the media's role was to "uphold the responsibility and accountability of government to the people". Meanwhile, individual citizens were guaranteed "the freedom to hold opinions and to receive and impart ideas and information without interference". By this time there were in Nigeria some 15 daily papers and 12 weeklies, together with 20 television stations. However, many of them had links with the federal or state governments, chief among them the ruling National Party of Nigeria. It was not long before political parties were accusing each other of abusing the power of the media.

Nor did it take long for the press, once again, to run into trouble with the government. The editor of the *Nigerian Tribune* was arrested and charged with sedition after he had run a story claiming that the government was bribing legislators. Similarly, senior staff of the *Nigerian Standard* were arrested after they had alleged that the National Party of Nigeria was planning to assassinate political opponents in Gongola state. It became an offence even to quote from a story considered defamatory. The government was supposedly trying to "persuade" journalists to distinguish between news and comment. At the same time legislators were entering broadcast studios in order to harass journalists, interrupt newscasts, and seize prerecorded programme tapes.

Nigeria returned to military rule, that of major general Muhammadu Buhari, on 31 December 1983. The new press law gave the government power to close newspapers and shut down radio stations for up to 12 months. The most draconian new legislation, though, was the Public Officers (Protection against False Accusation) Decree of 1984, otherwise known as Decree 4. Any journalist who published a story considered injurious to a public official was liable to a minimum of two years in jail, whether the story was true or false; he would be tried by a military tribunal. The first victim of this decree was *The Guardian* newspaper, and two of its journalists, Tunde Thompson and Nduka Irabor, who had written a story which predicted the posting abroad of certain Nigerian diplomats. Later, Lateef Jakande, managing editor of the *Nigeria Tribune*, and the governor of Lagos state, was placed in detention for 20 months, with no charges brought against him. In 1984 the State Security (Detention of Persons) Decree empowered government to detain people "for acts prejudicial to state security ... or in the preparation or instigation of such acts for a renewable period of six months at a time". Tony Upkong, a business journalist for the *Weekly Metropolitan*, who was detained for eight months without charge was one victim of this legislation. He was not even told the nature of his offence when released.

The seventh military coup in the country's history (1985) brought general Ibrahim Babangida to power. A journalist, Tony Momoh, was appointed minister of information and culture. He affirmed that the job of the press was to monitor the government on behalf of the people. Decree 4 was abolished and 20 detained journalists released. However, this was a false dawn. In 1986 Dele Giwa, a well-known investigative journalist and editor of *Newswatch*, who had previously been in trouble with the government for publishing classified information (and had subsequently been accused of importing arms), was killed by a parcel bomb. The government denied any involvement, but rejected the call by the Nigerian Union of Journalists for a commission of enquiry. The following year *Newswatch* was banned for six months after it had published a confidential government report on Nigeria's return to civilian government, which, it had been announced, would take place in 1990. Further arrests followed. Journalists on *The Republic* magazine were detained after they had published allegations that the chief of general staff, vice-admiral Augustus Aikhimu, had been involved in a financial scandal. The newspaper was subsequently closed down. Ikpe Ekotudo and Tunde Ogungbile of *New Horizon* magazine were arrested for having conducted an interview with chief Gani Fawehinni, a human rights lawyer. After an aborted coup in 1990, arrests became yet more random. Tolu Olanrewaju, a Radio Nigeria journalist who was believed to have been on duty when the rebels took over the radio station, was jailed. The *Lagos News*, *Evening News*, and *Sunday News* were closed down after an editorial on the coup in the last-named paper was judged "negative and critical".

Most people would regard the mid-1990s as the darkest period in Nigeria's short history as an independent nation. A return to civilian rule had been planned for 1994, but when general Babangida realized that the westerner chief Abiola was going to win the election, he arbitrarily and abruptly cancelled it, subsequently making way for general Sani Abacha in December 1994. Abiola stayed silent for a year, but when he then declared himself to be president he was arrested and imprisoned for treason. Further repressive legislation was introduced. Decree 43 of June 1993 declared that no person could own or publish a newspaper unless they were registered with the Newspapers Registration Board, for which they had to pay a considerable sum. The staff of publications which made "false statements" were liable to seven years imprisonment. Some 19 papers were proscribed, and the list of individual journalists who were made to suffer for what they had written is a long one, including Nosa Igiebor, Hola Ilori, Omone Osifo-Whiskey, Ayodele Akinkoku, and Chris Anyanwu. All five *Guardian* titles were closed down in August 1994 after an article, "The Battle to Rule Nigeria", had revealed divisions in the cabinet between conservatives and progressives. 50,000 copies of *Teal* were seized after a headline announced "The Return of Tyranny – Abacha Bares His Fangs". Ken Saro-Wiwa, the president of the Nigerian Association of Authors and leader of the Movement for the Survival of the Ogoni People, was arrested, tried, and executed. Wole Soyinka, the dramatist, supporter of Saro-Wiwa, and long-term opponent of Nigeria's military regimes, had his passport confiscated but managed to escape, via Benin, to Europe. Underground newspapers, run on "guerrilla" lines, held the fort for free expression.

After the death of Abacha and then Abiola in 1998, civilian rule finally returned, under the former president Olusegun Obasanjo, on 29 May 1999. The ever-versatile Nigerian press returned to the fray. There are around 100 newspapers and magazines today, some financed by federal and state governments, but an increasing number in private hands. The broadcast media, hitherto entirely in government hands (with 29 radio stations broadcasting in 13 local and regional languages, and television stations in 30 states as well as the Nigeria-wide service), looks set for some degree of private ownership. In 1987 there were 20 million radio receivers and 2 million TV sets. These represent the considerable potential for the dissemination of news and opinion as long as the media are now allowed to reflect the plural nature of Nigerian society. Commentators have observed that a formidable array of legislation capable of being used for the purpose of censorship has yet to be repealed, and, while applauding president Obasanjo's intentions, are reserving judgement on the regime until this takes place.

SAHEED A. ADEJUMOBI and
TOYIN FALOLA

Further Reading

Agbaje, A.A.B., *The Nigerian Press, Hegemony, and the Social Construction of Legitimacy, 1960–1983*, Lewiston, New York: Mellen, 1992

Amnesty International, *Unshackling the Nigerian Media: An Agenda for Reform*, London: Amnesty International, 1997

Ekru, Ray, "We Have Democratised the Press", *Index on Censorship*, 21/2 (February 1992)

Exeh, Peter, "Press Cancer, Not Council", *Index on Censorship*, 19/8 (September 1990)

Faringer, Gunilla L., *Press Freedom in Africa*, New York: Praeger, 1991

Mbachu, Dulue, "Owners and Censors", *Index on Censorship*, 21/2 (February 1992)

Ogbondah, Chris W., *Military Regimes and the Press in Nigeria, 1966–1993: Human Rights and National Development*, Lanham, Maryland: University Press of America, 1994

Omu, Fred I.A., *Press and Politics in Nigeria, 1880–1937*, London: Longman, and Atlantic Highlands, New Jersey: Humanities Press, 1978

Soyinka, Wole, "Nigeria: The Last Despot", *Index on Censorship*, 23/6 (November–December 1994)

NIGERIA: Guerrilla Journalism

The Nigerian version of guerrilla journalism evolved as a form of resistance to the censorship of the military dictatorships of generals Ibrahim Badamasi Babangida and Sani Abacha between 1985 and 1998. When, by 1990, Babangida had failed to honour his promise to restore democracy, the traditionally very lively Nigerian press ended the honeymoon that he had enjoyed since he had taken power. He, in turn, issued a barrage of decrees aimed at silencing them. Individual journalists were held down by the Nigeria Press Council Decree (1992), which provided for their compulsory registration. In parallel, Newspaper Decree no. 43 (1993) forced newspapers to register with the Ministry of Information, for which they had to pay a deposit of 250,000 naira (US$3125), and a non-refundable fee of 100,000 naira ($1250); failure to register would result in closure and court proceedings. These measures were still in force in 2001. Actually, however, Babangida and Abacha hardly needed formal legislation. Crude seizure, arbitrary arrest, and the invasion of newspapers by armed security guards were the order of the day.

Extreme daring and inventiveness were required if such draconian controls were to be subverted. Resistance began in 1991, with the foundation of the weekly news magazines *Tell* and *The News* (which also owned *Tempo*). Guerrilla journalism was their creation – a highly clandestine operation, by which news that otherwise would have been forbidden by the authorities actually reached the people who needed to know what was going on.

The three magazines were written, produced, and distributed "on the run"; normal administrative back up and journalistic status were swept aside. The first necessity for a guerrilla journalist was that he assume a fictitious name, and be ready to change it from time to time. He would then be issued with a fresh identity card, bearing the logo of a newly registered innocuous newspaper, which enabled him to enjoy the privileges of journalistic access where necessity dictated this. The official operational headquarters of the magazine was now a "no go" area, because it was always under official surveillance. (However, a skeleton staff was retained at the office, not only to pay the wages, but also to observe the movement of the government "goons", and to make them realize that, despite the absence of employees, the paper was still in being. As one might have expected, the "goons" were baffled.)

The guerrilla journalist working in the field, and never staying long at a single address, needed to know that the information he was collecting would see daylight. A relay system was devised which, though cumbersome, was effective:

(1) He was briefed by an editor on ideas, storylines, deadlines, and the venue for delivery. Stories were then researched and written undercover, and dropped at the agreed place, to be picked up by an agent who would not necessarily know anything about their content or purpose.

(2) The stories were then taken to a "strong room", whose location might well change, where the magazine was edited, proof-read, and designed. Senior editors were never all present at the same time, so that if there was a leakage, and arrests occurred, some of them would be free to continue the underground activities.

(3) Because there was round-the-clock surveillance at the regular commercial printers of the magazine, the layouts were then taken to a succession of less well known printers. Compromises on aesthetics were often necessary: if the A4 glossy print had to be sacrificed for a tabloid newspaper format, this at least had the advantages that it was quicker and cheaper to print.

(4) Clearly distribution could not be carried out in company vehicles! Other ingenious ways were devised for getting the magazines to vendors and thence to readers. When they reached the streets, they could still be seized by security guards, until the vendors themselves resorted to guerrilla tactics – quietly selling the magazines to known regular customers "under the counter", flatly denying copies to customers they did not recognize.

Guerrilla journalism can only be carried out by organizations that are small and flexible. Major daily newspapers with numerous correspondents scattered all over this vast country could hardly collate and edit reports from 36 states in 24 hours, let alone avoid leakages. On the other hand, radio, e-mail, and the Internet are now providing opportunities to extend the idea in the future. Already, Radio Kudirat broadcasts regularly from an unknown location.

OSA DIRECTOR

Further Reading
Unshackling the Nigerian Media, London: Article 19, 1996

ALEKSANDR NIKITENKO
Russian censor and diarist, 1804–1877

Nikitenko had a major influence in moderating censorship in Russia through the contrasting regimes and fluctuating policies of Alexander I, Nicholas I, and the relatively liberal reformer Alexander II, the emancipator of the serfs. Nikitenko exerted this influence from within the censorship system itself, and his diary chronicles the successes and frustrations he experienced in various governmental offices, including the Ministry of Education and the Censorship Department.

Nikitenko was born a serf in Ukraine in 1804, but received a grammar school education. Like his father, he was mainly an autodidact, and at 14 he became a schoolteacher. Taken up by liberal intellectuals, Nikitenko received his freedom in 1824 and was admitted to St Petersburg University, where he wrote a literary dissertation. Among his friends and patrons were several of the Decembrist conspirators of 1825, a year for which, unsurprisingly, Nikitenko burned his diary: surviving copies now begin in 1826 and end in 1877. Employed as secretary by the superintendent of the St Petersburg school district, K.M. Borozdin, Nikitenko was put to work on a new censorship code, which led to an official position in the Censorship Department in 1833.

Between 1804 and 1865 Russian publishing was regulated under a system of pre-publication censorship or licensing comparable to that deployed in England in the 16th and 17th centuries. The supervisory mechanism was the Ministry of Education, and the motivation for censorship was largely political. One difference between the systems, however, was that in Russia a censor himself could be punished for overlooking a suspect work or a dangerous subtext. Nikitenko himself was twice imprisoned briefly for such lapses. The intensity with which censorship was exercised fluctuated according to government policy and imperial whim. In 1848, the year of revolutions known at the time as "the springtime of nations", the notorious Buturlin Committee was created to establish a further, more stringent, level of oversight. Under the liberal Alexander II, however, the censorship was considerably relaxed. After 1865, when Nikitenko was promoted to the Privy Council, pre-publication censorship was partly replaced by the imposition of post-publication penalties, which Nikitenko saw as making the situation of writers only more hazardous. On 4 July 1872 Nikitenko wrote in his diary:

A new censorship law. *Finis* press! The minister of internal affairs can do as he pleases. Regardless of the specialized content of a book, he can confiscate it. If this law is applied, science and literature will be totally paralysed in Russia.

Having begun his civil service career as a moderate, probably shocked into that position by the fate of the Decembrists, Nikitenko constantly struggles in his diary to define what a moderate censorship should and should not do. He wanted, for the system, consistency and centralization; for writers, clear guidelines; and from writers of all kinds, social responsibility. Under the Buturlin Committee in 1848, he wrote in rage (as translated by Helen Saltz Jacobson) that:

censor Mekhelin is expurgating from ancient history the names of all great people who fought for the freedom of their country or were of a republican turn of mind in the republics of Greece and Rome . . . These people are blind: they don't see that by keeping learned ideas from being advanced through the printed word, they are forcing them to be transmitted by word of mouth. And this is far more dangerous, for bitterness born of irritation and indignation is unconsciously added in speech, while, in the press, it is restrained by censorship and decorum.

In December 1860, he wrote that the problem lay rather with the writers:

At the beginning of the present reign, our writers were not sufficiently tactful to benefit from the increased freedom bestowed on the press. They could have done a great deal to strengthen certain principles of society and incline the government towards various liberal measures, but instead they went to extremes and spoiled everything . . . forgetting that only a year or so ago they would scarcely have been allowed to hold a pen in their hands. They wanted everything at once and began to attack everything in sight . . . Instead of using the printed word, they abused it. I tried in vain to be the mediator between literature and the government, but literature had gone so far that it suddenly found itself in open and bitter opposition to the government, while the government shuddered and began in earnest to tighten the reins.

At the end of 1866, while observing that another reactionary period seemed to have begun, Nikitenko articulated a newly progressive principle:

Once a certain measure of free thought and speech has been permitted, there is no turning back. This freedom must be permitted and acknowledged as a new element in the life of our society in much the same way as the need for various social and administrative changes is acknowledged. Certain abuses of the printed word must then be regarded as a necessary evil.

Besides its record of the fluctuations in Russian censorship policy and the absurdities of censorship practice, Nikitenko's diary is a treasure house of intelligent commentary on the main events of European history, especially the relations between Russia and France. It is packed with anecdotes about Russian literary figures, especially Pushkin, Gogol', and Turgenev, but also with comments on the Russian absorption of the works of Balzac, Victor Hugo, and Sir Walter Scott, as well as John Stuart Mill's *On Liberty*.

In the end, perhaps the most telling of all Nikitenko's reflections is the following: "What is meant by the literary idea? In the main it means to arouse in the hearts of people a respect for intellectual and educational achievements."

ANNABEL PATTERSON

Writings

Dnevnik (Diary), 3 vols, 1955–56
The Diary of a Russian Censor, abridged and translated by Helen
    Saltz Jacobson, 1975

Further Reading

Balmuth, Daniel, *Censorship in Russia, 1865–1905*, Washington, DC:
    University Press of America, 1979
Choldin, Marianna Tax, *A Fence around the Empire: Russian
    Censorship of Western Ideas under the Tsars*, Durham: University
    of North Carolina Press, 1985

Dewhirst, Martin and Robert Farrell, *The Soviet Censorship*,
    Metuchen, New Jersey: Scarecrow Press, 1973
Monas, Sidney, *The Third Section: Police and Society in Russia under
    Nicholas I*, Cambridge, Massachusetts: Harvard University Press,
    1961
Ruud, Charles Arthur, *Fighting Words: Imperial Censorship and the
    Russian Press, 1804–1906*, Toronto: University of Toronto Press,
    1982
Stolbut Asov, S.A., *A.S. Pushkin po otzyvam A.V. Nikitenka* (Pushkin
    According to A.V. Nikitenko), Kharkov, 1900

PIUS NJAWE
Cameroonian editor and publisher, 1957–

Pius Njawe is well known both in Cameroon and abroad for
Le Messager (The Messenger), the French-language newspaper
he founded in 1979 and has managed to continue publishing in the face of frequent harassment from Cameroonian
politicians.

Njawe established the newspaper when he was in his early
twenties. It was printed in Bafoussam, the main city of the
Bamileke people to whom he belongs. In the first twenty years
after independence – during the regime of Ahmadou Ahidjo –
the press in Cameroon was kept under tight control with no
hint of dissent allowed. Independent publications were not outlawed, but they faced countless obstacles. In the early years of
Le Messager, Njawe encountered frequent problems with
the authorities. He also suffered constant financial difficulties.
The paper was founded with savings from freelance journalism, and while it started as a monthly it often came out irregularly due to the lack of financial support.

In 1982 president Ahidjo resigned. He was succeeded by Paul
Biya at the head of an otherwise unchanged one-party state.
The following year a political crisis between the two led to
Ahidjo's eclipse and exile, and there were hopes of a relaxation
of the regime under Biya. Njawe, who moved the offices of *Le
Messager* to Douala (the biggest city and main commercial
centre) in 1983, shared those hopes at first, and initially supported Biya's government even though its relaxation of one-
party rule was limited. With the government clinging to its
authoritarian ways, however, a clash with Njawe – who in 1985
declared his aim was the "denunciation of abuses and injustices of all sorts" – became inevitable. The paper was banned
after an article which noted the continued presence in the government of associates of Ahidjo and for a hostile review of the
book *Social Ideas of President Paul Biya* (May 1985).

In 1990 the government of Cameroon, like a number of other
governments in Africa, agreed reluctantly to the introduction
of multi-party democracy. However, it intended to keep democratic liberties within strict limits. This was shown in the "mass
communication" law of 19 December 1990, under which pre-
publication censorship was maintained and provision was made
for seizure, suspension, and banning of newspapers. Soon afterwards *Le Messager* published (issue no. 209, 27 December
1990) an article entitled "Open Letter to the President" by
Célestin Monga, a prominent banking official, economist, and
journalist (now working with the World Bank), in which Biya

was accused of implementing "fake democracy". The issue was
seized and Monga and the editor, Njawe, were charged. Their
trial in Douala in January 1991 was accompanied by a press
and media campaign against the "irresponsible" independent
press. It led to strong protests and was a key event in the transition to more democratic government. The defendants both
received six-month suspended prison sentences.

Events developed rapidly in Cameroon during 1991. Many
new parties were formed, but opposition calls for a national
conference with power to order major changes were rejected
by president Biya and his government, and this led to a serious
confrontation. Opposition forces declared a general strike and
total shutdown of activity in the cities ("villes mortes") and
enforced this in Douala, in the Bamileke homeland in Western
Province, and in the two ex-British provinces also in the west.
But the Biya government retained control of key areas of the
country and after three months the mass protests collapsed.
During this time *Le Messager* backed the opposition campaign
strongly despite frequent police action against it.

In the course of 1991 considerable freedom was won by the
press. This continued even though the RDPC (Rassemblement
Démocratique du Peuple Camerounais) government retained
power in multi-party elections in 1992. Although severe laws
against "sedition" and against "insults" to the president
remained in force, alongside other laws restricting press freedom, papers now operated virtually as though those laws did
not exist. There were occasional seizures and criminal charges,
but the opposition press continued to thrive. When issues were
seized, they were subsequently often sold clandestinely to a
public that had come to appreciate a free press. Repression had
not ended but it was now fitful and ineffective. Pius Njawe,
whose newspapers regularly denounced the "tropical dictator"
Biya and his policies, won the Gold Pen of Freedom of the
World Association of Newspaper Publishers (FIEJ) in 1993. By
1996 his venture had grown into a group of three publications,
including a successful satirical magazine, *Le Messager Popoli*.

In 1996 Njawe attended a conference in Cape Town organized by the Commonwealth Press Union (Cameroon having
joined the Commonwealth in 1995). Soon after his return, on
29 October 1996 he was arrested and gaoled for six months
for "spreading false news" and "insulting" the president and
members of the National Assembly. In prison he was denied
medical attention needed for his serious diabetes. Widespread

protests resulted in his release after some weeks in gaol. Meanwhile, the publishing group continued to flourish. By 1997 *Le Messager* was appearing three times a week.

On 22 December 1997 *Le Messager* published a short report entitled "Is the President Ill?" It described how president Biya, while attending Cameroon's football cup final in Yaoundé (the capital), had disappeared from public view for a good deal of the match, and quoted "senior sources" as saying that he had suffered a heart attack. Two days later Njawe was arrested, and on 13 January 1998 he was sentenced to two years in prison for publishing "false news" (the government claimed that the President had left his box at the stadium for urgent consultations on Cameroon's border dispute with Nigeria). The newspaper was fined 500,000 CFA francs (5,000 French francs) by the court, the Tribunal de Grande Instance in Douala.

The sentence was interpreted by some observers as an attempt to intimidate the opposition press and to curb its independence after the government had recently been forced to abolish pre-publication censorship. Similar actions had been taken against other opposition papers around the same time.

The punishment was seen to be way out of proportion to the "offence" and was widely condemned within Cameroon and abroad. After months of international protest, Pius Njawe was released on 12 October 1998, as an act of presidential clemency. His conviction and the fine remained in place.

JONATHAN DERRICK

Writings
"Cameroun: le combat du *Messager*", *Politique Africaine*
  (19 September 1985): 87–90
Bloc-notes du bagnard: prison de New Bell, Douala, Cameroun,
  1998

Further Reading
CPU News (November 1996 and January 1998)
Fombad, Charles Manga, "Freedom of Expression in the
  Cameroonian Democratic Transition", *Journal of Modern African
  Studies*, 33/2 (1995): 211–26
Norris, Carolyn, *Hollow Promises: Freedom of Expression in
  Cameroon since 1995*, London: Article 19, 1999

LEWIS NKOSI
South African novelist, dramatist, and essayist, 1936–

Lewis Nkosi grew up in Natal. While critical of colonialism and apartheid, he has viewed protest writing which reacts directly to oppression as somehow stunted and without the complexity and depth of memorable literature. These views were considered controversial but when the end of apartheid rendered protest literature obsolete, his views were echoed by the ANC constitutional expert Albie Sachs, as well as other figures in the liberation struggle and literary world.

Nkosi began his career in 1955 as a journalist for the Zulu–English weekly *Ilanga lasse Natal* (*Natal Sun*). In 1956 he joined the staff of *Drum* magazine as chief reporter and moved to Johannesburg. He later worked for the Sunday newspaper, *Post*. In 1960 he left on an exit visa for the United States where he studied at Harvard University on a Nieman Fellowship. He was among the writers banished in 1964 by the Government Gazette Extraordinary. This meant that all his past and future writings were prohibited.

Working as a journalist during the mid-1950s, Nkosi was able to follow and report on the tumultuous political events of the time. He saw the mass mobilization of the black population during the Defiance Campaigns organized by the African National Congress (ANC). He was still in the country on 21 March 1960 when a march on the Sharpeville police station organized by the Pan-Africanist Congress (PAC) resulted in 69 deaths and many injuries when the police opened fire on the unarmed gathering.

Home and Exile (1965) is a collection of essays that deals with his experiences in South Africa during the early years of apartheid, his exile in America, and his views on African and South African and African literature. It was first examined in terms of the Publications and Entertainment Act of 1963 and found undesirable. According to the Publication Control Board, "No reasons are available for this decision." It must therefore be assumed that the publication was deemed undesirable in the light of the fact that the author was a banned person.

In 1976 the publication was submitted for review under the Publications Act of 1974. The ban was not lifted and the status of "undesirable" was upheld by the committee. This time, however, six reasons were given for the decision.

The committee took exception to Nkosi's review of Alan Paton's novel *Cry the Beloved Country*. Nkosi had criticized the character Stephen Kumalo in Paton's novel. "His complaint," the report states,

> is against Paton for creating an absurdity like Kumalo. But in the goodness of Kumalo he sees the unconscious of the whites . . . the whites desire to survive the coming tragedy in South Africa. Because, Nkosi says, if the African is fundamentally as good and forgiving as Kumalo, "then the white South Africans might yet escape the immense penalty they would be required to pay".

The report concludes: "In this paragraph there is a concealed propagation of revenge by the black people against the whites in South Africa."

Nkosi had referred to the "brutal apartheid regime" as well as "Sharpeville and the brutal massacre of unarmed Africans marching to a local police station". He had accurately predicted the events of Sharpeville. This prompts the committee to conclude that Nkosi was part of a conspiracy. It states: "In the light of the circumstances at the time it is difficult to believe that this was a mere prediction."

The book was condemned for the "extremely bad light in which the South African police are cast". Phrases such as "fierce Boer policemen" and "a gun crazy police force" are cited as evidence.

References to the prime minister, J.G. Strydom, were said by the committee to be "in extreme bad taste". Nkosi had described how his fellow writer Can Themba once remarked that he would like to have a chat with Strydom over a drink. "It may very well be that after the umpteenth drink, even with the lowest of intelligence, a man may see reason." And perhaps he should "manoeuvre the Prime Minister's daughter under his all too protective arm. Who knows, with a little bit of luck I may yet be able to show her God's face".

More prosaically, the committee refers to Nkosi's chapter on apartheid, "a daily exercise in the absurd". It contains "many references which are true and correct, but the chapter is negative and many of the assertions are generalizations, which may be so or may not be so".

Finally, the report observes that although the following passage is written in jest, it is problematic: " 'What are you talking about man,' Sam objected. 'This cat is from South Africa. He don't need no standard of livin' What he needs is guns to fix them white crackers real good.' "

The report concludes that the first part of the book "is specifically aimed at cultivating grievances among the black people of the Republic". The idea of "revenge", "violence", and the "negative portrayal of the police" further made it "harmful for the safety of the state, general welfare and good order". These were common reasons provided for by the Publications Act, and used as justification for the prohibition of any publications critical of apartheid.

Nkosi's three-act play *The Rhythm of Violence* (1964), set in Johannesburg in the early 1960s, deals with personal and ideological struggles between blacks and whites who try to cooperate in a context of personal differences, police violence, and repression. His novel *Mating Birds* (1983) is the story of a black man who is on trial for raping a white woman. It explores the race and the sexual psychology of segregation. The book was examined and found to be "not undesirable".

With the liberalization of the 1980s, and the lifting of banning orders on persons and organizations in 1990, Nkosi's work became freely available in South Africa. Nkosi has lived in other parts of Africa well as in England, France, and Poland. Unlike many other exiles, he did not return to South Africa with the end of apartheid. Returning briefly for a conference in the early 1990s, he found that exiled writers of his generation were no longer on the lips of his fellow countrymen – a poignant illustration of the miseries of exile.

ANDRIES WALTER OLIPHANT

Writings

The Rhythm of Violence, 1964
Home and Exile and Other Selected Essays, 1965; revised edition 1983
The Transplanted Heart: Essays on South Africa, 1975
Tasks and Masks: Themes and Styles in African Literature, 1981
Mating Birds, 1983
South Africa: Black Consciousness, 1986

Further Reading

Lodge, Tom, *Black Politics in South Africa since 1945*, Johannesburg: Raven Press, and London and New York: Longman, 1983
Shava, Piniel, *A People's Voice: Black South African Writing in the 20th Century*, London: Zed, and Athens: Ohio University Press, 1989
Zell, Hans M. and Helene Silver (editors), *A Reader's Guide to African Literature*, New York: Africana, 1971; London: Heinemann, 1972

EMIL NOLDE
German painter, 1867–1956

The work of Emil Nolde, perhaps the most established of the German expressionist painters, was the subject of a great deal of critical acclaim during the years of the Weimar Republic (1919–33). In 1921, Max Sauerland discussed the epic and heroic quality of his paintings; and Rudolf Probst, who organized the Nolde retrospective in 1927, believed that Nolde's work was a timeless celebration of "the passion of nature". Nolde was elected to membership of the Prussian Academy of Arts in 1931.

Although Nolde was reclusive – he lived in a fisherman's cabin in Schleswig-Holstein – he sympathized with the extreme nationalism of the Nazi Party and was an early member of its North Schleswig branch. Having grown up in a farming community in Frisia, he was susceptible to the Nazis' myths of *Blut und Boden* ("blood and soil"), and shared their emphasis on national renewal and purification. Indeed, in his autobiography, *Jahre der Kämpfe* (1934, Years of Struggle), he attacks the paintings of "half-breeds, bastards, and mulattoes". Nolde had been championed by the Berlin Nazi newspaper *Der Angriff*, founded and edited by Hitler's propaganda chief Joseph Goebbels, who had entertained both Nolde and the sculptor Ernst Barlach at his house.

For a brief period after they came to power in 1933, the policy of the Nazis towards Nolde was contradictory. On the one hand, his work was championed by Otto-Andreas Schreiber, and other radical Nazi journalists writing in the periodicals *Kunst der Nation* and *Kunstkammer*, who believed that German expressionism and Nazism were aspects of the same ideology. They hoped to make political use of Goebbels, who was known, at that stage, to fear that the Nazi denial of artistic freedom would harm Germany's image abroad. Ranged against them were, among others, Wilhelm Frick, the Minister of the Interior, who closed down an exhibition of works by Nolde, Barlach, and Max Pechstein mounted by members of the National Socialist Students Association in the summer of 1933, and expelled its organizers from the party. *Kunst der Nation* was banned in 1935. Finally, in June 1937 an exhibition to be held at the National Gallery in Berlin, devoted to works by Nolde, Barlach, and Franz Marc, was prohibited, and the director of the gallery was dismissed, on the orders of

Schneitner-Mjolnar, the "Reich Plenipotentiary for Artistic Formulation".

Goebbels either lost the argument or simply had to bow before Hitler's denunciation of *entartete Kunst* ("degenerate art") and the adoption of a Nazi canon that froze German artistic development at about where it had stood in the 1870s. Goebbels had works by Nolde and Barlach removed from his home, and pictures by Nolde featured prominently in the list of 16,000 paintings, drawings, etchings, and sculptures ordered to be confiscated from museums throughout the country: in addition to the 1,000 items by Nolde, the list included 200 to 400 items each by Pechstein and Barlach, 400 by Oscar Kokoschka, and numerous works by such artists as Braque, Cézanne, Gauguin, Matisse, and Picasso. Some of them were burned in the courtyard of the headquarters of the Berlin fire brigade in 1939.

Twenty-seven of Nolde's works were included in the exhibition of Degenerate Art held in Munich from 19 July 1937: indeed, his nine-part altarpiece, *Life of Christ* (1912), was the centrepiece of the exhibition. A further 50 of his works had been rounded up and confiscated by 1940. Meanwhile, Nolde, who had previously declined invitations to resign from the Prussian Academy, had been expelled from it. Indignantly, Nolde appealed to Goebbels in a letter dated 2 July 1938:

> I . . . request . . . that the defamation against me cease. This I find especially cruel, particularly since, even before the National Socialist movement, I, virtually alone among German artists, fought publicly against foreign domination of German art, against the corruption of art dealers, and against the intrigue of the Liebermann and Cassirer era . . . When the National Socialists also labelled me and my art "degenerate" and "decadent", I felt this to be a profound misunderstanding because it is just not so. My art is German, strong, austere and sincere.

The letter remained unanswered, however, and the attacks on Nolde's work continued.

In 1941, the Reichskulturkammer (Reich Chamber of Culture) ordered Nolde to hand over all the work he had done in the previous two years for evaluation. On 23 August, he was informed by Arnold Ziegler, President of the Reich Chamber of Fine Arts, that his "lack of reliability" had resulted in an immediate ban on any other painting or other related artistic activities. Fifty-four of the works that he had submitted were forwarded to the police. The "painting ban" (*Malverbot*) was enforced over the next few years by means of regular visits by the Gestapo to Nolde's house at Seebull. Realizing that the use of oils would make it all too obvious that he had disobeyed the ban, he painted, between 1938 and 1945, more than 1,300 watercolours on scraps of paper small enough to be concealed, which he called "Unpainted Pictures". In October 1944, he wrote: "Only to you, my little pictures, do I sometimes confide my grief, my torment, my contempt."

The Nazi rejection of an artist who was willing to be a supporter was a rare phenomenon, but not really surprising. Expressionism, however German, had developed within Weimar Germany, a culture that they wholeheartedly despised. Emil Nolde and artists like him, however supportive they might wish to be, could not be expected to paint to order, and there was nothing in common between him and the painters Hitler really liked other than their nationality.

After 1945, "when the chains fell", as Nolde himself put it, he spent his remaining years transforming around 1,000 of the "Unpainted Pictures" into large oil paintings. He remained a major figure in German and European art, and was widely recognized by awards and honorary appointments.

LISA PINE

Writings

Jahre der Kämpfe, 1934
Das eigene Leben, 1976
Mein Leben, 1976

Further Reading

Bradley, William S., *Emil Nolde and German Expressionist Art: A Prophet in His Own Land*, Ann Arbor: UMI Research Press, 1986

Haftmann, W., *Emil Nolde: Unpainted Pictures*, revised edition, New York: Praeger, 1965

Miesel, Victor H. (editor), *Voices of German Expressionism*, Englewood Cliffs, New Jersey: Prentice Hall, 1970

Pois, R., "The Cultural Despair of Emil Nolde", *German Life and Letters*, 25 (1971–1972): 252–60

Pois, Robert, *Emil Nolde*, Washington, DC: University Press of America, 1982

Selz, Peter, *Emil Nolde*, New York: Museum of Modern Art, 1963

NORTHERN IRELAND

"Northern Ireland" is the official name of the "province" created when Ireland was partitioned in 1921; it comprises the six northeastern counties of Ireland. Unionists prefer the term "Ulster" even though the traditional province of that name consists of nine counties. Nationalists refer to "the North of Ireland", or merely "the North", while Republicans speak of "the Six Counties".

The failure to agree the name indicates a fundamental disagreement over the legitimacy of "Northern Ireland", which has its roots in a history of colonial domination from Britain and anti-colonial responses. British rule in Ireland rested, more often than not, on repression. For example, in the second half of the 19th century, 50 separate Coercion Acts were established. As Jenny Marx stated, the rule of law in Ireland was the exception rather than the norm. In opposition to a series of Home Rule Bills between 1886 and 1914, Irish unionists organized politically and militarily. Armed nationalists likewise mobilized throughout the country. At Easter 1916 republicans staged an unsuccessful uprising, which was followed, between 1919 and 1921, by a war of independence. Following a treaty, the island was partitioned in 1921.

Northern Ireland was founded on exclusion, its boundaries determined by the decision of unionists that six counties was the largest area in which their majority could be guaranteed. Within that area unionists had wide powers. Although it was subordinate to the British state, the Northern Ireland Administration had a great deal of independence in law and policy making. The Unionist Party was the sole governing party between 1921 and 1972. Conservative and often patrician in character, successive Unionist governments either opposed or reluctantly enacted legislation and policy deriving in London. Every Unionist MP in Westminster voted against the establishment of the welfare state in 1949; Northern Ireland was excluded from the 1967 Abortion Act; and homosexual law reform was not enacted in Northern Ireland until 1982, 15 years after reform in Britain, and only as a result of a successful case brought to the European Court of Human Rights. Matters of taxation and the army were confined to Westminster, but all other matters were left to the Unionist government. As a result, Northern Ireland was not discussed once in Westminster between partition in 1921and the civil rights agitation at the end of the 1960s.

Within Northern Ireland, governance through coercion prevailed. The armed police force, the Royal Ulster Constabulary (RUC), was almost entirely Protestant, its chief task conceived as controlling the large Roman Catholic minority, around one third of the population. At the RUC's disposal was the Special Powers Act, which allowed arrest without charge, internment without trial, flogging, prohibition of inquests, execution, destruction of buildings, and prohibition of meetings, organizations, and publications; in short, it permitted the Minister of Home Affairs, a member of Northern Ireland government, to make any regulation "he thinks necessary for the maintenance of order".

The minority was pushed to the political, social, and cultural margins. Its parties were destined to be in permanent opposition. Its workforce experienced lower status jobs and higher unemployment. And its sport, music, and the Irish language were relegated to private halls and grounds, while unionists could celebrate their past victories through annual marches and street paintings.

The mass media reflected these divisions, and continue to do so. The *News Letter*, founded in 1737, is bought mainly by Unionists. Its rival daily morning paper in Belfast, the *Irish News*, founded in 1892, is read for the most part by nationalists. The evening daily, the *Belfast Telegraph*, boasts a readership that matches neatly the sectarian ratio of the population, but is unashamedly unionist behind its liberal veneer. When broadcasting arrived in Northern Ireland in 1924, it quickly fell into the local sectarian pattern. Belfast was one of the first regions of the United Kingdom to have a local BBC station, 2BE. Its first station director, an Englishman named Geoffrey Beadle, was proud to be, in his own words, "a member of the establishment". Irish dance music appeared only in the refined guise of the Irish Rhythms Orchestra in the 1950s; results of Gaelic sports were not broadcast until the 1970s; local television weather forecasts until the 1970s showed a map of Northern Ireland disconnected from the Irish Republic; and the first Irish-language broadcast did not take place until 1981.

The policy of the BBC locally was, in effect, to ensure that there was no attack broadcast on the constitutional position of Northern Ireland. In pursuit of this policy, successive controllers of BBC Northern Ireland came to have immense power to vet all broadcasts relating to Ireland, whether produced locally or not. For example, George Marshall objected to the playing of the Irish National Anthem in a BBC North of England broadcast on Saint Patrick's Day 1937 on the grounds that "the song is essentially rebel". With such watchdogs, it was rarely necessary for the Unionist government to intervene directly.

Commercial television arrived in 1957 in the form of Ulster Television (UTV). Like the BBC before it, UTV was highly influential in determining overall coverage of Northern Ireland by the network of independent commercial television companies, ITV. At first this meant that UTV opted out of broadcasting programmes it judged to be sensitive. This was a situation that the regulatory body, the Independent Television Authority (ITA), found unsatisfactory. But instead of putting pressure on UTV to avoid opting out, it strove to ensure that none of its commercial companies broadcast programmes from which UTV would find it necessary to opt out. In the end, both UTV and BBC Northern Ireland were tails wagging their respective dogs.

In the late 1960s, the civil rights campaign began a non-violent agitation for reforms. In the face of communal violence from both sides, the British government sent in troops and intervened to push through reforms. By the early 1970s the Irish Republican Army (IRA) was militarily active against the British Army and the RUC. As civil disorder increased, the British government abolished the local parliament. With a brief exception in 1974, when a power-sharing local administration was brought down through a loyalist general strike, Britain maintained direct rule until 1998.

British journalists and broadcasters were initially sympathetic to the civil rights movement, but as peaceful protest turned to armed insurrection, they pulled back. The lesson was quickly learned that broadcasters and programmes could suffer. In 1971, Bernard Falk from the BBC *Tonight* programme was jailed for four days for contempt of court when he refused to identify an IRA man he had interviewed. In 1972, *A Question of Ulster*, a BBC programme that sought to examine the political conflict openly, was attacked in advance by the Unionist government; the BBC screened the programme, but the conclusion of top management and many programme-makers was that it was better to avoid such confrontations.

By the 1970s a pattern emerged in British broadcast reporting of Northern Ireland that remained intact for the next quarter of a century. It involved a number of elements. First, both BBC and ITV instituted "reference upwards" systems; all programmes on Northern Ireland had to be vetted, the decision often going to top management. In the BBC, this process had to be applied before a programme was made, whereas in ITV, with its more decentralized structure, fully or partially made programmes were vetted before broadcast. The BBC thus ended up strangling a number of projects at birth, while ITV has had a record of refusing to broadcast completed programmes. Over 70 programmes were directly censored between

1970 and the broadcasting ban of 1988. To take two examples: in 1971 ITV banned *South of the Border*, a programme that carried speeches from leading republicans, and *A Street in Belfast*, which focused on the small Catholic enclave of Short Strand in East Belfast, was commissioned by the BBC and completed in 1977, but never shown.

A second mechanism specified in official guidelines from both the BBC and the Independent Television Authority (ITA) was the demand that each programme be balanced. The result was the silencing of voices deemed to be more extreme, and the privileging of official voices as being moderate, no matter how extreme the policies they may support. Despite this, Lord Hill, the chairman of the BBC Board of Governors, stated in 1971: "as between the British army and the gunmen, the BBC is not and cannot be impartial." An over-reliance on official sources flowed from such sentiments.

Third, specific instructions related to interviews with "extremists". Republicans in particular were treated as hostile witnesses. Interviews with spokespersons for illegal organizations, while not banned outright, were rare: only six each on BBC and ITV between 1969 and 1979, since when there have been no others.

This strategy involved broadcasting organizations in a complicated game of self-policing. The end result, as the journalist Mary Holland put it, was that self-censorship became an art form in the British broadcasting media. That said, there were a number of serious confrontations between broadcasters and management: an interview on *Tonight* in 1979 with a spokesman for the Irish National Liberation Army (INLA) which had recently assassinated the Conservative Party spokesman for Northern Ireland, Airey Neave; the filming in 1979 by a BBC *Panorama* team of an IRA roadblock in Carrickmore, County Tyrone; the *Real Lives* controversy in 1985, which sympathetically portrayed leading Republican Martin McGuinness; and *Death on the Rock*, Thames Television's investigation of the killing of three Republicans by undercover soldiers in Gibraltar in 1988.

Real Lives was the only one of these in which the government directly intervened in advance. Home Secretary Leon Brittan wrote to the BBC governors stating that broadcasting the programme would be "contrary to the national interest", an intervention which undoubtedly influenced the governors' decision to postpone the programme and impose amendments.

On the face of it, there seems to be little evidence of what might be called classical censorship. A range of laws is available to the British government to curtail the independence of the media, but these have rarely been used in relation to Northern Ireland. Apart from the BBC Licensing Agreement and the Broadcasting Act (1981), which governs commercial broadcasting, there is the Official Secrets Act (1911); the Northern Ireland Criminal Law Act (1967), which makes it an offence to refuse to disclose information to the RUC; the Contempt of Court Act (1981); the Police and Criminal Evidence Act (1984), under which the police can demand, for example, newspaper photographs of a march or demonstration; the Emergency Provisions Act (1978), which prohibits publication of any information that could be of use to terrorists; and the Prevention of Terrorism Act (1989), which imposes on all citizens, media personnel included, the duty to provide

information to the police that could be of use in apprehending terrorists. The Prevention of Terrorism Act was used in 1988 against a German photographer in Northern Ireland, and again in 1992 against *Dispatches* (Channel 4) over its programme on collusion between the RUC and loyalist paramilitaries, *The Committee*.

With some exceptions, coverage of the conflict in the British media was, in the opinion of some commentators, remarkably formulaic: the problem was republicanism; loyalists were absent or only reacted to Republican violence; and the British army and RUC were "piggies in the middle". Many stories, especially those that were critical of the British government and its forces, were, on this view, ignored or played down; others, especially those that reflected badly on "extremists", were played up or told from an official viewpoint.

Foreign news coverage of the Irish conflict was less tied to this formula. Thus, at the time of the Republican hunger strike in 1981, when ten prisoners starved to death to achieve "political status", most international reporting was broadly sympathetic to the prisoners' demands and critical of British policy. That said, the British media's representation of the conflict was highly influential internationally, not least because of a reliance on official sources. In particular, as Miller (1994) reveals, the Northern Ireland press office, staffed by civil servants, has been a major source of many stories, some of which have been shown to be pure fiction. In addition, foreign news coverage is filtered through a few agencies, whose personnel have often been locally based journalists who subscribed to the formula summarized above.

In the aftermath of the 1981 hunger strike, Sinn Féin, the Republican party aligned with the IRA, grew in confidence and popularity. The propaganda battle became more intense, with the British prime minister, Margaret Thatcher arguing that the media were supplying "the oxygen of publicity" for terrorism. Finally, in 1988, the home secretary Douglas Hurd introduced a ban that forbade the broadcast of the voices of spokespersons for Sinn Féin and a number of other organizations. The broadcasting ban, was lifted after the Republican ceasefire of 1994.

Since the above was written, the Northern Ireland peace process has led to a number of substantial changes. The Republican ceasefire of August 1994 and the subsequent Loyalist ceasefire six weeks later created the space for all-party negotiations that led eventually to the Belfast agreement (also known as the Good Friday Agreement) in April 1998. A number of powers were devolved from Britain to a new Northern Ireland Assembly whose ministers came from across the political spectrum, including two each from Sinn Féin and the Democratic Unionist Party.

However, such developments did not usher in an instant new dawn as regards the North's political divisions. For many Unionists, Loyalists in particular, many of the changes – including the reform of the police force, the Royal Ulster Constabulary, the failure of the IRA to decommission its weaponry, and the holding of ministerial office by members of Sinn Féin – were a bitter pill to swallow. On the other hand, many Nationalists, in particular Republicans, became increasingly frustrated by the slow pace and relative paucity of political reforms, especially in relation to the release of prisoners, and the reform of policing. Sinn Féin's conviction was that many in the Unionist parties and the British establishment were still in combative mode, acting as if the war was still in progress.

Evidence of this legacy was apparent in many fields, not least in relation to the mass media. In February 2000, the United Nations Special Rapporteur on Freedom of Expression, Abid Hussain, issued a report in which he showed considerable sympathy with criticisms made of the media, including the following:

(1) the absence of public debate on how broadcasting in particular needed to change to enhance the peace process;

(2) the over-reliance of broadcasters and many press journalists on official sources;

(3) the tendency to bias in reports of confrontations between Orange Order marchers and nationalist residents opposed to their presence.

The relevance of at least one of these criticisms was confirmed throughout 2000 by the British government's successful blocking of stories in the *Sunday Times* and elsewhere revealing the covert operations of a special unit of the British Army, the FRU (Force Research Unit). In addition, in May 2001, the British government brought a successful legal action to prevent Ulster Television's *Insight* programme carrying an interview with a former British agent who claimed to have infiltrated the IRA and been involved in the targeting of British Army personnel.

At the same time, there were major structural changes facing broadcasters and journalists covering Northern Ireland. The *Belfast Telegraph*, the largest circulation daily newspaper and once the jewel in the crown of Thomson Newspapers, was bought by Tony O'Reilly, owner of both the *Independent* in Britain and Independent Newspapers in Dublin. At the same time Ulster Television purchased commercial radio stations in the Republic of Ireland. In terms of ownership, if nothing else, the Irish border became that bit less relevant as far as the media were concerned.

BILL ROLSTON

Further Reading

Cathcart, Rex, *The Most Contrary Region: The BBC in Northern Ireland, 1924–1984*, Belfast: Blackstaff Press, 1984

Curtis, Liz, *Ireland, the Propaganda War: The Media and the "Battle for Hearts and Minds"*, London: Pluto Press, 1984

Farrell, Michael, *Northern Ireland: The Orange State*, 2nd edition, London: Pluto Press, 1980

Miller, David, *Don't Mention the War: Northern Ireland, Propaganda and the Media*, London: Pluto Press, 1994

Rolston, Bill, "News Fit to Print: Belfast's Daily Newspapers" in *The Media and Northern Ireland: Covering the Troubles*, edited by Rolston, Basingstoke: Macmillan, 1991

Rolston, Bill and David Miller (editors), *War and Words: The Northern Ireland Media Reader*, Belfast: Beyond the Pale, 1996

United Nations, *Report Submitted by Mr Abid Hussain, Special Rapporteur, in Accordance with Commission on Human Rights Resolution 1999/39, Addendum Visit to the United Kingdom of Great Britain and Northern Ireland*, reference number E/CN.4/2000/63/Add. 3, February 2000

NORWAY

Population: 4,469,000	**Number of daily newspapers:** 83
Main religions: Evangelical Lutheran; Protestant; Roman Catholic	**Number of periodicals:** 71
	Number of radio receivers per 1000 inhabitants: 917
Official language: Norwegian	**Number of TV receivers per 1000 inhabitants:** 462
Other languages spoken: Lappish; Finnish	**Number of PCs per 1000 inhabitants:** 373.4

1300–1939

Early Norway – like Iceland: distinctive, independent, and the home of a considerable written culture – also shares with Iceland one of the earliest Scandinavian references to a form of censorship. A "national law" from the end of the 13th century, drawn up on the initiative of king Magnus, includes a ban on the use of swearing, slander, and insulting ballads; punishment took the form of fines and social ostracism.

Norwegian independence was by then nearing its end, however. From 1319 until 1355 Norway and Sweden shared the same king, and from 1380 Norway became the "junior partner" in a union with Denmark which lasted until 1814. In almost all respects – theological, legal, political – Copenhagen was the centre of power and administration, and the initiator of change. The Reformation, in the shape of Lutheranism, for instance, came first to Denmark, then to Norway, where it grew deep roots, still apparent in the Norway of Henrik Ibsen in the late 19th century. As in Denmark, the counter-Reformation made little headway in Norway. The Norwegian Jesuit Laurentius Nicolai (Lauritz Nielsson, alias Klosterlasse), attempting to commend Catholicism to his native land in *Confessio Christiana* (1606), had his work promptly banned; he himself was expelled – but it was to Copenhagen that he had directed his evangelical energies and from Copenhagen, not Oslo, that he was expelled. Ten years later, the so-called Oslo Humanists, said to be flirting with Catholicism, were also expelled after a series of trials initiated by Copenhagen.

Printing arrived in Norway in 1643, almost two centuries after it had been introduced in the rest of Europe, hindering the development of the territory's intellectual life. Few Norwegians stuck out for independent opinions in the manner of Anders Kemp, the pacifist who in 1674 was deported for his heretical opinions and publications. When the dual monarchy became an absolutist kingdom in 1687, the "Norwegian Law" was apparently accepted with less opposition than the similar "Danish Law". Enlightenment ideas might have penetrated more deeply in Norway through the Bergen-born playwright, historian, and philosopher Ludvig Holberg (1684–1754), but though several of his works were set in Norway he spent most of his life in Copenhagen, and wrote in Danish.

Danish control was epitomized in the declaration of 1772 that Danish was to be the official language of the two countries. Danish was to be taught in Norwegian grammar schools and all pupils were to study Danish history. The cabinet secretary Ove Høegh Guldberg declared: "There are no Norwegians. We are all citizens in the Danish state."

After several centuries of cultural deprivation, the beginning of a Norwegian consciousness emerged in the second half of the 18th century with the formation, albeit in Copenhagen, of Det norske Selskab (The Norwegian Society) in 1772. Norwegian-born authors, philosophers, and theologians discussed intellectual and political trends in the rest of Europe, not least events in France after 1789. How important the society was in shaping the desire for Norwegian independence is not yet clear, but certainly their discussions took place at the same time as a great increase in the production of periodicals, not only in Copenhagen, but also in Bergen, and Trondheim. *Hermoder*, published in Copenhagen, while printing with *Seip* ("the silent censorship", expressing oneself with care), carried several articles which implied a more independent political position from Norway – advocating its own university and bank, for example. Denmark–Norway had been the first country in the world to abolish censorship in 1770; the growth of the periodical press was presumably one result. Further liberalization was halted in 1799 – Europe was at war. In this war Denmark backed the losing side, and one result was its loss of Norway.

On 17 May 1814 an assembly at Eidsvoll declared Norway a sovereign constitutional monarchy. The constitution, which drew on those of Spain, the USA, and France, was one of the most liberal of its time, establishing the Storting (parliament) as the sole legislative body with no ultimate veto for the king, and proclaiming full liberty of the press. Full sovereignty was short-lived. Sweden had the power to enforce a new union on Norway, which they had long coveted. Nonetheless, Norway was able to hang on to a number of important gains: the constitution itself and the Storting. The union with Sweden (1815–1905) was of an entirely different character from its Norwegian–Danish predecessor. Sweden even admired parts of the Norwegian constitution. Samuel Laing reported that the Norwegians were a "free and happy people living under a liberal constitution"; he even declared this constitution "but the superstructure of a building of which the foundations had been laid and the lower walls constructed, eight centuries before" (*Journal of a Residence in Norway During the Years 1834, 1835 and 1836*). Nor was progress confined to the political level. Norway abolished the conventicle laws, establishing religious freedom in 1842.

The road to free expression in the area of sexuality was more rocky. Major debate followed the publication of Ibsen's *Et dukkehjem* (1879, A Doll's House) which challenged the conventional view of marriage, *Gengangere* (1881, Ghosts) which spoke openly of venereal disease, and Bjørnsterne Bjørn-

son's *En Handske* (1883, A Glove); Bjørnson, having been an advocate of free love, now blew moral hypocrisy wide open by suggesting that men as well as women should abstain from sexual intercourse before marriage. Though Ibsen had difficulty in getting his plays staged, and had to make compromises, for example, with *A Doll's House*, there was no wholesale ban on these works. With Hans Jæger's *Fra Kristiania-Bohêmen* (1885, From the Christiania Bohemian), things were different. An attack on the double standards of the middle class, it was seized and declared obscene causing Jæger to flee the country: nor was there any respite in Denmark or Sweden where the book was also banned. The scene was now set for further bans, most notably of Christian Krohg's *Albertine*, which dealt with prostitution and, perhaps more significantly, police corruption. *Albertine* was finally published in 1920, *From the Christiania Bohemian* not until 1953. These cases from the 1880s are significant for the history of censorship generally and for Norway in particular, illustrating the tension between a desire for national self-awareness built on Christian values (which then and subsequently have pulled in the direction of censorship) and a propensity for more radical thinking (which, drawing on international movements of moral change, has itself had influence well beyond Scandinavia).

The union of Sweden and Norway ended in 1905. Norway was now fully responsible for its own affairs for the first time in 600 years. Censorship has not played a major part in independent Norwegian history, but it has not been entirely absent. This entry records cases of political, religious, and moral censorship until 1939.

Two issues in the first half of the 20th century call for special attention: Norway's identity as a Christian country, and its relationship to the rise of German fascism. In 1933 Arnulf Øverland published the text of a talk he had given entitled *Kristendommen: den tiende landeplage* (Christianity: The Tenth Plague), which suggested that a belief in God and the practice of religion could be explained anthropologically. Such was the public outcry that Øverland was taken to court accused of blasphemy and when he was acquitted, steps had to be taken to tighten the blasphemy laws, now playfully known as the "Lex Øverland". It is of some significance, however, that in the 1990s Norway played a leading role in the campaign against the Salman Rushdie *fatwa* following his alleged "blasphemy".

Political censorship has rarely surfaced in Norway but in 1928 Didrik Brochmann published *Med norsk skib i verdenskrigen* (On a Norwegian Ship in the World War) which recorded the Germans' torpedoing of ships in World War I and the consequent loss of life. The German ambassador to Oslo requested that sales be stopped – and the Norwegians agreed to do so. (The book was not released again until 1960.) Then in the mid 1930s the Nobel committee considered awarding the Peace Prize to Carl von Ossietzky. It was evident that the Nazi government would regard this as an offensive act and Norway itself was divided on the subject. The minister for foreign affairs, Koht, a member of the Nobel committee, chose to resign from it, but "censorship" was narrowly avoided when the committee decided that Ossietzsky would indeed be awarded the 1935 prize; but the king, quite unprecedentedly, took no part in the prize giving in December 1936.

TEDDY K. PETERSEN

Further Reading

Andenæs, Johs, *Ordets frihet, ordets ansvar*, Oslo: Frittord Gyldendal, 1985

Benno, Joachim, *Ytringsfrihet*, Oslo: Institutt for Journalistikk, 1994

Bjørneboe, Jens, *Norge, mitt Norge: Essays on formyndermennesket*, Oslo: Pax, 1968; 4th edition, 1983

Gentikow, Barbara, *En skitten strøm: Samfunnskritikken i den "umoralske" litteraturen i Norge 1880–1960*, Oslo: Gyldendal Norsk, 1974

Haslund, Fredrik Juel, "Ytringsfriheten i Danmark–Norge, 1500–1814: En oversikt" (Freedom of Expression in Denmark-Norway, 1500–1814: An Outline) in *Literature as Resistance and Counter Culture*, edited by Andras Masát, Budapest: Hungarian Association for Scandinavian Studies, 1993

Holm, Edvard, *Den offentlige Mening og Statsmagten i den dansk-norske Stat i Slutningen af det 18de Aarhundrede, 1784–1799*, Copenhagen: Schultz, 1888; reprinted 1975

Raaum, Odd, "The Norwegian Secret Case" (letter), *Index on Censorship*, 8/1 (January–February 1979)

Rørdam, Holger, *Kjøbenhavns universitets historie fra 1537 til 1621* (The History of Copenhagen University), 4 vols, Copenhagen: Lunos, 1868–77

Seip, Jens Arup, "Teorien om det opinionstyrte enevelde", *Norsk Historisk Tidsskrift*, 5/38 (1958)

Singer, Isaac Bashevis, "Knut Hamsun, Artist of Scepticism", introduction to *Hunger*, by Knut Hansum, London: Duckworth, 1974

Stai, Arne, *Norsk kultur- og moraldebatt i 1930-årene*, Oslo: Gyldendal, 1954

Stothard, Blaine, "Norwegian Secret Case", *Index on Censorship*, 7/5 (September–October 1978)

Thuesen, Arthur, *Beslaglagte og supprimerte bøker vedrørende Norge*, Oslo: Gyldendal Norsk, 1960

Norway and the Nazis

Norway declared its neutrality at the beginning of World War II, but on 9 April 1940 was surprised by a German airborne and naval invasion, which seized the key ports and cities – Oslo, Kristiansund, Bergen, Trondheim, and Narvik. Resistance in the south of the country was quickly overcome. Britain and France responded with a hastily organized and ill-equipped expeditionary force which, nevertheless, succeeded in recapturing Narvik and inflicted significant naval losses on the Germans. Fighting continued in the north of Norway until 10 June 1940, when the Allies finally withdrew.

The political events which accompanied the German invasion of Norway are dominated by the notoriety of Vidkun Quisling who had met Hitler in 1939, discussed a coup d'état in Oslo, and revealed details of Norwegian defences. His name has become synonymous with treachery. Quisling, an ex-army officer who had been Norway's minister of defence between 1931 and 1933, was the founder of the Nasjonal Samling (National Unity) movement – an imitation of German National Socialism. Quisling believed in the "Nordic principle", the idea that the people of northern Europe shared a common historical and ethical heritage derived from the wanderings and colonizations of the Vikings. The Norwegian version of Nazism never appealed to more than a small minority of the electorate. (Estimates vary, but most historians agree that at most Nasjonal Samling had the support of about 5 per cent of the people.) Hitler appointed Josef Terboven as Reichskommissar für die besetzten Norwegischen Gebiete (Reich Commissioner for Occupied Norwegian Territory). Terboven was effectively in the same position as a minister of the Reich in Germany, in that he was responsible only to Hitler. Terboven disliked Quisling, and at first refused to work with him. Ultimately, however, the passive resistance of the civil servants, judges, and teachers obliged Terboven to turn to the even more unpopular Quisling, who in February 1942 was appointed "Minister-President" of a puppet government.

All political parties were declared illegal except for National Unity. Norway was subject to the same kind of oppressive censorship which the Nazis applied in other occupied countries. The media were controlled through the policy of *Gleichschaltung* (co-ordination). The press could only print official news (Nazi propaganda). Some 35 newspapers had been closed down by December 1940, while a number of journalists were arrested and sent to concentration camps in Germany without trial. Nazi authority was enforced by a state apparatus whose institutions were modelled on those in Germany itself: the Hird was organized on the model of the German Sturm Abteilung (the SA, or Brownshirts), while the Volksgerichtshof was a "people's court" which implemented a reign of terror through the use of informers and secret police.

The "Nazification" of Norway was embarked upon. All artists and artistic venues had to be licensed by the ministry of culture and enlightenment. Aspects of Norwegian culture which did not meet with official approval, such as the work of Norway's foremost novelist Sigrid Undset, were banned, as were all books written by foreign authors (except, of course, approved German writers). Most historians have concluded that the attempted "Nazification" of Norwegian society and culture was an outright failure:

> With a naive lack of psychological insight, the Nazis tried to force their *Kultur* upon an unwilling people by a continually growing use of imprisonment, torture, executions, concentration camps at home and in Germany, and a general policy of crafty, brutal terror. They were doomed to failure.

Karen Larsen wrote this immediately after the war, but her verdict has been corroborated by other scholars since.

Resistance in Norway was predominantly passive rather than military, and much of it was directed against Quisling's puppet government rather than at the Germans themselves. Professionals, such as teachers and doctors, refused to work with members of the National Unity appointed to positions for which they were not properly qualified. The judges of the Supreme Court resigned when they were denied the right to review legislation introduced by the Reichskommissar. And one particular aspect of censorship actually became a focus for passive resistance: when the sale of pictures of the royal family was banned, most households in Norway kept a portrait of the king.

Norway was still occupied when Germany surrendered on 7 May 1945. The occupying forces were disarmed by a small Allied force, Terboven committed suicide, while Quisling was arrested and later executed for treason. The exiled government returned to Oslo on 31 May and the king on 7 June.

JAMES CHAPMAN

Further Reading

Andenaes, Johs, *et al.*, *Norway and the Second World War*, Oslo: Tanum, 1966

Derry, T.K., *A History of Modern Norway, 1814–1972*, Oxford: Clarendon Press, 1973

Larsen, Karen, *A History of Norway*, Princeton, New Jersey: Princeton University Press, 1948

Milward, Alan S., *The Fascist Economy in Norway*, Oxford: Clarendon Press, 1972

Worm-Muller, Jacob, *Norway Revolts against the Nazis*, London: Drummond, 1941

Since 1945

After the war, a reckoning was made with those writers who were said to have supported or collaborated with the Nazis, notably the novelist Knut Hamsun (1859–1952). A Nobel Prize winner himself, he had demonstrated his sympathy with the Germans during the Ossietzky debate during the 1930s, and the Nazis read into his novels some support for their ideologies. Hamsun hoped that Nazism would spell the end of communism which he abominated, and had been pictured greeting Hitler. According to Isaac Bashevis Singer, another laureate, who admired Hamsun's novels, "In Norway, where strong opposition to Hamsun had always existed due to his isolation and his popularity with foreigners, he was quite properly anathematised." A great number of books, including Hamsun's, were burnt or seized: as often in the history of censorship, an author's own political sympathies were confused with his literary work.

A decade later, the issue of moral censorship again raised its head when, in 1957 two publishers imported a Danish translation of Henry Miller's *Sexus*. In a trial which has some parallels with the British treatment of *Lady Chatterley's Lover* three years later, a range of literary, psychological, aesthetic, and ethical opinions were heard. The importers were found guilty in the city court; but though acquitted in the high court, the seizure of the book was upheld. Meanwhile, in 1956 Agnar Mykle had published *Sangen om den røde rubin* (The Song of the Red Ruby), which, after a considerable sales success, was seized and prosecuted for its pornographic content. The author and publishers were acquitted in both the city court and the high court, bringing to an end a whole series of such prosecutions in Norway stretching back to the 1880s. But the price was high: Mykle withdrew from the public gaze and ceased writing altogether.

Politically, the major theme of postwar Norwegian censorship has been the issue of secrecy. During the war, Norway's geographical situation made it of key importance to the West. In September 1977, a member of parliament for the Socialist Left party (Sosialistisk Vensteparti, SV) alleged that the US Central Intelligence Agency (CIA) and Norwegian military intelligence were working together on the surveillance of certain Norwegian organizations. After official denials, two members of the party were charged with publishing military secrets. The party newsletter *Ny Tid* (New Times) announced that they had obtained a list of surveillance personnel, but subverted police raids by dispersing the relevant documents. The researcher's sentence of six months' imprisonment was quashed by the high court. With the exception of the liberal *Dagbladet*, the Norwegian press, whether warned off or through self-censorship, remained quiet on the issue. Odd Raaum claimed in a letter to *Index on Censorship*: "Norway does not have a very strong legal tradition in favour of press freedom." Yet when in 1979 four journalists were prosecuted for their possession of the "list", Tryve Moe, of the Norwegian Journalists' Guild asserted: "The press must have an absolute right to assess material even if it is classified on security grounds."

In August 1983 the pacifist magazine *Ikkevold* (Non Violence) published an article about US submarine listening devices in northern Norway. The magazine's subscriber list and the membership list of Folkereisning Mot Krig (FMT, the Norwegian Branch of War Resisters International) were confiscated, and the magazine charged with publishing classified information. Again, the high court overturned the conviction of lower courts: after all, the information was publicly available. Despite the end of the Cold War, these issues continue to be debated in Norway.

The Freedom of the Press Act (1971) allowed the Norwegian government to decree that any document was exempted from its provision – their agencies may even refuse access if documents would be "obviously misleading". A commission appointed by the ministry of justice in the late 1990s worked on possible changes to the Constitution to strengthen commitment to freedom of expression.

At a number of levels, Norwegian commitment has been exemplary. Their minister of culture was the first member of any government to meet Salman Rushdie officially after the pronouncement of the fatwa against him. Norway has played a leading role internationally in the campaign to get it reversed. In October 1993, William Nygaard the Norwegian publisher of *The Satanic Verses* was shot, presumably because of his government's active role in the affair. The Norwegian Forum for Freedom of Expression, to celebrate the opening of the new Bibliotheca Alexandria in 1999 has compiled a comprehensive international database on the censorship of books and newspapers, and of literature on freedom of expression. The database, funded by the Norwegian Ministry of Culture, was presented to the new library at its opening in September 1999.

TEDDY K. PETERSEN

Further Reading

Andenæs, Johs, *Ordets frihet, ordets ansvar*, Oslo: Frittord Gyldendal, 1985

Benno, Joachim, *Ytringsfrihet*, Oslo: Institutt for Journalistikk, 1994

Bjørneboe, Jens, *Norge, mitt Norge: Essays on formyndermennesket*, Oslo: Pax, 1968; 4th edition, 1983

Gentikow, Barbara, *En skitten strøm: Samfunnskritikken i den "umoralske" litteraturen i Norge, 1880–1960*, Oslo: Gyldendal Norsk, 1974

Seip, Jens Arup, "Teorien om det opinionstyrte enevelde", *Norsk Historisk Tidsskrift*, 5/38, Oslo (1958)

Thuesen, Arthur, *Beslaglagte og supprimerte bøker vedrørende Norge*, Oslo: Gyldendal Norsk Forlag, 1960

NOVAS CARTAS PORTUGUESAS (New Portuguese Letters)
Anthology by Maria Isobel Barreno, Maria Velho da Costa, and Maria Teresa Horta, 1971

To many observers, Portugal seemed the least likely country in Europe in the early 1970s to give birth to what has since come to be regarded as a classic of feminist literature. The country was intensely hierarchical in organization and patriarchal in attitude, and its brand of Catholicism was extremely traditionalist. The authors of *Novas cartas portuguesas* described the culture of their country thus: "O my Portugal, of machos, deceiving impotents, coverers, stallions, such bad lovers, so hurried in bed, only caring to show virility".

For nearly 50 years Portugal had been controlled by the authoritarian dictators of the Estado Novo (the "New State"): Antonio de Oliveira Salazar and, since 1968, Marcelo Caetano. Under pressure from international social change, and from the introduction of tourism and television to the country, opening it up to wider cultural pressures, by 1970 Caetano had embarked upon a process of cautious modernization and liberalization. Not the least of the factors driving him in this direction was Portugal's failing attempts to hold on to its African colonies of Angola, Guinea-Bissau, and Mozambique.

For Caetano, however, the publication of *Novas cartas portuguesas* was a step too far. The anthology discussed forbidden subjects, such as the colonial wars, the situation of Portuguese migrants in other countries, and the complaints of conscripts. Its treatment of these topics was highly unorthodox, reflecting a much broader conception of "politics" than that held by the men in charge of the country. Inspired by *Letters from a Portuguese Nun*, an account, written in the 17th century, of Mariana Alcoforado's desertion by a young French officer, the "Three Marias" addressed what Faith Gillespie called "actual *body* politics, social and biological, public and private", viewing it as the result of "power-structured relationships whereby one group of persons is controlled by another" (in the words of Kate Millett).

After the book had been "appreciated" at the National Information Office, it was decided that it would be expedient to charge its authors, not with direct subversion, but, by taking certain passages out of context, with obscenity and abuse of freedom of expression. As one of the authors told Faith Gillespie:

> It is not by accident that we are faced with an obscenity charge and not a political charge. A political charge carries dignity and some importance, but an obscenity charge is humiliating, degrading – and that is what the government wants to do to us.

These tactics would, it was considered, keep the book safely out of public view, since arrangements for the trial could be allowed to drag on for up to two years. It was also hoped that the solidarity of the three authors could be broken by forcing the one who had written the allegedly obscene passages to identify herself.

These tactics failed, on both counts. The women steadfastly refused to be separated: "We wrote this book together and we are all responsible." Their release on bail in mid-1972, far from allowing the issue to die, assisted the mobilization of protest by feminists, both in Portugal itself and abroad. In 1973, demonstrations against the Portuguese government's action took place in most European capitals, as well as in Brazil, Portugal's former colony. In New York a Broadway benefit evening was organized and in Paris there was a procession to the cathedral of Notre-Dame, with participants bearing effigies of the "Three Marias" and singing a suitably adapted version of the Catholic hymn *Dies irae* (Day of Wrath). The delays also made possible the mounting of an effective defence of the book in Lisbon. The writer Urbano Tavares Rodrigues described the work as of "high cultural value" and prophesied that it would "enter Portuguese literary history".

Ironically, this was not to be the case. The prosecution of the "Three Marias" was interrupted by the "Carnation Revolution", which broke out on 25 April 1974; the women received official pardons within a month. It was soon shown, however, that the feminist cause had still some way to go in Portugal. On 13 January 1974, 20 demonstrators from the incipient women's liberation movement were attacked by a Lisbon mob. Maria Velho da Costa then precipitated the breakup of the partnership when she distanced herself in the national press, not only from *Novas cartas portuguesas* but from radical feminism as a whole, in favour of a more orthodox Marxist approach. By the middle of 1975, the book was being condemned as elitist. It became, in the words of Graca Abranches of Coimbra University, "a text exiled in its own land", and was out of print in Portugal between 1980 and 1998.

ANTONIO DE FIGUEIREDO

Further Reading

Allan, Priscilla, "Unanswered Questions", *Index on Censorship*, 5/1 (Spring 1976)

Barreno, Maria Isabel, Maria Teresa Horta, and Maria Velho da Costa, *Novas cartas portuguesas*, Lisbon: Cor, 1972; as *New Portuguese Letters*, translated by Helen R. Lane and Faith Gillespie, London: Gollancz, 1976, Columbia, Louisiana: Readers International, 1994

Figueiredo, Antonio de, "The Three Marias", *Index on Censorship*, 3/2 (Summer 1974)

Owen, Hilary, "Exiled in Its Own Land", *Index on Censorship*, 22/1 (January–February 1999)

NOVI DANAS
See Danas

NIKOLAI NOVIKOV
Russian writer and publisher, 1744–1818

Nikolai Novikov was a key figure in Russian cultural life in the reign of Catherine II (1762–96). He was in turn a pioneering journalist, historiographer, educator, publisher, leading freemason, and philanthropist. His contributions in each of these fields shaped the particular course that the "Enlightenment" took in Russia. For most of his life he acted in concert with the empress, herself a spiritual child of the Enlightenment who took delight in corresponding with leading French *philosophes* such as Voltaire or Diderot. In 1792, however, Novikov fell victim to the reaction that followed the French Revolution. After interrogation by S.I. Sheshkovskii, Catherine's chief security investigator, Novikov was condemned to 15 years' imprisonment.

Before Catherine's accession in 1762, freedom of expression did not exist in Russia, even as a legal or philosophical principle. It was discussed publicly for the first time in Catherine's own "Great Instruction (*Nakaz*)" to her Legislative Commission, which during its existence (1767–69) was encouraged to demonstrate the principles of free speech in its debates. Novikov served as a minute-taker in the commission and so witnessed the novelty of a rudimentary "public opinion" being forged in argument.

In 1769 a moral weekly, *Vsiakaia vsiachina* (All Sorts), was published under imperial patronage as a model for other journals. Of the eight publications that came into being as a result, the most successful was Novikov's *Truten'* (The Drone). Most of these journals were printed on the presses of the Academy of Sciences, which was responsible for vetting the manuscripts that it printed. There was, therefore, an informal pre-publication censorship available, but there is no evidence that it was rigorously applied. Formal censorship by the state was directed against imported books. In an *ukaz* (edict) of September 1763, Catherine had decreed that booksellers should submit lists of proposed imports to the Academy of Sciences or the University of Moscow, which should reject works "contrary to religion, good morals, and ourselves". Novikov supported these three limits to publishing in a piece in his weekly journal *Zhivopisets* (The Painter) in 1773, which offered advice to a provincial governor who wished to establish a press attached to the Kharkov educational institutions. At this time, Novikov had begun to lay the foundations of his extensive publishing ventures by establishing his Society for the Printing of Books in support of the Imperial Society for the Translation of Foreign Books founded by Catherine in 1768. In his piece, he declares that:

> The general peace of the state and the security of each citizen in particular demand that there should be a prohibition on the publishing of books filled with refutations of divine law, opposed to the autocracy and fatherland, capable of harming the hearts and minds of young people, or changing innocence to wrongdoing.

Within this general consensus on the bounds to freedom of expression, Novikov flourished in the 1770s and the early 1780s. Access to Russia's hitherto closed imperial archives, granted to him by Catherine, allowed him to publish extensive historical material in a monthly periodical, *Drevniaia rossiiskaia vivliofika* (1773–75, Ancient Russian Library), which was augmented in a second revised edition in 1788–91. In 1779 Novikov, partly through his connections in freemasonry, of which he had become an enthusiastic adherent in 1775, acquired a ten-year lease on Moscow University's press. This allowed him to become Russia's most prolific and prosperous publisher. The university's press functioned, to Novikov's great profit, as an educational publishing house. Gary Marker writes that:

> Novikov, to be sure, did more than any other single individual to advance the publication of books and to establish networks for their distribution. In his prime, in the mid-1780s, he was responsible for publishing over a third of all Russian language books and he may have sold an even larger share.

Novikov also responded immediately to Catherine's liberal decree of 15 January 1783, permitting the establishment of private presses, by setting up his own presses, independent of the university's press and dedicated to the promotion of freemasonry. Another significant development was the founding in 1784 of the Typographical Company, a private joint stock company whose 15 shareholders were all freemasons allied to Novikov.

The 1783 decree, liberal as it was, established for the first time a system of censorship administered by the police authorities, who were to guard against infringements of the three generally accepted limits: religion, public decency, and government. In September 1784, *History of the Jesuit Order*, which had begun to appear in the university's journal *Moscow News*, was banned. In December 1785, an edict reflecting Catherine's distrust of masonic activity ordered an inspection of all books published by Novikov, on the grounds that his presses produced "many strange books". Furthermore, all books concerned with spiritual matters should henceforth be submitted for review by the church as well as by the police. Twenty-three suspect books were singled out for censure by Platon, Archbishop of Moscow, but Catherine banned only six, all of them concerned with freemasonry.

However, Catherine did not let matters rest there. A decree of July 1787 made books on religion and morals, as well as educational textbooks, a state monopoly. The profitability of private presses dedicated to these interests, such as Novikov's, was thereby undermined. Novikov's lease on Moscow University's press was not renewed in 1789, and by 1791 the Typographical Company had collapsed.

In 1792, as the atmosphere of reaction thickened in the aftermath of the French Revolution, Novikov finally fell from grace. A book containing the schismatic texts of the persecuted Old Believers had come to the notice of the authorities. Prozorovskii, the martinet governor-general of Moscow, received instructions to carry out a search of Novikov's properties for "such a book, or others similar to it". A number of books deemed "similar to it" were discovered, and Novikov was arrested and sent to the Schlüsselberg Fortress to face interrogation by Sheshkovskii. Novikov confessed to the crimes of having attempted to lure Paul, the heir to the throne, into freemasonry and having published banned books. Condemned to 15 years incarceration, Novikov was pardoned and released four years later after Paul's accession to the throne, but he never again played a significant role in Russia's literary life. Novikov was, as Georgii Plekhanov, then Russia's leading Marxist, acknowledged in 1888, the first in a long line of literary martyrs to the Russian state.

W. GARETH JONES

Writings

N.I. Novikov i ego sovremenniki: Izbrannye sochineniia, edited by I.V. Malyshev and L.B. Svetlov, 1961

Further Reading

Jones, W. Gareth, *Nikolay Novikov: Enlightener of Russia*, Cambridge and New York: Cambridge University Press, 1984

Madariaga, Isabel de, *Russia in the Age of Catherine the Great*, London: Weidenfeld and Nicolson, and New Haven, Connecticut: Yale University Press, 1981

Marker, Gary, *Publishing, Printing, and the Origins of Intellectual Life in Russia, 1700–1800*, Princeton, New Jersey: Princeton University Press, 1985

Papmehl, K.A., *Freedom of Expression in Eighteenth-Century Russia*, The Hague: Nijhoff, 1971

NOVYI MIR (New World)
Russian literary journal, founded 1925

It is safe to say that no other Soviet or Russian journal can boast such longevity and such a remarkable publication record as *Novyi mir*. This journal, publishing literature and articles of general interest, started publication in Moscow in 1925 under the editorship of Anatolii Lunacharskii, People's Commissar for Popular Enlightenment. During the 1920s *Novyi mir* published many works by Symbolists, Acmeists, and Futurists, as well as some of the best works in the socialist tradition by Vladimir Maiakovskii, Aleksei Tolstoi, and others.

After a few years of comparative freedom of expression, the first Five-year Plan (1928–32) brought many restrictions, and during the 1930s many writers, including some who had earlier contributed to *Novyi mir*, were silenced. During this decade major works by such Soviet icons as Aleksei Tolstoi, Maksim Gor'kii, and Mikhail Sholokhov appeared in *Novyi mir*. Ivan Gronskii was the editor-in-chief from 1935 up to his arrest and presumed execution in 1937; his disappearance was the result of his open support for the novelist Boris Pil'niak, who suffered the same fate. During World War II the journal declined under its editor Vladimir Shcherbina, a military man.

New energy was brought to *Novyi mir* by the poet Konstantin Simonov, who took over the editorship in 1946, but his efforts were frustrated by the many restrictive guidelines imposed to bring publishing into line with Andrei Zhdanov's "theses" on culture, issued in 1946. During this time Stalin took a personal interest in literature, in a way that was occasionally beneficial but on the whole destructive.

Simonov was moved to another editorial post in 1950 and was replaced by the poet Aleksandr Tvardovskii, who led the journal from 1950 to 1954 and again from 1958 to 1970. Simonov returned for the period 1954–58. Tvardovskii became the editor most closely identified with *Novyi mir* because of the intellectual and cultural turmoil of the years in which he held the post. Under his leadership, the journal frequently became the centre of controversy because of one or more controversial works that he published after slipping them past the censors. One of the major controversies in the early 1950s concerned Vasilii Grossman's novel *Za pravoe delo* (For the Just Cause). After coming to power in 1953, Khrushchev followed Stalin's example and interfered personally in literature. It was on Khrushchev's insistence that Tvardovskii was dismissed in 1954 for planning to publish his own verse satire *Terkin na tom svete* (Terkin in the Other World). In 1956 Simonov published Vladimir Dudintsev's novel *Ne khlebom edinym* (Not by Bread Alone), which became the best-known work of the "Thaw".

Surprised at the strong reaction to that novel, Simonov rejected Boris Pasternak's manuscript *Doktor Zhivago* (Doctor Zhivago) for publication in *Novyi mir*. When Tvardovskii came back to *Novyi mir* in 1958, he supported Simonov's rejection of Pasternak's novel, an action he later regretted. In the early 1960s he began bringing out the important and controversial memoirs of the novelist Il'ia Ehrenburg (1960–65), at the cost of many agonizing confrontations with the various levels of censorship.

Tvardovskii's major coup was the publication of Aleksandr Solzhenitsyn's novella *Odin den' Ivana Denisovicha* (1962, One Day in the Life of Ivan Denisovich). Tvardovskii bypassed the censor and went directly to Khrushchev, who had by then become his backer and now supported publication. Khrushchev even discussed with Tvardovskii the idea of abolishing censorship altogether, but he was deposed in 1964 before any action could be taken (if any was ever really intended).

After Khrushchev's removal Tvardovskii lost much of his influence, and in spite of immense efforts he failed to get permission to publish Solzhenitsyn's later novels. Other major publications in *Novyi mir* in the 1960s were Tvardovskii's own *Terkin na tom svete* (in 1963) and Mikhail Bulgakov's *Teatral'nyi Roman* (written 1936–37, published in *Novyi mir*

1965; Theatrical Novel), the first major work by that author to come out in his homeland. To get permission to publish this novella Tvardovskii appealed to the proper department of the Central Committee and benefited by a change of personnel there. He was unable to publish Bulgakov's *Master i Margarita* (written 1928–1940, The Master and Margarita), because by this time specially strict censorship restrictions had been placed on *Novyi mir* compared to other journals. (*Master i Margarita* was published in book form in 1966–67.) Tvardovskii nevertheless maintained high standards. During the 1960s, most of what was new and interesting in Soviet literature came out in *Novyi mir*, including works by Iurii Trifonov, Vasilii Shukshin, Iurii Dombrovskii, and others. Among the works that he did not succeed in pushing through were novels by Aleksandr Bek and Solzhenitsyn, diaries by Simonov, and his own poem "Po pravu pamiati" (By Right of Memory). In 1968 so much material was banned by the censor at the last moment that issue number 5 came out one signature short; the following issue, number 6, was correspondingly thicker.

After being hounded by the authorities for some time, Tvardovskii was finally forced to resign in early 1970. This event is sometimes referred to as the "death" or "disbanding" of *Novyi mir*, but although it was a setback, it was not the end of the journal. It experienced some eclipse after Tvardovskii's departure but it was led by competent editors, including the poet Sergei Narovchatov, and as glasnost emerged it was ultimately taken over by Tvardovskii's protégé, the novelist Sergei Zalygin, in 1986. Under Zalygin *Novyi mir* has published such major works as *Doktor Zhivago* (1988), Solzhenitsyn's *V kruge pervom* (completed 1968, published 1990; The First Circle) and his *Arkhipelag GULag* (1989, The Gulag Archipelago), and Dombrovskii's *Fakul'tet nenuzhnykh veshchei* (1988, Department of Useless Things). Important new works by Daniil Granin, Mikhail Kuraev, Tat'iana Tolstaia, and many others have also been published. Zalygin's major concern is no longer with the censor but with finding financial backers at a time when government funding has been cut off.

MARGARETA O. THOMPSON

Further Reading

Burtin, Iurii (editor), "Edva raskrylis pervye tsvety: Novyi mir i obshchestvennye umonastroeniia v 1954 godu" (The Flowers Have Barely Opened: *Novyi mir* and the Public Frame of Mind in 1954), *Druzhba narodov*, 11 (1993): 208–39

Frankel, Edith Rogovin, *Novyi mir: A Case Study in the Politics of Literature, 1952–1958*, Cambridge and New York: Cambridge University Press, 1981

Kondratovich, Aleksei (editor), *Novomirskii dnevnik 1967–1970* (A *Novyi mir* Diary), Moscow: Sovetskii pisatel, 1991

Lakshin, Vladimir, *Solzhenitsyn, Tvardovskii, and Novyi mir*, Cambridge, Massassachusetts. MIT Press, 1980

Lakshin, Vladimir, *Novyi Mir vo vremena Khrushcheva: dnevnik i poputnoe, 1952–1964* (*Novyi mir* in Khrushchev's Time: A Diary and Accompanying Notes), Moscow: Knizhnaia palata, 1991

Medvedev, Zhores A., *Ten Years after Ivan Denisovich*, New York: Knopf, 1973; Harmondsworth: Penguin, 1975

Miller, Tamara N. (editor), *Bibliographical Index of the Contributions to Novyi mir, 1925–1934*, Ann Arbor, Michigan: Ardis,1983

"Ob oshibkakh zhurnala *Novyi mir*," (On the Mistakes of the Journal *Novyi mir*), *Novyi mir* 9 (1954): 3–7

Solzhenitsyn, Aleksandr, *The Oak and the Calf: Sketches of Literary Life in the Soviet Union*, translated by Harry Willetts, New York: Harper and Row, and London: Collins Harvill, 1980

Spechler, Dina R., *Permitted Dissent in the USSR: Novyi mir and the Soviet Regime*, New York: Praeger, 1982

Thompson, Margareta O., "Years of Change: The Editorial Career of Aleksandr Tvardovskii" (dissertation), Chapel Hill: University of North Carolina, 1986

Tvardovskii, A.T., "Ot redkollegii" (From the Editorial Board), *Novyi mir*, 11 (1958): 1–11

Zaks, Boris, "Censorship at the Editorial Desk" in *The Red Pencil: Artists, Scholars, and Censors in the USSR*, edited by Marianna Tax Choldin and Maurice Friedberg, London and Boston: Unwin Hyman, 1989

ALBERT MUWALO NQUMAYO
Malawian politician, died 1976

The victims of censorship need not be heroes. Indeed, Albert Muwalo Nqumayo was a villain of the first order. He held the post of secretary-general of the ruling Malawi Congress Party (MCP) at the time of its most brutal repression of alleged opponents. Yet, among other reasons, he was eventually sent to the gallows because a copy of George Orwell's *Animal Farm* was found in his possession.

Muwalo and the head of the police Special Branch, Focus Martin Gwede, were prime movers in the violent persecution of the Jehovah's Witnesses in Malawi in the early 1970s. In addition, he was responsible for the detention without trial of hundreds of alleged opponents of the MCP regime – many of them distrusted primarily for their level of education. By 1976, however, Life President Hastings Kamuzu Banda feared, rightly or wrongly, that Muwalo and Gwede were plotting a coup d'état. They were arrested and charged with treason.

Malawi had two parallel judicial systems. One was modelled on the English system, with a magistrature, a High Court, and a Supreme Court. The other represented colonial notions of customary law and was intended initially to deal with civil disputes and minor criminal cases. In 1970, however, Banda had massively expanded the powers of the "traditional courts" to enable them to hear murder cases. This followed the decision of the High Court to acquit the accused in a politically sensitive murder case. The traditional court judges were chiefs – that is, low level administrators – with no legal training. The courts followed no rules of evidence and more or less made up their procedures as they went along. In a subsequent notorious political case, the head of the police investigation was allowed to give evidence as an "independent" handwriting expert. Defendants in the "traditional courts" were given no guarantee of legal representation. Over more than two decades, hundreds of Malawians were convicted of capital offences after unfair trials in these courts.

In 1976, at the time of Muwalo and Gwede's arrest, the traditional courts had no power to hear treason cases. No matter. The law was changed to allow their trial to be held in the Southern Region Traditional Court. There was one serious piece of evidence against the two men: they had been found in unauthorized possession of firearms. This was evidence of an offence, but that offence was not treason. Hence recourse was made to supposedly hallowed principles of traditional Malawian jurisprudence ("there is no smoke without fire") and a mass of bogus or irrelevant evidence. Two anonymous letters accused Muwalo and Gwede of plotting. Meanwhile, the fact that they were found to be in possession of photographs of exiled opposition leaders was held to be proof positive of their treasonous intent.

And then there were Muwalo's books. Excessive reading was always regarded as a symptom of political unreliability in Malawi – the party paper once memorably proclaimed that the country wanted "No graduates in Parliament" – but Muwalo had never previously been suspected of being a closet intellectual. Yet here he was with copies of *Animal Farm*, a historical study of the assassination of the Zulu leader Shaka, and various books on the politics and economics of the Soviet Union, Yugoslavia, and China. The Malawi Censorship Board had a banned list containing hundreds of publications but, as it happened, none of Muwalo's books other than *Animal Farm* was on it. This presented no obstacle to the judges, who declared

that: "if these books [had come] into the country in the regular manner they would no doubt [have been] declared banned publications."

It was the discovery of *Animal Farm* that most upset the judges. In vain did Muwalo plead that he had studied it as a set book at school and forgotten to throw it away when it was banned. According to the judges, it was "a satire on how a dictator's government was overthrown and the leaders killed". Clearly Muwalo was "a believer, convert or supporter of communist type of governments".

The irony, of course, is that *Animal Farm* was an apt comment on post-independence Malawi, yet for reasons quite different from those understood by the judges in the Muwalo case. His Excellency the Life-President Ngwazi Dr H. Kamuzu Banda was not Orwell's farmer, Mr Jones. He was "Our Leader Comrade Napoleon, Father of All Animals, Terror of Mankind, Protector of the Sheep-fold, Ducklings' Friend", who had seized power from the original leaders of the revolution and driven them to death or exile. Muwalo probably did not understand this. Indeed, there is no reason to doubt his claim that he had not opened the book since his O-levels. But this did not save his neck. He was sentenced to death and executed. First, however, he enacted a little scene worthy of Orwell himself, in which he thanked the bench for its conduct of his trial and apologized for his own ignorance in matters of procedure.

RICHARD CARVER

Further Reading

Carver, Richard, *Malawi under Banda: A Lost History*, forthcoming
Orwell, George, *Animal Farm*, London: Secker and Warburg, 1945, New York: Harcourt Brace, 1946; many reprints

NUEVA CANCIÓN (New Song)
Musicians and folklorists, Chile and elsewhere, from 1960s

Nueva canción grew up in the 1960s, as an inextricable part of the struggle for the election of the Chilean Popular Unity coalition, led by Salvador Allende. In a key speech, shortly after his victory in the 1970 presidential election, Allende appeared on stage, surrounded by musicians, in front of a banner that proclaimed: "There can be no revolution without song: we sing for the woman, the worker, the land worker, and the student." The musicians of *nueva canción* are notable in the history of Chilean censorship, not only for their resistance, mostly from exile, but also because they were among the thousands of Popular Unity supporters who were silenced by the regime of General Pinochet by means of exile, torture, imprisonment, and death.

The roots of *nueva canción* did not lie solely in political campaigning, but the movement certainly emerged at a time of great energy and hope for radical change to favour the poor, the voiceless, and the hitherto powerless. Inspired by collectivist values, most of the musicians who identified with the movement were actively involved in the struggle, as much for what

they sang and performed as whom they performed for and where. Like modern troubadours, they sang, accompanied by guitar and a variety of Latin American strings, wind and percussion instruments, at political meetings and outdoor cultural events, and were heard by masses of ordinary people, students, and factory workers in their lunch breaks.

Members of the most prominent groups dressed in the woven ponchos of the peasantry and took indigenous names. Quilapayún, formed in 1966, means "three beards" in the language of Chile's Mapuche people – although eventually there were six in the group. Inti Illimani derives from the Quechua name for sun-god and means "Over the mountain Illimani". Initially, Inti Illimani modelled themselves on the village panpipe bands of the *altiplano* of Bolivia and Peru, evoking South America's precolonial past, and its ancient community values and village economies, based on reciprocity and exchange.

After the coup d'état of 11 September 1973 officials of the military junta reportedly called together a group of noted folklorists to warn them that it would be "unwise" for anyone to play any music associated with *nueva canción*, or even to play instruments such as panpipes and *quenas* that could be identified with the *nueva canción* "sound" in the popular mind. For many, this was a warning too late. The *canto-autor* (songwriter) Victor Jara is the dominant figure of the history of *nueva canción*. Arrested at the Technical University on 11 September, he was taken, along with hundreds of others, to an improvised prison camp in a basketball stadium in downtown Santiago, where he was beaten, tortured, and finally shot. During his last hours in Estadio Chile, he managed to scribble a last poem, which began "Somos cinco mil" (We are 5000) and was later set to a haunting melody by Isabel Parra as "Ay canto, que mal me sales" (Oh, How Hard It Is to Sing, 1976).

Jara's career had evidently aroused the hostility and fear of the regime. His mother came from a family of *cantores* who sang at celebrations of birth, marriage, and harvest, and at *velorios* (wakes). A noted and innovative theatre director, he had pursued a parallel career as a folklorist, becoming one of the *canto-autores* who performed regularly at the Peña de los Parra, Calle Carmen 340, the crucible of the *nueva canción*. Jara followed in the footsteps of Violeta Parra (1917–67), whose songs were a key part of the repertoire of early *nueva canción* musicians; Jara's music was always rooted in popular tradition, but he also experimented freely with rock and pop. He courted controversy. His playful version of the traditional song "La Beata" (The Nun) caused complaints from some Catholics. "Preguntas par Puerto Montt" (1968, Questions about Puerto Montt), composed after a police massacre of an unarmed innocent group in southern Chile and named a government minister as responsible, was received with hostility when Jara sang it at an English school in Santiago. Work he composed in Popular Unity's last months, such as "Cuando voy al trabajo" (1973, When I Go to Work) and "Vientos del pueblo" (1973, Winds of the People), map many of the hopes and struggles of the time.

Jara had a close association with Inti Illimani and Quilapayún, or the Intis and Quilas, as they have become familiarly known. He was Quilas's artistic director between 1966 and 1969, and helped forge their dramatic presentation style. Both groups recorded a full range of work, from classically influenced pieces, a setting of the Popular Unity election programme, to the *canciones contingentes*, the lively songs sung at demonstrations, such as "El pueblo unido jamas sera vencido" (The People United Will Never be Defeated, 1973), a rallying cry in the last months of Popular Unity and during the years of exile.

At the time of the coup, Inti Illimani and Quilapayún happened to be on a tour in Europe as cultural ambassadors for Popular Unity, galvanizing support for the economically besieged government. Overnight they became the heart and soul of a worldwide movement of solidarity. During their extended "tour" of 15 years, they often made 200 or 300 appearances a year. Under their musical director, the composer Horacio Salinas, they created a new repertoire in exile, influenced by European traditions but never far removed from their roots in Chile, notably in songs such as "Vuelvo" (I Return) and "Cuando me acuerdo de mi país" (When I Remember my Country), both written with the composer Patricio Manns.

Many *nueva canción* albums that had first been issued by Discoteca del Cantar Popular (DICAP) in Chile were re-edited and licensed in exile. One such was *Chacabuco*, a recording of a concert in the eponymous makeshift concentration camp, situated in an old nitrate mine in the desert of northern Chile, made clandestinely by a prisoner just before the singer Angel Parra and others were released into exile. Parra and other musicians had organized music workshops with other prisoners. Parra joined his sister, the singer Isabel Parra, who had escaped first to Cuba, then to France.

Inti Illimani were eventually given permission to return home. Arriving on Chile's national day, 18 September 1988, they drove straight from the airport to take part in a historic concert in support of the "No" vote in the plebiscite called by general Pinochet to decide whether or not he should be allowed to stay in power.

Musicians of the *nueva canción* movement have shared and exchanged much with other musicians of their generation in Argentina, Brazil, Uruguay, Mexico, Nicaragua, Venezuela, and Cuba, some of whom have been imprisoned and exiled during times of dictatorship in their own countries.

JAN FAIRLEY

Further Reading

Jara, Joan, *Victor, an Unfinished Song: The Life of Victor Jara*, London: Jonathan Cape, and New York: Ticknor and Fields, 1983
Jara, Victor, *Victor Jara: His Life and Songs*, London: Elm Tree, 1976

Recordings

The independent record company Alerce has brought out many CD compilations of "new song" musicians in recent years. Into Illimani's CDs are distributed on Green Linnet, Xenophile label, ISA. Quilapayún, who officially disbanded in the 1980s, have reissued many of their LPs on CD.

O

EDNA O'BRIEN
Irish novelist, 1930–

All the novels published by Edna O'Brien during the 1960s were banned in Ireland by the Censorship of Publications Board: *The Country Girls* (1960); *The Lonely Girl* (1962) and its reprint *Girl with Green Eyes* (1964); *Girls in Their Married Bliss* (1964); *August Is a Wicked Month* (1965), which was also banned in Australia, Rhodesia, and South Africa; and *Casualties of Peace* (1966). O'Brien was hailed by *Esquire* as a "prophetess of sex"; she inspired an unprecedented campaign in Ireland, a campaign that was described by the Irish writer Benedict Kiely as "pathological" and a "determined persecution".

O'Brien's work gained notoriety in Ireland in the 1960s because of its detailed exploration of female sexuality. Her personal outspokenness and the range of sexual experience that she attributed to women in her fiction made her a scapegoat and reflected how far the foundations of Irish Catholic society were threatened by sexual permissiveness for women. O'Brien held both the Catholic church and its laity responsible for this reaction, viewing it as the product of a deep-seated fear of sexuality. "Sex is the factor here. The fear would be that the people would become libidinous, rampant."

In each of her novels O'Brien challenges what she describes as "the pedestal image" of women, "devoid of sexual desires, maternal, devout, attractive". She places her female characters' sexuality at the centre of their lives and represents in detail their sexual yearnings and encounters. Her first three novels follow the lives of two young Irish girls, Caithleen and Baba, as they leave their rural homes for the city, become involved with and mistreated by men, marry unhappily, and ultimately try to forge identities for themselves. *August is a Wicked Month* and *Casualties of Peace* focus upon the lives of women whose marriages have failed. In *August Is a Wicked Month*, O'Brien explores the promiscuity of Ellen Sage, who develops venereal disease and longs "to be free and young and naked with all the men in the world making love to her, all at once". In *Casualties of Peace*, Willa McCord tries to recover her self-esteem after a lesbian relationship and an abusive marriage; she eventually finds happiness with a black male lover before she is accidentally murdered by her maid's husband.

O'Brien felt acutely the impact of censorship at a personal level. Looking the image of an Irish colleen, she became identified in the popular mind with the characters in her fiction. Copies of her books were burned in her native village, where her family suffered public humiliation and was "appalled" by what she had written. O'Brien herself was accused of being a "smear on Irish womanhood". She never returned to live permanently in Ireland after the banning of her books, fearing that her psychological freedom as a writer would be jeopardized. She wrote in *Mother Ireland*: "I live out of Ireland because something in me worries that I might stop if I lived there."

In spite of the fact that five of her novels were banned, O'Brien never received the outpouring of public support accorded to John McGahern after the banning of his novel, *The Dark*. The absence of a strong feminist movement in Ireland in the early 1960s meant that O'Brien's representation of female sexuality was not adamantly defended. Critics who spoke in favour of her work were clear in their opposition to its censorship, but often offended by or ambivalent about her treatment of sexuality. Bruce Arnold, who called for the formation of a Censorship Reform Society in 1966, praised O'Brien for her depiction of "sexual failure" but at the same time called her work "exhibitionist". Sean McMahon argued for the availability of her work but described some of the scenes in *August is a Wicked Month* as "nauseating". He likened O'Brien's career to *The Pilgrim's Progress*: "Miss Pilgrim is finding it difficult to climb out of the Slough of Despond."

The most influential public support O'Brien received came, ironically, from within the Catholic Church. Father Peter Connolly, professor of English literature at St Patrick's College, Maynooth, took up her cause in the wake of the controversy that followed the banning of *The Dark*. At an emotionally charged public meeting in Limerick in April 1966, he appeared on a platform with O'Brien and delivered a paper arguing in favour of the moral character of her work. He praised *The Country Girls* and *The Lonely Girl* for their "cheerful, natural, rural ribaldry" which embodied "the spirit of the countryside". O'Brien's central character Caithleen was, he argued, "not amoral but premoral" and in possession of a kind of "original innocence". Like many of her supporters, he had difficulty with her later work. He was critical of her treatment of sexuality in *Girls in Their Married Bliss* and *August Is a Wicked Month*, which he found "indulgent", but praised the literary quality of her writing, concluding that he was "more interested in her work than in any other novels appearing at the moment in Ireland".

An editorial in *The Irish Times* praised Connolly for his courage and commented upon the absence of public protest against censorship in Ireland, commenting on "how many people in prominent places might, before this, have spoken out on behalf of Irish writers who have for so long been mangled by their own. This silence marks one of the more shameful aspects of the forty-odd years' existence of this State."

O'Brien was one of the few Irish writers to condemn Irish censorship openly and to campaign actively for changes in the censorship laws. She appeared at public meetings and brought her books across the border from Northern Ireland. Public protest against the banning of *The Dark* and of O'Brien's novels created a momentum which led to censorship reform in 1967.

JULIA CARLSON

Writings

The Country Girls, 1960
The Lonely Girl, 1962; as *Girl with Green Eyes*, 1964
Girls in Their Married Bliss, 1964
August Is a Wicked Month, 1965
Casualties of Peace, 1966

Further Reading

Adams, Michael, *Censorship: The Irish Experience*, University: University of Alabama Press, 1968

Arnold, Bruce, "Censorship and Edna O'Brien: A Special Case", *The Irish Times* (21 November 1966): 14

Carlson, Julia (editor), *Banned in Ireland: Censorship and the Irish Writer*, London: Routledge, and Athens: University of Georgia Press, 1990

"Censorship Reform Society Founded", *The Irish Times* (5 December 1966): 1, 11

Connolly, Peter, *No Bland Facility: Selected Writings on Literature, Religion, and Censorship*, edited by James H. Murphy, Gerrards Cross, Buckinghamshire: Smythe, 1991

Horgan, John, "Edna O'Brien Faces Limerick Audience", *The Irish Times* (23 April 1966): 7

Kiely, Benedict, "The Whores on the Half-Doors; or, An Image of the Irish Writer" in *Conor Cruise O'Brien Introduces Ireland*, edited by Owen Dudley Edwards. London: Deutsch, 1969; New York: McGraw Hill, 1970

McMahon, Sean, "A Sex by Themselves: An Interim Report on the Novels of Edna O'Brien", *Eire-Ireland*, 2/1 (1967): 79–87

"Now, Mr. Minister!", *The Irish Times* (25 April 1966): 9

KATE O'BRIEN
Irish novelist, 1897–1974
THE LAND OF SPICES
Novel, 1941

Kate O'Brien had three books banned during her lifetime. In Spain, her travel book, *Farewell, Spain* (1937) was banned because it criticized the Franco regime; O'Brien was barred from entering the country until 1957. In Ireland, two of her novels, *Mary Lavelle* (1936) and *The Land of Spices* (1941), were banned by the Censorship of Publications Board.

O'Brien's third novel, *Mary Lavelle* (1936), is a story of the sexual liberation of a young Irish woman who decides to take a married lover while living in Spain. When the novel was banned in Ireland in 1937, there was little surprise that it had been declared "indecent or obscene". Irish literary censorship was at its peak, Eamon de Valera's government was in power, and as a heroine, Mary Lavelle was far removed from his professed ideal of "comely maidens".

The banning of *The Land of Spices* was wholly unexpected, however. Its central character is Helen Archer, the Reverend Mother of an Irish convent, who rejects secular life at the age of 18 after discovering her father in a homosexual relationship with one of his music pupils. Helen is shocked and disgusted by their relationship and shifts from idealizing her father as a civilized man to rejecting him as a betrayer: "So that was the sort of thing that the most graceful life could hide! That was what lay around, under love, under beauty. That was the flesh they preached about, the extremity of what the sin of the flesh might be." She becomes obsessed with "the devilry of human love", and her adulthood is split between her highly successful professional career as a teacher and administrator (she eventually becomes the Mother Superior of her order), and her damaged emotional life, which is dominated by her inability to accept her father's sexuality and her subsequent reluctance to love and trust again.

The banning of *The Land of Spices* became the subject of a heated debate in the Irish Senate in November and December of 1942, when Sir John Keane put forward the motion that the Censorship Board "has ceased to retain public confidence, and that steps should be taken to reconstitute the board". His argument was based on the banning of *The Land of Spices* and two other books – *The Tailor and Ansty*, which consisted of the conversations of an elderly County Cork tailor and his wife as recorded by the scientist, Eric Cross, and *The Laws of Life* by Dr Halliday Sutherland, a book that, ironically, had received the sanction of the Catholic Church for its recommendation of natural methods of birth control. During the debate, it was revealed that *The Land of Spices* had been banned for the one sentence referring to the homosexual affair: "She saw Etienne and her father, in the embrace of love."

In defence of *The Land of Spices* Sir John Keane argued that he believed *male fides* could be proved with regard to the banning of the novel and that, technically, the board had acted without legal authority and outside the terms of the Censorship of Publications Act. The novel was, he argued, "a most astounding case": "a book about convent life" in which the "general motif is almost religious". He suggested that the banning of the novel was rooted in homophobia and that it probably never would have occurred if the reference had been to a heterosexual affair.

Sir John Keane's reasoned argument had little impact in the face of the emotionally charged argument put forth by senator professor William Magennis, who served on the Censorship Board from 1934 to 1946. He was a formidable debater and ultimately responsible for the rejection of Sir John Keane's motion. He argued against the dangers of "*lecher-ature*" and, when accused of Victorian prudery and of serving as a "literary Gestapo", he asserted that Christian values were being threatened by the forces of paganism and that his standards "do not date back to Queen Victoria's days; they date back to Moses". His focus was also anti-English, and he argued forcefully against the presence in Ireland of books that, "to suit the English publishers' demand", had been padded out "with sex and smut".

Magennis labelled *The Land of Spices* "the sodomy book", arguing that it was "dominated by the influence of the terrible theme" and that it was "unwholesome" and made "evil reading". He claimed: "That single sentence is a vivid account of what St Paul, the Apostle of the Gentiles, said was not to be mentioned amongst Christian men. This woman author chooses to make that the central and preponderating motif in a novel of convent life." Magennis was supported by Gerald Boland, the minister for justice, who banned the book on the recommendation of the board and agreed that its banning was justified by its "central theme".

The impact of the banning of *The Land of Spices* was considerable. In the short term, it drew attention to the extremes to which the Censorship Board went in recommending books to be banned, particularly those by Irish authors. In the long term, the 1942 Senate debate initiated the discussions that led to the creation of a Censorship of Publications Appeal Board in 1946.

Kate O'Brien was enraged by the banning of her work but, like most Irish authors, she never took political action. Instead, she responded through her fiction. In *Pray for the Wanderer* (1938), she focuses directly on the issue of censorship. Her central character, Matt Costello, is a banned writer who attacks Eamon de Valera's Ireland as "a dictator's country" and vehemently condemns censorship: "I reject censorship lock, stock, and barrel because it is a confession of failure. It is a denial of human judgement and understanding, and a gross intrusion on liberty."

JULIA CARLSON

Writings
Mary Lavelle, 1936
Farewell, Spain, 1937
Pray for the Wanderer, 1938
The Land of Spices, 1941

Further Reading
Adams, Michael, *Censorship: The Irish Experience*, University: University of Alabama Press, 1968
Seanad Éireann, *Parliamentary Debates*, 27 (1942)
Walshe, Eibhear (editor), *Ordinary People Dancing: Essays on Kate O'Brien*, Cork: Cork University Press, 1993

OBSCENITY AND INDECENCY

Indian Perspectives

Freedom of expression can be restricted in India on the grounds of "decency or morality" (article 19(2)). Though the word obscenity is rarely mentioned, courts in India have in most cases equated indecency with obscenity.

Section 292 of the Indian Penal Code (IPC) prohibits and penalizes the publication of obscene material. It provides that:

a book, pamphlet, paper, writing, drawing, painting, representation, figure or any other object, shall be deemed to be obscene if it is lascivious or appeals to the prurient interest or if its effect, or (where it comprises two or more distinct items) the effect of any one of its items, is, if taken as a whole, such as to tend to deprave and corrupt persons who are likely, having regard to all relevant circumstances, to read, see or hear the matter contained or embodied in it.

An exception is made whereby this section does not extend to any book, pamphlet, paper, writing, drawing, painting, representation, or figure, the publication of which is proved to be justified as being for the public good on the ground that such book, pamphlet, paper, writing, drawing, painting, representation, or figure is in the interest of science, literature, art, or learning or other objects of general concern; or which is kept or used *bona fide* for religious purposes. Another exception made is in respect of any representation sculptured, engraved, painted, or otherwise represented on or in any temple, or on any car used for the conveyance of idols, or kept or used for any religious purpose. The maximum sentence upon conviction is two years.

There are other statutory provisions that prohibit writings considered to be obscene. For example, the Indian Telegraph Act 1885 and the Post Office Act 1898 prohibit obscene writings. The Cinematograph Act 1952 provides that a film shall not be certified for public exhibition if, in the opinion of the authority competent to grant a certificate, it is against decency or morality (section 5(B)). Under section 11 of the Customs Act 1962, by the issue of a notification importation of books and other materials can be prohibited *inter alia* on the ground that they offend standards of decency or morality.

Another law, recently enacted, is the Indecent Representation of Women (Prohibition) Act 1986. Section 3 of this act prohibits the publication or exhibition of any advertisement that contains indecent representations of women in any form. Indecent representation of women is defined to mean "the depiction in any manner of the figure of a woman, her form or body or any part thereof in such a way as to have the effect of being indecent, or derogatory to, or denigrating women, or is likely to deprave, corrupt or injure the public morality or morals". Advertisement is defined to include "any notice, circular, label, wrapper or other document and also includes any visible representation made by means of any light, sound, smoke or gas". The sweep of the Act is wide. In recent times it has been frequently invoked by groups of women seeking to protect the dignity of women, much as Catharine A. MacKinnon and Andrea Dworkin have done in the United States.

"Obscenity", "indecency", "morality" are equivocal and relative concepts. Judges, despite valiant efforts, have failed to evolve a satisfactory definition of obscenity. The Federal Court of Appeal in Canada held that the expressions "immoral" and "indecent" are highly subjective and emotive and freedom of expression cannot be restricted on these grounds because uncertainty and vagueness are unconstitutional vices when they are used to restrict guaranteed rights and freedoms. The judicial predicament is vividly summed up in the lament of Justice Stewart of the US Supreme Court who confessed that he could not define obscenity but recognized it when he saw it (*Jacobellis* v. *Ohio*, 1964). Apparently, obscenity, like beauty, lies in the eyes of the beholder. The least unsatisfactory position would be to restrict the obscenity or indecency laws only to publications that are patently offensive and in which exploitation of the prurient interest in sex is the sole motive and object without the slightest redeeming feature in terms of art, literature, or any other discipline.

The Supreme Court of India has recognized that:

> the concept of obscenity would differ from country to country depending on the standards of morals of contemporary society. What is considered as a piece of literature in France may be obscene in England and what is considered in both countries as not harmful to public order and morals may be obscene in our country (*Chandratant* v. *State of Maharashtra*, 1970).

Sin, as Pascal reminds us, is geographical and the same is the case with obscenity. Nabokov's *Lolita* fell foul of the customs authorities and was rescued only after the personal intervention of the Indian prime minister, Jawarhalal Nehru, who found nothing objectionable in it. The same book surprisingly was branded indecent by a majority of New Zealand judges in 1961. Standards of morality and decency in the same society may also vary from time to time and from person to person and there is no uniform test of community standards of acceptance.

One reason for the failure to formulate a test for determining obscenity is that in adjudging issues of this kind the personal scale of values and the predilections of the judge inevitably play a part: D.H. Lawrence's *Lady Chatterley's Lover* fell foul of the Indian Supreme Court justices in the case of *Ranjit Udeshi*, decided on 19 August 1964. The Supreme Court adopted the 19th-century Hicklin test laid down by courts in Britain and came to the surprising conclusion that the book was obscene judged "from our community standards and there is no social gain to us which can be said to preponderate". Today the average English-speaking Indian has free and easy access, in libraries and bookshops, to books in whose company *Lady Chatterley's Lover* would blush like a tomato. In view of the changing standards of morality this judgement may well be regarded as anachronistic. The Supreme Court has noticed in a subsequent judgement that "the standards of contemporary society in India are also fast changing. The adults and adolescents have available to them a large number of classics, novels, stories and pieces of literature which have a content of sex, love and romance".

Later judgements of the Supreme Court reflect a liberal approach to the concept of obscenity. It has been emphasized that the work has to be considered as a whole, that there should be no undue emphasis on stray expressions or passages in isolation, and that the writing should not be considered "in the spirit of the lady who charged Dr Johnson with putting improper words in his dictionary and was rebuked by him 'Madam, you must have been looking for them'". To adopt such an attitude towards art and literature would make the Courts a board of censors" (*Chandratant* v. *State of Maharashtra*, 1970). The Supreme Court recognized that "if a reference to sex by itself is considered obscene, no books can be sold except those which are purely religious".

The Supreme Court has categorically stated that "a vulgar writing is not necessarily obscene. Vulgarity arouses a feeling of disgust and revulsion and also boredom but does not have the effect of depraving, debasing and corrupting the morals of any reader of the novel". Nor can a novel be pronounced obscene "merely because slang and unconventional words have been used in the book in which there have been emphasis on sex and description of female bodies and there are the narrations of feelings, thoughts and actions in vulgar language". However courts in India still adhere to the outdated Hicklin test and its ghost has not been fully exorcized.

In its judgement *Dr Ramesh Yeshwant Prabhoo* v. *Prabhakar K. Kunte* (1996) the Supreme Court ruled that indecency or morality that is one of heads on which freedom of expression can be restricted is not confined to sexual morality alone. Drawing upon the decision of the House of Lords in *Knuller (Publishing, Printing and Promotions) Ltd* v. *Director of Public Prosecutions* (1972) the Court held that "seeking votes at an election on the ground of the candidate's religion in a secular State, is against the norms of decency and propriety of the society". It thus upheld the constitutionality of Section 123(3) of the Representation of Peoples Act 1951 under which seeking votes at an election on the ground of religion is declared a corrupt practice resulting in the invalidation of the election of the successful candidate.

The contrast in Indian and Western perspectives of indecency is sharply brought out by the provisions of the Indecent Representation of Women (Prohibition) Act 1986 and its enforcement. Posters of women that would not cause even a mild flutter in the West occasion strong protests and agitation in India. According to the Indian ethos and mores, a woman's body must not be exploited for publicity purposes. She must be properly covered. Songs with sexual innuendoes and double meanings are considered objectionable and there are demands that they should be banned. Sustained kissing is not permitted in Indian films by the Censor Board. Equally the use of four-letter words and terms of abuse, although they are in common use, is frowned upon. Nudity has been anathema to the Indian censors and also to some judges irrespective of its context. In the film, *The Bandit Queen* there was a brief scene of frontal nudity of Phoolan Devi, the Bandit, lasting about 20 seconds. The High Court of Delhi ruled that this scene was indecent and should be deleted. The Supreme Court reversed the decision and ruled: "Nakedness does not always arouse the baser instinct". Portrayal of the sexual act is absolutely taboo.

Such a situation does seem incongruous in a country where the *Kama Sutra* has originated and where its celebrated caves and temples of Khajuraho and Konarak explicitly portray sexual activities in various manifestations through erotic sculp-

OBSCENITY AND INDECENCY: INDIAN PERSPECTIVES: Erotic stone carvings decorating one of the temples at Khajuraho in Madhya Pradesh, India, built during the Chandela dynasty, 950–1050. The explicitness of the subject matter here contrasts sharply with the strict legal censorship of sexual material in contemporary Indian culture. The Indian Penal Code makes exceptions for representations engraved or painted in any temple or used for religious purposes.

tures and representations. The fervent desire for the preservation of a "clean" society uncontaminated by immoral Western influences is the main motivation for the irresistible itch for censorship that extends beyond books and advertisements and paintings and seeks to ban female beauty contests. The attempted justification for such acts is rested *inter alia* on Article

51-A of the Indian Constitution which prescribes certain fundamental duties, one of which is "to renounce practices derogatory to the dignity of women".

The exceptions made in Section 292 of the Indian Penal Code with regard to any representation engraved or painted in any temple or used for any religious purposes reflects the schizophrenic Indian attitude smacking of prudery and hypocrisy. This aspect was adverted to by the Delhi High Court in *Neelam Mahajan Singh* v. *Commissioner of Police* (1996) wherein the petitioner sought an order from the High Court to ban *The Women and Men in My Life* by Khushwant Singh, an eminent Indian writer. The court, referring to the novelist Arthur Koestler, aptly and correctly observed that "Indians have a notoriously ambivalent attitude towards sex. On the one hand the cult of *lingam*, the erotic temple carvings, the *Kama Sutra*, and the other, prudery, hypocrisy, lip service to the ideal of chastity combined with spermal anxiety".

The reality is that in India the applicable legal principles in adjudging obscenity have in practice been totally overlooked. Vulgarity or erotic language is often treated as interchangeable with obscenity. Narrow mindedness and intolerance have been the order of the day and several books and other works have been indiscriminately and illegally banned.

SOLI J. SORABJEE

Further Reading

Committee on Obscenity and Film Censorship, *Report of the Committee on Obscenity and Film Censorship* (The Williams Report), London: HMSO, 1979

Copp, David and Susan Wendell (editors), *Pornography and Censorship*, Buffalo: Prometheus, 1983

Grace, Sharon, *Testing Obscenity: An International Comparison of Laws and Controls Relating to Obscene Material*, London: Home Office, 1996

Itzin, Catherine (editor), *Pornography: Women, Violence and Civil Liberties*, Oxford and New York: Oxford University Press, 1992

Lederer, Laura (editor), *Take Back the Night: Women on Pornography*, New York: Morrow, 1980; London: Bantam, 1982

Special Committee on Pornography and Prostitution, *Pornography and Prostitution in Canada*, Ottawa: Canadian Government Publishing Centre, 1985

Western Perspectives

Numerous methods of control have been used in Western societies to suppress or restrict the availability of obscene or indecent material, primarily pre-publication censorship (or prior restraint) and criminal law prosecutions against those who deal in various ways with such material. Several other methods have, however, been employed, including the seizure and forfeiture of material, fiscal controls, locational controls, licensing regulation, and civil actions.

Pre-publication censorship has been a common method of control, especially for certain types of material, notably films and video recordings. The degree of censorship, however, varies considerably from one country to another and, indeed, may well vary considerably within a particular country if control is exercised at a local rather than a national level. In some countries, such as Denmark and the Netherlands, for example, there is no censorship of films shown to adults and the role of censorship boards is limited to deciding whether films are suitable for public exhibition to children. But in other countries, such as Finland and Sweden, censorship extends to adults and all films require a classification certificate; if one is refused, the film cannot be shown in a public cinema. But even where adult censorship exists, it is not necessarily the case that all sexually explicit material that might be indecent or obscene cannot be

shown. In Finland, for instance, a classification certificate would be refused for films showing sexual violence, bestiality, or sexual activity involving children, but a certificate would be granted restricting viewing to persons aged 18 or over for films featuring other sexual activity even if of a "hard core" nature. Video recordings might also be treated in a similar manner to films and be subject to a pre-publication censorship system under which a classification certificate is required. This is the case in Britain where classification of both films and video recordings is undertaken by the British Board of Film Classification (BBFC). Similarly, in Finland, some types of video recordings (essentially fiction films) have to be examined and classified by the State Board of Film Classification, but others (e.g. educational and documentary) need not be, although they must be registered with the Board. Elsewhere, however, for example in Belgium and Luxembourg, video recordings have been left outside the scope of the regulatory system for dealing with publicly shown films.

Criminal sanctions will inevitably be provided where there is a failure to comply with a system of pre-publication censorship, but criminal liability may also result where persons deal in various ways with indecent or obscene material where no such system operates. The ambit of criminal liability in such cases can be wide and dealing can take many forms. It might encompass making material available to others through any one of a number of means; the English Obscene Publications Act 1959, for instance, makes it an offence if a person "publishes" an obscene article, which can occur where he or she

> (a) distributes, circulates, sells, lets on hire, gives, or lends it or who offers it for sale or for letting on hire; or (b) in the case of an article containing or embodying matter to be looked at or a record, shows, plays or projects it, or, where the matter is data stored electronically, transmits that data.

There will often be a prohibition on transferring material from one place to another; customs legislation may ban the importation (and perhaps exportation) of indecent or obscene material, while post office legislation may make it an offence to send it through the mail. There may also be a ban on public displays of such material, and perhaps advertisements for them, and mere possession itself of certain types of material, such as those featuring children and young persons, may give rise to liability.

An alternative method of control to criminal prosecution has been the empowerment of law enforcement authorities to seize under warrant obscene material, and to seek its destruction in judicial proceedings. Such proceedings are of a civil nature and result only in the forfeiture of the material if it is found to be obscene, the owners or persons in possession not themselves incurring any criminal or civil liability. The English police, for example, have such a power under section 3 of the Obscene Publications Act 1959, as do the Canadian police under section 160 of the Canadian Criminal Code. Similar powers may also be available to other law enforcement agencies such as customs and the post office.

Fiscal control is not a widely used method but a notable instance where it has been employed is in respect of pornographic films in France. Special fiscal legislation was introduced in 1975, which imposed a heavy tax on the importation of such films, a higher rate of Value Added Tax (VAT) on their sale and on the admission charge levied by cinemas showing them, and a special tax on the profits made from the films. Further, penalties were incurred by the makers and exhibitors of pornographic films in that they forfeited rights to government subsidies whether of an otherwise automatic kind or in the form of selective aid.

Additional controls have, in some jurisdictions, been imposed on businesses selling indecent and obscene material. These seek to minimize their environmental impact by regulating their location and/or the manner in which they are conducted. In the United States, particular towns and cities have, through municipal zoning ordinances, required "adult" bookshops, cinemas, and similar establishments either to maintain a minimum distance from each other, with a view to dispersing them over a wide area, or to concentrate within a particular area so as to keep the remainder of the town or city free from them. The former approach was adopted, for example, by the city of Detroit and the latter by the city of Boston. Similarly, in Britain, local authorities have since 1982 been able to adopt provisions for the licensing of sex shops and sex cinemas, and licences can be refused on locational grounds. Further, conditions can be attached to the grants of licences that regulate the manner in which such establishments are conducted. Matters in respect of which authorities have sought to impose conditions have included hours of opening, window displays, and the external appearance of the premises, and in some instances the nature of the products stocked by proscribing the sale or display of offensive material.

Censorship by means of zoning and licensing controls is essentially local in nature, but in some jurisdictions local controls have been virtually non-existent. This has been the case in the Netherlands, for instance, where local control has primarily been limited to regulations relating to the public display of objects such as sex aids. Such restricted control may well have been attributable to the protection afforded to freedom of expression in the Dutch constitution. Constitutional protection for freedom of expression and freedom of speech, which exists in a number of Western societies, can represent a powerful constraint on attempts to impose censorship. This has been particularly so in the United States, where freedom of speech is guaranteed by the First Amendment to the US constitution, and where the US Supreme Court has declared various legislative provisions concerned with obscene material to be constitutionally invalid for contravening this amendment. This occurred, for example, with the civil rights ordinance drafted in 1983 by Catharine A. MacKinnon and Andrea Dworkin, which differed from traditional criminal legislation against indecent or obscene material by creating a legal framework within which women themselves could bring civil actions against the publishers and distributors of pornography on the grounds of harm. Commissioned by the city of Minneapolis, but vetoed by the mayor, a modified form of the ordinance was introduced in the city of Indianapolis. However, its constitutional validity was immediately challenged and the challenge proved to be successful (*Hudnut* v. *American Booksellers Association* 1985). More recently, an attempt by Congress to censor indecency on the Internet, by making it an offence under the Communications Decency Act 1996 to put "adult

orientated" or "patently offensive" material online for computer access, was similarly held to contravene the First Amendment (*American Civil Liberties Union* v. *Reno* 1997).

However, the right to free speech under the First Amendment is not an absolute one and some restrictions might be imposed legitimately on indecent or obscene material. Thus the US Supreme Court has held that, although most of what can be called pornography is protected, really "hard core" pornographic material is not (*Miller* v. *California* 1973); locational restrictions on "adult book stores", cinemas, and similar establishments can be imposed by zoning ordinances to combat the undesirable secondary effects of sexually orientated businesses provided that the restrictions are not over-inclusive (*Young* v. *American Mini-Theaters* 1976); and legislation can prohibit the dissemination of material showing children engaged in sexual conduct, even though the dissemination of similar material featuring adults could not be prohibited (*New York* v. *Ferber* 1982). The constitutional protection provided for indecent or obscene material by the right to free speech, subject to legitimate restrictions such as those mentioned above, is in marked contrast to the position in other jurisdictions, notably Britain, where no such protection exists.

Controls on sexually explicit material in Western societies have traditionally been expressed in terms of indecency or obscenity, which are essentially moral concepts. The terms, in particular "obscene", might be variously defined (or in some cases left undefined, such as under English customs and post office legislation) as a tendency to deprave and corrupt (English Obscene Publications Act 1959); undue exploitation of sex, or of sex and any one of the following subjects, namely, crime, horror, cruelty, and violence (Canadian Criminal Code); appeal to prurient interest, depiction or description of sexual conduct in a patently offensive way, and lacking any serious literary, artistic, political, or scientific value (the United States' test laid down in *Miller* v. *California* 1973). Underlying all these definitions is the notion of an offence against the prevailing moral standards, but in recent years there have been attempts to move away from the concepts of indecency and obscenity, with committees in various jurisdictions, when examining this area, rejecting them in favour of alternative formulations. The Williams Committee in Britain (1979), for example, recommended that terms such as "obscene", "indecent", and "deprave and corrupt" should be abandoned, as having outlived their usefulness, and replaced with a test of whether material was offensive to reasonable people by reason of the manner in which it portrays, deals with, or relates to violence, cruelty or horror, or sexual, faecal, or urinary functions, or genital organs. Similarly, the Fraser Committee in Canada recommended that the term "obscenity" should no longer be used in the Criminal Code and that new offences relating to "pornography" should be created, "with care being exercised to ensure that the definition of the prohibited conduct, material, or thing is very precise".

Despite such recommendations, however, the terms "indecent" and "obscene" continue to have widespread application. It remains the case that in many Western societies, they still constitute the criteria for the various methods of control over sexually explicit or sexually orientated material that are employed and which have been outlined above.

Since the above was written, various developments have

occurred. Adult censorship of films and videos in Finland has been abolished and only those exhibited or distributed to persons under 18 now have to be classified. Not all such films and videos require classification and certain ones, e.g., those containing sport, educational, scientific, or culture-related material are exempt from classification, although they must be registered with the board. Some protection for free speech in Britain has been afforded by the Human Rights Act 1998. This gives further effect to rights and freedoms guaranteed under the European Convention on Human Rights, article 10 of which includes the right to freedom of expression. Following a declaration by the US Supreme Court that the Communications Decency Act 1996 was unconstitutional, the Child On Line Protection Act 1998 was passed, making it an offence to distribute commercially on the internet material deemed harmful to minors. This has been declared unconstitutional by the Third Circuit Court of Appeals, although as of May 2001, an appeal to the Supreme Court against this decision is pending (*Ashcroft v. American Civil Liberties Union*).

COLIN MANCHESTER

Further Reading

Copp, David and Susan Wendell (editor), *Pornography and Censorship*, Buffalo: Prometheus, 1983

Committee on Obscenity and Film Censorship, *Report of the Committee on Obscenity and Film Censorship*, London: HMSO, 1979 (Williams Committee)

Grace, Sharon, *Testing Obscenity: An International Comparison of Laws and Controls Relating to Obscene Material*, London: Home Office, 1996 (Research Study 157)

Itzin, Catherine (editor), *Pornography: Women, Violence, and Civil Liberties*, Oxford and New York: Oxford University Press, 1992

Lederer, Laura (editor), *Take Back the Night: Women on Pornography*, New York: Morrow, 1980; London: Bantam, 1982

Special Committee on Pornography and Prostitution, *Pornography and Prostitution in Canada*, Ottawa: Canadian Government Publishing Centre, 1985 (Fraser Committee)

Travis, Alan, *Bound and Gagged: A Secret History of Obscenity in Britain*, London: Profile, 2000

OBSERVATORIES

This entry examines two occasions, chronologically widely separate, but both in the Islamic world, on which observatories were destroyed for religious reasons. Both were acts of iconoclasm, and of censorship of both art and science. Liberal religious thinkers would say that there is nothing inherent in either Islam or Christianity that rules out scientific speculation. Historically, in any case, both religions have embraced both liberal and "fundamentalist" elements.

The birth of Islam in the 7th century CE inspired several generations of inquisitive and tolerant scholarship. Within 100 years Muslims had not only conquered Alexandria, the city of Ptolemy, of whose speculations on the universe they took careful note, but had also created at Baghdad a notable city of learning. Driven, it seems, by the crucial importance of time – the call to prayer – and space – the direction of Mecca – early Muslim scholars elaborated the astrolabe, with which they could determine latitude, sunrise, and sunset. Observatories as permanent institutions are a Muslim invention, one of the first being erected at Baghdad in 829 CE. This first golden age of Islamic science lasted until about the 11th century. As it faded, and with the simultaneous erosion of Islam's political power in the Crusades and other wars, in some circles rational enquiries began, for the first time, to be positively condemned as corrupting religious truths.

Science was not entirely eclipsed, however. In the last quarter of the 16th century, the Ottoman empire built its first observatory, Dar al-Rasad al-Jadid (The House of the New Observation) in Istanbul. Its founder, Takiyyüdin Mehmed (1520–78), was a native of Syria who was appointed chief astronomer (*munejjimbashi*) to sultan Selim II in 1571. Takiyyüdin wrote a memorandum to Selim's successor, Murad III (reigned 1574–95), drawing his attention to astronomy and suggesting the building of the observatory. Some historians trace the ruler's approval to his superstitious nature: after observing a comet in 1577, the astronomer had prophesied an Ottoman victory in the military campaign which was soon to be joined against Persia. Whatever the reasons for Takiyyüdin's initial success, the observatory appeared at the beginning to suggest a revival of ancient scholarly interest in the universe: among the instruments built was an astronomical clock as advanced as that of Tycho Brahe in western Europe. The observatory was complete no later than the 12th day of the lunar month Safar (20 April 1578), when its existence was mentioned in an official Ottoman document.

Takiyyüdin's luck seems to have deserted him quite rapidly. Reportedly, he failed to predict an outbreak of plague in Istanbul in 1578 and the deaths of various important people in the city, not to mention some heavy Ottoman losses on the battlefields. These failures fuelled the enmity felt towards him by the *sheih ul-Islam* (the supreme religious expert, head of the ʻulama'): Takiyyüdin's protector, Saʻddedin, the sultan's personal teacher, had previously removed the *sheih ul-Islam* from an official post. Besides personal motives and court intrigues, the *sheih ul-Islam* may also have sincerely feared for the conservative Islamic tradition he was charged to protect. Already disposed to regard astronomy (and astrology) as irreligious, the conservatives could also claim that the plague was a punishment for trying to penetrate God's secrets.

The *sheih ul-Islam* issued a fatwa (instruction in religious matters) which claimed that astronomical observations led empires to their doom. Murad III, having a strong belief in supernatural powers, seems to have been inclined to accept the recommendation and gave orders for the observatory to be demolished. This was carried out overnight on 21 January

1580; it was evidently planned as a military operation, with cannon the main agent of destruction.

The destruction was a fatal blow to Ottoman celestial sciences. No more observatories were constructed for three centuries. The discoveries of Copernicus, Kepler, and Galileo – themselves, of course, subject to rigorous Christian censorship, but soon widely accepted – passed the Ottoman world by. It was no wonder, perhaps, that the next observatory to be built in Istanbul, Rasadhāne-i 'Āmire (the Imperial Observatory, 1868) was formed not on Islamic, but on secular, western traditions. Its first director Coumbray was a French engineer, and its creation was seen as the result of an opening up towards western science (and astronomy in particular) that took place in the first half of the 19th century.

Housed on various sites, the Imperial Observatory was mainly used before 1909 for meteorological and seismographic observation; it aligned the public clocks in Dolmabashe and Tophane, quarters of Istanbul. However, shortly before its destruction in April 1909, preparations were under way for astronomical observations. It is nowhere stated that there was a connection between the observations and the zealously Muslim background of those who destroyed the observatory, but there is unanimity that antiwestern obscurantism was one of the motives for the vandalism. The "31 March Event" (the date corresponds to 13 April in the Gregorian calendar) was a bloody uprising of traditionalist Muslims, both civilian and military, against the reintroduction of the Ottoman constitu-

tion in 1908. Sultan 'Abdülhamid II (reigned 1876–1909) had previously abandoned this relatively liberal framework for the state, which had been inspired by the Belgian constitution, and attempted to reinstate Islam at the heart of Ottoman governance; but the forces of secularization, culminating in the Young Turk Revolution of 1909, had been too strong. The Muslim attempt at counter-revolution, of which the destruction of the observatory was one element, was suppressed by military units loyal to the constitution. The sultan then abdicated.

Several telescopes were saved and used again when the observatory was reopened on 1 July 1911. No longer "imperial", it has been variously named the Kandili Observatory, the Ministry of Education's Istanbul Observatory for Astronomy and Geophysics, and the Vaniköy Observatory. In 1982 all state links (i.e. with the Ministry of Education) were broken, and the observatory is now part of Boğaziçi University.

MICHAEL REINHARD HESS

Further Reading

Dolen, Emre, "Tanzimat 'tan Cumhuriyet 'e Bilim" (Science from the Age of Reforms to the Time of the Republic) in *Tanzimat'tan Cumhuriyet'e Turkiye Ansiklopedisi* (An Encyclopedia of Turkey from the Age of Reforms to the Time of the Republic), edited by Murat Belge, vol. 1, Istanbul: İletişim Yayınları, 1985

Sayıl, Aydın, *The Observatory in Islam and Its Place in the General History of the Observatory*, Ankara, 1960; New York: Arno Press, 1981

OCKHAM, WILLIAM OF
See **William of Ockham**

FRANK O'CONNOR
Irish fiction writer and critic, 1903–1966

In the 1940s Frank O'Connor's writings became a particular focus of literary censorship in the Irish Republic. His novel *Dutch Interior* was banned in 1940 and Eric Cross's *The Tailor and Ansty*, for which O'Connor had written an introduction, was banned in 1942. In 1946, *The Midnight Court* (1945) O'Connor's translation from the 18th-century Irish of Brian Merriman's poem *Cúirt an Mheán-Oíche*, was banned, and in 1961 the ban was repeated when the poem appeared in a collection of O'Connor's translations of Irish verse, *Kings, Lords and Commons* (1959). Two collections of short stories, *The Common Chord* (1947) and *Traveller's Samples* (1951), were also banned.

Throughout his career O'Connor was an outspoken critic of the Catholic establishment, a champion of Irish folk culture, and an Irish-language revivalist. He was deeply distrustful of the more extreme Gaelic nationalists, who, he believed, had hijacked native Irish culture in the name of Catholic middle-class respectability. By the 1940s he had developed a popular reputation as a renegade and had become effectively blocked

from employment in Dublin. For this reason, his weekly columns in the *Sunday Independent*, published from 1943 to 1945, were printed under the pseudonym "Ben Mayo".

The Irish Republic's Censorship Board was not required to state publicly why it banned individual books as "indecent or obscene", but it was widely believed that O'Connor's novel and short stories were so treated primarily because of their critique of the Irish Catholic middle class. In *Dutch Interior*, for example, O'Connor provides an exposé of an Irish town, with its bullying fathers, prostitutes, and adulterers.

In 1942 O'Connor's commitment to Irish folk culture led to his involvement in one of the most notorious cases of literary censorship in the Irish Republic, the banning of *The Tailor and Ansty* by Eric Cross, a scientist who had been born in Northern Ireland and educated in England. A book of amateur folklore, it offers an account of the life and conversation of an elderly couple in County Cork who, as O'Connor put it, "regarded sexual relations as the most entertaining subject for general conversation". The book does not pretend to be a documentary; rather, Cross recalls conversations he had with the couple and in particular focuses upon their lack of sexual inhibition. The book was banned almost immediately and it was generally assumed that O'Connor's well-publicized connection with the book had drawn it to the attention of the Censorship Board.

In November and December 1942, *The Tailor and Ansty* became the subject of a heated debate on censorship in the Irish Senate (Seanad Éireann), along with Kate O'Brien's novel *The Land of Spices* and Dr Halliday Sutherland's *The Laws of Life*. O'Connor wrote of the debate, in *The Backward Look: A Survey of Irish Literature*, that it was "an indispensable document for any student of our literature because it shows better than anything . . . to what depths the intellectual life of the country had sunk". Sir John Keane, who initiated the debate, defended *The Tailor and Ansty*, observing "that the book is Rabelaisian, but that it is not indecent". Few senators agreed: for the majority, the book was filled with "smut" and "the vilest obscenity".

Of particular concern was the image of Ireland that the book projected. Senator professor William Magennis, who also served as chairman of the Censorship Board, summed up this point of view. He argued that the book was "low, vulgar, blasphemous". To him the book embodied the kind of anti-Irish propaganda that he believed was being perpetrated by both Frank O'Connor and the British. After reading from O'Connor's introduction, he declared:

> There is Ireland! This sex-ridden, sex-besotted Tailor speaks of no subject whatsoever without spewing the foulness of his mind concerning sexual relations . . . It is propaganda, to show the English-speaking world what manner of man the Irish peasant is who is the citizen of Eire. It is propaganda, naked and unashamed.

The banning of *The Midnight Court* in 1946 was equally controversial. The poem, which is regarded as an Irish literary classic, tells the story of an elderly man who wakes to find himself at a court where a young woman is inveighing against the lack of available men in Ireland. The poem offers a critique of sexual repression, which it associates with the Catholic Church, and advocates a liberationist view of sexuality. The Irish poet Brendan Kennelly described O'Connor's translation as "vibrant with a kind of visionary bawdiness and uproarious spiritual gusto, perfectly capturing the curious mixture of verbal licence and emotional inhibition, of audacity and frustration, that Merryman discovered in 18th-century Gaelic Ireland". Ironically, the original Irish version of the poem was never banned, but O'Connor was reviled for blasphemy and even falsely accused of inventing a blasphemous passage that was not in the original. This accusation led him to suggest that the Censorship Board's decision was as much an attack on him as an attack on the contents of the poem: "I believe the best authorities hold that it is almost entirely my own work, the one compliment Ireland ever has paid me".

Throughout his career, O'Connor was one of the few Irish writers to raise his voice against censorship. He was a founding member of the Irish Academy of Letters, which was formed in 1932 to protest against the introduction of literary censorship. He was a constant critic of the policies pursued, over many years by the prime minister and later president, by Eamon de Valera, arguing repeatedly that the government's censorship during World War II, not only of books but also of newspapers, created a nation in which "the intellectual darkness of the country was almost palpable". On principle, O'Connor objected to the manner in which Irish literary censorship was conducted, by a Censorship Board rather than in a court of law:

> I don't want to depend for protection on any individual, whatever his taste and judgment. As a citizen of this country I want to depend for protection on the Constitution and the courts . . . When there was no pretence of law, the censorship represented everything with which I as a writer must deal – the bookless homes, the terrible libraries, each with its own little group of censors, sniffing out sex that the Censorship Board had failed to detect, the customs officials who try to give the censors a helping hand by seizing books whose name they knew and keeping them for months until they are no longer saleable.

JULIA CARLSON

Writings

Dutch Interior, 1940
Translator, *The Midnight Court: A Rhythmical Bacchanalia*, by Brian Merriman, 1945
The Common Chord: Stories and Tales, 1947
Traveller's Samples: Stories and Tales, 1951
Editor and translator, *Kings, Lords and Commons: An Anthology from the Irish*, 1959
The Backward Look: A Survey of Irish Literature, 1967; as *A Short History of Irish Literature*, 1967
Day Dreams and Other Stories and *The Holy Door and Other Stories*, edited by Harriet Sheehy, 2 vols, 1973
Collected Stories, 1981

Further Reading

Carlson, Julia, *Banned in Ireland: Censorship and the Irish Writer*, London: Routledge, and Athens: University of Georgia Press, 1990
Cross, Eric, *The Tailor and Ansty*, London: Chapman and Hall, 1964
Seanad Éireann, *Parliamentary Debates*, 27 (1942)
Sheehy, Maurice (editor), *Michael/Frank: Studies on Frank O'Connor*, Dublin: Gill and Macmillan, 1969

CLIFFORD ODETS
US dramatist, 1906–1963

WAITING FOR LEFTY
Play, 1935

The New York Stock Exchange crashed in October 1929, bringing about economic devastation for millions of US citizens. The resultant massive unemployment helped to stimulate significant social change. It accelerated the organization of trade unions, while pressure from many quarters led to legislation that shifted some responsibility for social welfare onto the shoulders of federal government. Activist organizations, including both amateur and professional theatre groups, used a variety of means to communicate the message that radical economic and social change was needed.

Waiting for Lefty is perhaps the most notable example of theatre with such a purpose. Odets had studied under Lee Strasberg, founder of the Group Theatre and exponent of Konstantin Stanislavski's "method acting"; his play was a realistic and powerful presentation, couched in the language of everyday working-class life, of a strike organized by a group of exploited taxi drivers.

The New Theatre Players (NTP) in Boston, Massachusetts, planned a production of *Waiting for Lefty* in March 1935. When the play opened, Boston's official censor was in the audience. The following week, their landlords having been visited by the police, the NTP were evicted from their rented space. Historically, Boston's censorship had focused on immorality, the censor responding primarily to perceptions of obscenity, profanity, and/or disrespect for Christianity. The initial justification for banning *Lefty*, however, was political: it was held to be "un-American". Boston soon reverted to type, however. When four of the cast were arrested, the charge was one of profanity, special mention being made of the expression "Goddamn", which by any standards was a fairly minor expletive even then. The change of tactics suggests that in 1935, the charge of being "un-American" would not have been regarded as valid justification for censorship. Odets commented that "'American' depends on your point of view. If you are afraid of the deepest truths about the class conflicts of our time, all liberal and radical activity may be so labelled."

The Unity Players' production of *Waiting for Lefty* won the George Pierce Baker Cup in the annual Yale Drama Tournament a month or two later. The Players applied for and received permission to give a repeat performance of the play in a public school building, but the New Haven Board of Education, perhaps intimidated by the events in Boston, withdrew permission. The police then issued an order that the play was not to be performed anywhere in New Haven. Battle was now joined by the American Civil Liberties Union (ACLU), the International Labor Defense, dean Charles Clark and students of Yale Law School, and professor Walter Pritchard Eaton of the Yale School of Drama, who fought to obtain an injunction against the ban. Under pressure from an effective campaign, police chief Smith announced that members of the police board would again read the text of *Waiting for Lefty*. The ban was subsequently dropped and the play was performed to large audiences in a leading New Haven theatre. The *Bridgeport* *Sunday Herald* had already printed the entire play, suggesting that the paper felt that the American people could be trusted to make their own judgements.

Supporters of the leftist theatre stressed the issue of free speech in an attempt to bring the argument about "appropriate" theatre back to politics. Susan Glaspell of the *New York Times* (9 August 1935) responded to attempts to suppress *Lefty* in Provincetown: "We are going back instead of ahead. What are they afraid of?" Eugene Meyer, a New York writer, remarked: "I hope the Board of Selection who banned the play has the consistency to tear down the memorial tablet at Town Hall, with its *Mayflower* compact drawn up by 41 men who fled from persecution to seek freedom of conscience in a foreign land."

What *were* they afraid of? From 1917 onwards, the US political establishment had feared that communist ideas would take hold or be imposed in the United States much as they had in the Soviet Union. Certainly, if ever there might have been a second American revolution, the 1930s was the period when it was most likely to take place. Yet there was little evidence of such an eventuality, despite the fact that it was during this decade that the US Communist Party was strongest – for it was never a real threat to the established government. Yet, 10 years later, "un-American activities" were at the centre of US politics. The House of Representatives had a committee devoted to investigating such activities (The House Committee on Un-American Activities, or HUAC) and considerations of freedom of conscience were not thought to apply to those holding "communist" ideas. In practice, these included the kind of ideas espoused by the taxi drivers in *Waiting for Lefty*, which are not communist at all, although they are profoundly subversive of American individualism.

BETH CHERNE

Writings
Waiting for Lefty, 1935
Six Plays, 1939, reprinted 1979; as *Waiting for Lefty and Other Plays*, 1993

Further Reading
"Author Protests Play Ban", *New York Times* (9 August 1935): 15
Bernstein, Irving, *The Turbulent Years: A History of the American Worker, 1933–1941*, Boston: Houghton Mifflin, 1970
Block, Anita, *The Changing World of Plays and Theatre*, Boston: Little Brown, 1939
"Boston Police Halt Play for Profanity; Arrest Four Members of Cast of 'Waiting for Lefty' in Premiere There", *New York Times* (7 April 1935): 37
"Censorship Conflict in the Theater", *Literary Digest*, 120/20 (1935): 20
Deacon, Ruth, letter to Alice Evans, 11 November 1938, Box 17, New Theatre League Records, New York Public Library Rare Books and Manuscripts
Evans, Alice, letter to Ruth Deacon, 30 November 1938, Box 17, New Theatre League Records, New York Public Library Rare Books and Manuscripts

Goldstein, Robert Justice, *Political Repression in Modern America from 1870 to the Present*, Boston: Hall, 1978

Himelstein, Morgan Yale, *Drama Was a Weapon: The Left-Wing Theatre in New York, 1929–1941*, New Brunswick, New Jersey: Rutgers University Press, 1963

Klehr, Harvey, *The Heyday of American Communism: The Depression Decade*, New York: Basic Books, 1984

Leuchtenberg, William, *Franklin D. Roosevelt and the New Deal*, New York: Harper and Row, 1963

Maltz, Albert, "The Left Wing Theatre in America", *New Republic* (24 July 1935): 302–04

The Nation, editorial (13 March 1935): 291

"On Mr Odets", *New York Times* (7 April 1935): 2–5

Ottanelli, Fraser M., *The Communist Party of the United States: From the Depression to World War II*, New Brunswick, New Jersey: Rutgers University Press, 1991

Pack, Richard and Mark Marvin, *Censored!*, New York: National Committee against Censorship of the Theatre Arts, 1935

"Prize Play Is Banned", *New York Times* (13 April 1935): 10

Walker, Samuel, *In Defense of American Liberties: A History of the ACLU*, New York: Oxford University Press, 1990

Zinn, Howard, "Second Thoughts on the First Amendment", *The Humanist*, 51/6: 15–19

ODI
Malawian magazine, 1972–77

Illustrating many of the tensions created by the use of censorship in Malawi during the 1970s, the *Odi* affair can be seen as a confrontation between the one-party state equipped with the machinery of repression, and an individual committed to freedom of expression. In trying to explain what happened in greater detail, I draw heavily on records kept at the time and my position as an "interested party" will become clear.

In May 1977 Robin Graham, a lecturer in the English Department at Chancellor College (part of the University of Malawi), edited and distributed a publication – *Odi*, volume two, number one – only some parts of which had been approved by the national Censorship Board. As a result, he was dismissed from his post and compelled to leave the country.

An energetic and creative scholar, Graham joined the English Department in October 1975. Keen to edit a "Journal of Literature from Malawi", he drew up a proposal for a publication that would move beyond the format of the existing Writers' Group/English Department publication, Volume One of *Odi* (published 1972–74), to something more substantial. It was to be a publication that was, in the words of the editorial he subsequently wrote, "self-questioning and self-defining". He invited three colleagues, Patrick O'Malley, Jack Mapanje, and myself to act as editors, and obtained financial support from the British Council and from the university's Research and Publications Committee (200 Malawian kwacha from each).

He then solicited articles and creative writing. Some of the articles, including an essay by O'Malley on the drama of John Pepper Clark, he submitted to the Censorship Board, only to have them rejected. The grounds given in the case of O'Malley's work were characteristically infuriating: that the paper referred to *Song of a Goat*, "an obscene play" that had already been refused a performance licence. The creative writing, including a play, *Cracks*, by Innocent Banda, and poems by Sam Chimombo, Mapanje, and Enoch Timpunza-Mvula, was also submitted to the Censorship Board, and was approved.

Correspondence between Graham and the Censorship Board dragged on for over a year, in an atmosphere of some tension. Graham, like many of his colleagues and students, was irritated by the operation of the board; the incursions it made into numerous aspects of life in the country, and the threat it posed to creative and academic projects such as *Odi*. Eventually, with the end of his contract approaching, and the government press facilities available, Graham had *Odi* printed. At the beginning of May 1977 he began distributing and selling copies.

Official reaction was almost instantaneous. In early May, the chairman of the Censorship Board, Tobias Banda, telephoned the English Department and spoke to Graham. He asked whether Graham knew that there were "references to rebels" in the journal and, when answered in the affirmative, queried: "What is the Government going to say about that?" Tobias Banda followed up this call by contacting J.Z.U. Tembo, the chairman of the University Council, to settle the matter. At this stage the "matter" focused on the references to a "rebel", the poet-playwright David Rubadiri, who had, in the immediate post-independence period, resigned from his post as Malawi's representative at the United Nations. Although he subsequently pursued a quiet academic career in East African universities, and although his novel *No Bride Price* was "not officially banned", Rubadiri was regarded by some, including Tobias Banda, as an opponent of president Hastings Banda's government, and therefore might be considered a "rebel."

In Banda's Malawi it was unwise even to mention "rebels". Two articles in *Odi* violated this convention of non-being. Adrian Roscoe, the professor of English, had examined one of Rubadiri's poems in his essay entitled "Comment", and I had referred to the same writer in my contribution "Theatre in Malawi". That brief survey also asserted that it was "frightening" to be in Malawi at that time "because the Censorship Board and other Government agencies [might] distort the whole national theatre movement". Both Roscoe and I were aware of the "taboo" we had broken. Indeed, Graham himself was aware of the problems that mentioning Rubadiri might cause. He had drawn my attention to the "provocative statement" and asked whether I wanted it left in. The particular compromise that I had come to was to refuse to anticipate Censorship Board decisions, and to obey the law of the land regarding publication. In line with this, I said that I wanted the sentence left in. Of course, I assumed, wrongly as it turned out, that Graham would submit the essay to Tobias Banda.

Following Tobias Banda's action, a series of meetings took place on the morning of Saturday 7 May 1977. Graham saw, first, the college principal, Brown Chimphamba, and then

Roscoe. Tembo arrived two hours late for an 11.30 appointment, but before summoning Graham spent 20 minutes with Chimphamba and the university registrar, S. Mbaya. When eventually called in to meet the chairman of the University Council, Graham was beginning to feel under considerable pressure.

After pointing out that he saw his role as being to intervene when necessary between the university and government agencies, Tembo asked Graham about the references to Rubadiri. Graham pointed out that they had been made in a literary, not a political, context. The grounds of the complaint then widened. Tembo suggested that Graham's conduct in the affair constituted a challenge to the Censorship Board. Graham apparently agreed that this was what he had intended and refused to apologize. Tembo said that he would take up the challenge, and, turning to Chimphamba, observed "Look what happens when I try to help!" The meeting ended on that note and a little later Graham was handed a two-line letter terminating his contract with the university. He was told that travel warrants would be ready on Monday.

Later the same Saturday, Chimphamba collected as many unsold copies of *Odi* as he could find. He also reported that Tembo had now read "Theatre in Malawi" and that "things looked worse". There was some discussion about whether or not Graham might be a scapegoat, but this idea seems to have been dismissed. The administration was satisfied that the "rotten apple" had been identified and was being removed.

When Graham's wife Brenda went to see the finance officer Geoffrey Chipungu to discuss the family's financial position, she was told that her husband was entitled to three months pay in lieu of notice and his gratuity. This was, I understand, because the deportation had been ordered in May, that is to say within a certain period of the end of Graham's contract. Had the deportation been ordered in April, the University would not have been obliged to pay the benefits. These calculations were of interest and importance.

On Monday 9 May Chimphamba summoned Roscoe and myself for help in compiling a report on the *Odi* affair. At this meeting, it was pointed out to the principal that *Odi* had not been on sale to the general public, and that it might therefore be considered exempt from consideration by the Censorship Board. Chimphamba did not think a defence along these lines was worth constructing and clearly felt Graham had invited termination of his contract and deportation. Evidence emerged that he had misled various groups and individuals by saying, or giving the impression, that material had been approved by the censor. His colleagues in the English Department and the members of the Research and Publications Committee felt they had been misled. The editorial board, which had not been consulted on any matter relating to the journal, and Ken Whitty, the British Council Officer who had secured financial support, felt particularly vulnerable as a result of Graham's action.

Looking back over events, it seems that during the period up to the end of April, Graham's anger mounted at what he called the "dictatorship of taste" by the Censorship Board. Early in the year, he discussed with a legal colleague, Bob Solomon, his financial position were he to be deported in April or in May, and he monitored his application for a teaching post at the University of Zimbabwe. With the benefit of hindsight, all this suggests a certain preparation for confrontation on a matter of principle. When the confrontation with the powerful Tembo came, Graham was, understandably, tense and, not surprisingly, sometimes caught off balance, but he made his point.

The affair had repercussions for the exercise of censorship in Malawi but it passed off with only one "casualty" – and he had somewhere to go. A poem by Jack Mapanje, "Gerrie's Season of Goodwill, 1975" which is "for Lan, Jim and Robin", celebrates defiance and catches a self-deprecating mood. It draws to a close with references to the moment when "Gerrie . . . summoned up enough/Courage to go it alone," and with a picture of a "precious neighbour" who is quoted as "subtly [declaring], 'You shouldn't have been so naughty/Really, you know, breaking other people's laws/Deserves imprisonment back home, you remember.'" Gerry is given the last word: it conceals much. He says: "I was only here for the beer!"

JAMES GIBBS

SEAN O'FAOLÁIN
Irish writer, 1900–1991

Sean O'Faoláin was independent Ireland's chief intellectual critic and a prolific writer in a number of genres. He is best known and regarded as a short story writer, but he was also a novelist, historian, literary critic and journalist, travel writer, editor, and essayist. Two of his works were banned, but his importance in the history of censorship lies primarily in the opposition he voiced, encouraged, and facilitated over four decades to the workings of the Irish literary censorship.

O'Faoláin's first collection of short stories, *Midsummer Night Madness and Other Stories*, was published in Britain, where he then lived, in 1932. It was critically acclaimed in Britain but banned in Ireland. The Catholic Truth Society of Ireland had complained about the book to the minister for justice, sending him a copy with over 20 marked pages that were deemed to be offensive. The story that caused most offence was "The Small Lady", which featured the seduction of a young rebel by an Anglo-Irish lady in a Trappist monastery. The banning genuinely shocked O'Faoláin. He received anonymous hate mail and his wife maintained that the experience made him introverted. O'Faoláin defended the individual's right to freedom of expression, declaring that the absence of intellectual freedom kept Ireland in a worse state of slavery than before independence. He returned to live in Ireland in 1933, hoping that the coming to power of Eamon de Valera and Fianna Fáil in 1932 would herald a new beginning in Irish life. He was to be disappointed, and grew disillusioned with the "dreary Eden" that was de Valera's Ireland.

O'Faoláin's first novel (he wrote four in all), *A Nest of Simple Folk*, was published in 1934. His second, *Bird Alone*, published two years later, was banned in Ireland. The banning caused a furore in Irish literary circles. Fellow Cork writer Frank O'Connor insisted that "There is not an indecent line in it. Yet O'Faolain is paraded before the public view as a common pornographer in company with the authors of *Women Had to Do It* and *A Lover Would be Nice*." It was alleged by some that the real reason for the ban was the fact that the novel's protagonist loses his Catholic faith but does not return to it in the end. The secretary of Irish PEN described the labelling of *Bird Alone* as indecent as "legalized slander" and called for the institution of an appeal board, a regular demand at the time. An appeal was lodged with the minister but the ban remained in force until 1947, when it was revoked by the newly established appeal board.

The onset of World War II in 1939, in which Ireland remained neutral, presented a new set of problems for Irish writers, who were denied access to the overseas markets that sustained them. They were forced to confront the Irish censorship and the mentality that drove it more directly, and chief vehicle for this opposition was *The Bell*, the journal founded in 1940 and edited by O'Faoláin until 1946. While O'Faoláin gave a forum to those like Lennox Robinson and Frank O'Connor, who were opposed on principle to censorship of any kind, his own position was more moderate and, in the circumstances of the time, more politic. He focused his criticism on the workings of the Censorship Board and its failure to distinguish between pornography and strong writing suitable for adult readers, and on the negative impact of censorship on Irish life. Censorship, he reminded his more libertarian colleagues, "is a permanent part of literature" and the proper response to the censors "is not to say that they are monsters but that they are naturals. In 20 years time the Dáil [the lower house of the Irish parliament] will be scratching its head to know how it can rescind the ban which now covers almost every known Irish writer . . . The Censor, like the Law, is always an ass." The wartime campaign spearheaded by O'Faoláin led to the first reform of the Censorship of Publications Act with the institution of an appeal board in 1946.

An additional censorious foe that faced O'Faoláin as editor of *The Bell* was the draconian wartime censorship that severely restricted comment on international and domestic affairs. He ran a series of "One World" editorials as "our modest contribution against Isolationism and Little Irelandism". These were frequently censored, leading a frustrated O'Faoláin to declare in 1944 that he would move to Belfast to publish if he was going to be silenced in the South. He did not carry out this threat and in the post-war period continued his campaign against literary censorship.

In 1946 with Frank O'Connor, he fought unsuccessfully against the banning of O'Connor's translation of *The Midnight Court*, the first Irish-published book to be banned. He continued his letter-writing campaign against the excesses of the board throughout the late 1940s and early 1950s. He was a leading figure in the newly established Irish Council for Civil Liberty and at a public meeting of that group which he chaired in 1956 he declared that: "The machinery of the Censorship of Publications Act does not need much alteration, but the attitude of mind of the censors themselves does . . ." It was precisely this change of attitude that occurred from 1957 when the board was reconstituted and began to act a little more sensibly.

In 1967, when the Minister for Justice was engaged in liberalizing the censorship laws in line with the changed atmosphere in Ireland, he consulted O'Faoláin about the changes he would make. The amended act meant that books were automatically unbanned after 12 years, which led to the immediate release of more than 5000 titles, including O'Faoláin's *Midsummer Night Madness*.

DONAL Ó DRISCEOIL

Writings
Midsummer Night Madness and Other Stories, 1932
Bird Alone, 1936
The Collected Stories, 3 vols, 1980–82

Further Reading
Adams, Michael, *Censorship: The Irish Experience*, University: University of Alabama Press, 1968
Brown, Terence, *Ireland: A Social and Cultural History, 1922–1979*, London: Fontana, 1981, Ithaca, New York: Cornell University Press, 1985
Carlson, Julia (editor), *Banned in Ireland: Censorship and the Irish Writer*, London: Routledge, and Athens: University of Georgia Press, 1990
Cork Review (O'Faolain issue, 1992)
Harmon, Maurice, *Sean O'Faolain: A Critical Introduction*, Notre Dame, Indiana: University of Notre Dame Press, 1966; Dublin: Wolfhound Press, 1984
Harmon, Maurice, *Sean O'Faolain* (biography), London: Constable, 1994
Irish University Review, 6 (O'Faolain issue, Spring 1976)
Woodman, Kieran, *Media Control in Ireland, 1923–1983*, Carbondale: Southern Illinois University Press, 1985

HUBERT OGUNDE
Nigerian dramatist, 1916–

From Dakar to Yaounde and Kano to Abidjan, somewhere out there, faded by time and memories of his audience, still float posters, graffiti, lyric and motion images of the stage magician from the heartland of the Nigerian Muse, a bewildering amalgam of myth, morality, history and the politics of human assertion. One moment he would domesticate the exotic world of Arabian nights, the next it was a head-on indictment of colonial inhumanity and a stirring summons for resistance (Wole Soyinka 1990).

In 1946 a 30-year old ex-teacher, church organist, and composer, Hubert Ogunde, resigned his job as a Lagos policeman to become a full-time producer of, as well as performer in, a form of quasi-dramatic musical entertainment then known as "Native Air Opera". In this time of relative prosperity, Ogunde proceeded to launch a professional troupe composed of male and female performers and musicians, the first professional modern theatre company in Nigeria, and the forerunner of the contemporary Yoruba Travelling Theatre movement.

Hubert Ogunde's early association with the traditional Alarinjo Theatre was linked to the anti-colonial movements that were emerging in Nigeria in the 1940s. Although he had received limited formal schooling, Ogunde was quick to join the new group of educated leaders in opposing colonial rule. Insurgent nationalism after World War II inevitably came to influence the forms of cultural expression being produced at this time. In particular, the period was marked by the desire to promote theatre as a channel through which political as well as cultural messages could be communicated to ordinary Nigerians.

Ogunde's plays, some of which were created in the form of opera, were often controversial. Because they specifically aimed to embarrass the government, Ogunde and his theatre became targets of official harassment. The British colonial authorities prevented him from staging his plays outside his western regional base, and he faced rigorous interrogation from immigration officials in Nigeria whenever he requested travel documents. In response to his mistreatment, the nationalist press in 1947 engaged in an extensive and vigorous press campaign to refute what they saw as the crudely inaccurate victimization of Ogunde by the Immigration Department. Ogunde's popularity grew, and he became something of a national hero. The principal Obas (traditional rulers of Yorubaland), would give Ogunde a royal welcome in their cities and towns during his tours of the western region.

Thirteen out of the 20 plays written by Ogunde between 1945 and 1950 were politically influenced. Seven of the *most* political ones drew upon the theme that freedom should be granted to Nigerians unconditionally. Ogunde also concentrated on what he considered to be the evils and inhumanity of colonial rule. The plays include: *Worse than Crime* (1945), which led British officials and police to arrest and detain Ogunde and another member of his troupe for two days; *Strike and Hunger* (1946); *Tiger's Empire* (1946); and *Towards Liberty* (1947), described as "the greatest political play ever produced by Hubert Ogunde", which called for the unity of the various anticolonial movements as a step towards total freedom from British overrule. A later historical play, *Bread and Bullets* (1950), was about the shooting down of miners during a demonstration for higher wages; the people asked for "bread" but were given "bullets." All these plays were banned by the British.

With independence from Britain in 1960, Ogunde wrote *The Song of Unity* (1960). It was meant to demonstrate the importance of ethnic cooperation in the formation of a stable postcolonial government in the complex society which was the new Nigeria. His final, and most important, political play was *Yoruba Ronu* (1963, Yoruba Think), which was inspired by the falling-out of the leading Yoruba politicians chief Obafemi Awolowo and chief S.L.A. Akintola. The quarrel eventually led to a split in the Action Group party, to which both chiefs belonged. Awolowo's imprisonment on a charge of treason and Akintola's subsequent formation of a splinter group, the Nigerian National Democratic Party, led to a period of unrest in Western Nigeria. *Yoruba Ronu* attacks Yoruba disunity and calls for a more reasoned approach.

At the time Akintola, who was prime minister of the western region, interpreted the play as an attack on him and his government, while being supportive of the position of chief Awolowo. As a result Akintola declared Ogunde's theatre "an unlawful society" whose intentions were "dangerous to the good government of Western Nigeria". Ogunde's plays were now banned from his home region. The ban made headline news. *The Daily Times* viewed it as shameful that it was an independent Nigerian government (as against the former colonial government) that had encroached on the "constitutional rights of Hubert Ogunde". It appealed to the Nigerian president to "repeat his admonition that all functionaries of the government should ensure that the freedoms entrenched in our constitution are not trampled underfoot". The *West African Pilot* observed: "The Western Nigeria Government can work itself up to the point where it believes that the concert party is an unlawful body. We doubt if . . . the populace shares this belief."

The law under which Ogunde was accused had hitherto been applied only to secret cults and organizations who engender disorder. Lawyers argued that the makers of the law never intended it to be applied to a group of artists. By declaring the concert party an unlawful body, the government was clearly restricting the performers' right to pursue a trade.

Ogunde responded to the ban with a protest play, *Otito Koro* (Truth Is Bitter). Ebun Clark records the venomous opening lines of the play as Ogunde recreated it for her: "We do not kill a dog because it barks/And we do not kill a ram because it butts/What have I done that you withhold my daily bread from me?/L-I-F-E/Help me ask the worthless elder/Help me ask the wicked one/The evil doer thinks that other people talk about him/The evil doer runs away, even when no one pursues him/We have made our promise to our God/That we shall tell the truth, even if it is bitter . . ."

The government of Western Nigeria made no effort to lift the ban on Ogunde and his theatre; indeed, it even extended its range to prohibit any of his works from being broadcast on government radio and television. Ironically, it was not until the military took over the national government in a coup d'état in 1966 that the ban was eventually lifted.

Saheed A. Adejumobi and
Toyin Falola

Writings (plays)

The Garden and the Throne of God, 1944
Worse than Crime, 1945
Tiger's Empire, 1946
Strike and Hunger, 1946
Towards Liberty, 1947
King Solomon, 1948
Swing the Jazz, 1948

Bread and Bullets, 1950
My Darling Fatima, 1951
Song of Unity, 1960
Truth Is Bitter, 1964
Yoruba Ronu, 1964
Aiye, 1972
Nigeria, 1976
Igba t'ode, 1977

Further Reading

Berber, Karin, "Popular Arts in Africa", *African Studies Review*, 30/3 (September 1987)
Clark, Ebun, *Hubert Ogunde: The Making of Nigerian Theater*, Oxford and New York: Oxford University Press, 1979
Laitin, David, *Hegemony and Culture: Politics and Religious Change among the Yoruba*, Chicago: University of Chicago Press, 1986

RON OLIVER
British photographer, 1959–

Ron Oliver took up a career as a professional photographer in about 1977. He specializes in family portraiture. Oliver's skills in the visualization and realization of images have put him among the greatest international practitioners in this area. To understand the nature of these skills and the consequent qualities of his photographs is to comprehend his success, and also to begin to gain insight into the reasons why he has been so ruthlessly targeted by the authorities.

Oliver is the most deliberate and careful of photographers. His is not an art of the accidental and casual, nor even of an illusion of fortuitousness. On the contrary, Oliver's image-making technique is one in which all factors, from the choice of negative emulsion and the format of the film to the methods of producing the final print, converge upon the achievement of the highest possible information density and the longest possible tonal scale between deepest shadow and peak highlight.

The decisions as to the choices of setting, content, and framing of Oliver's portraits are arrived at with equal care and industry. He spends time, perhaps days, with the family who have commissioned him. This enables him to become a familiar and accepted presence among them and to determine the sort of image which will best represent the appearances and relationships of the people he is to photograph. The actual portraiture is carried out in a setting which is either natural, or at least informal to the degree that there is no heavy presence of photo studio paraphernalia to cloud the communion between Oliver and his subjects. This ensures that they present the camera with a view of themselves as they are happiest to be seen.

The outcome is a set of images that, at the level of summary appearance, echo the still, perfectly proportioned, detached classicism of the paintings of Jacques Louis David. At the same time, by their minute description of form and surface and by the subtleties of expression and attitude precisely caught in the choice of moment, they are intense memorials to the individual sitters as they were at a certain point in the trajectories of their lives. Oliver's is a fertile visual poetic, embodying great joy and seriousness.

It can be no coincidence that other photographers who have experienced trouble with censorship, for example Sally Mann and Jock Sturges (both in the USA), have chosen to work in a similar technical idiom to Oliver's; they may therefore have suffered from the consequences of their representational expertise at least as much as from their choices of subject matter.

Oliver's choice may be conditioned towards nude subjects partly because he is himself a naturist, and so has naturist acquaintances, and towards children because parents, aware of the evanescence of childhood, like to ensure a record of their children's all too fleeting states of emotional and physical being. Also, of course, children enjoy their own nakedness. However, it should be understood that nudity appears in only a minority of the images in Oliver's body of work.

On 28 January 1993, the London Metropolitan Police Obscene Publications Squad raided Ron Oliver's premises and took away some 20,000 images, all his documents, and his computer. According to Oliver, this represented 18 years of work; the loss of the computer and documents brought his livelihood to a standstill. There had been no complaint against Oliver, and, according to the police themselves, only three of all the images seized might have been deemed indecent under the Child Protection Act of 1978. In police eyes, "indecent" and "posed" were, apparently, equivalents. It is possible that Oliver fell into police hands because he was noticed as a colleague of Graham Ovenden and Brian Partridge in mounting an internationally circulated exhibition on the *Alice in Wonderland* theme; the police believed they had bagged a paedophile "ring".

Oliver was well aware of the desirability of seeing the case through, in the hope of clearing his name and obtaining clarification of the various legal obscurities. However, after nearly a year, there were still no charges laid, and much of his property remained impounded. Consequently, the need to feed his family dictated a move to France, where he has rebuilt a fruitful practice.

Oliver collected the letters of support that he received from

OLIVER: *Laetitia, 9, and Veronique, Mother and Daughter, France 1993*, photograph by Oliver. Oliver's studio was raided by the London Metropolitan Police Obscene Publications Squad in 1993, in connection with his collaboration with the photographer Graham Ovenden and the artist Brian Partridge, with whom he had worked on an exhibition relating to *Alice in Wonderland*; Oliver's work was confiscated in its entirety. No charges were proved against Oliver, whose case was supported by museum curators, clients, models, and friends: his work remains in possession of the British police and Oliver now lives and works in France.
© Ron Oliver.

clients, models, and friends into a supplement which was issued with his book *As Far as the Eye Can See*. These letters make a plea for decency on the part of the authorities and express the pain which was gratuitously inflicted on Oliver's clients and subjects by the implication that they had in any sense been involved in obscene transactions. Further support came from museum curators, notably M. Jean-Claude Lemagny, Chief Curator of Prints and Photography at the Bibliothèque Nationale de Paris, which had acquired a number of Oliver's prints.

Oliver was one of the participants in the Channel 4 film *For the Sake of the Children*, which was transmitted in 1997 in their "Films of Fire" series. Although the necessities of his profession and the exigencies of police interest have dictated that he lives overseas, Oliver remains committed to the improvement of the British situation.

Recently, it has become abundantly clear that for all Oliver's desire to improve and ameliorate the understanding and practice of censorship, the British tabloid press in the form mainly of *The News of the World* (see especially the issue of 8 April 2001, p. 41) has every intention of enfolding him in its distasteful mix of prurience and puritanism – which activity allegedly involved the stalking of his children in the street and attempts to enter his house. This resulted in an article entitled "We snare celebrity photographer on run from child porn rap", part of a series of articles attacking the exhibition *I Am a Camera*, at the Saatchi Gallery, London, that included some of Oliver's photographs, with material by other photographers, notably Tierney Gearon. The attack scandalized the broadsheet press; the authorities took no action against the Saatchi gallery or any of the photographers.

PHILIP STOKES

Publications

The Secret Faces of Childhood: An Album to Mark Ten Years of Photographing Children, 1977–1987, 1987
Portraits, 1990
As Far as the Eye Can See: Photographs by Ron Oliver, 1994
Editor, *As Far as the Eye Can See: Supplement*, 1994 (pamphlet issued separately in conjunction with the publication of the book of photographs)
In the Eyes of a Child, 1995
Between Memories and Dreams, 1998

Further Reading

Adair, Gilbert, "Body of Evidence", *The Sunday Times* (The Culture section) (13 March 1994)
Bellos, Alex, "Propriety or Puritanism", *The Guardian* (5 February 1994)
Georgieff, Anthony, "As Far as the Eye Is Not Allowed to See", *European Photography*, 15/56 (Fall 1994): 48–52
Newnham, David and Chris Townsend, "Pictures of Innocence", *The Guardian Weekend* (13 January 1996)
O'Toole, Laurence, *Pornocopia: Porn, Sex, Technology and Desire*, 2nd edition, London: Serpent's Tail, 1999
Preston, Richard, "A Question of Taste", *The Independent Magazine* (4 September 1993)
"The Saatchi Gallery Should be Congratulated: It Is Standing Up for Childhood", *The Independent* (13 March 2001)
Stokes, Philip, *Notes on As Far as the Eye Can See*, 1994 (pamphlet of commentary issued with the book)
"Where do You Draw the Line", *Practical Photography* (August 1994)

HÉCTOR OLIVERA
Argentine film director, 1931–

LA PATAGONIA REBELDE (Rebellious Patagonia)
Film, 1974

A product of the brief cultural "thaw" experienced between the end of military rule (1966–73) and the renewal of state repression culminating in another military regime (1976–83), *La Patagonia rebelde* (Rebellious Patagonia) is considered by many to be the best film of Héctor Olivera's long and uneven career. The film's production history also stands as an excellent example of the censorial pressures that brought the Argentine film industry to a near-standstill in the mid-1970s.

The producing-directing team of Olivera and Fernando Ayala, founders of the highly successful production company Aries Cinematográfica Argentina (1956), has created some of Argentina's lightest comedies, musicals, and "for export" commercial films, and has strong ties to several Hollywood production companies, notably Roger Corman's New Horizons. However, the team has also produced and directed some of Argentina's most important "political" films, such as *No habrá más penas ni olvido* (1983, A Funny, Dirty, Little War), *La noche de los lápices* (1986, The Night of the Pencils, 1986), and *La Patagonia rebelde*, winner of the Berlin Silver Lion Award of 1975. Olivera's best work typically combines testimonial denunciation with excellent box-office timing.

La Patagonia rebelde tells the story of the Patagonian strikes of the early 1920s and the subsequent massacres of workers at the hands of the Argentine army. The workers of the British-owned sheep ranches go on strike for better living conditions; in response to pressure from the conservative oligarchy, President Yrigoyen calls on the armed forces to restore order. A wage contract is negotiated, and the army leaves, but when the owners fail to honour the contract, the workers organize another strike, which is violently repressed. The film's screenplay was based on Osvaldo Bayer's four-volume history by the same title discussed in the entry on Bayer. Bayer examines the various union positions taken during the strikes as well as their internal conflicts, and comes down firmly on the side of anarcho-syndicalist outsider, the Spaniard Antonio Soto. The film likewise rejects the violent *gaucho* response and the more conciliatory socialist position. The Patagonian rebellion resonates in 20th-century Argentine history as the moment when the armed forces began to assume "a more prominent political role than ever before as the arbiter in the fate of representative government" (Rock, 1987: 203). Both the book and screenplay were written just as the Argentine populace was beginning to mobilize itself after seven years of military rule.

The Argentine film industry had been heavily censored since the mid-1960s. Nevertheless, politicized "third cinema" filmmakers continued to work clandestinely, forming Raymundo Gleyzer's Cine de la Base and the Cine Liberación (Liberation Cinema) group of Octavio Getino, Fernando "Pino" Solanas, and Gerardo Vallejo. The best-known product was the Getino /Solanas four-hour, black-and-white documentary, *La hora de los hornos* (The Hour of the Furnaces), exhibited clandestinely throughout the years of Lanusse's dictatorship. After 1973 these filmmakers surfaced, and, during Juan Perón's brief presidency, leading Peronist leftists were given key, if calculatedly limited, cultural posts. Getino was appointed *interventor* (controller or censor) of the film classification board. During his 90-day appointment Getino lifted the bans on many films, attempted to "wipe out the existing rigid censorship, assist independent production, and establish an alternative system of film production financed and distributed by the state" (Kovacs, 1977), and approved several projects released in the following year. That year, 1974, was a "boom" year for the Argentine cinema in the number of high-quality, politically committed films for large audiences.

The previously established censorship laws were still in place when filming of *La Patagonia rebelde* began. In October 1973 Getino approved the script and shortly thereafter the film was classified as of "special national interest", which gave the producers greater advance funding. Shooting, which began in January 1974, was primarily on location in the province of Santa Cruz. Because of the production's special status, Olivera received the aid of the local police force, and the national gas, coal, petrol, and railway companies, as well as free lodging for the crew. The film was scheduled for an April release but did not premiere until 13 June. In May, with still no word from the film classification board and with the Defence Ministry vigorously opposing the screening, various film unions and associations petitioned for the film's release. Only after the intervention of national legislators and, reportedly, of Perón himself, was the film given a "14 years and older" rating and released. *La Patagonia rebelde* was an instant box-office success.

Nevertheless, in October 1974 the producers voluntarily withdrew the film from circulation, not re-releasing it until Argentina's 1983 return to democracy. In a 1975 interview published in *Crisis* magazine, Olivera explained his reasons for pulling the film:

> In October of last year [1974] when I was in Europe, with *La Patagonia rebelde* at the San Sebastián [Spain] festival, [Fernando] Ayala, over the phone, expressed his concern to me that, after what had happened in Catamarca, where they were killing military personnel almost on a daily basis, the film really constituted an irritant, considering that, among other things, it begins with an attempt on a military officer's life even though [the action] takes place in 1920. By mutual agreement, we decided to remove the film from circulation. Today . . . we would not [even try to make *La Patagonia rebelde*] because we don't feel like making a picture with such a dramatic climate when the situation in Argentina is so dramatic . . . *Rebellious Patagonia* is a film that came out of seven years of military government . . . [Today] the country is so convulsed that, even without censorship, one ends up censoring oneself" (quoted in Avellaneda, 1986, vol. 1: 131).

Despite Olivera's "voluntary" decision not to contribute to his country's increasing violence, throughout the subsequent military dictatorship he and Ayala had various film projects censored or denied. One project, *Matar al ángel* (Killing the Angel), was rejected because of fears that the relationship between a US executive and his security chief might drive away foreign investors. Another, *Tiernas hojas de almendro* (The Almond Tree's Tender Leaves), was turned down on the basis that its World War II love story between two teenagers living in a Buenos Aires German community might reinforce the reputation of Argentines as Nazi sympathizers. Even their more overtly commercial projects bowed to political pressure and threats. For example, Ayala and Olivera cut from the musical *El canto cuenta su historia* (1976, The Song Tells its Story) any scenes involving blacklisted folk-singer Mercedes Sosa.

Others involved in films in the early 1970s were more radically affected. In 1975 *La Patagonia rebelde*'s leading actors Héctor Alterio and Luis Brandoni exiled themselves to Spain after receiving death threats from the Argentine Anti-Communist Alliance (AAA), and the film's screenwriter, Bayer, was to spend most of his life in Germany. Others, such as the director Raymundo Gleyzer and the writer Rodolfo Walsh, "disappeared".

JEAN GRAHAM-JONES

Further Reading

Avellaneda, Andrés, *Censura, autoritarismo y cultura: Argentina, 1960–1983*, 2 vols, Buenos Aires: Centro Editor de América Latina, 1986

Barnard, Tim (editor), *Argentine Cinema*, Toronto: Nightwood, 1986

Bayer, Osvaldo, *La patagonia rebelde*, Mexico City: Editorial Nueva Imagen, 1980

Foster, David William, *Contemporary Argentine Cinema*, Columbia: University of Missouri Press, 1992

King, John and Nissa Torrents (editors), *The Garden of Forking Paths: Argentine Cinema*, London: British Film Institute, 1988

King, John, *Magical Reels: A History of Cinema in Latin America*, London: Verso, 1990

Kovacs, Steven, "Screening the Movies in Argentina", *New Boston Review*, 3/3 (December 1977): 19–20

Manrupe, Raúl and María Alejandra Portela, *Un diccionario de films argentinos*, Buenos Aires: Corregidor, 1995

Rock, David, *Argentina: 1516–1987: From Spanish Colonization to the Falklands War*, revised edition, Berkeley: University of California Press, 1987

Romano, Eduardo, "¿Una Patagonia rebelde o la Patagonia del rey?" in *Literatura/cine argentinos sobre la(s) frontera(s)*, by Romano, Buenos Aires: Catálogos, 1991

Viñas, David, *Los dueños de la tierra*, Buenos Aires: Losada, 1958

OMAN

(formerly Muscat and Oman)

Population: 2,538,000

Main religions: Ibadi Muslim; Sunni Muslim; Shia Muslim; Hindu

Official language: Arabic

Other languages spoken: English; Urdu; Indian dialects

Illiteracy rate (%): 19.8 (m); 38.4 (f)

Number of daily newspapers: 4

Number of radio receivers per 1000 inhabitants: 607

Number of TV receivers per 1000 inhabitants: 694

Number of PCs per 1000 inhabitants: 21

For many centuries Oman was a stable and prosperous mercantile community, linked by sea routes to India and east Africa, notably to Zanzibar, where it established a colony. Its decline began after the construction of the Suez Canal in 1860. A treaty of protection by Britain had been signed in 1798, but members of the Al bin Saʿid dynasty, notably the sultan Saʿid bin Taimur, allowed the territory to become gradually more impoverished. He turned his country's face against many modern developments: radio and books were banned, as well as music and dancing. He is said to have told the British: "That is why you lost India, because you educated the people." His son, Quabus bin Saʿid, assumed power after a palace coup in 1970. This was two years after oil reserves had been discovered, making it possible to modernize the economy, education, and the health services.

The sultanate is an autocracy. The sultan is regarded as provider for and protector of his people. The Islamic shariʿa is the basis of legislation. The family remains more important than the individual, and obedience to the hierarchy of the family is to some extent ingrained.

As the economic and social organization of the country has strengthened, sultan Quabus (or Qaboos) has introduced some

political changes, many of which bear on individual civil liberties in the western sense of the term. He has strengthened democratic aspects of his Consultative Council, for example. And in 1996 Oman received its first written constitution, or "Basic Law of the State". While such freedoms as those of assembly and the academy remain highly restricted, the new constitution appears to offer a long-range commitment to a degree of freedom of expression. Article 29 states that "Freedom of opinion and expression, whether spoken, written or in other forms, is guaranteed within the limits of the law". Article 30 adds that:

> Freedom of postal, telegraphic, telephonic and other forms of communication is sacrosanct and their confidentiality is guaranteed. Hence, it is not permitted to monitor or inspect them, reveal their contents, delay or confiscate them except in circumstances defined by the Law and in accordance with the procedures laid down therein.

According to article 31, "Freedom of the press, printing and publication is guaranteed in accordance with the conditions and circumstances defined by the Law." Yet article 41 states that, regarding the sultan, "his person is inviolable and must be respected and his orders must be obeyed".

Oman's 1987 Press and Publication Law authorized the Ministry of Information to censor domestic and imported publications for politically, culturally, or sexually offensive material. Foreign print media regarded as critical of Oman or containing inaccurate statements are prohibited. There can be no criticism of the sultan in any medium. Editorials, hardly surprisingly, continue to reflect government views.

Television and radio operate under the Ministry of National Heritage and Culture. There are no independently owned stations. The first radio station was established soon after the sultan came to power in 1970 and was promoted in order to reach citizens efficiently with information about national development efforts. Television transmission began in 1974. Egypt has in the past been Oman's main supplier of television-programmes but, as is the case with radio, emphasis has been on developing Omani production capability. During the early years of television the government placed large receivers in public places: by the late 1980s the need for public sets had disappeared, and 10 years later virtually all the people in a government survey had at least one colour television set. There is no airing of politically controversial material, although the questioning of government officials by members of the sultan's Consultative Council is televized. Satellite dishes are widely available and legal. The Omani authorities are, however, clearly aware that the growth of media technology threatens traditional culture and moral standards. In 1995 sheikh Hilal, director-general of culture, opened a censorship office at Seeb International Airport, primarily to exercise tighter control over the import of video cassettes.

In 2000–01 new legislation prohibited non-Omanis from selling audio and video tapes and also bans them from clerking in bookstores. These limits were instituted to increase job opportunities for Omani citizens, according to government sources.

BARBARA M. ROOS

Further Reading

Boyd, Douglas A., *Broadcasting in the Arab World: A Survey of the Electronic Media in the Middle East*, 2nd edition, Ames: Iowa State University Press, 1993

Freeman, Peter (editor), *Background Notes: Oman*, Washington, DC: US Department of State, Bureau of Public Affairs, 1994

Riphenburg, Carol J., *Oman: Political Development in a Changing World*, Westport, Connecticut: Praeger, 1998

US Department of State, *Oman: Report on Human Rights Practices of 1996*, section 2: *Respect for Civil Liberties*, Washington, DC: Bureau of Democracy, Human Rights and Labor, 1997

EUGENE O'NEILL
US dramatist 1888–1953

By the time Eugene O'Neill first ran foul of the censors in 1922 he had gained an international reputation for brilliance and innovation as a playwright. Seven of his plays had been produced in New York; two had won the venerated Pulitzer Prize. He had become a leader of a new drama of seriousness for a new century, his work an alternative to the bedroom farces, musical revues, and melodramas then endemic on the American stage.

While O'Neill's prestige grew, so did cries for the regulation of the theatre in the interest of public morality. Language and situation in plays, which now seem merely innocuous, or simply in bad taste, were then viewed with alarm. To John S. Sumner, the inheritor of the New York Society for the Suppression of Vice from the notorious Anthony Comstock, the stage "was worse today than it has ever been in its history". He and the district attorney, Joab Banton, along with New York's police commissioner, and the Episcopal Social Service Commission, bolstered by a conservative press, mounted successive censorship crusades throughout the 1920s.

By 1922, in an effort to deflect police action, while at the same time giving lip service to the principle of censorship, an arm of the Dramatists Guild called the Joint Committee Opposed to Political Censorship of the Theater, along with Actors Equity and the Producing Managers Association convinced a reluctant Banton to organize citizen play juries that would judge the quality of allegedly degenerate plays.

In April, the jury system not yet in force, the police threatened to close O'Neill's expressionistic play *The Hairy Ape* for being "indecent, obscene, and impure", a move that looked to the theatre community like harassment. "Such an idiotic attempt at suppression", O'Neill told the *New York World*, "will only bring ridicule on the poor dolts who started it." Several days later the city's chief magistrate dismissed the case without comment.

The spring of 1924 brought a far more serious challenge to O'Neill and his partners at the Provincetown Playhouse when it became known that *All God's Chillun Got Wings*, an exploration of a tragic interracial marriage, was being readied for performance. Mary Blair, a leading actress of the day, and the rising black star Paul Robeson would appear as the ill-fated couple. After Blair's photograph circulated across the country over a caption proclaiming "White Actress to Kiss Negro's Hand", the Ku Klux Klan threatened violence, and wild conjecture flooded the more rabid press, warning of the race riot that surely would occur if the drama went on. Since the play was open only to subscribers and was technically a private performance, the theatre could not be closed in the absence of immediate danger. On the opening night, crowds and police milled about outside the theatre, but the anticipated fracas never occurred. Just hours before the opening, however, the mayor made things as difficult as possible by refusing permission for child actors to perform in the first scene of the drama, which depicted black and white children playing happily together. That evening the director stepped before the curtain and read the scene, a practice that continued until the production expired of theatrical old age in October.

O'Neill's *Desire under the Elms* (1924), featuring incest and infanticide, became a major target for district attorney Banton's purity campaign the following year. "Too thoroughly bad", he told the press, "to be purified by a blue pencil". As word spread of a possible prosecution, box office receipts increased when a new sort of audience bent on salaciousness came to the theatre, flustering the actors with noisy comments. Faced with rising criticism from O'Neill's friends in the press, Banton agreed to activate the citizen play juries. Once again the district attorney would be frustrated in his attempt to save a degenerate stage. In March 1925, two separate juries unanimously acquitted *Desire under the Elms* and another accused play, Sidney Howard's *They Knew What They Wanted*, of any charge of immorality. This was hardly the result the district attorney wanted. Two years later Banton abolished the play jury system and worked with the state legislature to adopt a draconian law that gave police the power to padlock an offending theatre for a year.

Challenges to the performance of *Desire under the Elms* did not end. In Los Angeles, members of the cast were arrested and tried; the mayor banned the drama in Boston, and the Lord Chamberlain forbade its performance in England. O'Neill offered to change "whore" to "harlot" and "whorin'" to "sluttin'" to no avail. There would be no public performance of *Desire under the Elms* in Britain until 1940.

When Joab Banton tried to get his censors into the theatre to see O'Neill's *Strange Interlude* in 1928, he could not get tickets; the play had been sold out for weeks. An extraordinary hit by the standards of the 1920s, the drama won O'Neill a third Pulitzer Prize. However, just 17 days before the Boston opening, with an advance sale of some $40,000, the mayor forbade its performance. He had seen it in New York, he told the papers, and found it a "filthy, disgusting, degrading exhibition of utter filth". The management of the Theatre Guild, which had taken over the production of O'Neill's plays, reacted by marshalling a massive publicity campaign to put pressure on the mayor, but it had no success untangling the web of Boston politics, save learning that the play might possibly be performed if a "legal fee" of $10,000 were paid. In the end, the Theatre Guild achieved a publicity coup by ignoring the city altogether. "Banned in Boston" became merely a jocular phrase as Bostonians travelled in great numbers to see all nine acts of *Strange Interlude* in neighbouring Quincy.

There were no significant censorship challenges to O'Neill's plays during the 1930s. His *Mourning Becomes Electra* (1931) and *Ah, Wilderness!* (1933) were well received, and in 1936 he became the first US playwright to win the Nobel Prize for Literature. After a decade spent in relative seclusion and declining health, while absorbed in work on what were to become the greatest plays of his career, O'Neill saw the Theatre Guild produce his *The Iceman Cometh* in 1946. Once again the Boston censors struck, objecting to the play's "unclean" language. Irate, O'Neill would make no changes. The Theatre Guild dropped Boston from the tour.

When *The Iceman Cometh* reached Washington, DC, it was greeted with protests of a different sort. The National Theater had a racial segregation policy. The Guild was unable to break the contract, but O'Neill answered his critics by pledging to put a non-segregation clause in any future performance agreement.

The Theatre Guild's pre-Broadway tour of O'Neill's *A Moon for the Misbegotten* ended miserably because of casting and other difficulties in 1947, but not before it clashed with the police censor in Pittsburgh, who told the newspapers that the play was a slander on American motherhood, apparently objecting to the words "mother" and "prostitute" in the same sentence. "It isn't just a matter of profanity", he declared, "The whole play is obscene." In addition, he demanded that "tart" be substituted for "whore" and "louse" for "bastard." But after much negotiation, the performance continued; no more than eight words were ever actually changed.

The Iceman Cometh was the last O'Neill play produced on Broadway during the playwright's lifetime. Illness made it impossible for him to write. After his death in 1953 there would be renewed interest in his work. José Quintero produced what may very well be the definitive production of *The Iceman Cometh* at New York's Circle-in-the-Square Theatre in 1956. After the first performance of the O'Neill autobiographical masterwork, *Long Day's Journey Into Night* (1952) by the Royal Dramatic Theatre in Stockholm, Quinterro opened the play in New York to great acclaim, winning, O'Neill a fourth Pulitzer Prize.

It is a matter of some curiosity that in 1962 the dead hand of censorship fell once again on an O'Neill work. Responding to complaints of "blasphemous dialogue", the president of Baylor University in Texas closed *Long Day's Journey into Night* after its fourth performance at the university theatre. By contract no word of the play could be touched. Showing a deep respect for O'Neill and the integrity of their profession, the chairman of the drama department and eleven of the faculty resigned.

DAVID W. WILEY

Writings

The Hairy Ape, 1922
All God's Chillun Got Wings, 1924
Desire under the Elms, 1924
Strange Interlude, 1928
The Iceman Cometh, 1946
A Moon for the Misbegotten, 1947
Long Day's Journey into Night, 1956
Complete Plays, edited by Travis Bogard, 3 vols, 1988 (Library of America)

Further Reading

Alexander, Doris, *Eugene O'Neill's Creative Struggle: The Decisive Decade, 1924–1933*, University Park: Pennsylvania State University Press, 1992

Bogard, Travis, *Contour in Time: The Plays of Eugene O'Neill*, New York: Oxford University Press, 1972

Floyd, Virginia, *The Plays of Eugene O'Neill: A New Assessment*, New York: Ungar, 1985

Gelb, Arthur and Barbara, *O'Neill*, New York: Harper, and London: Jonathan Cape, 1962

Laufe, Abe, *The Wicked Stage: A History of Theater Censorship and Harassment in the United States*, New York: Ungar, 1978

Moorton, Richard F. Jr (editor), *Eugene O'Neill's Century: Centennial Views on America's Foremost Tragic Dramatist*, New York: Greenwood Press, 1991

Sheaffer, Louis, *O'Neill: Son and Artist*, Boston: Little Brown, 1973

Sisk, Robert F., "*Strange Interlude's* Bout with the Boston Censors", *Equity Magazine*, 32 (November 1929): 11–12

Wainscott, Ronald H., *Staging O'Neill: The Experimental Years, 1920–1934*, New Haven, Connecticut: Yale University Press, 1988

Wainscott, Ronald H., *The Emergence of the Modern American Theater, 1914–1929*, New Haven, Connecticut: Yale University Press, 1997

Witham, Barry B. "The Play Jury", *Theatre Journal* (December 1972): 430–35

MARCEL OPHULS
French film director, 1927–

LE CHAGRIN ET LA PITIÉ (The Sorrow and the Pity)
Documentary film, 1969

Marcel Ophuls's first documentary in a projected trilogy on World War II, *Munich; ou, la paix pour cent ans* (Munich; or, Peace for a Hundred Years), coproduced with André Harris and Alain de Sédouy and filmed in 1967, was well received. The second documentary, *Le Chagrin et la pitié* (The Sorrow and the Pity), encountered trouble soon after project planning began. French National Television (ORTF), which sponsored the project, understood it to be an account of the French Resistance struggle against the Germans during World War II. The authors, however, wanted to recount a history of the German Occupation that would include, but only in part, a look at the French Resistance. Following the disagreement, Ophuls left ORTF in 1968 and went to work for the Hamburg television station, Norddeutscher Rundfunk. The station, together with Swiss-French television and the Swiss publisher Éditions Rencontres supplied the necessary funds for producing *The Sorrow and the Pity*, which was completed in 1969.

Some 260 minutes long, *The Sorrow and the Pity* includes about 45 minutes of footage taken from contemporary French newsreels, spliced together with the accounts of witnesses 25 years after liberation. In unprecedented manner, it used witnesses from all sides of the divide: German soldiers, members of the Vichy government, Resistance members, spies, politicians, those imprisoned by the Germans, and those victimized by the liberators and ordinary citizens in the town of Clermont-Ferrand. Although acknowledged as lacking a certain balance (for example only one woman recounts her experiences during the years of Occupation), the film was none the less hailed as a breakthrough in seeking to present aspects of the Occupation years that had not been discussed previously.

Following completion, the film was shown on German, Swiss, Dutch, and American television stations. It would not, however, appear on French television until 1981. This delay represented, in Ophuls's words, "censorship by inertia". The initial justification given by the government for not broadcasting the documentary in France was that it might upset "myths necessary to Frenchmen" – including the "myth of the Resistance", the view, most strongly associated with the right-wing Gaullist party, that during the Occupation almost all French people had been solidly behind the Resistance. Although he was pro-Resistance himself, Ophuls's film showed that the myth was demonstrably false. At the time *The Sorrow and the Pity* was made, France was also living through the aftermath of the de Gaulle years – the massive upheavals of 1968–69. Control of the French airwaves, however, remained the same as it had been during the time of de Gaulle's presidency (1958–69). A central commission controlled what would be approved for projection on French national television. When *The Sorrow and the Pity* had come up for approval, the then Minister of Culture, André Malraux, had rejected it, not only because it might have revived memories which had been largely buried for 20 years, but also because the government was then trying to pick up the pieces of another rift in French society – that between the young seeking social change, who hardly born when the Occupation took place, and an uncomprehending older generation.

In France, the alternative to a television airing for Ophuls and his coproducers was to have the documentary shown in cinemas. After clearing the Censorship Commission, the film opened on 5 April 1971 in a small cinema near the student quarter of Paris and became a resounding success. Within a month, other cinemas began showing it. ORTF, however, declined to change its position. As Ophuls has noted, this did not constitute blatant censorship. Since ORTF had not produced the movie, it would have to buy the rights to show it; it simply chose not to do so. Thus, although the movie was shown several times in Parisian cinemas over 10 years, few French people outside the capital actually saw it.

Wartime Resistance members and collaborators criticized the documentary's contents. For example, Simone Veil, a concentration camp survivor and a minister in President Giscard d'Estaing's cabinet (1974–81), believed that a documentary that included so many negative accounts of the years of Occupation without an equal number of interviews of Resistance members amounted to a form of national masochism. This was in contrast to Ophuls's repeated statements that his documentary fell squarely on the side of the Resistance, but French television officials would not waver for over a decade.

The situation changed in 1981, when a Socialist President, François Mitterrand, was elected. Mitterrand was himself a former member of the Resistance. Within six months of the election, on 28–29 October 1981, *The Sorrow and the Pity* was shown on a French national television channel, FR3. Authorization was granted in part so that the Socialists could make a point about openness at a time when heavy suspicion surrounded their decision to appoint a limited number of Communist ministers. It also marked the first stage on the way to reform of French broadcasting, which would disband the governmental monopoly of the airwaves and grant French broadcasting rights similar to those enjoyed by the press through the law of 1881.

The Sorrow and the Pity marked a new phase in the assessment of French memory of World War II and the issue of national guilt. Although in itself just one of many documentaries made about the Occupation years, the censorship by inertia of the state broadcasting system ironically made The Sorrow and the Pity into the documentary of that period. Not only did it become a reference point for historians, but it also provided a starting point from which younger generations sought to shed light on the silence of their predecessors who had experienced the horrors and difficulties of World War II.

GUILLAUME DE SYON

Writings

The Sorrow and the Pity, script translated by Mireille Johnston, 1972
Le Chagrin et la pitié, 1980

Further Reading

Colombat, André Pierre, The Holocaust in French Film, Metuchen, New Jersey: Scarecrow Press, 1993

Conan, Eric and Henry Rousso, Vichy: un passé qui ne passe pas, 2nd edition, Paris: Fayard, 1994

Jacobsen, Kurt, "Memories of Injustice: Marcel Ophüls' Cinema of Conscience", Film Comment, 32 (July–August 1996): 61–67

Reynolds, Siân, "The Sorrow and the Pity Revisited; or, Be Careful, One Train Can Hide Another", French Cultural Studies, 1 (1990): 149–59

Rousso, Henry, The Vichy Syndrome: History and Memory in France since 1944, Cambridge, Massachusetts: Harvard University Press, 1991

Silverman, Michael, "Le Chagrin et la pitié", Film Quarterly, 25/4 (Summer 1972): 57–59

Sweets, John F., Choices in Vichy France: The French under Nazi Occupation, Oxford and New York: Oxford University Press, 1986

LA OPINIÓN
Argentine newspaper, founded 1971

La Opinión was founded during the presidency of general Alejandro Lanusse (1971–73), a period of industrial unrest, riots, and violence by rival groups of urban guerrillas. The state of the Argentine economy was ruinous. The publisher and editor of La Opinión, Jacobo Timerman, set out to produce the Argentine equivalent of Le Monde, claiming later that it was "a liberal newspaper . . . [that] every day committed what in Argentina was construed as a capital sin: . . . [using] precise language to describe actual situations so that its articles were comprehensible and direct". This programme was both laudable and relevant, but, arguably, was negated by an erratic series of changes in editorial policy, some of them over matters of principle, others dictated by changes in the political climate; and by a financial scandal that appeared to cast doubt on La Opinión's much trumpeted independence.

La Opinión initially attracted some of the best contemporary writers and journalists, including the poets Francisco Urondo and Juan Gelman. According to Andrew Graham-Yooll, then on the staff of the Buenos Aires Herald, "Timerman's paper was the best Argentina had. It was the best produced, [and] had the widest coverage and the best attempts to explain a complex social and political situation, self-censorship permitting". In a country still dominated by relatively large numbers of immigrants, it was courageous to announce that La Opinión was in favour of Zionism.

However, idealism soon gave way under the pressure of government manipulation. In particular, after it was announced that the placement of government advertising would in future depend on the extent to which newspapers supported the government, La Opinión became a fulsome supporter.

Daily bombings, kidnappings, and assassinations continued. In particular, a Peronist group, the Montoneros, were pitted against the Ejértcito Revolucionaria del Pueblo (ERP, Revolutionary Army of the People). In 1973 Lanusse stepped down in favour of Juan Perón, the populist leader of the 1940s and 1950s, whose return, it was thought, might help to restore some order. La Opinión promptly switched its allegiance to Perón and appeared to flourish, finding the money for the construction of a large printing works in 1974. Perón, having failed to quell the activities of the Montoneros and the ERP, while ignoring similar activity on the part of the secret organization known as the Argentine Anti-Communist Alliance (the "Triple A"), died on 1 July 1974. He was succeeded by his second wife, Maria Estela (Isabelita) Perón, a former night club dancer. She too received the support of Timerman's newspaper, at least initially.

By 1975 inflation had reached 183 per cent a year and was rising at a rate of 30 per cent a month. Once again La Opinión changed its stance. In February 1976 it was suspended for 10 days after it had suggested that both houses of Congress should meet to declare Madame Perón unfit to govern. It was now in favour of a military revolution, supporting general Jorge Videla, regarded as a moderate, who took power in March 1976. The new government embarked on a "process of national reconstruction", part of which was concerned with the removal of any who were opposed to its programme. Many thousands were "disappeared" (some 10,000, according to the Nunca Mas, the report of the National Commission on the Disappeared, published in 1985, although there may have been up to 30,000). Once again the approach of La Opinión could not be regarded as entirely heroic. Timerman even dismissed a journalist who had written an article on one Haroldo Conti, who had been abducted on 5 April 1976.

In November 1976 the paper published a letter from Madame Solari Irigoyen, the wife of a former senator who had been accused of collusion with guerrillas and detained for three months. The letter had previously been sent to general Videla, but had remained unanswered. Timerman was visited by a journalist from the Admiralty Information Services, who made the regime's displeasure clear. In yet another editorial turnaround, Timerman published a letter that was hostile to the senator. On 29 January 1977, on the other hand, all copies of the newspaper was seized before distribution after it had printed an article by the Jesuit Vicente Pellegrini on the issue of human rights violations. The military also prevented the publication of the following day's issue.

Most government repression was carried out in secret. Not so its seizure of *La Opinión* on 24 May 1977, which it justified by the promulgation of a decree allowing its administrators to run any organization while its affairs were subject to audit and inspection. It emerged that the newspaper and the SACI publishing company, which produced it at the printing works mentioned above, had been deeply involved in the "laundering" of money obtained from guerrilla groups from ransoms paid to free those whom they had abducted. The ensuing scandal became known as the "David Graiver affair", after the Jewish financier said to have been behind it. On 1 April 1977 Elgardo Sajón, the paper's production director and a former press secretary to general Lanusse, was "disappeared". On 14 April Timerman himself was arrested and taken to a military base at La Plata, where he was tortured and interrogated. It is said that, under torture, he blamed his deputies for the affair, and that in due course he was moved to more comfortable quarters. Meanwhile, Enrique Raab, a staff writer on the paper, was "disappeared".

La Opinión had continued to appear in Timerman's absence, latterly under the direction of Enrique Jara, who had been arrested at the same time as Timerman but later released. However, on 24 May 1977 a retired general, José Teofilo Goyret, was put in charge, with predictable results. The paper carried much less news and what it did print was subject to government approval. Many of the staff left.

Timerman was released from detention on 17 April 1978, but remained under house arrest until 15 September 1979, when, after representations from the Organization of American States, the order against him was rescinded. However, he was stripped of his citizenship, had his property confiscated, and was deported to Israel. Clearly, Timerman, despite his sufferings, cannot be regarded as a hero of Argentinian struggles against censorship.

According to Andrew Graham Yooll, "*La Opinión* was the best reflection of Argentine society, its changing sympathies and lack of political consistency". On the other hand, "the government said that its move against *La Opinión* was not an anti-Semitic measure, nor a crackdown on the press. But it was a bit of both."

LIRIA EVANGELISTA

Further Reading

Brysk, Alison, *The Politics of Human Rights in Argentina: Protest, Change, and Democratization*, Stanford, California: Stanford University Press, 1994

Hodges, Donald C., *Argentina's "Dirty War": An Intellectual Biography*, Austin: University of Texas Press, 1991

Jordán, Alberto R., *El Proceso, 1976–1983*, Buenos Aires: Emecé, 1993

Peleg, Ilan (editor), *Patterns of Censorship around the World*, Boulder, Colorado: Westview Press, 1993

RISTO ORKO
Finnish film director, 1899–1997
AKTIVISTIT (The Activists)
Film, 1939

T.J. SÄRKKÄ
Finnish film director, 1890–1975
HELMIKUUN MANIFESTI (The February Manifesto)
Film, 1939

For centuries the history of Finland has been dominated by its relationship to its big neighbour the Russian empire, and after 1917, the Soviet Union. After the Peace of Moscow (1944) the Finnish government adopted a policy known elsewhere as "Finlandization": having fought and lost two wars against the Soviet Union, the Winter War (1939–40) and the Continuation War (1941–44), Finland had preserved its independence, but the price was high; opting for neutrality in the Cold War, it had always to consider how its actions and policies would go down in the Soviet Union.

Censorship was obviously central to Finlandization. Foreign films thought to be hostile to the Soviet Union were regularly banned. *The Activists* and *The February Manifesto* are significant because they were products of the Finnish film industry, were both first released in 1939, several months before the outbreak of war with the Soviet Union, and because they had a "mythic" quality as descriptions of the struggle for Finnish independence.

Formally, *The February Manifesto* begins in 1807 when Napoleon and tsar Alexander I of Russia meet to decide Finland's fate. "Finland is a beautiful country," says the emperor to the tsar: "take it, it's yours." But both films concentrate on

the period between 1899 and Finland's independence in 1918. The so-called "February Manifesto" signed by Nicholas II in 1899 drastically reduced Finnish autonomy and was followed by a period of sharp conflict in Finland. The "compliants" were in favour of some degree of cooperation with the Russians, hoping that this would avoid Finland's complete incorporation into the empire. The "constitutionalists" were against any kind of collaboration; the so-called "Young Finns", social democrats and Swedish-speakers, they regarded Nicholas's action as unlawful, and were unwilling to compromise their position by taking any further part in the administration of the Finnish Grand Duchy. A further group, the "activists", took a yet more radical stance: they were ready to achieve Finnish independence by force; they were responsible for the murder of the Russian governor-general Bobrikov in 1904 and continued their armed struggle until independence was achieved.

Concentrating on the same period, these films take slightly different perspectives. *The February Manifesto*, produced by Oy Suomen Filmiteollisuus AS, concentrates on the historical process; *The Activists*, a Suomi-Filmi production, describes the role of individuals in the struggle for independence. *The February Manifesto* is focussed on judge Kotka and his family, his son Jaakko, and his son-in-law. The younger men collect a petition with half a million signatures against the tsar's action, but Russification continues unabated, inducing even the judge to more active resistance, resulting in his transportation to Siberia. Jaakko, meanwhile, makes links with working-class leader Sihvola; travelling together, they persuade people to refuse the conscription which the tsar had imposed on Finland in 1901. During the Russo–Japanese war of 1904–05 there is some temporary improvement for the Finns, and in 1905 a general strike forces the tsar to repeal most of the February Manifesto. The judge returns from exile, while Sihvola opts for socialist revolution, parting company from Jaakko.

Russian oppression is now intensified, judge Kotka is again banished to Siberia, concluding that a free Finland is now essential. Jaakko, still an active resister, avoids arrest, being saved by Aino, sister of Sihvola, with whom he falls in love. Aino promises to wait for him when he decides to become a "Jäger", one of those who, convinced that only armed resistance to the Russians could be effective, goes to Germany for military training in 1915–16. With Finnish independence in 1917, Sihvola turns up again, and demands his sister Aino choose between him (representing the "Reds") or "them" (Jaakko and his family, representing the "Whites" or bourgeois Finland). Aino remains with Jaakko, who plays a prominent role in the Civil War. The film ends on a note of reconciliation, with the end of the war, the defeat of the Reds, and Jaakko and Aino ready to build a new Finland.

In *The Activists* Jussi Virta leads a groups which steals an important map and a list of activists from the Russians. In a clash with a Russian patrol on Christmas Eve 1916 Jussi dies, but his group continues until late 1917 and the realization of their dreams. Their leader affirms "no sacrifice is too great when made for our fatherland."

Both films, completed in 1939, fuelled national feeling at a key moment in the history of Finno–Soviet relations. Särkkä, director of *The February Manifesto*, wrote: "the more clearly our youth learns to understand . . . our history and the threats we face, the better they will be able to fulfil their duty to the nation." In view of what happened after 1944, it was ironic that Särkkä had now to accede to German demands to restrict the distribution of American films imported to Finland during World War II. After 1944, the last thing the Soviet Union wanted was a revived anti-Russian Finnish nationalism, and the last thing the Finnish government wanted was any provocation of their neighbours. Both films were entirely banned until 1986 and 1987, despite three requests by Särkkä, who, for the sake of keeping his film in circulation had made cuts of 300 metres (around 11 minutes). Now period pieces, they had their postwar cinema airing in 1986, and their first TV showing in 1991.

A.M. VAN DER HOEVEN

Further Reading

Hakosalo, Heini, "Monumentaalista melodraamaa, 1930–ja 1940-luvun vaihteen isänmaallinen elokuva" (Monumental Melodrama: Patriotic Films at the Turn of the 1930s) in *Suomen kansallisfilmografia* vol. 2: *Vuosien 1936–1941 suomalaiset kokoillan elokuvat*, Helsinki: Suomen Elokuva-arkisto, 1995

Kivimäki, Ari, *Kriisi, kritiikki, konsensus: elokuva ja suomalainen yhteiskunta* (Crisis, Criticism, Consensus: Film and the Finnish Society), Turku, 1999

Nenonen, Markku, "Elokuvien ennakkotarkastuksen synty Suomessa" (The Birth of Preventive Censorship of Films in Finland), *Lähikuva*, 2 (1995): 5–13

Sedergren, Jari, *Poliittinen elokuvasensuuri Suomessa, 1939–1941* (Political Censorship of Films in Finland 1939–1941), Helsinki, 1991

Sedergren, Jari, "Elokuvasensuurin saksien politiikkaa" (Scissors Politics of Film Censorship) in *Rillumarei ja valistus: Kulttuurikahakoita 1950-luvun Suomessa.* ("Rillumarei and Enlightenment: Cultural Skirmishes in Finland of the 1950s", edited by Matti Peltonen, Helsinki: SHS, 1996

Uusitalo, Kari, *Suomalaisen elokuvan vuosikymmenet: Johdatus kotimaisen elokuvan ja elokuva-alan historiaan, 1896–1963* (Decades of Finnish Film: Introduction to the History of the Finnish Film and Film-Business, 1896–1963), Helsinki: Otava, 1965

GEORGE ORWELL
British novelist, essayist, and journalist (real name: Eric Blair), 1903–1950

Censorship was the subject of Eric Blair's first published article, "La Censure en Angleterre", which he wrote for *Le Monde* at the beginning of his two years in Paris in October 1928. It was a conventional discussion of "English puritanism which does not find filth repugnant but fears sexuality and detests beauty", but it foreshadowed his later interest in social observation: "Nowadays it is illegal to print a swearword and even to swear, but no race is more wont to swear than the English."

His draft of *Down and Out in London and Paris*, which he submitted to the publisher Victor Gollancz in 1932, was described by its reader Gerald Gould as "an extraordinarily forceful and socially important document" which "most certainly ought to be published". It was, Gould warned, also libellous, blasphemous, and obscene. Gollancz's solicitor Harold Rubinstein insisted that all names should be changed and that the word "fucking", which Blair had rendered "f—", should be replaced by a simple blank (—). Keen for the book to be published, Blair agreed to the cuts, but wrote to Gollancz: "If it is all the same to everybody I would prefer the book to be published pseudonymously. I have no reputation that is lost by doing this and if the book has any kind of success I can always use the same pseudonym again." It was, and he did: nearly always afterwards he was known as George Orwell.

By the beginning of World War II he was an established writer, who had nevertheless met with various forms of censorship. Like *Down and Out, A Clergyman's Daughter*, which Orwell later disowned, caused problems for Gould: "The author is so particular and exact in his geographical indicators" ("Southbridge about twelve miles from London" could easily have been identified with Uxbridge; and the school where "the clergyman's daughter" taught was apparently closely modelled on the one that Orwell himself had taught at in that town, a school he regarded as appalling.) The book was published after Orwell had agreed to "a little toning down".

However, it was his participation in the Spanish Civil War, first as a journalist and then as a member of the POUM (Partido Obrero de Unificación Marxista) militia and his attempt to tell the true story of the war, exposing what he saw as Communist duplicity in *Homage to Catalonia*, that foreshadowed most eloquently his later preoccupation with totalitarian censorship. Gollancz would not publish this book. He was, Orwell told Rayner Heppenstall:

> of course part of the Communist-racket, and as soon as he heard I had been associated with the POUM and Anarchists, and had seen the inside of the May riots in Barcelona, he said that he did not think he would be able to publish my book, though not a word of it was written yet.

It was accepted instead by Fredric Warburg, known then in some quarters, but without justification, as "the Trotskyite publisher".

While writing *Homage to Catalonia*, Orwell was asked by Kingsley Martin, editor of the *New Statesman and Nation*, to review Franz Borkenau's *Spanish Cockpit*. In a rare lapse from integrity, Martin rejected what Orwell wrote because "it too far contradicts the policy of the paper. It is very uncompromisingly said and implies that our Spanish correspondents are all wrong." Although Kingsley Martin's refusal was partly responsible for Orwell's permanent disillusion with intellectual "fellow-travellers", the two men were later to cooperate in defying the BBC censorship during World War II. The review appeared instead in *Time and Tide*.

Henry Miller wrote to Orwell on 20 April 1938: "You can't shoulder the responsibilities of the whole world (that's for guys like Hitler and Mussolini – they thrive on it)". It was advice that Orwell was constitutionally incapable of taking. Ironically, it was Miller who was the occasion of Orwell's next brush with censorship, in 1939, before the war began. The Orwells were knocked up by the police at his house in Wallingford, Oxfordshire early one morning. Apparently, the post office censors had come upon a letter of his to the Obelisk Press, Paris, requesting some of Miller's books. Obelisk were known as publishers of pornography, and Miller's reputation at the time was as an author of "dirty books", a regular matter of concern for the police, who were evidently set to confiscate some of Orwell's library. He protested, and wrote later to Gollancz: "the police were only carrying out orders and were very nice about it, and even the public prosecutor wrote and said that he understood that as a writer I might have a need for books that it was illegal to possess."

Orwell was already obsessed, intellectually and practically, with totalitarianism – reasonably, as the world's three "great dictators", Hitler, Mussolini, and Stalin, had entered into an alliance. He would modify his position later when Hitler reneged on the agreement, but continued to believe that despite ideological differences, dictators had much in common. Nor could he be so optimistic as Bertrand Russell, whose book *Power: A New Social Analysis* (1939) Orwell reviewed for the *Adelphi*. Russell had argued that dictatorships were inherently unstable – "the huge system of organized lying upon which dictators depend keeps their followers out of contact with reality and therefore tends to put them at a disadvantage as against those who know the facts". Orwell considered that these were unprecedented times. Shortly afterwards, in a review of N. de Basily's *Russia under Soviet Rule* for *The New English Weekly*, Orwell pointed out:

> The Inquisition failed, but then the Inquisition had not the resources of the modern state. The radio, press-censorship, standardized education and the secret police had altered everything. Mass suggestion is a science of the last 20 years and we do not yet know how successful it will be.

Nineteen Eighty-Four was already in embryo.

A further example will make this clear. In his 1940 essay "New Words" Orwell argued for the regular expansion of the language to ensure that as archaic words dropped out, new ones took their place. One immediately thinks of Syme, the fanatical philologist and Newspeak expert in the novel:

> The whole aim of Newspeak is to narrow the range of thought. In the end we shall make thoughtcrime literally impossible, because there will be no words in which to express it. Every concept that can ever be needed will be expressed by exactly *one* word, with its meaning rigidly defined and all its subsidiary meanings ruled out and forgotten.

In 1939 Orwell's wife Eileen Blair (*née* O'Shaughnessy) obtained work at the new Censorship Office. According to W.J. West, Orwell made considerable use of her inside knowledge for the detail of *Nineteen Eighty-Four*. There was, for instance, the "anti-lie bureau", which was responsible for finding out the names of those who started rumours considered harmful to the war effort; the title of the bureau had a distinct Orwellian ring. In Oceania, where Orwell's last novel was set, "by a routine that was not even secret all letters were opened in transit"; in the Britain of the early 1940s, all letters sent to foreign addresses were similarly opened and perused for interesting or suspicious information, which was duly noted down before the letter could proceed on its way – though of course anything which gave away vital information was altogether blacked out. It was ironical that Eileen worked in the very department that had to ensure that "red" newspapers like the *Daily Worker* and *Tribune* (for which Orwell wrote and which was in fact of a radically different socialist disposition than the *Worker*) were not exported.

In August 1941 Orwell himself got a job as a talks producer at the empire department of the BBC, putting together cultural programmes transmitted to India and Southeast Asia. In the 1920s Orwell had served in the Burmese colonial police service, and for some time now his *Burmese Days*, along with his essay *The Lion and the Unicorn*, had been banned in India, where the movement for independence, if partially silenced by the war, was working clandestinely to that end and might make use of Orwell's early espousal of anti-colonialism. It was thought, however, that this could be kept in check by confining him to cultural programmes, and in any case that the BBC's own strict system of control would be enough to see that nothing potentially seditious in the subcontinent would be aired. West has revealed the system to which Orwell had to sign up as a condition of service. Each script had to be referred upwards, and each page had to be stamped "BBC Passed for Security" and "BBC Passed for Policy" before it could be transmitted.

In general Orwell seems to have been philosophical about BBC censorship. He dug his heels in, however, when the Corporation hierarchy agonized over his proposal to broadcast a talk by J.B.S. Haldane, the geneticist and physiologist, who was also a committed Marxist. Orwell, who had no time for Haldane's politics, won the day, incidentally ensuring that the BBC's disingenuous profession that, in the words of J.B. Clarke, controller overseas, "there is no general ban on anyone . . . there is no blacklist" was recorded for posterity. However, their troublesome talks producer failed to persuade them to broadcast a talk by the left-wing Labour politician Aneurin Bevan, but then simply did not ask them if he could employ his old opponent Kingsley Martin, who had upset the BBC hierarchy in 1941, and was now unofficially banned (whatever they said about the absence of blacklists). Orwell put him on air regularly from the summer of 1943, on controversial subjects such as education (the Conservative politician R.A. Butler was preparing his Education Act), causing controllers to question whether he had the "discipline appropriate to an organization such as ours". Defiantly, Martin and Orwell planned a final challenge to authority in a talk called "The Freedom of the Press in Wartime" broadcast on 24 August 1943. Two weeks later, ostensibly because he believed that his programmes were not reaching audiences where they could make a difference, Orwell resigned.

His resignation letter appears to suggest that his departure was amicable : "On no occasion have I been compelled to say anything on the air that I would not have said as a private individual". But West claims:

> The fact that the establishment in the BBC could genuinely believe they were fighting for freedom of speech whilst censoring every word that they uttered over the air and all the while denying (and continuing to deny after the war was over) what they had been doing is one of the first examples of "doublethink".

Orwell was now appointed literary editor of *Tribune*, and continued to write widely for *The Observer*, and for the American *Partisan Review*, to which he contributed a regular "London Letter" from 1940. He was only conscious of a single act of censorship, when he had written that if German airmen had to make forced landings in Britain they would be lynched. In his final letter, he suggested that "a word of praise is due to the censorship department which has let these letters through with remarkably little interference". For *Tribune* (1 December 1944), on the other hand, he noted that, in deference to the Russians, the US government had ruled that Trotsky's *Life of Stalin* was to be withdrawn and reviewers asked to avoid "any comment whatsoever regarding the biography and its postponement". While understanding the reason for the censorship, which was also imposed in Britain, Orwell was disgusted by "the general willingness", on both sides of the Atlantic, "to suppress all mention of it".

He had himself been censored for an article which would have angered the Russians. The *Manchester Evening News* had refused to print his review of Harold Laski's *Faith, Reason and Civilization* because it was "anti-Stalin in tone". Orwell criticized Laski's failure to mention the USSR's "purges, liquidations, the dictatorship of a minority, suppression of criticism and so forth". The *Evening News*, stablemate of the reliably liberal and open *Manchester Guardian*, recognized that public opinion was, for the moment, mostly pro-Russian and was mindful of the USSR's regular complaints about what was written in the British press.

Orwell was increasingly preoccupied with the rewriting and falsification of history. In his essay "Looking Back on the Spanish War" written in 1942–43, he recalled:

> I saw great battles reported where there had been no fighting, and complete silence where hundreds of men had been killed. I saw troops who had fought bravely denounced as cowards and traitors and others who had never seen a short fired lauded as heroes of imaginary victories, and I saw newspapers in London retailing these lies, and eager intellectuals building emotional superstructures over events that never happened.

It was an insight which would once again inform *Nineteen Eighty-Four*:

> "Who controls the past" ran the party slogan, "controls the future: who controls the present controls the past" . . . All that was needed was an unending series of victories over our own memory. "Reality Control" they called it: in Newspeak, "double think".

Concretely, "Oceania was at war with Eurasia: therefore Oceania had always been at war with Eurasia".

Animal Farm, if not actually censored, was subject to a series of evasions by publishers who were not willing, in 1944, to publish Orwell's satirical treatment of communist political systems. Victor Gollancz turned it down summarily. At Nicholson and Watson, despite pressure by an enthusiastic André Deutsch, the chairman J.A.C. Roberts took exception to its anti-Sovietism. Cape considered that "it might be regarded as something which is ill advised at the present time". T.S. Eliot at Faber and Faber disguised his firm's political misgivings by turning it down on stylistic grounds. The book was finally bought by Secker and Warburg, who themselves delayed publication until after the 1945 general election, reckoning that the political wind might well soon blow in a different direction (aware, perhaps, as Orwell reports, that Aneurin Bevan, his boss at *Tribune* and putative member of a Labour government, was worried that a book like this would affect Labour's chances of victory). The book became an instant classic, and, needless to say, was banned entirely throughout the communist world until glasnost in the mid-1980s.

Of all Orwell's works, it is of course *Nineteen Eighty-Four* which deals most explicitly and extensively with censorship. Winston Smith, its "hero", works in the Ministry of Truth (Newspeak: *Minitrue*), whose formal role was to "supply the citizens of Oceania with newspapers, films, textbooks, telescreen programmes, novels", but only those which had passed through an "unseen labyrinth", where "a process of continual alteration was applied not only to newspapers but to books, periodicals, pamphlets, sound tracks, cartoons, photographs – to every kind of literature which might have political or ideological significance". On Winston's telescreen there appeared the instruction (one of many every day): "times 3.12.83 reporting bb dayorder doubleplus ungood refs unpersons rewrite fullwise upsub antefiling", which translated into Oldspeak, meant: "The reporting of Big Brother's Order for the Day in *The Times* of December 3rd 1983 is extremely unsatisfactory and makes references to non-existent persons. Rewrite it in full and submit your draft to higher authority before filing." The wretched "non-existent person" was Comrade Withers, who had fallen from favour, and had then "disappeared" or been "vaporized". As always, once Winston had rewritten the piece and had it passed, the original *Times* was also destroyed and the corrected version placed on file. Winston, who could not keep his dissidence secret, was cured of his thoughtcrime by a slow and painful process of manipulation and torture. Perhaps Comrade Withers had the better luck.

The poet, literary historian, and dissident Czesław Miłosz wrote revealingly in 1953 of the attitude of Polish Communist Party officials to *Nineteen Eighty-Four*:

> because it is both difficult to obtain and dangerous to possess it is known only to certain members of the Inner Party. Orwell fascinates them through his insight into details they know well, and through his Swiftian satire. Such a form of writing is forbidden by the New Faith, because allegory, by nature manifold in meaning, would trespass beyond the prescriptions of socialist realism and the demands of the censor.

By the time the real 1984 arrived, the writing was on the wall for at least some of the main communist totalitarianisms. Orwell's nightmare is in no way invalidated. It applied, as any wider reading of his work makes clear, to the centralizing and manipulative tendencies in all societies. In his essay "The Prevention of Literature" (1945) he noted that "any writer or journalist who wants to retain his integrity finds himself thwarted by the general drift of society rather than by active persecution". The ownership of the press "by a few rich men" was *ipso facto* censorship; 50 years later the world's press is in even fewer hands. Moreover, Orwell saw a future in which the writer was turned "into a minor official, working on themes handed to him from above and never telling what seems to him the whole of the truth"; many would see that as a not altogether inaccurate description of living with spin doctors.

DEREK JONES

Writings

Down and Out in Paris and London, 1933
Burmese Days, 1934
A Clergyman's Daughter, 1935
Homage to Catalonia, 1938
The Lion and the Unicorn: Socialism and the English Genius, 1941
Animal Farm: A Fairy Story, 1945
Nineteen Eighty-Four, 1949
The Collected Essays, Journalism and Letters, 1920–1950, edited by Sonia Orwell and Ian Angus, 4 vols, 1968
The War Broadcasts, edited by W.J. West, 1985
The War Commentaries, edited by W.J. West, 1985

Further Reading

Crick, Bernard, *George Orwell: A Life*, London: Secker and Warburg and Boston: Little Brown, 1980
Hewison, Robert, *Under Siege: Literary Life in London, 1939–1945*, London: Weidenfeld and Nicolson and New York: Oxford University Press, 1977
Meyers, Jeffrey (editor), *A Reader's Guide to George Orwell*, London: Thames and Hudson and Totowa, New Jersey: Littlefield Adams, 1975
Miłosz, Czesław, *The Captive Mind*, New York: Knopf, and London: Secker and Warburg, 1953
West, W.J., *The Larger Evils: Nineteen Eighty-Four: The Truth Behind the Satire*, Edinburgh: Canongate, 1992

JOHN OSBORNE
British dramatist, 1929–1994

A PATRIOT FOR ME
Play, 1965

John Osborne, an actor and playwright who had been one of George Devine's protégés in the English Stage Company (ESC) at the Royal Court Theatre, London, changed the face of British theatre with *Look Back in Anger* (1956). Even the Examiner of Plays recognized that this "impressive and depressing" drama broke "new psychological ground". With some fairly minor alterations of phrasing, it was recommended for licence, a decision that some considered showed a surprising degree of liberality on the part of the Lord Chamberlain, the official responsible for theatre censorship until 1968. Later plays by Osborne, such as *Luther* (1961), *The Blood of the Bambergs* (1962), and *Inadmissible Evidence* (1964), suffered more severe cuts, especially the last-named, because of the explicit, some-

times obscene, language that Osborne tended to use in preference to what he saw as the "thin and unexpressive" dramatic language used when he first started to write plays.

Osborne's greatest difficulties were reserved for *A Patriot for Me*, which, because of its pervasive homosexual content, touched a deep vein of resistance at the Lord Chamberlain's Office under Lord Cobbold, the last holder to exercise the power of censorship (1963–68). Although the issue of homosexuality on the stage had twice been reviewed by Lord Clarendon, then Lord Chamberlain, in 1946 and 1951, it was the case that until 1958, when some concessions were made by Lord Scarborough in response to the changes in the law recommended in the Wolfenden Committee's report, homosexuality as a dramatic theme was completely banned. Lillian Hellman's play *The Children's Hour* had been suppressed in 1935, on the grounds of its depiction of lesbianism, and in the case of Ronald Duncan's *The Catalyst* (1957), Scarborough was resolute that he was "not prepared to pick and choose between the good and the bad plays which deal with the subject of homosexuality and lesbianism".

Despite the concessions in 1958 to "sincere and serious" treatments of homosexuality, *A Patriot for Me* was refused a licence in September 1964 on the grounds that there were certain scenes that "exploit homosexuality in a manner that may tend to have corrupting influences". The most specific objections were to the drag ball and to a scene in which "men embrace each other and are seen in bed together". In Osborne's play, based on real events in the Austro-Hungarian empire in the period 1890–1913, colonel Redl is an army officer on the promotional ladder who is recruited into counterespionage. He gradually discovers from his unfulfilling sexual encounters with women that he is homosexual. By the end of act 1 his sexual induction with a young private has taken place and at the opening of act 2 he attends an extravagant homosexual ball. When his secret is found out by the Russians he is offered a way out by becoming a double agent, but Redl cannot comply and commits suicide.

As the play was unlicensed, the ESC was forced, in Osborne's words (quoted in the Joint Committee Report cited below, 1967), into "an act of desperation", the "elaborate farce of turning the theatre into a club", since private clubs were beyond the Lord Chamberlain's reach. *A Patriot for Me* opened at the Royal Court on 30 June 1965 and ran for nearly eight weeks, a total of 53 performances. It won the *Evening Standard* award for best drama of 1965, was well reviewed, and played to near-capacity audiences. It is now clear that Lord Cobbold would have liked to see the Royal Court prosecuted because it had found a way to get round his ban. However, government law officers instructed the Director of Public Prosecutions not to proceed, on the grounds that the play had "attracted a great deal of public support and has been running for some time". Being expensive to stage, it made a loss of nearly £16,000, half of which Osborne bore personally, but without a licence its transfer to a larger-capacity theatre in the commercial system of the West End was out of the question.

Outside the confines of the Lord Chamberlain's Office, there was a measure of agreement that, in refusing to sanction this play, Lord Cobbold had made an error of judgement. In the summer of 1965, on the initiative of Lord Goodman, Chairman of the Arts Council, Cobbold was asked to reconsider his decision. As the play's director with the ESC, Anthony Page visited St James's Palace to be informed what had to be done to secure a licence. Cobbold's requirements were extensive. In addition to several fairly minor cuts in phrasing, they included the deletion of three entire scenes: Redl's homosexual initiation with a private soldier (1:10); a similar bedroom scene in act 3, scene 5; and the drag ball scene set in Vienna (2:1). Additionally, Cobbold warned Page that Redl and the anonymous young man must not be seen in bed together (3:1), and a number of cuts in the dialogue in the same scene were requested. When the Countess announces her impending marriage to Stefan, one of Redl's ex-lovers, excisions were demanded of about 15 lines in which Redl argues that she will "never know

that body like I know it", along with the whole of the exchange between the Countess and Redl on the subject of gay men's bottoms being "quite different, much plumper and far wider than any ordinary man". Oddly, in the circumstances, although perhaps on the basis of some perverse notion of equality of treatment, Redl's sexual encounter with the Countess (1:4) was also labelled with a caution that they must not be seen in bed together.

The most damaging cut, covering about 18 pages of dialogue in the published text, was of the entire grandly decadent, highly colourful, and erotic Viennese ball, attended, mostly in drag (although not by Redl, who appears in uniform), by prominent members of the military and the aristocracy. For Osborne, this scene was at the heart of the play, which is not about homosexuality as such but about the evasions and hypocrisies at the centre of the establishment. Ronald Bryden argued in the *New Statesman* that the play provided "clinching evidence" that censorship was self-defeating. Without the drag ball scene the play loses its focus and becomes an apologia for homosexuality, whereas in fact the scene is "magnificently theatrical, the best thing in [the] play, . . . its centre, its validation, the image from which all else takes perspective and completeness".

That Osborne felt it impossible to accede to the censor's demands occasioned no surprise. There was no further movement on the part of Lord Cobbold and his intransigence caused the National Theatre to shelve its plans to stage the play in 1966. *A Patriot for Me* was not performed in the commercial theatre until after the ending of censorship.

In a speech to the House of Lords (17 February 1966) moving the appointment of a joint committee of the two houses of parliament to examine the whole issue of stage censorship, Noel Annan, a historian who was then provost of University College, London, cited Osborne's play in illustration of the kind of economic as well as artistic hardship that censorship could inflict on one of Britain's "better playwrights". When Osborne appeared before the joint committee (29 November 1966), he observed that "the present system of censorship is making life difficult for rather serious people"; and that, but for the attitude of the Lord Chamberlain over this play, he would have become much more commercially successful.

The published edition of *A Patriot for Me* (London, 1966) notes that:

> This play has not been licensed for public performance by the Lord Chamberlain. A list of the cuts and alterations requested by the Lord Chamberlain – and to which Mr Osborne refused to agree – is printed as an appendix to this volume.

Perhaps as a reminder of the struggles of the past, the notice was retained unaltered in subsequent editions, even after the abolition of censorship in September 1968.

In general, lesbianism was treated more sympathetically. *The Children's Hour* was eventually licensed by Lord Scarborough in 1960 (performed 1964); and Frank Marcus's *The Killing of Sister George*, a comedy about a lesbian actress in a radio soap opera, was, despite some misgivings on the part of the Examiner of Plays, licensed without a single cut in the very same year as *A Patriot for Me* was banned.

JOHN RUSSELL STEPHENS

Writings

Inadmissible Evidence, produced 1964; published 1965
A Patriot for Me, produced 1965; published 1966
A Better Class of Person: An Autobiography, 1929–1956, 1981
Almost a Gentleman: An Autobiography, 1955–1966, 1991
Plays, 3 vols, 1993–98 ("Introduction" by Osborne in vol. 1)
Damn You, England: Collected Prose, 1994

Further Reading

Browne, Terry, *Playwrights' Theatre: The English Stage Company at the Royal Court Theatre*, London: Pitman, 1975

De Jongh, Nicholas, *Not in Front of the Audience: Homosexuality on Stage*, London and New York: Routledge, 1992
De Jongh, Nicholas, *Politics, Prudery and Perversions: The Censoring of the English Stage, 1901–1968*, London: Methuen, 2000
Johnston, John, *The Lord Chamberlain's Blue Pencil*, London: Hodder and Stoughton, 1990
Joint Committee on Censorship of the Theatre, *Report, together with the Proceedings of the Committee, Minutes of Evidence, Appendices and Index*, London: HMSO, 1967
Sinfield, Alan, *Out on Stage: Lesbian and Gay Theatre in the Twentieth Century*, New Haven, Connecticut: Yale University Press, 1999

ŌSHIMA NAGISA
Japanese film director, 1932–

AI NO CORRIDA (In the Realm of the Senses)
Film, 1976

More than two decades after its Paris premiere in September 1976, the uncut version of *In the Realm of the Senses* continues to be banned in Japan. Based on the true story of Abe Sada, a poor prostitute who killed and castrated her lover, the film's many scenes of explicit sexual intercourse have caused it to be censored in numerous countries, including, briefly, the United States. Now generally regarded by film critics as a masterpiece of erotic art, *In the Realm of the Senses* is no less an investigation of the political repression of sexuality.

In both his films and his writings, Ōshima Nagisa has repeatedly challenged Japan's film industry and judicial system on the standards established for permissible film content. His fourth film, *Nihon no Yoru to Kiri* (1960, Night and Fog in Japan) was pulled from distribution after only four days by the production company, Shōchiku, ostensibly on the grounds that it had done poorly at the box office. However, Ōshima, and numerous others, have cited the overtly political nature of *Night and Fog in Japan* as the real reason for its being shelved. This disagreement inspired Ōshima to leave Shōchiku and begin working as an independent filmmaker. He has continued to explore political themes, and has pushed the linkage of politics and sexuality even further.

In the Realm of the Senses is his most thorough investigation of this linkage. It features two characters who attempt to escape from political repression through immersion in the sensual realm. It tells the story of an obsessive and fatal love affair between Abe Sada (Matsuda Eiko) and Kichizo (Fuji Tatsuya), the husband of her employer. At first just a servant whom he seduces, Sada quickly becomes a source of fascination for Kichizo. Her appetite for sex is insatiable, and he becomes obsessed with providing her pleasure. But her desire for pleasure escalates, and finally she resorts to strangling him to increase the size of his erection. Kichizo tells Sada not to hold back, and she strangles him to death. She then cuts off his penis and testicles with a knife, and writes in blood on his chest, "Sada, Kichi: together the two of us only." Ōshima's voice-over narration tells us that four days later she was found wandering the streets of Tokyo with Kichizo's genitals in her bag. She was arrested and tried, but her case inspired "a strange sympathy, and she was acquitted. This happened in 1936."

Set in the same year as an attempted coup d'état by extremists in the Japanese military, *In the Realm of the Senses* makes only one overt reference to the intense militarism of the 1930s. It is, however, a very powerful one. In a very brief scene, we see Kichizo walking through a narrow street wearing only his *yukata* (a light, unlined kimono also worn in bed). Suddenly a battalion of soldiers marches past him in the opposite direction. A crowd on the other side of the street waves miniature flags at the soldiers, while Kichizo struggles to keep from being swept along. Read against this scene, Sada and Kichizo's retreat into the sensual realm becomes a challenge to the militaristic repression and conformity of the 1930s. In the same way, the pornographic images in the film challenge the regulations that continue to dictate what can and cannot be seen in cinemas in Japan.

From the outset, Ōshima declared his intention to make *In the Realm of the Senses* a pornographic film in which the actors would engage in real sexual intercourse. Anatole Dauman, the French producer of Jean-Luc Godard's *Masculin, Feminin* (1965, *Maculine, Feminine*), Volker Schlöndorff's *Die Blechtrommel* (1979, *The Tin Drum*), and numerous other European "art house" films had been encouraging Ōshima to make a pornographic movie since 1972. After receiving Ōshima's treatment of the Abe Sada story, Dauman's company, Argos Films, agreed to finance its production, and gave Ōshima complete artistic freedom. In April 1975, France had relaxed its pornography laws, so, because of restrictions in Japan, the film stock had to be imported from France, shot in Japan, and then shipped back to France, where it was developed. Without this transnational collaboration, the film could not have been made in Japan.

After its premiere in Paris, *In the Realm of the Senses* was widely screened in European art houses. Despite this, it was seized while being imported into Japan under Article 21 of the Customs Tariff Law, which does not allow items that could

ŌSHIMA: Still from the explicitly erotic film *Ai no corrida* (In the Realm of the Senses). The film, based on a notorious 1930s murder case, was shot in Japan but completed in France, because of the liberal pornography laws there; it was premiered in Paris in 1976 and subsequently shown in European art-house cinemas. Ōshima was prosecuted for obscenity under the Japanese Penal Code and the film has never been shown uncut in Japan.

"injure public security or morals". Meanwhile, Ōshima was put on trial for obscenity under Section 175 of the Penal Code, which states that "A person, who distributes or sells an obscene writing, picture, or other thing of publicity, displays the same, shall be punished." As part of his defence, Ōshima stated that the repression of *In the Realm of the Senses* was in part "a prompt attack on the new method of using a collaboration with a foreign country to exceed the limits on sexual expression". Ōshima also accused the civil authorities of persecuting him directly, rather than his work. As the director of many controversial films, an outspoken social critic, and a frequent defence witness in the censorship trials of fellow filmmakers, Ōshima had made many enemies within the Japanese legal establishment. He had also provoked the judicial authorities by his statement that Article 175 was "a meaningless, bad law", in the book containing the script and stills of *In the Realm of the Senses*.

The film was also seized by US customs officials at the port of Los Angeles, on "moral" grounds, prior to its screening at the New York Film Festival in November 1976. A US district court later ruled the customs action "outrageous". In Japan, even with one-third of the entire film edited out, it has rarely been shown. Despite this, Ōshima continues to make films that challenge sexually repressive laws. He made *Gohatto*, a samurai drama of homosexual love, for Shōchiku in 1998.

JOSEPH CHRISTOPHER SCHAUB

Writings

Cinema, Censorship, and the State: The Writings of Nagisa Oshima, 1956–1978, edited by Annette Michelson, translated by Dawn Lawson, 1992

Further Reading

Desser, David, *Eros Plus Massacre: An Introduction to the Japanese New Wave Cinema*, Bloomington: Indiana University Press, 1988

Heath, Stephen, *Questions of Cinema*, Bloomington: Indiana University Press, 1981

Turim, Maureen, *The Films of Oshima Nagisa: Images of a Japanese Iconoclast*, Berkeley: University of California Press, 1998

OSLOBODJENJE (Freedom)
Newspaper published in Bosnia-Herzegovina since 1943

Oslobodjenje began its existence as a war newspaper: it was the organ of the Partisans in the republic of Bosnia-Herzegovina, who, after their victorious struggle against the Nazis and their Croatian collaborators, the Ustaše, during World War II, made it the party newspaper of the ruling Socialistički Savez Radnih Naroda (Socialist Alliance of Working People, or SAWP). As such, *Oslobodjenje* reflected the relative conservatism of the Bosnian party leadership, acquiring a reputation that it found hard to shed in the new conditions that followed the first multiparty elections in 1990.

The paper had always opposed Bosnian nationalism, in line with the ruling party's commitment to the Yugoslav federation. In 1979, it published extracts from a book by Derviš Sušić alleging links between senior Muslim clergy and the Ustaše during the war. The paper's intervention formed part of a concerted attack by the regime on what it called "pan-Islamism", which resulted in the imprisonment of Alija Izetbegović, the future president of Bosnia-Herzegovina, among others. In 1989 a survey revealed that, because of the newspaper's past history, only 26 per cent of the population of the republic turned to *Oslobodjenje* for reliable news.

Soon after Izetbegović's party, the Stranka Demokratske Akcije (Party of Democratic Action, or SDA), came to power in 1990, the new government set out to split *Oslobodjenje* into three newspapers along ethnic lines. Despite the fact that more than half the staff were Serbs by nationality, they unanimously opposed the reforms, defeated them, and set in motion the newspaper's re-establishment as an independent publication owned by a joint stock company. Nevertheless, despite the passage of 50 years, the staff of *Oslobodjenje* had not entirely forgotten how the paper had been born. During the Bosnian War (1991–93), they brought the paper out almost every day from a nuclear fallout shelter near the front line that was specially targeted by Serb forces, who realized the paper's growing importance as the only source of news in the besieged city of Sarajevo. Outside the city, the paper's Belgrade offices were taken over by the Bosnian Serb party, Srpska Demokratska Stranka (SDS), and, a month later, its Novi Sad bureau was attacked. Some regional correspondents were also threatened, and on 9 April 1992 the *Oslobodjenje* journalist Kjasif Smajoli was murdered at the door of the paper's Zbornik office.

After the formal end of the war, further attacks were reported to international journalists' organizations. Mate Bikić, a correspondent for ONASA, the news agency affiliated to *Oslobodjenje*, was beaten up at Tuzla on 6 October 1995; according to Reporters sans Frontières a journalist from *Zmaj od Bosne*, a newspaper close to the radical wing of the SDA, was suspected of carrying out this act. On 15 or 16 August 1996, Nedzad Mulahuseinović, a schoolteacher at Tesanj, close to Serb territory, was severely beaten by unidentified assailants. His wife, Azmina Mulahuseinović, was a correspondent for *Oslobodjenje* in this Muslim-controlled town, and had reported several stories about the harassment of local opposition parties. Her editors believed that the targeting of her husband was related to her coverage of the pre-election violence.

However, it was neither physical threat nor more direct censorship that conspired to bury *Oslobodjenje*, but the economic consequences of postwar political transformation. The war had restricted the paper's circulation to 5000 copies; its privatization had been stopped, and most of its assets destroyed. Newspapers could no longer cross borders, even within Bosnia-Herzegovina itself, and, in a situation where the purchase of a newspaper remained a luxury, the Muslim paper *Dnevni Azaz* commanded most of the reading public in the Muslim–Croat Federation.

Even as late as March 2001, the wages of the employees were lowered by 20 per cent. The director pointed to still unpaid war duties. The journalists went on strike, supported by the Organization of Independent Journalists of Bosnia-Herzegovina, demanding more insight into the financial operations and situation of the firm. Though constantly confronted with financial difficulties, the paper is still praised for its cultural reporting and its independent political standpoint.

ROBERT STALLAERTS

Further Reading

Camo, Mensur, "Sarajevo's Endless Siege", *Balkan War Report*, 17 (January 1993)

Dizdarević, Zlatko, *Sarajevo: A War Journal*, New York: Fromm, 1993

Dizdarević, Zlatko, Gérard Rondeau and Dominique Roynette, *Oslobodjenje, le journal qui refuse de mourir: Sarajevo, 1992–1996*, Paris: La Découverte, 1996

Fitzpatrick, Catherine A. and Amanda Onion, "Briefing Paper on Press Freedom in Bosnia and Herzegovina before the September 14th Elections", Committee to Protect Journalists, 1996

Lecompte, Christian, "Le Plus Vieux Quotidien bosniaque à bout de souffle: *Oslobodjenje*, journal réputé qui symbolisa la lutte de la capitale bosniaque contre le blocus serbe, est plongé dans une crise profonde" (The Oldest Bosnian Daily Runs Out of Breath: *Oslobodjenje*, the Famous Daily That Symbolized the Struggle of the Bosnian Capital against the Serbian Bloc, Is Plunged into Deep Crisis), *Le Monde*, 2 December 1997

Malcolm, Noel, *Bosnia: A Short History*, London: Macmillan, and New York: New York University Press, 1998

Mari, Jean-Paul, "De stem van de vrijkeid in Sarajevo" (The Voice of Freedom in Sarajevo), *Reader's Digest* and *Le Nouvel Observateur* (June 1993)

Ramet, Sabrina Petra, "The Role of the Press in Yugoslavia" in *Yugoslavia in Transition: Choices and Constraints: Essays in Honour of Fred Singleton*, edited by John B. Allcock *et al.*, New York and Oxford: Berg, 1992

Reporters sans Frontières, *Mission d'enquête à Banja Luka, Mostar, Sarajevo et Tuzla*, Paris: Reporters sans Frontières, 1996

"Strjk traje: Oslobodjenje izlazi" (The Strike Goes On: *Oslobodjenje* Comes Out), *Oslobodjenje* (19 May 2001)

Thompson, Mark, *Forging War: The Media in Serbia, Croatia and Bosnia-Hercegovina*, London: Article 19, 1994; revised edition, Luton: University of Luton Press, 1999

Wheeler, Mark, *What War Hath Wrought: The Media in Bosnia and Hercegovina*, London and Sarajevo: Institute for War and Peace Reporting, 1996

Website

http://www.oslobodjenje.com.ba

ALEKSANDR OSTROVSKII
Russian dramatist, 1823–1886

Outside the borders of Russia, Anton Chekhov is generally thought to be the preeminent playwright that country has produced. Within Russia, however, it is Aleksandr Ostrovskii who is widely beloved as the father of contemporary Russian drama. There can be little argument that such luminaries as Chekhov, Maksim Gor'kii, Vladimir Nemirovich-Danchenko, and Konstantin Stanislavskii are all heirs to the theatrical tradition fostered by Ostrovskii over the course of his career, a tradition fought for in the face of incessant government censorship and harassment.

Aleksandr Nikolaevich Ostrovskii was born and raised among the merchant middle class of imperial Moscow, the son of a judicial clerk who left government employment to represent the merchants of the city in the civil courts. The elder Ostrovskii prospered, and after the death of his first wife married a Swedish baroness, and so was elevated to nobility. As a child Ostrovskii was surrounded by literature, and was a frequent patron of the Moscow theatres. He enrolled in the school of law at the University of Moscow, but left after his second year and secured a clerkship at a court that considered commercial cases. Ostrovskii served as a civil servant for eight years, but also turned his hand to literary activities and began to see his work in print. Much of his later work was based on character studies that he made while working amidst the oppression and tyranny of the imperial bureaucracy.

In 1847 Ostrovskii's first play, a one-act piece entitled *Semeinaia kartina* (A Domestic Picture), was published in a Moscow literary magazine. The imperial censor forbade the staging of the play, the first of many such instances in Ostrovskii's career. His first full-length play, *Svoi liudi sochtemsya* (A Family Affair, previously The Bankrupt, also known as It's a Family Affair, We'll Settle It Ourselves), an exposé of the corruption of Moscow businessmen, received a public reading in 1849 before an audience that included Nikolai Gogol', and was then published in the journal *Moskvitianin* (Muscovite). This was a time when emperor Nicholas I, never particularly trustful of his intelligentsia, was reacting to the European revolutions of the previous year by arresting anyone perceived to be a dissenter, including, for example, Fedor Dostoevskii. As might have been expected in this atmosphere, *A Family Affair* ran foul of the censors, and eventually no less an authority than the emperor himself prohibited its production, finding subversion in its imperfect moral ending. This imperial ban not only kept the play from the theatres, but gave its author a place on the government's list of persons "of doubtful loyalty". He remained under police surveillance for seven years.

Ostrovskii spent the next several years of his life editing a Moscow literary journal, publishing the works of others, and practising his playwriting skills. This work paid off when, in 1853, three of his plays, *Bednaia nevesta* (The Poor Bride), *Ne v svoi sani ne sadis'!* (Stay in Your Own Lane), and *Bednost' ne porok* (Poverty is No Vice) were all produced in Moscow and St Petersburg. The three plays each featured Ostrovskii's new outlook on life, showing the Russian people in a flattering light.

Despite this success, Ostrovskii continued to struggle to have his plays produced on the Moscow stage, and found himself frequently in opposition to Pavel Federov, the director of repertory of the imperial theatres. During the course of his career, Ostrovskii completed several plays each year, working in a variety of different genres, including middle-class comedy, historical romance, fairy tales, and high tragedy. He was twice the winner of Russia's highest dramatic honour, the Uvarov Prize: in 1860, for perhaps his best known work, *Groza* (1859, *The Storm*), and in 1863, for *Grekh da beda na kogo ne zhivet* (Sin and Sorrow are Common to All). However, *Groza* was banned from production in 1860 for its depiction of adultery, and in 1863 a historical play, *Sukhoruk*, was rejected for production due to its farcical depiction of past Russian leaders. In 1866 another of Ostrovskii's historical plays, *Dmitrii Samozvanets* (The False Dmitry) was rejected for production in the same month that a previous ruling against his play *Minin* was reversed.

The last years of Ostrovskii's life were spent attempting to change the Russian theatre, first from without, finally from within. In 1863 he wrote a tract, *Circumstances Hindering the Development of Dramatic Art in Russia*, in which he listed censorship, the central playreading committee, and scarce financial rewards for playwrights as the main reasons for the dearth of high-quality Russian drama. Ostrovskii also wrote numerous memorandums to similar effect, lobbying in 1869, 1871, and 1881 for copyright laws that would guarantee playwrights some control over where and how their works were produced. In 1874 he aided in the formation of the Society of Dramatic Authors and Composers, and remained its president until his death. The plight of actors also concerned Ostrovskii, and he agitated for proper training at the imperial theatre school, which in 1871 had dropped all acting classes in favour of ballet training. After several fruitless years, he finally saw the task through himself from 1885, when he was named director of repertory for the imperial theatres in Moscow. With a mission to improve the quality of performance among all Russian theatre practitioners, Ostrovskii took office on 1 January 1886. Six months later, however, the father of modern Russian drama died of angina pectoris. There is a museum dedicated to his life and works in Berezhki, the village where he died, and in 1925 a bronze statue of him was erected in front of the Malyi Theatre in Moscow.

PATRICK JULIAN

Writings
Five Plays, translated by Eugene K. Bristow, 1969
Four Plays, translated by Stephen Mulrine, 1997

Further Reading
Hoover, Marjorie L., *Alexander Ostrovsky*, Boston: Twayne, 1981
Zohrab, Irene, "Problems of Translation: The Plays of A.N. Ostrovsky in English", *Melbourne Slavonic Studies*, 16 (1982)

OTTOMAN EMPIRE

1300–1831

At its height, under sultan Suleiman I (the "Magnificent", reigned 1520–66), the Ottoman empire stretched from central Europe to the Indian Ocean, and was thoroughly multinational: Arabs, Franks, Greeks, Kurds, Serbs, and Turks, together with many other smaller groups, were all under its control. Although dominated by Sunni Muslims, the empire also contained a variety of other faiths, notably Christianity, as well as several heretical forms of Islam itself.

According to Philip Mansel: "Constantinople had been taken by the sword; and, until the end of the Ottoman empire, 469 years later, force remained the Ottomans' principal means of control, as it did for other dynasties." An empire that was to last so long cannot have been uniformly repressive: Mehmet II (reigned 1444–81), the great conqueror of Constantinople, thereafter Istanbul, was just one example of a sultan who was open to a great variety of foreign, often liberalizing, impulses. Nevertheless, heresies, scholarship, music and dancing, painting, and popular religion were, at different times, subject to ruthless suppression, nearly all of it rooted in Islam, the religion of the state, and the sultan himself was subject to the shari'a (religious law).

None the less, György of Hungary could write in the 15th century: "The Turks do not compel anyone to renounce his faith, do not try to persuade anyone, and do not have a great opinion of renegades." The Ottoman treatment of Christianity was entirely opposite to that of western Europeans towards the people of other faiths; monsieur de la Motrage, a Huguenot whose Protestant beliefs had made necessary his escape from Catholic France, wrote in 1685: "There is no country on earth where the exercise of all sorts of religions is more free and less subject to being troubled than Turkey." Christians were regarded as "people of the Book", and Jesus revered as a great prophet. So long as Christians paid the poll tax laid down for those of other faiths, they were left in peace to practise their religion.

In theory, Christians were not supposed to build new churches, nor even to renew those in need of repair; in practice, they could certainly restore old buildings so long as they did so discreetly. For this, the Ottomans were praised. Gregory V, Orthodox patriarch of Constantinople (Christians continued to use the old place name) wrote in 1798 that the Ottomans were:

> to us, the people of the East, a means of salvation . . . [God] puts into the hearts of the Sultans of these Ottomans an inclination to keep free the religious beliefs of our Orthodox faith . . . to protect them even to the point of occasionally chastising Christians who deviate from the faith.

Suleiman I, trained in Islamic jurisprudence, briefly proposed that all churches should be turned into mosques, and that Christians who refused to embrace Islam should be killed. He was dissuaded by his mufti and grand vizier. Christians and Muslims lived side by side amicably enough until the Greek revolts of 1820 (in the Peloponnese, Epirus, Moldavia, and Wallachia), which entirely ruptured the accord of centuries (though many Greek folksongs lamented the fall of Constantinople): churches were looted and demolished, and Christian libraries sold and dispersed.

Dissidence within Islam was an entirely different matter, in part because unorthodox religious leaflets were increasingly held to be the focus of a more political opposition. The Dervish orders, for instance, which practised forms of mysticism, were suspected not only of "innovation", a cardinal sin for traditionalist Muslims, but of fomenting unrest. No wonder. Sheih Bedreddin (died 1416), for instance, was both an unorthodox mystic ("There is no here and no hereafter. Everything is a single moment"), but, according to Idris of Bitlis, writing a century later, believed that:

> at a signal from the unseen world, at the head of his disciples, he would distribute the lands among his followers. Then the secrets of God's unity would prevail in the world of reality . . . His own latitudinarian sect would make things lawful.

Bedreddin's latitude included a readiness to ignore differences between Muslims and non-Muslims, and an openness to wine and music. A popular revolt by one of his disciples, Börklüce Mustafa, was put down by force of arms; Börklüce and his captured dervishes refused to profess a "renewal of faith" and were executed. Around the same period, Nesimi (?1340–?1418), poet and mystic and follower of Fadl Allah, was flayed alive because the Hurufis, the sect to which he belonged, suggested that Islam, Judaism, and Christianity would all soon be united. The Kizilbash, who embraced an extreme form of Shiism, were persecuted in the 1520s and 1530s. The poet Pir Sultan Abdal wrote: "I gave my heart, I declared my faith to 'Ali/I shall stand firm if they cut me in pieces/They called me a heretic and hanged me/Strange, for where is my sin?" The Kizilbash exiled themselves to Persia, the main home of Shiism. Throughout the early 16th century the Ottomans kept a close watch on forbidden literature brought to their lands from Iran.

The specifically religious aspects of heresy were, from time to time, attacked by puritans not dissimilar to their western European counterparts. Mehmed of Birgi (1522–73) swore that he would "defend the people with my pen and my tongue from what God has prohibited". Among his targets were ceremonies to commemorate the dead, and even the practice of shaking hands. More traditional elements among the 'ulama' (senior scholars) regarded as blasphemous the decoration of mosques and the chanting of the Qur'an. Conservative faqihs (jurists) would allow no practice that had been introduced since Muhammad's death and were violently opposed to any kind of song or dance. The encyclopedist and madrasa (higher education) teacher Ahmed Tash Köprülzade (1495–1561), on the other hand, believed that music and dancing were to be condemned only if they aroused worldly desires. He wrote: "God preserve us from those who show fanaticism in religion." For him each Muslim was free to join the religious school to which he was drawn, but it was irreligious to regard his own truth as the only truth or to accuse any other Muslim of atheism. More moderate counsels prevailed in 1656, after fanatics had planned a general "final solution" to heresy through a massacre of its practitioners; their leaders were exiled by the grand vizier Köprülür Mehmed (died 1661).

The censorship of painting was similarly intermittent. Mehmet II had not only introduced Renaissance art from western Europe into his palaces, he had even had his portrait painted by the Venetian Gentile Bellini. His son, Bayezid II (reigned 1481–1512), took a dim view of his inheritance. His father had "by the counsel of mischief-makers and hypocrites . . . infringed the law of the Prophet". On his succession, he sold the Italian pictures and had the erotic frescoes painted over. The Qur'an does not prohibit painting, but popular feeling has often led to its suppression. On the other hand, as in Iran, there developed a strong Ottoman tradition of miniature painting, and it was not until 1609 that the final frescoes were removed from the former Christian cathedral of Ayia Sophia in Istanbul.

Treatment of the new science in the Ottoman empire closely paralleled that taking place almost contemporaneously in western Europe. In 1580 the mufti of Istanbul incited a mob to destroy a new observatory in Istanbul a mere three years after it had been erected. The sultan Murad III (reigned 1574–95) regarded such things as a "bad omen" and a source of calamity. This was an attitude to scholarship that had already surfaced in the beheading of the molla (mullah) Lutfi in 1494. Mainstream tradition was far from hostile to scholarship as such. Those who served the Ottoman state were expected to be well-read in literature, language, law, history, and geography. Libraries were revered, often being placed in mosques, hospitals, and private houses; some 200,000 manuscripts survive. However, speculative thinkers were tolerated only rarely. The basis of knowledge was said to be already enshrined in tradition; all that was really needed was annotation and commentary. Philosophy was allowed – the great 11th-century theologian Abu Hamid al-Ghazali (1058–1111) had taught that logic and mathematics helped to reveal religious truth – but only as a preparation for theology. Ideas that could not be reconciled with the Qur'an were ruled out. In 1716 the head of the ulama in Istanbul ordered the confiscation of Ali Pasha's books; works from his collection devoted to philosophy, astronomy, or history were not to be bequeathed to libraries.

Finally, printing. In Islamic thinking the "men of the pen" are given equal precedence with "men of the sword" and "men of religion". This triad was at the heart of Ottoman administration. The art of the calligrapher was protected, in part for reasons of security: it was a closed profession, unlikely to take kindly to mechanical reproduction. Calligraphers could also claim to be able to provide copies of work speedily and at low cost. So much for the practical reasons for the late introduction of printing to the Islamic world. At a deeper level lay the religious objections. If the Qur'an was the word of God, it should be reproduced in the finest possible way, with pen and ink. The use of the printing press seemed blasphemous. A 16th-century ambassador of the Holy Roman emperor, Baron de Busbecq, wrote: "They hold that their scriptures, that is their sacred books, would no longer be scriptures if they were printed."

Thus, as the new invention was sweeping through Europe early in the 16th century, sultan Selim I was, in 1515, threatening death to anybody who made use of it. Interestingly,

however, and in keeping with the general tolerance of non-Islamic religions, Jews and Christians were allowed – up to a point – to use the new technology. *The Four Columns*, a Jewish legal work written in Hebrew, was printed by David and Samuel Nahmiaas in 1493. Armenian Christians established a press at Yenkapi, Istanbul, in 1567. This establishment had a short life, but the Armenians had a permanent press from the late 17th century. On the other hand, when a Greek press began to produce anti-Catholic and anti-Jewish publications in 1627, the Ottoman authorities ordered its destruction, after they had listened to complaints by the French ambassador.

At length, printing was authorized by sultan Ahmed III (reigned 1703–30). A treatise on the topic was put before the grand vizier by Ibrahim Müteferrik, a Unitarian who originated from Transylvania. He argued that Europeans were already printing Islamic books, and that the development of an indigenous press would promote general education and literacy. Despite the arguments of the traditionalists, who said that printing would be "dangerous to public order and to the conduct of religion", and a demonstration by the calligraphers, a fatwa (legal opinion) was issued allowing the printing of books on any nonreligious subject. A press was established at Ibrahim Müteferrik's house and the ball was set rolling in 1729 with an Arabic dictionary, a book of Ottoman history, and a Turkish grammar for the use of French students and traders.

DEREK JONES

Further Reading

Inalcık, Halil, *The Ottoman Empire: The Classical Age, 1300–1600*, London: Weidenfeld and Nicolson, and New York: Praeger, 1973
Mansel, Philip, *Constantinople: City of the World's Desire, 1453–1924*, London: John Murray, 1995; New York: St Martin's Press, 1996

1831–1920

The final 100 years of Ottoman rule were marked, on the one hand by a gradual loss of territory – Greece won its independence in 1829, Serbia, Moldavia, and Wallachia gained autonomy, and the empire lost its Syrian provinces – and, on the other hand, by the gradual dissemination of modernizing ideas: the period of *Tanzimat* (reform) between 1838 and 1876 and the attempted reassertion of the authoritarian sultanate under 'Abdülhamid II (reigned 1876–1909), culminating in its demise following the constitutional revolution of 1908.

The first newspaper in Ottoman Turkish, *Takvim-i Vekayi* (The Calendar of Events), was published in November 1831 during the reign of Mahmud II, on the sultan's own initiative; it was merely a mouthpiece for official policies. The first private Ottoman Turkish newspaper, *Tercüman-i Ahval* (The Interpreter of Conditions), published by Agah Efendi and Ibrahim Şinasi, was also the first periodical to be suspended (for two weeks) by the Ottoman government in 1860. Şinasi went on to publish *Tasvir-i Efkar* (Illustration of Opinions) which attacked (but quite moderately) Ottoman authoritarianism. The paper grew more radical under Namık Kemal, arguing for representative democracy. Irritated by the paper's inclusion of a scathing open letter from Mustafa Fazil in 1865, the Ottoman government sent Kemal into internal exile.

The Press Regulation of 1864, which also contained articles on a Bureau of Administration of Press Affairs (Matbuat Müdürlüğü), was the first extensive attempt to provide a legal framework for the control of the press. It effectively endorsed the French 1852 Press Law enacted by the regime of Louis Napoleon Bonaparte, which was not known for its liberality. Individual publications were now required to obtain a licence from the Ministry of Education for Ottoman citizens, and the Ministry of Foreign Affairs for resident foreigners. In addition, a list of press offences and punishments was provided. The definitions were vague: the censors effectively had the authority to ban practically anything they found inappropriate.

Censorship mechanisms started to function systematically a few years later. *Muhbir* (The Informer), first published in 1866, became the first victim, because of an article written by its editor, Ali Suavi, who would eventually become an important figure in the Young Ottoman movement. Although Suavi had disguised his identity by publishing the article as a letter from an anonymous reader, *Muhbir* was closed down for a month in 1867 following an order issued by the Ministry of Education on the basis of article 27 of the Press Regulation; this gave the state the authority to change the due punishment for certain offences to a maximum of a month's closure. *Muhbir* was said to be perpetrating "lies and false statements against the government which become an instrument to confuse minds". This statement became the formula for dealing with other "harmful" publications. As the threat to the "sick man of Europe" from various irredentist movements began to increase, the government tightened its control over the press. A case in point was the ordinance of the grand vizier Ali Pasha, sent to all newspapers shortly after the closure of *Muhbir*, giving the government the authority to punish any publication that was found harmful. A memorandum was issued in the official gazette on 15 October 1867, warning the periodicals that they should apply to the Press Bureau for inspection before publishing anything concerning official proceedings, and the promotion and replacement of officials, unless it was already found in the official gazette.

As control over the press tightened, some intellectuals voluntarily exiled themselves to Europe, most of them to Paris, thus carrying political opposition abroad. Ali Suavi, for instance, restarted the *Muhbir* in London on 31 August 1867. Namık Kemal resurfaced with *Hürriyet* (Freedom) in London. Ottoman periodicals published outside the empire eventually became indispensable weapons of the political opposition. Pamphlets were also prepared and sent to the Ottoman empire: this later turned into a political activity over which the authorities never obtained total control. The problem was recognized by the Ottoman state in 1875, when the Ministry of Education sent an order to all the provinces defining a new category of censorship: that of foreign publications. A licence had now to be obtained for each translated book published within the empire. In addition, imported publications, including literary and scientific books, became subject to the scrutiny of government-appointed inspectors and interpreters. The Ottoman opposition in Europe countered this new provision by smuggling banned material through foreign mail companies, which were exempt from inspection by Ottoman authorities due to the privileges extended to certain European countries. The government made several unsuccessful attempts to gain an agreement that would grant customs officials the authority to inspect "suspicious" packages, but this leeway was used by the opposition abroad right until the end of the Young Turk period.

Further repressive measures were introduced during the term of the grand vizier Mahmud Nedim Pasha in the early 1870s. In addition to preliminary inspection, a financial disincentive in the form of a stamp duty was introduced. However, the Ottoman public sphere entered an irreversible process of transformation during the last decades of the 19th century. Theatre and satirical magazines, for example, were accessible to a wide audience since they did not require "literacy" in the strict sense of the word. Namık Kemal's play *Vatan yahut Silistre* (Fatherland, or Silistre), which attracted a hitherto unseen enthusiasm, alarmed the authorities about the explosive potential of a literary work for "mobilizing the masses", and its author was exiled to Cyprus in 1873 along with the writers of the paper that he had been editing.

The satirical press – which emerged as possibly the most lively representative of political opposition – was frequently censored, and ultimately silenced under the reign of ʿAbdülhamid II (1876–1908). As well as light verse, limericks, and articles, these magazines made extensive use of caricatures that required only a basic level of literacy, and they held great potential for publicizing social, economic, and political issues. One such magazine, *Hayal* (Dream), frequently used protagonists of the Ottoman shadow puppet theatre *Karagöz* and *Hacıvat* to criticize a wide array of policies; this was, after all, the primary function of this traditional folk art. When this tradition was carried from the puppet theatre to an inexpensive satirical magazine with a wide readership, the authorities were quick to see its potential to influence public opinion. *Hayal* was frequently suspended, and it was eventually closed down during the reign of ʿAbdülhamid II.

ʿAbdülhamid II's autocracy began with the promulgation of the 1876 Constitution, based on the (liberal) Belgian model but sufficiently authoritarian as to allow the sultan considerable power to extend censorship. Yet the reign of ʿAbdülhamid was far from being the apex of retrogression in late Ottoman history. The reforms of the period in the fields of communication, transport, and, especially, education made possible the wave of opposition that followed. One feature of the Hamidian period's press policy was that there was no significant effort to lay out a legal framework for the description of press offences and due punishments. In theory, a modified version of the 1864 Press Regulation remained in force, and the only legal arrangement made during this period was the 1888 Law of Printing Presses. All political discussion was now banned, especially mention of liberalism, nationalism, and constitutionalism. Newspapers and periodicals filled their pages instead with articles about science and technology, history, geography, and literature, a roundabout way of introducing their readers to the outside world.

An intricate network was devised for the collection of information on public gatherings, dangerous publications, and even the activities of the Ottoman opposition abroad. This system spread the task of the censors across all parts of public administration, rather than designating a separate body within the state, rendering the definition of "harmful" at the discretion of all the sultan's loyal subjects, official and unofficial alike. Everyone had an incentive to prove loyalty to the sultan by reporting acts that might be considered violations of his authority. The reign of ʿAbdülhamid II, therefore, gained its notoriety as a period in which censorship was ubiquitous not always because of formal restrictions, but through the promotion of a hierarchical system based purely on personal allegiances and heightened loyalty to the sultan. Censorship under ʿAbdülhamid II became a self-generating mechanism based on an etiquette of unwritten rules, making self-censorship the most prominent form of control.

It is difficult to classify Hamidian censorship as either preliminary or punitive. Although both types were used, the real control mechanism was that the press had been rendered incapable of producing anything that was worth censoring. All the newspapers that survived this period were state-subsidized, which implied that they were essentially turned into instruments of the regime. To be subsidized by the regime, however, was no guarantee of avoiding punishment, and even the official gazette and the official printing house were occasionally shut down. Even spelling mistakes could be interpreted as hidden attempts to attack the sultan.

Political writings or literary works were not the only materials subject to censorship during this period. Practically anything that was printed – tram tickets, advertisements, or cognac labels – could be considered dangerous. The obsession with eliminating "bad" words from public usage was a result not so much of ʿAbdülhamid's personal supervision of the censorship mechanism as of his officials' overzealous efforts to please the sultan. In addition to politically charged terms such as "socialism", "nihilism", "freedom", or "democrat", the list of tacitly banned words included anything that had a potential for upsetting ʿAbdülhamid such as "nose" (his was unusually large).

ʿAbdülhamid II attempted to re-establish the traditional concept of sultanic legitimacy that required the formation of a body of officials and subjects whose only allegiance would be to the sultan. Methods used by the sultan to silence opposition included putting certain journalists on the palace's payroll, or purchasing the publications of opposition groups abroad.

Abroad, the organized opposition was growing in coherence. The Young Turk revolution of 1908 brought the *ancien régime* to a close by reactivating the constitution of 1876 and opening the way for elections. An unprecedented atmosphere of freedom of expression characterized the first few months. However, hopes of a liberal parliamentary regime were very soon shattered, and Young Turk rule eventually proved itself to be at least as repressive as the autocracy it had overthrown.

The Party of Union and Progress (UP), emerged as the sole political power after the first elections. Broadly, opposition to UP consisted of two camps: moderate liberals, who supported the decentralization of the empire, and the conservatives, who were fundamentally against constitutionalism and demanded the suspension of the parliament on religious grounds. The festive climate of liberty was checked when religious conservatives staged demonstrations demanding the closure of theatres and the prohibition of photography. The UP aggravated the situation by demonstrating its determination to hold power exclusively. The assassination of Hasan Fehmi, the editor of an anti-UP paper, on 6 April 1909 sparked a counter-revolution on 13 April 1909, which was crushed by the Macedonia-based Hareket Ordusu (Action Army).

The abortive counter-revolution sharpened UP's intolerance towards opposition, and until 1911, when the opposition participated in the elections as a unified front, the UP ruled as the single authority. Another anti-UP journalist was killed on 9 June 1910. Although the assassin was never caught, it was widely believed that a Unionist gunman was responsible. Opposition to the UP centred around Hürriyet ve Itilaf Fırkası (Party of Freedom and Understanding, HI), also referred to as the Entente Libérale. Although HI's rights to propagate its agenda as a political party were guaranteed under law, party members and newspaper boys who sold its papers were harassed by UP's nonregistered "volunteer" corps in more than a few instances. The activities of HI's political clubs in the provinces were also placed under close police scrutiny.

The unified opposition against the UP took over the cabinet in July 1912, backed by a paramilitary group named Halaskar Zabitan (Saviour Officials). During the brief interval that they were in power, the same policy of repression was turned against the UP Several journalists, especially those known to have been pro-UP, were persecuted, their newspapers closed down, and some of the leading Unionists were forced to leave for western Europe. During the same period, an international crisis sprang up in the Balkans that resulted in the first Balkan War, and the disastrous circumstances allowed the Unionists to re-establish their authority.

A coup d'état led by the military wing of the UP brought the party back into full power on 23 January 1913. It remained in power until the end of World War I. After the assassination of the grand vizier Mahmud Şevket Pasha on 15 June 1913 by a supporter of HI, a reaction followed and the opposition was totally driven off the political scene. The outbreak of World War I aggravated the situation, and the military, who had been perpetually looming behind the Ottoman state's brief experience of multiparty parliamentarism, took complete control after 1914.

Between 1908 and 1914 the general policy towards the press did not include pre-publication censorship, which was considered anticonstitutional; the legal limit for pre-publication control was the licence requirement for periodicals and newspapers. The first Ottoman Press Law, which remained in effect until the end of the empire, was promulgated under the Unionist administration on 29 July 1909. In accordance with the state's increasing concern with regulating the flow of information – especially after the outbreak of the Balkan wars – "temporary" provisions supplemented the Press Law of 1909, giving it a restrictive character.

The most striking character of press censorship policy during this period was that it targeted circulation rather than production. It was relatively easy to control publication within the empire, but imported publications constituted a major challenge to state authority. The UP introduced two major legal/administrative devices for their regulation. The first one was article 35 of the Press Law, which required a ruling by the Council of Ministers for banning the importation of a specific publication. The second device was the formation of the General Management of Press Affairs, created by the merger of the separate administrations of Internal and Foreign Press Affairs. The essential task of this bureau, which was answerable to the Ministry of the Interior, was to estimate the "harmfulness" of contents when close inspection of a foreign publication was required. The Ministry of the Interior had total authority for controlling the press under the Young Turk regime, in significant contrast to the preceding period, when the authorities of different departments of state had overlapped.

The publications most frequently banned during this period were the nationalist periodicals of various ethnic groups; the conservative Islamist press; publishing organs of the political opposition groups; and publications offending religious feelings, Muslim and non-Muslim alike. Censorship under the Unionists had the exclusive purpose of eliminating political deviation, that is, practically any agenda that differed from that of the UP. Precisely because of the highly bureaucratized nature of the censorship process during this period, effective control was almost impossible to attain, and in most cases the publications in question had reached their destinations by the time a banning decision was issued.

From the outbreak of World War I in 1914 until the collapse of the empire, many forms of censorship of the press, literature, and theatre were in effect. The number of newspapers published within the empire had been around 70 before the war but had dropped to fewer than 10 by 1916. Although the circulation and number of papers gradually grew again, returning to their normal levels in 1918, the press had lost the character of an influential popular institution that it had started to acquire during the constitutionalist period.

In the immediate aftermath of World War I, when the Ottoman empire met its final defeat, the UP was disbanded and the parliament dissolved. Although censorship was nominally abolished on 11 June 1918, it was re-established after the conclusion of the British-administered Mudros Armistice of 31 October, while in Anatolia Turkish nationalists waged a war of independence.

İPEK K. YOSMAOĞLU

Further Reading

Berkes, Niyazi, *The Development of Secularism in Turkey*, new edition, New York: Routledge, 1998
Criss, Nur Bilge, *Istanbul under Allied Occupation, 1918–1923*, Leiden: Brill, 1999
Deringil, Selim, "Legitimacy Structures in the Ottoman State: The Reign of Abdülhamid II," *International Journal of Middle East Studies*, 23 (1991): 345–59
Hanioğlu, Şükrü, *The Young Turks in Opposition*, New York: Oxford University Press, 1995
Iskit, Server, *Türkiye'de Matbuât İdâreleri ve Politikalar* (Press Administrations and Policies in Turkey), Ankara: Başvekalet Basın ve Yayın Umum Müdürlüğü Yayınları, 1943
Kushner, David, *The Rise of Turkish Nationalism*, London: Frank Cass, 1977: chapter 1
Tunaya, Tarık Zafer, *Türkiye'de Siyasal Partiler* (Political Parties in Turkey), vol. 1, Istanbul: Hürriyet Vakfı Yayınları, 1984
Zürcher, Erik J., *Turkey: A Modern History*, London and New York: Tauris, 1993

GRAHAM OVENDEN
British photographer, 1943–

The first of Ovenden's major areas of artistic achievement is represented by the body of photographs which he began work on as a teenager in 1957 and continued with intermittently until 1964. These images of the East End of London, recorded with a box camera, show the streets and the street life, which had hardly changed in a century, but which were now on the verge of being swept away. Ovenden not only described his subjects among the buildings and people, but also captured their spirit, including an intimate sense of the ways in which children of that period occupied the streets in parallel with, but separately from, the adult world.

Then there is the work which Ovenden produced from about 1975 as a founder member of the Brotherhood of Ruralists, which owes its ethos both to the Pre-Raphaelite Brotherhood and also to the Brotherhood of Ancients, of whom William Blake was a member. In part, Ovenden's contribution was in the form of what might, albeit inadequately, be called realist or romantic paintings; he also contributed photographs realized by processes which were rediscoveries and reinterpretations of the oldest aspects of the photographic medium. His subject matter, for both the paintings and the photographs, tended to divide between landscape and portraiture; the principal subjects for Ovenden's portraiture were young girls. His whole body of work is underpinned by art and literary historical scholarship, and he has a special interest in Lewis Carroll and *Alice in Wonderland* studies.

Ovenden, his family, and their close friends espouse a philosophy which has its root in the delight in and respect for the physical and spiritual human body enunciated by William Blake. However, there is another world with a different view, tainted by the remnants of puritanism, which is fearful of sexuality and any other aspect of life that is resistant to prescription and regulation. This world impacted upon the Ovendens when the police, who were investigating the photographer Ron Oliver and the artist Brian Partridge, discovered that they were friends and colleagues of Graham Ovenden. They then considered Ovenden's work, and, because some of it involved images of nude children, they assumed that they could bring charges under the Protection of Children Act 1978 against the making and possession of indecent images of children.

Early in the morning of 10 March 1993, Ovenden's house was raided by a number of officers, some of whom were members of the London Metropolitan Police Obscene Publications Squad, who had travelled from London to participate. Of the many items thrown into dustbin sacks, some photographs were the property of national and regional museums, others were photographs of the royal family, and yet others were items from Ovenden's collection of *Titanic* memorabilia. All but one of the items were returned, up to two years later, some having been damaged by what Ovenden considers to be deliberate negligence. He further alleges that pieces of his work seized from Partridge were destroyed by the police; certainly, they have never been returned, and so represent both aesthetic and pecuniary loss.

OVENDEN: One of the nude studies of children taken by Ovenden which were confiscated by the London Metropolitan Police Obscene Publications Squad from Ovenden's home in March 1993. His collaboration with the artist Brian Partridge and the photographer Ron Oliver on an *Alice in Wonderland* exhibition alerted the police to his subject matter, which they assumed would lead to an indictment under the Protection of Children Act 1978. Ovenden remained on bail for two years after the raid but no further action was taken and most of his work was returned.
© G.S. Ovenden.

Much police effort was put into interviewing the now young adult models who had worked with Ovenden. Detailed reports of the interviews, and some independent interviews conducted later to cross-check the facts of the case, show the use of leading questions and frank intimidation, to the extent that it might be thought that the police were attempting to suborn the witnesses. Ovenden believes they had the impression that they were on the track of a paedophile "ring", because Ovenden, Oliver, and Partridge had collaborated on an *Alice* exhibition which had travelled internationally.

Ovenden remained on police bail for approximately two years before he was advised that no further action would be taken. During that time, he and his supporters took every opportunity to expose the legislative and judicial defects that had led up to his situation. One of the most significant events in this anti-censorship campaign was the Channel 4 film *For the Sake of the Children*, screened during 1997 in their "Films of Fire" series.

PHILIP STOKES

Writings

Editor, *Victorian Children*, 1971
Editor, *Victorian Erotic Photography*, London: Academy Editions, 1973
Satirical Poems and Others, 1983
The Marble Mirror, 1984
States of Grace, 1992
The Obscene Publications Squad versus Art: Scotland Yard Declares Child Nudity a Crime and Raids Artist/Photographer Graham Ovenden, with Rhona Rimmer, Philip Stokes, and A.D. Coleman, 1994
Street Children, 1998

Further Reading

Arwas, Victor *et al.*, *Graham Ovenden*, London: Academy Editions, and New York: St Martin's Press, 1987
Bellos, Alex, "In the Eye of the Beholder?", *The Sunday Telegraph* (2 January 1994)
Elliott, Valerie, "Artist Hounded over Nude Child Pictures", *The Sunday Telegraph* (12 November 1995)
Gale, Iain, "Portrait of the Artist as an Accused Man", *The Independent II* (15 February 1994)
Newnham, David and Chris Townshend, "Pictures of Innocence", *The Guardian Weekend* (13 January 1996)
O'Toole, Laurence, *Pornocopia: Porn, Sex, Technology and Desire*, 2nd edition, London: Serpent's Tail, 1999
Stokes, Philip, "When Indecency Is in the Eye of the Beholder", *LM*, 108 (March 1998)
Webb, Peter, *The Erotic Arts*, London: Secker and Warburg, and Boston: New York Graphic Society, 1975

OVID (Publius Ovidius Naso)
Roman poet, 43 BCE–17 CE

ARS AMATORIA (Art of Love)
Poem, c.1 BCE

The *Ars amatoria* is a didactic poem that was published in Rome at the end of the 1st century BCE. Despite its title it is not primarily a manual of sexual techniques (but see 2.703–32, 3.769–808). Written in three books, the poem instructs prospective lovers in the techniques of courtship and the plot-

ting of erotic intrigue. Books 1 and 2 instruct men how to select, meet, and seduce women; book 3 purports to give comparable advice to women, but the real beneficiaries remain the men. Ovid uses figures from Greek mythology and Roman history to explore the advantages and pitfalls of certain kinds of amatory behaviour. These figures from the legendary past offer models of a general sort. Ovid's intended students, however, are contemporary Romans, and Ovid provides his would-be lovers with "dos" and "don'ts".

In 8 CE Caesar Augustus banished Ovid to Tomis (now Constanta in Romania) on the Black Sea. Despite public and private pleading, neither Augustus nor his successor Tiberius were appeased, so the foremost and most urbane Roman poet of his day spent the remainder of his life at the far edge of the Roman frontier. Of the cause of exile (technically a relegation, since Ovid kept his property and estate), the poet himself says that there were two charges brought against him, a "poem" and a "mistake" (*carmen et error* [*Tristia* 2.207]). The offending "poem" is generally thought to have been his *Ars amatoria*, but some believe it was *Metamorphoses*. There is scant evidence about either charge and what we do have is difficult to interpret: most comes from Ovid's poetry itself, or from authors writing long after the fact.

Why this poem, if it was indeed the reason for Ovid's exile, could have so offended Augustus becomes intelligible in view of the moral and political climate of early imperial Rome. One of Augustus' aims throughout his career was the restoration of Roman morality. As part of his programme to encourage marriage and procreation among the upper classes, he passed, in 18 BCE, a law that made adultery a criminal offence (it had previously been considered a private injury). Ovid and Augustus would have agreed that poetry should be useful; but instead of instructing Roman youth about how to reverence the past and to be worthy of Rome, Ovid wrote a treatise that flew in the face of imperial mandates towards moral living.

Throughout the *Ars amatoria* one can detect subtle reminders of the emperor who would so deplore the subject of Ovid's poetry. Ovid seems to poke fun at Augustus' law on adultery when he reminds his readers that they do not get into bed "by order of the law" (2.157). Similarly, when advising husbands to keep an eye on their wives, Ovid reminds them that the "laws, leader [i.e. Augustus], and decency command this" (3.614). The poet repeatedly recommends as meeting places public buildings that have been refurbished by the imperial family. Pointing out that the theatre is a particularly advantageous spot for hunting women (2.89–134), Ovid digresses into

the story that Romulus, the legendary founder of Rome, forcibly procured women for the fledgling city while they were awaiting a theatrical performance. To associate moral laxity with Augustus' mythic "ancestor" was hardly calculated to please the emperor.

Adultery was in any case a touchy subject for Augustus. In 2 BCE his daughter Julia was alleged to have been involved in an adulterous affair. Shortly thereafter, Ovid circulated books 1 and 2 of the *Ars amatoria*. In 8 CE Augustus' grand-daughter, also named Julia, was convicted of adultery and exiled. It was then that Augustus sent Ovid into exile. The nature of the "mistake" which brought this about is a matter of considerable debate, but could easily have involved Ovid's unwitting complicity in the scandal. Whatever the specific offence, Ovid had not acted in a manner punishable in a court of law, but Augustus could banish him on his own authority (*Tristia* 2.131–32); it is possible that the emperor hoped by this act to divert attention from the scandal in his household.

Ovid's works were banned from public libraries, and it was imprudent to display personal copies (*Tristia* iii.1.59–74; *Epistulae ex Ponto* i.1.12). It was the beginning of long centuries of censorship. The *Ars amatoria* was among the books burnt by Savonarola in 1497, and was on the Roman Index of Prohibited Books from 1564. Christopher Marlowe's translation was destroyed at the Stationers Hall, London, in 1599 and the book was among the books proscribed in the American Library Association catalogue for 1904; it was still being banned by the US Customs in 1929.

G.M. SOTER

Writings

The Erotic Poems, translated by Peter Green, 1982
Ovid in English, edited by Christopher Martin, 1998

Further Reading

Mack, Sara, *Ovid*, New Haven, Connecticut: Yale University Press, 1988
Syme, Ronald, *History in Ovid*, Oxford: Clarendon Press, and New York: Oxford University Press, 1978
Thibault, John C., *The Mystery of Ovid's Exile*, Berkeley: University of California Press, 1964

OZ

British magazine, 1967–73

Oz was launched in Britain in January 1967 by Richard Neville, who had published a student magazine under the same name in his home town of Sydney, Australia, in 1963. Published irregularly but generally once a month, and achieving an average circulation of 30,000 copies, it became the chief organ of the British underground press movement until its demise in 1973.

The underground press movement itself can be seen to have originated in the counterculture of the 1950s, when, for the first time on any significant scale, greater access to higher education and improved provision of social security provided the financial means for many to "drop out". Middle-class protesters began to espouse, on the one hand, the intellectual

utopianism of the Beatniks and, on the other, the more radical ideologies of the New Left, including its opposition to political totalitarianism and to escalation in the numbers and firepower of nuclear weapons. During the late 1960s, magazines such as *Oz*, *International Times/IT* (1966–72), and *Black Dwarf* (1968–70) not only capitalized on such anti-establishment ideas but, influenced by Californian "flower power", also began to ally it to the drug-inspired culture of the hippies.

The editorial views and content of *Oz* were in permanent flux throughout its short life. In fact, it was a sensitive barometer of the counterculture, producing, for example, "psychedelic" issues (3 and 4) in 1967, as the hippie movement surfaced, and an *Angry Oz* (37) in the aftermath of the Angry Brigade's bombing campaigns of 1971. While political manifestos and passionate incitements to action appeared in numerous issues, particularly after 1968, the editors often took an irreverent and self-disparaging approach to such material. Following a rather bombastic article on the significance of the inevitability of revolution in *Oz* 19, they added an ironic coda "If the revolution means prose like this, let's LOSE!"

After a rather sober start, *Oz* also gained notoriety for its graphic invention and the format of the magazine constantly changed, sometimes appearing as a fold-out poster ("Plant a Flower Child", *Oz* 5) and at other times as a long, thin publication printed on glossy paper or in a larger, square format on newsprint. This playfulness in design could often draw fire from its own readers: Martin Sharp's regular use of day-glo colours and typographic overprinting led one correspondent to complain, "Because there is a clash of colours and it strains one's eyes to read . . . I passed on an article which I most likely should have enjoyed".

At the same time, Neville and the other owners of *Oz* were keen to encourage more democratic values in publishing. They thus eroded the usual capitalist division between producers and consumers by intermittently handing editorship of the magazine over to different groups.

It was this approach that led to the evolution of the "School Kids Issue" (28), containing articles and artwork by 20 teenage readers, and to the *Oz* obscenity trial in 1971. This issue was, for the most part, a rather jejune affair, containing insipid pieces about conditions and prejudice at the producers' schools. A few images and articles prepared by the guest editors, however, tackled the subject of sex in an uncompromising manner. Thus, the cover depicted scenes of lesbian sex and bestiality; a cartoon strip represented a priapic Rupert the Bear attempting to break the hymen of Robert Crumb's character Gipsy Granny; and another illustration, captioned "School Atrocities", portrayed a sexually aroused schoolmaster abusing a male pupil.

Although *Oz* had always been intent on testing the tolerance of the "permissive society", its own sexual politics were more often than not compromised and sometimes naive. "Cunt Power" *Oz* (19), edited by Germaine Greer, may be seen as a good example. The magazine, indeed, gradually became the victim of its own ideology. Consequently, on the strength of the content of the "School Kid's Issue" the magazine's editors, Richard Neville, Jim Anderson, and Felix Dennis, were indicted for corrupting the morals of children and young persons.

The *Oz* trial lasted for six weeks in the summer of 1971 and was presided over by judge Michael Argyle. Neville defended himself but was advised by a young Australian lawyer, Geoffrey Robertson; John Mortimer QC represented Anderson and Dennis; while the prosecution was led by Brian Leary. In turn, many liberal-minded individuals from Britain's academic and artistic communities came forward to testify on the magazine's behalf, including university professors such as Hans Eysenck, Richard Wollheim, and Ronald Dworkin; the writer Mervyn Jones; the artist Feliks Topolski; and the jazz musician, art critic, and Surrealist George Melly. Thus, the *Oz* trial became a test case for defining what constituted obscenity as opposed to art. Mervyn Jones, for example, invoked the strong language used in the many novels, newspapers, and plays that had not been arraigned, while Feliks Topolski referred to the sexual

content of Picasso's later etchings and Gillray's satires. The trial also served to demonstrate the discrepancies in cultural experience between different age groups. Two examples will suffice here to illustrate this point. After he had handed various documents to the jury before the trial began, Judge Argyle stated, "Don't worry at the moment if you don't understand them all. Nor do I. But as the case proceeds . . . no doubt we'll get a grip on it by the end." Later, as Leary was asking the mother of Vivian Berger, a 16-year-old boy who had contributed to "School Kids *Oz*" under the pseudonym Viv Kylastron, whether her son had been to see the musical *Hair*, the judge inquired "Is *Hair* an article?"

The three editors pleaded not guilty to the five charges that had been levelled against them: namely, conspiracy to corrupt the minds and morals of young children and other young persons; responsibility for the publication between 1 May 1970 and 8 June 1970 of *Oz* no. 28; the circulation by post of several indecent or obscene articles from the same; and the possession of both indecent and obscene articles and copies of *Oz* no. 28 for financial gain. After a difficult and fractious hearing, in which much was made of Rupert the Bear's genitalia ("Why is Rupert the Bear equipped with a large organ?", Leary inquired

Oz: Cover of the notorious "School Kids Issue" of *Oz*: its publication in 1970 led to the prosecution of its editors, Richard Neville, Jim Anderson, and Felix Dennis, on charges of conspiracy and obscenity. Neville, Anderson, and Dennis received fines and jail sentences but charges were later quashed on appeal after a public outcry.

of Edward De Bono; "What size do you think would be natural?" was the reply), the jury retired and returned twice – the first time to query the definition of obscenity and the second because they could not reach a unanimous verdict. Eventually, they found the defendants not guilty on the charge of conspiracy, but returned majority verdicts of guilty on the four remaining charges.

Neville was given a sentence of 15 months imprisonment and a recommendation for deportation back to Australia; Anderson got 12 months; and Dennis got nine months. Afterwards, the judge was burned in effigy. The sentences were quashed on appeal in October 1971, after Lord Widgery had pointed out that the obscenity could actually repel a reader rather than cause him to engage in it himself.

It is commonly believed that the trial was responsible for the demise of Oz. More realistically, however, we have to take into account the fact that sales of the magazine had been dwindling anyway. Its chronic financial crisis was exacerbated by the recession in the British economy during the early 1970s, which hit the underground press hard by increasing the cost of paper and diminishing its revenue from advertisers.

Home Office Papers published on 13 November 1999 have revealed that detective chief inspector George Fenwick, who was the head of the Metropolitan police's obscene publications squad in 1971, had used Oz as a stooge to deflect attention from police involvement in the Soho porn industry. Following an enquiry set up by the then home secretary, Reginald Maudling, systemic corruption at the heart of the Metropolitan's "dirty squad" was uncovered and Fenwick was sentenced to 10 years' imprisonment for accepting bribes from seven porn merchants.

PAUL JOBLING

Further Reading

Neville, Richard, *Play Power*, London: Jonathan Cape, and New York: Random House, 1970

Neville, Richard, *Hippie Hippie Shake: The Dreams, the Trips, the Trials, the Love-Ins, the Screw-Ups – the Sixties*, London: Bloomsbury, 1995

Palmer, Tony, *The Trials of Oz*, London: Blond and Briggs, 1971

P

PACIFISM
The example of Britain during World War I

The armoury of the Official Press Bureau and the Defence of the Realm Act (DORA, 1914) was applied in Britain with special zeal against any organization which opposed World War I for whatever reason. Some of these organizations were founded on religious or conscientious objection; others were based on political or socio-economic considerations. Peace movements had been gaining strength in Europe throughout the 19th century, the Society of Friends (Quakers) prominent among the leaders. The arms race and the rise of jingoism around the turn of the century engendered another form of protest on the grounds that, in terms of the national interest and as an instrument of policy, war defeated its own objects. Little attempt was made by the authorities to distinguish between these groups.

At the start of the war the most prominent of the dissenting organizations in Britain, and the targets of the most systematic surveillance and harassment, were the Union of Democratic Control (UDC), the Independent Labour Party (ILP), the No Conscription Fellowship (NCF), the National Council for Civil Liberties (NCCL), the Fellowship of Reconciliation (FoR), and the Women's International League (WIL), although these were by no means the only ones. The UDC was formed in August 1914 as a pressure group to try to secure a more democratic control over foreign policy in future and to bring about peace by negotiation at the earliest opportunity. The ILP was the only political party opposed to war both in principle and in practice. The NCF was formed as a support organization for men of military age "not prepared to take a combatant's part" in the war. The FoR was a primarily religious movement, and the WIL, as its name suggests, primarily a women's peace movement. The NCCL had evolved from an earlier organization, the National Council Against Conscription; when conscription was introduced in May 1916 the NCCL turned its attention to civil liberties, notably the treatment of conscientious objectors (over 16,000 of whom were registered) in prison, and to the threat posed to freedom of speech in the powers taken by the government.

Police informers regularly attended the meetings of such organizations and in some cases infiltrated them. Under Regulation 51 of DORA the police had the power, among others, to raid the premises and presses which printed pacifist literature, to confiscate it, and, when they could get a court order to do so, destroy it and break up the press. The state, it appeared, was even more afraid of the written than it was of the spoken word. After the introduction of conscription in 1916 chief constables were instructed to refer all suspect literature to the relevant local Authorized Competent Military Authorities (ACMAs), all of whom wrote weekly intelligence summaries on the basis of police reports and forwarded them to MI5. The police also wrote their own regular summaries for the Home Office on "Anti-Recruiting and Peace Proposals".

In the spring of 1917 anti-war feeling was growing and protest becoming audible. The government reacted by informing the Nobel Peace Prize Committee that no individual or organization involved in any branch of the peace movement in Britain should be considered for an award, and by setting up its own pro-war propaganda organization, the War Aims Committee. The dividing line between pacifist and socialist propaganda was further eroded by fear of the contagion of the Russian Revolution. In the autumn of 1917 the head of the Special Branch was asked to undertake an investigation of the suspect organizations in the hope of finding evidence that foreign money or "German gold" was supporting them. Some 30 premises were raided but no evidence was found, and not a single prosecution followed. What did follow, however, in November 1917 was DORA Regulation 27c.

This regulation required all pamphlets, from whatever source, to be submitted to the Press Bureau for approval at least 72 hours before printing, publication, or distribution, and to carry a stamp showing that this had been done. But it resulted in a storm of protest in which journalists and editors, members of parliament, and trade-union leaders were united. Regulation 27c was condemned as "the assassination of opinion", "a very important modification of our liberties", with constitutional implications which went far beyond any acceptable consideration of the influence of pacifist or socialist ideas. But the regulation was never withdrawn and DORA remained in force until 1920, although the police began to use their powers under it more sparingly in 1918. Pacifist literature struck at the heart of the government's foreign policy and in the period between the end of the war and the repeal of the act the Home Office continued to find regulation 27c useful against "seditious leaflets and pamphlets". Between August 1914 and August 1920 political censorship in Britain had, in effect, the force of law.

TANIA ROSE

Further Reading

Angell, Norman, *The Great Illusion: A Study of the Relation of Military Power in Nations to Their Economic and Social Advantage*, London: Heinemann, and New York: Putnam, 1910

Brockway, Fenner, *Inside the Left: Thirty Years of Platform, Press, Prison and Parliament*, London: Allen and Unwin, 1942

Brook, Peter, *Pacifism in Europe to 1914*, Princeton, New Jersey: Princeton University Press, 1971

Bussey, Gertrude and Margaret Tims, *Pioneers for Peace: Women's International League for Peace and Freedom, 1915–1965*, 2nd edition, London: WILPF, 1980

Ceadel, Martin, *Pacifism in Britain, 1914–1945: The Defining of a Faith*, Oxford: Clarendon Press, 1980

Crosby, G.R., *Disarmament and Peace in British Politics, 1914–1919*, Cambridge, Massachusetts: Harvard University Press, 1957

Kennedy, Thomas C., *The Hound of Conscience: History of the No-Conscription Fellowship, 1914–1918*, Fayetteville: University of Arkansas Press, 1981

Knock, Thomas J., *To End All Wars: Woodrow Wilson and the Quest for a New World Order*, New York: Oxford University Press, 1992

Martin, Laurence W., *Peace without Victory: Woodrow Wilson and the British Liberals*, New Haven, Connecticut: Yale University Press, 1958

Robbins, Keith, *The Abolition of War: The "Peace Movement" in Britain, 1914–1919*, Cardiff: University of Wales Press, 1976

Swanwick, Helena M., *Builders of Peace, Being Ten Years' History of the Union of Democratic Control*, London: Swarthmore Press, 1924; New York: Garland, 1973

Swartz, Marvin, *The Union of Democratic Control in British Politics during the First World War*, Oxford: Clarendon Press, 1971

Vellacott, Jo, *Bertrand Russell and the Pacifists in the First World War*, New York: St Martin's Press, and Hassocks, Sussex: Harvester Press, 1980

Wallis, Jill, *Valiant for Peace: A History of the Fellowship of Reconciliation, 1914–1919*, London: Fellowship of Reconciliation, 1992

HEBERTO PADILLA
Cuban poet, 1932–2000

In 1968 the award of the Casa de las Américas prize to Heberto Padilla for his volume of poetry *Fuera del juego* (Out of the Game), was met with stony disapproval by the Cuban government and the Cuban Writers Union (UNEAC). Early in 1971, Padilla was arrested, imprisoned, and, possibly, tortured, before being released to make a humiliating recantation to UNEAC in front of reporters and television crews. His "self-criticism", one day before an important congress on culture and education was to be opened, was intended as a deliberate and considered signal to the artists and intellectuals of Cuba that their relationship with the state was about to change.

Ten years earlier, in a speech at a gathering in the National Library, "Words to the Intellectuals", Fidel Castro, the Cuban head of state, had coined the slogan: "Within the Revolution, everything, outside the Revolution, nothing". This ambiguous phrase seemed to indicate that Castro saw intellectuals as having a special role to play. The regime had already, in 1960, clashed with the group identified with the cultural supplement *Lunes de revolución*, some of whom had produced the short film *PM*, which the state had banned as morally reprehensible for its portrayal of "bohemian" lifestyles in prerevolutionary Cuba. By the mid-1960s the condemnation of homosexuality had been added to the general official condemnation of "petit-bourgeois" lifestyles, presumably because it seemed to indicate a measure of individual independence of mind. At the same time, Cuba was beginning to feel internationally isolated as the US government tightened its siege. The country's growing absorption into the Soviet sphere threatened to lose Cuba some important friends; intellectuals might perhaps win support from international cultural circles. Casa de las Américas was one vehicle through which this was to be achieved. Writers and artists, Padilla among them, were despatched to Cuba's embassies to fly the revolutionary flag. The organization also employed international panels to award prizes to writers and artists in several categories.

Within the Communist world, the timing of Padilla's award could hardly have been less propitious: 1968 was the year of the invasion of Czechoslovakia by the forces of the Warsaw Pact, snuffing out the "Prague Spring". The Executive Committee of UNEAC took particular exception to a sequence of poems in *Fuera del juego*, "The Iron Beech Tree", in which Padilla criticized the state of Communism in Cuba and elsewhere in the world. Thus, for example, "Instructions on How to Enter a New Society" (as translated by John Butt):

One: be an optimist.
Two: be discreet, correct, obedient.
(Do well at sports – all of them.)
And, most of all, move
like all the other members:
one step forward, and
one (or two) steps back:
but never stop cheering.

The published book contained a critical preface by UNEAC condemning the author for his "ambiguity" and "antihistorical attitudes", and warning against "the presence among us of secret counterrevolutionaries who propose to cause the same problems here as in Czechoslovakia".

One reaction to this preface came from the Cuban novelist and essayist Guillermo Cabrera Infante, who had been a friend of Padilla's and was now an exile in Britain, having become disillusioned with the revolution. His article in the Buenos Aires magazine *Primera Plana* (Front Page) was clearly meant, in part, as a gesture of support for Padilla and others like him who had remained in the country:

The latest news shows that Padilla is now in a position in which every intelligent and honest person living in the Communist world finds himself, that of a spiritual exile who has only three choices before him: to opt for opportunism and demagogy by making a political recantation; jail; or genuine exile.

One can well understand that Padilla might have been irritated at such comments from one who was now removed from the action, but his response could have been written by a party ideologue and, if it was not, it certainly revealed the pressure he was now under to be "discreet, correct, obedient". Cabrera Infante, he claimed, had forfeited the right to speak about the progress of the Cuban revolution: "shirking responsibility, he renounces history; he has accepted the rules of the game. Instead of violent social change, he chooses irresponsibility, uncommitted placidity." Consciously or not, Padilla echoed Castro's original adage, but gave it an ominous twist: "For the revolutionary writer there is only one alternative: revolution or nothing".

Padilla's arrest came two years later, on 20 March 1971. It provoked the first indication that those intellectuals outside Cuba who had been well disposed to the Cuban revolution were beginning to have doubts, when 54 of them, including Hans Magnus Enzensberger, Carlos Fuentes, Juan Goytisolo, Jean-Paul Sartre, and Mario Vargas Llosa, wrote immediately to Fidel Castro:

> The use of repressive methods against intellectuals and writers who have exercised their right to criticize within the revolution can only have deeply negative repercussions among the anti-imperialist forces of the whole world, especially those in Latin America for all of whom the Cuban revolution is a symbol and a banner."

Padilla was released on 28 April, only to make a humiliating series of "confessions" to UNEAC the following day:

> I have discredited and defamed the revolution to Cubans and foreigners. I have gone ridiculously far in my mistakes and counterrevolutionary activities ... I acted against and harmed the revolution. I was much more concerned with my intellectual and literary importance than with the importance of the revolution.

The poems in *Fuera del juego* were, he said, "defeatist in spirit ... full of bitterness and pessimism". More followed, in a long litany of self-recrimination. Padilla even spoke of the security policemen who had interrogated him as "very intelligent people ... much more intelligent than I am".

On 30 April, in a speech to the National Congress of Education and Culture, Castro made a clear reference to the 54 signatories, whom he labelled "foreign bourgeois intellectuals":

> In Paris, London, Rome, West Berlin, and New York, the Pharisees find the best climate for their ambiguities, hesitations, and miseries generated by the colonial culture that they accept and profess. Among revolutionary peoples they will meet only the contempt that traitors and fugitives deserve.

The concluding document of the congress is reminiscent of those of the Soviet writers' congresses of 1928 and 1931, which enshrined "socialist realism" as the one approved cultural ideology. Not only should artists "serve the masses", they should also desist from the propagation of "snobbery, extravagance, homosexuality, and other social aberrations".

The parallels with the USSR were not lost on the 54 signatories, who now wrote an open letter to the Cuban leader that was published in the French newspaper *Le Monde*:

> We expect you in Cuba to avoid the dogmatic obscurantism, the cultural xenophobia, and the repressive system that Stalinism imposed on socialist countries ... The contempt for human dignity that presumes to force a man to accuse himself, in a ridiculous manner, of the worst kind of treachery and depravity does not alarm us just because it is a writer who is involved, but because any Cuban comrade – peasant, worker, technician or intellectual – might also fall victim to such violence and humiliation.

For many foreign intellectuals, the Padilla affair was the breaking point: they publicly disassociated themselves from the Cuban revolution. The Peruvian novelist Mario Vargas Llosa was the first to do so. He was predictably denounced as a tool of imperialism and a reactionary.

Padilla himself, clearly still acting under orders, replied to the 54 in much the same terms as he had used in responding to Cabrera Infante three years earlier:

> While we are concerned with work, study, and the plans that are transforming our country from one day to the next, you are concerned with aesthetics, Paris gossip, and the vain theorizing that led to my most hateful defect, and that you represent to the maximum degree.

Nonetheless, Padilla spent the next 10 years seeking permission to follow Cabrera Infante into exile before he was finally allowed to go. His subsequent career was predictably bitter and his politics, equally predictably, moved to the right.

The Padilla affair was important as an example of the lengths to which writers have sometimes had to go, in this case, perhaps, just to survive. Padilla's confession echoed, among others, that of the Soviet composer Dmitrii Shostakovich, who had in Stalin's time made his reply to the regime's "just criticism" of his Fourth Symphony with the more easily digestible Fifth. Shostakovich, however, did more than merely survive: he honed a musical language entirely his own, which was subversive without the authorities realizing it. Padilla was in some senses less fortunate. As for Cuba, the affair marked a vital turning point in relations between writers and the revolution: henceforth, they would be regarded as potential threats to its survival.

MIKE GONZALEZ

Writings

Fuera del juego, 1969
Sent Off the Field, translated by J.M. Cohen, 1972
Legacies: Selected Poems, translated by Alastair Reid and Andrew Hurley, 1982
Heroes Are Grazing in My Garden, translated by Andrew Hurley, 1984
Self-Portrait of the Other, translated by Alexander Coleman, 1990
A Fountain, a House of Stone, translated by Alastair Reid and Alexander Coleman, 1991

Further Reading

"A favor y en contra", *Cuadernos de Marcha*, (May 1971)

Article 19, *Cuba: World Report*, London: Article 19, 1991

Cabrera Infante, Guilermo, *Mea Cuba*, New York: Farrar Strauss, and London: Faber, 1994

Casal, Lourdes, *Literaturua y revolucion en Cuba: Documentos*, Miami: Universal, 1971

Castro, Fidel, *Palabras a los intelectuales*, Havana: Consejo Nacional de Cultura, 1961; as "Words to the Intellectuals" in *Radical Perspectives in the Arts*, edited by Lee Baxandall, Harmondsworth: Penguin, 1972

"Cuba: Revolution and the Intellectual: The Strange Case of Heberto Padilla", *Index on Censorship*, 1/2 (Summer 1972): 65–88, 101–34

Fornet, Ambrosio, introduction to "Bridging Enigma: Cubans on Cuba, special issue of *South Atlantic Quarterly* 96/1 (Winter 1997): 11

Núñez, Jiménez A., *Cuba, cultura, estado y revolución*, Mexico City: Presencia Latinoamericana, 1984

Ripoll, Carlos, *The Heresy of Words in Cuba*, New York: Freedom House, 1985

PAEDOPHILIA

Since the dawn of human history, no social structure has endorsed unlimited sexual freedom between its older and younger members. In Ancient Greece, pederasty (the love of an adult man for an adolescent boy) formed an integral part of everyday life, but paedophilia (sensual love for children) was as reprehensible as it is now by Western standards. In some Melanesian communities, young boys perform fellatio on older men and ingest the semen during an institutionalized sexual ritual, but this by no means implies that all types of sexual contact between adults and children are socially sanctioned.

Throughout history, numerous cases have been recorded of people being prosecuted for engaging in sexual acts with minors. Yet, until the 20th century, these offences were generally assimilated under broader categories like sodomy, buggery, and homosexuality. In many Western countries, laws stipulating an age of consent and defining "indecent assault" and "statutory rape" of minors were introduced only around the turn of the 19th century. Furthermore, the strictly moral censorship of paedophilia, whereby publications are banned and people are convicted because of the views they hold, has only gained momentum from the 1970s onwards.

Indeed, for centuries, poets and philosophers have been able to eulogize the beautiful bodies of young children without running the risk of being silenced, as long as they were not suspected of acting out their fantasies. In the slipstream of the social invention of "innocent childhood", the rudimentary establishment of the homosexual movement, and the generalized anti-sex atmosphere of the *fin de siècle*, this relative moral tolerance gradually changed during the first decades of the 20th century. However, until the 1970s, moral reactions were mainly directed against sexual (and especially homosexual) debauchery in general, rather than against paedophilia as such. Moral purity leagues rallying against cross-generational sex in particular are of a fairly recent date. During the 1980s and 1990s, their activities have escalated as a result of the international upsurge of knowledge about the extent of child sexual abuse, the distancing of traditional sexual minorities (gays and lesbians) from paedophile networks, the public success of the Recovered Memory Movement, the cooperative struggle of politicians of all shades of opinion against paedophilia, and the revelation of a number of ghastly cases of child abuse. The principle of this moral censorship was formulated by the right-wing philosopher Roger Scruton in *The Times* (London) of 13 September 1983: "We must not only foster those necessary virtues [modesty, restraint, chastity], but also silence those who teach the language which demeans them."

The extent to which moral censorship against paedophilia has increased since the 1970s can be illustrated by a score of examples. In 1979, six members of the British organization PIE (Paedophile Information Exchange) were charged with conspiracy to corrupt public morals. PIE had been created in 1975 as the successor to PAL (Paedophile Action for Liberation), its major goals being the abolition of the existing age of consent laws and the creation of civil (instead of criminal) provisions to protect children against sexual exploitation. The PIE newsletter contained no pornographic images and regularly urged its readers to remain within the boundaries of the law, but Tom O'Carroll, PIE's intellectual leader, was imprisoned for conspiracy to corrupt public morals in 1981. Two years later, new legal action was taken against the organization after the so-called "Brighton rape case", in which a young boy was sexually assaulted by three men. The real offenders were never found, but as a result of these new allegations, PIE disbanded in 1985.

In December 1977, the offices of the Canadian gay magazine *The Body Politic* were raided after the editorial collective had published a paper entitled "Men Loving Boys Loving Men". The editors were charged with obscenity and with using the mail "to distribute immoral, indecent and scurrilous materials", but they were acquitted on both counts. Three years later, they faced the same charges after publishing an article on "fisting" and were acquitted again. Soon afterwards, publication of the journal was terminated. In November 1996, Gerald Hannon, the author of the 1977 article on paedophilia in *The Body Politic*, was suspended from his teaching job at Toronto's Ryerson University, following allegations that "he was espousing his views on paedophilia in the classroom" and that he also worked as a prostitute. The university council decided that Hannon had not transgressed the limits of academic freedom, but it called his views abhorrent and placed a reprimand on his personal file.

After a 1978 conference on man–boy love and the age of consent in Boston, Massachusetts, a small group of radicals formed NAMBLA (North American Man–Boy Love Association), whose goals are largely similar to those of PIE. NAMBLA has been banned from the annual gay pride marches by the American homosexual community, and David Thorstad, NAMBLA's spokesman, has been scorned for trying to tear apart the gay movement. The *NAMBLA-Bulletin* contains scientific articles and reviews, and also pictures of half-nude adolescents. It has often been seized by law enforcers, in accordance with a federal US law which states that it is a felony to make photographs of nude persons under the age of 18. This law has also led to the withdrawal of *Show Me!*, a sex-education manual, by its publisher St Martin's Press, as well as to the prosecution of professional photographers like Jock Sturges, whose San Francisco studio was raided in 1990 by a team of FBI agents, who charged him with producing child pornography. The jury considered Sturges not guilty, and his books became immediate bestsellers.

Similar events have occurred in other countries. On 1 November 1991, a German group striving for the decriminalization of every type of consensual sex held its national meeting in Berlin. It was raided by police officers, who confiscated every document and recorded the names of all the participants. In France, the paedophile journal *Tantale* ceased publication after Christian Chardon, its editor, was prosecuted for publishing morally corrupt materials. Yet *Gaie France*, a magazine aimed at a homosexual readership which regularly shows pictures of nude prepubescent boys, can still be bought from ordinary newsagents. France's moral attitudes are ambiguous, but perhaps no more so than those of Britain and the US. In France, a journal like *Tantale* cannot be published, but some of the major French publishers have adopted the works of openly paedophile writers like Gabriel Matzneff. In the United States, *Doc and Fluff*, a novel by the lesbian sadomasochist activist Pat Califia, was banned by various bookshops because it allegedly celebrated lesbian paedophile activities; on the other hand, *The Blue Lagoon*, a 1980 film by Randal Kleiser starring a naked 14-year-old Brooke Shields, was shown nationwide.

One of the most recent examples of the impact of moral censorship in this area concerns Adrian Lyne's remake of Stanley Kubrick's film *Lolita*, which is based on Vladimir Nabokov's hugely successful 1955 novel about an ageing professor's infatuation with a 12-year-old girl. When Kubrick's film appeared in 1962, it was warmly commended by the critics and the public for its powerful portrayal of psychologically destructive love. Thirty-five years later, in 1997, public reactions to Lyne's remake of *Lolita* were completely different and had already flared up before the movie came into circulation. The American moral majority pressed Hollywood studios to decline purchase of the film from its producer, Pathé, because of its apparent defence of cross-generational sex. One of the film moguls declared in *Variety* that "paedophilia is a tough sell", to which Lyne retorted, "If I were making a movie about a 12-year-old getting chopped up by cannibals, there would be no problem." In Britain, there were similarly hostile reactions to the publication of A.M. Homes's *The End of Alice* in October 1997. The novel follows a paedophile serving his 23rd year in prison for sexually assaulting and killing a 12-year-old girl. The prisoner reflects upon his childhood and sexual inclinations, and conducts epistolary mind-games with a 19-year-old woman who is trying to seduce an underage boy. Defenders of the book claimed that it was an accurate reflection of how paedophiles justify their actions, but Jim Harding, the chief executive of the British National Society for the Prevention of Cruelty to Children (NSPCC), rejected it as a vile book which degraded and endangered children, and which tried to persuade the reader that paedophilia is somehow tolerable. Harding put pressure on booksellers not to stock copies of the novel, and the W.H. Smith chain decided to keep it off its shelves. Waterstones, on the other hand, decided to stock the novel commenting, "We recognise that some people would have problems with it, but we just don't censor material." Dillons stocked the book but did not promote it.

On the other hand, in Britain, photographers such as Graham Ovenden have been unjustifiably pursued for their serious studies of naked children. Since the mid-1990s, there have been campaigns to curtail the distribution of pornographic images depicting children via the Internet. In 1996, the American Congress passed a law prohibiting the dissemination of sexually explicit materials via easily accessible sites on the World Wide Web. In June 1997, however, the Supreme Court unanimously overruled the Congress's decision, stating that the law contradicted the First Amendment (which guarantees absolute freedom of speech), and that it is the task of parents, rather than Internet providers, to protect children against potentially harmful computer images. Obviously, the Supreme Court's ruling is only valid within the United States, but, since its inception, no country can take legal action against pornographic web images distributed by American providers, and these providers dominate the Internet scene.

The advantages of the Internet for accessing and distributing information are not only appreciated by paedophiles, however; they are equally well known to law-enforcers and vigilantes fighting against child abuse. In December 1996, an American man was arrested by FBI agents while waiting for a 13-year-old girl with whom he had previously exchanged sexually explicit messages on the Internet, unaware of the fact that her character had been created by FBI officers themselves in order to lure paedophiles. In June 1997, the Alaska state government agreed to create a website on which the names and addresses of recently released sex offenders are being published, thus extending to the Internet the applications of "Megan's Law", which says that citizens should have the right to know if a sex offender is living on their street. In Britain the *News of the World* newspaper has campaigned for similar listings.

It seems that the Netherlands is currently the only country where cross-generational sex has not been affected by moral censorship. At the University of Utrecht, Theo Sandfort pursues his research in this area and expresses nuanced views on paedophilia without being frowned upon. A scientific journal called *Paidika*, which is entirely devoted to the open investigation of paedophilia, is still being published, alongside other, more militant journals such as *OK* (*Ouderen–Kinderen*, Adults–Children).

DANY NOBUS

Further Reading

Bernard, Frits, *Paedophilia: A Factual Report*, Rotterdam: Enclave, 1985

Brongersma, Edward, *Loving Boys: A Multidisciplinary Study of Sexual Relations between Adult and Minor Males*, 2 vols, Elmhurst, New York: Global, 1986–90

Buffière, Félix, *Éros adolescent: la pédérastie dans la Grèce antique*, Paris: Belles Lettres, 1980

Bullough, Vern L., *Sexual Variance in Society and History*, Chicago: University of Chicago Press, 1976

Califia, Pat, "The Aftermath of the Great Kiddy-Porn Panic of '77

(1980)" in *Public Sex: The Culture of Radical Sex* by Califia, Pittsburgh: Cleis Press, 1994

Evans, David T., *Sexual Citizenship: The Material Construction of Sexualities*, London and New York: Routledge, 1993

Geraci, Joseph (editor), *Dares to Speak: Historical and Contemporary Perspectives on Boy-love*, Swaffham, Norfolk: Gay Men's Press, 1997

Hocquenghem, Guy, interview with David Thorstad in *Semiotext(e): Loving Boys* (Summer 1980): 18–35

Howitt, Dennis, *Paedophiles and Sexual Offences against Children*, Chichester and New York: Wiley, 1995

Kincaid, James R., *Erotic Innocence: The Culture of Child Molesting*, Durham, North Carolina: Duke University Press, 1998

Lautmann, Rüdiger, *Die Lust am Kind: Porträt des Pädophilen*, Hamburg: Klein, 1994

Li, C.K., D.J West and T.P. Woodhouse, *Children's Sexual Encounters with Adults*, London: Duckworth, 1990; Buffalo, New York: Prometheus, 1993

O'Carroll, Tom, *Paedophilia: The Radical Case*, London: Owen, 1980

PIE (Paedophile Information Exchange), *Paedophilia: Some Questions and Answers*, London: PIE, 1978

Rossman, Parker, *Sexual Experience between Men and Boys: Exploring the Pederast Underground*, New York: Association Press, 1979

Sandfort, Theo, *The Sexual Aspect of Paedophile Relations: The Experience of Twenty-Five Boys*, Amsterdam: Pan/Spartacus, 1982

Sax, Marjan and Sjuul Deckwitz (editors), *Op een oude fiets moet je het leren: erotische en seksuele relaties tussen vrouwen en jonge meisjes en jongens* (You Should Learn It on an Old Bike: Erotic and Sexual Relations between Women and Young Girls and Boys), Amsterdam: Schorer, 1992

Schérer, René and Guy Hocquenghem, "Co-ire: album systématique de l'enfance", *Recherches*, 22 (1976)

Taylor, Brian (editor), *Perspectives on Paedophilia*, London: Batsford, 1981

Tsang, Daniel (editor), *The Age Taboo: Gay Male Sexuality, Power, and Consent*, Boston: Alyson, and London: Gay Men's Press, 1981

Weeks, Jeffrey, *Sexuality and Its Discontents: Meanings, Myths, and Modern Sexualities*, London and Boston: Routledge, 1985

Wilson, Glenn D. and David N. Cox, *The Child-Lovers: A Study of Paedophiles in Society*, London: Owen, 1983

THOMAS PAINE
British pamphleteer and political thinker, 1737–1809

This restless revolutionary, the censorship of whose works is of central interest in the history of the practice, was the son of a religious nonconformist. Although Paine later rejected all forms of institutional religion, including such free accounts of Christianity as that of the Society of Friends (Quakers), of which his father was a member, his early indirect experience of the disadvantages of not belonging to the established Church of England cannot have been without their influence upon him.

Paine's political development was considerably shaped by his membership of the Headstrong Club of Lewes, East Sussex, where he worked as an exciseman from 1768. He was present in the town when John Wilkes passed through in 1770, and would have witnessed the cheering crowds which, in Lewes as elsewhere, applauded "Wilkes and Liberty". A letter signed "Common Sense" to the *Sussex Weekly Advertiser and Lewes Journal* on 1 April 1771 maintained that it was "better to cease to exist than to cease to be free"; Paine may well have written it.

Common Sense was the title of a series of highly influential pamphlets which Paine wrote in 1776, two years after his arrival in the American colonies. They variously espoused the cause of American independence, condemned hereditary monarchy, and denounced slavery. However, his main income at this stage came from his post as secretary of the committee on foreign affairs of the Continental Congress. Then, as now, it was difficult to write outspokenly when holding an official position, and when in 1779 he suggested that an official mission to France carried out by Silas Deane had been to the latter's financial advantage, Paine was forced to resign. He was said to be "a disturber of public peace, a spreader of falsehoods, and sower of dissension among the people".

In general, Paine felt at home in independent America, but he was not uncritical of certain developments. He quickly perceived, for instance, that the power of newspaper editors could be used for undemocratic ends, writing to David Claypole, editor of the *Pennsylvania Packet* on 22 March 1786: "If the freedom of the press is to be determined by the judgement of the printer of a newspaper in preference to that of the people, who, when they read, will judge for themselves, then freedom is on a very sandy foundation." Claypole had refused to print articles by Paine on certain aspects of governmental and business accountability.

Paine returned to Europe in 1787, his interest aroused by turmoil in France and the possibility that there at least a despotic monarchy could be removed. In Britain, he found that such a prospect was greeted with the utmost alarm by most political leaders, notably by his old friend Edmund Burke who, in 1790, published his *Reflections on the Revolution in France and on the Proceedings in Certain Socities in London Relative to That Event*, a classic defence of gradualism, but one permeated by class consciousness and the necessity, as Burke saw it, to maintain a system based on heredity and property. Paine replied in *The Rights of Man* (1791–92), written in language which many of the "lower orders" could understand, proclaiming that "despotism breeds a culture of despotism", and setting out a theory of equal natural rights.

The connection between Paine's programme and revolutionary rhetoric across the Channel was not difficult to discern. Joseph Johnson, who had agreed to publish the work, was subject to regular harassment by government agents during the typesetting, and he finally withdrew from the agreement on the day of publication. Paine promptly collected the unbound copies in a wheelbarrow and delivered them to J.S. Jordan, who published part 1 of *The Rights of Man* on 13 March 1791, selling copies at three shillings each. Sales were fast and furious and the work was quickly translated for distribution in France, Germany, and the Netherlands.

The British government considered the possibility of a straightforward ban on the book. The *Gazetteer and London Daily Advertiser* reported in April that "a consultation of law officers to determine whether the author could be prosecuted" had recommended that there should be no action for the moment. They may have thought that the book's relatively high cover price would prevent wide circulation (not realizing that it was being read aloud to poor or illiterate people). They noted that Paine had cleverly dedicated the book to George Washington, with whom the government was anxious to remain on good terms for reasons of trade.

Prosecution was not, however, by any means finally ruled out, as Burke revealed in his reply, *Appeal from the New to the Old Whigs* (August 1791): "I will not attempt in the smallest degree to refute [Paine's arguments]. This will probably be done (if such writings should be thought to deserve any other than the refutation of criminal justice) by others." As Joseph Johnson contemplated the publication of *The Rights of Man Part the Second*, he was warned: "if you wished to be hanged or inured in prison all your life, publish this book". A deal with Thomas Chapman fell through when Paine, suspicious that the text would be tampered with, refused to sell him the copyright, even for £1000. Paine's suspicions were vindicated when Chapman, again at the last minute, purported to find a "dangerous tendency" in the work. Paine returned to Johnson and Jordan, who agreed to print up to 200,000 copies within a year.

The response of the prime minister, William Pitt, was direct. In May 1792 he issued a proclamation against seditious writings. He told the House of Commons: "Principles had been laid down by Mr Paine which struck at hereditary nobility and which went to the destruction of monarchy and religion and the total subversion of the established form of government". Paine was now followed by government agents, booksellers were harassed if they were found to be stocking the work, bill-stickers prosecuted if they promoted Paine's ideas, and considerable anti-Paine propaganda was produced. Johnson was prosecuted and pleaded guilty. Finally Paine himself was summoned, on 21 May 1792, to answer charges of seditious libel. The hearing was continually postponed, perhaps in the hope that Paine would save trouble by going voluntarily into exile. Warned by his friend William Blake, he left for France on 13 September 1792.

He was tried *in absentia* during December, said by the prosecuting counsel, Spencer Perceval (later prime minister) to be a "wicked, seditious and ill-disposed person". He was defended by Thomas Erskine who maintained that "opinion is free and that conduct alone is amenable to law"; all had the right to "analyse the principles of [the] constitution, point out its errors and defects, examine and publicize its corruption, warning his fellow citizens against their ruinous consequences". None of this was admitted by the packed jury, who pronounced Paine guilty without further ado. He could never return to his native country.

Paine was granted French citizenship, elected to the Convention to represent the Pas de Calais, and was quickly plunged into debates about the treatment of Louis XVI. Paine was in favour of clemency and would have had the king shipped to America. He was then thought to be a revolutionary of a rather "traditional" stamp, and his arguments were not considered by the newly ascendant Jacobins. Danton told him

"Revolutions cannot be made with rosewater", and Louis was executed on 19 January 1793. Paine would "not abide with such sanguinary men", but was unable to leave France. He opted for semi-retirement in the village of St-Denis, but could not be silenced for long, as the Jacobins realized when they ordered his arrest and had him sentenced to a year's imprisonment from December 1793. The Terror was at its height and Paine was lucky to escape the guillotine. The political climate changed, and he was released, after American pressure, on 6 November 1794.

His writings had meanwhile moved in a new, and, it must have seemed in Britain, a surprising direction. It was less surprising in France where revolutionaries had turned to religious iconoclasm and the secularization of religious buildings, hoping to eradicate a further pillar of the *ancien régime*. Paine's recent biographer, John Keane, said of *The Age of Reason* (which first appeared in pamphlet form as *Le Siècle de la raison*, and was expanded for its first English edition of February 1794), that he "attempted something that many of his contemporaries (and a great many of his subsequent readers) thought to be impossible: to attack all forms of organized religion as pompous and obfuscatory, and at the same time to defend the idea of a benevolent Creator of the universe against those who were currently bent on decreeing the death of God".

Paine believed in "one God and no more". He despised "this thing called revelation, or revealed religion ... the most dishonorable belief against the character of the Divinity ... whence arose all those horrid assassinations of whole nations of men, women and infants with which the Bible is filled, and the bloody persecutions and tortures unto death and religious wars that since that time has laid Europe in blood and ashes". Jesus was "a virtuous and honourable man", but the supposed miracles concerning his life and death (the Virgin Birth and the Resurrection) had "every mark of fraud and imposition ... degrading the Almighty into the character of a showman".

The British authorities would now hardly have looked kindly on anything that Paine wrote. With little knowledge of the context addressed in *The Age of Reason*, and no willingness to make any distinctions, they launched proceedings against Thomas Williams for publishing a blasphemous book. Revealingly, the prosecutor (none other than Thomas Erskine, Paine's defender in *The Rights of Man* trial) argued that Paine's denial of Christianity would incite the "insolence and disobedience" of the "lowest classes". The jury hardly listened to the defending counsel Steward Kyd's argument that Jesus had been treated respectfully. They found Williams guilty; he was sentenced to a year's hard labour and made to deposit £1000 against his future good behaviour. Copies of the book were regularly burned in public.

The Age of Reason was nevertheless a bestseller in Europe and America, although after Paine again crossed the Atlantic in 1802 there were many who agreed with the *Gazette of the United States and Daily Advertiser*, which described him as "the infamous scavenger of all the filth that could be raked from dirty paths which have hitherto been trodden by all revilers of Christianity". His influence had declined, and America had changed in his absence. Paine noted early tendencies towards press sensationalism, and in his final reflections on these matters, "Liberty of the Press", quoted Jefferson with approval: "The licentiousness of the press produces the same effect as the restraint of the press was intended to do, if the restraint was to prevent things being told, and the licentiousness of the press prevents things being believed when they are told."

DEREK JONES

Writings

Common Sense, 1776, revised 1776
The American Crisis, 13 vols, 1776–83; *The Crisis Extraordinary*, 1780; *A Supernumerary Crisis*, 2 vols, 1783
The Rights of Man, 2 vols, 1791–92
Reasons for Wishing to Preserve the Life of Louis Capet [Louis XVI], 1793
The Age of Reason, 2 vols, 1794–95
Examination of the Passages in the New Testament, Quoted from the Old, and Called Prophecies Concerning Jesus Christ, 1807

Complete Writings, edited by Philip S. Foner, 1945
A Paine Reader, edited by Michael Foot and Isaac Kramnick, 1987
Political Writings, edited by Bruce Kuklick, 1989

Further Reading

Ayer, A.J., *Thomas Paine*, London: Secker and Warburg, and New York: Atheneum, 1988
Butler, Marilyn (editor), *Burke, Paine, Godwin, and the Revolution Controversy*, Cambridge and New York: Cambridge University Press, 1984
Conway, Moncure Daniel, *The Life of Thomas Paine*, 2 vols, New York: Putnam, 1892
Keane, John, *Tom Paine: A Political Life*, London, Bloomsbury, and Boston: Little Brown, 1995
Levy, Leonard W., *Blasphemy: Verbal Offence against the Sacred, from Moses to Salman Rushdie*, New York: Knopf, 1993

PAKISTAN

(formerly West Pakistan)

Population: 141,256,000	**Illiteracy rate (%):** 40.1 (m); 68.9 (f)
Main religions: Sunni Muslim; Shia Muslim; Christian; Hindu	**Number of daily newspapers:** 264
	Number of radio receivers per 1000 inhabitants: 94
Official language: Urdu	
Other languages spoken: English; Punjabi; Pushto; Sindhi; Siriki	**Number of TV receivers per 1000 inhabitants:** 22
	Number of PCs per 1000 inhabitants: 3.9

On 11 August 1947 in Karachi, Muhammad 'Ali Jinnah, the Father of the Nation, delivered what he considered to be the "greatest speech of his life", on the subject of religious freedom. He laid the basis for the newly independent state of Pakistan with these words:

> You are free; you are free to go to your temples, you are free to go to your mosques or to any other place of worship in this State of Pakistan. You may belong to any religion or caste or creed – that has nothing to do with the fundamental principle that we are all citizens and equal citizens of one State.

The Pakistani sociologist and media critic Zamir Niazi praises Jinnah, calling him an "untiring defender of freedom of expression and of conscience". Jinnah's associates, however, were less committed to such ideals. Immediately after Jinnah delivered these words to the first meeting of the Constituent Assembly of the newly created state, the history of censorship in Pakistan began. According to Hamid Jalal, certain secularist passages of the speech were excised from printed versions. Authorities censored some remarks on the grounds that they contradicted the "two-nation" theory, by which the very existence of an independent Muslim Pakistan was justified. If Pakistan was simply another secular state, then there would seem to be no logical reason to separate the Muslim sections of British India from the predominantly Hindu regions. Jinnah's secularist speech has suffered frequent alteration and suppression over the decades. According to Justice Muhammad

Munir, some detractors went so far as to denominate it "an inspiration of the devil."

Niazi, in his book *Press in Chains*, cites several occasions when Jinnah opposed closing down newspapers that took recalcitrant lines. Early in his tenure as head of state, Jinnah refused to sign an ordinance that would have provided for detention without trial and sharply curtailed press freedoms. According to Niazi, "Hardly a month had passed [since Jinnah died] when his successors trampled on the very principles for which he had struggled till his last breath." In October 1948 the draft ordinance on which he had refused to put his signature was decreed as the Safety Act Ordinance. In May 1952 the ordinance got permanent life with the backing of parliament. Later on it became part of the 1956 constitution. "People who refused to toe the official line were persecuted under this lawless law. Thus Jinnah's faith in liberalism, his regard for the sanctity of fundamental human rights and freedom of the press became a taboo for successive regimes who ruled, rather misruled, this unfortunate nation", writes Niazi.

Pakistan has known little else in its history but a succession of dictatorships. East Pakistan seceded in 1972 and the guidelines for the profession of Islam became increasingly narrow. Pakistan's press regime has been less restrictive than some other Islamic countries, such as Saudi Arabia. In this context it is important to stress that Islam, as a religious worldview, should not be blamed for the strict censorship regime that has been so prevalent in Pakistan. Contemporary Islamic scholars have plausibly demonstrated that virtually all modern human rights guarantees – including the rights to freedom of expression, free elections, and the right to practice one's own faith – are consistent with Islamic scripture, and with Islam's earliest intellectual traditions, going back to the Mu'tazilis or Rationalists of the 8th century (Bouamrane 1978). The Shari'a Court of Pakistan has argued that press freedoms can be guaranteed solely on the basis of Islamic thought. Nevertheless, strict censorship in one form or another has, since the proclamation of independence, been practised by each and every government of Pakistan.

The *New Orient*, edited by Ghayural Islam, was one of the first staunchly independent Karachi weeklies to suffer closure. The paper advocated "a strong, progressive, sovereign and democratic Pakistan where man-made inequalities will be eliminated ...", and argued for "a popular democratic constitution, [which enshrined] fundamental human rights." Not long after proclaiming these principles, the editor of the *New Orient* was interrogated by the police, the paper's offices were promptly searched and sealed, and remaining copies of the seven issues were confiscated.

During the first seven years of the existence of Pakistan as an independent state (1947–53),

> in the Punjab alone 31 newspapers were banned – 15 for one year each, nine for six months each, including literary magazines ... and nine for lesser periods. Security deposits of amounts ranging from 500 rupees to 10,000 rupees were demanded from another 15 newspapers.

Successive administrations employed a variety of means to control press organs that dared to criticize government policy: outright closure or censorship, the harassment of editors, and frivolous lawsuits (which drained independent papers of resources and forced them to close). Various governments also gave financial aid to subservient papers and colluded with financiers to monopolize a compliant publishing industry. When such measures failed, the authorities forcibly took over the management of the less amenable papers.

In 1960 (two years after the installation of general Ayub Khan's military government), four newspapers owned by Progressive Papers Limited (PPL) were taken over by the administration. It was alleged, though never proven in court, that these papers had "engaged in printing and publishing material which can be calculated to subvert the public mind and divert it on lines antagonistic to national interest." To counter the charge that the government was engaged in overt censorship, officials handed over the papers to a semi-private board. Niazi writes:

> The year 1964 saw the creation of the monstrosity known as the National Press Trust, in league with the industrial magnates, who purchased the PPL institution at a throwaway price. The once proud group of newspapers became the tame voice of successive governments.

Other newspapers fell into line and praised the government's move against papers which had formerly been "strangers in the house", a phrase frequently employed against papers deemed to be insufficiently "patriotic". The most vociferous criticisms of the move came from journalists and their affiliated unions. Unions argued that the PPL papers were the only media that "could claim near consistency in their struggle for freedom of the press and championing the cause of the down-trodden. The PPL papers had served," according to dissenters, "the cause of Pakistan's progress and the people's interest – not those of the ruling clique or any other elite group."

Over the years the government-created National Press Trust grew into a "virtual newspaper empire", until it controlled 12 papers in English, Urdu, and Bengali in six different cities. In 1970 Zulfiqar 'Ali Bhutto (executed 1979) came to power, and two years later the National Press Trust was dissolved. During the assembly debates on the matter, some champions of press freedom proposed that a new board should be created that would "include elected representatives of the people, of working journalists, and from other walks of life." There had been three previous attempts to run worker-owned, journalist-managed papers in Pakistan. These were *Javedan*, *Azad*, and *Kohistan*. All three had failed, presumably because of a shortage of money in the stages of initial investment. Opponents of a worker-run National Board argued that the failures of *Javedan*, *Azad*, and *Kohistan* proved that journalist-managed enterprises could not work. However, many journalists argued the rulers simply wanted the papers put under the total control of the business elite, to prevent the spread of egalitarian opinions such as those diffused by the PPL, which had been so effectively silenced.

The issue was rendered moot by the passage of the 1973 constitution which severely limited, both in theory and practice, the ability of any newspaper (whether run by working journalists or private corporations) to publish without restrictions. According to article 19: "Every citizen shall have the right to freedom of speech and expression, and there shall be freedom of the press, subject to any reasonable restrictions imposed by law in the interest of the glory of Islam or the integrity, security or defense of Pakistan." The article goes on to say that restrictions on freedom of expression can be made for the sake of friendly relations with foreign states, public order, decency, or morality.

To make matters worse article 269 strengthened the martial law proclamations made in 1971 and 1972, in response to the secession of East Pakistan. None of the executive judgments made during this period could be "called in question in any court on any ground whatsoever". The press were frightened into even deeper submission.

When Zia ul-Haqq seized power in a military coup, there appeared to be a brief honeymoon period between the government and the press. One foreign journalist wrote in July 1977: "Pakistan is now enjoying Press freedom for the first time in ten years or so." However, government actions against the press began to multiply within the first year of military rule, as the Chief Martial Law Administration (CMLA) began singling out its enemies. For example, in 1978 the editor of *The Sun* (Lahore) was sentenced to one year's imprisonment and 10 lashes for derogatory remarks against the CMLA. *Musawat* (Karachi) was banned for a day to prevent the publication of deposed president Bhutto's court appeal. One of the most infamous incidents occurred on 13 May 1978: 11 journalists were given prison sentences, and four of them were flogged for "organizing meetings at an open public place, raising slogans, displaying banners and starting a hunger strike". At about this time 11 papers were banned, and 13 others fined. During one two-month period 150 journalists were arrested for agitating for the "withdrawal of oppressive press laws". The CMLA stated, after canceling elections for a second time, that: "Only those newspapers and periodicals indulging in anti-state activities, in the garb of journalism and poisoning the mind of the people have been banned."

In 1979–80 the martial law regime instituted a practice of prior censorship of anything "which is prejudicial to Islamic ideology or the sovereignty, integrity and security of Pakistan, or morality and the maintenance of public order." A disturbing trend began to accelerate, that of mobs attacking journalistic establishments, as 300 students of the Islami-Jamiat-e-Tulba ransacked the offices of two Lahore dailies, *Jang* and *Nawa-i-Waqt*, damaging property and injuring eight workers. Such actions polarized Pakistani society: one group saw a free press as antithetical to Islam, while the other side believed the ideals of Islam to be fully consonant with modern notions of free expression.

In 1982 the All Pakistan Newspaper Society (APNS) argued, on the basis of the Qur'an, that government pressure on newspapers was "a direct violation of the principles of truth and justice that should prevail in an Islamic State". The government countered with more acts of suppression. They attacked the publication of a "lurid" article in *Jang* on Elvis Presley's life. The authorities stopped advertisements, filed a suit against *Jang*, and later withdrew it in August 1982.

Both the journalists under attack and the government claimed to be the legitimate interpreters of Islamic thought. The government defended its acts of suppression, arguing that "Only those journalists were penalized who were involved in unpatriotic and anti-national activities . . . The press should address itself to the Islamic ideology of Pakistan." Yet the government did not give a specific legal definition of Islam or of the national ideology. Any criticism of the government or of a government official could have conceivably been an attack against Islam or against Pakistan's "ideology."

In 1984 the Federal Shari'a Court was asked by a private individual to decide if the Press Ordinance and preventive press laws were in harmony with Islamic principles. Journalists' associations and private individuals presented evidence to prove that such repressive laws contravened the Qur'an and Islamic doctrine. The court, comprised of four Islamist jurists, concurred with the journalists and ruled against the government. Their unanimous judgment upheld "the right to protest and dissent". They affirmed the right of journalists to "express freely their opinions about the affairs of state with a view to ensuring that the authorities remain within the framework of law". Citing specific statements of the prophet Muhammad, they also urged the press to "raise their voice against oppression and tyranny", and said those who "see injustice and remain silent shall suffer the wrath of God".

Displeased with the judgment of the Shari'a Court, the information secretary, lieutenant-general Mujibur Rahman, made clear that government policy towards the press would continue as before. Relying on his own interpretation of religious dogma, the Chief Martial Law Administration president said of the military government: "Although we are not elected by the people, the Almighty has entrusted us with the responsibility of making Pakistan a citadel of Islam, and we will not leave unless we have carried out this task."

The Shari'a Court of Pakistan, while upholding the right of journalists to free expression, has not been as favourably disposed to defend freedom of religion. Some of the most serious abridgments of religious freedom in Pakistan have been perpetrated against members of the Ahmadi community. Ahmadis consider themselves to be Muslims; however they differ from the mainstream in asserting that a modern religious leader, Mirza Sahib, was "the promised Mehdi, the Promised Messiah, and a Prophet". A constitutional amendment categorized Ahmadis as non-Muslims, to be accorded the same status as members of other minority religions in Pakistan, such as Christians, Hindus, Sikhs, and Parsis. Furthermore a 1984 judgment of the Federal Shari'a Court made it a criminal offence for an Ahmadi to call himself a Muslim, to preach, or to call people to prayer. In 1997, 120 Ahmadis faced religious charges, including the charge of blasphemy, which carries a mandatory death penalty. By the end of the year more than 2500 Ahmadis had similar charges pending against them.

The election in 1988 of Pakistan's first female prime minister, Benazir Bhutto, gave hopes to the advocates of freer expression. Bhutto promised to repeal all laws that restricted press freedom, and to give autonomy to radio and television. During her first two-year term she abolished newspaper licensing, making possible a rapid growth in newspapers and periodicals – 1031 being established between January and June 1989 alone. A blacklist of writers denied access to the media was also torn up. Yet during the same period, Pakistan was the first country after Iran to ban Salman Rushdie's *The Satanic Verses* (15 February 1989). The Urdu weekly magazine *Takhear* – issued by Jamiat-i-Islami – was confiscated when it published extracts from the novel.

Hopes for greater press freedom dissipated when Bhutto was dismissed as prime minister by president Ghulam Ishaq Khan in August 1990. After Nawaj Sharif's Islamic Democratic Alliance came to power, an Islamic Shari Bill was passed in 1991 that compelled legislative, judicial, and bureaucratic decisions to conform with the Qur'an. As a result the media were further Islamicized. So-called informal censorship greatly increased during this time. Members of the Muhajir Quomi, a branch of the ruling party, attacked the offices of the *Dawn* preventing its distribution, beating the paper's street vendors, and burning remaining copies. They went on to burn down the offices of the blasphemous weekly magazine *Takhear*.

Between 1995 and 1998 journalistic freedom of expression continued to be suppressed by a variety of means. More than 10 journalistic establishments were bombed or subject to grenade attacks, overwhelmed by mobs, or ransacked. Several newspaper offices were raided by police. Some were subject to unfair taxation. Individual journalists were illegally detained, beaten, stabbed, assaulted by police, kidnapped, tortured, and subjected to sexual assault. The blasphemy laws were more rigorously enforced, and even Benazir Bhutto, who returned to power in 1995, announced that there were emphatically no plans to amend them. Three Christians who had been charged with blasphemy by an extremist Islamist party, Sepah-e-Sababa, were shot outside the high court in Lahore, and one of them died.

Groups such as the Pakistan Press Foundation, Article 19, the Committee to Protect Journalists (CPJ), and Reporters sans Frontières, issued at least 50 reports between 1995 and 1997 on violations of the basic right to freedom of expression in Pakistan. Perhaps the worst of these was "an unprecedented attack on freedom of the press", when the government closed down six Urdu-language dailies in 1995. Journalists responded almost immediately with a massive protest action.

In 1997 an attempt was made to film a version in Pakistan or India of Salman Rushdie's novel, *Midnight's Children*. "Permission to film in India and Pakistan had been refused on grounds it would offend Muslims in those countries and lead to communal antagonism", according to Reuters. During the same year *Dawn* accused the authorities of censoring and delaying their incoming and outgoing email messages through Paknet, indirectly government owned via the Pakistan Telecommunications Corporation. The CPJ's Year 2000 report cited a number of disturbing developments since the suspension of the constitution by general Musharraf in October 1999. The government decided to censor portions of the trial of deposed prime minister Nawaz Sharif on the grounds that the defendant's statements were "likely to tarnish and affect the security, integrity, and solidarity of the Islamic Republic of Pakistan". Other threats to free expression during 2000 included the assassinations of religious leaders and reporters, and the bombing of the headquarters of the newspaper *Nawa-i-Waqt*, which resulted in the deaths of two of the paper's managers and one computer operator. The press continues to be intimidated by religious extremists, drug traffickers who fear media exposure, and the government which on 27 September 2000 sent in the army to inspect the premises of *Dawn*.

PAUL WELLEN

Further Reading

Ahmed, Akbar S., *Resistance and Control in Pakistan*, London and New York: Routledge, 1991

Ahmed, Akbar S., *Jinnah, Pakistan and Islamic Identity*, London and New York: Routledge, 1997

Ahmed, Aziz, *Islamic Modernism in India and Pakistan, 1857–1964*, London: Oxford University Press, 1967

Amnesty International, *Pakistan: Use and Abuse of the Blasphemy Laws*, London and New York: Amnesty International, 1994

Bouamrane, Chikh, *Le Problème de la liberté humaine dans le pensée musulmane: solution mu'tazalite*, Paris: Vrin, 1978

"A Carrot for the Pakistani Press", *Index on Censorship*, 3/1 (Spring 1974)

Farhad, "Curbing Free Thought", *Index on Censorship*, 14/2 (April 1985)

Faroz, Ahmed, "Pakistan Curbs the Press", *Index on Censorship*, 9/4 (August 1980)

"Freedom of Religion and Religious Minorities in Pakistan: A Study of Judicial Practice", *Fordham International Law Journal*, 19 (1995)

Gauhar, Altef, "A Short Course on Blasphemy", *Index on Censorship*, 24/3 (May–June 1995)

Khan, Shafique Ali, *Freedom of Thought and Islam*, Karachi: Royal Book Company, 1989

Lodhi, Malenka, "Deterring Dissent in Education", *Index on Censorship*, 14/2 (April 1985)

Mayer, Ann Elizabeth, *Islam and Human Rights: Tradition and Politics*, 3rd edition, Boulder, Colorado: Westview Press, 1999

Melville, William J., "The Press in Pakistan", *Index on Censorship*, 7/5 (September–October 1978)

Niazi, Zamir, *Press in Chains*, Karachi: Karachi Press Club, 1986

Niazi, Zamir, *The Web of Censorship*, Oxford and New York: Oxford University Press, 1994

Pakistan Press Foundation, articles from IFEX Alert Service: International Freedom of Expression Clearing House, at www.ifex.org

"Persecuted Minorities and Writers in Pakistan", *Asia Watch*, (September 1993)

Ruthven, Malise, *Islam in the World*, 2nd edition, London: Penguin; New York: Oxford University Press, 2000

Scriptor, "Why the Press is Tame", *Index on Censorship*, 14/2 (April 1985)

Siddiq, Nadeen Ahmed, "Enforced Apostasy: *Zaheeruddin* v *State* and the Official Persecution of the Ahmadi Community in Pakistan", *Law and Equality* 14 (1995)

Ziring, Lawrence, *Pakistan in the Twentieth Century: A Political History*, Oxford and New York: Oxford University Press, 1997

PALESTINE PRESS SERVICE
Palestinian news agency, established 1978

In March 1978 Raymonda Tawil, who had been unofficially supplying news to foreign journalists and shepherding them to the scenes of important events, teamed up with Ibrahim Kar'ain (a Palestinian with a Jerusalem identity card) to establish the Palestine Press Service (PPS) in East Jerusalem. The service issued press releases through the Italian press service Interpress. What had started as a two-person operation soon became a respected news agency with a staff of 12, and changed the dynamics of communication between Israelis and Palestinians by giving the latter a voice that was heard by the international press. It has played a crucial part in the achievement of more balanced coverage of Palestinian affairs, previously dominated by the Israelis.

The PPS was hounded by Israeli officials from the moment it was established. The central court in Jerusalem refused to register the service because the word "Palestine" was likely to hurt the feelings of "the public". The feelings of the Arab public were not at issue under occupation. Yossi Arnon, the PPS's lawyer, attempted to persuade the court to order registration, but the court supported the Recorder. Arnon withdrew the case to avoid setting a precedent for further refusals.

On 2 March 1981 PPS's office was vandalized, and the names of its local and foreign subscribers were stolen. The Israeli chief of police did not rule out political motives for the break-in. In a solidarity visit to the PPS on 3 March 1981, progressive Israelis condemned the vandalism and theft.

Israeli authorities were especially hostile to the PPS during and after the Israeli invasion of Lebanon. They closed the office for six months on 14 September 1982 under the Emergency Regulations of 1945, article 129/1/B, and warned that anyone found inside the office would be arrested. On 7 April 1983 Israeli authorities banned the publication and distribution of the daily PPS newsletter which had become the primary source of information on the occupied territories for western journalists and diplomats. Raphel Levy, commissioner of Jerusalem, informed the PPS that the continued distribution of the newsletter violated the law because it was, in fact, a newspaper, and therefore required a licence and was subject to censorship. The London *Times* correspondent Christopher Walker reported that such a ban would be

> the end of a very useful round-up of the Israeli and Arab press comments on events in the Middle East, which certainly did not amount to a daily paper, merely a service to journalists and diplomats. They'll probably have to work harder to get the same information.

The PPS was forced to stop the circulation of the newsletter, but continued to offer its services to foreign agencies by telephone.

When the PPS resumed operation in 1983, official harassment continued in the form of three letters from the commissioner of Jerusalem threatening the PPS with punishment if it did not stop publication (on 4 May, 23 September, and 14 December 1983). Despite numerous applications, the Israeli authorities forbade the PPS from acquiring a telex until 1986. The technology finally enabled the PPS to contact Arab and foreign news agencies directly, instead of through Agence France Presse or the telephone.

When the first Palestinian uprising (the intifada) started in 1987, Israeli authorities clamped down on all media, and the PPS was no exception. Victor Cygielman wrote that the PPS was closed:

> for one reason: to silence those accurately reporting the events in the occupied territories; to silence a source that had become an indispensable tool for all serious journalists, Israeli and foreign; and to prevent all checking on the often incomplete and sometimes blatantly one-sided reports of the Israeli military spokesmen.

On 29 March 1988 Israeli authorities declared the occupied territories, excluding East Jerusalem, a closed military area, thus imposing a news blackout on events during Land Day (30 March). On that day Israel again closed the PPS for six months, invoking, as before, the 1945 British Emergency Regulations for "public safety and public order". Ibrahim Kar'ain, co-owner of the PPS, described the closure order as "an attempt to cut off the occupied territories from the international community". The closure order coincided with the three-day ban imposed by Israeli authorities on the entry of foreign journalists into the occupied territories, and with a large arrest campaign; 1000 arrests were made that week alone in a vain effort to stop the uprising.

A US State Department spokesman, Charles Redman, said in a 31 March 1988 briefing that:

> The Palestinian media in East Jerusalem, including the Palestine Press Service, play an important role in expressing Palestinian views and in providing information. We regret the government of Israel's decision to close the service and urge that it will be reconsidered soon.

Nevertheless, the Israeli authorities closed the office for one year, prompting the PPS to open an office in Athens on 13 March 1989. By that time, however, many other press agencies had opened in the West Bank. Journalists who worked for these shoestring operations, which were often closed shortly after opening, hired themselves out as stringers to foreign correspondents in need of West Bank contacts. Thus, the later closures of the PPS were not as damaging as the earlier ones, when it was the only Palestinian source on the scene. Furthermore, in the late 1980s Israeli West Bank reporters themselves increasingly depended on Palestinian sources, and that dependence in turn affected the operations of the western press which, before the PPS, had relied entirely on Israeli stringers.

ORAYB AREF NAJJAR

Further Reading

Abu Ayyash, Radwan, *The Press in the Occupied Homeland* (in Arabic), Jerusalem: Palestinian Press Services Office, 1987

Curtius, Mary, "Palestinian Press Walks a Tightrope", *Christian Science Monitor* (27 August 1987): 7–8

Cygielman, Victor, "When the Press is the Enemy", *New Outlook* (June 1988): 7

Friedman, Robert, "[Israeli] West Bank Reporters: 'The Gang of Four'", *The Press* (June 1982): 32–34

Geyer, Georgie Anne, "The Middle East Conundrum", *The Quill* (10–16 February 1983)

"Israelis Close Palestine Press Service Newsletter", *al-Fajr* (English) (29 April 1983): 3

Najjar, Orayb, "From Enemies to 'Colleagues': Relations between Palestinian Journalists and Israeli West Bank Beat Reporters, 1967–1994", *Gazette*, 55 (1995): 113–30

Negbi, Moshe, "Paper Tiger: The Struggle for Press Freedom in Israel", *Jerusalem Quarterly*, 39 (1986): 17–32

"New Restrictions in Areas", *al-Fajr* (English) (20 March 1989): 1, 2

"PPS Closed", *al-Fajr* (English) (3 April 1988): 1, 11

"PPS Opens Office in Athens", *al-Fajr* (English) (20 March 1989): 12

"Press Service Warned of Closure", *al-Fajr* (English) (21 September 1984): 1, 13

Schenker, Hillel, "Interview: David Shipler: A Certain Positive Evolution", *New Outlook* (May 1984): 20–24

Serrill, Michael, "In Israel, Wounding the Messenger", *Time* (11 April 1988): 56

Tawil, Raymonda Hawa, *My Home, My Prison*, New York: Holt Rinehart, 1980; London: Zed, 1983

PALESTINIAN NATIONAL AUTHORITY
(al-Sulta al-Wataniyya al-Filastiniyya)

The Palestinian National Authority (PNA) is an autonomous entity formed in non contiguous parts of the West Bank and Gaza Strip in 1994 as a result of the Oslo peace process between Israel and the Palestine Liberation Organization (PLO). The PNA possesses civil and municipal powers in most of the Palestinian-populated areas, but Israel retains full or shared rule over 70 per cent of the actual territory, pending a final agreement on status.

Under PNA rule Palestinians in Gaza and the West Bank have been able for the first time to publish newspapers and books, as well as operate radio and television stations, unchecked by Israeli control. Numerous new printed forms of media have appeared, while the PNA has inaugurated the Palestinian Broadcasting Corporation (PBC) to launch radio and television programmes. By 2001 more than 150 press publications, including three daily newspapers, 27 television stations, and eight radio stations were operating within Palestinian territories. In addition, already established newspapers such as *al-Quds* (Jerusalem) and *al-Nahar* (The Day), now free from many of Israel's strict press restrictions, appeared to have fresh opportunities too.

However, *al-Nahar* soon clashed with the PNA over its perceived pro-Jordanian bias. Established in East Jerusalem in 1986, it received subsidies from the Jordanian government. In July 1994 the PNA prohibited the newspaper's distribution after it printed articles on the Israeli–Jordanian peace talks, including a reproduction of the two countries' declaration recognizing special Jordanian rights over Islamic holy places in Jerusalem. Since Palestinians also claim these rights, the PNA charged the newspaper with printing information "harmful to Palestinian national interests". When publication resumed in September, *al-Nahar* was editorially more PNA-friendly. Yet repeated PNA interference with its distribution and the loss of Jordanian subsidies after 1996 forced *al-Nahar* to close down in January 1997.

In July 1995 the PNA enacted a comprehensive press law. It contains provisions for a "free press" and declares that "freedom of opinion is guaranteed to every Palestinian", who has "the right to express his opinion freely, orally, in writing, in photography or drawing in mediums of expression and information". Political parties are permitted to publish newspapers and the courts have been allotted review powers over the enforcement of the statute.

Other provisions qualified these rights, however. Modelled on the 1993 Jordanian Press and Publication Law, the Palestinian version contains rules for the licensing and printing of publications. They include the establishment of capital requirements for publishing companies, restrictions on the importation of non-Palestinian publications, and the listing of punitive measures for "press crimes". Books also fall under the statute's purview. Four copies of every book must be forwarded to the Ministry of Information before distribution and the ministry ultimately determines if the book will be circulated. The Press Law gives ample enforcement powers to this ministry, which also decides who is and who is not a journalist. The very creation of a Ministry of Information was condemned by Palestinian human rights groups as being contrary to the principle of freedom of expression. While the courts have review capacity over the law, the judicial system is still under development and its powers remain nebulous. Therefore, ultimate authority still rests in the Information Ministry, which reports to Yasser Arafat, president of the PNA.

The PNA has granted licences to scores of private newspapers and radio and television stations. Some of these new media outlets are owned by individuals or groups vehemently opposed to Arafat's policies. At times the PNA tolerates criticism, while at other times publications are suspended, licences revoked, and dissenting journalists arrested. Criticism of Palestinian officials is in many instances viewed as a personal attack on the individual. Journalists whose reports reflect a negative view of the PNA are frequently accused of violating the Press Law's article 8, which prohibits "publishing anything that may instigate violence, fanaticism and hatred or invite racism and sectarianism". These provisions often prompt publications to self-censor in order to stay in operation.

In late 1999, following riots in the West Bank and Gaza against the slow progress and scant gains of the peace talks with Israel, Palestinian police closed down four television and two radio stations. Bassan Eid of the Palestinian Human Rights Monitoring Group complained that the police were "continuously violating the press law without any intervention from the Ministry of Information". Signatories of a leaflet that accused the administration of "tyranny, corruption and political deceit" were arrested in November 1999, and kept in prison for 40 days.

These prohibitions also apply to the airing of unedited debates of the popularly-elected Palestinian Legislative Council. The council is constitutionally separate from the executive branch of the PNA. In March 1997 the independent al-Quds Educational Television started broadcasting live debates of the council, at which representatives often criticize Arafat's policies. While council meetings are open to the public, legislative news seldom appears on the official PBC unless Arafat is portrayed in a positive manner. The live debates were initially condoned but as the debates turned more captious, the broadcasts were jammed and the television service's director, Daoud Kuttab, arrested in May 1997. After some independent television stations aired taped versions of the debates and influential members of the Legislative Council intervened on Kuttab's behalf, he was released and the jamming ceased. Upon release Kuttab noted: "Arafat couldn't put the Council in jail, so he took me. But if that's the price of freedom of the press, I'm not at all sorry."

ROBERT J. BOOKMILLER

Further Reading

Gellman, Barton, "Palestinian Legislators' Telecasts Caught in a Jam", *Washington Post* (21 May 1997): A29

Immanuel, Jon, "Scent of Freedom", *Jerusalem Post*, International Edition (17 May 1997): 14

Levinson, Jay, "Death of a Newspaper", *Jerusalem Post*,
  International Edition (1 February 1997): 15
Najjar, Orayb Aref, "The 1995 Palestinian Press Law: A
  Comparative Study", *Communication Law and Policy*, 2 (1997):
  41–103

Schmemann, Serge, "Palestinians Free Reporter Held for Week",
  New York Times (28 May 1997): A7

Website

Palestinian National Authority homepage, http://www.pna.net

PANAMA

Population: 2,856,000	**Number of daily newspapers:** 7
Main religions: Roman Catholic; Protestant	**Number of radio receivers per 1000 inhabitants:** 299
Official language: Spanish	**Number of TV receivers per 1000 inhabitants:** 187
Other languages spoken: English	**Number of PCs per 1000 inhabitants:** 27.1
Illiteracy rate (%): 7.5 (m); 8.7 (f)	

Panama's geography has dominated its history. The isthmus through which the Panama Canal was built is both the lowest and the narrowest point in the southern Americas, a "strategic bridge" between the Atlantic and the Pacific, and the ideal route by which goods may be transported. The history of Panama has been dominated by the attempts of foreign powers to control, for their own economic purposes, the smallest country on the continent; this process culminated in the building of the Panama Canal, under US auspices, in 1905–14. Panamanians have struggled to reconcile the principle of political freedom with the need for economic and political stability.

Columbus traced the coastline of Central America on his fourth voyage between May 1502 and November 1504. Within four years, the isthmus had been invaded by raiders searching for slaves and the settlement of Darién had been established. By 1513 the Pacific had been reached and, in 1519, Pedro Arìas de Ávila had founded Panama City; the Spanish founded an *audiencia* (administrative and legal court) there in 1538. From 1564 Panama was formally administered from New Granada, but, because of the difficulty of travel between Santa Fé de Bogotá (in present-day Colombia) and Panama City, local government enjoyed rather more political autonomy than in other Spanish colonies in the region.

In general, however, the control of ideas was no different in Panama than in the rest of Spanish America. The Tribunal of the Inquisition was established at Cartagena, the bishop of Panama acting as local agent. The colony was dominated by the overwhelming conservatism of the Catholic Church, which controlled the education system. As Enlightenment ideas began to cross the Atlantic, towards the end of the 18th century, church and colonial government combined in a vain attempt to keep them out. Pedro de Mendinueta y Múzquiz (viceroy at Santa Fé de Bogotá, 1801–03) was particularly assiduous in banning literature and ideas that threatened Spanish interests, as well as religious texts at variance with Catholic orthodoxy.

The arrival of the new century coincided with news of countries to the south that had thrown off the colonial yoke. Amar y Borbon (viceroy, 1803–10) paid particular attention to events on Saint Domingue (1791–1804) and the subsequent establishment of the independent republic of Haiti, the first black republic in the Americas. He could hardly stem the tide, however, and, when trade ties with Jamaica were established in 1809, merchants were able, for the first time, to receive information censored by their home government in New Granada. Spain transferred its government to Panama City in 1812, with little effect on the rising demand for independence. During the last ten years of Spanish rule in Panama, military governors attempted to keep the lid on these demands, but at last, under Brigadier Pedro Ruiz de Porras, it became possible to publish *La Miscelánea*, a journal devoted to French and North American political ideas. Panama declared independence in 1821, joining the newly established republic of Gran Colombia. Freedom of the press and speech were confirmed in a string of trial constitutions.

In spite of enlightened policies, Panamanians chafed under Colombian rule, and the country declared itself completely independent during the Colombian civil war of 1839–41. This independence was shortlived. The status quo was restored in 1841 and, in the federal constitution of 1855, the isthmus was granted a considerable degree of political and economic autonomy.

Panama's oldest newspaper, *La Estrella de Panama* (The Star of Panama), owned by the Duque family, had been established in 1853. Under the new liberal republican Constitution, freedom of the press was guaranteed, but popular movements such as the independent Negro Liberal Party were feared by conservative-minded authorities. A black revolt of 1885, led by Pedro Prestán, was suppressed and Prestán was executed. Despite constitutional protection, Colombia regularly censored the Panamanian press, as, again in 1885, the Colombian general Santodomingo Vila suspended publication of the *Panama Star and Herald* for its alleged hostility to his government. The Colombian Constitution of 1886, moreover, placed limits on the freedom of the press in Panama, an action that was bound to play a part in once again fuelling the desire for complete Panamanian independence.

This was finally achieved with military assistance from the United States in 1903. The US was driven by the opportunity to control the Panama Canal, allowing for a dramatically shortened naval passage from the Atlantic to California: it was opened in 1914. The Canal Zone, eight kilometres on each side of the canal itself, together with its 60,000 inhabitants (the Zonians), became US property, administered under US law. From now on, Panama was economically dependent on the US. Meanwhile, the first Constitution of the Republic of Panama guaranteed freedom of the press and of religion; in its first 40 years, censorship was virtually unheard of in Panama. Musicians, artists, poets, and actors enjoyed encouragement and support from both government and people.

The second half of the 20th century, however, was characterized by a succession of presidents acutely conscious of their needs for security and dignity. Arnulfo Arías (president 1941–52), a member of a family that was to have continuing influence in Panamanian politics, began the succession. His censors kept a close eye on newspapers and the radio for any negative comments; *El País* was shut down for such an offence. Unprecendently, in 1952 the government demanded that radio commentators submit their scripts for review by a government legal representative before they were aired (the demand was later extended to newspapers). This was an election year; the radio broadcaster Italo Zuppi was arrested for predicting the fall of an Arías-supported candidate. By contrast, Arías's successor, José Remón (president 1952–68), was generally supported by the press. Censorship and surveillance were reduced, although Remón outlawed the Communist Party in 1953 in order to retain US support..

The novelist Graham Greene, in *The Captain and the Enemy* (1988), described the Panama of Omar Torrijos Herrera (dictator 1968–81) as "a little capitalist state with a socialist general, split in two by the Americas". A populist as well as a military leader, Torrijos established an official government radio station, named Radio Libertad (changed later to Radio Nacional). He also appropriated the Pan American SA Company, publishers of the weekly *Crítica Libre* and *El Siglo*, changing its name to Edición Renovación (ERSA), in 1970.

In the same year, Torrijos went so far as to have the national bank shut down opposition newspapers for supposed tax irregularities. The Spanish- and English-language editions of *Panama América*, *La Hora*, *El Mundo*, and *El Día* were terminated. A three-person censorship board, with power to ban any material considered "offensive", was established in 1971. Of considerable moment, because it continued to be used by Torrijos's successors into the 1990s, was law 11 of 1978, which laid down that fines, imprisonment, withdrawal of licences, and closure could be imposed on newspapers and radio stations if their reports were considered to be "false" or "slanderous". Arguments arose on the rightness or wrongness of the government's intention to impose such penalties directly rather than through the courts; yet the Supreme Court itself backed the law by six votes to three. Already, in 1975, Radio Impacto had had its licence revoked for criticizing the government. In 1979 several commentators were banned from the radio because they were said to have made anti-government statements. A report from the Organization of American States in 1978 declared that freedom of expression did not exist in Panama.

The military remained in control after Torrijos's mysterious death in 1981. Manuel Antonio Noriega took power and harsh censorship continued. Noriega was accused of complicity in Torrijos's assassination, but no legal proceedings took place. He was also said to have manipulated the 1984 elections to ensure the victory of his Democratic Revolutionary Party (PRD), the senior party in a coalition of pro-Noriega parties. Matters came to a head when his former second-in-command, colonel Roberto Diaz, repeated the charges in an interview for *La Prensa*, and called for Noriega's removal (after the election, Noriega had remained *de facto* leader). A state of emergency was declared on 11 June 1987. *La Prensa* and two other opposition papers, *Extra* and *El Siglo* (which had no connection with the paper of the same name that was now owned by ERSA) were now required to submit articles for approval before publication. They refused and did not appear for two weeks. Official news bulletins were issued, and had to be carried by radio and television. Only ERSA papers were allowed to publish without censorship. A watch was also kept on the foreign press: copies of the *New York Times*, the *Miami Herald*, and the *International Herald Tribune* were restricted, and a correspondent for the Spanish paper *El País* was censored after his reports on Noriega's private life.

Panama's fortunes were now increasingly tied to Noriega's personal fate. In July 1987 the Ministry of the Interior formally warned foreign reporters that writing that "destroyed the country's image abroad" would result in penal action. *La Prensa* was closed indefinitely. *Extra*, *El Siglo*, and the weeklies *Quibo* and *La Gazeta Financiera* were closed for "inciting rebellion". Radio was also put under threat: a decree laid down that no changes in the boards of directors of radio stations were permitted without the government's agreement. Radio Exitosa was subjected to arbitrary cuts in its electricity supply.

A further state of emergency was declared in March 1989. Radios Mundial, KW Continente, Noticias, and Exitosa, all of which had run anti-Noriega items, were closed down. Exitosa was briefly reprieved, only to be closed again, after its airwaves had been used to transmit news of the failed coup of 3 October. All radio stations were now required to air a networked "national information bulletin" from 11.45am until 12 noon each day.

Finally, on 20 December 1989, US troops invaded Panama to overthrow Noriega and instal a civilian government under Guillermo Endara, thought to have been the legitimate victor in the May 1989 elections. This was far from a bloodless invasion, but it was noted at the time that US newspaper reports were less than complete. It was finally shown that at least 556 people had been killed. Moreover, the headquarters of the National Radio were bombarded, and equipment at Radio Verbo and Nuevo Emperador was destroyed. Thirty journalists are said to have been prosecuted for "anti-invasion statements"; part of the penal code outlawing the "defence of crime" was invoked. By October 1990 there were just five daily newspapers, all of them pro-government.

Euclides Fuentes Arroya, vice-president of the Panamanian Union of Journalists, alleged in December 1990:

> In their desire not to ruffle the feathers of the looming northern giant, [Panamanian journalists] have omitted to condemn the abuses caused by invading troops; through self-imposed censorship, they have kept their mouths shut about the fact that the ruling triumvirate has sacked relatives of victims who perished under US machine-gun fire. Reporters praise the occupation and justify the handover of power to a government which is too cowardly to demand compensation for the damage inflicted.

Guillermo Endara was a lawyer and was acutely sensitive to what he considered attacks on his personal integrity. He invoked Noriega's slander law (no. 11) in 1991, after Joaquim Carraquila, cartoonist for *La Prensa*, portrayed him with two faces, standing next to two former colleagues of Noriega; the latter are shown running away with suitcases bulging with money, some of which is falling at Endara's feet. The case was finally dropped, but Endara remained adamant, saying that the cartoon "clearly attributes criminal acts to me". Later, Dagoberto Franco, columnist for *El Siglo*, was also accused of slander after he had commented on links between Endara and the national bank, Interbanca. Endara resolutely refused to change slander from a criminal to a civil offence.

The constitution of Panama now provides that "all individuals may freely express their thoughts in writing, and through any other medium, without subjection to prior censorship", but advertising and propaganda "must not be harmful to health, morality, education . . . or national consciousness". Manipulation of the press is now less overt, but is still effective. In March 1992 *Quibo* was closed after accusations of plagiarism. Old-style censorship by brutality also remains. Radical television stations have been attacked; in July 1992 Radio Continente was damaged by a bomb, and many blamed Noriega supporters for the blast.

Two issues have dominated discussions of censorship in recent years. The first is drugs. As in the rest of Central America, drug-trafficking is a major problem in Panama. In 1997 Gustavo Gorriti, a Peruvian journalist, was refused the renewal of his licence after filing stories about campaign donations to president Pérez Balladares from the Colombian drug-trafficker José Castilla Hernao. His licence was extended after the intervention of Hillary Clinton, wife of the president of the United States, but he was then accused of "slander, insult and falsehood" after he had charged that José Antonio Sousa, Attorney General of Panama, had received a cheque for US$5,000 from a Colombian drug-trafficker.

The second issue is the relationship between Panama and the United States, which remains, as always, high on the agenda. In 1997 Miguel Antonio Bernal, a law professor at the University of Panama, was charged with slander after comments made during an interview with United Press International. It was generally believed that the government was trying to stifle discussion of the future relationship with its ally to the north, not least the future of US bases after the return to the Canal Zone to Panama, which took place on 31 December 1999.

ERIC D. ANDERSON

Further Reading

Alba, M.M., *Cronología de los gobernantes de Panama, 1510–1967*, Panama: Imprenta Nacional, 1935

Alisky, Marvin, *Latin American Media: Guidance and Censorship*, Ames: Iowa State University Press, 1981

Arroya, Euclides Fuentes, "A Bleak Outlook for Journalism", *Index on Censorship*, 19/10 (December 1990)

Bamrud, Joachim, "No Slander Please", *Index on Censorship*, 31/1 (1992): 31–32

Bancroft, Hubert Howe, *History of Central America*, vol. 3, 1801–1887, San Francisco: Bancroft, 1887

Biesanz, John and Mavis Biesanz,, *The People of Panama*, New York: Columbia University Press, 1955

LaFeber, Walter, *The Panama Canal: The Crisis in Historical Perspective*, New York: Oxford University Press, 1978; expanded edition 1989

Mellander, G.A., *The United States in Panamanian Politics: The Intriguing Formative Years*, Danville, Illinois: Interstate, 1971

Niemeier, Jean Gilbreath, *The Panama Story*, Portland, Oregon: Metropolitan Press, 1968

Perez-Venero, Alex, *Before the Five Frontiers: Panama, from 1821–1903*, New York: AMS Press, 1978

Pierce, Robert N. and John Spicer Nicols, *Keeping the Flame: Media and Government in Latin America*, New York: Hastings House, 1979

Ropp, Steve C., *Panamanian Politics: From Guarded Nation to National Guard*, New York: Praeger, 1982

The U.S. Invasion of Panama: The Truth Behind Operation Just Cause (report of independent inquiry), Boston: South End Press, 1991

GLEB PANFILOV
Russian film director, 1934–

TEMA (The Theme)
Film, 1981

In Gleb Panfilov's first feature film, *V ogne broda net* (1967, No Ford under Fire), his wife, Inna Churikova, the leading actress in all of his films, plays a young woman of great energy and sincerity who becomes politically aware during the Bolshevik revolution, but also discovers her talent as a primitive painter. The theme of artistic talent and its fate was one that continued to preoccupy Panfilov and Churikova. Refused permission to make a film about Joan of Arc, they made *Nachalo* (1970, The Debut), in which Churikova plays a factory worker in a small town who is chosen to star as Joan in a film for a Moscow studio. Their hopes of making a film directly about Joan were not abandoned. After Filipp Ermash, whom Panfilov had known when both were working in Sverdlovsk, became chairman of the State Cinema Committee (Goskino) in 1972, their hopes were raised, but to no avail. In 1973, Churikova wrote a long and desperate letter of appeal to Ermash, relating her sacrifices of other roles, even of having children, in a desperate desire always to be ready to start work on the Joan of Arc project. Ermash did not reply. He told Panfilov later: "Make a film on a modern subject, and then you can have your Joan".

Panfilov and Churikova then made *Proshu slova* (1975, I Wish to Speak), but this tale of the leader of the executive committee running a provincial town (Churikova) whose passionate commitment to her job makes her unaware of the tragic unhappiness of her family ran into censorship trouble and was not immediately released. Panfilov started work on another contemporary subject, which was to become *Tema* (The Theme). He took care to disguise the main thrust of his screenplay, a crisis in the life of a successful writer, and to stress its interest in the significance of the cultural past. Ermash still would not countenance the film about Joan of Arc, but he gave permission for *Tema* "as long as certain accents are properly placed". Work continued on emendations to the script, with the result that Ermash received, in Panfilov's words, "something much more unpleasant. He brought it upon himself."

The main concern of *Tema* is with the behaviour, attitudes, and treatment of writers in late Soviet society. The hero is called Kim Esenin: his first name, an acronym of the Russian for "Communist International of Youth", places him as having been born in the 1920s. He is a highly successful writer who, at the start of the film, is driving to the ancient town of Suzdal to complete a play about the Old Russian prince, Igor, a play he has taken on, as he admits, because "the advance came along when my *dacha* needed mending". He is accompanied by another writer, Pashchin, the author of a string of successful adventure stories. In Suzdal both writers are lauded by their fans, Pashchin by a young traffic policeman, Esenin by an absurdly enraptured old schoolteacher, Mariia Aleksandrovna, whose indefatigable succession of dithyrambs in his praise finally infuriates him. He is also bemused by a young woman, Sasha (played by Churikova), a tour guide in the local museum, whose overt failure to be impressed by him he takes as a challenge. Sasha disdains Esenin's strategies of flirtation and despises his self-betrayal as an artist. She herself devotes much of her time to gathering together the writings of a local eccentric of the 1930s, Chizhikov, a fireman who wrote verses, whom she calls her "poor genius". Sasha is also, it transpires, unhappily in love with a young gravedigger, Andrei – unhappily because Andrei, formerly a gifted scholar at a literary research institute, was dismissed when he refused a compromise that would have advanced his career, and is now, in a fury of hatred ("everything here is lies"), on the point of emigrating to Israel or the United States. Shocked by what he has learned, Esenin drives away from Suzdal. After a change of heart, he turns back to see if Sasha is all right, but his car spins off the road and overturns. At the end of the film, Esenin's fate is left uncertain.

Tema is thus a film about writers and their readers. The contrast between the worldly success of the conformists and the oblivion or humiliation of the men of talent is eloquent. This assessment of the fates of writers in the Soviet Union, reminiscent of that provided 40 years previously by Mikhail Bulgakov in his novel *Master i Margarita* (*The Master and Margarita*), was anonymously denounced after it was shown to the Central Committee of the Communist Party, and openly attacked by the Writers Union, who angrily asserted that no writers like Esenin existed in their ranks.

In addition to its treatment of the Soviet intelligentsia, *Tema* touches upon a subject that had previously been taboo, that of emigration. These two themes were enough to get the film shelved, but there is something more pervasive about the film's unacceptability in the late Brezhnevite Soviet Union. Its picture of the falsity and banality of every aspect of people's lives, its unerring ear for the clichés and the fatuous rhetoric of their conversations, make it one of the most corrosive of all analyses of a society in crisis.

As was so often the case, the film's fate was not helped by external events. After it was made, Soviet troops invaded Afghanistan and Andrei Sakharov was exiled to the town of Gor'kii. *Tema* was shown out of competition at the Moscow Film Festival in 1981, but then disappeared again. It was finally released, after the intervention of the "conflict commission" set up by the fifth congress of the Filmmakers Union, in June 1986. It was seen by 3.9 million viewers in its first year of Soviet release and provoked passionate discussion about the state of Soviet society. It won the Grand Prix at the Berlin Film Festival in 1987.

JULIAN GRAFFY

Writings

Tema kinostsenarii (The Theme: Screenplay), with Aleksandr Chervinskii, 1989

Further Reading

Volchek, N.S. (editor), "Glavnaia tema – tvorchestvo: Khudozhestvennyi fil'm *Tema*" (The Main Theme is Creativity: The Feature Film *The Theme*), in *Kino, Vremia, Zritel'* (The Cinema, the Time, the Viewer), Moscow: Ruskii Iazyk, 1989

OSKAR PANIZZA
German dramatist, 1853–1921

Highly controversial and pugnacious, Oskar Panizza was best known for his "blasphemous" play *Das Liebeskonzil* (The Council of Love), for which in 1895 he was sentenced to a year in jail, the harshest punishment meted out to a writer in Imperial Germany.

Panizza and his siblings were baptized in the faith of their Catholic father, but after the father's death in 1855 their mother tried to raise them as Protestants. The church hierarchy – the dominant religious force in Bavaria – employed all legal means to force her to give the children a Catholic upbringing, but she hid them with friends and relatives until 1861, when the church gave up its claims. These experiences undoubtedly prepared the ground for Panizza's violently anti-Catholic attitudes in later life.

Panizza received a medical degree in 1881 and practised sporadically as a clinical psychologist. A generous annual stipend from his mother permitted him to devote time to writing, his preferred vocation. He was closely associated with Munich's naturalist circles in the early 1890s, and his viewpoints became increasingly radical: he became an atheist; he adopted anarchist beliefs that called for the right of the individual to challenge all social mores and legal strictures; and observations in his clinical work led him to write about "unconventional" sexual practices. He published a number of short stories and books, some of which were confiscated for being either too obscene or too hostile to the Catholic church. In 1894 he wrote a short play, *Der heilige Staatsanwalt* (The Holy Public Prosecutor), to protest against the repeated banning of his works.

Panizza's satirical streak, as well as his penchant for sexually risqué and anti-Catholic themes, came together in *Das Liebeskonzil*, which was published in Zürich in 1894. The play is set in 1495, during the papacy of Rodrigo Borgia (Alexander VI, 1492–1503), when the first outbreak of syphilis was reported in Europe. The drama explains the temporal coincidence of these events by suggesting that venereal disease was a form of divine retribution for papal iniquity. The first act opens in heaven, where we are introduced to a severely caricatured Holy Family: God the Father is an old doddering fool; Jesus is simpleminded and impotent; the Holy Spirit appears as a rocket streaking across the stage; and the Virgin Mary is vivacious, vain, and perpetually concerned with her sexual allure. To see what is transpiring on earth, the group inhales hashish and falls into a trance. What they witness is depicted in the ensuing act, which dramatizes sexual orgies at the papal court (Panizza provided footnotes purporting to document the historical veracity of what he depicted). Back in heaven, the Holy Family is outraged and summons the devil to concoct a suitable punishment. He invents syphilis, which he transmits first to the papal court via a stunningly beautiful woman he has fathered by Salome. In return for this favour, the devil demands that the Holy Family allow his books to be circulated freely on earth, since "when someone thinks and is not allowed to communicate his thoughts to others – that is the worst of all tortures".

The same freedom was not granted to Panizza. *Das Liebeskonzil* was confiscated and the author was prosecuted according to article 166 (blasphemy) of the German Penal Code. At the trial held in Munich on 30 April 1895, he was sentenced to a year in jail, a harsh punishment compared to the several weeks of fortress arrest which was the usual sentence applied to refractory writers in Imperial Germany. The trial sent shockwaves throughout Germany's literary community, including some who had little sympathy with Panizza's style or viewpoints. The imprisonment also took its toll on Panizza's health and sanity. After his release in 1896 he moved to Zürich, but was expelled as an undesirable alien two years later. He proceeded to Paris, where he wrote *Parisjana* (1899), a bitter work that included scatological poems about the Kaiser. German authorities promptly charged him with *lèse-majesté*, and confiscated the trust fund given him by his mother. Without income, Panizza was compelled to return to Munich in 1901. He was judged mentally unfit to stand trial, however, and eventually his family had him committed to an asylum in Bayreuth, where he died in 1921. His life seemed the fulfilment of a statement he had made while serving time in prison: "Today, when someone expresses a free thought, he is left with only three choices: the insane asylum, jail, or exile."

In terms of literary quality, Panizza's works were erratic, but his aggressive stance and his challenges to the censor made him a hero of the *avant-garde* well into the Weimar era, when Kurt Tucholsky and Walter Benjamin, like George Grosz, kept his memory alive. Indeed, his works continue to haunt the censors. As late as 1962 *Das Liebeskonzil* was confiscated in Germany, though it has been freely available since 1964. And in 1983 Bavarian authorities blocked the public funds that had been promised to Herbert Achternbusch for making his movie, *Das Gespenst* (The Ghost), which was strongly influenced by Panizza's work. Ninety years after Panizza's trial, however, Achternbusch was able to win his case in court.

PETER JELAVICH

Writings

Der heilige Staatsanwalt, 1894
Das Liebeskonzil: Eine Himmels-Tragödie, 1895; as *The Council of Love: A Celestial Tragedy*, translated by Oreste F. Pucciani, 1973

Further Reading

Bauer, Michael, *Oskar Panizza: Ein literarisches Porträt*, Munich: Hanser, 1984
Jelavich, Peter, "Oskar Panizza and *The Council of Love*" in his *Munich and Theatrical Modernism: Politics, Playwriting, and Performance, 1890–1914*, Cambridge, Massachusetts: Harvard University Press, 1985

ANDRZEJ PANUFNIK
Anglo–Polish composer, 1914–1991

Andrzej Panufnik's encounters with censorship – first in Poland and then, in effect, also in Britain – were for him doubly galling. A senior postwar composer and conductor who attempted to dedicate himself to the restoration of Polish musical excellence, he endured the political manipulation of his communist masters and the progressive emasculation of his creative spirit as a composer until he could bear the frustration no longer. In 1954, Panufnik escaped to the west only to find, within three or four years of his settling in Britain, that his music was being sidelined by the BBC and so, at least in the medium of broadcasting in Britain, being as effectively suppressed as it had been in Poland.

Panufnik had survived the appalling horrors and deprivations of wartorn Warsaw to become, in his early 30s, one of the most prominent and important musicians in postwar Poland, a figure from whom the Soviet-dominated government looked for compliant leadership. At first he contributed eagerly to the reconstruction of cultural life, although the brutality of Poland's Soviet "liberators" and the unashamed propaganda of the "people's government" allowed few illusions. For the first years of communist rule, however, composers could write more or less what they liked. In 1945 Panufnik helped to set up the state music publishing house, Polskie Wydawnictwo Muzyczne (PWM), and in 1946 was appointed director of the decimated Warsaw Philharmonic, charged with rebuilding Poland's most prestigious orchestra virtually from nothing. Frustrations and unfulfilled promises led to his resignation after only a year.

Despite his refusal to join the Communist Party, Panufnik was called upon by the Ministry of Culture and Art to represent Poland at the festivals of the International Society for Contemporary Music in London, Copenhagen, and Palermo, and, repeatedly, to conduct abroad. In accepting these engagements, he took the opportunity to promote fellow Polish composers, firmly rejecting the ministry's disapproval of his support for "fascist" composers who lived abroad. The ministry needed Panufnik as an international advertisement for Polish music, while Panufnik was glad to have such opportunities and eager to contribute to the re-establishment of a genuine Polish identity.

In 1948, when Panufnik was chosen by the ministry to join the governing body of the new Composers Union, by whom he was soon elected vice-president, he saw it as an opportunity to win for his colleagues more performances, publication of their music, and better royalties and commission fees. Instead, he found himself thwarted in his own composition while being ceaselessly paraded as a spokesman who was "drawn", as he wrote "into a propaganda machine that opened and shut my mouth for me, while gnawing away at my dwindling reserves of independence and objectivity". Repeatedly, he later reported, he was manoeuvred into situations that he found both humiliating and dishonest. Much against his will, he was forced to join other committees and contribute to conferences, such as the International Congress in Defence of Peace, held in Wrocław in August 1948, whose propaganda intent was all too obvious. Yet when, in 1950, Panufnik was elected vice-president of the Music Council of Unesco, along with Arthur Honneger, the ministry of culture and art accepted the honour on his behalf, but then prevented him from attending any of its meetings or visiting Unesco's headquarters in Paris.

The grimmest and most oppressive forms of artistic censorship were imposed across the whole of the Soviet bloc between 1948 and 1956. They were signalled from Moscow by Andrei Zhdanov, Stalin's cultural commissar, who, early in 1948, announced that "bourgeois" tendencies would be totally eliminated, and exhorted composers to write instead like Glinka and Tchaikovsky. This directive was quickly reinforced at an International Conference of Composers held in Prague during June 1948 and stage-managed by the Soviet delegates, led by the immensely powerful general secretary of the Russian Composers Union, Tikhon Khrennikov. Panufnik and his colleagues were, of course, required to attend this conference. In Poland the new policy was applied by the deputy minister of culture and art, Włodzimierz Sokorski, and pushed through meetings of the Composers Union by a voluble, passionate Marxist, the respected musicologist professor Zofia Lissa, who, like Sokorski and many other Poles now occupying positions of power, had spent the war years in Moscow and returned well attuned to Soviet demands. Immediately, Panufnik and the other 100 or so members of the Union, only one of whom belonged to the party, were ordered to enter a song competition, each having to set the same text, the "Song of the United Party". Panufnik's attempts to extricate himself were countered by threats from Professor Lissa that, if he failed to produce an entry, the Composers Union would lose state financial support. There being no escape, he dashed off at the last minute what he hoped would be recognized as an utterly inept setting, only to find himself awarded first prize.

More alarmingly, the music into which Panufnik had poured his heart and mind began to encounter disapproval. An early victim was *Nocturne* (1947), which he had already conducted successfully both in Poland and abroad, but which was condemned at a conference held in Łagów in 1949 for its failure to express "joyful life under socialism" and its "unsuitability for the masses". In a closing speech, minister Sokorski made it clear that the new rules would be relentlessly imposed, equating abstract, experimental, even faintly dissonant music with the dying convulsions of capitalism.

Soon afterwards, at a debate on recent music by Polish composers attended by Khrennikov as guest of honour, a Polish music critic and party member attacked Panufnik's *Sinfonia Rustica* for its "formalism", an accusation that nobody dared to question in front of Khrennikov. Panufnik later recalled how a colleague who had chaired the jury that awarded *Sinfonia Rustica* first prize in the Chopin Competition only a year before, now turned to criticism, declaring its content "alien to the socialist era". Finally, Sokorski, under the watchful eye of Khrennikov and "having listened attentively to the political condemnation of this patently innocent piece, announced his verdict: '*Sinfonia Rustica* has ceased to exist!'"

As the growing Sovietization of Poland isolated composers from the West, and Stalinist policies invaded every aspect of people's lives, Panufnik found it impossible "even to dream of tackling new, seriously creative compositions". Under the Nazis he had felt able to compose "for the drawer", for an eventual aftermath, but now faith in the future drained from him altogether. Rejecting the dictates of socialist realism, Panufnik resorted for a while to "restoring" 16th- and 17th-century Polish music, following the example of the architects painstakingly reconstructing the buildings of old Warsaw that had been destroyed in the war. His *Old Polish Suite* (1950) and *Concerto in modo antico* (1951) are among the results. Yet Sokorski was apparently not without humanity and could skilfully deploy his sense of humour with persuasive charm. Despite the frustrations, Panufnik could not help liking him. Understandably he felt ambivalent:

> part of me had become cynical about having to eat and breathe the system, but another part remained patriotic, needing – indeed, wanting profoundly – to remain a Polish composer able to function creatively in my own environment.

The likelihood of realizing this aspiration looked increasingly remote. While Panufnik was leading a delegation to the Soviet Union in 1950, a group of Soviet composers probed him about his composing plans, looking perhaps for endorsement of their own acquiescence. In an incautious moment, Panufnik said that he was considering writing a *Symphony of Peace*. At once he regretted the remark: it became a "promise" that he was not allowed to evade. Yet, to steer a path through the political minefield, "to walk the tightrope of honesty above the chasm of conflicting pressures", was virtually impossible. Eventually he completed a three-movement symphony, but it was too inwardly personal for the authorities. Although the audience's response to the premiere by the Warsaw Philharmonic, with the composer conducting, in the spring of 1951, was warm and enthusiastic, official reaction was frigid. The symphony was damned for being "weak in ideological eloquence" and Panufnik was accused of "praying" for peace instead of "fighting" for it.

Despite this condemnation, Panufnik embarked on a *Heroic Overture*, a work originally part-composed in 1939 in defiance of the Nazi invasion. The score had been lost during the destruction of Warsaw. Now, in reconstructing it, he saw his music as a symbolic stand against an invasion more psychological than physical. With its real meaning concealed, the *Heroic Overture* won a competition, the prize being performance by the Finnish Radio Orchestra at the Helsinki Olympic Games of 1952. The audience in Finland reacted positively, but before the work could be publicly performed in Poland, it had to be assessed politically in a private audition – this time performed by the Polish Radio Orchestra – before party faithful and a handful of composers assembled in Katowice. Again, Panufnik's music was torn to shreds, condemnation being led by two of the players, the composers and musicologists remaining "silent witnesses" to an attack that resulted in the *Heroic Overture* being banned as unfit for public performance.

For Panufnik, the awful reality was now clear:

> After the Katowice farce, I knew that if I wrote music true to myself it would only be banned again. I was warned that, unless I conformed, I might be excluded from all my professional activities, including film music.

Work for the Film Unit, in which Panufnik was now using reconstructed old Polish music, remained his only regular source of income. Yet, because of his stature, Panufnik continued to be used. Although his serious music was banned, he was still perceived as Poland's leading composer, and the authorities still wished to parade him as a symbol of respectability both at home and abroad. Panufnik was pressed to become President of the Composers Union, but Sokorski recognized that the composer was mentally and physically exhausted, and allowed him to refuse. Instead, he was ordered to another task. Who better than a vice-president of Unesco's Music Council to write a propaganda letter to all leading musical figures in the West, urging their support for the next stage-managed World Congress for Peace? Panufnik determined that he must escape.

Panufnik's arrival in Britain in July 1954 brought a sense of new birth, even though he had been transformed overnight, as he later wrote, from "number one to no one". Friends found him engagements to conduct and commissions to compose. Richard Howgill, then the BBC's controller of music, invited Panufnik to conduct his *Sinfonia Rustica* at one of the Promenade Concerts (Proms) in 1955 and to compose a work for the tenth anniversary of the BBC Third Programme the following year, capping this, during his final weeks in post, with a second commission for some Polish dances to be performed in a festival of light music. The result of this last commission, *Polonia*, did not, apparently, please Howgill's successor, William Glock, and Panufnik claimed that, when he subsequently asked to hear the tape, he was told that it had been destroyed. Its performance in August 1959 by the BBC Symphony Orchestra represented Panufnik's last invitation to conduct at the Proms for many years.

Panufnik's music now became a casualty of British musical fashion, rather than formal censorship as in Poland. Glock's artistic policy resulted in brilliantly imaginative programmes dedicated to the new canon of modernism. If Glock was concerned with balance, it was rather to reveal meaningful connections between earlier music and the Darmstadt-centred avant-garde. While it was undoubtedly inspired, Glock's vision tended to marginalize those who failed to match up to his agenda (though to be fair, no more so than the modernists themselves had been marginalized by previous BBC controllers of music, in a country then noted for its musical conservatism). Panufnik, with his distinctive personal solutions to structural and expressive issues, was one of these outcasts – and this at a time when the BBC's radio stations were the only ones legally permitted to broadcast in the UK.

For Panufnik, there followed a difficult period in which he sought to rediscover his true voice. Impecunious and lonely, he had accepted a position as music director of the City of Birmingham Symphony Orchestra (CBSO) (1957–59), which consumed much of his energy. Despite his success with the orchestra, Panufnik decided to return entirely to composing, but the artistic climate dominated by Glock's wind of change at the BBC was unsympathetic. Panufnik wrote a piano concerto for the CBSO, but its premiere, conducted by the composer in 1962, was never broadcast, even though the BBC had recorded it. This time, Panufnik was informed that the tape had been "lost".

Panufnik was still fulfilling conducting engagements in a number of countries, and his music had found an enthusiastic advocate in Leopold Stokowski. In 1963 came a major success, the award of the Prince Rainier of Monaco First Prize for his *Sinfonia Sacra*, which has since become Panufnik's most performed work. However, under the regime of William Glock and his leading assistant Hans Keller, the BBC denied the *Sinfonia Sacra* a British broadcast. The concert in Monte Carlo at which it received its premiere was broadcast, but with Panufnik's work excluded: the BBC's reading panel had rejected it, which explains why the *Sinfonia Sacra* was again omitted from the BBC's relay of a Unesco concert from Paris soon afterwards. Not until a decade later did it find its way into a broadcast from the Edinburgh Festival – "by some oversight", in Panufnik's opinion. This broadcast and a "Composer's Portrait" presented by a young producer, Martin Dalby, were the only exceptions to what amounted to an embargo on radio broadcasts of Panufnik's music that held sway for more than 10 years. A change of attitude was eventually triggered by the Arts Department of BBC Television, which relayed Stokowski's British premiere of Panufnik's *Universal Prayer* from Twickenham Parish Church and then invited Panufnik to compose a piece with his own screen visualization. The result was *Triangles*, premiered on television in 1972, after which radio broadcasts of his music resumed.

Glock later denied that he had excluded music that was either unfashionable or failed to meet with his approval, saying that he had merely allowed his staff to express their own attitudes and beliefs (he personally programmed only the Proms season), and that the composers whom he is accused of sidelining when he became controller of music are still ignored today (in this respect too, Glock accurately reported the situation – Panufnik was one of very few exceptions). In Britain, Panufnik no longer had to endure political denigration, yet the persistent exclusion of his music from radio broadcasts was censorship of a kind, though of course no-one was prevented from performing it, and many prominent musicians in Britain did, including Sir Georg Solti, Yehudi Menuhin, and André Previn. In Poland, Panufnik's music continued to be banned for 23 years after his departure, during which his name was to be neither written nor spoken. His tenure as conductor of the Warsaw Philharmonic was removed from the orchestra's records. Not until 1977, at the insistence of his Polish composer colleagues, was a work by Panufnik included in the Warsaw Autumn Festival. Thus Panufnik fell foul of two opposing ideologies, first "socialist realism", then the very "formalism" – to use the dismissive Stalinist term for it – that the exponents of the former reviled. Both ideologies were propounded by men in positions of power and influence, whose belief in an exclusive social and aesthetic agenda for new music was held no less passionately or sincerely because it was also, in each case, externally moulded – by Soviet cultural policy in the case of Sokorski, by the audacious yet prescriptive proclamations of the western avant-garde in the case of Glock. For the one, Panufnik's music was too modern, for the other it was too reactionary; for both it was too personal and independent.

RICHARD STEINITZ

Writings
Impulse and Design in My Music, 1974
Composing Myself, 1987

Further Reading

Jacobson, Bernard, *A Polish Renaissance*, London: Phaidon, 1996
Panufnik, Scarlett, *Out of the City of Fear*, London: Hodder and Stoughton, 1956

PAPUA NEW GUINEA

Population: 4.809,000
Main religions: Roman Catholic; Lutheran; Presbyterian; Methodist; Anglican; Evangelical Alliance; Seventh-Day Adventist; other indigenous religions
Official language: Pidgin; English; Motu

Illiteracy rate (%): 29.4 (m); 43.2 (f)
Number of daily newspapers: 2
Number of radio receivers per 1000 inhabitants: 91
Number of TV receivers per 1000 inhabitants: 9.3

An independent nation since 1975, Papua New Guinea consists of a mainland (the eastern half of the island of New Guinea) and a collection of smaller islands of varying sizes. The bulk of the population are Melanesian, but there are some 850 different tribes, and a similar number of languages and dialects, among which, however, English and Tok Pisin (Pidgin) are the most widely used.

Papua New Guinea was relatively undisturbed by European influence before the late 19th century. Around three million Stone Age people shared the belief that the affairs of this world are controlled by superhuman beings, often their ancestors, who needed regular acts of propitiation. Headhunting and cannibalism therefore had respected places in the lives of many of these peoples. Incest and adultery were punished by death; murder and theft were regularly avenged.

Sporadic European exploration and trading began under Portuguese auspices around 1512. The region was named New Guinea by the Dutch and, over 300 years, such individual explorers as Louis-Antoine Bougainville, Philip Carteret, and James Cook gave their names to places and districts. The practice of "blackbirding" – tricking or cajoling local people into forced labour in places as far away as Peru – was rife from the mid-19th century. Finally, at a constitutional conference held in Sydney in 1883, it was agreed that Germany should take the north of the territory as its colony and Britain the south (the western half of the island, now part of Indonesia, remaining in Dutch hands).

The colonial administrators and missionaries who now flooded into Papua New Guinea, especially in the British area, sought to censor those aspects of traditional belief that appeared shocking to European sensibilities, such as cannibalism. Magical and religious rituals were gradually replaced by a new form of supernatural belief, in the Christian Trinity, used as an agency of pacification as well as a moral force. However,

it was far from the case that belief in magic was eradicated. This is attested by the emergence, as early as the 1890s, of "cargo cults", millenarian movements that provided religious justification for resistance to white domination. These too were not easily censored, and emerged in various places as late as the 1930s, although each soon burned out.

The gap between Stone Age community organization and European liberal democracy was equally wide, and no attempts were made to bridge it in the German areas of Papua New Guinea. The British made their normal colonial arrangements for legislative and economic councils, inherited by the Australians, who, after World War I, were mandated by the League of Nations to administer large parts of Papua New Guinea (including the sector previously under German control). Education was largely carried out by missionaries, who, by the 1930s, had established more than 2,000 village schools, but, through lack of resources, had inculcated only minimal literacy in Tok Pisin and vernacular languages.

Whatever educational and political advances had been accomplished were thrown into confusion by the Japanese invasion of 1942. On the other hand, the presence in Papua New Guinea, for the rest of the war, of a great variety of "foreigners" finally drew a line under the territory's long past, and provided the impetus for its taking the road to independent nationhood.

In 1946, the United Nations appointed Australia as trustee of the territory, and obliged its administrators:

> to take into consideration the customs and usage of the inhabitants of New Guinea, and [to] safeguard the interests, both present and future, of the indigenous inhabitants of the Territory, ... [to] promote, as may be appropriate to the circumstances of the Territory, the educational and cultural advancement of its inhabitants,

. . . [and to] guarantee to the inhabitants of the Territory, subject only to the requirements of public order, freedom of speech, of the press, of assembly and petition, freedom of conscience and worship, and freedom of religious teaching.

At this stage most Australian administrators thought that independence was far away. They were under constant pressure from the United Nations, however, and embarked on programmes of mass literacy and progressively increased participation in the Legislative Council. A House of Assembly was elected in 1964 and political parties began to emerge in 1965. Ten years later, Papua New Guinea was independent, with a Westminster-style political system centred on a unicameral legislature. Many more political parties have emerged since then, many of them tribal or centred on individuals. Elections are held regularly, but cannot exactly be described as "fair", since considerable vote-buying, violence, and intimidation take place.

Section 46 of the Constitution extends to all citizens and noncitizens, subject to the provisions of laws on defamation, sedition, contempt, and obscenity, the rights of free speech and expression. These rights are, in general, jealously guarded by the media and the courts. The first major exception to the general absence of censorship was promoted by the activities of the Organazi Papua Mardeka (Free Papua Movement, or OPM), operating in neighbouring Irian Jaya, the former Dutch territory now ruled by Indonesia. The peoples of the two halves of the island are ethnically similar and there is an open border between the two. The OPM, however, is fighting for independence from Indonesia, and started a guerrilla war to that end in 1984. There is little doubt that the OPM has enjoyed considerable support in Papua New Guinea, which its guerrilla fighters have used as a sanctuary. Indonesia accused Papua New Guinea of covert support for the rebels and the government had little option but to dissociate itself from them. Inevitably, therefore, it had to expel in 1984 the resident correspondent of the Australian Broadcasting Corporation (ABC), Sean Dorney, after he had conducted an interview with an OPM leader inside Papua New Guinea. The foreign minister, Rubbie Nomaliu, declared: "This country is not to be trampled over by visiting journalists". Dorney was allowed to return in 1988, but in 1992 Per Eve Carlsson, a Swedish journalist and documentary filmmaker, was prevented from completing a film on the conflict.

Meanwhile, in 1988, secessionists on the resource-rich island of Bougainville staged a full scale revolt against the government. Bougainville was the the world's largest producer of copper, and the secessionists maintained that its exploitation brought them no economic benefits and caused great environmental damage. The Bougainville Revolutionary Army (BRA) came face to face with the Papua New Guinea Defence Force (PNGDF), a state of emergency was declared, and Bougainville was blockaded. A news blackout was imposed, journalists could not go to Bougainville without the PNGDF's permission, and they were expected to report the government's version of the conflict. Despite this, both local and foreign media began to report on atrocities committed against the civilian population in Bougainville. An Internal Security Act was swiftly rushed through parliament in 1993; it was targetted at the BRA and its supporters, but could also be used against journalists,

who, under section 6, are not allowed to meet proscribed organizations. In fact, however, such was the opposition to this provision that the government has never invoked it.

Bougainville remains a sensitive issue. In 1998, Sean Dorney was again in bad odour with the government when he reported that the then prime minister, Bill Skate, had been "continuously attacked" during a tour of the area. The offence was compounded by the ABC's allegations that Skate was involved in violent and corrupt activities. Protesting that he had been "unfairly treated", Skate declared that in future he would be interviewed only in Tik Pisin, so that Australian journalists would find it impossible to understand what he was saying.

There are half a dozen newspapers in Papua New Guinea. The three most influential – the *Post Courier*, owned by Rupert Murdoch's News International, the *National*, owned by the Malaysian timber giant Rimbuna Hijau, and the weekly *Independent*, owned by the mainstream churches – are published in English, both in print and on the internet. They regularly run stories on corruption and the misuse of public funds. In 1998, after the *National* published a critical editorial, it was threatened by the deputy prime minister, Michael Nali, who asserted that the right to free speech "did not permit foreigners to participate in the country's political destiny".

Public radio broadcasting is governed by an independent board, but has, in recent years, been transmitted only irregularly, owing to mismanagement and the lack of funds. In June 1995, the prime minister's senior media adviser, Franzalbert Jabu, directed Radio Kalong to withdraw an edition of the popular *Roger Hau'ofa Talkback Show* because it was due to discuss a new system of local government. Jabu maintained that "a key government agency should not be allowed to propagate information contrary to the majority view expressed in Parliament". If people wished to criticize, he said, they should buy advertising space on commercial radio. There are several private FM radio stations, which mostly play popular music and appeal to young people. Papua New Guinea's only television station, EM TV, owned by Australian interests, started broadcasting only in the late 1980s. Cable television, with dozens of overseas channels, is readily available at affordable prices.

Attempts to bring the media under firm control have been thwarted by the widespread opposition that they have engendered. A Mass Media Tribunal Bill, drafted in 1987, would have empowered the government to regulate and control both the press and broadcasting through a licensing system. The communications minister failed to dispel the popular conviction that the bill was intended to intimidate newspapers that ran unfavourable stories. A National Information and Communication Bill and, in 1997, a Media Commission Bill were also eventually shelved in favour of a system of self-regulation.

The Censorship Board is made up of representatives of the churches and community groups, together with government appointees. Formally, they are entitled to examine all printed and broadcast material, including imported films that may be shown on EM TV. However, they have neither the resources nor the personnel to enforce their rulings. Mostly preoccupied with pornography, they have banned such magazines as *Penthouse* and *Playboy*; *Cosmopolitan* and *Cleo* were banned between 1991 and 1998 because they contained nudity and advertisements for sex aids. Lifting the ban in 1998, the chairman of the Board declared that they contained some "useful articles". The only high-profile single incident of censorship occurred in 1993, when the chief censor ordered EM TV to cut a 16-minute segment of *60 Minutes*, the Australian current affairs programme, which dealt with sex abuse at a Catholic institution in Western Australia. The censor was widely condemned for this move.

Papua New Guinea has five internet service providers and the number of users is increasing rapidly. Newspapers run weekly features and primary schools have access to the Net.

The government actively encourages its use and most government departments have their own website.

JAMES CHIN

Further Reading

Chin, James, "The Media and Politics in Contemporary Papua New Guinea", *Point*, 24 (2000): 175–87
Dorney, Sean, *Papua New Guinea: People, Politics and History since 1975*, Sydney: Random House, 1990
Robie, David (editor), *Nius Bilong Pasifik: Mass Media in the Pacific*, Port Moresby: University of Papua New Guinea Press, 1995

PARAGUAY

Population: 5,496,000
Main religions: Roman Catholic; Mennonite; other Protestant
Official language: Spanish
Other languages spoken: Guarani

Illiteracy rate (%): 5.6 (m); 7.8 (f)
Number of daily newspapers: 5
Number of radio receivers per 1000 inhabitants: 182
Number of TV receivers per 1000 inhabitants: 101
Number of PCs per 1000 inhabitants: 9.6

One of only two landlocked countries in South America, Paraguay is often ignored or misunderstood because of its low profile, maintained since colonial times. Although its population has finally reached five million inhabitants, in its early years very few Spanish settlers moved there. The *mestizo* (mixed-race) population quickly grew as they took multiple Guaraní wives (as was the custom), and the native culture and language infiltrated daily life. Jesuit missionaries inhabited the country for nearly 200 years (until their expulsion in 1767), establishing large missions in which Guaraní was spoken exclusively while the Christian doctrine was amended to coincide with the indigenous belief system. From the beginning, Paraguay's isolationist spirit precluded peaceful relations with the viceroyalty of Río de la Plata, to which the territory was formally subordinate in the early 19th century. Because of the country's isolated state, a formal decree to abolish the *encomienda* (patronage) system in 1803 was largely ignored until after independence, and the practice of forced labor by the natives continued far longer than in the rest of Latin America. However, slavery was less widespread and harsh than in, for example, the mines of Bolivia and Peru. Colonial Paraguay was characterized by the imperviousness of its settlers to the outside world, the servility they imposed on the natives of the area, and the complete *mestizaje* (cross-breeding) of a culture whose majority would continue to communicate in the native tongue. These characteristics provided for the country's long history of dictatorship and consequent censorship.

Paraguayan distinctiveness continued well beyond the early achievement of independence in 1811. First, it refused incorporation into or cooperation with Argentina. In order to maintain the country's autonomy, the powerful José Gaspar Rodríguez de Francia, one of the founding fathers of Paraguay, was elected a member of the First Consulate. In 1814 he assembled a questionable congress which voted to give him absolute power for three years. Two years later, he declared himself dictator for life, with the title *El Supremo*. An austere man, with a doctorate in theology, Francia turned his back on the ideas

of Rousseau, which he had earlier imbibed, and – perhaps influenced by another of his earlier heroes, Napoleon Bonaparte – he established in Paraguay a long-lasting, personalized, and paternalistic rule, which lasted until his death in 1840. Francia, a typical hypochondriac dictator, feared that foreigners might exploit the country and undermine his position, so he carefully controlled all communications with the outside world.

Francia's control extended over the whole of Paraguayan life. The settlers' land, together with that of the Spanish crown and the church, was taken into public ownership. He set out to create a hybrid race, and to that end he forbade Spaniards to marry Spaniards, forcing them, under pain of imprisonment, to marry *mestizos*, indigenous people, or mulattos.

The publication of books and newspapers was forbidden, letters were censored, and meetings banned. Francia established an intricate network of informers, and instituted severe penalties for those who failed to denounce subversive activities. Literary and intellectual life were impossible, and great international exception was taken to the 10-year imprisonment of the French botanist Aimé Bonpland. He had entered Paraguayan territory without permission, which was considered an affront to national sovereignty. Fear was paramount, and the silence that reigned within Paraguay was so intense that even the guitar was muted, according to the Swiss doctor J.R. Rengger, trapped in Paraguay in 1819.

Despite the well-known "black" legend of Francia's dictatorship, he did create a certain stability within Paraguay during its long period of isolation from international confrontation. After Francia's death, Carlos Antonio López was elected president (1844–62) to continue a very different type of authoritarianism during the Nationalist period. Unlike Francia, López opened the country to foreign trade, established an army, initiated a republican form of government, and allowed some degree of freedom of expression. After his death, his son, Francisco Solano López, succeeded in power (1862–70). He recklessly led his country to ruin in the disastrous War of the Triple Alliance (1865–70) against Argentina, Brazil, and

Uruguay over disputed territory. This war was the bloodiest and most prolonged confrontation in post-independence South American history. In the Triple Alliance Treaty all three opposing countries declared war "not against Paraguay but against its tyrant, López". The war was devastating, reducing the Paraguayan population by half, shrinking Paraguayan territory by 26 per cent, and resulting in long-lasting economic and political paralysis. From 1870 until 1901, Paraguay was ruled by no fewer than 22 presidents. Another catastrophic war caused by a border dispute with Bolivia, the Chaco War (1932–35), again decimated the population.

In a situation of endemic war and dictatorship, it was surprising that any political or cultural life existed at all. But, in the immediate aftermath of the war, the Febrerista party was strong enough for their representative, colonel Rafael Franco, to assume the presidency (1936–37) and immediately to ban the activities of any other party or "vested interest". He declared that he had brought about a liberal revolution, "which is identical with the state". His "liberalism" included some redistribution of land, the right to form trade unions and to strike, and the guarantee of a wide range of social insurance benefits. The less liberal aspects of Franco's brief incumbency were institutionalized by his successor, marshal José Félix Estigarribia, who acted on the belief that dictatorship was necessary "to conquer anarchy which threatened to dissolve social ties". Political dissidents were arrested, and a tight censorship was imposed. His 1940 constitution aimed to give the executive limitless powers to suppress private association, suspend individual liberties, or impose a state of siege, and also allowed for the arbitrary arrest and the dispatch of dissidents into internal exile.

Estigarribia died in a suspicious plane crash less than a month after the promulgation of the constitution. General Higinio Morínigo, a Nazi sympathizer, became provisional president, then dictator (1940–48). All elements of liberalism were now eradicated. Liberal leaders were sent to detention camps, and their newspaper *El País* was confiscated and placed under the editorial control of a member of the German legation in the capital, Asunción. As Germany faced defeat in World War II, Nazis fleeing from Europe were given a home and enjoyed amenities not available to many Paraguayans.

In 1944 the United States pressured Morínigo to return to an acceptable state of democracy – allowing opposition parties to operate freely and holding national elections – or to forfeit economic benefits. Morínigo complied by proposing a democratization programme in 1946, during which he would restore freedoms of the press and of association. By late July, parties were denouncing the dictator in the name of "democratization". Consequently, Morínigo's minister of culture, Juan Natalicio González (a cultural historian and poet) organized the disruption of opposition meetings by squads of thugs (*Guión Rojo*, or Red Banner) who raided union meetings and attacked leaders. In September, the offices of *El País* were stormed, the staff beaten, and the presses damaged, it was said because they had accused Morínigo of plotting to stay in power. The Liberal and Febrerista party presidents were arrested, and Roque Gaona, editor of the Febrerista paper *El Pueblo*, along with Rafael Oddone, editor of *El País*, were forced to take refuge in the Brazilian embassy.

The civil war of 1947 followed, with the ruling Colorado Party restored after military aid from Argentine president Juan

Perón was offered to re-establish dictatorship. Remaining opposition newspapers were closed and the press and radio placed under government control. So oppressive was the atmosphere, dominated by the *Guión Rojo*, that tens of thousands of Paraguayans left the country over the next several months. A succession of dictators followed: Juan Natalicio González (1948–49), Federico Chaves (1949–54), and, notoriously, Alfredo Stroessner (1954–89), the most long-lasting in Paraguayan and Latin American contemporary history.

So far as history of Paraguayan censorship is concerned, the repression of previous centuries was but a prelude to that of general Stroessner. His censorship was severe, systematic and, in world terms, one of the most sustained of the second half of the 20th century. At its heart was the imposition of the "state of siege". This was already in place and had been used continuously since 1940, but Stroessner institutionalized the practice. Article 79 of his 1967 constitution allowed for its use in the case of "conflict or international war, or external invasion, internal disturbance or a grave threat from one of these". The condition of "internal disturbance" was evidently permanent, because the "state of siege" was renewed every 90 days, allowing people to be arrested, without access to trial, if suspected of participating in or causing such "internal disturbance".

Closely related to this provision was law 294, of 1955, entitled "the defence of democracy". It allowed Stroessner to accuse anybody who opposed him of espousing communism. Law 209, of 1970, said to have been enacted "for the defence of public peace and personal freedom", aimed to punish those "who foment class struggle and internal disorder". Stroessner had a simple view of democracy and of communism: he told his fellow dictator, general Pinochet of Chile, "Democracy exists in Paraguay because there is no Communism". The purpose of these laws was again catch-all – to persecute intellectuals.

From time to time, Stroessner would promise to lift the state of siege, only to find a pretext for keeping it in place. As early as 1959, such a promise included his intention to abandon press censorship. In May 1959, however, a student riot allowed him to re-impose the state of siege "in order to establish order". In Concepción, Catholic students who were caught painting anti-government slogans on walls were forced to scratch them off with their fingernails. In 1978, he lifted the emergency provisions in all areas of the country apart from Asunción, but the assassination of the exiled Nicaraguan dictator Anastasio Somoza in Asunción in September 1980 caused him to doubt his own security and the state of siege was re-imposed.

E. Pérez Barquín, a teacher, was expelled from Paraguay in 1977 because he was said to have been "educating potential supporters and implementers of the Marxist ideas of Communism". The evidence was in his library, where the authorities found copies of work by the educators Ivan Illich and Paolo Freire, and *A World History of the Communist Party*. Stroessner's censors took particular exception to journals published in Cuba such as *Casa de las Américas* and *Conjunto*, but the definitions of "Communism" and "Marxism" were left vague enough to ensure that libraries, bookshops, and publishers avoided making available any book that could be even remotely connected with the ideology.

Terror and suspicion were regularly used as weapons during the Stroessner regime. Like most modern dictators, he employed a corps of political police that prospered through involvement in contraband. In 1958 Father Ramón Talavera criticized the recent "elections" by which Stroessner had again been fraudulently returned to power. He was arrested, but released with a warning. Talavera then called for a protest rally, after which he "disappeared", to be found later on a country road, badly beaten and unable to speak – the official story read that he had suffered a nervous breakdown. The author Augusto Roa Bastos, living in exile since 1947, wrote in 1965 of "the brutality of the violence, the contempt for the spirit and for moral dignity" that "have contaminated the very air that is breathed, poisoning thought even before it is formulated . . . [I]t makes the rigour of official censorship superfluous."

Formally, article 73 of the constitution guaranteed freedom of the press, but press censorship of the most direct kind existed – that is, closure of those newspapers whose columns displeased the regime. The Liberal party newspaper *El Orden* made fun of Stroessner in late 1957 for his attempts to make the elections look legal; the paper was shut down. In the 1960s *El Enano*, the Febrerista Renovationists' weekly, often had to shut down because the authorities had seen to it that its electricity supply was reduced. And the police suppressed the Febreristas' *Prensa Campesina* after only one issue. By 1969 there was total press censorship, with police posted in every newspaper and radio station. Any criticism of police work, violations of human rights, corruption, or information about social problems was interpreted as encouraging subversion or preaching hatred between Paraguayans. *Comunidad* operated for some years as the weekly voice of radical Catholic protest, until the government closed it down in 1969; it was said to have promoted an anti-Stroessner campaign. The editor of *El Radical*, Miguel Angel Martínez, was arrested for "slandering a military officer" after the paper had accused general Otelo Carpinelli of abusing his powers; the paper was closed down between July and October 1974. During the 1970s and 1980s, the newspaper *ABC Color* was regularly harassed and its editors and journalists arrested and abused following its open denunciations of the government's corruption and incompetence. In March 1981 the journalists Humberto Paiva and Fernando Cazenave of *Ultima Hora* were arrested for their research into poverty in the city of Pilar. By 1987 *El Pueblo* was the only remaining opposition newspaper; it managed to survive until 1988, when Stroessner closed it during the year before his own removal from power. Severe criticism of the regime did get published in small opposition newspapers; however, absolutely no criticism of Stroessner was tolerated.

Radio and television also suffered from the complex net of censorship. In May 1986 Pedro Ferrari, an announcer for Teledifusora Paraguaya (Channel 13), was arrested and kept incommunicado for three weeks in the Department of Investigations for allowing copies of a film showing police violence to circulate. In May 1988 Radio Cáritas denounced obstacles placed to hinder reporting on the visit of pope John Paul II to Paraguay; later that year the station complained about the harassment and detention of its journalists. Similar treatment was meted out to its sister station, Radio Ñandutí.

It might have been thought from afar that the Film Censorship Board would operate like similar bodies elsewhere. But the standard reason given for its refusal of films ran along the lines of "films like this encourage Communists". Coming

under this rubric during the 1980s were all the films of the Greek director, Constantin Costa-Gavras (who admittedly had communist sympathies, and whose *L'Aveu* had been banned for a time even in Allende's Chile), Sidney Lumet's *Network*, and, along with the rest of Woody Allen's work, *Everything You Ever Wanted to Know about Sex but Were Afraid to Ask*. The dictatorship was also distrustful of the power of theatre. The Teatro Popular de Vanguardia, aiming to explore the lives of Paraguayan people as well as new ways of reaching them, was barred from the country's main theatre, the Municipal. The alleged lack of sanitation at the Teatro Caro in Asunción was blamed for the closure of Friedrich Dürrenmatt's *Romulus the Great*, immediately after its preview in 1971. At San Juan Bautista in 1975, an experimental theatre group run under the auspices of the Catholic Church was accused of "attacking Christian morality".

Religious repression was also rampant. The condition of Paraguay had naturally attracted the interest of the liberation theologians. Radical clergy and religious orders worked in rural areas to protect peasant rights with literacy programmes (thus the official unpopularity of Paolo Freire), welfare services, and small cooperatives. The regime responded by forbidding any contact between clergy and the people, effectively banning the celebration of Mass. In 1973 hundreds of Christian Agrarian League peasants occupied the churches in Coronel Oviedo to protest. Local Colorado peasant soldiers were ordered to storm the churches, which they did while chanting "death to the Christian Communists".

The large indigenous population of Paraguay also suffered during the Stroessner regime, which had a policy of genocide against them. In the mid 1970s professor Miguel Chase Sardi and his colleagues, who had created an Indian relief project, were arrested and tortured and the project closed in 1975. In 1976 six Catholic priests who denounced the genocide were deported and six Protestant missionaries doing relief work arrested. In 1962, 43 per cent of the population spoke only Guaraní, with a mere 5 per cent speaking only Spanish. However, Spanish was the official language, imposed on schoolchildren and university students alike. Consequently, Guaraní became the language of resistance to the regime. Julio Correa (1890–1953) presented plays in Guaraní which promoted awareness of peasant suffering. He was denied access to theatres and his plays were banned. José Asunción Flores, an exponent of Guaraní popular music, was expelled from the country after he had joined the Communist Party.

Poetry, always at the heart of Paraguayan culture, did not suffer direct censorship, although the poet's words could cost them dearly. Jorge Canese's *Paloma blanca; paloma negra* (1982, White Dove; Black Dove) contained the phrase "países de mierda como el nuestro" (shit countries like ours). Although the book was banned, it circulated widely to become the largest bestseller in the history of Paraguayan poetry. The generally repressive atmosphere caused such writers as Roa Bastos, Gabriel Casaccia, and Rubén Bareiro Saguier to live in voluntary or forced exile. Others such as Guido Rodríguez Alcalá and Renée Ferrer, chose to risk publishing while within the borders.

After 35 years in power, Stroessner was finally overthrown in a coup led by general Andrés Rodríguez, his right-hand man, on 3 February 1989. Elections were held, with all parties except the Communists allowed to stand. Most democratic freedoms were formally restored, but the legacy of Paraguay's long decades of dictatorship and corruption has not been easy to dispel, not least its treatment of journalists investigating the truth about the past. In 1991, for instance, the home of Francisco de Vargas, the vice-president of the Human Rights Commission of the Congress and Chamber of Deputies, was attacked. The police simply denied that torture, imprisonment, and "disappearances" of dissidents had ever taken place, until relevant documents were discovered buried in a police station yard. Lists, identity documents, and the transcripts of bugged telephone conversations provided concrete evidence of the abuses of Stroessner's political police, prompting the attorney general to initiate proceedings (ultimately unsuccessful) for the dictator's extradition from Brazil.

Paraguay's first free elections in May 1993 (although questions of fraudulence surfaced) brought the civilian Juan Carlos Wasmosy to power. But the military commander, general Lino Oviedo, announced that the armed forces would continue "co-governing the country with the glorious Colorado Party, whether the people liked it or not". Unrest was rife between Oviedo and Wasmosy as the president threatened to arrest Oviedo for coup attempts in 1996, and the military commander encouraged impeachment of the president. In March 1998 Oviedo was found guilty of insurrection and sentenced to ten years in prison.

In the May 1998 election, Raúl Cubas Grau, an Oviedo supporter, won the presidency and declared his intent to pardon Oviedo. His vice-president, Luis María Argaña, however, was an Oviedo opponent and deprived Cubas of a congressional majority. Cubas defied constitutional proceedings when he pardoned Oviedo, and Congress tried to have him impeached.

In March 1999 Argaña was assassinated by unknown assailants, but both Oviedo and Cubas were suspect. At the time of the assassination the services of the main cellular telephone company were interrupted for four hours, creating difficulties for the media. On 26 March six protesters were murdered while demonstrating for the resignation of Cubas. Two days later he resigned and fled to Brazil, while Oviedo left for Argentina. This political turmoil ended with Luis González Macchi, an Argaña supporter, in the presidency. His term was approved through 2003, but he has done little to improve the disastrous economic and political affairs of his country.

In May 2000 Macchi's government suffered an unsuccessful coup attempt by Oviedo supporters. Two radio stations were closed and four journalists arrested following the state of emergency declared by the government. The offices of Radio Asunción were ransacked and shut down and the owners Miguel and Adriana Fernández detained as suspected sympathizers with Oviedo. Other suspected Oviedo supporters were detained after the attempt. The vice-presidential elections of 13 August, 2000 were followed by attacks and threats against several media sources as the Colorado candidate lost by a narrow margin. Radio Primero de Marzo had its signal interrupted as it tried to report on the polls and received anonymous threats about blowing up the stations' transmitting equipment. In December a reporter for a Brazilian daily was beaten for reporting that young Brazilian men were serving in the Paraguayan army and National Police Force. On 5 January 2001, Salvador Medina, a reporter and chairman of the board of directors of a Capibary community radio station, was shot to death after exposing alleged local mafia activity. It is believed that the Colorado party is part of an orchestrated campaign against journalists.

BETSY J. PARTYKA

Further Reading

Amnesty International, *Paraguay: An Amnesty International Briefing*, London: Amnesty International, 1984

Blanch, José M. (editor), *El precio de la paz*, Asunción: CEPAG, 1991

Grow, Michael, *The Good Neighbor Policy and Authoritarianism in Paraguay: United States Economic Expansion and Great-Power Rivalry in Latin America during World War II*, Lawrence: Regents Press of Kansas, 1981

Inter-American Commission on Human Rights, *Report on the Situation of Human Rights in Paraguay*, Washington, DC: General Secretariat of the Organization of American States, 1978

Lewis, Paul H., *Paraguay under Stroessner*, Chapel Hill: University of North Carolina Press, 1980

Méndez-Faith, Teresa, *Paraguay: novela y exilio*, Somerville, New Jersey: SLUSA, 1985

Méndez-Faith, Teresa, *Breve diccionario de la literatura paraguaya*, 2nd edition, Asunción: El Lector, 1996

Méndez-Faith, Teresa, *Poesía paraguaya de ayer y de hoy*, 2 vols, Asunción: Intercontinental, 1997

Ñe-ëngatú lo dice todo: Información y análisis sobre el Paraguay (14 February 1984)

Nickson, R. Andrew, *Historical Dictionary of Paraguay*, 2nd edition, Metuchen, New Jersey: Scarecrow Press, 1993

Pendle, George, *Paraguay: A Riverside Nation*, London: Royal Institute of International Affairs, 1954

Rodríguez-Alcalá, Guido, *Ideología autoritaria*, Asunción: RP, 1987

Rodríguez-Alcalá, Guido, *Justicia penal de Francia*, Asunción: RP, 1997

Rodríguez-Alcalá, Hugo, *Historia de la literatura paraguaya*, Mexico City: Andrea, 1970

Roett, Riordan and Richard Scott Sacks, *Paraguay: The Personalist Legacy*, Boulder, Colorado: Westview Press, 1991

Saguier, Ruben Bareiro, "Culture of Fear", *Index on Censorship*, 8/1 (January–February 1973)

Saguier, Ruben Bareiro, "Guaraní: Rhetoric and Reality", *Index on Censorship*, 16/3 (March 1987)

PARAGUAY: Radio Ñanduti
Radio station, established 1962

Dictatorships fear spontaneity, in any medium. Radio broadcasting, much of it conducted in a conversational style and much of it also broadcast live, is anathema to such regimes, for which a script – prepared, checked, and cleared in advance – is a primary means of media control. Radio Ñanduti, a private broadcasting station, came into being precisely to challenge the status quo that was so comfortable for the Paraguayan authorities. The station's founder, Humberto Rubín, justified its emphasis on the live telephone interview as follows: "This idea has been around for years in other countries. We are convinced that everybody has the right to give their own opinion, so we introduced it into Radio Ñanduti."

The station's challenge to "order" first came to a head in the 1980s, during the final years of the dictatorship of general Alfredo Stroessner, who had been in power since 1954. Pressure was at first informal. The general secretary of the state communications agency (Administración Nacional de Telecomunicaciones, or Antelco), Dr Francisco Filizolla, telephoned Rubín on a number of occasions, demanding a change of journalistic line. Rubín recalled:

> He called me a subversive agitator. He said I interviewed only opposition politicians. I denied this, saying that I considered myself an independent journalist who allowed all shades of political opinion on my radio. I never make political distinctions as to who can and cannot speak.

Then, in July 1983, the minister of the interior, Sabino Montanaro, ordered a month's suspension of broadcasting by Radio Ñanduti, on the grounds that "its broadcasts systematically disrupt public order and create alarm . . . it has become the means by which unscrupulous persons confuse public opinion and put the nation at risk". Like all dictatorships, the Paraguayan regime had a low opinion of people's capacity to deal with "confusion" – that is, a variety of points of view that differ from what is officially authorized.

Broadcasts resumed on 9 August, but it was not long before the government again attempted to intervene. Rubín himself presented a popular, live phone-in programme called *Superonda*. After airing complaints from listeners on such topics as corruption, poor urban services, and the lack of democratic means to give voice to these complaints, Rubín was not only told to cut the programme, but was provided with a list of those who were authorized to appear. For once acting spontaneously rather than in response to pressure, the regime itself suddenly lifted the ban on 10 November 1983.

Two months later, the campaign against Rubín and Radio Ñanduti was widened to include the participation of the Department of Investigations. The journalist-proprietor was taken in for questioning and then told to "improve that radio station of yours". Later that year, Rubín was banned from using the microphone. Another department, the Ministry of Information, was now involved. When Rubín complained about the ban, he was informed of the reason: he had lent "the microphone to any number of irresponsible, unauthorized politicians".

On 10 August 1985 broadcasting was again suspended, this time for ten days. Antelco declared that the programmes "continued a line of thought towards subversion and embarrassment, and questioned the credibility and honesty of certain people and institutions, thereby motivating a state of latent moral violence". From the government's point of view, the "latent" soon became manifest. The year 1986 was one of demonstrations and protests in Paraguay. The Stroessner regime was on its last legs, and responded accordingly. Radio Ñanduti, which had reported on a strike for better wages and conditions at a hospital in Asunción, and had drawn attention to divisions in the ruling Colorado Party, was attacked by a crowd of 100 government supporters on the night of 29 April. Four days later five hooded vandals assaulted the radio transmitter in San Lorenzo, removing equipment and the mobile unit (the latter an obvious necessity for Radio Ñanduti's style of broadcasting). Further technical interference was engineered, causing frequent unexplained silences on air.

Finally, the interference became so chronic that Radio Ñanduti could no longer sell advertising. On 14 January 1987 Rubín decided to close down for 90 days because he no longer had the minimum funds to run the station. Antelco now moved swiftly, refusing to renew the station's licence.

However, Radio Ñanduti was never totally silenced. When it could not broadcast, it organized music festivals and public meetings, many of them impeded by the police. It also published the *Ñanduti vive* (Ñanduti Lives) series of books. It resumed broadcasting after the coup that swept Stroessner from power on 19 February 1989, and now transmits news 24 hours a day from ten stations across Paraguay. It also publishes a weekly newspaper, *Tiempo 14*.

Although the station now enjoys relative freedom in its broadcasts, it has suffered some disturbances. After the vice-presidential election results of August 2000, when the opposition Liberal Party won the vote, Colorado Party supporters attacked the offices of Radio Ñanduti. The station was one of few local media organizations to predict the Liberal victory prior to elections.

BETSY J. PARTYKA

Further Reading

"ABC Color and Radio Ñanduti", *Index on Censorship*, 16/4 (April 1987)

Nickson, R. Andrew, *Historical Dictionary of Paraguay*, 2nd edition, Metuchen, New Jersey: Scarecrow Press, 1993

El precio de la paz, Asunción: CEPAG, 1991

PARENTS MUSIC RESOURCE CENTER
US moral watchdog group, established 1985

The Parents Music Resource Center (PMRC) was founded by a group of American politicians' wives including Susan Baker, wife of the then treasury secretary James Baker and Tipper Gore, wife of then senator, and later-vice president, Al Gore. The organization was soon dubbed the "Washington Wives". In many ways Tipper Gore was the key figure within the PMRC. She is said to have become alarmed at the sexual content of much contemporary popular music after hearing her eight-year-old daughter playing the track "Darling Nikki" from Prince's *Purple Rain* album. This contains the line "I met her in a hotel lobby masturbating with a magazine". Appalled that tracks such as this were freely available to children of all ages, Gore sprang into action.

She and 19 other women allies wrote a letter on 31 May 1985 to the Recording Industry Association of America (RIAA). Sixteen of these signatories were married to congressmen. The letter accused the industry of promoting records about sex, violence, and drugs to children regardless of their age. Two months later, RIAA president Stanley Gortikov announced that the industry had agreed to put labels on relevant records warning about their content.

There are two points of view about labelling. One argues that it leads to a "chill factor" where some retailers (for example family stores such as Woolworth's) will not stock "stickered" records and some record companies in turn will not contract groups that are likely to get stickered. Here stickering is held to reduce sales. The opposite view is that a record will sell more if it is stickered, as some listeners – particularly adolescent youths – are drawn to buy records they would not otherwise buy purely because of their "naughty" content. Here stickering is held to increase sales. The situation is complicated by the fact that some records (such as Madonna's *Erotic* album) are issued in different formats – both clean (unstickered) and adult (stickered).

The campaigners denied that a voluntary code on labelling was censorship or that it infringed the principle of free speech as outlined in the First Amendment of the US constitution. Although there were soon reports that some record companies were not taking on groups who were likely to have their covers stickered, the Washington wives insisted that stickering was merely the provision of information for parents who could thereby influence their children's listening.

Encouraged by their early success, the letter-writers went further and became a full-fledged lobby group – the PMRC. It was funded in part by a donation from Mike Love, a member of the Beach Boys. The group soon called upon the industry to introduce a ratings system for records. Its main target at this point was heavy metal music, particularly that of Motley Crue, AC/DC, WASP, Judas Priest, and Twisted Sister.

The next step in the campaign came on 19 September 1985 when the US senate commerce committee held hearings on so-called "porn rock" following lobbying of the Committee by the PMRC. Five members of the committee were husbands of leading members of the PMRC. At the hearing PMRC supporters highlighted the ills of American society (such as abortion, crime, and drug abuse) and sought to put much of the blame for these phenomena upon the increasingly depraved content of much popular music. Susan Baker argued that there was a great deal of difference between Cole Porter proclaiming that "the birds and bees do it" and WASP's Exhortation to "Fuck like A Beast"; the PMRC posited a form of lost innocence within popular music.

Opponents of the PMRC at the hearing included Frank Zappa, John Denver, and Twisted Sister's lead singer, Dee Snider. Zappa argued that the issue was one of freedom of speech and insisted that there was no evidence to suggest that exposure to any form of music caused the listener to commit crime. Zappa also drew attention to the fact that it was fundamentalist Christians who were behind many of the arguments that the PMRC used. (The use by the PMRC of literature derived from Christian fundamentalist sources is well documented.) He also pointed out that many of the themes that the PMRC attacked were also present in country music. He suggested that the PMRC made no comments on country music because it had its home in Tennessee, where Al Gore was then senator.

The RIAA refused to meet the PMRC's demand to rate all records and to print all lyrics on sleeves. But on 1 November the industry and the PMRC announced that all future recordings that had explicit lyrics concerning sex, violence, or drugs would carry a sticker saying: "Explicit Lyrics – Parental Advisory". This now became common practice in both the US and Europe.

The PMRC continued its campaign via its newsletter which encouraged parents to monitor radio and television broadcasts, highlighting artists they approved of such as Phil Collins and U2. It encountered resistance from a number of anti-censorship groups such as the Free Music Coalition, Parents For Rock and Pop, and Rock Out Censorship. A newsletter called *No More Censorship* was started by Jello Biafra, leader of the New York punk band, The Dead Kennedys. Coincidentally or not, Biafra was subject to a censorship case himself in 1987, centring on a poster *Penis Landscape* by the Swiss artist H.R. Giger contained in the group's album *Frankenchrist*. After a protracted case the poster was declared to be not obscene by a 7–5 majority in a Los Angeles court in August 1987. But it led to the dissolution of the band.

Whether the case can be attributed to PMRC pressure or not, it is quite clear that, during the next few years, rap artists such as 2 Live Crew, Ice-T and NWA were subject to considerable censorial pressure. The PMRC was involved in many of such cases. However, since Tipper Gore left the organization in 1992, following her husband's election as vice-president, the organization has maintained a much lower profile.

MARTIN CLOONAN

Further Reading

Chastagner, Claude, "The Parents Music Resource Center: From Information to Censorship", *Popular Music*, 18/2 (1999):179–92

Denselow, Robin, *When the Music's Over: The Story of Political Pop*, London: Faber, 1989

Gore, Tipper, *Raising PG Kids in an X-Rated Society*, Nashville, Tennessee: Abingdon Press, 1987

Martin, Linda and Kerry Segrave, *Anti-Rock: The Opposition to Rock 'n' Roll*, Hamden, Connecticut: Archon, 1988

BLAISE PASCAL
French writer, 1623–1662
LETTRES ÉCRITES À UN PROVINCIAL (Provincial Letters)
Essays, 1656–57

The *Provincial Letters* were a series of 18 anonymous fly-sheets written by the brilliant young mathematician, physicist, and Jansenist Blaise Pascal with the help of a small team of Jansenist sympathizers between 23 January 1656 and 24 March 1657. Bound sets of the original quarto leaves were available in 1657. They were presented as the work of a fictitious author, Louis de Montalte, and were falsely declared to have been printed by a non-existent Pierre de la Vallée in Cologne. They were in fact printed in Paris by Denis Langlois for the bookseller Desprez. The formal first edition is considered to be the earlier of the two 1657 duodecimo printings, probably produced by Daniel Elzevir of Amsterdam, secretly imported, and on sale in Paris probably in July. The original full title, *The "Provinciales" or Letters written by Louis de Montalte to a Provincial among His Acquaintances and to the Reverend Jesuit Fathers on the Subject of the Moral Teaching and the Theology of Those Fathers* ("discovering the God of Abraham .. of Isaac .. of Jacob and not of philosophers and men of science") reflects something of Pascal's changes of purpose and tone as the composition of the "letters" progressed.

Pascal had undergone a spiritual experience in November 1654 which brought about a strong intensification of his devotional life and a growing closeness to the Jansenists which led him to take up residence at the Jansenist monastery and headquarters at Port-Royal in 1655 and to defend Jansenism so famously against the extremely powerful Catholic order of the Jesuits. In 1655 Antoine Arnauld (1612–94), the acknowledged leader of the Jansenists, wrote in his 250-page quarto manifesto of their position, the *Seconde Lettre à un duc et pair*, that when St Peter had denied Jesus, he sinned because the grace not to sin was withheld from him. That proposition had already been condemned in the first of the five propositions declared heretical by the papal bull *Cum occasione* condemning Jansen's *Augustinus*. Arnauld also denied that the five propositions listed by the papacy were to be found in Jansen's text.

The report of a commission set up by the theology faculty at the Sorbonne to examine Arnauld's work, delivered on 1 and 2 December 1655, led to the proposal, enforced by the administration, to strip Arnauld of his doctorate. A group of Arnauld sympathizers suggested a fly-sheet aimed at gaining public sympathy, and Arnauld drew one up and read it out, but to the scant applause of the sympathizers present. He then turned to Pascal, who had published very little, and nothing literary, suggesting that he draft something. Pascal promised a sketch, but produced overnight a first letter, attempting to rally the Dominicans to vote against the censure, since their views on grace appeared to him to be essentially the same as Arnauld's.

This first letter, dated 26 January, was a great public success, and not surprisingly infuriated the chancellor, Pierre Séguier. Séguier was to ensure Arnauld's condemnation both by his presence at the faculty meetings and by conniving at irregularities in the voting in favour of the regular clergy on whose votes he could count. Pascal, immediately suspected of the authorship

of the letter on the basis of what must have been leaked information, was careful not to return home, but stayed at first at various inns under an assumed name. He later hid with the Duc de Roannez, whom he had converted to the Jansenist cause, and probably also with the Duc de Luynes.

He also immediately wrote a second letter, dated 29 January 1656, the day on which Arnauld's full censure was voted. A third, in reply to answers to the first two, was dated 9 February. All three reduced the theological dispute, which concerned the human power of autonomous moral self-determination, to a farcically semantic quarrel of no apparent substance. The third letter argued ironically that "what is Catholic in the Fathers becomes heretical in M. Arnauld", presenting the debate as a vendetta against Arnauld personally.

From the fourth letter to the 10th the anonymous letter-writer changed direction and tone to attack first the Jesuit theology of grace (Molinism) and then the moral theology of the Jesuits, unfairly taking the leniency of their confessional practice as the measure of their moral teaching (Probabilism), and holding that it was the laxity of their moral teaching which was the cause of their doctrine on grace. The letters make much fun of the devices used by the Jesuits to alleviate the rigours of the moral law. Letters 11 to 16 were addressed directly to the Jesuits, defending their author against Jesuit counter-attacks, while the last two complete letters were a riposte addressed directly to Père Annat, the king's Jesuit confessor.

The letters were intensely subversive, clearly defending defined heresy, and might have got Pascal into severe trouble. On 2 February, the day after Le Petit printed the second letter, the police descended on the booksellers suspected of complicity, and arrested Savreux, merely searching the premises of Le Petit and Desprez. Savreux was released on 16 February. Le Petit's wife had removed the type-set formes in her apron, and a friend printed 1500 copies, distributed on 5 February. The first letters were paid for by friends of Port-Royal and distributed free. We know that the fifth letter was printed by Denis Langlois, at whose premises the police found the type after the printing had taken place. Langlois then reprinted the first four, and the impressions, originally 1500 in number, reached about 6000 copies. It is probable that the letters were printed simultaneously by different printers. They were distributed in at least one grand *salon*, and cardinal Mazarin had the seventh read out to him and the young king, Louis XIV.

Pascal's role was really as author-in-chief, working on material supplied by a whole team, of which Arnauld and his close associate Pierre Nicole were the principal members. We do not know whether Pascal remained in hiding for the whole campaign. His name was being widely circulated as the author of the letters by late May 1656, but at that date other names, too, were being put forward. A search for presses at the Port-Royal monastery in the Chevreuse valley near Paris had yielded nothing, and the official in charge of bookselling was indulgent, but by the date of the 16th letter, distributed about

Christmas 1656, it seemed probable that serious measures were being contemplated to stop the distribution of the letters. The 16th letter itself, probably written at Vaumurier, the residence of the Duc de Luynes, may partly have been the work of Nicole.

By the date of the 17th letter, 23 January 1657, printing the letters was clearly becoming dangerous, although the print run had increased to 10,000 copies. Official anti-Jansenist measures were tightened. The bull *Ad sacra beati Petri sedem*, signed on 16 October 1656, and declaring that the five propositions had been held by Jansen and had been condemned in the sense in which he had held them, was received by the clergy assembly on 17 March. The first 16 Provincial Letters had already been condemned to be burnt by the regional Parlement at Aix, and the cessation of the letters seems to have been the result of a collective political decision taken at Port-Royal. The work was condemned by the Congregation of the Index in 1657. Hostilities were to be resumed later, but by different means. Arnauld, meanwhile, was restored to his position at the Sorbonne, received by Louis XIV, and for a time acclaimed as a popular hero.

ANTHONY LEVI

Writings

Les Provinciales; ou, les lettres écrites par Louis de Montalte à un provincial de ses amis et aux RR. PP. Jesuites, edited by Louis Cognet, 1965
The Provincial Letters, translated by A.J. Krailsheimer, 1966
Pensées, translated by A.J. Krailsheimer, 1966; revised edition 1995
Pensées and Other Writings, translated by Honor Levi, edited by Anthony Levi, 1995

Further Reading

Broome, J.H., *Pascal*, London: Arnold, 1965
Duchêne, Roger, *L'Imposture littéraire dans les Provinciales de Pascal*, 2nd edition, Aix-en-Provence: Université de Provence, 1985
Miel, Jan, *Pascal and Theology*, Baltimore: Johns Hopkins Press, 1969
Parish, Richard, *Pascal's Lettres Provinciales: A Study in Polemic*, Oxford: Clarendon Press, and New York: Oxford University Press, 1989

PIER PAOLO PASOLINI
Italian writer and filmmaker 1922–1975

Pasolini was one of the most significant literary intellectuals (poet, novelist, journalist, critic, playwright) and filmmakers of the postwar generation in Italy. His earliest work, lyric poetry in the Friulan dialect and Italian, dates from the 1940s. He came to prominence in the mid-1950s with two novels, an influential collection of poetry *Le ceneri di Gramsci* (1957, The Ashes of Gramsci), and work in an important literary journal, *Officina* (Workshop). He started directing films in 1960. Over the course of the 1960s and 1970s, he became a prominent and notorious public figure, and an object of media scandal in a way that was relatively new for a recently modernized society such as Italy. In person and through his works, through legal but also physically violent means, by institutions, individuals, the press, and organized groups of neo-fascists, he was constantly under attack, or "lynched" as he put it; so much so that he seems now to illustrate many of the characteristic anxieties, repressions, and channels of power of Italian society of the time. He was killed in 1975, apparently by a rent boy, at the height of his vocal campaign in Italy's leading daily newspaper, *Corriere della sera*, lambasting the catastrophic consequences of late capitalist consumerism.

As was typical of his generation of writers, Pasolini was a self-declared if heterodox Marxist, dedicated to the values of the antifascist Resistance movement of 1943–45, and opposed to the Christian Democrat "regime" which held political sway in the Italian republic for almost 50 years after 1948. Marxism was one of an eclectic range of intellectual currents in his work, including psychoanalysis and later anthropology. Psychoanalysis, and through it his own homosexuality, inform many of his most controversial, and most censored works. He set great store by an elaborate and ideologically charged notion of "giving scandal" as a mode of writing and acting, and thus can

be said to have courted censorship to some degree. At the same time, he suffered from it personally and artistically, and the conditions created by constant persecution and prosecution over many years may well have led, directly or indirectly, to his death.

The history of Pasolini's confrontation with judicial and censoring authorities of various kinds is extensive and complex. Between 1949 and 1975 he or his work was prosecuted well over 30 times, and many of these cases took several years to resolve, each time ultimately in his favour. It is perhaps the climate of continual accusation that makes Pasolini's case such a striking and unusual one. It is also particularly important as an illustration of a distinct period in the history of censorship in Italy, in which the measures of the fascist state (1923) were adopted largely unchanged by the democratic Republic in 1948, and applied with varying rigour for political and moral reasons over the following 25 years, until they were finally reformed in the mid-1970s, since when Italy has been almost libertarian in its lack of formal censorship. Pasolini's work coincides almost precisely with this last gasp of state control.

As a student in wartime Bologna, he worked on two small GUF and GIL (fascist student groups) magazines, which were subject to the control of the local censors. In practice, these and many other similar youth magazines funded by the regime were the seedbed – even if in coded language – of critical and often antifascist views. Alongside poems and reviews, Pasolini contributed several more political articles of this kind, on the role of intellectuals and of the young as voices of dissent. These were all passed by the censors, after occasional debate, at least until the few weeks of final crisis of the regime in mid-1943 when rules were tightened.

After the war, Pasolini worked as a teacher in the northeastern region of Friuli, his mother's home. He became active in Friulan cultural and political movements, and in the local Communist Party (PCI). In 1949, after a sexual encounter with some local boys, he was accused of the "corruption of minors" and "obscene acts in a public place", sacked as a teacher, and expelled from the party. Local politics undoubtedly exacerbated the consequences of the encounter, just as fading interest meant that the charges collapsed, after two appeals, in 1952. He had, however, already left Friuli for Rome in 1950. It is important to note that Pasolini was as much a victim of PCI moralism (and homophobia) in this incident as of conservative political forces.

In Rome, he came to prominence in 1955 with his first novel, *Ragazzi di vita* (1955, The Ragazzi), which is a loosely linked collection of stories set in the shanty towns and slums on the periphery of Rome. The adolescent protagonists, members of an underclass unknown to the reading public, move through the city, stealing, gambling, being paid for sex, and so on. They speak in a hard, dialect argot, which is consistently but unremarkably obscene. On 21 July 1955 the book was denounced and banned by an order from the prime minister's office, and was brought to trial for its "pornographic character" a year later. For the defence, Pasolini's publisher Garzanti and his lawyers lined up the cream of Italy's literary intelligentsia – including Alberto Moravia, Giuseppe Ungaretti, Gianfranco Contini, and Carlo Bo. Pasolini himself claimed the book was "reportage, testimony . . . the perfect truth of one of Rome's most desolate areas". The charges were thrown out, and the book became a *succès de scandal*. Comparisons were made with the trial of Flaubert's *Madame Bovary* exactly a century earlier.

His next novel, *Una vita violenta* (1959, A Violent Life), set in the same Roman slumlands, was sued for defamation by the Milan branch of the private church organization Catholic Action. The suit was eventually dropped, but only in 1963. More significantly perhaps, the trial of *Ragazzi di vita* led Garzanti to pre-censor the new book in an attempt to avoid renewed legal troubles. This mechanism of preventive self-censorship was seen by Pasolini as the most insidious effect of all the attacks on his work, and encouraged him to go to the other extreme, "to expose himself utterly" as he put it. Several planned later works – written and filmed – were not completed because of hesitant support from publishers and producers.

Between 1959 and 1963 two distinct types of legal troubles beset Pasolini. He underwent a series of criminal or civil suits, most often on absurdly trumped-up charges, which indicate the form of his notoriety and the extent to which a preconceived association of him with lowlife criminality and immorality (i.e. homosexuality) was rooted in public perception. Life follows art very strangely here. These incidents included an episode in 1960 when two journalists set up two boys in Anzio to claim they were propositioned by Pasolini; a suit for defamation in 1959 against a town in Southern Italy, Cutro, following an article in a Milan magazine; a trial for helping a boy escape a gang fight in Rome in 1960; another, the most absurd of all, for armed robbery in November 1961, at a petrol station. For the last, newspapers used stills from a film in which Pasolini had acted the part of a gun-toting gangster to spice up the story. The appeals and counter-appeals dragged on until December 1968.

The second and certainly more important form of legal attack consisted of charges brought against Pasolini's films. The year 1960 saw the most authoritarian government in postwar Italy, led by Fernando Tambroni, and a tightening of often arbitrary censorship measures. The most famous victim of this was Luchino Visconti's *Rocco and His Brothers* (1960). A film partly scripted by Pasolini, Bolognini's *Una giornata balorda* (A Crazy Day) was also hit.

Pasolini's first films as a director were continuations of his Roman novels, and they ran into similar problems. *Accattone* (1961), the intense story of a pimp and his doomed life, was delayed for months by censors before release, banned for under-18s (the first time this measure had been specified by Italian censors), attacked violently by neofascist mobs, and sued by a former Christian Democrat member of Parliament in 1962 because one of the lowlife characters in the film had his name, Pagliuca.

Mamma Roma (1962), the story of a prostitute and her desperate attempts to save her son from the life she has led, became the first film in the history of the Venice film festival to be denounced by the Venetian town authorities, for "offence to common decency" and "obscene content".

His next film, a short entitled *La ricotta* (1963; Ricotta Cheese, part of *RoGoPaG*), an irreverent and satirical account of a film set during the shooting of a film about Christ, was prosecuted by a Roman magistrate for "contempt [*vilipendio*] for the state religion" (an offence dating to the concordat of 1930 between Mussolini and the church), and its trial is one of the crucial moments in the history of modern Italian censorship, coinciding with the tensions within the church brought about by John XXIII's liberalizing papacy. Some Catholic critics welcomed the film's modern spirituality; others saw it as a "Trojan horse" of pseudo-piety. Pasolini's statement used by his lawyer explains step by step the workings of the satire of the film industry in contrast to the sublime spirituality of the film's starving hero, Stracci, who dies of indigestion on the cross while playing one of the crucified thieves. The hearings and appeals lasted five years, and the film underwent important alterations, so that more than one version remains in circulation today.

All the cases mentioned thus far rumbled on for years, but the next new encounter with the courts was not until 1968. *Teorema* (Theorem), a fable of sexual and ideological awakening in which the members of a bourgeois family are one by one seduced and then abandoned by a god-like visitor, provoking existential crises in all, was the object of furious controversy at the Venice film festival (which that year was turned upside down by events related to the European movements of 1968), and was denounced by more than one local magistrate around Italy. Pasolini, and others who protested at Venice that year, would later be charged with "invading a public place" and other disorder offences. In 1971 and 1973 he would also be charged with "inciting criminal activity" for having supported formally, along with many other intellectuals, the extreme left-wing group-cum-newspaper *Lotta continua*.

All three films of Pasolini's Trilogy of Life of 1971–74 – *Decameron*, *The Canterbury Tales*, and *The Thousand and One Nights* – were also subject to lawsuits and censorship problems. The films retell three of the founding works of narrative in European and Arabic culture as explorations of free and joyous sexuality, across and within gender, as celebrations of the body and of body language. They coincided with a trend

PASOLINI: Still from Pasolini's last film, *Salò, o le centoventi giornate di Sodoma* (Salò; or, The 120 Days of Sodom), an adaptation of the marquis de Sade's novel, completed shortly before Pasolini's murder in 1975. The film was a shocking and sexually explicit allegory of fascism in wartime Italy which broke taboos and included scenes of torture and degradation such as this one. The film was refused a certificate for release by the Italian censors, and the producer was subjected to a lengthy prosecution before the film was released in a cut version in 1977.

towards such open sexuality in Italian cinema – see also Bertolucci's *Last Tango in Paris* (1972) – but also a growth in outright pornography and the then forthcoming collapse of the current censorship regime. The first two films were denounced by more than twelve separate magistrates and individuals throughout Italy.

Immediately following Pasolini's death in November 1975, and as his apparently lone assassin was going on trial, his last film *Salò, o le centoventi giornate di Sodoma* (Salò; or, The 120 Days of Sodom) was refused a release by the censors, and sequestered when shown in Milan. The film, an adaptation of the marquis de Sade's novel, is an exercise in starkly explicit sexual degradation and torture as an allegory for fascist ideology and power and the new fascism of the consumer society, in this instance quite clearly designed to break taboos and to appal. Trials of the producer, Alberto Grimaldi, continued until the film was finally released (with cuts) in Italy in 1977, although local actions continued for some time. *Salò* was also a key test-case for censors elsewhere in the world, including in Britain where it was finally granted a release certificate uncut in 2000.

Pasolini again and again pushed at the limits of a dying system of censorship in Italy, and for this alone, he is a central figure in the history of censorship in the post World War II age. From the perspective of his own aesthetic and ideological project, however, the encounter with censorship was one element in his broader strategy of self-construction, in which the juridically determined self intermingled with the media-determined public figure, and with the self constituted in the complex discourse of his poetry, prose, and films. Sexuality, sublimated or starkly explicit, is the most frequent token of these processes in his work, and the most frequent target of the censors' and their allies' attack. But sexuality was only a code for Pasolini, a terrain for an aesthetic and ideological battle. In the final months of his life he turned his lifelong experience of legal persecution against his political enemies in a rhetorical campaign to put the entire Christian Democrat ruling elite "on trial". The metaphor continued to resonate after his death, and became a reality when Italy's postwar regime collapsed amid massive corruption scandals in the early 1990s.

ROBERT S.C. GORDON

Writings

Ragazzi di vita, 1955; as *The Ragazzi*, translated by Emile Capouya, 1968

Una vita violenta, 1959; as *A Violent Life*, translated by William Weaver, 1968

Empirismo eretico, 1972; as *Heretical Empiricism*, translated by Louise Barnett and Ben Lawton, 1988

Lettere luterane, 1976; as *Lutheran Letters*, translated by Stuart Hood, 1983

Selected Poems, translated by Norman McAfee and Luciano Martinengo, 1982

Petrolio, 1992; as *Petrolio*, translated by Ann Goldstein, 1997

Films

Accattone, 1961
Mamma Roma, 1962
La ricotta episode of *RoGoPaG*, 1963
Teorema, 1968
Il decameron, 1971
I racconti di Canterbury, 1972
Il fiore delle mille e una notte, 1974
Salò, o le centoventi giornate di Sodoma, 1975

Further Reading

Baranski, Zygmunt (editor), *Pasolini Old and New*, Dublin: Irish Academic Press, 1997

Betti, Laura (editor), *Pasolini: cronaca giudiziaria, persecuazione, morte*, Milan: Garzanti, 1977

Brunetta, Gian Piero, *Storia del cinema italiano*, revised edition, Rome: Riunti, 1993

Gordon, Robert S.C., *Pasolini: Forms of Subjectivity*, Oxford: Clarendon Press, and New York: Oxford University Press, 1996
Greene, Naomi, *Pier Paolo Pasolini: Cinema as Heresy*, Princeton, New Jersey: Princeton University Press, 1990
Liehm, Mira, *Passion and Defiance: Film in Italy from 1942 to the Present*, Berkeley: University of California Press, 1984

Rohdie, Sam, *The Passion of Pier Paolo Pasolini*, Bloomington: Indiana University Press, and London: British Film Institute, 1995
Schwartz, Barth David, *Pasolini Requiem*, New York: Pantheon, 1992

BORIS PASTERNAK
Russian fiction writer and poet, 1890–1960

DOKTOR ZHIVAGO (Doctor Zhivago)
Novel, 1957

The scandal surrounding *Doctor Zhivago* and the award to Pasternak of the Nobel Prize for Literature in 1958 was apparently a matter of subsequent regret to Nikita Khrushchev. However, censorship was hardly a new experience for Boris Pasternak when it afflicted him in the 1950s. Although he was briefly courted by the cultural authorities in the 1930s as a prospective Soviet "poet laureate", his aesthetic preoccupations, the formal complexity of his work, and his political non-alignment had always marked him out as an awkward figure in the culture of the Soviet Union.

A number of Pasternak's earlier publications had been affected by the Glavlit censorship that had prevailed in Russia from 1922. His autobiography, *Okhrannaia gramota* (1931, *Safe Conduct*) was said to be marred by "subjective idealism". It was suggested that he withdraw the work "on the grounds that it had been ill received in literary quarters and it would be uncomradely of me to spurn their disapproval". *Safe Conduct* was not published in its original form until 1982. From the mid-1930s, while still writing in intervals between creative, psychological and personal crises, Pasternak could publish only translations (of Shakespeare, Goethe, Georgian poetry, and other works). Not the least traumatic experience of this period was the telephone call that he received from Stalin in 1934, following the arrest of Osip Mandel'shtam. It appears that only the abrupt ending to the purges in 1939 saved Pasternak from arrest. Andrei Zhdanov himself made him change his poem commemorating the liberation of Odessa in 1944, pruning its "involved imagery" and "excessive naturalism".

The seeds of *Doctor Zhivago* go back almost to the earliest stages of Pasternak's prose-writing career, surfacing every so often in fictional fragments, but the novel as we now know it was begun in earnest just after World War II, under the working title "Boys and Girls". In 1946 its composition took a new turn when Pasternak met Olga Ivinskaia at the offices of the journal *Novyi Mir*. In addition to becoming Pasternak's longstanding mistress, she was to become the prototype for the character of Lara. Press attacks on Pasternak, as on his friend Anna Akhmatova, were resumed in 1947–48 as part of the postwar Zhdanovite cultural clampdown, and his *Selected Works* was pulped in 1948. This period led to a considerable further hardening in Pasternak's attitude towards the Soviet system and its history. This was soon to be reflected in the novel.

At the centre of *Doctor Zhivago* is the love story of Iurii Zhivago and Lara Guichard (later Antipova), set against a revolutionary backdrop stretching from 1905 to the late 1920s,

in which Bolshevik power is depicted in an increasingly hostile manner as it becomes entrenched. Not only is Pasternak's novel far removed from "socialist realism", which demanded the foregrounding of positive heroes together with unstinting praise of the party, but it depicts the establishment of the Soviet state in a negative manner, while its protagonist, the unrecognized poet and erstwhile physician Zhivago, has the temerity to criticize Marxism from an individualist and religious perspective. At the same time, Pasternak's open scorn for the prerevolutionary era and his enthusiasm for certain of the ideals of the revolution made him equally unpopular in right-wing émigré and monarchist circles.

Doctor Zhivago was adopted as the final title in 1948 and the novel was completed by the end of 1955. After two years of inconclusive negotiations with Soviet publishers and officials, Pasternak lost patience and authorized the publication of a copy that he had handed to a representative of an Italian publishing house, Feltrinelli. This company proceeded to publish the novel in Russian; translations into Italian, English, and other languages soon followed. At first, the consequences of this action for Pasternak seemed relatively mild. However, the Nobel Prize announcement a year later unleashed a storm of officially inspired harassment. All Soviet publishing doors were closed to Pasternak, and *Novyi Mir* released a lengthy critical diatribe explaining why its editors had rejected the book in 1956. Vladimir Semichastnyi, then the head of the Komsomol (Communist Youth League) and later head of the KGB, claimed that Pasternak was "worse than a pig", because "a pig never befouls where it eats or sleeps", and suggested that he be expelled from the Soviet Union. Pasternak thereupon telegraphed his refusal of the prize to the Swedish Academy and the campaign against him died down. The short period of his life still remaining was relatively peaceful and he was able, to a limited extent at least, to bask in his sudden worldwide fame.

Pasternak died in 1960, still in official disgrace. A partial rehabilitation of his work soon followed, but *Doctor Zhivago* remained unmentionable in the Soviet Union for another quarter of a century. In the outside world its renown increased with the release in 1965 of David Lean's film, while the English translation of the novel has remained continuously in print since 1958. Some of the "Zhivago poems" that make up Part 17 of the novel were published or quoted surreptitiously in Soviet publications, but it was not until the advent of Gorbachev's policy of glasnost, in 1986, that a commission was set up to oversee the full publication of Pasternak's works.

Doctor Zhivago was finally printed in 1988 in *Novyi Mir*, the journal that had rejected it more than 30 years earlier; book editions, and a five-volume *Sobranie sochinenii* (Collected Works) soon followed. The novel was received by the reading public in the Soviet Union with some enthusiasm but, somewhat lost amid a sea of other previously banned or ignored treasures of Russian and world literature, it had much less impact than could have been expected if it had appeared in its author's lifetime.

In addition to the troubles and tribulations of its publishing history, *Doctor Zhivago* has given rise to formidable critical controversy ever since its first appearance, on both aesthetic and political grounds. Whatever the final verdict on it as a novel may be – although many have always considered it a true classic of Russian literature – it undoubtedly served as a litmus test for Soviet cultural policy. Just as the banning of *Doctor Zhivago* in 1956–57 advanced crucial testimony as to the false dawn of Khrushchev's "Thaw", its eventual publication in the Soviet Union proved to be an early harbinger of the death throes of the Soviet system itself.

NEIL CORNWELL

Writings

Doktor Zhivago, Milan: Feltrinelli, 1957; as *Doctor Zhivago*, translated by Max Hayward and Manya Harari, London: Collins, and New York: Random House, 1958

Further Reading

Barnes, Christopher, *Boris Pasternak: A Literary Biography*, 2 vols, Cambridge and New York: Cambridge University Press, 1989–98
Clowes, Edith W. (editor), *Doctor Zhivago: A Critical Companion*, Evanston, Illinois: Northwestern University Press, 1995
Conquest, Robert, *Courage of Genius*, London: Collins Harvill, 1961
Cornwell, Neil, *Pasternak's Novel: Perspectives on "Doctor Zhivago"*, Keele: Essays in Poetics, 1986
Fleishman, Lazar, *Boris Pasternak: The Poet and His Politics*, Cambridge, Massachusetts: Harvard University Press, 1990
Ivinskaya, Olga, *A Captive of Time: My Years with Pasternak*, London: Collins Harvill, and New York: Doubleday, 1978
Pasternak, Evgeny, *Boris Pasternak: The Tragic Years 1930–60*, translated by Michael Duncan, London: Collins Harvill, 1990

PATCHWORK TAPESTRIES
Chilean embroidery, 1970s–1990s

The Patchwork Tapestries (*arpilleras*) were embroidered by women whose relatives had "disappeared" during the years of the Pinochet dictatorship in Chile (1973–90). Beginning as a means of making a living and of dealing with grief, the tapestries developed into strong political statements. In a society where democratic institutions had been silenced, the *arpilleras* defied censorship in a unique way.

Following the 1973 coup, an estimated 3000 young men, presumed supporters of the deposed and murdered Salvador Allende, were removed. Strict censorship of the press having been instituted, no information on their whereabouts was available. Searches by their sisters, mothers, and grandmothers were to no avail.

The Vicariate of Solidarity, a human rights organization founded by the Catholic Church and situated in downtown Santiago and in 20 regional centres, offered the women legal aid, advice on health care, and, from 1974, sewing materials. Eventually some 300 women in 26 workshops engaged in purposeful needlework. In the first instance the women sewed in order to make money for their families now deprived of breadwinners. The painter Valentina Bonne then initiated handicraft workshops, in which women were encouraged not only to develop their skills but also to reflect imaginatively on their experiences.

Gradually a distinctive art form and a new politics came into being: tapestries that told the story of the women's sufferings, and their struggles for truth and justice. "I made my *arpilleras* because I have a double crime to denounce, the kidnapping of both my son and my brother. I joined the workshop to continue fighting, and so that the truth can be known, because my wounds are still open" (Violeta Morales, 1992).

The *arpilleras* became increasingly explicit. They depicted murder, torture, detention, and exile. They documented the resistance, including regular demonstrations outside the courts, in which women chained themselves together and had to be unlocked by the police. They featured the slogans of resistance – *No a la tortura* (No to torture), ¿Dónde están? (Where are they?). And – anathema to a deeply antisocialist regime – they demanded justice for the poor. The tapestries revealed what was censored and denied, what could not be articulated in other media. At the same time the tapestries were life-affirming: the sun appears in most of them and they celebrate hope, as well as documenting repression and fear.

The form of the *arpilleras* was greatly influenced by the Panamanian *mola*, and by "patchwork", then in fashion in Chile, made up of scraps and leftover fabric. A background – rooftops, the sky, the Andes – was first sewn onto sacking (*arpillera*). Then the theme, which was often decided on communally, was gradually assembled. Figures made of different shapes of patterned material were introduced and the story came to life. Although we now know the names of the individual women who did the sewing, the original work appeared without signatures.

The work was mostly carried out clandestinely in the basements of churches and in the women's own homes. Occasional displays were arranged in the inner courtyards of the churches, care being taken to keep the more overtly political pieces from being too prominent. The *arpilleras* were sold in gift shops as examples of popular craft, but, according to Irma Muller, "we know that Pinochet regards us as old madwomen who are stirring up his little chicks". If any of the work was found during raids on the women's homes it was destroyed. *Arpilleras* were

PATCHWORK TAPESTRIES: *Arpillera* (patchwork tapestry) from Chile, late 1970s. The work shows the women who chained themselves to the railings of the National Congress building in Santiago, one of the institutions of the former democratic government that were closed down by general Pinochet after the 1973 coup. Images of their disappeared relatives, abducted or murdered by the Pinochet regime, are placed over the women's hearts: they are demanding to know their whereabouts.

PATCHWORK TAPESTRIES: *Arpillera* from Chile, late 1970s. This work refers to two of the many men who disappeared during the Pinochet regime, Sergio Reyes and Modesto Espinosa: the legend reads: "Where are they?" There is a barred window on the left, and the four green shapes represent poplar trees (*alamos*): a well-known detention centre was called Cuatro Alamos. The black rectangle may refer to some unknown or secret place or to death itself.

smuggled abroad in visitors' suitcases but if any were discovered in customs, they were confiscated. Some got through, appeared in the European and North America press, helping to influence international opinion.

During the 1988 plebiscite the workshops ventured into explicit electioneering. One *arpillera* depicts two victims of the dictatorship, Newton Morales and Orlando Letelier, and it is captioned: "Did you forget? If you have no memory, you will vote for Pinochet."

Since 1989 the workshops have gradually declined, as the women get older and can no longer see well. Peter Winn has argued that the women's work has become a victim of the restored democracy's policy of "sanitizing the past". Certainly, the workshops have closed down and the art can now only be seen only in museums, but, according to Winn, the residents of Santiago's shanty town have begun the process of writing their own version of past events.

"We didn't understand a thing about politics. We were used to the fact that here in Chile it was the men who got involved in politics, while we women dedicated ourselves to our houses and children." Perhaps the greatest achievement of the *arpilleras* – like the Mothers of the Plaza de Mayo in Argentina – was to challenge that particular form of censorship.

MARJORIE AGOSÍN

PATCHWORK TAPESTRIES: *Arpillera* from Chile, late 1970s. It reads: "Never give in or stray from the path!" and shows five birds flying up to the sun. The three dark peaks represent the Andes, a common motif in the *arpilleras* of the Chilean resistance.

Further Reading

Agosín, Marjorie, *Tapestries of Hope, Thread of Love: The Arpillera Movement in Chile, 1974–1994*, Albuquerque: University of New Mexico Press, 1996

Brett, Guy, *Through Our Own Eyes: Popular Art and Modern History*, London: GMP, 1986; Philadelphia: New Society Publishers, 1990

Jacquette, Jane S. (editor), *The Women's Movement in Latin America: Participation and Democracy*, 2nd edition, Boulder, Colorado: Westview Press, 1994

Politzer, Patricia, *Fear in Chile: Lives under Pinochet*, New York: Pantheon, 1989

Rowe, William and Vivian Schelling, *Memory and Modernity: Popular Culture in Latin America*, London: Verso, 1991

Ruddick, Sara, *Maternal Thinking: Toward a Politics of Peace*, Boston: Beacon Press, 1989; London: Women's Press, 1990

JAN PATOČKA
Czech philosopher and dissident, 1906–1977

Jan Patočka is known in the west largely because he was one of the first three spokespersons for Charter 77 and because he died after police interrogation in March 1977. In the Czech Republic, however, he is also remembered as a philosopher in the phenomenological tradition, who did not compromise with the Nazi or communist regimes, and whose knowledge was transmitted to a small but committed group of disciples.

Thirty-two years of Patočka's working life were spent in conditions of strict censorship: first in the Nazi Protectorate of Bohemia and Moravia, then under the Stalinist regime of the 1950s, and again under Husák's system of "normalization" following the brief Prague Spring. Through all this time, he continued to develop his conception of what constitutes a civilized and tolerant society. In the conditions of the times, however, he couched these ideas in metaphors and analyses of historical cases.

When Patočka was born, the Czech lands of Bohemia and Moravia were still part of the Austro-Hungarian empire. In the years of the first Czechoslovak Republic (1918–39), he studied philosophy at the Charles University in Prague, spending the academic year 1928–29 at the Sorbonne in Paris. The two living philosophers who were to have the greatest influence on his thinking were Edmund Husserl, born in Moravia of a German-speaking Jewish family, whom Patočka met in Paris; and Husserl's pupil Martin Heidegger, whom Patočka met in Freiburg in 1933. Another important source of influence was the philosopher Tomáš Masaryk, president of Czechoslovakia from 1918 to 1936. For Patočka, and many other Czechs and Slovaks, Masaryk's death in 1937 marked the end of an era.

In the 1930s, the combination of the Depression and the influx of academics leaving Hitler's Germany created a critical situation in Prague, and, although Patočka started teaching at the Charles University in 1934 and became an associate professor in 1936, he did not obtain a permanent position. Nevertheless, he was secretary of the Prague Philosophy Circle, shared in the organization of the World Philosophy Congress in Prague in 1934, and invited Husserl to Prague in 1935. The publication in 1936 of *Přirozený svět jako filosofický problém* (The Natural World as a Philosophical Problem) created considerable interest and established him as a philosopher of European status. In this, his first book, Patočka argues that philosophy can be used by human beings as a tool for diagnosis, thus enabling them to recover their instinctive sense of the reality of the natural world, in the face of scientific concepts that alienate them from their actual environment.

In November 1939, the Nazi occupation authorities closed the Czech universities and Patočka went to work as a labourer. In spite of having no hope or expectation of publishing it, it was during this period that he worked on a text about pre-Socratic philosophy that, when it was eventually published in the 1990s, filled four volumes.

After the end of World War II, Patočka returned to the university. It was an extraordinary time to be teaching: the lecture halls were crowded with a five-year backlog of students, recent witnesses to the breakdown of society and shared values in almost every country in Europe. Patočka's intention was to deliver the essentials of philosophy as a basis for rebuilding an authentic way of life, concentrating on ancient Greek philosophy as a route to the rediscovery of the sources of European civilization.

Patočka initially escaped arrest when the communists seized power in 1948, but after a year of uncertainty he and many other teachers were expelled from the university. As far as the ideologists were concerned, his teaching was not to be allowed to reach disciples either by word of mouth or in writing. Over the following few years, only two of his studies were published (1949 and 1952) in the Protestant monthly *Křesťanské Noviny* (Christian News). For a short time, he worked in the Masaryk Library, then in the Comenius Archive of the Institute of Education, where initially his research was purely factual. Nevertheless, the study of Comenius's work was a contributing element in the development of his own philosophy, and, after 1958, when he began to work in the Institute of Philosophy as a librarian, he was able to write studies in the philosophy of science. At the same time, unknown to the authorities, he held seminars in his own home for a group of his former students, themselves now engaged in manual work.

In the mid-1960s, the political situation in Czechoslovakia began to ease. Official philosophy still followed the official, "Marxist-Leninist" line, and at first Patočka's work could not appear in academic publications. Articles could be placed, however, in cultural and intellectual journals, such as *Divadlo* (Theatre), in which, in 1963, Patočka wrote about the writer-performer Ivan Vyskočil; and in 1964 his analysis of an essay by Josef Čapek appeared in the avant-garde literary periodical *Tvář* (Face). In the same year, the Academy of Sciences published *Studie z dějin filosofie od Aristotela k Hegelovi* (Studies of the History of Philosophy from Aristotle to Hegel), for which Patočka was awarded the title of Doctor of Science. By 1965, the Communist Party was at war with itself, reform was in the air, and Patočka was able to publish his *Úvod do Husserlovy fenomenologie* (Introduction to Husserl's Phenomenology).

During the Prague Spring in 1968, Patočka was finally made a professor and returned to the Charles University, but the opportunity was short-lived. Four years later, he was forced into retirement and publication was closed to him. His original students, who were now more like fellow-philosophers, continued to meet at his home. They formed what was essentially a discussion group, often continuing late into the night, and including not only those forbidden to study, but also some who held positions in the Charles University. A separate series of underground lectures was published in France under the title *Platon et l'Europe* (Plato and Europe). In the mid-1970s, Patočka prepared a series of lectures that became his *Kacířské eseje o filosofii dějin* (Heretical Essays in the Philosophy of History); these, however, could only be published in translation, first in German and later in English. The meetings at Patočka's home are usually considered to be the beginning of the "underground university".

Patočka's original interest in individual human rights, influenced by Masaryk's philosophy and later by the dissident Czech philosopher Jiří Němec, as well as by the examples of Aleksandr

Solzhenitsyn, Andrei Sakharov, and Anna Akhmatova in the Soviet Union, developed into a life work. In late 1976, he was asked to become one of the three spokespersons for Charter 77, which, to some extent, had been influenced by his ideas and principles. He has occasionally been described as representing the "religious" strand of the Charter, although he himself was never a believer in the sense of accepting the creed of one or other of the churches. He did, however, represent those who had never accepted communism on any terms, and he had a natural sympathy with those individual Christians who had refused to compromise themselves in state-led movements.

The publication of the Charter provoked an immediate and aggressive reaction on the part of the authorities. Patočka collapsed after interrogation and was hospitalized. The police continued to interrogate him, and he died from a brain haemorrhage on 13 March 1977.

Even under the ferocious surveillance of the secret police, Patočka's colleagues and students managed to create an archive of everything that Patočka had written during his lifetime (27 volumes in all) and to smuggle duplicate copies to the Institut für Wissenschaft von Menschen in Vienna. After the "Velvet Revolution" of 1989, this became the Patočka archive (director: Ivan Chvatík), which is part of the Centre for Theoretical Study in Prague.

BARBARA DAY

Writings

An Introduction to Husserl's Phenomenology, translated by Erazim Kohák, 1996
Heretical Essays in the Philosophy of History, translated by Erazim Kohák, 1996
Body, Community, Language, World, translated by Erazim Kohák, 1998

Further Reading

Kohák, Erazim, *Jan Patočka: Philosophy and Selected Writings*, Chicago: University of Chicago Press, 1989

JEAN-JACQUES PAUVERT
French publisher and writer, 1926–

Within the French publishing world, Jean-Jacques Pauvert rose to fame as the first person to publish the complete works of the marquis de Sade, of which four volumes were banned by law in 1957. Despite the censorship, Pauvert continued to publish Sade's works during the 1960s and 1970s, as well as a score of other controversial books by such "erotologists" as Georges Bataille, Pierre Klossowski, and J.-M. Lo Duca. His commitment to the life and works of Sade eventually led to a massive three-volume biography, published between 1986 and 1990, which is widely considered as the principal source of reference for Sade scholars.

Jean-Jacques Pauvert decided to be a publisher and writer at the age of 15. His fate and fortune were sealed by one of the first lots of books he acquired. In a batch of miscellaneous erotica bought from a Parisian *bouquiniste*, he discovered a copy of *Les 120 Journées de Sodome* (The 120 Days of Sodom), originally written by Sade in autumn 1785 while imprisoned in the Bastille. Pauvert had accidentally purchased the three-volume edition of Sade published by Maurice Heine between 1931 and 1936. Well aware of the moral outrage that a full publication of Sade's work could create, Heine had taken great care to ensure the confidentiality of the books by limiting their production to 396 copies and by making them available only by private subscription.

In the midst of the political turmoil surrounding the ambiguous allegiance of the French Vichy regime to the German occupying forces in World War II, the adolescent Pauvert started reading *Les 120 Journées de Sodome*, a book whose minute descriptions of the most horrific sexual cruelties had managed to induce perplexity and exasperation even among "informed" adult readers. Remarkably, Sade's work affected Pauvert differently; he now wanted to read everything the "divine Marquis" had written, not so much out of a personal fascination with the sadistic contents of the work, but rather in order to understand the internal logic of its singular universe. Reflecting upon this period in a 1991 interview, Pauvert commented: "During my reading, I asked myself what the word literature meant. I talked about Sade to Paulhan, who said: he is a great philosopher; and with Camus, who said: he is a great moralist. Some people also said: he is great novelist. This was more interesting."

Partly because he wished the public to join him in his efforts to understand Sade, partly because he wanted to integrate Sade's oeuvre into the literary domain, thereby extending its boundaries, soon after World War II had ended Pauvert decided to publish Sade's complete works. Jean Paulhan, an established literary critic and the editor of the prestigious *Nouvelle Revue Française*, considered it a mad and dangerous idea, the plan of a 21-year-old rookie, but Pauvert was undeterred. He began the publication of the first-ever complete Sade edition, which would take up 27 volumes, with about 2000 copies of each printed. Unlike previous editions of individual works by Sade, Pauvert's volumes were utterly sober and austere, coming to the reader in an unusual, almost square paperback format, with a black and white cover and containing no illustrations. Each of Sade's major works – *Justine*, *Juliette*, *Aline et Valcour*, etc. – was prefaced by authorities like Paulhan, Bataille, Klossowski, and Lely (Sade's first biographer), who underlined the Marquis's perennial value as a revolutionary writer and philosopher.

Some seven years later, with only a couple of volumes to go, legal charges were brought against Pauvert under the French law of 29 July 1939 concerning offences against public decency in books and other printed material. In accordance with this law, a special Commission du Livre or book committee had investigated whether there was any reason to prohibit the publication of Sade's works on moral grounds and had concluded that four titles – *La Philosophie dans le boudoir*, *La Nouvelle Justine*, *Juliette*, and *Les 120 Journées de Sodome* – were reprehensible. For the trial, which opened on

15 December 1956, Pauvert had asked Maurice Garçon, one of the leading lawyers in France, to plead against censorship, defending his interests as a publisher as well as freedom of speech in writing. Garçon tried to nullify the charges by indicating the cultural-historical relativity of moral laws and by pointing out various procedural mistakes made during the investigation. Extra weight was added to his words by a score of Parisian intellectuals, including Jean Cocteau and André Breton, as well as Paulhan and Bataille, who tried to argue in favour of Sade's place within the history of ideas. However, the judge heeded the view of the prosecutor, and on 10 January 1957 ordered the confiscation and destruction of the incriminated books. Jean-Jacques Pauvert was fined 200,000 French francs and ordered to pay costs.

Pauvert now took the case to the Court of Appeal, where it was decided on 12 March 1958. Although the Court confirmed that the four volumes of Sade should be confiscated, the judge was much more lenient than his predecessor, merely ordering the works to be placed in the safe haven of the Bibliothèque Nationale (the so-called Enfer) and recognizing a special category of "adult literature".

Pauvert had reason to be fairly satisfied in the circumstances, but the story was not finished. In December 1958 censorship was officially re-introduced in France. This radical change of climate got worse under de Gaulle's regime during the 1960s, and it affected the French publishing scene in general, since legal action was no longer limited to sexually explicit and morally reprehensible publications (as under the law of 1939), but applied to all sources whose content was considered dangerous from a broad ideological point of view. Until the end of the 1970s many works falling within the category of "adult literature" had to be published anonymously and only circulated within clandestine and/or bibliophile networks. Despite this, Pauvert continued to publish subversive erotic works of fiction and non-fiction, such as the series entitled the *Bibliothèque Internationale d'Érotologie*. He regularly expressed his views on the problem of censorship in the media and in a number of theoretical writings, while at the same time assembling documents for a new biography of Sade, the first volume of which appeared in 1986.

Pauvert often wondered in which environment Sade's works would really thrive. Under severe moral censorship, it is an onerous task to publish controversial erotic works, but they surely maintain their subversive character. In a more liberal atmosphere, it is easier to distribute them, but they are more likely to be classified with banal pornography. Reflecting upon this dilemma in 1968, Pauvert wrote: "In a stubborn fashion, we must nevertheless try to use paper and ink in order to produce the most beautiful and surprising things, before the bookshop has disappeared from human life and before our children's children have forgotten what books are."

DANY NOBUS

Writings

"Le Vrai Problème de la censure" in *L'Enfer du sexe*, by Youl Belhomme, 1971
Sade vivant, 3 vols, 1986–90
Editor, *Osons le dire*, by the marquis de Sade, 1992
Nouveaux (et moins nouveaux) visages de la censure, suivi de l'affaire Sade, 1994

Further Reading

Brochier, Jean-Jacques, "Pauvert sous le signe de Sade", *Magazine littéraire*, 284 (1991): 23–25
Dean, Carolyn J., *The Self and Its Pleasures: Bataille, Lacan, and the History of the Decentered Subject*, Ithaca, New York: Cornell University Press, 1992
Garçon, Maurice (editor), *L'Affaire Sade*, Paris: Pauvert, 1957; 2nd edition 1963
Kearney, Patrick J., *A History of Erotic Literature*, London: Macmillan, 1982
Le Brun, Annie, *Soudain un bloc d'abîme, Sade: introduction aux oeuvres complètes*, Paris: Pauvert, 1986
Noël, Bernard, "Que peut la littérature?" in *Le Marquis de Sade et sa complice; ou, Les revanches de la pudeur*, edited by Jean Paulhan, Paris: Lilac, 1951

EDUARDO PAVLOVSKY
Argentine psychoanalyst, playwright, and actor, 1933–

Pavlovsky graduated with a degree in medicine in 1957. He started in child psychoanalysis, publishing his first book on the subject in 1966. From there he moved into psychodrama, and published his first findings in that field in 1970 and 1971, when he resigned from the Argentine Psychoanalytical Association for political reasons and founded a group known as Plataforma. By then he had also founded the Argentine Association of Psychodrama, and he later set up the Centre for Group Psychoanalytical Psychodrama, which he still headed in the late 1990s.

Pavlovsky has described his plays as belonging to the school of "exasperated realism". It was Samuel Beckett's *Waiting for Godot* (1952) that made him decide to go into theatre. He started a theatrical group, Yenesí (disbanded in 1965), which staged the work of Eugène Ionesco, Beckett, Harold Pinter, Fernándo Arrabal, and Griselda Gambaro. His own first plays, in the 1960s, include *Somos* (We are), *La espera trágica* (The Tragic Wait), *Camellos sin anteojos* (Camels without Glasses), *Robot*, and *Un acto rápido* (A Quick Act). His acting career outside the Yenesí group continued with plays by Pinter up to 1969, when his "political theatre" period began.

The immediate products were *La cacería* (The Hunt), *La mueca* (The Grimace), and *El Señor Galíndez* (1972). *Señor Galíndez* has been recognized as one of the strongest plays in the Spanish language, as it conveys the pathos of torture, which in the case of Argentina became a police and military institution. Galíndez is a mysterious character who telephones a torture training centre each day to give orders to Eduardo, his most competent trainee, who imbues torture and repression with an ideological content. *Señor Galíndez* and *Potestad*

(1983, Paternity) – about the military's abduction of the children of dead guerrillas who are then given up for adoption – are Pavlovsky's best-known plays.

A bomb explosion wrecked the Payró theatre during the staging of *El Señor Galíndez* in 1974. It is important to note that this was two years before the military takeover of March 1976, during the government of María Estela ("Isabelita") Perón, when paramilitary gangs of the "Argentine Anti-Communist Alliance" (known as the "Triple-A", and usually including off-duty police) were abducting and murdering, as well as bombing, left-wing suspects. Pavlovsky had been a candidate for Congress for the left-wing Socialist Workers' Party (PST) in the April 1973 elections. He wrote: "We did not dare to go back on stage. But we did have three special performances in the cellar, staged behind chicken wire, to give the audience the effect of looking into a chicken run". After *Señor Galíndez* was blown off the Payró stage it was taken as Argentina's entry to the Nancy Festival in France and toured Europe from there. In Madrid, Rodolfo Kuhn made a film of the play and it was one of Spain's entries at the Alternative Theatre Festival in Berlin in 1984.

In October 1977 Pavlovsky staged *Telarañas* (Cobwebs), a play about violence and authoritarian behaviour in the family. He had hoped that the dictatorship would not notice, but in fact only one performance took place. Further shows were not planned after telephoned threats were received. In March 1978, after two years of keeping a fairly low profile, Pavlovsky suddenly fled into exile. A military detachment went to his home, announcing themselves as gas fitters – a reference to the play in which Pavlovsky used gas fitters as surrogates for torturers – but he escaped through the neighbours' back yards. He went to Montevideo, then Rio de Janeiro, and finally Madrid, where he remained until the end of 1980, returning to Buenos Aires in 1981.

Pavlovsky's theatre work since then has included *Cámara lenta* (Slow Motion), about the last days of a former boxer, and *El Señor Laforgue*, a prescient depiction of the secret techniques of repression, including the throwing of drugged captives to their deaths in the South Atlantic. This was a practice often alleged, even as far back as 1976, in the *Buenos Aires Herald* and *Crónica* newspapers, and finally admitted by the Argentine army in 1996. These two, with *Potestad*, were published in 1983, after the Argentine defeat in the Malvinas (Falklands) War of 1982, and as the military dictatorship collapsed and made way for the return of constitutional rule in December 1983. In 1983 and 1989 Pavlovsky returned briefly to party politics, as a candidate for Congress for the Movement for Socialism (MAS), and was defeated on both occasions.

In 1988 Pavlovsky presented *Slow Motion* and *Potestad* at the Arts Festival of New York, with *Paso de Dos* (Pas de deux), about a love relationship between a torturer and his victim. His last production of the 1990s, *Rojos globos rojos* (1997, Red Balloons Red), was made into the film *La Nube* (1998, The Clouds), scripted and directed by Fernándo "Pino" Solanas.

Pavlovsky has acted in several Argentine films, his plays have been collected and published (by Búsqueda) in Argentina and in Spain (by Fundamentos), and his works are set texts at universities in Germany, Canada, Italy, the US, and Buenos Aires. His theatre has been included in festivals in France, Italy, Venezuela, Spain, the US, Canada, and Germany. He is sometimes called the "Dario Fo of under-development".

ANDREW GRAHAM-YOOLL

Writings
La mueca, El Señor Galíndez, Telarañas, 1980
Cámara lenta, El Señor Laforgue, Pablo, Potestad, 1989
Teatro completo, 1997–

PE THEIN
Burmese cartoonist, 1924–

Cartoons have long played an important part in Burmese political life. There are today around 50 full-time professional cartoonists, some of them contributing to the government-owned media, but others, well known for their convictions and integrity, being subjected to constant scrutiny by government censors. Pe Thein belongs to the second category. He has placed on record, sometimes at considerable personal risk, sometimes by using oblique references, his hostility to the violence and repression of his times.

It must be borne in mind that in Burma real political cartooning is not allowed (and has not been since about 1967); no government person may be caricatured, and anything suggesting criticism of the military will be banned. Men may not be depicted wearing trousers, unless they are foreigners. Daw Aung San Suu Kyi, however, can be cruelly and viciously satirized in the official media. It is said that by a glance at the cartoons a Burmese reader can assess the political attitude of a publication and so decide whether or not to buy it. This was offered as an explanation of why the Military Intelligence-sponsored pro-government monthly magazine, *Myet-khin-thit*, was carrying cartoons critical of corrupt local officials. This was, it was claimed, a cynical ploy to attract more readers by appearing to be critical of the government.

At the start of Pe Thein's career, in 1948, the newly independent Burma was engulfed in a civil war between the elected government of U Nu and those forces, including notably the Communist Party, that did not agree with the terms of the independence settlement. Nevertheless, there was considerable freedom of expression, and U Pe Thein's cartoons criticized government and rebels alike, reflecting his consistent opposition to violence and support for democracy. Although he was sometimes threatened, he was never harmed physically.

Newspapers – and their cartoonists – were largely free until 1958, when the ruling party split in two and general Ne Win was installed at the head of a caretaker military government. After the split and during the run-up to elections in 1960, Pe Thein drew cartoons in support of U Nu and against Ne Win, the only cartoonist bold enough to do so. Threatening letters were sent both to Pe Thein himself and to U Sein, the editor of the newspaper *Hanthawaddy*, who sent him the following note: "U Pe Thein, hold your horses for a bit! The men of violence have got it in for you. Take this as a warning."

U Nu won the election and resumed power for a short period, but in March 1962, following an army coup, Ne Win returned to power as head of the newly formed Revolutionary Council. Like the newspaper, censored from 1962 and nationalized from 1967, Pe Thein now had to comply with government policy. He could no longer produce a daily cartoon because "the only permitted topics for cartoons were the evil doings of the ethnic minority rebels [Karens, Kachins], of political opponents who had left the country, of the so-called 'economic saboteurs', and of 'capitalist imperialists'". Once again, he received a threatening note, but now the boot was on the other foot: "U Pe Thein, you are a famous cartoonist, ordinary people respect you and rely on you. You are no longer daring to criticize the government; instead you draw cartoons against us. Just you watch out!" He decided to cease drawing cartoons for the newspapers, confining himself to the columns of privately owned monthly magazines and journals.

Pe Thein continued to draw in support of the pro-democracy movement, including a most influential cartoon on the subject of Burma breaking loose from its chains, which also made a link with the anniversary of the bombing of Hiroshima. This cartoon appeared in *Cherry Magazine* on 1 August 1988. When the military resumed power in September 1988, Pe Thein was sent for and questioned many times, but he was not arrested.

The elections of May 1990 were won by the National League for Democracy, led by Aung San Suu Kyi, but the military prevented them from taking power. Pe Thein was banned from contributing to any form of publication – writings, illustrated storybooks, monthly comics, advertisements – and his name and photograph could no longer appear in print. He continued to draw cartoons, but only "for the drawer".

Pe Thein has since occasionally emerged from self-censorship, although in 1994 he refused the blandishments of the military regime, which wanted him to draw for government newspapers in return for the lifting of the ban. Later the same year, he prepared three topical cartoons for an exhibition sponsored by the Today publishing group in Rangoon. The most provocative, which showed a man in tattered clothing with railways lines for seams, wielding a pick, and working on a railway track – implying forced labour – was banned. However, it had served to distract attention from the other two, only slightly less provocative drawings, which were exhibited. One, about censorship, portrayed the author, carrying his pen, dressed in clothes made from newsprint, and walking across the page of an open book, showing one of Pe Thein's censored articles. All the printed text shown included blacked-out lines. The second cartoon showed a man reclining in front of a television set with a newspaper called *Yesterday* over his face, listening through earphones to a portable radio set – implying that the government's television and newspapers were of no value, and that the real news came from broadcasts by the BBC World Service, the Voice of America, or other foreign stations.

ANNA ALLOTT

Further Reading

Allott, Anna J., *Inked Over, Ripped Out: Burmese Storytellers and the Censors*, New York: PEN American Center, 1993

SAM PECKINPAH
US film director, 1925–1984

STRAW DOGS
Film, 1971

The early 1970s was an unhappy period for the British Board of Film Censors (BBFC). Within a short space of time it had to contend with a number of controversial films, including Ken Russell's *The Devils* (1971), Sam Peckinpah's *Straw Dogs* (1971), Stanley Kubrick's *A Clockwork Orange* (1971), and Bernardo Bertolucci's *Last Tango in Paris* (1972). All these can be seen, in retrospect, as pushing back the limits of what was permissible in the representation of sex and – in the cases of *Straw Dogs* and *A Clockwork Orange* – sexual violence on the cinema screen. The BBFC's handling of these films, and in particular of *Straw Dogs*, was widely criticized at the time, with a loud chorus of disapproval in the press threatening to undermine the authority of the Board. Public confidence in the practice of film censorship in Britain was severely affected. Although much of the criticism centred on Stephen Murphy, who had succeeded the highly respected John Trevelyan as secretary of the BBFC in 1971, it is unfair to blame the controversies which engulfed the BBFC during this period entirely on him. James C. Robertson and Guy Phelps have both argued that Murphy reaped a whirlwind not of his own making with these films; Robertson writes:

> The roots of growing disquiet with the BBFC lay in American film developments during the 1950s and 1960s when the Hollywood production code of the 1930s was first eaten away morsel by morsel, and then virtually collapsed. As a result the BBFC by the late 1960s was finding itself confronted by American material very different from what it had been accustomed to over a long period.

Straw Dogs was made in Britain by the American film director Sam Peckinpah, whose celebrated western *The Wild Bunch* (1969) had been a landmark in the representation of screen violence. *Straw Dogs* has often been described as a "Cornish western" in that it transposes a western-style "besieged homesteaders" plot to rural Cornwall. An equally valid comparison would be to John Boorman's *Deliverance* (1972), in that both films dramatize the conflict between urban and rural life, with unsuspecting city-dwellers finding a holiday in the country turning into a nightmare. In *Straw Dogs*, an American writer, David (Dustin Hoffman), and his English wife Amy (Susan George) are terrorized by vicious yokels while holidaying in a remote farmhouse. After Amy is gang-raped, David exacts a bloody revenge on her attackers. In the US, Pauline Keel described it as "the first American film that is a fascist work of art".

The BBFC's problems with *Straw Dogs* inevitably centred on the protracted and brutal rape sequence. They asked for cuts to be made, and the filmmakers duly obliged. Unfortunately, these cuts – which were supposed to reduce the degree of explicit sexual violence – altered the apparent nature of the violence. What had initially been a vaginal rape in which the victim was taken from behind by her attacker now appeared to be an anal rape. Whether this reduced or increased the apparent suffering of the victim is a moot point. Of the film as a whole, the BBFC reported that it was "tremendously enjoyable for the most part and compulsive viewing".

When *Straw Dogs* was released, it met with a barrage of criticism from the national press, which rounded on it for what they regarded as its gratuitous violence. Alexander Walker of the *Evening Standard* was highly critical of the BBFC for having passed it. "What the film censor has permitted on the screen in *Straw Dogs* makes one wonder whether he has any further useful role to play in the cinema industry", he declared. "To pass it on for public exhibition in its present form is tantamount to a dereliction of duty." Moreover, Walker was aware of the BBFC's role in altering the rape sequence, a "monstrous indecency [which] was not intended in this way but has been made to seem like it by censorship cuts". Thirteen leading critics wrote to *The Times* questioning the BBFC's judgement in passing the film. The critical reaction to the film is significant in several respects. First, the widespread condemnation of the BBFC for allowing the film to be shown illustrates the fact that, in the early 1970s, British critics believed that the relaxation of film censorship had gone too far. Second, many of the critics who wrote to *The Times* had their own agenda to pursue:

they were trying to persuade the Board to pass Andy Warhol's *Trash*, a film of which they approved but which the Board had banned. *Trash* (1971) was an account of the New York drugs subculture which most commentators agreed contained a strong anti-drugs message, but the BBFC had been unconvinced of this and did not pass the film for over a year, and then only after several cuts had been made.

The controversy which surrounded *Straw Dogs*, therefore, was due in part to the BBFC's own blunder in altering the rape scene so that it was made "worse" than it had been to begin with, and in part to the critical attitudes of the time, which rounded on this film for taking the screen representation of violence a step too far. It was soon being cited by the anti-permissive, pro-censorship lobby exemplified by the Festival of Light as an example of the depths to which the film industry had stooped, and it lent fuel to the criticisms levelled against the BBFC for what some critics perceived as failing in its duty. Shortly after *Straw Dogs*, the BBFC had to deal with *A Clockwork Orange*, which also featured scenes of rape and sexual violence, but which was passed uncut before being "censored" by the film's own director. The two films were often linked by commentators who deplored the escalation of screen violence and what they saw as the BBFC's *laissez faire* policy, although the reception of *A Clockwork Orange* from film critics (including many of those who had disliked *Straw Dogs*) was actually rather more favourable.

JAMES CHAPMAN

Further Reading

Barr, Charles, "*Straw Dogs, A Clockwork Orange* and the Critics", *Screen*, 13/2 (1972): 17–31

Mathews, Tom Dewe, *Censored*, London: Chatto and Windus, 1994

Phelps, Guy, *Film Censorship*, London: Gollancz, 1975

Robertson, James C., *The Hidden Cinema: British Film Censorship in Action, 1913–1975*, new edition, London and New York: Routledge, 1993

Trevelyan, John, *What the Censor Saw*, London: Joseph, 1973

Walker, Alexander, *National Heroes: British Cinema in the Seventies and Eighties*, London: Harrap, 1985

PELAGIANS
Christian dissidents, 5th century

Unlike such other heresies of the early Christian Church as Nestorianism and Monophysitism, Pelagianism had a direct impact on religious behaviour. It was a moral doctrine before it was a theological heresy, and its treatment at the hands of ecclesiastical authority, although superficially similar, involved a prior reduction of moral values to a series of heterodox propositions.

Pelagius was a Briton, ponderous, says Jerome, in body and mind, but ascetic, and scandalized by the moral laxity of upper-class Roman Christians. Living in Rome for a number of years, Pelagius had acquired followers, often young men of noble birth training for administrative careers. He held tenaciously to the view that, for the Christian God of love, there could be no punishable sin where there was no personal assent, and that it

was therefore always within human power to obey God's commandments.

He feared the infiltration of a Manichaean pessimism into Christianity, and rejected the view that sin was passed from parents to children in the reproductive process itself. Adam's sin was responsible for neither death nor, apart from the example it set, for sin in the world. Adam was not created immortal, and death is not a consequence of sin. Sin is the result of a voluntary choice in a world replete with bad examples and corrupted by the environmental ubiquity of wrong choices. Pelagius accepted that the forgiveness of sin required the action of unmerited grace in the soul, but felt that human nature could not itself be bad. It remained capable of the freely chosen acts that alone can be moral.

Trouble broke out on account of the now traditional practice of infant baptism. Pelagius could not accept that baptism was required for the remission of sin. He admitted only that the unbaptized could not be admitted to the kingdom of heaven, but held also that a just God could not consign unbaptized infants to an eternity of punishment. There had to be another solution, involving a state of natural felicity.

Pelagius and his disciple Caelestius had fled Rome when it was sacked by the Goths in 410, landing at Hippo in North Africa in 411, where Pelagius left his companion and continued by himself to the Holy Land. Caelestius preached that grace was the aid conveyed by moral exhortation and the example of Christ; that Adam would have died even if he had not sinned; that his sin was not transmitted; and that new-born children were born in the same state as Adam at the creation. He applied for ordination at Carthage, but the bishop had been warned against him, and was he denounced for heresy and formally censured by a Carthage synod for six propositions. Caelestius did not deny that he held the propositions, but he did deny that they were heretical. After a futile appeal to Rome, he went to Ephesus.

Pelagius, on arrival in the Holy Land, had been unwise enough to criticize the irascible Jerome, bringing on himself the considerable weight of Jerome's ill-will. When in 415 Augustine sent to Jerome a young friend from Spain, Orosius, to warn him against Pelagius, Jerome incited Orosius to report that the doctrines of Pelagius and Caelestius had been condemned as heretical in Africa for denying original sin and the human need for grace. Jerome then cited Pelagius before the bishop of Jerusalem.

The preliminary decision went in Pelagius' favour, as did that of a synod of Palestinian bishops at Diospolis, where neither of Pelagius' accusers was able to appear. The dispute was about the nature of the help required. Pelagius did not teach that man could avoid sin without God's help, but he continued to maintain that grace should not be such as to remove from a good action a free act of autonomous human will. Augustine, however, was not satisfied with Pelagius' notion of grace, and Pelagius was loudly condemned at African councils in Numidia and Proconsular Africa, which in 416 referred the matter to the pope, Innocent I, who replied that, on the evidence of the Africans, Pelagians must be held as excommunicated unless they recanted.

However, Innocent died, and three months later Caelestius put his case personally to the new pope, Zosimus. Pelagius sent the pope his new work explaining his doctrine of free will as the source of all moral acts. Zosimus reported to the Africans that their accounts of Pelagius' views were wrong, but was made hesitant by the resultant African clamour. Augustine profited from the delay to make representations directly to the emperor Honorius, who in 418 banished the Pelagians irrevocably from Rome, decreeing the confiscation of their goods. He saw them as a threat to peace, and it is not unlikely that Pelagius had indeed been the cause of social unrest by pointing to the irresponsibility of the rich.

Pelagius' theological beliefs were thought to have led to an icy and aristocratic asceticism in his followers, and also to the corollary that, if nature was free and capable of heroic virtue, then the general misery must be the result of reformable social conditions. Zosimus felt obliged to accept the imperial verdict, and issued a formal condemnation of Pelagius and Caelestius. Caelestius and his sympathizers then appealed to Alexandria and Constantinople, but the political relations involved made success impossible.

It was now that the argument reached its fiercest point, as Augustine began to elaborate a much more detailed psychology of grace than hitherto, notably connecting the transmission of original sin with the concupiscence (or lust) inherent in the reproductive process. Baptism was for the remission of sin, and it followed that babies dying unbaptized would be damned, however mild the form of damnation. All pagan acts, being devoid of grace, are sinful. God has predestined a select band of souls for salvation by a decree that does not rely on any human merit, but on the bestowal of irresistible grace. This doctrine was understandably attacked, its most notable opponent being the Pelagian Julian of Eclanum, for whom grace brings a nature of itself good to its perfection. Concupiscence is not sin, and leads to sin only when it takes the individual outside the limits laid down by God. Understandably, Julian thought that Augustine was importing views held in his Manichaean days.

Julian himself had to take refuge in the east, but his protest against an increasingly harsh Augustine had seeded opposition to Augustine even among non-Pelagians. Augustine had seemed to make moral effort otiose, since all human fate after death was predestined. The monastic communities held to the need for grace in all virtuous acts, but also to the need for the cooperation of the free will with proffered grace.

The immense importance of the condemnations of Pelagius, Caelestius, and Julian lies in the impetus they gave Augustine to refine his increasing insistence on man's absolute dependence on God for any good act, and for the doctrine of predestination by which alone a select few might be saved from among the human race. Augustine's doctrine, in only slightly attenuated forms, became normative for centuries.

ANTHONY LEVI

Further Reading

Augustinus Magister, 3 vols, Paris: Études Augustiniennes, 1954

Brown, Peter, *Augustine of Hippo: A Biography*, London: Faber, and Berkeley: University of California Press, 1967

Chadwick, Henry, *The Early Church*, revised edition Harmondsworth and New York: Penguin, 1993

Pelagius, *Expositions of Thirteen Epistles of St Paul*, introduction by Alexander Souter, 3 vols, Cambridge: Cambridge University Press, 1922–31

Pelagius, *Commentary on St Paul's Epistle to the Romans*, edited and translated by Theodore de Bruyn, Oxford: Clarendon Press, and New York: Oxford University Press, 1993

TeSelle, Eugene, *Augustine the Theologian*, London: Burns and Oates, and New York: Herder, 1970

PENG NING
Chinese film director

KU LIAN (Unrequited Love)
Film, 1980

Although the Cultural Revolution officially ended in 1976, the Chinese Communist Party (CCP) did not stop its strict censorship of the media, particularly films. The ban on Peng Ning's *Unrequited Love* in 1980 received national attention because it seemed at variance with the "open door" policy that the party was then promulgating. Under this new policy, open criticism of the excesses of the Cultural Revolution was not only tolerated, but also to some degree encouraged by top party officials. The fate of *Unrequited Love*, a film that depicted the sufferings caused by the Cultural Revolution, made it clear that the party would go so far but no further; it had a chilling effect on writers and artists.

Criticism of the film centred on the script, written by Bai Hua, which was completed in the spring of 1979. At the time, Bai served as the director of the propaganda department of Tianjin Municipality and the vice-chairman of the Tianjin Revolutionary Committee. Although he had been criticized earlier for his overtly frank writings during the Great Leap Forward, Bai was the featured speaker at the Fourth National Congress of Writers and Artists, which met in November 1979. *Unrequited Love*, based on Bai's script, was completed and released in 1980, but quickly withdrawn from circulation.

The film is set in a maze of overlapping flashbacks designed to illuminate the life and political fate of the hero, Ling Chenguang. Born in a small town in a mountainous area of China, he leaves home in 1937 to seek his fortune in the world and grows into manhood. He becomes an internationally famous artist. Out of patriotism, he returns to China after 1949, but suffers political persecution in the hands of leftist radicals. The film ends as Ling meets his death on a snowy plain, his errant footsteps forming a semicircle which his own corpse, a black dot on the white land, transforms into a giant question mark.

The most serious charge levelled was that the CCP was allowed no positive role in the pre-1949 revolution that had brought the communists to power; there was no mention of a single communist leader in a position of constructive authority. The film had described communist China as a modern feudalism, worse than that before the 1911 revolution. Furthermore, the film failed to separate its criticisms of the "bunch of scum" – Lin Biao and the Gang of Four – from its criticism of the motherland in general.

Unrequited Love was withdrawn from circulation and most people never had a chance to see it. Nationwide denunciation continued. In August 1981 the CCP's general secretary Hu Yaobang asserted that the film "was not good for the people and socialism and therefore should be criticized". Bai Hua and the production team were made to denounce the film and engage in self-criticism. The Changchun Film Studio proceeded to reshoot the film. The whole incident served as a warning to Chinese intellectuals: the party was not going to tolerate even the existence of any ideas that they did not endorse.

ZHIWEI XIAO

Further Reading

Chang, T.C. *et al.*, *Pai Hua's Cinematic Script Unrequited Love, with Related Introductory Materials*, Taipei: Institute of Current Chinese Studies, 1981
Clark, Paul, *Chinese Cinema: Culture and Politics since 1949*, Cambridge and New York: Cambridge University Press, 1987
Semsel, George Stephen, *Chinese Film: The State of the Art in the People's Republic*, New York: Praeger, 1987
Spence, Jonathan D., *Chinese Roundabout: Essays in History and Culture*, New York: Norton, 1992

THE PENTAGON PAPERS
US secret report, 1971

The Pentagon Papers was the popular name for the secret US Defense Department report entitled "History of US Decision-Making Process on Vietnam Policy". The report was commissioned in June 1967 by president Johnson's defense secretary, Robert McNamara, but not completed until shortly after President Nixon took office in January 1969. It traced the development of US policy towards Vietnam during the Truman, Eisenhower, Kennedy, and Johnson administrations. The report ran to some 7,000 pages and was classified "Top Secret – Sensitive".

In the US of the late 1960s, domestic opposition to the Vietnam War was intensifying. Daniel Ellsberg, one of the Defense Department analysts who had helped to compile the

report, had become increasingly concerned about the manner and degree of US involvement in Vietnam. In particular, the report made clear that the public had been deliberately misled as to the scale of US military involvement and its likely outcome. Knowing that to leak the report to the press would be a criminal offence under the Espionage Act, Ellsberg leaked it initially to several members of Congress whom he knew to be critical of the Vietnam policy, but who also had the necessary security clearance to see such sensitive material. When none of them acted on the information contained in it, Ellsberg passed parts of the report to Neil Sheehan, a journalist with the *New York Times*.

On 13 June 1971, a Sunday, the *Times* carried a front-page

lead under the anodyne headline "Vietnam Archive: Pentagon Study Traces Three Decades of Growing US Involvement". The story, written by Sheehan, indicated in broad terms the general scope of the report. It was followed the next day by a second article, and further revelations were promised for successive days.

At first the government appeared content to do nothing and let the *Times* run the story. It is quite likely that, prior to the leak, no one in the Nixon cabinet was aware of the report's existence. Since it dealt solely with the actions of previous governments it could contain nothing to embarrass the White House. On Tuesday, 15 June, however, the government expressed concern about the possible disclosure of military secrets, and immediately applied to the federal court in Manhattan for an injunction preventing the *Times* from publishing further extracts. This was the first time the federal government had ever sued to prevent disclosure of information on national security grounds.

From then on events moved apace. Judge Murray Gurfein granted a temporary restraining order and scheduled an evidentiary hearing for Friday 18 June. Before then, however, Ellsberg had passed the same extracts from the report to the *Washington Post*, which also went ahead with publication, prompting a second hearing in Washington. The government was now in the position of going to court to attempt to silence the country's two leading newspapers.

In New York the hearing went ahead as scheduled, Gurfein clearing the courtroom while he heard the government's evidence. In particular, the government claimed that further publication would endanger troop movements, harm diplomatic efforts then underway to end the conflict and to secure the return of US prisoners, and jeopardize the safety of intelligence agents. Apparently the government failed to make a convincing case, and on 19 June the judge turned down the request for a preliminary injunction. The US District Court in Washington, DC, came to a similar conclusion two days later.

The government promptly appealed against both judgements and on 23 June two appeals courts, in New York and Washington, came to different conclusions: the former that further hearings should be held, the latter that the papers could go ahead and publish. In the midst of such legal confusion, the government and the *New York Times* agreed to ask the Supreme Court for a speedy review.

On 30 June – just 17 days after the *Times* broke the Pentagon Papers story – the Supreme Court issued its ruling. By a vote of 6–3 the court denied the government its injunction. This was undoubtedly a great victory for the freedom of the press from prior restraints, but the court was extremely divided over the reasoning behind its judgement. Since the government had never before sought an injunction on national security grounds, there was no legal precedent to follow. There was no established standard that spelled out how much danger must ensue from disclosure for an injunction to be justified, or how soon after publication it should occur, or how likely it was to occur.

The court's confusion was indicated by the fact that it issued a *per curiam* opinion (unsigned, but intended to express the view of the court as a whole) in addition to the separate opinions of the nine justices. It said simply that "any system of prior restraints of expression comes to this court bearing a heavy presumption against its constitutional validity", and that the government had therefore had an especially heavy burden of proof. But it failed to indicate how the Court had weighed the government's evidence, or why it was found lacking.

The individual opinions showed the justices to be at odds on the question of whether prior restraints can ever be justified. Justice Brennan argued that only in a case where publication "must inevitably, directly and immediately cause the occurrence of an event kindred to imperilling the safety of a transport already at sea" could such an injunction be granted. Justice Black went further, ruling them out altogether in all cases. The minority opinions, on the other hand, objected primarily to being bounced into making a summary ruling on such a complex and sensitive matter. It is unclear, then, exactly what precedent the case set, other than that there is a very high standard of proof for injunctions to be granted in cases dealing with national security.

Ironically, it seems very unlikely that the newspapers were actually in possession of the particular parts of the report to which the government objected. One senior Nixon official has admitted that none of the information that posed a security risk was published until many years later, and dismissed the affair as "a tempest in a teapot". Nonetheless, the continued serialization of the Pentagon Papers did stimulate public debate over the conduct of the Vietnam War. In particular, revelations about the way president Johnson had publicly misrepresented the war certainly contributed to the breakdown in trust between people and politicians. It also fuelled Nixon's profound suspicions about the motives of the press.

ADAM NEWEY

Texts

United States–Vietnam Relations, 1945–1967: Study Prepared by Department of Defense (for use by the House Committee on Armed Services), 12 vols, Washington, DC: US Government Printing Office, 1971

The Pentagon Papers, as Published by the New York Times, Based on Investigative Reporting by Neil Sheehan, New York: Quadrangle, and London: Routledge, 1971

The Pentagon Papers: The Defense Department History of United States Decisionmaking on Vietnam (Senator Gravel edition), 5 vols, Boston: Beacon Press, 1971–72

The Secret Diplomacy of the Vietnam War: The Negotiating Volumes of the Pentagon Papers, edited by George C. Herring, Austin: University of Texas Press, 1983

The Pentagon Papers (selections), edited by George C. Herring, New York: McGraw Hill, 1993

Further Reading

Rudenstine, David, *The Day the Presses Stopped: A History of the Pentagon Papers Case*, Berkeley, California: University of California Press, 1996

Salter, Kenneth W., *The Pentagon Papers Trial*, Berkeley, California: Justa, 1975

Schuster, Joseph F., *The First Amendment in the Balance*, San Francisco: Austin and Winfield, 1993

Shapiro, Martin (editor), *The Pentagon Papers and the Courts: A Study in Foreign Policy-making and Freedom of the Press*, San Francisco: Chandler, 1972

Ungar, Sanford J., *The Papers and the Papers: An Account of the Legal and Political Battle over the Pentagon Papers*, New York: Dutton, 1972

PENTHOUSE
International men's magazine: censored in New Zealand, 1980–93

In New Zealand, from the passing of the Indecent Publications Act in 1963 until the comprehensive Films, Videos and Publication Classification Act of 1993, books and magazines went before their own censorship body, the Indecent Publications Tribunal. This collection of representative citizens appointed by parliament received regular submissions of two international magazines: *Playboy* and *Penthouse*. *Playboy* was not allowed into New Zealand until 1965 and *Penthouse* not until 1970. In May 1980, *Penthouse* was sent to the Tribunal. That month's issue and the subsequent one for June, which included a spread by the erotic artist, Jean-Marie Poumeyrol, and stills of lesbian love-making from the *Penthouse*-produced film *Caligula*, were declared indecent.

Gordon and Gotch, the commercial importers, then submitted, voluntarily, three consecutive issues (September, October, and November 1981) with the request that the Tribunal classify them as indecent in the hands of anyone under the age of 18. If such a ruling had been forthcoming, it could have covered all other issues for the next two years and made the business of importing the magazine much less erratic. This the Tribunal refused to do for they found the November issue to be unacceptable even in mature hands. Referring to a sequence entitled "To Rush in with Love" (*Penthouse*, November 1981, pp. 71–83) they stated that:

We find that the scenes are not only offensive and tasteless, but also that they are injurious to the public good because: (a) Of the mixture of sex and violence depicted; (b) Of the needless multiplicity of models and degree of intimacy among them; (c) Of the lesbian and prurient aspects of sex presented.

In addition they felt that *Penthouse* had been "on the borderline" since 1979 and that it was pushing the boundaries each month, so that there was no knowing where it might get to in two years. This ruling, which was applied as a check in future years, became known as the "tripartite test".

Customs then took the initiative. They were of the opinion that if they could obtain a ban on three sequential issues then all editions would be outlawed for two years. So, in early 1983, the Comptroller submitted all 12 editions that had been imported during 1982. This time the Indecent Publications Tribunal found material similar to that previously banned by the Tribunal in seven of the 12 issues for that year, but, even though four sequential editions (July to October), were found to be indecent the Tribunal still refused to give a blanket ban on future issues.

The situation for Gordon and Gotch, for whom *Penthouse* was a bestseller, was becoming increasingly difficult, as they could offer only an intermittent supply to retailers and when three more editions (for June, July, and August 1983) were sent to the Tribunal, Penthouse International, based in New York, sent Geoffrey Robertson of the English Bar to argue against the imposition of a serial ban. Robertson lodged affidavits that affirmed that the relevant issues were not indecent, including one by the author and QC John Mortimer. Robertson was particularly opposed to what Penthouse International regarded as too rigid an application of the "Tripartite Test". He went on to state that, "Unlike hard-core pornography, actual sexual connection is never photographed in *Penthouse*. Some acts may be simulated or suggested, but [they] are never actually committed in front of the camera . . .".

The chairman in his report observed that they had checked every issue of *Penthouse* for the previous two years (up to December 1983) and concluded that "if anything, (they) appear to be getting worse rather than better". Referring to the pictorial spread on pages 119–23 of the July issue in question, Walter Willis said that: "If the intimacy shown in those photographs was not actual intercourse it gives every appearance of being just that". He went on to reaffirm the relevance of the guidelines that had been laid down in previous decisions. The Tribunal found the three issues in question to be indecent in terms of this "Tripartite Test". Accordingly, they were not prepared to give a blanket R18 restriction (Restricted to people over 18) as requested by Robertson. Neither, since they had been told that the 1984 issues would be markedly different from the 1983 ones, would they be prepared to make a permanent ban. Needless to say, this was a finding that pleased neither Gordon and Gotch nor the Customs Department.

As the 1980s progressed video tapes containing matter more explicit than that to be found in *Penthouse* began to find their way into the country. Indeed, the treatment accorded to video tapes was about to become dramatically more free when, in 1987, the film censor, Arthur Everard, decided to pass hardcore pornography depicting consensual sexual acts. Nevertheless, the Indecent Publications Tribunal continued to take a firm line with *Penthouse*. Under Judge Richard Kearney, in 1994, the Tribunal had finally issued the two-year ban that campaigners against pornography had sought, and *Penthouse* was removed from the newsstands. It did not reappear until 1991 when the Tribunal, now led by Peter Cartwright, a former chairman of the Auckland Council for Civil Liberties, issued new guidelines for the treatment of sexually explicit materials, which opened the way for the sale of magazines even more forthright than *Penthouse*.

It was, once again, *Penthouse* that was pivotal to the decision. In 1990 the Bill of Rights Act had brought in a "freedom of expression" provision, albeit modified by "a reasonable limitation prescribed by law and demonstrably justified in a free and democratic society". In November, after evidence from 28 expert witness at a Tribunal hearing on *Penthouse* it was concluded that non-violent, sexually explicit material has no proved negative effect on male sexual behaviour or attitudes to women, which led the Tribunal to rule that while depictions of sexual activity "which demean or treat as inherently inferior or unequal any person or group of persons . . . are indecent; . . . explicit sex is no problem as long as those involved are shown as people willingly enjoying sex" (Kevin O'Connor, "People's Choice: Is it Erotic or is it Evil?, *Sunday Times*, May 1992).

There is obviously the potential for a great deal of disagreement about the interpretation of the words relating to "demeaning" and "treating as . . . . inferior" as the majority of sexual images show one person dominant and the other dominated, even when both are of the same gender.

Furthermore, the importers of *Penthouse* and *Knave*, among other titles, are still having problems with a meticulous interpretation of the Films, Videos and Publications Classification Act 1993 which considers advertisements for actions now specifically listed as "objectionable" to require the automatic banning of the whole publication in which they appear. This prohibition is based on the assumption that the publications are "promoting" the behaviour declared to be "objectionable". Thus, any reference in an advertisement to "Golden Showers" or "Water Sports" (which are code words for urination – one

of the eight categories of sexual behaviour listed as always objectionable by the act) will result in that issue being banned from sale.

So, although the law might have been tidied up, in some respects, as with all legislation seeking to rule on matters of obscenity, new anomalies have been created; new debates will arise.

CHRIS WATSON

Further Reading
Indecent Publications Tribunal, Decision 13/84, 29 November 1983

SPENCER PERCEVAL
British politician and prime minister, 1762–1812

THE BOOK (*An Inquiry or Delicate Investigation into the Conduct of Her Royal Highness The Princess of Wales*)
Report, 1813

In 1795 George, Prince of Wales (1762–1830), heir to the British throne, married his cousin Princess Caroline of Brunswick (1768–1821). The dissolute prince was already illegally married (under the terms of the Royal Marriages Act though the marriage was valid in the eyes of the Anglican and Roman Catholic churches) and during his life had a series of mistresses. The marriage was unhappy and the couple unofficially separated in 1798. Caroline left her husband's house and the prince gained principal control over their daughter. The arrangements for the princess's access to her daughter caused unhappiness and friction.

Caroline's subsequent indiscreet lifestyle generated rumours of lovers and allegations about an illegitimate son. When the "Delicate Investigation" by a secret commission of four cabinet ministers into these allegations began in May 1806, Caroline was no longer being received at court. In July the investigation cleared Caroline of the specific allegations but reported to the king that her general behaviour was questionable.

Caroline and her advisers believed the Whig cabinet (which included several of the prince's friends) was prepared to arrange a divorce, which she did not want. The rumours of her adultery still circulated, which suited the prince, and Caroline was keen to publish the transactions that exonerated her. Her mother also petitioned the king (her brother) for publication. But George III was averse to private quarrels being exposed to public scrutiny. Because of this, and from disapproval of Caroline's conduct, some Tories strongly opposed publication. However, one of Caroline's legal advisers, the Tory politician and former attorney general Spencer Perceval, thought publication would be acceptable if it were seen as Caroline's last resort. It was discussed over some time, but eventually, under pressure from Caroline, Perceval prepared *The Book*. It contained the evidence presented to the investigation, the investigation's findings, and a letter to George III, written for Caroline by Perceval, declaring her innocence and complaining about her treatment. Between 1500 and 2000 copies of *The Book* were printed. Francis Blagdon later argued that this number would

not have satisfied public demand and therefore indicated that Perceval had never intended to publish; however, once the book had been published it was likely that extracts would appear in newspapers and pamphlets which, being cheaper, had a wider circulation than books.

The threat of publication was intended to coerce the king into receiving Caroline at court and returning her to her apartments at her husband's residence. If that failed, publication would give Caroline public support by showing her as an injured woman. A similar kind of ultimatum was used in 1809 by Mary Anne Clarke, a printer's daughter who printed her love letters from one of George III's younger sons, the duke of York; her reward for destroying the copies – except for one she kept in a bank vault – was £7000 down and £400 a year for life.

In March 1807 Caroline sent Perceval's ultimatum to the king. Events then took an unexpected turn. The king, displeased with the Whigs, dismissed them and brought back the Tories – including Perceval. The threat of divorce was removed and the new cabinet immediately asked the king to receive Caroline. She was received at court for the first time in 18 months and given apartments at Kensington Palace, although the threat of publication had irreparably damaged the relationship between Caroline and the king. As the demands had been more or less met, Perceval decided not to publish and destroyed the books. However, he had lent out copies (strictly embargoed) to close colleagues. The printer had also loaned copies. *The Book* might now damage the new government's relationship with the king. "Lost" copies were advertised for anonymously and about £10,000 was spent on recovering them.

In 1808 Francis Blagdon launched a newspaper, the *Phoenix*, in which he promised to serialize an important publication. The editor of the *Morning Chronicle* told the prince of Wales's solicitor that this was *The Book*. The government was also told that Blagdon sought "to be *touch'd*" – that is, he wanted to be paid off (a not dissimilar strategy to Perceval's). The response was an injunction against publication on penalty of £5000. Blagdon complied and was later rewarded with a government subsidy to set up a second newspaper. However, the injunction also forbade him to give up the material he had which meant that he kept it in his possession.

From late 1809 onwards Caroline began to side with the opposition. In 1811 the prince became regent, retaining the same ministers as his father. However, the Tories found him a difficult master (rumour claimed that Perceval, then prime minister, stayed in office by blackmailing the regent with *The Book*). In early 1812, some Whigs discussed publishing *The Book* to embarrass the government.

The final development in the history of *The Book* began in early 1813. Caroline's very limited access to her daughter (now aged 17) was a cause of great discontent to her. Henry Brougham (1778–1868), a Whig lawyer temporarily barred from parliamentary politics, wrote Caroline a letter of complaint addressed to her husband. The regent refused to receive it and instead Brougham had it published in the *Morning Chronicle*. This revived interest in the findings of the "Delicate Investigation". Blagdon immediately started preparing a chancery injunction. This included the anonymized text of the injunction itself, some documents, and a series of letters from Blagdon to Caroline recounting the true history of *The Book* and emphasizing the importance of its publication. As Blagdon was rushing into print, a *Times* editorial claimed it would be "calamitous" for the princess if *The Book* were published (*The Times*, 11 February 1813). However, *The Times* was wrong. *The Book* was serialized in the press that year, followed by a pamphlet version from Blagdon and at least four other editions. Caroline, now seen as an injured woman, gained popular support, though she sank in the opinion of her daughter. The regent wanted to respond by publishing another document which would have condemned Caroline, but the government vetoed this as it would only increase his unpopularity. Caroline was allowed a pension and went abroad in 1813, returning in 1820 when her husband became George IV. Far from allowing her to become his queen, George attempted to get a divorce by act of parliament on the grounds of Caroline's adultery. However, she had the support of the country, including several thousand women; their demonstrations and petitions, supported by popular songs and a pamphlet, *The Queen and Magna Carta; or, The Thing That John Signed*, led to the bill being abandoned.

Although suppression of *The Book* was partly an exercise in self-censorship by its compiler, Spencer Perceval, its history shows some of the forces at work, including blackmail, in the absence of a system of state pre-publication censorship.

JOANNE C. STONE

Writings

Fairburn's Genuine Edition of The Book, Including the Defence of Her Royal Highness the Princess of Wales as Prepared by Mr Spencer Perceval, 1813

Further Reading

Blagdon, Francis, *Chancery Injunction: Letters to Her Royal Highness Caroline Princess of Wales, Comprising the Only True History of The Book*, London: Richardson, 1813
Colley, Linda, *Britons: Forging the Nation, 1707–1837*, New Haven, Connecticut and London: Yale University Press, 1992
Fraser, Flora, *The Unruly Queen: The Life of Queen Caroline*, London: Macmillan, and New York: Knopf, 1996
Gray, Denis, *Spencer Perceval: The Evangelical Prime Minister, 1762–1812*, Manchester: Manchester University Press, 1963
Smith, E.A., *George IV*, New Haven and London: Yale University Press, 1999

PERFORMANCE ART

Using the notion "end-of-art Art", coined by the contemporary philosopher of aesthetics Arthur Danto to refer to art practice in an age when virtually anything can be indexed as an artwork, an age in which historical linearity is abandoned, when both mimetic art and expressive art are overcome (or is it undertaken?) by a post-Enlightenment relativism, performance art can appear as a vivid form of philosophy enriched by reflexivity. Such a consideration of it takes it far from populist perceptions of a meaningless or elitist kind of theatre for the demented and closer to Joseph Beuys's view of his practice (which included many *actions*) as a purposeful form of historical and psychoanalytical action. Beuys's actions openly addressed a traumatized German subject and the "white guilt" of the West.

In performance, whenever the act has priority over the actor, or is severed from character development (which makes it unlike theatre, according to Laurie Anderson), we will be in the zone of artists' performance or "live art by artists" (RoseLee Goldberg). This zone encompassed the "happenings" of the 1960s, the name given to Allan Kaprow's development of collage environments as the site of chance, unexpected events where "something spontaneous . . . just happens to happen".

In addition, it takes in direct actions (ritualized political interventions), body art, and myriad unique blends of dance, painting, narrative, poetry, architecture, and projected images – elements ecstatic or controlled. Seeded in the margins of western art – as anti-art, by Dadaists – performance art too may be seen more recently in the forefront of moves to forge the way to a transnational culture or a postmodern consciousness. The performance work of Guillermo Gómez-Peña ranks as one of the finest examples of the latter, rooted as it is in "border experience", testing the capacity of rival communities for "the tolerance of otherness": Mexican, Chicano, Anglo-American, and "artworld" communities are his primary audiences, mixed or separate.

Although its history is a long one as an intermittent phenomenon spurred by fantasy and allegory, manifest in parades and processions, performance art flourished in Europe and the US in the 1960s and 1970s as part of the paradigmatic shift from formalist modernism. The latter, it might be ventured, sought to preserve the triumvirate of a linear history of art (with a teleology of abstraction), vanguard identities (progressive, conflictual movements in an era of manifestos), and a dialectical self-criticism made possible through formal autonomy and technical radicalism (an art dedicated to the purity of specific, critically fecund practices, especially painting): imaginative experience, aesthetic experience, or visual experience were upheld by critics (Roger Fry, Clive Bell, Clement Greenberg, and Michael Fried), as well as practitioners, as the saving, defining qualities to be preserved by the community of art specialists.

Performance art surged in that period now identifiable as awakening to the end of modernity. This is variously figured as the release from societies based on industrial production, from male-dominated forms of centralized authority or from colonial rule. The diversity of practices, confusing and chaotic as they must have appeared – happenings, actions, performances alongside tight conceptual work and Pop art – sought to challenge western artworld solipsism, long dominant aesthetic categories, the social and physical enclosures of the museum, and the reification of art as object. All of these issues were confronted unsparingly. At once anarchic and revitalizing, this performance art was also indicative of tremors in the wider culture: Victor Burgin, writing on the developments of conceptualism and 1970s postmodernism in an essay entitled "The Absence of Presence", advocated a wholesale challenge to narcissistic self-integrity (the "I" of humanist culture) in a call for a practice – seldom to be referred to as Art – suited to the active historical subject disclosed by Marx and warned against by Freud! Viewed in such a light, performance was perhaps the bodily, playful arena into which humanist *presence* collapsed, an arena perplexingly close to the everyday yet a potential conduit (or *conduct*, to draw upon the language of Gilles Deleuze) for transformatory energies.

Divergent tendencies can be seen in actions motivated by political priorities on the one hand – feminist, postcolonial, and ecological work – and explorations of ritual-play-spectacle on the other, which ranged from the humorous and entertaining to the spiritually esoteric. What links these is the turn towards an art without, or beyond, metaphysical values and that territory of transgression seen often in the form of acts enshrining sublime abjection. The paradoxical situation of affirmative transgressions by performance artists in an emergent nihilist culture of accumulation has often been misunderstood as perversion and crudity, leading to censorship of various kinds. The immediacy and bodily explicitness of much performance art has been driven by a craving for *is-ness*, the ever-out-of-reach power of Being as traced by Heidegger, later phenomenologists and the deconstructionism developed by Jacques Derrida, and the desire for *witness*, with a persistent devotion to pain, suffering, and taboo-crashing exposure. This can often appear, most often mistakenly, as sensationalism or irrationalism.

In North America and Europe, right-wing Christian groups, as well as conservative civic or national authorities in particular, tend to voice the strongest objections. This is done often via political lobbying in the United States, where the American Family Association along with others (Pat Robertson's 700 Club, Phyllis Schlafly's Eagle Forum, and Concerned Women for America) under the umbrella organization Taxpayers for Accountability have forced artists to mount counter-campaigns for free speech (Arts Coalition for Cultural Freedom, Artsave, National Campaign for Freedom of Expression) resulting in successful amendments to the Helms amendment (Public Law 101–121, legislating control of the content of artworks), a ban

in 1989 on "obscene" art which aimed at suppressing Robert Mapplethorpe's controversial photographs.

On another level, a form of critical prejudice survives whenever performance art is derided as a theatrical debasement of traditional practices. This institutional voice can, if dominant, marginalize "live art" in any number of ways – short of banning it. This mentality would link performance, as happens in practice, to video and then the order of mainstream telematics, the "debasement" being an attunement to large-audience *spectacle*, "public" normalization, and addiction to corporate *now-ness*, rather than the *is-ness* mentioned above as the code of an existential or corporeal consciousness.

RoseLee Goldberg, author of the perspicacious, conventional history of 20th-century performance by artists, cites three pieces by the young Chris Burden that may be instrumentally typical:

> Burden installed himself in a $2' \times 2' \times 3'$ locker for five days, his only supplies for this tight-fitting stay being a large bottle of water, the contents of which were pumped to him via the locker above. In the same year, in Venice, California, he asked a friend to shoot him in the left arm, in a work entitled *Shooting Piece*. The bullet, fired from fifteen feet away, should have grazed his arm, but instead blew away a large piece of flesh. *Deadman* of the following year was another all-too-serious game with death. He lay wrapped in a canvas bag in the middle of a busy Los Angeles boulevard. Luckily he was unhurt, and the police put an end to this work by arresting him for causing a false emergency to be reported.

There is a sense, in this last one, that the "crime" is the foolishly inaccurate calculation of risk – as opposed to blasphemy, obscenity, or sedition – in a society driven by risk management (Ulrich Beck) as its operational rationale. The first two pieces push endurance and pain (self-directed or self-inflicted) to the limit.

More subtle pieces involving physical harm, by Marina Abramovic (and her collaborator Ulay) in the 1970s, often transported audiences through frustration to a sublimated joy, or a feeling more credible than simple voyeuristic pleasure. *Light Dark* (1977) gave us slapping to excess, *Art Must be Beautiful* (1975) gave us hair-brushing to excess, *Bow and Arrow* (1978–79) had an arrow drawn, poised for an aching, life-threatening 90 minutes, and another work *Breathing In/ Breathing Out* turned a kiss into a panic sucking for life. One critic, Tim Martin, alludes to a special power – a wilful silence and a somatic presence – through which "her performances can become 'crowd crystals', to use Canetti's phrase". In a Freudian–Lacanian reading of her work with the audience, Martin describes it as "relational gratification" attuned to a non-Western belief in "God in Nature" – "Abramovic . . . inserts her body, thereby wrecking language to reveal the surplus that is pleasure and death".

While Burden's Los Angeles police officers simply brought things to a halt, Abramovic had an international artspace as a safe-haven from which to expose the political wounds of the bestial nationalisms of the former Yugoslavia: in the Venice Biennale of 1997 she wailed, atop a throne of rotting animal bones, for days on end, in a lament "distanced" but yet sure to shame her fellow Serbians.

Russians in the 1970s took to performance as an escape from official art and the attentions of the KGB (who must rank as both under- and over-sophisticated readers of symbolism). Performance groups such as Andrei Monastyrsky's Collective Actions "would perform ritualistic actions of an enigmatic nature not announced in advance" (Taylor 1995). Lev Nussberg's group Motion, who worked extensively in the Moscow, Leningrad, and Black Sea areas, were experiencing increased KGB and police surveillance as early as 1971: "Nussberg's projects weren't politically oriented or slanderous to the Soviet state but the group's independence and non-reliance on state agencies could not be ignored in the USSR" (Andrei Toluzakov), culminating in exclusion from the artistic establishment and public censure in a state-sponsored brochure "Against Abstractionism in Art", which attacked them as pro-Western, unofficial artists. Many such artists emigrated, Nussberg going via Vienna, to Paris for a time, then to the United States.

In Cuba between 1989 and 1992, the number of shows and events cancelled by the Ministry of Culture, together with government promotion of traditional fine art (paintings, drawings, and sculpture) for sale abroad – in the wake of the European communist collapse of 1989 – marked a dangerous time for performance artists. Jay Murphy cites the case of the conceptual art group ABTV (Angulo, Ballester, Toirac, and Villazon) whose show *Homage to Hans Haacke*, set to open in September 1989, was "never given the green light" by the visual arts council of the Ministry for Culture, or higher authorities. The intended satirical treatment of the Fondo Cubano de Bienes Culturales (which promoted the sales of Cuban art abroad) may have been the "problem", but more probably it was the official sense of some "seditious" streak: "The 'Hans Haacke' show was to have included a performance involving the sale of a copy of a famous photograph of Che Guevara, a satirical demonstration of the 'degradation of art' by exchange value" (Murphy). The ABTV artist Toirac, in 1991, stated: "censorship is not stable but shifts according to circumstances that set a specific limit at a specific time; our works are now playing with those limits". Toirac is a voice from the war of "institutional cultural politics", "mythmakers" at arms, with real consequences.

In Britain, the reasons behind the last minute cancellation, by the Scottish National Gallery of Modern Art in Edinburgh, of an internationally curated and exhibited show *Vienna 1960: From Action Painting to Action* that was to be held there in 1988–89, displayed a different kind of fear. This was to have been a retrospective on the Viennese Actionists (Brus, Frohner, Muhl, Nitsch, Schilling, and Schwarzkogler); these were performance artists dedicated to emotionally intense, orgiastic ritual ceremonies which often involved animal sacrifice, nudity, "buckets of blood", and mimicry of the gestures of the insane. The anthropology and psychology of ritual extremes toppled over the edge of tolerable creation into fatal self-mutilation with the death of Schwarzkogler in 1969 from successive injuries. The censorship of the Edinburgh exhibition, one might deduce, had a strange quality to it, as if a governing body had awakened too late to the degree of sado-masochistic ritual, of narcissistic non-narcissism, to be thrust at an unsuspecting audience. Yet, by 1988, such acts, "myths", and exposures were already finding widespread acceptance in the form of visual and literary documentation.

The raw horrors of such body art continue in regular festivals such as that held by the Institute of Contemporary Art in London (November–December 1995): *Rapture: The Body, Ritual and Sacred Practice*. This offered a list of contemporary performance art's least and most wanted artists: Abramovic; the Italian Franko B; the Americans Marcus Kuillard-Nazario and Mario Gardner, Fakir Musafar, Ron Athey and Company, the Sacred Naked Nature Girls, and Annie Sprinkle; and others from Britain and Europe. Other Live Art centres in Britain (Glasgow, Sheffield, and Hull are strong on this front) are more interesting on censorship issues, perhaps because of the greater gulf in familiarity between the local audience, organizing authorities, arts organizations, and performers over what is deemed tolerable within that ethical-cognitive-aesthetic triangle inhabited by performers. Tim Etchells, writing on the ROOT live art events in Hull of 1996, instanced what may be a common case:

> The German artist Trebor Scholz was supposed to hang naked in a net in the shopping centre, with an invitation to "Hurt me as much as you like for free", though only with water pistols. However, in the end the owners weren't keen, and the event was moved to another place, where a more circumscribed group of people, largely consisting of other artists, squirted water to the accompaniment of loud dance music, just like the crazy artists party scene from a 60s movie. It was one of the festival events representing a trend towards "performance *povera*", and provided a healthy antidote to the cyberfixation otherwise in evidence.

The feeble purchase on critique at the heart of the consumer spectacle – evident in such an example – signals a containment of performance art by deflection and marginalization (to a community of self-serving artists). Better work with similar aims has been done recently by the performance group Max Factory who target "Business-as-usual" as the force of estrangement to be disrupted by their orchestrated actions and architectural alterations.

In November 1991 Ian McKay took advantage of a Projects UK Conference on Censorship, "Where do we draw the line?", held in Newcastle-on-Tyne, by exposing the tendency towards self-censorship in the art world. He suggested that Annie Sprinkle's performance, during the week of Live Arts entitled *Burning the Flag*, was for a "carefully targeted audience" in order to minimize public concern. Similarly, he instanced the castigated performance artist Karen Finlay's hounding a journalist (Rosie Millard of *The Independent*) over her allegedly inaccurate and sensationalist reporting of events. Even the supporters of the festival and the conference, *New Statesman & Society*, were shown to have backed off from full-scale promotion, from the fear of negative publicity from the piece by an ex-Porn-Queen-turned-performance artist, Annie Sprinkle, described thus:

> Sprinkle had invited the audience to climb the stage and inspect her cervix with a speculum and torch. Delegates from the conference were among those who were invited to have a Polaroid photograph taken with Annie's cervix. Simulated oral sex followed, with Annie finally claiming

to have achieved orgasm on stage. Whilst the liberal-minded conference goers made cat-calls and wolf-whistles from the floor, the following day their voices turned harsher in successfully stopping Susan Edwards [concerned with issues of violence against women] from speaking on a pro-censorship tack.

McKay choked on the irony of seeing a political journal, the arts organization Projects UK, and the Arts Council of Great Britain mired in "self-censorship", gagging artists, journalists, and floor speakers.

Louise Wilson's reporting of the same weekend festival put the emphasis on the background concerning the American *NEA Four* (Karen Finley, Tim Miller, Holly Hughes, and John Fleck), those who had grants withdrawn by John Frohnmayer, chair of the National Endowment for the Arts (NEA). Between 1989 and 1991 obscenity charges brought by Jesse Helms and other conservative senators petitioned by Taxpayers for Accountability – first against Andres Serrano's work *Piss Christ*, then against a number of performance artists (Ron Athey, Karen Finlay, and Annie Sprinkle, for example) – led to president George Bush ordering a reauthorization review on the NEA itself, then to artists refusing funding awards as a protest against what they correctly perceived as a re-emergence of blacklisting.

The Americans are stormily divided over censorship of contentious art practice, at least that which is confrontationally explicit performance art – especially an art engaged in gender politics, women's rights, or sexuality and power (various issues including homoeroticism, AIDS, and abortion). Censorship of performance has been at the centre of legal and funding battles.

Elsewhere, typically, censorship in this field operates by less publicized means – by omission of artists' works from exhibitions and festivals; by various kinds of cultural deflection (factors of place, time, and audience and "damage limitation"); by institutional de-commissioning; and, by attrition, through lack of grant funding.

Cultural exclusion and negative opposition, the targets of Guillermo Gómez-Peña's efforts in the borderlands which, increasingly, we all inhabit, are the everyday soil for the double denial of "being-in-the-world . . . as possibility" (Milan Kundera) and the need to re-imagine justice in political worlds. Abjection, only part of the process, seems a necessary means for contemporary artists and might be defended for its honesty as well as the demands it places upon us to bring about responsibility for the other.

ALLAN HARKNESS

Further Reading

Anderson, Laurie, "Artists, Audiences and Censorship", *Dialogue (USA)*, 16/5 (September–October 1993): 12–13

Art Journal, censorship issue (Fall 1991): 6–86

Barber, Fionna, "Against the Act of Union: Censorship and Visual Imagery in Northern Ireland", *High Performance* (Spring 1992): 24–27

Becker, Carol (editor), *The Subversive Imagination: Artists, Society, and Responsibility*, New York and London: Routledge, 1994

Beuys, Joseph, *Energy Plan for the Western Man: Joseph Beuys in America* (writings and interviews), edited by Carin Kuoni, New York: Four Walls Eight Windows, 1990

Blumberg, Mark *et al.*, "Front Page", *Art in America*, censorship issue (May 1990): 41–43

Brett, Guy, "The Live Weekend", *Art Monthly* (September 1983): 10–12

"A Chronology of Actions, Protests, Lawsuits, Trials, Censorship and the NEA", *High Performance* (Winter 1990): 34–35

Danto, Arthur C., *The Philosophical Disenfranchisement of Art*, New York: Columbia University Press, 1986

Davis, Douglas, "Art and Contradiction: Helms, Censorship and the Serpent", *Art in America*, censorship issue (May 1990): 56–61

Diamond, Elin (editor), *Performance and Cultural Politics*, London and New York: Routledge, 1996

Dubin, Steven C., *Arresting Images: Impolitic Art and Uncivil Actions*, London and New York: Routledge, 1992

Fusco, Coco, "The Border Art Workshop/Taller de Arte Fronterizo", *Third Text*, 7 (Summer 1989): 53–76

Goldberg, RoseLee, *Performance Art: From Futurism to the Present*, New York: Abrams, 1988; revised edition London: Thames and Hudson, 1988

Gómez-Peña, Guillermo, "A Binational Performance Pilgrimage", *Third Text*, 19 (Summer 1992): 64–78

Gómez-Peña, Guillermo, "The New World (B)order: A Work in Progress", *Third Text*, 21 (Winter 1992–93): 71–79

Henry, Clare, *Arts Review*, 13 January 1989: 7

Heyd, Thomas, "Understanding Performance Art: Art beyond Art", *British Journal of Aesthetics*, 31/1 (January 1991): 68–73

McKay, Ian, "Art and Censorship", *Art Monthly* (November 1991): 30

Martin, Tim, "Marina Abramovic", *Third Text*, 33 (Winter 1995–96): 85–92

Murphy, Jay, "Notes from the Editor", *High Performance* (Fall 1990): 8

Murphy, Jay, "Report from Havana: Testing the Limits", *Art in America* (October 1992): 65–68

Pearlstein, Philip, "An Artist's Case", *Art in America*, censorship issue (May 1990): 61

Schneeman, Carolee, "The Obscene Body/Politic", *Art Journal*, 50/4 (Winter 1991): 28–35

Taylor, Brandon, *The Art of Today*, London: Weidenfeld and Nicolson, 1995

Toluzakov, Andrei, "The Artificial World of Lev Nussberg: A Post-National, Post-Ethnic Theater of the Spirit", *High Performance*, 32/8 (1985): 52–55

Vance, Carole S., "Misunderstanding Obscenity", *Art in America*, censorship issue (May 1990): 49–56

Wallach, Amei, "Censorship in the Soviet Bloc", *Art Journal*, 50/3 (Fall 1991): 75–83

Wijers, Louwrien *et al.*, "Fluxus Today and Yesterday", *Art & Design*, 28 (1993)

Wilson, Louise, "Burning the Flag", *Variant*, 10 (Winter 1991): 25–29

PERU

Population: 25,662,000	**Number of daily newspapers:** 74
Main religions: Roman Catholic	**Number of radio receivers per 1000 inhabitants:** 273
Official language: Spanish; Quechua	
Other languages spoken: Aymarà	**Number of TV receivers per 1000 inhabitants:** 126
Illiteracy rate (%): 5.3 (m); 14.6 (f)	**Number of PCs per 1000 inhabitants:** 18.1

The Conquest

The history of Peru, in particular the Spanish conquest headed by Francisco Pizarro, was in large part recorded by Spanish chroniclers. Although many of these, like Juan de Betanzos, used native Andean informants, there can be little doubt that these documents retained a western perspective. Unlike the case of Mexico, there is not a wealth of painted books to which scholars of Peruvian history can turn to attain an indigenous perspective. There are four principal native Andean texts – those by Guaman Poma de Ayala, Garcilaso de la Vega, and Joan Santacruz Pachacuti Yamqui, and the anonymous *Huarochirí* manuscript (the only account written exclusively in Quechua, and recorded by Francisco de Avila in 1598). These documents are recognized as being of paramount importance. The *Huarochirí* authors, moreover, grasp the significance of the written word to the preservation of history, and say so on the opening page of the manuscript.

Language played a central role in the conquest of Peru. In simple terms the arrival of the Spanish meant the imposition of a new alien language. Pizarro used *lenguas* (literally "tongues", but meaning translators) to facilitate communication. Schooled in Spain, following a preliminary expedition to Peru in 1526–27, these named interpreters, Felipillo and Martín, were often unable to transmit cultural and cosmological concepts. For example, Garcilaso recounts Felipillo as misunderstanding the notion of the Holy Trinity. Later, following severe criticism from the emperor Charles V, Spanish subjects were quick to blame distorted testimony by the interpreters for the death of *Sapa Inca* (ruler) Atahualpa.

The Inca did not have a written language, and this fact was used as part of Europe's efforts to portray the native Inca as technologically backward and thereby to justify cultural domination. However, forms of nonwritten, mnemonic notation were used in the Andes that were incomprehensible to the Spanish. The most significant of these systems was the *quipu*, a system of knotted strings on which information was stored. These were produced and deciphered by learned individuals called *quipucamayocs*, and kept in libraries. Numerous Spanish chroniclers, such as Agustín de Zárate, Miguel Cabello de Valboa, and José de Acosta, compared these with the painted books of Mexico, that is, as historical documents. Indeed, Guaman Poma de Ayala transcribed the historical section of his *Primer corónica y buen gobierno* from *quipucamayocs*. Yet the Spanish were unable to decipher the *quipu* and were undoubtedly nervous of the information they might record. The censoring of *quipu* took place relatively late in the conquest process. This followed the Taqui Onkoy ("dancing sickness") movement of the 1560s. This was a relatively short-lived messianic movement discovered in 1564 by Luis de Olivera, curate of the parish of Parinacocha. It gained widespread support by preaching the total withdrawal of Spanish settlers, customs, and goods and predicting the total elimination of the Spaniards through an alliance of the *huacas* (site or object of religious significance) and native Andeans against the European invaders. The Third (Catholic) Council of Lima (1582–83), fearful of preserved forms of Andean memory, ordered *quipus* to be destroyed. Huge numbers of these documents were subsequently burned. Records of the destruction of individual *quipu*, such as that carried out by Diego d'Avalos in Jauja in 1602 also exist.

Two further forms of notation were *tocapus* (abstract, geometric designs on boards and textiles) and *keros* (decorated drinking vessels). The *tocapu* and the *kero* are also known to have functioned together as mnemonic devices, forming a single signifying unit, in reference to historical events. The Spanish iconoclast Cristóbal de Albornoz appears to have understood the value of these items when, in his treatise written around 1580, he cautions priests against tolerating the use of *keros* and textiles in certain dances. The process of Spanish acculturation ruptured the manner in which these objects functioned: *keros*, for example, adopted European forms of representation.

As already noted, the *Huarochirí* manuscript reveals that native Andeans were quick to appreciate the importance of the written word. Yet initially they were unable to comprehend its usage. When presented with a printed breviary by the priest Vincente Valverde, at the fateful encounter with the Spanish forces of Pizarro at Cajamarca, Atahualpa is said to have thrown the book to one side when it did not speak to him. This act was later used to justify his execution.

Spoken language presented a number of difficulties for the invading Spanish forces. As with the invasion of Mexico, the conquest process was largely assumed by the church, which set out to cement the process of cultural transformation through evangelization. Garcilaso relates how Jesuits felt that the mysterious and divine concept of the holy scripture could not be explained in the barbarous language of Quechua. There was considerable debate about the use of indigenous language in the process of indoctrination. While some church representatives felt Quechua to be an inadequate language, others, such as Friar Domingo de Santo Tomás, author of *Grammática, o, arte de la lengua general de los indios del Perú* (1560, Grammar; or, The art of the Common Language of the Indians of Peru), a Quechua lexicon and grammar, appreciated the fine qualities of Quechua, and its ability to express ideas clearly and precisely. As a consequence, in 1545 the archbishop of Lima decreed that adults should be instructed in Quechua and children in Spanish. However, in 1550 Charles V banned the use of Quechua in indoctrination on the grounds that it failed to express ideas well and with the necessary decorum. Then, in

1578 under Charles's son Philip II, an ordinance required that priests be proficient in the native language of their mission. This was followed by the creation of academic posts in Quechua in Lima (1580) and Quito (1581) to assess the language skills of those who intended to minister to the native people. By the Third Council of Lima it was accepted that indigenous people should be taught in their own language. In 1612 the most celebrated Quechua study, *Gramática y arte nueva de la lengua general de todo el Perú llamada lengua Qquichua o lengua del Inca* by Diego González Holguín, was published in Lima. After much debate the Spanish authorities recognized the advantages of using existing native Andean languages. The church also established schools, such as the Royal School of San Francisco de Borja (founded by the Jesuits in 1621 in Cusco), to teach Spanish language and culture to the sons of *kuraca* (Andean nobles), mirroring earlier Inca practice.

However, the church was less understanding of native Andean religious worship. The extirpation of "idolatry", led by such figures as Francisco de Ávila and José de Arriaga, was pursued with vigour as the Spanish attempted to destroy Andean religious belief and replace it with the Catholic faith. Large numbers of religious shrines were desecrated and destroyed. Indeed, Ávila claimed that he had himself destroyed more than 30,000 idols and 3000 mummies during his missionary career. Participants in traditional ceremonies or beliefs were severely punished. For example, in Lima in 1609, the Andean religious teacher Hernando Paucar was tied to a stake and publicly flogged after being forced to witness the destruction, in a large bonfire, of sacred objects including the mummies of ancestors. As with language, knowledge was acquired by the Spanish authorities in order to confront these issues more efficiently. Viceroy Francisco de Toledo (governed 1569–81) organized a wide survey of Inca customs and administration for this purpose.

The Spanish conquest of Peru marked a prolonged period of censorship, waged through systematic campaigns aimed at eradicating specific practices or beliefs, and through the general process of acculturation. Native Andeans continued to resist these changes. The survival of the Neo-Inca state at Vilcamaba until 1572, the Taqui Onkoy movement, and the uprising of Tupac Amaru II in 1780–82 demonstrate that native Andeans continued to reject Spanish rule and culture, and testify to the fact that the Spanish conquest of Peru was never fully completed.

ADRIAN LOCKE

Further Reading

Adorno, Rolena, *Guaman Poma: Writing and Resistance in Colonial Peru*, 2nd edition, Austin: University of Texas Press, 2000

Cummins, Tom, "Representations in the Sixteenth Century and the Colonial Image of the Inca" in *Writing without Words: Alternative Literacies in Mesoamerica and the Andes*, edited by Elizabeth Hill Boone and Walter D. Mignolo, Durham: Duke University Press, 1994

Garcilaso de la Vega (El Inca), *Royal Commentaries of the Incas, and General History of Peru*, 2 vols, edited and translated by Harold V. Livermore, Austin: University of Texas Press, 1966

Harrison, Regina, *Signs, Songs, and Memory in the Andes: Translating Quechua Language and Culture*, Austin: University of Texas Press, 1989

Hemming, John, *Conquest of the Incas*, London: Macmillan, and New York: Harcourt Brace, 1970

The Huarochirí Manuscript: A Testament of Ancient and Colonial Andean Religion, edited and translated by Frank Salomon and George L. Urioste, Austin: University of Texas Press, 1991 (compiled c.1598)

Lockhart, James, *Spanish Peru, 1532–1560: A Social History*, 2nd edition, Madison: University of Wisconsin Press, 1994

MacCormack, Sabine, *Religion in the Andes: Vision and Imagination in Early Colonial Peru*, Princeton, New Jersey: Princeton University Press, 1991

Spalding, Karen, *Huarochirí: An Andean Society under Inca and Spanish Rule*. Stanford, California: Stanford University Press, 1984

Stern, Steve J., *Peru's Indian People and the Challenge of Spanish Conquest: Huamanga to 1640*, 2nd edition, Madison: University of Wisconsin Press, 1993

Modern

On paper, modern Peru is a democratic country, enjoying regular elections and a free, vigorous press. However, continuing economic difficulties, and the failure to close the enormous gap between the relatively few prosperous and well-educated Peruvians and the great mass of poor Indians has, in the last two decades, given rise to a crippling war with the Sendero Luminoso (Shining Path) guerrillas, to a society that is still influenced by military responses to dissidence, and to forms of censorship that go beyond the strictly legal.

Peru attained independence from Spain on 28 July 1821. During the 19th century its governments exercised control by various means, ranging from outright censorship to indirect guidance. Military presidents and *caudillos* outnumbered civilian presidents, and the executive overshadowed the legislative and judicial branches. The Democratic Party, elected to government in 1895, introduced direct suffrage, municipal elections, and public education. José Prado (president 1904–08) supported press freedom, but a decade later, with the election of Augusto Leguia, an 11-year dictatorship was inaugurated, in which his cabinet ministers defined what was news and could be printed, until he was forcibly ousted in 1930. Not until 1939–45 did press freedom return to Peru, and even then the press and radio were subject to official interference. A military coup by general Manuel Odría, in 1948, again resulted in dictatorship and censorship. In a general strike that brought the economy to a standstill in 1956, workers ended Odría's rule and former president Manuel Prado, now again in power, not only encouraged press and broadcasting freedom, but subjected himself to brutal criticism by the media without at any point resorting to his power to suppress it by decree. He even managed to resist the temptation to do so in 1958, when, at the age of 70 and after a first marriage that had lasted 43 years, he decided to marry his mistress, aged 39.

In early 1968 *El Comercial*, the leading daily newspaper in Peru, began to report in detail on a deal signed by the International Petroleum Company (IPC) with the government. IPC would return the largest oil fields in Peru to the government in exchange for a monopoly on refining all crude oil. *Oiga*, a national magazine, printed the secret agreement in full and a torrent of editorial criticism by the major dailies continued for some months. On 3 October 1968 senior generals and admirals ousted the elected civilian government of Fernando Belaúnde Terry, president since 1963, and named general Juan Velasco Alvaredo his successor, thus inaugurating a rare phenomenon: a left-wing military government, espousing both the language and the policies of revolution.

Freedom of the press, as understood hitherto, was immediately restricted. *El Comercio* and *La Cronica* were attacked as "counter-revolutionary", and, under a "Statute of the Freedom of the Press" (31 December 1969), the government took over the Lima daily newspapers *Expresso*, *Extra*, and *La Cronica*. All newspapers were obliged to print an "opinion column" written by the Comite de Asesoramienta o la Presidencia (Advisory Council to the Presidency). As the revolution proceeded its ideology developed and, in July 1974, an "integral solution" to the issue of press freedom was announced. "Freedom of the press is the right of the majority, not of the minority", it was declared. The regime found it unacceptable that newspapers should be vehicles only for the opinions and interests of their owners, and announced that in future they would reflect the opinions of the masses. Knowing that its proposals would be resisted, not least by editors and owners of periodicals, the government ordered the police to seize the offices and printing works of *El Comercio*, *Correa*, *Ogo*, *La Prensa*, and *Ultima Hora*, and to arrest their editors.

The expropriated papers would, it was announced, be controlled by "organized sectors" of society. Each "sector" would have responsibility for a single newspaper, appointing a general council of 30, most of whom would represent workers in the communications industry. The council would elect a seven-member management committee, which would appoint the editor. Even before the new statute had been implemented, the new "revolutionary" press was printing stories that would not have been allowed under previous regimes, such as news of trade union activities and international liberation movements. Criticism of the government, however, stopped short of attacking the revolution itself, and it was clear that, ultimately, the government controlled the content of newspapers. It was also in 1975 that the government closed down a leftist journal, *Marka*, after it had drawn attention to the growing number of arbitrary arrests.

The regime's "integral solution" did not last long, for it was overthrown in September 1975 in a bloodless coup led by general Morales Bermúdez. The rhetoric of revolution was not entirely discarded, but orders for the closure of newspapers and for the deportation of editors were revoked, and press criticism of the government was even permitted so long as "the principle of authority" was respected and the "revolutionary process" was not distorted or frustrated. By March 1976 the new government evidently felt that this had occurred: 12 journalists on *Expresso* were dismissed after they had criticized official economic policy from a position to the left of the government's. When a state of emergency was proclaimed on 1 July 1976, all political magazines, including even the pro-government *Momento*, were closed down. The editor of *Marka*, Carlos Urritia Bolana, was arrested after he had written a letter of protest complaining about the decline of press freedom.

The transfer of newspaper management to "organized sectors" was postponed indefinitely on 21 July 1976 and a press commission was appointed to consider its future. This lasted only a very short time, the government concluding that an unofficial agreement between the press and the minister of the interior, specifying that only "constructive journalism" would be pursued, was likely to be more effective. Seven of the political magazines that had been closed down were allowed to reappear, including even the Communist Party's journal *Unidad*. In keeping with the new agreement, editors were called in when a general strike was called in July 1977, to be warned that stories that could "undermine national unity" or "promote subversion" would not be acceptable. Moreover, a censorship commission was employed to read the magazines before they were distributed, and *Unidad* was again closed down after it had published an article analysing the results of the strike. The other magazines were again allowed to appear, but had to submit regularly to the withdrawal of pages displeasing to the government.

A further general strike led to a further declaration of a state of emergency on 19 January 1978. Publishing material in support of illegal acts, such as the strike, was made illegal and the weekly political magazines were closed down yet again. The National Assembly declared itself dissatisfied with government policy, and both *ABC* and *El Tiempo* complained that they had been unjustly closed: they had certainly opposed economic policy, but they had not supported the general strike. A month later the National Assembly called on the government to restore full freedom of the press and to reinstate the magazines.

The government allowed free elections in July 1980 and a civilian government under the former president Fernando Belaúnde Terry took office. Newspapers were returned to private hands and were compensated for their losses with credit for the purchase of new equipment. The two main television channels were privatized.

Some censorship remained in place, however. It was still an offence to publish information "tending to cause alarm, confusion or disorder". Heavier penalties for defamation and "disrespect towards a public official" were put in place. These were invoked by the vice-president, Javier Alva Orlandini, after the magazine *Kausachum* had accused him of being lenient towards drug traffickers. However, the censorship of private letters, which had been commonplace, was abolished, and film censorship was liberalized under a new board.

The emphasis changed with the emergence of the Sendero Luminoso (Shining Path) movement from 1982. Founded by Abimael Guzmán, a professor of philosophy at the University of Ayacucho, it arose out of disappointment at the failure of the revolutionary movements of the previous decade to deal with the problems of the peasants. Using these as its starting point, Sendero Luminoso espoused an extreme form of Maoism, in the belief that it could bring about a "long" revolution in favour of the Indians by the middle of the 21st century. Its tactics included sabotage, assassination, attacks on police stations, and raids on villages. By December 1982 the Senderistas had caused 1,600 deaths. A two-month state of emergency was declared, civil liberties were suspended, and the army was sent into the Ayacucho region, but it could make little headway in what was, effectively, guerrilla warfare. The army leadership's frustration with press reporting – hardly unusual in wars – began to make itself felt. According to general Clementi Noel y Moral, journalists were "intellectual terrorists" who had "succeeded in confusing public opinion by giving sensationalist reports of events and taking up the wildest rumours ... journalists get in the way when we are carrying out our operations."

On 26 January 1982 eight journalists were killed while trying to cover the conflict in Ayacucho. Although, eight years later, a commission of enquiry under the novelist and former presidential candidate Mario Vargas Llosa concluded that local villagers had carried out the murders, believing that they were carrying out police instructions to "defend yourselves and kill guerrillas", it was widely believed that the journalists had in fact been killed by the army's counterinsurgency unit. Certainly the army was not averse to using the bluntest instruments of censorship. President Belaúnde refused its request to close down *Marka* and *La Republica*, which had been particularly critical of military tactics. Instead, the army attempted to silence its opponents by accusing them of membership of the Sendero Luminoso. For example, Dr Jaime Urrutia, a lecturer in anthropology at the University of San Cristobal de Huamonga and a town councillor, belonged to a group opposed to Sendero Luminoso, but, because he contributed to *Marka* and was known to be active in the cause of human rights, he was abducted in May 1983, and his books and papers were confiscated. In January 1985 Amnesty International reported on 1000 such "disappearances": some believed this figure to be a considerable underestimation. It was difficult to say, however, whether the army or Sendero Luminoso itself was responsible for them.

Alan García Pérez was elected president in 1985, the first candidate of the Alianza Popular Revolucionaria American (APRA) ever to win the highest office in Peru. APRA had been formed in 1924 as a continent-wide movement against US imperialism; it believed in *indigenismo*, the creation of national identities based, in the case of Peru, on the revival of Inca communal traditions and the redistribution of land. García promised respect for human rights and proclaimed himself a champion of the working class, but he used the government printing press to create currency not backed by increased output. Inflation soared to 30 per cent a month, while the "disappearances" continued.

After several bomb attacks by Sendero Luminoso, the government proclaimed a further state of emergency in February 1986. Once again civil liberties were suspended as the army and Sendero Luminoso battled with each other for control of the media. The military insisted on the cancellation of a television programme presented by the campaigning journalist César Hildebrant on the grounds that it would have investigated reports of human rights abuses by a naval officer, Alvaro Artaza. In June, a programme about the killing of Sendero Luminoso guerrillas by members of the Republican Guard was blacked out during transmission. Members of Sendero Luminoso, on the other hand, briefly seized control of Radio Comercial in Chiclayo, 750 kilometres North of Lima, in July, forcing the station to transmit antigovernment propaganda; and this was far from an isolated occurrence.

Between October 1987 and October 1990 an estimated 15 journalists were murdered while covering the conflict. Nineteen eighty-nine was one of the worst years for political violence, with 2,085 deaths reported. Peru was declared to have the worst record in the world for disappearances during custody. The International Federation of Journalists charged the government with complicity in the murder of some of the journalists, such as that of Hugo Bustios of the Lima magazine *Caretas*. An investigation into his death had been swiftly abandoned, but *Caretas* then published accounts of the event by eyewitnesses. Lawyers attempting to reopen the investigation were threatened by a right-wing group, the Rodrigo Franco Commando (RFC). The RFC also attacked the home of Guillermo Lopez Salazar, who had been forced by Sendero Luminoso to broadcast one of their propaganda tapes.

Alberto Fujimori won the presidential election of 1990, and immediately sided with the military in its argument with *Caretas* about the magazine's disclosure of the names of military and security personnel working in the major areas of terrorist activity, the "exclusion zones". A supreme decree of 21 December 1990 prohibited the practice. After Fujimori had used a military coup to close down the Peruvian Congress for "violating constitutional norms" in 1992, it was inevitable that he should further strengthen the power of the army and the police. Military censors were installed in newspaper offices and broadcasting stations, and journalists could now be arrested and jailed for up to ten years for reasons of "national security". The censors were soon removed, but in 1993 Fujimori announced that the National Intelligence Service would "evaluate" reports that were at variance with the government's version of events.

By this time drug trafficking was a factor in attempted censorship. Vladimiro Monteciros, a senior adviser to Fujimori, was said to be involved, but when *Caretas* merely reported on his appointment it was charged with "publishing false information" and its editor was threatened with imprisonment if the report was repeated. After Cecilia Valenzuela uncovered evidence of army involvement in the trade, Fujimori threatened to remove advertising from the television channel that would have broadcast the information.

Fujimori was elected for a second term in 1995 and, by bending the rules, for an unprecedented third term in 2000, only to resign and take refuge in Japan later the same year. Throughout his unprecedently long period in power he displayed consistently firm support for the army's point of view in the continuing conflict with the Sendero Luminoso In 1997, for example, Baruch Ivcher, the owner of the television station Frequencia Latina, had his citizenship revoked after the station had reported on the alleged torture of journalists who had uncovered military plans and details of telephone tapping. It was said that he had harmed "the prestige and image of the armed forces", and he was forced to flee to Israel, his birthplace. Control of the station passed to minority shareholders, Samuel and Mendel Winter, who were said at the time to be supporters of Fujimori.

By late 1997 attacks on television stations and journalists had intensified. Cecilia Valenzuela received death threats, while Jaime Arrieta, who had broadcast news of the murder of an army intelligence agent on the television programme *Contrapunto* (Channel 4), had to seek political asylum in the United States. He told the Committee to Protect Journalists of threats to the lives of César Hildebrant and others. In 1999, from exile, Baruch Ivcher made public confidential documents including plans for 24-hour surveillance of journalists, especially correspondents of *El Comercio* and *La Republica*. Several tabloids that specialized in soft pornography were found to contain identical reports attacking Angel Paez of *La Republica*. As Peru entered the 21st century, there was no sign of a truce either in the real war or in the official campaign against those who report on it.

MARVIN ALISKY

Further Reading

Alisky, Marvin, *Latin American Media: Guidance and Censorship*, Ames: Iowa State University Press, 1981
"Dark Days in Lima", *Index on Censorship*, 4/1 (Spring 1975)
Harding, Colin, "Press Clampdown in Lima", *Index on Censorship*, 8/4 (July–August 1979)
Harding, Colin, "The Nationalisation of the Press", *Index on Censorship*, 9/1 (December 1980)
Harding, Colin, "Reporting the War in Ayaculco", *Index on Censorship*, 12/6 (December 1983)
Kirk, Robin, *Human Rights in Peru: One Year after Fujimori's Coup*, New York: Human Rights Watch, 1993
McClintock, Cynthia and Abraham F. Lowenthal (editors), *The Peruvian Experiment Reconsidered*, Princeton, New Jersey: Princeton University Press, 1983
Palmer, David Scott, *Peru: The Authoritarian Tradition*, New York: Praeger, 1980
Reid, Mike, "Fear of Media Scrutiny", *Index on Censorship*, 27/4 (June 1985)
Rudolph, James D., *Peru: The Evolution of a Crisis*, New York: Praeger, 1992
Ucedo, Ricardo, "Closure of the Exposure Factory", *Index on Censorship*, 27/4 (July–August 1998)

PETERBURGAS AVIZE (Petersburg Newspaper)
Latvian-language weekly newspaper, 1862–65

The *Peterburgas Avize* was not the first Latvian-language newspaper, nor was it even published in Latvia itself. Nevertheless, it would not be going too far to claim that it played a leading role in the Latvian national awakening of the mid-19th century.

Various newspapers, including the *Dienas Lapas* (Daily Pages) and the *Majas Vestnesis* (Home's Herald), had begun publishing news in the Latvian language during the first half of the 19th century. However, the harsh press censorship laws imposed by the Russian emperor Nicholas I denied these early Latvian-language periodicals the right to print stories about current events or to criticize the status quo in the Baltic provinces. In any case, these newspapers themselves were part of that status quo, since they were all controlled by Baltic Germans, members of the minority that had controlled every aspect of society in the Baltic provinces for centuries, in collaboration with successive foreign monarchies.

By the mid-19th century, however, the first generation of Latvian nationalists, who came together at the University of Tartu, were beginning to chafe at this arrangement, as were the Russian "Slavophiles", who wanted to reduce the autonomy of the Baltic provinces, or even russify them. Representatives of both the Latvian nationalists and the Russian Slavophiles united under the banner of the *Peterburgas Avize*. The newspaper was distinctive for two reasons: it was published outside the Baltic provinces; and those who produced it benefited from their close relations with Krišjanis Valdemars, a sympathetic censor based in St Petersburg. Valdemars was himself a graduate of the University of Tartu and one of the early Latvian nationalists. Juris Alunans, Krišjanis Barons, and Krišjanis Dinsbergs made their plans for their newspaper in the hope that Valdemars would be appointed the newspaper's censor, although they knew that his position as a government official meant that he had to compromise with the Slavophiles at the imperial court.

Most of the new paper's readers lived in the Baltic provinces, and it became a rallying point for the Latvian national awakening. Almost immediately, however, Baltic Germans demanded that the newspaper be closed, or at least transferred to the censorship in Latvia itself, which was under the control of Baltic Germans. Valdemars used his Slavophile connections to remain the newspaper's censor until 24 October 1862. Censorship functions were often transferred to Riga, but the paper continued to pursue its own agenda, particularly by calling for the introduction of Russian laws and decrees into the Baltic provinces. The inclusion of such Slavophile ideas kept the paper afloat for a time, but Baltic German pressure closed the paper for four months in 1863.

In October that year, the *Peterburgas Avize* returned, this time under the editorship of Valdemars – surely one of a very few examples of a newspaper's censor becoming its editor. He continued to campaign against Baltic German privileges, using the language of Slavophilism. In January 1864, a new Baltic German censor ordered the paper to cease publishing its satirical supplement *Zobu Gals* (The Tooth's End). Nevertheless, the paper continued to publish several articles about literature, science, philosophy, and economics to encourage the development of the Latvian national movement. Valdemars particularly championed the development of a Latvian and Estonian merchant marine, which it was hoped could escape Baltic German economic control. Finally, in late 1864 and early 1865, the *Peterburgas Avize* was accused of complicity in a series of pamphlets hostile to the landed aristocracy and local clergy. Valdemars and the editorial board were forced to close the paper permanently on 29 June 1865.

Ironically, the *Peterburgas Avize* appears to have been expurgated from most modern histories of Latvian nationalism. Its editors' decision to make common cause between Latvian nationalism and Russian Slavophilism may well have been appropriate in its time, but, especially after the decades of Soviet control, such a strategy now seems dangerously mistaken.

ALDIS PURS

Further Reading

Bilmanis, Alfred, *A History of Latvia*, Princeton, New Jersey: Princeton University Press, 1951
Thaden, Edward C. (editor), *Russification in the Baltic Provinces and Finland, 1855–1914*, Princeton, New Jersey: Princeton University Press, 1981
Treijs, Rihards (editor), *Latvijas Republikas Prese, 1918–1940* (The Press of the Republic of Latvia, 1918–1940) Riga: Zvaigzne ABC, 1996

RUMIANA PETKOVA
Bulgarian film and television director

GORI, GORI, OGANCHE (Flame, Flame, Little Spark)
Film/television serial, 1994

The action of *Flame, Flame, Little Spark* takes place in the 1960s, during a campaign launched by the communist government to force the Bulgarian Muslims (Pomaks) to remove distinctive Muslim elements from their names. The main character is a young woman, not herself a Pomak, who teaches in a remote village in the Rodopi Mountains and witnesses the violent disruption of community life under the pressure of the government's "homogenization" policy. The film tries to convey an understanding of "otherness" and to point up the implications of religious intolerance under totalitarian rule. It also challenges viewers to rethink their responsibilities as citizens under communism, by sketching out the Bulgarian participation in the Warsaw Pact invasion of Czechoslovakia in 1968.

Malina Tomova, a poet and literary editor, wrote the script proposal in 1979. The Bulgarian Arts Council rejected it, although in private many intellectuals praised it highly. In 1982, the Arts Council reviewed its assessment and approved the proposal, but further work was stopped again in 1984–85. The question of the treatment of minorities had again arrived at the top of the political agenda as the communist regime started another renaming campaign, this time affecting the Turkish minority.

The Arts Council finally authorized the shooting of the script after the collapse of communism in 1989. In 1993, the film received a grant from the National Film Centre and supplementary funding from the Open Society Fund in Sofia. In September 1994, the film was shown for the first time at the annual International Cinema Festival in Varna, Bulgaria, and received the Critic's Choice award.

The film was then adapted for television and scheduled for broadcast in four episodes. However, the National Television Service postponed it because an election campaign was under way. Channel 1 showed the first episode in 1995. The press then criticized the film for its "false reality", accused the authors of "national betrayal", and denied that the renaming campaign against the Pomaks had been carried out by force, as the film suggested. After the second episode had been transmitted, National Television announced that the third episode would be shown only if the filmmakers could defend themselves in the face of the increasing polemic against it. Yet Malina Tomova was prevented from taking part in the discussion programme *Extraordinary Studio*. Broadcasters who did not identify themselves asked her what she intended to say and, having heard her answer, decided to drop her from the programme. She was also not permitted to attend a press conference about the film, even though her accreditation as a journalist was valid. Her film crew received threatening phone calls and letters, and the door of Tomova's family apartment in Sofia was inscribed with swastikas, crosses, and red stars.

Meanwhile, the president of Bulgaria, Zhelu Zhelev, attended a special meeting on censorship where he sharply criticized the government of the Bulgarian Socialist Party (formerly the Communist Party) for imposing political control on the national media. He included the case of *Flame, Flame, Little Spark* in his criticisms. The press reported that the Commission for National Security had appealed to the Constitutional Court to sue the filmmakers for "national betrayal". Apparently, the charge was dropped by the court on the grounds that the film was fiction, not a documentary.

The national media continued to vilify the film in special reports that denied the existence of a distinct Pomak identity and affirmed the Bulgarian nationality of the villagers depicted in the film. The Arts Council remained silent and the editor in chief of the First Programme of National Radio was ordered not to cover the debate. Secondary school head teachers received an "unofficial" order from the Minister for Education that the film should be criticized in Bulgarian history lessons. Some film critics tried to depoliticize the debate by drawing a line between fictional treatment and nonfictional reality. Fifty-two journalists collected signatures in support of the film. Radio Free Europe interviewed the authors several times and gave them an opportunity to speak direct to listeners on the telephone.

Flame, Flame, Little Spark appeared during the difficult early years of transition from communism to democracy. It was drawn into the debate about the nature of Bulgarian communism, and fell victim to the alliance between the Socialist Party government and nationalist organizations.

MILENA MAHON BORDEN

Further Reading
Stefanova, Sylvia, article in *Vlast*, 21–27/2 (1997)
Tzanev, Ivan, article in *Literaturen Forum*, 9 (1995)
Waksberg, Tatiana, article in *Standart*, 20/2 (1995)

GYÖRGY PETRI
Hungarian poet, 1943–2000

Petri is one of the leading Hungarian poets of his generation. His ironic, outspoken, often abrasive style, in which paraphrases of classical rhetoric mingle with puns and colloquialisms, has greatly expanded the boundaries of modern Hungarian poetry.

Some of Petri's poems were published in the anthology *Költők egymás közt* (1969, Poets Among Themselves), but his own first book of verse, *Magyarázatok M. számára* (Explanations for M), appeared in 1971. This collection, which immediately established Petri as a talented young poet, contains politically challenging material, such as the poem "By an Unknown Poet from Eastern Europe, 1955", which ends with the lines: "Our terrible loneliness/crackles and flakes/like rust on iron rails in the heat of the sun" (as translated by Clive Wilmer and George Gömöri). Irony is a thread that runs through Petri's verse, and it is not only political taboos that are broken in his poetry, but also social and moral ones. In his second collection, *Körülírt zuhanás* (1974, Circumscribed Fall), there is a shift from the self-explanatory monologues of the first book towards more objective poems describing a social or private situation. Such are the sonnets "Now Only" and "Gratitude", the latter opening with the caustic lines: "The idiotic silence of state holidays / is no different/ from that of Catholic Sundays" (as translated by Wilmer and Gömöri). Disillusionment in the Marxist utopia is extended to the private sphere: Petri's love poems from this period can be read as somewhat cynical anti-love poems, impressing the reader not through empathy but through a cool analysis of the "love game".

Petri began to gain importance as a political poet in the late 1970s. The Warsaw Pact invasion of Czechoslovakia in 1968 had already undermined his youthful belief in socialism, and he made his loss of faith public at a poetry reading in 1976. The Hungarian democratic opposition provided a platform and a milieu for him. He was a signatory to the Hungarian protest against the trial of the organisers of Charter 77 in Czechoslovakia in 1979, and he started to write poems that openly challenged the regime. As he said later in an interview, when he handed in the typescript of his book *Örökhétfő* (Eternal Monday) to his publisher, in 1981, he was informed that around 30 of the poems in it were unacceptable, but that if they were cut, the book could still be published. This he refused to do, but soon afterwards the *samizdat* publisher AB (founded by Gábor Demszky, who is now mayor of Budapest) offered to publish the collection in its entirety. After its samizdat publication of 940 copies in 1981, a facsimile edition of *Örökhétfő* was published in Brussels in April 1982.

As Clive Wilmer has stated, *Örökhétfő* "exposed the limits of Kádárian liberalism". It is an exciting collection, and not only on political grounds. It contains poems that would certainly have been banned in some countries as "blasphemous" (for example, "Apocryphal") and others that offend conservative morality with their very explicit use of sexual taboo words or scatological expressions. Yet the gist of the book is against the political hypocrisy of "goulash Communism"; it challenges and defies the authorities. Petri's political satires from this period include small masterpieces such as "To Be Said Over and Over Again": "I glance down at my shoe and – there's the lace!/This can't be gaol then, can it, in that case" (as translated by Wilmer and Gömöri). The not unbridled yet continuous activity of the security police is exposed in the policeman's bitter monologue "Night Song of the Personal Shadow" and the rebellion of the Polish workers against the state, which erupted under the umbrella of Solidarity, is brilliantly captured in "The Under-Secretary Makes a Statement". The single most outspoken piece in *Örökhétfő* is the poem "On the 24th Anniversary of the Little October Revolution", which ends with the following indictment of post-Stalinist communism: "I say just two numbers: /56/68./ You can add them, subtract them,/ divide or multiply./Your innumerable doctrines, baseness is their basis,/have failed, are bankrupt" (as translated by Wilmer and Gömöri).

Although Hungarian censorship was, on the whole, less stringent than that in other countries in the Soviet bloc, and there was no central censorship agency in the 1970s and 1980s, Petri once again became unpublishable in 1984. The poems that he had written between 1982 and 1984 had been collected and published in a small edition by the Hungarian Human Rights Foundation in New York, and it was this poetic booklet, entitled *Hólabda a kézben* (Snowball in the Hand), that created the furore. In a short, biting poem, "To the Memory of Leonid Ilich Brezhnev", Petri had had the effrontery to denigrate the Soviet leader, who had died in 1982. This poem was considered so "strong" even by his *samizdat* publishers that it was left out of his next collection *Azt hiszik . . .* (1985, What They Think . . .). Not that Petri had decided to stop his regular baiting of the regime: *Azt hiszik . . .* contains a number of memorable political poems, among them a moving tribute to the memory of Imre Nagy, the reformist Prime Minister who was tried and executed in 1958 for his participation in the Hungarian uprising of 1956.

At the same time, Petri resented his "labelling" as just a political poet. From 1981 to 1989 he edited what was then a clandestine periodical, *Beszélő* (Talking through the Bars), which ranged across a variety of subjects (he briefly resumed the editorship in 1994–95). In the powerful poem, "Electra", he confesses his revulsion with the "populist" pretensions of the Kádár regime: Aegistus, "with his trainee-barber's face", is clearly János Kádár. In this poem Petri, assuming Electra's persona, states that: "revenge has become my dream and my daily bread" (as translated by Wilmer and Gömöri).

Revenge, in the form of the demise of the communist regime, arrived in 1989. In the spring of 1989, Szépirodalmi, Petri's former publisher, brought out a sizeable collection of his verse, *Valahol megvan* (It Exists Somewhere), and in the same year a small independent publisher collected all Petri's poems not included in the previous collection under the title *Ami kimaradt* (What Was Left Out). Since 1989, censorship has no longer been exercised in Hungary, but as recently as 1996 Petri was singled out for attack in Parliament for "blasphemy" by József Torggán, the leader of Hungary's Smallholders Party. Though he was awarded the Kossath Prize, Hungary's highest literary award, Petri remains a "controversial" figure for many conservative Hungarians.

GEORGE GÖMÖRI

Writings

Valahol megvan (It Exists Somewhere), 1989
Night Song of the Personal Shadow: Selected Poems, translated by Clive Wilmer and George Gömöri, 1991
Versei (Poems), 1991
In *The Faber Book of Modern European Poetry*, edited by A. Alvarez, 1992
Interview in *Poets Talking*, by Clive Wilmer, 1994
Beszélgetések Petri Györgyel (Conversations with György Petri), 1994
Versek, 1971–1995 (Poems, 1971–1995), 1996

Eternal Monday: New and Selected Poems, translated by Clive Wilmer and George Gömöri, 1999
Amíg lehet (While It Is Possible), 2000

Further Reading

Fodor, Géza, *Petri György költészete* (György Petri's Poetry), Budapest: Szépirodalmi, 1991
Gömöri, George, "György Petri", *The Independent* (9 August 2000)
McRobbie, Kenneth, "György Petri: The New Poetics of Tension in the Hungarian Context", *World Literature Today*, 62/1 (Winter 1988): 38–41
Radnóti, Sándor, "The First Hungarian Samizdat Poetry Collection", *Formations*, 3/1 (Spring 1986): 147–52
Várady, Szabolcs, "Poetry under the Weather: A Portrait of György Petri", *Hungarian Quarterly*, 36/137 (Spring 1995): 30–35

PHEIDIAS
Greek sculptor, active c.465–425 BCE

Pheidias son of Charmides was an Athenian, and easily the most renowned sculptor in antiquity. He was responsible for the principal works of religious art in classical Greece: the statues of Athena Parthenos and Promachos at Athens, the Marathon group at Delphi, and the Zeus Olympios at Olympia. He produced mainly cult images of gods and heroes, but ancient writers mention one individual portrait of an athlete at Olympia.

At Athens his main work was the statue of Athena Parthenos, made for the Parthenon on the Acropolis. In fact, Pheidias was overseer for the whole building project initiated at Athens by Pericles in the 440s BCE, and was responsible for the organization and commissioning of buildings and artworks. This was an ambitious attempt to remodel Athens using the profits of empire, creating both temples and public buildings on a magnificent scale. The Athena Parthenos was the patron figure of Athens, a huge chryselephantine statue of Athena standing with a figure of victory in one hand and a spear in the other, a snake and shield at her feet, placed in the great sanctuary of the Parthenon.

It was the work on this project that led Pheidias into conflict with Athens; all the sources agree that he became the object of jealousy because of his association with Pericles, at that time the effective leader of the city. Attempts were made to discredit him, perhaps first with rumours that he procured free women on his patron's behalf. Versions of the main charges differ, but the essentials are the same: Pheidias was accused of embezzling the material used in the construction of the statue, and required to stand trial, with an implication that Pericles was involved too. The accusation was more serious than it might seem: the gold and ivory were valuable in themselves, but were also materials dedicated to the god, and their theft was an act of impiety, temple robbery (*hierosylia*). Pheidias was also said to have caused ill-feeling by his inclusion of flattering portraits of Pericles and himself in the sculpture of the shield of Athena. The religious nature of the inquiry is emphasized by its unusual circumstances – the accusers asked first for immunity before bringing charges, and the trial was held before the popular assembly rather than in court.

Accounts of the circumstances of the trial are confused: one authority has Pheidias tried before the assembly and acquitted

on charges of the theft of the gold, since he was able to demonstrate that he had constructed the statue in such a way that the gold was removable, and thus could be weighed to discover whether the correct amount was there. He was nevertheless still jailed, and while in jail either died or was poisoned. This cannot be correct, since Pheidias carried out the Olympia commission after his trial, and motivation for his poisoning was weak. The dating is confused because it forms part of a long tradition tracing the origin of the Peloponnesian War in 431 BCE to Pericles' attempts to avoid trial, a theory originating in comedy which is undoubtedly wrong. The better version of events has Pheidias tried over embezzlement of the ivory for the statue, and exiled in 438 BCE, after the dedication of the Parthenon. Archaeology has confirmed that after his ejection from Athens, he went to Olympia, where he created the equally famous statue of Zeus Olympios for the Eleans. He died at Elis in exile.

The attack on Pheidias can be linked with attacks on other members of Pericles' circle, apparently for similar political motives. Pericles' teachers, Damon and Anaxagoras, suffered ostracism and indictment for impiety respectively, and both were exiled. Pericles' mistress, the famous Aspasia of Miletus, was traditionally also arraigned for impiety, although the source tradition here is very doubtful. Unlike the others, Pheidias was not a thinker or an intellectual, and his trial provides the clearest example of the use of religious charges for political purposes. His works were not censored as such, since they remained objects of admiration, and were to be very influential in the development of Greek sculpture, but he himself was not permitted to return to Athens. The whole set of trials demonstrates the power that an accusation of religious malpractice could have in mobilizing community opinion against a perceived offence. The strategic use of misinformation, especially if coloured by display, such as the informants seeking asylum before giving evidence, proved extremely difficult even for Pericles to oppose. Even so, the case remained internal to Athens, and Pheidias went on to work at the greatest religious sanctuary in Greece; censorship or conviction for impiety did not extend beyond the border of the state concerned.

SIAN LEWIS

Further Reading

Boardman, John, *Greek Sculpture: The Classical Period*, London and New York: Thames and Hudson, 1985

Parker, Robert, *Athenian Religion: A History*, Oxford: Clarendon Press, and New York: Oxford University Press, 1996

Plutarch, Life of Pericles in *Plutarch's Lives*, translated by Bernadotte Perrin, 11 vols, London: Heinemann, and New York: Macmillan, 1914–26 (Loeb edition; vol. 3)

Pollitt, J.J., *The Art of Ancient Greece: Sources and Documents*, Cambridge and New York: Cambridge University Press, 1990

CHARLES PHILIPON
French satirist and caricaturist, 1800–1862

The famous political satire, *La Poire*, was conceived by Charles Philipon in a courtroom in Paris, published widely in the satirical press, appropriated by many artists, and generally flaunted by the Republican Left as a sign of political resistance.

After the July Revolution of 1830, the constitutional charter of the new monarchy of King Louis-Philippe re-established freedom of the French press, promising that the rigorous censorship of the Bourbon Restoration (1815–30) would never be repeated. The expansive idealism of the summer of 1830 was rapidly tempered with the passage of more cautious laws in November of the same year, which made press attacks against royal authority or against the person of the king punishable by fines or imprisonment, or both. These laws did not dampen the spirit of the newly liberated press, however. Moreover, the development of the new medium of lithography was making possible the mass distribution of caricatures to members of an art-buying middle class with a taste for political humour and for affordable prints that could be displayed in the home. The temptation to test the new freedom and power of the press was irresistible.

Between 1830 and 1835 (when the far more severe "September" press laws were enacted), the opposition press staged an aggressive satirical campaign against the government. The king was a favourite target of caricaturists' potshots, and skirmishes with the new image police landed artists such as Philipon and Honoré Daumier in jail. On 14 November 1831, Philipon stood trial for one of his several violations of the press laws of 1830. The print in question, *Le Replâtrage* (The Replastering), had been published in his journal *La Caricature* on 30 June 1831, and represented Louis-Philippe as a mason plastering over the many promises he had made in 1830. In an attempt to clear himself at the trial, Philipon argued that because he had not depicted any royal insignia in this caricature, he had never portrayed the actual king. Instead, he maintained, he had relied only on the king's general resemblance to represent the government in a symbolic fashion. He argued passionately that the law could never control "the liberty of the crayon". To illustrate his point to the jury, he drew a quartet of images. In the first stage, he sketched an easily recognizable portrait of King Louis-Philippe. In the three subsequent stages, the face gradually mutated from a human face into a pear, with eyes, nose, and mouth that still firmly signified the physiognomy of the king. Philipon, brandishing the drawing, then asked the court whether the ultimate resemblance between king and pear meant that one could no longer draw simple pears.

This comparison of king and fruit was a clever insult that also turned on a pun, since *poire* meant both pear and fathead or dolt in the argot of the time. In its rotund contours,

and particularly in its bulbous cheeks, the affront of *La Poire* to the person of the king was twofold: first, the royal visage and body were demoted to the level of a common fruit, with its attendant punning implications of stupidity; and second, the shape of the pear's face bore a clear resemblance to the cheeks of buttocks, thus adding scatological fuel to the satirical fire. However brilliant Philipon's courtroom performance, he lost his case. He received a heavy sentence of six months in prison

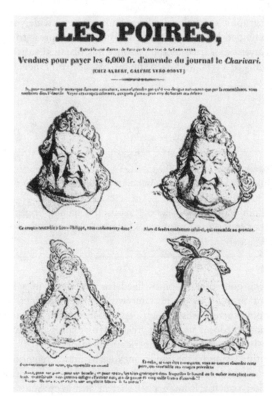

PHILIPON: *Les Poires* (Pears), satirical "portrait" of king Louis Philippe of France, which was published in a number of journals, including *Le Charivari* and *La Caricature*, between 1832 and 1835. The drawings were originally used by Philipon to illustrate his case during his 1831 trial for violating press laws and provoking contempt of the king's person. Philipon concluded his demonstration by asking: "Is it my fault, gentleman of the jury, if his Majesty's face looks like a pear?" The pun on the word *poire*, which also meant "fathead" or "dolt" in contemporary slang, was part of the joke. The image was subsequently used by a number of caricaturists of the period to ridicule the king until Louis Philippe retaliated with stringent restrictions on press freedom in 1835; the symbol of *La Poire* lived on as a potent image in graffiti and other unpublished contexts.

and a fine of 2000 francs. In protest, his journals *La Caricature* and *Le Charivari* both published the courtroom drawings of *La Poire* along with a description of the trial. Defiantly, Philipon proclaimed in his paper: "Yes, we have the right to personify power. Yes, we have the right to take, for this personification, whatever resemblance suits our needs! Yes, all resemblances belong to us!"

Between 1832 and September 1835 *La Poire* appeared in hundreds of satires published predominantly (but not exclusively) by Philipon's caricature shop, La Maison Aubert. Among the many artists who adopted the image in political critiques were Honoré Daumier (1808–79); Charles-Joseph Traviès de Villers (1804–59); Jean-Ignace-Isidore Gérard, known as Grandville (1803–47); Auguste Bouquet (1800–46); and Auguste Desperret (d. 1865). In their caricatures, the Pear-King appeared as pompous, greedy, lazy, fat, ambitious, stupid, treacherous, sated, corrupt, vain, and easily duped. It is no wonder that in 1835 the real king seized an opportunity, in the wake of a failed assassination attempt, to claim that freedom of the press had gone too far, and to restrict severely all criticisms of his person and his regime.

The graphic symbol of *La Poire* had caught on widely though, and extended beyond the pages of the satirical press to appear in locations as varied as the prison walls of jailed satirists, the city walls of Paris, and even the far reaches of French Empire.

A generation later, the writer Gustave Flaubert noted that among the graffiti sketched on the walls of the Great Pyramid in Egypt was none other than resilient form of *La Poire*.

ELIZABETH C. CHILDS

Further Reading

Cuno, James, "Charles Philipon, La Maison Aubert, and the Business of Caricature in Paris, 1829–41", *Art Journal*, 43/4 (Winter 1983): 347–54

Cuno, James, "Charles Philipon and 'la poire': Politics and Pornography in Emblematic Satire, 1830–1835" in *Consortium on Revolutionary Europe, 1750–1850: Proceedings 1984*, edited by Harold T. Parker, Athens, Georgia: Consortium on Revolutionary Europe, 1986

Goldstein, Robert Justin, *Censorship of Political Caricature in Nineteenth-Century France*, Kent, Ohio: Kent State University Press, 1989

Kenney, Elise K. and John M. Merriman, *The Pear: French Graphic Arts in the Golden Age of Caricature*, South Hadley, Massachusetts: Mount Holyoke College Art Museum, 1991 (exhibition catalogue)

Keshavjee, Serena, *The Pear and Its Pips: Auguste Bouquet and La Caricature*, Toronto: Art Gallery of Ontario, 1991 (exhibition catalogue)

Terdiman, Richard, *Discourse/Counter-Discourse: The Theory and Practice of Symbolic Resistance in Nineteenth-Century France*, Ithaca, New York: Cornell University Press, 1985

PHILIPPINES

Population: 75,653,000	**Illiteracy rate (%):** 4.5 (m); 4.8 (f)
Main religions: Roman Catholic; Protestant; Muslim; Buddhist	**Number of daily newspapers:** 47
	Number of radio receivers per 1000 inhabitants: 161
Official language: Filipino (based on Tagalog); English	**Number of TV receivers per 1000 inhabitants:** 52
Other languages spoken: Spanish; Cebuano; Ilocano; Hiligaynon; Bicol	**Number of PCs per 1000 inhabitants:** 15.1

A saying goes that Filipinos lived for 300 years in a Spanish convent and 48 more in Hollywood. The inference is that Philippine society was constrained under Spanish colonial rule, but that freedom, including freedom of expression, was also seriously abridged by the American liberators.

Printing came to the Philippines early, and a religious book was published as early as 1593, but the first use of print was to proselytize for Roman Catholicism and keep Spanish conquerors in touch with the mother country; the early books were meant to convert and control. When the first newspaper in the Philippines, *Del Superior Gobierno*, was started in 1811, it was governed by the censorship laws of 1750 and 1810; the latter, promulgated by the Real Audiencia, prohibited the printing of any "discouraging" information.

Only for a brief period from 1813 to 1824 did the islands experience constitutionalism and enlightenment. Governor Juan A. Martinez brought liberalization to a halt on 7 August 1824, when he abolished the constitution and reinstated press censorship. His successor in 1825 marked the end of the democratic period by dumping into the sea all political publications previously issued from Spain. Further orders on censorship

were issued by the Spaniards in 1827, 1834, 1839, and 1840. In 1856 and 1857, the repressive Comision Permanente de Censura and Reglamento de Asuntos del Imprenta were instituted. The all-encompassing Reglamento was divided into a number of articles dealing with printing, newspapers, books for sale, books for personal use, plays, clothing, and scapulars and other materials that were imprinted; it provided for pre-censorship and required publication licences.

For most of the Spanish colonial period, the Philippines were intellectually and culturally isolated from the outside world by both government and the church. Towards the end of the 19th century, liberal ideas were espoused covertly, many of them calling for revolution. After gaining independence from Spain in 1898, Filipinos promulgated the Malolos Constitution on 20 January 1899, guaranteeing no Filipino would be deprived "the right of expressing freely his ideas and opinions by word or by writing, availing himself of the press or any other similar means". Shortly after, as the Americans secured and henceforth occupied the archipelago, the US Congress passed the Philippine Act (1 July 1902), which gave assurances that "no law shall be passed abridging the freedom of speech or of the press, or of the people to peaceably assemble and petition the government for redress of grievances". The same freedoms were stated by the Jones Law in 1916, when an autonomous form of government was established prior to independence.

Yet, in the first years of liberation from the Spaniards, freedom of expression was denied by both Philippine general and president Emilio Aquinaldo and American general Arthur MacArthur. From 1898 to 1900, military censorship was in force, newspapers were suspended, and editors jailed. Individuals and institutions calling for independence from the United States were suppressed by the Second Philippine Commission, whose act of 1901 levied stiff penalties for dissension. Musical forms that, under the Spanish, had allowed servants to poke fun at their colonial masters, were frowned upon in the early US period, when the military authorities responded to satire and allegory by staging riots in the theatres and forcing playwrights to confine themselves to harmless love stories. Only after American rule was completely secured did freedom of expression result, and even then, those who spoke out were threatened by sedition laws, a flag ban, and the use and abuse of libel legislation by government officials. In 1908, the newspaper *El Renacimiento* was dissolved and its editors fined and jailed when the American secretary of the interior successfully filed a libel suit. In 1934, another serious threat occurred when delegates to the Constitutional Convention tried to limit freedom of expression guarantees to "good morals and public order".

After the demise of almost all intellectual and cultural life during World War II, freedom of expression flowered after February 1945, as many fly-by-night publishers set up periodicals and newspapers; radio stations mushroomed everywhere, and criticism was often tainted with sensationalism. Incidents in which the freedom of expression was denied were minor compared to the open mood that prevailed. In more cases than not, comment on the media and other cultural forms had to do more with irresponsible conduct than with government efforts to hamper them. In fact, a number of legislative and judicial decisions were extremely sympathetic to the cause of open discussion, such as those exempting journalists from revealing the sources of their stories, restricting the value of libel suits, and curbing the powers of the postmaster general to deny the media the use of the mails.

This euphoria was snuffed out on 22 September 1972, when Ferdinand Marcos, contemplating a constitutionally illegal third term as president, declared martial law. Citing the media as a prime enemy, Marcos wasted no time killing newspapers and broadcasting stations. Without warning, police entered newspaper offices and broadcasting studios, ordered the staff to leave, and sealed the premises under military control; in less than 24 hours, the government had wiped out the entire media of the Philippines in a fashion reminiscent of the Japanese occupation. Exempt were Marcos's own *Daily Express*, the Kanloan Broadcasting System (KBS) radio station, and a few other supporters.

Marcos immediately strengthened the publicly financed information structure he had built up in the late 1960s and early 1970s with his relatives and other cronies. These organs included the National Media Production Centre, the Malacañang (Presidential Palace) Press Office, and public information offices funded by all government departments. Additionally,

the Marcos forces had acquired KBS and the *Manila Bulletin* (renamed *Bulletin Today*) and its broadcasting outlets, and in April 1972, they established the *Philippines Daily Express*. A Department of Public Information was established to replace the Presidential Press Office. The new department quickly issued guidelines under which all media were expected to work, instituted a formidable array of government controls and censorship devices, and decreed that printers could not issue anything without prior approval of the department. The chief opponents of the Marcos regime were arrested, on charges that they had been involved in a communist conspiracy. A large number were released by mid-1973; some of them were placed under house arrest, while others fled the country.

By taking over cultural and media institutions, the Marcoses (the president, his wife Imelda, their children, and other relatives) controlled the production, distribution, and exhibition of virtually everything. Members of Pamulat Sa Kaunlaran ng Sombayenen (PAKSA, Writing for the Country's Progress), an association of progressive young writers formed in 1970, were imprisoned. Some wrote allegorical plays with political undertones. F. Sionel Jose's *Mass*, which described conditions in the late 1960s before martial law had been declared, was a frontal attack on Marcos and could not be published in the Philippines until 1982. Theatre and film personnel were urged to depict "national virtues" created by Imelda Marcos, who also established an international film festival and experimental theatre to curry international favour, while journalists were admonished by their publishers to write pro-government news and editorials, and downplay or totally exclude opposition viewpoints.

Nine major mechanisms of control were used for much of the Marcos regime: a series of presidential decrees allowed Marcos and the military to designate journalists and media as "subversives", to confiscate property, to detain journalists, or to bypass the civil judicial system; the firings of journalists and closure of media that refused to get on side; intimidating interrogation by intelligence officers; the filing of frivolous, excessively large libel suits by government officials; the purchase of journalists and cultural representatives with money bribes and other perks only at the disposal of the government; the stipulation of taboo subjects that critics dared not broach; the review and censoring by a board of all films and tapes meant for the theatre and television; the requirement of licensing for all television and radio stations; and the "busting" of media and theatre guilds.

Probably most effective were two other forms of control – the ownership of the media by Marcos forces, and self-censorship by editors and journalists. At the peak of the Marcos era, five relatives or close friends (Roberto Benedicto, US ambassador Benjamin Romualdez, general Hans Menzi, ambassador-at-large Eduardo Cojuangco, Jr, and Kerima Polotan) owned among them at least 11 dailies, chains of magazines, three of the largest broadcasting networks, and most of the telecommunications systems, as well as the sugar and coconut industries, and large chunks of banking, hotels, shipping, airlines, and the industries of processed foods, paper manufacture, agriculture, beer, soft drinks, utilities, engineering, and automobile assembly. In addition to family members, the leadership of these media included at least three former or present ambassadors, a governor, a presidential aide on military matters, and a presidential executive assistant.

This concentration of ownership and alignment of government, business, and media had disastrous repercussions for journalists. Because of warnings from their publishers and government higher-ups, and their dependence upon the media barons for employment, editors constantly censored themselves, choosing tame stories, and consulting with cabinet and military officials and even with supposedly competing newspapers.

Marcos remained keen to paint his administration in glowing colours abroad. The first Manila Film Festival in 1981 was supposed to "orient local movie audiences with the styles and genres of the cinema of other nations and prove that films are indeed the language of all men and nations". Such rhetoric masked the repressive actuality. Until then, film censorship had been carried out by the military. Their place was taken by a civil board that was, if anything, more capricious than before. Its chairwoman, Maria Kalaw-Katigbak, a former beauty queen, took to burning the negatives of films of which she disapproved, precluding any possibility of appeal or reconsideration. Local filmmakers were not taken in by the festival's public relations, nor did the decisions of the censorship board go without notice.

Indeed by no means all elements of Philippine society toed the government line: 22 journalists were killed between 1979 and 1985, presumably because of their critical writings and broadcasts, and many dissenters from academic, church, and women's circles disappeared or faced other harassments. An underground press operated at various times, and alternative (though not necessarily underground) media such as *Mr. and Ms.*, *We Forum*, *Malaya*, and Radio Veritas took aim at the authorities, especially after the assassination of the opposition leader Benigno Aquino in 1983. Even *Panorama*, the Sunday supplement of the pro-government *Bulletin Today*, became involved in opposition as its predominantly female staff braved libel suits, military interrogations, prior restraint, and numerous threats to get alternative views across. In the last years of the Marcos government, there was increased resistance, including public boycotts of government media groups, demonstrations calling for freedom of the press by the College Editors Guild, radio commentators, and newspapers generally, and increased support for alternative media.

When the Marcos government was toppled by the Philippine people in February 1986, the situation of the media changed considerably for the better. The new government of Corazon Aquino instituted a number of reforms that had a bearing upon media. Among them were the restoration of the power of writ of *habeas corpus*, the release of detainees (including media and cultural workers), the creation of the Presidential Committee on Human Rights and the Presidential Committee on Good Government (to investigate graft and corruption, including in the media), the reorganization of government-sponsored cultural and media groups, and the establishment of the Constitutional Commission, which recommended in 1987 guarantees for freedom of religion, the press, speech, and peaceful assembly. It recognized the "vital role of communication and information in nation building". Task forces, such as that "To Oversee and to Take Charge of All Film-Related Government Agencies", were developed: in this case, with recommendations that film boards should classify movies. The purpose of the Videogram Regulatory Board was to prevent piracy. The main function of neither of these bodies was to censor. Actions by the Presidential Committee on Good Government caused the first real government–media skirmish in 1986: newspapers viewed with alarm and indignation the committee's sequestration of media suspected of ownership links to Marcos and his friends.

In the heady air of freedom in 1986, media proliferated, and as they did, reverted to the practices that preceded martial law – close ties to oligarchies, and a go-for-the-jugular competitiveness that arguably led to irresponsible journalism. The ownership of media by large business groups, mainly for political leverage, predates World War II, when the Roces and Madrigal families controlled chains of print media and three studios dominated film. Although owners change at various times, the overall pattern, purposes, and implications do not. In the 1990s, the resurgent Manila press, consisting of about 30 dailies, returned to its generations-old tendency to serve corporate and political bosses, most recently, those of the Romualdez, Cojuangco, Yap, Lopez, Soriano, Zobel de Ayala, Ramos, Gokongwei, Gatchalian, and Enrile families. The journalism that has resulted is public relations-oriented, adversarially self-serving, sensationalist, and self-perpetuating. Meanwhile, readers are left in the dark on social issues.

Many of the expectations of the Aquino administration did not materialize. The arts community felt it suffered censorship by neglect, expressed by the acclaimed film director Lino Brocka, who blamed the president for not including culture and arts among her priorities. The media continued to experience repression, evidenced by 54 cases in Aquino's first 11 months in office. These included the murder of journalists (11 in 1987), death threats, closure of four radio stations in mid-1986 for confusing the public and leading to the destabilization of government, and direct and frequent governmental interference in news reporting. An October 1992 court decision convicting two well-known journalists of libelling Aquino sparked a lively discussion about the degree of freedom of expression permitted; there was no doubt the number of libel suits brought against critics of public officials had increased significantly.

Although president Fidel V. Ramos regularly railed against critics in the media, his administration was relatively free of censorship or other abuses of freedom of expression. This climate prevailed despite the fact that media exposés uncovered corruption in the Supreme Court, forced the resignation of Ramos's health secretary, and pressured the government into reforms on environment and corruption. Diversity of opinion finds a place in this highly opinionated society, which welcomes columnists and talk show hosts; most newspapers have at least 15 column writers, and in the mid-1990s, an entire newspaper, *Isyu* (Issues), was devoted to 80 columns.

Despite the overall positive picture, the Philippines remains a dangerous place to have differing opinions. Since 1986, at least 32 journalists have been killed, and many others threatened; one editor in the provinces was forced at gunpoint to eat his newspaper. Freedom of expression is also endangered by the fact that nearly all of the country's wealthiest tycoons own a medium, so that there is often a temptation not to write critically of the government officials who regulate business, while attacking corporate enemies and promoting political allies.

JOHN A. LENT

Further Reading

Abraham, Pedro R. Jr, "Aquino's First Months", *Index on Censorship* (September 1986): 9–10, 36

del Mundo, Clodualdo Jr (editor), *Philippine Mass Media: A Book of Readings*, Manila: Communication Foundation for Asia, 1986

Lent, John A., *Philippine Mass Communications: Before 1811, after 1966*, Manila: Philippine Press Institute, 1972

Lent, John A., "The Philippine Press under Martial Law", *Index on Censorship* (Spring 1974): 47–59

Lent, John A., "Press Freedom in the Philippines: The Final Months of Marcos", *Pilipinas* (Fall 1987): 35–49

Lent, John A., "Who Owns the Philippine Mass Media?", *Pilipinas* (Fall 1991): 1–33

National Press Club (Philippines), *The Philippine Press under Siege*, 2 vols, Manila: National Press Club, Committee to Protect Writers, 1984–85

Pineda-Ofreneo, Rosalinda, *The Manipulated Press: A History of Philippine Journalism since 1945*, Manila: Cacho Hermanos, 1984

Valenzuela, Jesus Z., *History of Journalism in the Philippine Islands*, Manila: The Author, 1933

PHOTOGRAPHY: Sexual Imagery

The general rule holds: just as on its emergence, photography was observed to spread in no time at all throughout the world, and once there to shape and be shaped in all its encounters, so the contenders in the photographic contest with censorship have found themselves writing and sometimes playing to a new set of rules. Under the camera's lens, neither the censored nor the censorious would ever be the same again.

This entry concentrates mainly on the censorship of sexual imagery in photographs in Britain. One of the first photographs to achieve much public notice in such a connection was shown at the Manchester Art Treasures Exhibition of 1857, the year in which Lord Campbell's Bill became law, as the Obscene Publications Act. The image was a large one, from some 30 negatives, staged individually and composed by O.G. Rejlander, the photographer, into an allegorical whole with marked affinities to the appearance of a Salon painting. That the direct sources should have been on the one hand philosophical, in the shape of Raphael's *School of Athens* (1509–10), and on the other hand at once moralizing and titillatory, following the *Romans of the Decadence* (1847) by Thomas Couture, may say much about Rejlander's art-historical sensibilities, but it could equally be seen as illuminating the reception of the photograph, which was entitled *Two Ways of Life*, or *Hope in Repentance*.

The debate concerned varying interpretations of the photograph's content. Rejlander himself spoke at length to describe the central figure, representing a father, who is leading his two sons into the world: as they enter it, one of them chooses the virtuous path of study and industry; the other veers sharply off to the left to join in with idlers, gamblers, and the partially draped, all too evidently loose women. It is clear that the virtuous spirit and solid, worldly success are made to manifest themselves in all the signs of grave austerity, whereas the siren calls of idleness and vice show through a congenial glow, and the display of female flesh. Rejlander's account typifies in principle, though maybe it surpasses in its floridity, many of the apologia for painterly allegories uttered in that period.

History is silent as to the aspect that drew queen Victoria towards *The Two Ways of Life*, and caused her to buy a copy for prince Albert, but there is no doubt at all regarding the side of the photograph that had to remain covered by a black drape for the duration of its exhibition in Edinburgh. The voices declaring the impropriety of "publicly exhibiting photographs of nude prostitutes, in flesh and blood truthfulness and minute-

ness of detail", co-exist with others offering enthusiastic, even fulsome praise; but there is a common thread of recognition that runs through all the views, that a difference exists between an image representing the human body through the transformative medium of paint, and one executed by a "mechanical contrivance", the camera, and thus lacking all idealization, since it proffers the squalor and imperfections of real day-to-day existence; and indeed is poised a mere hair's-breadth away from the actual life it depicts.

It will be noticed that the hand of authority manifested itself in none of these transactions, despite the newly enacted Obscene Publications Act. Indeed, legal attempts to control the dissemination of sexual material already had a long history, with 19th-century antecedents on the statute books in the forms of the Vagrancy Acts of 1824 and 1838 (photography made its first public appearance in 1839), which made it an offence to expose obscene material to public view, and the Town Clauses Act of 1847, which prohibited the sale of such material. These, and the Customs Consolidation Act of 1853, under which the import of obscene material was prohibited, were directed against the newly urbanized working classes, in the belief that, as Lord Campbell expressed it, the sale of obscene publications and indecent books was equivalent to the "sale of poison more deadly than prussic acid, strychnine or arsenic".

Partly, this articulated the fears expressed across the rest of society for the possible consequences in disorder arising from the formation of an energetic working class, then perceived as inchoate, both unmeasured and unregulated. In particular, moral, especially sexual turpitudes might break down the structures of social control even as they were being established, and render the working class less amenable to direction, and thus both politically and economically unhealthy, with added subjection to all the physical and mental diseases then known to be attendant upon debauch and general immorality.

The Obscene Publications Act offered a formal weapon to address this perception of a threat, including powers to order destruction; it was taken up joyfully by the Society for the Prevention of Vice and used in their attempt to cut down the pornographers, photographic and the rest, who brought infamy to Holywell Street and other locations in central London. The impact of this legislation was most severe at its inception, but it gradually steadied over time. One of the best known instances of police action involved a raid in 1874 upon the premises of one Hayler, a photographer, from whom, or so it was reported, there were recovered some 130,248 obscene photographs and 5000 stereoscopic slides. Surviving references to the case suggest that much if not all of this material showed explicit representations of sexual acts, but, equally certainly, the Holywell Street trade in images of persons unclothed included those that, like Rejlander's, had significant pretensions to the criteria of fine art, and stretched through further genres that claimed to provide material for the information of artists, or else to those promoted as vehicles of ethnographic and anthropological data.

As diffusion of information via the letterpress advanced, so authorities sought to control book and news publication, and the reactions to photographs we have noted here have an aspect as responses to mid-19th-century techniques of rapidly multiplying and distributing photographic images. The coming of film, television, and the Internet since then have each been accompanied by censorious peaks that have tended eventually to settle into intermittent skirmishing.

That, once the initial lines had been drawn, is how the state of affairs continued for photography into the 20th century. One may note that at the higher social levels, any tensions or disputes were brought to resolution privately, for instance, those arising from Lewis Carroll's photographing the little girls who were his friends. In the world of the urban masses, the Holywell streets across the country continued to be nagged by the organized opponents of vice and from time to time prosecuted by the police.

In 1901 postcards were permitted to bear both address and message on the same side, leaving the other side clear for illustrations, which gave greatly increased scope for the open mailing of images unconcealed by envelopes. While the mail traffic in discreetly sealed-away pornographic photographs was reputedly considerable, and had attracted its own legislation, the frankly indiscreet materials that formed a part of this vast cataract of open postcard images circulated for the most part without comment, let alone sanctions against them. That sanctions did not take place might indicate that at the time the development seemed a minor one, and the radical position of the erotically accented pictorial postcard has become evident only with a historical perspective.

As the 20th century progressed, rules were established, often tacitly, and applied to photographs that were expected to have a public currency. The airbrush came into its own for the overpainting of pubic hair and the removal of anything in a photograph that might be construed as genital. In the most publicly displayed imagery the same techniques were applied to turning photographed nipples into the merest hints of their actual selves; all of this conferred an extraordinary prurience upon the results. On the other hand, prepubertal children of both sexes from time to time appeared in the pages of naturist magazines, or on postcards, with every detail of their bodies fully rendered. It is observable that in the categories of photography that referred stylistically to Salon painting, photographers still found it expedient to be more cautious over the representation of sexual, or imaginably sexual parts, than was the case for gesturally made images of the same period.

Thus, the attitudes informing official reactions to photographic representation were set early and remained substantially unchanged. The photograph has been seen as separated

from reality by the thinnest of membranes, with an absoluteness of truth-telling that may repel or terrify those who fear the physical body. One of the notable changes that became evident from the 1960s on both sides of the Atlantic was in the acceptance that photographic illustrations in magazines directed towards the young male market could be anatomically very explicit indeed, provided they did not represent sexual activities. Limits of representation were nevertheless still tightly coded, but mapped variously between titles, with a discernible spectrum of practices from the relatively discreet pages of the openly sold *Playboy* and *Penthouse*, through a swathe of magazines that kept just within the law as it had become interpreted, to others that had to remain clandestine. It is reasonable to see this easing of restriction as consequent upon the climate of permissiveness; equally, the facilitations of developing print technologies created commercial pressures that moral regulators found it very hard to resist without the presence of a substantial crusading polemic to fuel them.

The first wave in the nay-saying recrudescence was provided by separatist feminists, who in both Britain and the US agitated against the appearance of women in the making of pornography on the grounds that they were thus demeaned, objectified, and exploited by the patriarchy in control of society. From the contexts of their writings, one may safely say that it was predominantly photographically originated imagery that the feminists had in mind. Efforts were made to restrict the distribution of magazines containing photographs defined as pornographic. In Britain there was an attempt in 1990 by the Labour MP Dawn Primarolo to introduce a Location of Pornographic Materials Bill, which would have restricted the sale of pornography to licensed premises; this failed. In the US there have been campaigns by various moralizing organizations to bring pressures to bear on distributors not to carry suspect titles. A reaction to this separatism and anti-sexualism has been the appearance in the feminist sector of women who propose the virtues of erotica for women, and disparage sexual censorship; this polarization has developed a powerful libertarian dynamic.

The second wave of polemic, however, proved even more significant and potentially damaging. It grew out of a generalized public concern centred on child abuse, and as a corollary, upon child pornography. While the best evidence on the matter shows that the commercial production of photographic child pornography was in decline by the mid-1970s, and the Williams Report of the Committee on Obscenity and Film Censorship of 1979 found "no evidence that child-pornography was a growing problem", US legislation against it, as the Protection of Children against Sexual Exploitation Act was enacted in 1977, became operative from 1 January 1978. Despite Home Office and other expert rebuttal of the notion that a special and increasing risk existed in the UK, legislative proposals went on their way to become the Protection of Children Act 1978.

It is worth noting that, during the debates, Lord Houghton of Sowerby's repeated pleas that actions should be properly informed by fact were brushed aside, and his examples of misinformation ignored. During the Report stage in the House of Lords, Lord Houghton said:

This Bill is surrounded by unhealthy attitudes and by vicious determination that, come what may, some evils in society must be put down, even though they create

PHOTOGRAPHY: Cover of the 10th anniversary issue of the American edition of *Playboy*, published in January 1964. *Playboy*'s images were relatively discreet compared with some of the more clandestine magazines of the period. The law allowed explicit anatomical representation in such publications, but not the representation of sexual activities.

greater ones in the process. I feel, with all my strength and heart, that this is a bad Bill. I said during the Second Reading that Parliament has been subjected to a campaign of hysteria and pressure unexampled in my experience of nearly 30 years in Parliament (*Debates in the House of Lords*, vol. 393, cc1060).

The Act's intention had been to stem the flow of commercial pornography; the debates made it quite clear that family, or other casually taken photographs that happened to show naked children, should not fall within its view. Yet *Regina* v. *Graham-Kerr* 1989 was the prosecution of a photographer who had happened to record a nude seven-year-old boy at a naturist swimming session, and in which the judge held that the context of making the photograph could not be considered in coming

to a decision as to the "indecency" or otherwise of the image. *Regina* v. *Cotterill* 1990 showed that the case of an artist charged with the possession of an archive of photographs recording nude children had to go to appeal to establish the force of the clause in the Act that exempted the possession of photographs for legitimate reason from prosecution under it.

In the US, intention, enactment, and prosecution twisted around one another in tighter and tighter spirals; the Act of 1977 was amended in 1984 to make it unnecessary for a depiction of a nude child to be obscene, or intended for commercial usage, for it to be prosecuted. Child pornography thus became a category of speech unprotected under the First Amendment. There does not appear to have been even lip-service to the legitimacy of family photographs showing naked children. *State* v. *Robinson*, no.85 CA 47. 85 CA 48 records the arrest of parents and consignment of their daughter to a foster home, with serious emotional effects, because of some nude sunbathing photographs of the child and her cousins: this is only one of many examples.

In Britain in 1995, there was the high-profile arrest of the TV newscaster Julia Somerville and her partner Jeremy Dixon for taking photographs of Ms Somerville's daughter in the bath. This followed a complaint to the police by an employee of the film processors; the complainant ignored the industry guidelines on questionable material. There was an immediate, scandalized public reaction to the arrests. The Crown Prosecution Service did not proceed with charges; but that could not expunge the fact of an intense inquisition into the personal lives of a law-abiding family, or justify the unrepentant attitude of the police.

The Criminal Justice Bill 1993 added a new offence to the provisions of the Protection of Children Act 1978; a new category of "pseudo-photograph" was to be included for anathema at every mention of "photograph" in previous legislation, a category which in both theory and practice is difficult to define.

Many of the prosecutions for photographic obscenity in the courts in both the US and Britain are brought in connection with material published in book form, and in both countries, allowing for the differences between the legal systems, the effect is similar: the same material may be complained against time after time, and so must be repeatedly defended until parties become tired, or recognize a consistency in judgement that renders further challenge futile.

One book will serve as an example. In 1974 *Zeig Mal!* was published in Germany. The joint authors were Dr Helga Fleischhauer-Hardt, who wrote the text, and Will McBride, who took the photographs. It was a book of sex education for children, based around photographic illustrations. The book was republished as *Show Me!* in the US; some 100,000 copies were sold in Germany, plus 240,000 copies of the US edition, which was distributed in Britain; distribution also took place in other countries. *Show Me!* has been showered with good opinions, from medical professionals, educators, literary authorities, religious leaders, and elected representatives, wherever it appeared. Nevertheless the pro-censorship faction challenged it in the US and Canadian courts. All of these challenges, three in the US and one in Canada, failed. In Britain, three photographs from *Show Me!* were held indecent in *Regina v. Stuart* 1995, while the book was acquitted in *Regina v. Moody* 1997. There is another point of interest in this latter case, since Roger Moody had his copy of *Show Me!* legitimately in terms of the law, for review purposes, and should thus have been exempted, by the provisions of the Protection of Children Act 1978, from any charges in connection with his possession of it.

It is characteristic also that for any given book, each police force, on each occasion, will have its own ideas of where the perceived indecency lies; so there tends to be discrepancy, rather than coherence, among the images examined from one court to another. Such variability, or arbitrariness, is typical too of actions by HM Customs, who are empowered to operate their own framings of indecency within the provisions of the Customs Consolidation Act 1876.

Whereas the foregoing examples have been of fragmentation in both censorious attack and in defence against it – and to that extent are at once typical examples of contemporary censorship and metaphors for the state of the law in both Britain and the US – the notion that there can also be censorship by control of funding raises possibilities that are potentially both discreet, focused, and draconian in their outcomes.

The work of the photographer Robert Mapplethorpe has provided a locus of contention for attempts at both sorts of censorship, and their convergence is perhaps best seen in the context of *The Perfect Moment*, a show of Mapplethorpe's work that first took place in the Institute of Contemporary Art, Philadelphia, from December 1988 to January 1989, whence it travelled to a number of other venues in the US and then to Britain and New Zealand.

A pursuit by moralists began. This did not affect the second venue, the Chicago Museum of Contemporary Art; but by the time the show reached Washington, where it was scheduled to open at the Corcoran Gallery, the possibility of a government move to limit the funding options allowed to the National Endowment for the Arts (NEA) had become sufficiently intimidating for the director to cancel the opening there, and so bring about its move to the Washington Project for the Arts. Senator Jesse Helms promoted an amendment to deny grants for "obscene or indecent" art. Although his full proposal was decisively defeated, Helms did manage a limited restriction on the NEA against their supporting "obscene" art for one year. At the Contemporary Arts Center, Cincinatti, the gallery was publicly raided and its director, Dennis Barrie, charged with obscenity and misuse of a minor in pornography. He was acquitted. Censorship instigated at the Hayward Gallery, London, venue was limited to the removal of a photograph of a small girl child, "Rosie", whose genitals are visible under her dress.

Wherever there is government funding, as in the US with the NEA, or in Britain with its Arts Councils, censorship either by politically directed choice or by legislative intervention necessarily generates a cluster of issues requiring vigilance over and above the general concerns over the constitution of the statutory framework for the regulation of discourse, especially when, as remarked above, the discourse is photographic and thus in a much more intense and problematic relation to reality than any of the gesturally originated modes of image making.

In recent years there has been much reiteration of well-worn, even worn-out attempts to limit public visual discourse in the UK. Looked at in retrospect, among the most important instances have been the police raids on the library of the University of Central England (1998) and the Saatchi Gallery (2001). The UCE raid had the purpose of destroying certain Robert Mapplethorpe images in books, and the Saatchi raid sought the removal of images of naked children from the gallery walls, some of which were family snapshots by the American photographer Tierney Gearon and some were child portraits by Ron Oliver. Reaction against these attempts was very strong, notably including the stand of the vice-chancellor of UCE, Peter Knight, backed by his senate and a significant cross-section of the academic world, and the rallying of press and intelligent opinion generally to the Saatchi cause. In neither case did proceedings follow. Nevertheless, it seems that police memories are thinning in respect of Roy Jenkins's warnings uttered in 1967 against precipitate acts in furtherance of censorship. The circumstances of Jenkins's intervention were well reviewed by Alan Travis in chapter 7 of his book *Bound and Gagged*.

PHILIP STOKES

Further Reading

Adler, Amy, "Photography on Trial", *Index on Censorship*, 25/3 (May–June 1996): 141–46

Beal, Graham, "But Is It 'Art'?: The Mapplethorpe/Serrano Controversy", *Apollo* (November 1990): 317–20

Dubin, Stephen C., *Arresting Images: Impolitic Art and Uncivil Actions*, London and New York: Routledge, 1992

Frascina, Francis and Jonathan Harris, "Social Control and Permissibility: A Case History", *Art Monthly* (March 1996): 40–41

Frascina, Francis and Jonathan Harris, "Power and Responsibility: A Retort", *Art Monthly* (June 1996): 46

Furedi, Ann, "Perverse Perceptions" in *Spiked on Line* at www.spiked-online.com

Furedi, Frank, *Culture of Fear: Risk-Taking and the Morality of Low Expectation*, London: Cassell, 1997

Georgieff, Anthony, "Concealed: Art or Kiddie Porn?", *Katalog* (Denmark), 9/2 (Winter 1997): 33–48

Hart, Janice, "Photography, Pornography and the Law: The First Fifty Years", *The Photographic Collector*, 4/3 (1983): 287–99

Hughes, Robert, *Culture of Complaint: The Fraying of America*, New York: Oxford University Press, 1993; revised edition, London: Harvill Press 1994

Hunter, Ian *et al.*, *On Pornography: Literature, Sexuality, and Obscenity Law*, New York: St Martin's Press, and London: Macmillan, 1993

Lucie-Smith, Edward, *Sexuality in Western Art*, revised edition, London and New York: Thames and Hudson, 1991

Lucie-Smith, Edward, "Eros and Innocence", *Index on Censorship*, 26/2 (March–April 1997): 139–44

Mavor, Carol, *Pleasures Taken: Performances of Sexuality and Loss in Victorian Photographs*, Durham: Duke University Press, 1995

Michelson, Annette, "Lolita's Progeny", *October*, 76 (Spring 1996): 3–14

Nead, Lynda, *Victorian Babylon: People, Streets, and Images in Nineteenth-Century London*, New Haven, Connecticut, and London: Yale University Press, 2000

O'Toole, Laurence, *Pornocopia: Porn, Sex, Technology and Desire*, 2nd edition, London: Serpent's Tail, 1999

Pearsall, Ronald, *The Worm in the Bud: The World of Victorian Sexuality*, New York: Macmillan, and London: Weidenfeld and Nicolson, 1969

Preston, Richard, "A Question of Taste", *The Independent Magazine*, 260 (4 September 1993): 28–32

Reardon, Valerie, "Whose Image Is It Anyway: A Reply", *Art Monthly* (April 1996): 45

"The Saatchi Gallery Should be Congratulated: It Is Standing Up for Childhood", *The Independent* (13 March 2001)

Stanley, Lawrence A, "The Child Porn Myth", *Cardozo Arts and Entertainment Law Journal*, 7/2 (1989): 295–358

Stokes, Philip, "When Indecency Is in the Eye of the Beholder", *LM*, 108 (March 1998)

Stone, Richard, "Extending the Labyrinth: Part VII of the Criminal Justice and Public Order Act 1994", *The Modern Law Review*, 58 (May 1995): 389–94

Strossen, Nadine, *Defending Pornography: Free Speech, Sex, and the Fight for Women's Rights*, New York: Scribner, 1995; London: Abacus 1996; 2nd edition, New York: New York University Press, 2000

Thompson, Bill, *Soft Core: Moral Crusades against Pornography in Britain and America*, London: Cassell, 1994

Townsend, Chris, "A Picture of Innocence?", *History Today*, 46/5 (May 1996): 8–11

Travis, Alan, *Bound and Gagged: A Secret History of Obscenity in Britain*, London: Profile, 2000

Webb, Peter, *The Erotic Arts*, London: Secker and Warburg, and Boston: New York Graphic Society, 1975

Williams, Bernard (chairman), *Home Office Report of the Committee on Obscenity and Film Censorship*, London: HMSO, 1979 (Cmnd 7772)

Wilson, Keith *et al.*, "A Campaign for Common Sense", *Amateur Photographer*, 187/46 (18 November 1995): 8–11 (on the Somerville case)

PHOTOGRAPHY: News Photography

The ideas and configurations of ideas around the making and censoring of news images are radically different from those that exist around the censorship of all other images, especially those that come under the category of "cultural" or "art" photography. Although there is some common ground between censorship of the news and in the culture, it is probably more useful to visualize two distinct, but overlapping subsets of circumstances than it is to think in terms of blending, or smooth transition across a spectrum.

The difference is found more in how the various sorts of photograph are read, rather than in what they typically show. It is adequate, or is habitually taken as adequate, to view the general run of photographs as representing moments to be seen as moments, or else fitted at will into a viewer's own fictional narrative about the world, or the medium: but photographic documentation, including news photography, is expected to fulfil much more severe truth criteria. At their root is the thought, even passionate belief, that news/documentary practice has as its objective the encapsulation and relaying of the truth of some event, complete in its flow of time like a fly in amber.

While popular myths about journalism do nothing to deny that view, the list of ways in which photographic/documentary truth is qualified is long indeed. The whole train of decisions – the selection of place, of time, of moment and angle, of technical parameters – together exclude, maybe of necessity, perhaps by choice, any number of the actions and aspects that go to make up an event in the world. And these selections, these inclusions and exclusions have an inevitable ideological vector: the photographer believes that the event has a meaning, that it signifies this rather than that, and that the process of making the image can be controlled to make such a meaning clear. Thus at the very heart of the documentary process are acts that shape the representation of the events recorded; one photographer might shape his or her record of an event differently from another's. Neither need distort, probably neither adds to the record, but both choose or submit to the inevitability of omissions, and both therefore involve, in some sense, acts of censorship.

The predisposition to entertain a notion, to install a vision even, that somewhere out there exists an ideal, total truth may receive its first denial in the making process, but it is in the contextualization and use of photographic images that all the varied aspects of censorship converge to bring about the greatest transformation; and they become most clearly evident when viewed in a historical perspective.

It is appropriate to take as a first example the Crimean War work of the British photographer Roger Fenton. The circumstances of his engagement to make a photographic record of that war are of considerable interest; on the one hand, Fenton had a commercial contract with the Manchester firm of Agnew and Sons who were to produce prints for sale; on the other, his way was smoothed by virtue of prince Albert's personal recommendations, which gave him entrée to the highest levels of command as a social equal. Fenton's own personal record is broadly compatible with the dispatches sent to *The Times* by William Howard Russell; chaos, disaster, and suffering are everywhere. In the photographs, however, there is much neatness and quiet; the unpleasant has been tidied away, leaving a sense of civilized leisure despite difficult conditions.

Agnew needed subjects that would sell; Albert needed to promote a photographer whose work would steady the public opinion already set in violent motion by Russell's dispatches. Their criteria may have been generated out of different circumstances, but Fenton's profile must have seemed equally admirable to both; an energetic man of good standing, technically skilled, aesthetically accomplished, who would above all know what was required of him, and tacitly accept it as an objective to be attained. While the dominant photographic process of the time – wet collodion negatives – did not allow action shots, Fenton, one of the best still-life photographers of his era, would have had every opportunity to memorialize the remains of the war in truly harrowing images; that he did not points to a powerful component of self-censorship in his work. One might also remark that, even so, Agnews' clients' threshold of the acceptable was yet higher, so that once the Crimean War was over, Fenton's prints were remaindered and his negatives sold off, since the market for war photographs collapsed in concert with an access of self-censorship in the public memory of the war.

It is worth noting that an independent British war artist (known as a "special artist"), William Simpson, was established in the Crimea before Fenton's arrival there, and that Simpson, whose work was directed to recording action, followed a routine of voluntarily submitting his output for the approval of the commander-in-chief or other senior officers, implying a kind of overt, though benign censorship that did not arise in Fenton's case, given his choice of subjects. The activities of war correspondents, who increasingly came to include photographers, became more and more of interest to censors as time progressed, and the submission of work for censorship before onward transmission grew to be a heavier obligation in most of the wars reported on during the second half of the 19th century.

In World War I a fully devised scheme of official censorship was introduced in the UK under the authority of the Defence of the Realm Act 1914. Correspondents were in fact treated similarly, give or take a few local variations, by all the main combatants: they needed accreditation; they could move only in the company of a conducting officer; they had to submit all they produced to the censor; and if they happened to be neutrals who by accident or design crossed the fighting lines, they ran a distinct risk of execution as spies. The threat of death was also applied to any soldier in the line who used a camera unofficially, though in reality, especially later in the war, such work might be tolerated or even encouraged if it served official purposes.

Traditional text-based journalists and war artists had a status somewhat above photographers. The opportunities for access to action and the manner of the application of censorship depended greatly on which service was involved, and, in the end, upon the personalities and agendas of those in authority with whom the photographer came into contact. The typical sequence of censorship began with the conducting officer, who exercised control of where the photographer went, and, so far as possible, what he recorded. The images were checked out at the field headquarters for anything considered immediately sensitive, and those that survived went on to the Press Bureau in London, popularly known as "Wellington House", where they were further censored and from which material was cleared for publication according to the perceived needs for news and propaganda. Finally, editors exercised their own filtration according to their papers' political agendas, and a desire not to do anything that might alienate their readers.

The net result was a set of published images that showed war as neater, less horrific and more sporting than either the best of the written dispatches or the memories of the combatants assured the world that it had been. Perhaps it was as a consequence of these imposed constraints that in 1934 Daily Express Publications brought out *Covenants with Death*, a book that can, without exaggeration, be called an explosion of the most extreme imagery of war to have been seen publicly in Britain. Whatever might be said about possible sensationalism, and some aspects of layout and editing, such as drawing attention to the section on atrocity photographs by segregating them in a special section, only to be reached by breaking a red seal around its pages, the book seems to be responding to a need to re-evaluate the past through extending public knowledge of it – surely a comment on the general principles of censorship, as well as on specific issues connected with the war.

The outbreak of World War II found the British government much more firmly convinced of the efficacy of overt, direct censorship than were its enemies. With the Emergency Powers Act in force, and the Ministry of Information to administer its provisions, journalists and photographers found the net of control ready for them. In its practicalities, the new censorship was much like the old, but more practised, and with the difference that by now the familiarity of photographic images, and the technical means to make and distribute them, had increased the supply and demand for visual material to an enormous degree, and so also the enormity of the censors' task.

These were the days of the great picture magazines, *Picture Post* and *Illustrated* in Britain, and *Life* in the US. Before television, they occupied unique positions as disseminators of visual information, and promoters of national ideology. Their circulations were huge, and their editors powerful; Tom Hopkinson of *Picture Post* enjoyed the confidence of Winston Churchill and many other prominent figures. *Picture Post* in particular had a deserved reputation for ethical, principled journalism, and would publish views critical of the Allies' conduct of the war.

It was the Korean War of 1950–53 that brought about the setting for one of the most serious conflicts of proprietorial versus editorial interests, to be played out in the pages of *Picture Post*. The post-war settlement of Korea had divided it into a client state of the USSR in the north and a US-supported state in the south, under Syngman Rhee. In the ensuing conflict a UN force intervened on South Korea's behalf, creating a situation in which separate, indigenous and UN armies fought in parallel towards similar general objectives.

On a number of occasions, both correspondents and personnel of the UN force observed South Korean forces acting in equal barbarity towards prisoners of war and the civilian population, imposing conditions of captivity and conducting arbitrary, mass executions. One of these occasions had been recorded by the *Picture Post* team of the writer James Cameron and the photographer Bert Hardy. Their dispatch was received in London by Tom Hopkinson, who recognized that it was a major news story. When he found that their material held up in every respect, he resolved that it was essential to publish, and laid out an article accordingly. Edward Hulton, the proprietor of *Picture Post*, on the other hand felt that to show such material would, irrespective equally of its truth and the existence of other similar reports then being published, be an act of disloyalty to the UN side. Hopkinson was forbidden to go ahead. Hopkinson told Hulton that, as editor, he had the right to decide on the contents of *Picture Post*, and since he had no intention of resigning, expected that Hulton would exercise his right to dismiss him, which is what happened. The article did not appear, and a *cause célèbre* was added to the history of British journalism.

A popular view is that the relatively uninhibited access by journalists, especially photojournalists, to the Vietnam War, with its concomitantly weak censorship, was a principal factor in establishing public discontent with its aims and progress. Whereas a reading focused on the evidence supportive of this thesis may seem to confirm it, an eclectic selection may induce doubts that with further study develop into a reversal of this position. Such an evolved view is cogently argued for by Caroline Brothers in *War and Photography* (1997). She questions not only the effects of specific photographs, but shows their contextualization into a much broader discourse that fostered the change of attitude to the Vietnam War.

A pointer of the eclectic sort comes with reading Joe Esterhas's paper, "The Selling of the Mylai Massacre", in the *Evergreen Review* (1971), which makes it clear that the photographs taken by Ron Haeberle of the Mylai killing caused no stir at all when shown in public lectures; it was only with the initiation of an investigation based upon the complaints of other witnesses that they were propelled into iconic status. The detailed account of the events around the emergence of the Mylai photographs is fascinating for the stories of the various close shaves the images had in escaping censorship; at different times elements of government, organs of the press, and individuals were after them to prevent publication. It is salutary to note that the fact of their publication as and where they did eventually appear had much more to do with the conduct of a squalid rights auction than it did with anyone's drive to establish the truth against all odds.

Even though the longer-term perspective has tended to reduce the power that had initially been ascribed to the Vietnam photographs, by the end of that conflict the British and US military and government authorities had no doubt that it had been excessive, and they resolved in advance that future wars should not be so freely documented, insofar as they had to be submitted to public documentation at all.

Thus in the Falklands/Malvinas War of 1982 only the British media were allowed a small contingent with the expeditionary force, and of those only two were photographers. It is claimed as significant that the photographer Don McCullin was refused a place among them, giving rise to the allegation that McCullin's exclusion constituted an attempt to censor the photographic record by preventing the presence of the best practitioner, with a long and famous track record for divining and communicating the nature of the wars he recorded.

One might also look at the accounts of the photographers who did reach the war zone, and note their difficulties both in reaching any action and in transmitting their images back to Britain. While the nature of single items from the catalogue of frustration and delay allows the possibility that they were the fortuitous result of military exigencies, mismanagement, or simple bad luck, together they take on the appearance of a more than tacit determination to permit only the barest minimum of imagery to enter the public domain. So we have a chain of events ranging from an extreme reluctance to allow photographers to land at all; when they eventually did, movement was circumscribed as much by inadequate personal kit as it was by the wishes of the command, and embodied in the presence of the minders. Then, because of the minimal provision of terminal equipment, most photographic images had to be sent physically to the UK via Ascension Island, rather than being wired out. The delays and the tiny volume of images arriving in Britain became notorious. Military photographers, meanwhile, had full access throughout – although it emerged later that even they had not been admitted to record the Argentinian surrender, on the grounds that their presence might have caused the event to be aborted.

The 20th century's traditions of pool journalism, minders, and controlled access were maintained and further refined in the Gulf War of 1991. Because their results in terms of photography could not be shifted off for blame onto logistic problems, as they had been at the time of the Falklands War, and because practice had polished their perfection even further, the visual representations of the news from the Gulf theatre began to look surreal, rather than merely inadequate, as the Falklands images had. Allied action was represented principally by stills from the missile-mounted cameras that showed the allegedly surgical precision with which Iraqi property was being destroyed, without even an allusion to the killing of human beings in the process. The massive land forces did not appear to be doing much beyond exercising and watching the desert, except, and it might seem it happened accidentally, when a single photograph of a carbonized Iraqi soldier was taken, published, and made to stand for the whole Basrah road massacre, which itself had perforce to stand in the public mind for other, hardly guessed at events of carnage and mass suffocation that passed unrecorded, except secretly, by the military, in the overrunning of the Iraqi lines.

While it is reasonable that there should be censorship in wartime of photographs showing events and places that have potential to interest the enemy, and it is to be expected that governments will wish to encourage images that support their current ideologies, it is notable, perhaps it becomes more notable, that editors for their part are on the whole disinclined to publish photographs that show the extremities of the events they refer to.

The media and their public tend to collude in allowing the complex and multivalent practices of censorship to run and develop without too much questioning; but there are points of friction where discreet agreement fails, and resort is made to draconian measures to forestall the possible ascendancy of an opposing view. Consider, for instance, the publication by *Time International*, on 21 June 1993 of an article entitled "Defiling the Children" (pp. 44–47). It dealt with child prostitution in Moscow, and was illustrated with Alexey Ostrovsky's photographs purporting to show boy prostitutes, one of whom is dressed as a girl, as they live and work with their pimp.

It happened that the Reuters chief photographer in Moscow, Richard Ellis, was aware that these images were staged, and he posted his concerns as a message in the *Compuserve Journalism Forum* on 23 and 25 June 1993. His concern was to draw attention to what he saw as a growing practice of marketing staged images as "news". Because of the way in which he did this, via a public channel rather than discreetly to *Time* via the Reuters management, there was a furore, in the course of which Ellis was moved to resign his post: a direct consequence of rejecting self-censorship and opting for open discourse around a topic of public interest.

Another issue here is that of the arguments currently in play around the notions of the staged versus the "real" image, which surely have echoes in the anathemas against "pseudo-photographs" expressed in the British Criminal Justice Act 1994. In other words, there are signs appearing across the culture that the photograph is expected to be the bearer of truth in ways that mere verbal utterances or gestural images can never be, and that photographs of which that is not the case require to be expunged, more in anger than in sorrow, and their protagonists punished.

There is no more dramatic example than the photograph, frame-grabbed from a British Independent Television News (ITN) bulletin, showing emaciated Bosnian Muslims standing behind barbed wire in a Serbian camp. It appeared first in the *Daily Mirror* of 7 August 1992 and was rapidly taken up as proof of Serb war crimes, including the establishment of concentration camps. However, a German journalist, Thomas Deichmann, claimed to have discovered that the picture had been staged to give this impression, with the camera behind the wire of a small utility compound, filming refugees looking in from outside, completely unconfined. Deichmann published this, with extensive documentation, in *Living Marxism* (no. 97, February 1997). ITN plunged into a libel action against *Living Marxism*, alleging "express malice" in their publication of Deichmann's article. *Living Marxism*, which argued that the action amounted to censorship of a possible interpretation, lost the case and was forced into liquidation.

Journalistic truth, like any other, is relative and mutable. But the manipulation of photojournalistic truth in particular has a long pedigree and many methods of accomplishing it. While pasteup and combination printing go back to the early history of photography, and airbrushing is far from novel, the computer and its image manipulation software are viewed with misgiving, despite the sophisticated and effective precedents.

Numerous examples exist of photographs altered to eliminate figures who had become politically embarrassing to the powerful. Even as early as the Russian Revolution, the most complex photographic re-formings assured the evanescence of Trotsky and innumerable others, as they established the seamless ubiquity of Lenin and Stalin. Exactly the same intentions and exercises of considerable skill may be seen recurring to the point of boredom in the photography of any of the totalitarian regimes, from Nazi Germany to modern China; there are those who argue that the only significant difference between practice in those states and the democracies is in the blatancy with which photographs are manipulated, or even invented.

PHILIP STOKES

Further Reading

Belsey, Andrew and Ruth Chadwick (editors), *Ethical Issues in Journalism and the Media*, London and New York: Routledge, 1992

Bilton, Michael and Kvein Sim, "My Lai: A Half-Told Story", *Sunday Times Magazine* (23 April 1989): 24–35

Brothers, Caroline, *War and Photography: A Cultural History*, London and New York: Routledge, 1997

Carmichael, Jane, *First World War Photographers*, London and New York: Routledge, 1989

Deichmann, Thomas, "The Picture That Fooled the World", *Living Marxism*, 97 (February 1997): 24–31

Esterhas, Joe, "The Selling of the Mylai Massacre", *Evergreen Review* (October 1971): 41–44, 63–71

Fenton, Roger, *Roger Fenton, Photographer of the Crimean War: His Photographs and His Letters from the Crimea*, with an essay by Helmut and Alison Gernsheim, London: Secker and Warburg, 1954; New York: Arno Press, 1973

Friedrich, Ernst and Douglas Kellner, *War against War*, Seattle: Real Comet Press, 1987 (as *Krug dem Kruge*, 1924)

Hopkinson, Tom, *Of This Our Time: A Journalist's Story, 1905–50*, London: Hutchinson, 1982

Hume, Mick, "There Are Camps, and Then There Are Concentration Camps", *Living Marxism*, 101 (June 1997): 20–22

Innes, T.A. and Ivor Castle (editors), *Covenants with Death*, London: Daily Express Publications, 1934

Johnson, Peter, *Front Line Artists*, London: Cassell, 1978

King, David, *The Commissar Vanishes: The Falsification of Photographs and Art in Stalin's Russia*, New York: Metropolitan Books, and Edinburgh: Canongate, 1997

Knightley, Phillip, *The First Casualty: The War Correspondent as Hero and Myth-maker from the Crimea to Kosovo*, revised edition, London: Prion, 2000

Lewinski, Jorge, *The Camera at War: A History of War Photography from 1848 to the Present Day*, London: W.H. Allen, and New York: Simon and Schuster, 1978

McCann, Paul, "You Can't Butcher Me, I've Got the Law on My Side", *Independent Media* (1 December 1997)

McCullin, Don and Lewis Chester, *Unreasonable Behaviour: An Autobiography*, London: Jonathan Cape, 1990; New York: Knopf, 1992

McCullin, Don, *Sleeping with Ghosts: A Life's Work in Photography*, London: Jonathan Cape, 1994; New York: Aperture, 1996

Rosler, Martha, "Image Simulations, Computer Manipulations: Some Considerations", *Ten8*, 2/2 (Autumn 1991): 52–63

Searle, Helen, "No Ordinary Libel Case", *Living Marxism*, 105 (November 1997): 15–17

Taylor, John, "Pictorial Photography in the First World War", *The History of Photography*, 6/2 (1982): 119–41

Taylor, John, *War Photography: Realism in the British Press*, London and New York: Routledge, 1991

Taylor, John, *Body Horror: Photojournalism, Catastrophe and War*, Manchester: Manchester University Press, and New York: New York University Press, 1998

Walsh, Jeffrey and James Aulich (editors), *Vietnam Images: War and Representation*, London: Macmillan, and New York: St Martin's Press, 1989

PHOTOGRAPHY: Fashion Photography

The relationship of fashion photography to censorship is somewhat marginal and hinges almost without exception on issues concerning sex and morality. While fashion photography had always allowed for the fetishistic display of the body (the work of Horst during the 1930s is a good example of this), it had managed largely to eschew censure through its association with various art movements. By the late 1960s, however, a discernible shift had begun to take place in attitudes towards fashion photography. The impact of youth culture and the changing sexual mores of the postwar period had generated a more knowing and ingenuous form of photographic realism which, in turn, led to a more volatile climate of public opinion, to the extent that Ernestine Carter could comment: "Pornography having taken over films, the theatre and literature, took over fashion photography too" (*The Changing World of Fashion*, 1977). Carter was, of course, referring to the work of such photographers as Helmut Newton, Guy Bourdin, Chris Von

Wangenheim, Jeanloup Sieff, and Deborah Turbeville, which had begun to appear in the American, French, and Italian editions of *Vogue* and in Britain in *Queen* and *Nova*. It is important to bear in mind here that such work was rarely censored officially, rather that it contributed to an arena of ongoing debate concerning sexual politics after it had been published.

One of the chief criticisms made of fashion photography during the 1970s centred on the exploitation by the photographer (who was usually male) of his subjects (who were usually female). As Helmut Newton himself put it, "we did a lot of naughty things and had a lot of fun". Newton, in particular, gained notoriety for the fashion work he produced for magazines such as *Nova* and the Continental editions of *Vogue*, with his images representing models ostensibly engaged in scenes of lesbian flirtation for French *Vogue* in March 1979 becoming something of a *succès de scandale*. In one scene, for example, we can perceive an interesting play on phallic symbolism as two women performing an intimate masquerade in a hotel lobby share a cigarette – one of them has long hair and wears a figure-revealing boob tube and split knee skirt, while the other, with slicked-back hair and dressed in a double-breasted suit, leans over her as their lighted cigarette ends provocatively touch. Feminists were quick to accuse Newton of producing work that was undeniably based on male fantasies of the psychosexuality of women (whether straight or gay) and that violated and degraded them.

But such criticism failed to take into account the meaning for the clothes intended by the designer – in this case Yves Saint Laurent, whose fashion at this time played deliberately on a "style androgyne" – and also overlooked the fact that even female photographers can objectify women in ambiguous terms. In American *Vogue* in May 1975, for instance, a photograph by Deborah Turbeville of five models in a communal shower wearing swimsuits and/or dressing gowns was attacked by readers not only for portraying an imputed scene of lesbianism (even though the models had been posed separately and in no way appear remotely interested in each other) but also for setting up a symbolic association with the gas chambers at Auschwitz. More recently, a fashion shoot for British *Vogue* in June 1993 entitled "Under Exposure", photographed by Corinne Day and consisting of eight images of Kate Moss wearing underwear in her own flat, met with similar controversy as soon as it was published by being implicated into debates on child pornography and drug culture by various writers and critics. Marion Hume writing in *The Independent* on 26 May 1993, for example, suggested that the spectator was "invited to stare at the crotch and breasts of a child" who in turn "looks back at the camera with the passivity of a victim", while a psychotherapist, Susie Orbach, insisted that Moss looked "paedophilic and almost like a junkie". In a similar vein, it should be noted that in 1995 Calvin Klein was forced to drop an advertising campaign for CK Jeans following complaints from the American Family Association, while President Clinton, following the death of the fashion photographer Davide Sorrenti from a drugs overdose in February 1997, rebuked the cult of "heroin chic", inveighing: "Glorifying death is not good for any society".

There are several important and interdependent points to observe concerning such criticisms of fashion photography in the context of censorship. First, the way that they appear to confuse and/or conflate photographic representation with reality itself. This kind of traduction tends to rehearse one of the commonest misconceptions concerning the ontological status of photography as nothing more than a spontaneous trace of what exists, as something that merely describes rather than interprets reality. Thus the image of five women modelling swimsuits in a shower can be seen to be one and the same thing as lesbianism or Auschwitz, while the photographic representation of Kate Moss modelling underwear is isologous with the reality of under-age sex itself. Such an attitude is obviously put into sharper relief when it comes to arguing the distinction between what may be regarded as erotic as opposed to pornographic forms of representation. We find this kind of thinking encoded in the Obscene Publications Act 1959 but it also subtends the logic of both the Williams Committee in Britain of 1979 and the Meese Commission of 1986 in the United States, which recommended that only the written word should be exempt from any censorship or legal control. Indeed, those who impugned Corinne Day's representation of Kate Moss appear to have been swayed by the hysterical rhetoric of censorship into seriously believing or wishing Moss to look as if she were less than the legal age of consent in Britain (in fact, she was 19 years old in 1993 and, as the pictures reveal, at the very least, had passed the age of puberty). More contentiously, they posited a somewhat spurious cause and effect between child pornography and publishing.

Second, such criticisms reveal the tension that ensues between the producer and his/her motives for carrying out the work in question and the consumer and his/her interests in viewing it. Alexandra Shulman, the editor of British *Vogue* in 1993, stated, for instance, that her intention in publishing "Under Exposure" was "to break the mould of the male photographer shooting a female model wearing black, lace lingerie at a hotel dressing table", while Corinne Day, who is a close friend of Moss, had also envisaged her photographs to be a humorous skit and, given both their *mise-en-scène* and circulation in *Vogue*, as making a statement against high fashion and the artificiality of studio photography. At the same time, those who have criticized fashion photography on the grounds of pornography and exploitation postulate a monolithic form of spectatorial pleasure that simply assumes the potential consumer of such imagery to be heterosexual and male, whereas most readers of *Vogue*, and roughly half the readers of other contemporary magazines featuring fashion photographs such as *The Face*, are female and not all of them are straight. In the final analysis, what seems to be at stake here is the right of editors to police their own iconography and to publish and be damned: witness Molly Parkin's decision to publish a photograph by Jeanloup Sieff of a model sitting on a toilet with her tights rolled down in *Nova* (1972), notwithstanding reservations expressed by the magazine's managers, or the publication of "Who's Shooting Who? – in Beirut It Pays To Know Your Terrorist" in *The Face* (July 1986), a polemical fashion feature thinly disguised as a guide to the different factions involved in the civil war between Christians and Muslims in the Lebanon.

PAUL JOBLING

Further Reading

Hall-Duncan, Nancy, *The History of Fashion Photography*, New York: Alpine, 1979

Jobling, Paul, *Fashion Spreads: Word and Image in Fashion Photography since 1980*, Oxford and New York: Berg, 1999

Williams, Val (editor), *Look at Me: Fashion and Photography in Britain 1960 to the Present*, London: British Council, 1998

PHOTOGRAPHY: The Altered Photograph

Whereas the current buzz and frisson is set to seethe about the digital manipulation of photographs, either pixel-by-pixel or through the application of algorithms to an encoded image, this stands merely as the most recent manifestation of a set of image-changing activities that have gone on since the earliest days of the medium.

In the context of censorship, the central criterion is believability. The care and artifice necessary to achieve this has varied. Sometimes, as with images produced via newsprint, the presumptions of photographic truth work with the obscuration brought about by cheap printing processes and coarse paper to prevent a casual viewer's detection of retouching. On other occasions, of clearer photographic renderings, it can only be those notions of the photograph as a true document that blind its viewers to the obvious signs of retouching that should have discredited it. More rarely, but nevertheless in a significant number of instances, a photograph is altered so effectively as to hide the alteration from any but the most skilful investigator, and its truthfulness reigns, effectively unchallengeable.

Occasions for political censorship by alteration most readily come to mind as those that are to be found in Soviet archives, especially from the Stalin period, when it became expedient to remove evidence that the purged had not only existed, but once participated in public life.

In 1924 there was no problem to be found in the photograph showing Trotskii and his wife as they sat in a car behind Sergo Ordjonikidze, on a visit to Georgia. But by 1936, when an illustration was required for a monograph on Ordjonikidze, Trotskii had fled into exile and utter disgrace; for him to be seen in the same frame as a heroic figure had become out of the question. Thus, for the later version, a certain "Comrade Masnikov" was brought across from the extreme right of the original picture and another man added beside him to ensure the Trotskiis were obscured from view, and out of mind.

By the time of Alexander Dubček's fall from grace in 1970, the physical consequences upon the person of the disgraced one tended to be less severe than they had been in Trotskii's time; nevertheless their images were pursued and extirpated from photographs with no less enthusiasm than the earlier generation had mustered. In the example shown, though the tactic

PHOTOGRAPHY: Left, photograph of Lev Trotskii and his wife Natal'ia Sedova in a car with the Soviet politician Sergo Ordjonikidze and others on a visit to Georgia, 1924. Right, the photograph used for a book celebrating Ordjonikidze's 50th birthday in 1936, by which time Trotskii was in exile in Norway, having been politically eclipsed by Stalin. Ordjonikidze had in the meantime become a close political ally of Stalin, so in order to obscure Trotskii and his wife the image was altered by moving across the figure of "Comrade Masnikov", originally positioned to the right of the car, and adding another figure, not in the original photograph.

PHOTOGRAPHY: The photograph on the right shows how the figure of Alexander Dubček has been removed from an original image after he fell from political favour in 1970. The effective elimination of the figure has been achieved here by cutting the picture down the middle and splicing it together again, with the result that the buildings in the background have been altered.

PHOTOGRAPHY: The front and back of an official Admiralty photograph from World War II, showing a Russian naval mission visit to Britain. The instructions from the Admiralty office, dated November 1941, are to obscure any evidence of identity of the equipment or location from the shot, as indicated in the shading, before reproduction, to avoid the use of the photograph for possible espionage or reconnaissance purposes.

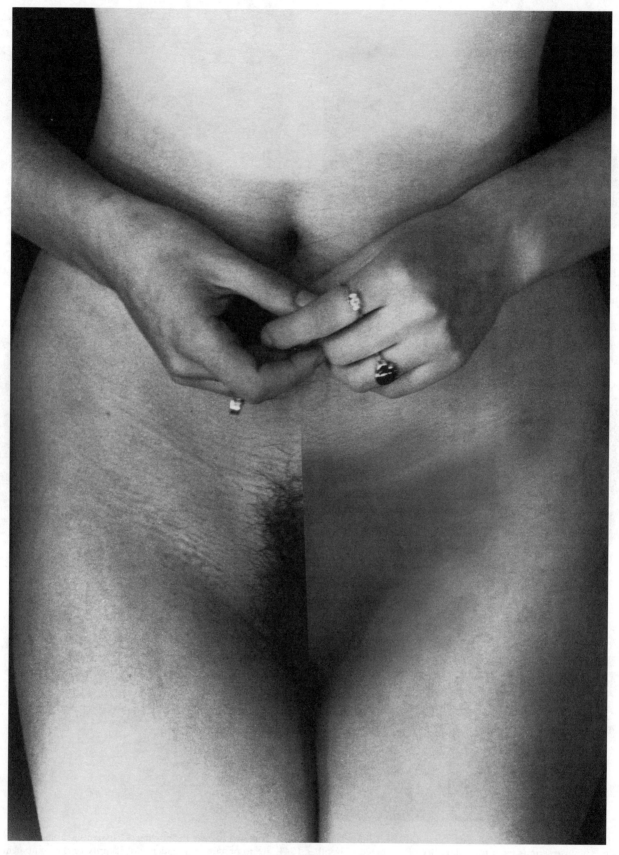

PHOTOGRAPHY: Demonstration print by Graham Bingham showing the effect of airbrushing a nude photograph in order not only to remove pubic hair detail but also to eliminate any reference to skin texture and quality.

employed was again to obscure Dubček by displacing a functionary to cover his image, the whole background has also been shifted, and much more nearly hides the intervention.

Military censorship may recognize its own need to deny the presence of some personage at a given time and place, but, more commonly, changes made to photographs in this sphere are addressed towards concealment of the technical details of equipment, or damage to it. Sometimes too, alterations may seek to confuse the location or other contextual aspects of an equipment's setting.

The caption to the next photograph states that it shows "Members of Russian Military Mission in the Conning Tower of the submarine after a practice dive." The annotations instruct that any published version removes a number of details from the vessel itself, obscuring both identity and equipment; and also deletes the background to prevent the event from being linked to its location.

The appearance of cultural censorship in photography is largely connected with a fear of the consequences of showing certain parts of the human body; what those consequences might be is largely unstated, and what human parts, might, if seen, lead to them, is a question that remains in flux. Whereas pubic hair, in its days of darkest implication, was removable from the person before photography took place, such nipples and genitalia as remained untucked away required elision by pencil, sable point or airbrush; the effect could on occasion be curiously prurient.

Whereas there are any number of nude photographs extant in books and as prints, that either clearly demonstrate or else hint at the possibility of anatomical veilings, the certitudes of direct comparison are not usually available. Thus the demonstration print produced by Graham Bingham provides a rare illustration of the scope of retouching regarding not only the more prominent features of a body, but also its potential in the suppression of the more subtle features of surface texture that might otherwise remind a viewer of the human realities behind a photographic image.

PHILIP STOKES

Further Reading

King, David, *The Commissar Vanishes: The Falsification of Photographs and Art in Stalin's Russia*, New York: Metropolitan, and Edinburgh: Canongate, 1997

PHRYNICHUS
Greek dramatist, active ?510–470 BCE

Phrynichus was a composer of tragedy at Athens, a successor to Thespis, and a slightly older contemporary of Aeschylus. His name is preserved by means of a few lines quoted from his tragedies and a limited historical record, which includes some details of what is probably the earliest incident of theatrical censorship in Europe, in which his play was banned from subsequent production.

The context for this incident is best understood by a combination of different kinds of evidence. Performances of tragedy at Athens took place at the city festival in honour of the god Dionysus, and had developed in a form now hidden from us over the years from c.535 BCE, apparently through the initiative and artistry of a composer called Thespis, about whom very little is known. Productions took place in a competition for a prize, which Phrynichus apparently won with an unknown play at some point in the years 511–508 BCE, according to a late classical encyclopedia. At this stage of its development, tragedy was predominantly a scripted song and dance by a chorus, which was differentiated from a comparable festival performance known as the *dithyramb* by the use of masks for characterization: tragedy also deployed a masked actor, who spoke verse, with a second actor introduced at some point in Phrynichus' lifetime. In the years following 510 BCE the city festival of Dionysus was reorganized as part of a new political order, which gave enhanced powers to the full assembly of citizen males in a nascent democracy.

One of the most significant acts of this new political order was to support, and then withdraw from, the revolt of the Greek cities in the eastern Aegean (an area known broadly as Ionia) from the dominion of Persia. The Ionian revolt took place from 499 to 494 BCE, when it ended in the capture and sack by the Persians of the Greek city of Miletus. Phrynichus composed a tragedy with the title *The Sack of Miletus*, and the historian Herodotus, who came from Ionia, recorded its reception in these words:

> The Athenians showed that they were extremely distressed by the sack of Miletus, most notably when Phrynichus composed and produced his play with that title: the audience in the theatre was reduced to tears, and the Athenians punished Phrynichus for reminding them of matters close to home with a fine of a thousand drachmas, adding an injunction that no one should ever again produce the drama (*Histories* 6.21).

This account suggests a legal act of the Athenian political assembly, almost certainly involving a public accusation and trial of an offence against the state. It is also likely to represent the aftermath of a continuing political debate about the merits of military involvement against Persia, evident in the initial support, and the subsequent refusal of further aid, for the Ionians.

Further aspects of a context are supplied by the association of Phrynichus with the politician Themistocles, who undertook the expense of training a chorus for a tragedy by Phrynichus in 476 BCE. It is likely that this tragedy was the *Phoenician Women*, and that its subject was the defeat of the Persian expedition against Greece in 480–479 BCE, in which Themistocles had played a leading part. Themistocles was the archon (leading annual magistrate) at Athens in 493–492 BCE, and the archon was the official who approved the selection of composers for performance at the festival of Dionysus. A reasonable supposition is that Themistocles accepted Phrynichus as a composer for the festival in that year (spring 492 BCE), and that this was the occasion of the performance of *The Sack of Miletus* recorded by Herodotus. Themistocles is firmly associated with the fortification of the port of Athens, the Piraeus, and with the development of the Athenian navy. A strong political context of patronage, in close association with an assertive role for Athens in Greek military and political hegemony, notably against Persia, seems almost certain.

Greek tragedy is normally understood to be concerned with figures from a mythical past. Yet the earliest surviving tragedy, *The Persians* by Aeschylus (472 BCE), has as its subject the defeat of Persia by the Greeks, and is said by a classical source to have been adapted from the *Phoenician Women* by Phrynichus. What is apparent is that in a revolutionary and critical period the emergent Athenian democracy was offered tragedies on themes from the recent past, notably concerning Athenian involvement with the non-Greek, or "barbarian" east. In *The Sack of Miletus*, the emotive qualities of tragic evocation and representation (the tears of the audience in Herodotus' account) were directed by Phrynichus towards sympathy with the inhabitants of a city that Athenian policy had left to its fate, and Athenian society signalled its refusal to tolerate this experience by enacting particular legislation. The eventual defeat of Persia by the Greeks, with Athens in a prominent role, was plainly less objectionable, despite the tragic treatment of the enemy and

the absence of the triumphalism that we find in Aeschylus' *Persians*: in fact, the Persian Wars rapidly took on the status of a myth in almost all the major art forms offered to the Athenians. But the course of Athenian tragedy into more remote mythical subjects was surely confirmed by this act of a radical democracy, defending its feelings from a sense of political guilt. Perhaps as a consequence, satirical invective was given considerable institutional licence in the development of the complementary dramatic form of comedy, recognized in the official festival in 486 BCE, but itself at least eventually subject to other forms of control or attempted censorship.

GRAHAM K.H. LEY

Further Reading

Hall, Edith, *Inventing the Barbarian: Greek Self-Definition through Tragedy*, Oxford: Clarendon Press, and New York: Oxford University Press, 1989

Herington, John, *Poetry into Drama: Early Tragedy and the Greek Poetic Tradition*, Berkeley: University of California Press, 1985

Lesky, Albin, *Greek Tragedy*, London: Benn, 1978

Lesky, Albin, *Greek Tragic Poetry*, New Haven, Connecticut: Yale University Press, 1983

Lloyd-Jones, Hugh, *Greek Epic, Lyric, and Tragedy*, Oxford: Clarendon Press, and New York: Oxford University Press, 1990

PABLO PICASSO
Spanish painter, 1881–1973

Picasso had the rare distinction of being denounced by the protagonists of no less than three dictatorships: the fascist regime of general Franco in his native Spain, the Nazis in Germany, who pronounced his art decadent, and the cultural ideologists of the USSR and other communist states, who welcomed Picasso as a member of their party but rejected his art as a typical product of "bourgeois formalism". He was not exactly popular among the real bourgeois – as the record of attempts to stop his exhibitions clearly shows. Picasso embodied some of the central issues of censorship in the 20th century.

Leaving Spain in 1904 to escape the chains of its artistic tradition, he remained in touch with his personal and cultural roots. In the Spanish Civil War (1936–39) he identified closely with the Republicans. He painted still lifes that were identified with specific battles and even believed that his art could affect the outcome of the war. *Dream and Lie of General Franco* (1937) is one of Picasso's most explicit statements. Ambiguities apart, it seems clear that he was depicting Franco as the destroyer of art.

The Republicans had previously recognized the power of Picasso's name in the struggle against fascism by naming him honorary director of the Prado Museum in September 1936. In 1937 they commissioned him to paint a mural-sized picture for the Spanish Pavilion at the World's Fair in Paris. On 26 April Nazi Germany's airforce bombed the Basque town of Guernica (population 10,000) in what they later justified as a "training exercise"; certainly the town had no military value. While Franco's troops occupied the town, Picasso got to work on a mural to mark the atrocity. Thus the genesis of *Guernica*, which

was to become a universal emblem of the inhumanity of war.

The Communist Party wished that Picasso had included a more explicit communist message, and, in fact, earlier studies had included the clenched fist of a Republican salute and the hammer and sickle. The Republicans wanted to include modernist art in the armoury of antifascist propaganda; Juan Negrín, the minister of finance, said: "In terms of propaganda for the Republic, the presence of the mural painted by Picasso is equivalent to military victory on the front." Picasso himself resisted the attempt to "programme" him. He agreed that *Guernica* was a piece of deliberate propaganda but did not confirm or deny that the bull represented Franco or fascism; it was clear that he had used similar images before with no political intent.

Picasso insisted that the mural should on no account hang in Spain while General Franco was alive. Between 1939 and 1981 *Guernica* was in the United States at the Museum of Modern Art (MOMA) in New York. Even there it could never be regarded as a neutral work of art. In the late 1960s, incensed at US atrocities in Vietnam, the Art Workers' Coalition wrote asking Picasso to remove the work from MOMA:

Tell the directors and trustees . . . that *Guernica* cannot remain on public view there as long as American troops are committing genocide in Vietnam. Renew the outcry of *Guernica* by telling those who remain silent in the face of My Lai that you remove from them the moral trust as guardian of your painting.

PICASSO: *Guernica*, 1937, mural-sized painting, commissioned by the Spanish Republican party to mark the bombing of the Basque town of Guernica by Nazi Germany's air force in April 1937 and exhibited to a mixed critical reception at the World's Fair in Paris that year. Picasso refused to allow the work to remain in Spain while general Franco was alive, and *Guernica* hung in New York's Museum of Modern Art from 1939 until 1981, six years after Franco's death. The controversial painting's symbolic power as a pacifist icon resulted in the Prado Museum in Madrid placing the work behind bulletproof glass; the painting was moved to the new Museo Nacional Reina Sofia in 1992 and the protective glass was removed in 1995. Further political controversy surrounded *Guernica* when the new Guggenheim Museum in Bilbao, 12 miles from the village of Guernica, requested the loan of the painting for its opening in 1997 and reserved a space in its galleries for the work. Despite campaigning by the museum and the Basque regional government the request was refused by the Museo Nacional Reina Sofia because the work was too fragile to transport.

The art critic Meyer Schapiro responded:

> A democratic republic is capable of great evils like a dictatorial state. But unlike the latter, it has a free press and free elections through which individuals and organized groups may criticize, resist, and act to change what they believe is wrong.

When the painting finally reached Spain, six years after Franco's death, in 1981, it was still sufficiently controversial to need exhibiting behind bullet-proof glass at the Prado. It is now in the Museo Nacional Reina Sofia.

For the Nazi government in Germany, only the most straightforward realism was acceptable. Quite apart from the message of *Guernica*, Picasso's entire output fell well within what they classified as "Degenerate Art". In 1937 Joseph Goebbels instructed Adolf Ziegler, president of the Reich Chamber of Art, to collect examples of the degenerate and the decadent from the museums of Germany for a major exhibition that was mounted, and subjected to deliberate ridicule, in Munich in July 1937. The works of Picasso were represented among the 16,000 works assembled; some were rescued by Baron Edmond van der Heydt, president of the Friends of the Nationgalerie, who, warned of the purge in advance, managed to get them stored in the vaults of the Thyssen Bank.

Further confiscations took place in 1938 and 1939, in preparation for a major auction that took place in Lucerne, Switzerland, on 30 June 1939. Among the works under the hammer were Picasso's *Absinthe Drinker*, described in the catalogue as "a masterpiece of the painter's Blue Period", and *Acrobat and Young Harlequin*. Art dealers were faced with a moral dilemma. Joseph Pulitzer Jr recorded: "To safeguard this art, I bought – defiantly"; Joseph Barr, director of MOMA, would not buy despite a major Picasso show that was forthcoming in New York. *Acrobat and Young Harlequin* was bought by a Belgian banker; 49 years later, the piece was sold for $49 million.

The Nazis attempted to continue their purge in occupied France, but the artists and their friends were often too clever for them. The Gestapo visited private bank vaults to inspect works deposited there, insisting that the artist be present. Picasso confused them by piling in so much of his own work and some belonging to others that they could not make a proper inspection; he also managed to persuade them that the neighbouring vault, which belonged to Braque, also belonged to him and contained nothing valuable.

An exhibition of "purified art" was mounted at the Jeu de Paume in Paris, and, strangely, contained some works by Picasso and Léger, which were, however, shown separately from those by Rembrandt and Vermeer. In July 1943 some of Picasso's works listed in the catalogue were marked *vernichtet* (destroyed), after they had been kicked, slashed, or burned by SS gangs. After the liberation, an exhibition at the Salon d'Automne in the Tokyo Museum, Paris, contained a retrospective of 74 works. Riots took place in protest at Picasso's modernism and his membership of the Communist Party.

Canvases were ripped from the walls and it became necessary to employ 20 gendarmes to protect the paintings.

Picasso joined the French Communist Party in 1944. It was "the logical outcome of my whole life . . . I have always been an exile, and now I am one no longer . . . I am again among my brothers." Brotherhood, however, did not extend to an appreciation of his art. John Berger says that Picasso had "asked for bread, but without any doubt what they offered him was a stone . . . they separated the man from his work. They honoured the former and equivocated about the latter." In 1947, as the gap between much modern art and the tenets of socialist realism widened and Zhdanov got into his stride, *Pravda* attacked the "bourgeois decaying art" of Matisse and Picasso. Vladimir Kamenov, editor-in-chief of the USSR Society for Cultural Relations with Foreign Countries, wrote: "He . . . renounced all the traditions of realistic art, Spanish included, and followed the line of cosmopolitanism, of empty, ugly geometric forms, which are as alien to Spanish as to any other democracy." Picasso's paintings were not shown.

Meanwhile in the United States the issue of *View* magazine of December 1943 was classified as unmailable by the Post Office in New York City, because it contained nudes by Picasso and Michelangelo; they later relented after protests by the editor. In 1955 a group of conservative women in Dallas, Texas, condemned Picasso and others for their modern style and communist sympathies. The Dallas Museum was urged to stop its sponsorship of the artist and replace him with more orthodox, patriotic painters, including some Texans! In 1969 visitors to the Chicago Art Institute protested against an exhibition of Picasso's prints, which included nudes and erotica.

DOUGLAS EDWARD LAPRADE

Writings

Picasso on Art: A Selection of Views, edited by Dore Ashton, 1972

Further Reading

Berger, John, *The Success and Failure of Picasso*, Harmondsworth and Baltimore: Penguin, 1965

Carmilly-Weinberger, Moshe, *Fear of Art: Censorship and Freedom of Expression in Art*, New York: Bowker, 1986

Clapp, Jane, *Art Censorship: A Chronology of Proscribed and Prescribed Art*, Metuchen, New Jersey: Scarecrow Press, 1972

Daniel, Marko, "Spain: Culture at War" in *Art and Power: Europe under The Dictators, 1930–45*, edited by Dawn Ades *et al.*, London: Thames and Hudson, 1995

Lehmann-Haupt, Hellmut, *Art under a Dictatorship*, New York: Oxford University Press, 1954

Nicholas, Lynn H., *The Rape of Europa: The Fate of Europe's Treasures in the Third Reich and the Second World War*, New York: Knopf, and London: Macmillan, 1994

Oppler, Ellen C. (editor), *Picasso's Guernica*, New York: Norton, 1988

Utley, Gertje R., *Picasso: The Communist Years*, New Haven and London: Yale University Press, 2000

GIOVANNI PICO DELLA MIRANDOLA
Italian philosopher, 1463–1494

Pico della Mirandola was born into a family of the petty nobility of eastern Lombardy who, as counts, ruled the small cities of Mirandola and Concordia in the Po valley. Trained in the Greek and Latin classics and groomed for an ecclesiastical career, Giovanni began the study of canon law at Bologna in 1477–78, where he helped Sebastian Brandt to prepare a series of conflicting interpretations of legal questions which anticipated, in form at least, his famous 900 theses. Following the early death of his father and mother, in 1479 Giovanni withdrew from Bologna and the study of canon law and undertook the study of philosophy at the University of Ferrara under the tutelage of Battista Guarini and as a friend of Girolamo Savonarola. The next year he moved to the University of Padua where he concentrated on the study of Aristotle and Averroës and developed an early interest in Hebrew and Arabic texts. At Pavia in 1483–84 he continued his studies of scholasticism, before transferring to Florence in 1484–85, where he became a friend of the Medicean court poet, Angelo Poliziano, and participated in discussions at Marsilio Ficino's Platonic Academy. Probably here, Pico conceived his project of reconciling Plato and Aristotle, and thus creating a new synthesis of philosophical truth. In July 1485 he moved to Paris, where he immersed himself in the scholasticism of the "northern barbarians" and developed deep interests in the great theological questions that were being discussed at Oxford and Basel as well as the Sorbonne. These studies all privileged Aristotelian philosophy, especially in the Arabic tradition as represented by Averroës, and were informed by a deepening interest in medieval Jewish philosophy.

Returning from Paris for Florence in the spring of 1486, Pico settled in Perugia in central Italy, where he composed his early attempt at reconciling Plato and Aristotle, *De ente et uno* (On Being and the One), which was eventually dedicated to Angelo Poliziano in 1492. Also at Perugia he began serious study of Hebrew and Arabic and prepared for public debate in Rome a number of theses, or propositions, on major theological and philosophical issues of the day. These *Conclusiones, sive Theses DCCCC* were published in Rome in December 1486, but the scheduled debate never took place. Instead the theses came under the scrutiny of a papal commission established by Innocent VIII, and 13 of the 900 theses, which seem to follow Averroistic or Cabbalistic doctrines, were condemned as heretical or dubious in March. Pico defended his position in an *Apologia* published in May 1487, but two months later declared his submission to church authority. Soon thereafter he left Rome for Florence and later Paris.

Angered, however, by the tone of the *Apologia*, pope Innocent VIII issued a bull in December 1487 that condemned all the 900 theses and ordered Pico's arrest in France, where he was briefly imprisoned. The intervention of powerful friends persuaded Charles VIII of France to release Pico, who returned to Florence where he spent the rest of life under Medici protection. The printed volume of Pico's theses was condemned to destruction, and many copies were publicly burned in 1491. A series of delicate negotiations led to the elevation of Giovanni's kinsman, Giovanni de' Medici, the future pope Leo X, to the cardinalate in 1492, and Pico's partial rehabilitation. Following the deaths of Lorenzo de' Medici and pope Innocent VIII, both late in 1492, Pico applied to the new pope, Alexander VI, for an official letter abolishing the prior condemnation of 13 of his theses. It seems that Pico was fully pardoned, but the exact legal status of the 900 theses remained unclear. Several condemned theses resembled Luther's famous 95 theses published at Wittenberg in 1517. In any case, Pico's name did not appear in the primitive index issued at Rome in 1499, or in later versions of the Index of Prohibited Books. On the other hand, his wide-ranging and free-thinking works have often been viewed with suspicion by orthodox Roman Catholic theologians. For example, as a result of discussions occasioned by the fourth centenary of his death in 1893, Catholic thinkers continued to condemn Pico for his seeming opposition to the reigning Thomism evidenced in some of his works.

The reasons for the distrust and sometime condemnation of Pico's views are not far to seek. His early works, the sevenfold interpretation of the first chapter of Genesis and the *Heptaplus*, dedicated to Lorenzo de' Medici in 1488, used suspected Platonizing and Cabbalistic concepts of biblical interpretation and ontology. But Pico's thought differed from that of the leader of the Florentine Platonic Academy, Marsilio Ficino, in his acceptance of certain features of Averroës's thought and deep interest in the Jewish Cabbala. To these sources, Pico added the use of ancient Hermeticism, and thus hoped to achieve a broad synthesis of non-Christian philosophical ideas. His differences from the Florentine Platonists were most pronounced in his *Oration on the Dignity of Man*, in which he denies the Platonic doctrine that man stands midway between the earthly and celestial worlds, and holds that human beings are outside the hierarchy and possess an infinite capacity for spiritual self-realization through the informed exercise of the will. Thus, philosophical truth allows the human soul to be cleansed of errors and achieve its perfection. In his *Oration*, which had been composed as a preface to the 900 theses, Pico repeatedly asserted the notion that all philosophies contain important truths, and that Christian thinkers should embrace the wisdom of the Arabs and the Jews. Thus, Giovanni Pico della Mirandola stood as a conspicuous early exponent of religious and philosophical syncretism, and implicitly challenged the belief that all theological truth must be contained only in the Bible and Christian authors. In addition to his acceptance of Platonic and Aristotelian thought, Pico especially valued Jewish Cabbalism which he viewed as an especially interpretative aid essential to the correct interpretation of the Bible, in particular the Old Testament. Pico's early death of natural causes on 17 November 1494 left unfinished his vigorous attack on astrology as an enemy of true religion, *Disputationes adversus astrologiam* (Disputations against Astrology). The drama of his life and the importance of his thought attracted a number of early biographers, including his nephew, Gianfrancesco Pico della Mirandola, and the English humanist Sir Thomas More, whose *Life of John Picus* (1505) established its subject as the paradigm of the freethinking Christian layman dedicated to the pursuit of a universal truth.

BENJAMIN G. KOHL

Writings

"Oration on the Dignity of Man", translated by E.L. Forbes in *The Renaissance Philosophy of Man*, edited by Ernst Cassirer *et al.*, 1948
Conclusiones, sive Theses DCCCC, edited by Bohdan Kieszkowski, 1973
Heptaplus, translated by Douglas Carmichael, 1998
On Being and the One, translated by Paul J.W. Miller, 1998
On the Dignity of Man, translated by Charles Glenn Wallis, 1998

Further Reading

Craven, William G., *Giovanni Pico della Mirandola, Symbol of His Age: Modern Interpretations of a Renaissance Philosopher*, Geneva: Droz, 1981
Garin, Eugenio, *Giovanni Pico della Mirandola: vita e dottrina*, Florence: Le Monnier, 1937
Kibre, Pearl, *The Library of Pico della Mirandola*, New York: Columbia University Press, 1936
Kristeller, Paul Oskar, *Eight Philosophers of the Italian Renaissance*, Stanford, California: Stanford University Press, 1964
Wirszubski, Chaim, *Pico della Mirandola's Encounter with Jewish Mysticism*, Cambridge, Massachusetts: Harvard University Press, 1989

BORIS PIL'NIAK
Russian novelist (real name: Boris Andreevich Vogau), 1894–1938

Boris Pil'niak had a huge influence on Soviet prose writing during the 1920s. He developed a style in which he successfully adapted many of the themes and forms of Symbolism to the post-revolutionary situation. However, his vocal assertion of the independence of literature from politics made him controversial and caused his work to be at the centre of two of the decade's most significant literary–political scandals.

The first surrounded the publication of his "Povest' nepogashennoi luny" (Tale of the Unextinguished Moon) in the May 1926 issue of the journal *Novyi Mir*. Almost the entire printrun was confiscated and the magazine was re-released with a different story in place of Pil'niak's. The work recounts how the People's Commissar for Military and Naval Affairs has a stomach ulcer and is forced to undergo surgery to remove it, against his own wishes, by an inhuman and bureaucratic "unbending man". The Commissar dies as a result of the operation and there are suggestions that he was murdered. Pil'niak prefaced the story with a claim that any resemblance between this character's fate and the death, during an operation in 1925, of Mikhail Frunze, the real Commissar for Military and Naval Affairs, was unimportant, since the story was a work of fiction, and warned readers not to look for "authentic facts and live persons". However, many of the details corresponded to the rumours that Stalin had had Frunze murdered in order to ease his own path to power. It is possible that Stalin, like many subsequent readers, recognized "the unbending man" as a caricature of himself.

The story bore a dedication to Aleksandr Voronskii, an influential communist critic, who wrote an angry letter to the magazine refusing the dedication and calling the story slanderous. Although Pil'niak was out of the country as press criticism of him mounted, in the January 1927 issue of the same journal he published a letter in which he apologized for the way in which the story had been received, and called its publication tactless, but did not actually accept the accusations levelled at him. This was possible in part because they were so vague: an attempt to examine the views expressed in the story would mean stating outright that the party and/or Stalin had effectively murdered Frunze, something that no one was willing to do. Subsequently, "Povest' nepogashennoi luny" was barely mentioned in the Soviet press. It was eventually republished in the Soviet Union in 1987.

In 1929, Pil'niak was targeted in the Soviet Union's first large-scale organized campaign to defame a writer. The case established a precedent, which was often to be repeated, of coercion through baseless accusation. Although the official reason for the attacks upon him was the publication in Berlin of his story "Krasnoe derevo" ("Mahogony"), publishing abroad had in fact already become standard practice. The true reasons for the scale and concentrated pitch of the attacks were more sinister: Pil'niak was the most vocal advocate of literature's independence from politics, and had earlier that year been elected chair of the Moscow section of the All-Russian Writers Union. That Leningrad's most articulate advocate of literary freedom, Eugenii Zamiatin, was also a target suggests that the actual purpose of the criticism was to intimidate writers into political submission, and force them to serve the state's need to muster public enthusiasm for the First Five-Year Plan and collectivization. (Zamiatin made a personal approach to Stalin for permission to emigrate; permission was granted.)

In August 1929 an article in *Literaturnaia Gazeta* criticized Pil'niak for his "apoliticism" – this now meant a failure to advocate the government point of view in every work of literature. With "the Pil'niak affair", political neutrality suddenly became a crime against the state. This article initiated the extensive campaign of defamation and abuse.

"Mahogany" undoubtedly presents a highly critical vision of a Soviet town rotten with bureaucracy, profiteering, and incompetence. The only true communists left in the story are the "outcasts": alcoholic tramps expelled from the party at the beginning of the NEP, and a Trotskyist who is powerless in a corrupt party. The destructiveness of this corruption is clearest in the scenes where bells are being torn from churches to be melted down. One of the story's most biting criticisms is of Soviet agricultural policy: in the Vasilii Vasilievich episode the government's antipathy towards the *kulaks* (affluent peasants) is presented as the counterproductive punishment of those who are enterprising and resourceful, whereas the incentives given to the poor peasantry are seen as subsidizing the drunken and wasteful. Finally, the episode of the canonization of a mystic can be interpreted as a satire of the already widespread cult of Lenin.

Later in 1929, Pil'niak started to incorporate "Krasnoe derevo" into a novel, *Volga vpadayet v Kaspiiskoe more* (*The Volga Falls into the Caspian Sea*). Although he often rewrote and incorporated one work into another, he claimed that in this case he was unwilling to accept the cuts proposed by the journal *Krasnaia Nov'*, and had decided instead to incorporate the story into a longer work. There are also claims that he was coerced into this. The rewriting of works according to party policy was later to become characteristic of Stalinist censorship. The effect of incorporating "Mahogany" into a novel about the building of a dam linking the Moskva and Volga rivers is to impart a sense of optimism about the new that outweighs the sense of the loss of the old. There are further significant changes: the young Trotskyist, the criticisms of agricultural policy, and the sexually liberated young woman have been removed, and statements about the eternally stagnant nature of Russia have been put into the mouths of negative characters. The novel uses the standard "socialist realist" opposition between positive and negative figures whose fates are determined by their political and sexual orthodoxy. Unlike "Mahogany", which was first published in the Soviet Union in 1989, *Volga vpadaet v Kaspiiskoye more* was published almost immediately, in 1930.

The novel's realist style was to become characteristic of Pil'niak's work of the 1930s. Although he was subsequently able to publish, he nevertheless continued to encounter censorship problems. *Dvoiniki* (1933, Twins) was published only in the form of a Polish translation and it was not until 1983 that the Russian text was reconstructed. In 1937, Pil'niak completed *Solianoi ambar* (The Salt Barn), a historical novel about the revolution, which was not published until 1990. The NKVD arrested Pil'niak in 1937 and executed him in 1938. He was rehabilitated in 1956.

JEREMY HICKS

Writings

Dvoiniki (Twins), edited by Mikhail Geller, 1983
Chinese Story and Other Tales, translated by Vera T. Reck and Michael Green, 1988 (includes "Mahogany" and "The Tale of the Unextinguished Moon")
Povesti i rasskazy 1915–29 (Tales and Stories), edited by B.B. Andronikashuili-Pil'niak, 1991
Sochineniia (Works), edited by B.B. Andronikashuili-Pil'niak, 3 vols, 1994

Further Reading

Andronikashvili-Pil'niak, Boris, "O moem ottse" (About My Father), *Druzhba narodov*, 1 (1989): 147–55
Boris Pil'niak: opyt segodniashnego prochteniia (Boris Pil'nyak: An Attempt to Read Him Today), Moscow: Nasledie, 1995
Browning, Gary, *Boris Pilniak: Scythian at a Typewriter*, Ann Arbor, Michigan: Ardis, 1985
Jensen, Peter Alberg, *Nature as Code: The Achievement of Boris Pilnjak, 1915–1924*, Copenhagen: Rosenkilde and Bagger, 1979
Pavlova, T.F., "'Pil'niak zhul'nichaet i obmanyvaet nas . . .': K istorii publikatsii 'Povesti nepogashennoi luny'" (Pil'nyak is Cheating and Deceiving Us . . .: The Publication History of "Tale of the Unextinguished Moon") in *Iskliuchit' vsiakie upominaniia . . .: Ocherki istorii sovetskoi tsenzury* (Eliminate All Reference to . . .: Studies in the History of Soviet Censorship), Minsk and Moscow: Staryi Svet-Print and Vremia i Mesto, 1995
Reck, Vera T., *Boris Pil'niak: A Soviet Writer in Conflict with the State*, Montreal: McGill–Queen's University Press, 1975
Shentalinsky, Vitaly, *The KGB's Literary Archive*, edited and translated by John Crowfoot, London: Harvill Press, 1995; as *Arrested Voices: Resurrecting the Disappeared Writers of the Soviet Regime*, New York: Free Press, 1996

VIRGILIO PIÑERA
Cuban poet, dramatist, and novelist, 1912–1979

Virgilio Piñera discerned his tragic fate early in life. As he states in his short autobiography, *La vida tal cual* (Life As It Is), first published in 1990:

> As soon as I was old enough for any thoughts to be expressed in something more than drooling and waving my arms about, I realized three things that were sufficiently dirty for me never to be able to wash them off myself. I learned that I was poor, that I was homosexual, and that I loved art.

Piñera began writing poetry and plays in the 1940s, and was closely associated with the review *Orígines*, and in particular with José Rodríguez Feo. Feo was also the friend and patron of José Lezama Lima, who was to suffer a fate similar to Piñera's. Such was Piñera's hostility to the Cuba of the 1940s and 1950s that he felt constrained to go into exile in Argentina (on three occasions between 1946 and 1958). The critic René Leal describes how, during these years, Piñera developed his "culture of negation", resisting in everything he wrote "the frozen values, the established rhetoric and lies . . . the superficial nature and . . . indifference to the intelligence" that characterized Cuban culture.

As a consequence, two of Piñera's major novels, *La carne de René* (1952; *René's Flesh*, 1989) and *Cuentos fríos* (1956; *Cold Tales*, 1988), had to be published in Argentina. The powerful Association of Theatre and Cinema Publishers prevented production of his play *Electra Garrigó* for 10 years; and young Catholics attempted to organize a boycott of another play, *La Boda* (The Wedding), in 1958, on the grounds of its immorality.

A month after Piñera's return from his third stay in Argentina, Fidel Castro's revolution was victorious. It was greeted enthusiastically by Piñera, who soon joined the supplement *Lunes de Revolución*. He began to receive recognition. *Lunes* published the first two acts of his most notable play, *Aire frío*, in March and April 1959, and the play had its premiere in 1962 (English translation published as *Cold Air*, 1985). Piñera's novel *Pequeñas maniobras* (1963, Small Manoeuvres) won the Casa de las Américas prize for 1967 and was quickly followed by the play *Dos viejos pánicos* (1968, Two Old Panics). His collected poems, *La vida entera* (Full Life), were published in 1969.

However, although Piñera had welcomed social change in Cuba, he had not abandoned his agonized vision of life. He continued to be the inconvenient and irreverent intellectual that he had always been, a world away from the new revolutionary art. After the Heberto Padilla case, when the poet was detained and then forced publicly to recant his previous beliefs, and the formulations of the Congress on Education and Culture in 1971, artists were obliged to work within specific boundaries, or abandon art altogether. The practice of homosexuality was entirely ruled out. Piñera's works were no longer to be published, or produced, or even referred to in studies or reports.

Officially silenced, he continued to write in the same style as before. Rehabilitated after his death, he was not present to enjoy the "Piñera cult" that ensued.

LEONARDO PADURA
translated by Rupert Capper

Writings

La carne de René, 1952; as *René's Flesh*, translated by Mark Schafer, 1988
Cuentos fríos, 1956; as *Cold Tales*, translated by Mark Schafer, 1988
Aire frío, 1959; as *Cold Air*, translated by María Irene Fornes, 1985
Teatro completo, 1960
La vida entera, 1960
Pequeñas maniobras, 1963
Dos viejos pánicos, 1968

Further Reading

Arrufat, Antón, *Virgilio Piñera: entre él y yo*, Havana: Unión Nacional de Escritores y Artistas de Cuba, 1994
Union Review, 10 (special issue: "Virgilio tal cual", April-May-June 1990)

FELIX PIRANI
British children's writer, 1928–

ABIGAIL AT THE BEACH
Picture book, illustrated by Christine Roche, 1988

Censorship of children's literature in late 20th-century Britain has rarely been overt. Rather, reading matter for children is controlled by pressures from powerful bookselling chains and a system of taxation and accounting which requires rapid results. Direct political pressure is rare and is seldom successful. However, because children's books are regarded as common intellectual property, censorship may occur very locally.

Abigail at the Beach is an example. This is a 32-page picture book, designed broadly for readers aged between four and eight, which was first published in Britain by Collins in 1988.

In the story, a father takes his young daughter Abigail to the beach. She builds a sand castle and fantasizes about its size; meanwhile, her father reads a book and drinks three cans of beer. Abigail defends her sand castle against destructive children with verbal threats, such as, "You touch one of my towers . . . and I'll get my daddy to hang you both upside down by the heels. He's in the Mafia." However, there is no actual depiction of violence, and the publisher, Rosemary Sandberg, felt that the book was "wise . . . honest [and] caring".

The first attempt to censor the book was made in 1988, when

54 members of the House of Commons signed an "early day motion" (a parliamentary device designed to draw attention to contentious issues) requesting that the book be withdrawn from sale. It was assumed that the book would encourage both violence and the consumption of alcohol. The publisher defended the book robustly, and it was not withdrawn.

In 1995, the book was reissued by the national supermarket chain Sainsbury's as part of a series of high-quality reprints. On this occasion, four complaints were received, the stress this time being on the implied violence, and the book was withdrawn. The case of *Abigail at the Beach* exemplifies how vulnerable children's books worldwide have been to simplistic views of cause-and-effect in reading. Equally, it demonstrates that these views can be used by most unlikely groups, such as supermarket chains, to restrict the availability of books.

PETER HUNT

Writings

Editor, *The ABC of Relativity*, by Bertrand Russell, revised edition, 1958, 1969, 1985
Abigail at the Beach, 1988
Triplets, 1990
The Universe for Beginners, illustrated by Christine Roche, 1993; as *Introducing the Universe*, 1999
Nuclear Power, illustrated by Christine Roche, 1997

Further Reading

Hunt, Peter, *Criticism, Theory and Children's Literature*, Oxford and Cambridge, Massachusetts: Blackwell, 1991
Sandberg, Rosemary, "Who Censors?", *Books for Keeps*, 59 (1989): 23

THE PLASTIC PEOPLE OF THE UNIVERSE
Czech rock group, formed 1968

The Czech rock group, the Plastic People of the Universe, were charged in September 1976 with "creating public disturbances", "jeopardizing the education of youth in a socialist spirit", and "singing indecent songs". The Plastic People's repertoire included a song addressed to an anonymous entity that concluded with the words: "What do you resemble in your greatness? Are you Truth? Are you God?/What do you resemble in your greatness? A piece of shit, a piece of shit . . ." (repeated eight times). Two Czech members of the Plastic People were sent to jail in September 1976 and the one non-Czech member, a Canadian, Paul Wilson (later a translator of Josef Škvorecký's novels), was expelled from the country. It was this trial that provided the immediate catalyst for the foundation of the human rights organization Charter 77. The fate of the Plastic People also draws attention to the particular significance of rock music in Czechoslovakia during the years of "normalization" that followed the Warsaw Pact invasion of 1968.

In the late 1960s, there had been a boom in rock music in Bohemia. The formation of the Primitives Group had marked the arrival of the "underground", playing music by Jimi Hendrix, Frank Zappa, the Animals, the Grateful Dead, the Doors, and other groups. The Plastic People, formed in 1968, consciously set out to be an extension of this tradition. As Ivan Jirous, the group's artistic director, put it, for the first time people who had had no access to art were now given an opportunity to express themselves. The aim of the underground, wrote Jirous in 1975, was "the creation of a second culture: a culture not dependent on official channels of communication, social recognition, and the hierarchy of values laid down by the authorities". It is important, however, to recognize that the Plastics were not protest singers. Their objectives were those of "absolute musical freedom".

In the early 1970s, the authorities took drastic steps to destroy rock music as a movement, including a ban on English names and songs sung in English. The Plastics refused to conform, arguing that it was better not to play at all than to play what the establishment dictated. Their work embraced poems by William Blake and the Czech artist and poet Jiří Kolář, and they also became identified with the work of the underground poet Egon Bondy.

Trouble began when, along with a dozen other rock groups, the Plastics and DG 307 played to 400 guests at Jirous's wedding in early 1976. More than 20 musicians were detained and over 100 people were interrogated. The Communist Party newspaper *Rudé pravo* (Red Rights) described the musicians and their followers as drug addicts, alcoholics, and criminals (8 April 1976).

The main trial was preceded by a trial of three young men in Plzen in July for organizing an illustrated lecture by Jirous on underground music. Held on the premises of the Socialist Union of Youth with the approval of its local committee at the village of Přeštice, near Plzeň, it had been attended by about 80 people. The "organizers" were Karel Havelka, a construction foreman; Miroslav Skalický, a carpenter; and František Stárek, a forester. They were sentenced to 32 months (Havelka), 18 months (Skalický), and eight months (Stárek). On appeal, these sentences were reduced by half in the cases of Havelka and Skalický, and to four months' conditional imprisonment, with immediate release, for Stárek.

If *Rudé pravo* found the musicians' "moral filth" repugnant, the situation had led Václav Havel to compose a *Letter to Heinrich Böll* (16 August), which was also signed by the poet Jaroslav Seifert, the literary historian Václav Černý, the philosophers Jan Patočka and Karel Kosík, and the writers Ivan Klíma and Pavel Kohout. Referring to the forthcoming trial, the *Letter* stated that the two rock groups had committed the "crime" of trying "to sing out their aversion to the established values of the world in which they live, to its hypocritical morality, to its conformity and bureaucratic stupidity, and to its consumer style of life". It also drew attention to the government's recent signing of the Helsinki agreements. On 8 September, Zdeněk Mlynář, a former member of Alexander Dubček's government, wrote his own open letter, condemning the abuse of the criminal code and calling not only for the release of these particular musicians, but also for the abolition of the administrative measures that had led to the banning of musical and artistic groups.

In the event, only four of the original 14 arrested in the main case were brought to trial in September – Jirous, Pavel Zajíček of DG 307, Svatopluk Karásek, a former Evangelical pastor who sang his own version of spirituals, and Vratislav Brabenec – and only Jirous received a significant sentence. The prosecution at the trial alleged that their antisocial performances had a negative influence on the lifestyle of young people. "The texts contained extreme vulgarity with an antisocialist and antisocial impact, most of them extolling nihilism, decadence, and clericalism". The defence attorney delivered a learned discourse on the function of scatological words in the language of the working class, quoting 17th-century folksong, the medieval English poet Geoffrey Chaucer, and Jaroslav Hašek's *The Good Soldier Švejk*. The judge nonetheless said that the use of the word "shit" in songs was a criminal offence under socialism. Despite the use of uncorroborated evidence, the four accused were sentenced to 18 months (Jirous), 12 months (Zajíček), and eight months (Brabenec, Karásek) on 23 September.

Havel's comments are reproduced in his *Selected Prose 1965–1990*. He described the trial of the musicians as an event that could become the precedent for "something truly evil". This was no longer an attack on political enemies, but an attack "on life itself, on the very essence of human freedom and integrity". The public prosecutor became

> the symbol of an inflated, narrow-minded power, persecuting everything that does not fit into its sterile notions of life, everything unusual, risky, self-taught, and unbribable, everything that is too artless and too complex, too accessible and too mysterious, everything in fact that is different from itself.

On 6 November, ten former lawyers, writing as "socialists", condemned the contravention of law and referred to the trials as "only the latest in a series of administrative interventions limiting and invalidating civil rights and freedoms".

At the trial, Jirous had been referred to by the prosecutor as the chief organizer of all unofficial cultural activities in the country. In 1977, he was rearrested within a few weeks of his release and again jailed for 18 months, this time for a speech at the opening of an unofficial art exhibition. In 1981, he was jailed for three and a half years on charges that he edited the undergound magazine *Vokno* (Window). He was awarded the 1986 Tom Stoppard Prize for his collection of poems written in prison, *Magorovy labutí písně* (Magor's Swan Songs) – a reference to his nickname, Magor, which is how Havel refers to Jirous in his *Dopisy Olze* (1983, Letters to Olga). In 1989, Jirous was again arrested, this time in connection with his signing of a petition protesting about the death of Pavel Wonka in pre-trial detention.

Brabenec was arrested again in 1981 after a Plastic People performance, which he had partly organized and which was based on his lyrics. Under pressure from the security police, he was given the choice of emigration or prison and left the country in 1982. He reported that 35 bands had been silenced in Prague, and that "the police don't merely stop them playing, they also wreck the places where the musicians practice, play, and live".

The Plastic People's roots in the music of the Velvet Underground, Zappa, and the Doors have frequently been noted, and their name is, in fact, derived from Zappa's lyrics. They were also influenced by free jazz and, on some recordings, by Czech baroque music. In the early years, observed the group's founder, Milan Hlavsa, "we were happy to play our instruments in the simplest way . . . We weren't great, we didn't want to be like Jimi Hendrix. It was more about the feeling." But the group's core lineup of Milan Hlavsa (bass guitar), Vratislav Brabenec (saxophone), Josef Janíček (guitar), Jan Brabec (drums), and Jiří Kabeš (viola) soon developed their own propulsive style matched by sardonic and witty lyrics.

The Plastic People's only professionally produced recording was *Egon Bondy's Happy Hearts Club Banned* (1973–74), which was released in the west four years later. A recording of their *Pašijově hry velikonoční* (Passion Play, 1978) was smuggled out of the country as was their performance of *Co znamená vésti koně* (What Does It Mean to Lead Horses?, 1981), which was first performed at a house belonging to friends at Česká Lípa. Several weeks later, the building was burned down by an organized gang and the security police all but admitted responsibility. The recording was subsequently made at Havel's country house. Other live recordings from this period include *Vožralej jak slíva* (Drunk as a Plum, 1973–75, released 1997), which includes recordings made at the First Festival of the Second Culture, held at Postupice in September 1974, and *Jak bude po smrtí* (Afterlife, 1979, released 1998), dedicated to the philosopher and novelist Ladislav Klíma on the 100th anniversary of his birth. Tracks from the Second Festival of the Second Culture, held at Bojanovice in February 1976 (Jirous's wedding), which gave rise to the group's arrest, are included on *Státu hanobení* (Dishonour to the State, concerts 1976–77, released 1998).

After various changes in lineup, the band finally broke up in 1987, when Hlavsa and others formed Půlnoc (Midnight), which was to tour the US in 1989. A reunion concert was held in Prague in 1992 and Havel persuaded the original lineup to perform again at a reunion concert at Prague Castle marking the 20th anniversary of Charter 77 in 1997. The group then re-formed and embarked on its first "overground" tour, subsequently touring the US and Canada in 1999. They were also the subject of the feature film documentary *The Plastic People of the Universe* (Jana Chytilová, 2001). Hlavsa died on 5 January 2001.

PETER HAMES

Further Reading

Brabenec, Vratislav, "Heroes or Madmen?", interviewed by Paul Wilson, *Index on Censorship*, 12/1 (February 1983): 30–32

Deutscher, Tamara *et al.* (editors), *Voices of Czechoslovak Socialists*, London: Merlin Press, 1977

Havel, Václav, *Disturbing the Peace: A Conversation with Karel Hvížd'ala*, London: Faber, and New York: Knopf, 1990

Havel, Václav, "The Trial" in his *Open Letters: Selected Prose 1965–1990*, edited by Paul Wilson. London: Faber, and New York: Knopf, 1991

Jirous, Ivan, "Underground Culture", *Index on Censorship*, 12/1 (February 1983): 32–34

Kriseová, Eda, *Václav Havel: The Authorized Biography*, New York: St Martin's Press, 1993

Patočka, Jan, "On the Matter of the Plastic People of the Universe and DG 307" in *Charter 77 and Human Rights in Czechoslovakia*, by H. Gordon Skilling, London: Allen and Unwin, 1981: 205–07
Seifert, Jaroslav *et al.*, "Letter to Heinrich Böll" in *Charter 77 and*

Human Rights in Czechoslovakia, by H. Gordon Skilling, London: Allen and Unwin, 1981
Skilling, H. Gordon, *Charter 77 and Human Rights in Czechoslovakia*, London and Boston: Allen and Unwin, 1981

PLATO
Greek philosopher, 429–347 BCE

Plato, one of the greatest classical Greek thinkers, lived almost all his life in Athens, where he enjoyed freedom of movement, ideas, and speech, yet the ideal state that he describes is one whose citizens experienced none of these. It is a great irony, when considering his involvement with Socrates and his own radical ideas, that Plato should ultimately have produced a blueprint for the ideal state where laws on religious orthodoxy were even more harsh than those that condemned Socrates. Some of his ideas strike a 20th-century audience as enlightened and before their time, such as his assertion that women as well as men should be educated as leaders, to play a full role in the state. But, in fact, as modern scholars have argued, there is a strong thread of conservatism and elitism running through his theories; his plans are intended to produce a static community divided into rulers and ruled.

Plato was born in Athens into a prominent family, and apart from a short exile between 399 and 387 BCE, he spent his life there as leader of a philosophical school, the Academy. According to the *Seventh Letter*, he began his career with the intention of entering Athenian politics, but became disillusioned after the civil wars of 403–401 BCE, seeing nothing but misgovernment even in the restored democracy. Instead he turned to philosophy, and after the death of his mentor, Socrates, became leader of a school himself, attracting pupils from all over Greece. He made at least one visit to Sicily in the 360s BCE, to the court of Dionysius II, in an attempt to apply his political theories about government in practice, although this ended in failure.

The most complete statement of Plato's ideas about censorship appears in his two political works, the *Republic* and the *Laws*. The *Republic*, written as a description of the ideal state, is the more theoretical; the *Laws* was written much later in Plato's life, as a more practical application of his ideas. It purports to be a design for a proposed colony in Crete. There is no sign that either constitution was ever put into effect, but both describe the organization of the state which will allow the best rule, the original and ideal form of the state.

Plato argued that the best state required the establishment of a system in which the citizen is educated in philosophical ways from birth through to adulthood, never encountering a divergent opinion. He suggests in *Republic* 540–41 that this could initially be achieved only by expelling all inhabitants of the city above the age of ten, and training the children in isolation. The foundation of the plan, which Plato expresses through his character "Socrates", is that the citizens must be prevented at all costs from hearing new or inappropriate ideas. This operates in several ways: in attitudes to literature, in contacts with outsiders, and in ideas about religion.

First, literature poses a problem for the ruler of the state. Poetry is to be considered dangerous because it is persuasive (poets are later said to be valuable to tyrannical rulers for their skill in persuasion), and because it presents an erroneous view of divine and heroic beings. "Socrates" proposes to establish censorship over all forms of poetry and music, from tales told to children by their nurses, to Homer, the most widely performed literature of Greece. Literature, for Plato, is harmful if not aimed at the moral good of its listeners, and only literature that reflects the values and beliefs of the state may be permitted. The gods in poetry, he submits, are shown as adulterous, quarrelsome, vindictive, and subject to fortune, ideas that fit badly with his concept of the perfection of the gods. Heroes, too, like Achilles, manifest cowardly and venal behaviour. Men may also be made cowardly through fear of death, because of the poets' depictions of the underworld. In order to promote harmony between citizens, "Socrates" declares that stories of quarrels and fights among the gods must not be mentioned, either in poetry, or, more surprisingly, in art (embroidered on clothes). This is a striking prohibition, since the battle between the gods and giants formed part of the civic art of Athens, most famously on the pediment of the temple of Athena on the Acropolis, and on the *peplos* presented to Athena every four years at the festival of the Panathenaia. Plato declares even the public monuments of his own city to be morally inappropriate.

It is notable that all the examples of harmful ideas in poetry are taken from Homer: this is an attack on the normal system of Greek education. Early on in the *Republic*, Plato proposes a censorship of poetry, allowing only depictions of virtue; by book 10 he is advocating the banning of all kinds of poetry, since poetry is an inferior imitation of reality. "Hymns to the gods and the praises of famous men are the only poetry which ought to be admitted into our state" (607). The *Laws* moderates this position somewhat, allowing poetry as an educational medium, and to encourage communal values, but the legislator is to put greater weight on the moral character of the poet than the content of the song. All poems are to be scrutinized by the authorities before performance, and no one is to sing an unauthorized song (*Laws* 829). This is perhaps an indirect criticism of Athenian dramatic performances, which had notoriously shown crimes such as those of Medea, who murdered her own children, and Phaedra, who attempted to seduce her stepson. Plato's principle seems to be the replacement of Homer as the cornerstone of Greek education by a new philosophical approach, complete with its own myths, designed to encourage conformity. Plato suggests at two points that manufactured "myths" should be used to instil the principle that men are not created equal: he describes the "noble lie" that should be told, that some individuals are created from iron and bronze, and are thus suitable to be labourers, and some from silver and gold, to be leaders (*Republic* 414–15). By banning all stories and myths apart from those approved by the state, Plato aims to induce complete obedience to the constitution.

On the same principle, concerns about allowing citizens contacts with other states are a continuous thread in both the *Republic* and the *Laws*. At *Laws* book 4 the Athenian adviser comments that a geographically isolated position is the best guarantee of stability, since contact with traders and outsiders leads to the introduction of dangerous novelties. There is an obvious concern that encountering different views would prevent single-minded acceptance of the laws, and that the citizens might become resistant. The *Republic* assumes a city that is closed to the outside, apart from contact through trade which is carried out by the trading class. The *Laws*, again a more practical application of ideas, admits that contacts between states must be allowed, for a city would be thought harsh and unreasonable if it cut itself off from all contact with the rest of the Greek world. This is a comment on Spartan attitudes, with their notorious expulsions of foreigners. But even so, strict laws provide for who is allowed to travel, and when. Four categories of visitor are allowed: spectators at religious festivals, merchants, ambassadors, and wise men from other similar states. All visitors are to be subject to state control: merchants are to remain outside the city, transacting their business in designated areas; ambassadors are to speak only to the magistrates and their hosts; and spectators are to be accommodated at the temples, leaving as soon as the festival is ended. None of these groups is to be allowed to speak to the ordinary citizens, whose contact with the outside world is thus strictly regulated. Visiting wise men, it is assumed, would converse only with wise and rich citizens, as befits their status.

Travel among the citizens is to be restricted to those over the age of 40, and no citizen is to travel abroad in a private capacity – they may travel only as a herald, ambassador, or sacred emissary (*theoros*). A select class of observers, over the age of 50, are the only ones permitted to go abroad for the purpose of learning about other constitutions. They may spend up to 10 years travelling and seeking out examples of good government, to add to the wisdom of their native city; on return, if an observer is judged to have been corrupted by what he has seen, he is to be kept apart from other citizens thereafter (a direct form of censorship). The thought behind this is that people seeing or hearing about the customs and laws of other states may want to change their own; they must be prevented from finding out any alternative until they have sufficient wisdom to adjudge their own ways the best. Again, the strongest contrast here in ancient Greece is with Athens, one of the most frequented cities because of its port, and one traditionally seen as open to all.

The ideas about religion in the *Laws* are the most troubling aspect of Plato's work, given his experience as a follower of Socrates. Socrates was tried in Athens in 399 BCE on a charge of religious unorthodoxy and executed, an event that Plato clearly regarded as unjust and tragic, yet in the ideal state he placed even stronger censorship on the expression of unorthodox views about the gods. Atheism is not to be allowed. Two kinds of atheist are distinguished: the man who is otherwise good, but refuses to worship the gods, and the man who is both impious and lawless. Different punishments are laid down for each, but the central plank of these laws is that all unsanctioned views must be suppressed. The "good" atheist is to be imprisoned for five years, and the leaders must attempt to persuade him of the error of his ways; if they cannot, he must be executed. The law is noteworthy as the first example of the idea of prison as corrective (rather than punitive), but what Plato demands is that all citizens conform to the beliefs of the state. The "bad" atheist must be permanently imprisoned and prevented from contact with any free man. This hostility towards rationalism is not necessarily as inconsistent as it sounds: neither Plato himself nor Socrates were atheists, and they reject philosophical argument if it is used to divert men's minds from proper worship. What was at stake was not belief in an absolute sense, but willingness to participate in and honour the worship and sacrifices made by the state.

In sum, in the ideal city devised by Plato, both rulers and ruled must know their place, and criticism of the constitution is not permitted, except among older men and in private. This is the deepest irony, since Plato lived his life as a citizen of Athens, under whose liberal regime he was able to criticize democracy as much as he wished, choosing to return even after the death of Socrates. The guiding principle of Plato's work is the oligarchic belief that the mass of the citizens are not fit to govern themselves, but require leadership from an intellectual and moral elite. Plato describes the creation of a class of "guardians" in his states who will take responsibility for the moral well-being of the citizens, and he says clearly that it is the leaders' prerogative to lie to their citizens. The state relies on the wisdom of its rulers; the role of the rest of the citizens is simply to obey: "no young man must consider which laws are right and which wrong: with one mouth and one voice they must all agree that the laws are all good" (*Laws* 633). What Plato seeks to avoid is change within the laws and constitution. He had seen Athens brought to disaster by changes in its constitution during the oligarchic revolution of 404 BCE; he comments unfavourably also on the actions of the restored democracy in changing laws and acting unjustly. Civil strife (*stasis*) was the besetting problem of the Greek polis in the 4th century BCE, and the *Laws* and *Republic* seem born out of this political turmoil. All his laws tend in this direction: the Athenian adviser in *Laws* (656) voices praise for the traditions of Egypt, where music and art have remained unchanged for thousands of years. The irony is that the ideal state can be attained only by the stifling of opposition or debate, and the demand for unquestioning obedience.

SIAN LEWIS

Writings

The Dialogues, translated by Benjamin Jowett, 4 vols, 1868–71; new edition, edited by D.J. Allan and H.E. Dale, 4 vols, 1953
Collected Dialogues, edited by Edith Hamilton and Huntington Cairns, 1961

Further Reading

Barrow, Robin, *Plato, Utilitarianism and Education*, London and Boston: Routledge, 1975
Fine, Gail (editor), *Plato 2: Ethics, Politics, Religion and the Soul*, Oxford: Oxford University Press, 1999
Levinson, Ronald Bartlett, *In Defense of Plato*, Cambridge, Massachusetts: Harvard University Press, 1953

Morrow, Glenn R., *Plato's Cretan City: A Historical Interpretation of the Laws*, Princeton, New Jersey: Princeton University Press, 1993

Murray, Penelope (editor), *Plato on Poetry*, Cambridge and New York: Cambridge University Press, 1995

Parker, Robert, *Athenian Religion: A History*, Oxford: Clarendon Press, and New York: Oxford University Press, 1996

Popper, K.R., *The Open Society and Its Enemies*, vol. 1, London: Routledge, 1945; revised edition Princeton, New Jersey: Princeton University Press, 1950

Saunders, T.J., "Plato's Later Political Thought" in *The Cambridge Companion to Plato*, edited by Richard Kraut, Cambridge and New York: Cambridge University Press, 1992

ANDREI PLATONOV

Russian novelist (real name: Andrei Platonovich Klimentov), 1899–1951

Before becoming a professional writer in 1927, Platonov had worked in civil engineering. Nevertheless, he had already developed a distinctive literary style, in which the social and political are entwined with, but ultimately subordinate to, ontological questions.

However, it was not this aspect of Platonov's work that first antagonized the literary authorities, but his satire on Soviet bureaucracy. An early short story cowritten with Boris Pil'niak and given the distinctive title "Che-Che-O" (1928; this is the Voronezh dialect pronunciation of the acronym for the Central Black-Earth Region), suggests that it is not the proletariat but the bureaucrats who are running things. Platonov was swiftly accused of falling under Pil'niak's influence, but in defending himself against criticism Platonov took full responsibility for the story.

In 1929 the printing of Platonov's only completed novel, *Chevengur*, was suddenly suspended, although it had already been typeset. No explanation was given and it was not until 1988 that it was published in the Soviet Union. One possible reason for the halting of publication was the hysterical atmosphere of the broader campaign against Pil'niak and those associated with him. The novel itself is a satire on utopianism, the story of how an attempt to build communism in one town leads to its destruction. It is written in Platonov's characteristic manner, suggestively ambivalent but apparently clumsy, which itself seems to suggest humanity's limitations. It was this style and the portrayal of revolutionaries as fools that caused Maksim Gor'kii, then one of the most influential writers in the country, to reject Platonov's appeals for help.

Platonov went on to intensify his satire on bureaucracy in another short story, "Usomnivshiisia Makar" (1929, Doubting Makar). It is the story of Makar, a peasant who comes to Moscow, in which the thwarting of his literal-mindedness and naive energies serves to show how bureaucratic Soviet society has become. However, the episode that shocked critics the most was a dream that Makar has in which he sees an inaccessible "scientific man" who can only think of the "overall picture" and not about "private Makar". The story was condemned by the influential Proletarian group of critics for its ambiguity in an age that demanded unequivocal allegiance.

Platonov's next story, *Kotlovan* (written 1929–30, The Foundation Pit), was probably written without any hope of publication, particularly in view of the climate created by the criticisms of "Doubting Makar". Probably as a consequence, Platonov's style is at its most oblique, and his representation of Soviet society and ideology is at its most pessimistic. The story recounts a worker's involvement in digging the foundations for a "common proletarian home". The plans for the final building become ever more fantastic and the foundation pit is dug ever deeper, yet the only part ever completed is the pit, which eventually serves as a grave. Collectivization is then represented as a series of senseless and cruel incidents, overseen by a terrified and confused "activist". The clichés of the Soviet construction novel are transformed into a grotesque parody and made to reveal the real destruction that they usually masked. *The Foundation Pit* is undoubtedly Platonov's masterpiece, and presents a damning fictional evocation of Soviet culture from a writer formed by and initially sympathetic to it. It has been available in the United States since 1973, but it was not published in the Soviet Union until 1987.

The story "Vprok" (1931, For Future Use: A Poor Peasant's Chronicle) was the work that provoked the fiercest criticism of Platonov. It was condemned in the government newspaper *Izvestiia* by A.A. Fadeev, the editor of *Krasnaia Nov'*, the journal in which it had appeared, as propaganda on behalf of the *kulaks* (the affluent peasants who were then the targets of state terror). Fadeev was probably attempting to vindicate himself and his journal in the eyes of Stalin, who had read and cursed the work. "For Future Use" was the result of a trip that Platonov made at the request of *Krasnaia Nov'* to survey the progress of collectivization. It is set in the immediate aftermath of Stalin's article, "Dizziness with Success", which was published in March 1930, and suggests that a *kulak* is virtually indistinguishable from a middle-ranking or poor peasant. This alone was enough to condemn the work, even though it also presents positive examples of well-functioning collective farms and makes concessions to the class war rhetoric with which the collectivization campaign was being conducted.

As a result of the criticism of this work, Platonov was unable to publish anything else until 1934, although he continued to write. He was now attempting to develop a style closer to the dominant norms of "socialist realism". During this period his rooms were searched by the security police, who confiscated the manuscript of *Tekhnicheskii roman* (The Technical Novel). A summary of this work was eventually discovered in the KGB archives during the glasnost era. Another unfinished novel, *Schastlivaia Moskva* (Happy Moscow), also dates from this period. Of the stories written but not published during these years of public silence, the more accomplished are "Iuvenil'noe more" (1934, The Sea of Youth), a story of socialist construction implicitly rather than explicitly doomed to failure, which was first published in the Soviet Union in 1986; and

"The Garbage Wind" (1934), which is about a German worker persecuted for his opposition to Hitler. This was not acceptable at the time because of its grotesque elements and the suspicion that Hitler was a cipher for Stalin; it was first published in 1966.

In 1934, Platonov participated in a writers brigade trip to Turkmenistan, as a result of which he wrote "Takyr", which did get into print. Throughout the late 1930s, Platonov worked as a literary consultant for various publications and continued to bring out work, particularly articles but also a trickle of stories. These are not as striking as his best, but they are often very good and stand out from much of the fiction of the period. Many of these stories were collected in *Reka Potudan'* (The Potudan River) in 1937, the year before Platonov's son was arrested and sent to the camps.

Platonov was able to publish more during World War II, as the climate of Soviet publishing became slightly less oppressive; he wrote a number of war stories, and also worked as a war correspondent. However, once Stalin had made Andrei Zhdanov his chief assistant on cultural matters Platonov again fell into disfavour. His story "Dre Kukli" (1948, Two Dolls) served as the pretext for attacks that reduced his remaining literary production to the retelling of folktales. In 1951, he died of tuberculosis, which he had caught from his son after the latter's return from the camps.

JEREMY HICKS

Writings

Kotlovan (written 1929–30), 1968; as *The Foundation Pit*, translated by Robert Chandler and Geoffrey Smith, 1996
Chevengur, 1989; as *Chevengur*, translated by Anthony Olcott, 1978
Collected Works, translated by Thomas P. Whitney *et al.*, 1978
Sobranie sochinenii (Collected Works), 3 vols, 1985
"Schastlivaia Moskva" (Happy Moscow), edited by M.V. Kornienko, *Novyi mir*, 9 (1991): 9–76
"The Technical Novel", translated by Geoffrey Smith, *Index on Censorship*, 20/8 (August–September 1991): 38–49, 58
Iuvenil'noe more, Kotlovan, Chevengur (The Sea of Youth; The Foundation Pit, Chevengur), 1995
The Portable Platonov, edited by Robert Chandler, 1999

Further Reading

Kornienko, N.V. and E.D. Shubina (editors), *Andrei Platonov: Mir tvorchestva* (Andrei Platonov: The Artistic World), Moscow: Sovremennyi pisatel', 1994
Kornienko, N.V. and E.D. Shubina (editors), *Andrei Platonov: Vospominaniia sovremmennikov: Materialy k biografii–Sbornik* (Andrei Platonov: Memoirs of His Contemporaries: Materials for a Biography–A Collection), Moscow: Sovremennyi pisatel', 1994
Seifrid, Thomas, *Andrei Platonov: Uncertainties of Spirit*, Cambridge and New York: Cambridge University Press, 1992
Shentalinsky, Vitaly, *The KGB's Literary Archive*, edited and translated by John Crowfoot, London: Harvill Press, 1995; as *Arrested Voices: Resurrecting the Disappeared Writers of the Soviet Regime*, New York: Free Press, 1996

PLAYBOY
International men's magazine, established 1953: banned in the Irish Republic (1959–95) and elsewhere

Playboy magazine has been one of the most controversial magazines of the 20th and early 21st centuries. With its mixture of nude pin-ups, slick journalism, serious fiction, and erotica, *Playboy* has repeatedly met with various forms of attempted or actual censorship, from action by vigilante groups to governmental bannings. In many countries, including the Irish Republic, it has served as a symbol of a corrupt, secular society posing a threat to "national morality".

Playboy was banned in the Irish Republic in 1959, and again in 1975, as "indecent or obscene" under the Censorship of Publications Act. It remained banned for 36 years, until Playboy Publications lodged a successful appeal in 1995. The Republic's Censorship Board was never required to provide a detailed explanation to the public for banning the magazine, but it was widely accepted that it was banned because of its erotica and nude centrefolds.

From the beginning of the Irish Free State (renamed the Irish Republic from 1949), many members of the country's Catholic majority were obsessed with national morality. This often took the form of targeting nudity. The poet and painter "AE" (George Russell), who edited the liberal journal *The Irish Statesman*, drew attention in 1928 to the way in which paintings and sculptures of nudes had been denounced, and the nude form was being unofficially banished from sight in a wave of fanaticism that operated in the name of "decency". By 1930,

all nudes had been removed from display in the Dublin Municipal Gallery, which was at the time Ireland's principal gallery of modern art.

A similar moral fervour was applied to the banning of British and US periodicals. Even before the original Censorship of Publications Act was passed, in 1929, British newspapers were being seized and burned by vigilantes who wished to block their importation into Ireland because of their discussion of divorce cases. In the 1930s, certain British newspapers, including *Thomson's Weekly News* and the *News of the World*, were banned, along with detective and confession magazines, such as *Real Detective* and *True Confessions*. In the 1950s, the focus expanded to include men's magazines, such as *Esquire*. Bans on other periodicals followed, including the *National Enquirer*, *Playgirl*, *Penthouse*, and *Hustler*. Recently, the focus has shifted to banning hard-core pornographic periodicals.

In theory, the banning of *Playboy* should have created debate about the challenge that the magazine presented to the Irish Republic's censorship legislation. At the very least, it should have drawn attention to the requirement that the Censorship Board consider the literary and artistic merits of a publication. In addition, it should have drawn attention to the vagueness of the definitions in the Censorship of Publications Act, in which "indecent" is defined "as including suggestive of, or inciting to sexual immorality or unnatural vice or likely in any other similar way to corrupt or deprave", and no definition is provided of "obscene". In practice, the moral consensus with regard to the threat presented by erotica and female nudity precluded a public challenge to the banning of the magazine.

The lifting of the ban on *Playboy* in 1995 occurred as a direct result of an appeal made to the Irish Censorship of Publications Appeal Board by Playboy Publications. An earlier appeal had been rejected in 1973. These appeals were notable because the mechanism had rarely been employed by those empowered to use it: authors, editors, publishers, and members of the Irish Parliament. A notable exception was Mitchell Beazley International, which in 1989 successfully appealed against the banning of Alex Comfort's book *The Joy of Sex*. As a result of the lifting of the ban on *Playboy*, other publishers began to lodge appeals and in 1998 Lancaster Publications successfully appealed against the banning of *Penthouse*.

The basis for the revocation of the ban on *Playboy* was that the magazine was readily available throughout member states of the European Union and of the Organization for Economic Cooperation and Development, while its website was accessible on the internet. The Irish Republic and Turkey were the only European countries where it remained officially prohibited. It was acknowledged that similar material was presented in a wide range of other readily available media, from tabloid newspapers to films and television programmes. In broader terms, the revocation reflected the rapid technological and social changes that Irish society was undergoing. In 1995 the country was preparing for its second constitutional referendum on divorce, which led to its legalization, and the obsession with national morality that lay behind the ban no longer had the support of the majority of Irish people.

The lifting of the ban on *Playboy* came at such a late stage in the Irish Republic's development away from a strict Catholic morality that it met with widespread approval and a striking absence of debate. The repeal of the ban was not used, as the rebanning of *The Joy of Sex* had been in 1987, as an occasion to promote censorship reform. Instead, organizations such as the Irish Council for Civil Liberties simply declared that the ban had been "silly".

The only serious commentary on the lifting of the ban on *Playboy* came from feminists. Olive Braiden of the Irish Rape Crisis Centre argued that the magazine portrays "fantasy nudes":

It objectifies women and portrays them as sexual objects. There is no research to show that it leads to violence but research does show [that] men think of women as objects, and [that it] leads men to thinking they are powerful and can have power over women.

The columnist Nuala O'Faolain observed that the unbanning of *Playboy* showed that the Irish Republic was joining the sexual consumer market: "the Republic of Ireland has signed up like the dutiful little consumer market it is for the Disneyfication of sexual arousal".

The threat that *Playboy* was perceived to pose in Ireland is now replicated in many countries where there is either a communist government or a dominant Muslim population. The magazine is currently not available, for example, in the People's Republic of China, Arab countries, India, Malaysia, Singapore, and Indonesia. It was also not available in the Soviet Union up to its collapse in 1991.

JULIA CARLSON

Further Reading

Magee, Audrey, "*Playboy* Arrives, Ending 36-year Ban in Republic", *The Irish Times* (27 September 1995)

O'Faolain, Nuala, "Sexual Impulse Wasted on *Playboy*", *The Irish Times* (9 October 1995)

Russell, George, "The Censorship Bill", *The Irish Statesman*, 10 (1928): 486–87; reprinted in *Banned in Ireland: Censorship and the Irish Writer*, edited by Julia Carlson, London: Routledge, and Athens: University of Georgia Press, 1990

JURIS PODNIEKS
Latvian filmmaker, 1950–1992

Juris Podnieks, one of Europe's greatest documentary filmmakers, was renowned for the observational insight of his films and his poetic use of images. His documentaries provide precious glimpses of the complexities and contradictions that racked the peoples of the former Soviet Union from the late 1970s to the early 1990s. The fact that he was able to make his films more or less in his own way, and often with the unwitting approval of the state, shows that it was possible for filmmakers to work within the limits set by Soviet censorship by using the traditions of propaganda, following the examples of such eminent predecessors as Sergei Eisenstein or Dziga Vertov.

Podnieks studied at the Soviet Film School, VGIK, in the 1970s. VGIK was renowned for its strong tradition of telling stories and conveying messages in films through a subtle and powerful use of imagery. On his graduation in 1975, Podnieks gained a reputation as a cameraman before starting to direct films in 1979. With the eye of an artist and a talent for engaging with people, Podnieks started to make subtle films that questioned the times he was living through and the role of the state. He first received wide recognition inside the Soviet Union for *Constellation of Riflemen* (1982), a film that looks at the Soviet army through the memories of old Latvian guards who had served in it.

International success came with the pioneering and timely *Vaivegli but jaunam?* (1986, Is It Easy to Be Young?), a film that exploded many official myths about Soviet youth by allowing young people to speak in their own words. Such a film would have been disallowed from the start in almost any earlier decade, but with the state itself promoting glasnost ("openness") Podnieks could more easily justify what he was doing to the censors and the studio bosses. The film pulled in extraordinarily high audiences when it was shown in cinemas throughout the Soviet Union. Thousands queued for tickets in sub-zero temperatures.

PODNIEKS: Scene from the documentary *Hello, Do You Hear Us?* (1990) depicting the Chernobyl disaster. Podnieks had gained access to the inside of the nuclear power plant. This scene in particular shows "the last pictures of the 4th reactor ... Afterwards it was filled and enclosed with concrete."

On a visit to Moscow as Controller of Features for the British company Central Independent Television, I became one of the first westerners to see *Is It Easy to Be Young?* I immediately commissioned Podnieks to produce a series of five hour-long documentaries, which was broadcast in Britain on Channel 4 and ITV in 1990 as *Hello, Do You Hear Us?* This series is likely to remain a seminal document for understanding the final years of the Soviet Union. Podnieks included all the major events of the period in these films, but it is the testimonies of individuals, from the Baltic provinces to Central Asia, that provide the most effective, eloquent accounts of human struggle. The struggles that Podnieks had in realizing these films were considerable. It was through a combination of shrewdness and guile, with a determination that it is always possible to get things done – it is always possible to be creative – that he managed to make the series under the noses of the censors, and indeed, astonishingly, with the full backing of the State Ministry for Cinematography (Goskino).

One example of creativity in the face of censorship came early in the production of the series. His determination to film the outbreak of fighting in Armenia brought us face to face with a potentially ruinous situation. We had been warned by a Goskino official that, if Podnieks went to Armenia to film, he would never be able to travel abroad again and I too would be banned from the USSR. There was to be "no coverage of the conflict". Podnieks travelled with me to Yalta to meet a deputy minister of Goskino. Together, we persuaded him that it was important that future historians should know what was happening. Censorship was subverted when the official agreed that Podnieks should "film the conflict for the state archives".

I was travelling to the Soviet Union a lot in those days, being keen to start up the Soviet–British Creative Association (SBCA), which was eventually established in 1989. The Soviet participants included Goskino and *Ogonek*, a radical magazine based in Moscow. The SBCA was unprecedented and, potentially, highly disturbing. These were chaotic times for the Soviet Union. No one knew quite what was happening. However, association with this small joint venture allowed Podnieks to film without major scrutiny. He used this smokescreen to the full in realizing *Hello, Do You Hear Us?*, opening the Latvian branch of the SBCA, which enabled him to draw on the authority of Goskino for access to highly sensitive locations. These included Unit 4 at Chernobyl, which he filmed minutes before it was turned into a sarcophagus. He also recorded an interview with Andrei Sakharov, the great dissident scientist, shortly after his release from detention, and another with Boris Yeltsin just after he had been removed from the Central Committee of the Communist Party by Mikhail Gorbachev.

After 1991, Podnieks became increasingly involved in documenting the struggle of the Baltic peoples to regain their independence. His film on the subject, *Kalvarii* (known in English as *Homeland*), was broadcast on Channel 4 in 1991. In January 1991, an attempt to repress this movement led to violence in Vilnius and Riga. While Podnieks and his team were filming in Riga his cameramen, Andris Slapins and Gvido Zvaigzne, were shot dead by troops. Their deaths were captured on film and shown in *Postscript* (1991). Podnieks held Andris Slapins in his arms as he died and then, at the cameraman's insistence, filmed his death. "He looked for the truth with the help of the camera. That was our only weapon", said Podnieks.

Podnieks's own career was cut short in its prime when he was drowned in a Latvian lake in June 1992. Podnieks, who said he never made films, but filmed life, was shooting *Unfinished Business* when he died.

RICHARD CREASEY

Films

Cradle, 1977
Brothers Kokari, 1978
Boys, to the Horses!, 1979
The White "Ave Sol", 1979
Under the Sign of Sagittarius, 1982
Commander, 1984

Sisyphus is Rolling the Stone, 1985
Vaivegli but jaunam? (Is It Easy to Be Young?), 1986
Hello, Do You Hear Us?, 1990
Kalvarii (Homeland), 1991
Homeland: Postscript, 1991
End of Empire, 1991
Moments of Silence, 1992

PODZEMNÍ UNIVERZITA (Underground University)
Resistance to censorship, Czechoslovakia, 1975–89

The concept of the "underground university" (also known as bytové semíndři or "home seminars") in Czechoslovakia developed from the private study groups that were organized by teachers expelled from the universities after the hard-line communist regime took power in 1948. During the 1950s, they tried (in circumscribed conditions of time and resources) to continue with their vocation: the study of their subject and the sharing of it with their students. Among them was the philosopher Jan Patočka. These early seminars, for friends who knew each other well, did not attract the attention of the authorities.

Under the more liberal regime of the mid-1960s, some teachers returned to the universities. However, in spring 1970 the purges began again. They were far more widespread than in earlier years, being extended to formerly committed communists, who were expelled from public life for their role in the reforms of the Prague Spring of 1968. There was also closer surveillance on the part of the authorities, who tried to extinguish all memory of 1968. This may have been the reason for greater thoroughness in the purges, in comparison with (for example) those in Poland and Romania, where most subjects were still taught in the universities. In spite (or because) of this, underground seminar activity was greater than before, and in many cases students registered at university still attended their former tutors' seminars as well as their official courses. However, the movement was fragmented; students were loyal to their own teachers, old rivalries survived, and for a long time the separate groups had little to do with each other.

In 1975 a new type of seminar began, led by Milan Machovec, a former communist and former philosophy professor at the Charles University, and his student Julius Tomin. This was open to anyone, essentially meaning those who found themselves outside the system, for the discussion of any topic on which someone was prepared to speak. This seminar contributed toward the ideas later incorporated into Charter 77.

The development of the underground university is inseparable from the development of the Charter. One led to the other, and the second validated and supported the first. Following the death, after police interrogation, of Patočka, the Chartists reviewed the concept of the home seminars. A major concern was the education of the children of dissident families, who, whatever their ability, were mostly forced to leave school at the age of 15 and take manual jobs. Some Chartists envisaged a structure (to be called the "Patočka University") within which young people would receive the basis of a full university education. Others feared that in the repressive conditions prevailing in Czechoslovakia this concept was potentially dangerous, as the setting up of an alternative organization was not the same as the right to free association.

The first of the new *teaching* seminars, as opposed to study and discussion groups, was on the history of philosophy, and took place in September 1977. It was led by Machovec and Tomin. However, other seminars still met, including one on a variety of philosophical topics at the home of the mathematician-philosopher Ivan Havel, brother of the future president Václav Havel. After harassment of the new seminar by the secret police, Machovec withdrew and for the next three years the seminar was led by Tomin, who worked with the students on texts by Plato and Aristotle. The seminar attracted some students from the Technical University, stimulated, like the dissidents' children, by Tomin's method of exposition, which was both lively and learned. In 1979, these Technical University students were expelled from their official courses.

In May 1978, Tomin took a new and decisive step in the development of the underground university by writing to invite teachers from four western universities. A positive response was received from philosophers at just one of these, Oxford, and the first Oxford visitor, Dr Kathy Wilkes, arrived in Prague in April 1979, creating a stir in dissident circles. Wilkes was impressed by the quality and enthusiasm of the students, for whom philosophy was a burning question of "how to live in this world of communism and lies". As a result, she founded the Jan Hus Educational Foundation; this foundation and the French Association Jan Hus, established later, were the only western organizations specifically committed to the support of the underground university in Czechoslovakia. Nevertheless, increasing numbers of western lecturers came by other routes, most notably Dutch Catholic theologians.

After Tomin's emigration in 1980, his philosophy seminar was taken over by Ladislav Hejdánek, while other important seminars continued to run on different subjects, such as political science or the concept of central Europe. One problem with teaching the students was always the shortage of literature, which the western visitors did their best to alleviate with donations of books and the support of *samizdat* publication. Another innovation was the introduction of courses essentially identical to western university courses, on, for example, Kant, Aristotle, and analytical philosophy, for which visiting teachers gave intensive teaching at approximately monthly intervals. In this way, the Jan Hus Educational Foundation initiated the teaching of the Cambridge diploma, believed to be the only case in which students of the underground university sat for outside examinations.

Police harassment was not uncommon, usually of such open seminars as those held by Tomin and Hejdánek. Use was made of the 48-hour detention law, both to prevent seminars being held and to deter students from future attendance. Among notorious events were the deportations of Anthony Kenny, master of Balliol College, Oxford, and the French philosopher Jacques Derrida. Seminar leaders recognized that there were likely to be police informers among their students, but maintained their stance that the discussion of philosophy, even in the presence of a foreigner, was not against the law.

Although there were cases in which students travelled to Prague to attend home seminars, seminars were also held in other cities. Brno, the capital of Moravia, was an important centre, being largely free from the rivalry prevalent in Prague. Through unified planning, the seminars were gradually incorporated into a network of semiofficial activities that also included exhibitions, performances, and festivals.

The underground university did not take root in Slovakia in the same way as in the Czech lands; conditions there were freer in many respects, and there were fewer dissident families. When, in 1986, a seminar was formed at the Bratislava home of the future prime minister Ján Čarnogurský, it was subjected to considerable police harassment.

In the last two years of the regime, seminar activity in the Czech lands increased considerably, and overflowed into some official institutions. A large part of the political, educational, and cultural leadership that emerged after the "Velvet Revolution" of 1989 owed its training in one form or another to the underground university.

BARBARA DAY

Further Reading

Day, Barbara, *The Velvet Philosophies*, London: Claridge Press, 1999

JORGE POLACO
Argentine film director, 1946–

KINDERGARTEN
Film, 1989

With the restoration of democracy in Argentina in 1983, censorship laws were repealed. Film production soared and directors were free to explore the horrors of the silent years (1976–83) of military dictatorship. Jorge Polaco's *Kindergarten*, however, was banned, unbanned, and banned again on numerous occasions over seven years, the only Argentine film of this period to be subjected to such treatment.

All of Polaco's films explore the dark side of sexuality, madness, and death. The plot of *Kindergarten* revolves around a teacher, Graciela (Graciela Borges), her new husband, Arturo (Arturo Puig), Arturo's young son, Luciano, who attends Graciela's class, and various other family members. It is a highly disturbing film in which the characters are haunted by the past (Arturo's dead wife; Graciela's dead father who is embalmed in a wheelchair), and consider suicide (Luciano, Graciela). Luciano is unhappy living with his stepmother and is constantly harassed by her. Graciela is tyrannized by the memory of her dead father and is depressed because she cannot bear children.

Moral critics took particular exception to scenes in which Graciela and Arturo make love in close proximity to minors, Graciela takes a bath with a child, and children between the ages of five and seven are shown naked. Catholic representatives on the Film Ratings Board denounced it for corruption of minors, indecent exposure, and "flagrant sexuality". Arguing that some limits to freedom were necessary in Argentina's newly restored democracy, the Prosecutor Jorge Vengara wrote, "Polaco has created an excess of obscenity and thus has taken advantage of the diminishing moral forces in our society during these last five years".

The film was first confiscated from the office of the producer, Argentina Sono Film, on 16 August 1989. It was returned after a few hours because definitive grounds for its permanent confiscation could not be found. In June 1990 a judge ruled in favour of its exhibition, but a month later, after a petition had been brought before the court, he overturned the ruling and banned the film. Polaco, the producer Salvador D'Antonio, the two main actors, and the parents of the child actors were each fined US$100,000.

Three years later, in 1993, the same judge lifted the ban on the grounds that a public screening would not now "personally endanger the mental health of the child actors". There was a further appeal by a juvenile court official, who petitioned "in defence of minors". The case was transferred to the civil court, which decided that the film could be shown as long as the "erotic scenes with minors" were omitted. The producers appealed, but the civil court confirmed its decision. Finally, in 1996, the ban was again overturned and the fines suspended.

Debates centred on the moral obligations of the parents of the child actors and on whether the state had the right to regulate moral standards. It was concluded that "parents had the right to guide and educate their children" and that "one dogma or religious doctrine could not determine the social mores of a society".

Some critics have considered that *Kindergarten* contains allegorical references to the terror of the dictatorship, such as the omnipresence of death and psychological trauma. Others have noted that "Polaco's films put traditional family values in crisis" because personal relationships "are the site where authoritarianism is located, such as between parents and children and between couples".

Despite the lifting of the ban, Polaco and his producer have decided not to release the film. He has said, "This film has made me suffer a lot, because it demonstrates that censorship still exists within art and society as a whole. Everything indicates that those who think are transgressors. This leads one to think that a cinema of authors [*cine de autor*] has almost disappeared" (*La Nacion*, 5 August 1995).

TAMARA L. FALICOV

Further Reading

España, Claudio (editor), *Cine argentino en democracia, 1983–1993*, Buenos Aires: Fondo Nacional de las Artes, 1994

Peña, Fernando Martín and Paula Félix-Didier, "Censura argentina, rigor cientifico" in *Film* (November 1997)

Torrents, Nissa, "Contemporary Argentine Cinema" in *The Garden of Forking Paths: Argentine Cinema*, by John King and Nissa Torrents, London: British Film Institute, 1988

POLAND

Population: 38,605,000	**Number of daily newspapers:** 55
Main religions: Roman Catholic; Eastern Orthodox; Protestant	**Number of periodicals:** 32
Official language: Polish	**Number of radio receivers per 1000 inhabitants:** 522
Other languages spoken: German	**Number of TV receivers per 1000 inhabitants:** 337
Illiteracy rate (%): 0.3 (m); 0.3 (f)	**Number of PCs per 1000 inhabitants:** 43.9

For much of its history Poland enjoyed the reputation of being, in Janusz Tazbir's phrase, "a state without stakes" – a realm in which neither people nor books were burned on the orders either of the secular government or of church authorities. Even before its dynastic union with Lithuania in 1386 (which led on to the Union of Lublin between the two countries, in 1569), Poland was a multiethnic state, whose rulers tended to respect religious and cultural diversity. Germans played a key role in developing towns in the Middle Ages; Armenians and Tatars were resident in the kingdom from at least the 15th century; the expansion of the kingdom eastwards under Casimir (Kazimierz) the Great (1333–70), during the 1340s, 1350s, and 1360s brought Orthodox dioceses into its orbit; and Jews from all over Europe, actively encouraged by Polish kings, sought refuge in Poland from the end of the 13th century. The pre-eminence of the Catholic Church in religious life did not equate with iron control over other faiths or the ruthless elimination of dissenting views.

Traditionally, the Cracow printer Szwajpolt Fiol has been seen as the first victim of censorship in the Polish lands. His printing of four books in Cyrillic script for the Orthodox Church in 1491, containing hymns, prayers, and psalms for religious services, appears to have been less important than some off-the-cuff heretical comments he was alleged to have made. Although the Catholic Church prohibited the distribution of these volumes and banned the printing of books in Cyrillic script, they continued to circulate in the eastern lands of the kingdom of Poland.

Around 50 years before the arrival of printing in Poland (1473), close historical links with Bohemia had exposed the kingdom to Hussite influences. Before the refoundation of the University of Cracow in 1400, Polish scholars were often educated, and went on to teach, at the Charles University in Prague. After the Council of Constance, Mikołaj Trąba, archbishop of Poznań, proscribed Hussitism and its works in his *Statuty* (1420). In 1424, king Ladislas Jagellon (Władysław Jagiełło, 1386–1434) reinforced the ban with his Edict of Wieluń, although this did not prevent him from undertaking a military operation with Prokop the Great against their common enemy, the Teutonic Knights, in 1432. The crushing of a Polish Hussite rebellion led by Spytek of Mełsztyń, Castellan of Bełz, in 1439

failed to extirpate the "contagion". Around 1449, Andrzej Gałka, sometime rector of the Jagiellonian University and author of the *Song on Wyclif*, faced charges of being a Hussite and fled to Silesia. Those persecuted for Hussitism may have seen their books burned, but they usually did not follow them to the stake, and compared to other European states Poland was remarkably lenient in its treatment of heretics.

The first expurgated book seems to have been Maciej Miechowita's *Chronica Polonorum* (1519), the earliest printed history of Poland. Sensing a potentially large audience for the work, its printer, Hieronim Wietor, sought to gain exclusive publication rights for six years while the book was still being printed. However, the Royal Chancellor, Jan Łaski, ordered the book's confiscation on the grounds of offence to the ruling dynasty, its government and other distinguished personages, and the Polish nation. The Senate questioned the doubts expressed in the book about the legitimacy of Jagiełło's sons by his fourth wife, Zofia, who was nearly 50 years younger. Criticism of the reigns of the two previous kings and the offence to the chancellor's own vanity caused by the book's diminution of his role in events led to the removal of several pages and a rewriting intended to enhance Łaski's reputation. Thus revised, the work appeared in 1521.

The Reformation and the Counter-Reformation, 1520–1795

Institutionalized controls commenced around this time in response to pope Leo X's bull *Exurge Domine* (1520). Sigismund (Zygmunt) I's Edict of Toruń (24 July 1520), which was re-issued several times, condemned Luther's writings, forbidding their importation, reading, and sale. This was followed by the burning of Luther's works in German and Latin at Toruń on 1 April 1521 – an action that proved extremely unpopular with the inhabitants. From the outset, the penalties for possession of Luther's works were severe, entailing confiscation of property and banishment; but in subsequent edicts, which extended the ban to works by Luther's followers, possession and printing could be punishable by death.

Sigismund's Edict of 1523 set up due process for the printing of works in Poland: the rector of Cracow University was to inspect every book before it was printed and distributed.

This privilege was confirmed in 1540, when a four-man committee was established at the university to deal with censorship. The Edict of 1523 signalled the introduction of both preventative and repressive censorship, and booksellers' and printers' premises were searched for heretical works.

As part of his general drive against Lutheranism, in 1522 Sigismund instructed the municipal council of Gdańsk not to disseminate works containing the new religious doctrines. In 1526, the council rose up in protest and declared Lutheranism to be the official religion of their city. Sigismund quickly put down the revolt, hanged the ringleaders, and restored Catholicism. In 1534 and 1540, young Poles were banned from going to study at German universities and from importing Lutheran works. In 1543, under pressure from the nobility, who zealously protected their rights, these restrictions were relaxed to allow travel to foreign universities if studies there did not contravene the Catholic Church's teachings. Nevertheless, as a face-saving formula for the king, the ban on the importation of books and any religious "novelties" remained in force. Although no "heretical" work was printed in Cracow in the first half of the 16th century, such works undoubtedly circulated illegally.

The accession of Sigismund Augustus (Zygmunt August, 1548–72) brought a significant relaxation in official repression of Protestantism. On the one hand, he confirmed the Catholic church's primacy in Polish life with an Edict issued in December 1550 against heresy, and another, issued in March 1556, that made the possession of "heretical" (no longer just Lutheran) works a crime – in whose pursuit the secular authorities should aid the church. On the other hand, Sigismund Augustus adopted very much a noninterventionist stance in matters of faith. He famously declared that he was "King of the people, not of their consciences", and he owned a substantial library of "heretical" works, often dedicated to him by their authors. In one famous case, he felt moved to protect the reformer Andrzej Frycz Modrzewski (1503–72) from persecution. Modrzewski's magnum opus, *De republica emendanda* (1551, On the Reform of the Republic), had earlier fallen foul of the ecclesiastical authorities in Poland. The author and the printer sought official opinion concerning the fourth book of the five originally to be published, which was devoted to the church. Printing was suspended while this fourth book was in the press and never completed. No action was taken against either man, but the work was not published in its entirety until 1554, and then in Basel (a second edition was published there in 1559). The fifth book, on schooling, was published with the first three in a Polish translation in Łosk (1577), but the book on the church never appeared in Poland–Lithuania. It has been suggested, however, that this was because events had made Modrzewski's proposals anachronistic, rather than because of censorship.

Calvinism found more followers in Poland–Lithuania than Lutheranism, perhaps owing to the greater compatibility of its partly democratic structures with the Polish nobility's political aspirations, and also because it was not a "German" faith. From the early 1550s, the nobility began to expel Catholic priests from their estates, refuse the payment of tithes, and set up Calvinist churches and presses. The first Calvinist synod took place in 1554, and the nobility's autonomy from the Catholic Church was officially confirmed at a session of the

Sejm (the legislature) of 1562–63, when they overthrew ecclesiastical jurisdiction. At the height of its popularity, around 20 per cent of the lesser nobility professed Calvinism, while among the lay magnates in the Senate there was an absolute majority. Religious equality for dissidents was definitively enshrined in the Act of Confederacy of Warsaw, passed by the Sejm in January 1573. This embodied a list of conditions, drawn up by the nobility for the first elected King of Poland and Grand Duke of Lithuania, Henri Valois (Henryk Walezy), which each subsequent ruler had to swear to observe at his coronation. Among many other provisions, these forbade mistreatment of "dissenters" (non-Catholics) on religious grounds, whether through violence, confiscation of property, imprisonment or banishment. Although books were not specified in the document, it later served as a basis for challenging censorship.

The one group explicitly excluded from the terms of the Act of Confederacy were Arians or Socinians, whose radical views, especially their rejection of the Trinity, had led them to break away from the Calvinists by the mid-1560s. After establishing a headquarters at Raków in 1569, under the protection of the magnate Michał Sienicki, they began to print protocommunist, pacifist, and dissident theological texts, including several versions of the Racovian Catechism (1575, 1601, 1605), which made their way, and were suppressed, all across Europe. The Arians were isolated even among their fellow Protestants. In 1595, the Synod of Toruń, intended to reconcile Calvinists, Czech Brethren (Hussites), and Lutherans, published a ban on accepting or reading any Arian works, and in January 1602, the Lutheran municipal council of Toruń banned the importation or sale of such works in the city. For their part, the Arians readily printed works by Catholics and Protestants alike, and reserved censorship largely for their own books, with the aim of preserving their own doctrinal purity. Their Synod of Lublin in 1579 decreed that no book should be published without preventative censorship, but Lithuanian delegates refused to accept this stipulation and acted as though it did not apply. One of the key figures of the less radical wing, Szymon Budny, who opposed the pacifist stance adopted by the Arians in Poland, published Jacob Palaeologus's attack on excessive radicalism, *Defensio verae sententiae de magistratu politico* (Defence of the True Understanding of Political Magistracy), at Łosk in 1580, in express defiance of such restrictions. In the more repressive times of the 16th century, which saw the closure of their centres at Nowogródek in Lithuania (now Novogrudok in Belarus) by royal decree (1618) and at Raków (1638) by order of the Sejm, Arians practised self-restraint, taking great pains to avoid antagonizing their religious opponents. Finally, in 1658, using their participation on the Swedish side during the invasion of 1654 as a pretext – a charge that applied equally well to the Calvinists, but they were not pursued – the monarch John Casimir (Jan Kazimierz, 1648–68) banned them from Polish territory.

The Bohemian Brethren, who started to arrive in Poland from 1550 and set up a centre at Leszno, proved even more cautious than the Arians. Their publishing house, established in 1631, was destroyed during the Swedish War in 1656, allegedly for printing a eulogy to the Swedish king, Charles Gustavus, written by Comenius.

The Act of Confederacy also covered the Orthodox Church, but, in effect, they merely confirmed the liberties that this church had enjoyed from the mid-15th century, when Władysław Warneńczyk granted the Privilege of Buda (1443) to Orthodox clergy in Hungary and Poland. In so doing, Warneńczyk had acknowledged the complete equality of the Orthodox with the Catholic rite, and also prohibited secular intervention in Orthodox jurisdiction. This position altered after 1596, when the Union of Brest formalized the schism developing within the church between those Orthodox who continued to acknowledge Constantinople and those, known as the Uniates, who transferred their allegiance to the pope. The Orthodox Church was thus disestablished and was not recognized again until 1633. This opened the way to censorship of Orthodox works, on the grounds that they posed a threat to the political system through their attacks on the Union of Brest, which they regarded as schismatic. In May 1610, Sigismund (Zygmunt) III banned the reading and distribution of books printed in Russian at the Russian printworks in Wilno (Vilnius), after the publication of Melecjusz Smotrycki's *Threnos*. This work's description of contemporary events, specifically the Union of Brest, caused it to be seen as presenting a challenge to ecclesiastical and secular authority. However, it was not until the Synod of Zamość, in 1720, that censorship in the Uniate community came to be regulated and unified. In 1640, by contrast, the Metropolitan of Kiev, who saw Uniate publications as heretical, provided direction for Orthodox censorship. By the 18th century, when Poland had fallen largely under Russian control, the defence of Orthodox religious rights provided an excuse for Russian intervention on a constitutional basis. The "Eternal" Treaty between Poland–Lithuania and Russia (1769) accorded responsibility for the protection of Greek Orthodox and dissident rights to the Russian empress, Catherine II.

In some respects, Jews found themselves in a position similar to that of the Uniates. They received privileges directly from the monarch, and, like the nobility, enjoyed considerable autonomy, which was crowned by the creation of their own separate governing body, the Vaad Arba Aratzot or Council of the Four Lands (c.1560–1764). The Jews sought state intervention in matters of religious dissent, as well as protection from anti-Semitic attacks. The *kahal* (Jewish commune) requested the prohibition of Sebastian Miczyński's *Mirror of the Polish Crown Expressing the Profound Insults and Great Anxieties that It Receives from the Jews* (1618), claiming that it incited public disorder. In 1628, however, Sigismund III issued a decree banning the publication and sale of Hebrew books, which caused the Jewish community to plead with the bishop of Cracow, Marcin Szyszkowski, to persuade the king to reverse his decision. In 1757, the burning of 1000 copies of the Talmud was ordered by the bishop of Kamieniec Podolski (Kamenets Podolskiy in Ukraine), who saw an opportunity to win converts to Catholicism from the Frankist controversy (over a movement proclaiming the validity of Catholic teaching on the Trinity and the errors of the Talmud). In 1758, the *kahal* successfully appealed to the monarch to restore order.

Concern for public order in respect of the defence of the realm lay behind some of the pronouncements made by Stephen (Stefan) Bathory (who reigned from 1575 to 1586) on the control of books and information. In July 1579, during his campaign against Ivan IV ("the Terrible"), tsar of Muscovy, he issued a ban on divulging military secrets, on pain of death.

In February 1580, he ordered printers and booksellers to ensure that history books, whether old or new, should honour Poland's good name, an order specifically aimed at counteracting the propaganda of the Habsburgs, who were allied with Ivan. Bathory even displayed a proactive information policy, by travelling with his own printer, who published not only royal edicts, but also descriptions of events and literary works in praise of Bathory, and his chancellor, Jan Zamoyski, written by the great Renaissance poet Jan Kochanowski.

Bathory was probably the last monarch to respect the Act of Confederacy fully, in letter and in spirit. Although Catholic attacks on their opponents were still taken seriously towards the end of the 16th century, if they were considered a threat to public order, the accession of the Swedish Catholic Sigismund (Zygmunt) III (1587–1632) saw the pendulum swing firmly back towards the Counter-Reformation. The Vatican's *Index Librorum Prohibitorum* (Index of Prohibited Books) was published for the first time in 1603 and rapidly went through a number of reprints, until the most extensive version appeared in 1617, with a list appended by bishop Szyszkowski devoted to works that he regarded as harmful to the church, indecent or libellous. Polish works banned under its terms included the Calvinist version of the Bible, published under the patronage of Mikołaj Radziwiłł in Brest in 1563; Kasper Twardowski's book of erotic verse, *Lekcje Kupidynowe* (Cupid's Lessons); and the *Postylla* of the great Calvinist writer Mikołaj Rej. In 1634, Cardinal Wężyk condemned the Gdańsk Bible (1632), the final revised version of the Radziwiłł Bible of 1563. Modrzewski came under proscription, as did Arian or Socinian works. Other categories of harmful works included the "Sowiźdrzał" (Eulenspiegel or Owlglass) genre of satires on the social order, written largely anonymously by university students throughout the 15th and early 16th centuries. In addition to the Indexes, papal nuncios provided guidance to the Curia. Given the multidenominational character of the country, the Catholicization of the whole of Poland–Lithuania was seen as a long-term project, as a Vatican instruction from December 1622 indicates (as cited in Buchwald-Pelcowa 1997: 204):

> Since in a country where Catholics may associate with heretics there can be no complete prohibition of reading evil books that may pollute the minds of Catholics, we must at least strive to ensure that such works are not printed or imported from other lands; and if they do come covertly, to ensure that they are not sold by having the King impose severe penalties . . . and so please remind the Lord Bishops that they are to carry out their duties in this regard, taking the Index as their guide and from time to time ordering searches of bookshops.

From the latter half of the 17th century, synods and pastoral letters became the most common channels for informing the laity of banned works. The bloodshed characteristic of the Counter-Reformation elsewhere in Europe was unknown to Poland–Lithuania, partly because of the country's renowned tradition of tolerance, but also because there was a gradual return by many Protestant noble families to the Catholic Church, a process that was undoubtedly facilitated by the marked preference displayed by Sigismund III and later monarchs for appointing only Catholics to senior positions.

In the first half of the 17th century the Catholic Church in Poland–Lithuania began to take a more vigorous approach to censorship. The Synod of Cracow (1621) condemned not only books, but also licentious and backward works of art. Bishop Szyszkowski strongly recommended the clothing of indecent (naked) portrayals of Adam and Eve and, especially, Mary Magdalene. His instructions were also applied to portrayals of the Virgin Mary, who appears fully clothed in Baroque art. The immodesty of figures of Adam and Eve on royal tapestries was also covered at this time. In 1632, the clergy introduced a clause enshrining respect for the rights of the Catholic Church. The Synod of Warsaw, convened under bishop Łubieński in 1643, consolidated preventative censorship in Poland by banning anonymous works on any subject, along with anti-Catholic and immoral works. Catholic bigotry reached its height in the first half of the 18th century. The Synod of Poznań (1720) codified heresy in all its forms, and the laws to be employed against it. In 1731, Jan Andrzej Załuski's tract *The Two Swords* whipped up Catholic antipathy towards non-Catholics, which went hand in hand with demands for ecclesiastical intrusion into individuals' choice of private reading matter. An Edict limiting the rights of non-Catholics was passed by the Sejm in 1717, and the expulsion of the last Protestant member of that body – the Calvinist Andrzej Piotrowski – soon followed in 1718. These events gave Poland–Lithuania's neighbours the pretexts they needed to justify their intervention in the country's affairs in the name of defending civil liberties against the country's own decision-makers.

The Baroque, particularly after the mid-17th century, is often referred to as the "age of manuscript", since major works frequently did not reach the press and often were not published until the 19th century. The greater restrictions imposed by the ecclesiastical authorities were only one of the factors responsible. In the aftermath of the Swedish War (1654–60), which devastated the country, publishing practice underwent a major change: the financial risks printing entailed meant that even magnates preferred to pay copyists than fund expensive editions. This encouraged authors and printers to seek the censors' approval, with increasing frequency after 1618, to avoid additional expense. Moreover, nobles preferred to sponsor three-dimensional works of art instead of literature as lasting monuments to themselves, except where the literary work magnified the clan's glory. Printworks belonging to collectives, and increasingly to religious groups, began to prevail over private printers. Varieties of self-censorship also played a part in authors' decisions to leave their works in manuscript, be it on grounds of personal taste – overlapping to a large degree with the readers' – or for the sake of their own political careers. The greatest writer of the age, Jan Andrzej Morsztyn (1620–93), who had written most of his works before becoming Crown Treasurer in 1661, let them circulate in manuscript rather than risk any publication damaging to his career. He was merely following in the footsteps of famous predecessors such as Andrzej Krzycki, the Renaissance bishop of Cracow and later cardinal, whose poems portraying various figures from his time at the court of Sigismund I remained unpublished. Readers themselves expurgated works: Catholics removed whole sections from the posthumous enlarged second edition (1574) of Mikołaj Rej's *Bestiary* in view of the offence to their religious sensibilities.

Defamation provided grounds for intervention in texts. Mikołaj Rej's epigram *Quarrel with a Neighbour*, the neighbour being a powerful magnate, was removed from the *Bestiary*. Foreign protests about works exported from Poland–Lithuania occasionally produced equally decisive action. James VI of Scotland and I of England sent his ambassador, John Dickenson, to demand the burning of Kasper Cichocki's polemic against non-Catholics, *Alloquiorum Oscensium sive variorum familiarium sermonum libri V* (1615, "Osiek Conversations"), and penalties for the author and printer, for comparing him to Nero and Julian the Apostate, and challenging his right to the throne. The author's natural death in 1616 brought the matter to a close. The tsar's emissaries were even more demanding: Muscovite ambassadors to Poland–Lithuania were required to study all works for unflattering comments or defamatory attacks on Muscovy, especially works relating to military campaigns. When the military situation lay in Muscovy's favour, these requests received greater sympathy. Grigorii Gavrilovich Pushkin required John Casimir's condemnation of Samuel Twardowski's *Władysław IV, Król Polski i Szwedzki* (Leszno, 1649, 1650, Ladislas V, King of Poland and Sweden), a book about John Casimir's brother and predecessor, who had once been a pretender to the throne of Muscovy, and several pages were burned in public, to considerable indignation among many Poles. In 1672, Muscovite complaints – this time ineffectual – extended to two ceilings decorated by Tomasso Donabella in the Senators' Chamber of the Royal Castle in Warsaw, which depicted the Polish–Lithuanian victory over Muscovite forces at Kłuszyn (Klushino) in 1610 and Stanisław Żółkiewski's presentation of the captured tsar and his brothers to Sigismund III at the Sejm in 1611.

Especially in the late 18th century, however, writers and publishers in Poland–Lithuania exhibited great caution regarding works that were potentially offensive to more powerful neighbours. In 1770, a reissue of Andrzej Frycz Modrzewski's *De republica emendanda . . .* omitted a passage dealing with 16th-century Prussia for fear of antagonizing Frederick II. Similarly, in 1788, Marshal Mniszek suspended publication of Jan Potocki's pamphlet *Essai de logique* (Essay on Logic) for 24 hours, since the monarch Stanislas Augustus Poniatowski thought that it might jeopardize relations with Russia. Although Potocki protested that he bore all responsibility, since his name appeared on the cover, he acceded to the work's withdrawal.

In the absence of any legislation specifically designed to curtail censorship, Poland–Lithuania's decentralized political system protected authors. The strong class unity that prevailed among the nobility, cutting across religious dividing lines, helped to offset the increasing stringency of ecclesiastical control. The condemnation of the expurgated version of Wespazjan Kochowski's *Nieprózujące próznowanie* (1674, Non-Idle Idleness) by Andrzej Trzebicki, bishop of Cracow, which stemmed from a power struggle between the Catholic Church and the Jagiellonian University over primacy in censorship matters, did not result in punitive action against the author, who had received the backing of the Sejm.

Another counterweight to the inexorable advance of the Counter-Reformation lay in the privileges granted to royal towns such as Gdańsk and Toruń, which continued to enjoy considerable autonomy. Their municipal councils, dominated by Lutherans, managed the local book culture by granting licences to printers and booksellers, as well as through specific interventions. There had been considerable freedom for publishers in Gdańsk until 1570, when the council introduced greater regulation in response to constant protests from various quarters – including English monarchs, the Elector of Prussia, and the Polish crown – about libellous works. Subsequently, repression of the works of other Protestant denominations came to be a regular occurrence. In July 1615, a magistrate banned all the works of the Calvinist Fabricius and, in 1645, an ordinance prohibited the printing of Mennonite and Socinian literature. As the Counter-Reformation gained ground, a ban on works attacking Catholicism appeared in the 1630s. Szymon Reiniger, the only Catholic printer permitted to operate in the city, gained the right to do so in 1662, but only after a lengthy struggle, and on condition that he published nothing hostile to Lutheranism. The Jesuits, however, were prevented from opening printworks in Gdańsk.

Like Gdańsk, Toruń had received a royal privilege from Sigismund Augustus in 1558, which enabled the Lutheran Church to enjoy religious liberties. Its city council was more overt in its hostility to Catholic works, banning "anything papist" in June 1601. Its manifest hostility towards other Protestants led it to obstruct the sale of Calvin's *De sacramentis* (On the Sacraments) in the 1620s. All mention of the Tumult of 1724 (the religious riots that culminated in the execution of 17 Protestants and the banishment of others, and subsquently blackened Poland's name across Europe) was banned in the city. Similarly, in private towns such as Leszno, or on the estates of Janusz Radziwiłł the Black, which were both Calvinist centres, the religious faith of the owner dictated publishing practice.

Commercial rivalry among publishers and booksellers also played its part in acts of repression, especially over the right to print profitable almanacs, the nobility's favourite reading matter. In 1617, rivals of the bookseller Jan Kownacki of Lublin, who had promised to convert to Catholicism and not to sell heretical works when granted the right to open his shop, instigated an action to have his privilege revoked on the pretext that he had failed to comply. Sigismund III confirmed the removal of his rights in 1618. Similar intentions lay behind calls to limit the number of printworks during the following century. In 1725, the firms of Kownacki and Różycki pleaded for such "regulation" in Warsaw, and in June 1789 the printer and publisher Pierre Dufour presented a memorandum to the Sejm on the management of printworks in the kingdom, arguing the same case.

The Jesuits, who had arrived in Poland in 1564, played a major role in church censorship, helping bishops to censor works and collaborating with them to defend their own reputation from attack. They also supervised book-burning, as in 1611, when the death of the local Calvinist protector led to the destruction of the press and the burning of heretical works in Kamieniec Podolski. Works written in Polish, and therefore comprehensible to wider circles of readers, constituted the Jesuits' main target. Yet, at the same time, they assisted the preservation of such books by assiduously amassing them in their libraries. At the time of the order's dissolution in 1773, 1,963 of the 9,952 volumes in the library of the Wilno Academy were heretical works.

The exercise of preventative censorship remained with the church. The secular authorities, in principle, operated only repressive censorship up to the 1790s, and after the 17th century monarchs issued fewer decrees on matters relating to books. Under the last monarch, Stanislas Augustus (Stanisław Poniatowski, who reigned from 1764 to 1795), the situation improved dramatically. Printing, the book trade, and the circulation of foreign works within Poland–Lithuania all increased considerably during his reign, and the massive growth in secular presses and publishing houses made the implementation of ecclesiastical censorship increasingly difficult. Stanislas Augustus's reform-minded regime largely restored the responsibility for censorship to municipal authorities alone. Wherever the monarch was in residence, the Grand Marshal of the Crown carried out chiefly repressive censorship with a view to preserving public order and peace.

The church none the less attempted to remove certain books. In 1776, the bishop of Płock published pope Pius VI's list of 34 works that Catholics should not read and several years later ordered the confiscation of 20 copies of a Polish version of John Locke's *Logic* (published in 1784 by the press of the Principal Royal School in Cracow) from schools in Pułtusk. The bulk of secular repressions concerned libel. In 1770, the publication in the leading journal, the *Monitor* (founded by the monarch five years earlier), of a satire on one of the leading opposition figures associated with the conservative nobility's revolt – the confederacy of Bar (1768–72) – led the grand marshal to make an example of the publisher Mitzler de Kolof with a fine and prison sentence. A later lampoon in a similar vein, *Polish Letters* (written in 1785), written under the pseudonym "Jan Wit", was impounded by the Grand Marshal's court and ordered to be burned in Warsaw on 15 March 1785. Where the authors or printers could not be punished, as in the case of the charges of corruption made by the *Gazette d'Utrecht* in June 1768 against the Royal Treasury Commission, the journal itself was destroyed.

The publication of the Cardinal Laws on 7 January 1791, which formed the basis of the liberal Constitution of 3 May that year, established freedom of speech in the modern sense. Paragraph XI extended freedom of expression to every citizen in printed and manuscript works. It marked the abolition of preventative censorship and the institution of a system of repressive censorship based on post-publication prosecution in the law courts in matters offensive to persons or religion.

The promulgation of the Constitution led to a conservative, Russian-backed revolt, launched at the Ukrainian town of Targowica. Its ultimate success saw the legal position revert to the position prevailing before 1791. The new conservative regime restored preventative censorship on 17 September 1792, requiring all manuscripts for approval prior to printing. The publication of a pamphlet, *Exposition*, by the French Ambassador to Poland, dealing with recent events in revolutionary France, provided the immediate pretext for instituting such controls. In November 1792, a ban on the importation of the *Parisian Monitor* followed, reflecting fear that news of the events in France might have a destabilizing effect. Freedom of speech continued to be observed during sessions of the Sejm – a considerable achievement considering the scale of Russian interference in political life – but this did not apply to print or writing. In pursuit of seditious works, a printer's fonts could be confiscated if an author's identity could not be discovered.

Other than the press, theatrical works caused the greatest concern to the authorities. In January 1793, for example, a production of Friedrich von Schiller's radical drama *Die Räuber* (1781, *The Robbers*) was banned. Polish plays were also stringently treated whenever they attempted to address the national crisis: Wojciech Bogusławski, the director of the National Theatre in Warsaw, was compelled to halt a production of his own play, *The Presumed Miracle; or, Cracovians and Highlanders* (1794), after just a few performances in March 1794, following "patriotic" demonstrations by members of the audience.

Poland partitioned, 1795–1918

The third and final partition of 1795 brought Poland–Lithuania under the almost uninterrupted rule of Austria, Prussia, and Russia for the next 123 years. Russian censorship had the deepest and most long-lasting effects. As Ryszard Nycz notes (in the article cited below), these entailed preventative censorship as a basic principle, but incorporated elements of repressive and (in practice) prescriptive censorship. A crucial distinction between Russian censorship and that practised in Prussia and Austria resided in its primarily extralegal, arbitrary character, and the general absence of any right to contest censorship decisions. The Russian authorities established multifarious bodies to control all aspects of literary, scientific, and artistic activity, from the moment of entrusting censorship to universities in the empire in July 1804.

Until the national insurrection of 1830, the local Polish authorities in the Russian-occupied lands performed a decisive and usually conservative role in controlling publications. Certain kinds of activity were excluded from the outset. In May 1817, for example, prince Adam Jerzy Czartoryski, the university "curator", declined to censor Yiddish newspapers for want of suitable experts, which served as a pretext for disallowing them altogether.

In the Kingdom of Poland established under emperor Alexander I by the Congress of Vienna in 1815, the emperor's adviser Nikolai Novosiltsov prevented draft bills defining and regulating censorship on the basis of the constitution from ever reaching the statute books. Control of publication fell under the remit of three separate bodies: the Government Commission for Religion and Education, the Commission for Internal Affairs and Police, and provincial commissions. However, it was the Polish viceroy, general Józef Zajączek, who first tightened the screw in May 1819, in an attempt to snuff out newspaper protests at Russian abuses.

From the start of the 1820s, Alexander I moved to more restrictive controls, establishing a central censorship committee to implement preventative press supervision, which gradually came to supervise all areas of publishing. Polish deputies in the legislature of the "Kingdom" strongly resisted the new legislation, but were outflanked by an official clampdown initiated in December 1821, which enforced pre-censorship and the confiscation of imported journals. Provisions for theatre censorship were issued in April 1821, bolstered in the 1830s by instructions as to precisely which Polish plays could be performed. From the latter half of the 1820s, reports on the proceedings of the legislature were prohibited. These developments culminated in Nicholas I's meticulously detailed, though never implemented, 230-article bill of 1826. However, despite the formal separation of control in the rest of the Russian empire from that in the "Kingdom", the Ministry of Education in St Petersburg provided lists of *prohibita* to guide the Polish censors. Historical works bore the brunt of these restrictions, which censored references to Poland's past, including the Constitution of 1791 and Tadeusz Kościuszko's uprising of 1794, as well as the works of French Enlightenment writers. The Polish insurrectionaries abolished the censorship committee as contrary to the constitution in December 1830.

When prince Ivan Paskievich restored Russian dominion in September 1831, preventative censorship returned in full force. The censorship committee established in February 1832 operated according to *ad hoc* instructions and directives issued by the supreme authorities. The post office and the customs service were enlisted to prevent the importation of forbidden works. The ensuing ban of 7 December 1832 on the direct importation of all foreign newspapers and periodicals, regardless of whether they were currently banned in the Kingdom, initiated a series of increasingly restrictive measures designed to isolate the Poles from subversive foreign influences. Every work imported from abroad, or else intended for publication, performance or presentation in the Kingdom, had henceforth to receive the censor's imprimatur before it could appear.

The rigors of censorship were eased after the death of Nicholas I (in 1855), so that Adam Mickiewicz's works, for instance, could appear for the first time since the 1830s. However, the uprising of January 1863 provoked more draconian measures. In its aftermath, the Russians reduced the Kingdom to a province, removed Poles from the administration, and banned Polish as a language of instruction in schools. These provisions were intended to destroy the Poles' sense of national identity, and the memory of ever having had an independent state. Censors rigorously eliminated the terms "Polish" and "Poland" from journalistic and literary works, replacing them by "domestic" (*krajowy*) or "our"; during periods of intensive repression, the term "fatherland" proved impermissible. Terms designating national dress and traditions disappeared from print, and Russian censors habitually degraded the Kings of Poland and Grand Dukes of Lithuania to the unspecific status of "prince". Polish writers responded by obliterating the Russian presence in their depictions of contemporary life, a practice that the National Democrat Roman Dmowski, who sought an accommodation with the Russians, criticized in Władysław Reymont's *Promised Land* (1899). Writers transmitted patriotic content to their readers by means of Aesopian language, or indirect expression in the form of allegory, symbols or ambiguous plots. It was, in effect, what Eliza Orzeszkowa termed a "prison language" in a letter to Malwina Blumberg, her translator, in 1887: "no date, nothing concerning the national struggle and suffering is given by name . . . And yet we understand each other – my reader and I – perfectly." This strategy produced some ingenious solutions. Walery Przyborowski cast his treatment of the uprising of 1863 as a historical novel, *Phantoms* (1902), set in medieval Spain, disguising Warsaw as Bilbao, changing Cracow Suburbs (a main street in Warsaw) to Madrid Suburbs, and presenting the leader of the uprising, Stanisław Traugutt, as Bona Fide. Over time, the circumlocutions dictated by the censors were transformed into badges of pride. Polish writers deliberately employed the term "our" in order to exclude others – understood as Russians,

Prussians or Austrians – from Polish discourse, thus subverting the censors' restrictions on political messages. References to "storms" or "ashes" signified the uprising; since exile to Siberia, the common punishment for participation in the uprising, could not be mentioned, the use of Russian constructions in letters or descriptions trailing away into dots, for instance, implied the character's fate – encouraging the reader to provide the missing information about historical or political events.

To some extent, the Russian censors, and those in the parts of Poland controlled by Austria and Prussia, tolerated such strategies, particularly if the work was intended for a narrow elite readership or the device was fairly opaque, and, occasionally, if a bribe was involved. Publications for the masses were invariably subject to tighter controls. The Aesopian strategy was in itself problematic, since editors and authors attempting to avoid the censor's response functioned as their own censors. Jerzy Pietrkiewicz has pointed out another pernicious dimension of self-censorship in 19th-century Polish literature, namely that it imposed on writers an overriding concern with the national cause – the failure to address which became synonymous with disloyalty.

In Prussia, Frederick Wilhelm II's edict of December 1788 had introduced preventative censorship, stipulating that all publications required prior approval from the pertinent administrative authorities. In the first decade after partition, Prussian attention focused on reportage of Napoleon's campaigns and specifically the creation of a Polish Legion in Italy under general Dąbrowski in 1797. The only permissible information related to lists of Polish casualties on San Domingo – an attempt to cast Napoleon in a bad light in Polish eyes. To counter this, Warsaw newspapers circulated handwritten reports of Napoleon's campaigns, which were complemented by secret patriotic meetings. At the Congress of Vienna in 1815, Pomerania and the province of Poznań (Posen to its increasingly numerous German inhabitants) were returned to Prussia, and were made subject to Frederick Wilhelm III's law of 18 October 1819, which re-established preventative censorship. Polish publishing in the 1820s and 1830s was limited to official announcements and regulations, and some modest religious works. After the defeat of the uprising in 1830, most of the major Polish writers went into exile, and an amendment of February 1834, devised to counteract conspiratorial activity, forbade the distribution of imported Polish works without the prior written agreement of the Oberzensurkollegium (the Higher Censorship Commission) in Berlin.

At the start of the 1840s, the more liberal regime of Frederick William IV affected publishing too. He set up an independent body to consider appeals against censorship decisions in the form of the Oberzensurengericht (Higher Censorship Court), which was subordinate to the Ministry of Justice (23 February 1843). The increasingly active Polish underground conspiracy led to more stringent censorship in 1845, when a complete ban on works likely to foment sedition, as well as those critical of Austrian and Russian policies on Poland, was instituted.

Throughout the "Springtime of the Nations" – the months in 1848–49 when most of Europe was swept by national uprisings – Prussian censorship practically ceased to function, and Polish publishing accordingly flourished. The first new Polish newspapers since 1795 began to appear. The resultant new liberal Constitution of January 1850 abolished preventative

censorship in principle, but the Prussian police harassed the Polish-language press, regarding its espousal of patriotic sentiments as subversive. The Press Law of 5 June 1850 allowed the suppression of both German and Polish oppositionist papers, as contributing to public disorder and hostility to the constitution and the king. Eventually, through the rescinding of this law in October 1858 and the promulgation of the new German imperial Press Code of 7 May 1874, repressive censorship came to be established as a principle, offering the possibility of challenging decisions in the courts.

Despite these increasingly liberal provisions, Polish publications continued to be regarded as subversive by the administrative authorities. Patriotic works, especially collections of hymns and songs (Alojzy Feliński's "Boże, coś Polskę" (O God Who through the Ages), Józef Wybicki's "Marsz Dąbrowskiego (The Dąbrowski March), and the "Varsovienne", which functioned as national anthems) found themselves on lists of prohibited works, and Polish works constituted a major part of those pursued by the police. References to the state that had existed before 1795 and to past Polish military glories – above all, the victory over the Teutonic Knights at Grunwald in 1410 – caused the Prussians to treat historical works with extreme suspicion. Works advancing the Poles' rights to their own state automatically amounted to sedition as defined by paragraph 85 of the penal code. Printers, editors, and journals were therefore under close police invigilation, yet devised ways of circumventing official restrictions. Typographers and publishers gave very low figures for print runs, meaning that by the time a court's verdict had been announced, a significant part of the edition had already reached the public, as in the case of the book *The Celebration of the 400th Anniversary of Copernicus's Birth in Toruń* (1873), which used Copernicus as a symbol of the indestructible vitality of the Polish spirit.

Prussia's creation of the German Empire (1871) could hardly be expected to lead to any significant relaxation of the repression, although the presence of Polish deputies in the new Reichstag at least allowed some issues to be raised and protested against. Catholic priests were specially targeted in the *Kulturkampf* ("cultural struggle") launched by Bismarck's government, and many were removed from teaching posts in 1872. After 1876, Polish as a school subject was restricted to the last three years of tuition. Ultimately, however, the assault on Polish culture had directly the opposite effect to that intended, serving to reinforce the Poles' sense of national difference and defiance within the Prussian state and the empire that it dominated.

Austrian attempts at Germanizing their Polish subjects generally proved halfhearted and shortlived. Instead, at least at times, the Habsburgs preferred to encourage ethnic discord between Poles and Ukrainians in their portion of the former Poland–Lithuania – known as Galicia – as the chief component of a policy of "divide and rule". The Poles' first experience of Austrian censorship had come even before the final partition, in the days of Maria Theresa, whose Court Chancellery in Vienna demanded the prompt despatch of 35 copies of every work published in Galicia as of 1776. Preventative censorship began with the instructions issued by her son Joseph II's Studien Commission in January 1790, stipulating that manuscripts be submitted for its approval before publication. Galicia and Cracow, which became a free city in 1815, were the main crossing points for Poles smuggling seditious literature into the

Russian-controlled "Kingdom". Invariably, individuals who gained official permission to publish Polish books engaged in some form of clandestine activity. In 1831, Konstanty Słotwiński became director of the Ossolineum Institute (founded 1827) in Lwów (or Lemberg; now L'viv in Ukraine). A year later, he set up a printing press and lithograph on which he printed 27 illegal works, including Adam Mickiewicz's patriotic *Księgi narodu i pielgrzymstwa polskiego* (Books of the Polish Nation and Pilgrimage) and revolutionary manuals. As was common practice, the provision of false places of publication or the absence of such information was designed to mislead the censors and the police. Arrested in 1833, Słotwiński was released after completing an eight-year sentence in the Tyrolean fortress of Kufstein, only to perish in the Austrian-sponsored *jacquerie* of 1846.

The Springtime of the Nations saw the introduction of more liberal policies, but Galicia began to enjoy true autonomous status only in the wake of the *Ausgleich*, the reform of 1867 that transformed the Habsburg lands into the Austro-Hungarian Empire, with separate administrations for the Hungarian-controlled and Austrian-controlled halves of the realm. Article 19 of the Fundamental Laws implemented in December 1867 guaranteed the nations of the empire the right to free development. Subsequent Polish pressure on the government in Vienna brought further concessions, specifically the raising of Polish to equality with German as a language of administration (1869), and the reinstatement of Polish as the principal language of instruction at the revitalized Jagiellonian University in Cracow (1870). In 1872, the Polish Academy of Learning (PAU), the forerunner of the Polish Academy of Sciences, was founded in Lwów. Poles received other concessions, in the form of permission to hold patriotic demonstrations, albeit, in the case of the most significant, such as the celebrations of the tercentenary of the Union of Lublin in Lwów in 1869, under duress.

From 1867, conditions in Galicia proved most conducive to the development of Polish culture. Exceptionally in the occupied Polish lands, émigré Romantic classics gradually reached the stage here, with the Stary Theatre in Cracow staging many of the premieres. In Lwów, the Viceroy allowed a performance of extracts (including the prison scenes, though without references to Russian cruelty towards the Poles) from Adam Mickiewicz's *Dziady* (Forefathers), part 3, in 1889, while Juliusz Słowacki's *Kordian* (1834), which depicted a conspiracy to assassinate Nicholas I in Warsaw, was permitted to be staged only in 1897. The Austrian regime was predicated upon the principle of loyalism and the censors in Lwów, who were often Polish, duly excised passages or banned plays containing anything that might inflame relations with Vienna or allied powers. In November 1870, the director of police prohibited the staging of the first version of Władysław Ludwik Anczyc's *Kościuszko at Racławice*, later to become the most popular patriotic play, because of its condemnation of the partitions and its expression of Polish revanchism. It was performed for the first time, in a considerably altered version, ten years later in Cracow, following a personal intervention by Stanisław Koźmian, director of the Stary Theatre, with the Viceroy's office, but at the cost of the complete removal of the derogatory term "Moskal" ("Muscovite"). The partition of what had been Poland–Lithuania remained the political status quo, which had to be

accepted by Poles, and any blame had to be sought in defects of the Polish character. Attacks on the Triple Alliance (1872–87) were thus restricted to fairly gentle allusions, especially where they concerned Prussia. An anti-Prussian historical play such as Lucjan Rydel's *Prisoners*, which was banned in Cracow and Lwów in 1902, could be performed later (1908) following the replacement of the Polish word for "German" throughout by an archaic term equivalent to our "Teuton", or the less specific "enemy". In the main, Austria–Hungary's competition with Russia in the Balkans allowed Polish authors slightly greater room for manoeuvre, and this carried over into translations of Russian classics that showed the full degradation of human beings under the autocracy, which were passed uncut.

The depiction of internal Galician affairs caused the censors' intervention when it was deemed likely to exacerbate Polish–Ukrainian relations. Włodzimierz Lewicki's *Wernyhora* was passed for performance in Lwów in 1894 after the removal of many passages addressing injustices committed by the Polish nobility against the Ukrainians and calls for Ukrainian national liberation. Plays with anti-Semitic or Zionist messages, as well as works endorsing proletarian revolution (particularly after 1905), were similarly prohibited because of fears for public order.

Liberalism, authoritarianism, and occupation, 1918–45

Immediately upon liberation in November 1918, preventative censorship was abolished in Poland. The registration of press titles replaced the licence system that had obtained under the partitioning powers. Repressive censorship had to be instigated through the courts by the public prosecutor, often at the behest of the Interior Ministry. Issues inspiring such motions included attacks on the government and perceived threats to public order or Poland's territorial integrity. The state of emergency prevailing over large sections of Polish territory, due to the numerous wars waged by Poland during the first few years of independence, led to the "temporary" suspension of democratic freedoms for long periods. The war against Soviet Russia launched in 1920 brought the introduction of preventative censorship in defence of military secrets. Vocal support by the communists and sections of the Jewish press for the Bolshevik cause led to their suppression, and in later years the authorities applied restrictive measures against Ukrainian and Belarusian separatist movements.

Press legislation in interwar Poland initially displayed great liberalism. The Constitution of March 1921 provided for a variety of liberties along the most democratic lines. Article 104 acknowledged the individual's right to free expression of his thoughts and convictions in any manner he saw fit as long as it did not infringe the rule of law, while Article 105 rejected both preventative censorship and any form of licensing for the press. The full implementation of these articles was dependent on the promulgation of further acts, which did not occur, therefore making mere desiderata of some of the guarantees of basic liberties. Until the coup that ended unfettered democracy in Poland in May 1926, more repressive moves foundered on the rapid changes of government, and the overturning of stringent legislation meant a return to the frequently more liberal provisions of Prussian and Austrian press laws from the previous century. Bills that had been vigorously supported by the right-wing National Democrats to suppress the left before 1926 were later used against their own publications.

After 1926 and the installation of the Sanacja governments, official thinking became increasingly authoritarian. The unified Press Law of 8 June 1927 provided for the use of economic sanctions to curtail press independence, a method that was adopted increasingly by the authorities during the 1930s. Although censorship applications still had to be referred to the courts case by case, measures were taken to reduce the independence of the judiciary, resulting in the abrogation of the irremovability of judges in 1932. The Constitution of 1935 no longer mentioned press liberties, while the Press Law of 21 November 1938 restricted *inter alia* the number of people who could become editors, formalized newspapers' obligations to publish official communiqués (or "corrections"), and increased the fines to be paid for violations.

The authorities also took a more proactive stance towards the press. During the election campaign of 1927–28, the Interior Ministry directed huge funds to the purchase of existing press titles (guaranteeing favourable coverage for the regime by directly appointing editors), setting up new papers or buying oppositionist papers' quiescence for the duration. The National Democrat (ND) organ in Lwów, *Słowo Polskie*, was taken over by young ND activists in December 1927 with 120,000 zlotys received from the Ministry's coffers. The regime also coerced editors to print favourable stories and even instructed pro-government newspapers on a daily basis about what they should print. Public institutions associated with the Sanacja government, such as the army, could wield massive influence through mass subscriptions to papers and journals. The political elite and their associates also strove to dominate the distribution network. On 6 March 1928, the Ministry of Communications signed an agreement with Ruch, the association of railway station bookshops, to exclude publications of a left-wing nature from its kiosks. In December 1935, it enabled Ruch to consolidate its position by granting it a *de facto* monopoly on distribution from the capital into the provinces. Despite this, the system of control was in no way as rigorous and complete as that of the totalitarian systems that followed. The nonpolitical press in particular enjoyed substantial freedom from interference, while even the most heavily censored papers continued to appear regardless of their political line towards the regime.

Authors were censored broadly along the lines established for the press: left-leaning writers suffered greater repression than supporters of the regime. Under the terms of the Press Agreement signed secretly with Nazi Germany in February 1934, works critical of Hitler and other leading Nazis were removed, and Hitler's *Mein Kampf* was allowed to circulate. The Catholic Church occasionally supported repressive measures against specific individuals and works that allegedly offended religious sentiment and public decency. The expressionist novels of Emil Zegadłowicz (1888–1941), which contain numerous graphic descriptions of sexual activity and scenes mocking Christian practices, fell prey to official sanctions. The second edition of his novel *Ghosts* (1935) was confiscated by the authorities and officially condemned by archbishop Sapieha of Cracow. The offending parts were removed from the third edition, but the original version was reprinted only in 1957. Zegadłowicz's *Motors*, published privately in October 1937

apparently by a nonexistent firm, Sirinx, was confiscated on the orders of the Grodsk district governor's office a month later. The ban affected both the text and the fairly graphic accompanying illustrations, which were not republished until 1981. Probably the most outstanding literary work banned during this period was a poem by Julian Tuwim (1894–1953), *Bal w operze* (1936, Ball at the Opera), an expressionist and apocalyptic vision of Poland studded with expletives, mockery of the military elite, and descriptions of decadent social excess, which was published for the first time in 1946.

While interwar literature sometimes radically challenged readers, interwar films rather pandered to viewers' tastes. Although the state showed no interest in developing a national film industry, it was very concerned to control films themselves in view of their impact upon the national imagination. For much of the interwar period, foreign films dominated the screen, and only by the late 1930s did domestic output exceed imports. Like the press, interwar cinema and theatrical productions came under the jurisdiction of the Interior Ministry. The Decree on Public Performances of 7 February 1919 introduced preventative censorship in respect of

> the showing of words or images [that are] (a) pornographic in content or generally offensive to morality or contrary to the law; (b) criminal in content, if the ways and means used to commit crimes are shown.

Around this time bans were imposed on displaying the insignia and uniforms of the modern Polish army. Before staging or distribution, theatres and cinemas had to demonstrate to the police that works were devoid of any such content. Having received the censor's warrant, any discrepancy between the content described and the actual performance could lead to prosecution. Officials in the Interior Ministry's press department thus functioned as the closest Poland then had to controllers of the mass imagination. The Instruction for Cinematographic Censors of 25 May 1920 provided far greater detail, banning the exhibition of scenes and images

> contrary to the law or public morality, especially: (1) scenes offensive to religious sensibilities; (2) images of saints, objects of religious cult in inappropriate locations (cemeteries and graves may be shown as long as the scene does not offend religious sensibilities); (3) the exhumation of corpses; (4) scenes offensive to Polish national sentiments; (5) scenes offensive to decency; (6) images based on the squalor of existence; (7) brutal murder scenes; (8) scenes showing torture, or the carrying out of death sentences; (9) detective and criminal images intending to give a showcase demonstration or incitement to commit various crimes; (10) images of a nihilistic or corrupting nature.

The revised law of February 1934 introduced no essential changes to these categories, but refined distribution procedures: cinematic works likely to offend the sensibilities of the minorities were often given restricted distribution. Imponderable criteria such as "taste" or "the public interest" caused censors to mangle foreign films, such as Luis Buñuel's *Tierra sin Pan* (1932) or Josef von Sternberg's *Morocco* (1930), which was never shown in its entirety. The most palpable consequence of film censorship was to encourage filmmakers and studios to develop pre-emptive strategies, watering down the literary originals in line with current tastes. Henryk Szaro's adaptation of Stefan Żeromski's *The History of Sin* (1933) updated the story of an adulterous affair and unwanted pregnancy to contemporary Poland, but softened scenes such as the killing of a baby.

Cinemas continued to survive under the German occupation that started in 1939, although the repertoire was changed to reflect Nazi policy. German films and weekly newsreels were shown, as well as a number of Polish films, including several begun before the outbreak of war, which the German Film and Propaganda Distributing Society completed, or works not previously shown. In 1941 Polish films formed 20 per cent of the repertoire, due to the receipts they brought in, a part of which went towards the German war effort. Cinemas themselves had been taken out of Polish hands and were managed by the German authorities. The underground resistance, the Home Army, attempted to disrupt performances, but without success. In line with Nazi policy in other spheres, an intention to "dumb down" audiences was evident through an emphasis on farce and comedy in the "homegrown" programmes.

After September 1939, the Nazis attempted the systematic destruction of Polish national identity. They razed statues honouring great Polish figures or marking famous victories in Polish history, plundered libraries and museums, and decimated the intelligentsia. At school, Polish children received only a very rudimentary education, encompassing basic reading and mathematical skills: the emphasis fell on a technical education fitting Poles for their role as a manual labour force. National holidays were banned, prewar history and geography textbooks were removed, and the teaching of Polish literature was proscribed. Anti-Bolshevik primers, such as *Ster* (The Rudder), which stressed the need for German–Polish collaboration, began to appear from 1940, and became a compulsory part of the syllabus. Although they included extracts from Polish classics – limited mainly to descriptions of nature, the seasons, and animal life – the emphasis fell upon the promotion of work as the key value in life. The Nazis' universal contempt for things Polish, which disqualified the Poles as potential collaborators, saved the populace from indoctrination, and, unlike the Soviets, the Nazis did not move to nationalize all commercial activity, which allowed a certain space to public life. Illegal publishing – which produced important works by Czesław Miłosz and Jerzy Andrzejewski – and secondhand bookshops helped to maintain the continuity of Polish culture, but the setting up of four underground universities, whose degrees were recognized after the war, served perhaps as the major symbol of cultural resistance.

Communist and postcommunist Poland, since 1945

Soviet control, established by the annexation of eastern Poland after 17 September 1939, displayed even greater rigidity than the Nazi occupation did. The Soviet authorities' contempt for Poles – universally termed "lords and masters" in Bolshevik propaganda – initially rivalled the Nazis': their policy instrumentalized Polish culture, determining that only those elements that could be adapted for the dissemination of socialist values would survive. The city of Lwów, which then had a large Polish population, served as a preliminary test site for the postwar experiment in manipulating Polish culture. School textbooks incorporated extracts from classic Polish literature that either implicitly criticized capitalist class relations or ostensibly promoted the propaganda ideals of Polish–Russian (and thus Polish–Soviet) friendship and cooperation. The revaluation of Adam Mickiewicz's work occupied a central place in this longterm strategy: the selective promotion and tacit censorship of parts of his oeuvre diminished its anti-Russian impact, which had sustained the Poles under oppression in the previous century. The marking of the 85th anniversary of Mickiewicz's death in Lwów in November 1940, and the broadcasting of the events into German-occupied Poland, then experiencing the Nazis' acts of cultural devastation, presented Soviet rule as intrinsically more benign and "cultured". Sovietization was therefore intended to penetrate Polish consciousness far more profoundly than Nazism.

After the creation of the Soviet-backed Lublin government in July 1944, the communists – formally, the Polish (or, after 1948, United) Workers' Party – moved quickly to control key areas of cultural activity. Legislation failed to keep pace with communist appropriation of such key activities as the regulation of paper production and the film industry. In December 1944, the government announced that attempts to circumvent or obstruct the application of prewar legislation requiring owners and producers of paper supplies to present personal and legal documentation would be punishable by death – a provision that remained in force until 1946. A regulatory body, the Central Bureau for Managing Printed Paper Supplies, was set up in the communist-dominated Ministry of Information and Propaganda in June 1945. After this ministry's abolition in April 1947, a body attached to the cabinet office took over its role, before the responsibility passed to the Ministry of Culture. The Sejm ratified the existence of Film Polski, set up in July 1945, only in January 1946. Control of these sectors represented merely the first stage of tightening communist control on cultural activity. Over the next five years, the party-state's gradual accumulation of printworks, enforcement of publishing plans, and development of absolute control over the whole film production process – from financing to distribution – came to determine in every respect the products made available to the public.

The misleading official division of publishing houses into state, collective, and private (church and, usually, surviving prewar publishers) began to be eroded from 1946. "Economic" arguments – "rationalization" and the democratization of access to culture through the decommercialization of publishing activity – gradually eliminated most private publishers from the market. A series of government decrees passed in 1949 introduced licensing for all firms seeking to publish books and non-periodicals (September), restricted publishing rights to enterprises subordinate to the state administration (November), and finally created a central distribution network, Dom Książki, in January 1950. This left the question of the availability of books solely to the state budget and storeroom capacity. The Ministry of Culture had by this time assumed responsibility for the shape of the annual publishing plan, which had to be supplied by publishers in advance, and its allocation of the film budget and paper supplies made it the technical censor of Polish culture. The net result was to make artistic production completely independent of audiences' preferences, which aided the subordination of culture to the communists' ideological programme. In July 1950, the Ruch conglomerate established a near-monopoly over the collection of subscriptions and distribution of periodical publications.

Institutional censorship entered postwar Poland with the Soviet Army. Usually women censors vetted soldiers' letters home for the disclosure of military secrets (the separate status of military censorship continued at least into the 1970s). At the end of 1944, two employees of Glavlit (the Soviet state censorship body) were delegated to the Workers' Party to help to set up a centralized office, which became known in July 1946 as the Main Office for Control of the Press, Publications, and Public Performances (GUKP). Hitherto "elementalness", an impromptu and inconsistent censorship, had operated as various agencies – the Ministries of Culture and Propaganda, the publishing houses, and newspapers – competed with each other over the right to control their products. Officially, non-state publishers and press did not have to submit to the censorship process, and the noncommunist press took advantage of this loophole to publish articles critical of the regime. The extension of GUKP's powers as the communists sought to suppress the principal political opposition, Stanisław Mikołajczyk's Peasant Party, stifled any dissenting voices.

Despite the clampdown on political opposition, this period has been termed the "gentle revolution", symbolized by the activities of the publishing collective Czytelnik, whose director, Jerzy Borejsza, attempted to win over wavering writers to the new system by publishing their works in substantial and attractively produced editions. At this time, the Catholic press, especially the newspaper *Tygodnik Powszechny* (Universal Weekly), experienced relatively little repression, as the government enlisted the aid of the church in stabilizing the internal situation, particularly on the newly acquired western territories. Catholic journalists, like most others, cooperated with the censors in producing their pieces. None the less, taboo subjects included any criticism of the Soviet Union, reports of the depredations carried out by Soviet troops, which the Polish authorities were largely powerless to prevent, and accounts of fraternization with the German inhabitants of the new Polish territories.

The decree of 5 July 1946 establishing the GUKP defined the status, duties, and general conditions under which censors would intervene in artistic works, the press, and performances. These criteria included attacks on the political system, disclosure of state secrets, "activity harmful to the Polish state's international relations" (usually meaning criticism of the Soviet Union and neighbouring "socialist" countries), and "misleading public opinion with false information". Their very lack of specificity gave the censors considerable freedom for manoeuvre in defending the ruling elite's interests, whose activity was in any case not democratically accountable.

The GUKP operated a three-stage procedure in relation to newspapers: *de facto*, the submission of the edition on which the censor indicated any necessary changes; *ex post*, immediately prior to publication, when the censor checked that the proposed changes had been made; and secondary, when a committee assessed the correctness of the decision in hindsight – the changing political situation and in view of any oversights – and adjusted practice accordingly. Because of the licensing system, newspapers were freed from a fourth stage of preliminary censorship, which books underwent: that is, the complete manuscript was submitted to the GUKP before printing.

The decree of 1946 failed to acknowledge the GUKP's part in purging public and even academic libraries of works considered politically undesirable after the war. These "clearances" initially helped to remove extreme right-wing publications, but with time they were extended to works by the regime's political opponents both within Poland and abroad – ultimately, to dissenters such as Władysław Gomułka within the party itself – and to works on history, literary history, and geography, as well as to scouting manuals, the works of émigré writers, and even Edgar Rice Burroughs's Tarzan novels. These publications were transferred to secondhand bookshops and sold at high prices, or else pulped. Print runs for the independent Catholic press were drastically reduced and administrative obstruction of its activity was increased. After Stalin's death in 1953, the editor of *Tygodnik Powszechny* refused to publish a flattering obituary, which led to the suspension of the newspaper and its transfer, until November 1956, to the state-promoted organization Pax. Effectively, over the next six years, Poland was cut off from western cultural, scientific, and political influence as the Soviet model dominated in all spheres.

Film elicited special treatment from the authorities. Initially, films were checked centrally at the Kinofikacja in Łódź and audiences' responses were monitored by GUKP officials on their distribution. From the late 1940s, screenwriters submitted scripts to the Ministry of Culture, which vetted them for political acceptability and granted funds. Once made, the films were viewed by various committees, which might include members of the Politburo, in order to determine the extent of distribution or whether they should be released at all. By 1981, the number of shelved feature films ran into double figures, costing the state millions of zlotys in lost revenues.

From 1949 onwards, the imposition of "socialist realism" as the obligatory creative method in the arts both advanced self-censorship and removed some of the responsibility for controlling works to earlier stages of the creative process. Editorial boards in publishing houses began to act as an additional screen. By funding "field trips" to industrial works, to stimulate the growth of a new literature hymning the achievements of the Six-year Plan (1950–56), the Ministry of Culture encouraged conformity with the party's aims, as did the various bodies set up within the artistic "trades unions". Most important of all, terror ensured either subservience or "inner emigration" on the part of the few who refused to comply.

The "Thaw", which took hold of Polish life from 1954, led to the gradual relaxation of these rigours. The main changes occurred, however, in the autumn of 1956, when Gomułka returned to the Politburo, to lead Poland until 1970. In September 1956, GUKP employees appealed for the abolition of censorship and, in the absence of institutional controls, an *ad hoc* review board consisting of journalists, party officials, and government representatives carried out the vetting of newspapers during the highly sensitive period of the Hungarian uprising in 1956. At this time, contacts with Polish émigré centres abroad were restored, and works by major writers such as Witold Gombrowicz and Miłosz began to appear in print within Poland.

The liberal hopes vested in Gomułka were dashed over the next few years as he sought to fasten his control on the party and Polish society. The GUKP was purged; the defiant newspaper *Po prostu*, which had been at the forefront of demands for change during the "Polish October", was closed down in November 1957; and while the revamped cultural policy ceased to require obeisance to a single artistic programme – so that the term "socialist realism" fell into disuse in official discourse – increasingly dogmatic trends within the party forced a cultural clampdown. The celebrated "Polish School" in cinema was stifled by the early 1960s, key "revisionists" such as Leszek Kołakowski, who advocated change from within the party, were expelled, and closer contacts with emigré publications such as the Paris-based journal *Kultura* were discouraged. In film and literature, the "black" version of social realism practised by Marek Hłasko faced official opprobrium from 1959. Aleksandr Ford's film version of Hłasko's short story "The Eighth Day of the Week" was banned from release in 1958 and did not appear until 1983.

In the main, a stand-off prevailed between artists and the authorities during the 1960s. A letter signed by 34 leading intellectuals and writers in March 1964 protesting about the growing power of censorship and paper shortages led to the repression of some of the signatories, but did not greatly affect the general situation. The closure of a production of Mickiewicz's *Dziady* (Forefathers) in January 1968 and the brutal suppression of the student revolts that followed produced complete disaffection with the party among the intelligentsia. These events also laid the foundations for the open opposition that was to produce the "Second Circulation" (see below) and, eventually, Solidarność (Solidarity).

A key difference between censorship in the 1960s and its development under Edward Gierek (General Secretary from 1970 to 1980) lay in the streamlining of the system. The lack of formality in the chain of command had led the GUKP to be "hijacked" to some extent by the chauvinist Partisan faction of the PUWP during the anti-Semitic campaign waged in the press after the Six Day War, in 1967–68. In the 1970s, however, relations became more formalized: the Press Secretary of the Central Committee was supposed to serve as the conduit for all requests for censorship services, be they from the Soviet ambassador, industrial interests, or other departments. The Censorship Office received ever more precise, and sometimes contradictory, instructions – contained in the *Black Book* – on a regular basis, in an attempt to guarantee the party's monopoly on information.

Access to information or limited freedom to criticize depended on the individual's status in the official hierarchy. After 1956 some highly placed party writers, such as Jerzy Putrament, received permission to tackle controversial issues such as Stalinism, which was otherwise taboo, in a more direct manner than most. Similarly, in 1973, after five years of official proscription, Sławomir Mrożek, the most renowned Polish playwright, premiered and published his new play *Szczęśliwe w darzenie* (A Happy Event) in People's Poland; it had first been published abroad. The turning point in the regime's treatment of emigré literature was the award of the Nobel Prize for Literature to Miłosz in 1980, which forced the authorities to conduct a radical review of their policy. Scholarly works were assessed on slightly less stringent criteria, since they were intended for a small and elite readership. In general, the popularity of the medium determined the degree of censorship:

television, which arrived in Poland in the mid-1950s, was, like film, subject to the strictest controls, with every item requiring prior approval. In the 1970s, much of Polish television was prerecorded.

From the mid-1970s, the opposition began to challenge the party's monopoly on information. The unregulated "Second Circulation" set up at the end of 1976 heralded an increasingly active underground publishing network. As a result, even before the rise of Solidarity, the total media blackout imposed after 1976 on certain writers began to be lifted. This also affected some emigré writers, such as Miłosz, whose translations of books of the Bible appeared in the monthly *Twórczość* (Creative Work) in the late 1970s.

Accountability and transparency of censorship were one of the 21 demands made by Solidarity in the Gdańsk Agreement of August 1980. The new law of July 1981 enabled editors to challenge the GUKP's decisions through the courts. The newspaper *Tygodnik "Solidarność"* mounted the first successful challenge in November 1981 to overturn the confiscation of readers' letters in praise of the "Second Circulation". The law also removed certain categories of publication from the censorship process, such as speeches by deputies at open sessions of the Sejm, textbooks approved by the Education Ministry, those approved by the church, publications of the Academy of Sciences, reissues of works previously published in "People's Poland" or before 1918, and information bulletins. The last provision covered most of Solidarity's own publications and, in principle, the legislation partly dismantled the censorship process. The imposition of martial law (itself a taboo subject) and the "normalization" of the early 1980s somewhat compromised these new freedoms, but the basic trend during the 1980s was towards increasing liberalization, particularly with the example of glasnost being set in the Soviet Union and eventually followed by the Polish regime. By 1989, about 25 per cent of all newspapers were exempt from preventative control and there was a substantial decrease in censorship interventions elsewhere. Following the Round Table talks in that year, a registration system was introduced instead of licensing, out of which the leading newspaper *Gazeta Wyborcza* emerged.

Changes accelerated after the collapse of communism. The GUKP was abolished in April 1990 and in March the Ruch conglomerate was broken up. The newspapers it had owned were sold off, while the distribution network survives and enjoys a considerable advantage over its competitors because governments have so far been unable to devise a privatization package satisfactory to all parties. Privatization came more slowly in television, and in effect new technology and European Union legislation has to some extent invalidated politicians' attempts to retain control over the medium. The radio landscape has also substantially altered. Nevertheless, the state still occupies a central position in the audiovisual market.

Since 1990, politicians have shown contradictory attitudes towards the new media freedoms, calling for a plurality of views while wishing to retain control. President Wałęsa deprived *Gazeta Wyborcza* of the Solidarity logo in June 1990, after it published articles that he regarded as critical of himself and the trade union, and he employed his considerable powers to nominate candidates to the National Radio and Television Council, the KRRiT. His successor, Aleksander Kwaśniewski, has taken a less interventionist approach to television, but the

KRRiT remains under the control of former communists. Slandering the president remains a criminal offence, punishable by a sentence of ten months to eight years imprisonment, but, although charges have been brought under this law, no one has yet been successfully prosecuted. In September 1997, Kwaśniewski took legal action against the newspapers *Życie* and *Dziennik Bałtycki* over articles alleging that he had had contacts with a Soviet agent. Within a week, the German owner of the Neue Passauer Presse, which publishes *Dziennik*, forced his journalists to withdraw their accusations and apologized to the president. Tomasz Wołek, the co-owner and chief editor of *Życie*, had previous experience of pursuing allegations against the president, when he was illegally ousted by the Italian owner, Grauso, from the editorship of the largest Warsaw daily *Życie Warszawy*, in December 1995, following accusations of a financial scam being run by the ex-communists then in government. The alacrity with which some foreign owners accommodate the government's views does not bode well for the future of independent Polish print media.

The Catholic Church has also tried to flex its muscles since 1990. Agreements with the government and the KRRiT gave it favourable access to both media as early as mid-1989. The church pays less than commercial stations for its radio licences because it carries little advertising. An ill-defined clause enshrining "respect for Christian values" was controversially forced through by the church's supporters in the Sejm as part of the new radio and television law passed in December 1992. The KRRiT can therefore revoke licences according to very vague criteria about safeguarding Christian values. In some respects, this merely continues the communist regime's deference towards ecclesiastical sensibilities: in the 1970s, Tadeusz Różewicz's play *Białe małżeństwo* (*Mariage Blanc*), condemned by the bishops for immorality, was never performed in Cracow.

In the absence of state censorship, however, the church and its allies have had to have recourse to the rather sparse provisions of the press and penal codes. Their main concern has been to combat what the church regards as pornography and obscenity. In the spring of 1991, the attorney general published a memorandum suggesting an urgent need to pursue pornography. Jerzy Urban, editor of the satirical weekly *NIE* (and formerly spokesman for the old regime during the 1980s), challenged the memorandum by reprinting a picture from *Penthouse*, and was subsequently vindicated. In November 1993, the Rzeszów municipal council attempted to ban screenings of the British director Antonia Bird's film *Priest*, on the grounds that it offended Catholics and contained obscenity. In August 1995, the ex-communist paper *Trybuna* reported the pressure exerted by the Białystok municipal authorities on Ruch kiosks to restrict the sale not only of pornographic magazines but even of *Gazeta Wyborcza*.

Journalists find themselves under attack from a number of angles. Despite the principle of drawing a "broad line under the past" (a phrase coined by the former prime minister Tadeusz Mazowiecki), many journalists who had worked in the official press before 1990 found themselves ousted. There is no code of practice for journalists. The controversy over disclosure of sources is gradually being resolved: the bill on state secrets (November 1998) now exempts journalists, in contrast to its original wording. At his inauguration as head of Polish Tele-

vision in April 1996, Ryszard Miazek declared that the task of television journalists was not to "express independent opinions, because opinions are formulated by the Sejm and other state representatives" – a statement that caused considerable consternation in the press and was widely viewed as harking back to communist times. The ex-communists took exception to state television programming under Miazek's predecessor, Wiesław Walendziak, which included a number of programmes critical of the past broadcast on 1 May 1995. A year later, programmes in a similar vein were removed from the schedule, including Ryszard Bugajski's feature film *The Interrogation*, which is about a woman imprisoned in Stalinist times. During the local government elections in September 1998, Polish Television refused to carry the election broadcasts of the right-wing party Ojczyzna, although the political parties themselves bear responsibility for the content of such broadcasts. This decision has led the procuracy to accuse the head of Polish Television of exceeding his powers (February 1999).

Despite the absence of official censorship, a number of authors have alleged book censorship. The most high-profile case concerns the Polish edition of Marco Politi and Carl Bernstein's biography of pope John Paul II, *His Holiness*. The US publisher Doubleday demanded that the book be destroyed following the removal of passages such as one implicitly praising recent Polish honesty about anti-Semitism (according to a report in the British newspaper the *Independent on Sunday*, 1 June 1997). The excised passages were to appear in a special appendix. Łukasz Gołębiowski commented (in *Rzeczpospolita Online*, 18 June 1997) that:

> Polish editors fairly often take little account of an author's rights on the principle that the writer should be grateful that his book appears on the market . . . [it also indicates] a lack of trust in the reader, on whose account the publisher attempts to decide what content may, or should not, be made available.

In this, as in certain other respects, the paternalistic controls of the postwar communist state and Catholic Church can still make their legacy felt.

Since the above was written, president Kwaśniewski's case against *Życie* has been resolved in his favour (27 February 2001), although Tomasz Wołek has promised to appeal against the decision. In March 2000 the Polish parliament introduced a bill completely banning pornography, without defining the term, which was subsequently vetoed by the president on the grounds that it violated freedom of expression and the right to privacy enshrined in the constitution. Klaus Bachman has defined criticism of the pope as the major taboo observed in journalism right across the political spectrum: in October 2000 Polish TV apologized for showing Helen Whitney's film on John Paul II following protests by cardinal Glemp and Polish bishops. He concludes that the political right holds the upper hand in the battle for minds ("rząd dusz") within Polish society, which can be seen, for instance, in the continuing marginalization of women's issues. Ultimately, this reflects the still dominant role of the church.

JOHN MICHAEL BATES

Further Reading

Anonymous, *The Nazi Kultur in Poland*, London: Polish Ministry of Information, by His Majesty's Stationery Office, 1945

Bachman, Klaus, "Nożyce w głowie" (Scissors inside the Head), *Polityka* (15 April 2000)

Bates, John M., "Freedom of the Press in Interwar Poland: The System of Control" in *Poland between the Wars, 1918–1939*, edited by Peter D. Stachura, Basingstoke: Macmillan, and New York: St Martin's Press, 1998

Buchwald-Pelcowa, Paulina, *Cenzura w dawnej Polsce: Między prasą drukarską a stosem* (Censorship in Old Poland: Between the Printing Press and the Stake), Warsaw: Wydawnictwo SBP, 1997

Choldin, Marianna Tax, *A Fence around the Empire: Russian Censorship of Western Ideas under the Tsars*, Durham, North Carolina: Duke University Press, 1985

Ciećwierz, Mieczysław, *Polityka prasowa 1944–1948* (Press Policy, 1944–1948), Warsaw: PWN, 1989

Davies, Norman, *God's Playground: A History of Poland*, 2 vols, Oxford: Clarendon Press, 1981, reprinted with corrections, 1982; New York: Columbia University Press, 1982

Davies, Norman, *Heart of Europe: A Short History of Poland*, Oxford: Clarendon Press, 1984

Garton Ash, Timothy (editor), *Freedom for Publishing, Publishing for Freedom: The Central and East European Publishing Project*, Budapest: Central European University Press, 1995

Goban-Klas, Tomasz, *The Orchestration of the Media: The Politics of Mass Communications in Communist Poland and the Aftermath*, Boulder, Colorado: Westview Press, 1994

Hobot, Joanna, *Gra z cenzurą w poezji Nowej Fali* (Playing with Censorship in the Poetry of the New Wave), Cracow: Wydawnictwo Literackie, 2000

Kawecka-Gryczkowska, Alodia and Janusz Tazbir, "The Book and the Reformation in Poland" in *The Reformation and the Book*, edited by Jean-François Gilmont, Aldershot, Hampshire: Ashgate, 1998

Kondek, Stanisław A., *Władza i wydawcy* (The Authorities and the Publishers), Warsaw: Narodowa, 1993

Kondek, Stanisław A., *Papierowa Rewolucja: Oficjalny obieg książek w Polsce w latach, 1948–1955* (The Paper Revolution: The Official Book Circulation in Poland, 1948–1955), Warsaw: Narodowa, 1999

Kostecki, Janusz and Alina Brodzka (editors), *Piśmiennictwo – systemy kontroli – obiegi alternatywne* (Literature–Systems of Control–Alternative Circulations), 2 vols, Warsaw: Narodowa, 1992

Madej, Alina, *Mitologie i konwencje* (Mythologies and Conventions), Cracow: Universitas, 1994

Miernik, Grzegorz (editor), *Granice wolności słowa* (The Limits of the Freedom of the Word), Kielce-Warsaw: KTN, 1999

Nałęcz, Daria, *Główny Urząd Kontroli Prasy: 1945–1949* (The Main Office of Press Control, 1945–1949), Warsaw: ISP PAN, 1994

Notkowski, Andrzej, *Prasa w systemie propagandy rządowej w Polsce, 1926–1939* (The Press in the System of Government Propaganda in Poland, 1926–1939), Warsaw and Łódź: PWN, 1987

Nycz, Ryszard, "Literatura polska w cieniu cenzury" (Polish Literature in the Shadow of Censorship), *Teksty Drugie*, 3 (1998): 5–27

Pelc, Janusz and Marek Prejs (editors), *Autor tekst cenzura* (Author Text Censorship), Warsaw: Wydawnictwo Uniwersytetu Warszawskiego, 1998

Pietrkiewicz, Jerzy, "'Inner Censorship' in Polish Literature", *Slavonic and East European Review*, 36/86 (1957): 294–307

Pietrzak, Michał, *Reglamentacja wolności prasy w Polsce, 1918–1939*, (State Control of Press Freedom in Poland, 1918–1939), Warsaw: KiW, 1963

Romek, Zbigniew (editor), *Cenzura w PRL: Relacje historyków* (Censorship in People's Poland: Historians' Personal Accounts), Warsaw: Wydawnictwo NERITON and Instytut Historyczny PAN, 2000

Stefaniak, Janusz, *Polityka władz państwowych PRL wobec prasy katolickiej w latach 1945–1953* (The Policy of the State Authorities in People's Poland towards the Catholic Press in the Years 1945–1953), Lublin: UMC-S, 1998

Szydłowska, Mariola, *Cenzura teatralna w Galicji w dobie autonomicznej, 1860–1918* (Theatre Censorship in Galicia in the Era of Autonomy 1860–1918), Cracow: Universitas, 1995

Szyndler, Bartłomiej, *Dzieje cenzury w Polsce do 1918 roku* (The History of Censorship in Poland to 1918), Cracow: KAW, 1993

Tazbir, Janusz, *A State without Stakes: Polish Religious Toleration in the Sixteenth and Seventeenth Centuries*, New York: Kosciuszko Foundation, 1972

Tenzer, Ewa, *Nation Kunst Zensur: Nationalstaatsbildung und Kunstzensur in Polen, 1918–1939*, Frankfurt: Campus, 1998

Zamoyski, Adam, *The Polish Way: A Thousand-Year History of the Poles and Their Culture*, London: John Murray, and New York: Watts, 1987

POLAND: The Powers
Russia, Prussia, and Austria in Poland, 1773–1918

Between 1773, the year of the first partition of what was once Poland–Lithuania, and 1918, the year when it became united and independent, Poland was captive territory, divided into sectors, and ruled and fought over by the Austrians, the Prussians, and the Russians. Despite the rivalry between "the Powers", however, they were not only influenced by each others' practice of censorship, but even cooperated with each other in the suppression of material that threatened their control.

All three powers relied on censorship not simply as a mode of thought control, but as a tool of occupation, vital to the policing of the partitioned territories. In the Królestwo, the Russian sector, which was the largest of the three, 23 major changes in the censorship apparatus occurred between 1815 and 1915. Despite the list of constitutional guarantees agreed

at the Congress of Vienna in 1815, including the right of free publication, the Russian censorship apparatus was already fully in place by 1819. Then, in the years immediately following the collapse of the uprising of November 1830, the constitution devised in 1815 was revoked, resulting in the tightening of censorship under the auspices of the Komisja Rządowa Wyznań Religijnych i Oświecenia Publicznego (KR WRiOP), which was now made responsible to the Ministry of the Interior.

In 1851, the censorship of sheet music was introduced, and then, in 1859, the Ministry of Education in St Petersburg ordered that nowhere on Russian territory could emigré writings be printed, sold or displayed. Five years later, the KR WRiOP was itself reorganized as the Komisja Rządowa Oświecenia Publicznego (KROP), following the collapse of the uprising of January 1863. There was a brief switch from preventative to retroactive censorship following Aleksander II's accession in 1865, but by 1868–69 the intensive and brutal russification campaign had reached a self-sustaining momentum. Russian became the official language of administration and of teaching in the schools, and censorship was reorganized to shift control directly to St Petersburg. Then, until the temporary relaxation of censorship throughout the Russian empire, between the revolution of 1905–06 and its full restoration in 1908, preventative censorship was applied to all publications, including commercial ones, appearing in the Królestwo.

However, censorship practices and policies in the other two sectors are similar enough to suggest that Russian censorship policy may well have been one of the models for them, particularly in the area of enforcement, which was also pursued in close cooperation with Russian authorities. For one thing, fear of revolutionary tendencies dominated censorship policies in all three sectors, especially following the revolutionary upheavals of 1789, 1830, and 1848. The Napoleonic wars and the rapid spread of revolutionary ideas across Europe had taught "the powers" that origin is less important than example. Similarly, any uprising, no matter which zone it occurred in, was viewed as a threat because it opened the door to similar rebellions in the other zones, at the same time creating the danger that it could spread across the borders that divided the territory in which a Polish majority continued to live.

Polish nationalist literature, regardless of where it had been written or printed, was correctly viewed as the spiritual source feeding the growing number of conspiracies in the years between the Congress of Vienna and the uprising of 1830. Such works, whether anti-Prussian, anti-Austrian, or anti-Russian, were viewed as nothing less than carriers of subversion, importing the idea of rebellion to their own territories the minute they entered any one of the three sectors. The repeated uprisings in the Królestwo, especially, produced a diligent effort to cordon off Polish nationalist writings, regardless of their point of origin. In Galicia, as the Austrian sector of Poland was known, possessing publications of the émigré press after the uprising in the Królestwo in 1830 became a crime against the state, while according to Stefan Dippel, "every freethinking writer was suspect and confiscations were the order of the day". While a "thaw" (odwilż) of several months in 1848 brought about an explosive growth of new printing establishments throughout the Austrian sector, as soon as the threat to the regime was over censorship returned in an even harsher form, and all censors' verdicts now became unappealable.

Austrian censors also kept obsessive track of literature considered contraband in the Russian sector, making sure that the latest list of books appearing on the censor's index in the Królestwo was sent to Galicia every two weeks. Just as in the Russian sector, where books from Cracow and Lwów were forbidden, and had to be smuggled across the unpatrolled border points known as the zielona granica, all kinds of printed material originating in the Królestwo, Lithuania, or the Prussian-controlled province of Poznań (Posen in German) were forbidden reading in Galicia. Writings by leading nationalist figures such as Piotr Wysocki, Adam Mickiewicz or Joachim Lelewel, or by other sympathetic western European figures such as the marquis de Lafayette, were perceived by the Austrians as being of the utmost danger. In regions of the Królestwo such

as the Wołyn in Podolia, underground editions of works by these writers and others, printed and published in the Austrian sector, were confiscated by the Russian police.

In Galicia, meanwhile, secret editions of contraband literature, such as those printed by the Ossolineum Press in Lwów, were hunted down during widespread searches of private homes. The fact that the publishers of such literature took vocal credit for laying the groundwork for the Cracow revolt in 1846 and the "Springtime of Nations" that swept most of Europe in 1848–49 bore out the authorities' worst fears.

During the years between 1815 and 1848, Prussian censors appeared to be far more sensitive than their Russian or Austrian counterparts, investing most of their efforts into building feelings of patriotism. However, the unrest of 1848–49 produced the same sort of panic in Prussia as it did in Austria, moving both regimes' policies even closer to the Królestwo model of censorship than previously. Thus, in 1850 a new provision, Article 63, purported to guarantee freedom of speech and of the press, but in reality gave the Prussian minister of state the right to impose any temporary restrictions on the press that he judged necessary. In effect, this provision not only outlawed all publications in opposition to the Prussian regime, but put most Polish-language newspapers out of business. Not until the 1870s were these laws liberalized by allowing retroactive censorship, restricting the grounds for confiscation by the government, and abolishing the "deposit and licence" system under which newspapers in the sector had been forced to operate, although the risks of publishing were now shifted to individual editors, and often resulted in large fines. In any case, by then the Polish press in Prussia had become a very tame affair.

In fact, censorship should be thought of as one of the weapons of occupation, with particularly heavy police involvement, both literally and, in a broader sense, in its function as the primary mechanism used to police identity itself. In the literal sense, for example, even after the Fundamental Laws of 1867 had guaranteed the nations of the Austro-Hungarian empire the right to free development, the police in the Austrian sector had the largest de facto influence on whether a work would or would not be allowed to circulate, despite the fact that censors were not supposed to judge a work by its political content but to limit themselves to assessing its moral and artistic worth. Indeed, the very structure of the censorship apparatus appeared to guarantee this, despite the governor's theoretical power to decide what could or could not be published or staged, since manuscripts were actually read by censors at the police headquarters in Cracow and Lwów, and their decisions were then sent on to the governor's office for virtually automatic approval. In the Russian sector, Russian soldiers undertook most of the searches of bookshops and at border points, and it was also common following an uprising for the authorities to send soldiers to bookshops to gather up any copies of banned books being sold.

While war and uprisings brought out the extremes of police involvement, the authorities' hostility to the Polish language itself was perhaps an even deeper, more serious instance of policing culture. As long as Polish was spoken and written, it not only pointed to ethnic differences, working counter to the intense efforts of "the powers" to impose russification and "germanization", but reminded its users of their identities as Poles, becoming during partition the sole container of that identity, which cut severely into the new identities being culti-vated in each sector. In that sense, Polish was the language in which the dream of an independent Poland was expressed, even when a book or article had nothing to do with the subject in the literal sense. This may in part explain the heavy-handed-ness of the Russian, Prussian, and Austrian authorities when censoring Polish manuscripts submitted to them.

In Galicia, following the collapse of the uprising of 1830, the Polish language could not be used either in schools or govern-ment offices until 1848, and one governor of Galicia tried to stamp out the very presence of Polish books in the province by having them removed from the Ossolińskich Library then ordering them burned in his presence as fuel for heating the garrison laundry room. As Ludwik Gocel puts it, *Wolność* ("freedom") was one word that could not be used in any text in the "Free City of Cracow". Indeed, "freedom" was not the only word that was taboo in the Austrian sector until the col-lapse of the Habsburg monarchy. Like their Russian counter-parts, Austrian censors also routinely blue-pencilled words such as *ojczyzna* ("fatherland") or *król* ("king"). The latter could not be used even in such expressions as "the master of the house is king at his own table", which was expunged from a Polish textbook by one of the censors in Cracow, in a way almost identical to that in the Królestwo until the collapse of the Habsburg monarchy.

In its own sector meanwhile, as Adam Zamoyski has described, Prussia, which retained direct control of its sector of Poland after forming the German empire in 1871, initiated a series of measures that not only made "German . . . the lan-guage of instruction in schools, but slowly outlawed the use of Polish altogether. By 1876, not only was . . . the use of Polish textbooks . . . forbidden by law, but German had become the exclusive administrative language . . . from a law-court to a post-office", while by 1887 "the study of Polish as a second language . . . [was] abolished throughout the educational system". Deeply connected to the broader, empire-wide policy of the *Kulturkampf*, the sustained religious and cultural strug-gle against Catholic Germans and regionalism generally, these severe restrictions on the Polish language were accompanied by policies of expropriating land owned by Poles and encourag-ing a massive emigration of Germans into the annexed territo-ries, giving further notice that such territories (not only the Prussian sector of Poland, but also Alsace–Lorraine) were solely German.

Interestingly enough, in Galicia, where an important rever-sal of policy had taken place in 1867, at least with regard to the language rights of national minorities (see above), raising the subject of partition itself remained a taboo that overrode any respect for Polish texts, and provoked a worrying, obses-sive attention to any mention of them found in manuscripts submitted to Galician censors during the 1870s. Galician censors were as adamant as their Austrian predecessors that the partitions be accepted as an unchangeable status quo, and automatically banned any literary works that raised partition as an issue in case they inflamed relations with Vienna. In 1870, for example, the police censor in Lwów refused to let a play by W.L. Anczyc, *Kościuszko pod Racławicami* (Kościuszko at Racławice), be staged in its original version on the grounds of its

condemnation of the partitions of Poland by the three powers, its praise of even the armed opposition against them, and its encouragement of taking back lands taken away from ancient Poland at the hands of the [other] . . . powers. Even though the author clearly speaks about Prussia and Russia there is not a doubt that it reflects on Austria, because the rebuilding of the old Poland without Galicia and Cracow is unthinkable.

Even Polish writers and historians dealing with the partitions as a historical event were free to do so only after first declar-ing their loyalty to the Austro-Hungarian empire and accept-ing the partitions, and even then were allowed to attribute the fall of Poland only to "the flaws of the Poles as a nation and the hostility of the other two partitioning powers".

Finally, between 1879 and 1882 Galician censors became even more anxious about not allowing any open criticism, not only of Austria's part in the partitions, but of her newfound allies Germany and Russia, with which Austria had signed two treaties – the first in 1879, between Austria and Germany, and, three years later, the Triple Alliance (known in Polish as the *Trójprzymierze*). Already, following the first treaty, works that touched on the *Kulturkampf* or were critical of the German chancellor Bismarck were discouraged, even though Austria, being a largely Catholic country, was opposed to Bismarck's anti-Catholic policies. From then on, Poles also had to be very careful how they used the word *Niemiec* ("German") in the Austrian sector. As late as 1901, censors in Cracow insisted that revisions of a novel by Henryk Sienkiewicz substitute the word *Krzyżak* ("Teuton") for *Niemiec*. In 1908, when Lucjan Rydel's play *Jeniec*, which had been banned in both Cracow and Lwów since 1902, was finally allowed to be staged, the censor recommended substituting for the noun or adjective "German" each time it occurred in Rydel's text, the "archa-isms" "Teuton" or "enemy". As for Russia, Austria's other partner in the Triple Alliance, after 1882 discussion of current conditions either in that country as a whole or the Królestwo were forbidden. In addition, offensive but popular expressions such as *precz z tyranem* ("down with the tyrant") or *precz z Moskalami* ("down with the Muscovites") continued to be taboo, even though plays about the uprisings of 1830 and 1863 were being allowed in Galicia.

All this might suggest that the circulation of Polish publica-tions was slowed and enfeebled to such a degree as to be vir-tually nonexistent. In fact, the Polish reading public was able to get almost anything it wanted, including the most revolu-tionary kind of writings imported from abroad, the sole crite-rion being not content but how much they were willing to pay. On the basis of a longstanding *modus vivendi* between pub-lishers and censors, as strictly worked out in its details as it was scrupulously adhered to by both parties, such relationships survived even during the most repressive periods and in the presence of the most stringent censors.

As a result, side by side with the small number of books cleared for official circulation by the censors of the Królestwo, and usually following a series of changes and omissions that often left manuscripts all but unrecognizable, large quantities of contraband writings were smuggled in from abroad, and from the other two sectors, throughout the partition era. Intellectuals such as Feliks Faleński complained that the verses of Mickiewicz, Juliusz Słowacki, and Zygmunt Krasiński could be read only in secret – in the case of Mickiewicz's usually only in handwritten copies – and at the risk of being sent to the Caucasus on forced military service if caught. Yet works by all three of these poets were being sold in complete, uncensored sets, and could be read virtually openly in such cities as Warsaw or Wilno (now Vilnius in Lithuania).

Wilno in particular was an important transit point for books coming in from abroad, and the most stringent efforts at cordoning off were supposed to be taking place there. The chief censor had ordered his staff to check even the wrapping paper around books so that not a single book got through before a censor had had the opportunity to examine it. Every day saw new shipments arriving of smuggled copies of the best-known of the thousands of manuscripts placed on the indexed list by the censor as either *zakazane* ("forbidden") or *niecenzuralne* ("uncensorable") – that is, formally incapable of being circulated no matter what degree of "correction" its author or publisher might agree to. The contraband included émigré manuscripts that were then reprinted in Warsaw and the provinces, or even sold sometimes, under false titles, in the capital's bookshops. Contraband sheet music might contain forbidden Polish anthems such as "Jeszcze Polska nie zginęła" (Poland Remains Undefeated) or "Boże coś Polskę" (God Protect Poland), which were not allowed to be sung in public, or might be smuggled in for the strictly commercial reason that, although scores from western Europe were better-printed and cheaper, Polish booksellers were not allowed to import many of them because they were also being published in Russia proper, a competing market.

Such smuggled reading matter and sheet music contributed significantly to many of the most successful booksellers' incomes. While the actual volume of such materials in circulation is unknown, by all accounts it was significant, and profitable enough for many booksellers to risk importing it even after they had been repeatedly jailed or exiled for it. For example, Jakub Mortkowicz, a leading bookseller and publisher who went on to become official printer for the Polish Socialist Party between the world wars, was jailed in 1908 and exiled in 1911 for smuggling and selling contraband. According to Dippel, Mortkowicz had "whole shipments of illegal books, containing editions of socialist and people's literature, and the literature of the pre-World-War-I underground military resistance", regularly arriving at his shop from Cracow, Lublin, and Piotrowka, which he then held for "trusted clients". Via Leipzig, the centre of the European book trade and another leading transit point for smuggled literature, contraband books, skilfully hidden underneath other books that the censors had cleared, or disguised to look like German prayer books, came in from Germany, France, Austria, Switzerland, and, more and more frequently, Galicia. Indeed, packaging contraband literature destined for long-distance and often circuitous transport was an art form that demanded physical dexterity, nerves of steel, and ingenuity, as well as many hours of unpacking, as Stanisław Arct explains:

> Since crates were opened in the presence of a censor supervising their unpacking, one had to lift off the packing paper swiftly and skilfully, and throw it under the table in such a way that the censor did not or was

not obliged to see its actual contents. After the crate had been searched, the contraband had to be returned to its former place within the crate before it was shut.

Even after the books had safely arrived in Warsaw, the censor could still sometimes catch a bookseller with contraband during an inspection. In one instance, when the censor had caught the Hoesick firm receiving a shipment from Leipzig containing complete sets of the works of Mickiewicz, Słowacki, and Krasiński, the Hoesicks, according to the memoirs of one family member, succeeded in

> calming him down by allowing Teodoridi, the censor in question, to confiscate the shipment and keep it in his office cupboard until little by little, the confiscated books, ransomed by the bookstore at a price of three rubles per lot, were returned in person by him.

Managing routine contacts with the censors constituted a second art form, practised no less assiduously or ingeniously by booksellers and publishers. This meant, once again, little more than judging how large or small a bribe a particular censor would accept. However, the offering of bribes was a delicate and time-consuming ritual, elaborately played out under the rules of guest and host, or sometimes even friend and confidant. Warsaw censors, for example, sat in a café waiting to read newspaper copy brought to their table from the *Kurier Warszawski* by Hoesick in his function as "the minister of bribes" – "a portfolio of a very delicate nature" – ready for a "working breakfast" paid for by Hoesick's paper. Hoesick concluded that: "The better the breakfast, the milder the censoring, the more alcohol imbibed, the less red ink".

As for the *prezes* or chief of the Warsaw Censors' Committee and his senior censors, they were entitled to a regular salary, as high as 300 rubles a month. Ludwig Fiszer, another leading Warsaw publisher, reports that he paid each of the three senior censors in Warsaw a quarterly salary of 200 rubles, supplemented by payments of 10 rubles for each crate found to contain any contraband books, while in cases in which the entire crate was found to be full of contraband, the censor inspecting it received 50 rubles extra. In return, each censor guaranteed that not a single book of Fiszer's would ever be confiscated, and that nothing shipped either from Galicia or from Poznań would ever be opened. Payments were made and each party kept up to date with the other at weekly breakfasts, also held at cafés.

How do such anecdotes square with the many arrests and confiscations that continued throughout partition? Both censors and publishers knew and accepted the fact that bribes did not guarantee publishers total immunity from prosecution. Publishers viewed this as an acceptable business risk from which they could often bounce back, either by switching ownership title to another member of the family, or by finding a partner whose name could be used to obtain a licence to open another bookshop. Sometimes, however, a ruling of political unreliability could be disastrous. For example, despite its leading role in the intellectual life of Wilno since the 1830s, Józef Zawadzki's bookshop, and the press associated with it, went into permanent decline following frequent searches by the authorities; orders that the bookstore be closed for intervals of several months following the uprising of 1863; a special commission's ruling in 1865 that its owners were politically unreliable; and the implementation of the law passed in 1866 forbidding the use of all Polish type by printers. Another Wilno bookshop, owned since 1879 by the writer Eliza Orzeszkowa, was closed down in 1882 and its liquidation was advertised by the authorities, while Orzeszkowa and her partner were placed under police surveillance for three years for running an illegal lending library containing banned Polish books. A bookseller named Jan Hussarowski acquired the shop and press, and hired one Bolesław Koreywo to work for him, until Koreywo was arrested on suspicion of participating in "patriotic activities" and Hussarowski's firm was shut down.

In the Prussian sector, where different rules applied, numerous publishers and booksellers were fined or subjected to confiscations, including Jan Konstanty Zupański, whose speciality was bringing out the Polish classics and critical works specializing in literary history; Walenty Maciej Stefański, who opened his bookshop in 1839; and Józef Chociszewski, who opened bookshops first in Chełmno, then in the city of Poznań, where he was accused of distributing patriotic songbooks. After that, Chociszweski was subjected to frequent confiscations for spreading "Polish propaganda", but continued operating under the authorities' constant surveillance. Yet none of these examples negates what seems to be their opposite, the equally powerful *modus vivendi* that censors and booksellers all lived by.

Perhaps a better way to think of the coexistence of accommodation and repression is that it kept the Polish book trade both flourishing and unhealthy. Considerable quantities of books did circulate illegally, but the catalogues were full of gaps, confusing, and issued irregularly or overprinted. Censors' bureaus added to the confusion by arbitrarily reversing decisions. Taken over a long period, even the distortion in cataloguing, a relatively minor inconvenience on the face of it, could be seen to produce chaos in the inventory process and, beyond that, potentially large losses for publishers, who had no clear sense of what they could deliver to their public.

As for the effects of such policies on book production, the strikingly small output of many respected publishers throughout the 18th and 19th centuries, directed to a tiny élite composed of the wealthy and educated, points to an industry virtually paralysed throughout this period. Between 1857 and 1875 there was no expansion at all in the number of bookshops in Warsaw (there were 35 altogether). The 500 publishers who were established enough during the 19th century to risk acknowledging themselves by name on their books together produced only 2,000 titles. Only 10 per cent of all firms brought out more than 10 titles throughout the 19th century.

Stanisław Arct has shown how the number of titles published in Warsaw rose slowly but surely until 1901, when they suddenly jumped spectacularly. It was not literary production that accounted for this boom but rather demand for school texts, one of the earliest signs of the *samouk* ("self-education") craze preceding the school strike of 1905–06, which centred on the demand for the restoration of Polish in schools. By 1904, 797 books had been published in Warsaw; by 1907 the figure was 1260. As mentioned above, preventative censorship had been replaced, temporarily, by retroactive censorship; the Russian authorities also allowed private schools to use Polish-language

textbooks. In 1910, however, the number of books produced in Warsaw dropped to 830, a fact that Arct attributes to yet another crackdown by the authorities against those writing and publishing progressive and patriotic works, accompanied by new strictures about what subjects could be taught in Polish. In particular, in history and geography it had once again become mandatory to use Russian texts. By 1913, all the growth experienced during the period of liberalization had vanished, and a record number of younger intellectuals, representing a sizeable readership, had emigrated to Russia proper to take up teaching posts.

One other aspect, virtually untouched in the current literature on censorship in partitioned Poland, is its impact on the large Jewish community living in the Russian sector, and publishing works in both Hebrew and Yiddish. The Russian authorities' fear and anxiety about access to and control over the Jewish minority caused them to set up a special system of censorship applying only to Jewish books. In the 1820s and 1830s in particular, stopping or at least slowing the circulation of such works became an obsession for the censors. Often themselves converts from Judaism, they went to extraordinary lengths to restrict Jewish publications. A striking instance is the case of Szaj Waks, a Jewish printer and publisher working in Józefów, who in 1822 approached the authorities with a plan to prohibit all imports of books, and prayer books in particular, from Russia proper, which, he argued, could not be understood by Jews living in the Królestwo in any case. Waks suggested that he himself be appointed as the sole printer of Hebrew books, with a state subsidy. At this point, a running battle between the censors and the Treasury was in full swing: the censors argued for a prohibitive import tax on Jewish books from Russia proper, similar to the one that regulated the flow of Jewish books from abroad, while the Treasury preferred to have the governor of the sector deal with the matter. While the governor was initially interested, the project fell apart when the censors refused to relax the conditions that they had imposed on Waks, including a security deposit of 20,000 zlotys, and a requirement that Waks bring each copy of the manuscript of any book he wished to print to Warsaw. The censors openly admitted that the purpose of these measures was to restrict the flow of Jewish books as far as possible.

Indeed, preventative censorship of Jewish books continued even during the "thaw" following the Congress of Vienna, when censors actively interfered with Jewish texts, almost destroying the work of Jewish writers with corrections and extractions. Phrases such as "well-known people speak and do not know what they are saying" in Salomon Ettinger's Yiddish play *Serkele* were taken to be slanders against the prominent. The word "monarch" was changed to "wealthy man" and the verb "kissed" was replaced by "stroked".

In some cases, however, members of the Jewish community actively sought to have certain publications censored. In March 1830, for example, a committee of prominent Jews whose own books had been so heavily censored that they were unreadable approached the censors with the request that they prevent the publication of a book by a convert and Catholic priest named Chiarini, *Théorie du judaïsme* (Theory of Judaism), but the censors refused to interfere. Another book, *Złość żydowska talmudowa* (Jewish Talmudic Spite), first published in 1739, which peddled the myth that Jews used Christian blood in their

Passover ceremonies, was also reissued during this period, despite protests to the censors from the Jewish community.

As late as the 1870s, the same policies were still at work, as shown in a short memoir by Christofor Emmauskij, who was chief censor in Warsaw from 1899 to 1901. (Hoesick identifies him as one of the worst bribetakers.) In 1870, the Warsaw committee was made responsible for publications written in the 10 Polish provinces, and those coming in from abroad, and for a second, separate division dealing with Jewish publications, both domestic and foreign. The latter was run by a convert, Wladimir Wasiliewicz Fiedorow, formerly Rabbi Hersz Birnbaum of Wilno, who had excellent knowledge of Hebrew and Yiddish. Fiedorow also censored Polish and German newspapers. According to Emmauskij, he frequently saw Fiedorow bent over Talmudic writings and commentaries, tearing whole sheets out, while scores of Jewish publishers and writers sat in an anteroom waiting patiently for him to finish. If any of them asked politely whether Fiedorow had had a chance to look at their books yet, Fiedorow responded by throwing one of the folios at their head.

Like other censors, Emmauskij was at pains to portray himself as an intermediary and peacemaker when ethnic tensions rose in Warsaw. Following a pogrom there in 1881, the censor's office took special steps to see to it that nothing provocative appeared in newspapers "either against Jews, or, on the other hand, against the [Królestwo] government", according to Emmauskij, whose perception of the mood of the Polish press in the early 1880s is equally frank and striking: "the entire Polish press is infected by Judeophobia".

The administration was equally alarmed by a phenomenon that should have raised hopes that ethnic relations between the two communities were improving. The coming together of Jewish assimilationists and sympathetic Poles, in particular the "Positivists" who openly promoted their integration into Polish society after the 1870s, alarmed them none the less. The work of Eliza Orzeszkowa, author of the groundbreaking novel *Meir Ezofowicz* (1878), the first literary work in Polish to forgo stereotyping and depict a Jewish character realistically, was of particular concern. Orzeszkowa was already being closely watched by authorities monitoring her book-smuggling activities in Wilno. When her novels also began being adapted as plays, they were quickly seen as being too dangerous for Warsaw's theatregoers. In 1889, one such play, *Eli Makower*, was forbidden to be staged because, according to the censor, it "develops the idea of the assimilation of Jews with the country's native-born population". The stage version of *Meir Ezofowicz* was likewise turned down for staging by the censors: "because of the situation prevailing at the moment, such propaganda is unwelcome by the public". Two years later, the censors refused permission to stage a third adaptation, *Syn judy*. At last, the censors' real reasons for not allowing these works to be performed surfaced in relation to a second attempt to stage *Eli Makower*. As the censors' reviewer put it, solidarity between Jews and Poles, based on the premise that "the same land nourished both", is "harmful to the Russian cause in our territory".

A shortage of bookshops, reduced book production, partic-ularly during the early years of partition, the lack of efficient, inexpensive book distribution, and all of the other byproducts of a literary community structured, not by its practitioners, but to evade the occupying powers: these were the symptoms of a prolonged, unmanageable crisis that had an enormous impact on Polish culture. The constantly changing policies of the censors over more than 120 years, enforced by three separate and often contradictory sets of regulations that were so byzantine that censors themselves had trouble keeping up with them, so closely parallel the ups and downs of book production that there is a strong case for the proposition that partition politics, rather than the broad generational and regional cultural developments and theories of readership taken for granted in the West, should serve as the landmarks for its historians.

HELENA K. KAMINSKI

Further Reading

Arct, Stanisław, *Okruchy wspomnień*, Warsaw: PIW, 1962

Cała, Alina, *Asymilacja Żydów w Królestwie Polskim 1864–1897: postawy, konflikty, stereotypy*, Warsaw: Panstwowy Instytut, 1989

Corrsin, Stephen D., *Warsaw before the First World War: Poles and Jews in the Third City of the Russian Empire, 1880–1914*, Boulder, Colorado: East European Monographs, 1989

Cywiński, Bohdan, *Rodowody niepokornych*, Warsaw: Wiezi, 1971

Dippel, Stefan, *O ksiegarzach którzy przeminęli*, Wrocław: Ossolińskich, 1976

Gąsiorowska, Natalia, *Wolność druku w Królestwie Kongresowym, 1815–1830*, Warsaw: Hoesicka, 1916

Gorski, Stefan. *Z dziejów cenzury w Polsce: Szkic historyczny*, Warsaw: GiW, 1906

Hoesick, F., *Ze wspomnień o cenzurze rosyjskiej w Warzawie*, Warsaw: Hoesicka, 1929

Kiepurska, Halina, *Warszawa 1905–1907* (Warsaw 1905–07), Warsaw: Wiedza Powszechna, 1974; Warsaw: PWN, 1991

Kostecki, Janusz and Alina Brodzka (editors), *Piśmiennictwo – systemy kontroli – obiegi alternatywne* (Literature–Systems of Control–Alternative Circulations), 2 vols, Warsaw: Narodowa, 1992

Kuszlejko, Jacek, *Książka polska w Rosji na przełomie XIX i XX wieku*, Warsaw: Narodowa, 1993

Łasiewiecki, Franciszek, *Pamiętniki woźnego cenzury*, Toruń: Uniwersytetu Kopernika, 1995

Lech, Marian J., "Książka i czytelnictwo w Warszawie w 1870 roku w świetle raportu inspektorów nadzoru w Komitecie Cenzury", *Rocznik Biblioteki Narodowej*, 2 (1967): 402

Lech, Marian J., *Drukarze i drukarnie w Królestwie Polskim 1869–1905: Materiały ze źródel archiwalnych*, Warsaw: Narodowa, 1979

Lewandowski, Stefan, *Poligrafia warszawska 1870–1914*, Warsaw: Książka i Wiedza, 1982

Mlekicka, Marianna, *Jakub Mortkowicz, księgarz i wydawca*, Wrocław: Ossolineum, 1974

Muszkowski, Jan, *Z dziejów firmy Gebethner i Wolff, 1857–1937*, Warsaw, 1938

Prussak, Maria, *Świat pod kontrolą: Wybór materiałów z archiwum cenzury rosyjskiej Warszawie*, Warsaw, 1994

Wandycz, Piotr S., *The Lands of Partitioned Poland, 1795–1918*, Seattle: University of Washington Press, 1974

Zamoyski, Adam, *The Polish Way: A Thousand-Year History of the Poles and Their Culture*, London: John Murray, and New York: Watts, 1987

POLITICAL CORRECTNESS

Although the term "political correctness" dates back to the 1960s when it was introduced by the New Left, the Black Panthers, and lesbian feminists, it gained wide currency only in the early 1990s as part of what was called the "culture wars" in the United States. Following on the heels of gay classicist Allan Bloom's jeremiad, *The Closing of the American Mind* (1987), American conservatives attacked the humanities faculties in higher education, whom they labelled "tenured radicals," composed of 1960s New Left holdovers – multiculturalists, feminists, Marxists, and deconstructionists, and the like. These former activists turned professors, conservatives maintained, had taken over the universities and politicized them, subordinating intellectual merit to supposedly democratic ends in programmes such as affirmative action (and gay rights legislation) and assaulting western culture and the literary canon, displacing Dante, Shakespeare, and Joyce with the likes of Zora Neale Hurston, Rigoberta Menchu, and Frantz Fanon. Western culture, conservatives argued, made up the basis of democratic values, values that were being drastically undermined by the left. The result of the leftist takeover, in the view of conservatives, was the imminent threat of the balkanization of the US. Furthermore, the introduction of campus speech codes forbidding racist or sexist speech was regarded by conservatives as a threat to free inquiry and unqualified debate, to the spirit of reasoned argument – censorship, in short. The university had forsaken "standards" for a dumbed-down, ideologically "pure" set of dogma. Truth, objectivity, merit, and so on, just didn't matter.

The Modern Language Association (MLA) in particular came in for major attack. The National Association of Scholars (formed in 1987) led the attack, and Dinesh De Souza's *Illiberal Education* (1991) and Roger Kimball's (of the *New Criterion*) *Tenured Radicals* (1990) were influential. Former radical turned reactionary David Horowitz started publishing a neotabloid newspaper called *Heterodoxy*. Cover articles on "p.c." appeared in mainstream magazines like *Newsweek*, and national media pundits like George F. Will entered the fray. Even the then president George Bush discussed the issue in a commencement address he gave in 1991 at the University of Michigan. A series of anthologies reproducing these texts and others quickly followed, including Patricia Aufderheide's *Beyond PC: Toward a Politics of Understanding* (1992). A counter-offensive from the left was quickly launched. The Teachers for a Democratic Culture circulated their own statement of principles and the MLA responded in 1991 with a panel at the annual conference. Stephen Greenblatt and Skip Gates, among others, defended the profession. Avowedly leftist critics claimed that the right was redefining "liberal" in a way that masked their own narrow set of conservative interests. The claims for merit and standards were really attempts to keep women, racial minorities, and gays (professors and writers) out of the profession and out of the culture.

Though critics differ about the origins of the term "politically correct", some locating it in the 1960s, others in the 1940s, all agree that it originated on the left and that it was often used ironically against other leftists as a critique of moralism and preachiness. In the 1990s, a term of self-criticism was then appropriated by the right. Despite the shared perception of vast differences among the participants in the debate, a remarkable rhetorical symmetry can be seen on both sides. Both are against political correctness and for tolerance; both are for democracy, and greater inclusion and against totalitarianism; both believe in intellectual merit, truth, standards; both believe in literary form; and so on. Each side accused the other of bad faith and McCarthyism; bad scholarship; deliberate distortion of the other's views; having a narrow political agenda; and so on.

Debates centred on whether censorship or disagreement was involved when Stephen Thernstrom of Harvard was alleged by his students to be guilty of insensitivity because his course on the history of race relations in the US failed to cover the testimony of slaves. Although, finally, Thernstrom and his students agreed to disagree, he withdrew the course. Yet, "there is no evidence", according to John Annetts, "that any academics today have been prevented from teaching or have been dismissed by the administration because of their perceived political views".

One has the sense that little of intellectual interest was happening here, in large part because debate over the term was a epiphenomenon, part of a narrowly political debate focused by the Reagan/Bush agenda, one that had a lot to do with PR and little to do with how criticism is practised, and courses taught. Whether cynically or altruistically motivated, people on both sides offered their services as political hacks and spin-doctors. In any case, the debate about political correctness in the US came to an end in the later 1990s when it was displaced by a debate (with far more lasting and drastic consequences) over the future of higher education itself, a future that, in some cases, appears to leave little room for full-time faculty and perhaps no room for faculty with tenure.

RICHARD BURT

Further Reading

Adlar, Jerry, "Taking Offense", *Newsweek* (24 December 1990): 48–50

Aufderheide, Patricia (editor), *Beyond PC: Toward a Politics of Understanding*, St Paul, Minnesota: Graywolf Press, 1992

Berman, Paul (editor), *Debating P.C.: The Controversy over Political Correctness on College Campuses*, New York: Dell, 1992

D'Souza, Dinesh, *Illiberal Education: The Politics of Race and Sex on Campus*, New York: Free Press, 1991

Dunant, Sarah (editor), *The War of the Words: The Political Correctness Debate*, London: Virago, 1994

Feldstein, Richard, *Political Correctness: A Response from the Cultural Left*, Minneapolis: University of Minnesota Press, 1997

Fish, Stanley, *There's No Such Thing as Free Speech, and It's a Good Thing, Too*, New York: Oxford University Press, 1994

Friedman, Marilyn and Jan Narveson, *Political Correctness: For and Against*, Lanham, Maryland: Rowman and Littlefield, 1995

Kimball, Roger, *Tenured Radicals: How Politics Has Corrupted Our Higher Education*, New York: Harper, 1990

Kurzweil, Edith and William Phillips (editors), *Our Country, Our Culture: The Politics of Political Correctness*, Boston: Partisan Review Press, 1994

POLITIKA
Serbian newspaper and related media group, established 1904

Writing to Mark Thompson in October 1993, Aleksandar Nenadović, a former editor-in-chief of *Politika*, described the newspaper as "much more in this country than a newspaper. It is an institution." One of many new publications that appeared as Serbia turned towards a limited form of parliamentary democracy in the early 1900s, it was founded by Bronislav Ribnikar as a liberal and independent publication. In general, it maintained that tradition for most of the 20th century.

The years of hardline communist rule must be excepted, however. At that time, the paper was declared "social property", which, although in principle it meant that it was owned by the staff, in practice made it subject to political interference by the Serbian branch of the Socialistički Savez Radnih Naroda (the Socialist Alliance of Working People). Thus, on 18 January 1975 it published a half-page editorial attacking Praxis, a group of communist philosophers at the University of Belgrade, which represented one step in the group's enforced dissolution (although some Praxis members reappeared some years later, as a rabidly nationalist chorus for the Serbian regime). Editors-in-chief of *Politika*, including Nenadović, were appointed by the Yugoslav League of Communists: Nenadović was dismissed as one of those who had been named "rotten liberals" by president Tito in 1972. Dragoljub Trailović, who had attacked government secrecy over the extent of foreign debt in 1983, was dismissed for "Serbian nationalism", a catch-all phrase during the communist years.

Politika's more populist stablemate, *Politika Ekspres*, was founded in 1970. The two papers were bought by 70 per cent of regular newspaper readers in Serbia during the late 1980s. The group also owned 18 other publications, a radio station, and a television channel. It thus formed a media empire that Slobodan Milošević needed to have on his side once he had risen to the leadership of the Serbian League of Communists, on a wave of nationalism, in September 1987. To that end, the Politika group's director-general, Ivan Stojanović, was replaced by Živorad Minović, who also became editor-in-chief of the newspaper. The editor of *Politika Ekspres*, Slobodan Jovanović, was also an ardent supporter of Milošević. Overnight, the newspapers lost their editorial independence. It was highly significant that an institution so central to the history of 20th-century Serbia now not only regularly excoriated the country's supposed external and internal enemies, but sang to the tune of its past glories (its medieval empire) and sufferings (its defeat at the hands of the Ottomans and the partly mythical forced migrations of its people).

The revolutionary changes at *Politika* were not achieved without journalistic resistance. Minović did not endear himself to *Politika*'s staff when, in April 1990, he reduced the salaries of 40 journalists, in an attempt to squeeze out those who opposed government policy. He resigned his post as editor-in-chief in March 1991, under pressure from the Independent Trade Union of *Politika*, which had been formed to oppose biased coverage. He remained director-general, however, with sufficient influence to ensure uncritical support for the government throughout the wars in Croatia and Bosnia-Herzegovina

(1991–95). Thus, for example, Croatian nationalists were said to be repeating the attacks on Serbs first committed 50 years previously, and the paper revived the wartime term *ustaše* to describe them. The demonstrations against Milošević in Belgrade in March 1991 were said to be "destroying the constitutional order". The Serb people, according to *Politika*, "were ready to fight barehanded" against Croatian forces after the events of June–July 1991. "In the pages of Serbia's most prestigious daily", writes Mark Thompson, the seizure and genocidal devastation of Zvornik (April 1992) "never happened". The "bread queue massacre" in Sarajevo on 27 May 1992 was said to have been perpetrated by the Croats, who had covered their tracks by removing Serb corpses from the street, and substituting those of Croats and Muslims.

Self-respecting journalists baulked at this kind of distorted coverage. In 1992, using the Federal Law of 1989, the staff attempted to buy out the paper. Without delay, the government brought forward a bill that would have given it direct control of the group. All 4,000 staff came out on official strike. Milošević retreated and the staff were allowed to proceed with their buy-out, ending up with 50 per cent of the company.

However, it made little real difference: the board of directors remained in effective control, and, through the agency of Živorad Minović, abolished *Politika*'s workers' council. Moreover, the papers continued faithfully to demonize external and internal enemies, following the changing priorities of the ruling party. For example, on 27 March 1996 *Politika* spearheaded the campaign against such alternative media as the press agency Beta, the review *Vreme*, the television company Studio B, and the periodical *Naša Borba*, which had broken loose from *Borba* when that publication was taken over by the government. It gave space to an interview with Milošević in which he accused all these media entities of being agents of foreign countries. During the local elections of November 1996, *Politika* was far less than even-handed, and failed to cover Milošević's attempted electoral fraud that followed. Two signatories of a letter of protest signed by 40 *Politika* journalists, Biserka Matić and Ivan Stojković, were dismissed by a disciplinary committee. As Aleksandar Nenadović wrote: "The regime took out everything that was good about us, and made the paper a launching pad for the nationalist offensive. They killed its liberal soul."

The elections of 24 September 2001 were finally fatal for Milošević. *Politika* remained under his control until the last day. But on 5 October the masses not only seized parliament, they also ran into the offices of the official media, including those of *Politika*, which were located downtown. Under armed protection, former director Hadži Dragan Antić escaped from his office and submitted his written resignation a few days later. On 6 October, the first page showed the victorious gesture of Kostunica before parliament and printed his speech, delivered to the paper by the previously bitterly criticized "alternative" Beta news agency.

Dragan Tomić, still leading the managing board of *Politika* of the pre-revolutionary period, appointed first Aleksandar Tijanic, a former head of TV Politika and information minister, as acting director of the *Politika* company. But there was another candidate, the *Politika* correspondent in the US, Darko Ribnikar. He had the support of the employees and the independent unions and was finally appointed as acting director on 20 October. As his ancestors founded the house, the circle seems to have been closed and the liberal tradition of *Politika* restored.

ROBERT STALLAERTS

Further Reading

Kišić, Milica and Branka Bulatović, *Srpska štampa, 1768–1995: Istorijsko-bibliografski pregled* (The Serbian Press, 1768–1995: Historical and Bibliographical Review), Belgrade: Medija Centar, 1996

Kuzmanović, Jasmina, "Media: The Extension of Politics by Other Means" in *Beyond Yugoslavia: Politics, Economics, and Culture in a Shattered Community*, edited by Sabrina Petra Ramet and Ljubiša S. Adamovich, Boulder, Colorado: Westview Press, 1995

Magaš, Branka, *The Destruction of Yugoslavia: Tracking the Break-up, 1980–92*, London: Verso, 1993

Mišović, Miloš, "Štampa i srpsko društvo 19. i 20. veka" (The Press and Serbian Society in the 19th and 20th Centuries) in *Srpska štampa, 1768–1995*, edited by Milica Kisić and Branka Bulatović, Belgrade: Medija Centar, 1996

Nikolić, Zoran B., "Postizborna Srbija: Oslobadjanje medija" (Post-electoral Serbia: Setting the Media Free), *AIM* (29 October 2000)

Ramet, Sabrina Petra, "The Role of the Press in Yugoslavia" in *Yugoslavia in Transition: Choices and Constraints: Essays in Honour of Fred Singleton*, edited by John B. Allcock *et al.*, New York and Oxford: Berg, 1992

Ramet, Sabrina Petra, *Balkan Babel: The Disintegration of Yugoslavia from the Death of Tito to the War for Kosovo*, 3rd edition, Boulder, Colorado: Westview Press, 1999

Robinson, Gertrude Joch, *Tito's Maverick Media: The Politics of Mass Communication in Yugoslavia*, Urbana: University of Illinois Press, 1977

Schöpflin, George (editor), *Censorship and Political Communication in Eastern Europe: A Collection of Documents*, London: Pinter, and New York: St Martin's Press, 1983

Thompson, Mark, *Forging War: The Media in Serbia, Croatia and Bosnia-Hercegovina*, London: Article 19, 1994; revised edition, Luton: University of Luton Press, 1999

Torov, Ivan, *Sunovrat srpskog novinarstva, 1987–1995* (The Eclipse of Serbian Journalism, 1987–95), Belgrade: Medija Centar, 1996

"Zaposleni u *Politici* podržali Darka Ribnikara: Upravni odbor danas bira direktora?" (Employees of *Politika* Support Darko Ribnikar: Does the Direction Committee Elect Today a Director?), *Danas* (18 October 2000)

Websites

http://www.mediacenter.org.yu
http://www.politika.co.yu
http://www.slavnet.com

GILLO PONTECORVO
Italian film director, 1919–

LA BATTAGLIA DI ALGERI (The Battle of Algiers)
Italian–Algerian film, 1966

The Battle of Algiers is a film about the Algerian war of independence. On its release in France it met with powerfully negative reactions from certain sections of the French population, partly, no doubt, because of its moving and sympathetic account of the Algerian fight for the end of French colonization. The loss of Algeria continued to be seen by many in France as humiliating or traumatic, and the suppression of books as well as films dealing with the Algerian war was widespread. Very few French films – indeed, as Pascal Ory points out, no "action" films at all – have taken the war as their subject.

The story starts in 1957, at the moment when the paras are about to achieve what they think is a conclusive victory. A prisoner has been tortured into giving away the hiding place of four resistance fighters, including ʿAli La Pointe (one of the leaders of the Front de Libération Nationale – FLN). The bulk of the film then takes place in a flashback beginning in 1954, when the war started. We follow the fate of ʿAli, a petty criminal who is politicized when he is sent to prison by the French, and who subsequently joins the FLN. He becomes a close associate of one of its leaders, Jafar (played by Yacef Saadi, president of Casbah Films, a former military commander in the Algerian resistance, and the film's co-producer). They work together in stamping out drugs, drunkenness, and prostitution in the Casbah, and then in a campaign of bombing and shooting against the French. The French react violently. In one scene, a group of settlers, including the chief of police, plants a bomb in the medina, causing terrible destruction. The FLN in turn organizes a succession of bombings. Again, the indiscriminate nature of the killing is apparent.

Shortly after this, in January 1957, colonel Mathieu – a fictional composite of various historical figures – arrives with his paras. The FLN, hoping (in vain) to persuade the United Nations to intervene, calls a week's general strike; and though on one level it provides an impressive display of solidarity, the strike rebounds against them when Matthieu uses it as the starting point of his fight to eliminate Algerian resistance. A crucial element of his strategy is the use of torture, which he defends calmly, and which is depicted graphically and disturbingly by Pontecorvo. We arrive at the point where ʿAli is the only leader left; and when he refuses to surrender, in the scene with which the film started, the building in which he and the others are hiding is blown to pieces. This marks the end of the "battle"; but in a coda, a huge, seemingly spontaneous, demonstration three years later signals the resurgence of Algerian resistance and the continuation of the war. A voiceover explains that on 2 July 1962 Algerian independence was finally won.

The Battle of Algiers was shot on location in Algiers in 1965, with the blessing and the assistance of the Algerian government. It was Saadi who initiated the project, choosing Pontecorvo to direct because he brought to the production not only his expertise (and that of Franco Solinas, a screenwriter who also worked with Rosi, Costa Gavras, Rossellini, Peckinpah, and Losey), but also political commitment and a willingness to work with inexperienced Algerian actors and technicians on the

PONTECORVO: Scene from the 1966 film *La battaglia di Algeri* (The Battle of Algiers). Controversy surrounded the film's release in France because of its sympathetic portrayal of the Algerian struggle for independence and the political issues it raised as a result. The film was not on general release in France until 1971; it provoked violent attacks in Rome, and was banned in Britain.

shoot (Pontecorvo had already been working on the idea for a film about Algeria, *Parà*, which was to approach colonialism through the eyes of an ex-para, a role for which both Paul Newman and Warren Beatty had been approached). However, Saadi's project, after a series of rewrites based on extensive research (and influenced, particularly in their treatment of Algerian women, by the work of Frantz Fanon, author of *The Wretched of the Earth*), provided a perspective which seemed at once balanced and sympathetic to the Algerian cause, and which presented the conflict less in terms of the motivations or even actions of any individual than in terms of inexorable historical forces.

Even before its release, the film caused controversy in France. Groups of *pieds noirs* (former settlers in Algeria who had returned to France) sought assurances from the government that it would not be released, nor extracts shown on television; and it was not granted a visa for distribution in France until 1970. It was presented at the 1966 Venice film festival, where it won first prize, an award which prompted the French delegation (who had boycotted the screening) to walk out. French papers such as *Le Figaro* and *Combat* expressed their disgust at the award, and *Le Monde* asserted that the jury's political opinions had determined the attribution of the prizes. If the

film remains emotionally powerful, though, this is partly thanks to its technical adroitness, particularly in its careful manipulation of music and of sound more generally.

By 1971 the French press, who had the opportunity to see the film in private screenings, started to review it more favourably. Its general release was further delayed by right-wing extremists who intimidated cinema-managers with threats, vandalism, and even bombs, but later that year the film was in circulation. Elsewhere in the world, meanwhile, there was also resistance to the film – a cinema in Rome was attacked in 1972, and Britain followed France's lead, banning it until 1971 – but its reputation continued to grow, culminating in two Oscar nominations and various other international accolades. Despite its global success, however, there were critics of the film inside Algeria, too, and on the political left, who rebuked Pontecorvo for being unduly sympathetic to the French (particularly in the person of Mathieu), or indeed for omitting or misrepresenting various other historical and ideological nuances of the struggle for independence (for instance in omitting to mention the MNA, a nationalist organization that was a rival of the FLN). The way the film (made in grainy black and white, with dialogue in French and Arabic) borrows formally from documentary-making was both a strength and a weakness in the face of its critics, of course, helping to make plausible its claims to historical accuracy but also disguising the respects in which it was a fictionalized, and at moments (most notably the sequence in the coda showing a woman dancing and taunting the police) even symbolic, account of historical events.

NICHOLAS HARRISON

Writings

"*The Battle of Algiers*: An Adventure in Filmmaking", *American Cinematographer* (April 1967)

Further Reading

Dine, Philip, *Images of the Algerian War: French Fiction and Film, 1954–1992*, Oxford: Clarendon Press, and New York: Oxford University Press, 1994

Ghirelli, Massimo, *Gillo Pontecorvo*, Florence: La Nuova Italia, 1974

Mellen, Joan, *Film Guide to the Battle of Algiers*, Bloomington: Indiana University Press, 1973

Michalczyk, John J., *The Italian Political Filmmakers*, Rutherford, New Jersey: Fairleigh Dickinson University Press, 1986

Ory, Pascal, "L'Algérie fait écran" in *La Guerre d'Algérie et les français*, edited by Jean-Pierre Rioux, Paris: Fayard, 1990

Solinas, Franco, *Gillo Pontecorvo's The Battle of Algiers* (includes English-language screenplay by Solinas), New York: Scribner, 1973

POPULAR CULTURE

Popular culture is notoriously difficult to define. As an academic subject, the area is of relatively recent origin, and its introduction has had the effect of broadening the ambit of many traditional disciplines, such as literature, while providing the impetus for newer ones such as media and communication studies. Once considered to be beneath serious academic investigation, it also now appears to be finding legitimacy in areas well beyond cultural studies; for example, the relationship between law and popular culture has become pertinent, because the study of popular culture is bound up with its ideological significance and consequent relationship to the state, and, as Strinati points out, "It therefore seems difficult to define popular culture independently of the theory which is designed to explain it." All of this has considerable implications for the study of censorship.

Burke, for example, in his analysis of popular culture in early modern Europe, concentrates on where it occurred, and defines it in a "negative way" as the unofficial culture of those Gramsci termed the "subordinate classes". Macdonald focuses on the audience for which artefacts are intended:

> For about a century, Western culture has really been two cultures: the traditional kind – let us call it "High Culture" – that is chronicled in the textbooks, and a "Mass Culture" manufactured wholesale for the market. In the old art forms, the artisans of Mass Culture have long been at work: in the novel, the line stretches from Eugène Sue to Lloyd C. Douglas; in music, from Offenbach to Tin-Pan Alley; in art from the chromo to Maxfield Parrish and Norman Rockwell; in architecture, from Victorian Gothic to suburban Tudor. Mass Culture has also developed new media of its own, into which the serious artists rarely ventures: radio, the movies, comic books, detective stories, science fiction, television (Macdonald 1957).

Those in the camp of high culture may have come to use the term "popular" pejoratively. Thus the popular or tabloid press may be viewed as inferior to the broadsheets or so-called quality press (though the British *Daily Mail* and *Daily Express* were once broadsheets); or popular fiction, music, or television may be described as intrinsically of lower quality (although television, for example, regularly transmits adaptations of high culture, from Shakespeare to Samuel Beckett). Those who take this view rarely consider whether the term "popular culture" refers to genuine people's culture, or to one imposed from above, for instance by commercial interests.

Even those who adopt a "theory neutral" definition run into problems when the more traditional boundaries merge. Berger provides some useful examples of this shifting mix:

> . . . works of elite culture influence works of popular culture (for example, many films draw upon myths), whereas in other cases, the influence is reversed (for instance, the cartoon character Krazy Kat was incorporated in a ballet, an elite art form). Some works originally seen as popular culture are later elevated to the status of elite culture (for example, Gershwin's *Porgy and Bess* has in

recent years attained the elite status of opera, whereas in the past it was often considered simply "folk opera" or a musical play).

Such mixing has, to say the least, muddied the waters for those moral guardians who would once have attempted censorship on the grounds of class or notions of what is "good" for people. Indeed, few would attempt overtly to censor on such grounds today.

Eileen and Stephen Yeo, after a study of popular culture embracing areas such as church bands, street football, and music halls, illustrate another perspective that what is both "popular" and "culture" is capable of development. They eloquently note that

> . . . the struggles mapped out in this book were also about control over time and territory. They were about social initiative, and who was to have it. They were about expected notions of what it is to be human and normal. They were struggles of substance in themselves. They were also struggles about *form*, the forms that association, mainly in the cultural and "leisure" branches of activity would take. When put together, they may be seen as struggles about the dominant styles and contours, constraints and opportunities of whole periods (Yeo and Yeo 1981).

Thus, as Burke demonstrates, the clergy of early modern Europe, Catholic and Protestant, objected on moral and theological grounds to miracle and mystery plays, popular sermons and religious festivals,

> denounced as occasions of sin, more especially of drunkenness, gluttony and lechery, and as encouraging servitude to the world, the flesh and the Devil – especially the Devil. It did not escape the godly that the maypole is a phallic symbol. Plays, songs and, above all dances were condemned for awakening dangerous emotions and as incitements to fornication (Burke 1978).

The Reformers were at first successful in their "censorship" of these activities, but as Ronald Hutton shows, people found other outlets, and in England, after a further reaction in favour of Protestant values in the 1640s, from 1660 "the attack on secular merry making was called off for half a century". It surfaced again with the activities of groups such as the Society for the Suppression of Vice in the 18th and 19th centuries, and it is still present in, for example, the uneasiness of moral guardians at television pictures of Elvis Presley, restricted to the upper half of his body because it was thought that images of his writhing hips would be too much for many young women to bear.

From the late 18th century onwards, state control has been directed at culture that is in mass circulation. Of *Lady Chatterley's Lover* by D.H. Lawrence (which most would place, if they had to make a choice, in the ranks of high culture), Sutherland has remarked, "Some custodians had been alarmed less at the four-letter words and 'bouts' . . . than at the fact that they were available to all in a 3s.6d book". He notes similarly that an expensive edition of John Cleland's *Fanny Hill* was tolerated, whereas the 3s.6d edition was subject to notorious litigation.

Political regimes may seek control over popular cultures because they see them as a contradiction of a national identity they are trying to create. Thus in communist Czechoslovakia, for example, four "long-haired, anti-social elements" of the pop group Plastic People of the Universe were imprisoned in the 1980s for "jeopardizing the education of youth in a socialist spirit". Censorship may also be related to the fact that certain kinds of popular culture are associated with ideologies considered hostile. After the 1979 revolution in Iran, for instance, popular art forms seen as reflecting western values suffered wholesale prohibition, and in Eastern bloc countries, Levi jeans were officially excluded because they were perceived as part of decadent (American) culture. In both these cases there was underground resistance, fed by the black market.

Frith points out that music has the necessary qualities to contribute to a more than individual cultural dimension: "Music, whether teenybop for young female fans, or jazz or rap for African-Americans or nineteenth century music for German Jews in Israel, stands for, symbolizes *and* offers the immediate experience of collective identity". Where such music has appeared to states as threatening to national unity and order, it has often been subject to restriction and suppression; the levels of control over rap in the US in the 1980s were as much attempts to control racial dissidents as an attack on "obscene music".

The censorship of sport should also be considered. Walvin has noted that even in pre-industrial societies public sport was conceived as a threat "to the life and limb of players and spectators and to the peace and property of the neighbourhood". The behaviour of football crowds was seen as so undermining of public order that, for instance, in 1840, the mayor of Derby in the English Midlands pronounced the game illegal. A 19th-century writer believed that spectator sports were "sowing the seeds of such a crop of weeds as the most elaborate treatment in the future will be unable to eradicate" (Abell quoted in Birley, 1995). As if to prove him right, in the 1980s football became again the chief folk devil of British popular culture, when hooliganism and serious disasters caused extreme political embarrassment which, if not censorship in a technical sense, at least altered the experience of attending a match. It is worth noting, in passing, that local authorities were similarly alarmed and took similar action to restrict the threat to disorder they thought was posed by the gathering of large crowds in the early cinemas.

It is interesting, finally, that British censorship has recently returned to an area last visited in early modern Europe – the festival. At Castle Martin in 1992, a huge, nonstop gathering lasting over 100 hours took place on a square mile of woodland in the Malvern Hills. It was seen by the "New Age travellers" who attended it as an occasion for spiritual growth, but, partly because the travellers adopted some of the culture of "raves" (unlicensed outdoor events that advocated hedonism and often outwitted the police), it led to the enactment of the Criminal Justice and Public Order Act (1994). This was described by the pressure group Liberty as "the most wide-ranging attack on human rights in the UK in years. If offends the basic principles of justice and is likely to increase harassment and intimidation . . . it tries to outlaw diversity and dissent". Unquestionably, the police, the press, and the local landowners would have disagreed, but effectively, the government was attempting to censor lifestyles.

STEVE GREENFIELD and GUY OSBORN

Further Reading

Berger, Arthur Asa, *Cultural Criticism: A Primer of Key Concepts*, Thousand Oaks, California: Sage, 1995

Birley, Derek, *Sport and the Making of Britain*, Manchester: Manchester University Press, 1993

Birley, Derek, *Land of Sport and Glory: Sport and British Society, 1887–1910*, Manchester: Manchester University Press, 1995

Blake, Andrew, *The Body Language: The Meaning of Modern Sport*, London: Lawrence and Wishart, 1996

Burke, Peter, *Popular Culture in Early Modern Europe*, London: Temple Smith, and New York: New York University Press, 1978

Collin, Matthew, *Altered State: The Story of Ecstasy Culture and Acid House*, London and New York: Serpent's Tail, 1997

Feldman, David, *Civil Liberties and Human Rights in England and Wales*, Oxford: Clarendon Press, and New York: Oxford University Press, 1993

Frith, S., "Music and Identity" in *Questions of Cultural Identity*, edited by Stuart Hall and Paul du Sage, London and Thousand Oaks, California: Sage, 1996

Greenfield, Steve and Guy Osborn, "When the Writ Hits the Fan: Panic Law and Football Fandom" in *Fanatics! Power, Identity and Fandom in Football*, edited by Adam Brown, London and New York: Routledge, 1998

Hebdige, Dick, *Hiding in the Light: On Images and Things*, London and New York: Routledge, 1988

Macdonald, D., "A Theory of Mass Culture" in *Cultural Theory and Popular Culture: A Reader*, edited by John Storey, New York: Harvester Wheatsheaf, 1994

Marqusee, Mike, *Anyone but England: Cricket and the National Malaise*, London and New York: Verso, 1994

Murray, Bill, *Football: A History of the World Game*, Aldershot, Hampshire: Scolar Press, and Brookfield, Vermont: Ashgate, 1994

Redhead, Steve, *Unpopular Cultures: The Birth of Law and Popular Culture*, Manchester: Manchester University Press, 1995

Strinati, Dominic, *An Introduction to Theories of Popular Culture*, London and New York: Routledge, 1995

Sutherland, John, *Offensive Literature: Decensorship in Britian, 1960–1982*, London: Junction, and Totowa, New Jersey: Barnes and Noble, 1982

Turner, Graeme, *British Cultural Studies: An Introduction*, 2nd edition, London and New York: Routledge, 1996

Walvin, James, *The People's Game: A Social History of British Football*, London: Allen Lane, 1975

Walvin, James, *The People's Game: The History of Football Revisited*, London: Mainstream, 1994

Yeo, Eileen and Stephen Yeo (editors), *Popular Culture and Class Conflict, 1590–1914: Explorations in the History of Labour and Leisure*, Brighton: Harvester Press, and Atlantic Highlands, New Jersey: Humanities Press, 1981

PORNOGRAPHY

Pornography is the depiction of sexual behaviour in the arts and media that is intended to cause or does cause sexual arousal. The term has traditionally been used to describe sex-related material that a dominant group does not wish to be available to a less powerful group. The US President's Commission on Obscenity and Pornography (1970) concluded, however, that the term "pornography" had no legal significance and primarily denoted subjective disapproval of certain materials rather than meaning anything specific about their content or effect.

Obscenity is the category of sexual content that is regulated by law; however, pornography is a broader popular term, not only for such content, but also for offensive and extreme representations of other content, such as violence and death, the expression of which is disturbing and provokes an intense emotional reaction; these matters are explored in the entry on violence. Pornography and obscenity are often distinguished from erotica, which presents sex or sexual love in a humanistic, tender or sensuous manner and/or has artistic claims or pretensions. The term "erotica" is generally used to describe materials that are not considered to be subject to censorship or other regulatory controls.

Explicit sexual material includes a whole range of depictions or descriptions in text or pictorial form, such as films, videotapes, postcards, peep booths, sound recordings, paintings, photographs, statuary, live performances, magazines, books, and, most recently, the Internet. Print is generally less likely to be censored than pictorial materials such as motion pictures and videotapes, as these are believed to be more provocative than print. Also, popular art materials such as photography are more likely to be censored than high art forms such as opera or ballet.

In modern times, a distinction is often made between soft-core and hard-core pornography, with most censorship or other regulation being directed at the latter. Hard-core usually signifies that the material depicts male erections or presents sexual organs interacting. Soft-core generally involves soft focus or implied sexual activity and fuzziness or ambiguity about its details. The same material may be prepared in a hard-core version for one market and a soft-core version for another.

Attitudes towards explicit pornography in any given society are closely related to that society's attitudes towards sexual behaviour. Western attitudes towards both the behaviour and the materials changed a great deal during the 20th century. World Wars I and II contributed to these changes, because of the enormous strains on the countries involved, the contact with other cultures, and the years of living with death. It is possible that the increasing awareness of the Holocaust by the late 1940s helped to make the world readier to accept representations of sex and other previously hidden aspects of human behaviour. Around this period, there emerged in many countries a growing interest in sex-related materials in both traditional and popular arts. This interest often led to a countervailing response of suppression and direct or indirect censorship. However, even in countries with strongly authoritarian governments, there were efforts to create and distribute sex-oriented materials clandestinely, as indeed there have been throughout history.

The nature and volume of pornography in a country is dependent on many factors, including the country's economy, degree of industrialization, the role of religion, gender roles, politics and government, literacy level, socioeconomic class structure, involvement in the threat or reality of military action, relative access to communications technology, cultural history, legal system, and national character. Similar national characteristics determine the nature of censorship, which may involve a system of prior restraint and deletion of unacceptable material or seizure by enforcement agencies like police, customs, or postal services. A government funding agency may refuse to support explicit works. Civil or criminal action may be taken in the courts.

Other forms of social control may be used to block explicit pornography: examples include the cancellation of exhibitions, lists of prohibited material, boycotts, picketing, and self-censorship by the artists. During the last few decades of the 20th century, mergers created enormous power for some international media conglomerates that exercise control over content and distribution. Officials in these conglomerates can modify or exclude materials that are believed to be pornographic, although there would be little or no record of such internal censorship. Similar kinds of informal control are increasingly replacing formal controls in many arenas.

Extent of the pornography business

Because of the large number of small producers, lack of trade associations, and the ambivalence with which the products are regarded in many countries, the extent of the pornography business is difficult to assess. Nonetheless, it has long been and continues to be a worldwide business. Some impression of its range may be derived from studies of the market for explicit materials in the United States, the world's largest producer of pornography, where the collection of market data is relatively advanced: here, in 1996, pornographic materials accounted for sales of over $8 billion, compared with $10 million in 1970. Another indication of the market's robustness is provided by the 8000 hard-core video titles released in 1995, compared with approximately 400 traditional films released in the same year by Hollywood.

In this market, new products emerge regularly. Telephone sex services are one example, illustrating the shift in the site of consumption of pornography from theatres and cinemas to people's own homes. In the US about $1 billion a year is spent on telephone sex, with the average call lasting about seven minutes, at a cost of $1 to $4 per minute. Other innovative services and products, such as cable television sex channels and hotel-room sex-film rentals, have been successfully introduced in other countries. Prior to the 1970s, Japan, Sweden, and Germany were the leading exporters, but the United States is now the world leader in pornography exports and new pornographic products.

In recent decades, there has been considerable movement in the relative sizes of the market for explicit materials in various countries. Denmark's experience with these materials is relevant here. It was the first country to legalize print and pictorial sex materials (1969). Soon thereafter, there was a dramatic increase in the sales, rental, and other uses of this material. Within a few years, however, sales dropped sharply: evidently, the novelty of the availability of explicit pornography had worn off. The market has since remained flat.

As worldwide distribution of pornography increases, there is no way of predicting which countries will continue to expand their interest, which will become bored, and which will maintain a consistent level of consumer demand. In every country, demographic, cultural, and social factors will influence the market trends, as will the number of new products that emerge. Other influential factors will include the extent to which pornography is perceived to be an important problem and the extent to which its regulation is given priority by the government and other watchdog groups.

Literary and artistic quality

Explicit material, like other aspects of high and popular cultures, has complex relationships to traditional criteria of literary and artistic quality. Pornography is not likely to be part of a country's official cultural canon and has involved many different formats. Like other artistic genres, the products may be well or poorly crafted. Few of the materials are reviewed regularly by the general media.

A number of celebrated artists have created artistically outstanding works that were at first considered to be obscene, although not necessarily pornographic. James Joyce's *Ulysses* (1922) is one of the world's great novels, but it could not be imported into the United States until a landmark 1933 decision by Judge John M. Woolsey. Similarly, the Academy Award-winning films *Ladri di biciclette* (1948, Bicycle Thieves) by Vittorio de Sica and *Jungfrukällen* (1960, The Virgin Spring) by Ingmar Bergman were found to be obscene in the United States. The banned film *Blue Movie* (1969) was directed by Andy Warhol, the key figure in Pop Art. In 1990, a Cincinnati museum's retrospective exhibition of photographs by the distinguished photographer Robert Mapplethorpe led to criminal charges against the museum and its director and demands for the elimination of the US government arts agency, the National Endowment for the Arts. *Memoirs of Hecate County*, a novel by Edmund Wilson, one of America's leading men of letters, was found to be obscene in 1948.

Practically every major writer or artist of the last two centuries has produced some work that has been described as pornographic. However, the typical creator of explicit works is not a major figure, and the work is not necessarily memorable. Most audiences are not responsive to the creator's unique vision or sensibility or to nuances of technique. The marketing of pornography seldom stresses the individual creator's artistry. Pornographic materials have increasingly become mass-market commodities that are sold competitively on the basis of price, with little or no emphasis on artistic dimensions. Even so, it is still difficult to draw lines between "real art" and even mass culture on the one hand, and pornography on the other. Opponents of censorship believe that to do so is likely to be more damaging to the former than to the latter.

Cultural context

In each country, the nature and vigour of the censorship of pornography reflects complex cultural, historical, and political forces. Government beliefs that licentious or obscene materials had to be controlled could be seen in the repressive totalitarian governments of the 20th century, whose leaders understood that people who have sexual freedom in the arts may be encouraged to seek personal and social liberty. In Nazi Germany, Hitler proscribed the "dark and sultry sensualism" of Jewish art and writings. In the Soviet Union, Jewish writers and artists were regularly denounced as pornographers and were often imprisoned.

Obscenity censorship has been relatively restrictive in East Asia, although it has become less common with the impact of modernization. In Japan, censorship of printed obscene material was ubiquitous in the 19th and early 20th centuries: between 1903 and 1917, the home minister blocked publication of 9960 books for reasons of public morality. Censorship continues in Japan today, as it does in China, where obscene films, videotapes, and music were prohibited in a 1982 resolution. In 1990, the death penalty was established in China for major pornography traffickers. Such severe measures are consistent not only with Chinese communism but also with the anti-sexual emphases of the larger culture and its concern about keeping the birth rate down.

Although independent India has never had formal censorship, its flourishing film industry is completely controlled by the state, and even screen kisses were prohibited until the 1990s, reflecting the country's traditional discouragement of public displays of affection. Such restrictions on sexual contact in films may have facilitated the films' acceptance by the multiple ethnicities and religious groups in India.

In the Soviet Union and the other communist countries, pornography was vigorously opposed, because it was believed to drain energies away from revolutionary goals. The Western countries were said to be infiltrating central and eastern European countries with pornography as a tactic to subvert communism. Any such materials had to be distributed clandestinely. In the communist countries, as elsewhere, pornography is regarded as a form of subversion.

Some western European countries have maximized access to sex-oriented materials for adults, while at the same time prohibiting obscenity and establishing machinery to safeguard children from exposure to it. In France, where the arts have enjoyed relative freedom since 1881, a commission evaluates materials for their impact on youth, and an obscene book can be re-evaluated after 20 years.

After the rigidities of the Hitler years, Germany permits adults great freedom – Germany probably has the largest per capita number of retail sex shops that sell explicit materials – but protects young people from exposure. Although less liberal, the Italian laws are also primarily concerned with the protection of the young. The Scandinavian countries, especially Sweden and Denmark, have consistently been liberal towards these materials.

In Britain, as in other European countries, the early 19th-century movement towards public education and inexpensive books was paralleled by concern about the obscenity of some of the materials that were available for the newly literate. A Society for the Suppression of Vice was established in 1802. In the Hicklin decision of 1868, the Lord Chief Justice noted that the obscenity test was intended to establish whether the

PORNOGRAPHY: Cover of the French journal *La Caricature*, May 1882, showing a drawing entitled *La Grande Epidémie de Pornographie* (The Great Epidemic of Pornography). France has maintained a liberal stance on artistic expression since 1881.

material could "deprave and corrupt those whose minds are open to such immoral influences", such as children. Obscenity prosecutions were actively pursued, along with seizures and destruction of materials by customs officers and police. A parliamentary committee reported that 167,000 books had been seized during 1954. The 1959 Obscene Publications Act made obscenity convictions more difficult by permitting expert testimony, requiring consideration of the work as a whole, and encouraging the consideration of scientific, literary, artistic, and educational criteria. The 1979 Williams Report recommended further relaxation of the rules.

For almost a century after the Hicklin decision, US obscenity law closely paralleled British practice. Then, in 1957 (*Roth v. United States*), the Supreme Court adopted a new and relatively liberal set of criteria, which may have influenced the 1959 British law. The relatively parallel progress in the two countries could be seen when the unexpurgated version of D.H. Lawrence's 1928 novel *Lady Chatterley's Lover* was declared not obscene in London in 1960, at just about the same time as the book was cleared by a New York court. US customs and post office authorities and the courts gave the green light to many other previously banned works between 1957 and 1973.

In the USA, as in a number of European countries, the 1960s was a decade in which liberal impulses were expressed in the youth movement, rock music, generational conflict, antiwar demonstrations, civil rights activities, and drug use. There was also greater acceptance of explicit materials and considerable opposition to censorship. Possibly because of concern about the implications of some liberation activities, a conservative Supreme Court handed down a more restrictive definition of obscenity. The case was *Miller v. California* (1973), and it set forth three criteria, all of which had to be met for materials to be found obscene: that the average adult, applying the standards of the contemporary community, would find the work, taken as a whole, to appeal to a prurient interest in sex; that sexual conduct was presented in a patently offensive manner; and that, taken as a whole, the work lacked serious literary, artistic, political, or scientific value. Standards of tolerance of acceptability for the materials were to be determined by each venue.

Between 1980 and 1992, anti-obscenity efforts were a major priority of the federal government, and they continue to play an important role. New legal weapons have been developed, including nuisance abatement laws, warning labels, anti-display laws, and re-zoning urban areas in order to avoid any concentration of sex-oriented theatres and bookshops. Opponents of censorship argue that such zoning provides a functional equivalent to censorship by making access to sex-related theatres and retail establishments either difficult or impossible.

Videotapes, magazines, and films are among the many pornographic materials that can be used in the privacy of one's home. In the last 20 years, there has been a greater expansion of the United States market for explicit pornography than any that occurred in the first 200 years of its history, in spite of the country's relatively restrictive laws and their vigorous enforcement. It is possible that enforcement activity has contributed to market growth by giving explicit materials a "forbidden fruit" dimension, which has added an oppositional appeal to their other selling points.

Gershon Legman has pointed out that the United States promotes the celebration of expressions of violence that would be censored in many other countries. The obscenity laws and "Adults Only" ratings for television programmes, magazines, movies, and popular music are overwhelmingly more likely to be applied in the United States against sex than against violence, although the reverse is true in many other countries.

Arguments for the censorship of pornography

The debate over censorship of explicit pornography has been extensive and continues today. Organized religion, some critics, some feminists, and other groups using the research findings of social scientists have called for its censorship for different reasons and at different times. Twentieth-century Catholic theologians have understood St Thomas Aquinas's writings as arguing that a work that arouses genital commotion and stimulates sexual passion outside marriage is obscene. Canon Law prohibits Catholics from reading books that "describe or teach impure or obscene matters". In Catholic moral theology, obscenity is said to degrade humans by reducing them to an animal level with a morally corrupt focus on body parts. Protestant asceticism has also been seen by some historians as contributing to negative attitudes toward sexual expression in the arts. Islamic countries tend to have substantial (if often ineffective) censorship of explicit materials.

Throughout the centuries, moralists, civic leaders, and political figures have interpreted a society's interest in the description and portrayal of sex as a reflection of cultural decline. Literary and social critics have denounced obscenity and pornography on various grounds. George Steiner has called pornography a totalitarian assault on the individual and an onslaught on human privacy. Norman Podhoretz has complained that it is boring and presents faceless creatures, not people. D.H. Lawrence denounced pornography's role in stimulating secretive masturbation. Ernest Van den Haag was concerned that it stimulated perverse forms of sexual satisfaction. Geoffrey Gorer feared that the young and immature would be precociously excited by it. Agnes Repplier noted pornography's negative impact on standards of taste and judgement and on the cultural environment.

The denunciation of pornography by certain feminists and political conservatives has received considerable attention in a number of countries, especially in the United States and Canada. Robin Morgan's epigram "Pornography is the theory, rape is the practice" has been cited frequently. In the last two decades of the 20th century, the most intense attacks came from the American feminist theorists Catharine MacKinnon and Andrea Dworkin, who define pornography as the sexually explicit subordination of women, graphically depicted in pictures or words. Women are said to be dehumanized and presented as sexual objects or commodities in such material. US federal courts have, in an Indianapolis case, found this approach to be unconstitutional, but in 1992 Canada's highest court determined that materials that are "degrading" or "dehumanizing" to women were illegal (Butler v. The Queen). To date, Canada is the only country where this approach has been implemented, although versions of the approach have been introduced in the legislatures of several countries.

Since the 1970s, substantial research in experimental psychology and other social sciences has been devoted to the investigation of the effects and functions of exposure to sexually explicit materials. Some research has found that such presentations can lead to potentially harmful imitation. Other studies suggest that an increase in sexual violence in the media can, under some conditions, promote antisocial behaviour and attitudes, such as the mistaken belief that women benefit from rape or other sexual violence. A number of researchers have reported that explicit materials have become more pro-rape in the last three decades.

Research has also been conducted into the role of the media in creating, enhancing, and sustaining sexual callousness in men and degrading women in the eyes of both men and women. One social-learning model suggests that violent and dehumanizing pornography is most likely to encourage sexual abuse in young males who are already sexually aggressive. The experimentally demonstrated effects of prolonged consumption of pornography have been said to include diminished desire for progeny and discontent with the appearance and sexual performance of intimate partners.

Arguments against the censorship of pornography

The pro-censorship arguments have been opposed by other critics and artists, some feminists, and groups that have cited social science research. Noted critics and writers like Susan Sontag, Norman Mailer, André Gide, James T. Farrell, Richard Brown, Albert Camus, Georges Bataille, Jean-Paul Sartre, and Arthur Knight have either attacked the censorship of artistic materials said to be obscene or testified at criminal trials on behalf of such materials.

These critics and artists cite various negative consequences of not permitting the arts and media to deal fully and openly with sexual matters. In testimony about such materials, critics and writers generally discuss the literary and artistic qualities of the work that is the subject of the trial. The British critic Kenneth Tynan argued that every artist hopes to stimulate the audience, so that explicit literature's arousal of sexual response is as legitimate as the arousal of other emotions or passions. He developed the nude theatre review Oh, Calcutta! (1969), which was designed to stimulate its audiences sexually, and which ran for four years in New York City and for extended periods in other cities and countries.

Some feminist writers, such as Sallie Tisdale, have identified positive dimensions of pornography. The Feminist Anti-Censorship Task-Force observed that explicit materials may empower women. Some feminists have produced explicit films and other materials, specifically for women or couples, that are sensitive to relationship and humanistic issues. Nadine Strossen of the American Civil Liberties Union (ACLU) has argued that the MacKinnon–Dworkin viewpoint represents only one feminist faction, the views of which would be likely to aggravate misogynistic violence and discrimination. Strossen reports that the 1992 Canadian Supreme Court decision has wreaked havoc on feminist bookshops and lesbian literature in Canada and has overlooked the actual concerns of real women by relying on an approach that represents a "quick fix" to complex problems.

A number of social science and psychiatric investigators have observed that the antisocial consequences attributed to pornography are not consistent with what is known about the complexity and multicausality of human behaviour. They also cite pro-social functions of pornography, both for people who are and for those who are not experiencing sexual difficulties. Such materials can stimulate fantasy, which may increase sexual satisfaction and, as psychoanalyst Otto Kernberg noted, "can be an antidote to stifled passion".

The US President's Commission on Obscenity and Pornography (1970) found that explicit materials, especially pictorial materials, provide very useful information on sexual behaviour to people who do not have access to traditional medical or other information sources or who are too embarrassed to pursue such sources. By desensitizing couples so that they can communicate more effectively with each other, such materials may improve the couples' sex lives. Explicit material provides a form of safe sex and offers information and gratification to a range of people, some of whom are without access to sex or are separated from their partners. Other reports have cited their use in the treatment of sexual dysfunctions, the diagnosis and treatment of some paraphilias, and other beneficial effects, such as the blocking of criminal impulses. Several studies, beginning with a Kinsey Institute report by Gebhard (1965),

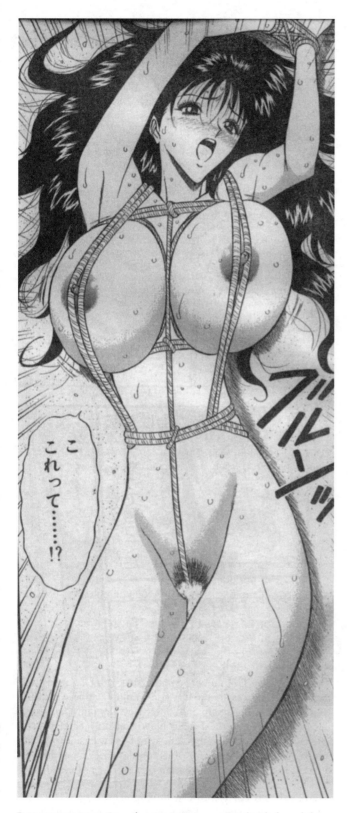

PORNOGRAPHY: Page from a Japanese comic book for adults showing a bondage scene. Bondage and rape have been common themes in Japanese pornography. A recent study, however, has found that despite this, the incidence of reported rape is surprisingly low in Japan.

have reported that convicted sex offenders are less likely than other offenders to have been exposed to explicit materials.

Cross-cultural investigations by Berl Kutchinsky have found that in Denmark, Sweden, and West Germany, the only three countries to have legalized pornography, rape rates declined or were constant between 1964 and 1984, although violent non-sexual crime increased substantially over the same 20-year period. In these countries and elsewhere, it is possible that the availability of explicit pornography provides a harmless safety valve for aberrant impulses. Another cross-cultural study found that, although bondage and rape are dominant themes in Japanese print and film pornography, the incidence of reported rape in Japan is extraordinarily low.

The lack of agreement on policy towards pornography can be seen in the divergent conclusions reached by the two official investigations in the United States in recent decades. The President's Commission of 1970 recommended that the obscenity laws be eliminated because of lack of evidence that pornography caused harm. By contrast, the Attorney General's Commission of 1986 argued that, because pornography could cause harm, there should be strict enforcement of existing obscenity laws.

New technology

Producers of pornography have regularly expanded their markets by using new technologies. In the 1970s, the Super 8mm home-movie projector provided a larger and clearer picture, and its inexpensive cartridge did not require users to thread the film. Around the same time, peep booths offered low-cost movies in private cubicles. The 1980s witnessed an explosion in the production of videotapes for home viewing and the development of telephone sex services. In the 1990s, the most dynamic new vehicle for disseminating explicit materials was provided by computers and the Internet. The vast expansion of both commercial and not-for-profit sexually explicit materials on the World Wide Web during the 1990s has led to criminal prosecutions in Germany, the United States, and other countries. Explicit materials proliferate on the Internet because of the low cost and ease of distribution, and because distributors can easily mask their identities, move out of electronic mailboxes, and destroy evidence that might lead to prosecution. Electronic distribution across borders is testing the limits of obscenity laws developed in a less technologically sophisticated era.

In cyberspace, pornography may be censored or criminalized by any venue in which it is received. Thus, a California couple was convicted in 1994 of distributing obscene material from their home-based computer bulletin board, after being indicted in Memphis, Tennessee, the site of the 1976 prosecution of *Deep Throat*. The problems inherent in efforts to censor and otherwise control explicit materials were underscored by a US Supreme Court decision unanimously overturning a federal law that attempted to criminalize "indecent" internet materials (*Reno* v. *American Civil Liberties Union*, 1997). The court noted the problems deriving from the substantial proportion of sex-related materials coming into the United States from other countries.

There is good reason to expect that the internet will represent the most rapidly growing vehicle for distribution of explicit materials in the next few decades, on a worldwide basis. The huge profits that are possible, the opportunity for multilateral interaction, and the international ramifications have not yet been fully addressed by the world's mechanisms for social control. Computer-mediated communication that permits actual back-and-forth discourse poses many new challenges for the existing mechanisms for censoring pornography.

CHARLES WINICK

Further Reading

Abramson, P.R. and H. Hayashi, "Pornography in Japan: Cross-cultural and Theoretical Considerations" in *Pornography and Sexual Aggression*, edited by Neil M. Malamuth and Edward Donnerstein, New York: Academic Press, 1984

Attorney General's Commission on Pornography: Final Report, 2 vols, Washington, DC: Department of Justice, 1986

De Grazia, Edward and Roger K. Newman, *Banned Films: Movies, Censors, and the First Amendment*, New York: Bowker, 1982

Donnerstein, Edward et al., *The Question of Pornography: Research Findings and Policy Implications*, New York: Free Press, and London: Collier Macmillan, 1987

Dworkin, Andrea, *Pornography: Men Possessing Women*, New York: Putnam, and London: Women's Press, 1981

Gardiner, Harold, *On Censorship*, New York: Hanover House, 1958

Gebhard, Paul et al., *Sex Offenders: An Analysis of Types*, New York: Harper, 1965

Gubar, Susan and Joan Hoff (editors), *For Adult Users Only: The Dilemma of Violent Pornography*, Bloomington: Indiana University Press, 1989

Hawkins, Gordon and Franklin E. Zimring, *Pornography in a Free Society*, Cambridge and New York: Cambridge University Press, 1988

Kappeler, Susanne, *The Pornography of Representation*, Minneapolis: University of Minnesota Press, 1986

Kendrick, Walter, *The Secret Museum: Pornography in Modern Culture*, New York: Viking, 1987

Kutchinsky, Berl, "Pornography and Rape: Theory and Practice?", *International Journal of Law and Psychiatry*, 14 (1991): 47–68

Legman, G., *Love and Death: A Study in Censorship*, New York: Breaking Point, 1949

MacKinnon, Catharine A., *Only Words*, Cambridge, Massachusetts: Harvard University Press, 1993; London: HarperCollins, 1994

Mitchell, Richard H., *Censorship in Imperial Japan*, Princeton, New Jersey: Princeton University Press, 1983

Rist, Ray C., *The Pornography Controversy: Changing Moral Standards in American Life*, New Brunswick, New Jersey: Transaction, 1975

Schlosser, Eric, "The Business of Pornography", *U.S. News and World Report*, 122/5 (1997): 42–50

Shah, A.B. (editor), *The Roots of Obscenity: Obscenity, Literature and the Law*, Bombay: Lalvani, 1968

Strossen, Nadine, *Defending Pornography: Free Speech, Sex, and the Fight for Women's Rights*, New York: Scribner, 1995; London: Abacus, 1996

Tisdale, Sallie, *Talk Dirty to Me: An Intimate Philosophy of Sex*, New York: Doubleday, 1994

United States Commission on Obscenity and Pornography, *The Report of the Commission on Obscenity and Pornography*, Washington, DC, 1970

Williams, Bernard, *Report of the Committee on Obscenity and Film Censorship*, London: HMSO, 1979

Winick, Charles, "From Deviant to Normative: Changes in the Social Acceptability of Sexually Explicit Material" in *Deviance and Social Change*, edited by Edward Sagarin, Beverly Hills, California: Sage, 1977

Winick, Charles, "A Content Analysis of Sexually Explicit Magazines Sold in Adult Bookstores", *Journal of Sex Research*, 21/2 (1985): 206–10

Zillmann, Dolf and Jennings Bryant (editors), *Pornography: Research Advances and Policy Considerations*, Hillsdale, New Jersey: Erlbaum, 1989

PORTUGAL

Population: 10,016,000	**Number of periodicals:** 182
Main religions: Roman Catholic; Protestant	**Number of radio receivers per 1000 inhabitants:** 306
Official language: Portuguese	**Number of TV receivers per 1000 inhabitants:** 336
Illiteracy rate (%): 5.2 (m); 10.0 (f)	**Number of PCs per 1000 inhabitants:** 81.3
Number of daily newspapers: 27	

In 1972, two years before the "Carnation Revolution" brought censorship in Portugal to an end, the novelist, playwright, and critic José Cardoso Pires calculated that "in the five centuries of its publishing history, Portugal has experienced 420 years of censorship". To the exceptionally long duration of the Portuguese Inquisition (1536–1821), he had added the years (1926–74) of the Estado Novo (New State) of Antonio de Oliveira Salazar and Marcelo Caetano; he also noted that censorship was by no means absent during the period of constitutional monarchy (1834–1910), and that the only real exception to the general rule had been under the First Republic (1910–26). Moreover, censorship was extensive in Portugal's overseas colonies (Brazil from c.1500 to independence in 1820; Angola and Mozambique up to 1974–75), and Portuguese censorship is bound up with such historical issues as slavery and

the slave trade. One might suppose that, after so many centuries of repression, the Portuguese would have been indelibly conditioned to censorship and self-censorship: indeed, Cardoso Pires describes how the Estado Novo transformed censorship into a "syntax of thought". In fact, however, since the late 1970s Portugal, unlike some of its former African colonies, has done little to arouse the attention of historians of censorship.

Medieval and early modern Portugal, to 1750

Like its neighbour Spain, Portugal was occupied by Arab forces under Walid I during the early eighth century, after which the Iberian peninsula became a fully independent Islamic state. Most of the population, with the exception of those in the far north of the territory, were converted, and for several centuries Iberian Islam was noted, not only for its scholarship, but also for its toleration of the Jewish and Christian minorities who remained. Christian attempts to recover what in due course became Portugal ("The Land of the Port") began with the forcible assertion by Robert Courte-Heuse, duke of Normandy, of a claim to the coastal region in 1097. Portugal's first king, Alfonso Henriques o Conquistador (Alfonso Henry the Conqueror), founder of the Burgundian dynasty, was installed in 1139, and Lisbon was conquered by English crusaders in 1147. Reconversion was undertaken by the Cistercians. It appears that, in general, the missionary Christians were less tolerant of Muslims than Muslims had been of Christians. By 1250, most of Portugal had been united under Alfonso III (1210–79), who also conquered the Algarve in 1256.

The Portuguese people rose in revolt against the Burgundian dynasty in 1383 and in 1385 the parliament elected John of Avis as king João I (reigned 1385–93). He inaugurated a dynasty that, until Portugal was taken over by Philip II of Spain in 1580, oversaw not only Portugal's emergence onto the world stage, in the great age of exploration, but also the evolution of forms of censorship that long characterized Portuguese regimes of all types.

João I's son, prince Henry the Navigator, a man of the Renaissance, and a student of the skies and the tides, sought the help of a Jew, Abraham Creques, a Majorcan cartographer, to guide his global journeys. Jews set up the country's first printing presses, at Lisbon, Faro, and Leiria, in the 1480s, publishing 11 works, including the Pentateuch, in Hebrew. Jews also suffered increasing intolerance from the 1490s onwards. The immediate occasion for this was the expulsion of Jews from Spain in 1492: 60,000 of them were allowed into Portugal for six months. It has been estimated that as a result Jews temporarily made up one fifth of the total population. After these six months, however, the Portuguese authorities imitated the Spanish policy: the Jews had either to convert to Christianity, or to depart. Some Jews were rich enough to buy themselves out of the ultimatum, but many of the poor had to take refuge in North Africa. In 1497, King Manuel I first promised not to persecute the *conversos* or "New Christians" for 20 years, then made public worship by Jews and Muslims illegal. There was a massacre of *conversos* in 1506.

Wealthy *conversos* had some influence in Rome and delayed the papacy's granting of permission to King João III to establish the Portuguese Inquisition. It started its work between 1532 and 1536, but the papal bull was not issued until 1547. Meanwhile, the first *auto da fé* had been "celebrated" in 1540, and a further 33 took place in Lisbon, Évora, and Coimbra between 1547 and 1580. At the same time, the Jesuits were invited into Portugal to establish their own university at Évora as a bastion against humanism. By the late 1570s, the persecution of *conversos* was, according to many accounts, more severe in Portugal than in Spain. At any rate, many *conversos* moved back to Spain, the land of their birth.

It was around this time that Antonio Ferreira (1528–69) wrote a verse that would have been equally applicable in 20th-century Portugal under Salazar:

> I live in fear
> I write and speak in fear
> I fear what I say to myself alone
> In fear I hold my tongue.

Even the poet Luís de Camões (1524–80), generally regarded as the greatest Portuguese poet, had to submit *Os Lusíadas* (*The Lusiads*), his epic celebration of the history of the Portuguese, to the Inquisition. Evidently, they permitted him to retain some very explicit descriptions of revels by nymphs and seamen, but warned him against the introduction of fictitious gods and goddesses. Garcia da Orta's *Colóquios dos Simples e Drogas da Índia* (Dialogue on Indian Herbs and Drugs), compiled during a visit to the Portuguese colony of Goa in southern India, passed unnoticed on its publication in 1563, but Orta's bones were dug up and burned after his death: inquisitiveness about how things work was not to be encouraged. The names of other scholars appeared from time to time in the *Index auctorum damnatae memoriae*.

The Spanish and Portuguese crowns were united under Philip II in 1580, but the persecution of Portuguese *conversos* did not lessen. The Cardinal Archduke Albert of Austria was appointed not only Governor of Portugal but also its Inquisitor-General. Between 1581 and 1600, a further 50 *autos da fé* took place. The emphasis everywhere was on conformity and obedience. The Jesuits took over the Portuguese theatre, which earlier, at the time of the great dramatist Gil Vincente (c.1460–1539), had been a scene of spectacle and provocation. Docrinal exposition of biblical and clerical themes took their place, and the theatre remained moribund at least until the early 18th century.

The Portuguese recovered their independence under João IV o Restaurador (John the Restorer) in 1640, inaugurating the house of Bragança, which lasted, in various forms, until the early 20th century. It is significant that, at a time when Portugal's old ally, England, was arguing about the divine right of kings, João (reigned 1640–56) was appointed by the Portuguese parliament. His adviser, the Jesuit, António Vieira, had only limited success in his pursuit of peace with the *conversos*. The Inquisition was opposed to a plan to abolish the admissibility of secret denunciations and had Vieira exiled to Rome.

Under João V (reigned 1706–50), Portugal enjoyed a considerable cultural flowering. Libraries were built and endowed, notably that at the University of Coimbra. The king himself composed motets, settings of the Mass, and madrigals, and employed Domenico Scarlatti as music teacher to his children. However, generally speaking, Portugal remained one of the most conservative societies in Europe. Annual trials and burnings still took place at the Church of St Vincent in Lisbon, and among those investigated by the Inquisition was the pioneer aviator Bartholomeu Lourenco de Gusmão (1685–1725), whose doubts about the Trinity apparently led him to convert to Judaism, although he returned to Christian belief before his death. (He is the subject of *Memorial do convento* (1982, *Baltasar and Blimunda*), a novel by the modern novelist and Nobel laureate José Saramago, which includes an imaginative reconstruction of the workings of the Portuguese Inquisition.)

The constitutional monarchy and the First Republic, 1750–1926

After the earthquake, which had destroyed three quarters of Lisbon, the Portuguese pundits could not think of any better way of preventing total ruin than to treat the people to a splendid *auto da fé*, for the University of

Coimbra had declared that the spectacle of a number of people being ceremoniously burnt over a slow fire was an infallible way of preventing an earthquake.

Voltaire's treatment of the Lisbon earthquake of 1755 in his novel *Candide* (1758) has Dr Pangloss and Candide arrested, "one for speaking and the other for listening with an air of approval". This is perhaps an indication of the notoriety of the Portuguese Inquisition elsewhere in Europe, not least in Enlightenment circles.

The beginnings of reform occurred under King José o Reformador (Joseph the Reformer, reigned 1750–77), mostly at the behest of Sebastião José de Carvalho e Melo, the Marquis of Pombal, who swept aside all those who stood in his path to supreme power. The Jesuits were expelled, and one of their number, Father Malagrida, was burned on charges of treason, blasphemy, impiety, and false prophecy. Alongside such echoes of the old Portugal, Pombal reformed the University of Coimbra, established schools, and encouraged the sciences. He cut the Inquisition down to size and, most notably of all, at last abolished the legal distinctions between "old" Christians and *conversos*. However, none of this endeared Pombal to the Portuguese elite, and after King José's death he was dismissed and banished.

Queen Maria I (reigned 1777–1816) began by continuing Pombal's educational and intellectual reforms. While the Church regained some of its former status, it had to accept, for instance, her establishment of academies of science and marine engineering. More fundamental changes were imposed by external events: the French Revolution from 1789, followed by Napoleon I's invasion of Portugal between 1808 and 1810. By the time of Maria's death, "the united kingdom of Portugal, Brazil, and the Algarve" was effectively a colony, ruled from Brazil, to which the royal family had fled, while its army was under the control of an Englishman, William Beresford.

A "liberal" revolution occurred in 1820. In a constitution that had been secretly drafted beforehand, the people of Portugal were accorded freedom of speech and of the press, while a minority of men were granted voting rights. The Inquisition was abolished and the Catholic Church lost its privileged position as the sole religion of the country. King João V, returning from Brazil, was inclined to accept the changes, but most Portuguese remained loyal to the Church and the idea of absolute monarchy. Liberal supporters of Pedro IV o Liberador (Peter the Liberator) fought against conservative supporters of Miguel o Usurpador (Michael the Usurper) until 1834, when constitutional monarchy was imposed.

A less democratic constitution, written by Pedro in 1826, was now adopted and further reforms were made, including the abolition of slavery. Resistance was directed primarily against an order issued by a minister, António Bernardo da Costa Cabral, for the abolition of the custom of burying the dead inside village churches, which he regarded as a danger to public health. Such was the uproar that Costa Cabral had to leave Portugal in disguise in 1840. After the protests had erupted into a peasant uprising, the government abolished the freedom of the press, imposed martial law, and curtailed civil liberties. Costa Cabral returned to power in 1848, but was deposed by a military coup in 1851. It appeared to many observers that Portugal was chronically unstable.

Nevertheless, during the second half of the 19th century Portugal not only modernized itself physically with the construction of railways and new roads, but evolved a two-party system of politics. Republicanism was widely regarded as subversive and until 1880 republicans were excluded from the political process, but, having taken the initiative in that year to organize a lavish celebration of the tercentenary of the death of Camões, the republican movement got its first member of parliament and founded a national newspaper, *O Trabalho*. In 1890, however, after republicans rose in revolt in Oporto, strict censorship was imposed on the press and the most influential republicans, accused of having provoked anarchy, were exiled to Portugal's African colonies. By 1901, the republican movement had been excluded from the Portuguese parliament.

Republicans continued to agitate underground, however, and were reasonably well prepared for the revolution of 1910, which was precipitated by the activities of the reformist but dictatorial Prime Minister João Franco, who had dismissed the parliament in 1906 and ruled by decree. King Carlos (Charles) was assassinated in 1908 and his successor, Manuel II, the last of Portugal's kings, was in no position to resist the revolution, which was launched by junior army officers on 11 October 1910. The First Republic was proclaimed the following day.

The new government was led initially by a philosopher and writer, Dr Teófilo Braga, but there were no fewer than seven other prime ministers up to 1915. Many reforms were carried out by Afonso Costa, the Minister of Justice, who cut the knot between church and state in the Law of Separation of 1911, legalized the right to strike, and made some improvements in the status of women (falling short of giving them the vote). New political parties emerged – the Democrats, the Unionists, and the Evolutionists – but Portugal's participation in World War I and its propensity for frequent changes of government hardly provided a basis for stability or sustained reform. It was not surprising that working-class newspapers such as *A Batalha* (The Battle) and *A Bandeira Vermelha* (The Red Flag) called for a more radical revolution; it was noteworthy that they were allowed to express their aspirations so openly.

The dictatorship, 1926–74

Reactionary forces were also at work, notably the Academic Centre for Christian Democracy (Centro Academico do Democracia Cristã, CADC). Its secretary was António de Oliveira Salazar, a graduate of the law school at Coimbra University who was greatly influenced by the French Catholic thinkers Charles Maurras and Léon Bloy. A believer in hierarchy, Salazar considered that such liberal reforms as the introduction of freedom of the press had sown "the seeds of subversion of established social and religious values". Salazar was elected to parliament in 1921 and, after a military coup in 1926, became Minister of Finance on condition that he exercise complete and unquestioned control over the country. This extended to all aspects of government when he became President of the Council of Ministers in 1932.

"Temporary" censorship was instituted in May 1926, and was progressively confirmed and strengthened throughout the years of Salazar's dictatorship. Article 8 of the Constitution proclaimed in 1933 granted "freedom of expression by any means whatever", yet Decree 22469, issued on 11 April 1933, maintained that censorship was necessary to prevent the perversion of public opinion as a social force; it shall be carried out in such a way as to defend public opinion from all factors that may misguide it against truth, justice, morals, efficient administration, and the common good, and to prevent any attack on the basic principles of the organization of society.

Decree 23203 referred to "crimes of rebellion committed by the press" against Portugal's territorial integrity and its president. Decree 23241 made it a crime to advocate the break-up of the empire, and gave colonial governors the authority to ban any journalist "whose presence may be thought to be undesirable from the point of view of security and public order". Salazar considered the colonies an integral part of Portugal, subject to all its laws and decrees, including censorship. Decree 23220 ordered the destruction "by fire" of "obscene publications or those that contain attacks upon Portuguese sovereignty or give offence to the government or its representatives or might promote crime or incite rebellion and disorder". In 1936, the government took power to refuse permission for individuals to establish new newspapers and to penalize papers without recourse to the courts.

As part of the apparatus of enforcement, it was laid down that publishers must pay for a deposit in respect of each periodical, which would be forfeited if the periodical was fined for non-compliance with the censorship rules. If a newspaper did not support the regime, it could not display government advertisements. Editors, journalists, or printers who did not obey the rules could be suspended, face prosecution, and have their businesses shut down. Nor was censorship confined to domestic publications: all cables and telephone calls sent abroad by foreign news agencies were to be scrutinized and censored. Salazar summed up the situation: "We will not discuss God; we will not discuss the country; we will not discuss authority; we will not discuss the family". These prohibitions remained in force in the Estado Novo throughout Salazar's years in power.

Like its neighbour Spain, itself intermittently a dictatorship from 1923 and firmly so from 1936, Portugal did not participate directly in World War II, but there was little doubt where the sympathies of the regime lay. A photograph of Salazar performing the Nazi salute was censored after the war. Like Hitler, Salazar had a pathological hatred for communism, and in particular for the Portuguese Communist Party (Partido Communista Português), which had been founded in 1921, and was the only group to resist his rule in a disciplined manner. In 1945, following the defeat of Nazi Germany, Salazar aligned himself with western anticommunism and significantly tightened the apparatus of censorship. The presentation of a national petition for free elections, and for the release of deportees and political prisoners, evidently convinced the regime of the need for strengthened controls. Salazar's security forces immediately confiscated the lists of signatories and made sure that any government employees among them were dismissed.

Over the long term, the most important development for censorship was the transformation of the established Police of Social Vigilance and Defence of the State into the yet more deeply repressive International and State Defence Police (Polícia Internacional de Defesa do Estado, or PIDE). PIDE officers could arrest without charge and detain for renewable periods of 180 days any dissident, Communist or otherwise. A decree of April 1945 stated:

> Those who consciously facilitate . . . subversive activities by providing the places for meetings or by subsidizing [these activities] or permitting their propaganda are subject to security measures of internment for an indefinite period of time, from six months to three years.

Even a stencilled sheet could be seized and regarded as a "crime against the security of the state". PIDE's methods were entirely comparable with those of the Inquisition: they encouraged denunciations, inflicted torture, and demanded that other institutions supply them with incriminating evidence. As Salazar had said in 1939:

> We came to the conclusion that the ill-treated prisoners were always, or almost always, fearless Communists, who resisted all attempts to make them confess where they had hidden their criminal and deadly weapons. Only after being subjected to these violent methods did they decide to tell the truth.

Given such extreme repression, more conventional censorship might seem to have been almost superfluous. It was, nevertheless, carried out. Censorship boards appointed by the Ministry of the Interior saw to it that, wherever a newspaper was published or a printing press operated, a censor, usually an army officer, was present to check its contents. Nothing was left to chance: the censors were issued with written instructions and guidelines. The following were not to be published:

> attacks on or criticism of the state, the government, personalities or institutions within it, or public services; statements that might cause alarm and public disquiet; writings that might offend religious creeds and practices; details of suicides or murders, as well as infanticide, when not followed up by news of the arrest of the delinquents or their punishment by the courts; articles or local reports or advertisements containing astrologers, witches or clairvoyants; . . . [reports on] issues that might prejudice diplomatic relations with foreign countries.

It was hardly possible for a newspaper not to transgress one or other of the prohibitions, and in due course the procedure was simplified by the expedient of demanding reader's proofs rather than typescripts, thereby ensuring that editors exercised self-censorship. According to Raul Rego, relations between the press and the censors became casual, "even cordial, with good manners and explanations on both sides . . . like the prisoner who gets used to his jailers and who talks to them with familiarity".

The press accepted even the most ludicrous of bans, such as those imposed on pessimistic horoscopes for Salazar's birth sign, Taurus, or on a report from the news agency Reuters about an outbreak of Colorado beetle that had led to restrictions on the import of vegetables into Britain. Newspapers could not show children with bare feet or drop even the faintest hint that the wars in Angola, Guinea-Bissau, and Mozambique were going badly.

Books did not have to be submitted to censorship, but they were often seized at the warehouse and publishers were held responsible for their contents. Surveillance of book publishing was pursued quite randomly, but if a book was banned any references to it in the press or in literary periodicals were automatically removed, as if the book did not exist. When in 1965 the Society of Writers had the temerity to award a literary prize to Luardina Vieira, who was in prison for collaborating with Angolan rebels, not only did the political police arrest all the members of the prize jury, but the government dissolved the society. The irony was that while about 60 per cent of the population could neither read nor write, Paulo Rodrigues, official censor from 1962 until 1968, instituted a separate "secret" council to reinforce literary censorship.

The director of the censorship system was also a member of the civic and moral section of the National Education Board, which examined textbooks and supervised the school curriculum. Special emphasis was placed upon instruction in Salazar's ideas and the teachings of the Catholic Church. Elsewhere, book censorship, formally illegal, was rigorously pursued in relation to works by the founding fathers of communism, pre-Soviet Russian writers, Émile Zola – once ubiquitously censored in Europe, North America, and the Antipodes, but now generally available in all these countries – and such contemporary writers as Albert Camus, André Malraux, Bertrand Russell, and John Steinbeck. The works of Castro Soromenho, a Portuguese novelist who wrote accounts of life in the colonies, also became a particular target for censorship.

Scholarship was equally under surveillance. The Centre of Archeology (Centro Portugues de Arqueologia, or CPA) prevented four Portuguese archeologists from conducting field-work during the early 1960s because they were said to have left-wing tendencies. Joaquim Barradas de Carvalho, a historian of "mentalities" who had been a member of the Portuguese Communist Party since 1940, had to go into exile, first in France and then in Brazil.

Broadcasting and the theatre were controlled by the National Propaganda Office. Up to 1945, theatre censorship targeted modernism, but for a brief period afterwards works by Jean Anouilh, Jean Giraudoux, Eugene O'Neill, and Bernard Shaw were allowed, together with those of José Regio (1901–69), widely considered to be one of the greatest Portuguese playwrights of the 20th century. The "thaw" lasted only until the early 1950s, when anticommunism was at its height: the films of the Marx brothers were banned because of the official hatred for their namesake. Works by Bertolt Brecht or Jean-Paul Sartre could not be performed, but neither could those of a succession of Portuguese playwrights. Thus, Bernardo Santareno's *A Promessa* (The Promise) was banned in 1958, and his *A Traicão do Padre Martinho* (Father Martin's Treason) in 1969. In the latter play, a socially and politically active priest angers both the church and the Estado Novo, which together agree that he be moved elsewhere; parishioners demonstrate in his support, the paramilitaries are called in, and a young girl is killed. *Estatua* (The Statue) by Luis de Sttau Monteiro, a left-wing journalist and novelist, was stopped in 1966, because it ridiculed hero worship in a manner wholly unacceptable to Salazar, the self-styled "father of the nation", whose agents had the play text confiscated during printing and its author

imprisoned. Any play that could interpreted as an incitement to opposition, even Shakespeare's *Julius Caesar*, was banned. *O Destino morreu de repente* (Destiny Died All of a Sudden), a play by Alves Redol (1911–69), implied that bureaucracy was collapsing under its own weight, and therefore could not be shown.

Edgar Rodrigues and Roberto dos Neves wrote in their *A Fome em Portugal* (1959, Hunger in Portugal):

> When we talk about politics in the street, we look around us in all directions to make sure there is no spy within earshot. Such is the terror that grips Portugal. In the cafés, public squares, factories, workshops, everywhere, there is fear planted by the Inquisition of Salazar and Cerejeira.

(Manuel Gonçalves Cerejeira was the Cardinal Patriarch of Lisbon, and thus head of the Catholic Church in Portugal, for many years under Salazar, whom he supported.) Despite the terrror, there was considerable clandestine resistance, expressed in literary forms as well as in action. An anonymous work, *Tarraful – Camp of Slow Death* (1945), describes a notorious concentration camp in the Cape Verde Islands; *A destruição sistematica de seres humanos* (1969, The Systematic Destruction of Human Beings) lists those who had been imprisoned for various periods. Radio Free Portugal operated wherever and whenever it could.

Following Salazar's death in 1968, he was succeeded by Marcelo Caetano, and it appeared that some liberalization would take place. It even became possible for newspapers to criticize the government, so long as their remarks were relatively mild. Two deputies first elected in 1969, Francisco de Sá Carneiro and Francisco Pinto Balsemão, felt emboldened to propose the abolition of censorship, or the requirement that "previous" government permission be given before a publication was established, and of the government's power to shut down newspapers. The government was forced to respond with vague proposals of its own. It declared that censorship would no longer be routine, but when a decree was drafted it reserved the right to restore its regular practice if "serious subversive acts" occurred; it also retained the right to seize troublesome newspapers and continued to demand that copies be deposited with the relevant authorities before a paper was distributed. All this was justified, it was said, "while the integrity of the fatherland is in danger", that is, while wars continued in Angola, Guinea-Bissau, and Mozambique. António dos Santos, general secretary of the Portuguese Union of Journalists and a writer for the newspaper *A Capital*, was sentenced to a year in prison and five years' loss of civil rights for "activities against the security of the state". A ban was imposed on *Portugal Gagged* by the future Prime Minister Mário Soares, who was deported to São Tomé in 1969, arrested at least 13 times in the late 1960s and early 1970s, and then exiled in Paris. In a different vein, *Novas Cartas Portugesas* (1971, New Portuguese Letters) was banned in 1973 and its authors, Maria Isobel Barreno, Maria Velho da Costa, and Maria Teresa Horta, were prosecuted for "outraging public morality" and "abusing the freedom of the press" in their highly original feminist critique of Portuguese politics and social life. Finally, *Portugal e o Futuro* (Portugal and the Future), by general António de Spínola, was banned because of its prognosis that the colonial wars could not be won by military means.

Since 1974

It was Spínola who, on 25 April 1974, led the coup by the Armed Forces Movement that toppled Caetano and brought almost 50 years of dictatorship to an end. On the following day, an amnesty for political prisoners was announced, and freedom of the press and assembly were proclaimed. The evening newspapers carried the legend "not submitted to censorship".

Portugal was not yet quite through the woods of censorship. The abolition of prior censorship was upheld by the Council of Ministers on 23 June, but a decree emphasized "the imperative need to avoid any abuse of freedom, which must be exercised responsibly so as to prevent the country from being dragged into a climate of anarchy through incitement to disorder and violence". The list of prohibitions sounded familiar: there was to be no incitement to strikes or unauthorized demonstrations, ideological aggression, or insulting Spínola, now President, or foreign heads of state, any of which might result in a fine of up to 500,000 escudos. *A Capital*, *República*, and *Diairio de Lisboa* were temporarily suspended because they had carried reports of a Maoist rally considered offensive to the Armed Forces Movement. However, when other papers decided not to publish, in sympathy, the order was withdrawn. The government announced none the less that the media had a "basic mission of actively cooperating in the reconstruction of the country in an essential spirit of responsibility", and of

> ensuring that the Portuguese people receive fully impartial information, based on truth, objectivity and respect for democratic legality, and the rights of individuals, which was not possible under the system of prior administrative censorship, which remains abolished.

Such strictures notwithstanding, it was thought desirable to celebrate what had been achieved so far by the "Carnation Revolution" in an exhibition held at the São Mamede Gallery in Lisbon at the end of 1974. On display were 186 works, by 87 artists, that had been banned under the dictatorship and never previously displayed in Portugal. No holds were barred, as denunciations of Salazar and Caetano appeared alongside criticisms of the Catholic Church and the wars in Africa.

Spínola resigned the presidency in September 1974, and the "Junta of National Salvation" was replaced by a Supreme Revolutionary Council. While the Socialist Party, under the former dissident Mário Soares, took the lead in forming a democratic government in April 1975, the atmosphere of "revolution" prevailed for some time, with attempts being made by workers' groups to take control of certain media, causing concern among some observers that the Communist Party was aiming for power and its own forms of censorship. The party, which dominated the printworkers' union, seized control of *República*, a pro-Socialist organ that by May 1975 was the only privately owned daily newspaper, since the others, unable to achieve solvency, had been nationalized. The communists justified the takeover on the grounds that the paper had claimed the party was planning to take control of radio

and television. The Press Council ruled that the seizure was illegal and the Revolutionary Council demanded that the paper be returned to its owners. Troops were employed to seal off the *República*'s offices, but they failed to prevent the workers from bringing out an alternative *Jornal do Caso República*. The Revolutionary Council made shorter work of the upheaval at Radio Renscenca, an organ of the Catholic Church: when it too was taken over by its staff, the building was bombarded and demolished.

From other perspectives, it seemed that the Portuguese media workers were simply relishing and experimenting with their newly achieved democracy. Some observers denied that the Communist Party was dominating these movements. Ben Pimlott and Jean Seaton, for example, pointed to the wholesale transformation of television: there was a doubling of the airtime devoted to news, discussions of contemporary issues were broadcast at peak times, the coverage of the general election in April 1974 was generally fair, and five episodes of the BBC's documentary series *The World at War*, previously banned, were broadcast. Diana Smith, on the other hand, refers to what she regarded as "hour upon hour of innumerable heads preaching garbled party propaganda".

Eventually, Portugal settled down, its people sobered perhaps by stirrings of right-wing reaction, such as the proposal by Commander Correia Jesuino, on 8 August 1975, that a "commission for the analysis of the media" be established. After an abortive coup on 17 November 1975, it seemed that everybody concerned realized the danger of a return to more repressive times. Thereafter, politics remained lively and, while the threat of censorship receded, it occasionally reappeared. In 1977, for example, the government threatened to reimpose censorship unless certain newspapers ceased to propagate "fascist and antidemocratic ideology", or to publicize "patently false and alarmist reports creating a climate of instability". The reference was to the publication of rumours that the value of the escudo was being forced downwards and that President António Ramalho Eanes, another former general, was about to dismiss Prime Minister Soares. In 1979, a television series *The Years of the Century*, announced as representing a personal view of the Estado Novo by a left-wing historian, attacked the Catholic hierarchy's support for repression in the colonies, and was cancelled after the church complained. In the same year, journalists at Radio Televisão Portuguesa (RTP) accused senior management of "systematic censorship of programmes", taking the view that "the return to past methods is gaining ground in the name of supposed consolidation of democracy". Television was then a public monopoly. Also in 1979, Mário António Paula, a journalist working for the national news agency, was prosecuted because he made a public statement that "abortion is not a crime". In fact, as in other Catholic countries at that time, it still was. It was also still possible in 1979 for police to confiscate copies of *Eanito the Unmoveable* and *Superman*, cartoons by the satirist Augusto Sidi considered to be "insulting and irreparably damaging" to President Eanes.

Over the past 20 years, the government has relinquished control of all the newspapers taken into public ownership in 1974. Television remained a government monopoly until 1992, when the Constitution was amended to allow three channels, one public and two private. The High Authority for Mass

Communications, and its regulatory body, is charged with the maintenance of "the pluralism, objectivity, and independence of the media in the face of economic and political forces".

ANTONIO DE FIGUEIREDO

Further Reading

Birmingham, David, *A Concise History of Portugal*, Cambridge and New York: Cambridge University Press, 1993

Boxer, C.R, "Some Notes on Portuguese Historiography", *History*, 6 (1954)

Camões, Luis de, *The Lusiads*, translated by William C. Atkinson, Harmondsworth: Penguin, 1952

Cardoso Pires, José, "Changing a Nation's Way of Thinking", *Index on Censorship*, 1/1 (Spring 1972)

Carvalho, Alberto A. and A. Monteiro Cardoso, "Press Censorship in Spain and Portugal", *Index on Censorship*, 1/2 (Summer 1972)

Figueiredo, Antonio de, "*New Portuguese Letters* and Other Literary Prosecutions", *Index on Censorship*, 3/2 (Summer 1974)

Figueiredo, Antonio de, *Portugal: Fifty Years of Dictatorship*, Harmondsworth: Penguin, and New York: Holmes and Meier, 1976

Kaplan, Marion, *The Portuguese: The Land and Its People*, revised edition, London: Viking Penguin, 1998

Kay, Hugh, *Salazar and Modern Portugal*, London: Eyre and Spottiswoode, and New York: Hawthorn, 1970

Lillios, K.T., "Nationalism and Copper Age Research in Portugal during the Salazar Regime, 1932–1974" in *Nationalism, Politics and the Practice of Archaeology*, edited by Philip L. Kohl and Clare Fawcett, Cambridge and New York: Cambridge University Press, 1995

Livermore, H.V., *A New History of Portugal*, Cambridge and New York: Cambridge University Press, 1977

Maxwell, Kenneth, *Pombal: Paradox of the Enlightenment*, Cambridge and New York: Cambridge University Press, 1995

Maxwell, Kenneth, *The Making of Portuguese Democracy*, Cambridge and New York: Cambridge University Press, 1995

Oliveira, A.H. de, *History of Portugal*, 2 vols, New York: Columbia University Press, 1972

Pimlott, Ben and Jean Seaton, "Sacking the Censor: Broadcasting, 1974–1976", *Index on Censorship*, 5/2 (Summer 1976)

Raby, D.L., *Fascism and Resistance in Portugal: Communists, Liberals and Military Dissidents in the Opposition to Salazar, 1941–1974*, Manchester: Manchester University Press, 1988

Robinson, R.A.H., *Contemporary Portugal*, London and Boston: Allen and Unwin, 1979

Saramago, José, *Baltasar and Blimunda*, New York: Harcourt Brace, 1987; London: Jonathan Cape, 1988

Smith, Diana, "What Next in Lisbon?", *Index on Censorship*, 4/3 (Autumn 1973)

Smith, Diana, "Turmoil in Portugal", *Index on Censorship*, 4/4 (Winter 1975)

Smith, Diana, "TV: No Room for Debate", *Index on Censorship*, 6/1 (January–February 1977)

Wheeler, Douglas, *Republican Portugal*, Madison: University of Wisconsin Press, 1975

PORTUGAL: Portuguese Empire

Far flung and long lasting, the Portuguese empire was, at its height, 25 times larger than Portugal itself, Mozambique and Angola alone covering an area equivalent to western Europe. The product of the 15th-century explorations by Vasco da Gama and Pedro Alvares Cabral, the empire long held the monopoly of maritime trade in the Indian Ocean (Goa and Mozambique), and was, from Macau, the pioneer of western trade in the Far East. So far as the Atlantic was concerned, Portugal was responsible for a considerable proportion of the slave trade (from Angola, Guinea-Bissau, Cape Verde, and São Tomé to Brazil). Brazil became independent in 1822. The Portuguese were ejected from Goa in 1961, and withdrew wholesale from its African colonies following the Carnatian Revolution of 1974–75; Macau was incorporated into China as recently as 1997.

For centuries, it was possible for a Portuguese to travel to and from its African colonies without ever touching foreign soil. Throughout the years of the Inquisition (1536–1820), censorship reinforced linguistic isolation, allowing for a veritable archipelago of serfdom and obscurantist repression. Perhaps for that reason, Portuguese bibliography on the subject is confined to a few dozen books, of which only a handful avoid nationalistic promotion and apology. For more comprehensive accounts, Portuguese historians have had to turn to the work of foreign colleagues, notably Charles Boxer, who, significantly, acquired an interest in Portuguese history by studying archives in Macau and Goa before he ever visited Portugal itself.

Boxer demonstrated that "so far as the overseas empire was concerned, virtually all potential authors had to send their manuscripts to Portugal for censorship and publication". A press was established at Goa in 1560, but it was soon commandeered by the Jesuits, who inevitably concentrated on works useful to their own mission and ministry. Of 40 books published there during the 16th and 17th centuries only two were written by laypeople. One of them, *Coloquios dos simples e drogas da India* (Colloquies of the Simples and Drugs of India) by Garcia d'Orta, the crypto-Jewish physician, "had far wider circulation abroad in the numerous translations and adaptations made by Carolus Clusius (1526–1609) than it ever obtained in the Portuguese world where it lay neglected for centuries". For drawing attention to the Portuguese record of literary, religious and educational control, Boxer was made *persona non grata* by the Salazar regime.

The American historian Joseph C. Miller similarly drew attention to a "conspiracy of silence" about the transport of slaves either between African buyers and sellers along the west coast of that continent, and, on an increasingly large scale, directly across the south Atlantic, without recourse to the "triangular route" that required other trading nations, including Britain, to take slaves through such European ports as Bristol and Liverpool, before transporting them across the ocean. Miller found that "the most important things were discussed least. Hence, the most profound dilemma for the historian: what becomes most obvious is never documented explicitly and is potentially hardest of all to render plausible to a reader who has not spent years immersed in the eloquent silences of governors' letters from Luanda". Miller warms to Mello e Castro, the minister for the colonies, who wrote to the Angolan governor Almeida e Vasconcelos on 7 August 1781, deploring the "extremely common, pernicious and inveterate abuse in Angola of telling this royal court not what it should know but only what it seems convenient there what ought to be known here".

The long tradition of government secrecy may have been rooted in the need to keep information about newly discovered sea routes, lands, and peoples from the eyes of the Spanish and other foreign rivals. Yet one of the earliest indictments of the slave trade is to be found in a classic nautical treatise, *A arte da guerra do mar* (The Art of War at Sea) by the *converso* Catholic priest Fernando Oliveira, who echoing the feelings of his fellow-Dominican Bartholomeu de las Casas, wrote in 1555: "There never will be, nor should human reason ever accept, the public and free exchange of free and peaceful men, as one who would buy and sell beasts, cattle and horses and their like." The captivity of slaves, wrote Oliveira was "more attached to the service of their masters than to that of God". Oliveira was to be prosecuted by the Inquisition on charges that were not specified, but these opinions were doubtless taken into consideration. They were not repeated for two centuries, when Manuel Ribeiro Rocha, long resident in Bahia, one of the main slavery ports in northern Brazil, ventured to propose in his *The Ethiopian Ransomed, Indentured, Sustained, Corrected, Instructed and Liberated* (Lisbon, 1758) that slavery be replaced by a system of indentured labour leading to eventual release.

After the loss of Brazil, Portugal fell into further decadence, turning gradually and grudgingly from slavery to colonial rule during the 19th century. Its influence in Africa was severely curtailed by British advances, and in several books of the early 1900s (notably Henry Nevinson's *A Modern Slavery*, 1905, Charles Swan's *The Slavery of Today*, 1908, and Dan Crawford's *Thinking Black*, 1909) played down the importance of Portuguese discoveries and colonizations. Reports to the Anti-Slavery Society and to the League of Nations were equally condemnatory. All these writings were dismissed as the work of "enemies of Portugal" by Manuel Heleno, director of the Lisbon Ethnology Museum in his *Os escravos em Portugal* (The Slaves in Portugal, 1933).

By then, Salazar's Estado Novo (established 1926) had formulated the ideology of "national colonialism", under which the colonies became "overseas provinces" of a single nation, subject to all the rules and guidelines on censorship then in force, including a clause in the Labour Code (1928), that stated:

> All Portuguese, as well as individuals of other nationalities residing in Portuguese territory, who intentionally, in public speeches, manifestos, books, booklets, newspapers or other periodicals to be sold or distributed free of payment to the public, propagate false information aiming at showing the existence of slavery or the traffic of slaves within the Portuguese colonies, will be punished with fines from escuda 20,000, or up to two years' imprisonment, and may still be liable to expulsion from Portuguese territory.

Under such laws, reinforcing the stringent security enforced by the International and State Defence Police (PIDE), few people dared to take notice of, let alone criticize, the living conditions of Africans. Henrique Galvao, member of the National Assembly and colonial inspector, was dismissed after his 1947 report had denounced comprehensively the system of forced labour from which "only the dead are exempted" as a new form of state slavery. The bishop of Beira (Mozambique) was the target of continuing pressure and was even subject to house arrest, after similar statements in his diocesan newspaper *Diario de Moçambique*. Those who gave information to foreign researchers were subject to detention and interrogation by PIDE. The books of international Africanist authors, such as Basil Davidson and René Pélissier, as well as those of political exiles such as myself, were included in a long list of books to be apprehended if imported into Portugal, or any of the "overseas provinces".

The negative consequences of censorship often increase in direct proportion to its duration, and end up self-defeating. The abolition of the Estatuto dos Indigenas da Guine-Bissau, Angola and Moçambique (1961) technically meant the abolition of forced labour. However, the regime was in no position to publicize this, as it would imply that mounting international pressure against the Portuguese colonial system was well-founded. By then, moreover, armed resistance was developing into colonial war on three fronts, providing new reasons for keeping the censors vigilant.

Those who create a fog end up by getting lost in it. In Portugal and its colonies, censorship forced the development of an oral subculture of resistance, a strategy of "pass the word", the title of a political tract published in Lisbon in 1965, exhorting the military to abandon what was by then a lost cause. The fact that the tract was distributed by the Communist Party, supported by the Soviet bloc countries, themselves under systematic repression, only added to the irony.

ANTONIO DE FIGUEIREDO

Further Reading

Birmingham, David, *Portugal and Africa*, London: Macmillan, and New York: St Martin's Press, 1999

Boxer, Charles, *The Portuguese Seaborne Empire, 1415–1825*, London: Hutchinson, and New York: Knopf, 1969

Chiavento, Julio J., *O negro no Brasil, da senzala à Guerra do Paraguai*, São Paulo: Brasiliense, 1987

Clarence-Smith, Gervase, *The Third Portuguese Empire, 1825–1975: A Study in Economic Imperialism*, Manchester: Manchester University Press, 1985

Figueiredo, Antonio de, *Portugal and its Empire: The Truth*, London: Gollancz, 1961

Figueiredo, Antonio de (editor), *Angola: Views of a Revolt*, London and New York: Oxford University Press, 1962

Figueiredo, Antonio de, "Censorship: The Shallow Grave of Empire", *Index on Censorship*, 28/1 (1999)

Heleno, Manuel, *Os Escravos em Portugal*, Lisbon: Anuário Comercial, 1933

Lopes, E. Correia, *A escravatura: subsídios para a sua história*, Lisbon: Agência Geral de Colónias, 1944

Maxwell, Kenneth, *The Making of Portuguese Democracy*, Cambridge and New York: Cambridge University Press, 1995

Miller, Joseph C., *Way of Death: Merchant Capitalism and the Angola Slave Trade, 1730–1830*, Madison: University of Wisconsin Press, and London: Currey, 1988

Nascimento, Abdias do, *Brazil: Mixture or Massacre?, Essays in the Genocide of a Black People*, 2nd edition, Dover, Massachusetts: Majority Press, 1989

Newitt, Malyn, *Portugal in Africa*, London: Longman, 1981

Núñez, Benjamin, *Dictionary of Portuguese–African Civilization*, London: Zell, 1995

Rodriguez, José Honório, *Brazil and Africa*, Berkeley: University of California Press, 1965

Saunders, A.C de C.M., *A Social History of Black Slaves and Freedmen in Portugal, 1441–1555*, Cambridge and New York: Cambridge University Press, 1982

DENNIS POTTER
British television and stage dramatist, 1935–1994

BRIMSTONE AND TREACLE
Television play, 1976

Dennis Potter's writing regularly probed into uncomfortable areas of the human psyche, especially cruelty and sexuality. On occasion, the discomfort was great enough to induce censorship. In 1966, for example, his television play *Almost Cinderella*, which retold the fairy tale in terms of sexual abuse, was commissioned and paid for by the BBC, and then rejected. After some desultory press controversy, Potter himself chose to suppress the play and it was never published or produced. This made a striking contrast with the case of *Brimstone and Treacle* ten years later.

Like many of Potter's television plays of the early 1970s, *Brimstone and Treacle* deals with a visitation. In a climate of incipient marital break-up, Mr and Mrs Bates care for their daughter Pattie, reduced to a vegetative state after a hit-and-run road accident. A charming and mysterious stranger, Martin, inveigles his way into their house, but, although he wins acceptance by playing on the couple's religiosity and sentimentality, he is evidently a demonic figure. Left alone in the house, he rapes Pattie and subsequently he becomes unpleasantly excited when discussing the logical consequences of Mr Bates's racist political beliefs. Interrupted during a second rape, he escapes into the night, leaving Pattie shocked back into normality. The play concludes with a flashback establishing that she ran out into the road after witnessing her father's adultery, a dark secret that Martin has enabled her to utter.

The play was made by the BBC for transmission in its series *Play for Today* at a cost of £70,000 and Bryan Cowgill, the controller of its main channel, BBC 1, scheduled it for transmission on 6 April 1976, although at a later than usual time and with broadcast warnings of possible offence. However, Cowgill remained concerned about the play's black-comedy tone, and referred it to his superior, Alasdair Milne, then the director of programmes for BBC Television. Nineteen days before the scheduled transmission, Milne decided that the play would not be transmitted: he found it "brilliantly written and made", he told Potter in a letter, "but nauseating".

The problem was fundamental and could not be resolved by selective cutting. Milne's objection was to the play's central juxtaposition of the diabolic intruder and the mentally handicapped girl, and its equation of rape with shock therapy. Milne considered this to be gratuitously offensive: "I believe that it is right in certain instances to outrage the viewers in order to get over a point of serious importance", his letter to Potter continued, "but I am afraid that in this case real outrage would be widely felt and that no such point would get across". It later emerged that an element in this assessment was the knowledge that Potter himself was suffering badly with psoriatic arthropathy. Recent commentators on *Brimstone and Treacle*, now widely regarded as one of the central works of Potter's canon, have seen a range of serious themes, from the justification of religious faith to the invasion of privacy, but Milne interpreted the play as expressing nothing more articulate than a scream of pain. As such, it seemed to him to be a private text disengaged from the world at large and there could be no justification for the offence that might be caused if it was broadcast. Another play by Potter, *Double Dare*, was shown instead, but it nearly became the subject of a private prosecution by the pro-censorship campaigner Mary Whitehouse over its "blasphemy"

POTTER: Michael Kitchen as Martin and Michelle Newell as Pattie in Dennis Potter's 1976 television play *Brimstone and Treacle*. The play, made by the BBC, was withdrawn from transmission shortly before the scheduled broadcast date by the BBC director general, Alasdair Milne, because he felt the play's theme and its treatment to be gratuitously offensive. Potter managed to publish the text of the play in the *New Review* later that year; the film version, starring Sting, Joan Plowright, and Denholm Elliott, was released in 1982, and the original television play was finally shown by the BBC in 1987 as part of a Dennis Potter retrospective series.

and "explicit" sex scenes. Potter was then commissioned to write a six-part series, *Pennies from Heaven*: "a smack and then a kiss", he commented in 1993.

The ban also reflected wider issues in the politics of broadcasting in the mid-1970s. The BBC was in retreat from the liberal identity it had established during the 1960s, having come under heavy pressure to censor its output of "offensive" programmes with the threat that, if it failed to do so, the forthcoming report of the Annan Committee on Broadcasting might recommend tighter external controls. In this connection, Milne's decision to withdraw *Brimstone and Treacle*, if not his decision to show *Double Dare* instead, could be advanced as the action of a "responsible" broadcaster. It is inevitably harder to verify speculation that Milne had also been primed by the security services, seeking to crack down on left-wing activists within the BBC Drama Group, among them the producer of *Brimstone and Treacle*, Kenith Trodd.

Although they had no formal right of appeal against Milne, Potter and Trodd went to great lengths to make the play available to the public. The text was published in the *New Review* in May 1976 and there were surreptitious screenings of the tape for the benefit of television critics, enabling them to challenge the ban in an informed way. Milne also received a telegram of protest after a showing on a closed circuit at the Edinburgh Television Festival in 1977. A stage adaptation opened in Sheffield in 1978 and a film version was released in 1982, with an accompanying "novelization" by Potter's daughter Sarah. The original television production was eventually shown in 1987, as part of a Potter retrospective.

MARTIN WIGGINS

Writings

Brimstone and Treacle, TV script published in *New Review* (May 1976); stage version produced and published 1978; film version shown 1982; TV version broadcast 1987

Further Reading

Carpenter, Humphrey, *Dennis Potter: A Biography*, London: Faber, 1998; New York: St Martin's Press, 1999
Cook, John R., *Dennis Potter: A Life on Screen*, Manchester: Manchester University Press, 1995
Gilbert, W. Stephen, *Fight and Kick and Bite: The Life and Work of Dennis Potter*, London: Hodder and Stoughton, 1995
Milne, Alasdair, *DG: The Memoirs of a British Broadcaster*, London: Hodder and Stoughton, 1988
Potter, Sarah, *Brimstone and Treacle* (adaptation), London: Quartet, 1982
Wiggins, Martin, "'Disgusted, Shepherd's Bush': *Brimstone and Treacle* at the BBC", *Essays and Studies*, 46 (1993): 131–43

EZRA POUND
US poet, essayist, translator, and literary critic, 1885–1972

Ezra Pound belongs in an encyclopedia of censorship almost entirely because of his behaviour during the second half of his life, when, after settling in Italy, he flaunted anti-Semitic attitudes and broadcast against US and Allied policies over fascist radio. Disgraced, he was returned to the United States to be tried for treason. Although only limited censorship of his writings took place, there were some who thought that Pound's work should be more thoroughly censored, and a debate of some moment to censorship studies, concerning Pound the poet versus Pound the man, continued during the late 1940s and on into the 1950s.

Pound was born in Hailey, Idaho, raised in Philadelphia, and educated at Hamilton College and the University of Pennsylvania. He briefly taught Romance languages at Wabash College in Crawfordsville, Indiana, before resigning under a cloud for what was called "Latin Quarter behaviour". In 1908, he left the United States for Europe, where he spent most of the rest of his life. Apart from producing his own works – he started the *Cantos*, "a cryselephantine poem of immeasurable length which will occupy me for the next four decades unless it becomes a bore" – he worked tirelessly on behalf of writers who were initially difficult to publish, such as T.S. Eliot, or who faced censorship, such as James Joyce. Interestingly, Pound was not averse to censoring some of the "dirtier" bits of Joyce's masterpiece, *Ulysses*.

As early as the English edition of *Lustra* (1916), censorship was an issue for Pound when publisher Elkin Mathews refused to publish several "indecorous" poems although they were already typeset. Four poems were omitted and 200 copies were sold as "almost unabridged." In the second edition, nine additional poems were omitted. For the US edition, Pound's friend, the New York lawyer and art patron John Quinn, saw that all but one poem were published; Quinn's privately printed edition included the omitted "The Temperaments".

In 1917 Pound precipitated a serious censorship incident involving Margaret Anderson's *Little Review*. Under the pseudonym Abel Sanders, he sent the journal a fake German document, which, although anti-German, brought attention to Wyndham Lewis's antiwar story "Cattleman's Spring-Mate". The New York Post Office suppressed the October 1917 issue on grounds of indecency.

In 1918 Pound met major C.H. Douglas, to whose ideas on "social credit" he remained attached: as Pound wrote, "any government worth a damn would pay dividends instead of collecting taxes". He also began to preach "contempt for the mob". He and other intellectuals should, he believed, fight "the dominant imbecilities of our time", including those perpetrated by modern journalism and publishing. A regular visitor to Italy, he felt some affinity with the ideas of Gabriele D'Annunzio, an artist and man of action but also a protofascist believer in "world hygiene". In 1924, Pound and his family settled permanently in Rapallo, near Genoa, just as Benito Mussolini was consolidating his power.

Pound again brushed with US censorship when, in 1926, James Joyce discovered that the American publisher Samuel Roth, having found loopholes in US copyright law, used Pound's name without permission as an editor of *Two Worlds* and announced a first installment and subsequent second installment of *Ulysses*. Joyce organized a signed protest which was cabled to 900 US papers. Although Pound offered advice and had his father Homer check into possible legal action (found too costly), Pound did not sign the protest; he eventually, however, gave testimony against Roth. The lawsuit dragged on for several years and can be followed in Joyce's letters. Pound believed the larger issue of copyright and pornography laws in the United States more important.

Pound wrote in 1932:

> Mussolini a great man, demonstrably in his effects on events . . . in the quickness of his mind, in the speed with which his real emotion is shown in his face, so that only a crooked man could misinterpret his meaning and his basic intention.

He prepared a film treatment on the history of fascism in 1932 and met the Duce himself on 30 January 1933. Later, Pound claimed that his book *Jefferson and/or Mussolini*, brought out by Stanley Nott in January 1935, had previously been rejected by 40 publishers. In this text, Pound asserts that the US founding father and the Italian dictator were alike in being shapers of a revolution in their own countries. At the same time, according to his friend and biographer, Noel Stock, "he never, so far as I have been able to discover, accepted the idea that people are there to be used by the government for purposes of its own, artistic or otherwise". In 1938, he visited the land of his birth for the first time since 1911, but was singularly unsuccessful in persuading president Roosevelt (who did not see him) or anybody else of the benefits either of Mussolini's system or of Pound's own social credit theories.

On his return to Italy, Pound's anti-Semitism erupted following the appearance in *Il Regime Fascista* (24 November 1939) of an article alleging that Jews were in control through the agencies of newspaper distribution. Pound's pamphlet, *Britain and Jewry*, supported the British fascist Sir Oswald Mosley's plan for a Jewish homeland in Madagascar. In the *Japan Times* (Pound's journalism was widely spread) of 12 August 1940, he wrote, "Democracy is now currently defined in Europe as 'a country governed by Jews'". He continued to write on economic issues, claiming later that the US mails had banned the distribution of two articles he had written for *Il Meridiano di Roma* for 24 November and 1 December 1941.

From January 1941 until July 1943, Pound broadcast regularly on Rome Radio. He appears to have taken at face value an announcement made before his talk on 29 January 1942 that

> Rome Radio, acting in accordance with the Fascist policy of intellectual freedom and free expression of opinion by those who are qualified to hold it, has offered Dr Ezra Pound the use of the microphone twice a week. It is understood that he will not be asked to say anything whatsoever that goes against his conscience or anything incompatible with his duties as a citizen of the United States of America.

Pound's talks, disorganized and wideranging, were peppered with anti-Semitic remarks. The fact that he accepted remuneration for them also caused his later accusers considerable indignation.

Pound remained a US citizen all his life, so certain remarks that he broadcast on 18 June 1942 were widely regarded as treasonable. Addressing his fellow citizens and their leaders (he was now particularly contemptuous of Roosevelt), he said: "You are not going to win this war . . . You never had a chance in this war". It was no wonder that the US Federal Communications Commission monitored his broadcasts from 1941 onwards. He was indicted for treason by a federal grand jury on 26 July 1943. He responded: "I do not believe that the simple fact of speaking over the radio, wherever placed, can itself constitute treason. I think that must depend on the motives for speaking." What, he asked, had happened to the idea of free speech?

Pound was in Rome when marshal Pietro Badoglio, Mussolini's successor, surrendered to the Allies in September 1943. With some difficulty he returned to Rapallo, where for two years he continued to propagandize for Mussolini's Salò Republic. Only a few copies of his *Orientamenti*, a collection of articles written between 1939 and 1943, saw the light of day, since the printer and publisher, in Venice, had decided that this was not the time to distribute such material. They similarly suppressed Pound's revised text of *Jefferson e Mussolini*. Copies of *The Unwobbling Pivot* (*Asse che non vacilla*) were published in February 1945; *asse*, however, means not "pivot" but "axis", and the book was therefore thought to be Axis propaganda. Copies were burned soon after the Liberation.

On 29 April 1945 Pound was arrested and turned over to the US authorities. Until November he was incarcerated (for the first three weeks in a reinforced outdoor cage) at the Detention Training Centre near Pisa, and then was returned to the United States for trial, charged with having written "broadcast texts, speeches, and announcements" that had been "useful to the Kingdom of Italy for propaganda purposes in the prosecution of the war", and generally to have undermined the confidence of the US government and its allies. No trial took place, however. Pound was declared to be "of unsound mind" and remanded to St Elizabeth's Hospital for the Criminally Insane in Washington, DC, where he remained until 1958.

Censorship continued. Angered over the bombing of the Tempio Malatestino in Rimini and saddened by the death of the futurist Marinetti, Pound had written Cantos LXXII and LXXIII in Italian during the war, sending copies to his daughter Mary and to Mussolini. In January 1945 lines 9–35, with the omission of line 18, of Canto LXXII were published in *Marina Repubblicana*, the naval journal of Mussolini's Salò republic, and the complete LXXIII in February. Reed Dasenbrach speculates that these shocking pieces begin a fascist Paradiso for the Cantos but were withheld from general publication and circulation in English (until 1986) in order to improve Pound's chances of regaining his freedom. However, a first copyright edition (25 copies) was published by the Estate of Ezra Pound in June 1973. Two copies were sold and two copies deposited with the US Copyright Office; the rest were distributed only upon the settlement of Pound's estate in 1978.

Meanwhile, the US publisher Random House had decided to drop the 12 poems by Pound that had been planned for reprinting in *An Anthology of Famous English and American Poetry*, edited by William Rose Benet and Conrad Aiken, and published in 1945. Aiken was said to have been in favour of their inclusion, and the Random House editor, Bennett Cerf, appears to have insisted that a note should make clear the publisher's refusal to publish the poems. A barrage of complaining letters followed. Cerf changed his mind, on the grounds that "it may be wrong to confuse Pound the poet with Pound the man", and the book was published with all 12 poems intact.

Then, in 1949, Pound won the first Bollingen Prize for Poetry, awarded by the Fellows of American Letters of the Library of Congress for *The Pisan Cantos* (1948). A furious controversy erupted on the old theme, man or poet. The poet Robert Hillyer led the attack in *The Saturday Review of Literature*. The rebuttal, *The Case against the Saturday Review*, included statements and reprints of articles by such prominent authors as Allen Tate, Malcolm Cowley, and Archibald MacLeish, together with a letter signed by John Berryman and 73 other writers accusing the *Review* of sanctioning a "prepared attack on modern poetry and criticism".

In 1958, after careful work by Archibald MacLeish and Robert Frost, the treason indictment against Ezra Pound was dismissed. He returned to Italy, and lived first at Schloss Brinnenburg in the Tyrol, and then in Venice. His papers are collected mostly in the Beinecke Rare Book and Manuscript Library at Yale University, New Haven, Connecticut.

JUDITH C. KOHL

Writings

Selected Prose, 1909–1965, edited by William Cookson, 1973
Selected Poems, 1908–1959, 1975
I cantos (bilingual edition), edited by Mary de Rachewiltz, 1985
The Cantos, 1986

Further Reading

Bagigalupo, Massimo, "The Poet at War: Ezra Pound's Suppressed Italian Cantos", *South Atlantic Quarterly*, 83/1 (1984): 69–79

Carpenter, Humphrey, *A Serious Character: The Life of Ezra Pound*, Boston: Houghton Mifflin, and London: Faber, 1988

The Case against the Saturday Review of Literature: The Attack of the Saturday Review on Modern Poets and Critics, Chicago: Poetry, 1949

Dasenbrach, Reed, "Cantos 72 and 73: What Kind of Textbook?", *Paideuma: A Journal Devoted to Ezra Pound Scholarship*, 19/3 (Winter 1990): 129–31

Heymann, C. David, *Ezra Pound, the Last Rower: A Political Profile*, New York: Viking, and London: Faber, 1976

Kenner, Hugh, *The Pound Era*, Berkeley: University of California Press, 1971

Levy, Alan, *Ezra Pound: The Voice of Silence*, Sag Harbor, New York: Permanent Press, 1983

Stock, Noel, *The Life of Ezra Pound*, London: Routledge, and New York: Pantheon, 1982

Torrey, E. Fuller, *The Roots of Treason: Ezra Pound and the Secret of St Elizabeths*, New York: McGraw Hill, 1984

MICHAEL POWELL
British film director and producer, 1905–1990

EMERIC PRESSBURGER
British screenwriter, 1902–1988

THE LIFE AND DEATH OF COLONEL BLIMP
Film, 1943

Winston Churchill's attempt to suppress the film *The Life and Death of Colonel Blimp* is one of the best-documented cases of film censorship in Britain during World War II and, as far as historians are concerned, one of the most controversial. The reasons for the prime minister's personal intervention in this case, and the implications of his actions for the role and nature of censorship in wartime Britain, have been subject to different interpretations, resulting in a degree of historical controversy.

By 1942 the relationship between the Ministry of Information (MOI) and the film industry in respect of film propaganda had achieved a degree of harmony. The MOI had adopted a policy of informal liaison with film producers, in which it advised them on the suitability of scripts and subject matter, while most producers, for their part, were willing to adhere to a patriotic line. The director-writer team of Michael Powell and Emeric Pressburger had already worked closely with the MOI on the production of *49th Parallel* (1941), the only feature film released during the war in which the British government invested public money. In 1942, however, Powell and Pressburger, now calling themselves The Archers and working under the aegis of the Rank Organisation, the largest and most powerful corporate body in the British film industry, decided that they wanted to make a film based on the character of "Colonel Blimp". A creation of the left-wing, New Zealand-born newspaper cartoonist David Low, "Colonel Blimp" was a military diehard and political reactionary who had appeared in Low's cartoons in the *Evening Standard* since 1934 and who was used to satirize what Low perceived as the muddleheaded attitude of the British "Establishment". The film treatment that Powell and Pressburger prepared focused on the military career of a British Army officer from the Boer War to World War II, showing how, with the passage of time, he is gradually transformed from a young firebrand into an old-fashioned fuddy-duddy who is out of touch with the reality of modern warfare. In particular, their screenplay suggested that, in order to beat the Germans, the British would have to disregard their gentlemanly codes of conduct and adapt to the more ruthless conduct of "total" war. The aim of the film, in Powell's words, was to show "that Colonel Blimp was a symbol of British procrastination and British regard for tradition, and all the things which we knew were losing the war".

It was not long before the film ran into opposition from official quarters. In particular, Sir James Grigg, the newly appointed secretary of state for war, disliked the proposed treatment. Grigg's opposition must be seen in the context of the political and military situation in 1942. Shortly after taking office he had been stung by accusations of "Blimpery" in the army, voiced both in press and in parliament. Furthermore, events such as the fall of Singapore, probably Britain's worst single military reversal of the war, lent substance to some of the charges of incompetence that were being levelled. Against a background of publicly expressed hostility to "Blimpery",

Grigg was never likely to be sympathetic to the film. Having failed to persuade Powell and Pressburger to change their treatment voluntarily, Grigg wrote to Churchill in September 1942 informing him of the film, telling him that "I think it of the utmost importance to get [it] stopped".

Churchill responded by despatching one of his many "prayers" to the minister of information, Brendan Bracken:

> Pray propose to me the measures necessary to stop this foolish production before it gets any further. I am not prepared to allow propaganda detrimental to the morale of the Army, and I am sure the Cabinet will take all necessary action.

Churchill's desire to suppress the film and even to adopt any additional powers of censorship that might be necessary to do so was not shared by Bracken. "I am advised that in order to stop it the Government would need to adopt powers of a very far-reaching kind", he replied, explaining that such powers would amount to "the imposition of a compulsory censorship of opinion upon all means of expression" and that "this could not be done without provoking infinite protest". The only way in which the MOI could obstruct the production was by withholding the provision of facilities, such as troops to appear as extras, and by refusing to allow Laurence Olivier to be released from his service in the Fleet Air Arm to play the main role. Roger Livesey, who was not in the services, was cast instead. Churchill continued to make loud noises about suppressing the film, but in the end left it to the MOI and the War Office to decide. When officials saw the finished film in May 1943, they decided that it was "unlikely to attract much attention or to have any undesirable consequences on the discipline of the Army". Accordingly it was released in the cinemas and became one of the most successful films at the British box office in 1943. The notoriety may have contributed to its success, in that some cinemas advertised it with the slogan "See the Banned Film". The overseas release of the film was delayed for several months at Churchill's instigation – the MOI even admitted that this amounted to an "illegal ban" – until he finally relented.

Churchill's intervention raises important questions that go right to the heart of the practice of censorship in wartime Britain. On the one hand, it shows that the prime minister took a personal interest in film propaganda and was quite prepared to consider suppressing a film that he considered was bad propaganda. On the other hand, however, it illustrates the fact that there were practical limitations on the extent of his power. The most important consequence of the *Colonel Blimp* controversy was that Churchill failed in his attempt to suppress the film. He was dissuaded from heavy-handed and arbitrary censorship by Brendan Bracken, who realized that to adopt the extensive censorship apparatus necessary to ban the film would have been a politically insensitive move for a democracy at war. Given

that so much British propaganda was based on showing how her democratic political culture differed from the tyranny of Nazi Germany, to suppress the film would have undone much of Bracken's good work in winning the confidence of the British media.

Official documentation relating to the attempted suppression of *Colonel Blimp* was released in the early 1970s, under the Thirty Year Rule, and can be found in the British Public Record Office (PREM 4 14/15). The "*Colonel Blimp* File" has also been published several times. The historians Nicholas Pronay and Jeremy Croft have argued that the controversy surrounding the film was in fact engineered by Bracken, who secretly approved of the film and used the furore as "a wonderful demonstration for the Americans that Britain was indeed a genuine democracy in which not even an apparently all-powerful Prime Minister such as Churchill had the power to suppress a privately made film". Other historians, however, have lent little support to this thesis, and nor, indeed, do the reminiscences and memoirs of Michael Powell himself.

JAMES CHAPMAN

Films
The Life and Death of Colonel Blimp (produced, directed, and written by The Archers), 1943
Peeping Tom (directed by Powell), 1960

Writings by Powell
A Life in Movies: An Autobiography, 1986

Further Reading
Badder, David, "Powell and Pressburger: The War Years", *Sight and Sound*, 48/1 (1978–79):8–12
Chapman, James, "*The Life and Death of Colonel Blimp* (1943) Reconsidered", *Historical Journal of Film, Radio and Television*, 15/1 (March 1995): 19–54
Chapman, James, *The British at War: Cinema, State and Propaganda 1939–1945*, London and New York: Tauris, 1998
Christie, Ian, "Blimp, Churchill and the State" in *Powell, Pressburger and Others*, edited by Christie, London: British Film Institute, 1978
Christie, Ian, "The *Colonel Blimp* File", *Sight and Sound*, 48/1 (1978–79): 13–14
Christie, Ian (editor), *Powell and Pressburger: The Life and Death of Colonel Blimp*, London: Faber, 1994
Macdonald, Kevin, *Emeric Pressburger: The Life and Death of a Screenwriter*, London: Faber, 1994
Pronay, Nicholas and Jeremy Croft, "British Film Censorship and Propaganda Policy during the Second World War" in *British Cinema History*, edited by James Curran and Vincent Porter, London: Weidenfeld and Nicolson, 1983
Richards, Jeffrey and Anthony Aldgate, *Best of British: Cinema and Society, 1930–1970*, Oxford: Blackwell, 1983
Robson, E.W. and M.M. Robson, *The Shame and Disgrace of Colonel Blimp: The True Story of the Film*, London: Sidneyan Society, 1944

EDUARDO PRADO
Brazilian writer, 1860–1901

The Constitution of the first Brazilian Republic (1889–1930) was largely modelled on that of the United States. Twenty self-governing states were linked to a national government under a directly elected president, who answered to a senate and a chamber of deputies. The republic was not without its critics: among them was Eduardo Prado.

In September 1889, two months before the monarchy's demise, Prado had published a leaflet in Leipzig, Germany, in which he praised the monarchy, in the person of Pedro II, and warned about what he regarded as harmful republican propaganda. In Paris when the Brazilian Republic was proclaimed, he wrote a series of critical articles, later published as a book, *Fastos da dictadura militar no Brasil*, in which he attacked press censorship, and the arrest and deportation of those considered enemies of the new republic. He continued his attacks in *A ilusão americana*, published in São Paulo in 1893. In this book he set out to show that there was nothing in common between Brazil and the other Iberian nations in South America, and also that its friendship with the United States was false and would lead to US domination and imperialism. Prado would have preferred the adoption of a British-style political system.

On 4 December 1893 the São Paulo police raided the few bookshops in the city to prevent sale of the book and, on the following day, the cavalry surrounded the printing works where the book had been produced in order to guarantee the confiscation of remaining copies. A citizen found reading the book on a streetcar was apparently arrested. Prado was not deterred. He bought the periodical *O Comércio de São Paulo* at the end of 1895, in order to continue his attacks. In March 1897 its office was broken into and its equipment destroyed by Prado's opponents. Many other Brazilian periodicals suffered the same treatment, with the connivance of the government. Prado continued his attacks while in Europe, between June 1897 and April 1898, publishing articles in *Revista Moderna*, owned by a Brazilian; US intervention in Cuba presented him with a strong argument against his country's reliance on that country.

Prado died in a yellow fever epidemic in 1901. His ideas did not die with him. It is significant that a further edition of *A ilusão americana* appeared in 1958, at a time when the Brazilian left was attacking the negative effects of capitalism and the considerable presence of the United States in Brazil.

NANCI LEONZO

Writings
Destinos políticos do Brasil, 1889
Fastos da dictadura militar no Brasil, 1890
A ilusão americana, 2nd edition, 1895
Anulação das liberdades políticas: comentário ao & 4 do art. 90 da Constituição da República, 1897

Further Reading
Leonzo, Nanci, *O mundo elegante de Eduardo Prado*, São Paulo: Tese de Livre-Docência, 1989
Levi, Darrel E., *A Família Prado*, São Paulo: Cultura 70 Livraria, 1977
Motta Filho, Cândido, *A vida de Eduardo Prado*, Rio de Janeiro: Olympio, 1967
Pagano, Sebastião, *Eduardo Prado e sua época*, São Paulo: O Centro, n.d.

PRAISE POETS
South African performance artists, 1940–90

Praise poets have deep roots in the richly textured oral culture of African society. Before the colonial era, this predominantly male profession responded to social and historical pressures through popular performances that articulated criticisms and praises of leaders and, at a broader level, referred to issues of local community concern. The poems ranged in style and length from short free-form verse to lengthy historical narratives. In the 20th century, praise poets drew upon this heritage and transformed their works into a modern form of political protest linked to trade unionism and urban workers' concerns about apartheid capitalism. The state censored and repressed praise poetry because of its message and popular appeal.

Praise poetry should be seen as an integrated performance art in which the writer, his or her political perspective, and the context of the actual performance all shape the meaning of the work. The state censored praise poets directly by preventing the publication of their work in written form under the 1963 Publications and Entertainment Act, and by banning them as political activists under a series of repressive measures including the Suppression of Communism Act (1950) and the Riotous Assemblies Act (1914, amended 1930) which prevented them from publishing material or being quoted publicly. To a certain extent, then, the public performances of praise poetry can be seen as a creative response to more direct censorship of written material, just as written poetry was a response to the banning of more explicit opposition in prose. The nature of performances and the allusive content of the material made it difficult for state police and censors to identify praise poetry itself for suppression.

From the 1950s, under the Public Safety Act (1953) the state also suppressed praise poets indirectly by making illegal any public gatherings, political rallies, and funerals where they sought to perform their work. This act also provided for states of emergency – which the government declared with increasing frequency from the 1960s through the 1980s – in which civil rights were suspended and the state could enforce draconian measures for the detention and banning of individuals and organizations which utilized praise poetry. During the 1980s the state used the Internal Security Act (1976, amended 1982) to attempt to ban praise poets from public gatherings. The police applied these measures frequently at rallies which commemorated the police killings in Soweto in 1960 and the Sharpeville massacre of children in 1976, at May Day workers' celebrations and trade union meetings, and at political funerals where praise poets would have performed.

During the 1960s and into the early 1970s, praise poets responded to the apartheid regime's pressure on rural African communities to accept the implementation of "homeland" (*bantustan*) institutions. In Transkei, for example, praise poets harkened back to heroic ancestral chiefs for their symbolic support during the 1960 "Peasants Revolt" against "Bantu Authorities". By the later 1960s, Transkeian bards were calling on the local African state-supported ruler, chief Kaiser Matanzima, to "return to the [ways of the ancestral] Thembu chiefs" and to abandon his support of "separate development".

By the 1970s, however, Bantustan leaders used their own state security systems to suppress local praise poets because of their role in supporting the emergent Black Consciousness Movement (BCM). Security legislation in the "independent" homelands mirrored or even exceeded that of the white state. In the Ciskei, for example, praise poets were regularly restrained for ridiculing and satirizing local chiefs and administrators. BCM poets such as O. Mtshali and A. Kumalo, however, succeeded at using venerated Africans from the past in favourable comparisons with contemporary activists. Their use of images of warrior leaders such as Shaka and Bambatha was intended to empower Africans in their struggle for liberation. In 1977 the state banned the BCM, and poets diffused their efforts to raise "Black consciousness" through exiled activists and new parties such as the Azanian People's Organization (AZAPO).

By the 1980s, and especially in industrial urban areas, praise poetry reflected a vibrant and growing trade union opposition movement. The academic and trade union activist Ari Sitas organized cultural groups within unions which performed drama and poetry to express concerns about working and living conditions. These organizations aimed to heighten workers' awareness of union activities and to popularize the role of unions in the struggle against apartheid. Worker praise poets performed material that championed the cause of banned unions and opposition political parties. The African National Congress (ANC) encouraged artists to direct their work toward the struggle for national liberation. Union leaders then acted as "cultural workers" and used poetry only as a "cultural weapon" against apartheid, until this policy was amended in 1990 to allow for free expression.

Praise poets, white and African alike, composed tributes and elegies to heroic political figures, past and present, and to opposition organizations. The white political poet-academics Jeremy Cronin and Peter Horn composed and performed poems such as Horn's *Civil War Cantos*, which highlighted their experiences of imprisonment and torture. Their works were taken up by African university students, and, in turn, applied to the oral culture of the townships. Christopher Tosie and Nkosinathi Yengwa composed and performed poems for Nelson Mandela and Albert Luthuli (president of the ANC from 1952 to 1967, who was banned in 1960). The white academic and poet Keith Gotschalk, who was detained for his political activities and writings, performed his *Emergency Poems*, which included a tribute to the Congress of South African Trade Unions (COSATU), at a May Day rally in 1990. In 1984–85 African

workers and praise poets Alfred Qabula and Mi S'dumo Hlatshwayo performed tributes to the Federation of South African Trade Unions (FOSATU) at union meetings and to African workers during a major industrial strike.

The performance of praise poetry at banned gatherings during the 1980s brought sharply into focus the purpose and meaning of this genre of opposition. For example, at a concert held to protest against the detention of political prisoners in 1985, the state forbade poets from praising or criticizing the form of government. Artists defiantly performed poems which condemned the state and celebrated opposition leaders while they and the audience endured police harassment and arrest. Similarly, police and protesters clashed during a banned gathering at which praise poetry was performed in Cape Town in 1985 when poets informed the audience of police brutality and the arrest of John Issel, leader of the United Democratic Front.

By the mid-1980s praise poetry performances at funerals were significant alternatives to illegal rallies and union meetings, where the state had effectively stifled public expressions of dissent. Under the 1985–90 state of emergency funerals were one of the few types of public gatherings which the government still permitted, albeit under strict police control. By 1984 many funerals had become more than simply gatherings for the outpouring of grief; they were also forums for praise poets to denounce the government. As Natal praise poetess Nise Malange called out at the funeral of a trade union leader, "I did not come here to open up a wound or mourn . . . I am here to challenge the minister of law and order."

At the height of violent tensions in the segregated townships in the mid-1980s, praise poetry took a bizarre and gruesome turn. Intense pressure and the infiltration of townships by state security informants led to increasing internal violence between the radical youth and those they perceived to be betraying the struggle. Sandile Dikeni not only performed poems at rallies which advocated revolutionary violence, he recounted the killing of informants and those who opposed the brutal methods of the struggle. While Dikeni's work *Guava Juice* was a tribute to the use of Molotov cocktails in political violence, he also described in a poem how his "comrades killed my granny with fire". Referring to the act of "necklacing", this poem highlighted how his grandmother became a "casualty" of the struggle when she was murdered by township youths ostensibly because she opposed their activities.

ARAN S. MACKINNON

Further Reading

Cobbett, William and Robin Cohen (editors), *Popular Struggles in South Africa*, Trenton, New Jersey: Africa World Press, 1988

Cronin, Jeremy, *Inside*, Johannesburg: Ravan Press, 1983; London: Jonathan Cape, 1987

Gerhart, Gail M., *Black Power in South Africa: The Evolution of an Ideology*, Berkeley: University of California Press, 1978

Gotschalk, Keith, *Emergency Poems*, Belleville, South Africa: Mayibuye/Snailpress, 1992

Gunner, Liz and Mafika Gwala (editors and translators), *Musho! Zulu Popular Praises*, East Lansing: Michigan State University Press, 1991

Horn, Peter, *Poems, 1964–1989*, Braamfontein: Ravan Press, 1991

Horn, Peter, "Struggle Poetry of Sandile Dikeni", *Southern African Review of Books*, (March 1993)

Horn, Peter, *Writing My Reading: Essays on Literary Politics in South Africa*, Amsterdam: Rodopi, 1994

Lange, Margreet de, *The Muzzled Muse: Literature and Censorship in South Africa*, Amsterdam: Benjamins, 1997

Lodge, Tom, *Black Politics in South Africa since 1945*, Joahannesburg: Ravan Press and New York: Longman, 1983

Mafeje, A., "The Role of the Bard in a Contemporary African Community", *Journal of African Languages*, 6/3 (1967)

Mbeki, Govan, *South Africa: The Peasants' Revolt*, London and Baltimore: Penguin, 1964

Merrett, Christopher, *A Culture of Censorship: Secrecy and Intellectual Repression in South Africa*, Cape Town: David Philip, and Macon, Georgia: Mercer University Press, 1995

Shava, P.V., *A People's Voice: Black South African Writing in the 20th Century*, London: Zed, and Athens: Ohio University Press, 1989

Sitas, Ari (editor), *Black Mamba Rising: South African Worker Poets in Struggle*, Durban: Worker Resistance and Culture Publications, 1986

Switzer, Les and Mohamed Adhikari (editors), *South Africa's Resistance Press: Alternative Voices in the Last Generation under Apartheid*, Athens: Ohio University Center for International Studies, 2000

PRAXIS
Yugoslav philosophical journal, 1964–75

The suppression of *Praxis*, and the dismissal from their academic posts of the philosophers and sociologists who made up its editorial board, constituted a remarkable attack on academic freedom during the last quarter of the 20th century. Those in the West who noticed it found it all the more surprising in that it arose in a communist society that had been internationally respected for its relative openness to intellectual development and new ideas, even extending to challenges to the very nature and practice of Marxism itself.

After Yugoslavia broke off relations with the Soviet Union, in 1948, it embarked on redefinitions of socialism that were unique in the communist world, formally adopting, most notably, the idea that workers should participate in the management and policy-making of the enterprises and services for which they worked. This was the starting point for the *Praxis* philosophers, but they went further than the architects of "self-management" had ever intended. (Indeed, it is now clearer than ever just how circumscribed self-management was in practice, and how little workers' councils could depart from centrally dictated policies.)

The *Praxis* group's studies of the writings of the young Karl Marx, whom they saw as a humanistic philosopher interested in such problems as the freedom of the individual in society, convinced them that political alienation still existed in Yugoslavia; that the working class was still exploited, now by bureaucratism and technocracy; and that a radical democratization, and ultimately the withering away of the party, were required if alienation was to be abolished. These ideas were published in *Praxis* magazine, published bimonthly, and in two other journals, *Filosofija* and *Gledišta*. The editorial board of *Praxis* was based in the philosophy department of the University of Zagreb, but academics at Belgrade and Ljubljana were also contributors, united in the belief that the concept of *praxis* was essential to Marxism and consisted in the radical criticism of "all existing reality", including both state and party structures, and the "self-management" system itself.

At first, the ideas of the *Praxis* group were apparently welcome. The Yugoslavia of the early 1960s was open to new ideas, and self-management could be applied to philosophy and sociology departments as much as it could to factories. The *Praxis* group's explicit rejection of any form of narrow nationalism was particularly welcome. However, *Praxis* was vulnerable to government interference because, like all other such journals, it was subsidized by the state. As early as 1968,

president Josip Broz Tito was demanding the removal of *Praxis* contributors from their academic positions. They were held responsible for the student uprisings of May and June 1968, in which some groups had displayed slogans that bore a close resemblance to some of the leading ideas explored in *Praxis*. The authorities at first wavered between outright hostility and pragmatism: professors in Ljubljana lost their teaching posts, but not their incomes; meanwhile, their counterparts in Zagreb were allowed to remain in post, because they provided a counterweight to the ideas of their nationalist colleagues. Predrag Vranički, a member of the *Praxis* group, was even elected rector of Zagreb University in 1972, and had his term prolonged for two more years from 1974.

Meanwhile, individual issues of *Praxis* were subject to confiscation, such as two in autumn 1971, one said to have contained "false reports" of the 1968 events, the other dedicated to "Yugoslav socialism today". The same happened to the issue of July 1972, in which the magazine criticized the trial of professor Mihajlo Djurić of Belgrade, which they considered an infringement of academic freedom. The regime was particularly irked at the ability of the *Praxis* philosophers to spread their ideas abroad, not only by maintaining an international subscription list, but also by attending international academic conferences. The authorities confiscated the passports of four members in 1972. Financial pressure was also applied. In its edition of September–December 1972, the editorial board complained that it had received only 47 per cent of its allowance for 1971, and that printing prices had increased by 50 per cent in comparison with the previous year.

By then, the university committee of the League of Communists had decided (9 October 1972) that the eight Belgrade philosophers linked with *Praxis* – Trivo Indjić, Mihailo Marković, Svetozar Stojanović, Ljubomir Tadić, Dragoljub Mičunović, Zagorka Pešić-Golubović, Nebojša Popov, and Miladin Životić – should no longer be allowed to teach at the university. This action, which had no legal basis, was in response to a speech by Tito on 17 September, attacking those who criticized "bureaucratism" and laying down that they would "have to go on pension or find another line of employment". *Politika* (1 November) accused the philosophers of "liberalism, defiance of central party guidance, and resistance to the efforts to rebuild a strong and disciplined party".

The Faculty Council hit back by asserting its rights to re-elect both Indjić and Popov, in defiance of party instructions.

The law was then changed to allow a person's political qualifications to be taken into account in faculty elections. A book
by Marković, *Reappraisal*, was banned because it would
"alarm citizens"; later, the ban was confined to the book's first
chapter, translated into English as "The Structure of Power in
Yugoslavia and Dilemmas of the Revolutionary Intelligentsia".
Mihajlo Djurić's sentence, meanwhile, was reduced from two
years to nine months. Pressure was reapplied in a law of 30
January 1973, allowing the police to search offices and apartments "when the situation requires it".

While resistance to the dismissal of the eight philosophers
continued – and extended to formal protests from Noam
Chomsky, Daniel Bell, Stanley Hoffman, and other western
sympathizers – in early 1974 the government withdrew its
subsidy to the Croatian Philosophical Society and the Yugoslav
Union of Philosophers, the two organizations that were the
formal publishers of *Praxis*. At first, the magazine was able to
continue because contributors agreed to write without remuneration, but then, in January 1975, the Communist Party,
acting through its printing branches, stopped printers from handling the magazine, in effect suppressing it. On 28 January the
Serbian legislature used powers that had been recently conferred upon it to remove the philosophers, on full pay, until
they either retired or obtained alternative employment.

On 24 March, the editorial board informed subscribers that
further publication had become impossible. A new journal,
Praxis International, was established outside Yugoslavia in
1981 and continued until 1994, publishing articles mainly in
English and drawing contributions from such thinkers as Jürgen
Habermas, but it could no longer reflect the living philosophical thought of Yugoslavia.

"Liberal Marxism" – as the *Praxis* group's line of thought
had come to be known – had been totally extinguished, even
within the informal gatherings of the "Free University" that
some former *Praxis* scholars organized in private homes in
Belgrade during the 1980s. In 1986, Marković, Tadić, and
Pesić-Golubović dumbfounded many of their former colleagues
by signing a nationalist petition supporting the claims of some
Serbs in Kosovo that the Albanians there were committing
"genocide" against them. Marković then went on to coauthor
a Memorandum of the Serbian Academy of Arts and Sciences
that endorsed the nationalist programme of the Serbian government under Slobodan Milošević. As another former editor
of *Praxis*, Rudi Supek, told the Croatian magazine *Danas* in
1987: "The normal evolution of our society was halted by the
absence of the left intelligentsia, which disintegrated or was
chased out of public life . . . or which, in protest, retired to
their studies".

In 1991 Marković became vice-president of the ruling
Serbian Socialist Party. In 1992–93, Stojanović served as a
special adviser to the nationalist writer Dobrica Ćosić during

his brief presidency of the rump of Yugoslavia (Serbia and
Montenegro). Finally, in 1996 Marković and Tadić organized
a petition in support of the Bosnian Serb leader and indicted
war criminal, Radovan Karadžić, whom they dubbed "the true
leader of all Serbs". They thus made it clear to all observers
just how far they, and several other former members of the
Praxis group, had travelled away from any form of Marxism,
or indeed liberalism. On the other hand, another former
member of the group, Zarko Puhovski, has consistently raised
his voice against censorship and other forms of repression, most
recently as vice-president of the Helsinki Committee on Human
Rights in Croatia; two others, Micunović and Popov, were
closely involved in the democratic opposition to Milošević in
the 1990s; and Zoran Djindjić, prime minister of Serbia since
late 2000, was both a student of Micunović's and a contributor to *Praxis International*. The formation, development, and
suppression of the *Praxis* group thus continue to resonate in
what was once Yugoslavia.

ROBERT STALLAERTS

Further Reading

"À quoi bon Praxis?" (What Use is *Praxis*?), *Praxis* 1 (1965)

Grlić, Danko, "Practice and Dogma", *Praxis* 1 (1965)

Kangrga, Milan, *Etika ili revolucija* (Ethics or Revolution), Belgrade:
Nolit, 1983

Kangrga, Milan, *Praksa, Vrijeme, Svijet* (Praxis, Time, World),
Belgrade: Nolit, 1984

Lovrić, Jelena, "Misljenje kao diverzija: Ima li protrebe da se o
Praxisu danas drugačije razmišlja. Intervju: Dr Rudi Supek"
(Thought as Diversion: Do We Have to Think Otherwise about
Praxis? Interview with Dr Rudi Supek), *Danas* 6 (1987)

Marković, Mihailo and Robert S. Cohen, *Yugoslavia: The Rise and
Fall of Socialist Humanism: A History of the "Praxis" Group*,
Nottingham: Spokesman, 1975

Petrović, Gajo, *Philosophie und Revolution*, Reinbek bei Hamburg:
Rowohlt, 1971

Secor, Laura, "Testaments Betrayed: Yugoslavian Intellectuals and the
Road to War", *Lingua franca* 9/6 (September 1999)

Sher, Gerson S., *Praxis: Marxist Criticism and Dissent in Socialist
Yugoslavia*, Bloomington: Indiana University Press, 1977

Sher, Gerson S. (editor), *Marxist Humanism and "Praxis"*, Buffalo,
New York: Prometheus, 1978

Steenbergen, Bart van, *Marxisme in theorie en praktijk: een keuze uit
het Joegoslavische tijdschrift "Praxis"* (Marxism in Theory and
Practice: A Selection from the Yugoslav Review *Praxis*), Assen,
Netherlands: Van Gorcum, 1975

Stojanović, Svetozar, "Contemporary Yugoslav Philosophy", *Ethics*
76/4 (July 1966)

Stojanović, Svetozar, *Kritik und Zukunft des Sozialismus*, Munich:
Hanser, 1970

Supek, Rudi and Branko Bošnjak (editors), *Jugoslawien denkt anders*
(Yugoslavia Thinks Otherwise), Vienna: Europa, 1971

"Yugoslav Philosophers under Fire", *Index on Censorship* 2/2
(Summer 1973): 61–64

OTTO PREMINGER
US film director, 1905–1986

THE MOON IS BLUE
Film, 1953

Otto Preminger's sex comedy successfully challenged the authority of the Motion Picture Producers of America (MPAA) to control the content and exhibition of films in the United States. The film also played a major role in undercutting the power of the Catholic Legion of Decency to function as the unofficial moral watchdog of the American cinema.

Preminger, Austrian by birth, deeply resented any interference with his artistic vision and did not adjust well to the Hollywood system of collaborative production and censorship which he described as absurd. After directing two films for 20th Century-Fox, he moved to Broadway where he had the control he demanded. In 1951 he re-negotiated his contract with 20th Century-Fox, demanding "the final cut", or complete control over all his films. *The Moon Is Blue* was his first film under the new freedom.

The plot of F. Hugh Herbert's sex farce was simple. A handsome New York architect named Don Gresham meets an attractive, struggling actress called Patty O'Neill on the observation platform of the Empire State Building. They are attracted to one another and he invites her to dinner, and she accepts. This young woman is neither shy nor demure – but rather startlingly direct. When they arrive at Don's apartment, Patty tells her date that she is glad he doesn't mind. Mind what? he asks. "Oh, men are usually so bored with virgins. I'm glad you're not." More sexual banter unfolds. Cynthia, Don's ex, lures him out of the apartment and sneeringly refers to Patty as a "professional virgin". Don is furious and storms back to the apartment where he discovers Patty's father, a tough old Irish cop, who promptly busts him in the jaw and drags his errant daughter home. The next day, the two meet again on the observation platform at the Empire State Building. Don proposes marriage and Patty accepts. The curtain drops and everyone lives happily ever after.

The play was a huge hit and ran for over three years on Broadway. It toured more than 35 cities throughout the United States with no objection from censors, churchmen, or public officials. The popularity of the play made it a natural for the movies. Preminger and Herbert formed an independent production company and struck a deal to release the film through United Artists. Preminger signed William Holden to play Don. David Niven, who specialized in playing suave, debonair playboys, was perfect for the role of David. For the *ingénue*, Patty, Preminger gambled on a Hollywood unknown, Maggie McNamara.

Everyone understood that the movie censors were sure to object to its frankness. In 1934, industry moguls had agreed not to exhibit any film that did not carry the seal of the industry censorship board, the Production Code Administration (PCA). After reviewing the script, PCA representatives expressed their objections based on the humour in the script regarding the subjects of seduction, virginity, divorce, and sexual relations. They were not as concerned about the use of the word virginity as they were about the context in which it was used. They objected to the line "You are shallow, cynical, selfish and immoral, and I like you". The industry censorship code, written by Father Daniel Lord in 1930, stated that sex "must *not* be the subject of *comedy* or *farce*, or treated as material for laughter".

Preminger and Herbert offered a few minor concessions but basically informed the PCA that they intended to shoot the picture more or less as it was written – which is what they did. Preminger remarked: "I am not a crusader or anything like that, but it gives me great pleasure to fight for my rights." When the final film was submitted to the PCA several months later, Breen accepted Preminger's challenge and rejected the film. He told Preminger that he could appeal against his decision to the MPAA board of directors. Preminger did this, but the MPAA board had no choice but to deny a seal to *The Moon Is Blue*. If the MPAA ruling body gave a PCA seal to Preminger, it would, in effect, completely undercut what was left of Breen's authority to cajole filmmakers to abide by it.

Everyone knew what was at stake. The MPAA action was, in 1953, no guarantee that the film would not be a box-office hit, but it was certainly going to make it more difficult to sell the film to distributors. Exhibitors were reluctant to book films that did not carry the seal. Nevertheless, the grip of the MPAA was weakening. Exhibitors could not help but notice that the play had packed theatres on its national tour and that preview audiences had loved the movie version.

The interesting question now was what the Legion of Decency would do. Executive secretary Father Patrick J. Masterson and his assistant monsignor Thomas F. Little announced on 9 June 1953 that *The Moon Is Blue* was condemned because "the subject matter . . . in its substance and manner of presentation seriously offends and tends to deny or ignore Christian and traditional standards of morality and decency and dwells hardly without variation upon suggestiveness in situations and dialogue". Little penned a long memorandum to the local legion directors advising them that *The Moon Is Blue*, while not outwardly salacious, was a danger to the moral well-being of movie audiences. New York's cardinal Spellman joined the attack when he declared *The Moon Is Blue* a violation of standards of morality and decency and demanded that all Catholics boycott the movie.

Behind the scenes, the legion worked furiously to make *The Moon Is Blue* a failure. Monsignor Little pressured distributors not to book the film into their movie theatres and implied that if they did, the legion would call for Catholics to boycott their movie theatres. He did meet with some success. The film was pulled from exhibition in Putnam, Connecticut, banned in Maryland, seized as obscene in New Jersey, and limited to adults in Chicago.

However, despite these victories the legion campaign against *The Moon Is Blue* fizzled out. The film was a box-office hit, grossing over $6 million and playing, according to Preminger, "in something like eight or nine thousand theatres in the US". In the end, the censors' victories were temporary. The courts eventually overturned as unconstitutional all the decisions to ban the film. Meanwhile, Preminger's next film *The Man with the Golden Arm* (1955), dealing with drug addiction, was also refused an MPAA seal. To avoid Legion of Decency condemnation, he cut a 30-second scene in which Frankie Machine (Frank Sinatra) prepared heroin for injection. For the first time, the legion failed to condemn a film without an MPAA seal.

GREGORY D. BLACK

Writings

"Your Taste, My Taste . . . and the Censors", *Films and Filming* (November 1959)
Preminger: An Autobiography, 1977

Further Reading

Black, Gregory D., *The Catholic Crusade against the Movies, 1940–1975*, Cambridge and New York: Cambridge University Press, 1998

Herbert, F. Hugh, *The Moon Is Blue*, New York: Random House, 1951

Randall, Richard S., *Censorship of the Movies: The Social and Political Control of a Mass Medium*, Madison: University of Wisconsin Press, 1968

Vizzard, Jack, *See No Evil: Life inside a Hollywood Censor*, New York: Simon and Schuster, 1970

Walsh, Frank, *Sin and Censorship: The Catholic Church and the Motion Picture Industry*, New Haven, Connecticut: Yale University Press, 1996

LA PRENSA
Argentine newspaper, established 1869

La Prensa has a history of principled opposition to authority and reasoned criticism of government since it was founded by José Clemente Paz on 18 October 1869. The founder of the paper, which from its launch was printed at 3 p.m. each afternoon, said that it was born "in response to a basic need of the Argentine people". The first issue stated that the newspaper would not publish a list of principles, because experience showed that they were usually broken. "Truth, honesty: that is our starting point. Freedom, progress, civilization, our only goal." It could be said that for much of its first half-century these aims were upheld.

Although conservative in the style of the Argentine establishment in the second half of the 19th century, *La Prensa* was essentially a liberal newspaper, and in the 20th century some of its leading writers were well-known socialists and staunch critics of the oligarchy. Its circulation between the two world wars was claimed to have reached 700,000 copies a day. However, it was clearly the paper of an educated elite, and the organ of a family that wanted to keep Argentina in the neocolonial role of exporter of farm produce and importer of manufactured goods.

Joseph Page, in his biography of Juan Perón, said of *La Prensa* in the 1930s (known as the "infamous decade" in Argentina because of widespread corruption):

> As liberals in the United States embraced *La Prensa*, the newspaper became a symbol of democracy, an ironic twist in view of the paper's tolerance of electoral fraud during the Infamous Decade. Of course, most *La Prensa* supporters in the United States had never read the paper (no easy task because of its poor layout and turgid style). They acted as though it were a paradigm of responsible journalism, whereas in reality, at least in its political coverage, it was more like a stuffy version of a contemporary Hearst newspaper or the *Chicago Tribune*.

Eighty-two years after *La Prensa* first made its appearance, the newspaper, and its editors, reached the highest and lowest points in the paper's history of international fame when general Perón, president of Argentina since 1946, engineered the paper's takeover in 1951. This was done by whipping up a vengeful frenzy among Péron's followers. The first stage was for Perón's supporters to present the public with the argument that the paper had broken distribution rules agreed with the news-vendors' network. In several speeches Perón had branded the paper as the mouthpiece of the oligarchy, who were against his populist reforms.

Perón hated the established press and from the time he took office in 1946 he set about combating it. Whatever press freedom had existed had vanished by 1947. The president's wife, Eva María Duarte de Perón – Evita – had organized the purchase of *Democracia, Crítica, La Razón, Noticias*, and *Epoca*, and three other papers had joined the Peronist camp through the forced sale of shares or outright seizure. The survivors were *La Nación*, founded on 4 January 1870 by Bartolomé Mitre, which more or less genuflected before the government in the name of survival; *Clarín*, founded by Roberto Noble on 28 August 1945, with Peronist support, to oppose the established press; and the socialist weekly *La Vanguardia*, which was seen by Perón as "establishment" because it challenged Peronist rule; and *La Prensa*.

La Prensa fell when it was singled out as a symbol of the landowning classes that opposed Perón. The paper was expropriated on 11 April 1951, after a lengthy labour dispute. The Argentine Congress, dominated by Perón's supporters, passed law number 14,021, which ordered the confiscation of all properties held by Ezequiel Paz, son of the founder, or by his wife and his heirs. The paper was declared anti-Argentine by parliament.

The atmosphere at the paper, and outside it, was by then one of pressure and conflict. *La Prensa*'s owners could not buy enough newsprint, so the paper had fewer and fewer pages. Outside the building, megaphones warned the public against buying copies of the paper, as did posters plastered throughout Buenos Aires. One employee was killed in a series of attacks on the newspaper's building on Avenida de Mayo and this death, it has been argued, was the point at which the editors gave in.

Perón had won the battle of *La Prensa*. He delivered the publication to "the workers" – in fact, a group of tame journalists who had been appointed with Eva Perón's authorization – and the newsroom now gathered together all the most loyal of the Peronist party's supporters through the Peronist-controlled General Confederation of Labour (CGT). According to Robert Crassweller, however, "his victory came at a terrible price. Alberto Gainza Paz [grandson of the founder] raging around the hemisphere, and receiving support of journalists and publishers everywhere, was more trouble to the government than he could ever have been in Argentina." *La Prensa* was returned to its owners by the government of general Pedro Eugenio Aramburu, who overthrew Perón in September 1955.

The newspaper's last moment of brilliance was also attributable to Perón. When the old general, who had always been referred to by *La Prensa* as "the deposed tyrant", died on 1 July 1974, the newspaper published an obituary containing all the venom of decades: in the text were allegations of corruption, cowardice, and abuse of power. Everything the editors had ever held against the dead president was there in print. Peronists went into the streets and burned copies of the newspaper in pavement ceremonies, and many small *autos da fé*. Partisans sang the "Peronist March" as the flames consumed the pages. By then, however, both Perón and *La Prensa* were part of the past.

Faced with mounting debts, the Paz family sold the paper in 1993 to Amalia Lacroze de Fortabat, a construction industry millionairess who wanted to enter the publishing world. The paper's circulation was slipping. In the 1970s it had fallen to 30,000 and it fell to 5000 copies by the late 1980s. The circulation had not grown when, in 1997, it was purchased by the owners of a small provincial newspaper chain based in the resort town of Mar del Plata.

ANDREW GRAHAM-YOOLL

Further Reading

Crassweller, Robert D., *Péron and the Enigmas of Argentina*, New York: Norton, 1987

Editors of La Prensa, *Defence of Freedom*, London and New York: Boardman, 1952

Page, Joseph A., *Perón: A Biography*, New York: Random House, 1983

LA PRENSA
Nicaraguan newspaper, established 1926

La Prensa, owned by the Chamorro family, has – like its proprietors – played a key role in Nicaragua's history. That role has changed dramatically, however, since January 1978, when the assassination of the paper's editor, Pedro Joaquín Chamorro, sparked a series of events that culminated in the overthrow of the dictatorship that had ordered his murder.

La Prensa was a trenchant vehicle of opposition to the Somoza dynasty, which ruled Nicaragua from 1937 to 1979. The Chamorro family represented a business community whose possibilities of independent economic development were constantly blocked by the interests of the corrupt and repressive Somoza regime, that enjoyed the support of a US government for whom it was an unconditional ally in a region grown particularly significant since the 1959 Cuban revolution.

La Prensa's criticisms of Somoza increased after the 1972 Managua earthquake, when the dictator appropriated all the aid designated for reconstruction, strengthening his economic position at the expense of the rest of the business community. From 1974 to 1978 *La Prensa* consistently denounced Somoza and supported all political opposition including the activities of the Sandinistas (FSLN), who were gaining support, particularly among the young. In 1977 Chamorro became president of a unified opposition front (UDEL), which called for human rights, democratic elections, and the resignation of Somoza. UDEL enjoyed broad support, but mainly expressed the opposition of bourgeois groups, and particularly business. When Chamorro was assassinated by Somoza's agents in 1978, the reaction to his death spread beyond his natural constituency. The population of Monimbó, a poor suburb of Masaya, for example, took to the streets and for a week held Somoza's National Guard at bay with home-made weapons. The US government began to distance itself from Somoza, and initially supported the protest demonstrations that followed Chamorro's murder. As the demonstrations changed seamlessly into the beginnings of a mass insurrection involving trade unions, popular organizations and, increasingly, the Sandinistas, the US rapidly changed course. On 19 July 1979 Somoza was overthrown and replaced by a government dominated by the Sandinistas.

While the US government was happy to see Somoza go, it was less happy about the balance of forces in the immediate aftermath of his overthrow. Without Chamorro, the conservative opposition could not challenge the Sandinistas for control of the state – and the echoes of the revolution were reverberating throughout Central America. The US honeymoon with Sandinista Nicaragua was extremely short-lived; by 1980 US intelligence began to gather former National Guards who had fled to Honduras into the core of an armed opposition to the Sandinistas known as the Contras. With Ronald Reagan in the White House, aid to the Contras increased dramatically: the president was determined to overthrow Sandinista Nicaragua at any cost. The declaration by the Sandinistas of the first of many states of emergency, early in 1980, was a response to the mounting economic, military, and propaganda campaign against Nicaragua. It was also an instrument for the consolidation of power in the new state as their erstwhile conservative allies, among them Pedro Joaquín's widow Violeta Chamorro, severed relations with the Sandinistas.

Within *La Prensa* the argument over the new Nicaragua led to a further division. Fernando Chamorro, Pedro Joaquín's brother, had already become editor of the new Sandinista daily *Barricada*. Then Xavier Chamorro took part of the family's assets to form *El Nuevo Diario*, with a position of critical support for the Sandinistas. By 1981 new regulations permitted direct censorship of the press, and *La Prensa* was subjected to their provisions with increasing severity. It was suspended five times before March 1982, and appeared regularly with blank sections thereafter. In June 1986 it was suspended for 16 months after receiving a grant from a US government-funded agency, and subsequently for shorter periods. According to the Sandinista Press and Propaganda Department, the paper "created a climate of fear" with provocative reports of shortages and mounting crime.

As Nicaragua found itself under an increasingly remorseless siege through the 1980s, *La Prensa*'s strident headlines and tabloid journalism formed part of a campaign of internal destabilization designed to complement US-supported military activity from outside. *La Prensa*'s political position was hostile to a Nicaraguan revolution under intensifying siege, but the problems it described did exist, even if it exploited them for its own political ends. The problem was that censorship itself became the core of a campaign against the Sandinistas. The real character of *La Prensa* was lost in the process – it had ceased to be an independent liberal newspaper seeking truth and justice through balanced reporting. It was now an unashamedly agitational sheet employing many of the techniques of the gutter press. The important issue – which *La Prensa*'s external supporters never considered – was the extent to which suppression of the paper gave legitimacy to a more generalized suppression of free speech and debate among the FSLN's grass-roots supporters. The fate of *La Prensa* was of far less concern to the mass of Nicaraguans than the economic crisis, the devastating war of attrition they were suffering, and the absence of a democratic debate with an increasingly remote and authoritarian Sandinista government.

In the elections of 1990 the Sandinistas were defeated. Violeta Chamorro came to power as the representative of National Opposition Union (UNO), a coalition that embraced the Contra organizations and other elements of the conservative opposition. She had the active political and economic support of the US and of her own newspaper, *La Prensa*. She also won the support of many people who believed that her election would bring an end to war and an influx of funds. In reality, few funds were forthcoming and her government's policies continued the war by other means through austerity measures and the return of rural and urban properties to their original, pre-revolutionary owners. The individual beneficiaries of the transition to the Chamorro presidency also included many leading members of the Sandinista government.

The Chamorro family retained the directorship of *La Prensa* until 1993. *Barricada* passed into new ownership in the same year and began to distance itself from the Sandinistas, while *El Nuevo Diario* remained an unconditional supporter of the FSLN throughout the decade. *La Prensa* entered the new millennium as the newspaper of highest circulation, having retained its characteristic tone and language.

MIKE GONZALEZ

Further Reading

Caistor, Nick, "A Day with *La Prensa*", *Index on Censorship*, 15/5 (May 1986)

Harris, Robert, "The Censor at Work on *La Prensa*", *Index on Censorship*, 6/6 (November–December 1977)

Sklar, Holly, *Washington's War on Nicaragua*, Boston: South End Press, 1988

Vilas, Carlos M., *The Sandinista Revolution: National Liberation and Social Transformation in Central America*, New York: Monthly Review Press, 1986

PRESS

The idea of press freedom in Europe and North America stemmed from that of religious freedom. The English philosopher John Locke (1632–1704) argued the natural right of freedom of conscience, a view reiterated a century later by the French novelist and critic Voltaire (1694–1778) who spoke for the more secular societies that were emerging. England had allowed prior restraint to elapse in 1694, but the first nation to grant explicit press freedom was Sweden by its Ordinance Concerning Freedom of Writing and Publishing issued in 1766. Following the sweeping laws of the French Revolution (1789) and the US First Amendment (1791), the idea of press freedom was unstoppable.

Sweden, the most consistently liberal European state, was the first nation to grant freedom of the press, with the King-in-Council Ordinance Concerning Freedom of Writing and Publishing in 1766. The law was the first to provide public access to official government documents, except secret ones. The French Revolution ushered in an era with sweeping laws granting freedom of the press. The US First Amendment explicitly renounced press censorship. Indeed, the French and American revolutions precipitated the recognition during the 19th century that the press had an essential role to play in democratic societies. As the journalism historian J. Herbert Altschull wrote of the First Amendment's worldwide impact in the 19th century:

The revolutionary idea embodied in the First Amendment has frequently summoned to the barricades men and women who believe that no liberty is genuine unless it contains the right to express one's opinion, however unpopular, hated, or inflammatory . . . It is doubtful in the extreme that the drafters of those sparse forty-five words [the First Amendment] could have imagined their impact, for, after all, there was nothing new in an assertion of the right of free expression. What was new, however, was the wide circulation of the declaration and the broad interpretation that came to be placed on the right, as well as the universal adulation that was to be heaped upon it.

On the other hand, also in the 19th century, the press evolved from a primarily political instrument to a commercial industry. About the same time that America was shifting to a commercial "Penny Press" in the third decade of the century, a similar trend occurred in Europe. Commercial newspapers that carried news about crime and sensational events were first introduced in New York. A few years later *La Presse* in France sharply reduced prices, sparking a circulation war. Scholars such as Altschull and Michael Schudson have noted that the commercial press, which was driven by profit, changed the nature of "news". In the United States, in particular, the first trace of the notion of journalistic "objectivity" started to take hold, developed from the press itself. This view contradicted even Enlightenment thinkers' views of the freedom of the press. They believed that the press should be free and unfettered to espouse its opinions and even advocate partisan causes. They hoped that the public would be able to grasp the "truth" by weighing all the contrasting ideas thrust into the marketplace.

Objectivity removed the press from the realm of partisan politics, since reporters now claimed to report "the facts". They distanced themselves and their opinions from their stories and allowed their news "sources" to speak for themselves. In theory, the practice of objectivity should have resulted in a relatively balanced view of "all sides" of public issues. In reality, "official" sources in government and industry exerted significant influence in shaping the news while non-official sources were "marginalized".

Objectivity gratified advertisers, who did not want to offend consumers who held different political views. The reliance of the American commercial press on advertising revenue, which by the end of the century surpassed economic reliance on subscriptions and sales, was a forewarning of the important role that advertisers would play in shaping the news. Advertisers did not have to flaunt their power to influence press coverage. Instead, the commercial press exercised self-censorship in reporting news that might offend advertisers. Throughout the 19th century, for example, few US newspapers covered the dangers of "patent medicines" that accounted for so much of their advertising revenue.

Despite potential advertising pressure, for a brief period during the first two decades of the 20th century US journalists working on national magazines were severely critical of the dishonest practices of big business. The "muckrakers", as these journalists were called, expressed moral outrage against the excesses of the "robber barons" who wielded their financial clout to limit competition, exploit workers, and sell inferior products. In particular, the journalist Ida Tarbell took on Standard Oil, headed by John D. Rockefeller, who, along with other entrepreneurs, had been praised by teachers and preachers as examples of the success that comes with hard work. Tarbell's "History of Standard Oil" series in *McClure's Magazine* exposed Rockefeller as a scoundrel who had built his economic empire on unscrupulous business practices. Rockefeller and his like did not know how to deal with the outraged press and public opinion. They aggravated their already bad reputations by openly adopting a social Darwinist ideology of the "survival of the fittest" applied to the marketplace, arguing that if they were more successful than other people it was because they were shrewder and more cunning than their competitors, a callous response which only fuelled further public wrath.

The evils of advertising were also targeted by the muckrakers. Will Irwin's series in *Colliers* in 1911 described advertising as "the main handicap on American journalism in its search for truth". He chronicled how rapacious publishers had allowed their newspapers to become corrupted by the dollars to be earned from advertising. But the muckrakers curtailed their attacks after the political system had responded to the most egregious industry abuses with modest reforms and the break-up of the largest monopolies. They were reformers – not revolutionaries. They wanted to correct – not destroy –

capitalism. Such aggressive reporting against industry never again occurred.

The muckrakers were successful, in part, because there were no countervailing communication messages from industry to challenge their reports. Indeed, despite their business acumen, the captains of industry were at first slow to recognize the importance of cultivating public opinion. In response, early 20th-century America witnessed the growth of public relations, in which corporations actively sought to curry favourable press coverage. Industrialists realized that they needed a hospitable environment in which to conduct business, so they sought advice from "councils" to improve their tarnished images. According to legend, Ivy Lee (known in press circles as "Poison Ivy"), a former journalist, successfully transformed Rockefeller's image from that of a despised tyrant to a philanthropist who established foundations and, on Lee's advice, handed out dimes to street urchins while the press reported his magnanimous deeds. Edward Bernays, who founded modern public relations, invented the press kit and taught the first university public relations course.

Scholarly study of press control and manipulation was first launched during the period between the two world wars, with the study of "propaganda". Many scholars include public relations under the rubric of propaganda. Three other lines of scholarly study related to press control and manipulation are the Four Theories of the Press; the New International Information Order; and behavioural approaches.

Early research on propaganda was largely anecdotal, summarizing coordinated propaganda efforts by nations that aimed to manipulate domestic and international news media during World War I. One of the few propaganda studies to offer an analytical framework was Alfred McClung Lee and Elizabeth Lee's *The Fine Art of Propaganda* (1939). Based on their analyses of the radio speeches of the "fascist priest" Charles Coughlin, they identified seven propaganda "techniques": name-calling, testimonial, the bandwagon effect, glittering generalities, plain folks, speech, transfer, and card stacking. The seven devices were so practical that they were incorporated into elementary school curricula in the United States so that children could recognize and decode propaganda in the press, entertainment, and advertising.

One of the earliest attempts to provide a press–government relations framework for understanding press censorship was *Four Theories of the Press* (1956) by Fred Siebert, Theodore Peterson, and Wilbur Schramm. The book, which offered a four-part typology, was widely adopted in international journalism courses. The theories or concepts were authoritarian, libertarian, communist, and social responsibility.

The two historical theories were the authoritarian and libertarian theories. The former conceived of a privately operated press subservient to state authority. Press control was accomplished by prior restraint and post-publication censorship. According to this concept, the press must serve – or at least not subvert – state policies. The libertarian concept, based on Enlightenment principles, envisioned absolute freedom of the press with no restraints or responsibilities. This belief held that if all media voices were unrestricted, then "the truth" would emerge from the cacophony. The libertarian concept may have been useful during the era of political pamphleteers. The problem was that this concept was not pertinent during the

1950s, with the rise of television networks and large newspapers and magazines where a few powerful corporate media organizations dominated the marketplace of ideas.

The two contemporary theories in the *Four Theories* book were the communist and social responsibility theories. The communist theory conceived of a press owned by the government "for the good of the people". Lenin mocked the notion of western press freedom, describing it as "freedom for the rich, systematically, unremittingly, daily, in millions of copies, to deceive, corrupt, and fool the exploited and oppressed mass of the people, the poor". The role of the press, Lenin argued, was as a collective agitator, propagandist, and organizer on behalf of the state. Siebert, Peterson, and Schramm conceded some validity to the communist criticisms that powerful media in Western nations essentially drowned out or marginalized alternative ideas. They disagreed, however, with the communist theory's "radical" solution of abolishing an independent press and, instead, offered another solution through social responsibility theory. This sought to rectify the admitted problems of libertarian theory by urging large media organizations to exercise their power responsibly.

The Four Theories were criticized in subsequent years for, among other things, putting forward a Eurocentric view of press–government relations, neglecting the possibly beneficial role of governments in fostering a marketplace of ideas, and minimizing the role of media conglomerates and advertisers in press censorship. These criticisms were especially fervent during the 1970s and 1980s, when developing nations put forward their ideas for what has been called a "New International Information Order" (NIIO) or "New World Information Order" (NWIO).

The NIIO consisted of a number of demands by nonaligned nations to exercise greater control on the flow and content of news into and out of their countries. The nonaligned nations advanced their ideas primarily through United Nations agencies and various international meetings. These countries became disappointed with the euphoria of independence during the 1960s, believing that they were victims of "media imperialism" because they had little control over the flow of the world's news and information. They claimed that their cultures were overwhelmed and shaped by foreign (mostly American and European) media messages.

The nonaligned nations demanded a number of remedies, including the establishment of Third World news agencies. The most controversial demands concerned what appeared to Western nations and journalists as efforts to impose authoritarian governmental controls over their domestic media under the benign cover of "developmental journalism". Developmental journalism, and related practices, involved government interventions in the news media for the stated goal of advancing social and political progress, or "nation building". The first attempt at developmental journalism came from the University of the Philippines in Los Baños in 1973, under the rubric of "development support communications". The programme received the endorsement of the Marcos dictatorship, which tended to erode its credibility.

By the late 1980s much of the impassioned rhetoric over the NIIO had subsided. The end of the Cold War contributed to the decline, and also caused confusion in Western journalism, since the press pondered on how to report international news in the absence of a Cold War threat. As a result press coverage of international news was even less than during the height of NIIO complaints about the neglect of developing nations in the Western press. Prestigious newspapers, national news magazines, and television networks reduced their resources and the attention paid to international news. The Western press in the post-Cold War era gave the impression that the world was a safer place; and this may have been true for western countries. But at any time there were 15 to 20 "hidden wars" or conflicts in places remote to American and European concerns, including the Sudan, Myanmar (Burma), Sri Lanka, Peru, Algeria, and Colombia.

Behavioural science researchers have not directly focused on governmental or corporate censorship of the press, but several popular "media effects" approaches have relevance to censorship including agenda setting, the third-person effect, and the spiral of silence.

Agenda-setting research has focused on the correspondence between the major issues in the news media (i.e. the media agenda) and the set of "salient" public issues among the public (i.e. the public agenda). The research generally reports significant associations between the media agenda of issues and those issues regarded as important and worthy of attention among the public. It is important to emphasize that social scientists do not regard agenda setting as the power of the press to change opinions or attitudes about issues. Rather, as researchers often stress, the media merely "set the agenda" of issues for what the public thinks about (thoughts and issue "salience"), not what the public thinks of public issues. Supporters of agenda setting embrace the approach as a pluralistic perspective valuable for a democratic society, in which the media take on the important role of focusing attention on important public issues of the day. Some critics, such as Oscar Gandy Jr in *Beyond Agenda Setting* (1982), take a political-economy approach to agenda setting. Gandy and other scholars claim that the narrow focus on the media and public agendas deflects attention from the role of largely unseen but powerful sources in government and industry in shaping the media and, ultimately, public agendas.

The third-person effect takes a psychological approach to explain the support of the public and policy makers for press censorship. The theory attempts to explain the censor's "mindset". The third-person effect is based on two hypotheses: a perceptual component hypothesis and a behavioural component hypothesis. Much empirical evidence supports the perceptual component hypothesis that people perceive the media to exert greater persuasive influence on other people than on themselves. Only recently have researchers investigated the behavioural component hypothesis for third-person perception to lead to greater public support for censorship. According to this hypothesis, people support censorship to "protect" other people judged less discerning than themselves from "harmful" media effects. Thus, the third-person effect argues that people support censorship for benign – almost paternalistic – reasons, to "protect" people from harmful media messages.

Another psychological approach, the spiral of silence, asserts that the news media exert censorship through enforcing social control. According to this approach, the news media reflect dominant public opinion about controversial issues. Individuals, eager to assess the "climate of opinion", look to the news media and other people not only for news about controversial issues but also to learn about the desirability of publicly supporting or opposing them in their interpersonal relations. If they learn that their opinion about a controversial issue is popular, they speak up and express their opinions, knowing that they will receive social approval. But if they hold an opinion that they perceive to be unacceptable or unpopular, they remain silent rather than risk censure from others. By speaking up or remaining silent, they become channels of communication and contribute to the upward or downward spiral of opinion.

Censorship, in its most brutal form of prior restraint and blatant post-publication punishment, is rare in contemporary democratic societies. Governments wishing to control or manipulate the press have had to take indirect approaches. Some methods that have developed include spin control, leaks and trial balloons, and photo-ops. Journalists are well aware that they are being used by politicians who employ such flagrant methods, but journalistic constraints to report the news objectively (i.e. what the government says) make it difficult for them to counter these methods effectively.

Spin control developed in the United States after televised presidential debates in the 1990s. Journalists focused their interpretations not on the content of the debates but rather on "who won and who lost". Politicians, recognizing the media's interest in "winners and losers", assembled their own spokespeople or "spin doctors", as the media dubbed them, to influence interpretations. Although the news media knew that the spin doctors offered biased opinions and were trying to influence news coverage, they nonetheless reported the spin doctoring as news, and the spin doctors got their opinions across.

Leaks and trial balloons involve passing unattributed or unidentified information to the media. The press, though aware of the self-serving nature of the information, still often finds the information useful. The value of leaks sparked a debate in American journalism when the Reagan administration authorized "disinformation" leaks to the press as part of a US government campaign of psychological warfare against Libyan leader Moammar al-Gadhafi. On 2 October 1986, Reagan confirmed a *Washington Post* story that he had authorized the disinformation campaign, the purpose of which was to make Gadhafi "go to bed every night wondering what we might do".

At the same time that the administration was sanctioning disinformation leaks, it was vigorously cracking down on unauthorized administration leaks. The defence secretary George Schultz, quoting Winston Churchill, defended the government's right to lie and mislead the press: "In time of war, the truth is so precious it must be attended by a bodyguard of lies." The CIA director William J. Casey even suggested that the administration might prosecute news organizations that reported unauthorized leaks. This led Jack Nelson, the Washington bureau chief of the *Los Angeles Times*, to comment: "The position they've taken is that if a journalist gets the truth through unofficial channels, it's a crime, but if he accepts disinformation through official channels, that's just fine."

Stephen Hess, of the Brookings Institution, described a typology of leaks and trial balloons. Trial balloons differ from leaks in that leaks refer to information about issues or events while trial balloons represent policy that is being ostensibly considered. If the public response to a trial balloon is negative, then officials can deny the press reports or claim that the policy was never seriously considered. If the trial balloon is warmly received, then it may lead to policy actions. Hess distinguished different types of leaks: "ego leaks", where officials provide information to show the press that they are people of consequence; "goodwill leaks" to win the favour of a journalist; "animus leaks" to undermine a policy or a rival; and "whistle-blower leaks", where a dedicated civil servant goes to the press with information about wrongdoing because he or she is unable to rectify the problem in any other way.

Photo opportunities or "photo-ops" arranged by politicians for the press represent efforts to gain favourable images in the news. Many politicians, journalists, and communication scholars believe that images can be more important than facts, given the importance of television news. Thus, politicians' handlers arrange suitable settings to "stage" the news for the press. Television journalists cynical of photo-ops often call attention to them in their stories. But handlers are not perturbed and believe that the images overshadow the journalists' cynical voice-overs. When president Clinton stopped in Costa Rica as part of a week-long visit to Latin America in May 1997, his signing of an accord pledging US technical support to Costa Rican conservation programmes was staged in a rain forest. After a reporter asked the interior secretary Bruce Babbitt whether a photo-op visit to the rain forest was needed, the response was: "What a shockingly cynical question!"

Governments regard news about national security as so risky that they often classify and restrict information. The United States and Britain have taken different approaches toward the publication of classified information. In the United States, the victory of the press in the landmark Supreme Court "Pentagon Papers" case (*New York Times* v. *United States* and *United States* v. *Washington Post*, 1971) recognized the government's right to maintain secrets and the right of the press to expose those secrets if it can.

In this landmark case, the Supreme Court ruled in favour of the right of the *New York Times* to publish government secrets pilfered by Daniel Ellsberg, a former deputy secretary of defence, who had sent the documents to the press. The 47-volume "History of the United States Decision-Making Process on Viet Nam Policy" (which came to be known as the "Pentagon Papers"), commissioned by the then secretary of defence in 1967, was brutally honest and showed that American policy did not follow public pronouncements.

The *New York Times* started to print parts of the document on 13 June 1971. The next day, the attorney general John Mitchell sent a telegram to the *New York Times* demanding that it cease publication. It refused. A few days later, it was enjoined from further publication after the Justice Department obtained a temporary restraining order. Meanwhile the *Washington Post* and other newspapers had joined in publishing the Pentagon Papers, claiming that the restraining order was an unconstitutional prior restraint on publication. In a rapid series of events, the Supreme Court heard the case and on 30 June, by a six-to-three decision, ruled in favour of the *New York Times*, even though some justices expressed anxiety that the reports could harm the nation. Justice Hugo Black (in an opinion joined by William O. Douglas), a First Amendment "absolutist" who believed in no press restrictions, praised the *New York Times* and the other newspapers for publishing the Pentagon Papers.

Britain has a clear policy regarding press publication of secrets: it is not permitted to. Secrecy has been described as a "British disease". The Official Secrets Acts of 1911 (amended in 1989) grants the government wide-ranging powers to suppress any mention of a subject in the press merely by issuing a "D notice". Among other things, the Act was enforced by the Thatcher government in 1987 temporarily to suppress the domestic publication of Peter Wright's *Spycatcher*, the memoirs of a former agent of British counterintelligence (MI5) even though the book was published abroad and brought into Britain by travellers. Margaret Thatcher continued to push for the prohibition as a "point of honour". The battle ended in October 1988 when the Law Lords ruled the case moot because of the book's publication in the United States and elsewhere.

While the United States has no official secrets act, government agencies such as the CIA found that they could restrain former government employees from publishing secret information through enforcement of contract law. In this way, rather than taking the legally difficult and unpopular path of censoring the press from publishing secret information, they could keep the information out of the press. In *Snepp* v. *United States* (1980) and *United States* v. *Marchetti* (1972) the courts recognized the legality of lifelong contractual agreements that require former employees to have their published works reviewed by their former employers. In the Snepp case, the government won the right to collect the royalties from the book of a former CIA agent because he failed to have his manuscript cleared before publication, as required in his secrecy agreement. When Victor Marchetti submitted the manuscript of his book, *The CIA and the Cult of Intelligence*, for review, the CIA demanded 339 deletions (almost one-fifth of the manuscript). Meetings between Marchetti's lawyers and the agency resulted in 168 deletions. The Fourth Circuit Court of Appeals held in favour of the agency and the book was eventually published with the boldface capital word DELETE where the deletions appeared.

Corporations have also made executives sign confidentiality agreements to withhold public disclosure of embarrassing information. In the most notorious case, the Brown & Williamson Tobacco Co. in the United States enforced a confidentiality agreement against Jeffrey Wigand, a former executive, to keep him from disclosing his charges that the company had doctored documents showing that it had known for many years that nicotine was addictive. Wigand made his charges in an interview to the *60 Minutes* programme on CBS. But in 1995 executives at CBS at first blocked *60 Minutes* from airing the interview because their lawyers feared the network might be slapped with a breach-of-contract suit. The lawyers feared that a jury might view CBS's consulting fee to Wigand for an earlier tobacco piece and its promise to indemnify him in the event of a lawsuit as a financial inducement to breach his contract. Although the interview was eventually aired, critics claimed that the case represented "corporate censorship" by CBS's parent company, Westinghouse, to censor news that was critical of corporations and capitalism.

Wartime represents a special case where even liberal democracies enforce press censorship. The Vietnam War was probably the last time that a country at war would permit virtually unrestricted freedom to journalists on the battlefield. In *The First Casualty* (1975, revised 2000) Phillip Knightley referred

to the period between the American Civil War and World War I as the "golden age" of war reporting, where colourful correspondents donned military regalia, carried arms, and covered the war from the trenches. For the most part, reporters supported their countries' policies so there was little reason to restrict their usually positive reports that contained only occasional mild criticisms.

World War I ushered in the age of systematized government propaganda and censorship. In America, president Woodrow Wilson established the Committee for Public Information (CPI). The CPI not only administered censorship but also supplied war news to the press. While the "mainstream" commercial press did not experience harsh prior restraint, antiwar socialist publications were prosecuted under the harsh measures of the Espionage Act of 1917 and the Sedition Act of 1918. A number of socialist publications lost their special mailing privileges and, in several instances, socialist leaders were jailed for expressing and publishing antiwar views.

Britain used the Official Censorship Act of 1911, passed during a period of anti-German spy fever, to muzzle war information. The government announced that it would take an expansive view of the Act. In 1919 a clerk who communicated details about army clothing contracts was prosecuted under the Act, even though he had communicated no military secrets. The British censors went to great efforts to keep the horrors of trench warfare out of the news. Fortunately for them, a cooperative press worked to support the war effort. In 1917 the prime minister David Lloyd George confided to the editor of the *Manchester Guardian*: "If the people really knew, the war would be stopped tomorrow. But of course they don't and can't know."

In France, censors were assigned to newsrooms to examine galleys before publication. Not even Germany, with an authoritarian tradition, exercised such pervasive censorship. The censors had the power to close the publications without trial; there were more than 170 censors in Paris alone.

The Vietnam War was a watershed because many US military officials blamed the press for America's defeat. The military itself, however, rejected this view with the US Army Center of Military History's report, *The Military and the Media, 1962–1968*. The report put the blame for public dissatisfaction on president Johnson's mishandling of the war and overly optimistic official statements. The government's optimistic statements and outright lies created cynicism among the journalists in the field, resulting in far less press–government cooperation than in previous wars. In 1961 the *New York Times* had willingly withheld reporting news about the CIA-sponsored invasion of Cuba, and in 1956 *The Times* of London had withheld reporting Britain's agreement with France and Israel to invade Egypt. In both cases the national leaders later regretted the newspapers' decisions to keep the failed missions secret.

The brief war between Britain and Argentina over the Falkland Islands/Malvinas served as a model for press control by the US military. The British re-introduced and refined the model of press "pools" during wartime. The concept of pooling all the journalists in one location was first implemented by the Japanese, in their conflict of 1904–05 with Russia. The reporters, who were promised a visit to the front, were sequestered in a Tokyo hotel under tight escort until they were taken to Manchuria; even there, they were kept far from the fighting. The British permitted only 17 carefully selected British reporters to accompany the military to cover the Falklands/Malvinas War. The correspondents had to sign forms agreeing to censorship by "public relations officers" from the Ministry of Defence. Presidents Reagan and later Bush were impressed by the wartime censorship policy. The US government experimented with and further refined British techniques on wartime press control during its Grenada and Panama invasions. The real test came with the American-led coalition invasion during the Gulf War of 1991. Reporters were kept away from the battlefield and learned about war news during carefully controlled briefings, which often involved misinformation. Further, their stories were subject to censorship. In one egregious example, a reporter who described US pilots as "giddy" had his copy changed to "proud" by the censors. As the ground war drew near, some irritated reporters bolted from the pools and tried to cover the war from the battlefield. They were almost all arrested, and some briefly jailed, by the coalition forces before they could reach the front lines.

Press censorship and control vary widely in non-Western nations. Most Latin American media have experienced greatly improved conditions since democratization spread through the region in the 1990s. The advances are uneven, with drug lords still making journalism dangerous in Colombia and criminal elements threatening the press in Guatemala, Argentina, and Mexico. Cuba has increased repressive acts against the small number of independent journalists on the island in recent years and, in 1997, enforced requirements of "objectivity" on foreign news organizations. The "Regulations for Foreign Media Work in Cuba" requires overseas correspondents to "act objectively" and "stick to the facts, in accordance with the ethical principles that govern the exercise of journalism".

Press "licensing", in the form of professional organizations known as *colegios*, has stirred much debate in Latin America. State-sanctioned, but organizationally controlled, *colegios* usually require membership and/or a university degree to practise journalism. The number of countries with *colegios* has increased with democratization, and several observers have noted that they may represent nothing more than efforts by journalists to increase their abysmally low salaries.

Until the region's privatization of state-run industries during the 1990s, many Latin American governments flagrantly wielded their power over the national economy to reward or punish news media with national advertising revenue. Nowhere has this been more pervasive than in Mexico. Government agencies regularly bribed journalists in an effort to attain positive coverage and would pay newspapers to insert their own news stories, which were indistinguishable from other stories. Although bribes and other shady practices are still practised, there has been movement toward a more critical press. In an effort to maintain their independence, several Mexican newspapers have adopted policies refusing contributions from political parties and prohibiting government advertising. Mexico's participation in the North American Free Trade Agreement (NAFTA) has forced the country to open its political system, and the press has used the opportunity to engage in criticisms. Even the powerful Televisa television network, once regarded as the unofficial organ of Mexico's ruling party, has had to become more aggressive as a result of a new competitor, TV Azteca.

The last Mexican government attempted to reassert control over its increasingly feisty press. In July 1996 the president, Ernesto Zedillo, issued an executive order raising the duty on imported newsprint (in violation of the spirit of the NAFTA agreement). Critics claim that this action was meant to make the press dependent on the state-owned newsprint company, which could wield its power to reward non-critical newspapers. On 13 September 1996, *El Universal*, one of Mexico's largest newspapers, was surrounded by armed police who arrested the publisher on tax evasion charges. The arrest came after the paper had begun to run front-page articles on government corruption and had added anti-government columnists to its opinion pages.

Many African and Middle Eastern nations practise blunt authoritarian press control. The press in much of sub-Saharan Africa is largely monopolized by governments, giving them easy control of information. The independent press of the sub-Saharan region experiences swings of on-again, off-again freedom and harsh censorship that depend on the whims of national leaders. Until recently Algeria was the most dangerous place for journalism. Harsh restrictions were imposed on the Islamic press in 1992, following the Declaration of the State of Emergency. Since then, the Armed Islamic Group, the most vigorous opposition, led a campaign that killed almost 50 journalists in three years and forced 200 more to flee abroad. Another nation in the Mediterranean region, Turkey, imprisoned the most journalists in 1996: 78. After Turkey, the other nations imprisoning journalists in significant numbers in 1996 were Ethiopia, 18; China, 17; Kuwait, 15; Nigeria, 8; and Myanmar (Burma), 8.

Middle Eastern nations such as Syria, Iraq, and Iran do not permit press freedom, and the major news media and national news agencies are widely read as official government voices. Israel has a generally free press, but as a country under siege it has security laws that permit censorship. The laws have been inordinately enforced against the Palestinian press. Ironically, the Israelis still retain Britain's Defence Regulations of 1945 permitting censorship, even though these unpopular laws were enforced against Jews fighting the British before Israel's independence.

There remains some question whether the newly emerging Palestinian press will enjoy press freedom or suffer the same restrictions as in other Arab states. Press freedom was not mentioned in the PLO's draft constitution and Yasser Arafat, who is known not to tolerate press criticism easily, has appointed loyal members of Fatah, Arafat's PLO faction, to the Palestinian Broadcasting Corporation (PBC). In May 1997 Daoud Kuttab, a leading Palestinian journalist who started an educational television station in competition with Arafat's official station, was detained without charges because Arafat was upset by his live broadcasts of the Palestinian Legislative Council, which regularly criticized him. When the assembly's debate focused on corruption among Arafat's cronies, raising the spectre of a scandal, Arafat had Kuttab's broadcasts blocked. But before he was arrested Kuttab kept filming the assembly sessions and distributing videos to television stations.

Asia has varying press systems, from official organs in China and North Korea, to harsh authoritarianism in Myanmar (Burma) and Indonesia, to self-censorship in Hong Kong on the eve of China's takeover of the island, to a coopted, syco-phantic press in Japan. Singapore enforces strict censorship against both domestic and foreign news media. As in the case of Israel and other countries influenced by British rule, Singapore has enforced its British-inspired laws to silence press criticism. The secrecy law was enforced in 1993 to prosecute a group of editors, security analysts, and economists who pub-lished government growth estimates without government approval.

In Japan, reporters have close relations with government offi-cials and no tradition of adversarial relations with the govern-ment. The press does little investigative reporting. A major scandal involving Lockheed aviation's Japanese contracts was not investigated or reported by the domestic press until a former prime minister mentioned it in a speech. The Japanese press exercises self-censorship with touchy issues. There is little criticism of the royal family and the press treads cautiously in reporting news about Japan's war crimes during World War II.

Although east European nations have generally enjoyed press freedom after the collapse of communism, vestiges of censorship remain. Eastern European governments have rarely enforced laws that restrict press freedom, but journalists are concerned that such laws might be enforced in the future. Poland, for example, has a law requiring the news media to reflect "Christian values". It still contains statutes from the communist era providing for up to eight years in prison for slandering the "supreme organs of the state". In Bulgaria, the government levies higher taxes on private newspapers than those operated by political parties. Slovakian law requires journalists to give "a truthful picture of the country". Meanwhile, in Russia, the economic circumstances for some of the independent news-papers are so dire that in order to survive some have become partisan newspapers sponsored by political parties.

In most liberal democratic societies, especially in the United States, much press control and censorship come from corpo-rate sources. During the 1980s and 1990s "critical" mass com-munication scholars shifted attention from press–government control issues to the role of media institutions, their structure and operations in framing and censoring the news.

The media mega-deals in the United States that resulted in the ABC, CBS, and NBC networks becoming parts of large con-glomerates in recent years have raised questions about how their news organizations report news that affect the parent companies and their subsidiaries. The General Electric–NBC merger has resulted in several incidents of self-censorship. In 1989 NBC's *Today* programme edited a segment to avoid men-tioning that GE had purchased defective parts for its nuclear plants. The programme mentioned the omission in a subsequent show after it received criticisms. In 1990, during a programme on consumer boycotts, the *Today* show conspicuously failed to report a national boycott of GE products because of its role as a nuclear arms producer.

Cases of corporate censorship in the United States rarely involve direct prohibitions. Rather, as Warren Breed noted in a classic article of 1955 in *Social Forces*, news organizations maintain "social control" over journalists by indirectly com-municating newsroom policy. Over time, journalists learn the unstated policies of their employers regarding political issues and local "sacred cows". They learn to handle such contro-versial issues delicately and practise self-censorship.

For example, while Congress was debating the first major overhaul of communications law in 60 years, the networks were lobbying to influence the legislation in their favour. Critics com-plained that the networks were giving scant attention to the legislation and neglecting the intense lobbying efforts of the net-works, although there was no evidence indicating that corpo-rate bosses ordered their news organizations either to avoid covering the issue or to cover it in any particular way. If there had been explicit corporate orders, this would have incited public condemnations and caused Congress to think twice about deregulating broadcasting. Ted Koppel of ABC began a *Nightline* programme on the proposed legislation by noting the pressure that the programme was under from the Walt Disney Co., which owns ABC, not to be too critical:

The major commercial networks, ABC among them, stand to make a great deal of money. You have proba-bly not heard a great deal about that, though, on televi-sion, not because anyone has told us not to cover the story – truly, the people we work for wouldn't do that – but neither is any one of us under the impression that they are especially happy that we have chosen to criti-cally examine the hand that feeds us.

Advertisers exert influence on editorial content in both large media conglomerates and local news organizations. Many local newspapers, for example, have relinquished entire sections to largely uncritical reports of local businesses. Some real estate sections, for example, carry news stories supplied by estate agents and developers that appear to be editorial content indis-tinguishable from the rest of the newspaper, although the word "advertising" is noted in small type somewhere. Similarly, many local newspapers and magazines have refrained from severely critical restaurant reviews for fear of hurting small local busi-nesses. Local car dealers who purchase entire pages pressure local newspapers to abstain from running "consumer" stories about how to negotiate purchases.

Advertisers have also become more assertive in wielding their power to shape the content of the news media. Nowhere is this more apparent than in the highly competitive American maga-zine industry. Recent moves by advertisers to demand fore-warning of controversial editorial content, and even to review content prior to publication, has sent shockwaves through the magazine industry. The Chrysler Corporation, the fifth largest purchaser of magazine advertising in the United States, issued an extraordinary memo to 100 magazines on 30 January 1996, through its advertising agency PentaCom: "Each and every issue that carries Chrysler advertising requires a written summary outlining major themes/articles appearing in upcom-ing issues. These summaries are to be forwarded to PentaCom prior to closing in order to give Chrysler ample time to review and reschedule if needed."

Several recent incidents show how advertisers influence the editorial content of magazines. A golf-ball manufacturer with-drew advertising from *Sports Illustrated* after the magazine's Golf Plus supplement of 7 April 1996 carried an article describ-ing how the Nabisco Dinah Shore Golf Tournament became an unofficial "spring break" for lesbians. After *People* magazine warned advertisers that it was running an article about the drug and alcohol abuse of the Grateful Dead rocker Jerry Garcia, cigarette and alcohol advertisers withdrew their advertising from the issue. After the *New Yorker* published explicit lyrics next to a Mercury car advertisement in its issue of 12 June 1995, Ford Motor Co. withdrew advertisements for six months as punishment. In response the *New Yorker* established a "sensitive advertiser list" to give certain advertisers advance warning about sensitive topics in forthcoming issues. The editor Tina Brown reluctantly supported the policy, adding that while the magazine would give advance warning this did not mean that it would change or withdraw editorial content.

Merchants also censor news and entertainment products, although this phenomenon is not new. Shops have often refused to carry books of which the owners disapproved. But these were small franchises, and with a little work consumers could find the books in other stores. What is relatively new is for large consumer chains, many of which have virtual local and regional monopolies, to exercise corporate censorship of news and entertainment products. Department store chains such as Wal-Mart and KMart have banned music compact discs, or successfully demanded music producers to produce edited versions of compact discs. Recently, even news products have been banned. When in June 1997 *The Globe* tabloid started running transcriptions of steamy accounts between Frank Gifford, husband of Kathie Lee Gifford, and a woman in a hotel, both Wal-Mart and KMart banned the issue. *The Globe* editor Tony Frost called the action "censorship" and "very un-American".

Current worldwide events offer a mixed picture of the future of press censorship. Many developing nations have sought to divest their government industries and spur free enterprise. Freedom of the press has emerged as a byproduct of this policy because free enterprise requires open, easy access to information, and international investors prefer to invest in "stable" nations that respect human rights. In fact, much of the worldwide pressure for increased freedom of the press and other civil liberties has come from the business sectors. This has certainly been the case in many Latin American nations, South Korea, and the former Soviet republics. But some Asian nations, including China, Vietnam, and Singapore, have tried to have both degrees of free enterprise and authoritarian press control.

The popularity of the internet also portends mixed blessings. It offers a potential source to unlimited news. At present, costs and telephone technology make it impossible for the internet to have a major worldwide impact. But as was the case with other technologies, there is reason to suspect that technical and cost impediments will be overcome. But governments such as China and Iran have tried to gain the national development promises associated with the internet while trying to control seditious material on the World Wide Web. In the west, many companies are investigating the business potential of the Web,

warning that this largely untapped frontier might become monopolized with information by media conglomerates. For western nations, issues of government censorship, while always a danger, should not overshadow the more immediate threat of corporate censorship. Too many civil libertarians and journalism professors are accustomed to thinking of censorship in press–government contexts while minimizing the dangers of corporate information control.

MICHAEL B. SALWEN

Further Reading

Altschull, J. Herbert, *Agents of Power: The Media and Public Policy*, 2nd edition, White Plains, New York: Longman, 1995

Blanchard, Margaret A., "Free Expression and Wartime: Lessons from the Past, Hopes for the Future", *Journalism Quarterly*, 69/1 (1991): 5–17

Curry, Jane Leftwich and Joan R. Dassin (editors), *Press Control around the World*, New York: Praeger, 1982

Gandy, Oscar H. Jr, *Beyond Agenda Setting: Information Subsidies and Public Policy*, Norwood, New Jersey: Ablex, 1982

Hohenberg, John, *Free Press/Free People: The Best Cause*, New York: Columbia University Press, 1971

Jansen, Sue Curry, *Censorship: The Knot That Binds Power and Knowledge*, New York: Oxford University Press, 1988

Knightley, Phillip, *The First Casualty: The War Correspondent as Hero and Myth-maker from the Crimea to Kosovo*, revised edition, London: Prion, 2000

Lent, John A., *The Asian Newspapers' Reluctant Revolution*, Ames: Iowa State University Press, 1971

Levy, Leonard Williams, *Legacy of Suppression: Freedom of Speech and Press in Early American History*, Cambridge, Massachusetts: Harvard University Press, 1960

Liston, Robert A., *The Right to Know: Censorship in America*, New York: Watts, 1973

Merrill, John C. (editor), *Global Journalism: Survey of International Communication*, 3rd edition, New York: Longman, 1995

Peleg, Ilan (editor), *Patterns of Censorship around the World*, Boulder, Colorado: Westview Press, 1993

Picard, Robert G., *The Ravens of Odin: The Press in the Nordic Nations*, Ames: Iowa State University Press, 1988

Ruud, Charles A., "Limits on the 'Freed' Press of the 18th- and 19th-Century Europe", *Journalism Quarterly*, 56/3 (1979): 521–30

Salwen, Michael B. and Bruce Garrison, *Latin American Journalism*, Hillsdale, New Jersey: Erlbaum, 1991

Seymour-Ure, Colin, *The Press, Politics, and the Public: An Essay on the Role of the National Press in the British Political System*, London: Methuen, 1968

Siebert, Fred S., *Freedom of the Press in England, 1476–1776*, Urbana: University of Illinois Press, 1952

Siebert, Fred S., Theodore Peterson and Wilbur Schramm, *Four Theories of the Press: The Authoritarian, Libertarian, Social Responsibility, and Soviet Communist Concepts of What the Press Should Be and Do*, Urbana: University of Illinois Press, 1956

Wilcox, Dennis L., *Mass Media in Black Africa: Philosophy and Control*, New York: Praeger, 1975

PRESS: Unstamped Press
Resistance to newspaper censorship, 19th-century Britain

The economic and social disruption caused by the slump after the Napoleonic Wars gave birth to considerable unrest, manifested in the attempt to assassinate the British Cabinet at Cato Street, London. The government's most repressive response to mass demonstrations was the Peterloo Massacre in Manchester (1819), but they also placed restrictions (collectively known as the "Gag Acts") upon meetings and introduced a draconian form of licensing of the press which aimed at undermining a platform that had been a powerful critic throughout the depression and the Queen Caroline affair. The government imposed a fourpenny stamp duty upon newspapers in an attempt to price potentially seditious material out of the hands of the urban working class.

The response of London radicals was to produce a number of papers intended, with varying degrees of subtlety, to flout the law. These were later joined by papers produced in Glasgow, Liverpool, Birmingham, Aberdeen, Hull, and Manchester. These were printed in secret and distributed by street vendors while the London papers were sent by post and other covert means (some concealed in coffins) to a considerable number of provincial locations. In response to the agitation preceding parliamentary reform in 1832, papers such as *The Destructive*, *A Slap at the Church*, *The Police Gazette* and *The Red Republican* openly defied the government by preaching a radical message aimed at reform of church, state, and society. However, not all unstamped papers were overtly political in tone and content. Some were literary and theatrical miscellanies that pandered to popular local taste and prejudice. Others were political scandal and satire sheets that attacked government and establishment attitudes in a much more oblique manner.

The most popular unstamped paper was the *Poor Man's Guardian* published by Henry Hetherington, who was to become a central figure in radical publishing. This paper's full title contained the defiant soubriquet "Established contrary to law to try the power of 'Might' against 'Right'" and at its peak it managed to sell an impressive 15,000 copies a week. Hetherington, formerly apprenticed to the parliamentary reporter, Luke Hansard, and his assistant James Watson were already veterans of other publishing ventures and their experience was supplemented by the talents of a remarkably gifted writer and editor – James Bronterre O'Brien, sometimes referred to in radical circles as the "English Robespierre". A glance at the content of this paper (available in a modern reprint) indicates that it not only argued articulately for parliamentary reform but analysed the class-based system introduced after 1832. The impressive style of the *Poor Man's Guardian* is best appreciated when read aloud and this increases the likelihood that the paper's influence extended beyond even its impressive sales.

Editors of other unstamped papers who were less intent on martyrdom and more concerned with fulfilling the burgeoning demand for the radical and populist products of the unregulated press found other ways of circumventing the law. Some avoided the use of paper at all by using linen or wood as a means of disseminating their message. Others still sought to avoid the title "newspaper" by providing cartoons, travelogues, and other ephemera. Committed radicals also sought such methods of circumventing the law: Hetherington himself once claimed that the failure to number one of his publications successively meant that it thus did not fall within the definition of a newspaper. Likewise, George Jacob Holyoake goaded the authorities by publishing a single-sheet paper with exactly the same stories borrowed from stamped papers reproduced in every edition. In the 1830s, the willingness of editors to flout the law led to a decline in the number and circulation of legitimate stamped papers as a result of this cheaper and racier competition.

Government attempts to attack the particularly radical papers were not always successful and may have been counterproductive. The prosecutions of destitute street vendors prompted many of the papers to establish subscription funds for the families of the victims. These were a successful feature of the "War of the Unstamped" and effectively trained many radicals who were later to be key figures in the Chartist movement in aspects of radical organization. The papers themselves also drew on this government action as a means to recruit and politicize other sections of the working class. *The Poor Man's Guardian* in 1831 offered its potential vendors "An honest and moral way of finding head and gaol shelter"; the determination of recalcitrant vendors could embarrass the government, while the spiky content of speeches from the dock could provide further useful copy.

When the government moved to imprison the printers and publishers such action was once again a double-edged sword. Although an important figure might be removed from the world of radical publishing, the boast of the unstamped that others would readily step forward to continue the work was regularly fulfilled. Moreover, as Hetherington repeatedly demonstrated, arrest, prosecution, and imprisonment could be an important method of boosting a flagging circulation. This cavalier attitude to imprisonment was an important aspect of Hetherington's charisma but also demonstrated his earnest belief that "Law is only the will of the aristocratic few". His arrests could even be used as a method of disseminating radical ideas to a still wider audience. Richard Carlile notoriously used his prosecution for selling Tom Paine's *Age of Reason* as an opportunity to read the whole book out loud as part of his defence.

In 1836 the Melbourne government decided to reduce the newspaper tax to one penny partly in response to the success of the unstamped, which had produced the *Daily National Gazette* by 1835. This should be set alongside the increasing clamour for action by the stamped periodicals who argued that their viability was threatened by this new departure. Moreover the reduction of the tax was also seen by the chancellor Thomas Spring Rice as a means to "shelter the law and the Government from odium and contempt". Although this measure effectively killed the unstamped press as a cohesive agitation many of those involved took the lessons they had learned about politics, government, and the practicalities of radicalism into the Chartist movement.

The issue of the so-called "Taxes upon Knowledge" remained a liberal radical cause until the stamp tax was abolished in

1861. Effective censorship, however, ended only in 1869 when the acts of George III's reign requiring publications to be licensed were finally removed.

DAVID NASH

Further Reading

Collet, Collet Dobson, *History of the Taxes on Knowledge: Their Origins and Repeal*, 2 vols, London: Unwin, 1899; reprinted Ann Arbor, Michigan: Gryphon, 1971

Hollis, Patricia, *The Pauper Press: A Study in Working-Class Radicalism of the 1830s*, Oxford: Oxford University Press, 1970
Wiener, Joel H., *The War of the Unstamped: The Movement to Repeal the British Newspaper Tax, 1830–1836*, Ithaca, New York: Cornell University Press, 1969

PRESS: Authoritarian Control

Fred Siebert, Theodore Peterson, and Wilbur Schramm, in their classic book *Four Theories of the Press* (1956), grounded authoritarian press theory in the writings of various philosophers. Plato had promoted benign – almost paternalistic – authoritarianism, where wise leaders (philosopher-kings) ruled as arbiters on matters of art and opinion for the good of society. The state would coordinate daily life, and all those who would not submit to authoritarian control Plato would "send to another city". In the 16th century Niccolò Macchiavelli was concerned with the ruler's maintenance of state power at any cost, for the continuance of the state was an end in itself. He advocated a pragmatic, amoral state policy to achieve political ends. Thomas Hobbes, in *Leviathan* (1651), claimed that the state must be obeyed because it provided protection against the inevitable chaos that results in the absence of authority. Later Georg Wilhelm Friedrich Hegel ridiculed the notion that the public should be involved in the operations of the state. "The state," Hegel wrote, "is the divine idea as it exists on earth."

While Siebert and his colleagues conceived of authoritarian press control as one of the "theories of the press", the theory was put forward largely as a contrast to other, better-conceived theories: libertarian, communist, and social responsibility. They noted that authoritarian theory "was almost automatically adopted" by autocratic states.

To understand authoritarian press theory, it is important to understand why it conceived of the monarchial ruler as all-wise and all-powerful. Monarchical rulers gained power when nomadic tribes came under attack from other tribes. A self-designated leader took charge, providing protection for the members of the tribe. For this he was revered. At some point, the tribe ceased its wanderings and put down roots in territories that would eventually become the fixed borders of the nation-state with the leader as king. The state provided protection and services. In return, the people recognized the king's authority and wisdom in all matters. He was not elected, but since the first king had enjoyed some degree of respect, he ruled with a degree of legitimacy.

Bureaucratic organizations formed around the king. It was in the interest of state bureaucrats to see that the monarchy continued after the king died, so hereditary rule was established. The bureaucrats fostered the belief in the monarch's authority by "divine rule" as a means of providing the monarchy with political legitimacy. Any criticism of monarchical authority was considered as sedition and resulted in severe punishment. The printing press, which appeared after the monarchical system had been established, had the potential to disseminate sedition on a large scale. A coterie of royal cronies and a bureaucracy enforced severe controls, including terror and violence, on speech or press that threatened the state.

The authoritarian model requires revision in modern societies because contemporary dictators cannot claim divine authority or, as (usually) unelected leaders, a popular mandate. One problem that authoritarian rulers face is legitimacy for their rule. Their lack of legitimacy makes them susceptible to pressures from various sectors of society – including the military, the business establishment, and even public opinion. It is not surprising that authoritarian leaders in some Islamic nations often claim lineal descent from Muhammad as a form of political legitimacy. Similarly, the late Ethiopian dictator Ras Tafari Makonnen crowned himself Haile Selassie ("The Power of the Trinity"), King of Kings, Lion of Judah, and claimed direct descent from the biblical ruler Solomon. To legitimize his rule, he held an elaborate and costly coronation in 1930.

Authoritarianism is sometimes incorrectly used interchangeably with totalitarianism (e.g., certain communist or fascist states). While there are similarities (they both suppress civil liberties for example), an authoritarian polity is dominated by an individual or small group exercising power broadly and often arbitrarily to silence criticism of the state. In contrast, a totalitarian polity is a complex bureaucracy with a state ideology that touches all aspects of life and institutions, including the press. While authoritarian governments do not try to create a new society, but rather seek to maintain the *status quo*, totalitarian Marxist or fascist societies advance grandiose revolutionary programmes and subscribe to ideological frameworks.

An important aspect that distinguishes authoritarian press theory from totalitarian press theory is that in authoritarian systems the press is privately owned, although access to the press may be restricted and subject to severe restraints, including licensing, physical threat, sedition laws, and the like. According to Siebert, Peterson, and Schramm: "The major problem in most authoritarian systems was establishing restraints and controls over the privately operated media." Totalitarian polities solve this problem by owning the press and not permitting independent initiatives. Journalists in totalitarian states are workers employed by the state to spread propaganda on behalf of state goals.

Another important difference distinguishing authoritarian press theory from totalitarian press theory is that while authoritarian systems restrict criticisms of the state, they do not demand support or propaganda to promote state policies. No demands are made on the press with regard to what it must publish, only what it cannot publish. Authoritarian societies may even permit wide-ranging political discussions, so long as these discussions do not challenge authority. As Siebert, Peterson and Schramm wrote, the authoritarian press may give an outward appearance of freedom:

> The authoritarians did not often object to a discussion of political systems in broad philosophical terms. Unlike the modern Communists, they did not demand complete conformance to a set of theoretical principles. They were usually content if the media avoided direct criticism of current political leaders and their projects, and with a benevolence uncommon in modern Communist and Fascist circles, they tolerated a wide divergence from the political principles upon which their system rested. What was not tolerated was an overt attempt to unseat the authorities themselves.

Today – although there are some signs of change – much of Africa, Asia, and the Middle East have authoritarian press systems. These systems may wrap themselves in the garbs of ideology, since an ideology is a form of legitimacy. But this feigned attempt at legitimacy is usually apparent. Like many authoritarian rulers, the Cuban dictator Fulgencio Batista (in power 1952–59), a classic Latin American *caudillo* (strongman) who came to power in a military coup against a weak and divided democratic government, tried to give the impression of an ideology, frequently referring to his "March 10 Revolution" (the date of his military coup in 1952).

Because Batista lacked legitimacy, he imposed on-again, off-again press censorship. He relaxed censorship periodically to curry favour with the press, placate the middle class, and leave the appearance of benign rule. A good deal of pressure came from Havana's conservative business community, which feared that censorship hampered international trade and investment. But Batista's limited liberalization efforts failed to win over either the press or the people, and may, in fact, have stiffened the opposition. The press despised Batista and criticized him whenever he loosened his grip on censorship, forcing the dictator to crack down again. Most media organizations, like most Cubans, welcomed Castro's ascent to power and celebrated when Batista fled into exile.

The brutal military dictatorship that ruled Argentina from 1976 to 1983 imposed severe censorship that included critical journalists as targets of government death squads. The government promulgated security laws that prohibited the news media from publishing the locations of detention camps and the names of *desaparecidos* (the disappeared ones) kidnapped by government authorities and never seen again. The government never dared to relax its grip on power. Ironically, it was censorship that led to its downfall during the war of 1982 with Britain over the Falklands / Malvinas Islands after the tightly controlled press misled public opinion about the progress of the war. Even many of the best educated Argentines had no idea that Argentina was losing the war until its end.

More recently, the Indonesian dictator Suharto, who ruled from 1967 until 1998, opened up the political system in 1990 with a policy of *keterbukaan* or openness, partly to assuage human rights groups, the military, and domestic and international corporations that believed authoritarian rule impeded Indonesia's economic development. The long-suppressed press immediately responded with a deluge of critical reports about political scandal, corruption, and ethnic unrest. The government responded by cracking down on the press again. The crackdown on *keterbukaan* led to public demonstrations and the formation of an independent press union in 1994. International outrage followed. The Indonesian example again demonstrated the many pressures that authoritarian governments feel to loosen their grip on power, and the difficulties they encounter when they do so, even briefly.

Because authoritarian systems do not involve coordinated press control, and permit a privately operated press to publish under tight restraints, the press and journalists are not socialized into the political ideology, unlike in totalitarian societies, and remain independent. Their oppositional status may in fact reinforce their belief in the valuable role of an independent press during a period of suppression. The fact that journalists in authoritarian societies are never socialized into the state ideology explains why the press can rebound so quickly after the fall of authoritarian governments. After the downfall of authoritarian leaders in Latin America and the Philippines in recent years, the once-suppressed press was able to bounce back quickly and thrive.

MICHAEL B. SALWEN

Further Reading

Hachten, William A., *The World News Prism: Changing Media of International Communication*, 3rd edition, Ames: Iowa State University Press, 1992

Ingelhart, Louis Edward, *Press Freedoms: A Descriptive Calendar of Concepts, Interpretations, Events, and Court Actions, from 4000 BC to the Present*, New York: Greenwood Press, 1987

Media Studies Journal, "Journalists in Peril", special issue: 10/4 (Fall 1996)

Merrill, John C. (editor), *Global Journalism: Survey of International Communication*, 2nd edition, New York: Longman, 1991

Pierce, Robert N., *Keeping the Flame: Media and Government in Latin America*, New York: Hastings House, 1979

Rugh, William A., *The Arab Press*, 2nd edition, Syracuse, New York: Syracuse University Press, 1979

Salwen, Michael B. and Bruce Garrison, *Latin American Journalism*, Hillsdale, New Jersey: Erlbaum, 1991

Salwen, Michael B., *Radio and Television in Cuba: The Pre-Castro Era*, Ames: Iowa State University Press, 1994

Siebert, Fred S., *Freedom of the Press in England, 1476–1776*, Urbana: University of Illinois Press, 1952

Siebert, Fred S., Theodore Peterson and Wilbur Schramm, *Four Theories of the Press: The Authoritarian, Libertarian, Social Responsibility, and Soviet Communist Concepts of What the Press Should Be and Do*, Urbana: University of Illinois Press, 1956

PRESS: Press Barons

Owners of newspapers have never been in any real doubt about the considerable potential power that they wield. To cite a famous example, in 1898, during the run-up to the Spanish–American war in Cuba, Frederic Remington, an artist on the *New York Journal*, wired the paper's proprietor, William Randolph Hearst, with the message: "There is no trouble here. There will be no war. Wish to return." Hearst, the model for Orson Welles's character Charles Foster Kane, swiftly replied: "Please remain. You furnish the pictures, and I'll furnish the war." His papers duly played their part in whipping-up pro-war sentiment, and the conflict soon followed.

In a similar vein, Alfred Harmsworth (later to become Lord Northcliffe, proprietor of the *Daily Mail*, *The Times*, and the *London Evening News*, and referred to by many of his contemporaries as "Northoleon") wrote in 1903: "every extension of the franchise renders more powerful the newspaper and less powerful the politician". In 1926 Lord Beaverbrook, whose press empire included the *Daily Express*, *Sunday Express*, and *Evening Standard* – and on whom Evelyn Waugh in *Scoop* based Lord Copper, proprietor of the *Daily Beast*, remarked of the press that "when skilfully employed at the psychological moment no politician of any party can resist it".

Given the undoubted power at their disposal, the crucial question is, have press proprietors actually intervened to influence the contents of their newspapers, insisting on the inclusion of certain stories and the exclusion of others? The latter would certainly constitute a form of censorship but, in practice, these different kinds of influence are hard to separate out. For example, when Hearst's newspapers were busy stoking up war fever it would clearly have been extremely difficult for any of his editors to run stories warning against or questioning the mood of increasing bellicosity. Similarly, in the 1930s when Beaverbrook used his papers to promote a British empire free trade zone, and Lord Rothermere, who succeeded Northcliffe, turned his (and especially the *Daily Mail*) into propaganda organs for the National Socialists in Germany and Oswald Mosley's Blackshirts at home – even going so far in 1934 as to pen the now infamous *Mail* leader headed "Hurrah for the Blackshirts!" – it is hard to imagine their giving space to opposing views on the subjects that so clearly obsessed them.

As early as the 1920s the power of the press barons to mould their newspapers and thus help to influence the political agenda was coming under fire. For instance, in *The Press and the Organisation of Society* James Angell branded them "the worst of all menaces to modern democracy". However, the most famous condemnation of press proprietors was uttered in 1930 by the Conservative prime minister Stanley Baldwin after Beaverbrook's and Rothermere's obsessive campaign on behalf of empire free trade had led their papers to back United Empire Party candidates, in preference to the Tories, in two London by-elections. As he put it forcefully:

> The newspapers attacking me are not newspapers in the ordinary sense. They are engines of propaganda for the constantly changing policies, personal wishes, personal dislikes of the two men . . . What the proprietorship of these papers is aiming at is power, and power without

responsibility – the prerogative of the harlot throughout the ages.

In October 1946 growing anxieties about the increasingly oligopolistic nature of the British press (the Beaverbrook/Rothermere axis having been augmented by Lord Kemsley, who owned the *Daily Sketch*, *Daily Graphic*, and *Sunday Times*) led to a House of Commons debate, which resulted in the setting up of the first Royal Commission on the Press. Called before it, Beaverbrook was typically forthright, arguing:

> My purpose originally was to set up a propaganda paper, and I have never departed from that purpose all through the years. But in order to make the propaganda effective the paper had to be successful. No paper is any good for propaganda purposes unless it has a thoroughly good financial position. So we worked very hard to build up a commercial position.

Asked what happened when his editors took a different line from him on empire free trade he replied: "I talked them out of it." As to why his papers echoed his own opposition to Britain's participating in the postwar Marshall Plan: "That comes from my co-operation with my colleagues. We are all thinking together and thinking alike". And while the Commission came to nothing, Beaverbrook, who was famously alleged to have issued 147 instructions in one day to the editor of the *Express*, and who was known by his staff as their "principal reader", launched his papers against new targets, such as the United Nations and the European Common Market.

Beaverbrook was hardly unique in acting thus, however, and in 1957 Francis Williams, in his classic study of the press, *Dangerous Estate*, having argued that "freedom of the journalist – freedom not only from censorship or intimidation by the State but from censorship or intimidation by anyone including his own employer – is an essential part of press freedom", went on to conclude that:

> The diminution in the status of the editor to no more than a paid servant of proprietorial interests, the mere tool of other men's whims and financial appetites, that has accompanied a good deal of the commercialisation of the last half century or so runs dangerously counter to the public interest and is contrary to the traditional role of journalism in public life.

Similarly Ralph Miliband was to claim a decade later that: "The right of ownership confers the right of making propaganda, and where the right is exercised, it is most likely to be exercised in the service of strongly conservative prejudices, either by positive assertion or by the exclusion of such matters as owners may find it undesirable to publish."

Of course, the press baron is hardly unique to Britain. In Germany, after World War I, Alfred Hugenberg, a former president of Krupp, co-founder of the Alldeutscher Verband, and leader of the ultra-conservative Deutschnationale Volkspartei, used his newspapers, along with the rest of his media empire, which included the Ufa film studios, to campaign remorselessly against the Weimar Republic. By the 1960s another German press magnate had emerged in Axel Springer, whose use of his considerable press empire, which included *Die Welt*, *Bild Zeitung*, and the Hamburg-based *Abendblatt*, to propagate his decidedly right-wing views, was the cause of considerable public and political concern. His activities were paralleled in France by the equally conservative Robert Hersant, a one-time Gaullist MP whose powerful Socpresse group included *France-Soir* and *Le Figaro* as well as a huge chain of local newspapers stretching from Le Havre to the Pyrenees, all of which clearly reflected their owner's views. Indeed, the sight of so much newspaper power in the hands of such a politically committed owner provoked the socialist government in 1981 into attempting to introduce, under the guise of anti-concentration legislation, what came to be known as the "anti-Hersant law".

As for the United States, the example of Hearst has already been cited, although, compared to its British counterpart, much of the American press has escaped the more baleful consequences of press barony by clinging firmly to the First Amendment and attempting, against admittedly powerful commercial odds, to preserve a spirit of independence. On the other hand, given British journalists' frequently envious glances across the Atlantic, it is sobering to note that, as far back as 1957, James Wechsler, editor of the New York *Post*, complained:

The American press is overwhelmingly owned and operated by Republicans who fix the rules of US political debate. And I use the word "fix" advisedly. I know it is a freer press than any prevailing in Communist or Fascist countries; but that is nothing to be complacent about. It is a press that has generally grown comfortable, fat, and self-righteous; and which with some noteworthy exceptions voices the prejudices and preconceptions of entrenched wealth rather than those qualities of critical enquiry and rebellious spirit we associate with our noblest journalistic traditions. It is a press that is generally more concerned with the tax privileges of any fat cat than with the care and feeding of any underdog. It is a press that sanctimoniously boasts of its independence and means by that its right to do what its Republican owners damn well please. The press used to be regarded as a public trust, not a private playground.

Wechsler's all-too-prescient remarks present a considerable challenge to the view that the increased commercialization of the press has actually helped to lessen the power of the press baron over his papers. For example, Stephen Koss in *The Rise and Fall of the Political Press in Britain* argued that the proprietor is now "a businessman first and foremost" whose prime aim was selling newspapers rather than supporting a political party, and thereby running the risk of alienating the all-important readers, who might support other parties or who might indeed find politics boring. Another argument, put forward by John Whale in *Journalism and Government*, is that today "the newspaper's staff is left to get on with the job" because the proprietors now have "global problems of trade and investment to occupy their minds". But while it may indeed be the case that purely party political partisanship on the part of proprietors

and their papers has become more fluid or conditional, this certainly does not mean that editors and journalists have a free hand in the broader ideological positioning of their papers: indeed, rather the opposite. As the third Royal Commission on the Press noted ruefully in 1977: "rather than saying that the press has other business interests, it would be truer to argue that the press has become a subsidiary of other interests". In such a situation, as James Curran concludes:

For some proprietors, newspaper ownership was little more than an investment in corporate public relations. It extended their range of business and political connections, increased their corporation's prestige, and, through judicious editorial appointments, contributed to the maintenance of public opinion favourable to public enterprise . . . The ownership of newspapers thus became one strategy by which large business organisations sought to influence the environment in which they operated . . . Owning (and in some cases subsidising) newspapers was merely another way of sustaining a political party providing it served their economic interests. It was also a way of buying political influence, and securing the relaxation of regulatory obstacles to business expansion.

In this view of things, owning a newspaper is no different from owning a car company; it is a purely commercial operation and, unlike public service broadcasting, carries with it no obligation to inform or duty to be impartial and accurate. A newspaper, in short, is its owner's private property, and theirs to do what they will with. As Lord Marsh, chairman of the Newspaper Publishers Association, put it in 1984 on the BBC:

I believe that the suggestion of editorial independence is a romantic myth dreamed up by editors. There is no doubt in my mind at all that proprietors, having spent a great deal of money on a newspaper, at the very least will not allow it to express views consistently with which they strongly disagree. Editors would rapidly find that if they wanted to do otherwise, they would be looking for a new job . . . If you buy a company and if the executives, that you hire and pay, pursue a policy to which you are strongly opposed, you will fire them before you accept someone else using your money and organisation to do something which you are opposed to.

The very model of a modern press baron is, of course, the multimedia magnate Rupert Murdoch, whose global record of political promiscuity demonstrates all too clearly that his newspapers will support any party that in turn will support his media interests. He is also the model for Lambert la Roux in David Hare's and Howard Brenton's coruscating stage satire on the British press, the aptly named *Pravda*.

When Murdoch acquired his first British newspaper, the *News of the World*, in 1969, he wanted, according to its then editor Stafford Somerfield, "to read proofs, write a leader if he felt like it, change the paper around and give instructions to staff". Remonstrations were met with the curt response: "I didn't come all this way not to interfere." Somerfield did not last long, nor did a subsequent editor, Barry Askew, who complained that Murdoch "would come into the office and literally re-write leaders which were not supporting the hard Thatcher monetarist line. That were not, in fact, supporting – slavishly – the Tory government." Over at the *Sun*, meanwhile, Murdoch changed the paper's allegiance from Labour to Conservative (in spite of the fact that most of its readers were Labour voters) in time for the General Election of 1974. Having acquired *The Times* and *Sunday Times* in 1981 in a deal that should have been referred to the Monopolies and Mergers Commission but was not, thanks to the pact that he had struck with Margaret Thatcher, he proceeded to make his hostility to the latter's liberal editor, Frank Giles, abundantly clear. According to Giles, he would spread the paper out before him and demand "What do you want to print rubbish like that for?", or, pointing to a particular by-line, snarl "That man's a commie". Needless to say, the unfortunate Giles's days at the paper were severely numbered. Meanwhile, at *The Times*, Murdoch was telling its veteran home affairs editor Fred Emery: "I give instructions to my editors all around the world, why shouldn't I in London?" This remark is reported in *Good Times, Bad Times* (1994) by Harry Evans, who edited the pre-Murdoch *Sunday Times* and *The Times* for one, he considered, distinctly unpleasant, year under the new proprietor. As he puts it in this seminal text on the Murdoch style:

The aura he created in 1981–2 was one of bleak hostility to Edward Heath and the Tory rebels, and contempt for the Social Democrats. He did this by persistent derision of them at our meetings and on the telephone, by sending me articles marked "worth reading!" which espoused right-wing views, by jabbing a finger at headlines which he thought could have been more supportive of Mrs Thatcher – "You're always getting at her" – and through the agency of his managing director, Long ... Murdoch himself came more and more to object to the balanced assessment of the Government I have described, calling later in my editorship for more "conviction", which meant more cheerleading. When he said that the leaders were "thoughtful" it was not a warming remark but a criticism. As the unemployment totals approached 3 million, both he and Long complained that *The Times* should be writing about the numbers of people who *were* employed. "We have more people in employment than they do in Europe!" became a refrain. None of this represented a reasonable exchange of views between editor and proprietor, unexceptional on any newspaper. The tone was assertive and hostile to debate. Such incidents were not isolated. They amounted to pressures to manipulate the independent editorial policy of *The Times* and they escalated into a campaign."

The unfortunate Frank Giles was replaced at the *Sunday Times* by Andrew Neil, a man very much in the Murdoch mould, but when this mutually beneficial relationship eventually came unstuck Neil published a memoir, *Full Disclosure* (1996), which, in spite of its self-serving tone, is also a key text not simply on the Murdoch *modus operandi* but on that of the modern press baron in general. In particular, he pinpoints how the owner allocates a fair degree of control over the day-to-day running of his papers to like-minded editors and managerial staff. Thus:

There is a common myth among those who think Rupert Murdoch has too much power and influence that he controls every aspect of his newspapers on three continents, dictating an editorial before breakfast, writing headlines over lunch and deciding which politician to discredit over dinner. He has been known to do all three. But he does not generally work like that: his control is far more subtle. For a start he picks as his editors people like me who are generally on the same wavelength as him: we started from a set of common assumptions about politics and society, even if we did not see eye to eye on every issue and have very different styles. Then he largely left me to get on with it.

Neil, however, continues:

Editorial freedom has its limits: Rupert has an uncanny knack of being there even when he is not. When I did not hear from him, and I knew his attention was elsewhere, he was still uppermost in my mind. When we did talk he would always let me know what he liked and what he did not, where he stood on an issue of the time and what he thought of a politician in the news. Such is the force of his personality that you feel obliged to take such views carefully into account. And why not? He is, after all, the proprietor.

Since Murdoch's staff are never sure when his next intervention will take place, or on what subject, "they live in fear of it and try to second-guess what he would want, even in the most unimportant of matters. It is a clever way of keeping his executives off balance: they live in a perpetual state of insecurity." Thus it was that Murdoch's worldview, neatly summed up by Neil as "a combination of right-wing Republicanism from America mixed with undiluted Thatcherism from Britain and stirred in with some anti-British Establishment sentiments as befits his colonial heritage", was able so thoroughly to infuse his newspapers without the constant need for direct intervention. Similarly his management methods, which Neil brands "autocratic" and "brutal", filtered through his own managers and "made life miserable for the shop floor".

That all this resulted in various forms of censorship, both direct and indirect, is undeniable, as James Curran and Jean Seaton illustrate in *Power without Responsibility*. Claire Tomalin, a former literary editor of the *Sunday Times* talks of "a reign of terror", Peter Wilby, a former education correspondent, remembers "a tone of fear, a horrible, 'totalitarian' atmosphere", and the renowned Latin American specialist Isabel Hilton states that:

The sense of intimidation was so strong that people actually started censoring themselves because it is very unpleasant to get into this kind of argument all the time. It is not just a collection of incidents, it's a collection of incidents *and* the atmosphere, which in the end is so depressing. You stop functioning as a journalist. There are things you just don't bother to pursue because you know you just won't get them into the paper.

In the first five years of the Murdoch/Neil regime, the *Sunday Times* lost at least 100 of its journalists, including most of its star names.

Nor is Murdoch's autocratic attitude confined only to his British newspapers. In the 1970s he insisted that his *New York Post* support Ed Koch over Mario Cuomo in the campaign for mayor of New York. When 80 of its reporters signed a petition that stated "we are dismayed to be manipulated into mere pamphleteers" and argued that the *Post* was their paper too, Murdoch replied: "Oh no it's not. When you pay the losses you can say it's your paper. It's my newspaper. You just work here, and don't you forget it." Meanwhile, in his native Australia Murdoch is notorious for having shifted around his newspapers' political allegiances in order to back whichever party he judges at the time will be the most friendly to his media interests. During the election campaign of 1975, for instance, Murdoch was in one of his anti-Labour phases and his paper the *Australian*, which had previously been pro-Labour, became so blatantly hostile that 75 of its journalists signed a letter complaining that the paper had been turned into a "propaganda sheet" and protesting at "the deliberate or careless slanting of headlines, seemingly blatant imbalance in news presentation and political censorship. Also on occasion the distortion of copy from senior, specialist journalists, the political management of news and features and the stifling of dissident and even unpalatable impartial opinion in the paper's columns." The letter was ignored, but thousands of copies of the paper were subsequently burned by demonstrators outside its Sydney offices.

In a lecture at the Edinburgh Film Festival in 1989, Murdoch stated:

> Government control will become increasingly impossible in the new age of television. The multiplicity of channels means that the government thought police, in whatever form, whether the benign good and the great in Britain, or the jackboot-in-the-night elsewhere, will find it hard to control more and more channels.

Two events in 1994, however, suggested that, in the modern media world, censorship, whether of television or the press, is as likely to be commercial as political in origin.

First, the *Sunday Times* ran a number of articles investigating possible links between British aid to Malaysia to enable it to build the Pergau dam and a vast Malaysian arms contract placed with Britain. These revelations of arms-for-aid infuriated the Malaysian prime minister, Mahathir Mohamed, and provoked what Andrew Neil states was the most bad-tempered call he ever had from Murdoch, who shouted: "You're boring people! You're doing far too much on Malaysia. Page after page of it, which nobody can understand. Malaysia doesn't merit all this coverage . . . It's my fault, I've been letting you get on with it. But it's too much, it has to stop." The following year, a British minister dining with the British high commissioner in Kuala Lumpur asked if the Malaysian government was still as hostile to British business interests as it had appeared to be in the wake of the Pergau revelations. The high commissioner replied: "Not since Murdoch fixed it with Mahathir. The Malaysian Prime Minister made it clear that Murdoch would never do business in his country as long as Andrew Neil was editor of the *Sunday Times*." Later, another British minister was told by Mahathir himself that when he protested to Murdoch about the articles the latter told him that he had a "rogue

editor" on his hands but that the matter was being "sorted out". The "business" about which Murdoch was so concerned was of course the expansion of his satellite television interests into Southeast Asia. It was for this reason too that, in March 1994, after certain news items about China on BBC World had upset the country's rulers, with whom Murdoch was also trying to do business, that he simply threw the channel off his Star satellite service. Similarly when, in 1998, he discovered that one of his publishing companies, HarperCollins, was publishing Chris Patten's account of his days as the last British governor of Hong Kong, an account not exactly flattering to the Chinese, he simply cancelled Patten's contract. The result, and not just in Britain, was a considerable media furore, although one in which Murdoch's own papers were singularly loath to join.

The Murdoch example illustrates particularly clearly just how press barons act as censors today. In Britain, however, Murdoch was hardly alone in using his papers to promote his own political views and to suppress or ridicule those of which he disapproved. After all, it was a former Conservative minister, Sir Ian Gilmour, who wrote of the Thatcher years, in *Dancing with Dogma*, that the press "could scarcely have been more fawning if it had been state controlled", and another who called it the "hallelujah chorus". Thus, for example, the owner of the *Express* group, Lord Matthews (who once delivered himself of the neo-Goldwynism that "by and large editors will have complete freedom as long as they agree with the policy I have laid down"), explicitly forbade the *Daily Star* from supporting Labour in the General Election of 1979 and, when faced with a leader that was critical of the Thatcher government's first budget, insisted on changes on the grounds that "there aren't any poor. You can take my word for it. There are no poor in this country." The group's next owner, Lord Stevens, was equally interventionist, penning the odd editorial and also stating:

> I think it would be very unlikely that I would have a newspaper that would support the socialist [sic] party. That isn't what some people would call press freedom, but why should I want a product I didn't approve of? I believe it is in the best interests of United Newspapers in terms of its profits and shareholders to support the Conservatives.

Not that interventionist proprietors are to be found only at the helm of right-wing newspapers. The day after Robert Maxwell had acquired the *Mirror* in 1984 he addressed a personal front-page message to his readers headed "Forward with Britain". Soon afterwards, during the coal dispute of 1984–85, he altered an article by Geoffrey Goodman, then one of Fleet Street's most highly respected industrial editors, to make it less critical of the Thatcher government. Owning newspapers, according to Maxwell, "gives me the power to raise issues effectively. In simple terms, it's a megaphone"; elsewhere he opined that "newspapers, if they are to be well run, have to be a dictatorship". Not for nothing was the in-house nickname of the paper, which carried endless stories of its owner's exploits, the *Daily Maxwell*.

Similarly when Tiny Rowland bought the liberal Sunday paper the *Observer* in 1981 it soon became abundantly clear that he was attracted by the paper's strong coverage of Africa, where his company Lonrho had important interests which he thought the *Observer* could further. In 1983, without consulting the editor, Donald Trelford, he hired Godwin Matatu as the paper's roving Africa correspondent; however, apart from being a journalist, Mutatu was also employed by Lonrho as a consultant and, as a mediator, by Robert Mugabe, the prime minister of Zimbabwe, where the company had huge mining interests. He was also related to Zimbabwe's minister of legal affairs. The foreign editor resigned, and editorial staff refused to handle his copy. In 1984 Trelford himself reported atrocities by government forces in Zimbabwe's Matabeleland province; Rowland found the reports distinctly unhelpful and pressured Trelford to spike them, withdrawing Lonrho advertising and even letting it be known that he was discussing selling the paper to Robert Maxwell. As a consequence the paper's five independent directors censured Rowland for "improper editorial interference". Nothing daunted, however, he was soon using the paper as a propaganda weapon in his battle against the al-Fayeds to acquire control over the House of Fraser, which owned Harrods. This culminated in March 1989 in the publishing of a special midweek edition that contained lengthy extracts from a leaked Department of Trade and Industry report which was highly critical of the al-Fayeds. The paper's independent directors concluded that its reputation had been "tarnished". After one proprietorial intervention too many, David Leigh, the respected head of the *Observer*'s investigative team, resigned, stating that it had become a "sick paper".

The fact is, then, that the power of the press baron over the content of the newspapers that he or she owns has not decreased since the days of Hugenberg, Hearst, Rothermere, and Beaverbrook. Indeed, quite the opposite. As Nicholas Coleridge notes, these fiefdoms "were in fact smaller by every criteria than the enormous, geographically diffuse, multi-lingual empires of the latest newspaper tycoons. The profits and total circulations of the old school proprietors were invariably lower, their papers thinner, the scope of their influence and newsgathering machines more local; none dominated so many world markets simultaneously." With the increasing commercialization of the press, its owners have acquired even more power, and the diminution of their influence that some predicted has conspicuously failed to materialize.

JULIAN PETLEY

Further Reading

Boyce, D.G., "Crusaders without Chains: Power and the Press Barons, 1896–1951" in *Impacts and Influences: Essays on Media Power in the Twentieth Century*, edited by James Curran et al., London and New York: Methuen, 1987

Coleridge, Nicholas, *Paper Tigers: The Latest, Greatest Newspaper Tycoons and How They Won the World*, London: Heinemann, 1993

Curran, James and Jean Seaton, *Power without Responsibility: The Press and Broadcasting in Britain*, 5th edition, London and New York: Routledge, 1997

Evans, Harold, *Good Times, Bad Times*, 3rd edition, London: Phoenix, 1994

Franklin, Bob, *Newszak and News Media*, London and New York: Arnold, 1997

Hollingsworth, Mark, *The Press and Political Dissent*, London: Pluto Press, 1986

Koss, Stephen, *The Rise and Fall of the Political Press in Britain*, 2 vols, London: Hamish Hamilton, and Chapel Hill: University of North Carolina Press, 1981–84

Leapman, Michael, *Treacherous Estate: The Press after Fleet Street*, London: Hodder and Stoughton, 1992

Miliband, Ralph, *The State in Capitalist Society*, New York: Basic Books, and London: Weidenfeld and Nicolson, 1969

Neil, Andrew, *Full Disclosure*, London: Macmillan, 1996

Snoddy, Raymond, *The Good, the Bad and the Unacceptable: The Hard News about the British Press*, London and Boston: Faber, 1992

Whale, John, *Journalism and Government*, London: Macmillan, and Columbia: University of South Carolina Press, 1972

Williams, Francis, *Dangerous Estate: The Anatomy of Newspapers*, London and New York: Longmans, Green and Co., 1957

Williams, Kevin, *Get Me a Murder a Day! A History of Mass Communication in Britain*, London and New York: Arnold, 1998

EMERIC PRESSBURGER
See **Michael Powell and Emeric Pressburger**

M. PHILIPS PRICE
British journalist, 1885–1973

The experience of M. Philips Price, the *Manchester Guardian*'s correspondent in Russia from 1914 to 1918, illustrates the way in which the machinery of censorship was used to support British foreign policy after the Russian Revolution. Between February and October 1918 Price kept copies of all but two of the 50 dispatches he sent to his paper by cable or wireless. It is therefore possible to compare these texts with the versions passed by the Official Press Bureau in London, and to see what news from Russia was completely suppressed.

In February 1918, the Soviet government that had come to power three months earlier was on the point of concluding a separate peace with Germany and Austria-Hungary. The motives of Russia's former allies for what followed were mixed. They wanted to keep Russia in the war, but the British and French were additionally alarmed by the possible effect of the Russian Revolution on their own people. Under the pretext of saving the Russians from themselves, they cast about for ways of overturning the Soviet government. For this they needed the support of public opinion, so it became necessary to ensure that no news from Russia was good news. Most British correspondents in Russia at that time were more or less hostile to the new government in any case and their copy provided no problems, rather the reverse. A few, however, remained open-minded, Price among them. His dispatches were censored with increasing severity and his last 21 dispatches, from 25 June 1918 onwards, were stopped altogether.

Since December 1917 the French and British had been financing counterrevolutionary forces assembling in southern Russia. By March 1918 plans were under consideration for landing Allied troops at Archangelsk and pressure was being put on Japan to intervene in the Russian Far East. In May and June British troops guarding stores at Murmansk that had been supplied to the previous Russian government were reinforced. Also in May, Austro-Hungarian prisoners of war in Russia, who had been allowed to form themselves into a specifically Czech Legion and who were supposedly on their way to France, began to advance eastward along the Trans-Siberian Railway instead. With French advisers and funds they overthrew the local Soviets on their way. The Soviets fought back. The Allies now had the excuse of invading Soviet territory to "rescue" the Czechs.

The British Official Press Bureau had three procedures for operating censorship: "D" notices, instructions to censors, and letters to editors. On 31 January 1918 censors received an instruction to delete, "when possible on grounds of military expediency", any reference to financial help given by the Allies to the counterrevolutionary forces in the South. Such a reference was the only piece cut out of Price's dispatch of 20 February. Throughout the spring, newspaper editors in Britain were receiving letters from the Press Bureau asking them to avoid the subject of Japanese or any other form of Allied intervention in Russia. A dispatch from Price on 12 March about the state of public opinion in Russia lost only its last sentence: "For the moment Japan assumed to be the chief enemy". A cable of 14 April reporting that the Japanese were supplying arms to "monarchist bands in Manchuria" was delayed until 19 July. A cable of 26 April was eventually printed on 1 June, but without a statement by the Soviet Commissariat of Foreign Affairs that Japanese, British, and French diplomats were known to have been negotiating with the counterrevolutionary "Siberian government" for military assistance against the Siberian Soviets. A cable of 16 June lost a number of sentences, including one beginning

Semiofficial statements reaching here from Paris that America has agreed with rest Allies to allow Japan free hand in Siberia are interpreted as meaning that the Allied governments see in Russia class enemy more dangerous to them than their national enemy German Imperialism.

The Czech Legion had begun its advance into Siberia in the second half of May. Three cables referring to their activities, sent on 5 and 7 June, were cut, and another, which chronicled the history of the Legion, was stopped. References to Allied support for the Legion were cut from cables of 11 and 14 June, and another, dated 28 June, belongs to the group that were stopped.

The censor's blue pencil was also applied to a wide variety of the many other topics mentioned in Price's cables. It is possible to give only a few examples here. Anything reporting criticism in Russia of aspects of Allied policy – such as the refusal to recognize the Soviet government – was cut. A report that the head of the American Red Cross in Russia was trying to persuade Washington to adopt a more constructive relationship with Moscow was cut. Reports of speeches by Russian leaders referring to the need for realism and self-discipline were cut, probably because they did not accord with the more popular picture of them as bloodthirsty anarchists. References to the fact that dissent within and between the parties then composing the Soviet government was expressed freely was also cut.

By the time of the Allied landings at Archangelsk in August 1918, Price had, as he put it himself, "abandoned objectivity", but he continued to try to present an alternative view of Soviet Russia to readers of the *Manchester Guardian*. Between August and October, his 14 unpublished dispatches contained detailed accounts of the improvements in food distribution, public order, transport, and education; the discipline and good progress of the newly founded Red Army, led by Lev Trotskii; the involvement of Britain's last remaining diplomatic representative in Russia in a plot to overthrow the government; and the provocations that had resulted in the "Red Terror", the existence of which Price did not deny. His last dispatch, dated 19 October 1918, begins:

After reading the English papers which have arrived here I am at a loss to decide whether the persons giving information on Russia are deliberately fabricating news for political ends, or whether they are merely the victims of chronic nervous breakdowns.

TANIA ROSE

Writings

My Reminiscences of the Russian Revolution, 1921
My Three Revolutions, 1969
Dispatches from the Revolution: Russia, 1916–18, edited by Tania Rose, 1997
Dispatches from the Weimar Republic: Versailles and German Fascism, edited by Tania Rose, 1999

Further Reading

Carley, Michael Jabara, *Revolution and Intervention: The French Government and the Russian Civil War, 1917–1919*, Kingston, Ontario: McGill–Queen's University Press, 1983
Kettle, Michael, *The Allies and the Russian Collapse, March 1917–March 1918*, London: Deutsch, and Minneapolis: University of Minnesota Press, 1981
Kettle, Michael, *The Road to Intervention, March–November 1918*, London and New York: Routledge, 1988
Knightley, Phillip, *The First Casualty: The War Correspondent as Hero and Myth-maker from the Crimea to Kosovo*, revised edition, London: Prion, 2000
Mawdsley, Evan, *The Russian Civil War*, London and Boston: Allen and Unwin, 1987
Rose, Tania, *Aspects of Political Censorship, 1914–1918*, Hull: University of Hull Press, 1995
Smele, Jonathen, "What the Papers Didn't Say: Unpublished Dispatches from Russia by M Philips Price, July 1918 to January 1919", *Revolutionary Russia*, 9/2 (1996)
Ullman, Richard H., *Anglo-Soviet Relations, 1917–1921*, 3 vols, Princeton, New Jersey: Princeton University Press, 1961–72

PRINTING

Invention of, China

Printing was developed in China by the 7th century using carved blocks of fine-grained wood such as jujube, catalpa, or pear. The text or illustration was written on a sheet of fine paper which was dampened so it stuck to the block face down, the Chinese characters therefore being carved proud. The block was then inked and a blank sheet of paper placed on top and smoothed with a brush.

Buddhists realized the potential of this new technology for the dissemination of their sacred texts and the earliest dated printed book in the world is a Buddhist text *The Diamond Sutra* dated 868, although this was clearly the product of a mature industry. Private printers and publishers became common throughout China and often flouted censorship laws in pursuit of profit. But printing was also a means to improve orthodoxy.

A study of metaphorical religious language used in the Tang dynasty (618–907) in China during the 7th century CE – when religious images were already being stamped from woodblocks on to paper – suggests that the Chinese of the time would have appreciated not only the speed and volume made possible by printing as a means of reproducing texts, but also its accuracy. It was probably the first two advantages that initially involved the Tang state – and certainly the 8th-century Japanese state – in undertaking printing itself, since short talismanic religious texts could with the new technology be multiplied and distributed on an unprecedented scale, so as to spread good fortune for the ruling regime across the land. But the dissemination of accurate normative texts (mainly of a religious nature) and the detection of distorted versions of such works were also important state concerns, since China was constantly threatened by religious groups inspired by heterodox millennarian beliefs.

The need for officials to detect, as soon as possible, writings stemming from such groups stimulated from the late 6th century onward both the increasingly careful compilation of canonical collections belonging to the state-recognized traditions of Buddhism and Daoism, with catalogues listing their hundreds of acceptable titles and marking out in supplementary sections those excluded works deemed heterodox, and also the diffusion from the capital to the provinces of carefully collated copies of works drawn from the contents of these orthodox canons. But in the age of manuscripts it was very difficult to guard against heterodox interpolations in the texts of orthodox titles. No chances were taken: when one such interpolation was confirmed in a Daoist work forwarded to the capital from the provinces in 648, the government, much to the chagrin of the priests who had established the illicit nature of the interpolation, decreed that all copies of the title should be burned, interpolated or not.

During the 8th century there were innovations that may be interpreted as being designed to ameliorate the problem of interpolation. One Buddhist catalogue of 730 lists pagination totals for each of its titles – numbering more than 1000 – so that, presumably, extensive interpolation became detectable, while plans also seem to have been drawn up around the

same time to carve the entire Buddhist canon on stone, so that a normative text could be checked against rubbings taken from this official source. Such an undertaking turned out to be beyond the resources of the state at this point, but by 776 the basic Confucian canonical writings, a mere five texts, had been carved on wood at the capital so that rubbings could be made, and by 837 the fuller set of nine Confucian texts had been engraved on stone.

By this time the spread of printing for simpler, shorter works in mass demand was threatening in a new way the government's control over the production of calendars: we find in 835 a request submitted by an official in west China that the circulation of privately printed calendars be banned, since entrepreneurs were putting such works on sale even before the government had promulgated its official version. Though this represents the first known attempt to censor printed materials in China, a yet more significant development during this century was probably the introduction of a device for the rapid retrieval of individual works from the massive canonical literature of Buddhism – and, though the corresponding details are scarce, presumably of Daoism too. In the wake of a destructive persecution of Buddhism culminating in 845, the government seems to have encouraged monasteries across the land to restock their manuscript canons according to a standard scheme, taking the order of the catalogue of 730 as normative, and assigning a character from the Thousand-Character Classic, a non-repeating series memorized in primary education (serving a purpose a bit like the western alphabet) as a tag for each group of texts stored in the same wrapper or box. Reading off this sequence against a similarly marked version of the catalogue allowed any text in any monastery to be located very rapidly for checking.

The production of a government-printed set of the Buddhist canon against which to check monastery holdings for interpolations had to wait until the next stable dynasty, the Song (960–1279), when experience in block cutting had progressed via the state printing of the most important Daoist text in 940 and the Confucian canon in 953 to the point where the tens of thousands of separate wooden blocks necessary for the entire Buddhist canon were eventually completed in 983. Distribution of the resulting prints was carefully controlled by the state. For example, a Japanese monk managed to obtain special imperial permission to take home a copy as early as 984, since at first the printed canon was entirely within the emperor's gift. What soon happened, however, may be surmised from a much later French missionary observation of 1728 on the Daoist canon, a compilation so full of magical texts that it could still only be printed under imperial control, a situation that lasted until the declaration of the Republic in 1911. The officials charged with taking copies from the blocks were then, says this observer, in the habit of printing extra sheets so that they could sell extra sets illicitly on the side. We may suppose that even in early Song times similar abuses caused the original distinction between official and private printing to collapse quite rapidly, even if the export of printed books remained for a while a more serious matter, so that in 1073 another Japanese seeking to send home some supplementary texts from the Buddhist canon still had to apply for official permission, though others (such as Koreans) were by this stage regularly flouting these regulations.

Even so, the state's vigilance with regard to printing religious literature would seem to have been vindicated (from their point of view) by events much later, in 1163, when an official in south China reported that he had detected Manichaeans (at that time seen as a heterodox and dangerous group in China) attempting to circulate their own printed texts, which for disguise copied the external format of a printed edition of the Daoist canon. This was precisely the type of deception that had worried the state since at least 648: the fact that a provincial official was now able to detect such impostures on his own initiative shows that the combination of measures described had had a certain effect. We must conclude that although we normally think of printing as a technology of liberation, to the Chinese state it probably commended itself in part also as a technology of control.

T.H. BARRETT

Further Reading

Barrett, T.H., "The Taoist Canon in Japan", *Taoist Resources*, 5/2 (1994): 71–77

Barrett, T.H., *Taoism under the T'ang: Religion and Empire during the Golden Age of Chinese History*, London: Wellsweep, 1996

Barrett, T.H., "The Feng-tao k'o and Printing on Paper in Seventh Century China", *Bulletin of the School of Oriental and African Studies*, 60/3 (1997): 538–40

Barrett, T.H., "Images of Printing in Seventh-Century Chinese Religious Literature", *Chinese Science*, 15 (1998): 81–93

Loon, Piet van der, *Taoist Books in the Libraries of the Sung Period: A Critical Study and Index*, London: Ithaca Press, 1984

McMullen, David, *State and Scholars in T'ang China*, Cambridge and New York: Cambridge University Press, 1988

Tsien, Tsuen-hsuin, *Chemistry and Chemical Technology*, part 1: *Paper and Printing*, Cambridge: Cambridge University Press, 1985 (Science and Civilisation in China)

Invention of, Europe

The origins of printing have been obscure since almost the first invention of the craft. Certainly, the ability to reproduce texts by some process of impression was not peculiarly European. As is clear from the preceding essay, China and Korea possessed techniques to do this hundreds of years before the first presses appeared in the West in the mid-15th century. And even in Europe itself the invention of the press soon became a matter of speculation rather than knowledge. A handful of cities laid claim to being the site for the first trials in printing, and rival stories of its discovery abounded. Some thought that those ancient Eastern techniques might have inspired the development of the craft; others considered that it had been a providential gift of a God eager to foster the coming of the Reformation. All that could be said for sure was that the first printed books had appeared in the north of Europe around 1440–50, and that presses had subsequently dispersed rapidly throughout the Low Countries, the Holy Roman empire, France, Italy, England and Scotland. By around 1480, printing was a recognized craft in more than 100 cities. It was beginning to transform the culture of western Europe in every respect. This essay surveys attempts by European regimes to understand, restrain, and perhaps even redefine print in the succeeding two centuries.

With each press, a pair of workers could produce perhaps 1000 sheets of printed paper every day. Labouring day after day, such workers soon produced books, images, and ephemera in previously unimaginable quantities. Within a generation, the number of printed books available exceeded, in all probability, the number ever produced in manuscript up to that time. It has been estimated that by 1500 there was already a printed book in existence for every five living Europeans – plenty indeed in an era of widespread illiteracy. Sheer quantity of this order had its own consequences. Relatively quickly, books – including, most importantly, *the* book, of scripture – became available in unprecedented numbers, in more places, and at lower cost. But more important still were a number of qualitative changes accompanying this transformation. These were of two main kinds, deriving respectively from alterations in the appearance of the page and from innovations in the uses of books. In the first place, after a brief period when Gutenberg and his successors tried to imitate the appearance of manuscripts, the printed page began to look markedly different from its handwritten equivalent. Typefaces became standardized, and the use of cross-referencing, indexes, errata, and notes grew commonplace. Woodcuts and engravings allowed the use of repeatable images, making possible accretive improvements in accuracy. On this basis the scientific diagram and the cartographic map became realizable. So did such authoritative tools for thinking as logarithmic tables, polyglot bibles, and exhaustive catalogues of legal statutes. The possibilities raised by print transformed the chances of making accurate, trustworthy, and enduring records of knowledge-claims in all fields, including religion, the sciences, and politics. In the second place, the very act of reading changed. With many books available, the social profile of readers was transformed. *How* they read changed too. The relation between reading, sociability, and knowledge was to be profoundly different in an age of print. For a ruler viewing this situation around 1500, the prospect must have been both exciting and troubling. How could he or she ensure that the coming changes would be beneficial?

The "printing revolution", as this transformation has been labelled, witnessed the advent of modern notions of openness, authorship, and collaboration. But print had to be made into a reliable medium before these could come into being. The press was rich in potential for many different uses, including piracy and sedition as well as creation and discovery. Which of these possibilities would be realized long remained in doubt. As a new practice of undoubted power but obscure origin, printing posed fundamental questions; and different answers to those questions were to be implicit in the various attempts that emerged to regulate and restrict the press. What was printing? What was it for? And who was best qualified to decide?

None of these questions was easy to answer. First and foremost, however, a printing house was a place in which practical work went on. In most cities such workplaces were made subject to the moral oversight of a defined craft community, as institutionalized in the form of a guild or company. In addition, they would be liable to regulation by governments (be they republics or monarchies) and by ecclesiastical bodies (whether Protestant or Catholic). Regulatory regimes based on these three premises began to emerge soon after the establishment of printing houses in the major European cities, and by the mid-16th century they were well entrenched. We may regard them as falling into six broad categories: internal trade regulation; regulation by prerogative, through proclamations and privileges; licensing regimes; indexes; civil, statute, and common law; and policing by deputed individuals. The distinctions between these were never hard and fast. In practice, most – with the exception of indexes, which were a peculiarly Catholic invention, and of common law, which was peculiarly English – intertwined in every European regime. None the less they may stand as useful categories of historical analysis. Most of this entry is devoted to an examination of their status, development, and impact.

Internal trade regulation

Printers, booksellers, and other participants in the book trades (for example, binders and warehouse keepers) were generally expected to adhere to the kind of moral conventions customary to any respectable craft or trade. Those conventions were typically local to a particular city, where they were the preserve of a guild or company dedicated to the trade and composed of its practitioners. In the Netherlands, for example, book traders belonged to the Guild of St Luke; in Paris, to that of St James; and in Madrid to that of St John. In London, the Stationers' Company, chartered in 1557, performed this role. The Company purported to embrace all members of the book trades, and insisted that they obey a comprehensive civility enshrined in its by-laws. That civility extended from minute niceties of personal manners right through to action against seditious, heretical, or piratical publishing. Company officers were empowered to search members' homes and workplaces for offending materials, and routinely did so from the Company's inception until its decline in the mid-18th century. The Company also maintained its own court, capable of exerting penalties against violators that included the confiscation and "damasking" (obliteration) of illicit works, the withdrawal of privileges, and the imposition of substantial fines. Serious offenders would be turned over to the state authorities for imprisonment (or worse, although scarcely ever was an English printer actually executed: we know of just three cases). Much the same machinery for detection and adjudication existed in most European cities possessed of a printing trade, and was also the commonest tool used by the state itself to seek out opposition printers and publishers. In an era before professional police forces, then, investigation, seizure, and adjudication were almost exclusively matters for participants. Printers and booksellers themselves sustained virtually the entire regulatory enterprise. They did so because the order of print that the guilds and companies fostered was one both polite and commercial. The alternative, if it were thinkable at all, would be at best anarchic. The interests of printers and the state coalesced in these craft collectives.

Two further points should be stressed. First, there was nothing whatsoever unusual about this to the early modern mind. All respectable trades and crafts had such organizations, and all such organizations provided for search-and-seizure practices under participant control – indeed, this was in large part what guaranteed their identity as respectable. It may be thought of (anachronistically) as a form of quality control. Only in the book trade, with its peculiar commerce in words, did such practices take on an appearance that to modern eyes is readily identifiable with censorship. Second, a particularly important aspect of the civility of trade custom related to the protection of individual members' livelihoods from interference, whether by other craftsmen or by outsiders. In the book trade, this meant the detection and prevention of what came to be called "piracy" – the unauthorized production of works already the preserve (in the eyes of this community) of a particular stationer. This concern was central to the motivation of the companies in policing the trade. But later the convention would be transferred from the craftsperson to the creator, and be renamed as copyright.

Regulation by prerogative

Monarchs could also act more directly, deploying what was called "royal prerogative" to restrict certain publishing activities or certain titles, by issuing proclamations against them. Royal prerogative was the ability of a monarch to act above and beyond common, civil, or statute law, and it was a crucial element in absolutist concepts of the state. In France, Austria, and the German principalities, prerogative regulation was the norm until the late 18th century, when it took on diverse forms of baroque complexity. In some cases it was even revived after Napoleon's reign in the 19th century. English press regulation likewise operated substantially on the basis of prerogative from the days of Henry VIII, and such regulation was formalized by the proclamation of licensers in 1586 (see below). The licensers derived their authority from Star Chamber, a court whose own legitimacy rested directly in royal power. But Star Chamber was abolished with the coming of civil war in 1641–42, and was not restored after the Restoration of 1660; thenceforth licensing rested on statutory foundations.

This was not the only component of prerogative employed to restrain printers and booksellers. To restrict work to particular individuals, a monarch (or equivalent authority) could sometimes exert prerogative by means of a patent or privilege. This was a royal gift issued on an *ad hoc* basis to grant particular freedoms, and concomitantly to restrict non-recipients in certain ways. For example, a single printer might be granted a privilege on news; this would mean that nobody else could then print news materials of any kind for the duration of the privilege. Other examples of patented texts included the Bible, astrological predictions, parliamentary proceedings, and specific learned works of all kinds. If detected (generally by the searches of the local company), a violator might be fined or even imprisoned, and a bond might be exacted for good behaviour in future. While the mechanism had roots far back in the Middle Ages, and was primarily deployed either to reward loyal courtiers (by granting them lucrative monopolies) or to protect investors from piratical competition, it could certainly have restrictive effects on printed knowledge – as the example of news implies. Moreover, a principal aim in issuing privileges was to create a group of powerful printer-publishers dependent on royal power for their well-being, and hence predisposed to favour the court side in its periodic interventions in craft politics. Implicitly, patentees were pioneers of a future print culture fundamentally different from that of the guilds.

Again, two points deserve emphasis. The first is that a privilege (or, for that matter, a proclamation banning a book) was effective only within the jurisdiction of its granter. A patent issued by a German prince-bishop, for example, would be of no power outside his dominion. Rivals in neighbouring principalities *might* follow suit; but on the other hand they might see a gap in the market and actively encourage their own printers to fill it. They would even grant their own patents to local workshops prepared to meet the challenge. The Holy Roman emperor could and did grant his own patents, however, and these were actionable across the empire. Second, the whole mechanism of patents embodied a view of the craft of printing that was fundamentally at odds with the concept of the customary guild or company. This view held that the monarch could legitimately intervene on a routine basis to reassign and restrict rights within a trade. Craft members generally took such rights to be customary properties, interference with which was one of the most tell-tale signs of "arbitrary government". So press regulation by patent was easily represented as unwarrantable not just because it restricted liberty of expression – in fact, objections on this ground were rare – but because the practice itself encapsulated tyranny. It is significant that both the English revolution of 1642–49 and the French of 1789–92 saw privileges swept away – only for them to return in scarcely modified form when the commercially catastrophic consequences of an unregulated book trade made themselves felt.

Licensing

The earliest attempts to impose pre-publication licensing occurred soon after 1500, and by the later 16th century most European regimes had some such system in operation. This meant that anyone wishing to publish a text in print had to submit it beforehand to a licenser nominated by the relevant authority. The licenser must put his name to a permission (or *imprimatur* – Latin for "it may be printed"), which would then be cited in full at the beginning or end of the published work. A book to be issued in several jurisdictions, or under secular and ecclesiastical authorities, might need several licences – in *Areopagitica*, Milton made ruthless fun of the multiplicity demanded by Catholic Italy in the mid-17th century. But although (as Milton pointed out) licensing was originally a Catholic device, Protestant states made use of it too. The system was all but ubiquitous. It was eliminated in England in 1695, but elsewhere in Europe it remained tenacious for much longer. And it seems to have enjoyed wide support as a mechanism for restraining expression that was deemed heretical or seditious.

Licensers were typically churchmen, and often of junior status. In certain spheres expertise was called for – universities sometimes had their own officers, for example – but for the most part a young chaplain would be called upon to do the work. It was arduous and unrewarding, and many licensers found it baffling too. In a world of rapidly shifting political allegiances and doctrinal verities, it could be hard to keep pace with orthodoxy. There are notorious cases of individual mistakes: of the hapless licenser of William Prynne's *Histriomastix*, for example, who suffered imprisonment for permitting the scandalous puritan text. Prynne's case also showed that an author could be punished even if the text had successfully passed a licenser. There are also instances of licensers who bent the rules to allow the circulation of materials formally beyond the pale: the best-known example is that of the 18th-century French censor Malesherbes, who actually hid copies of Diderot's and d'Alembert's *Encyclopédie* in his own house. But

the deeper point is that there were in fact no "rules" at all to licensing. Wherever it was practised, licensing was of unstable and unmeasurable efficacy; and many printers all but ignored it. It is impossible to provide quantitative data, but it seems clear enough that most printed works were never licensed at all. No action was taken against the vast majority, although lack of a licence did provide ready grounds for a prosecution if one were required for other reasons. By the 18th century, in France at least, this slightly absurd reality had come to be recognized as a matter of routine. Paris publishers could obtain "tacit" permits for works that were too unorthodox to be granted explicit licences, but which the police were in no mood to run to ground.

Indexes

It was not long before the variety of different licensing regimes, and the sheer number of books being published, generated such complexity that the status of a given title in a particular jurisdiction became difficult to determine. It was partly as a response to this situation that authorities began to compile indexes of proscribed titles. Popes Innocent VIII and Alexander VI set the stage by announcing protocols to limit impression sizes in particular locations. At first limited to certain episcopal regions (Mainz being one), in 1515 these protocols were made universal by Leo X. In succeeding generations the advent of the Reformation transformed the status and importance of such proclamations. The emperor Charles V and the Archbishop of Canterbury, among others, at first attempted to suppress Lutheran titles by proclamation. In Spain, the inquisitor-general Adrian of Utrecht (later pope Adrian VI) used his own authority to ban Lutheran texts in 1521, and the universities of Paris and Louvain likewise exerted themselves against reformers' tracts. These efforts gave rise to the first promulgation of an "index" by the theology faculty of the university of Paris in 1544. The faculty issued further indexes in 1545, 1547, 1548, 1551, and 1556, comprising more than 500 titles. From there the notion grew and spread across Catholic Europe. In 1546 Louvain followed suit, including more than 700 works in three successive indexes. In Venice – later in the century a relative haven for those named in such lists – the papal nuncio issued an index in 1549, and the Inquisition another in 1554, which included a total of some 6500 books. In Spain, the Inquisition generated a series of indexes from 1551 onwards, as did its counterpart in Portugal from 1547.

All these indexes, it is important to note, were essentially local. They had no claim to efficacy beyond the jurisdictions of their respective compiling authorities. In 1542, however, Pope Paul III created the Roman Inquisition, bringing into existence an authority that could transform what had been local regulations into universal ones. The first Roman index followed in 1559. It contained about 1000 entries, some of which ordered the suppression not just of individual titles but of *all* the works by a particular author. Erasmus, Rabelais, and Machiavelli fell under its censure, as did a number of editions of the Bible itself. The index also ordered that 61 named printers be banned from all printing activities. In 1564 this was succeeded by the first index to be issued in the context of the Council of Trent. With this index the system reached its mature form, which was formalized by Pius V's creation of a Congregation of the Index in 1571. Successive indexes thereafter added new titles but did not significantly extend or qualify the concept itself. By around 1600 some 2400 titles had been entered on the Roman index. Some were banned outright, others restricted pending substantial alterations. The system was to remain in being for three centuries.

The enforcement of the indexes was not as uniform as the papacy must have hoped for. In Portugal the Inquisition ensured adherence; in Spain, however, its counterpart continued to promulgate its own indexes and remained more concerned to enact these than the Roman version. In Italy, the Papal States were obviously most active in enforcing the indexes' bans, but Milan, Naples, and Sicily adopted Roman or Spanish indexes at different times, and in Florence policing was notably ambivalent. Most lax of all was Venice, which consistently chafed at Rome's stringency. In Germany, Bavaria was the region most notable for its enthusiasm, but even there enforcement fell off after around 1590. In the Spanish Netherlands, the index of 1564 was enforced for a while, but thereafter efficacy waned. In France the wars of religion effectively removed any possibility of real enforcement at all. And in Protestant realms, of course – principally England, Scotland, the Low Countries, Geneva, and parts of Germany – an entry in the index was not so much ignored as treated as a positive recommendation to print, buy, and read the book concerned. So across Europe the indexes were of mixed impact. But that did not mean that that impact was negligible, or (as some modern historians have implied) that the only major consequence of being placed on the index was that one's sales in Protestant countries boomed. Books, and the knowledge they contained, *were* effectively removed from circulation in large parts of Catholic Europe: historians of science have shown how Copernican texts, for example, were systematically censored of passages claiming that the heliocentric system was physically real. Assessing the consequences for the history of science in such regions is difficult for want of counterfactual comparisons – we cannot say how natural philosophy would have developed in Italy if Galileo Galilei's work had not been banned, for example – but it is difficult to believe that that development would not have been at least different. In that sense the system played an important role in shaping the transition to modernity in at least the consistently Catholic realms of southern and western Europe.

One other long-term consequence deserves to be mentioned here. It derives not so much from the concept of an index or its suppressive intent as from the practice of compilation itself. The devisors of indexes, faced with listing thousands of titles in a fashion permitting ready referencing, hit upon the tactic of organizing their lists by author. The tactic proved fruitful, and was adopted by bibliographers and booksellers with different aims. It has been claimed, not unreasonably, that the primacy of authorship in print culture derived in part from this innovation. Before authors were defined by property, then, they were defined by responsibility: the early modern author was the person whom the state or Church would seek out and prosecute if a work were deemed unacceptable. Not for the last time, creative individuality and the techniques for policing that individuality prove historically inseparable.

Civil, statute, and common law

Governments also had recourse to statute (and, in England, common) law. Although generally dating from before Guten-

berg's invention, laws to restrain other forms of communication could often be adapted to address the new medium. For example, the law could be used to prosecute the creators, printers, and distributors of allegedly treasonous tracts, although the relevant clauses of the laws of treason had originally been devised against spoken words. Similarly, libel law could be pressed into action against those involved in seditious, blasphemous, or (from around 1680) obscene publications, although the law's notion of "publishing" had originally possessed (and in part still retained) the meaning of "uttering aloud". In all cases, it is important to note, the measures invoked took effect after production of the offending book; there was no pre-publication restriction by these means except by the ineffable influence of fear. An exception to this rule obtained for a generation in England. The Restoration regime declined to resurrect Star Chamber and its prerogative system of licensers, and instead relied on a new Press Act passed by parliament in 1662. This act derived in large part from pre-civil war Star Chamber proclamations, reinstituting much of their licensing regime verbatim, but it avoided the stigma of prerogative rule. It was renewed periodically until 1695, but during the intervals when it was in abeyance the crown again resorted to prerogative regulation.

Policing by deputed individuals

States paying lip-service to early modern philosophies of royal governance were almost inevitably going to prove unsympathetic to the kinds of participant policing instantiated by printing and bookselling guilds. Thomas Hobbes likened such guilds to "lesser Common-wealths in the bowels of a greater, like wormes in the entrayles of a naturall man". In other words, the autonomous self-policing of a craft community ran counter to interests of state; if no actual conflict had yet occurred, that simply meant that the inevitable clash lay yet in the future. Concern at the implications was one motivation underlying attempts to regulate the press and literary property by prerogative, through proclamation and privilege. But to enforce those attempts, states increasingly saw the need to appoint individuals loyal not to the craft of printing and bookselling, but to the crown. In England such a figure – Sir Roger L'Estrange – made his appearance with the Restoration of monarchy in 1660. In alliance with the secretaries of state and a cohort of messengers of the press, this "Surveyor of Imprimery" masterminded most policing efforts for the next quarter of a century. Himself a talented Tory polemicist, L'Estrange tried to fund his efforts by means of a privilege in all printed news.

His success was never better than mixed – and this was very much the experience of his counterparts in France (like Malesherbes) and elsewhere. In fact, these ambiguous fortunes underline the fact that in early modern societies policing, even if undertaken by direct delegation from the crown, depended on the abilities, attitudes, and personalities of individual agents. L'Estrange himself was not just a regulator of the press and a suppresser of unwelcome publications, but an active and constant participant in pamphlet wars in his own right. He often encountered opposition from book-trade participants, not in the main because they were opposed to regulation itself (though a few were), but because they believed that regulation should be by participants and for participants. They resented what they perceived to be illegitimate intrusions into their craft customs by the court.

In sum, there were various practices developed in early modern Europe to regulate the printing craft and restrict the numbers and kinds of printed materials in circulation. Most depended to a substantial extent on participants in the book trades. Guilds of printers and book dealers acted to maintain standards and craft customs, and that included conventions for seizing illicit books. Licensers were appointed by church and state to oversee texts before publication, but they depended on friendly relations with the book traders themselves in order to maintain their role effectively. Monarchs could intervene in the trade directly, by proclamations or privileges, but this was not always effective, often aroused opposition from fiercely autonomous craft communities, and lacked all impact beyond the territorial bounds of the regime. In Catholic regions, however, indexes did transcend such territorial bounds. They made available lists of authors and titles to be abjured by all good Catholics. But again there was little by way of a "print police" to enforce these lists independent of the trade's own self-monitoring practices, and in zones of weak enforcement the indexes could almost become counterproductive.

Effects

What were the effects of these practices? Historians have advanced a wide range of arguments and appraisals, ranging from a claim that they altered the course of history in major ways to an insistence that they had virtually no consequences at all. Christopher Hill has made perhaps the most sweeping claims for the importance of censorship. Hill, a Marxist historian concerned to argue for the existence and transforming importance of an "English revolution" in the mid-17th century, maintains that censorship was a substantial impediment to the expression of radical ideas that dated back to the days of Lollardy. Those ideas were allegedly present over the long term, but remain largely undetectable to historians before the outbreak of civil war in 1642 because the censors prevented their airing. Then, the lapse of Star Chamber, and with it prerogative press regulation by licensers, allowed for a brief period when they could at last be voiced. The result was a short outpouring of political, religious, and social radicalism that was stifled under Cromwell's protectorate and censored almost out of existence at the Restoration. But once it had been given free voice the radical tradition could never again be silenced completely, and its moment of liberation marked a decisive turning-point in early modern history. The "revolution" of John Milton, Andrew Marvell, James Harrington, and Gerrard Winstanley was the transforming manifestation, then, of liberalizing and modernizing currents long artificially suppressed. In Hill's view, a high estimation of censorship's effects is central to an interpretation of the entire transition into the modern social order.

Strenuous criticisms have been made of this view. Not least, it tends to assume degrees of enforcement that are more suited to 20th-century states than 17th-century ones. Titles and the ideas they contained were indeed suppressed – revisionist historians occasionally go too far in questioning this – but not *all* titles were. Degrees of evasion were never less than substantial, and it is likely that no more than 30 per cent of published works were ever licensed at all. Of the remainder, very few were ever pursued by anyone. So it is difficult to defend a view of censorship that portrays it as uniform or consistently effective in suppressing ideas. Besides, licensers themselves were nervously aware of the difficulty of knowing what ideas they were supposed to suppress at any given juncture. When administrations, policies, and even religions themselves changed with the frequency encountered in the 16th and 17th centuries, this was no idle concern.

More subtly, an interpretation such as Hill's (and, in practice, Hill's opponents') misses the extent to which what modern historians see as "censorship" was in contemporary terms something rather different. Licensing, participant-policing, and the rest were seen as much in positive terms as in negative. To return to the questions posed at the beginning of this essay, they were important means to *make* print into a particular kind of enterprise: a reliable, trustworthy communicative practice suited to a civil society. A common analogy drawn by 17th-century writers was with the coinage. Money must be trusted, as must printed knowledge, and that trust could rest only on the validity guaranteed by the royal stamp or *imprimatur*. The modern notion of censorship fails to capture this sense that printed communication was not simply restricted by such practices, but defined and constituted by them. By protecting investments through the defence of literary properties, for example, regulatory systems made possible the publication of works otherwise too risky ever to be undertaken (mathematical treatises are a case in point). In that sense, it was only thanks to such systems – in the eyes of the vast majority of early moderns – that print constituted a civil enterprise at all. And that was again why so many printers and booksellers supported them.

In this spirit, it is possible to suggest some ways in which regulatory systems not only prevented communication, but actually contributed to the development of central elements in what we now know as "print culture". Some have already been mentioned: the relation between indexing and authorship, for example, and that between practitioner-policing and literary property. But a third very important element in print "culture" is the notion that identical texts, manufactured by printing, carry knowledge across confessional and political perimeters. They thereby make possible a transcultural "public sphere" capable of manifesting objectivity since its collective decisions are subject to no one controlling authority. Much modern criticism of censorship is based on its incompatibility with such a sphere – an incompatibility that is surely all too real today. But in the early modern period, when the representation of a public sphere (or a republic of letters) was still being forged, the relation between regulation and objective knowledge was far less one-sided. For example, it is sometimes asserted that printers voted with their feet to move into Protestant areas free of censorship. This is far too simplistic, since in fact the choice lay between different kinds of regulation rather than between its presence and absence. One might speculate that printers, if they voted at all, did so for intra-craft civility rather than (apparently absolutist) intrusions by church or state. They largely concurred that some regulation was essential to sustain a credit-worthy commerce in books. Moreover, such regulatory regimes as did exist were limited by political and confessional boundaries. They therefore gave those boundaries extra significance, in both commercial and epistemic terms, for the printers and booksellers of Europe. For example, operators in the Netherlands benefited from the combination of ready land-routes into France and the German principalities with freedom from the state oversight of either region. Later, the Société

Typographique de Neuchâtel thrived on the same basis, introducing into France much of the literature that constituted the Enlightenment. Again, one might observe in this context that the internationalism of the "republic of letters" actually depended on the national limits of regulatory regimes, inasmuch as traversing those limits was a central aspect of profitability for the printers as well as of objectivity for their authors. The relation between modern print culture and early modern practices of power is by no means as simple as we may suppose.

ADRIAN JOHNS

Further Reading

Bujanda, J.M. de et al., *Index des Livres Interdits*, 10 vols, Sherbrooke, Québec: Centre d'Études de la Renaissance, and Geneva: Droz, 1984–93

Chartier, Roger, *The Order of Books: Readers, Authors, and Libraries in Europe between the Fourteenth and Eighteenth Centuries*, Cambridge: Polity Press, and Stanford, California: Stanford University Press, 1994

Clegg, Cyndia Susan, *Press Censorship in Elizabethan England*, Cambridge and New York: Cambridge University Press, 1997

Darnton, Robert, *The Forbidden Best-Sellers of Pre-Revolutionary France*, New York: Norton, 1995; London: HarperCollins, 1996

Duke, A.C. and C.A. Tamse (editors), *Too Mighty to be Free: Censorship and the Press in Britain and the Netherlands*, Zutphen: De Walburg Pers, 1987

Eisenstein, Elizabeth L., *The Printing Press as an Agent of Change: Communications and Cultural Transformations in Early Modern Europe*, 2 vols, Cambridge and New York: Cambridge University Press, 1979

Febvre, Lucien, and Henri-Jean Martin, *The Coming of the Book: The Impact of Printing, 1450–1800*, London: Verso, 1990

Gingerich, Owen, "The Censorship of Copernicus' *De Revolutionibus*" in *The Eye of Heaven: Ptolemy, Copernicus, Kepler*, edited by Gingerich, New York: American Institute of Physics, 1993

Grendler, Paul F., *The Roman Inquisition and the Venetian Press, 1540–1605*, Princeton, New Jersey: Princeton University Press, 1977

Hill, Christopher, "Censorship and English Literature" in *The Collected Essays of Christopher Hill*, vol. 1, Brighton, Sussex: Harvester Press, and Amherst: University of Massachusetts Press, 1985

Johns, Adrian, *The Nature of the Book: Print and Knowledge in the Making*, Chicago: University of Chicago Press, 1998

Martin, Henri-Jean, *The French Book: Religion, Absolutism, and Readership, 1585–1715*, Baltimore: Johns Hopkins University Press, 1996

Myers, Robin, and Michael Harris (editors), *Censorship and the Control of Print: In England and France, 1600–1910*, Winchester: St. Paul's Bibliographies, 1992

Pinto Crespo, Virgilio, *Inquisición y control ideológico en la España del siglo XVI*, Madrid: Taurus, 1983

Santschi, Catherine, *La Censure à Genève au XVIIe siècle: de l'escalade à la révocation de l'Édit de Nantes*, Geneva: Tribune, 1978

Smith, Nigel (editor), *Literature and Censorship*, Cambridge: Brewer, 1993

Soman, Alfred, "Press, Pulpit and Censorship in France before Richelieu", *Proceedings of the American Philosophical Society*, 120 (1976): 439–63

PRINTING: The Venetian Press

Printing began in Venice in 1469, and, by 1500, the city was the largest and most important publishing centre in Europe. About 500 different publishers each issued at least one title in the 16th century. The Venetian press published in particular the Latin and Greek classics, which were at the heart of Renaissance humanism. Scholars throughout Europe sought these editions. Venice retained its European leadership in printing until the late 16th century, when Paris overtook it; thereafter, it continued to dominate Italian publishing until the 19th century.

The Venetian press operated with very little regulation before the Protestant Reformation. Publishers even ignored copyright laws in their zeal to publish as many books as possible. When Protestant literature began to appear in Italy around 1520, a few rulers and church leaders wished to impose censorship, but in Venice the civil and ecclesiastical authorities lacked both the will and the mechanism to censor an industry that could produce thousands of copies of a text.

Only after reconciliation efforts between Catholics and Protestants failed in the 1540s did the church authorities attempt to halt the publication and diffusion of heretical literature by promulgating lists of banned Protestant writers and titles. In 1547 Venice officially renewed its Inquisition, which had fallen into disuse. But since the Venetian government was not yet convinced of the gravity of the threat of heretics and their books, they gave only limited support to censorship efforts. The Venetian presses hence published some books in

the 1540s that guilefully propagated Protestant views. Such books lacked the name of the author or carried false names and title pages. Some booksellers smuggled Protestant works from abroad into the city in order to assist clandestine groups of Protestants.

The papacy proclaimed Indexes of Prohibited Books in 1554 and 1559, and tried to persuade the Venetian and other governments to enforce them, but the Venetian publishers, with the help of the state, strongly resisted this, and the papacy eventually withdrew them. The climate of opinion in Venice changed in the 1560s with the discovery that Protestantism had won converts among some younger members of the Venetian nobility, which roused the government to implement the censorship measures it had earlier disdained. The civil authority now helped the papacy to stamp out heresy by censoring the press. Censorship of the Venetian press was always a joint effort of church and state.

The Venetian government, in cooperation with the local Inquisition, erected a tripartite censorship procedure, which began with effective prepublication censorship. Three readers, a priest named by the local Inquisition and two laymen appointed by the state, examined each manuscript to be printed. They issued certificates stating that the book to be printed was free of religious error, did not advocate the overthrow of any government, and did not offend against good morals. No book could be published without these three certificates of approval. Because of this pre-publication censorship, with a handful of minor exceptions, publishers did not publish any prohibited books for the rest of the 16th century.

The government then tightened the inspection of imported books by stationing an inquisitorial representative at the customs house. Finally, at the end of the 1560s, the Inquisition began to make surprise inspection visits to bookshops. Thus state and church together ensured that the papal Indexes of Prohibited Books were enforced in Venice. Clandestine smuggling networks, however, involving some Venetian booksellers, continued to bring prohibited books from northern Europe into the city.

Censorship of the Venetian press was fairly effective so long as the Venetian state and the papacy agreed on policy. But this amity disintegrated in the 1590s when the Venetian state, urged on by its publishers, clashed with the papacy over a series of commercial press matters. The Venetian publishers particularly resented the papal practice of granting exclusive rights to print the revised liturgical and devotional books – the Breviary, the missal, etc. – essential to Catholic worship to non-Venetian publishers. Venetian publishers wanted a full share – and more – of this lucrative market. So long as the government perceived ecclesiastical censorship of the press as necessary to fight heresy, it accepted it, even at the expense of financial losses to the book trade. But, as heresy waned, the state moved to defend the economic viability of the Venetian press, particularly when Venetian publishers faced increasing competition from other cities. The Republic began to see papal press regulations as clerical incursion into civil jurisdictional territory.

A fight over the revised Index of Prohibited Books of 1596 brought matters to a head. The publishers felt that it was too restrictive, and its rules for the press too intrusive. Although the Republic eventually accepted the Index of 1596, enforcement waned. All areas of censorship, except political censorship, weakened, because the state would not permit the

Inquisition to do much. Probably more prohibited books entered Venice between 1590 and 1610 than at any time since the 1550s. The clandestine traffic in prohibited books became almost open in the first decade of the 17th century.

Although the papacy and Republic patched up some of their differences, religious censorship of the Venetian press never regained its former effectiveness. Some Venetian publishers printed, under transparent pseudonyms, writers who had long been banned in Italy. For example, in the 1630s the publisher Marco Ginammi printed Niccolò Machiavelli's *Discourses on the First Ten Books of Livy* under the title *De' discorsi politici e militari* attributed to "Amadio Niecollucci". Ginammi also issued many works of the banned pornographer Pietro Aretino under the name "Partenio Etiro". The Venetian press published works by anti-clerical, rationalist, and Enlightenment writers condemned by the papal Indexes of Prohibited Books in the later 17th and 18th centuries. The Venetian press was the least restricted press in Italy until the end of the Republic in 1797.

PAUL F. GRENDLER

Further Reading

Brown, Horatio F., *The Venetian Printing Press: An Historical Study Based upon Documents for the Most Part Hitherto Unpublished*, London: Nimmo, and New York: Putnam, 1891; reprinted Amsterdam: Heusden, 1969

Bujanda, J.M. de, *et al.*, *Index de Venise 1549, Venise et Milan 1554*, Sherbrooke, Québec: Centre d'Études de la Renaissance, and Geneva: Droz, 1987 (Index des livres interdits 3)

Bujanda, J.M. de, *et al.*, *Index de Rome 1590, 1593, 1596: avec étude des index de Parme 1580 et Munich 1582*, Sherbrooke, Québec: Centre d'Études de la Renaissance, 1994 (Index des livres interdits 9)

Grendler, Paul F., *The Roman Inquisition and the Venetian Press, 1540–1605*, Princeton, New Jersey: Princeton University Press, 1977

PRIOR RESTRAINT

Prior restraint is the heart and soul of censorship. It is far more inhibiting than subsequent punishment. Expression is snuffed out before its birth. The communication in question may never see the light of day. Suppression by the stroke of a pen is more common than that through a criminal process, in which case there is far less scope for public appraisal and discussion of the matter.

The individual most credited with advancing the doctrine against prior censorship was Sir William Blackstone, an English jurist of the 18th century. In his *Commentaries on the Laws of England* (1765) he wrote: "The liberty of the press is indeed essential to the nature of the free state, but this consists in laying no previous restraints upon publication, and not in freedom from censure for criminal matter when published." Blackstone condemns prior restraint, but he does not suggest that press freedom is absolute; a government has the right "to punish publishers of blasphemy, immoral, treasonable, schismatical, seditious or scandalous libels". Yet, to Blackstone, preventing the content of material prior to publication destroys the freedom to express any opinion, whether it is libellous or not.

The Blackstonian doctrine against prior restraint set in motion the legal precedents for press freedom not only in Britain, but also throughout the western world. By the end of the 19th century, most European countries had enacted laws against the practice, and in the US the constitution embodied a prohibition against it. It is, however, by no means absent from countries that are considered democratic, as the following survey shows; in non-democratic countries, on the other hand, the concept has little meaning.

Britain

Prior restraint orders are issued to prevent publications deemed harmful to national security. For example, in the *Spycatcher* cases (1988), despite the fact that information published in Peter Wright's book was already in the public domain, because it had been published in other countries and copies were imported into Britain, the courts continued injunctions against publication until the end of the litigation, when the House of Lords refused permanent injunctions against the newspapers. In a dictum of 1975, Lord Widgery had observed that in extreme cases involving matters affecting national security the courts could restrain publication, and, further, that "secrets relating to national security may require to be preserved indefinitely".

Although the doctrine of confidentiality is a matter for private law, it can be used by the state, and prior restraint orders may also be passed in cases of breach of confidence, as in *Attorney General* v. *Jonathan Cape Ltd* (1976). However, a prior restraint order is unlikely if the information is already in the public domain.

Restraint orders may also be passed by invoking the *sub judice* rule in order to ensure that no prejudice is caused to an accused or a defendant in a pending criminal or civil proceeding. In *Attorney General* v. *Times Newspapers* (1974), the House of Lords restrained the publication of a newspaper story about a pending trial in the thalidomide case, on the grounds that the publication created a risk of interference with the course of justice. The *Sunday Times* then approached the European Court, which laid down that the Lords ruling constituted a breach of the right of freedom of expression guaranteed by article 10(1) of the European Convention on Human Rights, because the injunction was not necessary, in a democratic society, for maintaining the authority of the judiciary under article 10(2) of the convention.

In actions for libel, an interlocutory injunction preventing publication will not be granted if the publishers indicate their intention to call evidence at the trial to prove the truth of the allegedly libellous statement. This rule is well settled and consequently "gagging libel writs" threatening an injunction to stop publication will not be accepted by the courts if the publishers or broadcaster pleads justification, except in the clearest cases, where any jury would say that the matter complained of was libellous.

Germany

Article 5 of the constitution prohibits pre-censorship: "Censorship shall not take place." The prohibition is confirmed in the regional laws enacted by the *Lander*. However, the press is subject to the criminal law, which serves to inhibit publication of any material considered treasonable, incites aggression, or betrays state secrets. Journalists and writers may not, moreover, publish "malicious defamation", even if they consider the material to be true.

India

Freedom of speech and expression is guaranteed as a fundamental right by article 19(1)(a) of the constitution. This freedom, like other fundamental rights, is not absolute, and was breached by the State of Emergency imposed by the prime minister Indira Gandhi in 1975. Free expression can also be restricted by a law that imposes restrictions under one or more heads specified under article 19(2), namely, state security, the sovereignty and integrity of India, friendly relations with foreign states, public order, decency or morality, contempt of court, defamation, or incitement to an offence. However, the restriction must be reasonable, not excessive or disproportionate; the procedure and manner of imposing the restriction must be just, fair, and reasonable.

The issue of pre-censorship arose in the case of *Brij Bhushan* v. *The State of Delhi* (1950). The court declared the statutory provision in question unconstitutional on the ground that the restrictions imposed were outside the purview of article 19(2) as it then stood. However, the court did not rule that prior censorship is *per se* unconstitutional. Thereafter, in 1957, the court upheld prior censorship imposed under the Punjab Special Powers (Press) Act (1956) for a limited period, which provided for a right of representation to the government. It is noteworthy that another statutory provision imposing censorship without any time limit and without providing any right of representation was struck down by the court in a judgement declared on the same day (*Virendra* v. *The State of Punjab*, 1971).

Prior restraint was upheld by the Supreme Court with regard to the exhibition of motion pictures in *K.A. Abbas* v. *Union of India* (1971), because "it has been almost universally recognized that the treatment of motion pictures must be different from that of other forms of art and expression. This arises from the instant appeal of the motion picture . . .". The court emphasized the necessity for a corrective machinery in the shape of an independent tribunal and also a reasonable time limit for the decision of the censoring authorities, ruling that "the standard that we must set for ourselves must make a substantial allowance in favour of freedom".

The question whether a newspaper can be injuncted from publishing any matter which is *sub judice* arose in *Reliance Petrochemicals Ltd* v. *Indian Express Newspapers, Bombay Pvt Ltd* (1988). The judgement implied a recognition that a "gagging order" can be passed "in such circumstances, providing the publication will clearly and obviously prejudice or tend to prejudice the course of pending proceedings". Apparently, the court is inclined to accept the Holmesian test of clear and present danger.

The Supreme Court of India in its path-breaking judgement in *R. Rajagopal* v. *State of TN* (1994) declared:

> neither the government nor the officials who apprehend that they may be defamed had the right to impose a prior restraint upon the publication of the autobiography of Auto Shankar, a convict serving sentence of death in jail and whose publication by his wife was likely to reveal nexus between criminals and high-ups in the police. The remedy of public officials/public figures, if any, will arise only after publication.

Israel

During the British Mandate, all publications were subject to the approval of a military censor. After independence in 1948, the new nation continued the practice, including the following regulation, confirmed by Military Order no. 5 (1967): "The censor may prohibit the importation or exportation or the printing or publishing of any publication . . . which, in his opinion, would be or be likely to become, prejudicial, for the defence [of Israel] or to the public safety or public order." Two copies of each publication were to be submitted to the censors on the day before they appeared, to be returned, amended where necessary, by midnight on the same day. For most of Israel's history pre-censorship has been applied much more stringently to the Arab press.

United States

Freedom of speech and the press are guaranteed by the First Amendment; any prior restraint bears a heavy presumption against its constitutional validity. The rationale is that prior restraint by its very definition and nature has an immediate and irreversible sanction: "If it can be said that a threat of criminal or civil sanctions after publication 'chills' speech, prior restraint 'freezes' it at least for the time" (*Nebraska Press Association* v. *Stuart*).

Immunity from prior restraint is not absolute. In *Near* v. *Minnesota* (1931) the court listed three exceptional cases that might justify it: (1) actual obstruction to the recruiting service or the publication of the sailing dates of transports or the number and location of troops; (2) enforcement of obscenity laws; and (3) enforcement of laws against incitement to acts of violence and overthrow by force of orderly government.

In *New York Times Co.* v. *United States* the government sought to prevent the publication by the *New York Times*, on grounds of national security, of the so-called Pentagon Papers, classified documents dealing with US activities in the Vietnam War before 1968. The court held that the government had not met the heavy burden of justifying prior restraint because the allegations could not be established as a matter of substantial certainty rather than speculation. Government in such cases must show that disclosure "will surely result in direct, immediate, and irreparable damage to our nation or its people".

Judicial protection of free speech weakens when questions of national security may raise questions of proximity and degree of danger. In *United States* v. *The Progressive Inc.* an injunction was granted preventing publication of an article allegedly exposing the "H-Bomb secret". The injunction remained in operation for seven months, even though it was admitted by the government that the information on which the article was based was already accessible to the general public and revealed nothing that would be new to a "competent scientist".

Earlier, the US had anticipated the Indian decision not to extend prohibitions on prior restraint to the medium of film. Likening film to such other media as the theatre and the cinema, the court ruled in *Mutual Film Corporation* v. *Industrial Commission of Ohio* (1915) that the new medium was exempt from the provisions of the First Amendment. The decision remained in force until it was reversed in *Joseph Burstyn Inc.* v. *Wilson* (1952).

Other forms of prior restraint

Elsewhere, prior restraint has been used by countries whose idea of democracy differs considerably from the countries named above (e.g., the former Soviet Union and the Chinese People's Republic, who identified democracy with the will of the party leadership and constructed elaborate systems of prior censorship to ensure that the party line is not breached); it has also, and more obviously, been used by other forms of dictatorship, where, without apology, pre-censorship is part of the armoury of control (e.g., in Burma – Myanmar – where the military junta empowers the Press Scrutiny Board to review, systematically, all news content before publication, and Nigeria under general Abacha, who, as well as resorting to the simple expedient of arresting journalists without charge, instituted Offensive Publications Decree no. 35, which allowed the government to confiscate any publication thought likely to "disturb the peace and public order of Nigeria"). More subtle forms of prior censorship have been practised in Singapore and Malaysia, whose political leaders, on occasion, censor *de facto* by the simple expedient of threatening to sue journalists believed to be ready to publish information damaging to their reputation.

SOLI J. SORABJEE
additional material by Christopher Rose

Further Reading

Blackstone, William, *Commentaries on the Laws of England*, 1765–69; reprinted 4 vols, New York: Legal Classics Library, 1983
Dunnett, Peter J.S., *The World Newspaper Industry*, London: Croom Helm, and New York: Methuen, 1988
Holsinger, Ralph L and Jon Paul Dilts, *Media Law*, 4th edition, New York: McGraw Hill, 1997
Lahav, Pnina (editor), *Press Law in Modern Democracies: A Comparative Study*, New York: Longman, 1985
Lord Lester of Herne Hill and Dawn Oliver, *Constitutional Law and Human Rights*, London: Butterworth, 1997
Nimmo, Dan and Michael W. Mansfield (editors), *Government and the News Media: Comparative Dimensions*, Waco, Texas: Baylor University, 1982
Ricciardi, Sherry, "Killing the Messenger", *American Journalism Review*, 17 (November 1995)

PRIORITAS
Indonesian newspaper, 1985–87

After Indonesia gained independence in 1945, its newspaper proprietors tended to be editors who worked exclusively in the press industry. However, from the mid-1980s the press began to attract successful entrepreneurs with diverse non-media holdings and established political connections. One of the earliest of this new breed was Surya Paloh, a long-time organizer in the New Order government's political organization, Golkar, which he represented in the national parliament, the People's Deliberative Assembly (MPR), from 1977 until 1982. A founder of an influential military-aligned lobby group Forum

Komunikasi Putra-Putri Purnawirawan ABRI (the Communication Forum for the Sons and Daughters of Retired Members of the Armed Forces), he was close to some of the nation's most powerful families and was frequently seen with Bambang Trihatmojo, son of the president general Suharto and head of the powerful Bimantara conglomerate.

In 1985 Surya Paloh diversified his successful catering business, PT Indocater, to establish PT Surya Persindo, a publishing holding company, and produce the controversial straight-talking daily *Prioritas*, the first Indonesian daily to publish regular colour photos on its front and back pages. To what extent he was assisted by Bambang Trihatmojo was a matter of muted speculation in the industry, but Bimantara's injection of capital into the firm in 1988 is documented.

Close friendships with the political elite did not prevent the revocation of *Prioritas*'s obligatory publication permit (SIUPP) by the minister of information, Harmoko, on 29 June 1987. The revocation order stated that *Prioritas* had published "reports which are not true and are not based on facts, and which are cynical, insinuative and tendentious", and that it had deviated from its permit provisions to publish 75 per cent economic news and only 25 cent general news. However, it was widely believed that the paper was closed because of its outspoken discussion of a number of corruption cases, its embarrassing interviews with high-ranking officials, and its ability to "anticipate" government economy policy with a frequency disconcerting to the authorities. Unsubstantiated claims by interests associated with the paper suggested that Harmoko had initially been keen to obtain complimentary shares in *Prioritas* but had been refused, leading the powerful minister to take a jaundiced view of the paper and its publisher.

After *Prioritas* was closed, Surya Paloh applied for a new publication permit for another paper, tentatively named *Realitas*, in August 1987. This was refused on the dubious grounds that the market would not sustain another "general daily". Documentation obtained by the Newspaper Publishers' Association (SPS) indicated that officially the application was still "being processed by the Department of Information" more than five years later. Meanwhile, to the consternation of those involved in *Prioritas*, licences were issued for other "general dailies" such as the Islamic *Republika*, associated with the minister for research and technology, B.J. Habibie, a protégé of president Suharto, and his successor as president.

After the *Prioritas* ban Surya Paloh became one of the most vocal opponents of the press permit provisions, particularly the 1984 ministerial regulations under which Harmoko cancelled *Prioritas*'s licence. *Prioritas* had been the second paper to have its permit withdrawn under these regulations, the first being the Protestant-oriented *Sinar Harapan*, closed down in October 1986. In October 1992 Paloh wrote an open letter to the People's Representative Council, requesting (unsuccessfully) that during its 1993 session the decision-making house, the People's Deliberative Assembly (MPR), cancel all press provisions and ministerial regulations governing the withdrawal of publication permits. He argued that they contravened the guarantees of freedom of the press outlined in the 1945 constitution, the New Order's "Broad Outlines of State Policy" (GBHN), and the 1982 Basic Law on the Press. He called for press transgressions and penalties to be determined in public by the Supreme Court rather than secretively by ministerial whim. In November 1992 he wrote to the Supreme Court requesting a judicial review to determine whether the 1984 ministerial regulations contravened the 1982 legislation. Acting for him voluntarily were six of the country's most prominent lawyers, including office-bearers of the Indonesian Bar Association (IKADIN) and leaders of the highly regarded Indonesian Legal Aid Institute Foundation.

The Supreme Court agreed to consider the issue at law, but chose to delay its verdict until after the March 1993 session of the MPR, which appointed the president for the following five-year term. With Suharto predictably re-elected unopposed, and Harmoko reappointed by the president as minister for information for a third successive term, the signal to the Supreme Court was clear: the president had full faith in his minister. Some observers speculated that it would be appointments to the Supreme Court that would be reconsidered should its legal determinations be critical of the government. In June 1993 the court rejected Surya Paloh's request, claiming he had not followed appropriate procedure in lodging his case – hardly surprising, since this was the first such request in Indonesian legal history and no procedures existed.

However, Surya Paloh's challenge forced the court to produce a ruling on procedures for appeals against government regulation (below the level of Acts of Parliament), the ramifications of which extend far beyond the press into all aspects of government regulation. As one attorney claimed, the Supreme Court ruling "is not only for the Press and the publication permit. Many more regulations below the level of Acts which have been forced through by the government can now be questioned." The precedent set by the *Prioritas* case paved the way for the editor, staff, and readers of the prestigious newsweekly *Tempo* to challenge the minister of information's decision to withdraw the magazine's publication permit in June 1994, by taking the case to the State Administrative Court.

After the loss of *Prioritas*, Surya Paloh took a controlling interest in another languishing daily paper, *Media Indonesia*, which he built into a significant publication within a couple of years. It became the flagship of a national network of linked provincial papers, which adopted a common block-style layout and typeface, modelled on *Media Indonesia* and its predecessor *Prioritas*, as if to demonstrate their shared progenitor.

DAVID T. HILL

Further Reading

Hill, David T., *The Press in New Order Indonesia*, Perth: University of Western Australia Press, 1994

Lubis, T. Mulya, *In Search of Human Rights: Legal-Political Dilemmas of Indonesia's New Order, 1966–1990*, Jakarta: Gramedia SPES, 1993

Vatikiotis, Michael, "Masses of Media", *Far Eastern Economic Review* (26 July 1990): 46–47

PRIVACY

Protection of privacy, as a right in itself, and as a ground for restricting freedom of expression, is of relatively recent origin in the Anglo-American tradition. While honour and reputation have been protected by law for centuries, privacy, as a further aspect of human dignity, has emerged only in the last 100 years. The first identification of privacy is usually attributed to two eminent American jurists, Warren and Brandeis, writing in the *Harvard Law Review* in 1890, in response to what they saw as the intrusiveness of the "yellow" press. They identified in broad terms a right to be left alone, not to have information about one's personal life exposed to the general public by the press.

The "new" right was developed to some extent through tort law but many difficulties were perceived with it, in particular the compatibility in the United States of such a right with the First Amendment and the freedom of the press. There, as in Britain, Australia, Ireland, and other common law countries, disagreement has centred not so much on whether to protect privacy as on what to protect and how to protect it. Difficulties have been experienced in defining privacy. There is some consensus as to the core of the right (intimacy), but not as to the penumbra. Closely aligned to intimacy in recent analysis are the concepts of autonomy and identity. All are aspects of human dignity and the individual personality, as recognized, for example, by the German constitution (articles 1 and 2).

Attempts at definition and protection to date have tended to focus on the methods used (deception, eavesdropping, bugging, and other forms of surveillance) and on the form of intrusion (publishing embarrassing private facts or pictures, causing unnecessary grief, and benefiting commercially from using a person's attributes or persona). That two-pronged approach may merely reflect the two-stage process involved in news-gathering and publication. In the US, professor Prosser identified four separate privacy-based torts: intrusion into another's seclusion; appropriation of another's image or person for trade or commercial purposes; knowingly or recklessly portraying another in a false light; and publication of private facts. In other common law countries, privacy continued to be protected only indirectly by existing torts, such as trespass and nuisance, and by the development in Britain of an action for breach of confidence. This incidental and haphazard protection was augmented in certain areas by legislation, for example broadcasting and copyright legislation. Since then, developments at European level, prompted by the widespread use of computers to store data, have led to the introduction of data protection legislation, which gives individuals a right of access to, and control over, personal data held about them by a whole range of agencies and institutions. Privacy considerations and a right of access to personal information are also commonly found in, or in tandem with, freedom of information legislation.

Awareness of the need for the effective protection of human rights generally and of the private lives of individuals, in particular, against intrusion by state authorities grew out of the atrocities of Nazism and World War II. The need for protection specifically aimed at intrusion by the media has been fuelled by the capabilities of modern technology and the growth of the tabloid media, with their appeal to prurience and their spotlight on intimate details and events of people's lives. Advances in technology have enhanced the media role in informing the public, and thereby benefited the public, but they have also increased the opportunity and capacity to intrude on the private lives of individuals. However, in a communications age, absolute protection is impossible. In a society that respects and values the role of the media in informing the citizenry, selective anonymity is likewise impossible, in theory and in practice. Hence, the formulation adopted by some legislatures of protecting from "unwarranted" or "unreasonable" intrusion. Such formulations also recognize that one should not legislate against all conscious intrusion, regardless of motive or circumstances, since there may be sufficient public interest grounds to justify intrusion in certain circumstances. All of these considerations are encapsulated in article 17 of the International Covenant on Civil and Political Rights (UN, 1966), which states that no one shall be subjected to arbitrary or unlawful interference with his privacy, home, or correspondence, or to unlawful attacks on his honour or reputation.

Article 17, therefore, links privacy and reputation but while the two overlap in many respects they are not synonymous. Injury to reputation arises from the publication of untruths about a person, while invasion of privacy usually results from the publication of truths about part of their life that is generally regarded by society or by the community in which they live as intimate and not for public consumption. In that respect, there is a clear cultural dimension to how privacy is protected, if at all, in different parts of the world. There is also an element of social judgement. For some, there must be a clearly defined harm involved in the invasion of privacy and a compelling interest to warrant its prevention (Zimmerman 1993). For others, some aspects of human relationships are beyond the reach of the law or unsuited to legal solution and to try to concoct or impose legal structures, theories, and remedies may lead to restrictions on the media without any corresponding social benefit.

In Britain, the Younger Committee Report (1972) recommended against a blanket declaration of a right to privacy on the grounds that it would introduce uncertainties into the law and affect freedom of information. It did, however, favour the introduction of a generally applicable tort of disclosure or other use of information unlawfully acquired. Almost 20 years later, the case of *Kaye* v. *Robertson* (1990), in which newspaper photographers took hospital pictures of a well-known actor, Gordon Kaye, who had been seriously injured in a car crash, confirmed that in British law there was no right to privacy as such and, accordingly, no right of action for breach of privacy by the press. The case prompted the British government to establish the Calcutt Committee, which recommended against the introduction of a tort of privacy and instead favoured the creation of specific criminal offences relating to surveillance. The proposals were not implemented; instead, the British press was given one more chance to make self-regulation work. The Press Council was replaced by the Press Complaints Commission, with a narrower remit, to implement a code of practice drawn up by newspaper editors. The code's provisions relating to privacy were reviewed and extended following the death in 1997 of Princess Diana.

In France, privacy is protected in the Civil Code and article 35 of the Press Law of 1881, which recognize the right of everyone to respect for private life and make it an offence to listen to, record, fix, or transmit words or pictures of a person in a private place without their consent. In France, case law was developed mainly in the 1960s and codified in the law of 17 July 1970. Actions for the invasion of privacy, with a moderate damages remedy, are taken frequently, particularly by celebrities and public figures. Unlike most countries that have privacy laws, France does not recognize a public interest defence. A damages remedy is not necessarily the most appropriate way to deal with invasion of privacy but the publication of private facts about a person that are true is more difficult to counter than publication of defamatory facts that are untrue and, therefore, alternative remedies such as corrections and clarifications are often of little or no avail.

In Germany, the right to privacy is recognized as part of the constitutional protection for the dignity and freedom of the individual, which together comprise the personality right. Different categories of privacy and of persons therefore enjoy different degrees of protection. Absolute protection is accorded to matters such as an individual's sexual behaviour, details of health, and confidential correspondence. An individual's family and home life and religious beliefs also receive a high level of protection. In relation to public persons, the law recognizes two distinct categories, namely absolute public persons, such as politicians, famous actors, or sports stars, who are continually or permanently in the public sphere, and relative public persons, such as someone who is propelled into the public spotlight by a particular issue or tragedy and who is, therefore, temporarily or to a limited extent in the public sphere.

The European Convention on Human Rights declares in article 8 that everyone has the right to respect for his or her private and family life, home, and correspondence, and that there shall be no interference by a public authority with the exercise of the right, except insofar as is in accordance with law and necessary in a democratic society, in support of certain specified interests. The interests specified are national security, public safety, or the economic well-being of the country, the protection of health or morals, the protection of the rights and freedoms of others. Privacy, as one of the "rights of others", is also included in article 10.2 of the convention as a legitimate ground for restricting freedom of expression. The convention, which is already part of the domestic law of most western European states, is due to be incorporated into law in Britain shortly. There is pressure on Ireland to follow suit, although in Ireland there is already protection for privacy in the written constitution of 1937. However, the Constitution Review Group recommended (1996) that the protection of freedom of expression in article 40.6 of the constitution should be replaced by an article closely modelled on article 10 of the convention, and, similarly, that the protection of privacy in the Irish constitution, which at present is an unspecified right included in article 40.3, should be strengthened by the incorporation of a formula modelled on article 8 of the convention. The convention has now been ratified by most central and eastern European states, and recently by Russia.

In June 1998 the European Parliament passed a resolution calling on member states that did not already have privacy legislation to introduce it. The Resolution acknowledges that a careful balancing of the rights to freedom of expression and privacy is involved, especially where public figures – those who play a role in public life whether in politics, the economy, the arts, the social sphere, sport, or any other domain – are concerned. They have to concede a degree of their privacy and accept that people have a right to know certain things about their private life. None the less, the Resolution calls for provision in the civil law and in media self-regulation (guidelines and complaints bodies) to allow aggrieved individuals effective redress.

The code of the International Federation of Journalists and journalists' codes in many countries enshrine principles advocating the use of fair and honest means to obtain news, pictures, films, tapes, and documents, respect for private grief and personal privacy. In New Zealand, for example, the journalists' code of ethics requires journalists *inter alia* to respect private grief and personal privacy and accords them the right to resist compulsion to intrude on them. The code of the British and Irish National Union of Journalists requires the use of straightforward means only to obtain information, photographs, and illustrations, emphasizing that the use of any other means can be justified only by "over-riding considerations of the public interest". Similar considerations apply in the case of intrusion into private grief and distress. Most codes also provide for corrections, apologies, or rights of reply in the case of harmfully inaccurate publication or criticism where the issue is of sufficient importance. Related issues of harassment, using listening devices or taking photographs without consent, are also provided for in the revised Code of Practice of the Press Complaints' Commission in Britain.

In addition to journalists' codes, some countries have Press Councils, created mainly in the 1960s, which oversee and adjudicate on privacy and other ethical issues. In Australia, the Press Council looks to see whether the private information obtained adds significantly to public knowledge so as to outweigh the privacy and ethical considerations, that is, whether there is a compelling public interest such as to outweigh any private interest.

Of particular concern in many countries is the protection of children, in accordance with article 16 of the International Convention on the Rights of the Child: "No child shall be subjected to arbitrary or unlawful interference with his or her privacy, family, home or correspondence . . ." This issue was brought into particular relief by the media attention to which Princess Diana's sons were subjected, both before and after her death in 1997. There are legal provisions and press conventions for not identifying children in the context of court cases, whether in relation to family disputes regarding custody, access, etc., or in relation to children's involvement in criminal proceedings. However, such measures, designed to protect the privacy of children, can create an information gap and act as a restriction on freedom of expression and information when they go beyond issues of identification and amount to a full clampdown on the reporting of family law cases. In the common law tradition, for example, family law cases were usually heard in private with no media presence permitted. However, there is now a trend towards more openness. In Australia and Canada, for example, family cases are now generally heard in public unless there are compelling reasons to hear them in private.

In practice, as far as it can be gauged, the track record of the media in relation to privacy in most countries is quite good. Although some of the British tabloid newspapers are regarded as persistent and blatant offenders, most complaints to the Press Complaints Commission in that country concern accuracy, rather than privacy. The same is true of Australia and Ireland, where only a very small percentage of complaints concern privacy, and even those are made generally by an unconnected third party. In addition, there is some evidence that issues of privacy are sometimes confused in the public mind with issues of offensiveness and taste.

In recent years, the Human Rights Act 1998 was passed in Britain, incorporating the European Convention on Human Rights into domestic law. In Ireland, a bill to incorporate the convention was published in 2001.

MARIE MCGONAGLE

Further Reading

Agre, Philip E. and Marc Rotenberg (editors), *Technology and Privacy: The New Landscape*, Cambridge, Massachusetts: MIT Press, 1997

Australian Press Council, annual reports

Boyle, Kevin and Marie McGonagle, *Media Accountability in Ireland: The Readers' Representative in Irish Newspapers*, Dublin: NNI, 1995

British Press Complaints' Commission, annual reports

Calcutt, David (chairman), *Report of the Committee on Privacy and Related Matters*, London: HMSO 1990

Calcutt, David, *Review of Press Self-Regulation*, London: HMSO, 1993

Emerson, Thomas I., "The Right of Privacy and Freedom of the Press", *Harvard Civil Rights – Civil Liberties Law Review*, 14 (1979): 329

Gerety, Tom, "Redefining Privacy", *Harvard Civil Rights – Civil Liberties Law Review*, 12 (1977): 233

Lorenz, Werner, "Privacy and the Press: A German Experience" in *Butterworths Lectures 1989–90*, London: Butterworth, 1990

McGonagle, Marie, *A Textbook on Media Law*, Dublin: Gill and Macmillan, 1996

McGonagle, Marie (editor), *Law and the Media: Views of Journalists and Lawyers*, Dublin: Round Hall Sweet and Maxwell, 1997

Markesinis, Basil S., "Our Patchy Law of Privacy: Time to Do Something about It", *Modern Law Review*, 53 (1990): 802

Markesinis, Basil S., *Protecting Privacy*, Oxford: Oxford University Press, 1999

Schauer, Frederick L., "Reflections on the Value of Truth" in *Privacy*, edited by Raymond Wacks, 2 vols, New York: New York University Press, 1993

Thwaite, Gregory and Wolfgang Brehm, "German Privacy and Defamation Law", *European Intellectual Property Review*, 16 (1994): 336

Warren, Samuel D. and Louis Brandeis, "The Right to Privacy", *Harvard Law Review*, 4 (1890): 193–220

Younger, Kenneth (chairman), *Report of the Committee on Privacy*, London: HMSO 1972

Zimmerman, Diane L., "Requiem for a Heavyweight: A Farewell to Warren and Brandeis's Privacy Tort", *Cornell Law Review*, 68 (1983): 291, 306, 365; reprinted in *Privacy*, edited by Raymond Wacks, 2 vols, New York: New York University Press, 1993

Zuckman, Harvey L., "The American Torts of Invasion of Privacy", *Entertainment Law Review*, 1 (1990): 173

PRIVATE CASE
Collection of forbidden books, British Library (formerly at the British Museum Library)

Most research libraries have collections of forbidden books. The content of these books, whether obscene, pornographic, or, as Alec Craig describes in *Banned Books of England*, dealing with "blasphemy, betrayal of masonic secrets, and unseemly truthfulness about royal families", has made it necessary to permit only limited access to the general reader. *L'Enfer* (or Hell) at the Bibliothèque Nationale, the British Library, the Bodleian at Oxford, the Library of Congress in Washington DC, and the Vatican *Inferno*, for example, all hold significant collections of such works, which are not normally available to the general public. Paradoxically such deliberate policies to restrict library access has protected forbidden books from readers who, from motives of moral outrage, religious fervour, or plain prurience may have felt moved to destroy, mutilate, or steal books regarded as offensive, controversial, or pornographic. By protecting such collections from hostile individuals as well as from book burnings during "orgies of cultural auto-destruction" as described by G. Legman, rare collections have been preserved in secret repositories. In the case of *L'Enfer* in Paris and the British Library in London, restriction has created two of the finest collections of rare forbidden books in the world.

Academics and bibliophiles have taken exception to protectionist policies which can blur into censorship and result in obstruction to scholarship. They have not, however, taken issue with libraries' need to protect their collections or to act responsibly toward readers, given the sensitive nature of some of the material in their care. It is for this reason that some libraries employ cautionary press-marks in their general catalogues to alert readers to the nature of certain books and to their restricted status, most amusing of which are the press-marks of the Bodleian Library which uses the Greek letter Φ to pun on "Fie".

Books on restricted access are usually kept under lock and key and are only issued at the discretion of the superintendent of books. Craig, writing in 1962, noted that "at the London Library certain books are kept 'in the Librarian's room' and a personal interview is necessary before they are issued to members". In the British Museum Library, too, numerous items in the old large green paste-up Catalogues of Printed Books (replaced by computers in the new British Library) could not be issued without an interview to satisfy the superintendent of books that the reader was a suitable person and serious scholar. The value or rarity of some books made this interview necessary, but more often the interview was connected with books of a sexual nature. Up to the mid-1960s, conditions for consulting such books, as described by Peter Fryer in *Private Case – Public Scandal*, usually meant sitting at prescribed tables in the North Library on the "front bench" in sight of the superintendent.

The British Library also had two other categories of books with more severely restricted access. One category, described as "the secret inferno" by Craig, is a collection of suppressed and uncatalogued books "whose very existence is not supposed to be known". These consist mainly of defamatory libels, criticisms of the royal family, and books revealing a variety of "secrets", including those of the police, officialdom, and masonic lodges. A British Museum Library document entitled "Information for those Superintending in the Reading Room" (1966) and quoted in Fryer tells us that also among the suppressed titles were "those which are confidential and are deposited on condition that they are not issued for a certain period". It appears from the "Information for Superintendents" that the suppression of books in the British Museum Library was far-reaching, for not only were readers denied access to certain books, they were also denied access to the hand-list which itemized those books. "Since none of the books in these classes is available to readers in any circumstances, the hand-list is also withheld from readers and readers may not be told whether a particular book is in the list."

The other category of suppressed books possessed by the British Museum Library was segregated into a special section, called the "Private Case", and they were locked away, along with incunabula (i.e. books printed before 1500) in the Arch Room. By the mid-1960s the Private Case contained some 5000 erotic and sexological volumes including a heavy preponderance of works on sadism and flagellation such as *Lady Gay Spanker's Tales of Fun and Flagellation* (1896), *Exhibition of Female Flagellants* (1860), and the marquis de Sade's *Justine; ou, les malheurs de la vertu* (1791).

While libraries operate restricted access to their forbidden collections, they have adopted, for the most part, a policy of free information toward the titles of forbidden books in their collection. These are openly and fully listed in their general, or special catalogues. In *L'Enfer*, for example, a complete catalogue of erotica has been in print since 1913. However, until the mid-1960s the British Museum Library collection of Private Case books and even the knowledge of their existence was deliberately withheld from the general reader. The Private Case was not listed in the general catalogue and no separate catalogue was published by the library for readers. A two-volume black folio catalogue of the Private Case housed in the keeper's office was not generally available. It was the library's attempts to censor scholarship which led to agitation, particularly in the 1960s, for the de-suppression of the Private Case.

The history of the Private Case may help to clear "the whole fog of furtiveness" which Fryer found to envelop "the subject of erotica at the British Museum". According to Legman, the Private Case was fully instituted between 1866 and 1870. However, Fryer sets the date earlier as 1856, the year John Winter Jones (1805–81) became keeper of printed books. Fryer believes that within a year of his appointment Winter Jones took sole responsibility for the decision to omit erotic titles from the general catalogue. He further believes that this decision was without the knowledge of the British Museum trustees nor Sir Antony Panizzi, the principal librarian. If this is so, then about 1857 Winter Jones began to press-mark books *within* the general catalogue as "Private Case" (a press-mark later erased and replaced by PC) but the books themselves were not transferred to the Private Case. Fryer argues that

books segregated into the Private Case were almost entirely newly acquired books and did not include books which already existed in the general catalogues. However, it should be noted that the British Museum Library did not actively purchase books to augment its collection; rather, the core of its collection came from bequests and donations.

The earliest gift was probably that of the antiquarian George Witt, who donated his collection of books on phallicism to the library in 1866 on condition "that a separate room be set apart for their reception, and that the public have access to them under certain restrictions". This collection was stored in some of the earliest cases, numbered PC 19 and 20. However, as Henry Spencer Ashbee, bibliographer of eroticism, noted in 1875, this meant "a dark room in the basement, difficult of access, and where the interesting specimens it comprises can be inspected only under the greatest disadvantages".

On Ashbee's death in 1900 he bequeathed to the British Museum Library a valuable collection of editions and translations of *Don Quixote* together with his collection of erotica comprising 15,229 volumes in all. Ashbee had been a fervent collector of erotica and especially 18th-century semi-erotic and "gallant literature". These titles went into the general catalogue but it was agreed that after duplicates had been destroyed, the erotica should be "kept specially locked up". A second large bequest was made to the British Museum Library in 1964, when Charles Reginald Dawes bequeathed his erotic library with its emphasis on French erotica of the period 1880–1930. Also in 1964, the American Beecher Moore donated his library, which covered the full spectrum of erotica from valuable leather-bound volumes to trashy pulp fiction.

Fryer argues that certainly until the end of the 19th century, the Private Case was "the preserve of a small circle of privileged men of letters, rich amateurs, and dilettanti" with connections to the higher officials of the British Museum. Such attitudes toward the Private Case held good until at least the 1950s. During the first half of the 20th century, books considered subversive of the throne or religion and those of an obscene nature remained uncatalogued, as did miscellaneous volumes classified as "rubbish". Some foreign works were catalogued but not their English translations. Uncatalogued books were available by special application to the keeper of printed books but the method and conditions of accessing such books, or of knowing of their existence, were still not published by the British Museum Library, and indeed some officials denied such books existed. By the 1940s access to the Private Case "required not only serious purpose but tact, patience, and persistence".

The censorship experienced by scholars is exemplified by an exchange of letters between Edward Carpenter and the keeper of printed books when Carpenter requested advice on how to access his own book *Intermediate Sex* (1908) which had still not been entered in the general catalogue in 1913 when the exchange of correspondence took place. A letter from the keeper read:

you ask me whether there are any printed instructions issued, and available for public use, by which the public may know of the existence of such books [i.e., Private Case books not in the general catalogue], and of the conditions under which they may be consulted. My reply to your question is that there are no printed instructions relating to such books.

Access to the Private Case gradually improved. According to Patrick Kearney, from about the 1960s:

> readers wishing to consult books that they thought might be in the Private Case had to ask at the enquiry desk, and, if the assistant confirmed that the Library had the book, the reader was obliged to write a letter to the Keeper stating his reasons for wishing to see it. Today [the 1980s] this regulation no longer applies and Private Case books may be called for in the same way as any other, except for a special form that has to be filled out in addition to the usual application slip.

Now that the British Library has moved to its new home in St Pancras, readers need only present themselves to the Rare Books Room to consult Private Case books, although they are still required to sit apart from other readers.

Where the British Museum Library was unwilling to assist, individual scholars tried to fathom the secrets of the Private Case in order to publish a complete catalogue. The *Registrum Librorum Eroticorum* which detailed the contents of the Private Case until about 1934 had been published posthumously in 1936 using catalogue cards and other materials taken from the estate of Rolf S. Reade, an anagrammatic pseudonym for the affluent collector of erotica, Alfred Rose. As a result of its publishing history, the *Registrum* was unreliable and it was not until the publication of Kearney's annotated bibliography in 1981 that a full and accurate description of the works listed in the Private Case as it stood up to 1975 became available.

From the mid-1950s there had been renewed agitation from readers and scholars for a liberalization in British Museum Library policy toward its erotic collections. A good example of earlier agitation is E.S.P. Haynes who, in 1913, had tried to expose the restrictions in an article entitled "The Taboos of the British Museum Library". In 1957, at a time when the library was undertaking the colossal task of revising its Catalogues of Printed Books for publication, Craig wrote to the *Times Literary Supplement* to complain of the damage being done to scholarship: "the omission from the general catalogue, however, of all books consigned to the purgatorial 'Private Case' or damned to the even deeper inferno beneath it is a serious limitation of the value and utility of this monumental work of reference." In *Public Case – Private Scandal*, Fryer railed against the censorship of subject indexes and the hindrance to free enquiry into sexual matters.

By 1965, the British Museum Library had bowed to pressure and had agreed to begin the laborious work of incorporating the titles of Private Case books into the general catalogue. Thus by 1981, when Kearney published his bibliography, almost half the books in the Private Case had been de-suppressed; 1920 remained. Although titles and press-marks were then freely accessible within the catalogues, before Kearney's bibliography, it was impossible to know what the Private Case contained without sifting through the millions of entries in the whole of the catalogues. Furthermore, details of the Private Case remain in constant need of updating as new titles are being added all the time. In the final stages of preparing his bibliography, Kearney stumbled across new press-marks and two shelves full of Private Case books. Time will tell if the computerized system in the new British Library will maintain an accurate and updated list, accessible through press-mark searches, or whether aspects of the Private Case will remain shrouded in mystery.

BARBARA WHITE

Further Reading

Craig, Alec, *The Banned Books of England*, foreword by E.M. Forster, London: Allen and Unwin, 1937

Craig, Alec, *Above All Liberties*, London: Allen and Unwin, 1942; Freeport, New York: Books for Libraries Press, 1972

Craig, Alec, "Letter to the Editor", *Times Literary Supplement* (1 March 1957): 129

Craig, Alec, *The Banned Books of England and Other Countries: A Study of the Conception of Literary Obscenity*, London: Allen and Unwin, 1962; Westport, Connecticut: Greenwood Press, 1977

Fryer, Peter, *Private Case – Public Scandal: On the "Private Case" Collection of Books in the British Museum*, London: Secker and Warburg, 1966

Kearney, Patrick J., *The Private Case: An Annotated Bibliography of the Private Case Erotica Collection in the British (Museum) Library*, with an introduction by G. Legman, London: Landesman, 1981

Young, Wayland, *Eros Denied: Sex in Western Society*, New York: Grove Press, 1964; London: Weidenfeld and Nicolson, 1965

PRIVATE PROPERTY

Arguments about the distribution of information in shopping centres: US, 1940s–90s

The legal battle over speech rights in privately owned shopping centres was one of the most constitutionally significant test cases for censorship in the US in second half of the 20th century, entailing attempts to find the appropriate balance between equally cherished Fifth Amendment rights to private property and First Amendment rights to freedom of expression.

The modern precedent for speech rights on private property came in *Marsh* v. *Alabama* (1944). In 1942, several Jehovah's Witness church members were arrested for handing out copies of *The Watchtower* magazine on a street corner in the town of Chickasaw, Alabama. Local officials claimed that because the town was owned by Gulf Shipbuilding Company for use by its employees, even its streets and sidewalks were effectively private property, and so not subject to protections of freedom of expression that held for public areas. The Supreme Court, however, upheld the church members' rights to distribute the literature, claiming that regardless of ownership, the streets and sidewalks effectively functioned as the public space of the town. As such, citizens of Chickasaw deserved the same freedom of information in the town's public areas as was available to citizens living in other towns.

Though based on the very particular circumstances of the

company town, a form of development then passing from existence, the *Marsh* decision would come to have broad applicability with the rapid proliferation of privately developed and privately owned shopping centres across the US in the 1950s and 1950s. In *Amalgamated Food Employees Union* v. *Logan Valley Plaza* (1968), the Supreme Court referred to *Marsh* as a precedent for extending speech-rights protections to shopping centres. In 1966, a labour union striking against the Weiss supermarket attempted to picket and distribute leaflets in the parking area of the Logan Valley Mall in Altoona, Pennsylvania. They were arrested for forming a picket on private property, and were advised to confine their protest to the public-access roads in front of the centre. The Supreme Court found that the shopping centre effectively served as the business district for its suburban area, and thus resembled the downtown area of Chickasaw, and thus should be subject to the same speech protections. In so doing, they found that First Amendment rights to freedom of expression were relatively more important than Fifth Amendment rights to private property.

However, the Court's liberal protections of speech rights proved to be short-lived. Changes in the Court, including three appointments by president Richard Nixon, shifted the political balance, and the Court now became more conservative. In *Lloyd Corporation* v. *Tanner* (1972), the Court reversed the precedent set in *Logan*. In 1970, Vietnam War protesters attempted to distribute handbills in the interior area of the Lloyd Center in Portland, Oregon, inviting the public to a meeting of the "Resistance Community" to protest the draft and the Vietnam War. The Lloyd Center owners asked the group to leave the shopping centre and conduct their leafletting on the public streets and pavements outside the Lloyd Center. The new conservative majority on the Supreme Court found in favour of the Lloyd Center owners, stating that the shopping centre was private property, and thus had no speech-right protections. The Court claimed that the *Marsh* decision applied only to company towns, and that *Logan* applied only to speech that was related to "regular uses of the property", which war protesting was not. A subsequent decision in 1976, *Hudgens* v. *National Labor Relations Board*, overturned *Logan* outright, claiming that *Lloyd* had overturned speech-rights protections for even normal uses of the property, such as labour protests. This occurred despite the greater protections for trade union protest actions accorded under the National Labor Relations Act.

Even after the *Lloyd* and *Hudgens* decisions, state court decisions on free speech in shopping centres continued to be appealed to the Supreme Court. In 1980, the Court decided in *Pruneyard Shopping Centre* v. *Robins* to allow the individual state courts to decide the issue for themselves. The case involved a group of local high school students who attempted to pass out literature and collect signatures for a petition protesting against a United Nations anti-Zionist resolution in the central courtyard of the Pruneyard Shopping Center in Campbell, California. The shopping centre owners ejected the students from their property; however, the California Supreme Court subsequently held that the state constitution protected speech rights even on private property. The US Supreme Court unanimously supported California's right to protect speech rights in shopping centres; yet rather than stating unequivocally that private property trumped speech rights in all shopping centre cases, the Court stated it would allow each state to decide for itself where the balance lay, based on its own state constitution.

As a result, since 1980, there has been a broad range of decisions on the speech versus property question in shopping centres. The majority of states, lacking specific clauses in their constitutions pertaining to speech protections on private property, have favoured property rights, exemplified in Connecticut's *Cologne* v. *Westfarms Associates* (1984) and New York's *Shad Alliance* v. *Smith Haven Mald* (1985) decisions. A handful of states, including California, Oregon, Washington, Colorado, and Massachusetts, have struck the balance in favour of protecting freedom of expression by drawing on varied protections in their constitutions for speech on private property or for political purposes. In *New Jersey Coalition Against War in the Middle East* v. *J.M.B. Realty Corporation* (1994), the New Jersey State Supreme Court revived the Logan precedent. In a conscious test case of state law, Gulf War protesters attempted to leaflet ten major shopping centres across the state, but were permitted to do so at only two of them. The state court found not only that speech rights were protected on private property under their state constitution, but that, per *Logan*, shopping centres functioned as the "downtowns" – the public spaces – of suburbia, and so it extended leafletting rights to all major regional shopping centres in New Jersey.

STEPHANIE DYER

Further Reading

Brownstein, Alan E. and Stephen M. Hankins, "Pruning *Pruneyard*: Limiting Free Speech Rights under State Constitutions on the Property of Private Medical Clinics Providing Abortion Services", *U.C. Davis Law Review*, 24/4 (Summer 1991):1073

Jacobs, Leslie Gielow, "Even More Honest than Ever Before: Abandoning Pretense and Recreating Legitimacy in Constitutional Interpretation", *University of Illinois Law Review*, (1995): 363

Linzer, Peter, "Why Bother with State Bills of Rights?", *Texas Law Review*, 68 (1989–90):1573

Vasquez, John Michael, "New Jersey Constitution, Article I, Paragraphs 6 & 18 – Free Speech – Regional Shopping Malls Must Permit Leafletting on Societal Issues Subject to Reasonable Time, Place, and Manner Constraints Created by the Mall Owners – New Jersey Coalition against War in the Middle East v. J.M.B. Realty Corp", *Constitutional Law Journal*, 6 (1995–96):389

PROJECT CENSORED
US campaign against censorship, established 1976

Project Censored is an annual review of important news stories that have been overlooked or under-reported by the national news media in the United States. It was founded in 1976 by Carl Jensen, professor emeritus of communication studies at Sonoma State University in California. It is now the longest-running annual news media censorship research project in the world.

The primary goal of Project Censored is to improve media coverage of important public issues. It identifies and publicizes critical stories that have not been given sufficient coverage by the mainstream media, and educates the public by raising questions about censorship and the role of the media in a democratic society. Project Censored was founded upon the principle that real and meaningful public involvement in public decisions is possible only if all ideas are allowed to compete daily in the media marketplace for awareness, acceptance, and understanding. In brief, Project Censored defines censorship as the suppression of information, whether purposeful or not, by any method – including bias, omission, under-reporting or self-censorship – that prevents the public from knowing fully what is happening in society.

When Project Censored was created in 1976, the discussion of censorship focused basically on three categories: religious censorship, political censorship, and the censorship of obscenities. By adding a fourth important category – the censorship of news – Project Censored has ensured that the issue of news media self-censorship is a major topic of discussion in journalism today. The project suggests that news media self-censorship has weakened or broken the efforts of progressive individuals and movements by preventing people from being fully aware of critical issues they have raised.

Project Censored's activities revolve around the selection of the top ten censored news stories of each year. The process starts with the solicitation of under-covered stories. This effort now produces more than 1000 nominations annually from journalists, librarians, educators, and the general public. The nominated stories are reviewed and rated using a standardized format by more than 70 Sonoma State University faculty and community volunteers. To qualify, stories must deal with an issue of significant national or international impact, affect a large number of people, be well-documented, be timely, and have received little or no coverage in the mainstream media.

The stories are ranked in importance and reviewed for credibility and clarity. The top-ranked stories are submitted to student researchers in the "Media Censorship" seminar offered at Sonoma State University each autumn term. Upper-division students, previously trained in library research methods, review each story for the amount of media coverage it has received. In November, faculty and student researchers jointly select the top 25 most important under-published stories for the year. Finally, these top 25 stories are submitted to a panel of national judges for the final ranking of the top ten censored news stories of the year. The final results are reported in a book Censored: The News That Didn't Make the News, published annually in March by Seven Stories Press, New York.

A statistical analysis of the top 200 stories from the first 20 years of the project, as reported in 20 Years of Censored News, reveals that, while there are some variations from year to year, there has been a systematic omission of a select number of issues. The subjects most often censored since 1976 are political, corporate, international, and military issues.

Following are the number and percentage of all 200 censored stories by subject matter from 1976 to 1995:

Subjects	No. of Stories	Percentage
(1) Political	64	32.0
(2) Corporate	37	18.5
(3) International	30	15.0
(4) Military	28	14.0
(5) Environmental	15	7.5
(6) Health	13	6.5
(7) Media	7	3.5
(8) Economic	5	2.5
(9) Educational	1	0.5

The analysis also revealed that many of the issues originally cited by Project Censored still have not been covered by the media since they were first raised. Of the 200 censored issues, more than three-quarters of them are still classified as overlooked or censored by the mainstream media. Just 46 of the original stories have received significant attention by the press.

Some of the issues from the late 1970s that have been covered include: acid rain, the fight for the oceans' resources, cutting off gas and electricity for non-payment of bills by elderly people, and the commercialization of the Public Broadcasting System (PBS) in the United States. Examples among the 154 issues that have not yet been widely addressed include hazardous over-the-counter drugs, the Indonesian repression in East Timor, corporate control of DNA research, dumping banned pesticides and drugs on the Third World, inadequate nuclear power accountability and waste disposal, international human rights violations, the ongoing infant formula scandal, and the dangers of genetic uniformity.

The project believes these failures are not a conspiracy on the part of the media elite. News is too diverse, fast-breaking, and unpredictable to be controlled by some sinister, conservative media cabal. Instead, there is a congruence of attitudes and interests on the part of the owners and managers of mass media organizations. That non-conspiracy conspiracy, when combined with a variety of other factors, leads to the systematic failure of the news media to inform the public fully. While it is not an overt form of censorship, such as the kind observed in some authoritarian societies, it is nonetheless real and often equally as dangerous to the public's well-being.

Factors accounting for censorship include the following: the source for a story is not considered reliable (an official government representative or corporate executive is a reliable source; a freelance journalist or eyewitness citizen is not); the story doesn't have an easily identifiable "beginning, middle, and end" (acid rain just seemed to go on for ever and ever); the stories are considered to be "too complex" for the general public (nobody would understand the intricacies of the savings-

and-loan débâcle); stories are ignored because they haven't been "blessed" by *The New York Times* or the *Washington Post* (reporters and editors at most of the more than 1600 daily newspapers in the United States know that their news judgement isn't going to be challenged when they write and publish fashionable "follow-the-leader" stories, a practice that leads to the "pack" or "herd" phenomenon in journalism).

One major factor contributing to media self-censorship is that some stories are considered potentially libellous. Long and costly jury trials, settlements out of court, and occasional multimillion dollar judgements against the media have produced a massive chilling effect on the press and replaced copy editors with copy attorneys. An equally ominous sign for freedom of the press in the United States is the chilling effect of SLAPP suits – Strategic Lawsuits Against Public Participation. In early 1997, the Food Lion supermarket chain in Florida sued ABC-TV after the network aired an exposé of the supermarket's meat-packing procedures. Food Lion sued on the basis of a false job application by a journalist seeking access to the company, rather than libel, thereby circumventing libel laws designed to protect the press. In another suit, the beef producers in Texas sued television talk-show host Oprah Winfrey and others for "disparaging" its product, beef. Winfrey had aired a segment about "Mad Cow Disease", which the beef producers said led to a loss of sales.

However, Project Censored argues that the "bottom line" explanation for much of the self-censorship that occurs in America's mainstream media is the media's own bottom line – that is, its profits and losses. Corporate media executives perceive their primary, and often sole, responsibility to be the need to maximize profits for the next quarterly statement and not, as some critics say, to inform the public. Many of the stories annually cited by Project Censored do not support the financial interests of media publishers, owners, stockholders, or advertisers.

Investigative journalism also is more expensive than the "public stenography" school of journalism practised at many media outlets. There is also the "don't rock the boat" mentality that pervades corporate media boardrooms and then filters down to the newsroom. The latter influence has been exacerbated by the number of megamedia mergers in the 1990s. The need to play it safe has become more pervasive as the stakes become increasingly higher.

Through the years Project Censored has generated queries from journalists, scholars, and concerned citizens throughout the world. It was the model for Project Censored Canada, launched by the Canadian Association of Journalists and the Communication Department at Simon Fraser University, Vancouver, in 1994. In 1996, Carl Jensen retired as director of Project Censored and turned the operation over to Peter Phillips, assistant professor of sociology at Sonoma State University.

CARL JENSEN

Further Reading

Goldstein, Robert Justin (editor), *Political Censorship*, Chicago and London: Fitzroy Dearborn, 2001 (The New York Times Twentieth Century in Review)

Jensen, Carl and Project Censored, *20 Years of Censored News*, New York: Seven Stories Press, 1997

Jensen, Carl, *Stories That Changed America: Muckrakers of the 20th Century*, New York: Seven Stories Press, 2000

Phillips, Peter and Project Censored (editors), *Censored, 2001: The News That Didn't Make the News – the Year's Top 25 Censored Stories*, New York: Seven Stories Press, 2001

SERGEI PROKOFIEV
Russian composer, 1891–1953

Precociously gifted as a musician, Prokofiev studied composition privately with Reinhold Glière and entered the St Petersburg Conservatoire at the age of 13. There he studied composition with Nikolai Rimskii-Korsakov and Anatolii Liadov. Graduating from the conservatoire in 1914, he was awarded the Anton Rubinstein prize as pianist-composer for his First Piano Concerto (opus 10). He then established a formidable reputation as a modernist who was particularly attracted to grotesque and satirical images. Prokofiev gained his first widespread success with the "Classical" Symphony (the Symphony no. 1, op. 25), which was first performed in 1918.

Prokofiev left Russia in May 1918, and now attempted to forge a career as a pianist and composer outside his native country. His opera *Liubov'z k trem apelsinam* (op. 33, written 1919, premiered 1921, *The Love for Three Oranges*) was first performed in the United States, but Prokofiev's main centre of activity was Paris. There he became associated with Sergei Diaghilev, for whom he composed the ballets *Chout* (op. 21, 1921, *The Tale of the Buffoon*), *Le Pas d'acier* (op. 41, 1927, *The Steel Step*), and *L'Enfant prodigue* (op. 46, 1929, *The Prodigal Son*), and with the conductor Sergei Kussevitskii, who published and promoted his concert works. During this period of exile, Prokofiev visited Russia in 1927 and 1929, but in 1935 he decided to return permanently to Moscow. One of the most celebrated of 20th-century composers, his output includes seven symphonies, five piano concertos, two violin concertos, nine piano sonatas, the "musical tale" *Petia i volk* (op. 67, 1936, *Peter and the Wolf*), the cantata *Aleksandr Nevskii* (op. 78, based on the music that he had composed for Sergei Eisenstein's film in 1939), the ballets *Romeo i Dzhuletta* (op. 64, 1938, *Romeo and Juliet*) and *Zolushka* (op. 87, 1945, *Cinderella*), and the operas *Igrok* (op. 24, written 1917, premiered 1929, *The Gambler*), *Ognennyi Angel* (op. 37, written 1923, premiered 1954, *The Fiery Angel*), and *Voina i mir* (op. 91, 1943, *War and Peace*).

In comparison with Dmitrii Shostakovich, whose musical development was inextricably linked to the vicissitudes of Soviet cultural policy, Prokofiev was far less concerned with political issues. In exile he remained aloof from the conflicts that raged between the two main opposing factions in Soviet music – the "progressive" Association for Contemporary Music (ACM) which applauded his modernist credentials, and the more condemnatory attitudes of the Russian Association of Proletarian Musicians (RAPM), for whom a work such as *Le Pas d'acier*, a ballet about life in a Soviet steel factory, seemed among the worst manifestations of bourgeois decadence. By the early 1930s the debate had been resolved largely in favour of the reactionary "proletarians," but Prokofiev had also modified his style by this time, embracing a more lyrical and direct mode of expression.

Presumably this change of outlook, coupled with the composer's homesickness, contributed greatly to his decision to return to Russia, the country where he felt that he would secure a more appreciative audience. It was therefore unfortunate that Prokofiev's homecoming coincided with Stalin's brutal purge of cultural life. In 1936, the *Pravda* article condemning Shostakovich's opera *Ledi Makbet mtsenskovo uezda* (*Lady Macbeth of the Mtsensk District*) for its modernisms sent shockwaves throughout the musical profession in the Soviet Union. Yet for a time Prokofiev believed that he could remain immune from similar censure. To a certain extent, the immediate success of occasional works such as the Suite from *Lieutenant Kijé* (op. 60, 1933, drawn from the score composed in 1933 for the film *Poruchik Kizhe*) or *Peter and the Wolf* cushioned him from the realities of musical life in the Soviet Union at this time. On the other hand, Prokofiev experienced considerable difficulty in promoting some of his other compositions. In the repressive cultural environment, much of his output from the modernist period of the 1920s was dropped by Soviet performers. Prokofiev subsequently devoted a considerable amount of energy to revising such works in order to make them more palatable.

However, some of Prokofiev's more recent concert works, such as the *Symphonic Song* (op. 57, 1933) or the first version of the Cello Concerto (op. 58, 1938), in which he had genuinely attempted to write in a more accessible style, also met with total incomprehension. Further problems arose in connection with the massive *Cantata for the 20th Anniversary of the October Revolution*, which Prokofiev wrote in 1937. This daringly original score failed to please the authorities and was banned. During this period, Prokofiev also received a commission to compose the music for the ballet *Romeo and Juliet*. This work also ran into difficulties: the dancers found the musical idiom too complex, and the censors even tried to alter the scenario of Shakespeare's play to make its conclusion optimistic.

During World War II, censorship of the leading Soviet composers was considerably relaxed as all efforts were devoted to defeating the Germans and their allies. Prokofiev made his own notable contribution to the propaganda campaign through his music for *Aleksandr Nevskii* and *Ballada o mal'zchike, Ostavshemsia neizvestnym* (op. 93, 1944, *Ballad of an Unknown Boy*). He also composed *Zdravitsa* (op. 85, 1939, *Hail to Stalin*), a cantata for Stalin's 60th birthday in 1939. At the same time, Prokofiev's concert music reverted to a darker and sometimes more aggressive modernism. In particular, the Piano Sonatas nos. 6 to 8 (opp. 82–84, 1940, 1942, 1944) betray both the scars of war and the harshness of life under Stalin.

After 1945, Prokofiev provided a suitably festive response to the ending of hostilities with his grandiose *Ode to the End of War* (op. 105, 1945), but the originality of his conception resulted once again in a hostile response from the authorities. This antipathy was further intensified after the premiere of the Sixth Symphony (op. 111) in 1947, as the work was deemed too introverted and pessimistic for the enforced climate of postwar optimism. The following year Prokofiev, Shostakovich, Nikolai Miaskovskii, and Aram Khatchaturian were publicly condemned as "formalists" by Stalin's "cultural commissar", Andrei Zhdanov. Prokofiev's music disappeared from all concert programmes, despite his writing what Shostakovich describes (in his memoir *Testimony*, 1979) as a "rather dry, cold letter in which he, as it were, argued that he was guilty of certain errors".

Whereas Shostakovich's response to such public humiliation was to withdraw several of the works that he was currently writing, Prokofiev, already a sick man, tried to appease the authorities by adopting a simpler, more optimistic style. Yet many of his efforts proved futile. The opera *Povest' o nastoiashchem cheloveke* (op. 117, written 1948, premiered 1960, *The Story of a Real Man*), based on the heroic deeds of a wartime Soviet pilot, was rejected, and progress on the ballet *Skaz o kammenom tsvetke* (op. 118, 1954, *The Tale of the Stone Flower*) was disrupted by problems with the scenario. Although Prokofiev found solace through the staunch support of younger performers such as the pianist Sviatoslav Richter and the cellist Mstislav Rostropovich, his revision of the Cello Concerto as the Sinfonia Concertante for Cello and Orchestra (op. 125), first performed in 1952, met with a cool response. Tikhon Khrennikov, the powerful secretary of the Composers Union, declared the work to be "a depressing manifestation of senile degeneration".

However, the Seventh Symphony (op. 131, 1952) proved to be a triumph and helped to secure Prokofiev's gradual rehabilitation. In 1957 the work was awarded the Lenin Prize, and the same year saw the official repudiation of the Zhdanov decrees. Yet this reversal came far too late: Prokofiev had died an embittered man four years earlier, ironically on the same day as Stalin.

ERIK LEVI

Writings
Selected Letters, edited by Harlow Robinson, 1998

Further Reading
Jaffé, Daniel, *Sergey Prokofiev*, London: Phaidon, 1998

Krebs, Stanley D., *Soviet Composers and the Development of Soviet Music*, London: Allen and Unwin, and New York: Norton, 1970

Nest'ev, I.V., *Prokofiev*, Stanford, California: Stanford University Press, 1960

Robinson, Harlow, *Sergei Prokofiev: A Biography*, London: Hale, and New York: Viking, 1987

Samuel, Claude, *Prokofiev*, London: Calder and Boyars, and New York: Grossman, 1971

Savkina, Natalia, *Prokofiev*, Neptune City, New Jersey: Paganiniana, 1984

PROTAGORAS
Greek philosopher and teacher, c.490–420 BCE

Protagoras was born in Abdera, a city in remote north-east Greece. The most famous of the sophists (a sort of itinerant professor), he travelled widely throughout the Greek world. In Athens he became part of the circle of Pericles, who invited him to write the constitution for the Athenian colony of Thurii in southern Italy. As a teacher Protagoras was well respected, and he demanded a high fee for his instruction. Plato, no admirer of Protagoras' views, clearly regarded the famous sophist as being on a high intellectual and moral level.

His interests included theology, ethics, politics, rhetoric, education, and cultural studies. None of Protagoras' works, however, survives intact; what we know of his thought is fragmentary and comes from what is alleged or quoted by later writers. Two of his major treatises were entitled *Truth*, and *Antilogiae* (Contradictory Arguments). The work known to posterity as *On the Gods* may be, in fact, part of another treatise instead of a separate work devoted specifically to divinity. It is this work that is said to have been subject to the Greek equivalent of censorship.

The theoretical foundation of Protagoras' thought (and his most famous dictum) is that "man is the measure of all things, of things that are, that they are, and of things that are not, that they are not", by which he suggests that what seems real to an individual is real only subjectively. Applying this principle to rhetoric, Protagoras taught his students to argue both sides of a case; he was notorious for his claim that he could "make the weaker argument the stronger".

In considering the possibility of knowledge about the gods, Protagoras observes: "Concerning the gods I cannot know either that they exist or that they do not exist, or what form they might have, for there is much to prevent one's knowing: the obscurity of the subject and the shortness of man's life." Though he merely suggested that we must suspend judgement on these matters, this statement earned him a reputation for atheism. According to an ancient tradition Protagoras was prosecuted for impiety (*asebeia*), exiled, and his books burned in the marketplace, but Plato records that Protagoras died with his reputation intact.

Whether or not Protagoras was himself prosecuted, we know that in the late 430s BCE a decree was passed to impeach those who did not respect divine things or who taught theories about the heavens. Anaxagoras, Socrates, Diagoras, and Euripides were among those who were prosecuted for such impiety.

G.M. SOTER

Writings

In *The Older Sophists*, edited by Rosamond Kent Sprague, Columbia: University of South Carolina Press, 1972

Further Reading

Farrar, Cynthia, *The Origins of Democratic Thinking: The Invention of Politics in Classical Athens*, Cambridge and New York: Cambridge University Press, 1988

Guthrie, W.K.C., *The Sophists*, London: Cambridge University Press, 1971

Kerferd, G.B., *The Sophistic Movement*, Cambridge and New York: Cambridge University Press, 1981

Ostwald, Martin, *From Popular Sovereignty to the Sovereignty of Law: Law, Society, and Politics in Fifth-Century Athens*, Berkeley: University of California Press, 1986

Wallace, R.W., "Private Lives and Public Enemies: Freedom of Thought in Classical Athens" in *Athenian Identity and Civic Ideology*, edited by Alan A. Boegehold and Adele C. Scafuro, Baltimore: Johns Hopkins University Press, 1994

Wallace, R.W., "The Athenian Laws against Slander" in *Symposion 1993: Vorträge zur griechischen und hellenistischen Rechtsgeschichte*, edited by Gerhard Thür, Cologne: Böhlau, 1994.

BOLESŁAW PRUS
Polish novelist (real name: Aleksander Głowacki), 1847–1912

A leading chronicler of events in Poland in his time, and one of its most important novelists, Aleksander Głowacki, who was to become famous as Bolesław Prus, very early came into conflict with the Russian authorities governing the part of Poland in which he grew up. He fought and was wounded at Kielce during the national uprising of January 1863, and was jailed for his activities until October that year. He was released for a short time to continue his studies in Siedlec, but in 1864 he was rearrested and tried for his underground activities, this time being deprived of his title as a member of the gentry. He was eventually released into his aunt's custody because of his age (his parents had died in his infancy). By the time he returned to his studies again, this time at the Liceum in Lublin, he had undergone a radical change. As he wrote to a friend in 1865,

In the past during which you knew me – I no longer exist. The former "I" is buried along with my hopes ... a "busted" head, frequent faintness, and attacks of high blood pressure to the brain – that's what my past has given me.

By 1870 Głowacki had started publishing his first articles under the pen-name Bolesław Prus in the newspaper *Przegląd Tygodniowy* and in *Niwa* (1872), originally founded as a student publication associated with that paper. He began to make a name for himself as a gifted satirist and humorist, publishing his first pieces, including *Kroniki tygodniowe* (Weekly Chronicles), in *Mucha* (Fly), a leading satirical journal, and giving a series of popular public readings. Although his work for *Mucha* lasted only a year, a longstanding association with the *Kurier Warszawski* (Warsaw Courier), and after 1887, with the *Kurier Codzienny* (Daily Courier), established Prus's reputation as a leading journalist and commentator, often on the most controversial issues of the day, including "the Jewish question", socialism, and women's suffrage. During longrunning public debates, conducted in the pages of *Nowiny* (News) until its closure in 1883, and then in the *Kurier Warszawski* and the *Kurier Codzienny*, Prus was often attacked and forced to defend himself. He also came under fire from the authorities and conservative circles for his strong support of the *bezpłatne czytelnie*, the free reading rooms organized by the Warszawskie Towarzystwo Dobroczynności (WTD, Warsaw Charitable Society) to raise the educational level and literacy rate among workers. By 1895 the reading rooms were becoming more strictly monitored by the authorities, following complaints by the WTD's conservative president, prince Radziwiłł, that some members were distributing antireligious and socialist literature. In 1899, the reading rooms were closed altogether and their leading members were arrested after persistent press attacks on them by a leading anti-Semite, Jan Jeleński, in his magazine *Rola*.

Prus began publishing fiction in the early 1880s. *Grzechy dzieciństwa* (The Sins of Childhood) and *Omyłka* (The Mistake) appeared between 1883 and 1885. In 1885, his first full-length novel, *Placówka* (The Outpost), which concerns the Polish peasants' struggles with the Germans over land, was serialized in the magazine *Wędriowiec*. It is not known to what extent these earlier works were censored, but a series of letters from Prus to his editor at *Kraj*, where instalments of *Omyłka* first appeared in 1884, give us a good sense of how intensive and intrusive censors were in scrutinizing his work generally. After pleading with his editors not to agree to any changes in work so intensely concentrated that "each paragraph bears an organic meaning", Prus revised the manuscript himself, twice changing its title, from *Szpieg* (The Spy) to *Vox populi* (The People's Voice) and then to the title by which it is known today. When the manuscript was returned by the censor Prus was horrified at the number of passages that had been cut wholesale, and asked his editors to allow him to publish the instalment simultaneously in the *Gazeta Lwówska* in Galicia, the Austrian sector of Poland, where the censors were far more liberal. However, while offering to let the piece run serially in the two papers, they refused to permit simultaneous publication.

Prus's next major work was *Emancypantki*, which began to appear in instalments in the *Kurier Codzienny* at the end of 1891 (it came out in book form in 1893). Its theme is the movement for the emancipation of women. Prus himself made extensive changes and cuts in the second edition, published in 1903, two years before the outbreak of the revolution of 1905–06. Whether these were intended to forestall the censors is not known.

It is now also thought that one of Prus's other works, *Z legend dawnego Egiptu* (1887, From the Legends of Ancient Egypt), which was a radical departure for so committed a realist as Prus, represents the transfer to ancient Egypt of the infighting in Germany between the liberal and reactionary wings of the government, as exemplified by Bismarck, William I, and his son Frederick III. Prus had followed the struggle between the two camps closely, as entries in his *Kroniki* for the years 1887–88 indicate. *Z legend dawnego Egiptu* is thus probably an important example of self-censorship.

Of all Prus's novels, none suffered as much from censorship as *Lalka* (The Doll). First serialized in the *Kurier Codzienny* between 1887 and 1899, it subsequently appeared in book form in 1890. The design of the work had been, for Prus, all-important, revisiting what was for him and many others the formative experience of his generation – the uprising of 1863 – together with its role in shaping the attitudes and fortunes of Poles of all classes living in the Russian sector. It was exactly the kind of work that censors were most likely to find offensive, and to alter radically. Anticipating such problems, Prus had already submitted a toned-down manuscript of *Lalka* to them, but excluded any description of the outbreak of the January uprising.

As Zygmunt Szweykowski points out, however, while censors often required the authors of serialized texts to change or even omit entire chapters before they went to press, forcing them to substitute entirely different material, the authorities had neither the time nor resources to apply the same level of care that they took with manuscripts to such work. It was therefore often possible to slip in whole passages of news copy that would never have made it into book form. As a result, when *Lalka* finally came out as a book, it had undergone even more extensive censorship, with new omissions that further deformed it. Szweykowski, who has made a detailed study of both the serialized and book versions of *Lalka*, points to several such important passages missing from the book but allowed to be printed in the *Kurier*.

One of the most important is a diary entry describing the contacts in revolutionary and nihilist circles made by a young Pole named Mraczewski while working in Moscow. Passages such as the following, recording Mraczewski's conversation with one of the revolutionaries, gives a powerful sense of the influence such ideas had on Polish youth, and not surprisingly the censors removed it:

> He also said that when the revolution begins . . . from that moment on we shall be working only an eight-hour day, while we use the rest of the day to have a good time, and moreover that everyone will get an old age pension and free burial. At last, he ended by saying that only then will there be Heaven on Earth, with everything being shared in common: land, buildings, machines, and even wives.

Likewise, all traces of one of the chief character's exile to Siberia, following his participation in the uprising, were systematically erased by the censors. Even a reference to this character's "red hands", which in the *Kurier* version are described as resulting from their having been "frozen . . . in Siberia", were omitted from the book, replaced by dialogue in which the resulting gap is obvious. Finally, no mention whatever of the participation in the uprising by two Jewish characters was allowed. (These scenes had been intended by Prus to demonstrate, not the loyalty of the Jews to the Polish cause, but rather their "gift for adaptability" – an indication that he was not free from what may politely be called a certain tendency to sterotyping.) Nor did the censors permit an instalment focused on a Russian administrator, portrayed sympathetically.

One of Prus's aims in *Lalka* was to illuminate the chaotic atmosphere in which the industrial boom of the latter part of the century had taken place; to do so, he had planned to portray three generations of the aristocracy, the gentry, the bourgeoisie, and the growing urban proletariat. In fact, as Prus always emphasized, the original title of *Lalka* had been *Trzy pokole-*

nia (Three Generations), and only later, and quite by accident, after Prus had read an excerpt from a trial involving the theft of a child's doll, had the latter title come to him. In design, *Lalka* was to be an epic, panoramic work, its temporal frame extending from 1840 to 1879, and the city of Warsaw was to play an especially important role. The experiences of its numerous characters were intended to offer a collective portrayal of the entire nation in crisis by "presenting a social portrait in cross-section in its entirety", as Szweykowski puts it. Increasingly pessimistic after 1883, Prus also meant to expose and dissect both the intelligentsia, "foreign to itself and to the nation", and the "dreamer syndrome" so fatal to Poland. A key element in the novel's success in carrying out these ambitious plans is Prus's ability to portray in detail the changing circumstances of his leading characters. The omission of such a central experience as exile to Siberia seriously damaged Prus's ability to evoke his chosen subjects, both thematically and atmospherically. Likewise, they interfered with his desire to demonstrate how the aristocratic values that had first been transferred to the gentry and were now filtering down to the bourgeoisie were harming the nation.

Self-censorship also played a crucial role in determining the book's final shape. As Józef Bachórz has pointed out, "people never discuss the occupation, but even behind the four walls of their own rooms they feel it". Whenever any topic that could be interpreted as political is discussed, it is in whispers. On one occasion, when a character mentions the arrest of a group of students, he does so in half-sentences and words only half-uttered. However, at a different and more sophisticated level, self-censorship was also used to great effect to signal the very repression that made it necessary. A complete absence of certain monuments and buildings indelibly associated in his readers' minds with the Russian occupation, including the Zamek (the official residence of the governor-general of Warsaw), the governor-general's palace, and the barracks of the Russian soldiers, is striking, while the Citadel and the Belvedere Palace, one of the other main centres of the Russian administration, are mentioned only to orient the reader topographically. Nor is there any reference to the fact that Warsaw's students are enrolled in a Russian university, or to the many Russian Orthodox churches found in the capital during this period. Such omissions signal not only the distaste that Prus felt for the Russian presence, but the ability of many residents of Warsaw to screen it out altogether.

HELENA K. KAMINSKI

Writings

"Co to jest socjalizm", in *Nowiny*, 1883
Lalka, 1890; as *The Doll*, translated by David Welsh, 1972
Faraon, 1897; as *Pharaoh*, translated by Christopher Kasparek, 1991
Pisma (Writings), edited by Zygmunt Szweykowski, 29 vols, 1948–52
Kroniki (Chronicles), edited by Zygmunt Szweykowski, 20 vols, 1953–70

Further Reading

Cała, Alina, *Asymilacja Żydów w Królestwie Polskim 1864–1897: postawy, konflikty, stereotypy*, Warsaw: PIW, 1989
Godlewski, Stefan *et al.*, *Śladami Wokulskiego: Przewodnik literacki po warszawskich realiach "Lalki"*, Warsaw: Czytelnik, 1957
Jeż, T.T., *W sprawie powieści ("Lalka" B. Prusa)*, *Świat*, 9 (1891)
Kott, Jan, *O "Lalce" "Bolesława Prusa"*, Warsaw: Ksizaka Wiedza, 1950
Kulczycka-Saloni, Janina, "Warszawa w oczach Prusa i Żeromskiego" in her *Pozytywizm i Żeromski*, Wrocław: Ossolińskich, 1977
Markiewicz, Henryk, "*Lalka*" Bolesława Prusa, Warsaw, 1951
Markiewicz, Henryk, *O Prusie i o Żeromskim: Prace Wybrane*, vol. 1, Cracow: Universitas, 1995
Tomkowski, Jan, "Neurotyczni bohaterowie powieści Prusa" *Pamiętnik Literacki*, 2 (1986)

WILLIAM PRYNNE
English barrister and pamphleteer, 1600–1669

Prynne is probably best known for his *Histriomastix* (1633), an attack on the "immoralities" of the English theatre and such other "intolerable mischiefs to churches, to republics, manners, minds, and souls of men" as hunting and dancing. However, such an attack would not necessarily have attracted much attention if it had not been accompanied by a denunciation of those "who now erect crucifixes and images in our churches, contrary to our articles, injunctions, homilies, canons, stations, and writing".

Prynne was in the right about the formal legal situation. Although Elizabeth I had kept a crucifix in her own chapel and had been appalled at the widespread violence against traditional imagery in the 1560s, her injunctions of 1559 had perhaps encouraged the violence, by ordering the destruction of

> all shrines, covering of shrines, all tables, candlesticks and rolls of wax, pictures, paintings, and all other monuments . . . so that there remains no memory of the same in walls, glasses, windows or elsewhere.

The memory often did remain, nevertheless, and, half a century later, a revival of interest in the decoration of churches was led by the archbishop of Canterbury, William Laud. He himself provided money for new stained glass at some of the Oxford colleges, the law courts, Lincoln's Inn in London, and his own London residence, Lambeth Palace. At Chester and Durham cathedrals, likewise, replacements were made for glass that had suffered at the hands of principled iconoclasts. To Prynne and his fellow puritans, it appeared that the English Reformation was being rolled back and the bishops restored to their former power. For Laud, however, Prynne's attack was not just against the episcopal nature of the Church of England but against king Charles I, who was a supporter of what has since become known as the "high church" movement.

Tried by the Star Chamber, England's highest judicial chamber, in February 1633, Prynne was given an extreme sentence: cropping of his ears, whipping, and imprisonment. This was not sufficient to silence him. While he was in prison, he started to write *News from Ipswich*, a further violent attack on

Laud's policies, which was published in 1636. This time Prynne was tried for "seditious libel", along with John Bastwick, whose recent pamphlet *Apologeticus ad Praesules Anglicanos* had attacked the High Commission, part of the apparatus of church and state censorship, and who had earlier declined to retract his views "till Doomsday, in the afternoon". Prynne's purpose in writing *News from Ipswich* had been to reveal "certain late detestable practices of some domineering lordly prelates", in particular Matthew Wren, bishop of Norwich (the diocese to which the town of Ipswich then belonged). Prynne had inveighed against "Romish innovations, whereat the whole kingdom cry shame, which breeds a general fear of a sudden alteration of our religion". It was also a cry for resistance:

> Wherefore, England, o England, if ever thou wilt be free from fasts and judgements, take notice of these thy anti-Christian prelates, desperate practices, innovations, and popish designs, to bewail, oppose, redress them with all thy force and power.

Prynne's punishment was even more severe than for *Histriomastix*: complete loss of his ears; branding of his cheeks with the initials "SL", meaning "seditious" or "schismatical libeller", but signifying, according to Prynne, *stigmata Laudis* ("wounds of Laud" or "wounds of praise"); and permanent imprisonment in Caernarvon Castle in northwest Wales.

Bans on his pamphlets had, however, been completely ineffective. We know, for instance, that Peter Ince, a Chester stationer, had stocked and sold copies, including some to Calvin Bruen of Bruen Stapleford, a fervent and active puritan like his father before him. Ince and Bruen met Prynne en route to Caernarvon. Extempore prayers were said and Bruen was later charged with "procuring the picture of the said Mr Prynne to be drawn by a limner in Chester". Five copies were made, which the authorities ordered to be "spoiled and defaced". They had, in fact, already been burned, but, so anxious were officials to make sure that no "relics" of Prynne's visits remained that the frames that had held the pictures were also publicly burned at Chester High Cross on 12 December 1637. This represented an interesting turning of the tables on the iconoclasts. Bruen, meanwhile, was fined £800, an enormous sum.

Prynne was released by the Long Parliament in November 1640, but continued to be an oppositionist, though now, it seems, with less reason or cogency. He alleged that Oliver Cromwell's New Model Army was being infiltrated by Catholics, and declared that the execution of the former king, Charles Stuart, in 1649 was "nothing else but the designs of Jesuits, popish priests, and recusants". In one of those reversals that occur regularly in the history of censorship, Prynne welcomed the restoration of Charles II in 1660 and was appointed keeper of the records of the Tower of London, the fortress in which he had been imprisoned in 1633.

DEREK JONES

Writings

Histriomastix: The Players Scourge or Actors Tragedy, 1633; reprinted, with a preface by Arthur Freeman, 1974
News from Ipswich, 1636

Further Reading

Aston, Margaret, "Puritans and Iconoclasts, 1560–1660" in *The Culture of English Puritanism, 1560–1700*, edited by Christopher Durston and Jacqueline Eales, Basingstoke: Macmillan, 1996
Coward, Barry, *The Stuart Age: England, 1603–1714*, 2nd edition, London: Longman, 1994
Lamont, William M., *Marginal Prynne*, London: Routledge, 1963

PSYCHIATRY USED IN CENSORSHIP
Soviet Union, 1950s to 1980s

The regular use of psychiatry to repress dissenters in the Soviet Union was inaugurated in the last years of Nikita Khrushchev's regime (1953–64). In the 1970s, under his successor Leonid Brezhnev, the system of "special" psychiatric hospitals became one of the standard tools to silence voices of criticism, although, as we shall see, ordinary psychiatric hospitals were also used for the same purpose. As the testimony of victims became known in the West, the practice was officially condemned by international groups, such as the World Psychiatric Association in 1977. Mikhail Gorbachev's policies of glasnost (openness) and perestroika (restructuring) led to repeal of the laws defining "anti-Soviet" crimes and the release of the "special" hospitals' inmates in 1988 and 1989. Nonetheless, even under Yeltsin in the 1990s, the Russian government did not remove the official stigma in the documents of survivors, nor did professional medical associations in Russia admit the extent of earlier misuse.

Khrushchev released political prisoners from Stalinist camps and began investigating the sporadic use of psychiatry to repress and censor. By 1959, however, the tide of reform had receded. Now Khrushchev blamed "mental disorders" for the resurgence of crime in Soviet society. Forensic psychiatrists, especially those in the Serbskii Institute in Moscow, took the cue to extend the diagnosis of schizophrenia to dissidents, who were said to be suffering from "reformist delusions". New facilities were added to the special psychiatric hospital system under the Ministry of Interior (the MVD).

Controls were tightened further in the Brezhnev era (1964–83). To muzzle critics while maintaining an aura of "socialist legality", officials either charged them with a crime such as "anti-Soviet agitation and propaganda" (under article 70 of the Russian criminal code), or used civil legal procedures to confine anyone found "dangerous to society or to himself". It went worse for those accused of political crimes. After being tried *in absentia*, they were routinely found nonaccountable by reason of insanity and sent for indefinite terms to one of about 15 special psychiatric hospitals. There they were incarcerated amid murderers and other violent psychotics. Their treatment had no recognized therapeutic effect; it consisted of injections with sulphazine, causing high fever; "wet wraps" of canvas strips, which constricted upon drying around an inmate's body until he lost consciousness; and insulin shock therapy.

Civil commitment for persons not accused of crimes was employed to brand dissidents as insane in order to discredit their ideas and provide a pretext to lock them up for relatively short periods in "ordinary" psychiatric hospitals. For example, the noted biologist Zhores Medvedev was forcibly taken to the Kaluga mental hospital because he had advocated free exchanges with western colleagues. Medvedev was released on 17 June 1970, after only 19 days, as a result of a campaign waged by his twin brother Roy among leading Soviet scientists. Aleksandr Solzhenitsyn declared at the time that "Soviet psychiatrists who break their Hippocratic oath are able to describe concerns for social problems as 'mental illness', [and] can declare a man insane for being too passionate or being too calm". He likened these practices to Nazi genocide, a kind of "spiritual murder", in which "the condemned suffer torments more fruitful and prolonged".

The spurious nature of diagnoses by expert psychiatric witnesses in criminal cases became evident to western observers in the spring of 1971, when Vladimir Bukovskii circulated dossiers on six nonviolent protesters, general Petr Grigorenko, Viktor Fainberg, Nataliia Gorbanevskaia, Vladimir Borisov, Viktor Kuznetsov, and Ivan Iakhimovich. Grigorenko had capped a distinguished military career by becoming a leader of the Democratic Movement in Moscow. A psychiatric commission of the Serbskii Institute had diagnosed him in April 1964 as having a "paranoid development of the personality, with reformist ideas". His forced hospitalization for this "condition" prevented him from making an articulate defence at a public trial. Grigorenko resumed his campaigns upon his release, and was rearrested while defending the Tatar movement in Tashkent. The local medical commission found him sane, but it was overruled by the Serbskii doctors, who ordered Grigorenko to undergo a new round of compulsory treatment in November 1969 for "reformist ideas, of which he is unshakeably convinced".

Fainberg, a philologist, and Gorbanevskaiia, a poet, were both arrested for demonstrating against the Warsaw Pact invasion of Czechoslovakia in August 1968. Both had records of emotional difficulties in their teenage years, which allowed Serbskii doctors to claim that they were justified in diagnosing them as having *vialotekushchaiia* (sluggish) schizophrenia. This clinical term had been coined by Dr Andrei Snezhnevskii, a senior figure among forensic psychiatrists, to account for the "outwardly correct behaviour" of persons who became dissidents, as shown by their "stubbornness and inflexibility of convictions".

The sanity of dissidents who had been released from special psychiatric hospitals has been attested, not only by western psychiatrists re-examining them, but also by Soviet observers, including Aleksandr Podrabinek, a Moscow paramedic who organized an unofficial "working commission to investigate the use of psychiatry for political purposes" in 1977. A number of Soviet psychiatrists also expressed their disagreement with official diagnoses. Dr Semen Gluzman was given a ten-year term in 1972, of which he served seven in a labour camp, the remaining three in internal exile. Dr Iuryii Novikov, a secretary of the All-Union Society of Neurologists and Psychiatrists, said in 1977, "There can be no doubt that psychiatric knowledge is abused in the USSR. In Soviet society any deviation from the officially prescribed norm is regarded as a symptom of mental illness." Dr Anatolii Koriagin was given a seven-year sentence in 1981 for finding that none of the 16 inmates of special psychiatric hospitals whom he had examined should have been hospitalized.

At its height, this misuse of psychiatry affected about a thousand inmates of special hospitals. It was frightening to many other potential dissidents, not as mass terror but as a deterrent. Virtually all such patients were released under Gorbachev, and a new mental health law enacted in Russia in 1992 brought "coercive psychiatry within the rule of law" and established "safeguards against violations of human rights", according to Richard J. Bonnie, a law professor at the University of Virginia. Yet no official apology has ever been issued for past abuses, and the survivors are still listed on police rosters as ex-patients.

HARVEY FIRESIDE

Further Reading

Bloch, Sidney and Peter Reddaway, *Psychiatric Terror: How Soviet Psychiatry Is Used to Suppress Dissent*, New York: Basic Books, 1977

Bukovsky, Vladimir, *To Build a Castle: My Life as a Dissenter*, New York: Viking, 1978

Fireside, Harvey, *Soviet Psychoprisons*, New York: Norton, 1979

Grigorenko, P.G., *The Grigorenko Papers*, Boulder, Colorado: Westview Press, and London: Hurst, 1976

Khodorovich, Tatyana (editor), *The Case of Leonid Plyushch*, Boulder, Colorado: Westview Press, and London: Hurst, 1976

Medvedev, Zhores A. and Roy A. Medvedev, *A Question of Madness*, New York: Knopf, and London: Macmillan, 1971

Nekipelov, Victor, *Institute of Fools: Notes from the Serbsky*, edited and translated by Marco Carynnyk and Marta Horban, New York: Farrar Straus, and London: Gollancz, 1980

Podrabinek, Alexander, *Punitive Medicine*, Ann Arbor, Michigan: Karoma, 1980

US Senate, Committee on the Judiciary, *Abuse of Psychiatry for Political Repression in the Soviet Union*, Washington, DC: US Government Printing Office, 1972

PSYCHOANALYSING DIANA
British television drama-documentary, 1996

On 2 May 1996, John Willis, director of programmes at Channel 4, one of the five national terrestrial television companies in Britain, issued a statement announcing the withdrawal of *Psychoanalysing Diana*, a half-hour drama-documentary on Diana, Princess of Wales, which had been scheduled for transmission on 7 May as part of the channel's *Without Walls* series on contemporary culture. The programme had been produced by Panoptic Productions and showed a Diana lookalike (played by Nicky Lilley) revealing details about her unhappy childhood, tumultuous royal marriage, and precarious mental state to a Freudian psychoanalyst (played by Dylan Evans). It was built around fragments of five on-the-couch sessions, interspersed with dramatized reconstructions of some traumatic events from Diana's childhood, such as the departure of her mother when she was six, and rounded off with added commentaries by the analyst, spoken directly to the camera. When writing the script of *Psychoanalysing Diana*, Dylan Evans (a psychoanalyst in private practice, who also worked for the clinical psychology department of an NHS trust in South London) relied mainly on statements made by Diana during a television interview with BBC journalist Martin Bashir on 20 November 1995. He supplemented these materials with quotations included in Andrew Morton's biographical accounts of the princess, and with his own views on how Diana would have replied to his psychoanalytic probings.

The official Channel 4 press release of 2 May stated that John Willis and chief executive Michael Grade had decided "after the normal editorial process of viewings within the Channel . . . that the idea did not work". Such self-imposed censorship was extremely unusual for Channel 4, a company which takes pride in its resistance to restrictions imposed by the moral majority. As a matter of fact, censorship within Channel 4 had not occurred since 1987, and it was unprecedented for a programme to be called off five days before its screening and after preview tapes had been sent to the media. In an attempt to explain the decision, some of the tabloids suggested that the programme was called off after Diana's personal feeling that the programme constituted "mental rape" had been conveyed to Michael Grade. Yet Grade was adamant that the cancellation had not been influenced by royal pressure from either the princess or the palace: he maintained that the concept had merely proved inadequate and that the whole thing was of limited significance.

Although there is no evidence to prove this, it may be that Willis and Grade gave way to the avalanche of blistering attacks in the media after news of the programme broke around the end of February 1996. In general, criticisms fell within one or more of the following categories: betrayal of the therapeutic profession, unauthorized intrusion into somebody's private life, unwarranted speculation about an individual's mental state, or the questionable reputation of the analyst. Representatives of the British Psychological Society, the British Confederation of Psychotherapists, and the British Association of Psychotherapists all scorned Dylan Evans for presenting psychotherapy in a misleading way and contributing to its already distorted public image. Investigating the psychoanalyst's motives for

engaging in such a programme, some journalists argued that he was only trying to cash in on the rampant Diana-hype, while others went further and questioned the value of Dylan Evans's own analytic training. A recurrent criticism was that some of the analyst's interpretations were extremely harsh and intrusive, especially when he postulated a link between Diana's marriage to Prince Charles and her unresolved maternal love for her brother, and when he explained her ambiguous relationship with men via the mechanism of consumption and regurgitation which purportedly governed Diana's notorious eating disorders. Raj Persaud, the UK's most popular "media shrink", vilified the way in which the programme presented psychoanalytic interpretations as certainties. This criticism was strengthened by fellow psychiatrists, who emphasized that *Psychoanalysing Diana* obviously staged an encounter between two people who had never really met.

On the day when the programme had been scheduled for screening, Dylan Evans published a reply to his critics in *The Guardian*, elucidating his motives and accusing the British press of hypocrisy. To the claim that it is wrong to put a person whom you do not know "on the couch", Evans retorted that this is common practice in the British media: indeed, in his *Daily Mail* column, Raj Persaud had considered the possibility of a borderline personality disorder in Diana after her 1995 interview. He concluded that the fuss was really about psychoanalysis rather than the invasion of privacy. He also reiterated that most of the words spoken by the Diana lookalike had been taken from sources which were in the public domain and which the princess had never repudiated. Tackling the vexed issue of consent, Evans referred to a statement by Lord Wakeham, chairman of the Press Complaints Commission, which was made shortly before Diana's 1995 interview with Bashir, in which he had conceded: "Where a member of the royal family seeks to put a matter into the public domain – through a public interview – that, too, becomes a matter of national interest on which comment and reporting are legitimate and predictable." Finally, Evans deplored the fact that, despite his explicit request, Channel 4 had not sent a copy of the programme to the princess a week before the broadcasting. In his view, this could only have confirmed the press's representation of the programme as a dubious, "sick" show, whereas it had actually been conceived as a defence of Diana's sanity.

The entire debate surrounding *Psychoanalysing Diana* raises a number of interesting questions, including the extent to which the media can be allowed to enter the lives of individuals, its role in inducing censorship, the relation between the private and the public, the boundary between truth and fiction, and the representation of psychoanalysis. Some of these issues resurfaced following the tragic death of Diana on 31 August 1997, for which a cohort of unscrupulous paparazzi was held partly responsible. However, Diana's demise did not revive any memories of the programme that was banned during the spring of 1996, and in which the lookalike at one point expressed her anger at the media by using the "F-word". Any reconsiderations of the programme's value were perhaps unpronounced for fear of being perceived as royal necrophilia. Until further notice, the tape of *Psychoanalysing Diana* remains buried in the archives of Channel 4.

DANY NOBUS

Further Reading

Morton, Andrew, *Diana: Her True Story*, London: O'Mara, and New York: Simon and Schuster, 1992; revised edition 1997

PSYCHOANALYSIS

Although it is rarely noted as such, censorship is a key psychoanalytic concept, which was introduced by Sigmund Freud (1856–1939) in the final chapter of *Studies on Hysteria*, his 1895 book written in conjunction with Josef Breuer (1842–1925). In an attempt to explain why his hysterical patients had difficulty recalling traumatic life events, Freud claimed that each time the memory of such an event was on the verge of entering consciousness, the patient's ego exercised a kind of defence or censorship (*Zensur*) against it, because of its incompatibility with the prevailing set of ideas in the ego. In *The Interpretation of Dreams* (1900), Freud extrapolated from this process of psychic censorship in hysteria to account for the bizarrerie of normal dream content, which he considered to be the result of an unconscious (repressed, sexual, and unpleasurable) wish seeking to express itself and a censoring agency countering this force. To Freud, censorship in dreams did not entail the complete eradication of the unconscious wish, but rather its recasting into a psychically acceptable format via various types of distortion (*Entstellung*), of which the most significant are displacement (*Verschiebung*, a central idea becoming peripheral and vice versa), condensation (*Verdichtung*, the creation of a new hybrid idea out of multifarious original ones), and secondary revision (*Sekundäre Bearbeitung*, adding elements to improve coherence). Summarizing the essence of this process, Freud asserted, "It lies in the very nature of every censorship that of forbidden things it allows those which are untrue to be said rather than those which are true" (*The Interpretation of Dreams*).

Within his first threefold topographical model of the psychic apparatus, which distinguished between the unconscious, the pre-conscious, and consciousness, Freud located censorship on the boundary of the unconscious and the pre-conscious, which explains why it is equally active during sleep, when consciousness is temporarily cancelled out. However, in a 1915 essay on *The Unconscious*, he also conjectured a form of censorship between the pre-conscious and consciousness, suggesting that before an unconscious idea can reach consciousness, it must pass through two distorting barriers, in accordance with the triune hierarchy in the mind. After 1923, when he devised the second topographical model of the Id, the Ego, and the Superego, Freud scarcely ever invoked censorship, and when he did draw attention to its mechanism, it was always in the context of a discussion on dream formation. Freud generally attributed censorship to the Ego, the agency that safeguards psychic integrity, although he also discerned a form of censorship exercised by conscience, a function that he ultimately allocated to the Superego. As in the previous framework, censorship seemed to impose itself under two avatars here, the first one acting upon impulses coming from the Id, the second restricting the freedom of expression of the Ego.

The broad Freudian definition of censorship, then, is an operation that distorts original but unpalatable ideas in such a way that they become acceptable and can be integrated into a reigning psychic and/or social ideology. Using this definition, it is remarkable how often Freudian psychoanalysis itself has suffered from censorship since its inception around the turn of the last century. Censorship, in a psychoanalytic sense, has affected psychoanalysis over the last 90 years in at least three different ways. First, Freud's theory has regularly been streamlined by his own pupils, sometimes giving rise to psychoanalytic frameworks that, apart from their inspiration, can no longer be classified as Freudian. Second, Freud's legacy has often been "purified", or even outlawed, following the patterns of cultural inheritance and the peremptory political decrees within a given social environment. Finally, many published sections of Freud's private correspondence with colleagues and friends, which are of particular historical significance, contain numerous omissions imposed by his descendants, and a large number of Freud documents have been placed under embargo at the Library of Congress in Washington DC, some until the end of the 21st century.

The first case of censorship of Freudian psychoanalysis by one of Freud's own pupils exploded around 1910, when Freud publicly criticized Alfred Adler (1870–1937) for trying to transform psychoanalysis into a new general psychology by ruling out sexuality and the unconscious, and by rephrasing radical insights (such as repression) in shallow, watered-down terms (such as masculine protest). The conflict escalated, and Adler eventually resigned from Freud's circle to develop his own theory of "individual psychology": this promoted the notions of "organ inferiority", "psychical compensation", and "community spirit", and was quite successful in the United States during the 1930s. Shortly after Adler's dissent, Freud had to deal with yet another attempt to decapitate his brainchild, this time by Carl Gustav Jung (1875–1961), the crown prince of the early movement on whom Freud had pinned all his hopes for the future of psychoanalysis. Like Adler, Jung was apprehensive about the central place accorded to sexuality in Freudian psychoanalysis, arguing instead that libido ought to be interpreted as general interest and that religious feelings are a more crucial component for mental health than sexual pleasures. After a long epistolary debate on these issues with his mentor, Jung withdrew from Freudian circles and devoted himself to the deployment of his "analytical psychology", the cornerstones of which are the "collective unconscious", the "archetypes", and the "animus/anima". Obviously, neither Adler nor Jung would have admitted that their lifework was based on an inaugural censorship of Freudian psychoanalysis, yet this is how their divergence was perceived by Freud himself: in his reply to Adler, Freud decried the distortion of his theory and the association of its controversial concepts with common-sense psychology. Both Adlerian and Jungian theories are still commonly regarded as stemming from a primary expunction of sex from the Freudian corpus.

From the 1930s, a new psychoanalytic paradigm started to take shape, which quickly passed as Freudian orthodoxy and which gathered momentum in the United States during the postwar years. Its chief proponents highlighted the function of the Ego in the mind and exchanged Freud's notion of the "death drive" for a less speculative and more clinically recognizable "destruction tendency". This repudiation of the death drive in "Ego psychoanalysis" constitutes yet another mordant example of how Freud's ideas have been censored by some of his most loyal followers. Freud must surely have anticipated this censorship when he adduced the concept in 1920, but he did not live to see its gradual rise to general acceptance.

The enormous boom of psychoanalysis in the US was to a high degree brought about by the pleiad of Jewish psychoanalysts who emigrated to the New World after Hitler's appointment as German chancellor, the public burning of Freud's books in Berlin on 10 May 1933, and the German Anschluss of Austria in March 1938. The political success of the Nazi Party affected the German Psychoanalytic Association (GPA) and the Berlin Psychoanalytic Institute, both of which were controlled by Max Eitingon (1881–1943), a Russian Jew who had been one of Freud's confidants for more than twenty years. When the Nazis decreed in the spring of 1933 that Jews were not allowed to sit on the council of any medical organization, Eitingon's responsibilities were taken over by Felix Boehm (1881–1958) and Carl Müller-Braunschweig (1881–1958), two of the few non-Jewish psychoanalysts in Berlin. Eitingon's forced resignation signalled the beginning of a progressive Aryanization of psychoanalysis in Germany. By the end of 1935, the GPA had lost all its Jewish members and trainees, and psychoanalysis itself was increasingly portrayed as a deleterious "Jewish science", despite Müller-Braunschweig's efforts to describe its potentially beneficial effects for the Nazi Volksgemeinschaft. After lobbying officials at the Interior Ministry for the protection of psychoanalysis, Boehm was offered the opportunity to liaise with other (Adlerian and Jungian) psychotherapeutic groups in a new institute directed by Matthias Göring (1879–1945), an established Adlerian psychotherapist and a cousin of the Reich Marshal Hermann Göring. The remaining members of the GPA agreed, but, rather than continuing as analysts, they found themselves obliged to practise "new German psychotherapy" (neue Deutsche Seelenheilkunde) and to change the bulk of their standard working vocabulary (integrating new terms such as "hereditary biology", and replacing psychoanalysis with "depth psychology" and the Oedipus complex with the "family complex"). Following the German invasion of Austria, the Vienna Psychoanalytic Institute was dissolved in August 1938, and Freud's works were officially banned in the entire Reich. During the war, the Göring Institute's mission statement included scientific research on public health, race, and psychic development; the psychotherapeutic treatment of war neurotics; the selection and training of soldiers; and the general assurance of Aryan health. In a devastating attack on Berlin in April 1945, allied bombers destroyed the institute and gave a final, lethal injection to the already waning Nazi state. Hardly inhibited by their former unsavoury Nazi sympathies, both Boehm and Müller-Braunschweig rapidly set out to restore psychoanalysis, an endeavour that proved more arduous than expected, despite the support of prominent figures in the International Psychoanalytic Association.

While psychoanalysis was condemned by Hitler for its degenerate Jewish roots, it was also driven out of Russia for its allegedly bourgeois inspiration by Stalin's ruthless purges of communist society in the 1930s. The fall of psychoanalysis in Russia – it was officially prohibited in 1936 – chimes with the political turmoil surrounding Stalin's repudiation of Lenin's New Economic Politics, and shows a number of peculiarities: the same psychological theories that had paved the way for the rise of Russian psychoanalysis between 1906 and 1925 were eventually used to debunk it; Russia was the first country to publish translations of Freud's works and also the first to ban them; and nowhere has the connection between politics and psychoanalysis been so strong as in Russia. Until Stalin's radical indictment of the practice, psychoanalysts ran treatment centres in major cities all over the country without being hindered by people in high places. Lenin's ideological criticism that psychoanalysis's glorification of the sexual drive was counter-revolutionary did not trigger any legal action, perhaps because most members of the Russian Psychoanalytic Society were active within the Communist Party, and also because Trotskii supported Freud's ideas. For Stalin, however, psychoanalysis was useless, wrong, and dangerous, and hence unacceptable. In Stalin's view, Soviet people did not require psychoanalysis, because they were supposed to work rather than dream and to direct their energy towards the achievement of common goals rather than towards self-realization. This ideological rejection of Freudianism escalated as psychoanalysis gained ascendancy in the US after World War II, because it was now also regarded as representative of Western capitalist imperialism. The relatively lenient communist doctrines of Khrushchev and Brezhnev enabled the central psychoanalytic notion of the unconscious to resurface in scientific publications, yet its interpretation bore little resemblance to Freud's, inasmuch as its conflictual dynamics were reduced to a set of reflexes. After Gorbachev's perestroika, the situation changed rapidly and dramatically: in no time, Freud's works were reissued, psychoanalytic organizations found their way to Moscow, and new psychoanalytic study groups were established. The latest token of psychoanalysis's rehabilitation occurred on 19 July 1996, when Boris Yeltsin decreed that the Russian Federation would give full support to its revival and development.

A final form of censorship of Freud's writings has been imposed by his descendants and most loyal followers. It involves the expurgation of his letters to colleagues, friends, and relatives, and the restriction of access to miscellaneous documents concerning the psychoanalytic movement. The prime example of spurious abridgement of Freud's correspondence for editorial purposes concerns his letters to Wilhelm Fliess (1858–1928), a German otolaryngologist with whom Freud discussed his discovery of psychoanalysis in myriad letters written between 1887 and 1904. Purchased in 1936 by princess Marie Bonaparte (1882–1962) from Reinhold Stahl, a German art dealer, the letters were first published in German in 1950 and translated into English four years later. Despite Freud's insistence that he did not want the letters to be preserved for posterity, Marie Bonaparte had convinced his daughter Anna Freud (1895–1982) that publication of her father's correspondence was invaluable for the history of psychoanalysis. However, it was believed to be inappropriate to release a full transcription, and therefore the first published version contained just over half of the letters, some of them severely edited. Some of these deletions were instigated by the editors' wish to preserve the confidentiality of patients, whereas others were clearly intended to preserve Freud's own integrity. The nature and scope of the latter decision could not be assessed until 1985, when a new complete edition of the Freud–Fliess correspondence was published by Jeffrey M. Masson, a dithyrambic Canadian sanskritologist and Freud scholar who later fell into disrepute for his renegade reading of the letters. For the first time, it became clear how the editors of the first version had carefully excised passages in which Freud had revealed aspects of his own sexual life and that of his family, including a suspicion that his father had sexually abused some of his sons. After the Freud–Fliess letters, other complete sections of the Freud correspondence were published, yet many are still available only in censored editions. Moreover, since the 1950s, most of the original manuscripts have been kept behind bars in the Library of Congress for rather dubious reasons. Harold P. Blum, the current director of the Sigmund Freud Archives, Inc., has promised "to release all letters and documents from restriction, as soon as possible, consistent with legal and ethical standards and obligations". In 2000 restrictions on many documents were indeed lifted, yet some manuscripts will remain under lock and key until well into the 21st century.

Setting the tone for a new era of Freud studies, Blum also took the initiative to organize a massive exhibition on "Freud, conflict, and culture" at the Library of Congress around the end of 1996. As a reaction against this initiative, Peter Swales, a former business associate of the Rolling Stones and a notorious independent Freud historian, launched a petition on 31 July 1995 scorning the organizers' unbalanced presentation of Freud and calling for the project to be cancelled unless a spokesperson for the Freud critical caucus was allowed to sit on their panel. Swales managed to gather some 50 signatures of illustrious academics – including Freud's granddaughter Sophie – who argued for the withdrawal of the exhibition in the name of absolute freedom of expression. When the supporters of the initiative got wind of the Swales petition, they accused its signatories of censorship, intellectual terrorism, and even anti-semitism. In France, the acclaimed psychoanalyst and historian Elisabeth Roudinesco started a counter-petition, which brought together some of the most respected Freudian scholars. However, this did not prevent the postponement of the exhibition until the autumn of 1998, a decision that the organizing committee ascribed to lack of funding rather than to compliance with the critics.

DANY NOBUS

Further Reading

Angelini, Alberto, *La psicoanalisi in Russia*, Naples: Liguori, 1988

Bertrand, Michèle (editor), *Psychanalyse en Russie*, Paris: Harmattan, 1992

Breuer, Josef and Sigmund Freud, *Studies on Hysteria*, London: Hogarth Press, 1955 (The Standard Edition of the Complete Psychological Works of Sigmund Freud, vol. 2; published in German 1895)

Cocks, Geoffrey, *Psychotherapy in the Third Reich: The Göring Institute*, 2nd edition, New Brunswick: Transaction, 1997

Colonomos, Fanny (editor), *On forme des psychanalystes: rapport original sur les dix ans de l'Institut psychanalytique de Berlin*, Paris: Denoël, 1985

"L'Engagement sociopolitique des psychanalystes", *Revue internationale d'Histoire de la Psychanalyse*, 5 (1992)

Etkind, Alexandre, *Eros of the Impossible: The History of Psychoanalysis in Russia*, Boulder, Colorado: Westview Press, 1997

Evard, Jean-Luc (editor), *Les Années brunes: la psychanalyse sous le IIIe Reich*, Paris: Confrontation, 1984

Freud, Sigmund, *The Interpretation of Dreams*, London: Hogarth Press, 1953 (The Standard Edition of the Complete Psychological Works, vols 4–5; German edition 1900)

Freud, Sigmund, "The Unconscious" in *On the History of the Psycho-Analytic Movement, Papers on Metapsychology, and Other Works*, London: Hogarth Press, 1957 (The Standard Edition of the Complete Psychological Works, vol. 14; published in German 1915)

Freud, Sigmund, *The Complete Letters to Wilhelm Fliess, 1887–1904*, edited and translated by Jeffrey Moussaieff Masson, Cambridge, Massachusetts: Harvard University Press, 1985

Jacoby, Russell, *The Repression of Psychoanalysis: Otto Fenichel and the Political Freudians*, New York: Basic Books, 1983

Katz, Chaim S. (editor), *Nazismo e psicanálise*, Rio de Janeiro: Taurus, 1985

Levine, Michael G., *Writing through Repression: Literature, Censorship, and Psycholoanalysis*, Baltimore: Johns Hopkins University Press, 1994

Lockot, Regine, *Die Reinigung der Psychoanalyse: Die Deutsche Psychoanalytische Gesellschaft im Spiegel von Dokumenten und Zeitzeugen, 1933–1951*, Tübingen: Diskord, 1994

Malcolm, Janet, *In the Freud Archives*, New York: Knopf, 1983; London: Jonathan Cape, 1984

"Psychanalyse et psychanalystes durant la deuxième guerre mondiale dans le monde", *Revue internationale d'Histoire de la Psychanalyse*, 1 (1988)

Reichmayr, Johannes, *Spurensuche in der Geschichte der Psychoanalyse*, Frankfurt am Main: Fischer, 1994

Roth, Michael S. (editor), *Freud: Conflict and Culture*, New York: Knopf, 1998

Roudinesco, Elisabeth, "Freud in der USSR: Die Psychoanalyse kann sich nur in einem Rechtsstaat entwickeln: Freuds Werk wird jetzt in Russland veröffentlicht", *Psyche: Zeitschrift für Psychoanalyse und ihre Anwendungen*, 46 (1992)

PUERTO RICO

Population: 3,915,000
Main religions: Roman Catholic; Protestant
Official language: Spanish; English
Illiteracy rate (%): 6.5 (m); 6.1 (f)

Number of daily newspapers: 3
Number of radio receivers per 1000 inhabitants: 714
Number of TV receivers per 1000 inhabitants: 270

The United States invaded and occupied Puerto Rico in 1898. José Luis González, in his book *Literatura y sociedad en Puerto Rico*, points out the island's unique status: "Unlike the rest of the Spanish-speaking countries, Puerto Rico is still fighting to achieve national independence." In his analysis of the impact of 1898 on Puerto Ricans, González suggests that "obscuring and deforming their cultural values came to be one of the most efficient means of impeding acts of emancipation." Over the past one hundred years the free speech rights of pro-independence activists have been violated, the free flow of pro-independence literature has been restricted, and the owners of the corporate media have cooperated with the colonial government to support Washington's primary aims. However, the education system has been the main tool employed to suppress culture, according to González.

José Luis Méndez, in the collection *La agresión cultural norteamericana en Puerto Rico* (US Cultural Aggression in Puerto Rico), provides a detailed account of the suppression of free speech and the deformation of the island's educational system. The US resorted to very heavy-handed tactics during the first few years of occupation. General Davis, the military governor, closed down several newspapers including *Combat*, *The Machine Gun*, and *The Bomb*, and also jailed journalists who openly advocated independence or criticized US rule of the island. According to historian Loida Figueroa, Davis threatened to shoot several reporters if they continued to speak out in favour of independence.

In 1900 the US Congress passed the Foraker Act, which created a department of instruction for Puerto Rico, that regulated from Washington the form that instruction would take. Under the new system all public school courses would be taught in English, rather than in the Spanish vernacular, which would now be taught as if it were a foreign language.

In Ponce in 1911 the Puerto Rican Teachers Association was formed, as part of a general movement against the imposition of English in schools and in the judicial system. The struggle came to a head in 1915, when Francisco Grovas was expelled from his school for asking people to sign a petition making the the use of Spanish obligatory in both the schools and the courts. When the students organized to protest, the commissioner of the day, Paul G. Miller, shifted the policy to bilingualism, with the motto "Conservation of Spanish and Acquisition of English".

In 1917 the US Congress imposed US citizenship on all Puerto Ricans, under the Jones Act. Puerto Ricans could reject US citizenship only if they were willing to give up their rights of free speech, freedom of association, and the right to vote. As a result, pro-independence agitation became more widespread. In 1921 governor E. Mont Reilly began a campaign to remove all *independentistas* from positions of public trust. Out of fear the Partido Unionista eliminated the demand for independence from its party platform.

During the 1920s and 1930s Pedro Albizu Campos became a central figure in the movement for independence. Despite Albizu's prominence, the Radio Corporation of Puerto Rico, a subsidiary of ITT, refused in 1931 to broadcast any of his speeches. Albizu's Nationalist Party became the target of systematic repression when Franklin D. Roosevelt named Robert H. Gore as governor in 1933. During this period the US American Civil Liberties Union issued a report in which they observed that "freedom of speech and assembly have repeatedly been denied, teachers have been summarily discharged or disciplined for their views, violence by the militarized police has resulted in deaths and in injuries running into the hundreds."

On 24 October 1935 four nationalists were killed by police in what came to be known as the Massacre of Río Piedras. Less than a year later Albizu and other leaders of the Nationalist Party were arrested and given sentences of between six and ten years for conspiring to overthrow the government of the United States by force.

Repression of the rights of association grew more severe over time, culminating in the 1937 Ponce Massacre. Police opened fire on peaceful protesters who marched against the imprisonment of Albizu. Nineteen people were killed and nearly 200 wounded. According to the writer Carmelo Delgado Cintrón, in addition to killing, wounding, and mutilating the participants in the march, the police had another purpose: "to terrorize the members of the Nationalist Party and others who believed in independence." The deaths should be seen in a larger geographical and historical context, in which the US had resorted frequently to armed intervention throughout the region. The worst contemporary example in the Caribbean basin had been the invasion of Haiti in 1915. The killing of an estimated 3250 Haitians led many to believe that Washington would not hesitate to use crushing force in Puerto Rico.

As most land, capital investment, and public funds came under the control of the colonial power (or those who agreed to cooperate with the colonial power), the need for overt censorship diminished over time. Freedom of the press became a rather abstract concept in the colonially and financially manipulated Puerto Rico of the mid-20th century. The journalist Pablo Tirado Mercado, author of *Anatomia del periodismo puertorriqueño* (The Anatomy of Puerto Rican Journalism), argues that "the only ones who enjoy press freedom are the owners of the newspapers." He goes on to state that press freedom in Puerto Rico is a kind of property, like any other, which can be bought and sold.

When financial pressures and colonial domination of the media were deemed insufficient to suppress dissent, the local authorities, at Washington's behest, resorted to special legislation. In 1948 the *ley de la mordaza* (muzzling law) was implemented, according to critics, to "silence the voices of the *independentistas* and the communists". The text of this law arrived in Puerto Rico already written in English, and was quickly translated into Spanish and circulated to local legislators with instructions from Washington. The law gave the government special powers to control dissent and detain reporters. The approved version, according to Paul Harrison of United Press International, was worded in such a way as to prevent anyone even from criticizing the government. Any criticism, Harrison noted, could be "interpreted as 'indirectly inciting' someone to use force against the government." The person voicing the criticism could be charged with a felony.

Students at the University of Puerto Rico attempted to challenge the law prior to its official enactment in 1948 by sponsoring a conference on the pro-independence fighter Albizu. When the university authorities prohibited the conference, students launched a general strike and the rector responded by ordering the shutdown of the entire university.

It was in this climate that the US Congress proposed a change in the constitutional status of the island. On 4 June 1951 a referendum was held on the issue, but the pro-independence factions challenged its validity arguing it was held under pressure, as the US "made use of its repressive apparatus and all the means of manipulation and dissuasion at its disposal". Large numbers boycotted the referendum or simply refrained from voting, out of distrust or apathy. The majority of eligible voters did not approve the new constitutional order. But since most of those who did vote favoured the Commonwealth (or Estado Libre Asociado), the new constitution was proclaimed on 25 July 1952. A subsequent UN investigatory report noted that during the period leading up to the referendum the Nationalist Party had been virtually prohibited from acting. During the 1940s and early 1950s more than 1300 nationalists and *independentistas* had been jailed, and freedom of speech and of association had been severely curtailed. Such conditions made a free airing of views and a free vote impossible. In 1953 the UN General Assembly demanded that Puerto Rico should cease to be a dependent territory.

Tirado Mercado notes several techniques used during the 1960s and early 1970s by the police to curtail the freedom of people working in the newspaper industry. According to a report in *El Imparcial*, police resorted to confiscating papers from street vendors attempting to sell *Claridad*, a pro-independence newspaper. *El Imparcial* also reported a case in which the police beat B. Ortiz Otero, the vice-president of a newspaper union, merely for trying to convince other reporters to join a strike.

In 1974 a group of terrorists attacked the National Printing Office and the offices of *Claridad*. One of the participants in the attack was wounded, and was treated in a US army hospital. He later left the country without ever facing charges, leaving the impression that there was US military complicity in the attacks. That same year the university fired nearly 100 professors, seriously compromising freedom of expression in the academic sphere. Most of the instructors had been *independentistas* or socialists who had participated in a strike the previous year.

According to a report issued by the UN Special Committee on Decolonization in 1987, there has been a systematic practice of discrimination and official persecution directed against tens of thousands of Puerto Ricans who support independence, in flagrant violation of their civil and political rights. The UN commission also noted that the most basic right of self expression and self-determination, the right to redact its own constitution, had been overridden by Washington. The original constitution, as formulated by the Constituent Assembly, enumerated numerous rights of free association, including the right of workers to organize themselves, to negotiate agreements collectively, and the right to strike. The assembly also sought a declaration of rights that would recognize the responsibility of the government to prevent illness and hunger, and to care for the aged. The US Congress ordered the more progressive articles eliminated from the constitution (*New York Times*, 2 July 1952).

Throughout the 1980s and 1990s the US government has maintained a climate inimical to free expression by imposing extremely harsh jail terms on leaders of the independence movement. During the early 1980s the US courts sentenced 15 dissidents to jail terms ranging from 30 to 90 years. Many imprisoned pro-independence fighters are considered by a number of US church groups, members of the House of Representatives, and by several international human rights groups to be prisoners of conscience. In 1997 the United Church of North America protested the length of the sentences because "none of the 15 prisoners was charged with or convicted of murder or any act of bloodshed". Ten of those arrested between 1980 and 1983 received an average sentence in excess of 70 years in jail, in spite of the fact that they had no prior criminal record. Such sentences are deemed to be political, designed to inhibit freedom of conscience (especially in light of the fact that the average sentence for murder during the same period was under 23 years).

During the late 1990s the local government of Puerto Rico came under attack from the Inter American Press Society (SIP), which monitors press freedom throughout the hemisphere. According to a report issued in March 1998 the governor of Puerto Rico had canceled the granting of official advertising as a reprisal against the newspaper *El Nuevo Día* for criticizing the government.

SIP also confirmed a pattern of "coercion and pressure exercised by the government of Puerto Rico, in February, 1998, against journalists working at *El Nuevo Día* and at other news outlets." The committee which visited Puerto Rico in 1998 reported that their efforts to point out the "hostility of the Puerto Rican Government toward the principles of freedom of the press were met with by obstruction from government officials." SIP also noted that official advertising belongs to the people and not to government officials, and that concessions of official advertising could not be used to reward or punish newspapers for their political lines. The visiting committee confirmed allegations of harassment made by the Asociación de Periodistas de Puerto Rico and the Overseas Press Club.

PAUL WELLEN

Further Reading

Acosta, Ivonne, *La mordaza: Puerto Rico, 1948–1957*, Rio Pedras: Edil, 1987

Beauchamp, José Juan *et al.*, *La agresión cultural norteamericana en Puerto Rico*, Mexico City: Grijalbo, 1980

Berríos Martínez, Rubén, *La independencia de Puerto Rico: razón y lucha*, Mexico City, Línea, 1983

Carrión, Juan Manuel *et al.* (editors), *La nación puertorriqueña: ensayos en torno a Pedro Albizu Campos*, San Juan: Universidad de Puerto Rico, 1993

Checa Godoy, Antonio, *Historia de la prensa en Iberoamérica*, Sevilla: Alfar, 1993

Delgado Cintrón, Carmelo, *Derecho y colonialismo: la trayectoria histórica del derecho puertorriqueño ensayos*, Río Piedras: Edil, 1988

Fernandez, Ronald, *Prisoners of Colonialism: The Struggle for Justice in Puerto Rico*, Monroe, Maine: Common Courage Press, 1994

Géigel Polanco, Vicente, *La farsa del estado libre asociado*, Río Piedras: Edil, 1972; 2nd edition 1981

González, José Luis, *Literatura y sociedad en Puerto Rico: de Los Cronistas de Indias a la Generación del 98*, Mexico City: Fondo de Cultura Económica, 1976

Maldonado-Denis, Manuel, *Puerto Rico: una interpretación histórico-social*, Mexico City: Siglo Veintiuno Editores, 1969

Negrón-Portillo, Mariano, *El autonomismo puertorriqueño: sa transformación idealógica, 1895–1914: la prensa en al análisis social, la Democracio de Puerto Rico*, Río Piedras: Huracán, 1981

Nelson, Anne, *Murder under Two Flags: The US, Puerto Rico and the Cerro Maravilla Cover-Up*, New York: Ticknor and Fields, 1986

Rúa, Pedro Juan, *Resistencia Nacional y Acción Universitaria*, Río Piedras: Edil, 1988

Tirado Mercado, Pablo, *Anatomia del periodismo puertorriqueño*, Mexico City, Costa Amic, 1974

MANUEL PUIG
Argentine novelist, 1932–1990

Born and raised in General Villegas, a small town in the province of Buenos Aires, Manuel Puig studied film direction at Cinecittá in Rome, and in 1965 moved to New York, where he finished his first novel, *La traición de Rita Hayworth* (Betrayed by Rita Hayworth). *La traición de Rita Hayworth* breaks with narrative conventions by blending different genres: monologues, conversations, letters, Hollywood musicals, and melodramas. Suzanne Jill Levine, who translated Puig's first three novels, suggests that "Manuel Puig subverted here the communicative function of spoken language by transforming it, with all its grammatical violations, into writing." The novel depicts everyday life in a small town in the Argentine pampas. Its main characters are oppressed housewives, children dealing with fears of sexual initiation and homosexuality, and lower-class girls who work as maids for middle-class families. Although the novel has no explicit ideology, it contains an implicit criticism of a system where identities are shaped by the media, which reproduce power relations and sexual repression. The book has no third-person narrator. Puig later declared that to be omniscient is to reproduce repression.

Puig originally intended to have *La traición de Rita Hayworth* published in Spain, while general Franco was still alive (although he said "I saw the manuscript after it came back from the censor, all underlined in red"). The Spanish censors did not reject the manuscript outright, however, and in December 1965 the novel was a finalist for the Seix Barral publishing house's Biblioteca Breve Prize. Puig signed a contract. Then, after a disastrous meeting with his Spanish editor, during which Puig unknowingly enraged the editor by criticizing Fidel Castro's policy towards homosexuality, he was told that the novel would not be published. According to Puig, "my first encounter with censorship was a confused affair. Dictator Franco wasn't entirely to be blamed. But it was an indication of things to come."

In 1967 Puig returned to Argentina after 11 years abroad, mostly in Britain and France, and signed another contract for *La traición de Rita Hayworth* with the publisher Paco Porrúa. At that time the country was under the military dictatorship of general Juan Carlos Onganía (1966–70). Although there was no central censorship office and publishers were "free" to sell anything, if a military officer claimed that a book was subver-sive or pornographic the author, publisher, printer, and bookseller could be incarcerated. The first galleys were passed, but a linotype operator noticed the abundance of foul language and reported the matter to the authorities at the publishing house. Printing was stopped. Puig recalls:

> If he had not concentrated on individual words he would have noticed that it was inexperienced and innocent 12- to 14-year-old boys talking and trying to live up to the *machismo* of their elders. Pathetically childish, but hardly pornographic.

La traición de Rita Hayworth was finally published in Buenos Aires in 1968 in by Jorge Alvarez, famous for not paying royalties to authors. This was a year of great political tension and social upheaval in Argentina, and there was some fear that the book would be seized by the police. This did not happen, but the novel was received with indifferent reviews and sold badly. The following year Gallimard published a French translation of the novel, which was selected by *Le Monde* as one of the five best foreign books of the year.

In 1969, Puig's second novel, *Boquitas pintadas* (published in English as *Heartbreak Tango* in 1973), was published in Argentina, becoming a bestseller. After a series of popular riots, general Onganía's regime was in decline and there were no censorship attacks. What Puig calls his "honeymoon" with Argentine audiences lasted until 1973, the year he published *The Buenos Aires Affair* and general Juan Domingo Perón returned to Argentina after 17 years' exile. In 1973 Perón was also the political choice of the left; the subtle criticism of Peronism in *The Buenos Aires Affair* led to a widespread rejection of Puig's novel. The book was banned on the grounds of pornography, and a bookseller imprisoned for selling it. According to Puig, members of the League of Mothers had seen the book on a stall and called the police. Puig left for New York in 1973, but was pursued and threatened by the fascist Argentine Anti-Communist Alliance in 1974: "I didn't want to go back and be killed, nor did I want to have to resort to self-censorship. But, on the other hand, I was losing contact with my people, my language."

El beso de la mujer araña (Kiss of the Spider Woman), his

internationally famous novel and the first that deals openly with homosexuality, was first published in post-Franco Spain in 1976. In this novel, a homosexual and a guerrilla meet in prison and discover their shared need for affection. Since the beginning of his writing career, Puig had demonstrated, metaphorically, the relationship between sexual repression and other forms of oppression. Puig has written that "the beginning of *Kiss of the Spider Woman* is all there in the boy's composition class from *Rita Hayworth*. In a repressive society some people dare to discuss matters only metaphorically."

Manuel Puig's novels and plays were banned not only in his native country during the last and most destructive of the of military dictatorships (1976–83), but also in Fidel Castro's Cuba, because, says Puig, "they were considered too concerned with sexuality, and worst of all, with homosexuality". After the fall of the Argentine dictatorship in 1983, Puig's work regained large audiences and also the appreciation of scholars and academics in his native country. In exile he wrote *Pubis angelical* (1986), an account of 1970s Argentina. Puig never returned home. After living for several years in Rio de Janeiro, Brazil, he died in Mexico in 1990.

LIRIA EVANGELISTA

Writings

La traición de Rita Hayworth, 1968; as *Betrayed by Rita Hayworth*, translated by Suzanne Jill Levine, 1971
Boquitas pintadas, 1969; as *Heartbreak Tango: A Serial*, translated by Suzanne Jill Levine, 1973
The Buenos Aires Affair (in Spanish), 1973; as *The Buenos Aires Affair*, translated by Suzanne Jill Levine, 1976
El beso de la mujer araña, 1976; as *Kiss of the Spider Woman*, translated by Thomas Colchie, 1979
Pubis angelical, 1979; as *Pubis angelical*, translated by Elena Brunet, 1986

Further Reading

Bacarisse, Pamela, *The Necessary Dream: A Study of the Novels of Manuel Puig*, Cardiff: University of Wales Press, and Totowa, New Jersey: Barnes and Noble, 1988
Bacarisse, Pamela, *Impossible Choices: The Implications of the Cultural References in the Novels of Manuel Puig*, Calgary: University of Calgary Press, and Cardiff: University of Wales Press, 1993
Swanson, Philip, *The New Novel in Latin America: Politics and Popular Culture after the Boom*, Manchester: Manchester University Press, 1995

ALEKSANDR PUSHKIN
Russian poet and prose writer, 1799–1837

Pushkin had already won fame as a literary prodigy at the Imperial Lycée at Tsarskoe Selo, when he arrived in St Petersburg in 1817 to take up a sinecure at the College of Foreign Affairs. In the course of the next three years he acquired a new set of friends, many of whom were active in what was to become the Decembrist conspiracy, and began composing verse of an overtly liberal and even seditious nature. This enjoyed a wide circulation in manuscript. One of Pushkin's Decembrist friends, the would-be regicide Ivan Iakushkin, later recalled that: "Not only did everyone know of all his unpublished poems . . . but there was scarcely a half-literate cornet or ensign in the entire army who could not recite them from memory." Strikingly, when the emperor Alexander I read the poem "Derevnia" (1819, "The Village"), with its message of opposition to serfdom, even he was moved to say that Pushkin should be thanked for the good feelings that his verses inspired. In fact, although Pushkin was vitriolic in his denunciations of tyranny in general and Alexander I in particular – see, in particular, the ode "Vol'nost'" (1817, "To Liberty") and "Skazki: Noël" (1818, "Fairy Tales: Noël") – his liberalism did not amount to a coherent doctrine, combining as it did violently revolutionary sentiments with a belief in constitutional monarchy and the rule of law. Yet the poet could be subversive not only in word, but also in deed. After the assassination of the duc de Berry, the heir to the French throne, he publicly displayed a portrait of the assassin bearing the inscription "A lesson to kings".

In 1820, Alexander I's patience with Pushkin's seditious activities, literary and otherwise, was finally exhausted, and only the intercession of the historiographer Nikolai Karamzin and of Petr Chaadaev, the future author of the *Filosoficheskoe pis'mo* (*Philosophical Letter*), saved Pushkin from confinement to the Solovetskii monastery, in the far north, or exile to Siberia. Instead, Pushkin was posted to the southern regions of the empire, where he served in a variety of minor capacities, first (1820–23) in Kishinev, under the indulgent general Inzov, the administrator of the southern colonies, and subsequently (1823–24) in Odessa, under the Anglicized snob count Vorontsov, viceroy of Bessarabia. These were the years of Pushkin's "Byronic period", which was inaugurated by the publication in book form of his first Romantic narrative poem, *Kavkazskii plennik* (1822, "Prisoner of the Caucasus"). Its text was disfigured by the censor, who excised the entire Dedication with its allusions to Pushkin's banishment from Petersburg, as well as a paean to "liberty's proud idol" in the main body of the poem. He even went so far as to order the removal of the author's portrait from all copies of the book. Incidents such as these gave Pushkin plenty of reasons to feel resentful. In the *Epistle to the Censor* (1822; see below), which could not appear in print, he compares his generic addressee to a "sour eunuch" who "stalks the muses".

Pushkin's own muse certainly suffered from the unwelcome attentions of the bureaucrats from the Department of Censorship. They made things so difficult that in August 1823 Pushkin complained to his brother that their depredations had made it impossible for him "to live by the pen". Indeed, several of his finest poems of the period were never published at all, among them "Kinzhal" (1821, "The Dagger"), with its sympathetic reference to the German student who had assassinated the playwright August von Kotzebue and "Svobody seiatel' pustynnyi . . ." (1823, "As freedom's sower in the wasteland . . ."), in which Pushkin, lamenting the loss of his liberal illusions, compares the "submissive nations" to bovine "herds",

"Their heritage each generation/The yoke with jingles, and the gall". Other verses were published with major excisions and changes–for example, "Napoleon" (1821), which appeared without the references to the French revolution, the execution of Louis XIV, and the "laurels" and "chains" that Frenchmen wore under the First Empire. The censor's pencil was not always guided by political considerations. In the printed version of the six-line poem "Nereida" (1820, "The Nereid"), a lip-smacking description of a bathing beauty, the penultimate line, "she raised her youthful swan-white bosom", was truncated to read "she raised . . .", much to the bemusement of those who liked this sort of thing.

During his time in Odessa, Pushkin had been quarrelling with count Vorontsov and sleeping with his wife. These circumstances made his position there increasingly precarious. When the police intercepted and read one of the poet's letters in which he mentioned the "lessons in pure atheism" that he had been taking, he was discharged from the civil service and confined to his father's estate of Mikhailovskoe in Pskov province. This time, the authorities did not use the fiction of an administrative transfer: Pushkin was now officially in disgrace and in exile. In Mikhailovskoe, he wrote the historical tragedy *Boris Godunov* (1825), which treats the touchy subject of the false pretender Grigorii Otrepiev's usurpation of the Russian throne in 1605, and resumed work on what has become his most famous work, the verse novel *Evgenii Onegin* (1823–31, *Eugene Onegin*). In the *Second Epistle to the Censor* (1824) he expresses the hope that the appointment of Aleksandr Shishkov as minister of popular education and head of the Department of Censorship would ease the political constraints on Russian literature: it did not.

It was during his exile in Mikhailovskoe that Pushkin learned of the Decembrist uprising (14–28 December 1825), the failure of which prompted him to try to reach some kind of accommodation with the new emperor, Nicholas I. The poet sent him a petition expressing "sincere remorse" over his former political views and was summoned to Moscow, where he arrived on 8 September 1826. That same day, he had an audience with the emperor at the Kremlin. No record of their conversation exists, but following it Alexander Benckendorff, the head of the newly created Third Section (the secret police), informed Pushkin that he would be exempt from the general rules governing the publication of literary works: "His Majesty the emperor shall be the first admirer of your writings and your censor". Pushkin could submit his writings to Nicholas via Benckendorff, although he also had the right to send them to the emperor directly. The poet was thrilled: the only writer who had enjoyed the same privilege had been his late patron, Karamzin.

The arrangement proved to be a decidedly mixed blessing: Nicholas, and by extension Benckendorff, now viewed the former liberal firebrand as the artistic property of the crown. Indeed, the emperor took the closest personal interest in every aspect of Pushkin's life and work. To Pushkin's disgust, in 1834 he even read one of the poet's letters to his wife, which had been intercepted by the postal authorities. Nicholas I was a dour but conscientious autocrat who "loved two things: dress parades and mathematics" (according to Henri Troyat). Like many men of this type, he was certain that he had excellent taste. When, in the autumn of 1826, Benckendorff rebuked the poet for giving private readings of *Boris Godunov*, Pushkin hastened to send a copy of the tragedy to Nicholas, whose considered judgement was that the author should turn this Shakespearean play "into a story or historical tale in the style of Walter Scott". Pushkin understandably refused to follow such asinine advice and was only able to publish the tragedy four years later, and then with major deletions and changes.

Despite enjoying the emperor's favour, Pushkin remained a suspect figure in the eyes of the government, as may be seen from the affair of *André Chénier* (1825). When this elegy to the martyred French poet was published in 1826, 44 of its lines were missing, having been deemed politically suspect by the censorship. Somehow the excised fragment found its way into private hands and was soon circulating, without the author's knowledge, under the provocative title "14 December". After a two-year investigation into the matter, the Council of State placed Pushkin under secret surveillance for having "a misguided attitude" to the Decembrist uprising, although the authorities could find no evidence that he had been responsible for disseminating the offending verses.

Meanwhile, Pushkin had become the subject of yet another government inquiry, this time involving the burlesque narrative poem, the *Gavriliada* (1821, "The Gabrieliad"), a copy of which had been discovered in the possession of a certain Captain Mitkov. Even today, this blasphemous account of the Annunciation, whose style is reminiscent of Voltaire's *La Pucelle d'Orléans* (*The Maid of Orleans*), retains its reputation as one of the most obscene works in the Russian language. Under questioning, Pushkin strongly denied his authorship, but then wrote a letter to the emperor in which he almost certainly admitted it (the letter has not survived). "I am aware of all the details of this affair. The matter is closed," was Nicholas's cryptic response to Pushkin's written explanation. The former student of atheism seems to have genuinely repented writing the *Gavriliada*. Beginning in the late 1820s, virtually every major female character in his works, whether poetic or prose, is called Maria. In 1832 he even gave the name to his firstborn child.

In February 1833 Pushkin had to endure another of Benckendorff's reprimands, this time for publishing the poem "Anchar" (1828, "The Upas Tree") and several other pieces with the consent of the regular censor but without that of the emperor. Ten months later, he managed to obtain the emperor's permission, conveyed to him orally by the secret police chief, to submit the works intended for Aleksandr Smirdin's new journal *Biblioteka dlia chteniia* (Library for Reading) through ordinary channels. During the same conversation, Benckendorff returned to him the manuscript of *Mednyi vsadnik* (1833, "The Bronze Horseman"), Pushkin's last – and greatest – narrative poem, which he had submitted for the emperor's consideration. This tale of the St Petersburg flood of 1824 foreshadowed Gogol''s and Dostoevskii's nightmare visions of the city on the Neva, and proleptically adumbrated much of the imagery and thematics of subsequent Russian poetry. The manuscript that Benckendorff now handed to Pushkin bore nine markings made by the imperial pencil. Nicholas, ever sensitive to real or metaphorical acts of lèse-majesté, had crossed out the lines "Outshone, old Moscow had to render/The younger sister pride of place,/As by a new queen's fresh-blown splendour/In purple fades Her Dowager Grace". Also judged inappropriate was the description of the climactic confrontation between Evgenii, the poem's tragic hero, and the eponymous statue of Peter the Great – "The dread Tsar's face,/With instantaneous fury burning,/It seemed to him, was slowly turning" – as well as the several references to the bronze figure as an "idol". As a result, Pushkin had to give up on the idea of publishing the poem.

After Pushkin's death, in a duel with Georges d'Anthès, the poet Vasilii Zhukovskii, instructed by Nicholas to go through Pushkin's papers, was able to thwart the emperor's intention of destroying any politically dubious writings that the dead man might have left behind. Over the next few years, Zhukovskii was able to publish several of the works that Pushkin had been unable or unwilling to get through the regular censorship, among them "The Bronze Horseman" and the mock-folktale "Skazka o pope i o rabotnike ego Balde" (1830, "The Tale of the Priest and His Workman Balda"); both nonetheless had to be brought out in altered form.

Pushkin's works continued to be censored in Russia, and then in the Soviet Union, until the latter collapsed in 1991. During the Soviet period, the complete texts of his "indecorous" (bawdy) poems were published only once, in the 17-volume Collected Works (1937–59), although the *Gavriliada* was made widely available to the reading public, probably because of its antireligious appeal. Pushkin's works have always suffered from the attentions of literary experts, be they politicians or pornographers. For example, Walter Arndt's translation of the *Gavriliada* appeared in the Christmas 1975 issue of *Playboy* with entire passages deleted or changed by the editors.

RICHARD TEMPEST

Writings

Polnoe sobranie sochinenii, 17 vols, 1937–59; reprinted 1994–
The Letters, edited and translated by J. Thomas Shaw, 3 vols, 1963
The Bronze Horseman: Selected Poems, translated by D.M. Thomas, 1982
Collected Narrative and Lyrical Poetry, translated by Walter Arndt, 1984

Further Reading

Briggs, A.D.P., *Alexander Pushkin: A Critical Study*, London: Croom Helm, and Totowa, New Jersey: Barnes and Noble, 1983
Eidel'man, N., *Pushkin: Iz biografii i tvorchestva, 1826–1837* (Pushkin: Details of His Biography and Creative Activity), Moscow: Khudozhestvennaia literatura, 1987
Lemke, Mikhail, *Nikolaevskie zhandarmy i literatura 1826–1855 gg.* (The Gendarmes of Nicholas I and Literature in 1826–55), 2nd edition, St Petersburg: Bunina, 1909
Ospovat, A.L. and R.D. Timenchik, *"Pechal'nuiu povest' sokhranit'..."* ("To Preserve the Sorrowful Tale..."), Moscow: Kniga, 1985
Troyat, Henri, *Pushkin*, New York: Doubleday, 1970; London: Allen and Unwin, 1974
Vatsuro, V.E. and M.I. Gillel'son, *Skvoz' "umstvennye plotiny"* (Through the "Barriers of the Mind"), Moscow: Kniga, 1985

"Poslanie tsenzoru" and "Vtoroe poslanie tsenzoru" (Epistle to the Censor and Second Epistle to the Censor)
Poems, written 1822 and 1824

"Poslanie tsenzoru", first written in 1822, circulated in manuscript and was not published until 1857, 20 years after the author's death. In it humour and wit alternate with passages of great seriousness. Pushkin depicts the censor in at least five ways: as "a gloomy guardian of the muses", as "a martyr", as "a citizen", as "a fool and a coward", and as "an unfortunate man" enslaved to his family. The poem begins and ends with a tongue-in-cheek humour that softens the invective at its core. Pushkin announces that he will resist the temptation to criticize the Russian censor, whom he calls a "gloomy guardian of the muses". The censor is to be pitied because he is obliged to read the drivel that passes for literature: the problem with literature, he argues, is the writers themselves, especially hack writers, who "sweat and grunt while writing odes". Hence, the censor is a "martyr": he wants to read Rousseau and Voltaire, but instead he is stuck reading paeans to woody groves and fields. The censor is also a "citizen", his charge is sacred, and he has sworn to perform his duties well. The ideal censor possesses both common sense and an enlightened outlook: he upholds custom and culture, defends "altar and throne", law and fatherland (*otechestvo*), and does not impede the progress of truth and justice. He is a friend to writers, not their enemy.

Reality, however, is far from ideal, and Pushkin reserves his strongest criticism for the fourth face of the censor, the "fool and coward". In the lengthy fifth stanza of the poem, Pushkin inveighs against the censor's ignorance and insensitivity: "On a whim you call black white, satire slander, poetry depravity, the word of truth rebellion". He blames the censor for lowering the standards of literacy and education. The poem alludes to numerous essays and narratives as targets of the censor's "murderous axe". Thanks to its repeated blows, "verse remains" the writer's sole resort. Yet, even here, the censor – that "meddling eunuch" – casts his dark shadow. Bereft of passion, wit, or taste, insensitive to Parnassian song, and suspicious of every word, the censor instills fear because he himself fears; he fears both signs of sedition and also the consequences were he to miss those signs in his examination of a work of art.

To support these charges, Pushkin engages a temporal polarity, marking the past as an oasis of enlightenment against the narrative present, a time of scepticism and sabotage. Thus, "in those days", great works escaped the censor's fatal touch: Ivan Barkov, Aleksandr Radishchev, Gavrila Romanovich Derzhavin, Ivan Khemnitser, Ippolit Bogdanovich and other Russian writers succeeded in publishing works that boldly unmasked Russian reality, "and censorship interfered with none of them". Pushkin views their work as the productions of a society in which freedom of expression fostered the expression of truth. Now, "in our most sage era", standards have fallen, thanks largely to censorship. Pushkin wonders why a minor poet such as Petr Shalikov is perceived to be a "dangerous man". He sees Russian literature poised to return to prohibitions against the use of such words as "fatherland" (*otechestvo*) – a reference to the emperor Paul I's edict of 1787 against 13 seditious words, including *otechestvo*, for which *gosudarstvo* was to be used instead; a world of moral turpitude engendered by the censor's amoral norms.

In juxtaposing a liberal past against a repressive present, Pushkin arranges the recent rulers of the Russian empire to suit his argument. He places in one corner Catherine II and Alexander I as paragons of civil freedom (the freedom to write); in the other corner he places Peter I. (Even emperors had circumvented the censor: the line "The Emperor himself ordered a publication to proceed in spite of you" refers to the publication, on Alexander I's command, of Nikolai Mihailovich Karamzin's *Istoriia Gosudarstva Rossiiskogo* (1816, History of the Russian State) without its first passing through the censorship system. Indeed, Pushkin portrays the "Alexandrine" period (the reign of Alexander I, 1801–25) as a time of open discussion and debate – "Just look at what the press accomplished then" – even though elsewhere in his writings he speaks less flatteringly of Alexander. This use of authority serves a strategic purpose: it allows Pushkin to value the past for its defence of the truth and its support of literature, and thus to imply that the present practice of censorship has been used, wilfully, to subvert this honoured tradition.

Pushkin sees in poetical satire an antidote to social vice and ignorance, and claims that even Catherine II knew this to be the case. Satire reveals ignorance and crushes it, but – according to one of Pushkin's letters – censorship undermines this effort because it substitutes "the arbitrary, summary dealings of a cowardly fool" for the writer's pursuit of truth and justice. Pushkin calls for an end to the reign of the censor. This is not necessarily the call of a rebel, however, for Pushkin was not opposed to the institution of censorship as such. "Give us a strict censorship, I agree," he wrote to Petr Viazemskii (6 February 1823), "but not a senseless one".

Some commentators have suggested that one line in the poem – "What's right for London is premature for Moscow" – expresses Pushkin's acceptance of his fate. Pushkin lived in a society that policed its best minds and hounded its writers. He himself was scrutinized, both before he wrote the poem and for a long time afterwards. He was forced to answer to the severest censor of all: the emperor Nicholas I. Perhaps he felt that it was pointless to criticize the censor, who like any writer risked displeasing the imperial court. The critical spirit reigned in some other parts of Europe, but in Russia it was silent.

Nevertheless, the line can be read in a different way. In the long central part of the poem, Pushkin describes an illustrious line of writers, including himself, who bypass censorship by self-publishing or by circulating handwritten copies of their work. His point may be that Russian writers find ways to circumvent the censor, and that this in itself constitutes a kind of civil disobedience. Russia is not Britain; parliamentary rule does not apply. Yet writers may salvage an authentic experience of literature, one that evades official channels and the censor, by seeking their ideal readers elsewhere.

Although Pushkin generalizes in commenting on Russian censors, he seems to have had in mind a particular person: Aleksandr Stepanovich Birukov, the primary censor of his works in the early 1820s, most notably of the poem *Kavkazskii plennik* (1822, *The Prisoner of the Caucasus*). Pushkin rails against Birukov in his letters, calling him "a cowardly fool" and "Birukov the Terrible", describing him as "unbearably stupid, arbitrary, and oppressive", and using his name as a collective term for all intrusive censors, "the Birukovs". At other times, however, Pushkin speaks less pejoratively, even warmly, of Birukov, describing him at one point as "an enlightened man . . . gracious and compassionate", and adding: "Now I submit myself unconditionally to his verdicts". Pushkin's target was probably the office, not the person, of the censor. In the letter to Viazemskii already quoted above, Pushkin commiserates with his fellow writer about the problems they were having with the censor, and then adds, more gravely: "We laugh, but it would be more sensible to take the Birukovs in hand. It is time to give weight to our opinion and to make the government esteem our voice – its disdain for Russian writers is unendurable."

In 1824, when A. S. Shishkov was appointed minister of education, Pushkin wrote a "Second Epistle to the Censor". It too is addressed to Birukov and, like the first "Epistle", makes a plea for freedom of expression. Pushkin hoped that Shishkov would loosen the grip of censorship on Russian writers, but he soon realized that this hope was in vain.

MARTHA KUCHAR

Further Reading

Bayley, John, *Pushkin: A Comparative Commentary*, Cambridge: Cambridge University Press, 1971

Bethea, David M. (editor), *Puškin Today*, Bloomington: Indiana University Press, 1993

Gessen, Arnold, *Zhizn' poeta*, Moscow: Detskaia Literatura, 1972

Todd, William Mills III, *The Familiar Letter as a Literary Genre in the Age of Pushkin*, Princeton, New Jersey: Princeton University Press, 1976

Q

HATEM ʿABDUL QADER
Palestinian journalist, 1953–

Hatem ʿAbdul Qader studied journalism at al-Azhar University in Cairo, returned to Jerusalem in 1980, started as a reporter and worked his way up to become managing editor of *al-Fajr* (The Dawn), the Arabic East Jerusalem daily newspaper, which from 1980 onwards also published a weekly English-language supplement for the benefit of foreign journalists who wanted to know the Palestinian point of view on current affairs.

Like the other Palestinian newspapers *al-Quds* (Jerusalem) and *al-Shaʿb* (The People), *al-Fajr* (The Dawn) had every day to send three copies of the following day's paper to the Israeli military censors who filed one copy for future police use, and checked the other and made deletions. The papers regularly appealed, but rarely got their way. Cheekily, in the early 1980s *al-Fajr* published in its English edition statistics of articles censored. Between 21 and 27 May 1982, it reported, 32 articles were submitted to the censor, of which 11 were totally censored, two were mutilated, and seven partially censored but used; only 12 escaped interference. On page 6 of the English edition for 26 March–1 April 1982 there is a blank editorial space on which is printed diagonally "we apologize".

In an interview with the present writer on 31 July 1989 ʿAbdul Qader said that editors had to learn that there were "red lines" that they were not allowed to cross. These included news of any announcement of strikes or sit-ins, regular arrests, Israeli army exercises, international censure of Israeli actions, and coverage of political initiatives outside the Occupied Territories. He further described the Israeli censorship's concern with the nuances of language. The words "soldiers sneaked in under cover of darkness" had to be removed because it was not acceptable to suggest that the Israeli military were in any way "sneaky"; the words "at night" had to be substituted. Israeli censors rejected the words "commandos", "fighters" or "resistance men", so Palestinians settled on "armed men" and the censors let it pass. Once the first intifada had begun, the paper had difficulty with the use of the words "was martyred"; very reluctantly, they had to write "was murdered" early in the uprising, which was very far from their understanding of what had taken place.

ʿAbdul Qader was placed under administrative detention (without trial) on four occasions. On one of them, in 1988, the Israeli authorities leaked to the press their suspicion that he was a prominent member of the Fatah movement and that he had planned (nonviolent) intifada, activities that "threatened the state of Israel". He was placed in solitary confinement for 93 days at Beersheba prison. He told the authorities that their treatment of him would not stop his resistance to occupation: "The facts on the ground did not change. The intifada continued because it belongs to the people and is not a trademark registered in the name of this or that individual."

ʿAbdul Qader, although he delighted in appealing against the more ridiculous and careless of censorship decisions (as when an item about the discovery of a treatment for baldness was crossed out), also used his imprisonment to reflect more deeply on the nature and particular circumstances of his experience of the practice:

> After occupation ends, we have to relearn to write freely. If I go to another country, and introduce myself, I have to say – to be honest with people who ask what I do for a living – "I am a journalist under occupation". I have to use "under occupation" as part of the job description. I have to say "I speak the language of occupation". In order to work elsewhere, I need to be retrained in the use of ordinary language to wake up from my journalistic coma. I have to say that up front because we deal with a different type of journalism when we are forced to censor ourselves.

Having been such an eloquent critic of Israeli censorship, ʿAbdul Qater was appointed head of the publication department of the Palestinian authority's Media Ministry in the early 1990s. He now had to defend the 1995 Palestinian Press Law, which journalists had criticized for being too restrictive. He replied: "We are not imposing restrictions on journalism; we organize it because total freedom means chaos." He was elected to the Palestinian Legislative Council in January 1996, and was harassed by the Israeli authorities when he opened his home to receive complaints from his Jerusalem constituents.

ORAYB AREF NAJJAR

Further Reading

Arnaut, Abdel Raouf, "New Harassment of Abdel Qader", *Jerusalem Times* (8 August 1997)

Benvenisti, Meron, *Israel's Censorship of Arab Publications*, Jerusalem: West Bank Data Project, 1983

Cohen, Akiba A. and Gadi Wolfsfeld (editors), *Framing the Intifada: People and the Media*, Norwood, New Jersey: Ablex, 1993

Johnson, Nels, *Islam and the Politics of Meaning in Palestinian Nationalism*. London and Boston: Kegan Paul, 1982

Najjar, Orayb Aref, "'The Editorial Family of *al-Kateb* Bows in Respect': The Construction of Martyrdom Text Genre in One Palestinian Literary and Political Magazine", *Discourse and Society*, 7/4 (October 1996): 499–530

Qous, Mousa, "Court Reviews Detention of *al-Fajr* Editor", *al-Fajr* 5 (English edition) (November 1990)

Rigby, Andrew and Tim Woodhouse, "Al Fajr", *Index on Censorship*, 11/4 (August 1982)

Shinar, Dov and Danny Rubinstein, *Palestinian Press in the West Bank: The Political Dimension*, Boulder, Colorado: Westview Press, 1987

Shinar, Dov, *Palestinian Voices: Communication and Nation Building in the West Bank*, Boulder, Colorado: Rienner, 1987

al-Zaru, Nawwaf, "Military Censorship Admits to 25 Arabic Letters: The Rest Is Scratched Out", *al-Sha'b* (Jordan) (21 July 1988)

QATAR

Population: 565,000	**Number of periodicals:** 1
Main religion: Sunni Muslim	**Number of radio receivers per 1000 inhabitants:** 450
Official language: Arabic	**Number of TV receivers per 1000 inhabitants:** 404
Other languages spoken: English	**Number of PCs per 1000 inhabitants:** 121
Illiteracy rate (%): 19.6 (m); 16.9 (f)	
Number of daily newspapers: 5	

Power in Qatar has remained, since independence in 1971, solely in the hands of the ruling family in the persons of the amir sheikh Khalifa bin Hamad Al Thani, and later his son, sheikh Hamad bin Khalifa. No political parties or other organizations critical of the government are allowed. Nor are any public religious gatherings for non-Muslims. Private meetings of the Shiite minority are also carefully monitored. While the ruling family has assiduously built up a range of modern communications, it has equally assiduously made sure that they are carefully controlled.

The press in Qatar is categorized by William Rugh (1987) as "loyalist". Given the authoritarian nature of the regime, the press appears to be guided first by the notion that the media should accept and help carry out development policies (defined by the Ministry of Information created in April 1972, and aimed at "building and developing the country and the citizens"). On this view, the media should give priority to content that links Qatar to other Gulf, Arab, and Muslim (all developing) countries that are geographically, politically, and culturally close to it. It is argued that as a matter of social responsibility both print and broadcast media in Qatar should "balance their aspirations to freedom with their obligations to their society". To ensure this balance the Qatari Public Commission for Improving the Quality of the Press reviews the performance of privately owned newspapers and magazines every three months, and presents its findings to the publishers and editors of those publications to be used as a guide.

Qatar's first paper, *al-Jaridah al-Rasmiyyah* (The Official Gazette) was established in 1961 and carried amirate decrees, official announcements, and state laws. After more than 30 years of independence it has the same form. The daily newspapers were started privately after independence. There are four privately owned daily newspapers: *al-'Arab* was established as a weekly in 1972 by the doyen of the Qatari press, 'Abd Allah Husayn Na'ma, and has appeared since 1974 as a broadsheet

daily newspaper. *Al-Rayah* (The Flag) was launched in 1979 by a group of Qatari businessmen and intellectuals. They recruited accomplished journalists from Egypt, Lebanon, Syria, and Sudan, and the paper was soon competing with other Middle Eastern newspapers. Although *Al-Rayah* presents itself as an independent political daily, it enjoys strong government support and the chairman of its board is a prominent member of the ruling Al Thani family. Not surprisingly, it promotes a Qatari viewpoint on major Arab, Islamic, and international issues and problems. *Al-Rayah* is also distributed in Saudi Arabia and Egypt, and is printed by the Gulf Publishing and Printing Organization. The third daily, *al-Sharq* (The Orient), was first published in 1985 by the al-Watan Printing and Publishing House under the name *al-Khalij al-Yawm* (The Gulf Today). Due to its initial lack of success it changed ownership, and the al-Sharq Printing, Publishing, and Distribution House was established. Determined to reach an audience that would include nationals and expatriates, men and women, professionals and nonprofessionals, the new owners added the subtitle "A political, general interest newspaper" to its masthead. Its staff includes mainly prominent writers of Egyptian, Sudanese, and Jordanian nationality, and only a few Qataris. It has foreign correspondents in such major news capitals as Washington, Moscow, London, and Cairo, and it has the right to publish Arab news derived from other big Arab dailies, such as the Egyptian *al-Ahram* (Pyramids). The fourth daily is *The Gulf Times*, published in English. It was established as a weekly in 1978 to serve the needs of the growing expatriate community from India, Pakistan, Britain, the United States, and other countries. It has a British editorial staff and has been published daily since 1981. It has gained some Qatari readers as well, mostly among those who have returned from studies abroad.

Freedom of the press and of expression are strictly limited, not least by the Press and Publication Law no. 8, which has remained in effect since its promulgation in 1979. Among other things, the law prohibits criticism of the amir, and publishing anything that will undermine established order, endanger the political regime, or jeopardize its relations with friendly nations. The authorities have the right to impose censorship to ensure adherence to these rules and principles. Government control and implementation of these limitations on the freedom of the press were enforced by the Ministry of Information until it was dissolved. In practice censorship was direct and straightforward within government-owned media. As virtually no paper is able to stand alone financially, the government subsidizes most of the private media considerably, thereby exercising indirect control; self-censorship is also practised.

According to articles 24 and 25 of the Press and Publishing Law the authorities (the Ministry of Information until 1995)

> may suspend for a maximum of a year, and/or confiscate, and/or close down any publication whose editing policy contradicts the national interests or serves the interests of a foreign country, or receives any financial support from any foreign entity, if such violations are proven.

The grip on the media is often dictated by the involvement of the Qatari state in regional or sometimes international politics. For example, the press was very carefully monitored during the Iraq–Iran War (1980–88); censors were stationed in all mass media organizations "to screen out any content that could violate public order, religion, or morals". It grew fiercer during the Gulf War, to suppress national unrest and safeguard Qatar's pro-Allied stand. Qatar has witnessed a general clampdown on the press since the 1980s. This can be attributed to the growing influence of Saudi Arabia since the establishment of the Gulf Cooperation Council (GCC, comprising the monarchies of Saudi Arabia, Kuwait, Bahrain, Qatar, the United Emirates, and Oman, and concerned with the security aspects of the Iraq–Iran War). However strict censorship may be, the media do test its limits. In 1995, for example, the concluding document in the Qatari signing of the GCC Security Agreement, which includes a clause prohibiting "hostile propaganda" among the members of the GCC, was published by the paper *al-Watan* (homeland). The paper was temporarily shut down, as was *al-Sharq* for publishing a poem considered offensive to Saudi Arabia.

Although the Ministry of Information was dissolved in 1995, censorship continues through the Ministry of Endowments and Islamic Affairs, in charge of censorship of radio, television, cable television, and videotapes.

Radio started in 1968 with the Voice of Qatar. In 1993 Qatari Radio had 11 large transmitters and the Qatar radio service comprised 15 radio studios. It reaches the Gulf, most of the Arab world, and parts of Europe and Asia. There are six channels: the first in Arabic, broadcasting news, music, government announcements, and religious programmes among others; the second in English, the bulk of its programming imported especially from Britain; next is the Folk channel, broadcasting folk music and programmes in local dialect; then the Urdu channel, Huna al-Doha, featuring Arabic music and concerts; and last the French channel.

Radio, like television, is regulated by law 20 of 1990. This law stipulates:

that radio and television provide the citizen with the political, economic, and social information that could enable him to understand local, regional, and international issues, develop and promote people's understanding [and awareness] within the framework of the vital principles guiding the state's policies, and entertain [audiences] within the limits of observed religious and traditional values.

Qatari television, Q-Tel, was set up by the government in 1970. In the 1990s it included an Arabic and an English channel. About 25 per cent of the programmes are locally produced; the rest are imported mainly from Egypt, but also from Syria, the United Arab Emirates, Kuwait, Jordan, the United States, the United Kingdom, and India. Educational programmes are imported from Japan, the Netherlands, and Sweden, and are provided with English and/or Arabic subtitles. Q-Tel accepts commercials, but they are tightly censored in order to block out any culturally or politically unfavourable images and ideas.

The Cable News Network (CNN) was brought to Qatar during the Gulf War but was taken off the air soon after. As Qataris now started tuning in to Bahraini television, which had retained the US-owned network, the government decided in 1992 to offer its people a package including CNN, the Middle East Broadcast Corporation (MBC), GCC State Television, Egyptian Satellite Channel (ESC), the BBC, the Indian ESPN, Pakistani Channel, and Islam Vision emanating from Muscat (Oman). CNN is back, this time, however, severely censored; images considered to be offensive are blacked out or sometimes the whole network is taken off the air for a period of time.

The first cinema in Qatar was opened in 1950 by the Shell Oil Company to entertain its employees. After independence the Qatar Cinema Company was formed to regulate and control all aspects of cinema operations. Films are strictly censored before being shown to a public or private audience, as stipulated by the Press and Printing Law and Law 20 of 1990, under which the authorities bear the responsibility for "censoring local and foreign artistic productions" – this includes imported video cassettes, audio tapes, books, and periodicals – and for licensing theatres, organizations, and shops selling and circulating these artistic productions.

Amir sheikh Hamad has taken major steps to improve the country's overall human rights situation. He has abolished a number of censorship measures and laws and has even dissolved the Ministry of Information. The first free elections of the Central Municipal Council took place in March 1999: women were allowed to participate, another first. Parliamentary elections have been announced and a draft permanent constitution is supposed to be ready by 2002. The establishment of Qatar's first non-governmental organizations for human rights was announced in 2001 as well.

Although self-censorship inside Qatar continues to a certain degree, the freedom of expression of the Qatari satellite station al-Jazeera has shocked the entire Middle East. In the last few years particularly, al-Jazeera, officially established in 1996, has developed itself into perhaps the only true independent and critical news organization in the Middle East. The station has broadcasted many controversial news programmes and interviews with various opposition groups in the region, but also a number of Israeli government officials, and has independently covered news in the entire area, including Iran, Iraq, and Israel. Al-Jazeera's outspokenness has already caused more than 400 complaints from other Middle Eastern countries. In the Palestinian Territories the office of the Qatari station was closed down after the station aired an interview with the Islamic opposition in the territories; in other countries, such as Algeria, broadcasts by al-Jazeera have been blocked.

As the station is sponsored completely by amir sheikh Hamad himself, criticism of Qatar itself remains limited, although some problematic issues, such as state subsidies for members of the royal family have been addressed.

The amir is adamantly and admirably defending liberal ideas in Qatari politics. He continues to sponsor al-Jazeera despite complaints in the region. He has also not hestitated to take strong measures to ensure, for example, women's liberation in the country. When an official of the Ministry of Education opposed the amir's decision to support female suffrage in the municipal elections, he had the official arrested and detained.

FERIDA JAWAD

Further Reading

Abu-Fadil, Magda, "Maverik Arab Satellite TV: Qatar's Al Jazeera Brings a Provocative New Brand of Journalism to the Middle East", *IPI Report*, 4 (1999)

Arafa, Mohamed M., "Qatar" in *Mass Media in the Middle East: A Comprehensive Handbook*, edited by Yahya R. Kamalipour and Hamid Mowlana, Westport, Connecticut: Greenwood Press, 1994

Gambill, Gary C., "Qatar's Al-Jazeera TV: The Power of Free Speech", *Middle East Intelligence Bulletin*, 2/5 (June 2000)

Mohammad H.A. and O. Saif el-Din, *Qatari Press: History and Evolution*, Doha: Authors, 1984

Rugh, William A., *The Arab Press*, revised edition, Syracuse, New York: Syracuse University Press, 1987

Zahlan, Rosemarie Said, *The Making of the Modern Gulf States: Kuwait, Bahrain, Qatar, the United Arab Emirates and Oman*, London: Unwin Hyman, 1989

Websites

http://www.state.gov/www/global/human_rights

World Press Freedom Report 2000: Qatar, at http://www.freemedia.at/wpfr/qatar.htm

QIANLONG EMPEROR
Chinese emperor, reigned 1730–1796

The tradition of state-sponsored literary compilations, encyclopedias, dictionaries, and other large works is a feature of Chinese culture. The *Book of Odes* (1st millennium BCE) was perhaps the earliest state compilation, but from the 3rd century CE onwards private and official compilations proliferated, and the development of printing resulted in even larger collections. And as such compilations necessarily involved an assessment of whether works were suitable for inclusion, they were associated with censorship. In the compilation of the Buddhist canon, for example, various emperors ordered the exclusion of certain sutras they held to be apocryphal and, at the same time, ordered these works to be destroyed. But no previous compilation compared in scale and scope with that initiated by the Qianlong emperor in 1772 when he ordered the collection of complete texts of works for the imperial library so that they might be preserved against loss and available for use in future historical works. At the same time the most important and unique literary works were to be compiled into a new publication, *Siku Quan Shu* (The Complete Works of the Four Treasuries). It was clear from the beginning of this enterprise that the works submitted were to be examined for loyalty to the Manchu state, and those found wanting were to be destroyed. This instruction is included in an edict of 1774 (after 10,000 books had been sent to the capital) in which the emperor voices his suspicion that so few seditious works have come to light, and reminds the provincial officials that they must send such works to the capital and not withhold any copies.

The next few years saw repeated edicts to this effect in which the methods decreed for searching out books became more detailed and effective. For example, an edict of 1777 reads:

I have appointed officials awaiting jobs, of whom there are not few at leisure, and commanded them each go to his own locality to make the search as relatives or friends of the families in question. This simplifies the search. By way of encouragement, if they discover many books we will place the finder at the top of the list [for an official appointment] and, if few, at the bottom, so that they will vie with each other in their search.

Those who withheld books were punished, usually by beatings and exile. However, the emperor sometimes intervened to lessen the penalty recommended by overzealous local officials. For example, one man refused to surrender a book of poems by his great-great-grandfather. The local governor recommended that the man be decapitated and his ancestor's body disinterred and dismembered. Officials in Beijing read the poems and found a number of suspicious lines, but the emperor rebuked the local official for his harsh recommendations and suggested lighter penalties. He then reduced the lighter penalties imposed by the Board of Punishments: the man received 100 strokes of the rod and three years' exile. The woodblocks for the poems were ordered to be found and destroyed.

Because of the Chinese dynastic system, it was usual for rulers at the start and end of a dynasty to use censorship to assert their legitimacy. The case of Tai Mingshi (1653–1713) was typical. Tai Mingshi was a Chinese historian and official who lived during the Manchu Qing, but whose work concerned the preceding (Chinese) dynasty, the Ming (1368–1644). Tai's crime was to use designations for late Ming reign periods other than those officially sanctioned by the Kangxi emperor (reigned 1662–1722), the founder of the Qing dynasty. This amounted, in the view of the Manchu conquering dynasty, to a challenge to their legitimacy in defeating the Ming.

The "crime" was discovered by the Head of the Censorate in 1711. The Board of Punishments recommended death by slicing for Tai and decapitation or exile for those who had contributed prefaces to the book. The sentence was revised, and Tai Mingshi was beheaded and his family and others involved sent into exile to the far north or made to enter military service. The body of a dead author deemed to have influenced Tai was exhumed and dismembered. (Punishments involving mutilation of the body, such as slicing, were considered more severe than the death penalty by strangulation because it was believed that it was an insult to one's ancestors to go to them after death with mutilated or missing body parts.) No mention is made in the contemporary records of what happened to the book, but it was banned later in the century under the Qianlong emperor along with six other works by Tai Mingshi. Only three of these are now extant.

In the case of the Qing dynasty, it is interesting that even when it was well established under the Qianlong emperor, imperial authority felt the need to continue using draconian measures to quell dissent. Censorship during the late imperial period in China has more parallels with that practised in post-1949 communist China than that in previous imperial dynasties. However, the books that were banned belonged to the same categories as those banned by previous rulers: books that incited rebellions; anti-Manchu works (as insulting either the Manchus themselves or previous northern rulers of China that they considered to be their dynastic ancestors); treatises on border and military affairs (unlike previous bans on this type of work, geographical works on the southeastern borders were included); and works considered heterodox against the neo-Confucian Cheng-Zhu tradition like those of Zhu Xi. The vast majority of works proscribed were by Ming and Qing authors, rather than older works.

In some cases, the works of certain individual authors were *opera non grata*, and the ban extended to all works by their immediate families and any of their inscriptions. One such example is Qian Qianyi (1582–1664), a famous Chinese literary figure and historian. Qian Qianyi served as an official under both the Ming and Qing dynasties. During the Ming he was dismissed twice, once being accused of being a member of the Donglin faction (a public academic institution considered seditious). He served briefly at the southern exile court of the Ming after the Qing dynasty had come to power, but then joined the Qing regime, where he was ordered by imperial decree to work on the history of the Ming. Despite being taken into custody several times accused of Ming loyalist sympathies, he died a natural death in retirement. The famous Ming loyalist Koxinga – Zheng Chenggong – had been one of his students.

His pre-Qing writings were compiled and published in 1643, and his post-Qing works in 1664. The latter included a history of the Ming. During the reign of the Qianlong emperor all such works were examined, and the emperor declared Qian's history to be "an insult to correct principles and a violation of loyalty", ordering that all his works be destroyed. In previous dynasties the effectiveness of such an edict would depend largely on the assiduity of local officials and was often not followed up; popular books, which existed in many widely dispersed copies, consequently escaped. This decree stated, as usual, that each provincial governor was responsible for collecting all copies of the books from bookshops and private libraries within his juris-

diction, and that the order was also to be passed to small places that might otherwise not hear of it. It also set a limit of two years for the collection and destruction of existing copies of the books and woodblocks for printing. What was unusual about this case was the thoroughness with which it was implemented: only some of Qian's works are extant. This case is interesting as Qian Qianyi became emblematic of those officials whose works were targeted by the Qianlong emperor. The fact that he had served the early Qing as well as the Ming was seen as an sign of his treacherous nature. His biography was placed at the head of a section in the dynastic history created specially by the emperor for such "traitors".

Not all books submitted by local officials as seditious were destroyed. Some works were returned uncensored to their owners, while others had only certain passages removed. For example, an edict dated 1780 notes that:

> Among the books of past generations which have arrived in Beijing from the provinces during the last few days, there was one item . . . in which all the characters expressing rebellious ideas had been obliterated. This book was turned over to [two officials] who have reviewed it and filled in the spaces [with other characters] . . . I command the high officials of all provinces to discover those volumes which need not be destroyed but have been printed with blank spaces, to mark them and send them to the capital. They will then be turned over to the commissioners to be deliberated upon, filled in, then returned. When there are woodblocks, the provincial officials should compare them with the revised works and engrave them afresh so that they may be precisely the same [as the censored version].

The final anthology contained 3460 works in 79,339 volumes. Eight sets were printed and distributed to different locations, of which two are still more or less extant. No single list of banned works survives, but a review of the various lists (first collected together and published in 1884) shows 2320 works listed for total suppression and over 300 for partial suppression. These include works of most of the major figures in the literary world. Many survive, complete or partially, some having been taken to Japan before the ban. In addition, it seems that the libraries of Manchu bibliophiles were left untouched; and the Christian missionaries also had sizeable libraries. One member of the imperial family, for example, retained books from the library of Qian Qianyi in his collection. But many other works on the list are no longer extant.

SUSAN WHITFIELD

Further Reading

Brook, Timothy, "Censorship in Eighteenth-Century China: A View from the Book Trade", *Canadian Journal of History*, 22 (August 1988): 177–96

Fang Chao-Ying, "Tai Ming-shih" in *Eminent Chinese of the Ch'ing Period, 1644–1912*, edited by Arthur W. Hummel, 2 vols, Washington, DC: Government Printing Office, 1943–44

Goodrich, L. Carrington, *The Literary Inquisition of Ch'ien-Lung*, Baltimore: Waverly Press, 1935

Spence, Jonathan D., *Treason by the Book*, London: Allen Lane, and New York: Viking, 2001

QIN GUI
Chinese official, 1091–1155

A chief minister (1139–55) during the factional politics of the late Northern Song dynasty (1127–1279) in imperial China, Qin Gui was not untypical in his resort to censorship to silence dissenting views. In 1138 a fellow minister had submitted a memorial to the emperor demanding Qin's execution as a traitor for his lack of opposition to the Jurchens (rulers of northern China). This was disregarded, and as chief minister, Qin was given complete power by the emperor. During his tenure, he banned all northern expeditions against the Jurchens (who had succeeded in driving the Chinese Song dynasty south in 1127), destroyed all government documents that were unfavourable to this view, and rewarded officials who divulged the critical opinions of others. This made the collection of private histories, which had started to proliferate during the Song, very difficult. The Jurchens also offered a large reward for anyone who could supply them with a copy of the 1138 memorial: they obtained it within three days.

Qin Gui's ruthlessness and power at this time is shown by his treatment of Yue Fei (1103–41), a general who had been successful against the Jurchens. Qin Gui summoned him back to the capital, had him imprisoned on a false charge, and then put to death in 1141. It is possible that he also had Yue Fei's writings destroyed at this time: certainly, very few survive.

From 1144 onwards he instituted a series of book-banning ordinances, mainly covering private histories which he deemed "insufficiently trustworthy". That the first such measure was not rigorously enforced is shown by the fact that provincial publishers continued to bring out new books by banned authors. An imperial edict directed at local officials was followed by a more comprehensive ban in 1150. Enforcement of the ban relaxed slightly after Qin Gui's death in 1155, but by this time it is probable that self-censorship was practised more widely. The grandson of the prominent and respected historian Sima Guang, for example, petitioned the emperor requesting that one of his grandfather's works be banned.

It was also at this time that there was a movement against Cheng studies – early neo-Confucianism (see Zhu Xi) – although scholars in northern China under Jurchen control discussed these works freely. Ways were found to avoid the bans, but some works mentioned in contemporary bibliographies are no longer extant. It also became usual practice at this time to punish others involved in censored works, such as the publisher and preface writer. The censorship continued with a new edict dated 1202 covering important writers since the Northern Song period.

SUSAN WHITFIELD

Further Reading
Gong, Wei Ai, "The Usurption of Power by Ch'in Kuei through the Censorial Organ, 1138–1155 AD", *Chinese Culture*, 15/3 (1974): 25–42

QIN SHIHUANGDI
Chinese emperor, 259–210 BCE

Qin Shihuangdi ascended the throne of the Chinese kingdom of Qin in 246 BCE as king Zheng. During the years 230–221 BCE, Qin defeated all competing Chinese kingdoms and the internecine Warring States period (463–221) thus came to an end with king Zheng assuming the title Qin Shihuangdi (The First Emperor of Qin), as ruler of a united empire.

He and his chief minister, Li Si (c.280–208 BCE), were responsible for the banning, burning, and (according to some) the near complete destruction of Chinese literary culture. It is recorded that the emperor personally gave orders for 460 scholars, accused of opposing him, to be buried alive. The great Han dynasty (206 BCE–220 CE) historian, Sima Qian, records that the punished scholars were those who "upheld the teachings of Confucius". Qin Shihuangdi's crackdown should be viewed in the broader context of struggle between the Confucian and Legalist political systems.

During the preceding centuries, referred to as the "Spring and Autumn" (722–464 BCE) and the "Warring States" (463–221 BCE) periods, many political and ethical philosophies were propounded and were therefore called the "Hundred Schools". The followers of Confucius (551–479 BCE) argued that the king should rule by moral example, whereas the Legalists believed that law should be used to control the populace, and that violators should be strictly and consistently punished.

Legalist ideas had first been developed by Shang Yang (died 338 BCE), chief minister of the kingdom of Qin, who lived nearly a hundred years before Qin Shihuangdi. Shang Yang believed Confucianism was a barrier to progressive thinking, and held the Confucian classics in such contempt that he suggested they all be burned. The most famous Legalist philosopher was Han Fei (280–233 BCE). Speaking of Han Fei's work, Qin Shihuangdi was reputed to have said: "If I could meet the author of this book and be friends with him, I would die without regrets." Han Fei argued that true knowledge can only be gained from the careful study of the present. The Confucianists, he argued, were obsessed with the past and old-fashioned ideas, using the past to criticize the present. They were the first of "the five vermin", and had to be eradicated otherwise they would cause the decline of the state. Han Fei advocated the abolition of all Confucian teachings and the shutdown of all private Confucian schools. He proposed that officials should be practical men and use modern legal texts rather than works of literature as their guides to rulership. The "rule of law", he said, should replace the old "rule by rites".

According to historian Sima Qian, during a discussion among scholars at an imperial banquet Li Si argued:

In antiquity all under Heaven was divided and in chaos and nobody could unify it, and it was for this reason that the feudal lords became active together, and all spoke of the past to injure the present, and made a display of empty rhetoric in order to throw the truth into confusion. People approved what they had learned in private in order to reject what their superiors had laid down. Now the August Emperor has unified and taken possession of all under Heaven . . . yet those who have studied privately collaborate with each other to reject the laws and teachings . . . disagreement they regard as noble, and they encourage the lower orders and fabricate slander. If such things are not prohibited, then the sovereign's power will decline above, and factions will form below.

"I humbly propose," Li said, "that all historical records except those of Qin be burned. If anyone who is not a court scholar dares to keep the *Book of Odes*, *Book of History* or writings of the hundred schools, these should be confiscated and burned by the provincial governors and army commanders. Those who in conversation dare to quote the *Book of Odes* and *Book of History* should be executed; those who use old precedents to oppose the new order should be wiped out together with their families; and officers who know of such cases but fail to report them should be punished in the same way."

The only books exempted were texts on practical matters, such as medicine and agriculture, as well as books on divination, including the *Yijing*. Qin Shihuangdi sanctioned the proposal. Sima Qian records that Qin Shihuangdi grew more tyrannical, condemning to death even those of his courtiers who spoke of where the emperor was. Two scholars, employed to find elixirs of life for the emperor, decided instead to go into hiding:

The Supreme One enjoys using punishments and executions as a sign of his authority, and since all under heaven

hang on to their salaries in fear of punishment, no-one dares to fulfil his loyal duties . . . When his greed for authority has reached such a pitch, the elixir of immortality can never be sought for him.

On hearing of their disappearance, Qin Shihuangdi ordered an investigation of all the scholars and 460 were buried alive as a warning to others.

In 1958 Mao Zedong, who likewise saw Confucian traditionalists as his political enemies, compared himself to Qin Shihuangdi in his treatment of intellectuals. Mao is reported to have boasted that he destroyed a hundred times as many intellectuals as Qin Shihuangdi. The rise of the Qin dynasty was interpreted, in accordance with Marxist historiography, as a progressive feudalist regime replacing the conservative Confucian slave-owners. However, the faction's political opponents were quick to point out that the Qin dynasty was short-lived, toppled by popular revolt because of its own harsh treatment of its subjects.

PAUL WELLEN

Further Reading

Li, Yu-ning (editor), "The First Emperor of China", *Chinese Studies in History* (Winter 1974–75)

Liang, Xiao, "Study the Historical Experience of the Struggle between the Confucian and Legalist Schools", *Beijing Review*, 2 (1975)

Luo, Si-ding, "Struggle between Restoration and Counter-Restoration in the Course of Founding the Chin Dynasty", *Beijing Review*, 17/18 (1974)

Szuma, Chien, "The First Emperor of China" in *Records of the Historian*, Beijing: Foreign Languages Press, 1979

Wei, Jin, "Qin Shi-huang's Burning of the Books Viewed from the Bamboo Documents of Yin-que shan", *Red Flag*, 7 (1974): 62–66

Wu, Tien-wei, *Lin-Biao and the Gang of Four: Contra-Confucianism in Historical and Intellectual Perspective*, Carbondale: Southern Illinois University Press, 1983

Yang, Jung-kuo, *Confucius: "Sage" of the Reactionary Classes*, Beijing: Foreign Languages Press, 1974

QIN ZHAOYANG
Chinese essayist and editor, 1916–

In the early 1950s, Qin Zhaoyang headed the fiction section of *Renmin Wenxue* (People's Literature), the official literary organ of the Chinese Communist Party. Following a series of controversial articles published early in 1953, the party decided that Liu would benefit from an extended period living among the peasants. This was a form of mild censure, aimed at eradicating any vestiges of "bourgeois thinking" that Qin was said to retain. The articles, including "Lixiang yu zhenshi" (Ideal and Truth), were critical of those writers who merely "fabricated stories according to formula" or, as Qin phrased it, went in for "formalism and abstract generalization". He also denounced what he saw to be the superficiality of contemporary writing, where scenery and characters were invented solely to serve

political ends. The main outcome of Qin's rustication was a series of sketches entitled *Nongcun sanji* (Village Vignettes). While these pieces were not entirely uncritical of rural collectivization, they expressed "an optimism that served as a motivating force during the early years of the People's Republic of China".

In the spring of 1956, Mao Zedong's "Hundred Flowers" policy heralded a more liberal cultural atmosphere. At the time, Qin Zhaoyang was appointed associate editor of *Renmin Wenxue*; because of the ill health of the chief editor Yan Wenjing, Qin assumed control of the journal's editorial decision making, sanctioning publication of highly provocative works by controversial young writers such as Wang Meng and

Liu Binyan. That Wang and Liu were to become such well-known figures on the literary stage of 1956–57 was the result in large part of Qin's patronage.

In the late summer of 1956, following wholehearted approval of the "Hundred Flowers" policy by the cultural authorities, Qin drafted an 18-point programme for "improving" the editorial policy of *Renmin Wenxue*. The programme supported the official stance that literature should adhere to the tenets of realism. However, writers should be encouraged to "delve into life" and to "face reality" rather than merely to toe the political line. Qin clarified that "we should not neglect or lower the artistic criteria because of political criteria". Furthermore, "it is not our task to perform an accompaniment to the current policies . . . [and] one should avoid strained, monotonous, dry and tasteless reflections." Although never published, the draft was cited as evidence of Qin's "rightism" in 1957.

In September 1956, under the pseudonym He Zhi, Qin Zhaoyang published his most celebrated essay, "Xianshi zhuyi: guangkuo de daolu" (Realism: The Broad Road). Holding similar views to those expressed by Konstantin Simonov, co-editor of *Novyi Mir*, at the Second Soviet Writers' Congress in 1954, Qin assailed socialist realism. Under the slogan "realism in the socialist era" Qin promoted the view that writers should be allowed to develop a broader realism, one that was honest both to life and to art. He suggested that all "administrative interferences" and "fixed formulas" be removed, and writers given the opportunity to explore their own themes and styles. The article concluded with the submission: "We are a country which has a deep realist tradition. How many masters of realism have emerged in our history! They all . . . broke through outdated rules and clichés. Let's follow their example."

Although he enjoyed support among many younger writers, Qin was opposed by the editors of other journals, who now published articles in support of socialist realism. Nonetheless, Qin continued to make his personal views known. His essay "Lun jianrui de feng" (On the Spirit of Sharpness) denounced the blanket criticism by cultural officials of all writers who did not follow the "correct" line. Similarly, the short story "Chenmo" (Silence) depicts party cadres putting opportunism and manipulation before the needs and rights of the people.

In the spring of 1957 Qin Zhaoyang was criticized on two counts. First, the debate on Wang Meng's short story "Zuzhi bu xinlai de qingnianren" (The Newcomer in the Organization Department) was aimed at Qin, the editor who had revised the draft and sanctioned publication, rather than Wang himself. Second, an article by the Propaganda Department of the People's Liberation Army indirectly singled out Qin as using the "Hundred Flowers" policy to engage in anti-party activity. Qin's essay of March 1957, "Guanyu xie zhenshi" (On "Writing the Truth"), however, was a renunciation of all his previous ideas on realism. Clearly under pressure and intimidation, Qin was also forced to condemn Wang Meng's story.

He concludes tritely: "We must increasingly study and reform ourselves and remember party principles in literature."

Criticism of Qin Zhaoyang reached a peak in the early spring of 1957. He was attacked for lacking ideological consciousness and for his inappropriate portrayal of party cadres. His exposure of the "dark side" of contemporary life was dismissed as unbalanced, and the conclusions drawn in his writings as negative. As a result of the denunciations, Qin was made to step down as editor of *Renmin Wenxue* and engage in "study". When the Anti-Rightist Campaign began in June 1957, Qin was forced to attend a series of meetings to witness his branding as a "rightist". Physically and mentally broken by consistent torment, he developed a stomach ulcer.

In 1958 the authorities firmly placed Qin among those intellectuals who, despite continued periods of "re-education", had refused to recant their "bourgeois ways". His self-criticism, published in response to the renewed attacks, was not totally contrite. He claimed that his publication of works by Wang Meng and Liu Binyan was meant to "stimulate discussion" in line with the "Hundred Flowers" policy and therefore had not strayed from Marxism-Leninism. A final series of meetings denouncing Qin was held in July 1958, during which he bowed to the inevitable and confessed to all his "crimes".

In 1959 Qin was sent to work in a factory in the southern province of Guangxi. Three years later he was given permission to work again in cultural organizations, and under a different name, as a professional writer, but not allowed to return to Beijing. At the outset of the Cultural Revolution, along with all the other writers branded "rightists" in 1957, Qin once again fell victim to changes in the party line. He was forced to undertake agricultural labour in a desolate region of Guangxi.

By 1975 Qin was given permission to return to the capital. He was officially rehabilitated in 1979 and shortly thereafter appointed editor of the influential literary journal *Dangdai* (Contemporary). His novel *Dadi* (The Big Land) won a literary prize in 1984. Qin continues to live and write in Beijing.

DESMOND A. SKEEL

Writings
Village Sketches, 1957

Further Reading
Børdahl, Vibeke, *Along the Broad Road of Realism: Qin Zhaoyang's World of Fiction*, London: Curzon Press, 1990

Fokkema, D.W., *Literary Doctrine in China and Soviet Influence, 1956–1960*, The Hague: Mouton, 1965

Goldman, Merle, *Literary Dissent in Communist China*, Cambridge, Massachusetts: Harvard University Press, 1967

Hsu, Kai-yu (editor), *Literature of the People's Republic of China*, Bloomington: Indiana University Press, 1980

McDougall, Bonnie S. and Louie Kam, *The Literature of China: The Twentieth Century*, London: Hurst, 1997

Nieh Hualing (editor), *Literature of the Hundred Flowers*, New York: Columbia University Press, 1981

QUAKERS (The Religious Society of Friends)
Christian dissenters, founded c.1652

This essay concerns both censorship within the Religious Society of Friends and censorship practised on the society and its members. However, it should be pointed out that although Quakers believe in "publishing truth" and in "speaking truth to power", they have never been much exercised by censorship and have suffered no more and no less from it than other groups of dissenters or libertarians. In the British context, there was one *cause célèbre*, which is considered later. However, in the United States there is no equivalent. This does not mean that either censorship of Friends by Friends or of Friends by outside bodies has never occurred in the US; only, its expressions have been so low-key that they have not found their way into that country's ample literature on the Religious Society of Friends.

What applies to the US applies also to other parts of the world. Thus Friends must today, of course, exercise prudence in authoritarian countries, just as in the past they had to live with the realities of censorship in, say, Nazi Germany, but neither then nor now have there been any special instances of censorship directed at them as a group. There are probably two reasons for this. First, being numerically very small, Friends are unlikely to be viewed as a threat to officialdom anywhere. Second, Quakers may be perceived as mildly cranky, but they generally elicit respect. Therefore, at the risk of appearing unashamedly Anglocentric, this article concentrates on censorship in Britain, and more precisely in England.

Over the past three-and-a-half centuries, Friends have been much more concerned with other issues. These, however, are not widely known since there are now only some 300,000 Friends in the world; one-third of them in Kenya, another third in the United States, and the remaining third scattered over the globe, sometimes in very small groups or even as isolated individuals. For these reasons, it is necessary to preface an account of censorship with a brief definition of this religious society and a synopsis of its history.

The Religious Society of Friends (Quakers) arose at a time of religious ferment in England when many dissenting groups were formed that were hostile to the absolute monarch, Charles I (1625–49). These were egalitarian and prelapsarian groups that wished to return to Paradise. Their utopian project was doomed, since what replaced the monarchy was Oliver Cromwell and his Protectorate; in other words, the squirearchy usurped power from the monarch and the aristocracy that had supported him. Friends were founded in the early 1650s by a mystic of a practical disposition, George Fox (1624–91). At first, they were drawn largely from the artisanal class and agricultural workers, and so it follows that their ways were plain. They were of egalitarian disposition, insisting on addressing even those in authority as "thou" (the informal mode of address) and refusing what was called "hat honour", that is, doffing one's hat or cap to those in authority when in their presence. All Friends, regardless of the form of Quakerism they practise, have in common basic testimonies. Of these the best-known is the peace testimony, but others, of equal importance to Friends themselves, are equality (Quakers are non-elitist), simplicity (of worship, dress, and lifestyle), honesty or integrity, and the social testimony which involved them, for example, in

feeding programmes in the USSR during the famine of the 1920s and in Germany after both world wars. Quakers were among the first to enter Belsen after this death camp was liberated, and the society was awarded the Nobel Peace Prize in 1947. Quakers were also early abolitionists, expelling members of the Barclay banking family from the society in 1761 when they refused to give up their interest in the slave trade. In addition, Friends have always been active in prison reform, partly because in the early years of the society – and also in World War I – they themselves had ample experience of the miseries of prison life.

Other points that should be made are that the original Quakers developed silent, unmediated worship and avoided any outward celebration of sacraments. They had preachers who travelled around England and in the American colonies, but never had resident pastors at their meeting houses since they believed in "the ministry of all believers". Moreover, women played a prominent part in the society from the beginning, and were accepted as preachers before the end of the 17th century.

It is said that one of the most important reasons why the Quakers were alone among the various radical religious groups in 17th-century England to stand the test of time was George Fox's insistence on group organization and sound administrative practices. Thus censorship of Friends by Friends arose in the early 1670s when the Second Day Morning Meeting of Ministers was established in London. This group had two duties: one was to ensure that preachers visited the various meetings for worship on a regular basis, and the other was to vet all the materials written by Friends before they were published. They were to formulate replies to hostile criticism aimed at Quakers, and they were to iron out questions of style.

The mid-17th century was one of intense religious and philosophical ferment, and naturally enough it produced a lunatic fringe. It was the task of Morning Meeting to control the cranks within their own society, with particular reference to the extravagances of style to be found in their writings. As previously mentioned, many of the early Quakers came from humble backgrounds and they were relatively unlettered. The titles of certain early pamphlets indicate an exuberance that any body of censors would frown on: *A Wren in the Burning Bush* and *Waving the Wings of Contraction to the Congregated Clean Fowls in the Ark of God* will serve to illustrate this point, even in an age of pamphleteers given to long and – to us – eccentric-sounding titles.

Not even George Fox or his wife Margaret Fell were spared the attentions of these censors, and when the former had a paper turned down, he responded huffily by writing: "I was not moved to set up that meeting to make orders against the reading of my papers." But the members of Morning Meeting were unrepentant and at a later point one of their members, Thomas Ellwood, excised from Fox's *Journal* passages on healing, "providential punishments", visions, and premonitions. Ellwood's edition of Fox's life remained the standard one until 1891. Quaker literature suffered through the censorship of Morning Meeting; its members tended to reject material of a highly mystical and prophetic nature, and directed the Society's mind-set towards the exclusiveness that was to characterize it in the 18th century.

The material printed for Quakers during the second half of the 17th century was unlicensed, although since they published more than 1800 books in the period 1660–1708, it cannot be said that the censors were unduly zealous in their pursuit of seditious publications. Among the printers bold enough to print and sell Quaker literature in the early years of the Restoration were several women. One of these, Mary Westwood, worked a private press at the "Black Spread Eagle". Two others were Widow Inman and Mrs Dover, the latter being described as a "common printer for all scandalous pamphlets".

The 18th century, known as the quietist period, was one in which Friends withdrew from society. However, since, like Jews, they were debarred from the professions, individual Quakers also devoted their energies to amassing wealth in banking and commerce. They also played an active part in the Industrial Revolution, something that accounts for their relative strength in the Midlands (the Darby family in Coalbrookdale and the Cadbury family in Birmingham) down to this day. But they were not to clash with the law of the land or to suffer censorship until World War I. When they did so, it was in earnest.

At their annual conference (known as Yearly Meeting) in 1916, Friends minuted their opposition to the introduction of conscription in Britain: "We take this, the earliest opportunity, of re-affirming our entire opposition to compulsory military service and our desire for the repeal of the Act" (i.e. the Military Service Act). It is not widely known that, despite official opposition, one-third of all Quakers of military age volunteered for army service or allowed themselves to be conscripted. This caused much anguish in those Quaker families in which parents felt obliged to break relations with any of their sons who entered willingly into the armed forces.

In 1917 a clause was added to the Defence of the Realm regulations, ordering that all publications dealing with the war or the making of peace should first be approved by the official censor. Quakers decided to defy the new regulation, and Meeting for Sufferings (their executive body) made the following declaration:

> We realize the rarity of the occasions on which a body of citizens find their sense of duty to be in conflict with

the law, and it is with a sense of the gravity of the decision that the Society of Friends must on this occasion act contrary to the regulations and continue to issue literature on war and peace without submitting it to the censor. It is convinced that in thus standing for spiritual liberty it is acting in the best spirit of the nation.

In January 1918 the Friends published a pamphlet about conscientious objectors in prison titled *A Challenge to Militarism*. Three Quakers who were directly responsible for its publication were tried and found guilty. These were Harrison Barrow, who in 1914 was mayor-elect of Birmingham, Edith Ellis, the daughter of the MP John Edward Ellis, and Arthur Watts. Barrow had withdrawn from the prospective mayorship so that it would not be his civic duty to participate in army recruitment. The two men were sentenced to six months' imprisonment, and Edith Ellis ended up serving a term of three months because she refused to pay the fine of £100 with 50 guineas costs.

Since then Friends in Britain have had no further brushes with authority over issues of censorship. However, they are concerned about secrecy in government, something that is made clear in *Questions of Integrity* (1993), a volume produced by the Committee for Truth and Integrity in Public Affairs (TIPA). In this volume 20 Quakers from various walks of life consider conflicts between openness and confidentiality, tact and truth, secrecy and irresponsibility. The introduction was written by Robin Robinson, a former civil servant who worked in the Cabinet Office. He asked himself the question: "What changed my views from actively enjoying the secrecy to finding it disturbing?" His conclusion is: ". . . my whole world view was shifting as a result of my spiritual experience. The concern that I took to Dover Meeting in 1988 was about the morality of spying."

VERITY SMITH

Further Reading

Boulton, David, *Objection Overruled*, London: MacGibbon and Kee, 1967

Committee for Truth and Integrity in Public Affairs, *Questions of Integrity*, London: London Yearly Meeting, 1993

Lloyd, Arnold, *Quaker Social History, 1669–1738*, London and New York: Longmans Green, 1950

Wright, Luella M., *The Literary Life of the Early Friends, 1650–1725*, New York: AMS Press, 1966

AL-QUDS (Jerusalem)
Palestinian/Jordanian newspaper, established 1967

Revised Jordanian press laws merged three East Jerusalem dailies into one to form *al-Quds* in March 1967. Quds is the Arabic name for Jerusalem. The launch of the Jordanian government-controlled newspaper was interrupted by the June 1967 Arab–Israeli war and the subsequent takeover of East Jerusalem by Israel. When it resumed publication in December 1968, *al-Quds* was subject to Israeli censorship regulations, although the Jordanian government continued to subsidize its operations.

The tacit Israeli–Jordanian cooperation over the newspaper was indicative of the overall relationship between these two countries regarding the occupied West Bank. Both countries sought to minimize the sway of Palestinian nationalism and the Palestine Liberation Organization (PLO) over the indigenous Palestinian population, who continued to hold Jordanian citizenship. *Al-Quds*, with its pro-Jordanian bias was one such vehicle used to enhance the kingdom's influence at the expense of the outlawed PLO, with the eventual goal of regaining control over the West Bank as part of an Israeli–Jordanian peace treaty.

By 1980 changes in Israeli policy as well as heightened Palestinian nationalism within the Occupied Territories signalled a switch in loyalties at *al-Quds*. Jordanian influence waned as the newspaper identified itself as pro-Palestinian. This shift was partly due to Israel's formal annexation of East Jerusalem in 1980. With annexation, Israeli law – and not military occupation ordinances – was applied to newspapers published in the city. While considerable censorship regulations remained, *al-Quds* and other publications enjoyed some leeway to express Palestinian sentiments. The paper straddled a fine line between its oblique backing of the PLO and strict Israeli punishments for any reference to or support of the outlawed organization. The newspaper was the most popular daily in the Occupied Territories, with a circulation between 15,000 and 20,000 copies.

With the start of the Palestinian uprising (the intifada) in December 1987, Israel tightened control on the Palestinian media. The government banned *al-Quds* and other newspapers from distributing in the West Bank and Gaza Strip for periods of up to 45 days at a time. During these periods *al-Quds* circulated only in East Jerusalem, and it was forced to cut the number of pages and the size of its press-run as readership and advertising dropped substantially. Israel routinely purged Arabic translations of news reports that had previously appeared in the Hebrew-language media on the grounds that such information would incite violence. New subjects were placed on the censorship list, including details of the killing of Palestinians by Israeli soldiers. The government restricted the movements of *al-Quds*'s editor during numerous occasions after 1987 and, in 1992, its Gaza correspondent was held in administrative detention for months and threatened with deportation.

Al-Quds encountered a new situation with the advent of the Palestinian National Authority (PNA) under Yasser Arafat in Gaza and parts of the West Bank after July 1994. While the newspaper continued to publish in Israeli-held East Jerusalem, much of its circulation was in the areas controlled by the PNA. It was in an untenable position; still under the watchful eye of the Israeli censor, it now also confronted pressures from the PNA. Despite *al-Quds*'s pro-Palestinian stance, the newspaper angered Arafat with its coverage and editorials on the Islamist opposition to the PNA, its criticism of some PNA policies, and its coverage of the Israeli–Jordanian relationship. At various times since 1994 the PNA has banned distribution of the newspaper or confiscated copies. In December 1995 PNA security officials summoned *al-Quds*'s editor, Mahir al-ʿAlami, for questioning about his refusal to publish a front-page article on Arafat. He was held without charge for a week. While *al-Quds* at times stakes out an independent line in its reporting, the newspaper exercises a great deal of self-censorship as it faces the scrutiny of both the Israeli government and the PNA.

ROBERT J. BOOKMILLER

Further Reading

Article 19, *Cry for Change: Israeli Censorship in the Occupied Territories*, London: Article 19, 1992

Website

http://www.alquds.com (*al-Quds* internet newspaper in Arabic)

AL-QUDS PALESTINIAN ARAB RADIO
Palestinian clandestine radio station, established 1988

The al-Quds Palestinian Arab Radio is operated by the Popular Front for the Liberation of Palestine–General Command (PFLP–GC). It began broadcasting from headquarters in Damascus in January 1988, following the outbreak of the Palestinian uprising, the intifada, in the Israeli occupied territories (al-Quds is Arabic for Jerusalem). The radio transmits on medium, short, and FM waves for approximately 10 hours a day. Al-Quds programmes, mixing music, news, and commentary are heard by their target audiences in the West Bank and Gaza, but are also received in Israel and Jordan.

While the Syrian-supported PFLP–GC is a Palestinian guerrilla organization operating outside the PLO umbrella, during the early phases of the intifada al-Quds's programming complemented the official PLO line. However, after the PLO indirectly recognized Israel in November 1988 and began to move towards peaceful accommodation, al-Quds struck an anti-PLO tone in addition to its already strident anti-Israeli proclivity. The radio also broadcasts communiqués from Hamas and other Palestinian or Arab groups opposed to peace with Israel.

The station's slogan "For the liberation of land and man" begins and ends most broadcasts. Its overall policy emphasizes its call for a return to Palestinian armed struggle against Israel. As a consequence, both the PLO and Jordanian peace treaties with Israel are vehemently condemned, while violence against Israeli targets is lauded.

Since its inaugural broadcasts, al-Quds's high reception quality within the West Bank and Gaza prompted Israeli officials to note that this was the "first time that the terrorists have such a powerful radio station . . . at their disposal". Because Israel did not permit Palestinians to broadcast in the occupied territories at that time, and heavily censored any printed materials distributed there, radio beamed from outside was the only way to make a Palestinian voice available without first passing through Israeli control. Israel began jamming the transmissions in 1988, a practice it rarely employed against other Arab broadcasts: al-Quds regularly changed frequencies to evade the jamming. Israel also hindered the radio's reception by broadcasting its own Arabic-language programming on the main medium-wave frequency (702 kHz) most often used by al-Quds.

After the 1994 inception of the Palestinian National Authority (PNA) in Gaza and some of the West Bank, Israel initially appropriated the al-Quds's medium-wave frequency for use by the PNA's broadcasting station in Ramallah. Another frequency was later assigned to the PNA. Al-Quds's pro-grammes also attack the PNA for cooperating with Israel. While the broadcasts are a constant irritant to president Yasser Arafat's government, the PNA does not possess the equipment necessary to jam the transmissions. Following stepped-up anti-Jordan programming from al-Quds, Amman joined Israel in regularly blocking the radio's broadcasts in 1996.

ROBERT J. BOOKMILLER

Further Reading

Article 19, *Cry for Change: Israeli Censorship in the Occupied Territories*, London: Article 19, 1992

Bookmiller, Kirsten Nakjavani and Robert J. Bookmiller, "Palestinian Radio and the Intifada", *Journal of Palestine Studies*, 19/4 (1990): 96–105

Fu'ad, Abir, "Al-Sabil Visits al-Quds Radio in Damascus", *Al-Sabil* (29 March–4 April 1994): 11; reprinted in *Foreign Broadcast Information Service: Near East and South Asia* (31 March 1994): 22

QUÉBEC

Censorship in Québec unfolded in two broad phases. From the 17th century, religion played a major role in its temporal as well as spiritual life. For French-Canadians, the majority ethnic group, no aspect of social being – entertainment, education, art, social service – could exist far from the church bell, and censorship was increasingly systematized as a tool for organizing public morality. Then, with the so-called Quiet Revolution, a modernist secular nationalist movement that coalesced during the 1960s, the alignment of censorial power was reshuffled, now deployed in organizing Québec as a collective entity or cultural unit. Religion began to cede its role to the market: gradually, church-state patterns of censorship would give way to a corporatist arrangement that allied the state with private enterprise.

In a New France where freedom of expression was an alien concept, few bans were imposed – the theatre was the exception, with a ban for example on Frontenac's mounting of Molière's *Tartuffe* (1694) – until Brown and Gilmore introduced the press in 1764, shortly after Britain replaced France as the dominant European power. Non-Catholics could now legally settle in Québec, heightening the church's key institutional role for the French-descended Catholic majority. Religious censorship's first period, from 1763 to 1840, would mark its learning years, followed by periods of prohibitive (1840–1900) and prescriptive (1900–50) censorship.

The *Gazette littéraire, pour la Ville & District de Montréal* was the first newspaper to pose a problem for the clergy. Led by the Enlightenment thinking of Valentin Jautard and Fleury Mesplet, friend and printer to Benjamin Franklin, it appeared for a year before the two were imprisoned. The same fate awaited Pierre Bédard, whose *Canadien* attacked the government ceaselessly: at a time when literate members of the public were a rarity, the controversial publisher was jailed in 1810. Thus far, clerical censorship had cloaked itself in civil power to accomplish its goals; it would soon overcome this limitation convincingly. Between 1805 and 1838, the newspaper sector had seen 104 publications opened and 85 closed. When, in 1837–8, journalists became involved with the revolt against British authorities, French-language newspapers were censored by a loose arrangement of state and church. English-language newspapers, on the other hand, were censored by market forces: in 1838, *The Advertiser*'s sponsors left after it expressed liberal ideas, forcing the paper to shut down. The market's dominance in English-language censorship would continue. But in the French-Québec sector, aligned with church-political power, censorship was becoming more organized. A religious conflict at the religious establishment's nerve centre between Québec City and Montréal was resolved by Montréal's institution as a separate bishopric in 1836. Freed from Québec City, Monseigneur Bourget became bishop of Montréal, ushering in a period of planned and proscriptive, or prohibitive, censorship.

Indeed, if 1763–1840 were its learning years, the period of prohibitive censorship that lasted from 1840 to 1900 reached its heights in Montréal, under Monseigneur Bourget (1840), Fabre (1876), and Bruchési (1897). Bourget generated his own material by founding Québec's first religious newspapers, *Les mélanges religieux* (1840), and *L'oeuvre des bons livres* (1844), while tightly controlling parish libraries, even as he took on oppositional voices. The Institut Canadien of Montréal (1844), in particular, was a secular mouthpiece of liberal ideas through Louis-Antoine Dessaulles until Bourget purged its library, banned its newspaper, *Le Pays*, and in 1868 and 1869, placed the Institut's *Annuaires* in the Vatican's Index.

Monseigneur Fabre's reign was punctuated by three cases. After having to ban written attacks against Laval University, a suspected liberalist hotbed (1882), religious authority emerged shaken from a civil suit brought by Aristide Filiatreault of the banned magazine *Canada-Revue*, despite Fabre's victory. Meanwhile, having tried in vain to oppose the accession of Wilfred Laurier to the post of Canadian prime minister in the 1896 election, the church establishment could do little more than relegate to the Catholic Index of Prohibited Books Laurent-Olivier David's *Le clergé canadien, sa mission son oeuvre* (1896), a treatise aimed at defending Laurier's Liberal Party in Rome.

An unprecedented parade of prohibition followed under Bruchesi: theatre (1903), newspapers *Les Débats* (1903) and *Le Combat* (1904), the novel *Marie Calumet* (Rodolphe Girard, 1904), and more – demonstrating, if nothing else, the limits of prohibitive censorship. Censorship in the second half of the 19th century had been organized around repression. Now, the onset of large-scale cultural production – mass-market newspapers whose dependence had shifted to publicity as source of funding; a wave of rebellious novelists (R. Girard, A. Bessette, A. Laberge); the arrival of cinema – led the clergy to a major strategic shift, prescriptive instead of prohibitive censorship: controlling thoughts before words.

In contrast to the prohibitive period of 1840–1900, this pre-scriptive turn (1900–50) saw the birth of Catholic movements such as the Association Catholique de la Jeunesse Canadienne-française (1904) and, especially, the Action Sociale Catholique (1907), which launched magazines, newspapers, and almanacs intended to reinforce public morality and mould thoughts and minds in the educational and popular milieux. Other publications such as the newspaper *Le Devoir* (1910) and the *L'action française* (1916), coordinated by historian Lionel Groulx, distributed in magazines, almanacs, and bookstores, shared similar goals. Few religious bans were imposed during the period, with the notable exception of Jean-Charles Harvey's *Les Demi-civilisés* (1934): the difficulties of preventing speech gave way to the more efficient method of compelling certain utterances. Even wartime news censorship during the first and second world wars was relatively uncontroversial.

More disputed was the celebrated Act to Protect the Province Against Communist Propaganda, or "Padlock Law", brought in by Premier Maurice Duplessis in 1937 after similar federal legislation was struck down. An effort by political, financial, and religious authorities to prevent French Québec from being contaminated by communist ideas, the law enabled the prohibition (1948) of the labour paper *Le Combat* and of *Le Progrès de Villeray*, on whose premises *Le Combat* were printed, and the padlocking of the United Jewish People's Order's premises (1950), before it was struck down in 1957.

Coordinated by church and state, the engineering of morality was proceeding apace. Censorship has already passed its high point, however. After its learning years and its prohibitive and prescriptive periods, 1950–60 would mark the decline of religious censorship. Certainly, the prescriptive turn had been successful as an initial response to the growth of the cultural and entertainment industries. But ongoing technological innovation, market growth, and information proliferation made the church's attempt to manage information supply increasingly difficult.

The encounter with "mass culture" had been developing for some time. The larger newspapers had been less and less dependent on the clergy since the 1930s; film, too, had been developing as a major art and entertainment form, leading the state to a more active role alongside the church. Indeed, the legislative framework for film censorship, first formalized in 1931, was already clearly established when, in 1950, a new morality law underscored the state's role in regulating public space. The ensuing crusade against crime comic books (1955–56) symbolized the campaign against popular culture's corrupting influence.

The campaign against a rapidly decentralizing, market-based mode of cultural production was an uphill battle, however. It was made even more difficult by a growing social movement seeking to modernize Québec life. Spurred on by declarations and actions such as the *Refus global* signed by Paul-Émile Borduas and other artists (1948), the clergy's influential voice began to give way to a different order. In the domain of censorship, the dogmas of religious power ceded to a new model which placed individual responsibility at its centre. Accountability for cultural and intellectual consumption moved from the author to the reader. It is this fundamental shift, in fact, that explains the abrogation of the Index in 1966: its disappearance signified not that moral individuals may read everything, but that they should be responsible for their choices.

For a century following its learning years, French-Canadian thought had been governed by an organized clerical censorship whose objects were the public mores of French-Canadian life in the province. The 1960s and the Quiet Revolution signalled both the end of this mode of control and the emergence of new powers. Driven by the desire for modernity, the object of governance shifted from French-Canadian Québécois to Québec as a whole. While morality would remain an issue, post-Quiet Revolution Québec would incorporate this question into a larger debate on cultural identity which, for both proponents and critics, would catalyze a shift in the very concept of censorship, from the relatively simple domain of prior restraint to a more complex form incorporating legal interdiction and political regulation in a heady mix. The very question of censorship's presence or absence became subject to heated debate.

Censorship would play its part in the Quiet Revolution itself. The censorship apparatus put into place to prevent the Front de libération du Québec (FLQ) terrorist group from gaining a platform following invocation of the War Measures Act in the 1970 October crisis is perhaps the most celebrated example. At the same time, accusations of censorship were at the centre of the unfolding conflict between the Quiet Revolution's nationalist protagonists and federally funded cultural institutions The National Film Board (NFB), whose origins lay in wartime propaganda, was scarred by a searing 1957 exposé of the inferior status accorded to French-language films, and became accused of acting as an instrument of Canadian-nationalist propaganda and fostering self-censorship in the francophone sector – a diagnosis not helped by the banning of Denys Arcand's *On est au coton* and Gilles Groulx's *24 heures ou plus* in the early 1970s. Radio-Canada, the federally funded and mandated French-language broadcaster, was also the object of criticism when its coverage of a 1968 nationalist parade steadfastly ignored police violence and when it ordered reporters to stop freelancing with a pro-independence news magazine.

The spectre of Radio-Canada censorship of national unity issues, made more concrete by legal provisions for reinforcing Canadian identity, has been the subject of much debate. A more subtle form of censorship has come from the lack of long-term planning and continuous decreases in the public broadcaster's budget, complicating media access for many Québécois, particularly in rural areas. Community radio and, to a lesser extent, community television – the "third sectors" of Québec and Canadian electronic media – have picked up the slack to some extent, but a certain degree of regulatory capture at the federal communications regulator, the Canadian Radio-Television and Telecommunication Commission (CRTC), has prevented community media from encroaching upon the space of private broadcasters which, in both radio and television, are heavily concentrated in the Montréal area.

While corporate concentration has reduced the diversity of voices in the broadcast sector, a licensing scheme that holds broadcast undertakings to a public-interest mandate has regulated market-place decision-making. According to CRTC regulations, 65 per cent of the playlists at French-language music radio stations must be sung in the French language, while 30 per cent of all radio music must be Canadian. These rules have been controversial – some have accused them of censoring broadcasting business people, while others have supported them as ways of interrupting censorship patterns imposed by the market – but are generally agreed to have stimulated the Québec and French-language music industry.

No such debate could exist in the newspaper industry, where regulation is limited to libel laws and to the private, nonprofit Conseil de presse du Québec (Québec Press Council, 1973). This does not mean that questions of censorship were not raised: in 1964, editors at *Le Soleil* and *L'Évenement* were ordered to play down criticism of the authorities; in 1965 the editor of *La Presse* was fired shortly after having criticized an enterprise directed by a member of the newspaper's board of directors; in 1975 a federal minister intervened to prevent government advertising from being published in the pro-independence newspaper *Le Jour*; in 1987 editorial writers at several UniMedia-owned newspapers were "reminded" of their owner's support of the Canada–US Free Trade Agreement then being hotly debated. Yet a high degree of press concentration has not resulted in state intervention in print media – two corporations control almost the entire French-language daily market – notwithstanding the recommendations of a federal Royal Commission which, in 1981, stated that

> [t]he ownership and control of most newspapers is today highly concentrated under interests whose business concerns extend far beyond the particular newspaper. Much of our press, consequently, is not itself dedicated exclusively to the purposes of the press, to the discharge of its public responsibility. Extraneous interests, operating internally, are the chains that today limit the freedom of the press.

The situation is similar for film, where distribution arrangements favouring Hollywood studios dominate local screens – albeit dubbed in French, as provided for by Québec law – and the former Bureau de censure des vues animées (Film Censorship Office), part of the public morality regulatory apparatus, was transformed into the Régie du cinéma (Cinema Board) which assigns movie ratings. In film as for newspapers and, to a lesser extent, broadcast media, organized church and state collaboration has given way to a more dispersed censorship coordinated by market structures, with the occasional cooperation through the state's action or inaction.

Just as its involvement in censorship had, in an earlier time, been based on decisions about public mores, the state's participation in the regulation of information and expression after the Quiet Revolution has proceeded from a concern with the cultural contours of public space and with the role of Québec as a cultural entity. A Canadian Charter of Rights and Freedoms has served as a baseline for ensuring freedom of expression since 1981, and the Québec Charter of Human Rights and Freedoms with similar guarantees has taken precedence over all other Québec laws since 1982. But French language use is the key to the cultural project championed by the state, and so it is appropriate that it be within public space that linguistic regulation be most organized, and most controversial. Following a Law to Promote the French Language in 1969 and an Official Language Law in 1974, the 1977 Charter of the French Language (Bill 101) legislated the primacy of French in the workplace and public areas, including store signs, and created two organizations, a French Language Office and French Language Council, to formulate and enforce strategies for meeting these goals.

Controversial as French-language legislation has been – it has undergone court challenges at every level of Québec and Canadian law, and even at the United Nations – it took on a layer of confusion when, in 1997, a Montréal-based computer store was issued a warning by the French Language Office, which felt that the store's English-language website violated the rule which obliged advertisements to be made available to customers in French. The networked space emerging from the convergence of broadcast and telecommunications media and computers has raised a number of as-yet unresolved issues regarding the regulation of information flow in the service of large-scale cultural projects.

While these are only now being addressed, a number of citizens' groups have been active in the area of new-media issues, ranging from little-known Fondation pour la Protection de L'Enfant, founded in Québec City in 1997, to English-language government watchdogs Electronic Frontier Canada (EFC), to various efforts attempting to counter the de facto censorship for non-English speakers posed by the predominance of English on the internet. Private sector privacy and data warehousing regulation by Québec and, more recently, Canadian law will play an increasing role in this sector's evolution, while the censorship abilities of Canadian customs inspectors, who serve as filters for obscenity and hate propaganda physically entering the country, will continue to diminish with the dematerialization of information.

BRAM DOV ABRAMSON and PIERRE HÉBERT

Further Reading

Elmer, Greg and Bram Abramson, "Excavating Ethnicity in Québécois", *Québec Studies*, 23 (1997): 13–28

Gagnon, Lysiane, "Journalism and Ideologies in Québec" in *The Journalists*, Ottawa: Royal Commission on Newspapers, 1981 (Research Publications 2)

Grenier, Line, "Policing French-language Music on Canadian Radio: The Twilight of the Popular Record Era?" in *Rock and Popular Music: Politics, Policies, Institutions*, edited by Tony Bennett *et al.*, London: Routledge, 1993

Hébert, Pierre and Patrick Nicol, *Censure et littérature au Québec: le livre crucifié, 1625–1919*, Montréal: Fides, 1997

Raboy, Marc, *Missed Opportunities: The Story of Canada's Broadcasting Policy*, Montréal: McGill–Queen's University Press, 1990

Royal Commission on Newspapers, Ottawa: Minister of Supply and Services, 1981

Trudel, Pierre *et al.*, *Droit du cyberespace*, Montréal: Université de Montréal, Centre de Recherche en Droit Public, 1997

QUIETISM
System of spirituality, 17th-century France

Strictly speaking, quietism lies in the practice of pure passivity in prayer. When expounded theoretically as a spiritual teaching, it becomes in the Catholic Church the heresy condemned by Innocent XI in the apostolic constitution *Coelestis pastor* of 19 November 1687. Its historical importance derives largely from its confusion with a controversy about the possibility of a "pure" or disinterested love of God which opposed François Fénelon, archbishop of Cambrai (1651–1715) who defended it, to Jacques Bossuet, bishop of Meaux (1627–1704) who regarded as posturings the subtle distinctions of mystical theology.

The ideal of passivity in prayer had recurred in the histories of both western and eastern ascetic teaching, and is obviously not unrelated to states regarded as spiritually advanced in many non-Christian religions. The ideal of pure love as it appeared in 17th-century France was also related to the dilemma of the devout Christian who, without either knowing it or being able to do anything about it, might, according to Jansenist theology, have been the subject of God's reprobation, condemned from the moment of his or her creation to the physical, moral, and spiritual torments of a hell that never ended. Passive acceptance was the only recourse.

The most important protagonist of passivity in prayer was the Spanish-born Miguel de Molinos (1628–96), a doctor of theology and noted spiritual director in Rome, where he was at the head of a Spanish confraternity, the Schola Christi. He believed that spiritual fulfilment could be attained only by a complete inertness in which all external works were to be disregarded. The body was at best a distraction from the perfection operated by God within the soul. In 1675 he published in Spanish his *Little Treatise on Daily Communion* and in the same year his main work, the much-translated *Spiritual Guide*, which he himself translated into Italian. It was published with all necessary ecclesiastical approval, but substituted as a mode of mental prayer what Molinos called "contemplation" for the more traditional discursive "meditation", itself an innovation relative to the chanted psalmody of the Church's official prayer, the divine office.

Objections to Molinos's teaching were soon raised. He issued a reply in letter form in 1676, leaving a *Defence of Contemplation* in manuscript. Strong opposition came from the Jesuits, formed on discursive, meditative prayer, with the *Value and Order of Ordinary and Mystical Prayer* (1678) by Gattardo Bell'huomo leading the attack, supported by père Segneri's work on the concord of tiredness and quiet in prayer published in 1680. Molinos remained in favour, and the works of both Jesuit opponents were placed on the Index of forbidden books on 28 November 1681.

Complaints were then levelled against Molinos on 30 January 1682 by the bishop of Marseilles, Inigo Caracciolo, who for the first time used the term "quietist". The documents for the period 1682 to 1685 have disappeared, but on 18 July 1685 Molinos was suddenly imprisoned, as were a number of like-minded associates. It looks as if one, Petrucci, was made a cardinal on 2 September 1686 to keep him out of prison. A total of 263 propositions attributed to Molinos was reduced to 68

for condemnation. Molinos abjured on 3 September 1687, and was condemned to life imprisonment. The 68 propositions, already condemned in a papal decree of 28 August, were formally included in *Coelestis pastor*.

Molinos was not only attacking centuries-old devotional practice, but also failing to guard against the possibility that spiritual perfection was compatible with activity contrary to the moral law – that not only God, but also Satan might enter and manipulate the passive soul. He believed in a prayer of pure faith, in untroubled recollection, in a perfectly orthodox abandonment to the divine will, and in a less usual omission of the customary thanksgiving after receiving communion. To explain the missing documents, it has been suggested, but never proved, that torture was used, although not on Molinos himself, to elicit confessions that the "contemplatives" had infringed the Church's laws on sexual morality.

The other important quietist was the highly connected Malaval (1627–1719) who, although blind from the age of nine months, became a doctor of theology and canon law. He received the necessary dispensation to be admitted to the clerical state, but was never ordained. His *Easy Way to Raise the Soul to Contemplation* (1664) exploiting a fashion for "easy ways", appeared in a second, augmented edition in 1673 and, although independent of Molinos, whose *Guide* did not appear until 1675, was implicated together with Molinos by Segneri in 1680. The Italian translation of Malaval's *Spiritual Poems* (1671) was then proscribed on 1 April 1688.

Malaval submitted, but Bossuet, at first favourable, became critical of Malaval's movement of the spiritual focus away from Christ's humanity. He condemned Malaval in a pastoral letter of 16 April 1695, associating him with Molinos and with Mme Guyon, who had attracted the admiration of Fénelon in 1688. He later referred to Malaval as "this layman with no theology", and Malaval's defence in a letter of 1695 to the vicar-general of Marseilles was put on the Index on 17 January 1703. Since Bossuet was by this time in disfavour at Rome, pointedly denied advancement to the bishopric of Lyons or Paris, and refused the cardinalate, the only serious censorship to which Malaval was subjected was the token censure of his poems.

Mme Jeanne-Marie Bouvier de la Mothe Guyon (1648–1717) scarcely belongs to the history of quietism. Married at 16, she was widowed in 1676, and entrusted by the bishop of Geneva with the direction of converts from Calvinism, when she formed an attachment to the Barnabite père La Combe, who lived in a state of spiritual exaltation; he finally went mad, but not before implicating Mme Guyon in serious misdemeanours, for which she was imprisoned. On her release, Mme Guyon impressed court society, especially Mme de Maintenon, and preached her view, in some ways analogous to that of Molinos, with whom she had corresponded, that perfection consisted of a continuous act of contemplation, with no obligation to defined acts, and that prayer required the elimination of distinct ideas.

The author of a *Short Method of Prayer* and an *Explanation of the Song of Songs*, she was interrogated by Bossuet, and demanded that her works should be judged by a commission.

She was allowed to nominate the two clerics who sat with Bossuet and held the celebrated "conferences of Issy" which, however, had no canonical standing. It was as a witness that Fénelon appeared to defend not quietism, but the possibility and desirability of the disinterested love of God. Mme Guyon's works were condemned by the bishop of Paris, annoyed at the apparent usurpation of his jurisdiction by Bossuet, and the hearings gave rise to the incidents marking the continued hostilities of Bossuet and Fénelon. Mme Guyon's works were also condemned in the dioceses of the two episcopal members of the commission and at Chartres. Her second imprisonment lasted nearly a year before she was exiled to her daughter's estate.

ANTHONY LEVI

Further Reading

Knox, R.A., *Enthusiasm: A Chapter in the History of Religion, with Special Reference to the XVII and XVIII Centuries*, Oxford: Clarendon Press, and New York: Oxford University Press, 1950

THE QUR'AN

The Qur'an is the Muslim holy book, containing God's revelations in Arabic to the prophet Muhammad; it is considered by Muslims to be the divine word of God as transmitted by the Angel Gabriel, a faithful reproduction of the original scripture in heaven. The Qur'an is part of the biblical tradition through which the Law was given to Moses and the Psalter to David. Hence Jews and Christians are *ahl al-kitab* (People of the Book).

The Qur'an, together with the *Sunna*, Muhammad's own daily practice, are, for Muslims, authoritative sources for living a holy and religious life. The Sunna, after which the main sect of Islam, the Sunnis, are named, was transmitted in the form of *Hadith* (Sayings), from those who had known the Prophet, which were handed down through a chain of authority (*Isnad*). The Qur'an and the Hadith lay down five religious duties: the *shahada*, the affirmation that "There is no god but God. Muhammad is the Prophet of God" (the Shias add "'Ali is the friend of God"); worship or prayer (*salat*); paying the compulsory alms tax (*zakat*); fasting during the holy month of Ramadan (*sawm*); and the Pilgrimage to Mecca (*hajj*).

Commanding good and forbidding evil (*al-amr bi'l-ma'ruf wa-l-nahy 'an al-munkar*) are seen by Muslims as the foundation stone of the essential freedom to express opinions. The concept lies at the heart of Shari'a law, and is commonly known as *hisbah* in Arabic. The principle Qur'anic authority for hisbah is the injunction "Let there be among you a group that calls others to good, commanding good and forbidding evil" (Qur'an III.104). The Qu'ran divides man's choice in life into that which is recommendable (*manduh*), that which is permissible (*mubah*) and that which is reprehensible (*makruh*). In a Hadith, Muhammad says "If any of you sees something evil, he should set it right with his hand; if he is unable to do so then with his tongue; and if he is unable to do even that (let him denounce it) in his heart. But this is the weakest form of faith." The Qur'an also refers to "sincere advice" (*nasihah*), a show of brotherhood that can be proffered to anyone, including the 'ulama' (scholars).

Further Islamic sanction for freedom of expression can be seen in *haqq al-mu'aradah*, the citizen's right to criticize government leaders. The Qur'anic principle of consultation, similarly, entitles ordinary Muslims to be consulted on public affairs. In Saudi Arabia, for instance, any man may, in principle, approach the king on allotted days and seek redress.

Hisbah involves both rights and duties at the same time. The Universal Islamic Declaration of Human Rights published by the Islamic Council of Europe sees Hisbah as involving the "right and duty of every person" to speak for and defend the rights of others, and those of the community when these are threatened or violated. Muslims see Hisbah as conferring on those who are capable of forming an opinion the liberty to express it. The Qur'an allows freedom of religion and does not compel non-Muslims to convert to Islam. But Muslims and non-Muslims may defend their religion from seditious provocation (*fitnah*). An important Qur'anic line reads: "Had thy Lord willed, everyone on earth would have believed. Do you then force people to become believers?" (X.99). The Universal Islamic Declaration of Human Rights reflects this: "Every person has the right to freedom of conscience and worship in accordance with his religious beliefs" (article XIII).

According to Muhammad Hashim Kamali, there are four degrees of hisbah: informing (*ta'rif*) the person who is committing a wrong of the seriousness of his conduct; kindly admonition (*wa'z*) to invoke the fear of God in him and appeal to his reason; harsh words, such as "oh tyrant", "oh ignorant one", "do you not fear God?"; and finally, the use of anger or even force. Only the first two can be applied to one's father or husband or to the head of state.

The key word *fitnah* (enticement, fascination, commotion, sedition, torture, strife) appears on 60 occasions in the Qur'an. Among its legal meanings is seditious speech, that which attacks the legitimacy of lawful government. It may also mean denying the faithful the right to practise their faith through verbal or physical aggression, according to Kamali its most usual meaning. Qur'an II.191 lays down: "And expel them from where they have expelled you. For oppression (fitnah) is worse than killing."

"The Qur'an is our constitution" is used ubiquitously by contemporary Islamists. They seek sources within the Qur'anic text to defend modern ideologies. The phrase *bi-ism Illahi* (In the name of God) is used to introduce even scientific facts. The emblem of the Muslim Brotherhood consists of the Qur'an placed between two swords. Even Iranian Marxists have used Qur'anic terminology. The ideas of revolutionary Iran also attempt to make Qur'anic concepts meaningful in a modern context. The former Iranian prime minister Abu 'l-Hasan Bani-Sadr, for example, equated the concept of *tawhid* (oneness) with a classless society and the *mustadafin* (wretched of the earth) with the proletariat. In 'Ali Shariati's works, similarly, Shia concepts take on a modern revolutionary hue. Qur'anic concepts such as *shura* (advisory council), made up of *ahl al-hall wa-l-'aqd* (those who have the power to bind and unbind) are used to claim democratic principles in Saudi Arabia. Many states use the Qur'an as the theoretical bedrock of their constitution. Article 2 of the Egyptian constitution of 1971 specifies that the shari'a is "the main source of legislation", while the Afghan constitution of 1987 specified that Islam was the state religion.

TREVOR MOSTYN

Further Reading

Ayubi, Nazih M., *Political Islam: Religion and Politics in the Arab World*, London and New York: Routledge, 1991

Kamali, Mohammad Hashim, *Freedom of Expression in Islam*, revised edition, Cambridge: Islamic Texts Society, 1997

Lewis, Bernard, *The Political Language of Islam*, Chicago: University of Chicago Press, 1988

Mayer, Ann Elizabeth, *Islam and Human Rights: Tradition and Politics*, 3rd edition, Boulder, Colorado, Westview Press, 1999

Ruthven, Malise, *Islam in the World*, 2nd edition, London: Penguin, and New York: Oxford University Press, 2000

QURRAT AL-AYN (Fatima Baraghani)
Iranian poet and religious leader, 1813–1852

Born into an important clerical family in the city of Qazvin and married at an early age to another cleric, Qurrat al-Ayn, also known as Tahira, was given a full education by her father and other family members in Quranic exegesis, jurisprudence, and Persian and Arabic literature. While this was not as unusual as it may seem, Qurrat al-Ayn achieved high standards of erudition. Even after her marriage, she was able to spend time studying at the Shiite colleges in Iraq, and in particular to attend the classes of a celebrated semi-heterodox cleric, Sayyid Kazim Rashti. On the latter's sudden death in January 1844, she remained in Karbala, where she began delivering lectures, addressing male students from behind a curtain.

Some months later Qurrat al-Ayn became one of dozens of Rashti's younger students to convert to a new formulation of Shiism being taught in Iran by Sayyid 'Ali Mohammad Shirazi, known as the Bab (1819–50). She rapidly became the leading exponent of the new teaching in Iraq, and – in a quite extraordinary move, given the time, the place, and her gender – she actually went much further than the Bab in pressing for the abolition of Islamic law and practice. It is arguable that if it had not been for her prompting, the Bab might not have moved as quickly as he did to abandon Islam and proclaim himself a new prophet.

Qurrat al-Ayn herself inevitably became embroiled in serious controversy, not only within the confines of Babism, but with a range of state dignitaries and religious personnel. She was hounded from Iraq in 1847, accompanied by a retinue of 30 mostly male followers, and returned to Qazvin. Following the murder of her anti-Babi uncle there in 1848, she was accused (probably falsely) of complicity and forced to flee the town. In the summer of that year she played the leading role at a Babi gathering (80 men and one woman were present) at which abrogation of the Qur'an and its laws was formalized. She is reputed to have announced this epochal decision by appearing before a male audience with her face unveiled.

There followed several years of hiding from the authorities until her arrest in 1851 and her confinement in Tehran. Following an attempt by some Babis to assassinate Nasir al-Din Shah, Qurrat al-Ayn was taken from prison and summarily executed by strangulation. The Persian term for strangulation, *Khafeh kardan*, often conveys "suffering, stifling, silencing". Tahireh's brother, Mirza Abdol-Vahab, is said to have observed: "The clergy have prevented all women from studying lest they should become believers like Tahireh." Sheikh Fazlullah Nuri declared

women's education to be against Islamic law, *haram* (forbidden).

In the years after her death, Qurrat al-Ayn became famous in some European literary circles. A play and numerous poems were written about her in France and Russia. In these she figures as a champion of women's rights against the forces of Muslim obscurantism. In the histories of the present-day Baha'i movement, she is vaunted as the "first suffragette martyr". This is really overembellishment, but there is no doubt that she did briefly signal wider possibilities for women in the Islamic world.

Significantly, much modern Muslim writing about Qurrat al-Ayn, in both Persian and Arabic, portrays her as a corrupted and corrupting libertine who used her physical charms to seduce men away from the true faith. The fact that this image remains popular says much about contemporary views of woman in Islam.

Qurrat al-Ayn was a prolific writer. Her prose, being of a sectarian nature, is of little interest to the general public. But her poetry, which has survived in decent quantities, although thoroughly religious in nature, owes much to the tradition of Persian erotic mystical verse, and is of wide appeal. Only a little has been translated into English. Yet, according to a contributor to *The Babi and Bahai Religions 1844–1944*:

> the odium which attaches to the name of Babi amongst Persian Mohammedans would render impossible the recitation of verses confessedly composed by her. If, therefore, she were actually the authoress of poems, the grace and beauty of which compelled an involuntary admiration even from her enemies, it would seem extremely probable that they should seek to justify their right to admire them by attributing them to some other author.

There is, however, a paradox in this. Qurrat al-Ayn's poetry has, over the years, been hard to come by, particularly in Iran, where the only printed texts have been two volumes issued by the Babi and Baha'i minorities, effectively in defiance of state publishing controls. Under the Islamic Republic, publication of such books could be punishable by death. The strange result is that, in Iran, every educated person knows of Qurrat al-Ayn and has read at least a few verses of her poetry, yet no-one can easily obtain even poorly edited editions of her work.

DENIS MACEOIN

Writings

In *Materials for the Study of the Bábí Religion*, edited by Edward G. Browne, Cambridge: Cambridge University Press, 1918, reprinted 1961: 342–47

Further Reading

Amanat, Abbas, *Resurrection and Renewal: The Making of the Babi Movement in Iran, 1844–1850*, Ithaca, New York: Cornell University Press, 1989

Momen, Moojan (editor), *The Babi and Bahai Religions, 1844–1944: Some Contemporary Western Accounts*, Oxford: Ronald, 1981

R

FRANÇOIS RABELAIS
French writer, c.1484–1553

Rabelais is one of France's major literary figures and one of its most provocative. Mention of his writings evokes images of a bawdy and festive world full of lavish meals, coarse laughs, and colourful language. But his stories were also full of more or less disguised satire and criticism aimed at many of the most influential groups in French society. Rabelais's works were subject to various forms of censorship, not only in his lifetime but also in succeeding centuries.

Rabelais was a true humanist scholar. He studied theology, law, and medicine at various French universities, made several visits to Rome, and published Hippocrates' *Aphorisms* and other erudite treatises. By the 1520s, however, humanist erudition was coming to be treated with the same hostility as Lutheran ideas in some quarters, not least among Catholic theologians. After Erasmus had published his commentaries on the Greek manuscripts of St Luke's Gospel, the Theology Faculty at the Sorbonne, fearing heresy, decided in 1523 to prohibit any further study of the Greek language. As a consequence, the superiors of the Franciscan monastery at Fontenay-le-Comte, where Rabelais lived for a time, confiscated his Greek books. With the help of his protectors, he was allowed to join the more liberal Benedictines, a change that gave him the right to recover his books.

After two years in Paris, Rabelais studied medicine at Montpellier and took an ill-paid medical post at Lyon, where he became a friend of Étienne Dolet, later burnt with his own books. Rabelais started to write stories inspired by already popular tales of giants that were sold during the annual fairs. In 1532, *Pantagruel* was published under the pseudonym Alcofribas Nasier, an anagram of Rabelais's own name. The novel immediately enjoyed a tremendous success – he wrote that more copies had been bought in two months than of all the Bibles that would be sold in nine years. However, the book's broad humour was condemned as obscene by the Sorbonne, perhaps not least because the Sorbonne was an important target of Rabelais's satire.

From then on, the ecclesiastical authorities never stopped their attacks on the writer's works. In 1534, Rabelais composed *Gargantua* to introduce his previous novel. The story of the education of Pantagruel's father was used by Rabelais as an opportunity to promote the new methods of the humanist teaching. The book was once again condemned by the Sorbonne. After a spell in Italy (1539–41) Rabelais returned to Lyon to arrange for an expurgated edition of his books, only to find that Étienne Dolet had just reprinted them in their original form.

In his *Tiers Livre*, the third book in his series of giants' tales, Rabelais's satire became much more subtle. To no avail. He was again condemned by the Sorbonne, although he was granted a royal licence to put his own name to the book. His *Quart Livre*, also much more scholarly and subtle than the first two works, was attacked by the monk Pritherbus, and, for the first time, the reformer John Calvin. Proceedings against Rabelais by the Parlement of Paris led to a rumour that he had been imprisoned. Soon after, in 1553, he died.

Although Rabelais's novels are at the junction of scholarly and popular culture, they were written at the very moment when these two worlds were gradually becoming more threateningly intertwined. As well as resisting satirical attacks upon themselves, the Sorbonne theologians wanted to censor Rabelais's coarse style and his insistence on bodily materiality. *Pantagruel* mocked hypocritical moralists and likened censors who read books in order to harm their authors to scoundrels who might dissect children's excrement to find the pips of the fruits they had stolen.

In succeeding centuries, Rabelais was far from rehabilitated. For Catholic polemicists, he was still regarded as an author beloved of freethinkers and libertines. For the compilers of the *Index Librorum Prohibitorum*, he was an author of the first class – that is, all his books were banned. Nicolas Bourbon, a scholar and poet who lived during the first half of the 17th century, reported with some humour in his *Memoirs*: "For a long time I used to have a book by Rabelais, but it was not mine. It was Mr. Guyer's who had left it in my office. Every year he used to confess that he owned a Rabelais that he did not have at home and I confessed that I had one which was not mine." Rabelais's writings continued to be widely viewed as dangerous.

Importantly, Rabelais's novels ran counter to the aesthetic norms of classicism that ruled for so long in France. Not only did their language become archaic, but their bawdy Gallic humour also transgressed the new rules of courtesy. By classical standards, there was no sense in the Rabelaisian attempt to express elevated thoughts in vulgar popular speech. La Bruyère wrote in the 17th century that "Rabelais is incomprehensible: whatever has been said about it, his work remains an inexplicable riddle. [. . .] It is a monstrous assemblage of a subtle and ingenious moral doctrine mingled with filthy corruption." Even during the Enlightenment, Rabelais's novels were still considered as an offence to good taste.

As a consequence, Rabelais was subjected to a form of aesthetic censorship by editors who, at best, produced versions written in modern French with the altered parts confined to footnotes. Most of the time, the original text was completely rewritten and the obscenities or outdated expressions removed. In 1776 a sanitized version appeared "aimed at ladies" and at the end of the 19th century softened-down versions of Rabelais were written for children. Although they had little in common with the original, they at least contributed to the survival of the image of Rabelais as a joyful storyteller. Outside France, some indication of the strength of the disapproval felt towards Rabelais's at times extremely coarse writing can be gauged from the fact that his books could not be imported into the USA until 1930, and were banned completely for a time from South Africa after 1938.

JEAN-CHRISTOPHE ABRAMOVICI

Writings
The Histories of Gargantua and Pantagruel, translated by
 J.M.Cohen, 1955
The Complete Works, translated by Donald M. Frame, 1991

Further Reading
Bakhtin, Mikhaïl, *L'Oeuvre de François Rabelais et la culture populaire au Moyen Age et sous la renaissance*, Paris: Gallimard, 1965; as *Rabelais and His World*, Cambridge, Massachusetts: MIT Press, 1968
Rigolot, François, "Les Langages de Rabelais", *Études rabelaisiennes*, 10 (1972)
Sainéan, Lazare, *L'Influence et la réputation de Rabelais*, Paris: Gamber, 1930
Saulnier, Verdun L., *Le Dessein de Rabelais*, Paris: Societé d'Édition d'Enseignement Supérieur, 1957

RACE AND ETHNICITY

Forms of discrimination based on race or ethnic origin have been present in most societies, ancient and modern, not all of them of direct relevance to the history of censorship. This essay, necessarily selective, confines itself to those notions of racial difference and superiority that entered history and gained ground in the extension of Western trading activities to full-scale imperialism between the 15th and 19th centuries, were then buttressed by theories of scientific racism, widespread in the 19th-century West, and reached their apogee in the doctrines embraced by Nazi Germany and, to some extent, by the Republic of South Africa in the 20th century, with some still held today by a few scholars and fringe political groups. These ideas are now discredited, not only because they are mostly regarded as false, but also as a result of the almost universal modern repulsion felt towards the slave trade and its aftermath, especially in the United States, towards the slaughter of European Jews by Germany and its allies between 1933 and 1956 (and the replication, if on a smaller scale, of "ethnic cleansing" in the former Yugoslavia), and towards the policy of apartheid, practised in South Africa between 1945 and 1989.

Censorship, in the broadest sense, has been used as one weapon in the armoury of repression. It was not usual (Jewish culture excepted) that the art, literature, music, and journalism of the so-called inferior races were directly silenced, despite the fact that such forms of expression defied the calumny of inferiority, resulting in work of the highest quality whose subject matter was precisely the sufferings of their fellows. The negative stereotype was therefore eloquently denied – and the work was censored for its manifest ability to subvert the racist *status quo*.

It might be thought that the roots of censorship by race lay in the early confrontations of white and black people, and in the sense of "otherness" that these encounters engendered. The early explorers came from societies in which the representation of nakedness was taboo, and sexual appetites were to be curbed. How then would Europeans respond to the culture and customs of peoples who, in the words of John Hawkins, the English explorer of South America, "go all naked, the men covering no part of their body but their yard, upon the which they wear a gourd, or piece of cane, made fast with a thread about their loins, leaving the other part of their members uncovered, whereof they take no shame. The women are also uncovered, saving with a cloth which they wear both before and behind"? As it happened, reactions were far from universally hostile, some travellers to Virginia even being moved to reflect on the Judeo–Christian myth of creation, describing the inhabitants of Virginia as "living after the manner of the golden age".

As for sexual appetite, there was certainly an early appearance of the notion that black Africans and other peoples of the Southern Hemisphere were both well-endowed and generous with their favours – as Iago tells Brabantio in Shakespeare's *Othello*, "an old black ram is tupping your white ewe". However, as V.G. Kiernan points out, a propos the behaviour of Tahitian women encountered in 18th-century explorations, those who used sexual encounters for the opportunities they presented for petty theft were given short shrift: the northerners "might admire a Noble Savage, but they wanted him to have solid bourgeois virtues as well".

Overall, according to Robert Miles:

hostile and negative European representations of the Other were discouraged, and the colonizers, anxious to develop profitable exchange networks, ensured that they studied the economic and social relations of those they met in the colonial situation, often to the point of adopting their customs.

The idea that black people were "savages", and in need of civilization, was never wholly absent from everyday practice and everyday speculation, but little was hard and fast. Paradoxically, later practitioners of racism and racial censorship would draw strength from "scientific" ideas that arose in the later 18th century, principally the idea of "race" itself, and the notion, in Miles's words, the "distinct 'races' of human beings had always existed and that the hierarchy of inferiority and superiority was therefore natural, inevitable and unalterable". For well over a century, biology appeared more important than culture, allowing H.F.K. Gunther, for instance, to argue in 1927 that ideas of racial hierarchy applied also to Europe; he feared "the running dry of the blood of the . . . Nordic race", and stood for "a world cleansing itself racially and eugenically". Six years later, a regime came to power in Germany that was ready to take him at his word.

The other root of racism and racial censorship was, of course, economic. By the middle of the 16th century, one tenth of the population of Lisbon, capital of Portugal, was said to be made up of slaves from Africa, Asia, and South America, a development considered necessary to make up gaps in the labour force. The estimated slave population in 1770 of the American colonies, North and South, was 2.5 million. In so far as the traders and slaveowners felt any need to justify the practice, the biological argument might eventually have proved useful, but it was not crucial. The habit of treating black people as mere tools for the production of white wealth was already ingrained and, especially in the southern United States, would not easily be relinquished even a century after slavery was abolished: the Moynihan report of 1965 maintained that the Negro had "no values or culture to guard and protect". In southern Africa, meanwhile, as Kiernan writes, "it was the misfortune of the Dutch settlers . . . which they have never outgrown, that they came at a time when slavery was, in European eyes, a natural institution". Later settlers of all nationalities were encouraged by E.S. Grogan and A.H. Sharp in 1900 to act on the belief that black Africans throughout the continent (and, for that matter, black Australians) were "fundamentally inferior in mental development and ethical possibilities (call it soul, if you will)". Only slightly more benevolent was the increasingly common characterization of black people everywhere as "child races", and therefore as infantile and dependent.

There was plenty in this mixture of commercial self-interest, pseudoscience, and patronage that could be used, in the 20th century, to justify the practice of censorship by skin colour. The protection of "children" was, of course, already one of the most commonly cited reasons in Europe and North America for more general censorship. From all that, it was a small step for the states of the American south, for example, to hinder the education of black people, lest they aspire to the condition of their "betters". A South Carolina law of 1834 prescribed a fine or whipping or both (depending on the race of the educator) for any person who taught a black person to read; a black school in North Carolina was closed down in 1862, and similar schools subjected to regular campaigns of arson and threats to educators. As late as the 1960s, sometimes violent resistance was offered to national programmes for the desegregation of schools.

Similar attitudes prevailed in white South Africa. The National Party Member of Parliament J.N. Le Roux, declared in 1945:

We should not give the natives an academic education as some people are too prone to do. If we do this, we shall later be burdened with a number of academically trained Europeans and non-Europeans, and who is going to do the manual labour in the country? . . . We should so conduct our schools that the native who attends these schools will know that, to a great extent, he must be the labourer in the country.

Le Roux was speaking to the already convinced. The Bantu Education Act (1953) was specifically designed to separate the education of whites from that of blacks, who were to have an education system that, in the words of "native affairs" minister Hendrik Verwoerd, was designed "so the native may be educated to his station". His successors would claim that schools in black areas were equal in facilities to those built in white areas; it is generally accepted that the quality of teaching was greatly inferior by design, and in 1980, half a million black adolescents were leaving school unable to read or write.

The southern United States, South Africa, and many other societies were, in other words, attempting censorship at source, making "scientific racism" a self-fulfilling prophecy: the blacks had "no culture". Their assumptions were by no means without effect, but were always subject to corporate and individual challenge by those who were the objects of their censorship. In 19th-century America, in the absence of black literacy, oral culture – mostly in the form of sermons and music, the Spirituals and the Blues – emerged as alternative methods of narrating and transmitting "black history". The Spirituals made skilful and selective use of biblical texts ("Let my people go", Exodus 10.3) and geography (the "Jordan river" as a metaphor for the Mississippi and the Ohio) to suggest connections that could hardly be "censored". Until the Blues were legitimized in the 20th century (the so-called "whitening" of black vernacular culture), they remained impenetrable to middle-class, white Americans who would certainly have found the lyrics obscene (and who later omitted the most explicit and ribald from their collections). The saying "got one mind for white folks to see, 'nother for what I know is me" summed up the culture of many generations of African Americans.

By the time Richard Wright wrote *Native Son* (1940), on the other hand, new pressures were in the way of "telling it how it is". A "black bourgeoisie" wished to distance itself from the past, to gain white acceptance. Wright wrote:

I felt a mental censor – product of the fears which a Negro feels from living in America – standing over me, warning me not to write. This censor's warnings were translated into my own thought processes thus: 'What will white people think if I draw the picture of such a Negro boy [Bigger Thomas, the novel's violent, but truthful, protagonist]. "See, didn't we tell you all along that niggers are like that? Now look, one of their own kind has come along and drawn the picture for us". . . And would not whites misread Bigger, and, doubting his authenticity, say, "This man is preaching against the whole white race"?

Wright also imagined black protests: "Why don't you portray in your fiction the best traits of our race, something that will show the white people what we have done in spite of oppression?" Wright resisted the temptation to self-censor. The novel was published, uncensored, but as Langston Hughes wrote in 1957, "Negro writers, just by being black, have been on the blacklist all our lives". Libraries would not willingly carry any books by black writers; in the deep south, Wright himself was reduced to pretending that he had been sent by a white person to borrow a copy of his *Black Boy* (1945). Copies of the increasingly political black newspapers, the *Chicago Defender* and the *Afro-American*, published in the North, had to be smuggled into the South on Pullman trains by black porters; they could not be sold openly.

The US Freedom of Information and Privacy Act (1974) made it possible to uncover the extent of surveillance carried out on black writers by US agencies between the 1930s and the 1970s. Wright was the subject of a 227-page dossier. James Baldwin (1924–87) had no less than 1700 pages devoted to his writings and opinions, some reflection of the successful political struggles of the 1960s. Eldridge Cleaver's *Soul on Ice* (1968) was one of the 10 works most often removed from the libraries of public institutions between 1966 and 1975; references to miscegenation were still unacceptable to many. Cleaver's book, along with *Black Boy* and Langston Hughes's collection *The Best Short Stories by Negro Writers* (1967), were removed from junior and senior high school libraries in Island Trees, New York, as late as 1982. Later works by Maya Angelou (*I Know Why the Caged Bird Sings*, 1970), and Alice Walker (*The Color Purple*, 1982) have suffered similar fates. Race is still a factor in US library censorship.

It is worth noting that the following classics of African-American struggle were banned, from both bookshops and libraries, in South Africa under apartheid: *Black Power* (1967), by Stokely Carmichael and Charles V. Hamilton; Cleaver's *Soul on Ice*; *The First Book of Africa* (1960), by Langston Hughes; *Why We Can't Wait* (1964), by Martin Luther King; and *The Autobiography of Malcolm X* (1965). Caliban's response to Prospero in Shakespeare's *The Tempest* may be appropriately applied to the United States, and to South Africa (indeed to all the countries of Africa during the colonial period): "You taught me language, and my profit on't is I know how to curse". The white South African novelist Nadine Gordimer concluded in 1979: "The black artist lives in a society that rejected his culture for hundreds of years. He has turned his alienation in the face of those who rejected him and made of his false consciousness the inevitable point of departure towards his true selfhood."

Thus, one of the earliest (1950s) generation of black South African writers, including such writers as Peter Abrahams (1919–), Can Themba (1924–69), and Bloke Modisane (1923–86), transformed the language of the townships into bitter satire against racial inequality and apartheid in their articles for *Drum* magazine, and in their novels. The "coloured" writer Dennis Brutus (1924–) determined to "state the bare fact and let it sing". Few of them escaped exile or other forms of silencing. Richard Rive (1931–) wrote of himself and others as "not allowed to read their own works in case they become influenced by them". The novelist Miriam Tlali wrote in the 1970s that, when preparing her major work, *Muriel at Metropolitan* (1975), "I could not dream of entering the Johannesburg public library to get hold of works by, for example, Ezekiel

Mphahlele, Lewis Nkosi, Alex La Guma, Peter Abrahams, Nelson Mandela".

South African race censorship was, as the white novelist André Brink wrote, "only one part of an overall strategy which also expressed itself in such forms as detention without trial, arbitrary bannings, job reservations, the Group Areas Act . . .", and so forth. The enforced separation of the races was well expressed in Donald Howarth's 1972 version of Shakespeare's *Othello*, *Othello Sleges Blankes* (Othello, Whites Only). Howarth had been told that he could not have a cast of one black person and the rest white; in his version, Othello's person is never on stage, but continually discussed. Howarth commented: "It's like the Bantustans. They are talked about but never allowed into parliament." The Serpent Players of Port Elizabeth – Athol Fugard (white), John Kani, and Winston Ntshona (black) – adopted a more combative strategy, and were regularly removed by the police while attempting to perform their plays before white audiences.

Unlike the US, South Africa had fully developed institutions of formal censorship, notably the Publications Control Board, established by law, and administered exclusively by white people, whose literary, musical, and filmic opinions were entirely based on racial assumptions. Thus, for example, it was assumed that most readers of black literature would be white, and therefore needing protection from work said to be undesirable on grounds it was "prejudicial to the safety of the state, the general welfare, or peace, and good order", or "harmful to the relations between any sections of the inhabitants of the Republic". On the one hand, the Board did not ban *Forced Landing* (1980), a collection of short stories by Mothobi Mutloatse, suggesting that it would "contribute towards a better understanding of the black man's problems, and create avenues and methods of dialogue in the pursuance of peaceful coexistence". On the other hand, having first rejected and then released Nadine Gordimer's *Burger's Daughter* (1979), complete with its school playground repetitions of the refrain "bloody Boers, dumb Dutchmen, thick Afrikaners", it rejected *Muriel at Metropolitan* because its narrator had spoken of an Afrikaans-speaking woman as a "lousy Boer". Gordimer asked, rhetorically, "Is it more insulting for a white South African to be abused by a black character in a book, than by a white one?" Far more works by black writers were found "undesirable" for what were considered, most ironically, incitements to racism, than those by whites. It did not take much for a work like Ayi Kwei Armah's *Two Thousand Seasons* (1973) to be so banned: ". . . it is quite clear that the novel has set out to create animosity against the whites. In the process, the white man's character, his religion, and his ways of life are all brought into ridicule, so as to add to the expression of hatred."

The chairman of the Publications Control Board, Judge Lannie Syman, could still suggest in 1980 that blacks were "inarticulate people, who, I am sure, are not interested in censorship". Es'kia (Ezekiel) Mphahlele, professor of African Literature at Witwatersrand University, was closer to the truth when he wrote in 1983: "People do not want for a novelist or a poet or playwright to play around with images and symbols to incite them to strike or march in the streets, or revolt. There are more immediate and direct forces to impel them to act against authorities". Notwithstanding that, of the 1808 publications submitted to the Publications Board between July 1982 and June 1983, 1070 were found to constitute a threat to state security.

In the end, and as apartheid evolved, its proponents were more concerned with self-interest – national security, the relative prosperity of white people, their need for a "race" who would do the dirty jobs – than with ideologies of racial superiority or purity. These were not absent – early National Party politicians professed some sympathy for Nazi ideas, parts of the Dutch Reformed Church adduced biblical support for the South African system, and, as apartheid entered its decline, according to J.M. Coetzee, "loss of hope manifested itself most markedly in an end-of-the-world fantasy of a 'total onslaught' of hostile powers against the South African state and against western civilization in Africa". This was embodied, not least, in "the construction of a bureaucracy of censorship entrusted with the task of scrutinizing every book, every magazine, every film, every stage performance, every T-shirt to appear in the land". However, nothing in South Africa approached in range, thoroughness, or ideological purity the genocide – of which censorship was only a minor component – inflicted on the Jews of Europe by the German National Socialist party between 1933 and 1945.

Eugen Fischer, who was installed as rector of the University of Berlin in 1933, had an established reputation as an advocate of racial hygiene; he had studied children of mixed race (Boer and Hottentot) in South Africa and now applied his thinking to Germany. He claimed:

> When a people wants, somehow or other, to preserve its own nature, it must reject alien racial elements, and when these have already insinuated themselves, it must suppress and eliminate them. The Jew is such an alien and, therefore, when he wants to insinuate himself, he must be warded off. This is self-defence. In saying this, I do not characterize every Jew as inferior, as Negroes are, nor do I underestimate the greatest enemy with whom we have to fight. But I reject Jewry with every means in my power, and without reserve, in order to preserve the hereditary endowment of my people.

This was relatively mild. An SS pamphlet declared that a Jew "only looks human, with a human face, but his spirit is lower than that of an animal. A terrible chaos runs rampant in this creature, an awful rage for destruction, primitive desires, unparalleled evil, a monster, subhuman".

The Nazis employed all the conventional means of censorship, racial and otherwise, but pursued them with unprecedented rigour: the exile or dismissal of individual Jewish writers, artists, and academics; the burning of their books; the destruction of their places of worship; the closure of their newspapers and their exclusion from the public education system. Censorship was not just the preserve of the professional censors; "Aryans" were expected to denounce their colleagues for alleged Jewish connections, to detect Jewish influences where none had been found before, as in "the German–Jewish novels of a Wasserman or a Feuchtwanger, or of the Jewish-assimilated Heinrich Mann". Lothar Muthel, ordered to direct Shakespeare's *The Merchant of Venice* in Vienna in 1942, at just the time when the mass deportation of Jews to Auschwitz was taking place, employed the critic H. Ihering to adapt the text so that it might conform with the race laws. Some German Christians were prepared to reduce "Jewish over-representation" in the Bible, and to cleanse the New Testament of "the scapegoat and inferiority theology of Rabbi Paul". The "final solution" – the Holocaust – was not enough; all traces of supposed Jewish influence were to be erased.

Fifty years later the force of Nazi racism is not yet spent. David Irving, who sued Deborah Lipstadt and Penguin Books in the British courts in 2000 for allegations of his Nazi and anti-Semitic opinions in her book *Denying the Holocaust* (1993), is only the latest in a series of writers who have claimed both that the Jews were largely responsible for their own misfortunes, and that accounts of the Holocaust grossly overestimate its extent – it was a "mistake", rather than the result of calculated policy. Irving lost the case, and, like his predecessors, suggested that his opinions and writings were being "censored". His American counterparts, such as Bradley Smith, put this down to another area of contemporary arguments about censorship – "political correctness": "The politically correct line on the Holocaust story is, simply, it happened. You don't debate it." Unlike in Germany, however, it is not illegal in America or in Britain to propagate such theories as Holocaust denial, however reprehensible they are thought to be. Deborah Lipstadt for one has stressed the importance of attending continually to their refutation. Others have embraced political correctness unashamedly in the belief that racism is so deeply embedded in the language and culture of western nations that some form of self-censorship, and perhaps even institutional censorship, is desirable to eradicate words and concepts that perpetuate it.

DEREK JONES

Further Reading

Banton, Michael, *The Idea of Race*, London: Tavistock, 1977; Boulder, Colorado: Westview Press, 1978

Carmichael, Stokely and Charles V. Hamilton, *Black Power: The Politics of Liberation in America*, New York: Random House, 1967; London: Jonathan Cape, 1968

Coetzee, J.M., *Giving Offense: Essays on Censorship*, Chicago: University Press of Chicago, 1996

Coggin, Theo, (editor), *Censorship: A Study of Censorship in South Africa by Five Distinguished Authors*, Johannesburg: South African Institute of Race Relations, 1983

Dawidowicz, Lucy S., *The War against the Jews, 1933–45*, New York: Holt Rinehart, and London: Weidenfeld and Nicolson, 1975

Friedman, John Block, *The Monstrous Races in Medieval Art and Thought*, Cambridge, Massachusetts: Harvard University Press, 1981

Gordimer, Nadine, *The Essential Gesture: Writings, Politics and Places*, edited by Stephen Clingman, London: Jonathan Cape, and New York: Knopf, 1988

Grunberger, Richard, *A Social History of the Third Reich*, London: Weidenfeld and Nicolson, 1971

Günther, Hans F.K., *The Racial Elements of European History*, London: Methuen, 1927; reprinted New York: Kennikat Press, 1970

Hakluyt, Richard, *The Principal Navigations, Voyages, & Discoveries of the English Nation, Made by Sea or Over Land, to the Most Remote and Farthest Corners of the Earth*, 1589, revised edition 3 vols, 1598–1600; Hakluyt Society edition, 12 vols, Glasgow: James MacLehose, 1903–05; edited and abridged by Jack Beeching, London: Penguin, 1972

Haller, John S., *Outcasts from Evolution: Scientific Attitudes of*

Racial Inferiority, 1859–1900, Urbana: University of Illinois Press, 1971

Jordan, Winthrop D., *White over Black: American Attitudes toward the Negro, 1550–1812*, Chapel Hill: University of North Carolina Press, 1968

Kiernan, V.G., *The Lords of Human Kind: European Attitudes towards the Outside World in the Imperial Age*, London: Weidenfeld and Nicolson, and Boston: Little Brown, 1969; new edition London: Serif, 1995

Lipstadt, Deborah E., *Denying the Holocaust: The Growing Assault on Truth and Memory*, New York: Free Press, 1993; London: Penguin, 1994

Malik, Kenan, *The Meaning of Race: Race, History and Culture in Western Society*, Basingstoke: Macmillan, and New York: NYUP, 1996

Miles, Robert, *Racism*, London and New York: Routledge, 1989

Rex, John, *Race and Ethnicity*, Milton Keynes: Open University Press, 1986

RACE AND IQ

If, as some scientists argue, intelligence is a phenotype, a distinct individual trait, which is not equally distributed, and one, moreover, that is correlated with many of our most intractable social problems, it is a public-policy issue of considerable importance. One might go further: in the paradigm of the knowledge-based economy, which seems set to dominate the 21st century, it may well be the most pressing public-policy issue of all. At this precise juncture, scientific research collides with Western society's most powerful taboo, that of race. The result is intellectual self-censorship, for across a whole range of social, educational, penal, and economic policies and outcomes, there is a refusal to consider any link with intelligence – openly at least – for fear of attracting the "racist" label.

Marxists have been at the forefront of attacking scientists involved in IQ-related research and pushing the belief that the science of mental ability is pseudo-science. Differences in individual achievements arise, Marxists argue, from the exploitation by a small capitalist class of a larger, politically and economically disenfranchised class, not from any inherent inequalities. From the Marxist perspective, environment is decisive. Change the environment and the differences between individuals will disappear. This assumption also underpins the huge federal spending on affirmative action and equal opportunities programmes in the US. IQ-related research, however, makes, potentially, a strong case for cutting back on welfare spending and threatens, therefore, the existence of federal bureaucracies whose role in dispensing this largesse is central.

Eugenics, founded by Sir Francis Galton and Karl Pearson, proceeded from the assumption that not all individuals and races were equal in abilities, and that the differences could be best explained by genetics. They believed, moreover, that dysgenic pressures were real and that measures designed to arrest dysgenic decline and actively to improve the quality of human stock was an obligation to the unborn. Of all the differences separating individuals and races, intelligence, insisted Galton and Pearson, was decisive, since its distribution determined the fate of the nation and the quality of life of its citizens.

When the Eugenics Education Society was founded at the beginning of the 20th century, Galton's views were not regarded as extreme. Even Beatrice Webb, who in the 1930s would write in support of Stalinism, accepted the thinking of the eugenicists. With the rise of National-Socialist Germany, support for Galton's views weakened. After 1945, eugenics was wrongly associated with the hideous experiments of Josef Mengele, and outside a very small group of scientists, the science was thor-

oughly discredited, or rather, there was widespread perception that it had been. Eugenics was the sort of word which one did not utter in polite company.

Notwithstanding the largely successful attempt to brand eugenics, and wider research into any kind of genetically-related human differences, as the work of neo-Nazis, later scientists have built on the work of the pioneers. Subsequent researchers have amassed a vast amount of raw data which, they believe, supports the importance of genetics in determining intelligence. In the mid-1960s Nobel-prizewinner William Shockley urged fellow scientists and policy makers to face up to the implications of this research; he was subjected to a prolonged campaign of abuse.

Similar methods, including even death threats, were deployed against Hans Eysenck, J. Philippe Rushton, Arthur Jensen, Richard Lynn, Sir Cyril Burt, Richard Herrnstein, Michael Levin, Charles Murray, and Christopher Brand for their willingness to discuss and to publish their findings in this field. Stanley Burnham, the pseudonymous author of *America's Bimodal Crisis: Black Intelligence in White Society*, has noted that: "If and when my identity is discovered by my colleagues, I can expect to be forced into early retirement, probably within the month."

Arthur Jensen's problems began after an invited article, "How Much Can We Boost IQ and Scholastic Achievement?", was published in the *Harvard Educational Review* in 1969 (Jensen's article subsequently became a citation classic, that is a book or article with a high number of citations in other books or journals). Jensen highlighted the importance of genetics in intelligence and maintained that the persistent difference in black/white IQ – approximately one standard deviation – could not entirely be explained by environmental factors. Two of Jensen's most ferocious detractors in the US were Richard Lewontin and Jerry Hirsch, who, drawing on a great deal of sympathy in the left-liberal media such as *Progressive Labour*, mounted considerable attacks on Jensen and his work.

Invited to address audiences in the US and in Britain, Jensen saw his lectures routinely disrupted by students and agitators. Prior to Jensen's addressing a conference, "Racial Variation in Man", organized by the Royal Geographical Society in Britain, Open University professor Steven Rose described Jensen's work as "social contempt theories". In the US hate calls were standard. Threats were also made against Jensen's life and his daughter and all mail had to be opened by the university's bomb squad.

Hans Eysenck attracted the attention of hate groups after the publication of his book, *Race, Intelligence and Education* (1971), which was, in part, a response to Jensen's article published in the *Harvard Educational Review*. Earlier in his academic career, Eysenck had accepted the view that intelligence and genetics were not related, but he became convinced that genetics might indeed be significant after studying the data and arguments in Audrey Shuey's book, *The Testing of Negro Intelligence* (1966).

Various methods were employed to discredit Eysenck's book. Initially it was ignored, but that option eventually became impossible to maintain as discussion of its contents had entered the public domain. It was now openly attacked as being based on poor science. The contents were misrepresented and conclusions were attributed to the author which could not be drawn from the book itself. Speaking at universities in Britain and in Australia, Eysenck encountered organized campaigns of verbal and physical intimidation. Such slogans as "Uphold genuine academic freedom: Fascist Eysenck has no right to speak" were on display. Eysenck responded:

> And, to be sure, if we *know* the truth – presumably through Marxological revelation – the end justifies the means: burn books, boycott publishers and book-sellers, break up meetings, threaten and persecute those who dare disagree with you. Force, not reason, becomes the measuring rod of truth.

Eysenck has also pointed out that the screaming and shouting, and the threats of physical violence directed at him and others, exercise a profoundly negative impact on the undecided and the scientifically curious who witness such scenes. Students are denied the opportunity to hear the arguments, so cannot make up their own minds, and some of them will become inured to seeing scientific arguments resolved by the application of intimidation and force. Since science progresses by the testing and discussion of arguments, any assault on this process, Eysenck argues, can only hinder scientific progress and understanding. Another consequence noted by Eysenck is the effect this may have on the civic courage of scientists and others. Scientists, who might agree with some propositions put forward, will, having seen the treatment meted out to those stating unpopular views, remain silent.

In 1989 J. Philippe Rushton, professor of psychology at the university of Western Ontario, advanced the hypothesis that those people who left Africa and headed to the Eurasian continent encountered a harsher environment and one that selected for higher intelligence and forward planning. In preparing his paper, he also gathered data on variables such as brain size, intelligence, and speed of maturation. Implicit in the later emergence of Caucasoids and Mongoloids, he argued, is an unequal development among the various racial groups.

In the immediate aftermath of his paper, Rushton was denounced by David Peterson, leader of the Ontario Liberal Party. Others followed suit and, as in the case of other scholar-victims, little attempt was made to address the arguments on their scientific merits. Among the flood of demands to dismiss Rushton and to censor him, there were some who recognized that the issue of academic freedom was crucial. An editorial published in *The London Free Press* noted that "the pressure for limits [to freedom of speech] is coming largely from those who present themselves as liberals." One consequence of the affair was the creation of the Society for Academic Freedom and Scholarship, modelled on the American National Association of Scholars (NAS), to defend academic freedom.

The most alarming aspect of the Rushton case, according to some commentators, was the use of the police to investigate and to evaluate Rushton's work under provisions of the federal criminal code of Canada. These are designed to proscribe the promotion of "hatred against any identifiable group". If found guilty, the accused can be imprisoned for up to two years. The police examination lasted six months. Though not found guilty, Rushton was judged to have made conclusions on "questionable source data". Police involvement in a purely academic matter represented an encroachment on academic freedom affecting all scholars. The Ontario Human Rights Commission attacked Rushton from 1991 onwards and copies of his book *Race, Evolution and Behaviour* (1995), were retained by Canadian customs for some nine months, while it was decided whether the book constituted "hate literature".

The Rushton case has recently been given a new twist. When Transaction Publishers distributed copies of the first printing of the abridged edition of his *Race, Evolution and Behaviour* (1999), they were threatened in certain academic circles with the loss of marketing opportunities at conferences and the withdrawal of advertising. Transaction gave way and published a letter of apology in their journal *Society*.

The general trend is also confirmed in the revelations of the former East German scientist Volkmar Weiss in an article for *The Mankind Quarterly* (1991), which affirmed the importance of genetics for intelligence. The article had been banned by the East German police, the Stasi, eight years previously, but when the results of his research reached the west, similar attitudes were in evidence. According to Weiss, a certain "S. Rose" asked an East German colleague whether there was any way of preventing further publication by Weiss in the west because "such publications printed in a socialist country were particularly disadvantageous to the propaganda of the radical left in the Western world".

The treatment of Jensen, Eysenck, and Rushton, to name a few, demonstrates that the long-established scientific ethos that obliges the scientist, first and foremost, to pursue the truth, wherever it may lead, will not always command universal support among non-scientists, nor even, surprisingly, among scientists themselves.

FRANK ELLIS

Further Reading

Burnham, Stanley, *America's Bimodal Crisis: Black Intelligence in White Society*, 3rd edition, Athens, Georgia: Foundation for Human Understanding, 1993

Ebling, F.J. (editor), *Racial Variation in Man*, London: Institute of Biology, and New York: Wiley, 1975

Herrnstein, Richard J. and Charles Murray, *The Bell Curve: Intelligence and Class Structure in American Life*, New York: Free Press, 1994; London: Simon and Schuster, 1996

Jensen, Arthur R., *The g Factor: The Science of Mental Ability*, Westport, Connecticut: Praeger, 1998

Levin, Michael, *Why Race Matters: Race Differences and What They Mean*, Westport, Connecticut: Praeger, 1997

Lewontin, R.C., Steven Rose, and Leon J. Kamin, *Not in Our Genes: Biology, Ideology, and Human Nature*, New York: Pantheon, and Harmondsworth: Penguin, 1984

Pearson, Roger, *Race, Intelligence, and Bias in Academe*, 2nd edition, Washington, DC: Scott Townsend, 1997

Rose, Steven, *Lifelines: Biology, Freedom, Determinism*, London: Allen Lane, 1997; New York: Oxford University Press, 1998

Rushton, J. Philippe, "The New Enemies of Evolutionary Science", *Liberty*, 11/4 (March 1998): 31–35

Snyderman, Mark and Stanley Rothman, *The IQ Controversy: The Media and Public Policy*, New Brunswick, New Jersey: Transaction, 1988

Taylor, Jared, *Paved with Good Intentions: The Failure of Race Relations in Contemporary America*, New York: Carroll and Graf, 1993

Weiss, Volkmar, "It Could be Neo-Lysenkoism, If There Was Ever a Break in Continuity!", *Mankind Quarterly*, 31/3, (Spring 1991): 231–53

RADIO

The first modern medium of mass communication, radio began during the last decade of the 19th century when Marconi, drawing on the work of earlier experimenters who had transmitted wireless signals over short distances, extended the process so greatly that by 1901 it became possible to transmit across the Atlantic. After two decades of mostly amateur "broadcasting", the medium came into its own in the early 1920s, as governments and commercial interests realized its potential for mass education and entertainment, and, not least, propaganda. Regional and national services, both commercial and "public service", quickly followed in developed countries and in their colonies, and for a quarter of a century, including the years of World War II, radio held sway as the medium most used to satisfy the appetite for "information, education and entertainment".

Television was in the wings from the late 1930s, but emerged on a mass scale only during the 1950s, when it was thought likely to displace radio entirely. This has proved to be far from the case. Not only was it soon realized that there were certain things that radio could do better and more economically than television; developments in high-fidelity equipment and the introduction of stereo music brought about a new interest in the medium. Moreover, the transistor radio had been invented in 1947, and was relatively cheap; and car radio became increasingly universal in the richer societies. In poorer countries, even more significantly, radio remained the predominant medium, accessible to nearly everybody, a prized possession, and even a means of resistance to censorship and other forms of repression.

The censorship of radio waves is technically difficult, costly, and time-consuming, never more so than at the present day when radio stations of all kinds – specialist, ethnic, and local as well as regional, national, and international – have proliferated, and forms of ownership become more diverse. Censorship has often been crude – setting fire to the studios, political takeover, jamming the signals – but sometimes more sophisticated. This entry surveys its history and geography.

Europe and North America

In Britain a nationalized monopoly was created to control the airwaves. The British Broadcasting Corporation was modelled by John Reith as a public service, subject to the highest standards in form and content. Censorship was ubiquitous in the sense that individual broadcasters were left in no doubt as to how far they could go – in the early days especially, not very far; the BBC could not at first even originate its own news, and across the radio output as a whole controversy was discouraged. The BBC Board of Governors, appointed by the govern-ment, were charged with the defence of the public interest and the general maintenance of standards, but in Reith's day at least, this was hardly necessary.

The USA had an entirely different view of the ownership of the industry, but its approach to the regulation of content was essentially similar. At first, anybody with the money and technical know-how could establish a radio station; the result was network anarchy in which rival stations were constantly interfering with each others' signals. The Federal Radio Commission (FRC, later known as the Federal Communications Commission, FCC), first charged with the regulation of the airwaves, soon acquired other tasks, but was not, in keeping with the provisions of the First Amendment, given powers of censorship. In the Federal Communications Act of 1934 the FCC was deputed to regulate radio "in the public interest, convenience or necessity", a wide-ranging phrase which was then, and is still now not defined, leaving the commission considerable discretion.

A middle way between what some in Europe considered the over-regulation of the British and the under-regulation of the USA was achieved first in Weimar Germany, where the state controlled radio transmission, but programmes remained in private hands, although subject to the laws of the land. In France, where state interference in radio was, in the event, to prove the longest lasting, radio was defined as a form of telegraphy, and was therefore subject at first to the Ministry of the Post, Telegraphy and Telephone (PTT). It licensed the country's first radio station, Radio Radiola, which was commercially owned, in 1922. The first state-owned outfit followed in 1923, and in 1926 the Ministry of Commerce and Industry confirmed that the airwaves were nationally owned. The ministry then created what they described as "a regime of liberty controlled by the state". Commercial radio stations could readily obtain licences to broadcast, but could be closed down if they threatened "public order" or "national security" – Europe's first intimations of formal radio censorship. It was envisaged that radio programmes would be made by "intellectual and artistic groups, the press, and listeners"; in this, France was far ahead of its time, but commercial interests soon prevailed, and by the early 1930s stations were censoring any news or information that redounded to the credit of left-wing parties.

It was otherwise from the beginning in the Soviet Union. Lenin had used the new medium to announce the installation of the revolutionary government in October 1917, and immediately saw the potential of radio for spreading knowledge of its ideology and decisions. Few Soviet citizens of course owned a radio set, but the regime installed them in factories and clubs, and dragooned workers into listening. Eschewing the self-censorship practised in western Europe, Soviet radio – transmission and content – was controlled by the party, and censors were soon present in every studio across a vast land, checking proposed schedules and contents against party directives and weeding out material that did not conform. Unlike in film, another major tool of agitprop, individual initiative was discouraged.

The situation was quickly similar in Nazi Germany, where radio manufacturers were encouraged, as an act of patriotism, to produce cheap radio sets for mass distribution; the liberal regulation of radio, pioneered during the 1920s, was swept aside, and the medium tightly censored and used for propaganda; by 1939 there were more radio sets than anywhere else in Europe.

By the mid-1930s it looked as if France was set to move towards the British model of radio regulation. Advertising was forbidden on the publicly owned channels, and the PTT took over Radio Paris, the most important commercial station. Government-appointed management boards were made the agents of public accountability. However, the right-wing Popular Front, elected in 1936, were the main beneficiary of this restructuring, and were soon taking leaves out of Nazi books – first using news bulletins for their own propaganda, and then placing the content of news bulletins under the direct control of the Centre Permanent de l'Information Génerale. Astonishingly, a group of government ministers met every day to decide on the content of bulletins. The transition to a fully-fledged Nazi system after the defeat of France in 1940 was, therefore, achieved without difficulty. The Vichy regime's control of broadcasting was equally draconian: daily guidance notes were issued to Radio Vichy, and the owners of private radio stations, no longer allowed to raise money by advertising, were paid to present government-originated material. Already, however, forms of resistance to radio censorship, which would develop considerably after World War II, were in place: in both Occupied and Vichy France, people were listening to the French-language services of the BBC and Radio Moscow, and, less extensively, to the Voice of America, established in 1942.

It was not, of course, that radio broadcasting in Britain and the USSR were free from censorship. Reith was still at the helm of the BBC, and the Communist Party made sure that Soviet citizens were shielded from the worst news of casualties and fed with propaganda about the outstanding military intelligence of marshal Stalin. In BBC Radio, now extended across the world, the limits of unsuitability were much more widely defined to include questions that went far beyond the conduct and progress of the war, as George Orwell found when he became a talks producer for Indian programmes in 1941.

As the Germans were driven out of France in 1944, one of the first actions of the Resistance was the establishment of Radiodiffusion de la Nation Française. The national anthem, the Marseillaise, which had been banned for four years, was played regularly, and the owners of radio sets turned up the volume and opened their windows so that everybody in the street could hear it. The radio was used similarly to call on priests to ring church bells (also banned by the Germans), as troops reached the Left Bank in Paris. Beginning with the bells of Notre Dame, the whole city was soon full of the sound. One of de Gaulle's first acts was the revocation of all commercial radio licences and the expropriation of their assets. The single

nationalized radio took their place, Radiodiffusion-Television Française (RTF), funded, like the BBC, by a licence fee. Even now, however, forms of censorship continued. The minister of information, and future president, François Mitterrand, told the National Assembly: "[Radio] makes policy every day, and its policy is the defence of the French national interests"; the government had the right, because it represented the popular will, to oversee what was being broadcast (not an argument that could possibly have been applied to newspapers).

France's more authoritarian model of broadcasting control would continue until the 1980s, but not without resistance. Thus, for instance, listeners tuned to the périfériques, notably Radio Luxemburg and Radio Monte Carlo, during the Algerian War of the late 1950s and early 1960s. Situated just outside French territory, the périfériques could, in most people's opinion, be relied upon for a more truthful description of the war of decolonization than was heard in the heavily censored official radio and television broadcasts. When de Gaulle returned to power in 1958, his government attempted to stifle these alternative sources of news by purchasing shares in them; the grand duchy of Luxemburg at first resisted this attempt, but finally succumbed to the efforts of Havas, France's national advertising agency. The RTF now became the ORTF (Office de Radiodiffusion-Television Française), which, despite a 1964 law promising that all "principal tendencies of thought and great currents of opinion" would have due airtime, was, to all intents and purposes, the mouthpiece of the Gaullist party. A wall poster composed during the revolutionary events of 1968 announced: "the police speak to you every night at 8 o'clock".

Radio broadcasts elsewhere in western Europe and the USA regarded themselves as being, on the contrary, in the forefront of the battle against censorship. The BBC World Service, Radio Free Europe, and Radio Liberty, although they were officially funded, the first by the British Foreign Office and the others by the US Central Intelligence Agency, nevertheless broadcast short-wave information on a variety of political, religious, and cultural topics to which the citizens of the Soviet Union and its satellites had no local access. In countries to which these services were directed, broadcasting engineers were instructed systematically to jam news that differed from their government's official line. During a heroic moment of history, the "Prague Spring", former dissidents made maximum use of radio, and it was significant that it was in a final radio broadcast, as Russian tanks occupied the Czech capital, that they appealed to the west not to forget them.

Radio Luxemburg, mentioned above, had been broadcasting since 1931, outside national laws and free from state censorship. The most famous and long-lasting of the "pirate" radio stations, it was subjected to an international campaign, led in the early 1930s by Britain and Germany, for its removal from the airwaves (interestingly, at that time France was much more liberal towards the station, in which, it hardly needs saying, there was considerable French investment). The campaign resumed after World War II, when Luxemburg, as well as transmitting more reliable news than French radio, became the focus for a desire among young people for radio that more closely reflected their culture, which, in their eyes, was censored by official broadcasters. A leaf out of Luxemburg's book was taken by such "offshore" initiatives as Radio Caroline, broadcasting from a ship near the coast of Essex, but outside British territorial waters, during the 1960s. The British government had the utmost difficulty in getting them removed from the airwaves, and public policy had finally to move away from the dismissal of popular culture as "trivial" to the culturally pluralist radio economy of the present day.

Attacks on radio "balance", regarded as the censorship of more "extreme" points of view, also came from a burgeoning movement for community radio. Active in the USA from the 1950s, this new arm of broadcasting gave voice to protests against the Vietnam War and to the opinions of leaders of the civil rights movement. The French Green Party established Radio Verte in 1977 to protest against government monopoly of the airwaves; it called for the licensing of local radio stations which would be empowered to reflect local activities and to hand over microphones to local voices. The Socialist Party joined the campaign, and its leader François Mitterrand, once, as has been noted, a defender of state censorship, was even arrested because he had made an illegal radio broadcast. By 1981, when Mitterrand won the presidential election, there were 130 such stations in Paris alone, with ethnic minorities, religious groups, women's groups, lesbians and gays, and many others all having uncensored access to radio. Their efforts were supported by a national organization, the Association pour la Libération des Ondes (ALO), and by a breakaway group, the Fédération Nationale des Radios Libres (FNRL). Mitterrand established the Holleaux Commission to allocate frequencies to them, but laid down that no community radio could broadcast advertising; few of the new stations could survive without it, and the movement soon collapsed. A smaller, but parallel movement in Britain, spearheaded by the Community Communications Group (COMCOM) and the Community Radio Group, suffered the same fate.

Mention has already been made of the censorship of popular music on radio. This has been the main theme of radio censorship in western Europe and North America since the 1980s. As the place where most new musics are publicly launched, radio can act as a gatekeeper barring tracks thought unsuitable by outside pressure groups or by the broadcasters themselves. Broadcasters may also be subject to pressure from governments who, in times of war (as with the Falklands/Malvinas and the Gulf) may indicate the inappropriateness of certain "unpatriotic" tracks. And, in the USA, the Parents Music Resource Center has been successful in the prevention of tracks it regards as too sexually explicit or violent.

Sub-Saharan Africa

As late as 1979 more than 70 per cent of the world's radio sets were in North America and Europe. Despite that, the growth of radio ownership worldwide had been exponential. In Africa, for instance, it grew from 6.5 million to 60 million between 1960 and 1980. On paper a public service, radio was, however, during that period mostly placed at the disposal of governments, and even at the sole disposal of heads of state. Broadcasting organizations were funded by governments, and their staff regarded as civil servants. Usually, he who paid the piper called the tune.

Radio censorship in the newly independent countries of Africa was often quite blatant, and was not always directed at the immediate domestic political situation. In newly independent Zimbabwe, radio broadcasters were instructed that there

were to be no references to the Soviet invasion of Afghanistan in 1979; North Korea, another "fraternal" socialist country, was to be praised for its achievements. Swaziland, the sole remaining outpost of monarchy, did not allow its broadcasting service to cover news critical of the institution in other countries.

Radio journalists who stood out of line could expect to be punished. In 1980, a Zaïrean radio reporter was arrested simply because he had reported on student disturbances. The Voix du Zaïre radio station was issued with no guidelines; it was impossible for a reporter to know, therefore, that such a report would be considered of an "insurrectional nature". A similar catch-all phrase was used in 1982, when three journalists on the French-backed *Africa Number One* were arrested in Gabon alleged to have been involved with "an illegal opposition group".

A senior Nigerian journalist reported at this time that broadcasting was "heavily mined politically, and one has to tread carefully". "Treading carefully" in Africa included at this time waiting for an official government response before transmitting the news – as with Radio Tanzania, who waited for its government's reaction before reporting news of the overthrow of Kwame Nkrumah, first president of Ghana, about whom it was notoriously possible to hold entirely opposite opinions. Similarly, in 1981, Radio Tanzania waited for an official go-ahead before it reported that one of the country's airliners had been hijacked on its way to London. As recently as 1997, Radio-Télévision Nationale Congolaise failed to carry the story of the death of the ousted dictator of Zaïre (now Congo), Mobutu Sese Seko.

The censorship and self-censorship in African radio so far described concerns state-owned services. When during the 1990s independent radio was at last allowed in various countries, more subtle forms of censorship had to be devised. In Uganda, as reported by Richard Carver and Adewale Maja-Pearce for *Index on Censorship* in 1995, licences were issued to Capital Radio and Radio Sanyu, which were partly owned by people who had a vested interest in the continuance of the government, one of them indeed the director-general of the internal security organization. Yet the station's licence only adjured them "to generally respect the cultural sensibilities of Ugandan society", and to avoid pornographic material. In Zambia, the first four licences were issued to Christian groups – the Baptist Communications Centre, the Roman Catholic diocese of Ndola, Uni Holdings Ltd, and the Christian Voice of Lusaka. Granted that few other Zambian organizations had the necessary capital to establish a radio station, Carver and Maja-Pearce speculate on how far the new stations could be regarded as truly independent – president Frederick Chiluba was a born-again Christian. It could at least be argued that, as in Namibia (where the churches own Channel 7), the government was likely to have an easier ride than otherwise.

In Kenya the manipulation of independent radio for government purposes has been more overt. A licence was issued to a body already active in the media field, the Kenya Television Network (KTN), "a whole owned subsidiary", reported Carver and Maja-Pearce, "of the Kenya Times Media Trust, publisher of one of the country's three daily newspapers, whose majority shareholder is none other than the ruling party, KANU". It is hardly surprising that the National Electoral Monitoring

Unit, reporting on the role of broadcasting in the 1992 elections, could conclude: "In general, both the TV and radio stations loudly and persistently broadcast news, events and reports to KANU's advantage."

Another important factor in the African context is the question of language. Many countries have a number of languages, some of which are understood by only a small number of people far from the capital cities. Carver and Maja Pearce suggest that the Malawi policy of broadcasting only in English and Chewa was deliberately formulated to maintain the government in power. In Mozambique, similarly, news bulletins are in Portuguese, which is only spoken by a small but powerful minority.

In March 1992 Radio Rwanda, the state-owned service, was prohibited from further incitement of anti-Tutsi hatred. In its place, Radio-Télévision des Milles Collines (RTML) waged an even more violent campaign. The use of independent radio for this kind of hate speech allowed the Rwandan government to distance itself from the campaign, with the aims of which it was at that time in entire agreement. The use of radio for hate speech now reached the international agenda – for once, censorship would have been regarded as benign.

Community radio, seen in Europe as an extension of democracy, was used in South Africa as a means of strengthening apartheid. Capital Radio (Umtate and Durban) and Radio 702 (Johannesburg) were private stations designed to serve the "homeland" governments of Transkei and Bophuthatswana, but could in no sense question the democratic existence of these homelands. On the face of it, the 22 South African Broadcasting Corporation (SABC) stations broadcasting in 11 languages seemed to be an extension of democratic radio; in practice it was a means of restricting the amount of information that could be broadcast to the linguistic groups concerned and of preventing them giving voice to their concerns for a wider audience.

After the end of apartheid, the Independent Broadcasting Authority (IBA) took it that one of its most important regulatory roles was the promotion of peace and reconciliation. Some commentators have seen this as a kind of censorship in reverse. Although, as in Europe, there has been a tendency to play down the bad news, Carver and Maja-Pearce commented: "An understandable desire to promote reconciliation can quickly spill over into suppression of 'divisive' points of view."

Southeast Asia

Here the censorship of radio has taken novel and subtle forms. During the 1970s and 1980s the medium was seen as an instrument of economic and social development, on the face of it quite unexceptional. John Lent reported in 1982 that in the Philippines, a Broadcast Media Development Programme had been established, which would guide the 200 radio stations "to assist and supplement the state in advancing the masses through development of education and culture in family planning and for wholesome family entertainment, help the advertising industry, promote truthful commercials". However, programmes soon began to arrive ready-made by the Voice of the Philippines Network, and these included news and current affairs as well as "development broadcasting". Programmes considered to be not in the national interest were dropped, and, in 1982, president Marcos evinced a new concern with the

levels of sex and violence on radio and television. He warned that stations would have their licences revoked if they persisted, and established a new board of censors to enforce his rulings. Most at stake, however, was his own political career. On the day of the assassination of Ninoy Aquino only one station, the Catholic Radio Veritas, reported the event. As Cory Aquino's election campaign drew to a close, the Radio Veritas building was stormed and destroyed by Marcos's troops.

Malaysian radio was similarly controlled, it seemed for identical motives. The Ministry of Information guidelines laid down that radio should:

> explain in depth and with full coverage, government policies and programmes to ensure maximum public understanding, stimulate public interest and opinions, assist in promoting civic consciousness and foster Malaysian arts and culture, provide suitable elements of popular education, general information and entertainment, and promote national unity.

There were some curious applications of these general admonitions, such as that no bad news was to be reported on radio before 12 noon in case it should disturb workers and prevent them carrying out their duties; and that air crashes should not be covered in case the stories upset intending pilgrims to Mecca.

Educational control was also at the heart of Singaporean radio, on which 34 per cent of material transmitted was devoted to the topic. In Indonesia, which has a formal national ideology – *pancasila* – little political news was broadcast, but Indonesian language broadcasts from Radio Australia could be heard, much to the disgust of the government, who called for their cessation in 1980.

Latin America and the Caribbean

For much of the 20th century the news media, including state-owned radio, were used as instruments of domination by most Latin American regimes. However, there more than anywhere else, the radio has been also used as a major means of resistance and self-help education, providing a contrast to Southeast Asia in this respect. Thus, for example, in Colombia, the "radio school" was developed from Canadian and Irish examples of the "farm forum" – groups of farmers met, listened to radio programmes, studied pamphlets, and used them to solve practical problems; and in the mountainous region of Sutatenza, radio provided a parish notice board, basic literacy training, and leadership in prayer. One result was the formation of Popular Cultural Action (ACPO), a provider of non-formal education throughout Colombia and beyond, organized by the Catholic Church. Not all those influenced by ACPO were willing to accept its hierarchical structure, opting instead for a more participatory role for listeners, with radio being used as a "voice for the voiceless", to organize the listener's own opinions rather than disseminating the ideas of others.

In Bolivia Miners Radio was established in direct opposition to the existing Catholic station (which, having been established to combat communism, was hardly likely to appeal to militant workers). Mining is at the heart of the Bolivian economy, and the government, therefore, could not push the miners too far; they did however, close down Miners Radio whenever they could safely do so.

In Paraguay Radio Charitas was the first Catholic station deliberately to oppose general Stroessner, in power since 1954; its director, Father Arrancon, was refused re-entry to the country after a visit to Argentina in 1983. Already, however, Radio Ñanduti, said by the regime to be "systematically disrupting public order and creating alarm", had been suspended for a month in 1983. Remarkably, the station's "open microphone" policy was the main issue bringing about its downfall. The government accorded to itself the right to decide who should be interviewed. It took exception to the station's practice of interviewing opposition politicians and holding radio phone-ins, by now commonplace throughout the world. In 1984, Ñanduti's owner Humberto Rubin was accused of "lending the microphone to any number of irresponsible, unauthorized politicians". The station was finally forced to close when, in April–May 1986, not only were its headquarters attacked by government-inspired demonstrators, but its broadcasting was subjected to continuous jamming. The government had evidently learned lessons from Nicaragua, where US-financed stations on the country's borders attempted to drown Sandinista signals after the successful revolution of 1979.

Haiti provides a further example of the use of radio to undermine a dictatorship but also of how, ultimately, a government can simply resort to its closure. The director of the Catholic-owned Radio Soleil was expelled during a crackdown on the media in the early 1980s. This did not prevent the station from organizing a boycott against a referendum to endorse the life-presidency of Jean-Claude Duvalier (Baby Doc) in 1985. The station was closed down, reopened after popular and international pressure, but then closed down again. During the unstable regimes that followed Duvalier's enforced departure, the station continued to be put under pressure, but, in a final twist, was made a propaganda tool for those who had overthrown Haiti's first democratically elected government in 1991.

Beyond transmission

Mention should finally be made of a remarkable development from radio, pioneered in the Middle East at the end of the 1970s. In countries where the government controlled the airwaves, banned artists could be widely heard through the unofficial distribution of audio cassettes, products that proved much more difficult to control. "Cassette Culture" was pioneered in Iran, where the technology was used to spread news and information about the Islamic Revolution. Elsewhere it was used for much more subversive ends, bringing to people's attention otherwise banned work in the fields of classical music, popular poetry (including that which was banned because it was spoken in non-official dialects), news, and political analysis, as well as education. Accessible, reasonably cheap, and easily passed from hand to hand, audio cassettes provided a "radio" service that did not need frequencies, in countries where the official media were strictly controlled, or even, as previously in Europe, considered out of touch with popular culture and need.

CANDELARIA VAN STRIEN-RENEY

Further Reading

Aldridge, Meryl and Nicholas Hewitt (editors), *Controlling Broadcasting: Access Policy and Practice in North America and Europe*, Manchester: Manchester University Press, 1994

Alger, Dean E., *The Media and Politics*, 2nd edition, Belmont, California: Wadsworth, 1996

Ansah, Paul A.V., "Blueprint for Freedom", *Index on Censorship*, 20/9 (October 1991)

Article 19, *Broadcasting Genocide: Censorship, Propaganda and State-Sponsored Violence in Rwanda, 1990–1994*, London: Article 19, 1996

Barbrook, Richard, *Media Freedom: The Contradictions of Communication in the Age of Modernity*, London: Pluto Press, 1995

Barnouw, Erik, *A History of Broadcasting in the United States*, 3 vols, New York: Oxford University Press, 1966–70

Black Radio Today for the 1990s, New York: Arbitron, 1992

Bredin, Andrew, "His Master's Voice: Radio and TV in Africa", *Index on Censorship*, 11/5 (October 1982)

Briggs, Asa, *The History of Broadcasting in the United Kingdom*, 6 vols, London and New York: Oxford University Press, 1961–96

Carver, Richard and Adewale Maya-Pearce, *Who Rules the Airwaves? A Report on Broadcasting in Africa*, London: Article 19, 1994

Carver, Richard, and Adewale Maya-Pearce, "Making Waves", *Index on Censorship*, 14/1 (January–February 1995)

Downing, John, Ali Mohammedi and Annabelle Sreberny-Mohammadi (editors), *Questioning the Media: A Critical Introduction*, Newbury Park, California: Sage, 1995

Foerstel, Herbert N., *Banned in the Media: A Reference Guide to Censorship in the Press, Motion Pictures, Broadcasting, and the Internet*, Westport, Connecticut: Greenwood Press, 1998

Girard, Bruce (editor), *A Passion for Radio: Radio Waves and Community*, Montreal: Black Rose, 1992

Huber, Peter W., *Law and Disorder in Cyberspace: Abolish the FCC and Let Common Law Rule in the Telecosm*, Oxford and New York: Oxford University Press, 1997

Khalafallah, Haifaa, "Unofficial Cassette Culture in the Middle East", *Index on Censorship*, 2/5 (October 1982)

Lent, John A., "How Broadcasting Operates in the ASEAN Countries", *Index on Censorship*, 11/5 (October 1982)

Lewis, Peter M. and Jerry Booth, *The Invisible Medium: Public, Commercial, and Community Radio*, Basingstoke: Macmillan, 1989; Washington, DC: Howard University Press, 1990

Price, Monroe E. (editor), *The V-Chip Debate: Content Filtering from Television to the Internet*, Mahwah, New Jersey: Erlbaum, 1998

Scupham, John, *Broadcasting and the Community*, London: Watts, 1967

Smith, Anthony, *The Shadow in the Cave: A Study of the Relationship between Broadcaster, His Audience and the State*, London: Allen and Unwin, and Urbana: University of Illinois Press, 1973

Summers, Harrison B. (editor), *Radio Censorship*, New York: Wilson, 1939; reprinted New York: Arno Press, 1971

Wedell, George and Philip Crookes, *Radio 2000: The Opportunities for Public and Private Radio Services in Europe*, Geneva: European Broadcasting Union, 1991

RADIO: Jamming

Jamming is the deliberate use of electronic interference to render an incoming broadcast signal intelligible. It may assume many forms, including a static sound, a repetitive Morse-code pattern, or the use of an alternative broadcast to overwhelm the arriving signal. Jamming is normally conducted by strategically located, land-based transmitters. A party must be highly determined to block broadcasts using this conventional method. To be effective, it requires tremendous financial, technical, and energy resources as well as manpower for a complex system of monitoring. As Julian Hale writes: "The incoming signal starts at one point, but it ends up over a huge area . . . This requires, in a country the size of Russia, innumerable transmitters directed against a single signal." Three transmitters may be required to neutralize one incoming transmission. In more recent developments, jamming may also originate from an airborne source, such as the US Air Force's Commando Solo plane. The EC-130 can block both radio and television broadcast signals or relay alternative programming on the same frequency.

Jamming is popularly associated with the superpowers and the Cold War, yet states have engaged in this practice almost since the inception of radio itself. The Italian physicist Guglielmo Marconi and others endeavoured to perfect wireless, radio wave communication during the late 19th century and the first two decades of the 20th. Early versions involved point-to-point sending and receiving stations with transmissions in Morse code only. "Broadcasting" – allowing for communication to the general public and carrying the human voice – was accomplished by 1920 in the US and Britain. Transmissions over globe-spanning distances became possible later that decade with the development of short-wave capability.

Debate exists as to when the first attempt to jam this new communication form occurred. During World War I Germany interfered with teletype signals between France and Russia by transmitting random characters. Berlin may have also tried to block Lenin's early cross-border telegraphic messages in 1918. In 1923 the French sought to drown out German broadcast programmes that denounced France's occupation of the Ruhr. There is also evidence of jamming during the Spanish Civil War, and its application by the Dollfuss government to block Nazi programming coming into Austria in 1934. Still, in its totality the pre-World War II period witnessed efforts that were highly sporadic and short-lived in nature. It was only during World War II that jamming came into its own as a common practice among belligerents, particularly for the Axis powers: Germany (where the process was referred to as "broadcast defence") and Italy. Among the Allied powers, the Soviet Union engaged in extensive electronic interference, but the US and Britain did not.

The Eastern bloc's jamming of the Western external services during the Cold War is now legendary. The Voice of America (VOA), the two US "surrogate services" Radio Liberty (RL) and Radio Free Europe (RFE), the British Broadcasting Corporation (BBC) World Service, and Deutsche Welle of Germany were by far the most common targets of communist transmitters until the late 1980s. The USSR and its eastern European counterparts maintained a complex and exceptionally expensive web of transmitters and monitors, according to Stanley Leinwoll: "Every city with a population of more than 250,000

had about 15 jamming transmitters, and large population centres such as Moscow had more than 75 of them. Each jamming station was guided by its own monitoring station, which was linked to a regional monitoring station. The regional station could call in additional jammers via sky-wave propagation if local equipment was overburdened." By the 1980s the Soviets were spending an estimated $1 billion to operate 3000 transmitters at 60 megawatts daily.

The extent of communist jamming reflected the larger ebb and flow of East–West relations. The general international news services, including the VOA and BBC, would gain the greatest latitude during periods of detente. Moscow suspended jamming of the major western stations in 1973 but resumed it in 1980 with the Solidarity crisis in Poland. RL and RFE, however, blocked from their inaugural broadcasts in 1951 and 1953 respectively, were rarely spared; as surrogate services their domestic news reports were considered highly threatening. Animosity toward the two services was so great that by most estimates they received 70 per cent of the Soviet jamming efforts in the final years of the bipolar rivalry, making them the most heavily blocked of any service in the world at that time. Mikhail Gorbachev unexpectedly ordered the complete cessation of all jamming in late 1988. It was considered an extraordinary move at the time, and it presaged the end of the Cold War.

While Eastern-bloc communist efforts were renowned, jamming was a global practice in the post-World War II period. Countries on every continent and for widely varying reasons found censorship through jamming desirable, despite the significant financial and technical costs. During the Algerian war of independence, France jammed the Voice of Free Algeria. Rhodesia did the same to a British station transmitting anti-Ian Smith programming from Botswana. Post-revolutionary Iran applied the technology against various official Western services as well as clandestine stations. Argentina employed it against the BBC during the Falklands/Malvinas War. Perhaps among the more intensive efforts in recent years has been Cuba's attempts – with notable success – to drown the American surrogate services Radio and TV Martí. It is also commonly used to combat pirate stations.

Jamming remains a vital part of the post-Cold War communications landscape. From 1996 the Serbian government jammed B92, the only remaining independent radio service in that part of the former Yugoslavia. The People's Republic of China engages in significant jamming activity of the VOA and the BBC, among others. In a historical irony, the British began to rely after 1992 on old Soviet transmitters to send its Mandarin programming into China. There has also been a controversial and heatedly debated proposal by a former United Nations official, Jamie Merzl, that the organization should employ jamming when hostile parties broadcast incitements to violence, as has been the case in many of the humanitarian crises of the 1990s, such as Rwanda and Liberia. Combined with more neutral UN programming under the heading "information intervention", Merzl contends that his approach may better achieve human rights goals than a costly large-scale military response.

Some communications analysts maintain that jamming may soon go the way of the Cold War, particularly with the arrival of direct broadcast satellite (DBS) technology. Direct broadcast satellite signals use a higher frequency than earth-bound transmitters and are therefore difficult to jam in conventional ways. However it will be some time before such advances are universally used. Either way, one principle of jamming is certain to remain constant. The more a party attempts to block an incoming message, the greater the curiosity and interest of its intended recipients.

K. NAKJAVANI BOOKMILLER

Further Reading

Briggs, Asa, *The History of Broadcasting in the United Kingdom*, vol. 3: *The War of Words*, Oxford and New York: Oxford University Press, 1961

"German Station Broadcasting Ruhr News and Music Is Drowned out by Eiffel Tower", *New York Times* (6 March 1923): A1

Hale, Julian, *Radio Power: Propaganda and International Broadcasting*, London: Elek, and Philadelphia: Temple University Press, 1975

"Jammed Belgrade Radio Defies the Buzz of Power", *New York Times* (3 December 1996): A3

Leinwoll, Stanley, "Jamming: The End of an Era?", *Radio Electronics*, 60 (June 1989): 75–77

Leinwoll, Stanley, "The Soviet Jamming System and the Future of Jamming", *Radio Electronics*, 60 (October 1989): 78–79

Lisann, Maury, *Broadcasting to the Soviet Union: International Politics and Radio*, New York: Praeger, 1975

Merzl, Jamie, "Rwandan Genocide and the International Law of Radio Jamming", *American Journal of International Law*, 91 (October 1997): 628–51

Merzl, Jamie, "Information Intervention: When Switching Channels Isn't Enough", *Foreign Affairs*, 76 (November–December 1997): 15

"Radio Free Europe–Radio Liberty: Free At Last", *Broadcasting* (5 December 1988): 39

"US Group Has 'Jam' Session in Cuba", *Broadcasting* (1 January 1990): 94

Whitton, John B. and Arthur Larson, *Propaganda towards Disarmament in the War of Words*, Dobbs Ferry, New York: Oceana, 1963

"Will Cuba Invade US radio?", *Broadcasting and Cable* (11 April 1994): 52

RADIO FREE ASIA

"Radio Free Asia had just better shut up, since the Asian people have become sick and tired of the endless harangue from America" complained the official *China Daily* after the United States introduced Radio Free Asia (RFA) on 29 September 1996. Launched with an inaugural two-hour programme in Mandarin Chinese, the service now broadcasts to seven locations, including Cambodia, China, Laos, Burma (Myanmar), North Korea, Tibet, and Vietnam. According to the US International Broadcasting Act of 1994 (Public Law 103–236), which established RFA, its purpose is "to provide accurate and timely information, news, and commentary about events in the respective countries of Asia and elsewhere; and to be a forum for a variety of opinions and voices from within Asian nations whose people do not fully enjoy freedom of expression".

A previous "Radio Free Asia" existed from 1950 to 1954. Transmitting only to China, its brief existence was attributed to the paucity of private radio ownership and difficulty in information gathering. A new "Radio Free China" proposal resurfaced in Congress after the Tiananmen Square massacre of 1989. The proposal gained further momentum after overwhelming testimony of the effectiveness of Radio Free Europe (RFE) and Radio Liberty (RL) following the fall of the Iron Curtain. By 1991 a presidential task force on international broadcasting, while recommending a scaling back of RFE/RL in the post-Cold War era, endorsed a new initiative for Southeast Asia. The US Commission on Broadcasting to the People's Republic of China of 1992 agreed, concluding in its report that "Though the Cold War is over, many millions around the world, particularly in Asia, remain under repressive rule. One of the shackles with which these regimes try to bind their people is the denial of information – about what is happening in the world and what is happening in their own countries."

The RFA plan prompted heated debate as Congress considered its authorization. The State Department under both the Bush (senior) and Clinton administrations disapproved of the project, on the grounds that the station would serve only to antagonize the Chinese government. The Voice of America also strongly objected, contending that expanded VOA programming tailored to each country would be sufficient, and more cost-effective, and build upon the sizeable audience the Voice already had in the area.

Prominent Chinese dissidents within the US were deeply divided. Many ardently supported the home service concept, drawing attention to Beijing's repressive grip on all internal media outlets and the pivotal role it would play in advancing the cause of democratization. "If Americans want to help China democratize, the most important and most effective thing they can do is this [Radio Free Asia]" declared Liu Binyan, a former reporter with the Communist Party newspaper, the *People's Daily*. Yet Nien Ching, the only ethnic Asian member on the Broadcasting to China Commission, campaigned against it. She was the dissident author of *Life and Death in Shanghai*, a journal covering her imprisonment for nearly seven years during the Cultural Revolution, and she told *Time* that RFA "might give hard-liners an excuse to crack down on dissidents" and endorsed the VOA option instead. Others feared that the project might backfire with pro-democratic but nationalistic activists within the target countries.

President Clinton, who had supported RFA as a presidential candidate in 1992, ended the VOA–RFA debate in 1994. In signing the International Broadcasting Act, he not only established RFA as a private non-profit-making US corporation but created a Broadcasting Board of Governors (BBG), which governed the VOA, Radio and TV Marti, Worldnet Television, RFE/RL, and RFA all under one bureaucratic roof. However the issue of the new service's name took longer to settle. When first envisaged in 1990–91, supporters tagged the concept "Radio Free China", patterning it on RFE. An expansion in the target audiences had swelled the name to "Radio Free Asia" by 1992; however, the US Commission on Broadcasting to China concluded that the title sounded too confrontational, and recommended that it be called instead "Asian Information Radio" or "Asia Democracy Radio". Yet the Act of 1994 retained the "Radio Free Asia" designation. By 1995 the new Broadcasting Board of Governors had changed the name to the more conciliatory "Asia Pacific Network" (APN). Congress, asserting that the Board did not possess the authority to alter the service's legally given name, succeeded in maintaining the name as "Radio Free Asia" just before broadcasting began.

RFA introduced its various language programmes gradually, but early problems have plagued its service. Simply hearing the broadcasts was difficult initially. Neighbouring countries, such as Thailand, refused to relay the programmes out of fear of diplomatic reprisals. The shortwave signal therefore travelled via satellite to relay stations further away from the Mandarin-speaking areas, including Armenia and Kazakhstan. Consequently the opening transmissions in Mandarin were either weak or non-existent in much of China. A difficulty in locating frequencies further complicated early reception. Intentional blocking has occurred in Vietnam, which jammed the first RFA broadcasts to the country starting in February 1997.

The problem of Chinese contributors has also surfaced. Dai Qing, a prominent Chinese journalist, agreed to report for the service in spring 1996, when the operation was still called the Asian Pacific Network and she was assured that moderates were in charge. However after hearing that the name would actually be Radio Free Asia, and that Liu Binyan, an ardent anticommunist would be a service host, Qing decided to quit. Explaining in a Beijing interview that "Any day, if the police were to come to take me, I would not be surprised at all", she later fled for Australia. Since then a number of other Chinese have faced harsh government treatment for cooperating with Radio Free Asia. The most extreme case to date may be that of Zhang Shanguang, who was sentenced in late 1998 to ten years in prison. He was charged with "providing intelligence to a foreign organization", in supplying RFA with information on internal labor protests.

It may be some time before it is known whether the latest American broadcast effort will find a stable and sizeable audience in the region. As US policy toward Beijing and other regimes in the area vacillates between accommodation and confrontation, RFA may be silenced before it has a chance to do so.

K. NAKJAVANI BOOKMILLER

Further Reading

Awanohara, Susumu, "Good Morning, Asia: US Debates Pains and Gains of New Radio Service", *Far Eastern Economic Review* (2 July 1992): 25–26

"China: Drop Plans for Radio Free Asia", *IPI Report*, 43/4–5 (May–June 1994): 31–32

Flint, Joe, "New US Radio Service to Asia Proposed", *Broadcasting*, 122 (28 September 1992): 34

Holloway, Nigel, "Nothing but Static: Radio Free Asia Is Hamstrung by Politics", *Far Eastern Economic Review* (2 March 1995): 25

Holloway, Nigel, "Troubled Persuader: Hard Knocks Await Radio Free Asia's Soft Line", *Far Eastern Economic Review* (1 August 1996): 22–23

Linter, Bertil, "Heavy Static: Washington's Radio Free Asia Runs into Trouble", *Far Eastern Economic Review* (24 March 1994): 26

Tuch, Hans N., "The Case against Radio Free China", *Foreign Service Journal*, 69 (July 1992): 23–24

Tyler, Patrick, "US Radio Aiming at China 'Tyranny' but Few Can Hear It", *New York Times* (27 December 1996): A1

United States, Presidential Commission on Broadcasting to the People's Republic of China, *The Commission on Broadcasting to the People's Republic of China*, Arlington, Virginia: Department of State, 1992

Website

http://www.rfa.org

RADIO FREE EUROPE/RADIO LIBERTY

The idea of the international radio stations Radio Free Europe (RFE) and Radio Liberty (RL) first arose in 1947–48. This was the time of the completion of Soviet domination of eastern Europe, the Berlin airlift, the Marshall Plan, and the Iron Curtain. Eastern, central, and western Europe were physically divided by barbed wire, armed patrols, land mines, and guard towers. There was a communist monopoly and censorship of the media. The free flow of information was cut off, not only from the outside, but also internally.

On 17 December 1947 the newly created United States National Security Council issued directive NSC 4-A, which directed the Director of the Central Intelligence Agency (CIA) to "initiate and conduct covert psychological operations designed to counteract Soviet and Soviet-inspired activities which constitute a threat to world peace". One aim of this campaign of psychological warfare was to create surrogate radio stations (home service) that would broadcast to countries under Soviet control yet not be officially connected with the United States government. These stations could broadcast programmes and take positions for which the United States could officially deny responsibility. By August 1948 in Europe, the CIA had acquired a radio transmitter, a printing plant, and had begun to assemble a fleet of weather balloons intended to carry and drop off propaganda leaflets, and other materials, over the Iron Curtain.

In 1949 the National Committee for a Free Europe (NCFE) was founded so that "émigrés from the satellite nations could find employment which would utilize their skills and, at the same time, document for the world at large the actions of the satellite governments and Soviet Russia".

The NCFE, in turn, established a Crusade for Freedom, with a former general, Lucius Clay, famous for his role in the Berlin airlift of 1948–49, as its chairman. In a US nation-wide radio broadcast on Labor Day in 1950, general Dwight D. Eisenhower made a passionate appeal for financial support for Radio Free Europe and for Americans to sign a "Freedom Scroll" with a "Declaration of Freedom". Some 16 million Americans from 20 cities signed the "Freedom Scrolls", and contributed $1,317,000 to the expansion of Radio Free Europe. The Crusade for Freedom culminated in the installation of the Freedom Bell at the Berlin City Hall on United Nations Day, 24 October 1950. The bell, eight feet high and weighing 10 tons, was inscribed: "That This World, Under God, Shall Have A New Birth of Freedom". Radio Free Europe transmitted its first programme, only 30 minutes long, on 4 July 1950, to Czechoslovakia. By August 1950 it was broadcasting to Romania, Poland, Hungary, and Bulgaria.

As the US foreign policy of "containment" changed to one of "liberation", the skies of central Europe from October 1951 to November 1956 were filled with more than 350,000 balloons carrying more than 300,000,000 leaflets, posters, books, and other printed matter. The balloon operations were coordinated with the radio programming and had colourful names: PROSPERO, VETO, FOCUS, and SPOTLIGHT. RFE constructed three major launching sites in Germany to send off the balloons around the clock in good weather.

During the Hungarian Revolution of 1956, Radio Free Europe was accused of encouraging the freedom fighters to battle on in the false understanding that they would receive reinforcements from the West. Investigations by the US Congress, the German government, and the Council of Europe exonerated the service of the charges.

The beginning of Radio Liberty contrasted dramatically with that of Radio Free Europe. The American Committee for Freedom of the Peoples of the USSR was founded in January 1951, also under CIA sponsorship and policy guidance. Unlike the NCFE, the American Committee chose not to raise public funds, which would have aided in providing a plausible cover for its activities. The CIA had difficulties in uniting the diverse Soviet émigré groups in Germany. The American Committee assumed that the most effective propaganda against the Soviet regime would be conducted by former Soviet nationals speaking in the name of a united emigration. There were two principal difficulties in the way of accomplishing this aim: one was the extreme hostility existing between Great Russian groups and those composed of the various non-Russian peoples of the Soviet Union. The other difficulty was the basic political differences between Marxist and non-Marxist elements in the emigration, regardless of nationality.

The radio station was called "Radio Liberation from Bolshevism" and first broadcast on 1 March 1953 to the Soviet armed forces in Germany and Austria. Within 10 minutes, the Soviet Union started jamming its broadcasts by transmitting signals on the same or adjacent frequencies. Soon the station was broadcasting in Ukrainian, Belorussian, Armenian, Azeri, Georgian, Kazakh, Kyrgyz, Tajik, Turkmen, Uzbek, Tatar-Bashkir, and other languages of the Caucasus and Central Asia. In keeping with the changing American foreign policy, the station was renamed Radio Liberation in 1956 and finally Radio Liberty in 1959.

A major turning point in RFE/RL's history occurred in 1967 when *Ramparts* magazine publicly revealed the RFE's relationship with the CIA. This subsequently led to a congressional decision that the CIA would no longer finance RFE and RL. Congressional debate began on the future of the two services. In 1973, a presidential commission under Milton Eisenhower published a report, *The Right to Know*, which formed the basis of congressional legislation to consolidate RFE and RL into one

new hybrid organization: a private, non-profit-making corporation but still funded by Congress. The final physical and administrative consolidation of the two radio stations took place in 1975–76 as a new corporation: RFE/RL.

During the 1980s this grew into a mature, productive radio station that played a major role in president Ronald Reagan's "Project Democracy". He explained RFE/RL's role as follows:

> It is impossible to resist oppression without having access to the truth and without being able to communicate with your fellow man. Radio Free Europe and Radio Liberty can help the people of Eastern Europe and the Soviet Union overcome their problems. They are indispensable – the closest thing to a domestic free press that outsiders can provide for them.

As the war in Afghanistan continued, a new broadcasting unit of RFE/RL, Radio Free Afghanistan, was created in October 1985. This unit broadcast from Munich in the two main languages of Afghanistan: Dari and Pashto. The collapse of communism in eastern Europe in 1989 brought about new challenges and opportunities: RFE/RL opened its first bureau in a broadcast-targeted country in Budapest in 1989, followed by bureaux in Prague and Warsaw. By comparison, in 1997, RFE/RL had 19 different bureaux in its broadcast areas.

In addition to jamming, the communist regimes reacted violently to effective RFE/RL programming by committing acts of intimidation, kidnapping, and even murder, of émigré employees and freelancers. Intelligence agents were infiltrated into the radio stations. And the RFE/RL headquarters building was seriously damaged in 1981 by a bomb attack directed by the infamous terrorist known as "Carlos the Jackal".

The effectiveness of RFE/RL can best be understood positively in the words and actions of its listeners. For example, on 29 January 1991 Lennart Meri, then foreign minister of Estonia, nominated RFE/RL for the Nobel Peace Prize. After the collapse of the Soviet Union in 1991, Russia's first president Boris Yeltsin said: "Radio Liberty was one of the very few channels through which it was possible to send information to the whole world and, most important, to the whole of Russia, because now almost every family in Russia listens to Radio Liberty." A few weeks later he signed a presidential decree allowing RFE/RL to operate an official news bureau in Moscow.

The 40th anniversary celebration of the first Radio Liberty broadcast took place in Moscow in March 1993. The ex-Soviet president Mikhail S. Gorbachev said that "in the dark years" of communist rule "before my own *perestroika* [reconstruction] reform programme began, Radio Liberty told the truth. We hope the radio station will continue in the future. I hope to be present at the 50th anniversary of Radio Liberty."

On 4 July 1994 the US president Bill Clinton formally accepted an offer from the Czech president Václav Havel and the Czech government to move RFE/RL headquarters to Prague. "With this move", he said, "the radios begin a new chapter in the continuing struggle for democracy throughout the former Communist bloc". Havel officially welcomed RFE/RL to Prague on 8 September 1995, saying, "I am not sure that I would have been in prison for another couple of years were it not for a certain amount of publicity which I had because of these radio stations." By 1997, RFE/RL in Prague was producing 700 hours of weekly programming in 23 languages.

The democratically elected president of Bulgaria Petr Stoyanov, visited the new RFE/RL headquarters in Prague in 1997. He praised its role in the Cold War: "We still remember sometimes how, through the interference on the short-wave range, we searched for the radio station we needed, the radio station to give us courage to go through the hardships of everyday life under communism, Radio Free Europe." The Romanian president Emil Constantinescu visited RFE/RL in 1997. He eloquently illustrated the importance of RFE and RL in the collapse of communism in eastern Europe:

> Communism could not exist, but by lies and lack of information. Communism could be torn apart, not by power of arms, but by power of words and especially of real beliefs. That is why Radio Free Europe has been much more important than the armies, the rockets, the most sophisticated equipment. The rockets that have destroyed Communism have been launched from RFE, and this was America's most important investment against the Cold War.

When asked about the importance of Radio Free Europe, Lech Wałęsa, the first directly elected president of Poland, answered: "Would there be earth without the sun?"

RICHARD H. CUMMINGS

Further Reading

Alexeyeva, Ludmilla, *U.S. Broadcasting to the Soviet Union*, New York: US Helsinki Watch Committee, 1986

Browne, Donald R., *International Radio Broadcasting: The Limits of the Limitless Medium*, New York: Praeger, 1982

Holt, Robert T., *Radio Free Europe*, Minneapolis: University of Minnesota Press, 1958

Lendvai, Paul, *The Bureaucracy of Truth: How Communist Governments Manage the News*, London: Burnett, and Boulder, Colorado: Westview Press, 1981

Michie, Allan Andrew, *Voices through the Iron Curtain: The Radio Free Europe Story*, New York: Dodd Mead, 1963

Mickelson, Sig, *America's Other Voice: The Story of Radio Free Europe and Radio Liberty*, New York: Praeger, 1983

Puddington, Arch, *Broadcasting Freedom: The Cold War Triumph of Radio Free Europe and Radio Liberty*, Lexington: University Press of Kentucky, 2000

Short, K.R.M. (editor), *Western Broadcasting over the Iron Curtain*, London: Croom Helm, 1986

Tyson, James L., *U.S. International Broadcasting and National Security*, New York: Ramapo Press, 1983

Washburn, Philo C., *Broadcasting Propaganda: International Radio Broadcasting and the Construction of Political Reality*, Westport, Connecticut: Praeger, 1992

Wettig, Gerhard, *Broadcasting and Détente: Eastern Policies and Their Implication for East–West Relations*, London: Hurst, and New York: St Martin's Press, 1977

RADIO MARTÍ

On 20 May 1985 the United States initiated "Radio Martí", a service broadcasting news, commentary, and music into Cuba. Authorized by the Radio Broadcasting to Cuba Act of 1983 (Public Law 98–111), the station was named after José Martí, a 19th-century Cuban independence hero and poet. Envisaged by the US as a "surrogate home-service" based on the model of Radio Free Europe (RFE) and Radio Liberty (RL) Martí's mission was to provide Cubans with information about their own country that the government in Washington believed they were denied in domestic media channels. The service operates 24 hours a day, seven days a week, and transmits on both short-wave and medium wave.

The Martí plan was first advanced at a meeting of international security specialists in 1980. Working through the Council on Inter-American Affairs in Washington, the "Committee of Sante Fe" recommended that the incoming Reagan administration consider a "Radio Free Cuba" as part of an overall plan to revitalize US–Latin American relations. On 22 September 1981 Reagan established a "Presidential Commission on Broadcasting to Cuba", which was charged with devising a broadcasting plan, with recommendations on programme content, an operating budget, and information gathering. On 28 September Radio Broadcasting to Cuba, Inc. was created as a private, non-profit-making organization. Incorporation made it possible for the station to accept private funding before receiving congressional authorization.

Negative reaction to the project was immediate. The US Interest section in Havana cabled the US Information Agency and the State Department, warning that a "Radio Free Cuba" would be counterproductive and that the Voice of America (VOA) general service to Cuba was adequate to satisfy the information needs of Cubans. Communications scholars contended that the underlying dynamics that made Radio Liberty and Radio Free Europe a success did not apply in the Cuban context: the presence of anti-US nationalism, indigenous support for Castro, and the fact that Cubans could hear American private radio stations transmitting out of Miami in Florida 90 miles away raised questions about need and viability.

A Radio Martí bill was introduced in Congress in November 1981. Hearings addressed concerns about Castro's possible retaliatory jamming of AM radio bands, the impact on US–Cuba relations, whether it would find sufficient listeners, and, most pivotally, whether or not to place the new service with RFE/RL or within the VOA structure. The Reagan administration argued strongly for making Radio Martí an independent "third leg" with RFE/RL, given their similar objectives, while many in Congress wanted the new service to be placed under more direct VOA oversight. The latter plan prevailed. In September 1983 Congress approved a new Radio Martí service for the Voice, broadcasting on VOA's 1180 AM frequency, which would disturb fewer commercial broadcasters.

Not surprisingly, Fidel Castro's response to the service was one of condemnation and retaliation, referring to the radio as "an instrument of psychological war and disinformation", and an infringement upon Cuban sovereignty. Shortly after the US House had voted for an early version of Martí in 1982, Castro responded angrily by transmitting radio interference on five AM frequencies heard in the US. The interference lasted for four continuous hours, and the Federal Communications Commission classified it as "stronger than any that previously originated in Cuba". After Radio Martí went on air in 1985, Castro took additional steps to show his displeasure. He immediately cancelled an important immigration agreement between Havana and Washington that had been in effect since 1984, and which had taken three years to negotiate. Cuba also jammed Martí's signals, although its regularity subsided after a few years. In 1990, however, Castro reinitiated radio jamming on a 24-hour basis after TV Martí took to the airwaves. The radio service is still intermittently blocked but nowhere to the extent of its television counterpart.

Internal dissension beset Martí's operations from the start. In 1987 the station's Miami bureau chief resigned, with the accusation that Martí staff had been ordered to engage in intelligence gathering during interviews with Cuban exiles newly arrived in the US. The first director, Ernesto Betancourt, was removed in 1990 after he maintained that powerful Cuban exile groups in the US had co-opted the service, especially the highly powerful Miami-based Cuban American National Foundation (CANF). In 1993 an anonymous staff memo identified ten members of staff as communist infiltrators sent by Castro. A former Radio Martí deputy director and four news analysts lodged complaints in 1995 after alleging that programming was enveloped in censorship, bias, and inaccuracy and was directly influenced by CANF and its leader, Jorge Mas Canosa. In 1997 the Clinton administration, citing cost-saving measures, moved the headquarters and operations of Radio and TV Martí from Washington, DC, to Miami. Critics argue that placing it in the heart of the country's largest Cuban exile community will further undermine the integrity and credibility of the station.

Audience response has varied from the start. In its early years a Reuters study revealed that Cubans found the programming "repetitive", "boring", "old-fashioned", and "out of touch". However, the service gradually improved and expanded its offerings so that by the mid-1990s it had garnered a 70 per cent audience share within the country. Even the *New York Times*, which denounced the project in many of its early editorials, changed its tune: "Contrary to our statement, the station appears to have found a responsive audience and filled a void in Cubans' information. Contrary to our fears . . . it has avoided propaganda and supplemented, not duplicated, commercial Spanish-language broadcasts from Florida." However in the waning years of the Clinton administration, Martí observers charged that the quality and level of objectivity of news reporting had declined again, and that the radio's audience had dropped back down to approximately 7 to 8 per cent of Cuban homes. The major remaining question is whether it will be the lack of listenership or the end of the Castro regime that will determine the future of Radio Martí.

K. Nakjavani Bookmiller

Further Reading

Frederick, Howard H., *Cuban–American Radio Wars: Ideology in International Telecommunications*, Norwood, New Jersey: Ablex, 1986

Howland, P.K., "Radio Martí and the US–Cuban Radio War", *Federal Communications Law Journal*, 36 (July 1984): 69–94

Maggs, John, "Weakening Signal from Radio Martí", *National Journal*, 32 (29 April 2000): 1356–57

Nichols, John Spicer, "Wasting the Propaganda Dollar", *Foreign Policy* (Fall 1984): 129–40

Salinas, José O., "Radio Martí: Meeting the Need for Uncensored Information in Cuba", *New York University Journal of International Law and Politics*, 19 (Winter 1987): 433–55

Smith, Wayne, "Pirating Radio Martí: The Shady Radio Voice of Right-Wing Cuban Exiles Is Pulling Another Fast One", *The Nation*, 264/3 (27 January 1997): 21–23

Yuom, Kyu-Ho, "The Radio and TV Martí Controversy: A Re-examination", *Gazette* 48/2 (1991): 95–103

ALEKSANDR RADISHCHEV
Russian prose writer and poet, 1749–1802

PUTESHESTVIE IZ PETERBURGA V MOSKVU
(A Journey from St Petersburg to Moscow)
Fictional travelogue, 1790

Radishchev had the misfortune to publish his travelogue in May 1790, in the aftermath of the French revolution, when empress Catherine II had become alarmed at the possible contagion of Russia by revolutionary ideas. The autocrat's response to the book can be gathered from the angry marginal notes written on her copy of it as she read it in June 1790. Her displeasure led directly to Radishchev's arrest and exile.

Ironically, Radishchev, director of the St Petersburg customs service, had benefited from Catherine's earlier enthusiasm for the western European Enlightenment. As a youth, he had studied at Leipzig University at imperial expense, absorbing the progressive thinking of the leading *philosophes* of the day. After

his return to Russia, his first literary venture, in 1773, was a translation of Gabriel Bonnot de Mably's *Observations sur l'histoire de la Grèce* (Observations on the History of Greece), which idealizes republican Sparta. His first significant original work, published in 1789, was an anonymous biography of Fedor Ushakov, a fellow student in Leipzig, which gave him an opportunity to excoriate evils such as war and despotism. His social criticism was further developed in his travelogue, which was to some extent modelled on the English novelist Laurence Sterne's *Sentimental Journey*. A sentimental traveller sets out from St Petersburg with little knowledge of the true nature of his country, but as episode follows episode, at each staging post, he becomes aware of the real state of affairs. The language of "sensibility" is used to express an increasingly impassioned criticism of social evils, particularly serfdom. The traveller arrives in Moscow, disabused of his innocence and conscious of the need for reform.

Radishchev printed his book on a press that he had bought for himself, benefiting from Catherine's liberal decree of 15 January 1783 that permitted private publishing. The same decree required books to be submitted to the police authorities for approval, and Radishchev had complied with this stipulation. The St Petersburg police official in charge of censorship, no doubt taking the book to be another example of the fashionable sentimental travelogue, gave it his official approval.

Censorship is itself the subject of one of the chapters in the book, which is set at the staging post of Torzhok, where the traveller meets an advocate of total press freedom. The traveller reminds this new acquaintance that everyone in Russia now has the freedom to maintain a printing press. However, the stranger insists that freedom from censorship is also essential, arguing that it is a form of official nannying that infantilizes and cripples the empress's subjects. Johann Gottfried von Herder is quoted in support: "In the domains of truth, in the realm of thought and spirit, no earthly power is capable of giving decisions, and it should not attempt to do so; a government is not capable, and a censor even less so." Further support for rejecting censorship is sought in Catherine's own *Nakaz* (Great Instruction) to her Legislative Commission of 1767–69, in which she had put forward the principle that: "Words are not always deeds, neither are thoughts crimes". The traveller's new acquaintance continues with his arguments. Libels can be fought in the courts; religious dissent can be challenged; sound governments can withstand criticism; prostitution is the evil that should not be tolerated, rather than pornographic writing; persecution of the written word only creates martyrs. In conclusion, he claims that the public alone should be the censor, with the ultimate power either to praise writers or else use their writings as wrapping paper. These general reflections on the folly of censorship end when the traveller is handed a manuscript containing a survey of the history of censorship in the civilized world.

Catherine's autocratic censoriousness was not inhibited by reading the chapter "Torzhok", as is shown by her extensive marginal refutations of its arguments. Other pencilled comments reject Radishchev's criticism of landowners and express scorn for his emotional portrayal of the oppression of the serfs, which she denies. The empress was particularly outraged by the book's warnings that the serfs might some day rise up against their oppressors. The book's encouragement to disregard the authority of rulers, emperors, magnates, and officials seemed to her to be particularly reprehensible. It is on this point that Catherine notes the "French poison" with which Radishchev was infected. The tense political atmosphere of the day focused Catherine's anger on this apparent attempt to inject French revolutionary principles into Russia and promote the violent overthrow of the established social order.

Her response was immediate. Radishchev was arrested and taken to the Peter and Paul Fortress for lengthy interrogation by S.I. Sheshkovskii, the empress's chief security investigator, who was head of the Secret Expedition of the Senate. Radishchev confessed that he had used intemperate language and literary conceit, but nevertheless did not renounce the substance of his argument. In a written confession addressed to Catherine from prison while he was awaiting the outcome of his interrogation, he defended his call for the emancipation of the serfs by attributing similar ideas to the empress herself. Similarly, on the question of censorship he wrote: "If I wrote against censorship it is because I thought I was doing the right thing; I believed it to be unnecessary: if it did not exist, then everyone would be answerable in person and would not have to depend on censors."

These appeals did not temper the verdict of the criminal court where Radishchev appeared on charges of sedition and treason. On 24 July 1790 he was sentenced to death, but in September Catherine commuted the penalty to 10 years' exile in Siberia. After the accession of emperor Paul, Radishchev was allowed to return to his estates in 1797. Five years later, still evidently "afflicted with the sufferings of mankind" (as he had described himself in the *Journey*), he committed suicide.

The observation in the "Torzhok" chapter that censorship may create martyrs was certainly borne out by Radishchev's own experience. The severity of his sentence ensured that his *Journey from St Petersburg to Moscow* enjoyed exceptional prestige among the Russian intelligentsia of his own time and in succeeding generations. Indeed, the extent of Radishchev's commitment to complete freedom of expression astonished later generations, who were accustomed to harsher censorship regimes. Aleksandr Pushkin, for example, responding to "Torzhok" in 1836, wrote: "It is concerned with the freedom of the press. It is curious to read ideas on this subject from a man who granted such freedom to himself by printing on his own press a book in which the boldness of thought and expression exceed all limits." For many Russians, Radishchev's martyrdom helped to keep alive their faith in the ideal of defending freedom of expression against the power of the autocratic state. However, the censors ensured that a complete edition of the *Journey* did not appear in Russia until after the revolution of 1905. Indeed, as the *Svodnyi katalog* points out, "The *Journey* is a great rarity: almost the whole edition (circa 650 copies were printed) was burned by the author when he learned of the investigation begun in connection with the publication of his book. Only 25 copies in total went on sale, and six copies were given by the author to various people."

W. GARETH JONES

Writings

Puteshestvie iz Peterburga v Moskvu, 1790; as *A Journey from St Petersburg to Moscow*, translated by L. Wiener, edited by R. Page Thaler, 1958

Further Reading

Lang, David Marshall, *The First Russian Radical: Alexander Radishchev, 1749–1802*, London: Allen and Unwin, 1959

McConnell, Allen, *A Russian Philosophe: Alexander Radishchev, 1749–1802*, The Hague: Nijhoff, 1964

Madariaga, Isabel de, *Russia in the Age of Catherine the Great*, London: Weidenfeld and Nicolson, and New Haven, Connecticut: Yale University Press, 1981

Papmehl, K.A., *Freedom of Expression in Eighteenth-Century Russia*, The Hague: Nijhoff, 1971

Svodnyi katalog russkoi knigi grazhdanskoi pechati XVIII reka 1725–1800 (Union Catalogue of 18th-Century Books), 5 vols, Moscow: Lenin Library Press–Kniga Press, 1963–67: vol.3, pp.7–8

RADNIČKA BORBA (Workers' Struggle),
BORBA (Struggle), NAŠA BORBA (Our Struggle)
Yugoslav/Serbian newspaper under three titles, 1920–41, 1941–94, and since 1994 respectively

Borba is an interesting example of a newspaper that was the mouthpiece of a political party, shared its fortunes for several decades, and then, as that party disintegrated, emancipated itself to become a dispassionate if cautious journal of record, resisting attempts by a new ruling group to bring it under control.

Borba's predecessor, *Radnička Borba* (Workers' Struggle), had first appeared in 1920, as the weekly paper of a party that then had no legal status: the Communist Party of the Kingdom of the Serbs, Croats, and Slovenes (as Yugoslavia was known until 1929). Taken aback by the party's relative success in the new country's first legislative elections, held in December 1920, the ruling Democrat–Radical Alliance immediately issued a decree, known as the *Obzvana* (Declaration), ordering the dissolution of all communist organizations and imposing a ban on propaganda advocating dictatorship or revolution. A Law for the Protection of the State, enacted in August 1921, effectively banned the party and imposed severe penalties for the propagation of "communist" ideas. This was hardly a propitious time, then, to found a paper with that precise intention, and it was no wonder that *Radnička Borba* was singled out to be banned in September 1924. However, it continued to appear occasionally, and the now clandestine party produced a number of other illegal papers, such as *Kommunist* (founded January 1925) and *Hammer and Sickle*, which was produced in Austria and secretly imported.

Its title shortened to *Borba*, the paper then appeared as the newspaper of the communist-led struggle against the German/Italian/Bulgarian/Hungarian occupation from 1941. The Partisans, as the communist-led fighters were known, placed great emphasis on propaganda, and *Borba* was produced every other day from the party headquarters at Ušice in western Serbia.

After the war and the communist victory, the print run of what was now the ruling party's newspaper rose quickly to 650,000 and, from 1954, the paper was published every day. *Borba* had become respectable, if not always respected, because it never deviated from the party's official line. From 1964, it was owned by the Socialisticki Savez Radnih Naroda (Socialist Alliance of Working People, or SSRN), a mass organization bringing together the official trade unions with youth, women's, and students' groups, which now appointed the paper's director, its editor-in-chief, and its managing editor.

Mass appeal still eluded *Borba* as it acquired an increasingly powerful intellectual profile, combining highly theoretical arguments with first-class cultural coverage. On the other hand, it was not above shady dealings, in complicity with the secret services. In 1993 the Croatian journalist Danko Plevnik drew attention to the fact that six years earlier a *Borba* correspondent in Serbia had been used to publicize an alleged economic scandal that disgraced a Bosnian politician, knowing full well that no such scandal had occurred.

It was as if an entirely new paper had come into being when, in 1988, *Borba* exposed the "decadent lifestyle" of senior members of the ruling party, including that of the federal prime minister, Branko Mikulić. Already, it had refused to take sides in the arguments between supporters and opponents of Slobodan Milošević after he had ridden the nationalist wave to the leadership of the Serbian League of Communists in September 1987. By April 1988 the SSRN, which had declared in favour of Milošević, was telling *Borba*'s editors amd journalists that "your editorial mistakes will not be tolerated". One such "mistake" was the paper's support for the new federal prime minister, Ante Marković, who had embarked on a series of economic and political reforms aimed at keeping Yugoslavia intact and afloat. *Borba* was privatized, 17 per cent of the shares being bought by the federal government, 15 per cent by banks, and 12 per cent by employees; 3,000 readers also bought shares and the balance was taken by private businesses.

As the communists lost power in the Croatian elections of 1990, and vast numbers of young people rioted against Milošević in Belgrade in early 1991, *Borba* had a more difficult path to tread. It maintained its impartiality for a year as the wars in Croatia and Bosnia–Herzegovina worsened. It was, to say the least, risky for its investigative reporter to trace, for example, the possible involvement of the Srpska Pokret Obnove (Serbian Renewal Movement, or SPO) in the killing of Croat civilians at Borovo Selo and Vukovar in April 1991. Yet its reports earned *Borba* no credit in Croatia, as gangs attacked its kiosks. Even more directly, after threats to kill its reporter Gradisa Katić the paper was forced to run an interview with the paramilitary leader "Arkan" (Željko Ražnatović) at the end of 1991. True to its now established impartiality, it published, alongside the piece about Arkan, an interview with Dobroslav Paraga of the Croatian Party of Right.

Under the pressure of events, however, *Borba*'s impartiality slipped in 1992, after Croatia and Slovenia had declared themselves independent. *Borba* was now isolated in Serbia and for a while carried headlines apparently provided by Srpska Republika Novinska Agencija, the news agency of the "Serb Republic of Bosnia-Herzegovina": "New genocide against the Serb people", "Pogroms of Serbs in Srebrenica", and the like. On the other hand, *Borba* was alone among Serbian media entities in attributing the "bread queue" massacre in Sarajevo on 27 May 1992 to those who had been "bombarding Sarajevo for 51 days already" – the Serbs.

It was, then, little wonder that *Borba* was accused of lack of patriotism by extremist political groups late in 1992. The paper reported on 17–18 July 1993 that its correspondent in Subotica had been taken to the police station for an "informal talk", and on 21 July that the names of those buying it at town-centre kiosks were being noted down. The paper was subjected to economic pressure as well: its cover price was frozen and it had to pay for newsprint at exorbitant prices. Moreover, the federal government, which, now that Marković was gone, was to all intents and purposes the creature of the Serbian government, still held 17 per cent of the shares in *Borba*. However, by this point 37 per cent of its stock was held by the Finagra Company, which took over the management of the newspaper, with government support. It appeared that, if the government could not force *Borba's* compliance by other means, it would, once again, take control of the newspaper.

In 1994, the paper's title was changed to *Naša Borba* (Our Struggle). On 4 February 1995 the journalists were prevented by court order from entering its offices in Belgrade: notices on the door forbade entry while liquidation procedures began. The authorities themselves now published a paper called *Borba*, while the journalists continued *Naša Borba*. With help from abroad, and despite Milošević's harassment of all independent media, the circulation of *Naša Borba* grew as it covered – and condemned – the electoral frauds of late 1996.

After the fall of Milošević and the change of regime, the editorial board underwent a change. Fifty journalists of *Naša Borba* tried on 8 October 2000 to return to their earlier positions at *Borba*, a process that was by no means automatic, though it was supported by the new authorities. Because of the difficult financial position of *Borba*, the commercial court ordered its liquidation on 19 October 2000. It appointed a new director in order to guarantee a new start to the paper.

ROBERT STALLAERTS

Further Reading

Carter, April, *Democratic Reform in Yugoslavia: The Changing Role of the Party*, London: Pinter, and Princeton, New Jersey: Princeton University Press, 1982

Kisić, Milica and Branka Bulatović, *Srpska štampa, 1768–1995: Istorijsko-bibliografski pregled* (The Serbian Press, 1768–1995: Historical and Bibliographical Review), Belgrade: Medija Centar, 1996

Kuzmanović, Jasmina, "Media: The Extension of Politics by Other Means" in *Beyond Yugoslavia: Politics, Economics, and Culture*

in a Shattered Community, edited by Sabrina Petra Ramet and Ljubiša S. Adamovich, Boulder, Colorado: Westview Press, 1995

Magaš, Branka, *The Destruction of Yugoslavia: Tracking the Break-up, 1980–92*, London: Verso, 1993

Malešić, Marjan (editor), *The Role of Mass Media in the Serbian–Croatian Conflict*, Stockholm: Styrelsen för Psykologiskt Försvar, 1993

Mišović, Miloš, "Štampa i srpsko društvo 19. i 20. veka" (The Press and Serbian Society in the 19th and 20th Centuries), in *Srpska štampa, 1768–1995*, edited by Milica Kisić, and Branka Bulatović, Belgrade: Medija Centar, 1996

Nikolić, Zoran B., "Postizborna Srbija: Oslobadjanje medija" (Post-electoral Serbia: Setting the Media Free), *AIM* (29 October 2000)

Plevnik, Danko, *Hrvatski obrat*, Zagreb: Durieux, 1993

Robinson, Gertrude Joch, *Tito's Maverick Media: The Politics of Mass Communication in Yugoslavia*, Urbana: University of Illinois Press, 1977

Schöpflin, George (editor), *Censorship and Political Communication in Eastern Europe: A Collection of Documents*, London: Pinter, and New York: St. Martin's Press, 1983

Thompson, Mark, *Forging War: The Media in Serbia, Croatia and Bosnia-Hercegovina*, London: Article 19, 1994; revised edition, Luton: University of Luton Press, 1999

"Zaposleni u Politici podržali Darka Ribnikara: Upravni odbor danas bira direktora?" (Employees of *Politika* Support Darko Ribnikar: Does the Direction Committee Elect Today a Director?), *Danas* (18 October 2000)

Websites

http://www.borba.co.yu
http://www.mediacenter.org.yu

GEORGI STOIKOV RAKOVSKI
Bulgarian revolutionary, writer, and journalist, 1821–1867

Georgi Stoikov Rakovski is a national hero of Bulgaria. His literary work, as well as his patriotic and revolutionary activities, set him apart as a patriot who did his best to forward the cause of Bulgaria's liberation from the Ottoman empire in the 19th century.

The Ottomans had ruled over the Bulgarian territories, as well as the rest of the Balkans, since the end of the 14th century. By the 19th century, as Ottoman authority was weakening and the government's political power was in a precipitous decline, liberation movements among the subject populations became increasingly widespread. Bulgarians also desired liberty but were not unanimous on how to achieve it. There emerged two basic divisions among Bulgarian patriots. One group sought to liberate the country through activism and, if necessary, revolutionary violence; the other believed that the ultimate goal of freedom should be achieved through patient, methodical steps taken within the existing Ottoman system. Rakovski belongs to the former group.

Even before Rakovski began his career as an active nationalist, he was punished for appearing to be disrespectful of persons in authority. He and his father were both imprisoned in 1844 when, following his return to his home village after an extended stay in France, he wore "foreign" French clothes and

incited the local youth to disregard the authority of the village elders. Such behaviour was regarded as revolutionary in a community where local notables were considered to have a legitimate share in authority under the Ottoman Sultan. They chose to report Rakovski to the authorities in the capital, Istanbul, as a subversive and unsettling influence, giving him a reputation that was to remain with him for the rest of his life.

As a Bulgarian nationalist, Rakovski was kept busy publishing several newspapers, the results of his historical research, numismatic studies, and compendiums of folklore. His experiences with censorship came from unusual quarters. The Ottoman authorities were not the only ones interested in suppressing his work; those members of the Bulgarian elites who had much to lose by the sudden disappearance of the state that supported them in their prominent positions were also instrumental in suppressing inflammatory prose.

In 1857, Rakovski was extradited from the Habsburg empire for his publication of a newspaper called the *Bulgarian Journal*. He had been editor, writer, and reporter for this project, and had received considerable support, both monetary and technical, from others. The goal of this publication was to elevate the national consciousness of the Bulgarian people by making them proud of their national past. He was given no notice of his forcible extradition, on the insistence of the Ottoman authorities, but he managed to convince the Austrians that they should extradite him to the autonomous Romanian principalities instead. He was thus saved from further persecution.

On another occasion Rakovski was pursued by no less than the Metropolitan of the Serbian Orthodox Church. In 1860–61 Rakovski lived and worked in Belgrade, publishing his second newspaper, *Danube Swan*, which was quite successful. It was widely read not only by his countrymen but also by other Europeans. At one point, the newspaper began publishing a number of articles in French as well as Bulgarian. In 1861, Rakovski took the precautionary step of acquiring Serbian citizenship because he feared that the Russian authorities would respond with severity to his newspaper's campaign to dissuade Bulgarians from emigrating to Russia. Rakovski was then threatened with censorship by the Serbian Metropolitan, who demanded that censors representing the church be permitted to review the newspaper's articles before they went to print.

In 1864, while publishing yet another newspaper, *Viitorul* (The Future), this time in Bucharest, Rakovski came up against censorship yet again. The Ottoman government forbade the distribution of the newspaper, and the possession of an issue was made punishable by law.

Rakovski did a great deal in his relatively short life to elevate Bulgarian language, literature, history, culture, and folklore, writing scholarly works on all these topics, seeking out ancient manuscripts, and trying in every way he could to help stimulate national consciousness. He believed that there were three essential requirements that would make a people great and also

free: a national church, a national education system, and a national press. These were consistent with the dominant line of thought in contemporary western Europe, which emphasized the power of such institutions to shape and unify national opinion. Rakovski also used the press most effectively, not only to sway Bulgarian public opinion but also as a critical means of turning Europe's attention to Bulgaria's problems. This was especially important in an era when the great powers had the capacity to support or destroy lesser nations. Rakovski was forced to spend his most productive years in exile because of the violent reaction to his work at home. In contemporary Bulgaria, he is still very much a hero who is larger than life: there is a bust of him in every park. Heroes of mythological proportions are perhaps necessary to a nation still trying to find its way in the modern world, especially one that has, in some important ways, been reborn very recently.

MARI A. FIRKATIAN

Further Reading

Firkatian, Mari A., *The Forest Traveler: Georgi Stoikov Rakovski and Bulgarian Nationalism*, New York: Peter Lang, 1996

Jelavich, Barbara, *History of the Balkans*, vol. 1: *Eighteenth and Nineteenth Centuries*, Cambridge and New York: Cambridge University Press, 1983

Jelavich, Charles and Barbara Jelavich (editors), *The Balkans in Transition: Essays on the Development of Balkan Life and Politics since the Eighteenth Century*, Berkeley: University of California Press, 1963

Meininger, Thomas A., *The Formation of a Nationalist Bulgarian Intelligentsia, 1835–1878*, New York: Garland, 1987

RAMBO FILMS
(*First Blood* directed by Ted Kotcheff; *Rambo: First Blood Part II* directed by George P. Cosmatos; *Rambo III* directed by Sylvester Stallone)
Films, 1982–88

Fears about the glamorization of screen violence and its harmful effects on British society were horrifically realized in the Hungerford massacre in the summer of 1987. The gunman Michael Ryan, wearing a camouflage jacket and a Rambo-style headband, indiscriminately opened fire on bystanders in the Berkshire town, murdering 16 people. The tabloid press, most notably the *Daily Mail*, linked Ryan's random killings to the incessant gunplay of the first two Rambo films, *First Blood* and *Rambo: First Blood Part II*. A year later, certain members of the public and press called for the banning of *Rambo III* in the belief that this might prevent the Hungerford atrocity from ever happening again.

First Blood, which was released in 1982, produced little outcry over the violence it depicted on the screen. A few local councillors, such as those at Malton, North Yorkshire, urged for a ban on the film, because it mirrored the crazed rampage of police killer Barry Prudom. However, the Rambo character would soon become a poster-child for some members of parliament and special interest groups, who saw him as an index for the increasing amount of violence bombarding British screens and streets.

Rambo hysteria took hold in Britain in 1985, shortly after the London newspapers began to cover the frenzy in the United States over *Rambo: First Blood Part II*. The film had been a box office hit in America, generating over $150 million in ticket sales, inspiring jingoism, and, as the film was released during the hijacking of a TWA jet by Lebanese guerrillas, rejuvenating an interest in patriotism and war. T-shirts proclaimed "Free the hostages. Send Rambo to Beirut." President Ronald Reagan (known affectionately as "Ronbo" during this time) declared, "After seeing Rambo last night, I know what to do the next time this happens." America even saw a dramatic increase in the sale of bows and arrows, knives, toy guns, and semi-automatic rifles that shoot water.

In Britain, however, some people and groups thought that "Rambo-mania" was detrimental to society as a whole, and they made their objections to its release known through the tabloid press. In the *Daily Express*, the "National Coalition on TV Violence" documented three copycat killings related to *First Blood* (this report, like many in the British tabloid press, was unfounded). Leading the campaign to ban the Hollywood blockbuster *Rambo II* (as the film became known) was James

RAMBO FILMS: Sylvester Stallone in the third Rambo film, *Rambo III*, released in Britain shortly after the horrific 1987 Hungerford massacre, described as a "Rambo-style rampage" by the British press. Calls for censorship of the film to prevent similar violent incidents occurring again prompted the British Board of Film Classification to make small cuts to the film and give it an "18" certificate.

Tye, director general of the British Safety Council. He claimed that the blood-and-guts movie, in which a death occurs every 2.1 minutes (44 murders in all), could spark a wave of copycat violence on the streets of Britain. Tye said that Sylvester Stallone's portrayal of Rambo "makes Irish extremists seem like 'gentle pacifists'". "It is violence for violence's sake", he argued, and it "speaks in a language that appeals to street gang mentality". Tye urged all members of parliament and council leaders to outlaw the film. The newspapers joined this banning fury. Headlines read "Rambo Keep Out" (*The Sun*) and "Ban Rambo – He's Too Brutal for Britain" (*The Star*). The *Sunday Mirror* wrote that teenagers interviewed after seeing the film made such comments as "It makes you want to go out and kill a Commie" and "I wish I could go and do stuff like that". The *Daily Mail* reported that, in the suburbs of New York, gangs of juveniles dressed like Rambo attacked people's houses, slashing bushes and turning on garden hoses to spray the inside of homes. Alexander Walker of the *Evening Standard* went so far as to call Rambo "the ugliest American in history".

Such press campaigns have often managed to get films banned somewhere in Britain (as in the case of *The Devils*) or cut by the British Board of Film Classification (BBFC) (as in the case of *Henry: Portrait of a Serial Killer*). However, *Rambo II* was shown throughout Britain uncut with a 15 certificate. Those councils which decided to consider Tye's request (the Greater London Council, Swansea, and Dundee) refused to ban the film after reviewing it. James Ferman, director of the BBFC, wrote to Tye about the film's supposed ability to inspire copycat violence, saying that "The simple cause and effect relationship which you postulate is not borne out by the evidence."

Nevertheless, fears of mob violence appeared to be confirmed on the very weekend of the film's release, as a gang of 50 youths rampaged at a late-night showing of *Rambo II* in Gloucester,

injuring two policeman; many of the youths wore headbands like Rambo. This isolated incident only added ammunition to Tye's case and to the anger against Hollywood's increasing gore-and-violence quotient. Later that year, the BBC removed *First Blood* from its Boxing Day schedule in response to rising public fears.

Demands for censorship did not go unheard during the lead-up to the release of *Rambo III* in 1988. People were still recovering from the Hungerford massacre, described in the press as a "Rambo-style rampage". Mary Whitehouse of the National Viewers' and Listeners' Association declared: "It is madness to project such a film into our increasingly violent society." The *Daily Mail* capitalized on this fear with headlines such as "New Rambo Film Could Spark Copycat Carnage". The article suggested that up to six per cent of the people who watched *Rambo III* could be tempted into copying the violence. Rising public disfavour did not subside when Stallone came to England to promote the film, brandishing the claim, "Rambo's okay. He never shoots first." In line with the mood of the country, the BBFC decided to give *Rambo III* an 18 certificate, even though the previous two instalments, which were no less violent, held a 15 certificate. Twenty-four brief cuts, amounting to just over a minute of film, were made to violent scenes and "glamorous displays of weaponry". Ferman announced, "We are not concerned about the film now the cuts have been made." In the event, the only "savagery" that occurred was the film's beating at the box office. During its first week, *Rambo III* only took in half a million pounds, about half as much as *Rambo II* did during its opening. After three weeks, *Rambo III* was playing to half-empty houses, echoing its similar fate in the United States.

KEVIN S. SANDLER

Further Reading

Hill, Patrick, "New Rambo Film 'Could Spark Copycat Carnage'", *Daily Mail* (4 July 1988): 9

Mathews, Tom Dewe, *Censored*, London: Chatto and Windus, 1994

Nurse, Keith, "BBC Bans Rambo from Christmas TV", *Daily Telegraph* (4 December 1985): 1

"Safety Chiefs Urge Ban Rambo", *The Star* (6 August 1985): 1

Willsher, Kim and John Kay, "Rambo Keep Out!", *The Sun* (6 August 1985): 1

RAND DAILY MAIL
South African newspaper, 1902–85

The *Rand Daily Mail* (RDM) was founded in 1902 and acquired in 1905 by the arch-imperialist mining magnate Sir Abe Bailey; his intervention prevented a bid by Afrikaner interests which was to be echoed 70 years later. The *RDM* was the first modern popular newspaper in South Africa. During the inter-war years it was closely identified with mining interests and attempted balanced coverage of the interests of capital and white labour. Collaboration with its main rival, *The Argus*, set the trend for cartels in the South African newspaper industry.

The *RDM* was threatened by the National Party before World War II for its outspoken criticism of fascism; the English-language press, it was implied, would have a hard time when they came to power. After the National Party victory in 1948, there was a long-running conflict between the paper and the government, particularly when Laurence Gandar assumed the editorship in 1957. The Gandar years were characterized by dissenting liberalism and crusading social protest; he published exposés on the pass laws and black labour conditions, and attached the paper to the cause of the Progressive Party. Internationally the paper was recognized as an upholder of human rights, ready to print a black perspective on South African events, bridge the racial divide, and act as an instrument of change. One of its achievements was to rescue blacks from press anonymity by abolishing the tradition of referring to them, namelessly, as "natives", a move that apparently led to the loss of a considerable number of subscribers. Gandar also appointed the first African affairs reporter on a white South African paper, Benjamin Pogrund. The *RDM*, the newspaper conscience of the nation, enjoyed considerable editorial independence and nurtured a generation of liberal journalists. Its support of full racial integration in the 1960s set it on a collision course with the authoritarian government of B.J. Vorster, who equated its liberalism with communism.

In 1962 the *RDM* announced its opposition to a self-regulating press code of conduct and Board of Reference which other newspapers accepted in preference to direct government control. A major conflict occurred in June and July 1965, when the *RDM* published a three-part series exposing conditions in South Africa's prisons, especially the use of electric-shock torture, and demanded an official inquiry, a call supported by other English-language papers. Its main informant, Harold Strachan, was banned for five years, the paper was raided on several occasions, and Gandar's and Pogrund's passports were seized. The paper was charged with publishing false information and became locked into a legal process that took four years and cost it £150,000. All its sources save one had made sworn statements and had been cross examined by a lawyer but, as a result of the perjury of numerous government witnesses, the

defendants were found guilty in July 1969 of contravening the Prisons Act (1959). The *RDM*'s crime, it appeared, had been to fail to consult the Prisons Department about the accusations in advance. The fines were nominal. The judgement left the press uncertain of its relationship to the state and the result was to inhibit not only reporting on prison conditions but also information on other sensitive topics for nearly 20 years.

A succession of liberal editors and journalists found themselves trapped between increasingly restrictive laws, such as the Defence and Police Acts, and nervous proprietors. The government harassed reporters during their exhaustive investigation of the forced removal of 2000 blacks in the Morsgat area of the northern Transvaal in October 1969; and in particular after black reporters provided inside information on the June 1976 Soweto uprising, of which the *RDM* was a major interpreter. Five *RDM* journalists, including the photographer Peter Magubane, were detained by police under the Terrorism Act.

Prime minister Vorster attacked the *RDM* in 1973 for publishing critical letters from black readers and warned it to put its house in order. In 1975, when a consortium of government supporters under Louis Luyt attempted to take over the paper, the English-speaking business establishment created the Advowson Trust to protect it. Investigations acutely embarrassing to the government continued. One concerned *The Citizen*, a right-wing paper set up with £7 million of taxpayers' money which inflated its circulation figures by 6,500 copies per day, and was under the editorial control of the Department of Information. This and other aspects of the Information Scandal (or "Muldergate"), an attempt to sell apartheid to the rest of the world, were exposed by the *RDM* and other titles in the South African Associated Newspapers (SAAN) group; the paper was charged for contempt of the Mostert Commission which, looking into exchange regulations, had uncovered financial irregularities. Muldergate effectively brought down the Vorster government; his successor P.W. Botha was determined that his government would not suffer in the same way. Although the *RDM* tried to outwit restrictive law, like all newspapers it was restrained by the voluntary code of self-censorship derived from threatened legislation in the wake of the Steyn Commission into the Mass Media (1982) whose proposals it described as fatal to a free press.

The *RDM*'s challenge to the authorities was conducted under increasingly difficult financial conditions. By 1977, 60 per cent of the readership was black with limited economic resources. Too few of the remaining readers were white women, and this adversely affected the advertising profile. Whites in general were resentful of the *RDM*'s tendency to bring them face to face with the less salubrious facts of the South African condition and, by 1982, its circulation had declined to only 106,000, although its readership, especially in the townships of Johannesburg, was far higher, and the following year rose to 219,000 whites and 715,000 blacks.

The sudden demise of the paper on 30 April 1985 is still clouded in controversy. While the *RDM* was apparently in a dire financial situation, the proprietors have been blamed for mismanagement, making decisions for reasons of political expediency and even in collusion with the government; the dismissal of editor Allister Sparks in 1981, for instance, was interpreted by some as a gesture of appeasement. Certainly the government hated the paper and greeted its closure with elation. In the late 1980s the vacuum was gradually filled by the independent (sometimes called the alternative) press such as *The New Nation*, *The Weekly Mail*, *Vrye Weekblad*, and *South*.

CHRISTOPHER MERRETT

Further Reading:

Hachten, William A. and C. Anthony Giffard, *Total Onslaught: The South African Press under Attack*, Johannesburg: Macmillan, and Madison: University of Wisconsin Press, 1984

Jackson, Gordon S., *Breaking Story: The South African Press*, Boulder, Colorado: Westview Press, 1993

Mervis, Joel, *The Fourth Estate: A Newspaper Story*, Johannesburg: Ball, 1989

Potter, Elaine, *The Press as Opposition: The Political Role of South African Newspapers*, London: Chatto and Windus, and Totowa, New Jersey: Rowman and Littlefield, 1975

Walker, Martin, *Powers of the Press: The World's Great Newspapers*, London: Quartet, 1982

RASTOKHEZ (Renaissance)
Tajik newspaper, 1990–92

Rastokhez was the unofficial mouthpiece of the cultural and political organization of the same name, which was established in 1989 by around 50 Tajik writers, academics, and political activists at a meeting at Tajikistan State University in Dushanbe, the capital city. The movement aimed to promote "cultural, economic, and environmental awareness" among the Tajik people; it was also in favour of privatization and the redistribution of land. The existence of such a movement was anathema to the Communist Party of Tajikistan, the slowest to undertake reform of all the ruling groups in the former Soviet republics, which was still espousing the principle of a command economy.

The newspaper began publication as a monthly from early 1990. Registered as an independent and private newspaper, it was printed in Vilnius, Lithuania, and edited first by Mirbobo Mirrahim and then Ahmadshah Komil. The paper aimed to shape a new national identity to replace that created by almost seven decades of Soviet rule. Along with Tajik history and language, exposure was given to Pan-Iranianism, and particularly to Iranian literature.

Issue 11 (March 1992) is typical of this four-page tabloid. The lead article, "If Renaissance Prevails . . ." attacks what it sees as the "lawlessness imposed upon Tajikistan by the government since September 1991". The paper is critical of the imprisonment of the reform-minded minister of internal affairs Mohammadayez Nojavonov, and of Maqsud Ikramov, the mayor of Dushanbe, who were said to have incited violence. On the centre pages, coverage is given to a mass sit-in at Shahidon Square in Dushanbe, otherwise known as Martyrs' Square after the demonstrators killed there by government forces in February 1990. *Rastokhez* reproduced the demonstrators' demands for the dissolution of the "inept legislature of Tajikistan", greater urgency in the passing of a new consti-

tution and in the organization of proper democratic elections, and an end to political repression. Provocatively, on the inside pages Mirbobo Mirrahim affirms that "Tajikistan is on the Road to Revolution", and Tohir Abdujabbar that "Independence is Sacred". On the back page, an article enquires "Oh Tajik, What will your banner and anthem be?" and there are three columns devoted to the historical and cultural ties between Tajikistan and Iran.

The staff of *Rastokhez* were aware that its existence was precarious. In March 1992 the newspaper expressed concern that "minor changes" made by the Supreme Assembly of Tajikistan in the Law on the Media (enacted 1990) could mean censorship and possible closure for newspapers that disseminated views different to those held by the government. Nine months later, in December 1992, with the country on the brink of civil war, *Rastokhez* was closed down along with many other independent newspapers.

SOLEIMAN M. KIASATPOUR

Further Reading

Brown, Bess, "The Media in the Countries of the Former Soviet Union", *RFE/RL Research Report*, 2/27 (2 July 1993): 1–15

Brown, Jeff L., "Mass Media in Transition in Central Asia", *Gazette*, 54 (1995): 249–65

Haghayeghi, Mehrdad, *Islam and Politics in Central Asia*, Basingstoke: Macmillan, and New York: St. Martin's Press, 1995

Mosalmanian Qobadiani, Rahim, *Tojikiston: Ozodi yo Marg* (Tajikistan: Freedom or Death), Tehran: Daftar-e Nashr-e Farhangi Eslami, 1994

Pannier, Bruce, "On the Front Lines in Tajikistan", *Transition*, 1/18 (6 October 1995): 78–79

Rubin, Barnett R., "The Fragmentation of Tajikistan", *Survival*, 35/4 (1993): 71–92

Tadjbakhsh, Shahrbanou, "Tajikistan: From Freedom to War", *Current History* (April 1994): 173–77

JAMES RAUTENBACH
South African film director

DIE KANDIDAAT (The Candidate)
Film, 1968

Who may call himself an Afrikaner? This question, explicitly raised in a pivotal scene in *Die Kandidaat*, has been central to the history and self-understanding of South Africans of Dutch descent from the late 19th until the late 20th century. Most Afrikaners had little difficulty in defining themselves in relation to black people – the latter were in every sense inferior, and were not entitled to the social and political rights of their betters. However, their attitudes to "Coloureds", descendants of liaisons between the Dutch and the indigenous Hottentots, was inherently more ambiguous.

In the 1870s the Afrikaner Bond (Afrikaner Society) under the Dutch Reformed Church minister S.J. du Toit, had confined the appellation "Afrikaner" to those who shared their religion and spoke their language, the vernacular Afrikaans as against High Dutch. In his *Die Geskiedenis van ous Land in die Taal van ons Volk* (1879), du Toit described his vision of a specially chosen and distinct people whose vocation was to "civilize" other peoples. An opposite point of view was developed by J.H. Hofmeyer (known as "Onze Jan", "our Jan"), for whom an Afrikaner was one who shared a love of the land, whatever their language or colour. When he was elected to the Cape Colony's legislature, Hofmeyer treated Coloureds as equal citizens, entitled to the same rights as "pure Afrikaners". Hofmeyer was a superior political tactician and, after the Anglo-Boer War had united all Afrikaners against the British, the Constitution of the Union of South Africa (1910) gave all Coloured men the franchise. This was entirely reversed when the National Party came to power after World War II. In 1954, under the prime ministership of J.G. Strijdom, Coloureds were deprived of full citizenship, including the vote, in the interests of racial purity and separate development.

The ambiguity of the Coloureds' position did not, however, go away. Many Afrikaners were aware that they had been crudely disenfranchised, and that this had been done by manipulation of parliament and the judiciary. Some thought that sooner or later their citizenship would have to be restored. The position of the Coloureds pervades the narrative of *Die Kandidaat*, which features a discussion on whether or not they are Afrikaners. Elsewhere, as in his previous film *Wild Season* (1967), Rautenbach portrays Afrikaners critically, subject to human weakness and failings. He reveals the divisions among them, their corrupt political pasts, their extramarital affairs. All this is hung on a plot in which a young Coloured "candidate" applies for membership of an exclusive Afrikaner cultural organization.

Hofmeyer had written: "I know that, whatever the future of South Africa may be, the English element will have to be tolerated along with the Dutch. And I am quite content with that." The Boer War had greatly exacerbated existing bitterness between English-speaking and Afrikaans-speaking peoples. Nearly 70 years later, the statement in *Die Kandidaat* that there was "no place for the English in Afrikaner organizations" still had currency.

Cuts were insisted on by the Publications Control Board on both counts. The scene in which the inclusion or exclusion of Coloureds was discussed was ordered to be entirely removed. Likewise, all anti-English commentary was deleted. That done, the film was awarded an "A" (adult viewing) certificate.

KEYAN GRAY TOMASELLI

Further Reading
Tomaselli, Keyan, *The Cinema of Apartheid: Race and Class in South African Film*, New York: Smyrna/Lake View Press, 1988; London: Routledge, 1989

MARK RAVENHILL
British dramatist, 1966–

SHOPPING AND FUCKING
Play, 1996

One of the new wave of young writers to emerge in British theatre in the 1990s, Mark Ravenhill came to prominence at the Royal Court Theatre in London in September 1996 with his first full-length play, *Shopping and Fucking*. The play concerns a group of "twentysomethings" – Robbie, Mark, and Lulu – who share a flat and become involved in various schemes to raise money. Two scenes in particular include shocking stage images: in one scene, Mark licks the anus of Gary, a teenage rentboy, and finds that it's bleeding; in another, the emotionally disturbed Gary, seeking "good hurt", asks to be penetrated by a knife. Content apart, however, the immediate controversy arose as a result of the play's title.

When the play was accepted for production by Max Stafford-Clark's Out of Joint touring theatre company, Sonia Friedman, the producer, was given legal advice that the word "fucking" could not appear on posters or in advertisements. Under the Indecent Advertisements Act 1889, as amended by the Indecent Displays (Control) Act 1981, the word "fuck" and its variants are banned from public display. Originally drafted to stamp out the explicit advertisements that prostitutes put in shop windows, the law was designed to curb a social nuisance and to protect polite society from "bad language". By 1996, its existence necessitated the "self-censorship" of advertisements for a play that represented, among other things, sexual activity. Friedman pointed out that the "F-word" could be used on stage, but "in anything unsolicited – posters, leaflets, direct-mail letters – we cannot print it without risking prosecution".

A passionate polemic about the play's title appeared on the Royal Court's website. Carl Miller pointed out how little had changed since the critic Kenneth Tynan became the first person to say "fuck" on British television, in 1965:

> Over 30 years later, we still can't tell people the name of one of the plays in the autumn season. If you see posters, leaflets, and advertisements for Mark Ravenhill's new play in the Theatre Upstairs, they will coyly censor the title ... [and] if you ring up to ask what the title is, the box office staff still cannot tell you. Thanks to the Indecent Advertisements Act of 1889, they lay the theatre open to prosecution if it is called anything more explicit than *Shopping and Effing* ... only once you have committed [yourself] to buy a ticket can the full horror of the title be revealed.

To solve the problem of using the "F-word" in advertisements for the play, the first posters for *Shopping and Fucking* used the image of a fork splintering the offending word. This was also used for the cover of the first edition of the playtext. The next solution involved asterisks, so the title became *Shopping and F**king*, and promotional postcards ironically advertised the play's transfer to Shaftesbury Avenue in 1997 with a quotation from the London *Evening Standard*: "Entert***ing, Sh**king and St*mulating". When the play went on a nationwide tour in October 1996, the splintered fork posters were found to be acceptable in seven towns, but three local authorities rejected even the asterisked version. As a result, in Bracknell, Warwick, and Newbury people were encouraged to see a play advertised as *Shopping and*. Other incidents involved more direct confrontation. In Swansea, a dozen members of a Christian organization, having made a block booking of seats, stood up and began singing hymns ten minutes after the show started. Police had to be called to eject them.

While such incidents helped make *Shopping and Fucking* notorious, and advertised the play more effectively than any display, they were rare. More common were heavy-handed jokes about alternative titles, such as *Shopping and Shagging* or *Shopping and Bonking*. In "polite" society, it was coyly called *Shopping and Flower Arranging*. Legends sprang up about spectators asking the box office if they could "watch the fucking and miss the shopping". In a way, the controversy emphasized the gap between what many young people consider normal – "Me and my friends never gave the play's title a second thought", said Ravenhill – and what the wider society (if the protesters were as representative as they claimed to be) may still feel is rude. The play's title is also a good example of the Royal Court's tradition of mischief-making: the theatre management was consciously using a provocative title to sell a provocative play. In a review for the *Sunday Express* that was reprinted in the programme for the play's transfer to the West

RAVENHILL: First edition of Mark Ravenhill's play *Shopping and Fucking*, produced by the Out of Joint touring theatre company at the Royal Court Theatre in London in September 1996. Under the Indecent Advertisements Act 1889, the word "fuck" could not be used on posters or advertisements. The problem was first solved by using the image of a fork shattering the offending word. The design was then used for the cover of the play's text. Subsequent advertising for the play used asterisks, resulting in the title *Shopping and F**king*.

End, the locale for mainstream theatre in London, James Christopher wrote that scandal was what made the Court "chic". However, as Stafford-Clark pointed out, there was also "a disparity between what journalists and critics thought would shock people, and what actually did shock people. In previous generations, the disparity was much smaller".

Shopping and Fucking became a highly successful play. It was put on twice at the Royal Court, toured Britain, and became, with help from the British Council, a cultural export to Sweden, the Irish Republic, Italy, Australia, and Israel. Productions were also mounted in New York, as well as in Germany and other European countries. In 1997–98, it came to the Gielgud Theatre and then the Queen's Theatre, both on Shaftesbury Avenue (and therefore in the West End). By this point, some older critics were noting ruefully that "the shocks of 50 years ago are no longer the shocks of today". Only its title continued, in the words of another such critic, Sheridan Morley, to give "typesetters and broadcasters headaches". When the play opened at the Gielgud Theatre, it was pointed out that the necessary coyness about the title contrasted with the explicit sexuality on display just around the corner in Soho, London's "red light" district. In *Time Out* magazine, Steve Grant noted the "nicely ironic twist" of the title's asterisks in a location "outside which people not only shout 'Fuck' but are often looking for one".

While the case of *Shopping and Fucking* shows how laws about one kind of activity (prostitution) can be deployed against another kind of activity (theatrical representation), it also suggests how much the public climate had changed during the 1990s. In 1994, the transfer to the West End of *Beautiful Thing*, a play by Jonathan Harvey first staged at the Bush, a pub theatre, was greeted by articles in the *Evening Standard* attacking a putative "plague of pink plays". Two years later, most of the critics who reviewed *Shopping and Fucking* appeared to regard the homosexual relationships in the play as unexceptional and did not categorize it as a "gay play". While

Sarah Kane's *Blasted*, staged at the Royal Court in January 1995, attracted some of the most negative reviews of the decade, Ravenhill's play was broadly welcomed, its shocking content widely seen as justified by its critical attitude to consumer culture and alienation.

ALEKS SIERZ

Writings

Shopping and Fucking, 1996; 2nd edition, 1997
Interview with Emma Freud on *Theatreland*, London Weekend Television (9 March 1997)

Further Reading

Christopher, James, *et al.*, programme for *Shopping and F***ing*, London: Gielgud Theatre, 1997
Eyres, Harry, "Sensation Stalks the Stage", *The Spectator* (9 May 1998): 45–46
Mortimer, John, "Diary", *The New Statesman* (27 March 1998): 6
"NB", *Times Literary Supplement* (27 March 1998): 16
Reviews in *Theatre Record*, 16/20 (1996); 17/13 (1997); 18/1–2 (1998)
Sierz, Aleks, *In-Yer-Face Theatre: British Drama Today*, London: Faber, 2001
Thornton, Michael, "A Shop Window for Outrage", *Punch* (21–27 September 1996): 70–71

GUILLAUME-THOMAS RAYNAL
French historian and journalist, 1713–1796

HISTOIRE DES DEUX INDES (A History of the Two Indies)
Critical history, 1770, revised 1774, 1780

Like the *Encyclopédie*, the *Histoire philosophique et politique des établissemens et du commerce des européens dans les deux Indes* (henceforth the *Histoire*) was a compendium of Enlightenment thought. Ostensibly a history of the discovery, conquest, and settlement of India and the West Indies up to the 18th century, the work was a monumental undertaking. Like its cousin, the *Histoire* contained "philosophical" criticisms of contemporary politics and society. It attacked the colonial enterprise, monarchy, and religion while suggesting the reform of many elements of the *ancien régime*. Such controversial themes made the work immensely popular. In the 20 years following its first publication in 1770, the *Histoire* was reprinted in 20 authorized editions, in more than 50 pirated editions, and under at least 24 different titles. Few literary or historical works of the 18th century saw comparable press-runs, and even fewer enjoyed as wide a reading audience. Sold throughout Europe as well as most of the Americas, the *Histoire* rivalled in popularity even the most celebrated works of Voltaire and Jean-Jacques Rousseau.

For nearly 10 years after its initial publication in 1770, the *Histoire* did not carry a byline. Nevertheless, many in Enlightenment circles believed that Guillaume-Thomas Raynal was the principal author of the work. Diderot, d'Alembert, the Baron d'Holbach, and Charles-Pinot Duclos, among others, were said to have assisted him. Born in Rodez in 1713, Raynal joined the Society of Jesus at a young age. In 1747 he left the Jesuits and, like many of his contemporaries, travelled to Paris

to seek his fortune. By the 1760s Raynal was writing official histories for ministers of state. After the success of his first large-scale work (1762), he devoted himself for the next 20 years to the *Histoire*.

Published initially in Amsterdam in a six-volume octavo edition, the *Histoire* remained unknown in France until March 1772. Taken over the borders clandestinely, it sold for the next five months without the permission of the French book trade authorities. Once its contents became generally known, however, critics of the work erupted in protest. Its charged rhetoric and its attacks on religion demonstrated a new brand of Enlightenment radicalism, a foretaste of the revolutionary extremism Raynal would later disavow. The clergy in particular found it galling that the man responsible for the work had once been a member of the Society of Jesus. Under the advice of the chancellor René-Nicolas de Maupeou, the government issued an *arrêt du conseil* on 19 December 1772 ordering the work's suppression and condemning it as "bold, dangerous, reckless, and contrary to good morals and to the principles of religion". Attacks on anticlerical books were nothing new in France, but the censoring of the *Histoire* coincided with a reinvigorated general campaign to suppress illicit works. In 1770, clerical leaders and opponents of the Enlightenment had called for a tightening of the controls over authors and the book trade.

As was the case with other Enlightenment works, official condemnation only increased the popularity of the *Histoire*. Despite the *arrêt du conseil*, and perhaps because of it, the 1770 edition sold vigorously. The publication of the first substantial revision of the text in 1774 further demonstrated the impotence of officials in stemming the tide of illicit books. With this new edition, Raynal took advantage of the work's popularity to lengthen the manuscript. Whereas the first edition had contained 2,100 pages in 18 books, the 1774 edition was a seven-volume octavo containing 19 books and slightly more than 3,000 pages. The official response to the 1774 edition was mixed. While book trade officials now turned a blind eye, the clergy renewed their attack. On 29 August 1774 the *Histoire* was placed on the *Index Librorum Prohibitorum*.

In the following year, two critics, François Bernard and Élie-Catherine Fréron, publicly attacked Raynal and his work. According to them, in the *Histoire* Raynal had encouraged rebellion against, and even the murder of legitimate sovereigns. Equally troubling to them was the work's advocacy of social and political liberty, the natural consequence of which, as they saw it, could only be disorder. In August 1775 Raynal was personally denounced by the Assembly of the Clergy. These concerted attacks on Raynal, along with the saturation of the market with authorized and pirated editions, brought about a sharp fall in sales of the *Histoire*.

Raynal, however, continued to carry out the second substantial revision of the work. A four-volume quarto printing from Geneva, the 1780 edition represented only a slight augmentation of the text. When printed in an octavo edition in 1781, this final revision contained only 35 more pages than the first revision of 1774. In private, Raynal maintained that the new edition would be a model of scientific research, true to the work's "philosophical and political" intentions. In fact this new version of the *Histoire* had only become more audacious in its attacks on monarchy and religion. Most daringly, the title page now cited Raynal as the work's sole author and the frontispiece bore his portrait. If Raynal was not the work's only author, he was nevertheless the one to suffer most from its publication. Anticipating the uproar which the appearance of the new edition would occasion and the mounting attacks of the clergy, Raynal had fled from Paris to Geneva, where he oversaw the publication of the 1780 quarto edition. He returned to Paris only at the close of the year. In early 1781 the revised *Histoire* followed him back to France.

In May 1781 the Parlement of Paris denounced the new edition as "impious, blasphemous, and seditious, tending to excite the people against the sovereign authority and to overturn the fundamental principles of the civil order". Raynal's enemies used the opportunity to issue an order for his arrest, although Raynal was ultimately afforded the opportunity once again to flee. On 25 May 1781, in a public display meant to discourage like-minded authors, the *Histoire* was publicly lacerated and burned. Not unexpectedly, the quarto and octavo editions of 1780 and 1781 sold vigorously, and for the rest of the 1780s the work appeared and reappeared in numerous abridgments and pirated editions.

With the coming of the Revolution, Raynal fell into popular disfavour. In part this was the result of the comte de Guibert's publication in Raynal's name of an open letter to the National Assembly that protested against the radicalism of the Revolution. In 1791, Raynal himself published an open letter repudiating the *Histoire*, strikingly foreshadowing similar repudiations occasioned by the Russian and Chinese Revolutions. Having suffered under the monarchy for nearly 20 years, Raynal now faced the fury of radical Republicans who believed he had betrayed his own revolutionary principles. In the ensuing years of the Revolution the *Histoire des deux Indes* fell from grace and into almost complete disrepute. Raynal himself became one of the *écrivains obscurs*, the forgotten writers of the 18th century.

SEAN C. GOODLETT

Writings

Histoire du Stathoudérat, 1747
Essai historique et politique sur le gouvernement présent de la Hollande, 1748
Histoire du Parlement d'Angleterre, 1748
Mémorial de Paris et de ses environs, 1749
Anecdotes historiques, militaires et politiques de l'Europe, 1753
L'École militaire, 1762
Histoire du divorce de Henry VIII, 1763
Histoire philosophique et politique des établissemens et du commerce des européens dans les deux Indes, 1770; translated as *A Philosophical and Political History of the Settlements and Trade of the Europeans in the East and West Indies*, 1777
Lettre à l'Assemblée nationale, 1791

Further Reading

Bancarel, Gilles, *Guillaume-Thomas Raynal: philosophe des Lumières*, Toulouse: CRDP Midi-Pyrénées, 1996
Bancarel, Gilles and Gianluigi Goggi (editors), "Raynal, de la polémique à l'histoire", *Studies on Voltaire and the Eighteenth Century*,12 (2000)
Darnton, Robert, *The Forbidden Best-Sellers of Pre-Revolutionary France*, New York: Norton, 1995; London: HarperCollins, 1996
Feugère, Anatole, *Un Précurseur de la Révolution: l'abbé Raynal, 1713–1796*, Angouleme: Imprimerie Ouvrière, 1922; reprinted Geneva: Slatkine, 1970
Guénot, Hervé, "La Réception de l'*Histoire dex deux Indes* dans la presse d'expression française, 1772–1781", *Studies on Voltaire and the Eighteenth Century*, 286 (1991): 67–84
Krauss, Werner, "L'Étude des écrivains obscurs du siècle des lumières", *Studies on Voltaire and the Eighteenth Century*, 26 (1963): 1019–24
Minois, Georges, *Censure et culture sous l'Ancien Régime*, Paris: Fayard, 1995
Wolpe, Hans, *Raynal et sa machine de guerre: l'histoire des deux Indes et ses perfectionnements*, Stanford, California: Stanford University Press, 1957

REAL LIVES: AT THE EDGE OF THE UNION
British television documentary, 1985

Real Lives: At the Edge of the Union focused on two politicians from either end of the political spectrum in Northern Ireland: Gregory Campbell of the Democratic Unionist Party (DUP), and Martin McGuinness of Sinn Féin. The cameras followed both these politicians in their daily lives. The style of the producer, Paul Hamann, was to ensure that the cameras and microphones were as unobtrusive as possible: there was no interruption from spoken commentary, nor any direct questioning of the participants. Critics later concluded that McGuinness came across as the more personable of the two politicians. But this alone was not the reason for the ire that the programme aroused in some quarters. The negative criticism concentrated on the fact that McGuinness, said by British intelligence sources to be a former chief of staff of the Provisional Irish Republican Army (IRA), was given a platform on which to put forward his views without criticism or interruption. This was said not only to offend against good taste, but also to run counter to specific instructions that broadcasters should present people like McGuinness in an unfavourable light.

From the point of view of the programme makers and BBC management, no rules had been broken in the making of the programme. In the aftermath of the 1981 republican hunger strike Sinn Féin had become increasingly involved in elections. By the time of the programme, the party had 59 elected local councillors. Martin McGuinness himself had been elected to the Northern Ireland Assembly. On this basis, it was concluded that it was legitimate to interview him. Moreover, with a few notable gaps, BBC management believed that their reference upwards system, instituted to police forthcoming programmes about the Irish conflict, had operated adequately.

The final ingredient in this explosive mix was the activity of journalists from the *Sunday Times*. They acquired details of the programme in advance and began feeding them to key government ministers, including the home secretary, Leon Brittan. They also approached prime minister Margaret Thatcher in New York with the hypothetical question: how would she react if she heard that the BBC was about to interview the Chief of Staff of the IRA? Needless to say, Thatcher replied that she would completely condemn such an action. As a result of what BBC management later referred to as the *Sunday Times* "stunt", the home secretary telephoned the chairman of the BBC governors, Stuart Young, stating that broadcasting the programme would be, in his (Brittan's) opinion, against the interests of national security. In a letter to the press, Brittan emphasized that as minister responsible for broadcasting, he did not wish to interfere with programme makers. However, as minister with responsibility for law and order, he could only conclude that such a programme would provide "the oxygen of publicity" for "terrorists". Later Brittan was to insist that he did not ban the programme. While this is technically correct, his unprecedented intervention was the catalyst for those who proceeded to ban it.

The BBC governors met hastily to respond to the crisis. They debated first whether they ought to view the film. BBC managers pointed out that such a move was not only virtually unprecedented – the last occasion on which a full board of governors had viewed a programme in advance had been in 1967 – but was also in effect a denial of the right of management to make independent professional judgements. Despite the warnings, the governors viewed the programme. They were almost unanimously negative in their conclusions and voted to ban the film.

On 7 August, the day on which the film should have been broadcast, National Union of Journalists (NUJ) members in the BBC and at Independent Television News (ITN) staged a one-day strike. No news was broadcast that day. For the first time ever, journalists in the BBC World Service also struck on the grounds that they could not easily speak out against censorship elsewhere in the world when it was so clearly present on their own doorstep. By the end of the summer the new BBC director general, Alasdair Milne, was able to raise the issue of broadcasting the programme. Some minor amendments were made, including the addition of 15 seconds' footage of exploding IRA bombs, and the film was finally screened on 16 October.

Real Lives represents the head-on clash between two views of dealing with dissident politics. On the one hand were those such as Margaret Thatcher and Leon Brittan and the majority of the BBC governors appointed by them who believed that broadcasting could not provide a platform for those in favour of "terrorism". Thatcher had used the memorable phrase "the oxygen of publicity" in July 1985 when condemning US coverage of the hijacking of a TWA aircraft. Brittan applied it to *Real Lives*. On the other hand were those, such as the programme makers and BBC management, who held that as professional broadcasters they had a right and a duty to examine the views and arguments of elected representatives, even those from a militant republican tradition.

Real Lives was the most serious conflict between government and broadcasters to that point. It was followed three years later by the controversy over *Death on the Rock* and finally by the broadcasting ban of late 1988. As with *Real Lives*, the government denied that it was attempting censorship; it merely left the broadcasters to squabble as to the most effective way to censor themselves.

Since the above was written, political developments have led to a devolved government in Northern Ireland in which Martin McGuinness became minister of education and Gregory Campbell minister of regional development. There was little sign, however, that the gulf between them was any less than when *Real Lives* was broadcast. In May 2001, McGuinness gave evidence to the Saville inquiry into the killing by British soldiers of 14 civil rights marchers in Derry in January 1972. In his evidence, he acknowledged that he had been second-in-command of the IRA in Derry at that time. Gregory Campbell was among the most vociferous people calling not just for his removal from ministerial office but also for his prosecution.

BILL ROLSTON

Further Reading

Leapman, Michael, *The Last Days of the Beeb*, London: Allen and Unwin, 1986

Miller, David, *Don't Mention the War: Northern Ireland, Propaganda and the Media*, London: Pluto Press, 1994

Milne, Alasdair, *DG: Memoirs of a British Broadcaster*, London: Hodder and Stoughton, 1988

Rolston, Bill and David Miller (editors), *War and Words: The Northern Ireland Media Reader*, Belfast: Beyond the Pale, 1996

RED CHANNELS

US report and listing on communist influence in radio and television, 1950s

Red Channels, published just as the television boom was getting under way, marked the official beginning of the blacklist in the US broadcast industry. This report listed 151 "subversive" writers, directors, and performers along with citations of their alleged communist or left-wing political affiliations (see complete list at end of article). Although many of the activities listed were either inaccurate or had nothing to do with the Communist Party, a mention in *Red Channels* proved devastating to one's career and personal life. Nobody who was mentioned in the pamphlet could be hired by a radio or television network until he or she was "cleared" by an official agency, and others in the industry were fearful of associating with them.

The political climate of the postwar US bred this type of ideological censorship was one beset by suspicion and anxiety. A "Red Scare" gripped the US, cultivating public hysteria over the threat of a communist presence in America. Television's rise coincided with the dramatic espionage case of Alger Hiss, the arrest and execution of accused Soviet spies Julius and Ethel Rosenberg, and senator Joseph McCarthy's hunt for "card-carrying Communists" in the State Department. These events solidified the menacing image of the undercover communist as an agent of enemy subversion. Federal agencies and opportunistic private organizations began investigating the military, government, academic, and entertainment industries for dissident elements in the late 1940s. The attorney general even compiled (and later published) a list of organizations with communist, fascist, totalitarian, or subversive views and used it to screen government employees. Additionally, the onset of the Korean War, coupled with the escalation of the Cold War, fuelled the country's attendant sense of paranoia.

The anticommunist crusade in the film and television sector found the spotlight in 1947, when the House Committee on Un-American Activities (commonly and derisively referred to as HUAC) reopened its investigations of Hollywood. Although HUAC dominated the news as the main instrument of blacklisting, however, there were other anticommunist forces with far-reaching impact. One notable example was American Business Consultants (ABC) in New York. ABC was created by three former FBI agents, Theodore Kirkpatrick, Kenneth Bierly, and John Keenan. The group published a regular edition of *Counterattack, the Newsletter of Facts on Communism*, as well as numerous special reports, from 1947 to 1955. In its early issues, the newsletter focused primarily on communism in the labour unions. Slowly, however, the attention shifted to the entertainment industry.

Red Channels, which suggested heavy communist infiltration of the US broadcast industry, became *Counterattack's* most famous special report. Its premise was that communists were rampant in the television business and should be removed, implying the otherwise impending destruction of America's social and political foundations. The index itemized all "subversive" organizations, petitions, meetings, and causes allegedly supported by each person. *Red Channels* also listed 192 organizations and publications that were considered to be communist-controlled, also known as "fronts". Among them were the American Committee of Jewish Writers, Artists and Scientists, the Hollywood Democratic Committee, and the National Negro Congress.

To compile the entries, the publishers and footsoldiers of ABC pored over transcripts from HUAC hearings and reports, back issues of the *Daily Worker*, and attendance lists from various meetings. *Red Channels* also frequently cited mention in *Counterattack* as proof of seditious activity. The resulting list totalled 151 people, all of whom were branded communists or "sympathizers" by virtue of their varying involvement with liberal political causes.

In some cases, however, the attributions were incorrect. Many listings were merely benign activities viewed by *Red Channels* as being subversive, such as attending a rally or signing a petition. There were also numerous instances of performers undertaking a pro-Soviet cause at the government's behest during World War II, which later came back to haunt them. Moreover, cases of mistaken identity caused many problems; the actress Martha Scott was confused with the listed singer Hazel Scott and both of their careers suffered greatly. For some, the pressure proved to be too much to handle. The deaths of Phillip Loeb, John Garfield, Mady Christians, and J. Edward Bromberg have all been attributed to the stress and persecution suffered during this period.

Red Channels soon became known as "the Bible of Madison Avenue", referring to its immense influence on the network offices and advertising agencies in New York City. All studio and ad agency executives had copies of *Red Channels* as part of their subscription to *Counterattack*. Many blindly honoured the judgements of these publications, effectively legitimizing them despite their questionable sources and misinformation.

The multiplicity of sponsors, advertising agencies, and networks, all with their own standards and hiring practices, combined with the various listing services like ABC, the American Legion, and Aware, Inc., to enact what was referred to as a "graylist". While not as clear-cut as the Hollywood blacklist, the graylist was a reservoir of names that were acceptable to some in broadcasting but not to others. Graylisting did not uniformly shut individuals out from working on every programme for every network, but it significantly diminished their prospects for employment.

The listing hysteria emerged in the wake of the HUAC trials as a means of attacking liberals in an effective yet unpublicized manner. An opening passage in *Red Channels* stated that the activities and associations described may have been innocent of subversive intent; this disclaimer made it nearly impossible for those singled out to seek legal damages for any professional ill-effects resulting from their inclusion in the pamphlet. The haphazard practice of blacklisting operated as if it were above the law, never formally discussed as deleterious to broadcasting professionals, nor outwardly claimed by its agents.

Nevertheless, listing was a mechanism of censorship that became part of the industrial fabric in the emerging days of American television. The CBS executive vice-president in charge of clearance ensured that the network did not hire any writer, actor, or director who was suspected of being a communist or "fellow traveller." Similarly, NBC's legal department checked previous political activities of network employees. The advertising agency Batten, Barton, Durstine and Osborn hired security officers to monitor the personnel of the shows they sponsored.

In rare cases, listed individuals were able to salvage their careers and return to work. The playwright Lillian Hellman was one of the few who managed to maintain her dignity *and* her job. She appeared before HUAC, refused to name names and, in a boldly worded statement, announced "I cannot and will not cut my conscience to fit this year's fashions." The careers of Lena Horne, Orson Welles, and Edward G. Robinson also rebounded after they were listed.

However, before any of the people who were identified by *Red Channels* could return to their positions in the industry, they were forced to sign loyalty oaths and statements prepared by the networks denouncing the political activities they were associated with in the booklet. Independent agencies, often referred to as "smear and clear" organizations, profited enormously by providing clearance services to sponsors and agencies on a consultant basis. Most of these, like ABC and Aware, Inc., also published lists of suspected communists that should be cleared before being allowed to work. Thus, they perpetuated their own cottage industry based on fear and became rich in the process.

The institutional structure of television in its developing stages rendered it particularly vulnerable to social pressures or outside threats. Advertisers still had control over the production of programmes, sponsoring entire shows instead of sharing the cost with dozens of other companies. They were reluctant to be associated with anything politically or socially controversial and took extreme care to craft programmes that were least likely to alienate any viewing segment. In their desire to appeal to the widest possible audience, the sponsors created a medium with a heightened sensitivity to the social climate. Content and plots of television shows were even affected; bankers and businessmen could no longer be suspects in mysteries, and law-and-order dramas became a staple output of the studios. As the networks remained under the control of the advertising agencies, sponsors also dictated hiring and funding decisions.

By 1952, those listed in *Red Channels* or cited in *Counterattack* were finding it impossible to find work without clearing themselves to the satisfaction of network and advertising executives. This clearance process could take years. Consequently, long after Senator Joseph McCarthy's downfall on Ed Murrow's television show *See It Now* in 1954, networks and sponsors still remained wary of anyone who had been named in *Red Channels*. All told, the elaborate censorship machinery that operated by unspoken agreement among networks, sponsors, and independent organizations endured well into the 1960s, maintaining its grip on the industry for almost 20 years and haunting its conscience ever since.

JENNIFER HOLT

Further Reading

Ceplair, Larry and Steven Englund, *The Inquisition in Hollywood: Politics in the Film Community, 1930–1960*, New York: Doubleday, 1980

Cogley, John, *Report on Blacklisting*, 2 vols, New York: Fund for the Republic, 1956

Foley, Karen Sue, *The Political Blacklist in the Broadcast Industry: The Decade of the 1950s*, New York: Arno Press, 1972

Hellman, Lillian, *Scoundrel Time*, Boston: Little Brown, 1976

McGilligan, Patrick and Paul Buhle, *Tender Comrades: A Backstory of the Hollywood Blacklist*, New York: St Martin's Press, 1997

Navasky, Victor S., *Naming Names*, New York: Viking, and London: Quartet, 1980

Red Channels: The Report of Communist Influence in Radio and Television, New York: American Business Consultants, 1950

Vaughn, Robert, *Only Victims: A Study of Show Business Blacklisting*, New York: Putnam, 1972

The complete list was Larry Adler, Luther Adler, Stella Adler, Edith Atwater, Howard Bay, Ralph Bell, Leonard Bernstein, Walter Bernstein, Michael Blankfort, Marc Blitzstein, True Boardman, Millen Brand, Oscar Brand, J. Edward Bromberg, Himan Brown, John Brown, Abe Burrows, Morris Carnovsky, Vera Caspary, Edward Chodorov, Jerome Chodorov, Mady Christians, Lee J. Cobb, Marc Connelly, Aaron Copland, Norman Corwin, Howard Da Silva, Roger De Koven, Dean Dixon, Olin Downes, Alfred Drake, Paul Draper, Howard Duff, Clifford J. Durr, Richard Dyer-Bennett, José Ferrer, Louise Fitch, Martin Gabel, Arthur Gaeth, William S. Gailmor, John Garfield, Will Geer, Jack Gilford, Tom Glazer, Ruth Gordon, Lloyd Gough, Morton Gould, Shirley Graham, Ben Grauer, Mitchell Grayson, Horace Grenell, Uta Hagen, Dashiell Hammett, E.Y. Harburg, Robert P. Heller, Lillian Hellman, Nat Hiken, Rose Hobart, Judy Holliday, Roderick B. Holmgren, Lena Horne, Langston Hughes, Marsha Hunt, Leo Hurwitz, Charles Irving, Burl Ives, Sam Jaffe, Leon Janney, Joe Julian, Garson Kanin, George Keane, Donna Keath, Pert Kelton, Alexander Kendrick, Adelaide Klein, Felix Knight, Howard Koch, Tony Kraber, Millard Lampell, John Latouche, Arthur Laurents, Gypsy Rose Lee, Madeline Lee, Ray Lev, Phillip Loeb, Ella Logan, Alan Lomax, Avon Long, Joseph Losey, Peter Lyon, Myron McCormick, Paul McGrath, Aline McMahon, Paul Mann, Margo, Burgess Meredith, Arthur Miller, Henry Morgan, Zero Mostel, Jean Muir, Meg Mundy, Lynn Murray, Ben Myers, Dorothy Parker, Arnold Perl, Minerva Pious, Samson Raphaelson, Bernard Reis, Anne Revere, Kenneth Roberts, Earl Robinson, Edward G. Robinson, William N. Robson, Harold Rome, Norman Rosten, Selena Royle, Coby Ruskin, Robert St John, Hazel Scott, Pete Seeger, Lisa Sergio, Artie Shaw, Irwin Shaw, Robert Lewis Shayon, Ann Shepherd, William L. Shirer, Allan Sloane, Howard K. Smith, Gale Sondergaard, Hester Sondergaard, Lionel Stander, Johannes Steel, Paul Stewart, Elliot Sullivan, William Sweets, Helen Tamiris, Betty Todd, Louis Untermeyer, Hilda Vaughn, J. Raymond Walsh, Sam Wanamaker, Theodore Ward, Fredi Washington, Margaret Webster, Orson Welles, Josh White, Ireene Wicker, Betty Winkler, Martin Wolfson, Lesley Woods, Richard Yaffe.

GEORGE ALEXANDER REDFORD
British theatre and film censor, died 1916

Redford was the Lord Chamberlain's examiner of plays from 1895 to 1911 and in 1912 became the first chairman of the British Board of Film Censors (BBFC). His terms of office came at a time when many firmly held moral assumptions were being called into question and the system of theatre censorship itself was being challenged. In 1909, as examiner of plays, Redford was brought before a Joint Select Committee of both houses of parliament to explain and justify his decisions. His difficulty in doing so led to calls for his post and, in particular, its connections with the Crown, to be abolished. When the BBFC was brought into being, another approach was favoured. The BBFC was not a government-appointed body, nor a royal office, but was brought into being by the film companies in response to government pressure; as a gesture towards accountability, it published its guidelines in its first annual report in 1913. These expressed the standards of behaviour which subjects of the British Empire were expected to uphold, standards which World War I (during which Redford died) did much to destroy.

Redford had few qualifications for his job as the examiner of plays. He had dabbled in writing plays, but his previous experience had mainly been in banking. He had his first experience as a licenser of plays in 1875, taking over from his friend and the then examiner of plays, Edward F.S. Pigott, who was away on holiday. He acted for some years as a deputy licenser, until Pigott retired in 1895, and in eight years, from 1902 to 1910, he read and censored 4233 plays, a monumental task. His very lack of qualifications commended him to one actor-manager, Sir George Alexander, who thought that the ideal censor should have some knowledge of literature and drama, but was "essentially . . . a man of the world".

Redford and Pigott believed that they were guided by the most broadminded principles of behaviour. "It may confidently be assumed," said Pigott in 1892, "that the mistakes of the Examiner of Plays [. . .] will always be in the direction of extreme indulgence, for the simple reason that if the reins were tightened, they would snap in his hands." "It has always been my effort," said Redford, "to take the broadest and most liberal view of every subject that came before me." The Joint Select Committee in 1909 noted examples of the censor's indulgences in allowing naughty farces translated "from the French" into the West End, because "it was the custom to allow a wider latitude to foreign plays".

The theatre profession was divided about whether censorship was desirable: the managers on the whole were in favour, the playwrights against. Some actors recalled how before the Theatres Act of 1843 they were described in law as "rogues and vagabonds" and treated accordingly. Local watch committees still had the power to harass them, and it was customary to give benefit performances for local charities to buy off the disapproval of the churches and other moral guardians. A play licence was like an official seal of approval and helped to combat the anti-theatrical prejudice. But in Britain towards the end of the 19th century, inspired by the examples of Ibsen in Norway, the Théâtre Libre in Paris and the Freie Bühne in Berlin, a new generation of professionals had emerged, who were unwilling to put up with this lowly status: they were not

mere entertainers but philosophers and social commentators as well. In London, the seasons run by Harley Granville Barker and J.E. Vedrenne at the Royal Court Theatre from 1904 until 1907, aroused much controversy. These included new plays by Shaw, Barker, and Galsworthy that were deeply critical of the British way of life, to the point, some might have thought, of undermining the authority of the state.

It was not the daring French farces or bloodbath melodramas but the social problem plays, such as Ibsen's *Ghosts*, Shaw's *Mrs Warren's Profession*, and Barker's *Waste*, that aroused Redford's alarm. He thought it improper to mention such subjects as venereal disease or prostitution, particularly when politicians, members of the royal family, or ministers of religion were concerned. He derived his authority as censor from the Theatres Act (1843) which provided that plays could be banned or censored for containing material considered detrimental to "the preservation of good manners, decorum or [. . .] public peace", but he extended his duties to apply to plays which were "immoral or otherwise improper for the stage". A discussion of venereal disease need not be immoral *per se* but only improper in the theatre, in front of mixed audiences, perhaps including children. There were wider laws against obscenity, which covered all the art forms, but the theatre was considered to require special treatment. It was the unfairness of this treatment which led to an open letter of protest in *The Times* from 71 writers and stage directors, addressed to the new Liberal prime minister, Sir Henry Campbell-Bannerman.

The writers protested against

> the power lodged in the hands of a single official, who judges without public hearing, and against whose dictum there is no appeal [. . .] They assert[ed] that the censorship has not been exercised in the interests of morality, but has tended to lower the dramatic tone by appearing to relieve the public of the duty of moral judgement. They ask[ed] to be freed from the menace hanging over every dramatist of having his work and the proceeds of his work destroyed at a pen's stroke by the arbitrary action of a single official, neither responsible to Parliament nor amenable to law. They ask[ed] that their art be placed on the same footing as every other art. They ask[ed] that they themselves be placed in the position enjoyed under law by every other citizen. To these ends, they claim[ed] that the licensing of plays should be abolished . . .

Their appeal to the prime minister came at an appropriate time. The Liberal Party had won a landslide victory in the 1906 general election and stood for greater personal freedom. The unelected court official, Redford, stood as a symbol for other anti-democratic elements in the British way of life, and so the matter was considered sufficiently important to warrant a Joint Select Committee. Shaw, who was called to give evidence, responded with a written statement which was rejected by the committee but published separately and later became part of the preface to *The Shewing-up of Blanco Posnet* (1910). Shaw distinguished between "immorality", which he defined as being against the customs of the day, and "sinfulness", and argued that while dramatists should avoid sinfulness, it was their duty to be immoral, that is, to criticize society.

This subtle distinction made little impact upon the committee, which was concerned to discover the guiding principles of stage censorship. Redford replied: "I simply bring to bear the official view and keep up the standard. It is really impossible to define what the principle may be. There are no principles that can be defined." His decisions were based on custom and precedent although "things [were] always changing". "Every case must be judged on its merits and every case is looked at from its merits." He was cross-examined by a member of the committee, Alfred Mason, who asked what he meant by "merits". "That is a bad term perhaps, I mean on what it contains", Redford replied. "We are trying," said Alfred Mason patiently, "to get at what is the guiding principle . . .". Redford did not reply and his silence was duly recorded in the committee's report.

Shaw and his comrades-in-arms against censorship poured scorn on him. They enquired whether in banning Maeterlinck's *Monna Vanna*, his insufficient knowledge of French had led him astray. Had he misread *nue sous un manteau* (naked under a cloak) for *nue sans un manteau* (naked without a cloak)? When the Joint Select Committee decided to appoint a committee to advise Redford, Shaw expressed the opinion that it was unconstitutional and advised its members to resign immediately "before the Lord Chamberlain gets them into trouble". It would be hard to dissent from Shaw's view that serious plays were more likely to get censored than trivial ones, but it must be admitted that Redford was placed in an unenviable position by the Joint Select Committee. He was asked to justify a range of taboos, which were not more extreme than those of earlier (or later) dates, but more under scrutiny.

Redford was expected to interpret what was meant by obscenity. The Obscene Publications Act of 1851 failed to contain a legal definition of obscenity, an omission rectified in 1868 by a formula which stated that "an article" may be deemed "obscene" if it tends "to deprave or corrupt persons who are likely . . . to read, see or hear matter contained or embodied therein". Few people admit that they have been depraved or corrupted by a book or a play and such an admission might be interpreted as a sign of their innocence. The censor was thus expected to prevent a crime which had not been committed and might well be unprovable, if it were. But the nature of obscenity was merely one of the imponderable questions which Redford had to bear in mind, others including blasphemy and undermining the authority of the state. Nor did Shaw's distinction between immorality and sinfulness help, for who could define "sin"?

When he became the chairman of the British Board of Film Censors, Redford felt the need to give guidance to the filmmakers. In his first annual report (1913), without mentioning films by name, he gave reasons why some had been banned or cut: for "indelicate or suggestive sexual situations", "indecent dancing", "holding a Minister of Religion to ridicule", "cruelty to animals", "subjects depicting procuration, abduction and seduction", "excessive drunkenness", "judicial executions", "native customs in foreign lands abhorrent to British ideas", "indelicate accessories in staging", "impropriety in conduct and dress", and "the materialization of Christ or the Almighty".

Redford was a hard-working, not well-paid, official, less bigoted than his predecessor, Pigott, who once said that he had "studied Ibsen's plays pretty carefully and all the characters in Ibsen's plays seem to me morally degraded". Redford was prepared to invite managers and playwrights to his office if there were problems to discuss. He may have been a figure of fun to Shaw and his friends, but he was supported, before the Joint Select Committee, by many actor-managers who, like Alexander, favoured his man-of-the-world approach. In common with others of his time, he believed that the theatre was a place for entertainment and should not bother with matters of moment; but he had the misfortune to encounter a new breed of dramatists who were as determined as Ibsen's Nora to bang the door on their particular kind of dolls' house.

JOHN ELSOM

Further Reading

Elsom, John, *Erotic Theatre*, London: Secker and Warburg, 1973; New York: Taplinger, 1974

Shaw, Bernard, *The Shewing Up of Blanco Posnet: A Sermon in Crude Melodrama*, New York: Brentano's, 1909; London: Constable, 1913

REPORTERS SANS FRONTIÈRES

An international, independent, and non-governmental organization that campaigns for the "freedom to inform, and to be informed" worldwide, Reporters sans Frontières (RSF) defends the rights of journalists, supports publications under threat, assists endangered writers, and raises awareness of censorship. In addition to its concern for writers, it takes an active interest in photographers and cartoonists under censorship and features their work in its publications.

Based in Paris, RSF receives financial support from the European Union, Unesco, personal subscriptions, and companies and institutions. It has national branches in Germany, Spain, Switzerland, Sweden, Belgium, Italy, the UK, and France, offices in Istanbul, Bangkok, Washington, and Abidjan, and members in more than 20 countries. It has consultative status with the Council of Europe, the UN Commission on Human Rights, and Unesco, and observer status with the African Commission on Human and People's Rights.

RSF was founded in 1985 by a radio journalist, Robert Ménard, in response to public complaints about poor press coverage of world news. Aiming to give space to those regions "forgotten" by the media, RSF supported coverage of some 60 topics, including Uganda (an RSF-sponsored piece appeared in

Liberation) and a French camp for Vietnamese refugees (published in *Le Matin de Paris*). The operation was haphazard, however, and some writers resented the organization.

Increasingly interested in the difficulties that many journalists faced in their work, RSF changed direction in 1989. Early reporting projects were closed down and a new programme was set up to secure the release of imprisoned journalists and to expose violations of press freedom. The focus was on those facing government repression and violence from armed groups or during open conflict.

RSF established its reputation quickly. Within a year it had produced a directory of principal international media, *L'Information dans le Monde* (News Worldwide), detailing their degree of independence and relative freedom to work; marked the bicentenary of the French Revolution with *Atlas mondiale des libertés* (World Atlas of Freedom); organized a seminar on China (in response to the Tianamen Square massacre); and initiated a monthly newsletter (*La Lettre de RSF*) and an annual report (*RSF Annual Report: Freedom of the Press Throughout the World*) listing violations of press freedom in more than 100 countries. In addition, it launched its long-running campaign to persuade newspapers and television and radio companies to sponsor journalists imprisoned for their work. So far some 40 news outlets have adopted jailed journalists, improving prison conditions for some and influencing the release of others.

RSF's strategy to engage Western media and use the free press to support the oppressed has been successful, and in 1997 it won the Ilaria Alpi prize for press freedom work for its weekly broadcasts on the Euronews channel. In November 1997 RSF took a film crew to Vietnam to film inside the prison where a dissident journalist, Doan Viet Hoat, was held. The footage was broadcast in France, Belgium, Switzerland, and Canada. Doan was released on 1 September 1998.

The correlation and dissemination of information about violations of press freedom are central to its work. The International Secretariat documents cases of censorship reported in the international press and by other human rights organizations, and conducts missions in the field (RSF has about 100 correspondents across the world and mounts about 20 investigations a year). Its findings and the results of its campaigns are published in French, English, Spanish, and Arabic in its annual report and also in its newsletter, Web pages, and fact files/country reports on censorship.

In 1990 RSF launched International Press Freedom Day, which has been recognized by the UN since 1994. Its annual publication *100 Photos pour défendre la liberté de la presse* (100 Photos for Press Freedom) not only publicizes the issue but also raises money (proceeds go to oppressed media and journalists). In 1992 it initiated an annual prize, awarded jointly with Fondation de France, for journalists who have contributed to press freedom. Worth FF50,000 ($10,000), its recipients have included Zlatko Dizdarevic of the Sarajevo daily *Oslobodenje*, Wang Juntao of China's *Economic Weekly*, the Rwandan editor André Sibomana, and Raul Rivero, founder of the independent Cuba Press news agency.

As well as publicizing censorship, RSF assists journalists in the field. In crises it has provided aid to media under threat, helping to keep papers such as *Oslobodenje* in print during the siege of Sarajevo and to relaunch the independent media in Rwanda after the genocide. In 1997 it was awarded the Organisation for Security and Cooperation in Europe's journalism prize for its work "for press freedom worldwide, and in particular during the war in Bosnia".

RSF's innovative work in Algeria, supported by Unesco, has been especially impressive. Between 1992 and 1994 it brought together journalists from the north and south of the country, to encourage professional solidarity by "twinning" newspapers. This idea was expanded in 1995 when links were established between the Algerian weekly *La Nation* and the French monthly *Le Monde diplomatique* and between the Algerian daily *El Watan* and the Swiss daily *Le Journal de Genève*. A year later, RSF arranged a conference in Madrid to encourage dialogue between journalists from opposite sides of the political divide in Algeria.

RSF's programme in 1995 provided material aid to *La Nation*, which had been economically weakened by the frequent seizure of issues. It also arranged for the editorial staff of the Algerian papers to spend time with their French counterparts. As a result of the programme two special issues of *La Nation* and *Le Monde diplomatique* were devoted to Algeria: one on human rights and the freedom of the press and another in commemoration of the assassination of the journalist Tahar Djaout. Copyright for the material published went to *La Nation*. Although *La Nation* has since ceased publishing as a newspaper, it is published on the Internet and RSF regularly reprints four articles from the electronic paper in its own "webzine".

Elsewhere RSF has provided practical help to journalists who are victims of repression, sending lawyers to represent defendants, paying legal costs, bail and medical costs, and assisting the families of those jailed and murdered. Recently it has publicized the plight of exiled journalists. It also supports those in danger in their own country and assists political exiles with entry to France, helping to secure *cartes de sejour* and visas.

RSF's concern for professional ethics also sets it apart. In 1990 it organized a seminar in response to the confused and contradictory international reporting of the Romanian revolution, publishing its findings in a book, *Roumanie: qui a menti?* (Romania: Who Lied?). It has held conferences on journalistic methods, professional standards, and relations with legal authorities. Since 1994 it has campaigned against hate speech in Rwanda, the former Yugoslavia, and the Caucasus, and in 1997 it debated the treatment of France's Front National and the extreme right in the media. Other recent areas of concern have been attempts to restrict press freedom on the internet (in the west as well as Asia and the Middle East) and the plight of journalists in Iran.

SARAH A. SMITH

Publications (selection)

La Lettre de RSF, monthly newsletter, 1989–
RSF Annual Report: Freedom of the Press throughout the World, annual report, 1989–
100 Photos pour defendré la liberté de la presse, annual publication, 1993–
Le Livre noir de l'Algérie, 1995
Rwanda: l'impasse? la liberté de la presse aprés de la genocide, 1995
Turquie: paroles interdits, 1995
Israel: Journalists in the Line of Fire, 1996

RHEINISCHE ZEITUNG/NEUE RHEINISCHE ZEITUNG
German newspaper, 1842–43, 1848–49

The *Rheinische Zeitung* was launched in Cologne on 1 January 1842 and suppressed by the Prussian Government on 17 March 1843. It was founded by progressive professionals and businessmen as a forum for liberal ideas, including the modernization and democratization of the government, constitutionalism, the advancement of personal liberties including trial by jury, freedom of religion (including civil equality for Jews), and freedom of the press. The conservative Protestant Government granted a licence to *Rheinische Zeitung* mostly because it provided competition to the influential Catholic newspaper, *Kölnische Zeitung*.

A week before the first issue was published, the Prussian cabinet promulgated a new censorship decree, which strengthened and expanded the relatively mild censorship law that had been in effect since 1819. Censors were instructed to suppress anything deemed critical to the "fundamental principles of religion" or "offensive to morality and good will". Censors were authorized to go beyond texts to surmise authors' intentions.

Throughout its short life, *Rheinische Zeitung* was heavily censored by the authorities and involved in fierce religious conflicts with its Catholic rival. Editors were subject to removal by authorities and none survived the pressure for long. The newspaper entered the annals of the history of censorship when in May 1842 it published a series of six articles on the debates over freedom of press in the Rhenish Landtag by a 24-year-old philosophy PhD. Permanently barred from an academic appointment by an intellectual censorship that purged anti-religious forces from German universities, the young Karl Marx turned to journalism. He made his journalistic debut with an essay entitled *Remarks on the Latest Prussian Censorship Instruction* that was censored by the authorities and was eventually published in Switzerland in an anthology edited by Arnold Ruge (*Anecdota on the Latest German Philosophy and Journalism*, 1843). To get his ideas past the censors, Marx changed the emphasis of the articles he submitted to *Rheinische Zeitung* from opposition to censorship *per se*, to an exploration of how the Berlin decree affected freedom of the press, the meaning of freedom, and the role of newspapers. Ruge described the articles as "without doubt the best work on freedom of the press written until now".

Before his Paris exile, Marx was not especially sympathetic to ideas that could be described as communist. His arguments for press freedom are Spinozian, even Jeffersonian. The sarcastic edge of his pen is pointed at "pseudo-Liberalism", not liberalism. Marx defines free expression as a natural right and claims that to oppose press freedom is to oppose freedom in general. He cites the American experiment as proof of his position: "You find the natural phenomenon of freedom of the press in North America in its purest and most natural form." Like the American revolutionaries, Marx conceives of the social role of the press as a peoples' watchdog: "And who is to censure the government except the people's press?" Under representative democracy, he maintains, the free press is the people's only protection against the emergence of a secret government within its parliament, court system, or administrative bureaucracy. He claims "the administration and the administered both need a third element, which is political without being bureaucratic . . . The complementary element, composed of a political head and civic heart, is a free press." Marx considers the free press to be at the cutting edge for enlightened ideas and argues that "the first freedom of the press consists in not being a trade". Although the journalist needs to make a living, the ethical practice of journalism must put the interests of freedom before the interests of shareholders.

Marx was appointed editor of *Rheinische Zeitung* when his college friend, Adolf Rutenberg, was forced out by pressure from the authorities. As editor, Marx made the paper a fiercely contentious critic of government as well as the relentless scourge of the cautious pieties of other newspapers. *Rheinische Zeitung* attracted considerable notice beyond Cologne, and the alarmed authorities in Berlin ordered the Cologne governor to instruct the publisher to submit the editor's name for approval. Marx responded that there was no provision in the law for such action and re-affirmed the paper's commitment to fearless criticism.

The paper was censored daily. In a letter to Ruge, Marx complained "We are burdened from morning to night with the most frightful censorship harassments, ministerial scribblings, gubernatorial complaints, Landtag accusations, shareholders' screamings, etc., etc." An article on tsarist military despotism produced what Marx describes as a "death sentence" for *Rheinische Zeitung*. Tsar Nicholas I wrote Frederick William IV a letter of protest. The King called his ministerial council into session and a royal order was issued suppressing the newspaper. The paper had nine weeks to cease publication, a delay intended to allow shareholders to try to recover their investments. In the interim the paper was subjected to double, then triple censorship. Marx resigned two weeks before the final issue appeared on 31 March 1843.

Marx left the country and joined the German exile community in Paris, where he studied economics. Expelled from Paris in 1845, he moved to Brussels. In collaboration with Friedrich

Engels, Marx completed the *Manifesto of the Communist Party* in January 1848. When revolutionary activity began in Germany later that year, Marx and Engels returned to Cologne to publish *Neue Rheinische Zeitung*. Unlike its namesake, *Neue Rheinische Zeitung* was a revolutionary paper committed to proletarian democracy. Troubles with the authorities began immediately. Engels was forced to leave Germany under threat of arrest, but continued his contributions to the paper from abroad. When revolution broke out in Cologne, the paper was suspended for two weeks under martial law. Shortly afterwards, Marx received a series of court summons: he was indicted for incitement to rebellion. The trial of Marx and his publisher took on a theatrical quality and drew capacity crowds. The jury found them not guilty. Three months later, however, Marx was expelled from Cologne by police order, and the *Neue Rheinische Zeitung* ceased publication. The last issue was printed in red ink on 11 May 1849 with an article by Marx that proclaimed

> We are ruthless, we demand no consideration from you. When our time comes, we will not gloss over our terrorism. But the royal terrorists, the terrorists by the Grace-of-God-and-of-Right, are brutal, contemptible, and vulgar in practice, cowardly, covert, and deceitful in theory, and dishonourable in both.

SUE CURRY JANSEN

Further Reading

Avineri, Shlomo, "Aspects of Freedom of Writing and Expression in Hegel and Marx", *Social Theory and Practice*, 4/3 (1977): 273–86

Berlin, Isaiah, *Karl Marx: His Life and Environment*, 2nd edition London and New York: Oxford University Press, 1948

Haye, Yves de la (editor), *Marx and Engels on the Means of Communication*, New York: International General, 1980

Jansen, Sue Curry, *Censorship: The Knot That Binds Power and Knowledge*, New York: Oxford University Press, 1988

McLellan, David, *Marx before Marxism*, New York: Harper and Row, and London: Macmillan, 1970

Marx, Karl, *On Freedom of the Press and Censorship*, translated and with an introduction by Saul K. Padover, New York: McGraw Hill, 1974 (Karl Marx Library, vol. 4)

Namier, Lewis, *1848: Revolution of the Intellectuals*, London: Oxford University Press, 1944

Padover, Saul K., *Karl Marx: An Intimate Biography*, New York: McGraw Hill, 1978

SAMUEL RICHARDSON
English novelist, 1689–1761

PAMELA
Novel, 1740

Through a fictional series of letters and journals, *Pamela; or, Virtue Rewarded* relates how the maidservant Pamela Andrews withstood the persistent advances of Squire B, the son of her late mistress, including virtual kidnap and several attempted rapes. Although in love with Mr B, Pamela remained chaste throughout her many ordeals and her virtue was rewarded by marriage when, despite her social inferiority, Mr B took her for his wife. The second part, published in 1742, described Mr B's continued reformation, Pamela's ideal marriage, despite Mr B's infidelity with Sally Godfrey, and offered Pamela's moral insights on a variety of subjects.

Pamela was an immediate and fashionable success, running to six editions by 1741, translated into the main European languages and inspiring many imitations and continuations. The novel's didactic morality won Richardson many admirers: it was recommended from a London pulpit and the villagers of Slough rang church bells when they read that Pamela had succeeded in reforming and marrying her would-be seducer. William Webster, whose praises Richardson included in the preface to the second edition, believed he had found in *Pamela* "all the *Soul* of Religion, Good-breeding, Discretion, Good-nature, Wit, Fancy, Fine Thought, and Morality".

And yet, four years after it was published, *Pamela* was placed on the *Index Librorum Prohibitorum* by pope Benedict XIV. Florian Schleck has pointed out that there was no mention of the English-language version of *Pamela* in an edition of the *Index* published in Rome in 1758. However, he noted that *Antipamela ou Memoires de M.D.* written by Claude Villaret in 1742 and an early French translation of *Pamela* were included in the Vatican's collection of "Editti" for the year 1745. These editions were still being cited in 1948. It was only when the *Index* was revised by Pope Leo XIII in 1900 that the English titles of *Pamela* and *Anti-Pamela* appeared. Although the Vatican process for banning books involved the submission of reports to consultative committees and committees of cardinals, the reasons for including *Pamela* are unknown. In conformity to the formulaic structure of the *Index*, *Pamela* was simply listed within a single alphabetical sequence.

In general terms, any book listed in the *Index* was believed to present a danger to faith or morals and it is likely that, as Bernard Kreissman has suggested, in the case of *Pamela*, "the surface lewdness of the novel" was the main reason for its inclusion rather than its subversion of social order by having a servant marry above her station. Charles Lamb, the 19th-century essayist and critic, imagined young men putting down the book "hastily with a deep blush" and Charles Povey in *Pamela Censured* (1741) referred to *Pamela*'s "warm scenes". Such critics responded to the highly charged eroticism of the rape scenes and were aware of Richardson's hypocrisy in writing prurient descriptions of attempted seduction while at the same time condemning such behaviour. For example, readers, in company with Mr B, become voyeurs as they watch Mrs Jervis and Pamela undress for bed or look at Pamela through the keyhole, outstretched on the floor, her gown ripped from the violence of her struggle to escape Mr B who had "by force kissed my neck and lips . . . [and] then put his hand in my bosom" (Letter XV). Kreissman, while accepting the sexual scenes were strong, nevertheless expresses surprise that *Pamela* deserved the extreme condemnation of being placed on the *Index* and another modern critic, Mark Kinkead-Weekes, has argued against the charge of prurience altogether in *Pamela*.

In addition to this perceived contradiction between the high moral purpose and the underlying gratuitous titillation were concerns that Pamela's innocence was feigned and calculated in order to buy her way into the upper classes. Thus, as the Danish dramatist Holberg noted in 1744, opinion on *Pamela* was divided into Pamelists and anti-Pamelists: "some look upon this young Virgin as an Example for Ladies to follow ... Others, on the contrary, discover in it, the Behaviour of an hypocritical, crafty Girl, in her Courtship; who understands the Art of bringing a Man to her Lure." The anonymous author of *Critical Remarks on Sir Charles Grandison, Clarissa and Pamela* (1754) echoed this view by describing Pamela as "a pert little minx whom any man of common sense or address might have had on his own terms in a week or a fortnight".

First among the many parodies and burlesques provoked by *Pamela* were Henry Fielding's *Shamela* (1741) and *Joseph Andrews* (1742). In *Shamela*, Fielding set out to prove that Richardson had confused virtue with the retention of virginity. Shamela's "vartue" exposed Pamela's virtue as based on nothing more than her good business sense of the negotiating value of her virginity. *Joseph Andrews* similarly began as a parody of *Pamela* but developed into a deeper study of the need for an active pursuit in everyday life of the Christian values of benevolence, tolerance, chastity, and charity. Pamela's brother Joseph, a footman in the service of Mr B's aunt, whose name Fielding expanded into Lady Booby, actively maintained his virtue against the advances of his widowed mistress.

The views of the anti-Pamelists have held sway for most of the 20th century: Shamela has been accepted as the true face of Pamela. However, critics such as Tassie Gwilliam are now defending Richardson and Pamela against charges of hypocrisy, arguing that attacks on both are echoes of similar attacks by Mr B and others in the novel, and that Richardson's concern in *Pamela* was to settle questions about the role of female duplicity in the 18th century and its relation to the complex interaction between appearance and reality, surface and depths. It is argued that Richardson explored differences between ideals of womanhood and woman as deceiver through the constant resurgence, and subsequent banishment, of charges of duplicity and hypocrisy throughout the novel.

By reclaiming Richardson in this manner, we may be inclined to agree with Richard Thornton, who commented in *English Authors Placed on the Roman Index* that "perhaps the oddest thing is the insertion of poor old Richardson's *Pamela*".

BARBARA WHITE

Writings

Pamela; or, Virtue Rewarded, 1740; *Pamela II*, 1741
Clarissa; or, The History of a Young Lady, 7 vols, 1747–48; augmented edition 1749, 1751
The History of Sir Charles Grandison, 7 vols, 1753–54
The Novels (Shakespeare Head edition), 18 vols, 1929–31

Further Reading

Gwilliam, Tassie, *Samuel Richardson's Fictions of Gender*, Stanford, California: Stanford University Press, 1993
Kinkead-Weekes, Mark, *Samuel Richardson: Dramatic Novelist*, London: Methuen, and Ithaca, New York: Cornell University Press, 1973
Kreissman, Bernard, *Pamela-Shamela: A Study of the Criticisms, Burlesques, Parodies, and Adaptations of Richardson's Pamela*, Lincoln: University of Nebraska Press, 1960
Schleck, Florian J., "Richardson on the Index", *Times Literary Supplement* (25 April 1935)
Thornton, Richard H., "English Authors Placed on the Roman 'Index' (1600–1750)", *Notes and Queries*, 11th series, 12 (1915)

YANNIS RITSOS
Greek poet, 1909–1991

Outside the old military prison in Navplion a marble column has been erected to commemorate those who were incarcerated there during the infamous dictatorship of the Colonels in Greece between 1967 and 1974. The column bears a four-line inscription by its most famous inmate, the Greek poet Yannis Ritsos, which in English translation reads: "May this place be sacred/to the memory of those who suffered,/who trod here barefoot on the snake of tyranny/and with their blood wrote its history."

Ritsos is one of the 20th century's great poets, but during much of his adult life he was at odds with successive Greek governments and, more seriously, dictatorships. His first experience of censorship as far as his own work was concerned occurred in 1936. In May that year workers in the tobacco industry in Thessalonica (Salonica) went on strike to protest at unfair wage restrictions. The police responded by opening fire on the unarmed strikers. Twelve were killed and many hundreds injured. The following day several newspapers carried a photograph of a mother, in black, weeping over her son's corpse as it lay in one of the city's streets. It was this image that prompted Ritsos's long elegiac poem, *Epitaphios* (Dirge), which, as Peter Bien has said, is "overtly political" and which is also a great poem of the people. (The *Epitaphios* is the lament sung in Greek Orthodox churches on Good Friday – Black Friday to the Greeks.) Ritsos uses the ballad form of 15-syllable couplets, "its verve engendered by weariness and hardship, its uncanny back-reaching into the racial and mythical past of a people continually invaded, cheated, and raped". Such ballads were also associated with protest against Turkish rule and often vowed vengeance. Hence, the mother's words: "My son, I'm off to join your comrades and add my wrath to theirs;/I've taken up your gun; sleep now, sleep, my son."

A few months after Ritsos's great poem was published the government of the day was overthrown and the Metaxas dictatorship established. Among general Metaxas's first acts was the public burning of books in front of the temple of Zeus in the centre of Athens. Naturally, *Epitaphios* was fed to the flames. From then on Ritsos was a marked man. A communist, he was unable to publish freely, first under Metaxas, then under the Nazis, then under the conditions of two civil wars and various post-war governments. The first civil war followed on the heels of Greece's liberation from Nazi control in 1944. The left, which had led the resistance to Hitler, was routed with the assistance of British arms. (One of the Yalta trade-offs was that Greece would not be allowed to become a communist state.) Out of Ritsos's bitter sense of the injustice suffered by the resistance fighters came his long poem *Romiosyni* (Greekness). Under the then prevailing conditions the poem could not be published, and in fact it saw the light of day for the first time only in 1954, after the second civil war had ended.

When the second civil war erupted in 1948 Ritsos was arrested and sent into detention on the island of Lemnos. From there he was transferred to Makronisos, where the officials used whatever physical and psychological means seemed to them appropriate to try to turn communists into good Greeks. Although at one point released because of ill-health, he was re-arrested in 1951 and served a further year's detention. During his four-year detention he went on composing poems which he famously buried in a bottle on Makronisos. Upon release he returned to Athens and produced a long poem called *Unsubjugated City*. He also wrote many shorter poems – he was astonishingly prolific – and during the 1950s the great Greek composer Mikis Theodorakis set to music both *Epitaphios* and *Romiosyni*; in the latter years of the same decade Ritsos became something of an international celebrity in socialist countries.

But trouble was never far away. In 1963 the parliamentary deputy Lambrakis was attacked by fascist thugs in the streets of Thessalonica. As he lay dying in hospital hundreds of students kept vigil and as they did so they sang Theodorakis's setting of the *Epitaphios*. The composer and poet both kept the vigil and were also in Athens when Lambrakis's funeral was held. Again the *Epitaphios* was sung, this time by thousands of mourners. Not surprisingly then, when the American-backed Colonels' junta took over Greece in 1967 Ritsos was promptly arrested, spent time in prison camps in Yiaros and Loros, and had his writings banned. International protest finally succeeded

in securing his release and he was even offered a passport to visit nations that wished to honour him. But the passport came with restrictions Ritsos would not accept. He chose to remain in Greece, living and working in Athens in the most modest of circumstances. After the Colonels were finally dismissed in 1974 Ritsos not surprisingly became openly venerated by many thousands of his countrymen and women, and when he died weeping crowds lined the streets of Greece's towns and villages to mourn the passing of a great poet and yet again sing Theodorakis's setting of Ritsos's most famous poem.

Whether it is his best is not so certain. A claim to supremacy can certainly be made for *The Fourth Dimension*. This series of linked soliloquies, at which Ritsos worked for some 20 years from the mid-1950s onwards, was published in Peter Green and Beverly Bardsley's superb English translation in 1993. *The Fourth Dimension* is, as the title suggests, about the interpenetration of time past, time present, past and present place; it is at once about the house of Atreus and the doings on the island of Makronisos, about the Athenian struggle for freedom against Xerxes' Persians and Hitler's stormtroopers. While it could only have been written by a very great poet, it is impossible to believe that *The Fourth Dimension* was not born out of Ritsos's first-hand experience of censorship and his embattled struggle to keep his spirit with the free.

JOHN LUCAS

Writings

Selected Poems, translated by Nikos Stangos, 1974
Exile and Return: Selected Poems, 1967–1974, translated by Edmund Keeley, 1985
Selected Poems, 1938–1988, edited and translated by Kimon Friar and Kostas Myrsiades, 1989
The Fourth Dimension, translated by Peter Green and Beverly Bardsley, 1993
Late into the Night: The Last Poems, translated by Martin McKinsey, 1995

Further Reading

Bien, Peter, *Three Generations of Greek Writers: Introductions to Cavafy, Kazantzakis, Ritsos*, Athens: Efstathiadis, 1983

GLAUBER ROCHA
Brazilian film director, 1939–1981

Described as "one of the great troublemakers of modern cinema" by the critic Serge Daney, Glauber Rocha was the creator and dominant force behind Brazil's Cinema Novo movement of the 1960s. At that time, half the population of the country was illiterate: "We realized that we were living in an undeveloped society, historically excluded from the modern world. We also realized that we must discover this reality more profoundly in order to find a way to emancipation." Profundity meant going beyond the political to the roots of violence in primitiveness and mysticism. Rocha's first feature-length film was *Barravento* (1962, The Storm), a study of exploited black fishermen in his native Bahia, who still practise an ancient sea-goddess cult, but whose faith is shaken when one of them takes

a more sceptical approach. The film was immediately banned, but was shown, to some acclaim, at foreign festivals.

Deus e o Diablo na Terra do Sol (Black God, White Devil) was released in 1964, just as the government of General Castello Branco had taken power after a military coup. Set in 1940, it portrays poverty and despair in the barren hinterlands of northeast Brazil. Having murdered his brutal master, the cowherd Manuel departs in search of the sea. The "black god" is a *beato*, who sacrifices children to make the ground fertile, and under whose influence Manuel falls. After the death of the *beato*, Manuel joins the "white devil", Corisco, a bandit who is also killed by Antônio dos Mortes, a bounty hunter who apparently stands for the view that people should seek freedom for themselves rather than have others do it for them. The new regime was much less willing to tolerate such provocation than had its predecessor. Rocha wrote:

> Copies of the film were promptly confiscated, and there were decisions and counter-decisions to have it burned or censored. However, as it was then at Cannes, being honoured by the Festival, the new regime ... had to pretend to accept it. Upon my return, I was followed by the Guanabara State Police, while articles and scornful reviews were written about me and my film.

Deus e o Diablo na Terra do Sol became the first part of "the trilogy of the earth", which presented a utopian and tormented vision of suffering in the developing world. One of Rocha's main theses, described in a manifesto called *The Aesthetic of Hunger*, was that hunger produces violence and that only popular mobilization can forestall social catastrophe. He was arrested, along with other intellectuals, during a protest against the regime in Rio de Janeiro. He and his comrades were released after an angry protest from European film directors, including Alain Resnais and François Truffaut. *Terra em Transe* (1966, Earth Entranced) is about the role of the artist in an unjust society. An intellectual leaves his life of privilege for radical politics, only to find that radicals are no closer to the masses than leftists in the elite. Rocha reported that the film was made semi-clandestinely, but that did not prevent visits by the police. Audiences were stunned, not only by its politics, but because of the dissonant appearance caused by Rocha's use of shock-montage, jump cuts, photographic distortion, an ironic use of sound, and film-within-film techniques. Rocha believed the film was more polemical than didactic and it was indeed even the subject of debate in the Senate and the Chamber of Deputies. Once again a ban was imposed; the Minister of Foreign Affairs also banned its exhibition at Cannes, but the film was smuggled out.

Antônio das Mortes (1969), the last of the trilogy, resurrects the bounty hunter of the first and explores similar themes. It too was banned in Brazil. Rocha was told that he would be imprisoned if he dared to protest. He then fled to Europe, where he was befriended by Jean-Luc Godard and other filmmakers, whose work influenced his oddly-titled *Der Leone Have sept cabeças* (The Lion Has Seven Heads, 1970), filmed in Brazzaville, Congo, and never released in Brazil. He also visited Cuba, where he directed the "Our America" film project. In 1978 his film *Cabeças Cortadas* (Severed Heads) was released by Brazil's Federal Censorship agency.

Rocha's last major film, *A Idade da Terra* (1980, The Age of the Earth), released after his return to Brazil, was in part inspired by Pasolini's *Gospel According to St Matthew*. Rocha's was a nonwhite Christ and this was, he believed, the main reason for its rejection by Italian critics, who were unable to accept that "my film says that Christ is African and not Roman". Once again, the film featured his trademark techniques, including juxtaposed images and stark visual effects. Eight years after his death in 1981, colleagues founded Tempo Glauber, a museum and film study centre in Rio de Janeiro.

ROBERT M. LEVINE

Films

Barravento, 1962
Deus e o Diablo na Terra do Sol, 1964
Terra em Transe, 1967
Antônio das Mortes, 1969

Further Reading:

Araújo, Vicente de Paula, *A bela época do cinema Brasileiro*, São Paulo: Perspectiva, 1976
Burns, E. Bradford, *Latin American Cinema: Film and History*, Los Angeles: UCLA Latin American Center, 1975
Hollyman, Burnes St Patrick, "Glauber Rocha and the Cinema Novo" (dissertation), Austin: University of Texas, 1977
Johnson, Randal, *Cinema Novo x 5: Masters of Contemporary Brazilian Film*, Austin: University of Texas Press, 1984
Johnson, Randal, *Culture and Power in Latin America*, Ann Arbor: University of Michigan Press, 1993
Johnson, Randal and Robert Stam (editors), *Brazilian Cinema*, 2nd edition New York: Columbia University Press, 1995
Levine, Robert M., *Brazilian Legacies*, Armonk, New York: Sharpe, 1997
Pick, Zuzana M., *The New Latin American Cinema: A Continental Project*, Austin: University of Texas Press, 1993
Sarno, Geraldo, *Glauber Rocha e o cinema latino-americano*, Rio de Janeiro, Centro Interdisciplinar, 1994

ROMANIA

Population: 22,438,000	**Illiteracy rate (%):** 1.0 (m); 2.8 (f)
Main religions: Romanian Orthodox; Roman Catholic; Protestant	**Number of daily newspapers:** 10
	Number of radio receivers per 1000 inhabitants: 319
Official language: Romanian	**Number of TV receivers per 1000 inhabitants:** 233
Other languages spoken: Hungarian; German	**Number of PCs per 1000 inhabitants:** 10.2

By the treaty of Trianon (1920), the territory of Romania (mostly formed by the union of Moldavia and Wallachia in 1861) was extended to include Transylvania, which had been at first an independent principality after the battle of Mohács (1529). The newly extended country was now home to peoples with different religious allegiances and cultural traditions: the populations of Moldavia and Wallachia were mostly Orthodox Christians; those of Transylvania were mostly Roman Catholic and Uniate, but there was also a Protestant minority. For clarity, this entry will discuss the history of censorship before 1920 in separate sections. The censorship of Hungarian literature in "Greater Romania" is covered in a further entry below.

Moldavia and Wallachia

These two chieftainships, which foreshadowed the future Romanian state, emerged in the 14th century, forming what was later known as the *Regat*, the Romanian kingdom. Moldavia also included Bessarabia and Bukovina. Among the chieftains, perhaps the most notorious was Vlad III of Wallachia, otherwise known as Vlad the Impaler, or "Dracula" (1431–76), a byword for cruelty and mass terror, who paid tribute to the Ottoman Turks soon after they had captured Constantinople in 1453. *Die Geschichte Drocole Waide*, published in 1488, is the "classical" account of religious fanaticism.

Both Moldavia and Wallachia owed allegiance to Orthodox Christianity, whose wholly traditional and restrictive attitude to new ideas is perhaps best epitomized in the words of patriarch Jeremias II of Constantinople in 1590:

> It is not the practice of our Church to innovate in any way whatsoever, whereas the Western Church innovates unceasingly … We do not dare to remove from the ancient books a single jot or title, as the saying goes. So we were taught and such is our purpose – to obey and to be subject to those who went before us.

Doubtless Orthodox leaders took account of the prototypical *Decretum Gelasianum* of 494 CE, which laid down which books Christians should or should not read, and which existed in several Slavonic–Byzantine versions. The only Romanian translation preserved in manuscript dates from 1667–69: *Cărtile ceale mincinoase pre care nu se cade a le tinea si a le citi drept credinciosii Hristiani* (The Untruthful Books, Which Christian Believers Ought Not to Keep and Read). The Orthodox hierarchy was particularly adamant that such "untruthful books" should not reach the hands of the laity.

Politically, Moldavia and Wallachia owed allegiance to the Turks for three centuries from around 1526. From 1711 to 1716 the Turks installed "phanariots", loyal to them, who kept order in these increasingly important buffer zones. The church, meanwhile, was allowed to order its own affairs. The metropolitan bishop in Wallachia could still censor books for most of the 18th century until M. Suţu, the ruler in 1785, laid down that he must be subordinate to the civil authorities – "nothing be printed … before notifying His Highness first". Suţu's successor, Alexandru Moruzi, was ready to allow that the publication of textbooks in "geography, physics, philosophy, and others of this kind" should be unrestricted; only "journals" and "books about the Turks" should be controlled. The church held on, however, citing its charter from 1749, when the phanariot had proclaimed, "without the will and the blessing of the metropolitan bishop, books could not be printed", and another from 1765, which had extended the episcopal monopoly to the circulation of books. At the end of the 18th century there were still texts that "anathematized" and "cursed" Roman Catholic and heretical books: "possessors of such books should expose them in order that all be gathered together and buried in the fire, lest those who read them should be led astray".

In July 1794, soon after the outbreak of the French Revolution, however, there appeared the first traces of a Romanian *samizdat*. Gherasim Adamovici, the Orthodox bishop of Sibiu (Transylvania), is said to have received some copies of a "Wallachian newspaper printed by someone named Paul Iorgovici in Vienna". It could spread "the dangerous ideas of freedom promoted by the French and would threaten to overthrow the public order". This was in any case a period of substantial political change for Wallachia and Moldavia. Russia seized Bessarabia in 1812, and encouraged further resistance to the Ottomans in the two territories. Both Russians and Turks installed *hospodars* (rulers) in place of the phanariots. On 3 November 1817 hospodar Ioan Caragea (Wallachia) granted Constantin Caracaş the right to set up the first secular printing house on Romanian territory. A brief liberal interval, marked by some separation of the powers of the church and civil authority, was now initiated. Church publications were still "under the blessing of the metropolitan bishop, but writings that have to do with the love of learning were now to be censored by the first counsellor".

Ten years later, at the end of the Russo-Turkish War (1828–29), censorship in the tsarist mode was introduced to Wallachia and Moldavia. The Commission for the Surveillance of Books (*Comisia de priveghere asupra cărtilor de cetit*) was established with power to approve, control, ban, or confiscate any type of publication. Such procedures as the following now became commonplace: the removal or alteration of titles, words, sentences, or whole passages; wholesale bans; blacklists; and – a pre-echo of Ceauşescu's Securitate – denunciation ("the Commission has discovered by roundabout ways …"). Any discussion of the idea of "independence" was notably taboo. Indeed, one of the main goals of censorship at this period was to isolate the Romanian principalities from the influence of western ideas; sealed book parcels from abroad were turned back by customs and all foreign newspapers were banned. Alecu Russo and three actors were sent away to a monastery to fast, pray, and repent after they had taken the liberty of staging the play *Pantry Administrator* in 1846.

Draconian the censorship may have been, but a tradition of resistance had been growing since the early years of the century. As early as 1804, tracts that terrified landowners, because they were inspired by recent events in France, were in circulation. In 1829 a Russian observer reported that there was a bookshop in Bucharest "in which I found many of the books banned in Russia". The Moldavian equerry Leonte Radu demanded explicitly in 1839 "the freedom of printing, of thought and writing, which should not be under censorship". The ground was thus to some extent prepared for 1848, and for "The Proclamation of Islaz", mostly written by I. Heliade Rădulescu, a putative Romanian constitution: "The Romanian people decrees freedom of printing, freedom of speech, freedom of association, in order to speak and write usefully, to show the truth. The freedom of printing can do no harm to anyone but the children of the dark." The revolutionary manifesto *Ce sunt meseriaşii* (Who are the Artisans?) demanded explicitly "the abolition of censorship".

In Moldavia, the revolution of 1848 was poorly planned and easily repressed, but strong seeds had been sown. V. Alecsandi's *In numele Moldovei, a omeniei şi a lui Dumnezeu* (In the Name of Moldavia, Decency, and God) demanded the lifting of censorship over all internal affairs and interests. "The wishes of the Moldavian National Party [*Dorinţele partidei nationale din Moldova*] states: 'Printing has always been free in Moldavia, and from now on there is no old or new law that can stop it or set limits to it' ".

By the end of 1848, however, it was "back to square one". Hospodar M. Sturza considered it his "duty to contain any tendency . . . to upheavals and anarchy" and compiled meticulous regulations for the compilation of blacklists and for police surveillance. The terminology of the modern police state was already in place in the "black book" and the "censor's stamp", to name only two familiar turns of phrase.

Some of censorship's timeless foolishness was also apparent in the reasons given for banning certain books. According to the Moldavian chief censor, Gh. Asachi, a certain play "ought to be banned, the more so because it has been translated by a woman". *Toderica* by Begruzzi was banned, not because it was dangerous, but because it was "a moralizing and worthless publication". Poems by A.I. Pelimon were said to contain "superficial lines". Actors were obliged not to introduce expurgated material or "seditious improvisations". It did not seem a propitious time for Prince Grigore Alexandru Ghica to declare the abolition of censorship in Moldavia on 12 May 1856 – and indeed, his successor, Teodor Bals, was quick to cancel the decree after Ghica stepped down the following month.

After the Crimean War (1853–56) the "powers" imposed a settlement by which Moldavia and Wallachia became two autonomous principalities with native rulers, under nominal Turkish overlordship. Nationalism had taken hold, however, and the notables of both principalities cleverly subverted "balkanization" by electing the same "prince", A.J. Cuza. Meanwhile, censorship continued, although the censor could no longer count on having the last word. C.D. Aricescu had originally been arrested in 1840 for some anti-Russian poems, and for "subversive" translations of J.P. Marat's *The Lamentations of Slavery* in 1859. In a distinctly modern kind of journalism, he produced a complete account of his trial (*Procesul si exilul mea la Snagov*, My Trial and Exile to Snagov). Then, when charged with "an apology for revolution", his *Oda la Grecia* (1863), he once again hit back with *Procesul meu pentru, Oda la Grecia* (1863, My Trial for *Ode to Greece*). B.P. Hașdeu was less fortunate. He was tried in 1863 for a licentious passage in his short play *Duduca Mamuca*, acquitted, but dismissed from his post as a history professor.

In 1861 the Union of Wallachia and Moldavia was proclaimed under the name of Romania. The constitution of 30 June 1866, modelled on the Belgian constitution of 1831, enshrined freedom of the press: "Neither censorship, nor any other measure preventing the printing, selling, or circulation of any publication can be re-introduced." Some hopes! The principle was continually challenged by conservatives, who demanded that "abuses" of press freedom be tried in the courts: "the licence of the press has become a real scandal in this country" (Iași Petition, 1871). The formal independence of Romania was declared in 1878, and in 1884 the legislative assembly changed the constitution so that it would be possible to try those who attacked the monarchy and other crowned heads in the civil courts; after writing *Omul periculos* (The Dangerous Man) against King Carol in April 1887, G. Panu was sentenced to two years' imprisonment and a fine of 5000 lei.

Censorship in early 20th-century Romania mirrored political developments, beginning with the uprising of 1907, after which the press was denounced as "anarchist". *România muncitoare* was confiscated and socialist publications denounced for "criminal tendencies". Romania allied itself with the forces opposing Germany and Austria–Hungary in World War I. All newspapers were made subject to the jurisdiction of military courts who could "censor the press and any publication [and] . . . block the release of any newspaper". After the war, the *Gazeta Bucureștilor* was tried for "high treason" and the demoralization of the Russian army at the front, because copies of the newspaper had been dropped into the trenches of Romanian troops; the defendants got sentences of between 10 and 15 years, but were freed within a year.

Transylvania

When the Turks destroyed the unified Hungarian state in 1526, Transylvania became a separate principality, subject to Ottoman tutelage, and remained so for two centuries. As in Wallachia and Moldavia, the church – in this case the Roman Catholic Church – was the prime mover in censorship. Transylvania was subject to the *Index Librorum Prohibitorum* of 1529, which listed heretical books that the faithful, however literate, were not permitted to read. The Jesuit College at Cluj maintained a secret store of such books that was accessible only to senior and trusted teachers – but the college itself was "censored" when Transylvania's Protestant prince, Sigismund Bathory, closed it down and dispersed its library in 1606; the *Index* was, of course, entirely disregarded by the relatively few Lutherans, Calvinists, and Unitarians.

Transylvania was incorporated into the Austrian dominions by the Treaty of Carlowitz (1699), and it is to Vienna that we must look for the next chapter in the history of censorship in the territory. With advancing secularization in the Habsburg empire, a more flexible – if, perhaps, more bureaucratic – system was put in place. Under Joseph II (reigned 1765–90) a raft of liberal measures was put in place – the emancipation of the serfs, the extension of religious toleration to the Uniate Church (which was strong in Transylvania), to the Orthodox (the allegiance of the Romanian minority), to Protestants, and to Jews. Censorship was centralized in the office of the Zensur-Hofkommission, and the number of banned titles reduced from 5000 to 900. Banned books were now placed in categories – pornographic literature, works with a superstitious content, anti-Christian writings, and, for the first time, politically dangerous works; but in the early years, only three or four new books a year were actually banned.

The new instructions were applied in Transylvania from June 1777 by the Commissio Regio Librorum Censoria. Liberal and secular in spirit, the Commission yet met under the presidency of the bishop, who was assisted by two assessors. They were mainly concerned to stem the progress of such Enlightenment writers as Montesquieu and Voltaire. Sixteen titles were purged from the Bathyaneum Library in Alba Iulia, and the first known purely "national" list of named books, the *Cathologus librorum prohibitorum*, had 38 titles listed in 1781. The word "censorship" was first used in 1791, when Gh. Șincai would have liked to have had a public debate with the Transylvanian Saxon scholar, I.C. Eder, who had attacked his *Supplex libellus Valachorum*, but "no one here will dare to publish it without the censorship of the government [*sine gubernii censura*]".

At the same time, the Uniate (Greek Catholic) Church carried out its own internal censorship, using the well-known formulae, *admittitur, imprimatur*, in cases of approval, and *erga schedam* for rejection; its competence ranged over all religious and domestic publications. The Uniates condemned works "infected by heresies" of the Calvinist churches, and took steps to ensure that Orthodox publications from Moldavia and Wallachia did not cross the border. By the end of the 18th century, it was common for the churches of Transylvania to censor each other on a reciprocal basis, entirely contrary to the spirit of Joseph II's Edict of Toleration of 1783.

Censorship in the 19th century is well documented and was in Transylvania well organized. It was operated through the printing office of the University of Buda, and had, by 1825, "royal censors in all the languages". The Romanian censor was extremely vigilant, even erasing from a text of 1845 a reference to "the honest office of censorship". Yet "the inhabitants of Buda know little about Transylvania and they care little about it; they allow the publication of such things that for Transylvanians are the venom of rebellion". Gh. Şincai came regularly to Buda's attention. As long ago as 1780, he had wanted to append a "dialogue" to his grammar *Elementa lingue Daco-Romanae sive valachicae*, "but the censorship at the emperor's court at Vienna did not allow me to". In 1812 he subjected his *Hronica Românilor* (The Chronicle of the Romanians) to considerable self-censorship (his introduction makes it clear that the book was not "the way I would like it to be"). An abridged edition was allowed, but was severely attacked by Joseph Mártonfi, bishop and censor, who alleged that it was "inept, ridiculous, full of false opinions, of bizarre conjectures".

Clearly books on "national" (i.e. Romanian *avant la lettre*) topics were specially vulnerable. The treatment of Petru Maior's *Istoria pentru începutul Romanilor în Dacia* (The History of the Beginnings of the Romanians in Dacia) is a good example. The Uniate bishop Ioan Bob complained that it had been printed with "I do not know whose approval". Four pages of the book would "disturb public order" and should be torn out from all copies. Printing of Maior's *Istoria Besericii Românilor* (The History of the Romanian Church) was stopped at page 192 – Ioan Bob having ordered that the remaining pages should be "erased, pure and simple". In the official investigation that followed, another Uniate bishop, S. Vulcan, was appointed arbitrator. He declared that "this work, thus cleansed and improved" could be put into circulation again, but urged Maior to apologize for the offending pages – and Maior complied. (A poacher-turned-gamekeeper, Maior himself censored a Lexicon by V. Colosi in 1819).

As was made clear in the above account of censorship in Wallachia and Moldavia, much of the rush for a Romanian identity and nation came from the Romanians of Transylvania, anxious to cast off the yoke of the Habsburgs and the dominance of the Hungarians. The idea of press freedom was regarded as a weapon in the service of these ideals. "Freedom" and "national emancipation" were always coupled together in the writings of Gh. Bariţiu, the most important journalist of the age, author of *Tiparul nostru român din punt politic* (1864, Our Romanian Printing Press from a Political Point of View), published just three years after the union of Wallachia and Moldavia had been achieved. His assertion that the press needed "an air of freedom and not a stifling air" was no doubt influenced by the Transylvanian record: *Espatriatul* (The Expatriate) was burned by the Austrians in 1848; *Gazeta Transilvaniei* (The Transylvanian Review) and *Foaie pentru minte, inimă, si literatură* (Review for the Mind, Heart and Literature) were obstructed, subjected to enquiries, and banned, and the editor charged with "obstinancy".

Censorship in Transylvania became no less repressive as the century wore on: a whole series of political trials are on the record – Georghe Bariţiu (1877), V. Lucaciu (1887), Ioan Slavici, imprisoned for a year (1888–89), and Aurel Mureşianu, sentenced for a "subversive article" in 1895. During the years 1893–1903, Romanian journalists served, between them, 17 years in jail and paid fines totalling 40,000 crowns. Early 20th-century Transylvania presented a scene of relentless censorship which continued until the creation of "Greater Romania" in the 1920s: the control of Romanian schools; the confiscation of publications that had originated in Bucharest; the strict surveillance of literary and cultural personalities from Romania, and of foreign scholars interested in Romanian language and literature; the banning of certain newspapers – all these were part of the landscape of the period. "Bardea" Gheorghe Cârţan specialized in the collection of Romanian books and journals, and regularly managed to get them through customs by using false covers and pages with altered titles; the exasperated authorities finally managed to confiscate the entire supply, comprising 4850 titles, which they listed meticulously and burned in 1907. In 1912 the Romanian consul in Budapest sought clarification of which Romanian publications were banned in Transylvania; a list of 230 titles was produced.

Romania since 1920

The Romanian state was rewarded for its World War I activities by the incorporation of Transylvania in 1920. It lost most of this territory during World War II, because Germany regarded its commitment as lukewarm. After the war, Bessarabia became Moldova, a Soviet Republic, which has voted to refuse overtures to rejoin Romania since the fall of communism. Much of Transylvania was returned in 1945.

The constitution of 1923 guaranteed "to all the right to communicate and publish their ideas and opinions by way of speech, writing, the press, everybody being responsible for the abuse of these liberties in cases defined by the Penal Code, which can by no means restrict the right in itself". But, almost immediately, the *Legea liniştii publice* (Law of Public Order) of 1924 dissolved the Romanian Communist Party, and suppressed all its publications. In 1927 the Legion of the Archangel Michael was formed. Also known as the Iron Guard, this organization grew into a Romanian form of fascism, deeply obscurantist and anti-Semitic. This was part of the background to the law of 1930 "for keeping public order and guarding the good name of the country" (known as "the law against alarmism"), which amounted to a re-introduction of some form of censorship. And, indeed, between 1933 and 1989, it was "downhill all the way" so far as censorship in Romania was concerned: first royalist, then fascist, and finally communist regimes exercised a near-total control of literature, the arts, and the media.

The regression began with the assassination of the prime minister, I.G. Duca, by members of the Iron Guard in December 1933 – just as, on the other side of Europe, Hitler's Nazi regime had come to power. Censorship was immediately re-introduced, and two far-right publications, *Calendarul* and *Cuvîtul*, were suspended. The writer and historian of religion Mircea Eliade, then associated with the right, complained that one of his articles had been "terribly mangled by censorship". The leftist press had already aroused official fear after its support of the strikes of February 1933. Violent attacks on them and the rest of the democratic press followed. *Adevǎrul* and *Dimineaţa*, daily papers, were burned in the street, their distribution stopped, and their editors molested. By 1936, on the verge of bankruptcy, they were forced to sell before being forcibly closed down by the rightist Goga-Cuza government of 1937.

The regimes of the Iron Guard and of general Antonescu were even more radical. The Ministry of Propaganda established a "department of the normative", whose role was to elaborate official communiques which the press was obliged to print. The royal dictatorship (king Carol II) introduced a new constitution on 10 February 1938, which banned "the exhortation of people by way of the spoken word or by wanting to change the form of government" – a provision that effectively cancelled out others that allowed press freedom. Looking back in 1946, Tudor Arghezi could say: "The pen was watched closely by a ministry, a censorship, and seven police departments, one of which, the secret service, would send to the press . . . [both] appreciations of the degree of conformism [required] as well as threats [for non-compliance]". It should also be noted that during World War II Jewish Romanians were subject to systematic discrimination and pogroms.

Nothing could compete, however, with the twists and turns, the extreme bureaucratization, the blind mistaking of the ideal for the real, that characterized Romania's very distinctive communist censorship between 1944 and 1989. The process began during the regime of Soviet occupation from 23 August 1944. Article 16 of the Truce Convention (12 September 1944) imposed general censorship, and a decree of 27 September prohibited any publication from the hands of those who had propagated fascist ideas. The censorship service was placed under the control of the Council of Ministers, who, over the next few years, instituted a barrage of further prohibitions. Noting the "refusal" of printers to touch the newspapers of the National Liberal Party, or the National Peasant Party, the Soviet authorities banned *Dreptatea* and *Viitorul* on 1 March 1945. On 2 May a law enjoined "the immediate withdrawal from circulation of all periodicals or other publications of a fascist Hitlerite nature". A law of 5 March 1946 changed the name of the Ministry of Propaganda to the Ministry of Information, whose task was to "direct, organize, and control all the activities of information through the press, radio, films, etc".

All was thus set for the coming of the communist regime in 1947. The constitutional framework was imposed in 1948, and amended in 1952 and 1965. It was administered successively by the Socialist Committee for Culture and the Arts (1952), the Department of the Press and Printed Matter (1964), and, finally, by the infamous Council for Culture and Socialist Education (1971). All of this was justified, ideologically, by the fight against "iron guardist, racist, chauvinistic" ideas, by the need for class struggle, and by the opposition of the Romanian regime to "bourgeois literature" and materials that were "anti-democratic, anti-Marxist, or hostile to peace".

Censorship was often retrospective: the communists set out to destroy work already in existence. A directive of 1945 stipulated that the Cluj-Sibiu University should "destroy all the materials and documents that can do harm to our good rela-

tions with the allied powers" (for instance, paintings, photography, and books). Public libraries elsewhere were instructed to withdraw from their shelves any data that "even if they are not state secrets, are not meant for publication" – a typically communist conspiratorial mentality. The first general list of banned publications (May 1945) was a relatively modest one, but, by 1 June 1946, the list had expanded to 2000 titles, and, a year later, with the indigenous communists firmly in place under Gh. Gheorghiu-Dej, the list had expanded to 8000 titles. By 1950–55, not only "chauvinistic, anti-Marxist" titles were targeted, but popular literature as well.

All the communist regimes of central and eastern Europe were subject to zigzags in policy, according to the political temperature. Arguably, Romania was the most quirkish, especially under Nicolae Ceauşescu. Lists of publications that "correspond no longer to the present circumstances" were prepared. Thus the name of Joseph Stalin was withdrawn from circulation under the influence of Khrushchev's speech to the 20th Congress of the Soviet Communist Party. But Ceauşescu soon also removed the name of his predecessor, Gheorghiu-Dej, and Khrushchev himself no longer "corresponded" after 1965. Ceauşescu then set out to be "independent" of the USSR and instituted, during the 1960s, what appeared to be a more "relaxed" policy, when, according to Paul Goma, "writers could at least negotiate with the censorship". It was possible, for a few short years, for such internationally known and respected poets as Marin Sorescu and Ana Blandiana to emerge.

Then, in 1968, Ceauşescu visited China, and came back with a new determination to build a distinctively Romanian communism. Censorship was considerably intensified, its bureaucracy extended, and up to six "filters" installed to ensure that no dissident ideas could reach the light of day. These included, according to Matei Călinescu, "pre-reading", "reading", and "post-reading committees", described by Goma as "a truly farcical labyrinth". Under the "New Press Law" of 1974, the Romanian press was called upon to "fight without cease for the implementation of the Romanian Communist Party policy, of the lofty principles of socialist ethics and equity, unabatedly to promote progress and progressive ideas in all fields of life and of social activity".

The "Party Programme" of July 1974 proclaimed: "Literature and Art are not the creation of chosen individuals who are above daily life . . . but the fruit of the creative forces of society, the expression of the genius and sensitivity of the people itself." Now "editorial control" was to prepare "general and unified projects . . . to be submitted for approval to the Commission on Socialist Culture and Education", which was entitled to "make periodical proposals in the light of current needs, concerning the inclusion of certain books in – or their exclusion from – already approved plans". A further bizarre justification for press control was also adumbrated in 1974 – "economizing paper consumption": this meant reducing the number of pages and copies printed as well as restricting the size and frequency of appearance of some newspapers and reviews. *Contemporanul*, a cultural weekly, was turned into "a political review whose main goal is to work for the mass propagation of Marxism-Leninism and our Party's doctrine of dialectical materialism"; book, theatre, and film reviews were dropped.

Then, at the end of the 1970s, censorship was "abolished", generally reckoned to be an entirely cynical move. At one level, the party was "sure" that after three decades of totalitarian rule people were conditioned to be self-censors, checking everything they wrote against everything they had imbibed; mutual surveillance could replace professional censors. At the same time, however, it was clear that the party had by no means such a high opinion of human nature; left to police themselves, people would beg for a return to the old system, where at least you knew where you were. And indeed it was not long before "corrective measures", in keeping with the last and most terrible decade of Romanian communism, were instituted. Norman Manea writes:

> Under the Council for Socialist Culture and Education – and its new Reading Service – censorship was "strengthened" by a great variety of intermediary measures. Censorship doubled, tripled, diversified, while the "purification" of texts took on new and ever more duplicitous methods.

Manea's own tortuous path to the publication of *The Black Envelope* is described in an entry devoted to that novel, and in "Censor's Report", as an essay in his volume *On Clowns: The Dictator and the Artist* (1992).

Practically all Romanian writers passed through censorship of one kind or another during the 45 years of communist rule. The following is an examination of its particular forms. A number of typical situations are arranged in rank order, depending on the interventions and punitive measures taken:

1. The most common situation involved the removal of a passage, of one or two poems, a chapter, a title. This was partial, almost benign censorship: the title of an essay on I.L. Cavagiale, by the playwright Mircea Iorgulescu, was changed from *The Big Chatter* to the harmless *Essay on Caragiale's World* (1988). Everything depended, in such circumstances, on the courage of the editors of reviews and publishing houses, who stood up for the authors.

2. Texts were "rejected", or withdrawn from circulation after publication because they contained material that had escaped the censor's vigilance. There are numerous examples: novels by V. Tănase, such as *Inchide ochii şi vedea orasul* (Close Your Eyes and You Will See the City), banned in 1950, were published only in 1970; *Sub zodia proletcultismului* (Under the Sign of the Prolecult), a literary history by M. Niţescu, submitted to the publisher in 1979, appeared only in 1995.

3. Bans on books were accompanied by "show trials" or public "unmasking" – for example, *Viata pe un peron* (Life on a Platform) by Octavian Paler in 1988.

4. All Romanian writers living abroad were automatically censored, however renowned: Eugene Ionesco, Emil Cioran, Mircea Eliade. Eliade's case is the most interesting. *La ţiganci şi alte povestiri* (With the Gypsies and Other Stories) got a Romanian publication with some difficulty in 1969. In 1981, astonishingly, his *History of Religious Belief and Ideas* was published in this "atheist" country – but was obtainable only through the party's "special channels".

5. Once a "dangerous" text had been published, the author could have his entire work banned. This happened to Ana Blandiana, whose poem *Arpagic* was a direct challenge to Ceauşescu; also to Adrian Păunescu, whose collection of poems published in the monthly *Familia* (1988) contained one

addressed directly to the *Analfabeti* (The Illiterate, apparatchiks).

6. Writers who published abroad had the rest of their work banned. The most notorious case was that of Paul Goma, whose *Ostinato* was published first in German and then in French. Similarly, there was Bujor Nedelcovici, whose *Le Second Messager* (1985) was an anti-totalitarian utopia. Constantin Dumitrescu, the author of the first systematic ideological criticism of the Ceauşescu regime, sent *La Cité Totale* to the Paris publishing house Seuil in 1980. By contrast, Petru Dumitriu, 20 years earlier, could publish his novel *Incognito* only by leaving the country secretly and abandoning his small child.

What of resistance? Norman Manea has said that the "reproach of passivity" was only partly justified:

> One shouldn't forget that in no other European Socialist country has surveillance been as tight and repression as severe . . . for years the whole nation was exposed to the repressive monotony of primitive, demagogic, cynical Party jargon, and to quick repression by the Securitate. Could that be why even the most virulent protests had an improvisatory, rhetorical character?

In 1973 A.E. Baconsby staged a protest in front of Ceauşescu against "inner censorship" – although formally he was constrained to accept the practice. In February 1988 M. Niţescu addressed petitions to the Writers' Union, the editor-in-chief, and Ceauşescu himself. Volume 1 of *Dictionarul sciitorilor români: Piese pentru o istorie a cenzurii* (1995, Dictionary of Romanian Writers: Specimens for a History of Censorship) comprises reports, notes, counter-reports, letters, addresses, and petitions made to the central authorities. Other episodes were linked with *Opinia studentească* and *Dialog*, the Iasi students' combative reviews, whose editors (A. Calinescu, Sorin Antohi, and Liviu Antonescu) were forced to step down.

I myself, as actor and spectator of this period, experienced all the situations described above: banned completely, deprived of the "right to sign" my works for two decades, my texts mangled, whole chapters deleted. I "ignored" censorship by publishing texts abroad without presenting them for approval or by contributing, under a pseudonym, to Radio Free Europe.

The path to a free society has not run entirely smoothly since Ceauşescu's downfall in 1989. The habit of censorship was hard to break. It was necessary for journalists to go on strike in 1990, in protest against the refusal of local presses to print articles critical of the National Salvation Front (NSF). The NSF blocked attempts to publish mass circulation papers; in a rather chilling echo of the above-mentioned measure to save paper, the officially inspired shortage of equipment could result in a print run of 600,000 taking 12 hours. An offer by the World Union of Free Romanians to set up a radio and television station for independent political parties, trade unions, and humanitarian bodies was said to have been refused by president Iliescu on the grounds that, if they had equipment, they could offer it to Romanian radio and television. *Romaniâ Librera* claimed that the NSF had obstructed the establishment of an independent news agency. The Group for Social Dialogue reported that vendors of their paper were beaten up by police, and were refused permission to set up kiosks.

The constitution of 21 November 1991 stipulates that "freedom of expression of thoughts, opinions, or beliefs and freedom of other means of communication in public are inviolable". It even states that "any censorship shall be suppressed". Yet Emanuel Valeriu, director of Romanian Radio and Television, could reiterate the old prohibition against slandering the nation: "People cannot say what they like. That is, they should be prevented from saying things that are offensive, vulgar, or provocative. Nothing against the state is permitted because the state is the people". It was proposed in 1993 that the criminal code be amended to allow for journalists who printed "insults and calumnies" or damaged "the reputation of a public official, or published false information that might damage state security" to be sentenced to two years in prison. In 1995 *Ziua* was charged with "defaming state authority" for publishing allegations that president Iliescu had been a KGB agent.

On the positive side, the resurgence of theatre, which began towards the end of the Ceauşescu period, and had often employed covert political messages, has continued. The director Silviu Purcărete staged *Decameron 645* in 1993. The theatre critic Marian Popescu wrote of its significance as an emblem of the end of censorship:

> Its wonderful theatre language, based on the mysterious secret of the human body, revealing the ambivalent nature of the human being, the joy of living, but also the inexorable path of fear and death, *Decameron 645* was one of the first post-1989 productions that dared to present naked actors to an audience accustomed, through 45 years of propaganda and censorship, to the human body as a kind of statistic. Love, sex, or abortion were prohibited entries in a never-published dictionary. The beauty of the production was not just sexuality, of which there was plenty, but the lonely mystery of being a man or woman created by God, but destined to find their own way out of the labyrinth.

ADRIAN MARINO

Further Reading

Bailey, Paul, "The Romanian Revolution That Never Was", *The Guardian* (18 December 1993)

Blandiana, Ana *et al.*, *Amintiri despre cenzura* (Remembrances on Censorship), *Agora*, 5 (1992): 22–47

Costea, Ionut *et al.*, *Fond Secret, Fond "S" special: (Secret Stok, Stok "S" Special)*, Cluj Napoca: Dacia, 1995

Deletant, Dennis, *Ceauşescu and the Securitate: Coercion and Dissent in Romania, 1965–1989*, London: Hurst, and Armonk, New York: Sharpe, 1989

Documente privitoare la cenzura in Muntenia, 1832–1833 (Documents about Censorship in Valachia, 1832–1833), *Arhivele Olteniei*, 8 (1929): 67–78

Jako, Klára, "History of the Library of Báthory University in Kolosvár/Cluj from 1579 to 1607", *Philobiblion* 1/1 (1996): 63–89

Manea, Norman, *On Clowns: The Dictator and the Artist*, New York: Grove Weidenfeld, and London: Faber, 1992

Marza, Iacob, "Une Liste de livres interdits en Transylvanie, second moitié du XVIIIe siècle", *Revue des études sud-est européennes*, 20/2 (1983): 177–81

Oprea, Marius, *Plimbare pe ulita tipografiei* (Trip on Printing House Street), Bucharest: Fundatiei Culturale Române, 1996

Rosetti, Radu, *Despre cenzura în Moldova* (About Censorship in Moldavia), *Analele Academiei Române*, 2/29 (1906–1907): 429–531; 4/30 (1907–1908): 1–109

Sashegyi, Oskár, *Zensur und Geistesfreiheit unter Josef II: Beitrag zur Kulturgeschichte der Habsburgischen Länder*, Budapest: Akademíai Kiadó, 1958

Siupiur, Elena, "Quelques documents militaires autrichiens relatifs á la fondation de la typographie grecque de Iassy (1812)", *Revue des études sud-est européennes*, 15/3 (1977): 509–14

Stan, Apostol, *Putere politica şi democraţie în România: 1859–1918* (Political Power and Democracy in Romania), Bucharest: Albatros, 1995

Stan, Apostol and Mircea Iosa, *Liberalismul politic în Romania: De la origini pânâ la 1918* (Political Liberalism in Romania: From the Beginnings to 1918), Bucharest: Enciclopedica, 1996

Vianu, Lidia, *Censorship in Romania*, Budapest: Central Europe University Press, 1998

Zaciu, Mircea *et al.*, *Dictionarul scriitorilor români* (Dictionary of Romanian Writers: Specimens for a History of Censorship), Bucharest: Fundaţiei Culturale Române, 1995

ROMANIA: Religion

When the communists took over Romania, the country was, though 23 per cent illiterate, deeply religious, with the most flourishing Orthodox Church in eastern Europe as well as substantial, influential, and efficient Hungarian and German minority Roman Catholic and Protestant churches. Although the communists provided legal recognition and minimum basic facilities for 14 denominations, they punished believers who tried to circumvent restrictions. After 1974, circulation of the Bible or other unauthorized literature was put in the same category as pornography; possession was made a punishable offence, for which dozens of believers, mainly from the expanding new Protestant churches, were sentenced.

The Orthodox press, three centuries old, was relatively favoured. The range and quality of its translations, theology, and spirituality was unparalleled in communist countries, but editions were limited with many copies sent to ecclesiastics abroad. Much of this ample scholastic press, as the Belgian scholar Olivier Gillet demonstrates, provided a model of self-censorship and pro-regime polemics and propaganda as authors distorted biblical and patristic theology to suit, in turn, Soviet foreign policy and the promotion of national ethnicity of the *neumul romanesc* (Romanian nation). They resorted to devious manoeuvres and dialectic to demonstrate the conformity of ecclesiastical canons to state laws, and subordination of the individual to the collective, consequently condemning all opposition to state and nation as against the laws of God and the church. Nine journals with a circulation of 30,000 had to suffice for 19 million believers including 9500 priests. The Bible of 1944 was reprinted several times in editions of up to 100,000, and the Department of Cults claimed to have imported around a million, some of them for other churches. If true, it rationed them stringently. How many reached their true destination is an interesting question. In 1972 and 1981 the World Reformed Alliance donated 200,000 Hungarian Bibles, of which only 200 copies actually reached any churches. The rest, according to papermill workers, were recycled as toilet paper, some of which was produced as evidence to challenge Romania's Most Favoured Nation Status in the US. As a disincentive, Bibles were made expensive and distributed by parish priests who had to reveal the identity of each recipient to officials. This could lead to harassment or discrimination.

The second largest church, the Roman Catholic, was denied a press because it rejected the Charter of 1948 that would have severed it from Rome; it was also largely Hungarian. As pressures to assimilate Hungarians and Germans escalated in the 1970s both their local language presses and imports were drastically reduced. The Department of Cults routinely scrutinized all circulars including those from abroad. The Hungarian diocese, Alba Iulia, with 450,000 members, was refused prayerbooks or catechisms until 1976 and even then was rationed to 3000. Although some Magyar and German Bibles were imported in 1980, complete Bibles for the growing Romanian Catholic minority were unobtainable.

Eight Seventh Day Adventists were arrested in 1979 for using state presses to print 14 titles of 10,000 copies, but regular *samizdat* of any kind barely existed. In the Hungarian cultural *Ellenpontok* (Counterpoints), which began in 1981, the Reformed priests László Tőkés (anonymously) and János Molnar contributed articles criticizing state control of churches. Molnar was tortured and imprisoned during the clampdown of 1983. Tőkés, photographed by the Securitate handing over an article, became one of their prime targets, suffering years of threats and harassment. From 1983 the police registered and scrutinized all private typewriters twice a year.

Most recognized churches had a regular magazine, but editors had to exercise self-censorship and it was obligatory to include sycophantic adulation of Ceauşescu. In 1989 a Catholic priest, Lucian Farcas, told the writer that Catholics had no journal because their bishops refused to do this; the faithful approved!

In 1948 the government banned the Bible-centred evangelical wing of the Orthodox Church, Oastea Domnului (Lord's Army), and brutally forced the Eastern Rite Catholic church (The Uniates) into "union" with the Orthodox Church. A nucleus of both churches survived clandestinely. Oastea Domnului cooperated with Evangelicals to obtain Bibles from abroad; for instance in 1981 two Oastea Domnului sisters were among 11 activists sentenced to six years for smuggling 600,000 Bibles. In 1982 its leader, the 75-year-old Traian Dorz, was imprisoned for two years for importing copies of a children's hymnbook that he himself had composed.

Protests demanding a free press and against Department of Cults censorship were circulated and smuggled abroad by courageous groups representing clergy and rank-and-file members of several confessions. The most comprehensive was the "Programme" of 1978 for a "free church in a free state", signed by the Romanian Christian Committee for the Defence of Believers' Rights (ALRC), mostly Evangelicals including the indefatigable Baptist pastor Pavel Nicolescu, but concerned with all denominations. They asked for regular publication of sufficient journals to meet public demand, and that these should contain reports of cases of persecution including that of people receiving religious news from abroad. Other demands were for the right for all confessions to own printing presses and duplicators; the right to disseminate and sell literature in several languages through bookshops and churches; the right to advertise religious events; and access to the media. Protests did not originate from church leaders, almost all of whom obeyed orders from the authorities – they had little choice to do otherwise – in suppressing just appeals and disciplining, often sacking, dissident clergy, such as the Orthodox priest Stefan Gavrila, author of the first *samizdat* letter, and five priests who wrote a "Testimony of Faith" in 1981. The demolition of 89 Bucharest churches and the threat of more in the late 1980s aroused many priests and intellectuals to belated dissent.

Thousands, mainly Evangelicals, were involved in the clandestine distribution of literature, prepared to risk arrest, fines, torture, interrogations, prison, internment in psychiatric hospital (as for instance in the case of Nestor Popescu, a Baptist film editor and novelist), and even contrived accidents, and death at the hands of the Securitate.

The most redoubtable Orthodox dissident priest until his expulsion in 1985, Gheorghe Calciu-Dumitreasa, was associated with the Evangelical appeal, the Lord's Army, and the Free Trade Union movement. He was sentenced to 10 years in 1978 for exposing the evils of totalitarianism and the oppression of religion in a series of Lent sermons for young people to packed congregations. An academic, Doina Cornea, an Eastern Rite Catholic, sacked for teaching the writings of Mircea Eliade, was almost a lone voice from 1982, combining dissent on political and religious grounds. In numerous letters to Radio Free Europe and pope John Paul II she urged the necessity of moral and spiritual regeneration. She faced death-threats to become the conscience of her nation when Ceauşescu threatened to obliterate 6000 villages. Support for Tokes, an outspoken champion of his church and national minority, sparked off the Revolution of 1989.

JANICE BROUN

Further Reading

Beeson, Trevor, *Discretion and Valour: Religious Conditions in Russia and Eastern Europe*, London: Fontana, 1974; revised edition, London: Collins, and Philadelphia: Fortress Press, 1982

Broun, Janice, "The Latin Rite Roman Catholic Church of Romania", *Religion in Communist Lands*, 12/2 (1984)

Broun, Janice and Grazyna Sikorska, *Conscience and Captivity: Religion in Eastern Europe*, Washington, DC: Ethics and Public Policy Center, 1988

Broun, Janice, *Romania: Religion in a Hardline State*, Washington, DC: Puebla Institute, 1989

Curry, Jane Leftwich (editor), *Dissent in Eastern Europe*, New York: Praeger, 1983

Deletant, Dennis, *Ceauşescu and the Securitate: Coercion and Dissent in Romania, 1965-1989*, London: Hurst, 1995

Deletant, Dennis, *Communist Terror in Romania: Gheorghiu-Dej and the Police State, 1948-1965*, London: Hurst, 1999

Gillet, Olivier, *Religion et nationalisme: l'idéologie de l'église orthodoxe roumaine sous le régime communiste*, Brussels: Éditions de l'Université de Bruxelles, 1997

Grossu, Sergiu, *La Calvaire de la Roumanie Chrétienne*, Paris: France-Empire, 1987

Ramet, Pedro (editor), *Eastern Christianity and Politics in the Twentieth Century*, Durham, North Carolina: Duke University Press, 1988

Ramet, Pedro (editor), *Catholicism and Politics in Communist Societies*, Durham, North Carolina: Duke University Press, 1990

Ramet, Sabrina Petra (editor), *Protestantism and Politics in Eastern Europe and Russia: The Communist and Postcommunist Eras*, Durham, North Carolina: Duke University Press, 1992

Romanian Christian Committee for the Defence of Believers' Rights, "Truths Which Cannot be Forgotten: ALRC, 1981", *Religion in Communist Lands*, 10/2 (Autumn 1982): 218–26

Scarfe, Alan, "Romanian Baptist Congress", *Religion in Communist Lands*, 5/2 (Summer 1977): 94–104 (includes documents)

Scarfe, Alan, "Dismantling a Human Rights Movement: A Romanian Solution", *Religion in Communist Lands*, 7/3 (Autumn 1979):166–77, (includes ALRC's Programme of Demands, 1978)

Skilling, H. Gordon, *Samizdat and an Independent Society in Central and Eastern Europe*, Basingstoke: Macmillan, and Columbus: Ohio State University Press, 1989

ROMANIA: Hungarian Literature in Romania

The Decree of Alba Iulia of 1919, which was issued after Transylvania's incorporation into the Greater Kingdom of Romania, promised "complete freedom for all the co-dwelling nationalities . . . [and] representation in the government according to their numerical proportion among the country's population". These promises were broken almost as soon as they were made. The Romanian state used all possible means to promote the use of Romanian and to suppress Hungarian (although in Transylvania more than 30 per cent of the population was Hungarian); while in theory there were Hungarian sections in Romanian state schools, in practice their numbers decreased year by year and the only schools where Hungarian could be taught were those maintained by the Roman Catholic and Protestant churches. The Hungarian-language university at Kolozsvár/Cluj was forced to move to Szeged in Hungary and a new Romanian-language university was created in its place, where only a very small number of ethnic Hungarian students could study. In spite of this, between 1919 and 1940 Hungarian journals flourished in Romania (censorship prevented the importation of papers from Hungary proper), although there were innumerable cases in which journalists were prosecuted and fined for their – not necessarily nationalistic, merely liberal or socialist – opinions. Among the Hungarian-language periodicals, *Korunk*, a left-wing journal devoted to culture and to the social sciences, appeared from 1926 to 1940, while most writers assembled around *Erdélyi Helikon*, which was first edited by Miklós Bánffy and later by Aladár Kuncz. (Kuncz's documentary novel *Fekete kolostor* (Black Monastery) of 1931 is considered one of the finest achievements of postwar Hungarian literature). There was also a Hungarian-language theatre at Cluj which regularly staged the work of Transylvanian writers. While some outstanding writers such as Lajos Áprily and Áron Tamási eventually moved to Budapest, many others (including the poets Sándor Remenyik and Jenő Dsida and the writer and architect Károly Kós) remained in Transylvania, where they tried to adapt to the changing political climate. In 1938 king Carol dissolved the political parties and declared a "royal dictatorship". The king promised a new "statute for the ethnic minorities", the realization of which was postponed indefinitely.

In the meantime Hungarian demands led to inconclusive negotiations with Romania on the reallocation of ethnic Hungarian territories to Hungary. In August 1940 Romania asked Hitler and Mussolini to arbitrate in this matter; the outcome was the so-called Vienna Award which assigned Northern Transylvania to Hungary. In consequence, between 1940 and 1944, though both countries were Germany's allies, Northern Transylvania (including the Sekler counties in the southeast) was under Hungarian rule, the Magyar university at Cluj was reinstated, and about 10,000 Romanians fled to the southern part of the country. The acquisition of Northern Transylvania by Hungary did not improve the situation of all the Hungarians in the region: *Korunk* was banned by the authorities and with Hungary's entry into the war in mid-1941 military censorship was imposed on all publications. Transylvanian Hungarian writers of left-wing leanings and Jewish writers were called up to labour battalions and many of them lost their lives in the war or died in concentration camps (Ernő Salamon, Benő Karácsony, and others).

The conclusion of World War II created a new situation. Although Romania switched sides in August 1944 and came out of the war as an ally of the USSR, it had earlier kept 25 divisions on the Soviet front and its occupation of the southern Ukraine (the so-called Transnistria) was characterized by the systematic murder of the local Jewish population. While the presence of the Soviet Army in Romania "guaranteed" the victory of left-wing forces in the long run, their traditional weakness forced them to forge an alliance with the ethnic minorities; and Petru Groza's left-wing coalition government had to rely on the Hungarian Popular Alliance (which won 29 parliamentary seats in the elections of 1946). For the first time since 1919 real concessions were made on the language issue: two laws were passed (the Statute of the National Minorities) that guaranteed the free use of Hungarian at all levels of education. In 1945 the University of Cluj was divided into the Romanian-language Babeş and the Magyar Bolyai universities; the latter existed until 1959 when it was forcibly merged with its Romanian counterpart.

Though the preconditions for the free development of Hungarian culture in Romania were created between 1945 and 1959, the period was marred (at least until 1953) by the inexorable process of Stalinization. In 1946 a new Hungarian-language cultural weekly, *Útunk* (Our Way) was launched at Cluj under the editorship of the prewar communist critic Gábor Gaál, and in 1953 the monthly *Igaz Szó* (True Word) came into being at Marosvásárhely/Tirgu-Mureş, capital of a region inhabited mostly by Hungarians. Yet in 1949 some leading Hungarian politicians of the Popular Alliance as well as several writers (Edgár Balogh, József Méliusz) were arrested and jailed as "Titoist agents", and even the staunchly Stalinist Gábor Gaál was attacked and humiliated, which contributed to his death in 1954. Another Hungarian poet, László Szabédi (1907–59), professor of literature at the Bolyai University, committed suicide in protest against the suppression of the university. None the less, the democratic impetus of the first period helped the emergence of writers and poets from the poorer classes, such as András Sütő (1927–), Gyula Szabó (1930–), and Sándor Kányádi (1929–), whose talents came to fruition only in the 1960s and 1970s.

Of these, Sütő's case is the most interesting. A committed supporter of Socialism, his first short stories glorified class warfare in an imaginative language reminiscent of Tamási's. In his later work he returned to his roots. The very popular *Anyám könnyű álmot igér* (1970, My Mother Promises a Light Dream) is a lyrical documentary of the "transformation of the Transylvanian village" since the last war, not concealing the abuses of power in the 1950s. Sütő's dramas are also important, ranging from the historical *Csillag a máglyán* (1974, Star at the Stake) to the moving ethnic protest of *Advent a Hargitán* (1985, Advent in the Hargita Mountain) – during the Ceauşescu regime the latter play could be staged only in Hungary.

Sándor Kányádi, who studied Hungarian literature at the Bolyai University, also came from a poor peasant family. His first book of verse published in 1955 reflected his socialist convictions, but his simple, optimistic poems turned sour under the relentless pressure of "homogenizing" Romanian nationalism. Between 1978 and 1989 the only collections he published in Romania were books for children or translations; on the other hand, his poetry was available in Hungary, where his collected poems *Fekete-piros* (1979, Black and Red) won great critical acclaim. His poems written in the 1980s are mostly protest-poems against Ceauşescu's tyranny, while in the poetic rhapsody "All Souls Day in Vienna" he bemoans the fate of Hungarians dispersed all over the world and daily discriminated against in the countries of their birth (e.g. Romania, where they were treated as second-class citizens). In 1987 Kányádi left the Romanian Writers' Association in protest against the regime's policies. In 1993 he won the Kossuth prize, Hungary's highest literary distinction, and in 1995 the Herder prize.

In the mid-1980s, when the last vestiges of Hungarian education and book publishing were being slowly eliminated, many Hungarian-language writers decided to emigrate to Hungary proper. Géza Páskándi (who was jailed for several years after 1956 for his participation in a political demonstration) had moved to Budapest already in 1974 and he was followed there some years later by Ádám Bodor, László Csiki, István Kocsis, and many others. From the point of view of the Hungarian ethnic minority in Romania the year 1977 was of crucial importance: it saw the publication of a long and detailed report (written by Sándor Tóth under a pseudonym) in the western press and also of the protest letter that Károly Király, an eminent Hungarian communist functionary, sent to the Romanian Communist Party's Central Committee. Both shed light on the increasing discrimination against Hungarians in Ceauşescu's Romania. Király immediately lost his position but wide western press coverage saved his life. The same was true for Géza Szőcs, who in 1982 with two other Hungarian intellectuals published the first *samizdat* journal in Romania, *Ellenpontok* (Counterpoints). When the secret police identified the editors, Szőcs was arrested, interrogated, and then expelled from the country. Having lived in Switzerland and the US for some time, Szőcs returned to Romania via Hungary after Ceauşescu's fall and in 1990 was elected senator to the Romanian parliament on the list of the Hungarian Democratic Alliance, though more recently he moved to Hungary.

In the last few years of Ceauşescu's rule censorship became almost intolerable. There was a triple net stretching from each editor through the County Party Committee to the Censors' Bureau in Bucharest, and year by year less and less worth reading could be published. In the 1980s *Korunk* was forbidden to print writers living in Hungary; even the classics were censored. Publication in Budapest, on the other hand, was punished by the withdrawal of favours enjoyed by the party *nomenklatura* (many Hungarian writers were Communist Party members) and sometimes by other administrative measures. In the 1980s the tone of polemics between Hungary and Romania became increasingly abrasive; the publication of a serious scholarly work, the three-volume *Erdély története* (History of Transylvania), by the Hungarian Academy of Sciences in 1986 was followed by hysterical attacks and denunciations by a number of Romanian historians. (The book was, naturally enough, banned in Romania.) The revolution of December 1989 created a new situation. Although the Iliescu regime managed to save the positions of many bureaucrats and generals who had served Ceauşescu, the press and the media became free. Now almost anything could be published in any language and many new Hungarian journals sprang up; *Korunk* was renewed and thoroughly transformed under the able editorship of Lajos Kántor, *Útunk* changed its name to *Helikon* and the Tirgu-Mureş-based *Igaz Szó* to *Látó*. Nevertheless, the media and most of the Romanian-language press remained in the hands of the government and was mercilessly manipulated, for example in March 1990 when a false rumour led to Securitate-organized anti-Hungarian riots in Tirgu-Mureş. Since the 1996 elections the level of objective information as regards the wishes and grievances of the Magyar minority has significantly risen in Romania, but there are still numerous right-wing publications that stir up national hatred and demand ethnic discrimination. At present there are plans to open a Hungarian-language university at Csikszereda (Miercurea Ciuc) but it still has not been approved by the relevant Romanian authorities.

GEORGE GÖMÖRI

Further Reading

Béládi, Miklós *et al.*, *A magyar irodalom története, 1945–1975*, volume 4: *A határon túli magyar irodalom*, Budapest: Akadémiai Kiadó, 1982

Biro, Sandor, *The Nationalities Problem in Transylvania, 1867–1940*, Boulder, Colorado: Social Science Monographs, 1992

Kocsis, Karoly and Eszter Kocsis-Hodosi, *Hungarian Minorities in the Carpathian Basin: A Study in Ethnic Geography*, Toronto: Corvinus, 1995

Mastny, Vojtech (editor), *Soviet/East European Survey, 1983–1984: Selected Research and Analysis from Radio Free Europe/Radio Liberty*, Durham, North Carolina: Duke University Press, 1985

Péter, László (editor), *Uj magyar irodalmi lexikon*, vols 1–3, 2nd edition, Budapest: Kiadó, 2000

Schöpflin, George, *The Hungarians of Rumania*, London: Minority Rights Group, 1978

Schöpflin, George (editor), *The Soviet Union and Eastern Europe: A Handbook*, 2nd edition, New York: Facts on File, and London: Muller Blond and White, 1986

Witnesses to the Cultural Genocide: First-Hand Reports on Rumania's Minority Policies Today, New York: American Transylvania Federation, 1979

Zsille, Zoltán (editor), *Független Fórum: Kéziratos tiltott magyar irodalom a Kárpát-medencében*, Cleveland, Ohio: Hungarian Central Committee for Books and Education, 1985

ROME, ANCIENT

By common convention, ancient Roman history is usually divided into three broad eras. The era of monarchy (traditionally 753–510 BCE) witnessed Rome's ascendancy over its immediate neighbours and the establishment of a rigid class system. The republican era (509–31 BCE) was generally marked by territorial expansion in Italy and abroad, increasing conflict between Rome's sharply defined social classes, and gradual and limited democratization. After nearly a century of civil wars, Rome entered its imperial era (31 BCE–476 CE), which was characterized by a concentration of autocratic power in the hands of the emperor and his agents, a homogenization of Roman society, and frequent foreign incursions on the frontiers of the vast empire.

The history and sociology of censorship in Roman antiquity make fascinating – if not crucial – study. Adequate evidence of official censorship, social censorship, and self-censorship survives, allowing us to make relatively informed judgements and sophisticated inferences about Roman attitudes on freedom and its abridgements. On the whole, the Romans made a clear distinction between a person's deeds (*acta* or *facta*) and his words (*verba*), the former always being viewed as more important, both from an individual and from a historical perspective. For example, the Roman historian Tacitus pointed out that deeds might be prosecuted, but a person's words traditionally enjoyed impunity. Of course, such distinctions, upon more careful scrutiny, can be found facile. Romans similarly distinguished between written words (*scripta*) and spoken words (*dicta*); social attitudes about this distinction changed as the society evolved from being pre-literate, to becoming proto-literate, and finally to being quite generally literate. So, too, the relative culpability of slander and libel changed as society changed from being strictly stratified to only loosely stratified.

A few notable qualities should be mentioned from the outset. First, the English word "censorship" is etymologically derived from a regular Roman magistracy. Two censors were elected from the Senate for 18-month terms. A minor duty of these censors was to protect the morals of the Roman people. This duty was officially performed quite seldom, since a censor's unofficial warning was usually sufficient to reform offending behaviours. Second, official censorship probably began at Rome because certain utterances and teachings (both religious and secular) were seen as subversive and punishable. Thenceforth censorship was extended to apply to the authors of literature (both formal and occasional), though notably not to their writings. The next development involved the destruction and/or suppression of the writings themselves if condemned as offensive – sometimes without any punishment of the authors. Finally, the official censorship enjoined the proscription of the writer and writings alike. When officially condemned, the offending writings typically met with a sentence of destruction either because they were regarded as socially or politically harmful to the state or because their obliteration was thought to bring an added punishment to their author and his memory. Once writings were officially banned, minor magistrates called *aediles* had the responsibility for collecting and destroying them; outside the capital, local authorities had the same responsibility. Persons caught owning or reading proscribed works

were liable to prosecution for treason. Individuals convicted under law for their speech or writings were punished with fines and/or exile or, in cases thought to pose the greatest threat to the social and political order, with death (a portion of the estate of the condemned was typically confiscated). Censorship against groups was often conducted differently from that against individuals, especially during the empire. A case against an individual could frequently be dispensed with summarily, whereas one against a group of people generally required a senatorial decree or an imperial edict. Last, most examples of censorship come from Rome or, less often, the rest of Italy; very rarely do they come from the provinces – until we reach the era of Christian persecutions.

A brief narration of Roman laws on treason bears directly on censorship. The crime of treason (*perduellio*) was originally treated as a capital offence in the oldest set of codified Roman law, the so-called Twelve Tables (451–450 BCE), and appears to have been defined as a hostile military act against the Roman state by a Roman. The law on *perduellio* was replaced by a law sponsored by the dictator Sulla in 81 BCE. This new law on treason (now called *maiestas*, short for *laesa* or *minuta maiestas*: "injured" or "diminished majesty") was passed to curb Roman provincial generals from taking any military actions unauthorized by the Senate in Rome. Treason was thus redefined to encompass any over-ambitious measures a general or magistrate might venture with revolutionary designs. Sulla's law also established a permanent court (*quaestio*) in Rome to hear cases of treason. A Julian law on treason, sponsored by Julius or Augustus Caesar, profoundly revised the Sullan law. Though the law continued to apply to public and military officials of the state, private citizens could also now be tried under it, since the definition of *maiestas* was extended to include conspiracy against the life of the emperor or his family members, defamation, and even adultery with someone in the imperial household. Under the Julian law, trials for *maiestas* were conducted by *quaestio*, by the Senate, or by the emperor himself. As the Roman concept of treason developed from the military crimes of an official against the state to any person's hostile words or deeds against the ruling family, we observe legal definition transformed from the very specific to the general, the potentially ambiguous and arbitrary, and the autocratic.

Speech

Any Roman would have regarded the notion that free speech is a natural, inalienable right, to be ratified by constitutional protections, as quite foreign. Moreover, Romans regarded the Greek conception of free speech (*parrhesia*) as bordering on mere licentiousness. To be sure, orators in the Roman courts and in the Roman Senate enjoyed free speech (*libertas*), but that was granted by convention alone. It might also be added that such speeches were delivered by and to members of Rome's upper classes. *Libertas* was not conferred on one by virtue of Roman citizenship, but by virtue of one's social rank and prestige (*auctoritas*): the greater one's *auctoritas*, the more *libertas* one was accorded. Many of the surviving speeches delivered by the famous orator Cicero are replete with outspokenness, invective, even scurrility.

Public harangues – whether political, military, funerary, or educational – were expected to be more circumspect. Ordinary citizens did not have the right to speak in popular assemblies, whether formal (*comitia*) or informal (*contiones*); only priests, senators, or magistrates were permitted to do so. Since criteria of truth and fiction were not rigorously applied at remembrances for the recently deceased, eulogists were conventionally accorded great freedom with facts and interpretations, but even a funeral could incur an emperor's displeasure if the eulogy contained open criticism of the regime. Philosophers or rhetoricians who gave public demonstrations of their skills could expose themselves to peril. In 155 BCE the head of the Academy in Athens, Carneades the Sceptic, visited Rome and gave public lectures at which he convincingly argued both sides of a particular debate. The Senate, at the stern urgings of Cato the Elder, banished him from Rome, finding his method educationally subversive and morally dangerous for Rome's youth. In 92 BCE Roman censors forbade certain Latin rhetoricians from practising their trade; the curriculum at their schools was regarded as too innovative and socially disruptive. In a later era, a certain teacher of rhetoric named Corvus, who held a public demonstration of debating skills, picked the unfortunate subject of childlessness – an all too common condition among Roman citizens which Augustus attempted to reverse by means of a body of legislation. The luckless Corvus was indicted for treason as a result of this staged debate (probably around 6 CE), but the outcome of the trial is unknown. During the early empire, philosophers of particular schools were occasionally persecuted, not so much because of their teachings but rather because of their attitudes toward authority (the Stoics) or biased misconceptions of their beliefs and lifestyles (the Epicureans). The Stoic philosopher Gaius Musonius Rufus, who lived in the 1st century CE, offers a useful case in point. He was banished from Rome at least three times. At fault, it appears, were neither writings nor even teachings (Musonius did propound some fairly radical notions): he simply associated with many of the leading citizens and thereby won imperial disfavour. It is probably worth observing here that most philosophers and rhetoricians at Rome were non-Roman, while their targeted audience was typically the Roman upper classes. Roman parents, on the other hand, were free to teach their children whatever and however they pleased; there is no recorded case of sanctions being imposed on parents for the education provided for their children.

During the republic, private conversations were immune from official censorship. Social censorship probably served to quash any vicious *bon mot* or salacious epigram which threatened to break out into wider currency. At the end of the republic, however, and during the early empire, Roman high society tended to produce and circulate (anonymously or pseudonymously) many defamatory tales and occasional verses about the political and military leaders of Rome. As their number and outrageousness increased, and as social censorship proved inadequate (or unwilling) to curb them, and as the political scene was turning more autocratic, it was virtually inevitable that official censorship would be imposed on licentious speech even when it occurred in private conversations. Two examples should suffice here.

A perennial annoyance for emperors was the critical epigram: short, memorable, invariably amusing and daring, this kind of lampoon could do much damage toward undermining imperial credibility. In 23 CE Aelius Saturninus was executed, in accordance with a grim old Roman tradition, by being hurled from the Tarpeian Rock after he had uttered libellous epigrams against Tiberius. A decade later, in 35 CE, after spending three years in prison, Sextius Paconianus was strangled in his cell, condemned for composing defamatory verses against the aged emperor.

This marks an opportune point to discuss the evolution of jurisprudential thought on defamation. Most ancient historians are agreed that defamation was covered by the Twelve Tables. Under that code, the composition or performance of defamatory verses was considered a capital offence. The prosecution of this law was conducted by the decemvirate, an extraordinary and extra-constitutional panel of ten senior magistrates; the enforcement of the law was overseen by the *tresviri capitales*, a board of three minor magistrates who carried out death sentences. Two points should be borne in mind here: though the codification of the Twelve Tables was an important step in the democratization of Roman society, the laws themselves usually protected the interests of the upper classes better than those of the lower classes; defamatory lampoons initially were non-literary and the common resort of non-Romans and lower-class Romans. In this context, the original law on defamation must be viewed as a mechanism of social control and class division. The application and enforcement of this law proved difficult (and perhaps unnecessary: we know of no one prosecuted under it after 204 BCE). It was probably replaced by the Cornelian law on injury, enacted during the dictatorship of Sulla (81 BCE). Under the law, slander and libel (for which no real distinction was made) would have been treated like any other personal injury that one party commits against another party; defamation thus was no longer necessarily a capital offence: liability would have been determined by the loss demonstrated by the defamed party. The enforcement and prosecution of this law was conducted by praetors, who unlike decemvirs were regular constitutional magistrates. The Cornelian law had only a brief span of application. During the reign of the emperor Augustus, defamation was covered under the law on treason (*maiestas*). This change implied two important points: that defamation, by legal definition, was a crime only against the emperor, his family, or his agents (i.e. those possessing *maiestas*); and that, *a priori*, defamation was a crime against the state, not simply against an individual (as the law on personal injury had defined it). Again, the enforcement and prosecution of defamation were the responsibilities of praetors, who officiated with and at the approval of the emperor. At first the law was employed only to combat the composition and distribution of occasional writings and lampoons critical of the emperor and his regime. Soon, however, its application was extended to counter criticisms of the emperor contained in *any* literature; thus, the law could be used in the suppression or punishment of practically any published work regarded as unsympathetic to the regime. For the remaining centuries of the Roman empire, this is how defamation was legally defined and dealt with.

To return to private conversations and how censorship was imposed under the empire, we will consider the following cases. Cassius Patavinus, a person of no particular note, was fined and exiled for casually boasting at the dinner-table that he was both willing and able to assassinate Augustus. In 17 CE a member of the imperial family itself, Appuleia Varilla, was tried for uttering insults against the deified Augustus, his widow Livia, and Tiberius; although Varilla was acquitted of these charges, she was convicted on a charge of adultery and exiled. The rhetorician Votienus Montanus was condemned in 25 CE for private remarks critical of Tiberius and exiled. Finally, we come to the case of Titius Sabinus (27 CE), a private citizen who in his own home spoke ill of the emperor Tiberius and his chief minister Aelius Sejanus in front of supposed friends. These "friends" in turn denounced Sabinus before the Senate on a charge of *maiestas*, and before a proper trial could be completed, Sabinus was summarily executed.

Literature

Even during the imperial era, a certain freedom of expression was tolerated in published writings. Books had a very limited distribution and circulation. Quite often readers of texts would be familiar, even sympathetic with the authors. Literature thus played a very small role in shaping popular opinion. So freedom of expression in literature was probably tolerated precisely because it had minimal consequences. Moreover, during the imperial era it suited most emperors to affect a certain forbearance toward outspoken literature: it suggested a sort of liberal enlightenment. Official postures and actual deeds did not invariably coincide, however.

The literary publication of plays and their reading were extremely rare: drama was performed rather than read in the Roman world. Compared with other genres, theatrical literature could play a considerable role in shaping popular opinion because many diverse members of the community attended theatrical performances. Therefore, more official controls appear to have been placed on free speech in dramas. The rationale, presumably, was that reading audiences for other genres of literature – being small and generally elite – could judge responsibly for themselves, while viewing audiences for the theatre were ill-equipped to judge critical comments. It should be added that most actors on the Roman stage were either non-Roman or of the lowest social class; the idea that such persons might criticize their social superiors from the stage was unthinkable to Romans of the upper classes. It is also important to note that the festivals at which dramatic performances took place were almost invariably state-sponsored and state-administered, a fact that distinguished theatre from all other literary genres. About 204 BCE the playwright Gnaeus Naevius was prosecuted under the Twelve Tables for criticizing from the stage the political talents of the Metelli, a very powerful family in Rome at that time. His censorship may have arisen because of high war-time anxieties (Rome was engaged in the Punic Wars at the time), or for purely political reasons (his literary patrons were staunch conservatives who opposed the recent ascendancy of certain more liberal leaders, including the Metelli), or simply to assert class superiority (Naevius' Italic origins were very humble). Naevius may well have been the first, last, and only playwright prosecuted under that law; he was convicted, imprisoned, and eventually exiled from Italy. There is some fragmentary evidence that a new law was introduced in the early 2nd century BCE, banning playwrights from criticizing individuals by name in their plays. This reversed a tradition of

unrestricted outspokenness adopted from the Greeks. Centuries later, soon after his son, Drusus, died in 23 CE, Tiberius banished actors from Rome, using their debased morals and their disruptive social influence as a pretext. Apart from inconclusive secondary evidence (cf. Curiatius Maternus in Tacitus' *Dialogue on Orators*), freedom of expression from the theatrical stage appears to have been effectively curtailed by the late republic or early empire, and there was virtually no original dramatic literature produced during the later empire.

Lampoons and occasional poetry, especially that of a defamatory character, have already been discussed. More formal poetry, while open to criticisms of form and content, was rarely proscribed. Verses of Lucilius, Catullus, and Martial, for example, were deprecated for their earthy language or prurient subjects, but they never elicited any official attempts at suppression or bowdlerization. The celebrated case of the poet Ovid represents an entirely different matter. He was banished from Rome by the emperor Augustus, in part because some of his writings (the *Ars Amatoria* or the *Metamorphoses*; scholars disagree) were viewed as incompatible with the regime's ideology. During Tiberius' reign, the poet Phaedrus offended the emperor's chief minister, Sejanus, with certain verses that were believed to allude to him. Phaedrus received a punishment unknown to us today. In 22 CE the hapless Clutorius Priscus prematurely composed and recited a funeral elegy for Tiberius' son, Drusus, anticipating his death. Priscus was tried by the Senate for treason, convicted, and sentenced to die: the first time in Roman history that such a penalty was handed down for a crime that was strictly literary. It is instructive to observe that in each of these cases only the writer was punished; his writings suffered no official proscription.

As discussed earlier, philosophers and rhetoricians were persecuted for their teachings and lifestyles. None is known to have been condemned specifically for his writings. The orators Titus Labienus and Cassius Severus incurred Augustus' disfavour because of their outspokenness and their invective fulminations against leading citizens; their writings were officially proscribed after they themselves had been condemned. Also in the era of Augustus, the orator Gaius Albucius Silus withdrew from public life and eventually committed suicide after he had displeased the emperor by invoking the memory of Marcus Brutus, assassin of Julius Caesar, in a bold, inflammatory manner. One of the most distinguished orators during the reign of Tiberius was Mamercus Aemilius Scaurus; his speeches from the floor of the Senate had frequently vexed the emperor. Scaurus was charged with treason, accused of adultery, of practising magic rites, and of writing subversive verses; he and his wife committed suicide before he could be sentenced, but his seven books of published orations were ordered by the Senate to be burned. Although it is uncertain whether he actually carried it out, the emperor Caracalla threatened in 212 CE to burn every book of Peripatetic philosophy.

Historiography and biography eventually became more precarious disciplines. During the republic, partisanship, prejudices, and even personal enmities were countenanced. Since most historians during this era were also active members of the ruling class, these sorts of literary drawbacks were generally understood and accepted even if the historians' analyses of fact were not. The historian Tacitus claims that the reign of Augustus Caesar was pivotal for historiography: in that period writers of any talent were deterred from taking up historiography because of the rising tide of adulation. On the other hand, the historian Cassius Dio observes the same dearth of historiographical talent, but he ascribes it to official suppression, sycophancy or fear of disfavour: probably both are right. The historian Cremutius Cordus committed suicide and his writings were banned because of certain pro-republican sentiments. Velleius Paterculus, another historian, won imperial favour for publishing a work, practically the only notable feature of which was its unctuous praise for the emperors Augustus and Tiberius. The biographer Suetonius, whose writings are striking for the inclusion of salacious and scurrilous details about past Roman emperors, lost the official patronage of the emperor Hadrian, but was permitted to continue publishing his biographies none the less. As long as historians and biographers limited their critiques to past emperors, their position was basically secure; living emperors wanted implicit contrasts, not explicit comparisons.

During the reign of Augustus, the Greek historian Timagenes, who had written a contemporary history, incited the emperor's ire because of certain gibes against him and his family. After Augustus had expressed his displeasure, as a gesture of defiance and revenge Timagenes burned those sections of his history that commemorated Augustus' exploits. When Timagenes subsequently approached a leading Roman for literary patronage, that person in turn went to the emperor and volunteered to reject Timagenes if Augustus so wished. This potential patron was clearly alarmed that the emperor had construed Timagenes' personal and intellectual opposition as posing a more significant political threat.

In 371 CE the emperor Valens demanded that several private libraries in Antioch be burned. Evidently, these collections contained a number of law books, which the emperor denounced as "illegal". One source informs us that in reaction to this incident, many people in the eastern provinces of the empire voluntarily torched their own libraries, either to avoid official censure or to show support for the emperor's actions.

Political pamphlets, especially common at the end of the republic and at the beginning of the empire, were hastily prepared, often anonymously published, probably not widely read, but were highly invective and thoroughly tendentious. We know, for example, that Cicero published a tract entitled *Cato* which, as an encomium to the deceased senator, espoused republican sentiments; Julius Caesar published his rejoinder, entitled *Anticato*, which fiercely refuted Cicero. Octavian published his own *Cato*, doubtless in response to a pamphlet published by his rival Marcus Brutus, the assassin of Julius Caesar. Such pamphlets were published during a brief era of competing propaganda, when official suppression – even if contemplated – would have proved impossible to implement and ultimately ineffective. Political rivalries in that era were decided on battlefields, not in any propagandistic forum. By the next generation, political treatises were handled very differently. Later in his reign, Augustus punished Junius Novatus with a fine and exile for publishing a political tract criticizing him; the tract was couched and disguised as a letter penned by the emperor's own grandson, Agrippa Postumus. Novatus' penalties were relatively lenient; considering the delicate and

uncertain role that Agrippa would play in his succession, the emperor was probably reluctant to turn the incident into a *cause célèbre*.

A genre that defies literary categorization is the fictional wills composed by Fabricius Veiento for leading senators and priests during the reign of Nero which exposed them and their associates to invective and ridicule. Veiento was banished in 62 CE, and his compositions were ordered to be burned. Tacitus notes that so long as the writings were banned they remained in great demand, but as soon as the ban was lifted they fell into absolute obscurity.

Romans took exceptional care in composing their wills, and the testaments of leading citizens were frequently read aloud in public. After a number of prominent individuals had attacked the emperor in their wills, the Senate passed a measure forbidding such testamentary criticisms. Augustus vetoed the measure, but his successor Tiberius evidently ratified it upon reintroduction. Obviously, from the state's standpoint, the criticisms *qua* criticisms were less threatening than the fact that they had been shared with the general populace.

Art

Roman public art was functional and subservient to the uses defined for it by the state. The artists who produced major public works were increasingly non-Roman, working on commission or under contract. We know of no individual artist who was censored for his artwork; but then again we know only a handful of artists by name for the entire Roman era. Even if the artists were not themselves censored, their works did undergo official opprobrium. A Roman town in Cisalpine Gaul, which displayed an especially fine statue of Marcus Brutus, received Augustus during one of his journeys abroad; when the emperor noticed this bronze statue, he accused the townspeople of harbouring a public enemy, and the people quailed. Our ancient source for this story portrays Augustus as only feigning disapproval, but the reaction he received verifies that this disapproval was not perceived as being altogether out of character. In 15 CE, a year after Tiberius assumed the throne, a provincial administrator named Marcus Granius Marcellus was indicted under the law on treason for elevating his own statue above those of the Caesars and for mutilating a statue of the deified Augustus by knocking off its head and replacing it with a bust of Tiberius; he was also accused of "sinister conversations about Tiberius". After the emperor displayed excessive zeal in prosecuting the case, he experienced second thoughts and decided to acquit Marcellus. Another story is told about how statues of Tiberius' chief minister Sejanus were found throughout Rome; within a day of his downfall in 31 CE, however, they were all upended and destroyed.

Noble families traditionally kept masks fashioned in the likeness of their illustrious ancestors. If a person was convicted of treason, declared an enemy of the state, or condemned posthumously, his family might be denied the right to display his death mask. During the reign of Tiberius, the death masks of Julius Caesar's assassins, Brutus and Cassius, were conspicuously absent from a kinsman's funeral procession. Since Brutus and Cassius were never officially denounced, the absence of their death masks at this procession probably represents an example of self-censorship on the part of their kinsmen. Some years later, the emperor Nero reproached a descendant of Cassius for displaying a likeness of his famous ancestor.

Religion

Typical of most polytheistic peoples, the Romans were generally tolerant of other religions. There were several notable exceptions, however, all of which involved the Romans' fear of religious practitioners achieving too much political power. Lest this connection between religion and politics seem strange, one must remember that there was no structural or even philosophical division between "church" and state, and that all public religion was state-sponsored and conducted by political magistrates and priests of the senatorial class.

The history of the Sibylline books makes a fascinating story. Tradition maintained that the Cumaean Sibyl originally produced nine of these books, all containing prophecies relevant to Rome. The king Tarquinius Priscus caused six of these books to be burned, but he preserved the remaining three. An accidental fire on the Capitoline hill destroyed these original three books in 83 BCE, but they were soon replaced with copies collated from various sources around the Mediterranean. The emperor Augustus spared only these books when he launched a campaign in 12 BCE to eradicate "spurious" books of Greek, Roman, and Etruscan soothsaying; it is reported that he destroyed more than 2000 of these volumes – an *auto da fé* unprecedented in Roman history. The emperor Tiberius interfered with the inclusion of an alleged Sibylline book in 32 CE. The general Stilicho, before his death in 408 CE, burned all the remaining Sibylline books. Throughout Roman history access to these books had been limited to a priestly college comprising 15 members of the upper classes and the high priest of Rome (the *pontifex maximus*), who during the imperial era was usually the emperor. Access was doubtless controlled because rulers considered that knowledge of prophecies might confer potential political power.

In 186 BCE the Senate vigorously opposed the introduction of Bacchic rites from Greece. This cult was spreading quickly throughout Italy, attracting followers mostly from the lower classes. The Senate's campaign reportedly resulted in the execution of thousands of cult followers. Since this growing religious movement could not really be quashed or stemmed, the Senate passed legislation legitimizing assemblies of believers (repeatedly characterized as "conspirators") only if they were officially registered with the state and were each composed of no more than five individuals.

In 181 BCE a collection of Greek and Latin books alleged to belong to Numa Pompilius, the second king of Rome and founder of most of its religious institutions, was discovered. After members of the Senate reviewed these books and considered them uncongenial to contemporary religious practices, the Senate voted to destroy them. (Contents aside, it must have been obvious to most of the senators that the collection was forged.) Coming so soon as it did after the controversy over Bacchic rites, this incident may in fact reflect a similar anti-Greek sentiment.

Astrologers and soothsayers were a common sight in ancient Rome. They sold their privileged knowledge for the most part to the lower classes. Frequently non-Roman, socially marginal, and behaviourally flamboyant, they were able to attract considerable attention with their dire predictions of woe, gloom, and doom – predictions commonly involving Rome's political leaders. Before 186 BCE, the Senate had on a number of occasions enjoined praetors to search out and destroy all published writings of soothsayers. Between the years 44 BCE and 180 CE, astrologers were expelled from Rome (or Italy) at least eight times and perhaps in fact twice that many times. Clearly, at particular times of crisis, they represented such a destabilizing force in Roman society that official suppression seemed warranted. In the year 11 CE, when Augustus was nearly 75 years old and had reigned for more than 40 years, legislation was passed prohibiting soothsayers from divining about any third-party individual or his death – clearly there must have been a thriving business in predicting Augustus' expected demise. In 16 CE, during Tiberius' reign, the nobleman Marcus Scribonius Libo Drusus was prosecuted for consulting astrologers, magicians, and dream-interpreters. Before a sentence could be handed down, Libo Drusus committed suicide, creating quite a stir. In the aftermath, all practitioners of the magic arts were expelled from Italy; two magicians, apparently Roman citizens, were tortured and executed.

Perhaps the greatest notoriety achieved by the Romans was their persecution of early Christians. The religious exclusivity of Christians and their refusal to take part in the Roman ruler-cult (an obligation imposed by citizenship throughout the Roman empire) guaranteed a climate of conflict and confrontation. After the great fire at Rome in 64 CE, to assuage widespread public unrest, Nero made scapegoats of the Christians. Thereafter, in isolated parts of the empire, under separate and individual circumstances, Christians were occasionally targeted for persecution – more for their retiring lifestyles and their unique practices, which at first the Romans misconstrued – than for their writings and doctrine. Not until the second half of the third century CE, under the reigns of such emperors as Decius and Diocletian, did the Romans undertake a systematic, empire-wide policy of suppressing Christianity. By this time, the pagan emperors had come to recognize that this new religion represented a considerable threat to their existing order. Diocletian's edict of 303 CE condemned all Christian writings; many stories were told of miraculous restorations of these texts, of martyrs who died for them, of curious evasions and open opposition to their destruction. Interestingly, there was also a conservative pagan backlash to this edict: some questioned why the emperor proscribed Christian texts, which were relatively innocuous, when certain non-Christian texts openly harmful to, or critical of, paganism were allowed to remain extant. (Diocletian did not only single out Christian texts; he also ordered the destruction of certain Egyptian volumes on alchemy.) Scholars estimate that during the so-called Great Persecution of 303 CE, about 3000 Christians were martyred.

After Roman emperors began converting and Christianity was adopted as the state religion, Christians deemed certain persons as heretics and their writings were officially condemned. Early Christians appear to have been somewhat more tolerant of pagan literature than of schismatic literature. The most notorious case involving the destruction of pagan literature occurred in 363 or 364 CE, when the Christian emperor Jovian torched a library founded by the pagan emperor Julian (the "Apostate") at Antioch.

Conclusion

A legitimate index of censorship may appropriately be found in contrary cases, too, where self-censorship was disallowed. For instance, in his will the poet Virgil insisted that his unfinished poem, the *Aeneid*, should remain unpublished and be destroyed; Augustus intervened and refused to allow the poet's testamentary wishes to be carried out. During the reign of Nero, the Stoic senator Publius Clodius Thrasea Paetus was condemned for retiring from the Senate in disgust over the conditions of the state. Because Paetus "could not say what he would, and would not say what he could" (Tacitus), he maintained a public silence. His absence from the Senate and his silence were treated as treasonous, since his civil disobedience was seen as tantamount to a wilful refusal both to swear oaths of loyalty to the emperor and to vote divine honours on his imperial person. Paetus himself felt compelled to commit suicide, while his outspoken son-in-law, Helvidius Priscus, was forced into exile. Priscus eventually would be recalled to Rome only to be banished again by the emperor Vespasian, who finally ordered that Priscus be executed (c.75 CE). Literary admirations for Paetus and Priscus published during the reign of Domitian cost their authors, Herennius Senecio and Quintus Junius Arulenus Rusticus, their lives and the writings themselves were put to the torch (c.93–95 CE). This case of father- and son-in-law and their admirers illustrates well the fact that freethinking and intellectual opposition to the regime – whether tacit or explicit – was at times not tolerated; of course eventually these conditions led to widespread sycophancy and acquiescence. Romans learned to live with the reality that individual rights as basic as testamentary instructions or the desire to remain silent could simply be abrogated by imperial authority.

Overall, the ancient Romans did not practice official censorship with great frequency. During the republic, censorship was imposed by the ruling classes as a mechanism for keeping the lower classes from organizing around formal criticisms of powerful individuals. Maintaining the existing class structure served as the primary incentive for censorship. Most cases involved a superior seeking to censor his social or political inferior; very infrequently did inferiors in Rome seek to censor their superiors. Censorship in Rome was very much about class, power, and status. Generally, censored persons (though theoretically vulnerable even to execution) were expelled from Rome (or less often Italy) and were thereby deprived of all their civil rights, while the speech or writing that had provoked the censorship was often simply ignored and left uncensored. Under the empire, when virtually all power resided with the Roman emperor, imperial agents, and the imperial family, their political and personal interests were preserved by various forms of censorship, including book burning. Censorship provides an interesting case study in how those in power maintained themselves in that position. That censorship did not occur frequently means that it was usually unnecessary and, in some cases, not altogether effective as a means for preserving social and political power.

Perhaps the most famous ancient dictum on censorship was offered by the historian Tacitus in his account of the fate of Cremutius Cordus:

One is all the more inclined to laugh at the stupidity of men who suppose that the despotism of the present can actually efface the remembrances of the next generation. On the contrary, the persecution of genius fosters its influence; foreign tyrants, and all who have imitated their oppression, have merely procured infamy for themselves and glory for their victims [*Annals* 4.35, Church and Brodribb translation].

This is a bold, if somewhat sanguine or naive statement. In some cases, Roman censorship was effective in effacing the remembrances of later generations (Cordus' own writings, for example, are no longer extant, having been expurgated and republished during the reign of Caligula); and certain "persecutors of genius" (e.g. the emperor Augustus) managed a good reputation with posterity.

As with many areas of Roman history, the reign of the emperor Augustus marked a dramatic turning-point in the development of Roman censorship. His predecessor, Julius Caesar, had shown remarkable forbearance (*clementia*) in the face of strong criticisms; in only one case, that of the scholar and pro-Pompey partisan Aulus Caecina, is there even a hint of possible official censorship (Caecina suffered banishment), but this case is far from clear. Augustus, however, who in his youth had himself composed scathingly scurrilous verses against Antony and his wife Fulvia and against his sometime rival Gaius Asinius Pollio, later in his career redefined legislation on treason and defamation to protect the dynastic aims of the imperial family. In effect, Augustus made the interests of the Roman state and the interests of the Roman emperor coextensive and equivalent. Free speech, never a concept fully naturalized in Rome, ceased to be practised. Not even the venerable Roman Senate preserved its *libertas*; by order of Augustus, the senatorial record (*acta senatus*) was no longer published as a verbatim transcript. (Although free speech was permitted within the Senate itself, and an unpublished *acta senatus* continued to be compiled until at least 438 CE, on most occasions senators exercised great discretion and self-censorship, particularly if the emperor was in attendance.) Augustus also extended the application of the *maiestas* law from pamphlets and occasional writings (*libelli*) to all published works (*libri*), setting a precedent for the destruction of important works of literature and oratory. Augustus reportedly told his future successor, Tiberius, that it was enough simply to have the power to control opposition (i.e. it was usually unnecessary actually to exercise that power). Interestingly, most examples of Roman censorship are found during Augustus' reign (especially in its later years) and that of Tiberius; we can safely infer that these emperors felt a greater need to impose censorship. But we should not conclude that these emperors encountered greater political opposition than later emperors did; evidence does not bear out such a conclusion. Instead, the increased incidence of censorship was probably due to the irregular frequency of intellectual opposition, which rarely required systematic elimination. Intellectual opposition was typically best dealt with quickly, quietly, and only as the individual need arose. In the case of Tiberius, if the testimony of Cassius Dio and others is to be trusted, that emperor had a particular sensitivity to criticisms and experienced considerable difficulty in restraining himself: he was frequently too ready to defend himself when prudence would have dictated simply keeping silent. Later emperors really did not need to employ censorship very often, since their subjects all knew what the imperial response to anti-regime statements might be. Most often, emperors benefited from a public attitude of tolerance, bolstered with the knowledge that, if needed, the law on *maiestas* could be invoked to counter virtually any critical utterance or writing.

PETER L. CORRIGAN

Further Reading

Bauman, Richard A., *Impietas in Principem: A Study of Treason against the Roman Emperor with Special Reference to the First Century AD*, Munich: Beck, 1974

Chilton, C.W., "The Roman Law of Treason under the Early Principate", *Journal of Roman Studies*, 45 (1955): 73–81

Cramer, Frederick H., "Bookburning and Censorship in Ancient Rome: A Chapter from the History of Freedom of Speech", *Journal of the History of Ideas*, 6 (1945): 157–96

Finley, Moses I., "Censorship in Classical Antiquity", *Times Literary Supplement*, 27 (July 1977): 923–25

Forbes, Clarence A., "Books for the Burning", *Transactions of the American Philological Association*, 67 (1936): 114–25

Momigliano, Arnaldo, "Review and Discussion: Robinson's *Freedom of Speech in the Roman Republic*", *Journal of Roman Studies*, 32 (1942): 120–24

Syme, Ronald, *The Roman Revolution*, Oxford: Clarendon Press, 1939; New York: Oxford University Press, 1960

Syme, Ronald, *The Augustan Aristocracy*, Oxford: Clarendon Press, and New York: Oxford University Press, 1986

ROME, ANCIENT: Sexual Representation

Modern views on sexual representation in ancient Rome can be best understood through a comprehension of the reception of classical sculpture in recent times, particularly of the nudity of that sculpture. Since the late 15th and early 16th centuries, collections of life-sized classical statuary have been built up in Rome as well as in other European centres. Many of the statues in these collections are marble copies, made during the Roman period, of Greek originals that were often in bronze and have since been lost. Pliny the Elder's discussion of famous Greek sculptors and sculptures (1st century CE) permits us to identify many of the Roman copies as those of specific lost Greek originals, and also provides us with some insights into Greek and Roman attitudes to such representations.

Roman statues in modern collections consist of a number of types, but the most prominent among them, as was probably the case among classical statues in general, are naked male figures. These usually represented young athletes, as it was the custom in ancient Greece to set up statues of victors in commemoration of their victories. Their nakedness was not only the mode in which they performed but was also seen as a heroic portrayal and as the conveyance of much admired qualities of naturalness. While it was also a Greek custom to depict gods as naked, this was not a traditional Roman custom and was initially frowned upon in Rome as one of the signs of the Greek "decadence" that was undermining Roman republican values. However, during the imperial period depictions of naked gods, emperors or generals became increasingly popular.

Statues of naked female figures were less common but still form a major group in the collections. While naked male figures were common in Greece from the 7th century BCE, their female counterparts were normally fully clothed. Those naked female figures in the collections of Roman sculpture that can be identified are generally copies of Greek depictions of the goddess Aphrodite. The earliest known naked representation of the goddess of love was the Aphrodite of Knidos, a statue made by Praxiteles in the mid-4th century BCE, which became very famous in its day.

During the late Roman Republic statues of naked male and female figures, which were frequently booty from campaigns in the Hellenic East, began to appear in public spaces, including temple areas. During the imperial period they also became popular in the private houses of the elite, particularly in their gardens. This is well attested in a number of houses in Pompeii and Herculaneum, and at the emperor Hadrian's villa complex at Tivoli, dating from the 2nd century CE, where the canal in the garden was surrounded by statues of young men and women, naked or seminaked. Apart from their apparent visibility in public and private spaces, and apart also from a few brief comments made by Pliny, it is difficult for us to assess the ancient Roman reception of nudity, beyond its association with the heroic and with nature. However, it seems that male and female nudity were viewed differently: while naked male figures represented a number of different types, most naked female figures were either of the goddess of love (Aphrodite in Greece, Venus in Rome) or of other mythological figures associated with love. Pliny provides us with anecdotes about Arellius of Rome, a painter in the late Republic, being heavily criticized for painting goddesses in the likeness of his mistresses, an undoubtedly inappropriate association, and about a painting of the naked figures of Atalanta and Helena that incited Claudius to attempt to remove the painting for lustful motives.

With the growing interest in classical art in the Renaissance, the leading aristocratic families of the Papal States, such as the Farnese, the Medici, the Ludovisi, and the Borghese, put together private collections of ancient sculptures, not only for their artistic appeal but also as repositories of accumulated and conspicuous wealth. Some of the leading Italian families also gave examples of this type of sculpture to members of other European aristocracies, while other examples were looted by foreign invaders during the Italian Wars. The largest and most significant collection of Roman statuary was that in the Vatican museums, which eventually set the standard for the display of classical art. This collection was built up by the popes, who by the time of the Renaissance were invariably members of the leading families of Rome. It was founded originally by pope Julius II in the late 15th century, in the specially adapted Villa Belvedere in the Vatican gardens. The statues in this collection were, and still are, displayed in a series of courts and long corridors. The impact of this collection on the world of art was considerable, but it did not receive unqualified support from all quarters. Some of the later popes considered the collection inappropriate for the home of a religious leader, and debates were waged concerning the conflict between the principles of the Christian faith, on the one hand, and, on the other, the significance of these Greek and Roman monuments, many of which were naked, as objects of idolatry. Pius V, who was elected pope in 1566, even ordered the dispersal of the Vatican collection. However, Renaissance thinkers defended the statues, arguing that they should be viewed not, or not primarily, as images of pagan gods, but as examples of "noble fine art" which should be distinguished from "corrupt art that flattered the senses". Despite Pius's orders, and later rumours that the Vatican was being stripped of its ancient statuary, few of these valuable pieces were actually removed. Instead, shutters were installed around some of them to conceal them from the visitors, and male genitals were removed from many of them and replaced with fig leaves, originally made of metal but later moulded in plaster. The example set by the popes was followed by most members of the nobility in their own collections. Such actions removed from the public gaze bodies and body parts that appear not to have been offensive to Roman viewers, whether in private or in public, and whether in a sacred or profane context.

Interest in the classical world and its artistic achievements was revived again in the 18th century, leading to the widespread reversal of censorship and a notable increase in the size and number of Roman collections. With the Enlightenment there developed a more academic interest in classical art, which was less concerned with the conflict between Christian principles and classical nudity or idolatry. Classical art came to be considered the highest accomplishment of art for all time. One of the principal purposes for the removal of such ancient works to European centres such as London, Paris, or Berlin was so that they could be used as models for sculptors and other artists, classical statuary being considered "ideal beauty". Thus, Lord Elgin claimed that it was necessary to remove the sculptures from the temples on the Acropolis at Athens so that British artists could see and learn from original Greek sculptures, rather than the Roman copies which Italian, French, and German artists had to be content with as models. From the late 18th century, both public and private collections have also been formed in centres outside Europe, such as in North America, Japan, Australia, and New Zealand. Increasing numbers of tourists from around the world also came to view the original collections. The prolific copying of such statues in the late 18th and 19th centuries bore witness to their acceptability in contemporary contexts. Thus, classical sculpture, whether draped or nude, was no longer censored. It was considered high art, was often conflated with romanticism, and was generally not considered erotic. With the rise of modernism, interest in classical sculpture in the 20th century has, in some quarters, become more a nostalgic interest in the romanticism of these representations. However, this does not apply to all classes of ancient works of art.

Pompeii and Herculaneum

Excavations at the Roman town of Herculaneum began in 1709; they commenced at neighbouring Pompeii in 1738 and are still continuing there. The objects unearthed during these excavations have included sculptures, pieces of furniture, decorated vessels, lamps, and smaller objects in stone, metal, and clay, many of which portray copulating couples (human, part-human – such as satyrs – and nonhuman), ithyphallic male figures, dwarf figures with enormous penises, or just the penis, sometimes augmented with limbs and ornamented with bells.

A large number of the wall-paintings and floor mosaics unearthed in these towns, particularly the figured paintings from the centre of the walls, depict scenes from Greek mythology, and include naked and seminaked couples, the naked female figures again being associated with love scenes. Other paintings and mosaics show sexually explicit scenes or copulating couples. These have generally been found in less central locations, in wall-painting schemes, on the walls of small buildings, in the smaller rooms of large buildings, and in public baths. This latter group has been considered to have been a more popular form of art, while the central panels based on Greek mythology have been considered "fine art". However, such perspectives rather reflect post-Renaissance attitudes than explicitly Roman ones.

For nearly two centuries after the first excavations, the finds were destined for the collections of the Neapolitan royal family, particularly in Portici, or as presents for distinguished and noble guests of the kings of Naples. Many also ended up on the black market, and many were copied. The objects in the royal collections, including paintings cut from the walls and parts of mosaic pavements, were displayed for visitors to see and admire. Information about the nature and manner of this display must be pieced together from the descriptions of such visitors and from contemporary paintings. This information does not provide evidence for the display of the types of objects listed above, confirming that such "erotic" items that might "flatter the senses", were hidden from visitors in secret rooms, such as in the Gabinetto Segreto in the Bourbon palace in Naples. In the academic climate of the 18th century, lavish books and extensive catalogues were published on the finds from the Herculaneum and Pompeian excavations but only the more comprehensive of these publications included any examples of such objects. Soon after the Kingdom of Italy was proclaimed, under king Victor Emmanuel II of Savoy, in 1861, the Bourbon palace and its collections were transformed into the National Museum of Naples. Père Dumas catalogued the "erotic" objects in the Gabinetto Segreto at this time, but the room remained closed to the public until 2000.

Not all the paintings and mosaics from Pompeii and Herculaneum were removed to these collections. Throughout the 19th century, and most of the 20th century, many that were considered erotic were left *in situ*, but the rooms in which they were found were locked and entry by tourists was forbidden. "Erotic" statuary was also sometimes removed from the place of its discovery, in gardens or public areas of the house, to be placed in such rooms. In situations where it was not possible to conceal such depictions from the public eye, wooden cabinets were constructed around the paintings to lock them away inside: these included, for example, a depiction of the phallic god Priapus weighing his penis in the entranceway to the House of the Vettii in Pompeii.

While many of these rooms remain closed even today, in the 1970s some of the secrecy was dropped. The wooden cabinet was removed from the Priapus painting in the House of the Vettii, for example, and it is now a major attraction for tourists. Tourists also queue in large numbers to be let into the closed room behind the kitchen in the same house, to be shown its wall-paintings of sexual scenes and an ithyphallic statue of a satyr, which is also locked away in this room but which originally served as a fountain in the garden of the house.

The easing of censorship in the 1970s also led to the publication of many books on the erotic art of Pompeii. A notable example is *Eros in Pompeii* (1975), by Michael Grant and Antonia Mulas, a photographic documentation of many of the objects in the Gabinetto Segreto. The appearance of such books led, in turn, to a belief, widely held not only among the general public but also among some scholars, that most of the art in Pompeii and Herculaneum had been "erotic" and "decadent". More recent works, such as those of Luciana Jacobelli, have struggled to dispel these views and to demonstrate that the viewers in Roman times interpreted such works of art in quite different ways from modern viewers: these works were concerned with fertility and prosperity, or perhaps represented puns that we no longer fully understand.

Nevertheless, a form of censorship still persists, and therefore continues to project contemporary ideas of the "erotic" and the "forbidden" onto the Roman past. For example, the chapter on the House of the Vettii in *Pompei, Pitture e Mosaici: Enciclopedia dell'Arte Antica* (1990 onwards) omits photographs or discussion of the paintings in the room behind the kitchen.

PENELOPE ALLISON

Further Reading

Baldassarre, Ida (editor): *Pompei, Pitture e Mosaici*, Rome: Istituto della Enciclopedia Italiana, 1990–99

Fehl, Philipp, *The Classical Monument: Reflections on the Connection between Morality and Art in Greek and Roman Sculpture*, New York: New York University Press, 1972

Grant, Michael and Antonia Mulas, *Eros in Pompeii: The Secret Rooms of the National Museum of Naples*, New York: Morrow, 1975; as *Erotic Art in Pompeii*, London: Octopus, 1975

Haskell, Francis and Nicholas Penny, *Taste and the Antique: The Lure of Classical Sculpture 1500–1900*, New Haven, Connecticut and London: Yale University Press, 1981

Jacobelli, Luciana, *Le pitture erotiche delle Terme Suburbane di Pompei*, Rome: Bretschneider, 1995

Pliny the Elder, *Natural History*, translated by H. Rackham, 10 vols, London: Heinemann, and Cambridge: Massachusetts: Harvard University Press, 1938–63 (Loeb edition; 9, books 34–35)

Trevelyan, Raleigh, *The Shadow of Vesuvius: Pompeii AD 79*, London: Joseph and The Folio Society, 1976

ABRAM ROOM
Russian film director, 1894–1976

STROGII IUNOSHA (A Stern Young Man)
Film, 1934: censored in Ukraine, 1936

Abram Room was a talented filmmaker and scriptwriter who had studied psychology, and then begun his career working in Vsevolod Meierkhol'd's theatre in 1923. His first two feature films, *Bukhta smerti* (Bay of Death) and *Predatel'* (The Traitor), had appeared in 1926, but he had been catapulted into notoriety in 1927 with *Tret'ia Meshchanskaia* (Third Meshchanskaya Street (also known as Bed and Sofa). In this study of an eternal triangle in the context of the New Economic Policy (NEP), traditional Russian gender roles are reversed and it is the woman who is presented as the decision-making pillar of strength. Room then made *Prividenie, kotoroe ne vozvrashchaetsia* (1930, The Ghost that Never Returns), a visually striking film set in a penal colony in Mexico and based on a novel by the Frenchman Henri Barbusse. In the same year Room also directed *Plan Velikikh rabot* (Plan for Great Works), the first sound feature film to be made in the Soviet Union. His next project, *Odnazhdy letom* (Once One Summer), was stopped during filming in 1932 and he was expelled from the Mosfilm studios.

A Stern Young Man was as controversial a project for the mid-1930s as *Bed and Sofa* had been for the late 1920s, but these were less tolerant times. The screenplay was written by Iurii Olesha, based on themes from his novel *Zavist'* (Envy); he dedicated it to Zinaida Raikh, an actress who was Meierkhol'd's wife. (All three suffered in the purges that engulfed the Soviet Union later in the 1930s, and only Olesha survived.) The screenplay provoked widespread controversy even before the film appeared, after it was published in the leading literary journal *Novyi Mir* in August 1934.

A Stern Young Man confronts the problem of equality in present and future socialist society, and the possible conflict between, on the one hand, the ideal of equal opportunity and treatment, and, on the other, the practical necessity of rewarding those whose talents and disposition make them particularly valuable contributors to that society. The principal characters are professor Stepanov and his wife Masha. Stepanov is a surgeon, trained before the revolution, who has placed his talents at the service of that revolution and been handsomely rewarded in material terms. He and his wife enjoy a lifestyle that, to contemporary Soviet readers and audiences, would have seemed like something out of Hollywood: they have a large villa and a car, items available only to the chosen few. Grisha, the stern young man of the title (which can also be translated as *The Strict Young Man* or *The Severe Young Man*), provides a stark contrast to this couple. He is a member of the communist youth movement, a "magic *Komsomolets*", puritanical in the extreme, even in his budding romance with Masha, who is old enough to be his mother. Indeed, Grisha can be interpreted as encapsulating the ideal morality of the future classless society. His developing relationship with Masha is used to explore the arguments about reward and equality in socialist society, both in the present and in the future that socialist realist art was instructed to explore through the techniques of "revolutionary romanticism", which had once been defined by

Anatolii Lunacharskii, the first People's Commissar for Popular Enlightenment, as "not reality as it is but reality as it will be". Eventually, Grisha renounces Masha, not because she is already married (which would be "bourgeois"), but because she is married to someone who is useful to society.

The treatment of a politically sensitive topic in Soviet cinema was always risky even at the best of times, but it was positively dangerous from the late 1920s until the mid-1980s, and doubly dangerous under Stalin, particularly when Communist Party policy was itself in a process of transition. Immediately after the Bolshevik revolution, all signs of social differentiation, such as noble titles and military ranks, had been abolished in the interests of the stated ideal of socialist equality. However, the revolutionary government had lacked the necessary expertise and experience to run a complex modern state, and Lenin had been forced to use the "old bourgeois specialists" typified by professor Stepanov. They had been tolerated because they were useful but by the 1930s they were beginning to seem anachronisms, as postrevolutionary society was producing its own specialists. The question that then arose was whether these new socialist specialists should be rewarded in the "bourgeois" manner, with material benefits, or whether their value should be judged by what they contributed to society voluntarily, and without extra material reward.

In 1935 military ranks were reintroduced into the Red Army and related measures were gradually introduced into civilian life, increasing inequalities in pay and access to facilities such as special shops, sanatoriums, and holiday centres, which were by then all controlled directly or indirectly by the state. By deliberately exposing the arguments for and against equality, the screenplay, and then the film made from it, raised questions that the government no longer wanted asked. Accordingly, on 10 June 1936 the film was banned from distribution by order of the Ukrainfilm studios where it had been made. Room was accused of basing A Stern Young Man on a screenplay that had "an alien 'philosophical' basis and a false system of characters". The deputy director of the studio was sacked and his two superiors were severely reprimanded for wasting 1.8 million roubles on the film. Room was told that he would never make a film for the studio again. By 1936 he was therefore effectively banned from filmmaking in both Moscow and Kiev, and his promising career went into a sharp decline.

Unusually for a Soviet director, Room had been relieved of his teaching responsibilities as early as 1934: others whose filmmaking ran into difficulties, such as Lev Kuleshov or Sergei Eisenstein (specifically over *Bezhin Lug*, Bezhin Meadow), nonetheless flourished as teachers. Room, however, continued to direct films, although these were largely literary adaptations of little historical interest or artistic distinction. *A Stern Young Man* effectively destroyed his career.

RICHARD TAYLOR

Further Reading

Graffy, Julian, *Bed and Sofa*, London and New York: Tauris, 2001

Grashchenkova, Irina, *Abram Room*, Moscow: Iskusstvo, 1977

Leyda, Jay, *Kino: A History of the Russian and Soviet Film*, 3rd edition, London: Allen and Unwin, and Princeton, New Jersey: Princeton University Press, 1983

Margolit, Evgenii and Viacheslav Shmyrov, *Iz"iatoe kino* (Withdrawn Cinema), Moscow: Double-D, 1995

Taylor, Richard and Derek Spring (editors), *Stalinism and Soviet Cinema*, London and New York: Routledge, 1993

Vincendeau, Ginette (editor), *Encyclopedia of European Cinema*, London: Cassell/British Film Institute, and New York: Facts on File, 1995

ALFRED ROSENBERG
German ideologue and censor, 1893–1946

Alfred Rosenberg was born in Reval (now Tallinn) in Estonia, of Baltic German bourgeois parentage. His ultranationalism was typical of many expatriate Germans from the border regions. Rosenberg joined the Nazi Party in 1919, the year it was founded, and became editor of its newspaper, the *Völkischer Beobachter*, in 1923. From the start, he was regarded as something of an outsider within the movement. His introverted and arrogant nature exacerbated the unfavourable attitudes of other Nazis towards him. Despite this, he established himself as the guardian of the Nazi *Weltanschauung* ("world view") in the early 1920s. His belief in Nazism as an ideology was all-encompassing, and he held on to his ideological tenets consistently and to the letter. He became the chief ideologue of the movement.

In 1929, Rosenberg established the Kampfbund für deutsche Kultur (Combat League for German Culture) to oppose what he and other Nazis regarded as *entartete Kunst* ("degenerate art"). He called for the encouragement and creation of a new *Volkskunst*, an "art of the people", in which the national spirit and national unity would be represented. This art was to be "healthy" and robust. It was the art of the artisan and the peasant, wholesome and ingenuous. He disliked what he saw as the decadence and self-centred individualism of modern art. According to Rosenberg, the *Volkskunst* was to be based upon Nazi criteria of beauty, and he proclaimed that all items displaying "cosmopolitan and Bolshevist symptoms" should be removed from German collections and museums, and burned. He further argued that "the names of those artists who have been swept along by the flood of Marxism and Bolshevism must never be mentioned again in public". Not all Nazis shared his opinions and, encountering unexpected resistance to his ideas, he made his attacks on modern art increasingly vitriolic. In July 1933, for example, within months of the Nazi seizure of power, he published an article in the *Völkischer Beobachter* entitled "Revolution in the Fine Arts?", in which he attacked the expressionist painter Emil Nolde and the sculptor Ernst Barlach, castigating Nolde's work in particular as "negroid, irreverent, raw, and devoid of true inner strength of form".

In Nazi Germany, control over censorship was divided between Joseph Goebbels, who represented the state, and

Rosenberg, who represented the party. From the start, major clashes arose between them. By encouraging such rivalry, and playing off party and state against each other, Hitler stimulated censorship policies. Although this meant that at first there were certain loopholes and inconsistencies in censorship, on the whole it strengthened the censorship procedure, as both Goebbels and Rosenberg redoubled their efforts to exceed each other's censorship activities.

In 1933, Rosenberg was placed in charge of the Reich Office for the Promotion of German Literature, known as the Reichsstelle. This was the largest of all the state and party organizations concerned with literature, employing 1400 editors to impose Nazi principles. Its members included Hans Hagemeyer and Günter Wismann, who also worked for the State Censorship Office. After the initial stages of suppression, the purpose of Rosenberg's machinery was not only to reject the undesirable, but also to promote desirable literature. His "white lists" of suitable and desirable books had considerable influence upon Bernhard Rust's Library Offices and the state censors of literature. The best-known of his "white lists" was the *Gutachtenanzeiger* (Review Indicator), which was published as a supplement to the journal *Die Bücherkunde* (Book News). In 1933, 2000 books were reviewed in this supplement, and by 1939 the annual number of book reviews had risen to 4250. Rosenberg carried out his spiritual and ideological leadership by means of a large administration, consisting of 32 state offices, 55 district offices, and between 800 and 1000 censors. He also controlled the censorship and book promotional activities of the Reich Youth Leadership Organization and the National Socialist Teachers Association.

From the start, Rosenberg's own interest in the German cultural community stemmed from his fascination with what he understood to be the Nordic Germanic folk heritage. He worked closely with the Nordic Society, and tried to promote cultural exchange programmes between German and Scandinavian writers and artists. He also worked with the Reich Office for German Prehistory to draw up plans for a national institute for Nordic Germanic folklore and history. In addition, he promoted the publication of folklore journals and had close links with the Institute for German Folklore.

In January 1934, Rosenberg was appointed the Führer's Commissioner for the Supervision of all Intellectual and Ideological Education and Instruction in the NSDAP (as the Nazi Party was formally known). He put his full title on each and every document he signed. Hence, he controlled the ideological education and training of party members. Although, at first, there were overlapping functions and structures of censorship within the party, by 1937 Rosenberg had succeeded in bringing every branch and division of all offices within his jurisdiction by making them all responsible to the Central Office that worked under his direct supervision within the Reichsstelle. Just nine years later, however, he was tried and hanged as a war criminal at Nuremberg.

LISA PINE

Writings

Der Mythus des 20. Jahrhunderts, 1933, 9th edition 1939; as *The Myth of the Twentieth Century: An Evaluation of the Spiritual-Intellectual Confrontations of Our Age*, 1982
Memoirs, translated by Eric Posselt, 1949
Selected Writings, edited by Robert Pois, 1970; as *Race and Race History, and Other Essays*, 1971

Further Reading

Bollmus, Reinhard, *Das Amt Rosenberg und seine Gegner: Studien zum Machtkampf im nationalsozialistischen Herrschaftssystem*, Stuttgart: Deutsche Verlags-Anstalt, 1970
Cecil, Robert, *The Myth of the Master Race: Alfred Rosenberg and Nazi Ideology*, London: Batsford, and New York: Dodd Mead, 1972
Hart, F.T., *Alfred Rosenberg: Der Mann und sein Werk*, Munich: Lehmanns, 1933

ROBERTO ROSSELLINI
Italian film director, 1906–1977

IL MIRACOLO/THE MIRACLE
Film, 1948 (Italy) and 1950 (US)

Il miracolo was produced in Italy in 1948 and was based on a story by Federico Fellini; it was also similar in theme to *Adega*, by the Spanish writer Ramón del Valle-Inclán, which had caused a sensation in 1901. Constructed in four short scenes, it starred Anna Magnani as Nanni, a poor, simple-minded goatherd who believes that a man (played by Federico Fellini) she encounters on a mountain path is St Joseph. When she first sees him he is wearing a cape-like coat and walks with the aid of a staff. She calls out to him: "St. Joseph. I knew you'd come." He says nothing, but offers Nanni some of his wine, which she drinks until she passes out. The scene fades to black.

Several months pass. Nanni is playing with a group of children in the courtyard of the village church and when she passes out a group of women realize she is pregnant. They know she is not married and is not mentally competent. The women begin to taunt her and laugh at her but she dismisses them and announces: "It is the grace of God." The news quickly spreads through the village that Nanni is pregnant and that she believes the father is St Joseph. Some of the older women are understanding and try to help her. But most of the villagers, especially the younger ones, make fun of her, faking a religious procession in her honour, singing hymns to "Mary", and crowning her with a bucket. Nanni is humiliated and leaves the village to live in the mountains where she gives birth in a deserted church.

Reception in Italy of *Il miracolo* was mixed. The film was approved by the Italian censorship board for public exhibition, but the Catholic Cinematographic Centre (CCC), the Italian counterpart to the US Legion of Decency, called the film an "abominable profanation" and advised "everyone, nobody excepted, not to see the film". The Vatican, however, made no attempt to suppress the film. The British Board of Film Censors (BBFC) was particularly concerned with Nanni's "labour pains" and refused a certificate.

Only when it began playing in the US did *The Miracle* become front-page news. The controversy began innocently enough. Booked into the Paris Theater on West 58th Street in New York City by film distributor Joseph Burstyn, the film had been cleared by US customs officials and approved for public exhibition on two different occasions by the New York state censorship board. The New York board, which was empowered to prohibit "sacrilegious" films, passed *The Miracle* in March 1949 without English subtitles and then approved a second version with subtitles in November 1949. In an effort to broaden the audience, *The Miracle* was combined with two short French films, Jean Renoir's *A Day in the Country* and Marcel Pagnol's *Jofroi*. The three films were released under the new title *The Ways of Love*.

This trilogy opened at the Paris Theater on 12 December 1950 without much public attention. Eleven days after the film opened, the Legion of Decency slapped a condemned rating on the film and charged that *The Miracle* was "a sacrilegious and blasphemous mockery of Christian and religious truth". It was, the legion director Father Patrick Masterson told Cardinal Francis Spellman, archbishop of New York, "a blasphemous mockery of the Virgin Birth". The controversy heated up when New York city's license commissioner Edward McCaffery informed the management of the Paris Theater that he found *The Miracle* "officially and personally blasphemous" and ordered it removed from the screen.

The Miracle was suddenly the hottest ticket in New York City. Newspapers chronicled the case on front pages. New York film critics registered their displeasure with the attempt to censor the film by voting *The Miracle* "Best Foreign Film" of the year. The publicity resulted in standing room only at the Paris Theater as curious movie fans braved miserable weather and Catholic pickets to see what all the fuss was about.

The drama continued on 5 January 1951 when the New York Supreme Court held that McCaffery had, in fact, overstepped his authority. The ruling infuriated Cardinal Spellman, who issued a stinging rebuttal which was read at every Mass in the New York archdiocese on 7 January 1951. The cardinal called the film "vile and harmful". It was, he charged, inspired by communists, and he demanded that all Catholics boycott it. Catholics rallied to Spellman's call to arms and the situation quickly turned ugly. Catholic picket lines at the Paris Theater swelled to over 1000 men and women. This was, according to Bosley Crowther, "the most distasteful and disturbing" aspect of the case.

By early 1951 it was very clear that the debate over *The Miracle* had moved far beyond anything that was on the screen. Perfectly intelligent people were arguing that in order to protect democracy, and the American way of life, the film had to be banned – not just censored. Catholics from Cardinal Spellman on down freely tossed the charge of communism at any who favoured showing the film. Pickets lines and bomb threats attempted to prevent people from seeing the film. Protestant and Catholic representatives argued over what was and was

ROSSELLINI: The British Board of Film Censors initially refused a certificate for the British release of *Il miracolo* (*The Miracle*) in 1948 because there were questions raised about the vivid depiction of the lead character, Nanni, giving birth. The film was eventually passed for release in Britain in January 1951 with the new "X" certificate, for screening to adults (over 16 years) only, which had been introduced that year.

not sacrilegious. No one, it seemed, could judge the film on its own merits – least of all the New York State censorship board, which was now under tremendous political pressure to revoke the licence it had originally granted to Burstyn.

On 15 February 1951 *The Miracle* was screened for a ten-member committee of the New York censorship board. After a brief deliberation they revoked the licence on the grounds that the New York law demanded that "men and women of all faiths respect the religious beliefs held by others". The film was sacrilegious, the committee held, because it associated the Protestant and Catholic versions of the Bible with "drunkenness, seduction and lewdness".

Burstyn was not surprised by the ruling. Determined to challenge the legality of movie censorship, Burstyn and his lawyer, Ephriam London, filed a petition with the US Supreme Court on 4 December 1951. The Supreme Court agreed to hear *Burstyn* v. *Wilson* and oral arguments were scheduled for 24 April 1952.

The legal precedent for government censorship of film rested with the US Supreme Court decision in 1915, *Mutual* v. *Ohio*, which upheld the constitutionality of state boards of film censorship. Justice Joseph McKenna, who wrote the opinion, stated that movies were "a business pure and simple," and not "regarded by the Ohio constitution . . . as part of the press". Burstyn was challenging this ruling. Prior to hearing the oral arguments, the Court screened *The Miracle*. At issue were two basic points: the constitutionality of government licensing of films prior to their exhibition; and more specifically, the constitutionality of a New York statute that gave authority to ban films that were held to be "sacrilegious".

A month after the oral arguments were presented, the Supreme Court handed down a reversal of the New York Court of Appeals decision. Justice Tom Clark wrote the unanimous decision for the Court. After summarizing the events that led up to the case, Clark wrote that "the present case is the first to present squarely to us the question whether motion pictures are within the ambit of protection which the First Amendment, through the Fourteenth, secures to any form of 'speech' or 'the press' ".

Clark looked at each element of *Mutual* v. *Ohio*. "It cannot be doubted", he wrote, "that motion pictures are a significant medium for the communication of ideas." Their ability to communicate ideas "is not lessened by the fact that they are designed to entertain as well as to inform", he wrote. Clark then addressed the issue that movies had a greater capacity for evil than other means of communication. They could, he understood, communicate ideas to "the youth of a community". But Clark countered that: "If there be capacity for evil it may be relevant in determining the permissible scope of community control, but it does not authorize unbridled censorship such as we have here." The New York statute, he argued, had set the censor "adrift upon a boundless sea amid a myriad of conflicting currents of religious views, with no charts but those provided by the most vocal and powerful orthodoxies". The state had "no legitimate interest in protecting any or all religions from views distasteful to them".

The Court concluded that motion pictures were "included within the free speech and the free press guarantee of the First and Fourteenth Amendments", but added that "a state may censor motion pictures under a clearly drawn statute designed and applied to prevent the showing of obscene films". Even with that added proviso that a carefully drawn censorship law to prevent obscene films might be legal, it was a stunning decision for freedom of the screen. In effect the Court ruled that the state censorship boards in New York, Ohio, Maryland,

Pennsylvania, and Kansas and the 200 or so municipal film censorship boards (Memphis, Atlanta, Chicago) were unconstitutional because they all included some type of statement that prohibited films on sacrilegious grounds. One by one over the next decade these institutions of censorship would fall by the wayside. It would take more than a decade for all the old remnants of film censorship to disappear from the American landscape, but *The Miracle* case was the beginning of the end for censorship of movies in the US.

Of the film itself, Rossellini argued that Nanni's belief "may be blasphemous ... but her faith is so strong that her faith redeems it. The last thing she does is completely human and normal: she gives her breast to the child. Some Catholics praised it."

GREGORY D. BLACK

Writings

Le Cinéma révélé, edited by Alain Bergala, 1984
Quasi un'autobiografia, edited by Stefano Roncoroni, 1987
My Method: Writings and Interviews, edited by Adriano Aprà, translated by Annapaola Cancogni, 1992

Further Reading

Black, Gregory D., *The Catholic Crusade against Hollywood, 1940–1975*, Cambridge and New York: Cambridge University Press, 1998
Giglio, Ernest D., "The Decade of the Miracle, 1952–1962: A Study in the Censorship of the American Motion Picture", (dissertation), Syracuse, New York: Syracuse University, 1964
Randall, Richard S., *Censorship of the Movies: The Social and Political Control of a Mass Medium*, Madison: University of Wisconsin Press, 1968
Westin, Alan F., *The Miracle Case: The Supreme Court and the Movies*, University: University of Alabama Press, 1961

EVDOKIIA ROSTOPCHINA
Russian poet and prose writer, 1812–1858

"NASIL'NYI BRAK" (The Forced Marriage)
Ballad, 1846

Countess Evdokiia Petrovna Rostopchina was a popular 19th-century Russian salon hostess and author. Her prose, dramas, and romantic lyrics featured high-society settings and emphasized women's perspectives. Contemporary critics lauded her work for its exemplary "feminine style". In 1846, an atypical ballad of Rostopchina's, "Nasil'nyi brak" (The Forced Marriage), appeared in the literary journal *Severnaia Pchela* (The Northern Bee). The idea for the ballad had emerged in 1845. As the Rostopchin family travelled through Poland to Italy, according to her daughter, Rostopchina reflected on the social and cultural plight of Jews in Poland. This the writer compared to an unhappy wife in a mismatched marriage. Written a year later, the ballad depicts an accusation by an old *barin* (landowner), followed by the reply of his younger wife.

The old *barin* asks his servants to judge the behaviour of his

wife, since she is not grateful for the protection and the riches he provides. The *barin* accuses her of scheming against him and siding with his enemies. In response, the wife asserts that the marriage was against her will. "Whether I am a slave or a spouse/God alone knows! Was it I who chose/For myself a cruel spouse?" she asks the servants. In her humiliating marriage she cannot speak in her native language nor display other forms of her culture. The *barin* exiled her servants, forced her into silence about her situation, and brought her "shame, persecution, and slavery" by wedding her. "Am I forbidden to grumble?/While suffering such a fate/Must a wife taken by force/Continue to conceal it from all others?"

Rostopchina's ballad became the subject of rumours and parlour conversations. Many believed that the countess was publicly describing her unhappy, incompatible marriage to count Andrei Fedorovich Rostopchin. This, though, was not the cause of the poem's censoring. The difficult plight of married noblewomen already belonged to the emerging Russian "woman question" polemic. More to the point was the popular pressure on women writers to keep their personal lives out of their publications. Most damaging was emperor Nicholas I's interpretation, seeing the old *barin* as representing him and the wife Poland, forcibly married to the Russian empire. The emperor summoned the Rostopchin family from Italy to St Petersburg and, in a private meeting, condemned the poet for her allegorical ballad.

Despite her pleas of innocence, Rostopchina was banned from all court activities. The Rostopchin family moved to Moscow in 1847. Around this time, the countess abandoned poetry in favour of writing prose, blank verse dramas, and stories. She re-established her literary salon in Moscow, gathering many of the foremost young writers and editors of the city. Although this helped Rostopchina's literary career, providing her with a publication outlet for new works, the young literatteurs were more interested in their association with the writer of the scandalous "Forced Marriage".

Meanwhile, the Third Section, which oversaw Russian censorship, confiscated all copies of the issue of *Severnaia pchela* to prevent circulation of Rostopchina's ballad. The ballad, however, was copied manually and passed around Russian educated society for many years. In Russian archives today scholars can find stray reproductions of "The Forced Marriage" in private collections and salon albums, demonstrating the elites' subversion of state censorship and the legacy of Rostopchina's poem.

LAURA SCHLOSBERG

Writings

"Nasil'nyi brak", 1846; as "The Forced Marriage," translated by Louis Pedrotti, *Slavic and East European Journal* 30/2 (1986): 202

"Stikhotvoreniia grafini E. Rostopchinyi" (The Poems of Countess E. Rostopchina), edited by V.G. Belinskii, in *Polnoe sobranie sochinenii* (Complete Collected Works), vol. 5, 1954

Stikhotvoreniia, proza, pis'ma (Verses, Prose, Letters), 1986

Talisman: Izbannaia lirika (Talisman: Collected Lyrics), 1987

Schastlivaia zhenshchina: literaturnye sochinenii (The Happy Woman: Literary Works), 1991

Palatstso Flori (Flora Palace), 1993

Further Reading

Choldin, Marianna Tax, *A Fence around the Empire: Russian Censorship of Western Ideas under the Tsars*, Durham, North Carolina: Duke University Press, 1985

Ernst, S., "Karolina Pavlova i gr. Evdokiia Rostopchina" (Karolina Pavlova and Countess Evdokiia Rostopchina), *Russkii bibliofil* (Russian Bibliophile), 6 (1916): 5–35

Fainshtein, M. Sh., *Pisatel'nitsy pushkinskoi pory: istoriko literaturnye ocherki* (Women Writers of Pushkin's Era), Leningrad: Nauka, 1989

Fuhrmann, Joseph T., Edward C. Bock and Leon I. Twarog, *Essays on Russian Intellectual History*. Austin: University of Texas Press, 1971

Khadasevich, V., "Grafina E.P. Rostopchina: Eë zhizn' i lirika" (Countess E.P. Rostopchina: Her Life and Lyrics) in his *Stat'i o russkoi poezii* (Essays about Russian Poetry), Petrograd: Epokha, 1922

Kiselev, V.S., "Poetessa i Tsar: Stranitsa istorii russkoi poezii 40-kh godov" (Poetess and Emperor: Pages from the History of Russian Poetry of the 1840s), *Russkaia literatura* (Russian Literature), 1 (1965): 144–56

Kiselev-Sergenin, V.S., "Po staromu sledu: o ballade E. Rostopchina 'Nasil'nyi brak'" (Along the Path of the Past: On the E. Rostopchina's Ballad "The Forced Marriage"), *Russkaia-Literatura: Istoriko-Literaturnyi Zhurnal*, 3 (1995): 137–52

Mersereau, John, Jr, *Russian Romantic Fiction*, Ann Arbor, Michigan: Ardis, 1983

Monas, Sidney, *The Third Section: Police and Society in Russia under Nicholas I*, Cambridge, Massachusetts: Harvard University Press, 1961

Nekrasova, E., "Grafinia E. P. Rostopchina, 1811–1858" (Countess E.P. Rostopchina, 1811–58), *Vestnik Evropy* (European Herald), 3 (1885): 42–81

Pedrotti, Louis, "The Scandal of Countess Rostopchina's Polish-Russian Allegory", *Slavic and East European Journal*, 30/2 (1986): 196–214

Rostopchina, Lidiia A., *Semeinaia khronika* (Family Chronicle), Moscow: Nauka, 1912

Ruud, Charles A., *Fighting Words: Imperial Censorship and the Russian Press, 1804–1906*, Toronto: University of Toronto Press, 1982

Squire, P.S., *The Third Department: The Establishment and Practices of the Political Police in the Russia of Nicholas I*, London: Cambridge University Press, 1968

Sushkov, D.P., "Vozrazhenie na stat'iu E. S. Nekrasovy" (Reply to E. S. Nekrasova's Essay) in *Vestnik Evropy* (European Herald), 2/2 (1888): 388–43

MSTISLAV ROSTROPOVICH
Russian cellist and conductor, 1927–

Mstislav Rostropovich is widely regarded as one of the great musicians of the 20th century. His career has been rewarded with every kind of success and honour that the Soviet, western, and now post-Soviet Russian worlds have been able to give. More than 100 compositions for the cello have been inspired or commissioned by him; he has founded festivals and competitions to highlight new cellists, many of whom are his students. Rostropovich also played a significant role in the battle for artistic freedom that raged during the last decades of the Soviet era.

Rostropovich's first teacher was his father, Leopold, himself a professional cellist. Mstislav attended the Moscow Conservatory (1943–1948), where he began a lifelong friendship with Dmitrii Shostakovich, who dedicated both of his cello concertos to the talented student, and also got to know Sergei Prokofiev, who wrote the Sinfonia Concertante for him. Rostropovich's brilliance and *joie de vivre* made him a star in a society that valued and richly rewarded its large number of gifted artists. He was allowed to undertake foreign tours, awarded Lenin and Stalin Prizes (the highest awards the Soviet state could grant), and given a *dacha* in the country. In 1955 Rostropovich married the brilliant soprano Galina Vishnevskaia, then the prima donna of the Bolshoi Theatre, where he later enjoyed a second and equally successful career as a conductor. Rostropovich also delighted in accompanying his wife at the piano in recitals. They had two daughters, talented musicians themselves. No man had more reason to be contented with life in the Soviet Union, or more to lose by defying its government, than Rostropovich.

In 1968, after a concert in the provincial city of Riazan, he introduced himself to the writer Aleksandr Solzhenitsyn, whose novella about life in the Soviet labour camps, *Odin den' Ivana Denisovicha* (1962, *One Day in the Life of Ivan Denisovich*), had shocked and thrilled the world. Solzhenitsyn was living in a rural shack, writing unpublishable novels and plays, and working on his encyclopedic testimony of the camps, *Arkhipelag GULag* (*The Gulag Archipelago*). His novels *V kruge pervom* (*The First Circle*) and *Rakovyi korpus* (*Cancer Ward*) had been published in the West, and the authorities were debating whether to expel him from the Writers Union (which they did in 1969). However different in personality, the two men became friends, and Rostropovich, having an unoccupied and newly renovated apartment at his *dacha*, offered it to the writer and the family he was establishing. (By the time Solzhenitsyn left in 1973, he and his wife had three sons, Ermolai, Ignat, and Stepan.)

In a interview in 1995, Rostropovich recalled that his offer had been purely humanitarian: Solzhenitsyn was simply a man who needed a place to live, whatever his politics. This seems disingenuous. Although he confirmed in that interview that "it was Solzhenitsyn's presence which triggered [my] hostility toward the Soviet regime", Rostropovich already knew full well the sort of regime he was living under. When his professors and friends Shostakovich and Prokofiev were anathematized in 1948 for "formalism" and stripped of their livelihoods, Rostropovich had dropped out of the Moscow Conservatory in solidarity with Shostakovich and moved in with Prokofiev. In 1958, when he was expected to speak at a meeting condemning Boris Pasternak's novel *Doktor Zhivago* (*Doctor Zhivago*), which neither he nor the other speakers had read, he instead fulfilled an out-of-town performance conveniently scheduled for the same day. The Warsaw Pact invasion of Czechoslavakia in 1968, which occurred when Rostropovich and Vishnevskaia were performing in London, so devastated them that they vowed never to perform in Czechoslavakia while their countrymen occupied it.

Thus, when Rostropovich invited the persecuted writer to live in his apartment, Rostropovich knew that his and Vishnevskaia's lives would surely be affected by his generosity. Rostropovich's openhandedness touched others in Solzhenitsyn's circle. He provided medical care for a dying professor who had hidden all the writer's work between 1962 and 1969; he offered his own house to two of Solzhenitsyn's former fellow *zeks* (camp inmates), who lived there for two winters; and from foreign tours he brought the writer a stencil machine, as well as other supplies unavailable in the Soviet Union.

The first governmental attempt at reprisal came when Vishnevskaia was forbidden to record *Boris Godunov*; she appealed to the deputy minister of culture, and was permitted to make the recording in 1970. That year, Solzhenitsyn received the Nobel Prize for Literature, but he was forbidden to go abroad to claim it, whereupon Rostropovich wrote a letter protesting the government's treatment of his friend. He mailed the letter from West Germany to four prestigious Soviet news-papers, which declined to print it, but it was immediately broadcast back to the Soviet Union on foreign radio stations. The government's response was to shelve a film biography of Vishnevskaia.

It was Rostropovich who suggested that Solzhenitsyn send five copies of his next novel, *Avgust chetyrnadtsatogo* (*August 1914*), to prominent Soviet officials, so that if they refused to read it, as they indeed did, Solzhenitsyn would have a reason to publish it in the West. Rostropovich himself took two copies of the novel to government officials, who also refused to look at it, and Vishnevskaia even pleaded with a Soviet diplomat in Vienna to give the book a chance. By this time, there was a KGB unit permanently parked in a car near their *dacha*, and, with the help of members of the household, the KGB were able to install listening devices inside their house.

After Rostropovich sent his letter, the reprisals increased. He was removed from his position as conductor at the Bolshoi, and Moscow orchestras were forbidden to invite him to conduct. He could not use Moscow halls for solo concerts. Gradually his foreign tours were cancelled. His and Vishnevskaia's appearances in a film on Shostakovich were not even officially cancelled; they were simply dropped from the project without so much as a phone call.

Rostropovich was allowed to perform as a soloist with the visiting San Francisco Symphony Orchestra, under Seiji Ozawa, and Vishnevskaya, as a People's Artist of the Soviet Union, could not be removed from her position as premier soloist with the Bolshoi. Nevertheless, neither her name nor Rostropovich's was ever mentioned in reviews, nor were their performances aired on radio or television. The government's punishment continued, sometimes in relatively petty ways, such as covering over posters announcing a performance, or not even asking Vishnevskaia if she wanted to step in for an ailing Tosca – one of her signature roles – during a visit from the La Scala company. Rostropovich was reduced to performing and conducting in the hinterlands, and to conducting *Die Fledermaus* at the less-than-first-class Moscow Operetta; even that job was eventually withdrawn. Sometimes the government tried the carrot instead of the stick. Rostropovich was told that he might return to the Bolshoi, and might even assume the directorship, if he would sign a letter condemning his country neighbour Andrei Sakharov. He refused.

When, in 1974, five prominent Bolshoi soloists, including one of her protégées, denounced Vishnevskaia – a ruse designed to cancel a recording of *Tosca* that she was making – she convinced Rostropovich that they must leave the Soviet Union. They wrote a letter to Leonid Brezhnev asking permission to take their family abroad for two years. The intention was never to emigrate, but to escape a situation that was increasingly destructive both personally and artistically. The prospect of leaving their homeland was so painful that Rostropovich unsuccessfully pleaded with an official to exile him to the provinces, if only he might work freely at his art. Their request to Brezhnev was granted instantly, due to the intercession of US senator Edward Kennedy and the composer and conductor Leonard Bernstein. Rostropovich flew to London, followed shortly by his wife and daughters.

In the west, Rostropovich and Vishnevskaia resumed their performing careers, becoming much honoured and much in demand. Among other responsibilities, Rostropovich became music director of the US National Symphony Orchestra, based in Washington, D.C., in 1977. Always, however, they both emphasized that they were "not defecting": they would return to the Soviet Union when its people had freedom and when its artists were allowed to perform anywhere in the world. In retaliation for their continued outspokenness, the Soviet authorities stripped the couple of their citizenship in 1978.

Rostropovich and Vishnevskaia met Mikhail Gorbachev at the White House in 1987. Their citizenship was restored in 1990, and Rostropovich brought the National Symphony Orchestra to Moscow. During the attempted coup of August 1991, he raced from Paris to Moscow to stand at the barricades with the opponents of the Soviet old guard. In 1993, to mark the centenary of Tchaikovskii's death, Rostropovich again led the National Symphony Orchestra in Moscow, this time in Red Square. Earlier the same day, he conducted the Orchestra in the hall of the Moscow Conservatory. They played Shostakovich's First Piano Concerto; the soloist was Ignat Solzhenitsyn.

HARRIET RAFTER

Further Reading

Campbell, Margaret, *The Great Cellists*, London: Gollancz, 1988

Samuel, Claude E., *Mstislav Rostropovich and Galina Vishnevskaya: Russia, Music, and Liberty*, Portland, Oregon: Amadeus Press, 1995

Scammell, Michael, *Solzhenitsyn: A Biography*, London: Hutchinson, and New York: Norton, 1984

Scammell, Michael (editor), *The Solzhenitsyn Files: Secret Soviet Documents Reveal One Man's Fight against the Monolith*, Chicago: Edition q, 1995

Slonimsky, Nicolas, Rostropovich entry in *Baker's Biographical Dictionary of Twentieth-Century Classical Musicians*, edited by Laura Kuhn, New York: Schirmer, 1997

Solzhenitsyn, Aleksandr, *Invisible Allies*, Washington, DC: Counterpoint, 1995; London: Harvill, 1997

Talbot, Joanne, "Shaping a Century", *The Strad* (1995): 1057–63

Thomas, D.M., *Alexander Solzhenitsyn: A Century in His Life*, London: Little Brown, and New York: St Martin's Press, 1998

Vishnevskaya, Galina, *Galina: A Russian Story*, London: Hodder and Stoughton, and New York: Harcourt Brace, 1984

SAMUEL ROTH
US publisher, 1894–1974

In the 1920s Samuel Roth delighted *aficionados* of pornography by publishing Charles Carrington's *Forbidden Books*. He gave James Joyce "the jawache" with his piracies of *Ulysses*, both in expurgated and complete editions. His "exposé" of Herbert Hoover occasioned secret investigations of his income sources by supporters of the US president. Similar scandal books, published in the 1950s, would galvanize the British embassy to protect the reputations of the duke and duchess of Windsor. Roth indignantly defended the titillating books and magazines that he mailed in great numbers, denying that they either reached or influenced teenagers. The Supreme Court's majority and dissenting opinions made his 1957 appeal of a five-year sentence and $5000 fine a landmark case in liberalizing obscenity law.

By his early twenties, Roth had established his credentials as a man of letters by publishing the literary magazine *The Lyric*, and founding The Poetry Bookshop. He reprinted the work of leading contemporary European writers whose works were not under copyright because of a lack of international accords. He made the acquaintance of Frank Harris, Harry Roskelenko, Sholem Asch, Edna St Vincent Millay, Floyd Dell, and Maxwell Bodenheim. He sold their works, and, as did many others, he sold or rented classics of under-the-counter pornography. In 1919, Boni and Liveright published his polemical verses about Jewish concerns past and present, *Europe: A Book for America*, in which the speaker assumes the tone of an Old Testament prophet. In Britain in 1921, he planned a history of contemporary US poetry, for which Ezra Pound was to supply marginal notes.

In that year, Roth founded a quarterly literary review, *Two Worlds*. He hoped to make a place for himself among other young Jewish publishers sponsoring the style and ideas of the European *avant-garde* and their American enthusiasts. It was sold by subscription only, thus corresponding to the way privately printed books were circulated. Having established a correspondence with Ezra Pound, Roth requested permission to serialize Joyce's *Ulysses*. There is some evidence that it was given, but Joyce did not think so. In 1926 and 1927, Roth published excerpts from *Finnegans Wake* in his quarterly *Two Worlds*, and, in *Two Worlds Monthly*, chapters from *Ulysses* that he had expurgated. Over 100 writers signed an International Protest against Roth; Pound did not sign, possibly because he had given Roth to believe that he could publish the *Ulysses* selections, although hardly in expurgated form, possibly because he now thought the main priority was a campaign against pornography laws headed by Joyce. Samuel Roth was no longer known as a man of letters. Indeed, for some of his editing and publishing ventures, he felt it necessary to adopt the alias of "Norman Lockridge", the first of several pseudonyms.

In 1928, the New York Society for the Suppression of Vice engineered Roth's arrest at his New York bookshop. One of the most incriminating items seized was a reprint of Charles Carrington's *Forbidden Books*, a 227-page annotated compilation of Carrington's best-selling sexology and erotology, probably acquired from St George Best, in Chicago. In mid-October, Roth was sentenced to 90 days in jail for selling by mail order a complete edition of Indian manuals of love, the *Kama Sutra* and *The Perfumed Garden*. Not long after his release, he was back behind bars. The Vice Society had raided his Golden Hind Press, finding bootleg copies of *Ulysses*, D.H. Lawrence's *Lady Chatterley's Lover*, *Forbidden Books*, and *Fanny Hill* – all proving Roth's heavy involvement with the distribution of erotica.

His photolithographed piracies of the Lawrence novel appeared early, and were ubiquitous in America. The *Ulysses* volume, printed between two and three years later than the serialized chapters in *Two Worlds Monthly*, has won Roth a dubious place in Joyce bibliography as the novel's first – and of course unauthorized – US publisher; Random House's authorized edition was inadvertently based on it. Many of the copies were destroyed in an incinerator at police headquarters. Nevertheless, Roth never ceased to point with pride to the contribution he felt he had made to the cause of modernist literature with his first US edition of *Ulysses*, even to the face of the contemptuous Estes Kefauver in his 1955 testimony before the senator's investigation of his mail-order sales to juveniles. Also found was a translation of a Boccaccio story, made more saleable by an unauthorized – and, by the standards of the day, obscene – set of Aubrey Beardsley illustrations (e.g. *Venus and Tannhauser*). His parole was revoked.

Roth founded William Faro Inc. in 1930 to publish books that could be sold openly in stores and through the mails, as well as stocked in the lending libraries, which were becoming increasingly popular during the Depression. He inaugurated his venture with "the Samuel Roth Edition" of *Lady Chatterley's Lover*, an expurgated and bowdlerized edition, although Roth's own term was "revised". "You may now place *Lady Chatterley's Lover* on your favourite reading shelf, beside the best of the modern classics," read one dust-jacket blurb. Roth set up a "ledger" in which to record funds in escrow until such time as Frieda Lawrence might authorize his edition, but Alfred Knopf offered a much larger sum. Faro did offer the public Roth's own dramatization of *Lady Chatterley*, as well as two "sequels", which transformed Lawrence's novel into the stuff of pulp romance.

The most notorious, and probably the most lucrative, Faro book was an exposé of Herbert Hoover, John Hamill's *The Strange Career of Mr Hoover Under Two Flags*, the first of several smear books that had some part in hindering Hoover's reelection bid. Hoover certainly took it seriously. His personal secretary dispatched three operatives to investigate Samuel Roth, and they found some powerful insiders who did not scruple to provide the president with confidential information. Late in 1931, a Democratic hanger-on who claimed to have supplied research to the book's author filed for an injunction against further sales. In granting the request, Judge Cotillo cast Roth in the role of the heartless "promoter" who would do anything for money.

By late 1932, the effects of the Depression had forced Roth to liquidate William Faro Inc. One outcome was his egregious anti-Semitic tract *Jews Must Live: An Account of the Persecution of the World by Israel on All the Frontiers of Civilization* (1934), which the Nazis sometimes cited, and for the existence of which Roth was deeply repentant. It was about this time that he began using the US mails to circulate, and Railway Express to ship, such materials as erotic playing cards and photograph sets. Some books carried his Black Hawk Press imprint. One of these was an expurgated *Ananga Ranga*. The more expensive copies featured pasted-in photographs like those in the aggressively pornographic "readers" of the period. Roth also risked mailing books that he could not advertise openly: these were the most strictly banned pornography of the period. In December 1936, the publisher and his wife were convicted of distributing obscene books through interstate commerce and of a conspiracy to do so. Roth served three years and 20 days; a fine of $2000 was suspended, to be enforced when and if he violated parole. Suspended also was his wife's three-year sentence. The sentence was, understandably, an extremely severe one for an obscenity conviction.

After World War II, Roth turned to mail-order advertising, and estimated that during this phase of his career, he sent out 10 million pieces of mail for borderline items advertised to appeal to prurience. The Post Office received so many complaints about his mailings – it claimed their number reached 5000 – that a special form letter was devised to answer them. His circulars got progressively bolder and more suggestive, and some of them contained sneering references to the "blue noses" who had repressed "vital" novels and magazines. After the well-publicized appearance before senator Kefauver's committee mentioned above, Roth was charged with 26 offences, sentenced to five years in prison and fined $5000 in 1956. Appeals to the district court and the Supreme Court failed, the latter upholding the conviction by six votes to three. On the other hand, William Brennan's definition of obscenity paved the way to a considerably more liberal definition of pornography. The British Hicklin rule of 1868 had concentrated on its "tendency . . . to deprave and corrupt those whose minds are open to such immoral influences". *Roth* v. *the USA* laid down that a publication was only obscene if "to the average person, applying contemporary community standards, the dominant theme of the material, taken as a whole, appeals to prurient interest". Within a few years, Barney Rossett of the Grove Press could market *Lady Chatterley's Lover* and Henry Miller's *Tropic of Cancer*, without fear that they would be prosecuted.

JAY A. GERTZMAN

Writings

Europe: A Book for America, 1919
Now and Forever: A Conversation with Mr Israel Zangwill on the Jew and the Future . . ., 1925
Stone Walls Do Not: The Chronicle of a Captivity, 2 vols, 1930
Jews Must Live: An Account of the Persecution of the World by Israel on All the Frontiers of Civilization, 1934

Further Reading

Bodenheim, Maxwell, *My Life and Loves in Greenwich Village*, New York: Bridgehead, 1954
Cacici, Dante, "A Note on the Author" in *Bumarap: The Story of a Male Virgin*, by Samuel Roth, New York: Arrowhead, 1947
Carrington, Charles, *Forbidden Books: Notes and Gossip on Tabooed Literature*, by an Old Bibliophile, Paris: The Author and His Friends, 1902; reprinted New York: Roth, 1928
de Grazia, Edward, *Girls Lean Back Everywhere: The Law of Obscenity and the Assault on Genius*, New York: Random House, 1992
Gertzman, Jay A., *Bookleggers and Smuthounds: The Trade in Erotica, 1920–1940*, Philadelphia: University of Pennsylvania Press, 1999
Hamalian, Leo, "Nobody Knows My Names: Samuel Roth and the Underside of Modern Letters", *Journal of Modern Literature*, 3 (1974): 889–921
Hamill, John, *The Strange Career of Mr Hoover under Two Flags*, New York: Faro, 1931
Kugel, Adelaide, " 'Wroth-Rackt Joyce' ", *Joyce Studies Annual*, 3 (Summer 1992): 242–48
Talese, Gay, *Thy Neighbor's Wife*, New York: Doubleday, and London: Collins, 1980

JEAN ROUCH
French film director, 1917–

LES MAÎTRES FOUS (The Mad Masters)
Film, 1954

Jean Rouch's anthropological and filmmaking activities, which began in the 1940s, have focused on the ethnographic study, analysis, and depiction of West African and French cultures. He has worked in France, where he held several national appointments, as well as Niger, Mali, Ghana, Ivory Coast, Nigeria, Burkino Faso, and Senegal. He has also produced a number of anthropological and fiction films in collaboration with many French and West African informants.

The events depicted in Les Maîtres fous are set in and around the city of Accra, which was then capital of the English colonial territory of the Gold Coast (now Ghana). The film features the annual possession ceremony performed by members of the Songhay and Zerma community in Accra, who had recently migrated from Niger, Mali, and Burkino Faso. Accra is portrayed as a developing city with a cosmopolitan population originating from various regions within West Africa. The Songhay and Zerma community featured in this film have migrated to Accra to share in the prosperity and economic growth in the region, bringing with them, along with a host of cultural beliefs and practices, their possession rituals and family of Hauka deities. The Hauka represent one of the recently arrived group of Songhay spirits in a historical succession of spirit possession cults which date back several hundred years. The specific origin of the Hauka cult occurred in French Niger during the mid-1920s. This family of spirits, consisting of "mad" colonial administrators, arose out of conditions created in 20th-century colonial West Africa.

Les Maîtres fous has generated controversy since its first screening in 1954 at the Museé de l'Homme, Paris. It has been both strongly criticized and enthusiastically extolled by western and African audiences. It was banned in Britain and in the Gold Coast after its release in 1955, but judged the best short film at the Venice Film Festival in 1957. This public ambivalence has resulted from differing reactions to the arresting and graphic images and scenes, and to the social and cultural significance of the activities depicted within the film.

The film opens with a brief explanation about the encounter between people from the northern and the southern regions and the discord created by the confluence of modern and traditional life in colonial Gold Coast. Accra is portrayed as a vibrant city where many groups and customs from West Africa have converged. This is the world the Songhay and Zerma must confront and adjust to after migration from their traditional homes in Niger, Mali, and Burkina Faso. We see migrants performing a range of daily work activities in the city. It is from this local urban context that the film moves to the bush where we see the compound where the Hauka ceremony will take place.

Rouch talks the viewer through corresponding images and sequences of the ceremony. The camera reveals the ceremonial activities performed by the high priest, initiates, musicians, and witnesses in close proximity. We witness the penance of initiates; a blood-stained altar; a caricatured fetish statue representing a colonial governor-general; the sacrifice of a chicken; the possession of Hauka spirit mediums and their wild flailing and marching; the entranced mediums foaming at the mouth; the bare-skinned handling of fire; the burlesquing of British military protocol; and the sacrifice, boiling, and consumption of a dog by the possessed mediums. As the ceremony comes to an end, it is pronounced a great success by the mediums and the Hauka spirits leave their mediums' bodies.

Rouch returns to the city the day after this extreme and physically demanding ceremony to show the contented participants back in their daily occupations. In closing, Rouch considers the possibility that their religion and practices are a psychological palliative for dealing with the alienating contradictions of modern society.

The British government banned Les Maîtres fous because it mocked the British governor-general and military protocol, which by extension was insulting to British society and ultimately the Queen. In addition, sacrificial acts in the film were considered violent and cruel to animals. Rouch admittedly held a critical posture towards the European colonization of African societies. Les Maîtres fous was consistent with his views on European colonial activities. However, the participants and the actual ceremony, ritual, and practices shown in the film were native expressions. The Hauka possessions of the Songhay and Zerma function as an interpretation and recasting of their social realities. The ceremonies enact the social and symbolic relationships existing within their immediate social realities. Thus Songhay religion and its practices help to delineate the social, political, and historical relationships which impinge on Songhay culture and society and also serve as a criticism and resistance to British and French control. As such, the British government was condemning not only the film, but also a community and set of cultural practices which stood against their political and economic agenda.

JOSEPH J. GONZALES

Writings
Les Songhay, 1954
"Migrations au Ghana", Journal de la Société des Africanistes, 26/1–2 (1956): 33–196
La Religion et la magie Songhay, 1960
Les Hommes et les dieux du fleuve: essai ethnographique sur les populations Songhay du moyen Niger, 1941–1983, 1997

Further Reading
Eaton, Mick (editor), Anthropology, Reality, Cinema: The Films of Jean Rouch, London: British Film Institute, 1979
Muller, Jean-Claude, "Review of Les Maîtres fous", American Anthropologist, 73 (1971): 1471–73
Naficy, Hamid, "Jean Rouch: A Personal Perspective", Quarterly Review of Film Studies (Summer 1979): 339–62
Predal, R. (editor), "Jean Rouch: un griot gaulois", special issue of CinemAction, 17 (1982)
Ruby, Jay (editor), "The Cinema of Jean Rouch", Visual Anthropology, 2/3–4 (1989)

Stoller, Paul, "Horrific Comedy: Cultural Resistance and the Hauka Movement in Niger", *Ethos*, 11 (1984): 165–67

Stoller, Paul, *Fusion of the Worlds: An Ethnography of Possession among the Songhay of Niger*, Chicago: University of Chicago Press, 1989

Stoller, Paul, *The Cinematic Griot: The Ethnography of Jean Rouch*, Chicago: University of Chicago Press, 1992

Yakir, Dan, "Ciné-transe: The Vision of Jean Rouch", *Film Quarterly*, 31/3 (1978): 1–10

JEAN-JACQUES ROUSSEAU
Swiss thinker and writer, 1712–1778

It comes as no surprise that the man who stated so famously that "L'homme est né libre, et partout il est dans les fers" (Man is born free, and everywhere he is in chains) should have suffered at the hands of the censors. Adopted after his death as one of the most influential political philosophers in modern history, Jean-Jacques Rousseau propounded views that were scarcely likely to appeal to the royal and ecclesiastical authorities of pre-Revolutionary France, where he spent much of his life. However, Malesherbes, the chief French royal censor when Rousseau was writing, did much behind the scenes to defend him.

Two of Rousseau's works in particular, *Émile* and *Du Contrat social*, would arouse the wrath of the Paris *Parlement*, the Catholic Church, and even the authorities in his native Geneva. Broadly, Rousseau argued that men were born happy and virtuous by nature, but were corrupted and made unhappy by the inequality, materialism, and despotism of the society in which they were forced to live. While other Enlightenment thinkers railed against the injustices of society, Rousseau objected to the existence of society itself, arguing that it was fundamentally unnatural. Such are the notions to emerge from Rousseau's major discourses and novels. Then in his best-known work, *Du Contrat social*, Rousseau imagined an ideal society where individuals, in signing the social contract, would surrender their rights to the collective general will, which would act for the common good. Rousseau died just over 10 years before the French Revolution. The heady mix of political idealism and emotional candour in his writings caused him to be regarded as a hero during the Revolution. His vision has influenced many theorists and politicians since, including, most notoriously, some totalitarian thinkers.

Descended from Huguenot exiles who had fled religious persecution in France, Jean-Jacques Rousseau spent his early years in Calvinist Geneva, a proudly autonomous city characterized by its puritanical morality. However, Rousseau left Geneva at a relatively young age, became a Catholic, and embarked on a restlessly itinerant life in Savoy, Piedmont, and finally, France, the scene of many of his encounters with censorship. He did, subsequently, rejoin the Calvinist Church, but the views he propounded on a new civil religion, where Christianity enjoyed no special status, was one of many distinctly unorthodox ideas that caused him trouble.

Rousseau's individuality is apparent in his first main work, his *Discours sur les sciences et les arts* (Discourse on the Sciences and the Arts, 1751). In total contrast to Diderot, he claimed that science was evil, both in its origins and in its effects. The generous-minded Diderot was willing to give Rousseau's view an airing, but Voltaire condemned it wholeheartedly. But it was not a view which would cause the censor to react. However, Malesherbes, the head of government censorship at the time, could not be expected to nod through Rousseau's next and more radical *Discours sur l'origine de l'inégalité* (Discourse on the Origin of Inequality, 1755) and demanded to see the whole text, despite the pleas of Marc-Michel Rey of Amsterdam, Rousseau's publisher, who stood to lose a lot of money if permission to publish was refused. Malesherbes finally gave his full authorization to a work which would cause Voltaire to dismiss Rousseau's views even more scornfully than before. But the *Discours sur l'origine de l'inégalité*, which accounted for the evolution of man and society, would have made Rousseau an object of suspicion at the Sorbonne.

Rousseau's next work, *Julie; ou, La Nouvelle Héloïse*, was a love story. He himself said of its possible effects: "My voluptuous imaginings would have lost all their grace if they had lacked the gentle colours of innocence." The novel challenged conventional sexual morality. Fellow writer Charles Duclos warned Rousseau that the church would not take kindly, for example, to a character who was an atheist, however virtuous. Early editions (printed abroad) sold well, but when it came to a French edition, Malesherbes, now having to do his job in a climate of rising religious intolerance, made it clear that some 50 cuts would be necessary. He indicated that there were some passages in the novel which would be offensive to Catholics and Protestants alike. Rousseau replied: "I confess I like her (Julie) better lovable, if heretical, than bigoted and narrow as they make her." He would accept some cuts but not any that would alter the purpose of the novel. In a letter to François Coidet, he wrote: "As for what Malesherbes calls a revolt against the Scriptures, I myself call it a submission to the authority of God and Reason, which ought to take priority over that of the Bible and serve as its basis." Malesherbes later claimed that he had done the best he could for Rousseau, but knew that "trivial" cuts were necessary for publication to take place.

It was not even deemed worth trying for a French publication of *Du Contrat social*, Rousseau's project for a political constitution, which was printed in the Netherlands in 1762 and banned from France. Rousseau himself had early doubts whether *Émile; ou, de l'éducation* could be published there "except with mutilations which I could not agree to". And indeed the road to publication of *Émile* would prove long and tortuous. Rousseau believed that the Jesuits were holding up the book in order to prepare their refutations. Malesherbes assured him that this was not the case. But, on this occasion, Malesherbes, otherwise felt to be a decent public official, played a double game. Realizing the likely impact of the book on

Church and *Parlement* alike, he distanced himself from his early promise to get it through, suggesting that the last two volumes be printed in the Netherlands so that he could claim that he had nothing to do with it. More intransigent than ever, Rousseau asserted that "no interdiction, no danger, no violence, no power on earth would ever make me retract a single syllable".

On 9 June 1762 the *Parlement* of Paris condemned the book as subversive of morals and decency, seditious, impious, and sacrilegious. Copies were to be seized, shredded, and burnt by the public executioner. Rousseau himself was to be arrested, but before the court officers arrived he had left, not for Geneva, where there was now a warrant for his arrest for blasphemy on account of the book, but for Berne. Both *Émile* and *Du Contrat social* were publicly burnt in Geneva in 1762. In 1763 both books were placed on the Catholic Index. Rousseau now fled to Neuchâtel, where he benefited from the protection of Frederick the Great, who had been elected prince of this Swiss canton. There he wrote his *Lettre à Christophe de Beaumont*, replying to the archbishop of Paris, who had issued a pastoral letter condemning Rousseau in August 1762; Rousseau's letter was itself put on the Index in 1766. His response to Geneva, defending *Émile* and *Du Contrat social*, was contained in his *Lettres écrites de la montagne* (1764, Letters from the Mountain).

Hostility followed Rousseau. Voltaire's *Le Sentiment des citoyens* expressed popular resentment at Rousseau's abandonment of his five children. Rousseau felt impelled to write (1764–70) his extremely frank autobiographical *Confessions*, and returned to France in the hope of reading them publicly; this was forbidden. But he did settle quietly at Ermenonville, north of Paris, until his death. Censorship of his works continued well after he had died. *Julie* was added to the Index in 1806, and, as late as 1929, the US Customs department was banning the import of the *Confessions* as injurious to public morals. Rousseau's writings were also banned for a brief time in the Soviet Union between 1935 and 1936.

J.D. LEIGH

Writings
The Collected Writings, edited by Roger D. Masters and Christopher Kelly, 1990–

Further Reading
Cranston, Maurice, *Jean-Jacques: The Early Life and Work of Jean-Jacques Rousseau, 1712–1754*, London: Allen Lane, and New York: Norton, 1983
Cranston, Maurice, *The Noble Savage: Jean-Jacques Rousseau, 1754–1762*, London: Allen Lane, and Chicago: University of Chicago Press, 1991
Dent, N.J.H., *A Rousseau Dictionary*, Oxford and Cambridge, Massachusetts: Blackwell, 1992
Gildin, Hilail, *Rousseau's Social Contract: The Design of the Argument*, Chicago: University of Chicago Press, 1983
Porter, Dennis, *Rousseau's Legacy: Emergence and Eclipse of the Writer in France*, Oxford and New York: Oxford University Press, 1995
Starobinski, Jean, *Jean-Jacques Rousseau: Transparency and Obstruction*, Chicago: University of Chicago Press, 1988
Thiéry, Robert (editor), *Rousseau, L'Émile et la Révolution*, Paris: Universitas, 1992
Wokler, Robert (editor), *Rousseau and Liberty*, Manchester: Manchester University Press, 1995

SALMAN RUSHDIE
British novelist, 1947–
THE SATANIC VERSES
Novel, 1988

The Satanic Verses tells the story of two Indians who fall 29,000 feet from an exploding plane and land unharmed in Britain. One of the two turns into a cloven-hoofed devil and the other into an archangel, complete with a sometimes-visible halo. In a loosely organized account of the dreams and real-life experiences of these two central characters, Rushdie examines the ambiguous relationship between fact and fiction, the compelling power of religious belief, and the fragmented nature of postcolonial identity. The fictional invocation of events and figures from the Qur'an, notably the Muhammad-like businessman/prophet named Mahound, led to the banning of the novel in many Muslim countries and the issuing of ayatollah Khomeini's death sentence against Rushdie on 14 February 1989.

Salman Rushdie is an Indian-born writer of English-language novels and essays who holds British citizenship. He has received a number of important awards, including the Booker Prize for his novel *Midnight's Children* (1981) and the Whitbread Prize for *The Satanic Verses* (1988). An author who claims that his chief literary influence in childhood was *The Arabian Nights*, Rushdie blends fantasy with political and social commentary in works that explore issues of national and cultural identity, the immigrant experience, and East–West relations.

Rushdie's writing first aroused the hostility of political authorities in his native India with the publication of *Midnight's Children*. The novel, which describes the life of a boy born at the exact moment that India achieved its independence, raised some controversy for its unflattering fictional presentation of the Nehru family. Indira Gandhi was so insulted with Rushdie's portrayal of her that she sued him for libel. However, due to her untimely death, the lawsuit was never resolved. In a similar manner, the publication of *Shame* (1983) angered the political elite in Pakistan, another country where Rushdie had lived for some time. Sale of the novel was ultimately banned in Pakistan, partly because of what was seen as its disparaging portrayal of then president Muhammad Ziaul-Haqq.

The Satanic Verses was published on 26 September 1988 in Britain by Viking Penguin. The initial reviews of the work in the western literary press were predominantly positive. Although some reviewers noted that the novel really consisted of two disparate story lines, one of the prophet Mahound and the other of the two crash victims, bound together in a loosely related narrative, for the most part its inventive blend of references to pop culture and historical allusions garnered it praise as a landmark work of magical realism. This critical acclaim culminated in the awarding of the Whitbread Prize for "best novel" on 8 November 1988. Most Muslim literary reviews, on the other hand, found the work offensive and blasphemous. 'Ali A. Mazrui, a well-known Muslim intellectual and director of the Institute of Global Cultural Studies at the State University of New York at Binghamton, suggested that references in the work were for Muslims as hurtful as would be the portrayal of the Virgin Mary as a prostitute or Jesus as the son of one of her clients.

The publication of *The Satanic Verses* provoked protests both in Britain and elsewhere. The rancour began before the work's actual publication date, when Muslims in India learned of it from excerpts in two Indian magazines. Syed Shahbuddin and Khurshid Alam Khan, Muslim members of the Indian parliament, moved to have the novel banned in India. On 5 October 1988 the Indian Finance Ministry prohibited the book. Shahbuddin had never read the work but defiantly claimed that it was unnecessary to wade through filth. South Africa banned the work the following month. Thereafter efforts began to have the book banned in Britian as well. Hesham al-Essawy, chairman of the Islamic Society for the Promotion of Religious Tolerance, wrote to Viking Press asking them to consider withdrawing the work from publication. On 20 October 1988 the Union of Muslim Organizations in Britain wrote to prime minister Margaret Thatcher requesting that *The Satanic Verses* be legally banned in Britain and Rushdie prosecuted on charges of blasphemy. The English legal system is distinctive among western nations in that it still has blasphemy laws on the books. However, as the Muslim community in Britain soon discovered, such laws applied only to Christian writings, and in any case were almost never enforced. Consequently, Mrs Thatcher rejected the request, opting instead to support freedom of expression.

The protests then began to take a more violent turn. In December 1988 Rushdie started to receive violent threats and Viking suffered two bomb scares (thereafter rumours circulated that Viking executives were wearing bulletproof vests to work). On 2 December 1988, after the Whitbread Prize ceremony, members of the Muslim community in Bolton (near Manchester) held a book burning at which 7000 were present. Another public book burning followed on 14 January 1989 in Bradford. Although only 1000 people attended, the latter event received extensive press coverage. Two weeks later a demonstration was held in Hyde Park, London, protesting against the work and its publisher.

These protests were eclipsed by the violence that accompanied subsequent demonstrations against the novel in the east. On 12 February 1989 some 10,000 people took to the streets in Islamabad, the capital of Pakistan, and marched on the American Cultural Centre. The protesters set fire to the building and threw stones at the windows. As the crowd surged towards the building, the police killed five demonstrators and about 100 more were injured; a Pakistani guard was shot. However, no British property was attacked or damaged during the rioting. The protests then spilled over into India. On 13

February 1989 one person was killed and more than 60 people were injured during street demonstrations in Srinagar.

Ultimately the work was banned in scores of countries with Muslim majorities or pluralities, including Papua New Guinea, Thailand, Sri Lanka, Kenya, Tanzania, Liberia, Sierra Leone, Malaysia, and Venezuela. It was uniformly banned in those countries with large Muslim populations, except for Turkey, where the work was greeted more ambivalently. Some govern-

RUSHDIE: Muslim demonstrators marching through Slough, Berkshire, in March 1989, to protest the publication of *The Satanic Verses*. The demonstration was one of a number that took place in British cities during late 1988 and early 1989 following the refusal of the British prime minister, Margaret Thatcher, to sanction the legal banning of the publication of the book in Britain.

ments in the Middle East went so far as to ban all books published by Viking and it was also common for magazines covering the controversy, including *Time*, *Newsweek*, and *The Far Eastern Economic Review*, to have issues banned.

Immediately following the violence in Pakistan ayatollah Khomeini issued his famous edict. As far as can be determined, his action was in response to news reports, perhaps on Iranian television or on a transistor radio, of the rioting. On 14 February 1989 he issued a *hukm* calling for Rushdie's death. Although commonly referred to as a *fatwa* (legal opinion) in the western press, the ayatollah's decree was substantially different. Unlike a *fatwa*, a *hukm* is a religious pronouncement that remains in place after the issuer's death. A *fatwa*, on the other hand, dies with its issuer. The edict stated:

> In the name of Him, the Highest. There is only one God, to whom we shall all return. I inform all zealous Muslims of the world that the author of the book entitled *The Satanic Verses* – which has been compiled, printed, and published in opposition to Islam, the Prophet, and the Qur'an – and all those involved in its publication who were aware of its content, are sentenced to death. I call on all zealous Muslims to execute them quickly, wherever they may be found, so that no one else will dare to insult the Muslim sanctities. God willing, whoever is killed on this path is a martyr. In addition, anyone who has access to the author of this book, but does not possess the power to execute him, should report him to the people so that he may be punished for his actions. May peace and the mercy of God and His blessing be with you. Ruhollah al-Musavi al-Khomeini, 25 Bahman 1367.

Rushdie's responses to the treatment of his work varied considerably. In September 1988 he stated openly that "one of my major themes is religion and fanaticism". However, a month later, when his work was first being protested against, he claimed that the book wasn't "actually about Islam, but about migration, metamorphosis, divided selves, love, death, London and Bombay". Then, in January 1989, Rushdie responded publicly to the sum of these events. In an editorial piece called "The Book Burning" he argued that Islam had been taken over by a "powerful tribe of clerics ... the contemporary Thought Police". At the same time he declared that his work was not antireligious, but rather addressed the issues attendant to migration. After the death threat was made public, on 17 February 1989, Rushdie offered a minimal apology in an attempt to take advantage of the Iranian president Khamenei's suggestion that the people might forgive him if he repented. The apology noted: "I recognize that Muslims in many parts of the world are genuinely distressed by the publication of my novel. I profoundly regret the distress that the publication had occasioned to sincere followers of Islam." This was flatly rejected by Khomeini on 19 February 1989; he made it clear that no apology could revoke the death edict. Rushdie's last public appearance for some time was on 14 February 1989; thereafter, he was under the protection of the police Special Branch and remained in hiding. Until 1996 his public appearances were unannounced and infrequent. Recent political events have led to greater freedom of movement for Rushdie.

Muslim critics found many aspects of the novel blasphemous. To begin with, they objected to the work's title, an important part of the controversy, as many people angered by the novel did not actually read the text. Although Rushdie argued that the title was derived from the writings of al-Tabari, a highly respected Islamic source, and described an event that took place between Muhammad and Gabriel in the Qur'an, al-Tabari never actually used the phrase "the satanic verses" to describe the incident. In fact, Rushdie probably borrowed the term from a work written by an English orientalist W. Montgomery Watt, *Muhammad at Mecca* (1953). Due to this connection, Muslim intellectuals familiar with orientalist positions reacted sharply against the title, perceiving it as part of a European effort to discredit Islam. What sparked the greatest outrage, however, may have been the manner in which the English title was translated into Eastern languages. For example, in Arabic the title was translated as *al-Ayat al-Shaytaniya*. Because *ayat* are specifically verses of the Qur'an, the title in translation literally meant "The Satanic Qur'an." Clearly, any work implying that the Qur'an was written by Satan would be inherently blasphemous to many Muslim readers, even though nowhere in the work did Rushdie suggest this to be the case. The versions of the novel in Persian and Turkish – the other two major languages of the Muslim world – bore titles with similar implications.

Perhaps the most objectionable aspect of the novel for many Muslims was its suggestion that the Qur'an could be incorrect or at least that its author, Muhammad, may have been fallible in writing it down. The controversy centres on the events from which Rushdie took the term *The Satanic Verses*. According to the writings of al-Tabari, Muhammad's initial teachings were not warmly greeted in Mecca. Before the rise of Islam, Mecca was a centre of polytheistic religions. Muhammad at first had trouble winning over converts to monotheism and consequently members of his clan, the Quraysh, suggested that he take a more flexible view towards their idols. In hopes of winning over his tribesmen, Muhammad then recited two lines from the Qur'an that made reference to the three most prominent Meccan goddesses, al-Lat, al-'Uzza, and Manat, and appeared to acknowledge their divine status. He declared, "These are the exalted birds [meaning the goddesses], And their intercession is desired indeed." At this moment, however, the archangel Gabriel (the Qur'an's source) interposed and questioned Muhammad's actions. According to al-Tabari, Gabriel revealed to the prophet that Satan had been the source of these lines and that they were therefore invalidated. As a result, they do not appear in the canonic Qur'anic text. In their place are lines indicating that the goddesses' names were only dreams and that "Allah vests no authority in them".

This incident is highly problematic for Islam. One of the central features of the faith is that the Qur'an is literally the word of God. To question this is to cast doubt upon the validity of Muhammad's mission and to imply that the entire religion is based on falsehood. For this reason, while a Muslim may criticize the mullahs, the religious establishment, and even the political leadership of Muhammad, he may not question the authenticity of the Qur'an. Consequently, al-Tabari's story of the missing lines, and the question of who spoke them, is a very sensitive one. Most Muslim historians avoid commenting on the issue altogether or try to steer a neutral course between an unlikely story and one of the major premises of the Islamic faith.

Rushdie, on the other hand, decided to tackle the complexities of this issue head-on. In his novel, the archangel Gibreel (Gabriel?) claims that both sets of verses came from his mouth: *"it was me both times, baba, me first and second also from me. From my mouth, both the statement and the repudiation, verses and converses, universes and reverses, the whole thing, and we all know how my mouth got worked."* One might infer from this statement either that God, through Gibreel, spoke two contradictory statements; that Gibreel himself was the source of both sets of lines; or that God and Satan are the same being. In any case, the passage would be troubling to Muslim readers. What is more, Gibreel later declares that he had been "obliged to speak by the overwhelming need of the Prophet, Mahound [Muhammad?]", which suggests that ultimately the Prophet – not God – was the source of the troubling lines. Whatever the truth of the situation (and it is far from clear in the text), the implication for many Muslim readers was that Rushdie had challenged the idea that the Qur'an is a literal and unambiguous transcription of God's words given to Muhammad by the archangel Gabriel. It must be remembered that the entire sequence is part of a dream and that the dreamer, Gibreel Farishta, suffers from a paranoid delusion of being an archangel. In the eyes of his Muslim critics, however, such fictional distancing failed to absolve Rushdie of responsibility for his blasphemy.

Other objections to the work centred on perceived back-handed insults to Islam. For example, the name "Mahound" was a pejorative term for Muhammad used by Christians in the medieval period; Mahound is portrayed as a rapacious businessman. But perhaps the most criticized section of the work describes a brothel in Mecca called "The Curtain", where the 12 prostitutes took on the names and personalities of the Prophet's 12 wives. In Rushdie's vision of Mecca, the visitors to the Curtain are the same men who prayed to Allah during the day. The insinuation for many Muslim readers was clear: the new religious converts are hypocrites who mock the religion's precepts each night through their visits to the brothel.

The initial western response to Khomeini's edict of 14 February 1989 wavered between silence and condemnation. The US government took a particularly low-key position on the subject, issuing no official statement and adopting no position on *The Satanic Verses* beyond a declaration that both the deaths in Pakistan and the edict were "regrettable". Later, however, the US Senate voted unanimously "to protect the right of any person to write, publish, sell, buy, and read books without fear of intimidation and violence", and to condemn Khomeini's death threat as "state-sponsored terrorism". Thatcher's government also initially kept quiet about Khomeini's threat, and even went so far as to agree to a judicial review of the Muslim Action Group's petition to try Rushdie and Viking under English blasphemy laws. A month later the government rejected the request, although some politicians appeared shamefaced and made disparaging remarks about the quality of the book. In contrast, the French government under president François Mitterrand roundly condemned the threat against Rushdie as "absolute evil" and the West German government recalled its head of mission from Iran on 17 February. Not long thereafter the European Community suspended all high-level contacts with Iran.

Despite being somewhat slow to respond, western intellectuals and journalists spoke out with near uniformity against both censorship and the threat on Rushdie's life. Even for those who condemned Rushdie, the issue of free speech was carefully differentiated from the quality of that speech. Especially in the US, most Rushdie critics felt that he had the right to free expression in keeping with their belief in the First Amendment of the constitution, but that his statements were nevertheless offensive to many in the Muslim community.

The Iranians also received little support for their position among other Muslim countries. Although authorities acknowledged that Rushdie's work was indeed blasphemous and quickly banned it, most were opposed to Khomeini's edict. Iraqi officials, for obvious political reasons, condemned the Iranian leader, declaring that his death threat was more harmful to Islam than the novel itself. Leaders in Kuwait, Bangladesh, Egypt, and Turkey similarly criticized Iran for overreacting. They saw the book as wrong, but felt that it did not warrant a death sentence. Public response in Muslim countries was not always so temperate; the book had enraged millions of Muslims. Violent demonstrations continued in the Indian subcontinent for a month after Khomeini's edict. On 24 February police opened fire on rioters who had burned cars, buses, and even a police station; 12 people were killed. A half-day nationwide strike in Bangladesh ended with 50 people injured. Numerous nonviolent protests were arranged in Malaysia, the Philippines, Japan, and Turkey.

On 24 September 1998, 10 years after *The Satanic Verses* was published, the Iranian foreign minister Kamal Kharrazi declared that the Iranian government had no intention "to threaten the life of the author of *The Satanic Verses* or anybody associated with his work, nor will it encourage or assist anybody to do so". This decision by the Iranian government was linked to a warming of relations between Britain and Iran that ultimately led to the resumption of full diplomatic relations between the two countries. Although the British government treated the foreign minister's statement as a change in policy, it was not. Kharrazi himself claimed that the 24 September statement signalled no change in Iranian policy. Indeed, a week later he proclaimed, "We did not adopt a new position with regard to the apostate Salman Rushdie, and our position remains the same as that which has been repeatedly stated by the Islamic Republic of Iran's officials." A majority of the Iranian parliament's members concurred, as evidenced by their signing an open letter pointing to the edict's irrevocability. Indeed, in 1998 the Association of Hizbollah University Students added $330,000 to the reward for Rushdie's assassin. The price remains on Rushdie's head and is considered irrevocable by the Iranian elite, since the Ayatollah did not revoke the *hukm* before his death.

Nonetheless, the nations of the European Union have warmed in their relations with Iran. The EU has concluded that the Iranian government's decision not to foment actions against Rushdie was enough to re-establish relations. This warming has been stoked by the election in May 1997 of the moderate president Mohammed Khatami. Although the edict against Rushdie remains in place, the west has generally decided to resume oil and other contracts with the Iranian government. Even the United States, which has had virtually no contact with Iran since 1979, and which has repeatedly reported that support for terrorism has not changed even with the election of Khatami, is pushing for rapprochement with the Islamic Republic. For both the US and the EU, commercial pressures – particularly related to the exploitation of the vast oil and gas reserves in the Caspian – have taken precedence. As Rushdie himself noted in 1997, "When it's Danish feta cheese or Irish halal beef against the European Convention on Human Rights, don't expect free expression to win."

In recent years Rushdie has come partially out of hiding. He made several public appearances in 2000 and in September of that year he moved to the United States, forsaking the protection that had been given to him for nearly a decade by the British Special Branch. When asked about the possible remaining threat to his life, Rushdie said, "To hell with that. This is my life, and I'll make my choices."

HEIDI LY BEIRICH and KEVIN R. HICKS

Writings

Grimus, 1975
Midnight's Children, 1981
Shame, 1983
The Jaguar's Smile: A Nicaraguan Journey, 1987
The Satanic Verses, 1988
Imaginary Homelands: Essays and Criticism, 1981–1991, 1991
The Wizard of Oz, 1992
East, West: Stories, 1994
The Moor's Last Sigh, 1995
The Ground beneath Her Feet, 1999
Conversations with Salman Rushdie, edited by Michael Reder, 2000

Further Reading

Appignanesi, Lisa and Sara Maitland (editors), *The Rushdie File*, London: Fourth Estate, 1989; Syracuse, New York: Syracuse University Press, 1990

Bedford, Carmel, *Fiction, Fact and the Fatwa: 2,000 Days of Censorship*, 5th edition, London: Article 19, 1994
Booker, M. Keith, (editor), *Critical Essays on Salman Rushdie*, New York: G.K. Hall, 1999
Clark, Roger Y., *Stranger Gods: Salman Rushdie's Other Worlds*, Montréal: McGill–Queens University Press, 2001
Cohn-Sherbok, Dan (editor), *The Salman Rushdie Controversy in Interreligious Perspective*, Lewiston, New York: Mellen, 1990
Goonetilleke, D.C.R.A., *Salman Rushdie*, New York: St Martin's Press, 1998
Hitchens, Christopher, *Unacknowledged Legislation: Writers in the Public Sphere*, London and New York: Verso, 2000
MacDonogh, Steve (editor), *The Rushdie Letters: Freedom to Speak, Freedom to Write*, Dingle, Ireland: Brandon and Lincoln: University of Nebraska Press, 1993
Pipes, Daniel, "Rushdie's False Reprive", *Harper's Magazine* (March 1990): 19–21
Pipes, Daniel, *The Rushdie Affair: The Novel, the Ayatollah, and the West*, New York: Carol, 1990
Ruthven, Malise, *A Satanic Affair: Salman Rushdie and the Rage of Islam*, London: Chatto and Windus, 1990; revised edition London: Hogarth Press, 1991
Travis, Alan, *Bound and Gagged: A Secret History of Obscenity in Britain*, London: Profile, 2000
Weatherby, William, *Salman Rushdie: Sentenced to Death*, New York: Carroll and Graf, 1990
Webster, Richard, *A Brief History of Blasphemy: Liberalism, Censorship and "The Satanic Verses"*, Southwold, Suffolk: Orwell Press, 1990

KEN RUSSELL
British film director, 1927–
THE DEVILS
Film, 1971

If there is one word which sums up Ken Russell's notorious film, from its production to the howls of outrage which greeted its release, that word is "hysterical".

Hysteria is what *The Devils* is all about. Set in the 17th century in the French walled town of Loudun, it charts the destruction of the partly Huguenot Protestant town by the emissaries and exorcists of cardinal Richelieu, the Catholic power broker to the effeminate Louis XIII. At the centre of the tale is the repressed love of Sister Jeanne (played by Vanessa Redgrave), the hunchbacked head of the town's Ursuline convent, for the worldly, womanizing priest Grandier (Oliver Reed), whom she accuses of filling her with demons and stoking her sexual desire. Jeanne's hysteria spreads to the entire convent, prompting the shaven-headed nuns to a "possessed" orgy of lesbian sex and sacrilege. Finally, the chief exorcist Barre and his inquisitors extract confessions via water enemas and other tortures, and Grandier is burnt at the stake.

Russell based his script on Aldous Huxley's historically accurate book *The Devils of Loudun* and John Whiting's play, *The Devils*, which had been produced nine years previously by the Royal Shakespeare Company. Shirley Russell, who was then Ken's wife, designed the costumes, and Derek Jarman did the astonishing anachronistic sets, some of which were based on Lang's *Metropolis*. When United Artists pulled out, the independent producer Bob Solo took the project to Warner's, who picked it up and became the film's first censors.

During 1970, Edward Heath's Conservative government came to power and was plunged into crisis, with the so-called permissive society facing a major backlash. The press saw Russell as the embodiment of permissiveness after his 1969 adaptation of D.H. Lawrence's *Women in Love*, with its famous nude male wrestling scene, and they saw *The Devils*'s potential for lurid copy immediately. Orgies were reported to have taken place on the closed set, female extras said they were abused in the naked orgy sequences (drawing an apology from Russell to Equity), and it was reported that a child actor was involved in an indecent scene, although this was later proved untrue. A list of the film's scenes, including the infamous "Rape of Christ", were enough to kick-start a campaign against the film before it had even been shot.

Russell kept hysteria on the set at fever pitch. Peter Thompson became the public relations officer for Mary Whitehouse and the Festival of Light after being released from Broadmoor; he had been sent there for knife attacks on two women, which he blamed on his exposure to "permissive" films. He orchestrated a campaign against *The Devils*. Meanwhile, Vanessa Redgrave tried, unsuccessfully, to bring the film crew out on strike in protest against Heath's anti-union policies.

Russell's final cut, which he had already self-censored to remove a sequence in which Jeanne masturbates with Grandier's charred thigh bone, was previewed by Ted Ashley, the head of Warner Brothers, and his fellow executives. The distributor compelled Russell's editor to remove for the American market all shots in which there was graphic nudity. It was Russell's cut, however, which was submitted to the BBFC (British Board of Film Censors, now Classification) in February 1971. The film split the BBFC: many of the examiners took against the film's "sensationalism" and favoured heavy cuts or a complete ban, but the then president, Lord Harlech, expressed the opinion that the film was a work of integrity. Russell made a first round of cuts at the BBFC's insistence, removing much of the fantasy sex scene between Sister Jeanne and Grandier as Christ descending from the cross. This failed to mollify the BBFC, and further cuts were made to scenes involving the torture of Grandier and the exorcism of Sister Jeanne, which Russell conceded to receive the X certificate. Two events intervened between this stage and the release of the film. The BBFC's secretary, John Trevelyan, retired, to be replaced by Stephen Murphy, and the Festival of Light's campaign was given extensive coverage in the press. Released in July 1971, the film was greeted with a flood of moralizing press criticism, and the Festival of Light asked the Greater London Council (GLC) to view it. The GLC upheld the BBFC's verdict and supported the cut version. The Festival of Light then picketed West End cinemas showing the film and sent circulars to churches encouraging them to protest to their local authorities, 17 of which responded to this protest by banning it in their areas.

The first video version of *The Devils* released in the UK was the heavily reduced US cut passed in 1984 by the BBFC. In 1995, BBC2 screened the 1971 X-rated version in their Forbidden Cinema season; in autumn 1997, Warner Home Video released the 1971 X-rated version – the longest extant version – as a "director's cut". Stephen Murphy, whose career as BBFC secretary was cut short by this and a number of other controversies, stood firmly behind this version. "In 30 years' time," he said in 1971, "people will be queuing at the National Film Theatre to see it revived."

RICHARD FALCON

Writings
A British Picture: An Autobiography, 1989

Further Reading
Atkins, Thomas R. (editor), *Ken Russell*, New York: Monarch Press, 1976

Baxter, John, *An Appalling Talent: Ken Russell*, London: Joseph, 1973

Falcon, Richard, "The Witch Report", *Neon* (September 1997): 108–13

Phelps, Guy, *Film Censorship*, London: Gollancz, 1975

Robertson, James C., *The Hidden Cinema: British Film Censorship in Action, 1913–1975*, new edition, London and New York: Routledge, 1993

Trevelyan, John, *What the Censor Saw*, London: Joseph, 1973

RUSSIA

Russian Federation
(formerly Russian Soviet Federative Socialist Republic)

Population: 145,491,000
Main religions: Russian Orthodox; Muslim; Buddhist; Jewish
Official language: Russian
Illiteracy rate (%): 0.3 (m); 0.6 (f)

Number of daily newspapers: 285
Number of radio receivers per 1000 inhabitants: 417
Number of TV receivers per 1000 inhabitants: 410
Number of PCs per 1000 inhabitants: 40.6

Russia seems to have been introduced to the idea of censorship after prince Vladimir and other warriors were converted to the Orthodox form of Christianity in 988–89, the eastern church having been the locus of many of the historic decrees against early heresies. This entry, however, is mostly concerned with the period between 1560, when Ivan IV, tsar of Muscovy, acquired Moscow's first printing press, and 1991, when Glavlit, the official censorship body of the Soviet Union, was formally abolished. Numerous continuities may be adduced, all of them relevant to the study of censorship in Russia, all of them still subject to controversy among historians: the growing attempts to impose uniformity on a vast region containing a great variety of cultures, languages and religions; the absence of a democratic tradition as it is understood in the West; the alternation of periods of extreme repression and relative thaw; and the presence of various forms of dissidence, from the religious nonconformity of the Old Believers in the 1650s to the social and political challenge of the "new journalism" of *Ogonek* and *Moscow News* in the late 1980s. The differences in the practice of censorship under the two systems were just as important, however. First, the Russian Orthodox Church was mostly under the direct control of successive rulers, yet, while it played an important part in the history of censorship before the Revolution, it was thereafter reduced to virtual impotence under a system that actively promoted atheism. Second, during the last half-century of the Russian empire, beginning with the reforms of Alexander II, the regime cautiously opened the doors of free expression, but in the Soviet Union, despite the early postrevolutionary semblances of freedom and the "thaw" that followed the death of Stalin, freedom of expression was generally considered an essentially western and bourgeois idea, until it was adopted as part of glasnost during communism's final decade.

Muscovy and the Russian empire, 1552–1917

Censorship began informally when Ivan IV, known as Groznyi ("the Terrible"), in the midst of his many wars of conquest, established a printing press and publishing house. In western Europe, printing had spread quickly, and printers had resisted attempts by churches and rulers to control the distribution of new ideas. In Russia, by contrast, there was only one publishing house until the end of the 17th century. Both this state press and the smaller presses that were later established in monasteries were confined to the production of prayer books, catechisms, and psalters. In great contrast to western Protestantism, there was no official translation of the Bible into Russian before the 1860s.

Ivan and his successors cultivated the myth of the "holy tsar", capable of, and justified in, the imposition of arbitrary, absolute power, exercised through censorship and other means of repression. Moreover, as part of his attempt to curb the power of the established nobility, the boyars, Ivan used the *oprichniki*, the officers of the monastic courts, to round up dissenters and have them tried for heresy or treason. Metropolitan Filipp, who protested against the "spilling [of] the innocent blood of faithful people and Christians", was arrested, imprisoned, and later strangled. Eventually, exhausted by the "Time of Troubles", Muscovy was united behind tsar Mikhail (or Michael) Fedorovich, the first of the Romanov dynasty (reigned 1613–45). With his father, metropolitan Filaret, Michael laid the foundations for a church–state partnership that, while it was increasingly unequal, lasted for 100 years.

The Russian Orthodox Church was galvanized into a form of "reformation" in the mid-17th century by the "Zealots of Piety" (*Revniteli blagochastiia*), and especially by Nikon, who became patriarch of Moscow in 1653. Changes were imposed and those who did not accept these changes, and called themselves "Old Believers", were anathematized by a church council of 1666–67. All these actions were enabled and supported by tsar Aleksei (or Alexis) Mikhailovich (reigned 1645–76). For their part, the Old Believers held that both church and state, corrupted by the "papist Latin heresy", were destroying Russia's unique position in Christendom. They resisted persecution, and continued to assert their own identity and orthodoxy throughout the 18th and 19th centuries.

The "papist Latin heresy" had little to do with Russia's transformation by Peter I (reigned 1692–1725) into a secular state on rough-and-ready western European lines, appropriate for the administration of a rapidly growing empire. To support his technological modernizations, Peter established schools, Russia's first public library, and an academy of sciences. Having abandoned the traditional title of "tsar of Muscovy" in favour of "emperor of All the Russias", Peter set out to control a considerable growth in publishing and the very necessary dissemination of practical information by expanding the crown's monopoly to include secular publishing. In 1702 he founded Russia's first newspaper, *Vedomosti* (Bulletin). This appeared 35 times a year, contained carefully selected and edited official documents, and promoted Peter and his programmes. Military victories such as those over the Ottoman empire and Sweden, were reported, but never reversals.

More general printing was also under Peter's control, sometimes quite directly. He founded new publishing houses, including the St Petersburg Press (1711), the senate presses at Moscow and St Petersburg (1719), and the naval academy press (1721). As in many other areas of his reforms, he sometimes involved himself personally, to the extent of approving copy, as with his official history of the Great Northern War. Day-to-day supervision, including the approval in advance of every book published, was placed in the hands of the printing section of the Department of Monasteries, but was then passed on to the newly created Holy Synod in 1721. Since Peter had abolished the patriarchate and declared himself the "supreme protector" of the church, the Synod was effectively another vehicle for his authority. The new doctrine of church–state relations was enshrined in archbishop Feofan Prokopovich's *The Right of the Monarch's Will*.

The demotion of the church to junior partner in the autocracy was reinforced when in 1750 empress Elizabeth I let the Academy of Sciences choose what to print and gave the same right to Moscow University at its founding in 1755. Four years later, the empress allowed citizens to pay for the printing and circulation of privately published works. Scholastic presses proliferated, usually overseen by committees of administrators and professors, together with, occasionally, a representative of the academy. The church, worried by the onset of new scientific ideas, retained the right only to approve books on religious themes. Even then, the academy might decline to bother about theological disputes. It took no action, for example, when the synod demanded the confiscation of issues of Aleksandr Sumarokov's magazine *Trudoliubivaia pchela* (Diligent Bee), which contained anti-Orthodox articles. Moreover, if a bookseller would not accede voluntarily to a request from the church to remove a book from his shelves, there was little that could be done, short of involving the emperor (or empress) or the police.

Vedomosti had appeared only infrequently towards the end of Peter's reign, and it was finally closed down in 1727. Within a year, the chancellery of the academy had filled the gap with the *Sanktpeterburgskie vedomosti* (St Petersburg News), which appeared twice weekly until 1817. It remained chiefly a publication for official announcements. Even so, in 1742 the Senate (an appointed body, not an elected one) complained about alleged inaccuracies and ordered that each issue be reviewed by its own press before distribution. In 1751, Elizabeth herself insisted that there should be no reference to herself or to the imperial family without her prior permission. Otherwise, the crown gave private publishers and their reviewers the sparest of guidelines, although the code of a previous ruler, Alexis, published in 1659, which had defined and forbidden *lèse-majesté* and treason, remained in force.

During most of her reign, Catherine II (reigned 1762–96) appears to have interfered only very sporadically in press affairs, and that usually for personal reasons. In 1764, she banned an ode by Sumarokov to king Stanislaus Augustus of Poland, one of her former lovers, and in 1769 she rebuked the satirical journal *Smes'* (Miscellany) for some translations that she considered offensive. Like her contemporaries Frederick II of Prussia and the Holy Roman emperor Joseph II, she saw herself as an Enlightenment monarch. She extended her patronage to the French *philosophe* Denis Diderot, even offering him printing facilities in Riga when the *Encyclopédie*, which he edited, was proscribed in Paris. While she had been shocked by the content of Jean-Jacques Rousseau's *Émile* and had, in 1763, forbidden its importation, an edition of his more radical *Discours sur les origines de l'inégalité* (*Discourse on the Origins of Inequality*), published by Moscow University's press, was circulated freely during the 1760s and 1770s. In her decree on "free publishing" (1783) Catherine entirely lifted the state monopoly on printing, requiring only that presses be officially registered. Between 1776 and 1801, 33 presses were established in Moscow and St Petersburg, and 8000 titles were published, most of them between 1783 and the promulgation of censorship in 1795. Nikolai Novikov leased Moscow University's press for ten years and his business boomed. Arguments by Soviet scholars that considerable indirect economic censorship took place during Catherine's reign have been discounted by most western historians for lack of firm evidence.

Press and printing issues, in any case, concerned only the literate. The revolt of Emel'ian Pugachev in the southeast of the empire, far from the centre of power, between 1773 and 1775 caused more concern, appealing as it did to a wider variety of discontented peoples, including Old Believers. It was not surprising that the church now attempted to have the Old Believers' printing press at the village of Klintskii closed down. It succeeded, temporarily, in 1787, but two Old Believer merchants operated a clandestine press for several years afterwards. The head of the Moscow police, meanwhile, had complained to Catherine in 1787 that the new law might make possible the publication of illegal and offensive books. The empress told him, in rather vague terms, to keep a watch on the situation. However, according to archbishop Platon, a review carried out in 1785 found only six books that were deemed to be against the teachings of the church.

Further complaints followed and, in 1787, Catherine restated the old guidelines, forbidding the publication of words against "the laws of God and the state" or of a "clearly seditious" nature. The Holy Synod was once again given a central role in censorship: it was to check all bookshops and publishing houses throughout the empire for any irreligious or offensive works. Once again, however, the instructions were vague and were interpreted with laxity or rigour according to the abilities or opinions of local clergy. In Moscow, on the other hand, some 313 titles and no fewer than 142,000 volumes were seized, yet when the synod subjected them to closer scrutiny, only 14 were found to require permanent confiscation, not as seditious, but as theologically unsound.

Why, then, did Catherine, on 11 October 1796, revoke the right of individuals to establish private presses? No single answer is possible. Certainly, the execution of the former king Louis XVI of France, on 21 January 1793, must have greatly disturbed her, and any text describing regicide, even Shakespeare's *Julius Caesar*, was proscribed. French books and newspapers could no longer be imported, and, turning away from her own previous intellectual interests, Catherine declared the writings of Diderot and the other Encyclopédistes seditious.

Fearing "enemies within", Catherine also turned against Novikov, who, during the previous decade, had become a veritable publishing tycoon. Much of his output was educational in nature, but he also dabbled in Freemasonry and Rosicrucianism. He was arrested and sentenced to 15 years in the Schlüssenberg Fortress; yet he had relentlessly attacked the atheism of the French *philosophes*. Aleksandr Radishchev, a social critic, presented Catherine with different problems. In his anonymously published *Puteshestvie iz Peterburga v Moskvu* (1790, *Journey from St Petersburg to Moscow*) he had reported on provincial corruption, superstition, drunkenness, and prostitution, and warned of the danger of peasant insurrection. He was sentenced to death, but this was commuted to 10 years in exile in Siberia; he returned in 1801, only to commit suicide a year later.

Despite these acts of individual repression, around 375 books were published each year. Coming to the end of her reign, and by no means entirely trusting her son and putative successor, Paul, Catherine took steps to perpetuate her *volte-face*. Following the 1796 edict, 12 private presses ceased active publication. Gary Marker has concluded that:

> For an empress who, for so long, had been inseparable from the leadership of literary life, and whose philosophy of rulership presupposed the virtue of the government's active intervention in civil society, the emancipation of intellectual life must have been hard to take. That it organized itself around institutions that could regulate themselves was simply intolerable.

Despite Catherine's fears, Paul (reigned 1796–1801) continued and even extended her policy on literature. Now, before a book could be imported, it had to be inspected by one of three new committees established at Riga in Latvia, Odessa in the Crimea, and Radzivilov (now Radekhov) in Ukraine, the first two for books entering the empire by sea and the third for those coming through Poland. Committees were also established at Moscow and St Petersburg. The effect was by no means uniform. Between 1797 and 1799, the committees at Moscow, St Petersburg, Odessa, and Radzivilov refused entry to a mere 87 titles; in Riga, the police censor, Fedor Tumanskii, turned away no less than 522 during the same period, including all books in Yiddish or Hebrew, and individual works by Goethe, Herder, Kant, Schiller, and Swift.

Before he came to the throne, Paul's successor Alexander I (reigned 1801–25) had declared to a Polish aristocrat, prince Adam Czartoryski, his "hatred of despotism, whenever and by whatever means it was executed". He "loved liberty" and believed that it was "owed equally to all men". However, as Geoffrey Hosking points out, granting liberty to all

> could only be done, if at all, by abolishing serfdom, that is by undermining the property and privileges of those who possessed the limited amount of civil liberty currently available in the Russian state ... he could only introduce liberty through despotism.

Some of that ambivalence is apparent in Alexander's immediate reinstatement of private presses, which was coupled with Russia's first, brief censorship statute. This is generally seen today as a major reform in a series intended to make state power more predictable and rational. Education was to be open to people at all levels of society, and to be aimed at preparing them to serve the state. The empire's four universities at Moscow, St Petersburg, Vilna (now Vilnius) in Lithuania, and Dorpat (or Iuriev, now Tartu) in Estonia, were each to be self-governing, but also had to provide censors. However, since, in the words of his "Preliminary Regulation for Public Education" (1803), publishing served "the cause of education", the new emperor placed the main burden of censorship upon the Main Administration of Schools within his new Ministry of Public Education.

Napoleon I's invasion in 1812 shook Russia's foundations and caused Alexander not only to tighten censorship, but also to embrace the intense religiosity that had spread during the war. In 1817, he recast the ministry that administered censorship as the Ministry of Spiritual Affairs and Popular Enlightenment, under one of his close friends, Aleksandr Golitsyn, the president of the Russian Bible Society, a branch of the British and Foreign Bible Society. Golitsyn used his role as chief censor to promote both the publication of his pietistic views and the wide dissemination of Bibles. His society had already published and distributed some 37,000 complete Bibles in Church Slavonic, French, German, Finnish, Estonian, Latvian, Lithuanian, Polish, Armenian, Georgian, Kalmyk, and Tatar. The Russian Orthodox Church opposed a Russian translation, arguing that only the Church Slavonic version, understood by hardly anybody, had the sanction of history and long usage. The Church was overruled by Alexander, but returned to contend that by law its censors still had the right to supervise all devotional publishing. Like his predecessors, Alexander was fearful of sedition, and he was now persuaded that the Bible Society was part of a conspiracy against him. Accordingly, he dismissed Golitsyn, replacing him with Serapion, metropolitan of Novgorod, who ordered that work on the Russian translation of the Bible was to cease.

At the outset of his reign Nicholas I (reigned 1825–55) put down the "Decembrist" revolt, led by army officers who had been influenced by French and Polish liberal ideas. The new emperor resolved that society should be permeated with Russian ideals; he wished to prove, through strong central rule, that autocracy was inherently right for Russia. Intending censorship to be a means to these ends, the emperor ordered the drafting of paired statutes to govern, respectively, secular and religious expression. He also established one committee to monitor theatrical performances and another to screen works from abroad. Within months he had promulgated a secular censorship law (June 1826). Credit for it went to A.S. Shishkov, head of the restored Ministry of Public Education, but the main drafter was his deputy P.A. Shirinskii-Shikhmatov. Rather than link censorship to education, Shishkov candidly announced that the new law would "direct public opinion into agreeing with present political circumstances and the views of the government".

In no fewer than 230 articles (five times as many as in the law of 1804), the new law set out the procedures, and made the author, not the censor, responsible if a duly censored text proved criminal once published (reversing the provisions of 1804). Bureaucrats in the Ministry of Education were now to replace professors as censors. When, however, many dismissed

this "cast iron" law as unworkable and counterproductive, Nicholas backed away, claiming to have signed the statute without reading it. A new drafting committee produced the substantially more liberal law of April 1828, intended to regulate all works of "literature, science, and art", whatever their language or source. A new ecclesiastical statute, issued on the same day, continued the administrative authority of the Holy Synod and its right to ban any book, artwork, ceremony, musical composition or performance counter to the precepts of the Orthodox Church; its censors were to be faculty members from ecclesiastical academies. In like spirit, the companion statute for secular censorship drew censors from universities once again, making them responsible for whatever they approved. As a concession to writers, censors were directed not to infer meanings from submitted texts or to change their wording without authorial assent. The censorship of foreign imprints was to be carried out by the Foreign Censorship Committee, responsible to the Main Administration of Censorship within the Ministry of Public Education in St Petersburg, with subordinate committees in Riga and Odessa, and individual censors when needed. Each month, the committee was to publish a list of banned foreign works.

Just three days after both censorship laws took effect, Nicholas secretly made censors of his new political police, the Third Section. To counter clandestine printing of illegal works and lax censorship of legal ones, he ordered this special corps to look for and report on anything "inclined to the spread of atheism, or which reflects, in the artist or writer, violations of the obligations of loyal subjects". In this period the liberal writer Aleksandr Herzen suffered regular political exile. Then, one year after the French and Belgian revolutions of 1830, Nicholas suppressed a similar rebellion in the "Congress Kingdom", the part of Poland that was under his control, abolished the special, semiautonomous status granted to the region by the Congress of Vienna in 1815, and subjected it to the laws and practices of his empire, including the censorship system. In 1833 he prescribed a system of ideas, known as "Official Nationality", to guide all his subjects, Russian, Polish or other, the institutions of society, and the array of agencies that now administered censorship:

> It is our common obligation to ensure that the education of the people be conducted according to the supreme intention of our August Monarch, in the joint spirit of Orthodoxy, Autocracy, and Nationality. I am convinced that every professor and teacher, being permeated by one and the same feeling of devotion to throne and fatherland, will use all his resources to become a worthy tool of government and to earn its complete confidence.

Private publishing was limited throughout this period. Nicholas I personally approved or rejected applications for the licensing of private periodicals, with the result that the total of 42 that circulated in 1825 had, by 1841, increased only modestly to 60, though it should be borne in mind that small readerships had also forced a number of licensed periodicals to close for lack of profits. As for books, the limited statistics available, which begin with the figures for 1837, show that secular censors in that year approved more titles (838) than in 1845 (804) or 1846 (810). Although the total for 1847 (862) went up a slight 6.49 per cent, annual figures for Russian book production remained minute compared to those for western Europe. Nikolai Gogol' had considerable trouble getting *Mertvye dushi* (1842, *Dead Souls*) into print, as it was considered to be both seditious and blasphemous.

News of the revolutions of 1848–49 in Paris, Vienna, Berlin, Budapest, and elsewhere prompted Nicholas I to re-examine security and to recruit a watchdog group, under D.P. Buturlin, to stiffen censorship. Buturlin's committee presided over a "censorship terror" that lasted for the remaining seven years of Nicholas's reign. The outbreak of the Crimean War in 1854 was used to justify even sterner limits. Thus, a typical order from Shirinskii-Shikhmatov, now education minister, required that all books for common readers be "penetrated with the living spirit of the Orthodox Church and with loyalty to the throne, state, and social order". The development of new printing technologies in the west had raised fears that cheap works might be produced in vast numbers, shaping public opinion, including that of the peasantry, among whom literacy was now increasing. Stringent licensing and customs requirements curbed the importation of this machinery. Censorship under Nicholas was more invasive and stricter than that imposed by any other Russian emperor. Even so, it has been argued, the system presented hurdles rather than roadblocks, especially for the most brilliant contemporary writers, such as Pushkin or Gogol'.

Assuming power in the last stages of the humiliating Crimean War, Alexander II (reigned 1855–81) blamed the debacle on the social and economic backwardness of the empire. Most at fault, he held, was the archaic system that kept 40 million peasants in chattel bondage. To prod landowners into negotiating a surrender that most of them opposed, Alexander quietly lifted the *de facto* ban on published comment about this issue. No law had specifically proscribed such comment, but the censors had disallowed it for decades. Alexander's action effected a seachange in the practice of censorship, even though, as a matter of politics, he stopped press commentary during 1859, while the Emancipation Proclamation was being drafted, but allowed "correct" debate on contingent reforms.

On the heels of the emancipation of the serfs, decreed in February 1861, Alexander named a new minister of the interior, P.A. Valuev, to implement the difficult reform of censorship. Valuev conceded that the phasing out of pre-publication censorship was inevitable, and that uncensored publications should not be kept in line solely through judicial prosecutions, but by an administrative system of warnings and penalties, curbing periodicals that published legal but dangerous material. In March 1862 Alexander freed all academic, scientific, and official publications from prepublication censorship, and abolished the special ministerial censorship offices inherited from his predecessor. Nikolai Chernyshevskii's *Chto delat'?* (*What is to be Done?*) was published in 1863 without censorial intervention, yet it is a call to prepare for revolution (and was to be a major source of inspiration for the young Lenin). Around the same time, N.A. Serno-Solovevich was able to open a bookshop and library in St Petersburg aiming to make political writings more widely available.

Early in 1863 both the censorship administration and its drafting committee were moved, at the emperor's insistence, from the Education Ministry to Valuev's Interior Ministry. The decree of 6 April 1865, a major reform, was designed to give "relief and convenience to the national press". It did, however, include Valuev's system of warnings and penalties (mainly fines, suspensions, and closures), to be imposed on uncensored publications that showed a "dangerous orientation". The system was to be monitored by the Ministry of the Interior's Chief Administration for Press Affairs. As before, shorter books were seen as having greater potential to do harm than more substantial works. All periodicals in Moscow and St Petersburg, and all translations of 320 pages or more, wherever published, were freed from censorship. Persons responsible for criminal content in any freed publication were to be subject to judicial prosecution. Among the press offences considered criminal were "justification of acts forbidden by law", "insulting an official person or establishment", "inciting one section of the population against another", and "calling into question the principles of property or the family unit".

In December 1866, the State Council added some supplementary rules, but termed them "temporary", like the statute of 1865, because full freedom to publish would "take place under the influence of judicial decisions". Eleven trials did go forward during the late 1860s, but judges handed down only four convictions. Critics within the government viewed the courts as lenient. During the next ten years, as mounting terrorism made the emperor wary of political mis-steps, the government all but abandoned press-related trials. Instead, it targeted freed periodicals that had consistently targeted the autocracy: new measures against them included limits on street sales and commercial advertisements, both of which could hurt them financially. Whereas the warning system was used, between 1865 and 1869, to suspend a mere ten freed periodicals, including *Sovremennik* (The Contemporary), closed down for its socialist opinions in 1866, those suspended between 1875 and 1879 numbered 27. Meanwhile, however, the number of periodicals increased, with the total number of journals rising from 12 in 1865 to 10 in 1879, and the total number of newspapers from 41 to 62 during the same period.

After the assassination of Alexander II in 1881, Alexander III (reigned 1881–94) cracked down hard on the press, creating a Supreme Commission of Press Affairs to discipline not just "dangerous" periodicals, but also their editors and publishers, through temporary banishment from the trade. *Golos* was warned three times in 1882 that it was pursuing a "dangerous orientation". A.A. Kraevskii's *Otechestvennye zapiski* was closed down after allegations that it was "an organ of the press that not only opens its pages to the spread of dangerous ideas, but also has as its collaborators people who belong to secret societies". The commission imposed closure, its harshest penalty, seven times between 1881 and 1889, a period when the overall number of journals and newspapers declined by just over 22 and 11 percentage points respectively.

From 1890 onwards, the apparent containment of what was called (depending on one's perspective) either "revolutionary violence" or "terrorism" allowed for an easing of restrictions that permitted the numbers of journals and newspapers to rise, reaching increasing numbers of literate people all over the empire. The total stood once more at the level of 1881 when Nicholas II (reigned 1894–1917) acceded to the throne. He opted to continue the controls he had inherited, despite calls from many quarters for solely judicial limits on the press. Ten years into his reign, however, as the dam of economic and political discontent broke in the strikes and demonstrations of the revolution of 1905–06, controls over a wide range of activities, including publishing, diminished.

In October 1905, following a government decree that no printing plant could be operated if its owners bypassed press regulations, the outlawed St Petersburg Soviet (or Council) of Workers' Deputies, chaired by Leo Trotskii, ordered members of the printworkers' union to refuse to work for owners who complied. Forced on all fronts to make concessions, Nicholas issued his Manifesto of 17 October 1905, promising imminent freedom of expression, a legislative assembly (the Duma), and other reforms. During the popular rebellion, known as the "days of freedom", that ensued in October and November, printers imposed their own censorship by setting in type only those texts that they approved, much of it radical in the extreme.

When he issued new rules for periodicals on 24 November 1905, the emperor claimed to have shifted wholly to judicial controls and therefore to have granted "one of the fundamental freedoms". Judicial prosecution was in itself, however, a means of punishment, for the new rules made possible the closure of an indicted publication pending what could be a protracted adjudication. No matter how feeble the charge against it, a closed periodical lost income and momentum.

The government also enacted supplementary rules that allowed pre-circulation screenings and seizures. Satirical journals, for example, were required to submit illustrations to a press committee at least 24 hours before publication, so that officials had time to send police armed with indictments to confiscate all copies as they came from the press. Legal closures of periodicals figured prominently in late 1905, the first sweep commencing after eight St Petersburg dailies published, on 2 December, the "Financial Manifesto" of the Workers' Soviet. The text urged people to withhold tax payments and to put pressure on Nicholas to grant more reforms. The government then closed the eight dailies, and secured the convictions of those found responsible for inciting illegal behaviour. By the end of the month, it had closed more than 50 periodicals on various grounds.

The promised new rules on book publishing took effect on 26 April 1906. These allowed most books to reach the public and the Committee on Press Affairs at the same time. However, works of up to 16 pages had to undergo inspection at least two days before publication, and those with between 17 and 80 pages at least seven days before. Book-related trials for the rest of 1906 reached an all-time high of 223, with 175 convictions. Those found guilty of circulating or attempting to circulate a work that had been ruled illegal mainly suffered fines, not imprisonment, for the main aim of the government was to identify criminal content and to keep it from the public judicially.

When two commercial "electric theatres" or cinemas opened in Moscow in 1903, the government had assigned the censorship of films to local police chiefs, officials who had long had a role in the monitoring of public morals. Each chief was authorized to establish an office for film censorship. The official in charge numbered each foreign or domestic film and entered it in a record book, along with a summary of its contents and a record of his decision. Constables on the beat made certain that only authorized films appeared on the screens. Bans could be imposed on any film that might "offend religious, patriotic or moral feeling" or that contained "pictures of a tendentious and political character", while films about revolutions, regicides, and other political upheavals were banned outright.

Criticism of press controls never ceased. For example, in a pronouncement issued in 1909, the first Congress of Russian Publishers and Booksellers declared that "the former censorship caused a mass of abuses of publishing, but it protected the editor and the bookseller from the annoyances of judicial prosecution". What was particularly odious, according to the congress, was the absence of a time limit on a book's liability to prosecution. In general, however, in those final peacetime years under the autocracy relations between the government and persons involved with legal publications were roughly as amicable as those of their western counterparts. There was an enormous expansion in the publication of books and newspapers alike. Illegal publications of a seditious nature – and especially such inflammatory papers as Lenin's *Iskra* (Spark), smuggled in from abroad – were another matter, and were dealt with by the political police. The Foreign Censorship Committee remained fully active right up to 1917, interdicting and banning illegal works from abroad at its own discretion.

In 1914, the outbreak of war with the Austro-Hungarian and German empires led to the imposition of military censorship on private publishing in Russia. Then followed a heightening of domestic turmoil, culminating in the revolutions of 1917 that brought imperial Russia to its end.

From 1865 onwards, the press in Russia had, arguably, gained a degree of genuine freedom and had continued to add to it, with some interruptions – notably in 1905–06 – right up until 1914. The novelist Vladimir Nabokov, an aristocrat who left Russia after the revolution, has sometimes been accused of indulging in excessive nostalgia for the imperial era, yet he seems to have described the situation accurately enough:

> Under the Tsars (despite the inept and barbarous character of their rule) a freedom-loving Russian had incomparably more possibility and means of expressing itself than at any time during Lenin's and Stalin's regime. He was protected by law. There were fearless and independent judges in Russia. The Russian *sud* (legal system) after the Alexander reforms was a magnificent institution, not only on paper. Periodicals of various tendencies and political parties of all possible kinds, legally and illegally, flourished ...

DEREK JONES

Further Reading
Balmuth, Daniel, *Censorship in Russia, 1865–1905*, Washington, DC: University Press of America, 1979

Choldin, Marianna Tax, *A Fence around the Empire: Russian Censorship of Western Ideas under the Tsars*, Durham, North Carolina: Duke University Press, 1985

de Madariaga, Isabel, *Russia in the Age of Catherine the Great*, London: Weidenfeld and Nicolson, and New Haven, Connecticut: Yale University Press, 1981

Foote, I.P., "Firing a Censor: The Case of N.V. Elagin, 1857", *Oxford Slavonic Papers*, new series, 29 (1986): 116–31

Foote, I.P., "In the Belly of the Whale: Russian Writers and the Censorship in the Nineteenth Century", *Slavonic and East European Review*, 98 (1990)

Foote, I.P., "The St Petersburg Censorship Committee", *Oxford Slavonic Papers*, new series, 24 (1991)

Foote, I.P., "Counter-Censorship: Authors versus Censors in 19th-century Russia", *Oxford Slavonic Papers*, new series, 27 (1994)

Goldstein, Robert Justin (editor), *The War for the Public Mind: Political Censorship in Nineteenth-Century Europe*, Westport, Connecticut: Praeger, 2000

Hosking, Geoffrey, *Russia: People and Empire, 1552–1917*, London: HarperCollins, and Cambridge, Massachusetts: Harvard University Press, 1997

Marker, Gary, *Publishing, Printing, and the Origins of Intellectual Life in Russia, 1700–1800*, Princeton, New Jersey: Princeton University Press, 1985

Monas, Sidney, *The Third Section: Police and Society in Russia under Nicholas I*, Cambridge, Massachusetts: Harvard University Press, 1961

Nikitenko, Aleksandr, *The Diary of a Russian Censor*, abridged and translated by Helen Saltz Jacobson, Amherst: University of Massachusetts Press, 1975

Papmehl, K.A., *Freedom of Expression in Eighteenth-Century Russia*, The Hague: Nijhoff, 1971

Rigberg, Benjamin F., "The Tsarist Press Law, 1894–1905", *Jahrbücher für Geschichte Osteuropas*, 13 (1965)

Rigberg, Benjamin F., "The Efficacy of Tsarist Censorship Operations, 1894–1917", *Jahrbücher für Geschichte Osteuropas*, 14 (1966)

Rigberg, Benjamin F., "Tsarist Censorship Performance, 1894–1905", *Jahrbücher für Geschichte Osteuropas*, 17 (1969)

Ruud, Charles A., *Fighting Words: Imperial Censorship and the Russian Press, 1804–1906*, Toronto: University of Toronto Press, 1982

The Soviet Union, 1917–89

The seizure of power by Lenin's Bolsheviks in Petrograd on 25 October 1917 (Russian calendar) was accompanied by three decrees of the utmost importance. The Decree on Peace called for an end to the war in Europe and the Decree on Land gave Russian peasants the right to control agriculture throughout the country. The Decree on the Press was not much noticed at the time, but its provisions were equally momentous. Right at the start of his rule, Lenin laid down that newspapers that published material hostile to the new revolutionary authorities were to be closed down. Thus, Soviet censorship was as old as the Soviet state.

The Bolsheviks had come to power with a number of basic assumptions. They thought that Marxism offered the only true set of doctrines for understanding the world, and they regarded even other variants of Marxism than their own as unscientific and misleading. They also argued that the inception of a communist society required a massive preliminary campaign of "popular enlightenment". The "toiling masses", argued Lenin and his comrades, had been systematically misled by decades of "bourgeois rule". The necessary corrective would be provided by the "dictatorship of the proletariat", a dictatorship that would not only suppress military and political enemies but would also set about the task of indoctrination so that a new kind of culture might arise in Russia and the rest of the world. From this standpoint, there could be no toleration of rival systems of thought. The only question for Lenin was pragmatic: how sensible was it to use a particular method of eliminating the other systems – cultural and religious as well as political – at any given time?

Initially, Lenin limited his regime to closing down conservative, liberal, and even several socialist newspapers. He also, in December 1917, established the Cheka, a political police force that arrested opponents of the regime. Some of the victims were writers. When the Civil War erupted in full intensity from mid-1918, the "Red Terror" eliminated nearly all the organs of alternative public opinion. Such few non-Bolshevik newspapers as survived belonged to the Menshevik Party, which took care to avoid too open an attack on the authorities. In the Civil War, too, there were violent campaigns against organized religion. The Russian Orthodox Church as well as other Christian denominations, Islam, and Judaism all suffered. Religious leaders were killed and religious buildings were seized, and the teaching and dissemination of the various faiths were severely curtailed.

Novelists and poets were simultaneously cowed. Only for a short while, in the winter of 1917–18, had it been possible to publish even satirical spoofs about the Bolshevik leadership. One such was produced by the writer Evgenii Zamiatin in the Socialist Revolutionary Party's newspaper. Thereafter, it was physically difficult to do so, for although some private presses continued to exist, they lacked the resources to support their authors. Paper was in short supply and, as the Civil War raged, the distribution network was disrupted.

Furthermore, neither writers nor anyone else in those years lived on money alone. Money lost its value as inflation rocketed, and the cardinal need of Soviet citizens was to obtain a ration card. They knew that otherwise they would starve. It was only state organizations and state enterprises that could issue such cards. Housing, heating fuel, and health care, as well as food supply, were declared state monopolies, and the indirect pressure on the intelligentsia to avoid giving offence to the regime grew ever more intense. Consequently, writers were obliged to take employment with the Soviet state regardless of their political principles. The Politburo of the Communist Party (as the Bolsheviks became) kept an eye on what was being published. It even reserved itself the power to decree whether particular writers, such as the great Russian poet Alexander Blok, should be allowed to travel abroad for a period of convalescence. In 1921 another poet, Nikolai Gumilev, was executed by the Petrograd Cheka on the trumped-up charge of belonging to a counter-revolutionary conspiracy.

Yet the Politburo had concentrated on winning the Civil War before it turned its repressive attention to the arts and "high" culture in general. In any case, it had hoped to pre-empt much intellectual criticism by offering substantial material reward to those writers who agreed to compose suitably favourable pieces for the authorities. Another source of income for intellectuals was translation work, as Gosizdat – the gigantic state publishing house – raced to get cheap editions of foreign classics into the hands of Soviet workers, soldiers, and peasants. Unfortunately for Lenin, however, it had become clear that there were extremely few talented writers who were willing to declare themselves unequivocally as supporters of the regime. Among those who did, furthermore, were some whose work he did not much like or understand. The futurist poetry of his own admirer, Vladimir Maiakovskii, was especially annoying to him, and he even tried to get the size of Maiakovskii's print-runs lowered.

After the Civil War it became feasible for the dictatorship to elaborate a more definite system of control over the media of public expression. In June 1922, the first Soviet censorship authority was created by the central party leadership: Glavlit (Main Administration for Affairs of Literature and Publishing Houses). Thenceforward, nothing could legally be published in the country without preliminary permission. Since 1906, even the Russian imperial regime had operated only a post-publication censorship, and after the revolution of February 1917 freedom of expression had existed for all citizens until the Bolshevik seizure of power in October. In keeping with its sinister purpose, the decree establishing Glavlit was kept secret, and was only printed after the fall of the Soviet Union. The specific function accorded to Glavlit was to prevent the publication of anything deemed antagonistic to the fundamental objectives of Leninist communism or to the current policies of the central party leadership. The Politburo thereafter felt able to leave the supervision of literary activity on political and other themes to Glavlit, and to the analogous organizations set up in relation to the cinema, theatre, and music.

The Politburo's confidence was bolstered by a measure of decisive intimidation. In summer 1922 dozens of outstanding noncommunist poets, philosophers, and scholars were deported en masse on the Moscow–Berlin train. Among them was the pioneering existentialist philosopher and Christian socialist Nikolai Berdiaev. Thereby a signal was given that, whatever economic and social relaxation had been introduced by the New Economic Policy in 1921 at the end of the Civil War, the militant cultural imperatives would remain in place. The USSR's political leaders aimed to insulate the country from every trend of thought they deemed hostile, flippant, or unhealthy.

In the meantime, there was considerable controversy among communists themselves. On Trotskii's suggestion, it was accepted that, for the foreseeable future, Glavlit should continue to permit works of art so long as they were not directly anti-communist. Novels by "fellow travellers" appeared in print. Several works that praised peasants and village life gained popularity, even though the party aimed to promote supposedly working-class, industrial and urban values. The poet-balladeer Sergei Esenin even sang verses in favour of bohemian escapism. Apart from the secret police and Glavlit, however, there was also always an indirect pressure on would-be rebels. Gosizdat enjoyed very close to a monopoly on printing presses. Not a single noncommunist newspaper survived and nearly all other cultural outlets were state-owned or state-subsidized. Without financial support from the authorities, it was virtually impossible for an author to get work published.

When Stalin initiated his first Five-Year Plan in 1928, the restrictions on cultural self-expression were instantaneously increased. Limits on what could be said, sung, or displayed were severely narrowed, and Glavlit was empowered to impose orthodoxy in the arts while the party secretariat controlled the output of the newspapers. Private printing presses vanished. Stalin's version of Marxism–Leninism was forced into every item of public discussion, and the image of Stalin as "the Lenin of today" became *de rigueur*.

The restrictions on political and cultural variety were extraordinary even by previous Soviet standards. Religious, literary, and national representatives who had been able to write material for their followers in the 1920s were vigorously suppressed. Show trials were common for the most prominent of them, and imprisonment, Siberian exile, or execution became

the fate of the many. There was a systematic campaign to eliminate all surviving bodies of alternative opinion. Lenin's policy of insulating his country from "alien", "reactionary", and "anti-Soviet" commentary was taken to an extreme, and the few opponents of the ascendant party leadership who dared to publicize their views were treated as traitors to their country and to the cause. By the mid-1930s, Stalin had arrested nearly all real and potential pamphleteers of this type.

Hostile literature thereafter had to be produced abroad and smuggled into the USSR, at huge personal risk to the carriers themselves. In exile, the Mensheviks continued their verbal tirades against Stalin in their journal *The Socialist Courier*. After his deportation in 1928, Trotskii produced a *Bulletin of the Opposition*. The readership in the USSR, however, was inevitably paltry. The NKVD (People's Commissariat of Internal Affairs), successor to the Cheka, was highly effective at eradicating most of the lines of contact between communist dissenters in Russia and the Menshevik and Trotskiite centres abroad.

In order to break the monolithic facade, there was a need for extreme bravery and not a little cunning. For example, Nikolai Bukharin, a former member of the Politburo, managed to write pieces in *Izvestiia* (News) that appeared to be castigating the nastiness of foreign political systems (such as Nazi Germany) but were understood by sophisticated readers to be offering a critique of Stalinism. Another example is afforded by Mikhail Sholokhov's *Tikhii Don* (*And Quiet Flows the Don*), which uses an ostensibly loyal political analysis as a means of describing the very variegated nature of Cossack life. Sholokhov got away with this mainly because he was transparently a supporter of Stalin. By contrast, Bukharin paid the ultimate price for his insouciance: he was executed in 1938. There was no room any longer for criticisms of the policies that were at the core of Stalin's programme. The struggle against unorthodoxy affected not only the political press and creative literature but the entire swathe of cultural self expression. Music, film, painting, hobbies, and sports: every single one of these activities was subjected to tight political control.

Four main methods were used for this purpose. The first was the enforcement of the production of a certain kind of art: "socialist realism". The main requirements were the elevation of working-class, communist heroes, and the portrayal of the material and social achievements of "socialism", as well as the grievous conditions of capitalism. Not only literature but also news broadcasting had to stay within such guidelines. The second method was to make it completely impossible to publicize anything in the Soviet Union except through the state-owned media. No newspaper, radio station, or printing press remained privately owned, and a vigorous central authority was imposed over local output. Thirdly, the regime established professional unions. For example, in 1934 it held the founding congress of the USSR Union of Writers. These unions organized and disciplined their members; they also provided them with security of employment and reward so long as they produced the kind of work officially demanded. Without membership of the unions, moreover, it was well nigh impossible to have one's work published.

The fourth method was the most direct form of preventative censorship: execution. Dozens of major writers, painters, and film directors perished in the Great Terror of 1937–38. Among them were some of the world's finest artists, such as the poet Osip Mandel'shtam and the short story writer Isaak Babel'. Those artists who were not arrested were nevertheless traumatized. The poet Anna Akhmatova saw her son taken off by the NKVD, and wrote her epic poem "Rekviem" (Requiem) on this theme (a poem that had to be kept secret). Other writers, journalists, and publicists were kept in constant fear, for it was not necessary to have written against the regime in order to fall foul of the police.

All through these years, official joy was expressed that the USSR was the brightest beacon of freedom for the contemporary world. Stalin authorized, part-wrote, and edited a book, *The Short Course*, which described the history of Soviet communism in the most glowing terms. Every issue of the central party newspaper *Pravda* (Truth) had to acknowledge his greatness, and Glavlit proceeded to check that the contents of each and every publication and broadcast conformed to the self-image that had been developed by Marxism–Leninism–Stalinism. By the time of Stalin's death nearly 800 million copies of his various works had been sold in the USSR and in the rest of the world. Glavlit removed all alternative opinions from public discussion and the resultant vacuum was filled by Stalinist ideology.

When Hitler's forces invaded the USSR in 1941, the authorities prudently accepted their need to widen the scope of what could be published. Patriotic themes in literature, which had begun to be allowed in the 1930s, were given even greater latitude. Newspaper journalists, too, could write more extensively about the war fronts. But this did not mean that the operations of the censorship were discontinued. On the contrary, Glavlit energetically ensured that the new limits were respected: not a scintilla of criticism of the regime or its practices was permitted. The fact was that the interests of the regime were served by patriotic poems and other artistic and informational output. Moreover, the Nazis were behaving so bestially in the German-occupied regions of the USSR that there was no longer any sense in requiring newspaper editors to print fantastic stories: the truth did the job better for the regime.

Through the wartime years the NKVD, too, was hard at work. In private conversation it was dangerous even to express admiration of the jeeps being supplied to the USSR by its military ally, the United States. A specific offence, "praise of American technology", was introduced. As the early Soviet military defeats gave way to victories, the state reverted to its prewar insistence on including a heavy dose of Stalinist ideology in its publications. Stalin intended to try and impose total control over Soviet citizens and the citizens of any conquered country.

This campaign reached its peak in the late 1940s, when Stalin's cultural affairs henchman Andrei Zhdanov made venomous attacks on any publication that did not openly support the regime. Akhmatova, the short story writer Mikhail Zoshchenko, and the composer Dmitrii Shostakovich were among the victims. The film director Sergei Eisenstein, who was working on a project about Tsar Ivan the Terrible, with whom Stalin identified himself, was reduced to a psychological wreck by Stalin's comment that the film did not sufficiently laud the efficacy of state terror. In contrast to prewar custom, these figures were not executed, but their public denigration was a lesson to every would-be author and artist that overt fealty to

the state authorities was an absolute demand if they wished to remain in public life.

Stalin died in 1953. His successors, led by Khrushchev, attacked his reputation. Khrushchev's closed-session speech to the 20th Party Congress in February 1956 marked a break with the Stalinist political and cultural heritage. Calls were made in the same period for the reintroduction of "sincerity" in literature, for greater plausibility in news reporting, and for a re-examination of party history. The snag was that Khrushchev's measures caused instability in eastern Europe and helped cause a Hungarian popular revolt in late 1956. As a result, Khrushchev was compelled to moderate his anti-Stalin campaign at home, even to the point of agreeing to the demand of his central party colleagues that his congress speech should not be published. It was not until 1990 that it appeared in print in the USSR.

However, the limits of officially approved public expression were nevertheless widened by Khrushchev. Lenin's dispute with Stalin was examined in detail, and the various blunders made by Stalin in World War II were recounted, even though the full scale of the Great Terror was never acknowledged. Most strikingly, Khrushchev sanctioned the publication of Aleksandr Solzhenitsyn's *Odin den' Ivana Denisovicha* (*One Day in the Life of Ivan Denisovich*), a story set in a postwar labour camp. Various other critiques of Stalinism were allowed, including poetry by Evgenii Evtushenko and Andrei Voznesenskii.

Under the surface of things, however, expectations had been raised. Writers were preparing material that they hoped would soon benefit from a further expansion of the limits. The material was held "in desk drawers", and as Khrushchev amplified his criticism of Stalin, there seemed a possibility that broader freedom would be granted. Yet Khrushchev dug in his heels. He created a scandal among the intellectuals by visiting an exhibition of contemporary art on the Manege in Moscow, and issuing a stream of obscenities about the paintings. His political associates would have clamped down even harder; most of them resented even the criticism of Stalin that he had been making. When Khrushchev fell from power in 1964, the scope of political discussion was narrowed again. The "thaw" was over. Winter began.

Even while Khrushchev ruled, there had been arrests of dissenting intellectuals and students. Maiakovskii Square in Moscow had attracted many such people, who wrote and passed their poems from hand to hand. Occasionally the KGB intervened and troublemakers were targeted. Prison sentences followed. It was a lighter punishment than under Stalin, but little love was left between Khrushchev and the intelligentsia when he was ousted from the Kremlin, and many dissenting figures predicted that his successors, led by Leonid Brezhnev, would be more "liberal". Their mistakenness was quickly exposed by the "show" trial of two satirists, Iulii Daniel' and Andrei Sinyavskii, in 1966. Their sentencing to the Gulag indicated a determination by the regime to tighten its grip on the media of public expression. The determination became still greater after the invasion of Czechoslovakia by the Soviet army and the armies of its Warsaw Pact allies (other than Romania's) in 1968. The slightest accusation of unorthodoxy could result in incarceration. Several works written in hope of publication were stopped from publication. Among them were Solzhenitsyn's novel *V kruge pervom* (*The First Circle*), Roy

Medvedev's *Let History Judge*, Vasilii Grossman's *Zhizn' i sud'ba* (*Life and Fate*), and Viktor Danilov's volumes on the forced collectivization of agriculture in the 1930s. Grossman was told in person by Mikhail Suslov, a member of the Politburo (see below), that his novel would not be published for several centuries. The official political line was rigidly enforced.

The key institutions remained Glavlit and its own watchdogs, the Department of Propaganda and the Department of Culture inside the Party Central Committee Secretariat; and Suslov was the Cerberus in chief, deciding every matter of ideological control that the departments did not find it easy to resolve by themselves. Suslov had risen to prominence under Stalin. His notions of Marxist–Leninist orthodoxy were much narrower than Khrushchev's, and there is no evidence that he ever enjoyed a work of art. A committed Marxist–Leninist, he hated ideological innovation, and whenever he needed to support his arguments for communist conservatism he consulted his personally compiled card-index of quotations from the collected works of Lenin.

However, Marxism–Leninism even under Stalin had already acquired a tinge – indeed a deep coloration – of Russian nationalism. The tendency had continued under Khrushchev and was retained by Brezhnev. This was not openly admitted, but the censors knew that they had to allow publication of a lot of material that would have exasperated Lenin. At the extreme, this included a lightly disguised tract of anti-Semitism, T. Kichko's *Judaism Without Veneer*, but it also embraced books that would have been unpublishable under not only Lenin but also Stalin. Members of a school of nationalist writers, the so-called *derevenshchiki* ("countrysiders"), wrote sympathetically about peasants, rural customs, and the Russian village. Hints were dropped that Orthodox Christianity had been a positive element in Russian national identity and that it should be accorded official acceptance. Even the cinema reflected this trend: cunning directors began to slip shots of onion-domed cathedrals into their films. Of course, the authorities were not oblivious to this, but many party leaders, including Brezhnev, who was no intellectual but knew what he liked, felt comfortable with this cultural tendency. A few Politburo members wanted to take the process still further in the direction of Russian nationalism. They had lost the Marxist–Leninist faith themselves and wanted the state ideology altered accordingly. They also recognized that Marxism–Leninism's grip was slipping even on the minds of many members of that minority of the population that felt positive about the Soviet political regime. Something else – more national, more avowedly moral and uplifting – had to be introduced into the growing vacuum.

Censorship even as a negative force, moreover, was no longer quite as efficacious as in the earlier years. The BBC World Service and Radio Liberty broadcast from the West into the USSR. Finnish television, which carried a lot of English-language programmes, could be picked up by Soviet citizens in Estonia and neighbouring areas. Official publishers in Moscow translated a large number of contemporary foreign novels. Soviet television relayed pictures of international sporting events. Soviet tourists, all of whom had been politically vetted, visited and made their observations of western Europe and North America. Foreign tourists came to Moscow, Leningrad, and the cities of the Volga. Copies of Beatles records were

smuggled into the country, and further copies were made on tape recorders. Even foreign communist newspapers were useful, at least occasionally, in purveying information about life under non-communist governments. Sources of alternative information were widening and deepening. Glavlit was still extremely oppressive, but no longer all-powerful.

It was still the case, however, that shops contained only those books and pamphlets that the regime allowed, and that authors hesitated before offering anything "risky" for the censor's perusal. Yet, clandestinely, there were a growing number of small-scale publications. These were referred to as "self publishing" (*samizdat*); if a tape was made of a speech or a piece of music, it was designated *magnitizdat*. Copies of both *samizdat* and *magnitizdat* were made very laboriously. No printing press was available. The basic technical equipment was the typewriter and carbon paper, or the tape recorder.

The KGB (Committee of State Security) could act against these illicit media, whereas Glavlit could only censor that which arrived in its offices. House searches were required. Police informers had to be employed and activated. If necessary, authors had to be imprisoned. In 1974, the recalcitrant Solzhenitsyn, who had released his works for publication in the West and who knew that copies were being illegally imported into the USSR, was deported against his will. Other writers endured the same fate. Still others, usually unknown abroad, languished in the Gulag. Solzhenitsyn was probably more of a problem for the Soviet regime when he was living in Vermont than he had been in the USSR. The KGB could restrict but not stop the flow of information around and into the country; it could not totally insulate all Soviet citizens from ideas that the regime found hostile or just uncongenial.

Always, in any case, the regime's uppermost leadership quietly allowed a broader discussion of ideas in its own midst than in *Pravda* or on television or radio. While Glavlit censored Roy Medvedev's works they were being read by several party leaders. A programme of reform, going far beyond Khrushchev's political and cultural "thaw", was the object of quiet debate. Medvedev was brusquely treated by the KGB and sometimes his manuscripts were confiscated, but he stayed clear of prison.

In 1985 a general secretary was appointed who increasingly accepted and tried to implement Medvedev's programme. This was Mikhail Gorbachev. From the start, he declared the need for glasnost. This Russian word, used by emperors and party leaders alike, is roughly translatable as "openness" or "publicity". It does not mean "freedom of the press". Gorbachev wished to encourage public discussion of sensitive matters of Soviet politics without relinquishing the party's political monopoly, or indeed the system of pre-publication censorship. In 1985–87, therefore, he quietly removed several matters from the official list of banned topics, while having Glavlit and the Secretariat Departments ensure both that the still more sensitive matters were not surreptitiously added by audacious authors, and that glasnost did not get out of hand by challenging the nature of the Soviet order itself.

Initially, this balancing act worked in Gorbachev's favour, and without much difficulty except from more conservative leaders. On his direct orders, several "blank spots" in the USSR's history were researched and described by loyal scholars. Among the "blank spots" were the mass abuses of the Stalin period, especially the Great Terror. Another topic of commentary was the "stagnation" in politics and economics in the Brezhnev period. Thus, Gorbachev aspired to manipulate glasnost as a means to gather popularity for his campaign to "return to Lenin". Gorbachev's opinion was that things had started to go badly wrong in the USSR under Stalin, not under Lenin, and that a great chance to build a humane, democratic socialism after Stalin's death had been lost until his own assumption of high office.

Films such as Tengiz Abuladze's *Pokayanie* (*Repentance*) and novels such as Anatolii Rybakov's *Deti Arbata* (*Children of the Arbat*) were given public circulation as being supportive of such an orientation. Gorbachev, moreover, indicated that no longer would a single interpretation of Soviet history – and Soviet history was the most controversial and important topic in the new period of glasnost – be mandatory for writers. Although he preferred his own particular view on Soviet history, he did not demand that a definitive textbook should be written to propagate it. Thus, he was allowing a fresh opportunity for writers to discuss historical events without having to remain within a tight framework of opinion.

This proved to be fatal for the practical primacy of any sort of Marxism-Leninism. Several authors in 1988 and after started to ask searching questions about the role of Lenin in the inception of dictatorship and terror. Vladimir Soloukhin's *Chitaia Lenina* (*Reading Lenin*), which previously had appeared only abroad and in samizdat, caused a sensation when it was printed, for it used the official edition of Lenin's collected works to indicate that Lenin had been an enthusiast for savage repressive policies soon after the October Revolution.

Fierce dispute broke out in the Politburo, and Gorbachev's deputy Egor Ligachev used Gorbachev's absence abroad to engineer a clampdown; he also connived in the publication of a tract by Nina Andreeva, who did not disguise either her Stalinist nostalgia or her anti-Semitism. On his return, Gorbachev reverted policy toward glasnost. However, although he could count on support from most professional historians, there were plenty of journalists, poets, and songwriters who insisted that the entire basis of Marxism-Leninism, the October Revolution, and the USSR should be subject to critical scrutiny. Even Gorbachev came to admit that abuses of power had occurred under Lenin, although he added that Lenin, despite being misguided in many matters, was essentially the greatest humanitarian of the century. In 1989–91 there was a degree of freedom to discuss all topics that exercised public opinion unprecedented since 1917.

True, practical limits remained to discussion. In particular, Glavlit continued to operate even though Gorbachev confined it to censoring material after, rather than before, publication. In addition, documents for debate could be and were withheld from scrutiny in the party and state archives. Even access to the text of the secret protocols of the Nazi–Soviet Pact of 1939, long known about in the west, was prohibited. In any case, authors wishing to publish criticisms tended to prefer to write short, snappy pieces for the newspapers. Lengthy works such as novels could not be produced in time to keep pace with the fast-changing public debate – and this in turn meant that Glavlit could not "censor" much material with any effectiveness. Gorbachev tried to upbraid newspaper editors, and threatened to sack one of them, but the flood of anticommunist material did not subside.

By the late 1980s, moreover, it was not just Soviet history that was being debated in a fashion unfavourable to the regime. The authoritarian form of rule, the ecological devastation, the poor provision of consumer goods, the judicial iniquities, the national and ethnic discrimination, the technological backwardness, the restrictions on foreign travel, the privileges of the party elite: all these topics were publicly aired, and the language was unbridled. Unless he opted to abandon glasnost and cultural pluralism, Gorbachev was helpless to curtail the criticism. He followed a pathway of zigzags in politics, but, by and large, he held to the notion that greater freedom was preferable to a return to clampdowns.

No longer were the critics operating as mere individuals. The Union of Writers in the Russian Federation, which was only one, albeit by far the largest, of the 15 Union Republics, had practically become a mouthpiece for Russian nationalism. Several of the other Soviet republics were led by communists who judged that the days of the USSR might be numbered and decided to cast their lots with the nationalists of their respective republics. Anti-Russian as well as anti-Soviet pieces began to appear in the non-Russian republics' media.

In August 1991 a coup d'état was attempted by conservatives against Gorbachev's programme. It did not succeed, but Gorbachev's power was debilitated by the fiasco and Boris Yeltsin, as president of the Russian Federation, engineered the breakup of the USSR. When the Russian Federation emerged in 1992 as a fully independent state, Yeltsin declared a commitment to total decommunization. Apart from the rapid introduction of a market economy, he dismantled the paraphernalia of formal censorship. Glavlit was abolished by him in October 1991, even before the USSR's disintegration. The Soviet party archives were taken into the possession of the newly independent Russian state, and scholars from Russia and abroad were invited to inspect them (see below). Freedom of the press was guaranteed by law. Secret materials, especially about Lenin and Gorbachev, were printed in newspapers. The horrors of the communist era, from start to finish, were exposed.

The state archives have become more accessible, but since the mid-1990s there has been a reluctance to keep up the pace of liberalization. In particular, the Presidential Archive established by Mikhail Gorbachev, which contained those materials thought to be politically very sensitive, was not made open to the public. Some items within it were declassified and published, but many of the holdings were kept secret. Declassification has a long way to go in other archives too, and the criticism of liberalization made by communist deputies and their allies in the State Duma has inhibited the progress of reform. Communists continue to argue that scholars who rummage in the archives are bent only upon denigrating the glorious achievements of the country's past.

ROBERT SERVICE

Further Reading

Choldin, Marianna Tax and Maurice Friedberg (editors), *The Red Pencil: Artists, Scholars, and Censors in the USSR*, London and Boston: Unwin Hyman, 1989

Churchward, L.G., *The Soviet Intelligentsia: An Essay on the Social Structure and Roles of Soviet Intellectuals during the 1960s*, London: Routledge and Kegan Paul, 1973

Conquest, Robert, *The Great Terror: A Reassessment*, Oxford and New York: Oxford University Press, 1990

Dewhirst, Martin and Robert Farrell, *The Soviet Censorship*, Metuchen, New Jersey: Scarecrow Press, 1973

Ermolaev, Herman, *Censorship in Soviet Literature, 1917–1991*, Lanham, Maryland: Rowman and Littlefield, 1997

Hosking, Geoffrey, *A History of the Soviet Union, 1917–1991*, final edition, London: Fontana Press, 1992

King, David, *The Commissar Vanishes: The Falsification of Photographs and Art in Stalin's Russia*, New York: Metropolitan, and Edinburgh: Canongate, 1997

Korsch, Boris, *The Permanent Purge of Soviet Libraries*, Jerusalem: Hebrew University of Jerusalem, 1983

Reddaway, Peter (editor), *Uncensored Russia – Protest and Dissent in the Soviet Union: The Unofficial Moscow Journal A Chronicle of Current Events*, London: Jonathan Cape, and New York: American Heritage Press, 1972

Rubinstein, Joshua, *Soviet Dissidents: Their Struggle for Human Rights*, London: Wildwood House, 1980

Service, Robert, *Lenin: A Political Life*, 3 vols, Basingstoke: Macmillan, and Bloomington: Indiana University Press, 1985–95

Service, Robert, *A History of Twentieth-Century Russia*, London: Allen Lane, 1997; Cambridge, Massachusetts: Harvard University Press, 1998

Shentalinsky, Vitaly, *The KGB's Literary Archive*, edited and translated by John Crowfoot, London: Harvill Press, 1995; as *Arrested Voices: Resurrecting the Disappeared Writers of the Soviet Regime*, New York: Free Press, 1996

Swayze, Harold, *Political Control of Literature in the USSR, 1946–1959*, Cambridge, Massachusetts: Harvard University Press, 1962

Mass Media after Gorbachev

Following the abortive coup against Mikhail Gorbachev in August 1991, thousands of newspapers and other periodicals formerly owned by the Communist Party were re-registered under new arrangements as the centralized press system collapsed. By 1997 post-Soviet Russia was producing an estimated 12,000 periodical publications, of which more than 2000 were state owned. It also boasted around 300 state owned and 500 privately owned television channels. If the communist heritage was not entirely dead, the range of topics that could be addressed in public had become far broader. Pornography was widely available. Publishers were operating according to increasingly commercial criteria and had run down their commitment to "serious" books and pamphlets. On television and radio, game shows and soap operas were the order of the day.

With the growing number of publications, the circulation of national periodicals decreased in the face of falling purchasing power, high printing and distribution costs, and readers' preferences for local newspapers. The newspaper *Trud* (Labour) had a circulation of 20 million in 1990, but seven years later only 1.2 million copies were being printed. In that time the circulation of *Izvestiia*, formerly the official newspaper of the Soviet government, fell from 10 million in 1990 to 600,000. As in most other countries, television's reach proved much broader: in the late 1990s ORT, the television station closest to the government, was broadcasting for 18 hours a day throughout Russia, reaching 98 per cent of the population.

Throughout Boris Yeltsin's presidency (1991–99) government influence on the state media remained strong. Yeltsin began this process by appointing his sympathizer Egor Iakortev to lead Gostelradio, the television and radio conglomerate. Direct interference in the activities of Moscow's privately owned media was generally avoided, but financial and administrative leverage was widespread. A virtual state monopoly on printing, transmitters, and distribution remained in force, and connections between regional businesses, sponsoring media outlets, and the administration were close.

In the late 1990s more than 80 per cent of printing plants were state owned. Publications critical of the state could face sudden increases in printing prices or unexpected annulments of contracts with printing houses. Regional, republican, and local administrations were in a position to issue and withdraw licences for broadcasting stations, while privately owned companies backing the authorities received licences more easily. Uncooperative media outlets were threatened with irritants such as defamation cases. In 1996, for example, the Moscow-based Glasnost Defence Foundation (GDF) reported that the editor of *Izvestiia* was continuously fighting up to 23 cases of this sort at once. The editor-in-chief of the independent Irkutsk newspaper *Sovetskaia molodezh* (Soviet Youth) said that his paper had been charged nearly 100 times between 1991 and 1996.

Regional newspapers retained close relations with the authorities. Financial privileges and subsidies often determined the political orientation of broadcast media outlets owned by regions and republics, which were well aware that any refusal to cooperate could end financial support. More independently inclined newspapers or television companies face repeated inspections or audits, and could have bank accounts seized, registrations cancelled, and editorial offices confiscated. A survey carried out by the GDF in 1994 found that 25 per cent of journalists questioned admitted that they had experienced pressure from the authorities; another 27 per cent said that they had been subject to harassment or threats from political, commercial, or criminal groups. In 1994–96 at least 10 journalists were killed either to prevent publication of their investigations or in retaliation for what they had published.

The two most widely publicized cases of violence against journalists in the mid-1990s were the murders of Dmitrii Kholodov and Vladislav Listiev. Kholodov was killed on 18 October 1993 when a booby-trapped briefcase, activated by a firing device commonly used by the military, exploded in his Moscow office. He had been investigating corruption among Russian forces still stationed in eastern Germany. Other journalists working on the same story had also received death threats. Listiev, director general of ORT, was shot on 1 March 1995. It was alleged that he had tried to cut out middlemen in the advertising industry who had links to organized crime. In November 2000, however, five former military intelligence officers and the head of a bodyguard agency went on trial for his killing. In mid-2001 investigations were still continuing.

Journalists and their families were threatened not only by criminal groupings but allegedly also by agencies associated with the Interior Ministry, regional or republican administrations, and local militias. For example, on 23 January 1996 Sergei Maltsev of *Sovetskaia molodezh* was molested and held by militia after attempting to photograph Irkutsk prison. Usually, however, perpetrators remained unidentified. In February 1996, Aleksandr Minkin of *Moskovskii komsomolets* and Aleksandr Krutov of *Moscow News* were both violently attacked; a bomb also exploded in the apartment of Viktor Antropov, who worked for *Novosibirskie Novosti* and

Vedomosti. He had been writing on criminality in Novosibirsk. The editor-in-chief of *Viatskii Nabliudatel'* was stabbed on 3 March the same year. In each case links with earlier publications were suspected. On 4 October, a bomb exploded outside the home of Vasilii Popok, of the regional paper *Kuznetskii Krai*, who had been investigating covert operations by businessmen and officials in Kemerovo.

By the late 1990s editorial self-censorship was taking root in post-Soviet Russia. Commentators have observed that journalists were reluctant to write on business and crime, or to engage in probing questioning and analysis. Fears of the possible consequences of writing critically about the mayor of Moscow, Iurii Luzhkov, were often mentioned. Luzhkov's office wielded huge financial leverage over Moscow-based print and electronic media, and the renting of offices and flats depended largely on his decisions.

Individuals have been imprisoned for alerting public opinion to instances of gross ecological damage. In 1997 naval captain and journalist Grigorii Pasko was charged with treason for leaking footage showing a Russian navy tanker dumping radioactive waste in the Sea of Japan to the Japanese television station NHK. Pasko spent 20 months in prison awaiting trial. He was then acquitted of treason but found guilty of abusing his authority as an officer and released under an amnesty programme. In November 2000 the Supreme Court's military bench announced that it would re-try Pasko in Vladivostok. The trial was postponed three times and was due to take place in July 2001.

Campaigners have argued that Pasko and other environmentalists imprisoned or harassed since the mid-1990s have been victims of attempts by military and nuclear agencies to scupper the work of ecological campaigners in general. Another victim who achieved wide publicity was Aleksandr Nikitin, a retired navy captain who in 1996 coauthored a report about the storage conditions of decommissioned submarine reactors and nuclear fuel on the Kola Peninsula. The report, funded by the Ecological Committee of the European Parliament, was the first book to be banned in Russia after the collapse of the Soviet Union. Nikitin was charged with high treason, arrested in February 1996, held on remand for 10 months, then released on bail and finally acquitted on 13 September 2000.

Most commonly in the 1990s journalists were simply refused access to information. Politically unreliable journalists were not admitted to press conferences, and background material was withheld. No law on access to information exists in Russia. During both Chechen wars the work of journalists was significantly hampered, notably through restrictions on accreditation and access, despite the fact that the Mass Media Law provided for freedom of press activity even during a state of emergency. In April 1995, for example, monitors were refused entry into the village of Samashki after reported massacres there. In January 1996 journalists were kept away from violent action in the villages of Kizliar and Pervomaiskoe, and only official reports from the authorities and the security services were released. As the first war in Chechnya raged in 1995, the GDF identified 350 cases of abuses of journalists' rights.

The elections to the Federal Assembly in 1993 saw instructions being given by the presidential apparatus to heads of the regional media, attempts to intervene in the campaign to gain extra coverage, and overt allegiance from government-appointed managements of radio and television stations. The results of the elections of 1993 proved disappointing for president Yeltsin, and four days later the chairman of the Russian state television and radio company Ostankino, Viacheslav Bragin, was dismissed. In February 1996, shortly before Yeltsin announced his candidacy for a second term, the president sacked Oleg Poptsov, the director of another broadcasting company, RTR, accusing the company of "lying", focusing on atrocities in Chechnya, and exaggerating economic hardships. In the run-up to the presidential election of 1996, the media supported Yeltsin's candidacy almost unanimously. His main rival, the communist candidate Gennadii Ziuganov, was given predominantly negative treatment, and other candidates were marginalized.

Economic hardship made sponsors and investors, including conglomerates, regional enterprises, and banks, into key players, dictating media orientation and political allegiance. With purchasing power low, limited advertising income, and high costs of production and distribution/transmission, only a handful of outlets could survive without government subsidy or financial support from enterprises. By 1997 the closeness of major media owners to the highest echelons of power was marked. Most Bank was said to be closely connected with mayor Luzhkov; in 1996 Igor' Malashenko, then head of NTV, Russia's largest privately owned television station, was a member of Yeltsin's campaign staff.

If media backing helped secure Yeltsin's re-election in 1996, immense media support also assured the victory of Vladimir Putin's Unity Bloc in the parliamentary elections of December 1999, and Putin's personal success in the subsequent election in March 2000.

Putin's first year in office saw the government take control of the majority of media outlets in Russia. Censorship of Chechen war coverage was stepped up, private media outlets were harassed, selected oligarchs removed, and the security services granted sweeping powers of surveillance. The state maintained its control of printing presses and its authority to issue and revoke broadcast and publishing licences. It also made use of its power to order tax inspections – a lever frequently used by regional authorities to encourage sympathetic coverage. Putin's policy of centralizing media control was marked by his struggle with the oligarchs on the one hand and by steps aimed at weakening the hold of regional forces over local media outlets. Responsibility for government subsidies distributed to regional newspapers was transferred from local politicians to the Media Ministry, affecting 2000 subsidized papers across Russia.

In Spring 2001 Putin divided Russia into seven federal districts and appointed his personal representatives to oversee them and take charge of the local implementation of a national Information Security Doctrine adopted in September 2000. This advocated strengthening state controlled media throughout the country by creating a pool of loyal journalists, giving favoured media better access to information and increasing direct financial support. It also argued that foreign countries are strengthening their media presence in Russia and threaten to take over the country's domestic media. In November 2000 Media Union, a new association apparently intended to undercut or replace the existing Journalists Union was formed. Its declared goals included: "precluding the selective 'human rights defence' of journalists that favours only 'democratic journalists'" and "the worthy presentation of the body of Russian journalists on the international stage, partly in order to end the constant, daily foreign control over the activity of our journalists".

Human rights groups were concerned also about the increase in official surveillance of the internet. The regulations of the government's Service for Operative-Investigative Measures (SORM) require internet service providers in Russia to route all their traffic through servers controlled by local law enforcement agencies including the FSB. In January 2001 an additional seven law enforcement bodies were authorized to monitor email and other electronic traffic, prompting anxiety that officials might not always bother with warrants when they investigate private internet communications. The Russian press was largely silent on the issue.

Putin's drive to centralize control of political life and the media met with little resistance from the Russian people who put little stock in oligarchs and local autocrats – widely reputed to be irresponsible and corrupt. The tight lid on information flow from Chechnya also ensured that opinion polls continued to show strong public support for the war effort.

Government restrictions on war reporting in Chechnya were far more severe than during the 1994–96 Chechnya campaign which was widely criticized in the media. After Russia's invasion of Chechnya in Autumn 1999, most Russian media offered overwhelming support to the government. Exceptions included the twice-weekly paper *Novaia Gazeta*, and the independent television network NTV, which is controlled by the oligarch Vladimir Gusinsky; this station revealed the high casualty figures and drew attention to the desperate condition of Chechen civilians. After the invasion, the Kremlin set up a Russian Information Agency to accredit and control the Chechen press corps. Russian military successes and Chechen terrorist atrocities were highlighted; the destruction of towns and villages, the plight of refugees, allegations of brutality and torture by Russian troops were downplayed.

In the war zone accreditation rules were strict, and no journalists were permitted to enter without military escort. Russian and international journalists faced often violent harassment. Fourteen journalists were killed in Chechnya between September 1999 and May 2000. Others were detained by the Russian military, questioned, beaten and deported. Anxiety over possible kidnapping by Chechen militants also restricted coverage of the conflict.

One Russian journalist who disobeyed government rules and travelled independently through the war zone reporting on the impact of the conflict on ordinary people was Andrei Babitskii, a Russian national who covered Chechnya for the US government-funded Radio Free Europe/Radio Liberty (RFE/RL). Babitskii disappeared on 16 January 2000 while on assignment in Grozny. After two weeks officials in Moscow acknowledged that he was being held by the Russian military. He was released on 25 February, following weeks of pressure from western governments and international press freedom groups, but remained confined to Moscow, under close official scrutiny while his case was being investigated.

Outside Chechnya, reports of house searches, death threats, arrests, beatings, even killings of journalists throughout Russia became more frequent. These appeared often to be related to their denunciation of corruption and organized crime or criticism of the authorities. Victims included Igor' Domnikov, a reporter for *Novaia Gazeta*, who was bludgeoned in the entryway to his Moscow apartment and died on 16 June 2000 after two months in a coma. *Novaia Gazeta* specializes in investigative journalism, including high-profile corruption cases. A colleague of Domnikov's, Oleg Sultanov, had earlier received repeated death threats which police failed to investigate. Another *Novaia Gazeta* reporter, Oleg Lurye, was brutally beaten outside his home in December 2000 after reporting on high level corruption scandals. The Committee to Protect Journalists (CPJ) reported that seven Russian journalists were killed in 2000. It was confirmed that three of these had died in connection with their profession.

Outside Moscow, where newspapers and broadcasting stations are dependent on local administrations for services such as access to printing presses and the leasing of premises, there were numerous reports of harassment, sometimes physical, and official retaliation against media outlets reporting on the authorities in an unflattering way. These included accounts of hot stories "lost" just before publication, television shows shut down, libel cases, and officials being instructed not to speak direct to the press.

The Kremlin's drive to achieve the fullest possible monopoly over the media attracted most attention when the Russian president came into conflict with the oligarch Vladimir Gusinskii. At the time of Putin's accession, most Moscow newspapers and broadcasters were controlled by one of three competing media groups: Gusinskii's Media-Most which owned NTV, the Ekho Moskvy radio station, and several newspapers including *Segodnia* and *Itogi*; Boris Berezovskii's conglomerate holding ORT and the publications *Kommersant-Daily*, *Novye Izvestiia*, and *Nezavisimaia Gazeta*; and Iurii Luzhkov's fiefdom consisting of TV-Tsentr and a few newspapers.

After Putin's accession, both Gusinskii and Berezovskii came under intense government pressure. On 11 May 2000, four days after Putin's inauguration, armed police and tax authorities raided the Moscow headquarters of Gusinskii's Media-Most Company. According to Kremlin officials the raid and subsequent investigations were motivated by the company's alleged violations of Russian tax law. On 13 June Gusinskii was arrested and charged with embezzlement of state property. Three days later he was released and over the next few months the federal prosecutor's office dropped charges, then announced new investigations and finally ordered Gusinskii's arrest for fraud. He was re-arrested in Spain in December 2000, detained pending a decision on extradition, then released in April 2001 while Russian prosecutors announced they would be filing charges for the laundering of US$97 million and submitting further extradition papers to Israel and the US.

Meanwhile, after almost a year of official harassment, threats, and pursuit through the courts, the state moved in on Media-Most. Its main creditor, the Kremlin-dominated energy monopoly, Gazprom, called in its debt in 2000 and with no repayment forthcoming, police and tax officials subjected the company to more than two dozen raids and inspections. In April 2001 Gazprom took over NTV in a boardroom coup removing Gusinskii, its founder, from its board of directors. Media-Most's respected Moscow paper *Segodnia* was also shut down, and the editor and staff of the weekly news magazine *Itogi* dismissed. Gazprom characterized the takeover as a straightforward effort to recoup its investment but the heavy-handed actions and the dismissal of the editor of *Itogi*, which was profitable and highly respected, suggest the motives may have been political.

The NTV takeover drew tens of thousands of demonstrators onto the streets of Moscow and provoked a stand-off with staff who refused to recognize the new Gazprom management. It took 11 days for Gazprom to occupy NTV headquarters. Many of NTV's best-known journalists moved to the small TV6 channel to try to build a new independent network. After the takeover, NTV significantly toned down its criticism of Putin himself, although it continued to give coverage to Chechnya and to take issue with the Kremlin and with government ministers.

Putin's brush with Boris Berezovskii was less dramatic but seemingly as decisive. Berezovskii came under investigation for alleged embezzlement of profits from the airline Aeroflot and in September 2000 claimed that an unnamed high-ranking Kremlin official gave him an ultimatum to sell his 49 per cent stake in ORT or go the way of Gusinskii. In December ORT's Moscow offices were raided and documents confiscated. Berezovskii chose to go into voluntary exile abroad, although he has remained an influential presence in the Russian media with a 75 per cent stake in TV6.

On 3 May 2001 Ekho Moskvy, now itself under investigation, reported a statement from the Russian Journalists Union warning that "attacks against freedom of speech are becoming more and more persistent and well prepared. We are being persuaded that certain things are more important than freedom. We are being urged to perceive the press as an enemy." Later that month the union published the findings of experts who concluded that Russia was not observing the provisions of the Unesco Sofia Declaration on media independence. The experts said the media were increasingly state owned, that the government was restricting the rights of journalists to do their jobs and obliging them to reveal their sources – all in violation of the declaration.

On the occasion of the 10th anniversary of the formation of the Glasnost Defence Foundation, in May 2001, its founder, Aleksei Simonov, remarked that "the state monopoly on the mass media is moving towards its apogee and . . . the press itself acknowledges that it has sold out". Public trust in the media had fallen drastically over the last decade, Simonov said,

and Russia lacked "the laws, traditions, and even the societal demand" for freedom of speech and of the press. That same month the GDF reported that, since 1991, 117 Russian journalists had been killed.

IRENA MARYNIAK

Further Reading

Belin. L., "Private Media Come Full Circle", *Transition*, 2/21 (18 October 1996)

Belin, I., "What Some Russian Journalists Were Afraid to Write in 1996", *OMRI Analytical Brief*, 1/156 (3 January 1997)

Index on Censorship: "Special Report: Russia", 4 (2000)

Jakubowicz, K., "Media Legislation as Mirror of Democracy", *Transition*, 2/21 (18 October 1996)

Lange, Yasha, *Media in the CIS*, Brussels: European Commission, 1997

Maryniak, Irena, "Notes from Prison", *Index on Censorship*, 1 (1996)

Maryniak, Irena, "Russian Roulette", *Index on Censorship*, 3 (1999)

Meek, James, "Who Pays the Piper Decides the News", *The Guardian* (12 September 1997)

Mickiewicz, Ellen, *Changing Channels: Television and the Struggle for Power in Russia*, Oxford and New York: Oxford University Press, 1997; revised edition, Durham, North Carolina: Duke University Press, 1999

Nivat, A., "The Vibrant Regional Media", *Transition*, 2/21 (18 October 1996)

Popstov, Oleg, "Capital Television", *Index on Censorship*, 3 (1996)

Simonov, Aleksei, "Censorship Yesterday, Today, Tomorrow", *Index on Censorship*, 3 (1996)

Simonov, Aleksei, "A Matter of Honour", *Index on Censorship*, 1 (1998)

Vartanova, E., "Corporate Transformation of the Russian Media", *Post-Soviet Media Law and Policy Newsletter*, 32 (September 1996)

Websites

Centre for Journalism in Extreme Situations, http://www.cjes.ru

Committee to Protect Journalists, http://www.cpj.org

Glasnost Defence Foundation, http://www.gdf.ru

Index on Censorship, http://www.indexoncensorship.org

Index-Dos'e na tzenzuru, http://www.index.org.ru

International Freedom of Expression Exchange (IFEX), http://www.ifex.org

Radio Free Europe / Radio Liberty (RFE / RL), http://www.rferl.org

Russian Media Bulletin, European Institute for the Media: http://www.eim.org

RUSSIA: Attitudes to Western Europe in the 19th Century

Western Europe was seen by the Russian authorities as a source of necessary inspiration but also of potential unrest. Russia needed western Europe's technical inventions to strengthen its military and economic potential; on the other hand, the Russian autocracy feared the spread of subversive ideas. The French Revolution of 1789 had been taken by Catherine II (1762–96) as a warning of the consequences of reforms slipping out of hand. She had therefore increased the controls on imported books, and for a short period even banned them altogether. The ban was lifted when Alexander I (1801–25) came to the throne.

A statute of 1828 established a special Foreign Censorship Committee, whose area of responsibility was censorship of material printed abroad. Every month this committee published an alphabetical list of forbidden books as a guide for the customs service. Another committee, set up at the Post Office Department, supervised foreign periodicals received on subscription. The distinction between domestic and foreign materials was retained in a new law on censorship enacted in 1865, but now the Foreign Censorship Committee censored all printed materials from abroad. It was, in effect, a branch of the customs service, which turned away any publication challenging the system of autocracy or the Russian Orthodox Church.

Anti-autocratic ideas from abroad found fertile soil among the intelligentsia. The Decembrist Uprising in 1825 was seen as having been inspired by the contact with western Europe during the Napoleonic wars. According to Petr Chaadaev, all Russia's problems were caused by its isolation from western European civilization and history: western Europe had benefited from Roman Catholicism and Latin as common denominators, while the Orthodox church had bolstered a self-centred and isolated Russia. Chaadaev's *Filosoficheskie pis'ma* (1836, Philosophical Letters) caused an outcry; Chaadaev was declared insane, and his publisher, Nadezhdin, was also penalized. Chaadaev himself later claimed that he had criticized Russia in order to facilitate reforms, clearly along a "European" path of development. Chaadaev's critique was a catalyst during the next decade for a split between "Slavophiles" and *zapadniki*, "westernizers".

In the middle of the 19th century, German romanticism became the main source of inspiration for the Russian intelligentsia. Other trends of western European thought that reached Russia during the century included utopian socialism, and later Marxism. The first Russian translation of Marx's *Das Kapital* was published in 1872, but it was not allowed to be republished for the next 30 years.

Developments in western Europe itself clearly influenced the attitude of the Russian rulers to Europe as an ideal and a reality. The more liberal the reforms, and the more profound the social transformation, the more the system of autocracy sought, for the sake of self-preservation, to shield Russia from foreign influence.

RIKKE HAUE

Further Reading

Andrew, Joe, *Writers and Society during the Rise of Russian Realism*, London: Macmillan, and Atlantic Highlands, New Jersey: Humanities Press, 1980

Barsht, Konstantin, *Podtsenzurnye strasti* (Censored Passions), Moscow: Izdatel'stvo "Pravda" Biblioteka Ogonek, 42, 1990

Firsov, V.R *et al.*, *Tsenzury v Rossii. Istoriia i sovremennost'* (Censors in Russia: Past and Present), St Petersburg: RNB 1995

Heltberg, Kristine *et al.*, *Kultur og censur i de slaviske lande* (Culture and Censorship in the Slavic Countries), Copenhagen: Centrum, 1983

Namazova, A.S. (editor), *Rossiia i Evropa: diplomatiia i kul'tura* (Russia and Europe: Diplomacy and Culture), Moscow: Nauka, 1995

Rantanen, Terhi, *Foreign News in Imperial Russia: The Relationship between International and Russian News Agencies, 1856–1914*, Helsinki: Soumalainen Tiedeakatemia, 1990

Ruud, Charles A., *Fighting Words: Imperial Censorship and the Russian Press, 1804–1906*, Toronto: University of Toronto Press, 1982

RUSSIA: Soviet Political Succession
Communist Party leaders from Lenin to Gorbachev

The role played by the Communist Party in censoring the expression of non-Marxist opinion about matters of public interest in the Soviet Union is familiar, and there is much information about the censorship of ideas inside the party itself. Internal party factions were formally banned at the 10th Party Congress in March 1921. Thenceforward, through to the late 1980s, the supreme party leader of the day had the power to lay down the orthodoxy for the rest of the party. Each of them, from Joseph Stalin to Mikhail Gorbachev, claimed to be following the precepts of Marxism–Leninism, which in turn they claimed were derived from the works of Vladimir Lenin himself.

What is less often appreciated is that this quasiapostolic succession involved recurrent censorship. First of all, Lenin censored himself. A supposedly full edition of his collected works started to appear in 1920. Removed from them were works, and especially political correspondence, that would have revealed his cynical attitudes towards terror, to the peasantry, and to the Russian people. By and large, however, he was willing, even keen, to reprint whichever of his previously published major works seemed to him to support the policies that he advocated in government. Thus he published himself according to a policy of pragmatic self-interest. Until 1922, when he fell terminally ill, he could choose what would appear.

This situation was changed by the disputes between Lenin and Stalin before Lenin's death in 1924. Stalin began to secrete items from the public domain that Lenin wished to ventilate. The most notorious example is the "political testament" written

by Lenin in 1922–23 and aimed at the removal of Stalin from the post of general secretary of the party. The testament was discussed by senior party leaders at the 12th Party Congress in 1923 – in Lenin's absence, because of his illness – and then banned altogether until after Stalin's death in 1953. When a foreign supporter of Trotskii referred to it, Trotskii was constrained by party discipline to deny that the testament even existed.

Thus began the tradition of censoring Lenin. Stalin not only codified Lenin's works; he exercised direct and constant control over which works of Lenin could be published. The "Lenin" promoted in this process was the product partly of the selection of appropriate texts and partly of the emasculation of the texts themselves. Where Lenin did not say quite what Stalin wanted him to have said, Stalin altered Lenin's words. The most notorious example occurred when Stalin fiddled with an article by Lenin so as to suggest that Lenin believed that socialism could be built in a single country, even if the socialist revolution had not spread to the rest of Europe. Such a belief was Stalin's and not Lenin's. It ought to be added that Stalin did not confine himself to censoring others. He also vigorously censored himself, banning certain texts from republication and tampering with other texts so as to fit the line of current policy as it changed.

However, after Stalin died, in 1953, his successors – most notably Nikita Khrushchev – applied the same treatment to him, and to an even greater extent. The collected works of Stalin, which at the time of his death had reached only what he wrote (or was attributed to him) during World War II, were suspended from publication. Once Khrushchev had denounced Stalin in the famous "closed session speech" at the 20th Party Congress in 1956, all Stalin's writings were withdrawn from public sale and became difficult to obtain in Soviet public libraries. At the same time, those works of Lenin's that had been secretly banned because of their anti-Stalin content were vigorously discussed and published, including the so-called political testament, whose very existence had hitherto been denied. Khrushchev instigated the preparation of a fifth edition of Lenin's collected works, which purported to be indeed "the complete collection of the works". Articles and books were dredged up from the archives for this purpose. Yet the "complete" collection was not complete at all. Although more material than ever appeared in print, it was not always published in unadulterated form. The names of Trotskii and Bukharin, for example, were often excised from documents.

Furthermore, only such material was published as was regarded as corroborating the current official version of the past. Anything that put Lenin in a poor light was kept secret in the Institute of Marxism–Leninism, and only a handful of archivists were permitted to inspect the full Lenin holdings. Even then, they were prohibited on pain of the most severe punishment from breathing a word about them in the outside world. Among the topics withheld from scrutiny were Lenin's cruel recommendations about class enemies after the revolution of October 1917, his medical problems, his difficulties in running the party after the Civil War, his zeal about using both armed force and financial subsidies to subvert capitalism in Europe, and his extramarital affair with Inessa Armand.

The close working relationship between Lenin and Stalin, until they fell out in 1922, was no longer a topic which could openly be discussed. The reason for this was evident. Khrushchev was trying to diminish the amount of repression used in the contemporary Soviet Union; it therefore behoved him to restrict the amount of attention paid to Lenin's enthusiasm for dictatorship, concentration camps, and mass terror. Censorship was maintained so as to offer a "Lenin" who had been, in every way possible, the benefactor of humanity for every waking hour of his life. Lenin, supposedly, had been pure as the driven snow.

Moreover, since Khrushchev was trying to emphasize the continuity of his own regime with the Lenin inheritance, he concurrently censored his own speeches in praise of Stalin and his policies before 1953. The campaign to present Khrushchev as a consistent anti-Stalinist was taken to the ultimate extent of issuing instructions to the KGB to incinerate archival documents from the 1930s and 1940s that demonstrated Khrushchev's deep complicity in the bloody purges undertaken in Moscow and Ukraine. Khrushchev consequently had to censor himself to an even sharper degree than Stalin had done to himself. Stalin, after all, had made no secret of his belief in the importance and desirability of state terror.

Khrushchev's fall from power in 1964 resulted in a further cycle of the censorship of the previous supreme leader by his successor. This time the new General Secretary, Leonid Brezhnev, did not carry out a campaign of personal denunciation. Instead, Khrushchev was treated as if he had not existed, and his works were quietly withdrawn from bookshops and libraries. His name was also removed from the official party history textbook, which came out in an annually updated edition. Although he lived until 1971 and received a substantial state pension, he became a "non-person" (to use a term invented by western journalists).

On the other hand, Brezhnev and his associates were nowhere near as keen as Khrushchev had been to criticize Stalin. Thus the party history textbook from the late 1960s began to include approving as well as hostile remarks about Stalin. In 1969 Brezhnev apparently even contemplated the full political rehabilitation of Stalin on the occasion of the 90th anniversary of Stalin's birth. Only the extraordinary pressure exerted by foreign communist leaders deflected him from this move.

The sole aspect of stability in this process was the continuing adulatory treatment of Lenin. Brezhnev, like Khrushchev, aimed to identify himself closely with Lenin, and he had no more reason than Khrushchev for allowing greater access to the full holdings of the central party archives. A few additional publications were made, but these added little to what was already available about Lenin. So determined was Brezhnev to control what Soviet citizens might independently know in detail about Lenin that from the late 1970s secondhand bookshops were specifically forbidden to sell the fifth edition of Lenin's collected works. The edition could still be consulted in libraries, but Brezhnev's Politburo preferred that the general public should have their "Lenin" served up to them in the still more carefully selected and presented segments prepared for them by the regime's official propagandists. Thus the object of the party's devotion, Lenin, was subjected to an even greater amount of censorship than had been applied to him by Khrushchev.

The public media meanwhile built up an extravagant "cult" of the personality and career of Brezhnev. His ghostwritten memoirs were sold in absolutely all bookshops. Concise biographies were published. His speeches, sometimes lasting over four hours, were carried on radio and television at prime time. *Pravda* and other newspapers obligatorily hailed his every policy innovation – not that there were many of these in his lengthy period of rule – as a stroke of political genius. His nearest rivals for political power, such as Aleksei Kosygin and Nikolai Podgorni, were gradually reduced to a shadowy status.

Brezhnev died in 1982. His successor, Iurii Andropov, edged towards various partial reforms in political, economic, and foreign policy; he also tried to root out the corruption that pervaded party and government under Brezhnev. Like Brezhnev before him, Andropov did not directly attack the record of his predecessor, but the barrage of contempt shown to several attitudes and practices of the 1970s made it obvious that Andropov felt no respect for Brezhnev and his supporters. Journalists and scholars ceased to eulogize Brezhnev. Further editions of his works were no longer printed. Andropov might eventually have proceeded to withdraw Brezhneviana from sale, but he himself was already mortally ill and died in 1984.

Andropov's successor was Konstantin Chernenko, Brezhnev's former personal assistant. Such a background made it unlikely that Chernenko would continue Andropov's policy of disrespect to Brezhnev. What was new about Chernenko, in fact, was that he shattered the convention of undermining the reputation of one's immediate political predecessor. Andropov's memory was cherished by Chernenko until his own death in 1985.

What then followed was an ideological earthquake. As general secretary, Mikhail Gorbachev called for a drastic review of party policies past and present. Only two of his predecessors, Lenin and Andropov, escaped without massive criticism. Glasnost involved the ventilation of matters that had previously been banned, and in the late 1980s Gorbachev instructed the Institute of Marxism–Leninism to publish dozens of Lenin documents – mainly letters and speeches – that had previously been hidden in the secret vaults. He also permitted increasingly open disputes about history.

Yet scholarly access to the most sensitive archives remained strictly controlled. It was Gorbachev's hope that he could channel glasnost in such a manner as to widen and strengthen affection for Lenin, the October revolution, and Marxism-Leninism among Soviet citizens. Glasnost therefore involved the maintenance of censorship. It also included other phenomena traditional to communist rulers. Gorbachev's speeches were treated as definitive statements of party and state policy. His works, suitably selected so as to exclude those that offered abundant praise for Brezhnev, were collected into a multivolume edition. His image was carried on posters. He appeared frequently and lengthily on radio, television, and the media. He also made himself editor in chief of the main journal that published revelations from the central party archives, *Izvestiia Tsentral'nogo Komiteta*. Aspects of party history showing Lenin in a poor light were kept secret, and although attacks on Stalin and Brezhnev were encouraged, not everything they did was permitted to be exposed. For example, until 1990 Gorbachev denied that the Nazi–Soviet Non-Aggression Pact of 1939 included secret protocols for the division of Poland into separate zones of interest.

Nevertheless, Gorbachev's ability to control public discussion steadily waned. He had gradually expanded the limits of glasnost so that anticommunist writings could be published, and his vision of an uncoerced Leninist society proved impractical as an ever greater number of writers denounced not only Stalin and Brezhnev but the entire Soviet period. By 1990–91 even Gorbachev was acknowledging that Lenin had made mistakes. When the Soviet Union was dismantled at the end of 1991, the ideological inheritance of Marxism–Leninism had long been discredited in the minds of most Soviet citizens. Even so, the censorship had yet to be lifted. Boris Yeltsin's Russian government announced that free scholarly access to archives would be maintained, and at last the most sensitive items of party history were revealed – or at least some of them were. By the mid-1990s Yeltsin, too, saw fit to limit access; and the Russian archival authorities remain under many constraints to this day.

ROBERT SERVICE

Further Reading

Djilas, Milovan, *Conversations with Stalin*, New York: Harcourt Brace, and London: Hart Davis, 1962

Hosking, Geoffrey, *A History of the Soviet Union*, final edition, London: Fontana Press, 1992

Service, Robert, *Lenin: A Political Life*, 3 vols, Basingstoke: Macmillan, and Bloomington: Indiana University Press, 1985–95

Service, Robert, *A History of Twentieth-Century Russia*, London: Allen Lane, 1997; Cambridge, Massachusetts: Harvard University Press, 1998

Service, Robert, *Lenin: A Biography*, London: Macmillan, and Cambridge, Massachusetts: Harvard University Press, 2000

RUSSIA: Archives of Soviet Censorship

The very fact that the Soviet Union practised censorship was itself censored. Accordingly, information on Soviet censorship was scarce until the opening of the archives in the late 1980s. Previous sources were limited to a few published legal decrees, one regional archive that ended up in the United States during World War II, and personal testimonies from various (mostly émigré) producers of texts, films, and works of art who had experienced censorship at first hand. One strategy to determine the specific targets of censorship involved the comparison of multiple editions of a text across time.

The gradual opening of archives in the late 1980s, and especially since the dissolution of the Soviet Union in 1991, has resulted in new studies that confirm earlier findings yet also offer a wealth of fresh information on the institutional history of Glavlit, the state agency chiefly concerned with controlling printed matter, on censorship practices at Glavlit and elsewhere, and on the censoring of specific texts. The greatest disappointment, however, has been the inability to gain access to the central, Moscow-based Glavlit archive for the period 1922–1937. This archive was either destroyed during World War II or is being concealed in still classified secret service archives. Given the absence of this vital depository, scholars have had to work in literary archives (notably RGALi, Russian State Archive for Literature and Art); in regional state or party archive Glavlit depositories, containing documents circulated from the centre; in the personal archives of Glavlit censors such as Pavel Lebedev-Polianskii, head of Glavlit from 1922 to 1931 and later a member of the Academy of Sciences, where his records are kept; and in various other state or party archives that house correspondence with Glavlit. In addition, at least one former censor, Vladimir Solodin, has come forward since the abolition of Glavlit in 1991 to give revealing interviews.

The censorship of printed matter in the Soviet period can be usefully broken down into five stages: 1922–1932, 1932–1956, 1956–1964, 1964–1985, and 1985–1991. During the first ten years of the Soviet regime, Glavlit was concerned first with institution-building, then, towards the end of the New Economic Policy period (1921–28), with the suppression of private publishing, and finally, during the transition to a centrally planned industrial economy (1928–1932), with the introduction of planning in censorship. During the 1920s, the primary mode of censorship was to excise what was deemed heretical.

The second stage was characterized by the tightening of Stalin's dictatorship following the completion of the First Five-year Plan in 1932. Censorship switched to a new master mode of reducing semantic ambiguity, in a totalizing drive towards *odnoznachnost'* (one-meaningness). For example, reproductions of canonical images of high-ranking Communists were censored if they could possibly be viewed as resembling a *persona non grata* and enemy of Stalin's such as Lev Trotskii. To take another example, in 1938 the censors prohibited the use by newspapers of hyphens within words such as "counter-revolutionary" or "anti-Bolshevik", lest the reader miss the negating prefix, which could be separated from the stem on another line, and invert the meaning. Ultimately, of course, the state's attempt to monopolize meaning proved unsuccessful, for signs – verbal, visual, and gestural – are inherently polysemic.

The later years of Stalin's rule have been characterized by Herman Ermolaev (1997) as witnessing the "peak" of Soviet censorship. Ermolaev's focus is on literature, but much the same could be said of other activities subject to censorship, especially in view of Andrei Zhdanov's far-reaching involvement in cultural politics between 1946, when a new wave of repression began, and his death in 1948 – although the repression continued even without Zhdanov. Yet, while it is certain that censorship increasingly targeted things western between the end of the war and the mid-1950s, it remains unclear whether the master mode of censorship practices changed.

The third stage began after Stalin's death in 1953 and is broadly associated with Khrushchev's "thaw", the loosening of censorship from 1956 onwards and the publication of works such as Aleksandr Solzhenitsyn's novella *Odin den' Ivana Denisovicha* (1962, *A Day in the Life of Ivan Denisovich*). Archival sources on this period have been slow to appear, though some informal revelations have made it clear that the release of sensitive writings by Solzhenitsyn and others involved not only numerous reworkings at the behest of editors and censors, but also the requirement to obtain Khrushchev's personal permission. This period also saw the rise of underground publishing (samizdat), on a significant scale.

The fourth stage – the period of "stagnation" (1964–85) – was marked by a certain strengthening of censorship and has yet to yield any archival sources. Studies of the final stage, associated with Mikhail Gorbachev's perestroika and glasnost, will some day provide an interesting window onto the relationship between party and censorship: what mechanisms of decision-making began the violation of former taboos and resurrected recently unspeakable names from silence?

Archival findings have confirmed the larger features of censorship practices. The central feature was the *Perechen'*, the "list of information constituting a state secret", which served as the (negative) canon and was centrally distributed from Moscow Glavlit to its branches. It was a top-secret list of authors and texts banned from circulation, a hierarchy of names subject to constant reshuffling in tune with the vagaries of party policy and, increasingly from 1927 onwards, Stalin himself, who could intervene whenever he pleased. Parts of the *Perechen'*, which was reissued regularly, were invariably superseded by irregular circulars.

The scope of censorship was also widened during the 1930s. A case study of Karelia, an autonomous republic bordering Finland, has revealed that censorship targeted ever new objects, from a hypnotist who failed to present his show to Glavrepertkom (Glavlit's counterpart for stage performances) before presenting it to the public, to newspapers used as wrapping paper in stores. In the latter case the fear was that Bolshevik leaders such as Trotskii, who had fallen from favour, might creep back into the public eye from the pages of a dated issue of *Pravda*.

The Soviet Union practised both pre-circulation and post-circulation censorship. More specifically, literary censorship included consultation with writers during the writing process for, in the words of a protocol issued by the party's Politburo in 1923, "censorship must have a pedagogic angle . . . authors must be worked with . . . [an author] must prophylactically be put in touch with a comrade who can really explain the reactionary elements of his text" (as quoted in Blium, 1994). Another method was the prefacing of a text with a Marxist foreword. After a text had been published but not yet circulated, it could be subjected to pulping and republication. Occasionally the censors found objections to texts that were already in circulation and instigated their confiscation by the security police. The archives document cases of security officers being sent to retrieve newspapers that a subscriber had used as wallpaper. Finally, the purging of libraries was a practice known before the opening of the archives: Glavlit circulated to libraries – including many in the West – lists of books to be purged, pages to be torn out, names to be blackened, and photographs to be replaced by sanitized ones from which individuals who had fallen from grace had been airbrushed.

Archival documents have revealed a striking saturation of all spheres of Soviet life during the 1930s by the discourses of centrally planned production, introduced during the period of the First Five-Year Plan (1928–1932), and the later campaigns of "socialist competition" and Stakhanovism. Censorship was no exception. Censors made alterations according to the *Perechen'*, collected these alterations in centrally distributed forms, and sent the completed forms back to the central Moscow office on a regular basis. They also kept statistics of who censored how much and submitted these to Moscow as well. Moscow sent out circulars to all its regional censorship boards with positive examples of particular "vigilance" and negative examples of particular negligence. As a result, censors worked in a pan-Soviet space and competed against their colleagues even in the most remote regions. Censors could be subjected to semipublic shaming or praise in front of these colleagues. To illustrate Moscow pointed out a case at Minsk radio censorship as a clear violation of the directive that "the character of radio programming must fit the political moment": "In spite of these instructions, in Minsk on 22 January, the anniversary of Lenin's death, the radio played several 'Gypsy romances' and foxtrots" (circular of 5 February 1937).

The archives also contain traces of what developed into a type of "swastikaphobia" in 1935–37: censors saw swastikas, imperial crowns, and the words "Hitler" and "Mussolini" in pictures where a contemporary eye would never detect them. For example, a circular issued by Moscow Glavlit in 1935 commented on a picture of Stalin and Georgi' Dmitrov, head of the Comintern, at a recent Comintern congress: "The curls on Comrade Dimitrov's forehead interweave in such a way that they create the impression of a drawn swastika . . . Glavlit categorically forbids further printing of this picture." Censors could be severely punished for missing these signs. Conversely, when the wave of "swastikaphobia" receded in 1937 they were subject to accusations that they had hallucinated swastikas.

How can observers outside the Soviet Union of the 1930s make sense of this phenomenon? Three speculative explanations come to mind. First, the Stalinist 1930s were characterized by violent purges of erstwhile and imagined "enemies of the people", the former being members of the various oppositions to Stalin in the 1920s, the latter constituting a malleable and often lethal label that could be attached to anyone. The purges culminated in "the Great Terror" of 1936–38. Historians are still struggling to reconstruct, let alone explain, the purges; many have had recourse to shallow psychological categories such as "mass hysteria". The imagining of subversive signs produced by imagined internal enemies might be filed under that rubric. "Swastikaphobia" may also have functioned as a mechanism of total control, whereby central censors at the top, and ultimately Stalin, encouraged the possible accusation of every censor by another censor. Finally, "swastikaphobia" was probably a sign of Stakhanovism in censorship: the overfulfilment of a plan. The logic of censorship's master mode in the 1930s – the reduction of semantic ambiguity – forced censors to see multiple meanings that people in a different political culture would never see.

In sum, despite their incompleteness the archives of Soviet censorship have furnished documents that will keep specialists busy interpreting for years to come. Apart from new information on the regime's interaction with famous cultural figures – a rich topic treated in other entries – archives tell us much that we did not know about practices of censorship. Censorship, to be sure, occupied a radically different place in the self-understanding of the Soviet regime than it had in imperial Russia. Soviet censorship censored its very existence, beginning in the 1930s, because, after the break from implementing the socialist utopia during the New Economic Policy period, Soviet society was supposed to have progressed to "socialism", an achievement officially proclaimed in 1936. Socialism was a condition in which, theoretically, censorship, the law, crime, and suicide would have "withered away". The fact that authors and their products still needed to "be worked on" was an embarrassment worth censoring. Ultimately, as unique windows into the processes of cultural production, the archives of Soviet censorship offer insights into some central theoretical questions about the Soviet "project". How was the utopian impulse to shape meaning played out in practice? What were the chances for its short-term and long-term success? What counterstrategies for the control of meaning were available to ordinary people?

JAN PLAMPER

Further Reading

Babichenko, D.L. (editor), *"Literaturnyi front": Istoriia politicheskoi tsenzury, 1932–1946gg.: Sbornik dokumentov* (The "Literary Front": A History of Political Censorship, 1932–1946. A Collection of Documents), Moscow: Entsiklopediia rossiiskikh dereven', 1994

Babichenko, D.L., *Pisateli i tsenzory: Sovetskaia literatura 1940-kh godov pod politicheskim kontrolem TsK* (Writers and Censors: Soviet Literature of the 1940s under the Political Control of the Central Committee), Moscow: Rossiia molodaia, 1994

Blium, A.V., *Za kulisami "ministerstva pravdy": Tainaia istoriia sovetskoi tsenzury, 1917–1929* (Behind the Scenes of "The Ministry of Truth": The Secret History of Soviet Censorship, 1917–1929), St Petersburg: Akademicheskii proekt, 1994

Blium, A.V., *Evreiskii vopros pod sovetskoi tsenzuroi, 1917–1991* (The Jewish Question in Soviet Censorship), St Petersburg: Peterburgskii evreiskii universitet, 1996

Blium, A.V., *Sovetskaia tsenzura v epokhu total'nogo terrora, 1929–1953* (Soviet Censorship in the Era of Total Terror, 1929–1953), St Petersburg: Akademicheskii proekt, 2000

Choldin, Marianna Tax and Maurice Friedberg (editors), *The Red Pencil: Artists, Scholars, and Censors in the USSR*, London and Boston: Unwin Hyman, 1989

Darnton, Robert, "Censorship, a Comparative View: France, 1789 – East Germany, 1989," *Representations*, 49 (1995): 40–60

Dewhirst, Martin and Robert Farrell (editors), *The Soviet Censorship*, Metuchen, New Jersey: Scarecrow, 1973

Ermolaev, Herman, *Censorship in Soviet Literature, 1917–1991*, Lanham, Maryland: Rowman and Littlefield, 1997

Fox, Michael S., "Glavlit, Censorship and the Problem of Party Policy in Cultural Affairs, 1922–28", *Soviet Studies*, 44/6 (1992): 1045–68

Goriaeva, T.M., (editor), *Iskliuchit' vsiakie upominaniia. . .: Ocherki istorii sovetskoi tsenzury* (Eliminate all References to. . .: Studies in the History of Soviet Censorship), Minsk and Moscow: Staryi Svet-Print and Vremia i Mesto, 1995

Goriaeva, T.M., (editor), *Istoriia sovetskoi politicheskoi tsenzury: Dokumenty i kommentarii* (The History of Soviet Political Censorship: Documents and Comments), Moscow: Rosspen, 1997

King, David, *The Commissar Vanishes: The Falsification of Photographs and Art in Stalin's Russia*, New York: Metropolitan, and Edinburgh: Canongate, 1997

Kostyrchenko, G.V., "Sovetskaia tsenzura v 1941–1952 godakh" ("Soviet Censorship 1941–1952), *Voprosy istorii*, 11–12 (1996): 87–94

Oleinikova, T.I., "Deiatel'nost' spetsial'nykh organov ideino-politicheskoi tsenzury literaturnykh proizvedenii v SSSR v kontse 1920-kh–nachale 1930-kh godov, po materialam Sibiri" (The Activity of the Special Institutions of Ideological-Political Censorship of Literary Works in the USSR Between the Late 1920s and the Early 1930s, on the Basis of Siberian Materials), in *Razvitie knizhnogo dela v Sibiri i na Dal'nem Vostoke*, Novosibirsk, 1993

Plamper, Jan, "Abolishing Ambiguity: Soviet Censorship Practices in the 1930s", *Russian Review*, forthcoming

Richmond, Steven, "'The Eye of the State': An Interview with Soviet Chief Censor Vladimir Solodin", *Russian Review*, 56 (October 1997): 581–90

Tsenzura v Rossii (Censorship in Russia), Ekaterinburg: Belinskogo, 1996

Valitov, O.K., *Pechat' i tsenzura* (Publishing and Censorship), Ufa: Kitap, 1995

Zelenov, M.B., "Glavlit i istoricheskaia nauka v 20–30-e gody," (Glavlit and Historical Scholarship during the 1920s and 1930s) *Voprosy istorii*, 3 (1997): 21–36

RUSSIA: Religion in the Soviet Union – Christianity, Islam, and Buddhism

From the first the Soviets rightly feared the power of religion and applied to it perhaps the most systematic censorship in world history. Lenin's Russian Constitution of 1918 granted the right to "religious propaganda", but this was to prove *de jure* only and Stalin's Soviet Constitution of 1936 removed even this fictitious right.

Christian churches

Between the revolution of October 1917 and the end of World War II, the single permitted exception to the total ban on religious literature was the publication of some 60,000 Bibles in the 1920s. Given that the modern Russian translation of the Bible from Old Church Slavonic was completed only in 1875, followed by a print-run of only 20,000, it was virtually impossible for private individuals to obtain copies even before this imposition of censorship.

As a thank-offering to the Russian Orthodox Church for its support in the war effort, Stalin personally granted a measure of religious liberty from 1943, and the end of the war saw the publication, irregular at first, of the monthly *Journal of the Moscow Patriarchate*. Naturally, this was subject to rigorous censorship, being limited to official – mostly propagandistic – pronouncements: the comings and goings of the hierarchy, attendances at peace conferences, permitted foreign travel, a few very formal sermons, and obituaries that omitted all reference to the prison sentences served by almost all prominent clerics earlier in the Stalin period. The journal was available only to priests and only on subscription. No printrun was ever stated and so many copies were exported that foreigners often received copies unrequested. Later there was an English-language edition, again clearly produced for propaganda purposes.

A church "history" published in 1942 might as well have been written by a communist, since it concealed the true nature of relations between church and state since 1917. Other Russian Orthodox publications appeared sporadically in tiny editions, but with increasing frequency after 1968: these included calendars and an occasional formal volume in the series *Theological Essays*. Most valuable were 250,000 copies of an Orthodox prayer book, *Pravoslavny Molitvoslov* issued for popular use in the early 1970s, followed in 1976 by a service and hymn book, *Bogosluzhebni sbornik*.

Given the Soviet policy of Russification, it is somewhat surprising that the *Orthodox Herald* began to appear in Ukrainian. However, not only were the contents of this journal censored, but the text waged uncompromising war against the underground Ukrainian Catholic Church. Other denominations fared worse. After the war, the Baptists could publish *Fraternal Messenger*, but it was restricted to 80 pages, six times a year; in the 1980s, they were allowed to produce inadequate print runs of a hymn book, vital to their worship, even including a very small music edition. The Armenian Apostolic and Georgian Orthodox churches, as well as the Old Believers, each published occasional official texts.

During the 20 years up to 1945 no single word of Christian scripture was published. Over the next three decades the Orthodox published small (and expensive) editions of the full Bible on four occasions, and of the New Testament and Psalms on three. The Baptists printed 10,000 Bibles in 1957, but thereafter had to wait 20 years for permission to receive imports from the Bible Society. Importing Bibles was always fraught with controversy. In the aftermath of World War II, the American Bible Society sent in 100,000 Gospels and 1,000 Greek New Testaments, as well as a few full Bibles, but then 30 years passed before the Baptists received 3,000 Bibles in German (for their numerous ethnic German believers) in 1976 and 25,000 Bibles in 1978. They printed 40,000 of their own in 1979–80. Unregistered Baptists printed some 40,000 Bibles on a secret press before it was confiscated in 1974. Meanwhile, Estonians, Latvians, and Lithuanians were working on new Bible translations, but only inadequate printruns appeared before the Gorbachev period. As for the great works of the Christian musical repertoire, these were virtually banned in the Soviet Union, while Christian composers were in constant conflict with the authorities. The Estonian Arvo Pärt adopted various stratagems to conceal the religious nature of the works he was writing.

This was the picture of deprivation for a literate, curious public of over 200 million people. Alongside this, there are many recorded instances in which items of "legitimate" religious literature, such as pre-revolutionary Bibles, were discovered by the security police and confiscated. Prisoners in the labour camps often petitioned in vain to receive Christian literature. No copy of a Bible or any other Christian literature could ever be sold or displayed in a bookshop. "Smuggling" of Bibles became a controversial international issue from the late 1960s, as Christian mission to communist countries increased. In fact, the Soviet regime never expressly outlawed the import of Bibles, so the term "smuggling" was not strictly correct. However, secret regulations and customs instructions certainly operated. The result was a huge demand on the black market, with a Bible often costing a month's average earnings. The huge range of religious literature from the church Fathers to the present remained unobtainable and unknown, with just an occasional volume of Russian Christian émigré writings (Nikolai Berdyaev, Semyon Frank, Vladimir Lossky) finding its way to Moscow in visitors' suitcases. Punishment for evading censorship was often severe.

Conversely, the ideological arm of the Communist Party sponsored thousands of titles in huge editions of mostly crude anti-religious propaganda.

Despite censorship, however, literary authors became able increasingly to incorporate religious references into their published works. This began with Aleksandr Solzhenitsyn's *Odin den' Ivana Denisovicha* (1962, *One Day in the Life of Ivan Denisovich*), and was a particularly noticeable feature of Vladimir Soloukhin's work, *Chernye doski* (1969, Black Boards; translated as *Searching for Icons in Russia*, 1971).

Islam

For the first decade after the Bolsehvik revolution there was a hiatus during which Islam, which numbered tens of millions of adherents, continued to enjoy some freedoms. In Tatarstan (the

Kazan region), for example, there was a youth league that published an explicitly religious newspaper, *Child of Islam*. However, the league's leading members were arrested and liquidated in 1929. From then until the Gorbachev era, Soviet state control of Islam was as complete as that of Christianity.

In Bashkiria (Bashkortostan), however, local Muslims devised an early form of samizdat, a "Testament of Mohammed", of which many copies were circulated in the 1920s warning the people against the sins of Soviet atheism. The text said that God would inflict terrible punishment upon the Soviets in 1937, but there would be protection for those who carried the document from town to town. In the event, it was those who obeyed who bore the punishment.

Throughout the vast territories of Soviet Central Asia the closure of Islamic schools carried with it the suppression of all the religious literature that they had contained. A ban on the teaching of Arabic meant that the younger generation could not even read the Qur'an, and the enforcement of a law under which the Turkic languages of Central Asia had to be printed in the Cyrillic alphabet further cut the people off from the roots of their culture. From the 1920s until they gained their independence from Moscow in 1991 there was no restitution of this loss, except that Arabic could be taught in the underfunded and relatively few *medressehs*, the religious schools newly opened after World War II. At the same time, the League of Militant Godless flooded the Islamic areas of the Soviet Union with books and pamphlets, produced in millions of copies, that held religion up to ridicule.

World War II saw the publication of appeals to Soviet Muslims to support the war effort. These quoted the Qur'an freely, but the substance of the texts was purely propagandistic. After the war the Soviet Union built up a new series of diplomatic links with such countries as Egypt, Iraq, and Syria. It was necessary, therefore, to demonstrate a certain number of open mosques as "proofs" of the religious liberty that existed under communism. The limited religious publishing programme that began around the same time was part of the same propaganda campaign. For local people the price constraints were such that it was virtually impossible to benefit from these publications, while foreign dignitaries travelled home with beautiful new editions of the Qur'an in their suitcases.

The Religious Board of Muslims of Central Asia and Kazakhstan began publication of a quarterly journal in 1946: it was in Uzbek, but was printed in Arabic script, knowledge of which was retained by few by this time. A Qur'an in Arabic followed in 1947 and there was an annual calendar in 10,000 copies, 12 pages also in Arabic, listing the principal civil and religious holidays. The Mufti of Ufa published a 68-page book, *Islam and Worship*, in 1957, and there were two further editions of the Qur'an, comprising fewer than 5000 copies each. In 1969 publication began of a magazine, *Muslims of the Soviet East*, in Uzbek, and from 1974 English and French editions appeared as well. Nevertheless, anti-Islamic propaganda in written form continued to appear sporadically in the postwar

period, reaching its peak, both in volume and intensity of aggression, during the later Khrushchev years (1959–64).

Buddhism

There were far fewer Buddhists than Christians or Muslims in the Soviet Union, and almost all were members of three nationalities, the Buryats, the Kalmyks, or (following the annexation of their homeland, Tuva Ulus, in 1944) the Tuvin. In Buryatia in the late 1920s, a pamphlet entitled "Erdem-Ba-Shadzhin" (Science and Religion) specifically attacked the Buddhist religion; various pamphlets in a similar mould followed in the 1930s, but the Soviet atheist agencies themselves criticized this literature for being primitive and ineffective. Nevertheless, religious oppression among these peoples was eventually more effective than among Muslims. Buddhism was all but destroyed during the Soviet period, its leaders even being accused of spying for the Japanese during World War II.

After the war even less religious literature was published for Buddhists than for Muslims. A Russian translation of the classic scripture, the *Dhammapada*, appeared in 1960, but only after a stir in Moscow. The authorities tried to ban this after it had gone to press, but those behind the project persuaded the Ambassador of Ceylon (now Sri Lanka) to hold a grand reception at his embassy to mark publication. The atheist agencies had to revoke their attempted act of censorship.

Bidya Dandaron, a remarkable Buddhist scholar of international repute, then published seven titles of scholarly works in the decade from 1963, which he probably managed by spreading publication around such widely scattered places as Tartu (Estonia), Moscow, and Ulan-Ude (Buryatia). Dandaron, however, was arrested and tried in 1972. Buryat Buddhist activists made a significant contribution to the early days of religious samizdat with a report on his trial. Implicated in the trial, either as codefendants or as supplying information under interrogation, was a network of oriental specialists from as far afield as Estonia, Leningrad, and Moscow. It was probably the interest Dandaron had aroused among intellectuals in other parts of the Soviet Union that primarily angered the authorities. Another facet of Dandaron's alleged crime was to have evaded Soviet censorship by contributing to an international *Encyclopaedia of Buddhism* (Colombo, 1963). Dandaron had already served a long sentence beginning in 1937. This time he did not survive: he died in one of the camps in 1974. Since the collapse of the Soviet Union there has been a remarkable revival both of Islamic and Buddhist culture in Russia.

MICHAEL BOURDEAUX

Further Reading

Beeson, Trevor, *Discretion and Valour: Religious Conditions in Russia and Eastern Europe*, London: Fontana, 1974; revised edition, London: Collins, and Philadelphia: Fortress Press, 1982

Kolarz, Walter, *Religion in the Soviet Union*, London: Macmillan, and New York: St Martin's Press, 1961

Sawatsky, Walter, "Bible Work in Eastern Europe since 1945", part 2 in *Religion in Communist Lands*, 3/6 (1975): 4–14

RUSSIA: Judaism and the Jewish Question

Imperial Russia

Until 1855, Russian imperial policy toward the Jews was exclusively a matter for the government. The press carried a few articles supporting official initiatives towards the Jews, such as the welcome extended by *Vestnik Evropy* (The Herald of Europe) in 1805 to a new law code for the Jews, the ethnographic material published in the official journals of the Ministries of Internal Affairs and Education, stories by Nikolai Gogol' and Ivan Turgenev, and a few articles, asserting Jewish self-worth, written by O.A. Rabinovich in 1847–48. However, any danger of a debate over the Jews developing was prevented by an instruction to the censors not to permit any discussion of the Jews in the press, lest this imply a lack of confidence in the government's intentions regarding its Jewish subjects.

Insofar as the censorship did deal with the Jews, its efforts were aimed at gaining control over the extensive trade in Jewish books of both domestic and foreign origin, especially those produced by the Hasidic movement. The censorship was primarily concerned that Jewish books might mock Christianity and spread anti-Christian sentiments among the Jews, or promote religious schisms within Jewry. A parallel fear was that Jews could promote sectarian movements among the Orthodox peasantry. Consequently, the censorship was always reluctant to permit the publication of Russian-language versions of Jewish scriptures and prayer books.

The "Jewish question" became a public issue in the Russian empire only in the second half of the 19th century, when the "Era of Great Reforms" (1855–81) witnessed the growth of a periodical press, a relaxation of press censorship, and a general if inconsistent commitment to openness in public debates. Censorship touching on the issue in the period from 1855 to 1914 focused on two areas: the actual content of periodical publications and books, and Jewish publishing ventures. The burgeoning underground literature engendered by Jewish political activism at the turn of the 19th and 20th centuries was, by its nature, outside the purview of the censorship.

The interdiction on discussion of the Jewish question was breached by the liberal newspaper *Russkii Invalid* (The Russian Veteran) in 1858, when it received permission to discuss the status of the Jews on a "case by case" basis. In the Ukraine, *Odesskii Vestnik* (The Odessa Herald), with the encouragement of the progressive administrator N.I. Pirogov, who was responsible for the local censorship, published articles that provoked a nationwide debate on the Jewish question. Pirogov's leniency was much criticized by officials in the Main Bureau of Press Affairs (the censorship) in St Petersburg, but the genie was out of the bottle. Discussion of the Jewish question grew, despite continual interventions by the censors, such as I.A. Brafman's attempts to suppress religious literature, and the restrictions imposed on reporting of the pogroms that took place in 1881–82, on coverage of the provincial committees on the Jewish question convoked by the Ministry of Internal Affairs in 1881, on reports of the expulsion of Jews from Moscow in 1891, and on materials linked to the Beilis "ritual murder" trial in 1913. As late as 1915, the authorities obstructed efforts by Leonid Andreev, Maksim Gor'kii, and Fedor Sologub to publish a collective work, *Shchit* (The Shield), as a rebuttal to Russian anti-Semites.

Despite these many exceptions, however, it can be stated as a general rule that, by the late 1860s, there were no effective limitations on press discussion of the Jewish question. At one extreme, authors called openly for the abolition of all legal restrictions on the Jews, such as the requirement to reside within the "Pale of Settlement". Both local and national officials were criticized individually for their treatment of Jews. All the accusations of the Judeophobes were refuted at length. Occasional interventions by the censor were easily circumvented. In the 1880s, when the censors forbade press discussion of the proto-Zionist movement Hoveve Zion (Lovers of Zion), authors discussed its activities under Hebrew pseudonyms. They also devised a (fairly transparent) code whereby criticism of Russia was expressed through negative comments about "Romania". Thus, H.N. Bialik's poem *In the City of Slaughter*, inspired by a pogrom in Kishinev in 1903, was passed by the censor when the title was changed to refer to the Cossack massacres of 1648; and, despite orders from above, the Kiev censor was signally unsuccessful in preventing the circulation of material devoted to the Beilis affair.

At the other end of the spectrum, Judeophobes in the press accused Jews of economic exploitation of Christians, widespread criminality, inspiration and domination of the revolutionary movement, leadership of an international conspiracy to subvert Christian civilization (culminating in the publication of the so-called *Protocols of the Elders of Zion*), and ritual murder. Virtually the only theme consistently banned by the censors was an open call for violence against the Jewish population.

Would-be publishers of Jewish periodicals, in any language, found the going rough. Their inevitable preoccupation with the Jewish question, and their critical response to anti-Semitism, caused them to be issued with official warnings for displaying "a harmful tendency", stirring up interethnic hostility, and placing the government in an unfavourable light. The editors of the first Russian-Jewish newspaper, *Rassvet* (1860–61), had to fight a lengthy battle over the content of their proposed publication before securing permission to publish. They were forced to eschew any discussion of religion or politics and their efforts to call for equal rights were continually blocked. The editors of a successor newspaper, *Sion* (1861–62), reportedly decided to close the paper when faced with the prospect of being subordinated to the religious censors as well as the secular censors. *Den', organ russkikh evreev* (1869–71, The Day, The Organ of the Russian Jews) was closed in part because the censor forbade a critical article about a pogrom that took place in Odessa in 1871. The critical tone of the Jewish Russian-language magazine *Voskhod* (1882–1906, Sunrise) ensured that it was warned and suspended by the censors on a regular basis.

Because books were thought to have smaller and more elite readerships, the censors often permitted material to appear in book form that was forbidden in the periodical press. The article on the Odessa pogrom that had been banned from *Den'* was published soon afterwards in a book of essays by its author,

I.G. Orshanskii. Nevertheless, works thought to be too critical of the government or too sympathetic to Jews were banned by the St Petersburg censorship in 1884, 1888, and 1891. The religious censors were particularly attentive. A miscellany devoted to Jewish religion and culture, approved by the secular censorship in 1866, was delayed by the religious censorship because of objections to small details. In 1893, a translation of Heinrich Graetz's *History of the Jews* was banned because it was held to "secularize sacred history". During the 1860s, the religious censorship repeatedly delayed publication of a Russian translation of the Jewish version of the Old Testament, for fear that it would have a subversive effect on the Christian masses.

JOHN D. KLIER

Further Reading

El'iashevich D.A., *Pravitel'stvennaya Politika i Evreiskaya Pechat' v Rossii, 1797–1917* (Government Policy and Jewish Printing in Russia, 1797–1917), St Petersburg: Gesharim, 1999

Gessen, Iulii., "K istorii tsenzury evreiskikh knig v Rossii" (On the History of the Censorship of Jewish Books in Russia), *Budushchnosti*, 2 (1901): 58–76

Gessen, Iulii, *Istoriia evreiskogo naroda v Rossii* (The History of the Jewish People in Russia), 2 vols, Leningrad: Gessen, 1925–27

Klier, John D., "*Odesskii vestnik*'s Annus Mirabilis of 1858", *Canadian Slavonic Papers*, 23/1 (1981): 41–55

Klier, John D., "*The Times* of London, the Russian Press, and the Pogroms of 1881–1882" in *Perspectives on the 1881–1882 Pogroms in Russia: The Carl Beck Papers in Russian and East European Studies*, 308 (1984)

Klier, John D., "1855–1894 Censorship of the Press and the Jewish Question", *Jewish Social Studies*, 48/3–4 (1986): 257–68

Klier, John D., *Russia Gathers Her Jews: The Origins of the "Jewish Question" in Russia, 1772–1825*, DeKalb: Northern Illinois University Press, 1986

Klier, John D., *Imperial Russia's Jewish Question, 1855–1881*, Cambridge and New York: Cambridge University Press, 1995

Orbach, Alexander, *New Voices of Russian Jewry: A Study of the Russian-Jewish Press of Odessa in the Era of the Great Reforms, 1860–1871*, Leiden: Brill, 1980

Tsinberg, S.L., *Istoriia evreiskoi pechati v Rossii v sviazi s obshchestvennymi techeniiami* (The History of the Jewish Press in Russia in the Light of Social Movements), St Petersburg: Fleitman, 1915

The Soviet Union

In March 1917 the provisional government of the Russian empire cancelled all official restrictions based on ethnicity and religion, and abolished all preliminary censorship (which had been revived at the start of World War I). Like other forms of expression, Jewish print production experienced an unprecedented growth. A great number of new magazines and newspapers were published, and some new publishing houses appeared. However, following the Bolshevik revolution of October–November 1917, general repression of the press, including the Jewish press, began once again. The first Jewish publication to fall victim to the new regime was a Yiddish newspaper *Togblatt* (Daily), which was closed down in Petrograd in January 1918 after publishing a private advertisement in Russian (advertisements having been declared a state monopoly).

Official censorship was carried out first by the Revolutionary Press Tribunal and then by the Chief Administration of Literature (Glavlit) and its local branches; both these organizations targeted much the same aspects of Jewish expression that had been suppressed before the revolution. The main blow was struck at Zionist publications in various languages. The Bolsheviks regarded Zionism as a reactionary bourgeois movement, to be fought against mercilessly. They had the same attitude towards the Hebrew language, whether in the modernized form promoted by Zionism or as used within the Jewish religion. The government recognized only Yiddish as a Jewish language, a policy influenced to some extent by former members of the Bund, the Jewish socialist movement that had long been politically antagonistic to the Zionist movement.

Prominent Jewish publishing houses, such as Safrut and Kadima (founded in 1906), had to close. By the mid-1920s, Hebrew print production had totally ceased. At around the same time all Zionist periodicals, whether published in Russian, Hebrew, or Yiddish, disappeared. The last newspaper to survive (until 1927) was that of the Poalei-Zion Party, which later renamed itself the Jewish Communist Party. In 1929 the Russian Jewish research publications of the old pre-revolutionary school were also abolished. Glavlit also prevented the penetration into Soviet territory of Jewish newspapers published in Berlin and Paris.

The Soviet authorities launched a campaign for Jewish territorial autonomy at the beginning of the 1930s, and a "Jewish autonomous region", centred on the Siberian town of Birobidzhan, was established in 1934. Yiddish was supposed to become its main spoken language, but the only authorized Yiddish literature was that of "socialist realism". Of all the works of Yiddish authors of the past, only officially selected texts by Sholom Aleichem, Mendele Mochez Sefazim, and I. Aksenfeld were permitted. Hebrew literature was still strictly prohibited. The few Soviet Hebrew writers, such as Chaim Lenskii, were subjected to repression. In 1934, the official Soviet newspaper *Der Emes* classified Chaim Nahman Bialik, who had moved to Palestine in the 1920s, as a "Jewish fascist imperialist".

From 1936 onwards, Joseph Stalin tried to write Jews out of Russian history. Jewish subject matter vanished from academic works and school textbooks, and every reference to the oppression of Jews in Russia before the revolution, especially pogroms, was censored. Existing books were subjected to considerable censorship in response to Stalin's policy, among them A. Kuprin's *Gambrinus*, Mikhail Zoshchenko's *Golubaia kniga* (The Blue Book), and even Gor'kii's essay "The Pogrom". The Moscow Literature Administration (Gorlit) banned S. Borovoii's books *Class Struggle in Ukraine in the 17th Century* and *Jewish Chronicle*, which is a study of the pogroms carried out by Bogdan Khmelnitskii. Censorship was accompanied by the persecution of Jewish culture and Jewish life in general. In the 1930s, all Jewish schools and professional colleges were closed, and the building of the Society for Providing Working Jews with Land was physically destroyed.

The nonexistence of Jewish subjects in Soviet books continued during World War II. As in other Allied countries, the Soviet people were given little information about what has since become known as the Holocaust. In the Soviet Information Bureau's reports, the mass exterminations of Jews in Nazi-occupied zones were reduced to "massacres of local residents". Jewish names were eliminated from the lists of decorated soldiers and officers usually published in newspapers (this was exactly what the Russian war censorship had practised in 1914–16). There was an officially organized Jewish Antifascist Committee, but, as Stalin's ideologists had planned, it was involved only in matters of foreign policy.

The censorship of Jewish literature and the "Jewish question" reached new levels of intolerance between 1946 and 1953. In 1947, *Chernaia kniga* (The Black Book) prepared by Vasilii Grossman and Il'ia Ehrenburg was finally prohibited. All Yiddish print production was forbidden – *Der Emes* was closed in 1948, and the few remaining Yiddish periodicals were also closed. In 1949, all but a few outstanding figures in Jewish Soviet culture were arrested – later they were shot or killed in prison – and publication of their books was prohibited for many years afterwards. Glavlit circulated a list of more than 500 titles "imbued with Zionism and Jewish nationalism" that were to be withdrawn from libraries and bookshops.

In the 1950s and 1960s the censorship of Jewish subject matter became less thorough. The KGB confiscated the manuscript of Grossman's novel *Zhizn' i sud'ba* (*Life and Fate*); and the publication of Evgenii Evtushenko's poem *Babii Iar'*, presenting a non-Jewish Russian's reflections on anti-Semitism, caused a scandal. Publications on Jewish history and culture, as well as publications in Hebrew, were still forbidden, although not formally, while Sholom Aleichem's books and popular atheistic essays against Judaism continued to be allowed. In the 1970s and early 1980s, the only Jewish subject one could hear mentioned was something referred to as the struggle against world Zionism. The importation of any Jewish books from abroad, including Israel, was prohibited. Glavlit and the KGB joined forces to hunt down Jewish samizdat, clandestine publications that began to appear in the 1980s.

Since 1991, there have been no formal obstacles to any Jewish publication, or publication on Jewish subjects, in any language in the Russian Federation.

DMITRY A. ELYASHEVICH

Further Reading

Anonymous, "Tsenzura" (Censorship) in *Evreiskaia Entsiklopedia* (Jewish Encyclopedia), vol. 15, St Petersburg: Brockhaus–Efron, n.d.

Blum, A.V., "The Jewish Question under Soviet Censorship, 1917–1991" in *The Holocaust and the Book: Destruction and Preservation*, edited by Jonathan Rose, Amherst: University of Massachusetts Press, 2001

El'iashevich D.A. and V.E. Kel'ner, (editors), *Literatura o Evreiakh na Russkom Iazyke, 1890–1947* (Literature on Jews in Russian, 1890–1947), St Petersburg: Akademicheskiy Projekt, 1995

El'iashevich D.A., *Evrei v Rossii: Istorija i Kul'tura* (Jews in Russia: History and Culture), St Petersburg: St Petersburg Jewish University Publishing House, 1998

Greenbaum Alfred Abraham, *Jewish Scholarship and Scholarly Institutions in Soviet Russia, 1918–1953*, Jerusalem: Hebrew University of Jerusalem, 1978

Kochan, Lionel (editor), *The Jews in Soviet Russia since 1917*, London and New York: Oxford University Press, 1970; 2nd edition 1972

RUSSIA: Religious Censorship after Gorbachev

A controversial bill on religion, originally vetoed by president Yeltsin following protests from US president Clinton and pope John Paul II, was passed by the Federal Assembly on 26 September 1997, leaving human rights groups and religious minorities perplexed and troubled. The new law limited the registration and activities of religious groups, and implicitly gave the Russian Orthodox Church the status of sole traditional Christian church in Russia. It made clear that religious bodies registered in Russia for less than 15 years could not enjoy full legal rights without undergoing a burdensome registration process every three years in order to qualify as "religious organizations". The process of registration demands detailed reports on each religious group and its history, giving ample opportunity for bureaucratic harassment and the suppression of minority sects with inadequate political links. "Religious organizations" can be founded only by Russian citizens, not by non-citizens legally resident in Russia. They are licensed to own buildings, and engage in teaching, charitable work, publishing, and worship in public places. In contrast, "religious groups" have the right only to conduct services in private locations and to teach their own followers. Groups that cannot or will not acquire full registration, such as the Baptist *initsiativniki* (schismatic, unregistered Baptists), will have no legal rights.

The new law also prohibited religious activities by representative bodies of foreign religious organizations. Had it been vigorously enforced in the late 1990s, it might have curtailed and potentially wiped out the missions and charitable activities of western churches that had flourished in Russia over the previous decade. There were fears that registered "religious organizations" might be forced to confine their activities to particular geographical areas, and that state policy on these would be determined in consultation with favoured bodies such as the Moscow patriarchate, which could dictate which towns or provinces should be off limits to Catholic activity, for example.

The law was apparently designed not only as protection for the Russian Orthodox Church from rival western denominations, but as a basis for state intervention in the struggle over the control of property by the Russian Orthodox and their rivals, notably the Ukrainian Orthodox Church, the Russian Orthodox Church Outside Russia, the Old Believers, and the Free Orthodox Church. In 1997 the Free Orthodox Church owned 15 churches in Suzdal and has 100 parishes in Russia under its jurisdiction, but it had registered with the authorities only in 1991 and so did not satisfy the 15-year rule. Consequently it was unable to continue operating religious schools or distributing religious literature.

Less than two months after the law was enacted, more than 20 religious and human rights groups formed a Movement for Freedom of Conscience and the Secular State to protest against increasing levels of religious discrimination. Instances cited then included attempts to revoke the registration of a Lutheran mission in Khakassia, the denial of registration to a Jewish congregation in Briansk, and efforts to remove a judge from a city court in the Tyumen region.

Over the next three years, however, the law was only loosely implemented. Fears for minority religious groups such as Jehovah's Witnesses or Mormons proved mostly unfounded and more than 90 per cent of communities of both confessions were re-registered. Reluctance to implement the law in a way that could be interpreted, internationally, as oppressive seemed to come from the highest level and non-traditional "religious groups" were more widely registered by federal than local authorities.

Pentecostals and charismatics experienced sporadic restrictions from provincial administrations. Registration or re-registration were refused on trivial pretexts and groups were not granted permission to rent state property. In 1999 and 2000, in Ekaterinburg, Russian Orthodox parishioners repeatedly picketed Pentecostal New Life Church services displaying "anti-sect" banners and distributing leaflets. Local media also ran items discrediting Pentecostals.

A re-registration deadline for all religious organizations was set for 31 December 2000 and, according to Ministry of Justice figures reported by the Keston Institute, 20,215 religious organizations were re-registered. These included 3048 Islamic groups and 3800 Protestant churches. A Russian Orthodox patriarchate spokesman, Viktor Malukhin, estimated that 30 per cent of religious organizations had been denied registration, but reportedly remarked that this was "normal". In Moscow, the Salvation Army was refused registration and had rental agreements curtailed and a programme cut as a result. A Keston Institute report dated April 2001 suggested that Russian provincial authorities could now put into play mechanisms to dissolve groups that had not re-registered, and subsequently prosecute them. A month earlier it had been reported that the parliament of the Voronezh region had proposed a draft law introducing additional grounds for liquidating religious organizations into the 1997 law on religion.

In 2000, the first year of Vladimir Putin's presidency, treatment of "traditional", non-Russian Orthodox confessions – Islam, Judaism, and Roman Catholicism – was dictated largely by pragmatic considerations. Putin condemned the "religious extremism" of Islamic fighters in Chechnya, but made no attempt to introduce legal controls on Islam that could alienate Muslims in the Russian Federation or in surrounding Islamic states. At the local level, registration of Islamic factions was apparently determined by their political allegiances within the locality.

Leaders of the Jewish community were also treated selectively by the presidential administration, according to their political loyalties. Chief rabbi Berl Lazar was given preference over chief rabbi Adolf Shayevich, whose links with the erstwhile oligarch and media magnate Vladimir Gusinskii probably contributed to his downfall.

Hostility to the Catholic presence in Russia was signalled by refusals and curtailments of visas for visiting clergy. Two Roman Catholic bishops were refused Russian citizenship in 2000 and, in March 2001, it was reported that the State Duma had requested information from the Ministry of Foreign Affairs about measures being taken to "prevent the spread of Catholicism". At the international level, however, Russia appeared to be making diplomatic efforts to create warmer relations with the Vatican: in June 2000 and February 2001, president Putin and prime minister Mikhail Kasianov paid visits to pope John Paul II in Rome.

The increased emphasis on state security under Putin's leadership encouraged growing concern in the security services and among experts on religion that foreign missionaries might be agents of western powers. This led to visa refusals and the expulsion of foreign missionaries in 2000 and the adoption of one new provincial decree regulating missionary activity.

But overall Putin's Russia seemed, in its first year, to move towards greater secularization. Under Boris Yeltsin, the presidential council on religion had been composed of clerics and a few nonspecialist state representatives. By March 2001 these had been replaced by secular academics, suggesting plans for the formation of some kind of Council for Religious Affairs to coordinate religious policy in the Russian Federation.

IRENA MARYNIAK

Further Reading
Religion State and Society (quarterly), 1992–

Websites
Keston News Service, http://www.keston.org
Radio Free Europe/Radio Liberty (RFE/RL), http://www.rferl

RUSSIA: Dictionaries

Tolkovyi slovar' zhivogo velikorusskogo iazyka (Explanatory Dictionary of the Living Russian Language)
Dictionary first compiled by Vladimir Ivanovich Dal' (1801–72) and continued by Jan Baudouin de Courtenay (1845–1929)

Lexicographers do not work in a void but within a specific culture with its own traditions, and each society has certain expectations for its dictionaries that cannot be ignored. For example, when the *Webster's Third New International Dictionary* appeared in the United States in 1961, it caused an emotional public debate about whether the new work was too permissive in its usage recommendations and whether it would undermine standard American English. As they pursue their main goal of presenting word meanings, lexicographers around the world are also constrained by the authority and prestige that societies attribute to dictionaries. On the other hand, the authority enjoyed by dictionaries puts lexicographers in a position to influence society, and this circumstance has not escaped the notice of governments with a strong desire to maintain social control.

The four-volume *Explanatory Dictionary* was first published in 1863–66 in St Petersburg. Dal' began collecting words in

1819, while he was still a naval school cadet, and continued to do so for the next 53 years. Throughout his life, Dal' was interested in the real speech of the Russian people; he estimated that 80,000 of the more than 200,000 words that he collected had not appeared in any previous Russian dictionary. His work contains a wealth of ethnographic detail, often relating to 19th-century peasant life. For example, in the entry *izba* (peasant's dwelling), Dal' gives detailed information on all the various types, including regional varieties, listing, for example, what kinds of windows, walls, and stoves they had. His dictionary also includes copious citations of proverbs and folk sayings.

Dal' meant his dictionary to make a strong statement. First, it advocates the development of the Russian standard language on the basis of Slavic roots and folk speech, rather than the borrowing of words from western European languages. Second, it demonstrates Dal's deep opposition to the compilation principles used in dictionary work carried out within the Russian Academy of Sciences. In particular, Dal' was reacting to the academy's dictionary of 1847.

Responses to Dal''s work were varied. Within the academy, he was criticized for his lack of linguistic training, for creating nonexistent words from Slavic roots as alternatives to foreign words, for parsimony of grammatical information, etymological errors, and for the use of nonstandard orthography. At the same time, however, he was highly praised for making available a wealth of information on Russian words, especially regional and dialectal ones. In 1868 he was unanimously elected an honorary Academician, and in 1869 he was awarded the academy's Lomonosov Prize. Outside the academy, Dal''s work was considered by "Slavophiles" (those seeking to define the Russian character in traditional, nonsecular, nonwestern terms) to reflect their views, and for this reason he was criticized by liberals. Given what was to come later, it is important to emphasize that many views were aired in the evaluation of Dal''s dictionary, and that his efforts were recognized and rewarded. After Dal''s death, a second edition, with corrections and additions, was printed in 1880–82.

The next edition of Dal''s dictionary had a very different fate from that of the first two. Jan Baudouin de Courtenay (1845–1929), a professor (from 1901) in the Department of Comparative Linguistics and Sanskrit at St Petersburg University, was invited by the publisher to prepare a new edition. Today Baudouin is better known for his ideas on phonology and morphology, developed while teaching at Kazan University, than he is for his lexicographic efforts. While at Cracow University, Baudouin had participated in the preparation of two Polish dictionaries. When he approached Dal''s work, Baudouin respected the spirit of the original, increasing grammatical indications, improving and correcting the system of nested entries, and expanding the word base by about 20,000 words. He added words missed by Dal', as well as new words that had appeared since the second edition.

However, Baudouin made two decisions that adversely affected the future of his dictionary. He included political words that had come into use around the Revolution of 1905, sometimes accompanied by expressions of his own political opinions, as well as words and expressions considered indecent (which he labelled "vulgar" when appropriate). An entry that combines both qualities – indecency and politics – is that for *zhopa*, (arse, rear end of a person). The definition reads in

part: "that part of the body that in France is free from corporal punishment". This perhaps reminds one more of the style of Ambrose Bierce's *The Devil's Dictionary* (1906) than of orthodox lexicographic practice. It is also reminiscent of N.S. Kirilov's *Karmannyi slovar' inostrannykh slov* (1845–46, Pocket Dictionary of Foreign Words), which was banned for propagating the teachings of French and English socialists under the guise of explaining foreign words.

It should be noted that, while Dal' was not facetious, he did not shun strong editorial statements in his original dictionary. Thus, he defines *nigilizm* (nihilism) as: "a disgraceful and immoral doctrine that rejects everything that cannot be felt", to which Baudouin adds the comment: "a naive definition from Dal'!", along with his own improved version.

After seven years of careful work, the third edition appeared in 1903–09. Even before all four volumes had been printed, Baudouin suffered scathing criticisms in Russian newspapers. In 1906 and 1907, Baudouin responded in the pages of *Vestnik literatury* (Literary Bulletin) and *Rech'* (Speech). Baudouin's Afterword to the fourth volume explains what drove him to include objectionable words, in a passage of great pertinence to debates about censorship:

> in order for an explanatory dictionary to demonstrate scholarly exactitude in its contents, it must reflect, to the extent possible, the real life and real opinions of a people ... If Russian reality is marred by some shameful activity, the compiler or editor of "a dictionary of the living Russian language" has a responsibility to provide appropriate explanations for the words invented for this activity. Similarly, complete lexicographic objectivity requires that a serious dictionary of "the living language" include the so-called "indecent" words, "foul language" [. . .] and the like. The lexicographer does not have the right to cut down and castrate "the living language". Once certain words are known to a huge majority of people and are continually expressed in public, the lexicographer has a responsibility to bring them into the dictionary – even if all the hypocrites rise in protest, feigning indignation. As a rule, such Tartuffes are great lovers of secret obscenity, and eagerly run toward any type of "swear words" or "foul language". Already Dal' himself brought into his dictionary many words that, while part of living speech, are nevertheless considered "indecent" [. . .] For all of these reasons, the editors considered it their duty to fill the [. . .] gaps – even in this part of Dal''s dictionary. We do not have the right to remake the Russian language, [. . .] to hide what is really a part of it, beating with its own intense life

Baudouin's work was reprinted in 1912–14, as the fourth edition. After that, in spite of his forceful arguments and his obvious improvements over the original two editions, his work was suppressed completely in the Soviet Union. The second edition of Dal''s dictionary was republished in 1935, even though it was already more than 50 years old, with its errors and faults intact. This took place despite the attention of the writer Maksim Gor'kii, who wrote to the publisher expressing a favourable opinion of Baudouin's work. In 1955, 1978–80, and 1989, Dal''s second edition was reprinted again in the

Soviet Union, while in Paris the Librairie des Cinq Continents reprinted Baudouin's third edition in 1954.

Toward the end of the Soviet period, "indecent" words began to appear for the first time in Soviet books and periodicals, as they had for some time in Russian-language publications abroad. A few of these words even received lexicographic treatment in the 1993 edition of the popular Russian dictionary by Ozhegov. The new political state of affairs has allowed Baudouin's work to be made available again in Russia, for the first time in more than 80 years. In 1994, the Baudouin edition of Dal"s dictionary at last appeared, printed by the publishing group Progress and Univers of Moscow.

DONNA M.T. CR. FARINA

Writings by Baudouin de Courtenay

"Po povodu 3-go izdaniia *Slovaria Dalia*" (Concerning the Third Edition of Dal's Dictionary), *Rech'*, 224 (1906)

"Gazetnaia travlia protiv 3-go izdaniia *Slovaria Dalia*" (Persecution by the Press of the Third Edition of Dal"s Dictionary), *Vestnik literatury*, 1 (1907)

Poslevlovie k 3-mu ispravlennomu i dopolnennomu izdaniiu slovaria Dalia" (Afterword to the Third Revised and Expanded Edition of Dal"s Dictionary) in *Tolkovyi slovar' zhivogo velikorusskago iazyka Vladimira Dalia*, 3rd edition, vol. 4, 1909

"Predislovie k novomu, ispravlennomu i dopolnennomu izdaniiu slovaria Dalia" (Foreword to the New Revised and Expanded Edition of Dal"s Dictionary) in *Tolkovyi slovar' zhivogo velikorusskago iazyka Vladimira Dalia*, 4th edition, vol. 1, 1912

Further Reading

Chernyshev, Vasilii Il'ich, "Vladimir Ivanovich Dal' i ego trudy v oblasti izucheniia russkogo iazyka i russkogo naroda" (Vladimir Ivanovich Dal' and His Works on Russian Language and Culture) in his *Izbrannye trudy*, vol. 1, 1970: 384–439

Chernyshev, Vasilii Il'ich, "Vospominaniia ob I. A. Boduèna de Kurtenè" (I. A. Baudouin de Courtenay: A Memoir) in his *Izbrannye trudy*, vol. 2, 1970: 675–90

Farina, Donna M.T. Cr., "The Meaning of Definition in Soviet Lexicography: The Leningrad Academic Dictionaries", *Lexicographica: International Annual for Lexicography*, 8 (1992): 69–99

Gove, Philip Babcock (editor), *Webster's Third New International Dictionary of the English Language*, 1961

Karmakova, O. E., "Slovar' V. I. Dalia" (The Dictionary of V. I. Dal') in *Entsiklopedicheskii slovar' iunogo filologa (iazykoznanie) dlia srednego i starshego shkol'nogo vozrasta*, edited by Mikhail Viktorovich Panov, Moscow: Pedagogika, 1984

Kirilov, N.S. (editor), *Karmannyi slovar' inostrannykh slov* (A Pocket Dictionary of Foreign Words), parts 1–2, St Petersburg, 1845–46

Leont'ev, A.A., "Tvorcheskii put' i osnovnye cherty lingvisticheskoi kontseptsii I. A. Boduèna de Kurtenè" (I. A. Baudouin de Courtenay's Career and the Basic Characteristics of His Linguistic Theory) in *I.A. Boduèn de Kurtenè (k 30-letiiu so dnia smerti)*, edited by S. B. Bernshtein, Moscow: Izdatel'stvo Akademii nauk SSSR, 1960

Morton, Herbert C., *The Story of Webster's Third: Philip Gove's Controversial Dictionary and Its Critics*, Cambridge and New York: Cambridge University Press, 1994

Nakoriakov, Nikolai Nikandrovich, "A. M. Gor'kii i izdatel'skoe delo" [A.M. Gor'kii and Publishing"], *Literaturnaia gazeta*, 32/668 (15 June 1937): 4

Ozhegov, S.I. and N. Iu. Shvedova (editors), *Tolkovyi slovar' russkogo iazyka* (Explanatory Dictionary of Russian), 3rd edition, Moscow: Az, 1995

Protchenko, Ivan Fedorovich, *Slovari russkogo iazyka: kratkii ocherk (posobie dlia uchitelia)* (Dictionaries of Russian: A Brief Outline [Teacher's Handbook]), 2nd edition, Moscow: Izd-vo ROU, 1995

Shcherba, Lev Vladimirovich, "I. A. Boduèn-de-Kurtenè i ego znachenie v nauke o iazyke (1845–1929)" (I. A. Baudouin de Courtenay and His Significance for Linguistic Science, 1845–1929), *Russkii iazyk v shkole*, 4, 1949: 83–91

Terras, Victor, (editor), *Handbook of Russian Literature*, New Haven, Connecticut: Yale University Press, 1985: notably the articles "Dal" by Joachim T. Baer, "Slavophilism" by Abbott Gleason

Tseitlin, Ralia Mikhailovna, *Kratkii ocherk istorii russkoi leksikografii* [A Short Outline of the History of Russian Lexicography], Moscow: Gosudarstvennoe uchebno-pedagogicheskoe izdatel'stvo Ministerstva prosveshcheniia RSFSR, 1958

Wertz, Christopher A., "Baudouín de Courtenáy" in *The Modern Encyclopedia of Russian and Soviet Literature*, edited by Harry B. Weber, vol. 2, Gulf Breeze, Florida: Academic International Press

Soviet Period

In the former Soviet Union, the reigning political ideology, as well as the related ideology within Soviet linguistics, directly affected every dictionary published. Most of the time, the strongest censorship operating on dictionaries was probably self-censorship by fearful lexicographers. Given that the vast Soviet bureaucracy of censorship achieved a degree of control over all printed material that could not have been imagined in imperial Russia, it is not surprising that lexicographers tried as much as possible to avoid official scrutiny. Nevertheless, dictionaries and lexicographers did get noticed from time to time, with unpleasant consequences. The unique qualities of dictionaries as compared to other printed texts make their censorship unique as well, and worthy of close examination.

Since all dictionaries are limited in the amount of space available, and not all the words of a language can be treated, censorship of vocabulary takes place when the inevitable selection process is based not on purely lexicographic principles (assuming that such principles exist), but on ideological or other principles. In Russian monolingual dictionaries of the Soviet period taboo words, politically charged words, religious terms, and other controversial words were often omitted. For example, as John Murray has pointed out, *feminizm* and *orgazm* do not appear in the 1977 or 1990 editions of the one-volume *Slovar' russkogo iazyka* (Dictionary of Russian) by Ozhegov; these words remain absent from the successor dictionary *Tolkovyi slovar' russkogo iazyka* (1993, Defining Dictionary of Russian) by Ozhegov and Shvedova. It is also telling that, as Morton Benson has noted, the abbreviation *GULAG* and the word *goluboi* ("homosexual"), and religious terms such as *uspenie* ("Assumption"), all made their first appearance in the 1993 version.

Entryword omission was also important in the bilingual dictionaries of the Soviet period. Words in any one of the Soviet national languages that conveyed cultural or religious notions that the state did not wish to foster were prime candidates for omission. Thus, Holger Nath notes that Soviet Yiddish dictionaries frequently omitted or misrepresented words relating to the Jewish religion, such as the Yiddish terms for "Jewish cemetery", *bejs-ojlem*, and for "non-Jewish cemetery", *svinter*. A 1932 Yiddish–Belorussian dictionary and a 1941 Russian–Yiddish dictionary do not list any word for "cemetery", and a 1940 Yiddish–Russian dictionary includes both Jewish and non-Jewish terms but does not differentiate their meanings. Much later, a 1984 Russian–Yiddish dictionary lists both terms with labels to distinguish Jewish from non-Jewish. Nash maintains that Soviet Yiddish shifted toward more secular and generic expression in the 1930s and 1940s, partially due to the adaptation in dictionaries of Slavic and international terms in place of Jewish religious ones. Furthermore, Nash notes that derogatory words such as *goj* ("gentile") or *shikse* ("gentile woman") were omitted from Soviet Yiddish dictionaries.

If one examines more than one edition of the same Russian dictionary, one can see how the ideological climate was also reflected both in the wording of definitions and in the ordering of different senses within definitions. Let us look at one leading example, the *Slovar' sovremennogo russkogo literaturnogo iazyka* (Dictionary of Modern Standard Russian). The first edition, in 17 volumes, was published from 1948 to 1965. The first two volumes of the second edition appeared in 1991; to date, six volumes of an eventual 20-volume work have appeared. The definition of *dusha* (soul) comprises eight senses in both editions. Of particular interest is the sixth sense in the first edition, which is moved up to become the second sense of the new, second edition. The first edition states: "In religious thought – the nonmaterial source in a person, which is the essence of his life and distinguishes him from animals . . ." The second edition reads: "In idealist philosophy – a specific nonmaterial substance, independent of the body; in religious thought – the nonmaterial immortal source in a person, which is the essence of his life and connects him with God . . ." Due to its religious content, this sense of *dusha* appeared much later in the first edition entry. What is more, by the second edition the lexicographers were not afraid to mention "nonmaterial substance" and "God", two concepts that were absolutely contrary to the philosophy of dialectical materialism. Note that, unlike in previous practice, they also write "God" with a capital letter. In the 1960 edition of the single-volume Ozhegov dictionary, by contrast, the definition of *dusha* comprises only four senses; not surprisingly, the religious meaning noted above is left out entirely. The 1989 edition of Ozhegov still does not include this meaning, but the post-Soviet 1993 successor, the Ozhegov/Shvedova dictionary, does not hesitate to include the formerly controversial meaning, listed as the third sense.

The censorship of quotations from authors considered undesirable, and (conversely) the inclusion of quotations from authors who were acceptable to the state, were pervasive practices in dictionaries of the Soviet period. In the first edition of the *Dictionary of Modern Standard Russian* mentioned above, *bezrabotitsa* (unemployment), is defined as: "An economic phenomenon typical in capitalist society, during which workers – deprived of the means of production and living by the sale of their labour – periodically find themselves out of work." Quotations from Stalin and Chekhov give examples of usage, and the inclusion of each provides interesting information. The quotation from Stalin illustrates the selection of a sanctioned and highly authoritative author; his words read in part: "If in bourgeois countries millions of unemployed endure need and suffering due to a lack of work, here there are no longer workers without work and pay." The quotation from Chekhov illustrates the selection of a "safe" author: as a classical Russian writer of the pre-Soviet period, Chekhov posed no ideological threat. The second edition contains a brand new definition: "A

socioeconomic phenomenon, during which some workers cannot find an application for their labour." Four brief unattributed examples and one 20th-century quotation (not from Stalin) follow. We can see that the new edition, by eliminating the references to "capitalist society" and "deprived" workers, is no longer alerting the reader to consider unemployment as a capitalist vice. In addition, the new examples of usage send a different message. The second edition uses a "neutral" 20th-century author instead of one such as Stalin or Lenin, and it does not use any "safe" pre-Soviet quotations. Indeed, the lexicographers are confident enough to include examples not attributed to any authors – and possibly of their own making.

The fate of another dictionary, the never-completed *Slovar' sovremennogo russkogo iazyka* (Dictionary of Modern Russian) makes clear what the consequences were for including authors considered unacceptable to the state. Work on this dictionary proceeded in Leningrad between 1928 and 1936; until 1937, releases were published for parts of several letters. It was to be a 56-volume work, the seventh edition in the long line of dictionaries produced in the Academy of Sciences that had begun with the *Slovar' Akademii Rossiiskoi* (St Petersburg, 1789–94, Dictionary of the Russian Academy). S.F. Beliaev notes that, in its content, the new dictionary was supposed to reflect Marxist–Leninist theory and the pseudo-Marxist linguistic theories of Nikolai Iakovlevich Marr. This meant that ideological quotations were to be used; besides making the dictionary Marxist–Leninist, they would presumably show the extent to which the revolution had created unprecedented change in words and their meanings, in line with the theories of Marr. However, the presidium of the Academy of Sciences resolved to stop further releases of the seventh edition in August 1937, stating that:

> work on the Dictionary of Modern Russian was neglected to the highest degree. The card file is poisoned with clearly counterrevolutionary words and quotations, as well as with vulgar, often pornographic and artificial language".

Beliaev gives examples of the "errors" that caused this project to be shut down; of interest here are those related to authors' citations. First, some citations from acceptable authors conveyed an erroneous impression of their views: a quotation from Saltykov-Shchedrin (a 19th-century satirist), meant to be ironic, about the "enemy of the Russian people", Arakcheev (Alexander I's despotic assistant), gives the uninitiated reader the impression that Arakcheev was a good Communist. Second, Beliaev notes that the compilers included prerevolutionary authors without choosing the quotations carefully enough: a citation by Marlinskii (the pseudonym of an acceptable writer, the Decembrist revolutionary Bestuzhev) for the word *analiz* (analysis), reads: "On them (the unmarried girls) were directed all lorgnettes, all mouths were occupied with their analysis". Third, some citations from revolutionary authors were taken out of context and sounded "counter-revolutionary" in the hands of the dictionary makers. Fourth, Beliaev maintains that the best Soviet writers were cited far too rarely; in particular, Maksim Gor'kii (considered a founder of "socialist realism") was hardly cited at all. Fifth, "enemies of the people", such as Bukharin, Radek, Zinov'ev, and Kamenev, were cited in the dictionary. This last criticism shows that, during the 1930s, good communists changed so quickly into enemies of the state that it was impossible to quote anyone safely in a dictionary. This inspired lexicographers to stick with 19th-century classics, as well as Lenin, Stalin, and a few others in their quotations, causing the representation of 20th-century language to suffer.

In Soviet dictionaries, a quotation sometimes appears in lieu of the definition itself: the words of a respected author such as Lenin are used to render the meaning. Thus, in the first edition of the *Dictionary of Modern Standard Russian*, the entry for *bol'shevizm* (Bolshevism), reads: "The same thing as Leninism, that is 'Marxism in the epoch of imperialism and the proletarian revolution. More exactly: Leninism is the theory and tactics of the dictatorship of the proletariat in particular' (Stalin)". This definition has the ultimate authority, as it is not merely a statement created by the lexicographer but a quotation from the Great Leader. While other quotations are italicized in this dictionary, this one is not. It appears in the same typeface as all the other definitions, but in quotation marks. In addition to Stalin's definition for "Bolshevism", there is a "real" quotation from Lenin in the first edition. The second edition contains a standard (not quoted) definition for this word, plus the same Lenin quotation carried over from the first edition, indicating a much lower but still visible degree of interference with the description of meaning.

The later editions of Russian dictionaries mentioned above show that the changed political situation in Russia after 1991 has directly affected the content of Russian dictionaries. Generally, this has resulted in improved descriptions of meaning and more informative illustrative examples of usage.

DONNA M.T. CR. FARINA

Dictionaries

Chernyshev, Vasilii Il'ich *et al.* (editors), *Slovar' sovremennogo russkogo literaturnogo iazyka* (Dictionary of Modern Standard Russian), 17 vols, 1948–65

Gorbachevich, Kirill Sergeevich (editor), *Slovar' sovremennogo russkogo literaturnogo iazyka* (Dictionary of Modern Standard Russian), 2nd revised edition, 6 vols, 1991–94

Ozhegov, Sergei Ivanovich, *Slovar' russkogo iazyka* (Dictionary of Russian), 1960

Ozhegov, Sergei Ivanovich, *Slovar' russkogo iazyka* (Dictionary of Russian), edited by Nataliia Iul'evna Shvedova, 1989

Ozhegov, Sergei Ivanovich and Nataliia Iul'evna Shvedova, *Tolkovyi slovar' russkogo iazyka* (Explanatory Dictionary of Russian), 1993

Further Reading

Beliaev, S.F., "'Akademicheskii' slovar' (*Slovar' russkogo iazyka*)" (The 'Academy' Dictionary [*The Dictionary of Russian*]), *Vestnik Akademii Nauk SSSR*, 4–5: (1937): 37–42

Benson, Morton, "A Step Forward in Russian Lexicography", *Slavic and East European Journal*, 39/3 (1995): 431–35

Blium, A.V., *Za kulisami "Ministerstva pravdy": Tainaia istoriia sovetskoi tsenzury, 1917–1929* (Behind the Scenes at the "Ministry of Truth": The Secret History of Soviet Censorship, 1917–29), St Petersburg: Akademicheskii proekt, 1994

Blium, Arlen Viktorovich, "Forbidden Topics: Early Soviet Censorship Directives", *Book History*, 1 (1998): 268–82

Farina, Donna M.T. Cr., "The Meaning of Definition in Soviet Lexicography: The Leningrad Academic Dictionaries", *Lexicographica: International Annual for Lexicography*, 8 (1992): 69–99

Farina, Donna M.T. Cr., "The Language of Terror", review of *Istoriia odnogo mifa: Marr i marrizm* (The History of a Myth: Marr and Marrism) by Vladimir M. Alpatov, 1991, and of *V nachale bylo slovo . . . Maloizvestnye stranitsy istorii sovetskoi lingvistiki* (Little-Known Pages From the History of Soviet Linguistics) by Mikhail V. Gorbanevskii, 1991, *Times Literary Supplement* (8 July 1994): 23

Farina, Donna M.T. Cr., "Marrism and Soviet Lexicography" in *Cultures, Ideologies, and the Dictionary: Studies in Honor of Ladislav Zgusta*, edited by Braj B. Kachru and Henry Kahane, Tübingen: Niemeyer 1995

Murray, John, "The Last Word on Glasnost", *Times Higher Education Supplement* (31 May 1991)

Nath, Holger, "National in Form, Socialist in Content: Translational Equivalence in Slavic–Yiddish Dictionaries" in *The Translational Equivalent in Bilingual Lexicography*, thematic part of *Lexicographica: International Annual for Lexicography*, 12, edited by Donna M. T. Cr. Farina, 1996

"Postanovleniia Prezidiuma" (Resolutions of the Presidium) in *Vestnik Akademii Nauk SSSR*, 7–8 (1937): 80–81

RUSSIA: *Bolshaia Sovetskaia Entsiklopediia* (The Great Soviet Encyclopedia)

Soviet Union, 1926–47, 1949–58, and 1970–78

The *Great Soviet Encyclopedia* is notable, throughout its three editions, for numerous reconsiderations of history, biography, and even geography. Each edition mirrors the censorial mood of its times and in so doing defines itself in terms of its predecessor(s). The first edition, which appeared in 65 volumes over the momentous years from 1926 to 1947, began as a novel attempt to present the world's knowledge through the filter of "Marxism–Leninism", while perpetuating the structure of its pre-revolutionary predecessors, but its content became increasingly subject to ideological adjustment by Joseph Stalin's minions, whose power was pervasive in all sectors of publishing. The mark of Stalinism is even more indelibly imprinted on

the 50 volumes of the second edition (1949–58), which is certainly one of the most blatantly manipulated general reference sources released to a reading audience in the 20th century. In comparison, the third edition (1970–78) is a more circumspect effort, produced in 30 volumes during the relatively staid but still repressive years of Leonid Brezhnev's regime.

It was the third edition that was translated into English and published by Macmillan (1973–83), under the title *The Great Soviet Encyclopedia*, in order to widen western access to a unique instrument of knowledge, and to the Soviet worldview expressed in it. In passing, it should perhaps be mentioned that the adjective "great" is not meant to aggrandize; it is merely the prevailing English translation of the word *bolshaia*, which could equally well be rendered as "big" or "large", and was employed by the publishers to convey its comprehensive nature, notably in contrast to the more compact *Malaia Sovetskaia Entsiklopediia*, a "small" work whose three editions averaged 10 volumes each as they shadowed the larger work over the years from 1928 to 1960.

The serial release of each of the three editions over a period of years allows a study of the ebb and flow of political manipulation. This is particularly evident in the protracted creation of the first two editions as their makers traversed some very difficult years in Soviet history. As the pre-eminent expression of official ideology for use in general education, the *Encyclopedia* reflected the regime's vital need to control its content and style, in order to guarantee a portrait of the world consistent with the propaganda reaching readers from many other directions in their daily lives.

Paralleling efforts to conceal or remove unwanted content during most of the years of the Soviet Union's existence, there was an industry devoted to the obfuscation of certain inconvenient yet manifest realities, Soviet and otherwise. While censorship certainly characterizes the *Encyclopedia* – Lev Trotskii, for example, is uniformly absent from all three editions, along with many other "enemies of the state" – it is also bolstered by propaganda and disinformation in the crafting of the work. The preface to the second edition quotes from a resolution of the Council of Ministers approving the new encyclopedia, which makes it clear that the goals of the enterprise could not be reached simply by means of excision or erasure. New ideas and accomplishments would need to be uncovered (or concocted) in order for the *Encyclopedia* to show socialist primacy in the world. Accordingly, it was required:

> broadly [to] illuminate the world-historical victories of socialism in our country, achieved in the USSR in the areas of economics, science, culture, and art. With comprehensive completeness it must show the superiority of socialist culture over that of the capitalist world. Guided by Marxist–Leninist theory, the encyclopedia should offer Party criticism of contemporary reactionary bourgeois tendencies in various areas of science and technology.

The trappings of socialist realism, engendered and perfected during the years when the first edition was being released, reach full fruition on the pages of the second edition, where right-thinking optimism, and the extolling of industrial and agricultural achievement, move beyond the realm of the arts and into the articles discussing history, the party, and state heroes. The central figure is an iconized Stalin, around whom swarm images and news of the progressive state in all its manifestations. His place alongside Lenin – whom he was always careful not to supplant in public – is nearly always in positions of relative prominence, which, of course, have no support in historical fact. The depiction of Stalin in the second edition projects his manifold attributes as "the Great Leader" throughout most of the first half of the set, but in the entry on the man himself – well into the second half, and published after Nikita Khrushchev's denunciation of the Stalinist cult of personality in 1956 – he is, ironically, shortchanged by the very ideology he himself had fostered. He is memorialized in a modest article

that takes him to task for his "mistakes" while acknowledging the leadership he exhibited in his early years, in marked contrast to the adulation accorded him in the first edition.

Stalin receives even more perfunctory coverage in the third edition, where, by another twist of fate, the now-disgraced Khrushchev merits a half-column biography noting that his leadership suffered from such faults as "subjectivism" and "voluntarism". These mild reprisals are typical of the relatively pragmatic approach adopted in the third edition, which none the less continued, as we have mentioned, to refuse amnesty to enemies of the state such as Nikolai Bukharin or Lev Trotskii. The dismissive article on Trotskyism offers only his name before going about the business of decrying the "ideological and political petit bourgeois trend" that he had allegedly inspired.

Possibly the best-known victim of outright censorship in the second edition of the *Encyclopedia* is Stalin's third state security chief, Lavrentii Pavlovich Beria. The article on him was the subject of a rather plodding postpublication revision. Feared and hated for his relentless victimization of innocent citizens during and after the purges of the 1930s, he was arrested and executed not long after Stalin's death in 1953, yet his despised name and face still haunted four pages of volume 5, which had been released in 1950. In 1954, in an attempt to remedy this now unseemly persistence, subscribers to the second edition were sent replacements for pages 21 to 24, which they were instructed to cut out. The new pages expanded the pictorial coverage of the adjoining article on the Bering Sea, while erasing any trace of Beria, his portrait, or the town in Armenia that was named in his honour at the height of his power – although it survives on the map of that Soviet republic in volume 3. This remarkable effort illustrates the strength of will characterizing some post-Stalinist censorship initiatives, which sometimes outdid their Stalinist antecedents. Beria's two equally dreaded predecessors at the helm of the NKVD (the forerunner of the KGB), Genrikh Grigor'evich Iagoda and Nikolai Ivanovich Ezhov, had both in turn lost Stalin's confidence and been eliminated, and were therefore already absent from the second edition. Notable also by their absence from these pages are many scores of senior military officers liquidated during the purges and the years just before World War II. In a curious exercise of internal damage control and indirect self-criticism by the *Encyclopedia*, a supplementary volume 51 was added to the second edition in 1958, featuring – along with the otherwise innocuous updating of earlier information on Soviet industries, scientific achievements, and the like – nearly all the most prominent poets, philosophers, writers, educators, political rivals, and military leaders purged by Stalin's increasingly paranoid state machinery, and therefore omitted from the first 50 volumes. Millions of other lost citizens could never be similarly rehabilitated, yet the attentive Soviet reader would readily comprehend the subtext and symbolic intent of this extraordinary publishing gesture.

Throughout all three editions of the work, the Russia of pre-Soviet times is generally given rather short shrift, relegated nearly to the status of a peculiar foreign country. In the careful sampling of Russian history, literature, arts, and culture presented over the three editions, the reader discovers accounts of Peter the Great, Ivan the Terrible, Aleksandr Nevskii, and numerous other characters and events convenient as mainstays to a universal Soviet memory, while the coverage of the creative process and its protagonists varies from edition to edition. The relative merits of writers such as Pushkin, Tolstoi, and Dostoevskii rise and fall according to prevailing ideological standards, and curious contradictions characterize the indirection employed in acknowledging certain well-known émigrés. Thus, the writer Vladimir Nabokov is listed as an American who emigrated from Russia, while Igor Stravinski is described as a Russian composer living in the United States. Ironically, a bourgeois figure saved the day for the second edition's discussion of aviation feats, wherein it was necessary to reach into the pre-revolutionary past to claim an aviator who flew before the Wright brothers. The naval officer Aleksandr Fedorovich Mozhaiskii (1825–90), absent from the first edition, is credited as "the inventor of the first aeroplane" in the second, having apparently achieved powered heavier-than-air flight during the summer of 1882. A considerably briefer sketch in the third edition notes only his research into, and development of, "flying contrivances", and reports that his first flight attempt (now redated to 1885) ended in a crash on takeoff.

The entries on aviation in all three editions feature photographs bearing the traces of standard Soviet retouching practices. In some cases employed to mask or enhance details, or to eliminate inconvenient persons from otherwise useful pictures, retouching clumsily alters images in such a way that its traces are usually apparent and unmistakable.

Maps and gazetteer sections were subjected to censorship and manipulation too. For example, in the third edition of the *Encyclopedia* the gazetteer entry for the Baikonur space launch complex describes it as being adjacent to the town of the same name in the Karaganda *oblast'* (region) of what was then the Kazakh Soviet Socialist Republic. In fact, the launch complex has always been some 300 kilometres to the southwest, in the Kyzyl Orda *oblast'*. It had been given the name "Baikonur" purely for reasons of state security – even though, while Soviet publications maintained the ruse, the true location of the complex had long been known in the West.

Each of the three editions of the *Encyclopedia* includes an article on censorship, varying in detail and length from the ten-page treatise in the first edition to the two-page sketches in the second and third. The first version focuses on a detailed history of the practice around the world; those who prepared the second edition updated but also truncated this, giving slightly less than half the text of the entry to a discussion of censorship in Russia and the Soviet Union. Both of the first two versions contain an unequivocal assertion that the October Revolution ended censorship, while the examination of censorship elsewhere includes consideration and criticism of its manifestations in Italy, France, Britain, and the United States. The newspaper publishers Lord Beaverbrook and William Randolph Hearst are cited as examples of imperialist and monopolist influences. The final version, in the third edition, allots more than half its space to domestic matters, having trimmed its foreign coverage of most specific examples. Gone is the claim that censorship had disappeared from the Soviet landscape, replaced now, towards the end of the article, by a description of the press freedoms enjoyed by all Soviet citizens.

This is followed by a statement that "state control has been established in order to prevent the publication of certain news items in the press and their dissemination through the mass media – namely, news items that reveal state secrets or that may be harmful to the interests of the working people" (quoted from the English-language edition, volume 28, p.36). This delayed but unattributed acknowledgment of Lenin's press edict of 1917 follows criticism of "vague" laws in both the United States and Britain regarding the abuse of press freedom and disregard for the "national interest".

The preface to the third edition of the *Encyclopedia* charts a course away from the chest-thumping didacticism of its predecessor, towards a more inclusive and conciliatory outlook:

> The encyclopedia articles are to give well-reasoned, scholarly criticism of the ideology of today's defenders of the bourgeois order and propaganda of anti-Communism, of right and left revisionism, and of contemporary bourgeois teachings in philosophy, sociology, history, and aesthetics. It is the duty of the *Great Soviet Encyclopedia* to show . . . the regularly developing process of rapprochement of the nationalist (in form) and socialist (in content) cultures of the peoples of the USSR.

This cautious and understated acknowledgment of the perennial nationalities problem signalled a shift by the state governing apparatus (and therefore, the *Encyclopedia*) away from past depictions of Soviet multiculturalism, which uniformly employed the notion of the "friendship of peoples", an ideological encoding of the officially imagined harmony among all the Soviet nationalities, especially as between the Russians and each of the other peoples. The final edition of the *Encyclopedia* lived up to these more modest aspirations: it had developed into a work more like its western counterparts than either of its predecessors. However, despite relative advances in candour and accuracy, it was still hostage to a political system more concerned with the control of knowledge than its dissemination, and it therefore remained fundamentally flawed by censorship, as well as by elision, disinformation, and propaganda.

GORDON E. HOGG

Further Reading

Benton, William, "The Great Soviet Encyclopedia", *Yale Review*, 47/4 (1958): 522–68

Havel, Václav *et al.*, *The Power of the Powerless: Citizens against the State in Central-Eastern Europe*, edited by John Keane, London: Hutchinson, and Armonk, New York: Sharpe, 1985

Hecker, Hans, "3 × Stalin: Die Darstellung Stalins in den drei Auflagen der Grossen Sowjetenzyklopadie", *Osteuropa*, 28/1 (1978): 50–55

Hogg, Gordon E., "*Bolshaia Sovetskaia Entsiklopediia*" in *Encyclopedia of Library and Information Science*, edited by Allen Kent *et al.*, vol. 61, New York: Dekker, 1998

Horecky, Paul Louis, *Libraries and Bibliographic Centers in the Soviet Union*, Bloomington: Indiana University Press, 1959

Matich, Vladimir, "Comparing the Three Editions of the *Large Soviet Encyclopedia*", *California Librarian*, 33/3 (1972), 169–79

RUSSIA: Proletarian Education and Culture in Bolshevik Russia: Proletkul't and RAPP

After the failure of the Russian revolution of 1905–06, some Bolsheviks believed that it would be necessary for the eventual dictatorship of the proletariat to shape its own culture. The key exponents of this view were Aleksandr Bogdanov (1873–1928) and his followers in the *Vpered* (Forward) group, which opposed Lenin's ideas on party organization and tactics. Bogdanov's view was that a working-class intelligentsia had to be brought into being that would control the Russian revolutionary movement and guide it from a strictly proletarian perspective. As a contribution to this, Bogdanov established party schools for workers at Bologna and Capri in 1909 and 1910, in collaboration with Maksim Gor'kii and Anatolii Lunacharskii. By 1910 Bogdanov was in open dispute with Lenin, arguing that it was a revolutionary necessity to create a distinct proletarian culture.

Bogdanov became the key figure in Organizatsiia Predstavitelei Proletarskoi Kul'tury (Organization of Representatives of Proletarian Culture), generally known by its Russian acronym Proletkul't, which was independent of the party, although it had the support of Lunacharskii even after he had settled his own disputes with Lenin. During and immediately after the Bolshevik revolution, and especially during the utopian fever of the Civil War years, the Proletkul't attracted large numbers of enthusiastic supporters, established a network of local clubs and branches, and gave support and encouragement to those poets, writers, artists, and actors that its decision-makers regarded as authentically "proletarian". It also founded newsletters and journals for the stimulation and dissemination of proletarian culture among the masses. Its example was to be invoked by revolutionaries elsewhere, notably by Antonio Gramsci (1891–1937), who helped to set up an affiliated Institute of Proletarian Culture in Turin at the time of the occupation of the factories there and elsewhere in Italy (1918–20). Gramsci regarded "proletarian culture" as part of an historically superior proletarian morality, based on the experience of productive work and on collaboration with others. It also echoed his belief in a new kind of educational system, in which the division between manual and intellectual labour would be erased.

The Soviet Proletkul't was not a specifically literary movement, but in 1920 it inspired the formation of a group of worker writers, known as Kuznitsa (The Forge), which issued a manifesto intended to be "The Red Flag of Proletarian Art". This group convened what was eventually to become the permanent Rossiiskaia Assotsiatsiia Proletarskikh Pisatelei (RAPP, All-Russian Association of Proletarian Writers). Other leading figures in the Proletkul't at this time were Valerian Pletnev, an authentic worker poet and dramatist; Lebedev Polianskii, a Marxist historian and literary critic; and Platon Kerzhentsev, an intellectual and member of the Central Institute of Labour. They reflected a tension within the Proletkul't between the new worker intellectuals and the middle-class enthusiasts for "proletarian culture".

Bogdanov's ideas continued to be dominant. He envisaged the "dictatorship of the proletariat" as a three-pronged activity, affecting politics, the economy, and culture alike. The Communist Party was to be the instrument of the political dictatorship, the trade unions of the economic, and the Proletkul't of the cultural. Bogdanov argued that it was mistaken to subordinate the cultural struggle to party control. In fact, he claimed that the distinctive proletarian perspective of the Proletkul't made it more advanced than the party, which had to take into account the necessity for political alliances. In a phrase which was later used against him, he described the proletarian writers as "immediate socialists" who should be regarded as the pacemakers of the revolution. Bogdanov did not in fact attack the culture of the past, although his enemies frequently accused him of doing so: he believed none the less that the proletariat should assume cultural leadership and direct cultural development from a clear proletarian perspective.

Lenin's opposition to Bogdanov's ideas was uncompromising, his own attitude having been made clear as early as 1905 in his pamphlet *Party Organization and Party Literature*, in which he said that cultural development should be a component part of organized, planned and integrated party work. Lenin's interpretation of Marxism treated culture as part of the superstructure of society built on the economic base, so that in his view it was absurd to treat culture as autonomous from economics and politics. Bogdanov's demands for cultural independence and his category of "immediate socialists" Lenin regarded as idealistic, divisive, and contrary to the doctrine of revolution that he had so carefully elaborated.

In 1919 Lenin declared the concept of "proletarian culture" an illusion of bourgeois intellectuals and, once victory in the Civil War was assured, moved against Bogdanov and the Proletkul't. At a conference of the Young Communist League (Komsomol) on 2 October 1920, Lenin asserted that communism could be built only on the basis of all the knowledge acquired from the old society, reminding his audience that Marx's achievement had been made possible through "making fully his own everything that earlier science could give". He scorned those people "who set up as specialists in proletarian culture" instead of working at the "development of those stores of knowledge" that humanity had accumulated over the centuries. Trotskii later developed the same argument in an article, "Proletarian Culture and Proletarian Art" (1923), arguing that the Russian proletariat had come to power before it had had time to assimilate bourgeois culture and should now concentrate on doing so.

Lenin instructed Lunacharskii, now People's Commissar of Popular Enlightenment, to bring the Proletkul't under control at its congress later the same month. It was to be incorporated as a subsidiary department of Lunacharskii's commissariat (Narkompros), making it an arm of the state and depriving it of its independent position. This Lunacharskii failed to do, thus betraying his sympathy for the ideas of his former associate Bogdanov. In fact, in a speech reported in the government newspaper *Izvestiia* on 8 October 1920, Lunacharskii stated explicitly that the movement should "preserve its quality of independent activity". This was the very opposite of what Lenin required and what, according to Lenin, Lunacharskii had previously agreed to say. Lenin's response was immediate. He drew up a draft resolution "On Proletarian Culture", to be approved by the Central Committee of the Communist Party and endorsed by the Proletkul't congress with the "utmost urgency . . . because the congress is closing today". The resolution made the party's authority clear, stating that the proletariat should play the leading role in the work of public education "through its vanguard – the Communist Party". The final paragraph called upon the Proletkul't congress to reject as "theoretically unsound and practically harmful all attempts to invent one's particular brand of culture in order to remain isolated in self-contained organization". Instead, activities should be carried out under "the general guidance of the Soviet authorities", and more specifically under Narkompros and the party organs concerned with cultural activities.

Nikolai Bukharin was given the task of ensuring that the congress accepted the resolution. This it did, and Bodganov resigned from the Central Committee of the Proletkul't. This was effectively the end of the matter: Bodganov had been overruled and the Proletkul't never resumed its former vitality or prestige. There was, however, an echo. Pletnev, one of the few genuinely proletarian writers, now replaced Bogdanov as the leading figure in the Proletkul't. On 29 September 1922 he published an article in the party newspaper Pravda, "On the Ideological Front", in which, while not demanding cultural autonomy from the party, he once more argued that the tasks of creating a proletarian culture could only be carried out by the proletariat itself. This prompted a bad-tempered letter from Lenin to Bukharin, complaining of the article's "stupidities" and asserting that Pletnev had "to learn, not proletarian science, but simply to learn".

A month later, on 25 October, Pravda printed a reply to Pletnev, who was accused of mechanically transferring to the sphere of culture the mistakes already made in the use of military and industrial experts. A further critical article was published on 1 January 1923, in the same newspaper, entitled "Menshevism in Proletkul't Garments". This made the point that the employment and integration into Soviet society of bourgeois intellectuals prepared to accept and serve it was a logical extension of the "correct" line of the New Economic Policy (NEP), as indeed it was. Lenin continued, even in his final writings, to drive home the case against Bogdanov, warning that much still had to be done "to attain the level of the ordinary civilized state of western Europe", which was "a menacing warning and reproach" to those who persisted in the idea of a "proletarian culture".

However, RAPP, the writers' organization mentioned above, was to have one more period of political significance, in 1928, when the party decided to enlist it as an instrument of its policy. At the April congress, Lunacharskii congratulated RAPP on its complete support for party directives and the socialist commitment of its membership. This was a preliminary to the use of RAPP as the Communist Party's monitor of literacy and cultural policy.

In December 1928, the Central Committee of the Communist Party issued a general directive requiring the publication of works of a "socially useful character", stating that publishers should depend "for the most part on communist authors". This was reinforced by regular Central Committee directives, issued

through the editorial pages of Pravda and Izvestiia, which called for a literature that could "mobilize the masses for the task of carrying out the general line of the party".

This policy was in line with the political decisions taken earlier to collectivize agriculture, and to begin the process of industrialization and modernization in pursuit of the Stalinist goal of "socialism in one country". This meant a massive accumulation of power by the central authorities of the party and the state. Material and human resources were now to be used, and disciplined, in pursuit of this objective, hastening the transition to a totalitarian system in a Soviet Union where most fundamental freedoms had already been lost. The consequences for creative freedom were profound, as the pragmatic was encouraged, and culture and the intellect were bent to the interests of the state.

In this atmosphere, "proletarianization" again became a cultural slogan. An editorial in Pravda on 18 May 1931 called for the literary artistic portrayal of "positive models of labour". Similarly, a Central Committee resolution, "On Publishing Work", issued later the same year, emphasized that the content and character of a book should meet the demands of "socialist construction". All this was orchestrated through RAPP, which, for four years, helped to obliterate the work of the few remaining noncommunist writers.

In June 1931 Stalin signalled a change of attitude towards bourgeois specialists employed in the Soviet economy: they were now to experience a lessening of officially orchestrated hostility. RAPP's monopoly of literary policy and its brutal, militant hectoring of "non-proletarian" writers was not brought to an end, however. It was dissolved by a Central Committee decree of 23 April 1932, only to be replaced by a single Writers Union, chaired by Maksim Gor'kii but controlled by a party faction. The liquidation of RAPP seemed to be a move towards greater freedom and, from exile in Paris, the writer Evgenii Zamiatin, author of the classic dystopian novel We, banned in Russia until 1988, even described the decision as "an unquestionable victory for the civilized". In practice it meant an even greater degree of centralization and direct party control. In 1932 "socialist realism" was announced as the guiding principle of Soviet literature, which, according to the statutes of the Writers Union, should aim to reflect "the great wisdom and heroism of the Communist Party".

W. JOHN MORGAN

Further Reading

Biggart, John, Georgii Gloveli and Avraham Yassour, Bogdanov and His Work: A Guide to the Published and Unpublished Works of Alexander A. Bogdanov (Malinovsky), 1873–1928, Aldershot: Ashgate, 1998

Claudin-Urondo, Carmen, Lenin and the Cultural Revolution, Hassocks, Sussex: Harvester Press, and Atlantic Highlands, New Jersey: Humanities Press, 1977

Conquest, Robert, The Politics of Ideas in the USSR, London: Bodley Head, and New York: Praeger, 1967

Fitzpatrick, Sheila, The Commissariat of Enlightenment: Soviet Organization of Education and the Arts under Lunacharsky, October 1917–1921, Cambridge: Cambridge University Press, 1970

Fitzpatrick, Sheila (editor), Cultural Revolution in Russia, 1928–1931, Bloomington: Indiana University Press, 1978

Forgacs, David and Geoffrey Nowell-Smith (editors), Antonio

Gramsci: Selections from Cultural Writings, London: Lawrence and Wishart, and Cambridge, Massachusetts: Harvard University Press, 1985

Gleason, Abbott *et al.* (editors), *Bolshevik Culture: Experiment and Order in the Russian Revolution*, Bloomington: Indiana University Press, 1985

Hingley, Ronald, *Russian Writers and Soviet Society, 1917–1978*, London: Weidenfeld and Nicolson, and New York: Random House, 1979

Kenez, Peter, *The Birth of the Propaganda State: Soviet Methods of Mass Mobilization, 1917–1929*, Cambridge and New York: Cambridge University Press, 1985

Koenker, Diane P. *et al.* (editors), *Party, State, and Society in the Russian Civil War: Exploration in Social History*, Bloomington: Indiana University Press, 1989

Lenin, V.I., *On Culture and Cultural Revolution*, Moscow: Progress, 1966

Trotskii, Lev, *On Literature and Art*, edited by Paul N. Siegel, 2nd edition, New York: Pathfinder Press, 1972

RUSSIA: Writers, Artists, and the Gulag

From its beginnings in 1918, writers and artists were among the many millions imprisoned in or deported to the Soviet system of forced labour camps, widely known as the Gulag – an acronym for the secret service organization that oversaw it, the Chief Administration of Corrective Labour Camps. Many were executed or died under the harsh conditions. According to estimates by Vitaly Shentalinsky, 2000 writers died in the Gulag, among them Isaak Babel', Daniil Kharms, Nikolai Gumilev, Nikolai Kliuev, Osip Mandel'shtam, and Boris Pil'niak. Among the countless others who were confined in the Gulag at some point in their lives were the philosopher Mikhail Bakhtin, the writer Iuz Aleshkovskii, the writer Evgeniia Ginzburg, the poet Natal'ia Gorbanevskaia, the historian Lev Gumilev, the avant-garde artist Gustav Klutsis, the Germanist Lev Kopelev, the historian Dmitrii Likhachev, the theatre director Vsevolod Meyerhold, the actor Solomon Michoels, the writers Andrei Siniavskii, and Aleksandr Solzhenitsyn, the avant-garde theoretician Sergei Tret'iakov, and the poet Nikolai Zabolotskii. Many victims of the Gulag – writers or not, famous or anonymous – were imprisoned for little or no apparent reason in the course of the regular purges of the 1930s and 1940s, which required arrests and detentions based on quotas fixed in advance.

It would be as wrong to put all writers and other cultural figures on the side of the repressed as to suggest that they were the only people repressed. Indeed, many writers willingly or otherwise supported the camps' existence. For example, in one infamous case during the 1930s a number of writers participated in a gigantic eulogy to the Gulag. The Belomor Kanal (White Sea Canal) project (1930–31), a 20-month construction effort that involved the labour of around 300,000 prisoners and left around one third dead, was visited by a group of more than 100 writers, who later published a collaborative volume on the project. Insensitive to the facts on the ground, this book, edited by Maksim Gor'kii, hailed the "reforging" of criminals and nonproletarians through socialist labour. Inside the camp, a "cultural and educational unit", employing many writers and artists, ran a theatre, conducted agitational poetry evenings, and staffed an orchestra to accompany convict labour with music. Belomor remained the only Gulag project with an official literary afterlife: once the canal had been completed, descriptions of Gulag operations were banned.

In 1938, Aleksandr Gerasimov, a painter who was an apologist for the regime and whose works included portraits of Stalin himself, summarized the results of the repressions of the 1930s in a report to the Union of Soviet Artists (quoted in Golomstock 1990):

> Enemies of the people, the Trotskyist–Bukharinite rabble, and fascist agents who have been active on the art front, and attempted in every way to brake and hinder the development of Soviet art, have been unmasked and neutralized by our Soviet intelligence service under the leadership of Stalin's comrade, Peoples' Commissar Ezhov. This has made the creative atmosphere more healthy and opened the way to a new wave of enthusiasm among the entire mass of artists.

The Gulag also gave rise to an entire new genre of memoirs and "camp literature", from a memoir of the earliest Soviet prison camp, on the Solovetskii Islands, written by a little-remembered escapee, Sergei Malsagov, to Solzhenitsyn's description of a typical prisoner's day, *Odin den' Ivana Denisovicha* (1962, *One Day in the Life of Ivan Denisovich*), which broke the taboo on discussing the camps in Soviet society. Arrested in 1945, when he was a captain in the Soviet army, Solzhenitsyn spent eight years in the camps and another three in exile. His encyclopedic study of the camp system, *Arkhipelag GULag* (1973–76, *The Gulag Archipelago*), has had worldwide resonance, not least by introducing the word "gulag" into other languages.

JAN PLAMPER

Further Reading

Conquest, Robert, *The Great Terror: A Reassessment*, Oxford and New York: Oxford University Press, 1990

Golomstock, Igor, *Totalitarian Art: In the Soviet Union, the Third Reich, Fascist Italy and the People's Republic of China*, New York: Icon, 1990

Kasack, Wolfgang, *Dictionary of Russian Literature since 1917*, New York: Columbia University Press, 1988

Malsagoff, S.A., *An Island Hell: A Soviet Prison in the Far North*, London: Philpot, 1926

Medvedev, Roy, "On Solzhenitsyn's *Gulag Archipelago*", *Index on Censorship*, 3/2 (Summer 1974)

Shentalinsky, Vitaly, *The KGB's Literary Archive*, edited and translated by John Crowfoot, London: Harvill Press, 1995; as *Arrested Voices: Resurrecting the Disappeared Writers of the Soviet Regime*, New York: Free Press, 1996

Solzhenitsyn, Aleksandr, *The Gulag Archipelago: An Experiment in Literary Investigation*, translated by Thomas P. Whitney and H.T. Willetts, 3 vols, New York: Harper and Row, and London: Collins and Harvill Press, 1974–78

RUSSIA: Treatment of Russian Literary Classics during the Soviet Period

Revolutionary iconoclasm was not generally characteristic of Bolshevik policy on the arts. Lenin, Trotskii, Bukharin, and the People's Commissar of Enlightenment, Anatolii Lunacharskii, all believed that the culture of the past could be employed selectively to educate Soviet society and further the cause of "cultural revolution". In the debates of the 1920s, the government consistently declined to come down in favour of the proletarian culture movement or the revolutionary avant-garde headed by the Futurists. Instead, it reminded the more militant literary groupings that Soviet culture was too immature to jettison the western and Russian cultural heritage.

Of all the cultural achievements of the past, the Russian literary classics of the 19th century were accorded a particularly high status. An early Bolshevik decree made the publication of "cheap popular editions of the Russian classics" one of the main tasks of the State Publishing House. In January 1918 the state established a monopoly on the publication of 57 "classic" authors for five years in the first instance (in 1922 it was duly extended). Even at the height of the Civil War, the government found the time and the resources to produce and distribute cheap editions of works of 19th-century literature. Great care was taken to make these "popular classics" accessible and digestible by publishing them in pamphlet form, with large print, illustrations, and sometimes even simplified content. These editions were accompanied by edifying forewords that offered simple assessments of the works' ideological significance – and hence provoked the opposition of a number of prominent intellectuals, who in 1918 refused to take any part in the project.

The Soviet regime was from the start highly selective about the writers it chose to canonize. Nekrasov, Saltykov-Shchedrin, Chekhov, and Turgenev were always favoured, while Dostoevskii, Leskov, Tiutchev, and Fet were regarded with great suspicion. The canon was filled out by using minor writers of the 1860s and 1870s whose "progressive" sympathies more than made up for their lack of talent.

During the period of the New Economic Policy (1921–29), the government was no longer prepared to throw money into the publishing of cheap books as it had during the Civil War. More editions of Russian classics were published in the first five years of the state monopoly than in the second; but the institutionalization of the classics continued nonetheless. Anniversaries of famous writers' births and deaths were celebrated with great pomp. From 1924 onwards, the State Publishing House produced collected works and other multivolume editions of the classics. Many of these were edited by renowned scholars and remained authoritative for several decades. They did not, on the whole, fall victim to political censorship or falsification; the government did, however, exercise censorship by limiting printruns. Any edition intended for a broad public had to meet strict ideological criteria. Public libraries, which were the main source of literature for the common reader, were purged of undesirable prerevolutionary classics. From about 1923, circulars were sent round instructing the removal of works by writers such as Leskov, Bunin or Dostoevskii from the open shelves.

In the 1930s, the publication of cheap popular editions of the classics was stepped up once again. The new mass Soviet reader, brought into being by the literacy campaigns that had been reintensified in the late 1920s, was to be presented with a filtered selection of 19th-century Russian literature. For example, the series Library for Beginners, which started in 1936, offered choice works by Pushkin, Lermontov, Gogol', Turgenev, Chekhov, and many others, all at low prices. For readers with greater cultural aspirations, expensive well-bound editions of classic authors were provided. The centenary of Pushkin's death, in 1937, spurred the regime to still greater publishing feats. By 1938 works by Pushkin had been published in 66 different languages, of which 40 were in use in the Soviet Union.

The popularization of the classics in the 1930s resulted in a cult of the author: it became inadmissible to suggest that Russia's "great writers" were anything other than ideologically exemplary. Author and work became indistinguishable under the pressure of hagiography. It was thus in the 1930s that the Soviet myth of prerevolutionary Russian literature truly took shape and hardened. Celebrated 19th-century authors were hitched to the ideological bandwagons of Stalin's Russia. The literary classics were made to play their part in the turn towards Great Russian nationalism in the 1930s. During and after the Great Patriotic War (as World War II was known), this role became even more pronounced. For example, in a 20-volume edition of Chekhov's collected works published between 1944 and 1951, several pro-Western or anti-Slav comments were omitted from the writer's letters. This characteristically selective treatment of the classics persisted into the post-Stalin period. In a long-awaited fourth volume of Dostoevskii's letters, published in 1959, anti-Semitic passages were systematically expunged.

By the mid-1950s, the Soviet selection of Russian classics had firmly established its canonical status. As of 1957, 1917 editions of works by Pushkin had been published, with a total printrun of 84 million, and the printruns for the works of Gor'kii, Tolstoi, and Chekhov were similarly enormous. Russia's literature formed an important part of a shared cultural heritage that was presented as if it underpinned a transnational Russified Soviet identity. The Russian classics were indeed used as weapons of Sovietization in the state's nationalities policy. The printruns of the Russian classics were boosted in all Soviet republics, and in the 1970s they gained much greater representation in school syllabuses.

The high priority granted the Russian classics by the Soviet publishing system had a definite impact on the habits of Soviet readers. Especially given the absence of popular entertainment literature such as we know it in the west, most Russian classics were avidly read right up to the end of the glasnost period. In the late 1980s, an edition of Pushkin in nearly 11 million copies did not exhaust demand for the works of Russia's national poet. The fall-away in demand for the Russian classics in the 1990s drew predictable assertions that there was a "crisis" in Russian culture.

STEPHEN LOVELL

Further Reading

Blium, A., *Za kulisami "Ministerstva pravdy": Tainaia istoriia sovetskoi tsenzury 1917–1929* (Behind the Scenes at the "Ministry of Truth": The Secret History of the Soviet Censorship 1917–29), St Petersburg: Akademicheskii proekt, 1994

Dobrynina, N., *Cherty dukhovnoi obshchnosti: Russkaia khudozhestvennaia literatura v chtenii mnogonatsional'nogo sovetskogo chitatelia* (Contours of Spiritual Community: Russian Fiction as Read by the Multinational Soviet Reader), Moscow, 1983

Friedberg, Maurice, *Russian Classics in Soviet Jackets*, New York: Columbia University Press, 1962

Goldstein, D., "Rewriting Dostoevsky's Letters", *American Slavic and East European Review*, 20/2 (1961)

Kenez, Peter, *The Birth of the Propaganda State: Soviet Methods of Mass Mobilization, 1917–1929*, Cambridge and New York: Cambridge University Press, 1985

Nazarov, A.I., *Oktiabr' i kniga: Sozdanie sovetskikh izdatel'stv i formirovanie massovogo chitatelia, 1917–1923* (October and the Book: The Creation of Soviet Publishing Houses and the Formation of the Mass Reader, 1917–23), Moscow: Nauka, 1968

O'Connor, Timothy Edward, *The Politics of Soviet Culture: Anatolii Lunacharskii*, Ann Arbor, Michigan: UMI Research Press, 1983

Struve, G., "Chekhov in Communist Censorship", *Slavonic and East European Review*, 33/81 (1955)

RUSSIA: Literature during World War II

Any Soviet writer who attempted to conceptualize or interpret the experience of World War II, or the Great Patriotic War (*Velikaia Otechestvennaia Voina*, 1941–45), beyond narrowly prescribed limits could expect to experience the full wrath of the regime's ideological watchdogs, both through prior censorship and, in the event of a change of policy after publication, savage personal criticism. In an early study of the rewriting of Soviet participation in World War II, Matthew Gallagher describes it as "one of the most audacious efforts ever undertaken by the Soviet leadership to tailor history to political prescription".

On all historical fronts, however, the official historians found themselves besieged by relentless historical truths. Numerous topics were never openly confronted until the very last days of the Soviet Union: the nature of the Molotov–Ribbentrop Pact of 1939, with its secret protocols; the disastrous consequences of the purges on the Soviet High Command, which became particularly apparent in the summer battles of 1941 and 1942; Stalin's stubborn refusal to heed repeated warnings from varied and impeccable sources concerning German military intentions in 1941; Soviet responsibility for the massacre of Polish officers at Katyn, finally acknowledged by Gorbachev in 1991; the desertion of huge numbers of Soviet soldiers to the enemy; the active assistance rendered by many Soviet citizens to the Germans in the occupied territories; the generally low level of Soviet military competence, even towards the end of the war; the brutal treatment of returning Soviet prisoners of war and civilians forced to work for the Germans, as members of both groups were regarded as traitors; the numbers of Soviet soldiers who served under general Vlasov, collaborating with the Germans; and, finally, the indifference, almost contempt, on the part of the Soviet leadership towards the lives of its soldiers and civilians. The open discussion of any one of these themes, let alone the combined weight of these revelations, would have put the survival of the party and its "leading role" in grave jeopardy well before the arrival of Gorbachev. Censorship of information about the war was thus a matter of the highest priority for the regime's survival.

Given the scale of official censorship, and the massive efforts expended internationally and domestically to sanitize the Soviet war record, it would be tempting to dismiss personal accounts as bearing the stamp of official approval and thus enjoying little merit. Fortunately, this is not the case. While it is true that far too much published material was crude, and unthinkingly conformed to the latest ideological directives, there were Soviet writers who tried to resist the historical certainties demanded of them. One can cite Viktor Nekrasov's *V okopakh Stalingrada* (1946, In the Trenches of Stalingrad), ironically the winner of a Stalin Prize; Emmanuel Kazakevich's *Zvezda* (1946, The Star), an eerie story of a Soviet reconnaissance patrol behind enemy lines; Grigorii Baklanov's *Iiul '41 goda* (1965, July 1941), which even now remains one of the best accounts of the early months of the war; Bulat Okudzhava's *Bud' zdorov, shkoliar* (1961, Take Care, Schoolboy), with its echoes of Erich Maria Remarque's *Im Westen nichts Neues* (1929, All Quiet on the Western Front); and Vasil Bykov's harrowing stories of partisan warfare, with their unflinching analysis of cowardice, treachery, and human weakness: *Sotnikov* (1970), *Volch'ia staia* (1975, The Wolf Pack), and *Znak bedy* (1983, The Sign of Disaster). It should be pointed out that all the writers mentioned experienced difficulties with literary officials. Okudzhava and Baklanov were accused of "Remarquism", that is, of having insufficient regard for ideological factors in their portrayal of war. Nekrasov was forced into exile, and the significance of Bykov's frequent juxtapositions of the horrors of collectivization and the Nazi occupation did not go unnoticed.

The personal standpoint from which these writers tackled the war may actually have assisted publication. Failures, it could be argued, were due to individuals: the system itself was essentially healthy. In the case of Baklanov (*July 1941*) and Bykov (*The Sign of Disaster*), flashbacks to the prewar period that indict Stalin were not totally at odds with the regime's attempts, after 1956, to come to terms with the "cult of personality", the curious euphemism used to describe Stalin's reign of terror. It was only after the ousting of Khrushchev in 1964 that the regime tried to retard and then to reverse the anti-Stalinist line.

Soviet censorship possessed an almost infallible instinct for recognizing the state's sworn enemies when confronted with their manuscripts. Bykov's stories were just about acceptable. Vasilii Grossman's Stalingrad epic, *Zhizn' i sud'ba* (Life and

Fate) was unpublishable. *Life and Fate* is the great literary rediscovery of the glasnost period. The manuscript of the novel was "arrested" by the KGB in 1961 and Grossman was told by Mikhail Suslov, the chief Soviet ideologist, that publication was out of the question for some 300 years. In *Life and Fate*, Grossman repeatedly draws parallels between Hitler's Nazi Germany and Stalin's Russia. The victory at Stalingrad, the Russian sacrifice, argued Grossman, merely saved Stalin, and indirectly strengthened totalitarianism in central and eastern Europe after 1945.

War waged on the scale of the Russo-German struggle, with millions of deaths and the ideologically sanctioned savagery of both combatants, leaves hideous memories. Soviet censorship prolonged and compounded the physical agony of the Russo-German war with denial, half-truths, lies, and silence.

FRANK ELLIS

Further Reading

Ellis, Frank, "The General and His Army: The Ghost of General Vlasov", *Modern Language Review*, 96/2 (April 2001):437–49

Gallagher, Matthew, *The Soviet History of World War II: Myths, Memories and Realities*, New York: Praeger, 1963

Garrard, John and Carol Garrard (editors), *World War 2 and the Soviet People*, New York: St Martin's Press, 1993

Higgins, Ian (editor), *The Second World War in Literature: Eight Essays*, Edinburgh: Scottish Academic Press, 1986

Klein, Holger *et al.* (editors), *The Second World War in Fiction*, London: Macmillan, 1984

Materski, Wojciech (editor), *Katyn: Documents of Genocide: Documents and Materials from the Soviet Archives Turned over to Poland on October 14 1992*, Warsaw: Institute of Political Studies, Polish Academy of Sciences, 1993

Rutherford, Andrew, *The Literature of War: Five Studies in Heroic Virtue*, London: Macmillan, and New York: Barnes and Noble, 1978

RUSSIA: Soviet Theatre

Along with films and other art forms, theatre was placed under the supervision of the Commissariat of Enlightenment (Narkompros) by a decree issued by the Soviet government on 9 November 1917. Theatre enjoyed a period of relative creative freedom during the 1920s, while the Bolsheviks struggled for complete power and the country was engulfed by civil war and famine. Vsevolod Meyerhold, appointed head of the theatre section of Narkompros, was active at the Theatre of the Revolution, and from 1922, directed his own Meyerhold Theatre. Aleksandr Tairov, who had founded the Kamerny Theatre in 1913, was allowed to continue in post and, in 1917, he directed the premiere of a Russian translation of Oscar Wilde's *Salome*, which had been banned in 1908. Theatre on a massive scale was encouraged as part of the regime's programme of "agitprop" (agitation and propaganda). Thus, Nikolai Evreinov's *The Storming of the Winter Palace* (1920) was staged with a cast of 10,000 in Petrograd (as St Petersburg was then known), and Nikolai Okhlopkov's *The Struggle between Capital and Labour* (1921), employing no less than 30,000 people, was performed in Irkutsk in Western Siberia. All theatres were nationalized and around 3,000 theatrical troupes came into being.

Nationalization, however, turned out to be one step towards censorship, embodied in 1922 by the creation of Glavlit, the Central Administration for Literary and Publishing Affairs, which in turn gave birth in 1923 to Glavrepertkom, the Central Repertory Committee, responsible for the censorship of all public performances. In 1927, moreover, the Department of Agitation and Propaganda of the Central Committee of the Communist Party held a theatre conference at which speakers demanded the further bending of theatre to the service of ideology, and of the proletariat (in practice, the regime claiming to act on the proletariat's behalf) in particular. Calls were made to strengthen the censorship of each theatre's productions. Each proposed production now had to pass the scrutiny of an in-house artistic council, made up of representatives of all the theatre's workers, and theatre managers were required to be members of the party. It was further asserted that drama criticism would be "the most important weapon against the independence of the theatre", legitimizing a strategy that was already being practised: the public vilification of a director and / or writer in the guise of a review, followed by the loss of the targeted artist's job, right to publish, freedom, or even life itself.

Among the first plays to be singled out for outright bans were two by Mikhail Bulgakov: *Dni Turbinykh* (The Days of the Turbins), which had been performed at the Moscow Arts Theatre in 1926, but was now condemned for its sympathetic portrayal of "White" (anti-Communist) army officers during the civil war; and *Zoikina Kvartira* (1926, Zoika's Apartment), which had been performed at the Vakhtangov Theatre and elsewhere in Moscow, but had skated on thin ice by satirizing the corruption of local administrators of the New Economic Policy. Bulgakov's *Beg* (1927, Flight), a sequel to *Dni Turbinykh*, was banned before any performances had taken place and thereafter none of his work was allowed to reach the stage.

This was only the beginning. As the theatre historian Aleksandr Gershkovich has written, "The martyrology of banned performances in the Soviet theatre is endless". Nikolai Erdman's *Samoubiitsa* (1928, The Suicide) was stopped at its dress rehearsal, being considered to have given too much attention to the activities of "class enemies" and "dreamers". Vladimir Maiakovskii's *Klop* (1928–29, The Bedbug) was staged at the Meyerhold Theatre, but was received badly by the official press; the playwright/director committed suicide in 1930, apparently for reasons quite unrelated to the treatment of his plays, but was rehabilitated by Stalin in 1935. Press attacks on "formalism" preceded the closure of the second studio of the Moscow Arts Theatre in 1936 and the Meyerhold Theatre in 1938; the Kamerny was subjected to close supervision, but managed to stay open until just before Tairov's death in 1950. Meyerhold was executed in 1940, and Isaak Babel', having been arrested after the seizure and probable destruction of his play *The Chekist* was secretly executed in 1940.

Meanwhile, in 1934 Andrei Zhdanov, one of Stalin's closest henchmen, had proclaimed the doctrine of "socialist realism", leading to the production of, among other works, Nikolai

Virta's "conflictless drama" and to the issuing of directions to playwrights to devise "positive heroes" who would enhance "party spirit". Aleksandr Korneichuk, a Ukrainian playwright, was among those who conformed, although Stalin himself took a hand in the censorship of Korneichuk's play *V stepiakh Ukrainy* (1941, On the Ukrainian Steppes), of which the dictator wrote:

> My only complaint is that [it] is too merry; there is a danger that this comedy's merry revelry might distract the reader's attention from its content ... I have added a few words on page 68. This is for greater clarity.

Opinions differ on the amount of protection afforded by the distance of provincial theatres from Moscow. Mark Zaitsev claims that theatres in the non-Russian republics "always enjoyed greater freedom of expression". Local languages may certainly have helped to disguise seditious themes. On the other hand, Viktor Savin of the Komi Autonomous Republic was sent to a "special camp" (*spetslager'*), where he died under torture, and the Ukrainian actor and director Aleksandr (Les) Kurbas was executed for "formalism" in 1937. Kurbas had been a marked man since 1928, when he produced his fellow-Ukrainian Mikola Kulish's play *The People's Malakhiy* which depicts a reformer who is declared insane. The Russian Drama Theatre in Riga was relegated to official non-being. According to V.A. Kumanev "Essentially, repression did not pass over any of the important centres of theatrical art."

Many plays, their authors, and their directors were rehabilitated during the "thaw" which followed Stalin's death in 1953. It again became possible to write and present plays about unheroic characters, as in the work of Victor Rozov and Aleksandr Volodin, and at the Sovremennik (Contemporary) Theatre Oleg Efremov was allowed to turn decisively away from the narrow "realism" of the Stalinist period towards more psychological themes. On the other hand, as the "years of stagnation" under Brezhnev approached, Aleksandr Solzhenitsyn's play *Olen' i shalashovka* (1962, The Love-Girl and the Innocent), based, like his novella *Odin den' Ivana Denisovicha* (1962, One Day in the Life of Ivan Denisovich), on his experiences in a labour camp, was suppressed after its dress rehearsal.

Other parts of the Soviet past remained forbidden territory, as was made clear to Iurii Liubimov, the artistic director of the Moscow Theatre of Drama and Comedy (the Taganka), in 1968, when he tried to stage Boris Mokhaev's *Alive*, a treatment of the collectivization campaign of the 1930s. "Normal" censorship continued until the mid-1980s, but it is noteworthy that after his expulsion from the Soviet Union in 1984, Liubimov remarked to a friend, "I have to thank them for not shooting me like Meyerhold".

Any playwright who hoped to have a play staged had first to submit the script to Glavlit, then wait for an interview with a censor, at which the playwright was told what revisions were necessary. After submitting the revisions in triplicate, he/she had to wait for approval, which was indicated by the return of the script with its pages sealed with wax, the number of authorized pages written on it by hand, and a note stipulating the maximum number of copies allowed. These copies could only be made at a special office designated for that purpose. Next,

the playwright had to submit the play to Glavrepertkom. If it was approved, he/she then took copies to the literary directors of various theatres, and might again be asked to make revisions. If the play was cleared in its latest revised version by the literary director, and had the approval of the theatre's chief director, who was often a genuine artist rather than a party functionary, the playwright was required to give a reading before the theatre's artistic council, who, in turn, could refuse the play, accept it as it was, or order yet more revisions. If the council approved the play, Glavrepertkom had still to be petitioned for permission to allow rehearsals. Even then, the censorship process continued until the very eve of public performance, and often beyond, although theoretically the final hurdle was the closed dress rehearsal for members of Glavrepertkom, the artistic council, the playwright, the director, and the designer. In December 1982, for instance, after the Taganka had held its dress rehearsal for Pushkin's *Boris Godunov*, directed by Liubimov, the play was vetoed by the artistic council, even though Pushkin's works were part of the official literary canon directed to be studied in Soviet schools.

From the 1970s onwards, many more topics could at least be broached in the theatre, if not allowed complete, uncensored treatment: teenage rebellion and pregnancy, family and neighbourhood relationships all had airings. A version of Edward Albee's *Who's Afraid of Virginia Woolf?* was presented at the Sovremennik in 1973. Iurii Trifonov's novellas *Obmen* (1976, The Exchange) and *Dom na naberezhnoi* (1980, The House on the Embankment) were dramatized for the Taganka, introducing to its audiences such themes as life in an apartment block and Stalinist guilt. Finally, under Gorbachev, it was even possible to perform Vladimir Gubarev's *Sarkofag* (1986, Sarcophagus), his account of the damage done to people and the environment by the Chernobyl explosion. Theatrical censorship ceased with the abolition of Glavlit in August 1990.

KATHERINE BLISS EATON

Further Reading

Braun, Edward, *Meyerhold: A Revolution in Theatre*, Iowa City: University of Iowa Press, and London: Methuen, 1995

Conquest, Robert, *The Great Terror: A Reassessment*, Oxford and New York: Oxford University Press, 1990

Dewhirst, Martin, "Censorship" in *The Cambridge Encyclopedia of Russia and the Former Soviet Union*, edited by Archie Brown *et al.*, New York and Cambridge: Cambridge University Press, 1994

Ermolaev, Herman, *Censorship in Soviet Literature, 1917–1991*, Lanham, Maryland: Rowman and Littlefield, 1997

Gershkovich, Alexander, "Censorship in the Theater" in *The Red Pencil: Artists, Scholars, and Censors in the USSR*, edited by Marianna Tax Choldin and Maurice Friedberg, Boston: Unwin Hyman, 1989

Gershkovich, Alexander, *The Theater of Yuri Lyubimov: Art and Politics at the Taganka Theater in Moscow*, New York: Paragon House, 1989

Gorchakov, N.A., *The Theater in Soviet Russia*, New York: Columbia University Press, 1957

Kumanev, V.A., *30-e gody v sud'bakh otechestvennoi intelligentsii* (The 30s in the Fates of our Country's Intelligentsia), Moscow: Nauka, 1991

Leach, Robert, *Revolutionary Theatre*, London and New York: Routledge, 1994

Liencourt, François de, "The Repertoire of the Fifties" in *Literature and Revolution in Soviet Russia, 1917–62*, edited by Max Hayward and Leopold Labedz, London and New York: Oxford University Press, 1963

Maggs, Peter B., *The Mandelstam and "Der Nister" Files: An Introduction to Stalin-era Prison and Labor Camp Records*, Armonk, New York: Sharpe, 1996

Richmond, Steven, "'The Eye of the State': An Interview with Soviet Chief Censor Vladimir Solodin", *Russian Review*, 56 (October 1997): 581–90

Shentalinsky, Vitaly, *The KGB's Literary Archive*, edited and translated by John Crowfoot, London: Harvill Press, 1995; as *Arrested Voices: Resurrecting the Disappeared Writers of the Soviet Regime*, New York: Free Press, 1996

Tamarchenko, Anna, "Theatre Censorship", *Index on Censorship*, 9/4 (August 1980)

Worrall, Nick, *Modernism to Realism on the Soviet Stage: Tairov–Vakhtangov–Okhlopkov*, Cambridge and New York: Cambridge University Press, 1989

Zaitsev, Mark, "Soviet Theater Censorship", *Drama Review*, 19 (June 1975): 119–28

RUSSIA: Historical and Factual Film

Film in Russia began with newsreel and many early fiction films treated Russian historical themes, for example Aleksandr Drankov's *Boris Godunov* (1907) and *Stenka Razin* (1908). However the pre-revolutionary cinema, while high in artistic value, was decadent and escapist in its subject matter, and the work of masters such as Evgenii Bauer eschewed realism and historical subjects. The cinema was relatively free of interference before World War I, largely because the authorities (including the tsar) looked upon moving pictures as ephemera.

By contrast, the Soviet regime realized the potential of cinema to be a vehicle for its (rewritten) version of history, past and present, a potential that even some of the great pioneers of the medium seemed willing to accept. Dziga Vertov could describe his documentary work as "life caught unawares" (*zhizn' vrasplokh*), but at the same time regard it as "the communist decoding of reality". Esfir Shub could re-edit her own *Velikii put'* (1927, The Great Way) as *Strana sovetov* (1937, Land of The Soviets) for differing political aims and with a completely different (Stalin-centred) perspective on the history of the Soviet Union.

During the Civil War (1918–22) vast amounts of scarce resources were expended on filmmaking and distribution. This was not least due to Lenin's belief that cinema was "the most important of all the arts". The Soviet leader hoped that most film production would be of an educational nature (the "Leninist film proportion"). Vertov dominated the early years of Soviet cinema with his "unplayed" films of "life caught unawares" but always with a clear political message; he wrote of "the communist decoding of reality". The first master of the Soviet fiction film, Sergei Eisenstein, began his career with two films on historical subjects: *Stachka* (1924, Strike) and *Bronenosets Potemkin* (1925, The Battleship Potemkin).

The 10th anniversary of the Revolution gave filmmakers (and the regime) a chance to celebrate the history and achievements of the Soviet state. In the documentary field Esfir Shub triumphed with *Padenie dinastii Romanovykh* (The Fall of the Romanov Dynasty) and *Velikii put'*, released in February and October 1927. Fiction films proved more problematic, with Eisenstein's *Oktiabr'* (1927, October) a victim of an organized campaign of vilification. The problems with *Oktiabr'* and Pudovkin's *Konets Sankt-Peterburga* (The End of St. Petersburg) were grist to the mill of those party functionaries who demanded – and got – much tighter control of the cinema at the end of the 1920s.

In the period after Stalin's rise to supreme power cinema joined in the campaigns to endorse crash industrialization. Thus Shub produced *Komsomol, shef elektrifikatsii* (1932, Komsomol, Chief of Electrification) or *KShE* and Vertov *Simfoniia Donbasa* (1931, Enthusiasm) while Aleksandr Medvedkin toured the factory and collective farm areas of the Ukraine in an "agitation" train making and showing short propaganda films. Sergei and Georgii Vasiliev's *Chapaev* (1934) was an enormously popular epic of the Civil War struggle and much praised for its simplicity of style. However, as Stalin's regime matured the need to create a national myth was largely superseded by a desire to mythologize the leader. Stalin's "cult of personality" was celebrated in film as in all the arts. The 20th anniversary of the Revolution was celebrated in Vertov's *Kolybel'naia* (Lullaby), which portrayed the great leader as father to all the people and Shub's *Strana sovetov* (1937, Land of the Soviets). Shub's film rewrote Soviet history to the greater glory of Stalin. This was done by re-editing her earlier films and rewriting the captions. The 1940 film *Den' novogo mira* (Day in the New World) typifies the air of unreality that permeated nonfiction film of the prewar period. The travesties continued in late Stalinism when those filmmakers who were allowed to work engaged in an act of revisionism. Mikheil Chiaureli's *Kliatva* (1947, The Vow) and *Padenie Berlina* (1949, Fall of Berlin) remain classics of their kind.

Under Khrushchev a relative relaxation took place. Films based on historical subjects tended to be restricted to the Great Patriotic War, for example Mikhail Kalatozov's *Letiat zhuravli* (1957, The Cranes are Flying) and Chukrai's *Balada soldata* (1959, Ballad of a Soldier). Many scripts continued to languish in the corridors of the cinema bureaucracy while whole finished films remained "on the shelf" because of the timidity of officials as much as central command. Documentary film still concentrated on the seemingly unlimited triumphs of Soviet science and technology.

In the "period of stagnation" (as Brezhnev's period in power came to be known) documentary films, seen mostly on TV, continued to focus on economic or foreign policy triumphs. Artistic historical films were made – as indeed were films about contemporary subjects – but only the most anodyne were shown.

Gorbachev recognized the power of the moving image in the massive task of changing Soviet society, especially as the printed word had become so untrustworthy. The urgent need for new

material in the cinema led to the formation of a special commission – under Elim Klimov – that found and released many
films suppressed during the previous decades. Feature films
dealing with painful memories of the past such as Aleksandr
Proshkin's *Kholodnoe leto 1953* (1989, Cold Summer of 1953)
attracted a mass audience. Documentary cinema experienced
something of a renaissance under perestroika (restructuring).
Both in the cinema and on television Soviet audiences were
allowed to see investigations of their past such as *Vlast'
Solovskaia* (Solovki Power), which dealt with the Soviet Union's
first prison camp; *Protsess* (The Trial); and *Bol'she sveta* (More
Light), which looked at the whole history of the Union, and of
contemporary social problems. In the latter category the work
of Juris Podnieks, such as *Vaivegli but jaunam?* (1986, Is it Easy
to be Young?) was particularly notable for its questioning tone.

The new critical glasnost (openness) became less and less
encouraged in the final years of the Soviet Union. Gorbachev
tried to reassert authority on what was becoming an increasingly out of control society and the media did not escape this
(failed) attempt. After the fall of the Soviet Union in 1991, the
increasing commercial pressures of the post-soviet period have
not been conducive to the production of quality historical/
factual film or television.

GRAHAM ROBERTS

Further Reading

Hosking, Geoffrey, *The Awakening of the Soviet Union*, Cambridge,
Massachusetts: Harvard University Press, and London:
Heinemann, 1990
Hosking, Geoffrey, *A History of the Soviet Union, 1917–1991*, final
edition, London: Fontana Press, 1992
Kenez, Peter, *Cinema and Soviet Society, 1917–1953*, Cambridge and
New York: Cambridge University Press, 1992
Lawton, Anna, *Kinoglasnost: Soviet Cinema in Our Time*, Cambridge
and New York: Cambridge University Press, 1992
Lawton, Anna, (editor), *The Red Screen: Politics, Society, Art in
Soviet Cinema*, New York and London: Routledge, 1992
Leyda, Jay, *Kino: A History of the Russian and Soviet Film*, 3rd
edition, London: Allen and Unwin, and Princeton, New Jersey:
Princeton University Press, 1983
Roberts, Graham, *Forward Soviet! History and Non-Fiction Film in
the USSR*, London and New York: Tauris, 1999
Taylor, Richard, *The Politics of Soviet Cinema, 1917–1929*,
Cambridge: Cambridge University Press, 1979
Taylor, Richard and Ian Christie (editors), *The Film Factory: Russian
and Soviet Cinema in Documents*, Cambridge, Massachusetts:
Harvard University Press, and London: Routledge, 1988
Taylor, Richard and Ian Christie (editors), *Inside The Film Factory:
New Approaches to Russian and Soviet Cinema*, London and
New York, Routledge, 1991
Taylor, Richard, and Derek Spring (editors), *Stalinism and Soviet
Cinema*, London and New York: Routledge, 1993

RUSSIA: Film during and about World War II

While very few foreign films were shown in the Soviet Union
at any time during World War II, the policy on the censorship
of domestic films varied in line with international relations.
Thus, during the first two years of the war, Nazi Germany and
the Soviet Union were officially at peace with each other.
Accordingly, films perceived as anti-German, most famously
Sergei Eisenstein's *Aleksandr Nevsky*, were shelved, and a few
anti-British and anti-Polish movies were released.

This pattern was reversed abruptly when the Nazis invaded
Soviet territory, on 22 June 1941. The film industry was enlisted
in the total mobilization of Soviet society. Eisenstein's film soon
reappeared on Soviet screens, as part of the industry's effort to
raise morale and promote a specific wartime version of patriotism, a mixture of national pride and proclamation of Stalin's
wise leadership, with very little emphasis on Marxist ideology.
Newsreels and documentaries, which together formed the
bulk of wartime cinema, emphasized German cruelty and Soviet
suffering. Feature films, some 70 of which were produced once
the studios established themselves in evacuation, did the same.
Filmmakers needed no coercion to portray the fortitude of the
population (most often embodied in female protagonists), love
of country, Nazi barbarity, the need for resistance, and the legitimacy of vengeance. Official intervention was rare. One of the
few proscriptions precluded showing Germans as other than
monsters, so that Vsevolod Pudovkin's *Ubiitsy vykhodiat na
dorogu* (Murderers Are Coming), depicting German victims of
Hitler, was not distributed.

After the war, as the Stalinist personality cult hypertrophied,
a succession of historical films portrayed Russia's past glory
and the greatness of its military leaders (Suvorov, Nevskii, Ivan
the Terrible) and artists (Mussorgskii and Rimskii-Korsakov),
who functioned as obvious analogues of Stalin. In *Kliatva*
(1946, The Oath), *Stalingradskaia bitva* (1949, The Battle of
Stalingrad), and, most notoriously, *Padenie Berlina* (1949, The
Fall of Berlin), Stalin replaced the protagonists of wartime films.
Several of these films explicitly state that "Comrade Stalin is
always with us", and he appeared to have "won the war single-
handedly". Russian losses were ignored in favour of military
triumphs, and the experience of "ordinary" Russians, which
had provided the material (however distorted) for films made
during the war, vanished. "The viewer got the impression,"
writes one western historian, "that in winning the war what
mattered was not the heroism of the simple soldier, who
remained faceless, but brilliant leadership."

One cornerstone of the revival of Soviet cinema in the 1950s
became the treatment of World War II. By 1956, especially after
Khrushchev declared that Stalin was partly responsible for
Soviet casualties, the war had become central in public attention. Readers welcomed a wave of memoirs and war fiction
that portrayed the defeat of Nazi Germany as having been
achieved not by the Kremlin leadership but by the Soviet
people, not just by Russians but by all the Soviet peoples, and
by civilians in the rear as much as by soldiers at the front.

A younger generation of directors, many of them army veterans, perceived the trauma of World War II as a ready-made context for depictions of kinds of heroism accessible to, and – more important – manifested by, millions of Soviet viewers. Beginning with *Bessmertnyi garnizon* (1956, Immortal Garrison) and culminating in Andrei Tarkovski's first feature film, *Ivanovo detstvo* (1962, Ivan's Childhood), films extended the definition of war far beyond military engagement, and identified its victims as including virtually all segments of Soviet society. In three enormously popular films – *Letiat zhuravli* (1957, Cranes are Flying), *Ballada o soldate* (1959, Ballad of a Soldier), and *Sud'ba cheloveka* (1960, Fate of a Man) – and a score of less distinguished ones, heroes were "deheroized", their crippling emotional scars as integral to them as their courage and endurance. (The special victimization of Jews remained off-screen until Aleksandr Askoldov's *Komissar* [The Commissar], made in 1968 but released only two decades later.)

Even in those years of relative freedom, filmmakers faced censorship if they got the balance wrong. Marlen Khutsiev's *Dva Fedora* (1958, Two Fyodors), for instance, was considered too "grim". Given the burnt-out postwar landscape of the film, punctuated by endless lines of people waiting for scarce food, and grubby, hungry, homeless children, critics wanted a hero less morose and bitter, more active and involved, than Big Fedor.

Aleksandr Alov and Vladimir Naumov's bleak *Mir vkhodiashchemu* (1961, Peace to Him Who Enters) fared even worse. Set on the last day of the war, *Peace* portrays the journey of three Russian soldiers assigned to transport an official dispatch and a heavily pregnant German woman to a town near Berlin. Language separates people, goodness is not reciprocated, and kindness proves inadequate to unite people. When bureaucrats from the Ministry of Culture of the Russian republic watched *Peace to Him Who Enters* in November 1960, they were outraged, regarding it as a slanderous insult to the Soviet army. Naumov claims that only the personal intervention of Ekaterina Furtseva, then minister of culture, saved the film. (Furtseva became notorious for her role in securing Aleksandr Solzhenitsyn's expulsion from the Writers Union a few years later.) Her predecessor had tried to block the film, but because Furtseva liked the directors – though not the film – she took *Peace* with her to the 1961 Venice Film Festival, where it won a special gold medal for "originality and innovation", and an award from Italian film critics. As a result, the film was released within the Soviet Union on a limited basis.

In the intensifying Cold War climate, *Peace* erred in both its compassionate portrayal of the Germans and its disquieting intimations of the fragility of peace. What awaited the newcomer was, one critic wrote, "not peace but an ongoing struggle ... the need to choose sides in this continuing battle in the world". The official animadversion was "pacifism", a charge levelled at art – poetry and songs, fiction and film – deemed philosophically antiwar for failing to distinguish between "just" and "unjust" wars, and for its focus on the irrationality and chaos of war.

Throughout the Brezhnev years, Soviet filmmakers continued to make war films in which the personal dominated the public, although the 40th anniversary of victory in 1985 prompted production of a large number of epic films. Censored or shelved war films included those that examined politically unacceptable themes, such as Soviet collaboration with the Nazis (for example, Aleksei German's *Proverka na dorogakh* [Road Test], made in 1971 and released in 1985), and those that failed to convey "the heroic spirit of the people", defined by the state film organization Goskino as incompatible with tragedy. Tarkovskii's script for *Zerkalo* (1975, Mirror) was criticized for its "tragic tonality"; Aleksei German, when he was working on *Dvadstat' dnei bez voiny* (1976, Twenty Days without War), was told to make sure that the final sequences demonstrated aggressive optimism.

World War II was inevitably a contentious subject. For the regime, it was a myth that could be manipulated to buttress its own authority, both by censoring unwelcome interpretations and by promoting its own version of the past (inflating Brezhnev's wartime service, for instance). For artists, the war signified a unifying if traumatic experience in the exceptionally divisive history of the Soviet Union, a source of authentic heroism and tragedy in a society dominated by spurious values. The most serious casualties were aborted projects, films conceived but never made. Yet if the bureaucrats had power on their side, the artists had time on theirs: most of the censored or shelved films eventually reached the audiences for which they were intended.

JOSEPHINE WOLL

Further Reading

Kenez, Peter, *Cinema and Soviet Society, 1917–1953*, Cambridge and New York: Cambridge University Press, 1992

Kenez, Peter, "Black and White: The War on Film" in *Culture and Entertainment in Wartime Russia*, edited by Richard Stites, Bloomington: Indiana University Press, 1995

Lazarev, Lazar, "Russian Literature on the War and Historical Truth" in *World War 2 and the Soviet People*, edited by John Garrard and Carol Garrard, New York: St Martin's Press, 1993

Woll, Josephine, *Real Images: Soviet Cinema and the Thaw*, London: Tauris, 2000

Youngblood, Denise, "Post-Stalinist Cinema and the Myth of World War II: Tarkovskii's *Ivanovo Detstvo* [*Ivan's Childhood*] (1962) and Klimov's *Come and See* (1985)" in *World War II, Film and History*, edited by John Whiteclay Chambers II and David Culbert, Oxford and New York: Oxford University Press, 1996

RUSSIA: The Shelf
Censorship of Soviet films under Brezhnev

Epoch-making changes came to the Soviet film industry in 1986, largely as a result of resolutions passed at the fifth congress of the Filmmakers Union, held in May that year at the Palace of Congresses in the Kremlin. Crucial among these resolutions was the sixth, which charged the Union's officials:

> to discuss the films that for one reason or another have not been released, and give detailed recommendations to the State Cinema Committee [Goskino] on each of these films; [and] to ask the State Cinema Committee of the USSR and the State Cinema Committees of the Union Republics to consider these recommendations when deciding on the distribution fate of the films under discussion.

As a result, the union immediately set up what came to be known as the "conflict commission", a group headed by Andrei Plakhov, formerly a film critic at the party newspaper *Pravda*.

The term *polka* (the shelf), had long been in use among filmmakers to describe the metaphorical and sometimes actual fate of their banned films. Banning had a long tradition in the Soviet and pre-Soviet film industry, in which ideological censorship had always been pervasive. A recently issued book, *Iz'iatoe kino* (1995, Removed Cinema) documents the banning of around 150 films in the years 1924–53, but during the Brezhnev period censorship mechanisms were further refined and developed.

As Plakhov recalls, he left for Tbilisi the day after the congress, and there he attended a clandestine screening of Tengiz Abuladze's allegory of Stalinist repression, *Monanieba* (*Repentance*). It was not until after his return to Moscow that he discovered that he had been made chairman of the "conflict commission". *Repentance* became the first film to benefit from the commission's activities and gain a release (in 1986). By August 1988, the commission had seen 159 films, a list of which was published in the last issue of the journal *Kinostsenarii* (Film Scripts) for 1988. The commission's work continued over the following years, and in December 1990 Andrei Smirnov, a former first secretary of the Filmmakers Union, put the number of films seen at "about 250".

Censorship could take several forms, from outright banning – with attempts, sometimes successful, to destroy the negative of the film in question – to release in a heavily censored form, or to absolutely minimal distribution. All the films that had suffered these fates were considered by the commission. Émigré directors were invited to return to the Soviet Union to re-edit their banned films for distribution. What the commission could not do was reconstitute lost films or sanction the making of the several films that had been banned at the script stage, such as Vasilii Shukshin's long-cherished project to film the life of the 17th-century Cossack rebel Stepan Razin.

As might be expected, the workings of the commission revealed that Goskino's vigilance had been particularly directed toward ideologically sensitive subjects, such as Russian and Soviet history. Films about the Bolsehvik revolution and the civil war that followed it, such as Aleksandr Askoldov's *Komissar* (1967, The Commissar) or the portmanteau film *Nachalo nevedomogo veka* (1967, The Beginning of an Unknown Era), thus fell foul of the system, as did films about the fate of the imperial family, notably Elem Klimov's *Agoniia* (*Agony*). However, Goskino's insistence upon an ideologically acceptable reading of history extended beyond great events, into the ordinary lives of Soviet citizens in the 1930s and 1940s, leading to the shelving of the work of Aleksei German and of Andrei Tarkovskii's *Zerkalo* (1975, The Mirror); as well as back into the past, where the axe also fell upon Tarkovskii's *Andrei Rublev*. Not for nothing was there a Soviet saying, "The future is certain. Only the past is still unclear."

Yet, as the work of the commission continued, it revealed that films that had no overt concern with history had also been banned. The desire for an ideologically acceptable picture, and the consequent tendency, in Soviet parlance, to "lacquer" that picture, extended to all aspects of life. Thus, Kira Muratova's dramas of small-town life were just as vulnerable, because their characters' uncertainties and confusions were deemed not to provide a positive "model" of Soviet life. The publication of a succession of censorship case histories, particularly by the film historian Valerii Fomin, has shown that films were censored for containing too much bad language, too much drunkenness, insufficient political awareness, or even, in the absurd case of Andrei Smirnov's *Osen'* (1974, Autumn), too much bad weather. Smirnov was required to reshoot the film and include a scene in which the protagonists take a sunlit walk in the woods.

The release of dozens of banned films had the effect of rewriting Soviet film history. Whole careers, especially those of Aleksei German, Kira Muratova, and Aleksandr Sokurov, had been submerged. The revelation of their work gained them national and international reputations. A poll of leading Soviet film critics in 1987 placed German's *Moi drug, Ivan Lapshin* (1984, My Friend Ivan Lapshin) ahead of Sergei Eisenstein's *Bronenosets Potemkin* (1925, Battleship Potemkin) as the best Soviet film of all time. The examples set by these directors have helped define the concerns and approaches of post-Soviet Russian films. German's influence is inescapable in the many films devoted to the re-examination of Soviet history as part of a general national attempt to understand the path taken to the final crisis. The bold stylistic innovations of Muratova and Sokurov have helped to shape post-Soviet "authorial" cinema, through the careers of a generation of younger filmmakers.

Although Goskino continues to exist in the Russian Federation, it is no longer performing a censorship function as it did in the Soviet period. For the present at least, Russian filmmakers, though they are now subject to the new rigours of the market, have escaped from the basilisk stare of the state censor.

JULIAN GRAFFY

Further Reading

Fomin, V.I., *"Polka": Dokumenty, Svidetel'stva, Kommentarii* (The "Shelf": Documents, Evidence, Commentaries), Moscow: Kinoiskusstva, 1992

Fomin, V.I., *Kino i vlast': Sovetskoe kino: 1965–1985 gody* (Cinema and Power: Soviet Cinema 1965–85), Moscow: Materik, 1996

Graffy, Julian, "The Arts" in *Gorbachev and Perestroika*, edited by Martin McCauley, London: Macmillan, and New York: St Martin's Press, 1990

Graffy, Julian, "Stripping the Well-stocked Shelves", *Index on Censorship*, 20/3 (March 1991)

Graffy, Julian, "Unshelving Stalin: After the Period of Stagnation" in *Stalinism and Soviet Cinema*, edited by Richard Taylor and Derek Spring, London and New York: Routledge, 1993

Lawton, Anna, *Kinoglasnost: Soviet Cinema in Our Time*, Cambridge and New York: Cambridge University Press, 1992

"List of Films 'Liberated' by the Conflict Committee" in *Lenfilm and the Liberation of Soviet Cinema*, edited by M. Müller and H. van der Meulen, Rotterdam: Rotterdam Film Festival, 1990

Margolit, E. and Shmyrov, V. (editors), *Iz'iatoe kino: Katalog sovetskikh igrovykh kartin, ne vypushchennykh vo vsesoiuznyi prokat po zavershenii v proizvodstve ili iz"iatikh iz deistvuiushchego fil'mofonda v god vypuska na ekran, 1924–1953* (Removed Cinema: A Catalogue of Soviet Feature Films That Were Not Released for All-Union Distribution upon Completion or Were Removed from the Film Archive in the Year of Their Release, 1924–53), Moscow: Dubl'-d, 1995

Plakhov, Andrei, "The 'Shelf' Yesterday and Today" in *Lenfilm and the Liberation of Soviet Cinema*, edited by M. Müller and H. van der Meulen, Rotterdam: Rotterdam Film Festival, 1990

"Reshenie V s"ezda kinematografistov SSSR" (Resolution of the Fifth Congress of Film-makers of the USSR), *Iskusstvo kino*, 10 (1986): 121–25

Rubanova, I., "Losses along the Way" in *Lenfilm and the Liberation of Soviet Cinema*, edited by M. Müller and H. van der Meulen, Rotterdam: Rotterdam Film Festival, 1990

RWANDA

(formerly part of Ruanda-Urundi)

Population: 7,609,000
Main religions: Animist; Roman Catholic; Protestant; Muslim
Official language: French; English; Kinyarwanda
Other languages spoken: Kiswahili

Illiteracy rate (%): 26.4 (m); 39.8 (f)
Number of daily newspapers: 1
Number of periodicals: 2
Number of radio receivers per 1000 inhabitants: 101
Number of TV receivers per 1000 inhabitants: 0.1

The modern history of Rwanda has been dominated by two massacres of the Tutsi people, carried out in 1959 and 1994. The killings of 1959 were described by the British philosopher Bertrand Russell in 1962 as "the most horrible and systematic massacre we have had occasion to witness since the extermination of the Jews by the Nazis". In 1992 the slaughter was equally systematic and conducted on an appalling scale. Over half a million people were killed, most of them Tutsi, although moderate Hutus were also targeted.

The precolonial period was one of Tutsi paramountcy. After the arrival of cattle-keeping Tutsi in the late 16th century resident Hutu agriculuralists became their clients in a feudal-type relationship. Tutsi dominance was maintained throughout the colonial period, during which Rwanda was first a part of German East Africa and then – after World War I – a Belgian protectorate. Cultural change ushered in by colonialism was not reflected in the political and administrative structures in the territory. The fact that Hutus, who constituted 86 per cent of the population, continued to be dominated by the Tutsi minority became increasingly problematic in the late 1950s as the prospect of self-rule became imminent. In 1959, three years before the country became independent, for reasons which are complex and still debated, Hutu militants turned on the Tutsi. The consequences of this outbreak of ethnic violence continue to reverberate in Rwanda and its neighbour Burundi (the entry for which should be read alongside this one) to the present day.

After the massacre, many Tutsi took refuge in Uganda. They harboured an understandable sense of injustice and posed a continuous threat to Rwanda, which became independent, under the Hutu president Grégoire Kayibanda, in 1962. The press was censored from the outset. Any comment on the massacre was not allowed. The Catholic *Kinyamateka*, which had been founded in 1935 as a monthly newspaper, and *Kanguaka*, founded in the 1960s, were both disposed to examine the causes and results of what had taken place. As a result, both were subject to suspension. Control tightened after the military takeover of general Juvénal Habyarimana in 1973, when Rwanda became a one-party state under the rule of the Mouvement Révolutionnaire National pour le Développement (MRND). All Rwandan citizens were now automatically members of the MRND, and political discussion was strictly censored. The government argued that continuing Hutu–Tutsi hostilities necessitated such policies. However, the government presided over institutional discrimination against the Tutsi such as the quota system for schools and universities. The quotas operated even in Butare, the one province left where the Tutsi were present in significant numbers (30 per cent). Needless to say, the publications of the Tutsi in exile were not allowed to circulate. The 1977 penal code declared it a crime to incite the population against the government. Journalists were regularly detained for threatening state security.

There was no formal press legislation. The Service Central de Renseignements (secret service) imposed its own rules. There was in any case no daily newspaper, and the daily bulletin of the Agence Rwandaise de Presse circulated only to public servants. The weekly *Imvaho* was owned by the state. Radio and television were also state controlled. The Catholic paper *Kinyamateka* continued to be published. However, the editor, Father Sindombue, was harassed after the paper had attacked government corruption. There was little scope for free expression in Rwanda, a fact made manifest by president Habyarimana's declaration in 1990 that journalists who published "false information" were to be prosecuted.

Yet in the late 1980s the government was actively pursuing

a cautious *rapprochement* with the exiled Tutsi. For many, though, it was too little too late. The Rwanda Patriotic Front (RPF), led by an ethnic Rwandese general in the Ugandan army, Fred Rwigena, was formed in 1990, and invaded northern Rwanda from Uganda. The invasion was repulsed with help from Zaire, and a ceasefire signed, only to be immediately broken. The government nevertheless pressed on with its plans for multi-party politics, and by 1992 some 12 parties had been officially recognized and a multi-party transitional government and national assembly was in place. The MRND retained only five out of 19 ministerial portfolios; party hardliners were excluded. None of this was enough to lessen the tension. The army issued the following warning:

> The enemy have set up a number of privately-owned papers . . . which vilify our government. They have given financial support to existing papers for the same purpose . . . [These papers] work openly for the enemy under cover of freedom of expression, but we want to put you on your guard against what you read in certain papers. Read them circumspectly. They preach hatred and regional and ethnic divisions.

Between 1990 and 1992, 24 journalists were arrested for penning articles alleged to be critical of the government. In 1991 the editor-in-chief of the independent satirical magazine *Byabarango* was arrested and accused of "insulting the head of state" after the publication of a cartoon figure throwing a map of the country into a hole in the ground. André Mameya, secretary of the Rwanda Journalists' Association, was arrested for suggesting that refugees from Burundi were members of a pro-Hutu group, Palipehutu, and were being trained for an attack on Burundi.

Such examples of the government's abuse of citizen's rights, however, are dwarfed by the events of 1994, when a barbarous campaign was launched against the Rwandese Tutsi population. The genocide was sparked by the death, in a plane crash, of president Habyarimana, as he was returning from peace talks in neighbouring Tanzania. It appears that his plane was shot down over Kigali by Hutu hardliners who were opposed to negotiation with the RPF. In the wake of Habyarimana's death, Hutu militia immediately launched a pogrom against Tutsi and Hutu "moderates". Within two months 500,000 people had been killed and 1,300,000 had fled to neighbouring countries. The Tutsi who had remained in the 1960s, 1970s, and 1980s were virtually exterminated. Evidence that emerged in the wake of the genocide indicated that there had been a large degree of prior planning. Meanwhile, the massacre was aided and abetted by Radio-Télévision Libre de Milles Collines (RTLM), which broadcast vicious propaganda, inciting Hutus to commit specific acts of violence against the Tutsi. Many international observers, including Reporters sans Frontières, who would in normal circumstances oppose all forms of censorship, called for the silencing of RTLM – to no avail.

Eventually the Hutu militias responsible for the slaughter retreated into Zaire in the face of an advance by RPF forces. By August 1994 the RPF had assumed control in Rwanda. The RPF government has since attempted to bring peace and stability to this troubled country. A seminar for journalists held in Kigali in January 1995 called for the end of ethnic hatred in the media, the granting of licences to private radio stations, and, above all, a recognition that to report on abuses of human rights was a service to the country rather than an act of subversion. The vice-president and military chief, Paul Kagame, endorsed these demands. Since then, incitement to ethnic hatred has lessened. When it has occurred, as in the case of *Le Partisan* and *Intego* in 1997, it has been firmly dealt with. However, the situation both within Rwanda itself and in the wider region remains highly volatile.

MARTINE K. MILLER

Further Reading

Ashworth, Lindsey and Liesl Fichardt, *Writers and Human Rights Abuses in Africa*, New York: Human Rights Watch, 1991

"Burying the Truth in the Name of Human Rights: The Case of Antoine Sibmorat and His Supporters", *African Rights* (September 1997)

Carver, Richard, *Truth from Below: The Emergent Press in Africa*, London: Article 19, 1991

Chrétien, J-P. *et al.* (editors), *Rwanda: les médias du génocide*, Paris: Karthala, 1995

Cone, Bruce and Jan Harris, *Human Rights in Africa 1981/1982/1983*, Wellington, New Zealand: African Information Center, 1981–83

Donnadieu, Jean-Louis, "Rwanda Takes Its Revenge on Journalists", *Index on Censorship*, 21/4 (April 1992)

Hammond, Peter, *Holocaust in Rwanda: The Roles of Gun Control, Media Manipulation, Liberal Church Leaders and the United Nations*, Newlands, South Africa: Frontline Fellowship, 1996

Kirschke, Linda, *Broadcasting Genocide: Censorship, Propaganda and State-Sponsored Violence in Rwanda, 1990–1994*, London: Article 19, 1996

Lemarchand, René, *Rwanda and Burundi*, New York: Praeger, 1970

Maquet, Jacques Jerome Pierre, *The Premise of Inequality in Ruanda: A Study of Political Relations in a Central African Kingdom*, London: Oxford University Press, 1961

Reporters sans Frontières, *L'Impasse? La Liberté de la presse après de la Génocide*, 1995

RWANDA: Radio-Télévision Libre des Mille Collines
Rwandan radio station, established 1993

Radio-Télévision Libre des Mille Collines (RTLM), the station which became notorious for its role in inciting the 1994 genocide in Rwanda, was established one year earlier, during a period of political transition in Rwanda. From April 1992 Rwanda was governed by a multi-party transitional coalition government, introduced following a campaign by recently created opposition political parties. This government negotiated a ceasefire with the Rwanda Patriotic Front (RPF), a rebel force composed of mainly Tutsi exiles, which had led a guerrilla war in northern Rwanda since October 1990. These discussions, and pressure from the international community, culminated in the signing of the Arusha Accords in August 1993. The peace agreement established a programme of widespread political and military reform. Most of president Juvénal Habyarimana's responsibilities were assumed by a transitional Council of Ministers in which the ruling party, the Mouvement Révolutionnaire National pour le Développement (MRND), would retain only five out of 19 positions. A transitional National Assembly was also to be created, with a strong opposition and RPF representation. Meanwhile, the Rwanda Patriotic Army would be integrated into the Rwandan Armed Forces on a 40/60 per cent basis.

RTLM was formally registered in April 1993 as a jointly funded company with 50 original shareholders, and began to broadcast in July that year. The emergence of RTLM at this time reflected the broader tensions between advocates of reform from opposition parties, as well as from an emerging civil society, and their hardline opponents within the MRND. The idea of creating an independent radio station devoted entirely to the agenda of extremists within the ruling party appears to have arisen in response to increasing pressure for Radio Rwanda to grant access to opposition parties. The main figure behind RTLM was Ferdinand Nahimana, who between 1990 and April 1992 had served as Director of the Rwandan Office of Information (ORINFOR) but was forced to resign by the multi-party government because of inflammatory communiqués which the national radio broadcast prior to the March 1992 Bugesera massacre. The other shareholders were mostly prominent figures linked to the MRND, including close relatives of the president, government officials, and army officers. Moreover, a number of the shareholders were high-level leaders of what has been called the "second power" in pre-genocide Rwanda: armed militias which emerged in 1992 and carried out state-sponsored violence against opposition supporters and government critics.

From July to October 1993 RTLM's broadcasts were apparently fairly innocuous, consisting mainly of popular music. The station introduced the concept of western-style radio talk shows, complete with audience participation, frequent studio guests, and even dirty jokes to attract its mostly urban audience. However, the station's extremist political leanings soon became evident following the death of Burundian president Melchior Ndadaye in October 1993. Broadcasts became inflammatory and began to incite ethnic hatred. Although the RPF had no connection with events in Burundi, RTLM accused the rebels of being behind the assassination, and claimed that the violence which ensued in the wake of Ndadaye's death represented a breach of the Arusha Accords.

RTLM further demonstrated its resistance to political reform when it began in late 1993 to denounce individual opposition leaders and human rights activists as "enemies". An opposition representative, Agathe Uwilingiyimana, who served as prime minister from July 1993 until she was killed on 7 April 1994, was repeatedly targeted by the station. A broadcast on 3 December 1993 warned: "The Prime Minister has created a bad atmosphere because she co-operates with the RPF. She should remember that the scar she has was previously a wound." This was a reference to injuries Uwilingiyimana suffered in 1992 when she was assaulted, allegedly by MRND representatives. The implicit menace of such statements was consolidated by the close links the station maintained with pro-MRND militias that regularly organized violent attacks during this period.

In early April RTLM suddenly announced that violence would soon sweep the country: "on the 3rd, the 4th, and the 5th, there will be a little something here in Kigali City. And also on the 7th and the 8th ... you will hear the sound of bullets or grenades explode". On 6 April the plane carrying president Habyarimana was hit with a missile as it approached Kigali. He had been returning from a regional meeting of heads of state in which he was pressured finally to implement the Arusha Accords, to which he had agreed in late 1993. Within half an hour of the crash, security forces and militias threw up roadblocks in Kigali and began the selective killing of Tutsis and opposition party members. One week later, military and paramilitary organizations had killed an estimated 20,000 in the Kigali area alone. Approximately 500,000 were slaughtered before the genocide came to an end with the RPF victory of 18 July.

Although reports in the international media claimed that RTLM incited the massacres by appealing to listeners to "help fill" mass graves, its message during the genocide was hardly so blunt. Rather than acknowledging that civilians were the main target in the killings, RTLM claimed that the RPF and its "accomplices", a term understood to mean the Tutsis generally, had prepared the *Simusiga* (final battle) against the Hutus. The station repeatedly told listeners that the only way to survive was for all Rwandans to engage in "self-defence". RTLM used this allegation to try to justify genocide. Yet more important was the station's role in assisting groups already involved in organizing the massacres. During the genocide RTLM announced the names, addresses, and in some cases car licence plate numbers of individuals who were targeted for killing. The station also served to direct militias or security forces to places where groups of people were hiding. In many cases, attacks on such individuals or groups were carried out by security forces shortly after the directions were announced by RTLM.

Following the 1994 genocide, an international campaign developed to ban "hate media" in the Great Lakes region. In March 1996 the UN Security Council adopted a resolution inviting member states to dismantle Radio Democracy, a Burundian radio station based in Zaire (now the Democratic Republic of Congo). Numerous African governments pointed to RTLM as an example of the "dangers" of opening up the airwaves, suggesting that some form of licensing or regulation was necessary. However, it has also been argued that the conclusion to be drawn from the Rwandan example is the need to address the problem of state-sponsored violence, and not for tighter controls on the independent media. It was RTLM's relationship to a larger network of pro-MRND militias and security forces, not its popular impact, which enabled the station to play its role in the genocide.

LINDA M. KIRSCHKE

Further Reading

African Rights, *Rwanda: Death, Despair and Defiance*, revised edition, London: African Rights, 1995

Chrétien, J-P., "'Presse Libre' et propagande raciste au Rwanda: Kangura et 'les 10 commandements des Hutu'", *Politique Africaine*, 42 (June 1991)

Chrétien, J-P., "Media and Propaganda in Preparation for and during the Rwandan Genocide", study submitted to Unesco by Reporters sans Frontières and produced in collaboration with the Centre de Recherches Africaines (Paris 1-CNRS), Paris: Unesco, 30 April 1995

Chrétien, J-P. et al., *Rwanda: les médias du génocide*, Paris: Karthala, 1995

Fédération Internationale des Droits de l'Homme, Africa Watch, Union interafricaine des Droits de l'Homme et des Peuples, Centre international des Droits de la Personne et du Développement démocratique, *Report of the International Commission of Investigation on Human Rights Violations in Rwanda since October 1, 1990 (January 7–21, 1993) Final Report*, New York: Human Rights Watch, March 1993

Genocide in Rwanda, April–May 1994, New York: Human Rights Watch, May 1994

Human Rights Watch, *Leave None to Tell the Story: Genocide in Rwanda*, New York: Human Rights Watch, 1999

Joint Evaluation of Emergency Assistance to Rwanda, *The International Response to Conflict and Genocide: Lessons from the Rwanda Experience*, Copenhagen: Steering Committee of the Joint Evaluation of Emergency Assistance to Rwanda, 1996

Kirschke, Linda, *Broadcasting Genocide: Censorship, Propaganda and State-Sponsored Violence in Rwanda, 1990–1994*, London: Article 19, 1996

Kirschke, Linda, "Multiparty Transitions, Elite Manipulation and the Media: Reassessing the Rwandan Genocide", *Vierteljahresschrift für Sicherheit und Frieden*, 18/3 (2000): 238–43

Kirschke, Linda, "Informal Repression, Zero-sum Politics and Late Third Wave Transitions", *Journal of Modern African Studies*, 38/3 (September 2000): 383–405

Mironko, C. and S. Cook, "Broadcasting Racism, Reaping Genocide: Radio Télévision Libre des Milles Collines (RTLM) and the Rwandan Genocide", paper presented at the annual conference of the American Anthropological Association, Washington, DC, 16 November 1995

Prunier, Gérard, *The Rwanda Crisis, 1959–1994: History of a Genocide*, London and New York: Hurst, 1995

Reporters sans Frontières, *Rwanda: médias de la haine ou presse démocratique? rapport de mission 16–24 septembre 1994*, Paris: Reporters sans Frontières, 1994

Reporters sans Frontières, *Rwanda – l'impasse: la liberté de la presse après le génocide, 4 juillet 1994–28 août 1995*, Paris: Reporters sans Frontières, 1995

Reyntjens, Filip, *L'Afrique des Grands Lacs en crise: Rwanda, Burundi, 1988–1994*, Paris: Karthala, 1994

Reyntjens, Filip, *Rwanda: trois jours qui ont fait basculé l'histoire*, Brussels and Paris: Institut Africain CEDAF/L'Harmattan, 1995 (Cahiers Africains 16)